ATHL[illegible]S
2018
THE INTERNATIONAL TRACK AND FIELD ANNUAL

BY PETER MATTHEWS
ASSOCIATION OF TRACK & FIELD STATISTICIANS

Published by SportsBooks Ltd

SportsBooks Limited
9 St Aubyns Place
York
YO24 1EQ
United Kingdom
Tel: 01904 613475
e-mail randall@sportsbooks.ltd.uk
Website www.sportsbooks.ltd.uk

This publication incorporates the ATFS Annual.

Front page photograph supplied by Mark Shearman, 22 Grovelands Road, Purley, Surrey, CR8 4LA. Tel: 0208 660 0156: mark@athleticsimages.com

British Library Cataloguing in Publication Data

Athletics: the international track and
field annual – 2018
1. Athletics. Track & Field events –
Serials
1. International athletics annual (London)
796.4′2′05

ISBN 9781907524554
Cover design: Kath Grimshaw

Printed arranged by Jellyfish Solutions, UK

CONTENTS

INTRODUCTION

THE DEATH OF Sir Roger Bannister in March reminded us of how his running of the first sub-4 minute mile captured the world's attention as no other single athletics achievement has done before or since. His run on 6 May 1954 was in an age of multiple world records every year when standards rapidly improved as the world recovered from the effects of World War II and the subsequent era of austerity. It was the beginning of rapid improvements in standards with improved knowledge, coaching and facilities together with the spread of competition to peoples all around the world. Nowadays world records are scarce commodities and world standards in depth are relatively stable, as can be seen in my analysis of Trends as can be seen on pages 106-107. In most events the huge improvements came from the 1950s to the 1980s. Even so it is staggering to see how few performances from 1954 would qualify for the 200 deep lists published here for 2017: for men just one mark each at 1 mile, 110mh, 400mh, LJ and DT, but five at 800m, and for women just the top shot mark. At distance events the world records of 13:51.2 for 5000m by Vladimir Kuts and 28:54.2 for 10,000m by Emil Zátopek are well short of the 200th best of this year. Bannister's times would not make it, but John Landy's 3:57.9 for 1 mile just makes the bottom of the 2017 list.

While Bannister's epic feat remains supreme for world attention, no athlete has transcended our sport in the way that Usain Bolt has done and following his retirement I detail his career achievements on pages 111-112. No one could match his ability and charisma, but there are plenty of men and women who will excite us in the years to come and a great feature of our sport is the way that new stars are constantly emerging. I hope that we will continue to be able to gather together the deeds of each year as is done in this Annual. The first ATFS publication was the Olympic Handbook by Don Potts and Roberto Quercetani, published by *Track & Field News* in 1948. This included the first deep all-time world lists and was followed in 1951 by the first International Athletics Annual. I bought, with great excitement, my first Annual in 1957. Nowadays, in the age of the Internet, information is much more readily available than it was in those days and it is a sign of the times that from this year the great American magazine *Track & Field News* is only published in electronic form. That follows, years earlier, of the change from print to email for its companion *Track Newsletter* and also *Athletics International* that I produce with Mel Watman. Nonetheless, I still see the place for books even though sales are in general decline. The discipline of gathering together comprehensive and accurate details of the year, particularly our annual world lists, remains vital in providing a permanent reference source while detail on the Internet may be more transitory.

The list of drugs bans in this Annual is the largest yet and there has never been such a rewriting of past results as we have seen over the past year or so. This can be depressing, but on a more positive note we can see that action is being taken on a large scale even though legal and practical issues can frustratingly delay this. Led by its president Lord Coe, the IAAF is pursuing its task of implementing decisions on a range of issues, often in difficult areas, with attempts to make the sport ever more attractive to its publics. The success of the World Championships both outdoors and indoors are testimony to the pre-eminence of real championships action. Long may this continue as well as maintaining the importance and attractiveness of the spectaculars such as seen at the highest level in the Diamond League. But we need to ensure that attention is concentrated on the athletics competitions and the needs of the athletes, rather than the increasing trend in some cases for putting on "a show".

Peter Matthews, March 2018.

ABBREVIATIONS

The following abbreviations have been used for meetings with, in parentheses, the first year that they were held.

AAU (USA) Amateur Athletic Union Championships (1888) (later TAC)
Af-AsG Afro-Asian Games (2003)
AfCh African Championships (1979)
AfG African Games (1965)
Af-J African Junior Championships (1994)
AmCp America's Cup (World Cup Trial) (1977)
APM Adriaan Paulen Memorial, Hengelo
AsiC Asian Championships (1973)
AsiG Asian Games (1951)
Asi-J Asian Junior Championships (1990)
ASV Weltklasse in Köln, ASV club meeting (1934)
Athl Athletissima, Lausanne (1976)
Balk Balkan Games (1929), C - Championships
Barr (Cuba) Barrientos Memorial (1946)
BGP Budapest Grand Prix (1978)
Bisl Bislett Games, Oslo (1965) (Bergen 2004)
Bol G Bolivar Games (1938)
BrGP British Grand Prix
CAC Central American and Caribbean Championships (1967)
CAG Central American and Caribbean Games (1926)
C.Asian Central Asian Championships
CAU Inter-counties, GBR (1934)
CG Commonwealth Games (1930)
C.Cup Continental Cup (2010)
Déca Décanation, Paris (C) (2005)
DL Diamond League (2010)
DNG DN Galan, Stockholm (1966)
Drake Drake Relays (1910)
EAF European Athletics Festival, Bydgoszcz (2001)
EAsG East Asian Games (1993)
EC European Championships (1934)
ECCp European Clubs Cup (1975)
EChall European Challenge (10,000m 1997, Throws 2001); see ET
ECp European Cup - track & field (1965), multi-events (1973)
EI European Indoor Championships (1970, Games 1966-9)
EICp European Indoor Cup (2003)
EJ European Junior Championships (1970)
ET European Team Championships (replaced European Cup, 2009)
EU23 European Under-23 Championships (1997) and European Under-23 Cup (1992-4)
FBK Fanny Blankers-Koen Games, Hengelo (formerly APM) (1981)
FlaR Florida Relays (1939)
FOT (USA) Final Olympic Trials (1920)
Franc Francophone Games (1989)
Gaz Gaz de France meeting, FRA (was BNP) (1968)
GGala Golden Gala, Roma (from 1980), Verona (1988), Pescara (1989), Bologna (1990)
GL Golden League (1998-2009)
GNR Great North Run – Newcastle to South Shields, GBR (1981)
GP Grand Prix
GPF IAAF Grand Prix Final (1985)
GS Golden Spike, Ostrava (1969)
Gugl Zipfer Gugl Grand Prix, Linz (1988)
GWG Goodwill Games (1986)
Gyulai István Gyulai Memorial, Budapest (2011-13), Székesfehérvár (2014-16)
Hanz Hanzekovic Memorial, Zagreb (1958)
Herc Herculis, Monte Carlo, Monaco (1987)
IAAF International Association of Athletics Federations
IAC IAC meeting (1968), formerly Coca-Cola
IAU International Association of Ultrarunners
IbAm Ibero-American Championships (1983)
Is.Sol Islamic Solidarity Games (2005)
ISTAF Internationales Stadionfest, Berlin (1921)
Jenner Bruce Jenner Classic, San Jose (1979)
Jerome Harry Jerome Track Classic (1984)
Jordan Payton Jordan U.S. Track & Field Open, Stanford (2004)
JUCO Junior Colleges Championships, USA
KansR Kansas Relays, Lawrence (1923)
Kuso Janusz Kusocinski Memorial (1954)
Kuts Vladimir Kuts Memorial (1978)
LGP London Grand Prix, Crystal Palace
LI Loughborough International (1958)
MAI Malmö AI Galan, Sweden (1958)
Mast Masters pole vault, Grenoble (1987), Donetsk
MedG Mediterranean Games (1951)
Mill Millrose Games, New York indoors (1908)
ModR Modesto Relays (1942)
MSR Mt. San Antonio College Relays (1959)
NA Night of Athletics, Heusden (2000) formerly Hechtel
NACAC North American, Central American & Caribbean Ch (2003)
NC National Championships
NC-w National Winter Championships
NCAA National Collegiate Athletic Association Championships, USA (1921)
NCAA-r NCAA Regional Championships (2003)
NCp National Cup
Nebiolo Memorial Primo Nebiolo, Torino (2000, originally 1963)
NG National Games
Nik Nikaïa, Nice (1976)
NM Narodna Mladezhe, Sofia (1955)
N.Sch National Schools
Nurmi Paavo Nurmi Games (1957)
NYG New York Games (1989)
OD Olympischer Tag (Olympic Day) (1963)
Oda Mikio Oda Memorial Meeting, Hiroshima (1967)
Odlozil Josef Odlozil Memorial, Prague (1994)
OG Olympic Games (1896)
OT Olympic Trials
Owens Jesse Owens Memorial (1981)
PAm Pan American Games (1951)
PArab Pan Arab Championships (1977) (G-Games 1953)
Pedro Pedro's Cup, Poland (2005)
PennR Pennsylvania Relays (1895)
PTS Pravda Televízia Slovnaft, Bratislava (1957) (later GPB)
Pre Steve Prefontaine Memorial (1976)

RdVin Route du Vin Half Marathon, Luxembourg (1962)
RomIC Romanian International Championships (1948)
RWC Race Walking Challenge Final (2007)
SACh South American Championships (1919)
SAsG South Asian Games (1984)
SEAG South East Asia Games (1959)
SEC Southeastern Conference Championships
SGP IAAF Super Grand Prix
Skol Skolimowska Memorial (2010)
Slovn Slovnaft, Bratislava (formerly PTS) (1990)
Spark Sparkassen Cup, Stuttgart (indoor) (1987)
Spart (URS) Spartakiad (1956)
Spitzen Spitzen Leichtathletik Luzern (1987)
Stra Stramilano Half marathon, Milan (1972)
Super Super Meet, Japan (Tokyo, Shizuoka, Yokohama, Kawasaki)
TexR Texas Relays (1925)
Tsik Athens Grand Prix Tsiklitiria (1998)
USOF US Olympic Festival (1978)
VD Ivo Van Damme Memorial, Brussels (1977)
Veniz Venizélia, Haniá, Crete (1936)
WAC Western Athletic Conference Championships (1962)
WAF World Athletics Finals (2003)
WCh World Championships (1983)
WCM World Challenge Meeting (2010)
WCp World Cup - track & field (1977), marathon (1985)
Walking – Lugano Trophy – men (1961), Eschborn Cup – women (1979)
WCT World Championships Trial
WG World Games, Helsinki (1961)
WI World Indoor Championships (1987), World Indoor Games (1985)
WJ World Junior Championships (1986)
WK Weltklasse, Zürich (1962)
WMilG World Military Games
WRly World Relays (2014)
WUG World University Games (1923)
WY World Youth Championships (1999)
Zat Emil Zátopek Classic, Melbourne
Znam Znamenskiy Brothers Memorial (1958)
-j, -y, -23 Junior, Youth or under-23

Dual and triangular matches are indicated by "v" (versus) followed by the name(s) of the opposition. Quadrangular and larger inter-nation matches are denoted by the number of nations and -N; viz 8-N designates an 8-nation meeting.

Events

CC cross-country
Dec decathlon
DT discus
h hurdles
Hep heptathlon
HJ high jump
HMar half marathon
HT hammer
JT javelin
LJ long jump
Mar marathon
Pen pentathlon
PV pole vault
R relay
SP shot
St steeplechase
TJ triple jump
W walk
Wt weight

Miscellaneous abbreviations

+ Intermediate time in longer race
= Tie (ex-aequo)
A Made at an altitude of 1000m or higher
b date of birth
D Made in decathlon competition
dnf did not finish
dnq did not qualify
dns did not start
exh exhibition
h heat
H Made in heptathlon competition
hr hour
i indoors
kg kilograms
km kilometres
m metres
M mile
m/s metres per second
mx Made in mixed men's and women's race
nh no height
O Made in octathlon competition
P Made in pentathlon competition
pb personal best
Q Made in qualifying round
qf quarter final (or q in lists)
r Race number in a series of races
sf semi final (or s in lists)
w wind assisted
WIR world indoor record
WR world record or best
y yards
* Converted time from yards to metres:
For 200m: 220 yards less 0.11 second
For 400m: 440 yards less 0.26 second
For 110mh: 120yh plus 0.03 second

Countries

From a founding membership of 17 nations in 1912, IAAF membership now stands at 214

AFG Afghanistan
AHO Netherlands Antilles #
AIA Anguilla
ALB Albania
ALG Algeria
AND Andorra
ANG Angola
ANT Antigua & Barbuda
ARG Argentina
ARM Armenia
ARU Aruba
ASA American Samoa
AUS Australia
AUT Austria
AZE Azerbaijan
BAH Bahamas
BAN Bangladesh
BAR Barbados
BDI Burundi
BEL Belgium
BEN Benin
BER Bermuda
BHU Bhutan
BIH Bosnia Herzegovina
BIZ Belize
BLR Belarus
BOL Bolivia
BOT Botswana
BRA Brazil
BRN Bahrain
BRU Brunei

BUL Bulgaria
BUR Burkina Faso
CAF Central African Republic
CAM Cambodia
CAN Canada
CAY Cayman Islands
CGO Congo
CHA Chad
CHI Chile
CHN People's Republic of China
CIV Côte d'Ivoire (Ivory Coast)
CMR Cameroon
COD Democratic Republic of Congo
COK Cook Islands
COL Colombia
COM Comoros
CPV Cape Verde Islands
CRC Costa Rica
CRO Croatia
CUB Cuba
CUR Curaçao
CYP Cyprus
CZE Czech Republic
DEN Denmark
DJI Djibouti
DMA Dominica
DOM Dominican Republic
ECU Ecuador
EGY Egypt
ENG England
ERI Eritrea
ESA El Salvador
ESP Spain
EST Estonia
ETH Ethiopia
FIJ Fiji
FIN Finland
FRA France
FRG Federal Republic of Germany (1948-90)
FSM Micronesia
GAB Gabon
GAM The Gambia
GBR United Kingdom of Great Britain & Northern Ireland
GBS Guinea-Bissau
GDR German Democratic Republic (1948-90)
GEO Georgia
GEQ Equatorial Guinea
GER Germany (pre 1948 and from 1991)
GHA Ghana
GIB Gibraltar
GRE Greece
GRN Grenada
GUA Guatemala
GUI Guinea
GUM Guam
GUY Guyana
HAI Haiti
HKG Hong Kong, China
HON Honduras
HUN Hungary
INA Indonesia
IND India
IRI Iran
IRL Ireland
IRQ Iraq
ISL Iceland
ISR Israel
ISV US Virgin Islands
ITA Italy
IVB British Virgin Islands
JAM Jamaica
JOR Jordan
JPN Japan
KAZ Kazakhstan
KEN Kenya
KGZ Kyrgyzstan
KIR Kiribati
KOR Korea
KOS Kosovo
KSA Saudi Arabia
KUW Kuwait
LAO Laos
LAT Latvia
LBA Libya
LBN Lebanon (LIB up to 2016)
LBR Liberia
LCA St Lucia
LES Lesotho
LIB Lebanon
LIE Liechtenstein
LTU Lithuania
LUX Luxembourg
MAC Macao
MAD Madagascar
MAR Morocco
MAS Malaysia
MAW Malawi
MDA Moldova
MDV Maldives
MEX Mexico
MGL Mongolia
MKD Former Yugoslav Republic of Macedonia
MLI Mali
MLT Malta
MNE Montenegro
MNT Montserrat
MON Monaco
MOZ Mozambique
MRI Mauritius
MSH Marshall Islands
MTN Mauritania
MYA Myanmar
NAM Namibia
NCA Nicaragua
NED Netherlands
NEP Nepal
NFI Norfolk Islands
NGR Nigeria
NGU Papua New Guinea
NI Northern Ireland
NIG Niger
NMA Northern Marianas Islands
NOR Norway
NRU Nauru
NZL New Zealand
OMA Oman
PAK Pakistan
PAN Panama
PAR Paraguay
PER Peru
PHI Philippines
PLE Palestine
PLW Palau
PNG Papua New Guinea
POL Poland
POR Portugal
PRK North Korea (DPR Korea)
PUR Puerto Rico
PYF French Polynesia
QAT Qatar
ROU Romania
RSA South Africa
RUS Russia
RWA Rwanda
SAM Samoa
SCG Serbia & Montenegro (to 2006)
SCO Scotland
SEN Sénégal
SEY Seychelles
SGP Singapore (SIN up to 2016)
SIN Singapore
SKN St Kitts & Nevis
SLE Sierra Leone
SLO Slovenia
SMR San Marino
SOL Solomon Islands
SOM Somalia
SRB Serbia
SRI Sri Lanka
SSD South Sudan
STP São Tomé & Principé
SUD Sudan
SUI Switzerland
SUR Surinam
SVK Slovakia
SWE Sweden
SWZ Swaziland
SYR Syria
TAN Tanzania
TCH Czechoslovakia (to 1991)
TGA Tonga
THA Thailand
TJK Tadjikistan
TKM Turkmenistan
TKS Turks & Caicos Islands
TLS East Timor
TOG Togo
TPE Taiwan (Chinese Taipei)
TTO Trinidad & Tobago
TUN Tunisia
TUR Turkey
TUV Tuvalu
UAE United Arab Emirates
UGA Uganda
UKR Ukraine
URS Soviet Union (to 1991)
URU Uruguay
USA United States
UZB Uzbekistan
VAN Vanuatu
VEN Venezuela
VIE Vietnam
VIN St Vincent & the Grenadines
WAL Wales
YEM Republic of Yemen
YUG Yugoslavia (to 2002)
ZAM Zambia
ZIM Zimbabwe

ceased to exist as a separate territory in 2010, and absorbed into the Netherlands.

ACKNOWLEDGEMENTS

MY THANKS, AS usual, to all those who have helped me to compile this Annual with lists or other information information. My valued correspondents remain much the same year on year. Perhaps many take for granted that information will be available via the Internet and surely that has transformed the collation of data, but there remains to need to check, correct and collate this. So a warm welcome to any newcomers who can help us in our work in producing definitive reference sources.

As usual I have worked up the world year lists in this annual from original compilations by Richard Hymans and Mirko Jalava with reference to those of many other experts. Mirko's superb web site www.tilastopaja.net provides great depth of worldwide results. I am also indebted to Pino Mappa for work on men's lists, Carlos Fernández for his expertise on the road lists and to Ray Herdt for the walks. I circulate draft lists to a number of ATFS experts and receive much valuable information from a worldwide circle of correspondents, most of whom have helped with information from their nations for many years. Juan Mari Iriondo checked the biographies most diligently, Børre Lilloe provided much index data and Ken Nakamura checked distance lists.

Both for this annual and throughout the year with *Athletics International* that I produce with Mel Watman, Winfried Kramer helps with widespread probing for results as do the area experts: *Africa*: Yves Pinaud, *Asia*: Heinrich Hubbeling, *Central and South America*: Eduardo Biscayart and Luis Vinker, and specialists: *Records* György Csiki, *Road racing*: Marty Post, *Ultrarunning* Andy Milroy, *Indoors* Ed Gordon, *Multi events:* Hans van Kuijen and Enn Endjärv, *Pole vault* Kenneth Lindqvist, *800m:* Nejat Kök.

Australia: Paul Jenes; *Austria*: Dr Karl Graf; Belgium: André de Hooghe and Alain Monet; *Bulgaria*: Aleksandar Vangelov; *China*: Mirko Jalava; *Cuba*: Alfredo Sánchez; *Czech Republic*: Milan Urban; *Denmark*: Erik Laursen; *Dominican Republic*: Arisnel Rodríguez; *Estonia*: Erlend Teemägi and Enn Endjärv; *Finland*: Mirko Jalava, Mikko Nieminen and Matti Hannus; *France*: Alain Bouillé, Carles Baronet and Patricia Doilin; *Germany:* Klaus Amrhein; *Greece*: Thomas Konstas and Nikos Kriezis; *Hungary*: György Csiki; *India*: Ram. Murali Krishnan; *Ireland*: Pierce O'Callaghan and Liam Hennessy; *Israel*: David Eiger; *Italy*: Enzo Rivas and Raul Leoni; *Japan*: Yoshimasa Noguchi, Akihiro Onishi, Tatsumi Senda and Ken Nakamura; *Latvia*: Andris Stagis; *Lithuania*: Steponas Misiunas; *Luxembourg*: Georges Klepper; *Malaysia*: Jad Adrian, *Montenegro*: Ivan Popovic; *New Zealand*: Murray McKinnon and Steve Hollings; *Norway*: Børre Lilloe; *Poland*: Zbigniew Jonik and Janusz Rozum; *Portugal:* Arons Carvalho; *Puerto Rico*: Pedro Anibal Diaz; *Russia*: Sergey Tikhonov; *Serbia*: Ozren Karamata, Roberto Camano and Olga Acic; *Slovakia*: Alfons Juck; *Slovenia*: Zdravko Peternelj; *South Africa:* Clyde Kinloch, Richard Meyer and Riël Hauman; *Spain*: José Luis Hernández, Miguel Villaseñor, Carles Baronet and the AEEA team; *Sweden*: Jonas Hedman, Lennart Julin and Peter Larsson; *Switzerland*: Alberto Bordoli and Antonin Hejda; *Trinidad & Tobago:* Bernard Linley, *Turkey*: Nejat Kök, *Ukraine*: Ivan Kachkivskiy; *UK*: Tony Miller,and Ian Hodge; *USA*: Tom Casacky, Garry Hill, Mike Kennedy, Sieg Lindstrom, Glen McMicken, Marty Post, Jack Shepherd and *Track Newsletter*. Also various national federation lists and to those who post results or ranking lists to various web sites.

Also to Marco Buccellato, Mark Butler, Carole Fuchs, Grzegorz Gladzikowski, Stan Greenberg, Alan Lindop, Rooney Magnusson (obituaries), Bill Mallon, David Monti, Jiri Ondrácek (European U23), Zdenek Procházka (hammer), and Rob Whittingham.

My apologies to anybody whose name I may have missed or who have corresponded with other key ATFS personnel, but all help, however small is deeply appreciated.

Keep the results flowing

During the year Mel Watman and I publish marks to ATFS standards (150-200 deep on world lists) in *Athletics International*, of which there are over 35 issues per year by email. This serves as a base from which the lists in this book can be compiled, together with information from web sites, especially Mirko Jalava's *Tilastopaja*, *Track & Field News* (USA) with its results spin-off *Track Newsletter* and newsletters, especially Alfons Juck's *EME News* and Carles Baronet's *Track in Sun*.

In order to ensure that the record of 2018 is as complete as possible I urge results contribution worldwide to AI, and then in turn our lists in *Athletics 2019* (if there is one) will be as comprehensive as we can make them.

Peter Matthews

THE ASSOCIATION OF TRACK & FIELD STATISTICIANS

The ATFS was founded in Brussels (at the European Championships) in 1950 and ever since has built upon the work of such key founding members as Roberto Quercetani, Don Potts and Fulvio Regli to produce authoritative ranking lists in the International Athletics Annual and elsewhere.

Current Executive Committee

President: Paul Jenes AUS
Vice-President: A.Lennart Julin SWE
Treasurer: Tom Casacky USA
Secretary: Michael J McLaughlin AUS
Past Presidents: Rooney Magnusson SWE, Dr Roberto Quercetani ITA
Committee: Giuseppa Mappa ITA, Peter J Matthews GBR, Yoshimasa Noguchi JPN, Yves Pinaud FRA

Website: www.atfs.org

Internet – Websites

IAAF	www.iaaf.org
IAU	www.iau-ultramarathon.org
Africa (CAA)	www.webcaa.org
Asian AA	athleticsasia.org
CAC Confederation	www.cacacathletics.org
European AA	www.european-athletics.org
NACAC	www.athleticsnacac.org
Oceania AA	www.athletics-oceania.com
South American Fed.	www.consudatle.org
WMRA	www.wmra.info
World Masters	www.world-masters-athletics.org
Marathon Majors	www.worldmarathonmajors.com
Africa	www.africathle.com
Andorra	www.faa.ad
Argentina	www.cada-atletismo.org
Australia	www.athletics.com.au
Austria	www.oelv.at
Bahamas	www.bahamastrack.com
Belarus	www.bfla.eu
Belgium	www.val.be
Bermuda	www.btfa.bm
Bosnia Hercegovina	www.asbih.org
Brazil	www.cbat.org.br
Bulgaria	www.bfla.org
Canada	www.athletics.ca
Chile	www.fedachi.cl
China	www.athletics.org.cn
Costa Rica	www.fecoa.org
Croatia	www.has.hr
Cyprus	www.koeas.org.cy
Czech Republic	www.atletika.cz
Denmark	www.dansk-atletik.dk
Dominican Republic	www.fedomatle.org
England	www.englandathletics.org
Estonia	www.ekjl.ee
Finland	www.sul.fi
France	www.athle.com
Germany	www.leichtathletik.de
Great Britain	www.britishathletics.org.uk
deep statistics	www.topsinathletics.info
	www.thepowerof10.info
Greece	www.segas.gr
Hong Kong	www.hkaaa.com
Hungary	www.masz.hu
Iceland	www.fri.is
India	www.indianathletics.org
Indonesia	www.indonesia-athletics.org
Ireland	www.athleticsireland.ie
Israel	www.iaa.co.il
Italy	www.fidal.it
Jamaica	www.trackandfieldja.com
Japan	www.jaaf.or.jp
running news	japanrunningnews.blogspot.co.uk
Kazakhstan	www.kazathletics.kz
Kenya	www.athleticskenya.or.ke
Latvia	www.lat-athletics.lv
Lithuania	www.lengvoji.lt
Luxembourg	www.fla.lu
Macedonia	www.afm.org.mk
Malaysia	www.maf.org.my
results	www.adriansprints.com
Mexico	www.fmaa.mx
Moldova	www.fam.com.md
Monaco	www.fma.mc
Montenegro	www.ascg.co.me
Morocco	www.moroccanathletics.com
Netherlands	www.atletiekunie.nl
New Zealand	www.athletics.org.nz
Northern Ireland	www.niathletics.org
Norway	www.friidrett.no
Peru	www.fedepeatle.org
Poland	www.pzla.pl
Portugal	www.fpatletismo.pt
	www.atletismo-estatistica.pt
Puerto Rico	www.atletismofapur.com
	www.pedroanibaldiaz.com
Romania	www.fra.ro
Russia	www.rusathletics.com
Scotland	www.scottishathletics.org.uk
	www.scotstats.net
Serbia	www.ass.org.rs
Singapore	www.singaporeathletics.org.sg
Slovakia	www.atletikasvk.sk
Slovenia	www.atletska-zveza.si
South Africa	www.athletics.org.za
Spain	www.rfea.es
Sweden	www.friidrott.se
Switzerland	www.swiss-athletics.ch
Taiwan	www.cttfa.org.tw
Trinidad & Tobago	www.ttnaaa.org
Turkey	www.taf.org.tr
Ukraine	www.uaf.org.ua
Uruguay	www.atlecau.org.uy
USA	www.usatf.org
collegiate results	www.ustfccca.org
Wales	www.welshathletics.org
	athleticsstatswales.webeden.co.uk

Other recommended sites for statistics and results

AIMS	www.aimsworldrunning.org
ARRS	www.arrs.net
British historical	www.gbrathletics.com
	www.athlos.co.uk
DGLD (German stats)	www.ladgld.de
French history etc.	http://cdm.athle.com
Marathons	www.marathonguide.com
Masters Track & Field	www.mastersathletics.net
Mirko Jalava	www.tilastopaja.org
NUTS/Track Stats	www.nuts.org.uk
Rankings etc	www.all-athletics.com
Runners World	www.runnersworld.com
Tracklion (NED/BEL)	sportslion.net/tracklion.html
Track & Field News	www.trackandfieldnews.com
Track in Sun results	trackinsun.blogspot.co.uk
Ultra marathon stats	statistik.d-u-v.org/index.php
World juniors	www.worldjuniorathleticsnewsnzl.co.nz
Olympic Games	www.aafla.org
	www.sports-reference.com

DIARY OF 2017
by Peter Matthews

A chronological survey of highlights in major events in the world of track and field athletics.
See Championships or National sections for more details. DL = Diamond League, WCM = World Challenge Meeting, WIT = World Indoor Tour.

January

4 **Glasgow**. Laura Muir made a spectacular debut at 5000m as her 14:49.12 smashed the 25 year-old Scottish record of 15:03.17 by Liz McColgan.

6 **San Giorgio su Legnano**, Italy. There were top quality fields for the 60th edition of the Campaccio Cross Country with wins by Muktar Edris from Imane Merga, and Hellen Obiri from Faith Kipyegon.

7 **Edinburgh**, GBR. The Simplyhealth Great Edinburgh International XCountry included a four-race match won by the USA (149) from Europe (152) and Britain (208), The senior men's 8k race was a thriller won by Leonard Korir in 24:03 by a second from Callum Hawkins, but there was a runaway women's winner in Yasemin Can. Also Laura Muir anchored the British team to victory in the mixed 4x1k relay, clocking 2:53 for her leg.

15 **Porto de Mos**, Portugal. The IAAF introduced world records for women's 50k walk from January 1, and Inês Henriques wasted no time in claiming the inaugural record. Her 4:08:26 compared to the previous best on record of 4:10:59 by Monica Svensson in 2007.

20 **Dubai**, United Arab Emirates. 18th Standard Chartered Marathon. Tamirat Tola broke the course record with 2:04:11, but Kenenisa Bekele fell at the start and sustained injuries that caused him to drop out at halfway. On her marathon debut Worknesh Degefa won the women's race in 2:22:36 from Shure Demise 2:22:36. Ethiopian women took places 1-9 and their men had 11 of the top 12 men.

28 **Boston (Roxbury)**, USA. A US team of Emma Coburn 1200m 3:18.40, Sydney McLaughlin 400m 52.42, Brenda Martinez 800m 2:01.94 and Jenny Simpson 1600m 4:27.66 set a world best of 10:40.31 for women's distance medley at the New Balance Indoor Grand Prix.

31 **Osaka**, Japan. 36th Women's Marathon. Risa Shigemoto won in 2:24:22, her fastest time since her win in 2:23:23 on the same course in 2012.

February

1 **Düsseldorf**, Germany. 11th PSD Bank meeting (WIT). The evergreen Kim Collins set world age-40 bests of 6.58 in his heat and 6.56 in the final behind Yunier Pérez, also 6.56.

4 **Melbourne**, Australia. The Coles Nitro Series was held here and on February 9 and 11. While the athletes enjoyed the meetings, the standard of this highly touted series was generally pretty poor and the crowds came mainly to see Usain Bolt, who ran in mixed 4x100m relays.

4 **Karlsruhe**, Germany (WIT). Laura Muir won an eagerly awaited clash at 3000m against Hellen Obiri, 8:26.41, a European and Commonwealth record, to 8:29.46, a Kenyan record. More world-leading times came at 60m hurdles from Andrew Pozzi 7.49 and 7.44 and Kendra Harrison 7.76.

4 **Mondeville**, France. Kim Collins added further M40 world bests for 60m with 6.54 and 6.52.

7 **Sabadell**, Spain. Miting Internacional de Catalunya. Genzebe Dibaba ran her sixth world indoor record with 5:23.75 for 2000m (1000m 2:42.66, 1 mile 4:21.3e). This is faster than the world outdoor mark.

10 **Ra's Al Khaymah**, United Arab Emirates. Peres Jepchirchir won the half marathon in 65:06 and both this and her 20k split of 61:40 were world records. Second was Mary Keitany 65:13 and the pair had set off fast, through 10k in 31:07. At 15k Keitany led by 2 secs in 46:30 before Jepchirchir pushed ahead. There were the fastest ever times for 1st to 3rd and 5th, so that now all the best times for women's places 1-11 have come on this course. Bidan Karoki surged to victory in 59:10 in the men's race over the last three kilometres. He was followed by Yigrem Demelesh 59:19 and Augustine Choge 59:26, all three setting personal bests.

10 **Torun**, Poland (WIT). Genzebe Dibaba provided the highlight with 3:58.80 for 1500m, the sixth fastest ever women's indoor 1500m, while the top men's mark was 6.46 for 60m by Ronnie Baker.

11 **New York (Armory)**, USA. 110th Millrose Games. Ajee' Wilson set a North American 800m record of 1:58.27 from Charlene Lipsey 1:58.64. As usual the Wanamaker Mile was the last event – and this year it was won by Eric Jenkins 3:53.23, while earlier the women's mile was won by Sifan Hassan 4:19.89.

11-12 **UK Indoor Championships**, Sheffield. Andrew Pozzi tied his world lead with 7.44 for 60m hurdles and Tom Bosworth improved the Commonwealth record for 5000m walk to 18:39.47.

18 **Birmingham**, GBR. Müller Indoor Grand Prix, the final meet of the World Indoor Tour, in which event winners earned $20,000 and a wild card for the 2018 World Indoor Championships. British athletes starred with European records: Mo Farah 13:09.16 at 5000m and Laura Muir 2:31.93 at 1000m, and Andrew Pozzi improved his 2017 world best for 60m hurdles to 7.43. National records were set by the women's 3000m 1-2 – Hellen Obiri 8:29.41 and Sifan Hassan 8:30.76 and Elaine Thompson ran the one women's sub-7 secs time for 60m in 2017, with 6.98.

18 **Russian Winter Walks Championships**, Sochi. As usual there were terrific times with Sergey Shirobokov, just a week after his 18th birthday, winning at 20k in 1:18:26 from Sergey Bakulin 1:18:51, and what remained the best times of the year at 35k: Sergey Sharipov 2:27:07, Dementiy Cheparev 2:28:00 and Denis Nizhegorodov 2:29:19, and women's 20k: Yelena Lashmanova 1:25:18 and Yekaterina Medvedyeva 1:25:22.

18-19 **Spanish Indoor Championships**, Salamanca. Ruth Beitia cleared a season's best 1.96 to win the her 16th title in succession from 2002 (plus 12 outdoor titles).

19-21 **Russian Indoor Championships**, Moscow. Top mark was the 2.03 high jump by Mariya Kuchina.

26 **Tokyo Marathon**, Japan. Race records were set by Wilson Kipsang 2:03:58 and Sarah Chepchirchir 2:19:47. Kipsang was 11 secs ahead of world record schedule at 30k in 1:27:27 and although he slowed from that he won clearly with his record eighth sub-2:05 performance from Gideon Kipketer 2:05:51 as Kenyans took the first six paces

March

3-5 **European Indoor Championships**, Belgrade, Serbia. The magnificent victory of local athlete Ivana Spanovic provided a wonderful finale. After7.16 and 7.17 her series culminated with 7.24, the longest indoor women's long jump for 28 years and third on the world-all-time list. Even higher was Kevin Mayer's 6479 European record heptathlon, a score beaten only by Ashton Eaton. Then there was an incredible 21.97 shot put by Konrad Bukowiecki, the best ever by a teenager, and completing seven world leading indoor marks for 2017 was the qualifying round TJ 17.52 by Max Hess, and by women's winners: Ekateríni Stefanídi, PV 4.85, Anita Márton, SP 19.28, and Nafi Thiam, 4870 pentathlon. Laura Muir won both 1500m (British record 4:02.39) and 3000m (8:35.6), both new championship records as was Meyer's heptathlon. There were unique third wins for Pavel Maslák at 400m and Adam Kszczot at 800m. *For report and leading results see Athletics 2017 p. 79-80.*

3-5 **US Indoor Championships**, Albuquerque. Noah Lyles, 31.87 for 300m, and Gwen Berry, 25.60 for the women's 20lb weight, set world indoor bests. Taking advantage of the 1561m altitude there were world-leading marks by Ronnie Baker, 6.45 for 60m, and Ajee' Wilson, 1:23.84 for 600m.

4-5 **Huangshan**, China. Wang Kaihua's 1:17:54 for 20k walk was to remain the world's fastest for 2017 as she led 46 men under 1:24 and Niu Wenbin won the national 50k title in 3:46:12. There were 13 women under 1:30 at 20k (and 49 under 1:38), led by Lu Xiuzhi 1:26:28.

10-11 **NCAA Indoor Championships**, College Station, USA. Christian Coleman won the sprint double, trying the collegiate record of 6.45 for 60m and running 20.11 for 200m, just 0.01 off Wallace Spearmon's US and collegiate record. More top sprinting came from Ariana Washington, 22.42 for 200m, and Fred Kerley, 44.85 for 400m. Kerley then teamed up with brother My'Lik to help Texas A&M win the 4x400m in a meeting record 3:02.80 and take the overall men's team title. Oregon retained the women's team title with a record 84 points total and were third for men, with Edward Cheserek again winning both 3000m and 5000m (and was 2nd in the mile). Kendell Williams won the pentathlon for a record fourth time, her score of 4681 just 22 short of her 2017 record. Her brother Devon was the men's heptathlon winner with 6177 from Tim Duckworth, who improved his British record to 6165. Raven Saunders achieved a collegiate record with 19.56 in the shot.

11-12 17th **European Cup Winter Throwing**, Las Palmas de Gran Canaria, Spain. The best marks included 85.85 javelin by Julian Weber and 65.73 discus by Lukas Weisshaidinger.

12 **Nagoya**, Japan. Eunice Jepkirui Kirwa won this women's marathon for the third successive year, running a Bahrain record 2:21:17.

14-17 **Copa Cuba** (Championships). Andy Díaz improved his pb by 60m with his 17.40 triple jump.

26 **World Cross-Country Champion-ships**, Kampala, Uganda. East Africans or East African-born women running for Bahrain won every individual or team medal. Geoffrey Kamworor defended the men's title he had won in 2015 and compatriot Irene Cheptai was the women's champion. Ethiopia beat Kenya by one point for the men's team prize but Kenyan women achieved the unique feat of raking the first six places. The new mixed relay was won by Kenya from Ethiopia and the all-Kenyan

transferee team of Turkey. *For report and leading results see Athletics 2017 p. 79-80*

26–Apr 2 **Australian Championships**, Sydney. Sally Pearson showed that she was back in top form, winning her eighth national title at 100m hurdles in 12.53w.

30-Apr 1 **Florida Relays**, Gainesville, USA. The third and fourth best ever times were run in the women's 4x200m, won by a 4-nation Tumblewood TC team 1:28.77 from Oregon whose 1:28.78 was a collegiate record as was the 42.34 by the same quartet at 4x100m.

30-Apr 1 90th **Texas Relays**, Austin, USA. After records indoors at 5.72, 5.75 and 5.82, the 17 year-old Armand ("Mondo") Duplantis set the world junior pole vault record with a third-time clearance at 5.90. Lindon Victor set a collegiate record with 8472 in the decathlon.

April

1 **Prague**, Czech Republic. Joyciline Jepkosgei broke four world records at the Sportisimo Prague Half Marathon when winning the IAAF Gold Label Road Race in 64:52. The 23 year-old, competing in just her fifth half marathon, set the road records at 10k 30:04, 15k 45:37 and 20k 45:40 en route to her victory with Violah Jepchumba 2nd in 65:22. Tamirat Tola was a convincing men's winner in 59:37.

3 **Paris Marathon**, France. The husband-wife duo of Paul Lonyangata (2:06:10) and Purity Rionoripo (course record 2:20:55) won their respective titles at the Schneider Electric Marathon de Paris. The 42,440 finishers (32,103 men and 10,337 women) was a record for a European marathon.

9 **Rotterdam Marathon**, Netherlands. Running in unseasonably warm conditions, winners were Marius Kimutai 2:06:04 and Meskerem Assefa 2:24:18.

13-15 16th **Gulf Countries Championships**, Jeddah, Saudi Arabia. Mutaz Essa Barshim started his outdoor campaign with 2.35 in the high jump.

14-16 59th **Mt SAC Relays**, Torrance, California, USA. Top performance of this huge meeting was Gwen Berry's 74.62 hammer throw. Deajah Stevens had a notable sprint double in 11.00 and 22.31 and top men's mark was 1:43.60 by Clayton Murphy at 800m.

17 121st **Boston Marathon**, USA. Winners were Kenyans – Geoffrey Kirui 2:09:37 from Galen Rupp 2:09:58, and Edna Kiplagat 2:21:52 from Rose Chelimo 2:22:51 and Jordan Hasay, who made a fine marathon debut with 2:23:00.

20-21 **South African Championships**, Potchefstroom (A). Luvo Manyonga added 3cm to the African long jump record that he had set five weeks earlier with 8.65 on his first jump (the stopping with a niggle in his hamstring) and behind him Rushwal Samaii added 11cm to his personal best, at 8.49. Despite a head-wind of 0.7 Akine Simbine ran 9.95 to win the 100m title on a cold evening (9.94 in his semi) and Caster Semenya had easy wins at 400m and 800m less than two hours apart. Chris Harmse won his 22nd South African title in the hammer to take him to the absolute world record for successive national titles at any event.

22-23 3rd **IAAF World Relays**, Nassau, Bahamas. At 4x200m Canada scored a clear men's win over the USA with 1:19.24 and Jamaica set a CAC and Commonwealth women's record with 1:29.04, but the USA were the clear winners of the Golden Baton for team standings. The meeting ended perfectly for the home crowd as the new gimmick of a 4x400m mixed relay was won by The Bahamas in 3:14.42 from the USA 3:17.29.

23 Virgin **London Marathon**, GBR. Mary Keitany went through halfway in 66:54, the fastest ever split by a woman in a marathon, and although she slowed to 70:07 for the second half, set a women's world record time of 2:17:01 with world bests en route at 25k 1:19:43 and 30k 1:36:05. In all she earned $305,000 in prize money and time bonuses. Tirunesh Dibaba was second in an Ethiopian record 2:17:56 in the second marathon of her career. The men's race also started fast but slowed between 25k and 30k before Daniel Wanjiru went away to win in 2:05:58 from Kenenisa Bekele 2:05:57. There were a record 39,406 finishers (23,912 men and 15,494 women).

26-29 108th **Drake Relays**, Des Moines, USA. Despite very cold weather Omar McLeod ran the 110mh hurdles in 13.06 and Kendra Harrison was also dominant at 100m hurdles, beating a world-class field comfortably in 12.56.

27-29 123rd **Penn Relays**, Philadelphia, USA. The USA v World relays match provided many of the highlights with the USA setting a world best of 1:35.59 for the women's medley relay. The US team was Morolake Akinosun 100m, English Gardner 100m, Dezerea Bryant 200m and Miki Barber 400m 50.90. Total attendance was 108,912 with a Saturday peak at 47,420.

29 **Berkeley**, USA. Emmanuel Korir ran an outstanding negative split (52.48 + 51.25) for 1:43.73 at 800m.

May

5 **Doha**, Qatar. On his seasonal debut Thomas Röhler threw the javelin 93.90, a German and Diamond League record and second to Jan Zelezny on the world all-time list. Performances throughout were of a very high standard in ideal conditions, including 7:28.73 at 3000m by Ronald Kwemoi, 2.36 high jump by Mutaz Essa Barshim and 1:56.61 800m by Caster Semenya. Hyvin Jepkemoi set a Commonwealth and African women's 3000m steeplechase record of 9:00.12 from 9:01.57 by

Beatrice Chepkoech and the fastest ever 3rd and 4th place times by Ruth Jebet 9:01.99 and Celliphine Chespol 9:05.70.

5 **Stanford**, USA. Payton Jordan Invitational. As usual there was great depth of distance times. Meraf Bahta set a Swedish record of 31:13.06 for 10,000m.

6 **Monza**, Italy. Eliud Kipchoge did not achieve Nike's "Breaking2" objective, but had a fantastic run to cover the marathon distance in 2:00:25, over two and a half minutes faster than the official world record of 2:02:57 set in Berlin in 2014 by his fellow Kenyan, Dennis Kimetto. Conditions were against the rules as well as the spirit of racing as a posse of pacemakers took turns, usually six at a time, to shield Kipchoge from any wind and closely follow an electric car programmed to operate at the 14:13 per 5k speed required to break 2 hours around the dead flat Monza motor racing circuit. The serene Kipchoge reached halfway in 59:57 and 30k in 1:25:20 and finished looking remarkably fresh well ahead of Zersenay Tadese 2:06:51.

10-14 **Collegiate Conference Championships**, USA. As usual the SEC (Southeastern Conference) provided easily the greatest depth of quality performances, including Lindon Victor with 8539 points for decathlon, adding 67 to his previous collegiate and Grenadian record, and Christian Coleman with a 9.97/19.98 sprint double ahead of Nethaneel Mitchell-Blake 9.99/20.09. Fred Kerley continued his brilliant unbeaten season with a world-leading 44.09 in his heat and 44.30 in the final of the 400m, adding the second leg on a world-leading 3:00.72 4x400m time by Texas A&M University. Deajah Stevens had another impressive sprint double with 11.05 and 22.09 at the Pacific-10 in Eugene, the latter a low-altitude collegiate best.

13 **Shanghai**, China (DL). Emily Thompson had a terrific win over Tori Bowie and Marie Josée Ta Lou at 100m, 10.78 to 11.04 and 11.07, and 19 year-old Noah Lyles won the 200m in 19.90, well clear of LaShawn Merritt 20.27. Other world-leading marks were set by Shaunae Miller-Uibo, 400m 49.77, Faith Kipyegon, 1500m 3:59.22 and Hellen Obiri, 5000m 14:22.47. In the field Luvo Manyonga long jumped a DL record 8.61 and Sam Kendricks beat Renaud Lavillenie 5.88 to 5.83 in the pole vault.

15 **Baie Mahault**, Guadeloupe. Top marks came in the triple jumps: Will Claye 17.40 and Yulimar Rojas 14.67.

16-20 4th **Islamic Solidarity Games**, Bake, Azerbaijan. Ruth Jebet won the 3000m steeplechase in 9:15.41 and had a notable victory at 5000m in 14:53.41, 0.09 ahead of Yasemin Can, who came back to win at 10,000m two days later in 31:18.20. Eda Tugsuz threw the javelin 67.21, a European under-23 record, adding 2.91m to the Turkish record that she had set four weeks earlier after national records at 59.21 and 59.68 in February and a pre-season best of 58.95.

20 **Halle**, Germany. 43rd Werfertage. Pawel Fajdek took a world lead in the hammer with 82.31, and other top winners included Daniel Ståhl, discus 68.07, and Anita Wlodarczyk, hammer 76.32.

20 **Kingston**, Jamaica Invitational (WCM). Kyron McMaster improved at 400m hurdles from 48.69 to 47.80, a time that remained the year's best and there were wins by Jamaican sprint stars, Yohan Blake, 100m 9.93, and Elaine Thompson's 200m 22.09.

21 **Kawasaki**, Japan. Golden GP. Liu Shiying improved the Asian javelin record to 66.47.

21 **European Race Walking Cup**, Podébrady, Czech Republic. Christopher Linke recorded 1:19:28 for his third successive win at 20k in 2017 and Antonella Palmisano was an impressive women's winner in 1:27:57. Spain won three of the five team awards,

25-27 **NCAA Regionals**, USA. The qualifying competitions for the NCAA Championships were held in Eastern and Western sections at Lexington and Austin. At Lexington Christian Coleman ran the 100m in 9.96 in his heat and 9.98 in his quarter-final before winning his 200m quarter in a world leading pb of 19.85. Next quickest was Jereem Richards in a big pb of 19.97. Fred Kerley improved the 400m collegiate record to 43.70 in Austin.

27 **European Clubs Cup**. Very sadly the 'A' group, planned for Mersin in Turkey was not held as an insufficient number of clubs confirmed their participation.

27 **Eugene**, USA. 43rd Prefontaine Classic (DL). Great rivals Christian Taylor and Will Claye had a terrific clash, Taylor winning with 18.11, the fourth longest jump in history, from Claye 18.05w (& 17.82). Mo Farah continued his dominance in the 5000m, winning in a world-leading 13:00.70 from Yomif Kejelcha 13:01.21 and Geoffrey Kamworor 13:01.35, Ronald Kwemoi won the Bowerman Mile in 3:49.04 with a last lap of 53.73 from Elijah Manangoi 3:49.08 and Timothy Cheruiyot 3:49.64, and Faith Kipyegon produced an equally dominant showing in the women's 1500m, having too much speed for her rivals on a final lap of 59.55 for 3:59.67 ahead of Hellen Obiri 4:00.46 and Laura Muir 4:00.47. There was a Diamond League record of 21.77 for the women's 200m by Tori Bowie, who was followed by Shaunae Miller-Uibo, Bahamas record 21.91, Elaine Thompson 21.98, Dafne Schippers 22.30 and Alyson Felix 22.33. Ryan Crouser put the shot 22.43, 72cm ahead of Tom Walsh, Mariya Lasitskene high jumped 2.03, and world-leading marks came from Omar McLeod, 110mh 13.01, Ashley Spencer, 400mh 53.38, and Celliphine Chespol whose 3000m

steeplechase time of 8:58.78 was an African, Commonwealth and world U20 record.

27-28 **Götzis**, Austria. 44th Hypo Meeting. Nafissatou Thiam shot to third on the world all-time list with 7013 points, the best by a woman for ten years with Carolin Schäfer 6836 taking second place and Laura Ikauniece-Admidina third with a Latvian record 6815. Damian Warner scored a world-leading 8591 to win the decathlon here for the third time. Eelco Sintnicolaas made a successful return from injury for second place with a Dutch record 8539, and Rico Freimuth was third with 8365. 15 men over 8000 points tied the most ever at Götzis, from 2000.

30-Jun 3 **Games of Small States of Europe**. Serravalle, San Marino.

June

2 **Andújar**, Spain. Yulimar Rojas produced world-leading triple jump marks with her last three jumps: 14.74, 14.82 and 14.96.

2-4 adidas Boost **Boston Games**, USA. The first two days featured track events at the Dilboy Stadium in Somerville, and the final day events on a special five-lane 200m straight track on a street in Boston. Tori Bowie won the 150m in 16.30, a time that bettered the previous world best on a straight track of 16.36 run by Allyson Felix at Manchester in 2013 (although FloJo ran 16.10 en route to her 200m world record at the 1988 Olympic Games). Other impressive straight track wins came at 200m from Wayde van Niekerk 19.84 and Shaunae Miller-Uibo 21.76. Muktar Edris won the 5000m in Somerville in 13:01.04.

3 **São Bernardo do Campo**: GP Brazil (WCM). Darlan Romani improved the South American shot record from 21.26 to 21.82.

3-4 **South American Junior Championships**, Leonora, Guyana.

5 **Prague**, Czech Republic. Jozef Odlozil Memorial. Antonio Alkana set an African record for 110m hurdles at 13.11 and Jakub Vadlejch threw the javelin 87.21.

7-10 **NCAA Championships**, Eugene, USA. Christian Coleman continued his impressive progress with a 100m/200m double. He ran a collegiate record 9.82 in his 100m semi but there were adverse winds in the finals won in 10.04 and 20.25. Fred Kerley maintained his unbeaten record for 2018, winning the 400m in 44.10 and anchoring Texas A&M to 4x400m victory with a 43.99 split. Even faster was 110mh winner Grant Holloway who ran a 43.88 final leg for Florida, who retained the men's team title with 61.5 points from Texas A&M 59.5 and Virginia 36, while Oregon 64 were the women's winners from Georgia 62.2 and USC 43, with the final results dependant on the final 4x400s. Doubles were also achieved by KeAndre Bates, LJ and TJ, and Filip Mihaljevic, SP and DT. Top women's marks came in the sprints from Mikiah Brisco 10.96 and Kyra Jefferson 22.02 and Raevyn Rogers at 800m, Keturah Orji at triple jump and Kendell Williams at heptathlon won third titles.

8 **Rome**, Italy. Golden Gala Pietro Mennea (DL). Sifan Hassan ran at 1500m in 3:56.22, clear of Winny Chebet 3:59.16 and Konstanze Klosterhalfen 3:59.30 with terrific depth as there was the fastest ever 17th place (4:08.04). Hellen Obiri set a Commonwealth and Kenyan record of 14:18.37 to come home alone in the 5000m as Genzebe Dibaba, who had been touted as going for the world record, faded to sixth. In the javelin Thomas Röhler beat Johannes Vetter 90.06 to 88.15 and in another important clash Yulimar Rojas beat Caterine Ibargüen 14.84 to 14.78.

10 **European Cup 10,000m**, Minsk, Belarus. Sara Moreira won the women's race for the third time (after 2011 and 2012).

10 **Szczecin**, Poland. The 63rd Kusocinski Memorial featured top throws, Andrius Gudzius, 68.16 discus, Pawel Fajdek, 80.43 hammer, and Anita Wlodarczyk, 77.07 hammer.

10 **Kingston**, Jamaica. Usain Bolt ran his last race in Jamaica in front of a 35,000 crowd with 10.03 for 100m, although Yohan Blake 9.97 and Akani Simbine 10.00 were faster in another race. Wayde van Niekerk ran a world-leading and South African record 19.84 for 200m.

10-11 **Hengelo**, Netherlands. 34th Fanny Blankers-Koen Games (WCM). Five world-leading marks were headed by a 2.04 high jump by Mariya Lasitskene, with 1500m times of 3:31.34 by Salah Mikhou and 3:56.14 by Sifan Hassan, and in 10,000m races, that were Ethiopian trials, 27:08.26 by Abadi Hadis and 30:40.87 by Gelete Burka. Luvo Manonga's 8.62 long jump meant he was over 8.60 for the fourth successive meeting.

13 **Turku**, Finland. 55th Paavo Nurmi Games. Elevated this year to a World Challenge Meeting, the javelin was as ever a great contest, Thomas Röhler winning with 88.26 from Johannes Vetter 87.88 and Keshorn Walcott 86.48, and Pawel Fajdek threw a world-leading 82.40 in the hammer. There was also a stadium record 65.03 by Tatyana Kholodovich in the women's javelin.

15 **Oslo**, Norway (DL). 52nd Bislett Games. Mutaz Essa Barshim cleared 2.38 in the high jump to add 1cm to the Bislett stadium record set by Javier Sotomayor back in 1989. There was no senior Dream Mile this year, but rather a 1500m that had an upset win in 3:34.17 by Jake Wightman, but there was an under-20 mile that was won in brilliant style by Jakob Ingebrigtsen in a world age-16 record of 3:56.29. That was great news for the locals as was Karsten Warholm's win in the 400m hurdles in a Norwegian record 48.25.

18 **Stockholm**, Sweden (DL). Andre De Grasse took advantage of a 4.8m/s following wind to win the 100m in 9.69w. This came just after a notable 1500m win by Timothy Cheruiyot in 3:30.77 and there were upsets in the discus events as Yaimi Pérez beat Sandra Perkovic 67.92 to 67.75 and Fedrick Dacres beat Daniel Ståhl 68.36 to 68.13.

22-25 **Jamaican Championships**, Kingston. As usual the sprint events took the headlines with Yohan Blake taking a double at 9.90 (his fastest time for five years) and 19.97, Elaine Thompson winning the women's 100m in 10.71 and Omar McLeod setting a Commonwealth record 12.90 for 110m hurdles.

22-25 **US Championships**, Sacramento. In very hot weather great performances at a wide range of events ensured that the US would have a strong team at the World Championships. Justin Gatlin handed Christian Coleman his first defeat of the year at 100m, 9.95 to 9.98, while Tori Bowie 10.94 dominated the women's 100m. Exceptional one-lap results included seven men under 44.8 for 400m, headed by Fred Kerley 44.03, Quanera Hayes was the women's winner in 49.72, and three women went under 53 secs in the hurdles: Dalilah Muhammad 52.64, Shamier Little 52.75 and Kori Carter 52.95 with the best-ever times for places 3-6, the last a world junior record 53.82 by Sydney McLaughlin. Will Claye topped a superb triple jump series with 17.91 as Christian Taylor, with a wild card entry for London and so only needing to compete, fouled his only attempt. There were world-leading marks in the field from Sam Kendricks, who became the 21st pole vaulter to clear 6m, and in the shot from Ryan Crouser, 22.65 the world's best since 2003, coming from behind with the last throw to beat Joe Kovacs 22.35, and Raven Saunders, 19.76.

24-24 **Kenyan Trials**, Nairobi. Ronald Kwemoi, 1500m 3:30.39, and Emmanuel Korir, 800m 1:43.86, headed classy middle-distance races and there were very impressive times at high altitude as four men, headed by Geoffrey Kamworor 27:35.9 (56.5 last lap) broke 27:50 at 10,000m.

23-25 **European Team Championships**, Villeneuve d'Ascq, France. With Russia not allowed to compete, German regained the title comfortably with 321.5 points from Poland 294.5, France 270 and Britain 269. The British men set a record for European Cup or Team competition with 38.08 for 4x100m. Regrettably the insulting format of just three attempts in the throws and horizontal jumps and just the top four then awarded one extra trial was continued. Also in the high jump and pole vault, athletes were eliminated if they had four failures during the competition as well as if they had three successive failures at any height.

The First League, held at Vaasa, Finland, was won by Sweden; the Second League at Tel Aviv, Israel, by Hungary; the Third League, at Marsa, Malta, by Luxembourg.

24-25 **Ratingen**, Germany. Rico Freimuth with a pb score of 8663, headed three decathletes over 8450 points in the annual IAAF Challenge multi-events meeting and Carolin Schäfer won the heptathlon by a margin of 484 points, 6667 to Nadine Visser 6183.

28 **Ostrava**, Czech Republic. 55th Golden Spike (WCM). Wayde van Niekerk stole the show by storming to 30.81 at 300m, a powerful display that bettered Michael Johnson's altitude assisted world best of 30.85 that had stood since 2000 and Usain Bolt's 30.97 meeting record as well. Isaac Makwala was second in 31.44. Bolt himself competed on this track for the ninth time, winning at 100m in 10.09, and other Olympic champions to excel were Christian Taylor with 17.57 for triple jump and Mo Farah 27:12.09 for 10,000m. Thomas Röhler dominated the javelin with a 91.53 in the second round and 91.02 in the third. IAAF Hammer Throw Challenge hammer competitions were held the precious day with Anita Wlodarczyk dominating as usual with 79.72 for her 37th straight victory and Pawel Fajdek adding more than a metre to his own world lead with 83.44, the third farthest of his career.

29 **Sollentuna**. Sweden. Highlight of the Folksam Grand Prix meeting was a 71.29 discus throw by Daniel Ståhl that improved the Swedish record from the 71.26 thrown by Ricky Bruch in 1984; it took Ståhl to ninth on the world all-time list.

29- Jul 2 **African Junior Championships**, Tiemcen, Algeria. Easily the best performance was 20.22 for 200m by Clarence Munyai, 0.89 ahead of the runner-up.

30- Jul 2 **Italian Championships**, Trieste. Chiara Rosa won her 13th successive shot title.

July

1 **Paris**, France. The DL meeting moved this year from the Stade de France in Saint-Denis to the more intimate Paris venue of Charléty (20,000 capacity). Two Olympic champions limped away from their events – Ruth Jebet after 4th in 9:10.95 in the 3000m steeplechase won by Beatrice Chepkoech in 9:01.69, and Omar McLeod who suffered cramp in his calves and came last in the 100m hurdles in which victory went to his compatriot Ronald Levy in a pb 13.05. Another champion Faith Kipyegon ran well at 1500m but was beaten 3:57.10 to 3:57.51 by Sifan Hassan. A strong finishing burst took Muktar Edris to victory in the 3000m in 7:32.31 from Ronald Kwemoi 7:32.88 and Yomif Kejelcha 7:33.37.

1-2 **European Combined Events Team Championships**, Tallinn, Estonia. Ukraine won, with 18 year-old Alina Shukh winning the women's heptathlon with 6208, from Estonia, for whom Janel Oiglane won the decathlon with 8170. The First and Second League were held at Monzón, Spain and won respectively by the Netherlands and Lithuania.

1-2 **UK Championships**, Birmingham. Highlights included a UK 5000m walk record of 18:43.28 by Tom Bosworth with 20 year-old Callum Wilkinson also inside Bosworth's old record of 19:00.73, and a 1.96 high jump by another 20 year-old, Morgan Lake. Nethaneel Mitchell-Blake ran 200m in 20.18 to break John Regis's 1987 championship record of 20.25 with Danny Talbot second in a pb 20.20.

1-2 **IAU World 24 Hours Championships**, Belfast, GBR. The women's race featured unprecedented times in depth. The winner Patrycia Bereznowska added 1.65k to her own world record with 258.339km and the next four went to 6th, 7th, 8th and 14th on the world all-time list as five women in one race running more than 240k beat the previous best of two. There was also record depth in the men's race with four over 260k, headed by Yoshihiko Ishikawa 267.566k.

1-2 **Zhukovskiy**, Russia. 59th Znamenskiy Memorial. Aleksandr Menkov long jumped 8.32.

3-4 **Székesfehérvár,** Hungary. 7th István Gyulai Memorial Meeting. Kendra Harrison beat most of the world's best by a huge margin as her 12.28 for 100m hurdles, her third best ever, was the year's best, and the men's sprint hurdles was also quick as Omar McLeod beat Sergey Shubenkov 12.96 to 13.01.

6 **Lausanne**, Switzerland. Athletissima (DL). Wayde van Niekerk ran a Diamond League record 43.62 for 400m, a time that was to remain the best recorded in 2017. Behind him the Botswana pair of Baboloki Thebe and Isaac Makwala ran 44.02 (pb) and 44.08. A further Diamond League record was set when Mariya Lasitskene cleared 2.06 on her second attempt in the high jump and further world leads came from Muktar Edris, 12:55.53 for 5000m as 17 year-old Selemon Barega was 2nd in 12:55.58, and Sara Kolak, who extended her Croatian javelin record to 66.65 and 68.43 after a great duel with Barbora Spotáková who had opened with 67.40. All ten finishers in the women's 800 metres broke 2 minutes, with Francine Niyonsaba the winner in 1:56.82. Sam Kendricks maintained his unbeaten pole vault record in 2017, winning on count-back as Pawel Wojciechowski also cleared the same height of 5.93, a Polish record. In just his third competition since 2015 Pedro Pablo Pichardo triple jumped 17.60 and beat Christian Taylor 17.49. There were best ever marks for places 7 and 8 in the shot while up front Ryan Crouser beat Tom Walsh 22.39 to 21.97. An athlete who won very easily was Genzebe Dibaba, back in form with 4:16.05 for the mile.

6 **Sotteville-lès-Rouen**, France. Yaimi Pérez came from behind Sandra Perkovic (68.30 and two more throws over 67.80) to throw a pb 69.19 in the last round of a discus clash between the world's top two women.

6-9 22nd **Asian Championships**, Bhubaneswar, India. The one new championships record was a 85.23 javelin throw by Neeraj Chopra, but all too many top Asian athletes were absent. Ehsan Hadadi's discus win with 64.54 was his fifth (first in 2005) to tie the men's record for any event and Dilshod Nazarov won the hammer with 76.69 for his fourth title and seventh medal to go with his three Asian Games titles.

8 **European Mountain Running Championships**, Kamnik, Slovenia. Italy took their 22nd men's team win in the 23 years of the event (21st successive) and Britain was the women's team winner.

8-9 **German Championships**, Erfurt. Johannes Vetter had a superb series in the javelin topped with 89.35 and 89.22 to be well ahead of Thomas Röhler 85.24. Robert Harting won his tenth discus title with 65.65. The fast-rising young star Konstanze Klosterhalfen ran away with the 1500m, her 3:59.58 being 11.13 ahead of the runner-up and Gesa Felicitas Krause was a class apart and enjoyed a 31.78 winning margin with 9:25.81 in the 3000m steeplechase.

9 **London (Olympic Stadium)**, GBR. Müller Anniversary Games (DL). Tom Bosworth campaigned to have a walk on the programme and rewarded the organisers and crowd by recording 5:31.08 for 1 mile, a rarely contested event, but improving the world best from 5:36.9 in 1990, Bosworth's year of birth. Kendra Harrison had set a world record here the previous year and again excelled to win the 100m hurdles in 12.39 from a resurgent Sally Pearson 12.48. Mo Farah won the 3000m in 7:35.15 and home fans enjoyed a Scottish 1 mile record of 4:18.03 from Laura Muir, but she was unable to hold off Hellen Obiri who strode on to a Commonwealth record 4:16.56. Behind them there were the best ever times for places 4-14 in a women's mile. World-leading marks came from Nijel Amos, 800m 1:43.18, and Alyson Felix, 400m 49.65. The remarkable Aries Merritt returned to the scene of his Olympic triumph and won the 110m hurdles in a season's best 13.09 and Barbora Spotáková gained immediate revenge over Sara Kolak after Lausanne, winning here 68.26 to 67.83.

11 **Luzern**, Switzerland. 31st Spitzen Leichtathletik meeting. From a previous javelin best of 89.68, Johannes Vetter made four successive improvements – 90.75, 91.06, 93.06 and 94.44, the last only exceeded (four times) by the great Jan Zelezny. Thomas Röhler again

threw well but his 89.45 left him five metres behind.

12-16 **World Youth (U18) Championships**, Nairobi, Kenya. This was the final edition of the IAAF World U18 Championships, the IAAF having determined that continental youth championships will suffice in future. Jordan Díaz set a world U18 record of 17.30 in the triple jump and Brittany Anderson ran the fastest ever girls' 100m hurdles time of 12.72, but aided by a strong tailwind of 4.1 m/s. There were other championship records by Dejour Russell, 110mh (91.4cm) 13.04, Yaroslava Mahuchikh, women's HJ (=) 1.92, and Marisleisys Duarthe, 500g javelin 62.92. The penultimate day attracted nearly 88,000 spectators – 37,600 in the morning and 50,300 in the evening – making it the best-attended session of any age-group athletics event in history. Australia, Canada, Great Britain, Japan, New Zealand, Switzerland and the USA did not send teams due to security concerns

13-16 **European U23 Championships**, Bydgoszcz, Poland. Polish shot putting prodigy Konrad Bukowiecki set three championship records as, after 21.26 in qualifying, he opened the final with 21.44 and improved to 21.59 in the final round. There were also championship records by Yasemin Can with 31:39.80 for 10,000m and, two days later, 15:01.67 for 5000m, and by Karsten Warholm, 48.37 for 400m hurdles. Germany headed the medal and points tables from Britain and France.

14 **Madrid**, Spain (WCM). In very hot weather (c. 40°C) and benefitting from the 640m altitude, Isaac Makwala became the first man to better 20 seconds and 44 seconds on one day. He won the A 400m race at 8:38 pm in 43.92, his second fastest ever time and only a little over an hour later, at 9:53pm, he won the 200m in 19.77, a 2017 world-leading time. 18 year-old Maykel Massó, was another to take advantage of the conditions, including a +2.0 tail wind, as he leapt to a CAC junior record 8.33 in the long jump, just 2cm short of the world junior record.

14-16 **French Championships**, Marseille. Mélina Robert-Michon won her 17th discus title in 18 years from 2000 and Renaud Lavillenie won his sixth pole vault with 5.80.

15-16 76th **Balkan Championships**, Novi Pazar, Serbia. Romania topped the points table.

16 **Padua, Italy**. (EA Classic**)**. Mariya Lasitskene cleared 2.00, her 12th high jump competition of 2017 at this height or higher.

16 **Rabat**, Morocco (DL). Ryan Crouser provided the field event highlight at the Meeting International Mohammed VI d'Athletisme as he improved throughout the competition from 22.21 to 22.44 and 22.47 for his tenth successive victory. In second place O'Dayne Richards added 27cm to his Jamaican record with 21.96. Elaine Thompson won her 14th successive 100m win, but with 10.87 she was only 0.03 ahead of Marie Josée Ta Lou, and Shaunae Miller-Uibo won the 400m in 49.80 by more than a second.

18 **Bellinzona**, Switzerland. Sandra Perkovic improved her Croatian record from 71.08 in 2014 to 71.41 on her second throw at the Galà dei Castelli meeting. This was the best women's discus throw since 1972 and she also threw over 70m (70.05) in the final round.

20-23 **European U20 Championships**, Grosseto, Italy. World U20 records were set by the German women's 4x100m quartet, whose 43.27 in a heat (43.44 in the final) took 0.02 off the mark set by the USA in 2006, and a 8415 points score by Nicklas Kaul in the (junior specification) decathlon. There were also championship records from Maksim Nedasekov, who added 3cm to Vladimir Yashchenko's 1977 high jump mark with a third-time 2.33 clearance, Armand Duplantis, 5.65 in the pole vault, and Hlib Piskunov, 81.75 with the 6kg hammer. A great women's competition came in the heptathlon, Alina Shukh beating Geraldine Ruckstuhl, 6381 to 6357. The prodigiously talented Jakob Ingebrigtsen won both 5000m and 3000m steeplechase but his bid to win three titles had been foiled when he fell with 300m to go in the 1500m final (he got up to finish 8th).

21 **Herculis, Monaco** (DL). Caster Semenya broke the South African record and Diamond League record that she had set here in 2016 by 0.06 with 1:55.27 for 800m, with Francine Niyonsaba again 2nd in a Burundi record 1:55.47 and Ajee' Wilson 3rd in an American record 1:55.61. The top races for men were the 400m in which Wayde van Niekerk beat Isaac Makwala 43.73 to 43.84 and the 1500m won by Elijah Manangoi 3:28.80 from Timothy Cheruiyot 3:29.10. Hellen Obiri again showed imperious form taking the 3000m in 8:23.14 as the nine women who followed her home all set pbs. In another great battle Catherine Ibargüen's 14.86 triple jump was just 3cm ahead of Yulimar Rojas's best and Marita Lasitskene maintained her marvellous high jumping form with 2.05. Evan Jager's 8:01.29 was to remain the world's best 3000m steeplechase time of the year and, while his opposition was not of the very best, Usain Bolt won the 100m in 9.95, 0.03 ahead of Isiah Young.

21-23 **Polish Championships**, Bialystok. Anita Wlodarczyk was over 80m in the women's hammer for the sixth time with 80.79 but there was was an upset in the men's event as Wojciech Nowicki beat Pawel Fajdek 80.47 to 78.64. Michal Haratyk produced a pb 21.53 to win the shot by 1.32m from Konrad Bukowiecki.

21-23 **Pan-American Junior Championships**, Trujillo, Peru. The US 4x400m team took 0.76 off the world junior record with 3:00.33. Jamal Walton retained his 400m title with 44.99.

22 **Heusden-Zolder**, Belgium. KBC Night of Athletics. There was the usual strong depth of times in the distance races, instanced by 15 pbs (and 26 season's bests) from the 30 men who broke 13:40 (15 sub 13:20) in the first two of the six men's 5000m races.

22-23 **Spanish Championships**, Barcelona. Ruth Beitia needed just 1.86m to win her 30th Spanish high jump title (14 outdoors, 16 indoors) and Berta Castells won her 14th at hammer.

23-27 8th **Francophone Games**, Abidjan, Ivory Coast.

28-30 **Russian Championships**, Zhukovskiy. Top marks came from Valeriy Pronkin, whose 79.32 consolidated his third place world ranking in 2017 at the hammer, and Aleksandra Gulyayeva, 1:58.34 for 800m. Artyom Primak had a winning double with 8.22 for the long jump and 17.17 for the triple jump and Mariya Lasitskene maintained her unbeaten record for 2017 with 1.96 in the high jump.

29 **Cetniewo**, Poland, Anita Wlodarczyk won the hammer with 82.87, just 11cm short of her world record and Michal Haratyk put the shot 21.88.

30 14th **WMRA Long Distance World Mountain Running Championships**, Premana, Italy. The men's race was a triumph for Uganda as their runners took the first three places with Viktor Kiplangat the winner and Oscar Chelimo led their junior team to victory. The USA were the women's team winners and Lucy Wambui Murigi of Kenya the individual champion.

August

4-13 **World Championships**, London. *See Championships section earlier.*

15 **Warsaw**, Poland. Kamila Skolimowska Memorial meeting. Renaud Lavillenie cleared a season's best of 5.91 in the pole vault and Tomás Stanek matched his Czech shot record with 22.01, beating Ryan Crouser by 33cm. In the hammer competitions that ended the meeting Anita Wlodarczyk, with 79.80, took her win-streak to 42 and Pawel Fajdek was back over 80m at 81.50.

20 **Birmingham**, GBR (DL). Mutaz Essa Barshim went to the top of the 2017 world lists with 2.40 in the high jump. The 1-2 in the women's 3000m both set national records – Sifan Hassan 8:28.90 and Konstanze Klosterhalfen 8:29.89. Elaine Thompson, recovered from the illness that ruined her World Champs bid, won the 100m in 10.93 into a 1.2m wind with Marie-Josée Ta Lou (10.94 heat) close behind in 10.97. There was a British winner of the Emsley Carr Mile for the first time since 2005 as Jake Wightman won in 3:54.92, 0.09 ahead of Chris O'Hare, and Mo Farah bade farewell to British track action with a 3000m win in 7:38.64.

22-26 29th **South East Asia Games**, Kuala Lumpur, Malaysia. 13 men and 7 women retained their titles from the previous Games two years ago.

24 **Zürich**, Switzerland. Weltklasse (DL). For the first time two women broke 9 minutes in the 3000m steeplechase as Ruth Jebet made up for her World Champs disappointment with a win in 8:55.29, a time bettered only by her 2016 world record, and Beatrice Chepkoech was 2nd in 8:59.84 with Norah Tanui taking over 10 secs from her pb for 3rd in 9:05.81. This was one of 16 Diamond Race titles decided here on a cool evening. Mo Farah ended his track career with a dramatic 5000m victory, beating World champion Muktar Edris by 0.04 in 13:06.05. After their exciting contests in 2017 Yulimar Rojas and Caterine Ibargüen had to settle for 2nd and 3rd behind Olga Rypakova, who won the triple jump with 14.55. Barbora Spotáková won her fifth Diamond trophy with 65.554 in the javelin. The women's pole vault, a non-DL event held the previous evening at the Hauptbahnhof was won on count-back by Ekateríni Stefanídi from Sandi Morris as both cleared 4.87 on their first attempts,

25-27 **Eberstadt**, Germany. Mutaz Essa Barshim 2.40 and Marie-Laurence Jungfleisch were the winners at the annual high jump competition. Second places were taken by Danil Lysenko 2.38 and Kamila Licwinko 1.96.

27 **Berlin**, Germany. 76th ISTAF (WCM). Caster Semenya set a world best for 600m with 1:21.77 (previous record 1:22.63 by Ana Fidelia Quirot in 1997) with Ajee' Wilson running a US record 1:22.39. Norah Tanui made further improvement at steeplechase to 9:03.70 followed by Gesa Felicitas Krause who smashed her German record with 9:11.85. Another German woman went one better as Konstanze Klosterhalfen won the 1500m in 3:58.92.

23-28 29th **World University Games**, Taipei, Taiwan. The highlight was the javelin competition in which when two men threw over 90m – just the second time this has ever happened. The Taiwanese pair Huang Shih-Feng and Cheng Chao-Tsun were 2nd and 3rd with their fourth round throws of 86.64 (pb) and 84.37 respectively, but then Cheng, whose previous pb was 86.92 in April, produced a massive Asian record of 91.36 in the last round to which Andreas Hofmann, leading until then with 88.59, replied with 91.07 to add 2.28m to his pb. There was also a Games record 76.85 by the fast-improving Malwina Kopron in the women's hammer, while Pawel Fajdek won a fourth hammer title (biennially from 2011) with 79.16. The Santos brothers were both winners – Luguelín at 400m in 45.24 and Juander at 400m hurdles in 48.65.

29 **Zagreb**, Croatia. 68th Boris Hanzekovic Memorial (WCM). Local star Sandra Perkovic threw over 70m twice as her last two discus throws were 70.83 and 70.44.

September

1 **Brussels**, Belgium. 41st Van Damme Memorial. Shaunae Miller-Uibo, who had won at 200m in Zürich, added a second DL title as she won the 400m in the year's fastest time of 49.46. Second placed Salwa Eid Naser made further progress to 49.88 for third on the all-time junior list. Elaine Thompson ended her season on a high note by winning a second consecutive Diamond Trophy in the 100m and steeplechaser Conseslus Kipruto edged past Soufiane El Bakkali to win his third Trophy in a time of 8:04.73. Better still was Christian Taylor, as with 17.49, he secured his sixth successive Trophy at triple jump, leaving him just one adrift of Renaud Lavillenie in the overall list, and Sandra Perkovic whose discus throw of 68.82 won her a women; record sixth consecutive Diamond Trophy. Perhaps the best race came in the women's 1500m in which Faith Kipyegon beat Sifan Hassan 3:57.04 to 3:57.22. Noah Lyles, in only his fourth 200m of the year produced a strong finish in the outside lane of the 200m for a narrow victory in 20.00 ahead of Ameer Webb and World champion Ramil Guliyev, who ran season's bests of 20.01 and 20.02 respectively. The greatest breakthrough by a winner came in the men's shot held in a city square the previous day as Darrell Hill threw 22.44 from a previous best of 21.91, and finished 7cm ahead of Ryan Crouser.

2-3 **Finland v Sweden**, Stockholm. Sweden had clear wins over Finland 216-188 for men and 232.5-177.5 for women in the annual Finnkampen.

2-7 **Chinese National Games**, Tianjin. Zhang Wenxiu won the women's hammer for the fourth time, following wins in 2003, 2009 and 2013, with a season's best 75.48.

9 **DécaNation**, Angers, France. The USA won with 122 points from France 103 and Poland 95.

9 **Prague**, Czech Republic. Joyciline Jepkosgei became the first woman to run 10k on the roads in under 30 minutes with 29:43, going through 5k in a world road best of 14:32, and finishing 23 secs ahead of Fancy Chemutai. Men's winner Benard Kimeli set a U20 world best of 27:10.

10 36th **Great North Run, Newcastle to South Shields**, GBR. Sir Mo Farah had his fourth win in the race in 60:06 and Marty Keitany beat Vivian Cheruiyot 65:59 to 67:44 in the women's race. There was a record number of 43,127 finishers from 140 countries.

10 **New York. 5th Avenue Mile**. Nick Willis won the race for the fourth time (after 2008, 2013 and 2015) in 3:51.3 on the slightly (8.23m) downhill course with 18 more men under 4 minutes. Jenny Simpson won for the sixth time in seven years and her 4:16.6 tied the race record set by PattiSue Plumer in 1990; 16 women broke 4:30.

16-17 **Talence**, France. Wins by Damien Warner and Anouk Vetter took them to second places in the IAAF World Combined Events Challenge behind Rico Freimuth and Carolin Schafer who had already sealed their first places.

17 **Copenhagen**, Denmark. Abraham Cheroben took eight seconds off his Bahrain record to win the half marathon in 58:40 for third on the world all-time list. There was terrific standard in depth as including the bests ever times for places 2 and 3 from Jorum Okombo 58:48 and Alex Korio 58:51. Nine of the top ten men and 17 of the top 20 women set pbs in the perfect conditions.

18-20 **Asian Indoor Games**, Ashgabat, Turkmenistan. Olga Rypakova was the top competitor, winning long jump 6.43 and triple jump 14.32, 18 Asian AA member federations did not enter teams so standards in several events were low.

24 BMW **Berlin Marathon**, Germany. Eliud Kipchoge confirmed his position as the world's number one marathon runner by taking a dramatic win. He ran the world's fastest time of 2017, 2:03:32 after coming from behind in difficult weather conditions, with rain and high humidity that cost him the chance of getting the world record after the lead pack had run the first half in 61:29. Guye Adola was second in 2:03:46, the fastest debut ever recorded on a record eligible course. The 2016 winner Kenenisa Bekele dropped out at 22k complaining afterwards about the poor conditions, particularly the very wet road, as did Wilson Kipsang at 30k. Gladys Cherono was the women's winner in 2:20:23 from Ruti Aga 2:20:41 and Valary Aiyabei 2:20:53. There were 39,101 finishers.

24-27 **Wuzhong**, China. The 4-day tour had high-class fields contesting walking races at 20k, 10k, 10.5k and 10k. Overall winners were (men) Dane Bird-Smith 3:27:30 and (women) Antonella Palmisano 3:44:45.

October

8 40th **Chicago Marathon**, USA. Galen Rupp became the first US male winner since 2002, surging over the final three miles to win in 2:09:20, 28 sec clear of the 2016 winner Abel Kirui. The women's race, however, had the best display of individual brilliance, with Tirunesh Dibaba winning in 2:18:31 from Brigid Kosgei 2:20:22 and Jordan Hasay 2:20:57, excellent

times in warm and windy weather. There was a record 44,511 finishers (22,908 men and 21,603 women).

15 **Amsterdam Marathon**, Netherlands. Lawrence Cherono 2:05:09 led five men under 2:06 and eleven under 2:09, while Tadelech Bekele was a clear women's winner in 2:21:53.

22 **Valencia**, Spain. Joyciline Jepkosgei took a second off her world half marathon record with 64:51, after falling behind the schedule that she had set in Prague in March as she was timed at 30:08 for 10k, 45:58 15k and 61:29 20k; second was Fancy Chemutai in 65:36. Abraham Cheroben secured his third win in four years in this race in 59:11.

29 **Frankfurt-am-Main**, Germany. Winners at the 36th Mainova Frankfurt Marathon were Shura Tola 2:05:50 and Vivian Cheruiyot 2:23:35.

November

5 47th TCS **New York City Marathon**, USA. A 4:31 25th mile helped Geoffrey Kamworor to win in 2:10:53, 3 seconds ahead of Wilson Kipsang, after a pedestrian early pace in cool and blustery conditions. Shalane Flanagan became the first American women's winner for 40 years in 2:26:53. She pulled clear from Mary Keitany and Mamitu Daska from three miles out. There were 50,766 finishers (29,678 men and 21,088 women) from 51,365 starters.

12 **Shanghai**, China. Roza Dereje 2:22:43 and Stephen Mokoka 2:08:35 won as they had done in 2016 and Mokoka had also won in 2013 and 2014. Second in the women's race was Lydia Cheromei, in her first marathon since 2013, with a women's over-40 record of 2:23:31. She had been the youngest ever world junior cross-country champion at age 13 in 1991!

19 **New Delhi**, India. Winners at the 12th Airtel Delhi Half Marathon were Berhanu Legesse 59:46 and Almaz Ayana, in her debut at the distance, 67:12.

21-25 18th **Bolivar Games**, Santa Marta, Colombia. Nine new Games records were set.

December

3 **Fukuoka**, Japan. Sondre Nordstad Moen took 4:19 off his Norwegian record and smashed the European record as he won the 71st Fukuoka Marathon in 2:05:48.

10 **European Cross-Country Championships**, Samorín-Cilistov, Slovakia. A record total of 560 athletes contested the seven championship races – from a record 37 nations. The two senior races were again won by Kenyan allegiance transferees competing for Turkey – Yasemin Can retaining her women's title and Kaan Kigen Özgilen the men's. Jakob Ingebrigtsen, who will still be a junior (U20) in 2018 and 2019, retained his U20 title. Britain again topped the medal table even before their victory in the new mixed relay event.

23 **Minsk**, Belarus. Mariya Lasitskene maintained her brilliant high jump form throughout the year with 2.00 here – and a close attempt at 2.08.

Retired in 2017/18

Men: Sebastian Bayer GER, Jamie Bowie GBR, Dwain Chambers GBR, Libor Charfreitag SVK, Willem Coertzen RSA, Bobby Curtis USA, Lee Emanuel GBR, Chris Erickson AUS, Iñaki Gómez CAN, Trey Hardee USA, Sergey Kirdyapkin RUS, Anton Kucmin SVK, Steve Lewis GBR, Markus Münch GER, Ross Murray GBR, David Oliver USA, Ruggero Pertile ITA, Jeff Porter USA, Robin Schembera GER, Retu Amara Schenkel SUI., Thomas Schmitt GER, René Stauss GER, Shinji Takahira JPN, Ingmar Vos NED, Shaquille Walker USA, Jeremy Wariner USA, Andrew Wheatibg USA, Rhys Williams GBR, Ryan Wilson USA, Johan Wissman SWE, Yves Zellweger SUI, Zhang Peimeng CHN.

Women: Ruth Beitia ESP, Lashinda Demus USA, Josefina Eisler GER, Bridget Franek USA, Marie Gayot FRA, Britney Henry USA, Carmelita Jeter USA, Lornah Kiplagat NED, Lucia Klocová Hrivnak SVK, Molly Ludlow USA, Barbara Madejczyk POL, Jessica Martin GBR, Kelly Massey GBR, Yuliya Nesterenko BLR, Jennifer Oeser GER, Christine Ohuruogu GBR, Maren Orth (née Kock) GER, Alexandra Plaza GER, Denisa Rosolová CZE, Goldie Sayers GBR, Risa Shigetomo JPN, Austra Skujyte LTU, Risa Takenaka JPN, Inna Weit GER, Zsenia Zadorina RUS, Zhang Wenxiu CHN

Transfer of Nationality/Allegiance

Of athletes who have made world lists

Name	*From*	*To*	*Noted*	*Eligible*
Men				
Mohsen Anani	EGY	TUN	1.1.17	30.3.17
Yaser Salem Bagharab	YEM	QAT	26.4.17	
Kevin Chelimo	KEN	USA	23.5.17	
Alexis Copello	CUB	AZE	26.4.16	24.4.17
Melvin Echard	USA	GRN	5.10.16	6.10.17
Dawit Fikadu	ETH	BRN	31.12.15	30.3.17
Miguel Francis	ANT	GBR	24.9.16	30.3.17
Derara Hurisa	BRN	ETH	3.5.16	4.5.17
Haron Kiptoo Lagat	KEN	USA	16.10.16	
Luke Lennon-Ford	GBR	IRL	5.1.16	30.3.17
Yunier Pérez	CUB	ESP	17.11.17	
Women				
Maggie Barrie	USA	SLE	25.7.17	
Olivia Ekponé	NGR	USA	17.1.17	30.3.17
Violah Jepchumba	KEN	BRN	1.7.16	2.7.17
Lyudmila Lyakhovich Kovalenko	UKR	BLR	2.11.15	30.3.17

The IAAF have frozen the consideration of athletes wanting to transfer national eligibility pending further consideration of this issue.

ATHLETES OF 2017

By Peter Matthews

FOR THE FIRST time since 1907 (!) no world record was set in a standard men's event in 2017. That is not to say however, that there was any diminution in the standards at the top, but further notice as to what a rare commodity a world record is these days – and it was also the case that the major outdoor event of the year, the World Championships, was held in temperate weather in London rather than in the heat at so many such meetings have been staged in recent years. Two performances are, however, of special note – as Wayde van Niekerk ran 300m in 30.81, to improve Michael Johnson's world best by 0.04, and Eliud Kipchoge amazingly took just 2:00:25 to cover the marathon distance although this was under highly irregular conditions in the Nike sub2 project on Monza race track.

Although he did not run as fast at 400m this year as in 2016, van Niekerk retained his position as the world's top 400m runner, winning his third successive global title and also ran that brilliant 300m and had just one loss in six 200m competitions. Kipchoge remained the top marathon runner, although he had just one true race in 2017 – running the year's fastest marathon time to win in Berlin in 2:03:32. Mention should also be made of Yohann Diniz, whose 3:33:12 for 50k walk at the World Championships had only ever been bettered by his own world record – and he won by the huge margin of 8:05.

Mo Farah vied with van Niekerk as the top male track athlete of the year. He won his third World 10,000m title in brilliant style, but could not quite complete the double at 5000m.

Selections for World Top Ten

	PJM	TFN	AI
*Mutaz Essa Barshim	1	1	1
Sam Kendricks	2	2	4
*Mo Farah	3	7	3
*Wayde van Niekerk	4	4	2
Luvo Manyonga	5	3	6
Yohann Diniz	6		10
Pawel Fajdek	7	6	7
Kevin Mayer	8	-	9
Johannes Vetter	9	10	5
Eliud Kipchoge	10	8	8
Christian Taylor	-	5	-
Omar McLeod	-	9	

** IAAF finalists, Barshim was their athlete of the year.*
Karsten Warholm was IAAF Rising Star of the Year.

Muktar Edris narrowly beat him in London, but Farah returned 12 days later to reverse that result in the Diamond League (DL) final in Zürich. Farah had three wins in four races at 5000m, won all three at 3000m, both at 10,0000m and his one half marathon, with a second at Eagle Rock in his one 1500m race.

Field eventers compiled the most perfect records as Mutaz Essa Barshim won all his 11 high jump competitions, Sam Kendricks all 18 at pole vault, and Luvo Manyonga all 9 at long jump with five jumps in four events over 8.60 compared to 8.49 by the next best athlete. Pawel Fajdek won 15 of 16 at hammer with the top ten performances of 2017 (22 when including all marks in a series, all over 80.50m). While not obtaining such dominance as he engaged in great rivalry with compatriot Thomas Röhler, Johannes Vetter threw the javelin 93.88, second only to Jan Zelezny on the world-all-time list. Christian Taylor also had another great year, with nine wins and two second places at triple jump, and, discounting those at which he only contested a selection of events, Kevin Mayer won both his multi-event competitions, clearly heading the world lists for indoor heptathlon to take the European Indoor title and decathlon to take the World title.

While it was a close decision, Barshim swept the polls for top place. He jumped 2.40 at Birmingham DL and Eberstadt – and was a clear winner each time, with Danil Lysenko getting closest, 2cm behind at Eberstadt, and Barshim's average winning margin was 8cm over his 11 events. He was also the most successful Diamond League competitor, winning at six of the seven meetings.

My top ten rankings are shown for each event – including indoor form (but also just on outdoor form where relevant), The rationale follows the well-developed system pioneered by Drs. Roberto Quercetani and Don Potts in *Track and Field News* from 1947. As usual the most difficult problems come from athletes with thin seasons or those who have been good for just part of the season, but the World Championships (Worlds) clearly provided the main focus, followed by the Diamond League meetings (with finals at Zürich and Brussels). However, not all athletes get the opportunity to contest DL meetings and these are dominated by the globetrotting professionals. These meetings regularly match a high proportion of top-ranked athletes and one can thus most readily judge form between them and get valuable win-loss records. But it has to be realised that a particular DL or Grand Prix event may not be especially valued by athletes just because they are up against top names nearly as much as a championship that provides a major target.

100 Metres

USAIN BOLT FINISHED his international career by running exclusively at 100m in 2017, but was restricted by injury to just three competitions. He won in Kingston and Ostrava, and although twice sub-10 at the World Championships, could manage only 3rd in the final, having to yield to Justin Gatlin, whom he had just held off the previous year at the Olympics, and the new star Christian Coleman. Then Bolt's marvellous career ended when he pulled up with a hamstring injury on the final leg of the sprint relay. Nothing can detract, however, from the majesty of his career achievements.

Gatlin, four and a half years older than Bolt, returned to the top ranking he had held in 2005 and 2014. Although 4th in Doha and Zürich and 5th in Eugene, Gatlin won five of his eight 100m competitions including the US and Worlds in both of which Coleman was 2nd for the latter's only losses at the event. Coleman's 9.82 in his semi at the NCAAs (before winning the final in 10.04 into a 2.1 wind) was easily the fastest wind-legal time of the year with Yohan Blake next fastest at 9.90, to win the Jamaican title. Blake went on to World 4th, his only loss in his six competitions. The year's fastest time under any conditions came at the Stockholm DL meeting when Andre De Grasse rode a +4.8 wind to 9.69w from Ben Youssef Meité 9.84. De Grasse was coming into top form but was unable to compete after June due to a hamstring injury. He was involved in the year's fastest DL race – when Ronnie Baker won in Eugene in 9.86w from Su Bingtian 9.92, Chijindu Ujah 9.95, De Grasse 9.96, Gatlin 9.97 and Michael Rodgers 9.98. Baker had two legal sub-10 times but after 6th in his semi at the US Champs did not run again until 3rd in the DL final in Zürich behind Ujah and Meité with Gatlin 4th, Isiah Young 5th and Akani Simbine 6th. Simbine had a strong, consistent season and matched Coleman with nine legal sub-10 times (five at high altitude) and he was 5th at the Worlds, a place ahead of lightly raced Jimmy Vicaut. Ujah was disappointed to miss the World final with 4th in his semi, but had further big wins in Rome, London, Rabat and Birmingham and was 3-0 v Meité and 1-1 v Simbine and De Grasse. Completing the World final were 7th Reece Prescod (UK champion) and 8th Su. Asafa Powell had hoped to achieve his target of 100 sub-10 times but had a best of 10.08.

Most times at 10.00/10.05 or faster: Coleman 9+1w/13+1w, Simbine 9/12, Gatlin 5+1w/8+1w; Blake 5/8, Meité 3+1w/6+2w, Bolt, Forte 3/4; I Young 3+1w/3+1w, Ujah 2+2w/6+2w, Baker 2+1w/5+1w, Kiryu 1/4, Belcher 1/3+1w, Vicaut, van Niekerk 1/3; Burrell 1+2w, Bacon 1+1w/3+2w, Pérez 1+1w/3+1w, Rodgers, Roto 1+1w/2+1w, De Grasse 2w/1+2w.

1. Gatlin, 2. Coleman, 3. Bolt, 4. Blake, 5. Simbine, 6. Ujah, 7. De Grasse, 8. Meité, 9. Baker, 10. Su.

The world indoor 60m list was headed at 6.45 by Ronnie Baker, to win the US title at high-altitude Albuquerque, and Coleman to win the NCAA title at College Station. Baker ran the year's other sub 6.50 time, with 6.46 at Torun, and Coleman had four of the year's eight times at 6.52 or better.

200 Metres

ONLY TWO OF the World finalists at 100m doubled up at 200m – and both, Yohan Blake and Akani Simbine, went out in the 200m semis. In sharp contrast to years gone by, only one man makes the top ten rankings at both 100m and 200m. That was Christian Coleman, who followed his NCAA double with 2nd place to Ameer Webb at the US Champs, but after a hectic unbeaten collegiate season decided to concentrate on just the 100m in London. He might have wondered what could have been as Ramil Guliyev, the only man to have run in a global 200m final before (8th 2016 Olympics and 9th 2007 and 6th 2016 Worlds), and Wayde van Niekerk took gold and silver. That was van Niekerk's one loss in six 200m competitions, while Guliyev was undefeated (11 wins) until his last race of the year, when he was third in the DL final in Brussels behind Noah Lyles and Webb. That was a third win at the event for Lyles but he had to withdraw due to a hamstring strain from the US semis in his only other 200m competition. He had, however, had a big win in 19.90 in Shanghai from LaShawn Merritt, Adam Gemili and Webb, so he was 2-0 v Webb, who was beaten 3-1 by Guliyev. The year's fastest times were run Isaac Makwala, 19.77 in Madrid before his traumatic Worlds experience that ended with his 6th in the 200m final (and his next two best times of the year 20.14w and 20.20), van Niekerk 19.84 in Kingston and 19.85 by Coleman in Lexington. Andre De Grasse only had four 200m competitions, but won them all: Kingston, Rome and Rabat as well as the Canadian Champs, and he was 2-0 v Webb, 3rd in Rome and 2nd in Rabat. 3-4-5 at the Worlds were the hugely promising Jereem Richards (3rd SEC and NCAA), Nethaneel Mitchell-Blake (2nd SEC and NCAA) and Webb, but Webb beat Mitchell-Blake 3-1. Isiah

Young was 5th at the US Champs, but made the World Champs after Coleman and Elijah Hall-Thompson dropped out of the team and, with 8th in the final, slips into the rankings in tenth place just ahead of Danny Talbot and Aaron Brown. Usain Bolt, who had ranked first on 8 of the last 9 years, did not run at 200m in 2017.

Most times at 20.10/20.30 or better: Guliyev 4+1w/10+2w, Coleman 4/8+1i+1w, Richards 3+1w/7+1w, Mitchell-Blake 3/4+2w/10+2w, van Niekerk 3/6, Webb 2/8, De Grasse 2+1w/3+1w, N Lyles 2/3, Simbine 1/4, Makwala 1+1w/2+1w, Munyai 1/4, Talbot 1w/2+1w, Young 0/5+1w, Dwyer 0/4+1w, Hughes 0/4, Lemaitre 0/3, Brown 0/2+1w.

1. Guliyev, 2. van Niekerk, 3. Coleman, 4. De Grasse, 5. Lyles, 6. Webb, 7. Mitchell-Blake, 8. Richards, 9. Makwala, 10. Young

400 Metres

WAYDE VAN NIEKERK RAN the 400m in just four competitions in 2017, but retained his top ranking with his third successive global title, although he did not run as fast as in 2015-16. Nonetheless he ran three of the eight sub-44 times – 43.62, 43.73 and 43.98 – of 2017. His main rival was Isaac Makwala who, controversially, and much to his chagrin, was barred from taking his place in the World final on medical grounds. Crucially Makwala had finished behind van Niekerk, 43.84 to 43.73 in Monaco and 44.08 to 43.82 in Lausanne, when Baboloki Thebe had split them with 44.02. The other men to beat 44 secs were Fred Kerley and Steven Gardiner. Kerley had a terrific unbeaten season in the USA with a best of 43.70 and wins in the NCAA 44.10 and US 44.03 Championships. However, he was unable to manage more than 7th at the Worlds, while Gardiner won five of his seven competitions, his best time being 43.89 in his World semi before 2nd in the final. He slipped and fell at the start in the DL final in Zürich, which Makwala won from Gil Roberts. Following as 3-6 in the World final were Abdelilah Haroun, Thebe, Nathon Allen, Dennish Gaye. The great rivals Kirani James and LaShawn Merritt were held back by injury and illness, so that James had a best of 45.12 and Merritt, with a best of 44.78 and who was 7th in his World semi, only just makes the top ten. Allen and Gaye, 1-2 in the Jamaican Champs, made substantial progress, Gaye from 45.30 in 2016 to 44.64 and Allen from 45.30 in 2015 to 44.19. in 2016 to 44.19. Roberts ran sub-45 in each of his competitions: 2nd US Champs 44.22, then 4th Monaco, 3rd semi Worlds, 2nd Zürich and 1st Zagreb. Allen did not contest a DL race, but NCAA, Jamaican and World Championships provided significant targets for him. Apart from the Worlds, Haroun's only other outdoor 400m race was a 45.17A, and he missed out on a ranking, with the final places contested by the Americans. Merritt, ranked for the 11th time in 12 years ,was 4-0 against the consistent Vernon Norwood (6th sf US), who was beaten 2-1 by Michael Cherry (6th US). Also running times in the US Champs final that took them into the world list top 11 were 3rd Will London (sf Worlds), 4th Bryshon Nellum and 5th Tony McQuay.

Most sub-45.00 times: Kerley 10+2i, Makwala, Gardiner, Thebe, Roberts 8; Allen 7, Cherry 6, Gaye 5, van Niekerk, Norwood, Norman 4; Merritt, McQuay, Bloomfield 3

1. van Niekerk, 2. Makwala, 3. Gardiner, 4. Kerley, 5. Thebe, 6. Allen, 7. Roberts, 8. Gaye, 9. Merritt, 10. Cherry

800 Metres

OVERALL STANDARDS AT the top were well down, with just 8 times by 5 men sub-1:44 compared to 30 in 2016 and 24 in 2015 and 10th best man at 1:44.44 is the worst since 1990.. However 1:46.26 for the 100th best man was a new record. David Rudisha, six times world number one, was restricted to just three races with a best of 1:44.90 and Nigel Amos returned to the top ranking he held in 2014 and 2015. He disappointed with 11th in Rome and surprisingly only 5th at the Worlds but he won all his other seven races, including five DL wins. Emmanuel Korir made an exciting breakthrough from 1:46.94 in 2016 and he was undefeated, including wins at the NCAAs and Kenyan Trials followed by the year's fastest time of 1:43.10 in Monaco before he was only 4th in his semi at the Worlds when bothered by a hip injury. Korir and Amos were joined as the men with the best collection of times by 19 year-old Kipyegon Bett, 2nd in the Kenyan Trials and 3rd at the Worlds, with a win and three second places in DL races. But the surprise World champion was Pierre-Ambrose Bosse, who following hip issues had just three races prior to that, with a 5th and a 7th before 4th in Monaco. He was unable to compete after London due to a severe assault. As usual Adam Kszczot used his finish to great effect including a win in Rome before 2nd at the Worlds and in Birmingham (behind Amos) before 3rd in the DL final at Brussels behind Amos and Marcin Lewandowski with Bett 4th and Ferguson Cheruiyot 5th. The US champion was Donavan Brazier, who had a best of 1:43.95 for 2nd in the London DL. But Brazier, Lewandowski and Cheruiyot all went out in the semis at the Worlds. Clayton Murphy ran 1:43.60 in April but was unable to run at the US Champs due to a hamstring injury sustained in the 1500m there. Brandon McBride peaked with 1:44.20 for 2nd in Monaco and was 8th at the Worlds, where the 2013 world number one Mohamed Aman came 6th – but had little to back that up so did not make the rankings that are completed by Antoine Gakémé (1st Madrid, 3rd Monaco, sf Worlds). Lewandowski was 3-2 v McBride and 2-1 v Cheruiyot.

Most times sub-1:45.0: Amos, K Bett 5, Brazier 4, Korir, Cheruiyot, Gakémé, Windle 3.

1. Amos, 2. Korir, 3. Bett, 4. Bosse, 5. Kszczot, 6. Brazier, 7. Lewandowski, 8. McBride, 9. Cheruiyot, 10. Gakémé

1500 Metres

THERE IS STILL no one man who dominates the event and the previous claimant to that, Asbel Kiprop had a disappointing year, no better than third in any race and 9th at the Worlds. However, after nine years in the top three he just made the ranking for the eleventh time. His younger compatriots Elijah Manangoi and Tim Cheruiyot took World gold and silver, with Manangoi, who had DL wins in Doha, Monaco and Brussels, holding an overall 4-2 advantage over Cheruiyot, who won in Stockholm and Zürich. They were the only men to better 3:30, respectively 3:28.80 and 3:29.10 in Monaco. Next fastest was Ronald Kwemoi, 3rd in Monaco, who had won the Kenyan Trials race in 3:30.89 from Cheruiyot and Manangoi. Kwemoi also ran the year's fastest mile with 3:49.04 in Eugene with Manangoi and Cheruiyot also under 3:50, so, although he was just 9th in his World semi, he clearly rates highly. Salah Mikhou started the year in great form with three runs under 3:32.5, but faded to 10th in Lausanne and Zürich and 6th at the Worlds, thus behind the 3-5 men: Filip Ingebrigtsen, Adel Mechaal and Jakub Holusa. Stronger performances in depth to those men were recorded by Kenyans Silas Kiplagat (who was 2-0 v Mikhou), Charles Simotwo and Vincent Kibet, although they had been 12th, 5th and 11th at the Kenyan Trials. Simotwo beat Kiplagat 3-2 and Kibet 3-0, while Kiplagat beat Kibet 3-2. Aman Wote had some top times and won in Lausanne; he had win-loss advantage over Simotwo, Kibet and Ingebrigtsen, but his programme was rather thin and he did not run at the Worlds. The order at the DL final in Zürich was Cheruiyot, Kiplagat, Manangoi, Kiprop, Simotwo, Kibet, Jake Wightman (who also had good wins in Oslo and Birmingham, but 8th semi at Worlds), Holusa, Marcin Lewandowski and Mikhou. There are seven Kenyans, including the top five, in the ranking.

Most times sub-3:35.0 or 3:52.0M: 7 Manangoi, Cheruiyot; 6 Kibet, 4 Wote, Ingebrigtsen; 3 Kwemoi, Kiplagat, Simotwo, Mikhou, Kiprop, Holusa, O'Hare, Tesfaye

1. Manangoi, 2. Cheruiyot, 3. Kwemoi, 4. Simotwo, 5. Kiplagat, 6. Mikhou, 7. Wote, 8. Kibet, 9. Ingebrigtsen, 10. Kiprop

3000 Metres/2 Miles

THE THREE FASTEST times of the year were run in Doha, as Ronald Kwemoi won in 7:28.73 from Paul Chelimo and Yomif Kejelcha with Caleb Ndiku 4th for fifth on the world list. The rest of the top 14 times of the year came in the DL races in Paris, where Muktar Edris (7:32.31) won from Kwemoi, Kejelcha, Joshua Cheptegei and Ben True, and London, won by Mo Farah (7:35.15) from Adel Mechaal, Andrew Butchart and Patrick Tiernan.

5000 Metres

AS IN 2016, sub-13 minute times were in short supply, and just three men achieved this in 2017: all in Lausanne where Muktar Edris won in 12:55.23 from Selemon Barega and Joshua Cheptegei. The next fastest race was in Eugene where five men broke 13:05, Mo Farah 13:00.70 from Yomif Kejelcha, Geoffrey Kamworor, Cheptegei and Albert Rop with Mohammed Ahmed, Paul Chelimo and Andrew Butchart 6th to 8th. Edris won in Somerville in 13:01.04 and his win over Farah in the closely contested but slow World Champs race ensured his top ranking, but Farah, who had ranked top five times at this event, gained some revenge when he won the last track race of his stellar career, holding off Edris 13:06.05 to 13:06.09 in the DL final in Zürich. The 3rd to 6th placers in the Worlds also featured in the top finishers in Zürich: Chelimo 3rd and dq (after finishing in the same time as Edris), Kejelcha 4th and 3rd, Barega 5th and 4th, Ahmed 6th and 5th. Barega, just 17 years old, had earlier won the African junior title, having improved from 13:21.21 in 2016, and apart from him six of the top seven men were also in the top seven in 2016. Kamworor had just that one 5000m race, but his placing at Eugene was enough to keep him ahead of the rest headed by Birhanu Yemataw (six wins and 12th Worlds), Butchart (8th Worlds), Yenew Alamirew (4th Lausanne, 6th Zürich) and Rop (14th ht Worlds. 7th Zürich). Aron Kifle was 7th at the Worlds, but 10th at Eugene was his only other 5000m race.

Most times under 13:15: Edris, Rop 3; Chelimo 2+1dq, Farah, Ahmed 2+1i.

1. Edris. 2. Farah, 3. Kejelcha, 4. Chelimo, 5. Barega, 6. Cheptegei, 7. Ahmed, 8. Kamworor, 9. Yemataw, 10. Butchart

10,000 Metres

THE WORLD CHAMPIONSHIP race was a magnificent one, and the top nine men ran the year's nine fastest times with three more in the top 14. The wonderful Mo Farah, unbeaten at the event for six years, ranks top for the fifth times as he won his fifth global 10,000m title and needed to run faster (26:46.57) than in any of his previous title races to do so. The times for places 11 to 14 were the best ever in any 10,000m race and the first 14 men were all born in East

Africa. Most of them ran two or three 10,000m races during the year, Farah also winning in Ostrava in 27:12.09, but runner-up Joshua Cheptegei ran just this one. Paul Tanui's bronze followed Olympic silver in 2016 and World bronze in 2013 and 2015. With such a class race the rankings follow the World Champs top ten exactly. Geoffrey Kamworor (6th) had beaten Bidan Karoki (4th) and Tanui at the Kenyan Trials, while Patrick Tiernan beat Mohammed Ahmed (8th) and Shadrack Kipchirchir (9th) at Stanford, but had no other 10,000m races. The Ethiopian Trial race at Hengelo was another fast one, with Hadis winning in 27:08.26 from Jemal Yimer (5th Worlds), Yenew Alamirew and Andamlak Belihu (10th Worlds).

1. Farah, 2. Cheptegei, 3. Tanui, 4. Karoki, 5. Yimer, 6. Kamworor, 7. Hadis, 8. Ahmed, 9. Kipchirchir, 10. Belihu

Half Marathon

THREE MEN BEAT 59 minutes to head the world list at Copenhagen, where Abraham Cheroben won in 58:40 from Jorum Okombo 58:48 and Alex Oloitiptip Korir 58:51. Cheroben also won in Valencia in 59:11 but had been 3rd in Yangzhou in 60:58 in a close finish behind Mosinet Geremew and Leonard Langat. 29 men completed the distance in under 1 hour and Okombo was the only other man to do so twice as he was 5th in the competitive New Delhi race in 59:58. That was won by Berhanu Legesse 59:46 from Andamlak Belihu, Leonard Korir and Asefa Mengistu. Seven men bettered 1 hour in Copenhagen and four did so in Ra's Al-Khaymah, won by Bidan Karoki 59:10, and in Valencia.

Marathon

HEADLINES IN THE spring were taken with the efforts of a group of Nike-sponsored runners to break the 2-hour barrier. Eliud Kipchoge got remarkably close on May 6 on the motor-racing track in Monza when he ran 2:00:25. Behind him Zersenay Tadese ran 2:06:51 and Lelisa Desisa 2:14:10. The runners were supported by a team of 30 pace-makers who rotated around the runners to reduce air resistance, specially designed shoes and clothes from Nike, plus a team providing additional nutrition when needed. By using pacers and handing drinks to the runners, the attempt did not qualify as an official world record attempt under IAAF regulations. This effort meant that Kipchoge, clearly the greatest marathoner of at least the current era, ran just one official marathon in 2017, instead of the two wins that he had in previous years, but was named as AIMS best marathon runner of 2017. He duly won in Berlin in 2:03:32, but conditions were not ideal for a world record attempt. Nonetheless this was the fastest time of the year and he was pushed surprisingly closely by Guye Adola, whose 2:03:46 was the fastest ever debut at the distance. Next fastest were the winners of three major races: Wilson Kipsang, Tokyo 2:03:58, Tamirat Tola, Dubai 2:04:11, and Lawrence Cherono, Amsterdam 2:05:08. The last had the best depth of times as five men broke 2:05:45. Kipsang did not finish in Berlin, so ran a month later in New York, where he was second to Geoffrey Kamworor, but they were outside 2:10 in a relatively slow race. Tola was 2nd in the World Champs, but his 2:09:49 meant that he was well behind winner Geoffrey Kirui's 2:08:27 and although that time left him outside the top 60 on the world list, Kirui's two major race wins (the first man to win Boston and the World title in one year) make him a major contender for top ranking. As usual a stellar cast featured in the London Marathon, and this was won in 2:05:48 by Daniel Wanjiru, 8th in the Worlds, from Kenenisa Bekele, who, however, did not finish in either Dubai or Berlin. Cherono ran 2:06:21 for 2nd to Marius Kimutai in Rotterdam and also won in Honolulu, The one man to run sub-2:06 twice was Amos Kipruto, 1st in Seoul and 5th Amsterdam. Felix Kandie had a pair of 2:06s, 2nd Seoul and 4th Berlin and Tola Shure won in Frankfurt (2:05:50 and Rome plus 3rd Xiamen. The World bronze medallist Alphonce Felix ran 2:09s in each of his races, also 1st Mumbai and 5th London.

1. Kipchoge, 2. Kirui, 3. Tola, 4. Kipsang, 5. Wanjiru, 6. Adola, 7. Cherono, 8. Kipruto, 9. Kandie, 10. Shura

3000 Metres Steeplechase

CONSESLUS KIPRUTO RETAINED his top ranking despite a thin season. His record was wins in Rome, Kenyan Trials , World Champs and DL final in Brussels with a dnf in Rabat; once again he missed his desire to get a sub-8 minute time, but was well short of his 8:00.12 in 2016 with his best of 8:04.63. He was held back, and indeed in pain at the Worlds, due to twisting his right ankle at the Kenyan Trials. The only man to run faster was Evan Jager with 8:01.29 in Monaco, the world's slowest top time since 2000. Jager was also US champion but was 3rd in the Worlds and DL final, when 2nd in each was Soufiane El Bakkali who has made rapid progress from 8:27.79 in 2015 and 8:14.35 in 2016 to 8:04.83, just 0.1 behind Kipruto in Brussels; he also won in Stockholm and Rabat and was 2nd in Rome. Julius Birech was only 12th at the Worlds and 9th in the DL final, but he had the next best set of times, with sub 8:08 for 3rd in Rome and 2nd in Monaco. As usual Mahiedine Mekhissi-Benabbad raced sparingly and his best was only 19th on the world list, but he was 4th at the Worlds, well ahead of the 5th to 9th: Stanley Kebenei

(2nd US, 3rd Monaco, 4th Brussels), Matthew Hughes, Tesfaye Diriba, Tafese Seboka and Getnet Wale. Ezekiel Kemboi came in 11th, a disappointing end to a marvellous career. Benjamin Kigen was 4th at the Kenyan Trials behind Conseslus and Brimin Kipruto and Birech, consolidating a strong ranking with a win in Ostrava, 4th in Monaco and 6th in Brussels, and Amos Kirui was 5th and 7th in those last two plus 4th in Rome. Seboka and Wale were 1-2 at the Ethiopian Champs and 2-2 overall and Nicholas Bett was 5th in Brussels. Notable absentees from the rankings were Paul Kipsiele Koech and Ezekiel Kemboi each of whom had 15 years.

Most times under 8:15: El Bakkali, Birech 4, C Kipruto, Kigen 3

1. C Kipruto, 2. El Bakkali, 3. Jager, 4. Birech, 5. Mekhissi-Benabbad, 6. Kebenei, 7. Kigen, 8. Kirui, 9. Seboka, 10. Wale

110 Metres Hurdles

AS IN 2015 Omar McLeod was the one man to break 13 seconds, with 12.90 and 12.96, and he ran 6 of the 11 times sub 13.10. He won six of his seven competitions, the exception being 7th in Paris when he cramped. Sergey Shubenkov was enabled to run as a neutral athlete and was a clear 2nd to McLeod at the Worlds before winning the DL final in Brussels, where Orlando Ortega was 2nd and Aries Merritt 3rd. Those two men were 7th and 5th respectively at the Worlds, when Balázs Baji was a surprise 3rd, Garfield Darien 4th, Shane Brathwaite 6th, and Hansle Parchment 8th. Just missing places in the final were Devon Allen and Andrew Pozzi. Merritt, after an inspiring recovery from his kidney transplant, takes third place in the rankings, with a 5-1 win-loss advantage over Allen, 3-1 v Darien and 1-1 v Baji, who also won the World University title. In the DL final 4th to 8th were Allen, Ronald Levy, Darien, Milan Trajkovic and Brathwaite. Aleec Harris had won the US title from Merritt and Allen but fell away in Europe including 6th semi at the Worlds. Win-loss helped determine rankings places with Allen 3-1 v Baji and Darien, Darien 3-1 v Baji, Baji 3-0 v Ortega. But Ortega was 1-1 v Allen and 3-1 v Darien. Levy did not finish his heat at the Worlds but was 2nd with Parchment 3rd behind McLeod at the Jamaican Champs, and won in Paris in 13.05 with 2nd in Eugene to McLeod. Pozzi had consistent results headed by 2nd in Paris in 13.14.

Most times under 13.30: Merritt 11, McLeod, Allen 10, Shubenkov 8+1w, Pozzi 7+2w, Baji 7, Darien 6, Ortega, Levy 5+1w; Harris 4, Parchment 3+1w, Trajkovic, Alkana 3.

1. McLeod, 2. Shubenkov, 3. Merritt, 4. Ortega, 5. Allen. 6. Darien, 7. Baji, 8. Levy, 9. Parchment, 10. Pozzi

At 60m hurdles indoors Pozzi had the three fastest times, 7.43 and 7.44 twice in an unbeaten season that culminated in his winning the European Indoor title from Dmitri Bascou and Garfield Darien with Orlando Ortega 7th after an unbeaten season. Omar McLeod was next fastest with 7.46 in his one race, at the Millrose Games and Aries Merritt win the US title from Aleec Harris

400 Metres Hurdles

KARSTEN WARHOLM EXCELLED at a wide variety of events as a youngster, but showed that he had found his event in 2017, as he won six of his seven outings at 400m hurdles, first making a major impact with a Norwegian record to win at the Oslo DL meeting in 48.25. He went on to win at the European Team I, European U23s and World Champs, but although he reduced his record to 48.22 at Zürich in the DL final, he was beaten there by 20 year-old Kyron McMaster 48.07, and the British Virgin Islander (who improved from 49.56 in 2016) had also run faster times with 47.80 in Kingston and 48.12 behind Kerron Clement 48.02 in the London DL for three of the year's four fastest times. However, McMaster's disqualification in his heat at the Worlds means that Warholm is preferred for the top ranking. Yasmani Copello and Clement were 2nd and 3rd at the Worlds and were 2-2 on win-loss. Apart from his races in London, Clement's record was fairly modest, only 7th, for instance at the US Champs, where the top seven all beat 49 secs – Eric Futch adding this title to the NCAAs and followed by Michael Stigler, T.J. Holmes, Bryon Robinson, Johnny Dutch and Quincy Downing. Holmes was 5th at the Worlds, but Futch was 3rd in his semi and Stigler was dq in his heat. Jaheel Hyde won the Jamaican title from Kemar Mowatt who was 3rd at the NCAAs (Holmes 6th), but Mowatt advanced with 4th at the Worlds (Hyde 3rd semi). Downing was third fastest in the world, with 48.13, but was down on win-loss to most of his rivals. The World final was completed by 6th Juander Santos (World University champion), 7th Abderrahmane Samba (winner at Doha and Zagreb) and Kariem Hussein, with the last adding an excellent 3rd in the DL final, ahead of Clement and Copello, after moderate early season form. Robinson has two good 2nd places in Europe, at Székesfehérvár and Lausanne. 109 men inside 50 seconds was a new record.

Most times to 49.00: Warholm 8, Downing 7, McMaster, Futch, Mowatt 6; Clement, Robinson 5; Copello, Samba, Stigler 4; Jackson, Hyde, Benjamin, Selmon 3.

1. Warholm, 2. McMaster, 3. Copello, 4. Clement, 5. Mowatt, 6. Futch, 7. Santos, 8. Samba, 9. Holmes, 10. Hussein

High Jump

AFTER SOME YEARS of fluctuating men's high jump standards, there was a downturn in 2017 as just three men went over 2.35 compared to ten in 2016. Back in 2014 six men cleared 2.40 or higher and all of them were in action in 2017, although Derek Drouin was held back by hamstring injuries and Aleksey Dmitrik had a best of only 2.25i. As in 2016 Mutaz Essa Barshim was the only one to clear 2.40 and he became the first to do so in five consecutive seasons. He did 2.40 at Birmingham and Eberstadt on successive weekends in August to conclude a brilliant season in which he won all his eleven competitions, including six DL events. Danil Lysenko was 2nd to Barshim at the Worlds (2.32 to 2.35) and improved his best from 2.34 to 2.38 at Eberstadt. Mateusz Przybylko was third on the world list with 2.35 but a next best of 2.31 in qualifying at the Worlds when a disappointing final meant that 3rd Majed El Dein Ghazal, 4th Edgar Rivera and 5th Przybylko cleared only 2.29 followed by four men at 2.25. Ghazal, one of 12 men with bests of 2.31 to 2.33 in the year, went on to be 2nd to Barshim in the DL final in Zürich and was 3-1 v Przybylko. Although below his form of 2013-15, Bohdan Bondarenko was consistent in his six competitions, over 2.30 four times and 9th Worlds and 3rd Zürich. Sylwester Bednarek jumped 2.33 indoors and won the European Indoor title with 2.32 from Robbie Grabarz 2.30 (Przybylko 7th), but Grabarz (6= Worlds, 4th Zürich) beat him 5-3 outdoors as Bednarek had a best of only 2.27 after June, having started outdoors with three marks at 2.30 or better. Ivan Ukhov was restricted to competing in Russia, where he had four competitions indoors and three outdoors 2.30-2.32 (after 2.35 in December 2016), but was only 4th in the Russian Champs outdoors. Erik Kynard won the US indoor title but was 3rd outdoors and no heighted at the Worlds, unable to match his form of recent years. Tihomir Ivanov cleared 2.31 and Wang Yu and Andriy Protsenko 2.29 in qualifying at the Worlds. Ivanov beat Protsenko and Bednarek 3-1 outdoors, although Bednarek was well ahead twice indoors. Rivera was consistent but 2.29 was his best. Pavel Seliverstov showed promise indoors, including European Indoor bronze and a pb 2.32, but had a best of only 2.28 outdoors.

Most competitions over 2.35/2.30m (outdoors + in): Barshim 9/12, Lysenko 1/7+3i, Przybylko 1/6, Bondarenko, Ghazal 4; Ukhov 3+4i, Bednarek 3+3i, Ivanov 3, Grabarz 2+1i, Kynard 1+2i, Seliverstov 3i.

1. Barshim, 2. Lysenko, 3. Ghazal, 4. Przybylko, 5. Bondarenko, 6. Grabarz, 7. Ivanov (9), 8. Rivera (10), 9. Wang Yu (-), 10. Protsenko (-). Bednarek (7), Ukhov (8). (Including indoors).

Pole Vault

RENAUD LAVILLENIE MADE a cautious start to the year after injury, but came back to good form (if not his very best) with nine marks at 5.80 or better headed by 5.91. However, after seven successive years at number one, he had to yield to Sam Kendricks, who had a brilliant season, winning all his 17 competitions including five DL. He was US champion, both indoors and out, the latter with 6.00. He also won a terrific World Champs clash with 5.95 with Piotr Lisek and Lavillenie taking silver and bronze with 5.89. That was just enough to give Lisek, who joined the 6m club with a Polish record 6.00 indoors, the edge for second ranking; he was 4-4 outdoors and 2-0 indoors v Lavillenie. Xue Changrui excelled with a Chinese record 5.82 for World 4th, but his next best was 5.70, while there were two more men over 5.90: former world champion Pawel Wojciechowski, who returned to his best including World 5th, and 17 year-old Armand Duplantis, who set world junior records indoors at 5.72, 5.75 and 5.82 and outdoors at 5.90. After a busy high school year in the USA, he won the European Junior title and was 9th at the Worlds. Medals at the European Indoors went to Lisek, Konstadínos Filippídis and Wojciechowski with Jan Kudlicka 4th, Raphael Holzdeppe 5th and Axel Chapelle 6th at 5.80. This was a peak of an excellent indoor season for Filippídis, but he missed most of the summer season through injury, with a best of 5.71. Shawnacy Barber was also best indoors with 5.83; outdoors he had a best of 5.72 and was 8th at the Worlds. Ahead of him there were Axel Chapelle 6th and Kurtis Marschall 7th with Holzdeppe no heighting. Kévin Menaldo, although not qualifying for the World final and 10th at the European Indoors, beat Chapelle 3-1 outdoors and 4-1 indoors. Chapelle was 2-0 v Marschall, who also did well in the GP final with 4th behind Kendricks, Lisek and Wojciechowski (2=), and ahead of Barber 5th, Menaldo 6th and Filippídis 7th. The 2016 Olympic champion Thiego Braz da Silva started well with 5.86 indoors followed by 5.71 and 5.70, but managed only a 5.60 best outdoors, troubled by a knee injury.

Most competitions over 5.70m (outdoors + in): Lisek 14+7i, Kendricks 14+2i, Lavillenie 12+1i, Wojciechowski 11+3i, Menaldo 6+3i, Duplantis 5+4i, Marschall 5, Nilsen 4+2i, Barber 4+1i, Holzdeppe, Kudlicka 3+3i; Chapelle, Morgunov 3+2i; Vloon 3, Filippídis 2+6i, Xue 2+1i, Horvat 1+3i, Braz da Silva 3i.

1. Kendrick, 2. Lisek, 3. Lavillenie, 4. Wojciechowski, 5. Duplantis, 6. Xue Changrui (7), 7. Menaldo (8), 8. Chapelle (9), 9. Marschall, 10. Barber (-). Filippídis (6). (Including indoors)

Long Jump

LUVO MANYONGA CONFIRMED his special talent with African records at 8.62 and 8.65 at altitude in South Africa, then 8.61 in Shanghai and 8.62 in Hengelo for four successive meetings over 8.60, going on to complete an unbeaten season of nine competitions with World and DL final victories. The other two men over 8.40, Ruswahl Samaai (8.49A) and Jarrion Lawson (8.44) were closely matched, finishing 2nd and 3rd at the Zürich DL final and 3rd and 2nd at the Worlds, with Samaai overall up 3-2. Aleksandr Menkov was 4th at the Worlds and otherwise undefeated, mainly in Russia, and overall form supports the World 5th to 8th to retain these rankings: 18 year-olds Maykel Massó and Shi Yuhao, then Wang Jianan and Michal Tornéus. After the top eight there is little between the next group. Huang Changzhou was dnq 24th at the Worlds, but won the Asian title and at the Chinese National Games, when Gao Xinglong was 2nd, Wang 3rd and Shi 6th. Huang and Gao were 2-2 overall. Marquis Dendy was 2nd to Lawson at the US Champs with 8.39w, but did not have much to back this up and Jeffrey Henderson (dnq 17th Worlds) was 5th. Emiliano Lasa was 9th at the Worlds and 10th was Radek Juska, who won the World Universities title. Although dnq 15th at the Worlds Juan Miguel Echevarría was otherwise 1st or 2nd in all his competitions and was 4-3 v Massó and 1-1 v Lasa. Greg Rutherford had just two competitions (8.18 and 7.95) before damaged ankle ligaments ended his season.

Most competitions over 8.10m: Manyonga, Samaai 10; Lawson, Shi 5; Lasa, Echevarría 4+1w; Menkov, Henderson, Wang 4; Zhang Yaoguang 3+2i, Massó, Tornéus, Huang, Juska, Gao, Tentóglou, Howard 3; Dendy 2+1w

1. Manyonga, 2. Samaai, 3. Lawson, 4. Menkov, 5. Massó, 6. Shi, 7. Wang, 8. Tornéus, 9. Juska, 10. Echevarría.

Triple Jump

CHRISTIAN TAYLOR HAD another outstanding season and is top for the fifth time. He had nine wins including the Worlds, two 2nd places and a no jump in a token effort at the US Champs. Both he (18.11) and Will Claye (18.05w) exceeded 18m at Eugene and Claye lost only to Taylor apart from when Pedro Paulo Pichardo beat them both at Lausanne. Pichardo made a welcome return, over 17m in each of his four meets, after missing 2016 but, seeking to represent Portugal in future, did not compete at the Worlds. These men were the top three at the DL final in Brussels, at 17.32 or better, with Troy Doris far behind, 16.64 for 4th, followed by Alexis Copello, Chris Benard, Jean-Marc Pontvianne (8th Worlds) and Omar Craddock. Nelson Évora was 3rd at the Worlds, but his 17.19 there was his only 17m plus jump outdoors, while Cristian Nápoles (4th Worlds) had five at 17m or better as did Andy Díaz (7th), and Benard (6th) had four. However, Copello had a very solid record; he was 1-1 v Évora and Nápoles and beat Benard (2nd US Champs) 4-0. After 3rd in Eugene with 17.28 (Copello 4th), Dong Bin missed much of the season with a thigh injury before returning to win at the Chinese National Games with 17.23. Max Hess produced a massive 17.52 in qualifying before placing 3rd at the European Indoors behind Évora and Fabrizio Donato, who went on record a world M40 record of 17.32 before injury meant he missed nearly all the outdoor season. Outdoors Hess was over 17m four times, but also had an injury-marred year, not competing at the Worlds. Just missing a top ten ranking are Pontvianne (8th Worlds, 6th European Indoors) and Nazim Babayev, who had major wins at the Islamic Solidarity Games, European U23s (Hess 3rd) and World University Games, and was dnq 14th Worlds.

Most competitions over 17.00: Taylor 10, Claye 8, Nápoles 5, Hess 4+2i, Díaz 4+1w, Pichardo, Benard 4; Babayev, O'Neal 3; Pontvianne 2+1w+1i, Dong Bin, Évora 2+1i i.

1. Taylor, 2. Claye, 3. Pichardo, 4. Nápoles, 5. Copello, 6. Benard, 7. Évora, 8. Díaz, 9. Dong, 10. Hess.

Shot

EVEN THOUGH HE slipped to 6th in the very high quality World final Ryan Crouser retains his top ranking. He had the top mark of the year, 22.63 to win the US title, and 8 of the top 17 marks of the mark, those over 22m. That compared to 4 by Tom Walsh, 2 each by Joe Kovacs and Tomás Stanek and 1 by Darrell Hill. Crouser won 10 of his 14 competitions, including the first 8 (including 3 DL at 22.39 or more), with three 2nds and that 6th. Crucially he was 5-2 v Walsh, 4-1 v Kovacs and 4-2 v Stanek. Kovacs, 2nd US and World's and 3rd DL final in Brussels but only one win, had the year's second best mark with 22.57 but was beaten 4-1 by Walsh, who had 8 wins and 4 2nds in his 13 competitions although only 6th in the DL final in Brussels that provided a surprise winner in Darrell Hill with 22.44 from a previous best of 21.63 in 2016, with Crouser 2nd. Stanek started the year with bests of 21.30i and 21.26 and improved to 21.43 indoors and 21.61 and 22.01 twice outdoors. He was 2nd to the prodigious Konrad Bukowiecki in the European Indoors, and 3-1 down to Kovacs but beat leading European rivals David Storl 6-1 and Michal Haratyk 5-0 outdoors (Storl was 3-1 up indoors). Storl was 10th at the Worlds but 4th in the DL final ahead of Stanek, Walsh, O'Dayne Richards and Bukowiecki and he was 4-2 v Hill and 4-1 outdoors v Haratyk, who was 5th Worlds, and 3-1 v Hill and Stipe Zunic, the surprise World bronze medallist. After his 21.97 at the European Indoors, Bukowiecki was inconsistent outdoors, when he had a best of 21.59 to win the European U23 title and was 8th Worlds and 2nd WUG. 8th. He was beaten 2-1 by Ryan Whiting, 3rd US and 7th Worlds. In this vintage year for shot putting there were 19 men over 21m and 10th best of 21.82 was easily an all-time record (21.63 in 1984 the only previous year over 21.50).

Most competitions over 21.00: Stanek 15+3i, Crouser 14, Storl 13 +4i, Walsh 13, Haratyk 10, Zunic 9+1i, Hill 8, Bukowiecki 7+3i, Whiting, Richards 6, Kovacs 4, Romani 3, Afonin 2+2i, Arnaudov 2+1i, Hassan 1+2i.

1. Crouser, 2. Walsh. 3. Kovacs, 4. Stanek, 5. Storl, 6. Haratyk, 7. Hill, 8. Zunic, 9. Whiting (10), 10, Bukowiecki (9).

Discus

IT WAS CLOSE at the top in 2017 and indeed a year of change with younger men replacing those who had mostly dominated in recent years. The top two marks were 71.29 by Daniel Ståhl and 69.21 by Andrius Gudzius. Ståhl had the better set of marks with 12 of the world's top 30 compared to 9 by Gudzius and 5 by Fedric Dacres. Ståhl and Gudzius went 4-4 on win-loss, but Ståhl won 15 of his 21 competitions while Gudzius won 10 of 18. There was little in it, but perhaps crucially Gudzius ended the year in style by winning both Worlds and DL final in Brussels, while Ståhl was 2nd and 7th. Other top men in those two events: Mason Finley (US champion) 3/-, Dacres 4/2, Piotr Malachowski 5/3, Robert Harting 6/5, Philip Milanov dnq 14/4, Robert Urbanek 7/6, Lukas Weisshaidinger 9/7. Dacres, like Gudzius a newcomer to the world top ten, beat Malachowski, who remained the best of the older brigade, 4-0. Olympic champion Christoph Harting struggled to recapture decent form, although he threw a season's best 64.55 for 5th in Brussels, but elder brother Robert had a solid season, including 3-3 v Malachowski and 5-1 v Urbanek, although he was beaten 4-1 by Milanov. Weisshaidinger and Urbanek were closely matched, with the former 4-3 up on win-loss. Travis Smikle, 8th Worlds, completes the ranking although US runner-up Andrew Evans (dnq 20th Worlds) had better marks, with Apostolis Parellis, (10th Worlds), the prolific Simon Pettersson (11th) and Gerd Kanter (12th) close behind.

Most competitions over 65m: Gudzius 16, Ståhl 14+2i, Dacres 12, Malachowski 9, R Harting, Milanov 7; Weisshaidinger 5, Finley, Urbanek 4; Evans 3.

1. Gudzius, 2. Ståhl, 3. Dacres, 4. Malachowski, 5. Milanov, 6. Finley, 7. R Harting, 8. Urbanek, 9. Weisshaidinger, 10. Smikle

Hammer

THERE WAS NO mistake this year by Pavel Fajdek as at the Olympics in 2016, so he retained his World title and is clearly the world no. 1 for the third year. Such was his superiority that he had the world's best ten performances of the year (80.53 up to a best of 83.44 in Ostrava). He lost just once – at the Polish Championships to Wojciech Nowicki, who, however, he beat 9-1. Nowicki was the only other man to throw (twice) over 80m, while the third longest was 79.32 by Valeriy Pronkin, who took World silver from Nowicki's bronze after seven wins in Russia. Quentin Bigot returned from a drugs ban to place 4th at the Worlds and he also won the European Throws event, but he did not contest the IAAF World Challenge, in which after the two Poles Dilshod Nazarov was 3rd, followed by Pavel Boreysha, Nick Miller, Bence Halász, Marcel Lomnicky and Marco Lingua. Bigot was 2-1 v Boreysha (2 Eur Team, 9 Worlds, 2 WUG), who was 2-1 v Nazarov (1 Asian Champs, 7 Worlds) and 3-1 v Miller (3 Eur Team, 6 Worlds). Miller was 3-3 v Nazarov. Aleksey Sokirskiy was 5th at the Worlds, but otherwise competed only in Russia. and further World placings were 8th Serghei Marghiev, 10th Lingua, 11th Halász with Marcel Lomnicky dnq 13th. Lomnicky was 3-2 v Lingua but beaten 4-1 by Marghiev and 3-1 by Halász. 10th best man at 77.72, although only 6cm behind 2016, was the worst since 1981.

Most competitions over 79m/76m: Fajdek 13/18, Nowicki 3/11, Pronkin 1/9, Bigot 0/10, Boreysha 0/9, Nazarov 0/5, Miller, Lomnicky, Lingua 0/4; Apak, Domingos 0/3

1. Fajdek, 2. Nowicki, 3. Pronkin, 4. Bigot, 5. Boreysha, 6. Miller, 7. Nazarov, 8. Sokirskiy, 9. Marghiev, 10. Halász

Javelin

THERE WAS CONSIDERABLE rivalry between Johannes Vetter and Thomas Röhler such that in their 14 clashes, they ended 7-7. It was Vetter, however, who came out on top as his first ever 90m throw was the year's best, 94.44 a distance ever exceeded only by the great Jan Zelezny, and he took the World title, when Röhler was also beaten by Jakub Vadljech (2nd) and Peter Frydrych (3rd), although Röhler had 5-4 and 4-1 win-loss advantage over these two Czechs. Both Vetter and Röhler had three 90m plus competitions. Tero Pitkämäki, who had missed a ranking in 2016, returned with a consistent season including Worlds 5th place, and 6th there was Ioánnis Kiriazís, who had won NCAA and European U23 titles. Two men surprisingly went over 90m at the World

University Games: Cheng Chao-Tsun with an Asian record 91.36 and Andreas Hofmann 91.07. While Cheng did not have much to support this and was dnq 22nd at the Worlds. Hoffman was 8th there and like Keshorn Walcott (7th Worlds) had a better set of marks than Frydrych. Other men to have strong seasons were Ahmed Bader Magour (2 Asian, 10 Worlds), Magnus Kirt (11 Worlds) and Lars Hamann, 1-1 v Kirt. The 10th man was at 87.97 for the all-time record, although 100th at 77.57 was down from the record 78.29 set in 2016.

Most competitions over 85m/83m: Vetter 15/18, Röhler 14/18, Vadlejch 13/15, Pitkämäki 6/11, Walcott 5/9, Kiriazís 5/5, Cheng 4/4, Kirt 3/10, Hofmann 3/9, Frydrych 3/4, Chopra 2/5, Magour 1/8, Hamann, Krukowski 1/4, Peacock 0/5, Devender Singh 0/4.

1. Vetter, 2, Röhler, 3. Vadlejch, 4. Pitkämäki, 5. Walcott, 6. Kiriazís, 7. Hofmann, 8. Frydrych, 9. Magour, 10. Kirt .

Decathlon

KEVIN MEYER STEPPED up from his Olympic silver to win the World title as the clear favourite. In this, his only decathlon of the year apart from taking part in just three events at the French Champs, he won by 204 points from Rico Freimuth, who had the year's second best score of 8663 at Ratingen and was also IAAF Challenge winner, adding his Götzis 3rd and Worlds 2nd. Following on the year list were Ilya Shkurenyov 8601 for the Russian title and Damien Warner 8591 to win at Götzis. Shkurenyov did not finish his other decathlons – Adler and Worlds – while Warner ended the year by winning at Talence but was unfortunate to be ill at the Worlds, although he struggled through to place 5th. The other top finishers at the Worlds were 3rd Kai Kazmirek (3rd Ratingen and 2nd Talence), 4th Janek Oiglane, youngest of the top men at 23 (14th Götzis, 1st European Team), 6th Oleksiy Kasyanov (7th Götzis, 2nd European Team, 3rd Talence), 7th Kurt Felix (2nd Ratingen, dnf Talence), 8th Adam Sebastian Helcelet (4th Götzis and Talence), 9th Jorge Ureña, 10th Devon Williams (2nd NCAA, 3rd US plus a pb of 8345 at Athens GA). Two non-finishers at the Worlds were Eelco Sintnicolaas, who had been 2nd at Götzis with 8539 and 6th at Talence, and Lindon Victor who had three wins in the US with top scores: 8462 Texas Relays, 8539 SEC and 8390 NCAA.

1. Meyer, 2. Freimuth, 3. Warner, 4. Kazmirek, 5. Victor, 6. Sintnicolaas, 7. Oiglane, 8. Kasyanov, 9. Felix, 10. Helcelet

Meyer also had easily the best indoor heptathlon score as he won the European title with 6479 from Ureña 6227 and Helcelet 6110. Those medallists were next on the year list, both with wins in Prague: Ureña 6249 and Helcelet 6188.

20 Kilometres Walk

WANG ZHEN, THE no. 1 in 2016, did not compete this year and the no. 2 Cai Zelin went dnf and dq in his two races, so the top Chinese man was Wang Kaihua, who recorded the year's best time of 1:17:54 in Huangshan and also won the Chinese title, but he came 8, 3, 7 in his other races, the last in the World Champs. That was typical of very mixed form by the top men, the exception being Eider Arévalo, whose World win was his fourth at 20k in 2017, a year he completed with an inconsequential 3rd at the Bolivar Games.. The World Champs race was obviously vital in the rankings and 2-8 were: Sergey Shirobokov, Caio Bonfim, Lebogang Shange, Christopher Linke, Dane Bird-Smith, Wang and Álvaro Martín. The Japanese pair of Eiki Takahashi and Isamu Fujisawa were 2nd and 3rd fastest on the world list (with Shirobokov 4th), but were 14th and 11th respectively at the Worlds. The European Cup was won by Linke from Miguel Ángel López (10th Worlds), Perseus Karlström (3th Worlds) and Tom Bosworth (dq Worlds) with Martín 31st, while major race winners included Bonfim at Taicang, Arévalo at Rio Maior and Martín at La Coruña. Sergey Bakulin raced only in the Russian champs, where he was 2nd to Shirobokov in the winter race and 1st in the summer.

1. Arévalo, 2. Shirobokov, 3. Bonfim, 4. Linke, 5. Shange, 6. Bird-Smith, 7. Wang, 8. Martín. 9. Takahashi, 10. López

50 Kilometres Walk

YOHANN DINIZ, WHO had a fractured rib earlier in the year, was magnificent at the Worlds, winning by a record margin of over 8 minutes from the Japanese pair of Hirooki Arai and Kai Kobayashi. This was a fast race with Diniz's 3:33:12 bettered only by his WR 3:32.33, and the times of the top 11 men made up all but 4 of the world top 15 times of the year. Naturally the rankings follow the World positions very closely as 4-11 were Ihor Hlavan, Satoshi Maruo, Maté Helebrandt, Robert Heffernan, Marco de Luca, Carl Dohmann and João Vieira. Håvard Haukenes did not finish but had an important win at Dudince in 3:43:22 from Rafal Augustyn. Just ahead of Haukenes on the world list in sixth place was Russian champion Dementiy Cheparev, who did not compete elsewhere. Ivan Banzeruk (19th Worlds) won the European Cup from Hlavan.

1. Diniz, 2. Arai, 3. Kobayashi, 4. Hlavan, 5. Maruo, 6. Augustyn, 7. Helebrandt, 8. Heffernan, 9. De Luca, 10. Haukenes

WOMEN

ALL THE OFFICIAL world records by women in 2017 came in endurance events. Joyciline Jepkosgei led the way with 64:52 and 64:51 for half marathon and with intermediate times at 15k and 20k although records will not in future be recognised at these distances. She also twice improved the world road best of 10k, although her final 29:43 is much slower than the track world record. Newly recognised as an official world record event for women at the beginning of the year, within a couple of weeks Inês Henriques had set an inaugural WR for 50k walk of 4:08:26 and she improved that to 4:05:56 to win the World title. Mary Keitany's 2:17:01 in London in April was the fastest ever in a women only marathon. Note also a world best for 600m: 1:21.77 by Caster Semenya. Indoors there were world best at two events not on the official IAAF list: Genzebe Dibaba ran 5:23.75 for 200m and Gwen Berry threw the 20lb weight 25.60m.

The closest that anyone came to a world record at a standard track and field event was the 82.87 hammer throw by Anita Wlodarczyk at Cetniewo, just 11 cm off her 2016 record. She had another superb unbeaten season as her 13 wins took her win streak to 43 from her last loss on 16 June 2014. She has reached a level of dominance at her event that has been very rare throughout athletics history. She had the 9 best performances of the year and now has the 14 top performances on the world all-time list and once again she is a major contender for athlete of the year. Also enjoying unbeaten seasons were Mariya Lasitskene (née Kuchina), 24 competitions at high jump with the top seven performances (2.06 to 2.02), and Caster Semenya, all eight finals at 800m, and Hellen Obiri, all six at 5000m, plus the very limited seasons of Nafi Thiam in her two heptathlons and Almaz Ayana, one race at 10,000m with a superb win at the Worlds. Other top rankers who got close to perfection were Sandra Perkovic, nine wins and two seconds at discus, Ekateríni Stefanídi, 15 of 16 at pole vault, Elaine Thompson, 8 wins in 9 finals at 100m as she was sick in the World final, and Faith Kipyegon, five wins and a second at 1500m. Although 3rd and 4th in the World Champs, Shaunae Miller-Uibo was top ranked at both 200m and 400m. Uniquely Lasitskene won all her seven DL competitions, while Perkovic had six wins.

I exclude Caster Semenya from my selections as I do not consider that she should be allowed to compete in women's races with her current testosterone balance.

100 Metres

UNFORTUNATELY ELAINE THOMPSON caught the sickness bug at the World Champs and struggled into 5th place in the final, unable to show her usual brilliant surge of pace. But she was clearly still the world's best and won all her other eight competitions, including five DL races. She ran the year's fastest times, with 10.71 in Kingston and 10.78 Shanghai. Torie Bowie beat Marie-Josée Ta Lou by 0.01 in the World final and was also US champion and 2nd in Shanghai. Ta Lou had an outstanding season with three wins, six 2nd places and a third; on win-loss she was ahead of all but Thompson (1-5) and Bowie (0-2), including 2-1 against the World bronze medallist Dafne Schippers. After the top four Murielle Ahouré, 4th Worlds, was the only woman with more than one wind-legal sub-11 time. Completing the World final were Michelle-Lee Ahye, Rosângela Santos (10.91 South American record in her semi) and Kelly-Ann Baptiste. Ahye was second on the year lists with 10.82 and was 4th in the DL final in Brussels behind Thompson, Ta Lou and Blessing Okagbare, who was 4th in her semi at the Worlds. but 4-2 v Ahye and 5-0 v Morolake Akinosun (US 4th, DL 6th). Deajah Stevens and Ariana Washington were US 2nd and 3rd (and NCAA 2nd and 4th) but were 8th and 7th respectively in their World semis. Jura Levy, 3rd to Thompson and Simone Facey at the Jamaican Champs, did better with World semi 5th and she was 7th in Brussels, a place behind Akinosun, with whom she was 1-1. Akinosun beat Santos 2-0.

Most times under 11.00/11.10: Thompson 11+1w/12+1w, Ta Lou 7/10+1w, Schippers 6/8, Bowie 4+1w/7+1w, Ahouré 3+2w/5+3w, Ahye 1+2w/10+2w, Baptiste 1+1w/5+1w, Hobbs 1/4+1w, R Santos 1/3+1w, Lückenkemper 1/3, Campbell-Brown 1/2+2w, Stevens 1w/6+2w, Levy 0/3, Facey 0/2+2w.

1. Thompson, 2. Bowie, 3. Ta Lou, 4. Schippers, 5. Ahouré, 6. Okagbare, 7. Ahye, 8. Baptiste, 9., Stevens, 10. Akinosun

At 60m indoors Elaine Thompson had just one competition but in that ran 6.98 in Birming-

Selections for World Top Ten

	PJM	*TFN*	*AI*
Mariya Lasitskene	1	2	1
Anita Wlodarczyk	2	1	2
*Nafissatou Thiam	3	4	4
Sandra Perkovic	4	7	5
* Ekateríni Stefanídi	5	3	3
Hellen Obiri	6	5	6
* Almaz Ayana	7	9	8
Joyciline Jepkosgei	8	-	-
Shaunae Miller-Uibo	9	-	-
Faith Kipyegon	10	8	-
Caster Semenya	-	6	7
Elaine Thompson	-	10	-
Mary Keitany	-		10

** IAAF finalists, Thiam was their athlete of the year. Yulimar Rojas was IAAF Rising Star of the Year.*

ham, much faster then the world's second fastest of the season, 7.06 by Asha Phillip to win the European Indoor title.

200 Metres

THE KEY RACES in determining the top of the rankings were the World Champs in London and DL final in Zürich. Dafne Schippers was 1st and 4th, Marie-Josée Ta Lou 2nd and 3rd, Shaunae Miller-Uibo 3rd and 1st, with Dina Asher-Smith 4th and Deajah Stevens 5th at the Words, and Elaine Thompson 2nd and Kyra Jefferson 5th in Zürich. Tori Bowie ran the year's fastest time, 21.77 in Eugene, but had only two other 200m competitions – a win in Gainesville and 3rd behind Stevens and Kimberlyn Duncan at the US Champs. Miller-Uibo had the next two best times, 21.88 in Zürich and 21.91 for 2nd in Eugene, and is narrowly favoured for top ranking. In all she had four wins in six 200m competitions. After wins in Doha and Kingston, Thompson was the third woman under 22.00 with 21.98 for 3rd in Eugene. Schippers was 4th in the race and had DL wins in Oslo and Lausanne. Asher-Smith made a brilliant return for that Worlds 4th place after breaking her foot earlier in the year. Jefferson was 2-1 v Duncan and won the NCAA title from Ariana Washington, as these two were 5th and 4th at the US Champs, with Gabrielle Thomas 3rd.

Washington was the fastest indoors, with 22.42 to win the NCAA title. After 13 successive years in the top eight Allyson Felix is not ranked as she concentrated on 400m; she ran sub-23 in her four races with a best of 22.33 for 5th in Eugene

Most times under 22.70: Jefferson 10, Schippers 9, Ta Lou 8, Miller–Uibo 7+1w, Stevens 6+2w, Duncan 6+1w, Washington 5+1w+2i,Thomas 5, Thompson, Bowie 4; Hill 3+1w, Jackson, Prandini, Wimbley 3; Henderson 2+2w.

1. Miller-Uibo, 2. Thompson, 3. Schippers, 4. Ta Lou, 5. Bowie. 6. Asher-Smith, 7. Stevens, 8. Jefferson, 9. Duncan, 10. Washington

400 Metres

SHAUNAE MILLER-UIBO misjudged the finish of the World final and came in 4th behind Phyllis Francis, Salwa Eid Naser and Allyson Felix, but she ran all her other 400m races in under 50 secs, ending with the year's top time of 49.46 to win the DL final in Brussels. There the 19 year-old Nigerian-born Naser was 2nd in a Bahrain record 49.88, having set previous records (50.57, 50.08 and 50.06) in each round at the Worlds. Courtney Okolo, who had missed the Worlds by her 8th place at the US Champs, was 3rd in Brussels followed by Natasha Hastings, Shericka Jackson, Novlene Williams-Mills and Stephenie Ann McPherson. Felix ran the world's second fastest of the year, 49.65 to beat Okolo at the London DL; she had just four meets but was also 2nd in Birmingham to Naser with Okolo 3rd and Francis 4th. Quanera Hayes was 3rd in her semi at the Worlds but had won the US title from Felix and Kendall Ellis with Hastings 4th. After five US athletes in the top seven, the three Jamaicans who were in the DL final follow. Jackson won at their championships, from Chrisann Gordon (3sf Worlds) and Williams-Mills, with McPherson a non-starter in the final. Ellis was only 6th in her heat at the Worlds, having also been 3rd at the NCAAs behind Gordon and Shakima Wimbley (NCAA champion indoors). The fastest European was Olha Zemlyak, 20th on the world list with 50.89.

Most times under 50.80: Miller-Uibo, Francis 6, Naser, Felix, Okolo, Williams-Mills, Gordon 5; Hayes, Jackson, Ellis, Wimbley 4; Hastings 3.

1. Miller-Uibo, 2. Naser, 3. Francis, 4. Felix, 5. Hayes, 6. Hastings, 7. Okolo, 8. Jackson, 9. Williams-Mills, 10. McPherson

800 Metres

LAST YEAR I wrote that the Olympic medallists Caster Semenya, Francine Niyonsaba and Margaret Wambui were in a different league from the rest, both medically it seems (released from testosterone control) and athletically. The situation was much the same in 2017 with no woman able to beat this trio until Ajee' Wilson ran superbly for third behind Semenya and Niyonsaba in Monaco and at the Worlds, as Wambui came in 8th and 4th in those races. We had expected an IAAF/CAS decision on the issue, but it did not come during the season and my opinion remains that it is grossly unfair on 'normal' women that intersex women should be allowed to compete without the testosterone control that had previously been introduced. As it was Semenya had a terrific record, winning all her eight meets with the year's two fastest times – South African records 1:55.16 at the Worlds and 1:55.27 in Monaco. Niyonsaba was 4-1 v Wambui and 2-0 v Wilson, who won her other three finals – US Champs, Padua and Zagreb. Sifan Hassan ran just three 800m races, but these were important ones: 4th in Lausanne and Monaco and 5th in Zürich, so she beat Melissa Bishop (5th Worlds) into 5th and 7th in the last two. Charlene Lipsey was the top newcomer in the rankings improving from 2:00.65 to 1:57.38 in the year; she was 2nd US, 8th Monaco, 7th Worlds and 6th Zürich. Lynsey Sharp (8th Worlds) had another consistent year and had much better times than the Worlds 6th placer Angelika Cichocka. Eunice Sum had 3rd places in Doha and Lausanne, and Lovisa Lindh also had good DL results with 4th Oslo, 2nd Stockholm and 4th Lausanne, but both missed the Worlds through injury. Youngest of the rankings contenders was Habitam Alemu (20 in July) whose best results were 4th places in Doha, Eugene and Zürich (for 7th on the world list), but 8th in her semi at the Worlds.

Most times under 1:59.5: Wilson 7 (+1i dq), Semenya, Niyonsaba 7, Lipsey 6+1i, Sharp 6, Wambui 5, Bishop, Martinez 4, Hassan, Alemu. Lindh 3.

1. Semenya, 2. Niyonsaba, 3. Wilson, 4. Wambui, 5. Hassan, 6. Bishop, 7. Lipsey, 8. Sharp, 9. Sum, 10. Lindh

1500 Metres

FOUR OF THE five fastest 1500m times of the year were run by Sifan Hassan, headed by 3:56.14 in Hengelo and 3:56.22 in Rome, but she ranks second to Faith Kipyegon. They met three times: Hassan won in Paris 3:57.10 to 3:57.51, but it was Kipyegon with 4:02.59 at the Worlds, where Hassan was only 5th in 4:03.34, and in Brussels 3:57.04 to 3:57.22. Kipyegon won all her other races – in Shanghai, Eugene and at the Kenyan Trials – and retains her top ranking. Genzebe Dibaba was fastest indoors with 3:58.80 and outdoors ran the year's fastest mile, 4:16.05 in Lausanne, but disappointed with 12th at the Worlds in her only other competition. Laura Muir had a brilliant double with 1500m and 3000m at the European Indoors and ran the year's fastest for 1000m. Outdoors she started with 3rd in Eugene and 2nd at 1 mile at the London DL, but was beaten in both these races by Hellen Obiri (2nd and 1st). Obiri did not have any other 1500m/1M races while Muir went on to 1st at Padua and 4th at the Worlds. Jenny Simpson once again showed her tactical nous with silver at the Worlds as Caster Semenya, in her only important 1500m race, stormed through to take the bronze. Simpson won the US title but was 8th in Eugene and 7th in Birmingham with her best times coming with 4:19.98 for 4th in the London Mile and 4:00.70 in 6th place at Brussels. Ahead of her in these races (and 3-1 up on win-loss) was Winny Chebet, only 7th in her World semi, but 3rd in the London mile, 2nd to Dawit Seyaum in Birmingham and 3rd in Brussels. 20 year-old Konstanze Klosterhalfen missed qualifying for the World final, but was under 4 minutes when 3rd in Rome and when winning at the German Champs and in Berlin. Gudaf Tsegay also missed making the World final but had been 5th in Eugene and Rome, plus winning in Ostrava and sub-4 for 3rd in Paris, ending with 4th in Birmingham and Brussels. 5th in both those races was Meraf Bahta, 9th at the Worlds and 4th in Rome. Actually the most prolific with sub-4:04 times was Angelika Cichocka, 7th Worlds, but beaten 3-1 by Bahta and Klosterhalfen and 4-1 by Tsegay. She was, however, 3-2 v Laura Weightman, 6th Worlds, and 5-2 v Arrafi, 8th Worlds.

Most times under 4:04.0 (or 4:23.6M): Cichocka 8, Kipyegon, Chebet 7, Hassan 6+1i, Tsegay, Arrafi 6; Sado 5, Muir 4+2i, Simpson, Klosterhalfen, Bahta 4; Semenya, Martinez 3; Dibaba 2+2i.

1. Kipyegon, 2. Hassan, 3. Obiri, 4. Muir, 5. Chebet, 6. Simpson, 7. Klosterhalfen, 8. Tsegay, 9. Bahta, 10. Cichocka

3000 Metres

HELLEN OBIRI RAN the year's fastest time with 8:23.14 in Monaco, with Beatrice Chepkoech also under 8:30 and a record ten women under 8:38. Laura Muir was third in this race, having run the year's best indoor time of 8:26.41 in Karlsruhe and also winning the European Indoor title. Two more women broke 8:30 in the Birmingham DL race: Sifan Hassan and Konstanze Klosterhalfen with Margaret Kipkemoi and Obiri just over 8:30. Running fast in both Birmingham and Monaco were Eilish McColgan 5th/4th, Lilian Rengeruk 6th/5th, Shannon Rowbury 9th/6th and Agnes Tirop 8th/7th; Susan Krumins was 7th in Birmingham.. Indoors in Birmingham Obiri ran 8:28.41, winning from Hassan and Dawit Seyaum.

5000 Metres

HELLEN OBIRI HAD a marvellous year as she won all her six 5000m races (and a heat at the Worlds). Her wins in DL races at Rome (14:18.37), Shanghai and Brussels were 1, 2 and 4 on the year list and she added two wins in Kenya and a clear success at the Worlds. Behind her, it was tricky to sort out a ranking. Almaz Ayana, who had no other 5000m competitions, was 2nd at the Worlds with Sifan Hassan (also 1st Stanford and 3rd Eugene) third. Second on the world list was Genzebe Dibaba, with 14:25.22 in Eugene (her other race was 6th in Rome), and third was Caroline Kipkirui, who made a startling breakthrough with 14:27.55 for 2nd in Brussels from a previous best of 14:51.87 for 5th in Shanghai (she also had two wins in Almaty). The 2-3-4 in Shanghai all rate highly as Teferi, Letesenbet Gidey and Margaret Kipkemboi went on to 4th, 11th and 5th at the Worlds. Teferi and Kipkemboi were also 3rd and 4th in the DL final in Brussels, followed by Beatrice Chepkoech, Lilian Rengeruk (2nd Eugene, 5th Kenyan Trials) and Gidey. Agnes Tirop (10th Brussels), Gidey, Yasemin Can and Etenesh Dido were 2nd to 5th in the fast race in Rome. Laura Muir had a fine debut at the event with 14:49.12 indoors and was 6th at the Worlds, doubling up with the 1500m.

Most times under 15:00: Obiri 5, Teferi, Kipkemboi, Gidey 4; Hassan, Rengeruk 3; Muir 2+1i.

1. Obiri, 2. Ayana, 3. Hassan, 4. Teferi, 5. G Dibaba, 6. Kipkemboi, 7. Kipkirui, 8. Rengeruk, 9. Gidey, 10. Muir

10,000 Metres

IT WAS HER first race since September 2016 due to an injury in April, but the 10,000m run by Almaz Ayana at the World Championships was utterly amazing as she won by a championship record margin of 46.37 secs from five times global champion Tirunesh Dibaba, with Agnes Tirop and Alice Aprot Nawowuna following. Ayana ran 15:51.38 for the first half and then an amazing 14:24.94 for the second. These four were joined by the first six in the Ethiopian trial race in Hengelo as the ten fastest of the year (all under 31:12). The Hengelo race was won by Gelete Burka from Senbere Teferi and Belaynesh Oljira, none of whom ran the 10,000m at the Worlds or indeed anywhere else in the year, so although they were 2-3-4 on the year list it is difficult to rate them against the World top women. Ethiopian champion Dera Dida was 4th at Hengelo but 14th at the Worlds., where 5th to 11th were: Susan Krumins, Emily Infield (2nd US), Irene Cheptai (2nd to Aprot at the Kenyan Trials), Molly Huddle (1st US), Emily Sisson (3rd US), Ayuko Suzuki (2nd JPN) and Yasemin Can (1st Islamic Solidarity and European U23s, There was also a fast race at Stanford won by Meraf Bahta from Amy Cragg, Goytatom Gebrselassie and Sisson.

1. Ayana, 2. T Dibaba, 3. Tirop, 4. Aprot Nawowuna, 5. Burka, 6. Teferi, 7. Oljira, 8. Infeld, 9. Krumins, 10. Cheptai.

Half Marathon

JOYCLINE JEPKOSGEI SET two world records for the event: 64:52 at Prague in April (with world road records en route for 10k 30:04, 15k 45:37, 20k 1:01:25) and 64:51 at Valencia in October. She also won with 67:44 at Gifu, having started the year with 66:08 for 3rd at Ra's Al-Khaymah. There the next two fastest times of the year were run by Peres Jepchirchir 65:06 and Mary Keitany 65:13. Keitany later won the Great North Run in 65:59. Second and 3rd in Prague were Violah Jepchumba (also 1st at Ustí and 2nd at Göteborg) 65:22, and Fancy Chemutai (2nd at Valencia in 65:36 and 1st at Göteborg). Lucy Cheruiyot was 3rd at both Ustí and Valencia and in all 13 women broke 67 minutes. One of those was Ruth Chepngetich, who started with year with four wins at the distance to 66:19 at Istanbul, when Eunice Jepkirui set an Asian record of 66:46 in 2nd place. There were records for standards in depth with 10th on the world list of 66:35 and 100th 70:12 easily better than records set in 2016 at 67:16 and 70:35.

Marathon

THERE WERE SEVEN different winners of the seven races in the World Marathon Majors series. Mary Keitany was named as AIMS best marathon runner of 2017 and the year's fastest times came from Keitany 2:17:01 and Tirunesh Dibaba 2:17:56 in London. Dibaba went on to run the year's next fastest time with 2:18:31 in Chicago, while Keitany's other marathon was 2nd in a much slower race to Shalane Flanagan in New York. Rose Chelimo and Edna Kiplagat were 1-2 at the World Champs after being in the reverse order in Boston, and Kiplagat was later 4th in New York. Amy Cragg was a fine third at the Worlds, but this was her only marathon and she ran 2:27:18, while 4th placer Filomena Cheyech, just 3 seconds behind, had run 2:21:22 in Paris behind Purity Rionoripo and Agnes Barsosio, The third fastest winning time of the year came from Sarah Chepchirchir in Tokyo, making it three women under 2:20 in the year and the fourth fastest was Berlin, won by Gladys Cherono (5th Boston) in 2:20:23, followed under 2:21 by Ruti Aga (19th Boston, 13th Dubai) and Valary Aiyabei (1st Prague in 2:21:57). Chepchirchir also had a win in Lisbon. After 8th in Boston Brigid Kosgei ran 2:20:22 for 2nd in Chicago, followed by Jordan Hasay, who had also been 3rd in Boston and Kosgei went on to a brilliant win in Honolulu, smashing the course record with 2:22:15. Vivian Cheruiyot won in Frankfurt after 4th London and Eunice Jepkirui won again in Nagoya and was 6th at the Worlds, a place behind Shure Demise, who was 2nd in Dubai to Worknesh Degafa.

1. Keitany, 2. T Dibaba, 3. Chelimo, 4. E Kiplagat, 5. Cherono, 6. Chepchirchir, 7. Aiyabei, 8. Rionroripo, 9. Cheyech, 10. Kosgei

3000 Metres Steeplechase

THE RESULT OF the World Championship was sensational in that it was 1-2 for the USA as Emma Coburn 9:02.58 and Courtney Frerichs 9:03.77 were both well inside Coburn's previous North American record and thus prevented the usual Kenyan domination. Beatrice Chepkoech, however, would surely have won but for running round the water jump after the first lap and having to go back to negotiate it and also falling later to end up fourth, a place behind Hyvin Jepkemoi with Ruth Jebet 5th and Celliphine Chespol 6th. Chepkoech beat Coburn on the other four occasions they met (all DL races) and had four of the best seven times of the year. Despite running a pb 8:59.84 she was, however, beaten in Zürich by Jebet, who returned to top form with 8:55.29, a time only ever bettered in her own world record of 2016. Chespol was a third women to break 9 minutes during the year as she set world junior records of 9:05.70 (4th in Doha behind Jepkemoi, Chepkoech and Jebet) and 8:58.78 in Eugene, when she beat Chepkoech, Jebet and Coburn. Chepkoech was

4-1 v Coburn and Jebet and 4-2 v Chespol, while her greatest challenge came from Jepkemoi with whom she was 2-2. Jepkemoi was 3-2 v both Coburn and Jebet. Norah Tanui was the closest to the top six, with three sub-9:06 times to end her season, including wins in Berlin and Zagreb and 3rd in the Zürich DL final. In that race 4th to 8th were Coburn, Jepkemoi, Gesa Felicitas Krause (9th Worlds), Sofia Assefa (5th heat Worlds), and Chespol. Apart from her World silver, Frerichs had been 16th in Doha, 5th in Eugene and 2nd to Coburn at the US Champs, with a dnf in Berlin. Etenesh Diro, beaten 2-1 by Assefa, was 7th at the Worlds and 9th in Zürich, while two more Kenyans Daisy Jepkemei and Purity Kirui were close to the top ten, and Karoline Bjerkeli Grøvdal ran a remarkable Norwegian record 9:13.25 in late August in her first steeplechase for six years. The 10th best of 9:13.25 was a record.

Most times under 9:25.0: Tanui 9, Jebet 8, Chepkoech, Coburn, Assefa, Krause 6; Jepkemoi, Chespol 5; Diro, Jepkemei 4; Frerichs, Kirui 3.

1. Chepkoech, 2. Jepkemoi, 3. Jebet, 4. Coburn, 5. Chespol, 6. Tanui, 7. Frerichs, 8. Krause, 9. Assefa, 10. Diro

100 Metres Hurdles

IN SOMEWHAT SIMILAR fashion to 2016, Kendra Harrison was clearly the woman for top ranking. She was undefeated prior to the World Champs (in seven competitions), and ran the year's fastest times with 12.28 at Székesfehérvár and 12.39 at the London DL and four of the top six, but managed only 12.74 at the Worlds for 4th place. Sally Pearson returned to the stadium where she had won Olympic gold in 2012 and ran her season's best of 12.48 for 2nd in the London DL meeting and won World gold in 12.59 by 0.03 from the 2012 Olympic runner-up (and 2008 champion) Dawn Harper Nelson with Pamela Dutkiewicz 3rd. This year the most notable casualty at the US Champs was Sharika Nelvis, who was only 5th there, behind K Harrison, Nia Ali, Christine Manning and Harper Nelson with Kristi Castlin 6th. But Nelvis had a great year, culminating with 2nd in the DL final in Zürich behind Pearson, and Nelvis overall beat Pearson 5-2 and Harper Nelson 4-2. She was also 8-3 v her great rival Jasmin Stowers, who had many good times but was only 8th at the US Champs and 7th in Zürich. However on win-loss she was 5-2 v Harper Nelson and 4-3 v Manning (5th Worlds). Danielle Williams was 5th in her semi at the Worlds, but was 4-1 v Ali (8th Worlds) and in their only meeting beat Dutkiewicz, 3rd to 7th in Monaco. That was Dutkiewicz's first loss of the year, having won at the European Team and German Champs. Both Ali (3-2) and Queen Harrison (2-1) had win-loss advantage over Castlin. Alina Talay 6th and Nadine Visser 7th completed the World finalists, but Q Harrison beat Talay 2-0.

Most times at 12.70 or faster: Nelvis 13, K Harrison 10+1w, Stowers 9, Manning 8, Pearson 5+1w, Williams 5, Ali 4, Harper-Nelson 3.

1. K Harrison, 2. Pearson, 3. Nelvis, 4. Stowers, 5. Manning, 6. Harper Nelson, 7. Williams. 8. Dutkiewicz, 9. Ali, 10. Q Harrison

At 60m indoors Kendra Harrison had the three fastest times, 7.74A, 7.75 and 7.76 with Dutkiewicz next, 7.79 to win the German title. Harrison won the US title from Stowers and the European Indoor medallists were Cindy Roleder, Talay and Dutkiewicz.

400 Metres Hurdles

THE YEAR'S FASTEST times came at the US Champs, as Dalilah Muhammad won in 52.64 from Shamier Little 52.75 and Kori Carter 52.96. Then 4th Ashley Spencer and 5th Georganne Moline ran the fifth and sixth bests of 2017. In 6th place 18 year-old Sydney McLaughlin ran her second world junior record of the year with 53.82 for seventh on the world list. The only woman to interrupt this US domination was Jamaican Ristanna Tracey, the world's sixth fastest with 53.74. That came at the World Champs when Carter took gold and Muhammad silver. In their other clashes Muhammad was 5th and Carter 7th in Eugene and Carter 1st and Muhammad 3rd at Székesfehérvár. While only eighth on the world list at 53.97, Zuzana Hejnová was 3-2 v Muhammad, 1-1 v Carter and 3-1 v Little, who was 4th in her semi at the World, while Hejnová was 4th in the final and 2nd in the DL final in Brussels to Muhammad. Following in Brussels were Spencer, Elidh Doyle (8th Worlds, 1st Eur Team), Sara Slott Peterson (4sf Worlds), Janeive Russell and Léa Sprunger (5th Worlds). Spencer had DL wins in Eugene and Lausanne, where Tracey was 7th in their only meeting. Moline had three wins then 3rd in Eugene, but did not run after the US Champs. Russell was 5-1v Doyle, who was also beaten 3-2 by Sprunger. Russell missed the Worlds by being 4th at the Jamaican Champs. Sage Watson did not contest any DL races, but was unbeaten, including at NCAA and Canadian Champs before 6th at the Worlds.

Most times under 54.0/55.0: Muhammad 4/11, Carter 3/10, A Spencer 3/6, Little 3/5, Moline 2/5, Hejnová, R Tracey 1/8; McLaughlin 1/4, Russell, Doyle 0/6; Sprunger, Watson 0/5; Petersen 0/4, Nel, Tate, Fontanive, Nugent, Whyte 0/3.

1. Carter, 2. Muhammad, 3. Hejnová, 4. Little, 5. A Spencer, 6. Tracey, 7. Russell, 8. Moline, 9. Sprunger, 10. McLaughlin

High Jump

MARIYA LASITSKENE (née Kuchina and top

ranked in 2014 and 2015) dominated women's high jumping in 2017, as she won all 7 of her indoor and all 17 of her outdoor contests, and cleared at least 2m in 3 of those indoors and 13 outdoors, with a best of 2.06 in Lausanne – she won all seven DL competitions. Otherwise 2m was cleared by Airine Palsyte (twice indoors), and once each by Yuliya Levchenko and Marie-Laurence Jungfleisch. Enabled to compete at the Worlds as a neutral athlete, Lasitskene did 2.03 ahead of Levchenko 2.01 and Licwinko 1.99. Licwinko had a narrow advantage as she was 3-2 v 19 year-old Levchenko, although at the European Indoors Levchenko was 3rd and Licwinko 9=. Licwinko had a better depth of performances and won at the European Team Champs from Jungfleisch, who was 4th at the Worlds and cleared 2.00 at Eberstadt. Blanka Vlasic did not compete in 2017 and super-veteran Ruth Beitia announced her retirement after a best of 1.94 outdoors and 1.88 for 12th at the Worlds, having had a fine indoor season, with a best of 1.98 and 2nd at the European Indoors behind Palsyte (3rd WUG), who cleared 2.01, but had an outdoor best of 1.92 for 7= at the Worlds due to leg problems. Vashti Cunningham won the US titles with 1.96 indoors and 1.99 outdoors and was 10th at the Worlds, also with 1.92. She had much better depth of marks than the two British women who did 1.95 at the Worlds: Katarina Johnson-Thompson 5th and UK champion Morgan Lake 6th. US 3rd placer Inika McPherson was 9th at the Worlds and was 1-0 v Michaela Hrubá (6 EI, 3= Eur Team, 1 Eur U20) and 3-1 v Oksana Okunova (4th EI, 6 Eur Team, 1 WUG), who was also beaten 3-0 outdoors by Sofie Skoog. Nafissatou Thiam jumped 1.98 and 1.95 in her heptathlons, but only contested two individual events outdoors and one indoors.

Most competitions over 2.00/1.95m: Lasitskene 13+2i/18+4i, Levchenko 1/3, Licwinko 10, Cunningham 4+1i, Jungfleisch, Okuneva 3; Thiam 2+1i, Palsyte 2i/3i, Beitia 3i.

1. Lasitskene, 2. Licwinko, 3. Levchenko, 4. Jungfleisch, 5. Cunningham, 6. Lake (7), 7. McPherson (9), 8. Hrubá (10), 9. Skoog (-), 10. Okuneva (-). Palsyte (6), Beitia (8). (Including indoors)

Pole Vault

IN 2016 SANDI MORRIS and Ekateríni Stefanídi had a considerable battle for the top rankings with the American getting the verdict. In 2017 the order was reversed as Stefanídi won all her 11 outdoor contests and four of her five indoors. Morris was the only one to beat her (at Clermont-Ferrand). Stefanídi, however, beat her American rival on the other time that they met indoors and on all seven occasions outdoors, including when both cleared the year's best height of 4.87 undercover in Zürich. Morris was also second at the Worlds and in the DL final in Brussels and was a clear choice for second ranking, being 6-1 with one tie against Yarisley Silva, who had win-loss advantage over all but the top two. Silva was tied for the World bronze by Rosbeilys Peinado, the 19 year-old South American champion, who with a best of 4.65 lacked the overall quality of marks of the other rankings contenders. The former Olympic champion Jenn Suhr cleared 4.81 indoors and 4.83 outdoors in April for third on the world list, but was mostly side-lined by injury after that and after 2nd in the US Champs no heighted at the Worlds and misses a rankings after ten years in the top ten. Holly Bradshaw was the only vaulter apart from the top two to go over 4.80 twice; she was 6th at both Worlds and DL final in Brussels and 3-2 with one tie against Lisa Rzhih, 5th and 7th in those two big events and 2nd at the European Indoors. New to the top ten was Alysha Newman, who set a Canadian record 4.65 indoors and four outdoors from 4.62 to 4.75 and who was 7th Worlds and 3rd in Brussels. She was beaten 5-1 in the outdoor season by Ryzih, but beat Katie Nageotte (3rd Zürich, 4th Brussels) 4-3 and was 2-2 v Eliza McCartney (9th Worlds), who was 1-1 v Nicole Büchler (11th Worlds, 5th Brussels). Anzhelika Sidorova had similar marks outdoors after a good indoor season but no heighted in qualifying at the Worlds and at the Russian Champs was 10= in the DL final.

Most competitions over 4.60m (outdoors + in): Morris 12+8i, Stefanídi 11+6i, Newman 8+3i, Silva 7+1i, Ryzih 5+4i, Büchler 5+3i, Bradshaw 5+1i, Sidorova 4+5i, Nageotte 4+4i, Suhr, Mullina 4+2i; Meijer, LeLeux 4; Krasnova 3+1i, McCartney 3

1. Stefanídi, 2. Morris, 3. Silva, 4. Bradshaw, 5. Ryzih, 6. Newman, 7. Nageotte. 8. McCartney, 9. Büchler, 10. Peinado. - Sidorova (10). (Including indoors)

Long Jump

BRITTNEY REESE CONSOLIDATED her position as one of the all-time greats with her eighth global title as she won a close competition with 7.02 from Darya Klishina 7.00, Tianna Bartoletta 6.97 and Ivana Spanovic 6.96. Spanovic could have won but for her bib number falling back into the sand on her final jump; she had the year's best mark of 7.24 to win the European Indoor title but missed the opening months of the outdoor season through a foot injury. She was 3-2 v Bartoletta, who had two competitions over 7m to three by Reese (and two indoors for Spanovic). Lorraine Ugen and Claudia Salman-Rath had their best marks indoors, 6.97 and 6.94 for 2nd and 3rd at the European Indoors (with Klishina 4th) and were respectively 5th and 10th at the Worlds. Two more US jumpers had good marks, Quanesha Burks and Sha'Keela Saunders, but after 4th and 3rd at the US Champs were dnq 14th and 21st at the Worlds. Saunders had jumped 6.90 to win the NCAA indoor title but both disappointed with Saunders 5th and Banks 11th at the NCAAs outdoors. Klishina beat Ugen 4-2, but one of those losses was at the DL final in Brussels, won by Spanovic from Ugen, Saunders, Bartoletta, Reese, Shara Proctor (dnq 13 Worlds) and Klishina. Brooke Stratton had a limited campaign but was 6th at the Worlds. Yelena Sokolova competed just three times in Russia, but won their two biggest events with 6.85 and 6.82.

Most competitions over 6.70m (outdoors + in): Bartoletta 7, Burks 6+2i, Reese 5, Spanovic 4+4i, Saunders 4+2i, Wester 4+1i, Ugen 3+4i, Klishina 3+1w, Proctor 3.

1. Reese, 2. Bartoletta (3), 3. Spanovic (2), 4. Klishina, 5. Ugen, 6. Saunders, 7. Stratton, 8. Salman-Rath. 9. Burks, 10. Sokolova.

Triple Jump

THERE WAS GREAT rivalry between two South Americans, with the 2016 rankings being reversed as Yulimar Rojas beat Caterine Ibargüen 3-2. They met five times, Rojas won the first, 14.84 to 14.78 in Rome, then Ibargüen won in Monaco 14.86 to 14.73, before Rojas won another close encounter, 14.91 to 14.89 to take the World title, Rojas was below par in Birmingham when she was 7th with 13.94 as Ibargüen won with 14.51 and finally Rojas was 2nd in the DL final in Zürich with 14.52 and Ibargüen 3rd 14.48. On that occasion Olga Rypakova, who had been 3rd 14.77 at the Worlds, beat them both with 14.55. Rojas also had the year's top mark, 14.96 at Andújar. Hanna Minenko was 4th at the Worlds, but competed only four times, including 5th in Zürich, a place behind Kimberley Williams (10th Worlds), a much more frequent competitor. 5th to 9th at the Worlds were Kristin Gierisch, Anna Jagaciak Michalska, Ana Peleteiro, Shanieka Ricketts and Patricia Mamona, while in Zürich 6th to 8th were Mamona, Michalska and Elena Panturoiu (dnq 14 Worlds). Gierisch won the European Indoor title from Mamona, Paraskévi Papahrístou (dnq 20 Worlds, 1st European Team), Jagaciak Michalska and Peleteiro. Last year's fourth placer Keturah Orji was again NCAA champion indoors and out, but her unbeaten season was ended by lingering calf pain after winning the US title. Fourth and sixth on the world lists were South American champion Nubia Soares, 14.56 to win the Brazilian title, and Liadagmis Povea, 14.45 at the Barrientos Memorial in Cuba, but Soares otherwise only had two wins in Brazil and 7th in Rabat while Povea was dnq 22 at the Worlds. Standards in depth fell as 100th on the world list, 13.56, was the worst since 1998.

Most competitions over 14.30m: Rojas 9+1i, Williams 6+1w, Ibargüen 6, Rypakova 5, Ricketts 4, Gierisch 2+1i, Mamona 1+1w+1i.

1. Rojas, 2. Ibargüen, 3. Rypakova, 4. Williams, 5. Minenko, 6. Gierisch, 7. Ricketts, 8. Mamona, 9. Jagaciak Michalska. 10. Papahrístou.

Shot

GONG LIJIAO WAS the one 20m thrower with 20.11 (the lowest world lead since 1970) and also had the year's second best, 19.94 to win the World title. There were just seven women over 19m, the least since 1971 and a very far cry from 30 years ago, 1987, when in that era of East European dominance, there were 22 women over 20m and 39 over 19m. Gong won all but one of her eleven meets, and in those the closest any woman came to her was Anita Márton, 45cm down with 19.49 at the Worlds. Michelle Carter took the bronze there and was 2-2 v Márton. Those were very clearly the top three. Next came Danniel Thomas-Dodd, the NCAA and Jamaican champion, who was 4th at the Worlds. Raven Saunders and Dani Bunch were second and third on the world list with 19.76 and 19.64 at the US Champs, but at the Worlds Saunders was 10th and Bunch managed only 17.30 for 18th in qualifying. Saunders also threw 19.56 to win the NCAA title indoors, but was only 4th outdoors. The seventh 19m woman was Alyona Dubitskaya with 19.01 and she won at the European Team Champs, but was dnq 14th at the Worlds. She improved a little, however, at the DL final in Zürich with 6th behind Gong, Márton, Yuliya Leontyuk (Worlds 7th and 4-3 v Dubitskaya outdoors), Carter and Bunch. Brittany Crew improved the Canadian record to 18.47 and 18.58 and was 6th at the Worlds and the World Universities champion, and Yaniuvis López was 8th Worlds after an unbeaten season in Cuba; both had better marks than Worlds 5th placer Gao Yang. Valerie Adams did not compete this year and Christina Schwanitz only indoors before giving birth to twins in July.

Most competitions over 18.70m: Gong 10+1i, Carter 7+1i, Márton 6+3i, Bunch 5, Thomas-Dodd 3, Saunders 2+3i.

1. Gong, 2. Márton, 3. Carter, 4. Thomas-Dodd (5), 5. Saunders (4), 6. Bunch, 7. Crew, 8. Leontyuk. 9. López, 10. Dubitskaya. (Including indoors).

Discus

SANDRA PERKOVIC HAD another terrific season. She ranks as number one and was the Diamond League discus winner, both for the sixth successive year. She won all 9 of her competitions (at 66.79 or better) for the top five and 12 of the best 17 performances of the year. Her top mark of 71.41 was the word's best since 1992. Her two losses were both to Yaimí Pérez, in Stockholm and Sotteville, but the world number two was Dani Stevens, who was second to Perkovic at both Worlds (in an Oceania and Commonwealth record 69.64) and DL final in Brussels and was 3-1 again both Cubans Pérez and Denia Cabellero, who were 4th and 5th at the Worlds. Again relishing a major event, Mélina Robert-Michon was 3rd at the Worlds but was beaten 5-2 by each of the Cubans, while Pérez beat Cabellero 6-4. Nadine Müller, 6th Worlds, had better marks and edged Robert-Michon 4-3, including when they were 4th and 5th in Brussels, where Cabellero was 3rd, Whitney Ashley 6th and Pérez 7th. Su Xinyue and Feng Bin were 7th and 8th at the Worlds and 1st and 2nd at the Chinese National Games. Gia Lewis-Smallwood beat Ashley for the US title and they were 3-3 on win-loss but Ashley was ahead at the Worlds, 13th to 17th as neither made the final. Julia Harting was 9th Worlds and 8th Brussels, and headed Anna Rüh (dnq 14th Worlds) and Claudine Vita (1st European U23s) at the German Championships. Just missing a top ten ranking was South American champion Andressa de Morais, 11th Worlds.

Most competitions over 63m: Pérez 13, Perkovic 12 (all over 66m), Stevens, Caballero 11, Müller 8, Su 6, Robert-Michon, Vita 3.

1. Perkovic, 2. Stevens, 3, Pérez, 4, Caballero, 5. Müller, 6. Robert-Michon, 7. Su Xinyue, 8. Feng Bin, 9. Ashley, 10. Harting

Hammer

ANITA WLODARCZYK WAS again in a league of her own. She ranks top for the sixth time and fifth in succession and had the best nine performances of the year (over 77m), her best throw of 82.87 just 11cm short of her world record. She won all her 13 competitions, including at the Worlds despite being below par on the day. The other World medals went to Wang Zheng and Malwina Kopron, who improved during the year by 4.11m and who also won the WUG title. Zhang Wenxiu was 4th at the Worlds and ended the year by winning at the Chinese National Games, but only had five competitions, whereas the Worlds 5th Hanna Skydan and 6th Joanna Fiodorow had much busier years, with Skydan 5-1 ahead on win-loss. Hanna Malyshik beat Kopron, with Sophie Hitchon 5th, at the European Team Champs, and was WUG 2nd, although 10th at the Worlds behind Hitchon 7th, Katarine Safránková 8th and DeAnna Price 9th. Gwen Berry just missed the World final (14th) but won the US title from Maggie Ewen (NCAA champion) and Price, and beat Price 5-1.

Most competitions over 73m: Wlodarczyk 13, Kopron 10, Berry 7, Skydan 5, Wang, Malyshik, Fiodorow 4. Hitchon, Berry, Price 3.

1. Wlodarczyk, 2. Wang Zheng, 3. Kopron, 4. Skydan, 5. Zhang Wenxiu, 6. Fiodorow, 7. Malyshik, 8. Berry, 9. Hitchon, 10. Price

Javelin

SARA KOLAK, 68.43 in Lausanne, and Barbora Spotáková, 68.26 in the London DL meeting, had the top throws of the year. Ten years after her previous win, the double Olympic champion Spotáková was a delighted winner of the World title. Although not back to her world record levels she regained the top ranking that she had in 2006-10, 2012 and 2014 with eight wins in ten competitions including the last three of the five DL events. Kolak, 4th at the Worlds, beat her in Lausanne, and at Eugene the order was Tatyana Kholodovich (6th Worlds), Liu Shying, Kolak and Spotáková. There Liu set an Asian record with 66.67, but that was improved to 67.59 in qualifying at the Worlds by Lu Huihu, and Lu went on to win the bronze medal while a third Chinese thrower Li Lingwei took the silver. The last ranks as the top Chinese thrower as she won at the Chinese Champs and National Games with Lu 2nd and Liu 5th at the latter, although this trio was very level on win-loss. Kolak was 4th at the Worlds and 3rd in the DL final and beat the prolific Kholodovich (6th Worlds, 4th DL) 4-1. Eva Tugsuz made a huge improvement from 58.95 in 2016 and her best of 67.21 meant that she joined the aforementioned sextet in the top seven of the world list. Although 4th at the European U23s and WUG, she was 5th at the Worlds, with Katharina Molitor 7th, Liu Shiying 8th, Martina Ratej (5th DL) 9th and Kelsey-Lee Roberts 10th. Tugsuz was 2-0 v Ratej, who maintained a 2-1 advantage over Roberts. German champion Molitor was 2-1 v Liz Gleadle (12th Worlds, 8th DL), who was 4-2 v US champion Kara Winger. World lists 10th at 65.37 and 100th at 56.20 were the best ever with the current specification javelin.

Most competitions over 62m: Kholodovich 14, Spotáková 12, Liu Shiying 10, Kolak, Tugsuz 9; Ratej 8, Li Lingwei 6, Lu Huihui, Roberts 5; Mitchell, Witek 4; Molitor, Winger, Gleadle, Palameika, Viljoen 3.

1. Spotáková, 2. Kolak, 3. Kholodovich, 4. Li Lingwei, 5. Lu Huihui, 6. Tugsuz, 7. Liu Shiying, 8. Ratej, 9. Roberts, 10. Molitor

Heptathlon

NAFISSATOU THIAM FOLLOWED her Olympic triumph by adding 203 points to her Belgian record total with 7013 at Götzis (for 3rd on the world all-time list) before going on to a clear World victory with 6784. Just two heptathlons meant that she could not feature in the IAAF Challenge that was won by Carolin Schäfer, who had a very solid season winning at Ratingen 6667 and 2nd at Götzis 6836 and Worlds 6696 As usual most of the world's best competed at those two major events: Anouk Vetter 7th and 3rd, Katarina Johnson-Thomson 4th and 5th, Yorgelis Rodríguez 8th and 4th, Claudia Salman-Rath 5th and 8th, Erica Bougard 6th and 18th, Nadine Visser 10th and 7th, Xénia Krizsán 9th in both and Ivona Dadic 14th and 6th. Laura Ikauniece-Admidina had the year's third highest score with 6816 for 3rd at Götzis but was a non-finisher at the Worlds due to injury in the first event. Kendall Williams (12th Worlds) won the US title from Bougard, both over 6500 points. Several women ensured a Challenge score by competing at Talence in September with Vetter winning from Krizsán and Rodríguez.

1. Thiam, 2. Schäfer, 3. Vetter, 4. Ikauniece-Admidina, 5. Johnson-Thompson, 6. Rodríguez, 7. Salman-Rath, 8. Williams, 9. Bougard, 10. Visser

The best indoor pentathlon scores were for the first three at the European Indoors: Thiam 4870, Dadic 4767 and Zsivoczky-Farkas 4723, followed by Williams who won the SEC with 4686 and NCAA with 4682 in the USA..

20 Kilometres Walk

RUSSIANS DOMINATE THE world lists, but only 21 year-old Klavdiya Afanasyeva was cleared to compete internationally. She won the European U23 title but was disqualified at the Worlds after placing 5th in both the Russian winter and summer championships. The former produced the world's fastest times – from Yelena Lashmanova 1:25:18 and Yekaterina Medvedyeva 1:25:22, and this pair were also 1-2 at the summer champs, where Mariya Ponomaryova was 3rd and Sofiya Brodatskaya 4th, with the latter 3rd at the winter champs.

Although she had been beaten by Lu Xiuzhi and Wang Na in the first big Chinese race at Huangshan, Yang Jiayu took the World title from María Guadeloupe González, who won her other races, Juárez, Pan-American Cup and Mexican Champs, and Antonella Palmisano. Indeed I also follow the World Champs order 4th to 8th in the rankings: Érica de Sena, Sandra Arenas, Ana Cabecinha, Kimberley García and Wang Na. Major wins were achieved by Palmisano in the European Cup (Cabecinha 2nd), de Sena at La Coruña and García at Rio Maior (Arenas 2nd). Lu won at Taicang from Yang, Wang, de Sena and Nie Jingjing, but then was 12th at Zhengzhou (won by Yang) and disqualified at the Worlds and Chinese National Games, won by Yang with Lu also dq.

1. Yang Jiayu, 2. González, 3. Palmisano, 4. de Sena, 5. Arenas, 6. Cabecinha, 7. García, 8. Wang Na, 9. Lu Xiuzhi, 10. Nie Jingjing. Russians not ranked.

50 Kilometres Walk

THE IAAF DETERMINED that women's walking would be brought into line with the men by making this a world record distance, and, close to the Worlds, that women would also be able to race there, a select few being included in the men's race. Inês Henriques made her mark early with a world record 4:08:26 in January and improved that to 4:05:56 to win the World title. Yin Hang won in Huangshan with 4:22:22 and then set the Asian record with 4:08:58 for World silver as she was followed home by Yang Shuqing and Kathleen Burnett. In November came a CAC record by Mayra Herrera with 4:15:40.

1. Henriques, 2.Yin Hang, 3. Yang Shuqing, 4. Burnett, 5. Herrera.

TOP JUNIORS 2018

EIGHT JUNIOR MEN and four junior women made the world top ten rankings on the previous pages. Of the men, the highest ranked was Kipyegon Bett (3rd), who was the World bronze medallist and ran four sub 1:44.4 800m races. Top woman was Salwa Eid Naser, 2nd at 400m, who took the World silver medal in 49.88 for third on the world junior all-time list. The other rankers were: Men: 5000m 5th Selemon Barega, 10,000m 10th Andamlak Belihu, 3000mSt 8th Amos Korir, PV 5th Armand Duplantis. LJ 5th Maykel Massó & 6th Shi Yuhao, TJ 4th Carlos Nápoles; Women: 5000m 9th Letesenbet Gidey, 3000mSt 5th Celliphine Chespol, 400mh 10th Sydney McLaughlin.

World junior records were set by four of these athletes. Duplantis improved the junior best three times (unratified) indoors with 5.72, 5.75 and 5.81, and outdoors set new records at 5.80 and 5.90; he had 8 performances at 5.70 or more while Chris Nilsen had 6. Chespol smashed the old steeplechase record of 9:20.37 with records at 9:05.70 and 8:58.78 and ran under the old mark six times. McLaughlin took her record down to 54.03 and 53,82 and from 2016 and 2017 now has 7 of the top 10 all-time junior performances at 400mh. Further world junior records were set in winning European Junior titles by Niklas Kaul, with 8435 points for the decathlon (junior specification) and the German women's 4x100m team who ran 43.27. The greatest domination of junior performances at any event came from Sofiya Palkina, with the top 12 marks in the women's hammer.

CROSS-COUNTRY - NATIONAL CHAMPIONS 2017

	Men (long distance)	**Women** (long distance)
Algeria	Rabah Aboud	Kenza Dahmani
Australia	Andrew Buchanan	Alex Peterson
Austria	Timon Theuer	Andrea Mayr
Belarus	Artyom Lohish	Nina Savina
(Nov)	Sergey Platonov	Nina Savina
Belgium	Isaac Kimeli	Louise Carton
Brazil	Gilberto Lopes	Tatiane da Silva
Bulgaria	Mitko Tsenov	Marinela Nineva
Canada (Nov)	Lucas Bruchet	Claire Sumner
Chile	Iván Chávez	Pauline Burdos
China	Dong Guojian	Zhang Deshun
Colombia	Javier Peña	Sandra Rosas
Croatia (Nov)	Dino Bosnjak	Bojana Bjeljac
Czech Republic (Nov)	Jakub Zemanik	Simona Vrzálová
Denmark	Peter Glans	Simone Glad
England	Ben Connor	Jessica Judd
Eritrea	Arom Kifle	Nazret Weldu
Ethiopia	Getaneh Tamire	Dera Dida
France	Hassan Chahdi	Christelle Daunay
Germany	Philipp Pflieger	Alina Reh
Greece	Ioánnis Zervákis	Ouranía Reboúli
Hungary	László Gregor	Lilla Böhm
India	Bugatha Srinu	Swathi Gadhave
Ireland (Nov)	Paul Pollock	Shona Heaslip
Israel	Demeke Teshala	Chamtai Korlima
Italy	Danielle Meucci	Federica Dal Ri
Japan	Syota Onitsuka	Mao Ichiyama
Kazakhstan	Andrey Leymanov	Tatyana Neroznak
Kenya	Leonard Barsoton	Irene Cheptai
Luxembourg	Christian Molitor	Liz Weiler
Morocco	Ali Chaif	Soukaina Atanane
Netherlands	Jesper van der Wielen	Andrea Deelstra
New Zealand	Craig Lautenslager	Ruby Muir
Northern Ireland	Aaron Doherty	Jessica Craig
Norway (Oct)	Okubamichael Mesfun ERI	Live Solheimdal
Poland	Tomasz Grycko	Katarzyna Rutkowska
Portugal	Rui Pinto	Jéssica Augusto
Romania (Oct)	Nicolae Sorae	Ancuta Boboce;
Russia	Igor Maksimova	Lyudmila Lebedeva
Saudi Arabia	Youssef Asiri	
Scotland	Callum Hawkins	Morag MacLarty
Serbia	Nemanja Cerovac	Olivera Jevtic
Slovakia (Nov)	Peter Durec	Silvia Schwaiger
Slovenia	Rok Puhar	Patricija Plazar
South Africa	Precious Mashele	Glenrose Xaba
Spain	Adel Mechaal	Trihas Gebre
Sri Lanka	Lionel Samarajeewa	Gayanthika Abeyrathne
Sweden (Oct)	Napoleon Salomon	Meraf Bahta
Switzerland	Matthias Kyburz	Flavia Stutz
Trinidad & Tobago	Shirvan Baboolal	Samantha Shukla
Uganda	Joshua Cheptegei	Mercyline Chelagat
Ukraine (October)	Yehor Zhukov	Viktoriya Kalyuzhna
USA	Leonard Korir	Aliphine Tuliamuk
Venezuela	Alexis Peña	Nubia Arteaga
Wales	Dewi Griffiths	Beth Kidger
Balkan (Nov)	Sedat Günen TUR	Roxana Bârca ROU
European Clubs	Yemaneberhan Crippa ITA	Irene Cheptai KEN
Team	Istanbul BBSK TUR	Üsküdar Belediye SK TUR
Gulf	Hassan Chani BRN	
NACAC	Abbabiya Simbasa USA	Sasha Gollish CAN
NCAA (USA)	Justin Knight CAN	Ednah Kurgat KEN
Nordic	Napoleon Salomon SWE	Sara Christiansson SWE
South American	René Champi PER	Carmen Toaquinza ECU
World Military	Ali Guerine ALG	

Short Course winners

Austria	Christian Steinhammer	
China	Dong Guojian	Zhang Xinyan
Denmark	Peter Glans	Anna Emili Møller
Estonia	Allar Lamp	Kelly Nevolihhin
France	Mohammed-Amine El Bouajaji	Élodie Normand
Germany	Florian Orth	
Morocco	Mohamed Tindoufte	Sanae El Otmani
Portugal	Samuel Barata	Daniela Cunha
Russia	Yegor Nikolayev	Yekaterina Sokolova
Scotland	Cameron Boyek	Laura Muir
South Africa	Mthobisi Baloyi	Glenrose Xaba
Sweden	Napoleon Solomon	Meraf Bahta
Switzerland	Jonas Schopfer	Fabienne Schlumpf
World Military	Djilali Bedrani ALG	Roxana Bârca ROU

Winners Major Cross-Country Races 2017

7 Jan	Edinburgh (EA)	Leonard Korir USA	Yasemin Can TUR
8 Jan	Amorebieta	Nguse Amsolom ERI	Jessica Martin GBR
14 Jan	Antrim (IAAF)	Conseslus Kipruto KEN	Caroline Kipkirui KEN
15 Jan	Kerkrade (EA)	David Nilsson SWE	Imane Truyers BEL
15 Jan	Santiponce, Seville (IAAF)	Aweke Ayalew BRN	Senbere Teferi ETH
15 Jan	Della Lagarina, Rovereto (EA)	Robert Ndiwa KEN	Sara Dossena ITA
22 Jan	San Vittore Olana (Cinque Mullina) (IAAF)	Selemon Barega ETH	Beyenu Degefa ETH
22 Jan	Elgóibar	Joshua Cheptegei UGA	Senbere Teferi ETH
22 Jan	Hannut (EA)	Andy Vernon GBR	Birtukan Adamu ETH
22 Jan	San Sebastián	Salah Mikhou BRN	Bontu Edao BRN
5 Feb	Albufeira (IAAF)	Yemaneberhan Crippa ITA	Irene Cheptai KEN
23 Sep	Lidingöloppet (EA) 30k	Napoleon Solomon SWE	Maria Larsson SWE
11 Nov	Middlefart (EA)	Napoleon Solomon SWE	Sara Christiansson SWE
11 Nov	Pforzheim-Huchenfeld (EA)	Jannik Arbogast GER	Elena Burkard GER
12 Nov	Burgos (Atapuerca) (IAAF)	Getaneh Tamire ETH	Senbere Teferi ETH
18 Nov	Salzburg (EA)	Richard Ringer GER	Simona Vrzálová CZE
19 Nov	Leffinckroucke (EA)	Birhanu Yemataw BRN	Margaret Chelimo KEN
19 Nov	Soria (EA)	Jacob Kiplimo UGA	Alice Aprot KEN
25 Nov	Istanbul (EA)	Benard Cheruiyot KEN	Meseret Asefa ETH
26 Nov	Darmstadt (EA)	Amanal Petros GER	Alina Reh GER
26 Nov	Alcobendas (EA)	Aron Kifle ERI	Alice Aprot KEN
26 Nov	Tilburg (EA)	Napoleon Solomon SWE	Mehraf Bahta SWE

IAAF – IAAF permit races, EA – European Athletics permit races

2017 WORLD ROAD RACE REVIEW

By Marty Post

JOYCILINE JEPKOSGEI PRESENTED a strong case for having run the greatest women's road race in history at Prague on April 1, 2017. The 23-year-old Kenyan's blistering pace at the Sportismo Half-Marathon carried her past 10k in 30:04, a remarkable 17 seconds faster than the standing world record for that distance set by Paula Radcliffe in 2003. Keeping up her unprecedented rhythm, her split times at 15k (45:37) and 20k (1:01:25) lowered the IAAF world records by 37 and 29 seconds respectively. The final strides on that day carried her to a historic first sub-65 minute half-marathon, stopping the clock in 1:04:52.

However, Jepkosgei was not finished breaking speed barriers. Returning to Prague on September 9, sub-30 minutes for a road 10k became reality when she crossed the finish in 29:43. Another rapid first half saw her reach 5k in 14:32, not an IAAF recognized record distance but still 14 seconds quicker than any other woman had every run on the roads. The final race in the Jepkosgei record trilogy was the Medio Maratón Ciudad de Valencia on October 22. Although her en route intervals were slightly slower (30:08/45:58/1:01:29) than Prague, a strong finishing kick resulted in one second off her previous WR with a 1:04:51.

In fact there were three women's half-marathon world records in 2017. At the always fast Ra's Al Khaymah race on February 10, Peres Jepchirchir won a stirring duel with Mary

Keitany, prevailing by seven seconds in 65:06. Besides the half-marathon WR, Jepchirchir set a new WR at 20k (61:40) as third place Jepksogei (66:08) and fifth place Tirunesh Dibaba (66:50) set all-time fastest marks for place. For Keitany it was a superb day with a new PR, but also a disappointing one with only her second loss at that distance ending a 13-race win streak dating back to October 2007. Violah Jepchumba, now representing Bahrain, set an Asian record of 65:22 in second place at Prague.

For years women had been threating to break 100 sub-70 minute half-marathons in a calendar year (96 in 2016, 91 in 2015, 92 in 2014). In 2017 this standard fell by mid-September as the year-end total reached 141 including splits en route in marathons and some point-to-point courses such as the Great North Run and Rome-Ostia.

The all-time 10k lists also underwent major revision. Prague was the site of new numbers one (Jepkosgei 29:47), two (Jepchumba 30:05 split), three (Fancy Chemutai, 30:06) and six (Sheila Kiprotich, 30:28). Excluding the downhill Madrid course, there were 15 sub-31s in 2017.

Mary Keitany ran not only the year's fastest times at 25k and 30k en route at the London Marathon but they were the fastest in history. Unfortunately, her former time of 1:19:43 came at a point exceeding the record-quality net elevation drop tolerance but the latter time of 1:36:05 was ratified as a new IAAF world record.

It was a banner year in the men's half marathon as well. The Copenhagen Half-Marathon produced the three fastest times of the year and only ones under 59 minutes as Abraham Cheroben's Asian record 58:40 held off Jorum Okombo (58:48, 19 years old on race date) and Alex Korio (58:51). There was a total of 30 sub-one hour runs turned in by 27 men. This included national records of 59:30 by Ismail Juma of Tanzania, and 59:48 by Sondre Moen of Norway – the fastest in history by a non-African born runner – plus just over an hour 1:00:17 by Yuta Shitara of Japan.

A pair of Kimelis topped the 10k rankings, Benard (27:10) and Matthew (27:11, a junior aged 19), with Rhonex Kipruto (27:13) third at the Prague race. Joshua Cheptegei lowered the Ugandan record to 27:29. Other 2017 leaders were Ben True at 5k (13:20, American record), Joshua Cheptegei at 15k (41:16, Uganda NR and number two all-time) and Rodgers Chumo at 10 miles (45:03).

WINNERS OF LEADING 2017 ROAD RACES

Date	Race	Men	Women
8 Jan	Adana HMar	Belay Tilahun ETH 63:34	Ruth Chepngetich KEN 69:06
8 Jan	Egmond aan Zee HMar	Dawit Wolde ETH 62:41	Desi Jisa BRN 72:08
8 Jan	Valencia Ibercaja 10k	Nicholas Kosimbei KEN 27:52	Marta Poveda ESP 33:49
15 Jan	Houston HMar	Leonard Korir USA 61:14	Veronica Nyaruai KEN 67:58
22 Jan	Santa Pola HMar	Peter Kirui KEN 60:56	Antonina Kwambai KEN 69:49
5 Fab	Coamo HMar	Clement Langat KEN 64:01	Gladys Tejeda PER 75:14
5 Fab	Granollers HMar	Mathew Kisorio KEN 61:30	Irene Pelayo ESP 72:11
5 Fab	Marugame HMar	Callum Hawkins GBR 60:00	Eunice Kirwa BRN 68:07
5 Fab	Naples HMar	Philip Tarbei KEN 61:21*	Eva Vrabcová Nyvltová CZE 71:54*
10 Fab	R'as Al Khaymah HMar	Bedan Karoki KEN 59:10	Peres Jepchirchir KEN 65:06*
12 Fab	Barcelona HMar	Leonard Langat KEN 60:52	Florence Kiplagat KEN 68:15
12 Fab	Verona HMar	Edwin Koech KEN 60:24	Mimi Belete BRN 69:15
12 Fab	Yamaguchi HMar	Abiyot Abinet ETH 61:21	Ami Utsonomiya JPN 70:47
19 Fab	Guadalajara HMar	Julius Keter KEN 63:55	Risber Gesabwa KEN 74:55
19 Fab	Ome 30k	Ezekiel Cheboitibin KEN 1:30:49	Ami Utsonomiya JPN 1:46:24
26 Fab	Gyeonggi HMar	Samuel Kariuki KEN 62:45	Jeong Da-eun KOR 74:46
26 Fab	San Juan 10k	Sam Chelanga USA 28:19	Mary Wacera KEN 31:41
5 Mar	Paris HMar	Morris Gachaga KEN 60:38	Ruth Chepngetich KEN 68:08
5 Mar	Verbania HMar	Reuben Kerio KEN 61:21	Brigid Kosgei KEN 67:35*
11 Mar	Jacksonville 15k (US Ch)	Leonard Korir USA 43:22	Jordan Hasay USA 49:28
12 Mar	The Hague HMar	Geoffrey Yegon KEN 59:56	Fabienne Schlumpf SUI 70:17
12 Mar	Rome-Ostia HMar	Guye Adola ETH 59:18	Gladys Cherono KEN 67:01
19 Mar	Eldoret HMar (A) (dh 110m)	Isaac Langat KEN 60:52	Esther Chesang KEN 70:08
19 Mar	Lisbon HMar	Jake Robertson NZL 60:01	Mare Dibaba ETH 69:43
19 Mar	Milan HMar	Frederick Moronga KEN 61:20	Ruth Chepngetich KEN 67:42*
19 Mar	New York City HMar	Feyisa Lilesa ETH 60:04	Molly Huddle USA 68:19
25 Mar	Mobile 10k	Dominic Ondoro KEN 28:04	Nancy Nzisa KEN 32:49
26 Mar	Venlo HMar	Meshack Koech KEN 60:19	Naomi Jebet Rotich KEN 70:03
26 Mar	Warsaw HMar	John Kipsang Lotiang KEN 61:12	Ayantu Gemechu ETH 70:26

1 Apr	Azkoitia HMar	Joseph Kiptum KEN 60:37	Desi Jisa BRN 69:25
1 Apr	Prague HMar	Tamirat Tola ETH 59:37	Joyceline Jepkosgei KEN 64:52*
2 Apr	Berkane HMar	El Hassan El Abbassi BRN 61:31	Salome Nyirukundo RWA 71:30
2 Apr	Berlin HMar	Gilbert Masai KEN 59:57	Joan Melly Chelimo KEN 68:45
2 Apr	Carlsbad 5k	Dejen Gebremeskel ETH 13:27	Violah Lagat KEN 15:35
2 Apr	Chicago 8k	Stephen Sambu KEN 22:47	Kim Conley USA 25:43
2 Apr	Madrid HMar	Moses Kibet UGA 61:54*	Joy Kemuna Loyce KEN 70:28
2 Apr	Washington DC 10M	Stanley Kebenei USA 46:36	Hiwot Gebrekidan ETH 53:37
9 Apr	New York City 10k	Sam Chelanga USA 28:21	Mamitu Daska ETH 31:37
15 Apr	Boston 5k	Ben True USA 13:20*	Buze Diriba ETH 14:54
15 Apr	New Orleans 10k	Jake Robertson NZL 27:55	Mamitu Daska ETH 32:19
15 Apr	Paderborn 10k	Benard Kimeli KEN 27:18*	Gladys Kimaina KEN 31:15*
23 Apr	Gifu HMar	Alexander Mutiso KEN 60:57	Joyciline Jepksogei KEN 67:44*
23 Apr	Yangzhou HMar	Mosinet Geremew ETH 60:56	Sutume Asefa ETH 70:30
30 Apr	Istanbul HMar	Ismail Juma TAN 60:09	Ruth Chepngetich KEN 66:19
30 Apr	Würzburg 10k	Benard Kimeli KEN 28:14	Fate Tola GER 32:47
1 May	Puy-en-Velay 15k	Mathew Kimeli KEN 42:00*	Yvonne Jelagat KEN 47:47
7 May	Casablanca 10k	El Hassan El Abassi BRN 27:55	Belaynesh Tsegaye ETH 32:09
7 May	Spokane 12k	Gabriel Geay TAN 34:31	Buze Diriba ETH 40:19
13 May	Grand Rapids 25k (US Ch)	Dathan Ritzenhein USA 1:14:27	Aliphine Tuliamuk USA 1:24:35*
14 May	Sendai HMar	Charles Ndirangu KEN 61:44	Hanae Tanaka JPN 71:07
20 May	Gothenburg HMar	Geoffrey Yegon KEN 60:19	Fancy Chemutai KEN 67:58*
20 May	Karlovy Vary HMar	Wilfred Kimitei KEN 60:54*	Yvonne Jelagat KEN 68:19*
21 May	Bengaluru 10k	Alex Korio KEN 28:12	Irene Cheptai KEN 31:51
21 May	Lugano HMar	Cosmas Kipchoge KEN 61:01	Muliye Dekebo ETH 69:59
21 May	San Francisco 12k	Philemon Cheboi KEN 34:48	Buze Diriba ETH 39:48
21 May	Vienna 5k	*women only*	Sara Moreira POR 15:36
27 May	Ottawa 10k	Leul Gebresilase ETH 28:43	Netsanet Gudeta ETH 31:35
28 May	Manchester 10k	Dathan Ritzenhein USA 28:06	Tirunesh Dibaba ETH 31:03
29 May	Boulder 10k	Gabriel Geay TAN 29:03	Mamitu Daska ETH 32:45
3 Jun	Ceské Budejovice HMar	Justus Kangogo KEN 62:47	Agnes Barsosio KEN 69:53*
4 Jun	San Diego HMar (dh 86.5m)	Tsegay Tuemay ERI 61:38	Biruktayit Degefa ETH 70:12
10 Jun	New York 10k	*women only*	Mary Keitany KEN 31:20
10 Jun	Zwolle HMar	Richard Mengich KEN 61:34	Flomena Chepchirchir KEN 70:38
17 Jun	Duluth HMar	Evans Kurui KEN 63:06	Biruktayit Degefa ETH 71:26
24 Jun	Appingedam 10k	John Langat KEN 28:06	Fancy Chemutai KEN 30:23*
24 Jun	Olomouc HMar	Josphat Kiptis KEN 61:50	Worknesh Degefa ETH 69:19
25 Jun	Boston 10k	Daniel Chebii KEN 27:58	Joan Melly Chelimo KEN 31:24
25 Jun	Hamburg HMar	Albert Kangogo KEN 61:07	Flomena Chepchirchir KEN 70:21*
4 Jul	Atlanta 10k (34m dh;US Ch)	Leonard Korir USA 28:16	Aliphine Tuliamuk USA 32:49
9 Jul	Utica 15k	Silas Kipruto KEN 43:55	Mary Wacera KEN 49:18
15 Jul	Kingsport 8k	Teshome Mekonen ETH 22:41	Stephanie Place USA 28:20
23 Jul	Capitola 6M	Teshome Mekonen ETH 27:33	Buze Diriba ETH 31:19
29 Jul	Davenport 7M (US Ch)	Sam Chelanga USA 32:53	Aliphine Tuliamuk USA 36:30
30 Jul	Bogotá (A) HMar	Feyisa Lilesa ETH 64:30	Brigid Kosgei KEN 72:16
5 Aug	Cape Elizabeth 10k	Stephen Kosgei Kibet KEN 27:55	Mary Keitany KEN 30:41*
19 Aug	Schortens 10M	Ezra Kering KEN 47:29	Naomi Jebet Rotich KEN 52:27*
20 Aug	Falmouth 7M	Stephen Sambu KEN 32:14	Caroline Chepkoech KEN 35:53
20 Aug	Klagenfurt HMar	Peter Kirui KEN 60:30	Viola Kibiwot KEN 70:15
26 Aug	Flint 10M	Julius Kogo KEN 47:01	Buze Diriba ETH 51:49
2 Sep	Lille HMar	Vincent Rono KEN 59:27	Gladys Cheshire KEN 67:49
3 Sep	Tilburg 10M/10k	Rodgers Kwemoi KEN 45:03	Senbere Teferi ETH 30:38
4 Sep	New Haven 20k (US Ch)	Galen Rupp USA 59:04	Jordan Hasay USA 66:35
9 Sep	Prague 10k	Benard Kimeli KEN 27:10*	Joyciline Jepkosgei KEN 29:43*
9 Sep	Waterloo, IA HMar	Sammy Rotich KEN 63:33*	Diana Kipyokei KEN 69:45*
10 Sep	New York 5th Avenue 1M	Nick Willis NZL 3:51.3 (dh 8.23m)	Jenny Simpson USA 4:16.6
10 Sep	South Shields HMar (dh 30m)		
		Mo Farah GBR 60:06	Mary Keitany KEN 65:59
16 Sep	Ustí nad Labem HMar	Barselius Kipyego 59:14*	Violah Jepchumba BRN 66:06*
17 Sep	Copenhagen HMar	Abraham Cheroben BRN 58:40*	Eunice Chumba BRN 66:11*
17 Sep	Krems HMar	Peter Kirui KEN 60:45	Polline Njeru KEN 70:38

17 Sep	Philadelphia HMar	Galen Rupp USA 62:18	Meseret Defar ETH 68:46
17 Sep	Porto HMar	Abraham Kiptum KEN 60:06	Monica Jepkoech KEN 69:23*
17 Sep	Udine HMar	Noah Kigen Kiprotich KEN 61:12	Wilfridah Moseti KEN 71:55
17 Sep	Zaandam 10M	Berhanu Legesse ETH 45:38	Mercyline Chelangat UGA 53:08*
23 Sep	Lynchburg 10M	Benard Ngeno KEN 47:26	Biruktayit Degefa ETH 54:31
24 Sep	Belfort-Montbéliard HMar	Wilson Too KEN 60:58	Dalilah Gosa BRN 72:30
24 Sep	Remich HMar	Zelalem Mengistu ETH 62:37	Peninah Kandie KEN 69:15
1 Oct	Breda HMar	Edwin Kiptoo KEN 60:42	Naomi Jebet Rotich KEN 68:44
1 Oct	Cardiff HMar	John Lotiang KEN 60:42	Edith Chelimo KEN 65:52*
1 Oct	Glasgow HMar	Chris Thompson GBR 62:44	Flomena Cheyech KEN 70:17
1 Oct	Minneapolis 10M (US Ch)	Shadrack Kipchirchir USA 47:33	Sara Hall 53:43
1 Oct	Turin HMar	Youssef Sbaai MAR 62:42	Winfridah Moseti KEN 69:39
1 Oct	Trento HMar	Justus Kangogo KEN 61:48*	Shitaye Eshete BRN 70:10
2 Oct	Utrecht 10k	Benard Kimeli KEN 27:57	Genet Gashie Beyene ETH 33:29
8 Oct	Berlin 10k	Mathew Kimeli KEN 27:32	Alina Reh GER 31:38
8 Oct	Boston HMar	Daniel Salel KEN 64:31	Joan Chelimo KEN 70:31
8 Oct	Durban 10k	Joshua Cheptegei UGA 27:29*	Mercyline Chelangat UGA 31:38
8 Oct	Groningen 4M	Victor Chumo KEN 17:31	Ruth Jebet BRN 19:16
14 Oct	Tokyo 20k	Wesley Ledama KEN 57:27	*men only*
15 Oct	Lisbon HMar	Birahan Nebebew ETH 62:02	Eunice Chumba BRN 68:48
15 Oct	Pettinengo 9.6k/4k	Yasin Haji ETH 27:56	Daisy Jepkemei KEN 12:03*
22 Oct	Valencia HMar	Abraham Cheroben BRN 59:11	Joyciline Jepkosgei KEN 64:51*
29 Oct	Arezzo HMar	James Mburugu KEN 62:14	Winfridah Moseti KEN 69:41
29 Oct	Marseille-Cassis 20k	Jemal Yimer ETH 59:16	Edith Chelimo KEN 65:58*
4 Nov	New York 5k (US Ch)	Shadrack Kipchirchir USA 13:57	Molly Huddle USA 15:24*
5 Nov	Morlaix 10k (dh 86m)	Paul Melly KEN 28:28	Mercyline Jeronoh KEN 32:46
19 Nov	Ageo HMar	Simon Kariuki JPN 61:25*	Chun Yu-Tsao TPE 65:51
19 Nov	Boulogne-Billancourt HMar	Hiskel Tewelde ERI 61:13	Rehima Tusa ETH 68:28*
19 Nov	New Delhi HMar	Berhanu Legesse ETH 59:46	Almaz Ayana ETH 67:12
19 Nov	Nijmegen 15k	Joshua Cheptegei UGA 41:16	Birke Debele ETH 48:52
23 Nov	Manchester, CT 4.75M	Paul Chelimo USA 21:32	Buze Diriba ETH 23:57*
26 Nov	Addis Ababa 10k	Selomon Barega ETH 28:37	Zeineba Yimer ETH 32:31
2 Dec	Geneva 7.32k	Julien Wanders SUI 20:59	Helen Bekele ETH 23:50
3 Dec	Kosa 10M	Yuta Shitara JPN 45:58	*men only*
3 Dec	s-Heerenberg 15k	Victor Chumo KEN 43:23	Mary Munanu KEN 49:08
17 Dec	Kolkata 25k	Kenenisa Bekele ETH 1:13:48*	Degitu Azimeraw ETH 1:26:01*
23 Dec	Okayama HMar	*women only*	Pauline Kamulu KEN 68:04*
31 Dec	Bolzano 10.05k/5.05k	Muktar Edris ETH 28:45	Agnes Tirop KEN 15:30*
31 Dec	Houilles 10k	Julien Wanders SUI 28:02	Stacy Ndiwa KEN 31:35
31 Dec	Madrid 10k (dh 55m)	Eric Kiptanui KEN 27:34	Geleta Burka ETH 30:55
31 Dec	Peuerbach 6.8k/5.1k	Victor Chumo KEN 19:08	Ruth Jebet BRN 15:38
31 Dec	São Paulo 15k	Dawit Fikadu BRN 44:17	Flomena Cheyech KEN 50:18

* = course record; dh = downhill course; A = altitude over 1000m

MARATHON REVIEW 2017

By Marty Post

ELIUD KIPCHOGE HAD the extraordinary accomplishment of running the fastest marathon of the year from two different perspectives in 2017. At Monza, Italy on May 6, the 63rd anniversary of Roger Bannister's historic first sub-four minute mile, Kipchoge challenged another mathematical landmark: the two hour marathon. While his performance in the Nike Breaking2 Challenge was ineligible for official world record sanction with the participation of rotating pacemakers, Kipchoge covered the marathon distance of 42.195 km in 2:00:25. He passed halfway in 59:57, and his splits for 25km (1:11:03) and 30km (1:25:20) were the fastest in history for road or track.

Kipchoge returned to Berlin in September where he won in 2015 and suffered the only loss of his marathon career in 2013. The race was promoted as a prospective world record showdown with defending champion Kenenisa Bekele and former world-record holder Wilson Kipsang in the field, but neither finished the race. In less than ideal weather conditions Kipchoge instead held off a late challenge from marathon novice Guye Adola of Ethiopia. The 2016 Olympic champion finished in 2:03:32 with Adola runner-up in 2:03:46, a debut world record. For the seventh year in a row Berlin produced the fastest time of the year.

The only other sub-2:04 of 2017 came when Kipsang set an Asian all-comer's record of 2:03:58 at the Tokyo Marathon. This was Kipgang's record fourth lifetime sub-2:04 and eighth sub-2:05 each one coming over eight consecutive years. Tsegaye Kebede chalked up his 16th sub-2:09 and 17th sub-2:10 in that race. And no annual review would be complete without a recap of where Japan's indefatigable Yuki Kawauchi stood at year's end with best ever career totals for breaking these time barriers: 2:12 (25), 2:13 (40), 2:14 (48), 2:15 (53), 2:16 (62) 2:17 (67), 2:18 (71), 2:19 (74); on January 1, 2018 he ran record number 76 for sub-2:20s.

Geoffrey Kirui became the first man with victories at Boston and the World Championships in the same year. Galen Rupp was second at Boston and six months later became the first non-African born champion in 35 years at the Bank of America Chicago Marathon. Geoffrey Kamworor's victory at New York City made him the first man with a "triple crown" of wins at a Marathon Major, IAAF Half-Marathon Championships and IAAF World Cross Country Championships (although Paul Tergat also did this before the launch of the Majors program in 2006). The European record was lowered to 2:05:48 at Fukuoka in December when Norway's Sondre Nordstad Moen became the first man from that continent to win there since 2005. Other notable national marathon records were set in 2017 for the Netherlands (2:08:16 Abdi Nageeye), Sudan (2:09:40 Aychew Bantie), Lesotho (2:09:47 Motloka Nkhabutlane), and Latvia (2:14:24 Valerijs Zolnerovics).

Mary Keitany had many moments of racing glory prior to the 2017 Virgin Money London Marathon but that race may stand out as the singular competition of her career. Accompanied by pacesetter Carolyn Chepkoech Kipkirui, she posted fastest ever splits of 15:31/31:17/47:15/63:26 as she reached halfway in 1:06:54. This was 62 seconds quicker than her New York City 2011 split (when she finished in 2:23:38) and even 1:06 ahead of Paula Radcliffe's 2:15:25 London pace. After Kipkirui dropped out, Keitany set more split records of 1:19:42 (25km) and 1:36:05 (30km). While Radcliffe's mixed race record would survive, her all-women's world record of 2:17:42 would not, as Keitany notched her third London victory in 2:17:01. It shattered her Kenyan record of 2:18:37 and along with Daniel Wanjiru's 2:05:48 broke the Chicago 2002 standard for fastest combined male/female race day winners by 25 seconds. In second place Tirunesh Dibaba of Ethiopia also set a national record of 2:17:56, the fastest losing time ever; despite stopping due to stomach woes late in race, she actually ran the second half five seconds faster than Keitany. In October, Dibaba prevailed at Chicago in 2:18:31, and her calendar year two race total of 4:36:27 was just 13 seconds shy of Radcliffe's sum in 2002.

Sarah Chepchirchir ran a breakthrough 2:19:47 to win the Tokyo Marathon and like her male counterpart Wilson Kipsang, she set a Japanese all-comers and month of February record. The year's biggest event, the TCS New York City Marathon (50,766 finishers), had its first home country champion in 40 years when American Shalane Flanagan sped away from Keitany late in the race to win by 61 seconds in 2:26:53. Eunice Jepkurui Kirwa set a Bahrain national record of 2:21:17 at Nagoya and other NRs included Mongolia, 2:32:59 by Munkhzaya Bayartsogt, and Paraguay, 2:35:17 by Carmen Patricia Martinez. Lydia Cheromei posted a 40-44 world age group record of 2:23:31 at Shanghai and Catherine Bertone a 45-49 record of 2:28:34 at Berlin. The husband-wife best combined time fell to Paul Lonyangata (2:06:10) and Purity Rionoripo (2:20:55) with 4:27:05 at Paris.

The three women sub-2:19s in 2017 was a new single year record, as were 11 sub-2:21s, 19 sub-2:22s and 29 sub-2:23s. There was also unprecedented depth with a new standard of 225 sub-2:30s, 19 more than in 2012. For the second consecutive year there were new indoor world records for men (2:21:48, Chris Zablocki) and women (2:42:30, Lauri Manninen) at the Armory in New York City.

NOTE: On January 28: Ron Hill, one of the great marathoners of the late 1960s/early 1970s with European, Commonwealth and Boston victories, did not run at least a mile, the end of a mind-boggling streak of 52 years and 39 days (19,032 days!) that began on 19 December 1964.

WINNERS OF 2017 INTERNATIONAL MARATHONS

2 Jan	Xiamen	Lemi Berhanu ETH	2:08:27	Meseret Mengistu ETH	2:25:58
6 Jan	TIberias	Habtamu Arega ETH	2:16:39	Hiwot Gebrekidan ETH	2:25:45*
15 Jan	Houston	Dominic Ondoro KEN	2:12:05	Meskerem Assefa ETH	2:30:18
15 Jan	Mumbai	Alphonce Felix TAN	2:09:32	Bornes Kitur KEN	2:29:02
20 Jan	Dubai	Tamirat Tola ETH	2:04:11*	Worknesh Degefa ETH	2:22:36
29 Jan	Marrakech	Gebretsadik Adhana ETH	2:08:55	Ashu Kasim Rabo ETH	2:30:18
29 Jan	Osaka	*women only*		Risa Shigetomo JPN	2:24:22
5 Feb	Beppu-Oita	Kentaro Nakamoto JPN	2:09:32	*elite men only*	
11 Feb	Lagos	Abraham Kiptum KEN	2:15:23	Rodah Tanui KEN	2:37:52
12 Feb	Hong Kong	Bizuneh Melaku ETH	2:10:31*	Gulume Tollesa ETH	2:33:39
19 Feb	Castellón	Abraham Girma ETH	2:12:18	Genet Getane ETH	2:36:49
19 Feb	Seville	Titus Ekiru KEN	2:07:43*	Paula González ESP	2:28:54
24 Feb	Tel Aviv	Belete Mekonen ETH	2:12:12	Margaret Wangui KEN	2:35:51*
26 Feb	Sanya	Abayneh Belachew ETH	2:14:53	Webalem Ayele ETH	2:35:06
26 Feb	Tokyo	Wilson Kipsang KEN	2:03:58*	Sarah Chepchirchir KEN	2:19:47*
5 Mar	Otsu	Ezekiel Chebii KEN	2:09:06	*elite men only*	
5 Mar	Rabat	Fikadu Kebede ETH	2:09:37	Worknesh Alemu ETH	2:30:04
12 Mar	Barcelona	Jonah Chesum KEN	2:08:57	Helen Tola ETH	2:25:04*
12 Mar	Brescia	Bernard Too KEN	2:09:47	Hayimanot Alemayehu ETH	2:40:28
12 Mar	Nagoya	*women only*		Eunice Kirwa BRN	2:21:17*
19 Mar	Chongqing	Afewerk Mesfin ETH	2:09:49	Rael Kiyara Nguriatukei KEN	2:26:22
19 Mar	Santa Monica (dh)	Elisha Barno KEN	2:11:52	Hellen Jepkurgat KEN	2:34:23
19 Mar	Seoul	Amos Kipruto KEN	2:05:54	Margaret Agai KEN	2:25:52
19 Mar	Taipei	Hillary Kipkogei Yego KEN	2:17:02	Munkhzaya Bayartsogt MGL	2:38:08
19 Mar	Wuxi	Khalid Yaseen BRN	2:13:13	Ayelu Abebe ETH	2:29:17
26 Mar	Zhengzhou	Titus Tuwei KEN	2:10:14*	Tigist Memuye ETH	2:27:39
2 Apr	Daegu	Matthew Kisorio KEN	2:07:32	Pamela Rotich KEN	2:27:48
2 Apr	Milan	Edward Koech KEN	2:07:13*	Sheila Chepkoech KEN	2:29:52
2 Apr	Rome	Shura Kitata ETH	2:07:28	Rahma Tusa ETH	2:27:21
2 Apr	Santiago	Luka Lobuwan KEN	2:09:37*	Ines Melchor PER	2:34:12
9 Apr	Gunsan	Elisha Rotich KEN	2:13:57	Munkhzaya Bayartsogt MGL	2:32:59
9 Apr	Hannover	Allan Kiprono KEN	2:09:52	Fate Tola GER	2:27:48
9 Apr	Linz	Anthony Maritim KEN	2:09:13	Danijela Kuna CRO	2:43:57
9 Apr	Paris	Paul Lonyangata KEN	2:06:10	Purity Rionoripo KEN	2:20:55*
9 Apr	Pyongyang	Pak Chol PRK	2:14:56	Jo Un-ok PRK	2:29:22
9 Apr	Rotterdam	Marius Kimutai KEN	2:06:04	Meskerem Assefa ETH	2:24:18
9 Apr	Zürich	Vincent Tonui KEN	2:12:58	Vera Nunes POR	2:34:18
16 Apr	Nagano	Taiga Ito JPN	2:14:39	Rachel Mutgaa KEN	2:33:00
17 Apr	Boston (dh)	Geoffrey Kirui KEN	2:09:37	Edna Kiplagat KEN	2:21:52
23 Apr	Hamburg	Tsegaye Mekonnen ETH	2:07:26	Jéssica Augusto POR	2:25:30
23 Apr	London	Daniel Wanjiru KEN	2:05:48	Mary Keitany KEN	2:17:01
23 Apr	Madrid	Bonsa Dida ETH	2:10:16	Elizabeth Rumokol KEN	2:33:55
23 Apr	Padua	Michael Njenga Kunyuga KEN	2:10:43	Fatna Maraoui ITA	2:32:52
23 Apr	Wien	Albert Korir KEN	2:08:40	Nancy Kiprop KEN	2:24:20
23 Apr	Warsaw	Felix Kimutai KEN	2:10:34	Anastasiya Ivanova BLR	2:28:44
30 Apr	Düsseldorf	Robert Chemonges UGA	2:10:32	Doroteia Peixoto POR	2:32:00
30 Apr	Kraków	Cosmas Mutuku Kyeva KEN	2:12:52	Stellah Barsosio KEN	2:33:01
7 May	Dongying	Husen Muhammedahin ETH	2:14:19	Letebrhan Gebreslase ETH	2:25:01*
7 May	Geneva (dh 46.4m)	William Yegon KEN	2:10:31	Megersa Motu ETH	2:40:46
7 May	Prague	Gebretsadik Adhana ETH	2:08:47	Valary Aiyabei KEN	2:21:57*
14 May	Riga	Joseph Munywoki KEN	2:12:15	Bekelech Daba ETH	2:31:23*
21 May	Copenhagen	Julius Karinga KEN	2:12:11*	Hana Teklu ETH	2:47:24
21 May	Lima (A)	Jeffrey Eggleston USA	2:15:25	Ayelu Lemma ETH	2:30:22
28 May	Ottawa	Eliud Kiptanui KEN	2:10:14	Guteni Shone ETH	2:30:18
3 Jun	Stockholm	Abrha Milaw ETH	2:11:36	Konjit Tilahun ETH	2:35:45
11 Jun	Lanzhou	Kelkile Gezahegn ETH	2:11:54	Ashete Bekere ETH	2:32:03
17 Jun	Duluth	Elisha Barno KEN	2:12:08	Hellen Jepkurgat KEN	2:32:09
18 Jun	Rio de Janeiro	Godfrey Kosgei KEN	2:17:41	Ednah Mukhwana KEN	2:38:30
2 Jul	Gold Coast	Takuya Noguchi JPN	2:08:59	Abebech Afework ETH	2:25:34*

27 Aug	Mexico City (A)	Fikadu Kebede ETH	2:17:28	Gladys Tejeda PER	2:36:16*
27 Aug	Sapporo	Akinobu Murasawa JPN	2:14:48	Honami Maeda JPN	2:28:48
10 Sep	Münster	Paul Maina KEN	2:11:22	Rose Maru KEN	2:33:05
10 Sep	Wroclaw	Abel Kibet Rop KEN	2:13:36	Stellah Barsosio KEN	2:28:14
17 Sep	Beijing	Salah-Eddine Bounasr MAR	2:11:18	Meselech Beyene ETH	2:27:24
17 Sep	Cape Town	Asefa Mengistu ETH	2:10:01	Betelhem Moges ETH	2:30:22
17 Sep	Sydney	Shota Hattori JPN	2:15:16	Makda Harun ETH	2:28:06
24 Sep	Berlin	Eliud Kipchoge KEN	2:03:32	Gladys Cherono KEN	2:20:23
24 Sep	Moscow	Artyom Alekseyenev RUS	2:14:15	Sardana Trofimova RUS	2:30:29*
24 Sep	Warsaw	Blazej Brzezinski POL	2:11:27	Bekelu Beji ETH	2:35:09
30 Sep	Hengshui	Michael Njenga Kunyuga KEN	2:12:31	Betty Lempus KEN	2:30:47
1 Oct	Kosice	Reuben Kiprop Kerio KEN	2:08:12	Sheilah Jerotich KEN	2:27:34*
1 Oct	St. Paul	Dominic Ondoro KEN	2:11:54	Jane Kibii KEN	2:30:26
8 Oct	Chicago	Galen Rupp USA	2:09:20	Tirunesh Dibaba ETH	2:18:31
8 Oct	Eindhoven	Festus Talam KEN	2:06:13	Eunice Jeptoo KEN	2:26:13
8 Oct	Zagreb	Wycliffe Biwott KEN	2:09:55*	Stellah Barsosio KEN	2:30:15*
15 Oct	Amsterdam	Lawrence Cherono KEN	2:05:09*	Tadelech Bekele ETH	2:21:54
.15 Oct	Bucharest	Duncan Koech KEN	2:13:13*	Almaz Gelana ETH	2:42:06
15 Oct	Buenos Aires	Barnabas Kiptum KEN	2:09:48*	Amelwork Fikadu ETH	2:35:32
15 Oct	Gyeongju	Felix Kiprotich KEN	2:06:54	Lee Sook-jeong KOR	2:39:59
15 Oct	Lisbon	Ismael Bushendich KEN	2:10:51	Sarah Chepchirchir KEN	2:27:57
15 Oct	Melbourne	Isaac Birir KEN	2:14:08	Celia Sullohern AUS	2:29:27
15 Oct	Sofia	Samson Barmao KEN	2:14:49	Ruth Matebo KEN	2:40:30
22 Oct	Rennes (dh)	Josphat Letting KEN	2:09:45	Viola Jelagat KEN	2:26:51*
22 Oct	Toronto	Philemon Rono KEN	2:06:52*	Marta Megra ETH	2:28:20
22 Oct	Toulouse	Dominic Kangor KEN	2:11:56	Merga Tesfanesh ETH	2:35:11
22 Oct	Venice	Eyob Gebrehiwet ITA	2:12:16	Gedo Sule Utura ETH	2:29:04
29 Oct	Casablanca	Evans Kipkoech KEN	2:09:42	Yiman Mengistu ETH	2:31:51
29 Oct	Chuncheon	Luka Kanda KEN	2:06:15*	Lee Yeon-jin KOR	2:41:02
29 Oct	Dublin	Bernard Rotich KEN	2:15:52	Nataliya Lehonkova UKR	2:28:57
29 Oct	Frankfurt	Shura Kitata Tola ETH	2:05:50	Vivian Cheruiyot KEN	2:23:35
29 Oct	Ljubljana	Marius Kimutai KEN	2:08:33	Shuka Genemo ETH	2:27:02
5 Nov	Cannes	Dejene Kelkilew ETH	2:12:09	Tejitu Siyum ETH	2:33:21
5 Nov	Hangzhou	Azmeraw Bekele ETH	2:10:33*	Muluhabt Tsega ETH	2:28:08*
5 Nov	New York City	Geoffrey Kamworor KEN	2:10:53	Shalane Flanagan USA	2:26:53
5 Nov	Porto	Jackson Limo Kibet KEN	2:11:34	Monica Jepkoech KEN	2:26:58*
5 Nov	Seoul	Thomas Kiplagat Rono KEN	2:09:13	Kim Do-yeon KOR	2:31:24
12 Nov	Athens	Samuel Kaleli KEN	2:12:17	Bedatu Hirpa ETH	2:34:18
12 Nov	Beirut	Dominic Ruto KEN	2:10:47*	Eunice Chumba BRN	2:28:43*
12 Nov	Hefei	Abdi Ibrahim BRN	2:12:00	Hayimanot Alemayehu ETH	2:36:20
12 Nov	Istanbul	Abraham Kiprotich FRA	2:11:22	Ruth Chepngetich KEN	2:22:36*
12 Nov	Saitama	Yuki Kawauchi JPN	2:15:54*	Flomena Cheyech KEN	2:28:39
12 Nov	Shanghai	Stephen Mokoka RSA	2:08:35	Roza Dereje ETH	2:22:43
19 Nov	Kobe	Khalil Lemciyeh MAR	2:12:49*	Maegen Krifchin USA	2:33:14
19 Nov	Valencia	Sammy Kitwara KEN	2:05:15*	Aberu Mekuria ETH	2:26:17
26 Nov	Florence	Zelalem Bacha BRN	2:14:41	Dire Tune ETH	2:28:55
26 Nov	La Rochelle	Workneh Tesfa ETH	2:11:07	Susan Jeptoo KEN	2:30:57
26 Nov	Nairobi (A)	Brimin Kipkorir Misoi KEN	2:12:39	Celestine Chepchirchir KEN	2:31:41
26 Nov	Osaka	Kaleab Solomon Ghilagabr ERI	2:12:03	Yumiko Kinoshita JPN	2:34:38
26 Nov	San Sebastián	Hosea Maiyo KEN	2:12:55	Rehima Serro ESP	2:44:23
3 Dec	Fukuoka	Sondre Nordstad Moen NOR	2:05:48	*men only*	
3 Dec	Macau	Felix Kiptoo Kirwa KEN	2:10:01*	Eunice Kirwa BRN	2:29:12*
3 Dec	Mersin	Hassane Ahouchar MAR	2:11:21*	Truphena Chepchirchir KEN	2:28:47*
3 Dec	Sacramento (dh)	Timothy Ritchie USA	2:11:55	Sara Hall USA	2:28:10
3 Dec	Singapore	Cosmas Koech Kimutai KEN	2:22:48	Pamela Rotich KEN	2:38:31
10 Dec	Guangzhou	Dickson Tuwei KEN	2:10:03	Rahma Tusa ETH	2:25:12*
10 Dec	Honolulu	Lawrence Cherono KEN	2:08:27*	Brigid Koskei KEN	2:22:15*
17 Dec	Hofu	Yuki Kawauchi JPN	2:10:03	Misaki Kato JPN	2:28:12*
17 Dec	Shenzhen	Peter Some KEN	2:14:49	Viktoria Poliudina KGZ	2:33:25

* course record; sc = short course; A = altitude over 1000m. dh = downhill course (Santa Monica 122.2m, Boston 136.3m, Rennes 65m, Sacramento 105m). See also Asian and World Championships

REVIEW OF ULTRARUNNING 2017

by Andy Milroy

ULTRARUNNING IS NEVER predictable, and 2017 was no exception. With no World Championships and unfortunately few continental championships to compensate, strength in depth was low in the 100k; there was a new male Japanese star however. The 24 hour event compensated for the temporary decline in the 100k. With several world records by the women, a strong World event and the emergence of China as a major force, the 24 came into its own. In the wider spectrum of the sport, the immediate post-war boom generation also began to show its strength in depth, as its members reached 70.

Although there was no World 100k in 2017, there was one stellar mark, set on the potentially wind aided Yubetsu course in Japan. Tatsuya Itagaki's 6:14:18 was the second fastest road mark of all-time, and third behind Don Ritchie's absolute track best of 6:10:20. With his nearest competition, fellow countrymen Yasuyuki Nakamura 6:29:52 and Nao Kazami 6:33:52, also in the Yubetsu race, Tatsuya Itagaki is the World No. 1 for 2017 with this big breakthrough, especially bearing in mind that his marathon pb is only 2:18:56.

The women's event was much closer with marks set in diverse races. Selecting the World No 1 is difficult. Nikolina Sustic CRO had the fastest time on the hilly Florence-Faenza course of 7:34:36, with Nele Alden-Baerens GER clocking 7:35:37 in Berlin and Yuri Kano JPN running 7:37:21 at Yubetsu, but there was no serious head to head competition. Camille Herron ran 7:36:39 as a split in her attempt on the world 100 mile track record when she set a new 12 hour world best. She also won the Comrades.

The 100 mile as an intermediate distance between the 100k and 24 hours has proved attractive, especially with no World 100k. Gina Slaby set a new world track record of 14:36:08 and later in the year, Camille Herron, former World 100k winner and winner of the Comrades ran 12:42:40 on the road. Just a few weeks later she attempted to break Gina Slaby's track record and broke the US 50 mile and 100k track records with 5:59:10 and 7:36:39 and set a new world 12 hour record of 149.130k. If the earlier road 100 mile had not still been in her legs, she would have almost certainly have demolished the world track 100 miles record. A feature of the 24 hour event was the emergence of Chinese runners. At Hangzhou Ying Shan ran a split of 15:02:29, the third fastest 100 mile of the year by a woman.

The 24 hour event was strong in 2017, as noted, with the women's best being improved twice by Patrycja Bereznowska POL, the obvious world No. 1. First she ran 256.246k in domestic competition and then became the first woman to cover 160 miles in 24 hours with 259.991k in the World 24 hours in Belfast in Northern Ireland, GBR, where there was intense USA v Poland competition. Aleksandra Niwinska POL 251.078k was second, followed by Katalin Nagy USA 250.622k, Gina Slaby USA 248.276k and Pam Smith USA 243.611k. Courtney Dauwalter had earlier set a new United States record of 250.079k and came back later in the year in Taiwan with a new world track record of 256.405k.

The men's event was also interesting with five men over 260k in Belfast. Yoshihiko Ishikawa JPN's 270.870k was the greatest distance of the year and ranks him first, but another Pole Sebastian Bialobrzeski took second with 267.187k, followed by the versatile Swede Johan Steene 266.515k, another Japanese Nobuyuki Takahashi 264.506k and the Frenchman Stéphane Ruel 260.077k.

This was not the end of the major competition. The Chinese Federation is keen to promote Ultrarunning. In September the currently fastest 100k runner in the world, Tatsuya Itagaki, was invited to the Chinese Fuxian Lake Highland Ultramarathon 100K where he ran 7:15 ahead of Jing Liang 7:32:07 which is probably a Chinese road record. In December the Federation put on a 24 hour track race, this time with significant prize money, $40,000 for first place and $20,000 for second. The race was at Hangzhou and Bereznowska was invited. There was a race-long struggle between Jing Liang and the top CHN 24 hour runner until then, Si Guosong. Jing Liang led at 100k 7:57:18 to 8:05:13 and by 100 miles had extended his lead to 13:18:54 to Si's 13:31:57. Both runners were pushed to their physical limits, highly motivated to win such a national prestigious event with significant prize money. Jing finished with the greatest track distance of 2017, 267.701k with Si second with 265.304k. Such hyper-competitive events produce marks that are seldom repeatable.

The 48 Hour event can be seen as an extended, more demanding, 24 hour race and the global spread of the event was intriguing. The greatest distance by a man was by the up and coming American Oliver Leblond with 421.939k with an Italian running in a French race ranked second, Tiziano Marchesi with 413.838k. The third best mark of the year was by Australian Michael Thwaites 404.560k. The women's event encompassed yet another continent. German Julia Fatton ran the greatest distance (378.082k) at Balatonfüred in Hungary and Shan Ying CHN and Chou Ling-Chun TPE were ranked second and third with 345.678k and 332.664k.

The 6 Day event showed another interesting development. The numbers contesting such events globally is growing and in recent years rankings have shown close to 400 performances. These are often older, more experienced runners, seeking to discover their limits in a prolonged test of endurance. Long time statistician Nick Marshall has begun documenting such performances over 100 miles by those who are over 70, even over 80! The numbers are growing. Over 200 over 70s, 50 plus over 75 and over a dozen over 80!

Of the elite runners, John Steene, third in the World 24 hours, covered 870.915k at Balatonfüred to beat Hungarian Peter Molnár 842.745k. In the largest 6 day race in the world, Privas in France, Christian Mauduit produced the third greatest distance of the year – 838.204k to finish first out a hundred competitors. The top women's marks of the year were also at Balatonfüred. Silke Gielen GER, a mere 59 years old, covered 782.336k ahead of Tina Andersen DEN 741.112k. The next best mark was in Glendale AZ, when Liz Bauer covered 674.106k.

As has been the case in recent years, the fastest 1000 mile marks of the year came in the 3100 mile race in New York. Nikolay Duzhiy ran 14:11:56:41 and in the same race Theresa Janáková clocked 15:16:49:31. This is the longest certified footrace in the world and Duzhiy went on to win with 46 days 17:38:22 with Janáková the first woman in 48:14:24:10 The race uniquely has a longer split of 5000k with Duzhiy first in 47 days 02:11:59 with Janáková 48:17:41:49. The race is longer than running from New York to Los Angeles!

The oldest ultra in the world is the 89k Comrades in South Africa, first held in 1921. The up race from Durban to Pietermaritzburg was won by Bongmusa Mthembu in 5:35:34 from Hatiwande Nyamande's 5:38:48 and Gift Kelehe with 5:41:48. First woman was American Camille Herron in 6:27:35. Herron appears frequently in this summary and was arguably the top ultrarunner of 2017. Alexandra Morozova took second in 6:31:45 with last year's winner, South African Charne Bosman third 6:39:51.

The Spartathlon, from Athens to Sparta, held in memory of Pheidippides, was won by Aleksandr Sorokin, who made such an exuberant attempt to win the European 24 hour championships in 2016. The LTU athlete took 22:04:04 to finish ahead of Radek Brunner CZE 22:49:37 and Nikolaos Sideridis GRE 22:58:40. Only Yiannis Kouros had run the course faster than the Lithuanian. The conditions must have been good, because the second and third placed athletes also set the fastest time yet for those positions. The women also had a remarkable race. Bereznowska, who had twice broken the 24 hour record in 2017, reduced the female record by close to 20 minutes to 24:48:18 (breaking Katalin Nagy's previous best set in 2015 of 25:07:12 for the 246k course). Behind her Zsuzsanna Maráz HUN ran the fastest ever second place time of 25:43:40 and Aleksandra Newinska's 26:28:48 was fastest ever third place.

There were no extended stage races in 2017 but the number of point-to-point extended races globally, particularly in the Far East, look to have blossomed. Races were held in China, India, Indonesia, Iran, Japan, Korea, Malaysia, Mongolia, Philippines and Taiwan. Often there were several such races in each country, the Japanese were particularly fond of them. There were also numerous 1000 miles races, including a 16 day race in RSA.

There is a well known saying, that an Ultrarunner is only limited by her or his imagination. There is now a virtual cornucopia of ultra events, world wide; crossing countries on foot seems particularly popular. This is not just for running tourists or elite ultrarunners, such races are organised and won by local runners. Interestingly there looks to be a move away from stage races, where runners tackle just a specific distance each day and can rest up and recover at the end of each session. Now tougher point-to-point non-stop races are becoming popular. The increasing number of ultra races widens the base of the pyramid and therefore is likely to raise the level of national performances. This looks to be happening in China for example as an increasing number of people have more leisure time, which they seek to spend on physical fitness.

As I said at the start of this summary, Ultrarunners are getting older and still seeking new challenges. 70 year old and even 80 year old are tackling extreme events of 100 miles and longer. Ultramarathons are now reaping the benefits of the running boom, as older runners seek to move away from pressure events like the 5k, 10k, half and full marathon.

IAAF WORLD CHAMPIONSHIPS 2017

August 4-13, London (Olympic Stadium)

THIS WAS A fascinating event in which 7 champions defended their titles from Beijing 2015 and 12 individual champions and two relay teams repeated their successes from the 2016 Rio Olympic Games. Also Justin Gatlin, Sally Pearson, Sandra Perkovic and Barbora Spotáková regained their world titles. It also featured a changing of the guard in many events as well as the thrills and spills of real championship action. There was terrific crowd support for the athletes – especially, but very far from exclusively, for the British competitors and it was marvellous to see capacity crowds, up to the 56,000 maximum figure for the morning sessions, in marked contrast to all too many major events around the world.

There was just one world record – in the new event, the women's 50k walk in which Inês Henriques took 2:30 off the inaugural mark for the event that she had set in January, while in the men's race Yohann Diniz got close with the second fastest time ever recorded. But conditions were not especially conducive to records – sprinters prefer 30-35°C rather than 15-20 °C. However the weather was generally reasonable apart from the incessant rain on the Wednesday (fortunately there was no high jump or pole vault on that day). As well as Diniz's 8 min 6 secs superiority in his walk, the most clear-cut win came from Almaz Ayana, whose brilliant run at 10,000m brought her home 46.37 secs ahead of the great Tirunesh Dibaba. World-leading marks were set 15 times and there were three Championship records: the two 50k walks and Emma Coburn in the women's steeplechase.

Usain Bolt and Mo Farah were the headline stars for the public and Farah duly delivered his sixth World gold but had to work harder and run faster than in any of his previous victories in the 10,000m, so he did extraordinarily well to return for the silver medal in the 5000m, when he could not quite match the finishing speed of the fresh Muktar Edris. That came on the penultimate day when Bolt, after his third place in the 100m, had his last competitive run. He had no problem in the heats, but so sadly pulled up in agony with cramp in the final of the 4x100m. Later he complained about being held up for 40 minutes, getting cold in the call room. At the end of the final day he walked round the track in an emotional farewell.

Brittney Reese won her fourth long jump title and Pawel Fajdek and Anita Wlodarczyk their third hammer titles. The USA were, as usual, easily the most successful nation with 30 medals including 11 gold although many of their team, particularly those who had peaked at their Trials after long collegiate seasons, underperformed. Kenya won five golds and France and South Africa three apiece, while host nation Britain came though with medals in each of the relays for six medals in all including two golds and were third in the placing table behind the USA and Kenya.

Men

100 Metres *(prelim, h 4th, sf, F 5th -0.8)*

1. Justin Gatlin USA	9.92
2. Christian Coleman USA	9.94
3. Usain Bolt JAM	9.95
4. Yohan Blake JAM	9.99
5. Akani Simbine RSA	10.01
6. Jimmy Vicaut FRA	10.08
7. Reece Prescod GBR	10.17
8. Su Bingtian CHN	10.27

A poor getaway cost Bolt the glorious finale to his championship career at 100m which most of of the 56,000 spectators were anticipating. Way down at halfway after a slow 0.183 reaction time compared to 0.123 for Coleman and 0.138 for Gatlin, he came close to salvaging the race but his top-end speed isn't what it used to be and with 9.95, equalling his season's best, he was 0.03 short. Inches ahead of him was Coleman, the world's quickest this year at 9.82, and the winner, regaining the title he won in 2015 was Gatlin, the world's oldest ever finalist, in his season's best time. Sub-10 times were run in the 1st round by Julian Forte 9.99 and in the 2nd by Coleman 9.97 just ahead of Bolt 9.98.

200 Metres *(h 7th, sf 9th, F 10th -0.1)*

1. Ramil Guliyev TUR	20.09
2. Wayde van Niekerk RSA	20.11
3. Jereem Richards TTO	20.11
4. Nethaneel Mitchell-Blake GBR	20.24
5. Ameer Webb USA	20.26
6. Isaac Makwala BOT	20.44
7. Abdul Sani Brown JPN	20.63
8. Isiah Young USA	20.64

The unexpected winner was Guliyev, but he was the only finalist to have previously run in a global 200m final (8th Olympics 2016, 7th 2009 and 6th 2015 Worlds). It was close as he won from van Niekerk 20.106 and Richards 20.107. Fastest in the heats were the impressive newcomer Richards 20.05 and Mitchell-Blake 20.08 and the fastest semi was the first, won by Young 20.12w from Makwala 20.14w, with

Medals and Points Table

Points: 8 for 1st to 1 for 8th place. 68 nations placed athletes in top eight, 43 won medals, and 19 won gold.

Nation	G	S	B	Points	2015	2013
USA	10	11	9	271.5	211	291
KEN	5	2	4	123	173	140
GBR	2	3	1	104.5	94	81
POL	2	2	4	86	66	43.5
CHN	2	3	2	81	93.5	43
GER	1	2	2	77.5	112.5	101.5
ETH	2	3	-	70	83	98
FRA	3	-	2	68	42	51
JAM	1	0	3	67.5	132	102
ANA*	1	5	-	55.5	RUS: 60	140
RSA	3	1	2	52	22	18
NED	1	-	3	40	28	24
CZE	1	1	1	37	13.5	38.5
CUB	-	-	1	34.5	30	33
CAN	-	-	-	30	65.5	41
BRN	1	1		26	10	3
JPN	-	1	2	25	13	31
AUS	1	1	-	23	19	28
TTO	1	-	1	22.5	22	13
TUR	1	1	-	21	8	-
BRA	-	-	1	20.5	13	18.5
CRO	1	-	1	19	14	8
BAH	-	1	1	19	16	8
COL	1	1	-	19	10	8
CIV	-	2	-	19	-	14
POR	1	-	1	17	11	6
QAT	1	-	1	16	10	7
HUN	-	1	1	16	13	9
UKR	-	1	-	15	29.5	50
NOR	1	-	1	14	-	5
ESP	-	-	-	14	12	23.5
BOT	-	-	-	14	4	7
VEN	1	-	1	13.5	-	-
BEL	1	-	-	13	19	19
MEX	-	1	-	12	-	8
GRE	1	-	-	11	6	-
ITA	-	-	1	10	10.5	18.5
LTU	1	-	-	9.5	2	-
NZL	1	-	-	9	9	8
SUI	-	-	-	8.5	3	-

MAR (1S), SWE (1S), AZE, BLR 8; UGA (1S) BDI (1S) 7; KAZ (1B), SYR (1B), TAN (1B) 6; EST, ISR, NGR, SRB 5; ERI, FIN 4; AUT, BAR, DOM 3; GRN, IVB, PER, TJK, ZAM 2; BUL 1.5; IRL, MDA 1. 43 nations won medals, 66 placed athletes in the top eight.

* *ANA = Russians who competed as authorised neutral athletes.*

Richards 20.14 and Guliyev 20.17 the other winners. Makwala was permitted to run in the semis after being barred from his heat on medical grounds but only after clocking 20.20 in a solo time trial to determine his fitness (and to run 20.53 or better). The only 100m finalists to double here were Blake and Simbine who went out in the semis.

400 Metres *(h 5th, sf 6th, F 8th)*

1. Wayde van Niekerk RSA 43.98
2. Steven Gardiner BAH 44.41
3. Abdelilah Haroun QAT 44.48
4. Baboloki Thebe BOT 44.66
5. Nathon Allen JAM 44.88
6. Demish Gaye JAM 45.04
7. Fred Kerley USA 45.23

dns. Isaac Makwala BOT –

Van Niekerk successfully defended his title, running away from the field through 100m 10.9, 200m 20.7 and 300m 31.6. Thebe was 2nd at 300m in 31.9 from Allen and Gardiner 32.0, but he was passed by Gardiner and Haroun, who came through from 300m in 32.7. Isaac Makwala coasted home in 44.55 for the fastest heat time and won the third semi in 44.30 but was not allowed to contest the final as he was withdrawn by the IAAF Medical Delegate as he had to undergo a 48-hour quarantine due to being diagnosed with an infectious disease (several athletes suffered from a Novovirus outbreak). Gardiner lowered his Bahamian record from 44.26 to 43.89 in the first semi from Allen 44.19 and van Niekerk won the second in 44.22, while for the USA LaShawn Merritt managed only 7th and Will London 5th as they were far from qualifying.

800 Metres *(h 5th, sf 6th, F 8th)*

1. Pierre-Ambroise Bosse FRA 1:44.67
2. Adam Kszczot POL 1:44.95
3. Kipyegon Bett KEN-J 1:45.21
4. Kyle Langford GBR 1:45.25
5. Nijel Amos BOT 1:45.83
6. Mohammed Aman ETH 1:46.06
7. Thiago André BRA 1:46.30
8. Brandon McBride CAN 1:47.09

Early shocks include the elimination in the semis of Kenyans Emmanuel Korir and Ferguson Cheruiyot plus the experienced Pole Marcin Lewandowski, and more followed as Bosse was the surprising gold medallist. He was 5th at 400m in 51.39 as McBride led in 50.78, and the Frenchman sped along the back straight to take the lead just before 600m (1:17.68) and maintained a strong finish ahead of Kszczot, who took silver as in 2015. Thijmen Kupers was fastest in the heats at 1:45.53 but did not start in the semis, where Aman was quickest in 1:45.40.

1500 Metres *(h 10th, sf 11th, F 13th)*

1. Elijah Manangoi KEN 3:33.61
2. Timothy Cheruiyot KEN 3:33.99
3. Filip Ingebrigtsen NOR 3:34.53
4. Adel Mechaal ESP 3:34.71
5. Jakub Holuša CZE 3:34.89
6. Sadik Mikhou BRN 3:35.81
7. Marcin Lewandowski POL 3:36.02
8. Nick Willis NZL 3:36.82
9. Asbel Kiprop KEN 3:37.24
10. John Gregorek USA 3:37.56
11. Fouad El Kaam MAR 3:37.72
12. Chris O'Hare GBR 3:38.28

After a slow start (400m 61.63), the final was a welcome truly run race. The second lap was fast at 55.96 so that at 800m Cheruiyot led In 1:57.59 from Manangoi 1:57.82 and Kiprop 1:58.07 (55.07 lap!) and this Kenyan trio was followed at a distance by Ingebrigtsen 1:59.04. The order stayed the same so that Cheruiyot led at the bell in 2:39.77 and 1200m 2:53.68. While Kiprop faded to 9th, Manangoi had the superior kick to beat his compatriot and Ingebrigtsen (after a 54.99 third lap) held on for 3rd. Holusa finished fastest (39.06 last 300m) to move from 8th to 5th. Olympic champion Matthew Centrowitz was the major casualty in the heats, as troubled by illness and injury for most of this season, he finished last.

5000 Metres *(h 9th, F 12h)*

1. Muktar Edris ETH	13:32.79
2. Mo Farah GBR	13:33.22
3. Paul Chelimo USA	13:33.30
4. Yomif Kejelcha ETH	13:33.51
5. Selemon Barega ETH-Y	13:35.34
6. Mohammed Ahmed CAN	13:35.43
7. Aron Kifle ERI-J	13:36.91
8. Andrew Butchart GBR	13:38.73
9. Justyn Knight CAN	13:39.15
10. Kemoy Campbell JAM	13:39.74
11. Patrick Tiernan AUS	13:40.01
12. Birhanu Yemataw BRN	13:43.25
13. Cyrus Rutto KEN	13:48.64
14. Awet Habte ERI	13:58.68
dns. Ryan Hill USA	–

After five global 5000m victories Farah could not quite manage another. At the end of a slowish race in which Farah was nearly tripped three times, he was outkicked by Edris, 11 years Farah's junior at age 23. Two younger still Ethiopians in Kejelcha (just turned 20) and 17 year-old Barega finished fourth and fifth, the bronze going to Chelimo, the Kenyan-born American who had placed second to Farah in Rio. The kilometre splits for the slow pace were 2:48.20, 5:48.08 and 8:32.93. Then Tiernan pushed ahead to 4k in 11:09.67, when he was followed by Farah 11:11.24, and was still 8m clear with two laps to go, but he was caught with 600m to go and finished 11th. In a furious finish in which Farah came through from third at the bell to pass Kejelcha on the inside and finish just ahead of Chelimo. Edris covered the last 200m in 26.34, 400m in 52.4, 800m in 1:50.4 and 1000m in 2:21.04 (against Chelimo 2:21.84 and Farah 2:21.98. The last 2000m took 4:59.86, 3000m 7:44.71. Barega's 13:21.50 was the fastest heat time.

10,000 Metres *(4th)*

1. Mo Farah GBR	26:49.51
2. Joshua Cheptegei UGA	26:49.94
3. Paul Tanui KEN	26:50.60
4. Bidan Karoki KEN	26:52.12
5. Jemal Yimer ETH	26:56.11
6. Geoffrey Kamworor KEN	26:57.77
7. Abadi Hadis ETH.	26:59.19
8. Mohammed Ahmed CAN	27:02.35
9. Shadrack Kipchirchir USA	27:07.55
10. Andamlak Belihu ETH-J	27:08.94
11. Aron Kifle ERI-J	27:09.92
12. Abraham Cheroben BRN	27:11.08
13. Leonard Korir USA	27:20.08
14. Timothy Toroitich UGA	27:21.09
15. Hassan Mead USA	27:32.49

This was the hardest and fastest of Farah's marvellous sequence of major wins as his East African rivals made it very hard for him. When Tanui edged ahead with 200m to go it looked ominous but once again Farah found that extra gear to pull away in the final straight for victory by 0.43 in a world leading mark of 26:49.51. His winning margins in his previous four global 10,000m titles have been similarly slim yet totally decisive: 0.48 in London 2012, 0.52 in Moscow 2013, 0.63 in Beijing 2015 and 0.47 in Rio 2016. The times for places 11 to 14 were the best ever in any 10,000m race and the first 14 men were all born in East Africa; 22 men finished from 24 starters. For much of the first half, with Karoki reaching 5000m in 13:33.74, Farah was content to run in mid-field. At the 6000m mark there was a lead pack of 14 but five dropped back as Cheptegei ran laps of 63.16 and 63.44 to reach 8000m in 21:40.97. Farah launched a long run for home from 600m out and he ran the last two laps in 61.92 and 55.63 with 13:13.31 for the second 5000m,

Marathon *(6th)*

1. Geoffrey Kirui KEN	2:08:27
2. Tamirat Tola ETH	2:09:49
3. Alphonce Felix Simbu TAN	2:09:51
4. Callum Hawkins GBR	2:10:17
5. Gideon Kipketer KEN	2:10:56
6. Daniele Meucci ITA	2:10:56
7. Yohannes Ghebregergis ERI	2:12:07
8. Daniel Wanjiru KEN	2:12:16
9. Yuki Kawauchi JPN	2:12:19
10. Kentaro Nakamoto JPN	2:12:41
11. Solomon Mutai UGA	2:13:29
12. Ezekiel Jafary Ngimba TAN	2:14:05
13. Abdi Hakin Ulad DEN	2:14:22
14. Kaan Kigen Özbilen TUR	2:14:29
15. Shumi Dechasa BRN	2:15:08

Kirui's win came with 65:28 for the first half and 62:59 for the second with a decisive 29:13 for the 10k from 20k to 30k by Kirui and Tola. Tola broke away after c.32k but Kirui gradually reeled him back in and the 5k to 35k was covered in 14:43 by Kirui and 14:44 by Tola, while Felix Simbu was now in third place alongside Kipketer over a minute in arrears and Hawkins another half a minute behind. Kirui slowed to 15:25 for the next 5k but by then he had drawn 52 sec clear of Tola and he increased his lead to 1:22 over the final 2.195k. 27 of the 98 starters failed to finish on a twisting four-lap course that started and finished on Tower Bridge.

3000 Metres Steeplechase *(h 6th, F 8th)*

1. Conseslus Kipruto KEN 8:14.12
2. Soufiane El Bakkali MAR 8:14.49
3. Evan Jager USA 8:15.53
4. Mahiedine Mekhissi-Benabbad FRA 8:15.80
5. Stanley Kebenei USA 8:21.09
6. Matthew Hughes CAN 8:21.84
7. Tesfaye Deriba ETH-J 8:22.12
8. Tafese Seboka ETH 8:23.02
9. Getnet Wale ETH-Y 8:25.28
10. Albert Chemutai UGA-J 8:25.94
11. Ezekiel Kemboi KEN 8:29.38
12. Jairus Birech KEN 8:32.90
13. Yoann Kowal FRA. 8:34.53
14. Jacob Araptany UGA 8:49.18

dq. Bilal Tabti ALG –

Kemboi, the four-time winner, could manage only 11th this time, but there was still a seventh consecutive win for Kenya as the favourite Kipruto won in a race that started slowly (Soboka 1k 2:51.81, Jager 2k 5:35.46) but finished with a final kilometre of 2:38.66. Kipruto powered home off the final water jump and celebrated flamboyantly in the last 30m. Heat winners were El Bakkali 8:22.60 and Jager 8:20.36, but Brimin Kipruto, the 2007 World and 2008 Olympic champion, was only 7th in his heat.

110 Metres Hurdles *(h & sf 6th, F 7th 0.0)*

1. Omar McLeod JAM 13.04
2. Sergey Shubenkov ANA/RUS 13.14
3. Balázs Baji HUN 13.28
4. Garfield Darien FRA 13.30
5. Aries Merritt USA 13.31
6. Shane Brathwaite BAR 13.32
7. Orlando Ortega ESP 13.37
8. Hansle Parchment JAM 13.37

Olympic champion McLeod won his heat in 13.23 and semi in 13.10, and in the final a great run-in from the last hurdle enabled him to win by a clear metre in 13.04. Defending champion Shubenkov had a shaky start, only third in his heat and qualifying for the final as a fastest loser in the semis, but led the final early on and matched strides with McLeod until the run-in. Merritt, returning to the scene of his Olympic triumph, impressed with the fastest heat of 13.16 and joint-fastest semi of 13.10 but couldn't reproduce that form in the final where the bronze went to the unheralded Baji, who had ranked equal ninth on this year's times. British medal hope Andy Pozzi led until the eighth barrier in his semi but in a very tight finish slipped back to 4th and elimination, while the US had only Merritt in the final, as Devon Allen (3rd) and Aleec Harris (6th) did not advance from the semis.

400 Metres Hurdles *(h 6th, sf 7th, F 9th)*

1. Karsten Warholm NOR 48.35
2. Yasmani Copello TUR 48.49
3. Kerron Clement USA 48.52
4. Kemar Mowatt JAM 48.99
5. TJ Holmes USA 49.00
6. Juander Santos DOM 49.04
7. Abderrahaman Samba QAT 49.74
8. Kariem Hussein SUI 50.07

In steady rain and on a cool night Warholm went out very fast in the final so that he was well clear at 300m and held on for a fine victory. Newcomer Samba was 2nd at halfway and still 3rd until he clobbered the final hurdle while Clement also lost a place with a clumsy clearance. Fastest heat was 49.13 from Copello and fastest semi 48.35 by Clement (from Warholm 48.43).

High Jump *(Q 2.31 11th, F 13th)*

1. Mutaz Essa Barshim QAT 2.35
2. Danil Lysenko ANA/RUS 2.32
3. Majed El Dein Ghazal SYR 2.29
4. Edgar Rivera MEX 2.29
5. Mateusz Przybylko GER 2.29

6= Ilya Ivanyuk ANA/RUS 2.25
6= Robert Grabarz GBR 2.25

8. Bryan McBride USA 2.25
9. Bohdan Bondarenko UKR 2.25
10. Eike Onnen GER 2.20

nh. Tihomir Ivanov BUL nh
dns. Wang Yu CHN –

Six men went over 2.31 in qualifying (and 17 over 2.29) but 2.29 was enough for the bronze in the final. Barshim was a big favourite to take his first global title and so it proved as he had a clean card at all heights to 2.35 before going close at 2.40. Lysenko also had just one failure (at 2.29) and secured silver at 2.32, going out with failures at 2.35. Ghazal went over 2.29 on his second attempt and Rivera and Przybylko on their third. A non-qualifier was injured Erik Kynard who retired after one failure at 2.17.

Pole Vault *(Q 5.75m 6th, F 8th)*

1. Sam Kendricks USA 5.95
2. Piotr Lisek POL 5.89
3. Renaud Lavillenie FRA 5.89
4. Xue Changrui CHN 5.82
5. Pawel Wojciechowski POL 5.75
6. Axel Chapelle FRA 5.65

7 Kurtis Marschall AUS 5.65

8. Shawnacy Barber CAN 5.65
9. Armand Duplantis SWE-J 5.50

nh Raphael Holzdeppe GER –
nh Arnaud Art BEL –
nh Yao Jie CHN –

On a cool night, Kendricks took gold by first-time clearances at 5.50, 5.65, 5.75, 5.82 and 5.89, then got over 5.95 at the third attempt and had one failure at 6.01. The other medals were decided at 5.89, with Wojciechowski and Xue (after a Chinese record at 5.82) failing, and Lisek going over on his first attempt and

Lavillenie on his second. Lavillenie tried to move up by taking a jump at 6.01 after two failures at 5.95, but he did not come close. Nine men qualified with 5.70 and then 3 of the 8 more who cleared 5.60 went through on count-back.

Long Jump *(Q 8.05m 4th, F 5th)*

1. Luvo Manyonga RSA	8.48/0.4
2. Jarrion Lawson USA	8.44/0.6
3. Ruswahl Samaai RSA	8.32/-0.1
4. Aleksandr Menkov ANA/RUS	8.27/0.0
5. Maykel Massó CUB-J	8.26/0.8
6. Shi Yuhao CHN-J	8.23/-0.3
7. Wang Jianan CHN	8.23/0.6
8. Michel Tornéus SWE	8.18/0.4
9. Emiliano Lasa URU	8.11/0.7
10. Radek Juska CZE	8.02/0.7
11. Fabrice Lapierre AUS	7.93/0.6
12. Damar Forbes JAM	7.91/0.6

Lawson had a great series (8.37, 8.43, 8.40, 8.11, 8.31, 8.44), but Manyonga's second round 8.48 (next best 8.32) held up for the win. Menkov was 2nd with 8.27 in the first round but followed that with five fouls and Samaai, 3rd with a first-round 8.25, moved to bronze with final jumps of 8.27 and 8.31. 18 year-olds Massó and Shi were 5th and 6th. Top US jumpers, Jeff Henderson (17th 7.84) and Marquis Dendy (20th 7.78) failed to advance from qualifying, which was led by Juska 8.24.

Triple Jump *(Q 17.00m 7th, F10th)*

1. Christian Taylor USA	17.68/0.2
2. Will Claye USA	17.63/-0.1
3. Nelson Évora POR	17.19/-0.1
4. Cristian Nápoles CUB-J	17.16 /0.2
5. Alexis Copello AZE	17.16/0.2
6. Chris Benard USA	17.16/0.2
7. Andy Díaz CUB	17.13/0.2
8. Jean-Marc Pontvianne FRA	16.79/0.1
9. Wu Ruiting CHN	16.66/0.7
10. Pablo Torrijos ESP	16.60/0.2
11. Yordanys Durañona DMA	16.42/-0.2
12. Lázaro Martínez CUB	16.25/0.6

The former team-mates at the University of Florida, Taylor and Claye, had a fascinating battle for supremacy, well ahead of the rest of the field. Claye took a first-round lead of 17.54 with Taylor 5th at 16.97. Taylor took over with 17.57 in the second round to 17.52 by Claye, only for the lead to change twice in round three – Claye 17.63 then Taylor 17.68. That's how it stayed, as Taylor closed with 17.26, 17.38 and 17.03 and Claye 17.49, 17.53 and foul. The win here took Taylor to a 21-20 career advantage over Claye. Just 6cm separated 3rd to 7th with Évora, the 2007 champion, taking the bronze with his second effort. Just three men made the automatic qualifying standard: Benard 17.20, Taylor 17.15 and Nápoles 17.06.

Shot *(Q 20.75m 5th, F 6th)*

1. Tomas Walsh NZL	22.03
2. Joe Kovacs USA	21.66
3. Stipe Zunic CRO	21.46
4. Tomás Stanek CZE	21.41
5. Michal Haratyk POL	21.41
6. Ryan Crouser USA	21.20
7. Ryan Whiting USA	21.09
8. Konrad Bukowiecki POL	20.89
9. Jacko Gill NZL	20.82
10. David Storl GER	20.80
11. Darrell Hill USA	20.79
12. Andrei Gag ROU	19.96

Walsh reached 22.14, the best in any shot qualification competition, and the standard was such that 12th (Gag 20.61) and 13th were the best ever, with Jakub Szyszkowski's 20.55 the best ever non-qualifying mark. Favourites Crouser 20.90 and Kovacs 20.67 were below par as also over 21m in qualifying were Storl 21.41, Haratyk 21.27 and Hill 21.11. The high standard was maintained in the final, in which for the first time seven men exceeded 21m, with best evers for places 5th to 11th. Kovacs 21.48 led from Walsh in the first round, before Walsh moved ahead with 21.64 and 21.75, following with 21.70 and 21.63 before his 22.03 to end the competition. In round two Zunic threw 21.46 and Stanek 21.41 and Kovacs sealed silver with a third-round 21.66. The 2015 1-2 Crouser and Storl were well below their best in 6th and 10th places.

Discus *(Q 64.50m 4th, F 5th)*

1. Andrius Gudzius LTU	69.21
2. Daniel Ståhl SWE	69.19
3. Mason Finley USA	68.03
4. Fedrick Dacres JAM	65.83
5. Piotr Malachowski POL	65.24
6. Robert Harting GER	65.10
7. Robert Urbanek POL	64.15
8. Traves Smikle JAM	64.04
9. Lukas Weisshaidinger AUT	63.76
10. Apostolos Parellis CYP	63.17
11. Simon Pettersson SWE	60.39
12. Gerd Kanter EST	60.00

Ståhl 67.64 and Gudzius 67.01 led the qualifying, but the order was reversed in a very close contest in the final. Finley led with a lifetime best of 67.07 in the first round, followed by Gudzius 67.52 with Ståhl having a foul. In round two Finley regained the lead with 68.03, only to be followed in the circle by Ståhl 69.19 and Gudzius 69.21. Ståhl had a fourth round 68.57 but that 2cm lead remained the winning margin. These three (average height 2.01m) stayed well clear of the next three men over 65m.

Hammer *(Q 75.50m 9th, F 11th)*

1. Pawel Fajdek POL	79.81
2. Valeriy Pronkin ANA/RUS	78.16

3. Wojciech Nowicki POL	78.03
4. Quentin Bigot FRA	77.67
5. Aleksey Sokirskiy ANA/RUS	77.50
6. Nick Miller GBR	77.31
7. Dilshod Nazarov TJK	77.22
8. Sergey Marghiev MDA	75.87
9. Pavel Boreysha BLR	75.86
10. Marco Lingua ITA	75.13
11. Bence Halász HUN	74.45
12. Özkan Baltaci TUR	74.39

He had the shortest winning mark in World Champs history, but Fajdek hardly minded as he took his third consecutive World title. He was over 79m in rounds 3-5: 79.73, 79.81 and 79.40 while Nowicki's third round 78.01 was passed in the last by Pronkin 78.16. Nowicki complained that the circle was very slow. The throwers coped well with pouring rain in qualifying, led by the Poles Nowicki 76.85 and Fajdek 76.82.

Javelin *(Q 83.00m 10th, F 12th)*

1. Johannes Vetter GER	89.89
2. Jakub Vadlejch CZE	89.73
3. Petr Frydrych CZE	88.32
4. Thomas Röhler GER	88.26
5. Tero Pitkämäki FIN	86.94
6. Ioánnis Kiriazís GRE	84.52
7. Keshorn Walcott TTO	84.48
8. Andreas Hofmann GER	83.98
9. Marcin Krukowski POL	82.01
10. Ahmed Bader Magour QAT	81.77
11. Magnus Kirt EST	80.48
12. Davinder Singh IND	80.02
13. Julius Yego KEN	76.29

13 men exceeded the automatic qualifying standard of 83m, and Vetter's 91.20 replaced Jan Zelezny's 90.76 in the 2001 World Champs as the longest ever qualifying throw. The best ever marks in any javelin competition were set for places 8th to 15th (at least) and Hamish Peacock's 82.46 was the best ever non-qualifying mark, but the most notable casualty was Vitezslav Vesely, who managed merely 75.50. Vetter did not throw as far in the final but his opener of 89.89 proved to be the winner. Röhler was second with 87.08, but was overtaken in the second round when Vadlejch threw a pb 89.73 to threaten Vetter's lead. However, Vetter responded with 89.78 and Röhler threw 88.26 for third place. His medal hopes were dashed when Frydrych, followed two efforts of 87.93 with a pb 88.32 in the final round.

Decathlon *(11th/12th)*

1. Kevin Mayer FRA	8768
2. Rico Freimuth GER	8564
3. Kai Kazmirek GER	8488
4. Janek Oiglane EST	8371
5. Damian Warner CAN	8309
6. Oleksiy Kasyanov UKR	8234
7. Kurt Felix GRN	8227
8. Adam Sebastian Helcelet CZE	8222
9. Jorge Ureña ESP	8125
10. Devon Williams USA	8088
11. Ashley Bryant GBR	8049
12. Martin Roe NOR	8040
13. Karl Robert Saluri EST	8025
14. Pau Tonnesen ESP	8006
15. Bastien Auzeil FRA	7922

Mayer was the clear favourite after his 2016 Olympic victory and was dominant throughout from reducing his 100m pb from 10.81 to 10.70, followed by a series of solid performances to a pb 400m of 48.28 which left him with a first day lead at 4478 points ahead of Kazmirek 4421, Freimuth 4361, Warner (battling against sickness) 4347 and Trey Hardee 4313. Mayer had another pb, 13.75 in the 110mh, and had a scare, needing three attempts to clearing his opening pole vault height of 5.10, and ended up with a 204 winning margin over the splendidly consistent Freimuth. Kazmirek was third and Oiglane improved his best from 8170 to 8371 for fourth, The 2009 and 2011 champion Hardee crashed out in the hurdles.

4 x 100 Metres Relay *(h, F 12th)*

1. GBR	37.47	Ujah, Gemili, Talbot, Mitchell-Blake
2. USA	37.52	Rodgers, Gatlin, Bacon, Coleman [ht: 3 B-J Lee]
3. JPN	38.04	Tada, Iizuka, Kiryu, Fujimitsu [ht: 4 Cambridge]
4. CHN	38.34	Wu Zhiqiang, Xie Zhenye, Su Bingtian, Zhang Peimeng
5. FRA	38.48	Dutamby, Vicaut, Zezé, Lemaitre
6. CAN	38.59	Smellie, Brown, Rodney, Ajomale
7. TUR	38.73	Hekimoglu, Harvey, Barnes, Guliyev
-. JAM	dnf	McLeod, Forte, Blake, Bolt [Ht: Tracey, Forte, Campbell, Bolt]

The British team showed splendid form with 37.76 in their heat, just behind the USA 37.70, while Jamaica won the other heat in 37.95. Usain Bolt anchored the Jamaican team and their strength was such that they could bring in Omar McLeod and Yohan Blake for the final. Thanks to super sprinting and slick baton passing, the British squad led throughout and was narrowly ahead of the USA at the last change. Amid a wall of noise Mitchell-Blake managed to hold off Coleman in the superb time of 37.47, a European record that only Jamaican and American teams have ever surpassed. Approx splits: Ujah 10.3 (turn), Gemili 9.0 (straight), Talbot 9.2 (turn) and Mitchell-Blake 9.0 (straight). Surely too far back, in his current form, for anything other than a bronze, Bolt ran the final leg for his final race of his unparalleled career, but to universal consternation his left hamstring tore early on and he fell to the track in pain and frustration. There was a more fitting farewell appearance the following night: a slow walking, emotional lap of honour to a standing ovation with Usain stopping to reflect at the start lines of the 100m and 200m. He is indeed the legend he always wanted to be and he will never be forgotten.

4 x 400 Metres Relay *(h 12th, F 13th)*

1. TTO	2:58.12	Solomon 46.1, Richards 43.5, Cedenio 44.41, L Gordon 44.08 (Quow ran in heat)
2. USA	2:58.61	London 44.8, Roberts 44.0, Cherry 44.91, Kerley 44.75 (Nellum and Cherry ran in heat)
3. GBR	2:59.00	Hudson-Smith 45.4, Cowan 44.2, Yousif 44.97, Rooney 44.42 (J Green ran in heat)
4. BEL	3:00.04	Venderbemden 46.4, J Borlée 44.7, D Borlée 45.36, K Borlée 43.60
5. ESP	3:00.65	Husillos 45.4, Búa 45.3, Echeverry 45.26, García 44.75
6. CUB	3:01.10	Collazo 46.6, Chacón 45.2, Pellicier 45.16, Lescay 44.21
7. POL	3:01.59	Duszynski 46.0, Omelko 44.8, Krawczuk 45.54, Zimny 45.26
8. FRA	3:01.79	Vaillant 45.6, Jordier 45.7, Hanne 45.09, Atine-Venel 45.45

Three teams broke 3 minutes in the heats (USA 2:59.23, TTO and BEL), and three did so in the final, in which the USA was denied a seventh successive title by Trinidad & Tobago who ran a national record time of 2:58.12. Crucial to their success was a magnificent second leg of 43.5 by Jereem Richards in taking them from a distant 7th to 3rd. He was followed by Machel Cedenio, 0.5 faster than the USA's Michael Cherry, and on the final leg Lalonde Gordon caught and passed a race-weary Fred Kerley. Martyn Rooney's typically excellent final leg took Britain to the bronze, although behind him Kevin Borlée's 43.60 was much the quickest anchor leg.

20 Kilometres Walk *(13th)*

1. Eider Arévalo COL	1:18:53
2. Sergey Shirobokov ANA/RUS-J	1:18:55
3. Caio Bonfim BRA	1:19:04
4. Lebogang Shange RSA	1:19:18
5. Christopher Linke GER	1:19:21
6. Dane Bird-Smith AUS	1:19:28
7. Wang Kaihua CHN	1:19:30
8. Alvaro Martin ESP	1:19:41
9. Alberto Amezcua ESP	1:19:46
10. Miguel Angel López ESP	1:19:57
11. Isamu Fujisawa JPN	1:20:04
12. Artur Brzozowski POL	1:20:33
13. Díego García ESP	1:20:34
14. Eiki Takahashi JPN	1:20:36
15. Nils Brembach GER	1:20:42

With ever-faster 5k splits of 19:56. 19:54, 19:43 and 19:20 for a South American record of 1:18:53, Arévalo, the 2012 World Junior champion, followed Luis Fernando López, the 20kW winner in 2011, as the only World golds ever for Colombia. He prevailed by just 2 secs over 'neutral' Shirobakov as times were excellent despite a temperature that seemed more than the listed 22°C. Shange moved up from 23rd at halfway to take the lead briefly and set a new South African record but struggled towards the end and was passed by Bonfim (in a Brazilian record) for the bronze. 58 of 64 men finished. One of the three men disqualified was home favourite Tom Bosworth, for the first time in his senior career, as he led rather over exuberantly at about 12k.

All the walks events were held on the same day on a 2k course up and down The Mall in the centre of London.

50 Kilometres Walk *(13th)*

1. Yohann Diniz FRA	3:33:12*
2. Hirooki Arai JPN	3:41:17
3. Kai Kobayashi JPN	3:41:19
4. Igor Hlavan UKR	3:41:42
5. Satoshi Maruo JPN	3:43:03
6. Maté Helebrandt HUN	3:43:56
7. Rafal Augustyn POL	3:44:18
8. Robert Heffernan IRL	3:44:41
9. Marco De Luca ITA	3:45:02
10. Carl Dohmann GER	3:45:21
11. João Vieira POR	3:45:28
12. Quentin Rew NZL	3:46:29
13. Karl Junghannss GER	3:47:01
14. Aleksi Ojala FIN	3:47:20
15. Evan Dunfee CAN	3:47:36

At his sixth World Championship, Diniz took the gold medal in magnificent style. His 3:33:12 is a time second only to his own world record of 3:32:33 (2014) and his winning margin of 8:05 is a World Champs record; at 39 he is the oldest ever winner of the event. Striking out alone, his 10k splits were 44:28, 42:50 (1:27:18), 42:33 (2:09:51), 41:40 (2:51:31) and 41:41. The Japanese pair broke away from the rest shortly after 36k. In 6th place Helebrandt set a Hungarian record of 3:43:56 that knocked a remarkable 9:58 off his previous best, 33 finished from 48 starters. Vieira contested his 10th World Championships

Women

100 Metres *(h 5th, sf, F 6th 0.1)*

1. Tori Bowie USA	10.85
2. Marie-Josée Ta Lou CIV	10.86
3. Dafne Schippers NED	10.96
4. Murielle Ahouré CIV	10.98
5. Elaine Thompson JAM	10.98
6. Michelle-Lee Ahye TTO	11.01
7. Rosângela Santos BRA	11.06
8. Kelly-Ann Baptiste TTO	11.09

Unfortunately Thompson, after winning her heat in 11,05 and semi in 10.84, was ill for the final, and in the circumstances did well to come 5th. But she lacked her usual scintillating pace and the way was clear for another champion,.

That was Bowie who came from behind to out-dip Ta Lou and win by just 0.01 with Schippers third, a metre behind. Ta Lou had been fastest in the heats with 11.00 and semi-final winners apart from Thompson were Ta Lou in 10.87 and Bowie in 10.91. Santos set a South American record of 10.91 behind Thomson.

200 Metres *(h 8th, sf 10th, F 11th 0.2)*

1. Dafne Schippers NED	22.05
2. Marie-Josée Ta Lou CIV	22.08
3. Shauna Miller-Uibo BAH	22.15
4. Dina Asher-Smith GBR	22.22
5. Deajah Stevens USA	22.44
6. Kimberlyn Duncan USA	22.59
7. Crystal Emmanuel CAN	22.60
8. Tynia Gaither BAH	23.07

Schippers retained her title, but her 22.05 was much slower then her 21.63 in Beijing, and she beat Ta Lou (20m shorter than the Dutch woman) by 0.03 as the Ivorian set a national record. Schippers was fastest in the heats with 22.63 and joint fastest in the semis with Miller-Uibo in 22.49. Miller-Uibo made up a little for her 400m mistake with the bronze here, overtaking Asher-Smith with 30m to go.

400 Metres *(h 6th, sf 7th, F 9th)*

1. Phyllis Francis USA	49.92
2. Salwa Eid Naser BRN-J	50.06
3. Allyson Felix USA	50.08
4. Shaunae Miller-Uibo BAH	50.49
5. Shericka Jackson JAM	50.76
6. Stephanie Ann McPherson JAM	50.86
7. Kabange Mupopo ZAM	51.15
8. Novlene Williams-Mills JAM	51.48

Felix and Miller-Uibo had been the 1-2 in Beijing, but were 3-4 here behind the surprising gold and silver medallists Francis and Naser. The latter had set Bahrain records as she was fastest in the heats with 50.57 and semis with 50.08, beating Felix 50.12, while the other semi-final winners were Miller-Uibo 50.36 and Francis 50.37. Run in pouring rain and cold weather, Felix was out fastest in the final (200m 23.1) but at 300m Miller-Uibo led in 35.5 from Felix 35.8, Francis 36.0 and Naser 36.3, and looked set to win but some 25m from the finish the Bahamian looked up at the giant screen, stumbled and lost her momentum – so much that she was pushed out of the medals. The first two finished strongly with 19 year-old Naser setting her third national record of the meeting. Felix made history by winning her 14th World Champs medal, equalling the record of Usain Bolt and Merlene Ottey.

800 Metres *(h 10th, sf 11th, F 13th)*

1. Caster Semenya RSA	1:55.16
2. Francine Niyonsaba BDI	1:55.92
3. Ajee' Wilson USA	1:56.65
4. Margaret Wambui KEN	1:57.54
5. Melissa Bishop CAN	1:57.68
6. Angelika Cichocka POL	1:58.41
7. Charlene Lipsey USA	1:58.73
8. Lynsey Sharp GBR	1:58.98

Semenya is pretty much unbeatable in women's 800m races these days, and she duly won here (as she had in 2009 and 2011), reducing her South African record to 1:55.16. Wilson ran well to split the Olympic medallists and take the bronze medal. She had shared the lead at 200m in 27.08 with Niyonsaba (Semenya 27.5) and at 400m it was Niyonsaba 57.98, Wilson 58.21, Wambui 85.36, and Semenya 6th 58.53. The top two stayed together to 600m in 1:27.07 by when Semenya had moved up third before finish and a last lap of 56.63 was much too strong. Niyonsaba 1:59.86 ran the one sub-2 min time of the heats and the semis were won by Semenya 1:58.90 and Wilson 1:59.21. Defending champion Marina Arzamasova went out in the heats.

1500 Metres *(h 4th, sf 5th, F 7th)*

1. Faith Kipyegon KEN	4:02.59
2. Jennifer Simpson USA	4:02.76
3. Caster Semenya RSA	4:02.90
4. Laura Muir GBR	4:02.97
5. Sifan Hassan NED	4:03.34
6. Laura Weightman GBR	4:04.11
7. Angelika Cichocka POL	4:04.16
8. Rabab Arrafi MAR	4:04.35
9. Meraf Bahta SWE	4:04.76
10. Malika Akkaoui MAR	4:05.87
11. Hanna Klein GER	4:06.22
12. Genzebe Dibaba ETH	4:06.72

Aggressive front-running by Jessica Judd led to the fastest heat in World Championships history, 4:02.67 by Dibaba from Semenya 4:02.84, and there was another fast heat win of 4:03.09 by Kipyegon who was also fastest with 4:03.54 in the first semi before Hassan took the second in 4:03.77. With Muir in front the final had a reasonable first lap of 65.34 but a depressingly slow second 400m of 71.77 to 800m in 2:17.11. After a third lap of 61.82 Hassan led in 3:18.93 from Kipyegon 3:18.94, Simpson 3:19.16), Muir 3:19.22 and Dibaba 3:19.38 with Semenya 3:19.86 some way back in ninth place. From the bell (3:04.55) Hassan led from Kipyegon and Muir until, in a dramatic finale to the race, Kipyegon stayed strong, Hassan faded, Simpson nipped past Muir on the inside and Semenya came through from far back. Kipyegon and Simpson each ran 57.9 for the last lap while Semenya ran 57.5. Dibaba trailed in last and withdrew from the 5000m heats due to a back problem.

5000 Metres *(h 10th, F 13th)*

1. Hellen Obiri KEN	14:34.86
2. Almaz Ayana ETH	14:40.35
3. Sifan Hassan NED	14:42.73
4. Senbere Teferi ETH	14:47.45

5. Margaret Chelimo KEN	14:48.74
6. Laura Muir GBR	14:52.07
7. Sheila Kiprotich KEN	14:54.05
8. Susan Krumins NED	14:58.33
9. Shannon Rowbury USA	14:59.92
10. Eilish McColgan GBR	15:00.43
11. Letesenbet Gidey ETH-J	15:04.99
12. Molly Huddle USA	15:05.28
13. Shelby Houlihan USA	15:06.40
14. Kalkidan Gezahegne BRN	15:28.21
dnf. Karoline Grøvdal NOR	–

The final started very slowly with a first lap of 1:21.77 and 1000m in 3:18.62. Soon afterwards Ayana and Obiri began to race in earnest. Ayana ran the second kilometre inside 2:49 to 6:07.41 at 2000m from Obiri 6:07.59 as they were 20m clear of the pack. The lead stretched to 50m by 3000m: Ayana 8:58.05, Obiri 8:58.28 and then Teferi 9:07.51. Ayana relentlessly ran 68+ sec laps but could not shake off her Kenyan opponent. At 4000m their times were 11:49.95 and 11:50.16. Some 60m behind, Teferi, Kipkemboi and Hassan were closely bunched in pursuit of the bronze medal. Ayana still led at the bell in 13:34.19 but had no answer when Obiri sprinted past with 250m to go. Covering the last lap in 60.6 she won by 30m. Her kilometre splits were 3:19.05, 2:48.54, 2:50.69, 2:51.88 and 2:44.70, which meant that she ran the last 3000m in 8:27.27. Hassan made up for her 1500m disappointment with the bronze medal, covering her final kilometre in a spectacular 2:42.04 and the last lap in 58,2. Seven women headed by Obiri 14:56.70 and Ayana 14:57.06 broke 15 minutes in the fastest of the two heats.

10,000 Metres *(5th)*

1. Almaz Ayana ETH	30:16.32
2. Tirunesh Dibaba ETH	31:02.69
3. Agnes Tirop KEN	31:03.50
4. Alice Aprop Nawowuna KEN	31:11.86
5. Susan Krumins NED	31:20.24
6. Emily Infeld USA	31:20.45
7. Irene Cheptai KEN	31:21.11
8. Molly Huddle USA	31:24.78
9. Emily Sisson USA	31:26.36
10. Ayuko Suzuki JPN	31:27.30
11. Yasemin Can TUR	31:35.48
12. Shitaye Eshete BRN	31:38.66
13. Mercyline Chelangat UGA	31:40.48
14. Dera Dida ETH	31:51.75
15. Desa Mokonin BRN	31:55.34

Racing for the first time since September 2016 due to injury, Ayana won the title by 46.37 sec, almost exactly double the previous widest margin of victory in this event. Her kilometre splits were: 3:30.38, 3:18.49, 3:10.60, 3:02.73, 2:49.18 (15:51.38 at 5000m, 6 sec ahead of Can), 2:51.59 (17 sec clear), 2:52.22 (27 sec up), 2:54.84 (37 sec), 2:56.80 (27:26.83 at 9000m with Tirop 28:12.18, Nawowuna 28:12.43 and Dibaba 28:12.71) and finally 2:49.49 for a world leading time of 30:16.32. She ran her second 5000m in 14:24.94 (better than her Championships record for 2015) and last 3000m in 8:41.13. Dibaba outkicked Tirop for second. 31 of 33 runners finished.

Marathon *(6th)*

1. Rose Chelimo BRN	2:27:11
2. Edna Kiplagat KEN	2:27:18
3. Amy Cragg USA	2:27:18
4. Flomena Cheyech KEN	2:27:21
5. Shure Demise ETH	2:27:58
6. Eunice Jepkirui Kirwa BRN	2:28:17
7. Helah Kiprop KEN	2:28:19
8. Mare Dibaba ETH	2:28:49
9. Jessica Trengrove AUS	2:28:59
10. Birhane Dibaba ETH	2:29:01
11. Serena Burla USA	2:29:32
12. Aselefech Mergia ETH	2:29:43
13. Charlotte Purdue GBR	2:29:48
14. Eva Nyvltová CZE	2:29:56
15. Kim Hye-gyong KOR	2:30:29

Kenyan-born Chelimo, who had taken Bahrain citizenship in 2015, won with halves of 74:53 and 72:18. First Catarina Ribeiro (to 10k) and then Alyson Dixon (to 29k) were allowed to build up substantial leads. Eventually Chelimo attempted to break away in the 38th kilometre, but Kiplagat caught her and led by a second at 40k in 2:20:06 and opened up a 15m lead, but Chelimo moved past her in decisive fashion over the last 800m to take Bahrain's first World Champs gold. Cragg overtook Cheyech in the final 100m and almost caught Kiplagat. There were 91 starters of whom 78 finished.

3000 Metres Steeplechase *(h 9th, F 11th)*

1. Emma Coburn USA	9:02.58*
2. Courtney Frerichs USA	9:03.77
3. Hyvin Jepkemoi KEN	9:04.03
4. Beatrice Chepkoech KEN	9:10.45
5. Ruth Jebet BRN	9:13.96
6. Celliphine Chespol KEN-J	9:15.04
7. Etenesh Diro ETH	9:22.46
8. Winfred Yavi BRN-J	9:22.67
9. Gesa Felicitas Krause GER	9:23.87
10. Purity Kirui KEN	9:25.62
11. Belén Casetta ARG	9:25.99
12. Genevieve LaCaze AUS	9:26.58
13. Geneviève Lalonde CAN	9:29.99
dq. Aisha Praught JAM	–
dns. Birtukan Fente ETH	–

Perhaps the biggest surprise of the Championships was this US 1-2 with East African-born athletes taking places 3-8. Chepkoech ran the fastest heat (9:19.03) and was the early leader in the final, but after the first full lap – losing concentration – she missed the turn-off leading to the water jump and by the time she realised her mistake and turned back the rest were far ahead. She stumbled and fell three barriers later and in the circumstances did remarkably well to work her way back to the leaders. After an even pace, with Jebet leading at 1000m 3:02.74 and 6000m 6:03.60, there were five in contention with a lap to go. Frerichs took the lead down the back straight before Coburn cleared the final water jump in masterful fashion and ran home strongly to set a North American record with Frerichs holding off the top Kenyan challenger Jepkemoi.

100 Metres Hurdles *(h & sf 11th, F 12th 0.1)*

1. Sally Pearson AUS	12.59
2. Dawn Harper Nelson USA	12.63
3. Pamela Dutkiewicz GER	12.72
4. Kendra Harrison USA	12.74
5. Christina Manning USA	12.74
6. Alina Talay BLR	12.81
7. Nadine Visser NED	12.83
8. Nia Ali USA	13.04

Word record holder Harrison was fastest, at 12.60, in the heats. Then the semis were won by Pearson 12.53, Harper Nelson 12.63 and Manning 12.71, but Harrison hit the first hurdle hard and only just qualified with her third place. A notable non-qualifier was Tiffany Porter, only 13.18 in her heat. Pearson, the 2011 World and 2012 Olympic champion, was off fast and led all the way in the final to complete a remarkable come-back with a well-deserved victory. The 2008 Olympic champion Harper-Nelson took the silver and Dutkiewicz excelled for the bronze, but Harrison hit hurdles 2, 3 and 4.

400 Metres Hurdles *(h 7th, sf 8th, F 10th)*

1. Kori Carter USA	53.07
2. Dalilah Muhammad USA	53.50
3. Ristananna Tracey JAM	53.74
4. Zuzana Hejnová CZE	54.20
5. Léa Sprunger SUI	54.59
6. Sage Watson CAN	54.92
7. Cassandra Tate USA	55.43
8. Eilidh Doyle GBR	55.71

Carter, running blind in lane nine, held the lead at 300m in the final but she and Muhammad were virtually level over the last hurdle. However, Carter had the superior speed and strength on the run-in and won quite clearly in the second quickest time of her career. Hejnová started fast but was overtaken by Tracey for the bronze medal. Muhammad was fastest in the heats with 54.59 and the semis, with Hejnová quickest at 54.59, were slower than expected.

High Jump *(Q 1.94 10th, F 12th)*

1. Mariya Lasitskene ANA/RUS	2.03
2. Yuliya Levchenko UKR	2.01
3. Kamila Licwinko POL	1.99
4. Marie-Laurence Jungfleisch GER	1.95
5. Katarina Johnson-Thompson GBR	1.95
6. Morgan Lake GBR	1,95
7= Mirela Demireva BUL	1.92
7= Airine Palsyte LTU	1.92
9. Inika McPherson USA	1.92
10, Vashti Cunningham USA-J	1.92
11, Michael Hrubá CZE-J	1.92
12. Ruth Beitia ESP	1.88

Exactly 12 women cleared 1.92 in qualifying to go though to the final. There the clear favourite Lasitskene had first time clearances at 1.84, 1.88, 1.92, 1.95 and 1.97, but a failure at 1.99 left her behind first-time clearances by Licwinko, who had four previous failures, and Levchenko who maintained a clear card. So Lasitskene passed, but then went over 2.01 and 2.03 on first attempts, eventually failing three times at 2.08, Licwinko failed twice at 2.01 and once at 2.03 but the 19 year-old Levchenko, from a pre-meet pb of 1.97, was thrilled to clear 2.01 on her second attempt for the silver medal.

Pole Vault *(Q 4.60m 4th, F 6th)*

1. Ekateríni Stefanídi GRE	4.91
2. Sandi Morris USA	4.75
3= Robeilys Peinado VEN	4.65
3= Yarisley Silva CUB	4.65
5. Lisa Ryzih GER	4.65
6. Holly Bradshaw GBR	4.65
7. Alysha Newman CAN	4.65
8. Olga Mullina ANA/RUS	4.55
9. Lisa McCartney NZL	4.55
10. Angelica Bengtsson SWE	4.55
11. Nicole Büchler SUI	4.45
12. Anicka Newell CAN	4.45

Of the two clear favourites, Morris entered at 4.45 and cleared that and 4.45, 4.55 and 4.65, while Stefanídi entered with a first attempt clearance at 4.65. Five other women cleared that height, but none were able to go higher and their placings were determined on count-back. Both the big two went over 4.75 first time, but while Stefanídi succeeded (just) first time at 4.82, Morris failed and then twice at 4.89. Sure then of the gold medal, Stefanídi failed her one try at 4.89, but went over for a Greek record at 4.91 and then tried 5.02 unsuccessfully. A surprise elimination in qualifying was Jenn Suhr, who entered and failed at 4.55.

Long Jump *(Q 6.70m 9th, F 11th)*

1. Brittney Reese USA	7.02/0.1
2. Darya Klishina ANA/RUS	7.00/-0.3
3. Tianna Bartoletta USA	6.97/-0.2
4. Ivana Spanovic SRB	6.96/0.1
5. Lorraine Ugen GBR	6.72/0.5
6. Brooke Stratton AUS	6.67/-0.9
7. Chantel Malone IVB	6.57/-0.1
8. Blessing Okagbare NGR	6.55/0.2
9. Lauma Griva LAT	6.54/1.0
10. Claudia Salman-Rath GER	6.54/0.8
11. Eliane Martins BRA	6.52/1.2
12. Alina Rotaru ROU	6.46/-0.3

Due to incessant rain nobody reached the automatic qualifying standard and 6.46 was enough to make the final. Klishina was best at 6.66 while Reese jumped only 6.50. But it was a different story in the final when there was a close battle for the medals. Reese managed only two valid jumps, starting with 6.75 and 7.02 in the third round. That proved just enough for her fourth World title (plus an Olympic and three World Indoor wins). Klishina led the first round with 6.78 and progressed to 6.88, 6.91 and 7.00 and Spanovic took the lead in the second round with 6.96 but was passed in the last by Bartoletta, the 2005 and 2015 champion, with 6.97. Responding to that Spanovic seemed to land beyond 7m, but replays showed that her flapping bib number had touched the sand at 6.91.

Triple Jump *(Q 14.20m 5th, F 7th)*

1. Yulimar Rojas VEN	14.91/0.4
2. Caterine Ibargüen COL	14.89/0.9
3. Olga Rypakova KAZ	14.77/0.9
4. Hanna Minenko ISR	14.42/1.2
5. Kristin Gierisch GER	14.33/0.3
6. Anna Jagaciak Michalska POL	14.25/0.7
7. Ana Peleteiro ESP	14.23/1.4
8. Shanieka Ricketts JAM	14.13/0.3
9. Patricia Mamona POR	14.12/0.1
10. Kimberly Williams JAM	14.01/0.2
11. Susana Costa POR	13.99/0.4
12. Neele Eckhardt GER	13.97/0.9

There was a terrific tussle between the two South Americans. Ibargüen led the first round with 14.67 to 14.55 by Rojas, who took over the lead with 14.82 in round 2, increasing it to 14.83 in round 3, just before Ibargüen jumped 14.89. The Colombian followed that with 14.80, 14.71 and 14.88, but it wax not quite enough for Rojas jumped 14.91 (15.01 from take-off to landing) in round 5. Rypakova was an isolated third with a third-round 14.77. Rypakova 14.57 and Rojas 14.52 had been best in qualifying.

Shot *(Q 18.30m 8th, F 9th)*

1. Gong Lijiao CHN	19.94
2. Anita Márton HUN	19.49
3. Michelle Carter USA	19.14
4. Danniel Thomas-Dodd JAM	18.91
5. Gao Yang CHN	18.25
6. Brittany Crew CAN	18.21
7. Yuliya Leontyuk BLR	18.12
8. Yaniuvis López CUB	18.03
9. Geisa Arcanjo BRA	18.03
10. Raven Saunders USA	17.86
11. Melissa Boekelman NED	17.73
12. Bian Ka CHN	17.60

It was cold and wet for the final, but just nine women over 18m (after eight in qualifying) showed how much standards have declined over the years. Gong opened with 19.61 and 19.35 and led at halfway from Carter 19.14 and Márton 18.89, and sealed her clear win with 19.94 and 19.89 in the last two rounds while Márton closed with 19.49 for the silver medal.

Discus *(Q 62.50m 11th, F 13th)*

1. Sandra Perkovic CRO	70.31
2. Dani Stevens AUS	69.64
3. Mélina Robert-Michon FRA	66.21
4. Yaimí Pérez CUB	64.82
5. Denia Caballero CUB	64.37
6. Nadine Müller GER	64.13
7. Su Xinyue CHN	63.37
8. Feng Bin CHN	61.56
9. Julia Harting GER	61.34
10. Chen Yang CHN	61.28
11. Andressa de Morais BRA	60.00
nm. Zinaida Sendriute LTU	–

Perkovic produced a mighty 69.67 in qualifying and had a terrific series in the final as her first four throws went out to 69.30, 70.31, 70.18 and 69.81 before two fouls. She regained her title but was given a much closer contest than expected by Samuels, who, secure in 2nd place after 66.82 and 66.59 in rounds 4-5, smashed the 13 year-old Commonwealth record with a final throw of 69.64. The ever reliable 38 year-old Robert-Michon started with 65.49 and improved in the final round to 66.21 for the bronze.

Hammer *(Q 71.50m 5th, F 7th)*

1. Anita Wlodarczyk POL	77.90
2. Wang Zheng CHN	75.98
3. Malwina Kopron POL	74.76
4. Zhang Wenxiu CHN	74.53
5. Hanna Skydan AZE	73.38
6. Joanna Fiodorow POL	73.04
7. Sophie Hitchon GBR	72.32
8. Katerina Safránková CZE	71.34
9. DeAnna Price USA	70.04
10. Hanna Malyshik BLR	69.43
11. Kathrin Klaas GER	68.91
12. Alexandra Tavernier FRA	66.31

Wlodarczyk was well below her best as she was throwing with a painful finger injury sustained in training and cramps but still outclassed the opposition. She had been behind compatriot Kopron 74.97 to 74.61 in qualifying and took a while to get going in the final. She was only 6th with 71.94 after three throws, when Wang led with 75.98 and Kopron 74.76, but then threw 77.39 and 77.90 to take her third title. Zhang was 4th in her seventh final.

Javelin *(Q 63.50m 6th, F 8th)*

1. Barbora Spotáková CZE	66.76
2. Li Lingwei CHN	66.25
3. Lu Huihui CHN	65.26
4. Sara Kolak CRO	64.95
5. Eda Tugsuz TUR	64.52
6. Tatyana Kholodovich BLR	64.05
7. Katharina Molitor GER	63.75
8. Liu Shiying CHN	62.84

9. Martina Ratej SLO	61.05
10. Kelsey-Lee Roberts AUS	60.76
11. Ásdís Hjálmsdóttir ISL	60.16
12. Elizabeth Gleadle CAN	60.12

She might have been surprised that 66.76 was enough for victory, but Spotáková was delighted to return to the venue of her 2012 Olympic title and regain the title she had won in 2007. Her winning throw came in round 2 and the Chinese throwers produced their best for Li 66.25 in round 3 and Lu 65.26 in round 5. None surpassed the Asian record 67.58 from Lu in qualifying.

Heptathlon *(5th/5th)*

1. Nafissatou Thiam BEL	6784
2. Carolin Schäfer GER	6696
3. Anouk Vetter NED	6636
4. Yorgelis Rodríguez CUB	6594
5. Katarina Johnson-Thompson GBR	6558
6. Ivona Dadic AUT	6417
7. Nadine Visser NED	6370
8. Claudia Salman-Rath GER	6362
9. Xénia Krizsán HUN	6356
10. Eliska Klucinová CZE	6313
11. Géraldine Ruckstuhl SUI	6230
12. Kendell Williams USA	6220
13. Grit Sadeiko EST	6094
14. Alina Shukh UKR-J	6075
15. Katerína Cachová CZE	6070

Thiam took the lead with 1.95 in the high jump, in which Johnson-Thompson managed only her opening height 1.80 as compared to 1.98 in Rio 2016. Thiam stretched her lead with 15.17 shot but only ran 24.57 for 200m. That left her behind Schäfer (200m 23.58) at the end of first day with the order Schäfer 4036, Thiam 4014, Rodríguez 3905, KJT (22.86 200m) 3838 and Vetter 38.32. Thiam regained the lead with 6.57 long jump and increased it to 172 points over Schäfer with 53.93 for javelin, in which Vetter improved her pb from 55.76 to 58.14. Thiam is no 800m runner, timed in 2:21.42 while four women broke 2:10, but still ended up taking the gold by an 88-point margin. Vetter set a Dutch record for 3rd and Rodríguez a CAC record for 4th.

4 x 100 Metres Relay *(h & F 12th)*

1. USA	41.82	A Brown, Felix, Akinosun, Bowie (ht: 4 A Washington)
2. GBR	42.12	Philip, Henry, Asher-Smith, Neita
3. JAM	42.19	Levy, Morrison, Facey, Forbes (ht: C Williams, Morrison, Levy, Forbes)
4. GER	42.36	Pinto, Mayer, Lückenkemper, Haase
5. SUI	42.51	Del Ponte, Atcho, Kambundji, Kora
6. TTO	42.62	Hackett, Ahye, St. Fort, Baptiste (ht: Baptiste, Ahye, Hackett, St. Fort)
7. BRA	42.63	Krasucki, A Silva, Rosa, R Santos
8. NED	43.07	van Schagen, Schippers, Sedney, Samuel (ht: 1 Ghafoor)

The USA team ran world-leading times in both heat (41.84) and final , while Britain followed them home, having run faster in the heat (41.93) than in the final. Jamaica took the bronze medal even though missing Elaine Thompson. Jamaica with Jura Levy led on the first leg in the final before they were caught by a blistering run on the back straight by AllysonFelix, who had a poor exchange with Morolake Akinosun and the final change was also poor, but Torie Bowie then streaked home as both she and Daryl Neita for Britain passed Jamaica.

4 x 400 Metres Relay *(h 12th, F 13th)*

1. USA	3:19.02	Hayes 50.5, Felix 48.7, Wimbley 49.58, Francis 50.28 (Ellis & Hastings ran in heat)
2. GBR	3:25.00	Clark 51.5, Laviai Nielsen 51.0, Doyle 51.56, Diamond 50.96 (Shakes-Drayton ran in heat)
3. POL	3:25.41	Holub 51.6, Baumgart 51.0, Gaworska 51.66, Swiety 51.17 (Wyciszkiewicz & Dabrowska ran in heat)
4. FRA	3:26.56	Perrossier 52.9, Sananes 51.4, Raharolahy 51.28, Diarra 51.01
5. NGR	3:26.72	P George 51.4, Egbeniyi 53.0, Nathaniel 51.45, Ajayi 50.93
6. GER	3:27.45	Spelmeyer 51.9, Müller 51.7, Gonska 52.43, Mergenthaler 51.47
7. BOT	3:28.00	Botlogetswe 52.3, Jele 52.1, Moroko 52.83, Montsho 50.71
dnf. JAM	–	Gordon 50.9, McLaughlin-Whilby, S Jackson, Williams-Mills

The USA were much the fastest in the heats with 3:21.66, helped by a brilliant lead off 49.97 by Quanera Hayes and a 3rd leg 49.20 by Shakima Wimbley. Jamaica were next quickest with 3:23.64, but in the final their second leg runner Anneisha McLaughlin-Whilby pulled up injured behind a typically marvellous leg by Allyson Felix, whose 48.7 gave the USA a huge lead that was stretched to some 50m by their final two runners for a record 5.98 winning margin. That gave Felix a new World Champs medal count record of 16, 11 of them gold to equal Bolt's tally.

20 Kilometres Walk *(13th)*

1. Yang Jiayu CHN	1:26:18
2. Maria Guadalupe González MEX	1:26:19
3. Antonella Palmisano ITA	1:26:36
4. Erica de Sena BRA	1:26:59
5. Sandra Arenas COL	1:28:10
6. Ana Cabecinha POR	1:28:57
7. Kimberly García PER	1:29:13
8. Wang Na CHN	1:29:26
9. Laura García-Caro ESP	1:29:29
10. Mária Pérez ESP	1:29:37
11. Mirna Ortíz GUA	1:30:01
12. Viktória Madarász HUN	1:30:05
13. Paula Pérez ECU	1:30:09
14. Eleonora Giorgi ITA	1:30:34
15. Valentina Trapletti ITA	1:30:35

With the tempo increasing throughout the race, Lu Xiuzhi was disqualified in a dramatic last 100m with three walkers together, leaving her 21 year-old team-mate Yang Jiayu to take gold by just a second from González. 52 of the 60 starters finished. The lead pack had been steadily whittled away through 5k splits for Yang of 22:22, 21:48, 21:23 and 20:45. National records were set by those finishing 4th (South American record for Sena), 5th, 7th and 12th.

50 Kilometres Walk *(13th)*

1. Ines Henriques POR 4:05:56*
2. Yin Hang CHN 4:08:58
3. Yang Shuqing CHN 4:20:49
4. Kathleen Burnett USA 4:21:51

stopped: Nair da Rosa BRA, Susan Randall USA; dq, Erin Talcott USA

50 kilometres walk for women was recognised as an official world record event from the start of the year and a very late decision (less than a month before the start of the Championships) was made to include it, incorporated into the men's event. Henriques took full advantage of this opportunity and she took 2:30 off her inaugural world record to earn a total of $160,000. There was an Asian record for Yin and North American record for Burnett. There was a 4:30 time limit and this meant that two walkers were prevented from finishing.

Prize money

Individual Events: Winner: US $60,000, 2nd $30,000, 3rd $20,000, 4th $15,000, 5th $10,000, 6th $6000, 7th $5000, 8th $4000. Relays: Winners $80,000, 2nd $40,000, 3rd $20,000, 4th $16,000, 5th $12,000, 6th $8000, 7th $6000, 8th $4000. $100,000 for a world record.

INTERNATIONAL CHAMPIONSHIPS 2017

IAAF World Indoor Tour

Overall winners (granted 2018 World Indoor Champs wild card): Men: Pavel Maslák CZE 400m, Bethwel Birgen KEN 1500m, Orlando Ortega ESP 60mh, Donald Thomas BAH HJ, Khotso Mokoena RSA LJ; Women: Gayon Evans JAM 60m, Joanna Józwik POL 800m, Hellen Obiri KEN 3000m, Patricia Mamona POR TJ, and Anita Martón HUN SP.

IAAF World Youth (U18) Championships 2017

At Nairobi, Kenya (1675m altitude) 12-16 July

Men

100m	1. Tshenolo Lemao RSA 10.57
(-0.3)	2. Retshiditswe Mlenga RSA 10.61
	3. Tyreke Wilson JAM 10.65
200m	1. Retshiditswe Mlenga RSA 21.03
(-0.7)	2. Tshenolo Lemao RSA 21.12
	3. Luís Brandner GER 21.23
400m	1. Antonio Watson JAM 46.59
	2. Daniel Williams GUY 46.72
	3. Colby Jennings TKS 46.77
800m	1. Melese Nberet ETH 1:47.12
	2. Tolesa Bodena ETH 1:47.16
	3. Japheth Kibiwott KEN 1:47.82
1500m	1. George Manangoi KEN 3:47.53
	2. Abebe Desasa ETH 3:48.65
	3. Belete Mekonen ETH 3:50.64
3000m	1. Selemon Barega ETH 7:47.16
	2. Edward Zakayo KEN 7:49.17
	3. Stanley Mburu Waithaka KEN 7:50.64
2000mSt	1. Leonard Bett KEN 5:32.52
	2. Cleophas Kandie KEN 5:33.07
	3. Alemu Kitessa ETH 5:42.10
110mh	1. Dejour Russell JAM 13.04*
(0.1)	2. Lu Hao-Hua TPE 13.41
91.4cm	3. Thomas Wanaverbecq FRA 13.55
400mh	1. Zazini Sokwakhana RSA 49.27
84cm	2. Moitalel Mboke KEN 52.06
	3. Baptiste Christophe FRA 52.21
HJ	1. Breyton Poole RSA 2.24
	2. Chima Ihenetu GER 2.14
	3. Vladyslav Lavskyy UKR 2.11
PV	1. Matthias Orban FRA 5.00
	2. Christos Tamanís CYP 4.85
	3. Illya Kravchenko UKR 4.70
LJ	1. Maykel Vidal CUB 7.88/-0.5
	2. Lester Lescay CUB 7.79/1.3
	3. Andreas-Samuel Bucsa ROU 7.47w/2.8
TJ	1. Jordan Díaz CUB 17.30/0.6*
	2. Frixon David Chila ECU 15.92/0.4
	3. Arnovis Dalmero COL 15.89/0.7
SP (5kg)	1. Timo Northoff GER 20.72
	2. Mikhail Samusov BLR 19.99
	3. Jonathan de Lacey RSA 19.93
DT (1.5kg)	1. Claudio Romero CHI 64.33
	2. Oleksiy Kyrylin UKR 63.98
	3. Morne Brandon RSA 58.34
HT (5kg)	1. Myhaylo Kokhan UKR 82.31
	2. Damneet Singh IND 74.20
	3. Raphael Winkelvoss GER 71.78
JT (700g)	1. Liu Zhekai CHN 77.54
	2. Johannes Schlebusch RSA 75.68
	3. Song Qingshu CHN 73.64
Yth Dec	1. Steven Fauvel Clinch FRA 7559 (10.82/1.3, 7.38/0.3, 14.09, 1.87, 49.09, 13.94/0.1, 34.14, 4.50, 48.08, 4:48.61)
	2. Olegs Kozjakovs LAT 7377
	3. Leo Neugebauer GER 7204
10,000mW	1. Zhang Yao CHN 41:12.01
	2. Salavat Ilkayev RUS 41:24.17
	3. Dominic Ndingiti KEN 41:25.78
Mixed 4x400	1. BRA 3:21.71
	2. JAM 3:22.23
	3. RSA 3:24.45

Women
100m (0.5)
1. Mizgin Ay TUR 11.62
2. Magdalena Stefanowicz POL 11.62
3. Kevona Davis JAM 11.67

200m (-0.7)
1. Talea Prepens GER 23.51
2. Jael Bestue ESP 23.61
3. Mizgin Ay TUR 23.76

400m
1. Barbora Maliková CZE 52.74
2. Mary Moraa KEN 53.31
3. Giovana dos Santos BRA 53.57

800m
1. Jackline Wamboi KEN 2:01.46
2. Lydia Cheruto KEN 2:02.06
3. Hirut Meshesha ETH 2:06.32

1500m
1. Hailu Lemlem ETH 4:20.80
2. Sindu Girma ETH 4:22.14
3. Edina Jebitok KEN 4:23.16

3000m
1. Abersh Minsewo ETH 9:24.62
2. Imaculata Chepkurui KEN 9:24.69
3. Yitayish Mekonene ETH 9:28.46

2000mSt
1. Caren Chebet KEN 6:24.80
2. Mercy Chepkurui KEN 6:26.10
3. Etalemahu Sintayehu ETH 6:35.79

100mh (4.1) 76.2cm
1. Brittany Anderson JAM 12.72w
2. Cyrena Samba-Mayela FRA 12.80
3. Daszay Freeman JAM 13.09

400mh
1. Zeney van der Walt RSA 58.23
2. Sanique Walker JAM 58.27
3. Gisele Wender GER 59.17

HJ
1. Yaroslava Mahuchikh UKR 1.92*=
2. Martyna Lewandowska POL 1.82
3. Lavinja Jürgens GRER 1.79

PV
1. Niu Chunge CHN 4.20
2. Leni Wildgrube GER 4.15
3. Anna Airault FRA 4.10

LJ
1. Gong Luying CHN 6.37/0.4
2. Lea-Sophie Klik GER 6.30w/2.2
3. Diane Mouillac FRA 6.28/1.4

TJ
1. Tan Qiujiao CHN 13.64/0.4
2. Aleksandra Nacheva BUL 13.54/0.5
3. Zulia Hernández CUB 13.29/1.6

SP (3kg)
1. Selina Dantzler GER 17.64
2. Yu Tianxiao CHN 17.62
3. Sun Yue CHN 17.59

DT
1. Silinda Morales CUB 52.89
2. Leia Braunagel GER 51.29
3. Liu Quantong CHN 50.10

HT (3kg)
1. Amanda Armendáris CUB 71.12
2. Yaritza Martínez CUB 69.75
3. Yekaterina Volodkevich BLR 68.17

JT (500g)
1. Marisleisys Duarthe CUB 62.92*
2. Cai Qing CHN 57.01
3. Dai Qianqian CHN 54.96

Yth Hep
1. María Vicente ESP 5612 (13.74/0.4, 1.73, 12.79, 24.00, 6.05/1.4, 30.90, 2:33.22)
2. Johanna Siebler GER 5602
3. Urté Bacianskaité LTU 5467

5000mW
1. Glenda Morejón ECU 22:32.30
2. Meryem Bekmez TUR 22:32.79
3. Elvira Khasanova RUS 22:35.72

Medal table leaders: RSA 5G-3S-3B, CHN 5-2-4, CUB 5-2-1, KEN 4-2-4, ETH 4-3-5, GER 3-5-5, JAM 3-2-3, FRA 2-1-4, UKR 2-1-2, 15 nations won gold medals, 28 medals of any colour.

Australia, Canada, Great Britain, Japan, New Zealand, Switzerland and the USA did not send teams due to security concerns.

IAAF World Relays 2017

At Nassau, Bahamas 22-23 April

Men

4x100 metres (a)
1. USA (L Collins, Rodgers, Baker, Gatlin) 38.43 (Bracy on leg 1 2h2 38.22)
2. BAR (Burke, Gittens, Deshong, B Ellis) 39.18
3. CHN (Tang Xingqiang, Xie Zhenye, Su Bingtian, Liang Jinsheng) 39.22

dnf. CAN (Haynes, Brown, Rodney, De Grasse) (1h2 38.21)

4x200 metres (b)
1. CAN (Smellie, Rodney, De Grasse, Brown) 1:19.42
2. USA (N Lyles, Lawson, I Young, Webb) 1:19.88
3. JAM (Ashmeade, O Bailey, Dwyer, Blake) 1:21.09

4x400 metres (b)
1, USA (Verburg 45.28, McQuay 45.26, Clemons 45.61, L Merritt 45.98) 3:02.13
2. BOT (Makwala 46.14, Thebe 44.95, Nkobolo 45.39, Sibanda 45.80) 3:02.28
3. JAM (P Matthews 45.43, D Gaye 45.39, Manley 45.76, S Gayle 46.28) 3:02.86

4x800 metres (b)
1, USA (Kidder 1:47.39, Sowinski 1:48.11, Loxsom 1:48.48, Murphy 1:49.18) 7:13.16
2. KEN (A Kipketer 1:47.52, K Bett 1:46.73, Kitum 1:49.76, F Cheruiyot 1:49.69) 7:13.70
3. POL (Kuciapski 1:49.14, Borkowski 1:49.29. Kszczot 1:49.80, Lewandowski 1:50.51) 7:18.74

Women – 4x100 metres (b)
1. GER (Burghardt, Mayer, Pinto, Haase) 42.84
2. JAM (Facey, Morrison, Evans, Forbes) 42.95
3. CHN (Liang Xiaojing, Wei Yongli, Tao Yujia, Yuin Qiqi) 43.11

4x200 metres (a)
1, JAM (Levy, Jackson, Forbes, Thompson) 1:29.04
2. GER (Matheis, Pinto, Haase, Lückenkemper) 1:30.68
3. USA (Bryant, Townsend, F Brown, Solomon) 1:30.87

4x400 metres (b)
1. USA (P Francis 50.42, A Spencer 50.92, Q Hayes 50.66, Hastings 52.36) 3:24.36
2. POL (Holub 51.80, Baumgart 51.59, Janowicz 52.81, Swiety 52.08) 3:28.28
3. JAM (Russell 51.72, McLaughlin-Whilby 51.91, Chambers 51.98, McPherson 52.88) 3:28.49

4x800 metres (b)
1, USA (Price 2:01.73, C Williams 2:03.72, Roesler 2:03.05, Lipsey 2:07.86) 8:16.36
2. BLR (Borisevich 2:02.64, I Usovich 2:04.37, Kushnir 2:04.54, Arzamasova 2:08.52) 8:20.07
3. AUS (Storey 2:02.07, de la Motte 2:02.66, Buckman 2:08.28, See 2:08.07) 8:21.08

Mixed 4x400m relay (b)
1, BAH (Gardiner 45.3, Miller-Uibo 49.60, Strachan, Mathieu) 3:14.42

IAAF World Combined Events Challenge

Men Decathlon

1	Rico Freimuth GER	25,592	8365 Götzis	8663 Ratingen	8564 Worlds
2	Damian Warner CAN	25,152	8591 Götzis	8309 Worlds	8252 Talence
3	Kai Kazmirek GER	24,986	8478 Ratingen	8488 Worlds	8020 Talence
4	Janek Oiglane EST	24,578	8037 Götzis	8177 Tallinn	8371 Worlds
5	Oleksiy Kasyanov UKR	24,531	8281 Götzis	8234 Worlds	8016 Talence
6	Adam Sebastian Helcelet CZE	24,506	8335 Götzis	8222 Worlds	7949 Talence
7	Martin Roe NOR	23,925	7741 Kladno	8144 Monzón	8040 Worlds
8	Pieter Braun NED	23,876	8334 Götzis	7890 Worlds	7652 Talence

Women Heptathlon

1	Carolin Schäfer GER	20,199	6836 Götzis	6667 Ratingen	6696 Worlds
2	Anouk Vetter NED	19,496	6497 Götzis	6636 Worlds	6363 Talence
3	Yorgelis Rodríguez CUB	19,134	6446 Götzis	6594 Worlds	6126 Talence
4	Xénia Krizsán HUN	19,028	6390 Götzis	6356 Worlds	6282 Talence
5	Nadine Visser NED	18,908	6355 Götzis	6183 Ratingen	6370 Worlds
6	Géraldine Ruckstuhl SUI	18,655	6291 Götzis	6134 Tallinn	6230 Worlds
7	Eliska Klucinová CZE	18,626	6285 Kladno	6313 Worlds	6028 Talence
8	Alina Shukh UKR	18,389	6106 Götzis	6208 Tallinn	6075 Worlds

Prize Money: 1st $30,000, 2nd $20,000, 3rd $15,000, 4th $10,000, 5th $8000, 6th $7000, 7th $6000, 8th $5000.
Best of three scores at qualifying meetings.

2. USA (Berry, Stepter, Dedewo, C Francis) 3:17.29
3, JAM (Bell, R Tracey, Goule, Rose) 3:20.26

World Relays Golden Baton (team standings): 1. USA 60, 2. JAM 39, 3. AUS 24, 4. POL 23, 5. TTO 17, 6= KEN, CHN 16, 8. GER 15

IAAF World Race Walking Challenge 2017

Results of walks at 10 meetings qualified. Walkers needed to compete at three or more of these to qualify and positions were based on the best positions from these races, with a sliding scale of points from three categories. Prize money: 1st $30,000, 2nd $20,000, 3rd $14,000, 4th $9000, 5th $7000, 6th $6000, 7th $4500, 8th $4000, 9th $3000, 10th $2000, 11th $1000, 12th $500. For the first time both titles went to South American walkers, World champion Yang Jiayu scored only twice.

Men: 1. Eider Arévalo COL 36, 2. Caio Bonfim BRA 25, 3. Andrés Chocho ECU 25, 4. Lebogang Shange RSA 20, 5. Evan Dunfee CAN 19, 6. Perseus Karlström SWE 19, 7. Álvaro Martín ESP 18, 8. Benjamin Thorne CAN 17, 9. Horacio Nava MEX 17, 10. Omar Pineda MEX 14. **Women:** 1. Érica de Sena BRA 34, 2. María Guadelupe González MEX 28, 3. Inês Henriques 24, 4. Ana Cabecinha POR 24, 5. Kimberly García PER 23, 6. Sandra Arenas COL 22, 7. Wang Na CHN 17, 8. Alana Barber NZL 13, 9. Ainhoa Pinedo ESP 12, 10. María Guadelupe Sánchez MEX 11.

IAAF Hammer Challenge 2017

The three best marks from the series of nine meetings in 2017 were totalled. Prize money from $30,000 for 1st to $500 for 12th. Anita Wlodarczyk was the women's winner for the fifth successive year (after 2nd in 2010 and 2012). Pawel Fajdek added to his wins in 2013 and 2015-16 (and 2nd in 2012 and 2014); his total is the all-time record for the Challenge that began in 2010.

Men: 1. Pawel Fajdek POL 248.48, 2. Wojciech Nowicki POL 236.32, 3. Dilshod Nazarov TJK 231.40, 4. Pavel Boreysha BLR 230.84, 5. Nick Miller GBR 229.56, 6. Bence Halász HUN 229.11, 7. Marcel Lomnicky SVK 227.52, 8. Marco Lingua ITA 226.08, 9, Serghei Marghiev MDA 224.97, 10, Ashraf Amjad El Seify QAT 224.46.

Women: 1. Anita Wlodarczyk POL 235.62, 2. Wang Zhang CHN 225.77, 3. Hanna Skydan AZE 221.75, 4. Malwina Kopron POL 220.03, 5. Sophie Hitchon GBR 219.97, 6. Joanna Fiodorow POL 217.73, 7. Amber Campbell USA 215.77, 8. Katerina Safránková CZE 209.54, 9. Kathrin Klaas GER 200.25, (10. Gwen Berry USA 147.50).

World University Games 2017

At Taipei, Taiwan August 23-28

100m	1. Yang Chun-Yan TPE 10.22
(-0.9)	2. Thando Roto RSA 10.24
	3. Cameron Burrell USA 10.27
200m	1. Jeffrey John FRA 20.93
(-3.8)	2. James Linde CAN 20.96
	3. Ján Volko SVK 20.99
400m	1. Luguelín Santos DOM 45.24
	2. Yoandys Lescay CUB 45.31
	3. Rafal Omelko POL 45.56
800m	1. Jesus López MEX 1:46.06
	2. Mohamed Belbachir ALG 1:46.73
	3. Aymeric Lusine FRA 1:47.18
1500m	1. Timo Benitz GER 3:43.45
	2. Alexis Miellet FRA 3:43.91
	3. Jonathan Davies GBR 3:43.99

5000m 1. François Barrer FRA 14:00.86
2. Jonathan Davies GBR 14:02.46
3. Andreas Vojta AUT 14:02.65

10,000m 1. Sadiq Bahati UGA 29:08.68
2. Nicolae Soare ROU 29:12.76
3. Kazuya Shiojiri JPN 29:20.96

HMar 1. Kei Katanishi JPN 66:09
2. Naoki Kudo JPN 66:23
3. Kengo Suzuki JPN 66:56

Teams: 1. JPN 3:19:28
2. RSA 3:31:38
3. TUR 3:34:42

3000mSt 1. Krystian Zalewski POL 8:35.88
2. Rantso Mokopane RSA 8:36.25
3. Ali Messaoudi ALG 8:37.149

110mh (-0.5) 1. Balázs Baji HUN 13.35
2. Chen Kuei-Ru TPE 13.55
3. Damian Czykier POL 13.56

400mh 1. Juander Santos DOM 48.65
2. Chen Chieh TPE 49.05
3. Abdelmalik Lahoulou ALG 49.30

HJ 1. Falk Wendrich GER 2.29
2. Marco Fassinotti ITA 2.29
3. Hsiang Chun-Hsien TPE 2.26

PV 1. Diogo Ferreira POR 5.55
2. Sergey Grigoryev KAZ 5.50
3. Claudio Stecchi ITA 5.40

LJ 1. Radek Juska CZE 8.02/0.8
2. Yasser Triki ALG 7.96/-0.3
3. Raihau Maiau FRA 7.91/-0.1

TJ 1. Nazim Babayev AZE 17.01/1.1
2. Fabrice Zango BUR 16.97/0.9
3. Ryoma Yamamoto JPN 16.80/1.7

SP 1. Francisco Belo POR 20.86
2. Konrad Bukowiecki POL 20.16
3. Andrei Gag ROU 20.12

DT 1. Reggie Jagers USA 61.24
2. Alin Firfirica ROU 61.13
3. Róbert Szikszai HUN 60.91

HT 1. Pawel Fajdek POL 79.16
2. Pavel Boreysha BLR 77.98
3. Serghei Marghiev MDA 74.98

JT 1. Cheng Chao-Tsun TPE 91.36*
2. Andreas Hofmann GER 91.07
3. Huang Shih-Feng TPE 86.64

Dec 1. Kyle Cranston AUS 7687
2. Juuso Hassi FIN 7566
3. Aaron Booth NZL 7523

20kW 1. Toshikazu Yamanishi JPN 1:27:30
2. Julio César Salazar MEX 1:28:20
3. Fumitaka Oikawa JPN 1:30:11

Teams: 1. JPN 4:28:41
2. MEX 4:29:14
3. UKR 4:41:34

4x100m 1. JPN 38.65
2. USA 38.69
3. TPE 39.06

4x400m 1. DOM 3:04.34
2. USA 3:06.68
3. CZE 3:08.14

Women

100m (-0.3) 1. Shashalee Forbes JAM 11.18
2. Irene Siragusa ITA 11.31
3. Salomé Kora SUI 11.33

200m 1. Irene Siragusa ITA 22.96
2. Gunta Latiseva-Cudare LAT 23.15
3. Anna Bongiorni ITA 23.47

400m 1. Malgorzata Holub POL 51.76
2. Justine Palframan RSA 51.83
3. Bianca Razor ROU 51.97

800m 1. Rose Mary Almanza CUB 2:02.21
2. Olha Lyakhova UKR 2:03.11
3. Dorcus Ajok UGA 2:03.22

1500m 1. Amela Terzic SRB 4:19.18
2. Dorcus Ajok UGA 4:19.48
3. Kristiina Mäki CZE 4:20.65

5000m 1. Hanna Klein GER 15:45.28
2. Jessica O'Connell CAN 15:50.96
3. Jessica Judd GBR 15:51.19

10,000m 1. Darya Maslova KGZ 33:19.27
2. Sanjivani Jadhav IND 33:22.00
3. Ai Hosoda JPN 33:27.89

HMar 1. Yuki Munehisa JPN 73:48
2. Esma Aydemir TUR 74:28
3. Saki Fukui JPN 74:37

Teams: 1. JPN 3:43:35
2. TUR 3:55:13
3. TPE 4:05:52

3000mSt 1. Tugba Güvenc TUR 9:51.27
2. Viktória Gyürkes HUN 9:52.17
3. Özlem Kaya TUR 9:52.59

100mh (-1.3) 1. Nadine Visser NED 12.98
2. Elvira German BLR 13.17
3. Luca Kozák HUN 13.19

400mh 1. Ayomide Folorunso ITA 55.63
2. Joanna Linkiewicz POL 55.90
3. Olena Kolesnychenko UKR 56.14

HJ 1. Oksana Okuneva UKR 1.97
2. Iryna Herashchenko UKR 1.91
3. Airine Palsyte LTU 1.91

PV 1. Iryna Zhuk BLR 4.40
2. Annika Roloff GER 4.40
3. Marta Onofre POR 4.40

LJ 1. Alina Rotaru ROU 6.65/0.3
2. Nektaria Panagi CYP 6.42/0.3
3. Anna Bühler GER 6.38/0.1

TJ 1. Neele Eckhardt GER 13.91/0.0
2. Fu Luna CHN 13.59/0.5
3. Mara Griva LAT 13.58/0.3

SP 1. Brittany Crew CAN 18.34
2. Klaudia Kardasz POL 17.90
3. Paulina Guba POL 17.76

DT 1. Kristen Pudenz GER 59.09
2. Valarie Allman USA 58.36
3. Taryn Gollshewsky AUS 58.11

HT 1. Malwina Kopron POL 76.85*
2. Hanna Malyshik BLR 74.93
3. Joanna Fyodorov POL 71.33

JT 1. Marcelina Witek POL 63.31
2. Marina Saito JPN 62.37
3. Jenni Kangas FIN 60.98

Hep 1. Verena Preiner AUT 6224
2. Alysha Burnett AUS 5835
3. Noor Vidts NED 5728

20kW 1. Inna Kashyna UKR 1:39:44
2. Zhang Xin CHN 1:41:18
3. Elisa Neuvonen FIN 1:42:50

Teams: 1. UKR 5:12:01
2. CHN 5:19:12 (only two teams)

4x100m 1. SUI 43.81

2. POL 44.19
3. JPN 44.56

4x400m 1. POL 3:26.75
2. MEX 3:33.98
3. ROU 3:34.16

Medal table leaders: JPN 7G, 2S, 7B, POL 6-4-4, GER 5-2-1, UKR 3-2-2, DOM 3-0-0, TPE 2-2-4, ITA 2-2-2, FRA 2-1-2, POR 2-0-1, USA 1-3-1, BLR & MEX 1-3-0, ROU 1-2-3, TUR 1-2-2, CAN 1-2-0, HUN 1-1-2. 27 nations won gold, 42 medals of any colour.

African U20 Championships

At Tlemcen. Algeria (A 1022m) June 29-July 2

Men: **100m**: Thembo Monareng RSA 10.41w, **200m** Clarence Munyai RSA 20.22, **400m**: Wogen Tucho ETH 47.65, **800m**: Solomon Lekuta KEN 1:48.04, **1500m**: Welde Tufa ETH 3:44.39, **5000m**: Selemon Barega ETH 13:51.43, **10,000m**: Nicholas Kipkorir Chelimo KEN 29:52.15, **3000mSt** Takele Nigatu ETH 8:31.36, 99m **110mh**: Mpho Tladi RSA 13.78w, **400mh**: Merid Alemu ETH 53.51, **HJ**: Fadi Chebeb TUN 2.00, **PV**: Réda Boudechiche ALG 4.30, **LJ**: Soufiane Zakour MAR 7.36, **TJ**: Chengetayi Mapaya ZIM 16.30, 6kg **SP**: Kayle Blignaut RSA 20.08, 1.75kg **DT**: Patrick Duvenage RSA 59.46, 6kg **HT**: Carel Haasbroek RSA 68.91, **JT**: Werner Dames RSA 72.75, Jnr **Dec**: Tarek Rahmani TUN 5770, **10,000mW**: Yohanis Wale ETH 44:43.47, **4x100m**: ZIM 40.64, **4x400m**: ETH 3:11.89, **Women**: **100m**: Gabri Mgbemena ZIM 12.08, **200m**: Ola Buwaro GAM 24.60, **400m**: Frehiywot Wondie ETH 54.43, **800m**: Tigist Ketema ETH 2:05.85, **1500m/3000m**: Joyline Cherotich KEN 4:30.57/9:27.11, **5000m**: Meskerem Haile ETH 15:37.13, **3000mSt**: Mekides Abebe ETH 10:11.80, **100mh**: Taylon Bieldt RSA 13.82, **400mh**: Sara Elhachimi MAR 60.62, **HJ**: Yvonne Robson RSA 1.74, **PV**: May Massika Mezioud ALG 2.80, **LJ**: Asdma Baya Araiba ALG 6.02, TJ: Fatimata Zougrana BUR 12.55w, **SP**: Jana Steinmann RSA 13.15, **DT**: Yolandi Stander RSA 49.13, **HT**: Samira Addi MAR 56.29, **Hep**: Joné Kruger RSA 4850, **10,000mW**: Ayalnesh Dejene ETH 52:14.73, **4x100m**: ALG 48.44, **4x400m**: ETH 3:48.19. **Medal Table leaders**: ETH 13G-13S-12B, RSA 12-4-1, ALG 4-8-8, KEN 4-4-2, 14 countries won medals.

20th Arab Championships

At Radès, Tunisia July 15-18

Men: 100m: Abdallah Abkar Mohamed KSA 10.19w, **200m** Ahmed Ali SUD 20.49, **400m**: Youssef Mohamed Daher Karam KUW 46.45, **800m**: Nabil Oussama MAR 1:47.24, **1500m/3000mSt**: Mohamed Ismail Ibrahim DJI 3:52.38/8:42.45, **5000m**: Zied Ben Othman TUN 14:33.02, **10,000m**: Hassan Touriss MAR 31:01.29, **HMar**: Atef Saad TUN 65:03, **110mh**: Yacoub Mohamed Al-Yoha KUW 13.48w, **400mh**: Abdelmalik Lahoulou ALG 49.05*, HJ: Hussein Faleh Al-Ibrahimi IRQ 2.16, **PV**: Hichem Cherabi ALG*, **LJ/TJ**: Mohamed Yasser Triki ALG 7.83/16.63, **SP**: Sultan Abdelmajid Al-Hebshi KSA 18.19, **DT**: Essa Mohamed Al-Zankawi KUW 59.75, HT: Ahmed Amjad El-Saify QAT 69.85, **JT**: Mohamed Ibrahim Kaida QAT 71.45, **Dec**: Majed Radhi Al-Zayed KUW 7118, **20kW**: Mohamed Ameur ALG 1:32:25, **4x100m**: KSA 40.08, **4x400m**: ALG 3:05.49, **Women: 100m/200m**: Assia Raziki MAR 11.63w/23.80, **400m**: Khadija Wardi MAR 53.97, **800m/1500m**: Oumaima Saoud MAR 2:16.83/4:30.45, **5000m/10000m**: Alia Mohamed Saeed UAE 16:39.41/ 38:53.31, **HMar**: Hayat Aloui MAR 1:20:34, **3000mSt**: Habiba Ghribi TUN 9:20.00*, **100mh**: Sanae Zouine MAR 14.38w, **400mh**: Tassabih Mohamed Sayed SUD 60.35, **HJ**: Yosra Arar ALG 1.71, **PV**: Dorra Mahfoudhi TUN 4.15*, **LJ**: Roumaissa Bellabiod ALG 6.30, **TJ**: Fatma Lahmadi TUN 12.60, **SP/JT**: Nada Cheroudi TUN 13.42/42.25, **DT**: Amina Mouadden MAR 47.49, **HT**: Zouina Bouzebra ALG 62.08, **Hep**: Nada Cheroudi TUN 5029w, **10kW**: Chahinez Nasri TUN 46:14*, **4x100m/4x400m**: MAR 46.69/3:44.22. **Medal Table leaders**: MAR 12G-11S-8B, TUN 9-13-12, ALG 9-5-4, KUW 4-1-3, KSA 3-6-3, SUD 2-3-3, 13 countries won medals (10 gold).

Asian Indoor Games

At Ashgabat, Turkmenistan 18-20 September

Men: 60m: Hassan Taftian IRI 6.55, **400m**: Abdelelah Haroun QAT 45.68*, **800m**: Jamal Al-Hairane QAT 1:49.33, **1500m**: Ajay Kumar Saroj IND 3:48.67, **3000m**: Govindan Lakshmanan IND 8:02.30, **60mh**: Ahmad Al-Moualed KSA 7.66*, **HJ**: Majid Eddin Ghazal SYR 2.26* (2, Ghanbarzadeh IRI 2.26*), **PV**: Sergey Grigoryev KAZ 5.40*, **LJ**: Nguyen Tien Trong VIE 7.48 rec, **TJ**: Arpinder Singh IND 16.21, **SP**: Ivan Ivanov KAZ 19.60*, **Hep**: Mohamed Al-Qaree KSA 5343, **4x400m**: PAK 3:11.40, **Women**: **60m**: Viktoriya Zyabkina KAZ 7.32, **400m**: Elina Mikhina KAZ 53.37, **800m** Gayanthika Thushari Abeyrathne SRI 2:05.12, **1500m**: Unnikkrishnan Chitra IND 4:27.77, **3000m**: Alia Mohammed Saeed UAE 9:25.03, **60mh**: Liu Lai Yiu HKG 8.41, **HJ**: Nadiya Dusanova UZB 1.86, **LJ/TJ**: Olga Rypakova KAZ 6.43/14.32, **SP**: Bian Ka CHN 17.34, **Pen**: Purnima Hembram IND 4062, **4x400m**: THA 3:43.41. **Medals and Points leaders**: THA (1-5-4) 116, CHN (1-2-2) 96; IND (5-2-1) 85, KAZ (6-1-3) 77, UZB (1-2-1) 57; QAT (2-1-1) 47, KSA (2-3-9) 46; IRI (1-1-1) 45, VIE (1-3-1) 36, HKG (1-0-2) 36, SRI (1-2-1) 30, KOR (0-1-2) 30

Asian Championships

At Bhubaneswar, India 6-9 July

100m	1. Hassan Taftian IRI 10.25
(0.7)	2. Femi Ogunode QAT 10.26
	3. Yang Chun-Han TPE 10.31
200m	1. Yang Chun-Han TPE 20.66
(0.0)	2. Park Bong-ko KOR 20.76
	3. Femi Ogunode QAT 20.79
400m	1. Muhammed Anas IND 45.77
	2. Arokia Rajiv IND 46.14
	3. Ahmed Al-Saadi OMA 46.39
800m	1. Ebrahim Al-Zofairi KUW 1:49.47
	2. Jamal Al-Hayrani QAT 1:49.94
	3. Jinson Johnson IND 1:50.07
1500m	1. Ajay Kumar Saroj IND 3:45.85
	2. Jamal Al-Hayrani QAT 3:46.90
	3. Moslem Niadost IRI 3:48.53
5000m	1. Govindan Lakshaman IND 14:54.48
	2. Yaser Salem Bagharab QAT 14:55.89
	3. Tariq Ahmed Al-Amri KSA 14:46.83
10,000m	1. Govindan Lakshmanan IND 29:55.87
	2. Thonakal Gopi IND 29:55.89
	3. Adilet Kyshtabekov KGZ 30:06.65
3000mSt	1. Hossein Keyhani IRI 8:43.82

2. Yaser Salem Bagharab QAT 8:46.16
3. Ali Ahmed Al-Amri KSA 8:52.64

110mh (-0.6) 1. Abdulaziz Al-Mandeel KUW 13.50
2. Yaqoub Al-Yoha KUW 13.59
3. Ahmad Al-Moualed KSA 13.61

400mh 1. Eric Cray PHI 49.57
2. Chen Chieh TPE 49.75
3. M P Jabir IND 50.22

HJ 1. Woo Sang-hyeok KOR 2.30
2. Zhang Guowei CHN 2.28
3. Majed El Dein Ghazal SYR 2.24

PV 1. Ding Bangchao CHN 5.65
2. Masali Ejima JPN-J 5.65
3. Ernest John Obiena PHI 5.50

LJ 1. Huang Changzhou CHN 8.09/-1.3
2. Chan Ming Tai HKG 8.03/-1.0
3. Shin-ichiro Shiroyama JPN 7.97/1.5

TJ 1. Zhu Yaming CHN 16.82w/2.8
2. Mark Henry Diones PHI 16.45/0.8
3. Xu Xiaolong CHN 16.45/-0.7

SP 1. Ali Samari IRI 19.80
2. Tejinder Pal Singh IND 19.77
3. Ivan Ivanov KAZ 19.41

DT 1. Ehsan Hadadi IRI 64.54
2. Mohd Irfan Shamsuddin MAS 60.96
3. Vikas Gowda IND 60.81

HT 1. Dilshod Nazarov TJK 76.69
2. Wang Shizu CHN 73.81
3. Lee Yun-chul KOR 73.77

JT 1. Neeraj Chopra IND 85.23*
2. Ahmed Bader Magour QAT 83.70
3. Davinder Singh IND 83.29

Dec 1. Suttisak Singkon THA 7732
2. Kazuya Kawasaki JPN 7584
3. Guo Qi CHN 7495

4x100m 1. CHN (Tang Xingqiang, Liang Jinsheng, Bie Ge, Xu Haiyang) 39.38
2. THA 39.38
3. HKG 39.53

4x400m 1. IND (Muhammed, Amoj Jacob, Anas, Rajov) 3:02.92
2. SRI 3:04.80
3. THA 3:06.48

Women

100m (1/0) 1. Viktoriya Zyabkina KAZ 11.39
2. Olga Safronova KAZ 11.45
3. Dutee Chand IND 11.52

200m -0.6) 1. Viktoriya Zyabkina 23.10
2. Rumeshika Rathnayake SRI 23.43
3. Olga Safronova KAZ 23.47

400m 1. Nirmala Sheoran IND 52.01
2. Quach Thi Lan VIE 52.78
3. Jisna Mathew IND 53.32

800m 1. Nimwali Konda SRI 2:05.23
2. Gayanthika Abeyrathne SRI 2:05.27
3. Fumika Omori JPN 2:06.50
dq. Archana Yadav IND (2:05.00) disqualified for pushing Konda

1500m 1. P.Unnikrishnan Chithra IND 4:17.92
2. Geng Min CHN 4:19.15
3. Ayoko Jinnouchi JPN 4:19.90

5000m 1. Darya Maslova KGZ 15:57.95
2. Alia Mohamed Saeed UAE 15:59.95
3. Sanjivani Jadhav IND 16:00.24

10,000m 1. Darya Maslova KGZ 32:21.21
2. Yuka Hori JPN 32:23.26
3. Mizuki Matsuda JPN 32:46.61

3000mSt 1. Sudha Singh IND 9:59.47
2. Ro Hyo-gyong PRK 10:13.94
3. Nana Sato JPN 10:18.11

100mh (-0.1) 1. Jung Hye-lim 13.16
2. Ayoko Kimura JPN 13.30
3. Wang Dou CHN 13.36

400mh 1. Nguyen Thi Huyen VIE 56.14
2. Anu Raghavan IND 57.22
3. Sayaka Aoki JPN 58.18

HJ 1. Nadezhda Dusanova UZB 1.84
2= Yeung Man Wai HKG 1.80
2= Wang Xueyi CHN 1.80
2= Liu Jingyi CHN 1.80

PV 1. Chen Qialoing CHN 4.40
2. Li Ling CHN 4.20
3. Sukanya Chomchuendee THA 4.10

LJ 1. Bui Thi Thu Thao VIE 6.54/-0.5
2. Narayanan Neena IND 6.54/0.5
3. Nayana James IND 6.42/1.6

TJ 1. Mariya Ovchinnikova KAZ-J 13.72/1.1
2. Irina Ektova KAZ 13.62/1.2
3. Nellickal Sheena IND 13.42/0.9

SP 1. Guo Tianqian CHN 17.91
2. Aya Ota JPN 15.45
3. Nanaka Kori JPN 15.33
drugs dq (1). Manpreet Kaur IND 18.28

DT 1. Chen Yang CHN 60.41
2. Subenrat Insaeng THA 56.82
3. Lu Xiaoxin CHN 55.27

HT 1. Luo Na CHN 69.92
2. Liu Tingting CHN 69.45
3. Hitomi Katsuyama JPN 60.22

JT 1. Li Lingwei CHN 63.06
2. Dilhani Lekamge SRI 58.11
3. Annu Rani IND 57.32

Hep 1. Swapna Burman 5942
2. Megu Hemphill JPN 5883
3. Purnima Hembram IND 5798

4x100m 1. KAZ (Kashafutdinova, Zyabkina, Ishanguliyeva, Safronova) 43.53
2. CHN 44.50
3. IND 44.57

4x400m 1. IND (Majumdar, Poovamma, Mathew, Sheoran) 3:31.34
2. VIE 3:33.22
3. JPN 3:37.84

Medal table leaders

Nat	*G*	*S*	*B*	*Nat*	*G*	*S*	*B*
IND	12	5	12	KGZ	2	0	1
CHN	8	7	5	SRI	1	4	0
KAZ	4	2	2	THA	1	2	2
IRI	4	0	1	PHI	1	1	1
VIE	2	2	0	TPE	1	1	1
KOR	2	1	1	QAT	0	6	1
KUW	2	1	0	JPN	0	5	9

14 nations won gold. 22 won medals.

Walks. *At Nomi City, Japan 19 March*
Men 20k: 1. Kim Hyun-sub KOR 1:19:50, 2. Georgiy Sheiko KAZ 1:20:47, 3. Irfan Kolothum Thodi IND 1:20:59; **Women 20k**: 1. Wang Na CHN 1:30:51, 2.

Throughout this section
** indicates Championships or Games record]*

Kuniko Okada JPN 1:33:21, 3. Jeaon Yeoung-eun KOR 1:34:35.

Marathon. *At Dongguan, China 26 November*
Men: 1. Thonakal Gopi IND 2:15:48, 2. Andrey Petrov UZB 2:15:51, 3. Byambajav Tseveenravdam MGL 2:16:14
Women: 1. Kim Hye-gyong PRK 2:28:35, 2. Keiko Nogami JPN 2:29:05, 3. Jo Un-ok PRK 2:30:01.

75th Balkan Championships

At Novi Pazar, Serbia 15-16 July
Men: **100m/200m:** Jak Ali Harvey TUR 10.11w/20.56, **400m**: Mateo Ruzic CRO 47.22, **800m**: Abedin Mujezinovic BIH 1:51.75; **1500m**: Mitko Tsenov BUL 3:50.81, **3000m**: David Nikolli ITA 8:31.45. **5000m**: Iolo Nikolov BUL 14:33.35, **3000mSt**: Osman Junuzovic 8:56.09, **110mh**: Cosmin Dumitrache ROU 14.06, **400mh**: Yann Senjaric CRO 51.42, **HJ**: Konstadínos Baniótis GRE 2.14, **PV**: Ivan Horvat CRO 5.50, **LJ**: Lazar Anic SRB 7.94w, **TJ**: Momchil Karailiev BUL 16.82w, **SP**: Mesud Pezer BIH 20.11, **DT**: Martin Maric CRO 61.20, **HT**: Özkan Baltici TUR 71.92, **JT**: Branko Paukovic SRB 75.82, **Dec**: Aleksandar Grnovic 7225, **4x100m**: ROU 40.62, **4x400m**: SRB 3:15.92; **Women**: **100m**: Milana Tirnanic 11.82, **200m**: Grigoría-Emmanouéla Keramidá GRE 23.35, **400m**: Bianca Razor ROU 52.76, **800m/1500m**: Amela Terzic SRB 2:07.25/4:19.00**,** **3000m**: Adelina Baltoi ROU 9:29.16, **5000m**: Cristina Negru ROU 16:36.98, **3000mSt**: Fatmir Demir TUR 10:35.12, **100mh**: Elisávet Pesirídou GRE 13.16, **400mh**: Elif Yildirim TUR 58.67, **HJ**: Tatiána Goúsin GRE 1.91, **PV**: Maria Aristotelous CYP 4.00, **LJ**: Háido Alexoúli GRE 6.41, **TJ**: Carmen Toma ROU 13.65w, **SP**: Dimitriana Surdu MDA 17.86, **DT**: Dragana Tomasevic SRB 59.35, **HT**: Zalina Petrivskaya MDA 69.03, **JT**: Marija Vucenovic SRB 56.41; **Hep**: Mladena Petrusic BIH 4796, **4x100m**: SRB 46.34, **4x400m**: ROU 3:37.29.

Half Marathon *at Pristina, Kosovo*. **Men**: Serkan Kaya TUR 67:43. **Women**: Seyma Yildiz 78:32. **Team:** TUR.
Marathon *at Zagreb, Croatia 8 Oct*. **Men**: Yavuz Agrali TUR 2:18:22. **Women**: Olivera Jevtic SRB 2:35:31. **Team:** TUR.
Walks *at Flórina, Greece 8 Apr.* **Men 20k**: Aléksandros Papamihaíl GRE 1:26:40. **Women 20k**: Antigóni Drisbióti GRE 1:34:00.

18th Bolivar(ianos) Games

At Santa Marta, Colombia 21-25 November
Men: **100m/200m**: Alex Quiñónez ECU 10.13*/20.27*, **400m**: Luguelín Santos DOM 45.44, **800m**: Rafith Rodríguez COL 1:46.84, **1500m/5000m**: Carlos Martín Díaz CHI 3:45.58/14:02.92, **10000m** José Luis Ostos PER 28:56.95, **HMar**: Jeison Suárez COL 66:53, **3000mSt**: José Gregorio Peña VEN 8:39.99, **110mh**: Javier Arturo McFarlane PER 13.72, **400mh**: Yeison Rivas COL 50.47, **HJ**: Eure Yáñez VEN 2.24, **PV**: Waler Viáfara COL 5.25*, **LJ**: Santiago Cova VEN 7.81, **TJ**: Jhon Murillo COL 16.16, **SP**: Eder Moreno COL 18.66, **DT**: Juan Caicedo ECU 57.99, **HT**: Hevert Alvarez CHI 62.08, **JT**: Arley Ibargüen COL 78.87*; **Dec**: José Gregorio Lemus COL 7762*, **4x100m**: VEN 39.40, **4x400m**: COL 3:06.14, **20kmW**: Manuel Soto COL 1:26:32; **50kW**: Andrés Chocho ECU 4:14:20. **Women**: **100m**: Ángela Tenorio ECU 11.25, **200m/400m**: Nercely Soto VEN 22.89/52.43, **800m**: Rosangélica Escobar COL 2:03.4, **1500m/5000m**: Muriel Coneo COL 4:15.64/16:08.29*, **10000m**: Inés Melchor PER 33:57.13, **HMar**: Gladys Lucy Tejeda PER 74:55; **3000mSt:** Katia Arenas PER 9:52.32, **100mh**: Genesis Romero VEN 13.19, **400mh**: Julieth Caballero COL 58.04, **HJ**: María Murillo COL 1.78, **PV**: Robeilys Peinado VEN 4.20, **LJ**: Nathalie Aranda PAN 6.46, **TJ**: Ana Lucía Tima DOM 13.50, **SP**: Natalia Ducó CHI 17.99*, **DT**: Karen Gallardo CHI 55.73, **HT**: Rosa Rodríguez VEN 66.31, **JT**: Flor Ruiz COL 62.48*, **Hep**: Luisarys Toledo VEN 5785*, **4x100m**: VEN 44.15, **4x400m**: CHI 3:37.93, **20kmW**: Sandra Arenas 1:32:39*.

11th Central American Games

At Managua, Nicaragua 9-11 December
Men: **100m**: Shermal Calimore CRC 10.39, **200m/400m**: Nery Brenes CRC 20.56/46.64, **800m**: Juan Diego Castro CRC 1:52.28, **1500m**: Mario Pacay GUA 3:49.52, **110mh**: Wienstan Mena GUA 14.24w, **400mh**: Gerber Blanco GAU 50.18, **HJ**: Alexander Bowen PAN 2.10, **PV**: Natán Rivera ESA 5.05, **LJ**: Becker Jarquín NCA 7.32, **TJ**: Jason Castro HON 15.80, **DT**: Winston Campbell HON 50.82, **HT**: Roberto Sawyers CRC 66.74, **JT**: Lusia Taracena GUA 71.78. **20kW**: Erick Barrondo GUA 1:26:41. **Women:** **100m**: Irma Harris Brown CRC 12.11, **200m**: Tracy Joseph CRC 23.91, **400m**: Desirée Bermúdez CRC 53.78, **800m/1500m/3000mSt**: Andrea Ferris PAN 2:06.75/4:23.69/10:04.19, **100mh**: Andrea Vargas CRC 13.12, **400mh**: Gianna Woodruff PAN 57.85, **LJ**: Natalie Aranda PAN 6.17, **TJ**: Estefany Cruz GUA 13.25, **SP**: Naomi Wint CRC 13.03, **DT**: Aixa Middleton PAN 54.58, **JT**: Dalila Rugama NCA 53.47 **Hep**: Ana María Porras CRC 4920, **4x100m/4x400m**: CRC 46.35/3:44.04, **20kW**: Mirna Ortíz GUA 1:35:13.

15th European Cup Winter Throwing

At Las Palmas de Gran Canaria, Spain 11-12 March
Men: SP: 1. Mesud Pezer BIH 20.69, 2. Carlos Tobalina ESP 20.57, 3. Francisco Belo POR 20.52; **DT**: 1. Lukas Weisshaidinger AUT 65.73, 2. Andrius Gudzius LTU 64.18, 3. Martin Kupper EST 62.86; **HT:** 1. Quentin Bigot FRA 76.55, 2. Pavel Boreysha BLR 74.41, 3. Simone Falloni ITA 74.37; **JT**: 1. Julian Weber GER 85.85, 2. Roberto Bertolini ITA 78.78, 3. Paraskevás Batzávalis GRE 78.40; **Women: SP**: 1. Anita Márton HUN 18.05, 2. Jessica Cérival FRA 17.50, 3. Yuliya Leontyuk BLR 17.48; **DT:** 1. Mélina Robert-Michon FRA 62.35, 2. Dragana Tomasevic SRB 59.60, 3. Hrisoúla Anagnostopoúlou GRE 59.47; **HT:** 1. Alexandra Tavernier FRA 71.71, 2. Kathrin Klaas GER 71.06, 3. Zalina Petrivskaya MDA 69.17; B: Ida Storm SWE 70.07; **JT**: 1. Martina Ratej SLO 60.66, 2. Ásdís Hjálmsdóttir ISL 59.20, 3. Christin Hussong GER 59.00

European Cup 10,000m

At Minsk, Belarus 10 June
Men: 1. Antonio Abadía ESP 28:31.16, 2. Juan Pérez ESP 28:35.69, 3. Carlos Mayo ESP 28:48.41; Team: 1. ESP 1:25:55.26, 2. UKR 1:29:03.26, 3. ITA

1:29:06.28; **Women: 1.** Sara Moreira POR 32:03.57, 2. Olga Mazuronak BLR 32:13.73, 3. Esma Aydemir TUR 32:41.03; **Team:** 1. BLR 1:37:57.33, 2. POR 1:39:56.65, 3. UKR 1:41:25.00.

European Cup Race Walking

At Podébrady, Czech Republic 21 May

Men 20km: 1. Christopher Linke GER 1:19:28, 2. Miguel Ángel López ESP 1:20:21, 3. Perseus Karlström SWE 1:20:40, 4. Tom Bosworth GBR 1:21:21, 5. Mariusz Ziukas LTU 1:21:38, 6. Alex Wright IRL 1:21:46, 7. Diego García ESP 1:21:56, 8. Giorgio Rubino ITA 1:22:05, 9. Artur Brzozowski POL 1:22:14, 10. Callum Wilkinson GBR 1:22:17, 59 of 68 finished, Team: 11. ESP 30, 2. GER 35, 3. IRL 45, 4. GBR 50, 5. POL 52, 6. BLR 59, 7. ITA 65, 8. UKR 80, 9. TUR 105, 10. LAT 143, 11. HUN 146. **50km**: 1. Ivan Banzeruk UKR 3:48:15, 2. Ihor Hlavan UKR 3:48:38, 3. Michele Antonelli ITA 3:49:04, 4. Brendan Boyce IRL 3:49:49, 5. Teodorico Caporaso ITA 3:52:14, 6. Maryan Zakalnytskyy UKR 3:53:50, 7. Nathaniel Seiler GER 3:55:13, 8. Pedro Isidro ESP 3:56:39, 9. Francisco Arcilla ESP 3:56:39, 10. Iván Pajuelo ESP 3:56:47, 23 of 28 finished, Team: 1. UKR 9, 2. ITA 19, 3. ESP 34, 4. GER 46. **U20 Men 10km**: 1. Leo Köpp GER 41:08, 2. Mikita Kallada BLR 41:19, 3. Lukasz Niedzialek POL 41:28, 37 of 38 finished, Team: 1. BLR 9, 2. FRA 11, 3. UKR 14, 12 nations scored. **Women 20 km**: 1. Antonella Palmisano ITA 1:27:57, 2. Ana Cabecinha POR 1:29:44, 3. Laura García-Caro ESP 1:29:57, 4. Inna Kashyna UKR 1:30:11, 5. Nadiya Borovska UKR 1:30:26, 6. María Pérez ESP 1:30:52, 7. Valentina Trapletti ITA 1:30:58, 8. Brigita Virbalyte-Dimsiene LTU 1:31:32, 9. Lidia Sánchez-Puebla ESP 1:32:09, 10. Émilie Menuet FRA 1:32:32, 43 of 52 finished, Team: 1. ESP 18, 2. ITA 34, 3. LTU 36, 4. UKR 37, 5. FRA 64, 6. GBR 75, 7. HUN 76, 8. BLR 77, 9. POL 89, 10. ROU 9. **U20 Women 10km**: 1. Yana Smerdova RUS (neutral) 46:39, 2. Meryem Bekmez TUR 46:48, 3. Teresa Zurek GER 46:51, 35 of 37 finished, Team: 1. ESP 10, 2. GRE 12, 3. GER 14, 11 nations scored.

European Team Championships

Super League *Villeneuve d'Ascq, France 23-25 June*

1. GER 321.5, 2. POL 294.5, 3. FRA 270, 4. GBR 269, 5. ESP 243, 6. UKR 236.5, 7. ITA 220, 8. CZE 213.5, 9. GRE 196.5, 10. BLR 188.5, 11. NED 175

100m (-0.7)
1. Harry Aikines-Aryeetey GBR 10.21
2. Julian Reus GER 10.27
3. Churandy Martina NED 10.30

200m (0.4)
1. Serhiy Smelyk UKR 20.53
2. Mickaël-Méba Zézé FRA 20.57
3. Likoúrgos-Stéfanos Tsákonas 20.59

400m
1. Dwayne Cowan GBR 45.46
2. Rafal Omelko POL 45.53
3. Davide Re ITA 45.56

800m
1. Thijmen Kupers NED 1:47.18
2. Giordano Benedetti ITA 1:47.94
3. James Bowness GBR 1:48.19

1500m
1. Marcin Lewandowski POL 3:53.40
2. Jake Wightman GBR 3:53.72
3. Timo Benitz GER 3:54.28

3000m
1. Jakub Holusa CZE 7:57.60
2. Marc Scott GBR 7:58.52
3. Carlos Mayo ESP 7:58.97

5000m
1. Antonio Abadía ESP 13:59.40
2. Nick Goolab GBR 13:59.72
3. Amanal Petros GER 13:59.83

3000mSt
1. Mahiedine Mekhissi-Benabbad 8:26.71
2. Sebastián Martos ESP 8:27.46
3. Krystian Zalewski POL 8:33.02

110mh (0.2)
1. Orlando Ortega ESP 13.20*
2. Aurel Manga FRA 13.35
3. David Omoregie GBR 13.36

400mh
1. Jack Green GBR 49.47
2. Sérgio Fernández ESP 49.72
3. Patryk Dobek POL 49.79

HJ
1. Mickaël Hanany FRA 2.26
2. Marco Fassinotti ITA 2.22
3. Eike Onnen GER 2.22

PV
1. Renaud Lavillenie FRA 5.80
2= Hendrik Gruber GER 5.55
2= Igor Bychkov ESP 5.55

LJ
1. Dan Bramble GBR 8.00/1.2
2. Eusebio Cáceres ESP 7.96/0.4
3. Radek Juska CZE 7.86/-1.1

TJ
1. Max Hess GER 17.02/0.3
2. Ben Williams GBR 16.73/1.5
3. Pablo Torrijos ESP 16.71/0.6

SP
1. Tomás Stanek CZE 21.63*
2. David Storl GER 21.23
3. Konrad Bukowiecki POL 20.83

DT
1. Robert Harting GER 66.30
2. Robert Urbanek POL 66.25
3. Lolasson Djouhan FRA 64.35

HT
1. Pawel Fajdek POL 78.29
2. Pavel Boreysha BLR 77.52
3. Nick Miller GBR 76.65

JT
1. Jakub Vadlejch CZE 87.95*
2. Ioánnis Kiriazís GRE 86.33
3. Thomas Röhler GER 84.22

4x100m
1. GBR (Ujah, Hughes, Talbot, Aikines-Aryeetey) 38.08*
2. GER (Reus, Hering, Schmidt, Platini Menga) 38.30
3. FRA (Bassaw, Dautremer, Zeze, Anouman) 38.68

4x400m
1. ESP (Husillos, Bua, Echeverry, García) 3:02.32
2. NED (Stuivenberg, Bonevacia, Agard, Blauwhof) 3:02.37
3. CZE (Tesar, Maslák, Müller, Sorm) 3:03.31

Women

100m (0.4)
1. Carole Zahi FRA 11.19
2. Gina Lückenkemper GER 11.35
3. Corinne Humphreys GBR 11.50

200m (0.4)
1. María Belibasáki GRE 22.6 (hand time)
2. Anna Kielbasinska POL 22.8
3. Rebekka Haase GER 22.8

400m
1. Lisanne de Witte NED 51.71
2. Olha Zemlyak UKR 51.88
3. Laura Müller GER 52.09

800m
1. Olha Lyakhova UKR 2:03.09
2. Yusneysi Santiusti ITA 2:03.56
3. Esther Guerrero ESP 2:03.70

1500m 1. Konstanze Klosterhalfen GER 4:09.57
2. Angelika Cichocka POL 4:12.16
3. Nataliya Pryshchepa UKR 4:13.51
3000m 1. Sofia Ennaoui POL 9:01.24
2. Hanna Klein GER 9:01.64
3. Simona Vrzalová CZE 9:02.77
5000m 1. Ana Lozano ESP 15:18.40
2. Yuliya Shmatenko UKR 15:30.36
3. Alina Reh GER 15:32.50
3000mSt 1. Gesa-Felicitas Krause GER 9:27.02
2. Lennie Waite GBR 9:43.33
3. Irene Sánchez ESP 9:43.51
100mh (0.4) 1. Pamela Dutkiewicz GER 12.75
2. Alina Talay BLR 12.91
3. Hanna Plotitsyna UKR 13.05
400mh 1. Eilidh Doyle GBR 54.60
2. Yadisleidy Pedroso ITA 55.39
3. Olena Kolesnychenko UKR 55.51
HJ 1. Kamila Licwinko POL 1.97
2. Marie-Laurence Jungfleisch GER 1.97
3= Michaela Hrubá CZE 1.94
3= Alessia Trost ITA 1.94
PV 1. Ekateríni Stefanídi GRE 4.70
2. Iryna Zhuk BLR 4.60
3. Ninon Guillon-Romarin FRA 4.45
LJ 1. Claudia Salman-Rath GER 6.66/1.2
2. Rougui Sow FRA 6.45/2.0
3. Maryna Bekh UKR 6.43/0.1
TJ 1. Paraskeví Papahrístou GRE 14.24/0.4
2. Kristina Gierisch GER 14.13/1.1
3. Jeanine Assani Issouf FRA 14.00/-0.6
SP 1. Alyona Dubitskaya BLR 18.39
2. Melissa Boekelman NED 17.72
3. Paulina Guba POL 17.67
DT 1. Mélina Robert-Michon FRA 62.62
2. Nadine Müller GER 62.57
3. Hrisoúla Anagnostopoúlou GRE 59.28
HT 1. Hanna Malyshik BLR 74.56
2. Malwina Kopron POL 73.06
3. Alyona Shamotina UKR 70.02
JT 1. Barbora Spotáková CZE 65.14
2. Tatyana Kholodovich BLR 64.60
3. Marcelina Witek POL 60.98
4x100m 1. GER (Matheis, Burghardt, Lückenkemper, Haase) 42.47*
2. POL (Ciba, Popowicz-Drapala, Kielbasinska, Swoboda) 43.07
3. UKR (Povh, Stuy, Kachur, Bryzgina) 43.09
4x400m 1. POL (Baumgart, Wyciszkiewicz, Dabrowska, Holub) 3:27.60)
2. UKR (Klymyuk, Lyakhova, Bryzgina, Zemlyak) 3:28.02
3. GER (Müller, Gonska, Mergenthaler, Spelmeyer) 3:28.47

First League *at Vaasa, Finland 23-25 June*

1. SWE 321.5, 2. FIN 315.5, 3. SUI 306.5, 4. TUR 303, 5. POR 286, 6. NOR 273.5, 7. ROU 247, 8. BEL 232.5, 9. IRL 227, 10. EST 204, 11. BUL 194.5, 12. DEN 187
Winners: **Men**: **100m**: Jonathan Quarco NOR 10.35, **200m**: Ramil Guliyev TUR 20.20, **400m**: Brian Gregan IRL 45.83, **800m**: Mark English IRL 1:47.02, **1500m**: Peter Callahan BEL 3:59.09, **3000m**: Hélio Gomes POR 7:55.94, **5000m**: Ali Kaya TUR 13:36.75, **3000mSt**: Ole Hesselbjerg DEN 8:37.02, **110mh**: Andreas Martinsen DEN 13.64, **400mh**: Karsten Warholm NOR 48.46, **HJ**: Tihomir Ivanov BUL 2.30, **PV**: Diego Ferreira POR 5.45, **LJ**: Michel Tornéus SWE 7.85w, **TJ**: Simo Lipsanen FIN 16.75, **SP**: Tsanko Arnaudov BUL 21.56, **DT**: Daniel Ståhl 66.41, **HT**: David Söderberg FIN 72.36, **JT**: Tero Pitkämäki FIN 88.27, **4x100m**: SUI 39.65, **4x400m**: TUR 3:08.01. **Women**: **100m**: Mujinga Kambunji SUI 11.45, **200m**: Ivet Lalova-Collio BUL 23.33, **400m**: Léa Sprunger SUI 51.61, **800m**: Lovisa Lindh SWE 2:02.36, **1500m**: Claudia Bobocea ROU 4:14.50, **3000m**: Linn Nilsson 9:08.97, **5000m/3000mSt**: Fabienne Schlumpf SUI 15:47.29/9:38.08, **100mh**: Noemi Zbären SUI 13.28, **400mh**: Petra Fontanive SUI 55.53, **HJ**: Sofie Skoog 1.90, **PV**: Nicole Büchler SUI 4.55, **LJ**: Khaddi Sagnia SWE 6.52, **TJ**: Patricia Mamona POR 14.02, **SP**: Emel Dereli TUR 17.97, **DT**: Irina Rodrigues POR 59.62, **HT**: Kivilcim Salman TUR 69.75, **JT**: Liina Laasma EST 57.93, **4x100m/4x400m**: SUI 43.77/3:33.10.

Second League *at Tel Aviv, Israel 23-25 June*

1. HUN 372.5, 2. SVK 306.5, 3. LTU 298.5, 4. SLO 296, 5. CYP 258, 6. LAT 258, 7. CRO 253.5, 8. ISR 243, 9. AUT 240.5, 10. SRB 238.5, 11. ISL 181.5, 12. MDA 166.5.
Winners: **Men**: **100m:** Jan Volko SVL 10.21, **200m/400m**: Luka Janezic SLO 20.60/45.47, **800m**: Zan Rudolf SLO 1:47.87, **1500m**: Simas Bertasius LTU 3:44.59, **3000m**: Benjamin Kovács HUN 8:07.25, **5000m**: Amine Khadiri CYP 14:13.22, **3000mSt**: Justinas Berzanskis LTU 8:53.29, **110mh**: Milan Trajkovic CYP 13.31, **400mh**: Tibor Koroknai HUN 49.74, **HJ**: Vasilios Constantinou CYP 2.21, **PV**: Ivan Horvat CRO 5.70, **LJ**: Lazar Anic SRB 7.91, **TJ**: Ton Ya-acobov ISR 16.38, **SP**: Sarunas Banevicius LTU 19.29, **DT**: Lukas Weisshaidinger AUT 65.66, **HT**: Serghei Marghiev MDA 73.37, **JT**: Andrian Mardare MDA 83.93, **4x100m**: HUN 39.97, **4x400m**: SLO 3:08.56. **Women**: **100m**: Viola Kleiser AUT 11.53, **200m**: Eleni Artymata CYP 23.39, **400m**: Iveta Putalová SVK 52.45, **800m**: Anita Hinriksdóttir ISL 2:02.57, **1500m/3000m**: Amela Terzic SRB 4:15.93/9:15.85, **5000m**: Krisztina Papp HUN 16:17.99, **3000mSt**: Zita Kácser HUN 10:06.80, **100mh**: Gréta Kerekes HUN 13.17, **400mh**: Agata Zupin SLO 56.80, **HJ**: Marusa Cernjul SLO 1.88, **PV**: Tina Sutej SLO 4.50, **LJ**: Jana Veldáková SVK 6.55, **TJ**: Hanna Minenko ISR 14.17, **SP**: Anita Márton HUN 18.09, **DT**: Dragana Tomasevic SRB 59.47, **HT**: Zalina Petrivskaya MDA 71.99, **JT**: Sara Kolak CRO 61.06, **4x100m**: HUN 44.81, **4x400m**: SVK 3:34.05.

Third League *at Marsa, Malta 23-25 June*

1. LUX 317, 2. BIH 266, 3. GEO 262, 4. MLT 261.5, 5. MNE 243.5, 6. ARM 217, 7. MKD 179, 8. AND 132, 9. AASSE 118, 10. AZE 90.

European Cup Combined Events

Super League *At Tallinn, Estonia 1-2 July*
1. UKR 40,085, 2. EST 39,779, 3. FRA 39,771, 4. GBR 38,382, 5. BLR 37,998, 6. SUI 37,893, no score POL (only 5 completed). **Men Dec:** 1. Janek Oiglane EST 8170, 2. Oleksiy Kasyanov UKR 7958, 3. Karl Robert Saluri EST 7837, 4. Vasyl Ivanytskyy UKR 7801, 5.

Jérémy Lelièvre FRA 7798; **Women Hep**: 1. Alina Shukh UKR 6208, 2. Géraldine Ruckstuhl SUI 6134, 3. Grit Sadeiko EST 5958, 4. Ellen Sprunger SUI 5813, 5. Esther Turpin FRA 5745

First League *At Monzón. Spain 1-2 July*
1. NED 39,386, 2. ESP 39,153, 3. SWE 38,376, 4. FIN 38,040, 5. CZE 37,566, 6. ITA 36,609, 7. POR 35,713, 8. ROU 31,861. **Men Dec**: 1. Jorge Ureña ESP 8121, 2. Marcus Nilsson SWE 7987, 3. Ben Markies NED 7624; **Women Hep**: 1. Nadine Broersen NED 6326. 2. Eliska Klucinová CZE 6003, 3. Lecabala Quaresma POR 5861.

Second League. *At Monzón. Spain 1-2 July*
1. LTU 36,838, 2. LAT 35,261, 3. DEN 35,026, 4. ISL 33,923, **Men Dec**: Martin Roe NOR 8144; **Women Hep**: Lucia Slanicková SVK 5816.

European Under-23 Championships

At Bydgoszcz, Poland 13-16 July

100m (0.0)
1. Ojie Edoburun GBR 10.14
2. Ján Volko SVK 10.18
3. Jonathan Quarcoo NOR 10.29

200m (1.6)
1. Ján Volko SVK 20.33
2. Gautier Dautremer FRA 20.66
3. Roger Gurski GER 20.70

400m
1. Luka Janezic SLO 45.33
2. Karsten Warholm NOR 45.75
3. Benjamin Lobo Vedel DEN 46.08

800m
1. Andreas Kramer SWE 1:48.15
2. Daniel Rowden GBR 1:48.16
3. Marc Reuther GER 1:48.66

1500m
1. Marius Probst GER 3:49.06
2. Filip Sasinek CZE 3:49.23
3. Michal Rozmys POL 3:49.30

5000m
1. Yemaneberhan Crippa ITA 14:14.28
2. Simon Debognies BEL 14:14.71
3. Carlos Mayo ESP 14:15.07

10,000m
1. Carlos Mayo ESP 29:28.06
2. Amanal Petros GER 29:34.94
3. Emmanuel Roudolff Lévisse FRA 29:42.85

3000mSt
1. Yohanes Chiappinelli ITA 8:34.33
2. Ahmed Abdelwahed ITA 8:37.02
3. Jamaine Coleman GBR 8:40.44

110mh (0.8)
1. Ludovic Payen FRA 13.49
2. Khai Riley-La Borde GBR 13.65
3. Dylan Caty FRA 13.66

400mh
1. Karsten Warholm NOR 48.37*
2. Dany Brand SUI 49.14
3. Ludvy Vaillant FRA 49.31

HJ
1. Dmitriy Nabokov BLR 2.24
2. Christian Falocchi ITA 2.24
3. Viktor Lonskyy UKR 2.24

PV
1. Ben Broeders BEL 5.60
2. Axel Chapelle FRA 5.60
3. Adrián Valles ESP 5.50

LJ
1. Vladyslav Mazur UKR 8.04/1.9
2. Filippo Randazzo ITA 7.98w/2.1
3. Thobias Nilsson Montler SWE 7.96/0.9

TJ
1. Nazim Babayev AZE 17.18/0.4
2. Simo Lipsanen FIN 17.14/-0.5
3. Max Hess GER 16.68/0.5

SP
1. Konrad Bukowiecki POL 21.59*
2. Denzel Comenentia NED 19.86
3. Sebastiano Bianchetti ITA 19.69

DT
1. Sven Martin Skagestad NOR 61.00
2. Alin Firfirica ROU 60.17
3. Clemens Prüfer GER 60.08

HT
1. Bence Halász HUN 73.30
2. Bence Pásztor HUN 71.51
3. Alexej Mikhailov GER 70.60

JT
1. Norbert Rivasz-Tóth HUN 83.08
2. Ioánnis Kiríazis GRE 81.04
3. Andrian Mardare MDA 78.76

Dec
1. Jiri Sykora CZE 8084
2. Fredrik Samuelsson SWE 8010
3. Elmo Savola FIN 7956

20kW
1. Diego García ESP 1:22:29
2. Karl Junghannss GER 1:22:52
3. Gabriel Bordier FRA 1:23:03

4x100m
1. GER (Gurski, Köllmann, Trutenat, Hoffmann) 39.11
2. GBR (Etienne de Escofet, Arthur, Edoburun) 39.11
3. FIN (Kajander, Lehtonen, S Samuelsson, Lehto) 39.70

4x400m
1. GBR (L Thompson, Snaith, Hazel, Chalmers) 3:03.65
2. POL (Suwara, Wascinski. Duszynski, Kowal) 3:04.22
3. FRA (Coroller, Biron, Merville.,Vaillant) 3:05.24

Women

100m (-0.6)
1. Ewa Swoboda POL 11.42
2. Kristina Tsimanovskaya BLR 11.54
3. Sina Mayer GER 11.58

200m (1.3)
1. Finette Agyapong GBR 22.87
2. Sarah Atcho SUI 22.90
3. Yana Kachur UKR 23.20

400m
1. Gunta Latiseva-Cudare LAT 52.00
2. Laura Müller GER 52.42
3. Laura de Witte NED 52.51

800m
1. Renée Eykens BEL 2:04.73
2. Anita Hinriksdóttir ISL 2:05.02
3. Hannah Segrave GBR 2:05.53

1500m
1. Konstanze Klosterhalfen GER 4:10.30
2. Sofia Ennaoui POL 4:13.54
3. Martyna Galant POL 4:17.91

5000m
1. Yasemin Can TUR 15:01.67*
2. Alina Reh GER 15:10.57
3. Sarah Lahti SWE 15:14.17

10,000m
1. Yasemin Can TUR 31:39.80*
2. Sarah Lahti SWE 32:46.91
3. Büsra Nur Koku TUR 33:33.22

3000mSt
1. Anna Emilie Møller DEN 9:43.05
2. Nataliya Strebkova UKR 9:44.52
3. Emma Oudiou FRA 9:50.30

100mh (2.3)
1. Nadine Visser NED 12.92w
2. Elvira German BLR 12.95
3. Luca Kozák HUN 13.06

400mh
1. Ayomide Folorunso ITA 55.82
2. Jessica Turner GBR 56.08
3. Arna Gudmundsdóttir ISL 56.37

HJ
1. Yuliya Levchenko UKR 1.96
2. Iryna Herashchenko UKR 1.92
3. Erika Furlani ITA 1.86

PV
1. Angelica Moser SUI 4.55

2. Maryna Kylypko UKR 4.45
3. Lucy Bryan GBR 4.40

LJ 1. Yanis David FRA 6.56/0.1
2. Anna Bühler GER 6.50/-0.8
3. Maryna Bekh UKR 6.48/0.3

TJ 1. Elena Panturoiu ROU 14.27/0.2
2. Ana Peleteiro ESP 14.19/0.6
3. Rouguy Diallo FRA 13.99w/3.7

SP 1. Fanny Roos SWE 18.14
2. Klaudia Kardasz POL 17.67
3. Alina Kenzel GER 17.46

DT 1. Claudine Vita GER 61.79
2. Daria Zabawska POL 59.08
3. Veronika Domjan SLO 58.48

HT 1. Alyona Shamotina UKR 67.46
2. Camille Sainte-Luce FRA 66.98
3. Beatrice Nedberge Llano NOR 66.74

JT 1. Sara Kolak CRO 65.12*
2. Anete Kocina LAT 64.47
3. Marcelina Witek POL 63.03

Hep 1. Caroline Agnou SUI 6330
2. Verena Preiner AUT 6232
3. Celina Leffler GER 6070

20kW 1. Klavdiya Afanasyeva RUS 1:31:15
2. Mária Pérez ESP 1:31:29
3. Ziviklé Vaiciukeviciuté LTU 1:32:21

4x100m 1. ESP (Sevilla, Petrirena, Gómez, Lara) 43.96
2. FRA (Pare, Leduc, Peltier, Brossier) 44.06
3. SUI (Dietsche, Atcho, Del Ponte, Frey) 44.07

4x400m 1. POL (Muraszewska, Janowicz, Karas, Gaworska) 3:29.66
2. GER (Richter, Müller, Schmidt, Mergenthaler) 3:30.18
3. UKR (Stavnycha, Kachur, Melnyk, Klymyuk) 3:30.22

Medal table and points (1-8) leaders

Nat	*G*	*S*	*B*	*Pts*	*Nat*	*G*	*S*	*B*	*Pts*
GER	4	6	8	185	FIN	-	1	2	46
GBR	3	4	3	148	BEL	2	1	-	42
FRA	2	4	7	140.5	ROU	1	1	-	31
POL	3	4	3	117	CZE	1	1	-	29
ITA	3	3	2	111	NED	1	1	1	26
UKR	3	3	4	86	SLO	1	-	1	22
ESP	3	2	2	84	SVK	1	7	-	20
SWE	2	2	2	88	LAT	1	1	-	19
BLR	1	2	-	65.5	ISL	-	1	1	19
TUR	2	-	1	57	DEN	1	-	1	18
SUI	2	2		55	LTU	-	-	1	14
NOR	2	1	2	52	POR	-	-	-	14
HUN	2	1	1	47	IRL	-	-	-	12

24 nations won gold. 29 medals. 34 scored points

European Under-20 Championships

At Grosseto, Italy 13-16 July

100m (-4.3) 1. Filippo Tortu ITA 10.73
2. Samuel Purola FIN 10.79
3. Oliver Bromby GBR 10.88

200m (-0.9) 1. Toby Harries GBR 20.81
2. Jona Efoloko GBR 20.92
3. Samuel Purola FIN 21.00

400m 1. Vladimir Aceti ITA 45.92
2. Tymoteusz Zimny POL 46.04
3. Jonathan Sacoor BEL 46.23

800m 1. Marino Bloudek CRO 1:48.70
2. Markhim Lonsdale GBR 1:48.82
3. John Fitzsimons IRL 1:49.15

1500m 1. Jake Heyward GBR 3:56.73
2. Dries De Smet BEL 3:56.98
3. Adrian Ben ESP 3:57.32

5000m 1. Jacob Ingebrigtsen NOR14:41.67
2. Tariku Novales ESP 14:44.66
3. Dorin Andrei Rusu ROU 14:46.07

10,000m 1. Dorin Andrei Rusu ROU 31:08.86
2. Sergiy Polikarpenko ITA 32:10.85
3. Sezgin Atac TUR 31:12.18

3000mSt 1. Jacob Ingebrigtsen NOR 8:50.00
2. Alexis Phelut FRA 8:53.73
3. Louis Gilavert FRA 8:57.12

110mh (0.0) 99cm 1. Jason Joseph SUI 13.41
2. Robert Sakala GBR 13.48
3. Luis Salort ESP 13.48

400mh 1. Wilfried Happio FRA 49.93
2. Alessandro Sibilio ITA 50.34
3. David José Pineda ESP 50.41

HJ 1. Maksim Nedasekov BLR 2.33*
2. Dmytro Nikitin UKR 2.28
3. Tom Gale GBR 2.28

PV 1. Armand Duplantis SWE 5.65*
2. Bo Kanda Lita Baehre GER 5.45
3. Romain Gavillon FRA 5.35

LJ 1. Miltiádis Tentóglou GRE 8.07/1.6
2. Jakub Andrzejczak POL 8.02/1.6
3. Héctor Santos ESP 7.96/0.8

TJ 1. Martin Lamou FRA 16.97/0.7
2. Andrea Dalla Valle ITA 16.87/0.5
3. Melvin Raffin FRA 16.82/-0.4

SP (6kg) 1. Marcus Thomsen NOR 21.36
2. Szymon Mazur POL 20.70
3. Odisséas Mouzenídis GRE 20.67

DT (1.75kg) 1. Oskar Stachnik POL 62.01
2. Hleb Zhuk BLR 60.16
3. George Evans GBR 59.05

HT (6kg) 1. Hlib Piskunov UKR 81.75*
2. Aleksandr Shymanovich BLR 77.74
3. Dániel Rába HUN 75.95

JT 1. Cyprian Mrzyglod POL 80.52
2. Aliaksei Katkavets BLR 76.91
3. Lukas Moutarde FRA 74.22

Jnr Dec 1. Niklas Kaul GER 8435*
2. Johannes Erm EST 8141
3. Karel Tilga EST 8002

10,000mW 1. Sergey Shirobokov RUS 43:21.29
2. José Manuel Pérez ESP 44:17.23
3. Eduard Zabuzhenko UKR 44:22.16

4x100m 1. GER (Skupin-Alfa, Barthel, Petzke, Stubican) 39.48
2. ITA (Zlatan, Artuso, Marchei, Tortu) 39.50
3. ESP (Troyano, Retamal, Ambros, S López) 39.59

4x400m 1. ITA (Aceti, Scotti, Gjetja, Sibilio) 3:08.68
2. FRA (Saidy, Andant, Mbaye, Happio) 3:09.04
3. POL (Rzezniczak, Walicki, Holub, Zimny) 3:09.32

Women

100m (-1.4)
1. Gina Akpe-Moses IRL 11.71
2. Keshia Kwadwo GER 11.75
3. Ingvild Meinseth NOR 11.77

200m (-1.0)
1. Maya Bruney GBR 23.04
2. Sophia Junk GER 23.45
3. Katrin Fehm GER 23.49

400m
1. Anastasiya Bryzhina UKR 52.01
2. Andrea Miklos ROU 52.31
3. Hannah Williams GBR 52.55

800m
1. Khahisa Mhlanga GBR 2:06.96
2. Ellie Baker GBR 2:07.01
3. Gabriela Gajanová SVK 2:07.15

1500m
1. Jemma Reekie GBR 4:13.25
2. Liliana Georgieva BUL 4:16.73
3. Harriet Knowles-Jones GBR 4:17.53

3000m
1. Delia Sclabas SUI 9:10.13
2. Mathilde Senechal FRA 9:20.05
3. Nadia Battocletti ITA 9:24.01

5000m
1. Miriam Dattke GER 16:39.81
2. Floor Doornwaard NED 16:41.71
3. Tamara Micevic SRB 16:57.71

Jasmijn Lau NED 16:38.85 was the original winner but lost the title due to a doping positive from drinking a tea that she could not have known contained a banned substance. She served no suspension for this.

3000mSt
1. Lisa Oed GER 10:00.79
2. Tatyana Shabonova BLR 10:03.32
3. Gülnaz Uskun TUR 10:19.44

100mh (0.1)
1. Solene Ndama FRA 13.15
2. Alicia Barrett GBR 13.28
3. Klaudia Siciarz POL 13.33

400mh
1. Yasmin Giger SUI 55.90
2. Agata Zupin SLO 55.96
3. Viivi Lehikoinen FIN 56.49

HJ
1. Michaela Hrubá CZE 1.93
2. Karina Taranda BLR 1.87
3. Maja Nilsson SWE 1.85

PV
1. Lisa Gunnarsson SWE 4.40
2. Molly Caudery GBR 4.35
3. Wilma Murto FIN 4.15

LJ
1. Milica Gardasevic SRB 6.46/0.6
2. Tabea Christ GER 6.41/1.0
3. Kaiza Karlén SWE 6.32/-0.1

TJ
1. Violetta Skvortsova BLR 14.21w/2.4
2. Ilionis Guillaume FRA 13.97w/2.2
3. Naomi Ogbeta GBR 13.68w/3.0

SP
1. Julia Ritter GER 17.24
2. Jorinde van Klinken NED 16.89
3. Anna Niedbala POL 16.32

DT
1. Alexandra Emilianov MDA 56.38
2. Karolina Urban POL 53.88
3. Kristina Rakocevic MNE 53.56

HT
1. Katerina Skypalová CZE 64.78
2. Eva Mustafic CRO 63.09
3. Michaela Walsh IRL 61.27

JT
1. Nikol Tabacková CZE 55.10
2. Carolina Visca ITA 53.65
3. Elina Kinnunen FIN 52.94

Hep
1. Alina Shukh UKR 6381
2. Géraldine Ruckstuhl SUI 6357
3. Sarah Lagger AUT 6083

10,000W
1. Yana Smerdova RUS 47:19.69
2. Teresa Zurek GER 47:33.20
3. Meryem Bekmez TUR 48:33.88

4x100m
1. GER (Fehm, Kwadwo, Junk, Montag) 43.44 (ht 43.27*)
2. FRA (De La Taille, Mingas, Raffai, Mignon) 44.03
3. GBR (Carr, Rees, Bruney, Okoli) 44.17

4x400m
1. UKR (Avramchuk, Koba, Marchak, Bryzhina) 3:32.82
2. GER (Aniteye, Gerlach, A Schmidt, Schwab) 3:33.08
3. GBR (M Edwards, Bruney, E Barrett, H Williams) 3:33.68

Medal and placing table:

Nat	*G*	*S*	*B*	*Pts*	*Nat*	*G*	*S*	*B*	*Pts*
GBR	5	6	8	188	TUR	-	-	3	44
GER	5	7	1	162.5	CZE	3	0	0	43
FRA	3	5	4	140.5	NED	1	1	1	40.5
ITA	3	5	1	111	IRL	1	-	2	40
ESP	0	2	5	106	SUI	3	1	0	38
POL	2	4	3	99.5	EST	-	1	1	31.5
BLR	2	5	0	69	ROU	1	1	1	26
SWE	2	-	2	65	CRO	1	1	-	25
FIN	-	1	3	56	GRE	1	-	1	24
NOR	3	0	1	54	BEL	-	1	1	21
UKR	4	1	1	47	HUN	-	-	1	19

28 nations won medals (19 won gold), 36 in top 8s.

Games of the Small States of Europe

At Serravalle, San Marino 30 May - 3 June

Men: **100m**: Paisios Dimitriades CYP 10.63, **200m**: Kolbeinn Hödur Gunnarsson ISL 21.20, **400m**: Téo Andant MON 47.52, **800m/1500m**: Christos Dimitriou CYP 1:50.45/4:00.36, **5000m**: Amine Khadiri CYP 14:21.35, **10,000m**: Pol Mellina LUX 30:46.61, **3000mSt**: Nikolas Fragkou CYP 9:08.18, **110mh/PV**: Nikandros Stylianou CYP 15.93/5.55*, **400mh**: Jacques Frisch LUX 52.16, **HJ**: Vasilios Constantinou CYP 2.21, **LJ**: Thorsteinn Ingvarsson ISL 7.54, **TJ**: Panayiotis Volou CYP 15.76, **SP**: Bob Bertemes LUX 19.33, **DT**: Gudni Valur Gudnason ISL 59.98, **JT**: Örn Davídsson ISL 74.81, **4x100m**: ISL 40.45, **4x400m**: LUX 3:15.03. **Women**: **100m/200m**: Charlotte Wingfield 11.62/23.78, **400m**: Christiana Katsari CYP 55.01, **800m**: Natalia Evangelidou CYP 2:06.62, **1500m**: Charline Mathias LUX 4:21.59, **5000m**: Sladana Perunovic MNE 17:04.10, **10,000m**: Arndís Yr Hafthorsdóttir 36:59.69, **100mh**: Natalia Christofi CYP 13.64, **400mh**: Arna Gudmundsdóttir ISL 59.14, **HJ**: Marija Vukovic MNE 1.91*, **PV**: Hulda Thorsteinsdóttir ISL 4.20, **LJ**: Ljiljana Matovic MNE 5.64, **TJ**: Eleftheria Christofi CYP 12.16, **SP**: Gavriella Fella CYP 15.81*, **DT**: Androniki Kriostina Rakocevic MNE 53.79*, **JT**: Asdis Hjálmsdóttir ISL 60.03*, **4x100m/4x400m**: ISL 45.31/3:47.64. **Medals**: CYP 14G-13S-5B, ISL 11-8-5, LUX 5-8-8, MNE 4-2-3, MLT 2-1-3, MON 1-1-3, AND 0-3-6, SMR 0-1-3.

8th Francophone Games

At Abidjan, Côte d'Ivoire 23-27 July

Men: **100m**: Dyland Sicobo SEY 10.33, **200m**: Wilfried Koffi CIV 20.73, **400m**: Ben Ayesu-Attah CAN 46.43, **800m**: Nabil Oussama MAR 1:46.14, **1500m**: Fouad El Kaam MAR 3:46.42, **5000m**: Younès Essalhi MAR 14:11.60, **10000m**: Soufiyan Bouqantar MAR 29:39.07, **Mar**: Makorobondo Salukombo COD 2:27:54. **3000mSt**: Mohammed Tindouft 8:44.69, **110mh**: Loïc Herkenrath

FRA 13.74, **400mh**: Jordin Andrade CPV 49.6, **HJ**: Sean Cate CAN 2.20, **PV**: Baptiste Boirie FRA 5.40, **LJ**: Raihau Maiau FRA 7.90w, **TJ**: Fabrice Zango BUR 16.92w, **SP**: Franck Elemba CGO 19.99, **DT**: El Bachir Mbarki MAR 57.14, **JT**: George Zaharia ROU 74.67, **Dec**: Taylor Stewart CAN 7852, **4x100m**: CIV 39.39, **4x400m**: SUI 3:10.70, **20kmW**: Antonin Boyez FRA 1:30:44. **Women**: **100m/200m**: Natacha Ngoye CGO 11.56/23.69, **400m**: Djénébou Danté MLI 52.23, **800m**: Malika Akkaoui MAR 2:00.71, **1500m**: Rabab Arrafi MAR 4:17.23, **5000m**: Soukaine Atanane MAR 16:00.36, **10000m**: Roxana Bârca ROU 35:31.13, **Mar**: Shelly Doucet CAN 2:51:14, **3000mSt**: Fadwa Sidi Madane MAR 9:44.11*, **100mh/LJ**: Marthe Yasmine Koala BUR 13.32/6.52, **400mh**: Maeva Contion FRA 57.38, **HJ**: Lissa Labiche SEY 1.91, **PV**: Pasacale Stöcklin SUI 4.10, **TJ**: Caroline Ehrhardt CAN 13.83w, **SP**: Auriole Dongmo CMR 17.68, **HT**: Bianca Ghelber-Perie ROU 67.79, **JT**: Pascale Dumont CAN 52.16, **4x100m**: CIV 44.22, **20kW**: Marine Quennehen FRA 1:45:35.

16th Gulf Countries Championships

At Jeddah, Saudi Arabia 13-15 April

Men: **100m**: Andrew Fisher BRN 10.31, **200m**: Mohamed Yacoub Salem BRN 20.35w, **400m**: Ali Khamis Abbas BRN 45.78, **800m**: Ibrahim Remaid Al-Zafari KUW 1:49.43, **1500m:** Benson Seurei Kiplagat BRN 3:44.89, **5000m:** Tarik Ahmed Al-Amri KSA 14:20.77, **10,000m**: Yimer Aweke Ayalew BRN 29:40.69, **3000mSt**: John Kibet Koech BRN 8:38.13, **110mh**: Abdulaziz Al-Mandeel KUW 13.66, **400mh**: Hamid Abdullah Salim KUW 51.61, **HJ**: Mutaz Essa Barshim QAT 2.35, PV: Ali Makki Al-Sabagha 5.00, **LJ**: Hamoud Ali Al-Wani KSA 7.55, **TJ**: Khaled Saeed Al-Subaie KUW 15.68w, **SP**: Sultan Abdulmajeed Al-Hebshi KSA 18.35, **DT**: Essa Al-Zankawi KUW 62.22, **HT**: Ashraf Amjad El-Seifi QAT 73.79, **JT**: Ahmed Bader Magour QAT 83.00, **Dec**: Majed Radhi Mubarak Al-Zayed KUW 7170**,** **10,000mW**: Mabrouk Saleh Nasser QAT 48:32.07, **4x100m**: BRN 40.04. **Medal table**: KUW 7-4-2, BRN 7-4-0, QAT 4-1-6, KSA 3-7-8, OMA 2-1-3, UAE 0-2-2.

Ibero-American Championships

Marathon:*15 October, Buenos Aires, Argentina*

Men: Antonio Lima BRA 2:17:42; **Women**: Andreia Hessel BRA 2:39:38

4th Islamic Solidarity Games

At Baku, Azerbaijan 16-20 May. Actually the 3rd Games as the 2nd due in Tehran, Iran in 2010 were cancelled.

Men: **100m/200m**: Ramil Guliyev TUR 10.06*/20.08*, **400m**: Ali Khamis Abbas BRN 45.54, **800m:** Mostafa Smaili MAR 1:45.78, **1500m:** Sadik Mikhou MAR 3:36.64*, **5000m:** Younès Essalhi MAR 13:27.64*, **10,000m**: Abraham Cheroben BRN 27:38.76, **3000mSt**: Mohammed M Tindouft MAR 8:26.26*, **110mh**: Ahmad Al-Moualed KSA 13.68*, **400mh**: Armando Machava Creve MOZ 50.73, **HJ**: Majid Del Dein Ghazal SYR 2.28*, **PV**: Hussain Asim Al-Hizam KSA-J 5.55*, **LJ**: Yahya Berrabah MAR 8.07, **TJ**: Nazim Babayev AZE 17.15*, **SP**: Osman Can Özdevici TUR 19.83*, **DT**: Essa Al-Zankawi KUW 62.22, **HT**: Ashraf Amjad El-Seifi QAT 73.79, **JT**: Ahmed Bader Magour QAT 83.45*, **4x100m**: BRN 39.55*, **4x400m**: TUR 3:06.83. **Women: 100m**: Gina Bass GAM 11.56*; **200m**: Ofonime Odiong BRN 22.96*, **400m**: Salwa Eid Nasser BRN 51.33*, **800m:** Malika Akkaoui MAR 2:01.04*, **1500m:** Rabab Arrafi MAR 4:18.82*, **5000m/3000mSt**: Ruth Jebet BRN 14:53.41*/9:15.41*, **10000m:** Yasemin Can TUR 31:18.20*; **100mh**: Odile Ahouanwanou BEN 13.55, **400mh**: Kemi Adekoya BRN 54.68*, **HJ**: Nadezhda Dusanova UZB 1.80 =*, PV: Buse Arikazan TUR & Demet Parlak TUR 4.15*, **LJ**: Romaissa Belbiod ALG 6.33*, **TJ**: Kandji Sangone SEN 13.05, **SP**: Auriole Dongmo CMR 17.75*, **DT**: Jessica Inchude GBS 50.23, **HT**: Hanna Skydan 75.29*, **JT**: Eda Tugsuz TUR 67.21*, **4x100m/4x400m**: BRN 44.98/3:32.96. **Medal table leaders**: BRN 11G-5S-3B, TUR 9-8-4, MAR 6-2-5, AZE 2-2-1, KSA 2-1-1. 16 nations won gold medals, 31 (from 47) won a medal.

NACAC Championships

Half Marathon:*19 November, Havana, Cuba*

Men: Richer Pérez CUB 66:18; **Women**: Dailin Belmonte CUB 78:44; **Team**: Cuba

Oceania Walks Championships

At Adelaide, Australia 21 February.

Men: **20k**: 1. Dane Bird-Smith AUS 1:19:37, 2. Quentin Rew NZL 1:21:12, 3, Rydian Cowley AUS 1:22:09; **W 20k**: 1, Regan Lamble 1:29:58, 2. Beki Smith AUS 1:31:23, 3, Alana Barber NZL 1:31:23.

Pan-American U20 Championships

At Trujillo, Peru 21-23 July

100m: T J Brock USA 10.45, **200m**: Christopher Taylor JAM 20.38, **400m**: Jamal Walton CAY 44.99*, **800m**: Ryan Sanchez PUR 1:46.41, **1500m** Eric van der Els USA 3:43.16*, **5000m**: Carlos Hernández COL 14:53.93, **10000m**: Steven Cross USA 32:09.66, **3000mSt**: Jean-Simon Desgagnés CAN 8:56.57, Jnr **110mh**: Eric Edwards USA 13.33, **400mh**: Quincy Hall USA 49.02*, **HJ**: Roberto Vilches MEX 2.21, **PV**: Tate Curran USA 5.20, **LJ**: Ja'Mari Ward USA 7.77w, **TJ**: Arturo Rodríguez CUB 15.93, 6kg **SP**: Jordan Geist USA 22.02*, 1.75kg **DT**: Claudio Romero CHI 62.09, 6kg **HT**: Joshua Hernandez USA 72.55, **JT**: Pedro Henrique Rodrigues BRA 74.58, Jnr **Dec**: George Patrick USA 7514, **4x100m/4x400m**: USA 39.33/3:00.33*, **10,000mW**: David Hurtado ECU 40:37.64; **Women: 100m**: Khalifa St. Fort TTO 11.32, **200m**: Ashlan Best CAN 23.27, **400m**: Roxana Gómez CUB 51.46*, **800m**: Victoria Tachinski CAN 2:04.22, **1500m**: Lucia Stafford CAN 4:21.70, **3000m**: Taylor Werner USA 9:16.12, **5000m**: Laura Dickinson CAN 16:39.50, **3000mSt**: Sarah Edwards USA 10:10.684, **100mh**: Tia Jones USA 13.01, **400mh**: Brandeé Johnson USA 56.65, **HJ**: María Fernanda Murillo COL 1.85, **PV**: Rachel Baxter USA 4.41*, **LJ**: Tara Davis USA 6.51w, **TJ**: Davisleidis Velazco CUB 13.59, **SP**: Alyssa Wilson USA 17.70, **DT**:

Laulauga Tausaga-Collins USA 59.29*, **HT**: Camryn Rogers CAN 63.42, **JT**: Yulesy Anahí Angulo ECU 52.30, **Hep**: Adriana Rodríguez CUB 5711, **10000mW**: Alegna González MEX 43:43.89*, **4x100m/4x400m**: USA 44.07/3:28.57*. **Medal table leaders**: USA 22G-14S-18B, CAN 6-9-7, CUB 4-3-0, MEX 2-5-0, ECU 2-1-3, COL 2-1-0, JAM 1-5-1, BRA 1-3-5.

Pan-American Race Walking Cup

At Lima, Peru 13-14 May

Men: **20k**: 1. Eider Arévalo COL 1:21:01, 2. Benjamin Thorne CAN 1:21:16, 3. Omar Pineda MEX 1:22:00; **50k**: 1. Claudio Villaneuva ECU 3:51:35, 2. Luis Fernando López COL 3:51:35, 3. José Montaña COL 3:58:27; **Women**: **20k**: 1. María Guadelupe González MEX 1:28:09, 2. Kimberley García PER 1:29:15, 3. Paola Pérez ECU 1:30:00.

South American Championships

Asunción, Paraguay 23-25 June

Men

100m	1. Diego Palomeque COL10.11*
(1.9)	2. Bruno de Barros BRA 10.22
	3. Felipe dos Santos BRA 10.29
200m	1. Bernardo Baloyes COL 20.36w
(2.2)	2. Alvaro Cassiani VEN 20.90
	3. Virjilio Griggs PAN 21.11
400m	1. Winston George GUY 45.42
	2. John Perlaza COL 45.77
	3. Yilmar Herrera COL 46.02
800m	1. Leandro Paris ARG 1:49.82
	2. Lutimar Paes BRA 1:50.27
	3. Jonathan Bolados CHI 1:50.3
1500m	1. Federico Bruno ARG 3:45.28
	2. Carlos Martín Díaz CHI 3:45.69
	3. Carlos San Martín COL 3:49.99
5000m	1. Víctor Aravena CHI 13:57.45
	2. Ederson Pereira BRA 13:59.20
	3. Iván González COL 14:15.76
10,000m	1. Bayron Piedra ECU 29:03.73
	2. José Luis Ostos PER 29:06.74
	3. Miguel Angel Amador COL 29:35.17
3000mSt	1. José Gregorio Peña VEN 8:45.93
	2. Gerald Giraldo COL 8:51.59
	3. Mario Bazán PER 8:51.97
110mh	1. Eduardo de Deus BRA 13.42w
(3.8)	2. Eder de Souza BRA 13.49
	3. Javier McFarlane PER 13.76
400mh	1. Guillermo Ruggeri ARG 49.72
	2. Albert Bravo VEN 50.36
	3. Alfredo Sepúlveda CHI 50.37
HJ	1. Eure Yáñez VEN 2.31*
	2. Talles Silva BRA 2.28
	3. Fernando Ferreira BRA 2.19
PV	1. Germán Chiaraviglio ARG 5.60
	2. Walter Viáfara COL 5.10
	3. Rubén Benítez ARG 5.00
LJ	1. Paulo Oliveira BRA 7.93w/2.3
	2. Emiliano Lasa URU 7.89/1.7
	3. Daniel Pineda CHI 7.87w/3.3
TJ	1. Miguel van Assen SUR 16.94/2.0
	2. Mateus de Sá BRA 16.70/3.9w
	3. Eduardo Landaeta ECU 16.30w/4.3
SP	1. Darlan Romani BRA 21.02*
	2. Willian Dourado BRA 19.95
	3. Germán Lauro ARG 19.91
DT	1. Mauricio Ortega COL 63.82*
	2. Germán Lauro ARG 61.70
	3. Douglas dos Reis BRA 58.83
HT	1. Wágner Domingos BRA 73.79
	2. Humberto Mansilla CHI 73.16
	3. Allan Wolski BRA 71.38
JT	1. Braian Toledo ARG 79.93
	2. Arley Ibargüen COL 75.97
	3. Víctor Fatecha PAR 74.57
Dec	1. Jefferson Santos BRA 8187w
	2. Geormis Jaramillo VEN 8126w
	3. José Lemus COL 7572(w)
4x100m	1. BRA (Barbosa, A G da Silva, de Barros, F dos Santos) 39.47
	2. COL 39.67
	3. VEN 39.74
4x400m	1 COL (Solís, Palomeque, Herrera, Perlaza) 3:05.02
	2. BRA 3:07.32
	3. VEN 3:07.74
20000mW	1. Mauricio Arteaga ECU 1:24:40.0
	2. John Alexander Castañada COL 1:25:04.5
	3. César Augusto Rodríguez PER 1:25:38.3

Women

100m	1. Angela Tenorio ECU 11.02w
3.4)	2. Ana Claudia Silva BRA 11.12
	3. Andrea Purica VEN 11.18
200m	1. Vitoria Rosa BRA 22.67w
(2.8)	2. Angela Tenorio ECU 22.90
	3. Nedian Vargas VEN 22.95
400m	1. Geisa Coutinho BRA 52.03
	2. Yennifer Padilla COL 52.68
	3. Maitté Torres PER 53.99
800m	1. Johana Arrieta COL 2:06.36
	2. Andrea Calderón ECU 2:07.25
	3. Déborah Rodríguez URU 2:07.41
1500m	1. Muriel Coneo COL 4:16.46
	2. Rosibel García COL 4:21.81
	3. Katia Arenas PER 4:23.37
5000m	1. Muriel Coneo COL 16:16.64
	2. Belén Casetta ARG 16:26.32
	3. Angela Figueroa COL 16:30.59
10,000m	1. Carmen Martínez PAR 34:08.2
	2. Clara Canchanya PER 35:01.47
	3. Jovana de la Cruz PER 35:06.24
3000mSt	1. Belén Casetta ARG 9:51.40
	2. Katia Arenas PER 10:09.2
	3. Tatiane da Silva BRA 10:34.23
100mh	1. Fabiana Moraes BRA 12.86w
(2.9)	2. Genesis Romero VEN 13.16
	3. Melissa González COL 13.46
400mh	1. Gianna Woodruff PAN 56.04*
	2. Melissa González COL 56.29
	3. Fiorella Chiappe ARG 57.02
HJ	1. María Murillo COL 1.82
	2. Lorena Aires URU 1.82
	3. Julia Cristina Silva BRA 1.79
PV	1. Robeilys Peinado VEN 4.50
	2. Joana Costa Ribeiro BRA 4.20
	3. Valeria Chiaraviglio ARG 4.15

LJ 1. Eliane Martins BRA 6.51w/3.9
2. Macarena Reyes CHI 6.51w/7.3
3. Joanmy Luque VEN 6.47w/4.0
TJ 1. Nubia Soares BRA 14.42w/4.2
2. Yulimar Rojas VEN 14.36/1.4
3. Yosiris Urrutia COL 13.64w/2.7
SP 1. Geisa Arcanjo BRA 18.06
2. Sandra Lemos COL 17.30
3. Livia Avancini BRA 16.75
DT 1. Andressa de Morais BRA 64.68*
2. Fernanda Borges BRA 60.80
3. Karen Gallardo CHI 59.73
HT 1. Mariana Marcelino BRA 66.83
2. Jennifer Dahlgren ARG 66.17
3. Eli Johana Moreno COL 63.09
JT 1. Flor Denis Ruiz COL 61.91*
2. Laila e Silva BRA 57.81
3. Laura Paredes PAR 54.86
Hep 1. Tamara de Souza BRA 5667w
2. Javiera Brahm CHI 5168w
3. Martina Corra ARG 5026w
4x100m 1. BRA (Krasucki, A C Silva, Rosa, R Santos) 43.12*
2. COL 44.50
3. ECU 44.53
4x400m 1, BRA (J de Lima, J da Silva, J dos Santos, Coutinho) 3:33.00
2. COL 3:33.92
3. CHI 3:40.00
20000mW 1. Paola Pérez ECU 1:32:26.0
2. Ángela Castro BOL 1:32:35.2
3. Johana Ordóñez ECU 1:38:13.3

Medal and points table

Nat	*G*	*S*	*B*	*Pts*	*Nat*	*G*	*S*	*B*	*Pts*
BRA	17	12	7	352	URU	0	2	1	34
COL	9	12	9	259	PAR	1	0	2	28
ARG	6	3	5	160	PAN	1	0	1	18
VEN	3	5	5	125	BOL	0	1	0	18
ECU	4	2	3	100	GUY	1	0	0	15
CHI	1	4	5	100	SUR	1	0	0	12
PER	0	3	6	62					

Half Marathon: *18 March, Montevideo, Uruguay*
Men: Damião de Souza BRA 65:52; **Women**: Clara Canchanya PER 75:39
Marathon: *19 March, Temuco, Chile*
Men: Enzo Yáñez CHI 2:18:28; **Women**: Mirella da Andrade BRA 2:44:41

42nd South American Junior (U20) Championships

At Leonora, Guyana, 3-4 June

Men: **100m**: Compton Caesar GUY 10.37, **200m**: Derick Silva BRA 20.92, **400m**: Miquel Shepper SUR 47.90, **800m/1500m**: Jefferson dos Santos BRA 1:56.35/4:00.95; **5000m/10,000m**: Daniel do Nascimento BRA 14:53.7/31:01.64, **3000mSt**: Walace Caldas BRA 9:26.40, Jnr **110mh**: Marcos Herrera ECU 13.58*, **400mh**: Caio Martins BRA 54.78, **HJ**: Luan de Souza BRA 1.95, **LJ**: José Luis Mandros PER 7.91, **TJ**: Frixon Chila ECU 15.76, 7.25k **SP**/1.75k **DT**: Saymon Hoffmann BRA 16.57, 6k **HT**: Alencar Pereira BRA 71.42, **JT**: Pedro Rodrigues BRA 69.71, **10,000mW**: Jhonathan Amores ECU 45:34.9, **4x100m**: BRA 41.29, **4x400m**: COL 3:20.85. **Women**: **100m/200m**: Lorraine Martins BRA 11.56/23.89, **400m**: Tiffani Marinho BRA 54.25, **800m**: Johana Arrieta COL 2:10.41, **1500m**: Pietra da Silva BRA 4:31.82, **3000m:** Micaela Levaggi ARG 9:58.15, **5000m**: Virginia Huatorongo PER 18:18.1, 3**000mSt**: Rina Cjuro PER 10:47.45, **100mh**: Maribel Caicedo ECU 14.32, **400mh**: Valeria Cabezas COL 60.27, **HJ**: María Fernanda Murillo COL 1.78, **LJ**: Chantoba Bright GUY 6.30, **TJ**: Mirieli Santos BRA 12.71, **SP/DT**: Ailén Armada ARG 14.34/47.43, **HT**: Mariana García CHI 60.42*, **JT**: Yuleisi Angulo ECU 54.00*, **10,000mW**: María Montoya COL 48:22.4, **4x100m**: ECU 46.47, **4x400m**: GUY 3:51.40. **Medal table**: BRA 18G-11S-3B, ECU 6-2-1, COL 5-7-6, PER 4-5-6, GUY 3-10-12, ARG 3-1-6, CHI 1-3-2, SUR 1-2-2, URU 0-0-2.

29th South East Asia Games

At Kuala Lumpur, Malaysia 22-26 August (Marathon at Putrajaya)

Men: **100m**: Khairul Hafiz Jantan MAS 10.38, **200m/400m**: Trenton Beram PHI 20.84/46.39, **800m/1500m**: Duong Van Thai VIE 1:48.97/3:51.44, **5000m**: Nguyen Van Lai VIE 14:55.15, **10000m**: Agus Prayogo INA 30:22.26, **Mar**: Soh Rui Yong SGP 2:29:29, **3000mSt**: Atjong Purwanto INA 9:03.94, **110mh**: Rayzam Sofian MAS 13.83, **400mh**: Eric Cray PHI 50.03, **HJ**: Nauraj Singh Randhawa MAS 2.24*=, **PV**: Porranot Poorahong THA 5.35*, **LJ**: Bui Van Dong VIE 7.83**, TJ**: Muhammad Ismail MAS 16.77***,** **SP**: Promrob Janthima THA 17.42, **DT**: Muhd Irfan Shamsuddin MAS 58.36, **HT**: Jackie Wong Siew Cheer MAS 65.90*, **JT**: Peerachet Janthra THA 71.49, **Dec**: Aries Toledo PHI 7433, **4x100m/4x400m**: THA 38.90*/3:07.25, **20000mW**: Hendro INA 1:32:11.27*. **Women**: **100m/200m**: Le Tu Chunh VIE 11.56/23.32, **400m/400mh**: Nguyen Thi Huyen VIE 52.48/56.06*, **800m**: Vu Thi Ly VIE 2:07.11, **1500m/5000m**: Nguyen Thi Oanh VIE 4:20.51/17:23.20, **10000m**: Triyaningsih INA 36:39.37, **Mar**: Mary Joy Tabal PHI 2:48:26 **100mh**: Tran Thi Yen Hoa VIE 13.40, **HJ**: Duong Thi Viet Anh VIE & Michelle Sng Suat Li SGP 1.83, **PV**: Sukanya Chomchuendee THA 4.10, **LJ**: Bui Thi Thu Thao VIE 6.68, **TJ**: Vu Thi Men VIE 14.15, **SP**: Eki Febri Ekawati INA 15.39, **DT**: Subenrat Insaeng THA 55.23, **HT**: Grace Wong Xiu Mei MAS 59.24*, **JT**: Natta Nachan THA 55.04, **Hep**: Sunisa Khotseemueang THA 5430, **4x100m/4x400m**: VIE 43.88*/3:33.40, **10000mW**: Elena Goh Ling Yin MAS 52:21.50. **Medals**: VIE 17G-11B-6B, THA 9-13-11, MAS 8-8-9, INA 5-7-3, PHI 5-3-10, SGP 2-2-4, LAO & MYA 0-0-1.

IAU World 24 Hours Championships

At Belfast, GBR 1-2 July

Men: 1. Yoshihiko Ishikawa JPN 270.870k, 2. Sebastian Bialobrzeski POL 267.187, 3. Johan Steene SWE 266.515, 4. Nobuyuki Takahashi JPN 264.506, 5. Stéphane Ruel FRA 260.077, 6. Florian Reus GER 258.662, 7. Olivia Leblond USA 258.172, 8. Tamás Rudolf HUN 255.375; Team: 1. JPN 783.159, 2. POL 763.630, 3. USA 755.458, 4. HUN 752.867, 5 FRA 752.813, 6. GER 731.356, 7. CZE 720.921, 8. GBR 715.582, 28 nations scored. **Women** – 1. Patrycia Bereznowska POL 259.991, 2. Aleksandra Niwinska POL 251.078, 3. Katalin Nagy USA 250.622, 4. Gina Slaby USA 248.276, 5. Pam Smith USA 243.611, 6.

Jess Baker GBR 238.713, 7. Antje Krause GER 237.841, 8. Julia Fatton GER 236.183; Team: 1. USA 740.856, 2. POL 740.234, 3. GER 689.622, 4. SWE 684.613, 5. JPN 658.904, 6. GBR 657.402, 7. CRO 657.357, 8. IRL 638.072, 24 scored.

15th European Mountain Running Championships

At Kamnik. Slovenia 8 July.

Men 12k: 1. Xavier Chevrier ITA 1:02:51. 2. Luís Saraiva POR 1:03:34. 3. Francesco Puppi ITA 1:03:35, Team: 1. FRA 17, 2. ITA 17, 3. POR 58, **Junior Men 8.3k**: Gabriel Bularda ROU 47:07, Team: ITA 12, **Women 8.3k**: 1. Maude Mathys SEU 49:30. 2. Sarah Tunstall GBR 50:51. 3. Andrea Mayr AUT 51:43, Team: 1. GBR 19, 2. ITA 33, 3. AUT 40, **Junior Women 4.4k**: Lisa Oed GER 23:16, Team: GBR 22

World Mountain Running Championships

At Premana, Italy 30 July.

Men 13k: 1. Victor Kiplangat UGA 52:31, 2. Joel Ayeko UGA 52:50, 3. Fred Musobo UGA 53:57, 4. Joseph Gray USA 55:35; drugs dq (5), Petro Mamu ERI 55:45; Team: 1. UGA 6, 2. ITA 25. 3. USA 34; **Jnr 6.5**k: 1. Oscar Chelimo UGA 26:46. 2. Daniel Pattis ITA 27:42, 3. Talon Hull USA 28:01; Team: UGA 13; **Women 13k**: 1. Lucy Wambui Murigi KEN 61:26, 2. Andrea Mayr AUT 62:44, 3. Sarah Tunstall GBR 64:16, 4. Maude Mathys SUI 66:02, 5. Allie McLaughlin USA 66:06; Team: 1. USA 26, 2. ITA 32, 3. CZE 41; **Jnr W 6.5k**: 1. Rispet Chebet UGA 31:46, 2. Bahar Atyalay TUR 33:02; Team: ROU 24.

IAAF DIAMOND LEAGUE

The IAAF's successor to the Golden League, the expanded and more globally widespread Diamond League, was launched in 2010 with 14 meetings spread across Asia, Europe, the Middle East and the USA. The total prize money was increased from $6.63 million (with a $50,000 bonus for any new world record) in 2010 to $8 million from 2011. In 2017 a new system was introduced.

DIAMOND LEAGUE – event winners 2017

D Doha May 5, **Sh** Shanghai May 13, **E** Eugene May 27, **Ro** Rome Jun 8, **O** Oslo Jun 15, **St** Stockholm Jun 18, **P** Paris (Charléty) Jul 1; **L** Lausanne Jul 6, **Lo** London Jul 9, **Ra** Rabat Jul 16, **M** Monaco Jul 21, **Bi** Birmingham Aug 20, Finals: **Z** Zürich Aug 24, **Br** Brussels Sep 1

Men:

100m: Final winner: Chijindu Ujah Z 9.97. Andre De Grasse O 10.01, St 9.69w; Akini Simbine D 9.99, Ronnie Baker E 9.86w, Justin Gatlin L 9.96; Usain Bolt M 9.95

200m: Final winner: Noel Lyles Bi 20.00, Sh 19.90; Andre De Grasse Ro 20.01, Ra 20.03; Ramil Guliyev P 20.15, Bi 20.17; Ameer Webb Lo 20.13

400m: Final winner: Isaac Makwala Z 43.95; Wayde van Niekerk L 43.62*, M 43.73; Steven Gardiner D 44.60, St 44.58; LaShawn Merritt E 44.79, Baboloki Thebe O 44.95.

800m: Final winner: Nijel Amos Br 1:44.53, P 1:44.24, Lo 1:43.18, R 1:43.91, Bi 1:44.50; Kipyegon Bett Sh 1:44.70, Adam Kszczot Ro 1:45.96

1500m/1M: Final winner: Timothy Cheruiyot Z 3:33.93, St 3:30.77; Elijah Manangoi D 3:31.90, M 3:28.80; Ronald Kwemoi E 3:49.04M, Jake Wightman O 3:34.17, Aman Wote L 3:32.20

3000m: Ronald Kwemoi D 7:28.73, Muktar Edris P 7:32.31

5000m: Final winner: Mo Farah Z 13:06.05, E 13:00.70; Muktar Edris L 12:55.23

3000mSt: Final winner: Conseslus Kipruto Br 8:04.73, Ro 8:04.63; Soufiane El Bakkali St 8:05.01, Ra 8:05.12; Evan Jager M 8:01.29

110mh: Final winner: Sergey Shubenkov Br 13.14; Aries Merritt Ro 13.13, Lo 13.09, Bi 13.29; Omar McLeod Sh 13.09, Orlando Ortega St 13.09w, Ronald Levy P 13.05

400mh: Final winner: Kevin McMaster Z 48.07; Karsten Warholm O 48.25, St 48.82; Bershawn Jackson Sh 48.63, Kerron Clement Lo 48.02

HJ: Final winner: Mutaz Essa Barshim Z 2.36, D 2.36, Sh 2.33, O 2.38, P 2.35, Bi 2.40; Andriy Protsenko Ra 2.29

PV: Final winner: Sam Kendricks Z 5.87, Sh 5.88, E 5.86, P 5.82, L 5.93; Pawel Wojciechowski Ra 5.85, Piotr Lisek M 5.82

LJ: Final winner: Luvo Manyonga Z 8.49, Sh 8.61*, St 8.36; Ruswahl Samaai Ra 8.35; Jarrrion Lawson Bi 8.19

TJ: Final winner: Christian Taylor Br 17.49, D 17.25, E 18.11*, P 17.29; Pedro Pablo Pichardo L 17.60

SP: Final winner: Darrell Hill 22.44; Ryan Crouser E 22.43, L 22.39, Ra 22.47; Tom Walsh Bi 21.83

DT: Final winner: Andrius Gudzius Br 68.16; Daniel Ståhl O 68.06, Lo 66.73; Philip Milanov Sh 64.94, Fedrick Dacres St 68.36

JT: Final winner: Jakub Vadlejch Z 88.50; Thomas Röhler D 93.90*, Ro 90.06, M 89.17; Johannes Vetter P 88.74

Women

100m: Final winner: Christania Williams Z 11.07; Elaine Thompson Sh 10.78, P 10.91, Lo 10.94, Ra 10.87, Bi 10.97; Dafne Schippers Ro 10.99

200m: Final winner: Shaunae Miller-Uibo Z 21.88; Dafne Schippers O 22.31, L 22.10; Tori Bowie E 21.77; Murielle Ahgouré St 22.69, Marie-Josée Ta Lou M 22.25

400m: Final winner: Shaunae Miller-Uibo Br 49.46, Sh 49.77, Ra 49.80; Natasha Hastings Ro 50.52, Novlene Williams-Mills P 51/03, Allyson Felix Li 49.65, Salwa Eid Naser Bi 50.59

800m: Final winner: Caster Semenya Z 1:55.84, D 1:56.61, E 1:57.78, O 1:57.59, M 1:55.27*; Francine Niyonsaba St 1:59.11, L 1:56.82

1500m: Final winner: Faith Kipyegon Br 3:57.04, Sh 3:59.22; Sifan Hassan Ro 3:56.22, P 3:57.10; Hellen Obiri L 4:16,56M, Angelika Cichocka Ra 4:01.93, Dawit Seyaum Bi 4:10.36

3000m: Hellen Obiri M 8:23.14; Sifan Hassan Bi 8:28.90

5000m: Final winner: Hellen Obiri Br 14:25.88, Sh 14:22.47, Ro 14:18.37
3000mSt: Final winner: Ruth Jebet Z 8:55.29; Hyvin Jepkemoi D 9:00.12, Norah Tanui O 9:17.27, Beatrice Chepkoech P 9:01.69, Gesa Felicitas Krause Ra 9:18.87
100mh: Final winner: Sally Pearson Z 12.55; Kendra Harrison D 12.59, Lo 12.39, M 12.51; Jasmin Stowers E 12.59, Pamela Dutkiewicz O 12.73, Sharika Nelvis L 12.53
400mh: Final winner: Dalilah Muhammad Br 53.89; Ashley Spencer E 53.38, L 53.90; Zuzana Hejnová Ra 54.22, Bi 54.18
HJ: Final winner: Mariya Lasitskene Br 2.02, E 2.03, Ro 2.00, St 2.00, L 2.06*, Lo 2.00, M 2.05
PV: Final winner: Ekateríni Stefanídi Br 4.85; D 4.80, Ro 4.85, Lo 4.81, Bi 4.75; Yarisley Silva O 4.81, Nicole Büchler St 4.65
LJ: Final winner: Ivana Spanovic Br 6.70; L 6.79; Tianna Bartoleta O 6.79, Lo 7.01; Brittney Reese E 7.01
TJ: Final winner: Olga Rypakova 14.55; Caterine Ibargüen Ra 14.51, M 14.86, Bi 14.51; Yulimar Rojas Ro 14.84
SP: Final winner: Gong Lijiao Z 19.60, Sh 19.46, Ro 19.56, P 19.14; Michelle Carter D 19.32
DT: Final winner: Sandra Perkovic Br 68.82, Sh 66.94, O 66.79, Bi 67.51; Yaime Pérez St 67.92
JT: Final winner: Barbora Spotáková Z 65.54, Lo 68.26, Ra 63.73; Tatyana Kholodovich E 66.30, Sara Kolak L 68.43
** Diamond League record*

Changes to Diamond League in 2017

IN A MAJOR restructure, the IAAF Diamond League adopted a championship-style model with the finalists competing for a prize pool of $3.2 million. Athletes earned points in the first 12 IAAF Diamond League meetings to qualify for two final meetings where $100,000 was at stake in each of the 32 Diamond disciplines, including $50,000 for each winner. In previous seasons, athletes accumulated points throughout the IAAF Diamond League season with the overall winner of each of the 32 events being the athlete with the most points, irrespective of whether they won the final.

The season is now a race to reach the finals with the winners of these crowned as IAAF Diamond League champions. Whereas in the past there were seven meetings for each event, this time the field events, in particular suffered, and the requirement unfortunately was reduced to a minimum of five events for each discipline this year. In the horizontal jumps and throwing events, there was a return in 2017 to six attempts for all athletes. This followed the disastrous experimental format in 2016 where all athletes were given three attempts but with only the top four athletes being given three further attempts.

Prize money structure for each of the 32 events at the finals (Zürich Aug 24 & Brussels Sep 1): 1st $50,000, 2nd $20,000, 3rd $10,000, 4th $6000, 5th $5000, 6th $4000, 7th $3000, 8th $2000. Prize money at the 12 qualification meetings: 1st $10,000, 2nd $6000, 3rd $4000, down to $1000 for 8th place.

Omitted in error from ATHLETICS 2017

World Junior Championships 2016

At Bydgoszcz, Poland 19-24 July

Men

100 Metres (19-20-20) (0.2)
1. Noah Lyles USA 10.17
2. Filippo Tortu ITA 10.24
3. Mario Burke BAR 10.26
4. Gift Leotlela RSA 10.28
5. Paulo A de Oliveira BRA 10.29
6. Raheem Chambers JAM 10.30
7, Derick Silva BRA 10.37
8. Rechmial Miller GBR 16.18

200 Metres (21-21-22): (1.2)
1. Michael Norman USA 20.17*
2. Tlotliso Leotlela RSA 20.59
3. Nigel Ellis JAM 20.63
4. Clarence Munyai RSA 20.77
5. Yang Chun-Han TPE 20.81
6. Roger Gurski GER 20.81
7. Cameron Tindle GBR 20.82
8. Jun Yamashita JPN 20.94

400 Metres (20-21-22)
1. Abdelilah Haroun QAT 44.81
2. Wilbert London III USA 45.27
3. Karabo Sibanda BOT 45.45
4. Godfrey Kiprotich KEN 45.64
5. Kahmaru Montgomery USA 46.48
6. Anthony Zambrano COL 46.50
7. Kazuki Matsukiyo JPN 46.69
8. Naoki Kitakani JPN 47.15

800 Metres (22-23-24)
1. Kipyegon Bett KEN 1:44.95
2. Willy Tarbei KEN 1:45.50
3. Mostafa Smaili MAR 1:46.02
4. Jesus López MEX 1:46.70
5. Robert Heppenstall CAN 1:47.33
6. Riad El Chenini TUN 1:47.38
7. Brian Bell USA 1:47.68
8. Gorata Gabanketse BOT 1:48.40

1500 Metres (21)
1. Kumari Taki KEN-Y 3:48.63
2. Teresa Tolosa ETH 3:48.77
3. Anthony Kiptoo KEN 3:49.00
4. Baptiste Mischler FRA 3:49.52
5. Ajay Kumar Saroj IND 3:49.52
6. Matthew Ramsden AUS 3:50.50
7. Jordi Torrents ESP 3:50.93
8. Asres Guadie ETH-Y 3:50.95

5000 Metres (23)
1. Selemon Barega ETH 13:21.21
2. Djamal Dirieh DJI 13:21.50
3. Wesley Ladema KEN-Y 13:23.34

4. Biyazen Alehegn ETH 13:28.41
5. Aron Kifle ERI. 13:31.09
6. Moses Koech KEN 13:35.10
7. Awet Habte ERI 13:50.60
8. Elzan Bibic SRB-Y 13:51.40

10,000 Metres (19)

1. Rodgers Chumo Kwemoi KEN 27:25.23*
2. Aron Kifle ERI 27:26.20
3. Jacob Kiplimo UGA-Y 27:26.68
4. Amdework Walelegn ETH-Y 28:00.14
5. Gizachew Hailu ETH 28:09.57
6. Ronald Kirui Klprotich KEN 28:13.53
7. Mogos Shumay ERI 28:23.76
8. Martin Musau UGA 28:34.33

3000 Metres Steeplechase (21-24)

1. Amos Kirui KEN 8:20.43
2. Yemane Haileselassie ERI 8:22.67
3. Getnet Wale ETH-Y 8:22.83
4. Vincent Kipyegon KEN 8:22.84
5. Yohanes Chiappinelli ITA 8:32.66
6. Abdelkarim Ben Zahra MAR 8:34.28
7. Albert Chemutai USA-Y 8:37.76
8. Kidanemariam Dessie ETH-Y 8:39.92

99cm **110 Metres Hurdles** (20-20-21): (0.2)

1. Marcus Krah USA 13.25
2. Amere Lattin USA 13.30
3. Takumu Furaya JPN 13.31
4. Dejour Russell JAM-Y 13.39
5. Dawid Zebrowski POL 13.45
6. Michael Nicholls BAR 13.45
7. James Weaver GBR 13.51
8. Matthew Treston GBR 13.55

400 Metres Hurdles (21-22-23)

1. Jaheel Hyde JAM 49.03
2. Taylor McLaughlin USA 49.45
3. Kyron McMaster IVB 49.56
4. Mikael de Jesús BRA 50.06
5. Tatsuhiro Yamamoto JPN 50.99
6. Gong Debin CHN 51.03
7. Yoshihiro Watanabe JPN 51.09
8. M Fares Jelassi TUN 52.14

High Jump (20-22)

1. Luis Zayas CUB 2.27
2. Darius Carbin USA 2.25
3. Hamdi Mahamat Allamine QAT 2.23
4. Oleksandr Barannikov UKR 2.21
5. John Dodds AUS-Y 2.21
6. Yuji Hiramatsu JPN 2.21
7. Jah-Nhai Perinchief BER 2.18
8. Maksim Nedosekov BLR 2.18

Pole Vault (21-23)

1. Deakin Volz USA 5.65
2. Kurtis Marschall AUS 5.55
3. Armand Duplantis SWE-Y 5.45
4. Emmanouil Karális GRE-Y 5.40
5. Adam Hague GBR 5.40
6. Masaki Ejima JPN-Y 5.35
7. Chris Nilsen USA 5.35
8. Muntaher Faleh Abdelwahid IRQ 5.30

Long Jump (19-20)

1. Maykel Massó CUB-Y 8.00/-1.8
2. Miltiádis Tentóglou GRE 7.91/-0.4
3. Darcy Roper AUS 7.88/-1.0
4. Yasser Triki ALG 7.81/-1.5
5. Juan Miguel Echevarría CUB 7.78/-1.1
6. Ja'Mari Ward USA 7.68/0.0
7. Shem James AUS 7.59/-1.6
8. Jakub Andrejczak POL 7.45/-1.1

Triple Jump (20-21)

1. Lázaro Martínez 17.06/-1.1
2. Cristian Atanay Nápoles CUB 16.62/-0.6
3. Melvin Raffin FRA 16.37/-2.4
4. Philipp Kronsteiner AUT 16.25/-0.3
5. Sung Jin-syuk KOR 16.11/-0.7
6. Jordan Scott JAM 16.01/0.2
7. Liu Mingxuan CHN 16.01/0.2
8. Miguel van Assen SUR 15.75/-1.9

6kg **Shot** (19)

1. Andrei Toader ROU 22.30
2. Bronson Osborn USA 21.27
3. Wictor Petersson SWE 20.65
4. Adrian Piperi USA-Y 20.62
5. Sszymon Mazur POL 20.40
6. Tobias Köhler GER 19.76
7. Burger Lambrechts RSA 19.61
8. Marcus Thomsen NOR 19.39

dq (1) Konrad Bukowiecki POL 23.34 (*)

1.75kg **Discus** (23-24)

1. Mohamed Ibrahim Moaaz QAT-Y 63.63
2. Oskar Stachnik POL 62.83
3. Hleb Zhuk BLR 61.70
4. Wictor Petersson SWE 61.23
5. Clemens Prüfer GER 59.10
6. Cheng Yilong CHN 58.81
7. Shin-ichi Yukinaga JPN 58.50
8. Merten Howe GER 58.16

dq (5) Konrad Bukowiecki 59.71

6kg **Hammer** (20-22)

1. Bence Halász HUN 80.93
2. Hlib Piskunov UKR 79.58
3. Aleksi Jaakkola FIN 77.88
4. Dániel Rába HUN 76.71
5. Alberto González ESP 75.52
6. Ahmed Tariq Ismail EGY 74.42
7. Ned Waetherly AUS 73.75
8. Adam Kelly USA 73.17

Javelin (22-23)

1. Neeraj Chopra IND 86.48
2. Johannes Grobler RSA 80.59
3. Anderson Peters GRN 79.65
4. Emin Öncel TUR 75.20
5. Alexandru Novac ROU 72.91
6. Márk Xavér Schmölcz HUN 72.66
7. Harry Hughes GBR 72.22
8. Zakhar Mishchenko UKR 71.21

Junior Decathlon (19/20)

1. Niklas Kaul GER 8162*
2. Maksim Andraloits BLR 8046
3. Johannes Erm EST 7879
4. Santiago Ford CUB 7819
5. Toralv Opsal NOR 7815
6. Jan Ruhrmann GER 7795
7. Rik Taam NED 7699
8. Cale Wagner USA 7510

4x100 Metres (22-23)

1. USA (M Norman. H Montgomery. B Taylor. N Lyles) 38.93
2. JPN (Q Takeda. J Yamashita. W Inuzuka. K Oshima) 39.01
3. GER (Gurski. Barthel, Giese, Eitel) 39.13

4. JAM 39.13
5. AUS 39.57
6. GBR 39.57
7. ITA 40. 02
8. POL 40.25

4x400 Metres 23-24)
1. USA (C Allison, A Cogdell, Montgomery, W London) 3:02.39
2. BOT (Poo, Thebe, Sibanda, Talane) 3:02.81
3. JAM (Carpenter, S Bailey, Thomas, Taylor) 3:04.83
4. JPN 3:07.02
5. GER 3:08.13
6. TTO 3:08.28
7. IND 3:09.14
dq. ITA

10,000 Metres Walk (23)
1. Callum Wilkinson GBR 40:41.62
2. Jonathan Javier Amorse ECU 40:43.33
3. Salih Korkmaz TUR 40:45.53
4. Yohanis Algaw ETH-Y 40:55.96
5. Zhu Guowen CHN 41:01.33
6. Bai Liga CHN 41:06.14
7. Noel Ali Chama MEX 41:29.28
8. Leo Köpp GER 41:33.10

Women

100 Metres (20-21-21): (0.9)
1. Candace Hill USA 11.07*
2. Ewa Swoboda POL 11.12
3. Khalifa St. Fort TTO 11.18
4. Imani Lansiquot GBR 11.37
5. Evelin Rivera COL 11.59
6. Hannah Brier GBR 11.60
7. Iman Isa Jassim BRN 11.60
8, Marcy Otia-Obong NGR 11.79

200 Metres (22-22-23) (0.6)
1. Ofonime Odiong BRN 22.84
2. Evelin Rivera COL 23.21
3. Estelle Raffai FRA 23.48
4. Jenae Ambrose BAH 23.53
5. Taylor Bennett USA 23.55
6. Ashlan Best CAN 23.68
7. Finette Agyapomg GBR 23.74
dnf. Sada Williams BAR

400 Metres (19-20-21)
1. Tiffany James JAM 51.32
2. Lynna Irby USA 51.39
3. Junelle Bromfield JAM 52.05
4. Jess Thornton AUS 52.05
5. Maureen Thomas KEN 52.09
6. Roxana Gómez CUB-Y 52.24
7. Natassha McDonald CAN 53.35
8. Dzhoys Koba UKR 53.74

800 Metres (19-20-21)
1. Samantha Watson USA 2:04.52
2. Aaliyah Miller USA 2:05.06
3. Tigist Ketema ETH 2:05.13
4. Elise Vanderelst BEL 2:05.82
5. Marat Hirpato BRN 2:06.04
6. Victoria Tachinski CAN 2:06.11
7. Sigei Betty Chepkemoi KEN 2:06.27
8. Mareen Kalis GER 2:06.32

1500 Metres (22-24)
1. Adanech Anbesa ETH 4:08.07
2. Fantu Worku ETH 4:08.43
3. Christiana Aragon USA 4:08.71
4. Winfredah Nzisa KEN 4:09.25
5. Alexa Efraimson USA 4:10.23
6. Beatha Nishimwe USA 4:10.23
7. Bobby Clay GBR 4:13.09
8. Harriet Knowles-Jones GBR 4:15.49

3000 Metres (20)
1. Beyenu Degefu ETH 8:41.76*
2. Dalilah Abdelkadir Gosa BRN 8:46.42
3. Konstanze Klosterhalfen GER 8:46.74
4. Fotyen Tesfay ETH 8:47.46
5. Sandra Tuei KEN 8:55.77
6. Sheila Chelangat KEN 8:59.89
7. Katie Rainsberger USA 9:00.62
8. Nozomi Tanaka JPN 9:01.16

5000 Metres (23)
1. Kalkidan Fente ETH 15:29.64
2. Imaculata Chepkurui KEN-Y 15:31.12
3. Bontu Edao BEN 15:31.93
4. Mercyline Chelangat UGA 15:34.09
5. Yatayis Mekonene ETH-Y 15:34.37
6. Catherine Syokau KEN-Y 15:37.79
7. Dalile Abdelkadir Gosa BRN 15:38.56
8. Rike Kaseda JPN-Y 15:39.66

3000 Metres Steeplechase (19-22)
1. Celliphine Chespol KEN-Y 9:25.15*
2. Tigist Mekonen BRN 9:34.08
3. Agrie Belachew ETH-y 9:37.17
4. Betty Kibet KEN-J 9:38.27
5. Anna Emilie Møller DEN 9:43.84
6. Charlotte Prouse CAN 9:44.62
7. Peruth Chemutai UGA-Y 9:49.29
8. Neha Asmerech ETH-Y 9:55.14

100 Metres Hurdles: (22-23-24) (2.0)
1. Elvira German BLR 12.85*
2. Rushelle Burton JAM 12.87
3. Tia Jones USA-Y 12.89
4. Alexis Duncan USA 12.93
5. Tobi Amusan NGR 12.9
6. Alicia Barrett GBR 13.15
7. Taylon Bieldt RSA 13.37
8. Laua Vallette FRA 13.42

400 Metres Hurdles (20-21-22)
1. Anna Cockrell USA 55.20
2. Shannon Kalawan JAM 56.54
3. Xahria Santiago CAN-Y 56.90
4. Eileen Demes GER 57.83
5. Michaela Pesková SVK 58.17
6. Aminat Yusuf Jamal BRN 58.23
7. Tetreza Vikálová CZE 59.08
8. Mariam Abdul-Rashid CAN 57.69

High Jump (24)
1. Michaela Hrubá CZE 1.91
2. Ximena Esquivel MEX 1.89
3. Yuliya Levchenko UKR 1.86
4. Lada Pejchalová CZE 1.86
5= Nicole Greene USA 1.83
5= Mareike Max GER 1.83
7. Salome Lang SUI 1.83
8. Nawal Meniker FGRA 1.83

Pole Vault (19-21)
1. Angelica Moser SUI 4.55*
2. Rosbeilys Peinado VEN 4.40
3. Wilma Murto FIN 4.40
4. Chen Qiaoling CHN-Y 4.30
5. Carson Dingler USA-Y 4.25
6. Li Chaoqun CHN 4.20
7= Lisa Gunnarsson SWE-Y 4.10
7= Thiziri Daci FRA 4.10
7= Amálie Svábíková-Y 4.10

Long Jump (22)
1. Yanis David FRA 6.42/0.6
2. Sophie Weissenberg GER 6.40/1.1
3. Hilary Kpatcha FRA 6.33/0.6
4. Kaiza Karlén SWE 6.25/1.0
5, Bria Matthews USA 6.24/0.9
6. Anna Bühler GER 6.21/0.5
7. Eszter Bajnok HUN 6.16/0.9
8. Samiyah Samuels USA 6.08/0.8

Triple Jump (22-23)
1. Chen Ting CHN 13.85/1.4
2. Konstadína Roméou GRE 13.55/0.7
3. Georgiana Anitei ROU-Y 13.49/1.7
4. Bria Matthews USA 13.49w/2.1
5. Norka Moretic CHI 13.40/1.8
6. Xu Ting CHN 13.23/1.6
7. Alexandra Mihai ROU 13.21/1.7
8. Mariya Ovchinnikova KAZ 13.17/1.2

Shot (20)
1. Alina Kenzel GER 17.58
2. Song Jiayuan CHN 16.36
3. Alyssa Wilson USA-Y 16.33
4. Sarah Schmidt GER 16.18
5. Maria Fernanda Oroczo MEX 15.94
6. Maja Slepowronsk POL 15.75
7. Elena Bruckner USA 15.73
8. Anna Nledbala POL 15.58

Discus (21)
1. Kristina Rakocevic MNE 56.36
2. Kirsty Williams AUS 53.91
3. Alexandra Emilianov MDA-Y 53.08
4. Serena Brown BAH 52.73
5. Kiana Phelps USA 52.60
6. Ailén Armada ARG 52.53
7. Elena Bruckner USA 53.83
8. Sun Kangping CHN 51.70

Hammer (21-23)
1. Beatrice Nedberge Llano NOR 64.33
2. Alex Hulley AUS 63.47
3. Suvi Koskinen FIN 62.49
4. Krista Tervo FIN 62.25
5. Mayra Gaviria COL 62.18
6. Kinga Lepkowska POL 60.86
7. Sara Fantini ITA 59.56
8. Greta Aljberg DSWE 58.65

Javelin (19-20)
1. Klaudia Maruszewska POL 57.59
2. Jo-Ané van Dyck RSA 57.32
3. Eda Tugsuz TUR 56.71
4. Nikol Tabacková CZE 56.19
5. Chang Chu TPE 55.35
6. Mikako Yamashita JPN 54.89
7. Géraldine Ruckstuhl SUI 53.38
8. Haruka Kitaguchi JPN 52.15

Heptathlon (21/22)
1. Sarah Lagger AUT-Y 5960
2. Adriana Rodríguez CUB-Y 5925
3. Hanne Maudens BEL 5881
4. Bianca Salming SWE 5849
5. Lovisa Östervall SWE 5723
6. Nina Schultz CAN 5639
7. Karin Strametz AUT 5579
8. Emma Fitzgerald USA 5577

4x100 Metres (23)
1. USA (Tia Jones. T Bennett. K Harris. C Hill) 43.69
2. FRA (Murcia. Leduc. Peltier. Raffai) 44.05
3. GER (Fehm. Kwadwo. Frommann. Butzek) 44.18
4. POL 44.81
5. IRL 44.82
6. ESP 44.99
7. AUS 45.15
8. ECU 45.72

4x400 Metres (23-24)
1. USA (L Irby, A Cockrell, K Winters, S Watson) 3:29.11
2. JAM (Kalawan, James, S-A Williams, Bromfield) 3:31.01
3. CAN (Santiago, Best, McDonald, Tachinski) 3:32.25
4. GER 3:32.63
5. UKR 3:33.95
6. POL 3:36.95
7. CZE 3:37.36
8. ITA 3:42.53

10,000 Metres Walk (19)
1. Ma Zhenxi CHN 45:18.45
2. Noemi Stella ITA 45:23.85
3. Yehualeye Belete ETH 45:33.69
4. Valeria Ortuño MEX 45:44.33
5. Jiang Shanshan CHN 45:51.27
6. Taika Nummi FIN 46:04.74
7. Karla Jaramillo ECU 46:15.24
8. Yukiho Mizoguchi JPN 46:19.49

Medals (G-S-B) and points leaders

Nation	*G*	*S*	*B*	*Total*	*Points*	*2014*
USA	11	6	4	21	213	206
KEN	5	2	2	9	108	124
ETH	4	2	4	10	101	74
GER	2	1	3	6	80	87
JAM	2	3	3	8	71	50
POL	2	2	-	4	58	34
CHN	2	1	-	3	53	69.5
CUB	3	2	-	5	50	57
AUS	-	3	1	4	49	55.5
FRA	1	1	3	5	42	39
JPN	-	1	1	2	42	83
GBR	1	-	-	1	39	78
BRN	1	2	1	4	39	28
RSA	-	3	-	3	34	3
SWE	-	-	1	1	33	0
CAN	-	-	2	2	31	16
FIN	-	-	3	3	26	2
UKR	-	-	2	2	25	14.5
CZE	1	-	-	1	24	26
ITA	-	2	-	2	23	9
MEX	-	1	-	1	23	2
QAT	2	-	1	3	22	8
ERI	-	2	-	2	22	8
BLR	1	1	1	3	22	9
GRE	-	2	-	2	19	11
HUN	1	-	-	1	18	17
COL	-	1	-	1	18	0
TUR	-	-	2	2	17	13
UGA	-	-	1	1	16	25

AUT (1G) 15, BOT, IND (1G) 14; NOR (1G), SUI (1G) 12; BRA, BEL 11; BAH, ECU 10; ESP, BAR, MAR, TTO 9; TPE, MNE (1G) 1; DJI, VEN 7; MDA, EST, GRN, IVB 6; ALG, NGR 5; KOR, SVK, TUN. CHI, DEN, IRL 4; EGY, ARG, RWA 3; NED, BER 2; IRQ, KAZ, SRB, SUR 1. 47 nations won medals (20 gold).

MAJOR MEETINGS 2017–2018

Diamond League, World Challenge and European Athletics Premium Meetings

DL – Diamond League, WC – World Challenge, EAP European Premium Meeting

2017 date		Meeting	2018 date	
5 May	DL	Qatar Super Grand Prix, Doha, QAT	4 May	DL
13 May	DL	Shanghai Golden Grand Prix, CHN	12 May	DL
20 May	WC	Jamaica International, KIngston JAM	19 May	WC
21 May	WC	Golden Grand Prix, Kawasaki 2017, Osaka 2018, JPN	20 May	WC
27 May	DL	Prefontaine Classic, Eugene, Oregon, USA	26 May	DL
3 Jun		GP Brasil, São Bernardo do Campo 2017, Braganca Paulista 2018	8 Jul	WC
8 Jun	DL	Golden Gala, Rome, ITA	31 May	DL
10-11 Jun	WC	Fanny Blankers-Koen Games, Hengelo, NED	3 Jun	WC
13 Jun	EAP	Paavo Nurmi Games, Turku, Finland	5 Jun	WC
15 Jun	DL	ExxonMobil Bislett Games, Oslo, NOR	7 Jun	DL
18 Jun	DL	Bauhaus, Stockholm, SWE	10 Jun	DL
28 Jun	WC	Golden Spike, Ostrava, CZE	13 Jun	WC
1 Jul	DL	Meeting de Paris (Charléty), FRA	30 Jun	DL
6 Jul	DL	Athletissima, Lausanne, SUI	5 Jul	DL
9 Jul	DL	Müller Anniversary Games, London (OS)	27/28 Jul	DL
11 Jul	EAP	Spitzen Leichtathletil Luzern, SUI	9 Jul	EAP
14 Jul	WC	Meeting Madrid, ESP	23 Jun	WC
16 Jul	DL	Mohammed VI d'Athlétisme, Rabat, MAR	10 Jul	DL
21 Jul	DL	Herculis, Monaco, MON	21 Jul	DL
20 Aug	DL	Müller Grand Prix, Birmingham, GBR	18 Aug	DL
24 Aug	DL	Weltklasse, Zürich, SUI	30 Aug	DL
27 Aug	WC	ISTAF, Berlin, GER	2 Sep	WC
29 Aug	WC	Boris Hanzekovic Memorial, Zagreb, CRO	3-4 Sep	WC
29 Aug	EAP	Palio Citta della Quercia, Rovereto, ITA	23 Aug	EAP
1 Sep	DL	Memorial Van Damme, Brussels, BEL	31 Aug	DL

INDOORS

WIT – IAAF World Indoor Tour; EAA – indoor permit meetings; US USATF series in USA.

2017 date		Meeting	2018 date	
28 Jan	WIT	New Balance Indoor GP, Boston (Roxbury), USA	10 Feb	WIT/US
1 Feb	EAA	International PSD Bank, Düsseldorf, GER	6 Feb	WIT
4 Feb	WIT	BW-Bank Meeting, Karlsruhe, GER	3 Feb	WIT
10 Feb	EAA	Copernicus Cup, Torun, POL	15 Feb	WIT
11 Feb		Millrose Games, New York (Armory), USA	3 Feb	US
18 Feb	WIT	Birmingham, GBR 2017, Glasgow GBR 2018	18 Feb	WIT
24 Feb		Madrid	8 Feb	WIT
3-5 Mar	US	USA Indoor Champs. Portland/Albuquerque	16-18 Feb	US

IAAF WORLD COMBINED EVENTS CHALLENGE 2016 & 2017

2017 date	Meeting	2018 date
28/29 Apr	Multistars, Firenze, ITA	27/28 Apr
27/28 May	Hypo-Mehrkampf Meeting, Götzis, AUT	26/27 May
17/18 Jun	TNT Express Meeting, Kladno, CZE	16/17 Jun
25/25 Jun	Stadtwerke Ratingen, GER	16/17 Jun
4/5 Jul	Pan-American CE, Ottawa, CAN	3/4 Jul
16/17 Sep	Decastar, Talence, FRA	15/16 Sep

Plus US and European Championships

IAAF WORLD RACE WALKING CHALLENGE 2017 & 2018

2017 date	Meeting	2018 date
19 Feb	Oceania Championships, Adelaide, AUS	11 Feb
12 Mar	Ciudad Juárez MEX	r
19 Mar	Monterrey, MEX	24-25 Feb
19 Mar	Asian Champs, Nomi, JPN	18 Mar
1 Apr	Rio Maior, POR	7 Apr
15 Apr	Taicang, CHN	
	IAAF Race Walking Cup, Taicang CHN	5 May
13/14 May	Pan-American Race Walking Cup, Lima PER	
3 Jun	Gran Premio Cantones de La Coruña, ESP	2 Jun
24-27 Sep	Suzhou (adound Taihu), CHN	22-26 Sep

Plus European Cup Race Walking and World Championships

European Athletics Race Walking Permit Meetings 2017 & 2018

Dudince, SVK 25/24 Mar, Podébrady, CZE 8/? Apr,

IAAF HAMMER THROW CHALLENGE 2017

To be confirmed

MARATHON MAJORS 2017–2018

Tokyo 26/25 Feb, Boston 17/16 Apr, London 23/22 Apr, Berlin 24 Sep, Chicago 8/7 Oct, New York 5/4 Nov.

ASIAN GRAND PRIX 2017

Jiaxing CHN 24 Apr, Jinhau CHN 27 Apr, Taipei City TPE 30 Apr.
2018 dates and vebues to be confirmed

EUROPEAN AA CLASSIC MEETINGS 2018 (with 2017 dates of these meetings first)

Bydgoszcz POL (European Athletics Festival) 1 Jun/29 May, Montreuil-sous-Bois FRA 1/13 Jun, Andújar ESP 2/1 Jun, Marseille 3/16 Jun, Prague, CZE (Josef Odlozil Memorial) 5/4 Jun, Gothenburg SWE 10 Jun/18 Aug, Huelva ESP (Iberoamerican) 14/8 Jun, Szczecin 2017, Chorzów 2018 POL (Janusz Kusocinski Memorial) 14/8 Jun, Copenhagen DEN 19/26 Jun, Tomblaine FRA 28/27 Jun, Sollentuna 29/28 Jun, Székesfehérvár HUN (István Gyulai Memorial) 3-4/1-2 Jul, Sotteville-lès-Rouen FRA 6/17 Jul, Liège (Naimette-Xhovément) 19/18 Jul, Padova ITA 16 Jul/2 Sep, Heusden-Zolder, BEL 22/21 Jul, Karlstad SWE 26/25 Jul
Special premium: Jun 1/24 Aug Athens GRE Street Pole Vault; 2017 only: Velenje SLO 20/- Jun

USATF CHAMPIONSHIP SERIES 2017–2018

Philadelphia (Penn Relays) 28-29/28 Apr, USA v The World at Penn Relays 27-29/26-28 Apr, Des Moines (Drake Relays) 26-29/25-28 Apr, Prefontaine Classic, adidas Boost Boston Games 2-3/20 May Jun, US Championships Sacramento 23-25 Jun 2017, Des Moines 21-24 Jun 2018
Track Town USA Summer Series 2017: Stanford CAL 29 Jun, Gresham (Portland) 2 Jul, New York 6 Jul.
2018 to be confirmed

NORTH AMERICA NACAC MEETINGS 2017–2018

St. George's GRN 8/21 Apr, George Town CAY -/1 Jun, Nassau BAH -/2 Jun, Kingston, JAM (Racers GP) 10/9 Jun, Guelph CAN 14/13 Jun, Vancouver (Harry Jerome Track Classic) CAN 28/27 Jun, Hamilton (Bermuda Invitational) Jul 1/11 May
2017: Baie Mahault, Guadeloupe 13 May

MAJOR INTERNATIONAL EVENTS 2017–2021

2018

Asian Indoor Championships – Tehran, Iran (1-3 February)
IAAF World Indoor Championships – Birmingham, GBR (2-4 March)
IAAF World Half Marathon Championships – Valencia, Spain (24 March)
Commonwealth Games – Gold Coast, Australia (8-15 April)
IAAF World Race Walking Cup – Taicang, China (5-6 May)
Asian Junior Championships – Gifu, Japan (7-10 June)
European U18 Championships – Györ, Hungary (5-8 July)
IAAF World Junior Championships – Tampere, Finland (10-15 July)
World Cup (national teams - London GBR (14-15 July)
Central American & Caribbean Games – Barranquilla, Colombia (29 Jul – 3 Aug)
African Championships – Assaba, Nigeria (1-5 August)
European Championships – Berlin, Germany (7-12 August)
NACAC Senior Championships, Canada (10-12 August)
Asian Games – Jakarta, Indonesia (22-29 August)
Ibero-American Championships – Trujillo, Peru (24-26 Aug)
IAAF Continental Cup – Ostrava, Czech Republic (8-9 Sep)
Youth Olympic Games – Buenos Aires, Argentina (11-17 Oct)
South American U23 Championships – Mendoza, Argentina (26-28 Oct)
European Cross Country Championships – Tilberg, Netherlands (9 Dec)

2019

European Indoor Championships – Glasgow, GBR (1-3 March)
IAAF World Cross Country Championships – Aarhus, Denmark (30 March)
IAAF World Relays – Nassau, Bahamas (4-5 May)
Pan-American Games ¬ Lima, Peru (26 Jul – 11 Aug)
World University Games – Brasilia, Brazil
Asian Games – Hanoi, Vietnam
IAAF World Championships – Doha, Qatar (28 Sep – 6 Oct)

2020

IAAF World Indoor Championships – Nanjing, China (13-15 Mar)
IAAF World Race Walking Cup – Minsk, Belarus (2-3 May)
European U18 Championships – Rieti, Italy
Olympic Games – Tokyo, Japan (31 July – 9 August)

2021

IAAF World Championships – Eugene, USA

EUROPEAN CHAMPIONSHIPS 2018

The first European Championships were staged at the Stadio Comunale, Torino, Italy in 1934 for men only. Women's championships were held separately in 1938, but men's and women's events were combined at one venue from 1946. The championships are held at four-yearly intervals, although there was a break in that pattern when they were held in 1969 and 1971, until a biennial pattern was set in 2012. The 24th Championships will be held in Berlin, Germany on 7-12 August 2018.

Championship Records

Men

100m	9.99	Francis Obikwelu POR	2006
	(9.96dq	Dwain Chambers GBR	2002)
200m	19.85	Konstadinos Kedéris GRE	2002
400m	44.52	Iwan Thomas GBR	1998
800m	1:43.84	Olaf Beyer GDR	1978
1500m	3:35.27	Fermín Cacho ESP	1994
5000m	13:10.15	Jack Buckner GBR	1986
10000m	27:30.99	Martti Vainio FIN	1978
Mar	2:10:31	Martín Fiz ESP	1994
3000mSt	8:07.87	Mahieddine Mekhissi FRA	2010
110mh	13.02	Colin Jackson GBR (s/F)	1998
400mh	47.48	Harald Schmid FRG	1982
HJ	2.36	Andrey Silnov RUS	2006
PV	6.00	Rodion Gataullin RUS	1994
LJ	8.47	Christian Reif GER	2010
TJ	17.99	Jonathan Edwards GBR	1998
SP	22.22	Werner Günthör SUI	1986
DT	68.87	Piotr Malachowski POL	2010
HT	86.74	Yuriy Sedykh USSR	1986
JT	89.72	Steve Backley GBR	1998
Dec	8811	Daley Thompson GBR	1986
4x100m	37.79	France	1990
4x400m	2:58.22	GBR	1990
20 kmW	1:18:37	Franc. J. Fernández ESP	2002
50 kmW	3:32:33	Yohann Diniz FRA	2014

Women

100m	10.73	Christine Arron FRA	1998
200m	21.71	Heike Drechsler GDR	1986
400m	48.16	Marita Koch GDR	1982
800m	1:55.41	Olga Minayeva USSR	1982
1500m	3:56.91	Tatyana Tomashova RUS	2006
3000m	8:30.28	Svetlana Ulmasova URS	1982
5000m	14:52.20	Alemitu Bekele TUR	2010
10000m	14:54.44	Elvan Abeylegesse TUR	2010
Mar	2:26:05	Maria Guida ITA	2002
3000mSt	9:17.57	Yuliya Zarudneva RUS	2010
100mh	12.38	Yordanka Donkova BUL	1986
400mh	52.92	Natalya Antyukh RUS	2010
HJ	2.03	Tia Hellebaut BEL	2006
	2.03	Venelina Veneva BUL	2006
	2.03	Blanka Vlasic CRO	2010
PV	4.81	Ekateríni Stefanídi GRE	2016
LJ	7.30	Heike Drechsler GDR	1990
TJ	15.15	Tatyana Lebedeva RUS	2006
SP	21.69	Viktoriya Pavlysh UKR	1998
DT	71.36	Diane Sachse GDR	1986
HT	78.76	Anita Wlodarczyk POL	2014
JT	67.47	Miréla Manjani GRE	2002
old spec	77.44	Fatima Whitbread GBR	q1986
Hep	6823	Jessica Ennis GBR	2010
4x100m	41.68	GDR	1990
4x400m	3:16.87	GDR	1986
20kmW	1:26:42	Olimpiada Ivanova RUS	2002
50kmW		*added for 2018*	

Four Successive Titles

Men

4 Janis Lusis USSR JT 1962-66-69-71
4 Steve Backley GBR JT 1990-94-98-2002
4 Colin Jackson GBR 110mh 1990-94-98-2002

Women

4 Nadezhda Chizhova USSR SP 1966-69-71-74
4 Heike Drechsler GDR/GER 1986-90-94-98
4 Sandra Perkovic CRO DT 2010-12-14-16

Most Gold Medals at all events

Men: 5 Harald Schmid FRG, Roger Black GBR

Women: 6 Marita Koch GDR, 5 Fanny Blankers-Koen NED, Irena Szewinska POL, Marlies Göhr GDR, Heike Drechsler GDR/GER, Grit Breuer GDR/GER

Most Medals

Men: 8 Christophe Lemaitre FRA 4/2/2 2010-14, 6 Harald Schmid FRG 1978-86, Pietro Mennea ITA 1971-4, Roger Black GBR 1986-94, Linford Christie GBR 1986-94, Mo Farah GBR 2006-14

Women: 10 Irena Szewinska POL 1966-78, 8 Fanny Blankers-Koen NED 1938-50, Renate Stecher GDR 1969-74; 7 Marlies Göhr GDR 1978-86, Myriam Soumaré FRA 2010-14; 6 Yevgeniya Sechenova USSR 1946-50, Marita Koch GDR 1978-86, Heike Drechsler GDR/GER 1986-98, Irina Privalova RUS 1994-8, Grit Breuer GDR/GER 1990-2002

Medals By Nation 2014

Nation	*Men*			*Women*			*Total*
	G	*S*	*B*	*G*	*S*	*B*	
GBR	8	3	3	4	2	3	23
FRA	5	3	4	4	5	2	23
RUS	1	3	8	2	3	5	22
POL	1	5	3	1	-	2	12
GER	2	1	-	2	-	3	8
UKR	1	1	1	1	4	-	8

Medals By Nation 2016

GBR	3	1	5	2	2	3	16
GER	2	0	3	3	4	4	16
POL	4	4	1	2	1	0	12
FRA	3	0	3	0	4	0	10
NED	1	0	2	3	1	0	7
ESP	2	3	1	1	0	0	7

Timetable and Qualifying Standards

QUALIFYING standards must be achieved in bona fide competition (indoors or outdoors) between 1 January 2017 to 30 July 2018. Each country can enter up to three athletes per event provided all of them have achieved the qualifying standard or one per event where the standard has not been achieved (at the discretion of the Technical Delegates). 16 natauional teams are permitted for each relay event. But additonally the current reigning European outdoor champions will be invited to oarticipate as a Wildcard – and this could allow four athletes form a member federation to compete in an event, The first three in the European Cup 10,000m in 2017 and 2018 automatically qualify for entry. Marathon Cups are incorporated; minimum of three and maximum of six per team. Six days of competition are scheduled. Dates of successive rounds (August) are shown for each event with the qualifying standards.

Event	*Days*	*Qual. standards*
Men		
100m	6-7-7	10.35
200m	8-8-9	20.90
400m	7-8-10	46.70
800m	9-10-11	1:47.60
1500m	8-10	3:40.00
5000m	11	13:42.00
10,000m	7	28:55.00
Mar	12	none
3000mSt	7-9	8:40.00
110mh	9-10-10	13.85
400mh	6-7-9	50.70
HJ	9-11	2.26
PV	10-12	5.55
LJ	6-8	7.95
TJ	10-12	16.60
SP	6-7	19.90
DT	7-8	63.50
HT	6-7	74.00
JT	8-9	80.00
Dec	7/8	7850
4x100m	12-12	none
4x400m	10-11	none
20 kmW	11	1:25:00
50 kmW	7	4:108:00
Women		
100m	6-7-7	11.50
200m	10-10-11	23.50
400m	8-9-11	53.40
800m	7-8-10	2:02.50
1500m	10-12	4:12.00
5000m	12	15:40.00
10,000m	8	33:20.00
Mar	12	none
3000mSt	10-12	9:55.00
100mh	8-9-9	13.25
400mh	7-8-10	57.70
HJ	8-10	1.90
PV	7-9	4.45
LJ	9-11	6.60
TJ	8-10	13.90
SP	7-8	16.50
DT	9-11	56.00
HT	10-12	69.00
JT	9-10	59.00
Hep	9/10	5900
4x100m	12-12	none
4x400m	10-11	none
20kmW	11	1:37:00
50kW	7	4:50:00

WORLD JUNIOR CHAMPIONSHIPS

The World Junior Championships have been held bienially from 1988 when they were staged in Athens, Greece. The 17th edition of the meeting will be held in Tampere, Finland on 10-15 July 2018.

Championship Records after 2016

Men

100m	10.05	Adam Gemili GBR	2012
200m	20.17	Michael Norman USA	2016
400m	44.66	Hamdam Al-Bishi KSA	2000
800m	1:43.79	Nijel Amos BOT	2012
1500m	3:35.53	Abdelati Iguider MAR	2004
5000m	13:08.57	Abreham Cherkos ETH	2008
10000m	27:25.23	Rodgers Kwemoi KEN	2016
3000mSt	8:06.10	Conseslus Kiprono KEN	2012
110mh 99cm	12.99	Wilhem Belocian FRA	2014
400mh	48.51	Kerron Clement USA	2004
HJ	2.37	Dragutin Topic YUG	1990
	2.37	Steve Smith GBR	1992
PV	5.71	Germán Chiaraviglio ARG	2006
LJ	8.20	James Stallworth USA q	1990
TJ	17.13	Lázaro Martínez CUB	2014
SP 6kg	22.30	Andrei Toader ROU	2016
DT 1.75kg	67.32	Margus Hunt EST	2006
HT 6kg	85.97	Ashraf Amjad El-Seify QAT	2012
JT	86.48	Neeraj Chopra IND	2016
Dec jnr	8162	Niklas Kaur GER	2016
4x100m	38.66	USA	2004
4x400m	3:01.09	USA	2004
10kmW	39:27.19	Daisuke Matsunaga JPN	2014

Women

100m	11.07	Candace Hill USA	2016
200m	22.53	Anthonique Strachan BAH	2012
400m	50.50	Ashley Spencer USA	2012
800m	2:00.06	Elena Mirela Lavric ROU	2008
1500m	4:04.96	Faith Kipyegon KEN	2012
3000m	8:41.76	Beyenu Degefu ETH	2016
5000m	15:08.06	Genzebe Dibaba ETH	2010
3000mSt	9:25.15	Celliphine Chespol KEN	2016
100mh	12.85	Elvira German BLR	2016
400mh	54.70	Lashinda Demus USA	2002
HJ	2.00	Galina Astafei ROM	1988
PV	4.55	Angelica Moser SUI	2016
LJ	6.82	Fiona May GBR	1988
TJ	14.62	Tereza Marinova BUL	1996
SP	18.76	Cheng Xiaoyan CHN	1994
DT	68.24	Ilke Wyludda GDR	1988
HT	70.62	Alexandra Tavernier FRA	2012
JT	63.01	Vira Rebryk UKR	2008
Hep	6470	Carolina Klüft SWE	2002
4x100m	43.40	Jamaica	2002
4x400m	3:27.60	USA	2004
10kmW	42:47.25	Anezka Drahotová CZE	2014

REFERENCE BOOKS 2017-18

My Life in Athletics by Mel Watman, 510 pages, 234 x 155mm. This is a marvellous book, in which Mel weaves what is a personalised history of athletics from the 1950s with his own story and reminiscences. The text includes much of his original writing from *Athletics Weekly, Athletics Today and Athletics International*. To order the book, write to Mel at 13 Garden Court, Stanmore HA7 4TE, UKwith your name and postal address. Cost, inclusive of postage, is £15 for customers in the UK, £20 or 20 euros to addresses in the rest of Europe, £20 or $25 by airmail to the rest of the world. Payment in cash or by cheque (on a UK bank) payable to M Watman or direct to his personal bank account (details on application). Sorry, no credit cards or PayPal.

NURMI – Athletics in the 19th Century, A Statistical Review Volume II 1885-1888 by Ari Törmä. A4 112 pages. This is the author's second book (part I covered 1881-84) that follows the great works of Hubert Hamacher in covering the years 1881-1900. As with the first Part he revises HH's lists and expands them. There were a variety of rules and specifications in that period and Ari brings together marks at different weights and distances to provide lists for the modern range of events. While showing the original mark, he converts performances so that for instance his 1500m lists contain mainly adjusted times for 1 mile marks, but also times in handicap races adjusted for the distance allowed, so converting times from about 1480m to 1610m in the lists. His hammer list contains marks with weights from 6kg to 11kg. Marks by both professional and amateurs are included in the lists for each year. See www.aritorma.net.

A Difference in Times by David Thurlow. A5 246 pages. The author interviewed more than forty former stars of British athletics, most of them Olympians, for "Track Stats" and these are now collected in this profusely illustrated, book. £9.99 plus postage. To order a copy, search for "A Difference In Times" on the lulu.com web-site or follow the link from the NUTS web-site at www.nuts.org.uk

Latvijas Vieflatletikas Vesture. Andris Stagis has written two handsome books (in a trilogy) detailing, in most comprehensive fashion. the history of Latvian athletics. These are 240x160m hardbacks and well illustrated with text in Latvian. Andris has done a wonderful job and can be contacted at andris.stagis@athletics.lv.

Part 1 1897-1944 (350 pages) covers the period from 1898 to 1917 when Latvia was part of Tsarist Russia, from 1918 to 1940 when it was independent, and then up to 1944 when it was incorporated in the USSR. The top athlete of this period was walker Janis Dalins.

Part 2 1944-1991 is a weighty tome of 696 pages, dealing with the time when Latvia was a republic within the USSR, contributing considerably to powerful Soviet success in international athletics. Latvia produced four Olympic champions in this era, all javelin throwers: Inesa Jaunzene, Elvira Ozolina, Janis Lusis and Dainis Kula.

The format in each book is to have a chapter reviewing the happenings of each year, all with a table of Latvian champions. Then follows complete details of all Latvian athletes in international championships and those to have won USSR titles plus details of all appearances in internationals. There are then Latvian progressive records for all events with accompanying text. The most prolific record-setter at any event is Janis Bojars who set 27 records at the shot from 18.80 in 1978 to 21.74 in 1984.

ANNUALS

L'Athlétisme Africain/African Athletics 2017. A5, 152 pages. By Yves Pinaud. Published by Éditions Polymédias (with Wayde van Niekerk on the cover). The 36th edition in this splendid series has 100 deep men's and women's lists for Africa for 2016, with all-time lists and official continental records. 25 euro, £20 or US $30 including postage from La Mémoire du Sport, 166 rue de Decize, 03000 Moulins, France. (Also available: booklist with very extensive list of athletics books and magazines for sale: librairie.polymedias@orange.fr

Asian Athletics 2016 Rankings. A5 100 pages. This is the 28th successive edition of Heinrich Hubbeling's great work in chronicling Asian athletics. This booklet contains top 30 lists for 2016 for athletes from Asian nations, with continuation lists for countries other than China and Japan (up to 4 best per country), national records set in 2016, and full lists of Asian records. Euro 20/US $22 in cash or by International Money Order from the author, Haaksbergener Str 25, 48691 Vreden, Germany. email hhubbeling@t-online.de. Copies also available for 1998, 2004-06, 2008-09, 2011-12 and 2014-15 and Asian all-time rankings as at 31.12.2000 at €15/US $17 each.

Athlérama 2016. A5 832pp. The latest edition of the French Annual, edited by Patricia Doilin with a strong team of compilers, is again a superb reference book and is 128 pages larger than the 2015 Annual. This is packed with information on French athletics – records, profiles of 85 top athletes, results, deep year lists for 2016 for all age groups plus all-time lists and indexes. Maintaining the sequence, there are French top ten lists and reviews for 1916 (limited by WW I) and 1966. Profiled athlete of the year is Kevin Mayer. 28 euros from the FFA, 33 avenue Pierre de Coubertin, 7540 Paris Cedex 13, France. email Patricia.Doilin@athle.org. See www.athle.fr.

British Athletics 2018. A5 438 pages. The 60th NUTS Annual, edited by Tony Miller, Rob Whittingham, and Peter Matthews. All the usual features are included: deep year lists in all age groups for 2017, all-time lists, records, major results, merit rankings, obituaries and index. Available from http://www.lulu.com/content/paperback-book/british-athletics-2018/22478482 at £15 plus postage (£2.99 in UK).

Combined Events Annual 2017 by Hans van Kuijen. The 25th edition of this splendid annual is c.200 pages containing outdoor and indoor all-time lists, 2017 years lists, national records, statistical profiles of 50 best women and women etc. Cost 30 EUR or £30 or $45 US if ordered before December 10 (after that €38, £38 or $55). Payments can be made to BIC-code: ABNANL2A, IBAN code: NL79ABNA0523127898, For more details contact Hans at j.kuijen4@upcmail.nl. He also has back numbers for each year 2005-16 available and his 1912-2012 100 years Olympic decathlon (€15)

Friidrott 2017. 170 x 240mm 487p Hardback. This, the 57th edition, features detailed reviews and results of World, Nordic and Swedish meetings and profiles of athletes of the year with top 50 world 2017 and all-time lists, top 25 Nordic and Swedish lists and records. It is most attractively produced with 373 photos. This book and others including "World's Greatest in Athletics" (now with 25% discount) and "Swedish Athletics Championships 1896–2005" are available from Jonas Hedman, Springarvägen 14, 142 61 Trånsgund, Sweden.
Friidrott 2017 is available for 495 Swedish crowns (52 EUR) plus postage – the same price as in 2015-16.
E-mail Jonas.hedman@textograf.com. website: www.textograf.com

Anuario Atlético Español 2016-2017. This amazing, massive work is available to download for free from the Spanish Federation website – http://www.rfea.es/revista/libros/rfea_rankingAL.htm. The heart of this 1536-page (30 MB) publication are the very deep Spanish lists for all ages for 2017 (and the end of 2016). There are also 300 pages of results, lists of Spanish records, deep all-time lists, and a large historical section with full lists of Spanish champions, biographies of Spanish athletes and a special 34-page section on their greatest ever athlete – Ruth Beitia.

Israel Athletics Annual 2017/18. 240 x 170mm, 58pp, illustrated. By David Eiger and Arit Cooks for the Israeli Athletic Association. Records, championship results, 2017 top 20s and all-time lists, with profiles of leading Israeli athletes. 8 euro or US $9 from David Eiger, 10 Ezra Hozsofer Str, Herzliya 46 371, Israel. Past editions from 1986 onwards are also available.

Latvijas Vieglatletikas Gadagramata 2018. A5 336 pp. Once again this is an exemplary example of a national annual with its most comprehensive coverage of Latvian athletics for 2017, including a chronology of the year, records, results, athlete profiles and year and all-time lists, compiled by ATFS member Andris Stagis. From the Latvian Athletic Association, Augsiela 1, Riga LV-1009, Latvia. email: lvs@lat-athletics.lv

Sverige Bästa 2016. A5 294 pages. Edited by Jonas Hedman. Detailed 2016 Swedish lists for seniors (100 deep), and younger age groups (20 deep). $20 (plus postage and shipping) from the Swedish Athletic Association: Svenska Friidrottsförbundet, Heliosgatan 3, 120 30 Stockholm, Sweden. Email: info@friidrott.se

Statistika 2017. A5 584 pp. The traditional Ukrainian Athletics annual compiled by Ivan Kachkivskyi and Serhiy Baranov has deep national lists in all age categories, with records and athlete profiles.

National Indoor Competitions. A5 45 pp. Compiled by Serhiy Baranov and Ivan Kachkivskyi. Handbook with statistics information about Ukrainian Indoor competitions since 2005: chronology, part-icipation, events, medals by regions, etc.
For the books contact: Ivan Kachkivskyi (ivan.work.mail@gmail.com). Also available on the web: http://uaf.org.ua/statistics/books/statistics2017.html and http://uaf.org.ua/statistics/books/national_indoor_competitions_2018.html

2016 USA Track & Field FAST Annual. General editor Tom Casacky. This is a heavyweight production, expanded again this year to 694 A5 pages. The 39th FAST Annual (in its 23rd year of collaboration with USA Track and Field), contains all its usual features: records, 50-70 deep US lists for 2016 and all-time, with 15-deep junior and college all-time lists. The final massive index section includes annual progressions and championships details for top American and resident foreign athletes. $25 post paid in the USA or $45 or 40 Euros airmail from Tom Casacky, PO Box 4288, Napa, CA 94558, USA. Payment is easiest by PayPal (to tom@interis.com).

Yleisurheilu 2017. A5 672pp. The Finnish Yearbook, published by Suomen Urheilulitto (Finnish Athletics) and compiled by Juhani and Mirko Jalava, contains every conceivable statistic for Finnish athletics (with results and deep year lists) in 2017 and also world indoor, outdoor and junior lists for the year. 20 euros plus 14 euros for postage and packaging. Orders by e-mail to juhani@tilastopaja.fi.

National Athletics Records for all countries in the world by Winfried Kramer with Heinrich Hubbeling, Yves Pinaud and Steffen Stübe. This latest edition is dedicated to Luigi Mengoni, who started the series of these valuable publications in 1963. Regrettably the ATFS has decided not to support the publication and Winfried has said that this will be the last, The contents are in alphabetic order of counries – not only all nations affiliated to the IAAF but also constituent parts of the United Kingdom and territories of major nations from Åland to Wallis and Futuna. for all of whom records are listed for all events. The book can be ordered via Paypal (kramer@saar.de) or you by cash to Winfried Kramer at Kohlrodweg 12, 66539 Neunkirchen-Kohlhof, GERMANY. Price is 30 Euros, incl. postage. Winfried also has various previous editions for sale at 10 Euroros each.

Scottish Athletics Record Book. By Arnold Black. 112 pages. Available as a pdf from the Scottish Athletics website. Link from scottishathletics.org.uk (go to the Record-breakers! page for the link). Progressive records are listed for men and women indoors and out with Scottish national records, native records and all-comers records with indexes of Scottish and non-Scottish athletes.

Statistical Bulletins

TRACK STATS. The NUTS quarterly journal edited by Bob Phillips comes with membership of the NUTS. £25 inc. postage to UK addresses, £30 to Europe, £35 to the rest of the world. Contact Liz Sissons at lizsissons9@gmail.com

February 2017 included an assessment of Mo Farah by Andy Milroy, an inquiry by editor Bob Phillips into whose idea was it to standardise the marathon distance as 26 miles and 385 yards, Steve Backley's career record (1985-2004) by Thomas S Hurst which indicates that he threw over 80m in 184 meetings (78 of them over 85m), a profile of Roy Beckett who beat Chris Chataway in a thrilling AAA 3 miles in 1951, and a review of an outstanding biography of Otto Peltzer.

May 2017 included a look back at the British showing at the 1924 Olympics, a profile of the late Buddy Edelen, the world record breaking American marathoner, Jacques Carmelli's revelation of a Chinese sprinter who tied the world best for 50 yards in Hawaii in 1908, Thomas Hurst's complete career record (1972-2000) for Judy Oakes and an appreciation by Peter Lovesey of NUTS stalwart Ian R Smith.

September 2017: Neil Shuttleworth examines the career of Harold Wilson (the first man, in 1908, to break 4 min for 1500m) and reveals that he was not killed in action in France in 1916 as previously supposed but in fact died in South Africa in 1932. Alan Lindop provides a complete career record of Britain's (American-born and raised) promising decathlete Tim Duckworth; the editor has listed Derek Ibbotson's 55 races during his world record year of 1957; and Jacques Carmelli describes the formative years of IAAF world records, including a re-discovered half hour mark of 9957m by Paavo Nurmi in 1924 (during his 30:06.2 10,000m), increasing the Finn's tally of world records, indoors and out, to 35.

November 2017: A compilation of Sally Gunnell's 106 races at 400m hurdles 1987-97; a list of 40 Olympians who died during the First World; how Parry O'Brien transformed shot putting; and the career record of Alberto Juantorena.

The **Spanish group, the AEEA** produces magnificent publications. Membership (four bulletins per year) is 55 euros per year (€61 outside Europe) from AEEA secretary Ignacio Mansilla, C/Encinar del Rey, 18 - 28450 Collado Mediano, Madrid, Spain. email: imansilla@rfea.es

Their **Bulletin No. 99** was a massive 418 pages. The biggest feature was a compilation by Eduardo Antonio Sánchez of top tens for 60 countries for each men's and women's event, ranked by the average of their marks. In all 116 nations managed to have at least one event in which they make the top 60. Top nations overall are: 1. USA, 2. GER, 3. RUS, 4, GBR, 5, FRA, 6. UKR, 7. POl, 8. AUS, 9, CHN, 10, ITA. Completing the list is Lesotho, who make the lists in just one event, men's 10,000m (in 60th place!). Then there is a compilation by Juan Maria Iriondo of the 763 men's 10,000m marks under 28 minutes, a survey by José María García of the longevity of national records for each event for Spain and for the rest of the world, and finally a massive listing of legal-wind 100m marks to 10.16 for each athlete (with the most 155 by Asafa Powell).

Bulletin No. 100 was a special 30th anniversary one. 400 A5 pages. The history of the AEEA is detailed with tributes from leading statisticians worldwide. Complete details are given of members and their annual gatherings and the contents are listed for each of the Bulletins from the first in June 1987 followed by the further 20 books that they have produced in association with the Spanish Federation (RFEA). This introduction is followed by complete career details of Ruth Beitia, and then the statistical profiles of leading Spanish athletes from the days before Spain became a leading athletics nation – 22 men mostly from the 1940s and 1950s and 25 women mostly from the 1960s and 1970s. Miguel Villaseñor provides an index of all Spanish athletes to have won medals at international championships. The final major section is a 120-page study of athletics in the Valencia region 1960-2016.

The **DGLD** – the **German** statistical group, Deutsche Gesellschaft für Leichtathletik-Dokumentation produces three annual bulletins plus an annual German lists book. The annual subscription is 55 euro per year. Contact Manfred Holzhausen, Bergheimer Str.33, 41515 Grevenbroich, Germany; manfred.holzhausen@gmx.de. Website: www.ladgld.de

Bulletin No. 77 contained 188 A5 pages with its usual features of athlete profiles (including most notably in this issue, Siegfried Herrmann) and a wide variety of articles with the major work being Part 3 of the survey of German international athletes with an alphabetic listing of women giving all their performances in internationals 1951-90.

Bulletin No. 78 A5 178pp. Amongst the usual profiles, was one for Armin Hary (for his 80th birthday); this included all his 100m races at 10.6 or better. There were also parts 4-5 of the survey of German international athletes (FRG & GDR) 1951-90 with part 6 that detailed the 599 men and 96 women internationals 1896-1942.

Bulletin No. 79 A5 168 pages including continuation of the surveys of German international athletes and an index of all German (DLV and DVfl) indoor champions from 1954 to 2017.

Deutsche Bestenliste 2016. A5 216 pages containing German lists for 2016 with deep lists of performances together with performers up to 100 per standard event. There are separate indoor lists.

Hammer Throw Stats History and News Bulletin No. 18. By Zdenek Procházka. pdf of 130 pages. The latest in this series features results and deep men's world hammer lists for 2016 for seniors (1030 men from 82 countries over 55m and 1039 performances over 68.41), juniors, youths and masters, and analysis including annual progression from 1960, plus national records, chronology of the 925 70m throwers (from 1960), and the all-time 'Top 2000' all hammer throwers over 64.90. Contact Zdenek at atlet2003@volny,cz. He expects to publish three bulletins this year, price 20 euro or $30.

IAAF Handbooks

Details of all IAAF publications are available on their website www.iaaf.org. The following can be downloaded from there.

The **IAAF World Championships London 2017 Statistics Handbook**. A5 810pp. The latest in the marvellous series edited by Mark Butler for the IAAF. The style follows that of previous edition including complete results of all World Championships.

IAAF World Cross Country Championships Kampala 2017 Facts & Figures. 12 pages

IAAF/BTC World Relays Nassau 2017 Facts & Figures. 36 pages.

Some Recent Marriages

Female	*Male*
Aleksandra Duliba BLR	Vitaliy Shafar UKR
Dovile Dzindzaletaite LTU	Richard Kilty GBR
Alina Kastrova BLR	Yuriy Shayunov BLR
Sarah Lahti SWE	Jesper van der Wielen NED
Lucia Slanícková SVK	Jakub Vadlejch CZE
Shevon Stoddart JAM	Jamie Nieto USA
Anastasiya Svechnikova UZB	Igor Zaytsev UZB
Irina Yakoltsevich BLR	Vitaliy Zhuk BLR

Further Recent Women's Name Changes

Original	*Married name*
Dami Bunch USA	Hill
Taylor Ellis-Watson	Washington
Halyna Obleshchuk UKR	Turchyn
Anastasiya Pilipenko KAZ	Vinogradova
Annie Rhodes USA	Johnigan
Mariya Shumilova RUS	Gromysheva
Lexi Weeks USA	Jacobus
Tori Weeks USA	Hoggard

OBITUARY 2017

See ATHLETICS 2017 for obituaries from early 2017: Horst Astroth, Don Campbell, Anne-Marie Colchen, Angela Cressi, Pamela Davies, Graham Everett, Roberto Galli, Ted Haggis, Siegfried Herrmann, Miroslav Horcic, Derek Ibbotson, Jirí Lansky, Jean-Paul Martin-du-Gard, Philip Morgan, Frank Murphy, Nadezhda Olizarenko, Jean Poczobut, Ilie Popa, Allan Steinfeld, István Tatár, Zoran Trifunovic, Mike Turner (d. 7 January), Ed Whitlock, Alice Whitty.

Fesseha ABEBE (Ethiopia) (b. 1964) in October. He won the IAAF World Junior CC in 1983 and also ran in the senior race in 1984-5 and 1991. He won the Cinque Mullini CC race in 1985.

Ingrid Margareta 'Pyret' **ALMQVIST** (Sweden) (b. 10 Oct 1927 Göteborg) on 9 November in Gothenburg. She competed at javelin at the Olympic Games of 1948 (10th), 1956 (5th) and 1960 (dnq 14) and at the European Championships of 1950 (8th), 1954 (10th) and 1958 (9th). She set 15 ratified Swedish records from 39.24 in 1947 to 52.32 in 1964 and won 15 Swedish titles: 1947, 1949-52, 1954-8 and 1960-4; 33 internationals. She also had 11 internationals for Sweden at handball 1951-9.

Vasilena Gerginova **AMZINA** (Bulgaria) (b. 29 Jun 1942) on 19 December. She was the European Indoor bronze medallist at 1500m in 1972, when she also was a semi-finalist at 1500m (and heat) 800m at the Olympic Games. At European Champs she ran at 1500m 1969 (heats) and 10th in 1971 (also heats 800m). She set Bulgarian records at 800m 2:05.2 & 2:04.8 (1971) and 1:59.9 (1972) and 1500m 4:12.59 & 4:09.12 (1972).

Márta ANTAL-RUDAS (Hungary) (b. 14 Feb 1937 Debrecen) on 4 June in Budapest. The Olympic javelin silver medallist of 1964, she was also 9th in 1960 and 6th in 1968, and at European Championships was 5th in 1962, 6th in 1966 and 8th 1971, 2nd European Cup 1965. She set eight Hungarian records from 52.79 (1961) to 58.36 (1965). HUN champion 1960-2 and 1964-5, 33 Internationals 1957-71.

Annual progression (position on world list): 1955- 36.54, 1956- 43.65 (72), 1957- 46.84 (43), 1958- 51.25 (22), 1959- 50.84 (20), 1960- 52.58 (15), 1961- 52.79 (12), 1962- 52.81 (14), 1963- 52.63 (14), 1964- 58.27 (4), 1965- 58.36 (3), 1966- 57.72 (5), 1967- 52.40 (37), 1968- 56.56 (10), 1969- 56.04 (10), 1970- 55.06 (17), 1971- 56.86 (20), 1972- 58.36 (29).

Lothar BECKERT (Germany) (b. 26 Mar 1931 St. Michaelis) on 28 April in Berlin. At the marathon he was 19th in 1956 and 56th in 1960 at the Olympic Games, 5th at the 1958 Europeans and GDR champion in 1958. He set a GDR record with 2:21:44.8 and a 10,000m pb of 30:47.0 in 1956.

Maud **Wivianne BERGH** (later **FREIVALD)** (Sweden) (b. 14 Feb 1939 Göteborg) on 19 June in Trollhättan. At the discus she was 12th at the 1960 Olympic Games; Swedish champion 1960, 1962-4 and 1967-8, Nordic 1963. 24 internationals. She set nine Swedish records from 44.40 (1959) to 52.65 (1964) that lasted for 26 years. Pb SP 12.42 (1964).

Her father Gunnar Bergh was 7th in the discus at the 1936 Olympic Games and Swedish champion at shot 1935-42, discus 1937-41 and 1943-4. Pbs: SP 15.84 (1936), DT 51.72 (1936).

Margaret **'Gretel' BERGMANN** (-LAMBERT) (Germany) (b. 12 Apr 1914 Laupheim) on 25 July in New York at the age of 103. Being Jewish, she was notoriously not allowed to compete at the 1936 Olympic Games in Berlin despite having equalled the German high jump record with 1.60 on 27 June 1936. She had won the WAAA title in Britain with 1.55 in 1934. She lived in the USA from 1937 and won US titles at HJ and SP in 1937 and HJ in 1938. She married Bruno Lambert, a Jewish long jumper in 1938.

Luigi BERTOCCHI (Italy) (b. 10 Jun 1965 Bergamo) on 17 November.. He had pbs for 60mh 7.80 (1987) and 110mh 13.69 (1991), and had 23 internationals, taking part at the World Championships 1987, World Indoors 1985 & 1987, European Indoors 1985-7 and at three Mediterranean Games (best 4th in 1991). He was national champion at 60mh indoors in 1986 & 1987.

Horst BEYER (FRG/Germany) (b. 5 Jan 1940 Neumünster) on 9 December in Hamburg. At the decathlon he had a pb of 7895 points (current tables) in 1972. He was 6th at the Olympic Games in 1964 and dnf in 1972, and won the European bronze medal in 1966, missing the 1969 Championships (due to the FRG boycott). FRG champion in 1969 and 1972 after 2nd in 1964-6 and 1969. 13 internationals 1963-72, pbs: 100m 10.9 (1964), 400m 49.2 (1965), 1500m 4:17.3 (1964), 110mh 14.6 (1963), HJ 2.01 (1964), PV 4.40 (1969), LJ 7.29 (1972), SP 15.38 (1968), 15.44i; DT 49.42 (1972), JT 60.82 (1971).

Martin Broomall **BILES** (USA) (b. 30 Mar 1919 San Diego) on 25 August in Houston. A member of the San Francisco Athletic Club, he was 6th at the 1948 Olympic Games for the javelin, having been NCAA champion in 1940-41 for the University of California and AAU champion 1943-44 (2nd 1941-42 and 1947-49). Pb 70.10 (1949). After the

War he continued his studies to earn a PhD in Nuclear Engineering at North Carolina State University. He left the Air Force with the rank of Lieutenant Colonel and worked for the Atomic Energy Commission until retirement in 1977 with the title of Director of Operational Safety. In this capacity he also served as Scientific Attaché with the US Embassies in Brussels and Paris.

Regina BRANNER (later EGGER) (Austria) (b. 5 Sep 1931 Rankweil) on 21 February in Rankweil. She was 7th in the shot at the 1956 Olympic Games, 11th at the 1954 Europeans and Austrian champion 1954-6, setting seven national records from 13.50 (1954) to 14.60 (1956 at the Olympics).

Birgit Margareta **BRINSLID** (Sweden) (b. 6 Dec 1945 Örnsköldsvik) on 7 December. She was 14th at 3000m at the 1982 Europeans and 69th in the 1985 World Cup marathon in 17 internationals. Swedish champion 3000m 1980, 10000m 1986, Half Mar 1990-91. Pbs: 1500m: 4:20.23 (1981), 3000m 9:05.71 (1981), 5000m 16:29.91 (1980), 10000m 33:38.01 (1987), HMar 72:03 (1986), Mar: 2:34:49 (1991)

Kathleeen A. '**Kathy**' **BRYANT/HADLER** (USA) (b. 25 Jul 1962 Columbus, Ohio) on 8 December in Columbus. She won the NCAA 5000m in 1982 for the University of Tennessee and was 42nd running on the winning US team at the 1983 World Cross. Pbs: 3000m 9:11.17 (1982), 5000m 15:37.73 (1982), 10000m 33:45.90 (1989).

James Stanley '**Jim**' **BUSH** (USA) (b. 15 Sep 1926 Cleveland, Ohio) in Culver City, California on 10 July. He went to the University of California before beginning a hugely successful coaching career in 1952. He then coached at Occidental College from 1962 and at UCLA 1965-84. He revived UCLA's record against their perennial rivals at USC (Trojans) so that his career record against them was 13-6 and his teams won five NCAA titles. He later worked at USC 1991-4.

Bernard '**Bernie**' **CASEY** (USA) (b. 8 June 1939 Wyco, West Virginia) on 19 September in Los Angeles. He was 4th in the NCAA 110m hurdles for Bowling Green State in 1960, when he had a best of 14.0 for 120yh. He then spent six seasons with the San Francisco 49ers and two with the Los Angeles Rams as a wide receiver at American Football, before a successful career as an actor. In 1983 he became the first black actor to play Felix Leiter of the CIA in the James Bond film series.

Milena CELESNIK (Slovenia) (b. 10 Aug 1933 Ljubljana) on 4 May in Ljubljana. She had 18 internationals for Yugoslavia at discus, was Yugoslav champion in 1957 and 1960-4 and was 22nd at the 1960 Olympic Games. Pb DT 49.46 (1960).

Nancy CONZ (USA) (b. 5 Jan 1957 Southampton) on 8 February in Southampton, Massachusetts. After 2nd in the Avon Marathon in London 1980 and winning the Avon Marathon in Ottawa in 1981, she was the women's winner at the 1982 Chicago marathon in her pb of 2:33:23. Other pbs: 5000m 16:13.8 (1986), 10000m 33:15.6mx (1981), 1Hr 17,488m (US rec 1981), 25k road 68:45 (US record 1982). Married Paul Conz in 1979.

Katalin CSÓKE (Hungary) (b. 1 Jul 1957 Fegyvernek) on 10 August. At discus she was 2nd in the European Juniors in 1975 and competed at the Olympic Games in 1980, setting a Hungarian record that year with 63.20. 30 internationals 1977-97, HUN champion 1979 and 1992-7. Pb SP 13.94 (1977).

Elizabeth Alyse '**Betty**' **CUTHBERT** (Australia) (b. 20 Apr 1938 Merrylands, Sydney) on 6 August in Mandurah, Western Australia. At the age of 18 she was the heroine of the Melbourne Olympics in 1956, when she won three gold medals. After her individual victories at 100m and 200m she helped the Australian team to two world records in the 4x100m relay. In all she was responsible for 18 world records, from her first, 23.2 for 200m in September 1956, to the 52.01 that she ran to win a fourth Olympic gold medal, at 400m in 1964.

In between her Olympic wins she had met with lesser success. At the Commonwealth Games she had been overshadowed by team-mate Marlene Mathews in 1958, when she was 4th at 100y and 2nd at 220y with silver also in the relay, and in 1962 although she took a relay gold, she was 5th at 220y and went out in the semis at 100y. She was injured at the 1960 Olympics when eliminated in the quarter-finals of the 100m and retired briefly after that. Australian champion 220y 1956 and 1960, 440y 1963. Other bests: 60m 7.2 (1960), 100y 10.4 (1958), 100m 11.4 and 11.2w (1956), 200m 23.55 auto (1956); 220y 23.2 (1960). It was revealed in 1979 that she was fighting multiple sclerosis.

Christa CZEKAY (née **EISLER**, later DRUST) (Germany) (b. 20 Mar 1944 Waldenburg) on 14 June in Wolfsburg. She ran the first leg on the FRG team that set a world record of 3:33.9 for 4x400m in 1969. That was the second of three national 4x400m records, going on to 3:32.7 for the bronze medal at the 1969 Europeans. She also ran on the national record 6:27.6 for 3x800m in 1971. At European Indoors, she won gold at 4x1 lap in 1968 and silver at 4x400m in 1971, and was 2nd in the European Cup in 1970. 11 internationals 1967-71, and German champion at indoor 200m in 1968. Pbs: 100m 11.7 (1971), 200m 23.7 (1969), 400m 53.9 (1969), 80mh 11.5 (1967), LJ 5.66 (1963), Pen 4199 (1964).

Judy DALY (née **HART**, later **TAPFIELD**) (Australia) (b. 30 Oct 1946) on 31 October. She was Australian cross-country champion 1967 and became a leading coach, married to national coach John Daly. Pbs: 400m 55.9 (1970), 800m 2.07.3 (1974), 1500m 4.28.7 (1980), 1M 4.50.8 (1982), 3000m 9.41.1 (1981), 80mh 11.6 (1968), 200mh 27.8 (1970), 400mh 64.4 (1973).

Isabelle Frances **DANIELS** (married name HOLSTON) (USA) (b. 31 Jul 1937 Jakin, Georgia) on 8 September in Atlanta, Georgia. As a teenager she was 2nd at 60m and won gold at 4x100m at the 1955 Pan-American Games and was 4th at 100m and ran the anchor leg for the US team that won bronze medals at the 1956 Olympic Games in a US record 44.9/45.04. She set a US 200m record at 23.8 in 1958 and improved to 23.6 (3rd equal on the world list that year) in 1959 behind Lucinda Williams 23.4 in the USA v USSR match at Philadelphia. She won further Pan-American Games medals with gold at 60m and 4x100m and silver at 200m in 1959. AAU champion at 60m 1959, 200m/220y 1957 & 1959 (2nd 1958) and indoors at 60m 1955, 50y 1956-8 and 220y 1958; 2nd 100y outdoors 1956-57. US Olympic Trials winner 100m 1956. Pbs: 60m 7.6 (1959), 100y 10.5w (1956), 100m 11.6 (1956), world indoor bests: 50y 5.8 (1956) and 5.7 (1957), 100y 11.1 (1956). Tennessee State University, she later worked as a teacher and coach.

Thomas DITTRICH (Germany) (b. 19 Aug 1954 Zwickau). At 110mh he was a semi-finalist at the 1980 Olympics after 4th in the European Juniors in 1973. He was 2nd in the GDR Champs in 1978-80 and 3rd in 1977. Pb 13.66 (1980).

William Jan **'Bill' DONAKOWSKI** (USA) (b. 21 Jun 1956 Flint, Michigan) on 15 October in Rochester, Michigan. His top performances came in 1980 with his marathon wins in Jersey City in 2:11:40 in May and in the Twin Cities race (US Championship) in a pb 2:10:42 in October. He also competed in the World Cross in 1979, 1981 (18th) and 1983. Pbs: 5000m 13:32.15 (1979), 10,000m 28:13.9 (1979), HMar 62:15 (1986). Graduate of the University of Michigan and an aerospace engineer.

Warren Oliver **DRUETZLER** (USA) (b. 8 Jun 1919 Chicago) in Indianapolis on 21 September. He was the 1950 American AAU 3000m steeplechase and 1951 NCAA mile champion, and was a member of the Michigan State College team that set an unratified world record of 7:31.8 for the 4x880y relay in 1950, then a finalist (12th) in the 1952 Olympic 1500m. He was commissioned as a lieutenant in the US Army. Pbs: 1500m 3:47.8 (1952), 1M 4:08.8 (1951), 2M 9:08.9 (1949), 5000m 14:53.4 (1953), 3000mSt 9:19.2 (1951). Also 2nd in the AAU 1500m 1951-52 and 3000mSt 1953-4 and the US Olympic Trials 1500 in 1952.

Eva Margareta **ERNSTRÖM** (Sweden) (b. 2 Sep 1961 Stockholm) on 8 November. She competed at 3000m (heat) at the 1984 Olympic Games, and at the World Championships in 1980 (8th) and 1983 (12th), and at two European Championships: 1982 (18th 3000m), 1986 (ht 3000m and 25th 10,000m). She was 9th at 1500m at the 1979 European Juniors. She also ran for Sweden at the World Cross 1983-7 with a best of 11th in 1984 and was 4th in the 1982 NCAA 5000m for San Diego State University in the USA. Swedish champion at 3000m 1982-3 and 1986, 4k CC 1983-4 and 1986, and 8k CC 1986. Pbs 1500m 4:13.92 (1980), 3000m 8:51.91 (1983), 5000m 15:34.76 (1983), 10,000m 32:51.59 (1986).

Johann **'Hans' FAHSL** (Germany/FRG) (b. 15 Aug 1941 Duisburg) on 1 August. At the hammer he set an FRG record with 63.94 in 1961 after a world junior record 61.34 in 1960, and competed at the Olympic Games in 1964 (dnq) and 1968 (11th) and was 9th at the Europeans in both 1962 and 1966. FRG champion in 1961-3 and runner-up to Uwe Beyer 1964-70. Pb 70.98 (1971).

Thomas **'Tom' FLEMING** (USA) (b. 23 Jul 1951) on 19 April in Verona, New Jersey while coaching high school track. His first marathon win was in New York in 1971 and he won the New York City Marathon in 1973 and 1975. He had a great record in the Boston Marathon; 2nd in 1973 & 1974, 3rd in 1975 in his pb of 2:12:05, and 6th in 1977, 10th in 1978; he was also 5th in the US Olympic Trial race in 1976, 4th Fukuoka 1977 and 6th Pan-American Games 1979 as well as winning marathons in Cleveland & Toronto (1978), Los Angeles (1981), and Washington, and ran 27 times in all under 2:20. He won the AAU 30km in 1977. He went to William Paterson State University and was a member of New York AC. He was USA Track & Field national distance coach in 1991-7. He set US records at 30k 1:30:27, 20M 1:40:21 and 50k 2:51.21; track pb: 6M 28:38.0 (1972).

John **GILBERT** (USA) (b. 16 Dec 1942 Santa Maria, California) on 28 October in Santa Maria. Only 1.65m (5'5") tall, in 1963 he ran 9.4 for 100y in his semi-final at the US Champs and was 2nd in 9.2w behind Bob Hayes (9.1w) in the final. Earlier that season he ran 10.0w for 100m behind Hayes (9.9) and Henry Carr (10.0), and he represented the USA in matches against the USSR and Poland. Pb 220y (straight) 20.9w (1963).

Calvin Errol **GREENAWAY** (Antigua) (b. 5 Nov 1948) on 14 January in Florida, USA. He competed at the 1970 Commonwealth Games at 100m, long jump and 4x100m, at the 1976 Olympic Games at long jump and 4x100m, and was 8th at long jump at the 1979 Pan-American Games. Pbs: LJ 7.45 (1973) & 7.65w (1972), HJ 1.95 (1972), ANT records: 100m 10.5 (1974), PV 3.80 (1973), Dec 6027 (1970). He went to the University of East London in Britain and on his return home was captain of the national team at volleyball. He was a vice president and then president of the Antigua & Barbuda Athletics Association and a member of the National Olympic Committee. He worked as a land surveyor.

Denise GUÉNARD (née LABORIE) (France) (b. 13 Jan 1934 Saint-Maurice) on 23 May. She was silver medallist at the European Championships in 1962 (8th 1966) at pentathlon, at which event she set French records of 4496 points (1961), 4556 and 4735 (1962). 47 internationals for France 1951-68, she competed at three Olympic Games: 1952– heat 100m & 4x100m, 1960– sf 80mh, 1964– 12 Pen, 8th 4x100m, and also at the 1954 Europeans (heats 80mh & 4x100m). She was French champion at 80mh 1954-5, 1960-2 & 1965; HJ 1953 & 1964, LJ 1965-6, DT 1959, Pen 1953-45, 1961, 1963-8. Pbs: 100m 11.7 (1963), 200m 24.4 (1962), 80mh 10.8 (1965), HJ 1.66 (1968), LJ 6.08 (1963), DT 43.26 (1959). Married Jacques Guénard (French decathlon champion 1954).

Gheorghe Calin **GUSET** (Romania) (b. 28 May 1968 Zalau) on 12 June in Cluj-Napoca. He set five Romanian shot records from 19.64 (1990) to 20.84 (1999) and improved indoors to national records at 20.93 in 2005 and 21.04 in 2006. He competed at two Olympic Games (dnq 1992 – 17th, 2000- 30th), at four World Champs (dnq 1999, 2001, 2003, 2005), and at four European Championships: 1990- dnq, 1998- 10th, 2002- 7th, 2006- dnq). He also made four major indoor finals: Worlds 9th 2001 and 4th 2006, Europeans 4th 2000, 5th 2005. He was Romanian champion 1990, 1992-4, and 1998-2007 with outdoor Balkan titles in 1990, 1992, 1999-2002 and 2004-05. Pb DT 63.82 (1991).

Catherine **'Cathy' HARDY** (- LAVENDER) (USA) (b. 8 Feb 1930 Carrolton, Georgia), on 8 September. She set world records for 4x100m, 45.9/46.14 auto, anchoring the US team to Olympic gold at Helsinki in 1952, and a week later for 4x220y for the US team that ran 1:40.0 at London (White City) (although well beaten by the composite British Empire team 1:38.7). She also ran at Helsinki at 100m (qf) and 200m (sf) after winning at 50m (6.4 = US record), 100m and 200m at the AAUs and winning the Final Trials 200m in a pb 24.3. Other pbs 50y 6.3i (won AAU 1951), 100m 11.8 (1952).

Bryan HAWKINS (Gt Britain & NI) (b. 16 Apr 1928 Clapton, London) on 22 December in Sussex, He was fifth in the 10,000m walk at the 1954 European Champs. Coached by Harold Whitlock, in AAA Champs walks he was 2nd at 2 miles in 1953 and at 7 miles in 1953-4, and was 3rd in the RWA 10 miles in 1953 and 1956. Walks pbs: 2M 14:05.8 (1953), 10000m 46:16.0 (1954), 7M 52:26.4/52:09R (1954), 10M 1:17:27 (1953. He competed successfully for many years as a veteran, setting a world M60 5000m walk record of 24:48 in 1988.

Luther HAYES (USA) (b. 7 Mar 1939 Houston) on 23 November in Palos Verdes Estates, California. He won the NCAA triple jump in 1960 and in 1961 when also 2nd at long jump for the University of Southern California, for whom he also starred at American football before playing for one season in the NFL for the San Diego Chargers. Pbs: LJ 7.78 and TJ 15.78 (both 1961).

Howard Neville **HEALEY** (New Zealand) (b. 3 May 1949 Gisborehe) on 21 May in Manukau City, Auckland. He competed at 3000m steeplechase at the Commonwealth Games in 1974 when he was 11th, a place behind his twin brother Nathan, and in 1978 when he was 5th. NZ champion in 1974 with a pb of 8:37.14 (1979). He ran in three World CC Championships with a best placing of 39th in 1977 after team bronze in 1973.

Rolf HERINGS (Germany) (b. 10 Jul 1940 Rheydt) on 29 September in Cologne. He ranked tenth in the world for the javelin in 1961 and 1962 and was 7th in 1964 and dnq 13th in 1968 at the Olympic Games, and 8th in 1962 at the European Championships. At the World University Games he was 3rd in 1961, 4th in 1963 and 1st in 1965, and won the World Military title in 1960. FRG champion in 1961 and 1965, he had 33 internationals for West Germany 1960-8 with his pb a national record 82.48 (1961). Club: 1.FC Köln.

Steve HOAG (USA) (b. 2 Apr 1947 Chicago) on 15 September in Shakopee, Minnesota. He was 3rd in the NCAA 10,000m for Minnesota in 1968 and runner-up in the 1975 Boston Marathon in his pb 2:11:54.

Monique JACQUET (France) (b. 26 Mar 1922) on 20 January in Paris. She was French champion at 100m 1954 and long Jump 1950 and 1953, with 14 internationals 1950-6, competing at the European Championships in 1950 (9 LJ) and 1954 (heats 100m & 4x100m).She ran on four French 4x100m records and had pbs; 100m 12.4 (1954), 80mh 12.0 (1953, LJ 5.64 (1952).

Ismail JUMA (Tanzania) (b. 3 Aug 1991) was killed when his motorbike collided with a lorry on the way to Arusha on 2 November. This was just six weeks after setting a national half marathon record of 59:30 for 3rd at Ústi nad Labem. Ninth in the World Cross and a non-finisher at 10,000m at the World Champs in 2015, he set his pb at that event with 28:13.46 for 7th in the African Championships. He had been selected to run in the 2018 Commonwealth Games.

Athanasios KALOYANNIS (Greece) (b. 10 Sep 1965 Volos) on 22 October in Athens. He set Greek records for 400m – 46.13 and 45.90 (1984) and 45.90 (1987) – and 400m hurdles 48.88 in 1986 and 48.80 in 1987. He went out in the 400mh heats of the Olympics 1984 and 1992, Worlds 1987 and Europeans 1982 and 1990, but was 8th in the European final in 1986. 2nd World

University Games 1987, and Balkan champion at 400m 1984 and 400mh 1988-9 and 1992. Having studied dentistry at Athens University, he worked as a fashion photographer.

Petra KANDARR (GDR/GER) (b. 20 Aug 1950 Halle) (née VOGT) on 12 March in Karlsruhe. She was triple European champion at 100m, 200m and 4x100m in 1969, 7th at 100m and 2nd 4x100m in 1971 and 8th at 200m in 1974, but never competed at the Olympic Games. She was 2nd at 60m at the European Indoors on 1973, 1st 4x100m European Cup 1973, and GDR champion at 100m & 200m in 1969 (2nd 100m 1973, 200m 1972, 3rd 200m 1974). She ran the first leg for the GDR team that set a world record (42.8) for 4x100m at Potsdam on 1 Sep 1973 and the anchor leg on a low altitude best at Athens in 1969. She set GDR records in 1969 at 100m (3) from 11.4 to 11.3 and 200m 23.3 and 23.0, and had pbs: 50m 6.2i, 60m 7.2/7.29i, 100m 11.0/10.9w, 200m 22.4 (all 1973), auto timed 200m 23.20 (1974). 16 internationals 1969-74. Her daughter Jana Kandarr was a tennis player who competed at the 2000 Olympic Games.

Sune Ferdinand **KARLSSON** (Sweden) (b. 20 Apr 1928 Helgesta) on 23 April. 1500m Swedish U21 champion in 1948, five years later he ran his best-ever time 3:44.2 (tied annual world leader with Wes Santee USA). Represented Sweden in 13 internationals. Swedish champion 1500m 1953 (2nd 1952 and 1955) and 4km cross 1953 and 1956. Other pbs: 800m 1:51.2 (1956), 1000m 2:23.1 (1953), 1 mile 4:04.4 (1953), 3000m 8:25.4 (1952).

Wolfgang KLEIN (Germany) (b. 26 Jan 1941 Hannover) on 15 September in Hamburg. At long jump he was 10th at the 1964 Olympic Games, and 5th in 1961 and 2nd in 1963 at the World University Games, also competing at the 1962 Europeans. German champion 1964 and indoor 1961-4. 20 internationals 1961-4, pbs: LJ 7.90 (1964), 100m 11.1 (1959), HJ 1.89i (1958).

Karel KOLÁR (Czech Republic) (b. 16 Dec 1955 Jindrichuv Hradec) on 4 October. He was the silver medallist at 400m at the 1978 Europeans (improving his national record from 46.13 to 45.77) and also anchored Czechoslovakia to bronze in the 4x400m. He was 1st in 1979 (in 46.21, world indoor best on auto timing) and 2nd in 1980 at the European Indoors and was a semi-finalist at 400m and 7th at 4x400m at the 1980 Olympic Games. Czechoslovak champion at 200m 1979-80 and 400m 1978-80. Pb 200m 21.16 (1980).

Johannes LAHTI (Finland) (b. 29 May 1952) on 1 March. As a high jumper, he was 4th at the 1970 European juniors, and in 1971 straddled over 2.16, which remained the Finnish junior record for 16 years. He concentrated on decathlon after a serious knee injury in 1972 and in 1978 became the first Finn to score over 8000 points on the current tables. He was 11th in both 1976 and 1980 at the Olympic Games and 7th at the 1978 Europeans. His career was ended by an Achilles tendon injury in 1982 Europeans. Finnish chanpion 1977-8, 1980, and 1982, with pbs: Dec 8090 (1978), 100m 10.76/10.67w (1978), 400m 48.93 (1978), 1500m 4:31.0 (1979), 110mh 14.83 (1977), PV 4.60 (1980), LJ 7.52 (1977), TJ 14.64 (1977), DT 43.84 (1979), JT 73.50 (1975), Hep 5866i (1980). He later became a distinguished nature photographer, publishing several books.

Murray LAMBDEN (GBR) (b. 14 Oct 1956) on 17 April in Douglas, Isle of Man. He had four internationals for Britain in 1981-2 and was 8th at 30k walk for the Isle of Man at the 1982 Commonwealth Games. Competing for Boundary Harriers, in RWA Championships he was 2nd at 100k in 1981 and 3rd at 50k in 1982, He set a UK record of 2:19:42 for 30k walk in 1981 and his other walks pbs were 20k 1:32:08 (1981), 35k 2:49:37 (1982), 50k 4:20:51 (1982), 50M 7:42:33 (1974) and 100k 9:38:38 (1981). After retiring from race walking due to a back injury he became a distance runner with a marathon best of 2:43:06 at age 48 in 2005. He made a huge contribution to athletics on the Isle of Man.

Allan Cleve Evan **LAWRENCE** (Australia) (b. 9 Jul 1930 Punchbowl, Sydney) on 15 May in Houston, USA. At the 1954 Empire Games he was 8th at 6 miles, 10th at 3 miles and dnf at marathon. Then he was a notable contender in the great Kuts v Pirie 10,000m duel at the 1956 Olympic Games, taking the bronze medal after being overtaken by József Kovács on the last lap, but after winning his heat, did not compete in the 5000m final due to injury. Four years later in Rome he competed at 5000m (ht), 10,000m (dnf) and marathon (55th). He set Australian records at 5000m: 14:01.8 (1956) and 13:54.2 (1957), and three at 10,000m in 1956: 29:50.8, 29:20.0 and 28:53.61 in that Olympic final; also 2M 8:48.2 (1956), 10M 51:46.0 (1956). Other pbs: 1M 4:09.6 (1955), 3000m 8:10.8 (1957), 6M 28:10.4 (1957), Mar 2:26:43 (1953). He was Australian champion at 6M 1954 and 1956. He went to the University of Houston and set world indoor bests at 2M 8:46.7 (1959) and 8:46.0 (1960) and 3M 13:26.3 (1960, 1 AAU) and was NCAA and AAU cross-country champion in 1959 and 1960, AAU 10,000m and NCAA 5000m champion in 1960. He became an American citizen in the 1980s and formed the Al Lawrence Running Club in Houston.

David LEECH (New Zealand) on 21 October in Christchurch at the age of 90. At the hammer he was 7th at the 1962 Commonwealth Games and NZ Champion in 1952, 1962 and 1964-5. He set NZ records with 53.90 (1962) and 54.10 (1964) and had a most successful career as a master. He was manager of the NZ athletics team at the 1976 Olympic Games.

Günther LEIN (Germany/GDR) (b. 22 Feb 1932 Leipzig) on 27 July. He set 12 GDR high jump records from 1.92 (1955) to 2.04 (1957), had 19 internationals 1953-60 and was GDR champion 1955-7.

Carina LILGE-LEUTNER (Austria) (b. 10 Jun 1960) (née Weber-Leutner) on 21 July in Vienna. She was the first Austrian winner of the Vienna City Marathon in 1987 and set national records for 10,000m with 34:28.7 (1988) and the marathon with 2:37:09 in Chicago 1986. Austrian champion at 10,000m in 1986, 15k road 1986 and 1991, HMar 1992 and 1995, Mar 1987, 1990-91 and 1993.

Raymond LORRE (France) (b. 31 May 1925) on 5 May. French champion at 4x400m in 1946 and 1948-9, he staged the inugural Leon Signoret Memorial, a forerunner of the Meeting de Paris, at the Jean Bouin Stadium in 1974, and founded the Paris Marathon in 1976.

Marjana LUZAR (Slovenia) (b. 26 May 1972 Ljubljana) on 9 August in Ljubljana. At 400mh she was 2nd in the 1990 World Juniors and 8th in 1991 at the European Juniors. Yugoslav champion 400m 1989. Pbs 200m 24.31, 400m 53.74 (1989), 400mh 56.74 (1990).

Germaine MASON (GBR) (b. 30 Jan 1983 Kingston, Jamaica) was killed in a motorcycling accident in Kingston on 20 April. He set six Jamaican high jump records from 2002 to 2.34 in 2003 and was 2nd in 2000 and 3rd in 2002 at the World Juniors, Pan-American Games champion in 2003, 5th at the 2002 Commonwealth Games and 2003 World Championships and 4th equal at the 2004 World Indoors as well as being Jamaican champion in 2000, 2002-03 and 2005. He then switched to compete for Britain (his father was born in London) from 8 March 2006, and, after not qualifying for the finals of the 2006 Europeans and 2007 Worlds, matched his best of 2.34 when he took the Olympic silver medal in 2008. UK champion 2009.

Walter MEIER (Germany/GDR) (b. 2 Aug 1927 Rogätz/Ohrekreis) on 25 March in Halle. He was ranked in the world top ten at decathlon each year 1953-9, placing 6th in 1956 and 16th in 1960 at the Olympic Games and winning European bronze in 1958. He was GDR champion at HJ 1950-2, and 1954; pentathlon 1951-2, decathlon 1952 and 1958 and set seven GDR records from 6194 (1953) to 7388 (1958) – on the 1952 tables. On the current tables his decathlon best was 7294 and other pbs included: 400m 47.9 (1958), HJ 1.90 (1952), PV 4.00 (1957), LJ 7.26 (1955). 19 internationals 1951-60.

Luigi MENGONI (Italy) (b. 21 Jun 1930) on 25 October in Ascoli Piceno. A great statistician and stalwart of the ATFS for decades, he was a founding compiler of national records books from 1957 including 'World and national leaders in track & field athletics 1860-1972', 'National athletics records at 1930, 1940, 1950' etc. He was also co-author of 'The ATFS Women's Track & Field Handbook' (1970 and 1974), 'Track and Field in Albania 1945-1986' and 'Chinese Track & Field Athletics 1910-1993'.

Robert 'Bob' **MIMM** (USA) (b. 18 Oct 1924) on 7 May at his home in Willingboro, New Jersey. He was 23rd at 20k walk at the Olympic Games in 1960, in which year he set his pb of 1:36:20. Millersville University, Penn AC, then Shore AC. He became a keen and very successful competitor at World Masters Championships.

Thomas William **'Tom' MISSON** (GBR) (b. 11 May 1930 Hendon, London) on 31 July in Havant, Hampshire. A pharmacist, who competed for Metropolitan Walking Club, he set a UK record for 50k walk with 4:20:31.8 when 4th in the 1958 European Championships in 1958 and was 5th in the 1960 Olympic Games. He had road pbs for 20k 1:35:16, 20M 2:37:30 and 50k 4:14:03, all in 1959. Three UK internationals 1958-60. He was RWA champion at 20 miles in 1959 and 2nd to Don Thompson at 50k each year 1958-60.

Eckart MÜLLER (Germany) (b. 25 Jan 1956 Mulheim) in June after a motorcycle accident in Berlin. He was the 1975 European Junior decathlon champion and had a pb of 8056 points in 1977. Other pbs: 110H 14.84 (1977), HJ 2.16 (1976), LJ 7.72 (1978), JT 69.10 (1977).

Hein-Direck NEU (Germany) (b. 13 Feb 1944 Bad Kreuznach) on 14 April in Wiesbaden. A regular on the international team he competed in 58 internationals for FRG 1964-82 and was FRG champion in 1966-9, 1974 and 1976. At major championships: OG: 1968- 9, 1972- dnq, 1976- 12; WCh: 1977- 3; EC: 1966- 11, 1971- dnq 13, 1974- 12; WUG: 1967- 2 (4 SP), 1970- 2; ECp: 1967- 4, 1970- 2, 1973- 5, 1975- 3, 1977- 4. He set eight FRG records from 60.27 (1967) to 68.08 (1977). Pbs: 100m 11.1 '61, SP 18.38 (1970). In 2003 he admitted to using steroids in the 1960s and 1970s.

Darel NEWMAN (USA) (b. 6 Aug 1943 Reedley, California) on 10 October in Bakersfield, California. The "Bald Bullet" was a top sprinter at Fresno State University. In 1964 he won the NCAA indoor 60y, ran 100y in 9.2 (Bob Hayes' world record was 9.1), 100m in 10.2 (& 10.1w) and placed fifth in the US Olympic Trials 100m. The following year he tied the world best for 60 yards indoors with 5.9 at San Francisco on 26 February, finished second in the NCAA and AAU 100y and ran 100m in 10.1 (a tenth outside the world record) when winning against the USSR in Kiev. After retiring from the track he became a high school teacher and coach. Pb 220y 21.2.

Cristina NICOLAU (Romania) (b. 9 Aug 1977 Bucharest) on 5 December. At triple jump she was 6th at the 2000 Olympics, 5th at the 2002

Europeans and, competing at four World Championships, was twice a finalist: 8th 1999 and 6th 2001. She was also 2nd in 2000 and 5th in 2002 at the European Indoors and won the World University Games bronze at long jump in 1997. Her first major medals came at long jump: bronze in 1993 and silver in 1995 at the European Juniors and silver at the 1996 World Juniors. At the European U23s she was 1st at TJ in 1997 and 1999 (2nd and 4th at LJ). Romanian champion at LJ 1996, 1999 and 2002, TJ 1999 and 2001, Balkan TJ 2003. Pbs: LJ 6.65 (2002), 6.69w (1999); TJ 14.94i (2000), 14.62 (2001).

Progress at TJ: 1996- 13.89, 1997- 14.22/14.23i, 1998- 14.20, 1999- 14.70, 2000- 14.94i/14.19/14.22w, 2001- 14.62, 2002- 14.40, 2003- 14.31, 2004- 14.04i/13.69, 2007- 13.59.

Dr. **Bernard** Jonathan **NOTTAGE** (Bahamas) (b. 23 Oct 1943 Nassau) on 29 June in Florida. He was a former minister of national security, education, health and consumer affairs, and described as a "political giant" in The Bahamas. Before his political career he competed as a sprinter at the 1968 Olympic Games (heat 100m, qf 200m, dnf 4x100m), Commonwealth Games 1966 (qf 100y and 220y) and 1970 (heat 100m and 200m), and he was 6th at 200m at the 1967 Pan-American Games. Pbs: 10.53 (1967), 200m 21.31 (1968). He studied medicine at Aberdeen University and qualified as a doctor in Britain in 1969, representing Scotland in four internationals. He became the longest-serving president of the Bahamas AAA, also being president of the Central American and Caribbean Athletics Confederation.

Zsuzsa NYITRAI (later **Sándorné PALLAY**) (Hungary) (b. 28 Sep 1948, Miskolc), on 25 August in Szikszó. She competed at the 1966 European Junior Games (SP 6th, DT 3rd). At discus: Hungarian champion 1974 and 1981, 18 internationals 1971-90. Pbs: SP 16.44 (1981), DT 62.36 (1981), HT 39.80 (1991).

Beth OBRUBA (USA) (b. 30 Apr 1977) on 20 October in Columbia, South Carolina. Kent State University. Pbs SP 16.54i (2001), DT 54.88 (2000), JT 55.36 (2000).

Brian Ray **OLDFIELD** (USA) (b. 1 Jun 1945 Elgin, Illinois) in Elgin on 26 March. He achieved astonishing world bests with 22.11, 22.55 and 22.86 at the shot as an ITA professional in 1975-6. At the time the world amateur record was 21.82. He also recorded four world indoor bests: 21.32, 21.57 and 21.60 in 1973 and 22.11 in 1975. Before turning professional he had a best of 20.97 and was sixth at the Olympics in 1972 (after 3rd at the US Olympic Trials) as well as AAU champion indoors in 1970. As a reinstated amateur he won the US title in 1980 (he was also 2nd in 1984 and 3rd in 1972 and 1981) and set two US records, 22.02 in 1981 and 22.19 in 1984 (when he topped the world list at the age of 39), but he was ineligible for the Olympics. A graduate of Middle Tennessee State, he used the rotational technique.

Annual progress: 1964- 16.38, 1965- 17.28, 1966- 18.03, 1968- 18.65, 1969- 1968, 1970- 19.47i/18.89, 1971- 18.59i, 1972- 20.97, 1973- 21.60i, 1974- 21.12, 1975- 22.86, 1976- 22.45, 1977- 19.95, 1979- 21.02, 1980- 21.82, 1981- 22.02, 1982- 20.71, 1983- 21.22, 1984- 22.19, 1985- 21.41, 1986- 20.63, 1987- 20.33, 1988- 19.15. Pb DT 62.26 (1975).

Henry Alexander **'Alec' OLNEY** (GBR) (b. 4 Jan 1922 Hampstead, London) on 25 April in Harrow, London. Joining Thames Valley Harriers in 1946 after wartime Army service, he achieved immediate cross-country success and was 6th in the 1947 International CC (later 7th in 1950 after 2nd in the National and 1951). On the track he had four internationals for Britain, including 1948 Olympic Games (heats) and 1950 Europeans 8th at 5000m. At 3 miles he was 2nd in the AAAs in 1947-8 and 1950 and 3rd in 1949, winning the CAU title in 1947-8 and 1950 and the Southern in 1948. Pbs: 1M 4:17.4 (1951), 2M 9:20.0u (1949), 3M 14:11.2 (1950), 5000m 14:41.0e (1950), 14:46.4 (1947).

Clement PARKER (New Zealand) (b. 31 Dec 1926 Hastings) on 6 November in Hamilton. He won a bronze medal at 4x110y and was a semi-finalist at 100y and 220y at the Empire Games in 1950, when his sister Dorothea was a 4x110y relay silver medallist. He had won the NZ 100y title in 1950 in 9.6w and was also 2nd in the NZ 220y each year 1948-50. Pbs: 100y 9.9, 220y 21.4 (both 1950).

Gabe PROCTOR (USA) (b. 29 Apr 1990) by suicide on 20 May in Lyndonville, Vermont. He had pbs of HMar 61:40 and Mar 2:13:45 in 2014 and in 2016 ran 10,000m in 28:33.76.

Katalin RÁCZ (Hungary) (b. 1 Aug 1965 Kapuvár) on 24 December in the USA. She was 6th at 1500m at the 1988 European Indoors and 1989 World University Games, set Hungarian records for 1500m 4:07.88i (1988), 1M 4:34.00 (1988) and 4:29.73 (1991), and 2000m 5:52.6 (1988), and was Hungarian champion at 1500m 1986-9 and indoors 1987-8, 1991 and 1993; 24 Internationals 1986-94. Other pbs: 800m 2:04.22 (1988), 1500m out 4:08.46 (1991), 3000m 9:12.60 (1990), 5000m 16:18.1 (1987), 10,000m 34:04.29 (1988), HMar 77:27 (1995).

James Arthur Noel **'Jim' RAILTON** (GBR) (b. 25 Dec 1935 Liverpool) on 16 August in Wallingford, Oxfordshire. Described in his Times obituary as a "Hell-raising rowing coach", he had been a promising young sprinter before a hamstring injury ended his career. He ran 440y in 49.2 at the age of 16 in 1952, twice equalled the British junior record with 9.9 for 100y in 1954 and ran 6.7 for 60y indoors in Germany in 1955 with outdoor pbs of 100y 9.8, 100m 10.8, 220y 21.8 (all in 1959). He graduated with a degree in modern jazz from Loughborough, having won the UAU 220y for them in 1957, and became a PE teacher and a talented rowing coach. He became a perceptive rowing correspondent of the Times and was director of the sports centre at Oxford University.

Stig Oskar Dalen **REKDAL** (Norway) (b. 9 Sep 1939 Larsnes, Møre & Romxdal) on 18 December in Larsnes. He was Norwegian champion at 800m and 1500m in 1965 and at 2k cross-country in 1964; heat European Champs 1500m 1966. Pbs: 800m 1:50.1 (1966), 1500m 3:40.6 (1966), 3000m 8:13.2 (1965).

Clarence ROBINSON (USA) (b. 9 Apr 1942, Atlanta, Mississippi) on 19 March in Albuquerque. He was the 1965 NCAA long jump and triple jump champion and that year ranked third in the world behind Ralph Boston and Igor Ter-Ovanesyan with 8.16 and triple jumped 16.06A. He also triple jumped 16.23w in 1966. He is not to be confused with Clarence "Arnie" Robinson, the 1976 Olympic long jump champion.

Philippa Kate **ROLES** (GBR) (b. 1 Mar 1978 Neath) on 21 May in London. Ranked in the top three in Britain at the discus every year from 1998 to 2010 (no.1 six times), she was the European Junior bronze medallist in 1997 and 4th in the European U23s in 1999 and competed at the Olympic Games in 2004 and 2008 but did not qualify for a final. She represented Britain in the European Cup six times with a best of 3rd in 2005. She was a member of Swansea H and Sale H Manchester and competed for Wales at four successive Commonwealth Games, placing 6/4/6/4 from 1998 to 2010. She was UK champion 2007 and 2009, AAA champion in 2002 and 2004-05 (with four 2nd places and 3rd) and in the shot was 2nd in the AAA Indoors in 1999 and 2000 (3rd 2001-02) after a great record through the age groups: winning shot and discus at the AAA U15s in 1992 and U17s in 1994, then shot 1995-6 and discus 1997 at the U20s and discus in 1999-2001 at the U23s. She won 14 Welsh discus titles between 1993 and 2001 and the shot in 1995, 1998 and 2001. Pbs: SP 15.95i (1999), 15.62 (2003); DT 62.89 (2003), HT 55.09 (1999).

Her sister Rebecca was Welsh discus champion in 2000 and 2003 with a best of 56.25 (2004).

Michael A.B. **RYAN** (Australia) (b. 19 Dec 1941) on 7 November. A member of Sandringham AC, Victoria, in 1964 he was Australian champion at 220y hurdles and 440y hurdles and competed at the Olympic Games (heat 400m hurdles). Pbs: 120yh 14.7 (1965), 220yh 23.7 (1964), 440yh 50.9 (1964).

Çetin SAHINER (Turkey) (b. 13 Oct 1934 Ankara) on 3 August in Ankara. He improved the Turkish high jump record, first with 1.98 in 1955 and finally with 2.02 in 1958 and for 110m hurdles with 14.6 in 1960 and 14.5 in 1963. In all he won 16 Turkish titles, competed in the Olympic Games at 110m hurdles in 1960 and 1964 and at high jump in 1960, and was 9th in the high jump at the Europeans in 1956, also competing at hurdles in 1962 and 1966. He also won the Balkan Games high jump in 1958.

Simo SALORANTA (Finland) (b. 12 Dec 1934 Lieto) on 8 November in Raisio. The third Finn to break 14 minutes at 5000m, he ran his pb 13:53.4 in 1962 and 1964. Finnish champion at 5000m in 1961, 1963 and 1964, 10000m 1960. He was 21st in the Olympic 10000m in 1960, and also ran in the heats of the 5000m in 1960 and 1964. He had 27 races in 21 international dual matches 1959-65 with six wins. Pbs: 1500m 3:45.4 (1959), 2000m 5:11.2 (FIN rec 1965), 3000m 8:03.6 (1962), 10,000m 29:38.4 (1964). In October 1959 his 1500m time of 3:54.2 was world best in a decathlon (4590 points, 1985 tables).

José Luis SÁNCHEZ Paraiso (Spain) (b. 21 Jul 1942 Lagunilla, Salamanca) on 18 July in Salamanca. He competed at the Olympic Games of 1968, 1972 and 1976 and at the European Championships of 1966, 1971 and 1974. He set 20 Spanish records for 100m (11 at 10.4 in 1965-70 and 9 at 10.3 in 1970-76) and 5 at 200m 21.6 (1963) to 21.3 (1966) plus 21 at 4x100m. Other pbs: 50m 5.7i (1967), 5.97i (1975); 60m 6.6 (1960), 6.87i (1976); 100m auto 10.69 (1968), 200m 21.60 (1971), LJ 7.10 (1964), Dec 4973 (1970). He was Spanish champion at 100m 1963-6, 1971- 3 and 1979, 200m 1962 and 1964-6 and indoors at 50m 1967-68 and 60m 1967-68 and 1972.

Dr. **Norbert** W. **SANDER. Jr.** (USA) (b. 21 Aug 1942 Yonkers, NY) on 17 March in Hudson, New York. He won the New York City Marathon in 1974 when it was run entirely within Central Park and led the way in converting the Fort Washington Avenue Armory in Upper Manhattan into a top class athletics facility from 1992.

Alan J. **SAYERS** (New Zealand) (b. 16 Dec 1915 Onehunga) on 19 August in Whangaparaoa, Auckland at the age of 101. He won a bronze medal on the NZ 4 x 440y team at the 1938 British Empire Games (also heats 220y and 440y). He won the NZ 440y in 1937 in his pb of 49.2. He became a successful coach and made a member of the New Zealand Order of Merit for services to sport and journalism in 2003.

Fredy SCHÄFER (Germany) (b. 10 Oct 1933) on 22 March in Koblenz. A Former long jumper (pb 6.78 in 1958) he was meeting director of the famous Rot-Weiss international meetings in Koblenz for many years.

Jarvis Lavonne **SCOTT** (-Jones) (USA) (b. 6 Apr 1947 Waco, Texas) in Lubbock, Texas on 29 September. She was AAU 400m champion in 1968 and 1st at 400m and 3rd at 800m at the Final Olympic Trials. Giving up her 800m place, she was sixth at 400m in the Olympic Games in a pb 52.79A. She was AAU indoor champion 1969 and 1971 and was 8th at the 1971 Pan-American Games and dnq at 1973 World University Games. She went to Cal State Los Angeles and ran for the L.A.Mercurettes. Other pbs: 200m 23.7 (1975), 800m 2:04.5 (1968), JT 43.90 (1972).

Elizete Gomes **da SILVA** (Brazil) (b. 2 May 1971 Londrina) in a car accident in Paraná on 22 September. She was South American heptathlon champion in 2001 and 2005-06 with a best score of 5766 (2007). BRA champion 2001, 2003 and 2008.

William G. '**Billy**' **SMITH** (USA) (b. 1933) on 15 December. A successful middle-distance runner while at Boston University 1951-5, after Army service he coached there for 16 years, most notably steering David Hemery to his marvellous Olympic triumph at 400m hurdles in 1968.

Christa SMOGER (later **GUTSCHE**) (Germany/GDR) (b. 8 Dec 1934) on 26 May. She set a GDR pentathlon record with 4514 points in 1960 and had six internationals 1955-6, with 6th in 1955 and 4th in 1957 at the UIE pentathlon. Pbs: 80mh 10.9 (1960), SP 13.48 (1962).

Julien SOUCOURS (France) (b. 7 Jun 1926 Tresses) on 15 June in Mureaux. He was French champion at 3000m steeplechase in 1955 and 1956 and had 28 internationals 1952-60 with 2nd at the Mediterranean Games in 1955. He set four French steeplechase records from 9:16.0 (1955) to 9:04.2 (1956) and had other pbs: 1M 4:19.0 (1956), 5000m 14:43.8 (1954), 10,000m 30:56.0 (1953).

Malcolm A.E. **SPENCE** (Jamaica) (b. 2 Jan 1936 Kingston) on 30 October in Fort Lauderdale, Florida. He won the bronze medal at 4x400m competing for the British West Indies at the 1960 Olympic Games, when he was also a semi-finalist at 400m, as he had been for Jamaica in 1956. He was 4th at 4x400m for Jamaica at the 1964 Games and teamed up with his twin brother Melville in both 1956 and 1964. Together they helped Jamaica to 4x440y gold at the 1962 Commonwealth Games, at which Mal was 5th at 440y. Mal also competed in the 440y heats at the 1958 (also 3rd at 4x440y) and 1966 Commonwealth Games. At the Pan-American Games he was 1st at 4x400m and 3rd at 400m in 1959 and 3rd at 4x400m in 1963 and at the CAC Games won gold at 4x400m in 1962 (3rd 400m) and 1966. Pbs 440y 46.7 (1959), 800m 1:51.1 (1957).

(Rev.) **Nicolas** David **STACEY** (GBR) (b. 25 Nov 1927 Belgravia, London) on 8 May near Canterbury, Kent. He made five international appearances for Britain in 1951-2, including at the 1952 Olympic Games (semis 200m, 5th 4x400m). He won a silver medal at 4x110y at the 1950 Empire Games (ht 100y, sf 220y) and was 2nd in the AAA 220y in 1951 and 3rd in 1950, and had pbs: 100y 9.9 (1949), 100m 10.7 (1950), 220y 21.6 (1951), straight 21.3w (1949), 200m 21.79 auto (1952), 400m 48.4 (1952). He ran on UK record-setting teams at 4x100m and 4x110y in 1951. After Oxford University, he took holy orders in 1952 and was later Dean of Greenwich, but his outspoken views brought his clerical career to an end at the age of 40 and he was the Deputy Director of Oxfam for two years and then a pioneering director of social services for the London Borough of Ealing, moving on to that job for Kent County Council 1974-85.

SUH Yun-bok (Korea) (b. 9 Jan 1923) on 27 June. He won the 1947 Boston Marathon in a world best time (point-to-point course) of 2:25:39, taking 1:03 off the time recorded in 1935 by his coach Sohn Kee-chung (the 1936 Olympic champion). A year later Suh competed at the 1948 Olympic Games but was only 27th in 2:59:36. He had also won the first All-Korea Marathon in 1946. He spent the next four decades as a sports administrator in South Korea, serving as an executive director and then vice president for the Korean AAF, and also as vice chairman for the Korean Olympic Committee.

Mona Coco **SULAIMAN** (Philippines) (b. 9 Jun 1942 Cotabato) on 21 December in Manila. She competed at 100m and 200m at the Olympic Games of 1960 and 1964 and won triple sprint gold at the 1962 Asian Games (also 4x100m). However she refused to take a sex test at the 1966 Asian Games. Pbs: 100m 11.8 (1961), 11.93 (1962); 200m 24.4 & 24.58 (1962); SP 13.86 (1966), Pen 3952 (1963).

János SZABÓ (Hungary) (b. 3 Mar 1945 Budapest) on 15 October in Budapest. He competed at the 1968 Olympic Games (ht 3000mSt). Pbs: 800m 1:52.0 (1967), 1000m 2:26.4 (1968), 1500m 3:45.4 (1968), 2000m 5:21.2 (1966), 3000m 8:08.0 (1967), 5000m 14:03.8 (1971), 10,000m 31:13.0 (1968), Marathon 2:53:50 (1972), 3000mSt 8:42.2 (1968).

József SZÉCSÉNYI (Hungary) (b. 10 Jan 1932, Szegvár), on 19 March in Budapest. He competed at the discus at the Olympic Games in 1960 (4th) and 1964 (5th); Europeans 1954 (3rd), 1958 (8th) & 1962 (6th); and World University Games 1957 (2nd), having been world student champion in 1954. He set a European record with 58.33 in 1959, one of eight HUN records from 56.02 in 1958 to 60.66 in 1962, when he was the first Hungarian over 60m. HUN champion 9 times (1955-56, 1958-63 and 1965). 50 internationals SP & DT 1953-66. Pb SP 16.21 (1958). He was head coach for the throws for the Hungarian team 1969-78 and coached the Kuwait team 1979-84. From 1989 he was a professor in the University of Physical Education.

Habib THIAM (France) (b. 21 Jan 1933) on 26 June in Dakar, Sénégal. He was French champion at 200m in 1954 and 1957 and had 11 internationals for France 1954-8. Pbs: 100m 10.6w (1957), 200m 21.5 (1958).

Willie THOMAS (USA) (b. 14 Jul 1950) in September in Chicago. While at the University of Tennessee in 1972 he won the NCAA 800m in 1:47.1 and set his pb of 1:47.6 for 880y. Also NCAA champion in 1974.

David TORRENCE (Peru) (b. 16 Nov 1985) was found dead at the bottom of a swimming pool in Scottsdale, Arizona on 28 August. The US junior champion and 8th at the World Juniors at 1500m in 2004, he had pbs of 800m 1:45.14 (2010), 1000m 2:16.76i (US indoor record, 2014), 2:17.46 (2012); 1500m 3:33.23 (2013), 1M 3:52.01 (2012), 2000m 4:56.99i (2014), 3000m 7:40.75 (2013), 5000m 13:16.53 (2012). He also ran on US relay teams that set a world record at 4x800m indoors (7:13.11 in 2014) and a North American record at 4x1500m (14:40.80 in 2014). Having been 6th in the US Olympic Trials 1500m in 2012 and 2nd in the Pan-American Games 5000m in 2015, he switched nationality to Peru (where his mother was from) in 2016 and competed for them at the Rio Olympic Games, 16th 5000m, and 2017 Worlds, heat 1500m.

Ivan ULLSPERGER (Czech Republic) (b. 20 Dec 1931 Svilengrad, Bulgaria) on 7 June. His mother came from Ljubljana, his father from Bohemia; through Slovenia, Maribor and Austria, he arrived in Jablonec nad Nisou in 1944. Inspired by Paavo Nurmi's book, he started running after the War. He ran on the Czech record team at 4x1500m 15:26.4 (1954), had six internationals 1954-7 and was Czechoslovakian champion at 10,000m in 1956 and 1957, managing to beat Emil Zátopek in several races. Pbs: 1500m 3:50.4. 3000m 8:12.8. 5000m 14:09.8, 10000m 29:29.2 (all in 1955, the last 10th on the world list that year).

Monte UPSHAW (USA) (b. 11 May 1936) on 26 July in Claremont, California. He broke Jesse Owens' national high school long jump record with 7.72m in 1954, second on the world list that year. In 1958 he was part of a University of California world record-breaking sprint medley relay quartet (3:18.8).

His daughter Grace was a world class long jumper: OG: 2004- 9, 2008- 8; WCh: 2003- 8, 2005- 6, US champion 2003, 2005, 2007; indoors 2002. Pb 6.88 '08, 6.99w '03.

Riana van NIEKERK (South Africa) (b. 18 Jun 1976) on 8 April. She won the Om die Dam 50k race six times: 2002, 2005, 2007 (in her best time on a standard course of 3:22:39), 2009, 2014 and 2017. She finished in the top ten in the Comrades four times (2004, 2006, 2008 and 2011), with a best of 6th in 2008 in 6:43:32 – the first South African behind five Russians. Her best marathon was 2:43:00 in 2007 and she was RSA champion in 2009.

Aleksandr VASILYEV (Belarus) (b. 26 Jul 1961 Shostka, Ukraine) on 30 October. Competing for the USSR, in 1985 he was 2nd in the European Cup 400m hurdles in Moscow in 47.92 (4th on the world list that year and then 6th on the world all-time list). This time was his third USSR record in 1985 and remains the BLR national record, He went on to 2nd in the World Cup in Canberra and also in the Goodwill Games and European Championships in 1986. USSR champion 1985 and a semi-finalist at the 1987 Worlds.

Progress at 400mh: 1977- 55.6, 1978- 53.69, 1979- 52.06, 1980- 51.51, 1981- 49.84, 1982- 49.64/49.4, 1983- 49.07, 1984- 48.45, 1985- 47.92, 1986- 48.24, 1987- 48.85, 1988- 49.00. pbs: 400m 46.76 '85, 110mh 14.31.

Zenon Romuald **WAZNY** (Poland) (b. 6 Dec 1929 Wilno) on 23 October. At the pole vault he set three Polish records with 4.46 and 4.47 in 1956 and 4.53 in 1958. Polish champion in 1951-2, 1956 and 1958, he competed at the Olympic Games in 1952 (dnq) and 1956 (6th) and at the European Championships in 1954 (11th) and 1956 (5th).

Kjellfred WEUM (Norway) (b. 30 Jul 1940 Hafslo) on 4 August in Luster, Sogn og Fjordane. At 110m hurdles he competed at the 1968 Olympic Games and was 7th at the 1969 Europeans. He set four Norwegian records from 14.2 in 1964 to 13.7 in 1967, as well as 14.08 and 14.04 auto-timed in 1968, and won eight successive Norwegian titles 1963-70. He worked as a police officer.

Cyrus J. **YOUNG** Jr (USA) (b. 23 Jul 1928 Modesto, California) on 6 December in Modesto. The 6ft 4½in (1.95m) tall Young won gold in Helsinki (the only US javelin winner ever) with a pb and Olympic record 73.78m on his 24th birthday, having been 2nd in the AAU and Olympic Trials that year. He was again 2nd in the AAUs in 1953 and 1955, and improved to his eventual pb 79.16 in 1956 also winning the AAU title and Olympic Trials but was only 11th at the 1956 Olympics when suffering from a sprained ankle. He had graduated from UCLA in 1951, having been 2nd in the NCAAs in 1950. Born into a farming family, he became a rancher.

Died in early 2018

Hassan AGABANI (Sudan) (b. Jan 1928) on 15 January. He was made an Honorary Life Member of the IAAF after serving as a Council member

1968–99. A former president of the Sudan Athletics Association, he worked as a technical delegate at several IAAF championships and was on the Jury of Appeal at various Olympics.

Horace 'Nip' ASHENFELTER III (USA) (b. 23 Jan 1923 Phoenixville, Pennsylvania) on 6 January in West Orange, New Jersey. His outstanding triumph was his surprise win in the 1952 Olympic Games 3000m steeplechase. He went there with a pb and US record of 9:06.4 (when he won at the US Olympic Trials) and improved in his heat to 8:51.0 before winning a terrific duel with Vladimir Kazantsev in the final in a world record 8:45.4 (8:45.68 on auto timing) with a powerful sprint finish that took him well clear of his rival. He won the Sullivan Award that year but it proved to be his only year in the world top rankings and he was 6th in his heat at the 1956 Olympics. A Penn State graduate, he joined the FBI in November 1951 before going into business after 1956. He won AAU titles at 5000m 1954-5 (2nd 1949) , 6 miles 1950 (3rd 1952) and 3000m steeple 1951, 1953, 1956 (2nd 1952, 1955, 1957, 3rd 1954), and was the AAU indoor 3 mile champion each year 1952-6. In those years he led the New York AC team to victory at cross-country, taking the individual title in 1955-6. NCAA champion at 2 miles 1949. Pbs: 1M 4:11.6 (1954), 2M 8:49.6 (1955), 3M 13:47.5i (1953), 10,000m 30:45.5 (1952).

His younger brother Bill was the AAU champion at cross-country in 1951 and steeplechase 1954. He ran the first leg for the US team that set a world 4x880y record against the British Empire at the White City, London in 1952.

Guy ARBOGAST (USA) (b. 6 Jun 1956 Woodland Hills, California) on 4 January in Eugene. His career highlight was placing fifth in the 1978 World Cross Country in Glasgow, leading the US team to second place. Track pbs included 14:03.6 5000m and 29:00.5 10,000m in 1979.

Étienne BALLY (France) (b. 17 Apr 1923 Vénissieux) on 10 January. After 4th at 100m in 1946, he won the 100m and took silver medals at 200m and 4x100m in 1950 at the European Championships. He competed at the Olympic Games in 1948 and 1952, 26 Internationals 1946-53. French champion at 100m 1947 and 1950, 200m 1946-7, 1950 and 1952. He equalled the French record for 100m of 10.5 eight times in 1947-50 and set 200m records with 21.6 (1947) and 21.3 (1949) plus two at 4x100m. Pb 400m 47.7 (1950).

Jarrod BANNISTER (Australia) (b. 3 Oct 1984 Townsville) on 9 February in the Netherlands. Second in the World Juniors in 2002, after 6th in 2006 he won the Commonwealth Games javelin in 2010. He was twice a global finalist, 6th at the Olympics in 2008 and 7th in the Worlds in 2011 and set the Australian record with 89.02 in 2008. He received a 20-month ban in 2013 for missing three anti-doping tests

Sir **Roger** Gilbert **BANNISTER** (b. 23 Mar 1929) died at his home in Oxford on 3 March. On 6 May 1954 he achieved one of the most celebrated deeds in the history of sport, with the first sub four-minute mile, running 3:59.4 at Iffley Road, Oxford. Six weeks later John Landy (Australia) improved the mile record to 3:57.9, but Bannister in this, his last season before concentrating on his medical career, beat Landy in a race dubbed 'The Mile of the Century' to win the Empire Games title at 1 mile in Vancouver. Bannister ran 3:58.8 and Landy 3:59.6, the first time two men had beaten four minutes in one race. Bannister then added the European title at 1500m. He set three British records at 1500m from 3:46.0 (3:46.30 auto) in 1952 to 3:42.2 in 1954 and three at 1 mile from 4:03.6 in 1953, plus unratified (assessed as a time trial) marks at both distances in 1953. He also ran the final leg (in 4:07.6) on the British team that set a world 4 x 1 mile record (16:41.0) in 1953. He had been 3rd in the European 800m in 1950 and a disappointed 4th at 1500m in the 1952 Olympics. AAA champion at 880y 1952, 1 mile 1951 and 1953-4. Other pbs: 880y 1:50.7 (1953); 3/4 mile 2:56.8 (1951), 2M 9:09.2 (1954). He had set UK junior 1 mile records at 4:18.7 and 4:17.2 in 1948. Other pbs: 880y 1:50.7 (1953), 3/4 mile 2:56.8 (1951), 2M 9:09.2 (1954).

He studied medicine at Oxford University and at St. Mary's Hospital Medical School in London, becoming a distinguished neurologist. He was awarded the CBE in 1955 and was knighted in 1975 for his services to medicine. He was Chairman of the Sports Council 1971-4, and was Master of Pembroke College, Oxford 1985-93. He was given the Companion of Honour in the 2017 New Year Honours

Clifford Frederick **BOURLAND** (USA) (b. 1 Jan 1921 Los Angeles) on 1 February. At the age of 97 he was the oldest living Olympic athletics gold medallist, having run on the US 4x400m team (47.3 for the second leg) in London in 1948 after he had been 5th at 200m. His peak year had come at the age of 20 in 1941 when on June 17 he ran a 46.0 third leg for the University of Southern California when they were 2nd to the University of California, both teams timed in 3:09.4, 1.1 secs inside the previous world record. On June 29 he was 3rd in 46.1 in the great AAU 400m at Philadelphia when winner Grover Klemmer tied Rudolf Harbig's world record at 46.0 and Hubie Kerns was 2nd in 46.1. Bourland won both NCAA and AAU titles in 1942 and 1943; he was also 3rd in 1941 and 4th in 1947 in the AAU 400m and 2nd in 1948 at 200m and 3rd at 220y in 1942 and 1943 in the NCAAs. Other pbs: 100y 9.7 (1948), 9.6w (1941), 100m 10.5 (1948), 200m 21.0 (1948). He served in the Navy in World War II.

Gerald (Eugene) COLE (USA) (b. 18 Feb 1928 New Lexington, Ohio) on 11 January. A former US high school record holder with 48.0 for 440y in 1948, he improved to a best of 47.0 in 1952. His best actual 400m time was 46.8 (46.94 auto) when placing fourth in his Olympic semi-final but on the second leg of an epic 4x400m relay, when the USA was 2nd to Jamaica, he was clocked at 45.5. Twelve days later he ran first leg for the US team which set a world record for the 4x440y of 3:08.8 at London's White City. Other pbs: 100y 9.7 (1951), 200m 21.2 (1952), 220ySt 20.7 (1952).

Christian FUCHS on 8 January aged 43. He was a journalist who was founder and first editor-in-chief of the German Athletics Federation website www.leichtathletik.de. His last international report was from the 2017 European Indoor Champs in Belgrade.

Jonathan GREY (USA) (b, 13 Feb 1988) on 10 February when he took his own life. A graduate of William & Mary University in his best year on the track he set pbs for 3000m 8:06.58i, 5000m 13.37.79 and 10,000m 27:59.88. On the roads he had a half marathon best of 62:25 (2012) and marathon 2:20.08 in December 2017 and he won the US Clubs cross-country title in 2011.

Sergey Nikolayevich **LITVINOV** (USSR/Russia) (b. 23 Jan 1958 Tsukarov, Krasnodar) on 19 February in Sochi. For over 30 years he has ranked second on the world all-time list for the hammer to Yuriy Sedykh and he may well stay there for many years to come. They are the only two men ever to have thrown the hammer more than 85 metres, yet Litvinov twice threw over this distance and lost to Sedykh, at Cork in 1984 and at the 1986 European Championships, when he opened with 85.74. However, he beat his great rival to gain the 1988 Olympic title and he was World champion in 1983 and 1987. He was also Olympic silver medallist in 1980 and was 3rd at the Europeans in 1982 in addition to his 2nd in 1986. He set three world hammer records, 81.66m in 1980, 83.98 in 1982 and 84.14 in 1983. His best ever was 86.04 in 1986.

He came to international prominence with bronze at the 1975 European Juniors and added a silver in 1977, with world junior records of 72.38 (1976) and 74.32 (1977). He was USSR champion in 1979 and 1983, and won the World Cup in 1979 and the European Cup in 1983 and 1987. He came back to form to take the Russian title and a third European Cup win and 7th in the World Champion-ships in 1993. A teacher, he competed for Rostov-on-Don VS. He coached the 2003 World hammer champion Ivan Tikhon (Belarus).

Annual progress: 1974- 60.68, 1975- 65.32, 1976- 72.38, 1977- 74.32, 1978- 76.22, 1979- 79.82, 1980- 81.66, 1981- 79.60, 1982- 83.98, 1983- 84.14, 1984- 85.20, 1985- 76.94, 1986- 86.04, 1987- 83.48, 1988- 84.80, 1990- 81.74, 1991- 79.42, 1992- 80.26, 1993- 82.16, 1994- 75.38, 1995- 67.92

His son **Sergey** (b. 27 Jan 1986 Rostov-on-Don) initially competed for Belarus, then took up his mother's German nationality and was 5th at hammer in the 2009 Worlds, before opting for Russia in 2011; In all he has competed at five World Championships, with a best of 5th in 2013, and he was the European bronze medallist in 2014. Pb 80.98 (2012).

Hazel Margaret **RIDER** (née Needham) (GBR) 2 Sep 1932) on 6 January. She won the 1951 WAAA mile title when aged 18 (2nd 1950 & 1952). Pbs: 880y 2:16.3 and 1M 5:12.6 (both 1952). A member of Cambridge Harriers, London and later its President. She was WAAA Hon Treasurer 1960-3 and a founder member of the Women's Veterans Association. Her younger sister Sylvia Needham (married name du Plessis) became in 1950 at 15 one of Britain's youngest ever internationals and was WAAA discus champion in 1957.

Aristídis ROUBÁNIS (Greece) (b. 9 Mar 1932 Tripolí) on 13 January. He set a Greek record for the javelin with 65.98 in 1952 and that year competed at the Olympic Games both at javelin (dnq 22nd) and at basketball, at which he was best known

Clyde Luther **SCOTT** (USA) (b. 29 Aug 1924 Dixie, Louisiana) on 30 January. He was 2nd at 110m hurdles at the 1948 Olympic Games after beating OG champion Bill Porter in the NCAA Championships and 3rd at the US Olympic Trials. Pbs: 100y 9.6, 110mh auto 14.18, 120yh 14.0/13.7w, 220yh St 22.8/22.6w (all 1948). He went to the University of Arkansas and starred with them and at the US Naval Academy as a running back at American Football before playing for five years in the NFL for Philadelphia Eagles and then Detroit Lions. Nicknamed "Smackover" after the Arizona town where he grew up.

John Desmond **'Jack' SINCLAIR** (New Zealand) (b. 14 Mar 1927) on 11 February in Auckland. He won the NZ mile title in 1949 and 1950 (in his pb of 4:13.5) and was 6th in the 1950 Empire Games. He became professor of physiology at the University of Auckland Medical School.

Jan Rolf **SMIDING** (Sweden) (b. 4 Feb 1932 Kristianstad, né Carlsson) on 3 January. After a first international in 1954 at triple jump he represented Sweden as a javelin throswer 32 times 1956-70. Swedish javelin champion 1962 and 1966. Pbs TJ 14.21 (1954), JT 78.02 (1966).

Osvaldo Roberto **SUÁREZ** (Argentina) (b. 17

Mar 1934 Sarandí) on 16 February. One of the greatest Argentine athletes, he was 9th in the 1960 Olympic marathon in a South American record 2:21:27 (and dnf 1964). He won a record four Pan-American Games gold medals: 5000m 1955 and 1963, and 10,000m 1955 and 1959 (with silver medals at 5000m 1959 and 10,000m 1963), and a record eleven gold medals at South American Championships: five at 10,000m, four 5000m and two marathon 1956-67, having first competed when he was 18 with 6th at 1500m in 1952. He was also Ibero-American champion in 1960 at 5000m, 10,000m and marathon and in 1962 at 5000m and 10,000m, and he won the famous São Silvestre road race in São Paulo each year 1958-60. He set South American records: 2000m 5:27.0 (1953) and 5:21.0 (1961), 3000m 8:15.4 & 8:12.0 (1959), 5000m: six 14:20.7 (1956) to 14:05.0 (1960), 10,000m: five 30:30.0 (1955) to 29:26.0 (1959) and in 1958: 10M 49:53.4, 20,000m 1:02:00, 1 hour 19,344.7m. Other pbs: 1500m 3:50.8 (1962), 1M 4:16.3 (1953).

Vasilios SYLLIS (Greece) (b. 9 Mar 1929 Athens) on 5 January. He ran in the heats of the Olympic Games at 200m and 400m in 1952 and at 400m in 1960, and ran at the European Championships of 1954, 1958 and 1962. He set seven Greek records at 400m from 49.2 in 1952 to 47.7 in 1962. Pb 200m 21.9 (1961).

Gerald Dietmar Eberhard **WEISS** (Germany/GDR) (b. 8 Jan 1960 Lübz) on 18 February. With 12 internationals 1980-9, at the javelin he was 6th at the 1988 Olympic Games, 11th Europeans 1986, 2nd World University Games 1981, 5th European Cup 1987 and GDR champion 1981 (2nd 1980, 1983, 1986-8; 3rd 1984, 1989-90). Pbs: old spec 90.06 (1984), new spec 83.30 (1988).

Peter WELLS (Gt Britain & NI/New Zealand) (b. 23 May 1929, Barnet) on 5 January in Christchurch, New Zealand. Three internationals for Britain at high jump 1952-6 with 11= in 1952 and 16th in 1956 at the Olympic Games. Coached in his younger days by Arthur Gold, he placed fifth for England at the 1950 British Empire Games in Auckland. He took such a shine to New Zealand that he did not travel back with the rest of the team but settled instead in Christchurch although he did return briefly to England in 1952 to qualify for the British Olympic team. In 1954 he finished fourth for New Zealand at that year's British Empire & Commonwealth Games in Vancouver. His highest jump of 6ft 7½ in (just short of 2.02) in Papakura in December 1954 was regarded both as a British and New Zealand record. He won seven NZ titles (1951 and 1953-8) and was runner-up in the AAA Champs of 1952 (3rd 1949.

Ken YOUNG (USA) (b. 9 Nov 1941 Petrolia, California) on 3 February in Petrolia, northern California. He started to run while at Arizona State University and took a Ph.D in geophysics at the University of Chicago. From 1969 he ran about 90 marathons with a best of 2:25 in Boston in 1974. In 1992 he set an American record of 4:08 for 40 miles 1974 and a 'world record' for an indoor marathon with 2:41:29 in Chicago. He founded the National Running Data Center in 1973 and was official record keeper from 1979 to 1988 for the USATF Long Distance Running Committee. In 2003 he co-founded the Association of Road Racing Statisticians (ARRS) and did much work on devising computer models to handle the effect of wind speed and course separation – which is where the 30% separation rule arose, and the effect of downhill courses.

Add to Obituary 2016

Alexandru BORIGA (Romania) (b. 2 Dec 1944 Bezdead) in April in Târgoviste. A civil engineer by profession, he was a valued contributor of information on Romanian athletics, joining the ATFS in 1999. His "History of Athletics in Romania" was published in 2005.

Harri PALOLA (Finland) (b. 29 Oct 1966) on 8 March. A pole vaulter, he had a best of 5.62 in 1988, was 4th in the European Juniors in 1985 and competed at the European Indoors 1988-9 and World Indoors 1989.

Hans PRINSLOO made a huge contribution to to South Africa athletics, editing the South African Athletics Annual from 1992 to 2002, working closely with Gert le Roux and Riël Hauman, having been a member of SAAS from 1981.

Börje Ingvar **RENDIN** (Sweden) (b. 12 Nov 1921 Malmö, né Nilsson) on 29 November. Malmö AI. In 1941 won the inaugural Swedish U21 110 m hurdles title, and at that event ran at the 1948 Olympic Games (heat), with three further internationals. At Swedish championships he was 2nd 3 times and 3rd. twice. Pbs: 110mh 14.6 (1948), 200mh 24.5 (1945).

Ian Reeves **SMITH** (b. 6 Aug 1931 Blackburn) in October. Before moving to Perth, Australia he was a leading NUTS compiler of junior rankings in the 1960s and joined the ATFS in 1964. He later produced world rankings for middle distance events, returning to Britain in 1985.

Burghild WIECZOREK (née NEUMANN) (Germany/GDR) (b. 4 May 1943 Dessau) on 28 November. A long jumper she had 21 internationals 1960–70, with 4th at the 1968 Olympic Games, 9th at the 1966 Europeans and 4th at the 1970 Eupean Indoors. She was GDR champion in 1966 and indoors in 1965-6 and 1970, setting GDR records at 6.48 and 6.57 in 1968. Other pbs: 200m 25.2, 80mh 11.5 , HJ 1.61, Pen 4558 (all 1968)

DRUGS BANS 2017

As announced by IAAF or national governing bodies. Suspension: L - life ban, y = years, m = months, W = warning and disqualification, P = pending hearing

Leading athletes

Men

Ryan Bailey USA (bobsleigh)	10 Jan	2y
Chris Carter USA	5 Mar	9m
Joseph Gitau KEN	8 Jan	4y
Marquise Goodwin USA	1 Apr	1y
Yevgeniy Labutov KAZ	30 Mar	4y
Nigel Levine GBR	Dec	P
Petro Mamu ERI	30 Jul	9m
Darien Moore USA	4 Mar	4y
Aziz Ouadai MAR	17 Apr	4y
Lhoussaine Oukhrid MAR	15 Oct	P
Oleksiy Semenov UKR	1 Jun	4y
Maksim Sidorov RUS	6 Jul	1y
Tiian Smit	22 Apr	4y
Rohit Yadev IND	Apr	P
Roman Yarko UKR	6 May	4y

Women

Margaret Bamgbose NGR	1 Jul	6m
Jo Blair GBR		P
Ding Changqin CHN	16 Apr	2y
Rosefline Chepngetich KEN	16 Jul	8m
Cassie Fien AUS	20 Apr	9m
Dawn Harper Nelson USA	8 Feb	3m
Lydia Jele BOT		P
Hanna Kasyanova UKR	21 Apr	9m
Manpreet Kaur IND	24 Apr	4y
Louise Leballo RSA	20 Mar	8y
Andreea Ograzeanu ROU	18 Feb	4y
Jessia Peris AUS		P
Olesya Povh UKR		P
Anastasiya Puzakova BLR	7 Jun	4y
Irina Sergeyeva RUS	? year	2.5y
Jemima Sumgong KEN	7 Apr	4y
Wang Jiali CHN	9 Aug	8y
Ajee' Wilson USA	11 Feb	W
Yang Xinli CHN	3 Sep	4y
Olha Zemlyak UKR		P
Zhang Yingying CHN	16 Apr	4y

8y: Simona Maxim ROU (23 May); **4y**: Abdullah Al-Khalifa KSA (4 Mar), Antonello Bassano ITA (18 Mar), Medeni Demr TUR (19 Apr), Gaetano Di Franco ITA (2 Jul), Mohammed El Sayed Eid Moustafa EGY (15 Mar), Abdelhadi Fettah FRA (5 Mar), Dmytro Harnyk UKR (14 Feb), Sabrina Kadasheva RUS (4 Aug), Ivan Khudyakov RUS (23 Mar), Lelia Koukhan IRI (25 Sep), Pradeep Kumara SRI (1 Jun), Damir Kusainov KAZ (12 Jun), Liu Baoqing CHN (5 Apr), Rakhat Magzamov KAZ (13 May), Jaromir Mazgal CZE (10 Jun), Francesco Megale ITA (12 Mar), Marco Moletto ITA (16 Jul), Mohamed Msandeki TAN (2 Jan), Robert Myring-Thompson GBR (20 Feb), Olga Nenahova RUS (7 Aug), Hadia Sharifi IRI (25 Sep), Simone van der Nest RSA (7 Apr), Verushka Woset RSA (7 Apr); **2y**: Adela Comor BIH (11 Jun), Danijela Kuna CRO (9 Apr), Yang Hua CHN (22 Feb); **1y**: Su Xueting CHN (26 Feb), Paulo Zilvetti ITA (2 Apr); **6m**: Aimine Bouriga MAR (9 Jul); **5m**: Geronimo Souza BRA (8 Jan); **W**: Talal Alzabarmawi KSA (4 Mar), Dulce García CHI (Jan), Dane Roets RSA (8 Feb), Lyudmila Rudzko BLR (23 Feb).

Coaches: Life ineligibility: Kenta Bell USA, Vladimir Kazarin RUS, Aleksey Melnikov RUS

Add to Drugs bans in 2016

Leading athletes

Men *Name*	*Date*	*Ban*
Konrad Bukowiecki POL	19 Jul	W
Jamel Chatbi ITA	30 Jun	8y
Abdellah Dacha MAR	14 Jul	2y
Amine El Manaoui MAR	11 Jun	4y
Jason Livermore JAM	16 Dec	2y
Iván López CHI	26 Feb	4y
Mauricio Valdivia CHI	26 Feb	4y
Jason Young USA	17 Nov	4y

Women

Saoud Aït Salem ALG	11 Mar	18m
Florence Chepsoi KEN	5 Nov	2y
Betelhem Desalegn UAE	22 Jul	2y
(results annulled 6 Mar 2014 to 13 Aug 2015)		
Yekaterina Doseykina RUS	1 Dec	2y
(results annulled 5 Aug 2015 to 21 Nov 2016)		
Manpreet Kaur IND	1 Jun	P
Molly Ludlow USA	21 Dec	W
Nataliya Lupu ROU	29 Jul	8y
Albina Mayorova RUS	14 Mar	4y
Imani Oliver USA	7 Jul	2y
(results annulled from 16 Mar 2016)		
Brianna Rollins USA	19 Dec	1y
Yekaterina Sharmina RUS	24 Sep	4y
née Martynova, (results annulled from 17 June 2011)		
Daniela Stanciu ROU	21 Feb	1y 8m

8y: Veysi Adslan TUR (9 Oct), Sorin Mineran ROU (9 Oct); **4y**: Cristobal Almudi ESP (14 May), Mónica Cajamarca ECU (10 Apr), Maurizio Carta ITA (5 Oct), Shieys Chepkosgei KEN (8 Oct), Martina Del Rosso SWE (23 Oct), Seref Dirli TUR (13 Mar), Nicholas Fernandez FRA (4 Dec), Riaf Guerfi FRA; Han Shunyuan CHN (27 Nov), Harkirat Kaur IND (30 Apr), Derya Kaya TUR (14 Aug), Mahesh Kale IND (4 Sep), Rahima Kolay TUR (22 May), Oleg Kramar UKR (2 Apr), Anna Lupke GER (9 Oct), Kevin Moore MLT (11 Jun), Fredrik Moraeus SWE (23 Mar), Sharon Muli KEN (29 Apr), Priyanka Panwar IND (2 Jul), Qin Zhan CHN (29 Jul), Latifa Schuster FRA (9 Oct), Eliya Daudi Sidame TAN (16 Oct), Haile Tolossa ETH (15 May), Vanesa Wohlgernuth ARG (30 Oct), Yang Yidi CHN (28 Jul), Yugant Singh IND (14 May); **3y**: Said Belharizi FRA (23 Oct); **2y 6m**: Giovana Da Mata BRA (25 Sep); **2y**: Dorjpalam Batbayar MGL (16 Oct), Samara de Camargo BRA (28 Aug), Patience Khumalo RSA (20 Feb), Sarah Klein AUS (13 Feb); **1y 6m**: Demet Dinc TUR (21 Mar); **1y 3m**: Ken Kirui Tele KEN (29 Apr) **1y**: Zilya Garipova RUS (15 Sep), Filipo Girardi ITA (25 Jul), Hsu Yu-Fang TPE (24 Jun), Ümmühan Karacadir TUR (20 Apr), Paul Matheka KEN (7 Aug), Jonathan Sanford (1 Apr); **6m**: Vladimir Brundukov BLR (3 Nov), Sara Cortez CHI (8 Apr); **4m**: Christel Dewalle FRA (22 Jul)

Silvia Danekova had been listed for a possible test failure in 2016, but the Bulgarian Olympic Committee cleared her in 2017.

Added to original bans as competed while ineligible on 25 Sep: 4y: Yevgeniy Khokhlov RUS, Larisa Kleymenova RUS; 1y: Tamara Schemtova RUS.

2015

Leading athletes

Men *Name*	*Date*	*Ban*
Nader Belhanbel MAR	14 Jul	21m
Benjamin Ngandu KEN	6 Jun	4y
Aleksandr Shelever AUS (5 Nov), RUS	22 May	4y
Stanislav Yemelyanov RUS	2 Jun	8y
(all results annulled from 2 Jun 2015)	11 Oct	Life
Women		
Mercy Kibarys KEN	8 Mar	W
Tori Polk USA	15 May	2y
Kenna Wolter USA	30 Nov	2y

8y: Narin Canbek TUR (27 Jul); **4y**: Nesebe Atacan TUR (23 May). Abdelmounaim Harroufi MAR (1 May), Andrey Kozhan BLR (15 May), Mujo Krakonja SWE (7 Dec), Samira Messad ALG (1 Aug), Hemen Talib Mustafa SWE (2 Mar), Omer Oti TUR (26 Dec), Talat Ovat SWE (23 Nov), Vikas Patel USA (1 Jun) Yuliya Smirnova RUS (12 Jul), Joel Vieira BRA (17 May), Atlanta Westbrook USA; **2y**: Zenia Almshdiny IRQ (25 Apr), Steve Camilleri MLT (15 Jan), Paul Chirchir KEN (30 Aug), Pak Hüseyin TUR (19 May), Nana Owusu-Nyantekyi GBR (25 Aug), Ignacio Rojas CHI (23 May); **1y**: Aihemaiti Ainikerjiang CHN (19 Oct), **W**: Elaine Arias ECU (28 Aug)

Coach: Life: Metin Sazak TUR; **4y**: Lyudmila Fedoriva (Belova) RUS (7 May), Valeriy Volkov RUS

2014

Men		
Kirill Sukharev RUS	15 Jul	2y
Women		
Batelhem Desalegn UAE	6 Mar	2y
(results annulled 6 Mar 2014 to 22 Jul 2016, when 2y ban started)		
Yekaterina Poistyogova RUS	21 Oct	2y

8y: Juliana Moreira BRA (28 Mar); **4y**: Mounir Acheriki FRA (1 Jan), Abdelmajid Hissou MAR (23 May), Cliff Nielsen USA (14 Aug); **2y**: Davide Inocenti ITA (30 Apr), Wang Dong CHN (15 Sep); **W**: Cécile Bennejean FRA (14 Dec)

Coaches: 8y: Jon Drummond USA; Eleven Turkish coaches (six lifetime, one 4-years)

2013

Men		
Hatem Mersal EGY	13 Nov	2y
Soslen Tsirikhov RUS	15 Aug	2y
Maksim Dyldin RUS	5 Aug	4y
(results annulled 5 Aug 2012 to 22 May 2015, when previous 4y ban started)		
Jason Young USA	24 Jan	4y
Women		
Kelly-Ann Baptiste TRI	24 Mar	1y 9m
Anna Bulgakova RUS	16 Aug	2y
(results annulled from 16 Aug 13 to 15 Aug 15)		
Anna Pyatykh RUS	6 Jul	4y
(results annulled from 6 Jul 2013 to 15 Dec 2016, and see 2007)		

4y: Riad Guerfi FRA (24 Apr); **2y**: David Edblad SWE (2 Dec), Abdulaziz Ladan Mohammed KSA (9 Aug)

2012

Men		
Aleksey Bartsaykin RUS	9 Sep	4y
(results annulled from 9 Sep 2012)		
Kirill Ikonnikov RUS	5 Aug	8y
(results annulled 5 Aug 2012 to 8 Oct 2016)		
Alex Schwazer ITA	30 Jul	3y 6m
(results annulled from 18 Mar 2012)		
Denys Yurchenko UKR	22 Aug	2y
Women		
Gulfita Khanafeyeva RUS	8 Aug	
Yuliya Chermoshanskaya RUS	20 Aug	2y
Viktoriya Gurova/Valyukevich RUS	5 Aug	2y
(results annulled 5 Aug 2012 to 4 Aug 2014)		
Svetlana Karamasheva RUS		2.5y
(results annulled 14 Jun 2012 to 16 Aug 2014)		
Lyudmila Kovalenko UKR	27 Jun	2y
(results annulled 27 Jun 2012 to 10 Apr 2016 (now Lyudmila Lyakhovich BLR, 2y from 31 Oct 2017)		
Vita Palamar UKR	23 Aug	2y
Marharyta Tverdohlib UKR	7 Aug	2y

2011

Men		
Recep Celik TUR	27 Aug	8y
Abdellah Falil MAR	9 Apr	4y
Andrey Krivov RUS	20 May	3y
(results annulled 20 May 2011 to 6 Jul 2013)		
Women		
Lyubov Kharlamova RUS	27 Jul	2y
Anna Omarova RUS	29 Aug	2y
Olena Shumkina UKR	20 May	3y 6m
Svetlana Vasilyeva RUS	18 Nov	4y
(results annulled 18 Oct 2011 to 14 Jul 2013 and 24 May to 12 Dec 2016)		

2010

Women		
Asli Cakir Alptekin TUR	29 Jul	Life

2009

Men		
Yevgeniy Borisov RUS	20 Aug	2y
Abdellah Tagharrafet MAR	10 Sep	4y
Women		
Tatyana Chernova RUS	15 Aug	3y 8m
(results annulled 15 Aug 2009 to 22 Jul 2013)		
Athanasía Pérra GRE	13 Aug	4y
(results annulled 15 Aug 2009 to 14 Aug 2011)		
Natalya Yevdokimova RUS	17 Aug	4y
(results annulled 17 Aug 2009 to 29 May 2012)		

2008

Men		
Denis Alekseyev RUS	23 Aug	4y
(also had 2-year ban from test on 27 Jun 2013)		
Samuel Francis QAT	13 Aug	2y
Pyotr Trofimov RUS	13 Aug	4y
(results annulled 13 Aug 2009 to 18 May 2013)		
Women		
Inga Abitova RUS	16 Aug	4y
Anna Chicherova RUS	24 Aug	2y
Anastasiya Kapachinskaya RUS	17 Aug	4y
Josephine Onyia ESP	18 Aug	L
Already banned for 2 years then and given a life ban in 2015, loses all results from this date		
Vita Palamar UKR	23 Aug	2y
Svetlana Usovich BLR	23 Aug	2y

2007

Women		
Darya Pishchalnikova RUS	29 Aug	2y
Already given 2-year ban for failed test on 10 Apr 2007 and 10-year ban from 20 May 2012 test,. Now loses results from 1.5.2011 to 20.5.12.		
Anna Pyatykh RUS	31 Aug	4y

WORLD LIST TRENDS - MEN

This table shows the 10th and 100th bests in the year lists for the last eight years, with previous bests.

10th Bests	**To 2009**	**2010**	**2011**	**2012**	**2013**	**2014**	**2015**	**2016**	**2017**
100m	9.95- 08	9.95	**9.89**	9.94	9.97	9.96	9.91	9.93	9.95
200m	20.03- 00	20.11	20.16	20.10	20.10	20.08	19.97	**19.96**	20.01
400m	44.51- 96	44.81	44.78	44.77	44.82	44.71	**44.36**	44.46	44.48
800m	1:43.66- 96	1:43.89	1:44.07	1:43.71	1:43.87	1:43.71	1:43.72	**1:43.55**	1:44.44
1500m	3:31.10- 04	3:32.20	3:31.84	3:31.61	3:31.94	3:30.98	**3:30.29**	3:32.30	3:32.66
5000m	**12:54.99- 03**	12:55.95	12:59.15	12:55.99	13:01.64	13:03.85	13:05.30	13:03.22	13:08.16
10000m	**27:00.30- 07**	27:17.61	26:52.84	27:03.49	27:21.50	27:28.27	27:18.86	27:05.64	27:08.94
Half Mar	59:30- 09	59:40	59:39	**59:15**	59:54	59:21	59:28	59:31	59:22
Marathon	2:06:25- 08	2:05:52	2:05:45!	**2:04:54**	2:05:16	2:05:13	2:06:00	2:05:21	2:05:39
3000mSt	**8:08.14- 02**	8:09.87	8:08.43	8:10.20	8:08.83	8:11.86	8:13.37	8:10.65	8:11.82
110mh	13.19- 07	13.28	13.23	**13.13**	13.18	13.19	**13.13**	13.20	13.15
400mh	**48.25- 02**	448.47	48.47	48.41	48.46	48.69	48.44	48.49	48.40
HJ	**2.36- 88**	2.32	2.33	2.32	2.34	2.34	2.33	2.35	2.32
PV	**5.90- 98**	5.80	5.80	5.73	5.80	5.76	5.82	5.80	5.83
LJ	**8.35- 97**	8.25	8.27	8.26	8.29	8.28	8.29	8.31	8.30
TJ	**17.48- 85**	17.29	17.35	17.31	17.26	17.27	17.24	17.16	17.27
SP	21.63- 84	21.29	21.16	21.14	21.09	21.37	21.14	21.30	**21.82**
DT	**68.20- 82**	66.90	67.21	67.50	65.98	66.11	66.40	67.13	66.52
HT	**81.88- 88**	78.73	79.27	79.56	79.16	78.27	78.22	77.78	77.72
JT	87.12- 96/97	85.12	84.81	84.72	84.61	85.92	86.21	86.48	**87.97**
Decathlon	**8526- 98**	8253	8288	8322	8390	8311	8398	8413	8345
20kmW	**1:18:30- 05**	1:20:36	1:19:57	1:19:20	1:19:36	1:19:42.1	1:19:14	1:19:24	1:19:12
50kmW	3:41:30- 05	3:47:54	3:44:03	**3:41:24**	3:43:38	3:43:02	3:44:17	3:42:57	3:44:35

Peak years shown in bold

Men 100th Bests									
100m	10.22- 09	10.26	10.21	10.20	10.21	10.18	10.16	**10.14**	10.17
200m	20.66- 99/00/07	20.71	20.63	20.57	20.60	20.51	20.51	**20.45**	20.49
400m	45.78- 00	45.92	45.91	45.79	45.87	45.69	**45.61**	45.71	45.65
800m	1:46.54- 99	1:46.76	1:46.50	1:46.56	1:46.44	1:46.60	1:46.51	1:46.44	**1:46.26**
1500m	3:38.42- 97	3:38.47	3:37.77	**3:36.84**	3:37.77	3:38.47	3:38.13	3:38.20	3:37.88
5000m	13:25.05- 08	13:25.88	13:26.29	**13:23.58**	13:27.29	13:28.60	13:27.10	13:24.13	13:26.67
10000m	**28:04.47- 08**	28:21.00	28:15.79	28:06.74	28:18.68	28:20.77	28:08.4	28:06.33	28:11.02
Half Mar	61:28- 09	61:38	61:31	61:19	61:25	61:17	**60:58**	61:21	61:04
Marathon	2:10:22- 08	2:09:31	2:09:19!	**2:08:32**	2:09:06	2:08:58	2:09:14	2:09:28	2:09:10
3000mSt	**8:31.06- 04**	8:35.29	8:35.45	8:31.2	8:34.42	8:35.05	8:33.69	8:32.63	8:32.03
110mh	13.67- 08	13.68	13.67	13.66	13.67	13.67	13.62	**13.61**	13.65
400mh	50.06- 00	50.41	50.28	50.15	50.16	50.21	50.06	49.89	**49.88**
HJ	**2.24- 84/88/89/92/96**	2.23	**2.24**	**2.24**	**2.24**	**2.24**	**2.24**	**2.24**	**2.24**
PV	**5.55- 00**	5.42	5.45	5.50	5.50	5.50	5.50	5.51	5.51
LJ	**7.96- 04**	7.91	7.94	7.93	7.92	7.89	7.90	7.94	7.93
TJ	**16.60- 88**	16.46	16.53	16.49	16.40	16.38	16.44	16.52	16.43
SP	19.48- 84	19.08	19.18	19.51	19.41	19.47	19.55	**19.56**	19.46
DT	60.96- 84	59.77	59.98	60.95	60.21	60.64	60.36	**61.36**	60.31
HT	**73.06- 84**	70.78	70.44	71.22	70.49	70.50	70.73	71.33	70.82
JT	77.14- 91	76.71	77.38	77.78	77.10	77.16	77.51	**78.29**	77.57
Decathlon	**7702- 88**	7526	7678	7648	7586	7559	7594	7620	7634
20kmW	1:22:48- 05	1:24:23	1:23:40	1:23:10	1:22:56	1:23:07	1:23:24	**1:22:25**	1:22:33
50kmW	4:03:49- 99	4:08:08	4:06:15	4:03:04	4:08:33	4:06:22	**4:02:23**	4:02:37	4:06:30

! From 2011 main marathon lists no longer include Boston or other such excessively downhill races

Number of athletes achieving base level standards for world lists:

Men		2012	2013	2014	2015	2016	2017
100m	10.25	148	132	163	168	203	187
200m	20.69	165	140	187	194	224	202
400m	46.19	184	177	202	216	228	201
800m	1:47.59	220	190	202	208	226	225
1500m	3:39.99	201	184	173	171	180	179
5000m	13:37.0	203	180	169	204	195	182
10000m	28:35.0	199	168	155	225	202	186
HMar	61:59	199	171	199	182	179	200
Mar	2:10:59	233	212	207	191	169	212
3000St	8:39.9	184	141	138	144	183	179
110mh	13.89	214	199	208	215	220	210
400mh	50.79	186	177	191	200	224	237

		2012	2013	2014	2015	2016	2017
HJ	2.20	216	197	211	216	212	213
PV	5.40	177	179	178	168	192	189
LJ	7.80	183	181	182	182	207	199
TJ	16.30	144	120	124	126	154	134
SP	18.70	181	180	180	180	196	191
DT	58.00	177	166	173	171	189	168
HT	68.00	158	146	149	156	171	173
JT	74.00	199	190	187	199	215	213
Dec	7400	173	143	150	157	145	168
20kmW	1:25:00	175	175	151	166	192	212
50kmW	4:10:00	132	106	113	134	142	11
Total		4251	3854	3992	4173	4448	4372

The 2017 numbers compared to those of 2016: for 10th best 8-15, 100th best 8-13 (2 tie), base level 7-16

WORLD LIST TRENDS - WOMEN

This table shows the 10th and 100th bests in the year lists for the last eight years, with previous bests.

10th Bests	**To 2009**	**2010**	**2011**	**2012**	**2013**	**2014**	**2015**	**2016**	**2017**
100m	10.92- 88	11.08	11.01	10.99	10.93	11.01	10.92	**10.90**	10.94
200m	22.24- 88	22.49	22.55	22.37	22.40	22.46	22.23	**22.16**	22.39
400m	**49.74- 84**	50.43	50.67	50.06	50.19	50.74	50.32	50.25	50.14
800m	**1:56.91- 88**	1:58.67	1:58.21	1:57.77	1:58.92	1:58.84	1:58.34	1:58.28	1:58.01
1500m	**3:58.07- 97**	4:00.25	4:01.73	3:59.71	4:01.48	4:00.17	4:01.26	4:00.18	4:00.52
5000m	14:49.86- 09	**14:38.64**	14:39.44	14:50.80	14:47.12	14:52.67	14:47.75	14:38.92	14:39.33
10000m	30:39.86- 08	31:29.03	31:10.02	30:59.19	31:04.85	31:48.6	31:13.29	**30:37.38**	31:11.86
Half Mar	68:23- 00	67:52	68:07	67:42	67:39	68:13	68:18	67:16	**66:35**
Marathon	2:23:22- 06	2:23:44	2:22:43!	**2:20:57**	2:23:00	2:22:30	2:22:51	2:22:40	2:20:59
3000mSt	**9:18.54-09**	9:24.84	9:25.96	9:23.52	9:27.49	9:23.43	9:20.64	9:18.85	**9:13.35**
100mh	**12.58- 08**	12.65	12.73	12.62	12.81	12.71	12.59	12.63	12.61
400mh	**53.99- 04**	54.58	54.69	54.21	54.38	54.74	54.37	54.15	54.29
HJ	**2.01- 03**	1.97	1.96	1.96	1.97	1.97	1.97	1.98	1.96
PV	4.70- 07/08	4.66	4.71	4.70	4.71	4.71	4.72	**4.81**	4.73
LJ	**7.07- 88**	6.89	6.88	6.97	6.91	6.90	6.93	6.93	6.83
TJ	**14.84- 08**	14.48	14.57	14.60	14.50	14.40	14.32	14.56	14.42
SP	**20.85- 87**	19.47	19.26	19.60	18.81	19.03	18.89	19.11	18.83
DT	**70.34- 88**	64.04	63.91	64.45	64.46	65.51	64.79	65.14	64.56
HT	74.40- 08	73.40	72.65	**75.59**	75.02	74.20	73.66	73.09	74.56
JT	64.89- 00	63.36	63.50	64.91	63.55	64.50	65.01	65.14	**65.37**
Heptathlon	**6540- 88**	6204	6338	6466	6345	6395	6458	6458	6421
20kmW	1:27:18- 08	1:29:20	1:28:41	**1:27:08**	1:27:53	1:27:54	1:27:09	1:27:18	1:27:538

Peak years shown in bold

Women 100th Bests									
100m	11.36- 00/08	11.40	11.36	11.34	11.35	11.32	11.31	**11.27**	11.29
200m	23.17- 08	23.27	23.21	23.10	23.19	23.17	23.08	**23.00**	23.03
400m	**52.08- 08**	52.52	52.33	52.16	52.25	52.36	52.25	52.13	52.15
800m	2:01.50- 84	2:02.14	2:01.86	**2:01.48**	2:02.05	2:02.05	2:02.06	2:01.80	2:02.14
1500m	4:10.22- 84	4:10.50	4:09.88	**4:09.06**	4:09.98	4:10.09	4:10.24	4:09.28	4:09.17
5000m	15:27.20- 04	15:37.45	15:31.67	15:32.88	15:35.74	15:33.42	15:32.67	**15:26.28**	15:30.28
10000m	32:30.10- 08	32:57.59	32:53.44	32:38.95	32:48.60	32:43.90	32:29.06	**32:21.98**	32:37.21
Half Mar	70:57- 09	70:59	71:06	70:48	70:44	70:45	70:43	70:35	**70:15**
Marathon	2:29:53- 08	2:29:36	2:28:32	**2:28:01**	2:29:10	2:29:17	2:28:24	2:28:49	2:28:15
3000mSt	9:56.48- 08	10:03.50	9:59.44	9:53.79	9:56.50	9:53.19	9:52.62	**9:46.86**	9:52.89
100mh	13.22- 00/08	13.23	13.16	13.11	13.19	13.14	13.17	**13.07**	13.14
400mh	57.21- 07	57.22	57.26	57.14	57.40	57.34	57.08	**56.85**	57.03
HJ	**1.88- 86/87/88/92/93**	11.87	1.86	1.87	1.87	1.86	1.86	1.87	1.86
PV	4.25- 08	4.25	4.30	4.31	4.30	4.30	4.32	**4.35**	4.33
LJ	6.53- 88	6.51	6.50	**6.55**	6.49	6.45	6.49	6.51	6.48
TJ	**13.75- 08**	13.67	13.70	13.71	13.69	13.60	13.62	13.60	13.56
SP	**17.19- 87**	16.46	16.60	16.82	16.65	16.60	16.84	16.96	16.92
DT	**58.50- 92**	55.55	56.12	56.94	55.70	56.27	56.26	56.83	55.99
HT	64.81- 08	64.12	64.79	**65.78**	64.65	64.79	65.67	65.75	64.86
JT	55.55- 00	54.98	55.34	55.97	55.10	55.78	55.95	56.19	**56.20**
Heptathlon	**5741- 88**	5568	5591	5702	5560	5668	5715	5735	5703
20kmW	1:34:11- 05	1:36:32	1:34:52	1:33:43	1:33:48	1:35:20	1:34:16	1:33:41	**1:33:32**

All-time record levels indicated in bold.

! From 2011 main marathon lists no longer include Boston or other such excessively downhill races.

Number of athletes achieving base level standards for world lists:

Women		2012	2013	2014	2015	2016	2017
100m	11.44	173	151	169	179	215	196
200m	23.29	152	140	138	174	198	183
400m	52.99	210	196	190	213	236	230
800m	2:03.50	196	166	184	191	211	188
1500m	4:13.5	197	167	169	164	195	202
5000m	15:45.0	201	167	172	192	224	187
10000m	33:00.0	151	131	133	169	176	154
HMar	72:00	199	204	193	200	212	237
Mar	2:32:00	212	170	171	195	196	230
3000mSt	10:05.0	167	144	161	166	195	164
100mh	13.39	198	175	195	191	228	212

		2012	2013	2014	2015	2016	2017
400mh	57.99	179	143	152	166	192	159
HJ	1.85	164	155	148	142	170	143
PV	4.25	131	123	133	143	169	140
LJ	6.35	212	171	168	186	189	175
TJ	13.30	199	184	171	169	189	158
SP	15.85	180	177	189	194	216	200
DT	53.65	172	159	152	165	180	174
HT	61.00	205	190	193	205	227	224
JT	53.00	177	159	172	176	188	202
Hep	5450	157	140	156	155	189	140
20kmW	1:38:00	173	194	148	176	198	192
TOTAL		3826	3463	3505	3745	4201	4107

TThe 2017 numbers compared to those of 2016: for 10th best 8-14, 100th best 5-17, base level 4-18

Olympic years continue to provide the top depth of performance, although it is notable that the drop off from 2016 to 2017 was much less than that from 2012 to 2013.

AMENDMENTS TO ATHLETICS 2017

p.11 Feb 3 Düsseldorf: Ortega 7.49 for 60mh
p.43-9 Running head should be 2016 not 2015
p.48 30 Oct Osaka Marathon winner: Hiroki Yamagishi JPN 2:12:59 (Ngandu drugs dq)
p.58-63 Olympic Games: drugs dq: 400m (7) Zemlyak, 4x100m (6) UKR Povh dq, 4x400m (5) UKR Zemlyak dq
p.70-71 European Champs: drugs 4x100m (4) UKR Povh dq, 4x400m (6) UKR Zemlyak dq
p.75 Ibero-American Champs. 1500m/3000m: Carlos Martin Díaz CHI 3:39.20/7:54.31 (as López drugs dq)
p.80 European Indoors 2017: W 60m: drugs dq (2) Povh. move up the rest
p.91 Obituaries in ATHLETICS 2016: Yeóryios Tsakaníkas
p.94 John Byron HOLT
p.97 Anne PASHLEY (b. 1934)
p.135 Franck Elemba is from the Republic of Congo (CGO).
p.142 EST Champs: delete W LJ: Balta 6.66 (6.51 is correct).
p.153 GER Champs. HJ: Eike Onnen
p.158 HUN Champs: W TJ: Krisztina Hoffer 13.02
p.183 NZ Champs: TJ: Anna Thomson 12.26,
p.198 RSA Champs: W Mar: Mapaseka Makhanya 2:51:32 as Khumalo drugs dq
p.201 Swedish Champs Women 20kW: Ellinor Hogrell 2:10:27.

2016 World Lists

Men

100m: 10.05/9.94w Forte b. 7.1.93 (& 200m 19.97); move to wa: 10.16w 3.0 Mothibi; 10.23w Jeremy Hicks. 10.24w Kurosawa 8.7.94, Iwasaki 14.6.96

200m: hand timed 20.2wA Maartens

400m: 45.66A Opiny 12.12.91; Junior: 46.17 Hooper

800m: 1:46.7A Oloirusha, 1:46.82A Abuu Mayanja 9.10.95, 1:47.2A Kipyegon 19.12.90, 1:47.3A Kipchirchir 1.9.97, 1:47.39 Labsir; Jnr: 1:47.53 Tadesse Lemi

1500m: 3:37.65 Hassan Mead 28.6.91 (also 3000m 7:38.85i, 5000m 13:04.17); Drugs dq 3:38.64 López (replace by 3:39.39i 15 Feb as best before ban). Jnr 3:42.3A Kiplangat 22.10.99

5000m: 13:05.59 Tamire 10.1.94, 13:23.03 Fikadu 29.12.95, 13:31.91 Niyonukiza J 10.12.98, delete 13:35.28 Kipchirchir (= Kiptoo at 13:30.3A)

5000m/10000m: 13:19.54/27:26.68 Kiplimo UGA-J.

Uncertainty over the John Maina: 5000m - b. 14.7.93 – may have 10000m 27:21.97 (for Fujitsu), b. 3.8.94 John Ndirangu Maina may have the 13:16.82 5000m. For Fujitsu: 1500m: 3:40.13, 5000m 13:17.93 2 Nobeoka 7 May, 27:21.97 and 27:43.70 1 Yokohama 23 Apr

10000m: 28:08.92 Jemal Yimer Mekonnen 11.9.96, 28:28.40 Mogusu 1.12.96; Jnr: 28:38.46 Kokeb Ghebru ERI-J 13.3.98 1 Yokohama 14 May; drugs dq 28:28.56 Gandu

HMar: 61:39+ M Teshome .93 (& Mar 2:09:24)

Mar: 2:08:55 Omullo .87, 2:09:05 B Teshome .93, 2:09:08 D Ruto 7.9.78, 2:11:01 Alex Chesakit UGA 18 Sep, 2:11:05 Girma Gebre ETH 29.12.92 17 Jan, 2:11:05 Emmanuel Sikuku KEN 25.12.93 23 Oct

100k: 6:44:24 Olsson SWE

3000mSt; 8:16.14 Girma J 24.1.97?? 8:18.28 Alex Kibet .20.10.94, 8:23.39 Alex Kibet KEN 20.10.90 or 10.11.90 4 Sotteville-lès-Rouen 18 Jul; 8:38.28 Madikizela 13.6.91

110mh: best low altitude 13.65 0.6 Rivas 15 Apr

400mh: 49.37 (not 49.27) Bultheel

HJ: 2.21A Blackham, 2.20 Laine 12.6.97, Hasegawa 15.11.96; Best out: 2.33 Grabarz 4= OG Rio de Janeiro 16 Aug

PV: 5.83 Jan Kudlicka CZE 29.4.88 1 Praha 22 Jun, 5.56 Chase Brannon 1 Atlanta 10 Jun (from 5.51), 5.52 Sean Young USA 27.12.85 1 Rock Hill 28 May (from 5.42i), 5.50 Paul Malquist 27 Aug (from 5.40), 5.40 Cheyne Rahme RSA 23.1.91 17 Mar

LJ: 8.38/8.40w Ruswahl Samaai; **TJ**: 17.13 Oke

SP: Walsh 22.20 in Zürich – series: 20.73, 21.12, 22.20, 21.25, 21.07, 21.43; 20.83i Geist (68'4") J, 19.82i Vena; 18.74i Silas Ristl GER 1.4.95 17 Dec; Jnrs: Bukowiecki add 20.80 1 NC Bydgoszcz 28 Jun, 18.18 Nathan Tharaldsen USA .91 1 Fargo 6 May; Jnr 6kg: 23.24 Bukowiecki # dq, so best is his 22.94

DT: 65.67 drugs dq Young

HT: delete the 77.26? by Winkler on 22 Jun; 69.90 Y Ivanov 21 Dec (from 69.50)?; drugs dq: 76.26 Ikonnikov, so 75.39 Pronkin (2), 73.83 Korolyov (3)

Dec: 7958 Jefferson Santos; Jnr: 8162 Niklas Kaul, delete 7260 Dolezal (not junior)

4x100m: drugs dq Povh for UKR 42.36 and 42.49, best pre ban 43.64 UKR (Strohova, Bryzgina, Povh, Pohrebnyak) 1 GGala Roma 2 Jun

4x400m: 3:06.52 RUS 23 Jun, drugs dq Zemlyak for UKR 3:24.54

3000mW: 11:10.03 Wayne Snyman RSA 8.3.85 1 Brisbane 6 Feb. **10,000mW**: Jnr: 40:33.33 Amores 29.8.98

Women

100m: 11.42 Rowe 19.9.92 . **200m**: 23.26 Sanni NGR

400m: drugs dq 50.75 Zemlyak (best pre-ban 51.60 1 NCp Kirovohrad 25 May)

800m: 2:00.00 Eykens 3h5, 2:00.0A 1 Nairobi 23 Apr Emily Jerotich Tuei 13.5.86 (& 1500m 4:12.47, 1M 4:29.55), 2:00.21 Assefa 4h5; Adele Tracey 2:00.24mx – then 2:01.24 1 Watford 28 May (delete the 2:01.16); Jnr: 2:03.5A Iveen Chepkemoi KEN 25.10.97 2 Eldoret 2 Sep

1500m: delete 4:21.8A Adanech Ana (same as 4:05.22). Jnr: 4:14.0A Medina Ibrahim ETH-Y .01 4 NC Addis Ababa 24 Apr. **5000m**: 15:39.27 Alema 19.7.95

10,000m: 32:47.30 LaRocco 15.2.96

HMar: 69:52 Njeru 12.12.88, 70:13 Wanjiru 4.10.86, 70:28 Rotich 5.4.94.70:45+ Aselefech Mergia ETH 23.1.85 in Mar London 24 Apr, 70:56 Etaferahu Temesgen ETH .89 20 Mar, 71:10 Alice Kimutai KEN 9.9.92 27 Mar, 71:45 Macharia 7.12.87, 71:51 Lempus .91. **Mar** 2:25:13 Kiprop 7.7.79

3000mSt: 8:59.97 Jebet 1, 9:50.9A Kemboi 8.8.94

60mh: drugs dq 8.11 Mokhnyuk (also 1.85i HJ, 6.66i LJ and 4847 Ind Pen (best acceptable her 4745)

400mh: Siefring 30.9.95 (4215i Pen , 5627(w) Hep)

LJ: 6.46 Reuwsaat 23.11.94; Irregular/doubtful marks: 6.72 0.8 Amalia Sharoyan ARM 19.6.88 1 Elbasan 21 May, 6.72 1.4 Yuliya Tarasova UZB 13.3.86 1 NC Dushanbe 13 Jun

TJ: drugs dq 14.02 Imani Oliver # (replace in main list by 13.59i 3 NC Portland 11 Mar). 13.34 Acquah 23.5.96

SP: 17.85 Dimitriana Surdu MDA 12.5.94 1 NC Toras[pol 29 May (delete 16.72i), 16.55i Wells 25.10.94. 16.34 Nicoll 2 Jul; drugs dq 16.78 Manpreet Kaur II (replace by 16.04 1 Jan). **Hep**: 5569 Cooks 6.12.93

3000mW: drugs dq 12:00.10 Svetlana Vasilyeva

20kW: 1:30:53 Galíková

4x100m: 44.34 RUS 1 Cheboksary 23 Jun, 45.13 ECU 24 Sep **4x400m**: 3:32.29 RUS 1 Cheboksary 23 Jun

Index changes are reflected in this year's Annual.

Amendments to World Indoor Lists 2017

400m: 46.16 Igbokwe, o/s 45.87: Tyler Terry 3.12.97; **800m**: 1:47.11 Borkowski; **TJ**: 17.13 drugs dq Carter, replace by 16.75 1 Houston 10 Feb; **SP**: 20.78 drugs dq Moore, so 1/2/3 Jones, Pless, Hill; **Women: 60m** drugs dq 7.10 Povh, **800m:** doping dq 1:58.27 Wilson so 1 Lipsey, 2 Sharp, 3 Fedronic, 4 Barowski, 5 Watson; **5000m**: 15:29.83 Rohrer 27.2.97 so not –J; **60mh:** 8.01A Johnson 20.7.96

Adjusted 4x400m splits at World Indoors (p.94): Men: 1. USA 3:02.45 Kyle Clemons 46.42, Calvin Smith 45.69, Chris Giesting 45.31, Vernon Norwood 45.03; 2. BAH 3:04.75 Michael Mathieu 46.71, Alonzo Russell 45.85, Shavez Hart 46.65, Chris Brown 45.84; 3. TTO 3:05.51 Jarrin Solomon 47.42, Lalonde Gordon 45.01, Ade Alleyne-Forte 46.80, Deon Lendore 46.28 **Women**: 1. USA 3:26.38 Natasha Hastings 51.88, Quanera Hayes 50.99, Courtney Okolo 50.80, Ashley Spencer 52.74, 2. 2 POL 3:31.15 Ewelina Ptak 54.61, Małgorzata Hołub 51.78, Magdalena Gorzkowska 53.02, Justyna Swiety 51.74, 3. ROU 3:31.51 Adelina Pastor 54.02, Mirela Lavric 53.12, Andrea Miklos 52.67, Bianca Razor 51.70

Amendments to Previous World Lists

2015: SP: 19.33 Comenentia 26 Jul, 19.20i McKelvey 28 Feb, 18.65i Cornelius 13.1.95
2014: SP: 19.88 Abramchuk 21 May, 19.23i Felpel 1 Mar, 18,99 Dacres 1 Feb, 18.97 Jeffrey 17.2.91, 18.65 Jake Deaton 26.6.90 13 Jun
2013: SP: 19.76 Dauphin 14 Jun, 19.53 Borodkin 25 Jun, 19.05 Miller 15 Mar
2012: SP: 20.25 Chang 3, 20.02 Pinkelman at Madison, 19.41 Brown 1 Jul
2011: SP: 20.42i Kokuyev 16 Feb, 18.39 Nazemi 24.12.88
2010: SP: 19,46 Bauer 4, 19.03 Millán 23 Jun, 18.95i Smith 16 Jan, 18.82 Haratyk 4 Sep,
2009: SP: 20.45 Martin on 8 Jul, 20.00 Belov 2, 19.10 Anastasópoulos 5 Aug, 19.04 Saad 27 Jul, 18.96 Shahrokhi 15 Oct; Best out: 19.65 Christensen 14 Jun, 19.24 Vanek 28 Jun

International Championships Changes.

Drugs dqs – move rest up accordingly
2016 European Champs: 3000mSt: (5) Jamel Chatbi
2016 World Indoors: W 3000m: (8) Betlhem Desalegn, Hep (2) Mokhnyuk
2015 World Champs: 800m: (7) Belhanbel
2015 Asian Champs: 1500m/5000m: (1) Desalegn
2015 World Military Games: HT: Kirill Ikonnikov, so winner Yevgen Vynogradov UKR 74.77
2015 European Indoors: W 1500: (2) Poistogova
2014 World Indoors: W 1500: (7) Karamasheva. 3000: (6) Desalegn; **European Champs**: 4x400: (2) RUS
2014 World Race Walking Cup: 50k: (4) Aleksey Bartsaykin
2013 World Champs: 4x400: (3) RUS; W 400: (6) Krivoshapka, TJ: (7) Pyatykh, 4x400: (2) RUS
2013 World University Games: 4x100: (1) RUS; W DT (1) Ganeyeva
2013 European U23 Champs: W 20kW: (1) Vasilyeva
2013 European Team Champs: W HT: (3) Bulgakova
2013 European Winter Throws: W SP: (1) Kolodko
2013 European Indoors: W 1500: (4) Karamasheva, SP: (2) Kolodko
2012 Olympic Games: HT: (5) Ikonnikov, 4x400: (5) RUS; W 400: (3) Krivoshapka, TJ: (8) Valyukevich, HT: (11) Bespalova; 4x400: (1) RUS
2012 European Champs: W 5000m: (2) Kovalenko, 4x100m: (4) RUS
2012 World Race Walking Cup: 20kW: (2): Krivov
2012 European Winter Throwing Cup: W DT: (2) Pishchalnikova
2011 World Champs: W 400m: (3) Kapachinskaya, 3000mSt: (8) Kharlamova; SP: (2) Ostapchuk, (10) Omarova, 4x400: (3) RUS, 20kW: (12) Shumkina UKR
2011 World University Games: 20kW: (1) Krivov
2011 European Team Champs: 4x400m: (1) RUS; W DT: (2) Pishchalnikova RUS, 4x400: (2) RUS
2011 European Race Walking Cup: 20kW: (6) Kanaykin, (8) Krivov; **European Indoors**: W TJ: (7) Pérra
2010 European Champs: W 200: (4) Kapachinskaya, SP: (1) Ostapchuk, (2) Mikhnevich; 4x400: (1) RUS, (7) BLR; **European Team Champs**: W 200m: (2) Chermoshanskaya, 400m: (3) S Usovich, TJ (2) Pérra, HT: (3) Pchelnik, 4x100m: (1) RUS
2010 Asian Indoor Champs: 60m: (1) Francis
2010 World Indoors: 60mh: (4) Borisov; W SP: (1) Ostapchuk, (3) Mikhnevich
2009 World Champs: W 400m: (7) Kapachinskaya, 1500m: (8) Yevdokimova, HJ: (2) Chicherova
2009 European Team Champs: 4x400m: (3) RUS; W 4x100m & 4x400m; RUS (1)
2009 World Athletics Final: W HJ: (2) Chicherova, HT: (5) Pchelnik; 2009 European Team Champs: 4x400m: (3) RUS; W 4x100m & 4x400m; RUS (1)
2009 World Half Marathon: (9) Abitova
2008 Olympic Games: PV: (3) Denys Yurchenko; W 400m: (5) Anastasiya Kapachinskaya, 10,000m: (6) Inga Abitova; HJ: (3) Chicherova, (4) Slesarenko. (5) Vita Palamar, SP: (3) Ostapchuk, HT: (1) Menkova; Hep: (3/4) Chernova
2008 European Cup 10,000m: (1) Abeylegesse
2008 World Indoors: W SP: (1) Ostapchuk
2007 World Athletics Final: W SP: (1) Ostapchuk
2007 World Champs: W TJ: (4) Pyatykh, SP (2) Ostapchuk
2007 European U23 Champs: W DT: (2) Pishchalnikova

Drugs disqualifications and annulled marks – IAAF Biological Passport Cases and othersd
Men
Denis Alekseyev RUS (18.8.08-24.7.11) 400m 2009- 46.21 (& RUS 4x400m 3:02.42), 2010- 46.12i, 2011- 45.73
Aleksey Bartsaykin RUS (results annulled from 9 Sep 2012) 2012- 10kW 39:31, 30/35kW: 2:07:13/2:29:15, 2013- 30/35kW: 2:06:24/2:27:42, 2014- 35kW 2:32:10, 50kW 3:46:34
Yevgeniy Borisov RUS (20.8.09-19.8.11) 2011- 60mh 7.51, 110mh 13.78/13.42w; 2011- 60mh 7.63i
Recep Celik TUR 20kW 2012- 1:23:10
Maksim Dyldin RUS (results annulled 5 Aug 2012 to 22 May 2015, when previous 4y ban started) 400m 2013- 45.55, 2014- 45.45, 2015- 45.56; loses 2013 & 2015 RUS titles
Abdellah Falil MAR 2011- Mar 2:08:18, 2012- Mar 2:10:44
Samuel Francis QAT (results annulled 13 Aug 2008 to 12 Aug 2010) 100m: 2009- 10.19/10.01w, 2010- 10.25/10.16w (& 60m ind 6.58)
Kirill Ikonnikov RUS (from 5 Aug 2012 to 8 Oct 2016) HT: 2015- 77.15, 2016- 76.26
Andrey Krivov RUS 2012- 20kW 1:18:25 (10kW 38:45) & 1:19:27
Pavel Lyzhin BLR (15 Aug 08 to 14 Aug 10) 2008- 20.98 (best pre ban 20.88 1 Staiki 7 Jun), 2009- 20.98, 2010- 21.21 & 21.12i
Wilfredo Martínez CUB: 2009- LJ 8.13
Maksym Mazuryk UKR (25 Jul 12 - 24 Jul 14) 2013- 5.55i
Oleksandr Pyatnytsa UKR JT: 2013- 77.46, 2014- 81.10 (best after ban 74.69 14 Aug)

Alex Schwazer ITA also loses 20kW 1:17:30 18 Mar & 50kW 3:40:58 24 Mar

Dmitriy Starodubtsev RUS 2013- 5.70i, 2014- 5.70 (replace by 5.60 1 ISTAF Berlin 31 Aug)

Kirill Sukharev RUS (15.7.14-14.7.16) LJ 2015- 7.98i/7.96, 2016- 8.07i

Pyotr Trofimov RUS (13 Aug 09 to 18 May 13): 2010- 20kW 1:20:44; 2011- 3000mW 19:32.8i, 20kW 1:20:31; 2012- 10kW 39:24, 20kW 1:19:20 (& 39:10 10k); 2013- 20kW 1:18:28 (replace with 1:23:30 8 Jun)

Soslan Tsirikhov RUS: SP: 2014- 20.58

Stanislav Yemelyanov RUS (from 2 Jun 2015): 2015- 1:20:10, 2016- 1:21:57

Jason Young USA (from 24 Jan 2013): DT: 2013- 63.08, 2014- 64.36, 2016- 65.67

Denys Yurchenko UKR (22.8.08-21.8.10) PV 2009- 5.52i/5.50, 2010- 5.72i/5.40

Women

Inga Abitova RUS 2008- 3000m 9:04.7, 5000m 15:11.6, 10000m 30:37.33 (best before ban 30:46.70); 2009- 10000m 31:40.00, HMar 69:53, 25k/30k 1:25:39/1:43:23, Mar 2:25:55; 2010- given before

Tatyana Andrianova RUS (26.7.10—25.7.12 as well as previous 9.8.-5- 8.8.07) 2011- 800m 2:01.62

Kelly-Ann Baptiste TTO 2013- 100m 10.83, 200m 22.60

Anna Bulgakova RUS (16.8.13-15.8.15) 2013- (74.83), 2014- 74.16, 2015- 72.15 (replace with 68.01 2 W.Mil Mungyeong 7 Oct)

Yuliya Chermoshanskaya RUS 2008- 22.57 (replace by 22.77 0.0 2s2 Kazan 19 Jul): 2009- 200m 22.99, 2010- 22.67

Tatyana Chernova RUS (15.9.09-22.7.13). In addition to those noted in previous Annuals. 2009- LJ 6.50 (best pre ban 6.39 21 Jun).

Anna Chicherova RUS (24.8.08- 23.8.10) 2008- 2.04 (best pre ban 2.03), 2009- 2.02

Betlhem Desalegn UAE (6.3.14-13.8.15 and from 22.7.16) 2014- 4:07.05 (replace by 4:08.79i 3 XL Stockholm 6 Feb), 2M 10:06.84, 3000mSt 9:53.19; 2015- 1500m 4:05.41/4:05.61i (add 4:05.73 5h1 WCh Beijing 22 Aug), 3000m 8:53.75 (add 8:54.32 5 Hanz Zagreb 8 Sep), 5000m 15:25.15

Anastasiya Kapachinsksya RUS 200m/400m: 2009- 22.92, 49.97, 2010- 22.47/50.16, 2011- 22.55/49.35, 2012- 50.37, 2013- 22.39/50.91

Svetlana Karamasheva (Podosyonova) RUS (14 Jun 2012 to 16 Aug 2014). 2012- 800m 2:00.69, 2013- 800m 2:00.32i/2:01.53, 1000m 2:38.73i, 1500m 4:04.01, 1M 4:34.06i; 2014- 800m 1:58.70 & 2:01.53i (replace by 2:01.66 6 Rieti 7 Sep), 1000m 2:39.16i, 1500m 4:04.45 & 4:10.91i (replace by 4:08.35 9 Zagreb 2 Sep)

Lyubov Kharlamova RUS: 2010- 3000mSt 9:29.82 (replace by 9:30.75 1 NC Saransk 12 Jul 10); 2011- 3000mSt 9:29.39; 2012- 3000mSt 9:36.81, Indoor 2000mSt 6:13.10.

Yevgeniya Kolodko RUS (6 Aug 12 to 5 Aug 2014) SP: 2012- 20.48 (best pre ban 20.22 1 Adler 27 May), 2013- 19.97i/19.96.

Lyudmila Kovalenko UKR (27 Jun 2012-10.4.16) 2013- 10k 32:35, 10M 52:32, 20k 66:05, HMar 69:59; 2014- Mar 2:31:31

Antonina Krivoshapka RUS (11 Aug 12-20 Aug 14): 2012- 200m 23.03, 400m (49.81 & 49.94), 4x400 RUS 3:20.23; 2013- 200m 23.01, 400m- 49.57 (& 49.78, 49.99), 4x400 RUS 3:20.19.

Oksana Menkova BLR (20 Aug 08 to 6 Aug 14) 2009- 76.32, 2010- 67.27, 2011- 67.78, 2012- 78.69, 2013- 75.45, 2014- 71.56 (best OK 66.92), 2016- 73.07

Natalya Mikhnevich BLR (16 Aug 08 to 15 Aug 10) 2009- 20.03, 2010- 20.42i/19.80m (best OK: 19.24i 3 WK Zürich 18 Aug)

Anna Omarova RUS SP: 2012- 18.80, 2013- 18.66

Josephine Onyia ESP 100mh: (all from 18.8.08) 2011- 12.94, 2014- 13.32, 2015- 12.98

Nadezhda Ostapchuk BLR all from 13 Aug 2005 to 5 Aug 2012.

Vita Palamar UKR (23 Aug 09 to 22 Aug 10): 2008 – 1.99 best out (replace by 1.95 3= Eberstadt 28 Jun), 2009- 1.95

Darya Pchelnik BLR (20 Aug 08 to 19 Aug 10) 2009- 73.98, 2010- 75.42

Athanasía Pérra GRE (15 Aug 09 to 14 Aug 11) TJ: 2010- 14.61 & 14.07i, 2011- 14.20i/14.05

Darya Pishchalnikova RUS loses all marks from Feb 2007, these are DT: 2007- 65.78, 2008- 67.28, 2011 63.91, 2012- 70.69

Yekaterina Poistogova RUS 2015: 800m 2:00.33 & 2:01.44i, 1000m 2:40.62i

Tori Polk USA: LJ: 2015- 6.70 (best before ban 6.426/51w 28 Mar), 2016- 6.68/6.77w

Anna Pyatykh RUS (31 Aug 2007 & 6 Jul 13-15 Dec 16): 2007- 14.88, more?, 2013- 14.40 (best pre ban 14.16 5 Sochi 26 May), 2014- 14.27

Olene Shumkina UKR (from May 2011): 20kW (10kW): 2011- 1:32:17 (best earlier 1:34:52 2 NC-w Yevpatoriya 26 Feb), 2012- 1:31:55 (44:22), 2013- 1:31:54 (45:50), 2014- 1:30:41 (46:04), 2015- 1:33:27 (45:26), 2016- 1:35:33 (46:15); 3000mW: 2012- 12:35.00i

Marharyta Tverdohlib UKR (25 Jul 12-6 Aug 14) 2013- 6.67i/6.53, 2014- 6.55

Svetlana Usovich BLR (15 Aug 08-14 Aug 10) 2008- 800m 2:00.42 (best pre-ban 2:01.35 5 Bydgoszcz 1 Jul), 2010- 400m 51.37, 800m 1:59.73, 4x400m BLR 3:28.74

Viktoriya Valyukevich (Gurova) (5 Aug 12 to 4 Aug 14) 2013- LJ 6.55, TJ 14.36, 2014- TJ 14.05

Svetlana Vasilyeva RUS 20kW: 2012- 1:28:30 (10k 43:20), 2013- 1:39:56 (10k 44:24)

Natalya Yevdokimova RUS: 2010- 1500m 4:04.56, 2011- 800m 2:02.8/2:02.94, 1500m 4:03.33;

Yuliya Zaripova RUS add to previous annuals 2012- 1500m 4:10.70, 3kSt 9:05.02 etc; 2013- 1500m 4:02.56, 5000m 15:38.1

Thanks for amendments to year and all-time lists to Norbert Heinrich (SP), Yves Pinaud and Peter Rule

USAIN BOLT - A TRIBUTE

USAIN BOLT WAS the greatest superstar there has ever been in the sport of athletics. The end of his career at the 2017 World Championships was something of an anti-climax as after taking the 100m bronze medal he pulled up with a hamstring injury on the final leg of the sprint relay. Nothing can detract, however, from the majesty of his career achievements.

"Lightning Bolt", an imposing figure at 1.96m tall and 86kg, was a junior phenomenon and in 2008 proved to be the super-star of the Beijing Olympic Games as he swept to the unique feat of winning the sprint treble with world records in each final. He went on to transcend the world of track and field athletics in a way that nobody else has ever done, adding eleven World titles and repeating his Olympic treble in both 2012 and 2016. Unfortunately he could be set to lose his relay gold from 2008 as his team-mate Nesta Carter tested positive for a banned stimulant on re-testing of his sample in 2016.

Usain St. Leo Bolt was born in Trelawny, Jamaica on 21 August 1986. From a best time for 200m of 21.73 in 2001, he ran 20.61 to win the 2002 CAC U17 title and became the youngest ever male world junior champion at 15 years 332 days, having set a world age best with 20.58 in his heat. In 2003 he was undefeated and ran a 200m world U18 record of 20.13 to win the Pan-American Junior title after taking the World Youth title; he was Jamaican senior champion but did not meet any of the world elite. He also ran a startling 45.35 in his only major race at 400m in 2003 and ran a 44.4 400m relay leg. He won the IAAF 'Rising Star' award for men in 2002 and in 2003.

Still only 17 years of age, he set a world junior record of 19.93 to win the Caribbean Junior title in April 2004. Unfortunately he was then injured, so did not compete again until the Olympics in August, when he went out in his heat. Still a junior he won the CAC title in 20.01 and ran 19.99 in 2005 just before the World Championships but there came in 8th in the 200m final after pulling up with an injury. In 2006 he ran a best time of 19.88 and was 2nd in the World Cup and he improved to a Jamaican record 19.75 in 2007, when he also took silver medals at 200m and 4x100m at the World Championships and, never having run the event before this year, ran a best of 10.03 for 100m.

From such a limited background at 100m it was extraordinary that he shot to second on the world all-time list with 9.76 at Kingston on 3 May 2008, and just four weeks later he took the world record when he ran 9.72 in Berlin on 1 June. All his previous feats were left behind, however, with his fantastic running in Beijing at the Olympic Games. First came the 100 metres, in which he sauntered through the preliminary rounds including easy 9.92 and 9.85 runs and then won the final in a world record 9.69. It was not just the time, nor the amazement that such a big man could unwind from the blocks with such haste, but the sheer power of his mid-race surge and the way he eased across the line with his arms raised high that left the watching world thrilled at such superb athleticism. He could clearly have taken several hundredths of a second off that time if he had pushed hard all the way. He did just that in his next final, as, powering through splits of 9.96 and 9.34 with his huge strides, he took his 200m best down from the CAC record that he had set at 19.67 earlier in the year to 19.30 to break Michael Johnson's 1996 world record of 19.32, a time that many felt would last our lifetimes. He had won the 100m title by 0.20 (two metres) and here his winning margin was 0.66, the widest margin in the event's Olympic history. The third world record and gold medal came when, in his tenth race of the Games, he ran the third leg for the Jamaican team that took 0.30 off the 4x100m mark with 37.10.

He left even those amazing times behind when he smashed the world records for 100m and 200m at the 2009 World Championships in Berlin, running 9.58 and 19.19, winning by margins of 0.13 and 0.62 secs, with the third leg on the 4x100m team. In recognition of these feats, in an unbeaten season, he was awarded the Order of Jamaica and the island's A-Z Highway 2000 was renamed the Usain Bolt Highway.

Held back by injuries in 2010, he had a restricted season, including just four races at 100m (best of 9.82 and losing once to Tyson Gay), two wins at 200m (19.56 best) and one each at 300m and 400m. By his own admission not in top shape in 2011, he still won all his three races at both 100m and 200m prior to the World Championships in Daegu. There he sensationally false started in the 100m final, but won the 200m in 19.40, the fourth fastest ever time, and then ended the championships by anchoring the Jamaican team to a world record 37.04 in the 4x100m. He then won two 100m races to end the year with a best time of 9.76.

There was again speculation in 2012 that, with some delays in his preparation, Bolt might be beaten at the Olympic Games by the man who had taken the World 100m title in 2011, his training companion Yohan Blake, and Blake beat him at both 100m and 200m at the Jamaican Championships. However, Bolt held off his young rival and won the Olympics titles with 9.63 to 9.75 and 19.32 to 19.44 and they once again combined with Nesta Carter and Michael Frater to smash the world record by running 36.84 for 4x100m. He also won the 2012 Diamond League 100m title.

In 2013 he won six of his seven finals at 100m and all four at 200m, sweeping to another sprint treble at the World Championships in Moscow. He had a quiet year in 2014 with just a couple of 100m races Wins in Rio and Warsaw), and running in the heat and final in ensuring the Jamaica won the Commonwealth Games 4x100m title. He also had only limited competition in 2015 due to injuries but he came back in time to remain undefeated and beat Justin Gatlin, who until then had had a great season, at both 100m (9.784 to 9.797) and at 200m (19.55 to 19.74) at the World Championships, where he also anchored the Jamaican 4x100m team victory and thus complete his third World triple.

He again had interrupted preparation for the Olympic Games in 2016 but in Rio de Janeiro he completed his successive wins at 100m and 200m, both by clear margins although some way short of his best form and he was very disappointed with his time in the 200m. But he was back in his pomp in the 4x100m two days before his 30th birthday as his long strides took him well clear of the mortals following him so that he completed his unique treble treble.

He finished his international career by running exclusively at 100m in 2017, but was restricted by injury to just three competitions. He won in Kingston and Ostrava, and although twice sub-10 at the World Championships, could manage only 3rd in the final. That and took his record World medal haul to 14 (11 gold, 2 silver and 1 bronze).

Bolt was a member of the MVP Track Club in Kingston, where he was coached by Glen Mills. He was IAAF Male Athlete of the Year in 2008, 2009, 2011-13 and 2016.

Usain Bolt – Best Times and Championships Placings Each Year

	100m	WL	WR	200m	WL	WR	400m	Championships
2001				21.73			48.28	5sf 200m, 4 MedR WY
2002				20.58	61	-	47.12	1 200m, 2 4x100m & 4x400m WJ 1 200m & 400m CAC-Y
2003				20.13	9	9	45.35	1 200m, dq MedR WY, 1 200m, 2 4x100m PAm-J
2004				19.93	2	-		5h OG 200m
2005				19.99	3	4		8 200m WCh, 1 200m CAC
2006				19.88	4	4	47.58	2 200m WCp
2007	10.03	12		19.75	3	3	45.28	2 200m & 4x100m WCh
2008	9.69	1	1	19.30	1	1	45.94	1 100m, 200m, 4x100m (dq?) OG
2009	9.58	1	1	19.19	1	1	45.54	1 100m, 200m, 4x100m WCh
2010	9.82	3	2	19.56	1	1	45.87	
2011	9.76	1	2	19.40	1	1		1 200m, 4x100m, dq (fs, final) 100m WCh
2012	9.63	1	1	19.32	1	1		1 100m, 200m, 4x100m OG
2013	9.77	1	1	19.32	1	1	46.44	1 100m, 200m, 4x100m WCh
2014	9.98	15=	-	19.66	1	-		1 4x100m CG
2015	9.79	2	1	19.55	1	1	46.38	1 100m, 200m, 4x100m WCh
2016	9.81	2	1	19.78	3	1		1 100m, 200m, 4x100m OG
2017	9.95	10=	3	—				3 100m, dnf 4x100m WCh

Jamaican Champion 100m 2008-09, 2013; 200m 2005, 2007-97

WL– position on the world lists for that year; WR – as ranked each year by Peter Matthews in the International Athletics Annual

World records100m: 9.72 New York 31.5.08, 9.69 Beijing 16.8.08, 9.58 Berlin 16.8.09
200m: 19.30 Beijing 20.8.08, 19.19 Berlin 20.8.09

Pbs at other events: pbs: 60m 6.31+ '09, 100y 9.14+ '11, 150m 14.35 straight & 14.44+ turn '09 (world bests), 300m 30.97 '10 (world low altitude best). (+ intermediate time).

Hall of Fame

Usain Bolt is already in our Hall of Fame. This contains a mix of past and current stars, taking special consideration of athletes who have just retired. Current stars can only be included if they have already had at least ten years in international competition. So several top athletes of today now meet this criteria, and added this year are:
Ezekiel Kemboi (Kenya), Renaud Lavillenie (France), David Rudisha (Kenya)
Allyson Felix (USA), Brittney Reese (USA)
Details of these stars can be found in the Biographies section with those already included who are still competing: Valerie Adams, Meseret Defar, Tirunesh Dibaba,

NATIONAL CHAMPIONS 2017 and BIOGRAPHIES OF LEADING ATHLETES

By Peter Matthews

THIS SECTION incorporates biographical profiles of 828 of the world's top athletes this year – 439 men and 389 women, listed by nation. Also listed are national champions at standard events in 2017 for the leading countries prominent in athletics (for which I have such details).

The athletes profiled have, as usual, changed quite considerably from the previous year. All entries have been updated, but also many newcomers have been included to replace those who have retired or faded a little from the spotlight. The choice of who to include is always invidious, but I have concentrated on those who are currently in the world's top 10-15 per event, those who have the best championship records and some up-and-coming athletes who I consider may make notable impact during the coming year.

Since this section was introduced in the 1985 Annual, biographies have been given for a total of 4956 different athletes (2799 men and 2163 women).

The ever continuing high turnover in our sport is reflected in the fact that there are many newcomers to this section (142 in all, 84 men, 58 women), as well as 11 athletes (5 men, 6 women) reinstated from previous Annuals. The athletes who now have the longest continuous stretch herein are Fabrzio Donato and Veronica Campbell-Brown on 18 years, 3 athletes at 16 years and 5 at 15 years. Athlees who have retired or who have been given drugs bans have generally been omitted.

No doubt some of those dropped from this compilation will also again make their presence felt; the keen reader can look up their credentials in previous Annuals, and, of course, basic details may be in the athletes' index at the end of this book.

Athletes included in these biographies are identified in the index at the end of this Annual by * for those profiled in this section and by ^ for those who were included in previous Annuals.

The biographical information includes:

a) Name, date and place of birth, height (in metres), weight (in kilograms).
b) Previous name(s) for married women; club or university; occupation.
c) Major championships record – all placings in such events as the Olympic Games, World Championships, European Championships, Commonwealth Games, World Cup and Continental Cup; leading placings in finals of the World Indoor Championships, European or World Junior Championships, European Under-23 Championships and other Continental Championships; and first three to six in European Indoors or World University Games. European Cup/Team Champs and IAAF Grand Prix first three at each event or overall. World Athletics Final (WAF) and Diamond League series (DL) winners
d) National (outdoor) titles won or successes in other major events.
e) Records set: world, continental and national; indoor world records/bests (WIR/WIB).
f) Progression of best marks over the years at each athlete's main event(s).
g) Personal best performances at other events.
h) Other comments.

See Introduction to this Annual for lists of abbreviations used for events and championships.

Information given is as known at 28 March 2018 (to include performances at the World Indoor Championships and World Half Marathon Championships as well as some other early indoor and outdoor events of 2018.

I am most grateful to various ATFS members who have helped check these details. Additional information or corrections would be welcomed for next year's Annual.

Peter Matthews

ALBANIA

Governing body: Federata Shqiptare e Atletikes. **National Championships** first held in 1945 (women 1946).

Luiza GEGA b. 5 Nov 1988 Dibër 1.66m 56kg.
At 800m: WCh: '11- h. At 1500m: WCh: '13- sf, '15- h; EC: '12- sf, '14- h; WI: '14- 6; EI: '17- 5; WUG: '13- 2. At 3000mSt: OG: '16- h; EC: '16- 2. Won Balkan 1500m 2011, 2015.
Albanian records: 800m (3) 2011-14, 1500m (4) 2013-15, 3000m (2) 2012-16, 5000m 2014, 3000mSt (4) 2011-16.
Progress at 1500m, 3000mSt: 2006- 4:38.0, 2010- 4:23.20, 2011- 4:14.22, 9:54.72; 2012- 4:08.65mx/ 4:09.76. 2013- 4:05.11, 2014- 4:03.12, 2015- 4:02.63, 2016- 4:06.89i, 9:28.52; 2017- 4:06.66i/4:09.76, 9:26.05. pbs: 800m 2:01.31 '14, 3000m 8:52.53i '17, 8:53.78 '16; 5000m 15:46.89 '14, 10000m 33:31.0 '17.

ALGERIA

Governing body: Fédération Algerienne d'Athlétisme.

National Champions 2017: Men: 100m/200m: Djamil Skandar Athmani 10.32/20.80, 400m: Miloud Laaredj 46.10, 800m: Mohamed Belbachir 1:47.24, 1500m: Abderrahmane Anou 3:45.67, 5000m: Rabah Khaouas 14:00.78, 10000m: Abdelghani Bensaadi 30:40.00, 3000mSt: Ali Messaoudi 8:49.25, 110mh: Amine Bouamani 13.93, 400mh: Admelmalik Lahoulou 49.41, HJ: Ryad Selloum 2.15, PV: Hichem Cherabi 5.00, LJ/TJ: Yasser Triki 8.03/16.75, SP: Mohamed Benzaaza 14.62, DT: Abdelmoumen Bourakba 50.24, HT: Abdelwahab Maamar 60.36, JT: Larbi Bouraada 64.04, 20kW: Mohamed Meddour 1:37:07; **Women**. 100m: Abir Barkaoui 12.17w, 200m/400m: Meriem Boulahsa 24.73/56.67, 800m/1500m: Nabila Sifi 2:09.39/4:22.20, 5000m: Kenza Dahmani 16:40.45, 10000m: Malika Benderbal 34:11.96, 3000mSt: Hadjer Soukhal 10:57.86, 100mh: Aina Hamida Zitouni 14.33w, 400mh: Dihia Haddas 58.92, HJ: Yousra Arrar 1.75, LJ: Romaissa Belbiod 6.03, TJ: Kaoutar Selmi 13.10, SP: Nadia Cheroudi 13.43, DT: Nabila Bounab 41.28, HT: Zouina Bouzebra 62.22, 20kW: Bariza Ghezalani 1:48:16.

Larbi BOURAADA b. 10 May 1988 Souk Ahras 1.87m 84kg.
At Dec (/PV): OG: '16- 5; WCh: '09-11-15-17: 13/ 10/5/dnf; AfG: '07- 3, '11- dnf/1; AfCh: '08- 1/2, '10- 1/2, '14- 1. Won ALG PV 2016, JT 2015-17.
Four African decathlon records 2009-16, ALG record 2014.
Progress at Dec: 2007- 7349, 2008- 7697, 2009- 8171, 2010- 8148A, 2011- 8302, 2012- 8332dq, 2014- 8311, 2015- 8461, 2016- 8521, 2017- 8120. pbs: 60m 6.89i '10, 100m 10.67 '10, 10.61w '11, 10.58dq '12; 400m 46.69 '09, 1000m 2:39.86i '10, 1500m 4:12.15 '09, 60mh 8.05i '10, 110mh 14.00 '15, HJ 2.10 '09, PV 5.00 '11, LJ 7.69 '09, 7.94w '11; SP 14.00i '10, 13.78 '16; DT 42.39 '16, JT 66.49 '16, 67.68dq '12; Hep 5911i '10. Two-years drugs ban from positive test 15 Jun 2012.

Taoufik MAKHLOUFI b. 29 Apr 1988 Souk Ahras 1.81m 66kg.
At (800m)/1500m: OG: '12- h/1, '16- 2/2; WCh: '09/11- sf, '15- 4; AfG: '11- 1/3, '15- (2); AfCh: '10- h, '12- (1), '14- (3).
Algerian records 800m 2016, 1000m 2015.
Progress at 800m, 1500m: 2008- 3:43.4, 2009- 1:49.40, 3:34.34; 2010- 1:48.39, 3:32.94; 2011- 1:46.32, 3:34.4; 2012- 1:43.71, 3:30.80; 2013- 3:36.30, 2014- 1:43.53, 3:30.40; 2015- 1:44.24, 3:28.75; 2016- 1:42.61, 3:31.35. pbs: 600m 1:16.5+ '16, 1000m 2:13.08 '15, 1M 3:52.16 '14.

ARGENTINA

Governing body: Confederación Argentina de Atletismo (CADA). Founded 1954 (original governing body founded 1919). **National Championships** first held in 1920 (men), 1939 (women). **2017 Champions**: **Men**: 100m: Matías Robledo 10.68, 200m: Jorge Caracassis 21.84, 400m: Martín Rojas 48.39, 800m: Franco Díaz 1:52.94, 1500m/5000m/3000mSt: Joaquín Arbe 3:50.40/14:27.50/9:05.24, 10000m: Javier Carriqueo 30:03.1, HMar: Mariano Mastromarino 64:43, Mar: Ulises Sanguinetti 2:20:50, 110mh: Agustín Carrera 14.09, 400mh: Jaime Rodríguez 53.35, HJ: Carlos Layoy 2.10, PV: Rubén Benítez 4.80, LJ: Julián Cherit 7.03, TJ: Maximiliano Díaz 15.38, SP/DT: Germán Lauro 18.85/57.45, HT: Joaquín Gómez 71.09, JT: Facundo Baudano 65.98, Dec: Sergio Pandiani 6790. **Women**: 100m: María Victoria Woodward 11.76, 200m/400m: Noelia Martínez 24.18/54.82, 800m: Mariana Borelli 2:09.78, 1500m: Carolina Lozano 4:25.63, 5000m: Fedra Luna 17:36.61, 10000m: Karen Cejas 37:48.6, HMar: Florencia Borelli 71:58, Mar: Karina Neipán 2:45:43, 3000mSt: Clara Baiocchi 10:59.16, 100mh: Agustina Zerboni 14.30, 400mh: Valeria Barón 61.96, HJ: Ana Celeste Sette 1.68, PV: Valeria Chiaraviglio 4.00, LJ: Camila Domínguez 5.63w, TJ: Yamila Levrino 11.95, SP/DT: Rocío Comba 13.93/56.59, HT: Jennifer Dahlgren 67.19, JT: Bárbara López 50.64, Hep: Martina Corrá 4862.

AUSTRALIA

Governing body: Athletics Australia. Founded 1897.

National Championships first held in 1893 (men) (Australasian until 1927), 1930 (women). **2017 Champions**: **Men**: 100m: Trae Williams 10.29, 200m: Alex Hartmann 21.19, 400m: Steven Solomon 46.66, 800m: Luke Mathews 1:46.71, 1500m: Ryan Gregson 3:52.86, 5000m: David McNeill 13:47.18, 10000m: Stewart McSweyn 28:37.28, HMar: Collis Birmingham 63:16, Mar: Jai Edmonds 2:29:28, 3000mSt: James Nipperess

8:52.89, 110mh: Nicholas Hough 13.53w, 400mh: Ian Dewhurst 49.77, HJ: Joel Baden 2.18, PV: Kurtis Marschall 5.45, LJ: Chris Mitrevski 7.78w, TJ: Alwyn Jones 16.13, SP: Damien Birkinhead 19.80, DT: Julian Wruck 61.56, HT: Matthew Denny 73.37, JT: Hamish Peacock 84.36, Dec: Cedric Dubler 7779, 10000mW/20kW: Dane Bird-Smith 38:34.23/1:19:37. **Women**: 100m: Melissa Breen 11.64, 200m: Ella Nelson 23.91, 400m: Morgan Mitchell 52.08, 800m: Lora Storey 2:05.56, 1500m/5000m: Heidi See 4:23.99/ 15:51.97, 10000m: Celia Sullohem 32:31.22, HMar: Linda Spencer 75:40, Mar: Makda Harun ETH 2:28:06, 3000mSt: Victoria Mitchell 9:44.09, 100mh: Sally Pearson 12.53w, 400mh: Lauren Wells 56.60, HJ: Eleanor Patterson 1.83, PV: Elizabeth Parnov 4.30, LJ: Naa Anang 6.50, TJ: Megan O'Riley 13.30, SP: Siiva Tafiti 14.23, DT: Dani Samuels 65.07, HT: Lara Nielsen 66.31, JT: Kelsey-Lee Roberts 61.40, Hep: Alysha Burnett 5817, 10000mW: Katie Hayward 45:51.09, 20kW: Regan Lamble 1:29:58.

Dane BIRD-SMITH b. 15 Jul 1992 Brisbane 1.78m 66kg. Racewalking Queensland. Uinversity of Queenland,
AtniOkW: OG: '16- 3; WCh: '13- 11, '15- 8, '17- 6; WCp: '14- 14, '16- 4; WUG: '15- 1; OCE Champion 2016-17; At 10000mW: WJ: '10- 5; WY: '09- 8. Won AUS 5000mW 2013, 10000mW 2014-17, 20kW 2013-14, 2017-18; OCE 20kW 2017.
Oceania 5000m walk record 2016.
Progress at 20kW: 2011- 1:26:38, 2012- 1:23:15, 2013- 1:22:03, 2014- 1:20:27, 2015- 1:20:05, 2016- 1:19:37, 2017- 1:19:28. pbs: 3000mW 10:56.23 '14, 5000mW 18:38.97 '16, 10000mW 38:34.23 '17.

Ryan GREGSON b. 26 Apr 1990 Bulli, NSW 1.84m 68kg. Glenhuntly.
At 1500m: OG: '12- sf, '16- 9; WCh: '09-11-15-17: h/sf/h/h; CG: '14- h; WJ: '08- 5 (12 5000m); WY: '07- 5. AUS champion 2010, 2016-18.
Oceania 1500m record 2010.
Progress at 1500m: 2003- 4:26.00, 2004- 4:20,00, 2005- 4:06.00, 2006- 3:57.00, 2007- 3:43.84, 2008- 3:41.14, 2009- 3:37.24, 2010- 3:31.06, 2011- 3:36.64, 2012- 3:33.92, 2013- 3:35.25, 2014- 3:36.17, 2015- 3:36.51, 2016- 3:32.13, 2017- 3:34.37. pbs: 800m 1:46.04 '10, 1000m 2:17.69 '10, 1M 3:52.24 '10, 3000m 7:42.19 '17, 5000m 13:56.83 '09, 10km Rd 29:09 '08.
Engaged to Genevieve LaCaze.

Fabrice LAPIERRE b. 17 Oct 1983 Réduit, Mauritius 1.79m 66kg. Westfields. Science graduate of Texas A&M University, USA.
At LJ: OG: '08- dnq 15, '16- 10; WCh: '09-11-13-15-17: 4/dnq 21/dnq/2/11; CG: '06- 3, '10- 1, '14- 4; WJ: '02- 2 (qf 100m); WI: '10- 1, '16- 2; WCp: '06- 8, '10- 7. Won WAF 2008-09, DL 2016, NCAA 2005, AUS 2006, 2009-10, 2013, 2016.
Oceania indoor long jump records 2010 & 2016.
Progress at LJ: 2000- 7.39, 2001- 7.31, 2002- 7.74, 2003- 7.66i/7.57/7.85w, 2004- 7.61i/7.52/7.94Aw, 2005- 7.90i/7.83/8.15w, 2006- 8.19, 2007- 7.98, 2008- 8.15, 2009- 8.35/8.57w, 2010- 8.40/8.78w, 2011- 8.02, 2012- 8.10/8.14w, 2013- 8.25, 2014- 8.00, 2015- 8.29, 2016- 8.31/8.36w, 2017- 8.03/ 8.50w. pbs: 60m 6.89i '06, 100m 10.56/10.48w '02, 200m 21.40 '00, TJ 15.24 '04.
Former football player.

Kurtis MARSCHALL b. 25 Apr 1997 North Adelaide 1.88m 78kg. Western District, Adelaide. Student at the University of South Australia.
At PV: OG: '16- dnq 15; WCh: '17- 7; WJ: '14- dnq 20=, '16- 2; WI: '18- 4. AUS champion 2016-18.
Progress at PV: 2013- 4.90, 2014- 5.35, 2015- 5.42, 2016- 5.70, 2017- 5.73, 2018- 5.80.

Jared TALLENT b. 17 Oct 1984 Ballarat 1.78m 60kg. Ballarat YCW. Graduate of University of Canberra.
At 20kW(/50kW): OG: '08- 3/2, '12- 7/1, '16- (2); WCh: '05- 18, '07- dq, '09- 5/6, '11- 23/2, 13- (3), '15- 26/2; CG: '06- 3, '10- 1; WCp: '06-08-10-12-14-16: 14/10/(3)/(1)/(3)/(1). At 10000mW: WJ: '02- 19; WY: '01- 7. Won AUS 5000mW 2012, 20kW 2008-13; 30kW 2004, 50kW 2007, 2009, 2011.
Commonwealth 5000m walk record 2009.
Progress at 20kW, 50kW: 2002- 1:40:21, 2003- 1:31:24, 2004- 1:27:02, 2005- 1:22:53, 2006- 1:21:36, 3:55:08; 2007- 1:21:25, 3:44:45, 2008- 1:19:41, 3:39:27; 2009- 1:19:42, 3:38:56; 2010- 1:19:15, 3:54:55; 2011- 1:19:57, 3:43:36; 2012- 1:20:02, 3:36:53; 2013- 1:20:41, 3:40:03; 2014- 1:20:55, 3:42:48; 2015- 1:24:05, 3:42.17; 2016- 1:21:50, 3:41:16; 2017- 1:32:01A. pbs: 3000mW 11:15.07 '09, 5000mW 18:41.83 '09, 10000mW 40:41.5 '06, 10kW 38:29 '10, 30kW 2:10:52 '13, 35kW 2:32:37 '12.
Won IAAF Walks Challenge 2008 and 2013. Married Claire Woods on 30 Aug 2008, she has 20kW pb 1:28:53 '12, 2 CG '10. Younger sister Rachel Tallent (b. 20 Feb 1993) has 20kW pb 1:31:33 to win OCE 2016, 34 WCh '15, 40 OG '16.

Women

Madeline HILLS b. 15 May 1987 Shellharbour, New South Wales 1.74m 53kg. Kembla Joggers – Wollongong. Was at Sydney University.
At (5000m)/3000mSt: OG: '16- 10/7; WCh: '15- h/h, '17- (h); CG: '14- 4. At 10000m: WCh: '17- 26. AUS champion 5000m 2015, 3000mSt 2016.
Progress at 5000m, 3000mSt: 2006- 9:56.54, 2014- 15:27.75, 9:34.01; 2015- 15:11.17, 9:21.56; 2016- 15:04.05, 9:20.38; 2017- 15:12.63. pbs: 800m 2:06.13 '16, 1500m 4:06.47 '16, 1M 4:41.89 '06, 3000m 8:44.20 '15, 10000m 31:41.10 '17.
Had an eight-year break from athletics, during which she established a career as a pharmacist. Married to Chris Hills.

Genevieve LaCAZE b. 4 Aug 1989 Benowa, Queensland 1.68m 54kg. Glenhuntly. Graduate

of the University of Florida, USA.
At 3000mSt: OG: '12- h, '16- 9 (12 5000m); WCh: '15- h, '17- 12; CG: '14- 5. At 1500m: WJ: '04- h. AUS champion 5000m 2016, 3000mSt 2013, 2015. Oceania records 2000mSt 2015, 3000mSt 2016.
Progress at 3000mSt: 2009- 10:26.92, 2010- 10:30.12, 2011- 9:59.44, 2012- 9:37.90, 2013- 9:37.62, 2014- 9:33.19, 2015- 9:35.17, 2016- 9:14.28, 2017- 9:24.52. pbs: 800m 2:04.05 '16, 1500m 4:10.20 '16, 1M 4:32.06 '17, 3000m 8:45.81i '17, 8:52.28 '16; 2M 9:52.21 '14, 5000m 15:06.67 '16, 10k Rd 34:51 '15, 2000mSt 6:16.86 '15.
Engaged to Ryan Gregson.

Kathryn MITCHELL b. 10 Jul 1982 Hamilton, Victoria 1.68m 72kg. Eureka AC.
At JT: OG: '12- 9, '16- 6; WCh: '13- 5, '15/17- dnq 17/25; CG: '06-10-14: 6/5/4; AUS champion 2008, 2018. Two Oceania javelin records 2018.
Progress at JT: 1999- 43.17, 2000- 51.44, 2001- 54.98, 2002- 54.72, 2003- 57.11, 2004- 48.10, 2005- 54.87, 2006- 58.81, 2007- 58.61, 2008- 58.77, 2010- 59.68, 2011- 59.47, 2012- 64.34, 2013- 63.77, 2014- 66.10, 2015- 63.70, 2016- 64.37, 2017- 66.12, 2018- 68.57.

Sally PEARSON b. 19 Sep 1986 Sydney 1.66m 60kg. née McLellan. Gold Coast Victory. Griffith University.
At (100m)/100mh: OG: '08- 2, '12- 1; WCh: '03- hR, '07- sf/sf, '09-11-13-17: 5/1/2/1; CG: '06- 7/ fell/3R, '10- dq/1, '14- 1; WJ: '04- 3/4; WY: '03- 1; WCp: '06- 8/4, '10- 1. At 60mh: WI: '12- 1, '14- 2. At 200m: WY: '03- 5; won DL 2017, AUS 100m & 100mh 2005-7, 2009, 2011, 2014-15; 100mh 2017-18, 200m 2011.
Records: Oceania 100mh (8) 2007-11, 60m 2009 & 60mh indoors (3) 2009-12; Commonwealth 100mh (2) 2011.
Progress at 100mh: 2003- 14.01, 2004- 13.30, 2005- 13.01, 2006- 12.95, 2007- 12.71, 2008- 12.53, 2009- 12.50, 2010- 12.57, 2011- 12.28, 2012- 12.35, 2013- 12.50, 2014- 12.5, 2015- 12.59, 2016- 13.14/ 12.92w, 2017- 12.48. pbs: 60m 7.16 '11, 100m 11.14 '07, 150m 16.86 '10, 200m 23.02/22.66w '09, 300m 38.34 '09, 400m 53.86mx '11, 200mh 27.54 '06, 60mh 7.73i '12, 200mh 26.96 '09, 400mh 62.98 '07.
Married Kieran Pearson on 3 April 2010. IAAF Female Athlete of the Year 2011.

Kelsey-Lee ROBERTS b. 21 Sep 1991 East London, South Africa 1.75m 70kg. South Canberra Tuggeranong.
At JT: OG: '16- dnq 28; WCh: '15- dnq 20, '17- 10; CG: '14- 3; AUS champion 2017.
Progress at JT: 2009- 46.10, 2010- 49.29, 2011- 52.01, 2013- 58.58, 2014- 63.92, 2015- 63.78, 2016- 59.02, 2017- 64.53.

Dani STEVENS b. 26 May 1988 Fairfield, Sydney 1.82m 82kg. née Samuels. Westfields, University of Western Sydney.
At DT/(SP): OG: '08- 8, '12- 11, '16- 4; WCh: '07-09-11-13-15-17: dnq 13/1/10/10/6/2; CG: '06-3/12, '14- 1; WJ: '06- 1/7; WY: '05- 1/3; WCp: '06- 6; WUG: '07- 2, '09- 1; CCp: '10- 4, '14- 2. AUS champion SP 2006-07, 2009, 2012; DT 2005-12, 2014-15, 2017-18.
Commonwealth & Oceania discus record 2017.
Progress at DT: 2001- 39.17, 2002- 45.52, 2003-47.29, 2004- 52.21, 2005- 58.52, 2006- 60.63, 2007-60.47, 2008- 62.95, 2009- 65.44, 2010- 65.84, 2011-62.33, 2012- 63.97, 2013- 64.46, 2014- 67.99, 2015-66.21, 2016- 67.77, 2017- 69.64, 2018- 66.02. pbs: SP 17.05 '14, HT 45.39 '05.
Added 1.65m to her pb to win World silver in 2017. Sisters Jamie and Casey played basketball for Australia. Married Joe Stevens (SP: pb 17.34 '88; 11 WJ '06).

Brooke STRATTON b. 12 Jul 1993 Box Hill, Melbourne 1.68m 58kg. Nunawading. Was at Deakin University, Melbourne.
At LJ: OG: '16- 7; WCh: '15- dnq 14, '17- 6; WJ: '10- 6, '12- 7; WY: '09- 10; WI: '16- 5. AUS champion 2014, 2018.
Oceania long jump record 2016.
Progress at LJ: 2004- 5.38, 2005- 5.40, 2006- 5.52, 2007- 5.90, 2008- 6.06, 2009- 6.13, 2010- 6.30, 2011-6.60, 2012- 6.56, 2013- 6.53, 2014- 6.70, 2015- 6.73, 2016- 7.05, 2017- 6.79. Pbs: 100m 11.98 '13, 200m 24.79 '16, 100mh 14.18 '10, TJ 13.34 '12.

AUSTRIA

Governing body: Österreichischer Leichtathletik Verband OLV). Founded 1902.
National Championships first held in 1911 (men), 1918 (women). **2017 Champions**: **Men**: 100m/200m: Markus Fuchs 10.45/21.23, 400m: Dominik Hufnagl 47.06, 800m: Dominik Stadlmann 1:53.51, 1500m/5000m: Andreas Vojta 3:50.81/13:33.76, 10000m: Hans Peter Innerhofer 31:13.89, HMar: Lemawork Kelema 64:30, Mar: Endris Seid 2:30:05, 3000mSt: Jürgen Aigner 9:05.15, 110mh: Florian Domenig 14.45, 400mh: Markus Kornfeld 51.59, HJ: Alexander Dengg 2.00, PV: Sebastian Ender 5.05, LJ: Julian Kellerer 7.75, TJ: Roman Schmied 15.91, SP: Georg Stamminger 15.45, DT/HT: Marko Cozzoli 45.60/61.91, JT: Matthias Kaserer 62.04, Dec: Severin Chum 6816, 20k: Dietmar Hirschmugl 1:51:26, 50kW: Roman Brzezowsky 5:12:17. **Women**: 100m/200: Viola Kleiser 11.52/ 23.66, 400m: Susanne Walli 54.39, 800m: Carina Schrepf 2:13.39, 1500m: Anna Baumgartner 4:48.16, 5000m: Julia Mayer 17:48.70, 10000m/ HMar: Sandrina Illes 35:46.17/75:12, Mar: Sandra Urach 2:45:24, 3000mSt: Lena Millonig 10:35.57, 100mh: Beate Schott 13.43, 400mh: Pena Pressler 61.61; HJ: Ekaterina Krasovskiy 1.83, PV: Brigitta Hesch 4.15, LJ: Sarah Lagger 6.28, TJ: Michaela Egger 12.80, SP: Ivona Dadic 14.44, DT: Veronika Watzek 51.51, HT: Christina Scheffauer 53.48, JT: Victoria Hudson 47.84, Hep: Sarah Lagger 5891, 10kW/20kW: Kathrin Schulze 51:53/1:52:14.

Lukas WEISSHAIDINGER b. 20 Feb 1992 Schärding 1.96m 136kg. ÖTB OÖ Leichtathletik.
At DT (SP): OG: '16- 6; WCh: '15- dnq 20, '17- 9; WJ: '10- dnq 16 (6); WY: '09- dnq 36 (4); EU23: '11- 7; EJ '11- 1 (5 SP). Won AUT SP 2012-15, DT 2015-16. Austrian discus record 2015.
Progress at DT: 2008- 43.47, 2009- 45.98, 2010- 54.21, 2011- 54.85, 2012- 58.00, 2013- 59.13, 2014- 60.68, 2015- 67.24, 2016- 66.00, 2017- 66.52. pb SP 18.90 '13.

Women

Ivona DADIC b. 29 Dec 1993 Weis 1.79m 65kg. PSV Hornbach Weiss
At Hep: OG: '12- 23, '16- 21; W Ch: '17- 6; EC: '16: 3; WJ: '12- dnf; WY: '09- 10; EU23: '13- 5, '15- 3; EJ: 11- 10 At Pen: WI: '18- 2; EI: '17- 2. Won AUT SP 2017, Hep 2012.
six Austrian heptathlon records 2012-16.
Progress at Hep: 2011- 5455, 2012- 5959, 2013- 5874, 2015- 6151, 2016- 6408, 2017- 6417. pbs: 200m 23.69 '17, 400m 56.27 '11, 800m 2:10.67 '12, 60mh 8.32i '18, 100mh 13.68 '17, HJ 1.87i/1.83 '17, LJ 6.49 '16, SP 14.44 '17, JT 52.48 '15, Pen 4767i '17.
Improved heptathlon pb by 212 points for 3rd EC '16 and pentathlon best by 247 for 2nd EI '17.

AZERBAIJAN

Governing body: Azerbaijan Athletics Association. Founded 1923, reorganised 1992.

Nazim BABAYEV b. 8 Oct 1997 Baku 1.85m 70kg.
At TJ: OG: '16- dnq 25; WCh: '17- dnq 14; EC: '16: dnq 23=; WJ: '16- dnq 15; EU23: '17- 1; EJ: '05- 1; YOG: '14- 3; WI: '16- 8; WUG: '17- 1. Won Is.Sol 2017.
Progress at TJ: 2013- 15.53, 2014- 16.18, 2015- 17.04, 2016- 16.83, 2017- 17.18. pbs: 60m 7.05i '17, LJ 7.49 '16.

Alexis COPELLO Sánchez b. 12 Aug 1985 Santiago de Cuba 1.85m 80kg.
At TJ: OG: '08- dnq 13, '12- 8; WCh: '09- 3, '11- 4, '17- 5; WI: '12- 7, '18- 4; PAmG: '11- 1; CAG: '06- 2; CCp: '10- 2. Won IbAm 2010, CAC 2009, Cuban 2009, 2011.
Progress at TJ: 2002- 15.38, 2003- 16.34, 2004- 16.90, 2005- 16.95/17.09w, 2006- 17.38, 2007- 16.87/17.15w, 2008- 17.50, 2009- 17.65/17.69w, 2010- 17.55, 2011- 17.68A/17.47, 2012- 17.17, 2014- 17.05, 2015- 17.15/17.24w, 2016- 16.99i/16.98, 2017- 17.16/17.17w, 2018- 17.17i. pb LJ 7.35 '04.
Former Cuban, Azeri citizenship 26 Apr 2016, cleared to compete for them from 24 Apr 2017. Elder brother Alexander (b. 19 Feb 1978) decathlon pb 7359 '02.

Women

Hanna SKYDAN b. 14 May 1992 Krasnyi Luch, UKR 1.83m 114kg.
At HT: OG: '12/16- dnq 14/13; WCh: '15- dnq 23, '17- 5; EC: '16- 3; WJ: '10- dnq 27; WY: '09- 12; EJ: 11- dnq; WUG: '15- 1; won Is.Sol 2017.
Eight AZE hammer records 2015-17.
Progress at HT: 2009- 56.90, 2010- 56.76, 2011- 67.56, 2012- 74.21, 2013- 68.44, 2014- 71.14, 2015- 72.31, 2016- 73.87, 2017- 75.29. pbs: SP 13.98 '17, DT 49.50 '15.
Competed for Ukraine to 2012, AZE citizenship 15 Jan 2015 and cleared to compete for them from 1 Jun 2015.

BAHAMAS

Governing body: Bahamas Association of Athletics Associations. Founded 1952.

National Champions 2017: **Men**: 100m: Warren Fraser 10.31, 200m: Shavez Hart 20.58, 400m: Steven 44.66, 800m: Rocky Jean-Louis 1:56.55, 400mh: Jeffrey Gibson 49.42, HJ: Jamal Wilson 2.25, LJ: Holland Martin 7.13, TJ: Leevan Sands 16.14, JT: Leonardo Romer 59.84, Dec: Ken Mullings 6500. **Women**: 100m: Tynia Gaither 11.47, 200m: Shaunae Miller-Uibo 22.21, 400m: Shaquania Dorsett 52.57, 800m: Mirian Byfield 2:35.68, 100mh: Devynne Charlton 12.95, HJ: Ashtoni Sands 1.65. LJ: Bianca Stuart 6.12, SP: Laquell Harris 11.88, DT: Serena Brown 50.60.

Steven GARDINER b. 12 Sep 1995 Moore's Island 1.88m 75kg.
At 400m: OG: '16- sf/3R; WCh: '15- sf, '17- 2; WJ: '14- 6R (sf 200m); BAH champion 2015-17.
Three Bahamas 400m records 2015-17.
Progress at 400m: 2013- 47.78, 2015- 44.27, 2016- 44.46, 2017- 43.89. pbs: 200m 20.64 '16, 20.35w '18; 300m 32.64 '16.

Donald THOMAS b. 1 Jul 1984 Freeport 1.90m 75kg. Lindenwood University, USA.
At HJ: OG: '08/12- dnq 21=/30=, '16- 7= WCh: '07-09-11-13-15-17: 1/dnq 15/11/6/6/dnq 22=; CG: '06-10-14: 4/1/9=; PAm: '07-11-15; 2/1/3; CAG: '06- 4=, '10- 1; CCp: '10- 2; WI: '18- 6=. Won WAF & NCAA indoors 2007, BAH 2007, 2010-11.
Progress at HJ: 2006- 2.24, 2007- 2.35, 2008- 2.28i/2.26, 2009- 2.30, 2010- 2.32, 2011- 2.32, 2012- 2.27, 2013- 2.32, 2014- 2.33i/2.25, 2015- 2.34, 2016- 2.37, 2017- 2.31i/2.29.
A basketball player, he made a sensational start by clearing 2.22 indoors in January 2006 with no high jump training since he had jumped at school five years earlier. 19 months later he was world champion.

Women

Shaunae MILLER-UIBO b. 15 Apr 1994 Nassau 1.85m 69kg. University of Georgia, USA.
At (200m)/400m: OG: '12- ht, '16- 1; WCh: '13- (4), '15- 2, '17- 3/4; CG: '14- 6; WJ: '10- 1, '12- 4; WY: '11- 1; WI: '14- 3. Won DL 200m & 400m 2017, BAH 200m 2017, 400m 2010-11, 2014-16; NCAA indoor 400m 2013.
Records: Tied world indoor 300m 2018, BAH 200m (4) 2015-17. CAC junior 200m 2013, 400m 2013.

Progress at 200m, 400m: 2009- 55.52, 2010- 24.09, 52.45; 2011- 23.70, 51.84; 2012- 22.70, 51.25; 2013- 22.45/22.41w, 50.70; 2014- 22.87, 51.63i/51.86; 2015- 22.14, 49.67; 2016- 22.05, 49.44; 2017- 21.88, 49.46. Pbs: 60m 7.59i '13, 100m 11.19 '16, 300m 35.45i '18, LJ 6.29 '17.
Married Estonian decathlete Maicel Uibo (qv) on 4 Feb 2017. Great-uncle Leslie Miller set BAH 400m record of 46.99 at 1968 Olympics.

Pedrya SEYMOUR b. 29 May 1995 Nassau 1.68m 57kg. Student at University of Illinois, USA.
At 100mh: OG: '16- 6. At 400mh: WJ: '12- h. Won BAH 400mh 2012.
Five Bahamas 100mh records 2016.
Progress at 100mh: 2016- 12.64, 2017- 13.06. pbs: 60m 7.58i '18, 200m 23.59 '16, 60mh 7.97i '17, 400mh 60.18 '16.
Having been a 300m/400m hurdler in 2010-13, she made an amazing breakthrough at 100mh in 2016 from her first race in 13.50 on April 9 to 6th in the Olympic final in 12.64.

Anthonique STRACHAN b. 22 Aug 1993 Nassau 1.68m 57kg.
At (100m)/200m: OG: '12- sf, '16- h (6 4x400m); WCh: '11/13/17- sf; WJ: '10- sf, '12- 1/1; PAm: '15- dnf; CCp: '14- 4; PAm-J: '11- 1. Won BAH 100m 2014, 200m 2013, 2015.
Two CAC junior 200m records 2011-12.
Progress at 200m: 2009- 23.95, 2010- 23.66, 2011- 22.70, 2012- 22.53, 2013- 22.32, 2014- 22.50, 2015- 22.69, 2016- 22.96, 2017- 22.84. Pbs: 60m 7.47 '18, 100m 11.20 '12, 400m 52.42 '16.
Won IAAF Female Rising Star Award 2012. Based in Auburn, USA.

BAHRAIN

Governing body: Bahrain Athletics Association. Founded 1974.

Ali Khamis ABBAS b. 30 Jun 1995 1.82m 70kg.
At 400m: OG: '16- 6; AsiC: '13- 2; At 400mh: WJ: '12- h, '14- 2; WY: '11- h; AsiG: '14- 1. Won Arab 400mh 2015, Is.Sol 2017.
Three Bahrain 400m records 2016,
Progress at 400m: 2013- 45.65, 2014- 46.13, 2015- 45.88, 2016- 44.36, 2017- 45.54. Pbs: 100m 10.69 '15, 200m 20.81 '15, 300m 32.0+ '16, 400mh 49.55 '14.

Abraham Naibei **CHEROBEN** b. 11 Oct 1992 1.76m 60kg.
At 10000m: OG: '16- 10; WCh: 17- 12; won Is.Sol 2017. At HMar: WCh: '18- 2. BRN records 10000m 2017, half marathon (61:00) 2016.
Progress at 10000m, HMar: 2012- 63:53, 2013- 60:38, 2014- 58:48, 2015- 59:10, 2016- 27:31.86, 60:35; 2017- 27:11.08, 58:40. Road pbs: 15k 41:55 '14, 20k 55:50 '14, 25k 1:11:47 '14.
Transferred from Kenya to Bahrain on 19 Aug 2015, with eligibility to compete for them from 1 Aug 2016.

Sadik MIKHOU b. 25 Jul 1990 Morocco 1.74 m 61kg.
At 1500m: WCh: '17- 6; won Is.Sol 2017.
Progress at 1500m: 2013- 3:33.31, 2014- 3:33.47, 2015- 3:33.45, 2016- 3:32.30, 2017- 3:31.34. pbs: 800m 1:46.55 '14, 1000m 2:22.28 '11, 3000m 7:39.02 '16, 10k Rd 28:05 '17.
Switched from Morocco to Bahrain in September 2015 with international eligibility from 17 Sep 2016.

Albert Kibichii **ROP** b. 17 Jul 1992 Kapsabet, Kenya 1.76m 55kg.
At 5000m: OG: '16- 7; WCh: '15- 11, '17- h; AsiG: '14- 3; AsiC: '15- 2; CCp: '14- 4; Won Arab 2013, WMilG & Gulf 2015. At HMar: WCh: '18- 13. World CC: '15- 11. Asian CC champion 2016.
Records: 1 Asian, 2 Bahrain 5000m and Bahrain 3000m 2013; Asian indoor 3000m (2) 2014 (if eligible), 5000m 2017.
Progress at 5000m: 2010- 14:15.81A, 2011- 13:03.70, 2012- 13:01.91, 2013- 12:51.96, 2014- 13:06.12, 2015- 13:06.74, 2016- 13:04.87, 2017- 13:04.82. Pbs: 1500m 3:45.7A '13, 2000m 5:01.4+ '16, 3000m 7:32.02 '16.
Bahrain citizen from 2 Apr 2013, international eligibility 1 Apr 2014.

Women

Oluwa**kemi ADEKOYA** b. 16 Jan 1993 Nigeria 1.68m 57kg. Accountancy graduate of University of Lagos.
At 400mh: WCh: '15- h (dq); AsiG: '14- 1 (1 400m); AsiC: '15- 1; CCp: '14- 3., won Is.Sol 2017. At 400m: OG: '16- sf; WI: '16- 1; Won Arab 400m & W.MilG 400mh 2015, Asi Ind 400m 2016.
Records: Asian indoor 400m (4) to 51.45 in 2016. Bahrain 400m (4) 2015-16, 400mh (3) 2014-15.
Progress at 400m, 400mh: 2012- 57.16H, 2013- 52.57, 55.30; 2014- 51.11, 54.59; 2015- 50.86, 54.12; 2016- 50.72, 54.87; 2017- 51.46, 54.57. pbs: 100m 11.55 '14, 400m 50.86 '15.
Switched nationality from Nigeria to Bahrain from 11 Sep 2013, with international eligibility from 10 Sep 2014.

Rose CHELIMO b. 12 Jul 1989 Kenya 1.62m 45kg.
At Mar: OG: '16- 8; WCh: 17- 1. World CC: '17- 9. At HMar: WCh: '18- 2.
Progress at HMar, Mar: 2010- 72:48, 2011- 69:45, 2012- 70:50, 2014- 68:40, 2015- 68:22 , 2016- 68:08, 2:24:14; 2017- 68:37, 2:22:51. Pbs: 10000m 31:37.81 '17, Road: 15k 49:08 '17, 20k 64:47 '15.
Transferred from Kenya to Bahrain on 19 Aug 2015, eligible to compete for them from 1 Aug 2016. Won in Seoul on marathon debut in 2016, 2nd Boston 2017.

Ruth JEBET b. 17 Nov 1996 Kenya 1.65m 49kg.
At 3000mSt: OG: '16- 1; WCh: '15- 11, '17- 5; WJ: '14- 1; AsiG: '14- 1; AsiC: '13- 1 but ineligible; CCp: '14- 3. Won DL 2016-17, WMilG 2015, Arab 2015, Arab-J 3000m 2014, Is.Sol 5000m & 3000mSt 2017. World CC: '15- 9J, '17- 7.

World 3000m steeplechase record 2016, four Asian 2014-16.
Progress at 3000mSt: 2013- 9:40.84, 2014- 9:20.55, 2015- 9:21.40, 2016- 8:52.78, 2017- 8:55.29. pbs: 1500m 4:13.4A '16, 3000m 8:47.24i '16, 9:09.8A '13; 5000m 14:53.41 '17, road 10k 32:01 '17, 2000mSt 6:17.33 '13 (5:54.16 in 3000mSt WR).
Switched nationality from Kenya to Bahrain from 19 Aug 2015, with international eligibility from 19 May 2014 and won Bahrain's first Olympic medal. Formerly known as Chebet.

Violah JEPCHUMBA b. 23 Oct 1990 1.72m 52kg.
Progress at HMar: 2014- 73:20, 2015- 69:30, 2016- 65:51, 2017- 65:22. pbs: Road: 10k 30:05 '17, 15k 45:40 '17, 20k 61:50 '17.
BRN citizen 1 Jul 2016, international eligibilty 2 Jul 2017.

Eunice JEPKIRUI Kirwa b. 20 May 1984 Kenya 1.65m 52kg.
At Mar: OG: '16- 2; WCh: '15- 3, '17- 6; AsiG: '14- 1. At 1500m: WY: '99/01- h.
Asian half marathon record 2017. Bahrain records: marathon (3) 2014-17, half marathon 2016 & 2017.
Progress at Mar: 2012- 2:21:41, 2013- 2:23:34, 2014- 2:25:37, 2015- 2:22:08, 2016- 2:22:40, 2017- 2:21:17. Pbs: 1500m 4:27.62 '99, 2000mSt 6:33.0A '03, 3000mSt 10:18.3A '05, Road: 10k 31:57 '12, 15k 48:37 '16, HMar 66:46 '17.
Won marathons in Asunción 2012, Lanzhou and Danzhou 2014, Nagoya 2015-17, Macao 2017. Transferred from Kenya 11 Dec 2013 with eligibility to compete for Bahrain from 15 Jul 2014. Married to Joshua Kiprugut Kemei (pb HMar 62:53 '11) with one son. Her brother Felix Kiptoo Kirwa KEN has pb 2:06:13 '17.

Salwa Eid NASER b. 23 May 1998 Nigeria 1.67m 50kg. Original name Ebele Egbapuonwu.
At 400m: OG: '16- sf; WCh: '17- 2; WY: '05- 1; Yth OG: '14- 2. Won Asi-Y & W.MilG 2015, Gulf & Isl Sol 2017.
Four Bahrain 400m records 2017.
Progress at 400m: 2014- 52.74, 2015- 51.39, 2016- 50.88, 2017- 49.88. pbs: 100m 11.70 '15, 200m 23.03 '15. Nigerian mother, Bahraini father – moved to Bahrain as a child,

BARBADOS

Governing body: Athletics Association of Barbados. Founded 1947.
National Champions 2017: **Men**: 100m: Mario Burke 10.17, 200m: Burkheart Ellis 20.37, 400m: Joshua Walcott 46.84, 800m: Anthonio Mascoll 1:47.49, 1500m: Jonathan Jones 3:55.08, 5000m: Joshua Hunte 16:22.42, 110mh: Shane Brathwaite 13.52, 400mh: Fabian Norgrove 50.24, HJ/LJ: Josiah Beckles 1.95/7.08, TJ: Hakeem Belle 15.25, SP/DT: Tristan Whitehall 16.09/54.53, JT: Kalvin Marcus 58.76. **Women**: 100m: Jade Bailey 11.39, 200m: Sada Williams 22.80, 400m/400mh: Tianna Bowen 55.96/60.47, 800m: Sonia Gaskin 2:09.01, 1500m: Krysta Maloney 5:16.56, 100mh: Kierre Beckles 13.15, HJ: Yuriko Harewood 1.70, LJ: Lisa Anne Barrow 5.73, TJ: Misha Nelson 10.23, SP/DT: Ashley Williams 15.00/43.98, JT: Jameila Artherly 42.25.

Shane BRATHWAITE b. 8 Feb 1990 Bridgetown 1.82m 75kg. Was at Texas Tech University, USA.
At 110mh: OG: '12- h; WCh: '15- sf, '17- 6; CG: '14- 3; PAm: '15- 3; won CAC 2013, BAR 2014-17. At Oct: WY: '07- 1. At 60mh: WI: '16- 8. At 400mh: WJ: '08- sf.
Progress at 110mh: 2008- 14.54, 2009- 13.83, 2010- 13.71A/13.80w, 2011- 13.58, 2012- 13.31A/13.46/13.43w, 2013- 13.44/13.43w, 2014- 13.24, 2015- 13.21, 2016- 13.51, 2017- 13.26/13.25w. pbs: 60m 6.85i '17, 100m 10.43 '09, 200m 20.51 '17, 400m 46.97 '11, 1000m 2:48.01 '07, 55mh 7.15i '13, 60mh 7.64i '16, 400mh 50.90 '12, HJ 1.86 '07, LJ 7.02/7.13w '08.
No relation to Ryan Brathwaite (1 WCh 110mh 2009).

Women

Akela JONES b. 21 Apr 1995 Saint Michael 1.86m 77kg. Student at Kansas State University, USA.
At Hep: OG: '16- 20 (dnq 31 HJ). At LJ: WJ: '12- dnq 18; '14- 1; WY: '11- 6; PAm: '15- 6 (3 HJ, h 100mh).
BAR records: 100mh 2016, HJ (2) 2015-16, LJ (2) 2015-16, Hep (3) 2015, CAC Indoor pentathlon record 2016.
Progress at HJ, LJ, Hep: 2008- 1.71, 2009- 1.81, 5.85w; 2010- 1.85, 2011- 1.75, 6.16; 2012- 1.81, 6.36; 2013- 1.85i/1.80, 6.26i/6.35w; 2014- 1.87i/1.85, 6.55; 2015- 1.91, 6.64i/6.60, 6371(w); 2016- 1.98i/1.95, 6.80i/6.75, 6307. pbs: 60m 7.47i '15, 100m 11.64 '15, 11.59w '13; 200m 23.28 '16, 800m 2:21.62 '15, 60mh 8.00i '16, 100mh 12.94 '16, SP 14.85 '15, JT 38.97 '16, Pen 4643i '16.

BELARUS

Governing body: Belarus Athletic Federation. Founded 1991.
National Champions 2017: **Men**: 100m: Denis Bliznets 10.63, 200m: Igor Popov 21.41, 400m: Maksim Graborenko 48.35, 800m: Yan Sloma 1:50.52, 1500m/5000m: Artyom Logish 3:49.88/14:15.85, 10000m: Vladislav Promov 29:13.14, 3000mSt: Sergey Litovchik 8:58.06, 110mh: Vitaliy Parakhonko 13.87, 400mh: Aleksandr Shaban 51.81, HJ: Maksim Nedasekov 2.26, PV: Vladislav Chemarmazovich 4.80, LJ: Konstantin Borichevskiy 7.50, TJ: Dmitriy Plotnitskiy 16.65, SP: Aleksey Nichipor 19.62, DT: Viktor Trus 58.27, HT: Zakhar Makrosenko 75.56, JT: Pavel Meleshko 82.21, Dec: Vitaliy Zhuk 7576, 20kW: Aleksandr Lyakhovich 1:23:40. **Women**: 100m/200m: Kristina Timanovskaya

11.52/23.13, 400m: Ilona Usovich 54.49, 800m: Yuliya Korol 2:04.81, 1500m: Tatyana Stefanenko 4:22.61, 5000m: Anastasiya Ivanova 15:51.58, 10000m: Nina Savina 33:14.17, 3000mSt: Tatyana Shabanova 10:17.29 (dq Anastasiya Puzakova 10:02.79), 100mh: Elvira German 12.99, 400mh: Viktoriya Shimanskaya 59.70, HJ: Karina Taranda 1.80, PV: Irina Zhuk 4.55, LJ: Anastasiya Metelskaya 6.09, TJ: Irina Vaskovskaya 14.00, SP: Yuliya Leontyuk 17.78, DT: Svetlana Serova 51.94, HT: Anastasiya Maslova 65.24, JT: Tatyana Korzh 54.54, Hep: Yuliya Rout 5565, 20kW: Anastasiya Yatsevich 1:35:21.

Pavel BOREYSHA b. 16 Feb 1991 1.93m 120kg. Grodno State University.
At HT: OG: '16- dnq 13; WCh: '15- dnq 25, '17- 9; EC: '14- 10, '16- dnq 14; WJ: '10- 6; EU23: '11- dnq 17; WUG: '15- 2; ET: '17- 2. Won BLR 2014.
Progress at HT: 2011- 69.62, 2012- 72.25, 2013- 75.62, 2014- 76.86, 2015- 77.03, 2016- 78.60, 2017- 78.04.

Women

Marina ARZAMASOVA b. 17 Dec 1987 Minsk 1.73m 57kg. née Kotovich. Minsk.
At 800m: OG: '12- h, '16- 7; WCh: '11/13- sf, '15- 1, '17- h; EC: '12- 2, '14- 1; WJ: '06- h; CCp: '14- 3; ET: '11-3, '13- 3; WI: '14- 3; EI: '13- 3. Won W.MilG 2011, BLR 800m 2008, 2013, 2015; 1500m 2013.
Progress at 800m: 2004- 2:09.37, 2005- 2:07.24, 2006- 2:06.39, 2007- 2:04.33, 2008- 2:02.67, 2009- 2:05.53i, 2011- 1:59.30, 2012- 1:59.63, 2013- 1:59.60, 2014- 1:58.15, 2015- 1:57.54, 2016- 1:58.36, 2017- 2:01.92. pbs: 400m 52.81 '12, 600m 1:27.05 '17, 1000m 2:37.93 '11, 1500m 4:15.99 '12.
Parents were Aleksandr Kotovich UKR (HJ 2.35i '85, 2.33 '84; 2 EI 85) and Ravilya Agletdinova BLR (800m 1:56.1 '82, 1500m 3:58.40 '85, 1 EC 86, 4 WCh 83). Married to Ilya, with daughter Sashenka born 2010.

Alyona DUBITSKAYA b. 25 Jan 1990 Grodno 1.82m 77k. née Hryshko. Grodnenskaya.
At SP: OG: '16- 8; WCh: '13- dnq 27, '15- 6, '17- dnq 14; EC: '14- 7, '16- 6; WJ: '08- 4; WY: '07- 1; EJ: '09- 1; WI: '16- 9; EI: '17- 7; ET: '15- 3, '17- 1. BLR champion 2009, 2014-15.
Progress at SP: 2007- 15.91, 2008- 16.55, 2009- 17.95, 2010- 18.12i/17.75, 2012- 16.63, 2013- 17.88, 2014- 19.03, 2015- 18.88, 2016- 18.78, 2017- 19.01. pb DT 46.30 '14. 6-month drugs ban 2014-15.

Tatyana KHOLODOVICH b. 21 Jun 1991 Brest 1.81m 83kg.
At JT: OG: '16- 5; WCh: '15- dnq 21, '17- 6; EC: '14- 5, '16- 1; WJ: '08/10- dnq 16/21; EU23: 13- dnq; WUG: '15- 1; ET: '15- 2, '17- 2. BLR champion 2012-16.
Three Belarus javelin records 2014-16.
Progress at JT: 2007- 46.12, 2008- 53.51, 2009- 46.80, 2010- 51.17, 2011- 55.94, 2012- 59.15, 2013- 59.37, 2014- 63.61, 2015- 62.00, 2016- 66.34, 2017- 66.30.

Yuliya LEONTYUK b. 31 Jan 1984 Pinsk 1.85m 80kg. Brest.
At SP: OG: '16- dnq 17; WCh: '13- dnq 15, '15- 7, '17- 7; EC: '14- 4, '16- 4; WJ: '02- 7; WY: '01- 3; EU23: '05- 4; EJ: '03- 2; WUG: '07- 2; ECp: '08- dq (1); WI: '14- 6; EI: '07-15-17: 4/2/3. BLR champion 2016-17.
Progress at SP: 2001- 15.16, 2002- 16.47, 2003- 17.44, 2004- 16.37, 2005- 17.91, 2006- 18.86, 2007- 18.86, 2008- 19.79, 2013- 18.47, 2014- 18.87, 2015- 19.00i/18.86, 2016- 18.92, 2017- 18.47. pb DT 48.72 '14. Two-year drugs ban 2008-10.

Hanna MALYSHIK b. 4 Feb 1994 1.75m 90kg. née Zinchuk.
At HT: OG: '16- 7; WCh: '17- 10; EC: '16- dnq 26; WJ: '12- dnq; WY: '11- dnq 15, EJ: '13- 1; WUG: '17- 2; ET: '17- 1. Won EY Oly 2011, BLR 2016.
Progress at HT: 2009- 50.70, 2010- 57.38, 2011- 60.11, 2012- 63.41, 2013- 66.36, 2014- 67.53, 2015- 66.50, 2016- 72.78, 2017- 74.94.

Olga MAZURONAK b. 14 Apr 1989 1.76m 56kg. Minsk.
At Mar: OG: '16- 5. At 5000m: ET: '15- 2. At 10000m: EC: '14- 7; ECp: '17- 2. At 10000mW: WJ: '06- 5; EJ: '07- dq. At 5000mW: WY: '05- 4. Won BLR 5000m 2013, 10000m 2013-14.
Belarus half marathon record 2018.
Progress at Mar: 2012- 2:33:56, 2013- 2:33:33, 2014- 2:27:33, 2015- 2:25:36, 2016- 2:23:54, 2017- 2:27:14. pbs: 3000m 9:11.68i '18, 5000m 15:33.06 '17, 10000m 32:13.73 '17, HMar 70:57 '18; 5000mW 22:36.55 '05, 10kW 44:30 '06.
Marathon wins: Debno & Siberia 2012, Sacramento 2014.

Alina TALAY b. 14 May 1989 Orsha, Vitebsk 1.64m 54kg.
At 100mh: OG: '12/16- sf; WCh: '13-15-17: sf/3/6; EC: '10-12-14-16: sf/1/5/2; WJ: '08- 4; EU23: '09- 3, '11- 1; WUG: '13- 2; ET: '11-15-17: 2/1/2; won W.MilG 2011, BLR 2009-10, 2013-17 (200m 2015). At 60mh: WI: '12- 3, '16- 6; EI: '11-13-15-17: 5/1/1/2.
Two BLR 100m hurdles records 2015-16.
Progress at 100mh: 2007- 14.38/14.01w, 2008- 13.31, 2009- 13.07, 2010- 12.87, 2011- 12.91, 2012- 12.71, 2013- 12.78, 2014- 12.89, 2015- 12.66, 2016- 12.63, 2017- 12.72. pbs: 60m 7.31i '15, 100m 11.48 '11, 200m 23.59 '11, 50mh 6.89i '11, 60mh 7.85i '15.

BELGIUM

Governing bodies: Ligue Royale Belge d'Athlétisme (KBAB/LRBA). Vlaamse Atletiekliga (VAL); Ligue Belge Francophone d'Athlétisme (LBFA). Original governing body founded 1889.

National Championships first held in 1889 (women 1921). **2017**: **Men**: 100m: Jean-Marie Louis 10.66, 200m: Robin Vanderbemden 20.84,

400m: Kevin Borlée 45.51, 800m: Aaron Botterman 1:49.21, 1500m: Pieter Claus 3:47.86, 5000m: Cédric Van De Putte 14:33.24, 10000m: Steven Casteele 29:31.32, Mar: Gerd Devos 2:22:07, 3000mSt: Mathijs Casteele 9:02.15, 110mh: Denis Hanjoul 14.29 (Dylan Caty FRA 13.67), 400mh: Arnaud Ghislain 50.73, HJ: Bram Ghuys 2.13, PV: Arnaud Art 5.50, LJ: Corentin Campener 7.85, TJ: Leopold Kapata 15.63, SP/DT: Philip Milanov 17.77/65.07, HT: Remi Malengreaux 58.03, JT: Jarne Duchateau 71.42, Dec: Jaan Bal 7011, 20000mW: Dirk Bogeart 2:00:16. **Women**: 100m/200m: Cynthia Bolingo Mbongo 11.69/23.57; 400m: Elis Lasser 53.24, 800m: Riet Vanfleteren 2:10.38, 1500m: Renée Eykens 4:13.50, 5000m: Hanne Verbruggen 16:59.59, 10000m: Ferihawat Gamachu Tulu 35:27.95, Mar: Hanna Vandenbussche 2:37:30, 3000mSt: Elke Godden 10:43.06, 100mh: Anne Zagré 13.22, 400mh: Axelle Dauwens 56.75, HJ: Hannelore Desmet 1.77, PV: Fanny Smets 4.25, LJ: Hanne Maudens 6.40, TJ: Elsa Loureiro 12.64, SP/HT: Jolien Boumkwo 15.50/63.75, DT: Babette Bandeput 50.75, JT: Sarah Vermeir 42.74, Hep: Ellen Hooyberghs 5165, 10000mW/20kW: Annelies Sarrazin 57:18.94/1:59:49.

Jonathan BORLÉE b. 22 Feb 1988 Woluwe-Saint Lambert 1.80m 70kg. Racing Club of Brussels. Was at Florida State University.
At 400m: OG: '08- sf/5R, '12- 6, '16- h (h 200m); WCh: '11-13-15-17: 5/4/sf/sf; EC: '10- 7/3R, '12- 1R, '14- dns, '16- h/1R; WJ: '06- 4; WY: '05- 5; EJ: '07- h; WI: '10- 2R, '18- 3R; EI: '11- 3R, '15- 1R. Won NCAA 2009. At 200m: EC: '12- 4. Won BEL 200m 2012-13, 400m 2006, 2011, 2015.
Four Belgian 400m records 2009-12, 300m 2012.
Progress at 400m: 2005- 47.50, 2006- 46.06, 2007- 47.85, 2008- 45.11, 2009- 44.78, 2010- 44.71, 2011- 44.78, 2012- 44.43, 2013- 44.54, 2014- 45.37, 2015- 44.67, 2016- 45.34, 2017- 45.09. pbs: 60m 6.81i '07, 100m 10.78 '07, 200m 20.31 '12, 300m 31.87 '12, 500m 1:00.76i '15, 600m 1:18.60i '11.
Twin brother of Kevin Borlée, their sister **Olivia** (b. 10 Apr 1986) has pbs 100m 11.39 '07, 200m 22.98 '06, 3 WCh '07, 2 OG '08 at 4x100mR. Younger brother **Dylan** (b. 20 Sep 1992) pb 45.57 '15 and 2 EI '15 (the three brothers ran on BEL 4x400m team 5th WCh 2013, 1st EI 2015 & EC 2016, 4th OG 2016, 3rd WI 2018). Their father Jacques was an international 400m runner (45.4 '79), mother Edith Demartelaere had pbs 200m 23.89 and 400m 54.09 in 1984.

Kévin BORLÉE b. 22 Feb 1988 Woluwe-Saint Lambert 1.80m 71kg. Racing Club of Brussels. Was at Florida State University.
At 400m: OG: '08- sf/5R, '12- 5, '16- h; WCh: '09- sf/4R, '11- 3, '13/15/17- sf; EC: '10- 1/3R, '12- 1R, '14- sf, '16- 4/1R; WJ: '06- sf; WI: '10- 2R, '18- 3R; EI: '11-15-17: 3R/1R/2R; CCp: '10- 4/2R. At 200m: WY: '05- sf. Won DL 2012, BEL 200m 2009, 2011; 400m 2007, 2013, 2017.
Belgian 400m records 2008 and 2012.
Progress at 400m: 2005- 47.86, 2006- 46.63, 2007- 46.38, 2008- 44.88, 2009- 45.28, 2010- 45.01, 2011- 44.74, 2012- 44.56, 2013- 44.73, 2014- 45.28, 2015- 44.74, 2016- 45.17, 2017- 44.79. pbs: 60m 6.85i '13, 100m 10.62 '07, 200m 20.72 '11, 300m 32.22 '17, 600m 1:15.65i '11.

Philip MILANOV b. 6 Jul 1991 Bruges 1.91m 118kg. Vilvoorde AC, Lille Metropole, FRA.
At DT: OG: '16- 9; WCh: '15- 2, '17- dnq 14; EC: '14- dnq 20, '16- 2; EU23: '13- 5; WUG: '15- 1. Won BEL DT 2011-17, SP 2016-17.
Six Belgian discus records 2014-16.
Progress at DT: 2011- 56.00, 2012- 57.66, 2013- 61.81, 2014- 66.02, 2015- 66.90, 2016- 67.26, 2017- 67.05. pb SP 18.33 '17.
His father Emil Milanov had DT pb 58.28 '82, moved from Bulgaria to Belgium in 1989.

Thomas VAN DER PLAETSEN b. 24 Dec 1990 Gent 1.85m 86kg. AC Deinze.
At Dec: OG: '16- 8; WCh: '11-13-15-17: 13/15/14/dnf; EC: '14- 10, '16- 1; EU23: '11- 1; EJ: '09- 1; WUG: '13- 1, '15- 1; Won BEL PV 2011, 2013; Dec 2010. At Hep: WI: '14- 3; EI: '11- 6.
Belgian decathlon record 2011.
Progress at Dec: 2010- 7564, 2011- 8157, 2013- 8255, 2014- 8184, 2015- 8035, 2016- 8332. pbs: 60m 7.13i '14, 100m 11.04 '14, 200m 22.34 '10, 400m 48.64 '11, 1000m 2:40.50i '14, 1500m 4:32.52 '11, 60mh 8.06i '14, 110mh 14.39 '16, HJ 2.17 '11, PV 5.41 '16, LJ 7.80 '13, SP 14.32i/14.12 '14, DT 44.48 '14, JT 65.31 '13, Hep 6259i '14.

Women

Nafissatou THIAM b. 19 Aug 1994 Namur 1.84m 69kg. RFCL. Student of geographical science at University of Liège.
At Hep: OG: '16- 1; WCh: '13-15-17: 14/11/1; EC: '14- 3; WJ: '12- 14; WY: '11- 4; EJ: '13- 1. At Pen: EI: '13-15-17: 6/2/1. At HJ: EC: '16- 4; EU23: '15- 2; WI: '14- 8=. Won BEL Hep 2012, LJ 2015.
Belgian records: heptathlon (4) 2013-17, javelin 2017. World junior heptathlon best 2013.
Progress at HJ, Hep: 2010- 1.74, 2011- 1.81, 2012- 1.88, 5916; 2013- 1.92, 6298, 2014- 1.97, 6508; 2015- 1.92, 6412; 2016- 1.98, 6810; 2017- 1.98, 7013. pbs: 60m 7.81i '13, 200m 24.40 '17, 800m 2:15.24 '17, 60mh 8.23i '17, 100mh 13.34 '17, LJ 6.58 '16, TJ 12.82 '14, SP 15.52i '18, 15.24 '15; JT 59.32 '17, Pen 4870i '17.
Tied high jump world best in a heptathlon with 1.97 at EC 2014 and improved that to 1.98 at the Olympic Games, when she set five events pbs en route to the gold medal and adding 319 points to her pb. IAAF female Rising Star award 2016, Female Athlete of the Year 2017. Won at Götzis 2017.

BOSNIA & HERZEGOVINA

Governing body: Atletski savez Bosne i Hercegovine (AsBIH). Founded 1948.

Mesud PEZER b. 27 Aug 1994 Zenica 1.98m 120kg. AK Zenica
At SP: OG: '16- dnq 24; WCh: '17: dnq 21; EC: '16: 12; WJ: '12- 5; WY: '11- 6; EU23: '15- 4; WJ: '13- 1; WI: '17- 5; EI: '17- 7; Won Balkan 2017.
BIH record 2017.
Progress at SP: 2012- 15.17, 2013- 18.86, 2014- 19.37, 2015- 19.99, 2016- 20.58, 2017- 21.40, 2018- 21.15i. Pb DT 57.08 '16.

Amel TUKA b. 9 Jan 1991 Kakanj 1.87m 77kg. AK Zenica. Mechanical engineering graduate.
At 800m: OG: '16- sf; WCh: '15- 3, '17- h; EC: '12-14-16: sf/6/4; EU23: '13- 3.
BIH records: 400m (4) 2012-16, 800m (5) 2013-15.
Progress at 800m: 2010- 1:51.04, 2011- 1:51.09, 2012- 1:48.31, 2013- 1:46.29, 2014- 1:46.12, 2015- 1:42.51, 2016- 1:44.54, 2017- 1:44.62. pbs: 300m 34.46 '16, 400m 46.63 '16, 600m 1:15.21 '16.

BOTSWANA

Governing body: Botswana Athletics Association.

Nijel AMOS b. 15 Mar 1994 Marobela 1.79m 60kg.
At 800m: OG: '12- 2, '16- h; WCh: '15- sf, '17- 5; CG: '14- 1; WJ: '12- 1, WY: '11- 5; AfG: '15- 1/2R; AfCh: '14- 1/1R, '16- 1; CCp: '14- 1; WUG: '13- 1. Won DL 2014-15, 2017.
World junior 800m and two Botswana 800m records 2012.
Progress at 800m: 2011- 1:47.28, 2012- 1:41.73, 2013- 1:44.71, 2014- 1:42.45, 2015- 1:42.66, 2016- 1:44.66, 2017- 1:43.18. pbs: 200m 21.34 '15, 400m 45.55 '17, 600m 1:15.0+ 12.

Isaac MAKWALA b. 29 Sep 1986 Tutume 1.83m 79kg.
At (200m)/400m: OG: '12- h, '16- sf; WCh: '09- h, '13- (h), '15- 5, '17- 6/dns; CG: '10- sf, '14- sf; AfG: '07- sf/1R, '11- 7, '15- 1/2R; AfCh: '08-10-12-14-16: 2/sf/1/1 & (2),1R/4; CCp: '14- 6/2/1R. Won DL 2017.
Records: Commonwealth 400m 2015, African 400m (2) 2014-15, Botswana 100m (2) 2013-14, 200m 2013-14, 300m 2017, 400m (4) 2014-15.
Progress at 200m, 400m: 2007- 46.48, 2008- 21.20, 45.64A; 2009- 20.73, 45.56; 2010- 21.33, 46.07; 2011- 21.17, 46.27; 2012- 20.87, 45.25; 2013- 20.21, 45.86; 2014- 19.96/19.7A, 44.01; 2015- 20.44A/20.77, 43.72; 2016- 20.42A, 44.85; 2017- 19.77, 43.84. Pbs: 100m 10.20A/10.14wA '14; 300m 31.44 '17.
Ran 43.92 & 19.77 double within two hours at Madrid 2017. Not permitted to run the 400m final at 2017 Worlds due to quarantine restriction, but allowed ro compete at 200m with a solo heat after missing the first round.

Karabo SIBANDA b. 2 Jul 1998 Shashe-Mooke 1.92m 79kg.
At 400m: OG: '16- 5; WCh: '17- h; WJ: '14- sf, 16- 3/2R; WY: '15- 5; AfCh: '16- 2/1R; Af-J: '15- 1/1R; Yth OG: '14- 2; Comm-Y: '15- 1 (1 4x100m).
Progress at 400m: 2014- 46.76, 2015- 45.83, 2016- 44.25, 2017- 45.05. Pb 200m 21.28A '16.

Baboloki THEBE b. 18 Mar 1997 Ramonake 1.86m 77kg.
At (200m)/400m: OG: '16- sf; WCh: '17- 4; WJ: '14- (sf), '16- dq sf/2R; AfCh: '16- 1/1R; Yth OG: '14- (2). Won BOT 200m & 400m 2016.
African junior 400m record 2016.
Progress at 200m, 400m: 2014- 20.85A, 2015- 20.56A, 2016- 20.21A, 44.22A/44.69; 2017- 44.02. Pb: 100m 10.29A '15.

Women

Amantle MONTSHO b. 4 Jul 1983 Mabudutsa 1.73m 64kg.
At 400m: OG: '04- h, '08- 6, '12- 4; WCh: '05-07-09-11-13-17: h/sf/8/1/2/sf; CG: '06-10-14: sf/1/4dq; AfG: '03-07-11: h/1/1; AfCh: '04-06-08-10-12: h/2/1/1/1; WI: '10- 4; CCp: '10- 1/3R. Won DL 2011-13.
Botswana records 100m 2011, 200m 2001-12, 400m 2003-13; African 300m 2010.
Progress at 400m: 2003- 55.03, 2004- 53.77, 2005- 52.59, 2006- 52.14, 2007- 50.90, 2008- 49.83A/50.54, 2009- 49.89, 2010- 49.89, 2011- 49.56, 2012- 49.54, 2013- 49.33, 2014- 50.37, 2017- 51.28, 2018- 50.66A. pbs: 100m 11.60 '11, 200m 22.89 '12, 22.88w '11, 300m 36.33i '10.
First Botswana woman to win a major title. Positive test at 2014 Commonwealth Games, for which she received a two-year ban.

BRAZIL

Governing body: Confederação Brasileira de Atletismo (CBAt). Founded 1914 (Confederação 1977).

National Championships first held in 1925. **2017**: **Men**: 100m: Paulo André de Oliveira 10.18, 200m: Aldemir Gomes da Silva 20.15, 400m: Lucas Carvalho 45.84, 800m/1500m: Thiago André 1:44.81/3:45.42, 5000m/3000mSt: Altobelli da Silva 13:46.72/8:26.06, 10000m: Daniel do Nascimento 29:13.34, 110mh: Éder de Souza 13.47, 400mh: Márcio Teles 48.94, HJ: Fernando Ferreira 2.25, PV: Thiago Braz da Silva & Augusto Dutra de Oliveira 5.52, LJ: PauloSérgio Oliveira 7.77, TJ: Alexsandro de Melo 16.42, SP: Darlan Romani 20.56, DT: Felipe Lorenzon 57.97, HT: Wágner Domingos 73.62, JT: Paulo Enrique da Silva 74.86, Dec: Jefferson Santos 7776, 20kW: Caio Bonfim 1:21:25, 50kW: José Alessandro Bagio 4:17:55. **Women**: 100m: Rosângela Santos 11.20, 200m: Vitória Rosa 22.93, 400m: Geisa Coutinho 51.97, 800m: Jéssica dos Santos 2:07.57, 1500m: Kleidiane Jardim 4:23.58, 5000m: Maria Aparecida Ferraz 16:31.98, 10000m: Tatiele de Carvalho 33:48.50, 3000mSt: Tatiane da Silva 10:22.00, 100mh: Fabiana de Moraes 13.26, 400mh: Jaílma de Lima 56.76, HJ: Júlia Cistina dos Santos 1.80, PV: Patrícia dos Santos & Juliana Campos 4.10, LJ: Eliane

Martins 6.69, TJ: Núbia Soares 14.56, SP: Geisa Arcanjo 18.08, DT: Andressa de Morais 58.57, HT: Mariana Marcelino 67.02, JT: Laila Ferrer e Silva Domingos 62.52, Hep: Tamara de Sousa 6040, 20000mW: Érica de Sena 1:37:34.

Caio BONFIM b. 19 Mar 1991 Brasília 1.70m 58kg. CASO.
At 20kW: OG: '12- 38, '16- 4 (50kW 9); WCh: '11-13-15-17: 18/dq/6/3; WCp: '12-14-16: 14/16/8; PAm: 15- 3, SACh: '13- 1; BRA champion 2012-17, IbAm 2016. At 10000mW: WJ: '08- 6, '10- 4; WY: '07- 12.
Brazil records: 20kW (2) 2016-17, 50kW 2016.
Progress at 20kW, 50kW: 2009- 1:30:17.9t, 2010-1:27:21.3t, 2011- 1:20:58.5t, 2012- 1:21:26, 2013-1:22:14, 2014- 1:20:28, 2015- 1:20:44, 4:02:20; 2016-1:19:42, 3:47:02; 2017- 1:19:04. Pbs: 5000mW 19:47.99 '11, 10000mW 40:00R '17, 40:40.0 '09.
National records at 20k and 50k walks at 2016 Olympics in Rio. His mother, Gianetti de Sena Bonfim (b. 13.3.65), won the 1996 Ibero-American 10,000m walk, and had pbs 5000m: 23:28.9 '96, 10000m: 47:42.0 '96, 20k: 1:41:07 '04.

Darlan ROMANI b. 9 Apr 1991 Concórdia 1.88m 140kg.
At SP: OG: '16- 5; WCh: '15-17: dnq 15/dnq 15; WJ: '10- 7; PAm: '15- 6; SACh: '13- 2, '17- 1; WI: '18- 4 won IbAm 2016, BRA 2012-17.
South American shot record 2017 and ten Brazilian records 2012-16. Two South American indoor shot records 2018.
Progress at SP: 2009- 4.60, 2010- 17.66, 2011-18.46, 2012- 20.48, 2013- 20.08, 2014- 20.84, 2015-20.90, 2016- 21.02, 2017- 21.82, 2018- 21.68.

Almir Cunha **dos SANTOS** b. 4 Sep 1993 Matupá 1.88m 79kg.
At TJ: WI: '18- 2. At HJ: WJ: '12; dnq 26=; won S.Am-Y 2010.
Progress at TJ: 2016- 15.89, 2017- 16.86, 2018-17.14i. Pbs: HJ 2.18 '14, LJ 7.96 '17.
Formerly a high jumper, he took up triple jumping in late 2016.

Thiago Braz da SILVA b. 16 Dec 1993 Marília 1.93m 84kg. Orcampi/Unimed.
At PV: OG: '16- 1; WCh: '13-15: dnq 14=/19; WJ: '12- 1; WI: '14- 4; PAm: '15- nh; SACh: '13- 1; Yth Oly: '10- 2, won BRA 2015-16, 2017 (=), PAm-J 2011.
Six South American pole vault records 2013-16, indoors (5) 2014-16.
Progress at PV: 2009- 4.60, 2010- 5.10, 2011- 5.31, 2012- 5.55, 2013- 5.83, 2014- 5.76i/5.73, 2015- 5.92, 2016- 6.03, 2017- 5.86i/5.60.
Married Ana Paula de Oliveira (HJ 1.86 '15) on 13 Dec 2014.

Women

Rosângela SANTOS b. 20 Dec 1990 Washignton DC 1.65m 55kg.
At 100m/(200m): OG: '08- 3R, 12- sf, '16- sf; WCh: '11- sf, '15- sf/sf, '17- 7/sf; WJ: '08- 4/3R; WY: '07- 2/4; PAm: '11- 1/1R, '15- 4. Won IbAm 2012, 2016, SAm U23 2008, U20 2007; BRA100m 2008, 20912, 2015-16, 200m 2012.
South American records 100m 2017, indoor 60m 2016.
Progress at 100m: 2005- 12.23, 2006- 11.82, 2007-11.44, 2008- 11.41/11.38w, 2009- 11.90, 2010-11.81, 24.14/13.71w; 2011- 11.22A/11.36, 2012-11.17/11.07w, 2013- 11.23, 2014- 11.32, 2015-11.04/11.01w, 2016- 11.23, 2017- 10.91. pbs: 60m 7.17i '16, 150mSt 17.12 '13, 200m 22.77 '15.

Érica Rocha **de SENA** b. 3 May 1985 Camaragibe, Pernambuco 1.68m 55kg. Orcampi Unimed.
At 20kW: OG: '16- 7; WCh: '15- 6, '17- 4; WCp: '16- 3; PAm: 15- 2; BRA champion 2011-17. Won IbAm 10000mW 2016.
S.American walk records 10k 2017. 20k (5) 2014-17; BRA records: 10000mW 2014, 10kW 2017, 20kW (7) 2012-16.
Progress at 20kW: 2006- 1:51:45.5t, 2007-1:44:52.96t, 2008- 1:44:14.6t, 2009- 1:44:27, 2010-1:38:59, 2011- 1:35:29.6t, 2012- 1:31:53, 2013-1:32:59, 2014- 1:30:43, 2015- 1:29:37, 2016- 1:27:18, 2017- 1:26:59. Pbs: 5000mW 23:10.59 '11, 10000mW 43:31.30 '14, 43:03 '17.
Won IAAF Walks Challenge 2017. Married to and coached by Ecuadorian Andrés Chocho (qv). Lives in Cuenca, Ecuador.

BRITISH VIRGIN ISLANDS

Kyron McMASTER b. 3 Jan 1997 1.87m 79kg. Student at Central Arizona University.
At 400mh: WCh: '17- dq h; WJ: '16- 3; won DL 2017. At 400m: WY: '13- h (h 200m).
Five IVB 400mh records 2015-17.
Progress at 400m: 2014- 53.26, 2015- 50.16, 2016-49.56, 2017- 47.80. pbs: 200m 21.24 '17, 21.14w '15; HJ 1.86.

BULGARIA

Governing body: Bulgarian Athletics Federation. Founded 1924.
National Championships first held in 1926 (men), 1938 (women). **2017 Champions**: **Men:** 100m/200m: Denis Dimitrov 10.35/21.04, 400m: Borislav Tonev 47.85, 800m/3000mSt: Mitko Tsenov 1:52.68/8:55.59, 1500m: Nikolai Parvanov 3:49.07, 5000m: Yolo Nikolov 15:06.34, HMar: Ivan Popov 68:25, Mar: Dmcho Mitsov 2:26:42, 110mh: Stanislav Stankov 14.64, 400mh: Nikolai Nikolov 52.82, HJ: Tikhomir Ivanov 2.25, PV: Plamen Piskov 4.60, LJ: Daniel Ankov 7.36, TJ: Momchil Karailiev 16.66, SP: Georgi Ivanov 19.34, DT: Rosen Karamfilov 52.52, HT: Aykhan Apti 66.82, JT: Mark Slavov 71.90, Dec: Kiril Zagorski 5314, 20kW: Nikolai Minkov 1:40:46. **Women**: 100m/200m/400m: Nadezhda Racheva 11.90/24.46/55.78, 800m/1500m: Monika Georgieva 2:09.54/4:38.44, 5000m: Dilyana Minkina 17:28.25, HMar: Marinela Nineva

1:19:58, Mar/3000mSt: Radosveta Simeonova 2:46:10/10:48.14, 100mh: Elena Miteva 13.98, 400mh: Kristina Borukova 60.94, HJ: Elena Petrova 1.73, PV: Polina Mitova 3.20, LJ/TJ: Gabriela Petrova 6.34/13.96, SP: Radoslava Mavrodieva 16.65, DT: Renata Petkova 49.12, HT: Ekaterina Dimova 49.62, JT: Rumyana Karapetrova 44.40, Hep: Iva Aleexandrova 3951, 20kW: Radosveta Simeonova 1:48:20.

Women

Mirela DEMIREVA b. 28 Sep 1989 Sofia 1.80m 58kg. Atletik Sf.
At HJ: OG: '16- 2; WCh: '13- dnq 26, '15- 9=, '17- 7=; EC: '12- 8, 14- dnq 17, '16- 2=; WJ: '06- dnq 16, '08- 2; EU23: '09- 7, '11- dnq 17; EJ: '07- 3; WI: '18- 6 EI: '13- 7. BUL champion 2007=08, 2011, 2013-14; Balkan 2015-16.
Progress at HJ: 2005- 1.76, 2006- 1.86, 2007- 1.88, 2008- 1.86, 2009- 1.86, 2011- 1.85i/1.84, 2012- 1.95, 2013- 1.92, 2014- 1.94, 2015- 1.94, 2016- 1.97, 2017- 1.92, 2018- 1.95i.
Her mother Valia Demireva (100m 11.34) was at 4x100m 4th at the 1987 Worlds and 5th at the 1998 Olympics. Her father Krasimir Demirev won EJ 400m hurdles in 1981; pb 49.48 '88, also setting a BUL 400m record with 46.34 '83.

Ivet LALOVA-COLLIO b. 18 May 1984 Sofia 1.68m 56kg. née Lalova. IL Sprint Academy.
At 100m/(200m): OG: '04- 4/5, '08- sf/qf, '12- sf/sf, '16- sf/8; WCh: '07- qf, '09- qf/h, '11- 7/sf, '13- sf/sf, '15- sf/7, '17- sf/sf; EC: '10- h, '12- 1/sf, '14- 5/sf, '16- 2/2; WJ: '02- sf; WY: '01- h/sf; EJ: '03: 1/1; EI: '05- (1). At 60m: WI: '12- 8; EI: '13- 3. Won BUL 100m 2004-05, 200m 2004; Balkan 100m 2011, 2013, 2016.
Bulgarian 100m record 2004.
Progress at 100m, 200m: 1998- 13.0, 27.2; 1999- 12.71, 2000- 12.14, 25.24; 2001- 11.72, 24.03; 2002- 11.59, 24.4; 2003- 11.14, 22.87; 2004- 10.77, 22.51/22.36w; 2005- 11.03, 22.76; 2007- 11.26/11.15w, 23.00; 2008- 11.31/11.28w, 23.13; 2009- 11.48/11.24w, 23.60; 2010- 11.43, 23.71; 2011- 10.96, 22.66; 2012- 11.06/11.01w, 22.98; 2013- 11.04, 22.78; 2014- 11.10, 23.17/22.92w; 2015- 11.09, 22.32; 2016- 11.11, 22.42; 2017- 11.25, 22.82. pbs: 50m 6.23i+ '12, 60m 7.12i '13.
Broke her leg in a warm-up collision with two athletes on 14 Jun 2005. Married Simone Collio (Italy, 60m 6.55 ITA record 2008, 100m 10.06 in 2009) on 20 Sep 2013. Her father Miroslav Lalov had 100m best of 10.4 and won BUL 200m in 1966, mother Liliya was a pentathlete.

Gabriela PETROVA b. 29 Jun 1992 Haskovo 1.67m 61kg. Lokomtiv Plovdiv.
At TJ: OG: '16- dnq 22; WCh: '15- 4, '17- dnq 17; EC: '14- 5, '16- dnq 20; WJ: '10- dnq 17; WY: '09- dnq 18; EU23: '13- 1; EJ: '11- 5; EI: '15- 2; BUL champion LJ 2017, TJ 2010, 2013, 2016-17.
Progress at TJ: 2007- 12.43, 2008- 12.72i, 2009- 12.64, 2010- 13.35, 2011- 13.27/13.44w, 2012- 13.45, 2013- 14.14i/13.92/13.96w, 2014- 14.13, 2015- 14.66/14.85w, 2016- 14.32i/13.92, 2017- 14.19. pb LJ 6.46 '15.

BURUNDI

Governing body: Fédération d'Athlétisme du Burundi.

Antoine GAKÉMÉ b. 24 Dec 1991 Musongati, Rutana 1.70m 57kg. Playas de Castellón, Spain
At 800m: OG: '16- h; WCh: '13/15/17- sf; AfCh: '14- 7; WI: '16- 2.
Progress at 800m: 2009 1:52.89, 2013- 1:45.39, 2014- 1:46.24, 2015- 1:44.09, 2016- 1:45.24, 2017- 1:44.44. pbs: 1000m 2:20.25i '16, 1500m 3:40.36 '16.

Women

Francine NIYONSABA b. 5 May 1993 Nkanda Bweru, Ruyiqi 1.61m 56kg.
At 800m: OG: '12- 5, '16- 2; WCh: '17- 2; AfCh: '12- 1; WI: '16- 1, '18- 1.
Seven Burundi 800m records 2012-17. 600m 2017.
Progress at 800m: 2012- 1:56.59, 2013- 1:56.72, 2015- 1:57.62, 2016- 1:56.24, 2017- 1:55.47. pbs: 400m 54.3 '13, 600m 1:23.18 '16.
Won World title on indoor debut in 2016 and first Olympic medal for a Burundi woman. Her 1:58.31 to win 2018 World Indoor title was the world's fastest indoor time since 2011.

CANADA

Governing body: Athletics Canada. Formed as Canadian AAU in 1884.

National Championships first held in 1884 (men), 1925 (women). **2017 Champions: Men**: 100m/200m: Andre De Grasse 10.11/19.96w, 400m: Ben Ayesu-Attah 46.27, 800m: Brandon McBride 1:45.23, 1500m: Charles Philibert-Thiboutot 3:45.32, 5000m: Mohammed Ahmed 14:02.36, 10000m: Evan Esselink 29:21.11, HMar: Kip Kangogo 66:27, Mar: Trevor Hofbauer 2:18:06, 3000mSt: Matthew Hughes 8:30.91, 110mh: Johnathan Cabral 13.61, 400mh: Kirema Macharia 51.30, HJ: Michael Mason 2.25, PV: Shawnacy Barber 5.40, LJ: Damian Warner 7.53, TJ: Patrick Hanna 15.43, SP: Tim Nedow 20.53, DT: Jordan Young 62.76, HT: Adam Keenan 69.81, JT: Evan Karakolis 73.71, Dec: Pierce LePage 7948, 20kW: Benjamin Thorne 1:22:12. **Women**: 100m/200m: Crystal Emmanuel 11.20/22.55w, 400m: Natasha McDonald 52.20, 800m: Melissa Bishop 2:00.26, 1500m: Gabriella Stafford 4:12.41, 5000m: Andrea Seccafien 15:30.66, 10000m: Victoria Coates 33:50.62, HMar: Rachel Hannah 77:16, Mar: Leslie Sexton 2:35:47, 3000mSt: Geneviève Lalonde 9:37.45, 100mh: Angela Whyte 13.02, 400mh: Sage Watson 54.97, HJ: Alyx Treasure 1.91, PV: Alysha Newman 4.65, LJ: Christabel Nettey 6.23, TJ: Caroline Ehrhardt 13.53, SP: Brittany Crew 18.32, DT: Agnes Esser 5095, HT: Sultana

Frizell 66.88, JT: Liz Gleadle 60.62, Hep: Miki Oudenaarden 6000, 20kW: Katelynn Ramage 1:45:12.

Mohammed AHMED b. 5 Jan 1991 Mogadishu, Somalia 1.82m 56kg. Niagara Olympic Club.
At (5000m)/10000m: OG: '12- 18, '16- 4/32; WCh: '13- 9, '15- (12), 17- 6/8; CG: '14- 5/6; PAm: '15- 1; WJ: '08- 9, '10- 4; PAm-J: '09- (1). At 3000m: WI: '16- 9. Won CAN 5000m 2016-17, 10000m 2012.
CAN records 3000m 2017, 10000m (3) 2015-17.
Progress at 5000m, 10000m: 2008- 14:26.71, 30:03.53; 2009- 14:11.84, 2010- 14:02.04, 28:57.44; 2011- 13:34.23, 29:08.29; 2012- 13:41.06, 27:34.64, 2013- 13:40.43i, 27:35.76; 2014- 13:18.88, 28:02.96; 2015- 13:10.00, 27:46.90; 2016- 13:01.74, 29:32.84; 2017- 13:04.60i/13:08.16, 27:02.35. pbs: 1500m 3:40.18 '15, 1M 3:56.60 '17; 3000m 7:40.11i '16, 7:40.49 '17; 2M 8:13.16i '17.
Moved to Canada at age 11. Younger twin brother Ibrahim 25 WJ 10000m 2012.

Shawnacy BARBER b. 27 May 1994 Las Cruces, New Mexico, USA 1.90m 82kg. Student at Akron University, USA.
At PV: OG: '16- 10; WCh: '13- dnq 27, '15- 1, '17- 8; CG: '14- 3; WJ: '12- 3; PAm: '15- 1; PAm-J: 13- 1; WI: '16- 4=; Won CAN 2013-14, 2016-17; NCAA 2015.
Pole vault records: Four Canadian 2013-15, indoors (7) 2014-16, N.American indoor 2016.
Progress at PV: 2010- 4.42, 2011- 5.03, 2012- 5.57, 2013- 5.71, 2014- 5.75Ai/5.65, 2015- 5.93, 2016- 6.00Ai/5.91, 2017- 5.83i/5.72.
He lost his Canadian title in 2016 following a positive test for cocaine (getting a Public Warning from the IAAF), but was cleared to compete at the Olympic Games. His father George vaulted 5.29 in 1985 and in 1983 competed for Canada at the Worlds (nh) and was Canadian champion.

Andre DE GRASSE b. 10 Nov 1994 Scarborough, Ontario 1.80m 73kg. University of Southern California (sociology).
At (100m)/200m: OG: '16- 3/2/3R; WCh: '15- (3=)/3R; CG: '14- sf; PAm: '15- 1/1; PAm-J: '13- 2/3. Won NCAA 100m & 200m 2015, CAN 100m 2015-17, 200m 2017.
Four Canadian 200m records 2015-16.
Progress at 100m, 200m: 2012- 10.59, 2013- 10.25/9.96w, 20.74A/20.57w; 2014- 10.15/10.03w, 20.38; 2015- 9.92/9.75w, 19.88/19.58w; 2016- 9.91, 19.80; 2017- 10.01/9.69w, 20.01/19.96w. pbs: 55m 6.21i '13, 60m 6.60i '15, 400m 47.93 '14.
Father came from Barbados and mother from Trinidad. IAAF male Rising Star award 2016.

Derek DROUIN b. 6 Mar 1990 Sarnia, Ontario 1.95m 80kg. Student of exercise science at Indiana University.
At HJ: OG: '12- 3=, '16- 1; WCh: '13- 3, '15- 1; CG: '14- 1; WY: '07- 10; PAm: '15- 1; CCp: '14- 4. Won PAmJ 2009, CAN 2012-16, NCAA 2013, Franc G 2013.
Commonwealth high jump record 2014, four Canadian high jump records 2013-14.
Progress at HJ: 2007- 2.07, 2008- 2.11, 2009- 2.27, 2010- 2.28i/2.26, 2011- 2.33i/2.23, 2012- 2.31, 2013- 2.38, 2014- 2.40, 2015- 2.37, 2016- 2.38, 2017- 2.33i/2.25. pbs: 60mh 7.98i '12, 1000m 2:45.06i '13, 110mh 14.04 '13, PV 4.15i '13. 3.65 '11; LJ 7.20i '13, 6.85 '11; Hep 5817i '13, Dec 7150 '17.
Decathlon high jump best ever 2.28 '17. Sister Jillian (b. 30 Sep 1986) heptathlon pb 5972w to win Pan-Am Cup in 2014; 6th CG 2010.

Evan DUNFEE b. 28 Sep 1990 Richmond, BC 1.86m 68kg. Was at University of British Columbia.
At (20kW)/50kW: OG: '16- 10/4; WCh: '13- 36, '15- 12/12, '17- 15; CG: '10- (6); PAm: '15- (1), WCp: '14- (11); won NACAC 2012. At 10000mW: WJ: '08- 10; WY: '07- 23. CAN champion 10000mW 2012, 2015, 20kW 2010-11, 2014.
N.American records: 20k & 20,000m 2014, 50kW (2) 2015-16.
Progress at 50kW: 2013- 3:59:28, 2014- 3:58:34, 2015- 3:43:45, 2016- 3:41:38, 2017- 3:46.03. pbs: 5000mW 18:53.06 '14, 10000mW 39:21.30 '16, 20kW 1:20:13 '14, 30kW 2:11:54 '14; HMar 70:44 '16.

Matthew HUGHES b. 3 Aug 1989 Oshawa, Ontario 1.80m 64kg. Was at University of Louisville, USA.
At 3000mSt: OG: '16- 10, WCh: '11-13-15-17: h/6/8/6; CG: '14- 4; WJ: '08- h; PAm: '15- 1; CCp: '14- 7; CAN champion 2013-15, 2017.
Canadian 3000m steeplechase record 2013.
Progress at 3000mSt: 2007- 9:20.61, 2008- 8:59.83, 2009- 8:47.36, 2010- 8:34.18, 2011- 8:24.87, 2012- 8:31.77, 2013- 8:11.64, 2014- 8:12.81, 2015- 8:18.63, 2016- 8:20.63, 2017- 8:21.84. pbs: 1500m 3:41.49 '15, 1M 4:01.98 '16, 3000m 7:51.87i '15, 8:11.64 '13; 5000m 13:19.56 '15.

Brandon McBRIDE b. 15 Jun 1994 1.95m 75kg. Was at Mississippi State University, USA.
At 8000m: OG: '16- sf, WCh: '17- 8; CG: '14- sf; WJ: '12- 6; WY: '11- h; NCAA champion 2014, CAN 2014, 2016-17. At 400m: PAm-J: 13- 1.
Progress at 800m: 2011- 1:48.41, 2012- 1:46.07, 2013- 1:46.38, 2014- 1:45.35, 2015- 1:45.87, 2016- 1:43.95, 2017- 1:44.41. pbs: 100m 10.29w '11, 400m 45.89 '13, 500m 1:01.40i '14, 1500m 3:41.55 '16, 1M 4:11.96 '16, 3000m 8:27.13i '17.

Tim NEDOW b. 16 Oct 1990 Brockville 1.98m 125kg. Ottawa Lions. Was at University of Tulsa and DePaul University, USA.
At SP: OG: '16- dnq 16; WCh: '13-15-17- dnq 24/20/16; CG: '14- 3; WI: '16- 7, '18- 9; PAm: '15- 2 (6 DT); PAm-J: '09- 3. Won CAN SP 2013-17, DT 2012-15
Progress at SP: 2010- 17.90, 2011- 19.18i/18.84, 2012- 20.51i/20.21, 2013- 20.74, 2014- 20.98, 2015-

20.78, 2016- 21.33i/20.88, 2017- 20.73, 2018- 20.82i. pb DT 61.49 '15.

Damian WARNER b. 4 Nov 1989 London, Ontario 1.85m 83kg. LWTF.
At Dec: OG: '12- 5, '16- 3; WCh: '11-13-15-17: 18/3/2/5; CG: '14- 1; PAm: '15- 1. Won Canadian 110mh 2014-15, LJ 2017, Dec 2011-13. At Hep: WI: '14- 7, '18- 2.
Two Canadian decathlon records 2015.
Progress at Dec: 2010- 7449, 2011- 8102A/7832, 2012- 8442, 2013- 8512, 2014- 8282, 2015- 8695, 2016- 8666, 2017- 8591. pbs: 60m 6.74i '10, 100m 10.15/10.09w '16, 200m 20.96 '13, 400m 46.36i '15, 46.54 '16, 1000m 2:37.12i '18, 1500m 4:24.73 '15, 60mh 7.63i '16, 110mh 13.27 '15, HJ 2.09 '13, PV 4.90 '16, LJ 8.04 '16, TJ 14.75w '08, SP 14.90i '18, 14.44 '15; DT 50.26 '16, JT 64.67 '13, Hep: 6343i '18 (CAN rec).
Made 340 points improvement on pb when 5th at 2012 Olympics, setting six pbs, and 70 more at 2013 Worlds, with three pbs. Won Götzis 2013, 2017, Talence 2013. Ran fastest ever in decathlons: 110mh 13.44 '15 and 100m 10.15 '16.

Women

Melissa BISHOP b. 5 Aug 1988 Eganville, Ontario 1.73m 57kg. Was at University of Windsor.
At 800m: OG: '12- h, '16- 4; WCh: '13- h, '15- 2, '17- 5; CG: '14- 8; PAm: '15- 1; CAN champion 2013-14, 2016-17. At 400m: WY: '05- h.
Two Canadian 800m records 2015-16.
Progress at 800m: 2007- 2:10.51 2008- 2:10.12, 2009- 2:06.77, 2010- 2:04.12, 2011- 2:02.69, 2012- 1:59.82, 2013- 1:59.76, 2014- 1:59.70, 2015- 1:57.52, 2016- 1:57.02, 2017- 1:57.01. pbs: 400m 56.27 '10, 600m 1:27.2+ '16, 1000m 2:38.75 '14, 1500m 4:09.58 '16. Expecting a baby in 2018.

Phylicia GEORGE b. 16 Nov 1987 Toronto 1.78m 65kg. Was at University of Connecticut, USA.
At 100mh: OG: '12- 5, '16- 8; WCh: '11- 7, '15/17- sf; PAm: '15- 5; Canadian champion 2014. At 200m: WJ: 06- h.
Progress at 100mh: 2006- 14.53w, 2007- 14.44w, 2008- 13.71/13.62w, 2009- 13.74, 2010- 13.39, 2011- 12.73, 2012- 12.65, 2013- 13.75, 2014- 13.08, 2015- 12.94, 2016- 12.74/12.67w, 2017- 12.85. pbs: 60m 7.35i '12, 100m 11.25 '12, 200m 23.10 '11, 50mh 6.90i '12, 55mh 7.69i '10, 60mh 7.93i '17.
Bronze medal at 2M bobsleigh at 2018 Winter Olympics.

Liz GLEADLE b. 5 Dec 1988 Vancouver 1.83m 95kg. Chinooks.
At JT: OG: '12- 12, '16- dnq 16; WCh: '15- 11, '17- 12; CG: '14- 5; PAm: '15- 1; WJ: '06- 12; WY: '05- 5; CCp: '14- 3. Canadian champion 2008-09, 2012, 2014-17.
Five Canadian javelin records 2009-15.
Progress at JT: 2005- 50.53, 2006- 50.86, 2007- 52.36, 2008- 54.13, 2009- 58.21, 2010- 57.84, 2011- 58.40, 2012- 61.15, 2013- 54.13, 2014- 64.50, 2015- 64.83, 2016- 62.59, 2017- 64.47.

Christabel NETTEY b. 2 Jun 1991 Brampton, Ontario 1.62m 59kg. Was at Arizona State University (justice studies).
At LJ: OG: '16- dnq 20; WCh: '13-15-17: dnq 19/4/dnq 19; CG: '14- 3; WY: '07- dnq 14 (8 100mh); WI: '18- 7; PAm: '15- 1; PAm-J: '09- 2; CCp: '14- 4. At 100mh: WY: '07- 8 (3 MedR). Won CAN LJ 2013-17, NACAC 2012
Three Canadian long jump records 2015, four indoor 2014-15.
Progress at LJ: 2006- 6.12, 2007- 6.14, 2008- 6.21, 2009- 6.05/6.10w, 2010- 6.42i/6.28, 2011- 6.49/ 6.55i, 2012- 6.58, 2013- 6.75, 2014- 6.73, 2015- 6.99, 2016- 6.75/6.88w, 2017- 6.92/6.94w. pbs: 60m 7.65A '17, 100m 12.14 '06, 60mh 8.25i '13, 100mh 13.42 '13, HJ 1.66 '11, TJ 12.80 '12, 12.90w '07; SP 12.16 '11, Hep 5068 '11.
Older sister Sabrina has LJ pbs 6.32i '14, 6.26 '12.

Alysha NEWMAN b. 29 Jun 1994 1.79m 67kg. Nike. Was at University of Miami
At PV: OG: '16- dnq 17; WCh: '17- 7; WJ: '12- dnq 25; WY: '11- 12; CG: '14- 3; WI: '18- 6; PAm-J: 13- 1; Canadian champion 2016-17.
Four Canadian pole vault records 2016-17.
Progress at PV: 2010- 3.91, 2011- 4.00i/3.91, 2012- 4.06, 2013- 4.40A, 2014- 4.41, 2015- 4.40, 2016- 4.61, 2017- 4.75, 2018- 4.70i. Pb 100mh 14.07 '14.

Sage WATSON b. 20 Jun 1994 Medicine Hat, Alberta 1.75m 62kg. Studied at Florida State, then University of Arizona, USA.
At 400mh: OG: '16- sf; WCh: '15- sf, '17- 6; PAm: '15- h/3R; WJ: '12- sf; WY: '11- 8 (3 MedR). Won NCAA 2017, CAN 2011, 2017.
Progress at 400mh: 2011- 59.00, 2012- 58.0 4, 2013- 56.81A/58.20, 2015- 55.97, 2016- 54.82, 2017- 54.52. pbs: 200m 23.80 '17, 300m 37.08i '18, 400m 51.62 '18, 500m 1:08.40i '17, 600m 1:28.31 '17.

CHILE

Governing body: Federación Atlética de Chile. Founded 1914.
2017 Champions: Men: 100m: Enrique Polanco 10.78, 200m/400m: Sergio Aldea 21.62/47.06, 800m: Jonathan Bolados 1:50.58, 1500m/5000m: Víctor Aravena 3:50.05/14:02.93, 10000m: Matías Silva 29:13.34, HMar: Patricio Uribe 67:07, 3000mSt: Roberto Tello 9:11.28, 110mh: Diego Lyon 14.61, 400mh: Alfredo Sepúlveda 52.18, HJ: Cristóbal Hurtado 2.12, PV: Felipe Fuentes 4.60, LJ: Daniel Pineda 7.41, TJ: Álvaro Cortez 15.92, SP: Matías López 18.34, DT: José Miguel Ballivian 50.71, HT: Patricio Palma 59.69, JT: Francisco Muse 65.00, Dec: César Jofre 6394, 20000mW: Fabricio Mitch Salas 1:39:01.7, 35kW: Yerko Araya 2:43:38. **Women**: 100m/200m: Isidora Jiménez 11.71/23.64, 400m: María Paula Goñi 56.41, 800m: Carmen Mansilla 2:08.62, 1500m: Stephanie Paradis 4:25.01, 5000m:

Jennifer González 17:32.63, HMar: Clara Morales 1:21:14, 3000mSt: Margaríta Masías 11:04.30, 100mh: María Ignacia Eguiguren 13.85, 400mh: María José Echeverría 59,86, HJ: Javiera Lazo 1.65, LJ: Macarena Reyes 6.32, TJ: Vanesa Mercado 11.89, SP: Natalia Ducó 17.00, DT: Karen Gallardo 58.60, HT: Leslie Torrejón 47.20, JT: María Paz Rïos 50.56, Hep: Javiera Brahm 50.41, 20kW: Anita Rico 1:49:09.

CHINA

Governing body: Athletic Association of the People's Republic of China.

National Championships first held in 1910 (men), 1959 (women). **2017 Champions**: **Men**: 100m: Xie Zhenye 10.19, 200m: Bie Ge 20.64, 400m: Guo Zhongze 46.12, 800m: Ma Junyi 1:53.17, 1500m: Luo Yuxi 3:52.38, 5000m: Liu Hongliang 14:06.61, 10000m: Duo Bujie 29:32.82, 3000mSt: Xu Pengcheng 8:51.78, 110mh: Ma Lei 13.55, 400mh: Cai Junqi 50.27, HJ: Zhang Guowei 2.31, PV: Ding Bangchao 5.70, LJ: Zhang Yaoguang 7.88, TJ: Zhu Yaming 17.17, SP: Tian Zhizhong 18.67, DT: Zhang Mengjie 57.31, HT: Wang Shizhu 72.20, JT: Liu Qizhen 79.15, Dec: Gong Kewei 7481, 50kW: Nu Wenbin 3:46:12. **Women**: 100m: Yuan Qiqi 11.30, 200m: Kong Lingwei 23.56, 400m: Tong Cenghuan 52.74, 800m: Zheng Xiaoqian 2:07.51, 1500m: Zhao Jing 4:28.37, 5000m: Li Zhixuan 15:56.83, 10000m: Wang Jiali 33:08.06, 3000mSt: Zhang Xinyan 10:07.04, 100mh: Wu Shuijiao 12.98, 400mh: Huang Yan 57.01, HJ: Wang Yang 1.84, PV: Ren Mengqian 4.50, LJ: Lu Minjia 6.36, TJ: Chen Ting 13.53, SP: Gong Lijiao 19.18, DT: Tan Jian 58.47, HT: Luo Na 70.44, JT: Li Lingwei 62.44, Hep: Wang Qingling 5743.

13th National Games: Men: 100m/200m: Xie Zhenye 10.04/20.20, 400m: Guo Zhongze 45.14, 1500m: Luo Yuxi 3:44.35, 10,000m: Duo Bujie 28:26.86, Mar: Dong Guojian 2:18:45, 110mh Xie Wenjun 13.52, 400mh: Feng Zhiqiang 49.66, HJ: Wang Yu 2.27, PV: Xue Changrui 5.60, LJ: Huang Changzhou 8.28, TJ: Dong Bin 17.23, SP: Tian Zhizhong 19.58, DT: Wu Jian 59.62, HT: Wang Shizhu 76.12, JT: Zhao Qinggang 80.04, Dec: Guo Qi 7666, 20kW: Wang Kaihua 1:20:52, 50kW: Xu Faguang 3:54:02. **Women**: 100m: Wei Yongli 11.31, 200m: Huang Guifen 23.24, 400m: Yang Huizhen 51.8, 800m: Wang Chunyu 2:03.49, 1500m: Zhao Jing 4:16.41, 5000m: Xu Qiuzi 15:46.42, 10000m: Li Dan 34:00.25, Mar: Wang Jiali 2:33:36, 100mh: Wu Shujiao 12.97, 400mh: Wang Huan 55.99, HJ: Wang Yang 1.90, PV: Xu Huiqin 4.40, LJ: Lu Minjia 6.63, TJ: Wang Wupin 13.88, SP: Gong Lijiao 19.46, DT: Su Xinyue 64.56, HT: Zhang Wenxiu 75.48, JT: Li Lingwei 64.07, Hep: Wang Qingling 6033, 20kW: Yang Jiayu 1:28:29.

CAI Zelin b. 11 Apr 1991 Dali, Yunnan 1.72m 55kg.
At 20kW: OG: '12- 4, '16- 2; WCh: '13- 26, '15- 5; AsiG: '14- 4; WCp: '14- 2, '16- 2. At 10000mW: WJ: '10- 2; WCp: '10- 2J. CHN 20kW champion 2012.
Progress at 20kW: 2010- 1:22:28, 2011- 1:21:07, 2012- 1:18:47, 2013- 1:18:55, 2014- 1:18:52, 2015- 1:19:45, 2016- 1:19:26, 2018- 1:20:38. Pbs: 5000mW 19:35.00 '14, 10,000mW 38:59.98 '12, 30kW 2:45:13 '09.

CAO SHUO b. 8 Oct 1991 Baoding, Hebei 1.80m 77kg.
At TJ: OG: '12- dnq 20, '16- 4; WCh: '15- dnq 15; AsiG: '10- 3, '14- 1; AsiC: '13- 1, '15- 2; CCp: '14- 5; WI: '14- 7. Won Asi-J 2010, CHN 2009, 2012-13, NG 2013.
World youth triple jump record 2009.
Progress at TJ: 2007- 15.82, 2008- 16.42, 2009- 17.13, 2010- 16.85, 2011- 16.86, 2012- 17.35, 2013- 17.26, 2014- 17.30, 2015- 16.77/16.98w, 2016- 17.13, 2017- 17.22.

DONG Bin b. 22 Nov 1988 Changshan. 1.79m 67kg.
At TJ: OG: '12- 10, '16- 3; WCh: '13- 9, '15- dnq 18; WJ: '06- dnq 14; AsiG: '14- 2; AsiC: '11- 5, '15- 4; WI: '12-16-18: 8/1/8. Won Asian indoors 2010, 2012, CHN NG 2017.
Asian indoor triple jump record 2016.
Progress at TJ: 2006- 16.22, 2007- 16.25, 2008- 16.54, 2009- 16.89i/16.65, 2010- 16.86, 2011- 17.01i/16.86, 2012- 17.38, 2013- 17.16i/16.98, 2014- 16.95, 2015- 17.12/17.21w, 2016- 17.58, 2017- 17.27. pb LJ 7.09 '07, 7.32w '06.

GAO Xinglong b. 12 Mar 1994 Heilongjiang Prov 1.81m 65kg.
At LJ: OG: '16- dnq nj; WCh: '15- 4; AsiG: '14- 3; AsiC: '15- 1. Won CHN 2014-15.
Progress at LJ: 2012- 7.27, 2013- 8.02i/7.98, 2014- 8.18/8.21w, 2015- 8.34, 2016- 8.23, 2017- 8.22.

HUANG Changzhou b. 20 Aug 1994 Sichuan Prov 1.83m 64kg.
At LJ: OG: '16- 11; WCh: '17- dnq 24; AsiC: '15- dnq, '17- 1; WI: '16- 3; Won CHN NG 2017.
Progress at LJ: 2012- 7.79, 2013- 7.97, 2014- 8.12, 2015- 8.17, 2016- 8.21i/8.12, 2017- 8.26.

SHI Yuhao b. 26 Sep 1998 Jiangsu Prov. 1.78m 61kg.
At LJ: WCh: '17- 6; WY: '15- 6 (6 TJ); WI: '18- 5. Asian indoor champion 2018.
Asian junior long jump records 2016 & 2017.
Progress at LJ: 2014- 7.39, 2015- 7.63, 2016- 8.30, 2017- 8.31. pb TJ 15.45 '16.

SU Bingtian b. 29 Aug 1989 Zhongshan, Guangdong Prov. 1.85m 65kg. Guandong.
At 100m: OG: '12- sf, '16- sf/4R; WCh: '13- sf, '15- 9/2R, '17- 8; AsiG: '14- 2/1R; AsiC: '11- 1, '13- 1, '15- 1R; WUG: '11- 3. Won Chinese 100m 2009, 2011-13, E.Asian G 2013. At 60m: WI: '14-16-18: 4/5/2; AsiG: '09- 1.
Records: Asian 4x100m 2016, indoor 60m (4) 2016-18, Chinese 100m (3) 2011-15 and 200m 2013.

Progress at 100m: 2006- 10.59, 2007- 10.45, 2008- 10.41, 2009- 10.28, 2010- 10.32, 2011- 10.16, 2012- 10.19/10.04w, 2013- 10.06, 2014- 10.10, 2015- 9.99, 2016- 10.08/10.04w, 2017- 10.03/9.92w. pbs: 60m 6.42i '18, 200m 21.23 '08.

WANG Jianan b. 27 Aug 1996 Shenyang, Liaoning prov. 1.78m 61kg.
At LJ: OG: '16- 5; WCh: '13-15-17: dnq 23/3/7; WJ: '14- 1; AsiC: '13- 1; WI '16- 8.
Asian junior long jump record 2015.
Progress at LJ: 2012- 8.04, 2013- 7.95, 2014- 8.10, 2015- 8.25, 2016- 8.24, 2017- 8.29. pbs: 60m 6.89i '12, 100m 10.88 '12, 60mh 8.46i '12, HJ 1.94 '12, PV 5.00 '12, Dec 7063 '12.
At 18 in 2015 he became the youngest ever male World Champs medallist at a field event.

WANG Kaihua b. 16 Feb 1994 Guangdong Prov. 1.80m 65kg.
At 20kW: WCh: '17- 7. Won CHN NG 2017.
Progress at 20kW: 2011- 1:26:48, 2013- 1:23:35, 2014- 1:26:54, 2015- 1:19:49, 2016- 1:19:51, 2017- 1:17:54. Pbs: 10000mW 41:50.75 '11, 39:50R '17 .

WANG Yu b. 18 Aug 1991 1.92m 73kg. Beijing
At HJ: OG: '16- dnq 32; WCh: '13-15-17: dnq 19/dnq 18=/dns; AsiG: '14- 4; AsiC: 15- 7; WUG: '11- 4, '13- 3. Won CHN 2015, NG 2013, 2017.
Progress at HJ: 2008- 2.08, 2009- 2.17, 2010- 2.24i/2.15, 2011- 2.28, 2012- 2.28, 2013- 2.33, 2014- 2.31, 2015- 2.31, 2016- 2.33, 2017- 2.30.

WANG Zhen b. 24 Aug 1991 Changzhou 1.80m 62kg. Heilongjiang.
At 20kW: OG: '12- 3, '16- 1; WCh: 11- 2, '13- dq, '15- 2; AsiG: '14- 1; WCp: '12-14-16: 1/6/1; CHN champion 2011, 2015; NG 2013. Won World Race Walking Challenge 2016 & Final 10k 2010-12.
Walks records: World junior 10k 2010, Asian 20k 2012, 10,000m track 2012 & 2015.
Progress at 20kW: 2008- 1:28:01, 2009- 1:22:10, 2010- 1:20:42, 2011- 1:18:30, 2012- 1:17:36, 2013- 1:19:08, 2014- 1:19:40. 2015- 1:18:00, 2016- 1:19:12. Pbs: 3000mW 11:23.2 14, 5000mW 18:49.10 '14, 10kW 37:44 '10, 38:23.73 '15; 30kW 2:08:46 '08, 50kW 3:53:00 '09.
Won IAAF Race Walking Challenge 2016.

XIE Wenjun b. 11 Jul 1990 Shanghai 1.88m 77kg, Shanghai
At 110mh: OG: '12- sf, '16- h; WCh: '13-15-17: h/sf/sf; AsiG: '14- 1; AsiC: '15- 1; CCp: '14- 4; Won CHN 2012, 2015-16; NG 2013, 2017.
Progress at 110mh: 2007- 14.09, 2008- 13.47, 2009- 13.53, 2010- 13.47, 2011- 13.45, 2012- 13.34, 2013- 13.28, 2014- 13.23, 2015- 13.36, 2016- 13.34, 2017- 13.31. pbs: 100m 11.04 '06, 60mh 7.60i '13.

XUE Changrui b. 31 May 1991 Shandong prov. 1.83m 60kg
At PV: OG: '16- 6; WCh: '13- 12, '17- 4; WI: '14- 5, AsiG: '14- 1; AsiC: '13- 1; CCp: '14- 2; Won CHN NG 2013, 2017.
Three Chinese pole vault records 2014-17.
Progress at PV: 2011- 5.30, 2012- 5.60, 2013- 5.75i/5.65, 2014- 5.80, 2015- 5.40, 2016- 5.81i/5.75, 2017- 5.82. pb LJ 7.15 '08

YU Wei b. 11 Sep 1987 1.80m 60kg. Shandong.
At 50kW: OG: '16- 5; WCh: '15- 7, '17- dnf. At 20kW: AsiC: '09- 2.
Progress at 50kW: 2008- 4:03:54, 2009- 3:58:00, 2010- 3:58:23, 2011- 3:51:46, 2014- 4:00:57, 2015- 3:45:21, 2016- 3:42:54. Pbs: 10000mW 40:30.50 '12, 20kW 1:19:07 '13.

ZHANG Guowei b. 4 Jun 1991 Binzhon, Shandong prov. 2.00m 77kg.
At HJ: OG: '12/16- dnq 21=/25=; WCh: '11-13-15-17: 10/9/2=/dnq 24; WI: '12-14-16: 4=/7/6, AsiG: '14- 2; AsiC: '11- 8, '17- 2; CCp: '14- 6. CHN champion 2011, 2017.
Progress at HJ: 2010- 2.23, 2011- 2.31, 2012- 2.31, 2013- 2.32i/2.29, 2014- 2.34, 2015- 2.38, 2016- 2.33, 2017- 2.31.

Women

CHEN Yang b. 10 Jul 1991 1.80m 97kg. Hebei.
At DT: OG: '16- 7; WCh: '17- 10; AsiC: '17- 1.
Progress at DT: 51.05- 53.79, 2011- 51.10, 2012- 53.10, 2013- 52.10, 2014- 58.53, 2015- 61.16, 2016- 63.61, 2017- 62.90.

FENG Bin b. 3 Apr 1994 1.84m 95kg. Shandong.
At DT: OG: '16- 8; WCh: '17- 8; WY: '11- 4. W. MilG 2015.
Progress at DT: 2010- 53.77, 2011- 55.94, 2012- 55.62, 2013- 58.14, 2014- 59.73, 2015- 62.07, 2016- 65.14, 2017- 64.46.

GAO Yang b. 1 Mar 1993. 1.78m 110kg. Army.
At SP: OG: '16- dnq 33; WCh: '15- 5, '17- 5; WJ: '12- 2; AsiC: '13- 3, '15- 2; WI: '16- 8, '18- 4. Won W.MilG 2015, CHN NG 2017.
Progress at SP: 2012- 17.07, 2013- 17.76, 2014- 17.52, 2015- 19.04, 2016- 19.20, 2017- 18.34, 2018- 18.77i.

GONG Lijiao b. 24 Jan 1989 Luquan, Hebei Prov. 1.74m 110kg. Hebei.
At SP: OG: '08- 3, '12- 2, '16- 4; WCh: '07-09-11-13-15-17: 6/3/3/3/2/1; WI: '10-14-18: 6/3/3; AsiG: '10- 2, '14- 1; AsiC: '09- 1; CCp: '10- 2, '14- 3. Won DL 2017, Chinese 2007-12, 2014, 2016-17; NG 2009, 2013, 2017; Asian indoor 2008.
Progress at SP: 2005- 15.41i, 2006- 17.92, 2007- 19.13, 2008- 19.46, 2009- 20.35, 2010- 20.13, 2011- 20.11, 2012- 20.22, 2013- 20.12, 2014- 19.65, 2015- 20.34, 2016- 20.43, 2017- 20.11, 2018- 19.53i. pb JT 53.94 '07.
Based at Neubrandenburg, Germany from 2013.

LI Ling b. 6 Jul 1989 Zhubo, Henan Province 1.80m 65kg. Zhejiang
At PV: OG: '08/12/16- dnq 27=/30/16; WCh: '09-11-13-15: dnq 18/dnq 29/11/9; WJ: '06- nh; AsiG: '10- 2, '14- 1; AsiC: '11-13-15-17: 2/1/1/2; CCp: '14- 1; WUG: '15- 1. Won CHN 2008-09, 2011-13, 2015-16; NG 2013, Asi Indoors 2009, 2012, 2016.

Asian PV records: 2013 & 2015, indoor (4) 2015-16, junior 2008.
Progress at PV: 2005- 3.90i/3.70, 2006- 4.15, 2007- 4.30, 2008- 4.45, 2009- 4.40, 2010- 4.45i/4.40, 2011- 4.40, 2012- 4.50i/4.40, 2013- 4.65, 2014- 4.61, 2015- 4.66, 2016- 4.70, 2017- 4.50.

LI Lingwei b. 26 Jan 1989 Yantai 1.72m 75kg.
At JT: OG: '12/16- dnq 30/15; WCh: '13-15-17: 8/5/2; WJ: '06- 8, '08- 2; AsiG: '10- 3, '14- 2; AsiC: '09-13-17: 2/1/1; won Asi-J 2008, CHN 2013, 2015-17; NG 2013, 2017.
Asian javelin record 2012.
Progress at JT: 2002- 49.60, 2003- 55.38, 2004- 51.19, 2005- 58.87, 2006- 58.87, 2007- 57.88, 2008- 59.25, 2009- 57.82, 2010- 60.60, 2011- 57.39, 2012- 65.11, 2013- 63.06, 2014- 62.56, 2015- 65.07, 2016- 62.89, 2017- 66.25.

LIU Hong b. 12 May 1987 Anfu, Jiangxi Prov. 1.61m 48kg. Guangdong.
At 20kW: OG: '08- 4, '12- 3, '16- 1; WCh: '07-09-11-13-15: 19/2/1/3/1; WCp: '06-14-16: 6/2/dq1; AsiG: '06- 1, '10- 1; won CHN 2010-11, NG 2009. At 10000mW: WJ: '06- 1; won IAAF Race Walking Challenge 10k 2012, 2014 (2nd 2011).
Walk records: World 20k 2015, Asian 5000m & 20k 2012.
Progress at 20kW: 2004- 1:35:04, 2005- 1:29:39, 2006- 1:28:26, 2007- 1:29:41, 2008- 1:27:17, 2009- 1:28:11, 2010- 1:30:06, 2011- 1:27:17, 2012- 1:25:46, 2013- 1:27:06, 2014- 1:26:58, 2015- 1:24:38, 2016- 1:25:56. pbs: 3000mW 12:18.18 '05, 5000mW 20:34.76 '12, 10kW 42:30R '10, 43:16.68t '12. Running: Mar 2:51:23 '15.
Won IAAF Race Walking Challenge 2011-12 and 2015. Failed drugs test when 'winning' the World Cup 20k race in 2016 and received a three-months ban. Expecting a baby in 2018.

LIU Shiying b. 24 Sep 1993 Shandong prov. 1.79m 76kg.
At JT: OG: '16- dnq 23; WCh: '17- 8; WJ: '12- 2; AsiC: '15- 1, Asi-J '12- 1.
Asian javelin record 2017.
Progress at JT: 2010- 50.92, 2011- 55.10, 2012- 59.20, 2013- 60.23, 2014- 62.72, 2015- 62.77, 2016- 65.64, 2027- 66.47.

LU Huihui b. 26 Jun 1989 Huwan, Henan 1.71m 68kg.
At JT: OG: '12- 5, '16- 7; WCh: '15- 2. '17- 3.
Three Asian javelin records 2012-17.
Progress at JT: 2005- 49.62, 2006- 49.96, 2010- 55.35, 2011- 58.72, 2012- 64.95, 2013- 64.48/65.62dq, 2015- 66.13, 2016- 64.03, 2017- 67.59. One-year drugs ban for positive test 27 Apr 2013.

LU Xiuzhi b. 26 Oct 1993 Chuzhou 1.67m 52kg.
At 20kW: OG: '12- 5, '16- 3; WCh: '15- 2, '17- dq; AsiG: '14- 1; WCp: '12-14-16: 3/6/5, won CHN 2014, NG 2013.
Asian 20k walk record 2015, junior 2012.
Progress at 20kW: 2011- 1:29:50, 2012- 1:27:01, 2013- 1:27:53, 2014- 1:27:15, 2015- 1:25:12, 2016- 1:28:07, 2017- 1:26:28. pb 10kW 43:16 '12.

QIEYANG Shenjie b. 11 Nov 1990 Haiyan, Qinghai Prov. 1.60m 50kg.
At 20kW: OG: '12- 2, '16- 5; WCh: '11- 4, '13- 15; WCp: '12- 13, '16- 2. CHN champion 2015. Tied first for IAAF Race Walking Challenge 2016.
Asian 20k walk record 2012.
Progress at 20kW: 2009- 1:35:54, 2010- 1:30:33, 2011- 1:28:04, 2012- 1:25:16, 2013- 1:28:05, 2015- 1:27:44, 2016- 1:26:49, 2017- 1:28:33. pbs: 5000mW 20:42.67 '12, 10kW 42:46 '17.
First athlete from Tibet to win an Olympic medal.

SU Xinyue b. 8 Nov 1991 1.79m 70kg. Hebei
At DT: OG: '16- 5; WCh: '13- dnq 19, '15- 8, '17- 7; AsiC: '13- 1, '15- 1; WJ: '10- dnq 13. Won CHN NG 2017.
Progress at DT: 2007- 48.29, 2009- 52.51, 2010- 56.11, 2011- 57.57, 2012- 60.32, 2013- 61.67, 2014- 61.31, 2015- 64.27, 2016- 65.59, 2017- 64.56.

WANG Na b. 29 May 1995 Heilongjiang Prov.
At 20kW: WCh: '17- 8; At 10000mW: WJ: '14- 2. Won AsiC 2017.
Progress at 20kW: 2013- 1:39:51, 2015- 1:30:19, 2016- 1:28:21, 2017- 1:26:29. Pbs: 10000mW 44:02.64 '14.

WANG Zheng b. 14 Dec 1987 Xian, Shanxi Province 1.74m 108kg.
At HT: OG: '08- dnq 30, '16- nt; WCh: '13- 4, '15- 5, '17- 2; WJ: '06- 9; AsiG: '10- 2, '14- 2; AsiC: '13- 1; CCp: '14- 4; won Asi-J 2006, E.Asian 2009, CHN 2014, 2016.
Asian hammer record 2014.
Progress at HT: 2000- 60.30, 2001- 66.30, 2002- 67.13, 2003- 70.60, 2004- 72.42, 2005- 73.24, 2006- 74.15, 2007- 74.86, 2008- 74.32, 2009- 74.25, 2010- 73.83, 2011- 75.65, 2012- 75.72, 2012- 76.99, 2013- 75.58, 2014- 77.68, 2015- 73.83, 2016- 74.50, 2017- 76.25.

YANG Jiayu b. 18 Feb 1996 1.63m 48kg.
At 20kW: WCh: '17- 1; WCp: '16- 7; WUG: '15- 5, won CHN NG 2017. At 10kW: WCp: '14- 2J.
Progress at 20kW. 50kW: 2013- 1:40:27, 2015- 1:36:50, 2016- 1:28:12, 2017- 1:26:18. Pbs: 5000mW 22:22.47 '14, 10000mW 45:59.81 '14, 43:19R '15.

YIN Hang b. 7 Feb 1997 1.61m 50kg. Army.
At 50kW: WCh: '17- 2.
Two Asian 50kW records 2017.
Progress at 20kW: 2016- 1:34:25, 2017- 1:31:23, 4:08:58. pb 10kW 44:52 '16.

ZHANG Wenxiu b. 22 Mar 1986 Dalian 1.82m 108kg. Army.
At HT: OG: '04- 7, '08- 2, '12- 3, '16- 2; WCh: '01-03-05-07-09-11-13-15-17: 11/dnq 14/4/3/5/3/3/2/4; WJ: '02- dnq 20; AsiG: '06-10-14: 1/1/1; AsiC: '05- 1, '09- 1; WCp: '06- 4, '10- 2. Won Asi-J 2002, W.Mil 2003, 2007, 2011, 2015; CHN 2004, 2006-10, 2012, 2015; NG 2003, 2009, 2013, 2017.

Nine Asian hammer records 2001-12, world youth 2003, two world junior 2004-05.
Progress at HT: 2000- 60.30, 2001- 66.30, 2002- 67.13, 2003- 70.60, 2004- 72.42, 2005- 73.24, 2006- 74.15, 2007- 74.86, 2008- 74.32, 2009- 74.25, 2010- 73.83, 2011- 75.65, 2012- 76.99, 2013- 75.58, 2014- 77.33, 2015- 76.33, 2016- 76.75, 2017- 5.48.
World age bests at 15-16-18. Originally lost third Asian Games title with a positive drugs test in 2014, but she was reinstated in May 2015 when it was ruled that her positive test was due to contaminated food. Baby born in 2016.

COLOMBIA

Governing body: Federación Colombiana de Atletismo. Founded 1937.

National Games Champions 2017: Men: 100m: Johnny Rentería 10.35, 200m: Bernardo Baloyes 20.11, 400m: Yilmer Herrera 45.48, 800m: Yelsin Robledo 1:49.07, 1500m: Carlos San Martín 3:48.83, 5000m: Iván Darío González 14:17.42, 10000m/3000mSt: Gerald Giraldo 29:40.02/ 8:57.36, Mar, 110mh/400mh: Yeison Rivas 13.65/51.10, HJ: Wanner Miller 2.15, PV: Walter Viáfara 5.10, LJ: Jheison Valois 7.52, TJ: Divie Murillo 16.07, SP: Jhon Zea 19.20, DT: Juan Benítez 51.75, HT: Fabián Serna 62.61, JT: Arley Ibargüen 70.07, Dec: José Gregorio Lemus 7530, 20000mW: Jhon Casteñada 1:26:14.0. **Women**: 100m/100mh: Eliecit Palacios 11.51w/13.73, 200m/400m: Yenifer Padilla 23.37/52.82, 800m: Johana Arrieta 2:07.22, 1500m: Rosibel García 4:28.77, 5000m: Ángela Fugueroa 17:00.78, 10000m: Angie Orjuela 35:27.11, 3000mSt: Grey Delgado 11:13.12, 400mh: Melisa González 57.84, HJ: María Fernanda Murillo 1.85, PV: Stefany Castillo 3.75, LJ: Evelis Aguilar 6.50, TJ: Giselly Landázuri 13.50w, SP: Sandra Lemus 17.02, DT: Johana Martínez 50.29, HT: Eli Johana Moreno 66.50, JT: Flor Dennis Ruiz 60.09, Hep: Damaris Palomeque 4794, 20000mW: Lorena Arenas 1:33:51.2.

Eider ARÉVALO b. 9 Mar 1993 Bogotá 1.65m 58kg.
At 20kW: OG: '12- 20, '16- 15; WCh: '13- dnf, '15- 7, '17- 1; PAm: 15- 5, SACh: '13- 2; Won PAmCp '17, COL 2012-13. At 10000mW: WJ: '12- 1; SAmJ & PAm-J: '11- 1; WCp: '10- 1J, '12- 1J.
Colombian 20k walk records 2013 & 2017.
Progress at 20kW: 2012- 1:21:49, 2013- 1:19:45, 2014- 1:21:28, 2015- 1:20:41, 2016- 1:20:47, 2017- 1:18:53. Pb 10000mW 39:56.01A '11.
Won IAAF Walks Challenge 2017.

Jhon Fredy **MURILLO** b. 13 Jul 1984 Apartadó, Antioquia 1.86m 85kg.
At HJ: OG: '16- 5; PAm: '15- 10; SACh: '06-07-13-15: 3/4/2/1. Won COL LJ 2008, 2011, 2014, TJ 2007-16; BolG 2017.
Colombia TJ record 2016.
Progress at TJ: 2006- 15.67A/16.33Aw, 2007- 15.93A, 2008- 16.02A, 2009- 16.20A, 2010- 15.61A, 2011- 16.18A, 2012- 16.37A, 2013- 16.58/16.82Aw, 2014- 16.47A, 2015- 16.55, 2016- 17.09, 2017- 16.95. pbs: 100m 10.42A '08. LJ 7.74A '11, 7.78w A '08.

Women

Sandra Lorena **ARENAS** b. 17 Sep 1993 Pereira, Risaralda 1.60m 50kg.
At 20kW: OG: 12- 31, '16- 32; WCh: '13-15-17: 21/19/5; WCp: '16- 10; PAm: 15- 4; SACh: '13- 1, '15- 1. COL champion 2012-14, 2016; SAm-J 2011, BolG 2017. At 10000mW: WJ: '12- 3; 10kW: WCp: '12- 1J.
S.American 20000m track walk record 2014. Six Colombia 20k walk records 2012-17.
Progress at 20kW: 2011- 1:48:36.0A, 2012- 1:32:36, 2013- 1:32:25, 2014- 1:30:18, 2015- 1:31:02.25t, 2016- 1:29:31, 2017- 1:28:10, 2018- 1:28:48. Pbs: 5000mW 23:01.4A '15, 10000mW 44:58.26 '14, 43:16R '17

Caterine IBARGÜEN b. 12 Feb 1984 Apartadó, Antioquia 1.81m 65kg. Studying nursing.
At TJ/(LJ): OG: '12- 2, '16- 1; WCh: '11-13-15-17: 3/1/1/2; WJ: '02: dnq 17; PAm: '11- 1/3; '15- 1; SACh: '03- 3/2, '05- 3/3, '06- 2/2, '07- (3), '09- 1, '11- 1/3; CAG: '02-06-10-14: 2/(2)/2/1; CCp: '14- 1. At HJ: OG: '04- dnq 27=; WCh: '09- dnq 28=; PAm: '07- 4; SACh: '99-05-06-07-09: 3/1/1/1/1; CAG: '02- 2, '06- 2. Won DL 2013-16, COL HJ 1999, 2001-03, 2005-12, 2015; LJ 2003-04, 2006-08, 2011-12, 2015; TJ 2002-05, 2007-12, 2014.
Records: South American triple jump (7) 2011-14, junior HJ 2003. Colombia HJ (7) 2002-05, LJ (7) 2004-11, TJ (15) 2004-14.
Progress at TJ: 2001- 12.90, 2002- 13.38A, 2003- 13.23A, 2004- 13.64A, 2005- 13.66A, 2006- 13.91A/13.98Aw, 2007- 12.66A, 2008- 13.79A, 2009- 13.96A/13.93, 2010- 14.29, 2011- 14.99A/ 14.84, 2012- 14.95A/14.85, 2013- 14.85/14.93w, 2014- 15.31, 2015- 14.90/15.18w, 2016- 15.17, 2017- 14.89. pbs: 200m 25.34 '08, 100mh 14.09 '11, HJ 1.93A '05, LJ 6.73A/6.87Aw/6.63/6.66w '12, SP 13.79 '10, JT 44.81 '09, Hep 5742 '09.
Formerly a high jumper, concentrating fully on TJ from 2010. First Colombian woman to win a medal in world champs. Unbeaten in 9 competitions in 2013, 11 in 2014 and 9 in 2015 plus her first 4 in 2016, taking her to 34 in succession 2012-16. She had 77 successive competitions over 14m from April 2010 to June 2017. She lives in Puerto Rico.

REPUBLIC OF CONGO

Franck Dannique **ELEMBA** Owaka b. 21 Jul 1990 Brazzaville 1.98m 130kg.
At SP: OG: '16- 4; WCh: '15-17- dnq 21/24; AfG: '11- 5, '15- 1 (3 DT); AfCh: '10-12-14-16: 4/5/3/2; CCp: '10- 7, '14- 7.
Congo shot records 2010-16, DT 2016.
Progress at SP: 2009- 15.09, 2010- 15.90, 2011- 16.44, 2012- 17.58, 2013- 19.02, 2014- 19.72, 2015-

20.25, 2016- 21.20, 2017- 20.86i/20.72. pb DT 54.30 '16.
Lives in Paris. His 2016 4th was the best Olympic place for an athlete from Congo.

CROATIA

Governing body: Hrvatski Atletski Savez. Founded 1912.

National Champions 2017 Men: 100m/200m: Zvonimir Ivaskovic 10.72/21.62, 400m: Mateo Ruzic 46.92, 800m: Marino Bloudek 1:48.16, 1500m: Daniel Ivanicic 4:00.57, 3000m: Dino Bosnjak 8:23.06, 5000m: Petar Bratulic 15:24.21, 10000m: Anton Rudolf Pavelic 30:56.2, HMar: Danifel Fac 70:51, Mar: Robert Radojkevic 2:40:05, 3000mSt: Filip Svalina 9:31.11, 110mh: Trpimir Siroki 15.02, 400mh: Yann Senjaric 51.65, HJ: Alen Melon 2.20, PV: Ivan Horvat 5.10, LJ: Dino Pervan 7.86, TJ: Ante Zuanovic 15.09, SP: Stipe Zunic 21.36, DT: Filip Mihaljevic 62.29, HT: Mirko Micuda 64.11, JT: Bartul Basic 72.72, Dec: Marko Culjak 5918, 20kW/50kW: Bruno Erent 1:54:54/4:45:59. **Women**: 100m: Daniela Pesic 12.12, 200m: Anita Banovic 24.52, 400m: Kristina Dudek 55.05, 800m: Ivona Zemunik 2:12.02, 1500m: Klara Andrijasevic 4:44.93, 3000m/HMar: Matea Parlov 9:39.77/76:12, 5000m: Matea Matosevic 17:04.78, 10000m: Kristina Hendel 35:10.3, Mar: Bojana Bjeljac 2:50:24, 3000mSt: Ljiljana Culibrk 11:23.80, 100mh: Dolores Cosic 14.59, 400mh: Valentina Juric 59.93, HJ: Ana Simic 1.88, PV: Elija Valentic 3.90, LJ/TJ: Paola Borvoic 6.15/13.25, SP: Marija Tolj 14.37, DT: Ivana Muzaric 51.20, HT: Anamari Kozul 62.12, JT: Franja Zelimorski 50.24, Hep: Ludja Cvitanovic 5339, 10kW/20kW: Ivana Renic 58:32/1:58:40.

Filip MIHALJEVIC b. 31 Jul 1994 Livno, Bosnia & Herzegovina 2.01m 113kg. University of Virginia, USA.
At SP/(DT): OG: '16- dnq 21; WCh: '17- dnq 14; EC: '16- dnq 22; EU23: '15- 1/4; EJ: '13- 2/11; WI: '16- 3. Won CRO SP 2013, DT 2015-17, NCAA SP 2016-17, DT 2017.
Progress at SP: 2012- 16.52, 2013- 17.54, 2014- 19.65, 2015- 20.16, 2016- 20.87i/20.71. 2017- 21.30. pb DT 63.11 '15.
Father Mirko was Yugoslav CC champion in 1987-8.

Stipe ZUNIC b. 13 Dec 1990 Zadar 1.88m 115kg. ASK Split. Sociology student at University of Florida, USA.
At SP: OG: '16- 11; WCh: '17- 3; EC: '14- 4, '16- 9; WY: '07- dnq 29; EI: '15- 7, '17- 5; NCAA indoor champion 2015. At JT: WJ: '08- dnq 18; WY: '07- 7; EJ: '09- 9 (11 DT); EU23: '11- 11; Croatian champion SP 2015-17, JT 2009-10.
Three Croatian shot records 2017.
Progress at SP: 2007- 15.36, 2008- 15.87, 2009- 16.83, 2011- 17.39i/16.60, 2012- 17.30i, 2014- 20.68, 2015- 21.11i/20.38, 2016- 20.61i/20.60, 2017- 21.48, 2018- 21.13i. pbs: DT 59.09 '15, JT 77.89 '12
Huge improvement at shot in 2014-15 after switching from javelin. Formerly world junior champion at kick-boxing.

Women

Sara KOLAK b. 22 Jun 1995 Koprivnica 1.70m 74kg. AK Kvarner Rijeka.
At JT: OG: '16- 1; WCh: '17- 4; EC: '14- dnq 21, 16- 3; WJ: '12- dnq 23, '14- 3; EU23: '17- 1EJ: '13- 3; Croatian champion 2012-14, 2016.
11 Croatian JT records 2013-17.
Progress at JT: 2008- 31.78, 2009- 43.13, 2010- 55.69, 2011- 45.94, 2012- 53.98, 2013- 57.79, 2014- 57.79, 2016- 66.18, 2017- 68.43.
National javelin records 63.50 for 3rd EC, and at OG 64.30 qualifying and 66.18 for gold in final.

Sandra PERKOVIC b. 21 Jun 1990 Zagreb 1.83m 80kg. Zagreb.
At DT(/SP): OG: '12- 1, '16- 1; WCh: '09-13-15-17: 9/1/2/1; EC: '10-12-14-16: 1/1/1/1; WJ: '06- dnq 21, '08- 3/dnq 13; WY: '07- 2/dnq 13; EJ: '07- 2, '09- 1/5; CCp: '10- 2, '14- 3. Won DL 2012-17, Med G 2013; CRO SP 2008-10, DT 2010, 2012.
9 Croatian DT records 2009-14, 2 SP 2010-11.
Progress at DT: 2004- 30.37, 2005- 36.21, 2006- 50.11, 2007- 55.42, 2008- 55.89, 2009- 62.79, 2010- 66.93, 2011- 67.96/69.99dq, 2012- 69.11, 2013- 68.96, 2014- 71.08, 2015- 70.08, 2016- 70.88, 2017- 71.41. pb SP 16.99i/16.40 '11.
First woman to win European and Olympic gold for Croatia. Won 62 of 70 competitions 2012-17. Five successive wins for Diamond Race, and won all seven competitions in 2016. Her 70.51 and 71.08 to win her third European title in 2014 and her 71.41 in 2017 were the women's world's best discus throws since 1992. Six months drugs ban 2011.

Ana SIMIC b. 5 May 1990 Gradacac, Bosnia 1.77m 58kg. Zagreb.
At HJ: OG: '12/16- dnq 29=/22=; WCh: '13/17- dnq 19/25, '15- 9=; EC: '10-12-16: dnq 22=/20/14, '14- 3; WJ: '08- dnq 14=; WY: '07- dnq 21=; EU23: '11- 7; EJ: '09- dnq 18; CCp: '14- 3; EI: '17- 7; Croatian champion 2006-09, 2011, 2015, 2017.
Progress at HJ: 2003- 1.66, 2004- 1.73, 2005- 1.69, 2006- 1.78, 2007- 1.73, 2008- 1.82, 2009- 1.87, 2010- 1.92, 2011- 1.92, 2012- 1.91i/1.88, 2013- 1.96, 2014- 1.99, 2015- 1.95i/1.94, 2016- 1.96, 2017- 1.92i/1.90.

CUBA

Governing body: Federación Cubana de Atletismo. Founded 1922.

National Champions 2017: Men: 100m: Roberto Skyers 10.06w, 200m: Reynier Mena 20.79, 400m: Yoandys Lescay 45.65, 800m: Andy González 1:47.28, 1500m: Francisco Estévez 3:59.15, 5000m: Jacinto Milanés 15:24.57, 10000m: Yumier Fouman 31:53.20, HMar: Richer Pérez 66:18, Mar: Henrry Jaen 2:28:42, 2000mSt: Alberto Carrero 6:14.78, 110mh: Yordan O'Farrill

13.33, 400mh: Leandro Zamora 49.94, HJ: Luis Zayas 2.16, PV: Eduardo Nápoles 5.00, LJ: Maykel Massó 7.93, TJ: Andy Díaz 17.40, SP: Lázaro Acosta 17.27, DT: Félix Valle 55.66, HT: Reinier Mejías 72.10, JT: Osmany Laffita 70.85, Dec: Briander Rivero 7633, 10kW/20kW: Ronaldo Hernández 44:14/1:35:57. **Women**: 100m/200m: Arialis Gandulla 11.33w/23.44, 400m: Roxana Gómez 54.01, 800m/1500m: Rose M. Almanza 2:00.12/4:16.00, 5000m: Yudileyvis Castillo 17:08.21, 10000m/HMar: Dailín Belmonte 34:59.9/76:44, Mar: Yudileyvis Castillo 2:46:36, 2000mSt: Milena Pérez 6:42.86, 100mh: Greisys Roble 13.76, 400mh: Zurian Hechavarría 56.79, HJ: Yorgelis Rodríguez 1.85, PV: Yarisley Silva 4.40, LJ: Paula Álvarez 6.59w, TJ: Liadagmis Povea 14.28w, SP: Yaniuvis López 17.22, DT: Yaimé Pérez 65.57, HT: Ayamey Medina 61.63, JT: Yulenmis Aguilar 58.90, Hep: Yusleidys Mendieta 5779, 10kW: Yuniabel Contreras 52:33.

Andy DÍAZ b. 25 Dec 1995 Guanabacoa, La Habana 1.91m 80kg.
At TJ: WCh: '17- 7; WJ: '14- 4. Won CUB 2017.
Progress at TJ: 2010- 13.29, 2012- 14.44, 2013- 15.70, 2014- 16.38/16.43w, 2015- 16.81, 2016- 16.80, 2017- 17.40. pb LJ 7.40 '17.

Juan Miguel ECHEVARRÍA b. 11 Aug 1998 Camagüey 1.86m 76kg.
At LJ: WCh: '17- dnq 15; WJ: '16- 5, WY: '15- 4; WI: '18- 1. Cuban champion 2016.
Progress at LJ: 2012- 5.69, 2013- 6.36, 2014- 7.47, 2015- 8.05, 2016-7.96/8.15w, 2017- 8.28/8.34w, 2018- 8.46i/8.40. Pb TJ 14.67 '14

Lázaro MARTÍNEZ b. 3 Nov 1997 Guantánamo 1.92m 85kg.
At TJ: OG: '16- 8; WCh: '17- 12; WJ: '14- 1, '16- 1; WY: '13- 1; CAG: '14- 2; PAm-J: '13- 1. Won CUB 2016. World youth triple jump record 2014.
Progress at TJ: 2011- 14.62, 2012- 15.38, 2013- 16.63, 2014- 17.24, 2015- 17.02, 2016- 17.06, 2017- 17.07.

Maykel Demetrio **MASSÓ** b. 8 May 1999 Santiago de Cuba 1.78m 69kg.
At LJ: OG: '16- dnq 15; WCh: '15- dnq 23, '17- 5; WJ: '16- 1; WY: '15- 1; CUB champion 2017.
CAC junior long jump record 2017.
Progress at LJ: 2013- 6.41, 2014- 7.59, 2015- 8.12, 2016- 8.28, 2017- 8.33.

Cristian Atanay **NÁPOLES** b. 27 Nov 1998 Marianao, La Habana 1.81m 80kg.
At TJ: WCh: '17- 4; WJ: '16- 2; WY: '15- 1.
Progress at TJ: 2013- 14.41, 2014- 15.42, 2015- 16.45, 2016- 16.92, 2017- 17.27. pb LJ 6.96 '16.

Leonel SUÁREZ b. 1 Sep 1987 Holguín 1.81m 78kg.
At Dec: OG: '08- 3, '12- 3, '16- 6; WCh: '09-11-13-17: 2/3/10/dnf; PAm: '07-11-15: 4/1/dnf. CAC champion 2009, Cuban 2009, 2015-16. At Hep: WI: '10- 7.
Decathlon records: 4 CUB 2008-09, CAC 2009.
Progress at Dec: 2005- 7267, 2006- 7357, 2007- 8156, 2008- 8527, 2009- 8654, 2010- 8328, 2011- 8501, 2012- 8523, 2013- 8317, 2015- 8027, 2016- 8460, 2017- 8214. pbs: 60m 7.11i '09, 100m 10.90 '08, 10.6w '06; 400m 47.65 '09, 1000m 2:36.12i '10, 1500m 4:16.70 '08, 60mh 7.90i '10, 110mh 14.12 '08, HJ 2.17 '08, PV 5.00 '09, LJ 7.52 '11, SP 15.20 '09, DT 47.32 '11, JT 78.29 '16, Hep 5964i '10.
Won at Talence 2010. Won IAAF Combined Events Challenge 2011.

Women

Rose Mary ALMANZA b. 13 Jul 1992 Camagüey 1.65m 55kg.
At 800m: OG: '12- sf, '16- h; WCh: '13/15/17- sf; WJ: '10- 4; WY: '09- 4; PAm: '11- 4, '15- 4; CAG: '14- 1. Won Cuban 800m 2010-11, 2014-15, 2017; 1500m 2013, 2015, 2017.
Two CAC junior 800m records 2010-11.
Progress at 800m: 2008- 2:11.1, 2009- 2:03.61, 2010- 2:02.04, 2011- 2:00.56, 2012- 1:59.55, 2013- 1:59.4, 2014- 1:59.48, 2015- 1:57.70, 2016- 1:58.49, 2017- 1:59.11. pbs: 400m 53.66 '17, 600m 1:26.33mx '14, 1:26.9 '13; 1000m 2:38.1 '14, 1500m 4:14.53 '14.

Denia CABALLERO b. 13 Jan 1990 Caibarién, Villa Clara 1.75m 80kg. VCL.
At DT: OG: '12- dnq 25, '16- 3; WCh: '11-13-15-17: 9/8/1/5; PAm: '11- 3, '15- 1; CAG: '14- 1. Won CAC 2011, Cuban 2015.
Progress at DT: 2006- 43.77, 2007- 46.08, 2008- 52.10, 2009- 57.21, 2010- 59.92, 2011- 62.94, 2012- 65.60, 2013- 63.47, 2014- 64.89, 2015- 70.65, 2016- 67.62, 2017- 67.04.

Yaimé PÉREZ b. 29 May 1991 Santiago de Cuba 1.72m 80kg.
At DT: OG: '12- dnq 28, '16- nt; WCh: '13- 11, '15- 4, '17- 4; WJ: '10- 1; PAm: '15- 2; CAG: '14- 2; CCp: '14- 5. Cuban champion 2013-14, 2016-17.
Progress at DT: 2007- 46.29, 2008- 51.80, 2009- 55.23, 2010- 59.30, 2011- 59.26, 2012- 62.50, 2013- 66.01, 2014- 66.03, 2015- 67.13, 2016- 68.86, 2017- 69.19. pbs SP 13.88 '08.

Yorgelis RODRÍGUEZ b. 25 Jan 1995 Guantánamo 1.71m 65kg.
At Hep: OG: '16- 7; WCh: '13- 12, '15- 21, '17- 4; WJ: '12- 1; '14- 2 (dnq 16= HJ); WY: '11- 2; PAm: '15- 1; At Pen: WI: '18- 3; won PAmCp 2013, 2015; CAG 2014, Cuban HJ 2017, Hep 2013, 2016.
Heptathlon records: CAC 2017, 2 Cuban 2016-17, 3 CAC junior 2012-14.
Progress at Hep: 2012- 5994, 2013- 6186, 2014- 6231, 2015- 6332, 2016- 6481, 2017- 6594. pbs: 200m 24.06 '16, 800m 2:10.48 '17, 60mh 8.57i '18, 100mh 13.52 '16, HJ 1.95 '17, LJ 6.41 '17, SP 14.64 '16, JT 48.89 '16, Pen 4637i '18.
Three HJ pbs with 1.89, 1.92 & 1.95 in World heptathlon 2017.

Yarisley SILVA b. 1 Jun 1987 Pinar del Rio 1.61m 62kg.

At PV: OG: '08- dnq 27=, '12- 2, '16- 7=; WCh: '11-13-15-17: 5/3/1/3=; WI: '12-14-18: 7/1/7; WJ: '06- dnq; PAm: '07-11-15: 3/1/1; CAG: '14- 1; Won CAC 2009, Cuban 2004, 2006-07, 2009, 2012-13, 2015, 2017.

Pole vault records: 19 Cuban & CAC 2007-15 (9 in 2011), 8 CAC indoor 2012 & 2013 (to 4.82).

Progress at PV: 2001- 2.50, 2002- 3.10, 2003- 3.70, 2004- 4.00, 2005- 4.10, 2006- 4.20, 2007- 4.30, 2008- 4.50, 2009- 4.50, 2010- 4.40, 2011- 4.75A/4.70, 2012- 4.75, 2013- 4.90, 2014- 4.70, 2015- 4.91, 2016- 4.84, 2017- 4.81.

CYPRUS

Governing body: Amateur Athletic Association of Cyprus. Founded 1983.

National Championships first held in 1896, 1952 (women). **2017 Champions**: **Men**: 100m/200m: Andreas Hadjitheoris 10.76/21.66, 400m: Onisforos Anastasiou 48.59, 800m/1500m: Christos Demetriou 1:53.36/3:52.07, 5000m: Amoine Khadiri 14:12.89, 3000mSt: Nikolas Frangou 9:01.47, 110mh: Milan Trajkovic 13.51, 400mh: Neofytos Georgiou 54.07, HJ: Vasilios Constantinou 2.04, PV: Nikandros Stylianou 5.20, LJ: Periclis Kleovoulou 7.43, TJ: Panagiotis Volou 15.67, SP:, Vasilis Mouamis 16.08, DT: Apostolos Parellis 62.00, HT: Alexandros Pousanides 71.84, JT: Michail Kakotas 67.68. **Women**: 100m: Olivia Fotopoulou 11.81, 200m/400m: Eleni Artymata 23.36/52.13, 800m/ 1500m: Natalia Evangelidou 2:05.21/4:15.95, 5000m: Meropi Panagiotou 17:30.73, 3000mSt: Chrystalla Hadjipolydorou 11:14.54, 100mh: Dafni Georgiou 14.21, 400mh: Christiana Katsari 61.57, HJ: Despina Charalambous 1.73, PV: Maria Aristotelous 3.80, LJ: Nektaria Panagi 6.54, TJ: Eleftheria Christofi 12.26, SP: Gabriella Fella 15.49, DT: Androniki Lada 51.38, HT: Chrytstalla Kyriakou 60.56, JT: Mariele Rousi 48.41.

Apostolos PARELLIS b. 24 Jul 1985 Limassol 1.86m 110kg.

At DT: OG: '12- dnq 13, '16- 8; WCh: '13-15-17: dnq 19/6/10; CG: '10- 4, '14- 2; EC: '10-12-14-16: dnq 17/13/16/18; EU23: '07- 3. Won CYP 2007-17. 17 CYP discus records 2007-16.

Progress at DT: 2004- 48.40, 2005- 50.88, 2006- 53.77, 2007- 58.16, 2008- 56.41, 2009- 61.07, 2010- 61.92, 2011- 61.44, 2012- 65.36, 2013- 62.48, 2014- 63.89, 2015- 65.04, 2016- 65.69, 2017- 65.13.

CZECH REPUBLIC

Governing body: Cesky atleticky svaz. AAU of Bohemia founded in 1897.

National Championships first held in 1907 (Bohemia), 1919 (Czechoslovakia), 1993 CZE. **2017 Champions**: **Men**: 100m: Zdenek Stromsík 10.29, 200m: Pavel Maslák 20.46, 400m: Patrik Sorm 46.33, 800m: Filip Snejdr 1:53.02, 1500m: Filip Sasinek 3:43.51, 5000m: Jakub Holusa 14:36.99, 10000m/HMar: Vit Pavlista 30:16.45/ 67:31, Mar: Petr Pechek 2:21:22, 3000mSt: Lukás Olejnicek 8:58.71, 110mh: Václav Sedlák 13.91, 400mh: Vit Müller 49.92, HJ: Jaroslav Bába 2.18, PV: Jan Kudlicka 5.60, LJ: Radek Juska 7.86, TJ: Jirí Vondrácek 15.75, SP: Tomás Stanek 21.61, DT: Jan Marcell 59.59, HT: Miroslav Pavlicek 67.21, JT: Jakub Vadlejch 87.07, Dec: Tomás Pulicek 6932, 20kW: Lukás Gdula 1:31:49, 50kW: Tomás Hlavenka 4:37:16. **Women**: 100m: Klára Seidlová 11.57, 200m: Nikola Bendová 23.38, 400m: Barbora Malíková 54.03, 800m: Katerina Hálová 2:08.81, 1500m: Kristiina Mäki 4:14.52, 5000m: Simona Vrzalová 16:45.54, 10000m: Moira Stewartová 34:26.11, HMar: Petra Kaminková 78:00, Mar: Petra Pastorová 2:46:34, 3000mSt: Eva Krchová 10:05.88 100mh: Katerina Cachová 13.28, 400mh: Denisa Rosolová 56.55, HJ: Michaela Hrubá 1.91, PV: Romana Malácová 4.50, LJ: Eva Klucinová 6.26, TJ: Lucie Májková 13.33, SP: Petra Klementová 15.48, DT: Eliska Stanková 56.95, HT: Katerina Skypalová 64.43, JT: Barbora Spotáková 64.09, Hep: Katerina Cachová 6637, 20kW: Anezka Srahotová 1:33:18

Petr FRYDRYCH b. 13 Jan 1988 Klatovy 1.98m 99kg. Dukla Praha.

At JT: OG: '12- dnq 33, '16- 12; WCh: '09- 10, '11-15: dnq 24/30, '17- 3; EC: '10- 10, '12/14- dnq 2/19; WJ: '06- dnq 16; WY: '05- 11; EU23: '09- 2; EJ: '07- 9; ET: '09- 6. Won CZE 2009.

Progress at JT: 2004- 57.89, 2005- 65.97, 2006- 70.91, 2007- 75.55, 2008- 74.13, 2009- 84.96, 2010- 88.23, 2011- 85.32, 2012- 81.14, 2013- 82.39, 2014- 85.07, 2015- 85.52, 2016- 84.10, 2017- 88.32.

Adam Sebastian HELCELET b. 27 Oct 1991 Turnov 1.87m 86kg. PSK Olymp Praha.

At Dec: OG: '16- 12; WCh: '15- 11, '17- 8; EC: '12-14-16: 8/11/2; EU23: '11- 4, '13- 3; WJ: '10- dnf; EJ: '09- 8. At Hep: WI: '12- 5, '16- 5; EI: 13-15-17: 4/5/3.

Progress at Dec: 2011- 7969, 2012- 8064, 2013- 8252, 2014- 8001, 2015- 8234, 2016- 8291, 2017- 8335. pbs: 60m 6.98i '15, 100m 10.81 '11, 400m 48.66 '11, 1000m 2:42.26i '13, 1500m 4:34.41 '16, 60mh 7.84i '17, 110mh 14.18 '12, 400mh 52.00 '11, HJ 2.07 '12, PV 5.10i '17, 5.00 '13; LJ 7.60i '15, 7.48/7.50w '12; SP 15.44i '16, 15.42 '15; DT 47.12 '16, JT 71.56 '17, Hep 6188i '17.

His partner Denisa Rosolová (400m 50.85 '10, 1 EI '11; 400mh 54.24 '12, 2/3R EC '12) has finished her career, awaiting the birth of her first child

Jakub HOLUSA b. 20 Feb 1988 Opava 1.83m 72kg. Dukla Praha.

At 800m: OG: '08/12- h; EC: '10/12: 5/5; EU23: '09- h; WI: '10- 5, '12- 2. At 1500m: OG: '16- sf; WCh: '15- h, '17- 5; EC: '14- dns, '16- dq h; EU23: '09- 3; WI: '14- 5, '16- 2; EI: '11- 5, '15- 1; ET: '14- 1 (2 3000m). At 3000m: ET: '17- 1. At 2000mSt: WY: '05- 7. At 3000mSt: EJ: '07- 1, Won CZE 800m 2008, 5000m 2014, 2017.

Czech 1500m records 2015 & 2016.

Progress at 1500m: 2003- 4:21.89, 2004- 4:04.47, 2005- 3:58.06, 2006- 3:56.23, 2007- 3:46.93, 2008- 3:41.88i/3:43.02, 2009- 3:42.15, 2010- 3:38.47, 2011- 3:38.10, 2012- 3:42.44i/3:42.79, 2013- 3:38.71, 2014- 3:35.26, 2015- 3:34.26, 2016- 3:33.36, 2017- 3:34.26. pbs: 400m 47.29 '10, 800m 1:45.12 '12, 1000m 2:16.79 '14, 1M 3:53.46 '14, 3000m 7:51.39 '17, 5000m 14:06.32 '14, 2000mSt 5:43.39 '05, 3000mSt 8:50.30 '07, 400mh 54.46 '07.

Has used devastating sprint finish to good effect in major championships.

Radek JUSKA b. 8 Mar 1993 Hustopece 1.95m 82kg. PSK Olymp Praha.

At LJ: OG: '16- dnq 13; WCh: '15- 11, '17- 10; EC: '16- 4; WJ: '12- dnq 24; EU23: '15- 2; WI: '18- 7; EI: '15- 2; WUG: '17- 1; ET: '17- 3. Czech champion 2014-15, 2017.

Two Czech long jump records 2017.

Progress at LJ: 2010- 6.60, 2011- 7.10/7.13w, 2012- 7.71, 2013- 7.60, 2014- 7.94, 2015- 8.15, 2016- 8.11, 2017- 8.31. pb TJ 15.18 '17.

Jan KUDLICKA b. 29 Apr 1988 Opava 1.84m 76kg. Dukla Praha.

At PV: OG: '08- 9, '12- 7, '16- 4=; WCh: '09-11-13-15-17 dnq 23=/9/7/13=/dnq 18=; EC: '10-12-14-16: 10/6/3=/2; WJ: '06- 5=; WY: '05- 6; EU23: '09- 8=; WI: '14- 3, '16- 4=; EI: '13-15-17: 5/7=/4; ET: '14- 2=; Won CZE 2008, 2010-17.

Czech pole vault record 2016.

Progress at PV: 2002- 3.65, 2003- 4.21, 2004- 4.80, 2005- 5.09, 2006- 5.30, 2007- 5.61/5.62ex, 2008- 5.70, 2009- 5.62, 2010- 5.65, 2011- 5.81ex/5.65, 2012- 5.73, 2013- 5.83ex/5.77i/5.76, 2014- 5.80i/5.72/5.76ex, 2015- 5.75, 2016- 5.83, 2017- 5.80i/5.72. pbs: 60m 7.11i '07, HJ 2.05i/2.03 '07, LJ 7.55 '07, TJ 14.41 '07.

Pavel MASLÁK b. 21 Feb 1991 Havírov 1.76m 67kg. Dukla Praha.

At 400m: OG: '12- sf (h 200m), '16- sf; WCh: '13- 5, '15- h, '17- sf; EC: '12- 1, '16- 2; WY: '07- h; WI: '12-14-16-18: 5/1/1/1; EI: '13- 1/3R, '15&17- 1/3R. At 200m: WCh: '11- sf; WJ: '10- 7; EU23: '11- 3, '13- 3; EJ: '09- 5/2R. At 100m: WJ: '08- h. Won CZE 200m 2012-13, 2015, 2017; 400m 2011.

European indoor 300m & 500m bests 2014. Czech records: 200m (5) 2012-17, 300m, 400m (5) 2012-14.

Progress at 400m: 2006- 50.41, 2007- 48.30, 2008- 47.60, 2009- 47.44, 2010- 46.89, 2011- 47.05i/47.43, 2012- 44.91, 2013- 44.84, 2014- 44.79, 2015- 45.09, 2016- 45.06, 2017- 45.10. pbs: 60m 6.65i '14, 100m 10.35 '16, 200m 20.46 '17, 300m 31.80 '17, 500m 1:00.35 '13.

European Athletics Rising Star Award 2012. Master of indoor running.

Tomás STANEK b. 13 Jun 1991 Prague 1.90m 127kg. Dukla Praha.

At SP: OG: '16- dnq 20; WCh: '15- dnq 19, '17- 4; EC: '14: dnq 14; EU23: '13- 5; WI: '18- 3; EI: 17- 2; ET: '17- 1. CZE champion 2016-17.

Two Czech records 2017.

Progress at SP: 2009- 15.01, 2010- 15.50, 2011- 17.16, 2012- 18.52, 2013- 19.50, 2014- 20.93, 2015- 20.94i/20.64, 2016- 21.30i/21.26, 2017- 22.01, 2018- 22.17i.

Jakub VADLEJCH b. 10 Oct 1990 Praha 1.90m 93kg. Dukla Praha.

At JT: OG: '12- dnq 24, '16- 8; WCh: '11/15- dnq 16/20, '17- 2; EC: '10/14- dnq 16/20, '16- 9; WJ: '08- 10; WY: '07- 12; EJ: '09- 8; ET: '17- 1. Won DL 2016-17, Czech 2014-15, 2017.

Progress at JT: 2006- 55.24, 2007- 66.12, 2008- 76.59, 2009- 81.95, 2010- 84.47, 2011- 84.08, 2012- 80.40A, 2013- 75.85, 2014- 82.97, 2015- 86.21, 2016- 88.02, 2017- 89.73.

Married Lucia Slanícková (SVK records: 400mh 56.96 '14, Hep 6103 '17) in October 2017.

Vitezslav VESELY b. 27 Feb 1983 Hodonin 1.86m 94kg. Dukla Praha.

At JT: OG: '08- 12, '12- 3, '16- 7; WCh: '09-11-13-15-17: dnq 28/4/1/8/dnq 26; EC: '10-12-14-16: 9/1/2/2; WJ: '02- 9; CCp: '14- 2. Won DL 2012-13, CZE 2008, 2010-12, 20-16.

Progress at JT: 2001- 66.18, 2002- 73.22, 2003- 66.95, 2004- 72.32, 2006- 75.98, 2007- 79.45, 2008- 81.20, 2009- 80.35, 2010- 86.45, 2011- 84.11, 2012- 88.34, 2013- 87.68, 2014- 87.38, 2015- 88.18, 2016- 84.82, 2017- 82.29.

Women

Zuzana HEJNOVÁ b. 19 Dec 1986 Liberec 1.70m 54kg. Dukla Praha.

At 400mh/4x400mR: OG: '08- 7, '12- 3, '16- 4; WCh: '05-07-09- sf, '11-13-15-17: 7/1/1/4; EC: '06- sf, '10- 4, 12- 4/3R; WJ: '02- 5, '04- 2; EU23: '07- 3; EJ: '03- 3; '05- 1; WY: '03- 1; WI: '10- 3R; ET: '09- 3, '11- 1. Won DL 2013, 2015. At 400m: EI: '13- 4/3R, '17- 2. At Pen: EI: '11- 7. Won CZE 400m 2006, 2009.

12 Czech 400mh records 2005-13. 3 world bests 300mh 2011 (38.91) and 2013 (38.75 & 38.16).

Progress at 400mh: 2002- 58.42, 2003- 57.54, 2004- 57.44, 2005- 55.89, 2006- 55.83, 2007- 55.04, 2008- 54.96, 2009- 54.90, 2010- 54.13, 2011- 53.29, 2012- 53.38, 2013- 52.83, 2014- 55.86, 2015- 53.50, 2016- 53.92, 2017- 53.93. pbs: 60m 7.64i '17, 150m 17.66 '13, 200m 23.65 '13, 300m 37.49A/37.80 '13, 400m 51.90/51.27i '13, 600m 1:28.04i '15, 800m 2:03.40i '16, 60mh 8.24i '17, 100mh 13.36 '11, 13.18w '10; 200mh 26.29 '17, 300mh 38.16 '13, HJ 1.80i '11, 1.74 '04; LJ 5.96i '11, 5.76 '07, SP 12.11i '11, JT 36.11 '10, Pen 4453i '11.

Unbeaten season at hurdles in 2013. Sister of Michaela Hejnová (b. 10 Apr 1980) pb Hep 6174w/6065 '04; OG: '04- 26; EC '02- 7; EU23: '01- 5; WJ: '98- 5; EJ: '97- 6/'99- 6 (100mh); WUG: '01- 5, '03- 3.

Michaela HRUBÁ b. 21 Feb 1998 Boskovice 1.91m 75kg. USK Praha.

At HJ: OG: '16- dnq 18; WCh: '17- 11; EC: '16- 12; WJ: '14- 2, '16- 1; WY: '15- 1; EJ: '17- 1; EI: '15- 8,

'17- 6; YOG: '14- 3; ET: '17- 3. Won CZE 2017.
Progress at HJ: 2011- 1.52, 2012- 1.66, 2013- 1.83, 2014- 1.91, 2015- 1.91i/1.90, 2016- 1.95i/1.93, 2017- 1.94. Pbs: 100mh 15.42 '12, 200mh 29.60 '13, LJ 6.02i '18, TJ 12.93 '17.

Eliska KLUCINOVÁ b. 14 Apr 1988 Prague 1.77m 69kg. USK Praha.
At Hep: OG: '12- 16, '16- 22; WCh: '09-13-15-17: 22/7/13/10; EC: '10-12-14: 6/7/dnf; WJ: '06- 8; WY: '05- 8; EU23: '09- 4, EJ: '07- 2; WUG: '13- 3. At Pen: WI: '18- 4; EI: '15- 3. Won CZE LJ 2012, 2014, 2017; Hep 2008-09.
Four CZE heptathlon records 2010-14.
Progress at Hep: 2004- 5006, 2005- 5074, 2006- 5468, 2007- 5844, 2008- 5728, 2009- 6015, 2010- 6268, 2012- 6283, 2013- 6332, 2014- 6460, 2015- 6349, 2016- 6182, 2017- 6313. pbs: 200m 24.41 '16, 800m 2:12.50 '13, 60mh 8.51i '18, 100mh 13.81 '14, HJ 1.90 '14, LJ 6.43 '14, SP 15.21 '16, JT 51.09 '15, Pen 4687i '15 (CZE rec).

Barbora SPOTÁKOVÁ b. 30 Jun 1981 Jablonec nad Nisou 1.82m 80kg. Dukla Praha.
At JT: OG: '04- dnq 23, '08- 1, '12- 1, '16- 3; WCh: '05-07-09-11-15-17: dnq 13/1/2/2/9/1; EC: '02-06-10-14-16: dnq 17/2/3/1/5; EU23: '03- 6; WUG: '03- 4, '05- 1; CCp: '14- 1; ET: '09-11-14-17: 2/3/1/1; won DL 2010, 2012, 2014-15, 2017; WAF 2006-08, Czech 2003, 2005-12, 2015-17. At Hep: WJ: '00- 4.
World javelin record 2008, two European records 2008, 11 Czech records 2006-08. World heptathlon javelin best (60.90) in 2012.
Progress at JT: 1996- 31.32, 1997- 37.28, 1998- 44.56, new: 1999- 41.69, 2000- 54.15, 2001- 51.97, 2002- 56.76, 2003- 56.65, 2004- 60.95, 2005- 65.74, 2006- 66.21, 2007- 67.12, 2008- 72.28, 2009- 68.23, 2010- 68.66, 2011- 71.58, 2012- 69.55, 2013- 62.33, 2014- 67.99, 2015- 65.66, 2016- 66.87, 2017- 68.26. pbs: 200m 25.33/25.11w '00, 800m 2:18.29 '00, 60mh 8.68i '07, 100mh 13.99 '00, 400mh 62.68 '98, HJ 1.78 '00, LJ 5.65 '00, SP 14.53 '07, DT 36.80 '02, Hep 5880 '12, Dec 6749 '04.
Son Janek born 24 May 2013. Will miss 2018 season as she is expecting her second child.

DENMARK

Governing body: Dansk Athletik Forbund. Founded 1907.
National Championships first held in 1894. **2017 Champions**: **Men**: 100m/200m: Kristoffer Hari 10.40/21.33, 400m: Nick Ekelund-Arenander 47.03, 800m/1500m: Nick Jensen 1:53.74/3:46.60, 5000m: Thijs Nijhuis 14:16.02, 10000m/HMar: Abdi Hakin Ulad 29:23.28/64:58, Mar: Jesper Faurschou 2:19:11, 3000mSt: Ole Hesselbjerg 9:18.97, 110mh/400mh: Christian Laugesen 14.79/53.51, HJ: Jonas Kløjgaard Jensen 2.10, PV: Michael Christiansen 4.75, LJ: Benjamin Gabrielsen 7.60, TJ: Peder P.Nielsen 14.73, SP: Kristoffer Thomsen 17.75, DT: Emil Mikkelsen 54.01, HT: Taj Murmann 59.57, JT: Mikkel Bach Garbrecht 63.80, Dec: Christian Laugesen 7028, 5000mW: , 20kW: Peer Jensen 2:13:39. **Women**: 100: Mathilde Kramer 11.99, 200m: Sara Slott Petersen 23.75, 400m/800m: Mia Helene Mørck 56.54/2:10.81, 1500m/10000m: Simone Glad 4:19.96/34:00.21, 5000m: Anna Emilie Møller 16:06.87, HMar: Anna Holm 72:56, Mar: Louise Langelund Batting 2:38:52, 100mh: Mette Graversgaard 13.87, 400mh: Liv Stæhr Rødtnes 63.20, HJ: Rikke Andersen 1.73, PV: Line Renée Jensen 4.01, LJ/Hep: Sandra Böll 5.90/5276, TJ: Janne Nielsen 12.63, SP: Trine Mulbjerg 14.97, DT: Lisa Brix Pedersen 54.03, HT: Celina Julin 58.60, JT: Marie Vestergaard 49.92, 10kW: Helle Jensen 72:45.

Sara SLOTT PETERSEN b. 9 Apr 1987 Nykøbing Falster, Sjælland 1.71m 57kg. Århus 1900 AM.
At 400mh: OG: 12- sf, '16- 2; WCh: '09/11/17- sf, '15- 4; EC: '10-12-14-16- h/sf/h/1; WJ: '04- h; WY: '03- 4; EU23: '07- 6, '09- 6; EJ: '05- 4; WUG: '09- 3, '11-4; Won Danish 400mh 2002-09, 2011-12, 2014-15; 100m 2007, 2009; 200m 2009, 2012, 2016-17; 400m 2008-09.
12 Danish 400m records 2007-16.
Progress at 400mh: 2002- 60.67, 2003- 59.42, 2004- 60.60, 2005- 58.21, 2006- 57.65, 2007- 57.01, 2008- 57.06, 2009- 56.40, 2010- 57.28, 2011- 55.97, 2012- 55.68, 2014- 56.44, 2015- 53.99, 2016- 53.55, 2017-54.35. pbs: 60m 7.62i '15, 100m 12.07 '07, 11.93w '09; 200m 23.59 '16. 400m 52.59i/53.55 '16, 1500m 4:27.96 '11, 60mh 8.58i '07, 100mh 14.25 '05.
Her silver was the best ever for a Danish woman at the Olympics. Partner of Thomas Cortebeeck, their son Tobias born 8 Oct 2013.

DJIBOUTI

Hassan **Ayanleh SOULEIMAN** b. 3 Dec 1992 Djibouti City 1.72m 60kg.
At (800m)/1500m: OG: '16- sf/4; WCh: '13- 3/sf, '15/17- h; WI: '12- 5; AfG: '11- 6; AfCh: '12- 2, '14- 1; CCp: '14- 1; WI: '14- 1, '16- 9; won DL 2013, Arab G 2011, Franc G 2013. At 3000m: WY: '09- h. Won Arab 5000m 2015.
World indoor 1000m record 2016. DJI records: 800m (5) 2012-15, 1000m (2) 2013-16, 1500m (3) 2011-14, 1M (3) 2012-14, 3000m 2012.
Progress at 800m, 1500m: 2011- 1:51.78A, 3:34.32; 2012- 1:47.45, 3:30.31; 2013- 1:43.63, 3:31.64; 2014- 1:43.69, 3:29.58; 2015- 1:42.97, 3:30.17; 2016- 1:43.52, 3:31.68; 2017- 1:45.01, 3:34.70. pbs: 1000m 2:13.49 '16, 1M 3:47.32 '14, 3000m 7:39.81i '13, 7:42.22 '12, 5000m 13:17.97 '15.
Djibouti's first ever world champion 2013 and first to set an official world record.

DOMINICAN REPUBLIC

Governing body: Federación Dominicana de Asociaciones de Atletismo. Founded 1953.

Luguelín SANTOS b. 12 Nov 1992 Bayaguana

1.73m 61kg. Universidad Interamericana de San Germán, Puerto Rico.
At 400m: OG: '12- 2, '16- sf; WCh: '13- 3 (h 200m), '15- 4, '17- h; WJ: '10- 6, '12- 1; PAm: '11- 2/2R, '15- 1; CCp: '14- 5; YthOG: '10- 1; WI: '18- dq (2); WUG: '15- 1, '17- 1. Won BolG 2017.
DOM records 200m 2013, 400m (5) 2011-15. CAC indoor 600m best 2015.
Progress at 400m: 2009- 47.88, 2010- 46.19, 2011- 44.71A, 2012- 44.45, 2013- 44.52, 2014- 44.53, 2015- 44.11, 2016- 44.71, 2017- 45.24. pbs: 200m 20.55A '13, 20.70 '16; 300m 32.0+, '15, 32.56 '12, 500m 59.75 '15, 600m 1:15.58 '16, 800m 1:48.67 '17.
Was over-age at the 2012 World Juniors. Younger brother **Juander** (b. 7 May 1995) has pbs 400m 45.93A '14; 400mh 48.59 '17, WCh '17- 6; WUG: '17- 1.

ECUADOR

Governing body: Federación Ecuatoriana de Atletismo. Founded 1925.

Andrés CHOCHO b. 4 Nov 1983 Cuenca 1.67m 67kg.
At 20kW: OG: '08- 38, '16- dq; WCh: '07-09-15-17: dq/37/dq/dq; WCp: '16- 6; SACh: '11- 1, '13- 3; WUG: '11- 2. At 50kW: OG: '12/16- dq; WCh: '11-13-15-17: 10/dq/8/dq; PAm: '15- 1; won BolG 2013, 2017. Won S.Am 20kW 2016, SAm-J 10,000W 2001.
Four S.American 50k records 2011-16.
Progress at 50kW: 2010- 3:54:42, 2011- 3:49:32, 2012- 3:49:26, 2013- 3:58:50, 2014- 3:57:00, 2015- 3:46:00, 2016- 3:42:57A, 2017- 3:47:37. pbs: 10kW 40:28 '16, 41:55.50tA '15, 20kW 1:20:07 '16, 30kW 2:16:46 '14, 35kW 2:36:56 '15.
Married to Érica de Sena (Brazil) (qv).

ERITREA

Governing body: Eritrean National Athletics Federation. Founded 1992.

Ghirmay GHEBRESLASSIE b. 14 Nov 1995 Kisadeka 1.62m 52kg..
At Mar: OG: '16- 4; WCh: '15- 1. World HMar: '14- 7; CC: '13- 7J; AfCC: 12- 9J.
Progress at Mar: 2014- 2:09:08, 2015- 2:07:47. 2016- 2:07:46, 2017- 2:09:57. pbs: 5000m 13:40.17 '12, 10000m 28:33.37 '12; Road: 10M 46:29 '12, HMar 60:09 '13, 25k 1:12:43 '16, 30k 1:28:13 '16.
Youngest ever world marathon champion at 19 in 2015 after 2nd in Hamburg Marathon. Won New York Marathon 2016.

Aron KIFLE Teklu b. 20 Feb 1998 1.70m 55kg.
At 5000m/(10000m): OG: '16- h; WCh: '15- h, 17- 7/11; AfG: '15- 8; WJ: 16- 5/2. At HMar: WCh: '18- 3. World CC: '17- 5, AfCC: 16- 3J.
Progress at 5000m, 10000m: 2015- 13:17.62, 28:18.44; 2016- 13:13.39, 27:26.20; 2017- 13:13.31, 27:09.92. pbs: 3000m 7:52.19 '17, 15k Rd 45:08 '15, HMar 60:31 '18.

ESTONIA

Governing body: Eesti Kergejôustikuliit. Founded 1920.
National Championships first held in 1917.
2017 Champions: Men: 100m/200m: Marek Niit 10.43/21.37, 400m: Rasmus Mägi 46.42, 800m: Rasmus Kisel 1:50.31, 1500m/10000m: Andi Noot 3:55.9/31:23.41, 5000m: Tiidrek Nurme 14:08.33, HMar: Roman Fosti 67:53, Mar: Argo Jöesoo 2:28:15, 3000mSt: Kaur Kivistik 9:25.45, 110mh: Andres Raja 14.61, 400mh: Jaak-Heinrich Jagor 49.38, HJ: Karl Lumi 2.13, PV: Janek Oiglane 5.10, LJ/TJ: Igor Syunin 7.60/16.50, SP: Kristo Galeta 18.78, DT: Martin Kupper 61.70, HT: Genro Paas 65.32, JT: Magnus Kirt 80.04, Dec: Taavi Tsernjavski 7561, 10000mW/ 20kW: Ruslan Sergatsjov 46:27.58/1:44:36. **Women**: 100m: Maarja Kalev 11.80, 200m: Öilme Vöro 24.00, 400m/400mh: Liis Roose 55.32/60.54, 800m/ 1500m: Liina Tsernov 2:06.16/4:15.95, 5000m: Jekaterina Patjuk 16:40.00, 10000m/HMar: Lily Luik 35:11.44/79:56, Mar: Olga Andrejeva 2:51:06, 3000mSt: Evelin Talts 11:14.30, 100mh/LJ: Grit Sadeiko 13.33/6.23, HJ: Grete Udras 1.76, PV: Lembi Vaher 3.75, TJ: Tähti Alver 13.50, SP: Kätlin Piirimäe 15.92, DT: Kätlin Töllasson 54.93, HT: Anna Maria Orel 67.39, JT: Liina Laasma 56.08, Hep: Margit Kalk 5334, 10000mW: Jekaterina Mirotvortseva 51:46.11, 20kW: Anna Tipukina 2:01:05.

Gerd KANTER b. 6 May 1979 Tallinn 1.96m 125kg. Tallinna SS Kalev. Business management graduate.
At DT: OG: '04- dnq 19, '08- 1, '12- 3, '16- 5; WCh: '03-05-07-09-11-13-15-17: dnq25/2/1/3/2/3/4/12; EC: '02-06-10-12-14-16: 12/2/4/2/2/3; EU23: '01- 5; CCp: '14- 1; WUG: '05- 1. Won WAF 2007-08, DL 2012-13, Estonian 2004-09, 2011-15.
Five Estonian discus records 2004-06.
Progress at DT: 1998- 47.37, 1999- 49.65, 2000- 57.68, 2001- 60.47, 2002- 66.31, 2003- 67.13, 2004- 68.50, 2005- 70.10, 2006- 73.38, 2007- 72.02, 2008- 71.88, 2009- 71.64, 2010- 71.45, 2011- 67.99, 2012- 68.03, 2013- 67.59, 2014- 66.28, 2015- 66.02, 2016- 65.27, 2017- 65.87. pb SP 17.31i '04, 16.11 '00.
Threw over 70m in four rounds at Helsingborg on 4 Sep 2006; a feat matched only by Virgilijus Alekna. Six successive seasons over 70m.

Magnus KIRT b. 10 Apr 1990 Törva 1.92m 89kg. Tallinn University of Technology. Tallinna TU SK.
At JT: OG: '16- dnq 23; WCh: '15- dnq 22, '17- 11; EC: '14/16- dnq 22/26, EU23: '11- dnq 18; EJ: '09- dnq 22; Won EST 2015, 2017.
Progress at JT: 2008- 54.40, 2008- 59.88, 2009- 72.97, 2010- 71.41, 2011- 70.07, 2012- 76.97, 2013- 79.82, 2014- 79.70, 2015- 86.65, 2016- 84.47, 2017- 86.06. Pbs: HJ 2.10 '09, LJ 6.96 '09, TJ 13.68 '09, DT 38.09 '09.

Rasmus MÄGI b. 4 May 1992 Tartu 1.88m 74kg. Tartu University ASK.
At 400mh: OG: '12- h, '16- 6; WCh: '13 & 15- sf; EC: '12-14-16: 5/2/sf; WJ: '10- h; EU23: '13- 3; EJ: '11- 4; CCp: '14- 4. Won EST 400m 2012, 2016-17; 400mh 2009, 2014-15.
S3v3n Estonian 400mh records 2012-16
Progress at 400mh: 2010- 52.79, 2011- 50.14, 2012- 49.54, 2013- 49.19, 2014- 48.54, 2015- 48.65, 2016- 48.40, 2017- 48.94. pbs: 200m 21.90 '11, 400m 46.40 '13, 200mh 24.01 '11, LJ 7.73 '12.
His sister Maris has won 22 Estonian titles in sprints and hurdles, pbs: 400m 52.21 '11, 400mh 56.56 '13 (EST record).

Janek OIGLANE b. 25 Apr 1994 1.82m 78kg. Audentese SK.
At Dec: WCh: '15- 19, '17- 4; EC: '16- 12; EU23: '15- 3; EJ: '13- 4; ET: '17- 1. At JT: WY: '17- 11.
Progress at Dec: 2014- 7815, 2015- 7945, 2016- 7762, 2017- 8371. pbs: 60m 7.33i '16, 100m 11.08 '17, 400m 49.58 '17, 1000m 2:44.37i '16, 1500m 4:34.41 '16, 60mh 8.16i '17, 110mh 14.50 '15, HJ 2.05 '17, PV 5.10 '17, LJ 7.42 '17, SP 15.15i '16, 15.13 '17; DT 44.62 '16, JT 71.73 '17, Hep 5739i '16.
Five pbs in his 8371 at 2017 Worlds,

Maicel UIBO b. 27 Dec 1992 Põlva 1.88m 86kg. Põlva. Was at Univerity of Georgia, USA.
At Dec: OG: '16- 24; WCh: '13- 19, '15- 10, '17- dnf; NCAA champion 2014-15. At Hep: WI: '18- 3. At HJ: WY: '09- dnq 19; EU23: '13- dnq 21.
Progress at Dec: 2012- 7548, 2013- 8223, 2014- 8182, 2015- 8356, 2016- 8315. 2017- 8371. pbs: 60m 7.16Ai '14, 7.18 '15; 100m 10.99 '13, 400m 50.24 '15, 1000m 2:38.51i '18, 1500m 4:25.53 '15, 60mh 8.19i '18, 110mh 14.61 '16, HJ 2.18 '15; PV 5.30i '18, 5.20 '15; LJ 7.82 '13, SP 14.98 '16; DT 49.14 '15, JT 64.51 '15, Hep 6265i '18.
Married Shaunae Miller (qv) on 4 Feb 2017.

ETHIOPIA

Governing body: Ethiopian Athletic Federation. Founded 1961.
2017 National Champions: **Men**: 100m/200m: Bedru Mehammed 10.6/21.3, 400m: Efrem Mekonnen 46.6, 800m: Tadesse Lemi 1:46.7, 1500m: Teresa Tolosa 3:37.9, 5000m: Getaneh Molla 13:42.4, 10000m: Andamlak Belihu 28:32.4, 3000mSt: Tafese Soboka 8:33.0, 110mh: Behailu Alemeshete 14.1, 400mh: Dadissa Bayo 51.4, HJ: Gemechu Tamiru 2.00, PV: Mezgebu Birara 4.40, LJ/TJ: Adir Gur 7.23/15.79, SP: Zegeye Moga 15.68, DT: Lemma Ketema 42.78, HT: Abrham Tocho 45.52, JT: Kerayo Bulala 65.18, 20kW: Yohannes Algeaw 1:26:50. **Women**: 100m: Ebide Kebede 12.0, 200m: Tegest Tamangnu 24.3, 400m: Hiwot Kinde 53.7, 800m: Mahelet Mulugeta 2:02.2, 1500m: Fantu Worku 4:07.8, 5000m: Senbere Teferi 15:12.2, 10000m: Dere Dida 33:58.5, 3000mSt: Birtukan Adamu 10:14.7, 100mh: Gebeyanesh Gedecha 14.4, 400mh: Deme Abu 58.8, HJ: Ariyat Dibo 1.74, LJ/TJ: Ariyat Dibo 5.81/12.94, SP: Zurga Usman 13.49, JT: Shura Utura 45.76, 20kW: Yehualeye Beletew 1:32:40.

Guye ADOLA Idemo b. 20 Oct 1990 Adola, Oromiya region 1.74m 54kg.
At Half Marathon: WCh: '14- 3, '15- 16; AfG: '15- 5; ETH champion 2015.
Progress at 10000m, Mar: 2016- 27:09.78, 2017- 28:14.19, 2:03:46. pbs: HMar 59:06 '14, 25k 1:12:50 '17, 30k 1:27:24 '17.
Ran world's fastest debut marathon when 2nd in Berlin 2017.

Yenew ALAMIREW b. 27 May 1990 Tilili 1.75m 57kg.
At 5000m: OG: '12- 12; WCh: '13- 9; AfG: '11- 2; AfCh: '14- 5; won DL 2013. At 3000m: WI: '12- 9, '16- 12.
Progress at 5000m, 10000m: 2010- 13:16.53, 2011- 13:00.46, 2012- 12:48.77, 2013- 12:54.95, 2014- 13:00.21, 2015- 13:05.53, 2016- 13:04.29, 2017- 13:06.81, 27:19.86. pbs: 1500m 3:35.09+ '11, 1M 3:50.43 '11, 3000m 7:27.26 '11, Road: 15k 42:30 '14, 10M 46:04 '15, Mar 2:08:56 '18.

Mohamed AMAN Geleto b. 10 Jan 1994 Asella 1.69m 55kg.
At 800m: OG: '12- 6, '16- sf; WCh: '11-13-15-17: 8/1/dq sf/6; WY: '11- 2; WI: '12-14-16: 1/1/4; AfCh: '14- 2; CCp: '14- 2; won DL 2012-13, Afr-J 2011, Yth OG 1000m 2010.
Records: Ethiopian 800m (6) 2011-13, 1000m 2014, world youth 800m indoors and out 2011, world junior 600m indoor 2013 (1:15.60), African indoor 800m 2014.
Progress at 800m: 2008- 1:50.29, 2009- 1:46.34, 2010- 1:48.5A, 2011- 1:43.37, 2012- 1:42.53, 2013- 1:42.37, 2014- 1:42.83, 2015- 1:43.56, 2016- 1:44.70, 2017- 1:45.40. pbs: 600m 1:15.0+ '12, 1000m 2:15.75 '14, 1500m 3:43.52 '11, 1M 3:57.14 '11.
Was disqualified from taking the African Junior 800m gold in 2009 for being under-age (at 15). Youngest ever World Indoor champion at 18 years 60 days in 2012. Beat David Rudishsa in the latter's last races in both 2011 and 2012.

Selemon BAREGA b. 20 Jan 2000 1.73m 59kg.
At 5000m: WCh: '17- 5; WJ: '16- 1; Af-J: '17- 1. At 3000m: WY: '17- 1; WI: '18- 2. World CC: '17- 5J.
Progress at 5000m: 2015- 13:58.8A, 2016- 13:21.21, 2017- 12:55.58. Pb 3000m 7:36.64i '18, 7:38.90 '17.

Kenenisa BEKELE b. 13 Jun 1982 near Bekoji, Arsi Province 1.62m 54kg.
At 5000m(/10000m): OG: '04- 2/1, '08- 1/1, '12- (4); WCh: '03- 3/1, '05- (1), '07- (1), '09- 1/1, '11- (dnf); WJ: '00- 2; AfG: '03- 1; AfCh: '06- 1, '08- 1. At 3000m: WY: '99- 2; WI: '06- 1; WCp: '06- 2. World CC: '99- 9J, 4k: '01- 1J/2 4k, '02-03-04-05-06: all 1/1, '08- 1. Won WAF 3000m 2003, 2009; 5000m 2006.
World records: 5000m 2004, 10000m 2004 & 2005, indoor 5000m (12:49.60) 2004, 2000m 2007,

2M 2008; World junior record 3000m 2001. ETH marathon record 2016.
Progress at 5000m, 10000m, Mar: 2000- 13:20.57, 2001- 13:13.33, 2002- 13:26.58, 2003- 12:52.26, 26:49.57; 2004- 12:37.35, 26:20.31; 2005- 12:40.18, 26:17.53; 2006- 12:48.09, 2007- 12:49.53, 26:46.19; 2008- 12:50.18, 26:25.97; 2009- 12:52.32, 26:46.31; 2011- 13:27e+, 26:43.16; 2012- 12:55.79, 27:02.59; 2013- 13:07.88, 27:12.08; 2014- 2:05:04, 2016- 2:03:03, 2017- 2:05:57. pbs: 1000m 2:21.9+ '07, 1500m 3:32.35 '07, 1M 3:56.2+ '07, 2000m 4:49.99i '07, 4:58.40 '09, 3000m 7:25.79 '07, 2M 8:04.35i '08, 8:13.51 '07; Road: 15k 42:42 '01, 10M 46:06 '13, 20k 57:19 '13, HMar 60:09 '13, 25k 1:12:47 '16, 30k 1:27:25 '16.
At cross-country has a record 16 (12 individual, 4 team) world gold medals. Unbeaten in 27 races from Dec 2001 to March 2007 when he did not finish in the Worlds. After winning all his 12 10,000m track races including five major gold medals, from a brilliant debut win over Haile Gebrselassie at Hengelo in June 2003, he had two years out through injury and then dropped out of World 10,000 in 2011 before running the year's fastest time to win at Brussels. 17 successive wins at 5000m 2006-09. Shared Golden League jackpot in 2009. Won Great North Run on half marathon debut 2013. Won in Paris on marathon debut 2014, then 4th Chicago; 3rd London and 1st Berlin 2016, 2nd London 2017. IAAF Athlete of the Year 2004-05. He married film actress Danawit Gebregziabher on 18 Nov 2007.

Andamlak BELIHU b. 20 Nov 1998 1.81m 62kg.
At 10000m: WCh: '17- 10. Won ETH 10000m 2017
Progress at 10000m: 2017- 27:08.94. Pb HMar 59:51 '17.

Lelisa DESISA Benti b. 14 Jan 1990 Shewa 1.70m 52kg.
At 10000m: Af-J: '09- 1. At: HMar: WCh: '10- 7, AfG: '11- 1. At Mar: WCh: '13- 2, '15- 7.
Progress at 10000m, HMar, Mar: 2009- 28:46.74, 2010- 59:39; 2011- 59:30, 2012- 27:11.98, 62:50; 2013- 2:04:45, 2014- 59:36, 2:11:06; 2015- 2:05:52, 2016- 60:37, 2:13:32dh, 2017- 2:11:32, 2018- 60:28. pbs: 5000m 13:22.91 '12, Road: 15k 42:25 '10, 10M 45:36 '11.
Brilliant marathon debut to win Dubai 2013 and then won Boston and 2nd Worlds. 2nd New York 2014 (3rd 2015, 2017), Dubai 2015. Won Boston again in 2015 (2nd 2016).

Muktar EDRIS Awel b. 14 Jan 1994 Adio 1.72m 57kg.
At 5000m: OG: '16- dq; WCh: '13- 7, '17- 1; WJ: '12- 1. At 10000m: WCh: '15- 10; Af-J: '11- 4. World CC: '11-13-15-17: 7J/3J/3/6; AfCC: 12- 1J.
Progress at 5000m, 10000m: 2011- 28:44.95A, 2012- 13:04.34, 2013- 13:03.69, 2014- 12:54.83, 2015- 13:00.30, 27:17.18; 2016- 12:59.43, 2017- 12:55.23, 27:20.60. pbs: 3000m 7:32.31 '17.
Disqualified for stepping inside kerb after finishing 4th in 2016 Olympic 5000m final.

Dejen GEBREMESKEL b. 24 Nov 1989 Adiqrat, Tigray region 1.78m 53kg.
At 5000m: OG: '12- 2, '16- 12; WCh: '11- 3; WJ: '08- 3; Af-J: '07- 2. At 10000m: WCh: '13- 16. At 3000m: WI: '10- 12-14: 10/5/3. World CC: '08- 18J.
Progress at 5000m, 10000m: 2007- 13:21.05, 2008- 13:08.96, 2009- 13:03.13, 2010- 12:53.56, 2011- 12:55.89, 2012- 12:46.81, 2013- 13:31.02, 26:51.02; 2014- 13:09.73, 2015- 13:00.49, 2016- 12:59.89. 2017- 13:25.95. pbs: 3000m 7:34.14i '12, 7:45.9+ '10, HMar 62:36 '14.
Fastest ever debut 10,000m at Sollentuna 2013.

Hagos GEBRHIWET Berhe b. 11 May 1994 Tsaedaenba, Tigray region 1.67m 55kg. Mesfen Engineering
At 5000m: OG: '12- 11, '16- 3; WCh: '13- 2, '15- 3; AfCh: '14- dnf; won DL 2016. At 3000m: WY: '11- 5; WI: '14- 5, '18- 4. World CC: '13- 1J, '15- 4, AfCC: '12- 4J.
World junior records 5000m 2012, indoor 3000m 2013.
Progress at 5000m: 2011- 14:10.0A, 2012- 12:47.53, 2013- 12:55.73, 2014- 13:06.88, 2015- 12:54.70, 2016- 13:00.20. pbs: 3000m 7:30.36 '13, 10k Rd 27:57dh '11.

Leul GEBRSELASSIE b. 20 Sep 1993 1.70m 55kg.
At 5000m: AfG: '15- 2. At HMar: WCh: '18- 10.
Progress at 10000m, Mar: 2012- 28:10.49. 2013- 28:05.66, 2015- 27:22.89, 2016- 27:17.91, 2017- 28:10.15, 2018- 2:04:02. pbs: 3000m 7:44.50i '16, 7:53.58 '14; 5000m 13:13.88 '16, Road: 15k 42:05 '17, 10M 47:18 '14, 20k 56:17 '17, HMar 59:18 '17, 25k 1:12:57 '18, 30k 1:27:37 '18.
2nd Dubai 2018 in 2:04:02, the third fastest ever marathon debut.

Mosinet GEREMEW b. 12 Feb 1992 1.74m 57kg.
At 10000m: WCh: '15- 11.
Progress at HMar, Mar: 2013- 62:47, 2014- 59:11, 2015- 59:21, 2016- 60:43, 2017- 60:56, 2:06:12; 2018- 2:04:00. pbs: 5000m 13:17.41 '12, 10000m 27:18.86 '15, Road: 25k 1:12:57 '18, 30k 1:27:38 '18.
Won Dubai marathon 2018, after 2nd Xiamen and 3rd Berlin 2017.

Abadi HADIS Embaye b. 6 Nov 1997 1.70m 63kg.
At 10000m: OG: '16- 15; WCh: '17- 7; won ETH 2016. World CC: '17- 3.
Progress at 5000m, 10000m: 2015- 13:13.17, 2016- 13:02.49, 26:57.88; 2017- 13:16.78, 26:59.19. pbs: 3000m 7:33.28 '16, HMar 60:25 '17.

Ibrahim JEYLAN Gashu b. 12 Jun 1989 Bale Province 1.68m 57kg. Muger Cement.
At 10000m: WCh: '11- 1, '13- 2; WJ: '06- 1, '08- 3; AfG: '11- 1; AfCh: '08- 2. At 3000m: WY: '05- 2. World CC: '06-08-17: 5J/1J/8. Won ETH 5000m 2014, 10000m 2006.
Two world youth 10,000m records 2006.

Progress at 5000m, 10000m: 2006- 13:09.38, 27:02.81; 2007- 13:17.99, 27:50.53; 2008- 13:15.12, 27:13.85; 2009- 13:19.70, 27:22.19; 2010- 13:21.29, 27:12.43; 2011- 13:09.95, 27:09.02; 2013- 13:09.16, 27:22.23; 2014- 13:09.67, 2015- 13:20.21, 2016- 13:03.22, 26:58.75. pbs: 3000m 8:04.21 '05, 15k 43:38 '08, HMar 61:47 '14.

Yomif KEJELCHA Atomsa b. 1 Aug 1997 1.86m 58kg. Nike.
At 5000m: WCh: '15- 4, '17-= 4; WJ: '14- 1; Af-J: '15- 1; won DL 2015. At 3000m: WY: '13- 1; Yth OG: '14- 1; WI: '16- 1, '18- 1. World CC: '17- 2 MxR.
World junior 3000m record 2016.
Progress at 5000m: 2014- 13:25.19, 2015- 12:53.98, 2016- 13:03.29, 2017- 13:01.21. pbs: 1500m 3:32.94 '17, 1M 3:56.95i '18, 2000m 4:57.74i '14, 3000m 7:28.19 '16, 10k Rd 28:13 '13.

Abera KUMA Lema b. 31 Aug 1990 Ambo 1.60m 50kg.
At 5000m: WCh: '11- 5; Af-J: '09- 1. At 10000m: WCh: '13- 5. At 3000m: WY: '07- 5.
Tied world 30km record 2014.
Progress at 5000m, 10000m, Mar: 2009- 13:29.40, 2010- 13:07.83, 2011- 13:00.15, 27:22.54; 2012- 13:09.32, 27:18.39; 2013- 26:52.85, 2014- 2:05:56, 2015- 2:06:47, 2016- 2:07:48, 2017- 2:06:44. pbs: 1500m 3:48.73 '09, 3000m 7:39.09i/7:40.85 '12, Road: 15k 42:01 '10, 10M 45:28 '11, HMar 60:19 '12, 25k 1:13:08 '14, 30k 1:27:38 '14.
3rd Berlin Marathon 2014, won Rotterdam 2015.

Hayle LEMI Berhanu b. 13 Sep 1994 Hasasa, 1.72m 56kg.
At Mar: OG: '16- 13; WCh: '15- 15.
Progress at Mar: 2014- 2:10:40, 2015- 2:05:28, 2016- 2:04:33, 2017- 2:08:27. pbs: HMar 61:37 '15, 30k 1:27:21 '16.
Marathon wins: Zürich & Taiyuan 2014, Dubai 2015 (2nd 2016), Warsaw 2015, Boston 2016, Xiamen 2017.

Sisay LEMMA Kasaye b. 12 Dec 1990 1.74m 57kg.
Progress at Mar: 2012- 2:11:58, 2013- 2:09:02, 2015- 2:06:26, 2016- 2:05:16, 2017- 2:08:04, 2018- 2:04:08. pbs: HMar 61:11 '16, 25k 1:12:49 '16, 30k 1:27:20 '16.
Marathon wins: Carpi 2012 (debut), Warsaw 2013, Vienna & Frankfurt 2015; 3rd Dubai 2017.

Feyisa LILESA Gemechu b. 1 Feb 1990 Tullu Bultuma 1.58m 50kg.
At Mar: OG: '16- 2; WCh: '11- 3, '13- dnf, World CC: 2008-09-10-11-13: 14J/12/25/17/9. Won ETH CC 2013.
Progress at Mar: 2009- 2:09:12, 2010- 2:05:23, 2011- 2:10:32, 2012- 2:04:52, 2013- 2:07:46, 2014- 2:08:26, 2015- 2:06:35, 2016- 2:06:56, 2017- 2:14:12, 2018- 2:07:30. pbs: 5000m 13:34.80 '08, 10000m 27:46.97 '08; Road: 15k 42:15+ '13, 20k 56:19+ '12, HMar 59:22 '12, 25k 1:13:22 '13, 30k 1:28:05 '13.
Marathons won: Dublin 2009, Xiamen 2010, Tokyo 2016. 3rd/2nd Chicago 2010/2012, 4th Rotterdam 2010 in then fastest ever by 20 year-old, 4th London 2013. Now living in the USA.

Tsegaye MEKONNEN Asefa b. 15 Jun 1995 1.74m 56kg.
At 5000m: WJ: '12- 5. At Mar: WCh: '17- 19.
World junior marathon record 2014.
Progress at Mar: 2014- 2:04:32, 2015- dnf, 2016- 2:04:46, 2017- 2:07:26. pbs: 5000m 13:44.43 '14; Road: 10k 28:36 '12, HMar 61:05 '15.
Marathons: 1st Dubai 2014 (3rd 2016), Hamburg 2017; 5th London 2014.

Samuel TEFERA b. 23 Oct 1999 1.71m 52kg.
At 1500m: WCh: '17- h; WI: '18- 1
World junior indoor 1500m record 2018.
Progress at 1500m: 2015- 13:58.8A, 2016- 3:43.0A, 2017- 3:33.78, 2018- 3:36.05i.

Adera **Tamirat TOLA** b. 11 Aug 1991 1.81m 59kg.
At 10000m: OG: '16- 3. At HMar: WCh: '16- 5. At Mar: WCh: '17- 2. World CC: '15- 6.
Progress at 10000m, Mar: 2014- 2:06:17, 2015- 27:22.64, 2016- 26:57.33, dnf; 2017- 2:04:11, 2018- 2:04:06. pbs: 15k 42:26 '17, 20k 56:36 '17, HMar 59:37 '17, 25k 1:12:54 '17, 30k 1:27:38 '18.
Won Dubai Marathon 2017 (3rd 2018).

Aman WOTE Fete b. 18 Apr 1984 Kabete 1.81m 64kg.
At 1500m: OG: '12- ht; WCh: 13- sf, '15- dnf; AfG: '11- 5; AfCh: '10- 7; WI: '12-14-16-18: 4/2/6/4. Won ETH 1500m 2014, 2016.
Ethiopian records 1500m (2) & 1M 2014.
Progress at 1500m: 2010- 3:38.89A 2011- 3:35.61, 2012- 3:35:38, 2013- 3:32.65, 2014- 3:29.91, 2015- 3:30.29, 2016- 3:34.58, 2017- 3:31.63. pbs: 800m 1:44.99 '13, 1M 3:48.60 '14, 3000m 7:43.99i '13.

Jemal YIMER Mekonnen b. 11 Sep 1996 1.63m 48kg.
At 10000m: WCh: '17- 5; AfCh: 16- 4. At HMar: WCh: '18- 4. World CC: 17- 4.
Progress at 10000m: 2016- 28:08.92, 2017- 26:56.11. pbs: 15k 41:14 '18, 20k 55:56 '18, HMar 59:00 '18.

Women

Habitam ALEMU b. 9 Jul 1997 1.71m 52kg.
At 800m: OG: '16- sf; WCh: '15- h, '17- sf; AfG: '15- 4; WI: '16- 6, '18- 4.
Ethiopian 800m record 2017.
Progress at 800m: 2014- 2:09.6A, 2015- 2:01.27, 2016- 1:58.99, 2017- 1:57.05. pb 1500m 4:05.51i '18, 4:14.67 '15.

Meskerem ASSEFA b. 20 Sep 1985 1.55m 43kg.
At 800m: WY: '10- h. At 1500m: OG: '12- h; WCh: '09- sf, '11- h; AfG: '07- 4, '11- 4; AfCh: '08- 2, '10- 5.
Progress at Mar: 2013- 2:25:17, 2014- 2:25:59, 2015- 2:25:11, 2016- 2:30:13, 2017- 2:24:18, 2018- 2:21:45. pbs: 800m 2:02.12 '08, 1500m 4:02.12 '11, 3000m 8:46.37 '09, 5000m 15:03.49i '10, Road: 10k: 31:43 '17, 15k 47:42 '17, 20k 64:18 '17, HMar 67:42 '17, 25k 1:24:37 '18, 30k 1:41:09 '18.

Marathon wins: Houston & Rotterdam 2017, Nagoya 2018.

Sofia ASSEFA Abebe b. 14 Nov 1987 Tenta District, south Wello 1.71m 58kg. Ethiopian Bank.
At 3000mSt: OG: '08- h, '12- 2, '16- 5; WCh: '09-11-13-15-17: 12/5/3/4/h; AfG: '15- 1; AfCh: '08-10-14: 4/2/2; CCp: '10- 3.
Three Ethiopian 3000mSt records 2011-17.
Progress at 3000mSt: 2006- 10:17.48, 2007- 9:48.46, 2008- 9:31.58, 2009- 9:19.91, 2010- 9:20.72, 2011- 9:15.04, 2012- 9:09.00, 2013- 9:12.84, 2014- 9:11.39, 2015- 9:12.63, 2016- 9:13.09, 2017- 9:07.06. pbs: 1000m 2:49.79 '07, 5000m 14:56.37 '17, 2000mSt 6:33.49 '07; Road: 10k 32:52 '17, 15k 48:56 '17, 10M 53:13 '17.

Almaz AYANA Eba b. 21 Nov 1991 Benshangul 1.65m 50kg.
At 5000m/(10000m): OG: '16- 3/1; WCh: '13- 3, '15- 1, 17- 2/1; AfCh: '14- 1; CCp: '14- 1. At 3000mSt: WJ: '10- 5; won DL 5000m 2016, ETH 5000m 2014, 3000mSt 2013.
World record 10000m 2016, junior 3000m steeplechase 2010.
Progress at 5000m, 10000m, 3000mSt: 2009- 10:03.75, 2010- 9:22.51, 2011- 15:12.24, 9:30.23; 2012- 14:57.97, 9:38.62; 2013- 14:25.84, 9:27.49; 2014- 14:29.19, 2015- 14:14.32; 2016- 14:12.59, 29:17.45; 2017- 14:40.35, 30:16.32. pbs: 2000m 5:35.10+ '15, 3000m 8:22.22 '15, HMar 67:12 '17.
Ran 30:07.00 on 10000m track debut to win ETH trial race at Hengelo, then smashed WR in Rio. Won 2017 World 10000m by record maregin of 46.37 secs. Married to Soresa Fida 1500m 3:34.72 '11, 3 AfCh '11). IAAF Female Athlete of the Year 2016.

Tadelech BEKELE Alemu b. 11 Apr 1991 Debre Birhan 1.54m 40kg.
Afr CC: 14- 5. Progress at 10000m, Mar: 2014- 2:23:02, 2015- 33:30.7A, 2:22:51; 2016- 30:54.61, 2:26:31; 2017- 2:21:54. pbs: 5000m 15:28.27 '12, 10k 30:38 '13, HMar 68:38 '13.
Won Amsterdam marathon after 3rd Prague and 4th Dubai all under 2:25 in 2017.

Gelete BURKA Bati b. 15 Feb 1986 Kofele 1.65m 45kg.
At 1500m: OG: '08- h; WCh: '05- 8, '09- 9 (fell), '11- sf, '13- h; WI: '08- 1, '10- 3; AfG: '07- 1; AfCh: '08- 1, '10- 2; CCp: '10- 6. At 3000m: WI: '12- 3. At 5000m: OG: '12- 5; WCh: '07- 9. At 10000m: OG: '16- 8; WCh: '15- 2; AfG: '15- 3. World CC: '03-05-06-07-08-09: 3J/1J/1 4k/4/6/8. Won ETH 800m 2011, 1500m 2004-05, 2007; 5000m 2005, 4k CC 2006.
African records: 1M 2008, 200m 2009, indoor 1500m 2008, junior 1500m 2005. World youth 1M best (4:30.81) 2003.
Progress at 1500m, 5000m, 10000m, Mar: 2003- 4:10.82, 16:23.8A, 2004- 4:06.10, 2005- 3:59.60, 14:51.47; 2006- 4:02.68, 14:40.92; 2007- 4:00.48, 14:31.20; 2008- 3:59.75i/4:00.44, 14:45.84; 2009- 3:58.79, 2010- 3:59.28, 2011- 4:03.28, 2012- 14:41.43, 2013- 4:04.36, 14:42.07, 2:30:40; 2014- 2:26:03, 2015- 14:40.50, 30:49.68; 2016- 14:52.4, 30:26.66; 2017- 15:06.01, 30:40.87; 2018- 2:20:45. pbs: 800m 2:02.89 '10, 1M 4:18.23 '08, 2000m 5:30.19 '09, 3000m 8:25.92 '06; Rd: 15k 49:26 '12, HMar 68:18 '17, 25k 1:23:10 '18, 30k 1:39:42 '18.
Married Taddele Gebrmehden in 2007.

Mamitu DASKA Molisa b. 16 Oct 1983 Liteshoa 1.64m 45kg.
At HMar: AfG: '11- 2, '15- 1. World CC: '09-10-15: 12/8/8.
ETH half marathon record 2015.
Progress at 10,000m, Mar: 20008- 32:45.46, 2009- 31:36.88, 2:26:38; 2010- 2:24:19, 2011- 2:21:59, 2012- 32:54.9A, 2:23:52; 2013- 2:23:23, 2014- 2:29:35, 2015- 30:55.56, 2016- 2:25:27, 2017- 2:28:08. pbs: Road: 5k 14:52 '15, 15k 49:26 '12, 10M 51:54 '14, HMar 66:28 '15, 30k 1:39:46 '11.
Marathon wins: Dubai 2010, Houston 2011, Frankfurt 2011 & 2016; 3rd New York 2017.

Meseret DEFAR b. 19 Nov 1983 Addis Ababa 1.55m 42kg.
At 5000m(/10000m): OG: '04- 1, '08- 2, '12- 1; WCh: '03- h, '05- 2, '07- 1, '09- 3/5, '11- 3/dnf, '13- 1; WJ: '00- 2, '02- 1; AfG: '03- 1, '07- 1; AfCh: '00-06-08-10: 2/1/2/2; WCp: '06- 1. At 3000m: WJ: '02- 1; WY: '99- 2; WI: '03-04-06-08-10-12-16: 3/1/1/1/1/2/2; CCp: '10- 1. Won WAF 3000m 2004-09, 5000m 2005, 2008-09; DL 5000m 2013. World CC: '02- 13J.
Records: World 5000m 2006 & 2007, 2M 2007 (2); indoor 3000m 2007, 2M 2008 (9:10.50) & 2009 (9:06.26), 5000m 2009; African 5000m 2005, Ethiopian 3000m (2) 2006-07. World 5k road best 14:46 Carlsbad 2006.
Progress at 3000m, 5000m, 10000m: 1999- 9:02.08, 33:54.9A; 2000- 8:59.90, 15:08.36; 2001- 8:52.47, 15:08.65; 2002- 8:40.28, 15:26.45; 2003- 8:38.31, 14:40.34; 2004- 8:33.44i/8:36.46, 14:44.81; 2005- 8:30.05i/8:33.57, 14:28.98; 2006- 8:24.66, 14:24.53; 2007- 8:23.72i/8:24.51, 14:16.63; 2008- 8:27.93i/8:34.53, 14:12.88; 2009- 8:26.99i/8:30.15, 14:24.37i/14:36.38, 29:59.20; 2010- 8:24.46i/8:36.09, 14:24.79i/14:38.87; 2011- 8:36.91i/8:50.36+, 14:29.52, 31:05.05; 2012- 8:31.56i/8:46.49, 14:35.85; 2013- 8:30.29, 14:26.90, 30:08.06; 2016- 8:30.83i. pbs: 1500m 4:02.00 '10, 1M: 4:28.5ei '06, 4:33.07+ '07; 2000m 5:34.74i/5:38.0 '06, 2M 8:58.58 '07, road 15k 47:30 '13, HMar 66:09 '13.
Married to Teodros Hailu. IAAF woman athlete of the year 2007. Record nine WAF wins. Record 45 times under 15 mins for 5000m. Daughter Gabriella born on 23 June 2014. In first race since 2013 won at 3000m indoors in 8:30.83 at Boston on 14 Feb 2016.

Worknesh DEGEFA b. 28 Oct 1990 1.59m 42kg.
At HMar: AfG: '15- 2.
Progress at HMar, Mar: 2012- 76:48, 2013- 67:49, 2014- 68:46, 2015- 67:14, 2016- 66:14, 2017- 68:10,

2:22:36; 2018- 2:19:53. pbs: 10k 31:53 '12, 25k 1:23:09 '18, 30k 1:39:41 '18.
Won at Dubai 2017 on marathon debut (4th 2018).

Shure DEMISE Ware b. 21 Jan 1996 Bore 1.59m 45kg.
At 10000m: AfCh: '16- 5. Won ETH 2016. At Mar: WCh: '17- 5. World junior marathon record 2015 (4th on debut at Dubai).
Progress at Mar: 2015- 2:20:59, 2016- 2:25:04, 2017- 2:22:57, 2018- 2:22:07. pbs: 10000m: 32:14.25 '16, 15k 49:22 '14, HMar 68:53 '14.
Won Toronto marathon 2015-16, 2nd Dubai 2017.

Roza DEREJE b. 6 May 1997 1.68m 52kg.
Progress at Mar: 2015- 2:34:02, 2016- 2:26:18, 2017- 2:22:43, 2018- 2:19:17. pbs: Road: 10k 31:43 '17, 15k 47:41 '17, 20k 63:59 '17, HMar 67:23 '17, 25k 1:23:09 '18, 30k 1:39:41 '18.
Marathon wins: Odense 2016, Shanghai 2016-17, Dubai 2018.

Birhane DIBABA b. 11 Sep 1993 Moyagajo 1.59m 44kg.
At Mar: WCh: '17- 10. Progress at Mar: 2012- 2:29:22, 2013- 2:23:01, 2014- 2:22:30, 2015- 2:23:15, 2016- 2:23:16, 2017- 2:21:19, 2018- 2:19:51. pbs: HMar 67:47 '16.
Won Valencia marathon 2012, Tokyo 2015 & 2018; 2nd São Paulo 2012, Nagoya 2013, Tokyo 2014 & 2017; 3rd Frankfurt 2013, Chicago 2014-15.

Genzebe DIBABA b. 8 Feb 1991 Bekoji. Muger Cement. 1.68m 52kg.
At 1500m: OG: '12- h, '16- 2; WCh: '13- 7, '15- 1, '17- 12; WI: '12- 1, '18- 1. At 3000m: CCp: '14- 1; WI: '14-16-18: 1/1/1. At 5000m: WCh: '09 -8, '11- 8, '15- 3; AfCh: '14- 2; WJ: '08- 2, '10- 1; Af-J: '09- 1. World CC: '07-08-09-10-11-17: 5J/1J/1J/11J/ 9/2 MxR. Won DL 5000m 2015, ETH 1500m 2010.
Records: World 1500m 2015, indoor 1500m, 3000m & 2M 2014, 5000m 2015, 1M 2016, 2000m 2017. Two African 1500m 2015. Ethiopian 1500m (3) 2012-15, 2000m 2014.
Progress at 1500m, 5000m: 2007- 15:53.46, 2008- 15:02.41, 2009- 14:55.52, 2010- 4:04.80i/4:06.10, 15:08.06; 2011- 4:05.90, 14:37.56; 2012- 3:57.77, 2013- 3:57.54, 14:37.68; 2014- 3:55.17i/4:01.00, 14:28.88; 2015- 3:50.07, 14:15.41; 2016- 3:56.46i+/ 3:57.31, 2017- 3:57.82, 14:25.22; 2018- 3:57.45i. pbs: 800m 1:59.37 '17, 1000m 2:33.06i '17, 2:35.6+ '15; 1M 4:13.31i/4:14.30 '16, 2000m 5:23.75i '17, 5:27.50 '14; 3000m 8:16.60i/8:26.21 '14, 2M 9:00.48i/ 9:14.28 '14.
Laureus World Sportswomen of the Year 2014, IAAF Woman Athlete of the Year 2015. Younger sister of Ejegayehu (2 OG 10000m 2004, 3 WCh 5000 & 10000m 2005) and Tirunesh Dibaba.

Mare DIBABA Hurssa b. 20 Oct 1989 Sululta, Oromia 1.52m 40kg.
At Mar: OG: '12- 22, '16- 3; WCh: '15- 1, '17- 8. At HMar: AfG: '11- 1. Won AZE 3000m and 5000m 2009.
AZE records (as Mare Ibrahimova) at 3000m, 5000m and HMar 2009.
Progress at HMar, Mar: 2008- 70:28, 2009- 68:45, 2010- 67:13, 2:25:27, 2011- 68:39, 2:23:25; 2012- 67:44, 2:19:52; 2014- 68:56, 2:21:36/2:20:35dh; 2015- 2:19:52, 2016- 67:55, 2:24:09; 2017- 69:43, 2:28:49. pbs: 3000m 9:16.94 '09, 5000m 15:42.83 '09, Road: 10k 31:55+ '10, 15k 48:04+ '10, 10M 51:29+ '10, 20k 63:47+ '10, 30k 1:39:19 '14.
She switched to Azerbaijan in December 2008 but back to Ethiopia as of 1 Feb 2010. Major marathons: won at Xiamen 2014 and 2015, Chicago 2014; 2nd Boston 2014, 3rd Dubai 2012.

Tirunesh DIBABA Kenene b. 1 Oct 1985 Chefa near Bekoji, Arsi region 1.60m 47kg.
At 5000m(/10000m): OG: '04- 3, '08- 1/1, '12- 3/1, '16- (3); WCh: '03- 1, '05- 1/1, '07- (1), '13- (1), '17- (2); WJ: '02- 2; AfG: '03- 4; AfCh: '06- 2, '08- (1), '10- (1). At 3000m: WCp: '06- 1. World CC: '01-02-03-05-06-07-08-10: 5J/2J/1J/1/1/2/1/4; 4k: '03-04-05: 7/2/1. Won WAF 5000m 2006, ETH 4k CC & 5000m 2003. 8k CC 2005.
Records: World 5000m 2008, indoor 5000m 2005 (14:32.93) & 2007, junior 5000m 2003-04, indoor 3000m & 5000m 2004, world road 5k best 14:51 2005, 15k 2009. African 10000m 2008, Ethiopian Mar 2017.
Progress at 5000m, 10000m, Mar: 2002- 14:49.90, 2003- 14:39.94, 2004- 14:30.88, 2005- 14:32.42, 30:15.67; 2006- 14:30.40, 2007- 14:27.42i/14:35.67, 31:55.41; 2008- 14:11.15, 29:54.66; 2009- 14:33.65, 2010- 14:34.07, 31:51.39A; 2012- 14:50.80, 30:20.75; 2013- 14:23.68, 30:26.67; 2014- 2:20:35, 2016- 14:41.73, 29:42.56; 2017- 31:02.69, 2:17:56. pbs: 2000m 5:42.7 '05, 3000m 8:29.55 '06, 2M 9:12.23i '10, road 15k 46:28 '09, 10M 51:49 '16, HMar 66:50 '17, 30k 1:39:14 '14.
In 2003 she became, at 17 years 333 days, the youngest ever world champion at an individual event and in 2005 the first woman to win the 5000m/10000m double (with last laps of 58.19 and 58.4) at a global event after earlier in the year winning both World CC titles. Now has women's record 21 World CC medals. Married Sileshi Sihine on 26 Oct 2008; son Natan Seleshi born 26 Mar 2015. Retained the Olympic 10,000m title and won the Great North Run on half marathon debut in 2012. Third in London on marathon debut 2014, second London and 1st Chicago in 2017. She ran eleven 10,000m track races – and won them all – before her 3rd in the 2016 Ethiopian Trial.

Buze DIRIBA Kejela b. 9 Feb 1994 Arsi 1.60m 43kg.
At 5000m: WCh: '13- 5; WJ: '12- 1. World CC: '11- 10J, '13- 9J
Progress at 5000m, 10000m: 2012- 14:53.06, 2013- 14:50.02, 2014- 15:16.83, 2015- 31:33.27, 2016- 31:38.61. pbs: 1500m 4:10.96 '12, 3000m 8:39.65

'12, 2M 9:29.03i '15, 9:40.01 '14; 10M Rd 51:38 '16, 15kRd 49:41 '17, HMar 66:50 '18.

Etenesh DIRO Neda b. 10 May 1991 Jeidu, Oromiya 1.69m 47kg.
At 3000mSt: OG: '12- 5, '16- 15; WCh: '13- 5, '15- h, '17- 7; AfG: '15- 6; AfCh: '14- 4; AfJ: '09- 2.
Progress at 5000m, 3000mSt: 2011- 15:21.51, 9:49.18, 2012- 15:19.77, 9:14.07, 2013- 9:16.97, 2014- 9:19.71, 2015- 9:29.10, 2016- 14:33.30, 9:16.87; 2017- 14:40.29, 9:13.25. pbs: 3000m 8:38.32 '16, Road: 10k 33:32A '11, 15k 51:21 '09, HMar 71:35 '10.

Axumawit EMBAYE Abraya b. 18 Oct 1994 1.60m 50kg.
At 1500m: WJ: '12- 7; AfCh: '14- 4; WI: '14- 2, '16- 4.
Progress at 1500m: 2012- 4:12.92, 2013- 4:05.16, 2014- 4:02.35, 2015- 4:02.92i/4:03.00, 2016- 4:03.05, 2017- 4:04.95i/4:09.17. pbs: 800m 2:03.27i '15, 2:05.67 '17; 1000m 2:37.43 '15, 1M 4:23.50i/4:26.84 '15, 3000m 8:49.52i '17, 8:51.82 '15.

Letesenbet GIDEY b. 20 Mar 1998 Endameskel, Tigray region 1.63m 48kg.
At 3000m: WY: '15- 4. At 5000m: WCh: '17- 11; World CC: '15- 1J, '17- 1J.
African junior 5000m record 2016.
Progress at 5000m: 2014- 16:19.3A, 2015- 15:39.83, 2016- 14:45.63, 2017- 14:33.32. pbs: 1500m 4:11.11 '17, 3000m 8:41.6 '17.

Amane GOBENA Gemeda b. 1 Sep 1982. 1.63m 48kg.
World 4k CC: '02- 8, '04- 11.
Progress at Mar: 2009- 2:26:53, 2010- 2:24:13, 2011- 2:31:49, 2012- 2:28:38, 2013- 2:23:50, 2014- 2:27:05, 2015- 2:23:30, 2016- 2:21:51, 2017- 2:23:09. pbs: 1500m 4:11.04 '04, 1M 4:41.57 '03, 3000m 9:01.46 '02, 5000m 15:19.50 '04, Road: 10km 31:44 '14, 15km 47:55 '10, HMar 68:16 '09, 30k 1:43:24 '09.
Marathon wins: Toronto 2009, Osaka and Seoul 2010, Xiamen 2011, Santa Monica 2014, Istanbul 2014-15, Mumbai 2018; 2nd Paris 2015, Tokyo 2016 (3rd 2017).

Netsanet GUDETA Kebede b. 12 Feb 1991 Bekoji 1.62m 45kg.
At 10000m: AfG; '15- dnf. At HMar: WCh: '14- 6, '16- 4, '18- 1. World CC: '15- 3.
ETH half marathon record 2015.
Progress at 10000m, HMar: 2014- 68:46, 2015- 31:06.53, 67:31; 2016- 30:36.75, 68:01; 2017- 67:26, 2017- 66:11. pbs: 5000m 15:25.0A '17, Rd: 5k 15:22 '15, 10k 31:35 '17, 15k 47:30 '18, 20k 62:53 '18, Mar 2:29:15 '17.

Yebrqual MELESE b. 18 Apr 1990 1.64m 55kg.
Won ETH 10000m 2015.
Progress at Mar: 2014- 2:26:21, 2015- 2:23:23, 2016- 2:24:49, 2017- 2:23:13, 2018- 2:19:36. pbs: 10000m: 32:40.3A '15, 10k 31:40 '13, HMar 68:21 '15, 25k 1:23:10 '18, 30k 1:39:41 '18.
Marathon wins: Hangzhou 2014, Houston & Prague 2015, 2nd Paris 2014, Chicago 2015; 3rd Dubai 2017-18.

Meselech MELKAMU b. 27 Apr 1985 Debre Markos, Amhara region 1.58m 47kg.
At 5000m(/10000m): OG: '08- 7; WCh: '05- 4, '07- 5, '09- 5/2, '11- (5); AfG: '07- 2, '11- (dnf); AfCh: '06- 6, '08- 1, '10- (2); WJ: '04- 1. At Mar: WCh: '13- dnf. At 3000m: WI: '08- 2. World CC: '03-04-05-06-07-08-09-10-11: 4J/1J/4 & 6/3 & 3/3/9/3/3/4 (17 medals). Won ETH 5000m 2004, 4k CC 2005, CC 2006-07.
African 10000m record 2009.
Progress at 5000m, 10000m, Mar: 2003- 15:27.93, 2004- 15:00.02, 2005- 14:38.97, 2006- 14:37.44, 2007- 14:33.83, 2008- 14:38.78, 31:04.93; 2009- 14:34.17, 29:53.80; 2010- 14:31.91, 31:04.52; 2011- 14:39.44, 30:56.55; 2012- 2:21:01, 2013- 2:25:46, 2014- 2:25:23, 2:21:28dh; 2015- 2:26:45, 2016- 2:21:54. pbs: 1500m 4:07.52 '07, 1M 4:33.94 '03, 2000m 5:39.2i+, 5:46.3+ '07; 3000m 8:23.74i '07, 8:34.73 '05, Road: 10M 53:12 '16, HMar 68:05 '13, 25k 1:23:23 '12, 1:22:27dh '14; 30k 1:39:58 '12, 1:39:21dh '14.
Third fastest ever marathon debut to win at Frankfurt 2012. 2nd Dubai 2014 (3rd 2016), won Daegu 2015, Hamburg & Amsterdam 2016.

Aselefech MERGIA b. 23 Jan 1985 Woliso 1.68m 51kg.
At Mar: OG: '12- 41; WCh: '09- 3, '11- dnf, '17- 12. HMar: WCh: '08- 2. World CC: '08- 16.
Ethiopian marathon record 2012.
Progress at HMar, Mar: 2006- 74:13, 2007- 74:50, 2008- 68:17, 2009- 67:48, 2:25:02; 2010- 67:22, 2:22:38; 2011- 67:21, 2:22:45; 2012- 69:42+, 2:19:31; 2014- 73:49, 2015- 71:42, 2:20:02; 2016- 2:23:57, 2017- 2:23:50. pbs: 1500m 4:14.85 '07, 3000m 8:54.42 '08; Road: 10k 31:25+ '08, 15k 47:53 '09, 20k 63:41 '09, 30k 1:41:52 '09.
2nd Paris Marathon 2009 on debut, won London 2010 (3rd 2017) and Dubai 2011-12 and 2015; 2nd New York 2015. Daughter Sena born July 2013.

Belaynesh OLJIRA Jemane b. 26 Jun 1990 Welek'a, Amhara 1.60m 47kg.
At 10000m: OG: '12- 5; WCh: '13- 3, '15- 9; AfCh: '14- 3. World CC: '11-13-15-17: 10/3/9/8; AfCC: '12- 5. Won ETH 10000m 2011.
Ethiopian 1500m record 2012.
Progress at 10000m, Mar: 2011- 31:17.80, 2012- 30:26.70, 2013- 30:31.44, 2:25:01; 2014- 32:49.39, 2:24:21dh; 2015- 30:53.69, 2016- 30:50.25, 2017- 30:44.57, 2018- 2:24:57. pbs: 1500m 4:33.14 '12, 3000m 8:38.55 '16, 2M 9:23.32 '14, 5000m 14:42.57 '16, Road: 15k 49:08 '14, 10M 52:40 '14, HMar 67:27 '11, 30k 1:39:33dh '14.

Besu SADO Beko b. 12 Jun 1996 1.72m 56kg.
At 1500m: OG: '16- 9; WCh: '15/17- sf; AfG: '15- 2; AfCh: '14- 7; Af-J: '15- 2; won ETH 2014.
Progress at 1500m: 2014- 4:07.59, 2015- 4:00.65, 2016- 3:59.47, 2017- 4:00.98. pbs: 800m 2:02.6A '14, 1000m 2:37.73 '15, 1M 4:39.27i '17.

Dawit SEYAUM Biratu b. 27 Jul 1996 Tumano 1.61m 49kg.
At 1500m: OG: '16- 8; WCh: '15- 4; WJ: '14- 1; WY: '13- 2; AfG: '15- 1; AfCh: '14- 2; Af-J: '13/15- 1; CCp: '14- 3; WI: '16- 2.
Progress at 1500m: 2013- 4:09.00, 2014- 3:59.53, 2015- 3:59.76, 2016- 3:58.09, 2017- 4:00.52. pbs: 1M 4:32.13i '15, 2000m 5:35.46i '15, 3000m 8:37.65i '17.

Feysa TADESE Boru b. 19 Nov 1988 Shirka 1.67m 53kg.
At Mar: WCh: '13- dnf. World HMar: '10- 4, '12- 2; CC: '10- 7.
Progress at Mar: 2009- 2:36:57, 2011- 2:25:20, 2012- 2:23:07, 2013- 2:21:06, 2014- 2:20:27, 2016- 2:25:03, 2017- 2:26:46, 2018- 2:19:30. pbs: 10000m 32:29.07 '10, Road: 10k 32:21 '13, 15k 48:51 '12, 20k 65:41 '12, HMar 68:35 '13, 25k 1:22:58 '14, 30k 1:39:18 '14.
Three wins in nine marathons: Seoul and Shanghai 2012, Paris 2013; 2nd Berlin 2014, Dubai 2018.

Senbere TEFERI Sora b. 3 May 1995 1.59m 45kg. Oromiya.
At 1500m: WCh: '13- h; WJ: '12- 3; WY: '11- 2; At 5000m: OG: '16- 5; WCh: '15- 2, '17- 4; ETH champion 2017; World CC: '15- 2, '17- 10.
Progress at 1500m, 5000m, 10000m: 2011- 16:09.0A, 2012- 15:36.74, 2013- 4:04.55, 16:21.0A, 2014- 4:08.49, 2015- 4:01.86, 14:36:44; 2016- 14:29.82, 30:40.59; 2017- 14:31.76, 30:41.68. pbs: 2000m 5:34.27 '14, 3000m 8:34.32 '15, 10kRd 30:38 '17, 10M Rd 52:51 '16, Mar 2:24:11 '18.

Gudaf TSEGAY Desta b. 23 Jan 1997 1.59m 45kg.
At 1500m: WCh: '17- sf; WJ: '14- 2; WI: '16- 3. At 800m: OG: '16- h.
World junior indoor 1500m record 2016.
Progress at 1500m: 2013- 4:07.27, 2014- 4:02.83, 2015- 4:03.09, 2016- 4:00.18, 2017- 3:59.55. pbs: 800m 1:59.77 '16, 1000m 2:38.05i '17, 1M 4:24.98i '16, 3000m 8:50.74i '17, 15k Rd 15:37 '15.

Tirfi TSEGAYE Beyene b. 25 Nov 1984 Bokoji 1.65m 54kg.
At Mar: OG: '16- 4; WCh: '15- 8. World HMar: '09- 6.
Progress at Mar: 2008- 2:35:32, 2009- 2:28:16, 2010- 2:22:44, 2011- 2:24:12, 2012- 2:21:19, 2013- 2:23:23, 2014- 2:20:18, 2015- 2:23:41, 2016- 2:19:41. pbs: 15k 49:48 '14, HMar 67:42 '12, 30k 1:39:17 '14.
Marathon wins: Porto 2008, Shanghai 2010, Paris 2012, Dubai 2013 & 2016, Tokyo & Berlin 2014. 3rd London 2015, 2nd Boston 2016.

Tigist TUFA Demisse b. 26 Jan 1987 1.55m 40kg.
At Mar: OG: '16- dnf; WCh: '15- 6.
Progress at Mar: 2011- 2:41:50, 2013- 2:29:24, 2014- 2:21:52, 2015- 2:23:22, 2016- 2:23:03. 2017- 2:25:52. pbs: 15k 51:05 '14, HMar 70:03 '08, 25k 1:24:13 '16, 30k 1:41:39 '16.
Marathon wins: Ottawa & Shanghai 2014, London 2015 (2nd 2016); 3rd New York 2015.

Genet YALEW b. 31 Dec 1992 1.46m 46kg. Defense.
At HMar: WCh: '14- 10, '16- 5. World CC: '10-11-13-15: 5J/2J/15/10; AfCC: '12- 8. At 3000m: WJ: '10- 6; WY: '09- 3. At 5000m: Af-J: '11- 3; AfG: '15- 5. At 10000m: AfCh: '14- 4.
Progress at 5000m, 10000m: 2009- 16:25.6A, 2010- 15:03.52, 2011- 15:10.45, 32:05.90; 2012- 14:48.43, 2013- 15:04.38, 2014- 32:45.1A, 2015- 15:43.77, 31:08.82; 2016- 14:51.04, 30:37.38. pbs: 8:49.6 '16, HMar 66:26 '16, Mar 2:27:46 '18.

FINLAND

Governing body: Suomen Urheiluliitto. Founded 1906.

National Championships first held in 1907 (men), 1913 (women). **2017 Champions**: **Men**: 100m/200m: Samuli Samuelsson 10.30/20.73, 400m/800m: Ville Lampinen 48.20/1:50.90, 1500m: Joonas Rinne 4:10.32, 5000m: Robin Ryynänen 14:20.09, 10000m/HMar: Jarkko Järvenpää 29:48.37/65:12, Mar: Jaakko Nieminen 2:23:06, 3000mSt: Topi Raitanen 8:50.32, 110mh: Elmo Lakka 13.82, 400mh: Oskaro Mörö 50.91, HJ: Jesse Huttunen 2.08, PV: Tomas Wecksten 5.35, LJ: Kristian Bäck 7.91w, TJ: Simo Lipsanen 16.82w, SP: Arttu Kangas 19.53, DT: Frantz Kruger 57.35, HT: Heri Liipola 72.71, JT: Tero Pitkämäki 82.80, Dec: Juuso Hassi 7591, 20kW/ 30kW: Aleksi Ojala 1:23:16/2:13:23. **Women**: 100m/200m: Hanna-Maari Latvala 11.59/23.68, 400m: Katri Mustola 54.40, 800m/1500m: Sara Kuivisto 2:03.95/4:14.27, 5000m: Kristiina Mäki 16:03.03, 10000m: Saara Nikander 35:07.08, HMar: Anne-Marie Hyryläinen 74:10, Mar: Paula Tukiainen 2:52:20, 3000mSt: Camilla Richardsson 9:58.36, 100mh: Lotta Harala 13.12w, 400mh: Jonna Berghem 58.05, HJ: Linda Sandblom 1.82, PV: Minna Nikkanen 4.45, LJ: Matilda Bogdanoff 6.09w, TJ: Kristiina Mäkelä 13.77, SP: Kaisa Kymäläinen 15.80, DT: Salla Sipponen 53.27, HT: Krista Tervo 67.18, JT: Jenni Kangas 5933, Hep: Jutta Heikkinen 5747, 10kW/ 20kW: Elisa Neuvonen 46:50/1:36:27.

Tero PITKÄMÄKI b. 19 Dec 1982 Ilmajoki 1.95m 92kg. Nurmon Urheilijat. Electrical engineer.
At JT: OG: '04- 8, '08- 3, '12- 4, '16- dnq 21; WCh: '05-07-09-11-13-15-17: 4/1/5/dnq 17/2/3/5; EC: '06-10-12-14-16: 2/3/11/3/dnq 14; EU23: '03- 3; EJ: '01- 6; ECp: '06- 1, '15- 1. Won WAF 2005, 2007; DL 2015, Finnish 2004-07, 2013, 2016-17.
Progress at JT: 1999- 66.83, 2000- 73.75, 2001- 74.89, 2002- 77.24, 2003- 80.45, 2004- 84.64, 2005- 91.53, 2006- 91.11, 2007- 91.23, 2008- 87.70, 2009- 87.79, 2010- 86.92, 2011- 85.33, 2012- 86.98, 2013- 89.03, 2014- 86.63, 2015- 89.09, 2016- 86.13, 2017- 88.27.

Partner is Niina Kelo (b. 26 Mar 1980) pb Hep 5956 (15 EC 2006).

Antti RUUSKANEN b. 21 Feb 1984 Kokkola 1.89m 86kg. Pielaveden Sampo.
At JT: OG: '12- 2, '16- 6; WCh: '09-11-13-15: 6/9/5/5; EC: '14- 1, '16- 3; EU23: '05- 2; EJ: '03- 3; CCp: '14- 8. Finnish champion 2012, 2014-15.
Progress at JT: 2002- 66.08, 2003- 72.87, 2004- 75.84, 2005- 79.75, 2006- 84.10, 2007- 82.71/ 87.88dh, 2008- 87.33, 2009- 85.39, 2010- 83.45, 2011- 82.29, 2012- 87.79, 2013- 85.70, 2014- 88.01, 2015- 88.98, 2016- 88.23.

David SÖDERBERG b. 11 Aug 1979 Vörå 1.85m 100kg. IF VOM Vöyri.
At HT: OG: '04-12: dnq 21/25, '16- 8; WCh: '07-09-17- dnq 20/18/15, '15- 6; EC: '02-06-10-12: dnq 18/16/13/dnq nt, '14-16: 8/7; EU23: '01- nt; WUG: '03- 3. Finnish champion 2013-16.
Progress at HT: 1997- 58.20, 1998- 61.02, 1999- 64.23, 2000- 68.53, 2001- 72.25, 2002- 76.51, 2003- 78.83, 2004- 75.56, 2005- 76.89, 2006- 75.58, 2007- 77.18, 2008- 75.82, 2009- 75.44, 2010- 76.05, 2011- 77.34, 2012- 77.53, 2013- 75.67, 2014- 77.57, 2015- 76.92, 2016- 77.60, 2017- 75.53.

FRANCE

Governing body: Fédération Française d'Athlétisme. Founded 1920.
National Championships first held in 1888 (men), 1918 (women). **2017 Champions: Men**: 100m: Christophe Lemaitre 10.34, 200m: Jeffrey John 20.66, 400m: Teddy Atine-Venel 45.39, 800m: Paul Renaudie 1:46.72, 1500m: Sofiane Selmouni 3:39.78, 5000m: François Barrer 14:23.12, 10000m: Emmanuel Roudolff-Levisse 29:08.24, HMar: Jean-Damascene Habarurema 63:53, Mar: Freffy Guimard 2:20:10, 3000mSt: Yoann Kowal 8:39.19, 110mh: Aurel Manga 13.41, 400mh: Mamadou Kasse Hann 49.22, HJ: Mickaël Hanany 2.24, PV: Renaud Lavillenie 5.80, LJ: Raihau Maiau 8.22w, TJ: Jean-Marc Pontvianne 17.13w, SP: Fréderíc Dagée 19.70, DT: Jordan Guehaseim 56.64, HT: Quentin Bigot 77.87, JT: Albert Reynolds LCA 78.99, Dec: Jérémy Lelièvre 7843, 5000mW/20kW: Kevin Campion 19:42.14/1:21:08, 50kW: Ugo Andrieu 4:06:42. **Women**: 100m: Carolle Zahi 11.13, 200m: Jennifer Galais 23.82, 400m: Elea Mariama Diarra 51.92, 800m: Noëlie Yarigo BEN 2.02.90, 1500m: Élodie Normand 4:16.56, 5000m: Liv Westphal 16:08.51, 10000m: Perrine Rosala-Humeau 35:47.06, HMar: Fanny Pruvost 74:20, Mar: Corinne Herbreteau 2:38:05, 3000mSt: Maeva Danois 10.01.65, 100mh: Pauline Lett 13.37, 400mh: Maeva Contion 56.56, HJ: Prisca Duvernay 1.87, PV: Marion Lotout 4.30, LJ: Éloyse Lesueur 6.93w, TJ: Jeanine Assani Issouf 14.48w, SP: Jessica Cérival 16.38, DT: Mélina Robert-Michon 63.40, HT: Alexandra Tavernier 64.76, JT: Alexia Kogut-Kobiak 55.90, Hep: Odile Ahouanwanou BEN 5986, 5000mW: Amandine Marcou 23.38.55, 20kW: Eilie Menuet 1:32:00

Dimitri BASCOU b. 20 Jul 1987 Schoelcher, Martinique 1.82m 79kg. Racing Club de France.
At 110mh: OG: '12- sf, '16- 3; WCh: '09/11- sf, '15- 5; EC: '10- 4, 14- dq, '16- 1; EU23: '07- h, '09- 4; EJ: '05- h; won FRA 2009-11, 2016. At 60mh: WI: '16- 3; EI: '11- 6, '15- 2.
Progress at 110mh: 2004- 14.61w, 2005- 14.35, 2006- 14.24, 2007- 13.76, 2008- 13.61/13.39w, 2009- 13.49, 2010- 13.41, 2011- 13.37/13.26w, 2012- 13.34, 2013- 13.51, 2014- 13.25, 2015- 13.16, 2016- 13.12/13.05w, 2017-13.55. pbs: 60m 6.88i '14, 100m 10.72 '07, 200m 21.62 '09, 50mh 6.57i '12, 60mh 7.41i '16.
Disqualified for obstruction after finishing 3rd at the 2014 Europeans.

Wilhem BÉLOCIAN b. 22 Jun 1995 les Abymes, Guadeloupe 1.78m 78kg. Stade Lamertin.
At 110mh: OG: '16- h; EC: '16- 3; WJ: '12- 3, '14- 1; WY: '11- 3 (3 Med R); EJ: '13- 1; At 60mh: EI: '15- 3. World junior record 99cm 110mh 12.99 in 2014, three European JR 2014-14.
Progress at 110mh: 2014- 13.54, 2015- 13.28, 2016- 13.25/13.15w, 2017- 13.89. pbs: 60m 6.82i '12, 100m 10.61 '16, 60mh 7.52i '15.

Quentin BIGOT b. 1 Dec 1992 Hayange 1.78m 95kg. Athlétisme Metz Metropole..
At HT: OG: '12- dnq 24; WCh: '13- dnq 13, '17- 4; EC: '12- dnq 24; WJ: '10- 7; WY: '09- dnq 13; EU23: '13- 3; EJ: '11- 1. FRA champion 2017.
Progress at HT: 2010- 64.81, 2011- 72.71, 2012- 78.28, 2013- 76.97, 2014- 78.58, 2016- 76.10, 2017- 77.87. 2-years drugs ban 2014-16.

Pierre-Ambroise BOSSE b. 11 May 1992 Nantes 1.85m 68kg. UA Gujan Mestras.
At 800m: OG: '12- sf, '16- 4; WCh: '13- 7, '15- 5, '17- 1; EC: '12-14-16: 3/8/5; WJ: '10- 8; EU23: '13- 1; EJ: '11- 1; ET: 15- 2; French champion 2012, 2014-15.
French 800m and European U23 1000m records 2014; European 600m record 2016.
Progress at 800m: 2007- 2:02.81, 2008- 1:56.05, 2010- 1:48.38, 2011- 1:46.18, 2012- 1:44.97, 2013- 1:43.76, 2014- 1:42.53, 2015- 1:43.88, 2016- 1:43.41, 2017- 1:44.67. pbs: 400m 47.80 '17, 600m 1:13.21 '16, 1000m 2:15.31 '14, 1500m 3:54.81 '09.
Real name Bossé, but has dropped the accent.

Axel CHAPELLE b. 24 Apr 1995 1.82m 77kg. Ea Cergy Pontoise Athlétisme.
At PV: WCh: '17- 6; WJ: '12- dnq 15, '14- 1; EU23: '15- 10=, '17- 2; EJ: '13- 2; EI: '17- 6.
Progress at PV: 2009- 3.90, 2010- 4.25. 2011- 4.90i/4.75, 2012- 5.12, 2013- 5.35i/5.32, 2014- 5.55, 2015- 5.55, 2016- 5.65, 2017- 5.80i/5.72, 2018- 5.88i.

Garfield DARIEN b. 22 Dec 1987 Lyon 1.87m 76kg. EA Chambéry.
At 110mh: OG: '12- sf; WCh: '09- sf, '15- 8, '17- 4; EC: '10- 2, '12- 2; WJ: '04- 7; EJ: '05- 1; CCp: '10- 4;

ET: '11- 2; French champion 2012, 2015. At 60mh: WI: '14- 3; EI: '09-11-17: 6/2/4.
Progress at 110mh: 2004- 14.03/13.98w, 2005- 13.73, 2006- 13.94/13.92w, 2008- 13.50/13.43w, 2009- 13.36, 2010- 13.34, 2011- 13.37, 2012- 13.15, 2013- 14.47, 2014- 14.01, 2015- 13.17, 2017- 13.09. pbs: 200m 22.05 '06, 60mh 7.47i '14, HJ 1.83 '04.
Father Daniel Darien had 110mh pb 13.76 '87.

Yohann DINIZ b. 1 Jan 1978 Epernay 1.85m 69kg. EFS Reims Athlétisme.
At 20kW: ECp: '07- 1, '15- 3; At 50kW: OG: '08- dnf, '12- dq, '16- 8; WCh: '05-07-09-11-13-17: dq/2/11/dq/10/1; EC: '06-10-14: 1/1/1; ECp: '05-13: 4/1. Won French 10000mW 2010, 2012, 2014; 20kW 2007-09, 2015; 50kW 2005, 2016.
World walks records: track 50,000m 2011, road 50k 2014, 20k 2015. French records 5000mW (3) 2006-08, 10000mW 2014, 20000mW 2014, 20kW (4) 2005-15, 50kW 2006 & 2009, 1 Hr 2010.
Progress at 20kW, 50kW: 2001- 1:35:05.0t, 2002- 1:30:40, 2003- 1:26:54.99t, 2004- 1:24:25, 3:52:11.0t; 2005- 1:20:20, 3:45:17; 2006- 1:23:19, 3:41:39; 2007- 1:18:58, 3:44:22; 2008- 1:22:31, 2009- 1:22:50, 3:38:45; 2010- 1:20:23, 3:40:37; 2011- 3:35:27.2t, 2012- 1:17:43, 2013- 1:23:17, 3:41:07; 2014- 1:19:42.1t, 3:32:33; 2015- 1:17:02, 2016- 3:37:48, 2017- 1:27:19, 3:33:12. pbs: 3000mW 10:52.44 '08, 5000mW 18:16.76i '14, 18:18.01 '08; 10000mW 38:08.13 '14, 20000mW 1:19:42.1 '14, 1HrW 15,395m '10, 35kW 2:32:24 '12.

Yoann KOWAL b. 28 May 1987 Nogent-le-Rotrou 1.72m 58kg. E. Périgueux Sarlat Trélissac.
At 1500m: OG: '12- sf; WCh: '09- h, '11- sf; EC: '10- 5; EU23: '09- 6; ET: '09- 3; EI: '09- 3. At 3000m: EI: '13- 4. At 3000mSt: OG: '16- 5; WCh: '13-15-17: 8/h/13; EC: '14- 1, '16- 3; WJ: '06- h; EU23: '07- 11; ET: '13- 3, '14- 1. Won FRA 1500m 2008, 2010; 3000mSt 2014-15, 2017.
Progress at 3000mSt: 2006- 8:56.54, 2007- 8:36.11, 2008- 8:34.66, 2009- 9:02.38, 2011- 8:41.07, 2012- 8:21.66, 2013- 8:12.53, 2014- 8:25.50, 2015- 8:18.38, 2016- 8:16.21, 2017- 8:15.60. pbs: 800m 1:47.95 '10, 1000m 2:20.43 '10, 1500m 3:33.75 '11, 2000m 5:04.18 '13, 3000m 7:44.26i '12, 7:45.11 '16; 5000m 14:40.02 '06, 10k Rd 29:01 '11.

Renaud LAVILLENIE b. 18 Sep 1986 Barbezieux-Saint-Hilaire 1.77m 69kg. Clermont Athl. Auvergne.
At PV: OG: '12- 1, '16- 2; WCh: '09-11-13-15-17: 3/3/2/3=/3; WI: '12-16-18- 1/1/1; EC: '10-12-14-16: 1/1/1/nh; EU23: '07- 10; EI: '09-11-13-15: 1/1/1/1; CCp: '10- 2, '14- 1; ET: '09-10-13-14-15-17: 1/1/1/1/1/1. Won DL 2010-16, French 2010, 2012-15, 2017.
World indoor pole vault record 2014. French record (indoors) 2011 and outdoors 2013.
Progress at PV: 2002- 3.40, 2003- 4.30, 2004- 4.60, 2005- 4.81i/4.70, 2006- 5.25i/5.22, 2007- 5.58i/5.45, 2008- 5.81i/5.65, 2009- 6.01, 2010- 5.94, 2011- 6.03i/5.90, 2012- 5.97, 2013- 6.02, 2014- 6.16i/5.93, 2015- 6.05, 2016- 6.03i/5.98, 2017- 5.91, 2018- 5.93i. pbs: 60m 7.23i '08, 100m 11.04 '11, 60mh 8.41i '08, 100m 11.04 '11, 110mh 14.51 '10, HJ 1.89i '08, 1.87 '07; LJ 7.31 '10, Hep 5363i '08.
Broke Sergey Bubka's 21 year-old absolute world pole vault record indoors in 2014. 23 successive wins 31 Aug 2013 to EC 2014, only man to win all seven Diamond League titles from 2010. IAAF Male Athlete of the Year 2014.
His brother **Valentin** (b. 16 Jul 1991) has PV pb 5.80i '15, 5.71 '16; 3rd EU23 and nh WCh in 2013; 6 EI '15, dnq 14 WCh '17.

Christophe LEMAITRE b. 11 Jun 1990 Annecy 1.89m 74kg. AS Aix-les-Bains.
At 100m/(200m): OG: '12- (6)/3R, '16- sf/3; WCh: '09- qf, '11- 4/3/2R, '13- 7, '15- sf/sf;, '17)sf) EC: '10- 1/1/1R, '12- 1/3R, '14- 2/2/3R; WJ: '08- (1); WY: '07- 4/5; EJ: '09- 1; CCp: '10- 1, '14- 5/4/2R; ET: '10- 2, '11- 1/1, '13- (1), '15- 1/2R. At 60m: EI: '11- 3. Won French 100m 2010-12, 2014, 2017; 200m 2010-15.
Records: European 4x200m 2014; French 100m (7) 2010-11, 200m (2) 2010-11, European junior 100m 2009. U23 100m 2010-11, 200m 2011.
Progress at 100m, 200m: 2005- 11.46, 2006- 10.96, 2007- 10.53, 21.08; 2008- 10.26, 20.83; 2009- 10.04/10.03w, 20.68; 2010- 9.97, 20.16; 2011- 9.92, 19.80; 2012- 10.04/9.94w, 19.91; 2013- 10.00/9.98w, 20.07; 2014- 10.10, 20.08; 2015- 10.07, 20.21; 2016- 10.07, 20.01; 2017- 10.18, 20.21. pbs: 60m 6.55i '10, 150m St 14.90 '13.
First Caucasian sub-10.00 100m runner and first to win sprint treble at European Champs; now has men's record eight EC medals.

Pascal MARTINOT-LAGARDE b. 22 Sep 1991 St Maur-des-Fossés 1.90m 80kg. Neuilly Plaisance Sport.
At 110mh: OG: '16- 4; WCh: '13- h, '15- 4; EC: '14- 3; WJ: '10- 1; EU23: '11- h; EJ: '09- 4; ET: '13-14-15: 2/3/2; won DL 2014, FRA 2014. At 60mh: WI: '12-14-16-18: 3/2/2/5; EI: '13-15-17: 3/1/2.
French 110m hurdles record 2014.
Progress at 110mh: 2008- 15.03, 2009- 14.13, 2010- 13.74, 2011- 13.94, 2012- 13.41/13.30w, 2013- 13.12, 2014- 12.95, 2015- 13.06, 2016- 13.12. pbs: 60m 7.07i '10, 100m 10.94 '13, 60mh 7.45i '14.
His brother **Thomas** (b. 7 Feb 1988) has 110mh pb 13.26, 7 WCh and French champion in 2013.

Kevin MAYER b. 10 Feb 1992 Argenteuil 1.86m 77kg. EA Tain-Tournon.
At Dec: OG: '12- 15, '16- 2; WCh: '13- 4, '17- 1; EC: '12- dnf, '14- 2; WJ: '10- 1; EJ: '11- 1; ECp: '13- 1. At Oct: WY: '09- 1. At Hep: WI: '18- 1; EI: '13- 2, '17- 1.
Records: European indoor heptathlon 2017, French decathlon 2016.
Progress at Dec: 2011- 7992, 2012- 8447w/8415, 2013- 8446, 2014- 8521, 2015- 8469, 2016- 8834, 2017- 8768. pbs: 60m 6.85i '18, 100m 10.70 '17, 200m 21.76 '17, 400m 48.28 '16, 1000m 2:37.30i '13, 1500m 4:18.04 '12, 60mh 7.79i '18, 110mh 13.75 '17, 400mh 54.57 '17, HJ 2.10i '10, 2.09 '12;

PV 5.60i '18, 5.40 '18; LJ 7.65 '14, SP 15.97i/15.76 '16, DT 50.13 '17, JT 70.54 '17, Hep 6479i '17.
Four individual event pbs when adding 313 points to his decathlon best for 2016 OG silver.

Mahiédine MEKHISSI-BENABBAD b. 15 Mar 1985 Reims 1.90m 75kg. EFS Reims.
At 3000mSt: OG: '08- 2, '12- 2, '16- 3; WCh: '07/09- h, '11- 3, '13- 3, '17- 4 (h 1500m); EC: '10-12-14-16: 1/1,dq (1 1500m)/1; WJ: '04- h; EU23: '05- h, '07- 1; CCp: '10- 3; ET: '07-08-17: 2/1/1. At 1500m: WI: '10- 8; EI: '13- 1; WCp: '06- 7, '14- 3. Won FRA 1500m 2014, 3000mSt 2008, 2012-13, 2016.
Records: World best 2000m steeplechase 2010. European 3000mSt 2013, French 1M 2014.
Progress at 3000mSt: 2003- 9:52.07, 2004- 9:01.01, 2005- 8:34.45, 2006- 8:28.25, 2007- 8:14.22, 2008- 8:08.95, 2009- 8:06.98, 2010- 8:02.52, 2011- 8:02.09, 2012- 8:10.90, 2013- 8:00.09, 2014- 8:03.23, 2016- 8:08.15, 2017- 8:14.67. pbs: 800m 1:53.61 '04, 1000m 2:17.14 '09, 1500m 3:33.12 '13, 1M 3:51.55 '14, 2000m 4:56.85 '13, 3000m 7:43.72i '13, 7:44.98 '10; 5000m 14:32.9 '05, 2000mSt 5:10.68 '10.
Disqualified after he took his vest off in the finishing straight when finishing well clear in 2014 EC steeplechase.

Kévin MENALDO b. 12 Jul 1992 Bordeaux 1.76m 66kg. E. Franconville Cesame Val d'Oise.
At PV: OG: '16- dnq 16=; WCh: '15- 6, '17- dnq 22=; EC: '14- 3=, '16- nh; WY: '09- 7; EU23: '13- dnq 15; EJ: '11- 2.
Progress at PV: 2007- 4.15i/4.00, 2008- 4.71, 2009- 5.05, 2010- 5.10i/5.05, 2011- 5.50, 2012- 5.43i/5.40, 2013- 5.65i/5.60, 2014- 5.75i/5.72, 2015- 5.81, 2016- 5.80. 2017- 5.83, 2018- 5.88i.

Teddy TAMGHO b. 15 Jun 1989 Paris 1.87m 82kg. Bordeaux
At TJ: WCh: '09- 11, '13- 1; EC: '10- 3; WI: '10- 1; WJ: '08- 1; EJ: '07- 4; EI: '11- 1 (4 LJ); ET: '10- 3, '13- 2. Won DL 2010, French 2009-10, 2013, 2016.
Four World indoor triple jump records 2010 (17.90) & 2011, four absolute French records 2009-13; three Eur U23 records 2010.
Progress at TJ: 2004- 12.56, 2005- 14.89, 2006- 15.58, 2007- 16.53i/16.35/16.42w, 2008- 17.19/ 17.33w, 2009- 17.58i/17.11, 2010- 17.98, 2011- 17.92i/ 17.91, 2013- 18.04, 2015- 17.24, 2016- 17.15. pbs: 60m 6.92i '06, 100m 10.60 '09, LJ 8.01i '11, 7.81 '13.
2011 season ended when broke ankle in warm-up for European U23s and also missed all of 2012. His 18.04 to win 2013 World title was third best ever and world's best for 17 years. Fractured his shin in November 2013 and missed all the 2014 season.

Jimmy VICAUT b. 27 Feb 1992 Bondy 1.88m 83kg. SCO Sainte-Marguerite de Marseille.
At 100m/(200m)/4x100mR: OG: '12- sf/3R, '16- 7; WCh: '11- 6/2R, '13- sf/sf, '15- 8, '17- 6; EC: '10- 1R, '12- 2/3R (res), '14- sf, '16- 3/2R; WJ: '10- 3; WY: '09- 7; EJ: '11- 1/1R; ET: '13- 1, '14- 1. At 60m: EI: '13- 1. Won French 100m 2013, 2015-16; 200m 2016.
Equalled European 100m record 2015.
Progress at 100m: 2005- 13.0, 2006- 12.50, 2007- 11.0, 2008- 10.75/10.69w, 2009- 10.56, 2010- 10.16, 2011- 10.07, 2012- 10.02, 2013- 9.95, 2014- 9.95/9.89w, 2015- 9.86, 2016- 9.86, 2017- 9.97. pbs: 60m 6.48i '13, 200m 20.30 '13.
His brother Willi was French U17 shot champion in 2012 and has senior pb of 17.33 '14.

Women

Cindy BILLAUD b. 11 Mar 1986 Coulommiers 1.65m 59kg. Athlé Sud 77.
At 100mh: OG: '16- sf; WCh: '09-11-13-15: sf/h/7/h; EC: '14- 2, '16- 7; WJ: '04- sf; EU23: '07- sf; EJ: '05- 3; ET: '14- 1; FRA champion 2013-16. At 60mh: WI: '14- 4; EI: '09- 7.
French 100mh record 2014.
Progress at 100mh: 2004- 13.48, 2005- 13.57, 2006- 13.49/13.46w, 2007- 13.25, 2008- 12.99/12.97w, 2009- 12.97, 2010- 13.11, 2011- 12.93, 2012- 12.97, 2013- 12.59, 2014- 12.56, 2015- 12.83, 2016- 12.83. pbs: 60m 7.64i '08, 100m 12.00 '05, 200m 24.68 '08, 50mh 7.14+i '12, 60mh 7.87i '14.
Had a baby in 2017.

Floria GUEI b. 2 May 1990 Nantes 1.68m 53kg. E.Sud Lyonnais.
At 400m: OG: '16- sf; WCh: '11- hR, 13- sf/3R, '15- sf; EC: '12- 2R, '14- sf/1R, '16- 2/2R; WJ: '08- h; EU23: '11- h/3R; EI: '11- 3R, '15- 1R, '17- 1; ET: '15- 1. French champion 2013, 2015-16.
Progress at 400m: 2008- 54.08, 2009- 52.90, 2010- 53.00, 2011- 52.77, 2012- 51.96, 2013- 51.42, 2014- 51.30, 2015- 50.89, 2016- 50.84, 2017- 51.51. Pbs: 50m 6.62i '09, 60m 7.56i '17, 100m 11.82 '09, 200m 23.00 '16, 300m 36.46i '16.
Brilliant anchor 400m legs including 49.71 at '14 EC, 49.95 at '15 WCh and 49.92 '16 EC.

Rénelle LAMOTE b. 26 Dec 1993 Annecy 1.68m 57kg. Annecy Haute Savoie.
At 800m: OG: '16- h; WCh: '15- 8; EC: '14- sf, '16- 2; WJ: '12- sf; EU23: '13- h, 15- 1; ET: '14- 2, '15- 1. French champion 2014, 2016.
Progress at 800m: 2009- 2:18.24, 2010- 2:14.53, 2011- 2:08.39, 2012- 2:05.23, 2013- 2:02.40, 2014- 2:00.06, 2015- 1:58.86, 2016- 1:58.01. Pbs: 400m 53.92 '16, 1500m 4:35.93 '13, 10k Rd 37:13 '14.

Antoinette NANA DJIMOU Ida b. 2 Aug 1985 Douala, Cameroon 1.74m 69kg. CA Montreuil.
At Hep: OG: '08- 17, '12- 4, '16- 11; WCh: '07-09-11-13-17: dnf/7/6/8/16; EC: '06-10-12-14-16: 21/ dnf/1/1/2; WJ: '04- 4; EU23: '05- 5, '07- 7; ECp: '08- 2, '14- 2. At Pen: WI: '10- 4; EI: '09-11-13-15: 3/1/1/5. Won French LJ 2008, Hep 2006-07.
CMR heptathlon record 2003, French indoor pentathlon record 2011.
Progress at Hep: 2003- 5360, 2004- 5649, 2005- 6089w/5792, 2006- 5981, 2007- 5982, 2008- 6204, 2009- 6323, 2010- 5994, 2011- 6409, 2012- 6576, 2013- 6326, 2014- 6551, 2016- 6458, 2017- 6311.

pbs: 60m 7.51i '11, 100m 11.78 '08, 200m 24.36 '11, 800m 2:15.22 '14, 60mh 8.11i '10, 100mh 12.96 '12, HJ 1.84i '10, 1.83 '11; LJ 6.44i '09, 6.43 '16, 6.61w '08; SP 16.17 '16, JT 57.27 '12, Pen 4723i '11.
Came to France at age 14, naturalised French citizen in 2004. Three pbs when winning European gold in 2012. Won IAAF CE Challenge 2012.

Mélina ROBERT-MICHON b. 18 Jul 1979 Voiron 1.80m 85kg. Lyon Athlétisme
At DT: OG: '00/04- dnq 29/30, '08- 7, '12- 5, '16- 2; WCh: '01-03-07-09-13-15-17: dnq 20/11/11/8/ 2/10/3; EC: '98-02-06-12-14-16: dnq 29/12/dnq 16/6/2/5; WJ: '98- 2; EU23: '99-12, '01- 1; WUG: '01- 3; CCp: '14- 4; ECp: '00-01-02-03-04-06-07-08-09-13-14-15-17: 5/6/8/2/4/7/5/4/2/1/1/1/1. French champion 2000-09, 2011-17; MedG 2009. Six French discus records 2000-16.
Progress at DT: 1997- 49.10, 1998- 59.27, 1999- 60.17, 2000- 63.19/63.61dh, 2001- 63.87, 2002- 65.78, 2003- 64.27, 2004- 64.54, 2005- 58.01, 2006- 59.89, 2007- 63.48, 2008- 62.21, 2009- 63.04, 2010- 56.52, 2011- 61.07, 2012- 63.98, 2013- 66.28, 2014- 65.51, 2015- 65.04, 2016- 66.73, 2017- 66.21. pbs: SP 15.23 '07, HT 47.92 '02.
Daughter Elyssa born in 2010, expecting second child in 2018. Broke her 11 year-old French record in winning 2013 World silver.

Alexandra TAVERNIER b. 13 Dec 1993 Annecy 1.70m 82kg. Annecy Haute Savoie.
At HT: OG: '16- 11; WCh: '15- 3, '17- 12; EC: '14- 6, '16- dnq; WJ: '12- 1; EU23: '15- 1; EJ: '11- 6; ET: '15- 3. French champion 2014, 2016-17.
Progress at HT: 2009- 44.96, 2010- 58.44, 2011- 62.13, 2012- 70.62, 2013- 70.79, 2014- 71.17, 2015- 74.39, 2016- 72.16, 2017- 72.69. Pbs: SP 11.81 '14, DT 41.58 '10.

GERMANY

Governing body: Deutscher Leichtathletik Verband (DLV). Founded 1898.
National Championships first held in 1891. **2017 Champions**: **Men:** 100m/200m: Julian Reus 10.10/20.29, 400m: Johannes Trefz 45.81, 800m: Benedikt Huber 1:48.21, 1500m: Timo Benitz 3:38.77, 5000m: Richard Ringer 14:15.90, 10000m: Simon Boch 29:13.60; HMar: Philipp Baar 64:57, Mar: Arne Gabius 2:09:59, 3000mSt: Tim Stegemann 8:43.40, 110mh: Matthias Bühler 13.50, 400mh: Luke Campbell 49.40, HJ: Mateusz Przybylko 2.30, PV: Bo Kanda Lita Baehre 5.60, LJ: Julian Howard 8.15, TJ: Max Hess 17.24w, SP: David Storl 20.98, DT: Robert Harting 65.65, HT: Alexander Ziegler 71.66, JT: Johannes Vetter 89.35, Dec: Felix Hepperle 7441, 20kW: Christopher Linke 1:20:26, 50kW: Nathaniel Seiler 4:00:43. **Women**: 100m: Gina Lückenkemper 11.10, 200m: Laura Müller 22.65, 400m: Ruth Sophia Spelmeyer 51.84, 800m: Christina Hering 2:04.05, 1500m: Konstanze Klosterhalfen 3:59.58, 5000m/3000mSt: Gesa-Felicitas Krause 16:20.10/9:25.81, 10000m/HMar: Sabrina Mockenhaupt 33:08.42/70:54, Mar: Katharina Heinig 2:29:29, 100mh: Pamela Dutkiewicz 12.82, 400mh: Djamila Böhm 56.92, HJ: Marie-Laurence Jungfleisch 1.94, PV: Lisa Ryzih 4.70, LJ: Claudia Salman-Rath 6.72, TJ: Kristin Gierisch 14.40, SP: Sara Gambetta 17.38, DT: Julia Harting 63.63, HT: Carolin Paesler 69.51, JT: Katharina Molitor 61.16, Hep: Mareike Arndt 5765, 20kW: Emilia Lehmeyer 1:36:20.

Arthur ABELE b. 30 Jul 1986 Mutlangen, Baden-Württemberg 1.84m 80kg. SSV Ulm 1846.
At Dec: OG: '08- dnf, '16- 15; WCh: '07- 9; EC: '14- 5; WJ: '04- 7; EJ: '05- 2; ECp: '04- 4. German champion 2013. At Hep: '15- 2.
Progress at Dec: 2006- 8012, 2007- 8269, 2008- 8372, 2013- 8251, 2014- 8477, 2016- 8605, 2017- dnf. pbs: 60m 6.93i '15, 100m 10.67 '14, 200m 22.41 '14, 400m 47.98 '08, 1000m 2:35.64i '15, 1500m 4:15.35 '08, 60mh 7.67i '15, 110mh 13.55 '14, 400mh 51.71 '04, HJ 2.04 '07, PV 5.01 '14, LJ 7.57 '16. SP 15.79 '16, DT 46.20 '16, JT 71.89 '16, Hep 6279i '15.
Five individual event absolute bests in 2015 European Indoor heptathlon, but Achilles injury cost him the summer season.

Rico FREIMUTH b. 14 Mar 1988 Potsdam 1.96m 92kg. SV Halle.
At Dec: OG: '12- 6, '16- dnf; WCh: '11-13-15-17: dnf/7/3/2; EC: '14- 7; EU23: '09- 10; EJ: '07- 3.
Progress at Dec: 2009- 7689, 2010- 7826, 2011- 8287, 2012- 8322, 2013- 8488w/8382, 2014- 8356, 2015- 8561, 2017- 8663. pbs: 60m 6.98i '12, 100m 10.40 '14, 10.36w '13; 200m 21.39 '12, 400m 47.51 '12, 1000m 2:48.22i '12, 1500m 4:34.60 '13, 60mh 7.83i '14, 110mh 13.63 '14, HJ 2.01 '17, PV 4.90 '12, LJ 7.60 '17, SP 15.62 '15, DT 51.56 '17, JT 65.04 '11, Hep 5715i '12.
Won IAAF Combined Events Challenge 2014, 2017. His father Uwe had decathlon best of 8794 (1984), and was 4th at 1983 Worlds and 1986 Europeans and twice winner at Götzis. Uwe and Rico are the highest scoring father-son combination. His uncle Jörg won the high jump bronze medal at the 1980 Olympic Games in a pb of 2.31.

Christoph HARTING b. 4 Oct 1990 Cottbus 2.07m 120kg. SCC Berlin. Police officer.
At DT: OG: '16- 1; WCh: '13- dnq 13, '15- 8; EC: '16- 4; EU23: '11- 5. German champion 2015.
Progress at DT: 2008- 52.00, 2009- 50.19, 2010- 61.19, 2011- 62.12, 2012- 61.22, 2013- 64.99, 2014- 63.78, 2015- 67.93, 2016- 68.37, 2017- 64.55. pb SP 17.75 '12.
The Hartings are the first siblings to win the same individual event in the history of the Summer Olympics.

Robert HARTING b. 18 Oct 1984 Cottbus 2.01m 127kg. SCC Berlin.

At DT: OG: 08- 4, '12- 1, '16- dnq 15; WCh: '07-09-11-13-17: 2/1/1/1/6; ECh: '06-10-12-14: dnq 13/2/1/1; CCp: '10- 1; ECp: '07-08-09-10-11-13-14-17: 2/2/2/1/1/1/1/1; WJ: '02- dnq 13; WY: '01- 2; EU23: '05- 1. GER champion 2007-14, 2016-17.
Progress at DT: 2002- 54.25, 2003- 59.54, 2004-64.05, 2005- 66.02, 2006- 65.22, 2007- 66.93, 2008-68.65, 2009- 69.43, 2010- 69.69, 2011- 68.99, 2012-70.66, 2013- 69.91, 2014- 68.47, 2016- 68.04, 2017-66.30. pb SP 18.63 '07.
35 successive wins 2011-13. Brother of Christoph (qv). His father Gert had pbs SP 16.05, DT 42.80 '88, and mother Bettina SP 15.04 and DT 43.06 '80. Married Julia Fischer (qv) on 17 Sep 2016.

Max HESS b. 13 Jul 1996 Chemnitz 1.86m 79kg. LAC Erdgas Chemnitz.
At TJ: OG: '16- dnq 15; EC: '16- 1; WJ: '14- 2; WY: '13- 8; EU23: '17- 3; WI: '16- 2; EI: '17- 3; ET: 17- 1. GER champion 2016-17.
Progress at TJ: 2012- 14.58, 2013- 15.52, 2014-16.55, 2015- 16.34i/16.07, 2016- 17.20, 2017- 17.52i/17.13/17.24w. pbs: 60m 6.93i '18, LJ 8.03i '16.

Andreas HOFMANN b. 16 Dec 1991 Heidelberg 1.95m 108kg. MTG Mannheim. Sports student.
At JT: WCh: '15- 6, '17- 8; EC: '14- 9; EJ: '09- 1; WUG: '17- 2; ET: '14- 1.
Progress at JT: 2008- 65.03, 2009- 77.84, 2010-66.75, 2011- 73.98, 2012- 80.81, 2013- 75.56, 2014-86.13, 2015- 86.14, 2016- 85.42, 2017- 91.07. pb SP 18.59i '17.

Raphael HOLZDEPPE b. 28 Sep 1989 Kaiserslautern 1.83m 77kg. LAZ Zweibrücken.
At PV: OG: 08- 7, '12- 3, '16- dnq 26; WCh: '11-13-15-17: dnq 20/1/2/nh; EC '10- 9, '12- 3; WJ: '06- 5, '08- 1; EU23: '09- 1, '11- 6; EJ: '07- dnq; ET: '15- 2; WI: '18- 5=; EI: '13- 8, '17- 5. GER champion 2015. World junior pole vault record (=) 2008 (and indoors 5.68).
Progress at PV: 2002- 3.45, 2003- 4.25, 2004- 4.50, 2005- 5.00, 2006- 5.42, 2007- 5.50, 2008- 5.80, 2009- 5.65, 2010- 5.80, 2011- 5.72, 2012- 5.91, 2013-5.91, 2014- 5.53, 2015- 5.94, 2016- 5.84i/5.70, 2017-5.80, 2018- 5.88i.

Daniel JASINSKI b. 5 Aug 1989 Bochum 2.07m 125kg. TV Wattenscheid.
At DT: OG: '16- 3; WCh: '15- dnq 15; EC: '14- 7, '16- 8; WJ: '08- dnq 24; EU23: '11- 6.
Progress at DT: 2008- 49.15, 2009- 55.01, 2010-59.02, 2011- 61.28, 2012- 64.37, 2013- 64.69, 2014-65.98, 2015- 65.93, 2016- 67.16, 2017- 62.20.

Kai KAZMIREK b. 28 Jan 1991 Torgau 1.89m 91kg. LG Rhein-Wied.
At Dec: OG: '16- 4; WCh: '15- 6, '17- 3; EC: '14- 6; WJ: '10- 6; EU23: '11- 6, '13- 1; EJ: '09- 3. German champion 2012. At Hep: WI: '14- 6, '18- 4.
Progress at Dec: 2011- 7802, 2012- 8130, 2013-8366, 2014- 8471, 2015- 8462, 2016- 8580, 2017-8488. pbs: 60m 7.01i '15, 100m 10.62 '16, 10.61w '13; 200m 21.40 '12, 400m 46.75 '11, 1000m 2:39.51i '14, 1500m 4:31.25 '16, 60mh 7.95i '18, 110mh 14.05 '14, HJ 2.15 '14, PV 5.20 '13, LJ 7.69 '16, SP 14.82 '17, DT 45.83 '15, JT 64.60 '16, Hep 6238i '18.
Won Götzis decathlon 2015, IAAF Combined Events Challenge 2016.

Christopher LINKE b. 24 Oct 1988 Potsdam 1.91m 66kg. SC Potsdam
At 20kW/(50kW): OG: '12- (21), '16- 5; WCh: '11-13-15'17: 17/9/38/5; EC: '10- (dnf), '14- 5; EU23: '09- 4; WCp: '12- (3), '16- 10; ECp: '11-13-15-17: (3)/10/7/1. At 10000mW: EJ: '07- 6. Won GER 10000W 2011, 2014-16, 20kW 2012, 2014, 2016-17; 50kW 2008.
Progress at 20kW, 50kW: 2008- 1:25:25, 4:03:59; 2009- 1:24:29, 2010- 1:27:25, 3:53:24; 2011- 1:20:51, 3:52:56; 2012- 1:20:41, 3:47:33; 2013- 1:22:36, 2014-1:21:00, 2015- 1:20:37, 2016- 1:19:19, 2017- 1:18:59. pbs: 3000mW 10:49.33i '18, 11:49.10A '10, 5000mW 18:44.32i '16, 20:37.47 '08; 10000W 38:40.25 '16.

Mateusz PRZYBYLKO b. 9 Mar 1992 Bielefeld 1.95m 72kg. TSV Bayer 04 Leverkusen
At HJ: OG: '16- dnq 28; WCh: '15- dnq 28=, '17-5; WJ: '10- dnq; WY: '09- 11; EU23: '13- 5; EJ: '11- 7; WI: '18- 3; EI: '17- 7. GER champion 2017.
Progress at HJ: 2009- 2.14i/2.10, 2010- 2.16, 2011-2.20, 2012- 2.20, 2013- 2.24, 2014- 2.24i/2.22, 2015- 2.30, 2016- 2.29, 2017- 2.35.

Thomas RÖHLER b. 30 Sep 1991 Jena 1.92m 92kg. LC Jena. Sports student.
At JT: OG: '16- 1; WCh: '13- dnq 29, '15- 4, '17- 4; EC: '12-14-16: dnq 13/12/5; WJ: '10- 9; EU23: '11-7, '13- 3; ET: '13- 2, '17- 3. Won DL 2014, German champion 2012-16.
German javelin record 2017.
Progress at JT: 2009- 61.26, 2010- 76.37, 2011-78.20, 2012- 80.79, 2013- 83.95, 2014- 87.63, 2015-89.27, 2016- 91.28, 2017- 93.90.

David STORL b. 21 Jul 1990 Rochlitz 1.98m 125kg. Leipzig SC DHfK. Federal police officer.
At SP: OG: '12- 2, '16- 7; ; WCh: '09-11-13-15-17: dnq 27/1/1/2/10; EC: '10-12-14-16: 4/1/1/1; WJ: '08- 1; WY: '07- 1; EU23: '11- 1; EJ: '09- 1; WI: '10-12-14-18: 6/2/2/2; EI: '11-15-17: 2/1/3; WCp: '14-1; ET: '11-13-14-15-17: 1/1/1/1/2. GER champion 2011-12, 2014-17.
World junior shot record and three with 6kg (to 22.73) 2009.
Progress at SP: 2008- 18.46, 2009- 20.43, 2010-20.77, 2011- 21.78, 2012- 21.88i/21.86, 2013- 21.73, 2014- 21.97, 2015- 22.20, 2016- 21.31, 2017- 21.87.
Nine major international titles and five second places.

Homiyu TESFAYE Heyi b. 23 Jun 1993 Debre Zeyit, Ethiopia 1.83m 66kg. LG Eintracht Frankfurt.
At 1500m: OG: '16- sf; WCh: '13- 5, '17- s; EC: '14- 5, '16- 10; WI: '14- 7; EI: '15- 4; ET: '14- 2.
European U23 1500m record 2014.
Progress at 1500m: 2011- 3:46.02, 2012- 3:38.56,

2013- 3:34.18, 2014- 3:31.98, 2015- 3:34.13i, 2016- 3:35.05, 2017- 3:33.47. pbs: 800m 1:46.08 '17, 1000m 2:17.56 '14, 1M 3:49.86 '14, 3000m 7:58.09i '14, 8:03.95 '12; 5000m 13:58.73 '13, 10000m 29:08.44 '13, Rd 10k 27:54 '15, HMar 62:58 '17.
Claimed asylum in Germany in 2010, and German citizen from 27 Jun 2013.

Johannes VETTER b. 26 Mar 1993 Dresden 1.88m 105kg. LG Offenburg.
At JT: OG: '16- 4; WCh: '15- 7, '17- 1; EC: '16- dnq 16; EU23: '15- 4; EJ: '11- 12; ET: '15- 2. GER champion 2017.
German javelin record 2017.
Progress at JT: 2010- 63.60, 2011- 71.60, 2012- 60.19, 2013- 76.58, 2014- 79.75, 2015- 85.40, 2016- 89.57, 2017- 94.44, 2018- 92.70.

Julian WEBER b. 29 Aug 1994 Mainz 1.90m 94kg. USC Mainz.
At JT: OG: '16- 9; EU23: '15- 5; EJ: '13- 1.
Progress at JT: 2012- 71.12, 2013- 79.68, 2014- 80.72, 2015- 81.15, 2016- 88.29, 2017- 85.85.

Martin WIERIG b. 10 Jun 1987 Neindorf 2.02m 127kg. SC Magdeburg. Federal police officer.
At DT: OG: '12- 6; WCh: '11-/15/17 dnq 18/19/nt, '13- 4; EC: '10-12-14-16: 7/dnq 14/11/dnq 14; WJ: '04- 8, '06- 3; EU23: '07- 1, '09- 3; EJ: '05- 3 (dnq SP); ET: '15- 2.
Progress at DT: 2005- 57.44, 2006- 57.37, 2007- 61.10, 2008- 63.09, 2009- 63.90, 2010- 64.93, 2011- 67.21, 2012- 68.33, 2013- 67.46, 2014- 66.59, 2015- 65.94, 2016- 67.16, 2017- 65.56. pb SP 17.30 '11.

Women

Shanice CRAFT b. 15 May 1993 Mannheim 1.85m 89kg. MTG Mannheim. Police officer.
At (SP)/DT: OG: '16- 11; WCh: '15- 7; EC: '14- 3, '16- 3; WJ: '12- 1/2; WY: '09- 3; EU23: '13- 2/2, '15- 2/1; EJ: '11- 1; ET: '14- 2. Won GER 2014, Yth Oly 2010,
Progress at DT: 2007- 44.86, 2008- 48.14, 2009- 50.57, 2010- 55.49, 2011- 58.65, 2012- 62.92, 2013- 60.77, 2014- 65.88, 2015- 64.79, 2016- 64.82, 2017- 63.18. Pb SP 17.75 '14. US father.

Pamela DUTKIEWICZ b. 28 Sep 1991 Kassel 1.70m 63kgkg. TV Wattenscheid 01.
At 100mh: OG: '16- sf, WCh: '17- 3; EC: '16- dnf; ET: '17- 1. GER champion 2017. At 60mh: EI: '17- 3.
Progress at 100mh: 2008- 14.13, 2009- 13.92, 2010- 13.37, 2011- 13.50/13.49w, 2012- 13.45, 2013- 13.39, 2014- 12.95, 2016- 12.85, 2017- 12.61. pbs: 60m 7.57i '14, 100m 12.21 '13, 200m 24.17i '14, 24.65 '13;, 60mh 7.79i '17.
Polish parents, mther Brygida Bak won POL 800m in 1984, pb 2:02.39 '86.

Kristin GIERISCH b. 20 Aug 1990 Zwickau 1.78m 59kg. LAC Erdgas Chemnitz. Police.
At TJ: OG: '16- 11; WCh: '15- 8, '17- 5; EC: '14- 9, '16- 8; WY: '07- 6; EU23: '11- dns; EJ: '09- 5; EI: '15- 4, '17- 1; ET: '15- 2, '17- 2; WI: '16- 2. German champion 2014-15, 2017.
Progress at TJ: 2006- 12.09, 2007- 13.00, 2008- 12.22, 2009- 14.02, 2010- 13.84, 2011- 14.10i/13.47, 2012- 14.19i/13.94, 2013- 13.91i/13.67, 2014- 14.31/14.34w, 2015- 14.46i/14.38/14.46w, 2016- 14.31, 2017- 14.40. pbs: 60m 7.59i '12, LJ 6.46i '15, 6.21 '14.

Julia HARTING b. 1 Apr 1990 Berlin 1.92m 95kg. née Fischer. SCC Berlin. Police officer.
At DT: OG: '12- dnq 20, '16- 9; WCh: '13- dnq 13, '15- 5, '17- 9; EC: '12-14-16: 5/5/2; WJ: '08- 2; WY: '07- 1; EU23: '11- 1; EJ: '09- 2; ET: '13- 2. GER champion 2015, 2017.
Progress at DT: 2005- 45.69, 2006- 50.23, 2007- 51.39, 2008- 55.92, 2009- 56.74, 2010- 57.49, 2011- 59.60, 2012- 64.22, 2013- 66.04, 2014- 66.46, 2015- 65.98, 2016- 68.49, 2017- 63.63.
Married Robert Harting (qv) on 17 Sep 2016.

Christin HUSSONG b. 17 Apr 1994 Zweibrücken 1.87m 82kg. LAZ Zweibrücken. Sports student.
At JT: OG: '16- 12; WCh: '15- 6, 17- dnq 17; EC: '14- 7, '16- dnq 17; WJ: '12- 7; WY: '11- 1; EU23: '15- 1; EJ: '13- 2, YthOG: '10- 4. Won GER 2016.
Progress at JT: 2009- 49.93, 2010- 55.35, 2011- 59.74, 2012- 55.74, 2013- 58.55, 2014- 63.34, 2015- 65.92, 2016- 66.41, 2017- 64.18. Pbs: SP 15.02i '14, 14.02 '11.

Marie-Laurence JUNGFLEISCH b. 7 Oct 1990 Paris, France 1.81m 68kg. VfB Stuttgart. Soldier.
At HJ: OG: '16- 7=; WCh: '13- nh, '15- 6, '17- 4; EC: '12-14-16: dnq 13=/5/5; EU23: '11- 8; EJ: '09- 6; ET: '17- 2; WI: '14- 8. Won GER 2013-17.
Progress at HJ: 2006- 1.70, 2007- 1.75, 2008- 1.78, 2009- 1.86, 2010- 1.90, 2011- 1.93, 2012- 1.95, 2013- 1.95, 2014- 1.97, 2015- 1.99, 2016- 2.00, 2017- 2.00.
Father from Martinique, mother German.

Kathrin KLAAS b. 6 Feb 1984 Haiger 1.68m 72kg. LG Eintracht Frankfurt. Police inspector.
At HT: OG: '08- dnq 22, '12- 4, '16- dnq 18; WCh: '05-07-13: dnq -/27/19, '09-11-15-17: 4/7/6/11; EC: '06-10-12-14-16: 6/dnq 15/4/4/dnq 25; EJ: '03-8, EU23: '05- 4; WUG: '09- 3. GER champion 2014.
Progress at HT: 2000- 44.24, 2001- 50.10, 2002- 57.74, 2003- 63.72, 2004- 68.01, 2005- 70.91, 2006- 71.67, 2007- 73.45, 2008- 70.39, 2009- 74.23, 2010- 74.53, 2011- 75.48, 2012- 76.05, 2013- 72.57, 2014- 74.62, 2015- 73.18, 2016- 71.78, 2017- 71.06.

Konstanze KLOSTERHALFEN b. 18 Feb 1997 Königswinter 1.74m 48kg. TSV Bayer 04 Leverkusen.
At 1500m: OG: '16- sf; WCh: '17- sf; EU23: '17- 1; EJ: '15- 3, EI: '17- 2; YthOG: '14- 4, ET: '17- 1. German champion 2016-17. At 3000m: WJ: '16- 3; WI: '18- 7. Eur CC: 14-15-16-17: 28J/1J/1J/2U23. German 3000m record 2017.
Progress at 1500m: 2012- 55.74, 2013- 4:26.58, 2014- 4:19.97, 2015- 4:09.58, 2016- 4:06.91, 2017- 3:58.92. Pbs: 800m 1:59.65 '17, 3000m 8:29.89 '17, 5000m 14:51.38 '17, 10kRd 32:24 '16.

Gesa Felicitas KRAUSE b. 3 Aug 1992 Ehringshausen 1.67m 55kg. LG Eintracht Frankfurt. Student.
At 3000mSt: OG: '12- 7, '16- 6; WCh: '11-13-15-17: 6/9/3/9; EC: '12-14-16: 3/5/1; WJ: '10- 4; EU23: '13- 1; EJ: '11- 1; ET: 15- 1, '17- 1; GER champion 2015-17 (& 5000m 2017). At 2000mSt: WY: '09- 7. At 1500m: EI: '15- 5.
Records: European junior 3000mSt 2011, German 2000mSt (2) 2015, 3000mSt (232016-17.
Progress at 3000mSt: 2010- 9:47.78, 2011- 9:32.74, 2012- 9:23.52, 2013- 9:37.11, 2014- 9:35.46, 2015- 9:19.25, 2016- 9:18.41, 2017- 9:11.85. pbs: 800m 2:03.09mx '17, 1000m 2:44.68 '10, 1500m 4:06.99 '16, 1M 4:29.58 '16, 3000m 8:49.43i '16, 9:02.04 '15; 5000m 15:24.53 '17; 10k Rd 33:26 '15, 2000mSt 6:04.20 '15.

Malaika MIHAMBO b. 3 Feb 1994 Heidelberg 1.70m 52kg. LG Kurpfalz. Political science student at Mannheim University.
At LJ: OG: '16- 4; WCh: '13- dnq 13, '15- 6; EC: '14- 4, '16- 3; WJ: '12- dnq 14; WY: '11- 9; EU23: '15- 1; EJ: '13- 1; WI: '18- 5; ET: '14- 1. GER champion 2016
Progress at LJ: 2008- 5.55, 2009- 5.81, 2010- 5.96, 2011- 6.40, 2012- 6.45i/6.32/6.50w, 2013- 6.70/ 6.80w, 2014- 6.90, 2015- 6.84, 2016- 6.95, 2017- 6.62, 2018- 6.72i. pbs: 200m 23.96 '15, HJ 1.78i/1.75 '10.
Tanzanian father, German mother.

Sosthene Taroum **MOGUENARA** b. 17 Oct 1989 Sarh, Moyen-Chari, Chad 1.82m 68kg. LG LAZ Saar 05 Saarbrücken.
At LJ: OG: '12- dnq 19, '16- 10; WCh: '11- dnq 31, '13- 11, '15- dnq 27; EC: '12- 4, '14- 9; EU23: '09- 4, '11- 3; ET: '15- 3; WI: '18- 3; EI: '15- 2. GER champion 2013.
Progress at LJ: 2007- 6.22, 2008- 6.37, 2009- 6.61/6.69w, 2010- 6.65, 2011- 6.83, 2012- 6.88, 2013- 7.04, 2014- 6.82, 2015- 6.94, 2016- 7.16, 2017- 6.61, 2018- 6.85i. pbs: 60m 7.66i '08, 100m 11.94 '10, 200m 24.85 '07.
Has lived in Germany from the age of nine.

Katharina MOLITOR b. 8 Nov 1983 Bedurg, Erft 1.82m 76kg. TSV Bayer 04 Leverkusen.
At JT: OG: '08- 7, 12- 6; WCh: '11-13-15-17: 5/dnq 13/1/7; EC: '10-12-14-16: 4/5/9/4; EU23: '05- 2; WUG: '07- 6, '09- 4. German champion 2010, 2015, 2017.
Progress at JT: 2000- 42.94, 2001- 48.53, 2002- 49.01, 2003- 48.03, 2004- 50.04, 2005- 57.01, 2006- 57.58, 2007- 58.87, 2008- 61.74, 2009- 62.69, 2010- 64.53, 2011- 64.67, 2012- 63.20, 2013- 63.55, 2014- 63.40, 2015- 67.69, 2016- 63.20, 2017- 65.37.
Played volleyball in the Bundesliga.

Nadine MÜLLER b. 21 Nov 1985 Leipzig 1.93m 90kg. Hallesche LA-Freunde. Federal police officer.
At DT: OG: '12- 4, '16- 6; WCh: '07-09-11-13-15-17: dnq 23/6/2/4/3/6; EC: '10-12-16: 8/2/4; WJ: '04- 3; EU23: '05- 10, '07- 8; EJ: '03- 2; ET: '10-11-17: 1/3/2. German champion 2010-13, 2016.
Progress at DT: 2000- 36.10, 2001- 46.27, 2002- 48.90, 2003- 53.44, 2004- 57.85, 2005- 59.35, 2006- 58.46, 2007- 62.93, 2008- 61.36, 2009- 63.46, 2010- 67.78, 2011- 66.99, 2012- 68.89, 2013- 66.89, 2014- 67.30, 2015- 65.72, 2016- 66.84, 2017- 65.76.
Father Hans-Joachim Muller was a 55m discus thrower.

Cindy ROLEDER b. 21 Aug 1989 Chemnitz 1.78m 68kg. SV Halle. Police officer.
At 100mh: OG: '12- sf, '16- 5, WCh: '11- sf, '15- 2; EC: '10-12-14-16: h/6/3/1; WJ: '08- sf; EU23: '09- sf, '11- 3; EJ: '07- 4; CCp: '14- 3; ET: '15- 3; GER champion 2011, 2015-16. At 60mh: WI: '14- 6, '18- 5; EI: '15- 4, '17- 1.
Progress at 100mh: 2007- 13.49, 2008- 13.72, 2009- 13.38, 2010- 12.97, 2011- 12.91, 2012- 12.91, 2013- 13.03/12.93w, 2014- 12.80, 2015- 12.59, 2016- 12.62, 2017- 12.90. pbs: 60m 7.34i '15, 100m 11.72 '13, 150m 17.40 '15, 200m 23.35 '15, 800m 2:15.49 '15, 50mh 7.14+i '10, 60mh 7.84i '17, HJ 1.66 '15, LJ 6.32i '14, 6.17 '13, 6.18w '15; SP 13.59i '16, 13.25 '15; JT 36.33 '15, Pen 4187i '14, Hep 6055 '15.

Anna RÜH b. 17 Jun 1993 Greifswald 1.86m 78kg. SC Neubrandenburg.
At DT: OG: '12- 9; WCh: '17- dnq 14; EC: '12- 4, '14- 4; WJ: '10- dnq 21, '12- 1; EU23: '13- 1, '15- 2; EJ: '11- 2 (3 SP).
Progress at DT: 2009- 44.43, 2010- 51.67, 2011- 59.97, 2012- 63.38, 2013- 64.33, 2014- 64.17, 2015- 66.14, 2016- 64.08, 2017- 63.90. pb SP 17.68i/17.20 '16.

Elisaveta **'Lisa' RYZIH** b. 27 Sep 1988 Omsk, Russia 1.79m 60kg. Formerly Ryshich. ABC Ludwigshafen. Psychology student.
At PV: OG: '12- 6=, '16- 10; WCh: '13- 8=, '15- 12, '17- 5; EC: '10-12-14-16: 3/7/4/2; WJ: '04- 1, '06- nh; WY: '03- 1; EU23: '09- 1; EJ: '07- 4; EI: '11- 7, '17- 2; CCp: '10- 2, '14- 3. German champion 2014-15, 23017.
Progress at PV: 2002- 3.92, 2003- 4.10, 2004- 4.30, 2005- 4.15, 2006- 4.35, 2007- 4.35, 2008- 4.52i/4.50, 2009- 4.50, 2010- 4.65, 2011- 4.65i, 2012- 4.65, 2013- 4.55, 2014- 4.71, 2015- 4.72i/4.70, 2016- 4.73, 2017- 4.75i/4.73. pb LJ 5.38w '06.
Set world age bests at age 13 in 2002 and 15 in 2004. Her sister 'Nastja' was World Indoor champion in 1999 and set four world junior and five European junior PV records in 1996 to 4.15, and three German records in 1999 to 4.50i/4.44 and had a pb of 4.63 in 2006. Their family left Omsk in Siberia in 1992 to live in Ulm; mother Yekaterina Ryzhikh (née Yefimova b. 20 Jan 1959) had HJ pb 1.91i '85 and 1.89 '81, and father Vladimir PV 5.30 '79.

Claudia SALMAN-RATH b. 25 Apr 1986 Hadamar, Hessen 1.75m 65kg. née Rath. LG Eintracht Frankfurt.

At Hep: OG: '16- 14; WCh: '11- 4, '15- 5, '17- 8 (10 LJ); EC: '10-12-14: 10/6/8. At WI Pen: '14- 5. At LJ: EI: '17- 3; ET: '17- 1. Won GER Hep 2010-11, LJ 2017.
Progress at LJ, Hep: 2003- 5.64, 5231; 2004- 5.99, 5353; 2005- 6.09, 5323; 2006- 6.13, 2007- 6.22, 5274; 2008- 6.29, 5697; 2009- 6.44, 5941; 2010- 6.50, 6107; 2011- 6.28. 6098; 2012- 6.44, 6210; 2013- 6.67, 6462; 2014- 6.46, 6314, 2015- 6.73/6.84w, 6458; 2016- 6.62, 6310; 2017- 6.94i/6.86, 6580. pbs: 200m 23.62 '17, 800m 2:05.54 '17, 60mh 8.43i '14, 100mh 13.44 '15, HJ 1.83 '13, SP 14.00 '17, JT 43.65 '16, Pen 4681i '14.

Carolin SCHÄFER b. 5 Dec 1991 Bad Wildungen 1.78m 64kg. TV Friedrichstein.
At Hep: OG: '16- 5; WCh: '15- dnf, '17- 2; EC: '12- 10, '14- 4; WJ: '08- 1; EU23: '11- 5, '13- 6; EJ: '09- 1. German champion 2013.
Progress at Hep: 2007- 5545, 2008- 5833, 2009- 5697, 2010- 5333, 2011- 5941, 2012- 6072, 2013- 5972, 2014- 6395, 2015- 6547, 2016- 6557, 2017- 6836. pbs: 60m 7.86i '07, 200m 23.27 '17, 800m 2:14.10 '15, 60mh 8.45i '16, 100mh 13.07 '17, HJ 1.86 '17, LJ 6.57 '17, SP 14.84 '17, JT 50.76 '12, Pen 4098i '09.
Won IAAF Combined Events Challenge 2016-17. Her elder brother Sebastian had 400m best 47.10 '08 and ran at 4x100m in EJ 2005 & 2007.

Christina SCHWANITZ b. 24 Dec 1985 Dresden 1.80m 103kg. LV 90 Erzebirge. Soldier.
At SP: OG: '08- 9, '12- 9, '16- 6; WCh: '05-09-11-13-15: 7/11/10/2/1; EC: '12-14-16: 5/1/1; WJ: '04- 3; EU23: '05- 2; WI: '08- 5, '14- 2; EI: '11- 2, '13- 1; CCp: '14- 1; ET: '08-13-14-15: 1/1/1/1. Won DL 2015, German 2011, 2013-16.
Progress at SP: 2001- 13.57, 2002- 14.26, 2003- 15.25, 2004- 16.98, 2005- 18.84, 2007- 17.06, 2008- 19.68i/19.31, 2009- 19.06, 2010- 18.28, 2011- 19.20, 2012- 19.15i/19.05, 2013- 20.41, 2014- 20.22, 2015- 20.77, 2016- 20.17. pb DT 47.27 '03.
Gave birth to twins in 2017.

Silke SPIEGELBURG b. 17 Mar 1986 Georgsmarienhütte 1.73m 64kg. TSV Bayer 04 Leverkusen. Economics student.
At PV: OG: '04- 13, '08- 7, '12- 4; WCh: '07-09-11-13-15-17: nh/4/9/4/dnq 17=/dnq 14; EC: '06-10-12: 6/2/4=; WJ: '02- 8; WY: '01- 1; EU23: '07- 4; EJ: '03- 1, '05- 1; WI: '06-12-14: 8/4/7; EI: '07-09-11: 5/2/2; ECp: '08-09-10-11-13-15: 3/3/2/2/1/1; Won WAF 2008, DL 2011-13, GER 2005-10, 2012.
PV records: World junior 2005, German 2012.
Progress at PV: 1998- 2.75, 1999- 3.30, 2000- 3.75, 2001- 4.00, 2002- 4.20, 2003- 4.20i/4.15, 2004- 4.40, 2005- 4.48i/4.42, 2006- 4.56, 2007- 4.60, 2008- 4.70, 2009- 4.75i/4.70, 2010- 4.71, 2011- 4.76i/4.75, 2012- 4.82, 2013- 4.79, 2014- 4.72i/4.50, 2015- 4.75, 2016- 4.56i/4.50, 2017- 4.55.
Brothers: Henrik PV pb 4.80, Christian (b. 15 Apr 1976) 5.51 '98; **Richard** (b. 12 Aug 1977) 5.85 '01; 6= WCh 01, 1 WUG 99.

Linda STAHL b. 2 Oct 1985 Steinheim 1.74m 72kg. TSV Bayer 04 Leverkusen. Doctor.
At JT: OG: '12- 3, '16- 11; WCh: '07-09-11-13-15: 8/6/dns/4/10; EC: '10-12-14-16: 1/3/3/2; EU23: '07- 1; CCp: '10- 4, '14- 5; ET: '14- 3. Won GER 2013-14.
Progress at JT: 2000- 42.94, 2001- 43.96, 2002- 47.23, 2003- 47.32, 2004- 50.11, 2005- 53.94, 2006- 57.17, 2007- 62.80, 2008- 66.06, 2009- 63.86, 2010- 66.81, 2011- 60.78, 2012- 64.91, 2013- 65.76, 2014- 67.32, 2015- 64.65, 2015- 65.25, 2016- 65.25. pb SP 13.91i '06.

Alexandra WESTER b. 21 Mar 1994 Bakau, The Gambia 1.80m 64kg. ASV Köln.
At LJ: OG: '16- dnq 34; WCh: '17- dnq 23; EC: '16- 7; WI: '16- 6; EI: '17- 8.
Progress at LJ: 2009- 6.19, 2010- 5.97i/5.86, 2011- 5.83, 2012- 5.82, 2013- 6.29, 2014- 6.13, 2015- 6.59, 2016- 6.95i/6.79/7.00w, 2017- 6.79. pbs: 60m 7.53i '15, 100m 12.00 '09, 200m 25.27i '10, 60mh 8.47i '15, HJ 1.68 '09, SP 11.51i '14, 11.42 '11; Hep 5523 '14. German father, Ghanian mother. Has lived in Germany from the age of 3.

GREECE

Governing body: Hellenic Amateur Athletic Association (SEGAS). Founded 1897.

National Championships first held in 1896 (men), 1930 (women). **2017 Champions**: 100m/200m: Likoúrgos-Stéfanos Tsákonas 10.18/20.26w, 400m: Mihaíl Pappás 47.02, 800m: Athanásios Kalákos 1:52.40, 1500m: Andréas Dimitrákis 3:47.80, 5000m/Mar: Konstadínos Gelaoúzos 14:33.00/2:27:21, 10000m: Dímos Maggínas 30:13.50, HMar: Ioánnis Zerbákis 69:03dh, 3000mSt: Nikólaos Gótsis 9:04.27, 110mh: Konstadínos Douvalídis 13.57, 400mh: Konstadínos Nákos 51.65, HJ: Yeóryios Tessaromátis 2.15, PV: Konstadínos Filippídis 5.75, LJ: Miltiádis Tentóglou 8.30, TJ: Dimítrios Tsiámis 16.39, SP: Kiriákos Zótos 19.34, DT: Iáson Thanópoulos 56.01, HT: Mihaíl Anastasákis 74.56, JT: Paraskevás Batzávalis 76.27, Dec: Paniótis Mántis 6738, 20kW: Aléxandros Papamihaíl 1:26:40; 50kW: Ioánnis Vaítsís 4:30:38. **Women**: 100m/200m: Grigoría-Emmanouéla Keramidá 11.39/23.16w, 400m: Iríni Vasilíou 52.33, 800m: Konstadína Yiannopoúlou 2:08.11, 1500m: Koraíni-Anthí Kiriakopoúlou 4:19.53, 5000m/HMar/Mar: Ouranía Reboúli 16:54.28/79:44dh/2:49:06, 10000m: Sonia Cekíni-Boudoúri 36:14.36, Mar:, 3000mSt: Marína Maniadáki 10:42.43, 100mh: Elisávet Pesirídou 13.23, HJ: Tatiána Goúsin 1.85, PV: Ekateríni Stefanídi 4.81, LJ: Haido Alexoúli 6.44w, TJ: Paraskevi Papahrístou 14.07, SP: Stamatía Skarvéli 16.76, DT: Hrisoúla Anagnostopoúlou 58.95, HT: Iliána Korosídou 64.65, JT: Sofía Ifantídou 59.23, Hep: Sofia Ifantídou 5745, 20kW: Antigóni Drisbióti 1:34:00.

Konstadínos FILIPPÍDIS b. 26 Nov 1986 Athens 1.88m 73kg. Panellínios YS Athens. Postgraduate student at Athens University of Economics and Business.
At PV: OG: '12- 6, '16- 7=; WCh: '05-09-11-13-15: dnq 14=/dnq 17/6/10/dnq 25=; EC: '06-10: dnq 26/21=, '12-14-16: 5/7/7=; WJ: '04- 4; WY: '03- 4; EJ: '05- 2; WI: '10-12-14-16-18: 4=/7/1/7/7=; EI: '11-13-15-17: 5/4/5/2; WUG: '05- 2; ET: '09/10- 4; Won MedG 2005, GRE 2005, 2009-17.
Ten Greek pole vault records 2005-15.
Progress at PV: 2001- 3.70, 2002- 4.80, 2003- 5.22, 2004- 5.50, 2005- 5.75, 2006- 5.55, 2007- 5.35i/5.30/5.40dq, 2009- 5.65, 2010- 5.70i/5.55, 2011- 5.75, 2012- 5.80, 2013- 5.83i/5.82, 2014- 5.80i/5.70, 2015- 5.91, 2016- 5.84i/5.72, 2017- 5.85i/5.75, 2018- 5.85i.
Two-year drugs ban (reduced to 18 months) from positive test on 16 June 2007.

Emmanouíl KARALÍS b. 20 Oct 1999 Athens 1.83m 75kg. G.S. Kifissia.
At PV: WCh: '17- dnq 21; WJ: '16- 4; WY: '15- 3; EJ: '17- dnq; WI: '18- 7=.
World junior indoor pole vault record (5.78) 2018, world youth records (2 indoor, 1 outdoor) 2016.
Progress at PV: 2014- 4.65, 2015- 5.25, 2016- 5.55, 2017- 5.70i/5.63, 2018- 5.80i.

Ioánnis KIRIAZÍS b. 19 Jan 1996 Athens 1.94m 98kg. Texas A&M University, USA..
At JT: WCh: '17- 6; EC: '16 - 12; WJ: '14- 7; WY: '13- dnq 16; EU23: '17- 2; EJ: '15- 4; ET: '17- 2. NCAA champion 2017.
Progress at JT: 2013- 69.30, 2014- 73.66, 2015- 78.41, 2016- 87.14, 2017- 88.01.

Women

Nikoléta KIRIAKOPOÚLOU b. 21 Mar 1986 Athens 1.67m 56kg. AYES Kámiros Rhodes.
At PV: OG: '08/12- dnq 27=/19=; WCh: '09-11-13-15: dnq 19/8/dnq 13=/3; EC: '10-12-14-16: dnq 13/3/7=/4; WJ: '04- 6; EJ: '05- 7; WI: '16- 6=; EI: '11- 9, '15- 5=. Won DL 2015, Balkan 2008, Med G 2009, Greek 2009, 2011-14.
Nine Greek pole vault records 2010-15.
Progress at PV: 2001- 2.90, 2002- 3.10, 2003- 3.70, 2004- 4.00, 2005- 4.10, 2006- 3.60, 2007- 4.00i/3.90, 2008- 4.45, 2009- 4.50, 2010- 4.55, 2011- 4.71, 2012- 4.60, 2013- 4.65, 2014- 4.72i/4.67, 2015- 4.83, 2016- 4.81i/4.75, 2018- 4.65i.
Married to Andreas Linardátos (400m pb 47.27 '90). Gave birth to daughter on 23 May 2017.

Paraskeví 'Voula' PAPAHRÍSTOU b. 17 Apr 1989 Athens 1.70m 53kg. AEK (Athens).
At TJ: OG: '16- 8; WCh: '09/11/17- dnq 28/16/20; EC: '12- 11, '16- 3; WJ: '08- 3; EU23: '09/11- 1/1; WI: '16- 3, '18- 6; EI: '17- 3; ET: '17- 1. Won Greek LJ 2011-12, 2016; TJ 2009, 2011, 2015, 2017.
Progress at TJ: 2005- 12.75, 2006- 12.81/13.13w, 2007- 12.98i/12.92, 2008- 13.86i/13.79/13.94w, 2009- 14.47i/14.35, 2010- 13.94i/13.85, 2011- 14.72, 2012- 14.58/14.77w, 2013- 14.21, 2015- 13.99/14.20w, 2016- 14.73, 2017- 14.24. pb LJ 6.60 '12.
Daughter Konstadína born Nov 2014.

Ekateríni STEFANÍDI b. 4 Feb 1990 Athens 1.72m 63kg. Was at Stanford University, USA and then MSc in cognitive psychology at Arizona State University.
At PV: OG: '12- dnq 24, '16- 1; WCh: '15- dnq 15, '17- 1; EC: '12-14-16: nh/2/1; WJ: '08- 3; WY: '05- 1, '07- 2; EU23: '11- 2; EJ: '07- 10; WI: '16- 3, '18- 3; EI: '15- 2, 17- 1; WUG: '11- 3; ET: '17- 1. Greek champion 2015-16, NCAA 2012, DL 2016-17.
World youth pole vault best 2005. Two Greek PV records 2016-17 and indoors 2016
Progress at PV: 2001- 2.30, 2002- 3.50, 2003- 3.90, 2004- 4.14, 2005- 4.37i/4.30, 2006- 4.10, 2007- 4.25, 2008- 4.25, 2009- 4.13, 2010- 4.30, 2011- 4.45, 2012- 4.51, 2013- 4.45Ai/4.40, 2014- 4.71, 2015- 4.77Ai/4.71, 2016- 4.90i/4.86, 2017- 4.91, 2018- 4.83i. Married to Mitchell Krier (PV 4.95i '16).

GRENADA

Governing body: Grenada Athletic Assocation. Founded 1924.

Kurt FELIX b. 4 Jul 1988 St. George's 1.90m 88kg. Was at Boise State University.
At Dec: OG: '12- dnf, '16- 9; WCh: '13- dnf, '15- 8, '17- 7; CG: '14- 3; PAm: '15- 2. At Hep: WI: '16- 6.
GRN records: decathlon (7) 2012-16, PV 2010-15.
Progress at Dec: 2008- 6946, 2009- 7091, 2010- 7412, 2012- 8062, 2013- dnf, 2014- 8070, 2015- 8302, 2016- 8323, 2017- 8509. pbs: 60m 7.00i '16, 100m 10.91 '15, 10.90w '12; 400m 48.63 '15, 1000m 2:42.91i '11, 1500m 4:30.53 '16, 60mh 8.31i '16, 110mh 14.58 '15, HJ 2.17i '11, 2.15 '09; PV 4.61i '16, 4.60 '12; LJ 7.74 '12, TJ 16.06 '09, SP 15.31 '17, DT 50.59 '15, JT 72.80 '17, Hep: 5986i '16.
Half brother of Lindon Victor (qv).

Kirani JAMES b. 1 Sep 1992 St George's 1.85m 74kg. Student at University of Alabama, USA
At (200m)/400m: OG: '12- 1, '16- 2; WCh: '11- 1, '13- 7, '15- 3; CG: '14- 1; WJ: '08- 2, '10- 1; WY: '07- 2, '09- 1/1; WI: '12- 6. Won DL 2011, 2015; PAm-J 400m 2009, 200m 2011; NCAA 2010-11.
Records: CAC & Commonwealth 400m 2012 & 2014, GRN 200m 2011, 400m (2) 2011-12; Indoor 400m: CAC & Commonwealth 2010 (45.24) &. 2011, World Junior (44.80) 2011.
Progress at 400m: 2007- 46.96, 2008- 45.70, 2009- 45.24, 2010- 45.01, 2011- 44.36, 2012- 43.94, 2013- 43.96, 2014- 43.74, 2015- 43.78, 2016- 43.76, 2017- 45.44. pbs: 200m 20.41A/20.53w '11, 20.76 '10; 300m: 31.3+ '16.
He set world age bests at 14 and 15. In 2011 he became the youngest ever World or Olympic champion at 400m and in 2012 the first Olympic medallist for Grenada at any sport. In January 2012 the 'Kirani James Boulevard' was opened in the Grenadan capital St. George. IAAF Rising Star award 2011.

Bralon TAPLIN b. 8 May 1992 St George's 1.80m 73kg. Was at Texas A&M University, USA
At 400m: OG: '16- 7; WCh: '15- h; CG: '14- sf; PAm: '15- h; WI: '16- 4.
Progress at 400m: 2008- 49.21, 2009- 47.25, 2010- 47.03, 2011- 46.79, 2012- 45.36, 2013- 46.85i/47.50, 2014- 45.18, 2015- 44.89, 2016- 44.38, 2017- 45.08, 2018- 44.88i. pbs: 100m 10.53A '12, 200m 20.80i '15, 20.83 '12; 300m 31.8+ '16, 31.97i '17; 600y 1:10.14i '11.

Lindon VICTOR b. 28 Feb 1993 St. George's 1.91m 90kg. Texas A&M University, USA.
At Dec: OG: '16- 16; WCh: '17- dnf; CG: '14- 9; PAm: '15- 7. Won NCAA 2017.
Grenada records: decathlon 2016 & 2017, pole vault (2) 2017.
Progress at Dec: 2014- 7429, 2015- 7453, 2016- 8446, 2017- 8539. pbs: 60m 6.94i '17, 100m 10.60 '16, 400m 48.24 '17, 1000m 2:51.14i '17, 1500m 4:43.81 '16, 60mh 8.24i '16, 110mh 14.45 '17, HJ 2.09 '17, PV 4.76i/4.70 '17, LJ 7.37 '17, SP 16.55i/16.52 '17, DT 55.22 '17, JT 71.23 '14, Hep: 5976i '17. Half brother of Kurt Felix.

HUNGARY

Governing body: Magyar Atlétikai Szövetség. Founded 1897.

National Championships first held in 1896 (men), 1932 (women). **2017 Champions. Men**: 100m: Dániel Szabó 10.49, 200m: László Szabó 21.38, 400m: Marcell Deák Nagy 47.55, 800m/1500m: Tamás Kazi 1:50.85/3:53.32, 5000m: István Szögi 14:50.65, 10000m: Benjamin Kovács 29:27.14, HMar: Gáspár Csere 67:19, Mar: Gábor Józsa 2:20:22, 3000mSt: Balázs Juhász 8:50.15, 110mh: Balázs Baji 13.29, 400mh: Tibor Koroknai 49.90, HJ: Péter Bakosi 2.16, PV: Csanád Simonváros 4.80, LJ: István Virovecz 7.69, TJ: Tibor Galambos 16.15, SP: Lajos Kürthy 17.54, DT: Zoltán Kövágó 63.06, HT: Bence Halász 75.32, JT: Norbert Rivasz-Tóth 80.50, Dec: Benedek Naszódi 6750, 20kW: Máté Helebrandt 1:23:11, 50kW: Dávid Tokodi 4:09:15. **Women**: 100m: Klaudia Sorok 11.64, 200m: Éva Kaptur 24.09, 400m: Evelin Nádházy 54.0, 800m: Bianka Kéri 2:03.80, 1500m/3000mSt: Viktória Gyürkés 4:13.52/9:48.67, 5000m/ 10000m: Krisztina Papp 16:03.83/33:19.99, HMar: Zita Kácser 76:59, Mar: Tünde Szabó 2:42:49, 100mh: Gréta Kerekes 13.13, 400mh: Mónika Zsiga 61.95, HJ: Barbara Szabó 1.87, PV: Zsófia Siskó 4.00, LJ: Petra Farkas 6.41, TJ: Krisztina Hoffer 13.34, SP/DT: Anita Márton 18.55/56.88, HT: Réka Gyurátz 68.76, JT: Annabella Bogdán 58.79, Hep: Luca Renner 5309, 20kW: Viktória Madarász 1:31:39.

Balázs BAJI b. 9 Jun 1989 Békéscsaba 1.92m 83kg. Budapewsti Honvéd SE.
At 110mh: OG: '12- h, '16- sf; WCh: '11-13-15-17: h/sf/sf/3; WJ: '08- 7; EC: '10-12-14-16: h/sf/4/2; EU23: '09- h,'11- 2; WUG: '11- 6; won HUN 200m 2009, 110mh 2007, 2011-17. At 60mh: WI: '16- 6; EI: '13- 4, '15- 7.
Seven Hungarian 110mh records 2014-17.
Progress at 110mh: 2007- 14.48, 2008- 14.44/14.43w, 2009- 13.96/13.88w, 2010- 13.79, 2011- 13.58, 2012- 13.50, 2013- 13.36, 2014- 13.29, 2015- 13.45, 2016- 13.28, 2017- 13.15. pbs: 60m 6.85i '13, 100m 10.60 '09, 200m 21.35 '13, 400m 49.6 '07, 60mh 7.53i '17, 400mh 56.38 '06.

Bence HALÁSZ b. 4 Aug 1997 Kiskunhalas 1.88m 86kg. Dobó SE.
At HT: WCh: '17: 11; WJ: '14- dnq 14, '16- 1 (dnq 35 DT); WY: '13- 7; EJ: '15- 1 (dnq 15 DT); EU23: '17- 1. Won HUN 2017.
Progress at HT: 2012- 51.56, 2013- 62.33, 2014- 68.55, 2015- 69.80, 2016- 73.97, 2017- 78.85. pbs: SP 16.12 '17, DT 54.31 '17.

Zoltán KÖVÁGÓ b. 10 Apr 1979 Szolnok 2.04m 127kg. Szolnoki Honvéd SE. Army lieutenant.
At DT: OG: '00- dnq, '04- 2, '08- dnq 21, '16- 7; WCh: '01-03-05-07-09-11-15-17: dnq 20/dnq 19/10/9/6/dnq 15/dnq 18/dnq 22; EC: '02-10-12-14-16: 7/dnq 21/dq (3)/dnq 14/6; WJ: '96- 4, '98- 1; EJ: '97- 3; EU23: '99- 6, '01- 1. HUN champion 2001, 2004-05, 2008-11, 2014-17; W.MilG 2015.
Progress at DT: 1995- 49.78, 1996- 59.70, 1997- 62.16, 1998- 60.27, 1999- 63.23, 2000- 66.76, 2001- 66.93, 2002- 65.98, 2003- 66.03, 2004- 68.93, 2005- 66.00, 2006- 69.95, 2007- 66.42, 2008- 68.17, 2009- 67.64, 2010- 69.69, 2011- 69.50, 2012- 68.21dq, 2014- 65.82, 2015- 67.39, 2016- 67.13, 2017- 65.67. pb SP 15.93 '01. 2-year drugs ban 2011-13.

Krisztián PARS b. 18 Feb 1982 Körmend 1.88m 113kg. Dobó SE.
At HT: OG: '04- 4, '08- 4, '12- 1, '16- 7; WCh: '05-07-09-11-13-15-17: 6/5/4/2/2/4/dnq 14; EC: '06-10-12-14: 5/3/1/1; WY: '99- 1; EJ: '01- 1; EU23: '03- 1; CCp: '14- 1. Won HUN 2005-16; World HT challenge 2011-12, 2014.
World junior records with 6kg hammer: 80.64 & 81.34 in 2001.
Progress at HT: 1998- 54.00, 1999- 61.92, 2000- 66.80, 2001- 73.09, 2002- 74.18, 2003- 78.81, 2004- 80.90, 2005- 80.03, 2006- 82.45, 2007- 81.40, 2008- 81.96, 2009- 81.43, 2010- 79.64, 2011- 81.89, 2012- 82.28, 2013- 82.40, 2014- 82.69, 2015- 79.91, 2016- 77.38, 2017- 76.84. pbs: SP 15.60 '05, DT 53.80 '06.

Women

Xénia KRIZSÁN b. 13 Jan 1993 Budapest 1.71m 62kg. MTK Budapest.
At Hep: OG: '16- 16; WCh: '15- 9, '17- 9; EC: '14- 9, '16- 4; WJ: '10- 7, '12- 2; WY: '09- 4; EU23: '13- 7, '15- 1; EJ: 11- 7. At Pen: WI: '18- 6; EI: '17- 4. Won HUN 100mh 2013,2015; LJ 2011-12, Hep 2013.
Progress at Hep: 2010- 5594, 2011- 5794, 2012- 5957, 2013- 5896, 2014- 6317, 2015- 6322, 2016- 6266, 2017- 6390. pbs: 200m 24.72 '15, 400m 56.48 '12, 800m 2:07.17 '17, 60mh 8.30i '15, 100mh 13.51 '16, 13.50w '17; HJ 1.82 '17, LJ 6.26 '17, TJ 11.83 '10,

SP 14.34 '17, JT 51.25 '17, Pen 4631i '17.

Anita MÁRTON b. 15 Jan 1989 Szeged 1.71m 84kg. Békéscsabai AC.
At SP (DT): OG: '12- dnq 22, '16- 3; WCh: '09-11-13: dnq 23/20/19, '15- 4, '17- 2 (dnq 24); EC: '10-12-14-16: 9/7/3/2; WJ: '06- dnq 15 (12), '08- 7 (6); WY: '05- 11 (dnq); EU23: '09- 5, (11) '11- 5 (3); EJ: '07- 7 (6); WUG: '13- 4; WI: '14-16-18: 5/2/1; EI: '11-15-17: 5/1/1; won HUN SP 2006-17, DT 2008-17. Three Hungarian shot records 2014-16.
Progress at SP: 2004- 13.88, 2005- 14.12i/13.90, 2006- 15.57, 2007- 15.68, 2008- 16.90, 2009- 17.27, 2010- 18.20, 2011- 18.15, 2012- 18.48, 2013- 18.18, 2014- 19.04, 2015- 19.48, 2016- 19.87, 2017- 19.63, 2018- 19.62i. pbs: DT 60.94 '16, HT 51.12 '17.
Improved pb from 18.48/18.63i to 19.04 to take EC bronze 2014, indoor best to 19.23i for EI gold and outdoor pb to 19.48 for World 4th 2015 and to 19.87 for Olympic silver 2016; HUN indoor record 19.33 for 2nd WI 2016 and again with 19.48 and 19.62 to become the first Hungarian to win a World Indoor title.

Györgyi ZSIVOCZKY-FARKAS b. 13 Feb 1985 Budapest 1.70m 58kg. Budapesti Honved SE.
At Hep: OG: '08- 27, '12- 20, '16- 8; WCh: '11-13-15-17: 22/15/6/17; EC: '12-14-16: 13/10/5; WJ: '02- 10, '04- 7; EU23: '05- 16; WUG: 13- 2/ At Pen: WI: '16- 4; EI: '15- 6, '17- 3. Won HUN LJ 2010, Hep 2008, 2010-11.
Progress at Hep: 2002- 5339, 2004- 5550, 2005-5342, 2006- 5033, 2008- 5842, 2009- dnf, 2010-5874, 2011- 6068, 2012- 6030, 2013- 6269, 2014-6180, 2015- 6389, 2016- 6442, 2017- 6050. pbs: 200m 25.21 '15, 40m 56.59 '16, 800m 2:11.76 '16, 60mh 8.44i '15, 100mh 13.79 '16, HJ 1.87 '16, LJ 6.38i '17, 6.32 '13; SP 14.95i '17, 14.62 '15; DT 42.06 '07, JT 50.73 '14, Pen 4723i '17.
Married to Attila Zsivoczky (Dec 8554 '00, 4/3 WCh 01/05, 8/6 OG 00/04. 2 EC 06).

ICELAND

Governing body: Frjálsíthróttasamband Islands. Founded 1947.
National Championships first held in 1927. **2017 Champions: Men:** 100m: Kolbeinn Hödur Gunnarsson 10.89, 200m: Ari Bragi Kárson 21.79, 400m: Kormákur Ari Haflidason 48.87, 800m/1500m: Kristin Thór Kristinsson 1:54.68/ 4:00.40, 5000m/10000m/Mar/3000mSt: Arnar Pétursson 15:27.91/32:25.87/2:28:17/9:43.73, HMar: Hlynur Andrésson 69:08, 110mh: Ísak Óli Traustason 15.26, 400mh: Ivar Kristinn Jasonarson 53.30, HJ: Bjarki Rúnar Kristinsson 1.90, PV: Ingi Rúnar Kristinsson 4.42, LJ/TJ: Kristinn Torfason 7.18/14.40, SP: Ódinn Björn Thorsteinsson 16.22, DT: Gudni Valur Gudnason 58.11, HT: Hilmar Örn Jónsson 69.16, JT: Dagbjatrur Dadi Jónsson 68.97. **Women:** 100m: Tiana Osak Whitworth 12.02, 200m: Gudbjörg Jóna Bjarnadóttir 24.68, 400m: Vilhelma Thór Óskarsdóttir 59.25, 800m: Idunn Björg Arnaldsdóttir 2:20.97, 1500m/3000m/ 5000m: Andrea Kolbeinsdóttir 4:54.87/10:37.32/ 18:40.57, HMar: Elín Edda Sigurdardóttir 1:21:25, Mar: Ásta Kristín R. Parker 3:11:07, 100mh: Arna Stefanía Gudmundsdóttir 14.13, 400mh: Sara Hlín Jóhannsdóttir 66.63, HJ: Thóranna Ósk Sigurjónsdóttir 1.72, PV: Karen Sif Ársælsdóttir 2.92, LJ: Gudrún Heida Bjarnadóttir 5.78, TJ: Hildigunnur Thórinsdóttir 11.62, SP/DT/JT: Ásdis Hjálmsdóttir 14.88/ 47.65/56.75, HT: Vigdis Jónsdóttir 55.67.

INDIA

Governing body: Athletics Federation of India. Founded 1946.
National Championships first held as Indian Games in 1924. **2017 Champions: Men**: 100m: Mohammad Sadath 10.57, 200m: Vidya Sagar 21.46, 400m: Jithu Baby 47.08, 800m/1500m: Ajay Kumar Saroj 1:49.05/3:41.93, 5000m/ 10000m: Govindan Lakshmanan 14:04.21/ 29:16.21, 3000mSt: Avinash Sable 8:39.81, 110mh: Thingalaya Siddhanth 14.06, 400mh: Santhosh Kumar 50.16, HJ: Siddharth Yadav 2.23, PV: Jayaraj Preeth 5.00, LJ: S.E.Shamsheer 7.74, TJ: K.Sreejith Mon 16.15, SP: Tejinder Pal Singh 18.86, DT: Dharam Raj Yadav 55.08, HT: Neeraj Kumar 65.42, JT: Davinder Singh Kang 75.12, Dec: Abhishek Shetty 6835, 20kW: Krishnan Ganapathy 1:27:33/Kolothum Thodi Irfan 1:22:44, 50kW: Sandeep Kumar 3:56:00. **Women**: 100m: Suseendran Archana 11.78, 200m: Hima Das 24.26, 400m: Soniya Baishya 53.98, 800m: Lili Das 2:04.51, 1500m: Archana Adhav 4:18.64, 5000m/10000m: Suriya Loganathan 16:02.85/ 32:42.62, 3000mSt: Chinta Yadav 9:49.23, 100mh/Hep: Purnima Hembram 13.89/5126, 400mh: Jauna Murmu 58.25, HJ: Jinu Maria Manuel 1.78, PV: Vakharia Khyati 3.90, LJ: Narayanan V. Neena 6.35, TJ: B. Aishwarya 13.03, SP: Navjeet Kaur 15.23, DT: Kamalpreet Kaur 54.25, HT: Sarita Prakash Singh 60.54, JT: Annu Rani 57.90, 20kW: Priyanka Goswami 1:40:43/1:37:59.

Neeraj CHOPRA b. 24 Dec 1997 Khandra Panipat, Haryana 1.84m 80kg.
At JT: WCh: '17- dnq 15; WJ: '16- 1; WY: '13- dnq 17, AsiC: '15- 9, '17- 1; AsiJ: '16- 2.
Javelin records: World junior 2016, two Asian junior & two Indian 2016.
Progress at JT: 2014- 70.19, 2015- 81.04, 2016-86.48, 2017- 85.63, 2018- 85.94.

Women

Lalita Shivaji **BABAR** b. 2 Jun 1989 Mohi, Satara district 1.60m 58kg.
At 3000mSt: OG: '16- 10; WCh: '15- 8; AsiG: '14-3; AsiC: '15- 1. At 10000m: CG: '10- 8. Won Indian 5000m 2010, 3000mSt 2015.
Indian records: HMar 2015, 3000mSt (5) 2014-16

Progress at 3000mSt: 2013- 10:33.40, 2014- 9:35.37, 2015- 9:27.86, 2016- 9:19.76. pbs: 5000m 15:46.73 '15, 10000m 34:54.37 '10, road: 10k 34::10 '10, HMar 70:52 '15, Mar 2:38:21 '15.
Married to Sandip Bhosale.

IRAN

Governing body: Amateur Athletic Federation of Islamic Republic of Iran. Founded 1936.

Ehsan HADADI b. 21 Jan 1985 Ahvaz 1.93m 125kg.
At DT: OG: '08- dnq 17, '12- 2, '16- dnq 24; WCh: '07-11-15-17: 7/3/dnq 24/dnq 15; WJ: '04- 1; AsiG: '06-10-14: 1/1/1; AsiC: '03-05-07-09-11-17: 8/1/1/ 1/1/1; AsiJ: '04- 1; WCp: '06- 2, '10- 3. Won W.Asian 2005. 8 Asian discus records 2005-08.
Progress at DT: 2002- 53.66, 2003- 54.40, 2004- 54.96, 2005- 65.25, 2006- 63.79, 2007- 67.95, 2008- 69.32, 2009- 66.19, 2010- 68.45, 2011- 66.08, 2012- 68.20, 2013- 66.98, 2014- 65.24, 2015- 65.22, 2016- 63.61, 2017- 65.66. pb SP 17.82i '08, 16.00 '06.
First Iranian athlete to win an Olympic medal.

IRELAND

Governing Body: The Athletic Association of Ireland (AAI). Founded in 1999. Original Irish federation (Irish Champions AC) founded 1873.
National Championships first held in 1873.
2017 Champions: **Men**: 100m: Jeremy Phillips 10.39, 200m: Eanna Madden 21.07, 400m: Brian Gregan 45.74, 800m: Mark English 1:50.89, 1500m: Seán Tobin 3:53.90, 5000m: Conor Dooney 14:25.60, 10000m/HMar: Kevin Dooney 29:30.16/66:50, Mar: Gary O'Hanlon 2:18:53, 3000mSt: Adam Kirk-Smith GBR 8:55.72, 110mh: Gerard O'Donnell 13.94w, 400mh: Thomas Barr 49.79, HJ: Ryan Carthy Walsh 2.11, PV: Thomas Houlihan 4.55, LJ: Adam McMullen 7.74, TJ: Denis Finnegan 15.39, SP: John Kelly 16.46, DT: Colin Quirke 55.12, HT: Ryan McCullough 65.84, JT: Stephen Rice 62.94, Dec: Shane Aston 6540, 10000mW: Joe Mooney 53:12.69, 20kW: Alex Wright 1:32:05. **Women**: 100m: Amy Foster 11.43, 200m: Phil Healy 23.56, 400m: Cliodhna Manning 53.25, 800m: Ciara Mageean 2:04.06, 1500m/5000m: Emma Mitchell 4:31.55/16:27.08, HMar: Gladys Ganiel 77:06, Mar: Laura Graham 2:39:06, 3000mSt: Kerry O'Flaherty 10:01.40, 100mh: Sarah Lavin 13.62, 400mh: Nessa Cooper Millet 61.34, HJ: Pippa Rogan 1.73, PV: Ellen McCartney 3.55, LJ/TJ: Sarah Buggy 5.87/13.01, SP/DT: Clare Fitzgerald 14.96/51.17, HT: Cara Kennedy 53.17, JT: Grace Casey 43.42, Hep: Amy McTeggart 4302, 5000mW: Kate Veale 23:22.15, 20kW: Veronica Burke 1:47:10.

Thomas BARR b. 24 Jul 1992 Waterford 1.83m 73kg. Ferrybank. Engineering graduate of University of Limerick.
At 400mh: OG: '16- 4; WCh: '15/17- sf; EC: '12/14/16- sf, EU23: '13- 8; EJ: '11- 6; WUG: '15- 1. Irish champion 2014-17.
Five Irish 400mh records 2014-16.
Progress at 400mh: 2009- 56.53, 2010- 56.47. 2011- 50.06, 2012- 50.22, 2013- 49.78, 2014- 48.90, 2015- 48.65, 2016- 47.97, 2017- 48.95. pbs: 200m 21.47i '16, 21.83 '17; 400m 46.87i '17, HJ 1.83 '09.
Sister Jessie Barr (b. 24 Jul 1989) pb 400mh 55.93 '12, 8 EC '12.

Robert HEFFERNAN b. 20 Feb 1978 Cork City 1.73m 55kg. Togher AC.
At 20kW/(50kW): OG: '00- 28, '04- dq, '08- 8, '12- 9/3, '16- (6); WCh: '01-05-07-09-13-15-17: 14/ dq/6/14/(1)/(5)/8; EC: '02- 8, '10- 3/4, '14- (dnf); WCp: '08- 9, '12- 8; ECp: '07-09-11-13-17: 5/4/6/ 9/13. At 10000mW: EJ: '97- 14; EU23: '99- 13. Won Irish 10000mW 2001-02, 2004-5, 2007-11; 20kW 2000-02, 2004, 2009; 30kW 2008.
Irish records: 3000mW 2013, 20kW (4) 2001-08, 50kW (3) 2010-12. World M35 3000mW 2013.
Progress at 20kW, 50kW: 1999- 1:26:45, 2000- 1:22:43, 2001- 1:21:11, 2002- 1:20:25, 2003- 1:23:03, 2004- 1:20:55, 2005- 1:24:20, 2006- 1:22:24, 2007- 1:20:15, 2008- 1:19:22, 2009- 1:22:09, 2010- 1:20:45, 3:45:30; 2011- 1:20:54, 3:49:28; 2012- 1:20:18, 3:37.54; 2013- 1:21:59, 3:37:56; 2014- 1:20:57, 2015- 3:44:17, 2016- 1:22:41, 3:43:55; 2017- 1:22:40, 3:44:41. pbs: 1MW 5:39.75i '14, 3000mW 11:09.08 14, 5000mW 18:51.46i '08, 18:59.37 '07; 10000mW 38:27.57 '08, 30kW 2:07:48 '11, 35kW 2:31:19 '00.
Married to Marian Andrews (b. 16 Apr 1982, Irish 400m champion 2008-09, pb 53.10 '11).

ISRAEL

Governing body: Israeli Athletic Association. Founded as Federation for Amateur Sport in Palestine 1931.
National Championships first held in 1935.
2017 Champions: **Men** 100m/200m Imri Pressiado 10.51/20.99, 400m: Maor Szeged 48.17, 800m: Necho Tayachew 1:54.61, 1500m/5000m: Yimer Getahun 3:44.09/14:15.65, 10000m/Mar: Girmaw Amare 28:43.11/2:17:20, HMar: Aimeru Almeya 67:51, 3000mSt: Noam Neeman 9:08.71, 110mh: Itamar Feiler 14.55, 400mh: Khai Cohen 53.06, HJ: Dmitriy Kroyter 2.22, PV: Lev Skorish 5.40, LJ: Gilron Tzavkevitz 7.30, TJ: Tom Yaacobov 16.23, SP/DT: Itamar Levi 18.07/55.15, HT: Viktor Zaginaiko 55.56, JT: Assa'el Arad 59.72, Dec: Konstantin Krinitzkiy 6121. **Women**: 100m: Diana Vaisman 11.85/24.25, 400m: Dariya Lokshin 57.33, 800m: Neri Gettreide 2:13.75, 1500m/5000m/3000mSt: Advah Cohen 4:24.49/ 17:05.91/10:16.20, 10000m: Chemtai Korlima 32:43.89, HMar: Yelena Dolinin 1:16:23, Mar: Mentamer Bikaya 2:53:24, 100mh: Allina Drozdov 14.19, 400mh: Dariya Lukshin 61.95, HJ: Yarden Delyahu 1.74, PV: Naama Bronstein 4.05, LJ: Yiff'at Zelikovitz 5.99, TJ: Noah Levi 12.19, SP: Anastasia Muchkaev 13.76, DT: Estelle Valeanu 48.61, HT: Margarita Belov 54.84, JT: Margaryta Dorozhon 55.77, Hep: Danielle Polster 4198.

Women

Hanna MINENKO b. 25 Sep 1989 Periaslav-Khmelnytskyi 1.78m 61kg. née Knyazyeva. Maccabi Tel Aviv.
At TJ: OG: '12- 4, '16- 5; WCh: '13- 6, '15- 2, '17- 4; EC: '16- 2; WJ: '08- 4; EJ: '07- 2; EU23: '11- 5; WUG: '11- 4; EI: '14- 3. Won UKR TJ 2012, ISR LJ 2014; TJ 2013-16.
Eight Israeli triple jump records 2013-15 and one long jump 2014.
Progress at TJ: 2005- 12.87, 2006- 13.28, 2007- 13.85, 2009- 13.61, 2010- 13.65, 2011- 14.20, 2012- 14.71, 2013- 14.58, 2014- 14.29, 2015- 14.78, 2016- 14.68, 2017- 14.42. pb LJ 6.52 '14.
Married Anatoliy Minenko (Dec 7046 '10) in November 2012 and switched from Ukraine to Israel on 12 May 2013.

ITALY

Governing Body: Federazione Italiana di Atletica Leggera (FIDA. First governing body formed 1896.
National Championships first held in 1897 (one event)/1906 (men), 1927 (women). **2017 Champions**: **Men**: 100m: Federico Cattaneo 10.24w, 200m: Eseosa Desalu 20.32w, 400m: Davide Re 46.07, 800m: Stefano Migliorati 1:49.85, 1500m: João Bussotti 3:46.12, 5000m: Najibe Marco Salami 14:06.59, 10000m: Ahmed El Mazoury 28:41.24, HMar: Yassine Rachik 62:13, Mar: Ahmed Nasef 2:16:52, 3000mSt: Ala Zoghlami 8:36.42, 110mh: Lorenzo Perini 13.54, 400mh: Lorenzo Vergani 49.36, HJ: Eugenio Meloni 2.21, PV: Giorgio Piantella 5.40, LJ: Filippo Randazzo 7.95, TJ: Daniele Cavazzani 16.40, SP: Sebastiano Bianchetti 19.74, DT: Hannes Kirchler 60.50, HT: Marco Lingua 73.84, JT: Mauro Fraresso 77.36, Dec: Jacopo Zanatta 7327, 10000mW: Federico Tontodonati 40:34.09, 20kW: Francesco Fortunato 1:22:04, 50kW: Stefano Chiesa 4:16:01; **Women**: 100m: Irene Siragusa 11.35, 200m: Gloria Hooper 23.14, 400m: Maria Benedicta Chigbolu 52.31, 800m: Yusneysi Santiusti 2:02.80, 1500m: Giulia Aprile 4:20.56, 5000m: Valeria Roffino 16:30.47, 10000m: Sara Dossena 33:11.98, HMar: Sara Brogiato 74:48, Mar: Federica Dal Ri 2:37:44, 3000mSt: Francesca Bertoni 9:56.96, 100mh: Micol Cattaneo 13.20, 400mh: Yadisleidy Pedroso 55.09, HJ: Erika Furlani 1.88, PV: Elisa Molinarolo 4.25, LJ: Laura Strati 6.59, TJ: Dariya Derkach 13.77, SP: Chiara Rosa 16.67, DT: Stefania Strumillo 56.15, HT: Sara Fantini 66.81, JT: Zahra Bani 59.01, Hep: Sveva Gerevini 5420, 10000mW: Eleonora Giorgi 43:58.95, 20kW: Valentina Trapletti 1:33:45.

Marco DE LUCA b. 12 May 1981 Rome 1.88m 69kg. Fiamme Gialle.
At 50kW: OG: '08- 19, '12- 14, '16- 21; WCh: 05-07-09-11-13-15-17: 13/dnf/7/11/15/16/9; EC: '06-10-14: 7/6/7; WCp: 06-08-10-12-16: 9/8/14/6/3; ECp: '07-09-11-15: 8/8/2/3. Won Italian 20kW 2011, 50kW 2006, 2009.
Progress at 50kW: 2002- 4:07:06, 2003- 4:13:24, 2004- 4:05:01, 2005- 3:55:30, 2006- 3:48:08, 2007- 3:47:04, 2008- 3:49:21, 2009- 3:46:31, 2010- 3:48:36, 2011- 3:49:40, 2012- 3:47:19, 2013- 3:48:05, 2014- 3:45:25, 2015- 3:46:21, 2016- 3:44:47, 2017- 3:45:02. pbs: 3000mW 12:03.79 '09, 5000mW 19:29.54i '15, 20:03.6 '05, 10000mW 40:48.0 '09, 20kW 1:22:38 '10, 30kW 2:09:37 '04, 35kW 2:28:53 '10.

Fabrizio DONATO b. 14 Aug 1976 Latina 1.89m 82kg. Fiamme Gialle.
At TJ: OG: '00/04/08/16: dnq 25/21/21/17, '12- 3; WCh: '03/07-09-13: dnq 13/32/41/15, '11- 10; EC: '02-06-10-12-14: 4/dnq 16/9/1/7; EJ: '95- 5; WI: '01-08-10-12: 6/4/5/4; EI: '00-02-09-11-17: 6/4/1/2/2; ECp: '00-02-03-04-06-14-15: 2/2/1/6/1/2/1. Won MedG 2001, Italian 2000, 2004, 2006-08, 2010-11, 2015.
Italian triple jump record 2000, world M40 records 16.60 & 17.13 at EI '17 and 17.32 outdoors.
Progress at TJ: 1992- 12.88, 1993- 14.36, 1994- 15.27, 1995- 15.81, 1996- 16.35, 1997- 16.40A, 1998- 16.73, 1999- 16.66i/16.53w, 2000- 17.60, 2001- 17.05, 2002- 17.17, 2003- 17.16, 2004- 16.90, 2005- 16.65/16.68w, 2006- 17.33i/17.24, 2007- 16.97/17.06w, 2008- 17.27i/16.91/17.29w, 2009- 17.59i/15.81, 2010- 17.39i/17.08, 2011- 17.73i/17.17, 2012- 17.53/17.63w, 2013- 16.86, 2014- 16.89/17.24w, 2015- 16.91/17.11w, 2016- 16.93, 2017- 17.32. pb LJ 8.03i '11, 8.00 '06.
Italian indoor record to win 2009 European Indoor title. Married Patrizia Spuri (400m 51.74 '98, 8 EC 98, 800m 1:59.96 '98) on 27 Sep 2003.

Marco FASSINOTTI b. 29 Apr 1989 Turin 1.90m 71kg. Aeronautica Militare.
At HJ: EC: '10- 9, '14- 7; WJ: '08- 7; EU23: '09- 6, '11- 5; WI: '14- 6; EI: '11- 6; WUG: '09- 4, '17- 2; ET: '15- 2. '17- 2; Italian champion 2013, 2015.
ITA high jump record 2015, indoors (3) 2014-16.
Progress at HJ: 2005- 1.70, 2006- 1.90, 2007- 2.08, 2008- 2.17, 2009- 2.22, 2010- 2.28, 2011- 2.29i/2.25, 2012- 2.26i/2.24, 2013- 2.27, 2014- 2.34i/2.30, 2015- 2.34i/2.33, 2016- 2.35i/2.29, 2017- 2.29.

Gianmarco TAMBERI b. 1 Jun 1992 Civitanove Marche 1.89m 71kg. Fiamme Gialle.
At HJ: OG: '12- dnq 21=; WCh: '15- 8=, '17- dnq 13=; EC: '12-14-16: 5/7=/1; WY: '09- dnq 18; EU23: '13- dnq 13=; EJ: '11- 3; WI: '16- 1; EI: '13- 5, '15- 7; Italian champion 2012, 2014, 2016.
Four Italian high jump records 2015-16 & three indoor 2016.
Progress at HJ: 2005- 1.52, 2006- 1.62i, 2007- 1.80, 2008- 2.01, 2009- 2.07, 2010- 2.14, 2011-2.25, 2012- 2.31, 2013- 2.30i/2.25, 2014- 2.29, 2015- 2.37, 2016- 2.39, 2017- 2.29.
Suffered serious injury, costing him Olympic chance, just after setting Italian records at 2.37 and 2.39 in Monaco 2016. His father Marco had pb 2.28i (Italian indoor record)/2.27 '83, elder brother Gianluca 4th EJ JT 2009, pb 78.61 '10.

Women

Eleonora GIORGI b. 14 Sep 1989 Cuneo 1.63m 52kg. Fiamme Azzurre. Social-economic law graduate of University "Bocconi" of Milan.
At 20kW: OG: '12- 13, '16- dq; WCh: '13-15-17: 10/dq/14; EC: '14- 5; EU23: '09- 11, '11- 3; WCp: '12- 12, '14- 5; ECp: '13- 6, '15- 2; won MedG 2013. At 10000mW: WJ: '08- 18.
Walk records: World best 5000m 2014, 25k & 30k 2016; Italian 20k (3) 2014-15.
Progress at 20kW: 2009- 1:34:27, 2010- 1:34:00, 2011- 1:33:46, 2012- 1:29:48, 2013- 1:30:01, 2014- 1:27:05, 2015- 1:26:17, 2016- 1:28:05, 2017- 1:30:34. pbs: 3000mW 11:50.08i/12:05.83 '13, 5000mW 20:01.80 '14, 10kW 44:33.56t '13, 43:51R '11; 25kW 1:56:12 '16, 30kW 2:19:43 '16.

Antonella PALMISANO b. 6 Aug 1991 Mottola, Taranto 1.66m 49kg. Fiamme Galle.
At 20kW: OG: '16- 4; WCh: '13-15-17: 13/5/3; EC: '14- 7; EU23: '11- 2, '13- 2; WCp: '14- 9; ECp: 17- 1. At 10000mW: WJ: '08- 9, '10- 4; EJ: '09- 2; WCp: '10- 1J; ECp: '09- 3J. At 5000mW: WY: '07- 5.
Italian 5000m walk record 2017.
Progress at 20kW: 2009- 1:38:47, 2010- 1:36:21, 2011- 1:34:31, 2012- 1:34:27, 2013- 1:30:50, 2014- 1:27:51, 2015- 1:28:40, 2016- 1:29:03, 2017- 1:26:36. pbs: 3000mW 11:55.30i '18, 10kW 41:57.29t '17.

Alessia TROST b. 8 Mar 1993 Pordenone 1.88m 68kg. Fiamme Gialle.
At HJ: OG: '16- 5; WCh: '13- 7=, '17- dnq 19; EC: '14- 9=, '16- 6=; WJ: '12- 1; WY: '09- 1; EU23: '13- 1, '15- 1; EJ: '11- 4; WI: '16- 7, '18- 3; EI: '13- 4=, '15- 2; ET: '13- 2, '17- 3=; YthOly: '10- 2. Italian champion 2013-14, 2016.
Progress at HJ: 2003- 1.37, 2004- 1.55, 2005- 1.62, 2006- 1.68, 2008- 1.81, 2009- 1.89, 2010- 1.90, 2011- 1.87, 2012- 1.92, 2013- 2.00i/1.98, 2014- 1.96i/1.91, 2015- 1.97i/1.94, 2016- 1.95i/1.94, 2017- 1.94. pbs: 100mh 15.5 '11, LJ 6.01 '14, SP 10.76i '14, Pen 4035i '14.

IVORY COAST

Governing Body: Fédération Ivoirienne d'Athlétisme, Abidjan. Founded 1960.

Ben Youssef MEITÉ b. 11 Nov 1986 Séguéla 1.79m 70kg.
At 100m/(200m): OG: '12- sf, '16- 6; WCh: '09-11-15-17- h & qf/11- h & h/sf/sf; AfG: '07- sf/sf, '11- 2/2, '15- 1; AfCh: '06- sf, '10- 1/2, '12- h/1, '16- 1; CCp: '10- 5/3.
CIV records 100m (7) 2012-16, 200m 2009.
Progress at 100m: 1002- 10.95, 2004- 10.5h, 2005- 10.40, 2006- 11.07, 2007- 10.49/10.46w, 2008- 10.49, 2009- 10.21/10.15w, 2010- 10.08A/10.25/10.19w, 2011- 10.21/10.14w, 2012- 10.06, 2015- 10.04, 2016- 9.96/9.95w, 2017- 9.97/9.84w. pbs: 60m 6.55i '18, 200m 20.37 '09, 300m 33.68i '07.
Lives in Canada. His brother Ibrahim (b. 18 Nov 1976) had pbs of 60m 6.58i '02 (CIV rec), 100m 10.24 '00, 200m 20.64 '94 and competed at Olympic Games of 1996 and 2000. Their father Amadou had 100m pb 10.32 '80 and competed at the Olympic Games in 1972 and 1976 and won 1978 African Games 100m.

Women

Murielle AHOURÉ b. 23 Aug 1987 Abidjan 1.67m 57kg. Graduated in criminal law from the University of Miami, USA.
At 100m/200m: OG: '12- 7/6, '16- sf/sf; WCh: '13- 2/2, '15- sf/-, '17- 4; AfCh: '14- 2/1, '16- 1. At 60m: WI: '12-14-18: 2/2/1. Won NCAA indoor 200m 2009.
Three African 60m indoor records 2013-18. CIV records 100m (8) 2009-16, 200m (3) 2012-13.
Progress at 100m, 200m: 2005- 11.96, 2006- 11.42, 23.33; 2007- 11.41/11.28w, 23.34; 2008- 11.45, 23.50; 2009- 11.09, 22.78; 2010- 11.41, 2011- 11.06/10.86w, 2012- 10.99, 22.42; 2013- 10.91, 22.24; 2014- 10.97, 22.36; 2015- 10.81, 22.29; 2016- 10.78, 22.52; 2017- 10.83, 22.68. pbs: 60m 6.97i '18, 300m 38.09i '07, 400m 54.77 '08.
Lived in Paris from age 2, then USA from age 12. Won first medals for Ivory Coast at World Champs.

Marie Josée TA LOU Gonerie b. 18 Nov 1988 1.59m 57kg.
At 100m/200m: OG: '16- 4/4; WCh: '15- sf/sf, '17- 2/2; AfG: '11- 7/6, 15- 1/1/3R; AfCh: '10- sf/-, '12- 4/3/3R, '14- 3/2/2R, '16- 3/1; CCp: '14- 4/5. At 60m: WI: '16- 7, '18- 2.
CIV 200m records 2016-17.
Progress at 100m: 2010- 12.10/11.6, 24.3; 2011- 11.56, 24.12; 2012- 11.53, 23.26; 2013- 11.58, 23.63; 2014- 11.20, 22.78; 2015- 11.02/10.95w, 22.56; 2016- 10.86, 22.21; 2017- 10.86, 22.08. pb 60m 7.05i '18.

JAMAICA

Governing body: Jamaica Athletics Administrative Association. Founded 1932.
2017 Champions: **Men**. 100m/200m: Yohan Blake 9.95/20.29, 400m: Nathon Allen 44.58, 800m: Daniel Glave 1:47.47, 1500m: Thaleetio Green 3:59.75, 5000m: Kemoy Campbell 13:53.61, 110mh: Omar McLeod 12.90, 400mh: Jaheel Hyde 48.53, HJ: Clayton Brown 2.15, PV: Akeem Kerr 4.20, LJ: Ramone Bailey 8.16, TJ: Clive Pullen 16.83, SP: O'Dayne Richards 21.29, DT: Fredrick Dacres 66.52, HT: Caniggia Raynor 70.93, JT: Adrien Mitchell 67.16. **Women**: 100m: Elaine Thompson 10.71, 200m: Shashalee Forbes 22.71, 400m: Shericka Jackson 50.05, 800m: Natolya Goule 2:00.90, 100mh: Danielle Williams 12.56, 400mh: Rhonda Whyte 54.29, HJ: Kimberly Williamson 1.88, LJ: Jessica Noble 6.46, TJ: Kimberly Williams 14.60w, SP: Danniel Thomas 18.80, DT: Kellion Knibb 62.73, HT: Niocky Grant 56.87, JT: Kateema Rietttie 48.53.

Nathon ALLEN b. 28 Oct 1995 1.78m 68kg. Auburn University, USA.
At 400m/4x400mR: OG: '16- 2R; WCh: '17- 5;

WJ: '14- sf/3R; WI: '16- 4R. JAM champion 2017. Progress at 400m: 2014- 46.11, 2015- 45.30, 2016- 45.39, 2017- 44.19. pb 200m 20.70 '16.

Nickel ASHMEADE b. 7 Apr 1990 Ocho Rios, Saint-Ann 1.84m 87kg.
At 200m/4x100mR (100m): OG: '16- sf/sf/1R; WCh: '11- 5, '13- 4/1R (5), '15- 8/1R (sf); CG: 14- (3)/1R; WJ: '08- 2/2R (2 4x400m); WY: '07- 3 (2, 3 MedR); PAm-J: '09- 1; won DL 2012, JAM 2015, CAC 2009.
World 4x200m record 2014.
Progress at 100m, 200m: 2006- 10.60, 21.30; 2007- 10.39, 20.76; 2008- 10.34, 20.80/20.16w; 2009- 10.37/10.21w, 20.40; 2010- 10.39, 20.63; 2011- 9.96, 19.91; 2012- 9.93, 19.85; 2013- 9.90, 19.93; 2014- 9.97/9.95w, 19.95; 2015- 9.91, 20.18; 2016- 9.94, 20.07; 2017- 10.18, 20.37. pbs: 60m 6.62i '14, 400m 47.19 '12.

Kemar BAILEY-COLE b. 10 Jan 1992 St. Catherine 1.95m 83kg. Racers TC.
At 100m/4x100mR (200m): OG: '12- res (1)R, '16- res 1R; WCh: '13- 4/1R; CG: '14- 1/1R; WY: '09- sf/sf.
Progress at 100m: 2008- 10.85, 2009- 10.41/10.38w, 2010- 10.53, 2011- 10.28, 2012- 9.97, 2013- 9.93, 2014- 9.96/9.95w, 2015- 9.92, 2016- 10.00, 2017- 10.06. pbs: 150mSt 15.00 '14, 200m 20.66 '15, 400m 47.20 '17.

Yohan BLAKE b. 26 Dec 1989 St. James 1.81m 79kg. Racers TC.
At 100m/4x100mR: OG: '12- 2/2/1R, '16- 4/sf/1R; WCh: '11- 1/1R, '17- 4/sf; WJ: '06- 3/1R, '08- 4/2R; WY: '05- 7; PAm-J: '07- 2 (3 4x400m); won CAC-J 100m & 200m 2006; JAM 100m & 200m 2012, 2016-17.
World record 4x100m 2012, 4x200m 2014.
Progress at 100m, 200m: 2005- 10.56, 22.10; 2006- 10.33, 20.92; 2007- 10.11, 20.62; 2008- 10.27/10.20w, 21.06; 2009- 10.07/9.93dq, 20.60; 2010- 9.89, 19.78; 2011- 9.82/9.80w, 19.26; 2012- 9.69, 19.44; 2013- 20.72, 2014- 10.02, 20.48; 2015- 10.12, 21.57; 2016- 9.93, 20.13; 2017- 9.90, 19.97. pbs: 60m 6.75i '08, 150mSt 14.71 '14, 400m 46.32 '13.
3-month drugs ban from positive test at Jamaican Champs 25 Jun 2009. Cut 200m pb from 20.60 to 19.78 in Monaco 2010 and then to 19.26 in Brussels 2011. Youngest ever World 100m champion at 21 in 2011.

Roxroy CATO b. 1 May 1988 Saint Mary 1.83m 76kg.Was at Lincoln University, Missouri, USA.
At 400mh: OG: '12-h, '16- sf; WCh: '15- h; PAm: '15- 3; CG: '14- dq h.
Progress at 400mh: 2007- 54.24; 2008- 52.75, 2009- 50.74, 2010- 49.45, 2011- 49.66, 2012- 49.03, 2013- 49.15, 2014- 48.48, 2015- 48.72, 2016- 48.56, 2017- 49.33. pbs: 100m 11.01 '08, 200m 21.36Ai '11, 21.38 '13, 400m 46.97 '14.

Fedrick DACRES b. 28 Feb 1994 Kingston 1.91m 104kg. Irvine.
At DT: OG: '16- dnq 34; WCh: '15- 7, '17- 4; PAm: '15- 1; WJ: '12- 1; WY '11- 1; won CAC-J 2012; JAM 2015-17.
Three Jamaican discus records 2017-18.
Progress at DT: 2011- 53.05, 2012- 55.45, 2013- 59.30, 2014- 66.75, 2015- 66.40, 2016- 68.02, 2017- 68.88, 2018- 68.84/69.75 light. pb SP 20.46 '17.

Rasheed DWYER b. 29 Jan 1989 St. Mary 1.88m 80kg. G.C.Foster College.
At 200m/4x100mR: WCh: '15- res 1R, '17- sf; CG: '10- sf/2R, '14- 1; WJ: '08- res2R; PAm: '15- 2; WUG: '11- 1, '13- 2; CCp: '14- 2. Won NACAC 2015. CAC 4x200m record 2014.
Progress at 200m: 2006- 21.67, 2007- 21.81, 2008- 21.84, 2009- 21.12/20.82w, 2010- 20.49, 2011- 20.20, 2012- 20.59, 2013- 20.15, 2014- 19.98, 2015- 19.80, 2016- 20.46, 2017- 20.11. pbs: 100m 10.10/10.08w '16, 400m 46.76 '16.

Damar FORBES b. 18 Sep 1990 Saint Ann 1.85m 77kg. Sports administration degree from Louisiana State University.
At LJ: OG: '12- dnq 19, '16- 12; WCh: '11/15- dnq 20/26, '13- 8, '17- 12; CG: '14- 9. Jamaican champion 2012-16, NCAA 2013.
Progress at LJ: 2009- 7.51i/7.48, 2010- 9.93, 2011- 8.23, 2012- 8.13, 2013- 8.25/8.35w, 2014- 8.10, 2015- 8.17, 2016- 8.23, 2017- 8.29. Pbs: 60m 6.73i '13, 100m 10.51 '13, 55mh 7.48i '09, 60mh 8.12i '09, TJ 16.11i '12, 15.85 '10.

Julian FORTE b. 1 Jul 1993 Saint Andrew 1.86m 73kg. University of Technology.
At 200m: WCh: '15- sf, '17 sf 100m; CG: '14- res 1R; WJ: '12- 8.
Progress at 100m, 200m: 2009- 10.75, 21.93; 2010- 10.49, 21.04; 2011- 10.70, 21.18; 2012- 10.19m 20.38; 2013- 10.12/9.98w, 20.79/20.22w; 2014- 10.03, 20.49; 2015- 10.06, 20.04; 2016- 10.05/9.94w, 19.97; 2017- 9.91, 20.41. pbs: 60m 6.55 '17, 400m 47.18 '14, LJ 7.25 '09, TJ 14.77.

Javon FRANCIS b. 14 Dec 1994 Bull Bay 1.83m 73kg. Akan TC.
At 400m/4x400mR: OG: '16- sf/2R; WCh: '13- sf/2R, '15- sf; WJ: '12- 9. JAM champion 2015-16.
Progress at 400m: 2012- 46.06, 2013- 45.24, 2014- 45.00, 2015- 44.50, 2016- 44.77, 2017- 45.94. Pb 200m 20.54 '16.
Brilliant anchor relay legs at Worlds: 2013- 44.05 to move JAM from 5th to 2nd, and 43.52 in 2015, when pipped for 3rd place.

Demish GAYE b. 20 Jan 1993 1.88m 77kg.
At 400m/4x400mR: WCh: '17- 6; WI: '16- 4R.
Progress at 400m: 2015- 46.15, 2016- 45.30, 2017- 44.55. pb 200m 20.48 '17.

Jaheel HYDE b. 2 Feb 1997 1.80m 74kg. University of West Indies
At 400mh: OG: '16- sf; WCh: '17- sf; WJ: '14- 1/3R, '16- 1. Won JAM 2017. At 110mh: WY: '13- 1; Yth OG: '14- 1.
Progress at 400mh: 2014- 49.29, 2015- 49.01, 2016- 48.81, 2017- 48.52. Pbs: 200m 20.78 '17, 400m 46.66 '16.

Scored a hat-trick for the Jamaican U17 football team against Bermuda in 2012. His father Lenworth played football for Jamaica.

Ronald LEVY b. 30 Oct 1992 1.81m 73kg. MVP.
At 110mh: WCh: '17-h.
Progress at 110mh: 2013- 14.42, 2015- 13.63, 2016- 13.50, 2017- 13.05. Pbs: 60m 6.62 '16, 100m 10.17 '17, 10.10w '16; 200m 20.81 '14, 800m 1:52.47 '16, 60mh 7.49i '18, 400mh 51.77 '13.

Rusheen McDONALD b. 17 Aug 1992 Mandeville, Manchester 1.75m 73kg. Utech.
At 400m/4x400mR: OG: '12- h, '16- sf/res 2R; WCh: '13- 2R, '15- sf; CG: '14- sf.
Jamaican 400m record 2015.
Progress at 400m: 2011- 47.32, 2012- 45.10, 2013- 45.28, 2014- 45.25, 2015- 43.93, 2016- 45.22, 2017- 45.19. Pbs: 100m 10.53 '17, 200m 20.57 '15, 300m 31.94 '15.

Omar McLEOD b. 25 Apr 1994 Kingston 1.80m 73kg. Studied business management at University of Arkansas, USA.
At 110mh: OG: '16- 1; WCh: '15- 6, '17- 1; WY: '11- 4 (8 400mh). At 60mh: WI: '16- 1. At 4x400m: WJ: '12-1. Won JAM 2015-17, NCAA 110mh 2015 (& 60mh indoors 2014-15).
Commonwealth 110m hurdles record 2017.
Progress at 110mh: 2014- 13.44, 2015- 12.97, 2016- 12.98, 2017- 12.90. Pbs: 60m 6.61i '17, 100m 9.99 '16, 200m 20.48i '17, 400m 47.41i '15, 60mh 7.41i '16, 400mh 49.98 '13.
First man ever to run under 10 secs for 100m as well as 13 secs for 110m hurdles,

Kemar MOWATT b. 12 Mar 1995 1.88m 77kg. University of Arkansas, USA.
At 400mh: WCh: '17- 4.
Progress at 400mh: 2014- 52.03, 2015- 51.13, 2016- 50.66, 2017- 48.49. Pbs: 200m 21.07i '17, 21.34 '15; 400m 47.15i '17, 60mh 7.93i '16, 110mh 13.90 '17, 13.75w 16.

Hansle PARCHMENT b. 17 Jun 1990 Saint Thomas 1.96m 90kg. Student of psychology at University of the West Indies.
At 110mh: OG: '12- 3; WCh: '13-15-17: sf/2/8; CG: '10- 5; WY: '07- sf; WUG: '11- 1. Won JAM 2012.
Three Jamaican 110mh records 2012-13.
Progress at 110mh: 2010- 13.71, 2011- 13.24, 2012- 13.12, 2013- 13.05, 2014- 12.94, 2015- 13.03, 2016- 13.10, 2017- 13.19. Pb 400mh 53.74 '08.

Asafa POWELL b. 23 Nov 1982 St Catherine 1.90m 88kg. MVP. Studied sports medicine at Kingston University of Technology.
At 100m/4x100mR: OG: '04- 5 (dns 200), '08- 5/dq1R, '12- 7, '16- 1R; WCh: '03- qf, '07- 3/2R, '09- 3/1R, '15- 7/1R; CG: '02- sf/2R, '06- 1/1R; PAm-J: '01- 2R. At 60m: WI: '16- 2. Won JAM 100m 2003-05, 2007, 2011, 2015; 200m 2006, 2010; WAF 100m 2004, 2006-08; 200m 2004; DL 100m 2011, 2016; GL 2006.
Four world 100m records, five CAC & Commonwealth 2005-07, seven JAM 2004-7; WR 4x100m 2008. Two world bests 100y 2010. Two CAC 60m indoor records 2016.
Progress at 100m, 200m: 2001- 10.50, 2002- 10.12, 20.48; 2003- 10.02/9.9, 2004- 9.87, 20.06; 2005- 9.77, 2006- 9.77, 19.90; 2007- 9.74, 20.00; 2008- 9.72, 2009- 9.82, 2010- 9.82/9.72w, 19.97; 2011- 9.78, 20.55; 2012- 9.85, 2013- 9.88, 2014- 9.87, 2015- 9.81, 2016- 9.92, 2017- 10.08. pbs: 50m 5.64i '12, 60m 6.42+ '09, 6.44i '16; 100y 9.07+ '10, 400m 45.94 '09.
Disqualified for false start in World quarters 2003 after fastest time (10.05) in heats. In 2004 he tied the record of nine sub-10 second times in a season and in 2005 he took the world record for 100m at Athens, tying that at Gateshead and Zürich in 2006, when he ran a record 12 sub-10 times and was world athlete of the year. Took record to 9.74 in Rieti 2007 and ran 15 sub-10 times in 2008, including seven sub-9.90 in succession after 5th place at Olympics. Now has record 97 sub-10 times (plus 8w and 1 while banned). IAAF Athlete of the Year 2006. He tested positive for a banned stimulant on 21 Jun 2013; an original 18-month ban was reduced to 6 months by the CAS. Elder brother Donovan (b. 31 Oct 1971): at 60m: 6.51i '96 (won US indoors '96, 6 WI '99); 100m 10.07/9.7 '95.

O'Dayne RICHARDS b. 14 Dec 1988 St. Andrew 1.77m 120kg. Data communications graduate. MVP TC.
At SP: OG: '16- 8; WCh: '13- dnq 20, '15- 3, '17- dnq 19; CG: '14- 1; PAm: '15- 1; WUG: '11- 1; CCp: '14- 2; won CAC 2011, 2013; JAM 2013-17.
Four CAC shot records 2014-17.
Progress at SP: 2008- 16.76, 2009- 18.05, 2010- 18.74, 2011- 19.93, 2012- 20.31, 2013- 20.97, 2014- 21.61, 2015- 21.69, 2016- 20.82, 2017- 21.96. pb DT 58.31 '12.

Andrew RILEY b. 6 Sep 1988 Saint Thomas 1.88m 80kg. Economics graduate of University of Illinois.
At 110mh: OG: '12- h, '16- sf; WCh: '11- sf, '13- 8, '15- sf; CG: 14- 1. Jamaican champion 2011, 2013-14; won NCAA 100m 2012, 110mh 2010 & 2012. At 60mh: WI: '14 dns final.
Progress at 110mh: 2009- 13.74/13.61w, 2010- 13.45, 2011- 13.32, 2012- 13.19, 2013- 13.14, 2014- 13.19, 2015- 13.28, 2016- 13.35, 2017- 13.33. Pbs: 60m 6.57i '12, 100m 10.02 '12, 200m 21.25w '12, 60mh 7.53i '12, HJ 2.10 '08.
First to win NCAA 100m and 110mh double 2012.

Annsert WHYTE b. 4 Oct 1987 Kingston 1.88m 86kg. Racers TC.
At 400mh: OG: '16- 5; WCh: 13/15: sf. Jamaican champion 2015-16. At 400m: PAm: '11- h.
Progress at 400mh: 2013- 49.17, 2014- 48.58, 2015- 48.90, 2016- 48.07, 2017- 50.18. pbs: 200m 21.03 '09, 400m 46.19 '09.

Women

Veronica CAMPBELL-BROWN b. 15 May 1982 Clarks Town, Trelawny 1.63m 61kg. Adidas. Was at University of Arkansas, USA.
At (100m)/200m/4x100mR: OG: '00- 2R, '04- 3/1/1R, '08- 1, '12- 3/4/2R, '16- h/2R; WCh: '05- 2/4/2R, '07- 1/2/2R, '09- 4/2, '11- 2/1/2R, '15- 4/3/1R; CG: '02- (2)/2R, '06- 2, 14- (2)/1R; WJ: '98- (qf), '00- 1/1/2R; WY: '99- (1)/1R; PAm-J: '99- 2R; CCp: '14- (1)/1R. At 60m: WI: '10-12-14: 1/1/5. Won WAF 100m 2004-05, 200m 2004; DL 100m 2014; CAC-J 100m 2000, JAM 100m 2002, 2004-05, 2007, 2011, 2014; 200m 2004-05, 2007-09, 2011.
Four CAC & Commonwealth 4x100m records 2004-15. CAC junior 100m record 2000.
Progress at 100m, 200m: 1999- 11.49, 23.73; 2000- 11.12/11.1, 22.87; 2001- 11.13/22.92; 2002- 11.00, 22.39; 2004- 10.91, 22.05; 2005- 10.85, 22.35/ 22.29w; 2006- 10.99, 22.51; 2007- 10.89, 22.34; 2008- 10.87/10.85w, 21.74; 2009- 10.89/10.81w, 22.29; 2010- 10.78, 21.98; 2011- 10.76, 22.22; 2012- 10.81, 22.32; 2013- 11.01/10.78w, 22.53/22.18w; 2014- 10.86, 22.94/22.30w, 2015- 10.89, 21.97; 2016- 10.83, 22.29; 2017- 10.84, 22.60. pbs: 50m 6.08i '12, 60m 7.00i '10, 100y 9.91+ '11 (world best), 400m 52.24i '05, 52.25 '11.
Has matched Merelene Ottey by winning medals at five Olympic Games. In 2000 became the first woman to become World Junior champion at both 100m and 200m. Unbeaten at 200m in 28 finals (42 races in all) from 11 March 2000 to 22 July 2005 (lost to Allyson Felix). Married Omar Brown (1 CG 200m 2006) on 3 Nov 2007. She received a public warning for a positive test for a banned diuretic on 4 May 2013 and was suspended for the season, but the CAS upheld her appeal in February 2014. Her brother Sean Bailey (b. 15 Jul 1997) has 400m pb 46.51 '16 and was 3rd at 4x400m at 2016 WJ.

Christine DAY b. 23 Aug 1986 St. Mary 1.68m 51kg. Cameron Blazers TC.
At 400m/4x400mR: OG: '12- sf/2R, '16- sf/res 2R; WCh: '09- sf, '15- 4/1R; CG: 14- 3/1R; CCp: '14- 1R. JAM champion 2015.
Progress at 400m: 2006- 55.33, 2007- 53.91, 2008- 53.10, 2009- 51.54, 2010- 52.43, 2011- 52.08, 2012- 50.85, 2013- 50.91, 2014- 50.16, 2015- 50.14, 2016- 50.29, 2017- 51.25. pb 200m 23.73 '13.

Simone FACEY b. 7 May 1985 Manchester 1.62m 53kg. Was at Texas A&M University.
At 200m/4x100mR: OG: '16- sf/res 2R; WCh: '07- 2R, '09- 6/1R, '17- sf/3R; PAm: '11- 2, '15- 3/2R; PAm-J: '03- 2R. At 100m: WCh: '17- sf; WJ: '02- 2; WY: '01- 4. Won JAM 200m 2016, NCAA 200m 2008, CAC-J 100m & 200m 2002.
CAC junior 200m record 2004.
Progress at 200m: 2000- 24.13, 2001- 23.67. 2002- 23.22, 2004- 22.71, 2005- 23.43i, 2006- 23.36, 2007- 22.49, 2008- 22.25, 2009- 22.58, 2010- 22.90, 2011- 22.86A/23.07, 2012- 23.12, 2013- 22.95, 2014- 22.67, 2015- 22.55, 2016- 22.50, 2017- 22.74. pbs: 60m 7.14i '16, 100m 10.95A '08, 11.04/11.00w '17, 11.0 '04.

Shelly-Ann FRASER-PRYCE b. 27 Dec 1986 Kingston 1.60m 52kg. MVP. Graduate of the University of Technology. née Fraser. Married Jason Pryce on 7 Jan 2011.
At 100m/(200m)/4x100mR: OG: '08- 1, '12- 1/2/2R, '16- 3/2R; WCh: '07- res (2)R, '09- 1/1R, '11- 4/2R, '13- 1/1/1R, '15- 1/1R; CG: '14- 1R. At 60m: WI: '14- 1. Won WAF 2008, DL 100m 2012-13, 2015; 200m 2013; JAM 100m 2009, 2012, 2015; 200m 2012-13.
CAC and Commonwealth records 100m 2009 & 2012, 4x100m (4) 2011-15; CAC 4x100m 4x200m 2014.
Progress at 100m, 200m: 2002- 11.8, 2003- 11.57, 2004- 11.72, 24.08; 2005- 11.72; 2006- 11.74, 24.8; 2007- 11.31/11.21w, 23.5; 2008- 10.78, 22.15; 2009- 10.73, 22.58; 2010- 10.82dq, 22.47dq; 2011- 10.95, 22.59/22.10w; 2012- 10.70, 22.09; 2013- 10.71, 22.13; 2014- 11.01, 22.53; 2015- 10.74, 22.37; 2016- 10.86, 23.15. pb 60m 6.98i '14, 400m 55.67 '15.
Double World and Olympic champion with eight global gold medals (and four silver). Huge improvement in 2008 and moved to joint third on world all-time list for 100m when winning 2009 world 100m title. 6-month ban for positive test for a non-performance enhancing drug on 23 May 2010. IAAF Athlete of the Year 2013. Son Zyon Price born 7 Aug 2017.

Chris-Ann GORDON b. 18 Sep 1994 1.64m 52kg. Student at University of Texas, USA.
At 400m/4x400mR: OG: '16- res2R; WCh: '15- res1R, '17- sf; WJ: '10- 3R, '12- 7; WY: 11- 7; PAm: '15- 4/2R; won PAm-J 2011, NCAA & JAM 2017.
Progress at 400m: 2009- 52.68, 2010- 53.62, 2011- 51.62, 2012- 52.31, 2013- 52.16, 2014- 51.39, 2015- 51.52. 2016- 51.02, 2017- 50.13. pbs: 60m 7.56i '17, 100m 11.87 '11, 200m 23.28A '15, 23.71w '17; 600m 1:29.19A '15, 800m 2:04.73 '14.

Shericka JACKSON b. 15 Jul 1994 1.74m 59kg. UTech.
At 400m/4x400mR: OG: '16- 3/2R; WCh: '15- 3/1R, '17- 5; won JAM 2017. At 200m: WJ: '12- 8/2R; WY: '11- 3/1 MedR; Yth OG: '10- 4.
CAC & Commonwealth 4x200m record 2017
Progress at 400m: 2008- 54.27, 2009- 53.13, 2010- 53.71, 2011- 52.94, 2012- 53.34, 2013- 51.60, 2014- 51.32, 2015- 49.99. 2016- 49.83, 2017- 50.05. pbs: 60m 7.31 '18, 100m 11.24 '17, 200m 22.46 '17.

Jura LEVY b. 4 Nov 1990 Trelawny 1.57m 50kg. Was at South Plains College, then Oklahoma Baptist University, USA.
At 100m/(200m)/4x100mR: WCh: '11- sf/res2R, '17- sf/3R; WJ: '08- (8)/2R; WY: '07- sf/sf/2 MedR; PAm-J: '09- 3/2R.
CAC & Commonwealth 4x200m record 2017
Progress at 100m: 2007- 11.64, 2008- 11.46, 2009- 11.41/11.33w, 2010- 11.28/11.15w, 2011- 11.10/

11.07w, 2014- 11.20, 2015- 11.99w, 2016- 11.25/ 11.11w, 2017- 11.06. pbs: 55m 6.81i '13, 60m 7.22i '17, 200m 22.76 '11, 400m 53.58 '11.

Stephenie Ann McPHERSON b. 25 Nov 1988 Westmoreland 1.68m 55kg. MVP. Was at Kingston University of Technology.
At 400m/4x400mR: OG: '16- 6/2R; WCh: '13- 3, '15- 5/1R, '17- 6; CG: 14- 1/1R; CCp: '14- 1R; WI: 14- 2R, '16- 4. Won DL 2016, JAM 2016.
Progress at 400m: 2006- 56.42, 2007- 55.77, 2008- 52.80, 2009- 51.95, 2010- 51.64, 2012- 52.98, 2013- 49.92, 2014- 50.12, 2015- 50.32, 2016- 50.04, 2017- 50.56. pbs: 100m 11.44 '10, 200m 22.93 '14, 800m 2:15.24 '12, 400mh 57.46 '12.

Natasha MORRISON b. 17 Nov 1992 1.70m 57kg. GGOF.
At 100m/4x100mR: WCh: '15- 7/1R, '17- sf/3R.
CAC and Commonwealth 4x100m record 2015.
Progress at 100m: 2007- 12.06, 2008- 12.00, 2010- 11.98/11.47w, 2011- 11.42, 2013- 11.17/11.12w, 2014- 11.06, 2015- 10.96, 2016- 11.27, 2017- 11.09. pbs: 60m 7.15i '16, 200m 23.08 '13.

Leah NUGENT b. 23 Nov 1992 Abington, Pennsylvania, USA 1.73m 66kg. Was at University of Kentucky.
At 400mh: OG: '16- 6; WCh: '17- sf.
Progress at 400mh: 2009- 60.72, 2010- 59.15, 2011- 57.72, 2012- 59.68, 2013- 58.47, 2014- 56.97, 2015- 55.63, 2016- 54.45, 2017- 54.54. pbs: 60m 7.39i '16, 200m 24.03 '16, 400m 53.09i '16, 60mh 7.96i '17, 100mh 13.11 '16, 12.83w '17.
She competed in the 2016 US Champs but then got clearance to compete for Jamaica from 22 July (her father came from Jamaica) and reduced her pb from 55.44 to 54.98 and 54.45 at the Olympic Games.

Shanieka RICKETTS b. 2 Feb 1992 Saint Andrew 1.82m 66kg. née Thomas.Was at San Diego State University, USA.
At TJ: OG: '16- dnq 14; WCh: '15- 11, '17- 8; CG: '14- 4; PAm: '15- 9; WI: '16- 8; Won NACAC 2015.
Progress at TJ: 2008- 11.83, 2011- 12.98i/12.90, 2012- 13.64, 2013- 14.15, 2014- 14.00, 2015- 14.23A/14.08, 2016- 14.57, 2017- 14.45. pbs: 100m 12.24 '17, 400m 55.38 '13, HJ 1.75 '10, LJ 6.63 '15.
Married coach Kerry-Lee Ricketts in 2016.

Janeive RUSSELL b. 14 Nov 1993 Manchester 1.75m 63kg. UTech.
At 400mh/4x400mR: OG: '16- 7; WCh: '15- 5; CG: '14- 3; WJ: '12- 1/2R. At 400m: WJ: '10- sf/3R. At LJ: WY: '09- 9. Won JAM Hep 2011, 400mh 2015.
Progress at 400mh: 2011- 57.71, 2012- 56.62, 2013- 56.30, 2014- 54.75, 2015- 54.64, 2016- 53.96, 2017- 54.02. pbs: 200m 24.10 '11, 400m 51.17 '16, 800m 2:11.5 '15, 100mh 13.80 '12, HJ 1.80 '09, LJ 6.20 '10, 6.26w '11; SP 10.86 '11, JT 26.53 '11, Hep 5361 '11.

Kaliese SPENCER b. 6 May 1987 Westmoreland 1.75m 63kg. Cameron Blazers TC. Was at University of Texas.
At 400mh/4x400mR: OG: '12- 4; WCh: '07-09-11-13-15: sf/4&res 2R/4/dq h/8; CG: 14- 1; WJ: '06- 1/3R; CCp: '14- 1; Won DL 2010-12, 2014; JAM 2011, 2014. At 400m: WI: '14- 2/2R.
Progress at 400mh: 2006- 55.11, 2007- 55.62, 2009- 53.56, 2010- 53.33, 2011- 52.79, 2012- 53.49, 2013- 54.22, 2014- 53.41, 2015- 54.15, 2016- 55.02, 2017- 55.38. pbs: 200m 23.11 '13, 400m 50.19 '13, 800m 2:03.01 '11.

Danniel THOMAS-DODD b. 11 Nov 1992 1.68m 91kg. née Thomas. PE student at Kent State University, USA. Married to Shane Dodd.
At SP: OG: '16- dnq 25; WCh: '15- dnq 22, '17- 4; PAm: '15- 5; WI: '18- 2; won NCAA 2017. At DT: CG: '14- 8. Won JAM SP 2014-17, DT 2015.
Four Jamaican shot records 2017.
Progress at SP: 2012- 14.58, 2013- 16.10, 2014- 16.97i/16.82, 2015- 17.76, 2016- 17.60, 2017- 19.15, 2018- 19.22i. pbs: DT 59.38 '14.

Elaine THOMPSON b. 28 Jun 1992 Manchester 1.69m 57kg. MVP. Kingston University of Technology.
At 100m: WCh: '17- 5; At 200m/4x100mR: OG: '16- 1/1/2R; WCh: '15- 2/1R; CG: '14- res 1R. Won DL 100m 2016-17, JAM 100m 2016-17, 200m 2015. At 60m: WI: '16- 3, '18- 4.
CAC and Commonwealth records 4x100m 2015, 100m 2016, 4x200m 2017.
Progress at 100m, 200m: 2008- 12.16, 25.56; 2009- 12.01, 24.35; 2010- 11.94w, 2012- 23.89, 2013- 11.41, 23.73; 2014- 11.17, 23.23; 2015- 10.84, 21.66, 2016- 10.70, 21.78; 2017- 10.71, 21.98. pbs: 60m 6.98i '17, 7.02 '17; 150mSt 15.00 '14, 400m 55.98 '17.

Ristananna TRACEY b. 9 May 1992 Kingston 1.73m 68kg. Racers TC.
At 400mh: OG: '16- 5; WCh: '11/13- sf, '15- h, '17- 3; PAm: '15- h; WJ: '10- 5; WY: '09- 8. Won CAC-J 2010, JAM 2013, 2016.
Progress at 400mh: 2009- 58.49, 2010- 57.77, 2011- 54.58, 2012- 55.64, 2013- 54.52, 2014- 55.12, 2015- 55.45, 2016- 54.15, 2017- 53.74. pbs: 200m 23.63 '11, 400m 51.95 '11, 800m 2:03.97 '11.
Sister Nikita (b. 18 Sep 1990) 400mh pb 55.18 '14, 8 WJ '08.

Christania WILLIAMS b. 17 Oct 1994 Saint Mary 1.65m 63kg. U.Tech.
At 100m/4x100mR: OG: '16- 8/2R; WCh: '17- res 3R; WJ: '12- dnf hR; WY: '11- 3 (1 MedR).
Progress at 100m: 2009- 12.01, 2011- 11.39, 2012- 11.54, 2014- 11.19, 2015- 11.11, 2016- 10.96, 2017- 11.03. pbs: 60m 7.05 '17, 200m 23.48 '15.

Danielle WILLIAMS b. 14 Sep 1992 St.Andrew 1.68m 59kg. Johnson C.Smith University, USA.
At 100mh: WCh: '13- sf, '15- 1, '17- sf; CG: '14- 4; WJ: '10- 4; WUG: '13- 3, '15- 1; PAm-J: '11- 2. JAM champion 2013, 2015, 2017.
CAC and Commonwealth 4x100m record 2015.
Progress at 100mh: 2010- 13.46/13.41w, 2011- 13.32/13.13w, 2012- 14.02, 2013- 12.69, 2014- 12.99, 2015- 12.57, 2016- 12.77/12.55w, 2017- 12.56. pbs:

60m 7.32i '14, 100m 11.24A '13, 11.25 '17; 200m 22.62A/23.43i '13, 23.48 '14; 60mh 8.02i '15.
Sister **Shermaine** (b. 4 Feb 1990) at 100mh: OG: '12/16- sf; WCh: '13- sf, '15- 7; WJ: '08- 2; WY: '05- 6, '07- 2; PAm-J: '09- 1; pb 12.78/12.65w '12.

Kimberly WILLIAMS b. 3 Nov 1988 Saint Thomas 1.69m 66kg. Florida State University, USA.
At TJ: OG: '12- 6, '16- 7; WCh: '09/11 dnq 15/14, '13-15-17: 4/5/10; CG: '14- 1; WJ: '06- dnq 15; WY: '05- dnq; CAG: '10- 1; PAm-J: '07- 2; CCp: '14- 4; WI: '12-14-18: 5/3/2. Won NCAA LJ & TJ 2009, JAM TJ 2010, 2012-17.
Progress at TJ: 2004- 12.53/12.65w, 2005- 12.63/13.09w, 2006- 13.18, 2007- 13.52, 2008- 13.82i/13.69/13.83w, 2009- 14.08/14.38w, 2010- 14.23, 2011- 14.25, 2012- 14.53, 2013- 14.62/14.78w, 2014- 14.59, 2015- 14.45, 2016- 14.56/14.66w, 2017- 14.54/14.60w. pbs: 100m 11.76 '12, 200m 24.55 '11, LJ 6.55i 11, 6.42/6.66w '09.

Novlene WILLIAMS-MILLS b. 26 Apr 1982 Saint Ann 1.70m 57kg. Studied recreation at University of Florida, USA.
At 400m/4x400mR: OG: '04- sf/3R, '08- sf/2R, '12- 5/2R, 16- 2R; WCh: '05-07-09-11-13-15-17: 2R/3&2R/4&2R/7&2R/7/6&1R/8; CG: '06- 3, '14- 2/1R; PAm: '03- 6/2R; WI: '06- 5; WCp: '06- 3/1R, '14- 2/1R. Won DL 2014, JAM 400m 2006-07, 2009-14.
World W35 400m record 2017
Progress at 400m: 1999- 55.62, 2000- 53.90, 2001- 54.99, 2002- 52.05, 2003- 51.93, 2004- 50.59, 2005- 51.09, 2006- 49.63, 2007- 49.66, 2008- 50.11, 2009- 49.77, 2010- 50.04, 2011- 50.05, 2012- 49.78, 2013- 50.01, 2014- 50.05, 2015- 50.47, 2016- 50.64, 2017- 50.14. pbs: 200m 23.25 '10, 500m 1:11.83i '03.
Married 2007. Younger sister Clora Williams (b. 26.11.83) joined her on JAM's 3rd place 4x400m team at 2010 WI; she has 400m pb 51.06 and won NCAA 2006.

JAPAN

Governing body: Nippon Rikujo-Kyogi Renmei. Founded 1911.
National Championships first held in 1913 (men), 1925 (women). **2017 Champions**: **Men**: 100m/200m: Abdul Hakim Sani Brown 10.05/20.32, 400m: Takamasa Kitagawa 45.76, 800m: Sho Kawamoto 1:47.00, 1500m: Ryoji Tatezawa 3:49.73, 5000m: Hiroki Matsueda 13:48.90, 10000m: Suguru Osako 28:35.47, Mar: Hiroto Inoue 2:08:22, 3000mSt: Hironori Tsuetaki 8:38.20, 110mh: Shun-ya Takayama 13.45, 400mh: Takatoshi Abe 49.32, HJ: Takashi Eto 2.25, PV: Seito Yamamoto 5.60, LJ: Yuki Hashioka 8.05, TJ: Ryoma Yamamoto 16.29, SP: Satoshi Hatase 18.26, DT: Yuji Tsutsumi 59.09, HT: Ryota Kashimura 71.36, JT: Ryohei Arai 82.13, Dec: Akihiko Nakamura 7873, 20kW: Eiki Takahashi 1:18:18, 50kW: Hirooki Arai 3:47:18. **Women**: 100m/200m: Kana Ichikawa 11.52/23.63, 400m: Yuna Iwata 53.65, 800m: Yume Kitamura 2:04.62, 1500m: Ayako Jinnouchi 4:15.71, 5000m: Rina Nabeshima 15:19.87, 10000m: Mizuki Matsuda 31:39.41, Mar: Reia Owada 2:31:10, 3000mSt: Chikako Mori 9:49.41 100mh: Ayako Kimura 13.12, 400mh: Sayaka Aoki 56.35, HJ: Haruka Nakano 1.80, PV: Tomomi Abiko 4.30, LJ: Ayaka Kora 6.14, TJ: Kaede Miyasaka 13.48, SP: Nanaka Kori 15.82, DT: Minori Tsujikawa 51.27, HT: Hitomi Katsuyama 63.32, JT: Yuki Ebihara 60.64, Hep: Meg Hemphill 5907, 20kW: Kumiko Okada 1:29:40.

Hirooki ARAI b. 18 May 1988 Obuse, Nagano pref. 1.80m 62kg. Japan Self-Defense Forces Physical Training School, was at Fukui University of Technology.
At 50kW: OG: '16- 3; WCh: '11-13-15-17: 9/11/4/2; JPN champion 2015, 2017.
Progress at 50kW: 2009- 4:04:01, 2010- 3:55:56, 2011- 3:48:40, 2012- 3:47:08, 2013- 3:45:56, 2014- 3:40:34, 2015- 3:40:20, 2016- 3:41:24, 2017- 3:41:17. Pbs: 3000mW 12:12.73 '09, 5000mW 19:05.46 '16, 10000m 39:17.66 '14, 20kW 1:19:25 '17, 30kW 2:13:02 '16, 35kW 2:34:53 '16.

Kai KOBAYASHI b. 28 Feb 1993 Odate, Akita pref. 1.64m 53kg. Bic Camera. Was at Waseda University.
At 50kW: WCh: '17- 3.
Progress at 20kW, 50kW: 2013- 1:22:47, 2014- 1:21:13, 2015- 1:19:12, 2016-1:19:57, 3:42:08; 2017- 1:19:13, 3:41:17. Pbs: 5000mW 19:11.94 '16, 10000m 39:06.86 '17, 30kW 2:13:10 '17, 35kW 2:35:20 '17.

Satoshi MARUO b. 28 Nov 1991 Kyoto pref. 1.75m 60kg. Aichi Steel Corporation. Was at Biwako Seikei Sport College.
At 50kW: WCh: '17- 5.
Progress at 20kW, 50kW: 2010- 1:30:56, 2011- 1:27:20, 2012- 1:25:09, 2013- 1:24:42, 2014- 1:24:57, 2015- 1:19:42, 2016-1:20:14, 4:02:36; 2017- 1:20:31, 3:43:03. Pbs: 5000mW 19:30.76 '15, 10000m 39:33.30 '15, 30kW 2:14:18 '17, 35kW 2:36:31 '18. Run: 3000m 8:53.7 '06.

Daisuke MATSUNAGA b. 24 Mar 1995 Yokohama, Kanagawa pref. 1.74m 58kg. Fujitsu, was at Iwate University.
At 20kW: OG: '16- 7; WCh: '17- 38; WUG: '15- 3. At 10000mW: WJ: '14- 1; As-J 12- 2; WCp: '14-2J.
Asian junior 10000m walk records 2013.
Progress at 20kW: 2013- 1:23:56, 2014- 1:21:17, 2015- 1:19:08, 2016- 1:18:53, 2017- 1:19:40, 2018- 1:17:46. pbs: 5000mW 19:28.91 '14, 10000mW 38:16.76 '16.

Abdul Hakim SANI BROWN b. 6 Mar 1999 Fukuoka 1.88m 78kg. University of Florida.
At (100m)/200m: WCh: '15- sf, '17- sf/7; WY: '15- 1/1. Won JPN 100m & 200m 2017.
Progress at 100m, 200m: 2010- 12.95; 2013- 10.88, 21.85; 2014- 10.45, 21.09; 2015- 10.28, 20.34; 2016- 10.22, 20.54; 2017- 10.05, 20.32.
Ghanaian father and Japanese mother.

Eiki TAKAHASHI b. 19 Nov 1992 Hanamaki, Iwate pref. 1.75m 56kg. Fujitsu, was at Iwate University.
At 20kW: OG: '16- 42; WCh: '15- 47, '17- 14; WCp: '14- 9, '16- 12; AsiG: '14- 7. Won JPN 2015-16.
Walk records: Asian 5000m & 10000m 2015, Japanese 20k 2015.
Progress at 20kW: 2011- 1:26:16, 2012- 1:22:33, 2013- 1:20:25, 2014- 1:18:41, 2015- 1:18:03, 2016- 1:18:26, 2017- 1:18:18, 2018- 1:17:26. pbs: 5000mW 18:37.60 '15, 10000mW 38:01.49 '15.

Takayuki TANII b. 14 Feb 1983 Namerikawa, Toyama pref. 1.67m 57kg. Japan Self-Defense Forces Physical Training School, was at Nihon University.
At (20kW)/50kW: OG: '04- 15/dq, '08- dq/29, '12- dnf, '16- 14; WCh: '05-07-09-11-13-15: (23)/(21)/dq/8/9/3; AsiG: '14- 1; WUG: '03- (6); At 10000mW: WJ: '02- 7; WY: '99- 3. Won Asian 20kW 2007, JPN 20kW 2004-05, 50kW 2013-14, 2016.
Japanese 50k walk record 2003.
Progress at 50kW: 2003- 3:47:54, 2006- 3:47:23, 2007- 3:50:08, 2008- 3:49:33, 2009- 3:52:22, 2010- 3:53:27, 2011- 3:48:03, 2012- 3:43:56, 2013- 3:44:25, 2014- 3:40:19, 2015- 3:42:01, 2016- 3:44:12, 2017- dnf. pbs: 5000mW 19:07.58 '16, 10000mW 40:03.42 '03, 20kW 1:20:39 '04, 30kW 2:11:34 '14, 35kW 2:33:37 '14.

KAZAKHSTAN

Governing body: Athletic Federation of the Republic of Kazakhstan. Founded 1959.
2017 National Champions: Men: 100m: Vitaliy Zems 10.65, 200m: Vladislav Grigoryev 20.79, 400m: Mikhail Litvin 47.59, 800m: Sergey Zaykov 1:50.85, 1500m: Aleksey Gusarov 3:52.23, 5000m: Mikhail Krasilov 15:11.13, 10000m: Andrey Leymenov 30:53.0, 3000mSt: Dmitriy Ivanchukov 9:10.18, 110mh: Vyacheslav Zems 14.13, 400mh: Igor Kondratyev 51.79, HJ: Roman Loshkaryev 2.16, PV: Nikita Filippov 5.40, LJ: Aleksandr Kiselyev 7.75, TJ: Roman Valiyev 16.08, SP: Ivan Ivanov 20.00, DT: Yevgeniy Milovatskiy 55.21, HT: Vladimir Torlopov 50.01, JT: Artur Gagner 65.08, Dec: Yevgeniy Marchenkov 6072, 20000mW: Georgiy Sheyko 1:29:24; **Women**: 100m: Viktoriya Zyabkina 11.52, 200m: Olga Safonova 23.17, 400m/400mh: Merjen Ishanguliyeva 54.87/57.72, 800m: Tatyana Neroznak 2:09.23, 1500m: Viktoriya Ryzhikova 4:32.37, 5000m: Irina Smolnikova 17:27.58, 10000m: Gulzhanat Zhanatbek 35:22.1, 3000mSt: Svetlana Saunina 11:40.00, 100mh: Anastasiya Vinogradova 13.43, HJ: Regina Kaysarova 1.80, PV: Anastasiya Yermakova 3.70, LJ/TJ: Mariya Ovchinnikova 6.13/13.25, SP: Yekaterina Nesterova 13.32, DT: Mariya Telushkina 54.08, HT: Diana Nusupbekova 60.25, JT: Asiya Rabayeva 46.80, Hep: Nadezhda Kimos 5190, 20kW: Polina Repina 1:45:37.

Women

Olga RYPAKOVA b. 30 Nov 1984 Kamenogorsk 1.83m 62kg. née Alekseyeva.
At TJ/(LJ): OG: '08- 2 (dnq 29), '12- 1, '16- 3; WCh: '07-09-11-15-17: 9/10/2/3/3; WJ: '00- (dnq 23); AsiG: '06- (3), '10- 1/2, '14- 1; AsiC: '07- 1/1, '09- 1; WI: '08-10-12: 3/1/2; WUG: '07- (1); WCp: '06- (8), '10: 1/3; won DL TJ 2012, Asian Indoor LJ 2008-09, 2017; TJ 2009, 2016-17; Pen 2005-06. At Hep: WJ: '02- 2; WY: '01- 4; AsiG: '06- 1; won DL 2017, C.Asian 2003. Won KAZ LJ 2005, 2008, 2011, 2015; TJ 2008, 2011, 2015; Hep 2006.
Four Asian TJ records 2008-10, five indoors 2008-10, seven KAZ records 2007-10.
Progress at LJ, TJ: 2000- 6.23, 2001- 6.00, 2002- 6.26, 2003- 6.34i/6.14, 2004- 6.53i, 2005- 6.60, 2006- 6.63, 2007- 6.85, 14.69; 2008- 6.52/6.58w, 15.11; 2009- 6.58i/6.42, 14.53/14.69w; 2010- 6.60, 15.25; 2011- 6.56, 14.96; 2012- 14.98, 2014- 14.37, 2015- 14.77, 2016- 14.74, 2017- 14.77. pbs: 200m 24.83 '02, 800m 2:20.12 '02, 60mh 8.67i '06, 100mh 14.02 '06, HJ 1.92 '06, SP 13.04 '06, JT 41.60 '03, Hep 6122 '06, Pen 4582i '06 (Asian rec).
Former heptathlete, concentrated on long jump after birth of daughter. Four KAZ and three Asian TJ records with successive jumps in Olympic final 2008, three Asian indoor records when won World Indoor gold in 2010. Son Kiril born June 2013.

KENYA

Governing body: Kenya Amateur Athletic Association. Founded 1951.
2017 National Champions: **Men**: 100m/200m: Mark Odhiambo, 10.14/20.41. 400m: Collins Omae 45.19, 800m: Peter Langat 1:45.00, 1500m: Timothy Cheruiyot 3:41.0, 5000m: Franklin Ngelel 13:36.7, 10000m: Mathew Kimeli 27:53.67, 3000mSt: Felix Kirongo 8:25.5, 110mh/400mh: William Mbevi 13.85/49.88, HJ: Mathew Sawe 2.25, PV: Robert Kipkoech 4.40, LJ: Kiplagat Ruto 7.43?, TJ: Elijah Kimitei 16.67, SP: Boaz Monyancha 15.52, DT: Charles Kipkemoi 47.56, HT: Dominic Abunda 60.10, JT: Alex Kiprotich 74.82, Dec: Gilbert Koech 6811, 20kW: Samuel Gathimba 1:23:49. **Women**: 100m/400m/TJ: Maximila Imali 11.57/51.18/12.90, 200m: Sabina Mukoswa 24.67, 800m: Margaret Wambui 2:00.05, 1500m: Beatrice Chepkoech 4:03.2, 5000m: Lilian Kasait Renguruk 15:53.7, 10000m: Alice Aprot Nawowuna 31:50.5, 3000mSt: Marion Kibor 9:50.4; 100mh: Priscila Tabunda 14.20, 400mh: Maureen Jelagat 58.53, HJ/PV: Caroline Chotich 1.70/2.90, DT: Rose Rakamba 46.68, HT: Lucy Omondi 51.54, JT: Damacline Nyakerui 47.88, Hep: Susan Murrey 4069, 20kW: Grace Wanjiru (17th successive title) 1:35:17.

Leonard Kiplimo **BARSOTON** b. 21 Oct 1994 1.66m 56kg.
At 10000m: AfG: '15- 2. At HMar: WCh: '18- 12. World CC: '13-15-17: 2J/5/2; AfCC: '14- 1. Won

KEN CC 2017.
Progress at 10000m: 2013- 27:33.13, 2014- 27:20.74, 2015- 27:27.55, 2016- 27:31.86, 2017- 27:47.4A. pbs: 1500m 3:47.95 '16,3000m 7:52.33 '17, 5000m 13:16.25 '15, HMar 59:28 '17.

Kipyegon BETT b. 2 Jan 1998 1.82m 70kg.
At 800m: WCh: '17- 3; WJ: '16- 1; WY: '15- 2. Won Afr-Y 2015.
Progress at 800m: 2014- 1:52.45A, 2015- 1:44.55A, 2016- 1:43.76, 2017- 1:44.04A.
Brother of Purity Kirui (qv).

Nicholas Kiptanui **BETT** b. 20 Dec 1996 1.72m 52kg.
At 2000mSt: WY: '13- 2.
Progress at 3000mSt: 2013- 8:52.1A, 2014- 8:28.83, 2015- 8:19.26, 2016- 8:10.07, 2017- 8:12.20. pbs: 5000m 14:33.6A '16, 2000mSt 5:20.92 '13.

Nicholas Kiplagat **BETT** b. 27 Jan 1990 1.86m 77kg. Kenya Police.
At 400mh/4x400mR: OG: '16- h; WCh: '15- 1; AfCh: '14- 3/3R.
Kenyan 400mh record 2015.
Progress at 400mh: 2010- 53.11A, 2011- 50.35A, 2012- 53.2A, 2013- 49.70A, 2014- 49.03, 2015- 47.79, 2016- 48.01, 2017- 49.70. pb 800m 1:49.34 '15.
Twin brother of Haron Koech.

Jairus Kipchoge **BIRECH** b. 14 Dec 1992 Uasin Gishu 1.70m 56kg.
At 3000mSt: WCh: '15- 4, '17- 12; CG: '14- 2; AfG: '11- 4; AfCh: '14- 1; Af-J: '11- 2; CCp: '14- 1. Won DL 2014-15, Kenyan 2014.
Progress at 3000mSt: 2010- 8:50.0A, 2011- 8:11.31, 2012- 8:03.43, 2013- 8:08.72, 2014- 7:58.41, 2015- 7:58.83, 2016- 8:03.90., 2017- 8:07.68 pbs: 2000m 4:58.76 '11, 3000m 7:41.83 '13, 5000m 13:38.4A '15, 10000m 28:35.7A '16, 10k Rd 28:14 '17.

Bethwel Kiprotich **BIRGEN** b. 6 Aug 1988 Eldoret 1.78m 64kg.
At 1500m: WCh: '13- sf; WI: '14- 8. At 3000m: WI: '18- 3.
Progress at 1500m, 5000m: 2010- 3:35.60, 2011- 3:34.59, 2012- 3:31.00, 14:01.0A; 2013- 3:30.77, 13:50.6A; 2014- 3:31.22, 2015- 3:34.62i, 2016- 3:33.94, 13:04.66; 2017- 3:32.27, 13:17.80. pbs: 800m 1:48.32 '11, 1M 3:50.42 '13, 3000m 7:32.48 '16, 5000m 14:01.0A '12.

Robert Kiptoo **BIWOTT** b. 28 Jan 1996 1.80m 68kg.
At 1500m: WY: '13- 1; Af-Y: '13-1 (1 800m).
Progress at 800m, 1500m: 2011- 3:41.2A, 2012- 3:43.81, 2013- 1:46.98, 3:36.77; 2014- 1:44.69, 3:43.91A; 2015- 1:43.56, 3:30.10; 2016- 3:33.05; 2017- 1:45.05, 3:34.30. pbs: 600m 1:15.91 '15, 1000m 2:13.89 '16, 1M 3:55.62 '16.

Stanley Kipleting **BIWOTT** b. 21 Apr 1986 1.76m 60kg.
At Mar: OG: '16- dnf.
World record 30k road 2016.
Progress HMar, Mar: 2006- 2:14:25, 2007- 61:20, 2010- 2:09:41, 2011- 60:23, 2:07:03; 2012- 59:44, 2:05:12; 2013- 58:56, 2014- 59:18, 2:04:55; 2015- 59:20, 2:06:41; 2016- 60:40, 2:03:51. Road pbs: 10k 28:00 '12, 15k 42:13 '13, 20k 56:02 '13, 25k 1:12:40 '16, 30k 1:27:13 '16.
Marathon wins: Säo Paulo 2010, Chunchon 2011, Paris 2012, New York 2015; 2nd London 2014, 2016. His brother Norris Biwott had a marathon best of 2:11:29 in 2013.

Evans Kiplagat **CHEBET** b. 10 Nov 1988 1.70m 60kg.
Progress at Mar: 2013- 2:11:26, 2014- 2:07:46, 2015- 2:08:50, 2016- 2:05:31, 2017- 2:05:30. pbs: 10M 45:06 '17, HMar 61:11+ '16.
Marathons: 2nd Prague 2014-15, Seoul Nov 2014 & Mar 2016, Valencia 2017, 3rd Berlin 2016.

Lawrence CHERONO b. 7 Aug 1988 1.70m 55kg.
Progress at Mar: 2014- 2:10:16, 2015- 2:09:39, 2016- 2:07:24, 2017- 2:05:09. pbs: 10M 45:06 '17, HMar 61:11+ '16.
Marathon wins: Seville 2015, Prague 2016, Honolulu 2016-17,Amsterdam 2017.

Ferguson Rotich CHERUIYOT b. 30 Nov 1989 1.83m 73kg.
At 800m: OG: '16- 5; WCh: '13-15-17: sf/4/sf; CG: '14- 4; AfCh: '14- 4. Won DL 2016, Kenyan 2014.
Progress at 800m: 2013- 1:43.22, 2014- 1:42.84, 2015- 1:43.60A, 2016- 1:43.43, 2017- 1:44.37. pb 1000m 2:16.88 '14, 1500m 3:49.0A '14.
Changed first name from Simon to Ferguson in honour of Manchester United manager Alex Ferguson.

Timothy CHERUIYOT b. 20 Nov 1995 1.78m 64kg.
At 1500m: WCh: '15- 7, '17- 2; AfCh: '16- 2. Won DL 2017, KEN 2017.
Progress at 1500m: 2015- 3:34.86A, 2016- 3:31.34, 2017- 3:29.10. pbs: 800m 1:45.92A '14, 1M 3:49.64 '17, 5000m 13:51.5A.

Edward CHESEREK b. 2 Feb 1994 Kenya 1.68m 57kg. Marakwet. Was at University of Oregon.
Won NCAA 5000m 2015-16, 10000m 2014-16, CC 2013-15, Ind 1M 2015, 3000m & 5000m 2014, 2016-17, Dist.Med R 2015-16.
Progress at 1500m (1M), 5000m: 2011- 4:03.29M, 14:02.33, 2012- 4:02.21iM, 13:57.04i; 2013- 3:48.89+, 2014- 3:36.50, 13:18.71; 2015- 3:37.08, 13:45.25; 2016- 3:41.57 (3:57.38iM), 13:25.59; 2017- 3:37.01i (3:52.01iM), 13:24.72; 2018- 3:33.76, 3:49.44Mi. pbs: 800m 1:49.98 '12, 1M 3:49.44i '18, 4:03.29 '11; 3000m 7:38.74i '18, 7:57.26 '16; 2M 8:39.15i '13, 10000m 28:30.18 '14, 3000mSt 9:00.11 '11 Record 17 NCAA titles.
Applying for US citizenship.

Augustine Kiprono **CHOGE** b. 21 Jan 1987 Kipsigat, Nandi 1.62m 53kg.
At 5000m: CG: '06- 1; WJ: '04- 1. At 3000m: WY: '03- 1; WI: '10-12-14-16: 11/2/9/3. At 1500m: OG:

'08- 9; WCh: '05- h, '09- 5. World CC: '03-05-06-08: 4J/1J/7 (4k)/12. Won KEN 1500m 2013, E.African Youth 800m/1500m/3000m 2003, Junior 1500m 2004.
Records: World 4x1500m 2009, world youth 5000m 2004, world junior 3000m 2005.
Progress at 1500m, 5000m: 2003- 3:37.48, 13:20.08; 2004- 3:36.64, 12:57.01; 2005- 3:33.99, 12:53.66; 2006- 3:32.48, 12:56.41; 2007- 3:31.73, 2008- 3:31.57, 13:09.75; 2009- 3:29.47, 2010- 3:30.22, 13:04.64; 2011- 3:31.14, 13:21.24; 2012- 3:37.47, 13:15.50; 2013- 3:33.21, 13:05.31; 2014- 3:35.5A, 13:06.12. At HMar: 2016- 60:01, 2017- 59:26. pbs: 800m 1:44.86 '09, 1000m 2:17.79i '09, 1M 3:50.01 '13, 2000m 4:56.30i '07, 3000m 7:28.00i/7:28.76 '11, 10000m 28:22.8A '16.
At 17 in 2004 he become youngest to break 13 minutes for 5000m.

Dickson Kiptolo **CHUMBA** b. 27 Oct 1986 1.67m 50kg. Nandi.
Progress at Mar: 2010- 2:09:20dh, 2011- 2:07:23, 2012- 2:05:46, 2013- 2:10:15, 2014- 2:04:32, 2015- 2:06:34, 2016- 2:07:34, 2017- 2:06:25, 2018- 2:05:30 pbs: 1500m 3:44.33 '10, 5000m 13:41.34 '10, road: 10k 28:09 '13, HMar 61:34 '12, 60:39dh '14; 30k 1:28:36 '12.
Marathon wins: Rome 2011, Eindhoven 2012, Tokyo 2014, 2018 (3rd 2015-17), Chicago 2015 (2nd 2016, 3rd 2014).

Geoffrey Kipsang KAMWOROR b. 22 Nov 1992 Chepkorio, Keiyo district 1.68m 54kg.
At 10000m: OG: '16- 11; WCh: '15- 2, 17- 6. World CC: '11-15-17: 1J/1/1; HMar: '14- 1, '16- , '18- 1. Won KEN 5000m 2015, CC 2016, 2018.
Tied world 30km record 2014.
Progress at 5000m, 10000m, HMar, Mar: 2010- 13:32.01, 2011- 13:12.23, 27:06.35, 59:31; 2012- 13:28.8A, 59:26, 2:06:12; 2013- 28:17.0A, 58:54, 2:06:26; 2014- 59:08, 2:06:39; 2015- 13:13.28A, 26:52.65, 2:10:48; 2016- 12:59.98, 27:31.94, 59:10; 2017- 13:01.35, 26:57.77, 2:10:53. pbs: 1500m 3:40.7A '15, 3000m 7:51.55 '17; Road: 15k 41:41 '16, 20k 56:02 '13, 30k 1:27:37 '14.
3rd in Berlin Marathon 2012 (on debut) and 2013 (4th 2014), won New York 2017 (2nd 2015). Won RAK half marathon 2013.

Felix Kipchirchir **KANDIE** b. 10 Apr 1987 1.78m 62kg.
Progress at Mar:2009- 2:18:31A, 2010- 2:19:06, 2012- 16:12, 2014- 2:10:37, 2015- 2:07:07, 2016- 2:06:25, 2017- 2:06:03. Road pbs: 10k 28:46 '14, HMar 60:04 '16.
Marathon wins: Athens 2014, Prague 2015 (2nd 2016). 2nd Seoul 2017.

Bedan KAROKI Muchiri b. 21 Aug 1990 Nyandarua 1.69m 53kg. S&B Foods, Japan.
At 10000m: OG: 12- 5, '16- 7; WCh: '13-15-17: 6/4/4; AfG: '11- 2. World CC: '15- 2; HMar: '16- 2. Won Kenyan CC 2012.
Progress at 10000m, HMar: 2010- 27:23.62, 2011- 27:13.67, 2012- 27:05.50; 2013- 27:13.12, 2014- 26:52.36, 59:23; 2015- 27:04.77, 59:14; 2016- 27:07.30, 59:32; 2017- 26:52.12, 59:10; 2018- 58:42. pbs: 1500m 3:50.91 '08, 3000m 7:37.68 '13, 5000m 13:15.25 '14, 15k 41:41 '16, 10M 45:02 '14, 20k 55:55 '18, Mar 2:07:41 '17.
Went to Japan in 2007. 3rd London 2017 on marathon debut. Won Ra's Al-Khaymah half marathon 2018, his sixth win in eight races at the distance, seven in under 1 hour.

Clement KEMBOI b. 1 Feb 1992 1.80m 65kg.
At 3000mSt: AfG: '15- 1.
Progress at 3000mSt: 2010- 9:03.4A, 2011- 8:28.13, 2012- 8:25.67, 2013- 8:17.18, 2014- 8:16.96, 2015- 8:12.68, 2016- 8:10.65, 2017- 8:23.98. pbs: 1M 4:02.19 '14, 3000m 7:51.65 '16, 10000m 29:07.55 '17, 10kRd 28:44 '14.

Ezekiel KEMBOI Cheboi b. 25 May 1982 Matira, near Kapsowar, Marakwet District 1.75m 62kg.
At 3000mSt: OG: '04- 1, '08- 7, '12- 1, '16- dq; WCh: '03-05-07-09-11-13-15-17: 2/2/2/1/1/1/1/11; CG: '02-06-10-14: 2/1/2/3; AfG: '03- 1, '07- 2; AfCh: '02-06-10-14: 4/dq/2/3; Af-J: '01- 1. Won WAF 2009, Kenyan 2003, 2006-07.
Progress at 3000mSt: 2001- 8:23.66, 2002- 8:06.65, 2003- 8:02.49, 2004- 8:02.98, 2005- 8:09.04, 2006- 8:09.29, 2007- 8:05.50, 2008- 8:09.25, 2009- 7:58.85, 2010- 8:01.74, 2011- 7:55.76, 2012- 8:10.55, 2013- 7:59.03, 2014- 8:04.12, 2015- 8:01.71, 2016- 8:14.19, 2017- 8:20.61. pbs: 1500m 3:40.8A '04, 3000m 7:44.24 '12, 5000m 13:50.61 '11, 10k Rd 28:38 '11.
Five gold and three silver medals from global 3000m steeplechase races. Disqualified after finishing third at 2016 Olympic Games for stepping inside lane one early in the race.

Stephen Kipkosgei **KIBET** b. 9 Nov 1986 1.72m 55kg.
At HMar: WCh: '12- 5.
Progress at HMar: 2009- 60:34, 2010- 60:09, 2011- 60:20, 2012- 58:54, 2013- 59:59, 2014- 59:21, 2015- 59:58, 2016- 59:27, 2017- 62:55A. pbs: 5000m 13:38.47 '15; road: 10k 27:44 '14, 15k 42:01+ '12, 20k 55:55+ '12, Mar 2:08:05 '12.
Six successive half marathon wins 2009-12.

Vincent KIBET b. 6 May 1991 Uasin Gishu 1.73m 57kg.
At 1500m: WI: '16- 7, '18- 9.
Progress at 1500m: 2010- 3:46.7A, 2011- 3:42.7A, 2012- 3:40.51A, 2013- 3:35.62, 2014- 3:31.96, 2015- 3:34.91i/3:36.80, 2016- 3:33.56, 2017- 3:32.66. pbs: 800m 1:46.71 '14, 1000m 2:19.93i '15, 1M 3:51.17 '17, 3000m 7:44.87i '16, 7:50.54 '17.

Abraham KIBIWOT b. 4 Jun 1996 1.75m 55kg.
At 3000mSt: AfCh: '16- 3; won Af-J 2015, Kenyan 2016.
Progress at 3000mSt: 2014- 8:52.36A, 2015- 8:22.10, 2016- 8:09.25, 2017- 8:10.62. pbs: 3000m 8:02.95 '16, 5000m 14:10.8A '15.

Benjamin KIGEN b. 5 Jul 1993 1.73m 57kg.
Progress at 3000mSt: 2017- 8:11:38. pbs: 800m 1:52.0A '16, 1500m 3:36.36 '17, 3000m 7:44.77i '18, 5000m 14:06.2A '13, 2000mSt 5:18.67 '17.

Dennis Kipruto **KIMETTO** b. 22 Jan 1984 near Kapngetuny 1.72m 57kg.
At Mar: WCh: '15- dnf.
World records 25km road 2012, marathon 2014.
Progress at Mar: 2012- 2:04:16, 2013- 2:03:45, 2014- 2:02:57, 2015- 2:05:50, 2016- 2:11:44, 2017- dnf. Road pbs: 10k 28:21 '12, 15k 42:46 '11, HMar 59:14 '12, 25k 1:11:18 '12, 30k 1:27:38 '14.
Second Berlin 2012 in fastest ever marathon debut after major road wins at half marathon and 25k in Berlin in 2012. Won Tokyo and Chicago marathons 2013. Dnf Boston before WR in Berlin marathon 2014. 3rd London 2015.

Eliud KIPCHOGE b. 5 Nov 1984 Kapsisiywa, Nandi 1.67m 52kg.
At Mar: OG: '16- 1; At 5000m: OG: '04- 3, '08- 2; WCh: '03-05-07-09-11: 1/4/2/5/7; CG: '10- 2. At 3000m: WI: '06- 3. World CC: '02-03-04-05: 5J/1J/4/5; HMar: '12- 6. Won WAF 5000m 2003, 3000m 2004, Kenyan CC 2005.
World junior 5000m record 2003. World road best 4M 17:10 '05 and WR 30k 2016.
Progress at 1500m, 5000m, 10000m: 2002- 13:13.03, 2003- 3:36.17, 12:52.61; 2004- 3:33.20, 12:46.53; 2005- 3:33.80, 12:50.22; 2006- 3:36.25i, 12:54.94; 2007- 3:39.98, 12:50.38, 26:49.02; 2008- 13:02.06, 26:54.32; 2009- 12:56.46, 2010- 3:38.36, 12:51.21; 2011- 12:55.72i/12:59.01, 26:53.27; 2012- 12:55.34, 27:11.93. At HMar, Mar: 2012: 59:25, 2013- 60:04, 2:04:05, 2014- 60:52, 2:04:11; 2015- 60:50, 2:04:00; 2016- 59:44, 2:03:05; 2017- 61:29, 2:03:32/2:00:25 irreg. pbs: 1M 3:50.40 '04, 2000m 4:59.?+ '04, 3000m 7:27.66 '11, 2M 8:07.39i '12, 8:07.68 '05; Road: 10k 26:55dh '06, 27:34 '05; 25k 1:12:39 '16, 30k 1:27:13 '16.
Kenyan Junior CC champion 2002-03, followed World Junior CC win by winning the World 5000m title, becoming at 18 years 298 days the second youngest world champion. Age 19 bests for 3000m & 5000m 2004. Ran 26:49.02 in 10,000m debut at Hengelo in 2007. All his seven marathons were in 2:05:30 or better until his Olympic win in 2:08:44; he won at Hamburg on debut then 2nd Berlin in 2013, 1st Rotterdam & Chicago 2014, London & Berlin 2015, London 2016 (in second fastest of all-time), Berlin 2017. Won World Marathon Majors 2015/16 & 2016/17. Ran 2:00:25 in Nike's carefully contrived 2-hour marathon bid at Monza racetrack on 6 May 2017 after seven months of preparation.

Kenneth Kiprop **KIPKEMOI** b. 2 Aug 1984 1.65m 52kg.
At 10000m: WCh: '13- 7; AfG: '17- 7; AfCh: '12- 1. Kenyan champion 2012, 2016. At HMar: World '14-10, AfG: '11- 2.
Progress at 10000m, HMar: 2009- 62:59A, 2011- 27:48.5A, 59:47; 2012- 26:52.65, 59:11; 2013- 27:28.50, 60:45; 2014- 27:30.94, 59:01; 2015- 60:17, 2016- 27:52.1A, 60:05; 2017- 60:24. pbs: 3000m 7:49.28+ '11, 5000m 13:03.37 '12, 15k 43:22 '12, 25k 1:22:32 '14.

Alfred KIPKETER b. 26 Dec 1996 1.69m 61kg.
At 800m: OG: '16- 7; WCh: '15- 7; WJ: '14- 1; WY: '13- 1.
Progress at 800m: 2013- 1:46.2A, 2014- 1:43.95, 2015- 1:44.07A, 2016- 1:42.87, 2017- 1:45.40. pb 600m 1:15.60 '15.

Gideon Kipkemoi **KIPKETER** b. 10 Nov 1992 1.78m 57kg.
At Mar: WCh: '17- 5. World CC: '10- 8J, AfCC: '11- 4J.
Progress at Mar: 2012- 2:08:14, 2013- 2:10:41, 2014- 2:10:36, 2015- 2:09:01, 2016- 2:08:35, 2017- 2:05:51. pbs: 3000m 7:52.11 '10, 5000m 13:15.77 '10, 10000m 28:25.31 '15, 10M Rd 46:36 '14, HMar 59:53 '12.
Won Mumbai marathon 2016, 2nd Tokyo 2017.

Nicholas KIPKOECH b. 22 Oct 1992 1.68m 57kg.
At 800m: WY: '09- 3.
Progress at 800m: 2009- 1:47.4A, 2010- 1:47.0A, 2011- 1:45.47, 2012- 1:45.02, 2013- 1:47.14, 2014- 1:45.7A, 2015- 1:44.9A, 2016- 1:43.37A, 2017- 1:44.9A. pbs: 600m 1:15.87 '15, 1000m 2:16.68 '16, 1500m 3:44.07 '11.

Silas KIPLAGAT b. 20 Aug 1989 Siboh village, Marakwet 1.70m 57kg.
At 1500m: OG: '12- 7; WCh: '11-13-15: 2/6/5; CG: '10- 1; AfCh: '10- 4; WI: '12- 6. Won DL 2012, 2014; Kenyan 2011. World 4x1500m record 2014.
Progress at 1500m: 2009- 3:39.1A, 2010- 3:29.27, 2011- 3:30.47, 2012- 3:29.63, 2013- 3:30.13, 2014- 3:27.64, 2015- 3:30.12, 2016- 3:33.68, 2017- 3:32.33. pbs: 800m 1:44.8A '12, 1000m 2:19.80 '16, 1M 3:47.88 '14, 3000m 7:39.94 '10, 5000m 13:54.05 '17, 10k Rd 28:00 '09.

Asbel Kipruto **KIPROP** b. 30 Jun 1989 Uasin Gishu, Eldoret. North Rift 1.86m 70kg.
At (800m)/1500m: OG: '08- 1, '12- 12, '16- 6; WCh: '07- 4, '09- sf/4, '11-13-15-17: 1/1/1/9; AfG: '07- 1; AfCh: '10- 1, '14- 2; CCp: '10- 6, '14- 2; Won DL 2010, 2015-16. At 800m: AfCh: '08- 3. World CC: '07- 1J, '17- 1 MxR. Won Kenyan 800m 2015, 1500m 2007, 2010.
World 4x1500m record 2014.
Progress at 800m, 1500m: 2007- 3:35.24, 2008- 1:44.71, 3:31.64; 2009- 1:43.17, 3:31.20; 2010- 1:43.45, 3:31.78; 2011- 1:43.15, 3:30.46; 2012- 1:45.91, 3:28.88; 2013- 1:44.8A, 3:27.72; 2014- 1:43.34, 3:28.45; 2015- 1:44.4A, 3:26.69; 2016- 1:44.6A, 3:29.33; 2017- 1:44.43, 3:33.17. pbs: 1000m 2:14.23 '16, 1M 3:48.50 '09, 3000m 7:42.32 '07, 5000m 13:48.43A '10.
Father David Kebenei had 1M pb 3:59.35 (1982), 4 AfG 1500m 1987.

Brimin KIPRUTO b. 31 Jul 1985 Korkitony, Marakwet District 1.76m 54kg.

At 3000mSt: OG: '04- 2, '08- 1, '12- 5, '16- 6; WCh: '05-07-09-11-15-17: 3/1/7/2/3/h; CG: '10- 3; Af-J: '03- 2; KEN champion 2011. At 1500m: WJ: '04- 3. At 2000St: WY: '01- 2. World 4k CC: '06- 18.
Commonwealth & African 3000mSt record 2011.
Progress at 3000mSt: 2002- 8:33.0A, 2003- 8:34.5A, 2004- 8:05.52, 2005- 8:04.22, 2006- 8:08.32, 2007- 8:02.89, 2008- 8:10.26, 2009- 8:03.17, 2010- 8:00.90, 2011- 7:53.64, 2012- 8:01.73, 2013- 8:06.86, 2014- 8:04.64, 2015- 8:10:09, 2016- 8:18.79, 2017- 8:19.87A. pbs: 1500m 3:35.23 '06, 2000m 4:58.76i '07, 3000m 7:39.07i '12, 7:47.33 '06; 5000m 13:58.82 '04, 2000mSt 5:36.81 '01.
First name is actually Firmin, but he stayed with the clerical error of Brimin, written when he applied for a birth certificate in 2001.

Conseslus KIPRUTO b. 8 Dec 1994 Eldoret 1.71m 55kg.
At 3000mSt: OG: '16- 1; WCh: '13- 2, '15- 2, '17- 1 WJ: '12- 1; won DL 2013, 2016-17. At 2000St: WY: '11- 1. World CC: 2013- 5J.
Progress at 3000mSt: 2011- 8:27.30, 2012- 8:03.49, 2013- 8:01.16, 2014- 8:09.81, 2015- 8:05.20, 2016- 8:00.12, 2017- 8:04.63. pbs: 800m 1:49.0A '15, 1000m 2:19.85 '12, 1500m 3:39.57 '13, 3000m 7:44.09 '12, 5000m 13:47.5A 16, 2000mSt 5:28.65 '11.

Wilson KIPSANG Kiprotich b. 15 Mar 1982 Keiyo district 1.78m 59kg.
At Mar: OG: '12- 3; WCh: '15- dnf; HMar: WCh: '09- 4. World marathon record 2013.
Progress at HMar, Mar: 2008- 59:16, 2009- 58:59, 2010- 60:04, 2:04:57; 2011- 60:49, 2:03:42; 2012- 59:06, 2:04:44; 2013- 61:02, 2:03:23; 2014- 60:25, 2:04:29; 2015- 61:23, 2:04:47; 2016- 61:11, 2:03:13; 2017- 61:29, 2:03:58. pbs: 5000m 13:55.7A '09, 10000m 28:37.0A '07; Road: 10k 27:42 '09, 15k 41:51+ '11, 10M 44:59+ '11, 20k 56:10+ '12, 25k 1:12:47 '16, 30k 1:27:26 '16.
Third in Paris in 2:07:13 on marathon debut and nine wins: Frankfurt in 2010 and 2011, Lake Biwa 2011, London 2012 and 2014 (2nd 2015), Honolulu 2012, Berlin 2013 (2nd 2016) and New York 2014 (2nd 2017), Tokyo 2017. Won World Marathon Majors 2013/14. Record six marathons inside 2:05. Won Great North Run 2012. His brother Noah Kigen HMar pb 60:25 '17.

Eliud KIPTANUI b. 6 Jun 1989 Kaplelach, Uasin Gishu 1.69m 55kg.
At Mar: WCh: '11- 5.
Progress at Mar: 2009- 2:12:17, 2010- 2:05:39, 2011- 2:09:08, 2012- 2:06:44, 2013- 2:15:10, 2014- 2:07:28, 2015- 2:05:21, 2016- 2:07:47, 2017- 2:07:25. pbs: 3000m 8:04.57 '09, Road: 25k 1:13:38 '14, 30k 1:29:18 '14; HMar 61:13 '16.
Won Safaricom Marathon in Kisimu in December 2009, then a stunning improvement to win Prague Marathon in 2010, Ottawa 2017; 3rd Seoul & 2nd Beijing 2012, 2nd Berlin 2015.

Abel KIRUI b. 4 Jun 1982 Bornet, Rift Valley 1.77m 62kg. Police.
At Mar: OG: '12- 2; WCh: '09- 1, '11- 1.
Progress at Mar: 2006- 2:15:22, 2007- 2:06:51, 2008- 2:07:38, 2009- 2:05:04, 2010- 2:08:04, 2011- 2:07:38, 2012- 2:07:56, 2014- 2:09:04, 2015- 2:10:55, 2016- 2:08:06, 2017- 2:07:45. pbs: 1500m 3:46.10 '05, 3000m 7:55.90 '06, 5000m 13:52.71 '05, 10000m 28:16.86A '08; Road: 10k 27:59 '09, 15k 42:22 '07, 10M 46:40 '11, HMar 60:11 '07, 25k: 1:13:41 '08, 30k 1:28:25 '08.
Brilliantly retained World marathon title with halves of 65:07 and 62:31 and a fastest 5k split of 14:18. Won Vienna Marathon 2008, Chicago 2016 (2nd 2017), 2nd Berlin 2007, 3rd Rotterdam 2009. Uncle Mike Rotich had marathon pb 2:06:33 '03.

Geoffrey Kipkorir **KIRUI** b. 16 Feb 1993 1.58m 50kg.
At Mar: WCh: '17- 1. At 10000m: WJ: '12- 3; AfG: '15- 5; Af-J: '11- 1. World CC: '13- 15
Progress at 10000m, Mar: 2011- 26:55.73, 2012- 27:08.44, 2014- 29:05.8A, 2015- 27:17.91, 2016- 29:08.6A, 2:06:27; 2017- 2:08:27. Pbs: 3000m 7:42.26 13, 5000m 13:16.68 13, Road: HMar 59:38 '15, 25k 1:14:42 '16, 30k 1:29:44 '16.
Won Boston marathon 2012 after 3rd Rotterdam & 7th Amsterdam 2016.

Jonathan Kiprotich **KITILIT** b. 24 Apr 1994 1.71m 61kg.
At 1500m: Af-J: '13- 2.
Progress at 800m: 2012- 1:47.8A, 2013- 1:48.03, 2015- 1:45.0A, 2016- 1:43.05, 2018- 1:44.64A. pbs: 2:13.95 '16, 1500m 3:39.81 '15.

Timothy KITUM b. 20 Nov 1994 Marakwet 1.72m 60kg.
At 800m: OG: '12- 3; WJ: '12- 2; WY: '11- 3; AfG: '15- 4.
Progress at 800m: 2011- 1:44.98, 2012- 1:42.53, 2013- 1:44.45, 2014- 1:43.65, 2015- 1:45.0A, 2016- 1:44.51A, 2017- 1:45.9A. pbs: 600m 1:14.4A '12, 1000m 2:17.62 '15.

Sammy Kiprop **KITWARA** b. 26 Nov 1986 Sagat village, Marakwet district 1.77m 54kg.
At 10000m: Kenyan champion 2009. World HMar: '09- 10, '10- 3.
Progress at 10,000m, HMar, Mar: 2007- 28:11.6A, 2008- 28:12.26A, 60:54; 2009- 27:44.46A, 58:58; 2010- 28:32.77A, 59:34; 2011- 58:47, 2012- 2:05:54, 2013- 61:53, 2:05:16; 2014- 60:24, 2:04:28; 2015- 60:25, 2:07:43; 2016- 59:47, 2:05:45; 2017- 2:05:15. pbs: 5000m 13:34.0A '08, Road: 10k 27:11 '10, 15k 41:54 '09, 10M 45:17 '08, 20k 57:42 '08, 25k 1:13:42 '14, 30k 1:28:46 '14.
Marathons: Won Taipei 2016, Valencia 2017, 2nd Chicago 2014-15 (3rd 2013, 4th 2012), 3rd Rotterdam 2013, Tokyo 2014

Haron KOECH b. 27 Jan 1990 1.88m 79kg. Central.
At 400mh/4x400mR: OG: '16- 7; WCh: '15/17- sf; AfCh: '16- 3/2R. Kenyan champion 2016.
Progress at 400mh: 2014- 51.14A, 2015- 49.38,

2016- 48.49, 2017- 49.39.
Twin brother of 400m hurdler Nicholas Bett.

Isiah Kiplangat **KOECH** b. 19 Dec 1993 Kericho 1.78m 60kg.
At 5000m: OG: '12- 5, '16- h; WCh: '11- 4, '13- 3, '15- 8; CG: '14- 2; AfCh: '14- 2; CCp: '14- 1; won DL 5000m 2012, Kenyan 2011, 2013. At 3000m: WY: '09- 1; WI: '16- 8. World CC: '10- 4J, '11- 10J.
World junior records indoors: 5000m 2011, 3000m 2011 & 2012.
Progress at 5000m, 10000m: 2010- 13:07.70, 2011- 12:53.29i/12:54.18, 2012- 12:48.64, 27:17.03; 2013- 12:56.08, 2014- 13:07.55, 2015- 13:07.33, 2016- 13:08.34. pbs: 1500m 3:38.7A '12, 3000m 7:30.43 '12, 2M 8:14.16 '11.

Paul Kipsiele **KOECH** b. 10 Nov 1981 Cheplanget, Buret District 1.68m 57kg.
At 3000mSt: OG: '04- 3; WCh: '05- 7, '09- 4, '13- 4; AfG: '03- 2; AfCh: '06- 1; WCp: '06- 2; won DL 2010-12, WAF 2005-08. At 3000m: WI: 08- 2.
Progress at 3000mSt: 2001- 8:15.92, 2002- 8:05.44, 2003- 7:57.42, 2004- 7:59.65, 2005- 7:56.37, 2006- 7:59.94, 2007- 7:58.80, 2008- 8:00.57, 2009- 8:01.26, 2010- 8:02.07, 2011- 7:57.32, 2012- 7:54.31, 2013- 8:02.63, 2014- 8:05.47, 2015- 8:10.24, 2016- 8:08.32. pbs: 1500m 3:37.92 '07, 2000m 5:00.9+i '08, 5:01.84 '14; 3000m 7:32.78i '10, 7:33.93 '05; 2M 8:06.48i/8:13.31 '08, 5000m 13:02.69i 12, 13:05.18 '10; 15k 42:44 '17, 20k 57:52 '17, HMar 61:03 '17, Mar 2:12:02 '17.
Younger brother John Koech (b. 23 Aug 1995) transferred to BRN 2013; 3000mSt: 8:14.75 '15; OG: '16- h; WCh: '15- 5, AsiC: '15- 1, CCp: '14- 5.

Emmanuel Kipkurui **KORIR** b. 15 Jun 1995 1.77m 64kg. University of Texas El Paso.
At 800m: WCh: '17- sf. Won NCAA indoors and out 2017.
World indoor best 600m 2017, African & Commonewealth 800m record 2018.
Progress at 800m: 2016- 1:46.94A, 2017- 1:43.10, 2018- 1:44.21i. Pbs: 44.53A '17, 600m 1:14.97Ai '17.

Ronald KWEMOI b. 19 Sep 1995 Mt. Elgon 1.80m 68kg.
At 1500m: OG: '16- 13; WCh: '17- sf; CG: '14- 2; AfG: '15- 4; AfCh: '14- 3; Kenyan champion 2014. World CC: '13- 9J.
World junior 1500m record 2014.
Progress at 1500m: 2013- 3:45.39, 2014- 3:28.81, 2015- 3:30.43, 2016- 3:30.49, 2017- 3:30.89A. pbs: 800m 1:49.7A '17, 1M 3:49.04 '17, 3000m 7:28.73 '17, 5000m 13:16.14 '15, 10000m 27:33.94 '16.

Thomas Pkemei **LONGOSIWA** b. 14 Jan 1982 West Pokot 1.75m 57kg. North Rift.
At 5000m: OG: '08- 12, '12- 3; WCh: '11- 6, '13- 4; AfG: '07- 6, '15- 3; . World CC: '06- 13J (but dq after birthdate found to be 1982). Won Kenyan 5000m 2007.
Progress at 5000m: 2006- 13:35.3A, 2007- 12:51.95, 2008- 13:14.36, 2009- 13:03.43, 2010- 13:05.60, 2011- 12:56.08, 2012- 12:49.04, 2013- 12:59.81, 2014- 12:56.16, 2015- 12:59.72, 2016- 13:01.69, 2017- 13:50.85. pbs: 1500m 3:41.92 '13, 2000m 5:01.6+ '10, 3000m 7:30.09 '09, 10000m 28:11.3A '06.

Wilson Erupe **LOYANAE** b. 20 Nov 1988 Lodwar, Turkana.
Progress at Mar: 2010- ?. 2011- 2:09:23, 2012- 2:05:37, 2015- 2:06:11, 2016- 2:05:13, 2017- 2:06:27, 2018- 2:06:57. pb HMar 61:46 '12.
Marathon wins: Mombasa 2011, Gyongju 2011-12, 2015; Seoul 2012, 2015-16, 2018. Two-year drugs ban for EPO 2013-15.

Elijah Motonei **MANANGOI** b. 5 Jan 1993 Narok 1.81m 65kg.
At 1500m: OG: '16- sf; WCh: '15- 2, '17- 1; CG: '14- 12. Kenyan champion 2015
Progress at 1500m: 2014- 3:35.0A, 2015- 3:29.67, 2016- 3:31.19, 2017- 3:28.80. pbs: 400m 46.5A '13, 47.33A '13; 800m 1:44.8A '17, 1000m 2:17.09i '16, 1M 3:49.08 '17.
His brother George won the World Youth 1500m title in 2017.

Boniface MUCHERU Tumuti b. 2 May 1992 Laikipia District 1.85m 75kg. Central.
At 400mh/4x400mR (400m): OG: '12- h, '16- 2; WCh: '15- 5; CG: '14- 6; AfCh: '10- h, '12- 3/3R, 14- (3)/3R, '16- 1; WJ: '10- 8 (h). Kenyan champion 2012, 2015.
Kenyan 400mh records 2015 & 2016.
Progress at 400mh: 2008- 52.79A, 2010- 51.04A, 2011- 50.35A, 2012- 49.45, 2013- 49.59A, 2014- 49.25A/49.67, 2015- 48.29, 2016- 47.78, 2017- 50.61. pbs: 200m 22.23 '15, 400m 45.07 '14, 800m 1:49.34 '15, 110mh 14.51A '15.

Caleb Mwangangi **NDIKU** b. 9 Oct 1992 Machakos 1.83m 68kg.
At 1500m: WJ: '10- 1; WY: '09- 2; AfG: '11- 1; AfCh: '12- 1; Kenyan champion 2012. At 3000m: CCp: '14- 1; WI: '14- 1, '16- 5. At 5000m: OG: '16- h; WCh: '15- 2; CG: '14- 1; AfCh: '14- 1; won DL 2014 World CC: '10- 1J.
Progress at 1500m, 5000m: 2009- 3:38.2A, 2010- 3:37.30, 2011- 3:32.02, 2012- 3:32.39, 2013- 3:29.50, 13:03.80; 2014- 3:35.8A, 12:59.17; 2015- 3:38.13, 13:05.30; 2016- 13:12.25, 2017- 13:31.45. pbs: 800m 1:52.6A '07, 1M 3:49.77 '11, 3000m 7:30.99 '12, 10000m 28:28.4A '14.
His father David was a javelin thrower.

Jonathan Muia **NDIKU** b. 18 Sep 1991 Machakos 1.73m 60kg. Hitachi Cable, Japan.
At 3000mSt: CG: '14- 1; AfCh: '14- 2; WJ: '08- 1, '10- 1; Af-J: '09- 1. At 2000mSt: WY: '07- 4.
Progress at 10,000m, 3000mSt: 2008- 28:08.28, 8:17.28; 2009- 27:37.72, 8:28.1A; 2010- 8:19.25A. 2011- 8:07.75, 2012- 8:17.88, 2013- 8:18.78, 2014- 8:10.44, 2015- 27:40.64, 8:11.64; 2016- 27:11.23, 2017- 27:39.40. pbs: 1500m 3:39.27 '10, 3000m 7:39.63 '14, 5000m 13:11.99 '09, HMar 62:07 '17, 2000mSt 5:37.30 '07.

David Lekuta **RUDISHA** b. 17 Dec 1988 Kilgoris 1.89m 73kg. Masai.

At 800m: OG: '12- 1, '16- 1; WCh: '09- sf, '11- 1, '15- 1; CG: '14- 2; WJ: '06- 1/4R; AfCh: '08- 1, '10- 1; Af-J: '07- 1; CCp: '10- 1. Won DL 2010-11, WAF 2009, Kenyan 2009-11.
Three world 800m records 2010-12, four African records 2009-10., Commonwealth & African 600m record 2016.
Progress at 800m: 2006- 1:46.3A, 2007- 1:44.15, 2008- 1:43.72, 2009- 1:42.01, 2010- 1:41.01, 2011- 1:41.33, 2012- 1:40.91, 2013- 1:43.87, 2014- 1:42.98, 2015- 1:43.58, 2016- 1:42.15. pbs: 400m 45.50 '10, 45.2A '13; 600m 1:13.10 '16.
IAAF Male Athlete of the Year 2010, won 26 successive 800m finals 2009-11. His father Daniel won 4x400m silver medal at 1968 Olympics with 440y pb 45.5A '67.

Stephen Kiptoo **SAMBU** b. 3 Jul 1988 Eldoret 1.69m 55kg. Was at University of Arizona.
Progress at 10000m: 2009- 28:37.96, 2010- 29:01.34, 2011- 27:28.64, 2012- 28:06.16, 2014- 26:54.61, 2016- 26:58.25. pbs: 1500m 3:43.56 '12, 3000m 7:51.59i/8:13.69 '12, 5000m 13:13.74i '12, 13:21.14 '16; 10M Rd 43:20 '15, HMar 60:41 '13, Mar 2:11:07 '17.

Michael Lotoromom **SARUNI** b. 18 Jun 1995 1.80m 78kg. University of Texas at El Paso.
At 800m: Won NCAA indoor 2018.
World best 600m indoors 2018.
Progress at 800m: 2017- 1:44.61A. pbs: 400m 45.69A '17, 600m 1:14.79Ai '18, 1500m 3:46.15A '17, 1M 4:03.32i '17.

Charles Cheboi **SIMOTWO** b. 6 May 1995 1.73m 59kg.
Progress at 1500m: 2015- 3:35.86A, 2017- 3:32.59. pb 800m 1:46.20 '17.

William Malel **SITONIK** b. 1 Mar 1994 1.65m 52kg. Honda, Japan.
At 3000m: WY: 11- 1. At 5000m: WJ: '12- 3.
Progress at 10000m: 2012- 29:29.3A, 2013- 27:48.55, 2014- 27:25.56, 2015- 27:22.12, 2016- 26:54.66, 2017- 27:22.79. pbs: 2000m 5:07.51 '11, 3000m 7:40.10 '11 '10, 5000m 13:19.83 '13.

Edwin Cheruiyot **SOI** b. 3 Mar 1986 Kericho 1.72m 55kg.
At 5000m: OG: '08- 3, '12- h; WCh: '13- 5, '15- 10; AfCh: '10- 1; CCp: '10- 4. At 3000m: WI: '08- 4, '12- 3; won WAF 3000m 2007, 5000m 2007-08. World CC: '06- 8 4k, '07- 9.
Progress at 5000m, 10000m: 2002- 29:06.5A, 2004- 13:22.57, 2005- 13:10.78, 2006- 12:52.40, 27:14.83; 2007- 13:10.21, 2008- 13:06.22, 2009- 12:55.03, 2010- 12:58.91, 2011- 12:59.15, 2012- 12:55.99, 2013- 12:51.34, 26:49.41; 2014- 12:59.82, 2015- 13:11.97, 2016- 13:03.26, 2017- 13:28.24. pbs: 1500m 3:40.52 '13, 2000m 5:01.4+ '10, 3000m 7:27.55 '11, 2M 8:14.10 '11, 10k Rd 28:13 '08.

Paul Kipngetich **TANUI** b. 22 Dec 1990 Chesubeno village, Moio district 1.72m 54kg. Kyudenko Corporation, Japan.
At 10000m: OG: '16- 2; WCh: '11-13-15-17: 9/3/3/3. World CC: '09-10-11: 4J/8/2. Won Kenyan CC 2010.
Progress at 5000m, 10000m: 2008- 13:59.2A, 2009- 13:37.15, 27:25.24; 2010- 13:14.87, 27:17.61; 2011- 13:04.65, 26:50.63; 2012- 13:19.18, 27:27.56; 2013- 13:16.57, 27:21.50; 2014- 13:00.53, 26:49.41; 2015- 12:58.69, 26:51.86; 2016- 13:15.22, 27:05.64; 2017- 13:14.09, 26:50.60. pbs: 1500m 3:43.97 '10, 3000m 7:46.61 '16, HMar 62:48 '14.

Daniel Kinyua **WANJIRU** b. 25 May 1992 Embu county 1.74m 58kg.
At Mar: WCh: '17- 8.
Progress at Mar: 2014- 2:08:18, 2016- 2:05:21, 2017- 2:05:48. pbs: 3000m 8:07.1A 10, 5000m 14:01.8A '16, 10000m 28:59.9A '16; Road: 10k 27:43 '16, 15k 42:16 '14, 20k 56:01 '16, HMar 59:20 '16, 30k 1:28:21 '17.
Marathon wins: Amsterdam 2016, London 2017.

Hillary Kipsang **YEGO** b. 2 Apr 1992 1.78m 60kg.
At 2000mSt: WY: '09- 1.
Progress at 3000mSt: 2009- 8:46.8A, 2010- 8:19.50, 2011- 8:07.71, 2012- 8:11.83. 2013- 8:03:57, 2014- 8:09.07, 2015- 8:13.10, 2016- 8:15.10, 2017- 8:31.54. pbs: 1500m 3:43.3 '10, 3000m 7:53.18 '10, 5000m 13:53.82 '16, 2000mSt 5:25.33 '09.

Julius Kiplangat **YEGO** b. 4 Jan 1989 Cheptonon, Nandi district 1.75m 90kg.
At JT: OG: '12- 11, '16- 2; WCh: '13- 4, '15- 1, '17- 13; CG: '10- 7, '14- 1; AfG: '11- 1; AfCh: '10-12-14: 3/1/1; CCp: '14- 4. Kenyan champion 2008-14.
Javelin records: Commonwealth & two African 2015, nine Kenyan 2011-15.
Progress at JT: 2008- 72.18A, 2009- 74.00A, 2010- 75.44, 2011- 78.34A, 2012- 81.81; 2013- 85.40, 2014- 84.72, 2015- 92.72, 2016- 88.24, 2017- 87.97.
His winning throw at the 2015 Worlds was the world's best javelin throw since 2001.

Solomon Kirwa **YEGO** b. 10 May 1987 1.75m 58kg. Af CC: 14- 4.
Progress at HMar: 2011- 64:40, 2012- 61:34, 2013- 61:56, 2014- 61:59, 2015- 60:04, 2016- 58:44, 2017- 59:50. pbs: 5000m 14:14.54 '12, 10000m 28:23.0A '15, Mar 2:08:31 '16.

Women

Alice APROT Nawowuna b. 2 Jan 1994 1.74m 55kg. Turkana.
At (5000m)/10000m: OG: '16- 4; WCh: '17- 4; WJ: '10- (3); AfG: '15- 3/1; AfCh: '16- 1. World CC: '10- 9J, '17- 2; AfCC: 14- 3. Won African & Kenyan CC 2016, KEN 10000m 2016-17..
Progress at 5000m, 10000m: 2010- 15:16.74, 2011- 16:36.8A, 2014- 16:22.8A, 2015- 15:31.82, 31:24.18; 2016- 14:39.56, 29:53.51; 2017- 31:11.86. pbs: 1500m 4:23.92 '14, 3000m 8:44.7 '16, 10M 51:59 '16.
Elder brother Joseph Ebuya won World CC in 2010, pb 5000m 12:51.00 '07.

Winny CHEBET b. 20 Dec 1990 1.65m 50kg.
At 800m: OG: '16- sf; WCh: '13- sf; CG: '10- 7;

AfG: '15- 5 (2- 4x400m); AfCh: '10- 5; WJ: '06- 2, '08- 5; WY: '05- 2, '07- dq (for obstruction after 2nd place); Af-J: '09- 2. At 1500m: WCh: '17- sf; WI: '18- 5.
Progress at 800m, 1500m: 2005- 2:08.15, 2006- 2:04.59, 2007- 2:04.10, 2008- 2:04.13, 2009- 2:01.36, 2010- 2:00.88A, 2011- 2:03.80A, 2012- 1:59.37, 4:16.0A; 2013- 1:59.30, 2015- 2:02.38A, 2016- 1:59.88, 4:02.66; 2017- 1:58.13, 3:59.16. pbs: 1000m 2:35.73 '13, 1M 4:19.55 '17.

Fancy CHEMUTAI b. 20 Mar 1995 1.63m 48kg.
Progress at HMar: 2016- 65:36, 2017- 64:52. pbs: 10k 30:09 '17, 15k 45:59 '17, 20k 61:35 '18, HMar 64:52 '18.
Won Ra's Al-Khaymah half marathon 2018.

Sarah CHEPCHIRCHIR b. 27 Jul 1984 1.65m 49kg. Lille metropole athletisme.
At HMar: WCh: '10- 11; AfG: '11- 5.
Progress at Mar: 2016- 2:24:13, 2017- 2:19:47. pbs: 3000m 9:40.37 '15, road: 10k 32:07 '11, 15k 49:28 '12, HMar 67:52 '16, 25k 1:23:35 '17, 30k 1:40:26 '17 '14.
Won Tokyo Marathon 2017, Lisbon 2016-17.

Joyce CHEPKIRUI b. 20 Aug 1988 Bureti 1.52m 48kg.
At 10000m: OG: '12- dnf; CG: '14- 1; AfCh: '14- 1. At 5000m: CCp: '14- 2. At 1500m: AfG: '11- 2; Af-J: '07- 5. At HMar: WCh: '10- 5. AfCC: '12- 1. Won Kenyan CC 2012, 10000m 2015.
Progress at 10000m, HMar, Mar: 2007- 75:11, 2009- 71:47, 2010- 69:25, 2011- 31:26.10, 69:04; 2012- 32:34.71A, 67:03; 2013- 68:15, 2:35:54; 2014- 32:09.35, 66:19, 2:30:23; 2015- 32:08.00A, 68:42, 2:24:11; 2016- 67:41, 2:29:08. pbs: 1500m 4:08.80A '11, 5000m 15:58.31 '14, 3000mSt 10:26.7A '08; Road: 10k 30:37 '11, 15k 46:49 '14, 10M 51:30 '15, 20k 62:55 '14.
Won Honolulu Marathon 2014-15, Amsterdam 2015; 3rd Boston 2016. Married Erick Kibet, pb HMar 61:10 '10, in 2009.

Beatrice CHEPKOECH b. 6 Jul 1991 1.71m 57kg.
At 3000mSt: OG: '16- 4; WCh: '17- 4. At 1500m: AfG: '15- 3; WI: '18- 7. World CC: '17- 1 MxR. Won KEN 1500m 2017.
Progress at 1500m, 3000mSt: 2011- 10:41.3A, 2013- 4:16.6A, 2014- 4:12.37A, 2015- 4:03.28, 2016- 4:18.0A, 9:10.86; 2017- 8:59.84. pbs: 800m 2:05.73 '15, 1500m 4:02.21i '18, 4:03.2A '17; 3000m 8:39.15i '18, 5000m 14:39.33 '17, 2000mSt 6:02.47 '15.
4th in 2017 Worlds despite missing the water jump after the first lap and having to run back to clear it and also later falling.

Irene Chebet **CHEPTAI** b. 4 Feb 1992 1.60m 45kg.
At 10000m: WCh: '17- 7. At 5000m: WCh: '15- 7. At 3000m: WY: '07- 7. World CC: '08-13-15-17: 2J/10/7/1. Won KEN CC 2017.
Progress at 5000m, 10000m: 2012- 16:02.0A, 2013- 14:50.99, 2014- 15:17.76, 2015- 14:53.32, 2016- 14:43.42, 2017- 31:21.11. pbs: 1500m 4:13.75 '14, 3000m 8:48.03 '15, 10k rd 31:45A '14.

Gladys Kiprono **CHERONO** b. 12 May 1983 Kericho 1.66m 50kg.
At 10000m: WCh: '13- 2; AfCh: '12- 1 (1 5000m). World HMar: '14- 1. Won Kenyan 5000m 2012.
Progress at 5000m, 10000m, Mar: 2005- 16:16.8A, 2007- 16:03.8A, 2008- 15:56.0A, 2012- 15:39.5A, 32:41.40; 2013- 14:47.12, 30:29.23; 2014- 16:49.8A, 34:13.0A; 2015- 15:50.3A, 32:24.10A, 2:19:25; 2017- 2:20:23; pbs: 1500m 4:25.13 '04, 3000m 8:34.05 '13, Road: 15k 47:43 '13, 20k 63:26 '13, HMar 66:07 '16.
Second Dubai Marathon (2:20:03, third fastest ever debut) and won Berlin in 2015 and 2017. Married to Joseph Bwambok (62:25 HMar 2010).

Vivian Jepkemoi **CHERUIYOT** b. 11 Sep 1983 Keiyo 1.55m 38kg. Police.
At 5000m (/10000m): OG: '04- 14, '08- 4, '12- 2/3, '16- 1/2; WCh: '07- 2, '09- 1, '11- 1/1, '15- (1); CG: '10- 1; WJ: '02- 3; AfG '99- 3; AfCh: '10- 1; Af-J: '01- 1; CCp: '10- 1; won DL 2010-12. At 3000m: WY: '99- 3; WI: '10- 2. World CC: '98-9-00-01-02-04-06-07-11: 5J/2J/1J/4J/3J/8 4k/8 4k/8/1. Won KEN 1500m 2009, 5000m 2010-11, 10000m 2011-12. African 2000m record 2009, Commonwealth 5000m 2009 & 2011, 10000m 2016, indoor 3000m (8:30.53) 2009; Kenyan 5000m 2007 & 2011, 10000m 2016.
Progress at 5000m, 10000m: 1999- 15:42.79A, 2000- 15:11.11, 2001- 15:59.4A, 2002- 15:49.7A, 2003- 15:44.8A, 2004- 15:13.26, 2006- 14:47.43, 2007- 14:22.51, 2008- 14:25.43, 2009- 14:37.01, 2010- 14:27.41, 2011- 14:20.87, 30:48.98; 2012- 14:35.62, 30:30.44; 2015- 14:46.69, 31:13.29; 2016- 14:26.17, 29:32.53. pbs: 1500m 4:06.6A '12, 4:06.65 '07; 2000m 5:31.52 '09, 3000m 8:28.66 '07, 2M 9:12.35i '10, 10M Rd 51:17 '15, HMar 67:44dh '17, Mar 2:23:35 '17.
Laureus Sportswomen of the Year for 2011. Married Moses Kiplagat on 14 Apr 2012; son Allan born 19 Oct 2013. Won Great North Run on half marathon debut 2016, and 4th London on marathon debut 2017, then 1st Frankfurt..

Celliphine Chepteek **CHESPOL** b. 23 Mar 1999 1.63m 48kg.
At 3000mSt: WCh: '17- 6; WJ: '16- 1; At 2000mSt: WY: '15- 1, World CC: 17- 3J, AfCC: '18- 1.
Two World junior records 3000mSt 2017.
Progress at 3000mSt: 2015- 10:18.3A, 2016- 9:24.73, 2017- 8:58.78. pbs: 1500m 4:11.1A '17, 2000St 6:17.15 '15.

Flomena Daniel **CHEYECH** b. 5 Jul 1982 West Pokot 1.68m 49kg.
At Mar: WCh: '17- 4; CG: '14- 1. World HMar: '09- 8; CC: 99- 10J.
Progress at Mar: 2006- 2:42:15A, 2012- 2:34:13, 2013- 2:24:34, 2014- 2:22:44, 2015- 2:24:38, 2016- 2:23:18, 2017- 2:21:22. pbs: 3000m 9:16.21 '07,

5000m 15:19.47 '09, 10000m 31:58.50 '08, road: 15k 48:26 '13, HMar 67:39 '13, 30k 1:40:33 '14. Marathon wins: Porto Alegre 2012, Vienna & Toronto 2013, Paris 2014, Saitama 2016-17; 2nd Amsterdam 2015.

Irene JELAGAT b. 10 Dec 1988 Samutet, Nyanza 1.62m 45kg.
At 1500m: OG: '08- h; WCh: '09- h; CG: '10- 6; AfG: '11- 1; AfCh: '08- 5, '10- 4; WJ: '06- 1; WY: '05- dns; WI: '10- 5. At 3000m: WI: 14- 4.
Two world 4x1500m records 2014.
Progress at 1500m: 2005- 4:21.3A, 2006- 4:08.88, 2007- 4:10.27, 2008- 4:04.59, 2009- 4:03.62, 2010- 4:03.76, 2011- 4:02.59, 2014- 4:04.07, 2015- 4:07.75. pb 800m 2:02.99 '06, 2000m 5:46.4 '14, 3000m 8:28.51 '14, 2M 9:12.90 '14, 5000m 14:55.49 '15.

Peres JEPCHIRCHIR b. 27 Sep 1993 Usain Gishu 1.53m 40kg.
World HMar: '16- 1.
World records 20k and half marathon 2017.
Progress at HMar: 2014- 69:12, 2015- 67:17, 2016- 66:39, 2017- 65:06. pbs: Road: 10k 30:55 '15, 15k 46:32 '17, 20k 61:40 '17, Mar 2:47:33A '13.
7 wins in 8 half marathons 2014-17, inc. RAK 2017.

Hyvin Kiyeng **JEPKEMOI** b. 13 Jan 1992 1.56m 45kg.
At 3000mSt: OG: '16- 2; WCh: '13- 6, '15- 1, '17- 3; AfG: '11- 1 (4 5000m); AfCh: '12- 3. Kenyan champion 2015. World CC: '17- 4.
African and Commonwealth 3000m steeplechase record 2016.
Progress at 3000mSt: 2011- 10:00.50, 2012- 9:23.53, 2013- 9:22.05, 2014- 9:22.58, 2015- 9:10.15, 2016- 9:00.01, 2017- 9:00.12. pbs: 1500m 4:19.4A '17, 4:19.44 '11; 3000m 9:07.51 '11, 5000m 15:40.37A '17, 10000m 35:14.0A '14.

Joyciline JEPKOSGEI b. 8 Dec 1993 Cheptil, Nandi 1.56m 52kg.
At 10000m: AfCh: '16- 3. At HMar: WCh: '18- 2. World road records in Prague Half Marathon 2017: 10k 30:04, 15k 45:37, 20k 1:01:25, HMar 1:04.52, improving at 10k to 29:43 in September and half marathon to 64:51 at Valencia in October 2017.
Progress at HMar: 2015- 74:06A, 2016- 69:07, 2017- 64:51. pbs: 5000m 15:40.0A '16, 10000m 31:28.38 '16, Road: 10k 29:43 '17, 15k 45:37 '17, 20k 61:25 '17.
Married to Nicholas Koech (10k Rd 28:39 '07), son Brandon born 2011. Member of the RunCzech Running Team from 2014.

Pauline Kaveke **KAMULU** b. 27 Sep 1993 Machakos county 1.54m 45kg.
World HMar: '18- 13, World CC: '13- 11J; AfCC: '16- 7.
Progress at HMar: 2011- 75:20, 2012- 68:37, 2015- 69:44, 2016- 72:52, 2017- 68:04, 2018- 66:56. pbs: 3000m 8:48.27 '17, 5000m 14:58,82 ''17, 10000m 31:47.13 '17, Road: 15k 47:34 '18, 20k 63:33 '18,

Mary Jepkosgei **KEITANY** b. 18 Jan 1982 Kisok, Kabarnet 1.58m 45kg.
At Mar: OG: '12- 4. World HMar: '07- 2, '09- 1.
Records: World 25km 2010, 10M, 20km, half marathon 2011, 30km 2017, women's only marathon 2017. Half marathon: African and Kenyan (2) 2009, marathon: Afrucan 2012 & 2017. Commonwealth 25k 1:19:43 & 30k 1:36:05 '17. World W35 HMar, 30k & Mar 2017.
Progress at HMar, Mar: 2000- 72:53, 2002- 73:01, 2003- 73:25, 2004- 71:32, 2005- 70:18, 2006- 69:06, 2007- 66:48, 2009- 66:36, 2010- 67:14, 2:29:01; 2011- 65:50, 2:19:19; 2012- 66:49, 2:18:37; 2014- 65:39dh, 2:25:07; 2015- 66:02, 2:23:40; 2016- 68:53, 2:24:26; 2017- 65:13, 2:17:01; 2018- 64:55. pbs: 1500m 4:24.33 '99, 10000m 32:18.07 '07; Road: 5k 15:25 '11, 10k 30:45 '11, 15k 46:40 '11, 10M 50:05 '11, 20k 61:34 '18, 25k 1:19:43dh '17, 30k 1:36:05 '17.
17 wins and 3 seconds in 20 half marathons 2006-18 (13 successive wins 2009-16) inc. Great North Run 2014-15 and 2017, RAK 2011-12, 2015. Marathons: won London 2011-12, 2017 (2nd 2015), New York 2014-16 (3rd 2010-11). Won World Marathon Majors 2011/12 & 2015/16. Married to Charles Koech (pbs 10k 27:56 & HMar 61:27 '07), son Jared born in June 2008 and daughter Samantha on 5 Apr 2013.

Viola Jelagat **KIBIWOT** b. 22 Dec 1983 Keiyo 1.67m 50kg.
At 1500m: OG: '08- h; WCh: '07- 5, '09/11- sf; CG: '06- 7, '10- 7; WJ: '02- 1. At 5000m: OG: '12- 6; WCh: '13- 4, '15- 4. World CC: '00-01-02-13: 3J/1J/1J/7; AfCC: '11-2.
Progress at 1500m, 5000m: 2003- 15:32.87, 2004- 4:06.64, 2006- 4:08.74, 2007- 4:02.10, 2008- 4:04.17, 14:51.59; 2009- 4:02.70, 2010- 4:03.39, 14:48.57; 2011- 4:05.51, 14:34.86; 2012- 3:59.25, 14:39.53; 2013- 4:00.76, 14:33.48; 2014- 4:00.46, 14:33.73; 2015- 4:01.41, 14:34.22; 2016- 4:18.7A, 14:29.50. pbs: 800m 2:04.7A '12, 1M 4:24.31 '15, 2000m 5:38.2+ '14, 3000m 8:24.41 '14, 2M 9:12.59 '14, 10000m 34:54.78A '17, 10k Rd 31:14 '16, HMar 70:15 '17, 30k 1:42:40 '17, Mar 2:25:32 '17.

Margaret Chelimo **KIPKEMBOI** b. 9 Feb 1993 1.62m 45kg.
At 5000m: WCVh: '17- 5; AfG '15-1; AfCh '16-2. At 800m: WY: '09- h. World CC: '15- 13.
Progress at 5000m, 10000m: 2014- 16:02.19A, 2015- 15:28.6A, 2016- 14:47.24, 31:16.38; 2017- 14:32.82. pbs: 1500m 4:10.8A '17, 3000m 8:30.11'17.

Valentine KIPKETER Jepkorir b. 5 Jan 1993 1.50m 40kg.
At Mar: WCh: '13- dnf.
Progress at Mar: 2012- 2:28:02, 2013- 2:23:02, 2016- 2:23:41. Pbs: 3000m 9:17.12 '10, 5000m 16:22.83 '10, Road: 10k 33:07 '11, HMar 68:21 '11. Won Mumbai and Amsterdam marathons 2013, 3rd Chicago 2016.

Caroline Chepkoech **KIPKIRUI** b. 26 May 1994 1.62m 47kg.

At 5000m: WJ: '12- 5; Af-J: '11- 1; At 3000m: WY: '11- 3. World CC: '13- 4J; AfCC: 11- 1J.
World road 10 miles record 2018.
Progress at 5000m: 2010- 16:09.0A, 2011- 15:24.66A, 2012- 15:49.1A, 2013- 15:28.34, 2015- 16:17.97A, 2017- 14:27.55. pbs: 1500m 4:21.0A '04, 3000m 8:51.28 '17, 10000m 31:16.38 '16, Road: 10k 30:45 '17, 15k 46:08 '18, 10M 49:29 '18, 20k 61:40 '18, HMar 65:07 '18, Mar 2:31:44A '12.

Edna Ngeringwony **KIPLAGAT** b. 15 Nov 1979 Eldoret 1.71m 54kg. Corporal in Kenyan Police.
At Mar: OG: '12- 19; WCh: '11-13-15-17: 1/1/5/2. At 3000m: WJ: '96- 2, '98- 3. World CC: '96-97-06: 5J/4J/13. African record 30km 2008.
Progress at Mar: 2005- 2:50:20, 2010- 2:25:38, 2011- 2:20:46, 2012- 2:19:50, 2013- 2:21:32, 2014- 2:20:21, 2015- 2:27:16, 2016- 2:22:36, 2017- 2:21:52dh. pbs: 3000m 8:53.06 '96, 5000m 15:57.3A '06, 10000m 33:27.0A '07; Road: 5k 15:20 '10, 10k 31:06 '16, 15k 47:57 '10, 10M 54:56 '09, HMar 67:41 '12, 30k 1:39:11 '14.
Won Los Angeles and New York Marathons 2010, London 2014 (2nd 2011-13), Boston 2017; 2nd Chicago & 3rd Tokyo 2016. Won World Marathon Majors 2010/11 & 2013/14. Married to Gilbert Koech (10000m 27:55.30 '01, 10k 27:32 '01, Mar 2:13:45 dh '05, 2:14:39 '09); two children.

Florence Jebet **KIPLAGAT** b. 27 Feb 1987 Kapkitony, Keiyo district 1.55m 42kg.
At 5000m: WJ: '06- 2. At 10000m: WCh: '09- 11; CG: '14- 2. World CC: '07- 5, '09- 1; HMar: '10- 1. Won Kenyan 1500m 2007, 10000m 2014, CC 2007 & 2009.
World records 20k and half marathon 2014 & 2015, 15k 2015.. Kenyan 10000m record 2009.
Progress at 5000m, 10000m, HMar, Mar: 2006- 15:32.34, 2007- 14:40.74, 31:06.20; 2009- 14:40.14, 30:11.53; 2010- 14:52.64, 32:46.99A, 67:40; 2011- 68:02, 2:19:44; 2012- 30:24.85, 66:38, 2:20:57; 2013- 67:13, 2:21:13; 2014- 31:48.6A, 65:12, 2:20:24; 2015- 65:09, 2:23:33; 2016- 69:19, 2:21:32; 2017- 68:15, 2:26:25. pbs: 1500m 4:09.0A '07, 3000m 8:40.72 '10, Road: 15k 46:14 '15, 20k 61:54 '15, 30k 1:39:11 '14.
Won half marathon debut in Lille in 2010, followed a month later by World title. Did not finish in Boston on marathon debut in 2011; won Berlin 2011 and 2013; Chicago 2015-16 (2nd 2014), 2nd London 2014 (3rd 2016). Formerly married to Moses Mosop, daughters Faith and Aisha Chelagat (born April 2008). Niece of William Kiplagat (Mar 2:06:50 '99, 8 WCh '07).

Helah KIPROP Jelagat b. 7 Apr 1985 Keiyo district 1.64m 48kg.
At Mar: OG: '16- dnf; WCh: '15- 2, '17- 7.
Progress at Mar: 2013- 2:28:02, 2014- 2:27:14, 2015- 2:24:03, 2016- 2:21:27, 2017- 2:25:59. Pbs: 1500m 4:19.14 '07, 3000m 9:21.02 '06, 5000m 15:33.90 '07, 10000m 33:03.8A '09, 3000mSt 10:25.6A '09, Road: 10k 31:44 '12, 15k 47:32 '13, 20k 64:10 '13, HMar 67:39 '13.
Won Seoul marathon 2014, Tokyo 2016 (2nd 2015). Baby born 2008.

Sheila Chepkirui **KIPROTICH** b. 27 Dec 1990 1.62m 48kg.
At 5000m: WCh: '17- 7; AfCh: '16- 1. At 1500m: WJ: '08- h; WY: 05- 1, '07- 3. Af CC: 16-2.
Progress at 5000m: 2016- 15:05.45, 2017- 14:54.05. pbs: 800m 2:06.2A '15, 1500m 4:12.29 '05, 3000m 8:45.94 '17, 10000m 32:35.0A '17, 10kRd30:28 '17.

Faith Chepngetich **KIPYEGON** b. 10 Jan 1994 Bornet 1.57m 42kg.
At 1500m: OG: '12- h, '16- 1; WCh: '13- 5, '15- 2, '17- 1; CG: '14- 1; AfCh: '14- 5; WJ: '12- 1; WY: '11- 1. Won DL 2017. World CC: '10-11-13-17: 4J/1J/1J/6; AfCC: '12- 1J, '14- 1.
Records: World 4x1500m 2014, African junior 1500m 2013, African & Commonwealth 1M 2015, Kenyan & Commonwealth 1500m (3) 2013-16.
Progress at 1500m, 5000m: 2010- 4:17.1A, 2011- 4:09.48, 2012- 4:03.82, 2013- 3:56.98, 2014- 3:58.01, 2015- 3:59.32, 14:31.95; 2016- 3:56.41, 2017- 3:57.04. pbs: 800m 1:58.02 '15, 1M 4:16.71 '15, 2000m 5:37.8+ '14, 3000m 8:23.55 '14.
Older sister **Beatrice Mutai** (b. 19 Apr 1987) 11 World CC 2013, HMar 69:30 '14.

Purity Cherotich **KIRUI** b. 13 Aug 1991 Kericho 1.62m 47kg.
At 3000mSt: WCh: '17- 10; CG: '14- 1; AfG: '15- 3; AfCh: '14- 6; WJ: '10- 1; Won KEN 2014-15.
Progress at 3000mSt: 2008- 10:27.19A, 2009- 10:05.1A, 2010- 9:36.34, 2011- 9:37.85, 2012- 9:35.61, 2013- 9:19.42, 2014- 9:23.43, 2015- 9:17.74, 2016- 9:22.47, 2017- 9:20.07. pbs: 800m 2:07.6A '14, 1500m 4:31.83 '08, 5000m 16:13.42 '11.
Sister of Kipyegon Bett (qv).

Janet KISA b. 5 Mar 1992 near Mount Elgon 1.60m 48kg.
At 3000m: CCp: '14- 4. At 5000m: WCh: '15- 6; CG: '14- 2; AfCh: '14- 3; Af-J: '11- 2. World CC: '11-13-15: 5J/6/12; AfCC: '14- 2.
Progress at 5000m: 2010- 16:02.2A, 2011- 15:24.75, 2012- 14:57.68, 2013- 15:05.89, 2014- 14:52.59, 2015- 15:02.68, 2016- 14:38.70. pbs: 1500m 4:14.77 '11, 2000m 5:41.4+ '16, 3000m 8:28.33 '16, 10k Rd 33:55 '13, HMar 71:01 '14.

Brigid Jepcheschir **KOSGEI** b. 20 Feb 1994 Kapsait 1.63m 46kg.
Progress at HMar, Mar: 2015- 2:47:59, 2016- 74:08, 2:24:45, 2017- 66:35, 2:20:22; 2018- 66:49. Pbs: Road: 10k 31:43 '17, 15k 47:24 '17, 20k 63:17 '17.
2nd Chicago Marathon 2017, won Honolulu 2016-17, Milan 2016. Married to Mathew Mitei, daughter Faith Jepchumba born 2014.

Cynthia Jerotich **LIMO** b. 18 Dec 1989 1.67m 52kg.
World HMar: '16- 2.

Progress at HMar: 2010- 73:19, 2011- 70:39, 2012- 70:06, 2013- 69:59, 2014- 68:24, 2015- 67:02, 2016- 66:04. pbs: Road: 1000m 32:25.18A '16, 10k 31:07 '15, 15k 47:11 '15, 20k 62:48 '16.
Won RAK Half marathon 2016.

Virginia Nganga **NYAMBURA** b. 20 Jul 1993 1.65m 48kg.
At 3000mSt: WCh: '15- 7; won DL 2015. 2000mSt: Yth OG: '10- 1.
World best 2000m steeplechase 2015.
Progress at 3000mSt: 2008- 10:27.46A, 2009- 10:13.6A, 2010- 10:28.19A, 2013- 9:58.08, 2014- 10:02.18, 2015- 9:13.85, 2016- 9:18.95. pbs: 1500m 4:10.0A '15, 2000m 6:05.45 '13, 5000m 16:38.6A '13, 2000mSt 6:02.16 '15.
Took 36.57 secs off pb at Doha 2015 after being the pacemaker and continuing to win.

Hellen Onsando **OBIRI** b. 13 Dec 1989 Nyangusu, Kisii 1.55m 45kg.
At 1500m: OG: '12- 8; WCh: '11- 10 (fell), '13- 3; CG: '14- 6; AfCh: '14- 1; CCp: '14- 4. At 3000m: WI: '12-14-18: 1/2/4. At 5000m: OG: '16- 2; WCh: '17- 1, won DL 2017. Won Kenyan 1500m 2011-14.
Two world 4x1500m records 2014. African & Commonwealth 3000m record 2014, Commonwealth 1M & 5000m record 2017.
Progress at 1500m, 5000m: 2011- 4:02.42, 2012- 3:59.68, 16:15.1A, 2013- 3:58.58, 15:49.7A; 2014- 3:57.05, 2016- 3:59.34, 14:25.78; 2017- 4:00.44, 14:18.37. pbs: 800m 2:00.54 '11, 1000m 2:46.00i '12, 1M 4:16.56 '17, 2000m 5:37.7+ '14, 3000m 8:20.68 '14. Daughter born in May 2015.

Lilian Kasait **RENGERUK** b. 3 May 1997 1.61m 44kg.
At 3000m: WJ: '14- 2; WY: '13- 1. World CC: '17- 3. Won KEN 5000m 2017.
Progress at 5000m: 2015- 16:04.61A, 2017- 14:36.80. pbs: 800m 2:07.6A '17, 3000m 8:32.73 '17.

Betsy SAINA b. 30 Jun 1988 Sokosik, Nandi 1.63m 48kg. Bowerman TC, USA. Graduate of Iowa State University, USA
At 10000m: OG: '16- 5; WCh: '15- 8; AfCh: '12- 3. At 3000m: WI: '16- 7. Won NCAA indoor 5000m & CC 2012, 10000m 2013.
Progress at 5000m, 10000m: 2009- 16:15.74, 36:34.94; 2010- 16:10.69, 33:13.13; 2011- 15:50.74i/ 16:06.05, 33:13.87; 2012- 15:36.09i, 31:15.97; 2013- 15:12.05, 31:37.22; 2014- 14:39.49, 30:57.30; 2015- 15:00.48, 31:51.35; 2016- 14:44.67, 30:07.78. pbs: 1M 4:40.98i '13, 2000m 5:45.7 '14, 3000m 8:38.01 '14, 2M 9:16.95 '14, Rd 10k 30:46 '14, 10M 51:55 '14, HMar 69:17 '148 67:22 short '16.

Eunice Jepkoech **SUM** b. 2 Sep 1988 Burnt Forest, Uasin Gishu 1.72m 53kg. Police.
At 800m: OG: '16- sf; WCh: '11- sf, '13- 1, '15- 3; CG: '14- 1; AfCh: '10- h,'12- 2, '14- 1; CCp: '14- 1; won DL 2013-15. At 1500m: OG: '12- h, Won Kenyan 800m 2012, 2014.
World 4x1500m record 2014, Commonwealth & African 4x800m 2014..

Progress at 800m, 1500m: 2009- 2:07.4A, 2010- 2:00.28, 2011- 1:59.66A, 4:12.41; 2012- 1:59.13, 4:04.26; 2013- 1:57.38, 4:02.05; 2014- 1:57.92, 4:01.54; 2015- 1:56.99, 4:09.7A; 2016- 1:57.47, 4:21.3A; 2017- 1:57.78, 4:13.2A. pb 3000m 8:53.12 '12.
Daughter Diana Cheruto born in 2008.

Norah Jeruto **TANUI** b. 2 Oct 1995 1.71m 57kg.
At 3000mSt: AfCh: '16- 1. At 2000mSt: WY: '11- 1.
Progress at 3000mSt: 2011- 9:45.1A, 2013- 10:11.4, 2014- 10:01.71A, 2015- 9:55.44, 2016- 9:25.07, 2017- 9:03.70. pbs: 1500m 4:30.0A '17, 3000m 8:49.89i '18, 2000mSt 6:16.41 '11.

Agnes Jebet **TIROP** b. 23 Oct 1995 Nandi, Chesumei 1.65m 50kg.
At 5000m: WJ: '12- 3, '14- 3; At 10000m: WCh: '17- 3. World CC: '13-15-17: 2J/1/5; AfCC: '12- 2J, '14- 1J.
Progress at 5000m, 10000m: 2011- 16:09.0A, 2012- 15:36.74, 2013- 14:50.36, 2014- 15:00.19, 2015- 32:55.41, 2016- 15:02.67, 2017- 14:33.09, 31:03.50. pbs: 1500m 4:12.68 '13, 2000m 5:48.65 '13, 3000m 8:35.23 '17, 10kRd 31:00 '17, 3000mSt 10:27.4A '12.

Mercy WACERA Ngugi b. 17 Dec 1988 1.55m.
World HMar: '14- 2, '16- 3. At 5000m: WJ: '06- 3; Af-J: 07- 1.
Progress at HMar: 2012- 70:54, 2013- 70:32, 2014- 67:44, 2015- 70:21, 2016- 66:29, 2017- 68:38. pbs: 1500m 4:24.4A '08, 3000m 8:55.89 '09, 5000m 15:20.30 '09, Road: 10k 31:28 '12, 15k 48:49 '15.
Widow of Samuel Wanjiru (2008 Olympic marathon champion). Daughter born 2010.

Margaret Nyairera **WAMBUI** b. 15 Sep 1995 Endarasha 1.75m 66kg.
At 800m: OG: '16- 3; WCh: '15- h, '17- 4; WJ: '14- 1; WI: '16- 3. At 400m: AfCh: '16- 2/3R. Won KEN 800m 2017.
Progress at 800m: 2014- 2:00.49, 2015- 2:01.32, 2016- 1:56.89, 2017- 1:56.87. pbs: 200m 24.1A '17, 400m 51.39A/51.97 '16, 600m 1:27.1 '16.

KOREA

Governing body: Korea Athletics Federation. Founded 1945.

National Champions 2017: **Men**: 100m: Kim Kuk-young 10.30, 200m: Lee Jae-ha 20.97, 400m: Mo Il-hwan 46.82, 800m: Lee Moo-young 1:52.86, 1500m/5000m: Baek Seung-ho 3:50.42/14:32.93, 10000m: Kim Young-jin 30:29.14, 3000mSt: Choi Dong-il 9:14.26, 110mh: Kim Byung-jun 13.70w, 400mh: Kim Hyun-Woo 50.93, HJ: Woo Sang-hyuk 2.30, PV: Jin Min-sub 5.50, LJ: Kim Sang-su 7.58, TJ: Kim Dong-han 16.08, SP: Jung Il-woo 18.48, DT: Choi Jong-bum 54.48, HT: Lee Yoon-chul 69.45, JT: Bae You-il 78.21, Dec: Bae Sang-hwa 7309, 20kW: Kim Hyun-sub 1:27:08; **Women**: 100m: Lee Sun-Ae 12.00, 200m: Shon Kyung-mi 24.31, 400m: Han Jung-mi 56.27, 800m/1500m: Shin So-mang 2:09.14/4:37.16, 5000m/10000m: Kim Do-yeon 15:57.01/34:57.48, 3000mSt: Jo Ha-rim 10:38.94,

100mh: Jung Hye-lim 13.18, 400mh: Jo Eun-ju 60.25, HJ: Suk Mi-young 1.76, PV: Choi Yun-hee 3.80, LJ: Jung Soon-ok 5.99, TJ: Park Min-hee 12.94, SP: Lee Mi-young 16.47, DT: Cho Hye-rim 49.49, HT: Park Hee-sun 60.65, JT: Kim Kyung-ae 54.60, Hep: Kim Chae-young 4885, 20kW: Jeon Yang-eun 1:36:33.

KIM Hyun-sub b. 31 May 1985 Sokcho 1.75m 53kg.
At 20kW: OG: '08- 23, '12- 17, '16- 17 (dnf 50kW); WCh: '07-09-11-13-15-17: 20/32/3/10/10;/26 AsiG: '06-10-14: 2/3/3; WUG: '05-07-09: 2/6/5. Asian champion 2011, 2014, 2017 (2nd 2015); KOR 2005-06, 2008-13, 2016-17. At 10000m/10kW: WJ: '04- 3; WCp: '04- 8.
Five Korean 20km road walk records 2008-15.
Progress at 20kW: 2004- 1:24:58, 2005- 1:22:15, 2006- 1:21:45, 2007- 1:20:54, 2008- 1:19:41, 2009- 1:22:00, 2010- 1:19:36, 2011- 1:19:31, 2012- 1:21:36, 2013- 1:21:22, 2014- 1:19:24, 2015- 1:19:13, 2016- 1:21:44, 2017- 1:19:50. Pbs 10000mW 39:30.56 '09, 38:13R '10; 50kW 4:01:06 '16.

LATVIA

Governing body: Latvian Athletic Association. Founded 1921.
National Championships first held in 1920 (men), 1922 (women). **2017 Champions**: **Men:** 100m: Janis Mezitis 10.74, 200m: Janis Leitis 21.43, 400m: Valerijs Valinscikovs 48.41, 800m/1500m: Dmitrijs Jurkevics 1:50.89/3:51.00, 3000m/5000m: Janis Girgensons 8:34.59/14:29.98, 10000m: Kristaps Kaimins 32:14.69, HMar/Mar: Valerijs Zolnerovics 69:23/2:14:23, 3000mSt: Arturs Niklavs Medveds 9:46.88, 110mh: Emils Rugums 14.66, 400mh: Maksims Sincukovs 51.46, HJ: Vladislavs Prosmickis 1.99, PV: Mareks Arents 5.45, LJ: Dairus Rincs 7.48, TJ: Elvijs Misans 16.55w, SP/DT: Maris Urtans 17.96/52.23, HT: Igors Sokolovs 75.86, JT: Rolands Strobinders 82.20, Dec: Didzis Siksalietis 6292, 10000mW: Raivo Saulgriezis 42:22.08. **Women**: 100m: Gunta Latiseva-Cudare 11.53, 200m: Sindija Buksa 23.89, 400m/400mh: Diana Daktere 56.93/61.10, 800m: Daira Deicmane 2:13.83, 1500m: Elena Miezava 4:41.77, 3000m/5000m/10000m: Gundega Heidingere 10:03.15/17:57.92/37:46.33, HMar/Mar: Anita Kazamaka 1:24:13/2:48:50, 3000mSt: Kristine Jevsejeva 11:43.90, 100mh: Paula Sprudzane 13.95, HJ: Madara Onuzane-Salina 1.74, PV: Ildze Bortascenoka 3.85, LJ/TJ: Mara Griva 6.11/13.61, SP: Kristine Strazdite 13.66, DT: Dace Steinerte 49.36, HT: Eva Rudzite 45.20, JT: Madara Palameika 61.11, Hep: Jolanta Kaupe 5048, 10000mW: Agnese Pastare 48:57.39.

Women

Laura IKAUNIECE-ADMIDINA b. 31 May 1992 Jürmala 1.79m 60kg. Jürmalas SS.
At Hep: OG: '12- 7, '16- 4; WCh: '13- 11, '15- 3, '17- dnf; EC: '12- 2, '14- 6; WJ: '10- 6; WY: '09- 2; EJ: '11- 3; WUG: '13- 1. At 100mh: EC: '16- h. Won LAT 100m 2012-13, 200m 2009, 2013; 100mh & HJ 2010.
Six Latvian heptathlon records 2012-17.
Progress at Hep: 2010- 5618, 2011- 6063, 2012- 6414, 2013- 6321, 2014- 6320, 2015- 6516, 2016- 6622, 2017- 6815. Pbs: 60m 7.58i '16, 100m 11.78 '16, 200m 23.49 '17, 800m 2:09.43 '16, 60mh 8.38i '14, 100mh 13.07 '16, HJ 1.85i '12, 1.84 '14; LJ 6.64 '17, SP 14.02 '17, JT 56.32 '17, Pen 4496i '14.
Won IAAF Challenge 2015. Her mother Vineta Ikauniece set Latvian records at 100m 11.34A '87, 200m 22.49A '87 and 400m 50.71 '88, and her father Aivars Ikaunieks had 110mh bests of 13.71A '87 and 13.4 '84. Married Rolands Admidins in 2014.

Madara PALAMEIKA b. 18 Jun 1987 Valdemarpils 1.85m 76kg. Ventspils.
At JT: OG: '12- 8, '16- 10; WCh: '09-13-15-17: dnq 27/27/13/21, '11- 11; EC: '10-12-14-16: 8/8/4/7; WJ: '06- dnq 16; EU23: '07- 3, '09- 1; EJ: '05- dnq 17. Won DL 2016, LAT 2009-11, 2014-15, 2017.
Three Latvian javelin records 2009-16.
Progress at JT: 2002- 42.31, 2003- 49.11, 2004- 51.50, 2005- 51.75, 2006- 54.19, 2007- 57.98, 2008- 53.45, 2009- 64.51, 2010- 62.02, 2011- 63.46, 2012- 62.74, 2013- 62.72, 2014- 66.15, 2015- 65.01, 2016- 66.18, 2017- 63.92.

LITHUANIA

Governing body: Athletic Federation of Lithuania. Founded 1921.
National Championships first held in 1921 (women 1922). **2017 Champions: Men** 100m: Rytis Sakalauskas 10.33, 200m: Ugnius Savickas 21.08w, 400m: Rokas Pacevicius 47.64, 800m: Benediktas Mickus 1:49.00, 1500m/5000m: Simas Bertasius 3:50.12/14:15.41, 10000m: Evaldas Gustaitis 32:27.92, HMar/3000mSt: Justinas Berzanskis 69:44/8:41.59, Mar: Mindaugas Virsilas 2:23:49, 110mh/400mh: Rapolas Saulius 13.76w/52,47, HJ: Raivydas Stanys 2.15, PV: Osvaldas Gedrimas 4.50, LJ: Tomas Lotuzis 7.52w, TJ: Darius Aucyna 15.77, SP: Sarunas Banevicius 19.64, DT: Andrius Gudzius 68.04, HT: Lukas Simonavicius 60.74, JT: Edis Matusevicius 74.80, Dec: Egidijus Zaniauskas 6925, 10kW/20kW: Marius Ziukas 41:33/1:28:36. **Women**: 100m: Karolina Deliautaite 11.59, 200m/400m: Eva Misiunaite 23.62/53.22, 800m: Egle Balcunaite 2:03.83, 1500m: Monika Saltenyte 4:32.05, 5000m/HMar: Monika Juodeskaite 17:10.51/1:20:47, 10000m: Gintare Zenkeviciute 36:45.94, Mar: Gitana Akmanaviciute 3:01:36, 3000mSt: Banga Balnaite 11:08.51, 100mh: Irma Maciukaite 13.79, 400mh: Gabija Galvydyte 59.42, HJ: Airine Palsyte 1.85, PV: Judita Kazlauskaite 3.20, LJ: Jogaile Petrokaite 6.42, TJ: Diana Zagainova 13.53w, SP: Austra Skujyte 16.11, DT: Zinaida Sendriute 60.50, HT: Aiste Ziginskaite

48.04, JT: Liveta Jasiunaite 60.24, 10kW/20kW: Brigita Virbalyte 45:36/1:33:54

Andrius GUDZIUS b. 14 Feb 1991 Vilkija, Kaunas district 2.00m 130kg. COSMA.
At DT: OG: '16- 12; WCh: '15- dnq 14, '17- 1; EC: '12- dnq 29, '14- 10, '16- dnq 13; WJ: '08- 6, '10- 1; WY: '07- 3; EU23: '11- dnq 13, '13- 1; EJ: '09- 5; WUG: '15- 3. Won DL 2017, LTU 2013-14, 2017.
Progress at DT: 2008- 54.72, 2009- 57.17, 2010- 61.85, 2011- 58.50, 2012- 63.39, 2013- 62.40, 2014- 66.11, 2015- 65.51, 2016- 65.18/67.96dh, 2017- 69.21.

Women

Airine PALSYTE b. 13 Jul 1992 Kaunas 1.86m 62kg. COSMA. Vilnius University.
At HJ: OG: '12- 11, '16- 13=; WCh: '13- 12, '15- dnq 14=, '17- 7=; WJ: '08- dnq 23, '10- 2; WY: '09- 4; EC: '10-12-14-16: dnq 18/9/13/2; EJ: '11- 2; EU23: '13- 2; WUG: '11- 2, '15- 1; WI: '16- 4; EI: '15- 4, '17- 1; Lithuanian champion 2010, 2012-17.
Three LTU high jump records 2011-14 and absolute records 2.00 & 2.01i 17.
Progress at HJ: 2003- 1.45, 2004- 1.40i, 2005- 1.60, 2006- 1.71, 2007- 1.70i/1.55, 2008- 1.80, 2009- 1.86i/1.83, 2010- 1.92, 2011- 1.96, 2012- 1.95, 2013- 1.95, 2014- 1.98, 2015- 1.98i/1.95, 2016- 1.97i/1.96, 2017- 2.01i/1.92. pb 200m 24.78 '12, TJ 12.70i '12.

Zinaida SENDRIUTE b. 20 Dec 1984 Klaisiai, Skuodas 1.88m 89kg. COSMA.
At DT: OG: '08- dnq 32, '12- 8, '16- 10; WCh: '09-11-13-15-17: dnq 31/11/9/dnq 13/nt; EC: '06-10-12-14-16: dnq 17/5/dnq 17/6/13; EJ: '03- 7; EU23: '05- 6; WUG: '11- 2; Lithuanian champion 2003, 2005-08, 2010-17.
Progress at DT: 2000- 33.37, 2001- 40.55, 2002- 48.66, 2003- 50.62, 2004- 51.38, 2005- 55.25, 2006- 57.26, 2007- 56.74, 2008- 59.42, 2009- 60.21, 2010- 60.70, 2011- 62.49, 2012- 64.03, 2013- 65.97, 2014- 65.83, 2015- 61.37, 2016- 61.89, 2017- 61.48. pbs: SP 14.15 '10, HT 33.19 '04.

LUXEMBOURG

Governing body: Fédération Luxembourgeoise d'Athlétisme. Founded 1928.
2017 National Champions: **Men**: 100m/200m: Olivier Boussong 10.87/21.80, 400m: Aymen Djazouli 50.86, 800m: Luc Hensgen 1:56.93, 1500m: Bob Bertemes 3:53.62, 5000m/10000m/HMar: Pol Mellina 15:25.34/33:18.48/69:07, Mar: Frank Schweitzer 2:32:26, 3000mSt: Luc Scheller 9:57.57, 110mh: Christopher Weber 16.14, 400mh: Philippe Hilger 56.61, HJ: Charel Gaspar 2.02, PV: Joe Seil 5.00, LJ: François Grailet 7.08, TJ: Sam Monners 12.52, SP: Bob Bertemes 19.99, DT: Steve Schneider 46.27, HT: Steve Tonizzo 46.91, JT: Tom Reuter 65.06, Dec: Sven Liefgen 4430, Women: 100m/200m: Anais Bauer 12.23/25.68, 400m: Fanny Arendt 59.88, 800m: Yana Have 2:22.18, 1500m: Fanny Gopy 4:43.06, 3000m/HMar: Martine Mellina 10:29.77/79:56, 10000m: Martine Nobili 38:52.81, Mar: Karin Schnak 2:51:21, 3000mSt: Liz Weiler 11:17.88, 100mh/LJ/TJ/Hep: Lara Marx 14.28/5.68/11.29/4611, 400mh: Kim Reuland 63.24, HJ: Cathy Zimmer 1.70, PV: Edna Semedo 3.70, SP: Ann Bertemes 13.10, DT/JT Noémie Pleimling 38.75/48.50, HT: Géraldine Davin 48.28.

MEXICO

Governing body: Federación Mexicana de Atletismo. Founded 1933.
National Champions 2017: Men: 100m/200m: Heber Gallegos 10.35/21.00, 400m: Valente Mendoza 46.68, 800m: Jesús López 1:46.05, 1500m: José Eduardo Rodríguez 3:48.84, 5000m: Ezau Arias 14:14.45, 10000m: Juan Carlos 30:02.78, 3000mSt: Christopher Endoqui 9:00.69, 110mh: Genaro Rodríguez 13.88, 400mh: Alejandro Orozco 51.22, HJ: Edgar Rivera 2.24, PV: Antonio Ruiz 5.15, LJ: Luis Rivera 7.56, TJ: Alberto Álvarez 16.67, SP: Uziel Muñoz 17.68, DT: Mario Cota 57.89, HT: Diego del Real 73.60, JT: Josué Menéndez 76.54, Dec: Felipe Ruiz 6924, 20000mW: Eder Sánchez 1:22:27.61. **Women:** 100m/200m: Iza Daniela Flores 11.85/23.24, 400m: Paola Morán 52.96, 800m: Ana Gómez 2:04.34, 1500m: Gabriela Eleno 4:24.86, 5000m: Brenda Flores 16:04.17, 10000m: Esmeralda Rebollo 35:25.70, 3000mSt: Azucena Rodríguez 10:47.15, 100mh: Mariaqueta Rodríguez 13.58, 400mh: Zudikey Rodríguez 56.75, HJ: Ximena Esquivel 1.81, PV: Carmelita Correa 4.25, LJ: Susana Hernández 6.36, TJ: Ivonne Rangel 13.06, SP: María Fernanda Orozco 16.61, DT: Alma Pollorena 51.13, JT: Luz Mariana Castro 55.25, Hep: Laura Montes 5138, 20000mW: María Guadelipe González 1:33:26.74.

Edgar RIVERA Morales b. 13 Feb 1991 Agua Prieta 1.91m 80kg. Pays de Colmar Athlétisme, FRA. Was at the University of Arizona, USA.
At HJ: OG: '16- dnq 35; WCh: '11-13: dnq 26/22, '17- 4; PAm: '11- 8, '15- 7=; WJ: '08- 10, '10- 6; WY: '07- 5. Won IbAm 2014, NACAC U23 2012, MEX 2009 (=), 2013-17.
Mexican HJ record indoors.
Progress at HJ: 2007- 2.14, 2008- 2.18A, 2009- 2.20A, 2010- 2.23i/2.20, 2011- 2.28, 2012- 2.25, 2013- 2.28, 2014- 2.28, 2015- 2.25, 2016- 2.30i/2.29, 2017- 2.30i/2.29.
Brother **Luis** (b. 21 Jun 1987) has LJ pb 8.47 '13 (MEX record) and 3 WCh and 1 WUG 2013

Women

María Guadalupe 'Lupita' **GONZÁLEZ** Romero b. 9 Jan 1989 Mexico City 1.62m 48kg.
At 20kW: OG: '16- 2; WCh: '17- 2; PAm: '15- 1; WCp: '14- 16, '16- 1. Won CAC 10kW 2013, PAmCp 20k 2015, 2017; MEX 20kW 2017, 10,000mW 2014. Tied first IAAF Race Walking Challenge 2016.
MEX 20k walk records 2014 & 2016 (& 20,000m track 1:33:26.8 '17), CAC 2016.
Progress at 20kW: 2013- 1:37:02, 2014- 1:28:48,

2015- 1:29:21, 2016- 1:26:17, 2017- 1:26:19. pbs: 10kW 43:49 '15.

MOLDOVA

Governing Body: Federatia de Atletism din Republica Moldova. Founded 1991.

Serghei MARGHIEV b. 6 Nov 1992 Vladikavkaz, North Osetia, Russia 1.94m 96kg.
At HT: OG: '12- dnq 30, '16- 10; WCh: '15- dnq 23, '17- 8; EC: '14 – 9, '16- 8; WJ: '10- dnq 14; WY: '09- dnq 28; EU23: '13- 5; EJ: '11- 2; WUG: '15- 4, '17- 3. Won Balkan 2013-14, MDA 2012-17.
Four MDA hammer records 2014-15
Progress at HT: 2011- 67.54, 2012- 75.20, 2013- 74.41, 2014- 78.27, 2015- 78.72, 2016- 78.48, 2017- 77.70.
Younger brother of Zalina (qv) and Marina.

Women

Zalina PETRIVSKAYA b. 5 Feb 1988 Vladikavkaz, North Osetia, Russia 1.74m 90kg. née Marghieva. AS-CSPLN.
At HT: OG: '08- dnq 35, '12- dq8, '16- 5; WCh: '09- dq dnq 26, '11- dq8, '15- 8, '17- dnq 19; EC: '10- dq5, '12- dq8, '16- 5; WJ: '06- 4; WY: '05- 7; EU23: '09- 1; EJ: '07- 5; WUG: '11- dq1, '13- dq3. Won Balkan 2015-17, MDA 2016.
Nine Moldovan hammer records 2005-16 (and 3 disqualified).
Progress at HT: 2005- 61.80, 2006- 65.50, 2007- 65.40, 2008- 70.22, 2009- 71.56, 2015- 73.97, 2016- 74.21, 2017- 73.80; DQ: 2010- 71.50, 2011- 72.93, 2012- 74.47, 2013- 74.28.
Drugs ban announced in 2013 with all results annulled from 2009 Worlds to 2013.
Sister **Marina** (now **Nikisenko**) (b. 28 Jun 1986) HT: 72.53 '09, seven MDA records 2007-09, OG: '08-16: dnq/41/24; WCh: '09/11/15/17- dnq 32/17/25/27; EC: '10- 5, '12/16- dnq 14/14; received a 3-year drugs ban from 24 July 2012. Brother **Serghei** (qv).

MOROCCO

Governing Body: Fédération Royale Marocaine d'Athlétisme. Founded 1957.

Soufiane EL BAKKALI b. 7 Jan 1996 1.88m 70kg.
At 3000mSt: OG: '16- 4; WCh: '17- 2; WJ: '14- 4; AfCh: '14- 10.
Progress at 3000mSt: 2013- 8:52.00, 2014- 8:32.66, 2015- 8:27.79, 2016- 8:14.35, 2017- 8:04.83. pbs: 1500m 3:45.36 '15, 3000m 7:41.88i '18, 7:49.68 '16, 5000m 13:10.60i '17, 13:47.76 '14.

Abdelaati IGUIDER b. 25 Mar 1987 Errachidia 1.70m 52kg.
At 1500m(/5000m): OG: '08- 5, '12- 3/6, '16- 5; WCh: '07-09-11-13-15-17: h/11/5/sf/3/sf; WJ: '04- 1, '06- 2; WI: '10-12-14-18: 2/1/3/3. At 3000m: WI: '16- 4.
Progress at 1500m, 5000m: 2004- 3:35.53, 2005- 3:35.63, 2006- 3:32.68, 2007- 3:32.75, 2008- 3:31.88, 2009- 3:31.47, 2010- 3:34:25, 2011- 3:31.60, 2012- 3:33.99, 13:09.17; 2013- 3:33.29, 2014- 3:29.83, 2015- 3:28.79, 12:59.25; 2016- 3:31.40, 13:08.61; 2017- 3:34.99. pbs: 800m 1:46.67 '15, 1000m 2:19.14 '07, 1M 3:49.09 '14, 2000m 4:59.20 '16, 3000m 7:30.09 '16.

Women

Malika AKKAOUI b. 25 Dec 1987 Zaida, Meknès-Tafilalet 1.60m 46kg.
At 800m/(1500m): OG: '12- sf, '16- h/sf; WCh: '11- (h), '13- sf, '15- sf/12, '17- (10); AfCh: '10-12-14-16: 3/3/6/2; WJ: '06- h. Won MAR 400m 2014, 800m 2007-08, MedG 800m 2013, Arab 800m 2015, Is.Sol 2017.
Progress at 800m: 2004- 2:09.2, 2005- 2:08.1, 2006- 2:06.29, 2007- 2:05.04, 2008- 2:04.25, 2009- 2:02.10, 2010- 2:00.6, 2011- 1:59.75, 2012- 1:59.01i/ 1:59.54, 2013- 1:57.64, 2014- 2:00.58, 2015- 1:59.03, 2016- 1:59.93, 2017- 2:00.71, 4:03.36. pbs: 400m 53.19 '13, 1000m 2:39.86 '13, 1500m 4:04.49 '15.

Rabab ARRAFI b. 12 Jan 1991 1.67m 54kg. ASOAK. 1.77m 64kg.
At (800m)/1500m: OG: '16- h/12; WCh: '13- sf, '15- 4/9, '17- 8; AfCh: 12- 1, '14- 3, '16- 5/2; WI: '14- dq after finishing 3rd; '18- 8; won Is.Sol 2017. At 3000m: WY: '07- 12. Won FrancG 2013, 2017.
Progress at 800m, 1500m: 2006- 24:21.59, 2011- 2:09.24, 2012- 2:04.60, 4:05.80; 2013- 2:00.58, 4:05.22; 2014- 2:03.18i, 4:02.71; 2015- 1:58.55, 4:02.94; 2016- 2:01.49, 4:03.95; 2017- 4:01.75. pbs: 1M 4:23.50 '15, 3000m 8:58.32i '13, 9:34.78 '07.

NETHERLANDS

Governing body: Koninklijke Nederlandse Atletiek Unie (KNAU). Founded 1901.
National Championships first held in 1910 (men), 1921 (women). **2017 Champions: Men**: 100m: Giovanni Codrington 10.42, 200m: Jorén Tromp 21.06, 400m: Leemarvin Bonevacia 45.61, 800m/1500m: Thijmen Kupers 1:49.10/3:43.29, 5000m: Mohamed Ali Mohamed 14:21.75, 10000m: Frank Futselaar 30:38.83, HMar: Michel Butter 65:04, Mar: Abdi Nageeye 2:08:16, 3000mSt: Simon Grannetia 9:02.57, 110mh: Koen Smet 14.11, 400mh: Jesper Arts 51.33, HJ: Sven van Merode 2.16, PV: Menno Vloon 5.70, LJ: Steven Nuytinck 7.49, TJ: Fabian Florant 16.54w, SP: Patrick Cronie 18.94, DT: Erik Cadée 58.19, HT: Sander Stok 58.21, JT: Daan Meijer 76.49, Dec: Rody de Wolff 7527, 20kW/50kW: Rick Liesting 1:33:00/4:44:39. **Women**: 100m: Jamile Samuel 11.46, 200m: Tessa van Schagen 23.40, 400m: Lisanne de Witte 52.12, 800m: Danaïd Prinsen 2:07.57, 1500m: Sanne Verstegen 4:15.23, 5000m: Irene van Lieshout, 10000m: Nesrine Leene 38:14.25, HMar: Ruth van der Meijden 73:52, Mar: Mireilla Baart 2:44:21, 3000mSt: Irene van der Reijken 10:30.51, 100mh: Eefje Boons 13.26, 400mh: Bianca Baak 58.80,

HJ: Marlies van Haaren 1.74, PV: Femke Pluim 4.21, LJ: Anouk Vetter 6.24, TJ: Patricia Krolis 12.75, SP: Melissa Boekelman 18.31, DT: Corinne Nugter 55.95, HT: Wendy Koolhaas 61.45, JT: Lisanne Schol 58.72, Hep: Michelle Oud 5539, 10kW: Loes van Bremen 1:07:27.

Churandy MARTINA b. 3 Jul 1984 Willemstad, Curaçao 1.78m 75kg. Rotterdam Atletiek. Studied civil engineering at University of Texas at El Paso, USA.

At 100m/(200m): OG: '04- qf, '08- 4/dq, '12- 5/5, '16- h/5; WCh: '03- h, '05- qf, '07- 5/5, '09- qf, '11/15- sf/sf, '13- sf/7; EC: '12- (1)/1R, '14- sf/4, '16- 1/dq(1); WJ: '00- h/h, '02- qf; WY: '99- sf; PAm: '03- sf, '07- 1; CAG: '06- 1/1R, '10- 1/1/3R; CCp: '10- (2)/1R; ET: '17- 3. Won PAm-J 2003; NED 100m 2011-16; 200m 2011, 2014, 2016.

Records: AHO 100m (8) 2004-08, 200m (6) 2005-10, 400m 2007; NED 100m (2) 2011-12, 200m (3) 2012-16.

Progress at 100m, 200m: 2000- 10.73, 21.73; 2001- 10.64A, 21.55; 2002- 10.30, 20.81; 2003- 10.29/ 10.26w, 20.71; 2004- 10.13, 20.75; 2005- 10.13/ 9.93Aw, 20.32/20.31w; 2006- 10.04A/10.06/9.76Aw/ 9.99w, 20.27A; 2007- 10.06, 20.20; 2008- 9.93, 20.11; 2009- 9.97, 20.76; 2010- 10.03A/10.07/9.92w, 20.08; 2011- 10.10, 20.38; 2012- 9.91, 19.85; 2013- 10.03, 20.01; 2014- 10.13, 20.25; 2015- 10.06, 20.20; 2016- 10.01, 19.81; 2017- 10.19/10.00w, 20.27. pbs: 60m 6.58i '10, 400m 46.13A '07.

At 2008 Olympics set three national records at 100m and one at 200m before crossing line in second place in final in 19.82 only to be disqualified for running out of his lane. Competed for Netherlands Antilles until 2010.

Eelco SINTNICOLAAS b. 7 Apr 1987 Dordrecht 1.86m 81kg. AV '34 (Apeldoorn). Economics student.

At Dec: OG: '12- 11, '16- dnf; WCh: '09-11-13-15-17: dnf/5/5/dnf/dnf; EC: '10-14-16: 2/4/16; WJ: '06- 8; EU23: '09- 1; EJ: '05- 14; ECp: '14- 1. At Hep: WI: '14- 4, '18- 5; EI: '11-13-15: 4/1/3.

Dutch decathlon records 2012 & 2017.

Progress at Dec: 2007- 7466, 2008- 7507w, 2009- 8112, 2010- 8436, 2011- 8304, 2012- 8506, 2013- 8391, 2014- 8478, 2015- 8298, 2017- 8539. pbs: 60m 6.88i '13, 100m 10.57 '15, 200m 21.62 '10, 400m 47.88 '10, 1000m 2:37.42i '06, 1500m 4:22.29 '11, 60mh 7.88i '13, 110mh 13.92/13.89w '13, 400mh 51.59 '10, HJ 2.08i/2.02 '13, PV 5.52i '11, 5.45 '10; LJ 7.65i, 7.76w '09, 7.65 '12; SP 14.67 '15, DT 43.38 '14, JT 63.59 '12, Hep 6372i '13.

Set six pbs in improving pb by 277 points for European silver 2010.

Women

Nadine BROERSEN b. 29 Apr 1990 Hoorn 1.71m 62kg. AV Sprint Breda.

At Hep: OG: '12- 11, '16- 13; WCh: '13-15-17: 10/4/dnf; EC: '14- 2, '16- dnf; EU23: '11- 9; EJ: '09- 5; ECp: '14- 1. At Pen: WI: '14- 1; EI: '17- 5. Won NED HJ 2010-11, 2014; LJ 2015; JT 2013.

Four Dutch high jump records 2013-14 and indoors 2014.

Progress at Hep: 2009- 5507, 2010- 5967, 2011- 5932(w)/5854, 2012- 6319, 2013- 6345, 2014- 6539, 2015- 6531, 2016- 6377, 2017- 6326. pbs: 200m 24.57 '14, 800m 2:11.11 '14, 60mh 8.32i '13, 100mh 13.39 '14, HJ 1.94 '14, LJ 6.39 '14, 6.40w '16; SP 14.93i '14, 14.82 '15; JT 54.97 '12, Pen 4830i '14.

Lost c.200 points in stumbling at last hurdle in first event of 2013 World heptathlon. Won IAAF Combined Events Challenge 2014.

Sifan HASSAN b. '1 Jan' 1993 Adama, Ethiopia 1.70m 49kg. Eindhoven Atletiek.

At 1500m/(5000m): OG: '16- 5 (h 800m); WCh: '15- 3 (sf 800m), '17- 5/3; EC: '14- 1/2, '16- 2; CCp: '14- 1; WI: '16- 1, '18- 3; EI: 15- 1; won DL 2015. At 3000m: WI: '14- 5, '18- 2; ET: '14- 1. Eur CC: '13- 1 U23, '15- 1.

Records: European U23 1500m (3) 2014-15, Dutch 1500m (3) 2014-15, 1M 2015, 3000m 2014 & 2017, 5000m (2) 2014-17.

Progress at 800m, 1500m, 5000m: 2011- 4:20.13, 2012- 4:08.74, 2013- 2:00.86, 4:03.73. 2014- 1:59.95, 3:57.00, 14:59.23; 2015- 1:58.50, 3:56.05; 2016- 2:00.27, 3:57.13; 2017- 1:56.81, 3:56.14, 14:41.24. pbs: 1000m 2:34.68 '15, 1M 4:18.20 '15, 2000m 5:46.1 '14, 3000m 8:28.90 '17, 10kRd 34:28 '12, HMar 77:10 '11.

Came to the Netherlands as a refugee at age 15. Dutch eligibility from 29 Nov 2013.

Maureen KOSTER b. 3 Jul 1992 Gouda 1.75m 56kg. Phanos.

At 1500m: OG: '16- h; WCh: '13/15- sf; EC: '14- h; WJ: '10- h. At 3000m: WI: '16- 4; EI: '15- 3, '17- 4. At 5000m: WCh: '15- h. Eur CC: '14- 5 U23, '15- 9. Won NED 1500m 2012-13, 2015.

Progress at 1500m: 2007- 4:37.38, 2008- 4:28.11, 2009- 4:24.32, 2010- 4:19.28, 2011- 4:17.64, 2012- 4:13.48; 2013- 4:06.50, 2014- 4:04.92, 2015- 3:59.79, 2016- 4:03.84, 2017- 4:03.77. pbs: 800m 2:02.15 '14, 1000m 2:40.09 '14, 3000m 8:44.63i '17, 8:48.46mx; 5000m 15:07.20 '16, 10kRd: 34:27 '14.

Susan KRUMINS b. 8 Jul 1986 Nijmegen 1.72m 54kg. née Kuijken. Zevenheuvelen. Was at Florida State University, USA.

At 1500m: WCh: '09- h; EC: '10- h; E23: '07- 4. At 3000m: WJ: '04- dnf; EJ: '05- 2; CCp: '14- 3. At 5000m/(10000m): OG: '16- 8/14; WCh: '13- 8, '15- 8/10, '17- 8/5; EC: '14- 3, '16- 4. Eur CC: '05- 3J, '08- 1 U23. Won NED 1500m 2014, 5000m 2016; NCAA 1500m 2009..

Progress at 5000m, 10000m: 2003- 16:41.31, 2006- 16:20.30, 2009- 16:31.68, 2013- 15:04.36, 2014- 15:32.82, 2015- 15:07.38, 31:31.97; 2016- 15:00.69, 31:32.43; 2017- 14:51.25, 31:20.24. pbs: 800m 2:02.24 '09, 1000m 2:38.01 '14, 1500m 4:02.25 '17, 1M 4:34.11i '09, 2000m 5:38.37 '13, 3000m 8:34.41 '17, HMar 70:32 '17, 3000mSt 10:42.93 '05.

In September 2016 married Andrew Krumins,

who competed for Australia at the 2001 World Youth Champs, pb 800m 1:47.16 '06.

Dafne SCHIPPERS b. 15 Jun 1992 Utrecht 1.79m 68kg. Hellas.
At (100m)/200m/4x100mR: OG: '16- 5/2; WCh: '11- sf, '15- 2/1, '17- 3/1; EC: 12- 5/2R, '14- 1/1, '16- 1/-/1R; WJ: '10- 3R; EU23: '13- (1) (3 LJ); CCp: '14- 3/1; ET: '14- 1. At 60m: WI: '16- 2, '18- 5; EI: '13- 4, 15- 1. At Hep: OG: '12- 10; WCh: '13- 3; WJ: '10- 1; EJ: '09- 4, '11- 1. Won DL 200m 2016, NED 100m 2011-12, 2014-15; LJ 2012, 2014.
European 200m record 2015, Dutch records: 100m (5) 2014-15, 200m (5) 2011-15, LJ 2014, Hep 2013 & 2014.
Progress at 100m, 200m, Hep: 2007- 12.09/12.08w, 2008- 12.26/12.01w, 2009- 11.79, 24.21, 5507; 2010- 11.56, 23.70/23.41w, 5967; 2011- 11.19/11.13w, 22.69, 6172; 2012- 11.36, 22.70, 6360; 2013- 11.09, 22.84, 6477; 2014- 11.03, 22.03, 6545; 2015- 10.81, 21.63; 2016- 10.83, 21.88; 2017- 10.95, 22.05. pbs: 60m 7.00i '16, 150m 16.93 '13, 800m 2:08.59 '14, 60mh 8.18i '12, 100mh 13.13 '14, HJ 1.80 '12, LJ 6.78 '14, SP 14.66 '15, JT 42.22 '15.
Added 117 points to pb and reduced 800m best from 2:15.52 to 2:08.62 in taking 2013 World heptathlon bronze. First Dutch woman to win a medal in World Championships and emulated Fanny Blankers-Koen (1950) by winning EC sprint double 2014. European Athlete of the Year 2014-15.

Anouk VETTER b. 4 Feb 1993 Amsterdam 1.77m 62kg. Sprint.
At Hep: OG: '16- 10; WCh: '15- 12, '17- 3; EC: '14- 7, '16- 1; WJ: '12- dnf; EJ: '11- dnf. At Pen: EI: '15- 8. Won NED LJ 2017.
Dutch heptathlon records 2016 & 2017.
Progress at Hep: 2011- 5549, 2012- 5764, 2013- 5872, 2014- 6316, 2015- 6458, 2016- 6626, 2017- 6636. pbs: 60m 7.46i '16, 100m 11.61 '16, 11.44w '17, 200m 23.70 '16, 800m 2:17.71 '16, 60mh 8.25i '16, 100mh 13.29 '16, HJ 1.81 '13, LJ 6.34 '15, 6.38w '16; SP 16.00 '17, JT 58.41 '17, Pen 4548i '15.
Mother Gerda Blokziel was NED javelin champion 1987-8. pb 58.22 '86.

Nadine VISSER b. 9 Feb 1995 Hoorn 1.75m 63kg. SAV.
At Hep/(100mh): OG: '16- 19 (h); WCh: '15- 8, '17- 7/7; EC: '14 (h), '16- (sf); WJ: '12- 11, 14- 3 (3); EU23: '15- (3, 11 LJ), '17- (1); EJ: '13- 4; WUG: '17- (1). At 60mh: WI: '18- 3; EI: '17- 7. Won NED 100mh 2015.
Progress at 100mh, Hep: 2011- 13.84, 5171; 2012- 13.50, 5475; 2013- 13.21, 5774; 2014- 12.99, 6110; 2015- 12.81, 6467; 2016- 12.89, 6190; 2017- 12.78/12.57w, 6370. pbs: 60m 7.38i '18, 100m 11.60 '14, 150m 17.69 '15, 200m 23.46, 22.83w '17, 800m 2:13.08 '15, 60mh 7.83i '18 (NED record), HJ 1.80 '14, LJ 6.48 '15, SP 13.89i, 13.64 '17, JT 44.01 '15, Pen 4428i '17.
Concentrating on 100mh hurdles in 2018.

NEW ZEALAND

Governing body: Athletics New Zealand. Founded as the New Zealand Amateur Athletic Association in 1887, current name from 1989.
National Championships first held in 1887 (men), 1926 (women). **2017 Champions: Men**: 100m/ 200m: Joseph Millar 10.18/20.37, 400m: Quin Hartley 48.63, 800m: Brad Mathas 1:50.66, 1500m: Eric Speakman 3:49.90, 3000m: Hamish Carson 8:05.25, 5000m: Daniel Balchin 14:15.88, 10000m: Aaron Pulford 29:38.98, HMar: Criag Lautenslager 64:58, Mar: Stephen Day 2:32:04, 3000mSt: Jack Beaumont 9:13.58, 110mh: Joshua Hawkins 14.31, 400mh: Cameron French 51.58, HJ: Hamish Kerr 2.15, PV: Nick Southgate 5.15, LJ: Jesse Bryant 7.22w, TJ: Ebuka Okpala 15.43, SP: Tom Walsh 21.51, DT: Marshall Hall 55.11, HT: Matt Bloxham 59.81, JT: Ben Langton Burnell 76.59, Dec: Max Attwell 6662, 3000mW: Bradyn Popow 16:35.31, 20kW: Graeme Jones 1:41:42. **Women**: 100m/200m: Zoe Hobbs 11.57/ 23.85, 400m: Megan Kikuchi 56.94, 800m/1500m: Angie Petty 2:03.35/4:19.54, 3000m: Laura Nagle 9:22.73, 5000m: Laura Nagel 16:04.45, 10000m: Sally Gibbs 36:38.69, HMar: Annika Pfitzinger 75:58, Mar: Alice Mason 2:48:36, 100mh: Fiona Morrison 13.35, 400mh: Anna Percy 60.23, HJ: Alex Hyland 1.76, PV: Eliza McCartney 4.55, LJ: Kelsey Berryman 6.40w, TJ: Anna Thomson 12.34, SP: Maddison-Lee Wesche 15.04, DT: TeRina Keenan 56.51, HT: Nicole Bradley 56.41, JT: Medeleine Chapman 50.98, Hep: Ariana Blackwood 4431, 3000mW: Laura Langley 13:36.76, 20kW: Roseanne Robinson 1:43:23.

Jacko GILL b. 20 Dec 1994 Auckland 1.90m 118kg. Takapuna.
At SP: OG: '16- 9; WCh: '15- 8, '17- 9; CG: '14- 11; WJ: '10- 1, '12- 1; WY: '11- 1, YthOG: '10- 2. Oceania champion 2014.
Five World youth shot records 5kg 23.86 '10, 24.35 and 24.45 '11; 6kg (4) 21.34 to 22.31, 7.26kg (3) in 2011. World junior 6kg record 23.00 '13. Three NZL records 2011.
Progress at SP: 2010- 18.57, 2011- 20.38, 2012- 20.05, 2014- 20.70, 2015- 20.75, 2016- 20.83, 2017- 21.01.
First name actually Jackson. World age 15 and 16 bests for 5kg, 6kg and 7.26kg shot. His father Walter was NZ champion at SP 1987 & 1989, DT 1975, pbs 16.57 '86 & 53.78 (1975); his mother Nerida (née Morris) had discus best of 51.32 and was NZ champion in 1990. His sister Ayla was 6th in WJ hammer 2010.

Tomas WALSH b. 1 Mar 1992 Timaru 1.86m 123kg. South Canterbury.
At SP: OG: '16- 3; WCh: '15- 4, '17- 1; CG: '14- 2; WJ: '10- dnq 16; WY: '09- 6 (dnq 31 DT), CCp: '14- 4; WI: '14-16-18: 3/1/1. Won DL 2016, NZ SP 2010-17, DT 2013.

Shot records: 8 Oceania 2016-18, 9NZL 2013-18 and 9 OCE indoor 2014-18, Comm 2016 (=) & 2018.
Progress at SP: 2010- 17.57, 2011- 18.83, 2012- 19.33, 2013- 20.61, 2014- 21.26i/21.16, 2015- 21.62, 2016- 22.21, 2017- 22.14, 2018- 22.67. pb DT 53.58 '14.
At World Indoors: set four NZ indoor records in 2014 and three Oceania records in both 2016 and 2018, when he beat the Championship record set in 1995.

Nick WILLIS b. 25 Apr 1983 Lower Hutt 1.83m 68kg. Economics graduate of University of Michigan, USA.
At 1500m: OG: '04- sf, '08- 2, '12- 9, '16- 3; WCh: '05- 07-11-13-15-17: sf/10/12/sf/6/8; CG: '06-1, '10- 3, '14-3 (10 5000m); WJ: '02- 4; WI: '08/14- dq, '16- 3; WCp: '06- 3, '14- 6 (4 3000m). Won NCAA indoor 2005, NZ 1500m 2006, 2015; 3000m 2013, 2016; 5000m 2011-12.
Records: NZ 1500m (6) 2005-15, 3000m 2014. Oceania 1500m (3) 2012-15 and indoors 1500m (3:35.80) 2010, 1M 2015 & 2016 (3:50.63).
Progress at 1500m: 2001- 3:43.54, 2002- 3:42.69, 2003- 3:36.58, 2004- 3:32.64, 2005- 3:32.38, 2006- 3:32.17, 2007- 3:35.85, 2008- 3:33.51, 2009- 3:38.85i, 2010- 3:35.17, 2011- 3:31.79, 2012- 3:30.35, 2013- 3:32.57, 2014- 3:29.91, 2015- 3:29.66, 2016- 3:34.29, 2017- 3:34.74. pbs: 800m 1:45.54 '04, 1000m 2:16.58 '12, 1M 3:49.83 '14, 3000m 7:36.91 '14, 5000m 13:20.33 '14, HMar 67:06 '14.
His brother Steve (b. 25 Apr 1975) had pbs: 1500m 3:40.29 '99, 1M 3:59.04 '00.

Women

Valerie ADAMS b. 6 Oct 1984 Rotorua 1.93m 123kg. Auckland City.
At SP: OG: '04- 7, '08- 1, '12- 1, '16- 2; WCh: '03-05-07-09-11-13: 5/2/1/1/1/1; CG: '02-06-10-14: 2/1/1/1; WJ: '02- 1; WY: '99- 10, '01- 1; WI: '04-08-10-12-14-16: dnq 10/1/1/1/1/3; WCp: '02- 6, '06- 1, '10- 1. Won WAF 2005, 2007-09, DL 2010-14, 2016; NZL SP 2001-11, 2013-14, 2016; DT 2004, HT 2003.
Nine Oceania & Commonwealth shot records 2005-11, 22 NZ 2002-11, 10 OCE indoor 2004-13.
Progress at SP: 1999- 14.83, 2000- 15.72, 2001- 17.08, 2002- 18.40, 2003- 18.93, 2004- 19.29, 2005- 19.87, 2006- 20.20, 2007- 20.54, 2008- 20.56, 2009- 21.07, 2010- 20.86, 2011- 21.24, 2012- 21.11, 2013- 20.98i/20.90, 2014- 20.67i/20.59, 2015- 18.73, 2016- 20.42. pbs: DT 58.12 '04, HT 58.75 '02.
Ten senior global shot titles. IAAF Female Athlete of the Year 2014. Matched her age with metres at the shot from 14 to 18 and missed that at 19 by only two months. 28 successive shot wins from September 2007 to World Indoor silver in March 2010, and another 56 from August 2010 to July 2015. The disqualification of Nadezhda Ostapchuk meant that the win streak for Adams lengtherned to 95.Her father came from England and her mother from Tonga. Married New Caledonia thrower Bertrand Vili (SP 17.81 '02, DT 63.66 '09, 4 ECp '07 for France) in November 2004 (divorced in 2010), and married Gabriel Price on 2 April 2016. She was made a Dame Companion of the New Zealand Order of Merit for services to athletics in the 2017 New Year's Honours. Daughter Kimoana born in October 2017.

Eliza McCARTNEY b. 11 Dec 1996 Auckland 1.79m 65kg. North Harbour Bays.
At PV: OG: '16- 3; WCh: '17- 9; WJ: '14- 3; WY: '13- 4; WUG: '15- 2; WI: '16- 5, '18- 4. NZ champion 2016.
Pole vault records: World junior 2015, Oceania & Commonwealth (2) 2016-17, 8 NZ 2014-17, Oceania indoor 2018.
Progress at PV: 2012- 3.85, 2013- 4.11, 2014- 4.45, 2015- 4.64, 2016- 4.80, 2017- 4.82, 2018- 4.75i.

NIGERIA

Governing body: The Athletic Federation of Nigeria. Founded 1944.

2017 National Champions: **Men**: 100m: Seye Ogunlewe 10.30, 200m: Emmanuel Arowolo 21.16, 400m: Samson Oghenewegba 46.10, 800m/1500m/3000mSt: Hamajan Soudi 1:48.97/3:48.61/9:13.95, 5000m/10000m: Emmanuel Gyang 14:40.97/29:15.97, 110mh: Ogieriakhi Martins 13.99, 400mh: Timothy Emo-Oghene 52.17, HJ: Tadius Okpara 2.05, LJ: Benjamin Arinze 7.54, TJ: Olajide Abiola 15.46, SP: Onwuka Kalu Eke 16.51, DT: Augustine Nwoye 52.24, HT: Olawale Olatunji 46.44, JT: Samuel Adams 71.24. **Women**: 100m: Aniekeme Alphonsus 11.52, 200m: Maria Thompson Omokwe 23.71, 400m: Patience George 51.06, 800m: Abike Egbeniyi 2:06.52, 1500m: Bamtefa Adeyinka 4:47.45, 5000m/10000m: Deborah Pam 17:35.59/36:47.03, 100mh: Grace Ayemoba 13.86, 400mh: Rita Ossai 58.83, HJ: Esther Issa 1.75, LJ: Ese Brume 6.40, TJ: Blessing Ibrahim 13.25, SP: Nkechi Chime 13.54, HT: Quween Obisesan 58.91, JT: Kelechi Nwangaa 53.04.

Women

Ese BRUME b. 20 Jan 1996 Ugheli, Delta State 1.67m 58kg. Student at University of Benin.
At LJ: OG: '16- 5; WCh: '17- dnq 17; CG: '14- 1; WJ: '14- dnq 33; AfG: '15- 4; Af Ch: '14- 1, '16- 1; CCp: '14- 5. Won Af-J LJ & 4x100m 2013 & 2015, TJ 2015; NGR LJ 2014, 2016-17.
Progress at LJ: 2012- 6.02, 2013- 6.53, 2014- 6.68, 2015- 6.61, 2016- 6.83, 2017- 6.64/6.68w. pbs: 100m 11.84 '14, 400m 55.53 '16, TJ 13.16A '15.

Blessing OKAGBARE b. 9 Oct 1988 Sapele 1.80m 68kg. Married name Ighoteguonor. Was at University of Texas at El Paso, USA.
At LJ/(100m): OG: '08- 2, '12- dnq 15/8; '16- (sf, sf 200m), WCh: '11- dnq 18/5, '13- 2/6 (3 200m), '15- (8), '17- 8/(sf); CG: '14- 1 100m & 200m/2R; AfG: '07- 2 (4 TJ), '11- 1/2; AfCh: '10- 1/1/1R,

'12- 1/2, '14- (1)/1R; WJ: '06- 16 (dnq 17 TJ); CCp: '10- 6/3/3R; Won Nigerian 100m 2009-14, 2016; 200m 2013-14, 2016; LJ 2008-09, 2011-13; TJ 2008; NCAA 100m & LJ 2010.

African records 100m (2) 2013, 2000m 2018, 4x200m 2015, Nigerian & African junior TJ record 2007.

Progress at 100m, 200m, LJ: 2004- 5.85 irreg, 2006- 6.16, 2007- 6.51, 2008- 23.76A, 6.91; 2009- 11.16, 6.73/6.90w; 2010- 11.00/10.98w/10.7Aw, 22.71, 6.88; 2011- 11.08/11.01w, 22.94, 6.78/6.84w; 2012- 10.92, 22.63, 6.97; 2013- 10.79/10.75w, 22.31, 7.00/7.14w; 2014- 10.85, 22.23, 6.86; 2015- 10.80, 22.67, 6.66; 2016- 11.02/10.92w, 22.58, 6.73; 2017- 10.99, 22.87, 6.77.; 2018- 22.04 pbs: 60m 7.18i '10, 300m 37.04 '13, 400m 53.34 '15, TJ 14.13 '07.

Majestic winner of Commonwealth Games sprint double in 2014. Married football international Jude Igho Otegheri on 7 Nov 2014.

NORWAY

Governing body: Norges Friidrettsforbund. Founded 1896.

National Championships first held in 1896 (men), 1947 (women, walks 1937). **2017 Champions**: **Men**: 100m/200m: Jonathan Quarcoo 10.33/20.76, 400m/400mh: Karsten Warholm 46.44/48.73, 800m: Thomas Roth 1:50.07, 1500m/5000m/3000mSt: Jakob Ingebrigtsen 13:53.29/13:35.84/8:44.12, 10000m: Bjørnar Sandnes Lillefosse 29:05.87 (Zeray Mezenghe ERI 28:56.95), HMar: Okubamichael Fissehatsion ERI 64:45, Mar: Frode Stenberg 2:43:39, 3000mSt: Tom Erling Kårbo 8:57.88, 110mh/ Dec: Martin Roe 15.28/7514, HJ: Kristoffer Nilsen 2.08, PV: Eirik Dolve 5.10, LJ: Amund Høie Sjursen 7.61, TJ: Jesper Vestbø 14.66, SP: Marcus Thomsen 19.40, DT: Sven Martin Skagestad 62.79, HT: Eivind Henriksen 74.27, JT: Christer Stenersrød 68.19, 5000mW: Håvard Haukenes 19:35.99, 10000mW: Fredrik Vaeng Røtnes 41:29.9. **Women**: 100m/200m: Helene Rønningen 11.75/23.81, 400m/400mh: Amalie Hammild Iuel 53.27/56.55, 800m: Yngvild Elvemo 2:09.76, 1500m: Sigrid Jervell Våg 4:25.75, 5000m: Maria Sagnes Wågan 16:21.99, 10000m: Vienna Dahle 34:29.32, HMar: Runa Skrove Falch 76:30, Mar: Mona Brundtland 3:28:10, 3000mSt: Karoline Bkerkelo Grøvdal 9:13.35, 100mh: Line Kloster 13.67, HJ: Tonje Angelsen 1.85, PV: Lene Retzius 4.20, LJ: Live Haugstad Hilton 6.14, TJ: Oda Utsi Onstad 13.12, SP: Charlotte Lund Abrahamsen 14.61, DT: Grete Etholm (17th title) 49,55, HT: Beatrice Nedberge Llano 64.65, JT: Sigrid Borge 60.93, Hep: Caroline Fleischer 5052, 3000mW/ 5000mW: Merete Heigheim 14:00.75/23:48.6.

Håvard HAUKENES b. 22 Apr 1990 Bergen 1.80m 68kg. IL Gular

At 50kW: OG: '16- 7; WCh: '13- dq, '15- 24, '17- dq; At 20kW: EC: '14- dq. Won NOR 5000mW 2017, 20kW 2014, 2016; 50kW 2012.

Progress at 50kW: 2011- 4:04:48, 2012- 3:56:38, 2015- 3:56:50, 2016- 3:46:33, 2017- 3:43:40. pbs: 3000mW 11:44.17 '15, 5000mW 19:19.79 '16, 10000mW 42:39.5 '16, 20kW 1:23:15 '16.

Filip INGEBRIGTSEN b. 20 Apr 1993 Stavanger 1.87m 75kg. Sandnes IL

At 1500m: OG: '16- h; WCh: '17- 3; EC: '14- h, '16- 1; WJ: '10- h, '12- 9; EU23: '13- 6. At 800m: WJ: '14- 7; EU23: '13- h; EJ: 11- h. Won NOR 800m 2016, 1500m 2013.

Progress at 1500m: 2011- 3:51.70, 2012- 3:44.04, 2013- 3:38.76, 2014- 3:40.48, 2015- 3:42.32, 2016- 3:32.43, 2017- 3:32.48. pbs: 800m 1:47.79 '16, 1000m 2:16.95 '16, 1M 3:53.23 '17, 3000m 7:49.70 '16, 2000mSt 5:46.15 '12,

Henrik INGEBRIGTSEN b. 24 Feb 1991 Stavanger 1.80m 69kg. Sandnes IL

At 1500m (3000m): OG: '12- 5, '16- sf; WCh: '13- 8, '15- h; EC: '10-12-14-16: h/1/2/3; WJ: '10- h; EU23: '11- h; EJ: '09- h; CCp: '14- 4; EI: '15- 6 (3), '17- (2). At 5000m: EC: '16- 4; EU23: '13- 1. Won NOR 800m 2013, 1500m 2010, 2012, 2014; 5000m 2015. Eur CC: '12- 1 U23, '17- 11.

Norwegian records: 1500m (4) 2012-14, 1M (3) 2012-14.

Progress at 1500m: 2004- 4:30.63, 2005- 4:22.48, 2006- 4:04.15, 2007- 3:54.08, 2008- 3:50.63, 2009- 3:44.53, 2010- 3:38.61, 2011- 3:39.50, 2012- 3:35.43, 2013- 3:33.95, 2014- 3:31.46, 2015- 3:32.85, 2016- 3:34.57, 2017- 3:38.96. pbs: 800m 1:48.09 '14, 1M 3:50.72 '14, 3000m 7:42.19 '13, 5000m 13:27.10 '15, 2000mSt 5:41.03 '09, 3000mSt 8:52.56 '09.

Younger brothers: **Filip** (qv) and **Jakob** (b. 19 Sep 00) European age 14 1500m bests to 3:48.37 '15, pbs in 2017: 800m 1:49.40, 3:39.92, 1M 3:56.29, 3000m 8:00.01, 5000m 13:35.84 European U17 rec, 3000mSt: h WCh 17, European junior record 8:26.81 '17, won EJ CC 2016-17, 5000m & 3000mSt 2017. NOR 1500m, 5000, 3000mSt 2017.

Sondre Nordstad MOEN b. 12 Jan 1991 1.78m 62kg. SK Vidar.

At Mar: OG: '16- 19. At 5000m: WCh: '17- h; EC: '10- h; WJ: '08- 14, EJ: '09- 5. At 10000m: EC: '10- 14, '14- 9; EU23: '11- 1; Eur CC: '07-08-09-10-11: 6J/2J/4J/5J/3 U23. Won NOR 5000m 2011, 10000 & HMar 2015, CC 2014.

European marathon record 2017, Norwegian records half marathon and marathon (2) 2017.

Progress at Mar: 2015- 2:12:43, 2016- 2:14:17, 2017- 2:05:48. Pbs: 1500m 3:48.65 '14, 3000m 7:52.55 '17, 5000m 13:20.16 '17, 10000m 28:15.12 '17, Road: 10M 47:32 '16, 10k 27:55 '17, 15k 43:52 '11, HMar 59:48 '17, 3000mSt 9:10.01 '08.

Won Fukuoka marathon 2017.

Karsten WARHOLM b. 28 Feb 1996 Volda 1.87m 78kg. Dimna IL.

At 400mh: OG: '16- sf; WCh: '17- 1; EC: '16- 6; EU23: '17- 1; At 400m: EC: '14- h; EU23: '17- 2; EJ: '15- 2; At Oct: WY: '13- 1; At Dec: WJ: '14- 10; EJ: '15- 2. Won NOR 400m & 400mh 2015-17, 110mh 2013-14.

NOR records; 400m (2) 2016-17, 400mh (6) 2016-17.

Progress at 400mh: 2014- 52.20, 2015- 51.09, 2016- 48.49, 2017- 48.22. pbs: 60m 6.75i '17, 100m 10.49i '17, 10.52 '16; 200m 20.92i/21.09 '16, 21.00w '15; 400m 44.87 '17, 1000m 2:45.80i '13, 1500m 4:44.73 '15, 60mh 8.10i '15, 110mh 14.30 '15, HJ 2.05 '14, PV 4.30 '15, LJ 7.66 '15, TJ 14.48i/14.33 '12, SP 9.18 '14, DT 29.40 '14, JT 45.82 '15.

Won multiple NOR age group titles at a wide range of events. EJ silver medals at 400m & Dec in 2015 even though 400m was in the middle of the decathlon first day. IAAF Rising Star of the Year 2017.

Women

Karoline Bjerkeli GRØVDAL b. 14 Jun 1990 Alesund1.67m 52kg. Sportsklubben Vidar.

At 1500m: WCh: '17- h; ET: '15- 2. At 5000m/ (10000m): OG: '12- h, '16- 7/9; WCh: 13- 13, '15- h, '17- dnf; (h 1500m) EC: '10- 9/dnf, '14- 12, '16- (3); EJ: '09- 1; ET: '10- 3. At 3000mSt: WCh: '09- h; EU23: '11- h; EJ: '07- 1, '09- 1. At 2000mSt: WY: '07- 3. Eur CC: '06-09-13-15-16-17: 2J/1J/ 5/3/3/3. Won NOR 1500m 2013, 2015; 5000m 2008, 2010, 2012, 2014; 3000mSt 2006, 2009-10.

NOR records 1M 2016, 3000mSt 2007 & 2017.

Progress at 5000m, 10000m, 3000mSt: 2005- 11:07.5, 2006- 9:55.95, 2007- 15:55.62, 9:33.19; 2008- 16:08.22; 2009- 15:29.82, 9:33.34; 2010- 15:25.40, 9:39.54; 2011- 15:44.92, 9:46.07; 2012- 15:24.86, 2013- 15:16.27mx, 2014- 15:47.63, 2015- 15:15.18; 2016- 14:57.53, 31:14.07; 2017- 15:00.44. 9:13.35. pbs: 800m 2:04.23 '16, 1500m 4:07.25 '17, 1M 4:26.23 '16, 3000m 8:37.58 '17, HMar 69:41 '12, 2000mSt 6:21.39 '08.

PANAMA

Governing body: Federación Panameña de Atletismo. Founded 1945.

Alonso EDWARD b. 8 Dec 1989 Ciudad de Panamá 1.83m 73kg. Was at Barton County CC.

At (100m)/200m: OG: '12- h, '16- 7; WCh: '09-11-13-15-17: 2/dnf/sf/4/h; WJ: '08- (h); PAm: '15- 3; SAG: '14- (1); SACh: '09- 1/1, SAm-J: '07- (1), SAm-Y: '06- 1/1; CCp: '14- 1. Won DL 2014-16, C.American 2012, C.AmG 100m 2010, 200m 2013; SAmG 100m 2014.

Records: S.American 200m 2009, Panama 100m (2) 2009-14, 200m (5) 2007-09; South American Junior 100m 2007.

Progress at 100m, 200m: 2006- 10.60, 21.18; 2007- 10.28/10.25w, 20.62; 2008- 10.63, 20.96; 2009- 10.09/9.97w, 19.81; 2010- 10.24/10.08w, 2011- 20.28, 2012- 21.23A, 2013- 10.13, 20.37/20.32w; 2014- 10.02, 19.84; 2015- 10.29, 19.87; 2016- 19.92, 2017- 10.00w, 20.61. pbs: 300m 34.17 '17, 400m 47.40i '10.

World age-19 best 19.81 in World final 2009. Younger brother Mateo (b. 1 May 1993): 60m 6.73i PAN record, 100m 10.29 & 200m 21.48 '14.

PERU

Governing body: Federación Peruana de Atletismo.

Kimberley GARCÍA b. 19 Oct 1993 Huancayo 1.67m 44kg.

At 20kW: OG: '16- 14; WCh: '13/15/17: 33/dnf/7; WCp: '16- 12; PAm: 15- 5; SACh: '14- 1. At 10000mW: WJ: '12- 10. At 5000mW: WY: '09- dnf; YOG: '10- 7.

S.American walks record 10k 2017, 20k 2014. Four Peru 20kW records 2013-17.

Progress at 20kW: 2013- 1:33:57, 2014- 1:29:44, 2015- 1:31:13, 2016- 1:29:38, 2017- 1:29:13. Pbs: 5000mW 22:57.4 '11, 10000mW 43:57.44 '14, 43:23R '17.

POLAND

Governing body: Polski Zwiazek Lekkiej Atletyki (PZLA). Founded 1919.

National Championships first held in 1920 (men), 1922 (women). **2017 Champions**: **Men**: 100m:/200m: Karol Zalewski 10.27/20.69, 400m: Rafal Omelko 45.67, 800m: Michal Rozmys 1:45.70, 1500m: Adam Kszczot 3:38.31, 5000m/ 3000mSt: Krystian Zalewski 13:53.45/8:34.89, 10000m/HMar: Arkadiusz Gardzielewski 29:09.16/63:32 , Mar: Artur Kozlowski 2:12:38, 110mh: Damian Czykier 13.44, 400mh: Patryk Dobek 49.53, HJ: Sylwester Bednarek 2.30, PV: Piotr Lisek 5.85, LJ: Adrian Strzalkowski 7.78, TJ: Karol Hoffmann 16.55, SP: Michal Haratyk 21.53, DT: Robert Urbanek 65.29, HT: Wojciech Nowicki 80.47, JT: Marcin Krukowski 88.09, Dec: Rafal Abramowski 7358, 10000mW: Artur Brzozowski 40:17.91/1:23:55, 50kW: Rafal Augustyn 3:44:42. **Women**: 100m: Ewa Swoboda 11.29, 200m: Anna Kielbasinska 23.27, 400m: Iga Baumgart 51.71, 800m: Angelika Cichocka 2:00.91, 1500m: Sofia Ennaoui 4:16.56, 5000m/ 10000m: Katarzyna Rutkowska 15:50.46/33:42.49, HMar: Ewa Jagielska 77:15, Mar: Dominika Stelmach 2:41:13, 3000mSt: Matylda Kowal 10:04.12, 100mh: Karolina Koleczek 13.17, 400mh: Joanna Linkiewicz 56.00, HJ: Kamila Licwinko 1.95, PV: Justyna Smietanka 4.30, LJ/ TJ: Anna Jagaciak Michalska 6.40/14.05, SP: Paulina Guba 17.92, DT: Lidia Augustyniak 58.43, HT: Anna Wlodarczyk 80.79, JT: Marcelina Witek 59.21, Hep: Izabela Mikolajczyk 5895, 5000mW/20kW: Paulina Buziak 22:20.99/1:36:08.

Rafal AUGUSTYN b. 14 May 1984 Chyki-Debiaki, near Mielec 1.78m 71kg. LKS Stal Mielec.

At 50kW: OG: '16- 22; WCh: '09- 21, '15- 28, '17- 7; EC: '14- 9; WCp: '12- 7; ECp: '11- 6. At 20kW: OG: '08- 29, '12- 29; WCh: '07-11-13: 26/20/19; EC: '10- 9; EU23: '05- 4; WCp: '10- 14; ECp: '09- 7, '13- 8. Won POL 20kW 2007, 50kW 2010-11, 2014-17.

Progress at 50kW: 2009- 3:52:16, 2010- 3:49:54,

2011- 3:46:56, 2012- 3:49:53, 2013- 3:51:33, 2014- 3:45:32, 2015- 3:43:55, 2016- 3:43:22, 2017- 3:44:18. pbs: 3000mW 11:17.82 '11, 5000mW 19:16.51i '14, 19:26.55 '11; 10kW 39:47 '10, 40:37.73t '06; 20kW 1:20:53 '12.

Sylwester BEDNAREK b. 28 Apr 1989 Glówno 1.98m 75kg. RKS Lódz.
At HJ: OG: '16- dnq 30=; WCh: '09- 3, '15/17- dnq 33=/20=; EC: '10- 10=, '16- dnq 16; WJ: '06- 4, '08- 2; WY: '05- 4; E23: '09- 1; EJ: '07- 6; WI: '18- 5; EI: '17- 1. Polish champion 2014-15, 2017.
Progress at HJ: 2003- 1.76, 2004- 2.06, 2005- 2.22, 2006- 2.26, 2007- 2.22, 2008- 2.24, 2009- 2.32, 2010- 2.26, 2012- 2.20, 2013- 2.22, 2014- 2.25, 2015- 2.30, 2016- 2.30, 2017- 2.33i/2.32, 2018- 2.33i.

Konrad BUKOWIECKI b. 17 Mar 1997 Olsztyn 1.91m 140kg. PKS Gwardia Szczytno.
At SP: OG: '16- nt; WCh: '15- dnq, '17- 8; EC: '16- 4; WJ: '14- 1, '16- dq1 & 5 DT; WY: '13- 5; EU23: '17- 1; EJ: '15- 1 (dnq 13 DT); Yth OG: '10- 1; WI: '16- 4, '18- 8; EI: '15- 6; WUG: '17- 2; ET: 17- 3. Polish champion 2016.
Shot records: Four world junior 7.26kg 2015-16, (6kg 23.34dq '16), indoor 6kg (4) 22.38 '15 to 22.96 '16, World youth 5kg 2 out to 22.24 & 5 indoor to 24.24 in 2014; European junior (5) 2015, indoor (3) 2016, U23 indoor 2017 & 2018.
Progress at SP: 2014- 17.29i, 2015- 20.78, 2016- 21.14, 2017- 21.97i/21.59, 2018- 22.00i. Pb DT 58.42 '17.
Lost his 2016 World Junior gold with a public warning for a banned stimulant.

Patryk DOBEK b. 13 Feb 1994 Koscierzyna 1.83m 75kg. SKLA Sopot.
At 400mh: OG: '16- h; WCh: '15- 7, '17- sf; EC: '14- sf; EU23: '15- 1/2R; ET: '15- 2, '17- 3; Polish champion 2014-17. At 400m: WJ: '12- sf/2R; WY: '11- 3; EJ: '13- 2/2R.
Progress at 400mh: 2012- 52.00, 2013- 50.67, 2014- 49.13, 2015- 48.40, 2016- 49.01, 2017- 49.15. pbs: 200m 21.38 '15, 300m 33.34 '13, 400m 46.15 '13, 600m 1:15.78 '14.

Pawel FAJDEK b. 4 Jun 1989 Swiebodzice 1.86m 118kg. KS Agros Zamosc.
At HT: OG: '12- dnq, '16- dnq 17; WCh: '11-13-15-17: 11/1/1/1; EC: 14- 2, '16- 1; WJ: '08- 4; EU23: '09- 8, '11- 1; WUG: '11-13-15-17: 1/1/1/1; CCp: '14- 3; ET: '11-13-14-15-17: 2/1/2/1/1. Won POL 2012, 2014-16; Franc G 2013, World HT challenge 2013, 2015-17.
Two Polish hammer records 2014-15.
Progress at HT: 2008- 64.58, 2009- 72.36, 2010- 76.07, 2011- 78.54, 2012- 81.39, 2013- 82.27, 2014- 83.48, 2015- 83.93, 2016- 82.47, 2017- 83.44. pb Wt 23.22i '14.
Won 16 of 17 competitions in 2015, 13/14 in 2016 and 15/16 in 2017, with respectively the top 12 /12/10 performances of the year at hammer. The clear favourite, he failed to qualify with only 72.00 for Olympic final 2016 after 29 successive wins, all over 78m.

Michal HARATYK b. 10 Apr 1992 Cieszyn 1.94m 136kg. KS AZS AWF Kraków.
At SP: OG: '16- dnq 18; WCh: '17- 5; EC: '16- 2. POL champion 2017.
Progress at SP: 2012- 17.72, 2013- 17.24, 2014- 19.95, 2015- 20.10i/19.95, 2016- 21.35i/21.23, 2017- 21.88. pb DT 53.53 '13.
Elder brother Lukasz SP 18.82 '10.

Karol HOFFMANN b. 1 Jun 1989 Warsaw 1.97m 80kg. MKS Aleksandrów Lódzki.
At TJ: OG: '16- 12; EC: '12- 6, '16- 2; WJ: '08- 10; EU23: '11- 10; EJ: '07- dnq 22; WI: '14- 5. Polish champion 2011-12, 2014, 2016-17.
Progress at TJ: 2006- 15.00/15.23w, 2007- 15.74/15.88w, 2008- 15.94, 2009- 16.00, 2010- 15.92, 2011- 16.50/16.87w, 2012- 17.09, 2013- 16.66, 2014- 16.89i/16.64, 2015- 16.29, 2016- 17.16, 2017- 16.59. pb LJ 7.76 '11.
His father Zdzislaw was TJ world champion in 1983, Polish record 17.53 '85.

Adam KSZCZOT b. 2 Sep 1989 Opoczno 1.78m 64kg. RKS Lódz. Studied organisation and management.
At 800m: OG: '12/16- sf; WCh: '09/13- sf, '11-15-17: 6/2/2; EC: '10-14-16: 3/1/1; WJ: '08- 4; EU23: '09/11- 1; EJ: '07- 3; WI: '10-12-14-18: 3/4/2/1; EI: '09-11-13-17: 4/1/1/1; CCp: '14- 3; ET: '11-13-14-15: 1/1/2/3. Won POL 800m 2009-10, 2012, 2014-15., 1500m 2017.
Polish 1000m record 2011 and 2014.
Progress at 800m: 2005- 1:59.57, 2006- 1:51.09, 2007- 1:48.10, 2008- 1:47.16, 2009- 1:45.72, 2010- 1:45.07, 2011- 1:43.30, 2012- 1:43.83, 2013- 1:44.76, 2014- 1:44.02, 2015- 1:43.45, 2016- 1:43.76, 2017- 1:44.84. pbs: 400m 46.51 '11, 600m 1:14.55 '10, 1000m 2:15.72 '14, 1500m 3:38.31 '17.

Marcin LEWANDOWSKI b. 13 Jun 1987 Szczecin 1.80m 64kg. SL WKS Zawisza Bydgoszcz. PE student.
At 800m: OG: '08/12- sf, '16- 6; WCh: '09-11-13-15-17: 8/4/4/sf/sf; EC: '10-14-16: 1/5/2; WJ: '06- 4; EU23: '07- 1, '09- 2; WI: '14- dq (3); EI: '09-11-15: 6/2/1; CCp: '10- 2; ECp: '08- 2, '10- 3; won W.MilG 2011. At 1500m: WCh: '17- 7; EJ: '05- 7; WI: '18- 2; EI: '13- 4, '17- 1; ET: '13-14-15-17: 3/3/2/1. Won Polish 800m 2011, 2016; 1500m 2008, 2010, 2014, 2016.
Polish 1000m record 2011 & 2016.
Progress at 800m: 2002- 1:57.86, 2003- 1:53.31, 2004- 1:51.73, 2005- 1:48.86, 2006- 1:46.69, 2007- 1:45.52, 2008- 1:45.84, 2009- 1:43.84, 2010- 1:44.10, 2011- 1:44.53, 2012- 1:44.34, 2013- 1:43.79, 2014- 1:44.03, 2015- 1:43.72, 2016- 1:43.73, 2017- 1:44.77. pbs: 400m 47.76 '09, 600m 1:15.17 '14, 1000m 2:14.30 '16, 1500m 3:34.04 '17.
Coached by brother Tomasz (1:51.00 '03).

Piotr LISEK b. 16 Aug 1992 Duszniki, Poznan 1.94m 96kg. OSOT Szczecin.

At PV: OG: '16- 4=; WCh: '15- 3=, '17- 2; EC: '14- 6, '16- 4=; EU23: '13- dnq 17; ET: '15- 3; WI: 16- 3; WI: '18- 3; EI: '15- 3, '17- 1. Won POL 2017.
Three Polish indoor pole vault records 2015-17.
Progress at PV: 2006- 3.20, 2007- 3.30, 2008- 4.10, 2009- 4.42, 2010- 4.70, 2011- 5.10i/5.00, 2012- 5.20, 2013- 5.60, 2014- 5.82, 2015- 5.90i/5.82, 2016- 5.77i/5.75, 2017- 6.00i/5.89.
6-months drugs ban in 2012.

Piotr MALACHOWSKI b. 7 Jun 1983 Zuromin 1.94m 135kg. WKS Slask Wroclaw.
At DT: OG: '08- 2, '12- 5, '16- 2; WCh: '07-09-11-13-15-17: 12/2/9/2/1/5; EC: '06-10-14-16: 6/1/4/1; WJ: '02- 6; EU23: '03- 9, '05- 2; EJ: '01- 5; CCp: '10- 4; ECp: '06-07-08-09-10-11-14: 1/1/3/1/2/3/2. Won DL 2010, 2014-16; POL 2005-10, 2012-15.
Nine Polish discus records 2006-13.
Progress at DT: 1999- 39.48, 2000- 52.04, 2001- 54.19, 2002- 56.84, 2003- 57.83, 2004- 62.04, 2005- 64.74, 2006- 66.21, 2007- 66.61, 2008- 68.65, 2009- 69.15, 2010- 69.83, 2011- 68.49, 2012- 68.94, 2013- 71.84, 2014- 69.28, 2015- 68.29, 2016- 68.15, 2017- 67.68.

Wojciech NOWICKI b. 22 Feb 1989 Bialystok 1.96m 112kg. KS Podlasie Bialystok.
At HT: OG: '16- 3; WCh: '15- 3, '17- 3; EC: '16- 3; EU23: '11- 5. Won POL 2017.
Progress at HT: 2008- 55.71, 2009- 64.41, 2010- 69.59, 2011- 72.72, 2012- 73.52, 2013- 75.87, 2014- 76.14, 2015- 78.71, 2016- 78.36, 2017- 80.87. pb Wt 22.72i '14.

Robert URBANEK b. 29 Apr 1987 Leczyca 2.00m 120kg. MKS Aleksandrów Lódzki.
At DT: OG: '12/16- dnq 32/17; WCh: '13-15-17: 6/3/7; EC: '12-14-16: 6/3/9; EU23: '09- 7; CCp: '14- 6; ET: '15- 1, 17- 2. Won POL 2017.
Progress at DT: 2004- 47.09, 2005- 47.83, 2006- 50.84, 2007- 56.18, 2008- 62.22, 2009- 60.54, 2010- 60.74, 2011- 64.37, 2012- 66.93, 2013- 65.30, 2014- 65.75, 2015- 66.31, 2016- 65.56, 2017- 66.73. pb SP 16.21 '07.

Pawel WOJCIECHOWSKI b. 6 Jun 1989 Bydgoszcz 1.90m 81kg. CWKS Zawisza Bydgoszcz. PE student.
At PV: OG: '12- dnq, '16- dnq 16=; WCh: '11- 1, '15- 3=, '17- 5; EC: '14- 2, '16- 7=; WJ: '08- 2; EU23: '11- 1; EJ: '07- dnq 16; EI: '11- 4, '17- 3; CCp: '14- 5. Won W.MilG 2011, POL 2015-16.
Polish pole vault record 2011 and 2017.
Progress at PV: 2001- 2.50, 2002- 2.70, 2003- 3.10, 2004- 3.50, 2005- 4.10, 2006- 4.70, 2007- 5.00, 2008- 5.51, 2009- 5.40i/5.22, 2010- 5.60, 2011- 5.91, 2012- 5.62, 2014- 5.80, 2015- 5.84, 2016- 5.84i/5.71, 2017- 5.93, 2018- 5.88i.

Women

Maria ANDREJCZYK b. 9 Mar 1996 Sejny 1.74m 77kg. LUKS Hancza Suwalki.
At JT: OG: '16- 4; WCh: '15- dnq 28; EC: '16- dnq 13; WJ: '14- 5; WY: '13- dnq 26; EJ: '15- 1. Polish champion 2016.
Polish javelin record 2016.
Progress at JT: 2010- 28.51, 2011- 41.21, 2012- 44.58, 2014- 56.53, 2015- 62.11, 2016- 67.11.

Angelika CICHOCKA b. 15 Mar 1988 Kartuzy 1.69m 54kg. SKLA Sopot.
At 800m: OG: '16- sf; WCh: '17- 6; EC: '10/14- h; EJ: '07- h; WI: '14- 2. At 1500m: WCh: '15- 8, '17- 7; EC: '12- h, '16- 1; E23: '09- 8; WI: '12- 5; EI: '15- 2; ET: 17- 2. Polish champion 800m 2011-13, 2016-17; 1500m 2011, 2014, 2016.
Polish 1M record 2017.
Progress at 800m, 1500m: 2005- 2:12.50, 2006- 2:06.50, 4:32.04; 2007- 2:06.51, 4:26.85; 2008- 2:04.24, 4:21.47; 2009- 2:03.24, 4:12.31; 2010- 2:00.86i/2:01.17, 4:10.54i/4:12.80; 2011- 2:00.20, 4:06.50; 2012- 2:01.32, 4:06.79; 2013- 2:00.60, 4:11.33; 2014- 2:00.30, 4:07.55; 2015- 1:59.55, 4:03.06; 2016- 1:58.97, 4:03.25; 2017- 1:58.41, 4:01.61. pbs: 400m 54.44 '10, 600m 1:28.38 '11, 1000m 2:34.84 '16, 1M 4:19.58 '17, 3000m 9:10.65 '12.

Sofia ENNAOUI b. 30 Aug 1995 Ben Guerir, Morocco 1.58m 43kg. MKL Szczecin.
At 1500m: OG: '16- 10; WCh: '15/17- sf; EC: '16- 7; WJ: '12- 10, '14- 5; EU23: '15- 2, '17- 2; EJ: '13- 2; EI: '17- 3. At 800m: WCh: '15- sf; WY: '11- h, At 3000m: WJ: '14- dnf; ET: '15- 1, '17- 1; EI: '15- 6; Eur CC: '13- 2J, '16- 1 U23. Won POL 1500m 2015, 2017.
Progress at 1500m: 2012- 4:13.68, 2013- 4:12.05, 2014- 4:07.34, 2015- 4:04.26. 2016- 4:01.00, 2017- 4:03.35. pbs: 400m 56.07 '15, 800m 2:00.11 '15, 1000m 2:35.15 '16, 1M 4:25.34 '16, 3000m 8:45.29i '17, 8:59.44 '14.
Moved to Poland with her Polish mother at the age of 2.

Joanna FIODOROW b. 4 Mar 1989 Augustów 1.69m 89kg. OS AZS Poznan.
At HT: OG: '12- 7, '16- 9; WCh: '11-15: dnq 21/17, '17- 6; EC: '14- 3, '16- 10; WJ: '08- dnq 19; EU23: '09- 4, '11- 2; ET: '14- 2; WUG: '15- 2, '17- 3.
Progress at HT: 2005- 40.96, 2006- 50.18, 2007- 55.93, 2008- 61.22, 2009- 62.80, 2010- 64.66, 2011- 70.06, 2012- 74.18, 2013- 68.92, 2014- 74.39, 2015- 72.67, 2016- 72.98, 2017- 75.09. pbs: SP 12.87 '10, JT 35.56 '09.

Anna JAGACIAK-MICHALSKA (née Jagaciak) b. 10 Feb 1990 Zielona Góra 1.76m 68kg. OS AZS Poznan.
At (LJ)/TJ: OG: '16- 10; WCh: '11- dnq 28, '13- 9, '17- 6; EC: '10- 10/dnq 15, '12- (dnq 22), '14- dnq 15, '16- 4; WJ: '08- 7/dnq 14; WY: '07- (dnq 13); EU23: '11- 4/3; EJ: '09- 3/4; EI: '17- 4; WUG: '13- 2, 15- 2/3. Won POL LJ 2010, 2016-17; TJ 2013-14, 2016-17; FrancG LJ & TJ 2013.
Progress at TJ: 2007- 12.62, 2008- 13.43, 2009- 13.55, 2010- 13.93/14.16w, 2011- 14.25, 2012- 13.87/14.06w, 2013- 14.21, 2014- 14.20, 2015- 14.17, 2016- 14.33/14.40w, 2017- 14.29. pb LJ 6.74 '10.
Married Lukasz Michalski (PV 5.85 '11, 4 WCh & 1 WUG 2011) in July 2014.

Joanna JÓZWIK b. 30 Jan 1991 Walbrzych 1.68m 53kg. AZS-AWF Warszawa.
At 800m: OG: '16- 5; WCh: '15- 7, '17- sf; EC: '14- 3, '16- 6; WJ: '10- sf; EU23: '11- h, '13- 8; ET: '15- 2; EI: '15- 3. Polish champion 2014-15.
Progress at 800m: 2007- 2:12.90, 2008- 2:11.55, 2009- 2:07.31, 2010- 2:05.09, 2011- 2:03.15, 2012- 2:05.87, 2013- 2:02.39, 2014- 1:59.63, 2015- 1:58.35, 2016- 1:57.37, 2017- 1:59.29i, 2:00.77. pbs: 200m 24.16 '14, 300m 39.83 '11, 400m 53.08 '14, 600m 1:25.04 '15, 1000m 2:34.93 '16.

Malwina KOPRON b. 16 Nov 1994 Pulawy 1.69m 89kg. AZS UMCS Lublin.
At HT: OG: '16- dnq 15; WCh: '15- dnq 14, '17- 3; EC: '16- 6; WJ: '12- dnq nt; WY: '11- 2; EU23: '15- 3; EJ: '13- 4; WUG: '17- 1; ET: '17- 2.
Progress at HT: 2011- 57.03, 2012- 64.88, 2013- 66.11, 2014- 69.30, 2015- 71.27, 2016- 72.74, 2017- 76.85. pb JT 51.66 '12.

Kamila LICWINKO b. 22 Mar 1986 Bielsk Podlaski 1.83m 66kg. née Stepaniuk. KS Podlasie Bialystok.
At HJ: OG: '16- 9; WCh: '09-13-15-17- dnq 16/7=/4/3; EC: '14- 9=; EU23: '07- 4; EJ: '05- 7; WI: '14- 1=,'16- 3; EI: '09- 8, '15- 3; ET: '13-14-15-17: 2/3=/3/1; WUG: '13- 1. Won POL 2007-09, 2015-17.
Polish high jump records 2013 & 2014, three indoor 2015.
Progress at HJ: 1999- 1.46, 2000- 1.61, 2001- 1.66, 2002- 1.75, 2003- 1.75, 2004- 1.84, 2005- 1.86, 2006- 1.85i/1.84, 2007- 1.90, 2008- 1.91, 2009- 1.93, 2010- 1.92i/1.89, 2011- 1.88i, 2012- 1.89, 2013- 1.99, 2014- 2.00i/1.97, 2015- 2.02i/1.99, 2016- 1.99, 2017- 1.99. Married her trainer Michal Licwinko in 2013. Expecting a baby in 2018.

Anita WLODARCZYK b. 8 Aug 1985 Rawicz 1.76m 90kg. RKS Skra Warszawa. PE student.
At HT: OG: '08- 4, '12- 1, '16- 1; WCh: '09-11-13-15-17: 1/5/2/1/1; EC: '10-12-14-16: 3/1/1/1; EU23: '07- 9; CCp: '14- 1; ET: '09-13-15: 1/2/1. Won POL 2009, 2011-12, 2014-17; Franc G 2013, IAAF HT challenge 2013-17.
Six world hammer records 2009-16, six Polish records 2009-14.
Progress at HT: 2002- 33.83, 2003- 43.24, 2004- 54.74, 2005- 60.51, 2006- 65.53, 2007- 69.07, 2008- 72.80, 2009- 77.96, 2010- 78.30, 2011- 75.33, 2012- 77.60, 2013- 78.46, 2014- 79.58, 2015- 81.08, 2016- 82.98, 2017- 82.87 pbs: SP 13.25 '06, DT 52.26 '08, Wt 20.09i '14.
In 2015 she had the eight best throws of the year, including when she became first woman to throw hammer over 80m with 81.08 at Cetniewo on 1 Aug 2015, and two 80m throws (80.27 and 80.85) later that month at the World Champs. She had the top 12 performances in 2016 and the top 9 in 2017, won all her competitions in 2015 – 11, 2016- 12 and 2017- 13 to take her win streak to 43 from a last loss on 16 June 2014.

PORTUGAL

Governing body: Federação Portuguesa de Atletismo. Founded 1921.
National Championships first held in 1910 (men), 1937 (women). **2017 Champions**: **Men**: 100m: Diego Antunes 10.10w, 200m: David Lima 20.47w, 400m: Vitor Ricardo Santos 48.34, 800m: Miguel Moreira 1:55.37, 1500m: Emanuel Rolim 3:57.62, 5000m: Samuel Barata 14:13.68, 10000m: Bruno Albuquerque 29:06.13, Mar: Bruno Paixão 2:26:24, 3000mSt: André Pereira 9:18.84, 110mh: Helio Vaz 13.87w, 400mh: Diogo Mestre 53.01, HJ: Pedro Pinheiro 2.02, PV: Diogo Ferreira 5.40, LJ: Marcos Chuva 7.99w, TJ: Nelson Évora 16.78, SP: Tsanko Arnaudov 20.79, DT: Francisco Belo 62.01, HT: Dário Manso 68.69, JT: Mário Marques 64.65, Dec: Eduardo Valério 5869w, 10,000mW/20kW: João Vieira 41:26.60/1:23:46, 50kW: Amaro Teixeira 4:56:53. **Women**: 100m/200m: Lorène Bazolo 11.16w/ 23.35w, 400m: Cátia Azevedo 53.87, 800m: Salomé Afonso 2:12.75, 1500m: Carla Mendes 4:35.54, 5000m: Ana Mafalda Ferreira 16:51.77, 10000m: Carla Salomé Rocha 32:17.73, Mar: Doroteia Piexoto 2:40:02, 3000mSt: Joana Soares 10:24.10, 100mh: Lecabela Quaresma 13.49w, 400mh: Vera Barbosa 59.11, HJ: Anabela Neto 1.83, PV: Catia Pereira 4.20, LJ: Evelise Veiga 6.27w, TJ: Patricia Mamona 14.40w, SP: Jessica Inchude 15.59, DT: Irina Rodrigues 59.29, HT: Vânia Silva 60.30, JT: Silvia Cruz 47.85, Hep: Catarina Fernandes 4992, 10000mW/20kW: Ana Cabacinha 43:18.72/1:32:14, 35kW: Inês Henriques 2:50:09.

Nelson ÉVORA b. 20 Apr 1984 Abidjan, Côte d'Ivoire 1.81m 70kg. Sporting CP.
At (LJ/)TJ: OG: '04- dnq 40, '08- 1, '16- 6; WCh: '05-07-09-11-15-17: dnq 14/1/2/5/3/3; EC: '06- 6/4, '14- 6, '16- dnq 17; WJ: '02- dnq 18/6; EU23: '05- 3; EJ: '03- 1/1; WUG: '09- 1, '11- 1; WI: '06-08-16-18: 6/3/4/3; EI: '07-15-17: 5/1/1; ECp: '09- 2/1; Won WAF TJ 2008, POR LJ 2006-07, 2016; TJ 2003-04, 2006-07, 2009-11, 2013-17.
Six Portuguese triple jump records 2006-07, Cape Verde LJ & TJ records 2001-02.
Progress at TJ: 1999- 14.35, 2000- 14.93i, 2001- 16.15, 2002- 15.87, 2003- 16.43, 2004- 16.85i/16.04, 2005- 16.89, 2006- 17.23, 2007- 17.74, 2008- 17.67, 2009- 17.66/17.82w, 2010- 16.36, 2011- 17.35, 2013- 16.68, 2014- 16.97, 2015- 17.52, 2016- 17.03, 2017- 17.20i/17.19, 2018- 17.40i. pbs: HJ 2.07i '05, 1.98 '99; LJ 8.10 '07.
Portugal's first male world champion in 2007. He suffered a serious injury in right tibia (in same place where he had an operation in February 2010) in January 2012 and missed season. Father from Cape Verde, mother from Côte d'Ivoire, relocating to Portugal when he was five. Switched nationality in 2002. Sister Dorothé (b. 28 May 1991) 400m pb 54.43 '14.

Pedro Pablo PICHARDO b. 30 Jun 1993 Santiago de Cuba 1.85m 71kg. SL Benfica.
At TJ: WCh: '13- 2, '15- 2; WJ: '12- 1; PAm: '15- 1; WI: '14- 3. Won CAC-J 2012, CUB 2014-15.
Three CAC triple jump records 2015.
Progress at TJ: 2009- 14.55, 2010- 15.35/15.45w, 2011- 16.09, 2012- 16.79, 2013- 17.69, 2014- 17.76, 2015- 18.08, 2017- 17.60., 2018- 17.19i pb LJ 7.81 '15.
Switched from Cuba to Portugal, effective from December 2017. Injured in 2016. Father Jorge was a 2.10 high jumper.

Women

Jéssica AUGUSTO b. 8 Nov 1981 Paris, France 1.65m 46kg. Sporting CP.
At Mar: OG: '12- 6, '16- dnf; EC: '14- 3. At HMar: EC: '16- 3; At 3000mSt: OG: '08- h (h 5000); WCh: '09- 10. At 5000m/(10000m): WCh: '05- h, '07- 14, '11- (10); EC: '10- 3/2; EU23: '03- dnf; WUG: '07- 1; CCp: '10- 7; ECp: '14- (2). At 3000m (1500m): WJ: '00- 8; EU23: '01- (10); EJ: '99- 6 (12); WI: '08- 8, '10- 7; EI: '09- 9. World CC: '07- 12, '10- 21; Eur CC: '98-99-00-02-04-05-06-07-08-09-10: 12J/8J/1J/16/18/30/9/11/2/4/1. Won POR 1500m 2007, 2011; 5000m 2006, 10000m 2014; IbAm 3000m 2004, 2006, 2010.
Two Portuguese 3000m steeplechase records 2008-10, European indoor 2M best 2010.
Progress at 5000m, 10000m, Mar, 3000mSt: 2003- 15:51.63, 2004- 15:15.76, 2005- 15:20.45, 2006- 15:37.55, 2007- 14:56.39, 2008- 15:19.67, 9:22.50; 2009- 9:25.25, 2010- 14:37.07, 31:19.15, 9:18.54; 2011- 15:19.60, 32:06.68, 2:24:33; 2012- 2:24:59, 2013- 15:38.73, 2:29:11; 2014- 31:55.56, 2:24:25; 2016- 15:52.53, 32:30.71, 2:28:53; 2017- 2:25:30. pbs: 800m 2:07.97i '02, 1500m 4:07.89i/ 4:08.32 '10, 1M 4:32.58i '09, 4:42.15 '99, 2000m 5:45.6i '09, 3000m 8:41.53 '07, 2M 9:19.39i '10, 9:22.89 '07; road 15k 48:40 '08, 10M 53:15 '08, HMar 69:08 '09, 30k 1:41:37 '11.
Won Great North Run 2009, Hamburg Marathon 2017. Daughter Leonor born 15 Jun 2015 (father is football goalkeeper Eduardo Carvalho).

Ana CABECINHA b. 29 Apr 1984 Beja 1.68m 52kg. CO Pechão.
At 20kW: OG: '08- 8, '12- 8, '16- 6; WCh: '11-13-15-17: 6/8/4/6; EC: '10- 7, '14- 6; EU23: '05- 4; WCp '08-10-12-14-16: 11/8/8/8/6; ECp: '13-15-17: 5/9/2. At 5000mW: WY: '01- 10. At 10000mW: WJ: '02- 12; EJ: '03- 3; won IbAm 2006, 2010; 2nd RWC 2012; POR 10000mW 2005, 2008, 2010, 2012, 2014-17; 20kW 2012-15, 2017.
POR records 10,000m and 20km walk 2008.
Progress at 20kW: 2004- 1:37:39, 2005- 1:34:13, 2006- 1:31:02, 2007- 1:32:46, 2008- 1:27:46, 2009- 1:33:05, 2010- 1:31:14, 2011- 1:31:08, 2012- 1:28:03, 2013- 1:29:17, 2014- 1:27:49, 2015- 1:28:28, 2016- 1:28:40, 2017- 1:28:57. pbs: 3000mW 12:17.50 '14, 5000mW 21:22.23 '15, 21:21R '12; 10000mW 43:08.17 '08; running 1500m 4:31.73 '07, 3000m 9:44.81i '17, 9:46.08 '13; 5000m 17:57.34 '12.

Inês HENRIQUES b 1 May 1980 Santarém 1.56m 48kg. CN Rio Maior.
At 50kW: WCh: '17- 1. At 20kW: OG: '04-12-16: 25/14/12; WCh: '01-05-07-09-11-13-15: dq/27/7/ 10/9/11/23; EC: '02-06-10-14: 15/12/8/13; EU23: '01- 10; WCp: '06-10-12-16: 13/3/9/8; ECp: '07- 7, '13- 8; Won POR 10000mW 2006, 2009, 2011, 2013; 20kW 2009, 2011, 2016, 35kW 2017. At 5000mW: EJ: '99- 12.
Two world records 50k walk 2017. POR record 35k walk 2018.
Progress at 20kW, 50kW: 2000- 1:41:09, 2001- 1:34:49, 2002- 1:34:46.5t, 2003- 1:36:03, 2004- 1:31:23.7t, 2005- 1:33:24, 2006- 1:30:28, 2007- 1:30:24, 2008- 1:31:06, 2009- 1:30:34, 2010- 1:29:36, 2011- 1:30:29, 2012- 1:29:54, 2013- 1:29:30, 2014- 1:29:33, 2015- 1:29:52, 2016- 1:29:00, 2017- 1:30:44, 4:05:56. pbs: 3000mW 12:25.36i '13, 12:38.75 '07; 5000mW 21:32.08 '14, 10000mW 43:22.05 '08, 43:09R '10; 35kW 2:45:51 '18.
Inaugural women's world record holder and world champion at 50k walk.

Patrícia MAMONA b. 21 Nov 1988 Lisbon 1.68m 53kg. Sporting CP. Was at Clemson University, USA.
At TJ: OG: '12- dnq 13, '16- 6; WCh: '11-15: dnq 27/16, '17- 9; EC: '10-12-14-16: 8/2/dnq 13;/1 WJ: '06- 4; WY: '05- 7; EU23: '09- 5; EJ: '07- dnq 15; WI: '14- 4; EI: '13-15-17: 8/5/2; WUG: '11- 2. POR champion 2008-17, NCAA 2010-11.
Nine Portuguese triple jump records 2009-16.
Progress at TJ: 2004- 12.71, 2005- 12.87, 2006- 13.37/13.38w, 2007- 13.24, 2008- 13.51, 2009- 13.83, 2010- 14.12, 2011- 14.42, 2012- 14.52, 2013- 14.02/14.07w, 2014- 14.36/14.49w, 2015- 14.32i/ 14.19, 2016- 14.65, 2017- 14.42. pbs: 200m 24.42 '10, 800m 2:19.70i '09, 60mh 8.41i '09, 100mh 13.53/13.49w '10, HJ 1.69 '04; LJ 6.28i '17, 6.16 '05; Pen 4081i '09, Hep 5293 '11.

Sara MOREIRA b. 17 Oct 1985 Santo Tirso 1.68m 51kg. Sporting CP.
At (5000m)/3000mSt: OG: '08- h; WCh: '07- 13, '09- 10/h, '11- dq; EC: '10- (2), '12- (2), '14- (6); EU23: '07- 3; WUG: '07- 4, '09- 1/1, '11- (2); ET: '11- 2. At 3000m: WI: '10- 5; EI: '09- 2, '13- 1; CCp: '10- 6. At 1500m: EI: '11- 7. At 10000m: OG: '12- 14; WCh: '15- 12; EC: '10/16- dnf, '14- 5; ECp: '10-11-12-14-17: 3/1/1/3/1. At HMar: EC: '16- 1. At Mar: OG: 16- dnf. Eur CC: '09-10-12: 10/9/12. Won IbAm 5000m 2016, POR 1500m 2010, 2012; 5000m 2014-15, 10000m 2015, 3000mSt 2007-09, 2011. POR 3000mSt record 2008.
Progress at 5000m, 10000m, Mar, 3000mSt: 2005- 10:27.72, 2007- 9:42.47, 2008- 9:34.30; 2009- 14:58.11, 9:28.64; 2010- 14:54.71, 31:26.55; 2011- 15:11.97, 31:39.11, 9:35.11; 2012- 15:08.33, 31:16.44; 2014- 15:20.01, 32:01.42, 2:26:00; 2015- 15:50.09,

31:12.93, 2:24:49; 2016- 15:34.93, 2:25:53; 2017- 15:39.95, 32:03.57. pbs: 1500m 4:07.11 '10, 3000m 8:42.69 '10, 2M 9:47.99i '10, 15kRd 48:48 '13, HMar 69:18 '15.
Third in New York on marathon debut 2014, 2nd Prague 2015. 6-months drugs ban 2011-12. Married to Pedro Ribeiro (POR 3000mSt champion 2010, pb 8:32.20 '06). Son Guillermo born 1 Nov 2013.

PUERTO RICO

Governing body: Federación de Atletismo Amateur de Puerto Rico. Founded 1947.
National Champions 2017: Men: 100m: Octavio Acevedo 10.60, 200m: Pedro Cruz 21.45, 400m: Josue Cuadrado 48.35, 800m: Félix Soto 1:54.82, 1500m: Nicholas Rivera 3:57.58, 5000m: Diego Rosario 15:44.90, 3000mSt: Luis Medina 9:14.27, 110mh: Ricardo Torres 13.92, 400mh: Ramfis Vega 52.52, HJ: Abiam Salas 1.95, PV: Kevin Sanchez 4.80, LJ: Michael Williams 7.43, TJ: Omahri Sturdinat 13.94, SP: Carlos Martinez 15.50, DT: Edilberto González 51.46, HT: Jerome Vega 66.62, JT: Kevin Ortiz 63.55, Dec: José Hernandez 5629. **Women**: 100m: Genoiska Cancel 11.97, 200m: Pariis Garcia 24.77, 400m: Grace Claxton 54.03, 800m: Priscila Morales 2:11.79, 1500m: Angelín Figueroa 4:29.25, 5000m: Beverly Ramos 16:04.58, 3000mSt: Loumarie Figuer 12:07.74, 100mh: Ericka Serrano 14.63, 400mh: Kathiria Benitez 66.11, HJ: Reina Hernández 1.55, PV: Yaritza Diaz 3.75, LJ: Jessica Acevedo 5.90w, TJ: Julissa Morales 10.34w, SP/DT: Taisha Ortiz 13.67/42.02, HT: Keyshia Luna 56.72, JT: Shakira Rosario 33.93.

Javier CULSON b. 25 Jul 1984 Ponce 1.98m 79kg.
At 400mh: OG: '08- sf, '12- 3, '16- dq; WCh: '07-09-11-13-15-17: sf/2/2/6/sf/h; PAm: '07- 6, '15- 2; CAG: '06- 5, '10- 2; PAm-J: '03- 3; WUG: '07- 3; CCp: '10- 2, '14- 3/3R; won DL 2012-13, IbAm 2006, CAC 2009, NACAC 2015.
Seven Puerto Rican 400mh records 2007-10.
Progress at 400mh: 2002- 54.47, 2003- 51.10, 2004- 50.77, 2005- 50.62, 2006- 49.48, 2007- 49.07, 2008- 48.87, 2009- 48.09, 2010- 47.72. 2011- 48.32, 2012- 47.78, 2013- 48.14, 2014- 48.03, 2015- 48.48, 2016- 48.46, 2017- 48.76. pbs: 200m 21.64w '07, 400m 45.99 '12, 600m 1:17.86 '18, 800m 1:49.83 '14, 110mh 13.84 '07.

QATAR

Governing body: Qatar Association of Athletics Federation. Founded 1963.

Mutaz Essa BARSHIM b. 24 Jun 1991 Doha 1.92m 70kg. Team Aspire.
At HJ: OG: '12- 3=, '16- 2; WCh: '11-13-15-17: 7/2/4/1; WJ: '10- 1; AsiG: '10- 1, '14- 1; AsiC: '11- 1, '15- 3; WI: '12-14-16-18: 9=/1/4/2; CCp: '14- 3; won DL 2014-15, 2017; Asian indoors 2010, 2012, 2014, 2016, 2018; Asi-J 2010, W.Mil G 2011, Arab 2011, 2013, 2015; Gulf 2013.
Five Asian high jump records 2012-14 and indoors (3) 2013-15, 14 Qatar records 2010-13.
Progress at HJ: 2008- 2.07, 2009- 2.14, 2010- 2.31, 2011- 2.35, 2012- 2.39, 2013- 2.40, 2014- 2.43, 2015- 2.41, 2016- 2.40, 2017- 2.40, 2018- 2.38i.
IAAF Male Athlete of the Year 2017. His 2.43 at Brussels in 2014 was the world's best since 1993, second only to Javier Sotomayor. Qatari father (who was a race walker), Sudanese mother. Younger brothers Muamer Aissa Barshim (b. 3 Jan 1994) has HJ pb 2.28 '14 and was 3rd 2014 Asian Games, and Hamdi Mahamat Alamine 2.26 '17.

Ashraf Amjad EL-SEIFY (Al-Saifi) b. 20 Feb 1995 Egypt 1.83m 100kg.
At HT: OG: '16- 6; WCh: '13- dnq 25, '15- 9, '17- dnq 23; WJ: '12- 1, '14- 1. Won Asi-J 2014.
Records: world youth 5kg 85.26 '11, world junior 6kg 85.57 '12, Asian junior 7.36k 2013, three Qatar 2013-16.
Progress at HT: 2013- 76.37, 2014- 71.81, 2015- 78.04, 2016- 78.19, 2017- 76.14. Former Egyptian.

Abdelilah HAROUN b. 1 Jan 1997 Sudan 1.78m 73kg.
At 400m: OG: '16- sf; WCh: '17- 3; AsiC: '15- 1/1R; WJ: '16- 1; WI: '16- 2. Won Asian indoor Champs 2016, 2018, Games 2017; Arab 2015.
Asian 400m records indoors and out 2015. World best 500m indoors 2016.
Progress at 400m: 2014- 45.74, 2015- 44.27, 2016- 44.81, 2017- 44.48. Pb 500m 59.83i '16.
Qatar citizen from 2 Feb 2015, having lived there from 2013.

Ahmed Bader MAGOUR b. 3 Mar 1996 Egypt 1.90m 90kg.
At JT: OG: '16- dnq 30; WCh: '17- dnq 10; AsiC: '17- 2. Gulf champion & Islamic Sol. 2017.
Four Qatar javelin records 2016-17.
Progress at JT: 2014-, 2015- 77.88, 2016- 84.74, 2017- 82.23. Formerly Egypt, eligible to compate for Qatar from 23 Apr 2016.

Femi Seun **OGUNODE** b. 15 May 1991 Nigeria 1.83m 79kg.
At (100m)/200m: OG: '16- h/h; WCh: '11- sf (8 400m), '15- sf/7; AsiG: '10- 1 (1 400m), 14- 1/1; AsiC: '11- 1, '15- 1/1, '17- 2/3; CCp: '14- 3/3; Won Arab 100m 2011, 100m/200m 2015; W.Asian 100m/200m 2010, W.MilG 100m/200m 2011. At 60m: WI: '14- 3.
Asian records 100m (3) 2014-16, 200m 2015, four Qatar 200m 2011-15.
Progress at 100m, 200m: 2010- 10.25, 20.43; 2011- 10.07, 20.30; 2014- 9.93, 20.06; 2015- 9.91, 19.97; 2016- 9.91, 20.10; 2017- 10.13, 20.77. pbs: 60m 6.51Ai/6.52i '14, 400m 45.12 '10.
Two-year drugs ban 2012-14. Switched allegiance from Nigeria to Qatar from 31 Oct 2009. Younger brother **Tosin** suddenly emerged with 6.50i for 60m in 2014 and has pb 100m 10.18 '16, 10.17w '17.

Abderrahmane SAMBA b. 5 Sep 1995 1.m kg.
At 400mh: WCh: '17- 7.
Progress at 400mh: 2017- 48.31A/48.44. Pbs: 200m 21.17, '16. 20.94w'15; 400m 46.04A/46.11 '16.
Tranferred from Mauritania to Qatar, when he has lived since 6 May 2015, citizen from 1 Oct 2015, cleared to compete from 6 May 2016.

ROMANIA

Governing body: Federatia Romana de Atletism. Founded 1912.

National Championships first held in 1914 (men), 1925 (women). **2017 Champions**: **Men**: 100m: Petre Rezmives 10.44, 200m: Ionut Neagoe 20.88, 400m/400mh: Zeno Moraru 46.76/52.38, 800m: Cosmin Trofin 1:49.16, 1500m: Nicolae Coman 3:49.20, 5000m/10000m/HMar: Nicolae Soare 14:22.02/30:26.74/66:02, Mar: Sorin Meneran 2:31:58, 3000mSt: Catalin Atanasoaei 8:55.86, 110mh: Cosmin Dumitrache 14.34, HJ: Dan Lazarica 2.24, PV: Andrei Deliu 5.00, LJ: Christian Staicu 7.85, TJ: Marian Oprea 16.37, SP: Andrei Gag 20.52, DT: Alin Firfirica 59.58, HT: Mihaita Micu 62.64, JT: Alexandru Novac 77.90, Dec: Razvan Roman 6982, 20kW: Marius Cocioran 1:27:46, 20000mW/50kW: Florin Stirbu 1:27:33.5/4:19:40. **Women**: 100m: Andreea Grecu 11.75, 200m/400m: Bianca Razor 23.43/51.62, 800m: Cloaudia Bobocea 2:02.05, 1500m: Florina Pierdevara 4:44.38, 5000m/10000m: Roxana Bârcâ 16:49.24/35:20.01, HMar: Ancuta Bobocel 73:37, Mar: Ana Rodean 2:57:42, 3000mSt: Adela Baltoi 10:19.22, 100mh: Anamaria Nesteriuc 13.25, 400mh: Sanda Belgyan 58.62, HJ: Ligia Damaris Bara 1.83, PV: Ionela Luca 4.05, LJ: Alina Rotaru 6.74, TJ: Carmen Toma 13.61, SP: Lenuta Burueana 14.98, DT: Ioana Toganasu 47.79, HT: Bianca Ghelber-Perie 69.44, JT: Nicoleta Anghelescu 50.69, Hep: Anamaria Ionita 5134, 20kW: Ana Rodean 1:38:44, 10000mW/20000mW: Andreea Arsine 46:45.9/ 1:35:43.52.

Andrei GAG b. 27 Apr 1991 Bocsig 1.95m 118kg. CSM Arad, University of Suceava.
At SP: OG: '16- dnq 13; WCh: '15- dnq 17, '17- 12; EC: '14-16: dnq 20/16, WUG: '15- 2, '17- 3; WI: '16- 2; At DT: WJ: '08- dnq 30, '10- 2; EU23: '11/13- dnq 19/11; EJ: '09- 10. Won ROU SP 2014-17, DT 2014; Balkan SP 2015.
Romanian shot records 2015 & 2016.
Progress at SP: 2008- 14.71i, 2009- 15.91, 2010- 16.00i/15.92, 2011- 16.95, 2012- 17.73, 2013- 18.41, 2014- 20.17i/19.64, 2015- 20.96, 2016- 21.06, 2017- 20.61. pb DT 61.27 '14.

Women

Elena Andreea **PANTUROIU** b. 24 Feb 1995 Ribeira 1.70m 57kg. CS Onesti.
At TJ: OG: '16- dnq 16; WCh: '15/17- dnq 18/14; EC: 16- dnq 16; WJ: '14- 5; WY: '11- dnq 24; E23: '15- 2, '17- 1; EJ: '13- 2; WI: '16- 5, 18- 4. Romanian champion 2016.
Progress at TJ: 2011- 12.79, 2012- 12.94i/12.67/ 13.08w, 2013- 13.26, 2014- 13.93i/13.81/14.20w, 2015- 14.13, 2016- 14.33, 2017- 14.43, 2018- 14.33i. pbs: 200m 25.94 '12, 800m 2:17.41 '14, 60mh 8.51i '16, 100mh 14.65 '13, HJ 1.80i '17, 1.71 '13; LJ 6.44i/6.14 '15, SP 11.61i '17; JT 31.09 '12, Pen 4309i '17, Hep 5102 '13.

Alina ROTARU b. 5 Jun 1993 Bucharest 1.75m 54kg. CSA Steaua Bucharest.
At LJ: OG: '16- dnq 18; WCh: '15- dnq 15, '17- 12; EC: '12- dnq 20, '14- 7; WJ: '10- dnq 19, '12- 5; WY: '09- 2 (4 HJ); Yth OG: '10- 2; EU23: '13- 5, '15- 3; EJ: '11- 2; WI: '18- 9; EI: '15- 4. ROU champion 2014-17.
Progress at LJ: 2008- 6.08i/5.99, 2009- 6.26, 2010- 6.40, 2011- 6.46, 2012- 6.57/6.58w, 2013- 6.63, 2014- 6.74, 2015- 6.75, 2016- 6.67, 2017- 6.78. pbs: 60m 7.63i '15, 60mh 8.86i '14, HJ 1.85i '12, 1.82 '09; TJ 13.24i/13.21 '12, Pen 4111i '12.

RUSSIA

Governing body: All-Russia Athletic Federation. Founded 1911.

National Championships first held 1908, USSR women from 1922. **2017 Champions**: **Men**: 100m: Denis Ogarkov 10.45, 200m: Aleksandr Yefimov 21.03, 400m: Pavel Ivashko 46.03, 800m: Konstantin Tolokonnikov 1:47.75, 1500m/ 5000m: Vladimir Nikitin 3:37.14/13:29.40, 100000m: Anatoliy Rybakov 28:01.93, HMar: Rinas Akhmadiyev 63:25, Mar: Stepan Kiselev 2:14:36, 3000mSt: Maksim Yakushev 8:19.19, 110mh: Konstantin Shabanov 13.79, 400mh: Timofey Chalyy 49.55, HJ: Danil Lysenko 2.32, PV: Timur Morgunov 5.65, LJ/TJ: Artyom Primak 8.22/17.17, SP: Aleksandr Lesnoy 21.31, DT: Aleksey Khudyakov 63.13, HT: Valeriy Pronkin 79.32, JT: Dmitriy Tarabin 80.40, Dec: Ilya Shkurenyov 8601, 20kW: Sergey Bakulin 1:20:38, 50kW: Dementiy Cheparev 3:43:05. **Women**: 100m: Kristina Sivkova 11.43, 200m: Anastasiya Polishchuk 23.36; 400m: Kseniya Aksyonova 51.62; 800m: Aleksandra Gulyayeva 1:58.34, 1500m: Yelena Korobkina 4:04.90, 5000m: Yekaterina Ishova 15:41.59, 10000m: Yelena Sedova 32:14.43, HMar: Marina Kovalyova 75:13, Mar: Natalya Starkova 2:30:45, 3000mSt: Yekaterina Sokolenko 9:37.53, 100mh: Anastasiya Nikolayeva 13.05, 400mh: Valeriya Khramova 55.75, HJ: Mariya Lasitskene 1.96, PV: Angelina Krasnova 4.60, LJ: Yelena Sokolova 6.85, TJ: Darya Nidbaykina 14.21, SP: Anna Avdeyeva 18.05, DT: Yelena Panova 60.59; HT: Yelizaveta Tsareva 70.30, JT: Vera Rebrik 61.40, Hep: Mariya Gromysheva 5888, 20kW: Yelena Lashmanova 1:27:43.

Lyukman ADAMS b. 24 Sep 1988 St. Petersburg 1.94m 87kg.
At TJ: OG: '12- 9; WCh: '15- 5; EC: '10- 6, '14- 2;

EJ: '07- 1; CCp: '14- 6; WI: '12- 3, '14- 1. Russian champion 2012, 2015-16.
Progress at TJ: 2005- 15.97, 2006- 15.16, 2007- 16.75, 2008- 16.86i/16.78, 2009- 16.22i/16.20, 2010- 17.17/17.21w, 2011- 17.32i/15.60, 2012- 17.53, 2013- 16.82, 2014- 17.37i/17.29, 2015- 17.34, 2016- 17.15, 2017- 17.20i/16.82. pb LJ 8.01 '15.
Married Yevgeniya Polyakova (60m 7.09 '08, 1 EI '09; 100m 11.09 '07; 4x100m 1 OG '08) on 5 Apr 2014.

Sergey BAKULIN b. 13 Nov 1986 Insar, Mordoviya. 1.69m 58kg. Mordoviya VS.
At 20kW: EC: '06- 5; EU23: '07- 3; WCp: '06- 6, '10- 7; WUG: '09- 1. At 50kW: OG: '12- dq6; WCh: '11- dq1; EC: '10- 3; WCp: '12-dq 4; ECp: '09- 4; Russian champion 2011, 2017.
Progress at 20kW, 50kW: 2006- 1:19:54, 2007- 1:19:14, 2008- 1:18:18, 3:52:38; 2010- 1:24:05, 3:43:26; dq: 2011- 3:38:46dq, 2012- 3:38:55dq, 2017- 1:18:51. pbs: 5000mW 18:26.82i '12, 10kW: 39:03 '06, 30kW: 2:05:19dq '13, 35kW 2:24:25 '09.
3 year 2 month ban announced in January 2015 for biological passport anomaly and with results annulled 25 Feb 2011 to 24 Dec 2012 lost 2011 World title and 2012 Olympic 5th place. Back competing in 2017.

Aleksey DMITRIK b. 12 Apr 1984 Slantsy. Leningrad reg, 1.91m 69kg. St Petersburg YR.
At HJ: WCh: '11- 2, '13- dnq 25=; EC: '10- 7, '14- dnq 23; WJ: '02- 14; WY: '01- 1; EJ: '03- 2; EU23: '05- 6; EI: '09- 2=, '13- 2; ECp: '05- 1, '11- 2. Russian champion 2011.
Progress at HJ: 2000- 2.08, 2001- 2.23, 2002- 2.26, 2003- 2.28, 2004- 2.30, 2005- 2.34i/2.30, 2006- 2.28, 2007- 2.30, 2008- 2.33i/2.27, 2009- 2.33, 2010- 2.32i/2.31, 2011- 2.36, 2012- 2.35i/2.33, 2013- 2.36i/2.30, 2014- 2.40i/2.30, 2015- 2.32, 2016- 2.28i/2.26, 2017- 2.25i/2.23.
Mother Yelana was a 1.75m high jumper.

Aleksandr LESNOY b. 28 Jul 1988 Krasnodar 1.94m 116kg.
At SP: WCh: '13-15-17: dnq 21/16/26; EC: '14- 10; WUG: '13- 1; WI: '14- 8; ET: '13-14: 3/3. RUS champion 2014, 2017.
Progress at SP: 2008- 16.46, 2009- 16.80, 2010- 19.09, 2011- 19.60, 2012- 20.05, 2013- 20.60, 2014- 21.40, 2015- 20.70i/20.55, 2016- 21.03, 2017- 21.36. pb DT 58.80 '12.

Sergey LITVINOV b. 27 Jan 1986 Rostov-on-Don 1.85m 110kg.
At HT: WCh: '09-11-13-15-17: 5/dnq 15/11/5/dnq 17; EC: '14- 3; WJ: '04- 9; EU23: '07- 11; EJ: '05- 9; WUG: '13- 3; ET: '14- 1. German champion 2009, Russian 2013, 2015-16.
Progress at HT: 2004- 60.00, 2005- 73.98, 2006- 66.46, 2007- 74.80, 2008- 75.35, 2009- 77.88, 2010- 78.98, 2011- 78.90, 2012- 80.98, 2013- 80.89, 2014- 79.35, 2015- 77.24, 2016- 77.67, 2017- 77.32.
Switched from Belarus to Germany 15 Jul 2008 and from 1 Jan 2011 to Russia. His father Sergey Litvinov (USSR) set three world records at hammer 1980-3 with a pb of 86.04 '86; he was Olympic champion 1988 (2nd 1980) and World champion 1983 and 1987. His mother was born in Germany.

Danil LYSENKO b. 9 Oct 1986 1.92m 73kg.
At HJ: WCh: '17- 2; WJ: '14- 6; EJ: '15- 5; YOG: '14- 1; WI: '18- 1. RUS champion 2017.
European junior indoor high jump record 2016.
Progress at HJ: 2013- 2.10, 2014- 2.24, 2015- 2.24i/2.22, 2016- 2.31i/2.30, 2017- 2.38, 2018- 2.37i.

Aleksandr MENKOV b. 7 Dec 1990 Minusinsk, Krasnoyarsk reg. 1.78m 74kg. Krasnoyarsk VS. Krasnoyarsk State University.
At LJ: OG: '12- 11; WCh: '09-11-13-15-17: dnq 32/6/1/6/4; EC: '14- dnq 13; WI: '12- 3, '14- 5; EU23: '11- 1; EJ: '09- 1; EI: '13- 1; WUG: '13- 2; ET: '11-13-15: 1/1/1. Won DL 2012-13, Russian 2012. Two Russian records 2013.
Progress at LJ: 2008- 6.98, 2009- 8.16, 2010- 8.10, 2011- 8.28, 2012- 8.29, 2013- 8.56, 2014- 8.30i/8.02, 2015- 8.27, 2016- 7.91, 2017- 8.32. pbs: HJ 2.15 '10, TJ 15.20 '09.

Timur MORGUNOV b. 12 Oct 1996 1.88m 77kg.
At PV: EJ: '15- 5. Russian champion 2017.
Progress at PV: 2014- 5.20, 2015- 5.50, 2016- 5.80i/5.55, 2017- 5.80, 2018- 5.85i. pbs: HJ 1.83 '17, LJ 7.25 '17, JT 51.68 '17. Dec 6856 '17.

Denis NIZHEGORODOV b. 26 Jul 1980 Saransk 1.80m 61kg. Saransk VS.
At 50kW: OG: '04- 2, '08- 3; WCh: '03-07-09-11: 5/4/dnf/1; EC: '06- dq; WCp: '06- 1, '08- 1; ECp: '09- 1, '11- 1; Russian champion 2003-04, 2007, 2016. At 20kW: EU23: '01- 5; WUG: '01- 4; ECp: '00- 17, '01- 7.
World record 50km walk 2008, best (no drugs test) 2004.
Progress at 20kW, 50kW: 2000- 1:21:47, 2001- 1:18:20; 2003- 1:23:23, 3:38:23; 2004- 3:35:29, 2005- dnf, 2006- 1:22:45, 3:38:02; 2007- 3:40:53, 2008- 3:34:14, 2009- 3:42:47, 2011- 3:42:45, 2016- 3:44:47, 2017- 3:53:25. pbs: 5000mW 18:58.81i '12, 30kW 2:05:08 '06, 35kW 2:24:50 '06.

Valeriy PRONKIN b. 15 Jun 1994 1.95m 115kg.
At HT: WCh: '17- 2; WJ: '12- 8; WY: 11- dnq 20 (10 DT); EU23: '15- 2; EJ: '13- 1. Won RUS 2017.
Progress at HT: 2012- 64.78, 2013- 73.50, 2014- 71.34, 2015- 76.80, 2016- 75.39, 2017- 79.32.

Sergey SHIROBOKOV b. 16 Feb 1999.
At 20kW: WCh: '17-2; ECp: '17- 12; At 10000mW: WY: '15-1; EJ: '17- 1.
Oceania 5000m walk record 2016.
Progress at 20kW: 2016- 1:22:31, 2017- 1:18:26, 2018- 1:18:53. pbs: 10000mW 40:58.0 '16, 39:50R '17.

Ilya SHKURENYOV b. 11 Jan 1991 Linevo, Volgograd reg. 1.91m 82kg. Volgograd Dyn.
At Dec: OG: '12- 16; WCh: '13- 8, '15- 4, '17- dnf;

EC: '12- 3, '14- 3; WJ: '10- 2; EU23: '11- 5, '13- 2; ECp: '15- 1. Russian champion 2013, 2016-17. At Hep: WI: '12- 4; EI: '13- 5, '15- 1.
Progress at Dec: 2011- 7894, 2012- 8219, 2013- 8370, 2014- 8498, 2015- 8538, 2016- 8292, 2017- 8601. pbs: 60m 6.98i '15, 100m 10.89 '17, 400m 47.88 '15, 1000m 2:41.65i '13, 1500m 4:24.98 '15, 60mh 7.86i '15, 110mh 13.95 '17, HJ 2.12 '17, PV 5.40 '13, LJ 7.78 '16, SP 14.84i '11, 14.24 '15; DT 46.04 '14, JT 63.58 '14, Hep 6353i '15.
Won IAAF Challenge 2015.

Sergey SHUBENKOV b. 4 Oct 1990 Barnaul, Altay Kray 1.90m 75kg. Tyumen State University.
At 110mh: OG: '12- sf; WCh: '11-13-15-17: h/3/1/2; EC: '12- 1, '14- 1; EU23: '11- 1; EJ: '09- 2, WUG: '13- 3; CCp: '14- 1; ET: '13-14-15: 1/1. Won DL 2017, WMilG 2015, Russian 2013, 20-16. At 60mh: EI: '13- 1.
Six Russian 110mh records 2012-15.
Progress at 110mh: 2010- 13.54, 2011- 13.46, 2012- 13.09, 2013- 13.16/13.10w, 2014- 13.13, 2015- 12.98, 2016- 13.20, 2017- 13.01. pb 60mh 7.49i '13.
Mother Natalya Shubenkova had heptathlon pb 6859 '04; 4th 1988 OG and 3rd 1986 EC.

Aleksey SOKIRSKIY b. 16 Mar 1985 Gorlivka, Ukraine 1.85m 108kg. Krim Sakhi.
At HT: OG: '12- 4; WCh: '09-11: dnq 22/17, '17- 5; EC: '10- 6, '12- nt; WJ: '04- 8, EU23: '07- 6; WUG: '09- 3; ET: '11- 3. UKR champion 2010-11.
Progress at HT: 2005- 70.23, 2006- 71.95, 2007- 73.44, 2008- 75.54, 2009- 76.50, 2010- 76.62, 2011- 78.33, 2012- 78.91, 2013- 77.38, 2014- 77.86, 2015- 75.29, 2016- 77.78, 2017- 77.50.
Switched from Ukraine to Russia 2015.

Dmitriy SOROKIN b. 27 Sep 1992 Khabarovsk 1.76m 73kg. Siberian Sate University of Physical Culture. Omsk.
At TJ: WCh: '15- 7; WY: 09- dnq 13; WUG: '15- 1; EI: '15- 6. Won WMilG 2015.
Progress at TJ: 2009- 15.62, 2010- 16.28/16.41w, 2011- 16.38dq, 2013- 15.30, 2014- 16.96, 2015- 17.29, 2016- 17.05i/16.49, 2017- 16.95. pb LJ 7.94i '16, 7.55 '10. 2-year drugs ban 2011-13.

Dmitriy TARABIN b. 29 Oct 1991 Berlin, Germany 1.76m 85kg. Student at Russian State University of Physical Education, Moscow
At JT: WCh: '11- 10, '13- 3, '15- dnq 25; EC: '14- 5; WJ: '10- 3; WY: '07- dnq 23; EU23: '11- 3; EJ: '09- dnq 13; WUG: '13- 1; ET: '13- 1, '14- 2. Won RUS 2013, 2015-17.
Progress at JT: 2007- 55.18, 2008- 67.39, 2009- 69.63, 2010- 77.65, 2011- 85.10, 2012- 82.75, 2013- 88.84, 2014- 85.92, 2015- 84.70, 2016- 81.56, 2017- 80.70.
Switched from Moldova to Russia 9 June 2010. Married Mariya Abakumova on 12 Oct 2012.

Daniyil TSYPLAKOV b. 29 Jul 1992 Khabarovsk reg. 1.78m 70kg. Khabarovskiy.
At HJ: WCh: '15- 5; EC: '14- 5; WY: '09- 3; EU23: '13- 2; EJ: '11- 4; ET: '15- 1; WUG: '15- 1; WI: '14- 5; EI: '15- 1. RUS champion 2014-15.
Progress at HJ: 2008- 2.11, 2009- 2.21, 2010- 2.21, 2011- 2.26, 2012- 2.31, 2013- 2.30, 2014- 2.34i/2.33, 2015- 2.33, 2016- 2.30i/2.28.

Ivan UKHOV b. 29 Mar 1986 Chelyabinsk 1.92m 83kg. Sverdlovsk TU.
At HJ: OG: '12- 1; WCh: '09-11-13-15: 10/5=/4/ dnq 24; EC: '06-10-14: 12=/2/3; WJ: '04- dnq 13; EJ: '05- 1; CCp: '14- 2; WUG: '05- 4; WI: '10-12-14: 1/3/2; EI: '09- 1, '11- 1. Won DL 2010, Russian 2009, 2012-13, 2016.
Russian high jump record 2014 (& 2 indoors, inc. one European).
Progress at HJ: 2004- 2.15, 2005- 2.30, 2006- 2.37i/2.33, 2007- 2.39i/2.20, 2008- 2.36i/2.30, 2009- 2.40i/2.35, 2010- 2.38i/2.36, 2011- 2.38i/2.34, 2012- 2.39, 2013- 2.35, 2014- 2.42i/2.41, 2015- 2.32, 2016- 2.35, 2017- 2.32, 2018- 2.35i.
Former discus thrower.

Women

Anna BULGAKOVA b. 17 Jan 1988 Stavropol 1.73m 90kg. Stavropol VS.
At HT: OG: '08- dnq 20; WCh: '13- dq5; EC: '12- 3, '14- dq nt; WJ: '04- 4, '06- 2; WY: '05- 2; EJ: '07- 4; ET: '14- dq3. RUS champion 2014.
Progress at HT: 2003- 57.24, 2004- 63.83, 2005- 64.43, 2006- 67.79, 2007- 68.49, 2008- 73.79, 2010- 66.29, 2011- 69.10, 2012- 74.02, 2013- 76.17, 2014- 74.16dq, 2015- 72.15dq, 2016- 72.07, 2017- 67.31. pb DT 44.19 '06.
Positve re-test of sample from 2013 Worlds, 2-year bon an and results annulled 16 Aug 2013 to 15 Aug20 15.

Irina GORDEYEVA b. 9 Oct 1986 Leningrad 1.85m 55kg. Yunost Rossii.
At HJ: OG: '12- 10; WCh: '13- 9=, '17- dnq 16; EC: '10- dnq 13=, '12- 3=; WJ: '04- 9; WY: '03- 7=; EJ: '05- 4; EI: '09- 5=.
Progress at HJ: 2001- 1.75, 2002- 1.82, 2003- 1.84, 2004- 1.88, 2005- 1.88, 2006- 1.88, 2007- 1.87i/1.83, 2008- 1.95, 2009- 2.02, 2010- 1.97, 2011- 1.94, 2012- 2.04, 2013- 1.99, 2014- 1.95, 2015- 1.96i/1.94, 2016- 1.94, 2017- 1.94.

Darya KLISHINA b. 15 Jan 1991 Tver 1.80m 57kg. Moskva. Model.
At LJ: OG: '16- 9; WCh: '11-13-15-17: 6/6/10/2; EC: '14- 3; WY: '07- 1; EU23: '11- 1; EJ: '09- 1; WI: '10-12-14: 5/4/7; EI: '11-13-17: 1/1/4, WUG: '13- 1; ET: '11-13-15: 1/2/1. RUS champion 2014.
Progress at LJ: 2005- 5.83, 2006- 6.33/6.47w, 2007- 6.49, 2008- 6.52i/6.20, 2009- 6.80, 2010- 7.03, 2011- 7.05, 2012- 6.93, 2013- 7.01i/6.90/6.98w, 2014- 6.90, 2015- 6.95, 2016- 6.84, 2017- 7.00.
The one Russian athlete permitted to compete (as a neutral) at OG '16 and EI 17.

Yekaterina KONEVA b. 25 Sep 1988 Khabarovsk 1.69m 55kg. Khabarovskiy.
At TJ: WCh: '13- 2, '15- 7; EC: '14- 2; WI: '14- 1; WUG: '11-13-15: 1/1/1; CCp: '14- 2; EI: '15- 1; ET:

'13-14-15: 2/1/1. RUS champion 2014-15, WMilG LJ & TJ 2015.

Progress at TJ: 2010- 13.93/14.00w, 2011- 14.46, 2012- 14.60i/14.36, 2013- 14.82, 2014- 14.89, 2015- 15.04, 2016- 14.42. pbs: 60m 7.39i '07, 100m 11.76 '09, 200m 23.89 '09, LJ 6.82i '15, 6.70/6.80w '11.

Married Sergey Polyanskiy (LJ 8.20 '15, 8 WCh '15) in October 2016, daughter Sofiya born 17 Apr 2017. Two-year drugs ban 2007-09. Baby born Aori 2017.

Yelena LASHMANOVA b. 9 Apr 1992 Saransk 1.70m 48kg. Biology student at Mordoviya State University.

At 20kmW: OG: '12- 1; WCh: '13- 1; WCp: '12- 1; won RUS 2016-17. At 10000mW: WJ: '10- 1; EJ: '11- 1; ECp: '11- 1J. At 5000mW: WY: '09- 1.

Official world 20km walk record 2012, world junior 10,000m walk record 2011.

Progress at 20kW: 2012- 1:25:02, 2013- 1:25:49, 2016- 1:24:58, 2017- 1:25:18, 2018- 1:26:23. pbs: 5000mW 20:15.6 '16, 10000mW 42:59.48 '11.

Best ever debut at 20k walk (1:26:30 in 2012) and has won all seven of her career 20k walks 2012-3. Won IAAF Walks Challenge 2013. Received two-year drugs ban from test on 4 Jan 2014.

Mariya LASITSKENE b. 14 Jan 1993 Prokhladny, Kabardino-Balkar 1.82m 60kg. née Kuchina. Moskovskaya.

At HJ: WCh: '15- 1, '17- 1; EC: '14- 2; WJ: '12- 3; WY: '09- 2=; EU23: '15- 12; EJ: '11- 1; WI: '14- 1=. '18- 1; EI: '15- 1; WUG: '13- 2; CCp: '14- 1; ET: '13-14-15: 1/1/1. Won DL 2014, 2017; Yth Oly 2010, RUS champion 2014, 2017; W.MilG 2015.

World junior indoor high jump record 2011.

Progress at HJ: 2009- 1.87, 2010- 1.91, 2011- 1.97i/1.95, 2012- 1.96i/1.89, 2013- 1.98i/1.96, 2014- 2.01i/2.00, 2015- 2.01, 2016- 2.00, 2017- 2.06, 2018- 2.04i.

Married journalist Vladas Lasitskas on 17 Mar 2017. 38 successive wins from 2016 to 2018 World Indoors and had the top seven performances of 2017.

Yekaterina MEDVEDYEVA b. 29 Mar 1994. Mordoviya.

At 10000mW: WJ: '12- 1; WCp: '12- 4J.

Progress at 20kW: 2015- 1:29:32, 2016- 1:26:40, 2017- 1:25:22. pbs: 10000mW 43:50.0 '13.

Marina PANDAKOVA 1 Mar 1989. Churvashkaya Region.

At 20kW: WCp: '14- 10. ECp: '13- 3, '15- 5; WUG: '15- 2.

Progress at 20kW: 2008- 1:38:19, 2011- 1:33:00, 2012- 1:28:29, 2013- 1:27:39, 2014- 1:27:54, 2015- 1:25:03, 2016- 1:27:18. pbs: 3000mW: 11:50.30 '16, 5000mW 21:40.41i '13, 10kW 43:29 '12.

Marina PONOMARYOVA 18 Jun 1995.

At 20kW: EU23: '15- 1.

Progress at 20kW: 2015- 1:27:17, 2016- 1:26:46, 2017- 1:27:53, 2018- 1:27:11. pbs: 3000mW: 12:05.91 '16, 10kW: 44:07 '16.

Vira REBRIK b. 25 Feb 1989 Yalta 1.76m 65kg.

At JT: OG: '08/12- dnq 15/19; WCh: '09- 11-13-15-17: 9/dnq 16/11/dnq 24/dnq nt; EC: '10- dnq 17, '12- 1; WJ: '06- 2, '08- 1; WY: '05- 2; EU23: '09- 2, '11- 2; EJ: '07- 1; WUG: '09- 2, '11- 4; ET: '13- 3. Won UKR 2010-12, RUS 2015-17.

World junior javelin record 2008; four UKR records 2010-12.

Progress at JT: 2003- 44.94, 2004- 52.47, 2005- 57.48, 2006- 59.64, 2007- 58.48, 2008- 63.01, 2009- 62.26, 2010- 63.36, 2011- 61.60, 2012- 66.86, 2013- 64.30, 2014- 61.57, 2015- 64.93, 2016- 67.30, 2017- 62.02.

Crimean athlete, transferred to Russia in 2015.

Anzhelika SIDOROVA b. 28 Jun 1991 Moskva 1.70m 52kg. Moskva Youth.

At PV: WCh: '15- nh, '17- dnq nh; EC: '14- 1; WJ: '10- 4; EU23: '13- 2; WI: '14- 2=, '18- 2; EI: '13- 3, '15- 1; ET: '13-14-15- 2/1/2. Won RUS 2014-15.

Progress at PV: 2007- 3.80, 2008- 4.00, 2009- 4.10i/4.00, 2010- 4.30, 2011- 4.40i/4.30, 2012- 4.50, 2013- 4.62i/4.60, 2014- 4.72i/4.70, 2015- 4.80i/4.79, 2016- 4.85, 2017- 4.75, 2018- 4.87i.

Yelena SOKOLOVA b. 23 Jul 1986 Staryi Oskol, Belgorod reg. 1.70m 61kg. née Kremneva. Krasnodarsk krai.

At LJ: OG: '12- 2; WCh: '09- dnq 13, '13- 8, '15- dnq 23; EU23: '07- 3; EI: '07- 5, '09- 2; WUG: '07- 2, '13- 2. Won DL 2012, RUS 2009, 2012, 2015, 2017.

Progress at LJ: 2002- 6.33, 2003- 6.39i?/6.31, 2006- 6.53, 2007- 6.71, 2008- 6.74, 2009- 6.92, 2010- 6.72/6.90w, 2011- 6.76, 2012- 7.07, 2013- 6.91, 2015- 6.70, 2016- 6.59, 2017- 6.85. pbs: 60m 7.34i '12, 100m 11.61 '12, TJ 13.15i/12.93 '03.

Son born on 23 Aug 2014.

SAINT KITTS & NEVIS

Governing body: Saint Kitts Amateur Athletic Association. Founded 1961.

Kim COLLINS b. 5 Apr 1976 Ogees, Saint-Peter 1.75m 64kg. Studied sociology at Texas Christian University, USA.

At 100m (/200m): OG: '96- qf, 00- 7/sf, '04- 6, '08- sf/6, '16- sf; WCh: '95- hR, '97- h, 99- h/h, '01- 5/3=, '03- 1, '05- 3, '07- sf, '09- qf/qf, '11- 3/sf/3R, '15- h; CG: '02- 1; PAm: '07- 5, '11- 2; PAm-J: '95- 2; CAC: '99- 2, '01- 1/1, '03- 1; WCp: '02- 2/2R, '14- 1R/3 4x400mR. At 60m: WI: '03-08-16: 2/2=/8. Won NCAA indoor 60m & 200m 2001.

SKN records: 100m from 1996 to 2016, 200m from 1998, 400m 2000. CAC indoor 60m 2015. M35 world records: 100m (3) 2013-16, indoor 60m (4) 2014-15; M40 100m 2016, 60m indoor (6) 2017.

Progress at 100m, 200m: 1995- 10.63, 21.85; 1996- 10.27, 21.06; 1998- 10.18/10.16w, 20.88/20.78w; 1999- 10.21, 20.43, 2000- 10.13A/10.15/10.02w, 20.31A/20.18w; 2001- 10.04A/10.00?/9.99w, 20.20/20.08w; 2002- 9.98, 20.49; 2003- 9.99/9.92w,

20.40w; 2004- 10.00, 20.98; 2005- 10.00, 2006- 10.33, 21.53; 2007- 10.14, 2008- 10.05, 20.25; 2009- 10.15/10.08w, 20.45; 2010- 10.20, 21.35/20.76w; 2011- 10.00A/10.01, 20.52; 2012- 10.01/9.96w, 2013- 9.97, 21.37i, 2014- 9.96, 2015- 9.98/9.94w, 2016- 9.93, 2017- 10.20. pbs: 60m 6.47i '15, 400m 46.93 '00.

The first athlete from his country to make Olympic and World finals and in 2003 the first to win a World Indoor medal and a World title; won a further medal in 2011 and has now competed in ten World Champs. Oldest man to have broken 10 secs for 100m. There is a 'Kim Collins Highway' in St Kitts.

ST LUCIA

Gov. body: Saint Lucia Athletics Association.

Levern SPENCER b. 23 Jun 1984 Cacao Babonneau 1.80m 54kg. Was at University of Georgia.

At HJ: OG: '08/12- dnq 24/19, '16- 6; WCh: '05-07-09-11-13-15-17: dnq 22/15=/dnq 23=/dnq 13/11/12=/dnq 13=; CG: '02-06-10-14: 12=/5/3/3; WJ: '02- 8; WY: '01- 3; PAm: '03-07-11-15: 5/3/6/1; CAG: '06-10-14: 3/1/1; WI: '14- 7, '16- 5=; CCp: '10- 3=, '14- 5. CAC champion 2001, 2005, 2008-09, 2011, 2013; NACAC 2007, 2015.

Nine St. Lucia high jump records 2004-10.

Progress at HJ: 2000- 1.80, 2001- 1.81, 2002- 1.83, 2003- 1.86, 2004- 1.88, 2005- 1.94, 2006- 1.90, 2007- 1.94, 2008- 1.93, 2009- 1.95, 2010- 1.98, 2011- 1.94, 2012- 1.91, 2013- 1.95A, 2014- 1.96, 2015- 1.94, 2016- 1.96, 2017- 1.92, 2018- 1.95i. pbs: 200m 24.22 '05, LJ 6.08 '14.

SERBIA

Governing body: Athletic Federation of Serbia. Founded in 1921 (as Yugoslav Athletic Federation).

National Championships (Yugoslav) first held in 1920 (men) and 1923 (women). **2017 Champions**: **Men**: 100m/200m: Aleksa Kijanovic 10.41w/21.25w, 400m: Stefan Vukadinovic 48.76, 800m/1500m: Bojan Stanisic 1:52.53/3:57.74, 3000m/5000m: Nemanja Stojanovic 8:47.53/15:26.62, 10000m: Elzan Bibic 30:32.87, HMar: Haris Ajdarevic 73:17, Mar: Aleksandar Adzic 2:42:00, 3000mSt: Milos Mitrovic 9:29.79, 110mh: Milan Ristic 13.67w, 400mh: Milos Markovic 54.42, HJ: Miodrag Djokic 2.13, PV: Mihail Dudas 4.90, LJ: Lazar Anic 7.82, TJ: Vukasin Zirojevic 14.86w, SP: Armin Sinancevic 18.53, DT: Marko Peric 53.27, HT: Vojislav Gvero 52.22, JT: Branko Paukovic 73.93, Dec: Aleksandar Grnovic 7177, 5000mW: Jovan Delcev 25:05.22, 5kW: Vladimir Savanovic 23:08. **Women**: 100m/200m: Zorana Barjaktarovic 11.55w/23.45w, 400m: Tamara Salaski 52.69, 800m/1500m: Amela Terzic 2:04.30/4:25.63, 3000m: Tamara Micevic 9:28.73, 5000m/HMar: Olivera Jevtic 16:22.66/73:30, 10000m: Teodora Simovic 36:09.50, Mar: Nora Trklja 3:01:59, 3000mSt: Ivana Petrovic 11:45.63, 100mh: Ivana Petkovic 13.66w, 400mh: Jelena Grujic 61.32, HJ: Zorana Bukvic 1.70, PV: Tamara Moravcevic 3.20, LJ: Milica Gardasevic 6.21, TJ: Biljana Topic 13.13, SP: Dijana Sefcic 13.19, DT: Dragana Tomasevic 61.57, HT: Aleksandra Ivanovic 57.32, JT: Tatjana Mirkovic 54.15, Hep: Sanja Ristovic 4566, 3000mW: Dusica Topic 13:52.52, 5kW: Danica Gogov 25:41.

Asmir KOLASINAC b. 15 Oct 1984 Skopje, Macedonia 1.86m 137kg. AC Partizan 4r5, Belgrade.

At SP: OG: '08- dnq 30, '12- 7, '16- dnq 15; WCh: '09-11-13-15: dnq 21/10/10/7; EC: '10-12-14-16: 7/3/5/5; EU23: '05- dnq; EI: '13- 1, '15- 2; Won Balkan 2011; SRB 2008, 2010-15.

Progress at SP: 2004- 15.50, 2005- 17.88, 2006- 17.85, 2007- 19.30, 2008- 19.99, 2009- 20.41, 2010- 20.52i/20.38, 2011- 20.50, 2012- 20.85, 2013- 20.80, 2014- 20.79, 2015- 21.58, 2016- 20.96, 2017- 20.87i/19.45.

Older brother Almir BIH had JT best 68.32 '09.

Women

Ivana SPANOVIC b. 10 May 1990 Zrenjanin 1.76m 65kg. AC Vojvodina, Novi Sad.

At LJ: OG: '08- dnq 30, '12- 9, '16- 3; WCh: '13- 3, '15- 3, '17- 4; EC: '10-12-14-16: 8/dnq 14/2/1; WJ: '06- 7, '08- 1; WY: '05- dnq, '07- 2; EU23: '11- 2; EJ: '07- 5, '09- 2; WUG: '09- 1; CCp: '14- 2; WI: '14-16-18: 3/2/1; EI: '13-15-17: 5/1/1. Won DL 2016-17, Serbian 2006, 2008, 2011-13, Balkan 2011, 2013.

11 Serbian long jump records 2009-16 (& 11 indoor 2007-17), indoor records 60m & Pen.

Progress at LJ: 2003- 5.36, 2004- 5.91, 2005- 6.43, 2006- 6.48i/6.38, 2007- 6.53i/6.41, 2008- 6.65, 2009- 6.71, 2010- 6.78, 2011- 6.71/6.74w, 2012- 6.64, 2013- 6.82, 2014- 6.92i/6.88, 2015- 7.02, 2016- 7.10, 2017- 7.24i/6.96, 2018- 6.96i. pbs: 60m 7.31i '15, 100m 11.90 '13, 60mh 8.49i '13, HJ 1.78i '13, 1.65 '05; TJ 13.78 '14, SP 12.40i '13, Pen 4240i '13.

Won first medal for Serbia at World Champs and Olympic Games. Her 7.24 at EI '17 was the world's longest indoor women's LJ for 28 years.

SLOVAKIA

Governing body: Slovak Athletic Federation. Founded 1939.

National Championships first held in 1939. **2017 Champions**: **Men**: 100m: Ján Volko 10.34, 200m: Roman Turcáni 21.86; 400m: Boris Pribil 49.32, 800m: Jozef Repcík 1:49.17, 1500m: Jozef Pelikán 3:L52.59, 5000m: Peter Durec 14:57.95, 10000m: Branislav Sarkan 31:21.82, HMar/Mar: Jozef Urbán 69:28/2:29:44, 3000mSt: David Mazuch 9:47.36, 110mh: Marco Adrien Drozda 14.84, 400mh: Jakub Bottlik 52.28, HJ: Matús Bubeník 2.23, PV: Ján Zmoray 5.00, LJ: Attila Toth 6.88, TJ: Martin Koch 15.51, SP: Matus Olej 18.98, DT: Michal Holica 54.07, HT: Marcel

Lomnicky 76.41, JT: Patrik Zenúch 74.30, 20kW: Matej Tóth 1:24:38, 50kW: Dusan Majdán 4:10:40. **Women**: 100m: Alexandra Bezeková 11.69, 200m: Iveta Putalová 24.17, 400m: Barbora Tomková 57.02, 800m: Alexandra Stuková 2:06.22, 1500m/3000mSt: Kristina Belová 4:33.13/ 11:29.85, 5000m: Zuzana Durcová 17:56.11, 10000m: Lucia Janecková 36:40.23, HMar: Sona Vnenacková 1:21:02, Mar: Michaela Mertová 2:51:49, 100mh: Stanislava Lajcáková 14.09, 400mh: Daniela Ledecká 60.81, HJ: Tána Dunajská 1.86, PV: Klaudia Kálnayová 3.60, LJ: Jana Veldáková 6.45, TJ: Dana Veldáková 13.63, SP: Ivana Kristoficová 15.08, DT: Patrícia Slosárová 42.36, HT: Nikola Lomnická 68.59, JT: Julia Hanuliaková 41.87, Hep: Stanislava Lajcaková 5660, 20kW: Maria Czaková 1:40:38.

Marcel LOMNICKY b. 6 Jul 1987 Nitra 1.77m 106kg. TJ Stavbár Nitra. Was at Virginia Tech University, USA.
At HT: OG: '12- dnq 14, '16- 5; WCh: '11-13-15-17: dnq 21/8/8/dnq 13; WJ: '04- dnq 17, '06- 3; EC: '10-12-14-16: dnq 24/11/7/5; EU23: '07- 3, '09- 6; EJ: '05- 8; WUG: '11- 2, '13- 2. SVK champion 2012-17, won NCAA HT 2009, indoor Wt 2012.
Progress at HT: 2005- 64.27, 2006- 69.53, 2007- 72.17, 2008- 72.66, 2009- 71.78, 2010- 74.83, 2011- 75.84, 2012- 77.43, 2013- 78.73, 2014- 79.16, 2015- 77.63, 2016- 77.48, 2017- 77.92. pbs: SP 15.73 '07, DT 43.82 '08, Wt 23.05i '12.
Sister Nikola Lomnická (b. 16 Sep 1988) has hammer best 71.58 '14, won NCAA 2010 and was 8th EC 2014.

Matej TÓTH b. 10 Feb 1983 Nitra 1.85m 73kg. Dukla Banská Bystrica.
At 20kW/(50kW): OG: '04- 32, '08- 26, '12- (5), '16- (1); WCh: '05- 21, 07- 14, '09- 8/9, '11- 10/dnf, '13- (5), '15- (1); EC: '06- 6, '10- 6, '14- (2); EU23: '03- 6; WCp: '10- (1); ECp: '09-11-13-15: 9/1/3/2. At 10000mW: WJ: '02- 16, WY: '99- 8; EJ: '01- 6. Won SVK 20kW 2005-08, 2010-12, 2015, 2017; 50kW 2011, 2018.
Four SVK 50k walk records 2009-15.
Progress at 20kW, 50kW: 1999- 1:34:29, 2000- 1:30:28, 2001- 1:29:33, 2003- 1:13:17, 2004- 1:23:18, 2005- 1:21:38, 2006- 1:21:39, 2007- 1:25:10, 2008- 1:21:24, 2009- 1:20:53, 3:41:32; 2010- 1:22:04, 3:53:30; 2011- 1:20:16, 3:39:46; 2012- 1:20:25, 3:41:24; 2013- 1:20:14, 3:41:07; 2014- 1:19:48, 3:36:21; 2015- 1:20:21, 3:34:38; 2016- 1:29:04, 3:40:58; 2017- 1:24:38, 2018- 3:42:46. pbs: 3000mW 10:57.32i '11, 11:05.95 '12; 5000mW 18:34.56i '12, 18:54.39 '11; 10000W 39:45.03 '06, 39:07R '10; 30kW 2:12:44 '13, 35kW 2:34:23 '13.
First ever World and Olympic gold medallist for Slovakia. Won IAAF Race Walking Challenge 2015. Had third win at Dudince in 2018 in first 50k race since 2016 Olympics

Women

Martina HRASNOVÁ b. 21 Mar 1983 Bratislava 1.77m 88kg. née Danisová. Dukla Banská Bystrica.
At HT: OG: '08- 6, '12/16- dnq 15/19; WCh: '01-07-13-15: dnq 23/12/20/16, '09- 3; EC: '02 & '06- dnq 26, '12—14-16: 2/2.7; WJ: '00- 5, '02- 2; EJ: '99- 4, '01- 2; CCp: '14- 3; WUG: '07- 5, '09- 2. Won SVK SP 2003, 2006; HT 2000-01, 2006, 2008-09, 2011-15.
14 Slovakian hammer records 2001-09.
Progress at HT: 1999- 58.61, 2000- 61.62, 2001- 68.50, 2002- 68.22, 2003- 66.36, 2005- 69.24, 2006- 73.84, 2007- 69.22, 2008- 76.82, 2009- 76.90, 2011- 72.47, 2012- 73.34, 2013- 72.41, 2014- 75.27, 2015- 74.27, 2016- 72.34, 2017- 67.86. pbs: 60m 7.96i '12, SP 15.60i '15, 15.02 '06; DT 43.15 '06, Wt 21.74i '11. Two-year drugs ban (nandrolone) from July 2003. Daughter Rebeka born on 4 July 2010. Brother of Branislav Danis (HT 69.20 '06).

SLOVENIA

Governing body: Atletska Zveza Slovenije. Current organisation founded 1948.
2017 National Champions: Men: 100m: Jan Kramberger 10.54w, 200m: Luka Marolt 21.39, 400m: Zan Rudolf 48.17, 800m: Lovrenc Valic 1:54.83, 1500m/3000m: Jan Kokalj 3:52.62/8:26.17, 5000m/10000m: Jan Bresan 14:55.39/30:43.11, HMar: Domen Hafner 71:07, Mar: Mitja Krevs 2:32:25, 3000mSt: Blaz Grad 9:36.55, 110mh: Aljaz Brlek 15.47, 400mh: Peter Hribarsek 52.58, HJ: Axel Luxa 2.00, PV: Robert Renner 5.40, LJ/ TJ: Ziga Vrscaj 7.37w/15.19w, SP: Blaz Zupancic 18.55, DT: Tadej Hribar 57.98, HT: Nejc Plesko 73.85, JT: Matija Kranjc 72.15, Dec: Urban Cehovin 6859. **Women**: 100m/200m: Anita Horvat 11.79/24.53, 400m/800m: Jerneja Smonkar 54.97/2:09.13, 1500m: Marusa Mismas 4:23.37, 3000m: Patricija Plazar 9:49.66, 5000m: Klara Ljubi 19:31.28, 10000m/HMar: Sonja Roman 34:35.12/77:25, Mar: Jasmina Pitamic Vojska 2:53:05, 3000mSt: Urska Arzensek 12:00.82, 100mh: Joni Tomicic Prezelj 13.45w, 400mh: Julija Praprotnik 60.24, HJ: Monika Podlogar 1.77, PV: Tina Sutej 4.30, LJ: Petra Rahne 5.63w, TJ: Petra Koren 13.21, SP/DT: Veronika Domjan 13.96/55.95, HT: Claudia Stravs 62.32, JT: Martina Ratej 63.15, Hep: Stasa Trajkovic 4516.

Women

Martina RATEJ b. 2 Nov 1981 Celje 1.78m 69kg. AD Kladivar Celje.
At JT: OG: '08- dnq 36, '12- 7, '16- dnq 18; WCh: '09-11-13-15-17: 11/7/dnq 20/dnq 23/9; EC: '06-10-12-14-16: dnq 21/7/dnq 21/6/6; WJ: '00- dnq 15. SLO champion 2005-14, 2016-17; MedG 2013, Balkan 2015. Five SLO javelin records 2008-10.
Progress at JT: 1999- 48.74, 2000- 46.83, 2005- 50.86, 2006- 57.49, 2007- 58.49, 2008- 63.44, 2009- 63.42, 2010- 67.16, 2011- 65.89, 2012- 65.24, 2013- 62.60, 2014- 66.13, 2015- 65.75, 2016- 61.03, 2017- 65.64. Mother of two.

SOUTH AFRICA

Governing body: Athletics South Africa. Original body founded 1894.

National Championships first held in 1894 (men), 1929 (women). **2017 Champions**: **Men**: 100m: Akani Simbine 9.95, 200m: Wade van Niekerk 19.90, 400m: Peter Conradie 45.15, 800m: Ryhardt van Rensburg 1:46.56, 1500m: Dumisani Hlaselo 3:41.63, 5000m: Thabang Mosiako 14:03.84, 10000m: Elroy Galant 29:09.87. HMar: Stephen Mokoka 61:21, Mar: Anele Dlamini 2:22:23, 3000mSt: Rantso Mokopane 8:34.47, 110mh: Antonio Alkana 13.49 (dq Tiaan Smit 13.42), 400mh: Le Roux Hamman 49.35, HJ: Chris Moleya 2.25, PV: Eben Beukes 5.00, LJ: Luvo Manyonga 8.65, TJ: Reneilwe Aphane 15.93, SP: Orazio Cremona 21.12, DT: Dewald van Heerden 56.61, HT: Chris Harmse 70.53 (22nd successive title), JT: Phil-Mar Janse van Rensburg 79.86, Dec: Friedrich Pretorius 7524, 20kW: Wayne Snyman 1:25:51, 50kW: Mthunzi Mnisi 4:36:40. **Women**: 100m/200m: Alyssa Conley 11.41/22.94, 400m/800m: Caster Semenya 51.60/2:01.03, 1500m: Simonay Weitsz 4:21.93, 5000m: Kesa Molotsane 16:22.30, 10000m: Glenrose Xaba 34:56.12, HMar: Cornelia Joubert 72:31, Mar: Danette Smith 2:54:59, 3000mSt: Cherise Sims 10:46.29, 100mh: Rikenette Steenkamp 13.02, 400mh: Wenda Nel 55.16, HJ: Julia du Plessis 1.85, PV: Nadja Fourie 3.70, LJ: Lynique Prinsloo 6.57, TJ: Kelly Kingwill 13.55, SP/DT: Ischke Senekal 16.97/51.92, HT: Letitia Janse van Vuuren 60.65, JT: Sunette Viljoen 63.49, Hep: Nienka Du Toit 4967, 20kW: Anél Oosthuizen 1:38:53, 50kW: Nalalie le Roux 4:54:33.

Anaso JOBODWANA b. 30 Jul 1992 Aberdeen, Eastern Cape 1.87m 71kg. Was at Jacksonville State University, USA.
At (100m)/200m: OG: '12- 8, '16- h; WCh: '13- sf/6, '15- 5/3; WUG: '13- 1/1. Won RSA 200m 2015. South African 200m record 2015.
Progress at 100m, 200m: 2009- 21.68A, 2010- 20.95A, 2012- 10.34/10.24w, 20.27; 2013- 10.10, 20.13/20.00w; 2015- 10.13, 19.87; 2016- 20.53, 2017- 10.16A/10.28, 20.62/20.10Aw; 2018- 20.07. pbs: 60m 6.60Ai '15, 6.66i '13; 150m 15.08A '18.

Luvo MANYONGA b. 18 Nov 1991 Mbekweni 1.85m 65kg. Tuks, University of Pretoria.
At LJ: OG: '16- 2; WCh: '11- 5, '17- 1; WJ: '10- 1; AfG: '11- 1, AfCh; '16- 2; Af-J: '09- 3; WI: '18- 2; won DL 2017, RSA 2018. Two African long jump records 2017, junior 2010, two indoor 2018.
Progress at LJ: 2009- 7.65, 2010- 8.19, 2011- 8.26, 2012- 8.00, 2016- 8.48, 2017- 8.65A/8.62, 2018- 8.44i. pb TJ 15.71A '10.
18 months drugs ban from positive test 20 Mar 2012. Unbeaten in nine LJ competitions 2017.

Godfrey Khotso MOKOENA b. 6 Mar 1985 Heidelberg, Gauteng 1.90m 73kg. University of Johannesburg.
At LJ/(TJ): OG: '04- (dnq 29), '08- 2, '12- 8, '16- (dnq 21); WCh: '05-07-09-11-13-15: 7/5/2/dnq 15=/7/dnq 13 & 9; CG: '06- 4/2, '14- (1); WJ: '02- 12, '04- 2/1; AfG: '03- 3/2, '07- 3; AfCh: '06- 2/2, '10- 1, '14- 2/1, '16- (3); CCp: '14- (2); WI: '06-08-10: 5/1/2. At HJ: WY: '01- 5. Won DL LJ 2014, RSA LJ 2005-07, 2009-11; TJ 2004-06, 2014-15, 2018.
Records: African LJ (3) 2009, RSA LJ (5) 2005-09, TJ (3) 2004-14, African junior TJ 2004.
Progress at LJ, TJ: 2001- 7.17A, 2002- 7.82A, 16.03A; 2003- 7.84A/7.83, 16.28; 2004- 8.09, 16.96A/16.77; 2005- 8.37A/8.22, 17.25; 2006- 8.39/8.45w, 16.95; 2007- 8.34A/8.28/8.32w, 16.75; 2008- 8.25/8.35w, 2009- 8.50, 2010- 8.23A/8.15/8.22w, 2011- 8.25/8.31w, 2012- 8.29A/8.24, 2013- 8.30, 15.68i; 2014- 8.19, 17.35; 2015- 8.16, 16.85; 2016- 16.77, 2017- 8.19, 16.55A; 2018- 16.74A/17.09wA. pbs: 100m 10.7A '09, HJ 2.10 '01.

Clarence MUNYAI b. 20 Feb 1998 Johannesburg 1.76m 66kg. Tuks, Pretoria.
At 200m: OG: '16- h; WCh: '17- dq h; WJ: 16- 4; AfCh: '16 sf; Af-J: 17- 1. Won RSA 200m 2016.
Records: World junior 300m 2017, African juniuor 200m 2017, South African 200m 2018.
Progress at 200m: 2014- 21.61A, 2015- 20.77A, 2016- 20.36A/20.40/20.33Aw, 2017- 20.10A/20.31, 2018- 19.69A. pbs: 100m 10.10A '18. 300m 31.61 '17.

Ruswahl SAMAAI b. 25 Sep 1991 Paarl 1.78m 73kg. Was at University of Johannesburg.
At LJ: OG: '16- 9; WCh: '15- dnq 20, '17- 3; CG: '14- 3; AfCh: '14- 3, '16- 1; WI: '16- 5, '18- 6; RSA champion 2015.
Progress at LJ: 2009- 6.93A, 2010- 7.41, 2011- 7.75/7.80w, 2012- 7.94A/7.61w, 2013- 7.96A/7.74, 2014- 8.13A/8.08, 2015- 8.38, 2016- 8.38/8.40w, 2017- 8.49A/8.35, 2018- 8.39. pb TJ 16.10A '14.

Lebogang SHANGE b. 1 Aug 1990 1.60m 56kg.
At 20kW: OG: '16- 44; WCh: '13-15-17: dnf/11/4; AfG: '15- 1; AfCh: '13-14-16: 1/1/3. RSA champion 2012-13, 2015-16
South African walks records: 3000m, 5000m & 20k 2017.
Progress at 20kW: 2011- 1:27:31, 2012- 1:25:48, 2013- 1:26:06, 2014- 1:24:09, 2015- 1:21:43, 2016- 1:20:06, 2017- 1:19:18. Pbs: 3000mW 11:14.49 '17, 5000mW 18:55.60 '17, 10000mW 41:16.23 '17, 39:48R '17.

Akani SIMBINE b. 21 Sep 1993 Kempton Park 1.74m 67kg. Tuks, was at University of Pretoria.
At 100m/(200m): OG: '16- 5; WCh: '13- h, '15- sf/sf, '17- 5/sf; CG: 14- sf/5; AfCh: '14- 8, 16- 3; WUG: '15- 1. Won RSA 100m 2015, 2017.
Three South African 100m records 2015-16.
Progress at 100m, 200m: 2010- 10.61A, 2011- 10.57A, 21.27A; 2012- 10.19A, 20.68A; 2013- 10.36, 20.79A/20.78w; 2015- 9.97, 20.23; 2016- 9.89, 20.16; 2017- 9.92A/9.99, 19.95A/20.21. pb 60m 6.60Ai '15, 6.66i '13.

Wayde van NIEKERK b. 15 Jul 1992 Cape Town 1.83m 73kg. University of the Free State, Bloemfontein.
At (200m)/400m: OG: '16- 1; WCh: '13- h, '15- 1, '17- 2/1; CG: '14- sf/2; AfCh: '14- 2, '16- (1); WJ: '10- (4); WUG: '13- 2R; CCp: '14- 4/1R. Won RSA 200m 2011, 2017, 400m 2013-15.
Records: World 400m 2016, 300m 2017, Commonwealth 400m 2015, African 300m (3) 2016-17. 400m (2) 2015, RSA 200m 2015 & 2017, 400m (2) 2015.
Progress at 200m, 400m: 2010- 21.02, 2011- 20.57, 2012- 20.91, 46.43; 2013- 20.84A, 45.09; 2014- 20.19, 44.38; 2015- 19.94, 43.48; 2016- 20.02, 43.03; 2017- 19.84, 43.62. pbs: 100m 9.94 '17, 300m 30.81 '17.
The only man to run under 10,0, 20.0 and 44.0, he ranks as the fourth best ever combination 100-200-400 man. Has won three successive global 400m titles.

Louis J. van ZYL b. 20 Jul 1985 Bloemfontein 1.86m 75kg. Tuks, University of Pretoria.
At 400mh/4x400mR: OG: '08- 5, '12- h, '16- sf; WCh: '05-07-09-11-13-15: 6/h/sf/3&2R/h/sf; CG: '06- 1/2R, '10- 2, '14- h; AfG: '07- 1; AfCh: '06-08-10-14-16: 1/1&1R/1/4/4&3R; WJ: '02- 1, '04- 4/2R; WY: '01- 3; WCp: '06- 2, '10- 5; RSA champion 2003, 2005-06, 2008, 2011, 2015.
Two RSA 400m hurdles records 2011. Tied world best for 200m hurdles straight 2015.
Progress at 400mh: 2001- 51.14A, 2002- 48.89, 2003- 49.22, 2004- 49.06, 2005- 48.11, 2006- 48.05, 2007- 48.24, 2008- 48.22, 2009- 47.94, 2010- 48.51A/48.63, 2011- 47.66, 2012- 49,42A, 2013- 49.11, 2014- 48.96A/48.97, 2015- 48.78, 2016- 48.67, 2017- 49.29A/49.35. pbs: 100m 10.62 '07, 10.3Aw '03, 10.5A '01; 200m 20.71A '15, 300m 32.32 '09, 400m 44.86A '11, 46.02 '08; 200mhSt 22.10 '15, 300mh 35.76 '04.
Ran world U18 record of 48.89 to win World Junior title in 2002 after world age record at 15 in 2001. Commonwealth Games record to win 400mh gold and ran brilliant final leg in 4x400m to take RSA from fifth to second in 2006. Married Irvette van Blerk (pbs HMar 70:56 '11, Mar 2:31:26 '13) on 29 Sep 2012.

Zarck VISSER b. 15 Sep 1989 Welkom 1.78m 70kg. University of Johannesburg.
At LJ: WCh: '13/15/17- dnq 13/19/25; CG: '14- 2; AfCh: '12- 2, '14- 1; CCp: '14- 3; RSA champion 2012-14.
Progress at LJ: 2007- 7.21A, 2008- 7.62A, 2009- 7.77, 2010- 7.76A/7.79Aw, 2011- 7.85, 2012- 8.15A/ 8.07/8.21w, 2013- 8.32, 2014- 8.31A/8.18, 2015- 8.41, 2016- 7.93A/7.81, 2017- 8.22/8.23w. pb 100m 10.68A '17, TJ 15.66A '08.

Women

Wenda NEL b. 27 May 1988 Worcester, Western Cape 1.69m 52kg. née Theron. Tuks, University of Pretoria.
At 400mh: OG: '16- sf; WCh: '11- sf, '15- 7, '17- sf; CG: '14- h; AfG: '11- 2; AfCh: '10-12-14-16: 7/5/1/1&1R; CCp: '14- 5. Won RSA 2011-2, 2014-18. At 100m/200m: WJ: '06- h/h; WY: '05: h/-.
Progress at 400mh: 2008- 60.23A, 2009- 56.45, 2010- 56.97, 2011- 56.13, 2012- 55.36A/55.79, 2013- 55.80, 2014- 54.82, 2015- 54.37, 2016- 54.47, 2017- 54.58. pbs: 100m 11.57Aw/11.80A '15, 200m 23.39A '17, 300m 37.59A '17, 400m 52.03A/52.97 '17, 600m 1:28.05A 15, 100mh 14.23 '07.

Caster SEMENYA b. 7 Jan 1991 Polokwane, Limpopo Province 1.70m 64kg. NWU Pukke. Student of sports science at North West University, Potchefstroom.
At 800m (/1500m): OG: '12- 1, '16- 1; WCh: '09- 1, '11- 1, '15- sf, '17- 1/3; AfG: '15- 1/8; AfCh: '16- 1/1/1R; WJ: '08- h; Afr-J: '09- 1 (1), won DL 2016-17. RSA 400m 2016-17, 800m 2011-12, 2014-18; 1500m 2011, 2016, 2018.
World best 600m 2017. Five RSA 800m records 2009-17, 600m 2012.
Progress at 800m, 1500m: 2007- 2:09.35, 2008- 2:04.23, 2009- 1:55.45, 4:08.01; 2010- 1:58.16, 2011- 1:56.35, 2012- 1:57.23, 4:12.93; 2013- 1:58.92, 2014- 2:02.66, 2015- 1:59.59, 4:21.63; 2016- 1:55.28, 4:01.99; 2017- 1:55.16, 4:02.84. pbs: 300m 37.22A '17, 400m 50.40 '16, 600m 1:21.77 '17, 1000m 2:35.43A '18, 1500m 4:01.99 '16, 3000m 9:36.29A '17.
Questions over her gender arose at the African Junior and World Champs in 2009, and she was barred from competing by Athletics South Africa until the IAAF determined whether she was free to compete again. They did so in July 2010 but saying that the medical details of her case remained confidential.

Sunette VILJOEN b. 6 Oct 1983 Johannesburg 1.70m 73kg. North West University, Potchefstroom.
At JT: OG: '04/08- dnq 35/32, '12- 4, '16- 2; WCh: '03/09- dnq 16/18, '11-13-15: 3/6/3; CG: '06-10-14: 1/1/2; AfG: '03- 3, '07- 3; AfCh: '04-06-08-10-14-16: 1/2/1/1/1/1; WUG: '07- 5, '09- 1, '11- 1; CCp: '10- 2, '14- 2. Won Afro-Asian Games 2003, RSA 2003-04, 2006, 2009-17.
Four African javelin records 2009-12, two Commonwealth 2011-12.
Progress at JT: 1999- 43.89A, 2000- 45.50A, 2001- 50.70A, 2002- 58.33A, 2003- 61.59, 2004- 61.15A, 2005- 57.31, 2006- 60.72, 2007- 58.39, 2008- 62.24A, 2009- 65.43, 2010- 66.38, 2011- 68.38, 2012- 69.35, 2013- 64.51, 2014- 65.32, 2015- 66.62, 2016- 65.14, 2017- 63.49A.
She played one Test and 17 ODIs for South Africa as an all-rounder at cricket 2000-02. Son Henré born in 2005.

SPAIN

Governing body: Real Federación Española de Atletismo (RFEA)/ Founded 1918.
National Championships first held in 1917 (men), 1931 (women). **2017 Champions**: **Men**:

100m: Ángel David Rodríguez 10.24, 200m: Samuel García 20.59, 400m: Óscar Husillos 45.42, 800m: Saul Ordóñez 1:47.03, 1500m/5000m: Adel Mechaal 3:47.17/14:07.93, 10000m: Juan Antonio Pérez 28:46.72, HMar: Javier Guerra 62:14, Mar: Pablo Villalobos 2:21:42, 3000mSt: Sebastián Martos 8:29.29, 110mh: Orlando Ortega 13.52, 400mh: Sergio Fernández 50.51, HJ: Miguel Ángel Sancho 2.17, PV: Adrián Valles 5.56, LJ: Jean Marie Okutu 7.54, TJ: Pablo Torrojos 16.88, SP: Borja Vivas 20.30, DT: Frank Casañas 59.75, HT: Miguel Alberto Blanco 70.59, JT: Odel Jainaga 73.50, Dec: Vicente Guardiola 7367, 10000mW/20kW: Alvaro Martín 39:47.17/1:21:11, 50kW: José Ignacio Díaz 3:58:52. **Women**: 100m: Christina Lara 11.40, 200m: Estela García 23.63, 400m: Laura Bueno 53.63, 800m: Esther Guerrero 2:03.58, 1500m: Solange Andreia Pereira 4:40.55, 5000m: Ana Lozano 16:02.27, 10000m: Trihas Gebre 32:11.67, HMar: Irena Pelayo 72:11, Mar: Clara Simal 2:37:22, 3000mSt: Irene Sánchez 9:48.45, 100mh: María Míujika 13.51, 400mh: Sara Gallego 57.88, HJ: Ruth Beitia 1.86, PV: Carla Franch 4.21, LJ: Olatz Arrieta 6.43w, TJ: Ana Peleteiro 13.67, SP: Úrsula Ruiz 18.28, DT: Sabina Asenjo 57.97, HT: Berta Castells 67.53, JT: Lidia Parada 57.97, Hep: Carmen Romero 5579, 10000mW: Julia Takacs 44:36.63, 20kW: Lidia Sánchez-Puebla 1:33:58.

Miguel Ángel LÓPEZ b. 3 Jul 1988 Murcia 1.81m 70kg. CA Llano de Brujas-Murcia.
At 20kW: OG: '12- 5, '16- 11 (dnf 50kW); WCh: '11-13-15-17: 13/3/1/10; EC: '10- 13, '14- 1; EU23: '09- 1; WCp: '10- 12, '14- 5; ECp: '11-13-15-17: 5/2/1/2. At 10kW: WJ: '06- 14; WY: '05- 6; EJ: '05- 9, '07- 8; WCp: '06- 2J; ECp: '07- 2J. Won Spanish 10000mW 2010, 2012-16; 20kW 2010, 2012, 2015; 50kW 2016.
Progress at 20kW: 2008- 1:23:44, 2009- 1:22:23, 2010- 1:23:08, 2011- 1:21:41, 2012- 1:19:49, 2013- 1:21:21, 2014- 1:19:21, 2015- 1:19:14, 2016- 1:20:34, 2017- 1:19:57. pbs: 3000mW 11:39.92 '13, 5000mW 18:46.95 '16, 10000mW 38:06.28 '16, 35kW 2:32:56 '15, 50kW 3:53:52 '16.

Alvaro MARTÍN b. 18 Jun 1994 Llerena 1.81m 62kg. Playas de Castellón.
At 20kW: OG: '16- 22; WCh: '13-15-17: 24/16/8; EC: '14- 6; EU23: '15- 2; WCp: '16- 3. At 10kW: WJ: '12- 5; WY: '11- 8; EJ: '13- 3; ECp: '11- 6J. Won Spanish 10000mW 2017, 20kW 2016-18.
Progress at 20kW: 2012- 1:22:12, 2013- 1:22:25, 2014- 1:20:39, 2015- 1:20:19, 2016- 1:19:36, 2017- 1:19:41. pbs: 5000mW 18:39.65 '15, 10000mW 39:23.51 '16, 35kW 2:37:17 '14.

Adel MECHAAL b. 5 Dec 1990 Tetouan, Morocco 1.84m 67kg. New Balance.
At 1500m: OG: '16- h; WCh: '15- h, '17- 4; EC: '14- h. At 3000m: WI: '18- 5; EI: '15- 6, '17- 1. At 5000m: OG: '16- h; EC: '16- 2; Eur CC: '15-16-17: 3/8/2. Won ESP 1500m & 2000m 2015, 2017.
Progress at 1500m, 5000m: 2010- 3:50.16, 2011- 3:42.77, 2012- 3:48.76i, 14:21.96; 2013- 3:36.78, 2014- 3:39.60, 2015- 3:36.55, 14:10.59; 2016- 3:35.24, 13:15.40 '16; 2017- 3:34.70, 13:27.37. pbs: 800m 1:49.51 '13, 3000m 7:35.28 '17, 10km Rd 29:25 '13.
Lived in Spain from 1995, gained Spanish citizenship Feb 2013. Younger brother Said is a Spanish junior CC international.

Orlando ORTEGA b. 29 Jul 1991 La Habana 1.85m 70kg. Club d'Atletisme de la Vall d'Albaida.
At 110mh: OG: '12- 6, '16- 2; WCh: '13- h, '17- 7; WJ: '10- h; PAm: '11- 3; ET: 17- 1. Won DL 2016, Cuban 2011, Spanish 2016-17. At 60mh: EI: '17- 7.
Two Spanish 110mh records 2016 & 60mh 2017.
Progress at 110mh: 2009- 14.11, 2010- 13.99, 2011- 13.29/13.1w, 2012- 13.09, 2013- 13.08, 2014- 13.01, 2015- 12.94, 2016- 13.04, 2017- 13.15/13.09w. pbs: 60m 6.71i '16, 100m 10.62 '11, 400m 47.84 '09, 50mh 6.66+i '12, 60mh 7.45i '15, 7.48i '17.
Left Cuba in 2013 and given Spanish citizenship on 9 Sep 2015 with eligibility confirmed just before 2016 Olympic Games.

Women

Ana PELETEIRO b. 2 Dec 1995 Ribeira, La Coruña 1.71m 52kg. FC Barcelona.
At TJ: WCh: '17- 7; WJ: '12- 1, '14- 5; WY: '11- 3; E23: '17- 2; EJ: '13- 3; WI: '18- 3; EI: '17- 5. Spanish champion 2015, 2017.
Two European youth bests at triple jump 2012.
Progress at TJ: 2011- 13.17, 2012- 14.17, 2013- 13.75i/13.29/13.30w, 2014- 14.07, 2015- 14.03, 2016- 13.91i/13.55, 2017- 14.23, 2018- 14.40i. pbs: 60m 7.56i '14, 100m 11,93 '14, LJ 5.99 '15.

SRI LANKA

Governing body: Athletic Association of Sri Lanka, n°33 Torrington Avenue, Colombo 7. Founded 1922.
National Champions 2017: **Men**: 100m: Yupin Abeykoon 10.52, 200m/400m: Dileep Ruwan 21.39/46.86, 800m: Indunil Herath 1:48.83, 1500m: Hemantha Kumara 3:49.99, 5000m: A.K.Tharanga 14:43.43, 10000m: Lionel Samarajeewa 31:37.7, 3000mSt: R.M.S. Pushpakumara 8:52.19, 110mh: Hasitha Nirmal 14.48, 400mh: A.Rathnasena 51.05, HJ: Manjula Wijesekara 2.21, PV: Ishara Sandaruwan 5.00, LJ: Dhanuka Pithirana 7.97w, TJ: Sanjaya Jayasinghe 16.36, SP: Joy Perera 15.35, DT: Gayan Jayawardana 50.77, HT: Rukshan Kumarasiri 49.21, JT: Sampath Ranasinghe 76.92, Dec: Ajith Kumara Karunathilake 7096. **Women**: 100m/200m: Rumeshika Rathnayake 11.82/24.40, 400m: Upamalika Rathnakumari 53.63, 800m/1500m: Gayanthika Abeyrathne 2:05.69/4:20.64, 5000m: Nilani Priyadarshani 17:20.4, 10000m: Anusha Lamahewage 36:02.56, 3000mSt: Nilani Rathnayake 10:25.25, 100mh: Lakshika Sugandi 14.36, 400mh: Kaushalya Madushani 60.89, HJ: Dulanjali Ranasinghe 1.76; PV: Aniththa Jegatheshwaran 3.47, LJ:

D.V.C.M.Thilakarathne 5.92, TJ: Vidusha Lakshani 13.43, SP: Tharika Kumudumali Fernando 14.52, DT/HT: Ayesha Maduwanthi 41.67/47.95, JT: Anne M De Silva 48.44, Hep: W.V.L. Sugandi 4879.

SWEDEN

Governing body: Svenska Friidrottsförbundet. Founded 1895.

National Championships first held in 1896 (men), 1928 (women). **2017: Men**: 100m: Austin Hamilton 10.18w, 200m: Henrik Larsson 20.71w, 400m: Nick Ekelund-Arenender DEN 47.01, 800m: Andreas Kramer 1:50.46, 1500m: Andreas Almgren 3:48.15, 5000m: Daniel Lundgren 14:08.35, 10000m/3000mSt: Napoleon Solomon 29:07.04/8:40.47, HMar: Mustafa Mohammed 65:18, Mar: Marton Öhman 2:24:11, 110mh: Anton Levin 14.31, 400mh: Isak Andersson 51.17, HJ: Jakob Thorvaldsson 2.13, PV: Melker Svärd-Jacobsson 5.45, LJ: Michel Tornéus 7.65, TJ: Simon Karlén 16.17w, SP: Leif Arrhenius 18.90, DT: Daniel Ståhl 67.80, HT: Oscar Vestlund 71.32, JT: Jiannis Smalios 77.05, Dec: Fredrik Samuelsson 7436, 10000mW: Anders Hansson 41:52.6, 20kW: Ato Ibáñez 1:26:38, 50kW: Perseus Karlsson 4:20:42. **Women**: 100m: Malin Ström 11.62, 200m: Elin Östlund 23.44w, 400m: Lisa Duffy 53.44, 800m/1500m: Meraf Bahta 2:07.29/4:18.25, 5000m: Linn Nilsson 16:13.05, 10000m: Charlotta Fougberg 35:13.97, HMar: Malin Strand 77:53, Mar: Mikaela Larsson 2:42:21, 3000mSt: Maria Larsson 9:58.59, 100mh: Elin Westerlund 13.72, 400mh: Hanna Palmqvist 58.68, HJ: Sofie Skoog 1.87, PV: Michaela Meijer 4.60, LJ: Khaddi Sagnia 6.47w, TJ: Aina Griksaite LTU 13.70, SP: Fanny Roos 17.64, DT: Vanessa Kamga 53.78, HT: Ida Storm 65.61, JT: Sofi Flink 58.29, Hep: Bianca Salming 5883, 5000mW/10kW/20kW: Monica Svensson 26:05.4/57:52/1:39:20.

Armand 'Mondo' DUPLANTIS b. 10 Nov 1999 Lafayette, LA, USA 1.81m 68kg. Upsala IF, Louisiana State University, USA.
At PV: WCh: '17- 9; WJ: '16- 3; WY: '15- 1; EJ: '17- 1; WI: '18- 7=.
World junior pole vault records (3 indoor unratified, 2 out) 2017, 2 indoor 2018.
Progress at PV: 2009- 2.89i, 2010- 3.86, 2012- 3.97i, 2013- 4.15, 2014- 4.60, 2015- 5.30, 2016- 5.51, 2017- 5.90, 2018- 5.88i. Pb LJ 7.15w '17.
Has dual citizenship Sweden/USA. Has been setting world age records from the age of 7 in 2007. His father Greg (USA) had pb 5.80 '93, his mother Helena was a Swedish heptathlete (5314 '83), and his brother Andreas (b. 2 May 1993) had PV pb 5.43i/5.36 '13, WJ: '12- 10, EJ: '11- 9.

Perseus KARLSTRÖM b. 2 May 1990 Eskilstuna né Ibáñez 1.84m 75kg. Eskilstuna FI.
At 20kW: OG: '16- dnf; WCh: '13- 38, '15- dnf, '17- 37; EC: '14-17; ECp: '15- 8, '17- 3. At 10000mW: WJ: '08- 30; WY: '07- 24; EJ: 09- 9. Won SWE 20k 2012-16, 50kW 2013, 2016, 10000mW 2008, 2015-16.
Swedish walks records: 10000m 2017, 20k 2016.
Progress at 20kW, 50kW: 2005- 1:53:39, 2008- 1:35:31, 2009- 1:31:22, 2010- 1:25:32, 2011- 1:26:20, 2012- 1:23:43, 2013- 1:24:55, 3:52:43; 2014- 1:21:54, 2015- 1:22:44, 2016- 1:19:11, 4:06:33; 2017- 1:20:20, 3:44:35. pbs: 1MW 5:38.18 '17, 5000mW 18:56.87 '16, 10000mW 38:57.45 '17.
His father Enrique Vera was 2nd in World 50kW 1976, pb 3:43:59 '79; mother Siw Gustavsson/ Ibáñez/Karlström was 3rd in European 10kW 1986. Brother Anatole Ibáñez (b. 14 Nov 1985) pbs 20kW 1:20:54 '16, 50kW 3:48:42 '14.

Daniel STÅHL b. 27 Aug 1992 Jarfalla 2.00m 155kg. Spårvägens FK.
At (SP)/DT: OG: '16- dnq 14; WCh: '15- 5, '17- 2; EC: '14- dnq 24, '16- 5; EU23: '13- 4; WJ: '10- (dnq 27); WY: '09- dnq 16/dnq 16; EJ: '11- (dnq 20). Won SWE SP 2015-17, DT 2014, 2016-17.
Swedish discus record 2017.
Progress at DT: 2008- 40.36, 2009- 44.34, 2010- 50.32, 2011- 55.60, 2012- 62.16, 2013- 61.29, 2014- 66.89, 2015- 64.73, 2016- 68.72, 2017- 71.29. pbs: SP 19.60i '17, 19.38 '16; HT 48.91 '16, JT 50.43 '16.
Father Jan had pbs SP 16.80 & HT 59.14 '80, mother Taina DT 51.90 '82, sister Annell HT 59.74 '13.

Michel TORNÉUS b. 26 May 1986 Botkyrka 1.84m 70kg. Hammarby IF.
At LJ: OG: '12- 4, '16- dnq 26; WCh: '09-11-13-15-17: dnq 28/27/19/dnq/8; EC: '10-12-14-16: 9/3/5/2; EU23: '07- 10; EJ: '05- 4; WI: '14- 3; EI: '11-13-15-17: 7/2/1/2; ET: '11- 2. Won Swedish LJ 2005, 2007-10, 2012-17 (indoor 2008, 2010-17); TJ 2012, 2016.
Swedish long jump records 2012 & 2016.
Progress at LJ: 2001- 6.48, 2002- 6.74/6.86w, 2003- 7.07, 2004- 7.41, 2005- 7.94, 2006- 7.68, 2007- 7.85, 2008- 7.86, 2009- 8.11, 2010- 8.12/8.21w, 2011- 8.19, 2012- 8.22, 2013- 8.29i/8.00/8.12w, 2014- 8.21i/8.09/8.10w, 2015- 8.30i/7.83/8.07w, 2016- 8.44A/8.07/8.21w, 2017- 8.30A/8.18. pbs: 60m 6.93i '12, 100m 10.71/10.63w '11, 400mh 55.48 '04, HJ 1.99i '05, 1.92 '04; TJ 16.10 '16, Dec 6115 '04.
Father came from DR of Congo.

Women

Meraf BAHTA Ogbagaber b. 24 Jun 1989 Dekishahay, Eritrea 1.76m 50kg. Hälle IF.
At 5000m: EC: '14- 1, '16- 6; ET: '14- 1. At 3000m: CCp: '14- 2. At 1500m: OG: '16- 6; WCh: '17- 9; WJ: '06- 5; EI: '17- 4. World CC: '06- 12J, '07- 6J; Eur CC: '14- 3. Won SWE 800m & 1500m 2017, 5000m 2011, 4k & 8k CC 2013-14.
Swedish records 3000m 2016 & 2017, 5000m 2014 & 2016, 10000m 2017.
Progress at 1500m, 5000m: 2006- 4:16.01, 2007- 4:15.12, 15:56.30; 2008- 4:12.52, 15:58.31; 2009-

4:28.93, 2010- 4:22.86, 16:28.77; 2011- 4:19.82, 16:29.08; 2012- 4:14.09, 2013- 4:05.11, 2014- 4:01.34, 14:59.49; 2015- 4:06.42i, 15:46.97; 2016- 4:02.62, 14:49.95; 2017- 4:00.49. pbs: 800m 2:04.41 '17, 1M 4:25.26 '16, 3000m 8:37.50 '17, 10000m 31:13.06 '17. Came from Eritrea to Sweden as a refugee in 2009; received Swedish citizenship on 23 Dec 2013.

Angelica BENGTSSON b. 8 July 1993 Väckelsång 1.64m 53kg. Hässelby SK.
At PV: OG: '12/16- dnq 19=/14=, WCh: '13- dnq 16, '15- 4=, '17- 10; EC: '12-14-16: 10/5/3; WJ: '10- 1, '12- 1; WY: '09- 1; EU23: '13- 3, '15- 1; EJ: '11- 1; YthOG: '10- 1; EI: '15- 3, '17- 3=; ET: '15- 3. SWE champion 2012, 2014-16.
Pole vault records: Two world youth 2010; four world junior indoors 2011, two world junior outdoor bests, six Swedish 2011-15.
Progress at PV: 2005- 3.10, 2006- 3.40, 2007- 3.90, 2008- 4.12, 2009- 4.37, 2010- 4.47, 2011- 4.63i/4.57, 2012- 4.58, 2013- 4.55, 2014- 4.62i/4.50, 2015- 4.70, 2016- 4.66i/4.65, 2017- 4.65. pbs: LJ 5.66 '16, JT 35.04 '17.
Rising Star Awards: IAAF 2010, European Athletics 2012. Her father Glenn had JT pb 67.08 '82, sisters Victoria (b. 1990) PV 4.00 '09 and Maria (b. 1988) DT 43.95 '07.

Khaddijatou **'Khaddi' SAGNIA** b. 20 Apr 1994 Helsingborg 1.73cm 63kg. Ullevi FK.
At LJ: OG: '16- dnq 27; WCh: '15- 7, '17- dnq 16; EC: '16- 6; WY: '11- 11; EU23: '15- 4; WI: '18- 6. At TJ: WY: '11- 9; YthOG: '10- 1. Won SWE TJ 2011, LJ 2015-17, 100m 2016.
Progress at LJ: 2007- 5.18i, 2008- 5.56, 2009- 6.03i/5.89/6.00w, 2010- 6.26, 2011- 6.32, 2014- 6.55, 2015- 6.78, 2016- 6.74, 2017- 6.72, 2018- 6.92i. Pbs: 60m 7.40i '15, 100m 11.48 '16, 200m 25.14 '14, 60mh 8.14i '18, 100mh 13.93 '15, 13.62w '14; HJ 1.78 '11, TJ 13.65/13.86w '11, JT 41.47 '14, Hep 5287 '11.

Sofie SKOOG b. 7 Jun 1990 Mora 1.81m 65kg. IF Göta Karlstad.
At HJ: OG: '16- 7; WCh: '15/17 dnq 14=/18; EC: '16- 9; WI: '16- 5. SWE champion 2015, 2017.
Progress at HJ: 2004- 1.55, 2005- 1.61, 2006- 1.64, 2007- 1.70, 2008- 1.71, 2009- 1.72, 2010- 1.78, 2011- 1.75i/1.65, 2012- 1.80, 2013- 1.90, 2014- 1.88i/1.87, 2015- 1.92, 2016- 1.94, 2017- 1.94. Pb TJ 11.05/11.29w '12.

SWITZERLAND

Governing body: Schweizerischer Leichtathletikverband (SLV). Formed 1905 as Athletischer Ausschuss des Schweizerischen Fussball-Verbandes.
National Championships first held in 1906 (men), 1934 (women). **2017**: **Men**: 100m: Alex Wilson 10.25, 200m: Silvan Wicki 20.70, 400m: Joel Burgunder 46.00, 800m: Jonas Schöpfer 1:53.79, 1500m: Julien Wanders 3:44.74, 5000m: Jonas Raess 14:22.28, 10000m: Sullivan Brunet 29:44.25, HMar: Abraham Tadesse 63:19, Mar: Fabian Anrig 2:27:23, 3000mSt: Adriamo Engelhardt 9:22.05, 110mh: Tobias Furer 14.13, 400mh: Alain-Hervé Mfomkpa 51.01, HJ: Loïc Gasch 2.26, PV: Mitch Greeley 5.00, LJ: Christopher Ullmann 7.61, TJ: Nils Wicki 15.63, SP: Gregori Ott 17.22, DT: Lukas Jost 50.88, HT: Martin Bingisser 62.74, JT: Laurent Carron 66.58, Dec: Dominik Alberto 7631, 10000mW: Quentin Macabrey 48:28.3, 20kW: Patrick Gavillet 1:59:22. **Women**: 100m/200m: Mujinga Kambundji 11.08/22.42, 200m: Léa Sprunger 22.38, 400m: Vanessa Zimmermann 52.89, 800m: Lore Hoffmann 2:13.64, 1500m: Stefanie Barmet 4:26.13, 5000m/10000m: Martina Tresch 16:28.58/33:38.30, HMar: Laura Hrebec 76:33, Mar: Franziska Inauen 2:52:49, 3000mSt: Fabienne Schlumpf 9:40.36, 100mh: Caroline Agnou 13.60, 400mh: Robine Schürmann 58.02, HJ: Salome Lang 1.80, PV: Angelica Moser 4.61, LJ/TJ: Fatim Affesi 6.19/12.53, SP: Lea Herrsche 14.16, DT: Chantal Tanner 44.17, HT: Nicole Zihlmann 60.67, JT: Nadja-Marie Pasternack 50.21, Hep: Elodie Jakob 5554, 5000mW: Laura Polli 23:41.0.

Tadesse ABRAHAM b. 12 Aug 1982 Asmara, Eritrea 1.78m 61kg. LC Uster.
At HMar: EC: '16- 1; at Mar: OG: '16- 7; WCh: '15- 19; EC: '14- 9. Won Swiss 10000m 2014, HMar 2015. Swiss records: half marathon 2015, marathon 2016.
Progress at Mar: 2009- 2:10:09, 2010- 2:09:24, 2011- 2:12:48, 2012- 2:10:26, 2013- 2:07:45, 2014- 2:15:05, 2015- 2:11:37, 2016- 2:06:40. pbs: 10000m 28:41.37 '15, Road: 10k 28:28 '13, 10 47:12 '12, HMar 60:42 '15.
Competed for Eritrea in World Junior CC in 2003 & 2004, but later disqualified when it was found that he was over-age. Lived in Switzerland from 30 Mar 2004, Swiss citizenship 10 Jun 2014. Won Zürich marathon 2009, 2013.

Kariem HUSSEIN b. 1 Apr 1989 Münsterlingen 1.90m 77kg. TV Amriswil
At 400mh: OG: '16- h; WCh: '15- sf, '17- 8; EC: '12- sf, '14- 1, '16- 3; EU23: '11- sf; CCp: '14- 2; Swiss champion 2011-15.
Swiss 300mh records 2014 & 2017.
Progress at 400mh: 2009- 52.33, 2010- 51.64, 2011- 51.09, 2012- 49.61, 2013- 49.78, 2014- 48.47, 2015- 48.45, 2016- 48.87, 2017- 48.45. pbs: 60mh 8.14i '11, 110mh 14.51 '11, 300mh 34.87 '17.
Successive pbs at end of 2014 from 49.08 to 48.96 EC, 48.70 WK, 48.47 CCp. Father Ehab came from Egypt to Switzerland in the early 1980s.

Women

Selina BÜCHEL b. 26 Jul 1991 Mosnang 1.68m 58kg. KTV Bütschwil
At 800m: OG: '16- sf; WCh: '15/17- sf; EC: '14- sf,

'16- 4; WJ: '10- sf; EU23: '11- 5, 13- 3; EJ: '09- 7; WI: '14- 4; EI: '15- 1, '17- 1. Won Swiss 400m 2016, 800m 2011, 2013.
Swiss 800m record 2015.
Progress at 800m: 2008- 2:11.68, 2009- 2:06.20, 2010- 2:05.95, 2011- 2:04.25, 2012- 2:04.02, 2013- 2:01.64i/2:01.66, 2014- 2:00.93i/2:01.42, 2015- 1:57.95, 2016- 1:58.77, 2017- 1:59.46. pbs: 400m 52.97 '17, 600m 1:25.45 '15, 1500m 4:08.95i '16, 4:18.57 '15.

Nicole BÜCHLER b. 17 Dec 1983 Biel 1.62m 56kg. LC Zürich.
At PV: OG: '08/12- dnq 22/25, '16- 6; WCh: '09-11-13-15: dnq 14/16/15/17=, '17- 11; EC: '14- dnq 17; EU23: '05- 12; WUG: '07- 3, '09- 2; WI: '12- 8, '16- 4. Won Swiss 400m 2016, 800m 2009, 2012-13, 2015.
12 Swiss pole vault records (and 14 indoors).
Progress at PV: 2004- 3.80, 2005- 4.15, 2006- 4.10, 2007- 4.35, 2008- 4.40, 2009- 4.50, 2010- 4.47i/4.00, 2011- 4.50, 2012- 4.60, 2013- 4.61, 2014- 4.67, 2015- 4.71, 2016- 4.80i/4.78, 2017- 4.73. pbs: 60mh 8.65i '09, 100mh 14.01 '09, LJ 5.65 '07.
She competed for Switzerland at two World and four European championships at rhythmic gymnastics, taking up pole vaulting at the age of 20. Married US pole vaulter Mitch Greeley (5.56sq '08, 5.55i '09) in 2010.

Mujinga KAMBUNDJI b. 17 Jun 1992 Uetendorf 1.68m 59kg. ST Bern.
At 100m/(200m): OG: '16- sf/sf; WCh: '15/17- sf/sf; EC: '12- h, '14- 4/5, '16- 3/sf; WJ: '10- sf/sf; WY: '09- sf/6; EU23: 13- 4/5; EJ: '11- 5/5; At 60m: WI: '18- 3; EI: '15- 5, '17- 3. Won Swiss 100m 2009, 2011-17; 200m 2009, 2012-15, 2017.
Swiss records: 100m (8), 200m (4) 2014-17.
Progress at 100m, 200m: 2007- 12.17, 2008- 12.02, 24.30; 2009- 11.66, 23.87; 2010- 11.70/11.57w, 23.68; 2011- 11.53, 22.70/23.31w; 2012- 11.62, 23.26; 2013- 11.50, 23.24; 2014- 11.20, 22.83; 2015- 11.07, 22.64; 2016- 11.14, 22.78; 2017- 11.07, 22.42. pbs: 60m 7.03i '18.
Congolese-Swiss father, Swiss mother.

Léa SPRUNGER b. 5 Mar 1990 1.83m 69kg. COVA Nyon.
At 400mh: OG:'16- h; WCh: '15- sf, '17- 5; EC: '16- 3; At Hep: WJ: '08-10; WY: '07- 13; EU23: '11- 16; EJ: '09- 3; At 200m: OG: '12- h; EC: '12/14- sf; At 400m: EI: '17- 5. Won Swiss 200m 2016-17, 400m 2014.
Swiss records: 200m 2016, 400m 2017.
Progress at 400mh: 2015- 55.60, 2016- 54.92, 2017- 54.29. pbs: 60m 7.37i '14, 100m 11.34 '14, 150m 17.06 '16, 200m 22.38 '16, 300m 35.70 '17, 400m 51.09 '17, 800m 2:23.94 '09, 60mh 8.65i '12, 100mh 14.31 '11, 300mh 39.29 '17, HJ 1.81 '08, LJ 6.14 '08, SP 12.77i '12, 12.63 '11; JT 38.73 '09, Pen 4047i '12, Hep 5651 '11.
Older sister Ellen Springer (b. 8 Aug 1986) Hep 6124 '12.

SYRIA

Majed El Dein GHAZAL b. 21 Apr 1987 Damascus 1.93m 72kg.
At HJ: OG: '08/12- dnq 24=/28=, 16- 7=; WCh: '09/11/13/15- dnq 28=/23=/21/15, '17- 3; AsiG: '10- dnq 13=, '14- 6; AsiC: '11- 2, '17- 3. Won WMilG 2015, Is.Sol & Asian Ind G 2017.
13 Syrian records 2007-16.
Progress at HJ: 2006- 2.09, 2007- 2.17, 2008- 2.21i/2.20, 2009- 2.16, 2010- 2.22, 2011- 2.28, 2012- 2.326, 2013- 2.23, 2014- 2.26, 2015- 2.31, 2016- 2.36, 2017- 2.32.

TADJIKISTAN

Governing body: Athletics Federation of Tadjikistan. Founded 1932.

Dilshod NAZAROV b. 6 May 1982 Dushanbe 1.87m 115kg.
At HT: OG: '08- 11, '12- 9, '16- 1; WCh: '05-07-09-11-13-15-17: dnq 15/dnq 21/11/10/5/2/7; WJ: '98- dnq 15, '00- 5, AsiG: '98-02-06-10-14: 7/9/1/1/1; AsiC: '03-05-07-09-13-15-17: 3/2/2/1/1/1/1; CCp: '10- 2, '14- 4. Won Asi-J 1999, 2001, C.Asian 2003.
Progress at HT: 1998- 63.91, 1999- 63,56, 2000- 66.50, 2001- 68.08, 2002- 69.86, 2003- 75.56, 2004- 76.58, 2005- 77.63, 2006- 74.43, 2007- 78.89, 2008- 79.05, 2009- 79.28, 2010- 80.11, 2011- 80.30, 2012- 77.70, 2013- 80.71, 2014- 80.62, 2015- 79.36, 2016- 78.87, 2017- 77.81.
President of national federation. In 2016 he won the first Olympic gold medal at any sport for Tadjikistan.

TAIWAN

Governing body: Chinese Taipei Athletics Association.

National Games 2017: **Men**: 100m/200m: Yang Chun-Han 10.29/20.56, 400m: Yang Lung-Hsiang 46.58, 800m/1500m: Hung Yu-Chao 1:51.94/3:58.38, 5000m/10000m/3000mSt: Chou Ting-Yin 14:37.14/31:40.94/8:58.90, Mar: Ho Chin-Ping 2:35:58, 110mh: Chen Kuei-Ju 13.58. 400mh: Chen Chieh 49.88, HJ: Hsiang Chun-Hsieng 2.14, PV: Yeh Yao-Wen 4.90, LJ: Lin Chia-Hao 7.72, TJ: Li Kuei-Lung 15.42, SP: Chang Ming-Huang 18.84, DT: Li Tzu-Yun 51.63, HT: Tzeng Hao-Chan 62.85, JT: Cheng Chao-Tsun 78.62, Dec: Chou Chun-Kai 6873. 20kW: Chang Wei-Lin 1:30:56; **Women**: 100m: Hu Chia-Chen 11.82, 200m: Liao Yen-Chun 24.38, 400m: Yang Jui-Hsuan 54.69, 800m/1500m: Chu Yun-Cheng 2:13.11/4:32.13, 5000m/10000m/Mar: Hsieh Chien-Ho 16:30.20/34:50.17/2:54:46, 3000m St: Chen Chao-Chun 10:35.97, 100mh: Hsieh His-En 13.64, 400mh: Luo Pei-Lin 58.15, HJ: Tsai Min-Ting 1.69, PV: Lin Ying-Tung 4.00, LJ: Liu Ya-Chun 5.93w, TJ: Chuang Chih-Han 12.32, SP: Lin Chia-Ying 15.99, DT: Li Tsai-Yi 52.20, HT: Hung Hsiu-Wen 54.69, JT: Li Huei-Chun 51.47,

Hep: Chu Chia-Ling 5396, 20kW: Lin Wen-Tzu 1:43:53.

CHENG Chao-Tsun b. 17 Oct 1993. 1.82m 88kg.
At JT: OG: 16- 5; WCh: '17- dnq 22; WJ: '10- 8; WY: '09- dnq 12; AsG: '14- 5; AsiC: '11-15-17: 11/7/6; WUG: '15- 4, '17- 1. Won Asi-J 2012.
Javelin records: 4 Taiwan 2010-17, Asian 2017.
Progress at JT: 2009- 71.71, 2010- 78.68, 2011- 77.07, 2012- 77.10, 2013- 71.22, 2014- 81.61, 2015- 81.78, 2016- 71.66, 2017- 91.36.

TANZANIA

Governing body: Tanzania Amateur Athletic Association. Founded 1954.

Alphonce FELIX SIMBU b. 14 Feb 1992 Singida region 1m kg.
At Mar: OG: 16- 5; WCh: '15- 12, '17- 3. At 10000m: AfG: '11- 8.
Progress at Mar: 2015- 2:12:01, 2016- 2:09:19, 2017- 2:09:10. pbs: 10000m 29:58.20 '11; Road: 10M: 46:05 '12, HMar 61:59 '16.
Marathon win: Mumbai 2017.

TRINIDAD & TOBAGO

Governing body: National Association of Athletics Administrations of Trinidad & Tobago. Founded 1945, reformed 1971.
National Championships first held in 1946 (men) and 1947 (women). **2017 Champions**: **Men**: 100m: Emmanuel Callender 10.10, 200m: Jereem Richards 20.15, 400m: Machel Cedonio 44.90, 800m: Jamaal James 1:49.38, 1500m: Mark London 4:06.81, 5000m: Colin Pereira 15:45.83, 110mh: Ruebin Walters 13.34, 400mh: Kern Alexis 50.52, HJ: Kareem Roberts 2.17, PV: Anderson Subero 3.20, LJ: Che Richards 7.80, TJ: Diamond Payne 14.19, SP: Hezekiel Romeo 18.19, DT: Quincy Wilson 54.56, HT: Ryan Samuel 19.35, JT: Tyriq Horsford 66.80, Dec: Jameel Joseph 4657. **Women**: 100m/200m: Michelle-Lee Ahye 10.82/22.50, 400m: Domonique Williams 52.74, 800m: Alena Brooks 2:05.44, 1500m: April Francis 5:15.83, 100mh: Deborah John 13.36, 400mh: Sparkle McKnight 55.61, HJ: Ayana Glasgow 1.60, LJ/TJ: Ayanna Alexander 5.97/13.63, SP: Portious Warren 15.42, DT: LaToya Gilding 42.83, HT: Sherselle Murray 28.84, JT: Chuntal Mohan 43.60, Hep: Khemani Roberts 5269.

Machel CEDENIO b. 6 Sep 1995 Pt. Fortin 1.83m 70kg. Simplex.
At 400m/4x400mR: OG: '16- 4; WCh: '15- 7/2R, '17- sf/1R; WJ: '12- 5/3R, '14- 1; WY: '11- 4; PAm: '15- 2/1R; WI: '16- res 3R. Won CAC-J 2014, TTO 2016-17. TTO 400m record 2016.
Progress at 400m: 2010- 48.12, 2011- 46.89, 2012- 46.02, 2013- 45.93, 2014- 45.13, 2015- 44.36, 2016- 44.01, 2017- 44.90. Pbs: 200m 21.15 '13, 300m 31.7+ '16.

Lalonde GORDON b. 25 Nov 1988 Lowlands, Tobago 1.88m 83kg. Tigers. Studied at Mohawk Valley CC.
At 400m/4x400mR: OG: '12- 3/3R, '16- sf; WCh: '15- sf/2R, '17- sf/1R; CG: '10- sf, '14- 3/3R; CAG: '10- 3R; WI: '12- 3R, '14- 5, '16- 6/3R. At 200m: WCh: '13- sf. Won NACAC 2015, TTO 200m 2013-14, 400m 2012.
Progress at 400m: 2009- 49.47, 2010- 46.33, 2011- 45.51, 2012- 44.52, 2013- 45.67, 2014- 44.78, 2015- 44.64A/44.70, 2016- 44.69, 2017- 45.02. pbs: 100m 10.45 '12, 200m 20.26 '13, 300m 31.92 '17.
Moved with his family to New York at the age of seven, and still lives there.

Jereem RICHARDS b. 13 Jan 1994 Pt. Fortin 1.83m 66kg. University of Alabama, USA.
At 200m/4x400mR: WCh: '17- 3/1R; WJ: '12- sf/3R, WY: '11- sf; CG: '14- h; WI: '12- 3R. Won TTO 2017.
Progress at 200m, 400m: 2011- 21.23, 47.32; 2012- 20.82, 47.17; 2013- 20.72/20.69w, 46.20; 2014- 20.58, 46.15; 2015- 20.72, 45.91; 2016- 46.02, 2017- 19.97, 45.21. Pbs: 300m 32.10i '18, 33.16 '16.

Keshorn WALCOTT b. 2 Apr 1993 Toco 1.88m 90kg. Rebirth.
At JT: OG: '12- 1, '16- 3; WCh: '13/15- dnq 19/26, '17- 7; CG: '14- 2; WJ: '10- dnq, '12- 1; WY: '09- dnq 13; PAm: '11- 7, '15- 1; CCp: '14- 3. Won CAC-J 2010, 2012; TTO 2012, 2015-16.
Javelin records: CAC 2015, nine TTO 2012-15, eight CAC junior 2011-12.
Progress at JT: 2009- 60.02, 2010- 67.01, 2011- 75.77A, 2012- 84.58, 2013- 84.39, 2014- 85.77, 2015- 90.16, 2016- 88.68, 2017- 86.61. pb TJ 14.28 '10.
First Caribbean Olympic champion and youngest ever Olympic champion in throwing events. Won IAAF Rising Star Award 2012. Elder brother Elton TJ pb 16.43/16.51w '11 & 4 WY '09, aunt Anna Lee Walcott Hep pb 5224 '00.

Women

Michelle-Lee AHYE b. 10 Apr 1992 Port of Spain 1.68m 59kg. Rebirth.
At 100m/(200m): OG: '12- sf, '16- 6/6; WCh: '11- sf, '13- sf, '15- 5/3R, '17- 6; CG: '14- sf; WY: '07- qf; CCp: '14- 2/1R; PAm-J: '11- 1. At 60m: WI: '14-16-18: 6/4/6. TTO champion 100m & 200m 2014, 2016-17.
TTO records: 100m 2017, 200m (2) 2016.
Progress at 100m, 200m: 2006- 11.94, 24.60; 2007- 11.76/11.63w, 24.30/24.23w; 2008- 11.48, 23.80; 2009- 11.69, 2010- 11.32, 24.14/23.71w; 2011- 11.20/11.15w, 22.92w; 2012- 11.19, 23.13; 2013- 11.06, 22.98; 2014- 10.85, 22.77; 2015- 10.97/10.87w, 23.19i, 22.01w; 2016- 10.90, 22.25; 2017- 10.82, 22.50. pbs: 50m 6.33i '13, 60m 7.09i '16.

Kelly-Ann BAPTISTE b. 14 Oct 1986 Plymouth, Tobago 1.68m 58kg. Zenith. Studied psychology at Louisiana State University.
At 100m/(200m): OG: '08- qf, '12- 6, '16- h; WCh: '05- qf, '09: sf/sf, '11- 3, '15- 6/3R, '17- 8; WJ: '02- sf, '04- (4); WY: '03- 3; PAm: '03- h, '15- 5; CCp:

'10- 1/1R. Won NCAA 100m & indoor 60m 2008, TTO 100m 2005-06, 2008-10, 2012-13, 2015; 200m 2005, 2013.
TTO records: 100m (6) 2005-14, 200m (5) 2005-13.
Progress at 100m, 200m: 2002- 11.71, 24.03; 2003- 11.48, 23.22; 2004- 11.40, 23.41/22.99w; 2005- 11.17/11.04w, 22.93; 2006- 11.08, 22.73; 2007- 11.22, 22.90i/22.95; 2008- 11.06/10.97w, 22.67; 2009- 10.94/10.91w, 22.60; 2010- 10.84, 22.78/ 22.58w; 2011- 10.90, 2012- 10.86, 22.33w; 2013- 10.83dq, 22.36bq; 2015- 10.84, 22.91w; 2016- 11.04, 22.73; 2017- 10.88. pbs: 55m 6.73i '06, 60m 7.13i '08.
Withdrawn from 2013 Worlds team after failing a drugs test and was given a 1y 9m ban and results annulled from 24 Mar 2013 by the IAAF.

Cleopatra BOREL b. 3 Oct 1979 Mayoro 1.68m 93kg. Rebirth. Was at University of Maryland; assistant coach at Virginia Tech University.
At SP: OG: '04- 9, '08- dnq 15, '12- dnq 11, '16- 7; WCh: '05-07-09-13: dnq 17/17/12/13, '11/15- 11/12; CG: '02-06-10-14: 4/3/2/2; PAm: '03-07-11-15: 6/3/2/1; CAG: '06-10-14: 3/1/1; CCp: '14- 5; WI: '04-06-08-16-18: dnq 11/7/6/4/9. Won NACAC 2007, CAC 2008, 2011, 2013; TTO 2002, 2004, 2006-10, 2012, 2014-16.
Eight TTO records at shot 2004-11.
Progress at SP: 2000- 14.64i, 2001- 16.44, 2002- 17.50i/16.90, 2003- 17.95i/17.79, 2004- 19.48i/18.90, 2005- 18.44, 2006- 18.81, 2007- 18.91, 2008- 18.87, 2009- 18.52, 2010- 19.30, 2011- 19.42, 2012- 18.82, 2013- 17.84, 2014- 19.13, 2015- 19.26, 2016- 18.78, 2017- 17.96. pb HT 51.28 '01.
Formerly competed under married name Borel-Brown. Her father Rayond Borel was TTO javelin champion 1973.

TUNISIA

Governing body: Fédération Tunisienne d'Athlétisme. Founded 1957.

Women

Habiba GHRIBI b. 9 Apr 1984 Kairouan 1.70m 57kg. Entente Franconville Cesame Va, FRA.
At 3000mSt: OG: '08- 12, '12- 1, '16- 12; WCh: '05-09-11-15: h/5/1/2; AfCh: '06- 2, '14- 5 (6 1500m). At 5000m: AfCh: '02- 11. Won FRA 1500m 2014, Arab 3000mSt 2017.
African 3000mSt record 2015, Tunisian: 1500m 2014, 3000m (3) 2008-13, 3000mSt (10) 2005-15.
Progress at 3000mSt: 2005- 9:51.49, 2006- 10:14.36, 2007- 9:50.04, 2008- 9:25.50, 2009- 9:12.52, 2011- 9:11.97, 2012- 9:08.37, 2014- 9:15.23, 2015- 9:05.36, 2016- 9:18.71, 2017- 9:20.00. pbs: 1500m 4:06.38 '14, 3000m 8:46.61i '15, 8:49.5+ '13; 5000m 16:12.9 '03, 10000m 35:03.83 '05, 10kRd 33:30 '04.
Missed 2010 season after toe surgery. Won first Olympic medal for a woman from Tunisia.

TURKEY

Governing body: Türkiye Atletizm Federasyonu. Founded 1922.

National Champions 2017: **Men**: 100m: Kayhan Özer 10.65, 200m: Alkin Özyürek 21.68, 400m: Yasin Süzen 48.14, 800m: Hasan Basri Güdük 1:50.90, 1500m: Süleyman Bekmezci 3:45.43, 5000m: Cihut Ulus 14:24.65, 10000m: Sezgin Ataç 30:23.30, 3000mSt: Turgay Bayram 8:54.52, 110mh: Mehmet Emin Bayram 14.45, 400mh: Sinan Ören 52.10, HJ: Enes Talha Senses 2.12, PV: Ümit Sungur 5.15; LJ: Alper Kulaksiz 7.84, TJ: Can Özüpek 15.78, DT: Talat Erdogan 52.47, HT: Özkan Baltaci 74.60, JT: Ahmet Talha Kiliç 68.38. Dec: Mustfa Yilmaz 6557, 10kW: Serkan Dogan 40:12, 20kW: Ersin Tacir 1:22:31. **Women**: 100m: Nimet Karakus 11.88, 200m: Yaren Açar 25.61, 400m: Emel Sanli 55.85, 800m/1500m: Semra Karaslan 2:07.45/4:26.49, 5000m: Emine Hatun Tuna 16:28.76, 3000mSt: Sümeyye Erol 10:07.52, 100mh: Özge Solu 13.79, 400mh: Emel Sanli 58.33, HJ: Kadriye Aydin 1.80, PV: Buse Ankazan 4.10; LJ: Ecem Çalagan 6.13w, TJ: Hayrunnisa Kazkayasi 12.23w, SP: Emel Dereli 17.63, DT: Elçin Kaya 48.77, HT: Kivilcim Salman-Kaya 70.77, JT: Aysel Boztas 43.43, 10kW/20kW: Elif Koç 48:41/1:42:13.

Polat Kemboi ARIKAN (ex Paul KEMBOI) b. 12 Dec 1990 Cheptirte, Kenya 1.73m 62kg.
At (5000m)/10000m: OG: '12- h/9, '16- 13; WCh: '13/17- dnf; EC: '12- 3/1, '14- 4, '16- 1; ECp: '12-14-15: 1/1/1; won Med G 2013. At 3000m: EI: '13- 10. Eur CC: '12-13-14-16-17: 7/2/1/2/9. World HMar: 14- 16, CC: '15- 22.
Turkish records 3000m 2012, 5000m 2011, HMar 2014.
Progress at 5000m, 10000m: 2006- 14:23.4A, 2009- 13:24.25, 2010- 13:18.12, 2011- 13:05.98, 2012- 13:12.55i/13:27.21, 27:38.81; 2013- 28:17.26, 2014- 28:11.11, 2015- 13:30.76, 28:05.64; 2016- 27:35.50, 2017- 13:19.20, 27:42.55. pbs: 1500m 3:47.05 '12, 3000m 7:42.31 '12, HMar 61:22 '14.
Became a Turkish citizen 9 Jun 2011, originally with 2-year wait for international eligibility, but waiting period ended in February 2012.

Yasmani COPELLO Escobar. b. 15 Apr 1987 La Habana, Cuba 1.96m 86kg. Fenerbahçe.
At 400mh: OG: '16- 3; WCh: '15- 6, '17- 2; EC: '16- 1; Ibero-American champion 2008, Balkan 2015, Cuban NG 2010.
Six Turkish 400mh records 2015-16.
Progress at 400mh: 2006- 52.30, 2007- 49.99, 2008- 50.08, 2009- 49.56, 2010- 51.23, 2011- 49.76, 2012- 50.28, 2013- 49.89, 2014- 50.62, 2015- 48.46, 2016- 47.92, 2017- 48.24. pbs: 200m 21.44 '09, 400m 46.77 '09, 110mh 14.35A '08.
Former Cuban, has lived in Turkey from 2012, acquired citizenship 21 Oct 2013, cleared to compete for them from 30 Apr 2014.

Ramil GULIYEV b. 29 May 1990 Baku, Azerbaijan 1.87m 73kg. Fenerbahçe. Student teacher
At (100m)/200m: OG: '08- qf, '16- 8; WCh: '09- 7,

'15- 6, '17- 1; EC: '14- h/6, '16- 6/2; WJ: '06- (h), '08- 5; WY: '07- 2; EJ: '09- 2/1; WUG: '09- 1, '15- 3/3; ET: '14- 3/2. At 60m: EI: '09- 7. Won Balkan 100m 2014, 2016; 200m 2014-16, TUR 100m 2012, 200m 2016; Is.Sol 100m & 200m 2017.
Records: European Junior 200m 2009; AZE 100m (2) 2009, 200m (4) 2007-09; TUR 100m (2) & 200m (4) 2011-15.
Progress at 200m: 2006- 21.74, 2007- 20.72, 2008- 20.66, 2009- 20.04, 2010- 20.73, 2011- 20.32, 2012- 20.53, 2013- 20.46, 2014- 20.38, 2015- 19.88, 2016- 20.09, 2017- 20.02/19.98w. pbs: 60m 6.58i '12, 100m 9.97/9.9 '17, 300m 32.61 '16.
Switched from Azerbaijan to Turkey on 26 Apr 2011, and cleared to compete for Turkey from 4 Apr 2013.

Jak Ali HARVEY b. 5 Apr 1989 Hanover Parish, Jamaica 1.82m 73kg. ENKA.
At 100m/(200m): OG: '16- sf/h; WCh: '15/17- sf; EC: '16- 2; WUG: '11- 1; Won Balkan 100m 2015, 2017, 200m 2017; TUR 2016.
Four Turkish 100m records 2015-16.
Progress at 100mh: 2007- 10.90, 2008- 10.53, 2009- 10.57/10.46w, 2010- 10.26, 2011- 10.09/10.03w, 2012- 10.08, 2013- 10.04, 2014- 10.17, 2015- 10.01, 2016- 9.92A/10.03, 2017- 10.10/10.03w. pb 200m 20.38 '15.
Born Jacques Montgomery Harvey. Turkey citizen from 25 Jul 2014, cleared to compete for them from 24 Jul 2015.

Ali KAYA b. 20 Apr 1994 Eldoret, Kenya 1.71m 55kg. Ex Stanley Kiprotich KEN. Fenerbahçe.
At 5000m/(10000m): OG: '16- h/dnf; WCh: '15- 9/7; EC: '14- 9/3. '16- (2); EU23: '15- 1/1; ECp: '14- 3/2; EJ: '13- 1/1; CCp: '14- 5. At 3000m: EI: '15- 1, '17- 9. World CC: '17- 3 MxR; Eur CC: '13- 1J, '14- 2, '15- 1.
Records: European U23 & Turkish 5000m & 10,000m 2015, HMar 2016; TUR 3000m & half marathon 2015.
Progress at 5000m, 10000m: 2013- 13:31.39, 28:31.16; 2014- 13:34.83, 28:08.72; 2015- 13:00.31, 27:24.09; 2016- 14:05.34, 28:21.42; 2017- 13:25.71, 27:54.41. pbs: 1500m 3:44.62 '16, 3000m 7:38.42i/ 7:38.65 '15, HMar 60:16 '16.
Moved to Turkey in 2010 and became a Turkish citizen on 6 Jun 2013.

Kaan Kigen ÖZBILEN (Mike Kipruto **KIGEN)** b. 15 Jan 1986 Keiyo district, Kenya 1.70m 54kg.
At 5000m/(10000m): AfCh: '06- 2/2; WCp: '06- 2. At HMar: WCh: '18- 9; EC: '16- 2. At Mar: OG: '16- 17; WCh: '17- 14. World CC: '06- 5; Eur CC: '16- 10, '17- 1. Won Kenyan 5000m 2006.
Progress at 5000m, 10000m, Mar: 2005- 13:22.48, 2006- 12:58.58, 28:03.70; 2008- 13:09.84, 2009- 13:04.38, 2011- 13:11.65, 27:30.53; 2012- 13:21.55A, 27:03.49; 2013- 13:36.51, 2:08:24; 2014- 13:26.6, 2:06:59; 2015- 2:07:42, 2016- 2:06:10, 2017- 14:04.50, 27:41.99, 2:14:29. pbs: 3000m 7:35.87 '06, 2M 8:20.09 '05, Road: 10M 45:34 '14, HMar 59:58 '11, 25k 1:14:17 '14, 30k 1:29:15 '14.
2nd Frankfurt marathon 2014, 3rd Amsterdam 2015. Acquired Turkish citizenship as Kaan Kigen Özbilen on 24 Jun 2015. 3rd Seoul Marathon 2016, but his 2:06:10 may not be eligible for European record.

Women

Yasemin CAN (formerly **Vivian Jemutai** KEN) b. 11 Dec 1996 Kenya. 1.66m 49kg. ENKA.
At 5000m/10000m: OG: 16- 6/7; WCh: '17- h/11; EC: '16- 1/1; EU23: '17- 1/1; At 3000m: EI: '17- 2. World CC: '17- 3 MxR; Eur CC: '16- 1, '17- 1. Won Balkan 5000m & 10000m 2017; TUR 10000m 2016, Is.Sol 2017.
European U23 records 10000m (3), 15k Rd 2016
Progress at 5000m, 10000m: 2015- 15:39.90, 32:42.31; 2016- 14:37.61, 30:26.41; 2017- 14:36.82, 31:18.20. pbs: 1500m 4:11.54i '17, 4:16.42- 16; 3000m 8:38.5 '17, 15k Rd 48:40 '16.
Became a Turkish citizen on 25 May 2015, cleared to compete for them from 13 Mar 2016.

Eda TUGSUZ b. 27 Mar 1997 1.71m 68kg.
At JT: WCh: '17- 5; EC: '16- 11; WJ: '14- dnq 21, '16- 3; WY: '13- 5; EU23: '17- 4; EJ: '15- 8. Won Isl. Sol 2017, Balkan 2016, TUR 2016
6 Turkish javelin records 2016-17, European U23 record 2017.
Progress at JT: 2013- 50.29, 2014- 52.53, 2015- 56.52, 2016- 58.95, 2017- 67.21.

UGANDA

Governing body: Uganda Athletics Federation. Founded 1925.

National Champions 2017: **Men:** 100m: Pius Adome 10.62w, 200m: Benson Okot 21.37, 400m: Leonard Opiny 46.05, 800m: Rashid Etiau 1:47.93, 1500m: Abu Salim Mayanja 3:46.93, 5000m: Moses Kurong 13:43.30, 10000m: Timothy Toroitich 28:37.78, 30000mSt: Benjamin Kiplagat 8:46.31, HJ: Francis Isaano 1.90, LJ/TJ: Francis Oketayot 7.17/14.40, SP: Jacob Wokorach 13.33, DT: Oscar Opio 37.03, JT: Robert Okello 59.77. **Women**: 100m: Maureen Banura 12.04, 200m/400m: Leni Shida 24.09/53.55, 800m/ 1500m: Docus Ajok 2:02.24/4:15.07, 5000m: Mercyline Chelangat 15:54.80, 10000m: Rachael Chemutai 33:51.69, 3000mSt: Sylvia Chelangat 10:51.67, HJ: Sharon Amito 1.50, LJ: Mary Unyuthfua 5.67, SP: Caroline Aber 11.27, JT: Nancy Lakot 43.11.

Joshua Kiprui **CHEPTEGEI** b. 12 Sep 1996 1.79m 61kg.
At (5000m)/10000m: OG: '16- 8/6; WCh: '15- 9, '17- 2; WJ: '14- 4/1; won Afr-J 2015. UGA champion 5000m 2014-16.
Ugandan 15k road record 2017.
Progress at 10000m: 2013- 28:53.52A, 2014- 13:32.84, 27:56.26; 2015- 13:28.50A, 27:27.57; 2016- 13:00.60, 27:10.06; 2017- 12:59.83, 26:49.94. pbs: 1500m 3:37.82 '16, 3000m 7:34.96 '17, 15k Rd 41:16 '17, 3000mSt 8:43.21A '13.

Had big lead at 3/4 distance in World Cross 2017, but faded badly to 30th.

Stephen KIPROTICH b. 27 Feb 1989 Kapchorwa 1.72m 56kg.
At Mar: OG: '12- 1, '16- 14; WCh: '11- 8, '13- 1, '15- 6. At 5000m: WCh: '07- h. At 10000m: WJ: '08- 5, AfCh: '10- 6, World CC: '08-11-17: 12J/6/17; AfChC: '11- 2.
Ugandan marathon records 2011 & 2015.
Progress at Mar: 2011- 2:07:20, 2012- 2:07:50, 2013- 2:08:05, 2014- 2:11:37, 2015- 2:06:33, 2016- 2:07:46, 2017- 2:07:31. Pbs: 3000m 7:48.06 '07, 5000m 13:23.70 '08, 10000m 27:58.03 '10, HMar 61:15 '13, 3000mSt 8:26.66 '10.
Won Enschede marathon on debut 2011. Became the second man ever to win Olympic and World titles at marathon. 2nd Tokyo 2015, Hamburg & Fukuoka 2017.

UKRAINE

Governing body: Ukrainian Athletic Federation (FLAU). Founded 1991.

National Champions 2017: **Men**: Serhiy Smelyk 10.25, 200m: Emil Ibrahimov 21.01, 400m: Vitaliy Butrym 46.48, 800m: Yevhen Hutsol 1:49.14, 1500m: Yuriy Kishchenko 3:50.34, 5000m: Volodymyr Kyts 14:10.47, 10000m: Dmytro Lashyn 29:15.51, Mar: Artem Piddubnyy 2:24:20, 3000mSt: Vasyl Koval 8:50.78, 110mh: Artem Shamatryn 13.95, 400mh: Anatoliy Synyanskyy, HJ: Viktor Lonskyy 2.28, PV: Ivan Yeryomin 5.40, LJ: Vladyslav Mazur 7.92, TJ: Oleksandr Malosilov 16.21, SP: Viktor Samolyuk 19.15, DT: Ivan Panasyuk 60.35, HT: Serhiy Reheda 73.73, JT: Dmytro Sheremet 73.38, Dec: Serhiy Yarokhovych 7134, 20kW: Ruslan Dmytrenko 1:22:35, 50kW: Andriy Hrechkovskyy 4:10:14. **Women**: 100m/100mh: Anna Plotitsyna 11.63/12.89, 200m: Alina Kalistratova 23.35, 400m: Kateryna Klymyuk 52.26, 800m: Anastasiya Tkachuk 2:03.14, 1500m: Olena Zhushman 4:26.38, 5000m: Yuliya Shmatenko 15:22.85, 10000m: Viktoriya Kaluzhna 33:35.96, Mar: Oksana Yurchuk 2:54:07, 3000mSt: Oksana Rayta 10:21.97, 400mh: Viktoriya Tkachuk 57.20, HJ: Oksana Okuneva 1.97, PV: Maryna Kylypko 4.60, LJ: Maryna Bekh 6.59, TJ: Olha Saladukha 13.90, SP: Viktoriya Klochko 16.07, DT: Nataliya Semenova 60.16, HT: Iryna Novozhylova 69.10, JT: Hanna Hatsko-Fedyusova 57.13, Hep: Anastasiya Cheremisina 5001, 20kW: Valentyna Myronchuk 1:35:22, 50kW: Khrystyna Yudkina 4:32:14.

Ivan BANZERUK b. 9 Feb 1990 1.77m 65kg. Volinska.
At 50kW: OG: '16- 39; WCh: '13-15-17: dq/15/19; EC: '14- 5; WCp: '14- 7, '16- 6; ECp: '13-15-17: 6/4/1.
Progress at 50kW: 2010- 4:21:57, 2011- 4:06:52, 2012- 3:56:20, 2013- 3:47:35, 2014- 3:49:02, 2015- 3:49:02, 2016- 3:51:57, 2017- 3:48:15. pbs: 5000mW 19:38.41i '15, 19:39.05 '14; 10000mW 40:37.5 '14, 10kW 40:01 '15, 20kW 1:22:08 '15, 35k 2:30:58 '14.

Bohdan BONDARENKO b. 30 Aug 1989 Kharkiv 1.97m 80kg.
At HJ: OG: '12- 7, '16- 3; WCh: '11-13-15-17: dnq 15=/1/2=/9; EC: '12- 11, '14- 1; WJ: '06- 3, '08- 1; EU23: '11- 1; EJ: '07- 9; WUG: '11- 1, CCp: '14- 1; ET: '13- 1. Won DL 2013.
Three UKR high jump records 2013-14.
Progress at HJ: 2005- 2.15, 2006- 2.26, 2007- 2.25i/2.19, 2008- 2.26, 2009- 2.27/2.15, 2010- 2.10, 2011- 2.30, 2012- 2.31, 2013- 2.41, 2014- 2.42, 2015- 2.37, 2016- 2.37, 2017- 2.32.
His father Viktor had decathlon pb of 7480 '87.

Igor HLAVAN b. 25 Sep 1990 Nazarivka, Kirovohrad 1.72m 62kg.
At (20kW)/50kW: OG: '12- 16, '16- 35/dnf; WCh: '13- 4, '15- 4/dq, '17- 4; EC: '14- 6; WCp: '12- 10, '14- (7), '16- 2; ECp: '13- 4, '15- (5), '17- 2. Won UKR 35kW 2013. UKR 50km walk record 2013.
Progress at 20kW, 50kW: 2010- 1:30:31, 4:08:08; 2011- 1:25:58, 4:03:18; 2012- 3:48:07, 2013- 1:22:32, 3:40:39; 2014- 1:19:59, 3:45:08; 2015- 1:20:29, 2016- 1:21:55, 3:44:02; 2017- 3:41:42. pbs: 5000mW 19:11.87 '14, 10000mW 39:15.1 '14, 35kW 2:31:15 '13.

Oleksiy KASYANOV b. 26 Aug 1985 Stakhanov, Lugansk 1.91m 87kg. Spartak Zaporozhye.
At Dec: OG: '08- 6, '12- 7, '16- dnf; WCh: '09-11-13-15-17: 4/12/dnf/9/6; EC: '10-12-14-16: dnf/2/8/4; EU23: '07- 4; WUG: '07- 4; ECp: '09-15-17: 3/2/2. UKR champion 2008. At Hep: WI: '10-12-14-16: 6/2/5/2; EI: '09- 2.
Progress at Dec: 2006- 7599, 2007- 7964, 2008- 8238, 2009- 8479, 2010- 8381, 2011- 8251, 2012- 8312, 2014- 8231, 2015- 8262, 2016- 8077, 2017- 8281. pbs: 60m 6.83i '09, 100m 10.50 '11, 200m 21.54 '15, 400m 47.46 '08, 1000m 2:39.44i '14, 1500m 4:22.27 '08, 60mh 7.85i '13, 110mh 13.92 '15, HJ 2.08i 14, 2.05 '09; PV 4.82 '09, LJ 8.04i/7.97 '10, SP 15.72 '09, DT 51.95 '10, JT 55.84 '07, Hep 6254i '10.
Won Talence decathlon 2009 & 2016. Married Hanna Melnychenko (qv) on 18 Oct 2014.

Andriy PROTSENKO b. 20 May 1988 Kherson 1.94m 80kg. Khersonskaya. Biotechnology graduate.
At HJ: OG: '12- 9, '16- 4=; WCh: '09-11-13-15-17: dnq 25/27/23=/17/13=; EC: '10-12: dnq 17/13=, '14- 2, '16= 9=; EU23: '09- 3; EJ: '07- 2; WI: '14- 3, '16- 7; EI: '15- 6; WUG: '13- 2; ET: '10- 3, '14- 1. UKR champion 2012.
Progress at HJ: 2005- 2.10, 2006- 2.18i/2.10, 2007- 2.21, 2008- 2.30, 2009- 2.25, 2010- 2.25, 2011- 2.31, 2012- 2.31, 2013- 2.32, 2014- 2.40, 2015- 2.33i/2.32, 2016- 2.33, 2017- 2.30.

Women

Yuliya LEVCHENKO b. 28 Nov 1997 1.79m 60kg.
At HJ: OG: '16- dnq 19; WCh: '15: dnq 24, '17- 2; WJ: '16- 3; WY: '13- 13; EU23: '17- 1; EJ: '15- 6;

YOG: '14- 1; WI: '18- 5; EI:'17- 3.
Progress at HJ: 2013- 1.77, 2014- 1.89, 2015- 1.92, 2016- 1.95, 2017- 2.01.

Oksana OKUNEVA b. 14 Mar 1990 Mykolaiv 1.75m 61kg. Mykolaivska.
At HJ: OG: '16- dnq 22=; WCh: '11-13-15-17: dnq 19/15/14=/dnq 20; EC: '14- 6, '16- 6=; WY: '07- 6; EU23: '11- 2; EJ: '09- 6; EI: '11- 7, '17- 4; WUG: '17- 1; ET: '14- 2. UKR champion 2011, 2013-14, 2016.
Progress at HJ: 2005- 1.60, 2006- 1.75, 2007- 1.78, 2008- 1.80, 2009- 1.90, 2010- 1.92, 2011- 1.94, 2012- 1.93i/1.87, 2013- 1.92, 2014- 1.98, 2015- 1.92, 2016- 1.97, 2017- 1.97.

Nataliya PRYSHCHEPA b. 11 Sep 1994 Kiev 1.63m 50kg. Rivnenska.
At 800m: OG: '16- sf; EC: '16- 1; WY: '11- sf. At 1500m: EC: '14- 10, '16- h; WJ: '12- h; E23: '15- 3; EJ: '13- 1; ET: '14- 3, '17- 3. Won UKR 800m 2016, 1500m 2013 & 2016.
Progress at 800m. 1500m: 2011- 2:08.02, 2012- 2:04.47, 4:22.63; 2013- 2:05.52, 4:13.81; 2014- 4:08.89, 2015- 2:05.22, 4:06.29; 2016- 1:58.60, 4:10.51; 2017- 1:58.82, 4:13.51.

Olha SALADUKHA b. 4 Jun 1983 Donetsk 1.75m 55kg.
At TJ: OG: '08- 7, '12- 3, '16- dnq 18; WCh: '07-11-13-15: 5/1/3/6; EC: '06-10-12-14-16: 4/1/1/1/6; WJ: '02- 5; EU23: '05- 4; EJ: '01- 9; WI: '08- 5, '14- 2; EI: '13- 1; WUG: '05- 2, '07- 1; WCp: '06-10-14: 6/2/3; ECp: '06-08-10-11-13-14: 1/1/1/1/1/2. Won DL 2011, UKR 2007-08, 2017.
Progress at TJ: 1998- 13.32, 1999- 12.86, 2000- 13.26, 2001- 13.48, 2002- 13.66i/13.63, 2003- 13.26i/13.03, 2004- 13.22, 2005- 14.04, 2006- 14.41/14.50w, 2007- 14.79, 2008- 14.84, 2010- 14.81, 2011- 14.98/15.06w, 2012- 14.99, 2013- 14.88i/14.85, 2014- 14.73, 2015- 14.62, 2016- 14.40, 2017- 14.02i/13.97. pb LJ 6.37 '06.
Married to professional road cyclist Denys Kostyuk with a daughter Diana born 2009.

Alina SHUKH b. 12 Feb 1999 Izmail, Odeksa region 1.75m 60kg. BVUFK Brovary.
At Hep: WCh: '17- 14; WY: '15- 3; EJ: 17- 1; EY: '16- 1; ET: '17- 1. At Pen: WI: '18- 7.
World youth spec heptathlon record 6186 in 2016, world indoor junior pentathlon record 2017.
Progress at Hep: 2016- 6099, 2017- 6381. pbs: 200m 25.97 '16, 800m 2:12.31 '17, 60mh 8.85i '17, 8.6 '18; 100mh 14.32/14.13w '17, 13.50w '17; HJ 1.92 '16, LJ 6.29 '17, TJ 12.70i '18, SP 14.27i/13.96 '17, JT 56.54 '17, Pen 4550i '17.

UNITED KINGDOM

Governing body: UK Athletics. Founded 1999 (replacing British Athletics, founded 1991, which succeeded BAAB, founded 1932). The Amateur Athletic Association was founded in 1880 and the Women's Amateur Athletic Association in 1922.

National Championships (first were English Championships 1866-79, then AAA 1880-2006, WAAA from 1922). **2017 UK Champions**: **Men**: 100m: Reece Prescod 10.09, 200m: Nethaneel Mitchell-Blake 20.18, 400m: Matthew Hudson-Smith 44.99, 800m: Elliot Giles 1:49.52, 1500m: Chris O'Hare 3:47.28, 5000m: Andrew Butchart 13:50.56, 10000m: Andrew Vernon 28:21.15, HMar (ENG): Mohammed Fraah 60:06, Mar: Josh Griffiths 2:14:53, 3000mSt: Rob Mullett 8:41.43, 110mh: David Kinbg 13.64w, 400mh: Jack Green 49.34, HJ: Robbie Grabarz 2.26, PV: Luke Cutts 5.45, LJ: Dan Bramble 8.02, TJ: Ben Williams 16.71, SP: Scott Lincoln 17.82, DT: Nick Percy 60.78, HT: Nick Miller 74.98, JT: Joseph Dunderdale 73.58, Dec: James Finney 7263, 5000mW/20kW: Tom Bosworth 18:43.28/1:24:59, 50kW: David Walker 5:29:12. **Women**: 100m: Asha Philip 11.21, 200m: Shannon Hylton 22.94, 400m: Zoey Clark 52.30, 800m: Shelayna Oskan-Clarke 2:01.54, 1500m: Laura Weightman 4:06.49, 5000m: Stephanie Twell 15:35.50, 10000m: Beth Potter 32:04.63, Mar: Alyson Dixon 2:29:06, 3000mSt: Iona Lake 9:57.83, 100mh: Alicia Barrett 13.07, 400mh: Eilidh Doyle 55.59, HJ: Morgan Lake 1.96, PV: Holly Bradshaw 4.45, LJ: Lorraine Ugen 6.59, TJ: Naomi Ogbeta 13.64, SP: Rachel Wallader 16.70, DT: Jade Lally 58.14, HT: Sophie Hitchon 67.58, JT: Laura Whittingham 52.07, Hep: Niamh Emerson 5801, 5000mW: Bethan Davies 21:21.52, 20kW: Gemma Bridge 1:32:33, 50kW: Jayne Farquhar 6:01:31.

Tom BOSWORTH b. 17 Jan 1990 Pembury, Kent 1.84m 64kg. Tonbridge, was at Leeds Metropolitan University.
At 20kW: OG: '16- 6, WCh: '15- 24, '17- dq; EC: '14- 12; CG: '10- 11; ECp: '17- 4 won RWA 2010-11, 2016-17; UK 50000mW 2011, 2014-16; 10kW 2011.
World bests: 1MW 2017, 3000m indoor 2018. UK walk records: 5000m (4) 2011-17, 10k road 2015, 20k (2) 2016.
Progress at 20kW: 2010- 1:28:24, 2011- 1:27:18, 2012- 1:24:49, 2013- 1:24:44, 2014- 1:22:20, 2015- 1:22:33, 2016- 1:20:13, 2017- 1:20:58. pbs: 1MW: 5:31.08 '17, 3000mW 10:30.28 '18, 11:29.54 '16; 5000mW 18:28.70i '18, 18:43.28 '17; 10kW 39:36 '15, 41:34.19t '15.

Andrew BUTCHART b. 14 Oct 1991 Dunblane 1.75m 64kg. Central.
At 5000m: OG: '16- 6; WCh: '17- 8; won UK 2016-17. At 3000m: ET: '15- 3. Eur CC: '16- 4, '17- 3.
Progress at 5000m: 2009- 14:49.93, 2010- 15:18.33, 2013- 15:14.18, 2014- 13:58.05, 2015- 13:29.49, 2016- 13:08.61, 2017- 13:11.45. pbs: 800m 1:51.39 '14, 1500m 3:37.58i '17, 3:44.57 '15; 1M 3:54.23i '17, 4:05.40 '13; 3000m 7:37.56 '17, 2M 8:12.63i '17, 10000m 29:32.43 '15, 10k Rd 28:28 '16, HMar 70:03 '17.

Mohamed FARAH b. 23 March 1983 Mogadishu, Somalia 1.71m 65kg. Newham &

Essex Beagles.
At 5000m (/10000m): OG: '08- h, '12- 1/1, '16- 1/1; WCh: '07- 6, '09- 7, '11- 1/2, '13- 1/1, '15- 1/1, '17- 2/1; EC: '06- 2, '10- 1/1, '12- 1, '14- 1/1; CG: '06- 9; WJ: '00- 10; EJ: '01- 1; EU23: '03 & '05- 2; ECp: '08-09-10-13: 1/1/1 &(1)/1. At 3000m: WY: '99- 6; WI: '08- 6, '12- 4; EI: '05-07-09-11: 6/5/1/1; ECp: '05-06: 2/2. World CC: '07- 11, '10- 20; HMar: '16- 3; Eur CC: '99-00-01-04-05-06-08-09: 5J/7J/2J/15/21/1/2/2. Won DL 5000m 2017, UK 5000m 2007, 2011; Mar 2014, HMar 2016.
Records: World indoor 2M 2015, European 10000m 2011, indoor 5000m 2011 (u) & 2017, 1500m 2013; indoor 2M 2012, 20k and half marathon 2015, 15k 2016; UK 3000m 2016, 2M 2014, 5000m 2010 & 2011, half mar (3) 2011-15.
Progress at 1500m, 5000m, 10000m: 1996- 4:43.9, 1997- 4:06.41, 1998- 3:57.67, 1999- 3:55.78, 2000- 3:49.60, 14:05.72; 2001- 3:46.1, 13:56.31; 2002- 3:47.78, 14:00.5; 2003-3:43.17, 13:38.41; 2004- 3:43.4, c.14:25; 2005- 3:38.62, 13:30.53; 2006- 3:38.02, 13:09.40; 2007- 3:45.2i+, 3:46.50, 13:07.00; 2008- 3:39.66, 13:08.11, 27:44.54; 2009- 3:33.98, 13:09.14; 2010- 12:57.94, 27:28.86; 2011- 12:53.11, 26:46.57; 2012- 3:34.66, 12:56.98, 27:30.42; 2013- 3:28.81, 13:05.88, 27:21.71; 2014- 13:23.42, 28:08.11; 2015- 3:28.93, 13:11.77, 26:50.97; 2016- 3:31.74, 12:59.29, 26:53.71; 2017- 13:00.70, 26:49.51. pbs: 800m 1:48.69 '03, 1M 3:56.49 '05, 2000m 5:02.1+ '16, 3000m 7:32.62 '16, 2M 8:03.40i '15, 8:07.85 '14; 2000mSt 5:55.72 '00; road 15k 42:03+ '16, 10M 45:32+ '15, 20k 56:27 '15, HMar 59:22dh/59:32 '15, Mar 2:08:21 '14.
Joined his father in England in 1993. Sixth man ever to win Olympic 5000m/10,000m double at same Games and uniquely repeated that in 2016; first British athlete to win either title and to win three/four Olympic golds. In 2013 became third man to win World 5000m/10000m double and he repeated that in 2015; now has record eight global distance running titles. Won in New York on his debut in 2011 and has seven wins, including Great North Run 2014-17, and three 2nds in his ten half marathons. He was knighted in the 2017 New Year's Honours

Miguel FRANCIS b. 28 Feb 1995 Montserrat 1.86m 75kg. Team Force 2000.
At 200m: WCh: '15- sf; WJ: '14- sf; CG: '14- 7R; PAm: '15- 6.
Three Antiguan 200m records 2015-16.
Progress at 100m: 2013- 20.60/20.58w, 2014- 20.71, 2015- 20.05/19.76dt, 2016- 19.88/19.67 doubtful, 2017- 20.44. pbs: 100m 10.28 '15, 150m 14.95 '16, 400m 46.48 '17.
Antigua to UK 24 Sep 2016. Eligible for international competition from 30 Mar 2017.

Adam GEMILI b. 6 Oct 1993 London 1.78m 73kg. Blackheath & Bromley.
At 100m/(200m)/4x100mR: OG: '12- sf, '16- (4); WCh: '13- (5), '17- 1R; EC: '14- (1)/1R, '16- 1R; CG: '14- 2/2R; WJ: '12- 1; EU23: '13- 1/4/1R; EJ: '11- 2/2R; ET: '13/14- 1R. Won UK 200m 2016. European 4x100m record 2017.
Progress at 100m, 200m: 2009- 11.2, 2010- 10.80/10.72w, 21.87w; 2011- 10.35/10.23w, 20.98; 2012- 10.05, 20.38; 2013- 10.06, 19.98; 2014- 10.04, 19.98; 2015- 9.97; 2016- 10.11, 19.97; 2017- 10.08/10.03w, 20.35. Pb 60m 6.59i '16.
Sixth equal all-time junior list 10.05 to win World Junior 100m in 2012, improved 200m best from 20.30 to 20.17 and 19.98 at 2013 Worlds before 5th in final in 20.08. At football he was a member of the Chelsea youth academy before playing for Dagenham & Redbridge. Won European Athletics Rising Star award 2014.

Robbie GRABARZ b. 3 Oct 1987 Enfield 1.92m 87kg. Newham & Essex Beagles.
At HJ: OG: '12- 3=, '16- 4=; WCh: '13- 8, '15- dnq 18=, '17- 6=; EC: '12- 1, '16- 2; WJ: '06- 12; EU23: '09- 11; EJ: '05- dnq 18; WI: '12- 6=, '16- 2; EI: '13- 6, '17- 2; won DL 2012, UK 2012-13, 2015-17.
UK high jump record 2012.
Progress at HJ: 2002- 1.75, 2004- 2.00, 2005- 2.22, 2006- 2.20i/2.14, 2007- 2.21, 2008- 2.27, 2009- 2.23i/2.22, 2010- 2.28, 2011- 2.28, 2012- 2.37, 2013- 2.31, 2014- 2.27i, 2015- 2.28, 2016- 2.33, 2017- 2.31. pb TJ 14.40 '09.

Matthew HUDSON-SMITH b. 26 Oct 1994 Wolverhampton 1.92m 79kg. Birchfield H.
At 400m/4x400mR: OG: '16- 8; WCh: '17- sf/3R; EC: '14- 2/1R, '16- 3R; CG: '14- 1R. At 200m: EJ: '13- 3/3R. Won UK 2016-17.
Progress at 400m: 2009- 52.09, 2011- 50.61, 2013- 48.76i, 2014- 44.75, 2015- 45.09, 2016- 44.48, 2017- 44.74. pbs: 60m 6.96i '12, 100m 10.9 '13, 10.8w '12; 200m 20.88 '13, 300m 32.3+ '16.

Zharnell HUGHES b. 13 Jul 1995 Sandy Ground, Anguilla 1.90m 79kg. Racers TC, Jamaica.
At (100m)/200m: WCh: '15- 5, '17- sf; EC: '16- h; WJ: '12- sf/h, '14- 5; ET: '17- 1R. Won CAC-J 2014, UK 2015, PAm-J 100m 2013.
Records: Anguilla: 100m (4), 200m (6) 2012-14.
Progress at 200m: 2012- 20.90, 2013- 20.79/20.77w, 2014- 20.32, 2015- 20.02, 2016- 20.62, 2017- 20.22. pbs: 100m 10.01 '18, 400m 46.95 '16.
Switched from Anguilla and cleared to compete for Britain from 19 June 2015.

Nick MILLER b. 1 May 1993 Carlisle 1.88m 112kg. Border H, Oklahoma State University, USA.
At HT: OG: '16- dnq 22/ WCh: '15: 11, '17- 6; EC: '16- dnq 25; CG: '14- 2; WJ: '12- dnq 25; EU23: '13- 9, '15- 1; ET: '15- 2, '17- 3. UK champion 2014-15, 2017; NCAA 2016. UK hammer record 2015.
Progress at HT: 2010- 49.86, 2011- 57.74, 2012- 67.56, 2013- 71.60, 2014- 74.38, 2015- 77.55, 2016- 76.93, 2017- 77.51. Pbs: DT 45.37 '13, Wt 22.46i '15.

Nethaneel MITCHELL-BLAKE b. 2 Apr 1994 Newham, London 1.86m 75kg. Ilford, Louisiana State University, USA.

At 200m/4x100mR: OG: '16- sf; WCh: '17- 4/1R; EC: '16- 5; WY: '11- sf; EJ: '13- 1/5R.
European 4x100m record 2017.
Progress at 200m: 2007- 25.4, 2011- 21.54, 2012- 21.49, 2013- 20.62, 2014- 20.69, 2016- 19.95, 2017- 20.04. Pbs: 60m 6.65i '16, 100m 9.99 '17, 400m 46.55 '16.
Moved when he was 13 with his family from London to Mandeville, Jamaica, where he went to Jamaica College, Kingston

Andrew POZZI b. 15 May 1992 Leamington Spa 1.86m 79kg. Stratford-upon-Avon. Bristol University.
At 110mh: OG: '12- h, '16- sf; WCh: '17- sf; EC: '16- dns; EJ: '11- 2. UK champion 2012, 2016. At 60mh: WI: '12-14-18: 4/4/1; EI: '17- 1.
Progress at 110mh: 2009- 14.8, 2011- 13.73/13.66w, 2012- 13.34, 2015- 13.62, 2016- 13.19, 2017- 13.14/13.13w. pbs: 100m 10.9 '11, 60mh 7.43i '17, LJ 6.73 '09.

Greg RUTHERFORD b. 17 Nov 1986 Milton Keynes 1.88m 84kg. Marshall Milton Keynes.
At LJ: OG: '08- 9, '12- 1, '16- 3; WCh: '09- 5, '15- 1, '07-11-13- dnq 21/15=/14; EC: '06-14-16: 2/1/1; CG: '06-10-14: 8/2/1; EJ: '05- 1; EI: '09- 6; ET: '13- 3, '14- 2. Won DL 2015, AAA 2005-06, UK 2008, 2012, 2015.
Three UK Long jump records 2009-14.
Progress at LJ: 1999- 5.04, 2001- 6.16, 2003- 7.04, 2004- 7.28, 2005- 8.14, 2006- 8.26, 2007- 7.96, 2008- 8.20, 2009- 8.30, 2010- 8.22, 2011- 8.27/8.32w, 2012- 8.35, 2013- 8.22, 2014- 8.51, 2015- 8.41, 2016- 8.31/8.36w, 2017- 8.18. pbs: 60m 6.68i '09, 100m 10.26 '10.
European Athlete of the Year 2015. Great-grandfather Jock Rutherford played 11 internationals for England at football 1904-08.

Danny TALBOT b. 1 May 1991 Trowbridge 1.84m 73kg. Birchfield H, bath University.
At 200m/4x100mR: OG: '12- dq hR, '16- sf; WCh: '15- sf, '17- sf/1R; EC: '12- 3, '14- sf/res 1R, '16- 3; CG: '14- 7/2R; WJ: '10- sf; E23: '11- 4/2R, '13- 2/1R; ET: '14- 2 100m; '15- 2/1R, '17- 1R. Won UK 2014. European 4x100m record 2017.
Progress at 200m: 2005- 24.8/24.6w, 2006- 22.96, 2007- 22.03/21.8, 2008- 21.64, 2009- 21.35, 2010- 20.97, 2011- 20.54, 2012- 20.52, 2013- 20.45, 2014- 20.36, 2015- 20.25, 2016- 20.25, 2017- 20.16/19.86w. Pbs: 60m 6.62i '14, 100m 10.14 '14, 150mSt 15/06 '16, 14.79w '15; 400m 47.84i '15.

Chijindu UJAH b. 5 Mar 1994 Enfield 1.80m 75kg. Enfield & Haringey.
At 100m: OG: '16- sf; WCh: '15- sf, '17- sf/1R; EC: '16- 1R; WJ: '12- 6; WY: '11- 8; EJ: '13- 1; ET: 17- 1R. UK champion 2015, DL 2017.
European 4x100m record 2017.
Progress at 2009- 11.61, 2010- 10.83, 2011- 10.58/10.49w, 2012- 10.26, 2013- 10.32, 2014- 9.96, 2015- 9.96, 2016- 10.01/9.97w, 2017- 9.97/9.95w. pbs: 60m 6.53i '15, 200m 20.39 '17.

Women

Dina ASHER-SMITH b. 4 Dec 1995 Farnborough 1.65m 55kg. Blackheath & Bromley. Student at King's College, London.
At 200m/4x100mR (100m): OG: '16- 5/3R; WCh: '13- 3R, '15- 5, '17- 4/2R; EC: '14- dnf, '16- 1/2R; WJ: '12- 7, '14- (1); EJ: '13- 1/1R. At 60m: WI: '16- dns; EI: '15- 2. Won UK 100m 2015.
UK recs 100m (2) & 200m 2015, 4x100m (2) 2016.
Progress at 100m, 200m: 2009- 12.10, 24.83; 2010- 12.00/24.50; 2011- 11.96, 24.16/24.11w; 2012- 11.54, 23.49; 2013- 11.38/11.30w, 23.14; 2014- 11.14/11.93w, 22.61; 2015- 10.99, 22.07; 2016- 11.08, 22.31; 2017- 11.13, 22.22. pbs: 60m 7.08i '15, 150mSt 16.70 '17, 400m 53.49 '14.

Holly BRADSHAW b. 2 Nov 1991 Preston 1.75m 68kg. née Bleasdale. Blackburn Harriers.
At PV: OG: '12- 6=, '16- 5; WCh: '11- dnq, '15- 7, '17- 6; WI: '12- 3, '14- 9; WJ: '10- 3; EU23: '11- 1; EI: '13- 1. UK champion 2011-12, 2015-17.
7 UK pole vault records 2011-17, 5 indoors 2011-12.
Progress at PV: 2007- 2.30, 2008- 3.10i, 2009- 4.05, 2010- 4.35, 2011- 4.71i/4.70, 2012- 4.87i/4.71, 2013- 4.77i/4.60, 2014- 4.73i, 2015- 4.70, 2016- 4.76i/4.70, 2017- 4.81. pbs: SP 11.81i '17, 11.32 '11; JT 37.60 '11.
World age-19 best 2011, age-20 best 2012. Married 800m runner Paul Bradshaw (1:47.37 '09) on 25 Oct 2014.

Eilidh CHILD/DOYLE b. 20 Feb 1987 Perth 1.72m 59kg. Pitreavie. PE degree from Edinburgh University.
At 400mh/4x400mR: OG: '12- sf, '16- 8/3R; WCh: '09/11- sf, '13- 5/2R, '15- 6/3R, '17- 8/2R; EC: '10- 8, '12- 4R, '14- 1/3R, '16- 1R; CG: '10- 2, '14- 2; EU23: '07- 5, '09- 2; CCp: '14- 2; ET: '09-10-13-14-15-17: 3R/2/1&1R/2/1/1; UK champion 2014-17. At 400m: WI: '14- 3R, '18- 3; EI: '13- 2/1R, '17- 2R.
Progress at 400mh: 2003- 59.8mx, 2004- 59.53, 2005- 59.78, 2006- 59.7/60.05, 2007- 57.11, 2008- 56.84, 2009- 55.32, 2010- 55.16, 2011- 55.67, 2012- 54.96, 2013- 54.22, 2014- 54.39, 2015- 54.46, 2016- 54.09, 2017- 54.36. pbs: 200m 24.51i '13, 24.56 '08; 300m 37.1i '13, 400m 51.45i/51.83 '13, 800m 2:24.2 '04, 60mh 8.89i '06, 100mh 14.51 '04, 14.38w '07, 200mhSt 25.84 '14.
Married Brian Doyle (400m 47.12 '06) Oct 2015.

Desiree HENRY b. 26 Aug 1995 Enfield, London 1.72m 60kg. Enfield & Haringey.
At 100m/(200m): OG: '16- sf/3R; WCh: '15- 4R, '17- sf/2R; EC: '14- 7/1R, '16- dnf; WJ: '12- (4), '14- 4; WY: '11- (1); EJ: '13- (2)/1R; WCp: '14- 2R.
Progress at 100m, 200m: 2007- 27.05i, 2008- 12.58/12.4w, 25.37/25.01w; 2009- 12.04/12.01w/ 12.0,24.18;2010-12.11/11.93w,23.93i/24.06/23.66w; 2011- 11.92/11.51w, 23.25; 2012- 11.84/11.48w, 23.28; 2013- 11.50/11.43w, 23.32; 2014- 11.13/ 11.04w, 23.29/23.16w; 2015- 11.11, 22.94; 2016- 11.06, 22.46; 2017- 11.09, 22.69. pbs: 60m 7.22i '14,

150mSt 16.57 '16 (UK best), 400m 52.27 '16.
One of the seven torchbearers who lit the cauldron at the Opening Ceremony of the 2012 Olympic Games.

Sophie HITCHON b. 11 Jul 1991 Burnley 1.70m 74kg. Blackburn H.
At HT: OG: '12- 8, '16- 3; WCh: '11-13: dnq 25/18, '15- 4, '17- 7; EC: '12- 10, '14- dnq 19, '16- 4; CG: '14- 3; WJ: '08- 7, '10- 1; WY: '07- dnq 17; EU23: '11- 3, '13- 1; EJ: '09- 3; ET: '13- 3; won Comm-Y 2008, UK 2011-12, 2014-17.
13 UK hammer records 2011-16.
Progress at HT: 2006- 40.98, 2007- 54.56, 2008- 60.73, 2009- 63.18, 2010- 66.01, 2011- 69.59, 2012- 71.98, 2013- 72.97, 2014- 71.53, 2015- 73.86, 2016- 74.54, 2017- 73.97. pbs: 100m 12.2/12.40 '09, 200m 25.2 '08, 25.51 '09; SP 10.75 '08.

Katarina JOHNSON-THOMPSON b. 9 Jan 1993 Liverpool 1.83m 70kg. Liverpool H.
At Hep: OG: '12- 13, '16- 6; WCh: '13-15-17: 5/28 & 11 LJ/5 & 5 HJ; WY: '09- 1; EU23: '13- 1; EJ: '09- 8, '11- 6. At LJ: WJ: '12- 1 (sf 100mh); WI: '14- 2. At Pen: WI: '18- 1; EI: '15- 1. Won UK LJ 2014.
UK indoor records: high jump (2) 2014-15, long jump & pentathlon 2015.
Progress at LJ, Hep: 2006- 5.11, 2007- 5.77i/5.65, 2008- 6.11i/5.90/6.07w, 5343; 2009- 6.31, 5481; 2010- 6.25i/5.58, 2011- 6.44, 5787; 2012- 6.51/ 6.81w, 6267; 2013- 6449, 6.56; 2014- 6.92, 6682; 2015- 6.93i/6.79, 5039; 2016- 6.84, 6523; 2017- 6.75, 6691. pbs: 60m 7.50i '14, 100m 12.35 '08, 12.2 '09, 11.30w '14; 200m 22.79 '16, 300m 38.56i '08, 400m 53.7 '14, 800m 2:07.64 '13, 60mh 8.18i '15, 100mh 13.37 '15, 200mhSt 25.31 '15, 400mh 58.3 '14, HJ 1.98 '16, TJ 12.83, 13.35w '14; SP 13.14 '16, JT 42.01 '15, Pen 5000i '12.
Set pbs in the each of the last four events when adding 182 points to her pb for 5th at the 2013 Worlds and 474 points to pentathlon best to win 2015 European Indoors, including 6.89 long jump, the best ever in a pentathlon. Three no-jumps (last by 1 cm) in 2015 WCh Hep LJ. World heptathlon best HJ 1.98 at 2016 OG. Won 29 English age-group titles U15 to U23.

Morgan LAKE b. 12 May 1997 Milton Keynes 1.78m 64kg. Windsor, Slough, Eton & Honslow.
At Hep/(HJ): OG: '16- (10=); WCh: '15- (dnq 14=), '17- (6); EC: '14- (dnq 17=), '16- dnf; WJ: '14- 1/1; WY: '13- dnf; EJ: '15- (1); WI: '18- (4). At Pen: WI: '16- 6; EI: '15- 9, '17- (8). Won UK HJ 2016-17.
World youth indoor pentathlon record 2014.
Progress at HJ, Hep: 2007- 1.28, 2008- 1.50, 2009- 1.57, 2010- 1.70, 2011- 1.76, 2012- 1.80, 2013- 1.90, 2014- 1.94, 6148; 2015- 1.94, 5082; 2016- 1.94, 5951; 2017- 1.96. pbs: 60m 7.98i '13, 200m 24.59 '14, 800m 2:18.53i '16, 2:21.06 '14; 60mh 8.63i '16, 100mh 14.25 '14, LJ 6.32 '14, TJ 12.35, 12.45w '13; SP 14.85 '14, JT 41.93 '17, Pen 4527i '15.
Record 31 English age-group titles 2010-17 (12 indoors, 19 out). Father Eldon had a TJ pb of 15.43 (1989).

Eilish McCOLGAN b. 25 Nov 1990 Dundee 1.76m 59kg. Dundee Hawkhill, was at Dundee University.
At 5000m: OG: '16- 13; WCh: '17- 10; EC: '16- 6. At 3000m: EI: '17- 3; At 3000mSt: OG: '12- h; WCh: '13- 10, CG: '14- 6; EU23: '11- 6; UK 2012-14.
Progress at 1500m, 5000m: 2002- 5:22.8, 2003- 4:58.14, 2004- 4:36.70, 2005- 4:37.78, 2006- 4:38.00, 2007- 4:35.56, 2008- 4:27.11, 2010- 4:21.38, 2011- 4:14.44, 15:52.69; 2012- 4:11.78mx/4:13.19, 15:44.62; 2013- 4:09.67, 2014- 4:15.23mx, 2016- 4:03.74, 15:05.00; 2017- 4:01.60, 14:48.49. pbs: 800m 2:12.22 '08, 2000m 5:43.1+ '17, 3000m 8:31.00 '17, 10000m 32:10.59 '17, 10kRd 31:53 '18, 2000mSt 6:42.24 '11, 3000mSt 9:35.82 '13.
Her mother Liz (10,000m OG: '88- 2, WCh: '91- 1, 30:57.07 '91), father Peter (3000mSt 8:27.93 '91).

Laura MUIR b. 9 May 1993 Milnathort, Kinross 1.62m 54kg. Dundee Hawkhill H. Was at Glasgow University.
At 1500m /(3000m): OG: '16- 7; WCh: '15- 5, '17- 4 (6 5000m); EC: '14- h; CG: '14- 11; WJ: '12- (16); EU23: '13- 3; WI: '18- 2/3; EI: '13- 6, '15- (4), '17- 1/1, won DL 2016. At 800m: WCh: '13- sf. Won UK 2015-16. Eur CC: '15- 4 U23.
Two UK 1500m records 2016, Indoor records: Commonwealth 30000m & European 1000m & 3000m 2017.
Progress at 1500m, 5000m: 2005- 5:33.16, 2006- 5:12.39, 2007- 4:48.97, 2008- 4:47.92, 2009- 4:58.77, 2010-4:50.91. 2011-4:38.90, 2012-4:14.52mx/4:17.81, 2013- 4:07.76, 15:53.68; 2014- 4:00.07, 2015- 3:58.66. 2016- 3:55.22, 2017- 4:00.35, 14:49.12i/14:52.07. pbs: 400m 55.36i mx '16, 55.71i '14, 56.78 '12; 800m 1:58.69 '17, 1000m 2:31.93i '17, 2:40.5 '16, 1M 4:18.03 '17, 2000m 5:41.5+i '17, 3000m 8:26.41i/8:30.64 '17, 10k Rd 38:23 '11.

Cindy OFILI b. 5 Aug 1994 Ypsilanti, USA 1.78m 68kg. University of Michigan.
At 100mh: OG: '16- 4; WCh: '15- sf. Won NCAA indoor 60mh 2016.
Progress at 100mh: 2012- 13.61, 2013- 13.34/13.30w, 2014- 12.93, 2015- 12.60, 2016- 12.63, 2017- 12.92. pbs: 60m 7.37i '14, 100m 11.39 '15, 200m 23.46/23.43w '16, 60mh 7.89i '16.
Sister of Tiffany Porter. Has dual British/US nationality.

Shelayna OSKAN-CLARKE b. 20 Jan 1990 London 1.67m 54kg. Windsor, Slough, Eton & Hounslow. Was at Brunel University.
At 800m: OG: '16- sf; WCh: '15- 5, '17- sf; WI: '18- 3; EI: '17- 2. Won UK 2016-17.
Progress at 800m: 2004- 2:23.1, 2005- 2:20.4, 2006- 2:21.4, 2007- 2:13.34, 2008- 2:09.20, 2009- 2:06.29, 2010- 2:08.25, 2011- 2:07.93i/2:08.02, 2012- 2:0771i/2:11.30, 2013- 2:03.52, 2014- 2:01.94. 2015- 1:58.86, 2016- 1:59.45, 2017- 1:59.82, 2018- 1:59.81i. pbs: 60m 7.96i '12, 200m 24.55 '11, 400m 53.20 '11, 600m 1:27.48mx '16, 1500m 4:28.29 '14.

Asha PHILIP b. 25 Oct 1990 Leytonstone, London 1.63m 54kg. Newham & Essex Beagles, was at Kingston University.
At 100m/4x100mR: OG: '16- sf/3R; WCh: '13- sf, '15- sf/4R, '17- sf/2R; EC: '14- sf/1R, '16- 4/2R; CG: '14- 4/3R; WJ: 06- 4/6R; WY: 07- 1; E23: 13- 4 200m; EJ: '07- 1R; ET: '15- 1. At 60m: WI: '14- 4, '16- 5; EI: '13- 5. '17- 1. Won UK 100m 2013-14, 2016-17.
Progress at 100m: 2004- 12.14/12.04w, 2005- 11.83, 2006- 11.45, 2007- 11.37, 2010- 12.0, 2011- 11.47, 2012- 11.53, 2013- 11.20, 2014- 11.18/11.11w, 2015- 11.10, 2016- 11.16, 2017- 11.14. pbs: 60m 7.06i '17, 150mSt 16.69 '14, 200m 23.45, 23.07w '13.
World U17 double-mini trampoline champion in 2006, but ruptured her knee in 2007 and unable to compete until 2010.

Tiffany PORTER b. 13 Nov 1987 Ypsilanti, USA 1.72m 62kg. née Ofili. Doctorate in pharmacy from University of Michigan.
At 100mh: OG: '12- sf, '16- 7; WCh: '11-13-15-17: 4/3/5/h; EC: '14- 1, '16- 3; CG: '14- 2; WJ: '06- 3 (for USA); CCp: '14- 2; ET: '13- 1. At 60mh: WI: '12-14-16: 2/3/3; EI: '11- 2. Won UK 100mh 2011, 2013-16; NCAA 100mh & 60mh indoors 2009.
Records: British 100mh (4) 2011-14, 50mh/55mh/60mh indoors; world best 4x100mh 2014 & 2015.
Progress at 100mh: 2005- 14.19, 2006- 13.37/13.15w, 2007- 12.80, 2008- 12.73, 2009- 12.77/12.57w, 2010- 12.85, 2011- 12.56, 2012- 12.65/12.47w, 2013- 12.55, 2014- 12.51, 2015- 12.56, 2016- 12.70, 2017- 12.75. pbs: 60m 7.41i '11, 100m 11.70 '09, 11.63w '08; 200m 23.90 '08, 400mh 61.96 '06, LJ 6.48 '09; UK records: 50mh 6.83i '12, 55mh 7.38i '12, 60mh 7.80i '11.
Opted for British nationality in September 2010; her mother being born in London (father born in Nigeria). Married US hurdler Jeff Porter (pb 13.08 '12, sf OG '12/16) in May 2011. Sister of Cindy Ofili (qv).

Shara PROCTOR b. 16 Sep 1988 The Valley, Anguilla 1.74m 56kg. Birchfield H. Was at University of Florida, USA.
At LJ: OG: '12- 7, '16- dnq 21; WCh: '07-09-11-13-15-17: dnq 29/6/dnq 20/5/2/dnq 13; WI: '12-14-16: 3/4/8; CG: '06- dnq 13, '14- nj; WJ: '06- dnq 16; WY: '05- 6; EI: '13- 4; ET: '13- 3. Won DL 2013, CAC 2009, UK 2011-13.
Records: Anguilla: LJ 2005-09, TJ 2007-09; UK LJ (4) 2012-15.
Progress at LJ: 2003- 5.64, 2004- 5.99A, 2005- 6.24, 2006- 6.17, 2007- 6.17, 2008- 6.54A/6.52/6.61w, 2009- 6.71, 2010- 6.69, 2011- 6.81, 2012- 6.95, 2013- 6.92, 2014- 6.82, 2015- 7.07, 2016- 6.91i/6.80, 2017- 6.73. pbs: 60m 7.36i '16, 100m 12.27 '08, 12.10w '10; TJ 13.88i '10, 13.82 '17.
Switched from Anguilla (a British Dependent Territory without a National Olympic Committee) to Britain from 16 Nov 2010. Younger sister Shinelle (b. 27 Jun 91) set Anguillan high jump records at 1.70 in 2009 and 2010 and 1.72i in 2014.

Jazmin SAWYERS b. 21 May 1994 Stoke-on-Trent 1.67m 52kg. City of Stoke. Studying law at Bristol University.
At LJ: OG: '16- 8; WCh: '17- dnq 20; EC: '16- 2; CG: '14- 2; WJ: '12- 3; EU23: '15- 2; EJ: '13- 2; EI: '17- 6. UK champion 2016. At Hep: WY: '11- 9.
Progress at LJ: 2005- 4.21/4.64w, 2006- 5.05, 2007- 5.65, 2008- 5.72, 2009- 5.96, 2010- 5.60i, 2011- 6.23/6.27w, 2012- 6.67, 2013- 6.63, 2014- 6.54, 2015- 6.71, 2016- 6.75/6.86w, 2017- 6.71i/6.53/6.55w. pbs: 200m 25.24 '11, 800m 2:28.71 '11, 100mh 14.29 '13, HJ 1.77i '08, 1.75 '11; SP 10.42 '11, JT 28.02 '11, Hep 5077 '11.
Silver medal for Britain at bobsleigh at 2012 Youth Olympics.

Lynsey SHARP b. 11 Jul 1990 Dumfries 1.75m 60kg. Edinburgh AC. Law graduate of Edinburgh Napier University.
At 800m: OG: '12- sf, '16- 6; WCh: '15- sf, '17- 8; EC: '12- 1, '14- 2; CG: '14- 2; WJ: '08- sf; WY: '07- sf; EU23: '11- 2; CCp: '14- 5. Won UK 2012, 2014-15.
Progress at 800m: 2000- 2:38.2, 2002- 2:25.97, 2003- 2:16.57, 2004- 2:09.98, 2005- 2:10.44, 2006- 2:10.91i, 2007- 2:06.92, 2008- 2:04.44, 2011- 2:00.65, 2012- 2:00.52, 2013- 2:02.63, 2014- 1:58.80, 2015- 1:57.71, 2016- 1:57.69, 2017- 1:58.01. pbs: 400m 54.43 '16, 600m 1:27.16i '17, 1:27.51 '14; 1500m 4:36.27 '11.
Father Cameron (1982: 4th 100m, 2nd 200m EC; 3rd 100m, 200m, 4x100m CG; pbs: 100m 10.20 '83, 200m 20.47 '82); mother Carol Lightfoot (800m 2:02.91 '82).

Lorraine UGEN b. 22 Aug 1991 London 1.78m 64kg. Blackheath & Bromley. Was at Texas Christian University, USA.
At LJ: OG: '16- 11; WCh: '13- dnq, '15- 5, '17- 5; EC: '16- dnq 18; CG: '14- 5; WJ: '10- dnq 17; EU23: '13- dns F; EJ: '09- dnq 21; WI: '16- 3; EI: 17- 2; won UK 2017, NCAA 2013.
Progress at LJ: 2007- 5.55, 2008- 5.79, 2009- 6.29, 2010- 6.35/6.42w, 2011- 6.54, 2012- 6.74/6.83w, 2013- 6.77, 2014- 6.73Ai/6.59i/6.39/6.40w, 2015- 6.92/6.96w, 2016- 6.93i/6.80/6.82w, 2017- 6.97i/6.78. pbs: 60m 7.50Ai '12, 7.51i '14; 100m 11.37 '18, 11.31w '17; 200m 23.81/23.71w '15, 100mh 15.2/15.42 '08, HJ 1.56 '08, Hep 4307 '08.

Laura WEIGHTMAN b. 1 Jul 1991 Alnwick 1.72m 58kg. Morpeth H. Leeds Met University.
At 1500m: OG: '12- 7, '16- 11; WCh: '13- h, '15- sf, '17- 6; EC: '14- 3; CG: '14- 2; WJ: '10- 6. Won UK 2012, 2014, 2017. At 3000m: ET: '13- 2. Eur U23 CC: '13- 8.
Progress at 1500m: 2004- 4:50.5, 2005- 4:44.0, 2006- 4:37.20, 2007- 4:26.02, 2008- 4:22.20, 2009- 4:14.9mx/4:19.9, 2010- 4:09.60mx/4:12.82, 2011- 4:07.94mx/4:15.51, 2012- 4:02.99, 2013- 4:05.36, 2014- 4:00.17, 2015- 4:04.70, 2016- 4:02.66, 2017- 4:00.71. pbs: 400m 58.43 '09, 800m 2:01.87 '17,

1000m 2:38.49 '13, 1M 4:20.88 '17, 2000m 5:44.22 '13, 3000m 8:43.46mx '13, 9:02.62 '12; 5000m 15:08.24 '17.

USA

Governing body: USA Track and Field. Founded 1979 as The Athletics Congress, when it replaced the AAU (founded 1888) as the governing body.

National Championships first held in 1876 (men), 1923 (women). **2017 Champions**: **Men**: 100m/: Justin Gatlin 9.95, 200m: Ameer Webb 20.09, 400m: Fred Kerley 44.03, 800m: Donavan Brazier 1:44.14, 1500m: Robby Andrews 3:43.29, 5000m: Paul Chelimo 13:08.62, 10000m: Hassan Mead 29:01.44, HMar: Leonard Korir 63:04, Mar: Tim Ritchie 2:11:55, 3000mSt: Evan Jager 8:16.88, 110mh: Aleec Harris 13.24, 400mh: Eric Futch 48.18, HJ: Bryan McBride 2.30, PV: Sam Kendricks 6.00, LJ: Jarrion Lawson 8.49w, TJ: Will Claye 17.91, SP: Ryan Crouser 22.65, DT: Mason Finley 63.03, HT: Alex Young 73.75, JT: Riley Dolezal 81.77, Dec: Trey Hardee 8225, 20kW: Emmanuel Corvera 1:26:43, 50kW: John Nunn 4:18:59. **Women**: 100m: Tori Bowie 10.94, 200m: Deajah Stevens 22.30, 400m: Quanera Hayes 49.72, 800m: Ajee' Wilson 1:57.78, 1500m: Jenny Simpson 4:06.33, 5000m: Shelby Houlihan 15:13.87, 10000m: Molly Huddle 31:19.86, HMar: Natosha Rogers 70:45, Mar: Sara Hall 2:28:10, 3000mSt: Emma Coburn 9:20.28, 100mh: Kendra Harrison 12.60, 400mh: Dalilah Muhammad 52.64, HJ: Vashti Cunningham 1.99, PV: Sandi Morris 4.80, LJ: Tianna Bartoletta 7.05w, TJ: Keturah Orji 14.26, SP: Raven Saunders 19.76, DT: Gia Lewis-Smallwood 62.65, HT: Gwen Berry 74.77, JT: Kara Winger 62.80, Hep: Kendell Williams 6564, 10000mW/20kW: Maria Michta-Coffey 45:31.40/1:33:20, 50kW: Katie Burnett 4:26:37.

NCAA Championships first held in 1921 (men), 1982 (women). **2017 Champions**: **Men**: 100m/200m: Christian Coleman 10.04/20.25, 400m: Fred Kerley 44.10, 800m: Emmanuel Korir KEN 1:45.03, 1500m: Josh Kerr GBR 3:43.03, 5000m: Grant Fisher 14:35.60, 10000m: Marc Scott GBR 29:01.54, 3000mSt: Edwin Kibichiy 8:28.40, 110mh: Grant Holloway 13.49, 400mh: Eric Futch 48.32, HJ: Christoffe Bryan 2.21, PV: Matthew Ludwig 5.60, LJ/TJ: KeAndre Bates 8.05/16.76w, SP/DT: Filip Mihaljevic CRO 21.30/63.76, HT: Rudy Winkler 74.12, JT: Ioánnis Kiriazis 82.58, Dec: Lindon Victor GRN 8390. **Women**: 100m: Mikiah Brisco 10.96, 200m: Kyra Jefferson 22.02, 400m: Chris-Ann Gordon JAM 50.51, 800m: Raevyn Rogers 2:00.02, 1500m: Jaimie Phelan CAN 4:13.78, 5000m: Karissa Schweizer 15:38.93, 10000m: Charlotte Taylor GBR 32:38.57, 3000mSt: Allie Ostrander 9:41.31, 100mh: Tobi Amusan NGR 12.57, 400mh: Sage Watson CAN 54.52, HJ: Madeline Fagan 1.91, PV: Olivia Gruver 4.50, LJ: Kate Hall 6.73, TJ: Keturah Orji 14.29w, SP: Danniel Thomas-Dodd JAM 19.15, DT: Shadae Lawrence JAM 61.37, HT: Maggie Ewen 73.32, JT: Irena Sedivá CZE 58.76, Hep: Kendell Williams 6265.

Devon ALLEN b. 12 Dec 1994 Phoenix, Arizona 1.83m 84kg. Student at University of Oregon.
At 110mh: OG: '16- 5; WCh: '17- sf; Won US 2014, 2016; NCAA 2014, 2016.
Progress at 110mh: 2014- 13.16, 2016- 13.03, 2017- 13.10. pbs: 60m 6.85Ai '14, 100m 10.36 '16, 200m 20.68 '16, 60mh 7.49Ai/7.50i '18, 400mh 51.19 '14.
On a football scholarship as a wide receiver., suffered a knee injury on the opening kickoff of the Rose Bowl at the end of 2014 and missed 2015 track season.

Ronnie ASH b. 2 Jul 1988 Raleigh NC 1.88m 86kg. Nike. Was at University of Oklahoma.
At 110mh: OG: '16- dq; WCh: '15- h; CCp: '14- 2; won NACAC 2010, NCAA 2009.
Progress at 110mh: 2008- 13.44, 2009- 13.27, 2010- 13.19/12.98w, 2011- 13.25/13.24w, 2012- 13.20/13.10w, 2014- 12.99, 2015- 13.13, 2016- 13.21, 2017- 13.65. pbs: 200m 22.08 '08, 60mh 7.55i '10.

Ronnie BAKER b. 15 Oct 1993 Louisville, Kentucky 1.78m 73kg. Texas Christian Univ.
At 100m: WUG: '15- 4. At 60m: WI: '18- 3; won NCAA indoor 2015-16, US 2017.
Progress at 100m: 2011- 10.57, 2012- 10.59/10.55w, 2013- 10.58/10.33w, 2014- 10.21/10.14w, 2015- 10.05/9.94w, 2016- 10.09/9.95w, 2017- 9.98. pbs: 60m 6.40Ai/6.44 '18, 200m 20.60Ai, 20.64 '16; 400m 46.18 '13.
Fastest in the world indoor 60m in 2016 & 2017.

Chris BENARD b. 4 Apr 1990 1.90m 79kg. Chula Vista Elite. Was at Arizona State University.
At TJ: OG: '16- dnq 16; WCh: '17- 6.
Progress at TJ: 2008- 15.09, 2009- 15.38, 2010- 15.52/16.20w, 2011- 15.80Ai/15.75, 2012- 16.74, 2013- 16.78, 2014- 17.10, 2015- 16.95, 2016- 17.21, 2017- 17.48. pb LJ 8.10Ai, 7.96 '14.

Boris BERIAN b. 19 Dec 1992 Colorado Springs 1.83m 71kg. Adams State University.
At 800m: OG: '16- 8; WI: '16- 1.
Progress at 800m: 2011- 1:52.18A, 2012- 1:48.93, 2013- 1:48.89, 2015- 1:43.34, 2016- 1:44.20. pbs: 400m 46.93A '11, 600m 1:15.51i '16, 1:16.14 '15.

Hillary BOR b. 22 Nov 1989 Eldoret, Kenya 1.68m 57kg. Was at Iowa State University.
At 3000mSt: OG: '16- 7; WCh: '17- h.
Progress at 3000mSt: 2008- 8:36.84, 2009- 8:35.12, 2010- 8:38.05, 2011- 8:40.83, 2012- 8:36.44, 2013- 8:32.41, 2014- 8:38.42, 2015- 8:45.94, 2016- 8:13.68, 2017- 8:11.82. pbs: 1500m 3:44.30 '07, 1M 4:03.43i '08, 3000m 8:10.77i '10, 5000m 14:03.45 '08, 10M Rd 48:31 '15.
US citizen from 31 December 2014 after joining the US Army with his brothers Emmanuel

(1500m: 4 WUG 3:41.65 in 2007, 3000m 7:44.93i '18, 5000m 13:28.79 '17) and Julius (1500m 3:41.11 '10).

Donavan BRAZIER b. 15 Apr 1997 Grand Rapids, Michigan 1.88m 73kg. Nike. Texas A&M University.
At 800m: WCh: '17- sf; won NCAA 2016, US 2017.
Progress at 800m: 2012- 2:06, 2013- 1:54.36, 2014- 1:48.61, 2015- 1:43.55, 2016- 1:44.14, 2017- 1:43.95. pbs: 400m 46.91i '18, 47.02 '16; 600m 1:16.02Ai '17, 1000m 2:21.79i '17, 1M 3:59.30i '17.

Trayvon BROMELL b 10 Jul 1995 St. Petersburg, Florida 1.75m 71kg. New Balance. Baylor University.
At 100m/4x100mR: OG: '16- 8; WCh: '15- 3=; WJ: '14- 2/1R; PAm-J: 13- 3/1R. At 60m: WI: '16- 1. Two world junior 100m records 2014.
Progress at 100m, 200m: 2012- 10.40, 21.01; 2013- 10.27/9.99Aw, 20.91/20.86w; 2014- 9.97/9.77w, 20.59/20.23w; 2015- 9.84/9.76w, 20.03/19.86w; 2016- 9.84, 20.30; 2017- 10.22. pb 60m 6.47i '16.
Fastest ever teenager with 9.84 for 100m in 2015.

Chris CARTER b. 11 Mar 1989 Austin 1.86m 80kg. Was at University of Houston.
At TJ: PAm: '11- 6; WI: '14- 6, '18- 5. Won US indoor 2014.
Progress at TJ: 2005- 14.43, 2006- 13.78/14.69w, 2007- 15.88, 2008- 15.41i/15.31/15.69Aw, 2009- 16.34, 2010- 15.98, 2011- 16.86, 2012- 16.61, 2013- 16.69, 2014- 17.15Ai/17.09, 2015- 16.71i/16.70, 2016- 17.18, 2017- 17.10Aidq/16.75i, 2018- 17.20Ai/ 17.18. pbs: 400mh 53.90 '07, LJ 7.67 '13.

Matthew CENTROWITZ b. 18 Nov 1989 Beltsville, Maryland 1.76m 61kg. Nike Oregon Project. Studied sociology at the University of Oregon.
At 1500m: OG: '12- 4, '16- 1; WCh: '11-13-15-17: 3/2/8/h; WI: '12- 7, '16- 1. At 5000m WJ: '08- 11. Won US 2011, 2013, 2015-16; NCAA 2011, PAm-J 2007.
Progress at 1500m: 2007- 3:49.54, 2008- 3:44.98, 2009- 3:36.92, 2010- 3:40.14, 2011- 3:34.46, 2012- 3:31.96, 2013- 3:33.58, 2014- 3:31.09, 2015- 3:30.40, 2016- 3:34.09, 2017- 3:33.41. pbs: 800m 1:44.62 '15, 1000m 2:16.67 '16. 1M 3:50.53 '14, 3000m 7:40.74i '16, 2M 8:21.07i '17, 8:40.55 '07; 5000m 13:20.06 '14.
Father Matt pbs: 1500m 3:36.60 '76, 3:54.94 '82, 5000m US record 13:12.91 '82, 10000m 28:32.7 '83; h OG 1500m 1976; 1 PAm 5000m 1979. Sister Lauren (b. 25 Sep 1986) 1500m pb 4:10.23 '09.

Paul Kipkemoi CHELIMO b. 27 Oct 1990 Iten, Kenya 1.71m 57kg. US Army. Went to the University of North Carolina.
At 5000m: OG: '16- 2; WCh: '17- 3; WUG: '13- 2 (1500m 6); won US 2017. At 3000m: WI: '16- 7.
Progress at 5000m: 2011- 13:53.02, 2012- 13:21.89, 2013- 13:36.27, 2015- 13:37.02, 2016- 13:03.90, 2017- 13:08.62. pbs: 1500m 3:39.33 '16, 1M 4:02.80i '12, 3000m 7:31.57 '17, 2M 8:28.53Ai '17, 10000m 29:44.42 '11, 15k Rd 43:46 '17, 10M Rd 48:19 '15.
Came to the USA in 2010, granted US citizenship on 23 Jul 2014 and cleared to compete for the US from 15 Jun 2015. Reduced his 5000m best from 13:19.54 to 13:03.90 at the 2016 Olympic Games.

Michael CHERRY b. 23 Mar 1995 1.86m 75kg. Wsa at Louisiana State University.
At 400m/4x400mR: WCh: '17- 2R; WJ: '14- 1R; WI: '18- 2/2R; Won US indoor 2018.
Progress at 400m: 2010- 49.25, 2011- 48.57, 2012- 46.37, 2013- 46.02, 2014- 45.17, 2015- 45.43, 2016- 44.81, 2017- 44.66. pbs: 200m 21.07 '17, 600m 1:17.17Ai '16.

Will CLAYE b. 13 Jun 1991 Phoenix 1.80m 68kg. Nike. University of Oklahoma, then Florida.
At (LJ)/TJ: OG: '12- 3/2, '16- 2; WCh: '11- 9/3, '13- 3, '15- dnq 19, '17- 2; WI: '12- 4/1, '18- 1; CCp: '14- 2/3; won US 2014, 2016-17; PAm-J and NCAA 2009.
Progress at LJ, TJ: 2007- 14.91/15.19w, 2008- 7.39/7.48w, 15.97; 2009- 7.89/8.00w, 17.19/17.24w; 2010- 7.30w, 16.30; 2011- 8.29, 17.50/17.62w; 2012- 8.25, 17.70i/17.62; 2013- 8.10, 17.52; 2014- 8.19/8.29w, 17.75; 2015- 8.07/8.11w, 17.48/17.50w; 2016- 8.14/8.42w, 17.76; 2017- 7.89, 17.91; 2018- 17.47i. pb 100m 10.64/10.53w '12.
Possibly youngest ever NCAA champion – he won 2009 title on his 18th birthday with 17.24w (and US junior record 17.19). First athlete to win Olympic medals at both LJ and TJ since 1936.

Kerron CLEMENT b. 31 Oct 1985 Port of Spain, Trinidad 1.88m 84kg. Was at University of Florida.
At 400mh/4x400mR: OG: '08- 2/res1R, '12- 8, '16- 1; WCh: '05-07-09-11-13-15-17: 4/1&res 1R/1&1R sf/8/4/3; WJ: '04- 1/1R; PAm: '15- 4/2R; WI: '10- res 1R; WCp: '06- 1. Won WAF 2008-09, DL 2016, US 2005-06, 2016; NCAA 2004-05.
World junior 4x400m record 2004, world indoor records: 400m 2005, 4x400m 2006.
Progress at 400mh: 2002- 49.77, 2003- 50.13, 2004- 48.51; 2005- 47.24; 2006- 47.39; 2007- 47.61; 2008- 47.79; 2009- 47.91; 2010- 47.86; 2011- 48.74; 2012- 48.12; 2013- 48.06; 2015- 48.18, 2016- 47.73, 2017- 48.02. pbs: 60m 6.89i '10, 100m 10.23 '07, 200m 20.40i '05, 20.49 '07; 300m 31.94i '06, 400m 44.48 '07, 55mh 7.28i '05, 60mh 7.80i '04, 110mh 13.78 '04. Born in Trinidad, moved to Texas in 1998, US citizenship confirmed in 2005. Ran 47.24, the world's fastest time since 1998, to win 2005 US 400mh title.

Christian COLEMAN b. 6 Mar 1996 Atlanta 1.75m 73kg. University of Tennessee (sport management).
At 100m: WCh: '17- 2/2R; OG: 16- resR; PAm-J: '15- 3. At 60m: WI: '18- 1. Won NCAA 100m & 200m, indoor 60m & 200m 2017.
Two world 60m indoor records 2018.

Progress at 100m, 200m: 2013- 22.43, 2014- 10.30/10.29w, 20.94; 2015- 10.18/10.16w, 20.61; 2016- 9.95, 20.26; 2017- 9.82, 19.85. pbs: 60m 6.34Ai/6.37i '18, LJ 7.21 '14.

Omar CRADDOCK b. 26 Apr 1991 Killeen, Texas 1.78m 79kg. Jump Corps. Was at University of Florida.
At TJ: WCh: '13- dnq 13, '15- 4; WJ: '10- 3; WI: '16- 5. Won US 2015, NCAA 2012-13.
Progress at TJ: 2006- 14.67, 2007- 15.16A, 2008- 15.53, 2009- 14.87i, 2010- 16.56, 2011- 16.57i/16.46, 2012- 16.75i/16.71/16.92w, 2013- 16.92/17.15w, 2014- 16.98/17.26w, 2015- 17.53, 2016- 17.16/17.42w, 2017- 17.08. pb LJ 7.63i '13, 7.60 '15, 7.70w '12.

Ryan CROUSER b. 18 Dec 1992 Portland 2.01m 127kg. University of Texas.
At SP(/DT): OG: '16- 1; WCh: '17- 6; WY: '09- 1/2. Won US SP 2016-17, NCAA SP 2013-14, indoors 2014.
Progress at SP: 2011- 19.48i, 2012- 20.29i/19.32, 2013- 21.09, 2014- 21.39, 2015- 21.14i/21.11, 2016- 22.52, 2017- 22.65. pbs: DT 63.90 '14, JT 61.16 '09. Set High School 1.62kg DT record 72.40 '11. His father Mitch SP 20.04i '83, 19.94 '82, DT 67.22 '85; uncle Dean SP 21.07 '82, DT 65.88 '83, won NCAA SP 1982 & DT 1982-3; uncle Brian JT 83.00 '87, old JT 95.10 '85, won NCAA 1982 & 1985, dnq OG 1988 & 1992; Dean's children: Sam SP 17.62 '13, JT 83.30 '15 (dnq 34 OG 16), US junior & HS record '10, won NCAA 2014-15; Haley US junior JT record 55.22 '12, 4 WY '11.

Marquis DENDY b. 17 Nov 1992 Middleton, Delaware 1.92m 75kg. Nike. Was at University of Florida.
At LJ/(TJ): WCh: '13-15-17: dnq 27/21 (13)/20; WI: '16- 1, '18- 3. At TJ: WJ: '10- 8; won US LJ 2015; NACAC LJ 2012, NCAA LJ 2015, TJ 2014-15, indoor LJ 2013, 2015-16; TJ 2015.
Progress at LJ, TJ: 2009- 7.20, 15.40; 2010- 7.45, 16.03; 2011- 7.47/7.56w, 15.62; 2012- 8.06i/7.81, 15.55; 2013- 8.28i/8.10/8.29w, 16.25i/16.03; 2014- 8.00, 16.52/17.05w; 2015- 8.39/8.68w, 17.50/17.71w; 2016- 8.42, 16.36; 2017- 8.18/8.39w, 2018- 8.42i. pbs: 60m 6.88i '14, 100m 10.31 '15.

Dedric DUKES b. 4 Feb 1992 Miami 1.80m 70kg. Was at University of Florida.
At 200m: WY: '09- 4/1 MedR. Won NCAA 2014.
Progress at 200m: 2007- 21.88/21.79w, 2008- 21.19/21.12w, 2009- 20.94, 2011- 20.88w, 2012- 20.47, 2013- 20.45/20.34w, 2014- 19.97/19.91w, 2015- 19.99/19.86w, 2016- 20.41/20.14w, 2017- 20.37. pbs: 60m 6.77i '14, 100m 10.13 '16, 10.06w '17; 400m 45.66 '14.
Football wide receiver in high school.

Johnny DUTCH b. 20 Jan 1989 Clayton NC 1.80m 82kg. Studied media arts at University of South Carolina.
At 400mh: WCh: '09/15- sf; WJ: '08- 2; PAm-J: '07- 1/2R. Won US 2014, NCAA 2010.
Progress at 400mh: 2005- 52.06, 2006- 51.72, 2007- 50.07, 2008- 48.52, 2009- 48.18, 2010- 47.63, 2011- 48.47, 2012- 48.90, 2013- 48.02, 2014- 48.93, 2015- 48.13, 2016- 48.10, 2017- 48.60. pbs: 400m 46.75 '13, 500m 1:03.25i '15, 55mh 7.31i '10, 60mh 7.71i '09, 110mh 13.50/13.30w '10.

Jarret EATON b. 24 Jun 1989 Philadelphia 1.83m 82kg. Was at Syracuse University.
At 60mh: WI: '16- 4, '18- 2. US indoor 60m champion 2016, 2018.
Progress at 110mh: 2008- 13.90, 2009- 14.06/13.99w, 2010- 13.83, 2011- 13.63, 2012- 13.44, 2014- 13.71, 2015- 13.41/13.40w, 2016- 13.25, 2017- 13.34. pbs: 55m 6.36i '16, 60m 6.83i '16, 100m 10.96 '17, 60mh 7.43Ai/7.47i '18, 400mh 53.26 '07.

Mason FINLEY b. 7 Oct 1990 2.03m 136kg. Was at University of Wyoming
At DT: OG: '16- 11; WCh: '17- 3; WUG: '11- 8 (3 SP). Won US 2016-17, PAm-J SP & DT 2009.
Progress at DT: 2010- 60.18, 2011- 60.65, 2012- 61.40, 2013- 62.48A, 2014- 64.17A, 2015- 64.80A, 2016- 66.72, 2017- 68.03. pbs: SP 20.71i '11, 19.89 '12; Wt 19.42i '14. His father Jared DT 58.34 '79.

Eric FUTCH b. 25 Apr 1993 Darby, Pennsylvania 1.75m 70kg. Student at University of Florida.
At 400mh: WCh: '17- sf; WJ: 12- 1/1R. Won NCAA 2016-17, US 2017.
Progress at 400mh: 2011- 51.67, 2012- 50.24, 2013- 50.66, 2015- 49.45, 2016- 48.91, 2017- 48.18. pbs: 200m 21.17 '15, 400m 46.16i/46.71 '17, 600y 1:11.10i '16.

Justin GATLIN b. 10 Feb 1982 Brooklyn, NY 1.85m 79kg. XTEP. Was at University of Tennessee.
At 100m/(200m)/4x100mR: OG: '04- 1/3/2R, '12- 3/dq2R, '16- 2/sf; WCh: '05- 1/1, '11- sf, '13- 2/2R, '15- 2/2, '17- 1/2R. At 60m: WI: '03- 1, '12- 1. Won DL 100m 2013-15, US 100m 2005-06, 2012, 2016; 200m 2005, 2015-16; (indoor 60m 2003), NCAA 100m & 200m 2001-02 (& indoor 60m/200m 2002).
N.American 4x100m record 2015. World M35 100m record 2017.
Progress at 100m, 200m: 2000- 10.36, 2001- 10.08, 20.29/19.86w; 2002: under international suspension 10.05/10.00w, 19.86; 2003- 9.97, 20.04; 2004- 9.85, 20.01; 2005- 9.88/9.84w, 20.00; 2006- 9.77dq, 2010- 10.09, 20.63; 2011- 9.95, 20.20; 2012- 9.79, 20.11; 2013- 9.85, 20.21; 2014- 9.77/9.76w, 19.68; 2015- 9.74, 19.57, 2016- 9.80, 19.75; 2017- 9.92. pbs: 60m 6.45i '03, 100y 9.10 '14, 55mh 7.39i '02, 60mh 7.86i '01, 110mh 13.41dq '02, 13.78/13.74w '01; LJ 7.34i '01, 7.21 '00.
Top hurdler in high school (110mh 13.66 and 300mh 36.74 on junior hurdles). Retained NCAA sprint titles while ineligible for international competition in 2002 after failing a drugs test in 2001 (when he won 100m, 200m and 110mh at the US Juniors) for a prescribed medication to treat Attention Deficit Disorder. Reinstated by IAAF in July 2002. Won 2005 World 100m title by biggest ever winning

margin of 0.17. and all five 100ms in 2006, including the US title and tying the world record with 9.77 in Doha, but had tested positive for testosterone before these races. He received a four-year drugs ban but returned to competition in August 2010. In 2014 he was unbeaten at 100m and 200m (the first man to do so since Usain Bolt in 2009) and in Brussels on 5 Sep recorded the best-ever one-day sprint double with 9.77 and 19.71. His run of successive wins (26 finals and 7 prelims) in 2014-15 ended by Usain Bolt in World 100m in 2015.

Tyson GAY b. 9 Aug 1982 Lexington 1.80m 73kg. adidas. Studied marketing at University of Arkansas.
At 100m/(200m)/4x100mR: OG: '08- sf, '12- dq(4/2R), '16- dq hR; WCh: '05- (4), '07- 1/1/1R, '09- 2, 15- 6; WCp: '06- 1/1R, '10- 1R. Won DL 2010, WAF 100m 2009, 200m 2005-06, US 100m 2007-08, 2013, 2015; 200m 2007, 2013; NCAA 100m 2004. Five N.American 100m records 2008-12, 4x100m 2015.
Progress at 100m, 200m: 1999- 10.81, 22.29i; 2000- 10.56, 21.27; 2001- 10.46/10.28w, 21.23; 2002- 10.27/10.08w, 20.88/20.21w; 2003- 10.01Aw/10.14w, 21.15/20.31w; 2004- 10.06/10.10w, 20.07; 2005- 10.08, 19.93; 2006- 9.84, 19.68; 2007- 9.84/9.76w, 19.62; 2008- 9.77/9.68w, 20.00; 2009- 9.69, 19.58; 2010- 9.78, 19.76; 2011- 9.79, 2012- 9.86/9.80dq, 20.21dq; 2013- 9.75dq, 19.74dq; 2014- 9.93, 20.22; 2015- 9.87/9.79w, 2016- 9.97, 20.16; 2017- 10.17/ 9.94w, 20.60/20.31w. pbs: 60m 6.39+ '09, 6.55i '05; 150mSt 14.51 '11, 200m/220ySt 19.41/19.54 '10, 400m 44.89 '10.
Ran four 200m races in under 19.85 in 2006. Then greatest ever sprint double (9.84 and 19.62) at 2007 US Champs and fastest ever 100m 9.68w/+4.1 (after US record in qf) to win US Olympic Trials in 2008 but pulled hamstring in 200m qf and unable to compete again until Olympics, where he was not back to top form. IAAF Athlete of the Year 2007. Positive test for a banned substance (later reported as a steroid) in May 2013 and withdrew from the World Championships; case resolved with a 1-year ban and annulment of results from 15 Jul 2012, thus including his Olympic 2012 results.

Elijah HALL (-THOMPSON) b. 22 Aug 1994 1.74m 69kg. Student at University of Houston.
Progress at 200m: 2010- 21.53, 2011- 21.12/20.76w, 2012- 20.86, 2013- 20.60, 2015- 10.18/10.16w, 21.16i, 2016- 20.37A/21.16i/20.69w; 2017- 9.82, 19.85. pbs: 60m 6.52i '18, 100m 10.11/10.00w '18.
Had to withdraw from World Champs team after 3rd in US Champs 20.17.

Aleec HARRIS b. 31 Oct 1990 Lawrenceville, Georgia 1.85m 77kg. adidas. Studied sociology at University of Southern California.
At 110mh: WCh: '15/17- sf. Won US 110mh 2017, indoor 60mh 2015. World 4x110mh best 2015.
Progress at 110mh: 2010- 14.15/13.88w, 2011- 13.65/13.55w, 2013- 13.69/13.55w, 2014- 13.14, 2015- 13.11, 2016- 13.43/13.32w, 2017- 13.18. pbs: 55mh 7.18i '11, 60mh 7.50i '15.

Mike HARTFIELD b. 29 Mar 1990 Manchester, Connecticut 1.90m 77kg. adidas. Was at Ohio State University.
At LJ: OG: '16- dnq 25; WCh: '15- nj.
Progress at LJ: 2007- 7.19w, 2008- 7.42/7.52w, 2009- 7.57, 2010- 7.61i, 2011- 7.91/7.95w, 2012- 7.96, 2013- 8.15, 2014- 8.15/8.17w, 2015- 8.27/8.42w, 2016- 8.34/8.39w, 2017- 8.21/8.22w pb TJ 15.84 '13.
Broke 77 year-old Ohio State University record set by Jesse Owens.

Jeffery HENDERSON b. 19 Feb 1989 Sherwood, Arkansas 1.78m 82kg. Was at Florida Memorial University and Stillman College.
At LJ: OG: '16- 1; WCh: '15- 9, '17- dnq 17; PAm: '15- 1; WI: '16- 4; US champion 2014, 2016; indoors 2012.
Progress at LJ: 2006- 7.14i, 2007- 7.51i/7.41, 2008- 7.74/7.77w, 2009- 8.15u/7.88/8.19w, 2010- 7.94Ai/ 7.90i, 2011- 7.78, 2012- 7.91w, 2013- 8.22, 2014- 8.43/8.52w, 2015- 8.52/8.54w, 2016- 8.38/8.59w, 2017- 8.28. pbs: 55m 6.31i '09, 60m 6.58i '16, 100m 10.18A '13, 10.25 '11, 10.19w '15; 200m 20.65A '13, TJ 14.90i '08.

Darrell HILL b. 17 Aug 1993 Darby, Pennsylvania 1.93m 135kg. Was at Penn State University.
At SP: OG: '16- dnq 23; WCh: '17- 11; PAm: '15- 4; WI: '18- 6. Won NCAA 2011-12, DL 2017.
Progress at SP: 2012- 17.62i/17.53, 2013- 19.13, 2014- 20.57, 2015- 20.86, 2016- 21.63, 2017- 22.44. pbs: DT 50.20 '15, Wt 19.12i '15.

Ryan HILL b. 31 Jan 1990 Hickory, North Carolina 1.76m 60kg. Bowerman TC. Was at North Carolina State University.
At 5000m: WCh: '13- 10, '15- 7, '17- dns. At 3000m: WI: '16- 2. Won US 5000m 2015.
Progress at 5000m: 2009- 14:09.63, 2010- 13:44.36, 2011- 13:31.67, 2012- 13:26.34, 2013- 13:14.22, 2014- 13:14.31, 2015- 13:05.69, 2016- 13:15.59, 2017- 13:07.61i/13:16.99. pbs: 800m 1:50.22iA '14, 1000m 2:20.26 '13, 1500m 3:35.59 '16, 1M 3:54.89i '14, 3:56.78 '12; 3000m 7:30.93 '16, 2M 8:11.56i '17, 10000m 29:32.28 '10.

Grant HOLLOWAY b. 19 Nov 1997 1.88m 82kg. Student at University of Florida.
Won NCAA 110mh 2017, 60mh ind 2017-18.
Progress at 110mh. LJ: 2015- 7.84, 2016- 7.91i/7.77, 2017- 13.39, 8.05i/8.04; 2018- 8.13i. pbs: 55m 6.22i '16, 200m 21.32 '16, 300m 32.80i '17, 500m 1:03.35i '16, 60mh 7.42i '18, HJ 2.16 '14.
Wide receiver at American football.

(Timothy Lamont) **T.J.HOLMES** b. 2 Jul 1995 1.82m 73kg. Sports medicine student at Baylor University.
At 400mh: WCh: '17- 5; WJ: 14- 3.
Progress at 400mh: 2013- 50.61, 2014- 49.90, 2015- 51.48, 2016- 49.31, 2017- 48.44. pbs: 400m

47.42i '17, 600y 1:10.53i '17, 800m 1:56.01 '17, 60mh 7.87i '18.

Bershawn JACKSON b. 8 May 1983 Miami 1.73m 69kg. Nike. Studied accountancy at St Augustine's University, Florida.
At 400mh/4x400mR: OG: '08- 3; WCh: '03- h (dq), '05- 1, '07- sf/res 1R, '09- 3/res 1R, '11- 6/1R, '13- sf, '15- h; WJ: '02- 3/1R; CCp: '10- 3/1R; won DL 2010, 2015; WAF 2004-05, US 2003, 2008-10, 2015. At 400m: WI: '10- 5/1R; won US indoor 2005, 2010.
Progress at 400mh: 1999- 54.53, 2000- 52.17, 2001- 50.86, 2002- 50.00, 2003- 48.23, 2004- 47.86, 2005- 47.30, 2006- 47.48, 2007- 48.13, 2008- 48.02, 2009- 47.98, 2010- 47.32, 2011- 47.93, 2012- 48.20, 2013- 48.09, 2014- 48.76, 2015- 48.09, 2016- 49.04, 2017- 48.63. pbs: 200m 21.03/20.46w '04, 400m 45.06 '07, 500m 1:00.70i '15, 600m 1:17.85i '16, 800m 1:53.40 '11, 200mhSt 22.26 '11.

Evan JAGER b. 8 Mar 1989 Algonquin, Illinois 1.86m 66kg. Bowerman TC. Was at University of Wisconsin.
At 3000mSt: OG: '12- 6, '16- 2; WCh: '13- 5, '15- 6, '17- 3; CCp: '14- 2; US champion 2012-17. At 1500m: WJ: '08- 8. At 5000m: WCh: '09- h.
3 N.American 3000m steeple records 2012-15.
Progress at 5000m, 3000mSt: 2009- 13:22.18, 2012- 8:06.81, 2013- 13:02.40, 8:08.60; 2014- 13:08.63, 8:04.71; 2015- 8:00.45, 2016- 13:16.86, 8:04.01; 2017- 8:01.29. pbs: 800m 1:50.10i '10, 1:51.04 '08; 1000m 2:20.29i '15, 1500m 3:32.97 '15, 1M 3:53.33 '14, 2000m 4:57.56 '14, 3000m 7:35.16 '12, 2M 8:14.95i '13.
Set US record in only his fifth steeplechase race, improving pb by 10.59 secs. In 2009 he had come 3rd in the US Champs in only his second race at 5000m.

Stanley Kipkoech **KEBENEI** b. 6 Nov 1989 Kenya 1.74m 61kg. Nike. Was at University of Arkansas.
At 3000mSt: WCh: '17- 5.
Progress at 3000mSt: 2011- 8:45.81, 2012- 8:24.45, 2014- 8:35.27, 2015- 8:23.93, 2016- 8:18.52, 2017- 8:08.30. pbs: 1000m 2:46.47i '14, 1500m 3:42.8 '11, 1M 4:04.37i '13, 4:05.79 '16; 3000m 7:49.74i '15, 7:54.21 '17; 5000m 13:51.85 '14, 10000m 27:58.56 '17, 15k Rd 43:29 '17.
US citizenship 28 Aug 2014, cleared to compete for USA 5 Mar 2015.

Sam KENDRICKS b. 7 Sep 1992 Oxford, Mississippi 1.89m 79kg. Nike. Army reservist (2nd Lt.). Was at University of Mississippi.
At PV: OG: '16- 3; WCh: '15- 9=, '17- 1; WUG: '13- 1; WI: '16- 2, '18- 2; Won DL 2017, US 2014-17, NCAA 2013-4.
Progress at PV: 2010- 4.68, 2011- 5.18, 2012- 5.50, 2013- 5.81, 2014- 5.75, 2015- 5.86Ai/5.82, 2016- 5.92, 2017- 6.00.

Fred KERLEY b. 7 May 1995 Taylor, Texas 1.905m 93kg. ALTIS. Texas A&M University.
At 400m/4x400mR: WCh: '17- 7/2R; WI: '18- 2R, Won NCAA & US 2017.
Progress at 400m: 2010- 52.30, 2014- 46.38, 2015- 47.15Ai/47.81, 2016- 45.10, 2017- 43.70. pbs: 100m 10.49A '15, 200m 20.24 '17, 300m 32.10+ '17, 600y 1:11.39i '14, TJ 13.90 '13.
Brother **My'Lik** (b. 6 Jun 1996) pb 400m 44.85 '17, sister Virginia 400m 54.38 '17.

Leonard Essau **KORIR** b. 10 Dec 1986 Iten, Kenya 1.73m 61kg. US Army. Studied political science at Iona College.
At 10000m: OG: '16- 14; WCh: '17- 13. Won US 10kRd & HMar 2017, CC 2017-18, NCAA 10000m 2011.
Progress at 10000m: 2011- 27:29.40, 2014- 28:01.85, 2015- 28:40.46, 2016- 27:35.65, 2017- 27:20.18. pbs: 1500m 3:43.65 '11, 1M 4:03.57i '12, 3000m 7:49.98i '13, 7:51.41 '17, 2M 8:22.44i '13, 5000m 13:15.4 '13, 15k 43:07 '18, HMar 59:52 '17.
Lived in the USA from 2014, US citizenship 3 May 2016.

Joe KOVACS b. 28 Jun 1989 Bethlehem, Pennsylvania 1.81m 132kg. Nike. Was at Penn State University.
At SP: OG: '16- 2; WCh: '15- 1, '17- 2; CCp: '14- 3; Won DL 2015, US 2014-15.
Progress at SP: 2007- 16.49, 2008- 16.86i, 2009- 18.53, 2010- 19.36i/18.73, 2011- 19.84i/19.15, 2012- 21.08, 2013- 20.82, 2014- 22.03. 2015- 22.56, 2016- 22.13, 2017- 22.57. pbs: DT 56.08 '11, HT 61.50 '11, Wt 19.07i '11.

Erik KYNARD b. 3 Feb 1991 Toledo, Ohio 1.93m 86kg. Nike Jordan. Was at Kansas State University.
At HJ: OG: '12- 2, '16- 6; WCh: '11-13-15-17: dnq 14/5/8=/dnq nh; WJ: '08- dnq 19=; CCp: '14- 5; WI: '14-16-18: 4/3/4; Won DL 2016, US 2013-14, 2016; NCAA 2011-12.
Progress at HJ: 2007- 2.13i/2.05, 2008- 2.23i/2.15, 2009- 2.24i/2.22, 2010- 2.25, 2011- 2.33i/2.31, 2012- 2.34, 2013- 2.37, 2014- 2.37, 2015- 2.37, 2016- 2.35, 2017- 2.31i/2.30. pb LJ 7.15i '09.

Jarrion LAWSON b. 6 May 1994 Texarcana, Texas 1.88m 75kg. University of Arkansas.
At LJ: OG: '16- 4 (res dqR); WCh: '17- 2; WJ: '12- 3 (dnq 22 TJ); WI: '18- 4. Won US LJ 2017, NCAA 100m, 200m & LJ 2016.
Progress at LJ: 2011- 7.26/7.46w, 2012- 7.82/7.89w, 2013- 7.93, 2014- 8.39Ai/7.92/8.13w, 2015- 8.34/ 8.36w, 2016- 8.58, 2017- 8.44/8.49w. pbs: 60m 6.60i '16, 100m 10.03 '17, 9.9/9.90w '15; 150mSt 15.25 '17, 200m 20.17 '16, TJ 15.80 '12.

Wil(bert) **LONDON** III b. 17 Aug 1997 Waco, Texas 1.83m 68kg. Kinesiology student at Baylor University.
At 400m/4x400mR: WCh: '17- sf/2R; WJ: '16- 2/1R.
Progress at 400m: 2013- 50.54, 2014- 47.66, 2015- 45.96, 2016- 45.27, 2017- 44.47. pb 200m 21.10 '16, 20.84w '17.

Noah LYLES b. 18 Jul 1997 Gainesville, Florida 1.80m 70kg.
At 100m: WJ: '16- 1/1R; PAm-J '15- 2 (1 200m); at 200m: WY: 13- sf/2Med R; Yth OG: '14- 1, won DL 2017. World indoor 300m record 2017.
Progress at 100m, 200m: 2013- 21.23; 2014- 10.45, 20.71; 2015- 10.14/10.07w, 20.18; 2016- 10.16/10.08w, 20.09/20.04w; 2017- 9.95w, 19.90. pbs: 60m 6.57i '18, 300m 31.87Ai/32.67i '17, 400m 47.04 '16, HJ: 2.03i '16.
His younger brother **Josephus** (b. 22 Jul 1998) 1 4x400m WJ '14, 3 200m & 2 400m WY '15; pbs 200m 20.74 '15, 20.73w '16; 400m 45.46 '15. Their father Kevin had a 400m pb 45.01 '95 and mother Keisha Caine 52.48 '94.

Tony McQUAY b. 16 Apr 1990 West Palm Beach, Florida 1.80m 70kg. adidas. Was at University of Florida.
At 400m: OG: '12- sf/2R, '16- 1R; WCh: '11- h, '13- 2/1R, '15- 1R, '17- res 2R; Won US 2011, NCAA 2012.
Progress at 400m: 2008- 48.09, 2009- 46.84, 2010- 45.37, 2011- 44.68, 2012- 44.49, 2013- 44.40, 2014- 44.92, 2015- 44.81, 2016- 44.24, 2017- 44.51. pbs: 100m 10.22 '13, 10.13w '14; 200m 20.60 '12, 300m 31.64 '16.

Aries MERRITT b. 24 Jul 1985 Marietta, Georgia 1.83m 74kg. Nike. Studied sports management at University of Tennessee.
At 110mh: OG: '12- 1; WCh: '09-11-13-15-17: h/5=/6/3/5; WJ: '04- 1. At 60mh: WI: '12-1, '18- 4, Won DL 110mh 2012, NCAA 60mh indoors & 110mh 2006, US indoor 60mh & 110mh 2012.
World 110mh record 2012.
Progress at 110mh: 2004- 13.47, 2005- 13.38/13.34w, 2006- 13.12, 2007- 13.09, 2008- 13.24, 2009- 13.15, 2010- 13.61, 2011- 13.12, 2012- 12.80, 2013- 13.09, 2014- 13.27, 2015- 13.04, 2016- 13.22, 2017- 13.09. pbs: 55m 6.43i '05, 60m 6.90i '10, 200m 21.31 '05, 50mh 6.54i '12, 55mh 7.02+i '12, 60mh 7.43Ai/7.44i '12, 400mh 51.94 '04.
Record 8 (and 2w) sub-13 second times in 2012. Revealed in 2015 that he had been suffering for two years from a kidney disorder and remarkably won World bronze medal just before undergoing a kidney transplant.

LaShawn MERRITT b. 27 Jun 1986 Portsmouth, Virginia 1.88m 82kg. Nike. Studied sports management at Old Dominion University, Norfolk, Virginia.
At 400m/4x400mR: OG: '08- 1/1R, '12- dnf ht, '16- 3/1R (6 200m); WCh: '05- res(1)R, '07- 2/1R, '09- 1/1R, '11- 2/1R, '13- 1/1R, '15- 2/1R, '17- sf; WJ: '04- 1/1R (1 at 4x100); WI: '06- 1R; WCp: '06- 1/1R, '14- 1/3R; won WAF 2007-09, DL 2013-14, 2016; US 2008-09, 2012-13, 2016.
World junior records 4x100m and 4x400m 2004, World indoor 400m junior best (44.93) 2005. World 4x110mh best 2015,
Progress at 200m, 400m: 2002- 21.46, 2003- 21.33, 47.69, 2004- 20.72/20.69w, 45.25; 2005- 20.38, 44.66; 2006- 20.10, 44.14; 2007- 19.98, 43.96; 2008- 20.08/19.80w, 43.75; 2009- 20.07, 44.06; 2011- 20.13, 44.63; 2012- 20.16, 44.12; 2013- 20.26, 43.74; 2014- 20.42, 43.92; 2015- 43.65, 2016- 19.74, 43.85; 2017- 20.27, 44.78. pbs: 55m 6.33i '04, 60m 6.68i '06, 100m 10.47/10.38w '04, 300m 31.23 '16, 500m 1:01.39i '12.
World age-18 400m record with 44.66 in 2005 and world low-altitude 300m best 2006 and 2009. Spent a year at East Carolina University before signing for Nike and returning home to Portsmouth. Two-year drugs ban for three positive tests from October 2009, reduced by three months after US arbitration panel declared that he had taken the steroid accidentally. Successfully challenged IOC rule preventing anyone serving 6 months or more from a drugs offence from competing in the next Games. Injured, he had to pull up in 2012 Olympic heat. Won six successive World 4x400m gold medals.

Clayton MURPHY b. 26 Feb 1995 New Madison, Ohio 1.82m 68kg. Nike. University of Akron.
At 800m: OG: '16- 3; WCh: '15- sf; PAm: '15- 1. Won US 800m 2016, NCAA 1500m 2016.
Progress at 800m, 1500m: 2013- 1600m 4:11.72, 2014- 1:50.03, 3:44.53; 2015- 1:45.59, 3:40.69; 2016- 1:42.93, 3:36.23; 2017- 1:43.60, 3:36.34. pbs: 600m 1:16.9+ '16, 1000m 2:17.17 '17, 1M 3:51.99 '17, 3000m 8:16.70i '17, 8:19.09 '16; 5000m 14:15.61 '15.

Bryshon NELLUM b. 1 May 1989 Los Angeles 1.83m 79kg. Was at University of Southern California.
At 400m/4x400mR: OG: '12- sf/2R; WCh: '15- sf/1R, '17- res 2R; WJ: '06- 1R; WY: '05- 3; PAm-J: '07- 1. Won NCAA 2013.
Progress at 400m: 2004- 47.27, 2005- 46.81, 2006- 46.20, 2007- 45.38, 2010- 45.94, 2011- 45.56, 2012- 44.80, 2013- 44.73, 2014- 48.19, 2015- 44.65, 2016- 45.50, 2017- 44.50. pbs: 200m 20.23/19.99w '13, 300m 32.07 '15.
Career seriously threatened when he was shot three times in the leg by gang in 2009.

Michael NORMAN b. 3 Dec 1997 San Diego 1.83m 73kg. University of Southern California.
At 200m: WJ: '16- 1/1R.
World indoor 400m record 2018.
Progress at 200m, 400m: 2013- 22.62, 49.54; 2014- 20.82, 46.94; 2015- 20.24, 45.19; 2016- 20.14/20.06w, 45.51; 2017- 20.75i, 44.60; 2018- 44.52i. pb 100m 10.27 '16.

Vernon NORWOOD b. 10 Apr 1992 New Orleans 1.87m 77kg. New Balance. Was at Louisiana State University.
At 400m/4x400mR: WCh: '15- sf/res1R; WI: '16- 1R, '18- 2R. Won NCAA indoors and out 2015, US indoor 2016.
Progress at 400m: 2011- 47.47, 2012- 45.72A/45.98, 2013- 45.56A/45.67, 2014- 45.02, 2015- 44.44,

2016- 45.00, 2017- 44.47. pbs: 200m 20.77 '15, 300m 32.07 '15, 500m 1:00.11i '17, 600y 1:08.80i '13, 600m 1:18.57Ai '15.

Gil ROBERTS b. 15 Mar 1989 Oklahoma City 1.88m 81kg. Nike. Was at Texas Tech University.
At 400m/4x400mR: OG: '16- sf/1R; WCh: '09- h, '17- sf/2R; WI: '12- 1R; US champion 2014, indoors 2012.
Progress at 400m: 2005- 47.47, 2006- 47.72A, 2007- 46.16, 2008- 46.14, 2009- 44.86, 2011- 45.22, 2012- 44.84, 2013- 45.73, 2014- 44.53, 2015- 45.29, 2016- 44.65, 2017- 44.22. pbs: 55m 6.26i '12, 100m 10.12/9.92w '14, 200m 20.22 '14, 300m 31.81 '16.

Kurt ROBERTS b. 20 Feb 1988 Lancaster, Ohio 1.91m 127kg. Nike, Was at Ashland University. Won NACAC 2010, US indoor SP 2016.
Progress at SP: 2007- 16.39, 2008- 17.81, 2009- 18.78, 2010- 19.80i/18.76, 2011- 19.55, 2012- 21.14, 2013- 20.98, 2014- 21.50i/21.47, 2015- 20.45, 2016- 21.57i/21.40, 2017- 20.73.

Michael RODGERS b. 24 Apr 1985 Brenham, Texas 1.78m 73kg. Nike. Studied kinesiology at Oklahoma Baptist University.
At 100m/4x100mR: OG: '16- dqR; WCh: '09-13-15-17: sf/6&2R/5/2R; CCp: '14- 2/1R. At 60m: WI: '08-10-16: 4/2/6. Won US 100m 2009, 2014; indoor 60m 2008.
N.American 4x100m record 2015.
Progress at 100m: 2004- 10.55/10.31w, 2005- 10.30/10.25w, 2006- 10.29/10.18w, 2007- 10.10, 10.07w, 2008- 10.06/10.01w, 2009- 9.94/9.9/9.85w, 2010- 10.00/9.99w, 2011- 9.85, 2012- 9.94, 2013- 9.90, 2014- 9.91/9.80w, 2015- 9.86, 2016- 9.97, 20.42; 2017- 10.00/9.98w. pbs: 60m 6.48Ai/6.50i '11, 150mSt 15.33 '14, 200m 20.24 '09.
Dropped out of US World Champs team after positive test for stimulant on 19 July 2011, for which he subsequently received a 9-month suspension. Younger sister Alishea Usery won US junior 400m 2009, pb 53.27 '09.

Galen RUPP b. 8 May 1986 Portland 1.80m 62kg. Nike Oregon Project. Studied business at University of Oregon.
At (5000/)10000m: OG: '08- 13, '12- 7/2, '16- 5 (3 Mar); WCh: '07- 11, '09- 8, '11- 9/7, '13- 8/4, '15- 5/5. At 5000m: WJ: '04- 9; PAm-J: '03- 1. At 3000m: WI: '10- 5, '14- 4; WY: '03- 7. Won US 5000m 2012, 10000m 2009-16, NCAA 5000m & 10000m (& indoor 3000m & 5000m) 2009, CC 2008.
N.American records: 10000m 2011 & 2014, junior 5000m 2004, 10000m 2005; indoor 5000m (13:11.44) 2011 & 2014, 3000m 2013, 2M 2012, 2014.
Progress at 5000m, 10000m, Mar: 2002- 14:34.05, 2003- 14:20.29, 2004- 13:37.91, 29:09.56; 2005- 13:44.72. 28:15.52; 2006- 13:47.04, 30:42.10; 2007- 13:30.49, 27:33.48; 2008- 13:49.8+, 27:36.99; 2009- 13:18.12i/13:42.59+, 27:37.99; 2010- 13:07.35, 27:10.74; 2011- 13:06.86, 26:48.00; 2012- 12:58.90, 27:25.33; 2013- 13:01.37, 27:24.39; 2014- 13:00.99, 26:44.36; 2015- 13:08.38, 27:08.91; 2016- 13:20.69, 27:08.92, 2:10:05; 2017- 13:54.88, 28:18.29. 2:09:20. pbs: 800m 1:49.87i/1:50.00 '09, 1500m 3:34.15 '14, 1M 3:50.92i/3:52.11 '13, 3000m 7:30.16i '13, 7:43.24 '10, 2M 8:07.41i '14, HMar 59:47 '18.
Won US Olympic Trials on marathon debut 2016, 2nd Boston & 1st Chicago 2017. Married to Keara Sammons (10000m 33:54.55 '07).

Michael STIGLER b. 5 Apr 1992 Canyon, Texas 1.78m 70kg. Studied communications at University of Kansas.
At 400mh: WCh: '17- dq h; WJ: 12- 1/1R. Won NCAA 2015, 2 NACAC U23 2012, 2014.
Progress at 400mh: 2011- 52.07, 2012- 49.45, 2013- 49.19, 2014- 49.34, 2015- 48.44, 2016- 49.68, 2017- 48.26. pbs: 400m 47.41i '15, 500m 1:02.11i '13, 600y 1:08.59i '14, 600m 1:18.38i '17, 800m 1:52.33 '17, 60mh 7.90i '15, 110mh 13.77 '14.

Christian TAYLOR b. 18 Jun 1990 Fayetteville 1.90m 75kg. Li Ning. Studied at the University of Florida.
At (LJ/)TJ: OG: '12- 1, '16- 1; WCh: '11-13-15-17: 1/4/1/1; WI: '12- 2; WJ: '08- 7/8 (res 1 4x400m); WY: '07- 3/1. Won DL 2012-17, NACAC 2010-11, US 2011-12, NCAA indoor 2009-10.
North American triple jump record 2015.
Progress at LJ, TJ: 2007- 7.29, 15.98; 2008- 7.79i/7.68/7.77w, 16.05; 2009- 8.02i/7.72, 16.98i/16.65/16.91w; 2010- 8.19, 17.18i/17.02/17.09w; 2011- 8.00/8.07w/17.96; 2012- 8.12, 17.81; 2013- 8.01/8.07w, 17.66; 2014- 8.09, 17.51; 2015- 8.18, 18.21; 2016- 7.96, 17.86; 2017- 18.11. pbs: 60m 6.79i '11, 200m 20.70 '13, 400m 45.17 '14.
His 18.21 in the final round of the 2015 World Champs was the second longest ever legal TJ mark; it was 18.32 from take-off to landing. Both parents came from Barbados.

Michael TINSLEY b. 21 Apr 1984 Little Rock, Arkansas 1.85m 74kg. adidas. Studied criminal justice at Jackson State University.
At 400mh: OG: '12- 2, '16- h; WCh: '13- 2, '15- 8; CCp: '14- 7; won DL 2014, NCAA 2008, US 2012-13.
Progress at 400mh: 2002- 52.5, 2004- 50.87, 2005- 48.55, 2006- 48.25, 2007- 48.02, 2008- 48.84, 2009- 48.53, 2010- 48.46, 2011- 48.45, 2012- 47.91, 2013- 47.70, 2014- 48.25, 2015- 48.34, 2016- 48.74, 2017- 49.00. pbs: 60m 6.92i '05, 200m 20.66 '09, 20.34w '13; 400m 46.02i '06, 46.05 '07; 55mh 7.39i '04, 60mh 7.84i '06, 110mh 13.86 '04.

Ben TRUE b. 29 Dec 1985 North Yarmouth, Maine 1.83m 70kg. Saucony. Studied art history and architecture at Dartmouth College.
At 5000m: WCh: '15- 6. World CC: '13- 6.
Progress at 5000m: 2006- 14:18.61, 2007- 13:14.85, 2010- 13:43.98, 2011- 13:24.11, 2012- 13:20.53, 2013- 13:11.59, 2014- 13:02.74, 2015- 13:05.54, 2016- 13:12.67, 2017- 13:06.74i/13:10.83. pbs: 800m 1:50.07 '07, 1500m 3:36.05 '16, 1M 3:57.31i '17, 4:02.61 '07; 3000m 7:35.53 '17, 2M 8:11.33i '17,

10000m 27:41.17 '12, road: 10M 46:48 '11, 15k 43:04 '14. Married to Sarah Groff, 4th 2012 Olympics in triathlon.

David VERBURG b. 14 May 1991 Oklahoma 1.68m 64kg. adidas. Was at George Mason University.
At 400m/4x400mR: OG: '16- sf/res 1R; WCh: '13- 1R, '15- sf/1R; WJ: 10- 1R; WI: '14- 4/1R. US champion 2015.
Progress at 400m: 2009- 47.15, 2010- 46.27, 2011- 46.09, 2012- 45.06, 2013- 44.75, 2014- 45.03, 2015- 44.41, 2016- 44.82, 2017- 45.85. pbs: 200m 20.63 '15, 300m 32.17 '15, 500m 1:01.29i '13, 600m 1:18.06i '12. Engaged to Cassandra Tate (qv).

Ameer WEBB b. 19 Mar 1991 Carson, California 1.75m 75kg. Nike, Was at Texas A & M Univ.
At 200m: OG: '16- sf; WCh: '17- 5; won US 2017, NCAA 2014 (indoor 2013-13).
Progress at 100m, 200m: 2008- 10.70w, 21.81w; 2009- 10.67, 21.25/21.24w; 2010- 10.37, 20.70; 2011- 10.37, 20.49; 2012- 10.17/10.05w, 20.46/20.20w; 2013- 10.14/10.07w, 20.20/20.05w; 2014- 10.37, 20.38; 2015- 10.04, 20.02; 2016- 9.94/9.90w, 19.85; 2017- 10.23, 20.01. pb 60m 6.60Ai/6.65i '16.

Ryan WHITING b. 24 Nov 1986 Harrisburg, Pennsylvania 1.91m 134kg. Nike. Studied civil engineering at Arizona State University.
At SP: OG: '12- 9; WCh: '11- 6, '13- 2, '17- 7; WI: '12-14-18: 1/1/7; PAm-J: '05- 1 (1 DT); Won DL 2013, US 2013, NACAC 2009, NCAA 2009-10, indoor 2008-10, DT 2010.
Progress at SP: 2006- 19.75, 2007- 20.35, 2008- 21.73i/20.60, 2009- 20.99, 2010- 21.97, 2011- 21.76, 2012- 22.00i/21.66, 2013- 22.28, 2014- 22.23i/21.31, 2015- 21.80i/21.37, 2016- 21.06, 2017- 21.65. pb DT 61.11 '08, Wt 18.94i '10.

Isiah YOUNG b. 5 Jan 1990 Junction City, Kansas 1.83m 75kg. Was at Univ. of Mississippi.
At 200m: OG: '12- sf; WCh: '13- sf, '15- h, '17- 8.
Progress at 100m, 200m: 2008- 10.96; 2009- 10.44, 21.22; 2010- 10.32, 20.98; 2011- 10.31, 20.81; 2012- 10.09/10.08w, 20.33/20.16w; 2013- 9.99/9.93w, 19.86; 2014- 10.23, 20.58/20.55w; 2015- 10.00/9.82w, 19.93/19.75w; 2016- 10.03, 20.24; 2017- 9.97/9.95w, 20.14/20.12w. pb 60m 6.61i '12.

Zachery ZIEMEK b. 23 Feb 1993 Itaska, Illinois 1.94m 88 kg. University of Wisconsin.
At Dec: OG: '16- 7; WCh: '15- 15, '17- dnf. At Hep: WI: '18- 6.
Progress at Dec: 2012- 7042, 2013- 7640, 2014- 7981, 2015- 8107, 2016- 8413, 2017- 8155. pbs: 60m 6.75i '16, 100m 10.57 '15, 400m 48.75 '17, 1000m 2:48.25i '13, 1500m 4:42.52 '16, 60mh 8.08i '18, 110mh 14.71 '16, HJ 2.10 '14, PV 5.45 '15, LJ 7.73 '14, SP 14.77 '15, DT 49.42 '16, JT 60.92 '16, Hep 6173i '16.

Women

Morolake AKINOSUN b. 17 May 1994 Lagos, Nigeria 1.63m 61kg. University of Texas.
At 100m/200m: OG: '16- res 1R; WCh: '17- 1R; PAm: '15- sf/1R. Won US Indoor 60m 2017.
Progress at 100m, 200m: 2010- 11.94, 24.58/24.07w; 2011- 11.42, 23.49/23.44w; 2012- 11.41, 24.34; 2013- 11.45/11.29w, 23.26/23.18w; 2014- 11.04/10.96w, 22.68/22.17w; 2015- 11.29/10.94w, 22.52; 2016- 10.95, 22.54; 2017- 10.98/10.94w. pbs: 60m 7.08Ai/7.17i '17.

Nia ALI b. 23 Oct 1988 Norristown 1.70m 64kg. ALTIS. Was at University of Southern California.
At 100mh: OG: '16- 2; WCh: '13- sf, '17- 8; WUG: '11- 1. Won NCAA 2011. At 60mh: WI: '14- 1, '16- 1; won US indoor 2013-14.
Progress at 100mh: 2005- 14.20, 2006- 13.63/13.55w, 2007- 13.25, 2008- 13.14, 2009- 13.17, 2011- 12.73/12.63w, 2012- 12.78, 2013- 12.48, 2014- 12.75, 2016- 12.55, 2017- 12.52. pbs: 60m 7.43i '14, 200m 23.90 '09, 800m 2:24.55 '07, 60mh 7.80i '14, HJ 1.86 '11, LJ 5.89 '09, SP 13.61 '09, JT 39.24 '09, Hep 5870 '16. Son Titus born to her and Michael Tinsley in May 2015.

Whitney ASHLEY b. 18 Feb 1989 1.83m 93kg. Nike. Was at San Diego State University.
At DT: OG: '16- dnq nt; WCh: '13- dnq 23, '15- 9, '17- dnq 13; NCAA champion 2012.
Progress at DT: 2008- 44.86, 2009- 46.05, 2010- 47.34, 2011- 54.75, 2012- 59.99, 2013- 61.64, 2014- 63.78, 2015- 64.80, 2016- 64.62, 2017- 63.85. pbs: SP 17.62i '16, 17.60 '17; HT 57.14 '11, Wt 19.19 '12.

Joanna ATKINS b. 31 Jan 1989 Stone Mountain, Georgia 1.80m 64kg. LifeSpeed. Was at Auburn University.
At 200m: CCp: '14- 2. At 400m: WCh: '13- res1R; WI: '14- 6/1R, '18- 1R; Won NCAA 400m 2009.
Progress at 200m, 400m: 2004- 24.25w, 56.12; 2005- 24.02, 54.32; 2006- 23.82, 55.42; 2007- 24.35i/23.69w, 53.93; 2008- 23.30, 52.94; 2009- 22.89, 50.39; 2010- 23.32, 51.52; 2011- 22.68, 51.50; 2012- 23.10/22.83w, 51.12; 2013- 23.27, 50.77; 2014- 22.27/22.19w, 50.74; 2015- 23.82i, 2016- 22.40, 52.39; 2017- 22.74/22.54w, 53.26i; 2018- 51.87Ai. pbs: 55m 6.91i '09, 600m 7.28i '09, 100m 11.02 '14, 10.99w '16; 300m 36.18Ai '17.

Tianna BARTOLETTA b. 30 Aug 1985 Elyria, Ohio 1.68m 60kg. née Madison. Nike. Studied biology at University of Central Florida, formerly at University of Tennessee.
At 100m/4x100mR: OG: '12- 4/1R, '16- sf/1R; won US 2014. At LJ: OG: '16- 1; WCh: '05- 1, '07- 10, '15- 1, '17- 3; CCp: '14- 3/1R; WI: '06- 1; PAm-J: '03- 4, won DL 2014-15, US 2015, 2017; NCAA indoors and out 2005. At 60m: WI: '12- 3, '14- 3; won US indoor 2012.
Progress at 100m, LJ: 2000- 5.73, 2001- 6.07, 2002- 11.98/11.91w, 6.20; 2003- 11.68, 6.28; 2004- 11.50/11.35w, 6.60; 2005- 11.41, 6.89/6.92w; 2006- 11.52/11.50w, 6.80i/6.60; 2007- 6.60/6.61w; 2008- 11.54, 6.53/6.58w; 2009- 11.05, 6.48; 2010- 11.20, 6.44; 2011- 11.29, 6.21/6.58w; 2012- 10.85, 6.48; 2013- 11.41; 2014- 10.92, 7.02; 2015- 10.94/10.90w,

7.14; 2016- 10.78, 7.17; 2017- 11.04, 7.01/7.05w. pbs: 55m 6.69i '09, 60m 7.02i '12, 200m 22.37/22.33w '12. Set long jump pbs in qualifying and final of 2005 Worlds. US bobsled team in 2012/13. Married John Bartoletta in 2012.

Gwen BERRY b. 29 Jun 1989 St. Louis, Missouri. 1.76m 80kg. New York AC. Was at University of Southern Illinois.
At HT: OG: '16- dnq 14; WCh: '17- dnq 14; Won US 2017, indoor weight 2013-14, 2017.
N.American hammer record 2017. World 20lb weight indoor record record 2017.
Progress at HT: 2008- 53.70, 2009- 59.58, 2010- 62.55, 2011- 70.52, 2012- 71.95, 2013- 73.81, 2014- 72.04, 2015- 72.326, 2016- 73.09/76.12dq, 2017- 76.77. Pbs: SP 16.99 '11, Wt 25.60i '17.
3-month ban from 29 Mar 2016 for use of a stimulant that cost her a North American 'record' of 76.31 and US indoor wight title.

Amanda BINGSON b. 20 Feb 1990 Victorville, California 1.70m 89kg. New York AC. Sports psychology graduate of University of Nevada, Las Vegas.
At HT: OG: '12- dnq 23; WCh: '13- 9, '15- 9; CCp: '14- 2; US champion 2013-14, NACAC 2012.
North American hammer record 2013.
Progress at HT: 2009- 55.19, 2010- 64.07, 2011- 69.79, 2012- 71.78, 2013- 75.73, 2014- 75.12, 2015- 72.35, 2016- 71.90, 2017- 72.06. Pbs: DT 46.08A '11, Wt 22.42i '14. Former gymnast.

Erica BOUGARD b. 26 Jul 1993 Memphis 1.73m 57kg. Was at Mississippi State University.
At Hep: WCh: '13-15-17: 24/dnf/18; WJ: '12- 13. At Pen: WI: '18- 5.
Progress at Hep: 2011- 5270?, 2012- 5547, 2013- 5990, 2014- 6118, 2015- 6288, 2016- 6170, 2017- 6502. pbs: 200m 23.28 '17, 400m 54.09 '11, 800m 2:08.39 '15, 60mh 7.98A '18, 8.03i '15; 100mh 12.93/12.90w '17, HJ 1.92 '17, LJ 6.59 '17, TJ 12.76i '18, 12.62 '13; SP 12.66 '17, JT 40.96 '17, Pen 4760Ai '18.

Tori BOWIE b. 27 Aug 1990 Jackson, Mississippi 1.75m 61kg. adidas. Studied psychology at University of Southern Mississippi.
At 100m/(200m): OG: '16- 2/3/1R; WCh: '15- 3, '17- 1/1R. At 60m: WI: '16- 6. Won US 100m 2015, 200m 2016. At LJ: won NCAA 2011.
Progress at 100m, 200m, LJ: 2008- 12.21w, 6.03w; 2009- 11.82, 23.99, 6.30/6.60w; 2010- 11.76/11.72w, 24.55/23.98w, 6.43/6.50w; 2011- 6.64, 2012- 11.28, 24.06, 6.78; 2013- 11.14/11.04w, 6.91, 2014- 10.80, 22.18, 6.95i/6.82; 2015- 10.81/10.72w, 22.23; 2016- 10.78/10.74w, 21.99; 2017- 10.85/10.80w, 21.77. pbs: 60m 7.11i '16, 150mSt 16.30 '17 (world best), TJ 13.09i/12.65 '14. First name Frentorish.

Tia BROOKS b. 2 Aug 1990 Saginaw, Michigan 1.83m 109kg. Nike. Was at University of Oklahoma.
At SP: OG: '12- dnq 19, WCh: '13- 7, '15- dnq 13. NCAA champion indoors and out 2012-13.
Progress at SP: 2008- 14.64, 2009- 14.13i/14.09, 2010- 17.37, 2011- 18.00, 2012- 19.00i/18.47, 2013- 19.22i/18.96, 2014- 18.83, 2015- 19.00, 2016- 19.73. pb DT 46.64 '08.

Quanesha BURKS b. 15 Mar 1995 Ozark, Alabama 1.60m 55kg. Was at University.of Alabama
At LJ: WCh: '17- dnq 14; WJ: 14- 5; PAm: '15- 8; WI: '18- 4; Won NCAA 2015, NACAC 2015-16.
Progress at LJ: 2012- 6.13, 2013- 5.84w, 2014- 6.38, 2015- 6.93A/6.84/6.91w, 2016- 6.80i/6.77, 2017- 6.83/6.90w. pbs: 60m 7.20i '18, 100m 11.21/11.18w '17.

Amber CAMPBELL b. 5 Jun 1981 Indianapolis 1.70m 91kg. Mjolnar. Was at Coastal Carolina University.
At HT: OG: '08/12- dnq 19/9, '16- 6; WCh: '05-11-13: dnq 18/13/12, '09- 11, '15- nt; PAm: '11- 3, '15- 2. Won NACAC 2015, US 2012, 2015-16; indoor Wt 2007-11.
Progress at HT: 2000- 49.16, 2001- 62.08, 2002- 63.76, 2003- 64.58, 2004- 67.23, 2005- 69.52, 2006- 67.52, 2007- 70.33, 2008- 70.19, 2009- 70.61, 2010- 71.94, 2011- 72.59, 2012- 71.80, 2013- 73.03, 2014- 73.61, 2015- 72.81, 2016- 74.03, 2017- 73.58. pbs: SP 14.81i '02, 14.42 '04; 20lb Wt 24.78i '12.

Kori CARTER b. 6 Mar 1992 Pasadena, California 1.65m 57kg. Nike. Studied human biology at Stanford University.
At 400mh: WCh: '15- sf, '17- 1; WJ: '08- h; CCp: '14- 7; Won US 2014, NCAA 2013. At 100mh: WY: '09- 2.
Progress at 400mh: 2007- 62.21, 2008- 60.22, 2009- 59.89, 2010- 60.47, 2011- 57.10, 2012- 57.60, 2013- 53.21, 2014- 53.84, 2015- 54.41, 2016- 54.47, 2017- 52.95. pbs: 100m 11.57 '11, 200m 23.07 '17, 60mh 8.00Ai '18, 8.11i '17; 100mh 12.76 '13.

Michelle CARTER b. 12 Oct 1985 San Jose 1.75m 110kg. Nike. Liberal arts graduate from University of Texas.
At SP: OG: '08- 13, '12- 4, '16- 1; WCh: '09-11-13-15-17: 5/8/4/3/3; WI: '12-14-16: 2/4/1; WJ: '04- 1; WY: '01- 2; PAm: '11- 3; PAm-J: '03- 1; CCp: '14- 2. Won US 2008-09, 2011, 2013-16; NCAA indoor 2006. North American shot records 2013 and 2016 and indoors (20.21) 2016.
Progress at SP: 2000- 14.76, 2001- 15.23, 2002- 16.25, 2003- 16.73, 2004- 17.55, 2005- 18.26, 2006- 17.98, 2007- 17.57, 2008- 18.85, 2009- 19.13, 2010- 18.80, 2011- 19.86, 2012- 19.60, 2013- 20.24, 2014- 19.84, 2015- 20.02, 2016- 20.63, 2017- 19.34. pbs: DT 54.06 '07.
First US woman to win Olympic shot. Her father Mike set a world junior shot record in 1979 and won the Olympic silver in 1984, seven NCAA titles (4 in, 3 out) (for a unique father-daughter double) and WUG gold in 1981 and 1983, pb 21.76 '84. Her younger sister D'Andra (b. 17 Jun 1987) won the NCAA discus in 2009, pb 57.73 '08.

Kristi CASTLIN b. 7 Jul 1988 Douglasville, Georgia 1.70m 75kg. adidas. Political science graduate of Virginia Tech University.
At 100mh: OG: '16- 3; won PAm-J 2007. At 60mh: won US indoors 2012.
World best 4x100mh 2014 & 2015.
Progress at 100mh: 2005- 13.85, 2006- 13.73, 2007- 12.91/12.82w, 2008- 12.81, 2009- 12.89, 2010- 12.83/12.59w, 2011- 12.83/12.68w, 2012- 12.56/ 12.48w, 2013- 12.61, 2014- 12.58, 2015- 12.71, 2016- 12.50, 2017- 12.61. pbs: 55m 7.04i '08, 60m 7.47i '08, 100m 11.60 '12, 11.49w '11; 200m 23.46 '12, 50mh 6.81+i '12, 55mh 7.37i '12, 60mh 7.84Ai/7.91i '12, 400mh 60.44 '07.
Married to Alonzo Nelson.

Emma COBURN b. 19 Oct 1990 Boulder 1.73m 55kg. New Balance. Marketing graduate of University of Colorado.
At 3000mSt: OG: '12- 8, '16- 3; WCh: '11- 8, '15- 5, '17- 1; CCp: '14- 1; US champion 2011-12, 2014-17; NCAA 2011, 2013.
Three North American 3000m steeple records 2014 (unratified as no doping test) & 2016-17 (3).
Progress at 3000mSt: 2009- 10:06.21, 2010- 9:51.86, 2011- 9:37.16, 2012- 9:23.54, 2013- 9:28.26, 2014- 9:11.42, 2015- 9:15.59, 2016- 9:07.63, 2017- 9:02.58. pbs: 800m 2:09.81 '10, 1500m 4:05.10 '15, 1M 4:29.86i '13, 4:33.24 '12; 2000m 5:41.11i '15, 3000m 8:41.16i '18, 8:48.60 '17.
Married Joe Bosshard on 14 Oct 2017.

Amy CRAGG b. 21 Jan 1984 Long Beaxh 1.62m 46kg. Nike Bowerman TC. née Hastings. Was at Arizona State University.
At 5000m: WCh: '11- 14. 10000m: WCh: OG: '12- 11; WCh: '13- 14; HMar: WCh: '09- 31; Mar: OG: '16- 9; WCh: '17- 3. Won US 10000m 2012.
Progress at Mar: 2011- 2:27:03, 2012- 2:27:17, 2013- 2:42:50, 2014- 2:27:03, 2016- 2:25:04, 2017- 2:28:20, 2017- 2:27:18, 2018- 2:21:42. pbs: 1500m: 4:15.77 '09, 1M 4:47.29 '06, 3000m 8:58.21 '12, 5000m 15:09.59mx '13, 15:14.31 '11; 10000m: 31:10.69 '12, HMar 68:27 '17, 3000mSt 10:17.67 '04.
Won Los Angeles marathon 2016, 3rd Tokyo 2018. Married Alistair Cragg IRL (1 EI 3000m 2005, pbs: 1M 3:55.04i '06, 3000m 7:32.49 '07, 5000m 13:03.53 '11) on 8 Nov 2014

Vashti CUNNINGHAM b. 18 Jan 1998 Las Vegas 1.85m 66kg. Nike. High school in Las Vegas, Nevada.
At HJ: OG: '16- 13=; WCh: '17- 10; WI: '16- 1, '18- 2; PAm-J: 15- 1; won US 2017, indoors 2016-17.
High jump records: World youth (=) 2015, World junior indoor 2016, North American junior 2017.
Progress at HJ: 2012- 1.76, 2013- 1.83, 2014- 1.90, 2015- 1.96, 2016- 1.99i/1.97, 2017- 1.99, 2018- 1.97Ai. Pb LJ 5.85w '15.
Father Randall Cunningham was a quarterback in the NFL. Her brother Randall (b. 4 Jan 1996) has HJ pbs 2.27i '17, 2.25 '16 and won PAm-J 2015 and NCAA 2016.

Kimberlyn DUNCAN b. 2 Aug 1991 Katy, Texas 1.73m 59kg. Nike. Was at Louisiana State University.
At 200m: WCh: '13- sf, '17- 6; won US 2013, NCAA 2011-13 (and indoors).
Progress at 100m, 200m: 2007- 24.54, 2008- 24.33, 2009- 23.46, 2010- 11.84, 23.08/22.96w; 2011- 11.09/11.02w, 22.24/22.18w, 2012- 10.96/ 10.94w, 22.19; 2013- 11.08/11.02w, 22.35/21.80w; 2014- 11.20, 22.53/22.10w; 2015- 11.13/11.08w, 22.83; 2016- 11.11, 23.01; 2017- 11.03, 22.54/22.41w. pb 60m 7.16i '13.

Kendall ELLIS b. 8 Mar 1996 Florida 1.73m 59kg. University of Southern California.
At 400m: WCh: '17- h/res1R. Won NCAA indoor 400m 2018.
North American indoor 400m record 2018.
Progress at 400m: 2011- 54.83i, 2012- 53.22, 2013- 53.80, 2014- 52.95, 2015- 52.32, 2016- 51.82, 2017- 50.00, 2018- 50.34i. pb 200m 22.79 '17.

Maggie EWEN b. 23 Sep 1994 St. Francis, Minnesota 1.78m 79kg. Arizona State Univ.
At HT: WCh: '17- dnq 21; won NCAA 2017. At DT: PAm-J: '13- 2.
HT Progress at SP, HT: 2011- 14.71, 2012- 14.78, 2013- 16.67, 2014- 15.90, 2015- 16.33, 60.54; 2016- 16.85i/16.82, 70.50; 2017- 18.12i/17.72, 74.56; 2018- 19.20i. 72.23. pbs: DT 60.51 '17, Wt 22.26i '18.

Allyson FELIX b. 18 Nov 1985 Los Angeles 1.68m 57kg. Nike. Elementary education graduate of University of Southern California.
At 400m/(4x100mR)/4x400mR: OG: '16- 21R/1R; At 200m: OG: '04- 2, '08- 2/1R, '12- 1/1R/1R; WCh: '03- qf, '05- 1, '07- 1/1R/1R, '09- 1/1R, '11- 3/1R/1R (2 400m), '13- dnf, '15- 1 400m/2R/2R, '17- 3 400m/1R/1R; WJ: '02- 5; PAm: '03- 3; WI: '10- 1R. At 100m: OG: '12- 5; WY: '01- 1 (1 Medley R). Won DL 200m 2010, 2014-15; 400m 2010, WAF 200m 2005-06, 2009; US 100m 2010, 200m 2004-05, 2007-09, 2012; 400m 2011, 2015-16.
World junior record 200m 2004 after unratified mark (no doping test) at age 17 in 2003.
Progress at 100m, 200m, 400m: 2000- 12.19/11.99w, 23.90; 2001- 11.53, 23.31/23.27w; 2002- 11.40, 22.83/22.69w, 55.01; 2003- 11.29/ 11.12w, 22.11A/22.51, 52.26; 2004- 11.16, 22.18, 51.83A; 2005- 11.05, 22.13, 51.12; 2006- 11.04, 22.11; 2007- 11.01, 21.81, 49.70; 2008- 10.93, 21.93/21.82w, 49.83; 2009- 11.08, 21.88, 49.83; 2010- 11.27, 22.03, 50.15; 2011- 11.26+, 22.32, 49.59; 2012- 10.89, 21.69; 2013- 11.06+, 22.30, 50.19; 2014- 11.01, 22.02, 50.81; 2015- 11.09, 21.98, 49.26; 2016- 22.02, 49.51; 2017- 11.03, 22.33, 49.65. pbs: 50m 6.43i '02, 60m 7.10i '12, 150mSt 16.36 '13 (world best), 300m 36.33i '07.
Women's record 6 Olympic gold medals from 9 medals to equal record. First teenager to won a World sprint title. Unbeaten in ten 200m competitions 2005 and five in 2007. Has women's records of 16 medals and 11 gold at

World Champs including three in 2007 when she had a record 0.53 winning margin at 200m and ran a 48.0 400m relay leg. Ran 47.72 relay leg at the 2015 Worlds. IAAF female Athlete of the Year 2012. Older brother Wes Felix won World Junior bronze at 200m and gold in WJR at 4x100m in 2002, pbs: 100m 10.23 '05, 200m 20.43 '04.

Shalane FLANAGAN b. 8 Jul 1981 Boulder 1.65m 50kg. Bowerman TC. Was at University of North Carolina.
At 5000m/(10000m): OG: '04- h, '08- 9/2; WCh: '05- h, '07- 8, '09- (13), '11- (7), '13- (8), '15- (6). At Mar: OG: '12- 9, '16- 6. World CC: '10- 12, '11-3; 4k: '04- 14, 05- 20. Won US 5000m 2005, 10000m 2008, 2011, 2013; HMar 2010, Mar 2012, CC 2008, 2010-11, 2013; 4km CC 2004-05, indoor 3000m 2007, NCAA CC 2002-03, indoor 3000m 2003.
N.American records: 5000m and indoor 3000m 2007, 10000m (2) 2008, 15km & 25km road 2014.
Progress at 5000m, 10000m, Mar: 2001- 16:29.68, 2003- 15:20.54, 2004- 15:05.08, 2005- 15:10.96, 2007- 14:44.80, 2008- 14:59.69, 30:22.22; 2009- 14:47.62i/15:10.86, 31:23.43; 2010- 14:49.08, 2:28:40; 2011- 14:45.20, 30:39.57; 2012- 31:59.69, 2:25:38; 2013- 31:04.85, 2:27:08; 2014- 2:21:14, 2015- 15:10.02, 31:09.02, 2:27:47dh; 2016- 2:25:26, 2017- 14:58.99, 31:31.12, 2:26:53. pbs: 800m 2:09.28 '02, 1500m 4:05.86 '07, 1M 4:33.81i '11, 4:48.47 '00; 3000m 8:33.25i/8:35.34 '07, Road: 15k 47:03 '14, 10M 51:45 '10, HMar 67:51dh '16, 68:31 '13, 25k 1:22:36 '14, 30k 1:39:15 '14.
2nd New York 2010 on marathon debut and won Olympic Trials 2012 and New York 2017; 3rd Berlin 2014. Married to Steve Edwards. Mother, Cheryl Bridges, set marathon world best with 2:49:40 in 1971 and was 4th in 1969 International CC, father Steve ran in World Cross 1976-7, 1979.

Phyllis FRANCIS b. 4 May 1992 New York 1.78m 61kg. Nike. Was at University of Oregon.
At 400m/4x400mR: OG: '16- 5/1R; WCh: '15- 7/res2R, '17- 1/1R; PAm-J: '11- 3/1R. Won NCAA indoors 2014.
Progress at 400m: 2010- 55.82i, 2011- 52.93, 2012- 51.22, 2013- 50.86, 2014- 50.46Ai/50.59, 2015- 50.50, 2016- 49.94, 2017- 49.92. pbs: 60m 7.30i '17, 100m 11.55 '17, 11.34w '16; 200m 22.50 '16, 300m 36.15Ai '17, 36.85i '18; 600m 1:27.38i '11, 800m 2:04.83 '08.
Younger sister Claudia pbs 400m 51.55 '16, 800m 2:02.92 '15, 400mh 55.55 '16.

Courtney FRERICHS b. 18 Jan 1993 Nixa, Missouri 1.70m 62kg. Studied biology at University of New Mexico.
At 3000mSt: OG: '16- 11; WCh: '17- 2; NCAA champion 2016.
Progress at 3000mSt: 2009- 10:06.21, 2010- 9:51.86, 2011- 9:37.16, 2012- 10:34.48, 2013- 9:55.02, 2014- 9:43.07, 2015- 9:31.36, 2016- 9:20.92, 2017- 9:03.77. pbs: 1500m 4:18.92 '16, 3000m 8:53.99 '17, 5000m 15:31.62i '15, 16:22.98 '13.
Improved pb by 15.32secs to win 2017 World silver medal at 3000mSt.

Stephanie GARCIA b. 3 May 1988 Austin, Texas 1.68m 52kg. New Balance. Was at University of Virginia.
At 3000mSt: WCh: '11- h, '15- 9.
North American 3000m steeple record 2014 (unratified as no doping test), & 2000mSt best.
Progress at 3000mSt: 2007- 10:15.83, 2008- 10:17.38, 2009- 10:08.48, 2010- 10:05.05, 2011- 9:41.12, 2012- 9:47.76, 2013- 9:45.78, 2014- 9:24.28, 2015- 9:23.48, 2016- 9:19.48, 2017- 9:25.04. pbs: 800m 2:05.65i '17, 1500m 4:04.63 '17, 1M 4:24.68 '17, 2000m 5:48.25i '14, 3000m 8:52.74 '17, 2M 10:04.14i '15, 5000m 15:16.56 '16, 2000mSt 6:14.66 '14.

English GARDNER b. 22 Apr 1992 Philadelphia 1.62m 50kg. Nike. Was at University of Oregon.
At 100m/4x100mR: OG: '16- 7/1R; WCh: '13- 4/2R, '15- sf/2R; Won US 100m 2016, NCAA 100m 2013, indoor 60m 2012.
Progress at 100m, 200m: 2005- 11.99, 24.53; 2007- 11.61, 24.01; 2008- 11.82/11.49w, 24.27/24.19w; 2011- 11.03, 23.02; 2012- 11.10/11.00w, 22.82; 2013- 10.85, 22.62; 2014- 11.01, 22.81; 2015- 10.79/10.76w, 22.74; 2016- 10.74, 2017- 11.04, 22.97. pbs: 60m 7.12i '12, 400m 53.73 '12.

Kate GRACE b. 24 Oct 1988 Sacramento 1.73m 55kg. Oiselle. Was at Yale University.
At 800m: OG: '16- 8. US champion 2016. At 1500m: WCh: '17- sf.
Progress at 800m, 1500m: 2007- 2:10.18, 2008- 2:06.12, 4:32.29; 2009- 2:04.72i/2:05.82, 4:30.31; 2010- 2:04.22, 4:24.57; 2011- 2:03.41, 4:20.66; 2012- 2:01.63, 4:10.57; 2013- 1:59.47, 4:07.40; 2014- 2:01.22, 4:07.35; 2016- 1:58.28, 4:05.65; 2017- 1:59.30, 4:03.59. pbs: 400m 55.96 '06, 600m 1:27.8 '16, 1000m 2:36.97i '17, 1M 4:22.93i, 4:24.01 '17, 3000m 8:47.26i '17, 5k Rd 16:03 '16.

Dawn HARPER NELSON b. 13 May 1984 Norman, Oklahoma 1.68m 61kg. Nike. Studied psychology at UCLA.
At 100mh: OG: '08- 1, '12- 2; WCh: '09-11-13-15-17: 7/3/4/sf/2; CCp: '14- 1; won DL 2012-15, PAm-J 2003, US 2009, 2014-15.
World best 4x100mh 2015.
Progress at 100mh: 2002- 13.63, 2003- 13.33/13.21w, 2004- 13.16/12.91w, 2005- 12.91, 2006- 12.80A/12.86, 2007- 12.67, 2008- 12.54, 2009- 12.48/12.36w, 2010- 12.77w, 2011- 12.47, 2012- 12.37, 2013- 12.48, 2014- 12.44, 2015- 12.48, 2016- 12.65, 2017- 12.63. pbs: 60m 7.70i '05, 100m 11.66 '07, 200m 23.97 '06, 50mh 6.96i '12, 60mh 7.98i '06.
Married Craig Everhart (b. 13 Sep 1983, 400m 44.89 '04) in October 2007, and then Alonzo Nelson on 27 March 2013. Given 3-months drugs suspension from 1 Dec 2016 for inadvertent use of a masking agent.

Kendra 'Keni' HARRISON b. 18 Sep 1992 Clayton, North Carolina 1.63m 52kg. University of Kentucky.
At 100mh: WC: '15- sf, '17- 4. Won DL 100mh 2016, US 2017, NCAA 100mh (& 60mh indoors) 2015. At 60mh: WI: '16- 8, '18- 1.
Records: World and two N.American 100m hurdles 2016, N.American 60mh (=) 2018.
Progress at 100mh, 400mh: 2010- 13.79, 59.19; 2011- 13.49, 59.13; 2012- 13.03/13.02w, 56.72; 2013- 12.88/12.87w, 55.75; 2014- 12.71/12.68w, 54.76; 2015- 12.50/12.46w, 54.09; 2016- 12.20, 2017- 12.28. pbs: 60m 7.31i '14, 100m 11.35 '16, 200m 23.00 '16, 22.85w '17; 300m 37.84i '15, 400m 53.82i '13, 60mh 7.7oi '18.

Queen HARRISON b. 10 Sep 1988 Loch Sheldrake, New York 1.70m 60kg. Studied of business marketing at Virginia Tech.
At 100mh: WCh: '13- 5; PAm: '15- 1. At 400mh: OG: '08- sf; WCh: '11- sf; PAm-J: '07- 1 (2 100mh); won NCAA 100mh, 400mh & 60mh indoors 2010. World best 4x100mh 2014 & 2015.
Progress at 100mh, 400mh: 2007- 12.98, 55.81; 2008- 12.70, 54.60; 2009- 13.14/12.98w, 56.03; 2010- 12.61/12.44w, 54.55; 2011- 12.88, 54.78; 2012- 12.62, 55.32; 2013- 12.43, 2014- 12.46, 2015- 12.52/ 12.50w, 2016- 12.57/12.54w, 2017- 12.64. pbs: 400m 52.88 '08, 60mh 7.74Ai/7.75i 17, LJ 5.82i '06.

Jordan HASAY b. 21 Sep 1991 Fontana, California 1.63m 45kg. Nike. Was at University of Oregon.
At 1500m: WJ: '08- 4, '10- 4 (9 3000m); Won PAm-J 2009, NACAC U23 2012. WY: '07- 2. At 10000m: WCh: '13- 12.
Progress at 10000m, Mar: 2013- 31:46.42, 2014- 31:39.67, 2015- 32:46.04, 2016- 31:58.33, 2017- 2:20:57. pbs: 800m 2:08.32 '12, 1000m 2:41.08i '15, 1500m 4:07.70 '14, 1M 4:28.27i '15, 4:42.21 '06; 3000m 8:46.89 '13, 2M 9:35.05 '14. 5000m 15:28.56 '14; road: 10k 31:39 '14, 15k 48:21 '17. 20k 64:32 '17, HMar 67:55 '17.
3rd in Boston in 2:23:00 for fastest ever US marathon debut 2017, then 3rd Chicago.

Natasha HASTINGS b. 23 Jul 1986 Brooklyn, New York 1.73m 63kg. Under Armour. Studied exercise science at University of South Carolina.
At 400m/4x400m: OG: '08- res 1R, '16- 4/1R; WCh: '07- sf/res 1R, '09/11- res 1R, '13- 4/1R, '15- sf/2R, '17- res 1R; WJ: '04- 1/1R; WY: '03- 1; WI: '10/14/16- 1R, '12- 3/2R; PAm-J: '03- 1R, '05- 1/1R. Won US 2013, NCAA indoors and out 2007.
World junior 500m indoor best 2005, North American indoor 4x400m record 2014.
Progress at 400m: 2000- 54.21, 2001- 55.06, 2002- 53.42, 2003- 52.09, 2004- 52.04, 2005- 51.34, 2006- 51.45, 2007- 49.84, 2008- 50.80, 2009- 50.89, 2010- 50.53, 2011- 50.83Ai/50.97, 2012- 50.72, 2013- 49.94, 2014- 50.53, 2015- 50.24, 2016- 49.90, 2017- 50.14. pbs: 55m 7.08i '02, 60m 7.26i '13, 100m 11.24 '13, 11.08w '14; 200m 22.57 '16, 22.55w '14, 22.50St '17; 300m 35.9+ '07, 36.25i '16; 500m 1:10.05i '05.
Father from Jamaica, mother Joanne Gardner was British (ran 11.89 to win WAAA U15 100m at 14 in 1977).

Quanera HAYES b. 7 Mar 1992. Hope Mills, North Carolina 1.72m 59kg. Was at Livingstone College.
At 400m/4x400mR: WCh: '17- sf/1R; WI: '16- 3/1R, '18- 1R.
North American indoor 300m record 2017.
Progress at 400m: 2010- 56.46, 2012- 54.18A, 2013- 51.54A, 2014- 51.91, 2015- 50.84, 2016- 49.91, 2017- 49.72. pbs: 60m 7.34i '17, 100m 11.27 '16, 200m 22.55 '17. 300m 35.71i '17.

Candace HILL b. 11 Feb 1999 Conyers, Georgia. 1.75m 59kg.
At 100/(200m): WJ: '16- 1/1R; WY: '15- 1/1.
World youth records 100m & 200m 2015, world indoor junior 300m record 2017.
Progress at 100m, 200m: 2013- 11.81, 23.85; 2014- 11.44/11.34w, 23.14; 2015- 10.98, 22.43A/23.05; 2016- 11.07, 22.76/22.38w; 2017- 11.23, 22.68. Pbs: 60m 7.30i '17, 300m 36.56Ai/36.86i '17, 400m 52.70 '17.

Daniella HILL b. 16 May 1991 Mahomet, Illinois 1.78m 95kg. née Bunch. Nike. Was at Purdue University.
At SP: WCh: '17- dnq 18.
Progress at SP: 2008- 15.10, 2009- 15.20, 2010- 15.22, 2011- 16.07i/15.72, 2012- 16.65i/16.46, 2013- 17.13, 2014- 17.39, 2015- 18.89, 2016- 18.87i/18.18, 2017- 19.64. pbs: DT 48.86 '13, HT 58.36 '14, Wt: 22.35i '14. Married Zachary Hill (SP 19.25i/18.87 '12) on 7 Oct 2017

Aleai HOBBS b. 24 Feb 1996 New Oreeans 1.72m 59kg. Student at Louisiana State University.
At 100m: PAm-J: '15- 2/1R. Won NCAA 60m ind 2018.
Progress at 100m: 2010- 11.95, 2011- 11.756, 2012- 11.77, 2013- 11.68, 2014- 11.49, 2015- 11.13, 2016- 11.34, 2017- 10.85. pbs: 60m 7.07i '18, 200m 23.80 '13.

Shelby HOULIHAN b. 8 Feb 1993 sioux City, Iowa 1.60m 54kg. Nike Bowerman TC. Was at Arizona State University.
At 1500m/3000m: WI: '18- 4/5. At 5000m: OG: '16- 11; WCh: '17- 13. Won NCAA 1500m 2014, NACAC U23 800m 2014.
Progress at 1500m, 5000m: 2010- 4:31.21, 2011- 4:26.39, 2012- 4:22.95, 2013- 4:13.64, 16:15.85; 2014- 4:10.89, 16:11.63; 2015- 4:09.62, 15:49.72; 2016- 4:03.39, 15:06.14; 2017- 4:06.22, 15:00.37. pbs: 800m 2:01.12 '14, 1M 4:24.16i '17, 4:31.79 '15, 3000m 8:36.01i '18, 8:37.40 '17.

Molly HUDDLE b. 31 Aug 1984 Elmira, New York 1.63m 48kg. Saucony. Was at University of Notre Dame.
At 5000m: OG: '12- 11; WCh: '11-13-17: h/6/12;

CCp: '10- 3. At 10000m: OG: '16- 5; WCh: '15- 4, '17- 8. Won US 5000m 2011, 2014, 2016; 10000m 2015-17. World CC: '10- 19, '11- 17.
North American 5000m (2) records 2010-14, 10000m 2016, 10M, 20k & HMar 2018.
Progress at 5000m, 10000m: 2003- 15:36.95, 2004- 15:32.55, 2005- 16:12.17i, 2006- 15:40.41, 32:37.87; 2007- 15:17.13, 33:09.27; 2008- 15:25.47, 31:27.12; 2009- 15:53.91, 32:42.11; 2010- 14:44.76, 31:27.12; 2011- 15:10.01, 31:28.66; 2012- 15:01.32, 2013- 14:58.15, 2014- 14:42.64, 30:47.59; 2015- 14:57.23, 31:39.20; 2016- 14:48.14, 30:13:17; 2017- 15:01.64i/15:03.60, 31:24.78. pbs: 1500m 4:08.09 '13, 1M 4:26.84 '14, 3000m 8:42.99 '13, Rd: 15k 48:52 '14, 10M 50:52 '18, 20k 63:48 '18, HMar 67:25 '18, Mar 2:28:13 '16.
Married Kurt Benninger CAN (pbs 1500m 3:38.03 '08, 1M 3:56.99 '08, 5000m 13:30.27 '09) in 2009. Won US road running titles in 2014 at a women's record four distances and now has won 26 national titles. 3rd New York 2016 on marathon debut.

Emily INFELD b. 21 Mar 1990 University Heights, Ohio 1.63m 48kg. Saucony. Was at Georgetown University.
At 10000m: OG: '16- 11; WCh: '15- 3, '17- 6. World CC: '13- 21. Won NCAA ind 3000m 2012.
Progress at 10000m: 2015- 31:38.71, 2016- 31:26.94, 2017- 31:20.45. pbs: 800m 2:06.05 '09, 1000m 2:44.56i '09, 1500m 4:07.77 '12, 1M 4:30.78 '17, 3000m 8:41.43 '13, 5000m 14::56.33 '17.
Older sister Maggie (b.10 Apr 1986) has pb 1500m 4:08.31 '12.

Kyra JEFFERSON b. 23 Sep 1994 Detroit 1.65m 57kg. Student at University of Florida.
At 200m/4x400mR: PAm: '15- 2/1R. Won NACAC 2015, NCAA 2017.
North American 4x200m indoor record 2018.
Progress at 200m: 2009- 24.27, 2010- 24.24/24.07w, 2011- 23.53, 2012- 24.11i/24.27, 2013- 23.43i, 2014- 22.78, 2015- 22.24, 2016- 22.56, 2017- 22.02. pbs: 60m 7.34i '14, 100m 11.73 '12, 11.66w '10; 300m 37.74i '18, 400m 51.50 '15.

Gia LEWIS-SMALLWOOD b. 1 Apr 1979 Urbana, Illinois 1.83m 93kg. Nike. Was at University of Illinois.
At DT: OG: '12- dnq 15; WCh: '11- dnq 14, '13- 5, '15- 11, '17- dnq 17; PAm: '11- 4, '15- 3; CCp: '14- 1. US champion 2013-15, 2017.
North American discus record 2014.
Progress at DT: 2000- 53.52, 2001- 57.76, 2002- 52.28, 2003- 54.95, 2004- 57.88, 2005- 50.85, 2006- 49.95, 2007- 52.02, 2008- 59.96, 2009- 60.32, 2010- 65.58, 2011- 62.26, 2012- 63.97, 2013- 66.29, 2014- 69.17, 2015- 64.01, 2016- 57.15, 2017- 65.81. pb Wt 18.91i '02.

Charlene LIPSEY b. 16 Jul 1991 1.68m 57kg. adoidas. Was at Louisiana State University.
At 800m: WCh: '17- 7; won US indoor 1000m 2017.. World indoor 4x800m record 2018.
Progress at 800m: 2008- 2:07.46, 2009- 2:05.83, 2010- 2:05.34, 2011- 2:03.73, 2012- 2:01.40, 2013- 2:01.80, 2014- 2:00.91, 2015- 2;00.60, 2016- 2:00.65, 2017- 1:57.38. pbs: 400m 55.14 '15, 600m 1:29.85i '09, 1000m 2:37.97iA '17, 1500m 4:10.68 '17, 1M 4:30.13i '17.

Shamier LITTLE b. 20 Mar 1995 Louisville, Kentucky 1.63m 52kg. Texas A&M University.
At 400mh: WCh: '15- 2, '17- sf; WJ: '12- dnf, '14- 1/1R; PAm: '15- 1/1R.
Progress at 400mh: 2011- 57.83, 2012- 57.44, 2013- 58.80, 2014- 55.07, 2015- 53.74, 2016- 53.51, 2017- 52.75. pbs: 60m 7.65i '17, 200m 23.17 '16, 23.01w '17; 300m 36.98i '18; 400m 50.40 '17, 60mh 8.43i '14, 100mh 13.77 '14.
Mother Tiffany Mayfield had HJ pb 1.73.

Chaunté LOWE b. 12 Jan 1984 Templeton, California 1.75m 59kg. née Howard. Nike. Economics graduate of Georgia Tech University.
At HJ: OG: '04- dnq 26=, '08- 3, '12- 6, '16- 4; WCh: '05- 2, '09- 6=, '15- dnq; PAm-J: '03- 3; CCp: '14- 2; WI: '06-10-12: 8/3/1; Won DL 2012, US 2006, 2008-10, 2012, 2014-16; NCAA 2004, indoors 2004-05.
N.American HJ records (3) 2010, indoors 2012.
Progress at HJ: 2000- 1.75, 2001- 1.84, 2002- 1.87, 2003- 1.89, 2004- 1.98A, 2005- 2.00, 2006- 2.01, 2008- 2.00, 2009- 1.98, 2010- 2.05, 2011- 1.78, 2012- 2.02Ai/2.01, 2014- 1.97, 2015- 1.91, 2016- 2.01, 2017- 1.94. pbs: 100m 11.83 '05, 200m 24.47 '16, 100mh 13.78 '04, LJ 6.90 '10, TJ 12.93 '04, 12.98w '05; Hep 5133 '16.
Married Mario Lowe (b. 20 Apr 1980, TJ pb 16.15 '02) in 2005, daughters Jasmine born 30 Jul 2007 and Aurora in 4 Apr 2011 and son Mario Josiah in August 2013.

Francena McCORORY b. 20 Oct 1988 Hampton, Virginia 1.70m 60kg. adidas. Psychology graduate of Hampton University.
At 400m/4x400mR: OG: '12- 6/1R, '16- res 1R; WCh: '11- 3/1R, '13- 5/1R, '15- 2R; CCp: '14- 1/1R; WI: '14- 1/1R; won DL 2015, US 2014, NCAA indoors 2009-10, out 2010.
World junior indoor 300m best 2007, North American indoor 4x400m record 2014.
Progress at 400m: 2004- 54.54, 2005- 55.26i, 2006- 51.93i, 2008- 51.54, 2009- 50.58, 2010- 50.52, 2011- 50.24, 2012- 50.06, 2013- 49.86, 2014- 49.48, 2015- 49.83, 2016- 50.23. pbs: 55m 6.86i '06, 60m 7.43i '07, 100m 11.55 '16, 200m 22.92 '10, 300m 35.7+ '13, 500m 1:09.01i '12, 600m 1:29.07i '13, 800m 2:20.25i '07.

Candyce McGRONE b. 24 Mar 1989 Indianapolis 1.68m 59kg. adidas. Was at Florida State University, then Oklahoma.
At 200m: WCh: '15- 4; won NCAA 100m 2011.
Progress at 100m, 200m: 2007- 11.54/11.29w, 23.82/23.24w; 2008- 11.50/11.37w, 23.47; 2009- 11.44, 23.30/23.17w; 2010- 22.84; 2011- 11.08/11.07w, 22.81; 2012- 11.38, 23.49; 2013-

11.19, 22.85; 2014- 11.26/11.20w, 23.43; 2015- 11.00/10.91w, 22.01; 2016- 11.13/11.06w, 22.98; 2017- 11.20/10.83w 22.95/22.39w. pbs: 60m 7.21Ai/7.27i '12, 400m 55.34 '11.

Sydney McLAUGHLIN b. 7 Aug 1999 New Brunswick, New Jersey. 1.74m 61kg. University of Kentucky.
At 400mh: OG: '16- sf; WY: '15- 1.
Three World junior 400mh records 2016-17, indoor 300m 2017 & 400m (3) 2018; world youth records 400mh (2) and 400m indoors 2016.
Progress at 400mh: 2014- 55.63; 2015- 55.28; 2016- 54.15, 2017- 53.82. pbs: 200m 22.95i '18, 22.96w '17; 300m 36.12i '17, 400m 50.36i '18, 51.87 '16; 600m 1:28.85 '18, 55mh 7.66i '15, 60mh 8.17i '15, 100mh 13.34 '14, 300mh 38.90 '17, LJ 5.89i '15. 5.81w '14.
Her brother Taylor (b. 3 Aug 1997) was 2nd at the 2016 World Juniors.

Inika McPHERSON b. 29 Sep 1986 Galveston, Texas 1.63m 55kg. Was at Univ. of California.
At HJ: OG: '16- 10=; WCh: '11/13- dnq 26/18, '17- 9; WJ: '04- 11; PAm: '07- 11; WI: '18- 7=.
Progress at HJ: 2002- 1.83, 2004- 1.83, 2005- 1.88, 2006- 1.80i/1.78, 2007- 1.84, 2008- 1.78, 2009- 1.83, 2011- 1.86, 2012- 1.95, 2013- 1.92, 2014- 2.00dq/1.96, 2016- 1.94, 2017- 1.96. pb LJ 5.69 '04.
Before the mark was annulled her 2.00 US women's high jump in 2014 was a world record height differential for a woman of 37cm. She tested positive for a banned substance at this meeting and received 21-month ban.

Christina MANNING b. 29 May 1990 Waldorf, Maryland 1.63m 54kg. adidas. Was at Ohio State University.
At 100mh: WCh: '17- 5; WUG: '11- 3/2R. At 60mh: WI: '18- 2. Won NCAA 100mh & 60mh ind 2012.
Progress at 100mh: 2008- 13.86, 2009- 13.08, 2010- 13.10, 2011- 12.86/12.72w, 2012- 12.68/ 12.57w, 2014- 13.61, 2015- 13.04, 2016- 12.87/12.67w, 2017- 12.54. pbs: 60m 7.23i '12, 100m 11.29 '11, 200m 23.27 '12, 60mh 7.73Ai/7.77i '18, LJ 5.75 '08.

Brenda MARTINEZ b. 8 Sep 1987 Upland, California 1.63m 52kg. New Balance. Studied sociology and law at University of California - Riverside.
At 800m: WCh: '13- 2, '15/17- sf. At 1500m: OG: '16- sf; WI: '16- 5.
N.American 4x800m & 4x1500m records 2014.
Progress at 800m, 1500m: 2007- 2:04.22, 4:21.18; 2008- 2:02.34, 4:17.09; 2009- 2:00.85, 4;09.52; 2010- 2:04.76, 4:18.17; 2011- 2:01.07, 4:10.77; 2012- 1:59.14, 4:06.96; 2013- 1:57.91, 4:00.94; 2014- 1:58.84, 4:01.36; 2015- 1:59.06; 2016- 1:59.64, 4:03.57; 2017- 1:58.43, 4:02.75. pbs: 1000m 2:38.48 '12, 1M 4:26.76 '12, 3000m 9:07.99+i '13, 2M 9:51.91i '13, 5000m 15:30.89mx '13, 15:41.50 '14; 5km Rd 15:24 '14.
Married coach Carlos Handler in October 2012.

Georganne MOLINE b. 6 Mar 1990 Phoenix, Arizona 1.78m 59kg. Nike Psychology and communications student at University of Arizona.
At 400mh: OG: '12- 5; WCh: '13- h. At 4x400m: WI: '18- 1R.
Progress at 400mh: 2010- 57.88, 2011- 57.41, 2012- 53.92, 2013- 53.72, 2014- 54.00, 2015- 54.24, 2016- 53.97, 2017- 53.14. pbs: 200m 23.23i '18, 23.37 '13; 400m 51.39i '18, 51.93 '17; 500m 1:08.84i '15, 600m 1:26.70Ai '16, 1:27.15 '15; 800m 2:08.67i '13. 2:09.58 '14.
Seven 400mh pbs in 2012 to 53.92 in OG final.

Sandi MORRIS b. 8 Jul 1992 Downers Grove, Illinois 1.74m 65kg. Student at University of Arkansas, formerly North Carolina.
At PV: OG: '16- 2; WCh: '15- 4=, '17- 2; WI: '16- 2, '18- 1; PAm-J: 11- 2. Won NACAC 2014, US 2017.
Three North American outdoor pole vault records 2016.
Progress at PV: 2009- 3.81, 2010- 4.05, 2011- 4.30, 2012- 4.23i/4.15, 2013- 4.43i/4.02, 2014- 4.55, 2015- 4.76, 2016- 5.00, 2017- 4.87i/4.84, 2018- 4.95i.

Dalilah MUHAMMAD b. 7 Feb 1990 Jamaica, Queens, New York 1.70m 62kg. Nike, Business graduate of University of Southern Califormia.
At 400mh: OG: '16- 1; WCh: '13- 2, '17-21; WY: '07- 1; PAm-J: '09- 2; US champion 2013, 2016-17, DL 2017.
World best 200mh 2018.
Progress at 400mh: 2005- 61.25, 2006- 59.82, 2007- 57.09, 2008- 57.81, 2009- 56.49, 2010- 57.14, 2011- 56.04, 2012- 56.19, 2013- 53.83, 2014- 58.02, 2015- 55.76, 2016- 52.88, 2017- 52.64. pbs: 60m 7.64i '10, 100m 11.42 '13, 200m 23.61 '16, 400m 52.64 '16, 500m 1:09.66i '17, 600m 1:30.70 '18,60mh 8.23i '12, 100mh 13.33 '12, 200mh 25.20 '18, HJ 1.75 '10.

Katie NAGEOTTE b. 30 Jun 1991 1.68m 59kg. New York AC. Was at Ashland University.
At PV: WI: '18- 5.
Progress at PV: 2008- 3.76, 2009- 3.96, 2010- 3.90, 2011- 4.00i, 2012- 3.81, 2013- 4.44, 2014- 4.48, 2015- 4.55, 2016- 4.63i, 4.60, 2017- 4.73, 2018- 4.91Ai.

Sharika NELVIS b. 10 May 1990 Memphis 1.78m 64kg. adidas. Sociology student at Arkansas State University.
At 100mh: WCh: '15- 8. At 60mh: WI: '18- 4. Won NCAA 100mh & indoor 60mh 2014.
World best 4x100mh 2015. North American indoor 60mh record 2018.
Progress at 100mh: 2008- 14.23, 2009- 14.03, 2011- 13.45, 2012- 13.22/12.99w, 2013- 12.84, 2014- 12.71/12.52w, 2015- 12.34, 2016- 12.60, 2017- 12.52. pbs: 60m 7.28i '14, 100m 11.27/11.17w '14, 200m 23.19 '15, 22.70w '14; 400m 54.62 '13, 60mh 7.70Ai/7.80i '18, LJ 6.32i '13, 6.27 '14.

Barbara NWABA b. 18 Jan 1989 Los Angeles 1.75m 64kg. Santa Barbara TC .Was at UC Santa Barbara.

At Hep: OG: '16- 12; WCh: '15- 27 (dnf 100mh). US champion 2016. At Pen: WI: '16- 3.
Progress at Hep: 2009- 5039, 2010- 5552, 2011- 5733, 2012- 5986, 2014- 6307, 2015- 6500, 2016- 6494. pbs: 200m 23.76 '15, 800m 2:07.13 '15, 60mh 8.40i '15, 100mh 13.38 '15, 400mh 60.51 '10, HJ 1.90 '16, LJ 6.23 '15, SP 15.00i /14.81 '16, JT 49.19 '16, Pen 4661i '16.

Courtney OKOLO b. 15 Mar 1994 Carrolltown, Texas 1.68m 54kg. Student at Univ. of Texas.
At 400m/4x400mR: OG: '16- 1R; WI: '16- 1R, '18- 1/1R; PAm-J: '13- 1/1R. Won NACAC 2015, NCAA 2014, 2016.
US indoor 500m record 2017.
Progress at 400m: 2009- 56.50, 2010- 54.34, 2011- 53.03, 2012- 52.40, 2013- 51.04, 2014- 50.03, 2015- 50.82A/50.99, 2016- 49.71, 2017- 50.29. pbs: 60m 7.52i '14, 100m 11.53 '16, 200m 22.93 '15, 22.79i '16; 300m 35.74 '16, 500m 1:07.34i '17, 600y 1:18.24i '15, 600m 1:24.00Ai/1:25.21 '17.

Keturah ORJI b. 5 Mar 1996 Mount Olive, New Jersey 1.66m 61kg. University of Georgia.
At TJ: OG: '16- 4; WJ: '14- 9; WY: '13- 3 (2 LJ); WI: '16- 4, '18- 5; won US 2016-17, NCAA 2015-17
North American and 3 US triple jump records 2016, N.Am indoors 2017 & 2018.
Progress at TJ: 2012- 12.46/12.51w, 2013- 13.69, 2014- 13.46, 2015- 14.15, 2016- 14.71, 2017- 14.32i/ 14.31, 2018- 14.53i. pbs: 60m 7.53i '18, 100m 12.13/12.07w '14, LJ 6.72i '17, 6.63 '15.

Barbara PIERRE b. 28 Apr 1987 Port-au-Prince, Haiti 1.75m 60kg. Nike. Was at St. Augustine's College.
At 100m/4x100mR: OG: '08- qf; PAm: '11- 2/2R, '15- 3/1R. Won NACAC 2015. At 60m: WI: '12- 4, '16- 1. Haiti records 100m 2009, 200m 2008-09.
Progress at 100m: 2003- 11.98, 2005- 11.78, 2006- 11.66, 2007- 11.30, 2008- 11.40A, 2009- 11.18, 2010- 11.35, 2011- 11.14, 2012- 11.34, 2013- 10.85, 2014- 11.05, 2015- 10.92, 2016- 11.07/11.01w, 2017- 10.99. pbs: 50m 6.22+i '12, 55m 6.89i '07, 60m 7.00i '16, 100y 10.38y '11, 200m 23.23 '10, 400m 57.04 '08.
With dual citizenship, she switched from US to Haiti on 31 Dec 2007, and back to US on 24 Mar 2010.

Jenna PRANDINI b. 20 Nov 1992 Clovis, California 1.72m 59kg. Student of psychology at University of Oregon.
At 200m/4x100mR: OG: '16- sf; WCh: '15- sf/2R. Won NCAA 100m 2015, LJ 2014; US 200m 2015.
Progress at 100m, 200m, LJ: 2008- 12.18/11.74w, 5.86; 2009- 11.81, 24.48/24.02w; 2010- 11.34, 24.61, 6.15/6.29w; 2011- 11.51/11.44w, 23.75/23.51w, 6.20; 2012- 24.07, 2013- 11.31/11.14w, 23.15, 6.15; 2014- 11.11, 22.60, 6.55; 2015- 10.92, 22.20/22.18w, 6.80; 2016- 10.95/10.81w, 22.39; 2017- 11.05, 22.54. pbs: 60m 7.15i '15, TJ 12.73/12.98w '10.

DeAnna PRICE b. 8 Jun 1993 Moscow Mills, Missouri 1.72m 109kg. Was at Southern Illinois University.
At HT: OG: '16- 8; WCh: '15- dnq 18, '17- 9; WJ: '12- dnq 11; PAm: '15- 4. NCAA champion 2015-16, US indoor 20lb Wt 2018.
North American hammer record 2013.
Progress at HT: 2011- 55.20, 2012- 62.62, 2013- 65.18, 2015- 72.30, 2016- 73.09, 2017- 74.91. Pbs: SP 16.30 '15, DT 53.46 '15, Wt 24.51i '18.

Colleen QUIGLEY b. 20 Nov 1992 St. Louis, Missouri 1.73m 59kg. Nike Bowerman TC. Was at Florida State University.
At 3000mSt: OG: '16- 8; WCh: '15- 12, '17- h; NCAA champion 2015. At 1500m: WI: '18- 9.
Progress at 3000mSt: 2012- 10:02.53, 2013- 9:38.23, 2014- 9:56.96, 2015- 9:24.92, 2016- 9:20.00, 2017- 9:15.97. pbs: 800m 2:08.69i '15, 1500m 4:03.93 '17, 1M 4:24.88i '17. 3000m 9:13.79i '13, 5000m 15:58.90 '13.

Brittney REESE b. 9 Sep 1986 Gulfport, Mississippi 1.73m 64kg. Nike. English graduate of University of Mississippi.
At LJ: OG: '08- 5, '12- 1, '16- 2; WCh: '07-09-11-13-15-17 8/1/1/1/dnq 24/1; WI: '10-12-16: 1/1/1; won DL 2010-11, WAF 2009, US 2008-12, 2014, 2016 (& 3 indoors); NCAA 2007-08.
North American indoor long jump record 2012.
Progress at LJ: 2004- 6.31, 2006- 5.94, 2007- 6.83, 2008- 6.95, 2009- 7.10, 2010- 6.94/7.05w, 2011- 7.19, 2012- 7.23i/7.15, 2013- 7.25, 2014- 6.92, 2015- 6.97, 2016- 7.31, 2017- 7.13. pbs: 50m 6.23i '12, 60m 7.24i '11, 100m 11.40 '17, 11.20w '11; HJ 1.88i/1.84 '08, TJ 13.16 '08.
Concentrated on basketball at Gulf Coast Community College in 2005-06.

Brianna ROLLINS b. 18 Aug 1991 Miami 1.64m 55kg. Nike. Was at Clemson University.
At 100mh: OG: '16- 1; WCh: '13- 1, '15- 4; Won US 2013, 2016; NACAC 2012. At 60mh: WI: '16- 2; won US indoor 60mh 2016, NCAA 100mh 2013, indoor 60mh 2011 & 2013.
North American 100m hurdles record 2013, world best 4x100mh 2014 & 2015.
Progress at 100mh: 2007- 14.48, 2008- 13.93, 2009- 13.83, 2011- 12.99/12.88w, 2012- 12.70/ 12.60Aw, 2013- 12.26, 2014- 12.53, 2015- 12.56, 2016- 12.34. pbs: 60m 7.29Ai '16, 200m 23.04/ 23.02w '13, 300m 37.90i '10, 400m 53.93 '13, 60mh 7.76i '16, 400mh 60.58 '09.
Undefeated in 2013: inc. heats 200m- 7, 400m- 1, 60mh- 8, 100mh- 18.
Received a one-year ban due to missing three drugs test in 2016, dated from 19 Dec 2016.

Shannon ROWBURY b. 19 Sep 1984 San Francisco 1.65m 52kg. Nike Oregon Project. Was at Duke University.
At 1500m: OG: '08- 7, '12- 4, '16- 4; WCh: '09- 3, '11- sf, '15- 7; CCp: '14- 2; Won US 2008-09, NCAA indoor mile 2007. At 3000m: WI: '14- 7, '16- 3; CCp: '10- 2. At 5000m: WCh: '13- 7, '17- 9. WR distance medley 2015, North American records: 2M 2014, 1500m 2015, 5000m 2016.

Progress at 1500m, 5000m: 2004- 4:17.41, 2005- 4:14.81, 2006- 4:12.31, 15:38.42; 2007- 16:59.97i, 2008- 4:00.33, 2009- 4:00.81, 15:12.95; 2010- 4:01.30, 15:00.51; 2011- 4:05.73, 2012- 4:03.15, 2013- 4:01.28, 15:06.10, 2014- 3:59.49, 14:48.68; 2015- 3:56.29, 2016- 3:57.78, 14:38.92; 2017- 4:04.56i/4:04.61, 14:57.55. pbs: 800m 1:59.97 '16, 1000m 2:40.25i '15, 1M 4:20.34 '08, 2000m 5:46.2 '14, 3000m 8:29.93 '14, 2M 9:20.25 '14, 3000mSt 9:59.4 '06.

Former ballet and Irish dancer. Married Pablo Solares (Mexican 1500m record 3:36.67 '09) on 11 April 2015. Expecting a baby in the summer of 2018.

Raven SAUNDERS b. 15 May 1996 Charleston, SC 1.65m 125kg. Student at Southern Illinois University.

At SP: OG: '16- 5; WCh: '17- 10; WJ: 14- 2. Won PAm-J 2015, NCAA 2016.

Progress at SP: 2014- 17.82, 2015- 18.62i/18.35, 2016- 19.35, 2017- 19.76. pbs: DT 56.85 '16, HT 56.91 '16, Wt 21.67i '17.

4 indoor and 4 outdoor US junior records 2015.

Sha'Keela SAUNDERS b. 18 Dec 1993 Elizabeth City, North Carolina 1.68m 59kg. University of Kentucky.

At LJ: WCh: '17- dnq 21; PAm: '15- 3.Won NACAC U23 2014, NCAA indoor2017.

Progress at LJ: 2008- 5.92w, 2011- 5.65/5.90w?, 2012- 6.00i, 2014- 6.43, 2015- 6.75, 2016- 6.89, 2017- 6.90i/6.79/6.92w. pbs: 55m 7.04i '09, 60m 7.54i '16, 100m 11.88 '17, 200m 23.80 '17, 300m 39.08 '09, 400m 55.47 '09, 100mh 13.99 '16, TJ 13.32i '17, 13.03/13.34w '16.

Jennifer SIMPSON b. 23 Aug 1986 Webster City, Iowa 1.65m 50kg. née Barringer. New Balance. Studied political science at University of Colorado.

At 1500m: OG: '12- sf, '16- 3; WCh: '11-13-15-17: 1/2/11/2; won DL 2014. At 3000mSt: OG: '08- 8; WCh: '07- h, '09- 4; won NCAA 2006, 2008-09. Won US 1500m 2014-17, 5000m 2013, 3000mSt 2009. North American records: 3000m steeplechase (3) 2008-09, indoor 2 miles 2015.

Progress at 1500m, 5000m, 3000mSt: 2006- 16:15.23, 9:53.04, 2007- 4:21.53, 15:48.24, 9:33.95; 2008- 4:11.36, 9:22.26; 2009- 3:59.90, 15:01.70i/ 15:05.25, 9:12.50; 2010- 4:03.63, 15:33.33; 2011- 4:03.54, 15:11.49; 2012- 4:04.07, 2013- 4:00.48, 14:56.26; 2014- 3:57.22, 2015- 3:57.30, 2016- 3:58.19, 2017- 4:00.70. pbs: 800m 2:00.45 '13, 1M 4:19.98 '17, 2000m 5:45.7 '14, 3000m 8:29.58 '14, 2M 9:18.35i '15. Married Jason Simpson on 8 Oct 2010. Won 5th Avenue Mile 2011.

Emily SISSON b. 12 Oct 1991 Chesterfield, Missouri 1.65m 47kg. New Balance. Was at Providence University.

At 10000m: WCh: '17- 9. At 3000m/5000m: WJ: '10- 10/6. World CC: '10- 18J. Won NCAA 5000m indoors and out 2015.

Progress at 10000m: 2011- 35:07.35, 2013- 33:02.88, 2014- 32:31.06, 2015- 31:38.03, 2016- 32:54.06, 2017- 31:25.64. pbs: 1M 4:38.49i '13, 4:44.02 '10; 3000m 8:52.60i/9:09.12 '15, 5000m 15:02.10i/15:10.90 '17, HMar 68:21 '17.

Shalonda SOLOMON b. 19 Dec 1985 Inglewood, California 1.69m 56kg. Reebok. Was at University of South Carolina.

At (100m)/200m/4x100m: WCh: '11- 4/res (1)R; WJ: '04- 1/1R; PAm-J: '03- 1/1/1R; CCp: '10- (2)/1R. Won NCAA 200m 2006, NCAAC 100m & 200m 2006.

Progress at 100m, 200m: 2001- 11.57/11.37w, 23.65/23.22w; 2002- 11.51/11.46w, 23.31; 2003- 11.35/11.25w, 22.93; 2004- 11.41/11.32w, 22.82; 2005- 11.29, 22.74/22.72w; 2006- 11.09/11.07w, 22.36/22.30w; 2007- 11.33, 22.77; 2008- 11.16, 22.48/22.36w; 2009- 11.04/11.00w, 22.41; 2010- 10.90, 22.47; 2011- 11.08/10.90w, 22.15; 2012- 11.26, 22.82; 2013- 11.04/10.97w, 22.41/22.33w; 2014- 11.12, 22.64/22.54w; 2015- 11.06/10.97w, 22.56; 2016- 11.16/11.05w, 22.63/22.58w; 2017- 11.35/ 11.19w, 22.64/22.21w. pbs: 55m 6.72i '09, 60m 7.15Ai '11, 7.21i '06; 300m 36.45i '09, 400m 52.83 '16.

Ashley SPENCER b. 8 Jun 1993 Indianapolis 1.68m 54kg. Student at University of Texas, formerly Illinois.

At 400mh: OG: '16- 3. At 400m/4x400mR: WCh: '13- sf/1R; WJ: '12- 1/1R; WI: '16- 2/1R. Won NCAA 2012-13.

Progress at 400m, 400mh: 2012- 50.50, 59.43; 2013- 50.28, 56.32; 2014- 51.38, 59.78; 2015- 51.72, 2016- 51.09, 53.72; 2017- 52.81, 53.11. pbs: 60m 7.42i '13, 100m 11.34/11.27w '14, 200m 22.92/ 22.69w '14, 300m 36.27i '17, 100mh 14.40/14.28w '11.

Deajah STEVENS b. 19 May 1995 Tarrytown, New York 1.72m 60kg. University of Oregon.

At (100m)/200m: OG: '16- 7; WCh: '17- (sf)/5. US champion 2017.

North American 4x200m indoor record 2018.

Progress at 100m, 200m: 2008- 25.54, 2009- 24.48, 2011- 12.11, 24.20; 2012- 12.10w, 24.38; 2013- 12.05, 24.15; 2015- 23.18, 2016- 11.18/11.04w, 22.25; 2017- 11.00/10.89w, 22.09. Pbs: 60m 7.17i '17, 300m 37.90i '13, 400m 53.63 '15. LJ 5.95 '15.

Jeneva STEVENS b. 28 Oct 1989 Dolton, Illinois 1.78m 102kg. née McCall. Was at Southern Illinois University.

At HT: WCh: '11- dnq 14, '13- 8; WUG: '13- 1. At SP: WCh: '15- 10; PAm: '15- 6; WI: '14- 7, '18- 8. Won NCAA DT 2010, HT 2012.

Progress at SP, HT: 2009- 15.22, 55.83; 2010- 17.25i/16.54, 64.17; 2011- 17.22i/16.96, 69.55; 2012- 17.97i/17.89, 69.38; 2013- 19.10i/18.47, 74.77; 2014- 18.45i/17.86, 70.78; 2015- 18.84, 72.69; 2016- 19.11, 71.10; 2017- 18.54i/18.48, 71.56. Pbs: DT 59.45 '12, Wt 24.24i '18.

Daughter of 1994-5 WBC world heavyweight boxing champion Oliver McCall.

Jasmin STOWERS b. 23 Sep 1991 Pendleton, SC 1.75m 64kg. Degree in nutrition from Louisiana State University.
At 100mh: WY: '07- 4; won NCAA indoor 60mh 2013, US 2015. World best 4x100mh 2015.
Progress at 100mh: 2005- 14.27w, 2006- 14.05/13.82Aw, 2007- 13.69/13.68w, 2008- 13.66/13.46w, 2009- 13.59/13.32Aw, 2010- 14.47, 2011- 12.88/12.86w, 2012- 12.92, 2013- 13.00/12.88w, 2014- 12.71/12.54w, 2015- 12.35, 2016- 12.55, 2017- 12.47. pbs: 60m 7.51i '12, 100m 11.82 '11, 60mh 7.82Ai '17, 7.84i '15; 400mh 61.17 '08.

Jennifer SUHR b. 5 Feb 1982 Fredonia, New York 1.80m 64kg. adidas. née Stuczynski. Graduate of Roberts Wesleyan University, now studying child psychology.
At PV: OG: '08- 2, '12- 1, '16- 7=; WCh: '07-11-13-15-17: 10/4/2/4=/dnq nh; PAm: '15- 3; WI: '08-14-16: 2/5=/1; WCp: '06- nh; US champion 2006-10, 2012-16; indoors 2005, 2007-09, 2011-13.
Records: world indoors 2013 & 2016, four North American pole vault records 2007-08, four indoors 2009-13.
Progress at PV: 2002- 2.75, 2004- 3.49, 2005- 4.57i/4.26, 2006- 4.68i/4.66, 2007- 4.88, 2008- 4.92, 2009- 4.83i/4.81, 2010- 4.89, 2011- 4.91, 2012- 4.88i/4.81, 2013- 5.02Ai/4.91, 2014- 4.73i/4.71, 2015- 4.82, 2016- 5.03i/4.82, 2017- 4.83, 2018- 4.82. pbs: 55mh 8.07i '05, JT 46.82 '05.
All-time top scorer at basketball at her university, then very rapid progress at vaulting.

Cassandra TATE b. 11 Sep 1990 Hammond, Louisiana 1.74m 64kg. Management graduate of Louisiana State University.
At 400m/4x400m: WI: '14- 1R. At 400mh: WCh: '15- 3, '17- 7; won DL 2016, NCAA & NACAC 2012.
Progress at 400mh: 2010- 56.87, 2011- 55.99, 2012- 55.22, 2013- 55.45, 2014- 54.70, 2015- 54.01, 2016- 54.47, 2017- 54.59. pbs: 60m 7.49i '11, 100m 11.79 '08, 11.47w '10; 200m 23.37i '10, 23.68 '09; 400m 52.40Ai '14, 52.51 '15; 60mh 8.61i '09, 100mh 14.21 '08, 14.08w '07.
Engaged to David Verburg (qv).

Jasmine TODD b. 23 Dec 1993 San Diego 1.65m 55kg. Student of psychology at University of Oregon.
At 100m/LJ/4x100m: WCh: '15- sf/dq 19, 2R.
Progress at 100m, LJ: 2010- 11.99/11.64Aw, 6.08i/6.07; 2011- 11.80/11.73w, 6.01; 2012- 11.76, 6.13; 2013- 12.02/12.00w, 5.95; 2014- 11.25, 6.50Ai/6.06; 2015- 10.92/10.86w, 6.84; 2016- 11.20, 6.47; 2017- 11.29, 6.83/6.84w. pbs: 60m 7.15i '15, 200m 22.89 '15, TJ 13.10 '15.

Ariana WASHINGTON b. 4 Sep 1996 Signal Hill, California 1.75m 59kg. Student at University of Oregon.
At 100/(200m): WCh: '17- sf/res 1R; WJ: '14- 7/1R; WY: '13- 2/3. Won NCAA 100m & 200m 2016.
Progress at 100m, 200m: 2010- 12.78/12.55w, 25.176; 2011- 12.07, 24.01; 2012- 11.47, 23.41; 2013- 11.39/11.18Aw, 23.18/23.05Aw; 2014- 11.22, 22.96; 2015- 23.07i; 2016- 11.01/10.95w, 22.21; 2017- 11.06/10.97w, 22.39. pbs: 60m 7.20i '17, HJ 1.57 '11, LJ 5.79 '11.

Charonda WILLIAMS b. 27 Mar 1987 Richmond, California 1.67m 55kg. adidas. Was at Arizona State University.
At 200m: WCh: '09- sf, '13- 6. Won DL 2012.
Progress at 200m: 2006- 24.19/24.08w, 2007- 23.53, 2008- 23.09, 2009- 22.55/22.39w, 2010- 22.97, 2011- 22.85/22.78w, 2012- 22.52, 2013- 22.71, 2014- 23.41, 2015- 22.32, 2016- 23.44/23.08w, 2017- 23.00/22.54w. pbs: 55m 6.99Ai '08, 60m 7.29Ai '09, 7.36i '11; 100m 11.07 '13, 10.95w '12; 300m 37.04i '11, 400m 52.71 '11, LJ 5.91 '07, 6.03w '00.

Kendell WILLIAMS b. 14 Jun 1995 Marietta 1.73m 64kg. Student at University of Georgia.
At Hep: OG: '16- 17; WCh: '17- 12; WJ: '12- 8; WY: '11- 11; won US 2017, NCAA 2016-17, indoor Pen 2014-17. At Pen: WI: '16- 5, 18- 9. At 100mh: WJ: '14- 1; WY: '11- 3.
Progress at Hep: 2011- 5169, 2012- 5578, 2013- 5572A, 2014- 6018, 2015- 6223, 2016- 6402, 2017- 6564. pbs: 200m 23.50 '17, 800m 2:15.31 '16, 60mh 8.34i '17, 100mh 12.82 '17, 400mh 58.63 '10, HJ 1.88Ai '14, 1.84 '16; LJ 6.54i '15, 6.49 '17; SP 13.55i '16, 13.01 '17; JT 46.48 '17, Pen 4703i '16.
Her brother Devon (b. 17 Dec 1994) has decathlon pb 8345 '17, 10th WC and won NCAA indoor heptathlon with 6177 in 2017.

Ajee' WILSON b. 8 May 1994 Neptune, New Jersey 1.69m 55kg. adidas. Student of kinesiology at Temple University, Philadelphia.
At 800m: OG: '16- sf; WCh: '13- 5. '17- 3; WJ: '10- 5, '12- 1; WY: 11- 1; CCp: '14- 2; WI: '16- 2, '18- 2; won US 2014, 2017; indoor 2013-14, 2016.
Records: WR distance medley 2015, World indoor 4x800m 2018, North American 4x800m 2014, 600m 2017, world junior 600m & North American junior 800m 2013.
Progress at 800m: 2008- 2:11.43, 2009- 2:07.08, 2010- 2:04.18, 2011- 2:02.64, 2012- 2:00.91, 2013- 1:58.21, 2014- 1:57.67, 2015- 1:57.87, 2016- 1:59.44, 2017- 1:55.61. pbs: 400m 53.63 '14, 500m 1:09.63i '17, 600m 1:22.39 '17, 1000m 2:42.71i '16, 1500m 4:12.10 '14, 1M 4:33.57 '16, 3000m 10:13.41 '07.
Positive test for zeranol at the Millrose Games on 11 Feb 2017 meant that her result from then, when she had run a North American indoor 800m record of 1:58.27, was annulled, although it was announced in June she will not face a ban as it was deemed likely that the test result was due to contaminated meat. Elder sister Jade has 400mh pb 59.90 '12.

Shakima WIMBLEY b. 23 Apr 1995 Fort Lauderdale, Florida 1.88m 61kg. Univ of Miami.
At 400m/4x400mR: WCh: '17- 1R; WJ: '14- 1R; PAm: '15- 2/1R; WI: '18- 2/1R.
Progress at 400m: 2012- 55.11, 2013- 53.67, 2014-

51.68, 2015- 50.84, 2016- 50.90, 2017- 50.36. pbs: 100m 11.99 '13, 200m 22.43 '15, 300m 36.71 '17.

Kara WINGER b. 10 Apr 1986 Seattle 1.83m 84kg. née Patterson. Studied interior design at Purdue University.
At JT: OG: '08/12/16- dnq 40/31/13; WCh: '09/11/17- dnq 29/21/15, '15- 8; PAm: '15- 2; PAm-J: '05- 2; CCp: '10- 6, '14- 7. Won NACAC 2015, US 2008-11, 2014-15, 2017.
North American javelin record 2010.
Progress at JT: 2003- 44.75, 2004- 48.51, 2005- 52.09, 2006- 56.19, 2008- 61.56, 2009- 63.95, 2010- 66.67, 2011- 62.76, 2012- 60.49, 2013- 57.12, 2014- 62.90, 2015- 66.47, 2016- 61.86, 2017- 64.80. Pb DT 35.17 '11.
Married Russ Winger (SP 21.29i '08, 21.25 '10; DT 66.04 '11, dnq 26 WCh 15) on 28 Sep 2014.

UZBEKISTAN

Governing body: Athletic Federation of Uzbekistan.

Svetlana RADZIVIL b. 17 Jan 1987 Tashkent 1.84m 61kg
At HJ: OG: '08- dnq 16, '12- 7, '16- 13=; WCh: '09- dnq 21=, '11- 8=, '15- 9=; AsiG: '06-10-14: 7/1/1; AsiC: '09-11-13-15: 3/2/2/1; WJ: '02- dnq, '04- 13, '06- 1; WY: '03- dnq; CCp: '14- 4; WI: '12- 8. Won Asi-J 2006, Asian indoor 2014, 2016.
Progress at HJ: 2002- 1.84, 2003- 1.78, 2004- 1.88, 2005- 1.85, 2006- 1.91, 2007- 1.91, 2008- 1.93, 2009- 1.91, 2010- 1.95, 2011- 1.95, 2012- 1.97, 2013- 1.94, 2014- 1.96, 2015- 1.94, 2016- 1.95.

VENEZUELA

Governing body: Federación Venezolana de Atletismo. Founded 1948.

National Champions 2017: **Men**: 100m/200m: Rafael Vásquez 10.42/21.00, 400m: Alberto Aguilar 46.53, 800m/1500m: Lucirio Garrido 1:48.12/3:47.35, 5000m: Marvin Blanco 14:34.63, 3000mSt: José González 9:12.21, 110mh: Yefferson González 14.67, 400mh: Wilson Bello 51.35, HJ: Eure Yáñez 2.20, PV: Ronny Sevilla 4.90, LJ/TJ: Santiago Cova 7.89/15.96, SP: Mario González 15.20, DT: Kendrick Rojas 40.52, HT: Giordy Álvarez 54.21, JT: Billy Julio 72.15, Dec: Geormis Jaramillo 7917, 20000mW: Yerenman Salazar 1:31:07, 20kW: Jefferson Chacón 1:25:15. **Women**: 100m/100mh/400mh: Génesis Romero 11.79/13.66/61.36, 200m: Nercely Soto 23.31, 400m: María Simancas 54.06, 800m: Ydanis Navas 2:10.89, 1500m: María Garrido 4:37.29, 5000m/10000m: Nubia Arteaga 17:04.92/36:46.30, 3000mSt: Yazilu Montes 11:43.83, HJ: Thaylor Vergara 1.78, PV: Carmen Villanueva 3.85, LJ: María Parra 5.49, TJ: Estefany Pérez 11.32, SP: Ahymara Espinoza 16.50, DT: Yerilda Zapata 43.37, HT: Rosa Rodríguez 61.40, JT: Estefany Chacón 57.95, Hep: Luisaris Toledo 5439, 20000mW: Lilian Bentancourt 1:51:00, 20kW: Milángela Rosales 1:37:29.

Women

Robeilys PEINADO b. 26 Nov 1997 Caracas 1.78m 62kg. OSOT Szczecin, Poland.
At PV: WCh: '15- dnq 23, '17- 3=; WJ: '14- nh, '16- 2; WY: '13- 1; PAm: '15- 6; Yth OG: '14- 2; SACh: '15- 1, '17- 1; SAG: '14- 2. Won S.Am-U23 & -Y 2014, –J 2015.
Four South American pole vault records 2015-17, 3 SAm U20 records 2014-15.
Progress at PV: 2011- 3.90, 2012- 4.15, 2013- 4.40A, 2014- 4.31, 2015- 4.60, 2016- 4.56, 2017- 4.65.

Yulimar ROJAS b. 21 Oct 1995 Caracas 1.89m 75kg. FC Barcelona, Spain.
At TJ (LJ): OG: '16- 2; WCh: '17- 1; WJ: '14- dnq 17 (11); PAm: '15- 4 (11); SACh: '15- 1, '17- 2; WI: '16- 1, '18- 1. Won SAu23 LJ & TJ 2014, SAmJ HJ 2011.
Venezuelan records: LJ 2015, TJ (5) 2015-16. Four South American indoor TJ records 2016-17.
Progress at TJ: 2014- 13.65, 2015- 14.20, 2016- 15.02, 2017- 14.96. Pbs: 100m 11.94 '13, HJ 1.87 '13, LJ 6.57 '15.
Lives in Guadalajara, Spain and coached by Iván Pedroso. First woman to win an Olympic medal for Venezuela. IAAF Rising Star of the Year 2017.

ZAMBIA

Kabange MUPOPO b. 21 Sep 1992 1.70m 57kg.
At 400m: OG: '16- sf; WCh: '15- sf, '17- 7; CG: '14- sf; AfG: '15- 1; AfCh: '14- 2, '16- 1; CCp: '14- 4/3R.
Zambian records 100m 2014 & 2016, 200m 2014 & 2017, 400m (4) 2014-15.
Progress at 400m: 2014- 50.87, 2015- 50.22, 2016- 51.04A/51.35, 2017- 50.60. pb: 100m 11.68A '16, 200m 23.03A '17.
Before turning to athletics in the spring of 2014, Mupopo captained the Zambian football team.

IAAF Council Statements March 2018

IAAF President Sebastian Coe presented the following at the IAAF Council meeting in March 2018.

Hyperandrogenism

In July 2015 the Court of Arbitration for Sport asked the IAAF to provide further evidence as to the degree of performance advantage that hyperandrogenic female athletes have over athletes with normal testosterone levels. Based on the collected evidence, Council approved a request to revise the competition regulations for track events from 400m up to and including one mile. Following some further drafting, the regulations will be communicated to CAS before being released. It is anticipated that the regulations will go into effect on 1 November 2018

"This is one of the toughest subjects my Council and I are discussing," Coe said. "This is not about cheating. No hyperandrogenic athlete has cheated. This is about our responsibility as a sport federation to ensure a level playing field. It is for us to decide the rules, to draw the lines for competition. We choose to have two classifications for our competition – men's events and women's events. This means we need to be clear about the competition criteria for these two categories. We have always believed that testosterone, either naturally produced or artificially inserted into the body, provides significant performance advantages."

Transfer Of Allegiance

Following the recommendations from the Working Group, Council agreed to a set of principles regarding transfers of allegiance in athletics, which include: a minimum three-year waiting period for athletes wanting to transfer from one country to another… the establishment of a review panel that will determine the credibility of applications… evidence that countries are offering full citizenship and associated rights… the provision that an athlete can transfer only once in their career… and that no transfers take place before the age of 20. While the specific rules are being drafted for approval at the July meeting of Council in Buenos Aires, the IAAF's current freeze on transfers remains in effect.

RUSAF Suspension Extended

Rune Andersen delivered the IAAF Taskforce's latest report on the reinstatement of the Russian Athletics Federation (RusAF). The Taskforce's recommendation, which Council unanimously approved, was that RusAF was not ready for reinstatement. While some conditions have been met, several key areas have still not been satisfied by RusAF and RUSADA including providing a plan for 2018 that shows an adequate amount of testing and demonstrating that is has fixed legal issues making it unable to enforce provisional doping bans of athletics coaches. Additionally, RUSADA has still not yet been reinstated by WADA as a fully compliant independent body.

Council has agreed that if progress is not made, further measures should be discussed at the July Council meeting as a means of prompting greater efforts in Russia, including withdrawing permission for Russian athletes to compete as neutral athletes, and ultimately taking the steps necessary to recommend to Congress that RusAF be expelled from IAAF membership.

Global Calendar Update

Following extensive consultation with groups including athletes and fans, Council agreed to a calendar framework that helps provide an understandable and set rhythm for our sport. This, with fixed dates for IAAF World Athletics Series events, is as follows:

- The World Cross Country Championships on the second weekend of February.
- The World Indoor Championships on the second weekend of March.
- The World Half Marathon Championships on the last weekend of March.
- The Race Walking Team Championships, allowed some flexibility, in either April or May.
- The World Relays on the first weekend in May.
- The World U20 Championships, allowed some flexibility, to be held in July.
- The World Championships on the last weekend of August or first weekend of September, to officially end the season.

INTRODUCTION TO WORLD LISTS AND INDEX

Records

World, World U20 and U18, Olympic, Area and Continental records are listed for standard events. In running events up to and including 400 metres, only fully automatic times are shown. Marks listed are those which are considered statistically acceptable by the ATFS, and thus may differ from official records. These are followed by 'odd events', road bests and bests by over 35/40 masters.

World All-time and Year Lists

Lists are presented in the following format: Mark, Wind reading (where appropriate), Name, Nationality (abbreviated), Date of birth, Position in competition, Meeting name (if significant), Venue, Date of performance.

In standard events the best 30 or so performances are listed followed by the best marks for other athletes. Position, meet and venue details have been omitted beyond 100th in year lists.

In the all-time lists performances which have been world records (or world bests, thus including some unratified marks) are shown with WR against them (or WIR for world indoor records).

Juniors (U20) are shown with-J after date of birth, and Youths (U18) with -Y.

Indexes

These contain the names of all athletes ranked with full details in the world year lists for standard events (and others such as half marathon). The format of the index is as follows:

Family name, First name, Nationality, Birthdate, Height (cm) and Weight (kg), 2016 best mark, Lifetime best (with year) as at the end of 2016.

* indicates an athlete who is profiled in the Biographies section, and ^ one who has been profiled in previous editions.

General Notes

Altitude aid

Marks set at an altitude of 1000m or higher have been suffixed by the letter "A" in events where altitude may be of significance.

Although there are no separate world records for altitude assisted events, it is understood by experts that in all events up to 400m in length (with the possible exclusion of the 110m hurdles), and in the horizontal jumps, altitude gives a material benefit to performances. For events beyond 800m, however, the thinner air of high altitude has a detrimental effect.

Supplementary lists are included in relevant events for athletes with seasonal bests at altitude who have low altitude marks qualifying for the main list.

Some leading venues over 1000m

Addis Ababa ETH	2365m
Air Force Academy USA	2194
Albuquerque USA	1555
Antananarivo MAD	1350
Ávila ESP	1128
Bloemfontein RSA	1392
Bogotá COL	2644
Boulder USA	1655
Bozeman USA	1467
Calgary CAN	1045
Cali COL	1046
Ciudad de Guatemala GUA	1402
Ciudad de México MEX	2247
Cochabamba BOL	2558
Colorado Springs USA	1823
Cuenca ECU	2561
Denver USA	1609
El Paso USA	1187
Flagstaff USA	2107
Fort Collins USA	1521
Gabarone BOT	1006
Germiston RSA	1661
Guadalajara MEX	1567
Harare ZIM	1473
Johannesburg RSA	1748
Kampala UGA	1189
Krugersdorp RSA	1740
La Paz BOL	3630
Levelland USA	1069
Logan USA	1372
Medellín COL	1541
Monachil ESP	2302
Nairobi KEN	1675
Orem USA	1455
Pietersburg RSA	1230
Pocatello USA	1361
Potchefstroom RSA	1351
Pretoria RSA	1400
Provo USA	1380
Pueblo USA	1487
Reno USA	1369
Roodepoort RSA	1623
Rustenburg RSA	1215
Salt Lake City USA	1321
San José CRC	1200
Sasolberg RSA	1488
Secunda RSA	1628
Sestriere ITA	2050
Soría ESP	1056
South Lake Tahoe USA	1909
Sucre BOL	2750
Toluca MEX	2680
Windhoek NAM	1725
Xalapa MEX	1356
Some others over 500m	
Albertville FRA	550
Almaty KZK	847
Ankara TUR	902
Bangalore, IND	949
Bern SUI	555
Blacksburg USA	634
Boise USA	818
Canberra AUS	581

La Chaux de Fonds SUI	997
Caracas VEN	922
Edmonton CAN	652
Jablonec CZE	598
Las Vegas USA	619
Lausanne SUI	597
Lubbock USA	981
Madrid ESP	640
Magglingen SUI	751
Malles ITA	980
Moscow, Idaho USA	787
München GER	520
Nampa, Idaho USA	760
Salamanca ESP	806
Santiago de Chile CHI	520
São Paulo BRA	725
Sofia BUL	564
Spokane USA	576
Trípoli GRE	655
Tucson USA	728
Uberlândia BRA	852
350m–500m	
Banská Bystrica SVK	362
Fayetteville USA	407
Genève SUI	385
Götzis AUT	448
Johnson City USA	499
Rieti ITA	402
Sindelfingen GER	440
Stuttgart GER	415
Tashkent UZB	477
Zürich SUI	410

Automatic timing
In the main lists for sprints and hurdles, only times recorded by fully automatic timing devices are included.

Hand timing
In the sprints and hurdles supplementary lists are included for races which are hand timed. Athletes with a hand timed best 0.01 seconds or more better than his or her automatically timed best has been included, but hand timed lists have been terminated close to the differential levels considered by the IAAF to be equivalent to automatic times, i.e. 0.24 sec. for 100m, 200m, 100mh, 110mh, and 0.14 sec. for 400m and 400mh. It should be noted that this effectively recognises bad hand timekeeping, for there should be no material difference between hand and auto times, but badly trained timekeepers anticipate the finish, having reacted to the flash at the start.

In events beyond 400m, auto times are integrated with hand timed marks, the latter identifiable by times being shown to tenths. All-time lists also include some auto times in tenths of a second, identified with '.

Indoor marks
Indoor marks are included in the main lists for field events and straightway track events, but not for other track events as track sizes vary in circumference (200m is the international standard) and banking, while outdoor tracks are standardised at 400m. Outdoor marks for athletes with indoor bests are shown in a supplemental list.

Mixed races
For record purposes athletes may not, except in road races, compete in mixed sex races. Statistically there would not appear to be any particular logic in this, and women's marks set in such races are shown in our lists – annotated with mx. In such cases the athlete's best mark in single sex competition is appended.

Field event series
Field event series are given (where known) for marks in the top 30 performances lists.

Tracks and Courses
As well as climatic conditions, the type and composition of tracks and runways will affect standards of performance, as will the variations in road race courses.

Wind assistance
Anemometer readings have been shown for sprints and horizontal jumps in metres per second to one decimal place. If the figure was given to two decimal places, it has been rounded to the next tenth upwards, e.g. a wind reading of +2.01m/s, beyond the IAAF legal limit of 2.0, is rounded to +2.1; or -1.22m/s is rounded up to -1.2.

Drugs bans
The IAAF Council may decertify an athlete's records, titles and results if he or she is found to have used a banned substance before those performances. Performances at or after such a positive finding are shown in footnotes. Such athletes are shown with ¶ after their name in year lists, and in all-time lists if at any stage of their career they have served a drugs suspension of a year or more (thus not including athletes receiving public warnings or 3 month bans for stimulants etc., which for that year only are indicated with a #). This should not be taken as implying that the athlete was using drugs at that time. Nor have those athletes who have subsequently unofficially admitted to using banned substances been indicated; the ¶ is used only for those who have been caught.

Venues
Place names occasionally change. Our policy is to use names in force at the time that the performance was set. Thus Leningrad prior to 1991, Sankt-Peterburg from its re-naming.

Amendments
Keen observers may spot errors in the lists. They are invited to send corrections as well as news and results for 2018.

Peter Matthews
Email p.matthews121@btinternet.com

WORLD & CONTINENTAL RECORDS

As at 1 April 2018. **Key**: W = World, Afr = Africa, Asi = Asia, CAC = Central America & Caribbean, Eur = Europe, NAm = North America, Oce = Oceania, SAm = South America, Com = Commonwealth, W20 = World Junior (U20), W18 = World Youth (U18, not officially ratified by IAAF). h hand timed.
Successive columns show: World or Continent, performance, name, nationality, venue, date.
A altitude over 1000m, + timing by photo-electric-cell, # awaiting ratification, § not officially ratified

100 METRES

W,CAC,Com	9.58	Usain BOLT	JAM	Berlin	16 Aug 2009
NAm	9.69	Tyson GAY	USA	Shanghai	20 Sep 2009
Afr	9.85	Olusoji FASUBA	NGR	Doha	12 May 2006
Eur	9.86	Francis OBIKWELU	POR	Athína	22 Aug 2004
	9.86	Jimmy VICAUT	FRA	Saint-Denis	4 Jul 2015
	9.86	Jimmy VICAUT	FRA	Montreuil-sous-Bois	7 Jun 2016
Asi	9.91	Femi Seun OGUNODE	QAT	Wuhan 4 Jun 15 & Gainesville	22 Apr 2016
Oce	9.93	Patrick JOHNSON	AUS	Mito	5 May 2003
SAm	10.00A	Róbson da SILVA	BRA	Ciudad de México	22 Jul 1988
W20	9.97	Trayvon BROMELL	USA	Eugene	13 Jun 2014
W18	10.15	Anthony SCHWARTZ	USA	Gainesville	31 Mar 2017

200 METRES

W,CAC,Com	19.19	Usain BOLT	JAM	Berlin	20 Aug 2009
NAm	19.32	Michael JOHNSON	USA	Atlanta	1 Aug 1996
Afr	19.68	Frank FREDERICKS	NAM	Atlanta	1 Aug 1996
Eur	19.72A	Pietro MENNEA	ITA	Ciudad de México	12 Sep 1979
SAm	19.81	Alonso EDWARD	PAN	Berlin	20 Aug 2009
Asi	19.97	Femi Seun OGUNODE	QAT	Bruxelles	11 Sep 2015
Oce	20.06A	Peter NORMAN	AUS	Ciudad de México	16 Oct 1968
W20	19.93	Usain BOLT	JAM	Hamilton, BER	11 Apr 2004
W18	20.13	Usain BOLT	JAM	Bridgetown	20 Jul 2003

400 METRES

W, Afr, Com	43.03	Wayde van NIEKERK	RSA	Rio de Janeiro	14 Aug 16
NAm	43.18	Michael JOHNSON	USA	Sevilla	26 Aug 1999
CAC	43.74	Kirani JAMES	GRN	Lausanne	3 Jul 2014
Asi	43.93	Yousef Ahmed AL-MASRAHI	KSA	Beijing	23 Aug 2015
SAm	44.29	Sanderlei PARRELA	BRA	Sevilla	26 Aug 1999
Eur	44.33	Thomas SCHÖNLEBE	GER	Roma	3 Sep 1987
Oce	44.38	Darren CLARK	AUS	Seoul	26 Sep 1988
W20	43.87	Steve LEWIS	USA	Seoul	28 Sep 1988
W18	45.14	Obea MOORE	USA	Santiago de Chile	2 Sep 1995

800 METRES

W, Afr, Com	1:40.91	David RUDISHA	KEN	London (OS)	9 Aug 2012
Eur	1:41.11	Wilson KIPKETER	DEN	Köln	24 Aug 1997
SAm	1:41.77	Joaquim CRUZ	BRA	Köln	26 Aug 1984
NAm	1:42.60	Johnny GRAY	USA	Koblenz	28 Aug 1985
Asi	1:42.79	Youssef Saad KAMEL	BRN	Monaco	29 Jul 2008
CAC	1:42.85	Norberto TELLEZ	CUB	Atlanta	31 Jul 1996
Oce	1:44.3+ h	Peter SNELL	NZL	Christchurch	3 Feb 1962
W20	1:41.73	Nijel AMOS	BOT	London (OS)	9 Aug 2012
W18	1:43.37	Mohamed AMAN	ETH	Rieti	10 Sep 2011

1000 METRES

W, Afr, Com	2:11.96	Noah NGENY	KEN	Rieti	5 Sep 1999
Eur	2:12.18	Sebastian COE	GBR	Oslo	11 Jul 1981
NAm	2:13.9	Rick WOHLHUTER	USA	Oslo	30 Jul 1974
SAm	2:14.09	Joaquim CRUZ	BRA	Nice	20 Aug 1984
Asi	2:14.72	Youssef Saad KAMEL	BRN	Stockholm	22 Jul 2008
Oce	2:16.09	Jeff RISELEY	AUS	Ostrava	17 Jun 2014
CAC	2:17.0	Byron DYCE	JAM	København	15 Aug 1973
W20	2:13.93 §	Abubaker KAKI	SUD	Stockholm	22 Jul 2008
W18	2:17.44	Hamza DRIOUCH	QAT	Sollentuna	9 Aug 2011

1500 METRES

W, Afr	3:26.00	Hicham EL GUERROUJ	MAR	Roma	14 Jul 1998
Com	3:26.34	Bernard LAGAT	KEN	Bruxelles	24 Aug 2001
Eur	3:28.81	Mo FARAH	GBR	Monaco	19 Jul 2013
Asi	3:29.14	Rashid RAMZI	BRN	Roma	14 Jul 2006
NAm	3:29.30	Bernard LAGAT	USA	Rieti	28 Aug 2005

Oce	3:29.66	Nick WILLIS	NZL	Monaco	17 Jul 2015
SAm	3:33.25	Hudson Santos de SOUZA	BRA	Rieti	28 Aug 2005
CAC	3:35.03	Maurys CASTILLO	CUB	Huelva	7 Jun 2012
W20	3:28.81	Ronald KWEMOI	KEN	Monaco	18 Jul 2014
W18	3:33.72	Nicholas KEMBOI	KEN	Zürich	18 Aug 2006

1 MILE

W, Afr	3:43.13	Hicham El GUERROUJ	MAR	Roma	7 Jul 1999
Com	3:43.40	Noah NGENY	KEN	Roma	7 Jul 1999
Eur	3:46.32	Steve CRAM	GBR	Oslo	27 Jul 1985
NAm	3:46.91	Alan WEBB	USA	Brasschaat	21 Jul 2007
Asi	3:47.97	Daham Najim BASHIR	QAT	Oslo	29 Jul 2005
Oce	3:48.98	Craig MOTTRAM	AUS	Oslo	29 Jul 2005
SAm	3:51.05	Hudson de SOUZA	BRA	Oslo	29 Jul 2005
CAC	3:56.13	Daniel HERRERA	MEX	Concord, MA	1 Jun 2017
W20	3:49.29	William Biwott TANUI (now ÖZBILEN)	KEN	Oslo	3 Jul 2009
W18	3:54.56	Isaac SONGOK	KEN	Linz	20 Aug 2001

2000 METRES

W, Afr	4:44.79	Hicham EL GUERROUJ	MAR	Berlin	7 Sep 1999
Com	4:48.74	John KIBOWEN	KEN	Hechtel	1 Aug 1998
Oce	4:50.76	Craig MOTTRAM	AUS	Melbourne	9 Mar 2006
Eur	4:51.39	Steve CRAM	GBR	Budapest	4 Aug 1985
NAm	4:52.44	Jim SPIVEY	USA	Lausanne	15 Sep 1987
Asi	4:55.57	Mohammed SULEIMAN	QAT	Roma	8 Jun 1995
SAm	5:03.34	Hudson Santos de SOUZA	BRA	Manaus	6 Apr 2002
CAC	5:03.4	Arturo BARRIOS	MEX	Nice	10 Jul 1989
W20	4:56.25	Tesfaye CHERU	ETH	Reims	5 Jul 2011
W18	4:56.86	Isaac SONGOK	KEN	Berlin	31 Aug 2001

3000 METRES

W, Afr, Com	7:20.67	Daniel KOMEN	KEN	Rieti	1 Sep 1996
Eur	7:26.62	Mohammed MOURHIT	BEL	Monaco	18 Aug 2000
NAm	7:29.00	Bernard LAGAT	USA	Rieti	29 Aug 2010
Asi	7:30.76	Jamal Bilal SALEM	QAT	Doha	13 May 2005
Oce	7:32.19	Craig MOTTRAM	AUS	Athína	17 Sep 2006
CAC	7:35.71	Arturo BARRIOS	MEX	Nice	10 Jul 1989
SAm	7:39.70	Hudson Santos de SOUZA	BRA	Lausanne	2 Jul 2002
W20	7:28.19	Yomif KEJELCHA	ETH	Saint-Denis	27 Aug 2016
W18	7:32.37	Abreham CHERKOS Feleke	ETH	Lausanne	11 Jul 2006

5000 METRES

W, Afr	12:37.35	Kenenisa BEKELE	ETH	Hengelo	31 May 2004
Com	12:39.74	Daniel KOMEN	KEN	Bruxelles	22 Aug 1997
Eur	12:49.71	Mohammed MOURHIT	BEL	Bruxelles	25 Aug 2000
Asi	12:51.96	Albert ROP	BRN	Monaco	19 Jul 2013
NAm	12:53.60	Bernard LAGAT	USA	Monaco	22 Jul 2011
Oce	12:55.76	Craig MOTTRAM	AUS	London	30 Jul 2004
CAC	13:07.79	Arturo BARRIOS	MEX	London (CP)	14 Jul 1989
SAm	13:19.43	Marilson dos SANTOS	BRA	Kassel	8 Jun 2006
W20	12:47.53	Hagos GEBRHIWET	ETH	Saint-Denis	6 Jul 2012
W18	12:54.19	Abreham CHERKOS Feleke	ETH	Roma	14 Jul 2006

10,000 METRES

W, Afr	26:17.53	Kenenisa BEKELE	ETH	Bruxelles	26 Aug 2005
Com	26:27.85	Paul TERGAT	KEN	Bruxelles	22 Aug 1997
Asi	26:38.76	Abdullah Ahmad HASSAN	QAT	Bruxelles	5 Sep 2003
NAm	26:44.36	Galen RUPP	USA	Eugene	30 May 2014
Eur	26:46.57	Mohamed FARAH	GBR	Eugene	3 Jun 2011
CAC	27:08.23	Arturo BARRIOS	MEX	Berlin	18 Aug 1989
Oce	27:24.95	Ben ST LAWRENCE	AUS	Stanford	1 May 2011
SAm	27:28.12	Marilson dos SANTOS	BRA	Neerpelt	2 Jun 2007
W20	26:41.75	Samuel WANJIRU	KEN	Bruxelles	26 Aug 2005
W18	27:02.81	Ibrahim JAYLAN Gashu	ETH	Bruxelles	25 Aug 2006

HALF MARATHON

W, Afr	58:23	Zersenay TADESE	ERI	Lisboa	21 Mar 2010
Com	58:33	Samuel WANJIRU	KEN	Den Haag	17 Mar 2007
Asi	58:40	Abraham CHEROBEN	BRN	København	17 Sep 2017
Eur	59:32	Mohamed FARAH	GBR	Lisboa	22 Mar 2015
SAm	59:33	Marilson dos SANTOS	BRA	Udine	14 Oct 2007

NAm	59:43	Ryan HALL	USA	Houston	14 Jan 2007
Oce	59:47	Zane ROBERTSON	NZL	Marugame	1 Feb 2015
CAC	60:14	Armando QUINTANILLA	MEX	Tokyo	21 Jan 1996
W20	59:16	Samuel WANJIRU	KEN	Rotterdam	11 Sep 2005
W18	60:38	Faustin BAHA Sulle	TAN	Lille	4 Sep 1999

MARATHON

W, Afr, Com	2:02:57	Dennis KIMETTO	KEN	Berlin	28 Sep 2014
NAm	2:05:38	Khalid KHANNOUCHI (ex MAR)	USA	London	14 Apr 2002
SAm	2:06:05	Ronaldo da COSTA	BRA	Berlin	20 Sep 1998
Asi	2:06:16	Toshinari TAKAOKA	JPN	Chicago	13 Oct 2002
Eur	2:05:48	Sondre Nordstad MOEN	NOR	Fukuoka	3 Dec 2017
Oce	2:08:16	Steve MONEGHETTI	AUS	Berlin	30 Sep 1990
CAC	2:08:30	Dionicio CERÓN	MEX	London	2 Apr 1995
W20	2:04:32	Tsegaye MEKONNEN	ETH	Dubai	24 Jan 2014
W18	2:11:43	LI He	CHN	Beijing	14 Oct 2001

3000 METRES STEEPLECHASE

W, Asi	7:53.63	Saïf Saaeed SHAHEEN	QAT	Bruxelles	3 Sep 2004
Afr, Com	7:53.64	Brimin KIPRUTO	KEN	Monaco	22 Jul 2011
Eur	8:00.09	Mahiedine MEKHISSI-BENABBAD	FRA	Saint-Denis	6 Jul 2013
NAm	8:00.45	Evan JAGER	USA	Saimt-Denis	4 Jul 2015
Oce	8:14.05	Peter RENNER	NZL	Koblenz	29 Aug 1984
SAm	8:14.41	Wander MOURA	BRA	Mar del Plata	22 Mar 1995
CAC	8:25.69	Salvador MIRANDA	MEX	Barakaldo	8 Jul 2000
W20	7:58.66	Stephen CHERONO (now Shaheen)	KEN	Bruxelles	24 Aug 2001
W18	8:12.28	Getnet WALE	ETH	Hengelo	11 Jun 2017

110 METRES HURDLES

W, NAm	12.80	Aries MERRITT	USA	Bruxelles	7 Sep 2012
CAC	12.87	Dayron ROBLES	CUB	Ostrava	12 Jun 2008
Asi	12.88	LIU Xiang	CHN	Lausanne	11 Jul 2006
Com	12.90	Omar McLEOD	JAM	Kingston	24 Jun 2017
Eur	12.91	Colin JACKSON	GBR/Wal	Stuttgart	20 Aug 1993
Afr	13.11	Antonio ALKANA	RSA	Praha	5 Jun 2017
SAm	13.27A	Paulo César VILLAR	COL	Guadalajara	28 Oct 2011
Oce	13.29	Kyle VANDER-KUYP	AUS	Göteborg	11 Aug 1995
W20	13.12	LIU Xiang (with 3'6" hurdles)	CHN	Lausanne	2 Jul 2002
W20 99cm h	12.99	Wilhem BELOCIAN	FRA	Eugene	24 Jul 2014
W18	13.43	SHI Dongpeng	CHN	Shanghai	6 May 2001
W18 91cm h	12.96	Jaheel HYDE	JAM	Nanjing	23 Aug 2014

400 METRES HURDLES

W, NAm	46.78	Kevin YOUNG	USA	Barcelona	6 Aug 1992
Afr, Com	47.10	Samuel MATETE	ZAM	Zürich	7 Aug 1991
CAC	47.25	Felix SÁNCHEZ	DOM	Saint-Denis	29 Aug 2003
Eur	47.37	Stéphane DIAGANA	FRA	Lausanne	5 Jul 1995
Asi	47.53	Hadi Soua'an AL-SOMAILY	KSA	Sydney	27 Sep 2000
SAm	47.84	Bayano KAMANI	PAN	Helsinki	7 Aug 2005
Oce	48.28	Rohan ROBINSON	AUS	Atlanta	31 Jul 1996
W20	48.02	Danny HARRIS	USA	Los Angeles	17 Jun 1984
W18	48.89	L.J. VAN ZYL	RSA	Kingston	19 Jul 2002
W18 84cm	48.84A	Sokwakhana ZAZINI	RSA	Pretoria	17 Mar 2017

HIGH JUMP

W, CAC	2.45	Javier SOTOMAYOR	CUB	Salamanca	27 Jul 1993
Asi	2.43	Mutaz Essa BARSHIM	QAT	Bruxelles	5 Sep 2014
Eur	2.42	Patrik SJÖBERG	SWE	Stockholm	30 Jun 1987
	2.42 i§	Carlo THRÄNHARDT	FRG	Berlin	26 Feb 1988
	2.42i	Ivan UKHOV	RUS	Praha	25 Feb 2014
	2.42	Bohdan BONDARENKO	UKR	New York	14 Jun 2014
NAm	2.40 i§	Holis CONWAY	USA	Sevilla	10 Mar 1991
	2.40	Charles AUSTIN	USA	Zürich	7 Aug 1991
NAm=, Com	2.40	Derek DROUIN	CAN	Des Moines	25 Apr 2014
Afr	2.38	Jacques FREITAG	RSA	Oudtshoorn	5 Mar 2005
Oce	2.36	Tim FORSYTH	AUS	Melbourne	2 Mar 1997
SAm	2.33	Gilmar MAYO	COL	Pereira	17 Oct 1994
W20	2.37	Dragutin TOPIC	YUG	Plovdiv	12 Aug 1990
		Steve SMITH	GBR	Seoul	20 Sep 1992
W18	2.33	Javier SOTOMAYOR	CUB	La Habana	19 May 1984

POLE VAULT

W, Eur	6.16 i	Renaud LAVILLENIE	FRA	Donetsk	15 Feb 2014
	6.14 A	Sergey BUBKA (best outdoor mark)	UKR	Sestriere	31 Jul 1994
Oce, Com	6.06i	Steve HOOKER	AUS	Boston (R)	7 Feb 2009
	6.05	Dmitriy MARKOV	AUS	Edmonton	9 Aug 2001
NAm	6.04	Brad WALKER	USA	Eugene	8 Jun 2008
Afr	6.03	Okkert BRITS	RSA	Köln	18 Aug 1995
Asi	5.92i	Igor POTAPOVICH	KAZ	Stockholm	19 Feb 1998
	5.90	Grigoriy YEGOROV	KAZ	Stuttgart	19 Aug 1993
	5.90	Grigoriy YEGOROV	KAZ	London (CP)	10 Sep 1993
	5.90	Igor POTAPOVICH	KAZ	Nice	10 Jul 1996
SAm	6.03	Thiago BRAZ da SILVA	BRA	Rio de Janeiro	15 Aug 2016
CAC	5.90	Lázaro BORGES	CUB	Daegu	29 Aug 2011
W20	5.92	Armand DUPLANTIS	SWE	Austin	31 Mar 2018
W18	5.55	Emmanouil KARALÍS	GRE	Ostrava	20 May 2016

LONG JUMP

W, NAm	8.95	Mike POWELL	USA	Tokyo	30 Aug 1991
Eur	8.86 A	Robert EMMIYAN	ARM	Tsakhkadzor	22 May 1987
SAm	8.73	Irving SALADINO	PAN	Hengelo	24 May 2008
CAC	8.71	Iván PEDROSO	CUB	Salamanca	18 Jul 1995
Afr, Com	8.65A	Luvo MANYONGA	RSA	Potchefstroom	22 Apr 2017
Oce	8.54	Mitchell WATT	AUS	Stockholm	29 Jul 2011
Asi	8.48	Mohamed Salim AL-KHUWALIDI	KSA	Sotteville	2 Jul 2006
W20	8.35	Sergey MORGUNOV	RUS	Cheboksary	20 Jun 2012
W18	8.28	Maykel D MASSÓ	CUB	La Habana	28 May 2016

TRIPLE JUMP

W, Eur, Com	18.29	Jonathan EDWARDS	GBR/Eng	Göteborg	7 Aug 1995
NAm	18.21	Christian TAYLOR	USA	Beijing	27 Aug 2015
CAC	18.08	Pedro Pablo PICHARDO	CUB	La Habana	28 May 2015
SAm	17.90	Jadel GREGÓRIO	BRA	Belém	20 May 2007
Asi	17.59	LI Yanxi	CHN	Jinan	26 Oct 2009
Oce	17.46	Ken LORRAWAY	AUS	London (CP)	7 Aug 1982
Afr	17.37	Tareq BOUGTAÏB	MAR	Khémisset	14 Jul 2007
W20	17.50	Volker MAI	GDR	Erfurt	23 Jun 1985
W18	17.32	Jordan A. DIAZ	CUB	La Habana	17 Feb 2018

SHOT

W, NAm	23.12	Randy BARNES	USA	Los Angeles (Westwood)	20 May 1990
Eur	23.06	Ulf TIMMERMANN	GER	Haniá	22 May 1988
Oce, Com	22.67	Tom WALSH	NZL	Acckland (Waitakere)	25 Mar 2018
Com	22.21	Dylan ARMSTRONG	CAN	Calgary	25 Jun 2011
AfC	21.97	Janus ROBBERTS	RSA	Eugene	2 Jun 2001
CAC	21.96	O'Dayne RICHARDS	JAM	Rabat	16 Jul 2017
SAm	21.82	Darlan ROMANI	BRA	São Bernardo do Campo	3 Jun 2017
Asi	21.13	Sultan Abdulmajeed AL-HEBSHI	KSA	Doha	8 May 2009
W20	21.14	Konrad BUKOWIECKI	POL	Oslo	9 Jun 2016
W18	20.38	Jacko GILL	NZL	Auckland (North Shore)	5 Dec 2011
W20 6kg	23.34	Konrad BUKOWIECKI	POL	Bydgoszcz	19 Jul 2016
W18 5kg	24.45	Jacko GILL	NZL	Auckland (North Shore)	19 Dec 2011

DISCUS

W, Eur	74.08	Jürgen SCHULT	GDR	Neubrandenburg	6 Jun 1986
NAm	72.34 ¶	Ben PLUCKNETT	USA	Stockholm	7 Jul 1981
	71.32 §	Ben PLUCKNETT	USA	Eugene	4 Jun 1983
CAC	71.06	Luis DELIS	CUB	La Habana	21 May 1983
Afr, Com	70.32	Frantz KRUGER	RSA	Salon-de-Provence	26 May 2002
Asi	69.32	Ehsan HADADI	IRI	Tallinn	3 Jun 2008
Oce	68.20	Benn HARRADINE	AUS	Townsville	10 May 2013
SAm	66.32	Jorge BALLIENGO	ARG	Rosario	15 Apr 2006
W20	65.62 §	Werner REITERER	AUS	Melbourne	15 Dec 1987
W18/20	65.31	Mykyta NESTERENKO	UKR	Tallinn	3 Jun 2008
W20 1.75kg	70.13	Mykyta NESTERENKO	UKR	Halle	24 May 2008
W18 1.5kg	77.50	Mykyta NESTERNKO	UKR	Koncha Zaspa	19 May 2008

¶ Disallowed by the IAAF following retrospective disqualification for drug abuse, but ratified by the AAU/TAC

HAMMER

W, Eur	86.74	Yuriy SEDYKH	UKR/RUS	Stuttgart	30 Aug 1986
Asi	84.86	Koji MUROFUSHI	JPN	Praha	29 Jun 2003

NAm	82.52	Lance DEAL	USA	Milano	7 Sep 1996
Afr	81.27	Mostafa Hicham AL-GAMAL	EGY	Al-Qáhira	21 Mar 2014
Com	80.63	Chris HARMSE	RSA	Durban	15 Apr 2005
Oce	79.29	Stuart RENDELL	AUS	Varazdin	6 Jul 2002
SAm	78.63	Wagner DOMINGOS	BRA	Celje	19 Jun 2016
CAC	78.02	Roberto JANET	CUB	La Habana	28 May 2015
W20	78.33	Olli-Pekka KARJALAINEN	FIN	Seinäjoki	5 Aug 1999
W18	73.66	Vladislav PISKUNOV	UKR	Kyiv	11 Jun 1994
W20 6kg	85.57	Ashraf Amgad EL-SEIFY	QAT	Barcelona	14 Jul 2012
W18 5kg	87.16	Bence HALÁSZ	HUN	Baku	31 May 2014

JAVELIN

W, Eur	98.48	Jan ZELEZNY	CZE	Jena	25 May 1996
Afr, Com	92.72	Julius YEGO	KEN	Beijing	26 Aug 2015
Asi	91.36	CHENG Chao-Tsun	TPE	Taipei	26 Aug 2017
NAm	91.29	Breaux GREER	USA	Indianapolis	21 Jun 2007
CAC	90.16	Keshorn WALCOTT	TTO	Lausanne	9 Jul 2015
Oce	89.02	Jarrod BANNISTER	AUS	Brisbane	29 Feb 2008
SAm	84.70	Edgar BAUMANN	PAR	San Marcos	17 Oct 1999
W20	86.48	Neeraj CHOPRA	IND	Bydgoszcz	23 Jul 2016
W18 700g	89.34	Braian Ezequiel TOLEDO	ARG	Mar del Plata	6 Mar 2010

DECATHLON

W, NAm	9045	Ashton EATON	USA	Beijing	29 Aug 2015
Eur	9026	Roman SEBRLE	CZE	Götzis	27 May 2001
Com	8847	Daley THOMPSON	GBR/Eng	Los Angeles	9 Aug 1984
Asi	8725	Dmitriy KARPOV	KAZ	Athína	24 Aug 2004
CAC	8654	Leonel SUÁREZ	CUB	La Habana	4 Jul 2009
Afr	8521	Larbi BOURAADA	ALG	Rio de Janeiro	18 Aug 2016
Oce	8490	Jagan HAMES	AUS	Kuala Lumpur	18 Sep 1998
SAm	8393	Carlos Eduardo CHININ	BRA	São Paulo	8 Jun 2013
W20 Jnr spec	8435	Niklas KAUL	GER	Grosseto	23 Jul 2017
Snr spec	8397	Torsten VOSS	GDR	Erfurt	7 Jul 1982
W18	8104h	Valter KÜLVET	EST	Viimsi	23 Aug 1981
	7829	Valter KÜLVET	EST	Stockholm	13 Sep 1981

4 X 100 METRES RELAY

W, CAC, Com	36.84	JAM (Carter, M Frater, Blake, Bolt)	London (OS)	11 Aug 2012
NAm	37.38	USA (Demps, Patton, Kimmons, Gatlin)	London (OS)	10 Aug 2012
	37.38	USA (Rodgers, Gatlin, Gay, Bailey)	Nassau	2 May 2015
Eur	37.47	GBR (Ujah, Gemili, Talbot, Mitchell-Blake)	London (OS)	12 Aug 2017
Asi	37.60	JPN (Yamagata, Iizuka, Kiryu, Cambridge)	Rio de Janeiro	19 Aug 2016
SAm	37.90	BRA (V Lima, Ribeiro, A da Silva, Cl da Silva)	Sydney	30 Sep 2000
Afr	37.94	NGR (O Ezinwa, Adeniken, Obikwelu, D Ezinwa)	Athína	9 Aug 1997
Oce	38.17	AUS (Henderson, Jackson, Brimacombe, Marsh)	Göteborg	12 Aug 1995
	38.17	AUS (Alozie, Ntiamoah, McCabe, Ross)	Ldon (OS)	10 Aug 2012
W20	38.66	USA (Kimmons, Omole, Williams, Merritt)	Grosseto	18 Jul 2004
W18	39.97	JAM (Everett, Wilson, Powell, Stephens)	Willemstad	16 Apr 2017

4 X 400 METRES RELAY

W, NAm	2:54.29	USA (Valmon, Watts, Reynolds, Johnson)	Stuttgart	22 Aug1993
Eur	2:56.60	GBR (Thomas, Baulch, Richardson, Black)	Atlanta	3 Aug 1996
CAC, Com	2:56.72	BAH (Brown, Pinder, Mathieu, Miller)	London (OS)	10 Aug 2012
SAm	2:58.56	BRA (C da Silva, A J dosSantos, de Araújo, Parrela)	Winnipeg	30 Jul 1999
Afr	2:58.68	NGR (Chukwu, Monye, Bada, Udo-Obong)	Sydney	30 Sep 2000
Oce	2:59.70	AUS (Frayne, Clark, Minihan, Mitchell)	Los Angeles	11 Aug 1984
Asi	3:00.76	JPN (Karube, K Ito, Osakada, Omori)	Atlanta	3 Aug 1996
W20	3:01.09	USA (Johnson, Merritt, Craig, Clement)	Grosseto	18 Jul 2004
W18	3:11.66A	TTO (Guevara, Cedenio, Walters, Lewis)	Morelia	1 Jul 2012

20 KILOMETRES WALK

W, Asi	1:16:36	Yusuke SUZUKI	JPN	Nomi	15 Mar 2015
Eur	1:17:02	Yohann DINIZ	FRA	Arles	8 Mar 2015
	1:16:43 §	Sergey MOROZOV	RUS	Saransk	8 Jun 2008
SAm	1:17:21	Jefferson PÉREZ	ECU	Saint-Denis	23 Aug 2003
CAC	1:17:25.6 t	Bernardo SEGURA	MEX	Bergen (Fana)	7 May 1994
Oce, Com	1:17:33	Nathan DEAKES	AUS	Cixi	23 Apr 2005
Afr	1:19:02	Hatem GHOULA	TUN	Eisenhüttenstadt	10 May 1997
NAm	1:19:20	Inaki GÓMEZ	CAN	Nomi	20 Mar 2016
W20	1:18:06 §	Viktor BURAYEV	RUS	Adler	4 Mar 2001
W18	1:18:07	LI Gaobo	CHN	Cixi	23 Apr 2005

20,000 METRES TRACK WALK

W, CAC	1:17:25.6	Bernardo SEGURA	MEX	Bergen (Fana)	7 May 1994
Asi	1:18:03.3	BU Lingtang	CHN	Beijing	7 Apr 1994
Eur	1:18:35.2	Stefan JOHANSSON	SWE	Bergen (Fana)	15 May 1992
Oce, Com	1:19:48.1	Nathan DEAKES	AUS	Brisbane	4 Sep 2001
SAm	1:20:23.8	Andrés CHOCHO	ECU	Buenos Aires	5 Jun 2011
NAm	1:21:57.0	Evan DUNFEE	CAN	Moncton	27 Jun 2014
Afr	1:22:51.84	Hatem GHOULA	TUN	Leutkirch	8 Sep 1994
W20	1:20:11.72	LI Gaobo	CHN	Wuhan	2 Nov 2007
W18	1:24:28.3	ZHU Hongjun	CHN	Xian	15 Sep 1999

50 KILOMETRES WALK

W, Eur	3:32:33	Yohann DINIZ	FRA	Zürich	15 Aug 2014
Oce, Com	3:35:47	Nathan DEAKES	AUS	Geelong	2 Dec 2006
Asi	3:36:06	YU Chaohong	CHN	Nanjing	22 Oct 2005
CAC	3:41:09	Erick BARRONDO	GUA	Dudince	23 Mar 2013
NAm	3:41:38	Evan DUNFEE	CAN	Rio de Janeiro	19 Aug 2016
SAm	3:42:57	Andrés CHOCHO	ECU	Ciudad Juárez	6 Mar 2016
Afr	3:54:12	Marc MUNDELL	RSA	Melbourne	13 Dec 2015
W20	3:41:10	ZHAO Jianguo	CHN	Wajima	16 Apr 2006
W18	3:45:46	YU Guoping	CHN	Guangzhou	23 Nov 2001

50,000 METRES TRACK WALK

W, Eur	3:35:27.2	Yoahnn DINIZ	FRA	Reims	12 Mar 2011
CAC	3:41:38.4	Raúl GONZÁLEZ	MEX	Bergen (Fana)	25 May 1979
Oce, Com	3:43:50.0	Simon BAKER	AUS	Melbourne	9 Sep 1990
Asi	3:48:13.7	ZHAO Yongshen	CHN	Bergen (Fana)	7 May 1994
NAm	3:52:21.0	Tim BERRETT	CAN	Victoria	29 Oct 2000
SAm	3:57:58.0	Claudio dos SANTOS	BRA	Blumenau	20 Sep 2008
Afr	4:21:44.5	Abdelwahab FERGUÈNE	ALG	Toulouse	25 Mar 1984

World Records at other men's events recognised by the IAAF

20,000m	56:25.98+	Haile GEBRSELASSIE	ETH	Ostrava	27 Jun 2007
1 Hour	21,285 m	Haile GEBRSELASSIE	ETH	Ostrava	27 Jun 2007
25,000m	1:12:25.4	Moses MOSOP	KEN	Eugene	3 Jun 2011
30,000m	1:26:47.4	Moses MOSOP	KEN	Eugene	3 Jun 2011
U18 Octathlon	6491	Jake STEIN	AUS	Villeneuve d'Ascq	7 Jul 2011
4 x 200m	1:18.63	National team	JAM	Nassau	24 May 2014
		(Nickel Ashmeade, Warren Weir, Jermaine Brown, Yohan Blake)			
4 x 800m	7:02.43	National Team	KEN	Bruxelles	25 Aug 2006
		(Joseph Mutua, William Yiampoy, Ismael Kombich, Wilfred Bungei)			
4 x 1500m	14:22.22	C Cheboi, A Kiplagat, Magut, A Kiprop	KEN	Nassau	25 May 2014
Distance Medley	9:15.50	Merber,Spratting,Johnson,Blankenship	USA	Nassau	3 May 2015

Walking

2 Hours track	29,572m+	Maurizio DAMILANO	ITA	Cuneo	3 Oct 1992
30km track	2:01:44.1	Maurizio DAMILANO	ITA	Cuneo	3 Oct 1992
U20 10,000m track	38:46.4	Viktor BURAYEV	RUS	Moskva	20 May 2000
U20 10km road	37:44	WANG Zhen	CHN	Beijing	18 Sep 2010
W18 10km road	38:57	LI Tianlei	CHN	Beijing	18 Sep 2010

WOMEN

100 METRES

W, NAm	10.49	Florence GRIFFITH JOYNER	USA	Indianapolis	16 Jul 1988
CAC, Com	10.70	Shelly-Ann FRASER	JAM	Kingston	29 Jun 2012
	10.70	Elaine THOMPSON	JAM	Kingston	1 Jul 2016
Eur	10.73	Christine ARRON	FRA	Budapest	19 Aug 1998
Afr	10.78	Murielle AHOURÉ	CIV	Montverde	11 Jun 2016
Asi	10.79	LI Xuemei	CHN	Shanghai	18 Oct 1997
SAm	10.91	Rosângela SANTOS	BRA	London (OS)	6 Aug 2017
Oce	11.11	Melissa BREEN	AUS	Canberra	9 Feb 2014
W20	10.88	Marlies OELSNER/GÖHR	GDR	Dresden	1 Jul 1977
W18	10.98	Candace HILL	USA	Shoreline	20 Jun 2015

200 METRES

W, NAm	21.34	Florence GRIFFITH JOYNER	USA	Seoul	29 Sep 1988
Eur	21.63	Dafne SCHIPPERS	NED	Beijing	28 Aug 2015
CAC, Com	21.64	Merlene OTTEY	JAM	Bruxelles	13 Sep 1991
Asi	22.01	LI Xuemei	CHN	Shanghai	22 Oct 1997
Afr	22.04	Blessing OKAGBARE	NGR	Abilene	24 Mar 2018
Oce	22.23	Melinda GAINSFORD-TAYLOR	AUS	Stuttgart	13 Jul 1997

SAm	22.48	Ana Cláudia da SILVA	BRA	São Paulo	6 Aug 2011
W20	22.18	Allyson FELIX	USA	Athína	25 Aug 2004
	22.11A §	Allyson FELIX (no doping control)	USA	Ciudad de México	3 May 2003
W18	22.43A	Candace HILL	USA	Cali	19 Jul 2015

400 METRES

W, Eur	47.60	Marita KOCH	GDR	Canberra	6 Oct 1985
Oce, Com	48.63	Cathy FREEMAN	AUS	Atlanta	29 Jul 1996
NAm	48.70	Sanya RICHARDS	USA	Athína	16 Sep 2006
CAC	48.89	Ana GUEVARA	MEX	Saint-Denis	27 Aug 2003
Afr	49.10	Falilat OGUNKOYA	NGR	Atlanta	29 Jul 1996
SAm	49.64	Ximena RESTREPO	COL	Barcelona	5 Aug 1992
Asi	49.81	MA Yuqin	CHN	Beijing	11 Sep 1993
W20	49.42	Grit BREUER	GER	Tokyo	27 Aug 1991
W18	50.01	LI Jing	CHN	Shanghai	18 Oct 1997

800 METRES

W, Eur	1:53.28	Jarmila KRATOCHVÍLOVÁ	CZE	München	26 Jul 1983
Afr,W20,Com	1:54.01	Pamela JELIMO	KEN	Zürich	29 Aug 2008
CAC	1:54.44	Ana Fidelia QUIROT	CUB	Barcelona	9 Sep 1989
Asi	1:55.54	LIU Dong	CHN	Beijing	9 Sep 1993
NAm	1:55.61	Ajee' WILSON	USA	Monaco	21 Jul 2017
SAm	1:56.68	Letitia VRIESDE	SUR	Göteborg	13 Aug 1995
Oce	1:58.25	Toni HODGKINSON	NZL	Atlanta	27 Jul 1996
W18	1:57.18	WANG Yuan	CHN	Beijing	8 Sep 1993

1000 METRES

W, Eur	2:28.98	Svetlana MASTERKOVA	RUS	Bruxelles	23 Aug 1996
Afr	2:29.34	Maria Lurdes MUTOLA	MOZ	Bruxelles	25 Aug 1995
Com	2:29.66	Maria Lurdes MUTOLA	MOZ	Bruxelles	23 Aug 1996
NAm	2:31.80	Regina JACOBS	USA	Brunswick	3 Jul 1999
SAm	2:32.25	Letitia VRIESDE	SUR	Berlin	10 Sep 1991
CAC	2:33.21	Ana Fidelia QUIROT	CUB	Jerez de la Frontera	13 Sep 1989
Asi	2:33.6 §	Svetlana ULMASOVA	UZB	Podolsk	5 Aug 1979
	2:40.53	ZHAO Jing	CHN	Changbaishan	2 Sep 2014
Oce	2:37.28	Angie PETTY	NZL	Chiba	15 Aug 2015
W20	2:35.4a	Irina NIKITINA	RUS	Podolsk	5 Aug 1979
	2:35.4	Katrin WÜHN	GDR	Potsdam	12 Jul 1984
W18	2:38.58	Jo WHITE	GBR	London (CP)	9 Sep 1977

1500 METRES

W, Afr	3:50.07	Genzebe DIBABA	ETH	Monaco	17 Jul 2015
Asi	3:50.46	QU Yunxia	CHN	Beijing	11 Sep 1993
Eur	3:52.47	Tatyana KAZANKINA	RUS	Zürich	13 Aug 1980
Com	3:55.22	Laura MUIR	Sco/GBR	Saint-Denis	27 Aug 2016
NAm	3:56.29	Shannon ROWBURY	USA	Monaco	17 Jul 2015
Oce	4:00.93	Sarah JAMIESON	AUS	Stockholm	25 Jul 2006
CAC	4:01.84	Yvonne GRAHAM	JAM	Monaco	25 Jul 1995
SAm	4:05.67	Letitia VRIESDE	SUR	Tokyo	31 Aug 1991
W20	3:51.34	LANG Yinglai	CHN	Shanghai	18 Oct 1997
W18	3:54.52	ZHANG Ling	CHN	Shanghai	18 Oct 1997

1 MILE

W, Eur	4:12.56	Svetlana MASTERKOVA	RUS	Zürich	14 Aug 1996
Afr	4:14.30	Genzebe DIBABA	ETH	Rovereto	6 Sep 2016
NAm	4:16.71	Mary SLANEY	USA	Zürich	21 Aug 1985
Com	4:16.56	Hellen OBIRI	KEN	London (OS)	9 Jul 2017
Asi	4:17.75	Maryam Yusuf JAMAL	BRN	Bruxelles	14 Sep 2007
Oce	4:22.66	Lisa CORRIGAN	AUS	Melbourne	2 Mar 2007
CAC	4:24.64	Yvonne GRAHAM	JAM	Zürich	17 Aug 1994
SAm	4:30.05	Soraya TELLES	BRA	Praha	9 Jun 1988
W20	4:17.57	Zola BUDD	GBR	Zürich	21 Aug 1985
W18	4:30.81	Gelete BURKA	ETH	Heusden	2 Aug 2003

2000 METRES

W, Eur	5:25.36	Sonia O'SULLIVAN	IRL	Edinburgh	8 Jul 1994
Com	5:26.93	Yvonne MURRAY	GBR/Sco	Edinburgh	8 Jul 1994
Afr	5:27.50	Genzebe DIBABA	ETH	Ostrava	17 Jun 2014
Asi	5:29.43+§	WANG Junxia	CHN	Beijing	12 Sep 1993
	5:31.88	Maryam Yusuf JAMAL	BRN	Eugene	7 Jun 2009
NAm	5:32.7	Mary SLANEY	USA	Eugene	3 Aug 1984

Oce	5:37.71	Benita JOHNSON	AUS	Ostrava	12 Jun 2003
W20	5:33.15	Zola BUDD	GBR	London (CP)	13 Jul 1984
W18	5:46.5+	Sally BARSOSIO	KEN	Zürich	16 Aug 1995

3000 METRES

W, Asi	8:06.11	WANG Junxia	CHN	Beijing	13 Sep 1993
Afr, Com	8:20.68	Hellen OBIRI	KEN	Doha	9 May 2014
Eur	8:21.42	Gabriela SZABO	ROU	Monaco	19 Jul 2002
NAm	8:25.83	Mary SLANEY	USA	Roma	7 Sep 1985
Oce	8:35.31	Kimberley SMITH	NZL	Monaco	25 Jul 2007
CAC	8:37.07	Yvonne GRAHAM	JAM	Zürich	16 Aug 1995
SAm	9:02.37	Delirde BERNARDI	BRA	Linz	4 Jul 1994
W20	8:28.83	Zola BUDD	GBR	Roma	7 Sep 1985
W18	8:36.45	MA Ningning	CHN	Jinan	6 Jun 1993

5000 METRES

W, Afr	14:11.15	Tirunesh DIBABA	ETH	Oslo	6 Jun 2008
Com	14:18.37	Hellen OBIRI	KEN	Roma	8 Jun 2017
Eur	14:23.75	Liliya SHOBUKHOVA	RUS	Kazan	19 Jul 2008
Asi	14:28.09	JIANG Bo	CHN	Shanghai	23 Oct 1997
NAm	14:38.92	Shannon ROWBURY	USA	Bruxelles	9 Sep 2016
Oce	14:45.93	Kimberley SMITH	NZL	Roma	11 Jul 2008
CAC	15:04.32	Adriana FERNÁNDEZ	MEX	Gresham	17 May 2003
SAm	15:18.85	Simone Alves da SILVA	BRA	São Paulo	20 May 2011
W20	14:30.88	Tirunesh DIBABA	ETH	Bergen (Fana)	11 Jun 2004
W18	14:45.71	SONG Liqing	CHN	Shanghai	21 Oct 1997

10,000 METRES

W, Afr	29:17.45	Almaz AYANA	ETH	Rio de Janeiro	12 Aug 2016
Asi	29:31.78	WANG Junxia	CHN	Beijing	8 Sep 1993
Com	29:32.53	Vivian CHERUIYOT	KEN	Rio de Janeiro	12 Aug 2016
Eur	30:01.09	Paula RADCLIFFE	GBR	München	6 Aug 2002
NAm	30:13.17	Molly HUDDLE	USA	Rio de Janeiro	12 Aug 2016
Oce	30:35.54	Kimberley SMITH	NZL	Stanford	4 May 2008
CAC	31:10.12	Adriana FERNANDEZ	MEX	Brunswick	1 Jul 2000
SAm	31:47.76	Carmen de OLIVEIRA	BRA	Stuttgart	21 Aug 1993
W20	30:26.50	Linet MASAI	KEN	Beijing	15 Aug 2008
W18	31:11.26	SONG Liqing	CHN	Shanghai	19 Oct 1997

HALF MARATHON

W, Afr, Com	64:51	Joyciline JEPKOSGEI	KEN	Valencia	22 Oct 2017
Asi	65:22	Violah JEPCHUMBA	BRN	Praha	1 Apr 2017
Eur	66:25	Lornah KIPLAGAT	NED	Udine	14 Oct 2007
Oce	67:11	Kimberley SMITH	NZL	Philadelphia	18 Sep 2011
NAm	67:25	Molly HUDDLE	USA	Houston	14 Jan 2018
CAC	68:34 dh	Olga APPELL	MEX	Tokyo	24 Jan 1993
	69:28	Adriana FERNÁNDEZ	MEX	Kyoto	9 Mar 2003
SAm	70:14	Gladys TEJEDA	PER	Cardiff	26 Mar 2016
W20	67:57	Abebu GELAN	ETH	Ra's Al Khaymah	20 Feb 2009
W18	72:31	LIU Zhuang	CHN	Yangzhou	24 Apr 2011

MARATHON

W, Eur, Com	2:15:25	Paula RADCLIFFE	GBR/Eng	London	13 Apr 2003
Wo only, Afr	2:17:01	Mary KEITANY	KEN	London	23 Apr 2017
Asi	2:19:12	Mizuki NOGUCHI	JPN	Berlin	25 Sep 2005
NAm	2:19:36	Deena KASTOR	USA	London	23 Apr 2006
Oce	2:22:36	Benita JOHNSON	AUS	Chicago	22 Oct 2006
CAC	2:22:59	Madai PÉREZ	MEX	Chicago	22 Oct 2006
SAm	2:26:48	Inés MELCHOR	PER	Berlin	28 Sep 2014
W20	2:20:59	Shure DEMISE	ETH	Dubai	23 Jan 2015

3000 METRES STEEPLECHASE

W, Asi	8:52.78	Ruth JEBET	BRN	Sant-Denis	27 Aug 2016
Eur	8:58.81	Gulnara GALKINA	RUS	Beijing	17 Aug 2008
Afr,Com,W209	8:58.78	Celliphine CHESPOL	KEN	Eugene	26 May 2017
NAm	9:02.58	Emma COBURN	USA	London (OS)	11 Aug 2017
Oce	9:14.28	Genevieve LaCAZE	AUS	Saint-Denis	27 Aug 2016
SAm	9:25.99	Belén CASETTA	ARG	London (OS)	11 Aug 2017
CAC	9:27.21	Mardrea HYMAN	JAM	Monaco	9 Sep 2005
W18	9:24.73	Celliphine CHESPOL	KEN	Shanghai	14 May 2016

100 METRES HURDLES

W, NAm	12.20	Kendra HARRISON	USA	London (OS)	22 Jul 2016
Eur	12.21	Yordanka DONKOVA	BUL	Stara Zagora	20 Aug 1988
Oce, Com	12.28	Sally PEARSON	AUS	Daegu	3 Sep 2011
Asi	12.44	Olga SHISHIGINA	KAZ	Luzern	27 Jun 1995
Afr	12.44	Glory ALOZIE	NGR	Monaco	8 Aug 1998
	12.44	Glory ALOZIE	NGR	Bruxelles	28 Aug 1998
	12.44	Glory ALOZIE	NGR	Sevilla	28 Aug 1999
CAC	12.45	Brigitte FOSTER	JAM	Eugene	24 May 2003
SAm	12.67	Yvette LEWIS	PAN	Lahti	17 Jul 2013
W20	12.74	Dior HALL	USA	Eugene	13 Jun 2015
W18	12.84	Tia JONES	USA	Clovis	25 Jun 2016

400 METRES HURDLES

Eur, W	52.34	Yuliya PECHONKINA	RUS	Tula	8 Aug 2003
CAC, Com	52.42	Melaine WALKER	JAM	Berlin	20 Aug 2009
NAm	52.47	Lashinda DEMUS	USA	Daegu	1 Sep 2011
Afr	52.90	Nezha BIDOUANE	MAR	Sevilla	25 Aug 1999
Oce	53.17	Debbie FLINTOFF-KING	AUS	Seoul	28 Sep 1988
Asi	53.96	HAN Qing	CHN	Beijing	9 Sep 1993
	53.96	SONG Yinglan	CHN	Guangzhou	22 Nov 2001
SAm	55.76	Gianna WOODRUFF	PAN	Tucson	20 May 2017
W20	53.82	Sydney McLAUGHLIN	USA	Sacramento	25 Jun 2017
W18	54.15	Sydney McLAUGHLIN	USA	Eugene	10 Jul 2016

HIGH JUMP

W, Eur	2.09	Stefka KOSTADINOVA	BUL	Roma	30 Aug 1987
Afr, Com	2.06	Hestrie CLOETE	RSA	Saint-Denis	31 Aug 2003
NAm	2.05	Chaunté HOWARD-LOWE	USA	Des Moines	26 Jun 2010
CAC	2.04	Silvia COSTA	CUB	Barcelona	9 Sep 1989
Asi	1.99	Marina AITOVA	KAZ	Athína	13 Jul 2009
Oce	1 98	Vanessa WARD	AUS	Perth	12 Feb 1989
	1.98	Alison INVERARITY	AUS	Ingolstadt	17 Jul 1994
SAm	1.96	Solange WITTEVEEN	ARG	Oristano	8 Sep 1997
W20	2.01	Olga TURCHAK	KAZ	Moskva	7 Jul 1986
	2.01	Heike BALCK	GDR	Chemnitz	18 Jun 1989
W18	1.96A	Charmaine GALE	RSA	Bloemfontein	4 Apr 1981
	1.96	Olga TURCHAK	UKR	Donetsk	7 Sep 1984
	1.96	Eleanor PATTERSON	AUS	Townsville	7 Dec 2013
	1.96	Vashti CUNNINGHAM	USA	Edmonton	1 Aug 2015

POLE VAULT

W, Eur	5.06	Yelena ISINBAYEVA	RUS	Zürich	28 Aug 2009
NAm	5.03i	Jennifer SUHR	USA	Brockport	30 Jan 2016
	5.00	Sandi MORRIS	USA	Bruxelles	9 Sep 2016
CAC	4.91	Yarisley SILVA	CUB	Beckum	2 Aug 2015
SAm	4.87	Fabiana MURER	BRA	ßão Bernardo do Campo	3 Jul 2016
Com	4.87i	Holly BLEASDALE	GBR	Villeurbanne	21 Jan 2012
Com, Oce	4.82	Eliza McCARTNEY	NZL	Auckland (NS)	26 Feb 2017
Asi	4.70i	LI Ling	CHN	Doha	19 Feb 2016
	4.66	LI Ling	CHN	Wuhan	6 Jun 2015
Afr	4.42	Elmarie GERRYTS	RSA	Wesel	12 Jun 2000
W20	4.71i	Wilma MURTO	FIN	Zweibrucken	31 Jan 2016
	4.64	Eliza McCARTNEY	NZL	Auckland	19 Dec 2015
W18	4.50	Lisa GUNNARSSON	SWE	Pézenas	28 May 2016
	4.50	Lisa GUNNARSSON	SWE	Angers	25 Jun 2016

LONG JUMP

W, Eur	7.52	Galina CHISTYAKOVA	RUS	Sankt-Peterburg	11 Jun 1988
NAm	7.49	Jackie JOYNER-KERSEE	USA	New York	22 May 1994
	7.49A §	Jackie JOYNER-KERSEE	USA	Sestriere	31 Jul 1994
SAm	7.26A	Maurren MAGGI	BRA	Bogotá	26 Jun 1999
CAC, Com	7.16A	Elva GOULBOURNE	JAM	Ciudad de México	22 May 2004
Afr	7.12	Chioma AJUNWA	NGR	Atlanta	1 Aug 1996
Oce	7.05	Brooke STRATTON	AUS	Perth	12 Mar 2016
Asi	7.01	YAO Weili	CHN	Jinan	5 Jun 1993
W20	7.14	Heike DAUTE/Drechsler	GDR	Bratislava	4 Jun 1983
W18	6.91	Heike DAUTE/Drechsler	GDR	Jena	9 Aug 1981

TRIPLE JUMP

W, Eur	15.50	Inessa KRAVETS	UKR	Göteborg	10 Aug 1995
Afr, Com	15.39	Françoise MBANGO Etone	CMR	Beijing	17 Aug 2008
SAm	15.31	Caterine IBARGÜEN	COL	Monaco	18 Jul 2014
CAC	15.29	Yamilé ALDAMA	CUB	Roma	11 Jul 2003
Asi	15.25	Olga RYPAKOVA	KAZ	Split	4 Sep 2010
NAm	14.71	Keturah ORJI	USA	Rio de Janeiro	14 Aug 2016
Oce	14.04	Nicole MLADENIS	AUS	Hobart	9 Mar 2002
	14.04	Nicole MLADENIS	AUS	Perth	7 Dec 2003
W20	14.62	Tereza MARINOVA	BUL	Sydney	25 Aug 1996
W18	14.57	HUANG Qiuyan	CHN	Shanghai	19 Oct 1997

SHOT

W, Eur	22.63	Natalya LISOVSKAYA	RUS	Moskva	7 Jun 1987
Asi	21.76	LI Meisu	CHN	Shijiazhuang	23 Apr 1988
Oce, Com	21.24	Valerie ADAMS	NZL	Daegu	29 Aug 2011
CAC	20.96	Belsy LAZA	CUB	Ciudad de México	2 May 1992
NAm	20.63	Michelle CARTER	USA	Rio de Janeiro	12 Aug 2016
SAm	19.30	Elisângela ADRIANO	BRA	Tunja	14 Jul 2001
Afr	18.43	Vivian CHUKWUEMEKA	NGR	Walnut	19 Apr 2003
W20	20.54	Astrid KUMBERNUSS	GDR	Orimattila	1 Jul 1989
W18	19.08	Ilke WYLUDDA	GDR	Karl-Marx-Stadt	9 Aug 1986

DISCUS

W, Eur	76.80	Gabriele REINSCH	GDR	Neubrandenburg	9 Jul 1988
Asi	71.68	XIAO Yanling	CHN	Beijing	14 Mar 1992
CAC	70.88	Hilda RAMOS	CUB	La Habana	8 May 1992
Oce, Com	69.64	Dani STEVENS	AUS	London (OS)	13 Aug 2017
NAm	69.17	Gia LEWIS-SMALWOOD	USA	Angers	30 Aug 2014
Afr	64.87	Elizna NAUDE	RSA	Stellenbosch	2 Mar 2007
SAm	64.68	Andressa de MORAIS	BRA	Asunción	23 Jun 2072
W20	74.40	Ilke WYLUDDA	GDR	Berlin	13 Sep 1988
W18	65.86	Ilke WYLUDDA	GDR	Neubrandenburg	1 Aug 1986

HAMMER

W, Eur	82.98	Anita WLODARCZYK	POL	Warszawa	28 Aug 2016
Asi	77.68	WANG Zheng	CHN	Chengdu	29 Mar 2014
NAm	76.77	Gwen BERRY	USA	Oxford, USA	6 May 2017
CAC	76.62	Yipsi MORENO	CUB	Zagreb	9 Sep 2008
NAm, Com	75.73	Sultana FRIZELL	CAN	Tucson	22 May 2014
SAm	73.74	Jennifer DAHLGREN	ARG	Buenos Aires	10 Apr 2010
Oce	71.12	Bronwyn EAGLES	AUS	Adelaide	6 Feb 2003
Afr	69.70	Amy SÈNE	SEN	Forbach	25 May 2014
W20	73.24	ZHANG Wenxiu	CHN	Changsha	24 Jun 2005
W18	70.60	ZHANG Wenxiu	CHN	Nanning	5 Apr 2003
W18 3kg	76.04	Réka GYURÁTZ	HUN	Zalaegerszeg	23 Jun 2013

JAVELIN

W, Eur	72.28	Barbora SPOTÁKOVÁ	CZE	Stuttgart	13 Sep 2008
CAC	71.70	Osleidys MENÉNDEZ	CUB	Helsinki	14 Aug 2005
Afr, Com	69.35	Sunette VILJOEN	RSA	New York	9 Jun 2012
Asi	67.59	LU Huihui	CHN	London (OS)	6 Aug 2017
Oce	68.57	Kathryn MITCHELL	AUS	Melbourne	3 Mar 2018
NAm	66.67	Kara PATTERSON	USA	Des Moines	25 Jun 2010
SAm	63.84A	Flor Dennis RUIZ	COL	Cali	25 Jun 2016
W20	63.86	Yulenmis AGUILAR	CUB	Edmonton	2 Aug 2015
W18	62.93	XUE Juan	CHN	Changsha	27 Oct 2003

HEPTATHLON

W, NAm	7291	Jackie JOYNER-KERSEE	USA	Seoul	24 Sep 1988
Eur	7032	Carolina KLÜFT	SWE	Osaka	26 Aug 2007
Com	6955	Jessica ENNIS	GBR/Eng	London (OS)	4 Aug 2012
Asi	6942	Ghada SHOUAA	SYR	Götzis	26 May 1996
Oce	6695	Jane FLEMMING	AUS	Auckland	28 Jan 1990
CAC	6594	Yorgelis RODRIGUEZ	CUB	London (OS)	6 Aug 2017
Afr	6423	Margaret SIMPSON	GHA	Götzis	29 May 2005
SAm	6270A	Evelis AGUILAR	COL	Cali	26 Jun 2016
W20	6542	Carolina KLÜFT	SWE	München	10 Aug 2002
W18	6185	SHEN Shengfei	CHN	Shanghai	18 Oct 1997
U18 spec	6186	Alina SHUKH	UKR	Tbilisi	15 Jul 2016

DECATHLON

W, Eur	8358	Austra SKUJYTE	LTU	Columbia, MO	15 Apr 2005
Asi	7798 §	Irina NAUMENKO	KAZ	Talence	26 Sep 2004
NAm	7577 §	Tiffany LOTT-HOGAN	USA	Lage	10 Sep 2000
CAC	7245 §	Magalys GARCÍA	CUB	Wien	29 Jun 2002
Afr, Com	6915	Margaret SIMPSON	GHA	Réduit	19 Apr 2007
SAm	6570	Andrea BORDALEJO	ARG	Rosario	28 Nov 2004
Oce	6428	Simone CARRÉ	AUS	Melbourne	11 Mar 2012

4 X 100 METRES RELAY

W, NAm	40.82	USA (Madison, Felix, Knight, Jeter)	London (OS)	10 Aug 2012
CAC, Com	41.07	JAM (Campbell-Brown, Morrison, Thompson, Fraser-Pryce)	Beijing	29 Aug 2015
Eur	41.37	GDR (Gladisch, Rieger, Auerswald, Göhr)	Canberra	6 Oct 1985
Asi	42.23	Sichuan CHN (Xiao Lin, Li Yali, Liu Xiaomei, Li Xuemei)	Shanghai	23 Oct 1997
SAm	42.29	BRA (E dos Santos, Silva, Krasucki, R Santos)	Moskva	18 Aug 2013
Afr	42.39	NGR (Utondu, Idehen, Opara-Thompson, Onyali)	Barcelona	7 Aug 1992
Oce	42.99A	AUS (Massey, Broadrick, Lambert, Gainsford-Taylor)	Pietersburg	18 Mar 2000
W20	43.27	GER (Fehm, Kwadwo, Junk, Montag)	Grosseto	23 Jul 2017
W18	44.05	GDR (Koppetsch, Oelsner, Sinzel, Brehmer)	Athína	24 Aug 1975

4 X 400 METRES RELAY

W, Eur	3:15.17	URS (Ledovskaya, Nazarova, Pinigina, Bryzgina)	Seoul	1 Oct 1988
NAm	3:15.51	USA (D.Howard, Dixon, Brisco, Griffith Joyner)	Seoul	1 Oct 1988
CAC, Com	3:18.71	JAM (Whyte, Prendergast, N Williams-Mills, S Williams)	Daegu	3 Sep 2011
Afr	3:21.04	NGR (Bisi Afolabi, Yusuf, Opara, Ogunkoya)	Atlanta	3 Aug 1996
Oce	3:23.81	AUS (Peris, Lewis, Gainsford-Taylor, Freeman)	Sydney	30 Sep 2000
Asi	3:24.28	Hebei CHN (An X, Bai X, Cao C, Ma Y)	Beijing	13 Sep 1993
SAm	3:26.68	BRA (Coutinho, de Oliveira, Souza, de Lima)	São Paulo	7 Aug 2011
W20	3:27.60	USA (Anderson, Kidd, Smith, Hastings)	Grosseto	18 Jul 2004
W18	3:36.98	GBR (Ravenscroft, E McMeekin, Kennedy, Pettett)	Duisburg	26 Aug 1973

10 KILOMETRES WALK

W, Eur	41:04	Yelena NIKOLAYEVA	RUS	Sochi	20 Apr 1996
Asi	41:16	WANG Yan	CHN	Eisenhüttenstadt	8 May 1999
Oce, Com	41:30	Kerry SAXBY-JUNNA	AUS	Canberra	27 Aug 1988
CAC	42:42	Graciela MENDOZA	MEX	Naumburg	25 May 1997
SAm	43:03	Erica de SENA	BRA	Suzhou	25 Sep 2017
NAm	44:09+	Maria MICHTA-COFFEY	USA	St. Louis	3 Apr 2016
Afr	45:02	Chahinez NASRI	TUN	La Coruña	28 May 2016
W20	41:52 §	Tatyana MINEYEVA	RUS	Penza	5 Sep 2009
	41:57 §	GAO Hongmiao	CHN	Beijing	8 Sep 1993
W18	43:28	Aleksandra KUDRYASHOVA	RUS	Adler	19 Feb 2006

10,000 METRES TRACK WALK

W, Asi	41:37.9 §	GAO Hongmiao	CHN	Beijing	7 Apr 1994
W, Eur	41:56.23	Nadyezhda RYASHKINA	RUS	Seattle	24 Jul 1990
Oce, Com	41:57.22	Kerry SAXBY-JUNNA	AUS	Seattle	24 Jul 1990
SAm	43:41.30	Erica de SEÑA	BRA	São Paulo	1 Aug 2014
NAm	44:30.1 m	Alison BAKER	CAN	Bergen (Fana)	15 May 1992
	44:06 no kerb	Michelle ROHL	USA	Kenosha	2 Jun 1996
CAC	44:16.21	Cristina LÓPEZ	ESA	San Salvador	13 Jul 2007
Afr	44:41.8A	Grace Njue WANJIRU	KEN	Thika	5 Mar 2016
W20	42:47.25	Anezka DRAHOTOVÁ	CZE	Eugene	23 Jul 2014
W18	42:56.09	GAO Hongmiao	CHN	Tangshan	27 Sep 1991

20,000 METRES TRACK WALK

W, Eur	1:26:52.3	Olimpiada IVANOVA	RUS	Brisbane	6 Sep 2001
Asi, W20	1:29:32.4 §	SONG Hongjuan	CHN	Changsha	24 Oct 2003
SAm	1:31:02.25	Sandra Lorena ARENAS	COL	Lima	13 Jun 2015
CAC	1:31:53.8A	Mirna ORTIZ	GUA	Ciudad de Guatemala	9 Aug 2014
NAm, Com	1:32:54.0	Rachel SEAMAN	CAN	Moncton	27 Jun 2014
Oce	1:33:40.2	Kerry SAXBY-JUNNA	AUS	Brisbane	6 Sep 2001
Afr	1:36:18.22	Nicolene CRONJE	RSA	Durban	17 Apr 2004
W18	1:34:21.56	WANG Xue	CHN	Wuhan	1 Nov 2007

20 KILOMETRES WALK

W,Asi	1:24:38	LIU Hong	CHN	La Coruna	6 Jun 2015
Eur	1:24:47 §	Elmira ALEMBEKOVA	RUS	Sochi	27 Feb 2015
	1:25:02	Yelena LASHMANOVA	RUS	London	11 Aug 2012
CAC	1:26:17	María Guadeloupe GONZÁLEZ	MEX	Roma	7 May 2016

SAm	1:26:59	Erica de SENA	BRA	London	13 Aug 2017
Oce, Com	1:27:44	Jane SAVILLE	AUS	Naumburg	2 May 2004
NAm	1:29:54	Rachel SEAMAN	CAN	Nomi	15 Mar 201
Afr	1:30:43	Grace Njue WANJIRU	KEN	Durban	26 Jun 2016
W20	1:25:30	Anisya KIRDYAPKINA	RUS	Adler	23 Feb 2008
W18	1:30:35	ZHOU Tongmei	CHN	Cixi	23 Apr 2005

50 KILOMETRES WALK

W, Eur	4:05:56	Inês HENRIQUES	POR	London	13 Aug 2017
Asi	4:08:58	YIN Hang	CHN	London	13 Aug 2017
CAC	4:15:42	Mayra Carolina HERRERA	GUA	Owego	9 Sep 2017
NAm	4:21:51	Kathleen BURNETT	USA	London	13 Aug 2017
SAm	4:19:43A	Magal BONILLA	ECU	Sucua	10 Mar 2018
Com	4:50:51	Sandra BROWN	GBR	Basildon	13 Feb 1991
Afr	4:54:33	Natalie le ROUX	RSA	George, RSA	21 Oct 2017

World Records at other track & field events recognised by the IAAF

1 Hour	18,517 m	Dire TUNE	ETH	Ostrava	12 Jun 2008
20,000m	1:05:26.6	Tegla LOROUPE	KEN	Borgholzhausen	3 Sep 2000
25,000m	1:27:05.84	Tegla LOROUPE	KEN	Mengerskirchen	21 Sep 2002
30,000m	1:45:50.0	Tegla LOROUPE	KEN	Warstein	6 Jun 2003
4x200m	1:27.46	L Jenkins, L Colander, N Perry, M Jones	USA	Philadelphia	29 Apr 2000
4x800m	7:50.17	Olizarenko, Gurina, Borisova, Podyalovskaya	USSR	Moskva	5 Aug 1984
4x1500m	16:33.58	M Cherono, Kipyegon, I Jelagat, Obiri	KEN	Nassau	24 May 2014

WORLD BESTS AT NON-STANDARD EVENTS

Men

50m	5.47+e	Usain Bolt	JAM	Berlin (in 100m)	16 Aug 2009
60m	6.31+	Usain Bolt	JAM	Berlin (in 100m)	16 Aug 2009
100 yards	9.07	Asafa Powell	JAM	Ostrava	27 May 2010
150m turn	14.44+	Usain Bolt	JAM	Berlin (in 200m)	20 Aug 2009
150m straight	14.35	Usain Bolt	JAM	Manchester	17 May 2009
300m	30.81	Wayde van Niekerk	RSA	Ostrava	28 Jun 2017
500m	59.32	Orestes Rodríguez	CUB	La Habana	15 Feb 2013
600m	1:12.81	Johnny Gray	USA	Santa Monica	24 May 1986
2 miles	7:58.61	Daniel Komen	KEN	Hechtel	19 Jul 1997
2000m Steeple	5:10.68	Mahiedine Mekhissi	FRA	Reims	30 Jun 2010
200mh	22.55	Laurent Ottoz	ITA	Milano	31 May 1995
	22.55	Yoshiro Watanabe	JPN	Izumi	1 Oct 2017
(hand time)	22.5	Martin Lauer	FRG	Zürich	7 Jul 1959
200mh straight	22.10	Andrew Turner	GBR	Manchester	15 May 2011
	22.10	L.J. van Zyl	RSA	Manchester	9 May 2015
220yh straight	21.9	Don Styron	USA	Baton Rouge	2 Apr 1960
300mh	34.48	Chris Rawlinson	GBR	Sheffield	30 Jun 2002
35lb weight	25.41	Lance Deal	USA	Azusa	20 Feb 1993
Pentathlon	4282 points	Bill Toomey	USA	London (CP)	16 Aug 1969
(1985 tables)		(7.58, 66.18, 21.3, 44.52, 4:20.3)			
Double decathlon	14,571	Joe Detmer	USA	Lynchburg	24/25 Sep 2010
	10.93w, 7.30, 200mh 24.25w, 12.27, 5k 18:25.32, 2:02.23, 1.98, 400m 50.43, HT 31.82, 3kSt 11:22.47 15.01, DT 40.73, 200m 22.58, 4.85, 3k 10:25.99, 400mh 53.83, 51.95, 4:26.66, TJ 13.67, 10k 40:27.26				
4x110mh	52.94	USA Richardson, Harris, Merritt, Oliver		Des Moines	25 Apr 2015
1 mile walk	5:31/08	Tom Bosworth	GBR	London (OS)	9 Jul 2017
3000m track walk	10:47.11	Giovanni De Benedictis	ITA	San Giovanni Valdarno	19 May 1990
5000m track walk	18:05.49	Hatem Ghoula	TUN	Tunis	1 May 1997
10,000m track walk	37:53.09	Francisco Javier Fernández	ESP	Santa Cruz de Tenerife	27 Jul 2008
10 km road walk	37:11	Roman Rasskazov	RUS	Saransk	28 May 2000
30 km road walk	2:01:13+	Vladimir Kanaykin	RUS	Adler	19 Feb 2006
35 km road walk	2:21:31	Vladimir Kanaykin	RUS	Adler	19 Feb 2006
100 km road walk	8:38:07	Viktor Ginko	BLR	Scanzorosciate	27 Oct 2002

Women

50m	5.93+	Marion Jones	USA	Sevilla (in 100m)	22 Aug 1999
60m	6.85+	Marion Jones	USA	Sevilla (in 100m)	22 Aug 1999
100 yards	9.91	Veronica-Campbell-Brown	JAM	Ostrava	31 May 2011
150m	16.10+	Florence Griffith-Joyner	USA	Seoul (in 200m)	29 Sep 1988
300m	34.1+	Marita Koch	GDR	Canberra (in 400m)	6 Oct 1985
500m	1:05.9	Tatána Kocembová	CZE	Ostrava	2 Aug 1984
600m	1:21.77	Caster Semenya	RSA	Berlin	27 Aug 2017
2 miles	8:58.58	Meseret Defar	ETH	Bruxelles	14 Sep 2007
2000m Steeple	6:02.16	Virginia Nyambura	KEN	Berlin	6 Sep 2015
200mh	24.8	Yadisleidis Pedroso	ITA	Caserta	6 Apr 2013
	25.20	Dalilah Muhammad	USA	Northridge	10 Mar 2018

300mh	38.16	Zuzana Hejnová	CZE	Cheb	2 Aug 2013
Double heptathlon	10,798	Milla Kelo	FIN	Turku	7/8 Sep 2002
	100mh 14.89, HJ 1.51, 1500m 5:03.74, 400mh 62.18, SP 12.73, 200m 25.16, 100m 12.59				
	LJ 5.73w, 400m 56.10, JT 32.69, 800m 2:23.94, 200mh 28.72, DT 47.86, 3000m 11:48.68				
4x100mh	50.50	USA Castlin, Q Harrison, Harper-Nelson, Rollins		Des Moines	24 Apr 2015
3000m track walk	11:35.34i	Gillian O'Sullivan	IRL	Belfast	15 Feb 2003
	11:48.24	Ileana Salvador	ITA	Padova	29 Aug 1993
5000m track walk	20:01.80	Eleonora Giorgi	ITA	Misterbianco	18 May 2014
25 km road walk	1:56:12+	Eleonora Giorgi	ITA	Catania	31 Jan 2016
30 km road walk	2:19:43	Eleonora Giorgi	ITA	Catania	31 Jul 2016
35 km road walk	2:45:51	Inês Henriques	POR	Porto de Mos	7 Jan 2018
100 km road walk	10:04:50	Jolanta Dukure	LAT	Scanzorosciate	21 Oct 2007

LONG DISTANCE WORLD BESTS – MEN TRACK

	hr:min:sec	*Name*	*Nat*	*Venue*	*Date*
15,000m	0:42:18.7+	Haile Gebrselassie	ETH	Ostrava	27 Jun 2007
10 miles	0:45:23.8+	Haile Gebrselassie	ETH	Ostrava	27 Jun 2007
15 miles	1:11:43.1	Bill Rodgers	USA	Saratoga, Cal.	21 Feb 1979
20 miles	1:39:14.4	Jack Foster	NZL	Hamilton, NZ	15 Aug 1971
30 miles	2:42:00+	Jeff Norman	GBR	Timperley, Cheshire	7 Jun 1980
50 km	2:48:06	Jeff Norman	GBR	Timperley, Cheshire	7 Jun 1980
40 miles	3:48:35	Don Ritchie	GBR	London (Hendon)	16 Oct 1982
50 miles	4:51:49	Don Ritchie	GBR	London (Hendon)	12 Mar 1983
100 km	6:10:20	Don Ritchie	GBR	London (CP)	28 Oct 1978
150 km	10:34:30	Denis Zhalybin	RUS	London (CP)	20 Oct 2002
100 miles	11:28:03	Oleg Kharitonov	RUS	London (CP)	20 Oct 2002
200 km	15:10:27+	Yiannis Kouros	AUS	Adelaide	4-5 Oct 1997
200 miles	27:48:35	Yiannis Kouros	GRE	Montauban	15-16 Mar 1985
500 km	60:23.00+ ??	Yiannis Kouros	GRE	Colac, Aus	26-29 Nov 1984
500 miles	105:42:09+	Yiannis Kouros	GRE	Colac, Aus	26-30 Nov 1984
1000 km	136:17:00	Yiannis Kouros	GRE	Colac, Aus	26-31 Nov 1984
1500 km	10d 17:28:26	Petrus Silkinas	LTU	Nanango, Qld	11-21 Mar 1998
1000 mile	11d 13:54:58+	Petrus Silkinas	LTU	Nanango, Qld	11-22 Mar 1998
2 hrs	37.994 km	Jim Alder	GBR	Walton-on-Thames	17 Oct 1964
12 hrs	162.400 km +	Yiannis Kouros	GRE	Montauban	15 Mar 1985
24 hrs	303.506 km	Yiannis Kouros	AUS	Adelaide	4-5 Oct 1997
48 hrs	473.797 km	Yiannis Kouros	AUS	Surgères	3-5 May 1996
6 days	1036.8 km	Yiannis Kouros	GRE	Colac, Aus	20-26 Nov 2005

LONG DISTANCE ROAD RECORDS & BESTS – MEN

Where superior to track bests (over 10km) and run on properly measured road courses. (I) IAAF recognition.

10 km (I)	0:26:44	Leonard Patrick Komon	KEN	Utrecht	26 Sep 2010
15 km (I)	0:41:13	Leonard Patrick Komon	KEN	Nijmegen	21 Nov 2010
10 miles	0:44:24 §	Haile Gebrselassie	ETH	Tilburg	4 Sep 2005
	0:44:45	Paul Koech	KEN	Amsterdam-Zaandam	21 Sep 1997
20 km (I)	0:55:21+	Zersenay Tadese	ERI	Lisboa	21 Mar 2010
25 km (I)	1:11:18	Dennis Kimetto	KEN	Berlin	6 May 2012
30 km (I)	1:27:13+	Eliud Kipchoge	KEN	London	24 Apr 2016
	1:27:13+	Stanley Biwott	KEN	London	24 Apr 2016
20 miles	1:35:22+	Steve Jones	GBR	Chicago	10 Oct 1985
30 miles	2:37:31+	Thompson Magawana	RSA	Claremont-Kirstenbosch	2 Apr 1988
50km	2:43:38+	Thompson Magawana	RSA	Claremont-Kirstenbosch	2 Apr 1988
40 miles	3:45:39	Andy Jones	CAN	Houston	23 Feb 1991
50 miles	4:50:21	Bruce Fordyce	RSA	London-Brighton	25 Sep 1983
100 km (I)	6:13:33	Takahiro Sunada	JPN	Yubetsu	21 Jun 1998
200km	15:08:53+	Denis Zhalybin (at 202.5k)	RUS	Sankt-Peterburg	2-3 Sep 2006
500km	58:00:50	Yiannis Kouros	GRE	Colac, AUS	20-23 Nov 2005
1000 miles	10d:10:30:35	Yiannis Kouros	GRE	New York	21-30 May 1988
12 hrs	162.543 km	Yiannis Kouros	GRE	Queen's, New York	7 Nov 1984

LONG DISTANCE WORLD BESTS – WOMEN TRACK

15 km	0:48:54.91+	Dire Tune	ETH	Ostrava	12 Jun 2008
10 miles	0:54:21.8	Lorraine Moller	NZL	Auckland	9 Jan 1993
20 miles	1:59:09 !	Chantal Langlacé	FRA	Amiens	3 Sep 1983
30 miles	3:12:25+	Carolyn Hunter-Rowe	GBR	Barry, Wales	3 Mar 1996
50 km	3:18:52+	Carolyn Hunter-Rowe	GBR	Barry, Wales	3 Mar 1996
40 miles	4:26:43	Carolyn Hunter-Rowe	GBR	Barry, Wales	7 Mar 1993
50 miles	5:48:12.0+	Norimi Sakurai	JPN	San Giovanni Lupatoto	27 Sep 2003
100 km	7:14:05.8	Norimi Sakurai	JPN	San Giovanni Lupatoto	27 Sep 2003
150 km	12:49.23	Mami Kudo	JPN	Soochow	10-11 Dec 2011

100 miles	13:45:49	Gina Slaby	USA	Phoenix	11-12 Dec 2016
200 km	17:52.18+	Mami Kudo	JPN	Soochow	10-11 Dec 2011
200 miles	39:09:03	Hilary Walker	GBR	Blackpool	5-7 Nov 1988
500 km	77:53:46	Eleanor Adams	GBR	Colac, Aus.	13-16 Nov 1989
500 miles	130:59:58+	Sandra Barwick	NZL	Campbelltown, AUS	18-23 Nov 1990
1000 km	8d 00:27:06+	Eleanor Robinson	GBR	Nanango, Qld	11-19 Mar 1998
1500 km	12d 06:52:12+	Eleanor Robinson	GBR	Nanango, Qld	11-23 Mar 1998
1000 miles	13d 02:16:49	Eleanor Robinson	GBR	Nanango, Qld	11-24 Mar 1998
2 hrs	32.652 km	Chantal Langlacé	FRA	Amiens	3 Sep 1983
12 hrs	149.208 km	Camille Herron	USA	Phoenix	10 Dec 2017
24 hours	256,405 km	Courtney Dauwalter	USA	Taipei	3 Dec 2017
48 hrs	385.130 km	Mami Kudo	JPN	Surgères	22-24 May 2010
6 days	883.631 km	Sandra Barwick	NZL	Campbelltown, AUS	18-24 Nov 1990

! Timed on one running watch only

LONG DISTANCE ROAD RECORDS & BESTS - WOMEN

	hr:min:sec	*Name*	*Nat*	*Venue*	*Date*
10 km (l)	0:29:43	Joyciline Jepkosgei	KEN	Praha	9 Sep 2017
15 km (l)	0:45:37	Joyciline Jepkosgei	KEN	Praha	1 Apr 2017
10 miles	0:50:05+	Mary Keitany	KEN	Ra's Al-Khaymah	18 Feb 2011
	0:50:01+ dh	Paula Radcliffe	GBR	Newcastle	21 Sep 2003
20 km (l)	1:01:25	Joyciline Jepkosgei	KEN	Praha	1 Apr 2017
25 km (l)	1:19:53	Mary Keitany	KEN	Berlin	9 May 2010
30 km (l)	1:36:05	Mary Keitany	KEN	London	23 Apr 2017
20 miles	1:43:33+	Paula Radcliffe	GBR	London	13 Apr 2003
30 miles	3:01:16+	Frith van der Merwe	RSA	Claremont-Kirstenbosch	25 Mar 1989
50 km	3:08:39	Frith van der Merwe	RSA	Claremont-Kirstenbosch	25 Mar 1989
40 miles	4:26:13+	Ann Trason	USA	Houston	23 Feb 1991
50 miles	5:40:18	Ann Trason	USA	Houston	23 Feb 1991
100 km (l)	6:33:11	Tomoe Abe	JPN	Yubetsu	25 Jun 2000
100 miles	12:42:39	Camille Herron	USA	Vienna, Illinois	10-11 Nov 2017
200 km	18:45:51	Mami Kudo	JPN	Steenbergen	11-12 May 2013
1000 km	7d 01:11:00+	Sandra Barwick	NZL	New York	16-23 Sep 1991
1000 miles	12d 14:38:40	Sandra Barwick	NZL	New York	16-29 Sep 1991
12 hours	144,840 km	Ann Trason	USA	PQueens, New York	4 May 1991
24 hours	259.991 km	Patrycja Bereznowska	POL	Belfast	1 Jul 2017
48 hrs	401.000k	Patrycja Bereznowska	POL	Athína	26-28 Jan 2018

100 KILOMETRES CONTINENTAL RECORDS

Men

W, Asi	6:13:33	Takahiro SUNADA	JPN	Yubetsu	21 Jun 1998
Eur	6:16:41	Jean-Paul PRAET	BEL	Torhout	24 Jun 1989
SAm	6:18:09	Valmir NUNES	BRA	Winschoten	16 Sep 1995
Afr	6:24:06	Bongmusa MTHEMBU	RSA	Los Alcazares	27 Nov 2016
NAm	6:27:43	Maxwell KING	USA	Doha	21 Nov 2014
Oce	6:29:26	Tim SLOAN	AUS	Ross-Richmond	23 Apr 1995

Women

W, Asi	6:33:11	Tomoe ABE	JPN	Yubetsu	25 Jun 2000
NAm	7:00:48	Ann TRASON	USA	Winschoten	16 Sep 1995
Eur	7:10:32	Tatyana ZHYRKOVA	RUS	Winschoten	11 Sep 2004
SAm	7:20:22	Maria VENÂNCIO	BRA	Cubatão	8 Aug 1998
Afr	7:31:47	Helena JOUBERT	RSA	Winschoten	16 Sep 1995
Oce	7:34:35	Kirstin BULL	AUS	Los Alcazares	27 Nov 2016

WORLD INDOOR RECORDS

Men

50 metres	5.56A	Donovan Bailey	CAN	Reno	9 Feb 1996
60 metres	6.34A	Christian Coleman	USA	Albuquerque	18 Feb 2018
100 metres	9.98	Usain Bolt	JAM	Warszawa	23 Aug 2014
200 metres	19.92	Frank Fredericks	NAM	Liévin	18 Feb 1996
400 metres	44.52	Michael Norman	USA	College Station	10 Mar 2018
800 metres	1:42.67	Wilson Kipketer	KEN	Paris (Bercy)	9 Mar 1997
1000 metres	2:14.20	Ayanleh Souleiman	DJI	Stockholm	17 Feb 2016
1500 metres	3:31.18	Hicham El Guerrouj	MAR	Stuttgart	2 Feb 1997
1 mile	3:48.45	Hicham El Guerrouj	MAR	Gent	12 Feb 1997
2000 metres #	4:49.99	Kenenisa Bekele	ETH	Birmingham	17 Feb 2007
3000 metres	7:24.90	Daniel Komen	KEN	Budapest	6 Feb 1998
2 miles #	8:04.35	Kenenisa Bekele	ETH	Birmingham	16 Feb 2008
5000 metres	12:49.60	Kenenisa Bekele	ETH	Birmingham	20 Feb 2004

10000 metres #	27:50.29	Mark Bett	KEN	Gent	10 Feb 2002
50 m hurdles	6.25	Mark McKoy	CAN	Kobe	5 Mar 1986
60 m hurdles	7.30	Colin Jackson	GBR	Sindelfingen	6 Mar 1994
110 m hurdles	13.03	Orlando Ortega	CUB	Warszawa	23 Aug 2014
High jump	2.43	Javier Sotomayor	CUB	Budapest	4 Mar 1989
Pole vault	6.16	Renaud Lavillenie	FRA	Donetsk	15 Feb 2014
Long jump	8.79	Carl Lewis	USA	New York	27 Jan 1984
Triple jump	17.92	Teddy Tamgho	FRA	Paris (Bercy)	6 Mar 2011
Shot	22.66	Randy Barnes	USA	Los Angeles	20 Jan 1989
Javelin #	85.78	Matti Närhi	FIN	Kajaani	3 Mar 1996
35 lb weight #	25.86	Lance Deal	USA	Atlanta	4 Mar 1995
3000m walk #	10:30.28	Tom Bosworth	GBR	Glasgow	25 Feb 2018
5000m walk	18:07.08	Mikhail Shchennikov	RUS	Moskva	14 Feb 1995
10000m walk #	38:31.4	Werner Heyer	GDR	Berlin	12 Jan 1980
4 x 200m	1:22.11	United Kingdom		Glasgow	3 Mar 1991
		(Linford Christie, Darren Braithwaite, Ade Mafe, John Regis)			
4 x 400m	3:01.39	USA (Texas A&M University)		College Station	10 Mar 2018
		(Ilolo Izu, Robert Grant, Devin Dixon, Mylik Kerley)			
4 x 800m	7:11.30	USA (Hoka New Jersey/New York TC)		Boston (Allston)	25 Feb 2018
		(Joe McAsey, Kyle Merber, Chris Giesting, Jesse Garn)			
Distance Med	9:19.93	USA		New York (Armory)	31 Jan 2015
		(Matthew Centrowitz, Mike Berry, Erik Sowinski, Pat Casey)			
Heptathlon	6645 points	Ashton Eaton	USA	Istanbul	9/10 Mar 2012
		(6.79 60m, 8.16 LJ, 14.56 SP, 2.03 HJ, 7.68 60mh, 5.20 PV, 2:32.77 1000m)			

Women

50 metres	5.96+	Irina Privalova	RUS	Madrid	9 Feb 1995
60 metres	6.92	Irina Privalova	RUS	Madrid	11 Feb 1993 & 9 Feb 1995
200 metres	21.87	Merlene Ottey	JAM	Liévin	13 Feb 1993
400 metres	49.59	Jarmila Kratochvílová	CZE	Milano	7 Mar 1982
800 metres	1:55.82	Jolanda Ceplak	SLO	Wien	3 Mar 2002
1000 metres	2:30.94	Maria Lurdes Mutola	MOZ	Stockholm	25 Feb 1999
1500 metres	3:55.17	Genzebe Dibaba	ETH	Karlsruhe	1 Feb 2014
1 mile	4:13.31	Genzebe Dibaba	ETH	Stockholm	17 Feb 2016
2000 metres #	5:23.75	Genzebe Dibaba	ETH	Sabadell	7 Feb 2017
3000 metres	8:16.60	Genzebe Dibaba	ETH	Stockholm	6 Feb 2014
2 miles #	9:00.48	Genzebe Dibaba	ETH	Birmingham	15 Feb 2014
5000 metres	14:18.86	Genzebe Dibaba	ETH	Stockholm	19 Feb 2015
50 m hurdles	6.58	Cornelia Oschkenat	GDR	Berlin	20 Feb 1988
60 m hurdles	7.68	Susanna Kallur	SWE	Karlsruhe	10 Feb 2008
100 m hurdles	12.64	Ludmila Engquist	SWE	Tampere	10 Feb 1997
High jump	2.08	Kajsa Bergqvist	SWE	Arnstadt	4 Feb 2006
Pole vault	5.03	Jenn Suhr	USA	Brockport	30 Jan 2016
Long jump	7.37	Heike Drechsler	GDR	Wien	13 Feb 1988
Triple jump	15.36	Tatyana Lebedeva	RUS	Budapest	5 Mar 2004
Shot	22.50	Helena Fibingerová	CZE	Jablonec	19 Feb 1977
Javelin #	61.29	Taina Uppa/Kolkkala	FIN	Mustasaari	28 Feb 1999
20 lb weight #	25.60	Gwen Berry	USA	Albuquerque	4 Mar 2017
3000m walk	11:35.34 un	Gillian O'Sullivan	IRL	Belfast	15 Feb 2003
	11:40.33	Claudia Iovan/Stef	ROU	Bucuresti	30 Jan 1999
5000m walk #	20:37.77	Margarita Turova	BLR	Minsk	13 Feb 2005
10000m walk	43:54.63	Yelena Ginko	BLR	Mogilyov	22 Feb 2008
4 x 200m	1:32.41	Russia		Glasgow	29 Jan 2005
		(Yekaterina Kondratyeva, Irina Khabarova, Yuliya Pechonkina, Yuliya Gushchina)			
4 x 400m	3:23.37	Russia		Glasgow	28 Jan 2006
		(Yuliya Gushchina, Olga Kotlyarova, Olga Zaytseva, Olesya Krasnomovets)			
4 x 800m	8:05.89		USA	New York (Armory)	3 Feb 2018
		(Chrishuna Williams, Raevyn Rogers, Charlene Lipsey, Ajee' Wilson)			
Distance Med	10:42.57	Newa Balance TC	USA	Boston(Roxbury)	7 Feb 2015
		(Sarah Brown, Mahogany Jones, Megan Krumpoch, Brenda Martinez)			
Pentathlon	5013 points	Nataliya Dobrynska	UKR	Istanbul	9 Mar 2012
		(8.38 60mh, 1.84 HJ, 16.51 SP, 6.57 LJ, 2:11.15 800m)			

events not officially recognised by the IAAF

WORLD INDOOR JUNIOR (U20) RECORDS

First approved by IAAF Council in 2011. **Men**

60 metres	6.51	Mark Lewis-Francis	GBR	Lisboa	11 Mar 2001
200 metres	20.37	Walter Dix	USA	Fayetteville	11 Mar 2005
400 metres	44.80	Kirani James	GRN	Fayetteville	27 Feb 2011
800 metres	1:44.35	Yuriy Borzakovskiy	RUS	Dortmund	30 Jan 2000
1000 metres	2:15.77	Abubaker Kaki	SUD	Stockholm	21 Feb 2008

1500 metres	3:36.05 §	Samuel Tefera	ETH	Val-de-Reuil	27 Jan 2018
One mile	3:55.02	German Fernandez	USA	College Station	28 Feb 2009
3000 metres	7:32.87	Hagos Gebrhiwet	ETH	Boston (Roxbury)	2 Feb 2013
5000 metres	12:53.29	Isiah Koech	KEN	Düsseldorf	11 Feb 2011
60mh (99cm)	7.40	Trey Cunningham	USA	New York (Armory)	12 Mar 2017
High jump	2.35	Volodymyr Yashchenko	URS	Milano	12 Mar 1978
Pole vault	5.88	Armand Duplantis	SWE	Clermont-Ferrand	25 Feb 2018
Long jump	8.22	Viktor Kuznetsov	UKR	Brovary	22 Jan 2005
Triple jump	17.20	Melvin Raffin	FRA	Belgrade	3 Mar 2017
Shot (6kg)	22.48	Konrad Bukowiecki	POL	Torun	8 Jan 2016
Heptathlon	6022	Gunnar Nixon	USA	Fayetteville	27/28 Jan 2012
(jnr imps)		(7.10, 7.53, 13.97, 2.15, 8.21, 4.50, 2:40.15)			
Women					
60 metres	7.07	Ewa Swoboda	POL	Torun	12 Feb 2016
200 metres	22.40	Bianca Knight	USA	Fayetteville	14 Mar 2008
400 metres	50.36	Sydney McLaughlin	USA	Colleger Station	10 Mar 2018
800 metres	2:01.03	Meskerem Legesse	ETH	Fayetteville	14 Feb 2004
1000 metres	2:35.80	Mary Cain	USA	Boston (Roxbury)	8 Feb 2014
1500 metres	4:01.81	Gudaf Tsegay	ETH	Glasgow	20 Feb 2016
One mile	4:24.10	Kalkidan Gezahegne	ETH	Birmingham	20 Feb 2010
3000 metres	8:33.56	Tirunesh Dibaba	ETH	Birmingham	20 Feb 2004
5000 metres	14:53.99	Tirunesh Dibaba	ETH	Boston	31 Jan 2004
60m hurdles	7.98	Tara Davis	USA	College Station	10 Mar 2018
High jump	1.99	Vashti Cunningham	USA	Portland	12 Mar 2016
Pole vault	4.71	Wilma Murto	FIN	Zweibrücken	31 Jan 2016
Long jump	6.88	Heike Daute	GDR	Berlin	1 Feb 1983
Triple jump	14.37	Ren Ruiping	CHN	Barcelona	11 Mar 1995
Shot	20.51	Heidi Krieger	GDR	Budapest	8 Feb 1984
Pentathlon	4635A	Kendell Williams	USA	Albuquerque	15 Mar 2014
		(8.21, 1.88, 12.05, 6.32, 2:17.31)			
	4550 §	Alina Shukh	UKR	Zaporizhzhya	27 Jan 2017
		(8.85, 1.88, 14.27, 6.04, 2:17.69)			

WORLD VETERANS/MASTERS RECORDS

MEN – aged 35-39

100 metres	9.92	Justin Gatlin (10.2.92)	USA	London (OS)	5 Aug 2017
200 metres	20.11	Linford Christie (2.4.60)	GBR	Villeneuve d'Ascq	25 Jun 1995
400 metres	44.54	Chris Brown (15.10.78)	BAH	Eugene	30 May 2015
800 metres	1:43.36	Johnny Gray (19.6.60)	USA	Zürich	16 Aug 1995
1000 metres	2:18.8+	William Tanui (22.2.64)	KEN	Rome	7 Jul 1999
1500 metres	3:32.45	William Tanui (22.2.64)	KEN	Athína	16 Jun 1999
1 mile	3:51.38	Bernard Lagat (12.12.74)	USA	London (CP)	6 Aug 2011
2000 metres	4:58.3+ e	William Tanui (22.2.64	KEN	Monaco	4 Aug 1999
	4:54.74i	Bernard Lagat (12.12.74)	USA	New York	15 Feb 2014
3000 metres	7:29.00	Bernard Lagat (12.12.74)	USA	Rieti	29 Aug 2010
5000 metres	12:53.60	Bernard Lagat (12.12.74)	USA	Monaco	22 Jul 2011
10000 metres	26:51.20	Haile Gebrselassie (18.4.73)	ETH	Hengelo	24 May 2008
20000 metres	57:44.4+	Gaston Roelants (5.2.37)	BEL	Bruxelles	20 Sep 1972
1 Hour	20,822m	Haile Gebrselassie (18.4.73)	ETH	Hengelo	1 Jun 2009
Half Marathon	59:10 dh	Paul Tergat (17.6.69)	KEN	Lisboa	13 Mar 2005
	59:31	Gilbert Masai (20.5.81)	KEN	København	18 Sep 2016
Marathon	2:03:59	Haile Gebrselassie (18.4.73)	ETH	Berlin	28 Sep 2008
3000m steeple	8:04.95	Simon Vroemen (11.5.69)	NED	Bruxelles	26 Aug 2005
110m hurdles	12.96	Allen Johnson (1.3.71)	USA	Athína	17 Sep 2006
400m hurdles	48.10	Felix Sánchez (30.8.77)	DOM	Moskva	13 Aug 2013
High jump	2.31	Dragutin Topic (12.3.71)	SRB	Kragujevac	28 Jul 2009
	2.31	Jamie Nieto (2.11.76)	USA	New York	9 Jun 2012
Pole vault	5.90i	Björn Otto (16.10.77)	GER	Cottbus	30 Jan 2013
	5.90i	Björn Otto		Düsseldorf	8 Feb 2013
	5.90	Björn Otto		Eugene	1 Jun 2013
Long jump	8.50	Larry Myricks (10.3.56)	USA	New York	15 Jun 1991
	8.50	Carl Lewis (1.7.61)	USA	Atlanta	29 Jul 1996
Triple jump	17.92	Jonathan Edwards (10.5.66)	GBR	Edmonton	6 Aug 2001
Shot	22.67	Kevin Toth ¶ (29.12.67)	USA	Lawrence	19 Apr 2003
Discus	71.56	Virgilijus Alekna (13.2.72)	LTU	Kaunas	25 Jul 2007
Hammer	83.62	Igor Astapkovich (4.1.63)	BLR	Staiki	20 Jun 1998
Javelin	92.80	Jan Zelezny (16.6.66)	CZE	Edmonton	12 Aug 2001
Decathlon	8241	Kip Janvrin (8.7.65)	USA	Eugene	22 Jun 2001
		(10.98, 7.01, 14.21, 1.89, 48.41, 14.72, 45.59, 5.20, 60.41, 4:14.96)			
20 km walk	1:17:02	Yohann Diniz (1.1.78)	FRA	Arles	8 Mar 2015

20000m t walk	1:19:42.1	Yohann Diniz (1.1.78)	FRA	Bogny-sur-Meuse	25 May 2014
50 km walk	3:32:33	Yohann Diniz (1.1.78)	FRA	Zürich	15 Aug 2014
50000m t walk	3:49:29.7	Alain Lemercier (11.1.57)	FRA	Franconville	3 Apr 1994

MEN – aged 40 or over

100 metres	9.93	Kim Collins (5.4.76)	SKN	Bottrop	29 May 2016
200 metres	20.64	Troy Douglas (30.11.62)	NED	Utrecht	9 Aug 2003
400 metres	46.96	Sandro Viana ((26.3.77)	BRA	São Bernardo do Campo	1 Jul 2017
800 metres	1:48.05	Anthony Whiteman (13.11.71)	GBR	Manchester (Stretford)	12 Jul 2014
1000 metres	2:24.93i	Vyacheslav Shabunin (27.9.69)	RUS	Moskva	10 Jan 2010
1500 metres	3:40.20i+	Bernard Lagat (12.12.74)	USA	New York (Armory)	14 Feb 2015
	3:41.87	Bernard Lagat		Birmingham	7 Jun 2015
1 mile	3:54.91i+	Bernard Lagat		New York (Armory)	14 Feb 2015
	3:57.91	Bernard Lagat		London (OS)	25 Jul 2015
3000 metres	7:37.92i+	Bernard Lagat (12.12.74)	USA	Metz	25 Feb 2015
	7:42.75	Bernard Lagat		Luzern	14 Jul 2015
5000 metres	13:06.78	Bernard Lagat		Rio de Janeiro	20 Aug 2016
10000 metres	27:49.35	Bernard Lagat		Stanford	1 May 2016
10 km road	27:48	Bernard Lagat (12.12.74)	USA	Manchester	10 May 2015
1 Hour	19.710k	Steve Moneghetti (26.9.62)	AUS	Geelong	17 Dec 2005
Half marathon	60:41 dh	Haile Gebrselassie (18.4.73)	ETH	South Shields	15 Sep 2013
	61:04	Mark Kiptoo KEN (21.6.76)	KEN	Azpeitia	24 Mar 2016
Marathon	2:08:38	Kenneth Mungara KEN (7.9.73)	KEN	Milano	3 Apr 2016
3000m steeple	8:38.40	Angelo Carosi (20.1.64)	ITA	Firenze	11 Jul 2004
110m hurdles	13.97	David Ashford (24.1.63)	USA	Indianapolis	3 Jul 2004
	13.79 ?	Roger Kingdom (26.8.62)	USA	Slippery Rock	23 Jun 2004
400m hurdles	49.69	Danny McFarlane (14.2.72)	JAM	Kingston	29 Jun 2012
High jump	2.28	Dragutin Topic (12.3.71)	SRB	Beograd	20 May 2012
Pole vault	5.71i	Jeff Hartwig (25.9.67)	USA	Jonesboro	31 May 2008
	5.70	Jeff Hartwig		Eugene	29 Jun 2008
Long jump	7.68A	Aaron Sampson (20.9.61)	USA	Cedar City, UT	21 Jun 2002
	7.59i	Mattias Sunneborn (27.9.70)	SWE	Sätra	3 Feb 2013
	7.57	Hans Schicker (3.10.47)	FRG	Kitzingen	16 Jul 1989
Triple jump	17.32	Fabrizio Donato (14.8.76	ITA	Pierre=Bénite	9 Jun 2017
Shot	21.41	Brian Oldfield USA (1.6.45)	USA	Innsbruck	22 Aug 1985
Discus	70.28	Virgilijus Alekna (13.2.72)	LTU	Klaipeda	23 Jun 2012
Hammer	82.23	Igor Astapkovich (4.1.63)	BLR	Minsk	10 Jul 2004
Javelin	85.92	Jan Zelezny (16.6.66)	CZE	Göteborg	9 Aug 2006
Pentathlon	3510	Werner Schallau (8.9.38)	FRG	Gelsenkirchen	24 Sep 1978
		6.74, 59.20, 23.0, 43.76, 5:05.7			
Decathlon	7525	Kip Janvrin (8.7.65)	USA	San Sebastián	24 Aug 2005
		11.56, 6.78, 14.01, 1.80, 49.46, 15.40, 42.70, 4.70, 58.43, 4:25.87			
20 km walk	1:20:20	Andriy Kovenko (25.11.73)	UKR	Alushta	28 Feb 2014
20000m t walk	1:24:46.1	Ivan Trotskiy (27.5.76)	BLR	Grodno	23 Jun 2016
50 km walk	3:40:46	Yuriy Andronov (6.11.71)	RUS	Moskva	11 Jun 2012
50000m t walk	3:51:54.5	José Marín (21.1.50)	ESP	Manresa	7 Apr 1990
4x100m	42.20	SpeedWest TC	USA	Irvine	2 May 2004
		(Frank Strong, Cornell Stephenson, Kettrell Berry, Willie Gault)			
4x400m	3:20.83	S Allah, K Morning, E Gonera, R Blackwell	USA	Philadelphia	27 Apr 2001

WOMEN – aged 35-39

100 metres	10.74	Merlene Ottey (10.5.60)	JAM	Milano	7 Sep 1996
200 metres	21.93	Merlene Ottey (10.5.60)	JAM	Bruxelles	25 Aug 1995
400 metres	50.14	Novlene Williams-Mills (26.4.82)	JAM	Kingston	25 Jun 2017
800 metres	1:56.53	Lyubov Gurina (6.8.57)	RUS	Hechtel	30 Jul 1994
1000 metres	2:31.5	Maricica Puica (29.7.50)	ROU	Poiana Brasov	1 Jun 1986
1500 metres	3:57.73	Maricica Puica (29.7.50)	ROU	Bruxelles	30 Aug 1985
1 mile	4:17.33	Maricica Puica (29.7.50)	ROU	Zürich	21 Aug 1985
2000 metres	5:28.69	Maricica Puica (29.7.50)	ROU	London (CP)	11 Jul 1986
3000 metres	8:23.23	Edith Masai (4.4.67)	KEN	Monaco	19 Jul 2002
5000 metres	14:33.84	Edith Masai (4.4.67)	KEN	Oslo	2 Jun 2006
10000 metres	30:30.26	Edith Masai (4.4.67)	KEN	Helsinki	6 Aug 2005
Half Marathon	65:13	Mary Keitany (18.1.82)	KEN	Ra's Al-Khaymah	10 Feb 2017
Marathon	2:17:01	Mary Keitany (18.1.82)	KEN	London	23 Apr 2017
3000m steeple	9:24.26	Marta Domínguez (3.11.75)	ESP	Huelva	7 Jun 2012
100m hurdles	12.40	Gail Devers (19.11.66)	USA	Lausanne	2 Jul 2002
400m hurdles	52.94	Marina Styepanova (1.5.50)	RUS	Tashkent	17 Sep 1986
High jump	2.01	Inga Babakova (27.6.67)	UKR	Oslo	27 Jun 2003
	2.01	Ruth Beitia (1.4.79)	ESP	Zürich	17 Aug 2014
Pole vault	4.87	Fabiana Murer (16,3,81)	BRA	São Bernardo do Campo	3 Jul 2016
Long jump	6.99	Heike Drechsler (16.12.64)	GER	Sydney	29 Sep 2000
Triple jump	14.68	Tatyana Lebedeva (21.7.76)	RUS	Cheboksary	3 Jul 2012

	14.82i	Yamilé Aldama (14.8.72)	GBR	Istanbul	10 Mar 2012
Shot	21.46	Larisa Peleshenko (29.2.64)	RUS	Moskva	26 Aug 2000
	21.47i	Helena Fibingerová (13.7.49)	CZE	Jablonec	9 Feb 1985
Discus	69.60	Faina Melnik (9.6.45)	RUS	Donetsk	9 Sep 1980
Hammer	74.03	Amber Campbell (5.6.81)	USA	Eugene	6 Jul 2016
Javelin	68.34	Steffi Nerius (1.7.72)	GER	Berlin (Elstal)	31 Aug 2008
Heptathlon	6533	Jane Frederick (7.4.52)	USA	Talence	27 Sep 1987
		13.60, 1.82, 15.50, 24.73; 6.29, 49.70, 2:14.88			
5000m walk	20:12.41	Elisabetta Perrone (9.7.68)	ITA	Rieti	2 Aug 2003
10km walk	41:41	Kjersti Tysse Plätzer (18.1.72)	NOR	Kraków	30 May 2009
10000m t walk	43:26.5	Elisabetta Perrone (9.7.68)	ITA	Saluzzo	4 Aug 2004
20km walk	1:25:59	Tamara Kovalenko (5.6.64)	RUS	Moskva	19 May 2000
20000m t walk	1:27:49.3	Yelena Nikolayeva (1.2.66)	RUS	Brisbane	6 Sep 2001
50km walk	4:05:56	Inês Henriques (1.5.80)	POR	London	13 Aug 2017
4x100m	47.65	Stafford, Springer, Hutchinson, Baird	TTO	Lyon	16 Aug 2015
4x400m	3:50.80	Mitchell, Mathews, Beadnall, Gabriel	GBR	Gateshead	8 Aug 1999

WOMEN – aged 40 or over

100 metres	10.99	Merlene Ottey (10.5.60)	JAM	Thessaloniki	30 Aug 2000
200 metres	22.72	Merlene Ottey (10.5.60)	SLO	Athína	23 Aug 2004
400 metres	53.05A	María Figueirêdo (11.11.63)	BRA	Bogotá	10 Jul 2004
	53.14	María Figueirêdo (11.11.63)	BRA	San Carlos, VEN	19 Jun 2004
800 metres	1:59.25	Yekaterina Podkopayeva (11.6.52)	RUS	Luxembourg	30 Jun 1994
1000 metres	2:36.16	Yekaterina Podkopayeva (11.6.52)	RUS	Nancy	14 Sep 1994
	2:36.08i	Yekaterina Podkopayeva	RUS	Liévin	13 Feb 1993
1500 metres	3:59.78	Yekaterina Podkopayeva (11.6.52)	RUS	Nice	18 Jul 1994
1 mile	4:23.78	Yekaterina Podkopayeva (11.6.52)	RUS	Roma	9 Jun 1993
3000 metres	9:01.1+	Jo Pavey (20.9.73)	GBR	Roma	5 Jun 2014
	8:58.20i	Nuria Fernández (16.8.76)	ESP	Beograd	3 Mar 2017
5000 metres	15:04.87	Jo Pavey (20.9.73)	GBR	Roma	5 Jun 2014
10000 metres	31:31.18	Edith Masai (4.4.67)	KEN	Alger	21 Jul 2007
1 hour	16.056k	Jackie Fairweather (10.11.67)	AUS	Canberra	24 Jan 2008
Half Marathon	69:37	Deena Kastor (14.2.73)	USA	Philadephia	21 Sep 2014
Marathon	2:23:31	Lydia Cheromei (11.5.77)	KEN	Shanghai	12 Nov 2017
3000m steeple	10:00.75	Minori Hayakari (29.11.72)	JPN	Kumagaya	22 Sep 2013
100 m hurdles	13.20	Patricia Girard (8.4.68)	FRA	Paris	14 Jul 2008
400 m hurdles	58.35	Barbara Gähling (20.1.65)	GER	Erfurt	21 Jul 2007
	58.3 h	Gowry Retchakan (21.6.60)	GBR	Hoo	3 Sep 2000
High jump	1.94i	Venelina Veneva-Mateeva (13.6.74)	BUL	Dobrich 15 Feb & Praha	6 Mar 2015
	1.90	Venelina Veneva-Mateeva	BUL	Plovdiv 12 Jul & Pitesti	27 Jul 2014
Pole vault	4.10	Doris Auer (10.5.71)	AUT	Innsbruck	6 Aug 2011
	4.11 §	Doris Auer	AUT	Wien	5 Jul 2011
Long jump	6.64	Tatyana Ter-Mesrobian (12.5.68)	RUS	Sankt-Peterburg	31 May 2008
	6.64i	Tatyana Ter-Mesrobian	RUS	Sankt-Peterburg	5 Jan 2010
Triple jump	14.06	Yamilé Aldama (14.8.72)	GBR	Eugene	1 Jun 2013
Shot	19.05	Antonina Ivanova (25.12.32)	RUS	Oryol	28 Aug 1973
	19.16i	Antonina Ivanova	RUS	Moskva	24 Feb 1974
Discus	67.89	Iryna Yatchenko (31.10.65)	BLR	Staiki	29 Jun 2008
Hammer	67.57	Iryna Sekachyova (21.7.76)	UKR	Kyiv	14 Jun 2017
Javelin	61.96	Laverne Eve (16.6.65)	BAH	Monaco	9 Sep 2005
Heptathlon	5449	Tatyana Alisevich (22.1.69)	BLR	Staiki	3 Jun 2010
		14.80, 1.62, 13.92, 26.18, 5.55, 45.44, 2:24.39			
5000m walk	21:46.68	Kelly Ruddick (19.4.73)	AUS	Brisbane	29 Mar 2014
10000m t walk	44:50.19	Susana Feitor (28.1.75)	POR	Leiria	25 Jul 2015
20km walk	1:31:58	Susana Feitor		Rio Maior	18 Apr 2015
	1:31:58	Susana Feitor		Murcia	17 May 2015
20000m t walk	1:33:28.15t	Teresa Vaill (20.11.62)	USA	Carson	25 Jun 2005
50km walk	4:54:12	Susan Randall (6.9.74)	USA	Santee	28 Jan 2017
4x100m	48.01	Mogentale, Brims, Bezuidenhout, Strong	AUS	Lahti	8 Aug 2009
4x400m	3:56.28	Roberts, Henderson, Brooker, Clark	USA	Philadelphia	25 Apr 2008

WORLD AND CONTINENTAL RECORDS SET IN 2017

OUTDOORS – MEN

§ Not ratified

1100	W18	10.15	Anthony SCHWARTZ	USA	Gainesville	31 Mar 17
	W35	9.92	Justin GATLIN	USA	London (OS)	5 Aug 17
300	W, Afr	30.81	Wayde van NIEKERK	RSA	Ostrava	28 Jun 17
	W20	31.61	Clarence MUNYAI	RSA	Ostrava	28 Jun 17
400	W40	46.96	Sandro VIANA	BRA	São Bernardo do Campo	1 Jul 17
1M	CAC	3:56.13	Daniel HERRERA	MEX	Concord, MA	1 Jun 17
15k	W20	42:00	Mathew KIMELI	KEN	Le Puy-en-Velay	1 May 17
	Asi	41:53+	Abraham CHEROBEN	BRN	København	17 Sep 17

20k	Oce	56:38	Zane ROBERTSON	NZL	Lisboa	19 Mar 17
	Asi	55:51+	Abraham CHEROBEN	BRN	København	17 Sep 17
HMar	Asi	58:40	Abraham CHEROBEN	BRN	København	17 Sep 17
Mar	Eur	2:05:48	Sondre Nordstad MOEN	NOR	Fukuoka	3 Dec 17
3000mSt	W18	8:12.28	Getnet WALE	ETH	Hengelo	11 Jun 17
110mh	Afr	13.11	Antonio ALKANA	RSA	Praha	5 Jun 17
	Com	12.90	Omar McLEOD	JAM	Kingston	24 Jun 17
200mh	W, Asi=	22.55	Yoshiro WATANABE	JPN	Izumi	1 Oct 17
400mh/84	W18	48.84A	Sokwakhana ZAZINI	RSA	Pretoria	17 Mar 17
HJ (in Dec)	W	2.28)	Derek DROUIN (in 7150 Dec)	CAN	Santa Barbara	8 Apr 17
PV	W20	5.80 & 5.90	Armand DUPLANTIS	SWE	Austin	1 Apr 17
LJ	Afr, Com	8.62A	Luvo MANYONGA	RSA	Pretoria	17 Mar 17
	Afr, Com	8.65A	Luvo MANYONGA	RSA	Potchefstroom	22 Apr 17
TJ	W40	17.32	Fabrizio DONATO	ITA	Pierre-Bénite	9 Jun 17
	W18	17.30A	Jordan A. DÍAZ	CUB	Nairobi	14 Jul 17
SP	SAm	21.82	Darlan ROMANI	BRA	São Bernardo do Campo	3 Jun 17
	CAC	21.96	O'Dayne RICHARDS	JAM	Rabat	16 Jul 17
JT	Asi	91.36	CHENG Chao-Tsun	TPE	Taipei	26 Aug 17
Dec U20	W20	8435	Niklas KAUL	GER	Grosseto	23 Jul 17
		(11.48, 7.20, 15.37, 2.05, 48.42 / 14.55, 48.49, 4.70, 68.05, 4:15.52)				
4x100 R	W18	39.97	Everett, Wilson, Powell, Stephens	JAM	Willemstad	16 Apr 17
	Eur	37.47	Ujah, Gemili, Talbot, Mitchell-Blake	GBR	London (OS)	12 Aug 17
4x400 R	W20	3:00.33	Schinnick, Lyles, Herron, Hooper	USA	Trujillo	23 Jul 17
1M Walk	W	5:31.08	Tom BOSWORTH	GBR	London (OS)	9 Jul 17

Under exceptional conditions, ineligible for ratification

25k	W, Afr	1:11:03+ §	Eliud KIPCHOGE	KEN	Monza	6 May 17
30k	W, Afr	1:25:20+ §	Eliud KIPCHOGE	KEN	Monza	6 May 17
Mar	W, Afr	2:00:25 §	Eliud KIPCHOGE	KEN	Monza	6 May 17

OUTDOORS – WOMEN

100	SAm	10.91	Rosângela SANTOS	BRA	London (OS)	6 Aug 17
300	Eur=	35.70	Lea SPRUNGER	SUI	Langenthal	25 May 17
400	W35	50.14	Novlene WILLIAMS-MILLS	JAM	Kingston	25 Jun 17
600	W, Afr	1:21.77	Caster SEMENYA	RSA	Berlin	27 Aug 17
800	NAm	1:55.61	Ajee' WILSON	USA	Monaco	21 Jul 17
1M	Com	4:16.56	Hellen OBIRI	KEN	London (OS)	9 Jul 17
5000	Com	14:18.37	Hellen OBIRI	KEN	Roma	8 Jun 17
10k	W	30:04+	Joyciline JEPKOSGEI	KEN	Praha	1 Apr 17
	Asi	30:05+	Violah JEPCHUMBA	BRN	Praha	1 Apr 17
	W	29:43	Joyciline JEPKOSGEI	KEN	Praha	9 Sep 17
15k	W35	46:30+	Mary KEITANY	KEN	Ra's Al-Khaymah	10 Feb 17
	W	45:37+	Joyciline JEPKOSGEI	KEN	Praha	1 Apr 17
	Asi	45:40+	Violah JEPCHUMBA	BRN	Praha	1 Apr 17
20k	W	61:40+	Peres JEPCHIRCHIR	KEN	Ra's Al-Khaymah	10 Feb 17
	W	61:25+	Joyciline JEPKOSGEI	KEN	Praha	1 Apr 17
	Asi	61:50+	Violah JEPCHUMBA	BRN	Praha	1 Apr 17
HMar	W,Afr,Com	65:06	Peres JEPCHIRCHIR	KEN	Ra's Al-Khaymah	10 Feb 17
	W35	65:13	Mary KEITANY	KEN	Ra's Al-Khaymah	10 Feb 17
	W,Afr,Com	64:52	Joyciline JEPKOSGEI	KEN	Praha	1 Apr 17
	Asi	65:22	Violah JEPCHUMBA	BRN	Praha	1 Apr 17
	W,Afr,Com	64:51	Joyciline JEPKOSGEI	KEN	Valencia	22 Oct 17
25k	NAm	1:22:19+	Jordan HASAY	USA	Chicago	8 Oct 17
25k downhill	W, W35	1:19:43+	Mary KEITANY	KEN	London	23 Apr 17
30k	W40	1:42:09+	Lucy KARIMI	KEN	Rotterdam	9 Apr 17
	W, W35	1:36:05+	Mary KEITANY	KEN	London	23 Apr 17
	NAm	1:39:11+	Jordan HASAY	USA	Chicago	8 Oct 17
Mar	W,Afr,W35	2:17:01 (Mx)	Mary KEITANY	KEN	London	23 Apr 17
	W40	2:23:31	Lydia CHEROMEI	KEN	Shanghai	12 Nov 17
100M	W, NAm	12:42:39	Camille HERRON	USA	Vienna, USA	11 Nov 17
12Hr	W, NAm	149.208k	Camille HERRON	USA	Phoenix	10 Dec 17
24Hr Rd	W	256.246k	Patrycja BEREZNOWSKA	POL	Lódz	9 Apr 17
road	W	259.991k	Patrycja BEREZNOWSKA	POL	Belfast	2 Jul 17
track	W	256.405k	Courtney DAUWALTER	USA	Taipei	3 Dec 17
3000mSt	W20	9:05.70	Celliphine CHESPOL	KEN	Doha	5 May 17
	CAC	9:19.29	Aisha PRAUGHT-LEER	JAM	Doha	5 May 17
	Afr,Com,W20	8:58.78	Celliphine CHESPOL	KEN	Eugene	26 May 17
	SAm	9:35.78	Belém CASETTA	ARG	London (OS)	9 Aug 17
	NAm	9:02.58	Emma COBURN	USA	London (OS)	11 Aug 17
	SAm	9:25.99	Belén CASETTA	ARG	London (OS)	11 Aug 17
200mh	W=	25.79	Lauren WELLS	AUS	Canberra	21 Jan 17

Event	Record	Mark	Athlete	Nat	Venue	Date
400mh	SAm	55.76	Gianna WOODRUFF	PAN	Tucson	20 May 17
	W20	54.03	Sydney McLAUGHLIN	USA	Egg Harbor	2 Jun 17
	W20	53.82	Sydney McLAUGHLIN	USA	Sacramento	25 Jun 17
PV	Oce, Com	4.82	Eliza McCARTNEY	NZL	Auckland (NS)	26 Feb 17
DT	SAm	64.68	Andressa de MORAIS	BRA	Asunción	23 Jun 17
	Oce, Com	69.64	Dani STEVENS	AUS	London (OS)	13 Aug 17
HT	NAm	76.77	Gwen BERRY	USA	Oxford, USA	6 May 17
	W40	65.08	Iryna SEKACHYOVA	UKR	Koncha-Zaspa	21 May 17
	W40	65.87 & 67.57	Iryna SEKACHYOVA	UKR	Kyiv	14 Jun 17
JT/500	W18	65.44	Marisleisys DUARTHE	CUB	La Habana	25 May 17
JT	Asi	66.47	LIU Shiying	CHN	Kawasaki	21 May 17
	Asi	67.59	LU Huihui	CHN	London (OS)	6 Aug 17
Hep	CAC	6594	Yorgelis RODRIGUEZ	CUB	London (OS)	6 Aug 17
		(13.60, 1.95, 13.45, 24.42 / 6.23, 47.41, 2:10.48)				
4x100 R	W20	43.27	Fehm, Kwadwo, Junk, Montag	GER	Grosseto	23 Jul 17
4x200 R	CAC,Com	1:29.04	Levy, Jackson, Forbes, Thompson	JAM	Nassau	22 Apr 17
	Asi	1:33.99	Tao Xijia, Zhou Yanbing, Tian Wen, Wei Yongli	CHN	Nassau	22 Apr 17
Sprint Med R	W	1:35.59	Akinosun, Gardner, Bryant, Barber	USA	Philadelphia	29 Apr 17
5kW	SAm	21:16A	Glenda MOREJÓN	ECU	Sucua	15 Apr 17
10kW	SAm	43:52+	Kimberley GARCIA	PER	Lima	13 May 17
	SAm	43:03	Erica de SENA	BRA	Suzhou	25 Sep 17
20kW	SAm	1:26:59	Erica de SENA	BRA	London	13 Aug 17
30kW	SAm	2:24:33	Paola PEREZ	ECU	Hauppauge	22 Oct 17
50kW	W,Eur,W35	4:08:26	Inés HENRIQUES	POR	Porto de Mos	15 Jan 17
	NAm	4:26:37	Katie BURNETT	USA	Santee	28 Jan 17
	W40	4:54:12	Susan RANDALL	USA	Santee	28 Jan 17
	Asi	4:22:22	YIN Hang	CHN	Huangshan	5 Mar 17
	SAm	4:39:28	Nair Da ROSA	BRA	Lima	14 May 17
	W,Eur,W35	4:05:56	Inês HENRIQUES	POR	London	13 Aug 17
	Asi	4:08:58	YIN Hang	CHN	London	13 Aug 17
	NAm	4:21:51	Katie BURNETT	USA	London	13 Aug 17
	CAC	4:15:42	Mayra HERRERA	GUA	Owego	9 Sep 17
	Afr	4:54:33	Natalie le ROUX	RSA	George, RSA	21 Oct 17

See ATHLETICS 2017 for Indoor Records set in January - March 2017 – and add

INDOORS – MEN

Event	Record	Mark	Athlete	Nat	Venue	Date
1000	W18	2:23.01	Colin SCHULTZ	USA	Boston (Allston)	5 Mar 17

INDOORS – WOMEN

Event	Record	Mark	Athlete	Nat	Venue	Date
800	NAm	1:58.27 §	Ajee' WILSON	USA	New York (Arm)	11 Feb 17
	NAm	1:58.64	Charlene LIPSEY	USA	New York (Arm)	11 Feb 17
Pen	W20	4550 §	Alina SHUKH	UKR	Zaporizhzhya	27 Jan 17
		(8.85, 1.88, 14.27, 6.04, 2:17.69)				
	W20	4542	Alina SHUKH	UKR	Tallinn	4 Feb 17
		(8.98, 1.89, 13.81, 6.12, 2:16.84)				
4x200 R	Oce	1:42.34A	Mucci, Andrew, Boyle, Cairns	AUS	Pocatello	18 Feb 17

WORLD AND CONTINENTAL RECORDS SET IN JAN-MAR 2018

INDOORS – MEN # on oversized track

Event	Record	Mark	Athlete	Nat	Venue	Date
60	W, NAm	6.37 §	Christian COLEMAN	USA	Clemson	19 Jan 18
	Asi	6.47	SU Bingtian	CHN	Karlsruhe	3 Feb 18
	Asi	6.43	SU Bingtian	CHN	Düsseldorf	6 Feb 18
	W, NAm	6.34A	Christian COLEMAN	USA	Albuquerque	18 Feb 18
	Asi	6.42	SU Bingtian	CHN	Birmingham	3 Mar 18
200	W18	20.95	Brian HERRON	USA	Birmingham USA	30 Dec 17
	W40	21.48	Alexander KOSENKOW	GER	Leipzig	10 Feb 18
	NAm	20.02	Elijah HALL	USA	College Station	10 Mar 18
300	W20	32.64	Brian HERRON	USA	Lynchburg	19 Jan 18
400	Oce	45.44	Steven SOLOMON	AUS	Clemson	23 Feb 18
	SAm	46.14	Alejandro PERLAZA	COL	Boston (Allston)	4 Mar 18
	W, NAm	44.52	Michael NORMAN	USA	College Station	10 Mar 18
600	W,Afr,Com	1:14.79A	Michael SARUNI	KEN	Albuquerque	19 Jan 18
800	Afr, Com	1:44.21	Emmanuel KORIR	KEN	New York (Armory)	3 Feb 18
1500	W20	3:36.05 §	Samuel TEFERA	ETH	Val-de-Reuil	27 Jan 18
1M	Com	3:49.44	Edward CHESEREK	KEN	Boston (Allston)	9 Feb 18
	W18	4:04.94	Colin SCHULTZ	USA	Boston (Allston)	3 Mar 18
Mar	WB	2:19:02	Malcolm RICHARDS	USA	New York	17 Mar 18
60mh	SAm =	7.60	Gabriel CONSTANTINO	BRA	São Caetano do Sul	17 Feb 18
300mh	WB	34.26 (o/s)	Karsten WARHOLM	NOR	Tampere	10 Feb 18
PV	W20 #	5.83A	Armand DUPLANTIS	SWE	Reno	12 Jan 18
	W20	5.78	Emmanouil KARÁLIS	GRE	Pireás	11 Feb 18

	W20	5.81, 5.88	Armand DUPLANTIS	SWE	Clermont-Ferrand	25 Feb 18
LJ	Afr	8.40	Luvo MANYONGA	RSA	Metz	11 Feb 18
	Afr	8.44	Luvo MANYONGA	RSA	Birmingham	2 Mar 18
TJ	Afr	17.23	Hugues-Fabrice ZANGO	BUR	Val-de-Reuil	27 Jan 18
SP	W18	18.86	Aleksey ALEKSANDROVICH	BLR	Gomel	23 Jan 18
	Oce	22.13, 22.13, 22.31	Tomas WALSH	NZL	Birmingham	3 Mar 18
	SAm	21.23, 21.37	Darlan ROMANI	BRA	Birmingham	3 Mar 18
Wt	W20	22.49	Alex HILL	USA	Allendale	24 Feb 18
4x200 R	Asi	1:26.70	Vi.Zems, Grigoryev, Vy.Zems, Efremov	KAZ	Ust-Kamenogorsk	15 Jan 18
4x400 R	W,Eur	3:01.77	Zalewski, Omelko, Krawczuk, Krzewina	POL	Birmingham	4 Mar 18
	CAC	3:02.52	Lendore, Richards, Guevara, Gordon	TTO	Birmingham	4 Mar 18
	W,Nam	3:01.39	Izu, Grant, Dixon, M Kerley	USA	College Station	10 Mar 18
4x800 R	W,NAm	7:11.30	McAsey, Merber, Giesting, Gam	USA	Boston (Allston)	25 Feb 18
3000mW	W	10:30.28	Tom BOSWORTH	GBR	Glasgow	25 Feb 18
5000mW	W40	19:30.20	João VIEIRA	POR	Pombal	17 Feb 18
	Afr	19:39.92	Hédi TÉRAOUI	TUN	Liévin	18 Feb 18

INDOORS – WOMEN

60	Afr	6.97	Murielle Ahouré	CIV	Birmingham	2 Mar 18
200	SAm	23.15	Brenessa THOMPSON	GUY	College Station	24 Feb 18
300	W20	36.12	Sydney McLAUGHLIN	USA	Bloomington	8 Dec 17
	W=	35.45	Shaunae MILLER-UIBO	BAH	New York (Armory)	3 Feb 18
400	W20	50.52	Sydney McLAUGHLIN	USA	College Station	25 Feb 18
	NAm	50.34	Kendall ELLIS	USA	College Station	10 Mar 18
	W20	50.36	Sydney McLAUGHLIN	USA	College Station	10 Mar 18
1500	CAC	4:04.95	Aisha PRAUGHT-LEER	JAM	Boston (Roxbury)	10 Feb 18
3000	CAC	8:41.10	Aisha PRAUGHT-LEER	JAM	New York (Armory)	3 Feb 18
5000	W18	15:37.12	Katelyn TUOHY	USA	Lynchburg	20 Jan 18
Mar	WB	2:40:56	Lindsey SCHERF	USA	New York	17 Mar 18
60mh	NAm =	7.72	Kendra HARRISON	USA	Clemson	9 Feb 18
	W18	8.12	Grace STARK	USA	Lexington	17 Feb 18
	NAm	7.70A	Sharika NELVIS	USA	Albuquerque	18 Feb 18
	NAm =	7.70	Kendra HARRISON	USA	Birmingham	3 Mar 18
	W20	7.98	Tara DAVIS	USA	College Station	9 Mar 18
	W18	8.05	Grace STARK	USA	New York (Arm)	11 Mar 18
PV	W35	4.71, 4.81	Jenn SUHR	USA	Toronto	20 Jan 18
	W35 =	4.81A	Jenn SUHR	USA	Albuquerque	18 Feb 18
	Oce	4.75	Eliza McCARTNEY	NZL	Birmingham	3 Mar 18
TJ	NAm	14.53	Keturah ORJI	USA	Clemson	20 Jan 18
Pen U18	W18	4371	Maria VICENTE	ESP	Antequera	10 Mar 18
			(8.33, 1.75, 13.06, 6.11, 2:22.77)			
4x200 R	NAm	1:32.67	Jefferson, Stevens, Harper, Ruth	USA	New York (Arm)	27 Jan 18
	CAC	1:34.83	Chambers, Ellington, Walker, Hodges	JAM	New York (Arm)	27 Jan 18
	Sam	1:40.14	King, Amsterdam, Hooper, McCammon	GUY	New York (Arm)	27 Jan 18
4x400 R	NAm	3:23.85	Hayes, Moline, Wimbley, Okolo	USA	Birmingham	4 Mar 18
4x800 R	W,NAm	8:05.89	Williams, Rogers, Lipsey, Wilson	USA	New York (Arm)	3 Feb 18
3000mW	CAC	12:47.16	Mirna ORTIZ	GUA	Bratislava	28 Jan 18
	CAC	12:40.33	Mirna ORTIZ	GUA	Liévin	18 Feb 18

OUTDOORS – MEN

HMar	W40	61:04	Mark KIPTOO	KEN	Azpeitia	24 Mar 18
PV	W20	5.92	Armand DUPLANTIS	SWE	Austin	31 Mar 18
TJ	W18	17.32	Jordan A. DIAZ	CUB	La Habana	17 Feb 18
SP	Oce, Com	22.67	Tomas WALSH	NZL	Auckland (Waitakere)	25 Mar 18

OUTDOORS – WOMEN

200	Afr	22.04	Blessing OKAGBARE	NGR	Abilene	24 Mar 18
HMar	NAm	67:25	Molly HUDDLE	USA	Houston	14 Jan 18
HMar	W-Wo	66:11	Netsanet GUDETA	ETH	Valencia	24 Mar 19
48Hr Road	W	401.000k	Patrycja BEREZNOWSKA	POL	Athína	28 Jan 18
200mh	W	25.20	Dalilah MUHAMMAD	USA	Northridge	10 Mar 18
JT	Oce	67.58	Kathryn MITCHELL	AUS	Melbourne	11 Feb 18
	Oce	68.57	Kathryn MITCHELL	AUS	Melbourne	3 Mar 18
35kW	W	2:45:51	Inês HENRIQUES	POR	Porto de Mos	7 Jan 18
50kW	SAm	4:19:43A	Magaly BONILLA	ECU	Sucua	10 Mar 18

WORLD MEN'S ALL-TIME LISTS

100 METRES

Mark	Wind	Name		Nat	Born	Pos	Meet	Venue	Date
9.58 WR	0.9	Usain	Bolt	JAM	21.8.86	1	WCh	Berlin	16 Aug 09
9.63	1.5		Bolt			1	OG	London (OS)	5 Aug 12
9.69 WR	0.0		Bolt			1	OG	Beijing	16 Aug 08
9.69	2.0	Tyson	Gay ¶	USA	9.8.82	1		Shanghai	20 Sep 09
9.69	-0.1	Yohan	Blake	JAM	26.12.89	1	Athl	Lausanne	23 Aug 12
9.71	0.9		Gay			2	WCh	Berlin	16 Aug 09
9.72 WR	1.7		Bolt			1	Reebok	New York (RI)	31 May 08
9.72	0.2	Asafa	Powell	JAM	23.11.82	1rA	Athl	Lausanne	2 Sep 08
9.74 WR	1.7		Powell			1h2	GP	Rieti	9 Sep 07
9.74	0.9	Justin	Gatlin ¶	USA	10.2.82	1	DL	Doha	15 May 15
9.75	1.1		Blake			1	NC	Kingston	29 Jun 12
9.75	1.5		Blake			2	OG	London (OS)	5 Aug 12
9.75	0.9		Gatlin			1	GGala	Roma	4 Jun 15
9.75	1.4		Gatlin			1	Athl	Lausanne	9 Jul 15
9.76	1.8		Bolt			1		Kingston	3 May 08
9.76	1.3		Bolt			1	VD	Bruxelles	16 Sep 11
9.76	-0.1		Bolt			1	GGala	Roma	31 May 12
9.76	1.4		Blake			1	WK	Zürich	30 Aug 12
9.77 WR	1.6		Powell			1	Tsik	Athína	14 Jun 05
9.77 WR	1.5		Powell			1	BrGP	Gateshead	11 Jun 06
9.77 WR	1.0		Powell			1rA	WK	Zürich	18 Aug 06
9.77	1.6		Gay			1q1	NC/OT	Eugene	28 Jun 08
9.77	-1.3		Bolt			1	VD	Bruxelles	5 Sep 08
9.77	0.9		Powell			1h1	GP	Rieti	7 Sep 08
9.77	0.4		Gay			1	GGala	Roma	10 Jul 09
9.77	-0.3		Bolt			1	WCh	Moskva	11 Aug 13
9.77	0.6		Gatlin			1	VD	Bruxelles	5 Sep 14
9.77	0.9		Gatlin			1s2	WCh	Beijing	23 Aug 15
9.78	0.0		Powell			1	GP	Rieti	9 Sep 07
9.78	-0.4		Gay			1	LGP	London (CP)	13 Aug 10
9.78	0.9	Nesta	Carter ¶?	JAM	10.11.85	1		Rieti	29 Aug 10
9.78	1.0		Powell			1	Athl	Lausanne	30 Jun 11
9.78	-0.3		Gatlin			1	Herc	Monaco	17 Jul 15
		(34 performances by 6 athletes)							
9.79 WR	0.1	Maurice	Greene	USA	23.7.74	1rA	Tsik	Athína	16 Jun 99
9.80	0.4	Steve	Mullings ¶	JAM	29.11.82	1	Pre	Eugene	4 Jun 11
9.82	1.7	Richard	Thompson	TTO	7.6.85	1	NC	Port of Spain	21 Jun 14
9.82	1.3	Christian	Coleman	USA	6.3.96	1s1	NCAA	Eugene	7 Jun 17
		(10)							
9.84 WR	0.7	Donovan	Bailey	CAN	16.12.67	1	OG	Atlanta	27 Jul 96
9.84	0.2	Bruny	Surin	CAN	12.7.67	2	WCh	Sevilla	22 Aug 99
9.84	1.3	Trayvon	Bromell	USA	10.7.95	1h4	NC	Eugene	25 Jun 15
9.85 WR	1.2	Leroy	Burrell	USA	21.2.67	1rA	Athl	Lausanne	6 Jul 94
9.85	1.7	Olusoji	Fasuba	NGR	9.7.84	2	SGP	Doha	12 May 06
9.85	1.3	Michael	Rodgers	USA	24.4.85	2	Pre	Eugene	4 Jun 11
9.86 WR	1.2	Carl	Lewis	USA	1.7.61	1	WCh	Tokyo	25 Aug 91
9.86	-0.4	Frank	Fredericks	NAM	2.10.67	1rA	Athl	Lausanne	3 Jul 96
9.86	1.8	Ato	Boldon	TTO	30.12.73	1rA	MSR	Walnut	19 Apr 98
9.86	0.6	Francis	Obikwelu	NGR/POR	22.11.78	2	OG	Athína	22 Aug 04
		(20)							
9.86	1.4	Keston	Bledman	TTO	8.3.88	1	NC	Port of Spain	23 Jun 12
9.86	1.3	Jimmy	Vicaut	FRA	27.2.92	2	DL	Saint-Denis	4 Jul 15
9.87	0.3	Linford	Christie ¶	GBR	2.4.60	1	WCh	Stuttgart	15 Aug 93
9.87A	-0.2	Obadele	Thompson	BAR	30.3.76	1	WCp	Johannesburg	11 Sep 98
9.88	1.8	Shawn	Crawford ¶	USA	14.1.78	1	Pre	Eugene	19 Jun 04
9.88	0.6	Walter	Dix	USA	31.1.86	2		Nottwil	8 Aug 10
9.88	0.9	Ryan	Bailey	USA	13.4.89	2		Rieti	29 Aug 10
9.88	1.0	Michael	Frater	JAM	6.10.82	2	Athl	Lausanne	30 Jun 11
9.89	1.6	Travis	Padgett	USA	13.12.86	1q2	NC/OT	Eugene	28 Jun 08
9.89	1.6	Darvis	Patton	USA	4.12.77	1q3	NC/OT	Eugene	28 Jun 08
		(30)							
9.89	1.3	Ngonidzashe	Makusha	ZIM	11.3.87	1	NCAA	Des Moines	10 Jun 11
9.89	1.9	Akani	Simbine	RSA	21.9.93	1	Gyulai	Székesfehérvár	18 Jul 16
9.90	0.4	Nickel	Ashmeade	JAM	7.4.90	1s2	WCh	Moskva	11 Aug 13
9.91	1.2	Dennis	Mitchell ¶	USA	20.2.66	3	WCh	Tokyo	25 Aug 91
9.91	0.9	Leonard	Scott	USA	19.1.80	2	WAF	Stuttgart	9 Sep 06
9.91	-0.5	Derrick	Atkins	BAH	5.1.84	2	WCh	Osaka	26 Aug 07

Mark	Wind	Name		Nat	Born	Pos	Meet	Venue	Date
9.91	-0.2	Daniel	Bailey	ANT	9.9.86	2	GL	Saint-Denis	17 Jul 09
9.91	0.7	Churandy	Martina	NED	3.7.84	2s1	OG	London (OS)	5 Aug 12
9.91	1.1	James	Dasaolu	GBR	5.9.87	1s2	NC	Birmingham	13 Jul 13
9.91	1.8	Femi Seun	Ogunode ¶	QAT	15.5.91	1	AsiC	Wuhan	4 Jun 15
		(40)							
9.91	0.2	Andre	De Grasse	CAN	10.11.94	3	OG	Rio de Janeiro	14 Aug 16
9.91	1.0	Julian	Forte	JAM	7.1.93	1	ISTAF	Berlin	27 Aug 17
9.92	0.3	Andre	Cason	USA	20.1.69	2	WCh	Stuttgart	15 Aug 93
9.92	0.8	Jon	Drummond	USA	9.9.68	1h3	NC	Indianapolis	12 Jun 97
9.92	0.2	Tim	Montgomery ¶	USA	28.1.75	2	NC	Indianapolis	13 Jun 97
9.92A	-0.2	Seun	Ogunkoya	NGR	28.12.77	2	WCp	Johannesburg	11 Sep 98
9.92	1.0	Tim	Harden	USA	27.1.74	1	Spitzen	Luzern	5 Jul 99
9.92	2.0	Christophe	Lemaitre	FRA	11.6.90	1	NC	Albi	29 Jul 11
9.92	-0.8	Kemar	Bailey-Cole	JAM	10.1.92	3	DL	London (OS)	24 Jul 15
9.92A	0.9	Jak Ali	Harvey	JAM/TUR	5.4.89	1		Erzurum	12 Jun 16
		(50)	100th man 9.98, 200th 10.05, 300th 10.09, 400th 10.12, 500th 10.15						

Doubtful timing

Mark	Wind	Name		Nat	Born	Pos	Meet	Venue	Date
9.88A	0.2	Sydney	Siame	ZAM	7.10.97	1		Lusaka	8 Apr 17

Doubtful wind reading: 9.91 -2.3 Davidso Ezinwa NGR 22.11.71 1 Azusa 11 Apr 92

Wind-assisted – performances to 9.76, performers listed to 9.89

Mark	Wind	Name		Nat	Born	Pos	Meet	Venue	Date
9.68	4.1	Tyson	Gay ¶	USA	9.8.82	1	NC/OT	Eugene	29 Jun 08
9.69A	5+	Obadele	Thompson	BAR	30.3.76	1		El Paso	13 Apr 96
9.69	4.8	Andre	De Grasse	CAN	10.11.94	1	DL	Stockholm	18 Jun 17
9.72	2.1		Powell			1	Bisl	Oslo	4 Jun 10
9.74	w	Richard	Thompson	TTO	7.6.85	1		Clermont	31 May 14
9.75	3.4		Gay			1h1	NC	Eugene	25 Jun 09
9.75	2.6		Powell			1h2	DL	Doha	14 May 10
9.75	4.3	Darvis	Patton	USA	4.12.77	1rA	TexR	Austin	30 Mar 13
9.75	2.7		De Grasse			1	NCAA	Eugene	12 Jun 15
9.76A	6.1	Churandy	Martina	AHO	3.7.84	1		El Paso	13 May 06
9.76	2.2		Gay			1	GP	New York	2 Jun 07
9.76	2.7		Gatlin			1	Pre	Eugene	31 May 14
9.76	3.7	Trayvon	Bromell	USA	10.7.95	1s1	NC	Eugene	26 Jun 15
9.78	5.2	Carl	Lewis	USA	1.7.61	1	NC/OT	Indianapolis	16 Jul 88
9.78	3.7	Maurice	Greene	USA	23.7.74	1	GP II	Stanford	31 May 04
9.79	5.3	Andre	Cason	USA	20.1.69	1h4	NC	Eugene	16 Jun 93
9.80	4.1	Walter	Dix	USA	31.1.86	2	NC/OT	Eugene	29 Jun 08
9.80	2.7	Michael	Rodgers	USA	24.4.85	2	Pre	Eugene	31 May 14
9.82	3.0	Isiah	Young	USA	5.1.90	1		Clermont	16 May 15
9.82	4.9	Remontay	McClain	USA	21.9.92	1h3	NC	Eugene	25 Jun 15
9.83	7.1	Leonard	Scott	USA	19.1.80	1r1	Sea Ray	Knoxville	9 Apr 99
9.83	2.2	Derrick	Atkins	BAH	5.1.84	2	GP	New York	2 Jun 07
9.84	5.4	Francis	Obikwelu	NGR/POR	22.11.78	1		Zaragoza	3 Jun 06
9.84	4.8	Ben Youssef	Meité	CIV	11.11.86	2	DL	Stockholm	18 Jun 17
9.85	4.8	Dennis	Mitchell ¶	USA	20.2.66	2	NC	Eugene	17 Jun 93
9.85A	3.0	Frank	Fredericks	NAM	2.10.67	1		Nairobi	18 May 02
9.85	4.1	Travis	Padgett	USA	13.12.86	4	NC/OT	Eugene	29 Jun 08
9.85	3.6	Keston	Bledman	TTO	8.3.88	1rA		Clermont	2 Jun 12
9.85	3.2	Charles	Silmon	USA	4.7.91	1s1	NC	Des Moines	21 Jun 13
9.85A	3.0	Kemar	Hyman	CAY	11.10.89	1s2	NACAC	San José, CRC	7 Aug 15
9.86	2.6	Shawn	Crawford ¶	USA	14.1.78	1	GP	Doha	14 May 04
9.86	3.6	Michael	Frater	JAM	6.10.82	2h4	NC	Kingston	23 Jun 11
9.86	3.2	Rakieem "Mookie"	Salaam	USA	5.4.90	2s1	NC	Des Moines	21 Jun 13
9.86	3.7	Diondre	Batson	USA	13.7.92	2s1	NC	Eugene	26 Jun 15
9.86	2.4	Ronnie	Baker	USA	15.10.93	1	Pre	Eugene	27 May 17
9.87	11.2	William	Snoddy	USA	6.12.57	1		Dallas	1 Apr 78
9.87	4.9	Calvin	Smith	USA	8.1.61	1s2	NC/OT	Indianapolis	16 Jul 88
9.87	2.4	Michael	Marsh	USA	4.8.67	1rA	MSR	Walnut	20 Apr 97
9.87	3.3	Yoshihide	Kiryu	JPN	15.12.95	1r1	TexR	Austin	28 Mar 15
9.87	2.1	Tevin	Hester	USA	10.1.94	1	ACC	Tallahassee	16 May 15
9.88	2.3	James	Sanford	USA	27.12.57	1		Los Angeles (Ww)	3 May 80
9.88	5.2	Albert	Robinson	USA	28.11.64	4	NC/OT	Indianapolis	16 Jul 88
9.88	4.9	Tim	Harden	USA	27.1.74	1	NC	New Orleans	20 Jun 98
9.88	4.5	Coby	Miller	USA	19.10.76	1		Auburn	1 Apr 00
9.88	3.6	Patrick	Johnson	AUS	26.9.72	1		Perth	8 Feb 03
9.88	3.0	Darrel	Brown	TTO	11.10.84	1	NC	Port of Spain	23 Jun 07
9.88	3.7	Ivory	Williams #	USA	2.5.85	1	TexR	Austin	3 Apr 10
9.89	4.2	Ray	Stewart	JAM	18.3.65	1s1	PAm	Indianapolis	9 Aug 87
9.89	4.4	Henricho	Bruintjies	RSA	16.7.93	1		Gavardo	29 May 16
9.89	4.8	Ryan	Shields	JAM	12.5.83	3	DL	Stockholm	18 Jun 17

Mark	Wind	Name		Nat	Born	Pos	Meet	Venue	Date
Hand **timing**	and three men at 9.7w								
9.7	1.9	Donovan	Powell ¶	JAM	31.10.71	1rA		Houston	19 May 95
9.7	1.9	Carl	Lewis	USA	1.7.61	2rA		Houston	19 May 95
9.7	1.9	Olapade	Adeniken	NGR	19.8.69	3rA		Houston	19 May 95
Drugs disqualification									
9.75	1.1		Gay ¶			(1)	NC	Des Moines	21 Jun 13
9.77	1.7		Gatlin ¶	USA	10.2.82	(1)	SGP	Doha	12 May 06
9.78	2.0	Tim	Montgomery ¶	USA	28.1.75	(1)	GPF	Paris (C)	14 Sep 02
9.79	1.1	Ben	Johnson ¶	CAN	30.12.61	(1)	OG	Seoul	24 Sep 88
9.87	2.0	Dwain	Chambers ¶	GBR	5.4.78	(2)	GPF	Paris (C)	14 Sep 02
9.7w ht	3.5		Johnson	CAN	30.12.61	(1)		Perth	24 Jan 87
9.75w	2.4		Gay			(1s2)	NC	Des Moines	21 Jun 13

200 METRES

Mark	Wind	Name		Nat	Born	Pos	Meet	Venue	Date
19.19	WR-0.3	Usain	Bolt	JAM	21.8.86	1	WCh	Berlin	20 Aug 09
19.26	0.7	Yohan	Blake	JAM	26.12.89	1	VD	Bruxelles	16 Sep 11
19.30	WR-0.9		Bolt			1	OG	Beijing	20 Aug 08
19.32	WR0.4	Michael	Johnson	USA	13.9.67	1	OG	Atlanta	1 Aug 96
19.32	0.4		Bolt			1	OG	London (OS)	9 Aug 12
19.40	0.8		Bolt			1	WCh	Daegu	3 Sep 11
19.44	0.4		Blake			2	OG	London (OS)	9 Aug 12
19.53	0.7	Walter	Dix	USA	31.1.86	2	VD	Bruxelles	16 Sep 11
19.54	0.0		Blake			1	VD	Bruxelles	7 Sep 12
19.55	-0.1		Bolt			1	WCh	Beijing	27 Aug 15
19.56	-0.8		Bolt			1		Kingston	1 May 10
19.57	0.0		Bolt			1	VD	Bruxelles	4 Sep 09
19.57	0.4	Justin	Gatlin ¶	USA	10.2.82	1	NC	Eugene	28 Jun 15
19.58	1.3	Tyson	Gay ¶	USA	9.8.82	1	Reebok	New York	30 May 09
19.58	1.4		Bolt			1	Athl	Lausanne	23 Aug 12
19.59	-0.9		Bolt			1	Athl	Lausanne	7 Jul 09
19.62	-0.3		Gay			1	NC	Indianapolis	24 Jun 07
19.63	0.4	Xavier	Carter	USA	8.12.85	1	Athl	Lausanne	11 Jul 06
19.63	-0.9		Bolt			1	Athl	Lausanne	2 Sep 08
19.65	0.0	Wallace	Spearmon	USA	24.12.84	1		Daegu	28 Sep 06
19.66	WR1.7		M Johnson			1	NC	Atlanta	23 Jun 96
19.66	0.0		Bolt			1	WK	Zürich	30 Aug 12
19.66	0.0		Bolt			1	WCh	Moskva	17 Aug 13
19.67	-0.5		Bolt			1	GP	Athína	13 Jul 08
19.68	0.4	Frank	Fredericks	NAM	2.10.67	2	OG	Atlanta	1 Aug 96
19.68	-0.1		Gay			1	WAF	Stuttgart	10 Sep 06
19.68	-0.1		Bolt			1	WAF	Thessaloníki	13 Sep 09
19.68	-0.5		Gatlin			1	Herc	Monaco	18 Jul 14
19.68	0.9		Gatlin			1	Pre	Eugene	30 May 15
19.69	0.9		Dix			1	NCAA-r	Gainesville	26 May 07
		(30/9)							
19.72A	WR 1.8	Pietro	Mennea (10)	ITA	28.6.52	1	WUG	Ciudad de México	12 Sep 79
19.73	-0.2	Michael	Marsh	USA	4.8.67	1s1	OG	Barcelona	5 Aug 92
19.75	1.5	Carl	Lewis	USA	1.7.61	1	NC	Indianapolis	19 Jun 83
19.74	1.4	LaShawn	Merritt ¶	USA	27.6.86	1s3	NC/OT	Eugene	8 Jul 16
19.75	1.7	Joe	DeLoach	USA	5.6.67	1	OG	Seoul	28 Sep 88
19.77	0.7	Ato	Boldon	TTO	30.12.73	1rA		Stuttgart	13 Jul 97
19.77	0.0	Isaac	Makwala	BOT	29.9.86	1		Madrid	14 Jul 17
19.79	1.2	Shawn	Crawford ¶	USA	14.1.78	1	OG	Athína	26 Aug 04
19.79	0.9	Warren	Weir	JAM	31.10.89	1	NC	Kingston	23 Jun 13
19.80	0.8	Christophe	Lemaitre	FRA	11.6.90	3	WCh	Daegu	3 Sep 11
19.80	2.0	Rasheed	Dwyer	JAM	29.1.89	1s1	PAm	Toronto	23 Jul 15
		(20)							
19.80	-0.3	Andre	De Grasse	CAN	10.11.94	2s2	OG	Rio de Janeiro	17 Aug 16
19.81	-0.3	Alonso	Edward	PAN	8.12.89	2	WCh	Berlin	20 Aug 09
19.81	0.4	Churandy	Martina	NED	3.7.84	1	Athl	Lausanne	25 Aug 16
19.83A	WR 0.9	Tommie	Smith	USA	6.6.44	1	OG	Ciudad de México	16 Oct 68
19.84	1.7	Francis	Obikwelu	NGR/POR	22.11.78	1s2	WCh	Sevilla	25 Aug 99
19.84	1.2	Wayde	van Niekerk	RSA	15.7.92	1		Kingston	10 Jun 17
19.85	-0.3	John	Capel ¶	USA	27.10.78	1	NC	Sacramento	23 Jul 00
19.85	-0.5	Konstadínos	Kedéris ¶	GRE	11.7.73	1	EC	München	9 Aug 02
19.85	0.0	Nickel	Ashmeade	JAM	4.7.90	2	WK	Zürich	30 Aug 12
19.85	1.9	Ameer	Webb	USA	19.3.91	1	DL	Doha	6 May 16
		(30)							
19.85	-0.5	Christian	Coleman	USA	6.3.96	1q1	NCAA-E	Lexington	27 May 17
19.86A	1.0	Don	Quarrie	JAM	25.2.51	1	PAm	Cali	3 Aug 71

Mark	Wind	Name		Nat	Born	Pos	Meet	Venue	Date
19.86	1.6	Maurice	Greene	USA	23.7.74	2rA	DNG	Stockholm	7 Jul 97
19.86	1.5	Jason	Young	JAM	21.3.91	1	Spitzen	Luzern	17 Jul 12
19.86	1.6	Isiah	Young	USA	5.1.90	1	NC	Des Moines	23 Jun 13
19.87	0.8	Lorenzo	Daniel	USA	23.3.66	1	NCAA	Eugene	3 Jun 88
19.87A	1.8	John	Regis	GBR	13.10.66	1		Sestriere	31 Jul 94
19.87	1.2	Jeff	Williams	USA	31.12.65	1		Fresno	13 Apr 96
19.87	-0.1	Anaso	Jobodwana	RSA	30.7.92	3	WCh	Beijing	27 Aug 15
19.88	-0.3	Floyd	Heard	USA	24.3.66	2	NC	Sacramento	23 Jul 00
		(40)							
19.88	0.1	Joshua 'J.J'	Johnson	USA	10.5.76	1	VD	Bruxelles	24 Aug 01
19.88	-0.4	Ramil	Guliyev	AZE/TUR	29.5.90	1		Zagreb	8 Sep 15
19.88	1.2	Miguel	Francis	ANT	28.2.95	1		Kingston	11 Jun 16
19.89	-0.8	Claudinei	da Silva	BRA	19.11.70	1	GPF	München	11 Sep 99
19.89	1.3	Jaysuma	Saidy Ndure	NOR	1.1.84	1	WAF	Stuttgart	23 Sep 07
19.90	1.3	Asafa	Powell	JAM	23.11.82	1	NC	Kingston	25 Jun 06
19.90	-0.4	Noah	Lyles	USA	18.7.97	1	DL	Shanghai	13 May 17
19.92A	WR 1.9	John	Carlos	USA	5.6.45	1	FOT	Echo Summit	12 Sep 68
19.95	0.4	Nethaneel	Mitchell-Blake	GBR	2.4.94	1	SEC	Tuscaloosa	14 May 16
19.95A	1.7	Akani	Simbine	RSA	21.9.93	1		Pretoria	4 Mar 17
		(50)	100th man 20.09, 200th 20.21, 300th 20.30, 400th 20.36, 500th 20.40						

Wind-assisted 2 performances to 19.69, performers listed to 19.90

Mark	Wind	Name		Nat	Born	Pos	Meet	Venue	Date
19.58	2.4	Andre	De Grasse	CAN	10.11.94	1	NCAA	Eugene	12 Jun 15
19.61	>4.0	Leroy	Burrell	USA	21.2.67	1	SWC	College Station	19 May 90
19.73	3.3	Shawn	Crawford ¶	USA	14.1.78	1	NC	Eugene	28 Jun 09
19.75	4.1	Isiah	Young	USA	5.1.90	1rA		Clermont	16 May 15
19.83	9.2	Bobby	Cruse	USA	20.3.78	1r2	Sea Ray	Knoxville	9 Apr 99
19.86	4.6	Roy	Martin	USA	25.12.66	1	SWC	Houston	18 May 86
19.86	2.4	Dedric	Dukes	USA	2.4.92	2	NCAA	Eugene	12 Jun 15
19.86	2.4	Trayvon	Bromell	USA	10.7.95	3	NCAA	Eugene	12 Jun 15
19.86	2.9	Danny	Talbot	GBR	1.5.91	1r2		Clermont	15 Apr 17
19.87	5.7	Malik	Moffett	USA	11.4.94	1	Big 10	University Park	14 May 17
19.90	3.8	Steve	Mullings ¶	JAM	29.11.82	1		Fort Worth	17 Apr 04

Low altitude mark for athletes with lifetime bests at high altitude

19.94 0.3 Regis 2 WCh Stuttgart 20 Aug 93 19.96 0.0 Mennea 1 Barletta 17 Aug 80

Hand timing

19.7A James Sanford USA 27.12.57 1 El Paso 19 Apr 80, 19.7A 0.2 Robson C. da Silva BRA 4.9.64 1 AmCp Bogotá 13 Aug 89, 19.7A 1.4 Isaac Makwala BOT 29.9.86 1 Germiston 15 Mar 14

300 METRES

In 300m races only, not including intermediate times in 400m races

Mark	Name		Nat	Born	Pos	Meet	Venue	Date
30.81	Wayde	van Niekerk	RSA	15.7.92	1	GS	Ostrava	28 Jun 17
30.85A	Michael	Johnson	USA	13.9.67	1		Pretoria	24 Mar 00
30.97	Usain	Bolt	JAM	21.8.86	1	GS	Ostrava	27 May 10
31.23	LaShawn	Merritt ¶	USA	27.6.86	2		Kingston	11 Jun 16
31.44	Isaac	Makwala	BOT	29.9.86	2	GS	Ostrava	28 Jun 17
31.48	Danny	Everett	USA	1.11.66	1		Jerez de la Frontera	3 Sep 90
31.48	Roberto	Hernández	CUB	6.3.67	2		Jerez de la Frontera	3 Sep 90
31.56	Doug	Walker ¶	GBR	28.7.73	1		Gateshead	19 Jul 98
31.61	Anthuan	Maybank	USA	30.12.69	1		Durham	13 Jul 96
31.61	Clarence	Munyai	RSA	20.2.98	3	GS	Ostrava	28 Jun 17
31.64	Tony	McQuay	USA	16.4.90	3		Kingston	11 Jun 16
31.67	John	Regis	GBR	13.10.66	1	Vaux	Gateshead	17 Jul 92

400 METRES

Mark	Name		Nat	Born	Pos	Meet	Venue	Date
43.03 WR	Wayde	van Niekerk	RSA	15.7.92	1	OG	Rio de Janeiro	14 Aug 16
43.18 WR	Michael	Johnson	USA	13.9.67	1	WCh	Sevilla	26 Aug 99
43.29 WR	Butch	Reynolds ¶	USA	8.6.64	1	WK	Zürich	17 Aug 88
43.39		Johnson			1	WCh	Göteborg	9 Aug 95
43.44		Johnson			1	NC	Atlanta	19 Jun 96
43.45	Jeremy	Wariner	USA	31.1.84	1	WCh	Osaka	31 Aug 07
43.48		van Niekerk			1	WCh	Beijing	26 Aug 15
43.49		Johnson			1	OG	Atlanta	29 Jul 96
43.50	Quincy	Watts	USA	19.6.70	1	OG	Barcelona	5 Aug 92
43.50		Wariner			1	DNG	Stockholm	7 Aug 07
43.62		Wariner			1rA	GGala	Roma	14 Jul 06
43.62		van Niekerk			1	Athl	Lausanne	6 Jul 17
43.65		Johnson			1	WCh	Stuttgart	17 Aug 93
43.65	LaShawn	Merritt ¶	USA	27.6.86	2	WCh	Beijing	26 Aug 15
43.66		Johnson			1	NC	Sacramento	16 Jun 95
43.66		Johnson			1rA	Athl	Lausanne	3 Jul 96
43.68		Johnson			1	WK	Zürich	12 Aug 98
43.68		Johnson			1	NC	Sacramento	16 Jul 00

Mark	Wind	Name		Nat	Born	Pos	Meet	Venue	Date
43.71			Watts			1s2	OG	Barcelona	3 Aug 92
43.72		Isaac	Makwala	BOT	29.9.86	1		La Chaux-de-Fonds	5 Jul 15
43.73			van Niekerk			1	Herc	Monaco	21 Jul 17
43.74			Johnson			1	NC	Eugene	19 Jun 93
43.74			Merritt			1	WCh	Moskva	13 Aug 13
43.74		Kirani	James	GRN	1.9.92	1	Athl	Lausanne	3 Jul 14
43.75			Johnson			1		Waco	19 Apr 97
43.75			Merritt			1	OG	Beijing	21 Aug 08
43.76			Johnson			1	GWG	Uniondale, NY	22 Jul 98
43.76			James			2	OG	Rio de Janeiro	14 Aug 16
43.78			James			3	WCh	Beijing	26 Aug 15
43.81		Danny	Everett	USA	1.11.66	1	NC/OT	New Orleans	26 Jun 92
		(31/10)							
43.86A	WR	Lee	Evans	USA	25.2.47	1	OG	Ciudad de México	18 Oct 68
43.87		Steve	Lewis	USA	16.5.69	1	OG	Seoul	28 Sep 88
43.89		Steven	Gardiner	BAH	12.9.95	1s1	WCh	London(OS)	6 Aug 17
43.93		Youssef	Al-Masrahi	KSA	31.12.87	1h2	WCh	Beijing	23 Aug 15
43.93		Rusheen	McDonald	JAM	17.8.92	2h2	WCh	Beijing	23 Aug 15
43.97A		Larry	James	USA	6.11.47	2	OG	Ciudad de México	18 Oct 68
44.01		Machel	Cedenio	TTO	6.9.95	4	OG	Rio de Janeiro	14 Aug 16
44.02		Baboloki	Thebe	BOT	18.3.97	2	Athl	Lausanne	6 Jul 17
44.05		Angelo	Taylor	USA	29.12.78	1	NC	Indianapolis	23 Jun 07
44.09		Alvin	Harrison ¶	USA/DOM	20.1.74	3	NC	Atlanta	19 Jun 96
		(20)							
44.09		Jerome	Young ¶	USA	14.8.76	1	NC	New Orleans	21 Jun 98
44.10		Gary	Kikaya	COD	4.2.78	2	WAF	Stuttgart	9 Sep 06
44.11		Luguelín	Santos	DOM	12.11.92	4	WCh	Beijing	26 Aug 15
44.13		Derek	Mills	USA	9.7.72	1	Pre	Eugene	4 Jun 95
44.14		Roberto	Hernández	CUB	6.3.67	2		Sevilla	30 May 90
44.15		Anthuan	Maybank	USA	30.12.69	1rB	Athl	Lausanne	3 Jul 96
44.16		Otis	Harris	USA	30.6.82	2	OG	Athína	23 Aug 04
44.17		Innocent	Egbunike	NGR	30.11.61	1rA	WK	Zürich	19 Aug 87
44.18		Samson	Kitur	KEN	25.2.66	2s2	OG	Barcelona	3 Aug 92
44.19		Nathon	Allen	JAM	28.10.95	2s1	WCh	London (OS)	6 Aug 17
		(30)							
44.20A		Charles	Gitonga	KEN	5.10.71	1	NC	Nairobi	29 Jun 96
44.21		Ian	Morris	TTO	30.11.61	3s2	OG	Barcelona	3 Aug 92
44.22		Gil	Roberts	USA	15.3.89	2	NC	Sacramento	24 Jun 17
44.24		Tony	McQuay	USA	16.4.90	1s1	NC/OT	Eugene	2 Jul 16
44.25		Karabo	Sibanda	BOT	2.7.98	5	OG	Rio de Janeiro	14 Aug 16
44.26		Alberto	Juantorena	CUB	21.11.50	1	OG	Montreal	29 Jul 76
44.27		Alonzo	Babers	USA	31.10.61	1	OG	Los Angeles	8 Aug 84
44.27		Antonio	Pettigrew ¶	USA	3.11.67	1	NC	Houston	17 Jun 89
44.27		Darold	Williamson	USA	19.2.83	1s1	NCAA	Sacramento	10 Jun 05
44.27		Abdelilah	Haroun	QAT	1.1.97	2		La Chaux-de-Fonds	5 Jul 15
		(40)							
44.28		Andrew	Valmon	USA	1.1.65	4	NC	Eugene	19 Jun 93
44.28		Tyree	Washington	USA	28.8.76	1		Los Angeles (ER)	12 May 01
44.29		Derrick	Brew	USA	28.12.77	1	SEC	Athens, GA	16 May 99
44.29		Sanderlei	Parrela	BRA	7.10.74	2	WCh	Sevilla	26 Aug 99
44.30		Gabriel	Tiacoh	CIV	10.9.63	1	NCAA	Indianapolis	7 Jun 86
44.30		Lamont	Smith	USA	11.12.72	4	NC	Atlanta	19 Jun 96
44.31		Alejandro	Cárdenas	MEX	4.10.74	3	WCh	Sevilla	26 Aug 99
44.33		Thomas	Schönlebe	GDR	6.8.65	1	WCh	Roma	3 Sep 87
44.34		Darnell	Hall	USA	26.9.71	1	Athl	Lausanne	5 Jul 95
44.35		Andrew	Rock	USA	23.1.82	2	WCh	Helsinki	12 Aug 05
		(50)	100th man 44.57, 200th 44.83, 300th 45.01, 400th 45.19, 500th 45.30						
Drugs disqualification									
44.21		Antonio	Pettigrew ¶	USA	3.11.67	1		Nassau	26 May 99
Hand timing			** 440 yards time less 0.3 secs*						
44.1		Wayne	Collett	USA	20.10.49	1	OT	Eugene	9 Jul 72
44.2*		John	Smith	USA	5.8.50	1	AAU	Eugene	26 Jun 71
44.2		Fred	Newhouse	USA	8.11.48	1s1	OT	Eugene	7 Jul 72

600 METRES

Mark	Name		Nat	Born	Pos	Meet	Venue	Date
1:12.81	Johnny	Gray	USA	19.6.60	1		Santa Monica	24 May 86
1:13.10	David	Rudisha	KEN	17.12.88	1	DL	Birmingham	5 Jun 16
1:13.2 + ?	John	Kipkurgat	KEN	16.3.44	1		Pointe-à-Pierre	23 Mar 74
1:13.21	Pierre-Ambroise	Bosse	FRA	11.5.92	2	DL	Birmingham	5 Jun 16
1:13.28	Duane	Solomon	USA	28.12.84	1		Burnaby	1 Jul 13
1:13.49	Joseph	Mutua	KEN	10.12.78	1		Liège (NX)	27 Aug 02

800 METRES

Mark	Wind	Name		Nat	Born	Pos	Meet	Venue	Date
1:40.91	WR	David	Rudisha	KEN	17.12.88	1	OG	London (OS)	9 Aug 12
1:41.01	WR		Rudisha			1rA		Rieti	29 Aug 10
1:41.09	WR		Rudisha			1	ISTAF	Berlin	22 Aug 10
1:41.11	WR	Wilson	Kipketer	DEN	12.12.70	1	ASV	Köln	24 Aug 97
1:41.24	WR		Kipketer			1rA	WK	Zürich	13 Aug 97
1:41.33			Rudisha			1		Rieti	10 Sep 11
1:41.51			Rudisha			1	NA	Heusden-Zolder	10 Jul 10
1:41.54			Rudisha			1	DL	Saint-Denis	6 Jul 12
1:41.73	!WR	Sebastian	Coe	GBR	29.9.56	1		Firenze	10 Jun 81
1:41.73	WR		Kipketer			1rA	DNG	Stockholm	7 Jul 97
1:41.73		Nijel	Amos	BOT	15.3.94	2	OG	London (OS)	9 Aug 12
1:41.74			Rudisha			1	adidas	New York	9 Jun 12
1:41.77		Joaquim	Cruz	BRA	12.3.63	1	ASV	Köln	26 Aug 84
1:41.83			Kipketer			1	GP II	Rieti	1 Sep 96
1:42.01			Rudisha			1	GP	Rieti	6 Sep 09
1:42.04			Rudisha			1	Bisl	Oslo	4 Jun 10
1:42.12A			Rudisha			1	OT	Nairobi	23 Jun 12
1:42.15			Rudisha			1	OG	Rio de Janeiro	15 Aug 16
1:42.17			Kipketer			1	TOTO	Tokyo	16 Sep 96
1:42.20			Kipketer			1	VD	Bruxelles	22 Aug 97
1:42.23		Abubaker	Kaki	SUD	21.6.89	2	Bisl	Oslo	4 Jun 10
1:42.27			Kipketer			1	VD	Bruxelles	3 Sep 99
1:42.28		Sammy	Koskei	KEN	14.5.61	2	ASV	Köln	26 Aug 84
1:42.32			Kipketer			1	GP II	Rieti	8 Sep 02
1:42.33	WR		Coe			1	Bisl	Oslo	5 Jul 79
1:42.34			Cruz			1r1	WK	Zürich	22 Aug 84
1:42.34		Wilfred	Bungei	KEN	24.7.80	2	GP II	Rieti	8 Sep 02
1:42.37		Mohammed	Aman	ETH	10.1.94	1	VD	Bruxelles	6 Sep 13
1:42.41			Cruz			1	VD	Bruxelles	24 Aug 84
1:42.45			Amos			1	Herc	Monaco	18 Jul 14
1:42.47		Yuriy	Borzakovskiy	RUS	12.4.81	1	VD	Bruxelles	24 Aug 01
		(31/10)		*! photo-electric cell time*					
1:42.51		Amel	Tuka	BIH	9.1.91	1	Herc	Monaco	17 Jul 15
1:42.53		Timothy	Kitum	KEN	20.11.94	3	OG	London (OS)	9 Aug 12
1:42.53		Pierre-Ambroise	Bosse	FRA	11.5.92	2	Herc	Monaco	18 Jul 14
1:42.55		André	Bucher	SUI	19.10.76	1rA	WK	Zürich	17 Aug 01
1:42.58		Vebjørn	Rodal	NOR	16.9.72	1	OG	Atlanta	31 Jul 96
1:42.60		Johnny	Gray	USA	19.6.60	2r1		Koblenz	28 Aug 85
1:42.61		Taoufik	Makhloufi	ALG	29.4.88	2	OG	Rio de Janeiro	15 Aug 16
1:42.62		Patrick	Ndururi	KEN	12.1.69	2rA	WK	Zürich	13 Aug 97
1:42.67		Alfred	Kirwa Yego	KEN	28.11.86	2	GP	Rieti	6 Sep 09
1:42.69		Hezekiél	Sepeng ¶	RSA	30.6.74	2	VD	Bruxelles	3 Sep 99
		(20)							
1:42.69		Japheth	Kimutai	KEN	20.12.78	3	VD	Bruxelles	3 Sep 99
1:42.79		Fred	Onyancha	KEN	25.12.69	3	OG	Atlanta	31 Jul 96
1:42.79		Youssef Saad	Kamel	KEN/BRN	29.3.83	2	Herc	Monaco	29 Jul 08
1:42.81		Jean-Patrick	Nduwimana	BDI	9.5.78	2rA	WK	Zürich	17 Aug 01
1:42.82		Duane	Solomon	USA	28.12.84	4	OG	London (OS)	9 Aug 12
1:42.84		Ferguson	Cheruiyot	KEN	30.11.89	4	Herc	Monaco	18 Jul 14
1:42.85		Norberto	Téllez	CUB	22.1.72	4	OG	Atlanta	31 Jul 96
1:42.86		Mbulaeni	Mulaudzi	RSA	8.9.80	3	GP	Rieti	6 Sep 09
1:42.87		Alfred	Kipketer	KEN	26.12.96	1	DL	Saint-Denis	27 Aug 16
1:42.88		Steve	Cram	GBR	14.10.60	1rA	WK	Zürich	21 Aug 85
		(30)							
1:42.91		William	Yiampoy	KEN	17.5.74	3	GP II	Rieti	8 Sep 02
1:42.93		Clayton	Murphy	USA	26.2.95	3	OG	Rio de Janeiro	15 Aug 16
1:42.95		Boaz	Lalang	KEN	8.2.89	2rA		Rieti	29 Aug 10
1:42.95		Nick	Symmonds	USA	30.12.83	5	OG	London (OS)	9 Aug 12
1:42.97		Peter	Elliott	GBR	9.10.62	1		Sevilla	30 May 90
1:42.97		Ayanleh	Souleiman	DJI	3.12.92	3	Herc	Monaco	17 Jul 15
1:42.98		Patrick	Konchellah	KEN	20.4.68	2	ASV	Köln	24 Aug 97
1:43.03		Kennedy/Kenneth	Kimwetich	KEN	1.1.73	2		Stuttgart	19 Jul 98
1:43.05		Jonathan	Kitilit	KEN	24.4.94	3	DL	Saint-Denis	27 Aug 16
1:43.06		Billy	Konchellah	KEN	20.10.62	1	WCh	Roma	1 Sep 87
		(40)							
1:43.07		Yeimer	López	CUB	20.8.82	1		Jerez de la Frontera	24 Jun 08
1:43.08		José Luiz	Barbosa	BRA	27.5.61	1		Rieti	6 Sep 91
1:43.09		Djabir	Saïd-Guerni	ALG	29.3.77	5	VD	Bruxelles	3 Sep 99
1:43.10		Emmanuel	Korir	KEN	15.6.95	1	Herc	Monaco	21 Jul 17

Mark	Wind	Name		Nat	Born	Pos	Meet	Venue	Date
1:43.13		Abraham Kipchirchir	Rotich	KEN	26.6.93	1	Herc	Monaco	20 Jul 12
1:43.15		Mehdi	Baala	FRA	17.8.78	5	GP II	Rieti	8 Sep 02
1:43.15		Asbel	Kiprop	KEN	30.6.89	2	Herc	Monaco	22 Jul 11
1:43.16		Paul	Ereng	KEN	22.8.67	1	WK	Zürich	16 Aug 89
1:43.17		Benson	Koech	KEN	10.11.74	1		Rieti	28 Aug 94
1:43.20		Mark	Everett	USA	2.9.68	1rA	Gugl	Linz	9 Jul 97
		(50)	100th man 1:43.81, 200th 1:44.56, 300th 1:44.96, 400th 1:45.28, 500th 1:45.55						

1000 METRES

Mark	Wind	Name		Nat	Born	Pos	Meet	Venue	Date
2:11.96	WR	Noah	Ngeny	KEN	2.11.78	1	GP II	Rieti	5 Sep 99
2:12.18	WR	Sebastian	Coe	GBR	29.9.56	1	OsloG	Oslo	11 Jul 81
2:12.66			Ngeny			1	Nik	Nice	17 Jul 99
2:12.88		Steve	Cram	GBR	14.10.60	1		Gateshead	9 Aug 85
2:13.08		Taoufik	Makhloufi	ALG	29.4.88	1		Tomblaine	1 Jul 15
2:13.40	WR		Coe			1	Bisl	Oslo	1 Jul 80
2:13.49		Ayanleh	Souleiman	DJI	3.12.92	1	Athl	Lausanne	25 Aug 16
2:13.56		Kennedy/Kenneth	Kimwetich	KEN	1.1.73	2	Nik	Nice	17 Jul 99
2:13.62		Abubaker	Kaki	SUD	21.6.89	1	Pre	Eugene	3 Jul 10
2:13.73		Noureddine	Morceli	ALG	28.2.70	1	BNP	Villeneuve d'Ascq	2 Jul 93
2:13.89		Robert	Biwott	KEN	28.1.96	2	Athl	Lausanne	25 Aug 16
2:13.9	WR	Rick	Wohlhuter	USA	23.12.48	1	King	Oslo	30 Jul 74
2:13.95		Jonathan	Kitilit	KEN	24.4.94	3	Athl	Lausanne	25 Aug 16
2:13.96		Mehdi	Baala	FRA	17.8.78	1		Strasbourg	26 Jun 03
		(12)	50th man 2:15.81, 100th 2:16.58, 200th 2:17.51						

1500 METRES

Mark	Wind	Name		Nat	Born	Pos	Meet	Venue	Date
3:26.00	WR	Hicham	El Guerrouj	MAR	14.9.74	1	GGala	Roma	14 Jul 98
3:26.12			El Guerrouj			1	VD	Bruxelles	24 Aug 01
3:26.34		Bernard	Lagat	KEN/USA	12.12.74	2	VD	Bruxelles	24 Aug 01
3:26.45			El Guerrouj			1 rA	WK	Zürich	12 Aug 98
3:26.69		Asbel	Kiprop	KEN	30.6.89	1	Herc	Monaco	17 Jul 15
3:26.89			El Guerrouj			1	WK	Zürich	16 Aug 02
3:26.96			El Guerrouj			1	GP II	Rieti	8 Sep 02
3:27.21			El Guerrouj			1	WK	Zürich	11 Aug 00
3:27.34			El Guerrouj			1	Herc	Monaco	19 Jul 02
3:27.37	WR	Noureddine	Morceli	ALG	28.2.70	1	Nik	Nice	12 Jul 95
3:27.40			Lagat			1rA	WK	Zürich	6 Aug 04
3.27.52			Morceli			1	Herc	Monaco	25 Jul 95
3:27.64			El Guerrouj			2rA	WK	Zürich	6 Aug 04
3:27.64		Silas	Kiplagat	KEN	20.8.89	1	Herc	Monaco	18 Jul 14
3:27.65			El Guerrouj			1	WCh	Sevilla	24 Aug 99
3:27.72			Kiprop			1	Herc	Monaco	19 Jul 13
3:27.91			Lagat			2	Herc	Monaco	19 Jul 02
3:28.12		Noah	Ngeny	KEN	2.11.78	2	WK	Zürich	11 Aug 00
3:28.21+			El Guerrouj			1	in 1M	Roma	7 Jul 99
3.28.37			Morceli			1	GPF	Monaco	9 Sep 95
3:28.37			El Guerrouj			1	Herc	Monaco	8 Aug 98
3:28.38			El Guerrouj			1	GP	Saint-Denis	6 Jul 01
3:28.40			El Guerrouj			1	VD	Bruxelles	5 Sep 03
3:28.45			Kiprop			2	Herc	Monaco	18 Jul 14
3:28.51			Lagat			3	WK	Zürich	11 Aug 00
3:28.57			El Guerrouj			1rA	WK	Zürich	11 Aug 99
3:28.6+			Ngeny			2	in 1M	Roma	7 Jul 99
3:28.73			Ngeny			2	WCh	Sevilla	24 Aug 99
3:28.75		Taoufik	Makhloufi	ALG	29.4.88	2	Herc	Monaco	17 Jul 15
3:28.79		Abdelaati	Iguider	MAR	25.3.87	3	Herc	Monaco	17 Jul 15
3:28.80		Elijah	Manangoi	KEN	5.1.93	1	Herc	Monaco	21 Jul 17
3:28.81		Mohamed	Farah	GBR	23.3.83	2	Herc	Monaco	19 Jul 13
3:28.81		Ronald	Kwemoi	KEN	19.9.95	3	Herc	Monaco	18 Jul 14
		(31/11)							
3:28.95		Fermín	Cacho	ESP	16.2.69	2rA	WK	Zürich	13 Aug 97
3:28.98		Mehdi	Baala	FRA	17.8.78	2	VD	Bruxelles	5 Sep 03
3:29.02		Daniel Kipchirchir	Komen	KEN	27.11.84	1	GGala	Roma	14 Jul 06
3:29.10		Timothy	Cheruiyot	KEN	20.11.95	2	Herc	Monaco	21 Jul 17
3:29.14		Rashid	Ramzi ¶	MAR/BRN	17.7.80	2	GGala	Roma	14 Jul 06
3:29.18		Vénuste	Niyongabo	BDI	9.12.73	2	VD	Bruxelles	22 Aug 97
3:29.29		William	Chirchir	KEN	6.2.79	3	VD	Bruxelles	24 Aug 01
3:29.46	WR	Saïd	Aouita	MAR	2.11.59	1	ISTAF	Berlin	23 Aug 85
3:29.46		Daniel	Komen	KEN	17.5.76	1	Herc	Monaco	16 Aug 97
3:29.47		Augustine	Choge (20)	KEN	21.1.87	1	ISTAF	Berlin	14 Jun 09

Mark	Wind	Name		Nat	Born	Pos	Meet	Venue	Date
3:29.50		Caleb	Ndiku	KEN	9.10.92	3	Herc	Monaco	19 Jul 13
3:29.51		Ali	Saïdi-Sief ¶	ALG	15.3.78	1	Athl	Lausanne	4 Jul 01
3:29.53		Amine	Laâlou ¶	MAR	13.5.82	2	Herc	Monaco	22 Jul 10
3:29.58		Ayanleh	Souleiman	DJI	3.12.92	4	Herc	Monaco	18 Jul 14
3:29.66		Nick	Willis	NZL	25.4.83	5	Herc	Monaco	17 Jul 15
3:29.67	WR	Steve	Cram	GBR	14.10.60	1	Nik	Nice	16 Jul 85
3:29.77		Sydney	Maree	USA	9.9.56	1	ASV	Köln	25 Aug 85
3:29.77		Sebastian	Coe	GBR	29.9.56	1		Rieti	7 Sep 86
3:29.77		Nixon	Chepseba	KEN	12.12.90	2	Herc	Monaco	20 Jul 12
3:29.91		Laban	Rotich	KEN	20.1.69	2rA	WK	Zürich	12 Aug 98
		(30)							
3:29.91		Aman	Wote	ETH	18.4.84	6	Herc	Monaco	14 Jul 14
3:30.04		Timothy	Kiptanui	KEN	5.1.80	2	GP	Saint-Denis	23 Jul 04
3:30.07		Rui	Silva	POR	3.8.77	3	Herc	Monaco	19 Jul 02
3:30.10		Robert	Biwott	KEN	28.1.96	7	Herc	Monaco	17 Jul 15
3:30.18		John	Kibowen	KEN	21.4.69	3rA	WK	Zürich	12 Aug 98
3:30.20		Haron	Keitany	KEN	17.12.83	2	ISTAF	Berlin	14 Jun 09
3:30.24		Cornelius	Chirchir	KEN	5.6.83	4	Herc	Monaco	19 Jul 02
3:30.33		Ivan	Heshko	UKR	19.8.79	2	VD	Bruxelles	3 Sep 04
3:30.34		Collins	Cheboi	KEN	25.9.87	9	Herc	Monaco	17 Jul 15
3:30.40		Matthew	Centrowitz	USA	18.10.89	10	Herc	Monaco	17 Jul 15
		(40)							
3:30.46		Alex	Kipchirchir	KEN	26.11.84	3	VD	Bruxelles	3 Sep 04
3:30.54		Alan	Webb	USA	13.1.83	1	Gaz	Saint-Denis	6 Jul 07
3:30.55		Abdi	Bile	SOM	28.12.62	1		Rieti	3 Sep 89
3:30.57		Reyes	Estévez	ESP	2.8.76	3	WCh	Sevilla	24 Aug 99
3:30.58		William	Tanui	KEN	22.2.64	3	Herc	Monaco	16 Aug 97
3:30.61		James	Magut	KEN	20.7.90	5	DL	Doha	9 May 14
3:30.67		Benjamin	Kipkurui	KEN	28.12.80	2	Herc	Monaco	20 Jul 01
3:30.72		Paul	Korir	KEN	15.7.77	3	VD	Bruxelles	5 Sep 03
3:30.77	WR	Steve	Ovett	GBR	9.10.55	1		Rieti	4 Sep 83
3:30.77		Bethwel	Birgen	KEN	6.8.88	4	Herc	Monaco	19 Jul 13
		(50)	100th man 3:31.96, 200th 3:33.73, 300th 3:34.61, 400th 3:35.57, 500th 3:36.15						
Drugs disqualification: 3:30.77			Adil Kaouch ¶	MAR	1.1.79	1	GGala	Roma	13 Jul 07

1 MILE

Mark	Wind	Name		Nat	Born	Pos	Meet	Venue	Date
3:43.13	WR	Hicham	El Guerrouj	MAR	14.9.74	1	GGala	Roma	7 Jul 99
3:43.40		Noah	Ngeny	KEN	2.11.78	2	GGala	Roma	7 Jul 99
3:44.39	WR	Noureddine	Morceli	ALG	28.2.70	1		Rieti	5 Sep 93
3:44.60			El Guerrouj			1	Nik	Nice	16 Jul 98
3:44.90			El Guerrouj			1	Bisl	Oslo	4 Jul 97
3:44.95			El Guerrouj			1	GGala	Roma	29 Jun 01
3:45.19			Morceli			1	WK	Zürich	16 Aug 95
3:45.64			El Guerrouj			1	ISTAF	Berlin	26 Aug 97
3:45.96			El Guerrouj			1	BrGP	London (CP)	5 Aug 00
3:46.24			El Guerrouj			1	Bisl	Oslo	28 Jul 00
3:46.32	WR	Steve	Cram	GBR	14.10.60	1	Bisl	Oslo	27 Jul 85
3:46.38		Daniel	Komen	KEN	17.5.76	2	ISTAF	Berlin	26 Aug 97
3:46.70		Vénuste	Niyongabo	BDI	9.12.73	3	ISTAF	Berlin	26 Aug 97
3:46.76		Saïd	Aouita	MAR	2.11.59	1	WG	Helsinki	2 Jul 87
3:46.78			Morceli			1	ISTAF	Berlin	27 Aug 93
3:46.91		Alan	Webb	USA	13.1.83	1		Brasschaat	21 Jul 07
3:46.92			Aouita			1	WK	Zürich	21 Aug 85
3:47.10			El Guerrouj			1	BrGP	London (CP)	7 Aug 99
3:47.28		Bernard	Lagat	KEN/USA	12.12.74	2	GGala	Roma	29 Jun 01
3:47.30			Morceli			1	VD	Bruxelles	3 Sep 93
3:47.32		Ayanleh	Souleiman (10)	DJI	3.12.92	1	Pre	Eugene	31 May 14
3:47.33	WR	Sebastian	Coe	GBR	29.9.56	1	VD	Bruxelles	28 Aug 81
		(22/11)							
3:47.65		Laban	Rotich	KEN	20.1.69	2	Bisl	Oslo	4 Jul 97
3:47.69		Steve	Scott	USA	5.5.56	1	OsloG	Oslo	7 Jul 82
3:47.79		José Luis	González	ESP	8.12.57	2	Bisl	Oslo	27 Jul 85
3:47.88		John	Kibowen	KEN	21.4.69	3	Bisl	Oslo	4 Jul 97
3:47.88		Silas	Kiplagat	KEN	20.8.89	2	Pre	Eugene	31 May 14
3:47.94		William	Chirchir	KEN	6.2.79	2	Bisl	Oslo	28 Jul 00
3:47.97		Daham Najim	Bashir	KEN/QAT	8.11.78	1	Bisl	Oslo	29 Jul 05
3:48.17		Paul	Korir	KEN	15.7.77	1	GP	London (CP)	8 Aug 03
3:48.23		Ali	Saïdi-Sief ¶	ALG	15.3.78	1	Bisl	Oslo	13 Jul 01
		(20)							
3:48.28		Daniel Kipchirchir	Komen	KEN	27.11.84	1	Pre	Eugene	10 Jun 07

Mark	Wind	Name		Nat	Born	Pos	Meet	Venue	Date
3:48.38		Andrés Manuel	Díaz	ESP	12.7.69	3	GGala	Roma	29 Jun 01
3:48.40	WR	Steve	Ovett	GBR	9.10.55	1	R-W	Koblenz	26 Aug 81
3:48.50		Asbel	Kiprop	KEN	30.6.89	1	Pre	Eugene	7 Jun 09
3:48.60		Aman	Wote	ETH	18.4.84	3	Pre	Eugene	31 May 14
3:48.78		Haron	Keitany	KEN	17.12.83	2	Pre	Eugene	7 Jun 09
3:48.80		William	Kemei	KEN	22.2.69	1	ISTAF	Berlin	21 Aug 92
3:48.83		Sydney	Maree	USA	9.9.56	1		Rieti	9 Sep 81
3:48.95		Deresse	Mekonnen	ETH	20.10.87	1	Bisl	Oslo	3 Jul 09
3:48.98		Craig	Mottram	AUS	18.6.80	5	Bisl	Oslo	29 Jul 05
		(30)							
3:49.04		Ronald	Kwemoi	KEN	19.9.95	1	Pre	Eugene	27 May 17
3:49.08		John	Walker	NZL	12.1.52	2	OsloG	Oslo	7 Jul 82
3:49.08		Elijah	Manangoi	KEN	5.1.93	2	Pre	Eugene	27 May 17
3:49.09		Abdelaati	Iguider	MAR	25.3.87	4	Pre	Eugene	31 May 14
3:49.20		Peter	Elliott	GBR	9.10.62	2	Bisl	Oslo	2 Jul 88
3:49.22		Jens-Peter	Herold	GDR	2.6.65	3	Bisl	Oslo	2 Jul 88
3:49.29		William	Biwott/Özbilen	KEN/TUR	5.3.90	2	Bisl	Oslo	3 Jul 09
3:49.31		Joe	Falcon	USA	23.6.66	1	Bisl	Oslo	14 Jul 90
3:49.34		David	Moorcroft	GBR	10.4.53	3	Bisl	Oslo	26 Jun 82
3:49.34		Benjamin	Kipkurui	KEN	28.12.80	3	VD	Bruxelles	25 Aug 00
		(40)							
3:49.38		Andrew	Baddeley	GBR	20.6.82	1	Bisl	Oslo	6 Jun 08
3:49.40		Abdi	Bile	SOM	28.12.62	4	Bisl	Oslo	2 Jul 88
3:49.43		James	Magut	KEN	20.7.90	5	Pre	Eugene	31 May 14
3:49.45		Mike	Boit	KEN	6.1.49	2	VD	Bruxelles	28 Aug 81
3:49.50		Rui	Silva	POR	3.8.77	3	GGala	Roma	12 Jul 02
3:49.56		Fermín	Cacho	ESP	16.2.69	2	Bisl	Oslo	5 Jul 96
3:49.56		Collins	Cheboi	KEN	25.9.87	6	Pre	Eugene	31 May 14
3:49.60		José Antonio	Redolat	ESP	17.2.76	4	GGala	Roma	29 Jun 01
3:49.64		Timothy	Cheruiyot	KEN	20.11.95	3	Pre	Eugene	27 May 17
3:49.70		Mekonnen	Gebremedhin	ETH	11.10.88	4	Pre	Eugene	4 Jun 11
		(50)	100th 3:50.98, 200th 3:53.13, 300th 3:54.78, 400th 3:55.84						

2000 METRES

Mark	Wind	Name		Nat	Born	Pos	Meet	Venue	Date
4:44.79	WR	Hicham	El Guerrouj	MAR	14.9.74	1	ISTAF	Berlin	7 Sep 99
4:46.88		Ali	Saïdi-Sief ¶	ALG	15.3.78	1		Strasbourg	19 Jun 01
4:47.88	WR	Noureddine	Morceli	ALG	28.2.70	1		Paris (JB)	3 Jul 95
4:48.36			El Guerrouj			1		Gateshead	19 Jul 98
4:48.69		Vénuste	Niyongabo	BDI	9.12.73	1	Nik	Nice	12 Jul 95
4:48.74		John	Kibowen	KEN	21.4.69	1		Hechtel	1 Aug 98
4:49.00			Niyongabo			1		Rieti	3 Sep 97
4:49.55			Morceli			1	Nik	Nice	10 Jul 96
4:50.08		Noah	Ngeny	KEN	2.11.78	1	DNG	Stockholm	30 Jul 99
4:50.76		Craig	Mottram	AUS	18.6.80	1		Melbourne (OP)	9 Mar 06
4:50.81	WR	Saïd	Aouita	MAR	2.11.59	1	BNP	Paris (JB)	16 Jul 87
4:51.30		Daniel	Komen	KEN	17.5.76	1		Milano	5 Jun 98
4:51.39	WR	Steve	Cram (10)	GBR	14.10.60	1	BGP	Budapest	4 Aug 85
Indoors									
4:49.99		Kenenisa	Bekele	ETH	13.6.82	1		Birmingham	17 Feb 07

3000 METRES

Mark	Wind	Name		Nat	Born	Pos	Meet	Venue	Date
7:20.67	WR	Daniel	Komen	KEN	17.5.76	1		Rieti	1 Sep 96
7:23.09		Hicham	El Guerrouj	MAR	14.9.74	1	VD	Bruxelles	3 Sep 99
7:25.02		Ali	Saïdi-Sief ¶	ALG	15.3.78	1	Herc	Monaco	18 Aug 00
7:25.09		Haile	Gebrselassie	ETH	18.4.73	1	VD	Bruxelles	28 Aug 98
7:25.11	WR	Noureddine	Morceli	ALG	28.2.70	1	Herc	Monaco	2 Aug 94
7:25.16			Komen			1	Herc	Monaco	10 Aug 96
7:25.54			Gebrselassie			1	Herc	Monaco	8 Aug 98
7:25.79		Kenenisa	Bekele	ETH	13.6.82	1	DNG	Stockholm	7 Aug 07
7:25.87			Komen			1	VD	Bruxelles	23 Aug 96
7:26.02			Gebrselassie			1	VD	Bruxelles	22 Aug 97
7:26.03			Gebrselassie			1	GP II	Helsinki	10 Jun 99
7:26.5 e			Komen			1	in 2M	Sydney	28 Feb 98
7:26.62		Mohammed	Mourhit ¶	BEL	10.10.70	2	Herc	Monaco	18 Aug 00
7:26.69			K Bekele			1	BrGP	Sheffield	15 Jul 07
7:27.18		Moses	Kiptanui	KEN	1.10.70	1	Herc	Monaco	25 Jul 95
7:27.26		Yenew	Alamirew	ETH	27.5.90	1	DL	Doha	6 May 11
7:27.3+			Komen			1	in 2M	Hechtel	19 Jul 97
7:27.42			Gebrselassie			1	Bisl	Oslo	9 Jul 98
7:27.50			Morceli			1	VD	Bruxelles	25 Aug 95

Mark Wind	Name		Nat	Born	Pos	Meet	Venue	Date
7:27.55	Edwin	Soi (10)	KEN	3.3.86	2	DL	Doha	6 May 11
7:27.59	Luke	Kipkosgei	KEN	27.11.75	2	Herc	Monaco	8 Aug 98
7:27.66	Eliud	Kipchoge	KEN	5.11.84	3	DL	Doha	6 May 11
7:27.67		Saïdi-Sief			1	Gaz	Saint-Denis	23 Jun 00
7:27.72		Kipchoge			1	VD	Bruxelles	3 Sep 04
7:27.75	Thomas	Nyariki	KEN	27.9.71	2	Herc	Monaco	10 Aug 96
7.28.04		Kiptanui			1	ASV	Köln	18 Aug 95
7:28.19	Yomif	Kejelcha	ETH	1.8.97	1	DL	Saint-Denis	27 Aug 16
7:28.28		Kipkosgei			2	Bisl	Oslo	9 Jul 98
7:28.28	James	Kwalia	KEN/QAT	12.6.84	2	VD	Bruxelles	3 Sep 04
7:28.37		Kipchoge			1	SGP	Doha	8 May 09
	(30/15)							
7:28.41	Paul	Bitok	KEN	26.6.70	3	Herc	Monaco	10 Aug 96
7:28.45	Assefa	Mezegebu	ETH	19.6.78	3	Herc	Monaco	8 Aug 98
7:28.67	Benjamin	Limo	KEN	23.8.74	1	Herc	Monaco	4 Aug 99
7:28.70	Paul	Tergat	KEN	17.6.69	4	Herc	Monaco	10 Aug 96
7:28.70	Tariku	Bekele	ETH	21.1.87	1		Rieti	29 Aug 10
	(20)							
7:28.72	Isaac K.	Songok	KEN	25.4.84	1	GP	Rieti	27 Aug 06
7:28.73	Ronald	Kwemoi	KEN	19.9.95	1	DL	Doha	5 May 17
7:28.76	Augustine	Choge	KEN	21.1.87	4	DL	Doha	6 May 11
7:28.93	Salah	Hissou	MAR	16.1.72	2	Herc	Monaco	4 Aug 99
7:28.94	Brahim	Lahlafi	FRA/MAR	15.4.68	3	Herc	Monaco	4 Aug 99
7:29.00	Bernard	Lagat	USA	12.12.74	2		Rieti	29 Aug 10
7:29.09	John	Kibowen	KEN	21.4.69	3	Bisl	Oslo	9 Jul 98
7:29.34	Isaac	Viciosa	ESP	26.12.69	4	Bisl	Oslo	9 Jul 98
7:29.45 WR	Saïd	Aouita	MAR	2.11.59	1	ASV	Köln	20 Aug 89
7:29.92	Sileshi	Sihine	ETH	29.1.83	1	GP	Rieti	28 Aug 05
	(30)							
7:30.09	Ismaïl	Sghyr	MAR/FRA	16.3.72	2	Herc	Monaco	25 Jul 95
7:30.09	Thomas	Longosiwa	KEN	14.1.82	2	SGP	Doha	8 May 09
7:30.09	Abdelaati	Iguider	MAR	25.3.87	2	DL	Saint-Denis	27 Aug 16
7:30.15	Vincent	Chepkok	KEN	5.7.88	5	DL	Doha	6 May 11
7:30.36	Mark	Carroll	IRL	15.1.72	5	Herc	Monaco	4 Aug 99
7:30.36	Hagos	Gebrhiwet	ETH	11.5.94	1	DL	Doha	10 May 13
7:30.43	Isiah	Koech	KEN	19.12.93	1	DNG	Stockholm	17 Aug 12
7:30.50	Dieter	Baumann ¶	GER	9.2.65	6	Herc	Monaco	8 Aug 98
7:30.53	El Hassan	Lahssini	MAR/FRA	1.1.75	6	Herc	Monaco	10 Aug 96
7:30.53	Hailu	Mekonnen	ETH	4.4.80	1	VD	Bruxelles	24 Aug 01
	(40)							
7:30.62	Boniface	Songok	KEN	25.12.80	3	VD	Bruxelles	3 Sep 04
7:30.76	Jamal Bilal	Salem	KEN/QAT	12.9.78	4	SGP	Doha	13 May 05
7:30.78	Mustapha	Essaïd	FRA	20.1.70	7	Herc	Monaco	8 Aug 98
7:30.84	Bob	Kennedy	USA	18.8.70	8	Herc	Monaco	8 Aug 98
7:30.93	Ryan	Hill	USA	31.1.90	4	DL	Saint-Denis	27 Aug 16
7:30.95	Moses	Kipsiro	UGA	2.9.86	1	Herc	Monaco	28 Jul 09
7:30.99	Khalid	Boulami	MAR	7.8.69	1	Nik	Nice	16 Jul 97
7:30.99	Caleb	Ndiku	KEN	9.10.92	2	DNG	Stockholm	17 Aug 12
7:31.13	Julius	Gitahi	KEN	29.4.78	6	Bisl	Oslo	9 Jul 98
7:31.14	William	Kalya	KEN	4.8.74	3	Herc	Monaco	16 Aug 97
	(50)	100th man 7:34.70, 200th man 7:39.02, 300th 7:41.39, 400th 7:43.21, 500th 7:44.98						
Indoors								
7:24.90 WIR		Komen			1		Budapest	6 Feb 98
7:26.15 WIR		Gebrselassie			1		Karlsruhe	25 Jan 98
7:26.80		Gebrselassie			1		Karlsruhe	24 Jan 99
7:27.80		Alamirew			1	Spark	Stuttgart	5 Feb 11
7:27.93		Komen			1	Spark	Stuttgart	1 Feb 98
7:28.00	Augustine	Choge	KEN	21.1.87	2	Spark	Stuttgart	5 Feb 11
7:30.16	Galen	Rupp	USA	8.5.86	1		Stockholm	21 Feb 13

2 MILES

Mark Wind	Name		Nat	Born	Pos	Meet	Venue	Date
7:58.61 WR	Daniel	Komen	KEN	17.5.76	1		Hechtel	19 Jul 97
7:58.91		Komen			1		Sydney	28 Feb 98
8:01.08 WR	Haile	Gebrselassie	ETH	18.4.73	1	APM	Hengelo	31 May 97
8:01.72		Gebrselassie			1	BrGP	London (CP)	7 Aug 99
8:01.86		Gebrselassie			1	APM	Hengelo	30 May 99
8:03.50	Craig	Mottram	AUS	18.6.80	1	Pre	Eugene	10 Jun 07
8:03.54 WR		Komen			1		Lappeenranta	14 Jul 96

A – mark made at an altitude of 1000m or higher, i – indoors, Q – in qualifying competition, WR – world record

Mark	Wind	Name		Nat	Born	Pos	Meet	Venue	Date
Indoors									
8:03.40		Mohamed	Farah	GBR	23.3.83	1	GP	Birmingham	21 Feb 15
8:04.35		Kenenisa	Bekele	ETH	13.6.82	1	GP	Birmingham	16 Feb 08

5000 METRES

Mark	Wind	Name		Nat	Born	Pos	Meet	Venue	Date
12:37.35	WR	Kenenisa	Bekele	ETH	13.6.82	1	FBK	Hengelo	31 May 04
12:39.36	WR	Haile	Gebrselassie	ETH	18.4.73	1	GP II	Helsinki	13 Jun 98
12:39.74	WR	Daniel	Komen	KEN	17.5.76	1	VD	Bruxelles	22 Aug 97
12:40.18			K Bekele			1	Gaz	Saint-Denis	1 Jul 05
12:41.86	WR		Gebrselassie			1	WK	Zürich	13 Aug 97
12:44.39	WR		Gebrselassie			1	WK	Zürich	16 Aug 95
12:44.90			Komen			2	WK	Zürich	13 Aug 97
12:45.09			Komen			1	WK	Zürich	14 Aug 96
12:46.53		Eliud	Kipchoge	KEN	5.11.84	1	GGala	Roma	2 Jul 04
12:46.81		Dejen	Gebremeskel	ETH	24.11.89	1	DL	Saint-Denis	6 Jul 12
12:47.04		Sileshi	Sihine	ETH	29.9.83	2	GGala	Roma	2 Jul 04
12:47.53		Hagos	Gebrhiwet	ETH	11.5.94	2	DL	Saint-Denis	6 Jul 12
12:48.09			K Bekele			1	VD	Bruxelles	25 Aug 06
12:48.25			K Bekele			1	WK	Zürich	18 Aug 06
12:48.64		Isiah	Koech	KEN	19.12.93	3	DL	Saint-Denis	6 Jul 12
12:48.66		Isaac K.	Songok	KEN	25.4.84	2	WK	Zürich	18 Aug 06
12:48.77		Yenew	Alamirew (10)	ETH	27.5.90	4	DL	Saint-Denis	6 Jul 12
12:48.81		Stephen	Cherono/Shaheen	KEN/QAT	15.10.82	1	GS	Ostrava	12 Jun 03
12:48.98			Komen			1	GGala	Roma	5 Jun 97
12:49.04		Thomas	Longosiwa	KEN	14.1.82	5	DL	Saint-Denis	6 Jul 12
12:49.28		Brahim	Lahlafi	MAR	15.4.68	1	VD	Bruxelles	25 Aug 00
12:49.50		John	Kipkoech	KEN	29.12.91	6	DL	Saint-Denis	6 Jul 12
12:49.53			K Bekele			1	Aragón	Zaragoza	28 Jul 07
12:49.64			Gebrselassie			1	WK	Zürich	11 Aug 99
12:49.71		Mohammed	Mourhit ¶	BEL	10.10.70	2	VD	Bruxelles	25 Aug 00
12:49.87		Paul	Tergat	KEN	17.6.69	3	WK	Zürich	13 Aug 97
12:50.16			Sihine			1	VD	Bruxelles	14 Sep 07
12:50.18			K Bekele			1	WK	Zürich	29 Aug 08
12:50.22			Kipchoge			1	VD	Bruxelles	26 Aug 05
12:50.24		Hicham	El Guerrouj	MAR	14.9.74	2	GS	Ostrava	12 Jun 03
		(30/17)							
12:50.25		Abderrahim	Goumri ¶	MAR	21.5.76	2	VD	Bruxelles	26 Aug 05
12:50.55		Moses	Masai	KEN	1.6.86	1	ISTAF	Berlin	1 Jun 08
12:50.72		Moses	Kipsiro	UGA	2.9.86	3	VD	Bruxelles	14 Sep 07
		(20)							
12:50.80		Salah	Hissou	MAR	16.1.72	1	GGala	Roma	5 Jun 96
12:50.86		Ali	Saïdi-Sief ¶	ALG	15.3.78	1	GGala	Roma	30 Jun 00
12:51.00		Joseph	Ebuya	KEN	20.6.87	4	VD	Bruxelles	14 Sep 07
12:51.34		Edwin	Soi	KEN	3.3.86	1	Herc	Monaco	19 Jul 13
12:51.45		Vincent	Chepkok	KEN	5.7.88	2	DL	Doha	14 May 10
12:51.96		Albert	Rop	KEN/BRN	17.7.92	2	Herc	Monaco	19 Jul 13
12:52.33		Sammy	Kipketer	KEN	29.9.81	2	Bisl	Oslo	27 Jun 03
12:52.45		Tariku	Bekele	ETH	21.1.87	2	ISTAF	Berlin	1 Jun 08
12:52.80		Gebre-egziabher	Gebremariam	ETH	10.9.84	3	GGala	Roma	8 Jul 05
12:52.99		Abraham	Chebii	KEN	23.12.79	4	Bisl	Oslo	27 Jun 03
		(30)							
12:53.11		Mohamed	Farah	GBR	23.3.83	1	Herc	Monaco	22 Jul 11
12:53.41		Khalid	Boulami	MAR	7.8.69	4	WK	Zürich	13 Aug 97
12:53.46		Mark	Kiptoo	KEN	21.6.76	1	DNG	Stockholm	6 Aug 10
12:53.58		Imane	Merga	ETH	15.10.88	3	DNG	Stockholm	6 Aug 10
12:53.60		Bernard	Lagat	USA	12.12.74	2	Herc	Monaco	22 Jul 11
12:53.66		Augustine	Choge	KEN	21.1.87	4	GGala	Roma	8 Jul 05
12:53.72		Philip	Mosima	KEN	2.1.77	2	GGala	Roma	5 Jun 96
12:53.84		Assefa	Mezegebu	ETH	19.6.78	1	VD	Bruxelles	28 Aug 98
12:53.98		Yomif	Kejelcha	ETH	1.8.97	1	VD	Bruxelles	11 Sep 15
12:54.07		John	Kibowen	KEN	21.4.69	4	WCh	Saint-Denis	31 Aug 03
		(40)							
12:54.15		Dejene	Berhanu	ETH	12.12.80	3	GGala	Roma	2 Jul 04
12:54.19		Abreham	Cherkos	ETH	23.9.89	5	GGala	Roma	14 Jul 06
12:54.46		Moses	Mosop	KEN	17.7.85	3	Gaz	Saint-Denis	8 Jul 06
12:54.58		James	Kwalia	KEN/QAT	12.6.84	5	Bisl	Oslo	27 Jun 03
12:54.70		Dieter	Baumann ¶	GER	9.2.65	5	WK	Zürich	13 Aug 97
12:54.83		Muktar	Edris	ETH	14.1.94	1	DNG	Stockholm	21 Aug 14
12:54.85		Moses	Kiptanui	KEN	1.10.70	3	GGala	Roma	5 Jun 96
12:54.99		Benjamin	Limo	KEN	23.8.74	3	Gaz	Saint-Denis	4 Jul 03

Mark Wind		Name	Nat	Born	Pos	Meet	Venue	Date
12:55.06	Lucas	Rotich	KEN	16.4.90	4	Bisl	Oslo	4 Jun 10
12:55.52	Hicham	Bellani	MAR	15.9.79	7	GGala	Roma	14 Jul 06
	(50)	100th man 13:00.36, 200th 13:07.95, 300th 13:11.99, 400th 13:15.19, 500th 13:17.97						
Indoors: 12:49.60		K Bekele			1		Birmingham	20 Feb 04

10,000 METRES

Mark Wind		Name	Nat	Born	Pos	Meet	Venue	Date
26:17.53 WR	Kenenisa	Bekele	ETH	13.6.82	1	VD	Bruxelles	26 Aug 05
26:20.31 WR		K Bekele			1	GS	Ostrava	8 Jun 04
26:22.75 WR	Haile	Gebrselassie	ETH	18.4.73	1	APM	Hengelo	1 Jun 98
26:25.97		K Bekele			1	Pre	Eugene	8 Jun 08
26:27.85 WR	Paul	Tergat	KEN	17.6.69	1	VD	Bruxelles	22 Aug 97
26:28.72		K Bekele			1	FBK	Hengelo	29 May 05
26:29.22		Gebrselassie			1	VD	Bruxelles	5 Sep 03
26:30.03	Nicholas	Kemboi	KEN/QAT	25.11.83	2	VD	Bruxelles	5 Sep 03
26:30.74	Abebe	Dinkesa	ETH	6.3.84	2	FBK	Hengelo	29 May 05
26:31.32 WR		Gebrselassie			1	Bisl	Oslo	4 Jul 97
26:35.63	Micah	Kogo	KEN	3.6.86	1	VD	Bruxelles	25 Aug 06
26:36.26	Paul	Koech	KEN	25.6.69	2	VD	Bruxelles	22 Aug 97
26:37.25	Zersenay	Tadese	ERI	8.2.82	2	VD	Bruxelles	25 Aug 06
26:38.08 WR	Salah	Hissou	MAR	16.1.72	1	VD	Bruxelles	23 Aug 96
26:38.76	Abdullah Ahmad	Hassan (10)	QAT	4.4.81	3	VD	Bruxelles	5 Sep 03
	(Formerly Albert Chepkurui KEN)							
26:39.69	Sileshi	Sihine	ETH	29.9.83	1	FBK	Hengelo	31 May 04
26:39.77	Boniface	Kiprop	UGA	12.10.85	2	VD	Bruxelles	26 Aug 05
26:41.58		Gebrselassie			2	FBK	Hengelo	31 May 04
26:41.75	Samuel	Wanjiru	KEN	10.11.86	3	VD	Bruxelles	26 Aug 05
26:41.95		Kiprop			3	VD	Bruxelles	25 Aug 06
26:43.16		K Bekele			1	VD	Bruxelles	16 Sep 11
26:43.53 WR		Gebrselassie			1	APM	Hengelo	5 Jun 95
26:43.98	Lucas	Rotich	KEN	16.4.90	2	VD	Bruxelles	16 Sep 11
26:44.36	Galen	Rupp	USA	8.5.86	1	Pre	Eugene	30 May 14
26:46.19		K Bekele			1	VD	Bruxelles	14 Sep 07
26:46.31		K Bekele			1	WCh	Berlin	17 Aug 09
26:46.44		Tergat			1	VD	Bruxelles	28 Aug 98
26:46.57	Mohamed	Farah	GBR	23.3.83	1	Pre	Eugene	3 Jun 11
26:47.89		Koech			2	VD	Bruxelles	28 Aug 98
26:48.00		Rupp			3	VD	Bruxelles	16 Sep 11
	(30/16)							
26:48.35	Imane	Merga	ETH	15.10.88	2	Pre	Eugene	3 Jun 11
26:48.99	Josphat	Bett	KEN	12.6.90	3	Pre	Eugene	3 Jun 11
26:49.02	Eliud	Kipchoge	KEN	5.11.84	2	FBK	Hengelo	26 May 07
26:49.20	Moses	Masai	KEN	1.6.86	2	VD	Bruxelles	14 Sep 07
	(20)							
26:49.38	Sammy	Kipketer	KEN	29.9.81	1	VD	Bruxelles	30 Aug 02
26:49.41	Paul	Tanui	KEN	22.12.90	2	Pre	Eugene	30 May 14
26:49.55	Moses	Mosop	KEN	17.7.85	3	FBK	Hengelo	26 May 07
26:49.90	Assefa	Mezegebu	ETH	19.6.78	2	VD	Bruxelles	30 Aug 02
26:49.94	Joshua	Cheptegei	UGA	12.9.96	2	WCh	London (OS)	4 Aug 17
26:50.20	Richard	Limo	KEN	18.11.80	3	VD	Bruxelles	30 Aug 02
26:51.02	Dejen	Gebremeskel	ETH	24.11.89	1		Sollentuna	27 Jun 13
26:51.11	Yigrem	Demelash	ETH	28.1.94	1	OT	Hengelo	29 Jun 16
26:51.16	Emmanuel	Bett	KEN	30.3.83	1	VD	Bruxelles	7 Sep 12
26:51.49	Charles	Kamathi	KEN	18.5.78	1	VD	Bruxelles	3 Sep 99
	(30)							
26:51.68	Vincent	Chepkok	KEN	5.7.88	2	VD	Bruxelles	7 Sep 12
26:52.12	Bedan	Karoki	KEN	21.8.90	4	WCh	London (OS)	4 Aug 17
26:52.23 WR	William	Sigei	KEN	14.10.69	1	Bisl	Oslo	22 Jul 94
26:52.30	Mohammed	Mourhit ¶	BEL	10.10.70	2	VD	Bruxelles	3 Sep 99
26:52.33	Gebre-egziabher	Gebremariam	ETH	10.9.84	4	FBK	Hengelo	26 May 07
26:52.65	Kenneth	Kipkemoi	KEN	2.8.84	3	VD	Bruxelles	7 Sep 12
26:52.65	Geoffrey	Kamworor	KEN	28.11.92	3	Pre	Eugene	29 May 15
26:52.85	Abera	Kuma	ETH	31.8.90	2		Sollentuna	27 Jun 13
26:52.87	John Cheruiyot	Korir	KEN	13.12.81	5	VD	Bruxelles	30 Aug 02
26:52.93	Mark	Bett	KEN	22.12.76	6	VD	Bruxelles	26 Aug 05
	(40)							
26:54.25	Mathew	Kisorio ¶	KEN	16.5.89	7	Pre	Eugene	3 Jun 11
26:54.61	Stephen	Sambu	KEN	3.7.88	4	Pre	Eugene	30 May 14
26:54.64	Mark	Kiptoo	KEN	21.6.76	8	Pre	Eugene	3 Jun 11
26:54.66	William Malel	Sitonik	KEN	1.3.94	2	Pre	Eugene	27 May 16
26:55.29	Leonard Patrick	Komon	KEN	10.1.88	9	Pre	Eugene	3 Jun 11

Mark	Wind	Name		Nat	Born	Pos	Meet	Venue	Date
26:55.73		Geoffrey	Kirui	KEN	16.2.93	6	VD	Bruxelles	16 Sep 11
26:56.11		Jemal	Yimer	ETH	11.9.96	5	WCh	London(OS)	4 Aug 17
26:56.74		Josphat	Menjo	KEN	20.8.79	1		Turku	29 Aug 10
26:57.33		Tamirat	Tola	ETH	11.8.91	3	Pre	Eugene	27 May 16
26:57.36		Josphat	Muchiri Ndambiri	KEN	12.2.85	1		Fukuroi	3 May 09
		(50)	100th man 27:12.39, 200th 27:27.87, 300th 27:36.60, 400th 27:42.84, 500th 27:47.97						

20,000 METRES & 1 HOUR

Mark	Distance	Name		Nat	Born	Pos	Meet	Venue	Date
56:25.98+	21 285m	Haile	Gebrselassie	ETH	18.4.73	1	GS	Ostrava	27 Jun 07
56:55.6+	21 101	Arturo	Barrios	MEX	12.12.63	1		La Flèche	30 Mar 91
57:24.19+	20 944	Jos	Hermens	NED	8.1.50	1		Papendal	1 May 76
57:18.4+	20 943	Dionísio	Castro	POR	22.11.63	1		La Flèche	31 Mar 90

HALF MARATHON

Included are the slightly downhill courses: Newcastle to South Shields 30.5m, Tokyo 33m, Lisboa (Spring to 2008) 69m

Mark	Wind	Name		Nat	Born	Pos	Meet	Venue	Date
58:23	WR	Zersenay	Tadese	ERI	8.2.82	1		Lisboa	21 Mar 10
58:30			Z Tadese			1		Lisboa	20 Mar 11
58:33	WR	Samuel	Wanjiru	KEN	10.11.86	1		Den Haag	17 Mar 07
58:40		Abraham	Cheroben	KEN/BRN	11.10.92	1		København	17 Sep 17
58:44		Solomon	Yego	KEN	10.5.87	1		Ostia	13 Mar 16
58:46		Mathew	Kisorio ¶	KEN	16.5.89	1		Philadelphia	18 Sep 11
58:47		Atsedu	Tsegay	ETH	17.12.91	1		Praha	31 Mar 12
58:48		Sammy	Kitwara	KEN	26.11.86	2		Philadelphia	18 Sep 11
58:48			Cheroben			1		Valencia	19 Oct 14
58:48		Jorum	Okumbo	KEN	10.12.97	2		København	17 Sep 17
58:51		Alex	Oloitiptip Korio	KEN	20.12.90	3		København	17 Sep 17
58:52		Patrick	Makau (10)	KEN	2.3.85	1		Ra's Al Khaymah	20 Feb 09
58:53	WR		Wanjiru			1		Ra's Al Khaymah	9 Feb 07
58:54		Stephen	Kibet	KEN	9.11.86	1		Den Haag	11 Mar 12
58:54		Geoffrey	Kamworor	KEN	28.11.92	1		Ra's Al-Khaymah	15 Feb 13
58:55	WR	Haile	Gebrselassie	ETH	18.4.73	1		Tempe	15 Jan 06
58:56			Makau			1		Berlin	1 Apr 07
58:56	dh	Martin	Mathathi	KEN	25.12.85	1	GNR	South Shields	18 Sep 11
58:56		Stanley	Biwott	KEN	21.4.86	2		Ra's Al-Khaymah	15 Feb 13
58:58			Kitwara			1		Rotterdam	13 Sep 09
58:58		Geoffrey	Mutai	KEN	7.10.81	3		Ra's Al-Khaymah	15 Feb 13
58:59			Z Tadese			1	WCh	Udine	14 Oct 07
58:59		Wilson	Kipsang	KEN	15.3.82	2		Ra's Al Khaymah	20 Feb 09
59:01		Kenneth	Kipkemoi	KEN	2.8.84	2		Valencia	19 Oct 14
59:02			Makau			2	WCh	Udine	14 Oct 07
59:02		Jonathan	Maiyo	KEN	5.5.88	2		Den Haag	11 Mar 12
59:05	dh		Tadese			1	GNR	South Shields	18 Sep 05
59:05		Evans	Cheruiyot (20)	KEN	10.5.82	3	WCh	Udine	14 Oct 07
59:05		Ezekiel	Chebii	KEN	3.1.91	1		Lille	1 Sep 12
59:06	dh	Paul	Tergat	KEN	17.6.69	1		Lisboa	26 Mar 00
59:06	dh		Kipsang			1	GNR	South Shields	16 Sep 12
59:06			G Mutai			1		Udine	22 Sep 13
59:06		Guye	Adola	ETH	20.10.90	1		New Delhi	23 Nov 14
		(33/23)							
59:07		Paul	Kosgei	KEN	22.4.78	1		Berlin	2 Apr 06
59:07	dh	Micah	Kogo	KEN	3.6.86	2	GNR	South Shields	16 Sep 12
59:07		James	Wangari	KEN	23.3.94	1		København	18 Sep 16
59:09		James Kipsang	Kwambai	KEN	28.2.83	3		Rotterdam	13 Sep 09
59:10		Bernard	Kipyego	KEN	16.7.86	4		Rotterdam	13 Sep 09
59:10		Bernard	Koech	KEN	31.1.88	2		Lille	1 Sep 12
59:10		Bedan	Karoki	KEN	21.8.90	1		Ra's Al-Khaymah	10 Feb 17
		(30)							
59:11		Mosinet	Geremew	ETH	12.2.92	3		New Delhi	23 Nov 14
59:12		Cyprian	Kotut	KEN	.92	4		New Delhi	23 Nov 14
59:14		Dennis	Kimetto	KEN	22.1.84	1		Berlin	1 Apr 12
59:14		Leonard Patrick	Komon	KEN	10.1.88	1		Berlin	30 Mar 14
59:14		Barselius	Kipyego	KEN	23.7.93	1		Ústí nad Labem	16 Sep 17
59:15		Deriba	Merga	ETH	26.10.80	1		New Delhi	9 Nov 08
59:15		Wilson	Chebet	KEN	12.7.85	5		Rotterdam	13 Sep 09
59:15		Wilson	Kiprop	KEN	14.4.87	2		Berlin	1 Apr 12
59:18		Leonard	Langat	KEN	7.8.90	2		Ostia	13 Mar 16
59:18		Leul	Gebrselassie	ETH	20.9.93	2		Valencia	22 Oct 17
		(40)							
59:19		Tilahun	Regassa	ETH	18.1.90	1		Abu Dhabi	7 Jan 10
59:19		Robert	Chemosin	KEN	1.2.89	2		Ostia	3 Mar 13

Mark	Wind	Name		Nat	Born	Pos	Meet	Venue	Date
59:19		Yigrem	Demelash	ETH	28.1.94	2		Ra's Al-Khaymah	10 Feb 17
59:20	dh	Hendrick	Ramaala	RSA	2.2.72	2		Lisboa	26 Mar 00
59:20		Moses	Mosop	KEN	17.7.85	1	Stra	Milano	21 Mar 10
59:20		Simon	Cheprot	KEN	2.7.93	3		Ostia	3 Mar 13
59:20		Berhanu	Legesse	ETH	11.9.94	1		New Delhi	29 Nov 15
59:20		Daniel	Wanjiru	KEN	25.5.92	1		Praha	2 Apr 16
59:21	dh	Robert Kipkoech	Cheruiyot	KEN	26.9.78	2		Lisboa	13 Mar 05
59:21		Samuel	Tsegay	ERI	24.2.88	2	WCh	København	29 Mar 14
		(50)	100th man 59:41, 200th man 60:09, 300th 60:29, 400th 60:49, 500th 61:02						
Short course:		58:51 Paul	Tergat	KEN	17.6.69	1	Stra	Milano 49m sh	30 Mar 96
Excessively downhill:		58:42 Bernard	Koech	KEN	31.1.88	1		San Diego (dh 86m)	2 Jun 13

MARATHON

Mark	Wind	Name		Nat	Born	Pos	Meet	Venue	Date
2:02:57	WR	Dennis	Kimetto	KEN	22.1.84	1		Berlin	28 Sep 14
2:03:03		Kenenisa	Bekele	ETH	13.6.82	1		Berlin	25 Sep 16
2:03:05		Eliud	Kipchoge	KEN	5.11.84	1		London	24 Apr 16
2:03:13		Emmanuel	Mutai	KEN	12.10.84	2		Berlin	28 Sep 14
2:03:13		Wilson	Kipsang	KEN	15.3.82	2		Berlin	25 Sep 16
2:03:23	WR		W Kipsang			1		Berlin	29 Sep 13
2:03.32			Kipchoge			1		Berlin	24 Sep 17
2:03:38	WR	Patrick	Makau	KEN	2.3.85	1		Berlin	25 Sep 11
2:03:42			W Kipsang			1		Frankfurt	30 Oct 11
2:03:45			Kimetto			1		Chicago	13 Oct 13
2:03.46		Guye	Adola	ETH	20.10.90	2		Berlin	24 Sep 17
2:03:51		Stanley	Biwott	KEN	21.4.86	2		London	24 Apr 16
2:03:52			Mutai			2		Chicago	13 Oct 13
2:03:58			W Kipsang			1		Tokyo	26 Feb 17
2:03:59	WR	Haile	Gebrselassie	ETH	18.4.73	1		Berlin	28 Sep 08
2:04:00			Kipchoge			1		Berlin	27 Sep 15
2:04:05			Kipchoge			2		Berlin	29 Sep 13
2:04:11			Kipchoge			1		Chicago	12 Oct 14
2:04:11		Tamirat	Tola (10)	ETH	11.8.91	1		Dubai	20 Jan 17
2:04:15		Geoffrey	Mutai	KEN	7.10.81	1		Berlin	30 Sep 12
2:04:16			Kimetto			2		Berlin	30 Sep 12
2:04:23		Ayele	Abshero	ETH	28.12.90	1		Dubai	27 Jan 12
2:04:24		Tesfaye	Abera	ETH	31.3.92	1		Dubai	22 Jan 16
2:04:26	WR		Gebrselassie			1		Berlin	30 Sep 07
2:04:27		Duncan	Kibet	KEN	25.4.78	1		Rotterdam	5 Apr 09
2:04:27		James Kipsang	Kwambai	KEN	28.2.83	2		Rotterdam	5 Apr 09
2:04:28		Sammy	Kitwara	KEN	26.11.86	2		Chicago	12 Oct 14
2:04:29			W Kipsang			1		London	13 Apr 14
2:04:32		Tsegaye	Mekonnen	ETH	15.6.95	1		Dubai	24 Jan 14
2:04:32		Dickson	Chumba	KEN	27.10.86	3		Chicago	12 Oct 14
2:04:33		Hayle	Lemi Berhanu	ETH	13.9.94	2		Dubai	22 Jan 16
2:04:38		Tsegaye	Kebede	ETH	15.1.87	1		Chicago	7 Oct 12
		(32/20)							
2:04:45		Lelisa	Desisa	ETH	14.1.90	1		Dubai	25 Jan 13
2:04:48		Yemane	Tsegay Adhane	ETH	8.4.85	1		Rotterdam	15 Apr 12
2:04:48		Berhanu	Shiferaw	ETH	31.5.93	2		Dubai	25 Jan 13
2:04:49		Tadesse	Tola	ETH	31.10.87	3		Dubai	25 Jan 13
2:04:50		Dino	Sefir	ETH	28.5.88	2		Dubai	27 Jan 12
2:04:50		Getu	Feleke	ETH	28.11.86	2		Rotterdam	15 Apr 12
2:04:52		Feyisa	Lilesa	ETH	1.2.90	2		Chicago	7 Oct 12
2:04:52		Endeshaw	Negesse	ETH	13.3.88	4		Dubai	25 Jan 13
2:04:53		Bernard	Koech	KEN	31.1.88	5		Dubai	25 Jan 13
2:04:54		Markos	Geneti	ETH	30.5.84	3		Dubai	27 Jan 12
		(30)							
2:04:55	WR	Paul	Tergat	KEN	17.6.69	1		Berlin	28 Sep 03
2:04:56		Sammy	Korir	KEN	12.12.71	2		Berlin	28 Sep 03
2:04:56		Jonathan	Maiyo	KEN	5.5.88	4		Dubai	27 Jan 12
2:05:03		Moses	Mosop	KEN	17.7.85	3		Rotterdam	15 Apr 12
2:05:04		Abel	Kirui	KEN	4.6.82	3		Rotterdam	5 Apr 09
2:05:09		Lawrence	Cherono	KEN	7.8.88	1		Amsterdam	15 Oct 17
2:05:10		Samuel	Wanjiru	KEN	10.11.86	1		London	26 Apr 09
2:05:13		Vincent	Kipruto	KEN	13.9.87	3		Rotterdam	11 Apr 10
2:05:13		Wilson	Loyanae ¶	KEN	20.11.88	1		Seoul	20 Mar 16
2:05:13		Nobert	Kigen	KEN	24.1.93	2		Amsterdam	15 Oct 17
		(40)							
2:05:15		Martin	Lel	KEN	29.10.78	1		London	13 Apr 08
2:05:16		Levi	Matebo Omari	KEN	3.11.89	2		Frankfurt	30 Oct 11

Mark	Wind	Name		Nat	Born	Pos	Meet	Venue	Date
2:05:16		Sisay	Lemma	ETH	12.12.90	4		Dubai	22 Jan 16
2:05:21		Eliud	Kiptanui	KEN	6.6.89	2		Berlin	27 Sep 15
2:05:21		Daniel	Wanjiru	KEN	26.5.92	1		Amsterdam	16 Oct 16
2:05:25		Bazu	Worku	ETH	15.9.90	3		Berlin	26 Sep 10
2:05:25		Albert	Matebor	KEN	20.12.80	3		Frankfurt	30 Oct 11
2:05:26		Abraham	Kiptum	KEN	.89	3		Amsterdam	15 Oct 17
2:05:27		Jaouad	Gharib	MAR	22.5.72	3		London	26 Apr 09
2:05:27		Wilson	Chebet	KEN	12.7.85	1		Rotterdam	10 Apr 11
2:05:27		Tilahun	Regassa	ETH	18.1.90	3		Chicago	7 Oct 12
		(51)	100th man 2:06:18, 200th 2:07:12, 300th 2:07:52, 400th 2:08:29, 500th 2:08:52						

Downhill point-to-point course – Boston marathon is downhill overall (139m) and sometimes 1trongly wind-aided.

Mark	Wind	Name		Nat	Born	Pos	Meet	Venue	Date
2:03:02		Geoffrey	Mutai	KEN	7.10.81	1		Boston	18 Apr 11
2:03:06		Moses	Mosop	KEN	17.7.85	2		Boston	18 Apr 11
2:04:53		Gebre-egziabher	Gebremariam	ETH	10.9.84	3		Boston	18 Apr 11
2:04:58		Ryan	Hall	USA	14.10.82	4		Boston	18 Apr 11

Illegally paced

Mark	Wind	Name		Nat	Born	Pos	Meet	Venue	Date
2:00:25		Eliud	Kipchoge	KEN	5.11.84	1		Monza	6 May 17

2000 METRES STEEPLECHASE

Mark	Wind	Name		Nat	Born	Pos	Meet	Venue	Date
5:10.68		Mahiedine	Mekhissi-Benabbad	FRA	15.3.85	1		Reims	30 Jun 10
5:13.47		Bouabdellah	Tahri	FRA	20.12.78	1		Tomblaine	25 Jun 10
5:14.43		Julius	Kariuki	KEN	12.6.61	1		Rovereto	21 Aug 90
5:14.53		Saïf Saaeed	Shaheen	QAT	15.10.82	1	SGP	Doha	13 May 05
5:16.22		Phillip	Barkutwo	KEN	6.10.66	2		Rovereto	21 Aug 90
5:16.46		Wesley	Kiprotich	KEN	31.7.79	2	SGP	Doha	13 May 05
5:16.85		Eliud	Barngetuny	KEN	20.5.73	1		Parma	13 Jun 95

3000 METRES STEEPLECHASE

Mark	Wind	Name		Nat	Born	Pos	Meet	Venue	Date
7:53.63	WR	Saïf Saaeed	Shaheen	KEN/QAT	15.10.82	1	VD	Bruxelles	3 Sep 04
7:53.64		Brimin	Kipruto	KEN	31.7.85	1	Herc	Monaco	22 Jul 11
7:54.31		Paul Kipsiele	Koech	KEN	10.11.81	1	GGala	Roma	31 May 12
7:55.28	WR	Brahim	Boulami ¶	MAR	20.4.72	1	VD	Bruxelles	24 Aug 01
7:55.51			Shaheen			1	VD	Bruxelles	26 Aug 05
7:55.72	WR	Bernard	Barmasai	KEN	6.5.74	1	ASV	Köln	24 Aug 97
7:55.76		Ezekiel	Kemboi	KEN	25.5.82	2	Herc	Monaco	22 Jul 11
7:56.16		Moses	Kiptanui	KEN	1.10.70	2	ASV	Köln	24 Aug 97
7:56.32			Shaheen			1	Tsik	Athína	3 Jul 06
7:56.34			Shaheen			1	GGala	Roma	8 Jul 05
7:56.37			P K Koech			2	GGala	Roma	8 Jul 05
7:56.54			Shaheen			1	WK	Zürich	18 Aug 06
7:56.58			P K Koech			1	DL	Doha	11 May 12
7:56.81		Richard	Mateelong	KEN	14.10.83	2	DL	Doha	11 May 12
7:56.94			Shaheen			1	WAF	Monaco	19 Sep 04
7:57.28			Shaheen			1	Tsik	Athína	14 Jun 05
7:57.29		Reuben	Kosgei	KEN	2.8.79	2	VD	Bruxelles	24 Aug 01
7:57.32			P K Koech			3	Herc	Monaco	22 Jul 11
7:57.38			Shaheen			1	WAF	Monaco	14 Sep 03
7:57.42			P K Koech			2	WAF	Monaco	14 Sep 03
7:58.09			Boulami			1	Herc	Monaco	19 Jul 02
7:58.10			S Cherono			2	Herc	Monaco	19 Jul 02
7:58.41		Jairus	Birech (10)	KEN	14.12.92	1	VD	Bruxelles	5 Sep 14
7:58.50			Boulami			1	WK	Zürich	17 Aug 01
7:58.66			S Cherono			3	VD	Bruxelles	24 Aug 01
7:58.80			P K Koech			1	VD	Bruxelles	14 Sep 07
7:58.83			Birech			1	DL	Saint-Denis	4 Jul 15
7:58.85			Kemboi			1	SGP	Doha	8 May 09
7:58.98			Barmasai			1	Herc	Monaco	4 Aug 99
7:59.03			Karoki						
Kemboi			1	DL	Saint-Denis	6 Jul 13			
		(30/10)							
7:59.08	WR	Wilson	Boit Kipketer	KEN	6.10.73	1	WK	Zürich	13 Aug 97
8:00.09		Mahiedine	Mekhissi-Benabbad	FRA	15.3.85	2	DL	Saint-Denis	6 Jul 13
8:00.12		Conseslus	Kipruto	KEN	8.12.94	1	DL	Birmingham	5 Jun 16
8:00.45		Evan	Jager	USA	8.3.89	2	DL	Saint-Denis	4 Jul 15
8:01.18		Bouabdellah	Tahri	FRA	20.12.78	3	WCh	Berlin	18 Aug 09
8:01.67		Abel	Mutai	KEN	2.10.88	2	GGala	Roma	31 May 12
8:01.69		Kipkirui	Misoi	KEN	23.12.78	4	VD	Bruxelles	24 Aug 01
8:03.41		Patrick	Sang	KEN	11.4.64	3	ASV	Köln	24 Aug 97
8:03.57		Ali	Ezzine	MAR	3.9.78	1	Gaz	Saint-Denis	23 Jun 00
8:03.57		Hillary	Yego	KEN	2.4.92	3	DL	Shanghai	18 May 13
		(20)							

Mark	Wind	Name		Nat	Born	Pos	Meet	Venue	Date
8:03.74		Raymond	Yator	KEN	7.4.81	3	Herc	Monaco	18 Aug 00
8:03.81		Benjamin	Kiplagat	UGA	4.3.89	2	Athl	Lausanne	8 Jul 10
8:03.89		John	Kosgei	KEN	13.7.73	3	Herc	Monaco	16 Aug 97
8:04.83		Soufiane	El Bakkali	MAR	7.1.96	2	VD-DLF	Bruxelles	1 Sep 17
8:04.95		Simon	Vroemen ¶	NED	11.5.69	2	VD	Bruxelles	26 Aug 05
8:05.01		Eliud	Barngetuny	KEN	20.5.73	1	Herc	Monaco	25 Jul 95
8:05.35 WR		Peter	Koech	KEN	18.2.58	1	DNG	Stockholm	3 Jul 89
8:05.37		Philip	Barkutwo	KEN	6.10.66	2		Rieti	6 Sep 92
8:05.4 WR		Henry	Rono	KEN	12.2.52	1		Seattle	13 May 78
8:05.43		Christopher	Kosgei	KEN	14.8.74	2	WK	Zürich	11 Aug 99
		(30)							
8:05.51		Julius	Kariuki	KEN	12.6.61	1	OG	Seoul	30 Sep 88
8:05.68		Wesley	Kiprotich	KEN	1.8.79	4	VD	Bruxelles	3 Sep 04
8:05.75		Mustafa	Mohamed	SWE	1.3.79	1	NA	Heusden-Zolder	28 Jul 07
8:05.88		Bernard	Mbugua Nganga	KEN	17.1.85	2	ISTAF	Berlin	11 Sep 11
8:05.99		Joseph	Keter	KEN	13.6.69	1	Herc	Monaco	10 Aug 96
8:06.13		Tareq Mubarak	Taher	BRN	24.3.84	3	Tsik	Athína	13 Jul 09
8:06.16		Roba	Gari	ETH	12.4.82	3	DL	Doha	11 May 12
8:06.77		Gideon	Chirchir	KEN	24.2.66	2	WK	Zürich	16 Aug 95
8:06.88		Richard	Kosgei	KEN	29.12.70	2	GPF	Monaco	9 Sep 95
8:06.96		Gilbert	Kirui	KEN	22.1.94	2	DL	London (OS)	27 Jul 13
		(40)							
8:07.02		Brahim	Taleb	MAR	16.2.85	2	NA	Heusden-Zolder	28 Jul 07
8:07.13		Paul	Kosgei	KEN	22.4.78	2	GP II	Saint-Denis	3 Jul 99
8:07.18		Obaid Moussa	Amer ¶	KEN/QAT	18.4.85	4	OG	Athína	24 Aug 04
8:07.44		Luis Miguel	Martín	ESP	11.1.72	2	VD	Bruxelles	30 Aug 02
8:07.59		Julius	Nyamu	KEN	1.12.77	5	VD	Bruxelles	24 Aug 01
8:07.62		Joseph	Mahmoud	FRA	13.12.55	1	VD	Bruxelles	24 Aug 84
8:07.75		Jonathan	Ndiku Muia	KEN	18.9.91	6	Herc	Monaco	22 Jul 11
8:07.96		Mark	Rowland	GBR	7.3.63	3	OG	Seoul	30 Sep 88
8:08.02 WR		Anders	Gärderud	SWE	28.8.46	1	OG	Montreal	28 Jul 76
8:08.12		Matthew	Birir	KEN	5.7.72	3	GGala	Roma	8 Jun 95
		(50)	100th man 8:11.82, 200th 8:17.09, 300th 8:20.70, 400th 8:23.16, 500th 8:25.4						

7:53.63 Shaheen formerly Stephen Cherono KEO

Drugs disqualification: 7:53.17 Brahim Boulami ¶ MAR 20.4.72 1 WK Zürich 16 Aug 02

110 METRES HURDLES

Mark	Wind	Name		Nat	Born	Pos	Meet	Venue	Date
12.80 WR	0.3	Aries	Merritt	USA	24.7.85	1	VD	Bruxelles	7 Sep 12
12.87 WR	0.9	Dayron	Robles	CUB	19.11.86	1	GS	Ostrava	12 Jun 08
12.88 WR	1.1		Liu Xiang	CHN	13.7.83	1rA	Athl	Lausanne	11 Jul 06
12.88	0.5		Robles			1	Gaz	Saint-Denis	18 Jul 08
12.89	0.5	David	Oliver	USA	24.4.82	1	DL	Saint-Denis	16 Jul 10
12.90	1.1	Dominique	Arnold	USA	14.9.73	2rA	Athl	Lausanne	11 Jul 06
12.90	1.6		Oliver			1	Pre	Eugene	3 Jul 10
12.90	0.7	Omar	McLeod	JAM	25.4.94	1	NC	Kingston	24 Jun 17
12.91 WR	0.5	Colin	Jackson	GBR	18.2.67	1	WCh	Stuttgart	20 Aug 93
12.91 WR	0.3		Liu Xiang			1	OG	Athína	27 Aug 04
12.91	0.2		Robles			1	DNG	Stockholm	22 Jul 08
12.92 WR	-0.1	Roger	Kingdom	USA	26.8.62	1	WK	Zürich	16 Aug 89
12.92	0.9	Allen	Johnson	USA	1.3.71	1	NC	Atlanta	23 Jun 96
12.92	0.2		Johnson			1	VD	Bruxelles	23 Aug 96
12.92	1.5		Liu Xiang			1	GP	New York	2 Jun 07
12.92	0.0		Robles			1	WAF	Stuttgart	23 Sep 07
12.92	-0.3		Merritt			1	OG	London (OS)	8 Aug 12
12.93 WR	-0.2	Renaldo	Nehemiah (10)	USA	24.3.59	1	WK	Zürich	19 Aug 81
12.93	0.0		Johnson			1	WCh	Athína	7 Aug 97
12.93	-0.6		Liu Xiang			1	WAF	Stuttgart	9 Sep 06
12.93	0.1		Robles			1	OG	Beijing	21 Aug 08
12.93	1.7		Oliver			1	NC	Des Moines	27 Jun 10
12.93	-0.3		Oliver			1	WK	Zürich	19 Aug 10
12.93	1.2		Merritt			1	NC/OT	Eugene	30 Jun 12
12.93	0.6		Merritt			1	LGP	London (CP)	13 Jul 12
12.93	0.0		Merritt			1	Herc	Monaco	20 Jul 12
12.94	1.6	Jack	Pierce	USA	23.9.62	1s2	NC	Atlanta	22 Jun 96
12.94	1.8		Oliver			1	Pre	Eugene	4 Jun 11
12.94	0.1		Merritt			1s2	OG	London (OS)	8 Aug 12
12.94	0.8	Hansle	Parchment	JAM	17.6.90	1	DL	Saint-Denis	5 Jul 14
12.94	0.5	Orlando	Ortega	CUB/ESP	29.7.91	1	DL	Saint-Denis	4 Jul 15
		(31/13)							

Mark	Wind	Name		Nat	Born	Pos	Meet	Venue	Date
12.95	1.5	Terrence	Trammell	USA	23.11.78	2	GP	New York	2 Jun 07
12.95	0.2	Pascal	Martinot-Lagarde	FRA	22.9.91	1	Herc	Monaco	18 Jul 14
12.97	1.0	Ladji	Doucouré	FRA	28.3.83	1	NC	Angers	15 Jul 05
12.98	0.6	Mark	Crear	USA	2.10.68	1		Zagreb	5 Jul 99
12.98	1.5	Jason	Richardson	USA	4.4.86	1s3	NC/OT	Eugene	30 Jun 12
12.98	0.2	Sergey	Shubenkov	RUS	4.10.90	1	WCh	Beijing	28 Aug 15
12.99	1.2	Ronnie	Ash	USA	2.7.88	1s1	NC	Sacramento	29 Jun 14
		(20)							
13.00	0.5	Anthony	Jarrett	GBR	13.8.68	2	WCh	Stuttgart	20 Aug 93
13.00	0.6	Anier	García	CUB	9.3.76	1	OG	Sydney	25 Sep 00
13.01	0.3	Larry	Wade ¶	USA	22.11.74	1rA	Athl	Lausanne	2 Jul 99
13.02	1.5	Ryan	Wilson	USA	19.12.80	3	GP	New York	2 Jun 07
13.02	1.7	David	Payne	USA	24.7.82	3	WCh	Osaka	31 Aug 07
13.03	-0.2	Greg	Foster	USA	4.8.58	2	WK	Zürich	19 Aug 81
13.03	1.0	Reggie	Torian	USA	22.4.75	1	NC	New Orleans	21 Jun 98
13.03	1.0	Devon	Allen	USA	12.12.94	1	NC/OT	Eugene	9 Jul 16
13.05	1.4	Tony	Dees ¶	USA	6.8.63	1		Vigo	23 Jul 91
13.05	-0.8	Florian	Schwarthoff	GER	7.5.68	1	NC	Bremen	2 Jul 95
		(30)							
13.05	-0.1	Ronald	Levy	JAM	30.10.92	1	DL	Paris (C)	1 Jul 17
13.08	1.2	Mark	McKoy	CAN	10.12.61	1	BNP	Villeneuve-d'Ascq	2 Jul 93
13.08	0.0	Stanislav	Olijar	LAT	22.3.79	2	Athl	Lausanne	1 Jul 03
13.08	1.2	Jeff	Porter	USA	27.11.85	3	NC/OT	Eugene	30 Jun 12
13.09	2.0	Antwon	Hicks	USA	12.3.83	2s2	NC/OT	Eugene	6 Jul 08
13.09	0.6	Garfield	Darien	FRA	22.12.87	1	GS	Ostrava	28 Jun 17
13.11	0.5	Aleec	Harris	USA	31.10.90	4	DL	Saint-Denis	4 Jul 15
13.11	1.8	Antonio	Alkana	RSA	12.4.90	1	Odlozil	Praha	5 Jun 17
13.12	1.5	Falk	Balzer ¶	GER	14.12.73	2	EC	Budapest	22 Aug 98
13.12	1.0	Duane	Ross ¶	USA	5.12.72	3	WCh	Sevilla	25 Aug 99
		(40)							
13.12	1.9	Anwar	Moore	USA	5.3.79	1	ModR	Modesto	5 May 07
13.12	0.0	Dimitri	Bascou	FRA	20.7.87	2	Herc	Monaco	15 Jul 16
13.13	1.6	Igor	Kovác	SVK	12.5.69	1	DNG	Stockholm	7 Jul 97
13.13	2.0	Dexter	Faulk	USA	14.4.84	2	GS	Ostrava	17 Jun 09
13.14	0.1	Ryan	Brathwaite	BAR	6.6.88	1	WCh	Berlin	20 Aug 09
13.14	0.0	Andrew	Riley	JAM	6.9.88	4	DL	Saint-Denis	6 Jul 13
13.14	-0.1	Andrew	Pozzi	GBR	15.5.92	2	DL	Paris (C)	1 Jul 17
13.15	0.3	Robin	Korving	NED	29.7.74	5rA	Athl	Lausanne	2 Jul 99
13.15	0.1	Dwight	Thomas	JAM	23.9.80	2	Bisl	Oslo	9 Jun 11
13.15	-0.3	Garfield	Darien	FRA	22.12.87	1s3	EC	Helsinki	1 Jul 12
13.15	0.3	Balázs	Baji	HUN	9.6.89	4	Gyulai	Székesfehérvár	4 Jul 17
		(53)	100th man 13.26, 200th 13.39, 300th 13.47, 400th 13.53, 500th 13.58						

Rolling start but accepted by race officials

Mark	Wind	Name		Nat	Born	Pos	Meet	Venue	Date
13.10A	2.0	Falk	Balzer ¶	GER	14.12.73	1	WCp	Johannesburg	13 Sep 98

Doubtful timing: Scheessel 4 Jun 95 +1.3 1. Mike Fenner GER 24.4.71 13.06, 2. Eric Kaiser ¶ GER 7.3.71 13.08

Wind-assisted marks *Performances to 12.94, performers to 13.14*12.87 2.6
Roger Kingdom USA 26.8.62 1
WCp Barcelona 10 Sep 89

Mark	Wind	Name		Nat	Born	Pos	Meet	Venue	Date
12.87	2.4		Liu Xiang	CHN	13.7.83	1	Pre	Eugene	2 Jun 12
12.89	3.2	David	Oliver	USA	24.4.82	1s1	NC/OT	Eugene	6 Jul 08
12.91	3.5	Renaldo	Nehemiah	USA	24.3.59	1	NCAA	Champaign	1 Jun 79
12.94A	2.8		Jackson			1rA		Sestriere	31 Jul 94
12.98	3.1	Ronnie	Ash	USA	2.7.88	1	NACAC	Miramar	9 Jul 10
13.00	2.6	Anwar	Moore	USA	5.3.79	1	DrakeR	Des Moines	28 Apr 07
13.05	3.6	Ryan	Brathwaite	BAR	6.6.88	1		Austin	2 May 09
13.05	2.1	Dimitri	Bascou	FRA	20.7.87	1	NC	Angers	26 Jun 16
13.06	2.1	Mark	McKoy	CAN	10.12.61	1	Gugl	Linz	13 Aug 92
13.12	2.4	Dexter	Faulk	USA	14.4.84	4	Pre	Eugene	2 Jun 12
13.13	5.8	Andrew	Pozzi	GBR	15.5.92	1		Clermont	15 Apr 17
13.14	2.9	Igor	Kazanov	LAT	24.9.63	1r1	Znam	Leningrad	8 Jun 86
13.14	4.7	Lawrence	Clarke	GBR	12.3.90	1h1		Madrid	7 Jul 12
13.14	3.8	Wayne	Davis	TTO	22.8.91	1	NCAA	Eugene	8 Jun 13
13.15	2.1	Courtney	Hawkins	USA	11.7.67	1		Salamanca	10 Jul 98
13.15	2.1	Wilhem	Bélocian	FRA	22.6.95	2	NC	Angers	26 Jun 16

Hand timing

Mark	Wind	Name		Nat	Born	Pos	Meet	Venue	Date
12.7		Sergey	Shubenkov	RUS	4.10.90	1		Barnaul	2 Jul 16
12.8	1.0	Renaldo	Nehemiah	USA	24.3.59	1		Kingston	11 May 79
12.9	0.0	Yordan	O'Farrill	CUB	9.2.93	1	Barr	La Habana	23 May 14

Wind-assisted

Mark	Wind	Name		Nat	Born	Pos	Meet	Venue	Date
12.8	2.4	Colin	Jackson	GBR	18.2.67	1		Sydney	10 Jan 90
12.9	4.1	Mark	Crear	USA	2.10.68	1rA	S&W	Modesto	8 May 93
12.9	3.1	William	Sharman	GBR	12.9.84	1r2		Madrid	2 Jul 10

400 METRES HURDLES

Mark	Wind	Name		Nat	Born	Pos	Meet	Venue	Date
46.78	WR	Kevin	Young	USA	16.9.66	1	OG	Barcelona	6 Aug 92
47.02	WR	Edwin	Moses	USA	31.8.55	1		Koblenz	31 Aug 83
47.03		Bryan	Bronson ¶	USA	9.9.72	1	NC	New Orleans	21 Jun 98
47.10		Samuel	Matete	ZAM	27.7.68	1rA	WK	Zürich	7 Aug 91
47.13	WR		Moses			1		Milano	3 Jul 80
47.14			Moses			1	Athl	Lausanne	14 Jul 81
47.17			Moses			1	ISTAF	Berlin	8 Aug 80
47.18			Young			1	WCh	Stuttgart	19 Aug 93
47.19		Andre	Phillips	USA	5.9.59	1	OG	Seoul	25 Sep 88
47.23		Amadou	Dia Bâ	SEN	22.9.58	2	OG	Seoul	25 Sep 88
47.24		Kerron	Clement	USA	31.10.85	1	NC	Carson	26 Jun 05
47.25		Félix	Sánchez	DOM	30.8.77	1	WCh	Saint-Denis	29 Aug 03
47.25		Angelo	Taylor	USA	29.12.78	1	OG	Beijing	18 Aug 08
47.27			Moses			1	ISTAF	Berlin	21 Aug 81
47.30		Bershawn	Jackson (10)	USA	8.5.83	1	WCh	Helsinki	9 Aug 05
47.32			Moses			1		Koblenz	29 Aug 84
47.32			Jackson			1	NC	Des Moines	26 Jun 10
47.35			Sánchez			1rA	WK	Zürich	16 Aug 02
47.37			Moses			1	WCp	Roma	4 Sep 81
47.37			Moses			1	WK	Zürich	24 Aug 83
47.37			Moses			1	NC/OT	Indianapolis	17 Jul 88
47.37			Young			1	Athl	Lausanne	7 Jul 93
47.37		Stéphane	Diagana	FRA	23.7.69	1	Athl	Lausanne	5 Jul 95
47.38			Moses			1	Athl	Lausanne	2 Sep 86
47.38		Danny	Harris ¶	USA	7.9.65	1	Athl	Lausanne	10 Jul 91
47.38			Sánchez			1rA	WK	Zürich	17 Aug 01
47.39			Clement			1	NC	Indianapolis	24 Jun 06
47.40			Young			1	WK	Zürich	19 Aug 92
47.42			Young			1	ASV	Köln	16 Aug 92
47.43			Moses			1	ASV	Köln	28 Aug 83
47.43		James	Carter	USA	7.5.78	2	WCh	Helsinki	9 Aug 05
		(31/13)							
47.48		Harald	Schmid	FRG	29.9.57	1	EC	Athína	8 Sep 82
47.53		Hadi Soua'an	Al-Somaily	KSA	21.8.76	2	OG	Sydney	27 Sep 00
47.54		Derrick	Adkins	USA	2.7.70	2	Athl	Lausanne	5 Jul 95
47.54		Fabrizio	Mori	ITA	28.6.69	2	WCh	Edmonton	10 Aug 01
47.60		Winthrop	Graham	JAM	17.11.65	1	WK	Zürich	4 Aug 93
47.63		Johnny	Dutch	USA	20.1.89	2	NC	Des Moines	26 Jun 10
47.66A		L.J. 'Louis'	van Zyl	RSA	20.7.85	1		Pretoria	25 Feb 11
		(20)							
47.67		Bennie	Brazell	USA	2.6.82	2	NCAA	Sacramento	11 Jun 05
47.69		Jehue	Gordon	TTO	15.12.91	1	WCh	Moskva	15 Aug 13
47.70		Michael	Tinsley	USA	21.4.84	2	WCh	Moskva	15 Aug 13
47.72		Javier	Culson	PUR	25.7.84	1		Ponce	8 May 10
47.75		David	Patrick	USA	12.6.60	4	NC/OT	Indianapolis	17 Jul 88
47.78		Boniface Mucheru	Tumuti	KEN	2.5.92	2	OG	Rio de Janeiro	18 Aug 16
47.79		Nicholas	Bett	KEN	14.6.92	1	WCh	Beijing	25 Aug 15
47.80		Kyron	McMaster	IVB	3.1.97	1		Kingston	20 May 17
47.81		Llewellyn	Herbert	RSA	21.7.77	3	OG	Sydney	27 Sep 00
47.82	WR	John	Akii-Bua	UGA	3.12.49	1	OG	München	2 Sep 72
		(30)							
47.82		Kriss	Akabusi	GBR	28.11.58	3	OG	Barcelona	6 Aug 92
47.82		Periklis	Iakovákis	GRE	24.3.79	2	GP	Osaka	6 May 06
47.84		Bayano	Kamani	PAN	17.4.80	2s1	WCh	Helsinki	7 Aug 05
47.84		David	Greene	GBR	11.4.86	2	DL	Saint-Denis	6 Jul 12
47.89		Dai	Tamesue	JPN	3.5.78	3	WCh	Edmonton	10 Aug 01
47.91		Calvin	Davis	USA	2.4.72	1s2	OG	Atlanta	31 Jul 96
47.92		Aleksandr	Vasilyev	BLR	26.7.61	2	ECp	Moskva	17 Aug 85
47.92		Yasmani	Copello	CUB/TUR	15.4.87	3	OG	Rio de Janeiro	18 Aug 16
47.93		Kenji	Narisako	JPN	25.7.84	3	GP	Osaka	6 May 06
47.93		Jeshua	Anderson	USA	22.6.89	1	NC	Eugene	26 Jun 11
		(40)							
47.93		Omar	Cisneros	CUB	19.11.89	1s3	WCh	Moskva	13 Aug 13
47.94		Eric	Thomas	USA	1.12.73	1	GGala	Roma	30 Jun 00
47.97		Maurice	Mitchell	USA	14.5.71	2rA	WK	Zürich	14 Aug 96
47.97		Joey	Woody	USA	22.5.73	3	NC	New Orleans	21 Jun 98
47.97		Thomas	Barr	IRL	24.7.92	4	OG	Rio de Janeiro	18 Aug 16
47.98		Sven	Nylander	SWE	1.1.62	4	OG	Atlanta	1 Aug 96

Mark	Wind	Name		Nat	Born	Pos	Meet	Venue	Date
48.00		Danny	McFarlane	JAM	14.2.72	1s2	OG	Athína	24 Aug 04
48.02A		Ockert	Cilliers	RSA	21.4.81	1		Pretoria	20 Feb 04
48.04		Eronilde	de Araújo	BRA	31.12.70	2	Nik	Nice	12 Jul 95
48.05		Ken	Harnden	ZIM	31.3.73	1	GP	Paris (C)	29 Jul 98
48.05		Kemel	Thompson	JAM	25.9.74	1	GP	London (CP)	8 Aug 03
48.05		Isa	Phillips	JAM	22.4.84	1	NC	Kingston	27 Jun 09
48.05		Emir	Bekric	SRB	14.3.91	3	WCh	Moskva	15 Aug 13
48.05		Denis	Kudryavtsev	RUS	13.4.92	2	WCh	Beijing	25 Aug 15
		(54)	100th man 48.41, 200th man 48.91, 300th man 49.15, 400th 49.36, 500th 49.53						

Best at low altitude: 47.66 van Zyl 1 GS Ostrava 31 May 11
Drugs disqualification 47.15 Bronson ¶ 1 GWG Uniondale, NY 19 Jul 98

HIGH JUMP

Mark	Wind	Name		Nat	Born	Pos	Meet	Venue	Date
2.45 WR		Javier	Sotomayor ¶	CUB	13.10.67	1		Salamanca	27 Jul 93
2.44 WR			Sotomayor			1	CAC	San Juan	29 Jul 89
2.43 WR			Sotomayor			1		Salamanca	8 Sep 88
2.43i			Sotomayor			1	WI	Budapest	4 Mar 89
2.43		Mutaz Essa	Barshim	QAT	24.6.91	1	VD	Bruxelles	5 Sep 14
2.42 WR		Patrik	Sjöberg	SWE	5.1.65	1	DNG	Stockholm	30 Jun 87
2.42i WR		Carlo	Thränhardt	FRG	5.7.57	1		Berlin	26 Feb 88
2.42			Sotomayor			1		Sevilla	5 Jun 94
2.42i		Ivan	Ukhov	RUS	29.3.86	1		Praha	25 Feb 14
2.42		Bohdan	Bondarenko	UKR	30.8.89	1	adidas	New York	14 Jun 14
2.42			Barshim			2	adidas	New York	14 Jun 14
2.41 WR		Igor	Paklin	KGZ	15.6.63	1	WUG	Kobe	4 Sep 85
2.41i			Sjöberg			1		Pireás	1 Feb 87
2.41i			Sotomayor			1	WI	Toronto	14 Mar 93
2.41			Sotomayor			1	NC	La Habana	25 Jun 94
2.41			Sotomayor			1	TSB	London (CP)	15 Jul 94
2.41			Bondarenko			1	Athl	Lausanne	4 Jul 13
2.41			Bondarenko			1	WCh	Moskva	15 Aug 13
2.41i			Ukhov			1		Chelyabinsk	16 Jan 14
2.41			Ukhov			1	DL	Doha	9 May 14
2.41			Barshim			1	GGala	Roma	5 Jun 14
2.41			Barshim			1		Eberstadt	22 Aug 14
2.41i			Barshim			1		Athlone	18 Feb 15
2.41		(24/7)	Barshim			1	Pre	Eugene	30 May 15
2.40 WR		Rudolf	Povarnitsyn	UKR	13.6.62	1		Donetsk	11 Aug 85
2.40		Sorin	Matei	ROU	6.7.63	1	PTS	Bratislava	20 Jun 90
2.40i		Hollis	Conway (10)	USA	8.1.67	1	WI	Sevilla	10 Mar 91
2.40		Charles	Austin	USA	19.12.67	1	WK	Zürich	7 Aug 91
2.40		Vyacheslav	Voronin	RUS	5.4.74	1	BrGP	London (CP)	5 Aug 00
2.40i		Stefan	Holm	SWE	25.5.76	1	EI	Madrid	6 Mar 05
2.40i		Aleksey	Dmitrik	RUS	12.4.84	1		Arnstadt	8 Feb 14
2.40		Derek	Drouin	CAN	6.3.90	1	DrakeR	Des Moines	25 Apr 14
2.40		Andriy	Protsenko	UKR	20.5.88	2	Athl	Lausanne	3 Jul 14

2.40 27 more performances: Sotomayor 13, Barshim 3
5, Bondarenko 4, Sjöberg, Ukhov 2, Thränhardt1 for (58/16)

Mark	Wind	Name		Nat	Born	Pos	Meet	Venue	Date
2.39 WR			Zhu Jianhua	CHN	29.5.63	1		Eberstadt	10 Jun 84
2.39i		Dietmar	Mögenburg	FRG	15.8.61	1		Köln	24 Feb 85
2.39i		Ralf	Sonn	GER	17.1.67	1		Berlin	1 Mar 91
2.39		Gianmarco (20)	Tamberi	ITA	1.6.92	1	Herc	Monaco	15 Jul 16
2.38i		Gennadiy	Avdeyenko	UKR	4.11.63	2	WI	Indianapolis	7 Mar 87
2.38		Sergey	Malchenko	RUS	2.11.63	1		Banská Bystrica	4 Sep 88
2.38		Dragutin	Topic ¶	YUG	12.3.71	1		Beograd	1 Aug 93
2.38i		Steve	Smith	GBR	29.3.73	2		Wuppertal	4 Feb 94
2.38i		Wolf-Hendrik	Beyer	GER	14.2.72	1		Weinheim	18 Mar 94
2.38		Troy	Kemp	BAH	18.6.66	1	Nik	Nice	12 Jul 95
2.38		Artur	Partyka	POL	25.7.69	1		Eberstadt	18 Aug 96
2.38i		Matt	Hemingway	USA	24.10.72	1	NC	Atlanta	4 Mar 00
2.38i		Yaroslav	Rybakov	RUS	22.11.80	1		Stockholm	15 Feb 05
2.38		Jacques (30)	Freitag	RSA	11.6.82	1		Oudtshoorn	5 Mar 05
2.38		Andriy	Sokolovskyy	UKR	16.7.78	1	GGala	Roma	8 Jul 05
2.38i		Linus	Thörnblad	SWE	6.3.85	2	NC	Göteborg	25 Feb 07
2.38		Andrey	Silnov	RUS	9.9.84	1	LGP	London (CP)	25 Jul 08
2.38			Zhang Guowei	CHN	4.6.91	2	Pre	Eugene	30 May 15
2.38		Danil	Lysenko	RUS	19.5.97	2		Eberstadt	27 Aug 17
2.37		Valeriy	Sereda	RUS	30.6.59	1		Rieti	2 Sep 84

Mark	Wind	Name		Nat	Born	Pos	Meet	Venue	Date
2.37		Tom	McCants	USA	27.11.62	1	Owens	Columbus	8 May 88
2.37		Jerome	Carter	USA	25.3.63	2	Owens	Columbus	8 May 88
2.37		Sergey	Dymchenko	UKR	23.8.67	1		Kyiv	16 Sep 90
2.37i		Dalton	Grant	GBR	8.4.66	1	EI	Paris	13 Mar 94
		(40)							
2.37i		Jaroslav	Bába	CZE	2.9.84	2		Arnstadt	5 Feb 05
2.37		Jesse	Williams	USA	27.12.83	1	NC	Eugene	26 Jun 11
2.37		Robbie	Grabarz	GBR	3.10.87	3	Athl	Lausanne	23 Aug 12
2.37		Eric	Kynard	USA	3.2.91	2	Athl	Lausanne	4 Jul 13
2.37		Donald	Thomas	BAH	1.7.84	1	Gyulai	Székesfehérvár	18 Jul 16
2.36	WR	Gerd	Wessig	GDR	16.7.59	1	OG	Moskva	1 Aug 80
2.36		Sergey	Zasimovich	KZK	6.9.62	1		Tashkent	5 May 84
2.36		Eddy	Annys	BEL	15.12.58	1		Gent	26 May 85
2.36i		Jim	Howard	USA	11.9.59	1		Albuquerque	25 Jan 86
2.36i		Jan	Zvara	CZE	12.2.63	1	vGDR	Jablonec	14 Feb 87
		(50)	100th man 2.34, 200th 2.31, 300th 2.30, 400th 2.28, 500th 2.27						

Mark	Name		Nat	Date
2.36	Gerd	Nagel	FRG	17 Mar 89
2.36	Nick	Saunders	BER	1 Feb 90
2.36	Doug	Nordquist	USA	15 Jun 90
2.36	Georgi	Dakov	BUL	10 Aug 90
2.36	Lábros	Papakóstas	GRE	21 Jun 92
2.36i	Steinar	Hoen	NOR	12 Feb 94
2.36	Tim	Forsyth	AUS	2 Mar 97
2.36	Sergey	Klyugin	RUS	12 Aug 98
2.36	Konstantin	Matusevich	ISR	5 Feb 00
2.36	Martin	Buss	GER	8 Aug 01
2.36	Aleksander	Walerianczyk	POL	20 Jul 03
2.36	Michal	Bieniek	POL	28 May 05
2.36i	Andrey	Tereshin	RUS	17 Feb 06
2.36A	Dusty	Jonas	USA	18 May 08
2.36	Aleksandr	Shustov	RUS	23 Jul 11
2.36i	Chris	Baker	GBR	13 Feb 16
2.36	Majed El Dein	Ghazal	SYR	18 May 16
	(67)			

Best outdoor marks for athletes with indoor bests

Mark	Name	Pos	Meet	Venue	Date
2.41	Ukhov	1	DL	Doha	9 May 14
2.39	Conway	1	USOF	Norman	30 Jul 89
2.38	Avdeyenko	2=	WCh	Roma	6 Sep 87
2.37	Thränhardt	2		Rieti	2 Sep 84
2.37	Smith	1	WJ	Seoul	20 Sep 92
2.37	Holm	1		Athína	13 Jul 08
2.36	Mögenburg	3		Eberstadt	10 Jun 84
2.36	Howard	1		Rehlingen	8 Jun 87
2.36	Zvara	1		Praha	23 Aug 87
2.36	Grant	4	WCh	Tokyo	1 Sep 91
2.36	Hoen	1		Oslo	1 Jul 97
2.36	Bába	2=	GGala	Roma	8 Jul 05
2.36	Dmitrik	1	NC	Chelyabinsk	23 Jul 11

Ancillary jumps – en route to final marks

Mark	Name	Date
2.40	Sotomayor	8 Sep 88
2.40	Sotomayor	29 Jul 89
2.40	Sotomayor	5 Jun 94
2.40	Bondarenko	14 Jun 14
2.40	Barshim	14 Jun 14
2.40	Barshim	5 Sep 14

POLE VAULT

Mark	Wind	Name		Nat	Born	Pos	Meet	Venue	Date
6.16i	WR	Renaud	Lavillenie	FRA	18.9.86	1		Donetsk	15 Feb 14
6.15i	WR	Sergey	Bubka	UKR	4.12.63	1		Donetsk	21 Feb 93
6.14i	WIR		Bubka			1		Liévin	13 Feb 93
6.14A	WIR		Bubka			1		Sestriere	31 Jul 94
6.13i	WIR		Bubka			1		Berlin	21 Feb 92
6.13	WR		Bubka			1	TOTO	Tokyo	19 Sep 92
6.12i	WIR		Bubka			1	Mast	Grenoble	23 Mar 91
6.12	WR		Bubka			1		Padova	30 Aug 92
6.11i	WIR		Bubka			1		Donetsk	19 Mar 91
6.11	WR		Bubka			1		Dijon	13 Jun 92
6.10i	WIR		Bubka			1		San Sebastián	15 Mar 91
6.10	WR		Bubka			1	MAI	Malmö	5 Aug 91
6.09	WR		Bubka			1		Formia	8 Jul 91
6.08i	WIR		Bubka			1	NC	Volgograd	9 Feb 91
6.08	WR		Bubka			1	Znam	Moskva	9 Jun 91
6.08i			Lavillenie			1		Bydgoszcz	31 Jan 14
6.07	WR		Bubka			1	Super	Shizuoka	6 May 91
6.06	WR		Bubka			1	Nik	Nice	10 Jul 88
6.06i		Steve	Hooker	AUS	16.7.82	1		Boston (R)	7 Feb 09
6.05	WR		Bubka			1	PTS	Bratislava	9 Jun 88
6.05i			Bubka			1		Donetsk	17 Mar 90
6.05i			Bubka			1		Berlin	5 Mar 93
6.05			Bubka			1	GPF	London (CP)	10 Sep 93
6.05i			Bubka			1	Mast	Grenoble	6 Feb 94
6.05			Bubka			1	ISTAF	Berlin	30 Aug 94
6.05			Bubka			1	GPF	Fukuoka	13 Sep 97
6.05		Maksim	Tarasov	RUS	2.12.70	1	GP II	Athína	16 Jun 99
6.05		Dmitriy	Markov	BLR/AUS	14.3.75	1	WCh	Edmonton	9 Aug 01
6.05			Lavillenie			1	Pre	Eugene	30 May 15
6.04		Brad	Walker	USA	21.6.81	1	Pre	Eugene	8 Jun 08
6.04i			Lavillenie			1		Rouen	25 Jan 14
6.04i		(32/6)	Lavillenie			1	EI	Praha (O2)	7 Mar 15

Mark	Wind	Name		Nat	Born	Pos	Meet	Venue	Date
6.03		Okkert	Brits	RSA	22.8.73	1	ASV	Köln	18 Aug 95
6.03		Jeff	Hartwig	USA	25.9.67	1		Jonesboro	14 Jun 00
6.03		Thiago	Braz da Silva	BRA	16.12.93	1	OG	Rio de Janeiro	15 Aug 16
6.02i		Rodion	Gataullin	RUS	23.11.65	1	NC	Gomel	4 Feb 89
		(10)							
6.01		Igor	Trandenkov	RUS	17.8.66	1	NC	Sankt Peterburg	4 Jul 96
		Hit bar hard, but kept it on with his hand illegally. Next best 5.95				1		Dijon	26 May 96
6.01		Tim	Mack	USA	15.9.72	1	WAF	Monaco	18 Sep 04
6.01		Yevgeniy	Lukyanenko	RUS	23.1.85	1	EAF	Bydgoszcz	1 Jul 08
6.01	sq	Björn	Otto	GER	16.10.77	1		Aachen	5 Sep 12
6.00		Tim	Lobinger	GER	3.9.72	1	ASV	Köln	24 Aug 97
6.00i		Jean	Galfione	FRA	9.6.71	1	WI	Maebashi	6 Mar 99
6.00i		Danny	Ecker	GER	21.7.77	1		Dortmund	11 Feb 01
6.00		Toby	Stevenson	USA	19.11.76	1eA	CalR	Modesto	8 May 04
6.00		Paul	Burgess	AUS	14.8.79	1		Perth	25 Feb 05
6.00Ai		Shawnacy	Barber	CAN	27.5.94	1		Reno	15 Jan 16
		(20)							
6.00i		Piotr	Lisek	POL	16.8.92	1		Potsdam	4 Feb 17
6.00		Sam	Kendricks	USA	7.9.92	1	NC	Sacramento	24 Jun 17
5.98		Lawrence	Johnson	USA	7.5.74	1		Knoxville	25 May 96
5.97		Scott	Huffman	USA	30.11.64	1	NC	Knoxville	18 Jun 94
5.96		Joe	Dial	USA	26.10.62	1		Norman	18 Jun 87
5.95		Andrei	Tivontchik	GER	13.7.70	1	ASV	Köln	16 Aug 96
5.95		Michael	Stolle	GER	17.12.74	1	Herc	Monaco	18 Aug 00
5.95		Romain	Mesnil	FRA	13.6.77	1		Castres	6 Aug 03
5.94i		Philippe	Collet	FRA	13.12.63	1	Mast	Grenoble	10 Mar 90
5.94		Raphael	Holzdeppe	GER	28.9.89	1	NC	Nürnberg	26 Jul 15
		(30)							
5.93i	WIR	Billy	Olson	USA	19.7.58	1		East Rutherford	8 Feb 86
5.93i		Tye	Harvey	USA	25.9.74	2	NC	Atlanta	3 Mar 01
5.93		Alex	Averbukh	ISR	1.10.74	1	GP	Madrid (C)	19 Jul 03
5.93		Pawel	Wojciechowski	POL	6.6.89	2	Athl	Lausanne	6 Jul 17
5.92		István	Bagyula	HUN	2.1.69	1	Gugl	Linz	5 Jul 91
5.92		Igor	Potapovich	KAZ	6.9.67	2		Dijon	13 Jun 92
5.92		Dean	Starkey	USA	27.3.67	1	Banes	São Paulo	21 May 94
5.91	WR	Thierry	Vigneron	FRA	9.3.60	2	GGala	Roma	31 Aug 84
5.91i		Viktor	Ryzhenkov	UZB	25.8.66	2		San Sebastián	15 Mar 91
5.91A		Riaan	Botha	RSA	8.11.70	1		Pretoria	2 Apr 97
		(40)							
5.91		Malte	Mohr	GER	24.7.86	1		Ingolstadt	22 Jun 12
5.91		Konstadinos	Filippídis ¶	GRE	26.11.86	1	DL	Saint-Denis	4 Jul 15
5.90		Pierre	Quinon	FRA	20.2.62	2	Nik	Nice	16 Jul 85
5.90i		Ferenc	Salbert	HUN/FRA	5.8.60	1	Mast	Grenoble	14 Mar 87
5.90		Miroslaw	Chmara	POL	9.5.64	1	BNP	Villeneuve d'Ascq	27 Jun 88
5.90i		Grigoriy	Yegorov	KAZ	12.1.67	1		Yokohama	11 Mar 90
5.90		Denis	Petushinskiy ¶	RUS	28.6.67	1	Znam	Moskva	13 Jun 93
5.90i		Pyotr	Bochkaryov	RUS	3.11.67	1	EI	Paris (B)	12 Mar 94
5.90		Jacob	Davis	USA	29.4.78	1	TexR	Austin	4 Apr 98
5.90		Viktor	Chistyakov	RUS/AUS	9.2.75	1		Salamanca	15 Jul 99
		(50)							
5.90		Pavel	Gerasimov	RUS	29.5.79	1		Rüdlingen	12 Aug 00
5.90		Nick	Hysong	USA	9.12.71	1	OG	Sydney	29 Sep 00
5.90		Giuseppe	Gibilisco	ITA	5.1.79	1	WCh	Saint-Denis	28 Aug 03
5.90i		Igor	Pavlov	RUS	18.7.79	1	EI	Madrid	5 Mar 05
5.90		Lázaro	Borges	CUB	19.6.86	2	WCh	Daegu	29 Aug 11
5.90i		Dmitriy	Starodubtsev	RUS	3.1.86	1		Chelyabinsk	18 Dec 11
5.90		Armand	Duplantis	SWE	10.11.99	1	TexR	Austin	1 Apr 17
		(57)	100th man 5.82, 200th 5.73, 300th 5.70, 400th 5.62, 500th 560						

Best outdoor marks for athletes with lifetime bests indoors

Mark	Name	Pos	Meet	Venue	Date
6.00	Gataullin	1		Tokyo	16 Sep 89
6.00	Hooker	1		Perth	27 Jan 08
5.98	Galfione	1		Amiens	23 Jul 99
5.93	Ecker	1		Ingolstadt	26 Jul 98
5.93	Barber	2	DL	London (OS)	25 Jul 15
5.90	Yegorov	2	WCh	Stuttgart	19 Aug 93

Exhibition or Market Square competitions

Ancillary jump: 6.05i Bubka 13 Feb 93

Mark	Name		Nat	Born	Pos	Venue	Date
6.00	Jean	Galfione	FRA	9.6.71	1	Besançon	23 May 97
5.95	Viktor	Chistiakov	RUS/AUS	9.2.75	1	Chiari	8 Sep 99
5.90	Pyotr	Bochkaryov	RUS	3.11.67	1	Karlskrona	28 Jun 96

LONG JUMP

Mark	Wind	Name		Nat	Born	Pos	Meet	Venue	Date
8.95 WR	0.3	Mike	Powell	USA	10.11.63	1	WCh	Tokyo	30 Aug 91
8.90A WR	2.0	Bob	Beamon	USA	29.8.46	1	OG	Ciudad de México	18 Oct 68
8.87	-0.2	Carl	Lewis	USA	1.7.61	*	WCh	Tokyo	30 Aug 91

Mark	Wind	Name		Nat	Born	Pos	Meet	Venue	Date
8.86A	1.9	Robert	Emmiyan	ARM	16.2.65	1		Tsakhkadzor	22 May 87
8.79	1.9		Lewis			1	TAC	Indianapolis	19 Jun 83
8.79i	-		Lewis			1		New York	27 Jan 84
8.76	1.0		Lewis			1	USOF	Indianapolis	24 Jul 82
8.76	0.8		Lewis			1	NC/OT	Indianapolis	18 Jul 88
8.75	1.7		Lewis			1	PAm	Indianapolis	16 Aug 87
8.74	1.4	Larry	Myricks ¶	USA	10.3.56	2	NC/OT	Indianapolis	18 Jul 88
8.74A	2.0	Erick	Walder	USA	5.11.71	1		El Paso	2 Apr 94
8.74	1.2	Dwight	Phillips	USA	1.10.77	1	Pre	Eugene	7 Jun 09
8.73	1.2	Irving	Saladino	PAN	23.1.83	1	FBK	Hengelo	24 May 08
8.72	-0.2		Lewis			1	OG	Seoul	26 Sep 88
8.71	-0.4		Lewis			1	Pepsi	Los Angeles (Ww)	13 May 84
8.71	0.1		Lewis			1	OT	Los Angeles	19 Jun 84
8.71	1.9	Iván	Pedroso	CUB	17.12.72	1		Salamanca	18 Jul 95
8.71i		Sebastian	Bayer (10)	GER	11.6.86	1	EI	Torino	8 Mar 09
8.70	0.8		Myricks			1	NC	Houston	17 Jun 89
8.70	0.7		Powell			1		Salamanca	27 Jul 93
8.70	1.6		Pedroso			1	WCh	Göteborg	12 Aug 95
8.68	1.0		Lewis			Q	OG	Barcelona	5 Aug 92
8.68	1.6		Pedroso			1		Lisboa	17 Jun 95
8.67	0.4		Lewis			1	WCh	Roma	5 Sep 87
8.67	-0.7		Lewis			1	OG	Barcelona	6 Aug 92
8.66	0.8		Lewis			*	MSR	Walnut	26 Apr 87
8.66	1.0		Myricks			1		Tokyo	23 Sep 87
8.66	0.9		Powell			1	BNP	Villeneuve d'Ascq	29 Jun 90
8.66A	1.4		Lewis			*		Sestriere	31 Jul 94
8.66	0.3		Pedroso			1		Linz	22 Aug 95
8.66	1.6	Loúis	Tsátoumas	GRE	12.2.82	1		Kalamáta	2 Jun 07
		(31/11)							
8.65A	1.3	Luvo	Manyonga ¶	RSA	18.11.91	1	NC	Potchefstroom	22 Apr 17
8.63	0.5	Kareem	Streete-Thompson	CAY/USA	30.3.73	1	GP II	Linz	4 Jul 94
8.62	0.7	James	Beckford	JAM	9.1.75	1		Orlando	5 Apr 97
8.59i		Miguel	Pate	USA	13.6.79	1	NC	New York	1 Mar 02
8.58	1.8	Jarrion	Lawson	USA	6.5.94	2	NC/OT	Eugene	3 Jul 16
8.56i	-	Yago	Lamela	ESP	24.7.77	2	WI	Maebashi	7 Mar 99
8.56	0.2	Aleksandr	Menkov	RUS	7.12.90	1	WCh	Moskva	16 Aug 13
8.54	0.9	Lutz	Dombrowski	GDR	25.6.59	1	OG	Moskva	28 Jul 80
8.54	1.7	Mitchell	Watt	AUS	25.3.88	1	DNG	Stockholm	29 Jul 11
		(20)							
8.53	1.2	Jaime	Jefferson	CUB	17.1.62	1	Barr	La Habana	12 May 90
8.52	0.7	Savanté	Stringfellow	USA	6.11.78	1	NC	Stanford	21 Jun 02
8.52	1.8	Jeff	Henderson	USA	19.2.89	*	PAm	Toronto	22 Jul 15
8.51	1.7	Roland	McGhee	USA	15.10.71	2		São Paulo	14 May 95
8.51	1.7	Greg	Rutherford	GBR	17.11.86	1		Chula Vista	24 Apr 14
8.50	0.2	Llewellyn	Starks	USA	10.2.67	2		Rhede	7 Jul 91
8.50	1.3	Godfrey Khotso	Mokoena	RSA	6.3.85	2	GP	Madrid	4 Jul 09
8.49	2.0	Melvin	Lister	USA	29.8.77	1	SEC	Baton Rouge	13 May 00
8.49	0.6	Jai	Taurima	AUS	26.6.72	2	OG	Sydney	28 Sep 00
8.49	0.7	Christian	Reif	GER	24.10.84	1		Weinheim	31 May 14
		(30)							
8.49A	-0.8	Ruswahl	Samaai	RSA	25.9.91	2	NC	Potchefstroom	22 Apr 17
8.48	0.8	Joe	Greene	USA	17.2.67	3		São Paulo	14 May 95
8.48	0.6	Mohamed Salim	Al-Khuwalidi	KSA	19.6.81	1		Sotteville-lès-Rouen	2 Jul 06
8.47	1.9	Kevin	Dilworth	USA	14.2.74	1		Abilene	9 May 96
8.47	0.9	John	Moffitt	USA	12.12.80	2	OG	Athína	26 Aug 04
8.47	-0.2	Andrew	Howe	ITA	12.5.85	2	WCh	Osaka	30 Aug 07
8.47	0.0		Li Jinzhe	CHN	1.9.89	1		Bad Langensalza	28 Jun 14
8.46	1.2	Leonid	Voloshin	RUS	30.3.66	1	NC	Tallinn	5 Jul 88
8.46	1.6	Mike	Conley	USA	5.10.62	2		Springfield	4 May 96
8.46	1.8	Cheikh Tidiane	Touré	SEN/FRA	25.1.70	1		Bad Langensalza	15 Jun 97
		(40)							
8.46	0.3	Ibrahin	Camejo	CUB	28.6.82	1		Bilbao	21 Jun 08
8.46	1.3	Luis	Rivera	MEX	21.6.87	1	WUG	Kazan	12 Jul 13
8.45	2.0	Nenad	Stekic	YUG	7.3.51	1	PO	Montreal	25 Jul 75
8.45	0.8	Marquise	Goodwin	USA	19.11.90	1		Baie Mahault	14 May 16
8.44	1.7	Eric	Metcalf	USA	23.1.68	1	NC	Tampa	17 Jun 88
8.44A	1.8	Michel	Tornéus	SWE	26.5.86	1		Monachil	10 Jul 16
8.43	0.8	Jason	Grimes	USA	10.9.59	*	NC	Indianapolis	16 Jun 85
8.43	1.8	Giovanni	Evangelisti	ITA	11.9.61	1		San Giovanni Valdarno	16 May 87
8.43i	-	Stanislav	Tarasenko	RUS	23.7.66	1		Moskva	26 Jan 94

Mark	Wind	Name		Nat	Born	Pos	Meet	Venue	Date
8.43	0.1	Luis Felipe	Méliz	CUB/ESP	11.8.79	2	OD	Jena	3 Jun 00
8.43	-0.2	Ignisious	Gaisah	GHA/NED	20.6.83	2	GGala	Roma	14 Jul 06
		(51)	100th man 8.34, 200th 8.24, 300th 8.18, 400th 8.14, 500th 8.10						

Best at low altitude: 8.62 0.8 Manyonga 1 FBK Hengelo 11 Jun 17
8.61 1.3 Emmiyan 1 GWG Moskva 6 Jul 86 8.58 1.8 Walder 1 Springfield 4 May 86

Wind-assisted marks performances to 8.70, performers to 8.43

Mark	Wind	Name		Nat	Born	Pos	Meet	Venue	Date
8.99A	4.4	Mike	Powell	USA	10.11.63	1		Sestriere	21 Jul 92
8.96A	1.2+	Iván	Pedroso	CUB	17.12.72	1		Sestriere	29 Jul 95
8.95A	3.9		Powell			1		Sestriere	31 Jul 94
8.91	2.9	Carl	Lewis	USA	1.7.61	2	WCh	Tokyo	30 Aug 91
8.90	3.7		Powell			1	S&W	Modesto	16 May 92
8.79	3.0		Pedroso			1	Barr	La Habana	21 May 92
8.78	3.1	Fabrice	Lapierre	AUS	17.10.83	1	NC	Perth	18 Apr 10
8.77	3.9		Lewis			1	Pepsi	Los Angeles (Ww)	18 May 85
8.77	3.4		Lewis			1	MSR	Walnut	26 Apr 87
8.73	4.6		Lewis			Q	NC	Sacramento	19 Jun 81
8.73	3.2		Lewis			Q	NC	Indianapolis	17 Jun 83
8.73A	2.6		Powell			1		Sestriere	31 Jul 91
8.73	4.8		Pedroso			1		Madrid	20 Jun 95
8.72	2.2		Lewis			1	NYG	New York	24 May 92
8.72A	3.9		Lewis			2		Sestriere	31 Jul 94
8.70	2.5		Pedroso			1		Padova	16 Jul 95
8.68	4.9	James	Beckford	JAM	9.1.75	1	JUCO	Odessa, Tx	19 May 95
8.68	3.7	Marquis	Dendy	USA	17.11.92	1	NC	Eugene	25 Jun 15
8.66A	4.0	Joe	Greene	USA	17.2.67	2		Sestriere	21 Jul 92
8.64	3.5	Kareem	Streete-Thompson	CAY/USA	30.3.73	2	NC	Knoxville	18 Jun 94
8.63	3.9	Mike	Conley	USA	5.10.62	2	NC	Eugene	20 Jun 86
8.59	2.9	Jeff	Henderson	USA	19.2.89	1	NC/OT	Eugene	3 Jul 16
8.57	5.2	Jason	Grimes	USA	10.9.59	1	vFRG,AFR	Durham	27 Jun 82
8.53	4.9	Kevin	Dilworth	USA	14.2.74	1		Fort-de-France	27 Apr 02
8.51	3.7	Ignisious	Gaisah	GHA	20.6.83	1	AfCh	Bambous	9 Aug 06
8.49	2.6	Ralph	Boston	USA	9.5.39	1	OT	Los Angeles	12 Sep 64
8.49	4.5	Stanislav	Tarasenko	RUS	23.7.66	2		Madrid	20 Jun 95
8.48	2.8	Kirill	Sosunov	RUS	1.11.75	1		Oristano	18 Sep 95
8.48	3.4	Peter	Burge	AUS	3.7.74	1		Gold Coast (RB)	10 Sep 00
8.48	2.1	Brian	Johnson	USA	25.3.80	1	Conseil	Fort-de-France	8 May 08
8.48	2.8	Lamont Marcell	Jacobs	ITA	26.9.94	1	NC-23	Bressanone	10 Jun 16
8.46	3.4	Randy	Williams	USA	23.8.53	1		Eugene	18 May 73
8.46		Vernon	George	USA	6.10.64	1		Houston	21 May 89
8.44		Keith	Talley	USA	28.1.64	Q		Odessa, Tx	16 May 85
Exhibition: 8.46		Yuriy	Naumkin	RUS	4.11.68	1		Iglesias	6 Sep 96

Best outdoors
8.56 1.3 Lamela 1 Torino 24 Jun 99 8.49 1.6 Bayer 1 NC Ulm 4 Jul 09
8.46A 0.0 Pate 1 Cd. de México 3 May 03 and 8.45 1.5 2 NC Stanford 21 Jun 02, 8.48w 5.6 1 Fort Worth 21 Apr 01

Ancillary marks – other marks during series (to 8.67/8.70w)

8.84	1.7	Lewis	30 Aug 91	8.89Aw	2.4	Pedroso	29 Jul 95	8.75w	2.1	Lewis	16 Aug 87
8.71	0.6	Lewis	19 Jun 83	8.84Aw	3.8	Powell	21 Jul 92	8.75Aw	3.4	Powell	21 Jul 92
8.68	0.3	Lewis	18 Jul 88	8.83w	2.3	Lewis	30 Aug 91	8.73w	2.4	Lewis	18 May 85
8.68	0.0	Lewis	30 Aug 91	8.80Aw	4.0	Powell	21 Jul 92	8.73w		Powell	16 May 92
8.67	-0.2	Lewis	5 Sep 87	8.78Aw		Powell	21 Jul 92	8.71Aw		Powell	31 Jul 91

TRIPLE JUMP

Mark	Wind	Name		Nat	Born	Pos	Meet	Venue	Date
18.29 WR	1.3	Jonathan	Edwards	GBR	10.5.66	1	WCh	Göteborg	7 Aug 95
18.21	0.2	Christian	Taylor	USA	18.6.90	1	WCh	Beijing	27 Aug 15
18.11	0.8		Taylor			1	Pre	Eugene	27 May 17
18.09	-0.4	Kenny	Harrison	USA	13.2.65	1	OG	Atlanta	27 Jul 96
18.08	0.0	Pedro Pablo	Pichardo	CUB	30.6.93	1	Barr	La Habana	28 May 15
18.06	0.8		Pichardo			1	DL	Doha	15 May 15
18.06	1.1		Taylor			1	Athl	Lausanne	9 Jul 15
18.04	0.3	Teddy	Tamgho	FRA	15.6.89	1	WCh	Moskva	18 Aug 13
18.04	0.8		Taylor			2	DL	Doha	15 May 15
18.01	0.4		Edwards			1	Bisl	Oslo	9 Jul 98
18.00	1.3		Edwards			1	McD	London (CP)	27 Aug 95
17.99	0.5		Edwards			1	EC	Budapest	23 Aug 98
17.99	1.8		Pichardo			2	Athl	Lausanne	9 Jul 15
17.98 WR	1.8		Edwards			1		Salamanca	18 Jul 95
17.98	1.2		Tamgho			1	DL	New York	12 Jun 10
17.97 WR	1.5	Willie	Banks	USA	11.3.56	1	TAC	Indianapolis	16 Jun 85
17.96	0.1		Taylor			1	WCh	Daegu	4 Sep 11
17.96	-0.4		Pichardo			1	GGala	Roma	4 Jun 15

Mark	Wind	Name		Nat	Born	Pos	Meet	Venue	Date
17.94	0.0		Pichardo			1		La Habana	8 May 15
17.93	1.6		Harrison			1	DNG	Stockholm	2 Jul 90
17.92	1.6	Khristo	Markov	BUL	27.1.65	1	WCh	Roma	31 Aug 87
17.92	1.9	James	Beckford	JAM	9.1.75	1	JUCO	Odessa, TX	20 May 95
17.92i	WIR -		Tamgho			1	EI	Paris (Bercy)	6 Mar 11
17.92	0.7		Edwards			1	WCh	Edmonton	6 Aug 01
17.91i	WIR -		Tamgho			1	NC	Aubière	20 Feb 11
17.91	1.4		Tamgho			1	Athl	Lausanne	30 Jun 11
17.91	0.9	Will	Claye	USA	13.6.91	1	NC	Sacramento	23 Jun 17
17.90	1.0	Vladimir	Inozemtsev (10)	UKR	25.5.64	1	PTS	Bratislava	20 Jun 90
17.90	0.4	Jadel	Gregório	BRA	16.9.80	1	GP	Belém	20 May 07
17.90i			Tamgho			1	WI	Doha	14 Mar 10
17.89A	WR 0.0	João Carlos	de Oliveira	BRA	28.5.54	1	PAm	Ciudad de México	15 Oct 75
		(31/12)							
17.87	1.7	Mike	Conley	USA	5.10.62	1	NC	San José	27 Jun 87
17.86	1.3	Charles	Simpkins	USA	19.10.63	1	WUG	Kobe	2 Sep 85
17.85	0.9	Yoelbi	Quesada	CUB	4.8.73	1	WCh	Athína	8 Aug 97
17.83i	WIR -	Aliecer	Urrutia	CUB	22.9.74	1		Sindelfingen	1 Mar 97
17.83i	WIR -	Christian	Olsson	SWE	25.1.80	1	WI	Budapest	7 Mar 04
17.81	1.0	Marian	Oprea	ROU	6.6.82	1	Athl	Lausanne	5 Jul 05
17.81	0.1	Phillips	Idowu	GBR	30.12.78	1	EC	Barcelona	29 Jul 10
17.78	1.0	Nikolay	Musiyenko	UKR	16.12.59	1	Znam	Leningrad	7 Jun 86
		(20)							
17.78	0.6	Lázaro	Betancourt ¶	CUB	18.3.63	1	Barr	La Habana	15 Jun 86
17.78	0.8	Melvin	Lister	USA	29.8.77	1	NC/OT	Sacramento	17 Jul 04
17.77	1.0	Aleksandr	Kovalenko	RUS	8.5.63	1	NC	Bryansk	18 Jul 87
17.77i	-	Leonid	Voloshin	RUS	30.3.66	1		Grenoble	6 Feb 94
17.75	0.3	Oleg	Protsenko	RUS	11.8.63	1	Znam	Moskva	10 Jun 90
17.74	1.4	Nelson	Évora	POR	20.4.84	1	WCh	Osaka	27 Aug 07
17.73i		Walter	Davis	USA	2.7.79	1	WI	Moskva	12 Mar 06
17.73i	-	Fabrizio	Donato	ITA	14.8.76	2	EI	Paris (Bercy)	6 Mar 11
17.72i		Brian	Wellman	BER	8.9.67	1	WI	Barcelona	12 Mar 95
17.72	1.3	Sheryf	El-Sheryf	UKR	2.1.89	1	EU23	Ostrava	17 Jul 11
		(30)	El-Sheryf now Seref Osmanoglou TUR						
17.70i		Daniele	Greco	ITA	1.3.89	1	EI	Göteborg	2 Mar 13
17.69	1.5	Igor	Lapshin	BLR	8.8.63	1		Stayki	31 Jul 88
17.69i		Yoandri	Betanzos	CUB	15.2.82	2	WI	Doha	14 Mar 10
17.68	0.4	Danil	Burkenya	RUS	20.7.78	1	NC	Tula	31 Jul 04
17.68A	1.6	Alexis	Copello	CUB	12.8.85	1		Ávila	17 Jul 11
17.66	1.7	Ralf	Jaros	GER	13.12.65	1	ECp	Frankfurt-am-Main	30 Jun 91
17.65	1.0	Aleksandr	Yakovlev	UKR	8.9.57	1	Znam	Moskva	6 Jun 87
17.65	0.8	Denis	Kapustin	RUS	5.10.70	2	Bisl	Oslo	9 Jul 98
17.64	1.4	Nathan	Douglas	GBR	4.12.82	1	NC	Manchester (SC)	10 Jul 05
17.63	0.9	Kenta	Bell	USA	16.3.77	1c2	MSR	Walnut	21 Apr 02
		(40)							
17.62i	-	Yoel	García	CUB	25.11.73	2		Sindelfingen	1 Mar 97
17.62	-0.2	Arne David	Girat	CUB	26.8.84	3	ALBA	La Habana	25 Apr 09
17.60	0.6	Vladimir	Plekhanov	RUS	11.4.58	2	NC	Leningrad	4 Aug 85
17.59i	-	Pierre	Camara	FRA	10.9.65	1	WI	Toronto	13 Mar 93
17.59	0.3	Vasiliy	Sokov	RUS	7.4.68	1	NC	Moskva	19 Jun 93
17.59	0.8	Charles	Friedek	GER	26.8.71	1		Hamburg	23 Jul 97
17.59	0.9	Leevan	Sands	BAH	16.8.81	3	OG	Beijing	21 Aug 08
17.59	0.0		Li Yanxi	CHN	26.6.84	1	NG	Jinan	26 Oct 09
17.58	1.5	Oleg	Sakirkin	KZK	23.1.66	2	NC	Gorkiy	23 Jul 89
17.58	1.6	Aarik	Wilson	USA	25.10.82	1	LGP	London (CP)	3 Aug 07
17.58	-1.7	Ernesto	Revé	CUB	26.2.92	2		La Habana	7 Feb 14
17.58	-0.2		Dong Bin	CHN	22.11.88	3	OG	Rio de Janeiro	16 Aug 16
		(52)	100th man 17.41, 200th 17.20, 300th 17.03, 400th 16.92, 500th 16.82						

Wind-assisted marks – performances to 17.91, performers to 17.59

Mark	Wind	Name		Nat	Born	Pos	Meet	Venue	Date
18.43	2.4	Jonathan	Edwards	GBR	10.5.66	1	ECp	Villeneuve d'Ascq	25 Jun 95
18.20	5.2	Willie	Banks	USA	11.3.56	1	NC/OT	Indianapolis	16 Jul 88
18.17	2.1	Mike	Conley	USA	5.10.62	1	OG	Barcelona	3 Aug 92
18.08	2.5		Edwards			1	BrGP	Sheffield	23 Jul 95
18.05	2.4		Claye			2	Pre	Eugene	27 May 17
18.03	2.9		Edwards			1	GhG	Gateshead	2 Jul 95
18.01	3.7		Harrison			1	NC	Atlanta	15 Jun 96
17.97	7.5	Yoelbi	Quesada	CUB	4.8.73	1		Madrid	20 Jun 95
17.93	5.2	Charles	Simpkins	USA	19.10.63	2	NC/OT	Indianapolis	16 Jul 88
17.92	3.4	Christian	Olsson	SWE	25.1.80	1	GP	Gateshead	13 Jul 03
17.91	3.2		Simpkins			1	NC	Eugene	21 Jun 86

Mark	Wind	Name		Nat	Born	Pos	Meet	Venue	Date
17.82	2.5	Nelson	Évora	POR	20.4.84	1	NC	Seixal	26 Jul 09
17.81	4.6	Keith	Connor	GBR	16.9.57	1	CG	Brisbane	9 Oct 82
17.76A	2.2	Kenta	Bell	USA	16.3.77	1		El Paso	10 Apr 04
17.75		Gennadiy	Valyukevich	BLR	1.6.58	1		Uzhgorod	27 Apr 86
17.75	7.1	Brian	Wellman	BER	8.9.67	2		Madrid	20 Jun 95
17.73	4.1	Vasiliy	Sokov	RUS	7.4.68	1		Riga	3 Jun 89
17.71	2.4	Marquis	Dendy	USA	17.11.92	1	NCAA	Eugene	12 Jun 15
17.69	3.9	Alexis	Copello	CUB	12.8.85	1	ALBA	La Habana	25 Apr 09
17.63	4.3	Robert	Cannon	USA	9.7.58	3	NC/OT	Indianapolis	16 Jul 88
17.59	2.1	Jerome	Romain	DMA/FRA	12.6.71	3	WCh	Göteborg	7 Aug 95

Best outdoor marks for athletes with indoor bests

17.79	1.4	Olsson	1	OG	Athína	22 Aug 04
17.75	1.0	Voloshin	2	WCh	Tokyo	26 Aug 91
17.71	-0.7	Davis	1	NC	Indianapolis	25 Jun 06
17.70	1.7	Urrutia	1	GP II	Sevilla	6 Jun 96
17.67w	3.4	Greco	1	NC	Bressanone	8 Jul 12
17.65	1.4	Betanzos	2	ALBA	La Habana	25 Apr 09
17.67w	5.4		1		Bilbao	1 Jul 06
17.62A	0.1	Wellman	1		El Paso	15 Apr 95
17.60	1.9	Donato	1		Milano	7 Jun 00
17.63w	2.8		1	EC	Helsinki	30 Jun 12

Low altitude best: 17.65 0.1 Copello 1 Barr La Habana 30 May 09

Ancillary marks – other marks during series (to 17.90)

18.16 WR	1.3	Edwards	7 Aug 95
18.02	0.8	Taylor	9 Jul 15
17.99	0.1	Harrison	27 Jul 96
17.93	0.2	Pichardo	28 May 15
17.92i		Tamgho	6 Mar 11
18.39w	3.7	Edwards	25 Jun 95
18.06w	4.9	Banks	16 Jul 88
17.90w	2.5	Edwards	25 Jun 95

SHOT

Mark	Name		Nat	Born	Pos	Meet	Venue	Date
23.12 WR	Randy	Barnes ¶	USA	16.6.66	1		Los Angeles (Ww)	20 May 90
23.10		Barnes			1	Jenner	San José	26 May 90
23.06 WR	Ulf	Timmermann	GDR	1.11.62	1	Veniz	Haniá	22 May 88
22.91 WR	Alessandro	Andrei	ITA	3.1.59	1		Viareggio	12 Aug 87
22.86	Brian	Oldfield	USA	1.6.45	1	ITA	El Paso	10 May 75
22.75	Werner	Günthör	SUI	1.6.61	1		Bern	23 Aug 88
22.67	Kevin	Toth ¶	USA	29.12.67	1	KansR	Lawrence	19 Apr 03
22.66i		Barnes			1	Sunkist	Los Angeles	20 Jan 89
22.65	Ryan	Crouser	USA	18.12.92	1	NC	Sacramento	25 Jun 17
22.64 WR	Udo	Beyer	GDR	9.8.55	1		Berlin	20 Aug 86
22.62 WR		Timmermann			1		Berlin	22 Sep 85
22.61		Timmermann			1		Potsdam	8 Sep 88
22.60		Timmermann			1	vURS	Tallinn	21 Jun 86
22.57	Joe	Kovacs	USA	28.6.89	1		Tucson	18 May 17
22.56		Timmermann			1		Berlin	13 Sep 88
22.56		Kovacs			1	Herc	Monaco	17 Jul 15
22.55i		Timmermann			1	NC	Senftenberg	11 Feb 89
22.54	Christian	Cantwell (10)	USA	30.9.80	1	GP II	Gresham	5 Jun 04
22.52	John	Brenner	USA	4.1.61	1	MSR	Walnut	26 Apr 87
22.52		Crouser			1	OG	Rio de Janeiro	18 Aug 16
22.51		Timmermann			1		Erfurt	1 Jun 86
22.51	Adam	Nelson	USA	7.7.75	1		Gresham	18 May 02
22.47		Timmermann			1		Dresden	17 Aug 86
22.47		Günthör			1	WG	Helsinki	2 Jul 87
22.47		Timmermann			1	OG	Seoul	23 Sep 88
22.47		Crouser			1	DL	Rabat	16 Jul 17
22.45		Oldfield			1	ITA	El Paso	22 May 76
22.45		Cantwell			1	GP	Gateshead	11 Jun 06
22.44	Darrell	Hill	USA	17.8.93	1	VD-DLF	Bruxelles	31 Aug 17
22.43		Günthör			1	v3-N	Lüdenscheid	18 Jun 87
22.43	Reese	Hoffa	USA	8.10.77	1	LGP	London (CP)	3 Aug 07
22.43		Crouser			1	Pre	Eugene	27 May 17
	(31/14)							
22.28	Ryan	Whiting	USA	24.11.86	1	DL	Doha	10 May 13
22.24	Sergey	Smirnov	RUS	17.9.60	2	vGDR	Tallinn	21 Jun 86
22.21	Dylan	Armstrong	CAN	15.1.81	1	NC	Calgary	25 Jun 11
22.21	Tom	Walsh	NZL	1.3.92	2	Hanz	Zagreb	5 Sep 16
22.20	John	Godina	USA	31.5.72	1		Carson	22 May 05
22.20	David	Storl	GER	27.7.90	1	Athl	Lausanne	9 Jul
15	(20)							
22.10	Sergey	Gavryushin	RUS	27.6.59	1		Tbilisi	31 Aug 86
22.10	Cory	Martin	USA	22.5.85	1		Tucson	22 May 10
22.09	Sergey	Kasnauskas	BLR	20.4.61	1		Stayki	23 Aug 84
22.09i	Mika	Halvari	FIN	13.2.70	1		Tampere	7 Feb 00
22.02i	George	Woods	USA	11.2.43	1	LAT	Inglewood	8 Feb 74
22.02	Dave	Laut	USA	21.12.56	1		Koblenz	25 Aug 82
22.01	Tomás	Stanek	CZE	13.6.91	1		Schönebeck	2 Jun 17

Mark	Wind	Name		Nat	Born	Pos	Meet	Venue	Date
22.00	WR	Aleksandr	Baryshnikov	RUS	11.11.48	1	vFRA	Colombes	10 Jul 76
21.98		Gregg	Tafralis ¶	USA	9.4.58	1		Los Gatos	13 Jun 92
21.97		Janus	Robberts	RSA	10.3.79	1	NCAA	Eugene	2 Jun 01
		(30)							
21.97i		Konrad	Bukowiecki	POL	17.3.97	1	EI	Beograd	4 Mar 17
21.96		Mikhail	Kostin	RUS	10.5.59	1		Vitebsk	20 Jul 86
21.96		O'Dayne	Richards	JAM	14.12.88	2	DL	Rabat	16 Jul 17
21.95		Tomasz	Majewski	POL	30.8.81	1	DNG	Stockholm	30 Jul 09
21.93		Remigius	Machura ¶	CZE	3.7.60	1		Praha	23 Aug 87
21.92		Carl	Myerscough ¶	GBR	21.10.79	1	NCAA	Sacramento	13 Jun 03
21.88		Michal	Haratyk	POL	10.4.92	1		Cetniewo	29 Jul 17
21.87		C.J.	Hunter ¶	USA	14.12.68	2	NC	Sacramento	15 Jul 00
21.85	WR	Terry	Albritton	USA	14.1.55	1		Honolulu	21 Feb 76
21.83i		Aleksandr	Bagach ¶	UKR	21.11.66	1		Brovary	21 Feb 99
		(40)							
21.82	WR	Al	Feuerbach	USA	14.1.48	1		San José	5 May 73
21.82		Andy	Bloom	USA	11.8.73	1	GPF	Doha	5 Oct 00
21.82		Darlan	Romani	BRA	9.4.91	1		São Bernardo do Campo	3 Jun 17
21.81		Yuriy	Bilonog ¶	UKR	9.3.74	1	NC	Kiev	3 Jul 03
21.78	WR	Randy	Matson	USA	5.3.45	1		College Station	22 Apr 67
21.78		Dan	Taylor	USA	12.5.82	1		Tucson	23 May 09
21.77i		Mike	Stulce ¶	USA	21.7.69	1	v GBR	Birmingham	13 Feb 93
21.77		Dragan	Peric	YUG	8.5.64	1		Bar	25 Apr 98
21.76		Michael	Carter	USA	29.10.60	2	NCAA	Eugene	2 Jun 84
21.76		Stephen	Mozia	NGR	16.8.93	1		Ustí nad Labem	19 Jul 16
		(50)	100th man 21.26, 200th 20.79, 300th 20.50, 400th 20.20, 500th 19.99						

Not recognised by GDR authorities: 22.11 Rolf Oesterreich GDR 24.8.49 1 Zschopau 12 Sep 76

Drugs disqualification

Mark	Name		Nat	Born	Pos	Venue	Date
22.84		Barnes			1	Malmö	7 Aug 90
22.10	Andrey	Mikhnevich ¶	BLR	12.7.76	1	Minsk	11 Aug 11
21.82	Mike	Stulce ¶	USA	21.7.69	1	Brenham	9 May 90

Best outdoor marks for athletes with indoor bests

21.70 Stulce ¶ 1 OG Barcelona 31 Jul 92 | 21.63 Woods 2 CalR Modesto 22 May 76

Ancillary marks – other marks during series (to 22.45)

22.84 WR	Andrei	12 Aug 87	22.72 WR	Andrei	12 Aug 87	22.55	Barnes	20 May 90
22.76	Barnes	20 May 90	22.70	Günthör	23 Aug 88	22.49	Nelson	18 May 02
22.74	Andrei	12 Aug 87	22.58	Beyer	20 Aug 86	22.45	Timmermann	22 May 88

DISCUS

Mark	Wind	Name		Nat	Born	Pos	Meet	Venue	Date
74.08	WR	Jürgen	Schult	GDR	11.5.60	1		Neubrandenburg	6 Jun 86
73.88		Virgilijus	Alekna	LTU	13.2.72	1	NC	Kaunas	3 Aug 00
73.38		Gerd	Kanter	EST	6.5.79	1		Helsingborg	4 Sep 06
72.02			Kanter			1eA		Salinas	3 May 07
71.88			Kanter			1eA		Salinas	8 May 08
71.86	WR	Yuriy	Dumchev	RUS	5.8.58	1		Moskva	29 May 83
71.84		Piotr	Malachowski	POL	7.6.83	1	FBK	Hengelo	8 Jun 13
71.70		Róbert	Fazekas ¶	HUN	18.8.75	1		Szombathely	14 Jul 02
71.64			Kanter			1		Kohila	25 Jun 09
71.56			Alekna			1		Kaunas	25 Jul 07
71.50		Lars	Riedel	GER	28.6.67	1		Wiesbaden	3 May 97
71.45			Kanter			1		Chula Vista	29 Apr 10
71.32		Ben	Plucknett ¶	USA	13.4.54	1	Pre	Eugene	4 Jun 83
71.29		Daniel	Ståhl	SWE	27.8.92	1		Sollentuna	29 Jun 17
71.26		John	Powell (10)	USA	25.6.47	1	NC	San José	9 Jun 84
71.26		Rickard	Bruch	SWE	2.7.46	1		Malmö	15 Nov 84
71.26		Imrich	Bugár	CZE	14.4.55	1	Jenner	San José	25 May 85
71.25			Fazekas			1	WCp	Madrid (C)	21 Sep 02
71.25			Alekna			1	Danek	Turnov	20 May 08
71.18		Art	Burns	USA	19.7.54	1		San José	19 Jul 83
71.16	WR	Wolfgang	Schmidt	GDR	16.1.54	1		Berlin	9 Aug 78
71.14			Plucknett			1		Berkeley	12 Jun 83
71.14		Anthony	Washington	USA	16.1.66	1eA		Salinas	22 May 96
71.12			Alekna			1	WK	Zürich	11 Aug 00
71.08			Alekna			1		Réthimno	21 Jul 06
71.06		Luis Mariano	Delís ¶	CUB	12.12.57	1	Barr	La Habana	21 May 83
71.06			Riedel			1	WK	Zürich	14 Aug 96
71.00			Bruch			1		Malmö	14 Oct 84
70.99			Alekna			1		Stellenbosch	30 Mar 01
70.98		Mac	Wilkins	USA	15.11.50	1	WG	Helsinki	9 Jul 80

Mark	Wind	Name		Nat	Born	Pos	Meet	Venue	Date
70.98			Burns			1	Pre	Eugene	21 Jul 84
		(31/17)							
70.82		Aleksander	Tammert	EST	2.2.73	1		Denton	15 Apr 06
70.66		Robert	Harting	GER	18.10.84	1	Danek	Turnov	22 May 12
70.54		Dmitriy	Shevchenko ¶	RUS	13.5.68	1		Krasnodar	7 May 02
		(20)							
70.38	WR u	Jay	Silvester	USA	27.8.37	1		Lancaster	16 May 71
70.32		Frantz	Kruger	RSA/FIN	22.5.75	1		Salon-de-Provence	26 May 02
70.06		Romas	Ubartas ¶	LTU	26.5.60	1		Smalininkay	8 May 88
70.00		Juan	Martínez ¶	CUB	17.5.58	2	Barr	La Habana	21 May 83
69.95		Zoltán	Kövágó ¶	HUN	10.4.79	1		Salon-de-Provence	25 May 06
69.91		John	Godina	USA	31.5.72	1		Salinas	19 May 98
69.90		Jason	Young ¶	USA	27.5.81	1		Lubbock	26 Mar 10
69.70		Géjza	Valent	CZE	3.10.53	2		Nitra	26 Aug 84
69.62		Knut	Hjeltnes ¶	NOR	8.12.51	2	Jen	San José	25 May 85
69.62		Timo	Tompuri	FIN	9.6.69	1		Helsingborg	8 Jul 01
		(30)							
69.50		Mario	Pestano	ESP	8.4.78	1	NC	Santa Cruz de Tenerife	27 Jul 08
69.46		Al	Oerter	USA	19.9.36	1	TFA	Wichita	31 May 80
69.44		Georgiy	Kolnootchenko	BLR	7.5.59	1	vUSA	Indianapolis	3 Jul 82
69.40		Art	Swarts ¶	USA	14.2.45	1		Scotch Plains	8 Dec 79
69.36		Mike	Buncic	USA	25.7.62	1		Fresno	6 Apr 91
69.32		Ehsan	Hadadi	IRI	21.1.85	1		Tallinn	3 Jun 08
69.28		Vladimir	Dubrovshchik	BLR	7.1.72	1	NC	Staiki	3 Jun 00
69.26		Ken	Stadel	USA	19.2.52	2	AAU	Walnut	16 Jun 79
69.21		Andrius	Gudzius	LTU	14.2.91	1	WCh	London (OS)	5 Aug 17
68.94		Adam	Setliff	USA	15.12.69	1		Atascadero	25 Jul 01
		(40)							
68.91		Ian	Waltz	USA	15.4.77	1		Salinas	24 May 06
68.90		Jean-Claude	Retel	FRA	11.2.68	1		Salon-de-Provence	17 Jul 02
68.88		Vladimir	Zinchenko	UKR	25.7.59	1		Dnepropetrovsk	16 Jul 88
68.88		Fedrick	Dacres	JAM	28.2.94	1		Kingston	11 Feb 17
68.76		Jarred	Rome	USA	21.12.76	2cA		Chula Vista	6 Aug 11
68.64		Dmitriy	Kovtsun ¶	UKR	29.9.55	1		Riga	6 Jul 84
68.58		Attila	Horváth	HUN	28.7.67	1		Budapest	24 Jun 94
68.52		Igor	Duginyets	UKR	20.5.56	1	NC	Kyiv	21 Aug 82
68.50		Armin	Lemme	GDR	28.10.55	1	vUSA	Karl-Marx-Stadt	10 Jul 82
68.49A		Casey	Malone	USA	6.4.77	1		Fort Collins	20 Jun 09
		(50)	100th man 67.22, 200th 65.46, 300th 64.48, 400th 63.38, 500th 62.46						

Subsequent to or at drugs disqualification ! recognised as US record

Mark	Wind	Name		Nat	Born	Pos	Meet	Venue	Date
72.34!		Ben	Plucknett ¶	USA	13.4.54	(1)	DNG	Stockholm	7 Jul 81
71.20			Plucknett			(1)	CalR	Modesto	16 May 81
70.84		Kamy	Keshmiri ¶	USA	23.1.69	(1)		Salinas	27 May 92

Sloping ground

Mark	Wind	Name		Nat	Born	Pos	Meet	Venue	Date
72.08		John	Powell	USA	25.6.47	1		Klagshamn	11 Sep 87
69.80		Stefan	Fernholm	SWE	2.7.59	1		Klagshamn	13 Aug 87
69.44		Adam	Setliff	USA	15.12.69	1		La Jolla	21 Jul 01

Ancillary marks – other marks during series (to 70.98)

72.35 Alekna 3 Aug 00 72.30 Kanter 4 Sep 06 71.08 Plucknett 4 Jun 83

HAMMER

Mark	Wind	Name		Nat	Born	Pos	Meet	Venue	Date
86.74	WR	Yuriy	Sedykh	RUS	11.6.55	1	EC	Stuttgart	30 Aug 86
86.66	WR		Sedykh			1	vGDR	Tallinn	22 Jun 86
86.34	WR		Sedykh			1		Cork	3 Jul 84
86.04		Sergey	Litvinov	RUS	23.1.58	1	OD	Dresden	3 Jul 86
85.74			Litvinov			2	EC	Stuttgart	30 Aug 86
85.68			Sedykh			1	BGP	Budapest	11 Aug 86
85.60			Sedykh			1	PTG	London (CP)	13 Jul 84
85.60			Sedykh			1	Drz	Moskva	17 Aug 84
85.20			Litvinov			2		Cork	3 Jul 84
85.14			Litvinov			1	PTG	London	11 Jul 86
85.14			Sedykh			1	Kuts	Moskva	4 Sep 88
85.02			Sedykh			1	BGP	Budapest	20 Aug 84
84.92			Sedykh			2	OD	Dresden	3 Jul 86
84.90		Vadim	Devyatovskiy ¶	BLR	20.3.77	1		Staiki	21 Jul 05
84.88			Litvinov			1	GP-GG	Roma	10 Sep 86
84.86		Koji	Murofushi	JPN	8.10.74	1	Odlozil	Praha	29 Jun 03
84.80			Litvinov			1	OG	Seoul	26 Sep 88
84.72			Sedykh			1	GWG	Moskva	9 Jul 86
84.64			Litvinov			2	GWG	Moskva	9 Jul 86

Mark	Wind	Name		Nat	Born	Pos	Meet	Venue	Date
84.62		Igor	Astapkovich	BLR	4.1.63	1	Expo	Sevilla	6 Jun 92
84.60			Sedykh			1	8-N	Tokyo	14 Sep 84
84.58			Sedykh			1	Znam	Leningrad	8 Jun 86
84.51		Ivan	Tikhon ¶	BLR	24.7.76	1	NC	Grodno	9 Jul 08
84.48		Igor	Nikulin	RUS	14.8.60	1	Athl	Lausanne	12 Jul 90
84.46			Sedykh			1		Vladivostok	14 Sep 88
84.46			Tikhon			1		Minsk	7 May 04
84.40		Jüri	Tamm	EST	5.2.57	1		Banská Bystrica	9 Sep 84
84.36			Litvinov			2	vGDR	Tallinn	22 Jun 86
84.32			Tikhon			1		Staiki	8 Aug 03
84.26			Sedykh			1	Nik	Nice	15 Jul 86
		(30/8)							
84.19		Adrián	Annus ¶	HUN	28.6.73	1		Szombathely	10 Aug 03
83.93		Pawel	Fajdek	POL	4.6.89	1	Kuso	Szczecin	9 Aug 15
		(10)							
83.68		Tibor	Gécsek ¶	HUN	22.9.64	1		Zalaegerszeg	19 Sep 98
83.46		Andrey	Abduvaliyev	TJK/UZB	30.6.66	1		Adler	26 May 90
83.43		Aleksey	Zagornyi	RUS	31.5.78	1		Adler	10 Feb 02
83.40 @		Ralf	Haber	GDR	18.8.62	1		Athína	16 May 88
		82.54				1		Potsdam	9 Sep 88
83.38		Szymon	Ziólkowski	POL	1.7.76	1	WCh	Edmonton	5 Aug 01
83.30		Olli-Pekka	Karjalainen	FIN	7.3.80	1		Lahti	14 Jul 04
83.04		Heinz	Weis	GER	14.7.63	1	NC	Frankfurt	29 Jun 97
83.00		Balázs	Kiss	HUN	21.3.72	1	GP II	Saint-Denis	4 Jun 98
82.78		Karsten	Kobs	GER	16.9.71	1		Dortmund	26 Jun 99
82.69		Krisztián	Pars	HUN	18.2.82	1	EC	Zürich	16 Aug 14
		(20)		*@ competitive meeting but unsanctioned by GDR federation*					
82.64		Günther	Rodehau	GDR	6.7.59	1		Dresden	3 Aug 85
82.62		Sergey	Kirmasov ¶	RUS	25.3.70	1		Bryansk	30 May 98
82.62		Andrey	Skvaruk	UKR	9.3.67	1		Koncha-Zaspa	27 Apr 02
82.58		Primoz	Kozmus	SLO	30.9.79	1		Celje	2 Sep 09
82.54		Vasiliy	Sidorenko	RUS	1.5.61	1		Krasnodar	13 May 92
82.52		Lance	Deal	USA	21.8.61	1	GPF	Milano	7 Sep 96
82.40		Plamen	Minev	BUL	28.4.65	1	NM	Plovdiv	1 Jun 91
82.38		Gilles	Dupray	FRA	2.1.70	1		Chelles	21 Jun 00
82.28		Ilya	Konovalov ¶	RUS	4.3.71	1	NC	Tula	10 Aug 03
82.24		Benjaminas	Viluckis	LIT	20.3.61	1		Klaipeda	24 Aug 86
		(30)							
82.24		Vyacheslav	Korovin	RUS	8.9.62	1		Chelyabinsk	20 Jun 87
82.23		Vladislav	Piskunov ¶	UKR	7.6.78	2		Koncha-Zaspa	27 Apr 02
82.22		Holger	Klose	GER	5.12.72	1		Dortmund	2 May 98
82.16		Vitaliy	Alisevich	BLR	15.6.67	1		Parnu	13 Jul 88
82.08		Ivan	Tanev	BUL	1.5.57	1	NC	Sofia	3 Sep 88
82.00		Sergey	Alay ¶	BLR	11.6.65	1		Stayki	12 May 92
81.88		Jud	Logan ¶	USA	19.7.59	1		State College	22 Apr 88
81.81		Libor	Charfreitag	SVK	11.9.77	3	Odlozil	Praha	29 Jun 03
81.79		Christophe	Épalle	FRA	23.1.69	1		Clermont-Ferrand	30 Jun 00
81.78		Christoph	Sahner	FRG	23.9.63	1		Wemmetsweiler	11 Sep 88
		(40)							
81.70		Aleksandr	Seleznyov	RUS	25.1.63	2		Sochi	22 May 93
81.66		Aleksandr	Krykun	UKR	1.3.68	1		Kiev	29 May 04
81.64		Enrico	Sgrulletti	ITA	24.4.65	1		Ostia	9 Mar 97
81.56		Sergey	Gavrilov	RUS	22.5.70	1	Army	Rostov	16 Jun 96
81.56		Zsolt	Németh	HUN	9.11.71	1		Veszprém	14 Aug 99
81.52		Juha	Tiainen	FIN	5.12.55	1		Tampere	11 Jun 84
81.49		Valeriy	Svyatokho	BLR	20.7.81	1	NCp	Brest	27 May 06
81.45		Esref	Apak ¶	TUR	3.1.82	1	Cezmi	Istanbul	4 Jun 05
81.44		Yuriy	Tarasyuk	BLR	11.4.57	1		Minsk	10 Aug 84
81.35		Wojciech	Kondratowicz	POL	18.4.80	1		Bydgoszcz	13 Jul 03
		(50)	100th man 80.12, 200th 77.72, 300th 75.96, 400th 74.61, 500th 73.56						

Drugs disqualification

Mark	Wind	Name		Nat	Born	Pos	Meet	Venue	Date
86.73		Ivan	Tikhon ¶	BLR	24.7.76	1	NC	Brest	3 Jul 05

Ancillary marks – other marks during series (to 84.85)

86.68	Sedykh	30 Aug 86	85.82	Sedykh	22 Jun 86	85.42	Sedykh	11 Aug 86	85.20	Sedykh	3 Jul 84
86.62	Sedykh	30 Aug 86	85.52	Sedykh	13 Jul 84	85.28	Sedykh	30 Aug 86	85.04	Sedykh	13 Jul 84
86.00	Sedykh	3 Jul 84	85.46	Sedykh	30 Aug 86	85.26	Sedykh	11 Aug 86	84.98	Sedykh	4 Sep 88
86.00	Sedykh	22 Jun 86	85.42	Litvinov	3 Jul 86	85.24	Sedykh	11 Aug 86	84.92	Litvinov	3 Jul 86

JAVELIN

Mark	Wind	Name		Nat	Born	Pos	Meet	Venue	Date
98.48 WR		Jan	Zelezny	CZE	16.6.66	1		Jena	25 May 96
95.66 WR			Zelezny			1	McD	Sheffield	29 Aug 93

Mark	Wind	Name		Nat	Born	Pos	Meet	Venue	Date
95.54A	WR		Zelezny			1		Pietersburg	6 Apr 93
94.64			Zelezny			1	GS	Ostrava	31 May 96
94.44		Johannes	Vetter	GER	26.3.93	1		Luzern	11 Jul 17
94.02			Zelezny			1		Stellenbosch	26 Mar 97
93.90		Thomas	Röhler	GER	30.9.91	1	DL	Doha	5 May 17
93.88			Vetter			1		Thum	18 Aug 17
93.09		Aki	Parviainen	FIN	26.10.74	1		Kuortane	26 Jun 99
92.80			Zelezny			1	WCh	Edmonton	12 Aug 01
92.72		Julius	Yego	KEN	4.1.89	1	WCh	Beijing	26 Aug 15
92.61		Sergey	Makarov	RUS	19.3.73	1		Sheffield	30 Jun 02
92.60		Raymond	Hecht	GER	11.11.68	1	Bisl	Oslo	21 Jul 95
92.42			Zelezny			1	GS	Ostrava	28 May 97
92.41			Parviainen			1	ECp-1A	Vaasa	24 Jun 01
92.28			Zelezny			1	GPF	Monaco	9 Sep 95
92.28			Hecht			1	WK	Zürich	14 Aug 96
92.12			Zelezny			1	McD	London (CP)	27 Aug 95
92.12			Zelezny			1	TOTO	Tokyo	15 Sep 95
91.82			Zelezny			1	McD	Sheffield	4 Sep 94
91.69		Kostadínos	Gatsioúdis	GRE	17.12.73	1		Kuortane	24 Jun 00
91.68			Zelezny			1	GP	Gateshead	1 Jul 94
91.59		Andreas	Thorkildsen	NOR	1.4.82	1	Bisl	Oslo	2 Jun 06
91.53		Tero	Pitkämäki (10)	FIN	19.12.82	1		Kuortane	26 Jun 05
91.53			Röhler			1	GS	Ostrava	28 Jun 17
91.50			Zelezny			1	Kuso	Lublin	4 Jun 94
91.50A			Zelezny			1		Pretoria	8 Apr 96
91.50			Hecht			1		Gengenbach	1 Sep 96
91.46	WR	Steve	Backley	GBR	12.2.69	1		Auckland (NS)	25 Jan 92
91.40			Zelezny			1	BNP	Villeneuve d'Ascq	2 Jul 93
		(30/11)							
91.36			Cheng Chao-Tsun	TPE	17.10.93	1	WUG	Taipei	26 Aug 17
91.29		Breaux	Greer	USA	19.10.76	1	NC	Indianapolis	21 Jun 07
91.07		Andreas	Hofmann	GER	16.12.91	2	WUG	Taipei	26 Aug 17
90.73		Vadims	Vasilevskis	LAT	5.1.82	1		Tallinn	22 Jul 07
90.60		Seppo	Räty	FIN	27.4.62	1		Nurmijärvi	20 Jul 92
90.44		Boris	Henry	GER	14.12.73	1	Gugl	Linz	9 Jul 97
90.16		Keshorn	Walcott	TTO	2.4.93	1	Athl	Lausanne	9 Jul 15
89.73		Jakub	Vadlejch	CZE	10.10.90	2	WCh	London (OS)	12 Aug 17
89.21		Ihab	Abdelrahman ¶	EGY	1.5.89	1	DL	Shanghai	18 May 14
		(20)							
89.16A		Tom	Petranoff	USA	8.4.58	1		Potchefstroom	1 Mar 91
89.15			Zhao Qinggang	CHN	24.7.85	1	AsiG	Incheon	2 Oct 14
89.10	WR	Patrik	Bodén	SWE	30.6.67	1		Austin	24 Mar 90
89.02		Jarrod	Bannister ¶	AUS	3.10.84	1	NC	Brisbane	29 Feb 08
88.98		Antti	Ruuskanen	FIN	21.2.84	1	NC	Pori	2 Aug 15
88.90		Aleksandr	Ivanov	RUS	25.5.82	1	Znam	Tula	7 Jun 03
88.84		Dmitriy	Tarabin	RUS	29.10.91	1	NC	Moskva	24 Jul 13
88.75		Marius	Corbett	RSA	26.9.75	1	CG	Kuala Lumpur	21 Sep 98
88.70		Peter	Blank	GER	10.4.62	1	NC	Stuttgart	30 Jun 01
88.36		Matthias	de Zordo	GER	21.2.88	1	VD	Bruxelles	16 Sep 11
		(30)							
88.34		Vitezslav	Vesely	CZE	27.2.83	Q	OG	London (OS)	8 Aug 12
88.32		Petr	Frydrych	CZE	13.1.88	3	WCh	London (OS)	12 Aug 17
88.29		Julian	Weber	GER	29.8.94	2	ISTAF	Berlin	3 Sep 16
88.24		Matti	Närhi	FIN	17.8.75	1		Soini	27 Jul 97
88.22		Juha	Laukkanen	FIN	6.1.69	1		Kuortane	20 Jun 92
88.20		Gavin	Lovegrove	NZL	21.10.67	1	Bisl	Oslo	5 Jul 96
88.09		Marcin	Krukowski	POL	14.6.92	1	NC	Bialystok	21 Jul 17
88.01		Ioánnis	Kiriazis	GRE	19.1.96	1	TexR	Austin	31 Mar 17
88.00		Vladimir	Ovchinnikov	RUS	2.8.70	1		Tolyatti	14 May 95
87.83		Andrus	Värnik	EST	27.9.77	1		Valga	19 Aug 03
		(40)							
87.82		Harri	Hakkarainen	FIN	16.10.69	1		Kuortane	24 Jun 95
87.60		Kazuhiro	Mizoguchi	JPN	18.3.62	1	Jenner	San José	27 May 89
87.40		Vladimir	Sasimovich ¶	BLR	14.9.68	2		Kuortane	24 Jun 95
87.34		Andrey	Moruyev	RUS	6.5.70	1	ECp	Birmingham	25 Jun 94
87.23		Teemu	Wirkkala	FIN	14.1.84	1		Joensuu	22 Jul 09
87.20		Viktor	Zaytsev	UZB	6.6.66	1	OT	Moskva	23 Jun 92
87.20		Peter	Esenwein	GER	7.12.67	1		Rehlingen	31 May 04
87.20A		Guillermo	Martínez	CUB	28.6.81	1	PAm	Guadalajara	28 Oct 11
87.17		Dariusz	Trafas	POL	16.5.72	1		Gold Coast (RB)	17 Sep 00

Mark	Wind	Name		Nat	Born	Pos	Meet	Venue	Date
87.12		Tom	Pukstys	USA	28.5.68	2	OD	Jena	25 May 97
87.12		Emeterio	González	CUB	11.4.73	1	OD	Jena	3 Jun 00

(51) 100th man 84.95, 200th 82.62, 300th 80.62, 400th 79.56, 500th 78.54

Ancillary marks – other marks during series (to 91.48) new javelin introduced in 1986

95.34	Zelezny	29 Aug 93	92.30	Zelezny	26 Mar 97	91.67	Vetter	18 Aug 17
93.06	Vetter	11 Jul 17	92.26	Zelezny	26 Mar 97	91.48	Zelexny	15 Sep 95
92.88	Zelezny	25 May 96	91.88	Zelezny	27 Aug 95			

Javelins with roughened tails, now banned by the IAAF

Mark	Wind	Name		Nat	Born	Pos	Meet	Venue	Date
96.96	WR	Seppo	Räty	FIN	27.4.62	1		Punkalaidun	2 Jun 91
94.74	Irreg		Zelezny			1	Bisl	Oslo	4 Jul 92
91.98	WR		Räty			1	Super	Shizuoka	6 May 91
90.82		Kimmo	Kinnunen	FIN	31.3.68	1	WCh	Tokyo	26 Aug 91
87.00		Peter	Borglund	SWE	29.1.64	1	vFIN	Stockholm	13 Aug 91

MEN All-time

DECATHLON

9045 WR Ashton Eaton USA 21.1.88 1 WCh Beijing 29 Aug 15
10.23/-0.4 7.88/0.0 14.52 2.01 45.00 13.69/-0.2 43.34 5.20 63.63 4:17.52
9039 WR Eaton 1 NC/OT Eugene 23 Jun 12
10.21/0.4 8.23/0.8 14.20 2.05 46.70 13.70/-0.8 42.81 5.30 58.87 4:14.48
9026 WR Roman Sebrle CZE 26.11.74 1 Götzis 27 May 01
10.64/0.0 8.11/1.9 15.33 2.12 47.79 13.92/-0.2 47.92 4.80 70.16 4:21.98
8994 WR Tomás Dvorák CZE 11.5.72 1 ECp Praha 4 Jul 99
10.54/-0.1 7.90/1.1 16.78 2.04 48.08 13.73/0.0 48.33 4.90 72.32 4:37.20
8902 Dvorák 1 WCh Edmonton 7 Aug 01
10.62/1.5 8.07/0.9 16.57 2.00 47.74 13.80/-0.4 45.51 5.00 68.53 4:35.13
8900 Dvorák 1 Götzis 4 Jun 00
10.54/1.3 8.03/0.0 16.68 2.09 48.36 13.89/-1.0 47.89 4.85 67.21 4:42.33
8893 Sebrle 1 OG Athína 24 Aug 04
10.85/1.5 7.84/0.3 16.36 2.12 48.36 14.05/1.5 48.72 5.00 70.52 4:40.01
8893 Eaton 1 OG Rio de Janeiro 18 Aug 16
10.46/-0.1 7.94/1.7 14.73 2.01 46.07 13.80/0.7 45.49 5.20 59.77 4:23.33
8891 WR Dan O'Brien USA 18.7.66 1 Talence 5 Sep 92
10.43w/2.1 8.08/1.8 16.69 2.07 48.51 13.98/-0.5 48.56 5.00 62.58 4:42.10
8869 Eaton 1 OG London (OS) 9 Aug 12
10.35/0.4 8.03/0.8 14.66 2.05 46.90 13.56/0.1 42.53 5.20 61.96 4:33.59

8847 WR Daley Thompson GBR 30.7.58 1 OG Los Angeles 9 Aug 84
10.44/-1.0 8.01/0.4 15.72 2.03 46.97 14.33/-1.1 46.56 5.00 65.24 4:35.00
8844w O'Brien 1 TAC New York 13 Jun 91
10.23 7.96 16.06 2.08 47.70 13.95W/4.2 48.08 5.10 57.40 4:45.54
8842 Sebrle 1 Götzis 30 May 04
10.92/0.5 7.86w/3.3 16.22 2.09 48.59 14.15/0.3 47.44 5.00 71.10 4:34.09
8837 Dvorák 1 WCh Athína 6 Aug 97
10.60/0.8 7.64/-0.7 16.32 2.00 47.56 13.61/0.8 45.16 5.00 70.34 4:35.40
8834 Kevin Mayer FRA 10.2.92 2 OG Rio de Janeiro 18 Aug 16
10.81/-0.4 7.60/0.1 15.76 2.04 48.28 14.02/0.7 46.78 5.40 65.04 4:25.49
8832 WR Jürgen Hingsen FRG 25.1.58 1 OT Mannheim 9 Jun 84
10.70w/2.9 7.76/-1.6 16.42 2.07 48.05 14.07/0.2 49.36 4.90 59.86 4:19.75
8832 Bryan Clay USA 3.1.80 1 NC/OT Eugene 30 Jun 08
10.39/-0.4 7.39/-1.6 15.17 2.08 48.41 13.75/1.9 52.74 5.00 70.55 4:50.97
8825 WR Hingsen 1 Bernhausen 5 Jun 83
10.92/0.0 7.74 15.94 2.15 47.89 14.10 46.80 4.70 67.26 4:19.74
8824 O'Brien 1 OG Atlanta 1 Aug 96
10.50/0.7 7.57/1.4 15.66 2.07 46.82 13.87/0.3 48.78 5.00 66.90 4:45.89
8820 Clay 2 OG Athína 24 Aug 04
10.44w/2.2 7.96/0.2 15.23 2.06 49.19 14.13/1.5 50.11 4.90 69.71 4:41.65

8817 O'Brien 1 WCh Stuttgart 20 Aug 93
10.57/0.9 7.99/0.4 15.41 2.03 47.46 14.08/0.0 47.92 5.20 62.56 4:40.08
8815 Erki Nool EST 25.6.70 2 WCh Edmonton 7 Aug 01
10.60/1.5 7.63/2.0 14.90 2.03 46.23 14.40/0.0 43.40 5.40 67.01 4:29.58
8812 O'Brien 1 WCh Tokyo 30 Aug 91
10.41/-1.6 7.90/0.8 16.24 1.91 46.53 13.94/-1.2 47.20 5.20 60.66 4:37.50
8811 Thompson 1 EC Stuttgart 28 Aug 86
10.26/2.0 7.72/1.0 15.73 2.00 47.02 14.04/-0.3 43.38 5.10 62.78 4:26.16
8809 Eaton 1 WCh Moskva 11 Aug 13
10.35/-0.5 7.73/0.3 14.39 1.93 46.02 13.72/0.4 45.00 5.20 64.83 4:29.80
8807 Sebrle 1 Götzis 1 Jun 03
10.78/-0.2 7.86/1.2 15.41 2.12 47.83 13.96/0.0 43.42 4.90 69.22 4:28.63
8800 Sebrle 1 Götzis 2 Jun 02
10.95/0.5 7.79/1.8 15.50 2.12 48.35 13.89/1.6 48.02 5.00 68.97 4:38.16

Mark	Wind	Name			Nat	Born	Pos	Meet	Venue		Date
8800			Sebrle				1	EC	München		8 Aug 02
		10.83/1.3	7.92/0.8	15.41	2.12	48.48	14.04/0.0	46.88	5.10	68.51	4:42.94
8792		Uwe	Freimuth (10)		GDR	10.9.61	1	OD	Potsdam		21 Jul 84
		11.06/0.4	7.79/1.2	16.30	2.03	48.43	14.66/1.9	46.58	5.15	72.42	4:25.19
8791			Clay				1	OG	Beijing		22 Aug 08
		10.44/0.3	7.78/0.0	16.27	1.99	48.92	13.93/-0.5	53.79	5.00	70.97	5:06.59
		(30/10)									
8790		Trey	Hardee		USA	7.2.84	1	WCh	Berlin		20 Aug 09
		10.45/0.2	7.83/1.9	15.33	1.99	48.13	13.86/0.3	48.08	5.20	68.00	4:48.91
8784		Tom	Pappas		USA	6.9.76	1	NC	Stanford		22 Jun 03
		10.78/0.2	7.96/1.4	16.28	2.17	48.22	14.13/1.7	45.84	5.20	60.77	4:48.12
8762		Siegfried	Wentz		FRG	7.3.60	2		Bernhausen		5 Jun 83
		10.89	7.49/	15.35	2.09	47.38	14.00	46.90	4.80	70.68	4:24.90
8735		Eduard	Hämäläinen		FIN/BLR	21.1.69	1		Götzis		29 May 94
		10.50w/2.1	7.26/1.0	16.05	2.11	47.63	13.82/-3.0	49.70	4.90	60.32	4:35.09
8727		Dave	Johnson		USA	7.4.63	1		Azusa		24 Apr 92
		10.96/0.4	7.52w/4.5	14.61	2.04	48.19	14.17/0.3	49.88	5.28	66.96	4:29.38
8725		Dmitriy	Karpov		KAZ	23.7.81	3	OG	Athína		24 Aug 04
		10.50w/2.2	7.81/-0.9	15.93	2.09	46.81	13.97/1.5	51.65	4.60	55.54	4:38.11
8709		Aleksandr	Apaychev		UKR	6.5.61	1	vGDR	Neubrandenburg		3 Jun 84
		10.96/	7.57/	16.00	1.97	48.72	13.93/	48.00	4.90	72.24	4:26.51
8706		Frank	Busemann		GER	26.2.75	2	OG	Atlanta		1 Aug 96
		10.60/0.7	8.07/0.8	13.60	2.04	48.34	13.47/0.3	45.04	4.80	66.86	4:31.41
8698		Grigoriy	Degtyaryov		RUS	16.8.58	1	NC	Kiyev		22 Jun 84
		10.87/0.7	7.42/0.1	16.03	2.10	49.75	14.53/0.3	51.20	4.90	67.08	4:23.09
8695		Damian	Warner		CAN	4.11.89	2	WCh	Beijing		29 Aug 15
		10.31/-0.4	7.65/0.2	14.44	2.04	47.30	13.63/-0.2	44.99	4.80	63.50	4:31.51
		(20)									
8694		Chris	Huffins		USA	15.4.70	1	NC	New Orleans		20 Jun 98
		10.31w/3.5	7.76w/2.5	15.43	2.18	49.02	14.02/1.0	53.22	4.60	61.59	4:59.43
8680		Torsten	Voss		GDR	24.3.63	1	WCh	Roma		4 Sep 87
		10.69/-0.3	7.88/1.2	14.98	2.10	47.96	14.13/0.1	43.96	5.10	58.02	4:25.93
8670		Michael	Schrader		GER	1.7.87	2	WCh	Moskva		11 Aug 13
		10.73/-0.5	7.85/0.2	14.56	1.99	47.66	14.29/0.4	46.44	5.00	65.67	4:25.38
8667	WR	Guido	Kratschmer		FRG	10.1.53	1		Bernhausen		14 Jun 80
		10.58w/2.4	7.80/	15.47	2.00	48.04	13.92/	45.52	4.60	66.50	4:24.15
8663		Rico	Freimuth		GER	14.3.88	1		Ratingen		25 Jun 17
		10.44w/3.3	7.60/1.5	14.87	2.01	48.76	13.87/0.7	51.56	4.90	62.33	4:37.04
8654		Leonel	Suárez		CUB	1.9.87	1	CAC	La Habana		4 Jul 09
		11.07/0.7	7.42/0.8	14.39	2.09	47.65	14.15/-0.6	46.07	4.70	77.47	4:27.29
8644		Steve	Fritz		USA	1.11.67	4	OG	Atlanta		1 Aug 96
		10.90/0.8	7.77/0.9	15.31	2.04	50.13	13.97/0.3	49.84	5.10	65.70	4:38.26
8644		Maurice	Smith		JAM	28.9.80	2	WCh	Osaka		1 Sep 07
		10.62/0.7	7.50/0.0	17.32	1.97	47.48	13.91/-0.2	52.36	4.80	53.61	4:33.52
8634	WR	Bruce	Jenner		USA	28.10.49	1	OG	Montreal		30 Jul 76
		10.94/0.0	7.22/0.0	15.35	2.03	47.51	14.84/0.0	50.04	4.80	68.52	4:12.61
8627		Robert	Zmelík		CZE	18.4.69	1		Götzis		31 May 92
		10.62w/2.1	8.02/0.2	13.93	2.05	48.73	13.84/1.2	44.44	4.90	61.26	4:24.83
		(30)									
8626		Michael	Smith		CAN	16.9.67	1		Götzis		26 May 96
		11.23/-0.6	7.72/0.6	16.94	1.97	48.69	14.77/-2.4	52.90	4.90	71.22	4:41.95
8617		Andrey	Kravchenko		BLR	4.1.86	1		Götzis		27 May 07
		10.86/0.2	7.90/0.9	13.89	2.15	47.46	14.05/-0.1	39.63	5.00	64.35	4:29.10
8605		Arthur	Abele		GER	30.7.86	1		Ratingen		26 Jun 16
		10.95/-0.6	748/0.4	1579	198	49.43	14.07/-0.94620	490		7189	4:24.12
8603		Dean	Macey		GBR	12.12.77	3	WCh	Edmonton		7 Aug 01
		10.72/-0.7	7.59/0.4	15.41	2.15	46.21	14.34/0.0	46.96	4.70	54.61	4:29.05
8601		Ilya	Shkurenyov		RUS	11.1.91	1	NC	Smolensk		10 Jun 17
		10.89/0.7	7.58/0.9	14.15	2.12	49.00	13.95/1.4	44.91	5.30	60.29	4:28.35
8583w		Jón Arnar	Magnússon		ISL	28.7.69	1	ECp-2	Reykjavik		5 Jul 98
		10.68/2.0	7.63/2.0	15.57	2.07	47.78	14.33W/5.2	44.53	5.00	64.16	4:41.60
		8573					3		Götzis		31 May 98
		10.74/0.5	7.60/-0.2	16.03	2.03	47.66	14.24/0.7	47.82	5.10	59.77	4:46.43
8580		Kai	Kazmirek		GER	28.1.91	4	OG	Rio de Janeiro		18 Aug 16
		10.78/-0.1	7.69/-1.0	14.20	2.10	46.75	14.62/0.7	43.25	5.00	64.60	4:31.25
8574		Christian	Plaziat		FRA	28.10.63	1	EC	Split		29 Aug 90
		10.72/-0.6	7.77/1.1	14.19	2.10	47.10	13.98/0.7	44.36	5.00	54.72	4:27.83
8574		Aleksandr	Yurkov		UKR	21.7.75	4		Götzis		4 Jun 00
		10.69/0.9	7.93/1.8	15.26	2.03	49.74	14.56/-0.9	47.85	5.15	58.92	4:32.49
8571		Lev	Lobodin (40)		RUS	1.4.69	3	EC	Budapest		20 Aug 98
		10.66w/2.2	7.42/0.2	15.67	2.03	48.65	13.97/0.9	46.55	5.20	56.55	4:30.27

Mark	Wind	Name		Nat	Born	Pos	Meet	Venue	Date
8566		Sebastian	Chmara	POL	21.11.71	1		Alhama de Murcia	17 May 98
		10.97w/2.9	7.56/1.2 16.03	2.10	48.27	14.32/1.8		44.39 5.20 57.25	4:29.66
8558		Pascal	Behrenbruch	GER	19.1.85	1	EC	Helsinki	28 Jun 12
		10.93/0.8	7.15/-0.8 16.89	1.97	48.54	14.16/0.2		48.24 5.00 67.45	4:34.02
8554		Attila	Zsivoczky	HUN	29.4.77	5		Götzis	4 Jun 00
		10.64w/2.1	7.24/-1.0 15.72	2.18	48.13	14.87/-0.9		45.64 4.65 63.57	4:23.13
8548		Paul	Meier	GER	27.7.71	3	WCh	Stuttgart	20 Aug 93
		10.57/0.9	7.57/1.1 15.45	2.15	47.73	14.63/0.0		45.72 4.60 61.22	4:32.05
8547		Igor	Sobolevskiy	UKR	4.5.62	2	NC	Kiyev	22 Jun 84
		10.64/0.7	7.71/0.2 15.93	2.01	48.24	14.82/0.3		50.54 4.40 67.40	4:32.84
8539(w)		Lindon	Victor	GRN	28.2.93	1	SEC	Columbia, SC	12 May 17
		10.64w/3.6	7.35w/2.1 15.18	2.05	48.74	14.45/1.8		55.22 4.70 68.97	4:55.91
8539		Eelco	Sintnicolaas	NED	7.4.87	2	Hypo	Götzis	28 May 17
		10.57/0.5	7.61/0.6 14.62	1.91	48.37	14.16/-1.2		43.52 5.40 62.13	4:30.32
8534		Siegfried	Stark	GDR	12.6.55	1	OT	Halle	4 May 80
		11.10w	7.64 15.81	2.03	49.53	14.86w		47.20 5.00 68.70	4:27.7
8534w/8478		Antonio	Peñalver	ESP	1.12.68	1		Alhama de Murcia	24 May 92
(7.19w/4.0)		10.76w/3.9	7.42W/6.2 16.50	2.12	49.50	14.32/0.8		47.38 5.00 59.32	4:39.94
8528		Aleksandr	Pogorelov ¶	RUS	10.1.80	3	WCh	Berlin	20 Aug 09
		10.95/-0.3	7.49/-0.4 16.65	2.08	50.27	14.19/0.3		48.46 5.10 63.95	4:48.70
		(50)	100th man 8357, 200th 8192, 300th 8090, 400th 8000, 500th 7922						

4 x 100 METRES RELAY

Mark	Nat	Team	Pos	Meet	Venue	Date
36.84 WR	JAM	N Carter 10.1, Frater 8.9, Blake 9.0, Bolt 8.8	1	OG	London (OS)	11 Aug 12
37.04 WR	JAM	N Carter, Frater, Blake, Bolt	1	WCh	Daegu	4 Sep 11
37.10 WR	JAM	N Carter, Frater, Bolt, Powell	1	OG	Beijing	22 Aug 08
37.27	JAM	Powell, Blake, Ashmeade, Bolt	1	OG	Rio de Janeiro	19 Aug 16
37.31	JAM	Mullings, Frater, Bolt, Powell	1	WCh	Berlin	22 Aug 09
37.36	JAM	Carter, Bailey Cole, Ashmeade, Bolt	1	WCh	Moskva	18 Aug 13
37.36	JAM	Carter, Powell, Ashmeade, Bolt	1	WCh	Beijing	29 Aug 15
37.38	USA	Demps, Patton, Kimmons, Gatlin	1h2	OG	London (OS)	10 Aug 12
37.38	USA	Rodgers, Gatlin, Gay, R.Bailey	1	W.Rly	Nassau	2 May 15
37.39	JAM	Carter, Frater, Blake, Bailey-Cole	1h1	OG	London (OS)	10 Aug 12
37.40 WR	USA	Marsh, Burrell, Mitchell, C Lewis	1	OG	Barcelona	8 Aug 92
37.40 WR	USA	Drummond, Cason, D Mitchell, L Burrell	1s1	WCh	Stuttgart	21 Aug 93
37.41	JAM	Carter, Powell, Dwyer, Ashmeade	1h2	WCh	Beijing	29 Aug 15
37.45	USA	Kimmons, Spearmon, Gay, Rodgers	1	WK	Zürich	19 Aug 10
37.47	GBR	Ujah, Gemili, Talbot, Mitchell-Blake	1	WCh	London (OS)	12 Aug 17
37.48	USA	Drummond, Cason, D Mitchell, L Burrell	1	WCh	Stuttgart	22 Aug 93
37.50 WR	USA	Cason, Burrell, Mitchell, C Lewis	1	WCh	Tokyo	1 Sep 91
37.52	USA	Rodgers, Gatlin, Bacon, Coleman	2	WCh	London (OS)	12 Aug 17
37.58	USA	'Red' Silmon, Rodgers, Salaam, Gatlin	1	Herc	Monaco	19 Jul 13
37.58	JAM	Livermore, Bailey-Cole, Ashmeade, Bolt	1	CG	Glasgow	2 Aug 14
37.59	USA	Drummond, Montgomery, B Lewis, Greene	1	WCh	Sevilla	29 Aug 99
37.59	USA	Conwright, Spearmon, Gay, Smoots	1	WCp	Athína	16 Sep 06
37.60	JPN	Yamagata, Iizuka, Kiryu, Cambridge	2	OG	Rio de Janeiro	19 Aug 16
37.61	USA	Drummond, Williams, B Lewis, Greene	1	OG	Sydney	30 Sep 00
37.61	USA	Kimmons, Gatlin, Gay, Bailey	1	Herc	Monaco	20 Jul 12
37.62	TTO	Brown, Burns, Callander, Thompson	2	WCh	Berlin	22 Aug 09
37.64	CAN	Haynes, A.Brown, Rodney, DeGrasse	3	OG	Rio de Janeiro	19 Aug 16
37.65	USA	Drummond, Williams, C Johnson, Greene	1	ISTAF	Berlin	1 Sep 00
37.65	USA	Rodgers, Coleman, Gay, Lawson	1h1	OG	Rio de Janeiro	18 Aug 16
37.66	USA	Silmon, Rodgers, Salaam, Gatlin	2	WCh	Moskva	18 Aug 13
37.67 WR	USA	Marsh, Burrell, Mitchell, C Lewis	1	WK	Zürich	7 Aug 91
	(31 performances by teams from 6 nations)	Further bests by nations:				
37.79 WR	FRA	Morinière, Sangouma 8.90, Trouabal, Marie-Rose	1	EC	Split	1 Sep 90
37.82	CHN	Tang, Xie, Su, Zhang	2h1	OG	Rio de Janeiro	18 Aug 16
37.90	BRA	de Lima, Ribeiro, A da Silva, Cl da Silva	2	OG	Sydney	30 Sep 00
37.94	NGR	O Ezinwa, Adeniken, Obikwelu, D Ezinwa	1s2	WCh	Athína	9 Aug 97
	(10)					
38.00	CUB	Simón, Lamela, Isasi, Aguilera	3	OG	Barcelona	8 Aug 92
38.01	ANT	Walsh, D.Bailey, Jarvis, Francis	4h2	WCh	Beijing	29 Aug 15
38.02	URS	Yevgenyev, Bryzgin, Muravyov, Krylov	2	WCh	Roma	6 Sep 87
38.02	GER	Reus, Unger, Kosenkow, Jakubczyk	1		Weinheim	27 Jul 12
38.12	GHA	Duah, Nkansah, Zakari, Tuffour	1s1	WCh	Athína	9 Aug 97
38.17	AUS	Henderson, Jackson, Brimacombe, Marsh	1s2	WCh	Göteborg	12 Aug 95
38.17	ITA	Donati, Collio, Di Gregorio, Checcucci	2	EC	Barcelona	1 Aug 10
38.29	NED	Mariano, Martina, Codrington, van Luijk	3h1	OG	London (OS)	10 Aug 12
38.30	TUR	Safer, Harvey, Barnes, Guliyev	4h1	OG	Rio de Janeiro	18 Aug 16
38.31	POL	Masztak, Kuc, Kubaczyk, Krynski (20)	6h2	OG	London (OS)	10 Aug 12

Mark	Wind	Name	Pos	Meet	Venue	Date
38.35	RSA	Bruintjies, Magakwe, Titi, Simbine	4	CG	Glasgow	2 Aug 14
38.41	SKN	Lestrod, Rogers, Adams, Lawrence	6h1	OG	London (OS)	10 Aug 12
38.45	AHO	Goeloe, Raffaela, Duzant, Martina	6	WCh	Helsinki	13 Aug 05
38.46	URS/RUS	Zharov, Krylov, Fatun, Goremykin	4	EC	Split	1 Sep 90
38.46	ESP	Viles, Ruiz, Hortelano, Rodríguez	4h1	WCh	Moskva	18 Aug 13
38.47	HKG	Tang Yik Chun, Lai Chun Ho, Ng Ka Fung, Tsui Chi Ho	1		Taipei	26 May 12
38.52	BAH	Griffith, Fraser, Hart, T.Smith	3h1	CG	Glasgow	1 Aug 14
38.52	DOM	De Oloe, Andujar, Del Carmen, Martinez	1	IbAm	Rio de Janeiro	16 May 16
38.53	UKR	Rurak, Osovich, Kramarenko, Dologodin	1	ECp	Madrid	1 Jun 96
38.54	SUI	Mancini, Schenkel, Somasundaran, Wilson (30)	2h1	EC	Zürich	18 Aug 14
38.55A	BAR	Cadogan, Gittens, Deshong, Ellis	3	NACAC	San José, CRC	9 Aug 15
38.60	CIV	Meité, Douhou, Sonan, N'Dri	3s1	WCh	Edmonton	12 Aug 01
Multi-nation team						
37.46	Racers TC	Bailey/ANT, Blake JAM, Forsythe JAM, Bolt JAM	1	LGP	London (CP)	25 Jul 09
Hand timed						
38.2 A	TUR	Hekimoglu, Harvey, Barnes, Guliyev	1		Erzurum	10 Jun 17
38.3 A	UKR	Kravtsov, Smelyk, Suprun, Ibrahimov	2		Erzurum	10 Jun 17
One man disqualified for drugs						
37.04	USA	Kimmons 10.1, Gatlin 8.9, Gay ¶ 9.0, Bailey 9.0	(2)	OG	London (OS)	11 Aug 12
37.91	NGR	Asonze ¶, Obikwelu, Effiong, Aliu	(3)	WCh	Sevilla	29 Aug 99

4 x 200 METRES RELAY

Mark	Nat	Name	Pos	Meet	Venue	Date
1:18.63 WR	JAM	Ashmeade 20.5, Weir 19.2, J Brown 19.6, Y Blake 19.4	1	WRly	Nassau	24 May 14
1:18.68 WR	USA – Santa Monica Track Cluc	Marsh 20.0, Burrell 19.6, Heard 19.7, C Lewis 19.4	1	MSR	Walnut	17 Apr 94
1:19.10	World All-Stars	Drummond USA 20.4, Mitchell USA 19.3, Bridgewater USA 20.3, Regis GBR 19.1	2	MSR	Walnut	17 Apr 94
1:19.11 WR	Santa Monica TC/USA	M.Marsh, L Burrell, Heard, C Lewis	1	Penn	Philadelphia	25 Apr 92
1:19.16	USA	Red Team Crawford, Clay, Patton, Gatlin	1	PennR	Philadelphia	26 Apr 03
1:19.20	CAN	Smellie, Rodney, DeGrasse, A.Brown	1	FlaR	Gainesville	2 Apr 16
1:19.38 WR	Santa Monica TC/USA	Everett, Burrell, Heard, C Lewis	1	R-W	Koblenz	23 Aug 89
1:19.39	USA Blue	Drummond, Crawford, B Williams, Greene	1	PennR	Philadelphia	28 Apr 01
1:19.42	CAN	Smellie, Rodney, De Grasse, Brown	1	W.Rly	Nassau	23 Apr 17
1:19.45	Santa Monica TC/USA	DeLoach, Burrell, C.Lewis, Heard	1	Penn	Philadelphia	27 Apr 91
1:19.47	Nike Int./USA	Brokenburr, A Harrison, Greene, M Johnson	1	Penn	Philadelphia	24 Apr 99
Best non-US nations						
1:20.51	SKN	A Adams, L Roland, BJ Lawrence, A Clarke	2	WRly	Nassau	24 May 14
1:20.66	FRA	Lemaitre, Fonsat, Bassaw, Romain	3	WRly	Nassau	25 May 14
1:21.10	ITA	Tilli, Simionato, Bongiorno, Mennea	1		Cagliari	29 Sep 83
1:21.22	POL	Tulin, Balcerzak, Pilarczyk, Urbas	2		Gdansk	14 Jul 01
1:21.29	GBR	Adam, Mafe, Christie, Regis	1	vURS	Birmingham	23 Jun 89

4 x 400 METRES RELAY

Mark	Nat	Name	Pos	Meet	Venue	Date
2:54.29 WR	USA	Valmon 44.5, Watts 43.6, Reynolds 43.23, Johnson 42.94	1	WCh	Stuttgart	22 Aug 93
2:55.39	USA	Merritt 44.4, Taylor 43.7, Neville 44.16, Wariner 43.18	1	OG	Beijing	23 Aug 08
2:55.56	USA	Merritt 44.4, Taylor 43.7, Williamson 44.32, Wariner 43.10	1	WCh	Osaka	2 Sep 07
2:55.74 WR	USA	Valmon 44.6, Watts 43.00, M Johnson 44.73, S Lewis 43.41	1	OG	Barcelona	8 Aug 92
2:55.91	USA	O Harris 44.5, Brew 43.6, Wariner 43.98, Williamson 43.83	1	OG	Athína	28 Aug 04
2:55.99	USA	L Smith 44.62, A Harrison 43.84, Mills 43.66, Maybank 43.87	1	OG	Atlanta	3 Aug 96
2:56.16A WR	USA	Matthews 45.0, Freeman 43.2, James 43.9, Evans 44.1	1	OG	Ciud. México	20 Oct 68
2:56.16 WR	USA	Everett 43.79, S Lewis 43.69, Robinzine 44.74, Reynolds 43.94	1	OG	Seoul	1 Oct 88
2:56.60	GBR	I Thomas 44.92, Baulch 44.19, Richardson 43.62, Black 43.87	2	OG	Atlanta	3 Aug 96
2:56.65	GBR	Thomas 44.8, Black 44.2, Baulch 44.08, Richardson 43.57	2	WCh	Athína	10 Aug 97
2:56.72	BAH	Brown 44.9, Pinder 43.5, Mathieu 44.25, Miller 44.01	1	OG	London (OS)	10 Aug 12
2:56.75	JAM	McDonald 44.5, Haughton 44.4, McFarlane 44.37, Clarke 43.51	3	WCh	Athína	10 Aug 97
2:56.91	USA	Rock 44.7, Brew 44.3, Williamson 44.40, Wariner 43.49	1	WCh	Helsinki	14 Aug 05
2:57.05	USA	Nellum 45.2, Mance 43.5, McQuay 43.41, Taylor 44.85	2	OG	London (OS)	10 Aug 12
2:57.25	USA	Verburg 44.8, McQuay 44.1, C Taylor 44.6, L Merritt 43.8	1	WRly	Nassau	25 May 14
2:57.29	USA	Everett 45.1, Haley 44.0, McKay 44.20, Reynolds 44.00	1	WCh	Roma	6 Sep 87
2:57.30	USA	Hall 45.3, McQuay 43.2, Roberts 44.79, Merritt 43.97	1	OG	Rio de Janeiro	20 Aug 16
2:57.32	USA	Ramsey 44.9, Mills 44.6, Reynolds 43.74, Johnson 44.11	1	WCh	Göteborg	13 Aug 95
2:57.32	BAH	McKinney 44.9, Moncur 44.6, A Williams 44.43, Brown 43.42	2	WCh	Helsinki	14 Aug 05
2:57.53	GBR	Black 44.7, Redmond 44.0, Regis 44.22, Akabusi 44.59	1	WCh	Tokyo	1 Sep 91
2:57.57	USA	Valmon 44.9, Watts 43.4, D.Everett 44.31, Pettigrew 44.93	2	WCh	Tokyo	1 Sep 91
2:57.59	BAH	L Williams 45.0, Pinder 43.8, C Brown 44.2, Mathieu 44.6	2	WRly	Nassau	25 May 14
2:57.82	USA	Verburg 45.0, McQuay 44.3, Nellum 44.38, Merritt 44.18	1	WCh	Beijing	30 Aug 15
2:57.86	USA	Taylor 45.4, Wariner 43.6, Clement 44.72, Merritt 44.16	1	WCh	Berlin	23 Aug 09
2:57.87	USA	L Smith 44.59, Rouser 44.33, Mills 44.32, Maybank 44.63	1s2	OG	Atlanta	2 Aug 96
2:57.91	USA	Nix 45.59, Armstead 43.97, Babers 43.75, McKay 44.60	1	OG	Los Angeles	11 Aug 84
2:57.97	JAM	McDonald, Haughton McFarlane, D Clarke	1	PAm	Winnipeg	30 Jul 99

Mark	Wind	Name	Nat	Born	Pos	Meet	Venue	Date
2:58.00	POL	Rysiukiewicz 45.6, Czubak 44.2, Haczek 44.0, Mackowiak 44.2			2	GWG	Uniondale, NY	22 Jul 98
2:58.03	BAH	Bain 45.9, Mathieu 44.1, A Williams 44.02, Brown 44.05			2	OG	Beijing	23 Aug 08
2:58.07	JAM	Ayre 44.9, Simpson 44.9, Spence 44.48, Clarke 43.81			3	WCh	Helsinki	14 Aug 05
	(30/5	plus 7 times for teams that contained an athlete who was subsequently banned for drugs abuse						
2:58.12	TTO	Solomon 46.1, Richards 43.4, Cedenio 44.41, L. Gordon 44.08			1	WCh	London (OS)	13 Aug 17
2:58.52	BEL	Watrin 46.0, J.Borlée 44.1, D.Borlée 44.71, K.Borlée 43.67			4	OG	Rio de Janeiro	20 Aug 16
2:58.56	BRA	Cl. da Silva 44.6, A dos Santos 45.1, de Araújo 45.0, Parrela 43.9			2	PAm	Winnipeg	30 Jul 99
2:58.68	NGR	Chukwu 45.18, Monye 44.49, Bada 44.70, Udo-Obong 44.31			1	OG	Sydney	30 Sep 00
2:58.96	FRA	Djhone 45.4, Keita 44.7, Diagana 44.69, Raquil 44.15			2	WCh	Saint-Denis	31 Aug 03
	(10)							
2:59.06	BOT	Makwala 44.9, Sibanda 43.9, Nkobolo 44.94, Maotoanong 45.28			5	OG	Rio de Janeiro	20 Aug 16
2:59.13	CUB	Martínez 45.6, Herrera 44.38, Tellez 44.81, Hernández 44.34			1h2	OG	Barcelona	7 Aug 92
2:59.21	RSA	Pistorius 45.58, Mogawane 43.97, de Beer 44.46, Victor 45.20			3h1	WCh	Daegu	1 Sep 11
2:59.45	RUS	Denmukhametov 46.0, Trenikin 44.5, Kudryavtsev 44.63, Ivashko 44.29			4h1	WCh	Beijing	29 Aug 15
2:59.63	KEN	D Kitur 45.4, S Kitur 45.13, Kipkemboi 44.76, Kemboi 44.34			3h2	OG	Barcelona	7 Aug 92
2:59.70	AUS	Frayne 45.38, Clark 43.86, Minihan 45.07, Mitchell 45.39			4	OG	Los Angeles	11 Aug 84
2:59.86	GDR	Möller 45.8, Schersing 44.8, Carlowitz 45.3, Schönlebe 44.1			1	vURS	Erfurt	23 Jun 85
2:59.95	YUG	Jovkovic, Djurovic, Macev, Brankovic 44.3			2h3	WCh	Tokyo	31 Aug 91
2:59.96	FRG	Dobeleit 45.7, Henrich 44.3, Itt 45.12, Schmid 44.93			4	WCh	Roma	6 Sep 87
3:00.15	DOM	Cuesta 45.4, Soriano 43.8, J.Santos 46.58, L.Santos 44.36			6h2	WCh	Beijing	29 Aug 15
	(20)							
3:00.64	SEN	Diarra 46.53, Dia 44.94, Ndiaye 44.70, Faye 44.47			4	OG	Atlanta	3 Aug 96
3:00.65	ESP	Husillos 45.4, Búa 45.3, Echeverry 45.26, García 44.75			5	WCh	London (OS)	13 Aug 17
3:00.76	JPN	Karube 45.88, Ito 44.86, Osakada 45.08, Omori 44.94			5	OG	Atlanta	3 Aug 96
3:00.79	ZIM	Chiwira 46.2, Mukomana 44.6, Ngidhi 45.79, Harnden 44.20			2h3	WCh	Athína	9 Aug 97
3:00.82A	VEN	A Ramírez 45.7, Aguilar 45.3, Acevedo 44.7, Longart 45.2			3	PAm	Guadalajara	28 Oct 11
3:00.91	IND	Kunhu, Anas, Dharun, Rajiv			1		Bengaluru	10 Jun 16
3:01.12	FIN	Lönnqvist 46.7, Salin 45.1, Karttunen 44.8, Kukkoaho 44.5			6	OG	München	10 Sep 72
3:01.16 A	COL	Zambrano, Lemos, Palomeque, Perlaza			1		Medellín	10 Jul 16
3:01.26	IRL	Gregan 46.1, Murphy 45.2, Barr 45.05, English 44.96			8h2	WCh	Beijing	29 Aug 15
3:01.37	ITA	Bongiorni 46.2, Zuliani 45.0, Petrella 45.3, Ribaud 44.9			4	EC	Stuttgart	31 Aug 86
	(30)							

Including subsequently banned athlete

Mark	Nat	Name	Pos	Meet	Venue	Date
2:54.20(WR)	USA	Young 44.3, Pettigrew ¶ 43.2, Washington 43.5, Johnson 43.2	(1)	GWG	Uniondale, NY	22 Jul 98
2:56.35	USA	A Harrison 44.36, Pettigrew 44.17, C Harrison 43.53, Johnson 44.29	(1)	OG	Sydney	30 Sep 00
2:56.45	USA	J Davis 45.2, Pettigrew 43.9, Taylor 43.92, M Johnson 43.49	(1)	WCh	Sevilla	29 Aug 99
2:56.47	USA	Young 44.6, Pettigrew 43.1, Jones 44.80, Washington 44.80	(1)	WCh	Athína	10 Aug 97
2:56.60	USA Red	Taylor 45.0, Pettigrew 44.2, Washington 43.7, Johnson 43.7	(1)	PennR	Philadelphia	29 Apr 00
2:57.54	USA	Byrd 45.9, Pettigrew 43.9, Brew 44.03, Taylor 43.71	1	WCh	Edmonton	12 Aug 01
2:58.06	RUS	Dyldin 45.5, Frolov 44.6, Kokorin 44.34, Alekseyev ¶ 43.56	3	OG	Beijing	23 Aug 08

4 x 800 METRES RELAY

Mark	Nat	Name	Pos	Meet	Venue	Date
7:02.43	KEN	Mutua 1:46.73, Yiampoy 1:44.38, Kombich 1:45.92, Bungei 1:45.40	1	VD	Bruxelles	25 Aug 06
7:02.82	USA	J Harris 1:47.05, Robinson 1:44.03, Burley 1:46.05, Krummenacker 1:45.69	2	VD	Bruxelles	25 Aug 06
7:03.89 WR	GBR	Elliott 1:49.14, Cook 1:46.20, Cram 1:44.54, Coe 1:44.01	1		London (CP)	30 Aug 82
7:04.70	RSA	van Oudtshoorn 1:46.9, Sepeng 1:45.2, Kotze 1:48.3, J Botha 1:44.3	1		Stuttgart	6 Jun 99
7:06.66	QAT	Sultan 1:45.81, Al-Badri 1:46.71, Suleiman 1:45.89, Ali Kamal 1:48.25	4	VD	Bruxelles	25 Aug 06
7:07.40	URS	Masunov, Kostetskiy, Matvetev, Kalinkin	1		Moskva	5 Aug 84
7:08.5 WR	FRG	Kinder 1:46.9, Adams 1:47.5, Bogatzki 1:47.9, Kemper 1:46.2	1		Wiesbaden	13 Aug 66
7:08.89	POL	Konieczny 1:48.9, Krawczyk 1:49.1, Lewandowski 1:45.9, Kszczot 1:44.8	2	WRly	Nassau	24 May 14

4 x 1500 METRES RELAY

Mark	Nat	Name	Pos	Meet	Venue	Date
14:22.22 WR	KEN	C Cheboi 3:38.5, S Kiplagat 3:32.4, Magut 3:39.0, A Kiprop 3:32.3	1	WRly	Nassau	25 May 14
14:36.23 WR	KEN	W Biwott 3:38.5, Gathimba 3:39.5, G Rono 3:41.4, Choge 3:36.9	1	VD	Bruxelles	4 Sep 09
14:38.8 WR	FRG	Wessinghage 3:38.8, Hudak 3:39.1, Lederer 3:44.6, Fleschen 3:36.3	1		Köln	16 Aug 77
14:40.4 WR	NZL	Polhill 3:42.9, Walker 3:40.4, Dixon 3:41.2, Quax 3:35.9	1		Oslo	22 Aug 73
14:40.80	USA	Casey 3:38.2, Torrence 3:36.6, Leer 3:39.3, Manzano 3:46.7	2	WRly	Nassau	25 May 14
14:41.22	ETH	Gebremedhin 3:39.9, Fida 3:37.5, Z Alemayehu 3:46.5, Wote 3:37.3	3	WRly	Nassau	25 May 14
14:45.63	URS	Kalutskiy, Yakovlev, Legeda, Lotarev	1		Leningrad	4 Aug 85
14:46.04	AUS	Gregson 3:39.1, McEntee 3:44.9, Birmingham 3:38.3, Williamsz 3:43.7	4	WRly	Nassau	25 May 14
14:46.16	Larios, ESP	Jiménez 3:40.9, Pancorbo 3:41.2, A García 3:43.9, Viciosa 3:40.2	1		Madrid	5 Sep 97
14:48.2	FRA	Bégouin 3:44.5, Lequement 3:44.3, Philippe 3:42.2, Dien 3:37.2	2		Bourges	23 Jun 79

Mixed Team: 14:44.31 Ali BRN, Birgen KEN, N Kemboi KEN, Campbell IRL 2 VD Bruxelles 4 Sep 09

4 x 1 MILE RELAY

Mark	Nat	Name	Pos	Meet	Venue	Date
15:49.08	IRL	Coghlan 4:00.2, O'Sullivan 3:55.3, O'Mara 3:56.6, Flynn 3:56.98	1		Dublin	17 Aug 85
15:59.57	NZL	Rogers 3:57.2, Bowden 4:02.5, Gilchrist 4:02.8, Walker 3:57.07	1		Auckland	2 Mar 83

4 x 110m/120y HURDLES

Mark	Nat	Name	Pos	Meet	Venue	Date
52.94	USA Blue	Richardson, Harris, Merritt, Oliver	1	DrakeR	Des Moines	25 Apr 15

Mark	Wind	Name		Nat	Born	Pos	Meet	Venue	Date
53.08	All Stars Riley JAM, R Brathwaite BAR, Parchment JAM, Swift BAR					2	DrakeR	Des Moines	25 Apr 15
53.31y	USA Red Oliver, Herring, Brown, Merritt					1	PennR	Philadelphia	25 Apr 08
53.36	USA Bramlett, Moore, Payne, Merritt					1	DNG	Stockholm	7 Aug 07

3000 METRES TRACK WALK

Mark	Name		Nat	Born	Pos	Meet	Venue	Date
10:47.11	Giovanni	De Benedictis	ITA	8.1.68	1		S.Giovanni Valdarno	19 May 90
10:52.44+	Yohann	Diniz	FRA	1.1.78	1	in 5k	Villeneuve d'Ascq	27 Jun 08
10:54.70	Dane	Bird-Smith	AUS	15.7.92	1		Brisbane	11 Feb 17
10:56.22	Andrew	Jachno	AUS	13.4.62	1		Melbourne	7 Feb 91
10:56.34+	Roman	Mrázek	SVK	21.1.62	1	in 5k	Bratislava	14 Jun 89
10:58.16	Kevin	Campion	FRA	23.5.88	2		Cork	8 Jul 14
10:58.47	Alex	Wright	IRL	19.12.90	3		Cork	8 Jul 14
10:59.04	Luke	Adams	AUS	22.10.76	1		Cork	3 Jul 10
11:00.2+	Jozef	Pribilinec	SVK	6.7.60	1	in 10k	Banská Bystrica	30 Aug 85
11:00.50+	Francisco Javier	Fernández ¶	ESP	6.3.77	1	in 5k	Villeneuve d'Ascq	8 Jun 07
Indoors								
10:31.42	Andreas	Erm	GER	12.3.76	1		Halle	4 Feb 01
10:50.0	Denis	Nizhegorodov	RUS	26.7.80	1		Saransk	4 Dec 06
10:53+	Mikhail	Shchennikov	RUS	24.12.67	1	in 5k	Moskva	14 Feb 95
10:53.3	Igor	Yerokhin	RUS	4.9.85	2		Saransk	4 Dec 06
10:54.61	Carlo	Mattioli	ITA	23.10.54	1		Milano	6 Feb 80
10:56.77+	Ivano	Brugnetti	ITA	1.9.76	1	in 5k	Torino	21 Feb 09
10:56.88	Reima	Salonen	FIN	19.11.55	1		Turku	5 Feb 84
10:57.32	Matej	Tóth	SVK	10.2.83	1		Wien	12 Feb 11

5000 METRES TRACK WALK

Mark	Name		Nat	Born	Pos	Meet	Venue	Date
18:05.49	Hatem	Ghoula	TUN	7.6.73	1		Tunis	1 May 97
18:17.22	Robert	Korzeniowski	POL	30.7.68	1		Reims	3 Jul 92
18:18.01	Yohann	Diniz	FRA	1.1.78	1		Villeneuve d'Ascq	27 Jun 08
18:27.34	Francisco Javier	Fernández ¶	ESP	6.3.77	1		Villeneuve d'Ascq	8 Jun 07
18:28.80	Roman	Mrázek	SVK	21.1.62	1	PTS	Bratislava	14 Jun 89
18:30.43	Maurizio	Damilano	ITA	6.4.57	1		Caserta	11 Jun 92
Indoors								
18:07.08	Mikhail	Shchennikov	RUS	24.12.67	1		Moskva	14 Feb 95
18:08.86	Ivano	Brugnetti	ITA	1.9.76	1	NC	Ancona	17 Feb 07
18:11.41	Ronald	Weigel	GDR	8.8.59	1mx		Wien	13 Feb 88
18:11.8	Valeriy	Borchin ¶	RUS	11.9.86	1		Saransk	30 Dec 10
18:15.25	Grigoriy	Kornev	RUS	14.3.61	1		Moskva	7 Feb 92
18:15.54	Andrey	Ruzavin	RUS	28.3.86	1		Samara	30 Jan 14
18:16.54 ?	Frants	Kostyukevich	BLR	4.4.63	2	NC	Gomel	4 Feb 89
18:16.76	Yohann	Diniz	FRA	1.1.78	1		Reims	7 Dec 14
18:19.97	Giovanni	De Benedictis	ITA	8.1.68	1	EI	Genova	28 Feb 92
18:21.76	Ruslan	Dmytrenko	UKR	22.3.86	2		Samara	30 Jan 14
18:22.25	Andreas	Erm	GER	12.3.76	1	NC	Dortmund	25 Feb 01
18:23.18	Rishat	Shafikov	RUS	23.1.70	1		Samara	1 Mar 97
18:24.13	Francisco Javier	Fernández ¶	ESP	6.3.77	1		Belfast	17 Feb 07
18:27.15	Alessandro	Gandellini	ITA	30.4.73	1	NC	Genova	12 Feb 00
18:27.80	Jozef	Pribilinec	SVK	6.7.60	2	WI	Indianapolis	7 Mar 87
18:27.95	Stefan	Johansson	SWE	11.4.67	3	EI	Genova	28 Feb 92
18:28.54	Igor	Yerokhin	RUS	4.9.85	1		Samara	31 Jan 13
Drugs dq: 18:17.13	Vladimir	Kanaykin ¶	RUS	21.3.85	(2)	Winter	Moskva	5 Feb 12
18:26.82	Sergey	Bakulin ¶	RUS	13.11.86	(3)	Winter	Moskva	5 Feb 12

10,000 METRES TRACK WALK

Mark	Name		Nat	Born	Pos	Meet	Venue	Date
37:53.09	Francisco Javier	Fernández ¶	ESP	6.3.77	1	NC	Santa Cruz de Tenerife	27 Jul 08
37:58.6	Ivano	Brugnetti	ITA	1.9.76	1		Sesto San Gioavnni	23 Jul 05
38:01.49	Eiki	Takahashi	JPN	19.11.92	1		Isahaya	13 Dec 15
38:02.60	Jozef	Pribilinec	SVK	6.7.60	1		Banská Bystrica	30 Aug 85
38:06.6	David	Smith	AUS	24.7.55	1		Sydney	25 Sep 86
38:06.28	Miguel Ángel	López	ESP	3.7.88	1	NC	Gijón	24 Jul 16
38:08.13	Yohann	Diniz	FRA	1.1.78	1	NC	Reims	12 Jul 14
38:10.23	Yusuke	Suzuki	JPN	2.1.88	1		Abashiri	16 Jul 15
38:12.13	Ronald	Weigel	GDR	8.8.59	1		Potsdam	10 May 86
38:16.76	Daisuke	Matsunaga (10)	JPN	24.3.95	1		Yokohama	21 May 16
38:18.0+	Valdas	Kazlauskas	LTU	23.2.58	1		Moskva	18 Sep 83
38:20.0	Moacir	Zimmermann	BRA	30.12.83	1		Blumenau	7 Jun 08
38:23.73		Wang Zhen	CHN	24.8.91	1		Genova	8 Feb 15
38:24 0+	Bernardo	Segura	MEX	11.2.70	1	SGP	Fana	7 May 94
38:24.23	Dane	Bird-Smith	AUS	15.7.92	1	NC	Sydney	31 Mar 17
38:24.31	Hatem	Ghoula	TUN	7.6.73	1		Tunis	30 May 98
38:26.4	Daniel	García	MEX	28.10.71	1		Sdr Omme	17 May 97

Mark Wind	Name		Nat	Born	Pos	Meet	Venue	Date
38:26.53	Robert	Korzeniowski	POL	30.7.68	1		Riga	31 May 02
38:27.57	Robert	Heffernan	IRL	20.2.78	1	NC	Dublin	20 Jul 08
38:32.0	Erik	Tysse	NOR	4.12.80	1	NC	Bergen (Fana)	13 Jun 08
38:37.02	Kevin	Campion	FRA	23.5.88	1	NC	Paris (C)	13 Jul 13
Indoors: 38:31.4	Werner	Heyer	GDR	14.11.56	1		Berlin	12 Jan 80

20 KILOMETRES WALK

Mark Wind	Name		Nat	Born	Pos	Meet	Venue	Date
1:16:36WR	Yusuke	Suzuki	JPN	2.1.88	1	AsiC	Nomi	15 Mar 15
1:16:43	Sergey	Morozov ¶	RUS	21.3.88	1	NC	Saransk	8 Jun 08
1:17:02	Yohann	Diniz	FRA	1.1.78	1	NC	Arles	8 Mar 15
1:17:16WR	Vladimir	Kanaykin ¶	RUS	21.3.85	1	RWC	Saransk	29 Sep 07
1:17:21WR	Jefferson	Pérez	ECU	1.7.74	1	WCh	Saint-Denis	23 Aug 03
1:17:22WR	Francisco Javier	Fernández ¶	ESP	6.3.77	1		Turku	28 Apr 02
1:17:23	Vladimir	Stankin	RUS	2.1.74	1	NC-w	Adler	8 Feb 04
1:17:24		Diniz			1		Lugano	15 Mar 15
1:17:25.6t	Bernardo	Segura	MEX	11.2.70	1	SGP	Bergen (Fana)	7 May 94
1:17:33	Nathan	Deakes	AUS	17.8.77	1		Cixi	23 Apr 05
1:17:36		Kanaykin			1	NC	Cheboksary	17 Jun 07
1:17:36		Wang Zhen (10)	CHN	24.8.91	1		Taicang	30 Mar 12
1:17:38	Valeriy	Borchin ¶	RUS	11.9.86	1	NC-w	Adler	28 Feb 09
1:17:40		Chen Ding	CHN	5.8.92	2		Taicang	30 Mar 12
1:17:41		Zhu Hongjun	CHN	18.8.83	2		Cixi	23 Apr 05
1:17:43		Diniz			1		Lugano	18 Mar 12
1:17:46	Julio	Martínez	GUA	27.9.73	1		Eisenhüttenstadt	8 May 99
1:17:46	Roman	Rasskazov	RUS	28.4.79	1	NC	Moskva	19 May 00
1:17:52		Fernández			1		La Coruña	4 Jun 05
1:17:53		Cui Zhide	CHN	11.1.83	3		Cixi	23 Apr 05
1:17:54		Wang Kaihua	CHN	16.2.94	1		Huangshan	4 Mar 17
1:17:55		Borchin			1	NC-w	Adler	23 Feb 08
1:17:56	Alejandro	López	MEX	9.2.75	2		Eisenhüttenstadt	8 May 99
1:18:00		Fernández			2	WCh	Saint-Denis	23 Aug 03
1:18:00		Wang Zhen			1		La Coruña	6 Jun 15
1:18:03	Eiki	Takahashi	JPN	19.11.92	1	NC	Kobe	15 Feb 15
1:18:03.3tWR		Bo Lingtang (20)	CHN	12.8.70	1	NC	Beijing	7 Apr 94
1:18:05	Dmitriy	Yesipchuk	RUS	17.11.74	1	NC-w	Adler	4 Mar 01
1:18:06	Viktor	Burayev ¶	RUS	23.8.82	2	NC-w	Adler	4 Mar 01
1:18:06	Vladimir (30/23)	Parvatkin	RUS	10.10.84	1	NC-w	Adler	12 Mar 05
1:18:07		Li Gaobo	CHN	4.5.89	4		Cixi	23 Apr 05
1:18:12	Artur	Meleshkevich	BLR	11.4.75	1		Brest	10 Mar 01
1:18:13WR	Pavol	Blazek	SVK	9.7.58	1		Hildesheim	16 Sep 90
1:18:13		Wang Hao	CHN	16.8.89	1	NG	Jinan	22 Oct 09
1:18:14	Mikhail	Khmelnitskiy	BLR	24.7.69	1	NC	Soligorsk	13 May 00
1:18:14	Noé	Hernández	MEX	15.3.78	4	WCh	Saint-Denis	23 Aug 03
1:18:16	Vladimir (30)	Andreyev	RUS	7.9.66	2	NC	Moskva	19 May 00
1:18:17	Ilya	Markov	RUS	19.6.72	2	NC-w	Adler	12 Mar 05
1:18:18	Yevgeniy	Misyulya	BLR	13.3.64	1		Eisenhüttenstadt	11 May 96
1:18:18	Sergey	Bakulin ¶	RUS	13.11.86	2	NC-w	Adler	23 Feb 08
1:18:20WR	Andrey	Perlov	RUS	12.12.61	1	NC	Moskva	26 May 90
1:18:20	Denis	Nizhegorodov	RUS	26.7.80	3	NC-w	Adler	4 Mar 01
1:18:22	Robert	Korzeniowski	POL	30.7.68	1		Hildesheim	9 Jul 00
1:18:23	Andrey	Makarov	BLR	2.1.71	2	NC	Soligorsk	13 May 00
1:18:24	Alex	Schwazer ¶	ITA	26.12.84	1		Lugano	14 Mar 10
1:18:25	Erick (40)	Barrondo	GUA	14.6.91	3		Lugano	18 Mar 12
1:18:26	Sergey	Shirobokov	RUS	16.2.99	1	NC-w	Sochi	18 Feb 17
1:18:27	Daniel	García	MEX	28.10.71	2	WCp	Podebrady	19 Apr 97
1:18:27		Xing Shucai	CHN	4.8.84	5		Cixi	23 Apr 05
1:18:30		Yu Chaohong	CHN	12.12.76	6		Cixi	23 Apr 05
1:18:31		Han Yucheng	CHN	16.12.78	7		Cixi	23 Apr 05
1:18:32		Li Zewen	CHN	5.12.73	4	WCp	Podebrady	19 Apr 97
1:18:33		Liu Yunfeng ¶	CHN	3.8.79	8		Cixi	23 Apr 05
1:18:34	Eder	Sánchez	MEX	21.5.86	3	WCp	Cheboksary	10 May 08
1:18:35.2t	Stefan	Johansson	SWE	11.4.67	1	SGP	Bergen (Fana)	15 May 92
1:18:36	Mikhail	Shchennikov	RUS	24.12.67	1	NC	Sochi	20 Apr 96
1:18:37	Aleksandr	Pershin	RUS	4.9.68	2	NC	Moskva	26 May 90
1:18:37	Ruslan	Shafikov	RUS	27.6.75	1	NC-w23	Adler	11 Feb 95
1:18:37	Ruslan (53)	Dmytrenko	UKR	22.3.86	1	WCp	Taicang	4 May 14

100th man 1:19:20, 200th 1:20:15, 300th 1:210:57, 400th 1:21:37, 500th 1:22:05

Mark	Wind	Name		Nat	Born	Pos	Meet	Venue	Date
Probable short course									
1:18:33		Mikhail	Shchennikov	RUS	24.12.67	1	4-N	Livorno	10 Jul 93
Drugs disqualification									
1:16:53		Vladimir	Kanaykin ¶	RUS	21.3.85	(2)	NC	Saransk	8 Jun 08
1:17:30		Alex	Schwazer ¶	ITA	26.12.84	(1)		Lugano	18 Mar 12
1:17:47		Andrey	Ruzavin ¶	RUS	28.3.86	(1)	NC-w	Sochi	18 Feb 12
1:17:52			Morozov ¶			(2)	NC-w	Sochi	18 Feb 12
1:18:25		Andrey	Krivov ¶	RUS	14.11.85	(3)	NC-w	Sochi	18 Feb 12
1:18:28		Pyotr	Trofimov ¶	RUS	28.11.83	1	NC-w	Sochi	23 Feb 13
1:18:29		Stanislav	Yemelyanov ¶	RUS	23.10.90	(4)	NC-w	Sochi	18 Feb 12

30 KILOMETRES WALK

Mark	Wind	Name		Nat	Born	Pos	Meet	Venue	Date
2:01:13+		Vladimir	Kanaykin ¶	RUS	21.3.85	1	in 35k	Adler	19 Feb 06
2:01:44.1t		Maurizio	Damilano	ITA	6.4.57	1		Cuneo	3 Oct 92
2:01:47+			Kanaykin			1	in 35k	Adler	13 Mar 05
2:02:27+			Kanaykin			1	in 35k	Adler	8 Feb 04
2:02:41		Andrey	Perlov	RUS	12.12.61	1	NC-w	Sochi	19 Feb 89
2:02:45		Yevgeniy	Misyulya	BLR	13.3.64	1		Mogilyov	28 Apr 91
2:03:06		Daniel	Bautista	MEX	4.8.52	1		Cherkassy	27 Apr 80
2:03:50+		Vladimir	Parvatkin	RUS	10.10.84	2	in 35k	Adler	19 Feb 06
2:03:56.5t		Thierry	Toutain	FRA	14.2.62	1		Héricourt	24 Mar 91
2:04:00		Aleksandr	Potashov	BLR	12.3.62	1		Adler	14 Feb 93
2:04:24		Valeriy	Spitsyn	RUS	5.12.65	1	NC-w	Sochi	22 Feb 92
2:04:30		Vitaliy	Matsko (10)	RUS	8.6.60	2	NC-w	Sochi	19 Feb 89
2:04:49+		Semyon	Lovkin	RUS	14.7.77	1=	in 35k	Adler	1 Mar 03
2:04:49+		Stepan	Yudin	RUS	3.4.80	1=	in 35k	Adler	1 Mar 03
2:04:50+		Sergey	Kirdyapkin ¶	RUS	16.1.80	2	in 35k	Adler	13 Mar 05
2:04:55.5t		Guillaume	Leblanc	CAN	14.4.62	1		Sept-Iles	16 Jun 90
2:05:01		Sergey	Katureyev	RUS	29.9.67	2	NC-w	Sochi	22 Feb 92
2:05:05		Pyotr	Pochenchuk	UKR	26.7.54	2		Cherkassy	27 Apr 80
2:05:06		Nathan	Deakes	AUS	17.8.77	1	NC	Hobart	27 Aug 06
2:05:08+		Denis	Nizhegorodov	RUS	26.7.80	3	in 35k	Adler	19 Feb 06
2:05:09		Mikhail	Shchennikov	RUS	24.12.67	1	NC-w	Adler	11 Feb 96
2:05:12		Valeriy	Suntsov (20)	RUS	10.7.55	3		Cherkassy	27 Apr 80

35 KILOMETRES WALK

Mark	Wind	Name		Nat	Born	Pos	Meet	Venue	Date
2:21:31		Vladimir	Kanaykin ¶	RUS	21.3.85	1	NC-w	Adler	19 Feb 06
2:23:17			Kanaykin			1	NC-w	Adler	8 Feb 04
2:23:17			Kanaykin			1	NC-w	Adler	13 Mar 05
2:24:25		Semyon	Lovkin	RUS	14.7.77	1	NC-w	Adler	1 Mar 03
2:24:25		Sergey	Bakulin ¶	RUS	13.11.86	1	NC-w	Adler	1 Mar 09
2:24:50		Denis	Nizhegorodov	RUS	26.7.80	2	NC-w	Adler	19 Feb 06
2:24:56			Nizhegorodov			2	NC-w	Adler	1 Mar 09
2:25:19		Andrey	Ruzavin ¶	RUS	28.3.86	3	NC-w	Adler	1 Mar 09
2:25:38		Stepan	Yudin	RUS	3.4.80	2	NC-w	Adler	1 Mar 03
2:25:54		Mikhail	Ryzhov	RUS	17.12.91	1	NC-w	Sochi	27 Feb 15
2:25:57			Kirdyapkin			2	NC-w	Adler	13 Mar 05
2:25:58		German	Skurygin ¶	RUS	15.9.63	1	NC-w	Adler	20 Feb 98
2:25:59			Kanaykin ¶			1	NC-w	Adler	23 Feb 08
2:25:59			Ryzhov			1	NC-w	Sochi	18 Feb 12
2:26:16		Alex	Schwazer ¶	ITA	26.12.84	1		Montalto Di Castro	24 Jan 10
2:26:25		Aleksey	Voyevodin ¶ (10)	RUS	9.8.70	2	NC-w	Adler	8 Feb 04
2:26:29		Yuriy	Andronov	RUS	6.11.71	4	NC-w	Adler	1 Mar 09
2:26:33		Ivan	Noskov	RUS	16.7.88	2	NC-w	Sochi	18 Feb 12
2:26:36		Igor	Yerokhin ¶	RUS	4.9.85	1	NC-w	Sochi	26 Feb 11
2:26:46		Oleg	Ishutkin	RUS	22.7.75	1	NC-w	Adler	9 Feb 97
2:27:02		Yevgeniy	Shmalyuk	RUS	14.1.76	1	NC-w	Adler	20 Feb 00
2:27:07		Dmitriy	Dolnikov	RUS	19.11.72	2	NC-w	Adler	20 Feb 98
2:27:07		Sergey	Sharipov	RUS	14.4.92	1	NC-w	Sochi	18 Feb 17
2:27:21		Pavel	Nikolayev	RUS	18.12.77	3	NC-w	Adler	20 Feb 98
DQ: 2:25:42		Sergey	Kirdyapkin ¶	RUS	18.6.80	(1)	NC-w	Sochi	18 Feb 12

50 KILOMETRES WALK

Mark	Wind	Name		Nat	Born	Pos	Meet	Venue	Date
3:32:33	WR	Yohann	Diniz	FRA	1.1.78	1	EC	Zürich	15 Aug 14
3:33:12			Diniz			1	WCh	London	13 Aug 17
3:34:14	WR	Denis	Nizhegorodov	RUS	26.7.80	1	WCp	Cheboksary	11 May 08
3:34:38		Matej	Tóth	SVK	10.2.83	1		Dudince	21 Mar 15
3:35:27.2t	WR		Diniz			1		Reims	12 Mar 11
3:35:29			Nizhegorodov			1	NC	Cheboksary	13 Jun 04
3:35:47		Nathan	Deakes	AUS	17.8.77	1	NC	Geelong	2 Dec 06
3:36:03	WR	Robert	Korzeniowski	POL	30.7.68	1	WCh	Saint-Denis	27 Aug 03

Mark	Wind	Name		Nat	Born	Pos	Meet	Venue	Date
3:36:04		Alex	Schwazer ¶	ITA	26.12.84	1	NC	Rosignano Solvay	11 Feb 07
3:36:06			Yu Chaohong	CHN	12.12.76	1	NG	Nanjing	22 Oct 05
3:36:13			Zhao Chengliang	CHN	1.6.84	2	NG	Nanjing	22 Oct 05
3:36:20			Han Yucheng	CHN	16.12.78	1	NC	Nanning	27 Feb 05
3:36:21			Tóth			2	EC	Zürich	15 Aug 14
3:36:39	WR		Korzeniowski			1	EC	München	8 Aug 02
3:36:42		German	Skurygin ¶ (10)	RUS	15.9.63	2	WCh	Saint-Denis	27 Aug 03
3:36:53		Jared	Tallent	AUS	17.10.84	1	OG	London	11 Aug 12
3:37:04			Schwazer			2	WCp	Cheboksary	11 May 08
3:37:09			Schwazer			1	OG	Beijing	22 Aug 08
3:37:16			Si Tianfeng	CHN	17.6.84	2	OG	London	11 Aug 12
3:37:26	WR	Valeriy	Spitsyn	RUS	5.12.65	1	NC	Moskva	21 May 00
3:37:41	WR	Andrey	Perlov	RUS	12.12.61	1	NC	Leningrad	5 Aug 89
3:37:41		Ivan	Noskov ¶	RUS	16.7.88	3	EC	Zürich	15 Aug 14
3:37:46		Andreas	Erm	GER	12.3.76	3	WCh	Saint-Denis	27 Aug 03
3:37:48			Diniz			1	NC	St.Sebastien-sur-Loire	13 Mar 16
3:37:54		Robert	Heffernan	IRL	20.2.78	3	OG	London	11 Aug 12
3:37:56			Heffernan			1	WCh	Moskva	14 Aug 13
3:37:58			Xing Shucai	CHN	4.8.84	2	NC	Nanning	27 Feb 05
3:38:01		Aleksey	Voyevodin ¶	RUS	9.8.70	4	WCh	Saint-Denis	27 Aug 03
3:38:02			Nizhegorodov			1	WCp	La Coruña	14 May 06
3:38:08		Sergey	Kirdyapkin ¶ (20)	RUS	16.1.80	1	WCh	Helsinki	12 Aug 05
3:38:08		Igor	Yerokhin ¶	RUS	4.9.85	1	NC	Saransk	8 Jun 08
3:38:08			Kirdyapkin			1	WCp	Saransk	13 May 12
		(31/21)							
3:38:17	WR	Ronald	Weigel	GDR	8.8.59	1	IM	Potsdam	25 May 86
3:38:29		Vyacheslav	Ivanenko	RUS	3.3.61	1	OG	Seoul	30 Sep 88
3:38:43		Valentí	Massana	ESP	5.7.70	1	NC	Orense	20 Mar 94
3:38:58		Mikhail	Ryzhov ¶	RUS	17.12.91	2	WCh	Moskva	14 Aug 13
3:39:01			Li Jianbo	CHN	14.11.86	4	OG	London	11 Aug 12
3:39:17			Dong Jimin	CHN	10.10.83	4	NC	Nanning	27 Feb 05
3:39:21		Vladimir	Potemin	RUS	15.1.80	2	NC	Moskva	21 May 00
3:39:22		Sergey	Korepanov	KAZ	9.5.64	1	WCp	Mézidon-Canon	2 May 99
3:39:34		Valentin	Kononen	FIN	7.3.69	1		Dudince	25 Mar 00
		(30)							
3:39:45		Hartwig	Gauder	GDR	10.11.54	3	OG	Seoul	30 Sep 88
3:39:54		Jesús Angel	García	ESP	17.10.69	1	WCp	Podebrady	20 Apr 97
3:40:02		Aleksandr	Potashov	BLR	12.3.62	1	NC	Moskva	27 May 90
3:40:07		Andrey	Plotnikov	RUS	12.8.67	2	NC	Moskva	27 May 90
3:40:08		Tomasz	Lipiec ¶	POL	10.5.71	2	WCp	Mézidon-Canon	2 May 99
3:40:12		Oleg	Ishutkin	RUS	22.7.75	2	WCp	Podebrady	20 Apr 97
3:40:12		Yuki	Yamazaki	JPN	16.1.84	1		Wajima	12 Apr 09
3:40:13		Nikolay	Matyukhin	RUS	13.12.68	3	WCp	Mézidon-Canon	2 May 99
3:40:19		Takayuki	Tanii	JPN	14.2.83	2	AsiG	Incheon	1 Oct 14
3:40:20		Hirooki	Arai	JPN	18.5.88	1	NC	Wajima	19 Apr 15
		(40)							
3:40:23			Gadasu Alatan	CHN	27.1.84	3	NG	Nanjing	22 Oct 05
3:40:39		Igor	Hlavan	UKR	25.9.90	4	WCh	Moskva	14 Aug 13
3:40:40		Vladimir	Kanaykin ¶	RUS	21.3.85	1	NC	Saransk	12 Jun 05
3:40:46	WR	José	Marin	ESP	21.1.50	1	NC	Valencia	13 Mar 83
3:40:46		Yuriy	Andronov ¶	RUS	6.11.71	1		Moskva	11 Jun 12
3:40:57.9t		Thierry	Toutain	FRA	14.2.62	1		Héricourt	29 Sep 96
3:41:02		Francisco Javier	Fernández ¶	ESP	6.3.77	1	NC	San Pedro del Pinatar	1 Mar 09
3:41:02			Wang Zhendong	CHN	11.1.91	1		Huangshan	6 Mar 16
3:41:09		Érick	Barrondo	GUA	14.6.91	1		Dudince	23 Mar 13
3:41:10			Zhao Jianguo	CHN	19.1.88	1	AsiC	Wajima	16 Apr 06
		(50)	100th man 3:43:59, 200th 3:48:24, 300th 3:51:35, 400th 3:54:20, 500th 3:56:18						
Drugs disqualification			Russians – Noskov, Ryzhov, Strelkov and Yargunkin suspended pending investigation						
3:35:59		Sergey	Kirdyapkin ¶	RUS	16.1.80	(1)	OG	London	11 Aug 12
3:36:55		Vladimir	Kanaykin ¶	RUS	21.3.85	(2)	WCp	Cheboksary	11 May 08
3:37:54		Igor	Yerokhin ¶	RUS	4.9.85	(5)	OG	London	11 Aug 12
3:38:46		Sergey	Bakulin ¶	RUS	13.11.86	(1)	NC	Saransk	12 Jun 11

100 KILOMETRES WALK

Mark	Name		Nat	Born	Pos	Venue	Date
8:38.07	Viktor	Ginko	BLR	7.12.65	1	Scanzorosciate	27 Oct 02
8:43:30		Ginko			1	Scanzorosciate	29 Oct 00
8:44:28		Ginko			1	Scanzorosciate	19 Oct 03
8:48:28	Modris	Liepins	LAT	30.8.66	1	Scanzorosciate	28 Oct 01
8:54:35	Aleksey	Rodionov	RUS	5.3.57	1	Scanzorosciate	15 Nov 98
8:55:12	Pascal	Kieffer	FRA	6.5.61	1	Besançon	18 Oct 92

WOMEN'S ALL-TIME WORLD LISTS

100 METRES

Mark	Wind	Name		Nat	Born	Pos	Meet	Venue	Date
10.49WR	0.0	Florence	Griffith Joyner	USA	21.12.59	1q1	NC/OT	Indianapolis	16 Jul 88
		@ Probably strongly wind-assisted, but recognised as a US and world record							
10.61	1.2		Griffith Joyner			1	NC/OT	Indianapolis	17 Jul 88
10.62	1.0		Griffith Joyner			1q3	OG	Seoul	24 Sep 88
10.64	1.2	Carmelita	Jeter	USA	24.11.79	1		Shanghai	20 Sep 09
10.65A	1.1	Marion	Jones ¶	USA	12.10.75	1	WCp	Johannesburg	12 Sep 98
10.67	-0.1		Jeter			1	WAF	Thessaloníki	13 Sep 09
10.70 (WR)	1.6		Griffith Joyner			1s1	NC/OT	Indianapolis	17 Jul 88
10.70	-0.1		Jones			1	WCh	Sevilla	22 Aug 99
10.70	2.0		Jeter			1	Pre	Eugene	4 Jun 11
10.70	0.6	Shelly-Ann	Fraser-Pryce	JAM	27.12.86	1	NC	Kingston	29 Jun 12
10.70	0.3	Elaine	Thompson	JAM	28.6.92	1	NC	Kingston	1 Jul 16
10.71	0.1		Jones			1		Chengdu	12 May 98
10.71	2.0		Jones			1s2	NC	New Orleans	19 Jun 98
10.71	-0.3		Fraser-Pryce			1	WCh	Moskva	12 Aug 13
10.71	0.5		Thompson			1	OG	Rio de Janeiro	13 Aug 16
10.71	0.8		Thompson			1	NC	Kingston	23 Jun 17
10.72	2.0		Jones			1	NC	New Orleans	20 Jun 98
10.72	0.0		Jones			1	Herc	Monaco	8 Aug 98
10.72	0.0		Jones			1	Athl	Lausanne	25 Aug 98
10.72	-0.3		Fraser-Pryce			1	VD	Bruxelles	6 Sep 13
10.73	2.0	Christine	Arron	FRA	13.9.73	1	EC	Budapest	19 Aug 98
10.73	0.1		Fraser-Pryce			1	WCh	Berlin	17 Aug 09
10.74	1.3	Merlene	Ottey	JAM/SLO	10.5.60	1	GPF	Milano	7 Sep 96
10.74	0.2		Fraser-Pryce			1	DL	Saint-Denis	4 Jul 15
10.74	1.0	English	Gardner	USA	22.4.92	1	NC	Eugene	3 Jul 16
10.75	0.6		Jones			1	GGala	Roma	14 Jul 98
10.75	0.4	Kerron	Stewart	JAM	16.4.84	1	GGala	Roma	10 Jul 09
10.75	0.1		Stewart			2	WCh	Berlin	17 Aug 09
10.75	1.5		Fraser-Pryce			1	OG	London (OS)	4 Aug 12
10.76 WR	1.7	Evelyn	Ashford (10)	USA	15.4.57	1	WK	Zürich	22 Aug 84
10.76	0.9		Jones			1	VD	Bruxelles	22 Aug 97
10.76	0.3		Jones			1q4	WCh	Sevilla	21 Aug 99
10.76	1.1	Veronica	Campbell-Brown	JAM	15.5.82	1	GS	Ostrava	31 May 11
10.76	-0.3		Fraser-Pryce			1	WCh	Beijing	24 Aug 15
		(33 performances by11 athletes)							
10.77	0.9	Irina	Privalova	RUS	22.11.68	1rA	Athl	Lausanne	6 Jul 94
10.77	0.7	Ivet	Lalova-Collio	BUL	18.5.84	1	ECp-1A	Plovdiv	19 Jun 04
10.78A	1.0	Dawn	Sowell	USA	27.3.66	1	NCAA	Provo	3 Jun 89
10.78	1.8	Torri	Edwards ¶	USA	31.1.77	1s2	OT	Eugene	28 Jun 08
10.78	1.6	Murielle	Ahouré	CIV	23.8.87	1		Montverde	11 Jun 16
10.78	1.0	Tianna	Bartoletta '	USA	30.8.85	2	NC	Eugene	3 Jul 16
10.78	1.0	Tori	Bowie	USA	27.8.90	3	NC	Eugene	3 Jul 16
10.79	0.0		Li Xuemei	CHN	5.1.77	1	NG	Shanghai	18 Oct 97
10.79	-0.1	Inger (20)	Miller	USA	12.6.72	2	WCh	Sevilla	22 Aug 99
10.79	1.1	Blessing	Okagbare	NGR	9.10.88	1	DL	London (OS)	27 Jul 13
10.81 WR	1.7	Marlies	Göhr'	GDR	21.3.58	1	OD	Berlin	8 Jun 83
10.81	-0.3	Dafne	Schippers	NED	15.6.92	2	WCh	Beijing	24 Aug 15
10.82	-1.0	Gail	Devers	USA	19.11.66	1	OG	Barcelona	1 Aug 92
10.82	0.4	Gwen	Torrence	USA	12.6.65	2	GPF	Paris	3 Sep 94
10.82	-0.3	Zhanna	Pintusevich-Block ¶	UKR	6.7.72	1	WCh	Edmonton	6 Aug 01
10.82	-0.7	Sherone	Simpson	JAM	12.8.84	1	NC	Kingston	24 Jun 06
10.82	0.9	Michelle-Lee	Ahye	TTO	10.4.92	1	NC	Port of Spain	24 Jun 17
10.83	1.7	Marita	Koch	GDR	18.2.57	2	OD	Berlin	8 Jun 83
10.83	-1.0	Juliet (30)	Cuthbert	JAM	9.4.64	2	OG	Barcelona	1 Aug 92
10.83	0.1	Ekateríni	Thánou ¶	GRE	1.2.75	2s1	WCh	Sevilla	22 Aug 99
10.84	1.3	Chioma	Ajunwa ¶	NGR	25.12.70	1		Lagos	11 Apr 92
10.84	1.9	Chandra	Sturrup	BAH	12.9.71	1	Athl	Lausanne	5 Jul 05
10.84	1.8	Kelly-Ann	Baptiste ¶	TTO	14.10.86	1		Clermont	5 Jun 10
10.85	2.0	Anelia	Nuneva	BUL	30.6.62	1h1	NC	Sofia	2 Sep 88
10.85	1.0	Muna	Lee	USA	30.10.81	1	OT	Eugene	28 Jun 08
10.85	2.0	Barbara	Pierre	HAI/USA	28.4.87	1s1	NC	Des Moines	21 Jun 13
10.85	2.0	Aleia	Hobbs	USA	24.2.96	1		Baton Rouge	29 Apr 17
10.86	0.6	Silke	Gladisch'	GDR	20.6.64	1	NC	Potsdam	20 Aug 87
10.86	1.2	Chryste	Gaines ¶ (40)	USA	14.9.70	1	WAF	Monaco	14 Sep 03

Mark	Wind	Name		Nat	Born	Pos	Meet	Venue	Date
10.86	2.0	Marshevet	Hooker/Myers	USA	25.9.84	2	Pre	Eugene	4 Jun 11
10.86	0.5	Marie Josée	Ta Lou	CIV	18.11.88	4	OG	Rio de Janeiro	13 Aug 16
10.87	1.8	Octavious	Freeman	USA	20.4.92	2	NC	Des Moines	21 Jun 13
10.88	0.4	Lauryn	Williams	USA	11.9.83	2	WK	Zürich	19 Aug 05
10.89	1.8	Katrin	Krabbe ¶	GDR	22.11.69	1		Berlin	20 Jul 88
10.89	0.0		Liu Xiaomei	CHN	11.1.72	2	NG	Shanghai	18 Oct 97
10.89	1.5	Allyson	Felix	USA	18.11.85	5	OG	London (OS)	4 Aug 12
10.90	1.4	Glory	Alozie	NGR/ESP	30.12.77	1		La Laguna	5 Jun 99
10.90	1.8	Shalonda	Solomon	USA	19.12.85	2		Clermont	5 Jun 10
10.91	0.2	Heike	Drechsler'	GDR/GER	16.12.64	2	GWG	Moskva	6 Jul 86
10.91	1.1	Savatheda	Fynes	BAH	17.10.74	2	Athl	Lausanne	2 Jul 99
10.91	1.5	Debbie	Ferguson McKenzie	BAH	16.1.76	1	CG	Manchester	27 Jul 02
10.91	1.7	Alexandria	Anderson	USA	28.1.87	3s2	NC	Des Moines	21 Jun 13
10.91	-0.2	Rosângela	Santos	BRA	20.12.90	2s2	WCh	London (OS)	6 Aug 17
		(54)	100th women 11.00, 200th 11.10, 300th 11.16, 400th 11.22, 500th 11.26						
Doubtful wind reading									
10.83	0.0	Sheila	Echols	USA	2.10.64	1q2	NC/OT	Indianapolis	16 Jul 88
10.86	0.0	Diane	Williams	USA	14.12.60	2q1	NC/OT	Indianapolis	16 Jul 88
Probably semi-automatic timing: 10.87	1.9	Lyudmila	Kondratyeva	RUS	11.4.58	1		Leningrad	3 Jun 80
Low altitude best: 10.91	1.6		Sowell			1	NC	Houston	16 Jun 89
Wind-assisted performances to 10.74 and performers to 10.88									
10.54	3.0		Griffith Joyner			1	OG	Seoul	25 Sep 88
10.60	3.2		Griffith Joyner			1h1	NC/OT	Indianapolis	16 Jul 88
10.68	2.2		Jones			1	DNG	Stockholm	1 Aug 00
10.70	2.6		Griffith Joyner			1s2	OG	Seoul	25 Sep 88
10.71	2.2		Fraser-Pryce			1	Pre	Eugene	1 Jun 13
10.71	2.4		Thompson			1		Kingston	7 May 16
10.72	3.0		Jeter			1s1	NC	Eugene	26 Jun 09
10.72	3.2	Tori	Bowie	USA	27.8.90	1s2	NC	Eugene	26 Jun 15
10.72	4.5	Tawanna	Meadows	USA	4.8.86	1		Lubbock	6 May 17
10.74	2.7		Jeter			1	NC	Eugene	24 Jun 11
10.74	3.1		Bowie			1s1	NC	Eugene	3 Jul 16
10.74	2.5		Gardner			1s3	NC	Eugene	3 Jul 16
10.75	2.2	Blessing	Okagbare	NGR	9.10.88	2	Pre	Eugene	1 Jun 13
10.76	3.4	Marshevet	Hooker/Myers	USA	25.9.84	1q1	NC/OT	Eugene	27 Jun 08
10.77	2.3	Gail	Devers	USA	19.11.66	1	Jen	San José	28 May 94
10.77	2.3	Ekateríni	Thánou ¶	GRE	1.2.75	1		Rethymno	28 May 99
10.78	5.0	Gwen	Torrence	USA	12.6.65	1q3	NC/OT	Indianapolis	16 Jul 88
10.78	3.3	Muna	Lee	USA	30.10.81	2	NC	Eugene	26 Jun 09
10.79	3.3	Marlies	Göhr'	GDR	21.3.58	1	NC	Cottbus	16 Jul 80
10.80	2.9	Pam	Marshall	USA	16.8.60	1	NC	Eugene	20 Jun 86
10.80	2.8	Heike	Drechsler'	GDR	16.12.64	1	Bisl	Oslo	5 Jul 86
10.81	3.6	Jenna	Prandini	USA	20.11.92	1h4	NC	Eugene	2 Jul 16
10.82	2.2	Silke	Gladisch/Möller	GDR	20.6.64	1s1	WCh	Roma	30 Aug 87
10.83	3.9	Sheila	Echols	USA	2.10.84	1h2	NC/OT	Indianapolis	16 Jul 88
10.83	4.5	Candyce	McGrone	USA	24.3.89	2		Lubbock	6 May 17
10.84	2.9	Alice	Brown	USA	20.9.60	2	NC	Eugene	20 Jun 86
10.86	3.4	Lauryn	Williams	USA	11.9.83	2q1	NC/OT	Eugene	27 Jun 08
10.86	3.2	Jasmine	Todd	USA	23.12.93	3s2	NC	Eugene	26 Jun 15
10.87	3.0	Me'Lisa	Barber	USA	4.10.80	1s1	NC	Carson	25 Jun 05
10.88	5.9	Alexandria	Anderson	USA	28.1.87	1		Austin	14 Apr 12
Hand timing: 10.6	0.1	Zhanna	Pintusevich ¶	UKR	6.7.72	1		Kiev	12 Jun 97
Drugs disqualification									
10.75	-0.4		Jones			(1)	OG	Sydney	23 Sep 00
10.78	0.1		Jones			(1)	ISTAF	Berlin	1 Sep 00
10.83	1.6	Kelly-Ann	Baptiste ¶	TTO	14.10.86	1	NC	Port of Spain	22 Jun 13
10.85	0.9	Kelli	White ¶	USA	1.4.77	(1)	WCh	Saint-Denis	24 Aug 03
10.79w	2.3	Kelli	White ¶	USA	1.4.77	(1)		Carson	1 Jun 03

200 METRES

Mark	Wind	Name		Nat	Born	Pos	Meet	Venue	Date
21.34WR	1.3	Florence	Griffith Joyner	USA	21.12.59	1	OG	Seoul	29 Sep 88
21.56WR	1.7		Griffith Joyner			1s1	OG	Seoul	29 Sep 88
21.62A	-0.6	Marion	Jones ¶	USA	12.10.75	1	WCp	Johannesburg	11 Sep 98
21.63	0.2	Dafne	Schippers	NED	15.6.92	1	WCh	Beijing	28 Aug 15
21.64	0.8	Merlene	Ottey	JAM	10.5.60	1	VD	Bruxelles	13 Sep 91
21.66	-1.0		Ottey			1	WK	Zürich	15 Aug 90
21.66	0.2	Elaine	Thompson	JAM	28.6.92	2	WCh	Beijing	28 Aug 15
21.69	1.0	Allyson	Felix	USA	18.11.85	1	NC/OT	Eugene	30 Jun 12
21.71WR	0.7	Marita	Koch	GDR	18.2.57	1	v CAN	Karl-Marx-Stadt	10 Jun 79
21.71WR	0.3		Koch			1	OD	Potsdam	21 Jul 84

Mark	Wind	Name		Nat	Born	Pos	Meet	Venue	Date
21.71WR	1.2	Heike	Drechsler'	GDR	16.12.64	1	NC	Jena	29 Jun 86
21.71WR	-0.8		Drechsler			1	EC	Stuttgart	29 Aug 86
21.72	1.3	Grace	Jackson	JAM	14.6.61	2	OG	Seoul	29 Sep 88
21.72	-0.1	Gwen	Torrence (10)	USA	12.6.65	1s2	OG	Barcelona	5 Aug 92
21.74	0.4	Marlies	Göhr'	GDR	21.3.58	1	NC	Erfurt	3 Jun 84
21.74	1.2	Silke	Gladisch'	GDR	20.6.64	1	WCh	Roma	3 Sep 87
21.74	0.6	Veronica	Campbell-Brown	JAM	15.5.82	1	OG	Beijing	21 Aug 08
21.75	-0.1	Juliet	Cuthbert	JAM	9.4.64	2s2	OG	Barcelona	5 Aug 92
21.76	0.3		Koch			1	NC	Dresden	3 Jul 82
21.76	0.7		Griffith Joyner			1q1	OG	Seoul	28 Sep 88
21.76	-0.8		Jones			1	WK	Zürich	13 Aug 97
21.77	-0.1		Griffith Joyner			1q2	NC/OT	Indianapolis	22 Jul 88
21.77	1.0		Ottey			1	Herc	Monaco	7 Aug 93
21.77	-0.3		Torrence			1	ASV	Köln	18 Aug 95
21.77	0.6	Inger	Miller	USA	12.6.72	1	WCh	Sevilla	27 Aug 99
21.77	1.5	Tori	Bowie	USA	27.8.90	1	Pre	Eugene	27 May 17
21.78	-1.3		Koch			1	NC	Leipzig	11 Aug 85
21.78	-0.1		Thompson			1	OG	Rio de Janeiro	17 Aug 16
21.79	1.7		Gladisch			1	NC	Potsdam	22 Aug 87
21.80	-1.1		Ottey			1	Nik	Nice	10 Jul 90
21.80	0.4		Jones			1	GWG	Uniondale, NY	20 Jul 98
		(31/16)							
21.81	-0.1	Valerie	Brisco-Hooks	USA	6.7.60	1	OG	Los Angeles	9 Aug 84
21.83	-0.2	Evelyn	Ashford	USA	15.4.57	1	WCp	Montreal	24 Aug 79
21.85	0.3	Bärbel	Wöckel'	GDR	21.3.55	2	OD	Potsdam	21 Jul 84
21.87	0.0	Irina	Privalova	RUS	22.11.68	2	Herc	Monaco	25 Jul 95
		(20)							
21.88	0.1	Shaunae	Miller-Uibo	BAH	15.4.94	1	WK-DLF	Zürich	24 Aug 17
21.93	1.3	Pam	Marshall	USA	16.8.60	2	NC/OT	Indianapolis	23 Jul 88
21.95	0.3	Katrin	Krabbe ¶	GDR	22.11.69	1	EC	Split	30 Aug 90
21.97	1.9	Jarmila	Kratochvílová	CZE	26.1.51	1	PTS	Bratislava	6 Jun 81
21.99	0.9	Chandra	Cheeseborough	USA	10.1.59	2	NC	Indianapolis	19 Jun 83
21.99	1.1	Marie-José	Pérec	FRA	9.5.68	1	BNP	Villeneuve d'Ascq	2 Jul 93
21.99	1.1	Kerron	Stewart	JAM	16.4.84	2	NC	Kingston	29 Jun 08
22.00	1.3	Sherone	Simpson	JAM	12.8.84	1	NC	Kingston	25 Jun 06
22.01	-0.5	Anelia	Nuneva'	BUL	30.6.62	1	NC	Sofia	16 Aug 87
22.01	0.0		Li Xuemei	CHN	5.1.77	1	NG	Shanghai	22 Oct 97
		(30)							
22.01	0.6	Muna	Lee	USA	30.10.81	4	OG	Beijing	21 Aug 08
22.01	0.2	Candyce	McGrone	USA	24.3.89	4	WCh	Beijing	28 Aug 15
22.02	1.1	Kyra	Jefferson	USA	23.9.94	1	NCAA	Eugene	10 Jun 17
22.04A	0.7	Dawn	Sowell	USA	27.3.66	1	NCAA	Provo	2 Jun 89
22.06A	0.7	Evette	de Klerk'	RSA	21.8.65	1		Pietersburg	8 Apr 89
22.07	-0.1	Mary	Onyali	NGR	3.2.68	1	WK	Zürich	14 Aug 96
22.07	0.2	Dina	Asher-Smith	GBR	4.12.95	5	WCh	Beijing	28 Aug 15
22.08	0.8	Marie Josée	Ta Lou	CIV	18.11.88	2	WCh	London (OS)	11 Aug 17
22.09	-0.3	Sanya	Richards-Ross	USA	26.2.85	1	DL	New York	9 Jun 12
22.09	-0.2	Shelly-Ann	Fraser-Pryce	JAM	27.12.86	2	OG	London (OS)	8 Aug 12
		(40)							
22.09	1.5	Deajah	Stevens	USA	19.5.95	1	Pac 12	Eugene	14 May 17
22.10	-0.1	Kathy	Cook'	GBR	3.5.60	4	OG	Los Angeles	9 Aug 84
22.11	1.0	Carmelita	Jeter	USA	24.11.79	2	NC/OT	Eugene	30 Jun 12
22.11	0.1	Myriam	Soumaré	FRA	29.10.86	2	VD	Bruxelles	5 Sep 14
22.13	1.2	Ewa	Kasprzyk	POL	7.9.57	2	GWG	Moskva	8 Jul 86
22.14	-0.6	Carlette	Guidry	USA	4.9.68	1	NC	Atlanta	23 Jun 96
22.15	1.0	Shalonda	Solomon	USA	19.12.85	1	NC	Eugene	26 Jun 11
22.17A	-2.3	Zhanna	Pintusevich-Block ¶	UKR	6.7.72	1		Monachil	9 Jul 97
22.18	-0.6	Dannette	Young-Stone	USA	6.10.64	2	NC	Atlanta	23 Jun 96
22.18	0.9	Galina	Malchugina	RUS	17.12.62	1s2	NC	Sankt Peterburg	4 Jul 96
22.18	0.5	Merlene	Frazer	JAM	27.12.73	1s2	WCh	Sevilla	25 Aug 99
22.18	1.9	Dezerea	Bryant	USA	27.4.93	1	NCAA	Eugene	13 Jun 15
		(52)	100th woman 22.32, 200th 22.56, 300th 22.70, 400th 22.81, 500th 22.88						
Wind-assisted			*Performers listed to 22.16*						
21.80	3.2	Kimberlyn	Duncan	USA	2.8.91	1	NC	Des Moines	23 Jun 13
21.82	3.1	Irina	Privalova	RUS	22.11.68	1	Athl	Lausanne	6 Jul 94
21.91	2.8	Muna	Lee	USA	30.10.81	1		Fort-de-France	10 May 08
22.01	2.9	Michelle-Lee	Ahye	TTO	10.4.92	1		San Marcos	25 Apr 15
22.06	3.8	Jeneba	Tarmoh	USA	27.9.89	1	NC	Sacramento	29 Jun 14
22.16	3.1	Dannette	Young-Stone	USA	6.10.64	2	Athl	Lausanne	6 Jul 94
22.16	3.2	Nanceen	Perry	USA	19.4.77	1		Austin	6 May 00

Mark	Wind	Name		Nat	Born	Pos	Meet	Venue	Date
22.16	3.2	Kamaria	Brown	USA	21.12.92	4	NC	Des Moines	23 Jun 13
Hand timing									
21.9	-0.1	Svetlana	Goncharenko	RUS	28.5.71	1		Rostov-na-Donu	31 May 98
21.6w	2.5	Pam	Marshall	USA	16.8.60	1	NC	San José	26 Jun 87
Drugs disqualification									
22.05	-0.3	Kelli	White ¶	USA	1.4.77	1	WCh	Saint-Denis	28 Aug 03
22.18i		Michelle	Collins ¶	USA	12.2.71	1	WI	Birmingham	15 Mar 03

300 METRES

Times in 300m races only

Mark	Wind	Name		Nat	Born	Pos	Meet	Venue	Date
35.30A		Ana Gabriela	Guevara	MEX	4.3.77	1		Ciudad de México	3 May 03
35.46		Kathy	Cook'	GBR	3.5.60	1	Nike	London (CP)	18 Aug 84
35.46		Chandra	Cheeseborough	USA	10.1.59	2	Nike	London (CP)	18 Aug 84
Indoors									
35.45		Irina	Privalova	RUS	22.11.68	1		Moskva	17 Jan 93
35.48	#	Svetlana	Goncharenko	RUS	28.5.71	1		Tampere	4 Feb 98

400 METRES

Mark	Wind	Name		Nat	Born	Pos	Meet	Venue	Date
47.60 WR		Marita	Koch	GDR	18.2.57	1	WCp	Canberra	6 Oct 85
47.99 WR		Jarmila	Kratochvílová	CZE	26.1.51	1	WCh	Helsinki	10 Aug 83
48.16 WR			Koch			1	EC	Athína	8 Sep 82
48.16			Koch			1	Drz	Praha	16 Aug 84
48.22			Koch			1	EC	Stuttgart	28 Aug 86
48.25		Marie-José	Pérec	FRA	9.5.68	1	OG	Atlanta	29 Jul 96
48.26			Koch			1	GO	Dresden	27 Jul 84
48.27		Olga	Vladykina'	UKR	30.6.63	2	WCp	Canberra	6 Oct 85
48.45			Kratochvílová			1	NC	Praha	23 Jul 83
48.59		Tatána	Kocembová'	CZE	2.5.62	2	WCh	Helsinki	10 Aug 83
48.60 WR			Koch			1	ECp	Torino	4 Aug 79
48.60			Vladykina			1	ECp	Moskva	17 Aug 85
48.61			Kratochvílová			1	WCp	Roma	6 Sep 81
48.63		Cathy	Freeman	AUS	16.2.73	2	OG	Atlanta	29 Jul 96
48.65			Bryzgina'			1	OG	Seoul	26 Sep 88
48.70		Sanya	Richards	USA	26.2.85	1	WCp	Athína	16 Sep 06
48.73			Kocembová			2	Drz	Praha	16 Aug 84
48.77			Koch			1	v USA	Karl-Marx-Stadt	9 Jul 82
48.82			Kratochvílová			1	Ros	Praha	23 Jun 83
48.83		Valerie	Brisco	USA	6.7.60	1	OG	Los Angeles	6 Aug 84
48.83			Pérec			1	OG	Barcelona	5 Aug 92
48.83			Richards			1	VD	Bruxelles	4 Sep 09
48.85			Kratochvílová			2	EC	Athína	8 Sep 82
48.86			Kratochvílová			1	WK	Zürich	18 Aug 82
48.86			Koch			1	NC	Erfurt	2 Jun 84
48.87			Koch			1	VD	Bruxelles	27 Aug 82
48.88			Koch			1	OG	Moskva	28 Jul 80
48.89 WR			Koch			1		Potsdam	29 Jul 79
48.89			Koch			1		Berlin	15 Jul 84
48.89		Ana Gabriela (30/9)	Guevara	MEX	4.3.77	1	WCh	Saint-Denis	27 Aug 03
49.05		Chandra (10)	Cheeseborough	USA	10.1.59	2	OG	Los Angeles	6 Aug 84
49.07		Tonique	Williams-Darling	BAH	17.1.76	1	ISTAF	Berlin	12 Sep 04
49.10		Falilat	Ogunkoya	NGR	12.5.68	3	OG	Atlanta	29 Jul 96
49.11		Olga	Nazarova ¶	RUS	1.6.65	1s1	OG	Seoul	25 Sep 88
49.16		Antonina	Krivoshapka ¶	RUS	21.7.87	1	NC	Cheboksary	5 Jul 12
49.19		Mariya	Pinigina'	UKR	9.2.58	3	WCh	Helsinki	10 Aug 83
49.24		Sabine	Busch	GDR	21.11.62	2	NC	Erfurt	2 Jun 84
49.26		Allyson	Felix	USA	18.11.85	1	WCh	Beijing	27 Aug 15
49.28 WR		Irena	Szewinska'	POL	24.5.46	1	OG	Montreal	29 Jul 76
49.28		Pauline	Davis-Thompson	BAH	9.7.66	4	OG	Atlanta	29 Jul 96
49.28		Yuliya (20)	Gushchina	RUS	4.3.83	2	NC	Cheboksary	5 Jul 12
49.29		Charity	Opara ¶	NGR	20.5.72	1	GGala	Roma	14 Jul 98
49.30		Petra	Müller'	GDR	18.7.65	1		Jena	3 Jun 88
49.30		Lorraine	Fenton'	JAM	8.9.73	2	Herc	Monaco	19 Jul 02
49.32		Shericka	Williams	JAM	17.9.85	2	WCh	Berlin	18 Aug 09
49.33		Amantle	Montsho ¶	BOT	4.7.83	1	Herc	Monaco	19 Jul 13
49.40		Jearl	Miles-Clark	USA	4.9.66	1	NC	Indianapolis	14 Jun 97
49.41		Christine	Ohuruogu	GBR	17.5.84	1	WCh	Moskva	12 Aug 13
49.42		Grit	Breuer ¶	GER	16.2.72	2	WCh	Tokyo	27 Aug 91
49.43		Kathy	Cook'	GBR	3.5.60	3	OG	Los Angeles	6 Aug 84
49.43A		Fatima	Yusuf (30)	NGR	2.5.71	1	AfG	Harare	15 Sep 95

Mark	Wind	Name		Nat	Born	Pos	Meet	Venue	Date
49.44		Shaunae	Miller-Uibo	BAH	15.4.94	1	OG	Rio de Janeiro	15 Aug 16
49.47		Aelita	Yurchenko	UKR	1.1.65	2	Kuts	Moskva	4 Sep 88
49.48		Francena	McCorory	USA	20.10.88	1	NC	Sacramento	28 Jun 14
49.49		Olga	Zaytseva	RUS	10.11.84	1	NCp	Tula	16 Jul 06
49.53		Vanya	Stambolova ¶	BUL	28.11.83	1	GP	Rieti	27 Aug 06
49.56		Bärbel	Wöckel'	GDR	21.3.55	1		Erfurt	30 May 82
49.56		Monique	Hennagan	USA	26.5.76	1	NC/OT	Sacramento	17 Jul 04
49.57		Grace	Jackson	JAM	14.6.61	1	Nik	Nice	10 Jul 88
49.58		Dagmar	Rübsam'	GDR	3.6.62	3	NC	Erfurt	2 Jun 84
	(40)								
49.59		Marion	Jones ¶	USA	12.10.75	1r6	MSR	Walnut	16 Apr 00
49.59		Katharine	Merry	GBR	21.9.74	1	GP	Athína	11 Jun 01
49.61		Ana Fidelia	Quirot	CUB	23.3.63	1	PAm	La Habana	5 Aug 91
49.63		Novlene	Williams-Mills	JAM	26.4.82	1		Shanghai	23 Sep 06
49.64		Gwen	Torrence	USA	12.6.65	2	Nik	Nice	15 Jul 92
49.64		Ximena	Restrepo	COL	10.3.69	3	OG	Barcelona	5 Aug 92
49.64		Deedee	Trotter	USA	8.12.82	1	NC	Indianapolis	23 Jun 07
49.64		Debbie	Dunn ¶	USA	26.3.78	1	NC	Des Moines	26 Jun 10
49.65		Natalya	Nazarova	RUS	26.5.79	1	NC	Tula	31 Jul 04
49.65		Nicola	Sanders	GBR	23.6.82	2	WCh	Osaka	29 Aug 07
		(50)	100th woman 50.14, 200th 50.75, 300th 51.11, 400th 51.3, 500th 51.593						
Hand timing									
48.9		Olga	Nazarova ¶	RUS	1.6.65	1	NP	Vladivostok	13 Sep 88
49.2A		Ana Fidelia	Quirot	CUB	23.3.63	1	AmCp	Bogotá	13 Aug 89
Drugs disqualification									
49.35		Anastasiya	Kapachinskaya ¶	RUS	21.11.79	(1)	NC	Cheboksary	22 Jul 11

600 METRES

Mark	Wind	Name		Nat	Born	Pos	Meet	Venue	Date
1:22.63		Ana Fidelia	Quirot	CUB	23.3.63	1		Guadalajara, ESP	25 Jul 97
1:22.87		Maria Lurdes	Mutola	MOZ	27.10.72	1		Liège (NX)	27 Aug 02
1:23.35		Pamela	Jelimo	KEN	5.12.89	1		Liège (NX)	5 Jul 12
1:23.5A		Doina	Melinte	ROU	27.12.56	1		Poiana Brasov	27 Jul 86

800 METRES

Mark	Wind	Name		Nat	Born	Pos	Meet	Venue	Date
1:53.28	WR	Jarmila	Kratochvílová	CZE	26.1.51	1		München	26 Jul 83
1:53.43	WR	Nadezhda	Olizarenko'	UKR	28.11.53	1	OG	Moskva	27 Jul 80
1:54.01		Pamela	Jelimo	KEN	5.12.89	1	WK	Zürich	29 Aug 08
1:54.44		Ana Fidelia	Quirot	CUB	23.3.63	1	WCp	Barcelona	9 Sep 89
1:54.68			Kratochvílová			1	WCh	Helsinki	9 Aug 83
1:54.81		Olga	Mineyeva	RUS	1.9.52	2	OG	Moskva	27 Jul 80
1:54.82			Quirot			1	ASV	Köln	24 Aug 97
1:54.85	WR		Olizarenko			1	Prav	Moskva	12 Jun 80
1:54.87			Jelimo			1	OG	Beijing	18 Aug 08
1:54.94	WR	Tatyana	Kazankina ¶	RUS	17.12.51	1	OG	Montreal	26 Jul 76
1:54.97			Jelimo			1	Gaz	Saint-Denis	18 Jul 08
1:54.99			Jelimo			1	ISTAF	Berlin	1 Jun 08
1:55.04			Kratochvílová			1	OsloG	Oslo	23 Aug 83
1:55.05		Doina	Melinte	ROU	27.12.56	1	NC	Bucuresti	1 Aug 82
1:55.1 '			Mineyeva			1	Znam	Moskva	6 Jul 80
1:55.16			Jelimo			1	VD	Bruxelles	5 Sep 08
1:55.16		Caster	Semenya	RSA	7.1.91	1	WCh	London (OS)	13 Aug 17
1:55.19		Maria Lurdes	Mutola	MOZ	27.10.72	1	WK	Zürich	17 Aug 94
1:55.19		Jolanda	Ceplak ¶ (10)	SLO	12.9.76	1rA	NA	Heusden	20 Jul 02
1:55.26		Sigrun	Wodars/Grau	GDR	7.11.65	1	WCh	Roma	31 Aug 87
1:55.27			Semenya			1	Herc	Monaco	21 Jul 17
1:55.28			Semenya	RSA	7.1.91	1	OG	Rio de Janeiro	20 Aug 16
1:55.29			Mutola			2	ASV	Köln	24 Aug 97
1:55.32		Christine	Wachtel	GDR	6.1.65	2	WCh	Roma	31 Aug 87
1:55.33			Semenya			1	Herc	Monaco	15 Jul 16
1:55.41			Mineyeva			1	EC	Athína	8 Sep 82
1:55.41			Jelimo			1	Bisl	Oslo	6 Jun 08
1:55.42		Nikolina	Shtereva	BUL	25.1.55	2	OG	Montreal	26 Jul 76
1:55.43			Mutola			1	WCh	Stuttgart	17 Aug 93
1:55.45			Semenya			1	WCh	Berlin	19 Aug 09
		(30/13)							
1:55.46		Tatyana	Providokhina	RUS	26.3.53	3	OG	Moskva	27 Jul 80
1:55.47		Francine	Niyonsaba	BDI	5.5.93	2	Herc	Monaco	21 Jul 17
1:55.54		Ellen	van Langen	NED	9.2.66	1	OG	Barcelona	3 Aug 92
1:55.54			Liu Dong	CHN	24.12.73	1	NG	Beijing	9 Sep 93

Mark Wind		Name	Nat	Born	Pos	Meet	Venue	Date
1:55.56	Lyubov	Gurina	RUS	6.8.57	3	WCh	Roma	31 Aug 87
1:55.60	Elfi	Zinn	GDR	24.8.53	3	OG	Montreal	26 Jul 76
1:55.61	Ajee'	Wilson	USA	8.5.94	3	Herc	Monaco	21 Jul 17
1:55.68	Ella	Kovacs	ROU	11.12.64	1	RomIC	Bucuresti	2 Jun 85
	(20)							
1:55.69	Irina	Podyalovskaya	RUS	19.10.59	1	Izv	Kyiv	22 Jun 84
1:55.74	Anita	Weiss'	GDR	16.7.55	4	OG	Montreal	26 Jul 76
1:55.87	Svetlana	Masterkova	RUS	17.1.68	1	Kuts	Moskva	18 Jun 99
1:55.96	Lyudmila	Veselkova	RUS	25.10.50	2	EC	Athína	8 Sep 82
1:55.96	Yekaterina	Podkopayeva'	RUS	11.6.52	1		Leningrad	27 Jul 83
1:55.99	Liliya	Nurutdinova ¶	RUS	15.12.63	2	OG	Barcelona	3 Aug 92
1:56.00	Tatyana	Andrianova	RUS	10.12.79	1	NC	Kazan	18 Jul 08
1:56.0 WR	Valentina	Gerasimova	KAZ	15.5.48	1	NC	Kyiv	12 Jun 76
1:56.0	Inna	Yevseyeva	UKR	14.8.64	1		Kyiv	25 Jun 88
1:56.04	Janeth	Jepkosgei	KEN	13.12.83	1	WCh	Osaka	28 Aug 07
1:56.09	Zulia	Calatayud	CUB	9.11.79	1	Herc	Monaco	19 Jul 02
	(30)							
1:56.1	Ravilya	Agletdinova'	BLR	10.2.60	2	Kuts	Podolsk	21 Aug 82
1:56.2 ‘	Totka	Petrova ¶	BUL	17.12.56	1		Paris (C)	6 Jul 79
1:56.2	Tatyana	Mishkel	UKR	10.6.52	3	Kuts	Podolsk	21 Aug 82
1:56.21	Martina	Kämpfert'	GDR	11.11.59	4	OG	Moskva	27 Jul 80
1:56.21	Zamira	Zaytseva	UZB	16.2.53	2		Leningrad	27 Jul 83
1:56.21	Kelly	Holmes	GBR	19.4.70	2	GPF	Monaco	9 Sep 95
1:56.24		Qu Yunxia	CHN	8.12.72	2	NG	Beijing	9 Sep 93
1:56.40	Jearl	Miles-Clark	USA	4.9.66	3	WK	Zürich	11 Aug 99
1:56.42	Paula	Ivan	ROU	20.7.63	1	Balk	Ankara	16 Jul 88
	(40)							
1:56.43	Hasna	Benhassi	MAR	1.6.78	2	OG	Athína	23 Aug 04
1:56.44	Svetlana	Styrkina	RUS	1.1.49	5	OG	Montreal	26 Jul 76
1:56.51	Slobodanka	Colovic	YUG	10.1.65	1		Beograd	17 Jun 87
1:56.53	Patricia	Djaté	FRA	3.1.71	3	GPF	Monaco	9 Sep 95
1:56.56	Ludmila	Formanová	CZE	2.1.74	4	WK	Zürich	11 Aug 99
1:56.57	Zoya	Rigel	RUS	15.10.52	3	EC	Praha	31 Aug 78
1:56.59	Natalya	Khrushchelyova	RUS	30.5.73	2	NC	Tula	31 Jul 04
1:56.60	Natalya	Tsyganova	RUS	7.2.71	1	NC	Tula	25 Jul 00
1:56.6	Tamara	Sorokina'	RUS	15.8.50	5	Kuts	Podolsk	21 Aug 82
1:56.61	Yelena	Afanasyeva	RUS	1.3.67	3	WK	Zürich	13 Aug 97
	(50)	100th woman 1:57.42, 200th 1:58.45, 300th 1:59.21, 400th 1:59.66, 500th 2:00.1						
Indoors: 1:55.85	Stephanie	Graf	AUT	26.4.73	2	EI	Wien	3 Mar 02
Drugs disqualification								
1:54.85	Yelena	Soboleva ¶	RUS	3.10.82	(1)	NC	Kazan	18 Jul 08
1:55.87	Mariya	Savinova ¶	RUS	13.8.85	1	WCh	Daegu	4 Sep 11

1000 METRES

Mark Wind		Name	Nat	Born	Pos	Meet	Venue	Date
2:28.98 WR	Svetlana	Masterkova	RUS	17.1.68	1	VD	Bruxelles	23 Aug 96
2:29.34 WR	Maria Lurdes	Mutola	MOZ	27.10.72	1	VD	Bruxelles	25 Aug 95
2:30.6 WR	Tatyana	Providokhina	RUS	26.3.53	1		Podolsk	20 Aug 78
2:30.67 WR	Christine	Wachtel	GDR	6.1.65	1	ISTAF	Berlin	17 Aug 90
2:30.85	Martina	Kämpfert'	GDR	11.11.59	1		Berlin	9 Jul 80
2:31.50	Natalya	Artyomova ¶	RUS	5.1.63	1	ISTAF	Berlin	10 Sep 91
2:31.5 A	Maricica	Puica	ROU	29.7.50	1		Poiana Brasov	1 Jun 86
2:31.51	Sandra	Gasser ¶	SUI	27.7.62	1		Jerez de la Frontera	13 Sep 89

1500 METRES

Mark Wind		Name	Nat	Born	Pos	Meet	Venue	Date
3:50.07 WR	Genzebe	Dibaba	ETH	8.2.91	1	Herc	Monaco	17 Jul 15
3:50.46 WR		Qu Yunxia	CHN	8.12.72	1	NG	Beijing	11 Sep 93
3:50.98		Jiang Bo	CHN	13.3.77	1	NG	Shanghai	18 Oct 97
3:51.34		Lang Yinglai	CHN	22.8.79	2	NG	Shanghai	18 Oct 97
3:51.92		Wang Junxia	CHN	9.1.73	2	NG	Beijing	11 Sep 93
3:52.47 WR	Tatyana	Kazankina ¶	RUS	17.12.51	1	WK	Zürich	13 Aug 80
3:53.91		Yin Lili ¶	CHN	11.11.79	3	NG	Shanghai	18 Oct 97
3:53.96	Paula	Ivan'	ROU	20.7.63	1	OG	Seoul	1 Oct 88
3:53.97		Lan Lixin	CHN	14.2.79	4	NG	Shanghai	18 Oct 97
3:54.11		Dibaba			1		Barcelona	8 Jul 15
3:54.23	Olga	Dvirna (10)	RUS	11.2.53	1	NC	Kyiv	27 Jul 82
3:54.52		Zhang Ling	CHN	13.4.80	5	NG	Shanghai	18 Oct 97
3:55.0 ‘ WR		Kazankina ¶			1	Znam	Moskva	6 Jul 80
3:55.01		Lan Lixin			1h2	NG	Shanghai	17 Oct 97
3:55.07		Dong Yanmei	CHN	16.2.77	6	NG	Shanghai	18 Oct 97
3:55.22	Laura	Muir	GBR	9.5.93	1	DL	Saint-Denis	27 Aug 16

Mark Wind		Name	Nat	Born	Pos	Meet	Venue	Date
3:55.30	Hassiba	Boulmerka	ALG	10.7.68	1	OG	Barcelona	8 Aug 92
3:55.33	Süreyya	Ayhan ¶	TUR	6.9.78	1	VD	Bruxelles	5 Sep 03
3:55.38		Qu Yunxia			2h2	NG	Shanghai	17 Oct 97
3:55.47		Zhang Ling			3h2	NG	Shanghai	17 Oct 97
3:55.60		Ayhan			1	WK	Zürich	15 Aug 03
3:55.68	Yuliya	Chizhenko ¶	RUS	30.8.79	1	Gaz	Saint-Denis	8 Jul 06
3:55.82		Dong Yanmei			4h2	NG	Shanghai	17 Oct 97
3:56.0 WR		Kazankina ¶			1		Podolsk	28 Jun 76
3:56.05	Sifan	Hassan	ETH/NED	.93	2	Herc	Monaco	17 Jul 15
3:56.14	Zamira	Zaytseva	UZB	16.2.53	2	NC	Kyiv	27 Jul 82
3:56.14		Hassan			1	FBK	Hengelo	11 Jun 17
3:56.18	Maryam	Jamal	BRN	16.9.84	1	GP	Rieti	27 Aug 06
3:56.22		Ivan			1	WK	Zürich	17 Aug 88
3:56.22		Hassan			1	GGala	Roma	8 Jun 17
3:56.29	Shannon	Rowbury	USA	19.9.84	3	Herc	Monaco	17 Jul 15
	(31/20)							
3:56.31		Liu Dong	CHN	24.12.73	5h2	NG	Shanghai	17 Oct 97
3:56.41	Faith	Kipyegon	KEN	10.1.94	1	Pre	Eugene	28 May 16
3:56.43	Yelena	Soboleva ¶	RUS	3.10.82	2	Gaz	Saint-Denis	8 Jul 06
3:56.50	Tatyana	Pozdnyakova	RUS	4.3.56	3	NC	Kyiv	27 Jul 82
3:56.54	Abeba	Aregawi	ETH/SWE	5.7.90	1	GGala	Roma	31 May 12
3:56.63	Nadezhda	Ralldugina	UKR	15.11.57	1	Drz	Praha	18 Aug 84
3:56.65	Yekaterina	Podkopayeva'	RUS	11.6.52	1		Rieti	2 Sep 84
3:56.7 '	Lyubov	Smolka	UKR	29.11.52	2	Znam	Moskva	6 Jul 80
3:56.7	Doina	Melinte	ROU	27.12.56	1		Bucuresti	12 Jul 86
3:56.77+	Svetlana	Masterkova	RUS	17.1.68	1	WK	Zürich	14 Aug 96
	(30)							
3:56.8 '	Nadezhda	Olizarenko'	UKR	28.11.53	3	Znam	Moskva	6 Jul 80
3:56.91	Lyudmila	Rogachova	RUS	30.10.66	2	OG	Barcelona	8 Aug 92
3:56.91	Tatyana	Tomashova ¶	RUS	1.7.75	1	EC	Göteborg	13 Aug 06
3:56.97	Gabriela	Szabo	ROU	14.11.75	1	Herc	Monaco	8 Aug 98
3:57.03		Liu Jing	CHN	3.2.71	6h2	NG	Shanghai	17 Oct 97
3:57.05	Svetlana	Guskova	MDA	19.8.59	4	NC	Kyiv	27 Jul 82
3:57.05	Hellen	Obiri	KEN	13.12.89	1	Pre	Eugene	31 May 14
3:57.12	Mary	Decker/Slaney	USA	4.8.58	1	vNord	Stockholm	26 Jul 83
3:57.22	Maricica	Puica	ROU	29.7.50	1		Bucuresti	1 Jul 84
3:57.22	Jennifer	Simpson	USA	23.8.86	2	DL	Saint-Denis	5 Jul 14
	(40)							
3:57.40	Suzy	Favor Hamilton	USA	8.8.68	1	Bisl	Oslo	28 Jul 00
3:57.4 '	Totka	Petrova ¶	BUL	17.12.56	1	Balk	Athína	11 Aug 79
3:57.41	Jackline	Maranga	KEN	16.12.77	3	Herc	Monaco	8 Aug 98
3:57.46		Zhang Linli	CHN	6.3.73	3	NG	Beijing	11 Sep 93
3:57.71	Christiane	Wartenberg'	GDR	27.10.56	2	OG	Moskva	1 Aug 80
3:57.71	Carla	Sacramento	POR	10.12.71	4	Herc	Monaco	8 Aug 98
3:57.72	Galina	Zakharova	RUS	7.9.56	1	NP	Baku	14 Sep 84
3:57.73	Natalya	Yevdokimova ¶	RUS	17.3.78	2	GP	Rieti	28 Aug 05
3:57.90	Kelly	Holmes	GBR	19.4.70	1	OG	Athína	28 Aug 04
3:57.92	Tatyana	Samolenko/Dorovskikh ¶	UKR	12.8.61	4	OG	Barcelona	8 Aug 92
	(50)	100th woman 3:59.9, 200th 4:02.20, 300th 4:03.98, 400th 4:05.30, 500th 4:06.30						
Indoors: 3:55.17 WIR		G Dibaba			1		Karlsruhe	1 Feb 14
Drugs disqualification: 3:56.15		Mariem Alaoui Selsouli ¶	MAR	8.4.84	(1)	DL	Saint-Denis	6 Jul 12
3:56.62	Asli	Çakir Alptekin ¶	TUR	20.8.85	(2)	DL	Saint-Denis	6 Jul 12
3:57.65	Anna	Alminova ¶	RUS	17.1.85	(1)	DL	Saint-Denis	16 Jul 10

1 MILE

Mark		Name	Nat	Born	Pos	Meet	Venue	Date
4:12.56 WR	Svetlana	Masterkova	RUS	17.1.68	1	WK	Zürich	14 Aug 96
4:14.30	Genzebe	Dibaba	ETH	8.2.91	1		Rovereto	6 Sep 16
4:15.61 WR	Paula	Ivan'	ROU	20.7.63	1	Nik	Nice	10 Jul 89
4:15.8	Natalya	Artyomova ¶	RUS	5.1.63	1		Leningrad	5 Aug 84
4:16.56	Hellen	Obiri	KEN	13.12.89	1	DL	London (OS)	9 Jul 17
4:16.71 WR	Mary	Slaney (Decker)	USA	4.8.58	1	WK	Zürich	21 Aug 85
4:16.71	Faith	Kipyegon	KEN	10.1.94	1	VD	Bruxelles	11 Sep 15
4:17.25	Sonia	O'Sullivan	IRL	28.11.69	1	Bisl	Oslo	22 Jul 94
Indoors								
4:13.31 WIR	Genzebe	Dibaba	ETH	8.2.91	1	Globen	Stockholm	17 Feb 16
4:17.14 WIR	Doina	Melinte	ROU	27.12.56	1		East Rutherford	9 Feb 90
Drugs dq: 4:15.63	Yelena	Soboleva ¶	RUS	3.10.82	1		Moskva	29 Jun 07

2000 METRES

Mark		Name	Nat	Born	Pos	Meet	Venue	Date
5:25.36 WR	Sonia	O'Sullivan	IRL	28.11.69	1	TSB	Edinburgh	8 Jul 94
5:26.93	Yvonne	Murray	GBR	4.10.64	2	TSB	Edinburgh	8 Jul 94

Mark	Wind	Name		Nat	Born	Pos	Meet	Venue	Date
5:27.50		Genzebe	Dibaba	ETH	8.2.91	1	GS	Ostrava	17 Jun 14
5:28.69	WR	Maricica	Puica	ROU	29.7.50	1	PTG	London (CP)	11 Jul 86
5:28.72	WR	Tatyana	Kazankina ¶	RUS	17.12.51	1		Moskva	4 Aug 84
5:29.43+			Wang Junxia	CHN	9.1.73	1h2	NG	Beijing	12 Sep 93
5:29.64		Tatyana	Pozdnyakova	UKR	4.3.56	2		Moskva	4 Aug 84
5:30.19		Zola	Budd'	GBR	26.5.66	3	PTG	London (CP)	11 Jul 86
5:30.19		Gelete	Burka	ETH	15.2.86	1	VD	Bruxelles	4 Sep 09
5:30.92		Galina	Zakharova	RUS	7.9.56	3		Moskva	4 Aug 84
Indoors:									
5:23.75		Genzebe	Dibaba	ETH	8.2.91	1		Sabadell	7 Feb 17
5:30.53		Gabriela	Szabo	ROU	14.11.75	1		Sindelfingen	8 Mar 98

3000 METRES

Mark	Wind	Name		Nat	Born	Pos	Meet	Venue	Date
8:06.11	WR		Wang Junxia	CHN	9.1.73	1	NG	Beijing	13 Sep 93
8:12.18			Qu Yunxia	CHN	8.12.72	2	NG	Beijing	13 Sep 93
8:12.19	WR		Wang Junxia			1h2	NG	Beijing	12 Sep 93
8:12.27			Qu Yunxia			2h2	NG	Beijing	12 Sep 93
8:16.50			Zhang Linli	CHN	6.3.73	3	NG	Beijing	13 Sep 93
8:19.78			Ma Liyan	CHN	6.9.68	3h2	NG	Beijing	12 Sep 93
8:20.68		Hellen	Obiri	KEN	13.12.89	1	DL	Doha	9 May 14
8:21.14		Mercy	Cherono	KEN	7.5.91	2	DL	Doha	9 May 14
8:21.26			Ma Liyan			4	NG	Beijing	13 Sep 93
8:21.42		Gabriela	Szabo	ROU	14.11.75	1	Herc	Monaco	19 Jul 02
8:21.64		Sonia	O'Sullivan	IRL	28.11.69	1	TSB	London (CP)	15 Jul 94
8:21.84			Zhang Lirong	CHN	3.3.73	5	NG	Beijing	13 Sep 93
8:22.06	WR		Zhang Linli			1h1	NG	Beijing	12 Sep 93
8:22.20		Paula	Radcliffe (10)	GBR	17.12.73	2	Herc	Monaco	19 Jul 02
8:22.22		Almaz	Ayana	ETH	21.11.91	1		Rabat	14 Jun 15
8:22.34			Ayana			1	WK	Zürich	3 Sep 15
8:22.44			Zhang Lirong			2h1	NG	Beijing	12 Sep 93
8:22.62	WR	Tatyana	Kazankina ¶	RUS	17.12.51	1		Leningrad	26 Aug 84
8:23.11			Ayana			1	DL	Doha	6 May 16
8:23.14			Obiri			1	Herc	Monaco	21 Jul 17
8:23.23		Edith	Masai	KEN	4.4.67	3	Herc	Monaco	19 Jul 02
8:23.26		Olga	Yegorova ¶	RUS	28.3.72	1	WK	Zürich	17 Aug 01
8:23.55		Faith	Kipyegon	KEN	10.1.94	3	DL	Doha	9 May 14
8:23.75			Yegorova			1	GP	Saint-Denis	6 Jul 01
8:23.96			Yegorova			1	GGala	Roma	29 Jun 01
8:24.19			Szabo			2	WK	Zürich	17 Aug 01
8:24.27			Obiri			1	Herc	Monaco	15 Jul 16
8:24.31			Szabo			1	GP	Paris (C)	29 Jul 98
8:24.41		Viola	Kibiwot	KEN	22.12.83	4	DL	Doha	9 May 14
8:24.51+		Meseret (30/17)	Defar	ETH	19.11.83	1	in 2M	Bruxelles	14 Sep 07
8:25.40		Yelena	Zadorozhnaya	RUS	3.12.77	2	GGala	Roma	29 Jun 01
8:25.56		Tatyana	Tomashova ¶	RUS	1.7.75	3	GGala	Roma	29 Jun 01
8:25.62		Berhane	Adere (20)	ETH	21.7.73	3	WK	Zürich	17 Aug 01
8:25.83		Mary	Slaney	USA	4.8.58	1	GGala	Roma	7 Sep 85
8:25.92		Gelete	Burka	ETH	15.2.86	2	DNG	Stockholm	25 Jul 06
8:26.21		Genzebe	Dibaba	ETH	8.2.91	6	DL	Doha	9 May 14
8:26.48		Zahra	Ouaziz	MAR	20.12.69	2	WK	Zürich	11 Aug 99
8:26.53		Tatyana	Samolenko' ¶	UKR	12.8.61	1	OG	Seoul	25 Sep 88
8:26.78	WR	Svetlana	Ulmasova	UZB	4.2.53	1	NC	Kyiv	25 Jul 82
8:27.12	WR	Lyudmila	Bragina	RUS	24.7.43	1	v USA	College Park	7 Aug 76
8:27.15		Paula	Ivan'	ROU	20.7.63	2	OG	Seoul	25 Sep 88
8:27.62		Getenesh	Wami	ETH	11.12.74	4	WK	Zürich	17 Aug 01
8:27.83		Maricica (30)	Puica	ROU	29.7.50	2	GGala	Roma	7 Sep 85
8:28.33		Janet	Kisa	KEN	5.3.92	3	Herc	Monaco	15 Jul 16
8:28.41		Sentayehu	Ejigu	ETH	21.6.85	1	Herc	Monaco	22 Jul 10
8:28.51		Irene	Jelagat	KEN	10.12.88	7	DL	Doha	9 May 14
8:28.66		Vivian	Cheruiyot	KEN	11.9.83	2	WAF	Stuttgart	23 Sep 07
8:28.66		Beatrice	Chepkoech	KEN	6.7.91	2	Herc	Monaco	21 Jul 17
8:28.80		Marta	Domínguez	ESP	3.11.75	3	WK	Zürich	11 Aug 00
8:28.83		Zola	Budd'	GBR	26.5.66	3	GGala	Roma	7 Sep 85
8:28.87		Maryam	Jamal	BRN	16.9.84	1	Bisl	Oslo	29 Jul 05
8:28.90		Sifan	Hassan	NED	1.1.93	1	DL	Birmingham	20 Aug 17
8:29.02		Yvonne (40)	Murray	GBR	4.10.64	3	OG	Seoul	25 Sep 88
8:29.06		Priscah	Cherono	KEN	27.6.80	3	WAF	Stuttgart	23 Sep 07

Mark	Wind	Name		Nat	Born	Pos	Meet	Venue	Date
8:29.14		Lydia	Cheromei ¶	KEN	11.5.77	5	WK	Zürich	11 Aug 00
8:29.36		Svetlana	Guskova	MDA	19.8.59	2	NC	Kyiv	25 Jul 82
8:29.52		Mariem Alaoui	Selsouli ¶	MAR	8.4.84	1	Herc	Monaco	25 Jul 07
8:29.55		Tirunesh	Dibaba	ETH	1.10.85	1	LGP	London (CP)	28 Jul 06
8:29.58		Jennifer	Simpson'	USA	23.8.86	4	VD	Bruxelles	5 Sep 14
8:29.89		Konstanze	Klosterhalfen	GER	18.2.97	2	DL	Birmingham	20 Aug 17
8:29.93		Shannon	Rowbury	USA	19.9.84	5	VD	Bruxelles	5 Sep 14
8:30.00		Mimi	Belete	BRN	9.6.88	8	DL	Doha	9 May 14
8:30.11		Margaret	Kipkemboi	KEN	9.2.93	3	DL	Birmingham	20 Aug 17
		(50)	100th woman 8:35.34, 200th 8:42.2, 300th 8:46.71, 400th 8:49.69						
Indoors:									
8:16.60	WIR	Genzebe	Dibaba	ETH	8.2.91	1		Stockholm	6 Feb 14
8:23.72	WIR	Meseret	Defar	ETH	19.11.83	1	Spark	Stuttgart	3 Feb 07
8:23.74		Meselech	Melkamu	ETH	27.4.85	2	Spark	Stuttgart	3 Feb 07
8:25.27		Sentayehu	Ejigu	ETH	21.6.85	2	Spark	Stuttgart	6 Feb 10
8:26.41		Laura	Muir	GBR	9.5.93	1		Karlsruhe	4 Feb 17
8:27.86	WIR	Liliya	Shobukhova ¶	RUS	13.11.77	1	NC	Moskva	17 Feb 06
8:28.49		Anna	Alminova ¶	RUS	17.1.85	2	Spark	Stuttgart	7 Feb 09
8:29.00		Olesya	Syreva ¶	RUS	25.11.83	2	NC	Moskva	17 Feb 06

5000 METRES

Mark	Wind	Name		Nat	Born	Pos	Meet	Venue	Date
14:11.15	WR	Tirunesh	Dibaba	ETH	1.10.85	1	Bisl	Oslo	6 Jun 08
14:12.59		Almaz	Ayana	ETH	21.11.91	1	GGala	Roma	2 Jun 16
14:12.88		Meseret	Defar	ETH	19.11.83	1	DNG	Stockholm	22 Jul 08
14:14.32			Ayana			1	DL	Shanghai	17 May 15
14:15.41		Genzebe	Dibaba	ETH	8.2.91	1	DL	Saint-Denis	4 Jul 15
14:16.31			Ayana			1		Rabat	22 May 16
14:16.63	WR		Defar			1	Bisl	Oslo	15 Jun 07
14:18.37		Hellen	Obiri	KEN	13.12.89	1	GGala	Roma	8 Jun 17
14:18.89			Ayana			1	VD	Bruxelles	9 Sep 16
14:19.76			G Dibaba			1	Pre	Eugene	30 May 15
14:20.87		Vivian	Cheruiyot	KEN	11.9.83	1	DNG	Stockholm	29 Jul 11
14:21.29			G Dibaba			1	Bisl	Oslo	11 Jun 15
14:21.97			Ayana			2	DL	Saint-Denis	4 Jul 15
14:22.47			Obiri			1	DL	Shanghai	13 May 17
14:22.51			Cheruiyot			2	Bisl	Oslo	15 Jun 07
14:23.46			T Dibaba			1	GP	Rieti	7 Sep 08
14:23.68			T Dibaba			1	DL	Saint-Denis	6 Jul 13
14:23.75		Liliya	Shobukhova ¶	RUS	13.11.77	1	NC	Kazan	19 Jul 08
14:24.53	WR		Defar			1		New York (RI)	3 Jun 06
14:24.68	WR	Elvan	Abeylegesse ¶	TUR	11.9.82	1	Bisl	Bergen (Fana)	11 Jun 04
14:25.22			G Dibaba			1	Pre	Eugene	26 May 17
14:25.43			Cheruiyot			1	VD	Bruxelles	5 Sep 08
14:25.52			Defar			2	VD	Bruxelles	5 Sep 08
14:25.78			Obiri			2	VD	Bruxelles	9 Sep 16
14:25.84			Ayana			2	DL	Saint-Denis	6 Jul 13
14:25.88			Obiri			1	VD-DLF	Bruxelles	1 Sep 17
14:26.17			Cheruiyot			1	OG	Rio de Janeiro	19 Aug 16
14:26.83			Ayana			1	WCh	Beijing	30 Aug 15
14:26.90			Defar			1	Bisl	Oslo	13 Jun 13
14:27.41			Cheruiyot			1	DL	Saint-Denis	16 Jul 10
14:27.55		Caroline	Kipkirui	KEN	26.5.94	2	VD-DLF	Bruxelles	1 Sep 17
14:28.09	WR		Jiang Bo	CHN	13.3.77	1	NG	Shanghai	23 Oct 97
		(32/10)							
14:28.39		Sentayehu	Ejigu	ETH	21.6.85	2	DL	Saint-Denis	16 Jul 10
14:29.11		Paula	Radcliffe	GBR	17.12.73	1	ECpS	Bydgoszcz	20 Jun 04
14:29.32		Olga	Yegorova ¶	RUS	28.3.72	1	ISTAF	Berlin	31 Aug 01
14:29.32		Berhane	Adere	ETH	21.7.73	1	Bisl	Oslo	27 Jun 03
14:29.50		Viola	Kibiwot	KEN	22.12.83	2		Rabat	22 May 16
14:29.82			Dong Yanmei	CHN	16.2.77	2	NG	Shanghai	23 Oct 97
14:29.82		Senbere	Teferi	ETH	3.5.95	3	VD	Bruxelles	9 Sep 16
14:30.42		Sally	Kipyego	KEN	19.12.85	2	WK	Zürich	8 Sep 11
14:30.88		Getenesh	Wami	ETH	11.12.74	1	NA	Heusden-Zolder	5 Aug 00
14:31.14		Linet	Masai	KEN	5.12.89	2	DL	Shanghai	23 May 10
		(20)							
14:31.20		Gelete	Burka	ETH	15.2.86	2	GS	Ostrava	27 Jun 07
14:31.48		Gabriela	Szabo	ROU	14.11.75	1	ISTAF	Berlin	1 Sep 98
14:31.91		Meselech	Melkamu	ETH	27.4.85	3	DL	Shanghai	23 May 10
14:31.91		Sylvia	Kibet	KEN	28.3.84	4	DL	Shanghai	23 May 10
14:31.95		Faith	Kipyegon	KEN	10.1.94	2	Pre	Eugene	30 May 15

Mark Wind		Name	Nat	Born	Pos	Meet	Venue	Date
14:32.08	Zahra	Ouaziz	MAR	20.12.69	2	ISTAF	Berlin	1 Sep 98
14:32.33		Liu Shixiang ¶	CHN	13.1.71	3h1	NG	Shanghai	21 Oct 97
14:32.74	Ejagayehu	Dibaba	ETH	25.6.82	3	Bisl	Bergen (Fana)	11 Jun 04
14:32.82	Margaret	Kipkemboi	KEN	9.2.93	4	VD-DLF	Bruxelles	1 Sep 17
14:33.04	Werknesh (30)	Kidane	ETH	21.11.81	2	Bisl	Oslo	27 Jun 03
14:33.09	Agnes	Tirop	KEN	23.10.95	2	GGala	Roma	8 Jun 17
14:33.13	Gulnara	Galkina'	RUS	9.7.78	2	NC	Kazan	19 Jul 08
14:33.30	Etenesh	Diro	ETH	10.5.91	4	VD	Bruxelles	9 Sep 16
14:33.32	Letesenbet	Gidey	ETH	20.3.98	3	GGala	Roma	8 Jun 17
14:33.49	Lucy Wangui	Kabuu	KEN	24.3.84	2	Bisl	Oslo	6 Jun 08
14:33.84	Edith	Masai	KEN	4.4.67	3	Bisl	Oslo	2 Jun 06
14:33.95	Mercy	Cherono	KEN	7.5.91	2	GGala	Roma	2 Jun 16
14:35.30	Priscah	Jepleting/Cherono	KEN	27.6.80	4	Bisl	Oslo	2 Jun 06
14:36.45 WR	Fernanda	Ribeiro	POR	23.6.69	1		Hechtel	22 Jul 95
14:36.52	Mariem Alaoui (40)	Selsouli ¶	MAR	8.4.84	1	G Gala	Roma	13 Jul 07
14:36.80	Lilian	Rengeruk	KEN	3.5.97	2	Pre	Eugene	26 May 17
14:36.82	Yasemin	Can	TUR	11.12.96	4	GGala	Roma	8 Jun 17
14:37.07	Jéssica	Augusto	POR	8.11.81	5	DL	Saint-Denis	16 Jul 10
14:37.33 WR	Ingrid	Kristiansen'	NOR	21.3.56	1		Stockholm	5 Aug 86
14:38.09	Mariya	Konovalova ¶	RUS	14.8.74	3	NC	Kazan	19 Jul 08
14:38.21	Isabella	Ochichi	KEN	28.10.79	4	VD	Bruxelles	26 Aug 05
14:38.44	Wude	Ayalew	ETH	4.7.87	5	Bisl	Oslo	3 Jul 09
14:38.70	Janet	Kisa	KEN	5.3.92	4		Rabat	22 May 16
14:38.92	Shannon	Rowbury	USA	19.9.84	5	VD	Bruxelles	9 Sep 16
14:39.19	Ines	Chenonge	KEN	1.2.82	6	DL	Saint-Denis	16 Jul 10
	(50)	100th woman 14:47.20, 200th 15:02.48, 300th 15:08.61, 400th 15:14.67, 500th 15:19.0						
Indoors:								
14:18.06		G Dibaba			1	XL-G	Stockholm	19 Feb 15
14:24.37 WIR		Defar			1		Stockholm	18 Feb 09
14:24.79		Defar			1	GE Galan	Stockholm	10 Feb 10
14:27.42 WIR		T Dibaba			1	BIG	Boston (R)	27 Jan 07
14:39.89	Kimberley	Smith	NZL	19.11.73	1		New York (Armory)	27 Feb 09
Drugs disqualification: 14:36.79	Alemitu	Bekele ¶	TUR	17.9.77	4	VD	Bruxelles	27 Aug 10

10,000 METRES

Mark Wind		Name	Nat	Born	Pos	Meet	Venue	Date
29:17.45 WR	Almaz	Ayana	ETH	21.11.91	1	OG	Rio de Janeiro	12 Aug 16
29:31.78 WR		Wang Junxia	CHN	9.1.73	1	NG	Beijing	8 Sep 93
29:32.53	Vivian	Cheruiyot	KEN	11.9.83	2	OG	Rio de Janeiro	12 Aug 16
29:42.56	Tirunesh	Dibaba	ETH	1.10.85	3	OG	Rio de Janeiro	12 Aug 16
29:53.51	Alice Aprot	Nawowuna	KEN	2.1.94	4	OG	Rio de Janeiro	12 Aug 16
29:53.80	Meselech	Melkamu	ETH	27.4.85	1		Utrecht	14 Jun 09
29:54.66		T Dibaba			1	OG	Beijing	15 Aug 08
29:59.20	Meseret	Defar	ETH	19.11.83	1	NC	Birmingham	11 Jul 09
30:01.09	Paula	Radcliffe	GBR	17.12.73	1	EC	München	6 Aug 02
30:04.18	Berhane	Adere (10)	ETH	21.7.73	1	WCh	Saint-Denis	23 Aug 03
30:07.00		Ayana			1	OT	Hengelo	29 Jun 16
30:07.15	Werknesh	Kidane	ETH	21.11.81	2	WCh	Saint-Denis	23 Aug 03
30:07.20		Sun Yingjie ¶	CHN	3.10.77	3	WCh	Saint-Denis	23 Aug 03
30:07.78	Betsy	Saina	KEN	30.6.88	5	OG	Rio de Janeiro	12 Aug 16
30:08.06		Defar			1		Sollentuna	27 Jun 13
30:11.53	Florence	Kiplagat	KEN	27.2.87	2		Utrecht	14 Jun 09
30:11.87	Wude	Ayalew	ETH	4.7.87	3		Utrecht	14 Jun 09
30:12.53	Lornah	Kiplagat (KEN)	NED	1.5.74	4	WCh	Saint-Denis	23 Aug 03
30:13.17	Molly	Huddle	USA	31.8.84	6	OG	Rio de Janeiro	12 Aug 16
30:13.37		Zhong Huandi	CHN	28.6.67	2	NG	Beijing	8 Sep 93
30:13.74 WR	Ingrid	Kristiansen'	NOR	21.3.56	1	Bisl	Oslo	5 Jul 86
30:15.67		T Dibaba			1		Sollentuna	28 Jun 05
30:16.32		Ayana			1	WCh	London (OS)	5 Aug 17
30:17.15		Radcliffe			1	GP	Gateshead	27 Jun 04
30:17.49	Derartu	Tulu	ETH	21.3.72	1	OG	Sydney	30 Sep 00
30:18.39	Ejegayehu	Dibaba (20)	ETH	25.6.82	2		Sollentuna	28 Jun 05
30:19.39		Kidane			1	GP II	Stanford	29 May 05
30:20.75		T Dibaba			1	OG	London (OS)	3 Aug 12
30:21.67	Elvan	Abeylegesse ¶	TUR	11.9.82	1	ECp	Antalya	15 Apr 06
30:22.22	Shalane	Flanagan	USA	8.7.81	2	OG	Beijing	15 Aug 08
30:22.48	Getenesh (31/24)	Wami	ETH	11.12.74	2	OG	Sydney	30 Sep 00
30:22.88	Fernanda	Ribeiro	POR	23.6.69	3	OG	Sydney	30 Sep 00

Mark	Wind	Name		Nat	Born	Pos	Meet	Venue	Date
30:23.07		Alla	Zhilyayeva	RUS	5.2.69	5	WCh	Saint-Denis	23 Aug 03
30:24.36			Xing Huina	CHN	25.2.84	1	OG	Athína	27 Aug 04
30:26.20		Galina	Bogomolova	RUS	15.10.77	6	WCh	Saint-Denis	23 Aug 03
30:26.37		Sally	Kipyego	KEN	19.12.85	2	OG	London (OS)	3 Aug 12
30:26.41		Yasemin	Can	TUR	11.12.96	7	OG	Rio de Janeiro	12 Aug 16
30:26.50		Linet	Masai	KEN	5.12.89	3	OG	Beijing	15 Aug 08
		(30)							
30:26.66		Gelete	Burka	ETH	23.1.86	8	OG	Rio de Janeiro	12 Aug 16
30:26.70		Belaynesh	Oljira	ETH	26.6.90	3	Pre	Eugene	1 Jun 12
30:29.21mx		Philes	Ongori	KEN	19.7.86	1mx		Yokohama	23 Nov 08
30:29.23		Gladys	Cherono	KEN	12.5.83	2	GS	Ostrava	27 Jun 13
30:29.36		Liliya	Shobukhova ¶	RUS	13.11.77	1	NC	Cheboksary	23 Jul 09
30:30.26		Edith	Masai	KEN	4.4.67	5	WCh	Helsinki	6 Aug 05
30:31.03		Mariya	Konovalova ¶	RUS	14.8.74	2	NC	Cheboksary	23 Jul 09
30:31.42		Inga	Abitova ¶	RUS	6.3.82	1	EC	Göteborg	7 Aug 06
30:32.03		Tegla	Loroupe	KEN	9.5.73	3	WCh	Sevilla	26 Aug 99
30:32.36		Susanne	Wigene	NOR	12.2.78	2	EC	Göteborg	7 Aug 06
		(40)							
30:32.72		Lidiya	Grigoryeva ¶	RUS	21.1.74	3	EC	Göteborg	7 Aug 06
30:35.54		Kimberley	Smith	NZL	19.11.81	2		Stanford	4 May 08
30:35.91		Birhane	Ababel	ETH	10.6.90	4	GS	Ostrava	27 Jun 13
30:36.75		Netsanet	Gudeta	ETH	12.2.91	4	OT	Hengelo	29 Jun 16
30:37.38		Genet	Yalew	ETH	31.12.92	5	OT	Hengelo	29 Jun 16
30:37.68		Benita	Johnson	AUS	6.5.79	8	WCh	Saint-Denis	23 Aug 03
30:38.09			Dong Yanmei	CHN	16.2.77	1	NG	Shanghai	19 Oct 97
30:38.33		Mestawat	Tufa	ETH	14.9.83	1		Nijmegen	25 Jun 08
30:38.78		Jelena	Prokopcuka	LAT	21.9.76	6	EC	Göteborg	7 Aug 06
30:39.41			Lan Lixin	CHN	14.2.79	2	NG	Shanghai	19 Oct 97
		(50)	100th woman 31:07.88, 200th 31:28.43, 300th 31:42.8, 400th 31:53.83, 500th 32:01.88						
Drugs dq: 29:56.34		Elvan	Abeylegesse ¶	TUR	11.9.82	(2)	OG	Beijing	15 Aug 08

HALF MARATHON

Slightly downhill courses included: Newcastle-South Shields 30.5m, Tokyo 33m (to 1998), Lisboa (Spring to 2008) 69m

Mark	Wind	Name		Nat	Born	Pos	Meet	Venue	Date
64:51		Joyciline	Jepkosgei	KEN	8.12.93	1		Valencia	22 Oct 17
64:52			Jepkosgei			1		Praha	1 Apr 17
65:06		Peres	Jepchirchir	KEN	27.9.93	1	RAK	Ra's Al-Khaymah	10 Feb 17
65:09	WR	Florence	Kiplagat	KEN	27.2.87	1		Barcelona	15 Feb 15
65:12	WR		F Kiplagat			1		Barcelona	16 Feb 14
65:13		Mary	Keitany	KEN	18.1.82	2	RAK	Ra's Al-Khaymah	10 Feb 17
65:22		Violah	Jepchumba	BRN	23.10.90	2		Praha	1 Apr 17
65:36		Fancy	Chemutai	KEN	20.3.95	2		Valencia	22 Oct 17
65:39	dh		Keitany			1	GNR	South Shields	7 Sep 14
65:40	dh	Paula	Radcliffe	GBR	17.12.73	1	GNR	South Shields	21 Sep 03
65:44	dh	Susan	Chepkemei	KEN	25.6.75	1		Lisboa	1 Apr 01
65:45	dh	Priscah	Jeptoo	KEN	26.6.84	1	GNR	South Shields	15 Sep 13
65:50	WR		Keitany			1		Ra's Al Khaymah	18 Feb 11
65:51			Jepchumba	KEN	23.10.90	1		Praha	2 Apr 16
65:52		Edith	Chelimo (10)	KEN	16.7.86	1		Cardiff	1 Oct 17
65:59	dh		Keitany			1	GNR	South Shields	10 Sep 17
66:02			Keitany			1		Ra's Al-Khaymah	13 Feb 15
66:04		Cynthia	Limo	KEN	18.12.89	1		Ra's Al-Khaymah	12 Feb 16
66:06			Jepchumba			1		Ústí nad Labem	16 Sep 17
66:07		Gladys	Cherono	KEN	12.5.83	2		Ra's Al-Khaymah	12 Feb 16
66:08			Jepkosgei			3	RAK	Ra's Al-Khaymah	10 Feb 17
66:09		Lucy Wangui	Kabuu	KEN	24.3.84	1		Ra's Al-Khaymah	15 Feb 13
66:09	dh	Meseret	Defar	ETH	19.11.83	2	GNR	South Shields	15 Sep 13
66:11			P Jeptoo			2		Ra's Al-Khaymah	15 Feb 13
66:11		Eunice	Chumba	BRN	23.5.93	1		København	17 Sep 17
66:14		Worknesh	Degefa	ETH	28.10.90	2		Praha	2 Apr 16
66:19		Joyce	Chepkirui	KEN	20.8.88	1		Praha	5 Apr 14
66:19		Ruth	Chepngetich	KEN	8.8.94	1		Istanbul	30 Apr 17
66:25		Lornah	Kiplagat	NED	1.5.74	1	WCh	Udine	14 Oct 07
66:25		Joan	Chelimo	KEN	10.11.88	2		København	17 Sep 17
		(30/20)		* uncertain course measurement					
66:26		Genet	Yalew	ETH	31.12.92	3		Ra's Al-Khaymah	12 Feb 16
66:27		Rita	Jeptoo ¶	KEN	15.2.81	3		Ra's Al-Khaymah	15 Feb 13
66:28		Mamitu	Daska	ETH	16.10.83	2		Ra's Al-Khaymah	13 Feb 15
66:29		Mercy Wacera	Ngugi	KEN	17.12.88	1		Houston	17 Jan 16
66:35		Brigid	Kosgei	KEN	20.2.94	3		København	17 Sep 17
66:40*		Ingrid	Kristiansen	NOR	21.3.56	1	NC	Sandnes	5 Apr 87

Mark	Wind	Name		Nat	Born	Pos	Meet	Venue	Date
66:43	dh	Masako	Chiba	JPN	18.7.76	1		Tokyo	19 Jan 97
66:43		Jemima	Sumgong ¶?	KEN	21.12.84	4	RAK	Ra's Al-Khaymah	10 Feb 17
66:44		Elana	Meyer	RSA	10.10.66	1		Tokyo	15 Jan 99
66:46		Eunice	Jepkirui	BRN	20.5.84	2		Istanbul	30 Apr 17
		(30)							
66:49		Esther	Wanjiru	KEN	27.3.77	2		Tokyo	15 Jan 99
66:50		Tirunesh	Dibaba	ETH	1.10.85	5	RAK	Ra's Al-Khaymah	10 Feb 17
66:53+		Caroline	Kipkirui	KEN	26.5.94		in Mar	London	23 Apr 17
66:56		Meseret	Hailu	ETH	12.9.90	4		Ra's Al-Khaymah	15 Feb 13
66:57	dh	Kara	Goucher	USA	9.7.78	1	GNR	South Shields	30 Sep 07
66:57		Gladys	Chesire	KEN	20.2.93	5		Ra's Al-Khaymah	12 Feb 16
67:03	dh	Derartu	Tulu	ETH	21.3.72	3		Lisboa	1 Apr 01
67:07		Elvan	Abeylegesse	TUR	11.9.82	1		Ra's Al Khaymah	19 Feb 10
67:08		Sharon	Cherop	KEN	16.3.84	2		New Delhi	21 Nov 11
67:11	dh	Liz	McColgan	GBR	24.5.64	1		Tokyo	26 Jan 92
		(40)							
67:11		Kimberley	Smith	NZL	19.11.81	1		Philadelphia	18 Sep 11
67:12	dh	Tegla	Loroupe	KEN	9.5.73	1		Lisboa	10 Mar 96
67:12		Almaz	Ayana	ETH	21.11.91	1		New Delhi	19 Nov 17
67:13		Mare	Dibaba	ETH	20.10.89	2		Ra's Al Khaymah	19 Feb 10
67:16		Edith	Masai	KEN	4.4.67	1		Berlin	2 Apr 06
67:16		Angela	Tanui	KEN	27.7.92	2		Ostia	13 Mar 16
67:17		Pasalia	Kipkoech	KEN	22.12.88	1		Rio de Janeiro	19 Aug 12
67:18		Dire	Tune	ETH	19.6.85	1		R'as Al Khaymah	20 Feb 09
67:19	dh	Sonia	O'Sullivan	IRL	28.11.69	1	GNR	South Shields	6 Oct 02
67:21		Aselefech	Mergia	ETH	23.1.85	3		New Delhi	21 Nov 11
67:21		Yeshaneh	Ababel	ETH	10.6.90	2		New Delhi	19 Nov 17
		(51)	100th woman 67:59, 200th 68:56, 300th 69:27, 400th 69:52, 500th 70:13						

MARATHON

P = point-to-point or start and finish more than 30% apart, 2nd column

Mark		Name		Nat	Born	Pos	Meet	Venue	Date
2:15:25 WR		Paula	Radcliffe	GBR	17.12.73	1		London	13 Apr 03
2:17:01		Mary	Keitany	KEN	18.1.82	1		London	23 Apr 17
2:17:18 WR			Radcliffe			1		Chicago	13 Oct 02
2:17:42			Radcliffe			1		London	17 Apr 05
2:17:56		Tirunesh	Dibaba	ETH	1.10.85	2		London	23 Apr 17
2:18:37			Keitany			1		London	22 Apr 12
2:18:31			Dibaba			1		Chicago	8 Oct 17
2:18:47 WR		Catherine	Ndereba	KEN	21.7.72	1		Chicago	7 Oct 01
2:18:56			Radcliffe			1		London	14 Apr 02
2:18:58		Tiki	Gelana	ETH	22.10.87	1		Rotterdam	15 Apr 12
2:19:12		Mizuki	Noguchi	JPN	3.7.78	1		Berlin	25 Sep 05
2:19:19		Irina	Mikitenko	GER	23.8.72	1		Berlin	28 Sep 08
2:19:19			Keitany			1		London	17 Apr 11
2:19:25		Gladys	Cherono	KEN	12.5.83	1		Berlin	27 Sep 15
2:19:26			Ndereba			2		Chicago	13 Oct 02
2:19:31		Aselefech	Mergia	ETH	23.1.85	1		Dubai	27 Jan 12
2:19:34		Lucy Wangui	Kabuu (10)	KEN	24.3.84	2		Dubai	27 Jan 12
2:19:36		Deena	Kastor	USA	14.2.73	1		London	23 Apr 06
2:19:39			Sun Yingjie ¶	CHN	3.10.77	1		Beijing	19 Oct 03
2:19:41		Yoko	Shibui	JPN	14.3.79	1		Berlin	26 Sep 04
2:19:41		Tirfi	Tsegaye	ETH	25.11.84	1		Dubai	22 Jan 16
2:19:44		Florence	Kiplagat	KEN	27.2.87	1		Berlin	25 Sep 11
2:19:46 WR		Naoko	Takahashi	JPN	6.5.72	1		Berlin	30 Sep 01
2:19:47		Sarah	Chepchirchir	KEN	27.7.84	1		Tokyo	26 Feb 17
2:19:50		Edna	Kiplagat	KEN	15.11.79	2		London	22 Apr 12
2:19:51	P		Zhou Chunxiu	CHN	15.11.78	1	Dong-A	Seoul	12 Mar 06
2:19:52		Mare	Dibaba (20)	ETH	20.10.89	3		Dubai	27 Jan 12
2:19:52			M Dibaba			1		Xiamen	3 Jan 15
2:19:55			Ndereba			2		London	13 Apr 03
2:19:57		Rita	Jeptoo ¶	KEN	15.2.81	1		Chicago	13 Oct 13
		(30/21)							
2:20:14		Priscah	Jeptoo	KEN	26.6.84	3		London	22 Apr 12
2:20:22		Brigid	Kosgei	KEN	20.2.94	2		Chicago	8 Oct 17
2:20:27		Feyse	Tadesse	ETH	19.11.88	2		Berlin	28 Sep 14
2:20:30		Bezunesh	Bekele	ETH	29.1.83	4		Dubai	27 Jan 12
2:20:30		Aberu	Kebede	ETH	12.9.89	1		Berlin	30 Sep 12
2:20:41		Ruti	Aga	ETH	16.1.94	2		Berlin	24 Sep 17
2:20:42		Berhane	Adere	ETH	21.7.73	1		Chicago	22 Oct 06
2:20:43 WR		Tegla	Loroupe	KEN	9.5.73	1		Berlin	26 Sep 99

Mark	Wind	Name		Nat	Born	Pos	Meet	Venue	Date
2:20:47		Galina	Bogomolova	RUS	15.10.77	2		Chicago	22 Oct 06
		(30)							
2:20:48		Jemima Jelagat	Sumgong	KEN	21.12.84	2		Chicago	13 Oct 13
2:20:48		Amane	Beriso	ETH	13.10.91	2		Dubai	22 Jan 16
2:20:53		Valary	Aiyabei	KEN	8.6.91	3		Berlin	24 Sep 17
2:20:55		Purity	Rionoripo	KEN	10.6.93	1		Paris	9 Apr 17
2:20:57		Jordan	Hasay	USA	21.9.91	3		Chicago	8 Oct 17
2:20:59		Shure	Demise	ETH	21.1.96	4		Dubai	23 Jan 15
2:20:59		Agnes	Barsosio	KEN	5.8.82	2		Paris	9 Apr 17
2:21:01		Meselech	Melkamu	ETH	27.4.85	1		Frankfurt	28 Oct 12
2:21:06 WR		Ingrid	Kristiansen	NOR	21.3.56	1		London	21 Apr 85
2:21:09		Meseret	Hailu	ETH	12.9.90	1		Amsterdam	21 Oct 12
		(40)							
2:21:14		Shalane	Flanagan	USA	8.7.81	3		Berlin	28 Sep 14
2:21:17		Eunice	Jepkirui	BRN	20.5.84	1		Nagoya	12 Mar 17
2:21:19		Birhane	Dibaba	ETH	11.9.93	2		Tokyo	26 Feb 17
2:21:21		Joan	Benoit'	USA	16.5.57	1		Chicago	20 Oct 85
2:21:22		Filomena	Cheyech	KEN	5.7.82	3		Paris	9 Apr 17
2:21:27		Helah	Kiprop	KEN	7.4.85	1		Tokyo	28 Feb 16
2:21:29		Lyudmila	Petrova	RUS	7.10.68	2		London	23 Apr 06
2:21:30		Constantina	Dita	ROU	23.1.70	2		Chicago	9 Oct 05
2:21:30		Lydia	Cheromei ¶	KEN	11.5.77	6		Dubai	27 Jan 12
2:21:31		Svetlana	Zakharova	RUS	15.9.70	4		Chicago	13 Oct 02
2:21:31		Askale	Tafa	ETH	27.9.84	2		Berlin	28 Sep 08
		(51)	100th woman 2:23:19, 200th 2:25:03, 300th 2:26:13, 400th 2:27:07, 500th 2:28:00						
Downhill point-to-point course –		Boston marathon is downhill overall (139m) and sometimes strongly wind-aided.							
2:19:59	D	Buzunesh	Deba	ETH	8.9.87	2		Boston	21 Apr 14
2:20:41	D	Jemima Jelagat	Sumgong	KEN	21.12.84	4		Boston	21 Apr 14
2:20:43	D	Margaret	Okayo	KEN	30.5.76	1		Boston	15 Apr 02
Drugs disqualification									
2:18:20		Liliya	Shobukhova ¶	RUS	13.11.77	1		Chicago	9 Oct 11
2:20:15			Shobukhova			2		London	17 Apr 11
2:20:23			Wei Yanan ¶	CHN	6.12.81	1		Beijing	20 Oct 02
2:18:57	D	Rita	Jeptoo ¶	KEN	15.2.81	1		Boston	21 Apr 14
2:21:29	D	Aleksandra	Duliba ¶	BLR	9.1.88	6		Boston	21 Apr 14

2000 METRES STEEPLECHASE

Mark	Name		Nat	Born	Pos	Meet	Venue	Date
6:02.16	Virginia	Nyambura	KEN	20.7.93	1	ISTAF	Berlin	6 Sep 15
6:02.47	Beatrice	Chepkoech	KEN	6.7.91	2	ISTAF	Berlin	6 Sep 15
6:03.38	Wioletta	Janowska	POL	9.6.77	1		Gdansk	15 Jul 06
6:04.20	Gesa-Felicitas	Krause	GER	3.8.92	3	ISTAF	Berlin	6 Sep 15
6:04.46	Dorcus	Inzikuru	UGA	2.2.82	1	GP II	Milano	1 Jun 05
6:10.82	Magdalene	Masai	KEN	4.4.93	4	ISTAF	Berlin	6 Sep 15

3000 METRES STEEPLECHASE

Mark	Name		Nat	Born	Pos	Meet	Venue	Date
8:52.78 WR	Ruth	Jebet	KEN/BRN	17.11.96	1	DL	Saint-Denis	27 Aug 16
8:55.29		Jebet			1	WK-DLF	Zürich	24 Aug 17
8:58.78	Celliphine	Chespol	KEN	23.3.99	1	Pre	Eugene	26 May 17
8:58.81 WR	Gulnara	Samitova/Galkina	RUS	9.7.78	1	OG	Beijing	17 Aug 08
8:59.75		Jebet			1	OG	Rio de Janeiro	15 Aug 16
8:59.84	Beatrice	Chepkoech	KEN	6.7.91	2	WK-DLF	Zürich	24 Aug 17
8:59.97		Jebet			2	DL	Shanghai	14 May 16
9:00.01	Hyvin	Jepkemoi	KEN	13.1.92	2	Pre	Eugene	28 May 16
9:00.12		Jepkemoi			1	DL	Doha	5 May 17
9:00.70		Chepkoech			2	Pre	Eugene	26 May 17
9:01.57		Chepkoech			2	DL	Doha	5 May 17
9:01.59 WR		Samitova/Galkina			1		Iráklio	4 Jul 04
9:01.69		Chepkoech			1	DL	Paris (C)	1 Jul 17
9:01.96		Jepkemoi			2	DL	Saint-Denis	27 Aug 16
9:01.99		Jebet			3	DL	Doha	5 May 17
9:02.58	Emma	Coburn	USA	19.10.90	1	WCh	London (OS)	11 Aug 17
9:03.52		Jebet			3	Pre	Eugene	26 May 17
9:03.70	Norah	Tanui	KEN	2.10.95	1	ISTAF	Berlin	27 Aug 17
9:03.77	Courtney	Frerichs	USA	18.1.93	2	WCh	London (OS)	11 Aug 17
9:04.03		Jepkemoi			3	WCh	London (OS)	11 Aug 17
9:04.56		Tanui			1	Hanz	Zagreb	29 Aug 17
9:04.78		Jebet			1	DL	Shanghai	13 May 17
9:05.31		Tanui			3	WK-DLF	Zürich	24 Aug 17
9:05.36	Habiba	Ghribi	TUN	9.4.84	1	VD	Bruxelles	11 Sep 15
9:05.70		Chespol			4	DL	Doha	5 May 17

Mark	Wind	Name		Nat	Born	Pos	Meet	Venue	Date
9:06.00			Jepkemoi			2	DL	Paris (C)	1 Jul 17
9:06.57		Yekaterina	Volkova ¶ (10)	RUS	16.2.78	1	WCh	Osaka	27 Aug 07
9:06.72			Jepkemoi			2	DL	Shanghai	13 May 17
9:07.00			Jebet			1	WK	Zürich	1 Sep 16
9:07.06		Sofia	Assefa	ETH	14.11.87	1	FBK	Hengelo	11 Jun 17
9:07.08			Chespol			3	DL	Shanghai	13 May 17
9:07.12			Jepkemoi			2	OG	Rio de Jáneiro	15 Aug 16
9:07.14		Milcah	Chemos Cheywa	KEN	24.2.86	1	Bisl	Oslo	7 Jun 12
9:07.41		Eunice	Jepkorir	KEN	17.2.82	2	OG	Beijing	17 Aug 08
9:07.42			Jepkemoi			1	DL	Shanghai	14 May 16
9:07.54			Chespol			3	DL	Paris (C)	1 Jul 17
9:07.63			Coburn			3	OG	Rio de Janeiro	15 Aug 16
9:07.96			Coburn			4	Pre	Eugene	26 May 17
9:08.21			Galkina			1	NC	Kazan	18 Jul 08
9:08.33	WR		Samitova			1	NC	Tula	10 Aug 03
		(30/13)							
9:08.39		Yuliya	Zaripova' ¶	RUS	26.4.86	2	WCh	Berlin	17 Aug 09
9:09.19		Tatyana	Petrova	RUS	8.4.83	2	WCh	Osaka	27 Aug 07
9:09.39		Marta	Dominguez ¶	ESP	3.11.75	1		Barcelona	25 Jul 09
9:09.61		Hiwot	Ayalew	ETH	6.3.90	3	Bisl	Oslo	7 Jun 12
9:11.85		Gesa-Felicitas	Krause	GER	3.8.92	2	ISTAF	Berlin	27 Aug 17
9:12.50		Jennifer	Simpson'	USA	23.8.86	5	WCh	Berlin	17 Aug 09
9:12.55		Lydia	Chepkurui	KEN	23.8.84	2	WCh	Moskva	13 Aug 13
		(20)							
9:13.16		Ruth	Bisibori	KEN	2.1.88	7	WCh	Berlin	17 Aug 09
9:13.22		Gladys	Kipkemboi	KEN	15.10.86	2	GGala	Roma	10 Jun 10
9:13.25		Etenesh	Diro	ETH	10.5.91	6	DL	Paris (C)	1 Jul 17
9:13.35		Karoline Bjerkeli	Grøvdal	NOR	14.6.90	1	NC	Sandnes	26 Aug 17
9:13.53		Gülcan	Mingir	TUR	21.5.89	1	Pavlov	Sofia	9 Jun 12
9:13.85		Virginia	Nyambura	KEN	20.7.93	3	Herc	Monaco	17 Jul 15
9:14.28		Genevieve	LaCaze	AUS	4.8.89	6	DL	Saint-Denis	27 Aug 16
9:15.04		Dorcus	Inzikuru	UGA	2.2.82	1	SGP	Athína	14 Jun 05
9:16.51	WR	Alesya	Turova	BLR	6.12.79	1		Gdansk	27 Jul 02
		(30)							
9:16.85		Cristina	Casandra	ROU	21.10.77	4	OG	Beijing	17 Aug 08
9:16.94		Mercy	Njoroge	KEN	10.6.86	2	DL	Doha	6 May 11
9:17.15		Wioletta	Frankiewicz/Janowska	POL	9.6.77	1	SGP	Athína	3 Jul 06
9:17.74		Purity	Kirui	KEN	13.8.91	5	VD	Bruxelles	11 Sep 15
9:17.85		Zemzem	Ahmed	ETH	27.12.84	7	OG	Beijing	17 Aug 08
9:18.03		Lydia	Rotich	KEN	8.8.88	3	Bisl	Oslo	4 Jun 10
9:18.35		Donna	MacFarlane	AUS	18.6.77	3	Bisl	Oslo	6 Jun 08
9:18.54		Antje	Möldner-Schmidt	GER	13.6.84	9	WCh	Berlin	17 Aug 09
9:18.54		Jéssica	Augusto	POR	8.11.81	1		Huelva	9 Jun 10
9:18.85		Leah	O'Connor	USA	30.8.92	6	Pre	Eugene	28 May 16
		(40)							
9:19.29		Aisha	Praught Leer	JAM	14.12.89	8	DL	Doha	5 May 17
9:19.48		Stephanie	Garcia	USA	3.5.88	8	DL	Saint-Denis	27 Aug 16
9:19.68		Daisy	Jepkemei	KEN	13.2.96	2	Hanz	Zagreb	29 Aug 17
9:19.76		Lalita	Babar	IND	2.6.89	4h2	OG	Rio de Janeiro	13 Aug 16
9:20.22		Joan	Chepkemoi	KEN	24.11.93	3	Hanz	Zagreb	29 Aug 17
9:20.23		Mekdes	Bekele	ETH	20.1.87	2		Huelva	13 Jun 08
9:20.37		Birtukan	Adamu	ETH	29.4.92	4	GGala	Roma	26 May 11
9:20.38		Madeline	Heiner/Hills	AUS	15.5.87	7	OG	Rio de Janeiro	15 Aug 16
9:20.64		Salima	El Ouali	MAR	29.12.83	7	Herc	Monaco	17 Jul 15
9:20.65		Tigist	Mekonen	BRN	7.7.97	8	Herc	Monaco	17 Jul 15
		(50)	100th woman 9:28.86, 200th 9:40.51, 300th 9:48.01, 400th 9:54.86, 500th 9:59.29						
Drugs disqualification									
9:05.02		Yuliya	Zaripova	RUS	26.4.86	(1)	DNG	Stockholm	17 Aug 12
9:06.72			Zaripova			(1)	OG	London (OS)	6 Aug 12
9:07.03			Zaripova	RUS	26.4.86	(1)	WCh	Daegu	30 Aug 11
9:07.32		Marta	Dominguez ¶	ESP	3.11.75	(1)	WCh	Berlin	17 Aug 09
9:07.64			Volkova			3	OG	Beijing	17 Aug 08

100 METRES HURDLES

Mark	Wind	Name		Nat	Born	Pos	Meet	Venue	Date
12.20	WR 0.3	Kendra	Harrison	USA	18.9.92	1	DL	London (OS)	22 Jul 16
12.21	WR 0.7	Yordanka	Donkova	BUL	28.9.61	1		Stara Zagora	20 Aug 88
12.24	0.9		Donkova			1h		Stara Zagora	28 Aug 88
12.24	0.5		K Harrison			1	Pre	Eugene	28 May 16
12.25	WR 1.4	Ginka	Zagorcheva	BUL	12.4.58	1	v TCH,GRE	Drama	8 Aug 87
12.26	WR 1.5		Donkova			1	Balk	Ljubljana	7 Sep 86

Mark	Wind	Name		Nat	Born	Pos	Meet	Venue	Date
12.26	1.7	Lyudmila	Narozhilenko ¶	RUS	21.4.64	1rB		Sevilla	6 Jun 92
		(later Ludmila Engquist SWE)							
12.26	1.2	Brianna	Rollins	USA	18.8.91	1	NC	Des Moines	22 Jun 13
12.27	-1.2		Donkova			1		Stara Zagora	28 Aug 88
12.28	1.8		Narozhilenko			1	NC	Kyiv	11 Jul 91
12.28	0.9		Narozhilenko			1rA		Sevilla	6 Jun 92
12.28	1.1	Sally	Pearson'	AUS	19.9.86	1	WCh	Daegu	3 Sep 11
12.28	0.1		K Harrison			1	Gyulai	Székesfehérvár	4 Jul 17
12.29	WR-0.4		Donkova			1	ASV	Köln	17 Aug 86
12.32	1.6		Narozhilenko			1		Saint-Denis	4 Jun 92
12.33	1.4		Donkova			1		Fürth	14 Jun 87
12.33	-0.3	Gail	Devers	USA	19.11.66	1	NC	Sacramento	23 Jul 00
12.34	-0.5		Zagorcheva			1	WCh	Roma	4 Sep 87
12.34	1.9	Sharika	Nelvis	USA	10.5.90	1h3	NC	Eugene	26 Jun 15
12.34	1.2		Rollins			1	NC	Eugene	8 Jul 16
12.35	WR 0.1		Donkova			1h2	ASV	Köln	17 Aug 86
12.35	-0.2		Pearson			1	OG	London (OS)	7 Aug 12
12.35	0.9	Jasmin	Stowers	USA	23.9.91	1	DL	Doha	15 May 15
12.36	WR 1.9	Grazyna	Rabsztyn (10)	POL	20.9.52	1	Kuso	Warszawa	13 Jun 80
12.36	WR-0.6		Donkova			1	NC	Sofia	13 Aug 86
12.36	1.1		Donkova			1		Schwechat	15 Jun 88
12.36	0.3		Pearson			1s2	WCh	Daegu	3 Sep 11
12.36	1.4		K Harrison			1	Towns	Athens GA	8 Apr 16
12.37	1.4		Donkova			1	ISTAF	Berlin	15 Aug 86
12.37	0.7		Devers			1	WCh	Sevilla	28 Aug 99
12.37	1.5	Joanna	Hayes	USA	23.12.76	1	OG	Athína	24 Aug 04
12.37	-0.2	Dawn	Harper Nelson	USA	13.5.84	2	OG	London (OS)	7 Aug 12
12.37	2.0		Nelvis			1s1	NC	Eugene	27 Jun 15
		(33/12)							
12.39	1.5	Vera	Komisova'	RUS	11.6.53	1	GGala	Roma	5 Aug 80
12.39	1.8	Natalya	Grigoryeva ¶	UKR	3.12.62	2	NC	Kyiv	11 Jul 91
12.42	1.8	Bettine	Jahn	GDR	3.8.58	1	OD	Berlin	8 Jun 83
12.42	2.0	Anjanette	Kirkland	USA	24.2.74	1	WCh	Edmonton	11 Aug 01
12.43	-0.9	Lucyna	Kalek (Langer)	POL	9.1.56	1		Hannover	19 Aug 84
12.43	-0.3	Michelle	Perry	USA	1.5.79	1s1	NC	Carson	26 Jun 05
12.43	0.2	Lolo	Jones	USA	5.8.82	1s1	OG	Beijing	18 Aug 08
12.43	1.2	Queen	Harrison	USA	10.9.88	2	NC	Des Moines	22 Jun 13
		(20)							
12.44	-0.5	Gloria	Uibel (-Siebert)	GDR	13.1.64	2	WCh	Roma	4 Sep 87
12.44	-0.8	Olga	Shishigina ¶	KAZ	23.12.68	1	Spitzen	Luzern	27 Jun 95
12.44	0.4	Glory	Alozie	NGR/ESP	30.12.77	1	Herc	Monaco	8 Aug 98
12.44	0.6	Damu	Cherry ¶	USA	29.11.77	2rA	Athl	Lausanne	11 Jul 06
12.45	1.3	Cornelia	Oschkenat'	GDR	29.10.61	1		Neubrandenburg	11 Jun 87
12.45	1.4	Brigitte	Foster-Hylton	JAM	7.11.74	1	Pre	Eugene	24 May 03
12.45	1.5	Olena	Krasovska	UKR	17.8.76	2	OG	Athína	24 Aug 04
12.45	1.4	Virginia	Powell/Crawford	USA	7.9.83	1	GP	New York	2 Jun 07
12.46	0.7	Perdita	Felicien	CAN	29.8.80	1	Pre	Eugene	19 Jun 04
12.47	1.1	Marina	Azyabina	RUS	15.6.63	1s2	NC	Moskva	19 Jun 93
		(30)							
12.47	1.1	Danielle	Carruthers	USA	22.12.79	2	WCh	Daegu	3 Sep 11
12.48	-0.2	Kellie	Wells	USA	16.7.82	3	OG	London (OS)	7 Aug 12
12.48	1.2	Nia	Ali	USA	23.10.88	3	NC	Des Moines	22 Jun 13
12.49	0.9	Susanna	Kallur	SWE	16.2.81	1	ISTAF	Berlin	16 Sep 07
12.49	1.0	Priscilla	Lopes-Schliep	CAN	26.8.82	2	VD	Bruxelles	4 Sep 09
12.50	0.0	Vera	Akimova'	RUS	5.6.59	1		Sochi	19 May 84
12.50	-0.1	Delloreen	Ennis-London	JAM	5.3.75	3	WCh	Osaka	29 Aug 07
12.50	0.8	Josephine	Onyia ¶	NGR/ESP	15.7.86	1	ISTAF	Berlin	1 Jun 08
12.50	1.2	Kristi	Castlin	USA	7.7.88	2	NC	Eugene	8 Jul 16
12.51	1.4	Miesha	McKelvy	USA	26.7.76	2	Pre	Eugene	24 May 03
		(40)							
12.51	0.7	Tiffany	Porter'	USA/GBR	13.11.87	2	C.Cup	Marrakech	14 Sep 14
12.52	-0.4	Michelle	Freeman	JAM	5.5.69	1s1	WCh	Athína	10 Aug 97
12.53	0.2	Tatyana	Reshetnikova	RUS	14.10.66	1rA	GP II	Linz	4 Jul 94
12.53	-0.4	Svetla	Dimitrova ¶	BUL	27.1.70	1	Herc	Stara Zagora	16 Jul 94
12.53	1.0	Melissa	Morrison	USA	9.7.71	1	DNG	Stockholm	5 Aug 98
12.54	0.4	Kerstin	Knabe	GDR	7.7.59	3	EC	Athína	9 Sep 82
12.54	0.9	Sabine	Paetz/John'	GDR	16.10.57	1		Berlin	15 Jul 84
12.54	1.7	Nichole	Denby	USA	10.10.82	2s2	OT	Eugene	6 Jul 08
12.54	1.3	Jessica	Ennis	GBR	28.1.86	1H5	OG	London (OS)	3 Aug 12
12.54	1.4	Christina	Manning	USA	29.5.90	1	ISTAF	Berlin	27 Aug 1712.56
		(50)	100th woman 12.66, 200th 12.81, 300th 12.90, 400th 12.99, 500th 13.06						

Mark	Wind	Name		Nat	Born	Pos	Meet	Venue	Date
Wind assisted performances to 12.36, performers to 12.53									
12.28	2.7	Cornelia	Oschkenat'	GDR	29.10.61	1		Berlin	25 Aug 87
12.29	3.5		Donkova			1	Athl	Lausanne	24 Jun 88
12.29	2.7	Gail	Devers	USA	19.11.66	1	Pre	Eugene	26 May 02
12.29	3.8	Lolo	Jones	USA	5.8.82	1	NC/OT	Eugene	6 Jul 08
12.30	2.8		Rollins			1s1	NC	Des Moines	22 Jun 13
12.33	2.3		Rollins			1h3	NC	Des Moines	21 Jun 13
12.35	2.4	Bettine	Jahn	GDR	3.8.58	1	WCh	Helsinki	13 Aug 83
12.35	3.7	Kellie	Wells	USA	16.7.82	1		Gainesville	16 Apr 11
12.36	2.2	Dawn	Harper Nelson	USA	13.5.84	1	NC	Eugene	28 Jun 09
12.37	2.7	Gloria	Uibel/Siebert'	GDR	13.1.64	2		Berlin	25 Aug 87
12.37	3.4	Danielle	Carruthers	USA	22.12.79	1s1	NC	Eugene	26 Jun 11
12.40	2.1	Michelle	Freeman	JAM	5.5.69	1	GPF	Fukuoka	13 Sep 97
12.41	2.2	Olga	Shishigina ¶	KAZ	23.12.68	1rA	Athl	Lausanne	5 Jul 95
12.42	2.4	Kerstin	Knabe	GDR	7.7.59	2	WCh	Helsinki	13 Aug 83
12.43	2.7	Yvette	Lewis	USA/PAN	16.3.85	1	MSR	Walnut	20 Apr 13
12.44	2.6	Melissa	Morrison	USA	9.7.71	1		Carson	22 May 04
12.45	2.1	Perdita	Felicien	CAN	29.8.80	1	NC	Victoria	10 Jul 04
12.47	3.0	Tiffany	Porter	USA/GBR	13.11.87	1		Gainesville	21 Apr 12
12.48	3.8	Kristi	Castlin	USA	7.7.88	1		Clermont	2 Jun 12
12.50	2.7	Svetla	Dimitrova ¶	BUL	27.1.70	1		Saint-Denis	10 Jun 94
12.51	3.2	Johanna	Klier'	GDR	13.9.52	1	NC	Cottbus	17 Jul 80
12.51	3.6	Sabine	Paetz/John'	GDR	16.10.57	1		Dresden	27 Jul 84
12.51A	3.3	Yuliya	Graudyn	RUS	13.11.70	1		Sestriere	31 Jul 94
12.52	3.1	Angela	Whyte	CAN	22.5.80	2		Edmonton	29 Jun 13
12.53	2.2	Mihaela	Pogacian	ROU	27.1.58	1	IAC	Edinburgh	6 Jul 90
Probably hand timed Officially 12.36, but subsequent investigations showed this unlikely to have been auto-timed									
12.4	0.7	Svetla	Dimitrova ¶	BUL	27.1.70	1		Stara Zagora	9 Jul 97
Hand timed									
12.3 WR	1.5	Anneliese	Ehrhardt	GDR	18.6.50	1	NC	Dresden	22 Jul 73
12.3		Marina	Azyabina	RUS	15.6.63	1		Yekaterinburg	30 May 93
12.0w	2.1	Yordanka	Donkova	BUL	28.9.61	1		Sofia	3 Aug 86
12.1w	2.1	Ginka	Zagorcheva	BUL	12.4.58	2		Sofia	3 Aug 86

400 METRES HURDLES

Mark	Wind	Name		Nat	Born	Pos	Meet	Venue	Date
52.34 WR		Yuliya	Nosova-Pechonkina'	RUS	21.4.78	1	NC	Tula	8 Aug 03
52.42		Melaine	Walker	JAM	1.1.83	1	WCh	Berlin	20 Aug 09
52.47		Lashinda	Demus	USA	10.3.83	1	WCh	Daegu	1 Sep 11
52.61 WR		Kim	Batten	USA	29.3.69	1	WCh	Göteborg	11 Aug 95
52.62		Tonja	Buford-Bailey	USA	13.12.70	2	WCh	Göteborg	11 Aug 95
52.63			Demus			1	Herc	Monaco	28 Jul 09
52.64			Walker			1	OG	Beijing	20 Aug 08
52.64		Dalilah	Muhammad	USA	7.2.90	1	NC	Sacramento	25 Jun 17
52.70		Natalya	Antyukh	RUS	26.6.81	1	OG	London (OS)	8 Aug 12
52.73			Walker			2	WCh	Daegu	1 Sep 11
52.74 WR		Sally	Gunnell	GBR	29.7.66	1	WCh	Stuttgart	19 Aug 93
52.74			Batten			1	Herc	Monaco	8 Aug 98
52.75		Shamier	Little	USA	20.3.95	2	NC	Sacramento	25 Jun 17
52.77		Faní	Halkiá ¶ (10)	GRE	2.2.79	1s2	OG	Athína	22 Aug 04
52.77			Demus			2	OG	London (OS)	8 Aug 12
52.79		Sandra	Farmer-Patrick	USA	18.8.62	2	WCh	Stuttgart	19 Aug 93
52.79		Kaliese	Spencer	JAM	6.5.87	1	LGP	London (CP)	5 Aug 11
52.82		Deon	Hemmings	JAM	9.10.68	1	OG	Atlanta	31 Jul 96
52.82			Halkiá			1	OG	Athína	25 Aug 04
52.82			Demus			1	GGala	Roma	10 Jun 10
52.83		Zuzana	Hejnová	CZE	19.12.86	1	WCh	Moskva	15 Aug 13
52.84			Batten			1	WK	Zürich	12 Aug 98
52.88			Muhammad			1	NC	Eugene	10 Jul 16
52.89		Daimí	Pernía	CUB	27.12.76	1	WCh	Sevilla	25 Aug 99
52.90			Buford			1	WK	Zürich	16 Aug 95
52.90		Nezha	Bidouane	MAR	18.9.69	2	WCh	Sevilla	25 Aug 99
52.90			Pechonkina			1	WCh	Helsinki	13 Aug 05
52.92			Antyukh			1	EC	Barcelona	30 Jul 10
52.94 WR		Marina	Styepanova'	RUS	1.5.50	1s	Spart	Tashkent	17 Sep 86
52.95		Sheena	Johnson/Tosta	USA	1.10.82	1	NC/OT	Sacramento	11 Jul 04
52.95		Kori	Carter	USA	3.6.92	3	NC	Sacramento	25 Jun 17
		(31/19)							
53.02		Irina	Privalova (20)	RUS	22.11.68	1	OG	Sydney	27 Sep 00
53.11		Tatyana	Ledovskaya	BLR	21.5.66	1	WCh	Tokyo	29 Aug 91

Mark Wind	Name		Nat	Born	Pos	Meet	Venue	Date
53.11	Ashley	Spencer	USA	8.6.93	4	NC	Sacramento	25 Jun 17
53.17	Debbie	Flintoff-King	AUS	20.4.60	1	OG	Seoul	28 Sep 88
53.20	Josanne	Lucas	TTO	14.5.84	3	WCh	Berlin	20 Aug 09
53.21	Marie-José	Pérec	FRA	9.5.68	2	WK	Zürich	16 Aug 95
53.21	Kori	Carter	USA	6.3.92	1	NCAA	Eugene	7 Jun 13
53.22	Jana	Pittman/Rawlinson	AUS	9.11.82	1	WCh	Saint-Denis	28 Aug 03
53.24	Sabine	Busch	GDR	21.11.62	1	NC	Potsdam	21 Aug 87
53.25	Ionela	Târlea-Manolache	ROU	9.2.76	2	GGala	Roma	7 Jul 99
53.28	Tiffany	Ross-Williams	USA	5.2.83	1	NC	Indianapolis	24 Jun 07
	(30)							
53.32	Sandra	Glover	USA	30.12.68	3	WCh	Helsinki	13 Aug 05
53.36	Andrea	Blackett	BAR	24.1.76	4	WCh	Sevilla	25 Aug 99
53.36	Brenda	Taylor	USA	9.2.79	2	NC/OT	Sacramento	11 Jul 04
53.37	Tetyana	Tereshchuk	UKR	11.10.69	3s2	OG	Athína	22 Aug 04
53.47	Janeene	Vickers	USA	3.10.68	3	WCh	Tokyo	29 Aug 91
53.48	Margarita	Ponomaryova'	RUS	19.6.63	3	WCh	Stuttgart	19 Aug 93
53.55	Sara Slott	Petersen	DEN	9.4.87	2	OG	Rio de Janeiro	18 Aug 16
53.58	Cornelia	Ullrich'	GDR	26.4.63	2	NC	Potsdam	21 Aug 87
53.63	Ellen	Fiedler'	GDR	26.11.58	3	OG	Seoul	28 Sep 88
53.65A mx	Myrtle	Bothma'	RSA	18.2.64	mx		Pretoria	12 Mar 90
	53.74A				1		Johannesburg	18 Apr 86
	(40)							
53.67	Perri	Shakes-Drayton	GBR	21.12.88	2	DL	London (OS)	26 Jul 13
53.68	Vania	Stambolova ¶	BUL	28.11.83	1		Rabat	5 Jun 11
53.72	Yekaterina	Bikert	RUS	13.5.80	2	NC	Tula	30 Jul 04
53.74	Ristananna	Tracey	JAM	9.5.92	3	WCh	London (OS)	10 Aug 17
53.77	Irina	Davydova	RUS	27.5.88	1	EC	Helsinki	29 Jun 12
53.82	Sydney	McLaughlin	USA	7.8.99	6	NC	Sacramento	25 Jun 17
53.84	Natasha	Danvers	GBR	19.9.77	3	OG	Beijing	20 Aug 08
53.85	Angela	Morosanu	ROU	26.7.86	2	DL	Shanghai	18 May 13
53.86	Anna	Jesien	POL	10.12.78	1s3	WCh	Osaka	28 Aug 07
53.88	Debbie-Ann	Parris	JAM	24.3.73	3s1	WCh	Edmonton	6 Aug 01
	(50)	100th woman 54.45, 200th 55.28, 300th 55.74, 400th 56.08, 500th 56.38						
Drugs disqualification: 53.38		Jiang Limei ¶	CHN	.3.70	(1)	89	Shanghai	22 Oct 97

HIGH JUMP

Mark Wind	Name		Nat	Born	Pos	Meet	Venue	Date
2.09 WR	Stefka	Kostadinova	BUL	25.3.65	1	WCh	Roma	30 Aug 87
2.08 WR		Kostadinova			1	NM	Sofia	31 May 86
2.08i	Kajsa	Bergqvist	SWE	12.10.76	1		Arnstadt	4 Feb 06
2.08	Blanka	Vlasic	CRO	8.11.83	1	Hanz	Zagreb	31 Aug 09
2.07 WR	Lyudmila	Andonova ¶	BUL	6.5.60	1	OD	Berlin	20 Jul 84
2.07 WR		Kostadinova			1		Sofia	25 May 86
2.07		Kostadinova			1		Cagliari	16 Sep 87
2.07		Kostadinova			1	NC	Sofia	3 Sep 88
2.07i	Heike	Henkel'	GER	5.5.64	1	NC	Karlsruhe	8 Feb 92
2.07		Vlasic			1	DNG	Stockholm	7 Aug 07
2.07	Anna	Chicherova ¶	RUS	22.7.82	1	NC	Cheboksary	22 Jul 11
2.06		Kostadinova			1	ECp	Moskva	18 Aug 85
2.06		Kostadinova			1		Fürth	15 Jun 86
2.06		Kostadinova			1		Cagliari	14 Sep 86
2.06		Kostadinova			1		Wörrstadt	6 Jun 87
2.06		Kostadinova			1		Rieti	8 Sep 87
2.06i		Kostadinova			1		Pireás	20 Feb 88
2.06		Bergqvist			1		Eberstadt	26 Jul 03
2.06	Hestrie	Cloete	RSA	26.8.78	1	WCh	Saint-Denis	31 Aug 03
2.06	Yelena	Slesarenko	RUS	28.2.82	1	OG	Athína	28 Aug 04
2.06		Vlasic			1		Thessaloníki	30 Jul 07
2.06		Vlasic			1	ECp-1B	Istanbul	22 Jun 08
2.06		Vlasic			1	GP	Madrid	5 Jul 08
2.06	Ariane	Friedrich	GER	10.1.84	1	ISTAF	Berlin	14 Jun 09
2.06i		Vlasic			1		Arnstadt	6 Feb 10
2.06i		Chicherova			1		Arnstadt	4 Feb 12
2.06	Mariya	Lasitskene' (10)	RUS	14.1.93	1	Athl	Lausanne	6 Jul 17
2.05 WR	Tamara	Bykova	RUS	21.12.58	1	Izv	Kyiv	22 Jun 84
2.05	Inga	Babakova	UKR	27.6.67	1		Tokyo	15 Sep 95
2.05i	Tia	Hellebaut	BEL	16.2.78	1	EI	Birmingham	3 Mar 07
2.05	Chaunté	Lowe'	USA	12.1.84	1	NC	Des Moines	26 Jun 10

(60/14) with Further 2.05 performances: Kostadinova 10, Vlasic 10, Bergqvist, Chicherova 2, Hellebaut, Henkel, Cloete, Friedrich, Lasikskene 1

Mark Wind	Name		Nat	Born	Pos	Meet	Venue	Date
2.04	Silvia	Costa	CUB	4.5.64	1	WCp	Barcelona	9 Sep 89
2.04i	Alina	Astafei	GER	7.6.69	1		Berlin	3 Mar 95
2.04	Venelina	Veneva ¶	BUL	13.6.74	1		Kalamáta	2 Jun 01
2.04i	Antonietta	Di Martino	ITA	1.6.78	1		Banská Bystrica	9 Feb 11
2.04	Irina	Gordeyeva	RUS	9.10.86	1		Eberstadt	19 Aug 12
2.04	Brigetta	Barrett	USA	24.12.90	1	NC	Des Moines	22 Jun 13
	(20)							
2.03 WR	Ulrike	Meyfarth	FRG	4.5.56	1	ECp	London (CP)	21 Aug 83
2.03	Louise	Ritter	USA	18.2.58	1		Austin	8 Jul 88
2.03	Tatyana	Motkova	RUS	23.11.68	2		Bratislava	30 May 95
2.03	Níki	Bakoyiánni	GRE	9.6.68	2	OG	Atlanta	3 Aug 96
2.03i	Monica	Iagar/Dinescu	ROU	2.4.73	1		Bucuresti	23 Jan 99
2.03i	Marina	Kuptsova	RUS	22.12.81	1	EI	Wien	2 Mar 02
2.03	Svetlana	Shkolina	RUS	9.3.86	3	OG	London (OS)	11 Aug 12
2.02i	Susanne	Beyer'	GDR	24.6.61	2	WI	Indianapolis	8 Mar 87
2.02	Yelena	Yelesina	RUS	4.4.70	1	GWG	Seattle	23 Jul 90
2.02	Viktoriya	Styopina	UKR	21.2.76	3	OG	Athína	28 Aug 04
	(30)							
2.02	Ruth	Beitia	ESP	1.4.79	1	NC	San Sebastián	4 Aug 07
2.02i	Kamila	Licwinko'	POL	22.3.86	1	NC	Torun	21 Feb 15
2.01 WR	Sara	Simeoni	ITA	19.4.53	1	v Pol	Brescia	4 Aug 78
2.01	Olga	Turchak	UKR	5.3.67	2	GWG	Moskva	7 Jul 86
2.01A	Desiré	du Plessis	RSA	20.5.65	1		Johannesburg	16 Sep 86
2.01i	Gabriele	Günz	GDR	8.9.61	2		Stuttgart	31 Jan 88
2.01	Heike	Balck	GDR	19.8.70	1	vUSSR-j	Karl-Marx-Stadt	18 Jun 89
2.01i	Ioamnet	Quintero	CUB	8.9.72	1		Berlin	5 Mar 93
2.01	Hanne	Haugland	NOR	14.12.67	1	WK	Zürich	13 Aug 97
2.01i	Tisha	Waller	USA	1.12.70	1	NC	Atlanta	28 Feb 98
	(40)							
2.01	Yelena	Gulyayeva ¶	RUS	14.8.67	2		Kalamáta	23 May 98
2.01	Vita	Palamar	UKR	12.10.77	2=	WK	Zürich	15 Aug 03
2.01	Amy	Acuff	USA	14.7.75	4	WK	Zürich	15 Aug 03
2.01	Iryna	Myhalchenko	UKR	20.1.72	1		Eberstadt	18 Jul 04
2.01	Emma	Green Tregaro	SWE	8.12.84	2	EC	Barcelona	1 Aug 10
2.01i	Airine	Palsyte	LTU	13.7.92	1	EI	Beograd	4 Mar 17
2.01	Yuliya	Levchenko	UKR	28.11.97	2	WCh	London (OS)	12 Aug 17
2.00 WR	Rosemarie	Ackermann'	GDR	4.4.52	1	ISTAF	Berlin	26 Aug 77

2.00 by 22 others (70) 100th woman 1.98, 200th 1.95, 300th 1.93, 400th 1.92, 500th 1.90

Best outdoor marks

Mark	Name	Pos	Meet	Venue	Date
2.05	Henkel	1	WCh	Tokyo	31 Aug 91
2.05	Hellebaut	1	OG	Beijing	23 Aug 08
2.03	Di Martino	1	ECp-1B	Milano	24 Jun 07
2.02	Iagar/Dinescu	1		Budapest	6 Jun 98
2.02	Kuptsova	1	FBK	Hengelo	1 Jun 03
2.01	Astafei	2		Wörrstadt	27 May 95
2.00	Kositsyna, Quintero, Bilac, Waller				

Ancillary jumps: 2.06 Kostadinova 30 Aug 87, 2.05i Henkel 8 Feb 92, 2.05i Bergqvist 4 Feb 06, 2.05 Vlasic 31 Aug 09

POLE VAULT

Mark Wind	Name		Nat	Born	Pos	Meet	Venue	Date
5.06 WR	Yelena	Isinbayeva	RUS	3.6.82	1	WK	Zürich	28 Aug 09
5.05 WR		Isinbayeva			1	OG	Beijing	18 Aug 08
5.04 WR		Isinbayeva			1	Herc	Monaco	29 Jul 08
5.03 WR		Isinbayeva			1	GGala	Roma	11 Jul 08
5.03i WIR	Jennifer	Suhr	USA	5.2.82	1		Brockport	30 Jan 16
5.02Ai WIR		Suhr			1	NC	Albuquerque	2 Mar 13
5.01 WR		Isinbayeva			1	WCh	Helsinki	12 Aug 05
5.01i WIR		Isinbayeva			1	XL Galan	Stockholm	23 Feb 12
5.01i		Suhr			1		Fredonia	1 Oct 16
5.00 WR		Isinbayeva			1	LGP	London (CP)	22 Jul 05
5.00i		Isinbayeva			1		Donetsk	15 Feb 09
5.00	Sandi	Morris	USA	8.7.92	1	VD	Bruxelles	9 Sep 16
4.95 WR		Isinbayeva			1	GP	Madrid	16 Jul 05
4.95i		Isinbayeva			1		Donetsk	16 Feb 08
4.95i		Morris			1	NC	Portland	12 Mar 16
4.93 WR		Isinbayeva			1	Athl	Lausanne	5 Jul 05
4.93		Isinbayeva			1	VD	Bruxelles	26 Aug 05
4.93i		Isinbayeva			1		Donetsk	10 Feb 07
4.93		Isinbayeva			1	LGP	London (CP)	25 Jul 08
4.93		Morris			1		Houston	23 Jul 16
4.92 WR		Isinbayeva			1	VD	Bruxelles	3 Sep 04
4.92		Stuczynski/Suhr			1	NC/OT	Eugene	6 Jul 08
4.91 WR		Isinbayeva (this jump on 25 Aug)			1	OG	Athína	25 Aug 04
4.91i		Isinbayeva			1		Donetsk	12 Feb 06

Mark	Wind	Name		Nat	Born	Pos	Meet	Venue	Date
4.91			Isinbayeva			1	LGP	London (CP)	28 Jul 06
4.91			Isinbayeva			1	Gaz	Saint-Denis	6 Jul 07
4.91			Suhr			1		Rochester, NY	26 Jul 11
4.91			Suhr			1		Lyndonville	14 Jun 13
4.91		Yarisley	Silva	CUB	1.6.87	1		Beckum	2 Aug 15
4.91i			Suhr			1		Kent	16 Jan 16
4.91		Ekateríni	Stefanídi	GRE	4.2.90	1	WCh	London (OS)	6 Aug 17
		(31/5)							
4.90i		Demi	Payne	USA	30.9.91	2	Mill	New York (A)	20 Feb 16
4.88	WR	Svetlana	Feofanova	RUS	16.7.80	1		Iráklio	4 Jul 04
4.87i		Holly	Bleasdale/Bradshaw	GBR	2.11.91	1		Villeurbanne	20 Jan 12
4.87		Fabiana	Murer	BRA	16.3.81	1	NC	São Bernardo do Campo	3 Jul 16
4.85i		Anna	Rogowska	POL	21.5.81	1	EI	Paris (Bercy)	6 Mar 11
		(10)							
4.85		Anzhelika	Sidorova	RUS	28.6.91	2	NC	Cheboksary	21 Jun 16
4.83		Stacy	Dragila	USA	25.3.71	1	GS	Ostrava	8 Jun 04
4.83		Nikoléta	Kiriakopoúlou	GRE	21.3.86	1	DL	Saint-Denis	4 Jul 15
4.82		Monika	Pyrek	POL	11.8.80	2	WAF	Stuttgart	22 Sep 07
4.82		Silke	Spiegelburg	GER	17.3.86	1	Herc	Monaco	20 Jul 12
4.82		Eliza	McCartney	NZL	11.12.96	1		Auckland (NS)	26 Feb 17
4.81		Alana	Boyd	AUS	10.5.84	1		Sippy Downs	2 Jul 16
4.80		Martina	Strutz	GER	4.11.81	2	WCh	Daegu	30 Aug 11
4.80i		Nicole	Büchler	SUI	17.12.83	4	WI	Portland	17 Mar 16
4.78		Tatyana	Polnova	RUS	20.4.79	2	WAF	Monaco	19 Sep 04
		(20)							
4.77		Annika	Becker	GER	12.11.81	1	NC	Wattenscheid	7 Jul 02
4.76		Jirina	Ptácníková'	CZE	20.5.86	1		Plzen	4 Sep 13
4.75		Katerina	Badurová	CZE	18.12.82	2	WCh	Osaka	28 Aug 07
4.75i		Yuliya	Golubchikova	RUS	27.3.83	1		Athína (P)	13 Feb 08
4.75Ai		Kylie	Hutson	USA	27.11.87	2	NC	Albuquerque	2 Mar 13
4.75i		Lisa	Ryzih	GER	27.9.88	2	EI	Beograd	4 Mar 17
4.75		Alysha	Newman	CAN	29.6.94	2		Beckum	27 Aug 17
4.73		Chelsea	Johnson	USA	20.12.83	1		Los Gatos	26 Jun 08
4.73		Anastasiya	Savchenko	RUS	15.11.89	1	NCp	Yerino	15 Jun 13
4.73		Katie	Nageotte	USA	30.6.91	2		Rottach-Egern	15 Jul 17
		(30)							
4.72i		Kym	Howe	AUS	12.6.80	2		Donetsk	10 Feb 07
4.72i		Jillian	Schwartz	USA/ISR	19.9.79	1		Jonesboro	15 Jun 08
4.72		Carolin	Hingst	GER	18.9.80	1		Biberach	9 Jul 10
4.71i		Tina	Sutej	SLO	7.11.88	1		Moskva	2 Feb 14
4.71Ai		Mary	Saxer Sibears	USA	21.6.87	1	NC	Albuquerque	23 Feb 14
4.71i		Marion	Fiack	FRA	13.10.92	1		Aubière	10 Jan 15
4.71i		Wilma	Murto	FIN	11.6.98	1		Zweibrücken	31 Jan 16
4.71		Michaela	Meijer	SWE	30.7.93	1		Göteborg	2 Jul 17
4.70		Yvonne	Buschbaum	GER	14.7.80	1	NC	Ulm	29 Jun 03
4.70		Vanessa	Boslak	FRA	11.6.82	2	ECp-S	Málaga	28 Jun 06
		(40)							
4.70		Angelina	Zhuk/Krasnova	RUS	7.2.91	1	EU23	Tampere	13 Jul 13
4.70i		Angelica	Bengtsson	SWE	8.7.93	3	EI	Praha (O2)	8 Mar 15
4.70i			Li Ling	CHN	6.7.89	1	AsC	Doha	19 Feb 16
4.70		Kristen	Brown	USA	26.5.92	1		Chula Vista	26 Jun 16
4.70		Lexi	Weeks	USA	20.11.96	3	NC	Eugene	10 Jul 16
4.68		Anna	Battke	GER	3.1.85	5	ISTAF	Berlin	14 Jun 09
4.67i		Kellie	Suttle	USA	9.5.73	1		Jonesboro	16 Jun 04
4.67		Olga	Mullina	RUS	1.8.92	1		Kuortane	17 Jun 17
4.66i		Christine	Adams	GER	28.2.74	1	IHS	Sindelfingen	10 Mar 02
4.66i		Lacy	Janson	USA	20.2.83	1		Fayetteville	12 Feb 10
4.66i		Kristina	Gadschiew	GER	3.7.84	1		Potsdam	18 Feb 11
		(51)	100th woman 4.56, 200th 4.42, 300th 4.35, 400th 4.30, 500th 4.23						

Outdoor bests

4.83	Rogowska	2	VD	Bruxelles	26 Aug 05
4.81	Bradshaw	1		Rottach-Egern	15 Jul 17
4.78	Büchler	2	DL	Doha	6 May 16
4.75	Golubchikova	4	OG	Beijing	18 Aug 08
4.73	Ryzih	3		Rottach-Egern	15 Jul 17
4.71	Payne	1		Hammond	8 May 15
4.70	Hutson	1		Terre Haute	15 Jun 13
4.70	Saxer	1		Chula Vista	6 Jun 13
4.70	Bengtsson	4=	WCh	Beijing	26 Aug 15
4.66	Li Ling	1	AsiC	Wuhan	6 Jun 15

Ancillary jumps: Isinbayeva: 4.97 15 Feb 09, 4.96 WR 22 Jul 05, 4.95 18 Aug 08, 4.93 29 Jul 08, 4.92i 23 Feb 12

Exhibition: 4.72 Anastasiya Shvedova RUS 3.5.79 1 Aosta 5 Jul 08

LONG JUMP

Mark	Wind	Name		Nat	Born	Pos	Meet	Venue	Date
7.52 WR	1.4	Galina	Chistyakova	RUS	26.7.62	1	Znam	Leningrad	11 Jun 88
7.49	1.3	Jackie	Joyner-Kersee	USA	3.3.62	1	NYG	New York	22 May 94

Mark	Wind	Name		Nat	Born	Pos	Meet	Venue	Date
7.49A	1.7		Joyner-Kersee			1		Sestriere	31 Jul 94
7.48	1.2	Heike	Drechsler	GER	16.12.64	1	v ITA	Neubrandenburg	9 Jul 88
7.48	0.4		Drechsler			1	Athl	Lausanne	8 Jul 92
7.45 WR	0.9		Drechsler'			1	v USSR	Tallinn	21 Jun 86
7.45 WR	1.1		Drechsler			1	OD	Dresden	3 Jul 86
7.45 WR	0.6		Joyner-Kersee			1	PAm	Indianapolis	13 Aug 87
7.45	1.6		Chistyakova			1	BGP	Budapest	12 Aug 88
7.44 WR	2.0		Drechsler			1		Berlin	22 Sep 85
7.43 WR	1.4	Anisoara	Cusmir/Stanciu	ROU	28.6.62	1	RomIC	Bucuresti	4 Jun 83
7.42	2.0	Tatyana	Kotova ¶	RUS	11.12.76	1	ECp-S	Annecy	23 Jun 02
7.40	1.8		Daute' (Drechsler)			1		Dresden	26 Jul 84
7.40	0.7		Drechsler			1	NC	Potsdam	21 Aug 87
7.40	0.9		Joyner-Kersee			1	OG	Seoul	29 Sep 88
7.39	0.3		Drechsler			1	WK	Zürich	21 Aug 85
7.39	0.5	Yelena	Byelevskaya'	BLR	11.10.63	1	NC	Bryansk	18 Jul 87
7.39			Joyner-Kersee			1		San Diego	25 Jun 88
7.37i	-		Drechsler			1	v2N	Wien	13 Feb 88
7.37A	1.8		Drechsler			1		Sestriere	31 Jul 91
7.37		Inessa	Kravets ¶	UKR	5.10.66	1		Kyiv	13 Jun 92
7.36	0.4		Joyner			1	WCh	Roma	4 Sep 87
7.36	1.8		Byelevskaya			2	Znam	Leningrad	11 Jun 88
7.36	1.8		Drechsler			1		Jena	28 May 92
7.35	1.9		Chistyakova			1	GPB	Bratislava	20 Jun 90
7.34	1.6		Daute'			1		Dresden	19 May 84
7.34	1.4		Chistyakova			2	v GDR	Tallinn	21 Jun 86
7.34			Byelevskaya			1		Sukhumi	17 May 87
7.34	0.7		Drechsler			1	v USSR	Karl-Marx-Stadt	20 Jun 87
7.33	0.4		Drechsler			1	v USSR	Erfurt	22 Jun 85
7.33	2.0		Drechsler			1		Dresden	2 Aug 85
7.33	-0.3		Drechsler			1	Herc	Monaco	11 Aug 92
7.33	0.4	Tatyana	Lebedeva	RUS	21.7.76	1	NC	Tula	31 Jul 04
		(33/8)							
7.31	1.5	Yelena	Kokonova'	UKR	4.8.63	1	NP	Alma-Ata	12 Sep 85
7.31	1.9	Marion	Jones ¶	USA	12.10.75	1	Pre	Eugene	31 May 98
		(10)							
7.31	1.7	Brittney	Reese	USA	9.9.86	1	NC	Eugene	2 Jul 16
7.27	-0.4	Irina	Simagina/Meleshina	RUS	25.5.82	2	NC	Tula	31 Jul 04
7.26A	1.8	Maurren	Maggi ¶	BRA	25.6.76	1	SACh	Bogotá	26 Jun 99
7.24	1.0	Larisa	Berezhnaya	UKR	28.2.61	1		Granada	25 May 91
7.24i		Ivana	Spanovic	SRB	10.5.90	1	EI	Beograd	5 Mar 17
7.21	1.6	Helga	Radtke	GDR	16.5.62	2		Dresden	26 Jul 84
7.21	1.9	Lyudmila	Kolchanova	RUS	1.10.79	1		Sochi	27 May 07
7.20 WR	-0.5	Valy	Ionescu	ROU	31.8.60	1	NC	Bucuresti	1 Aug 82
7.20	2.0	Irena	Ozhenko'	LTU	13.11.62	1		Budapest	12 Sep 86
7.20	0.8	Yelena	Sinchukova'	RUS	23.1.61	1	BGP	Budapest	20 Jun 91
		(20)							
7.20	0.7	Irina	Mushayilova	RUS	6.1.67	1	NC	Sankt-Peterburg	14 Jul 94
7.17	1.8	Irina	Valyukevich	BLR	19.11.59	2	NC	Bryansk	18 Jul 87
7.17	0.6	Tianna	Bartoletta'	USA	30.8.85	1	OG	Rio de Janeiro	17 Aug 16
7.16		Iolanda	Chen	RUS	26.7.61	1		Moskva	30 Jul 88
7.16A	-0.1	Elva	Goulbourne	JAM	21.1.80	1		Ciudad de México	22 May 04
7.16	1.6	Sosthene	Moguenara	GER	17.10.89	1		Weinheim	28 May 16
7.14	1.8	Nijole	Medvedeva ¶	LTU	20.10.60	1		Riga	4 Jun 88
7.14	1.2	Mirela	Dulgheru	ROU	5.10.66	1	Balk G	Sofia	5 Jul 92
7.13	2.0	Olga	Kucherenko ¶	RUS	5.11.85	1		Sochi	27 May 10
7.12	1.6	Sabine	Paetz/John'	GDR	16.10.57	2		Dresden	19 May 84
		(30)							
7.12	0.9	Chioma	Ajunwa ¶	NGR	25.12.70	1	OG	Atlanta	2 Aug 96
7.12	1.3	Naide	Gomes	CPV/POR	10.11.79	1	Herc	Monaco	29 Jul 08
7.11	0.8	Fiona	May	GBR/ITA	12.12.69	2	EC	Budapest	22 Aug 98
7.11	1.3	Anna	Nazarova	RUS	3.2.86	1	Mosc Ch	Moskva	20 Jun 12
7.10	1.6	Chelsea	Hayes	USA	9.2.88	2	NC/OT	Eugene	1 Jul 12
7.09 WR	0.0	Vilhelmina	Bardauskiené	LTU	15.6.53	Q	EC	Praha	29 Aug 78
7.09	1.5	Ljudmila	Ninova	AUT	25.6.60	1	GP II	Sevilla	5 Jun 94
7.08	0.5	Marieta	Ilcu ¶	ROU	16.10.62	1	RumIC	Pitesti	25 Jun 89
7.08	1.9	Anastasiya	Mironchik-Ivanova	BLR	13.4.89	1		Minsk	12 Jun 12
7.07	0.0	Svetlana	Zorina	RUS	2.2.60	1		Krasnodar	15 Aug 87
		(40)							
7.07	0.5	Yelena	Sokolova	RUS	23.7.86	2	OG	London (OS)	8 Aug 12
7.07	0.4	Shara	Proctor	AIA/GBR	16.9.88	2	WCh	Beijing	28 Aug 15
7.06	0.4	Tatyana	Kolpakova	KGZ	18.10.59	1	OG	Moskva	31 Jul 80

Mark	Wind	Name		Nat	Born	Pos	Meet	Venue	Date
7.06	-0.1	Niurka	Montalvo	CUB/ESP	4.6.68	1	WCh	Sevilla	23 Aug 99
7.06		Tatyana	Ter-Mesrobyan	RUS	12.5.68	1		Sankt Peterburg	22 May 02
7.05	0.6	Lyudmila	Galkina	RUS	20.1.72	1	WCh	Athína	9 Aug 97
7.05	-0.4	Eunice	Barber	FRA	17.11.74	1	WAF	Monaco	14 Sep 03
7.05	1.1	Darya	Klishina	RUS	15.1.91	1	EU23	Ostrava	17 Jul 11
7.05	2.0	Brooke	Stratton	AUS	12.7.93	1		Perth	12 Mar 16
7.04	0.5	Brigitte	Wujak' (50)	GDR	6.3.55	2	OG	Moskva	31 Jul 80
7.04	0.9	Tatyana	Proskuryakova'	RUS	13.1.56	1		Kyiv	25 Aug 83
7.04	2.0	Yelena	Yatsuk	UKR	16.3.61	1	Znam	Moskva	8 Jun 85
7.04	0.3	Carol	Lewis	USA	8.8.63	5	WK	Zürich	21 Aug 85
		(53)	100th woman 6.93, 200th 6.82, 300th 6.76, 400th 6.71, 500th 6.65						
Wind assisted			*Performances to 7.35, performers to 7.05*						
7.63A	2.1	Heike	Drechsler	GER	16.12.64	1		Sestriere	21 Jul 92
7.45	2.6		Joyner-Kersee			1	NC/OT	Indianapolis	23 Jul 88
7.39	2.6		Drechsler			1		Padova	15 Sep 91
7.39	2.9		Drechsler			1	Expo	Sevilla	6 Jun 92
7.39A	3.3		Drechsler			2		Sestriere	31 Jul 94
7.36	2.2		Chistyakova			1	Znam	Volgograd	11 Jun 89
7.35	3.4		Drechsler			1	NC	Jena	29 Jun 86
7.23A	4.3	Fiona	May	ITA	12.12.69	1		Sestriere	29 Jul 95
7.22	4.3	Anastasiya	Mironchik-Ivanova	BLR	13.4.89	1	NC	Grodno	6 Jul 12
7.19A	3.7	Susen	Tiedtke ¶	GER	23.1.69	1		Sestriere	28 Jul 93
7.17	3.6	Eva	Murková	SVK	29.5.62	1		Nitra	26 Aug 84
7.15	2.8	Janay	DeLoach-Soukup	USA	12.10.85	Q	NC/OT	Eugene	29 Jun 12
7.14A	4.5	Marieke	Veltman	USA	18.9.71	2		Sestriere	29 Jul 95
7.14	2.2	Blessing	Okagbare	NGR	9.10.88	2	DL	Doha	10 May 13
7.12A	5.8	Níki	Xánthou	GRE	11.10.73	3		Sestriere	29 Jul 95
7.12A	4.3	Nicole	Boegman	AUS	5.3.67	4		Sestriere	29 Jul 95
7.09	2.9	Renata	Nielsen	DEN	18.5.66	2		Sevilla	5 Jun 94
7.08	2.2	Lyudmila	Galkina	RUS	20.1.72	1		Thessaloniki	23 Jun 99
7.07A	5.6	Valentina	Uccheddu	ITA	26.10.66	5		Sestriere	29 Jul 95
7.07A	2.7	Sharon	Couch	USA	13.9.67	1		El Paso	12 Apr 97
7.07A	w	Erica	Johansson	SWE	5.2.74	1		Vygieskraal	15 Jan 00
7.06	3.4		Ma Miaolan	CHN	18.1.70	1	NG	Beijing	10 Sep 93

Best outdoors

7.10 0.3 Spanovic 1 Beograd 11 Sep 16

Best at low altitude:

7.06 0.8 Maggi ¶ 1 Milano 3 Jun 03 | 7.12w 3.4 May 1 NC Bologna 25 May 96
7.17w 2.6 1 São Paulo 13 Apr 02

Ancillary marks – other marks during series (to 7.34/7.36w)

7.45 1.0 Chistyakova 11 Jun 88 | 7.47Aw 3.1 Drechsler 21 Jul 92 | 7.38w 2.2 Chistyakova 11 Jun 88
7.37 Drechsler 9 Jul 88 | 7.39Aw 3.1 Drechsler 21 Jul 92 | 7.36w Joyner-Kersee 31 Jul 94

TRIPLE JUMP

Mark	Wind	Name		Nat	Born	Pos	Meet	Venue	Date
15.50 WR	0.9	Inessa	Kravets ¶	UKR	5.10.66	1	WCh	Göteborg	10 Aug 95
15.39	0.5	Françoise	Mbango	CMR	14.4.76	1	OG	Beijing	17 Aug 08
15.36i		Tatyana	Lebedeva ¶	RUS	21.7.76	1	WI	Budapest	6 Mar 04
15.34	-0.5		Lebedeva			1		Iráklio	4 Jul 04
15.33	-0.1		Kravets			1	OG	Atlanta	31 Jul 96
15.33	1.2		Lebedeva			1	Athl	Lausanne	6 Jul 04
15.32	0.5		Lebedeva			1	Super	Yokohama	9 Sep 00
15.32	0.9	Hrisopiyi	Devetzí ¶	GRE	2.1.76	Q	OG	Athína	21 Aug 04
15.32	0.5		Lebedeva			2	OG	Beijing	17 Aug 08
15.31	0.0	Caterine	Ibargüen	COL	12.2.84	1	Herc	Monaco	18 Jul 14
15.30	0.6		Mbango			1	OG	Athína	23 Aug 04
15.29	0.3	Yamilé	Aldama	CUB/SUD/GBR	14.8.72	1	GGala	Roma	11 Jul 03
15.28	0.3		Aldama			1	GP	Linz	2 Aug 04
15.28	0.9	Yargelis	Savigne	CUB	13.11.84	1	WCh	Osaka	31 Aug 07
15.27	1.3		Aldama			1	GP	London (CP)	8 Aug 03
15.25	-0.8		Lebedeva			1	WCh	Edmonton	10 Aug 01
15.25	-0.1		Devetzí			2	OG	Athína	23 Aug 04
15.25	1.7	Olga	Rypakova	KAZ	30.11.84	1	C.Cup	Split	4 Sep 10
15.23	0.8		Lebedeva			1		Réthimno	23 Jun 04
15.23	0.6		Lebedeva			1	Tsik	Athína	3 Jul 06
15.21	1.2		Aldama			2		Réthimno	23 Jun 04
15.20	0.0	Sarka	Kaspárková	CZE	20.5.71	1	WCh	Athína	4 Aug 97
15.20	-0.3	Tereza	Marinova (10)	BUL	5.9.77	1	OG	Sydney	24 Sep 00
15.20	1.3		Savigne			1	Vard	Réthimno	14 Jul 08
15.19	0.5		Lebedeva			1	Athl	Lausanne	11 Jul 06
15.18	0.3	Iva	Prandzheva ¶	BUL	15.2.72	2	WCh	Göteborg	10 Aug 95

Mark	Wind	Name		Nat	Born	Pos	Meet	Venue	Date
15.18	-0.2		Lebedeva			1	WCh	Saint-Denis	26 Aug 03
15.17	0.4		Ibargüen			1	OG	Rio de Janeiro	14 Aug 16
15.16	0.1	Rodica	Mateescu ¶	ROU	13.3.71	2	WCh	Athína	4 Aug 97
15.16i WIR	-	Ashia	Hansen	GBR	5.12.71	1	EI	Valencia	28 Feb 98
15.16	0.7	Trecia	Smith	JAM	5.11.75	2	GP	Linz	2 Aug 04
		(31/14)							
15.14	1.9	Nadezhda	Alekhina	RUS	22.9.78	1	NC	Cheboksary	26 Jul 09
15.09 WR	0.5	Anna	Biryukova	RUS	27.9.67	1	WCh	Stuttgart	21 Aug 93
15.09	-0.5	Inna	Lasovskaya	RUS	17.12.69	1	ECCp-A	Valencia	31 May 97
15.08i		Marija	Sestak	SLO	17.4.79	1		Athína (P)	13 Feb 08
15.07	-0.6	Paraskeví	Tsiamíta	GRE	10.3.72	Q	WCh	Sevilla	22 Aug 99
15.04	1.7	Yekaterina	Koneva	RUS	25.9.88	2	Pre	Eugene	30 May 15
		(20)							
15.03i		Iolanda	Chen	RUS	26.7.61	1	WI	Barcelona	11 Mar 95
15.03	1.9	Magdelin	Martinez	ITA	10.2.76	1		Roma	26 Jun 04
15.02	0.9	Anna	Pyatykh ¶	RUS	4.4.81	3	EC	Göteborg	8 Sep 06
15.02	-0.4	Yulimar	Rojas	VEN	21.10.95	1		Madrid	23 Jun 16
15.00	1.2	Kène	Ndoye	SEN	20.11.78	2		Iráklio	4 Jul 04
14.99	0.2	Olha	Saladukha	UKR	4.6.83	1	EC	Helsinki	29 Jun 12
14.98	1.8	Sofia	Bozhanova ¶	BUL	4.10.67	1		Stara Zagora	16 Jul 94
14.98	0.2	Baya	Rahouli	ALG	27.7.79	1	MedG	Almeria	1 Jul 05
14.96	0.7	Yelena	Hovorova	UKR	18.9.73	4	OG	Sydney	24 Sep 00
14.94i	–	Cristina	Nicolau	ROU	9.8.77	1	NC	Bucuresti	5 Feb 00
		(30)							
14.94i		Oksana	Udmurtova	RUS	1.2.82	1		Tartu	20 Feb 08
14.90	1.0		Xie Limei	CHN	27.6.86	1		Urumqi	20 Sep 07
14.85	1.2	Viktoriya	Gurova' ¶	RUS	22.5.82	3	NC	Kazan	19 Jul 08
14.83i	-	Yelena	Lebedenko	RUS	16.1.71	1		Samara	1 Feb 01
14.83	0.5	Yelena	Oleynikova	RUS	9.12.76	1	Odlozil	Praha	17 Jun 02
14.79	1.7	Irina	Mushayilova	RUS	6.1.67	1	DNG	Stockholm	5 Jul 93
14.78i		Adelina	Gavrila	ROU	26.11.78	1		Bucuresti	3 Feb 08
14.78	-0.1	Hanna	Minenko	UKR/ISR	25.9.89	2	WCh	Beijing	24 Aug 15
14.76	0.9	Galina	Chistyakova	RUS	26.7.62	1	Spitzen	Luzern	27 Jun 95
14.76	1.1	Gundega	Sproge ¶	LAT	12.12.72	3		Sheffield	29 Jun 97
		(40)							
14.76	0.4	Kseniya	Detsuk	BLR	23.4.86	*	NCp	Brest	26 May 12
14.73	-1.3	Paraskeví	Papahrístou	GRE	17.4.89	1		Athína (F)	8 Jun 16
14.72	1.8		Huang Qiuyan	CHN	25.1.80	1	NG	Guangzhou	22 Nov 01
14.71	1.4	Athanasía	Pérra	GRE	2.2.83	1	NC	Athína	16 Jun 12
14.71	0.0	Keturah	Orji	USA	5.3.96	4	OG	Rio de Janeiro	14 Aug 16
14.70i		Oksana	Rogova	RUS	7.10.78	1		Volgograd	6 Feb 02
14.69	1.2	Anja	Valant	SLO	8.9.77	3		Kalamáta	4 Jun 00
14.69	1.2	Simona	La Mantia	ITA	14.4.83	1		Palermo	22 May 05
14.69	2.0	Teresa	N'zola Meso	ANG/FRA	30.11.83	1	ECp-S	München	23 Jun 07
14.68i		Anastasiya	Taranova-Potapova	RUS	6.9.85	1	EI	Torino	8 Mar 09
		(50)	100th woman 14.46, 200th 14.16, 300th 14.00, 400th 13.84, 500th 13.71						

Wind assisted *Performances to 15.14, performers to 14.75*

Mark	Wind	Name		Nat	Born	Pos	Meet	Venue	Date
15.24A	4.2	Magdelin	Martinez	ITA	10.2.76	1		Sestriere	1 Aug 04
15.18	2.1		Ibargüen			1	Pre	Eugene	30 May 15
15.17	2.4	Anna	Pyatykh ¶	RUS	4.4.81	2	SGP	Athína	3 Jul 06
15.10	2.7	Keila	Costa	BRA	6.2.83	1		Uberlandia	6 May 07
15.06	2.6	Olga	Saladukha	UKR	4.6.83	1	DNG	Stockholm	29 Jul 11
14.99	6.8	Yelena	Hovorova	UKR	18.9.73	1	WUG	Palma de Mallorca	11 Jul 99
14.85	2.5	Gabriela	Petrova	BUL	29.6.92	1	ET-2	Stara Zagora	20 Jun 15
14.84	4.1	Galina	Chistyakova	RUS	26.7.62	1		Innsbruck	28 Jun 95
14.83	8.3		Ren Ruiping	CHN	1.2.76	1	NC	Taiyuan	21 May 95
14.83	2.2	Heli	Koivula-Kruger	FIN	27.6.75	2	EC	München	10 Aug 02
14.81	2.4	Kseniya	Detsuk	BLR	23.4.86	1	NCp	Brest	26 May 12
14.78	2.7	Kimberly	Williams	JAM	3.11.88	3	Pre	Eugene	1 Jun 13
14.77	2.3	Paraskeví	Papahrístou	GRE	17.4.89	1		Ankara	5 Jun 12
14.75	4.2	Jelena	Blazevica	LAT	11.5.70	1	v2N	Kaunas	23 Aug 97

Best outdoor mark for athlete with all-time best indoors

Mark	Wind	Name	Pos	Meet	Venue	Date
15.15	1.7	Hansen	1	GPF	Fukuoka	13 Sep 97
15.03	1.1	Sestak	6	OG	Beijing	17 Aug 08
14.97WR	0.9	Chen	1	NC	Moskva	18 Jun 93
14.85	1.4	Udmurtova	1		Padova	31 Aug 08
14.75	1.1	Gavrila	3	GP II	Rieti	7 Sep 03
14.70	1.3	Nicolau	1	EU23	Göteborg	1 Aug 99

Ancillary marks – other marks during series (to 15.19)

Mark	Wind	Name	Date
15.30	0.5	Mbango	23 Aug 04
15.21	-0.2	Mbango	23 Aug 04
15.28	-0.3	Ledebeva	4 Jul 04
15.19	1.0	Lebedeva	3 Jul 06
15.25i		Ledebeva	6 Mar 04
15.19	1.3	Mbango	17 Aug 08

Drugs disqualification

Mark	Wind	Name	Pos	Meet	Venue	Date
15.23	1.6	Devetzí ¶	3	OG	Beijing	17 Aug 08
15.22	1.5	Devetzí ¶	1		Thessaloníki	9 Jul 08

SHOT

Mark Wind		Name	Nat	Born	Pos	Meet	Venue	Date
22.63 WR	Natalya	Lisovskaya	RUS	16.7.62	1	Znam	Moskva	7 Jun 87
22.55		Lisovskaya			1	NC	Tallinn	5 Jul 88
22.53 WR		Lisovskaya			1		Sochi	27 May 84
22.53		Lisovskaya			1		Kyiv	14 Aug 88
22.50i	Helena	Fibingerová	CZE	13.7.49	1		Jablonec	19 Feb 77
22.45 WR	Ilona	Slupianek' ¶	GDR	24.9.56	1		Potsdam	11 May 80
22.41		Slupianek			1	OG	Moskva	24 Jul 80
22.40		Slupianek			1		Berlin	3 Jun 83
22.38		Slupianek			1		Karl-Marx-Stadt	25 May 80
22.36 WR		Slupianek			1		Celje	2 May 80
22.34		Slupianek			1		Berlin	7 May 80
22.34		Slupianek			1	NC	Cottbus	18 Jul 80
22.32 WR		Fibingerová			1		Nitra	20 Aug 77
22.24		Lisovskaya			1	OG	Seoul	1 Oct 88
22.22		Slupianek			1		Potsdam	13 Jul 80
22.19	Claudia	Losch	FRG	10.1.60	1		Hainfeld	23 Aug 87
22.14i		Lisovskaya			1	NC	Penza	7 Feb 87
22.13		Slupianek			1		Split	29 Apr 80
22.06		Slupianek			1		Berlin	15 Aug 78
22.06		Lisovskaya			1		Moskva	6 Aug 88
22.05		Slupianek			1	OD	Berlin	28 May 80
22.05		Slupianek			1		Potsdam	31 May 80
22.04		Slupianek			1		Potsdam	4 Jul 79
22.04		Slupianek			1		Potsdam	29 Jul 79
21.99 WR		Fibingerová			1		Opava	26 Sep 76
21.98		Slupianek			1		Berlin	17 Jul 79
21.96		Fibingerová			1	GS	Ostrava	8 Jun 77
21.96		Lisovskaya			1	Drz	Praha	16 Aug 84
21.96		Lisovskaya			1		Vilnius	28 Aug 88
21.95		Lisovskaya			1	IAC	Edinburgh	29 Jul 88
	(30/4)							
21.89 WR	Ivanka	Khristova	BUL	19.11.41	1		Belmeken	4 Jul 76
21.86	Marianne	Adam	GDR	19.9.51	1	v URS	Leipzig	23 Jun 79
21.76		Li Meisu	CHN	17.4.59	1		Shijiazhuang	23 Apr 88
21.73	Natalya	Akhrimenko	RUS	12.5.55	1		Leselidze	21 May 88
21.69	Viktoriya	Pavlysh ¶	UKR	15.1.69	1	EC	Budapest	20 Aug 98
21.66		Sui Xinmei ¶	CHN	29.1.65	1		Beijing	9 Jun 90
	(10)							
21.61	Verzhinia	Veselinova	BUL	18.11.57	1		Sofia	21 Aug 82
21.60i	Valentina	Fedyushina	UKR	18.2.65	1		Simferopol	28 Dec 91
21.58	Margitta	Droese/Pufe	GDR	10.9.52	1		Erfurt	28 May 78
21.57 @	Ines	Müller'	GDR	2.1.59	1		Athína	16 May 88
	21.45				1		Schwerin	4 Jun 86
21.53	Nunu	Abashidze ¶	UKR	27.3.55	2	Izv	Kyiv	20 Jun 84
21.52		Huang Zhihong	CHN	7.5.65	1	NC	Beijing	27 Jun 90
21.46	Larisa	Peleshenko ¶	RUS	29.2.64	1	Kuts	Moskva	26 Aug 00
21.45 WR	Nadezhda	Chizhova	RUS	29.9.45	1		Varna	29 Sep 73
21.43	Eva	Wilms	FRG	28.7.52	2	HB	München	17 Jun 77
21.42	Svetlana	Krachevskaya'	RUS	23.11.44	2	OG	Moskva	24 Jul 80
	(20)	*@ competitive meeting, but unsanctioned by GDR federation*						
21.31 @	Heike	Hartwig'	GDR	30.12.62	2		Athína	16 May 88
	21.27				1		Haniá	22 May 88
21.27	Liane	Schmuhl	GDR	29.6.61	1		Cottbus	26 Jun 82
21.24	Valerie	Adams	NZL	6.10.84	1	WCh	Daegu	29 Aug 11
21.22	Astrid	Kumbernuss	GDR/GER	5.2.70	1	WCh	Göteborg	5 Aug 95
21.21	Kathrin	Neimke	GDR	18.7.66	2	WCh	Roma	5 Sep 87
21.19	Helma	Knorscheidt	GDR	31.12.56	1		Berlin	24 May 84
21.15i	Irina	Korzhanenko ¶	RUS	16.5.74	1	NC	Moskva	18 Feb 99
21.10	Heidi	Krieger	GDR	20.7.65	1	EC	Stuttgart	26 Aug 86
21.09	Nadezhda	Ostapchuk ¶	BLR	12.10.80	1		Minsk	21 Jul 05
21.06	Svetlana	Krivelyova ¶	RUS	13.6.69	1	OG	Barcelona	7 Aug 92
	(30)							
21.05	Zdenka	Silhavá' ¶	CZE	15.6.54	2	NC	Praha	23 Jul 83
21.01	Ivanka	Petrova-Stoycheva	BUL	3.2.51	1	NC	Sofia	28 Jul 79
21.00	Mihaela	Loghin	ROU	1.6.52	1		Formia	30 Jun 84
21.00	Cordula	Schulze	GDR	11.9.59	4	OD	Potsdam	21 Jul 84
20.96	Belsy	Laza	CUB	5.6.67	1		Ciudad de México	2 May 92
20.95	Elena	Stoyanova ¶	BUL	23.1.52	2	Balk	Sofia	14 Jun 80

Mark	Wind	Name		Nat	Born	Pos	Meet	Venue	Date
20.91		Svetla	Mitkova	BUL	17.6.64	1		Sofia	24 May 87
20.80		Sona	Vasícková	CZE	14.3.62	1		Praha	2 Jun 88
20.77		Christina	Schwanitz	GER	24.12.85	1		Beijing	20 May 15
20.72		Grit	Haupt/Hammer	GDR	4.6.66	3		Neubrandenburg	11 Jun 87
		(40)							
20.70		Natalya	Mikhnevich' ¶	BLR	25.5.82	2	NC	Grodno	8 Jul 08
20.63		Michelle	Carter	USA	12.10.85	1	OG	Rio de Janeiro	12 Aug 16
20.61		María Elena	Sarría	CUB	14.9.54	1		La Habana	22 Jul 82
20.61		Yanina	Korolchik' ¶	BLR	26.12.76	1	WCh	Edmonton	5 Aug 01
20.60		Marina	Antonyuk	RUS	12.5.62	1		Chelyabinsk	10 Aug 86
20.54			Zhang Liuhong	CHN	16.1.69	1	NC	Beijing	5 Jun 94
20.53		Iris	Plotzitzka	FRG	7.1.66	1	ASV	Köln	21 Aug 88
20.50i		Christa	Wiese	GDR	25.12.67	2	NC	Senftenberg	12 Feb 89
20.47		Nina	Isayeva	RUS	6.7.50	1		Bryansk	28 Aug 82
20.47			Cong Yuzhen	CHN	22.1.63	2	IntC	Tianjin	3 Sep 88
		(50)	100th woman 19.73, 200th 18.89, 300th 18.28, 400th 17.87, 500th 17.56						

Best outdoor marks

21.58	Ostapchuk ¶	1	Minsk	18 Jul 12
21.08	Fedyushina	1	Leselidze	15 May 88
20.82	Korzhanenko ¶	1	Rostov na Donu	30 May 98
	21.06 drugs dq	(1) OG	Athína	18 Aug 04

Ancillary marks – other marks during series (to 22.09)

22.60	Lisovskaya (WR)	7 Jun 87
22.40	Lisovskaya	14 Aug 88
22.34	Slupianek	11 May 80
22.33	Slupianek	2 May 80
22.20	Slupianek	13 Jul 80
22.19	Lisovskaya	5 Jul 88
22.14	Slupianek	25 May 80
22.14	Slupianek	13 Jul 80
22.12	Slupianek	13 Jul 80
22.11	Slupianek	7 May 80
22.10	Slupianek	25 May 80
22.09	Slupianek	7 May 80

Drugs disqualification

21.70i		Nadezhda	Ostapchuk ¶	BLR	12.10.80	(1)	NC	Mogilyov	12 Feb 10

DISCUS

Mark	Wind	Name		Nat	Born	Pos	Meet	Venue	Date
76.80	WR	Gabriele	Reinsch	GDR	23.9.63	1	v ITA	Neubrandenburg	9 Jul 88
74.56	WR	Zdenka	Silhavá' ¶	CZE	15.6.54	1		Nitra	26 Aug 84
74.56		Ilke	Wyludda	GDR	28.3.69	1	NC	Neubrandenburg	23 Jul 89
74.44			Reinsch			1		Berlin	13 Sep 88
74.40			Wyludda			2		Berlin	13 Sep 88
74.08		Diana	Gansky'	GDR	14.12.63	1	v USSR	Karl-Marx-Stadt	20 Jun 87
73.90			Gansky			1	ECp	Praha	27 Jun 87
73.84		Daniela	Costian ¶	ROU	30.4.65	1		Bucuresti	30 Apr 88
73.78			Costian			1		Bucuresti	24 Apr 88
73.42			Reinsch			1		Karl-Marx-Stadt	12 Jun 88
73.36	WR	Irina	Meszynski	GDR	24.3.62	1	Drz	Praha	17 Aug 84
73.32			Gansky			1		Neubrandenburg	11 Jun 87
73.28		Galina	Savinkova'	RUS	15.7.53	1	NC	Donetsk	8 Sep 84
73.26	WR		Savinkova			1		Leselidze	21 May 83
73.26			Sachse/Gansky			1		Neubrandenburg	6 Jun 86
73.24			Gansky			1		Leipzig	29 May 87
73.22		Tsvetanka	Khristova ¶	BUL	14.3.62	1		Kazanlak	19 Apr 87
73.10		Gisela	Beyer	GDR	16.7.60	1	OD	Berlin	20 Jul 84
73.04			Gansky			1		Potsdam	6 Jun 87
73.04			Wyludda			1	ECp	Gateshead	5 Aug 89
72.96			Savinkova			1	v GDR	Erfurt	23 Jun 85
72.94			Gansky			2	v ITA	Neubrandenburg	9 Jul 88
72.92		Martina	Opitz/Hellmann	GDR	12.12.60	1	NC	Potsdam	20 Aug 87
72.90			Costian			1		Bucuresti	14 May 88
72.78			Hellmann			2		Neubrandenburg	11 Jun 87
72.78			Reinsch			1	OD	Berlin	29 Jun 88
72.72			Wyludda			1		Neubrandenburg	23 Jun 89
72.70			Wyludda			1	NC-j	Karl-Marx-Stadt	15 Jul 88
72.54			Gansky			1	NC	Rostock	25 Jun 88
72.52			Hellmann			1		Frohburg	15 Jun 86
72.52			Khristova			1	BGP	Budapest	11 Aug 86
		(31/10)							
72.14		Galina	Murashova	LTU	22.12.55	2	Drz	Praha	17 Aug 84
71.80	WR	Maria	Vergova/Petkova	BUL	3.11.50	1	NC	Sofia	13 Jul 80
71.68			Xiao Yanling ¶	CHN	27.3.68	1		Beijing	14 Mar 92
71.58		Ellina	Zvereva' ¶	BLR	16.11.60	1	Znam	Leningrad	12 Jun 88
71.50	WR	Evelin	Schlaak/Jahl	GDR	28.3.56	1		Potsdam	10 May 80
71.41		Sandra	Perkovic	CRO	21.6.90	1		Bellinzona	18 Jul 17
71.30		Larisa	Korotkevich	RUS	3.1.67	1	RusCp	Sochi	29 May 92
71.22		Ria	Stalman	NED	11.12.51	1		Walnut	15 Jul 84
		Disallowed as Dutch record in 2016 after Stalman admitted drugs use							
70.88		Hilda Elia	Ramos ¶	CUB	1.9.64	1		La Habana	8 May 92

WOMEN All-time

Mark	Wind	Name		Nat	Born	Pos	Meet	Venue	Date
70.80		Larisa	Mikhalchenko	UKR	16.5.63	1		Kharkov	18 Jun 88
		(20)							
70.68		Maritza	Martén	CUB	16.8.63	1	Ib Am	Sevilla	18 Jul 92
70.65		Denia	Caballero	CUB	13.1.90	1		Bilbao	20 Jun 15
70.50	WR	Faina	Melnik	RUS	9.6.45	1	Znam	Sochi	24 Apr 76
70.34	@	Silvia	Madetzky	GDR	24.6.62	3		Athína	16 May 88
		69.34				1		Halle	26 Jun 87
70.02		Natalya	Sadova ¶	RUS	15.7.72	1		Thessaloniki	23 Jun 99
69.86		Valentina	Kharchenko	RUS	.49	1		Feodosiya	16 May 81
69.72		Svetla	Mitkova	BUL	17.6.64	2	NC	Sofia	15 Aug 87
69.68		Mette	Bergmann	NOR	9.11.62	1		Florø	27 May 95
69.64		Dani	Stevens	AUS	26.5.88	2	WCh	London (OS)	13 Aug 17
69.51		Franka	Dietzsch	GER	22.1.68	1		Wiesbaden	8 May 99
		(30)							
69.50		Florenta	Craciunescu'	ROU	7.5.55	1	Balk	Stara Zagora	2 Aug 85
69.19		Yaimé	Pérez	CUB	29.5.91	1		Sotteville-lès-Rouen	7 Jul 17
69.17		Gia	Lewis-Smallwood	USA	1.4.79	1	Déca	Angers	30 Aug 14
69.14		Irina	Yatchenko ¶	BLR	31.10.65	1		Staiki	31 Jul 04
69.08		Carmen	Romero	CUB	6.10.50	1	NC	La Habana	17 Apr 76
69.08		Mariana	Ionescu/Lengyel	ROU	14.4.53	1		Constanta	19 Apr 86
68.92		Sabine	Engel	GDR	21.4.54	1	v URS,POL	Karl-Marx-Stadt	25 Jun 77
68.89		Nadine	Müller	GER	21.11.85	1	ECp-w	Bar	18 Mar 12
68.80A		Nicoleta	Grasu	ROU	11.9.71	1		Poiana Brasov	7 Aug 99
68.64		Margitta	Pufe'	GDR	10.9.52	1	ISTAF	Berlin	17 Aug 79
		(40)							
68.62			Yu Hourun	CHN	9.7.64	1		Beijing	6 May 88
68.62			Hou Xuemei	CHN	27.2.62	1	IntC	Tianjin	4 Sep 88
68.60		Nadezhda	Kugayevskikh	RUS	19.4.60	1		Oryol	30 Aug 83
68.58		Lyubov	Zverkova	RUS	14.6.55	1	Izv	Kyiv	22 Jun 84
68.52		Beatrice	Faumuiná	NZL	23.10.74	1	Bisl	Oslo	4 Jul 97
68.49		Julia	Fischer/Harting	GER	1.4.90	1	Werfer	Halle	21 May 16
68.38		Olga	Burova'	RUS	17.9.63	2	RusCp	Sochi	29 May 92
68.18		Tatyana	Lesovaya	KAZ	24.4.56	1		Alma-Ata	23 Sep 82
68.18		Irina	Khval	RUS	17.5.62	1		Moskva	8 Jul 88
68.18		Barbara	Hechevarría	CUB	6.8.66	2		La Habana	17 Feb 89
		(50)	100th woman 65.96, 200th 63.88, 300th 62.00, 400th 60.36, 500th 59.16						

Unofficial meeting: Berlin 6 Sep 88: 1. Martina Hellmann 78.14, 2. Ilke Wyludda 75.36

Downhill: 69.44 Suzy Powell USA 3.9.76 1 La Jolla 27 Apr 02

Drugs disqualification:

70.69 Darya Pishchalnikova ¶ RUS 19.7.85 (1) NC Cheboksary 5 Jul 12

Ancillary marks – other marks during series (to 72.92)

73.32	Reinsch	13 Sep 88	73.28	Gansky	27 Jun 87	73.10	Reinsch	9 Jul 88
73.28	Gansky	11 Jun 87	73.16	Wyludda	13 Sep 88	73.06	Gansky	27 Jun 87
						72.92	Hellmann	20 Aug 87

HAMMER

Mark	Wind	Name		Nat	Born	Pos	Meet	Venue	Date
82.98	WR	Anita	Wlodarczyk	POL	8.8.85	1	Skol	Warszawa	28 Aug 16
82.87			Wlodarczyk			1	Skol	Cetniewo	29 Jul 17
82.29	WR		Wlodarczyk			1	OG	Rio de Janeiro	14 Aug 16
81.08			Wlodarczyk			1	Skol	Cetniewo	1 Aug 15
80.85			Wlodarczyk			1	WCh	Beijing	27 Aug 15
80.79			Wlodarczyk			1	NC	Bialystok	23 Jul 17
80.26			Wlodarczyk			1		Cetniewo	12 Jul 16
79.80			Wlodarczyk			1	Skol	Warszawa	15 Aug 17
79.73			Wlodarczyk			1	DL	Doha	6 May 17
79.72			Wlodarczyk			1	GS	Ostrava	27 Jun 17
79.61			Wlodarczyk			1	Kuso	Szczecin	18 Jun 16
79.58	WR		Wlodarczyk			1	ISTAF	Berlin	31 Aug 14
79.48			Wlodarczyk			1	Werfer	Halle	21 May 16
79.45			Wlodarczyk			1		Forbach	29 May 16
79.42	WR	Betty	Heidler	GER	14.10.83	1		Halle	21 May 11
78.80		Tatyana	Lysenko ¶	RUS	9.10.83	1	WCh	Moskva	16 Aug 13
78.76			Wlodarczyk			1	EC	Zürich	15 Aug 14
78.69			Wlodarczyk			1	NC	Bydgoszcz	26 Jun 16
78.54			Wlodarczyk			1	GS	Ostrava	19 May 16
78.51			Lysenko			1	NC	Cheboksary	5 Jul 12
78.46			Wlodarczyk			2	WCh	Moskva	16 Aug 13
78.30	WR		Wlodarczyk			1	EAF	Bydgoszcz	6 Jun 10
78.28			Wlodarczyk			1	ET	Cheboksary	21 Jun 15
78.24			Wlodarczyk			1	NC	Kraków	21 Jul 15

Mark	Wind	Name		Nat	Born	Pos	Meet	Venue	Date
78.22			Wlodarczyk			1		Dubnica nad Vahom	21 Aug 13
78.18			Lysenko			1	OG	London (OS)	10 Aug 12
78.17			Wlodarczyk			1		Cetniewo	26 Jul 14
78.16			Wlodarczyk			1	Skol	Warszawa	13 Sep 15
78.15			Lysenko			1	NC	Moskva	24 Jul 13
78.14			Wlodarczyk			1	EC	Amsterdam	8 Jul 16
		(30/3)							
77.68			Wang Zheng	CHN	14.12.87	1		Chengdu	29 Mar 14
77.33			Zhang Wenxiu ¶	CHN	22.3.86	(1)	AsiG	Incheon	28 Sep 14
77.26	WR	Gulfiya	Khanafeyeva ¶	RUS	4.6.82	1	NC	Tula	12 Jun 06
77.13		Oksana	Kondratyeva	RUS	22.11.85	1	Znam	Zhukovskiy	30 Jun 13
76.90		Martina	Hrasnová' ¶	SVK	21.3.83	1		Trnava	16 May 09
76.85		Malwina	Kopron	POL	16.11.94	1	WUG	Taipei	26 Aug 17
		(10)							
76.83		Kamila	Skolimowska	POL	4.11.82	1	SGP	Doha	11 May 07
76.77		Gwen	Berry	USA	29.6.89	1		Oxford, USA	6 May 17
76.72		Mariya	Bespalova ¶	RUS	21.5.86	2		Zhukovskiy	23 Jun 12
76.66		Olga	Tsander	BLR	18.5.76	1		Staiki	21 Jul 05
76.63		Yekaterina	Khoroshikh ¶	RUS	21.1.83	2	Znam	Moskva	24 Jun 06
76.62		Yipsi	Moreno	CUB	19.11.80	1	GP	Zagreb	9 Sep 08
76.56		Alena	Matoshko	BLR	23.6.82	2		Minsk	12 Jun 12
76.33		Darya	Pchelnik ¶	BLR	20.12.81	2		Staiki	29 Jun 08
76.21		Yelena	Konevtsova	RUS	11.3.81	3		Sochi	26 May 07
76.17		Anna	Bulgakova ¶	RUS	17.1.88	2	NC	Moskva	24 Jul 13
		(20)							
76.07	WR	Mihaela	Melinte ¶	ROU	27.3.75	1		Rüdlingen	29 Aug 99
76.05		Kathrin	Klaas	GER	6.2.84	5	OG	London (OS)	10 Aug 12
75.73		Amanda	Bingson	USA	20.2.90	1	NC	Des Moines	22 Jun 13
75.73		Sultana	Frizell	CAN	24.10.84	1		Tucson	22 May 14
75.68		Olga	Kuzenkova ¶	RUS	4.10.70	1	NCp	Tula	4 Jun 00
75.29		Hanna	Skydan	UKR/AZE	14.5.92	1	Isl.Sol	Baku	16 May 17
75.09		Yelena	Rigert'	RUS	2.12.83	1	Kuts	Moskva	15 Jul 13
75.09		Joanna	Fiodorow	POL	4.3.89	2	Skol	Cetniewo	29 Jul 17
75.08		Ivana	Brkljacic	CRO	25.1.83	2	Kuso	Waszawa	17 Jun 07
74.94		Hanna	Malyshik	BLR	4.2.94	1	NCp	Brest	1 Jun 17
		(30)							
74.91		DeAnna	Price	USA	8.6.93	1		Sacramento (CS)	10 Jun 17
74.77		Jeneva	McCall/Stevens	USA	28.10.89	2		Dubnica nad Vahom	21 Aug 13
74.66		Manuèla	Montebrun	FRA	13.11.79	1	GP II	Zagreb	11 Jul 05
74.65		Mariya	Smolyachkova	BLR	10.2.85	2		Staiki	19 Jul 08
74.56		Maggie	Ewen	USA	23.9.94	2	NC	Sacramento	25 Jun 17
74.54		Sophie	Hitchon	GBR	11.7.91	3	OG	Rio de Janeiro	15 Aug 16
74.52		Iryna	Sekachyova	UKR	21.7.76	1	NC	Kyiv	2 Jul 08
74.39		Alexandra	Tavernier	FRA	13.12.93	Q	WCh	Beijing	26 Aug 15
74.21		Zalina	Petrivskaya' ¶	MDA	5.2.88	1	NC-w	Chisinau	6 Feb 16
74.20		Jessica	Cosby Toruga	USA	31.5.82	3		Tucson	22 May 14
		(40)							
74.17		Tugçe	Sahutoglu ¶	TUR	1.5.88	1		Izmir	19 May 12
74.10		Iryna	Novozhylova	UKR	7.1.86	1		Kyiv	19 May 12
74.03		Amber	Campbell	USA	5.6.81	1	NC	Eugene	6 Jul 16
73.90		Arasay	Thondike	CUB	28.5.86	1		La Habana	18 Jun 09
73.87		Erin	Gilreath	USA	11.10.80	1	NC	Carson	25 Jun 05
73.74		Jennifer	Dahlgren	ARG	21.4.84	1		Buenos Aires	10 Apr 10
73.64		Rosa	Rodríguez	VEN	2.7.86	1		Barquisimeto	16 May 13
73.59		Ester	Balassini	ITA	20.10.77	1	NC	Bressanone	25 Jun 05
73.52		Bianca	Ghelber-Perie	ROU	1.6.90	1	NC	Bucuresti	16 Jul 10
73.44		Éva	Orbán	HUN	29.11.84	2	Werfer	Halle	25 May 13
		(50)	100th woman 70.67, 200th 67.56, 300th 65.21, 400th 63.91, 500th 62.99						
Downhill: 75.20		Manuéla	Montebrun	FRA	13.11.79	1		Vineuil	18 May 03

Ancillary marks – other marks during series to 78.80 – all by Wlodarczyk

81.77	28 Aug 16	80.73	29 Jul 17	80.31	28 Aug 16	79.67	12 Jul 16	79.39	12 Jul 16
81.74	14 Aug 16	80.69	29 Jul 17	80.27	27 Aug 15	79.62	12 Jul 16	79.31	27 Aug 15
81.63	29 Jul 17	80.42	29 Jul 17	79.68	28 Aug 16	79.60	14 Aug 16	79.27	27 Jun 17
81.27	28 Aug 16	80.40	14 Aug 16	79.68	27 Jun 17	79.58	12 Jul 16	79.23	15 Aug 17

Drugs disqualification

78.69	Oksana	Menkova ¶	BLR	28.3.82	(1)		Minsk	18 Jul 12
78.61		Lysenko			(1)		Sochi	26 May 07
78.19		Menkova			(1)		Brest	28 Apr 12
78.19		Menkova			(1)		Minsk	12 Jun 12
77.36	Gulfiya	Khanafeyeva ¶	RUS	4.6.82	(2)		Sochi	26 May 07
74.47	Zalina	Marghieva ¶	MDA	5.2.88	(1)	Univ Ch	Chisinau	7 May 12

JAVELIN

Mark	Wind	Name		Nat	Born	Pos	Meet	Venue	Date
72.28	WR	Barbora	Spotáková	CZE	30.6.81	1	WAF	Stuttgart	13 Sep 08
71.99		Mariya	Abakumova ¶	RUS	15.1.86	1	WCh	Daegu	2 Sep 11
71.70	WR	Osleidys	Menéndez	CUB	14.11.79	1	WCh	Helsinki	14 Aug 05
71.58			Spotáková			2	WCh	Daegu	2 Sep 11
71.54	WR		Menéndez			1		Réthimno	1 Jul 01
71.53			Menéndez			1	OG	Athína	27 Aug 04
71.42			Spotáková			1	OG	Beijing	21 Aug 08
70.53			Abakumova			1	ISTAF	Berlin	1 Sep 13
70.20		Christina	Obergföll	GER	22.8.81	1	ECp-S	München	23 Jun 07
70.03			Obergföll			2	WCh	Helsinki	14 Aug 05
69.82			Menéndez			1	WUG	Beijing	29 Aug 01
69.81			Obergföll			1		Berlin (Elstal)	31 Aug 08
69.75			Abakumova			1		Berlin (Elstal)	25 Aug 13
69.57			Obergföll			1	WK	Zürich	8 Sep 11
69.55			Spotáková			1	OG	London (OS)	9 Aug 12
69.53			Menéndez			1	WCh	Edmonton	7 Aug 01
69.48	WR	Trine	Hattestad	NOR	18.4.66	1	Bisl	Oslo	28 Jul 00
69.45			Spotáková			1	Herc	Monaco	22 Jul 11
69.35		Sunette	Viljoen	RSA	6.1.83	1	DL	New York	9 Jun 12
69.34			Abakumova			1	ECp-w	Castellón	16 Mar 13
69.15			Spotáková			1		Zaragoza	31 May 08
69.09			Abakumova			Q	WCh	Moskva	16 Aug 13
69.05			Obergföll			1	WCh	Moskva	18 Aug 13
68.94			Abakumova			1	WK	Zürich	29 Aug 13
68.92			Abakumova			Q	WCh	Berlin	16 Aug 09
68.91			Hattestad			1	OG	Sydney	30 Sep 00
68.89			Abakumova			1	DL	Doha	14 May 10
68.86			Obergföll			1	NC	Kassel	24 Jul 11
68.81			Spotáková			1	Odlozil	Praha	16 Jun 08
		(30/6)							
68.43		Sara	Kolak	CRO	22.6.95	1	Athl	Lausanne	6 Jul 17
68.34		Steffi	Nerius	GER	1.7.72	2		Berlin (Elstal)	31 Aug 08
67.69		Katharina	Molitor	GER	8.11.83	1	WCh	Beijing	30 Aug 15
67.67		Sonia	Bisset	CUB	1.4.71	1		Salamanca	6 Jul 05
		(10)							
67.59			Lu Huihui ¶	CHN	26.6.89	Q	WCh	London (OS)	6 Aug 17
67.51		Miréla	Manjani/Tzelíli	GRE	21.12.76	2	OG	Sydney	30 Sep 00
67.32		Linda	Stahl	GER	2.10.85	1	adidas	New York	14 Jun 14
67.30		Vera	Rebrik	RUS	25.2.89	1	NC-w	Adler	19 Feb 16
67.29		Hanna	Hatsko-Fedusova	UKR	3.10.90	1	NC	Kirovohrad	26 Jul 14
67.21		Eda	Tugsuz	TUR	27.3.97	1	Isl.Sol	Baku	18 May 17
67.20		Tatyana	Shikolenko	RUS	10.5.68	1	Herc	Monaco	18 Aug 00
67.16		Martina	Ratej	SLO	2.11.81	3	DL	Doha	14 May 10
67.11		Maria	Andrejczyk	POL	9.3.96	Q	OG	Rio de Janeiro	16 Aug 16
66.91		Tanja	Damaske	GER	16.11.71	1	NC	Erfurt	4 Jul 99
		(20)							
66.83		Kimberley	Mickle	AUS	28.12.84	1		Melbourne	22 Mar 14
66.80		Louise	McPaul/Currey	AUS	24.1.69	1		Gold Coast (RB)	5 Aug 00
66.67		Kara	Patterson/Winger	USA	10.4.86	1	NC	Des Moines	25 Jun 10
66.47			Liu Shiying	CHN	24.9.93	1		Kawasaki	21 May 17
66.41		Christin	Hussong	GER	17.4.94	1	NC	Kassel	19 Jun 16
66.34		Tatyana	Kholodovich	BLR	21.6.91	1	EC	Amsterdam	9 Jul 16
66.25			Li Lingwei	CHN	26.1.89	2	WCh	London (OS)	9 Aug 17
66.18		Madara	Palameika	LAT	18.6.87	1	VD	Bruxelles	9 Sep 16
66.17		Goldie	Sayers	GBR	16.7.82	1	LGP	London (CP)	14 Jul 12
66.12		Kathryn	Mitchell	AUS	10.7.82	3	Athl	Lausanne	6 Jul 17
		(30)							
65.91		Nikola	Brejchová'	CZE	25.6.74	1	GP	Linz	2 Aug 04
65.47			Zhang Li	CHN	17.1.89	1	AsiG	Incheon	1 Oct 14
65.30		Claudia	Coslovich	ITA	26.4.72	1		Ljubljana	10 Jun 00
65.29		Xiomara	Rivero	CUB	22.11.68	1		Santiago de Cuba	17 Mar 01
65.17		Karen	Forkel	GER	24.9.70	2	NC	Erfurt	4 Jul 99
65.08		Ana Mirela	Termure ¶	ROU	13.1.75	1	NC	Bucuresti	10 Jun 01
64.90		Paula	Huhtaniemi'	FIN	17.2.73	1	NC	Helsinki	10 Aug 03
64.89		Yekaterina	Ivakina	RUS	4.12.64	4	Bisl	Oslo	28 Jul 00
64.87		Kelly	Morgan	GBR	17.6.80	1	NC	Birmingham	14 Jul 02
64.83		Christina	Scherwin	DEN	11.7.76	3	WAF	Stuttgart	9 Sep 06
		(40)							
64.83		Liz	Gleadle	CAN	5.12.88	1		Kawasaki	10 May 15

Mark	Wind	Name		Nat	Born	Pos	Meet	Venue	Date
64.75		Brittany	Borman	USA	1.7.89	2		Kawasaki	10 May 15
64.62		Joanna	Stone	AUS	4.10.72	2		Gold Coast (RB)	5 Aug 00
64.62		Nikolett	Szabó	HUN	3.3.80	1		Pátra	22 Jul 01
64.61		Oksana	Makarova	RUS	21.7.71	2	ECp	Paris (C)	19 Jun 99
64.56		Margaryta	Dorozhon	UKR/ISR	4.9.87	1	Bisl	Oslo	11 Jun 15
64.53		Kelsey-Lee	Roberts	AUS	21.9.91	2	WK	Zürich	24 Aug 17
64.51		Monica	Stoian	ROU	25.8.82	4	WCh	Berlin	18 Aug 09
64.49		Valeriya	Zabruskova	RUS	29.7.75	1	Znam	Tula	7 Jun 03
64.47		Anete	Kocina	LAT	5.2.96	2	EU23	Bydgoszcz	16 Jul 17
		(50)	100th woman 62.23, 200th 59.23, 300th 57.36						

Drugs dq: 70.78 Abakumova 2 OG Beijing 21 Aug 08

Ancillary marks – other marks during series (to 68.90)

71.25	Abakumova	2 Sep 11	69.32	Abakumova	21 Aug 08	68.95	Obergföll	8 Sep 11
69.42	Menéndez	7 Aug 01	69.22	Spotáková	21 Aug 08	Spec. changed from 1 May 1999.		
69.35	Abakumova	25 Aug 13	69.08	Abakumova	21 Aug 08			

WOMEN All-time

HEPTATHLON

Mark	Wind	Name		Nat	Born	Pos	Meet	Venue		Date
7291 WR		Jackie	Joyner-Kersee	USA	3.3.62	1	OG	Seoul		24 Sep 88
		12.69/0.5	1.86 15.80		22.56/1.6		7.27/0.7	45.66	2:08.51	
7215 WR			Joyner-Kersee			1	NC/OT	Indianapolis		16 Jul 88
		12.71/-0.9	1.93 15.65		22.30/ 0.0		7.00/-1.3	50.08	2:20.70	
7158 WR			Joyner-Kersee			1	USOF	Houston		2 Aug 86
		13.18/-0.5	1.88 15.20		22.85/1.2		7.03w/2.9	50.12	2:09.69	
7148 WR			Joyner-Kersee			1	GWG	Moskva		7 Jul 86
		12.85/0.2	1.88 14.76		23.00/0.3		7.01/-0.5	49.86	2:10.02	
7128			Joyner-Kersee			1	WCh	Roma		1 Sep 87
		12.91/0.2	1.90 16.00		22.95/1.2		7.14/0.9	45.68	2:16.29	
7044			Joyner-Kersee			1	OG	Barcelona		2 Aug 92
		12.85/-0.9	1.91 14.13		23.12/0.7		7.10/1.3	44.98	2:11.78	
7032		Carolina	Klüft	SWE	2.2.83	1	WCh	Osaka		26 Aug 07
		13.15/0.1	1.95 14.81		23.38/0.3		6.85/1.0	47.98	2:12.56	
7013		Nafissatou	Thiam	BEL	19.8.94	1	Hypo	Götzis		28 May 17
		13.34/-0.7	1.98 14.51		24.40/-1.6		6.56/0.8	59.32	2:15.24	
7007		Larisa	Nikitina ¶	RUS	29.4.65	1	NC	Bryansk		11 Jun 89
		13.40/1.4	1.89 16.45		23.97/1.1		6.73w/4.0	53.94	2:15.31	
7001			Klüft			1	WCh	Saint-Denis		24 Aug 03
		13.18/-0.4	1.94 14.19		22.98/1.1		6.68/1.0	49.90	2:12.12	
6985		Sabine	Braun	GER	19.6.65	1		Götzis		31 May 92
		13.11/-0.4	1.93 14.84		23.65/2.0		6.63w/2.9	51.62	2:12.67	
6979			Joyner-Kersee			1	NC	San José		24 Jun 87
		12.90/2.0	1.85 15.17		23.02/0.4		7.25/2.3	40.24	2:13.07	
6955		Jessica	Ennis-Hill	GBR	28.1.86	1	OG	London (OS)		4 Aug 12
		12.54/1.3	1.86 14.28		22.83/-0.3		6.48/-0.6	47.49	2:08.65	
6952			Klüft			1	OG	Athína		21 Aug 04
		13.21/0.2	1.91 14.77		23.27/-0.1		6.78/0.4	48.89	2:14.15	
6946 WR		Sabine	Paetz'	GDR	16.10.57	1	NC	Potsdam		6 May 84
		12.64/0.3	1.80 15.37		23.37/0.7		6.86/-0.2	44.62	2:08.93	
6942		Ghada	Shouaa	SYR	10.9.72	1		Götzis		26 May 96
		13.78/0.3	1.87 15.64		23.78/0.6		6.77/0.6	54.74	2:13.61	
6935 WR		Ramona	Neubert	GDR	26.7.58	1	v USSR	Moskva		19 Jun 83
		13.42/1.7	1.82 15.25		23.49/0.5		6.79/0.7	49.94	2:07.51	
6910			Joyner			1	MSR	Walnut		25 Apr 86
		12.9/0.0	1.86 14.75		23.24w/2.8		6.85/2.1	48.30	2:14.11	
6906			Ennis			1		Götzis		27 May 12
		12.81/0.0	1.85 14.51		22.88/1.9		6.51/0.8	47.11	2:09.00	
6897			John'			2	wOG	Seoul		24 Sep 88
		12.85/0.5	1.80 16.23		23.65/1.6		6.71/ 0.0	42.56	2:06.14	
6889		Eunice	Barber (10)	FRA	17.11.74	1		Arles		5 Jun 05
		12.62w/2.9	1.91 12.61		24.12/1.2		6.78w/3.4	53.07	2:14.66	
6887			Klüft			1	WCh	Helsinki		7 Aug 05
		13.19/-0.4	1.82 15.02		23.70/-2.5		6.87/0.2	47.20	2:08.89	
6878			Joyner-Kersee			1	NC	New York		13 Jun 91
		12.77	1.89 15.62		23.42		6.97/0.4	43.28	2:22.12	
6875			Nikitina			1	ECp-A	Helmond		16 Jul 89
		13.55/-2.1	1.84 15.99		24.29/-2.1		6.75/-2.5	56.78	2:18.67	
6861			Barber			1	WCh	Sevilla		22 Aug 99
		12.89/-0.5	1.93 12.37		23.57/0.5		6.86/-0.3	49.88	2:15.65	
6859		Natalya	Shubenkova	RUS	25.9.57	1	NC	Kyiv		21 Jun 84
		12.93/1.0	1.83 13.66		23.57/-0.3		6.73/0.4	46.26	2:04.60	

Mark Wind	Name		Nat	Born	Pos	Meet	Venue	Date
6858	Anke	Vater/Behmer	GDR	5.6.61	3	OG	Seoul	24 Sep 88
	13.20/0.5	1.83	14.20	23.10/1.6	6.68/0.1		44.54	2:04.20
6847		Nikitina			1	WUG	Duisburg	29 Aug 89
	13.47	1.81	16.12	24.12	6.66		59.28	2:22.07
6845 WR		Neubert			1	v URS	Halle	20 Jun 82
	13.58/1.8	1.83	15.10	23.14/1.4	6.84w/2.3		42.54	2:06.16
6845	Irina	Belova ¶	RUS	27.3.68	2	OG	Barcelona	2 Aug 92
	13.25/-0.1	1.88	13.77	23.34/0.2	6.82/0.0		41.90	2:05.08
	(30/13)							
6836	Carolin	Schäfer	GER	5.12.91	2	Hypo	Götzis	28 May 17
	13.09/1.0	1.86	14.76	23.36/0.7	6.57/0.9		49.80	2:14.73
6832	Lyudmila	Blonska ¶	UKR	9.11.77	2	WCh	Osaka	26 Aug 07
	13.25/0.1	1.92	14.44	24.09/0.3	6.88/1.0		47.77	2:16.68
6831	Denise	Lewis	GBR	27.8.72	1		Talence	30 Jul 00
	13.13/1.0	1.84	15.07	24.01w/3.6	6.69/-0.4		49.42	2:12.20
6815	Laura	Ikauniece-Admidina	LAT	31.5.92	3	Hypo	Götzis	28 May 17
	13.10/1.0	1.77	13.53	23.49/-2.9	6.64/0.8		56.17	2:11.76
6808	Brianne	Theisen-Eaton	CAN	18.12.88	1	Hypo	Götzis	31 May 15
	13.05/-0.2	1.89	13.73	23.34/1.4	6.72/0.9		42.96	2:09.37
6803	Jane	Frederick	USA	7.4.52	1		Talence	16 Sep 84
	13.27/1.2	1.87	15.49	24.15/1.6	6.43/0.2		51.74	2:13.55
6778	Nataliya	Dobrynska 20)	UKR	29.5.82	2	EC	Barcelona	31 Jul 10
	13.59/-1.6	1.86	15.88	24.23/-0.2	6.56/0.3		49.25	2:12.06
6768w	Tatyana	Chernova ¶	RUS	29.1.88	1		Arles	3 Jun 07
	13.04w/6.1	1.82	13.57	23.59w/5.2	6.61/1.2		53.43	2:15.05
6765	Yelena	Prokhorova	RUS	16.4.78	1	NC	Tula	23 Jul 00
	13.54/-2.8	1.82	14.30	23.37/-0.2	6.72/1.0		43.40	2:04.27
6750		Ma Miaolan	CHN	18.1.70	1	NG	Beijing	12 Sep 93
	13.28/1.5	1.89	14.98	23.86/	6.64/		45.82	2:15.33
6741	Heike	Drechsler	GER	16.12.64	1		Talence	11 Sep 94
	13.34/-0.3	1.84	13.58	22.84/-1.1	6.95/1.0		40.64	2:11.53
6735(w)	Hyleas	Fountain	USA	14.1.81	1	NC	Des Moines	26 Jun 10
	12.93w/2.6	1.90	13.73	23.28w/3.3	6.79w/2.7		42.26	2:17.80
6703	Tatyana	Blokhina	RUS	12.3.70	1		Talence	11 Sep 93
	13.69/-0.6	1.91	14.94	23.95/-0.4	5.99/-0.3		52.16	2:09.65
6702	Chantal	Beaugeant ¶	FRA	16.2.61	2		Götzis	19 Jun 88
	13.10/1.6	1.78	13.74	23.96w/3.5	6.45/0.2		50.96	2:07.09
6695	Jane	Flemming	AUS	14.4.65	1	CG	Auckland	28 Jan 90
	13.21/1.4	1.82	13.76	23.62w/2.4	6.57/1.6		49.28	2:12.53
6691	Katarina	Johnson-Thompson	GBR	9.1.93	4	Hypo	Götzis	28 May 17
	13.29/1.2	1.95	12.72	22.81/-2.9	6.53/0.7		39.98	2:11.12
6683	Jennifer	Oeser	GER	29.11.83	3	EC	Barcelona	31 Jul 10
	13.37/-1.0	1.83	13.82	24.07/-0.3	6.68/-0.3		49.17	2:12.28
	(30)							
6681	Kristina	Savitskaya	RUS	10.6.91	1	NC	Cheboksary	3 Jun 12
	13.52/0.0	1.88	15.27	24.61/0.0	6.65/0.0		46.83	2:14.73
6660	Ines	Schulz	GDR	10.7.65	3		Götzis	19 Jun 88
	13.56/0.4	1.84	13.95	23.93w/2.8	6.70/0.7		42.82	2:06.31
6658	Svetla	Dimitrova ¶	BUL	27.1.70	2		Götzis	31 May 92
	13.41/-0.7	1.75	14.72	23.06w/2.4	6.64/1.9		43.84	2:09.60
6649	Lilli	Schwarzkopf	GER	28.8.83	2	OG	London (OS)	4 Aug 12
	13.26/0.9	1.83	14.77	24.77/0.9	6.30/-0.7		51.73	2:10.50
6646	Natalya	Grachova	UKR	21.2.52	1	NC	Moskva	2 Aug 82
	13.80	1.80	16.18	23.86	6.65w/3.5		39.42	2:06.59
6636	Anouk	Vetter	NED	4.2.93	3	WCh	London (OS)	6 Aug 17
	13.31/0.0	1.77	15.09	24.36/-0.4	6.32/-1.0		58.41	2:19.43
6635	Sibylle	Thiele	GDR	6.3.65	2	GWG	Moskva	7 Jul 86
	13.14/0.6	1.76	16.00	24.18	6.62/1.0		45.74	2:15.30
6635	Svetlana	Buraga	BLR	4.9.65	3	WCh	Stuttgart	17 Aug 93
	12.95/0.1	1.84	14.55	23.69/0.0	6.58/-0.2		41.04	2:13.65
6633	Natalya	Roshchupkina	RUS	13.1.78	2	NC	Tula	23 Jul 00
	14.05/-2.8	1.88	14.28	23.47/-0.2	6.45/0.4		44.34	2:07.93
6623	Judy	Simpson'	GBR	14.11.60	3	EC	Stuttgart	30 Aug 86
	13.05/0.8	1.92	14.73	25.09/0.0	6.56w/2.5		40.92	2:11.70
	(40)							
6619	Liliana	Nastase	ROU	1.8.62	4	OG	Barcelona	2 Aug 92
	12.86/-0.9	1.82	14.34	23.70/0.2	6.49/-0.3		41.30	2:11.22
6616	Malgorzata	Nowak'	POL	9.2.59	1	WUG	Kobe	31 Aug 85
	13.27w/4.0	1.95	15.35	24.20/0.0	6.37w/3.9		43.36	2:20.39
6604	Remigija	Nazaroviene'	LTU	2.6.67	2	URSCh	Bryansk	11 Jun 89
	13.26/1.4	1.86	14.27	24.12/0.7	6.58/0.9		40.94	2:09.98

Mark	Wind	Name		Nat	Born	Pos	Meet	Venue		Date
6604		Irina	Tyukhay	RUS	14.1.67	3		Götzis		28 May 95
		13.20/-0.7	1.84 14.97		24.33/1.7	6.71/0.5		43.84	2:17.64	
6599A		Jessica	Zelinka	CAN	3.9.81	1	NC	Calgary		28 Jun 12
		12.76/-0.6	1.77 14.74		23.42w/2.1	5.98w/2.9		46.60	2:08.95	
6599		Austra	Skujyté	LTU	12.8.79	33	OG	London (OS)		4 Aug 12
		14.00/0.7	1.92 17.31		25.43/0.9	6.25/-0.6		51.13	2:20.59	
6598		Svetlana	Moskalets	RUS	22.1.69	1	NC	Vladimir		17 Jun 94
		13.20/0.8	1.82 13.78		23.56/0.1	6.74/0.8		42.48	2:14.54	
6594		Yorgelis	Rodríguez	CUB	25.1.95	4	WCh	London (OS)		6 Aug 17
		13.60/-0.3	1.95 13.45		24.42/-0.4	6.23/-0.6		47.41	2:10.48	
6591		Svetlana	Sokolova	RUS	9.1.81	1	NC	Tula		23 Jun 04
		13.56/1.1	1.82 15.09		24.02/0.6	6.26/0.3		45.07	2:07.23	
6586		Anna	Melnychenko	UKR	24.4.83	1	WCh	Moskva		13 Aug 13
		13.29/-0.6	1.86 13.85		23.87/0.0	6.49/0.2		41.87	2:09.85	
		(50)	100th woman 6423, 200th 6223, 300th 6102, 400th 6021, 500th 5938							

Drugs disqualification

Mark	Wind	Name		Nat	Born	Pos	Meet	Venue		Date
6880		Tatyana	Chernova ¶	RUS	29.1.88	(1)	WCh	Daegu		30 Aug 11
		13.32/0.9	1.83 14.17		23.50/-1.5	6.61/-0.7		52.95	2:08.04	
6618		Lyudmyla	Yosypenko ¶	UKR	24.9.84	4	OG	London (OS)		4 Aug 12
		13.25/0.9	1.83 13.90		23.68/0.6	6.31/-0.6		49.63	2:13.28	

DECATHLON

Mark	Name		Nat	Born	Pos	Venue	Date
8358 WR	Austra	Skujyte	LTU	12.8.79	1	Columbia, MO	15 Apr 05
	12.49/1.6 46.19 3.10	48.78 57.19	14.22w/2.4	6.12/1.6	16.42 1.78	5:15.86	
8150	Marie	Collonvillé	FRA	23.11.73	1	Talence	26 Sep 04
	12.48/0.4 34.69 3.50	47.19 56.15	13.96/0.4	6.18/1.0	11.90 1.80	5:06.09	

4 x 100 METRES RELAY

Mark	Nat	Team	Pos	Meet	Venue	Date
40.82 WR	USA	Madison (-Bartoletta), Felix, Knight, Jeter	1	OG	London (OS)	10 Aug 12
41.01	USA	Bartoletta, Felix, Gardner, Bowie	1	OG	Rio de Janeiro	19 Aug 16
41.07	JAM	Campbell-Brown, Morrison, Thompson, Fraser-Pryce	1	WCh	Beijing	29 Aug 15
41.29	JAM	Russell, Stewart, Calvert, Fraser-Pryce	1	WCh	Moskva	18 Aug 13
41.36	JAM	C.Williams, Thompson, Campbell-Brown, Fraser-Pryce	2	OG	Rio de Janeiro	19 Aug 16
41.37 WR	GDR	Gladisch, Rieger, Auerswald, Göhr	1	WCp	Canberra	6 Oct 85
41.41	JAM	Fraser-Pryce, Simpson, Campbell-Brown, Stewart	2	OG	London (OS)	10 Aug 12
41.47	USA	Gaines, Jones, Miller, Devers	1	WCh	Athína	9 Aug 97
41.49	RUS	Bogoslovskaya, Malchugina, Voronova, Privalova	1	WCh	Stuttgart	22 Aug 93
41.49	USA	Finn, Torrence, Vereen, Devers	2	WCh	Stuttgart	22 Aug 93
41.52	USA	Gaines, Jones, Miller, Devers	1h1	WCh	Athína	8 Aug 97
41.53 WR	GDR	Gladisch, Koch, Auerswald, Göhr	1		Berlin	31 Jul 83
41.55	USA	Brown, Williams, Griffith, Marshall	1	ISTAF	Berlin	21 Aug 87
41.56	USA	B Knight, Felix, Myers, Jeter	1	WCh	Daegu	4 Sep 11
41.58	USA	Brown, Williams, Griffith, Marshall	1	WCh	Roma	6 Sep 87
41.58	USA	L.Williams, Felix, Lee, Jeter	1		Cottbus	8 Aug 09
41.60 WR	GDR	Müller, Wöckel, Auerswald, Göhr	1	OG	Moskva	1 Aug 80
41.60	JAM	Simpson, Morrison, Thompson, Fraser-Pryce	1	WK	Zürich	3 Sep 15
41.61A	USA	Brown, Williams, Cheeseborough, Ashford	1	USOF	USAF Academy	3 Jul 83
41.62	GER	Pinto, Mayer, Lückenkemper, Haase	1		Mannheim	29 Jul 16
41.63	USA	Brown, Williams, Cheeseborough, Ashford	1	v GDR	Los Angeles	25 Jun 83
41.64	USA	Madison, Tarmoh, Knight, L Williams	1h1	OG	London (OS)	9 Aug 12
41.65	USA	Brown, Bolden, Cheeseborough, Ashford	1	OG	Los Angeles	11 Aug 84
41.65	GDR	Gladisch, Koch, Auerswald, Göhr	1	ECp	Moskva	17 Aug 85
41.65	JAM	C.Williams, Thompson, Facey, Campbell-Brown	1	WK	Zürich	1 Sep 16
		(25 performances by 4 nations) from here just best by nation				
41.77	GBR	Philip, Henry, Asher-Smith, Neita	3	OG	Rio de Janeiro	19 Aug 16
41.78	FRA	Girard, Hurtis, Félix, Arron	1	WCh	Saint-Denis	30 Aug 03
41.92	BAH	Fynes, Sturrup, Davis-Thompson, Ferguson	1	WCh	Sevilla	29 Aug 99
42.03	TTO	Baptiste, Ahye, Thomas, Hackett	3	WCh	Beijing	29 Aug 15
42.04	UKR	Povh, Stuy, Ryemyen, Bryzgina	3	OG	London (OS)	10 Aug 12
42.04	NED	Samuel, Schippers, van Schagen, Sedney (10)	1	EC	Amsterdam 10 Jul 16	42.08mx
BUL		Pavlova, Nuneva, Georgieva, Ivanova	mx		Sofia	8 Aug 84
		42.29 Pencheva, Nuneva, Georgieva, Donkova	1		Sofia	26 Jun 88
42.23	CHN	(Sichuan) Xiao Lin, Li Yali, Liu Xiaomei, Li Xuemei	1	NG	Shanghai	23 Oct 97
42.29	BRA	E dos Santos, Silva, Krasucki, R Santos	2h3	WCh	Moskva	18 Aug 13
42.39	NGR	Utondu, Idehen, Opara-Thompson, Onyali	2h2	OG	Barcelona	7 Aug 92
42.50	SUI	Del Ponte, Atcho, Kambundji, Kora	3h1	WCh	London (OS)	12 Aug 17
42.54	BEL	Borlée, Mariën, Ouédraogo, Gevaert	2	OG	Beijing	22 Aug 08
42.56	BLR	Nesterenko, Sologub, Nevmerzhitskaya, Dragun	3	WCh	Helsinki	13 Aug 05
42.59	FRG	Possekel, Helten, Richter, Kroniger	2	OG	Montreal	31 Jul 76
42.60	CAN	Emmanuel, Hyacinthe, Fofanah, Bingham	3h1	WCh	Beijing	29 Aug 15

Mark Wind Name Nat Born Pos Meet Venue Date

Mark	Wind	Nat	Name	Pos	Meet	Venue	Date
42.67		GHA	Owusu-Agyapong, Acheampong, Gyaman, Amponsah	1		Cape Coast	8 Jul 16
		(20)					
42.68		POL	Popowicz, Korczynska, Jeschke, Wedler	3	EC	Barcelona	1 Aug 10
42.89		CUB	Ferrer, López, Duporty, Allen	6	WCh	Stuttgart	22 Aug 93
42.92		KAZ	Kashafutdinova, Zyabkina, Rakhmanova, Safronova	1		Almaty	4 Jul 16
42.98		CZE/TCH	Sokolová, Soborová, Kocembová, Kratochvilová	1	WK	Zürich	18 Aug 82
42.99A		AUS	Massey, Broadrick, Lambert, Gainsford-Taylor	1		Pietersburg	18 Mar 00
43.03A		COL	M.Murillo, Palacios, Obregón, D Murillo	2	SAm-r	Bogotá	10 Jul 04
43.04		ITA	Pistone, Calí, Arcioni, Alloh	3	ECp-S	Annecy	21 Jun 08
43.07		GRE	Tsóni, Kóffa, Vasarmídou, Thánou	2	MedG	Bari	18 Jun 97
43.25A		RSA	Hartman, Moropane, Holtshausen, Seyerling	2		Pietersburg	18 Mar 00
43.28		DOM	M Sánchez, Chala, Mejía, Manzueta (30)	5h1	WCh	Moskva	18 Aug 13
Best at low altitude							
43.03		COL	M.Murillo, Palacios, Obregón, N.González	3h2	WCh	Helsinki	12 Aug 05
43.18		AUS	Wilson, Wells, Robertson, Boyle	5	OG	Montreal	31 Jul 76
One or more athlete susbsequently drugs dq							
41.67		USA	A Williams, Jones ¶, L Williams, Colander	(1)	3-N	München	8 Aug 04
41.67		USA	A Williams, Jones ¶, L Williams, Colander	(1h1)	OG	Athína	26 Aug 04

4 x 200 METRES RELAY

Mark	Wind	Nat	Name	Pos	Meet	Venue	Date
1:27.46	WR	USA Blue	Jenkins, Colander-Richardson, Perry, M Jones	1	PennR	Philadelphia	29 Apr 00
1:28.15	WR	GDR	Göhr, R.Müller, Wöckel, Koch	1		Jena	9 Aug 80
1:28.77		Tumbleweed, TC	Henry GBR, Onuora GBR, Bartoletta USA, Schippers NED	1	FlaR	Gainesville	1 Apr 17
1:28.78		Un of Oregon USA	Dunmore, Cunliffe, Stevens, Washington	2	FlaR	Gainesville	1 Apr 17
1:29.04		JAM	Levy, Jackson, Forbes, Thompson	1	W.Rly	Nassau	22 Apr 17
1:29.42		Texas A & M (USA)	Tarmoh, Mayo, Beard, Lucas	1	Penn R	Philadelphia	24 Apr 10
1:29.45		USA	Solomon, Meadows, Knight, K Duncan	1	WRly	Nassau	25 May 14
1:29.61		GBR	Henry, A Onuora, B Williams, A Philip	2	WRly	Nassau	25 May 14
Drugs dq:		1:29.40 USA Red	Colander, Gaines, Miller, M Jones ¶	1	Penn	Philadelphia	24 Apr 04

4 x 400 METRES RELAY

Mark	Wind	Nat	Name	Pos	Meet	Venue	Date
3:15.17	WR	URS		1	OG	Seoul	1 Oct 88
			Ledovskaya 50.12, O.Nazarova 47.82, Pinigina 49.43, Bryzgina 47.80				
3:15.51		USA		2	OG	Seoul	1 Oct 88
			D.Howard 49.82, Dixon 49.17, Brisco 48.44, Griffith Joyner 48.08				
3:15.92	WR	GDR	G.Walther 49.8, Busch 48.9, Rübsam 49.4, Koch 47.8	1	NC	Erfurt	3 Jun 84
3:16.71		USA	Torrence 49.0, Malone 49.4, Kaiser-Brown 49.48, Miles 48.78	1	WCh	Stuttgart	22 Aug 93
3:16.87		GDR	Emmelmann 50.9, Busch 48.8, Müller 48.9, Koch 48.21	1	EC	Stuttgart	31 Aug 86
3:16.87		USA	Trotter 50.3, Felix 48.1, McCorory 49.39, Richards-Ross 49.10	1	OG	London (OS)	11 Aug 12
3:17.83		USA	Dunn 50.5, Felix 48.8, Demus 50.14, Richards 48.44	1	WCh	Berlin	23 Aug 09
3:18.09		USA	Richards-Ross 49.3, Felix 49.4, Beard 49.84, McCorory 49.52	1	WCh	Daegu	3 Sep 11
3:18.29		USA		1	OG	Los Angeles	11 Aug 84
			Leatherwood 50.50, S.Howard 48.83, Brisco-Hooks 49.23, Cheeseborough 49.73				
3:18.29		GDR	Neubauer 50.58, Emmelmann 49.89, Busch 48.81, Müller 48.99	3	OG	Seoul	1 Oct 88
3:18.38		RUS		2	WCh	Stuttgart	22 Aug 93
			Ruzina 50.8, Alekseyeva 49.3, Ponomaryova 49.78, Privalova 48.47				
3:18.43		URS	Ledovskaya 51.7, Dzhigalova 49.2, Nazarova 48.87, Bryzgina 48.67	1	WCh	Tokyo	1 Sep 91
3:18.54		USA	Wineberg 51.0, Felix 48.6, Henderson 50.06, Richards 48.93	1	OG	Beijing	23 Aug 08
3:18.55		USA	Trotter 51.2, Felix 48.0, Wineberg 50.24, Richards 49.07	1	WCh	Osaka	2 Sep 07
3:18.58		URS	I.Nazarova, Olizarenko, Pinigina, Vladykina	1	ECp	Moskva	18 Aug 85
3:18.63		GDR	Neubauer 51.4, Emmelmann 49.1, Müller 48.64, Busch 49.48	1	WCh	Roma	6 Sep 87
3:18.71		JAM	Whyte 50.0, Prendergast 49.6, Williams-Mills 49.84, Williams 49.22	2	WCh	Daegu	3 Sep 11
3:19.01		USA	Trotter 49.8, Henderson 49.7, Richards 49.81, Hennagan 49.73	(1)	OG	Athína	28 Aug 04
			Note team was disqualified as Crystal Cox (subject of retrospective drugs ban) ran for them in the heat				
3.19.02		USA	Hayes 50.4, Felix 48.7, Wimbley 49.58, Francis 50.28	1	WCh	London (OS)	13 Aug 17
3:19.04	WR	GDR	Siemon' 51.0, Busch 50.0, Rübsam 50.2, Koch 47.9	1	EC	Athína	11 Sep 82
3.19.02		USA	Hayes 50.4, Felix 48.7, Wimbley 49.58, Francis 50.28	1	WCh	London (OS)	13 Aug 17
3:19.06		USA	Okolo 50.3, Hastings 49.2, Francis 49.82, Felix 49.66	1	OG	Rio de Janeiro	20 Aug 16
3:19.12		URS	Baskakova, I.Nazarova, Pinigina, Vladykina	1	Drz	Praha	18 Aug 84
3:19.23	WR	GDR	Maletzki 50.05, Rohde 49.00, Streidt 49.51, Brehmer 49.79	1	OG	Montreal	31 Jul 76
3:19.49		GDR	Emmelmann, Busch, Neubauer, Koch 47.9	1	WCp	Canberra	4 Oct 85
		(25/5 with USSR and Russia counted separately)					
3:20.04		GBR	Ohuruogu 50.6, Okoro 50.9, McConnell 49.79, Sanders 48.76	3	WCh	Osaka	2 Sep 07
3:20.32		CZE/TCH		2	WCh	Helsinki	14 Aug 83
			Kocembová 48.93, Matejkovicová 52.13, Moravcíková 51.51, Kratochvílová 47.75				
3:21.04		NGR	Afolabi 51.13, Yusuf 49.72, Opara 51.29, Ogunkoya 48.90	2	OG	Atlanta	3 Aug 96
3:21.21		CAN	Crooks 50.30, Richardson 50.22, Killingbeck ¶ 50.62, Payne 50.07	2	OG	Los Angeles	11 Aug 84
3:21.88		BLR	Yushchenko 51.40, Khlyustova 50.7, I Usovich 49.97, S Usovich 49.78	5	WCh	Osaka	2 Sep 07
		(10)					
3:21.94		UKR	Dzhigalova, Olizarenko, Pinigina, Vladykina	1	URS Ch	Kyiv	17 Jul 86

Mark	Nat	Team	Pos	Meet	Venue	Date
3:22.34	FRA	Landre 51.3, Dorsile 51.1, Elien 50.54, Pérec 49.36	1	EC	Helsinki	14 Aug 94
3:22.49	FRG	Thimm 50.81, Arendt 49.95, Thomas 51.50, Abt 50.23	4	OG	Seoul	1 Oct 88
3:23.21	CUB	Díaz 51.1, Calatayud 51.2, Clement 50.47, Terrero 50.46	6	OG	Beijing	23 Aug 08
3:23.81	AUS	Peris-K 51.71, Lewis 51.69, Gainsford-T 51.06, Freeman 49.35	4	OG	Sydney	30 Sep 00
3:24.28	CHN (Hebei)	An X, Bai X, Cao C, Ma Y	1	NG	Beijing	13 Sep 93
3:24.49	POL	Guzowska 52.2, Bejnar 50.2, Prokopek 50.47, Jesien 51.59	4	WCh	Helsinki	14 Aug 05
3:25.16	ITA	Chigbolu 52.1, Spacca 51.3, Folorunso 51.44, Grenot 50.18	4h2	OG	Rio de Janeiro	19 Aug 16
3:25.68	ROU	Ruicu 52.69, Rîpanu 51.09, Barbu 52.64, Tîrlea 49.26	2	ECp	Paris (C)	20 Jun 99
3:25.7a	FIN	Eklund 53.6, Pursiainen 50.6, Wilmi 51.6, Salin 49.9	2	EC	Roma	8 Sep 74
	(20)					
3:25.81	BUL	Ilieva, Stamenova, Penkova, Damyanova	1	v Hun,Pol	Sofia	24 Jul 83
3:26.33	GRE	Kaidantzi 53.2, Goudenoúdi 51.6, Boudá 51.76, Halkiá 49.75	3	ECpS	Bydgoszcz	20 Jun 04
3:26.36	BAH	L Clarke 52.4, Strachan 51.9, Cox 50.91, Amertil 51.07	6h2	OG	Rio de Janeiro	19 Aug 16
3:26.68	BRA (Bovespa)	Coutinho, de Oliveira, Sousa, de Lima	1	NC	São Paulo	7 Aug 11
3:26.89	IND	R Kaur 53.1, Beenamol 51.4, Soman 52.51, M Kaur 49.85	3h2	OG	Athína	27 Aug 04
3.26.90	BOT	Botlogetswe 52.5, Jele 51.0, Moroko 52.12, Montsho 51.25	3h1	WCh	London (OS)	12 Aug 17
3:26.98	NED	Ghafoor 52.4, Lisanne de Witte 51.0, van Leuveren 50.99, Laura de Witte 52.49	6h1	OG	Rio de Janeiro	19 Aug 16
3:27.08	CMR	Nguimgo 51.7, Kaboud 52.1, Atangana 51.98, Béwouda 51.35	7	WCh	Saint-Denis	31 Aug 03
3:27.14	MEX	Rodríguez 53.3, Medina 51.2, Vela 52.94, Guevara 49.70	4h2	WCh	Osaka	1 Sep 07
3:27.48	IRL	Andrews 53.4, Cuddihy 49.9, Bergin 52.60, Carey 51.54	4h3	WCh	Daegu	2 Sep 11

Drugs disqualification

Mark	Nat	Team	Pos	Meet	Venue	Date
3:18.82	RUS	Gushchina 50.6, Litvinova 49.2, Firova 49.20, Kapachinskaya 49.82	(2)	OG	Beijing	23 Aug 08
3:19.36	RUS	Krivoshapka 50.3, Antyukh 50.0, Litvinova 49.96, Kapachinskaya ¶ 49.22	(3)	WCh	Daegu	3 Sep 11
3:21.85	BLR	Kozak 52.0, Khlyustova 50.3, I Usovich 49.85, S Usovich 49.69	(4)	OG	Beijing	23 Aug 08

4 x 800 METRES RELAY

Mark	Nat	Team	Pos	Meet	Venue	Date
7:50.17 WR	USSR	Olizarenko, Gurina, Borisova, Podyalovskaya	1		Moskva	5 Aug 84
7:51.62	USSR II	Ruchayeva, Agletdinova, Zvagintseva, Zhukova	2		Moskva	5 Aug 84
7:52.24	USSR	Podkopayeva, Zvyagintseva, Olizarenko, Agletdinova	1		Leningrad	4 Aug 85
7:52.3 WR	USSR	Providokhina 1:58.4, Gerasimova 1:59.2, Styrkina 1:57.3, Kazankina ¶ 1:57.4	1		Podolsk	16 Aug 76
7:54.10 WR	GDR	Zinn, Hoffmeister, Weiss, Klapezynski	1	NC	Karl-Marx-Stadt	6 Aug 76
8:00.62	USA	Price 2:01.30, Vessey 2:00.92, Ludlow 1:59.50, Montaño 1:58.90	1	WRly	Nassau	3 May 15

4 x 1500 METRES RELAY

Mark	Nat	Team	Pos	Meet	Venue	Date
16:33.58 WR	KEN	M Cherono 4:07.5, Kipyegon 4:08.5, Jelagat 4:10.5, Obiri 4:07.1	1	WRly	Nassau	24 May 14
16:55.33	USA	Kampf 4:09.2, Mackey, Grace, Martinez 4:10.2	2	WRly	Nassau	24 May 14
17:08.65	AUS	Buckman 4:08.1, Delaney 4:15.5, McGowan, Duncan 4:16.0	3	WRly	Nassau	25 May 14

5000 METRES WALK (TRACK)

Mark		Name	Nat	Born	Pos	Meet	Venue	Date
20:01.80 WR	Eleonora	Giorgi	ITA	14.9.89	1		Misterbianco	18 May 14
20:02.60 WR	Gillian	O'Sullivan	IRL	21.8.76	1	NC	Dublin (S)	13 Jul 02
20:03.0 WR	Kerry	Saxby-Junna	AUS	2.6.61	1		Sydney	11 Feb 96
20:07.52 WR	Beate	Anders/Gummelt	GDR	4.2.68	1	vURS	Rostock	23 Jun 90
20:11.45	Sabine	Zimmer/Krantz	GER	6.2.81	1	NC	Wattenscheid	2 Jul 05
20:12.41	Elisabetta	Perrone	ITA	9.7.68	1	NC	Rieti	2 Aug 03
20:15.71	Lyudmyla	Olyanovska ¶	UKR	20.2.93	1		Kyiv	4 Jun 14
20:18.87	Melanie	Seeger	GER	8.1.77	1	NC	Braunschweig	10 Jul 04
20:21.69	Annarita	Sidoti	ITA	25.7.69	1	NC	Cesenatico	1 Jul 95
20:27.59 WR	Ileana	Salvador	ITA	16.1.62	1		Trento	3 Jun 89

10 KILOMETRES WALK

Mark		Name	Nat	Born	Pos	Meet	Venue	Date
41:04 WR	Yelena	Nikolayeva	RUS	1.2.66	1	NC	Sochi	20 Apr 96
41:16		Wang Yan	CHN	3.5.71	1		Eisenhüttenstadt	8 May 99
41:16	Kjersti	Plätzer (Tysse)	NOR	18.1.72	1	NC	Os	11 May 02
41:17	Irina	Stankina	RUS	25.3.77	1	NC-w	Adler	9 Feb 97
41:24	Olimpiada	Ivanova ¶	RUS	26.8.70	2	NC-w	Adler	9 Feb 97
41:29 WR	Larisa	Ramazanova	RUS	23.9.71	1	NC	Izhevsk	4 Jun 95
41:30 WR	Kerry	Saxby-Junna	AUS	2.6.61	1	NC	Canberra	27 Aug 88
41:30		O Ivanova			2	NC	Izhevsk	4 Jun 95
41:31	Yelena	Gruzinova	RUS	24.12.67	2	NC	Sochi	20 Apr 96
41:37.9t		Gao Hongmiao	CHN	17.3.74	1	NC	Beijing	7 Apr 94
41:38	Rossella	Giordano (10)	ITA	1.12.72	1		Naumburg	25 May 97
41:41		Nikolayeva			2		Naumburg	25 May 97
41:41		Tysse Plätzer			1		Kraków	30 May 09
41:42	Olga	Kaniskina ¶	RUS	19.1.85	2		Kraków	30 May 09
41:42.5t	Lyudmyla	Olyanovska ¶	UKR	20.2.93	1		Mukachevo	1 Nov 14
41:45		Liu Hongyu	CHN	11.1.75	2		Eisenhüttenstadt	8 May 99

Mark	Wind	Name		Nat	Born	Pos	Meet	Venue	Date
41:46		Annarita	Sidoti	ITA	25.7.69	1		Livorno	12 Jun 94
41:46			O Ivanova			1	NC/w	Adler	11 Feb 96
41:47			Saxby-Junna			1		Eisenhüttenstadt	11 May 96
41:48		(20/15)	Li Chunxiu	CHN	13.8.69	1	NG	Beijing	8 Sep 93
41:50		Yelena	Arshintseva	RUS	5.4.71	1	NC-w	Adler	11 Feb 95
41:51		Beate	Anders/Gummelt	GER	4.2.68	2		Eisenhüttenstadt	11 May 96
41:52		Tatyana	Mineyeva ¶	RUS	10.8.90	1	NCp-j	Penza	5 Sep 09
41:52		Tatyana	Korotkova	RUS	24.4.80	1		Buy	19 Sep 10
41:53		Tatyana	Sibileva	RUS	17.5.80	1	RWC-F	Beijing	18 Sep 10
		(20)							
41:56		Yelena	Sayko	RUS	24.12.67	2	NC/w	Adler	11 Feb 96
41:56.23t		Nadezhda	Ryashkina	RUS	22.1.67	1	GWG	Seattle	24 Jul 90
41:57.29t		Antonella	Palmisano	ITA	6.8.91	1		Orvieto	23 Apr 17
41:59		Marina	Pandakova	RUS	1.3.89	1		Podolsk	8 May 16
42:01		Tamara	Kovalenko	RUS	5.6.64	3	NC-w	Adler	11 Feb 95
42:01		Olga	Panfyorova	RUS	21.8.77	1	NC-23	Izhevsk	16 May 98
42:03		Lina	Bikulova	RUS	1.10.88	1		Bui	13 Sep 14
42:04+		Vera	Sokolova ¶	RUS	8.6.87	1=	in 20k	Sochi	26 Feb 11
42:04+		Anisya	Kirdyapkina	RUS	23.10.89	1=	in 20k	Sochi	26 Feb 11
42:04+		Tatyana	Shemyakina	RUS	3.9.87	1=	in 20k	Sochi	26 Feb 11
		(30)							
42:05+		Margarita	Turova	BLR	28.12.80	1+	in 20k	Adler	12 Mar 05
42:06		Valentina	Tsybulskaya	BLR	19.2.68	4		Eisenhüttenstadt	8 May 99
42:07		Ileana	Salvador	ITA	16.1.62	1		Sesto San Giovanni	1 May 92
42:09		Elisabetta	Perrone	ITA	9.7.68	4		Eisenhüttenstadt	11 May 96
42:11		Nina	Alyushenko	RUS	29.5.68	3	NC	Izhevsk	4 Jun 95
42:12+		Elmira	Alembekova ¶	RUS	30.6.90	1	in 20k	Sochi	27 Feb 15
42:12+		Svetlana	Vasilyeva	RUS	24.7.92	3	in 20k	Sochi	27 Feb 15
42:13		Natalya	Misyulya	BLR	16.4.66	5		Eisenhüttenstadt	8 May 99
42:13.7t		Madelein	Svensson	SWE	20.7.69	2	SGP	Fana	15 May 92
42:14.12t		Raquel	González	ESP	16.11.89	1	NC	Gijón	23 Jul 16
		(40)	50th woman 42:29, 100th 43:02.3, 200th 43:51.6, 300th 44:26, 400th 44:51.8						

Best track times

Mark	Wind	Name		Nat	Born	Pos	Meet	Venue	Date
41:57.22		Kerry	Saxby-Junna	AUS	2.6.61	2	GWG	Seattle	24 Jul 90
42:11.5		Beate	Anders/Gummelt	GER	4.2.68	1	SGP	Fana	15 May 92

20 KILOMETRES WALK

Mark	Wind	Name		Nat	Born	Pos	Meet	Venue	Date
1:24:38 WR			Liu Hong	CHN	12.5.87	1		La Coruña	6 Jun 15
1:24:47		Elmira	Alembekova ¶	RUS	30.6.90	1	NC-w	Sochi	27 Feb 15
1:24:50		Olimpiada	Ivanova ¶	RUS	26.8.70	1	NC-w	Adler	4 Mar 01
1:24:56		Olga	Kaniskina ¶	RUS	19.1.85	1	NC-w	Adler	28 Feb 09
1:24:58		Yelena	Lashmanova ¶	RUS	9.4.92	1	NC	Cheboksary	25 Jun 16
1:25:02 WR			Lashmanova			1	OG	London	11 Aug 12
1:25:03		Marina	Pandakova	RUS	1.3.89	2	NC-w	Sochi	27 Feb 15
1:25:04		Svetlana	Vasilyeva	RUS	24.7.92	3	NC-w	Sochi	27 Feb 15
1:25:08 WR		Vera	Sokolova	RUS	8.6.87	1	NC-w	Sochi	26 Feb 11
1:25:09		Anisya	Kirdyapkina ¶	RUS	23.10.89	2	NC-w	Sochi	26 Feb 11
1:25:11			Kaniskina			1	NC-w	Adler	23 Feb 08
1:25:11			Kirdyapkina			1	NC-w	Sochi	20 Feb 10
1:25:12			Lu Xiuzhi (10)	CHN	26.10.93	1	WCT	Beijing	20 Mar 15
1:25:16			Qieyang Shenjie	CHN	11.11.90	2	OG	London	11 Aug 12
1:25:18		Tatyana	Gudkova	RUS	23.1.78	1	NC	Moskva	19 May 00
1:25:18			Lashmanova			1	NC-w	Sochi	18 Feb 17
1:25:20		Olga	Polyakova	RUS	23.9.80	2	NC	Moskva	19 May 00
1:25:22		Yekaterina	Medvedyeva	RUS	29.3.94	2	NC-w	Sochi	18 Feb 17
1:25:26			Sokolova			2	NC-w	Adler	28 Feb 09
1:25:26			Kirdyapkina			3	NC-w	Adler	28 Feb 09
1:25:27			Alembekova			1	NC-w	Sochi	18 Feb 12
1:25:29		Irina	Stankina	RUS	25.3.77	3	NC	Moskva	19 May 00
1:25:30			Kirdyapkina			2	NC-w	Adler	23 Feb 08
1:25:32		Yelena	Shumkina ¶	RUS	24.1.88	4	NC-w	Adler	28 Feb 09
1:25:35			Sokolova			2	NC-w	Sochi	20 Feb 10
1:25:38			Sokolova			4	NC-w	Sochi	27 Feb 15
1:25:41 WR			Ivanova			1	WCh	Helsinki	7 Aug 05
1:25:42			Kaniskina			1	WCp	Cheboksary	11 May 08
1:25:46		Tatyana	Shemyakina	RUS	3.9.87	3	NC-w	Adler	23 Feb 08
1:25:46			Liu Hong			1		Taicang	30 Mar 12
		(30/18)							
1:25:52		Larisa	Yemelyanova	RUS	6.1.80	5	NC-w	Adler	28 Feb 09
1:25:52		Tatyana	Sibileva	RUS	17.5.80	3	NC-w	Sochi	20 Feb 10

Mark	Wind	Name		Nat	Born	Pos	Meet	Venue	Date
1:25:59		Tamara	Kovalenko	RUS	5.6.64	4	NC	Moskva	19 May 00
		(20)							
1:26:11		Margarita	Turova	BLR	28.12.80	1	NC	Nesvizh	15 Apr 06
1:26:14		Irina	Petrova	RUS	26.5.85	2	NC-w	Adler	19 Feb 06
1:26:16		Lyudmila	Arkhipova	RUS	25.11.78	5	NC-w	Adler	23 Feb 08
1:26:17		Eleonora	Giorgi	ITA	14.9.89	2	ECp	Murcia	17 May 15
1:26:17		María Guadalupe	González	MEX	9.1.89	1	WCp	Roma	7 May 16
1:26:18			Yang Jiayu	CHN	18.2.96	1	WCh	London	13 Aug 17
1:26:22	WR		Wang Yan	CHN	3.5.71	1	NG	Guangzhou	19 Nov 01
1:26:22	WR	Yelena	Nikolayeva	RUS	1.2.66	1	ECp	Cheboksary	18 May 03
1:26:23			Wang Liping	CHN	8.7.76	2	NG	Guangzhou	19 Nov 01
1:26:27		Sofiya	Brodatskaya	RUS	4.10.95	3	NC-w	Sochi	18 Feb 17
		(30)							
1:26:28		Iraida	Pudovkina	RUS	2.11.80	1	NC-w	Adler	12 Mar 05
1:26:29			Wang Na	CHN	29.5.95	2	NGP	Huangshan	4 Mar 17
1:26:34		Tatyana	Kalmykova	RUS	10.1.90	1	NC	Saransk	8 Jun 08
1:26:35			Liu Hongyu	CHN	11.1.75	3	NG	Guangzhou	19 Nov 01
1:26:36		Antonella	Palmisano	ITA	6.8.91	3	WCh	London	13 Aug 17
1:26:46			Song Hongjuan	CHN	4.7.84	1	NC	Guangzhou	20 Mar 04
1:26:46		Mariya	Ponomaryova	RUS	18.6.95	3	NC	Cheboksary	25 Jun 16
1:26:47		Irina	Yumanova ¶	RUS	6.11.90	3	NC-w	Sochi	18 Feb 12
1:26:47		Klavdiya	Afanasyeva	RUS	15.1.96	4	NC	Cheboksary	25 Jun 16
1:26:50		Natalya	Fedoskina	RUS	25.6.80	2	ECp	Dudince	19 May 01
		(40)							
1:26:53		Anezka	Drahotová	CZE	22.7.95	4	ECp	Murcia	17 May 15
1:26:57		Lyudmila	Yefimkina	RUS	22.8.81	3	NC-w	Adler	19 Feb 06
1:26:59		Erica	de Sena	BRA	3.5.85	4	WCh	London	13 Aug 17
1:27:07		Kjersti	Tysse Plätzer	NOR	18.1.72	2	OG	Beijing	21 Aug 08
1:27:09		Elisabetta	Perrone	ITA	9.7.68	3	ECp	Dudince	19 May 01
1:27:09		Lyudmyla	Olyanovska ¶	UKR	20.2.93	7	ECp	Murcia	17 May 15
1:27:12		Elisa	Rigaudo	ITA	17.6.80	3	OG	Beijing	21 Aug 08
1:27:14		Antonina	Petrova	RUS	1.5.77	1	NC-w	Adler	1 Mar 03
1:27:18		Alena	Nartova	RUS	1.1.82	6	NC-w	Adler	23 Feb 08
1:27:19			Jiang Jing	CHN	23.10.85	1	NC	Nanning	25 Feb 05
		(50)	100th best woman 1:28:38, 200th 1:30:31, 300th 1:31:51, 400th 1:33:09						
Drugs dq: 1:25:09			Kaniskina			(2)	OG	London	11 Aug 12
1:27:08		Anna	Lukyanova ¶	RUS	23.4.91	(5)	NC-w	Sochi	18 Feb 12

50 KILOMETRES WALK

Mark	Name		Nat	Born	Pos	Meet	Venue	Date
4:05:56	Inês	Henriques	POR	1.5.80	1	WCh	London	13 Aug 17
4:08:26		Henriques			1		Porto de Mós	15 Jan 17
4:08:58		Yin Hang	CHN	7.2.97	2	WCh	London	13 Aug 17
4:10:59	Monica	Svensson	SWE	26.12.78	1		Scanzorosciate	21 Oct 07
4:12:16	Yelena	Ginko	BLR	30.7.76	1		Scanzorosciate	17 Oct 04
4:14:27		Svensson			1		Scanzorosciate	18 Oct 09
4:15:42	Mayra Carolina	Herrera	GUA	20.12.88	1		Owego	9 Sep 17
4:16:27	Jolanta	Dukure	LAT	20.9.79	1		Paralepa	9 Sep 06
4:17:29		Svensson			1		Scanzorosciate	15 Oct 06
4:18:53		Ginko			1		Scanzorosciate	19 Oct 08
4:19:13		Ginko			1		Scanzorosciate	27 Oct 02
4:20:49		Yang Shuqing	CHN	30.8.96	3	WCh	London	13 Aug 17
4:21:51	Kathleen	Burnett	USA	10.7.88	4	WCh	London	13 Aug 17
4:22:00		Ginko			1		Scanzorosciate	19 Oct 03
4:22:20		Svensson			2		Scanzorosciate	19 Oct 08
4:22:22		Yin Hang			1	NGP	Huangshan	5 Mar 17
4:25:22	Brigita	Virbalyte-Dimsiene	LTU	1.2.85	1		Villa di Serio	17 Oct 10
4:26:37		Burnett			1	NC	Santee	28 Jan 17
4:27:24		Yang Shuqing			2	NGP	Huangshan	5 Mar 17
4:28:13	Evaggelía	Xinoú	GRE	22.11.81	2		Scanzorosciate	17 Oct 04
	(20/10)							
4:28:53	Neringa	Aidietyté	LTU	5.6.83	1		Ivano-Frankivsk	1 Oct 06
4:28:59	Kora	Boufflért	FRA	23.4.66	1		Charly-sur-Marne	18 Feb 07
4:29:33	Erin	Talcott'	USA	21.5.78	2	NC	Santee	28Jan 17
4:29:56	Natalia	Bruniko	ITA	23.2.73	2		Scanzorosciate	27 Oct 02
4:32:14		Jiang Shanshan	CHN	28.2.97	3	NGP	Huangshan	5 Mar 17
4:32:14	Khrystyna	Yudkina	UKR	4.12.84	1	NC	Ivano-Frankivsk	15 Oct 17
4:32:25	Lyudmyla	Shelest	UKR	4.10.74	3		Scanzorosciate	18 Oct 09
4:33:45	Lyudmila	Yegorova	UKR	4.10.74	3		Scanzorosciate	17 Oct 04
4:34:01		Zhou Kang	CHN	24.12.89	1	NGP	Huangshan	6 Mar 16
4:34:49	Kseniya	Radko	UKR	18.8.94	2	NC	Ivano-Frankivsk	15 Oct 17
	(20)							

WOMEN All-time

JUNIOR MEN'S ALL-TIME LISTS

100 METRES

Mark	Wind	Name		Nat	Born	Pos	Meet	Venue	Date
9.97	1.8	Trayvon	Bromell	USA	10.7.95	1	NCAA	Eugene	13 Jun 14
10.00	1.6	Trentavis	Friday	USA	5.6.95	1h1	NC-j	Eugene	5 Jul 14
10.01	0.0	Darrel	Brown	TTO	11.10.84	1q3	WCh	Saint-Denis	24 Aug 03
10.01	1.6	Jeffery	Demps	USA	8.1.90	2q1	NC/OT	Eugene	28 Jun 08
10.01	0.9	Yoshihide	Kiryu	JPN	15.12.95	1h3	Oda	Hiroshima	29 Apr 13
10.03	0.7	Marcus	Rowland	USA	11.3.90	1	PAm-J	Port of Spain	31 Jul 09
10.04	1.7	DeAngelo	Cherry	USA	1.8.90	1h4	NCAA	Fayetteville	10 Jun 09
10.04	0.2	Christoph	Lemaitre	FRA	11.6.90	1	EJ	Novi Sad	24 Jul 09
10.04	1.9	Abdullah Abkar	Mohammed	KSA	.97	1	MSR	Norwalk	15 Apr 16
10.05		Davidson	Ezinwa	NGR	22.11.71	1		Bauchi	4 Jan 90
10.05	0.1	Adam	Gemili	GBR	6.10.93	1	WJ	Barcelona	11 Jul 12
10.05	0.6	Abdul Hakim	Sani Brown	JPN	6.3.99	1	NC	Osaka	24 Jun 17

Wind assisted to 10.02

Mark	Wind	Name		Nat	Born	Pos	Meet	Venue	Date
9.77	4.2	Trayvon	Bromell	USA	10.7.95	1	Big 12	Lubbock	18 May 14
9.83	7.1	Leonard	Scott	USA	19.1.80	1		Knoxville	9 Apr 99
9.96	4.5	Walter	Dix	USA	31.1.86	1rA	TexR	Austin	9 Apr 05
9.96	5.0	André	De Grasse	CAN	10.11.94	1	JUCO	Hutchinson, KS	18 May 13
9.97	??	Mark	Lewis-Francis	GBR	4.9.82	1q3	WCh	Edmonton	4 Aug 01
9.98	5.0	Tyreek	Hill	USA	1.3.94	2	JUCO	Hutchinson, KS	18 May 13
10.02	2.8	DeAngelo	Cherry	USA	1.8.90	1h2	NC-j	Eugene	26 Jun 09
10.02	2.4	Marcus	Rowland	USA	11.3.90	1	NC-j	Eugene	26 Jun 09

200 METRES

Mark	Wind	Name		Nat	Born	Pos	Meet	Venue	Date
19.93	1.4	Usain	Bolt	JAM	21.8.86	1		Hamilton, BER	11 Apr 04
20.04	0.1	Ramil	Guliyev	AZE	29.5.90	1	WUG	Beograd	10 Jul 09
20.07	1.5	Lorenzo	Daniel	USA	23.3.66	1	SEC	Starkville	18 May 85
20.09	1.6	Noah	Lyles	USA	18.7.97	4	NC/OT	Eugene	9 Jul 16
20.10A	1.7	Clarence	Munyai	RSA	20.2.98	2		Pretoria	4 Mar 17
20.13	1.7	Roy	Martin	USA	25.12.66	1		Austin	11 May 85
20.14	1.8	Tyreek	Hill	USA	1.3.94	1		Orlando	26 May 12
20.14	1.6	Michael	Norman	USA	3.12.97	5	NC/OT	Eugene	9 Jul 16
20.16A	-0.2	Riaan	Dempers	RSA	4.3.77	1	NC-j	Germiston	7 Apr 95
20.18	1.0	Walter	Dix	USA	31.1.86	1s2	NCAA	Sacramento	9 Jun 05
20.20A	0.5	Tlotliso Gift	Leotlela	RSA	12.5.98	3	NC	Potchefstroom	22 Apr 17
20.21A	1.4	Baboloki	Thebe	BOT	18.3.97	1	NC-j	Gaborone	22 May 16

Wind assisted to 20.16

Mark	Wind	Name		Nat	Born	Pos	Meet	Venue	Date
19.86	4.0	Justin	Gatlin	USA	10.2.82	1h2	NCAA	Eugene	30 May 01
20.01	2.5	Derald	Harris	USA	5.4.58	1		San José	9 Apr 77
20.03	2.9	Trentavis	Friday	USA	5.6.95	1	NC-j	Eugene	6 Jul 14
20.04	3.3	Noah	Lyles	USA	18.7.97	1h1	NC/OT	Eugene	7 Jul 16
20.06	2.8	Michael	Norman	USA	3.12.97	1h4	NC/OT	Eugene	7 Jul 16
20.07	3.4	Maxwell	Willis	USA	2.9.98	1h1	Big 12	Lawrence	13 May 17
20.08	9.2	Leonard	Scott	USA	19.1.80	2r2		Knoxville	9 Apr 99
20.10	4.6	Stanley	Kerr	USA	19.6.67	2r2	SWC	Houston	18 May 86
20.16	5.2	Nickel	Ashmeade	JAM	4.7.90	1	Carifta	Basseterre	24 Mar 08

400 METRES

Mark	Name		Nat	Born	Pos	Meet	Venue	Date
43.87	Steve	Lewis	USA	16.5.69	1	OG	Seoul	28 Sep 88
44.22A	Baboloki	Thebe	BOT	18.3.97	1	NC-j	Gaborone	21 May 16
44.25	Karabo	Sibanda	BOT	2.7.98	5	OG	Rio de Janeiro	14 Aug 16
44.27	Abdelilah	Haroun	QAT	1.1.97	2		La Chaux-de-Fonds	5 Jul 15
44.36	Kirani	James	GRN	1.9.92	1	WK	Zürich	8 Sep 11
44.66	Hamdam Odha	Al-Bishi	KSA	5.5.81	1	WJ	Santiago de Chile	20 Oct 00
44.66	LaShawn	Merritt	USA	27.6.86	1		Kingston	7 May 05
44.69	Darrell	Robinson	USA	23.12.63	2	USOF	Indianapolis	24 Jul 82
44.71A	Luguelín	Santos	DOM	12.11.93	2	PAm	Guadalajara	26 Oct 11
44.73A	James	Rolle	USA	2.2.64	1	USOF	USAF Academy	2 Jul 83
44.75	Darren	Clark	AUS	6.9.65	4	OG	Los Angeles	8 Aug 84
44.75	Deon	Minor	USA	22.1.73	1s1	NCAA	Austin	5 Jun 92

800 METRES

Mark	Name		Nat	Born	Pos	Meet	Venue	Date
1:41.73	Nijel	Amos	BOT	15.3.94	2	OG	London (OS)	9 Aug 12
1:42.37	Mohammed	Aman	ETH	10.1.94	1	VD	Bruxelles	6 Sep 13
1:42.53	Timothy	Kitum	KEN	20.11.94	3	OG	London (OS)	9 Aug 12
1:42.69	Abubaker	Kaki	SUD	21.6.89	1	Bisl	Oslo	6 Jun 08
1:43.13	Abraham Kipchirchir	Rotich	KEN	26.6.93	1	Herc	Monaco	20 Jul 12
1:43.40	Leonard	Kosencha	KEN	21.8.94	2	Herc	Monaco	20 Jul 12
1:43.55	Donavan	Brazier	USA	15.4.97	1	NCAA	Eugene	10 Jun 16

Mark	Wind	Name		Nat	Born	Pos	Meet	Venue	Date
1:43.56		Robert	Biwott	KEN	28.1.96	2		Barcelona	8 Jul 15
1:43.64		Japheth	Kimutai	KEN	20.12.78	3rB	WK	Zürich	13 Aug 97
1:43.76		Kipyegon	Bett	KEN	2.1.98	2	ISTAF	Berlin	3 Sep 16
1:43.81		Edwin	Melly	KEN	24.3.94	2		Rieti	9 Sep 12

1000 METRES

Mark	Wind	Name		Nat	Born	Pos	Meet	Venue	Date
2:13.93		Abubaker	Kaki	SUD	21.6.89	1	DNG	Stockholm	22 Jul 08
2:15.00		Benjamin	Kipkurui	KEN	28.12.80	5	Nik	Nice	17 Jul 99
2:16.84		Ali	Hakimi	TUN	24.4.76	1		Lindau	28 Jul 95

1500 METRES

Mark	Wind	Name		Nat	Born	Pos	Meet	Venue	Date
3:28.81		Ronald	Kwemoi	KEN	19.9.95	3	Herc	Monaco	18 Jul 14
3:30.10		Robert	Biwott	KEN	28.1.96	7	Herc	Monaco	17 JUl 15
3:30.24		Cornelius	Chirchir	KEN	5.6.83	4	Herc	Monaco	19 Jul 02
3:31.13		Mulugueta	Wondimu	ETH	28.2.85	2rA	NA	Heusden	31 Jul 04
3:31.42		Alex	Kipchirchir	KEN	26.11.84	5	VD	Bruxelles	5 Sep 03
3:31.54		Isaac	Songok	KEN	25.4.84	1	NA	Heusden	2 Aug 03
3:31.64		Asbel	Kiprop	KEN	30.6.89	1	GGala	Roma	11 Jul 08
3:31.70		William	Biwott	KEN	5.3.90	3	GGala	Roma	10 Jul 09
3:32.02		Caleb	Ndiku	KEN	9.10.92	4	FBK	Hengelo	29 May 11
3:32.48		Augustine	Choge	KEN	21.1.87	1	ISTAF	Berlin	3 Sep 06
3:32.68		Abdelaati	Iguider	MAR	25.3.87	5	VD	Bruxelles	25 Aug 06
3:32.91		Noah	Ngeny	KEN	2.11.78	9	Herc	Monaco	16 Aug 97

1 MILE

Mark	Wind	Name		Nat	Born	Pos	Meet	Venue	Date
3:49.29		William	Biwott	KEN	5.3.90	2	Bisl	Oslo	3 Jul 09
3:49.77		Caleb	Ndiku	KEN	9.10.92	5	Pre	Eugene	4 Jun 11
3:50.25		Alex	Kipchirchir	KEN	26.11.84	2	GP II	Rieti	7 Sep 03
3:50.39		James	Kwalia	KEN	12.6.84	1	FBK	Hengelo	1 Jun 03
3:50.41		Noah	Ngeny	KEN	2.11.78	2	Nik	Nice	16 Jul 97
3:50.69		Cornelius	Chirchir	KEN	5.6.83	5	GGala	Roma	12 Jul 02
3:50.83		Nicholas	Kemboi	KEN	18.12.89	6	Bisl	Oslo	6 Jun 08

2000 METRES

Mark	Wind	Name		Nat	Born	Pos	Meet	Venue	Date
4:56.25		Tesfaye	Cheru	ETH	2.3.93	1		Reims	5 Jul 11
4:56.86		Isaac	Songok	KEN	25.4.84	6	ISTAF	Berlin	31 Aug 01
4:58.18		Soresa	Fida	ETH	27.5.93	4		Reims	5 Jul 11
4:58.76		Jairus	Kipchoge	KEN	15.12.92	7		Reims	5 Jul 11

3000 METRES

Mark	Wind	Name		Nat	Born	Pos	Meet	Venue	Date
7:28.19		Yomif	Kejelcha	ETH	1.8.97	1	DL	Saint-Denis	27 Aug 16
7:28.78		Augustine	Choge	KEN	21.1.87	2	SGP	Doha	13 May 05
7:29.11		Tariku	Bekele	ETH	21.1.87	2	GP	Rieti	27 Aug 06
7:30.36		Hagos	Gebrhiwet	ETH	11.5.94	1	DL	Doha	10 May 13
7:30.43		Isiah	Koech	KEN	19.12.93	1	DNG	Stockholm	17 Aug 12
7:30.67		Kenenisa	Bekele	ETH	13.6.82	2	VD	Bruxelles	24 Aug 01
7:30.91		Eliud	Kipchoge	KEN	5.11.84	2	VD	Bruxelles	5 Sep 03
7:32.37		Abreham	Cherkos	ETH	23.9.89	2	Athl	Lausanne	11 Jul 06
7:32.72		John	Kipkoech	KEN	29.12.91	4		Rieti	29 Aug 10
7:33.00		Hailu	Mekonnen	ETH	4.4.80	2		Stuttgart	6 Jun 99
7:33.01		Levy	Matebo	KEN	3.11.89	2	GP	Rieti	7 Sep 08

5000 METRES

Mark	Wind	Name		Nat	Born	Pos	Meet	Venue	Date
12:47.53		Hagos	Gebrhiwet	ETH	11.5.94	2	DL	Saint-Denis	6 Jul 12
12:48.64		Isiah	Koech	KEN	19.12.93	3	DL	Saint-Denis	6 Jul 12
12:52.61		Eliud	Kipchoge	KEN	5.11.84	3	Bisl	Oslo	27 Jun 03
12:53.66		Augustine	Choge	KEN	21.1.87	4	GGala	Roma	8 Jul 05
12:53.72		Philip	Mosima	KEN	2.1.77	2	GGala	Roma	5 Jun 96
12:53.81		Tariku	Bekele	ETH	21.1.87	4	GGala	Roma	14 Jul 06
12:53.98		Yomif	Kejelcha	ETH	1.8.97	1	VD	Bruxelles	11 Sep 15
12:54.07		Sammy	Kipketer	KEN	29.9.81	2	GGala	Roma	30 Jun 00
12:54.19		Abreham	Cherkos	ETH	23.9.89	5	GGala	Roma	14 Jul 06
12:54.58		James	Kwalia	KEN	12.6.84	5	Bisl	Oslo	27 Jun 03
12:55.58		Selemon	Barega	ETH	20.1.00	2	Athl	Lausanne	6 Jul 17
12:56.15		Daniel	Komen	KEN	17.5.76	2	GG	Roma	8 Jun 95

10,000 METRES

Mark	Wind	Name		Nat	Born	Pos	Meet	Venue	Date
26:41.75		Samuel	Wanjiru	KEN	10.11.86	3	VD	Bruxelles	26 Aug 05
26:55.73		Geoffrey	Kirui	KEN	16.2.93	6	VD	Bruxelles	16 Sep 11
26:57.56		Yigrem	Demelash	ETH	28.1.94	4	VD	Bruxelles	7 Sep 12
27:02.81		Ibrahim	Jeylan	ETH	12.6.89	4	VD	Bruxelles	25 Aug 06

Mark	Wind	Name		Nat	Born	Pos	Meet	Venue	Date
27:04.00		Boniface	Kiprop	UGA	12.10.85	5	VD	Bruxelles	3 Sep 04
27:04.45		Bernard	Kipyego	KEN	16.7.86	4	FBK	Hengelo	29 May 05
27:06.35		Geoffrey	Kipsang	KEN	28.11.92	10	Pre	Eugene	3 Jun 11
27:06.47		Habtanu	Fikadu	ETH	13.3.88	8	FBK	Hengelo	26 May 07
27:07.29		Moses	Masai	KEN	1.6.86	7	VD	Bruxelles	3 Sep 04
27:08.94		Andamlak	Belihu	ETH	20.11.98	10	WCh	London(OS)	4 Aug 17
27:09.92		Aron	Kifle	ERI	20.2.98	11	WCh	London (OS)	4 Aug 17
27:11.18		Richard	Chelimo	KEN	21.4.72	1	APM	Hengelo	25 Jun 91

HALF MARATHON

Mark	Wind	Name		Nat	Born	Pos	Meet	Venue	Date
59:16		Samuel	Wanjiru	KEN	10.11.86	1		Rotterdam	11 Sep 05
59:31		Geoffrey	Kipsang	KEN	28.11.92	2		New Delhi	27 Nov 11
59:36		Tilahun	Regassa	ETH	18.1.90	1		Lille	6 Sep 08
59:38		Faustin	Baha	TAN	30.5.82	4		Lisboa	26 Mar 00
59:51		Andamlak	Belihu	ETH	20.11.98	2		New Delhi	19 Nov 17
59:57		Eric	Ndiema	KEN	28.12.92	4		Den Haag	14 Mar 10
60:09		Ghirmay	Ghebrselassie	ERI	14.11.95	1		Paderborn	30 Mar 13
60:10		Jonathan	Maiyo	KEN	5.5.88	5		Rotterdam	9 Sep 07
60:22		Terefa	Deleba	ETH	20.4.98	2		Istanbul	30 Apr 17
60:30		Lawrence	Kiprotich	KEN	20.8.86	3	Stra	Milano	10 Apr 05

MARATHON

Mark	Wind	Name		Nat	Born	Pos	Meet	Venue	Date
2:04:32		Tsegaye	Mekonnen	ETH	15.6.95	1		Dubai	24 Jan 14
2:06:07		Eric	Ndiema	KEN	28.12.92	3		Amsterdam	16 Oct 11
2:06:15		Bazu	Worku	ETH	15.9.90	2		Paris	5 Apr 09
2:08:17		Edwin	Kibet	KEN	7.7.96	5		Eindhoven	11 Oct 15
2:08:51		Berhanu	Shiferaw	ETH	31.5.93	1		Taiyuan	2 Sep 12
2:08:53		Tola	Shira	ETH	9.6.96	3		Shanghai	8 Nov 15
2:09:08		Ghirmay	Gebrselassie	ERI	14.11.95	6		Chicago	12 Oct 14
2:09:12		Feyisa	Lilesa	ETH	1.2.90	1		Dublin	26 Oct 09
2:10:00		Samuel	Rutto	KEN	?.95	1		Torino	16 Nov 14
2:10:01		Ernest	Ngeno	KEN	20.5.95	2		Torino	16 Nov 14

3000 METRES STEEPLECHASE

Mark	Wind	Name		Nat	Born	Pos	Meet	Venue	Date
7:58.66		Stephen	Cherono	KEN	15.10.82	3	VD	Bruxelles	24 Aug 01
8:01.16		Conseslus	Kipruto	KEN	8.12.94	1	DL	Shanghai	18 May 13
8:03.74		Raymond	Yator	KEN	7.4.81	3	Herc	Monaco	18 Aug 00
8:05.52		Brimin	Kipruto	KEN	31.7.85	1	FBK	Hengelo	31 May 04
8:06.96		Gilbert	Kirui	KEN	22.1.94	2	DL	London (OS)	27 Jul 13
8:07.18		Moussa	Omar Obaid	QAT	18.4.85	4	OG	Athína	24 Aug 04
8:07.69		Paul	Kosgei	KEN	22.4.78	5	DNG	Stockholm	7 Jul 97
8:07.71		Hillary	Yego	KEN	2.4.92	3	DL	Shanghai	15 May 11
8:08.37		Amos	Kirui	KEN	9.2.98	4	GGala	Roma	8 Jun 17
8:09.37		Abel	Cheruiyot/Yugut	KEN	26.12.84	2	NA	Heusden	2 Aug 03
8:11.22		Yemane	Haileselassie	ERI	21.2.98	5	GGala	Roma	8 Jun 17
8:11.31		Jairus	Birech	KEN	15.12.92	5	DL	Saint Denis	8 Jul 11

110 METRES HURDLES (106cm)

Mark	Wind	Name		Nat	Born	Pos	Meet	Venue	Date
13.12	1.6		Liu Xiang	CHN	13.7.83	1rB	Athl	Lausanne	2 Jul 02
13.23	0.0	Renaldo	Nehemiah	USA	24.3.59	1r2	WK	Zürich	16 Aug 78
13.32	0.7	Dejour	Russell	JAM	1.4.00	4	NC	Kingston	24 Jun 17
13.40	-1.0		Shi Dongpeng	CHN	6.1.84	1	NC	Shanghai	14 Sep 03
13.44	-0.8	Colin	Jackson	GBR	18.2.67	1	WJ	Athína	19 Jul 86
13.46	1.8	Jon	Ridgeon	GBR	14.2.67	1	EJ	Cottbus	23 Aug 85
13.46	-1.6	Dayron	Robles	CUB	19.11.86	1	PAm-J	Windsor	29 Jul 05
13.47	1.9	Holger	Pohland	GDR	5.4.63	2	vUSA	Karl-Marx-Stadt	10 Jul 82
13.47	1.2	Aries	Merritt	USA	24.7.85	4	NCAA	Austin	12 Jun 04
13.47	0.2		Xie Wenjun	CHN	11.7.90	2	GP	Shanghai	20 Sep 08
13.49	0.6	Stanislav	Olijar	LAT	22.3.79	1		Valmiera	11 Jul 98
13.49	1.2	Booker	Nunley	USA	2.7.90	2	SEC	Gainesville	17 May 09

Wind assisted

Mark	Wind	Name		Nat	Born	Pos	Meet	Venue	Date
13.41	2.6	Dayron	Robles	CUB	19.11.86	2	CAC	Nassau	10 Jul 05
13.42	4.5	Colin	Jackson	GBR	18.2.67	2	CG	Edinburgh	27 Jul 86
13.42	2.6	Antwon	Hicks	USA	12.3.83	1	WJ	Kingston	21 Jul 02
13.47	2.1	Frank	Busemann	GER	26.2.75	1	WJ	Lisboa	22 Jul 94

99 cm Hurdles

Mark	Wind	Name		Nat	Born	Pos	Meet	Venue	Date
12.99	0.5	Wilhem	Belocian	FRA	22.6.95	1	WJ	Eugene	24 Jul 14
13.06	0.5	Tyler	Mason	JAM	15.1.95	2	WJ	Eugene	24 Jul 14
13.08	2.0	Wayne	Davis	USA	2.7.90	1	PAm-J	Port of Spain	31 Jul 09
13.14	1.6	Eddie	Lovett	USA	25.6.92	1	PAm-J	Miramar	23 Jul 11
13.17	-0.7	David	Omoregie	GBR	1.11.95	1	NC-j	Bedford	22 Jun 14

Mark	Wind	Name		Nat	Born	Pos	Meet	Venue	Date
13.18	1.0	Yordan	O'Farrill	CUB	9.2.93	1	WJ	Barcelona	12 Jul 12
13.20	0.6	Dejour	Russell	JAM	1.4.00	1s3	WJ	Bydgoszcz	20 Jul 16
13.21	1.5	Misana	Viltz	USA	21.2.96	1	NC-j	Eugene	25 Jun 15
Wind assisted to 13.20									
13.03	2.9	Eddie	Lovett	USA	25.6.92	1h1	PAm-J	Miramar	23 Jul 11
13.15	2.7	Brendan	Ames	USA	6.10.88	1	NC-j	Indianapolis	21 Jun 07
13.18		Arthur	Blake	USA	19.8.66	1	GWest	Sacramento	9 Jun 84
13.19	3.8	Chad	Zallow	USA	25.4.97	1		Greensboro	20 Jun 15
Hand timed: 12.9y		Renaldo	Nehemiah	USA	24.3.59	1		Jamaica, NY	30 May 77

400 METRES HURDLES

Mark	Wind	Name		Nat	Born	Pos	Meet	Venue	Date
48.02		Danny	Harris	USA	7.9.65	2s1	OT	Los Angeles	17 Jun 84
48.26		Jehue	Gordon	TTO	15.12.91	4	WCh	Berlin	18 Aug 09
48.51		Kerron	Clement	USA	31.10.85	1	WJ	Grosseto	16 Jul 04
48.52		Johnny	Dutch	USA	20.1.89	5	NC/OT	Eugene	29 Jun 08
48.62		Brandon	Johnson	USA	6.3.85	2	WJ	Grosseto	16 Jul 04
48.68		Bayano	Kamani	USA	17.4.80	1	NCAA	Boise	4 Jun 99
48.68		Jeshua	Anderson	USA	22.6.89	1	WJ	Bydgoszcz	11 Jul 08
48.72		Angelo	Taylor	USA	29.12.78	2	NCAA	Bloomington	6 Jun 97
48.74		Vladimir	Budko	BLR	4.2.65	2	DRZ	Moskva	18 Aug 84
48.76A		Llewellyn	Herbert	RSA	21.7.77	1		Pretoria	7 Apr 96
48.79		Kenneth	Ferguson	USA	22.3.84	1	SEC	Knoxville	18 May 03

HIGH JUMP

Mark	Wind	Name		Nat	Born	Pos	Meet	Venue	Date
2.37		Dragutin	Topic	YUG	12.3.71	1	WJ	Plovdiv	12 Aug 90
2.37		Steve	Smith	GBR	29.3.73	1	WJ	Seoul	20 Sep 92
2.36		Javier	Sotomayor	CUB	13.10.67	1		Santiago de Cuba	23 Feb 86
2.35i		Vladimir	Yashchenko	UKR	12.1.59	1	EI	Milano	12 Mar 78
		2.34				1	Prv	Tbilisi	16 Jun 78
2.35		Dietmar	Mögenburg	FRG	15.8.61	1		Rehlingen	26 May 80
2.34		Tim	Forsyth	AUS	17.8.73	1	Bisl	Oslo	4 Jul 92
2.33			Zhu Jianhua	CHN	29.5.63	1	AsiG	New Delhi	1 Dec 82
2.33		Patrik	Sjöberg	SWE	5.1.65	1	OsloG	Oslo	9 Jul 83
2.33		Maksim	Nedosekov	BLR	21.1.98	1	EJ	Grosseto	22 Jul 17
2.32i		Jaroslav	Bába	CZE	2.9.84	3		Arnstadt	8 Feb 03
2.32			Huang Haiqiang	CHN	8.2.88	1	WJ	Beijing	17 Aug 06

POLE VAULT

Mark	Wind	Name		Nat	Born	Pos	Meet	Venue	Date
5.90		Armand	Duplantis	SWE	10.11.99	1	TexR	Austin	1 Apr 17
5.80		Maksim	Tarasov	RUS	2.12.70	1	vGDR-j	Bryansk	14 Jul 89
5.80		Raphael	Holzdeppe	GER	28.9.89	2		Biberach	28 Jun 08
5.75		Konstadínos	Filippídis	GRE	26.11.86	2	WUG	Izmir	18 Aug 05
5.75		Chris	Nilsen	USA	13.1.98	3	NC	Sacramento	24 Jun 17
5.72		Andrew	Irwin	USA	23.1.93	1	SEC	Baton Rouge	13 May 12
5.71		Lawrence	Johnson	USA	7.5.74	1		Knoxville	12 Jun 93
5.71		Germán	Chiaraviglio	ARG	16.4.87	1	WJ	Beijing	19 Aug 06
5.71		Shawnacy	Barber	CAN	27.5.94	2	TexR	Austin	29 Mar 13
5.70		Viktor	Chistyakov	RUS	9.2.75	1		Leppävirta	7 Jun 94
5.70		Artyom	Kuptsov	RUS	22.4.84	1	Znam	Tula	7 Jun 03
5.70		Kurtis	Marschall	AUS	25.4.97	1		Mannheim	26 Jun 16
5.70i		Emmanouíl	Karalís	GRE	20.10.99	2	NC	Piréas	19 Feb 17
5.70		Vladyslav	Malykhin	UKR	15.1.98	1		Zary	27 May 17

LONG JUMP

Mark	Wind	Name		Nat	Born	Pos	Meet	Venue	Date
8.35	1.1	Sergey	Morgunov	RUS	9.2.93	1	NC-j	Cheboksary	19 Jun 12
8.34	0.0	Randy	Williams	USA	23.8.53	Q	OG	München	8 Sep 72
8.33	2.0	Maykel	Massó	CUB	8.5.99	1		Madrid	14 Jul 17
8.31	0.8		Shi Yuhao	CHN	26.9.98	1		Beijing	25 Jun 17
8.30	1.8	Miltiádis	Tentóglou	GRE	18.3.98	1	NC	Pátra	18 Jun 17
8.28	0.8	Luis Alberto	Bueno	CUB	22.5.69	1		La Habana	16 Jul 88
8.28	0.8	Juan Miguel	Echevarría	CUB	11.8.98	2		Madrid	14 Jul 17
8.27	1.7	Eusebio	Cáceres	ESP	10.9.91	Q	EC	Barcelona	30 Jul 10
8.25	0.9		Wang Jianan	CHN	27.8.96	3	DL	Shanghai	17 May 15
8.24	0.2	Eric	Metcalf	USA	23.1.68	1	NCAA	Indianapolis	6 Jun 86
8.24	1.8	Vladimir	Ochkan	UKR	13.1.68	1	vGDR-j	Leningrad	21 Jun 87
Wind assisted									
8.40	3.2	Kareem	Streete-Thompson	CAY	30.3.73	1		Houston	5 May 91
8.35	2.2	Carl	Lewis	USA	1.7.61	1	NCAA	Austin	6 Jun 80
8.34	2.3	Juan Miguel	Echevarría	CUB	11.8.98	1		Padova	16 Jul 17
8.29	2.3	James	Beckford	JAM	9.1.75	1		Tempe	2 Apr 94

Mark	Wind	Name		Nat	Born	Pos	Meet	Venue	Date
TRIPLE JUMP									
17.50	0.4	Volker	Mai	GDR	3.5.66	1	vURS	Erfurt	23 Jun 85
17.42	1.3	Khristo	Markov	BUL	27.1.65	1	Nar	Sofiya	19 May 84
17.40A	0.4	Pedro	Pérez	CUB	23.2.52	1	PAm	Cali	5 Aug 71
17.40	0.8	Ernesto	Revé	CUB	26.2.92	1		La Habana	10 Jun 11
17.31	-0.2	David	Girat Jr.	CUB	26.8.84	Q	WCh	Saint-Denis	23 Aug 03
17.30A	0.6	Jordan	Diaz	CUB	23.2.01	1	WY	Nairobi	14 Jul 17
17.29	1.3	James	Beckford	JAM	9.1.75	1		Tempe	2 Apr 94
17.27		Aliecer	Urrutia	CUB	22.9.74	1		Artemisa	23 Apr 93
17.27	1.6	Cristian	Nápoles	CUB	27.11.98	2	NC	La Habana	17 Mar 17
17.24	0.7	Lázaro	Martínez	CUB	3.11.97	2		La Habana	1 Feb 14
17.23	0.2	Yoelbi	Quesada	CUB	4.8.73	1	NC	La Habana	13 May 92
Wind assisted									
17.33	2.1	Teddy	Tamgho	FRA	15.6.89	1	WJ	Bydgoszcz	11 Jul 08
17.24	2.5	Will	Claye	USA	13.6.91	1	NCAA	Fayetteville	13 Jun 09
SHOT									
21.14		Konrad	Bukowiecki #	POL	17.3.97	2	Bisl	Oslo	9 Jun 16
21.05i		Terry	Albritton	USA	14.1.55	1	AAU	New York	22 Feb 74
		20.38				2	MSR	Walnut	27 Apr 74
20.83i		Jordan	Geist	USA	21.7.98	1		Greensburg	22 Dec 16
		20.62				1		Tucson	9 Dec 17
20.65		Mike	Carter	USA	29.10.60	1	vSU-j	Boston	4 Jul 79
20.54	?	Andrei	Toader	ROU	26.5.97	1	ROU IC	Pitesti	4 Jun 16
20.43		David	Storl	GER	27.7.90	2		Gerlingen	6 Jul 09
20.39		Janus	Robberts	RSA	10.3.79	1	NC	Germiston	7 Mar 98
20.38		Jacko	Gill	NZL	10.12.94	1		Auckland (NS)	5 Dec 11
20.20		Randy	Matson	USA	5.3.45	2	OG	Tokyo	17 Oct 64
20.20		Udo	Beyer	GDR	9.8.55	2	NC	Leipzig	6 Jul 74
6 kg Shot									
23.00		Jacko	Gill	NZL	10.12.94	1		Auckland	18 Aug 13
22.94		Konrad	Bukowiecki	POL	17.3.97	1	NC-j	Suwalki	3 Jul 16
		23.34 drugs dq				(1)	WJ	Bydgoszcz	19 Jul 16
22.73		David	Storl	GER	27.7.90	1		Osterode	14 Jul 09
22.30 dq?		Andrei	Toader	ROU	26.5.97	2	WJ	Bydgoszcz	19 Jul 16
22.02		Jordan	Geist	USA	21.7.98	1	PAm-J	Trujillo	23 Jul 17
21.96		Edis	Elkasevic	CRO	18.2.83	1	NC-j	Zagreb	29 Jun 02
21.90		John	Maurins	USA	3.8.96	1	NC-j	Eugene	25 Jun 15
21.79		Mustafa Amer	Ahmed	EGY	16.12.95	1	Arab	Cairo	23 Feb 14
21.78		Krzysztof	Brzozowski	POL	15.7.93	2	WJ	Barcelona	11 Jul 12
23.34 dq		Konrad	Bukowiecki	POL	17.3.97	1	WJ	Bydgoszcz	19 Jul 16
DISCUS									
65.62		Werner	Reiterer	AUS	27.1.68	1		Melbourne	15 Dec 87
65.31		Mykyta	Nesterenko	UKR	15.4.91	3		Tallinn	3 Jun 08
63.64		Werner	Hartmann	FRG	20.4.59	1	vFRA	Strasbourg	25 Jun 78
63.26		Sergey	Pachin	UKR	24.5.68	2		Moskva	25 Jul 87
63.22		Brian	Milne	USA	7.1.73	1		State College	28 Mar 92
62.58		Matthew	Denny	AUS	2.6.96	2	WUG	Gwangju	11 Jul 15
62.52		John	Nichols	USA	23.8.69	1		Baton Rouge	23 Apr 88
62.43		Martin	Markovic	CRO	13.1.96	1	NC-w	Split	8 Mar 15
62.36		Tulake	Nuermaimaiti	CHN	8.3.82	2	NG	Guangzhou	21 Nov 01
62.16		Zoltán	Kövágó	HUN	10.4.79	1		Budapest	9 May 97
1.75kg Discus									
70.13		Mykyta	Nesterenko	UKR	15.4.91	1		Halle	24 May 08
68.48		Martin	Markovic	CRO	13.1.96	1	NC-j	Varazdin	28 Jun 15
68.02		Bartlomiej	Stój	POL	15.5.96	1	EJ	Eskilstuna	19 Jul 15
67.32		Margus	Hunt	EST	14.7.87	1	WJ	Beijing	16 Aug 06
66.88		Traves	Smikle	JAM	7.5.92	1		Kingston	31 Mar 11
66.81		Matthew	Denny	AUS	2.6.96	1		Brisbane	23 Nov 14
66.45		Gordon	Wolf	GER	17.1.90	1		Halle	23 May 09
66.41		Roje	Stona	JAM	26.2.99	1	Carifta	Willemstad	15 Apr 17
66.27		Clemens	Prüfer	GER	13.8.97	1		Wiesbaden	15 May 16
65.88		Omar	El-Ghazaly	EGY	9.2.84	1		Cairo	7 Nov 03
HAMMER									
78.33		Olli-Pekka	Karjalainen	FIN	7.3.80	1	NC	Seinäjoki	5 Aug 99
78.14		Roland	Steuk	GDR	5.3.59	1	NC	Leipzig	30 Jun 78
78.00		Sergey	Dorozhon	UKR	17.2.64	1		Moskva	7 Aug 83
76.54		Valeriy	Gubkin	BLR	3.9.67	2		Minsk	27 Jun 86
76.42		Ruslan	Dikiy	TJK	18.1.72	1		Togliatti	7 Sep 91

Mark	Wind	Name		Nat	Born	Pos	Meet	Venue	Date
76.37		Ashraf Amjad	El-Seify	QAT	20.2.95	1		Doha	10 Apr 13
75.52		Sergey	Kirmasov	RUS	25.3.70	1		Kharkov	4 Jun 89
75.42		Szymon	Ziolkowski	POL	1.7.76	1	EJ	Nyíregyhazá	30 Jul 95
75.24		Christoph	Sahner	FRG	23.9.63	1	vPOL-j	Göttingen	26 Jun 82
6kg Hammer									
85.57		Ashraf Amjad	El-Seify	QAT-Y	20.2.95	1	WJ	Barcelona	14 Jul 12
82.97		Javier	Cienfuegos	ESP	15.7.90	1		Madrid	17 Jun 09
82.84		Quentin	Bigot	FRA	1.12.92	1		Bondoufle	16 Oct 11
82.64		Bence	Halász	HUN	4.8.97	1	NC-j	Szombathely	25 Jun 16
82.62		Yevgeniy	Aydamirov	RUS	11.5.87	1	NC-j	Tula	22 Jul 06
81.75		Hlib	Piskunov	UKR	25.11.98	1	EJ	Grosseto	21 Jul 17
81.73		Aleksandr	Shimanovich	BLR	9.2.98	1		Brest	28 Apr 17
81.34		Krisztián	Pars	HUN	18.2.82	1		Szombathely	2 Sep 01
81.16		Özkan	Baltaci	TUR	13.2.94	1		Ankara	31 Jul 13
81.15		Ákos	Hudi	HUN	10.8.91	1		Veszprém	7 Jul 10

JAVELIN

Mark	Wind	Name		Nat	Born	Pos	Meet	Venue	Date
86.48		Neeraj	Chopra	IND	24.12.97	1	WJ	Bydgoszcz	23 Jul 16
84.69		Zigismunds	Sirmais	LAT	6.5.92	2		Bauska	22 Jun 11
84.58		Keshorn	Walcott	TTO	2.4.93	1	OG	London (OS)	11 Aug 12
83.87		Andreas	Thorkildsen	NOR	1.4.82	1		Fana	7 Jun 01
83.55		Aleksandr	Ivanov	RUS	25.5.82	2	NC	Tula	14 Jul 01
83.07		Robert	Oosthuizen	RSA	23.1.87	1	WJ	Beijing	19 Aug 06
82.52		Harri	Haatainen	FIN	5.1.78	4		Leppävirta	25 May 96
82.52		Till	Wöschler	GER	9.6.91	1	WJ	Moncton	23 Jul 10
81.95		Jakub	Vadlejch	CZE	10.10.90	1		Domazlice	26 Sep 09
81.91		Patriks	Gailums	LAT	10.5.98	1		Valmiera	12 Jul 17
81.80		Sergey	Voynov	UZB	26.2.77	1		Tashkent	6 Jun 96

DECATHLON

Mark	Name		Nat	Born	Pos	Meet	Venue	Date
8397	Torsten	Voss	GDR	24.3.63	1	NC	Erfurt	7 Jul 82
	10.76 7.66 14.41 2.09 48.37 14.37 41.76 4.80 62.90 4:34.04							
8257	Yordani	García	CUB	21.11.88	8	WCh	Osaka	1 Sep 07
	10.73/0.7 7.15/0.2 14.94 2.09 49.25 14.08/-0.2 42.91 4.70 68.74 4:55.42							
8114	Michael	Kohnle	FRG	3.5.70	1	EJ	Varazdin	26 Aug 89
	10.95 7.09/0.1 15.27 2.02 49.91 14.40 45.82 4.90 60.82 4:49.43							
8104	Valter	Külvet	EST	19.2.64	1		Viimsi	23 Aug 81
	10.7 7.26 13.86 2.09 48.5 14.8 47.92 4.50 60.34 4:37.8							
8082	Daley	Thompson	GBR	30.7.58	1	ECp/s	Sittard	31 Jul 77
	10.70/0.8 7.54/0.7 13.84 2.01 47.31 15.26/2.0 41.70 4.70 54.48 4:30.4							
8041		Qi Haifeng	CHN	7.8.83	1	AsiG	Busan	10 Oct 02
	11.09/0.2 7.22/0.0 13.05 2.06 49.09 14.54/0.0 43.16 4.80 61.04 4:35.17							
8036	Christian	Schenk	GDR	9.2.65	5		Potsdam	21 Jul 84
	11.54 7.18 14.26 2.16 49.23 15.06 44.74 4.20 65.98 4:24.11							
7992	Kevin	Mayer	FRA	10.2.92	8		Kladno	16 Jun 11
	11.23/0.1 7.34/0.2 12.44 2.01 48.66 14.74/-2.0 38.64 4.90 60.96 4:19.79							
7938	Frank	Busemann	GER	26.2.75	1		Zeven	2 Oct 94
	10.68/1.6 7.37/1.1 13.08 2.03 50.41 14.34/-1.1 39.84 4.40 63.00 4:37.31							
IAAF Junior specification with 99cm 110mh, 6kg shot, 1.75kg Discus								
8435	Niklas	Kaul	GER	11.2.98	1	EJ	Grosseto	23 Jul 17
	11.48/-1.3 7.20/1.6 15.37 2.05 48.42 14.55/-0.2 48.49 4.70 68.05 4:15.51							
8141	Johannes	Erm	EST	26.3.98	2	EJ	Grosseto	23 Jul 17
	11.06/0.7 7.42/-0.3 13.44 1.92 48.17 14.66/0.9 43.61 4.50 54.19 4:28.96							
8135	Jiri	Sykora	CZE	20.1.95	1	WJ	Eugene	23 Jul 14
	10.92/0.5 7.35/2.0 15.50 1.94 49.00 14.23/-0.1 48.55 4.40 60.56 4:42.10							
8131	Arkadiy	Vasilyev	RUS	19.1.87	1		Sochi	27 May 06
	11.28/-0.8 7.70/2.0 14.59 2.00 49.17 14.67/0.6 46.30 4.70 56.96 4:32.10							
8126	Andrey	Kravchenko	BLR	4.1.86	1	WJ	Grosseto	15 Jul 04
	11.09/-0.5 7.46-0.2 14.51 2.16 48.98 14.55*/0.4 43.41 4.50 52.84 4:28.46							
8124	Kévin	Mayer	FRA	10.2.92	1	EJ	Tallin	24 Jul 11
	11.40/-1.7 7.52/1.5 14.65 2.04 49.41 14.09/0.7 41.00 4.80 56.60 4:25.23							

10,000 METRES WALK

Mark	Name		Nat	Born	Pos	Meet	Venue	Date
38:46.4	Viktor	Burayev	RUS	23.8.82	1	NC-j	Moskva	20 May 00
38:54.75	Ralf	Kowalsky	GDR	22.3.62	1		Cottbus	24 Jun 81
38:58.21	Vasiliy	Mizinov	RUS	29.12.97	1	NC-j	Cheboksary	25 Jun 16
39:08.23	Daisuke	Matsunaga	JPN	24.3.95	1		Tama	14 Dec 13
39:28.63	Toshizaku	Yamanishi	JPN	15.2.96	2		Osaka	13 Sep 15
39:28.45	Andrey	Ruzavin	RUS	28.3.86	1	EJ	Kaunas	23 Jul 05
39:30.15	Yuga	Yamashita	JPN	6.2.96	1		Tama	12 Dec 15
39:35.01	Stanislav	Yemelyanov	RUS	23.10.90	1	WJ	Bydgoszcz	11 Jul 08

20 KILOMETRES WALK

Mark	Wind	Name	Nat	Born	Pos	Meet	Venue	Date
1:18:06		Viktor Burayev	RUS	23.8.82	2	NC-w	Adler	4 Mar 01
1:18:07		Li Gaobo	CHN	23.7.89	4		Cixi	23 Apr 05
1:18:26		Sergey Shirobokov	RUS	16.2.99	1	NC-w	Sochi	18 Feb 17
1:18:44		Chu Yafei	CHN	5.9.88	5		Yangzhou	22 Apr 06
1:18:52		Chen Ding	CHN	5.8.92	3		Taicang	22 Apr 11
1:18:57		Bai Xuejin	CHN	6.6.87	7		Yangzhou	22 Apr 06
1:19:02		Éder Sánchez	MEX	21.5.86	11		Cixi	23 Apr 05
1:19:14		Xu Xingde	CHN	12.6.84	3	NC	Yangzhou	12 Apr 03
1:19:34		Li Jianbo	CHN	14.11.86	16		Cixi	23 Apr 05

4 x 100 METRES RELAY

Mark	Nat	Team	Pos	Meet	Venue	Date
38.66	USA	Kimmons, Omole, I Williams, L Merritt	1	WJ	Grosseto	18 Jun 04
38.97	JAM	Tracey, Skeen, Minzie, Murphy	2	WJ	Barcelona	14 Jul 12
39.01	JPN	Oseto, Hashimoto, Cambridge, Kanamori	1h1	WJ	Barcelona	13 Jul 12
39.05	GBR	Edgar, Grant, Benjamin, Lewis-Francis	1	WJ	Santiago de Chile	22 Oct 00
39.13	GER	Gurski, Vartel, Giese, Eitel	3	WJ	Bydgoszcz	23 Jul 16
39.17	TTO	Simpson, Burns, Holder, Brown	3	WJ	Kingston	21 Jul 02
39.29	BRA	de Araújo, Monteiro, R dos Santos Jnr, Rocha	2h1	WJ	Barcelona	13 Jul 12
39.31	POL	Bijowski, Slowikowski, Zalewski, Jabłonski	3h1	WJ	Barcelona	13 Jul 12

4 x 400 METRES RELAY

Mark	Nat	Team	Pos	Meet	Venue	Date
3:00.33	USA	Herron 45.1, Shinnick 45.1, Hooper 44.73, J Lyles 45.36	1	PAm-J	Trujillo	23 Jul 17
3:02.81	BOT	Poo, Thebe, Sibanda, Talane	2	WJ	Bydgoszcz	24 Jul 16
3:03.77	JAM	Chambers, Carpenter, James, C Taylor	2	PAm-J	Trujillo	23 Jul 17
3:03.80	GBR	Grindley, Patrick, Winrow, Richardson	2	WJ	Plovdiv	12 Aug 90
3:04.11	JPN	Walsh, Yui, Kitagawa, Kato	2	WJ	Eugene	27 Jul 14
3:04.22	CUB	Cadogan, Mordoche, González, Hernández	2	WJ	Athína	20 Jul 86
3:04.50	RSA	le Roux, Gebhardt, Julius, van Zyl	2	WJ	Grosseto	18 Jul 04
3:04.58	GDR	Preusche, Löper, Trylus, Carlowitz	1	EJ	Utrecht	23 Aug 81

JUNIOR WOMEN'S ALL-TIME LISTS

100 METRES

Mark	Wind	Name	Nat	Born	Pos	Meet	Venue	Date
10.88	2.0	Marlies Oelsner	GDR	21.3.58	1	NC	Dresden	1 Jul 77
10.89	1.8	Katrin Krabbe	GDR	22.11.69	1rB		Berlin	20 Jul 88
10.98	2.0	Candace Hill	USA	11.2.99	1		Shoreline	20 Jun 15
10.99	0.9	Angela Tenorio	ECU	27.1.96	2	PAm	Toronto	22 Jul 15
11.03	1.7	Silke Gladisch	GDR	20.6.64	3	OD	Berlin	8 Jun 83
11.03	0.6	English Gardner	USA	22.4.92	1	Pac10	Tucson	14 May 11
11.04	1.4	Angela Williams	USA	30.1.80	1	NCAA	Boise	5 Jun 99
11.06	0.9	Khalifa St. Fort	TTO	13.2.98	3	NC	Port of Spain	24 Jun 17
11.07	0.7	Bianca Knight	USA	2.1.89	4q2	NC/OT	Eugene	27 Jun 08
11.08	2.0	Brenda Morehead	USA	5.10.57	1	OT	Eugene	21 Jun 76
11.10	0.9	Kaylin Whitney	USA	9.3.98	1	NC-j	Eugene	5 Jul 14

Wind assisted to 11.08

Mark	Wind	Name	Nat	Born	Pos	Meet	Venue	Date
10.96	3.7	Angela Williams	USA	30.1.80	1		Las Vegas	3 Apr 99
10.97	3.3	Gesine Walther	GDR	6.10.62	4	NC	Cottbus	16 Jul 80
11.01	5.4	Kaylin Whitney	USA	9.3.98	3	Athl	Lausanne	9 Jul 15
11.02	2.1	Nikole Mitchell	JAM	5.6.74	1	Mutual	Kingston	1 May 93
11.03	2.2	Dina Asher-Smith	GBR	4.12.95	1		Mannheim	5 Jul 14
11.04	5.6	Kelly-Ann Baptiste	TTO	14.10.86	1rB	TexR	Austin	9 Apr 05
11.04	3.1	Desiree Henry	GBR	26.8.95	1		Clermont	26 Apr 14
11.06	2.2	Brenda Morehead	USA	5.10.57	1s2	OT	Eugene	21 Jun 76

200 METRES

Mark	Wind	Name	Nat	Born	Pos	Meet	Venue	Date
22.11A	-0.5	Allyson Felix	USA	18.11.85	1		Ciudad de México	3 May 03
		22.18 0.8			2	OG	Athína	25 Aug 04
22.19	1.5	Natalya Bochina	RUS	4.1.62	2	OG	Moskva	30 Jul 80
22.37	1.3	Sabine Rieger	GDR	6.11.63	2	vURS	Cottbus	26 Jun 82
22.42	0.4	Gesine Walther	GDR	6.10.62	1		Potsdam	29 Aug 81
22.43	0.8	Bianca Knight	USA	2.1.89	1	Reebok	New York (RI)	31 May 08
22.43A	-0.7	Candace Hill	USA	11.2.99	1	WY	Calí	19 Jul 15
22.45	0.5	Grit Breuer	GER	16.2.72	2	ASV	Köln	8 Sep 91
22.45	0.9	Shaunae Miller	BAH	15.4.94	2	NC	Freeport	22 Jun 13
22.47	0.4	Kaylin Whitney	USA	9.3.98	4	NC	Eugene	28 Jun 15
22.51	2.0	Katrin Krabbe	GDR	22.11.69	3		Berlin	13 Sep 88
22.52	1.2	Mary Onyali	NGR	3.2.68	6	WCh	Roma	3 Sep 87

Indoors

Mark	Wind	Name	Nat	Born	Pos	Meet	Venue	Date
22.40		Bianca Knight	USA	2.1.89	1r2	NCAA	Fayetteville	15 Mar 08
22.49		Sanya Richards	USA	26.2.85	2rA	NCAA	Fayetteville	12 Mar 04

Mark	Wind	Name		Nat	Born	Pos	Meet	Venue	Date
Wind assisted									
22.25	5.6	Bianca	Knight	USA	2.1.89	5	NC/OT	Eugene	6 Jul 08
22.34	2.3	Katrin	Krabbe	GDR	22.11.69	1	WJ	Sudbury	30 Jul 88
22.38	2.1	Candace	Hill	USA	11.2.99	1		Montverde	11 Jun 16
22.41	3.1	Shaunae	Miller	BAH	15.4.94	1		Athens, GA	13 Apr 13
22.41	2.6	Gina	Lückenkemper	GER	21.11.96	1	EJ	Eskilstuna	18 Jul 15
22.44	2.5	Lauren Rain	Williams	USA	25.7.99	1		Norwalk	21 May 16

400 METRES

Mark	Name		Nat	Born	Pos	Meet	Venue	Date
49.42	Grit	Breuer	GER	16.2.72	2	WCh	Tokyo	27 Aug 91
49.77	Christina	Brehmer	GDR	28.2.58	1		Dresden	9 May 76
49.89	Sanya	Richards	USA	26.2.85	2	NC/OT	Sacramento	17 Jul 04
50.01		Li Jing	CHN	14.2.80	1	NG	Shanghai	18 Oct 97
50.19	Marita	Koch	GDR	18.2.57	3	OD	Berlin	10 Jul 76
50.46	Kendall	Baisden	USA	5.3.95	2	Big 12	Lubbock	18 May 14
50.50	Ashley	Spencer	USA	8.6.93	1	WJ	Barcelona	13 Jul 12
50.59	Fatima	Yusuf	NGR	2.5.71	1	HGP	Budapest	5 Aug 90
50.70	Shaunae	Miller	BAH	15.4.94	2	NCAA	Eugene	7 Jun 13
50.74	Monique	Henderson	USA	18.2.83	1		Norwalk	3 Jun 00
50.78	Danijela	Grgic	CRO	28.9.88	1	WJ	Beijing	17 Aug 06

800 METRES

Mark	Name		Nat	Born	Pos	Meet	Venue	Date
1:54.01	Pamela	Jelimo	KEN	5.12.89	1	WK	Zürich	29 Aug 08
1:55.45	Caster	Semenya	RSA	7.1.91	1	WCh	Berlin	19 Aug 09
1:56.59	Francine	Niyonsaba	BDI	5.5.93	1	VD	Bruxelles	7 Sep 12
1:57.18		Wang Yuan	CHN	8.4.76	2h2	NG	Beijing	8 Sep 93
1:57.45	Hildegard	Ullrich	GDR	20.12.59	5	EC	Praha	31 Aug 78
1:57.62		Lang Yinglai	CHN	22.8.79	1	NG	Shanghai	22 Oct 97
1:57.63	Maria	Mutola	MOZ	27.10.72	4	WCh	Tokyo	26 Aug 91
1:57.74	Sahily	Diago	CUB	26.8.95	1	Barr	La Habana	25 Jul 14
1:57.77		Lu Yi	CHN	10.4.74	4	NG	Beijing	9 Sep 93
1:57.86	Katrin	Wühn	GDR	19.11.65	1		Celje	5 May 84
1:58.16		Lin Na	CHN	18.1.80	3	NG	Shanghai	22 Oct 97

1000 METRES

Mark	Name		Nat	Born	Pos	Meet	Venue	Date
2:35.4	Irina	Nikitina	RUS	16.6.61	5	Kuts	Podolsk	5 Aug 79
2:35.4	Katrin	Wühn	GDR	19.11.65	3		Potsdam	12 Jul 84

1500 METRES

Mark	Name		Nat	Born	Pos	Meet	Venue	Date
3:51.34		Lang Yinglai	CHN	22.8.79	2	NG	Shanghai	18 Oct 97
3:53.91		Yin Lili	CHN	11.11.79	3	NG	Shanghai	18 Oct 97
3:53.97		Lan Lixin	CHN	14.2.79	4	NG	Shanghai	18 Oct 97
3:54.52		Zhang Ling	CHN	13.4.80	5	NG	Shanghai	18 Oct 97
3:56.98	Faith	Kipyegon	KEN	10.1.94	2	DL	Doha	10 May 13
3:59.53	Dawit	Seyaum	ETH	27.7.96	1		Marrakech	8 Jun 14
3:59.60	Gelete	Burka	ETH	15.2.86	5	GP	Rieti	28 Aug 05
3:59.81		Wang Yuan	CHN	8.4.76	7	NG	Beijing	11 Sep 93
3:59.96	Zola	Budd	GBR	26.5.66	3	VD	Bruxelles	30 Aug 85
4:00.05		Lu Yi	CHN	10.4.74	8	NG	Beijing	11 Sep 93
4:00.18	Gudaf	Tsegay	ETH	23.1.97	3	Pre	Eugene	28 May 16

3000 METRES

Mark	Name		Nat	Born	Pos	Meet	Venue	Date
8:28.83	Zola	Budd	GBR	26.5.66	3	GG	Roma	7 Sep 85
8:35.89	Sally	Barsosio	KEN	21.3.78	2	Herc	Monaco	16 Aug 97
8:36.45		Ma Ningning	CHN	1.6.76	4	NC	Jinan	6 Jun 93
8:36.87	Alemitu	Haroye	ETH	9.5.95	14	VD	Bruxelles	5 Sep 14
8:38.61	Kalkedan	Gezahegn	ETH	8.5.91	5	WAF	Thessaloníki	13 Sep 09
8:38.97	Linet	Masai	KEN	5.12.89	5	GP	Rieti	9 Sep 07
8:39.13	Agnes	Tirop	KEN	23.10.95	3		Rieti	8 Sep 13
8:39.65	Buze	Diriba	ETH	9.2.94	3	Herc	Monaco	20 Jul 12
8:39.90	Gelete	Burka	ETH	15.2.86	3	SGP	Doha	13 May 05
8:40.08	Gabriela	Szabo	ROU	14.11.75	3	EC	Helsinki	10 Aug 94
8:40.28	Meseret	Defar	ETH	19.11.83	10	VD	Bruxelles	30 Aug 02

5000 METRES

Mark	Name		Nat	Born	Pos	Meet	Venue	Date
14:30.88	Tirunesh	Dibaba	ETH	1.10.85	2	Bisl	Bergen (Fana)	11 Jun 04
14:33.32	Letesenbet	Gidey	ETH	20.3.98	3	GGala	Roma	8 Jun 17
14:35.18	Sentayehu	Ejigu	ETH	21.6.85	4	Bisl	Bergen (Fana)	11 Jun 04
14:39.96		Yin Lili	CHN	11.11.79	4	NG	Shanghai	23 Oct 97
14:43.29	Emebet	Anteneh	ETH	13.1.92	5	Bisl	Oslo	9 Jun 11
14:45.33		Lan Lixin	CHN	14.2.79	2h2	NG	Shanghai	21 Oct 97
14:45.71		Song Liqing	CHN	20.1.80	3h2	NG	Shanghai	21 Oct 97

Mark	Wind	Name		Nat	Born	Pos	Meet	Venue	Date
14:45.90			Jiang Bo	CHN	13.3.77	1		Nanjing	24 Oct 95
14:45.98		Pauline	Korikwiang	KEN	1.3.88	7	Bisl	Oslo	2 Jun 06
14:46.71		Sally	Barsosio	KEN	21.3.78	3	VD	Bruxelles	22 Aug 97
14:47.13		Mercy	Cherono	KEN	7.5.91	7	DL	Shanghai	23 May 10

10,000 METRES

Mark	Wind	Name		Nat	Born	Pos	Meet	Venue	Date
30:26.50		Linet	Masai	KEN	5.12.89	4	OG	Beijing	15 Aug 08
30:31.55			Xing Huina	CHN	25.2.84	7	WCh	Saint-Denis	23 Aug 03
30:39.41			Lan Lixin	CHN	14.2.79	2	NG	Shanghai	19 Oct 97
30:39.98			Yin Lili	CHN	11.11.79	3	NG	Shanghai	19 Oct 97
30:59.92		Merima	Hashim	ETH	.81	3	NA	Heusden-Zolder	5 Aug 00
31:06.20		Lucy	Wangui	KEN	24.3.84	1rA		Okayama	27 Sep 03
31:11.26			Song Liqing	CHN	20.1.80	7	NG	Shanghai	19 Oct 97
31:15.38		Sally	Barsosio	KEN	21.3.78	3	WCh	Stuttgart	21 Aug 93
31:16.50		Evelyne	Kimwei	KEN	25.8.87	1		Kobe	21 Oct 06
31:17.30			Zhang Yingying	CHN	4.1.90	1		Wuhan	2 Nov 07
31:20.38		Tigist	Kiros	ETH	8.6.92	4	GS	Ostrava	31 May 11

HALF MARATHON

Mark	Wind	Name		Nat	Born	Pos	Meet	Venue	Date
67:57		Gelana	Abebe	ETH	18.1.90	4		R'as Al Khaymah	20 Feb 09
68:21		Valentine	Kipketer	KEN	5.1.93	1		Lille	3 Sep 11
68:36		Merima	Mohamed	ETH	10.6.92	2		New Delhi	21 Nov 10
68:41		Evelyne	Kimwei	KEN	25.8.87	1		Kobe	19 Nov 06
68:53		Shure	Demise	ETH	21.1.96	4		Ostia	2 Mar 14
69:05		Delillah	Asiago	KEN	24.2.72	1	GWR	Exeter	5 May 91
69:10		Muliye	Dekebo	ETH	13.3.98	5		Ostia	12 Mar 17
69:21		Ann	Wamuchi	KEN	29.9.78	5		Tokyo	19 Jan 97
69:45		Meseret	Mengistu	ETH	6.3.90	1		Reims	18 Oct 09
69:48		Yuka	Hata	JPN	3.2.79	4	WJ	Lisboa (U)	15 Mar 98

MARATHON

Mark	Wind	Name		Nat	Born	Pos	Meet	Venue	Date
2:20:59		Shure	Demise	ETH	21.1.96	4		Dubai	23 Jan 15
2:22:38			Zhang Yingying	CHN	4.1.90	1	NC	Xiamen	5 Jan 08
2:23:06		Merima	Mohamed	ETH	10.6.92	3		Toronto	26 Sep 10
2:23:37			Liu Min	CHN	29.11.83	1		Beijing	14 Oct 01
2:23:57			Zhu Xiaolin	CHN	20.4.84	4		Beijing	20 Oct 02
2:25:23		Azmera	Abreha	ETH	.98	3		Amsterdam	15 Oct 17
2:25:48			Jin Li	CHN	29.5.83	6		Beijing	14 Oct 01
2:26:34			Wei Yanan	CHN	6.12.81	1		Beijing	15 Oct 00
2:27:05			Chen Rong	CHN	18.5.88	1		Beijing	21 Oct 07

3000 METRES STEEPLECHASE

Mark	Wind	Name		Nat	Born	Pos	Meet	Venue	Date
8:58.78		Celliphine	Chespol	KEN	23.3.99	1	Pre	Eugene	26 May 17]
9:20.37		Birtukan	Adamu	ETH	29.4.92	4	GGala	Roma	26 May 11
9:20.55		Ruth	Chebet	KEN/BRN	17.11.96	4	WK	Zürich	28 Aug 14
9:20.65		Tigist	Mekonen	BRN	7.7.97	8	Herc	Monaco	17 Jul 15
9:22.51		Almaz	Ayana	ETH	21.11.91	3	VD	Bruxelles	27 Aug 10
9:22.67		Winfred	Yavi	BRN	–.99	8	WCh	London (OS)	11 Aug 17
9:24.51		Ruth	Bisibori	KEN	2.1.88	1		Daegu	3 Oct 07
9:25.91		Rosefline	Chepngetich	KEN	17.6.97	3h2	WCh	Beijing	24 Aug 15
9:26.25			Liu Nian	CHN	26.4.88	1		Wuhan	2 Nov 07
9:27.72		Penuth	Chemutai	UGA	10.7.99	7	DL	Shanghai	13 May 17
9:29.52		Korahubish	Itaa	ETH	28.2.92	1		Huelva	10 Jun 09

100 METRES HURDLES

Mark	Wind	Name		Nat	Born	Pos	Meet	Venue	Date
12.74	1.7	Dior	Hall	USA	2.1.96	3	NCAA	Eugene	13 Jun 15
12.83A	0.4	Tobi	Amusan	NGR	23.4.97	1		El Paso	30 Apr 16
12.84	1.5	Aliuska	López	CUB	29.8.69	2	WUG	Zagreb	16 Jul 87
12.84	1.2	Tia	Jones	USA	8.9.00	1h1	NC-j	Clovis	25 Jun 16
12.85	2.0	Elvira	German	BLR	19.6.97	1	WJ	Bydgoszcz	24 Jul 16
12.87	2.0	Kendell	Williams	USA	14.6.95	1	NC-j	Eugene	6 Jul 14
12.87	2.0	Rushelle	Burton	JAM	4.12.97	2	WJ	Bydgoszcz	24 Jul 16
12.88	1.5	Yelena	Ovcharova	UKR	17.6.76	2	ECp	Villeneuve d'Ascq	25 Jun 95
12.89	1.3	Anay	Tejeda	CUB	3.4.83	1		Padova	1 Sep 02
12.91	1.8	Kristina	Castlin	USA	7.7.88	1	NCAA-r	Gainesville	26 May 07
12.92	0.0		Sun Hongwei	CHN	24.11.79	6	NG	Shanghai	18 Oct 97
Wind assisted to 12.89									
12.79	3.8	Tobi	Amusan	NGR	23.4.97	2	NCAA	Eugene	11 Jun 16
12.81	3.4	Anay	Tejeda	CUB	3.4.83	1	WJ	Kingston	21 Jul 02
12.82	2.1	Kristina	Castlin	USA	7.7.88	1		College Park	21 Apr 07
12.83	3.7	Tara	Davis	USA	20.5.99	1		Clovis	3 Jun 17

Mark	Wind	Name		Nat	Born	Pos	Meet	Venue	Date

400 METRES HURDLES

Mark	Wind	Name		Nat	Born	Pos	Meet	Venue	Date
53.82		Sydney	McLaughlin	USA	7.8.99	6	NC	Sacramento	25 Jun 17
54.40			Wang Xing	CHN	30.11.86	2	NG	Nanjing	21 Oct 05
54.58		Ristananna	Tracey	JAM	5.9.92	2	NC	Kingston	24 Jun 11
54.70		Lashinda	Demus	USA	10.3.83	1	WJ	Kingston	19 Jul 02
54.93			Li Rui	CHN	22.11.79	1	NG	Shanghai	22 Oct 97
55.07		Shamier	Little	USA	20.3.95	1	NCAA	Eugene	13 Jun 14
55.11		Kaliese	Spencer	JAM	6.4.87	1	WJ	Beijing	17 Aug 06
55.15			Huang Xiaoxiao	CHN	3.3.83	2	NG	Guangzhou	22 Nov 01
55.20		Lesley	Maxie	USA	4.1.67	2	TAC	San Jose	9 Jun 84
55.20A		Jana	Pittman	AUS	9.11.82	1		Pietersburg	18 Mar 00
55.20		Anna	Cockrell	USA	28.8.97	1	WJ	Bydgoszcz	22 Jul 16
Drugs disqualification:		54.54	Peng Yinghua ¶	CHN	21.2.79	(2)	NG	Shanghai	22 Oct 97

HIGH JUMP

Mark	Wind	Name		Nat	Born	Pos	Meet	Venue	Date
2.01		Olga	Turchak	UKR	5.3.67	2	GWG	Moskva	7 Jul 86
2.01		Heike	Balck	GDR	19.8.70	1	vURS-j	Karl-Marx-Stadt	18 Jun 89
2.00		Stefka	Kostadinova	BUL	25.3.65	1		Sofia	25 Aug 84
2.00		Alina	Astafei	ROU	7.6.69	1	WJ	Sudbury	29 Jul 88
1.99i		Vashti	Cunningham	USA	18.1.98	1	NC	Portland	12 Mar 16
		1.99				1	NC	Sacramento	23 Jun 17
1.98		Silvia	Costa	CUB	4.5.64	2	WUG	Edmonton	11 Jul 83
1.98		Yelena	Yelesina	RUS	5.4.70	1	Druzh	Nyiregyháza	13 Aug 88
1.97		Svetlana	Isaeva	BUL	18.3.67	2		Sofia	25 May 86
1.97i		Mariya	Kuchina	RUS	14.1.93	1		Trinec	26 Jan 11
1.96A		Charmaine	Gale	RSA	27.2.64	1	NC-j	Bloemfontein	4 Apr 81
1.96i		Desislava	Aleksandrova	BUL	27.10.75	2	EI	Paris (B)	12 Mar 94
1.96		Marina	Kuptsova	RUS	22.12.81	1	NC	Tula	26 Jul 00
1.96		Blanka	Vlasic	CRO	8.11.83	1	WJ	Kingston	20 Jul 02
1.96		Airine	Palsyte	LTU	13.7.92	2	WUG	Shenzhen	21 Aug 11
1.96		Eleanor	Patterson	AUS	22.5.96	1	N.Sch	Townsville	7 Dec 13

POLE VAULT

Mark	Wind	Name		Nat	Born	Pos	Meet	Venue	Date
4.71i		Wilma	Murto	FIN	11.6.98	1		Zweibrücken	31 Jan 16
		4.52				2	PNG	Turku	29 Jun 16
4.64		Eliza	McCartney	NZL	11.12.96	1		Auckland	19 Dec 15
4.63i		Angelica	Bengtsson	SWE	8.7.93	2		Stockholm	22 Feb 11
		4.58				1		Sollentuna	5 Jul 12
4.61		Alyona	Lutkovskaya	RUS	15.3.96	1		Irkutsk	21 May 15
4.60i		Hanna	Shelekh	UKR	14.7.93	3		Donetsk	11 Feb 12
4.60i		Roberta	Bruni	ITA	8.3.94	1	NC	Ancona	17 Feb 13
4.60		Robeilys	Peinado	VEN	26.11.97	1		Barquisimeto	20 May 15
4.59		Nina	Kennedy	AUS	5.4.97	1		Perth	14 Feb 15
4.57		Angelica	Moser	SUI	9.10.97	1		Frauenkappelen	1 Aug 16
4.55i		Lisa	Gunnarsson	SWE	20.8.99	6=	EI	Beograd	4 Mar 17
4.52i		Katie	Byres	GBR	11.9.93	2		Nevers	18 Feb 12

LONG JUMP

Mark	Wind	Name		Nat	Born	Pos	Meet	Venue	Date
7.14	1.1	Heike	Daute	GDR	16.12.64	1	PTS	Bratislava	4 Jun 83
7.03	1.3	Darya	Klishina	RUS	15.1.91	1	Znam	Zhukovskiy	26 Jun 10
7.00	-0.2	Birgit	Grosshennig	GDR	21.2.65	2		Berlin	9 Jun 84
6.94	-0.5	Magdalena	Khristova	BUL	25.2.77	2		Kalamáta	22 Jun 96
6.91	0.0	Anisoara	Cusmir	ROU	28.6.62	1		Bucuresti	23 May 81
6.90	1.4	Beverly	Kinch	GBR	14.1.64	*	WCh	Helsinki	14 Aug 83
6.88	0.6	Natalya	Shevchenko	RUS	28.12.66	2		Sochi	26 May 84
6.84		Larisa	Baluta	UKR	13.8.65	2		Krasnodar	6 Aug 83
6.83	1.7	Kate	Hall	USA	12.1.97	1		Greensboro NC	21 Jun 15
6.82	1.8	Fiona	May	GBR	12.12.69	*	WJ	Sudbury	30 Jul 88
6.81	1.6	Carol	Lewis	USA	8.8.63	1	TAC	Knoxville	20 Jun 82
6.81	1.4	Yelena	Davydova	KZK	16.11.67	1	NC-j	Krasnodar	17 Jul 85
Wind assisted to 6.82									
7.27	2.2	Heike	Daute	GDR	16.12.64	1	WCh	Helsinki	14 Aug 83
6.93	4.6	Beverly	Kinch	GBR	14.1.64	5	WCh	Helsinki	14 Aug 83
6.88	2.1	Fiona	May	GBR	12.12.69	1	WJ	Sudbury	30 Jul 88
6.84	2.8	Anu	Kaljurand	EST	16.4.69	2		Riga	4 Jun 88

TRIPLE JUMP

Mark	Wind	Name		Nat	Born	Pos	Meet	Venue	Date
14.62	1.0	Tereza	Marinova	BUL	5.9.77	1	WC	Sydney	25 Aug 96
14.57	0.2		Huang Qiuyan	CHN	25.1.80	1	NG	Shanghai	19 Oct 97
14.52	0.6	Anastasiya	Ilyina	RUS	16.1.82	q	WJ	Santiago de Chile	20 Oct 00

Mark	Wind	Name		Nat	Born	Pos	Meet	Venue	Date
14.46	1.0		Peng Fengmei	CHN	2.7.79	1		Chengdu	18 Apr 98
14.43	0.6	Kaire	Leibak	EST	21.5.88	1	WJ	Beijing	17 Aug 06
14.38	-0.7		Xie Limei	CHN	27.6.86	1	AsiC	Inchon	1 Sep 05
14.37i	-		Ren Ruiping	CHN	1.2.76	3	WI	Barcelona	11 Mar 95
		14.36	0.0			1	NC	Beijing	1 Jun 94
14.36	0.0	Dailenys	Alcántara	CUB	10.8.91	3	Barr/NC	La Habana	29 May 09
14.35		Yana	Borodina	RUS	21.4.92	1J	Mosc Ch	Moskva	15 Jun 11
14.32	-0.1	Yelena	Lysak ¶	RUS	19.10.75	1		Voronezh	18 Jun 94
14.29	1.2	Mabel	Gay	CUB	5.5.83	1		La Habana	5 Apr 02
14.28	0.9	Valeriya	Kanatova	UZB	29.8.92	3	NCp	Tashkent	12 Jun 11
Wind assisted									
14.83	8.3		Ren Ruiping	CHN	1.2.76	1	NC	Taiyuan	21 May 95
14.55	3.7	Dailenis	Alcántara	CUB	10.8.91	1	Barr/NC	La Habana	21 Mar 10
14.43	2.7	Yelena	Lysak ¶	RUS	19.10.75	1	WJ	Lisboa	21 Jul 94

SHOT

Mark	Wind	Name		Nat	Born	Pos	Meet	Venue	Date
20.54		Astrid	Kumbernuss	GDR	5.2.70	1	vFIN-j	Orimattila	1 Jul 89
20.51i		Heidi	Krieger	GDR	20.7.65	2		Budapest	8 Feb 84
		20.24				5		Split	30 Apr 84
20.23		Ilke	Wyludda	GDR	28.3.69	1	NC-j	Karl-Marx-Stadt	16 Jul 88
20.12		Ilona	Schoknecht	GDR	24.9.56	2	NC	Erfurt	23 Aug 75
20.02			Cheng Xiaoyan	CHN	30.11.75	3	NC	Beijing	5 Jun 94
19.90		Stephanie	Storp	FRG	28.11.68	1		Hamburg	16 Aug 87
19.63			Wang Yawen	CHN	23.8.73	1		Shijiazhuang	25 Apr 92
19.57		Grit	Haupt	GDR	4.6.66	1		Gera	7 Jul 84
19.48		Ines	Wittich	GDR	14.11.69	5		Leipzig	29 Jul 87
19.46			Gong Lijiao	CHN	24.1.89	Q	OG	Beijing	16 Aug 08
19.42		Simone	Michel	GDR	18.12.60	3	vSU	Leipzig	23 Jun 79

DISCUS

Mark	Wind	Name		Nat	Born	Pos	Meet	Venue	Date
74.40		Ilke	Wyludda	GDR	28.3.69	2		Berlin	13 Sep 88
		75.36 unofficial meeting				2		Berlin	6 Sep 88
67.38		Irina	Meszynski	GDR	24.3.62	1		Berlin	14 Aug 81
67.00		Jana	Günther	GDR	7.1.68	6	NC	Potsdam	20 Aug 87
66.80		Svetla	Mitkova	BUL	17.6.64	1		Sofia	2 Aug 83
66.60		Astrid	Kumbernuss	GDR	5.2.70	1		Berlin	20 Jul 88
66.34		Franka	Dietzsch	GDR	22.1.68	2		Saint-Denis	11 Jun 87
66.30		Jana	Lauren	GDR	28.6.70	1	vURS-j	Karl-Marx-Stadt	18 Jun 89
66.08			Cao Qi	CHN	15.1.74	1	NG	Beijing	12 Sep 93
65.96		Grit	Haupt	GDR	4.6.66	3		Leipzig	13 Jul 84
65.22		Daniela	Costian	ROU	30.4.65	3		Nitra	26 Aug 84
65.20			Liu Fengying	CHN	26.1.79	Q	NC	Chengdu	1 Jun 97
64.52		Martina	Opitz	GDR	12.12.60	3	NC	Karl-Marx-Stadt	12 Aug 79

HAMMER

Mark	Wind	Name		Nat	Born	Pos	Meet	Venue	Date
73.24			Zhang Wenxiu	CHN	22.3.86	1	NC	Changsha	24 Jun 05
71.71		Kamila	Skolimowska	POL	4.11.82	1	GPF	Melbourne	9 Sep 01
70.62		Alexandra	Tavernier	FRA	13.12.93	1	WJ	Barcelona	14 Jul 12
70.39		Mariya	Smolyachkova	BLR	10.2.85	1		Staiki	26 Jun 04
70.39		Réka	Gyurátz	HUN	31.5.96	1		Budapest	23 May 15
69.73		Natalya	Zolotukhina	UKR	4.1.85	1		Kyiv	24 Jul 04
69.63		Bianca	Perie	ROU	1.6.90	1	NC-j	Bucuresti	14 Aug 09
69.32		Sofiya	Palkina	RUS	9.6.98	2		Zhukovskiy	16 Jun 17
69.25		Audrey	Ciofani	FRA	13.3.96	1		Gagny	10 May 15
68.98		Ayamey	Medina	CUB	21.2.98	2	Barr	La Habana	27 May 16
68.74		Arasay	Thondike	CUB	28.5.86	2	Barr	La Habana	2 May 05
68.50		Martina	Danisová	SVK	21.3.83	1		Kladno	16 Jun 01

JAVELIN

Mark	Wind	Name		Nat	Born	Pos	Meet	Venue	Date
63.86		Yulenmis	Aguilar	CUB	3.8.96	1	PAm-J	Edmonton	2 Aug 15
63.01		Vira	Rebryk (now RUS)	UKR	25.2.89	1	WJ	Bydgoszcz	10 Jul 08
62.93			Xue Juan	CHN	10.2.86	1	NG	Changsha	27 Oct 03
62.11		Maria	Andrejczyk	POL	9.3.96	1	Skol	Cetniewo	1 Aug 15
62.09			Zhang Li	CHN	17.1.89	1		Beijing	25 May 08
61.99			Wang Yaning	CHN	4.1.80	1	NC	Huizhou	14 Oct 99
61.96		Sofi	Flink	SWE	8.7.95	Q	WCh	Moskva	16 Aug 13
61.79		Nikolett	Szabó	HUN	3.3.80	1		Schwechat	23 May 99
61.61			Chang Chunfeng	CHN	4.5.88	1	NC-j	Chengdu	4 Jun 07
61.49			Liang Lili	CHN	16.11.83	1	NC	Benxi	1 Jun 02
61.38		Annika	Suthe	GER	15.10.85	1-j		Halle	23 May 04
61.38		Haruka	Kitaguchi	JPN	16.3.98	3		Kawasaki	8 May 16

Mark	Wind	Name		Nat	Born	Pos	Meet	Venue	Date

HEPTATHLON

Mark	Wind	Name		Nat	Born	Pos	Meet	Venue	Date
6768w		Tatyana	Chernova	RUS	29.1.88	1		Arles	3 Jun 07
	13.04w/6.1	1.82	13.57	23.59w/5.2		6.61/1.2		53.43	2:15.05
		6227				1	WJ	Beijing	19 Aug 06
	13.70/1.6	1.80	12.18	24.05/0.3		6.35/-0.4		50.51	2:25.49
6542		Carolina	Klüft	SWE	2.2.83	1	EC	München	10 Aug 02
	13.33/-0.3	1.89	13.16	23.71/-0.3		6.36/1.1		47.61	2:17.99
6465		Sibylle	Thiele	GDR	6.3.65	1	EJ	Schwechat	28 Aug 83
	13.49	1.90	14.63	24.07		6.65		36.22	2:18.36
6436		Sabine	Braun	FRG	19.6.65	1	vBUL	Mannheim	9 Jun 84
	13.68	1.78	13.09	23.88		6.03		52.14	2:09.41
6428		Svetla	Dimitrova ¶	BUL	27.1.70	1	NC	Sofia	18 Jun 89
	13.49/-0.7	1.77	13.98	23.59/-0.2		6.49/0.7		40.10	2:11.10
6403		Emilia	Dimitrova	BUL	13.11.67	6	GWG	Moskva	7 Jul 86
	13.73	1.76	13.46	23.17		6.29		43.30	2:09.85
6381		Alina	Shukh	UKR	12.2.99	1	EJ	Grosseto	21 Jul 17
	14.46/-1.7	1.87	13.87	25.97/0.3		6.33w/3.2		54.51	2:13.52
6357		Géraldine	Ruckstuhl	SUI	24.2.98	2	EJ	Grosseto	21 Jul 17
	13.98/-1.5	1.81	13.54	24.74/0.1		5.97/1.1		54.32	2:12.56
6298		Nafissatou	Thiam	BEL	19.8.94	1	EJ	Rieti	19 Jul 13
	13.87/1.2	1.89	14.26	25.15/-0.6		6.37/0.1		46.94	2:24.89
6276		Larisa	Nikitina	RUS	29.4.65	8	URS Ch	Kiyev	21 Jun 84
	13.87/1.6	1.86	14.04	25.26/-0.7		6.31/0.1		48.62	2:22.76
6267		Katarina	Johnson-Thompson	GBR	9.1.93	15	OG	London (OS)	4 Aug 12
	13.48/0.9	1.89	11.32	23.73/-0.3		6.19/-0.4		38.37	2:10.76
6231		Yorgelis	Rodríguez	CUB	25.1.95	1		La Habana	22 Feb 14
	14.01/0.0	1.84	14.21	24.93/0.0		6.03/0.0		47.58	2:17.93
Drugs disqualification: 6534		Svetla	Dimitrova	BUL	27.1.70	(3)	ECp	Helmond	16 Jul 89
	13.30/1.0	1.84	14.35	23.33/-2.2		6.47/-1.4		39.20	2:13.56

10 KILOMETRES WALK

Mark	Wind	Name		Nat	Born	Pos	Meet	Venue	Date
41:52		Tatyana	Mineyeva	RUS	10.8.90	1	NCp-j	Penza	5 Sep 09
41:55		Irina	Stankina	RUS	25.3.77	1	NC-wj	Adler	11 Feb 95
41:57			Gao Hongmiao	CHN	17.3.74	2	NG	Beijing	8 Sep 93
42:15+		Anisya	Kirdyapkina	RUS	23.10.89	1=	in 20k	Adler	23 Feb 08
42:29		Tatyana	Kalmykova	RUS	10.1.90	1	NC-wj	Adler	23 Feb 08
42:31		Irina	Yumanova	RUS	17.6.90	2	NC-wj	Adler	23 Feb 08
42:43.0	t	Svetlana	Vasilyeva	RUS	24.7.92	1	NC-wj	Sochi	27 Feb 11
42:44			Long Yuwen	CHN	1.8.75	3	NC	Shenzen	18 Feb 93

20 KILOMETRES WALK

Mark	Wind	Name		Nat	Born	Pos	Meet	Venue	Date
1:25:30		Anisya	Kirdyapkina	RUS	23.10.89	2	NC-w	Adler	23 Feb 08
1:26:36		Tatyana	Kalmykova	RUS	10.1.90	1	NC	Saransk	8 Jun 08
1:27:01			Lu Xiuzhi	CHN	26.10.93	2		Taicang	30 Mar 12
1:27:16			Song Hongjuan	CHN	4.7.84	1	NC	Yangzhou	14 Apr 03
1:27:34			Jiang Jing	CHN	23.10.85	2	WCp	Naumburg	2 May 04
1:27:35		Natalya	Fedoskina	RUS	25.6.80	2	WCp	Mézidon-Canon	2 May 99
1:28:08		Anezka	Drahotová	CZE	22.7.95	3	EC	Zürich	14 Aug 14
1:28:23			Song Xiaoling	CHN	21.12.87	2		Yangzhou	22 Apr 06

4 X 100 METRES RELAY

Mark	Nat	Team	Pos	Meet	Venue	Date
43.27	GER	Fehm, Kwadwo, Junk, Montag	1h3	EJ	Grosseto	23 Jul 17
43.29	USA (Blue)	Knight, Tarmoh, Olear, Mayo	1		Eugene	8 Aug 06
43.40	JAM	Simpson, Stewart, McLaughlin, Facey	1	WJ	Kingston	20 Jul 02
43.44A	NGR	Utondu, Iheagwam, Onyali, Ogunkoya	1	AfrG	Nairobi	9 Aug 87
43.68	FRA	Vouaux, Jacques-Sebastien, Kamga, Banco	3	WJ	Grosseto	18 Jul 04
43.81	GBR	Miller, Asher-Smith, S Wilson, Henry	1	EJ	Rieti	21 Jul 13
43.87	URS	Lapshina, Doronina, Bulatova, Kovalyova	1	vGDR-j	Leningrad	20 Jun 87
43.98	BRA	Silva, Leoncio, Krasucki, Santos	2	PAm-J	São Paulo	7 Jul 07
44.04	CUB	Riquelme, Allen, López, Valdivia	2	WJ	Sudbury	31 Jul 88

4 X 400 METRES RELAY

Mark	Nat	Team	Pos	Meet	Venue	Date
3:27.60	USA	Anderson, Kidd, Smith, Hastings	1	WJ	Grosseto	18 Jul 04
3:28.39	GDR	Derr, Fabert, Wöhlk, Breuer	1	WJ	Sudbury	31 Jul 88
3:29.66	JAM	Stewart, Morgan, Walker, Hall	1	PennR	Philadelphia	28 Apr 01
3:30.03	RUS	Talko, Shapayeva, Soldatova, Kostetskaya	2	WJ	Grosseto	18 Jul 04
3:30.38	AUS	Scamps, R Poetschka, Hanigan, Andrews	1	WJ	Plovdiv	12 Aug 90
3:30.46	GBR	Wall, Spencer, James, Miller	2	WJ	Kingston	21 Jul 02
3:30.72	BUL	Kireva, Angelova, Rashova, Dimitrova	3	v2N	Sofia	24 Jul 83
3:30.84	NGR	Abugan, Odumosu, Eze, Adesanya	2	WJ	Beijing	20 Aug 06
3:31.57	ROU	Petrea, Florea, Tîrlea, Nedelcu	1	WJ	Seoul	20 Sep 92

MEN'S WORLD LISTS 2017

60 METRES INDOORS

Mark	Name		Nat	Born	Pos	Meet	Venue	Date
6.45A	Ronnie	Baker	USA	15.10.93	1	NC	Albuquerque	5 Mar
6.45	Christian	Coleman	USA	6.3.96	1	NCAA	College Station	11 Mar
6.46		Baker			1		Torun	10 Feb
6.50		Coleman			1h1	NCAA	College Station	11 Mar
6.51		Coleman			1		Blacksburg	3 Feb
6.51	Kendal	Williams	USA	23.9.95	1		Clemson	17 Feb
6.52	Kim	Collins	SKN	5.4.76	1		Mondeville	4 Feb
6.52		Coleman			1	SEC	Nashville	25 Feb
6.53	Yunier	Pérez	CUB	16.2.85	1		Lódz	16 Feb
6.53	Cameron	Burrell	USA	11.9.94	2h1	NCAA	College Station	10 Mar
		(10/6)						
6.54	Richard	Kilty	GBR	2.9.89	1	EI	Beograd	4 Mar
6.54A	LeShon	Collins	USA	11.12.93	2	NC	Albuquerque	5 Mar
6.55	Hasan	Taftian	IRI	4.5.93	1	AsiC	Ashgabat	19 Sep
6.56	Chijindu	Ujah	GBR	5.3.94	2		Torun	10 Feb
	(10)							
6.56	Sean	Safo-Antwi	GHA	31.10.90	1		Athlone	15 Feb
6.56	Ryan	Shields	JAM	12.5.83	2		Lódz	16 Feb
6.56	Jaylen	Bacon	USA	5.8.96	3	NCAA	College Station	11 Mar
6.57	Everton	Clarke	JAM	24.12.92	3		Düsseldorf	1 Feb
6.57	James	Dasaolu	GBR	5.9.87	1	ISTAF	Berlin	10 Feb
6.57	Andrew	Robertson	GBR	17.12.90	1	NC	Sheffield	11 Feb
6.57	Andrew	Fisher	BRN	15.12.91	1		Ostrava	14 Feb
6.57	Warren	Fraser	BAH	8.7.91	2		Clemson	17 Feb
6.57A	Desmond	Lawrence	USA	19.12.91	1h2	NC	Albuquerque	5 Mar
6.57	Kyree	King	USA	9.7.94	3h1	NCAA	College Station	10 Mar
	(10)							
6.58	Christophe	Lemaitre	FRA	11.6.90	1r1		Tignes	5 Jan
6.58	Riak	Reese	USA	23.11.94	1		Akron	4 Feb
6.58A	Ameer	Webb	USA	19.3.89	1		Flagstaff	4 Feb
6.58	Ján	Volko	SVK	2.11.96	2	EI	Beograd	4 Mar
6.58	Joseph	Dewar	GBR	27.1.96	1		Eton	5 Mar
6.59	Rafael	Scott	USA		1		Nashville	21 Jan
6.59	Brandon	Carnes	USA	6.3.95	1		Iowa City	21 Jan
6.59	Hakim	Montgomery	USA	23.6.97	1h2		Clemson	27 Jan
6.59	Kyle	de Escofet	GBR	4.10.96	2h1		Mondeville	4 Feb
6.59	Darryl	Haraway	USA	19.3.97	1		Fayetteville	10 Feb
	(30)							
6.59	Theo	Etienne	GBR	3.9.96	2	NC	Sheffield	11 Feb
6.59	Julian	Forte	JAM	1.7.93	5		Birmingham	18 Feb
6.59	Senoj-Jay	Givans	JAM	30.12.93	1	Big12	Ames	25 Feb
6.59	Mario	Burke	BAR	18.3.97	1		Birmingham AL	25 Feb
6.59A	Dentarius	Locke	USA	12.12.89	2h2	NC	Albuquerque	5 Mar
6.60	Giovanni	Cellario	ITA	22.11.94	1h4		Modena	14 Jan
6.60	Massimiliano	Ferraro	ITA	6.2.91	1		Modena	21 Jan
6.60A	Shavez	Hart	BAH	6.9.92	2		Flagstaff	4 Feb
6.60	D'Angelo	Cherry	USA	1.8.90	2h1		Athlone	15 Feb
6.60	Ramon	Gittens	BAR	20.7.87	2		Athlone	15 Feb
	(40)							
6.60	Eric	Cray	PHI	6.11.88	3		Lódz	16 Feb
6.60A	Wilfried	Koffi Hua	CIV	12.10.89	1		Flagstaff	17 Feb
6.60		Mi Hong	CHN	8.7.93	1h13		Xianlin	23 Feb
6.60	Odean	Skeen	JAM	28.8.94	2	SEC	Nashville	25 Feb
6.60A	Cordero	Gray	USA	9.5.89	2h3	NC	Albuquerque	5 Mar
6.60A	Marqueze	Washington	USA	29.9.93	4	NC	Albuquerque	5 Mar
6.60	Mobolade	Ajomale	CAN	31.8.95	1	NCAA II	Birmingham AL	11 Mar
6.61	Omar	McLeod	JAM	25.4.94	1		Fayetteville	17 Feb
6.61		Yang Yang	CHN	26.6.93	1		Beijing	19 Feb
6.61A	Quentin	Butler	USA	18.9.92	3h2	NC	Albuquerque	5 Mar
	(50)							
6.61A	Tevin	Hester	USA	10.1.94	3h3	NC	Albuquerque	5 Mar
6.61	Kenzo	Cotton	USA	13.5.96	4h2	NCAA	College Station	10 Mar
6.62	Michael	Rodgers	USA	24.4.85	3		Paris	8 Feb
6.62	Reece	Prescod	GBR	29.2.96	5		Torun	10 Feb
6.62	Dwain	Chambers	GBR	5.4.78	3	NC	Sheffield	11 Feb
6.62	Clayton	Vaughn	USA	15.5.92	1	Mill	New York (Armory)	11 Feb
6.62		Gao Ze	CHN	20.10.94	2		Beijing	19 Feb

Mark	Wind	Name		Nat	Born	Pos	Meet	Venue	Date
6.62		Solomon	Bockarie	NED	18.5.87	2		Madrid	24 Feb
6.62		Keitavious	Walter	LCA	16.4.96	1h2	JUCO	Pittsburg	3 Mar
6.62A		Blake	Smith	USA	28.5.93	4h3	NC	Albuquerque	5 Mar
		(60)							
6.63		Gerald	Phiri	ZAM	6.10.88	1		Frisco	10 Feb
6.63		Noah	Lyles	USA	18.7.97	3	Mill	New York (Armory)	11 Feb
6.63			Tang Xingqiang	CHN	11.8.95	1rA		Xianlin	27 Feb
6.63		Austin	Hamilton	SWE	29.7.97	3	EI	Beograd	4 Mar
6.63		Odain	Rose	SWE	19.7.92	4	EI	Beograd	4 Mar

Best at low altitude

6.56	Collins	2	Düsseldorf	1 Feb
6.59	Lawrence	1	Montreal	18 Feb
6.62	Hester	1h1	Clemson	7 Jan
6.62	Washington	1	Pittsburg	28 Jan
6.63	Butler	2	Frisco	10 Feb
6.63	Locke	3	Clemson	17 Feb

100 METRES

Mark	Wind	Name		Nat	Born	Pos	Meet	Venue	Date
9.82	1.3	Christian	Coleman	USA	6.3.96	1s1	NCAA	Eugene	7 Jun
9.90	0.9	Yohan	Blake	JAM	26.12.89	1	NC	Kingston	23 Jun
9.91	1.0	Julian	Forte	JAM	7.1.93	1	ISTAF	Berlin	27 Aug
9.92A	1.2	Akani	Simbine	RSA	21.9.93	1		Pretoria	18 Mar
9.92	-0.8	Justin	Gatlin	USA	10.2.82	1	WCh	London (OS)	5 Aug
9.93A	2.0		Simbine			1		Pretoria	4 Mar
9.93	0.4		Blake			1		Kingston	20 May
9.93	0.8	Cameron	Burrell	USA	11.9.94	1s2	NCAA	Eugene	7 Jun
9.93	1.6	Chris	Belcher	USA	29.1.94	1s3	NCAA	Eugene	7 Jun
9.93	0.2		Coleman			1h2	NC	Sacramento	22 Jun
9.94A	0.2		Simbine			1s1	NC	Potchefstroom	21 Apr
9.94	0.9	Wayde	van Niekerk	RSA	15.7.92	1		Velenje	20 Jun
9.94	-0.8		Coleman			2	WCh	London (OS)	5 Aug
9.95A	1.2	Thando	Roto	RSA	26.9.95	2		Pretoria	18 Mar
9.95A	-0.7		Simbine			1	NC	Potchefstroom	21 Apr
9.95	-0.7		Gatlin			1	NC	Sacramento	23 Jun
9.95	0.7	Usain	Bolt (10)	JAM	21.8.86	1	Herc	Monaco	21 Jul
9.95	-0.8		Bolt			3	WCh	London (OS)	5 Aug
9.96	1.7		Coleman			1h6	NCAA-E	Lexington	25 May
9.96	0.2		Gatlin			1	Athl	Lausanne	6 Jul
9.97	0.6		Coleman			1	SEC	Columbia, SC	13 May
9.97	0.5	Jimmy	Vicaut	FRA	27.2.92	1		Dijon	21 May
9.97	0.6		Blake			1		Kingston	10 Jun
9.97	1.5	Isiah	Young	USA	5.1.90	1h3	NC	Sacramento	22 Jun
9.97	1.5	Ramil	Guliyev	TUR	29.5.90	1		Bursa	6 Jul
9.97	0.4		Coleman			1s3	WCh	London (OS)	5 Aug
9.97	0.0	Chijindu	Ujah	GBR	5.3.94	1	WK-DLF	Zürich	24 Aug
9.97	0.0	Ben Youssef	Meité	CIV	11.11.86	2	WK-DLF	Zürich	24 Aug
9.98A	1.1		Simbine			1h3		Pretoria	18 Mar
9.98	2.0	Odean	Skeen	JAM	28.8.94	1h4		Auburn	22 Apr
9.98	0.4	Ronnie	Baker	USA	15.10.93	2		Kingston	20 May
9.98	-0.2		Coleman			1q1	NCAA-E	Lexington	26 May
9.98	-0.7		Coleman			2	NC	Sacramento	23 Jun
9.98	0.9		Gatlin			1	Gyulai	Székesfehérvár	4 Jul
9.98	0.2		Meité			2	Athl	Lausanne	6 Jul
9.98	-0.3		Ujah			1	DL	Rabat	16 Jul
9.98	0.7		Young			2	Herc	Monaco	21 Jul
9.98	0.4		Bolt			2s3	WCh	London (OS)	5 Aug
9.98	1.8	Yoshihide	Kiryu	JPN	15.12.95	1		Fukui	9 Sep
		(39/18)							
9.99	0.6	Nethaneel	Mitchell-Blake	GBR	2.4.94	2	SEC	Columbia, SC	13 May
10.00	2.0	Jaylen	Bacon	USA	5.8.96	1		Arlington	14 May
		(20)							
10.00	1.3	Kyree	King	USA	9.7.94	2s1	NCAA	Eugene	7 Jun
10.00	1.2	Michael	Rodgers	USA	24.4.85	2h4	NC	Sacramento	22 Jun
10.00	2.0	Yunier	Pérez	CUB/ESP	16.2.85	1h1		Madrid	14 Jul
10.00	0.2	Ryota	Yamagata	JPN	10.6.92	1		Osaka	24 Sep
10.01	0.2	Andre	De Grasse	CAN	10.11.94	1	Bisl	Oslo	15 Jun
10.02	1.6	Senoj-Jay	Givans	JAM	30.12.93	3s3	NCAA	Eugene	7 Jun
10.03	0.2	Jeff	Demps	USA	8.1.90	2h2	NC	Sacramento	22 Jun
10.03	1.5	Jarrion	Lawson	USA	6.5.94	3h3	NC	Sacramento	22 Jun
10.03	0.0	Reece	Prescod	GBR	29.2.96	3h3	WCh	London (OS)	4 Aug
10.03	-0.2		Su Bingtian	CHN	29.8.89	1h4	WCh	London (OS)	4 Aug
		(30)							

Mark	Wind	Name		Nat	Born	Pos	Meet	Venue	Date
10.04	2.0	Clayton	Vaughn	USA	15.5.92	1h4		Clermont	15 Apr
10.04	0.3		Xie Zhenye	CHN	17.8.93	1	NG	Tianjin	3 Sep
10.05	0.8	Cejhae	Greene	ANT	6.10.95	3s2	NCAA	Eugene	7 Jun
10.05	1.2	Beejay (Bernard)	Lee	USA	5.3.93	3h4	NC	Sacramento	22 Jun
10.05	0.6	Abdul Hakim	Sani Brown	JPN-J	6.3.99	1	NC	Osaka	24 Jun
10.05	2.0	David	Lima	POR	6.9.90	2h1		Madrid	14 Jul
10.06	0.4	Kemar	Bailey-Cole	JAM	10.1.92	1		Kingston	11 Mar
10.06	1.4	Kendal	Williams	USA	23.9.95	1h2	TexR	Austin	31 Mar
10.06	1.3	Brandon	Carnes	USA	6.3.95	1		Iowa City	22 Apr
10.06	1.5	Henricho	Bruintjies	RSA	16.7.93	2	PNG	Turku	13 Jun
		(40)							
10.06	0.3	James	Dasaolu	GBR	5.9.87	2	DL	London (OS)	9 Jul
10.06	0.5	Jak Ali	Harvey	TUR	5.4.89	2		Angers	9 Sep
10.07	-0.4	Marqueze	Washington	USA	29.9.93	1		Mesa	10 Jun
10.07	0.9	Michael	Campbell	JAM	29.11.96	4	NC	Kingston	23 Jun
10.07	0.8		Kim Kuk-young	KOR	19.4.91	1		Jeongseon	27 Jun
10.07	1.8	Shuhei	Tada	JPN	24.6.96	2		Fukui	9 Sep
10.08	1.8	Adam	Gemili	GBR	6.10.93	1	Clay	Azusa	14 Apr
10.08	-1.2	Asafa	Powell	JAM	23.11.82	2	DL	Doha	5 May
10.08A	2.0	Emile	Erasmus	RSA	3.4.92	1		Pretoria	13 May
10.08	1.9	Shota	Iizuka	JPN	25.6.91	1		Fuse	4 Jun
		(50)							
10.08	-0.9	Aska	Cambridge	JPN	31.5.93	1h4	NC	Osaka	23 Jun
10.08	1.8	Keston	Bledman	TTO	8.3.88	2h9	NC	Port of Spain	23 Jun
10.10	-1.1	Charles	Silmon	USA	4.7.91	1		Houston	25 May
10.10	1.8	Emmanuel	Callender	TTO	10.5.84	1	NC	Port of Spain	24 Jun
10.10	0.2	Julian	Reus	GER	29.4.88	1	NC	Erfurt	8 Jul
10.11	1.2	LeShon	Collins	USA	11.12.93	1	PennR	Philadelphia	29 Apr
10.11	1.0	Elijah	Hall	USA	22.8.94	1h3		Houston	13 May
10.11	0.7	Alex	Wilson	SUI	19.9.90	1h2		Weinheim	27 May
10.11	0.4	Mosito	Lehata	LES	8.4.89	1	Odlozil	Praha	5 Jun
10.11	1.3	Kenzo	Cotton	USA	13.5.96	3s1	NCAA	Eugene	7 Jun
		(60)							
10.11	1.9	Diego	Palomeque	COL	5.12.93	1	SAmC	Asunción	23 Jun
10.12	-1.6	Zharnel	Hughes	GBR	13.7.95	1rB		Kingston	11 Mar
10.12A	1.1	Tlotliso Gift	Leotlela	RSA-J	12.5.98	1h1		Pretoria	18 Mar
10.12	-0.6	Everton	Clarke	JAM	24.12.92	1		Kingston	8 Apr
10.12	0.5	Andrew	Fisher	BRN	15.12.91	1		Manama	10 May
10.12	0.8	Damarcus	Simpson	USA	14.7.93	4s2	NCAA	Eugene	7 Jun
10.12	1.6	Tony	Brown	USA	13.7.95	5s3	NCAA	Eugene	7 Jun
10.12	0.2	Ojie	Edoburun	GBR	2.6.96	1	NC-23	Bedford	17 Jun
10.12	2.0	Gavin	Smellie	CAN	26.6.86	1q1		Windsor	17 Jun
10.12	0.5	Tyquendo	Tracey	JAM	10.6.93	4s1	NC	Kingston	23 Jun
		(70)							
10.13	1.2	Femi Seun	Ogunode	QAT	15.5.91	1		Doha	25 Apr
10.13	1.4	Andre	Ewers	USA	7.6.95	1		Arkansas City, KS	6 May
10.13	1.9	Shota	Hara	JPN	18.7.92	3		Fuse	4 Jun
10.13	0.2	Sean	McLean	USA	23.3.92	3h1	NC	Sacramento	22 Jun
10.13	1.6	Harry	Aikines-Aryeetey	GBR	29.8.88	1	LEAP	Loughborough	22 Jul
10.13	1.6	Alex	Quiñónez	ECU	11.8.89	1	Bol G	Santa Marta	21 Nov
10.14	1.4	Just'N	Thymes	USA	24.1.94	2h2	TexR	Austin	31 Mar
10.14A	0.8	Mark	Otieno	KEN	11.5.93	1	NC	Nairobi	9 Jun
10.14	1.5	Remontay	McClain	USA	21.9.92	5h3	NC	Sacramento	22 Jun
10.15	2.0	Anthony	Schwartz	USA-Y	5.9.00	1	FlaR-HS	Gainesville	31 Mar
		(80)							
10.15A	1.0	Julius	Morris	MNT	14.4.94	1		El Paso	14 May
10.15	0.9	Filippo	Tortu	ITA-J	15.6.98	1		Savona	25 May
10.15	0.2	Jevaughn	Minzie	JAM	20.7.95	2r2		Kingston	10 Jun
10.15	0.2	Aaron	Brown	CAN	27.5.92	5	Bisl	Oslo	15 Jun
10.15	1.8	Rondell	Sorrillo	TTO	21.1.86	3	NC	Port of Spain	24 Jun
10.15	2.0	Kemar	Hyman	CAY	11.10.89	3h1		Madrid	14 Jul
10.15	0.9	Ján	Volko	SVK	2.11.96	1p3	WCh	London (OS)	4 Aug
10.16	2.0	Diondre	Batson	USA	13.7.92	1		San Marcos	16 May
10.16	1.5	Ryan	Shields	JAM	12.5.83	1		Oordegem	27 May
10.16	1.5	Chadadyne	Walker	JAM	14.4.97	1		Kingston	3 Jun
		(90)							
10.16	0.3	Dentarius	Locke	USA	12.12.89	4		Marseille	3 Jun
10.16	0.5	Likoúrgos-Stéfanos	Tsákonas	GRE	8.3.90	2		Gavardo	4 Jun
10.16	0.4	Ramon	Gittens	BAR	20.7.87	4	Odlozil	Praha	5 Jun
10.16	1.8	Kyle	Greaux	TTO	26.4.88	4	NC	Port of Spain	24 Jun
10.16A	1.1	Anaso	Jobodwana	RSA	30.7.92	1		Pretoria	11 Nov

Mark	Wind	Name		Nat	Born	Pos	Meet	Venue	Date
10.17	1.6	Reynier	Mena	CUB	21.11.96	1s1	NC	La Habana	15 Mar
10.17	-0.6	Ronald	Levy	JAM	30.10.92	2		Kingston	8 Apr
10.17		Egwero	Ogho-Oghene	NGR	26.11.88	1		Dubai	25 May
10.17	0.6	Mobolade	Ajomale	CAN	31.8.95	1	NCAA-2	Bradenton, FL	27 May
10.17	1.9	Emre Zafer (100)	Barnes	TUR	7.11.88	3		Erzurum	11 Jun
10.17	0.2	Tyson	Gay	USA	9.8.82	3h2	NC	Sacramento	22 Jun
10.17	0.8	Nigel	Ellis	JAM	8.8.97	4s2	NC	Kingston	23 Jun
10.17	1.0	Chevaughn	Walsh	ANT	29.12.87	1r1	TTO Ch	Port of Spain	24 Jun
10.17	0.2	Mario	Burke	BAR	18.3.97	1	NC	Bridgetown	24 Jun

Mark	Wind	Name		Nat	Born	Date
10.18	0.5	Joseph	Millar	NZL	24.9.92	17 Mar
10.18	0.7	Warren	Fraser	BAH	8.7.91	8 Apr
10.18	0.9	Christophe	Lemaitre	FRA	11.6.90	1 Jun
10.18	0.5	Richard	Kilty	GBR	2.9.89	4 Jun
10.18	1.6	Maxwell	Willis	USA-J	2.9.98	7 Jun
10.18	0.5	Paulo André	de Oliveira	BRA-J	20.8.98	9 Jun
10.18	0.2	Nickel	Ashmeade	JAM	7.4.90	10 Jun
10.18	0.2	Reuben	Arthur	GBR	12.10.96	17 Jun
10.18	nwi	Jason	Rogers	SKN	31.8.91	17 Jun
10.18	0.8	Brendon	Rodney	CAN	9.4.92	7 Jul
10.18	1.8	Emmanuel	Matadi	LBR	15.4.91	7 Jul
10.19	1.7	Tatenda	Tsumba	ZIM	12.11.91	31 Mar
10.19	2.0	Hanoj	Carter	USA	26.6.94	14 May
10.19	0.6	Lester	Miller	USA	24.10.95	27 May
10.19	0.2	Churandy	Martina	NED	3.7.84	15 Jun
10.19	0.6	Meba-Mickaël	Zézé	FRA	19.5.94	18 Jun
10.19	1.2	Desmond	Lawrence	USA	19.12.91	22 Jun
10.19	1.0	Arthur Gue	Cissé	CIV	29.12.96	24 Jun
10.19	1.8	Moriba	Morain	TTO	8.10.92	24 Jun
10.19	-0.3	Walter	Dix	USA	31.1.86	22 Jul
10.19	0.1	Rohan	Browning	AUS	31.12.97	16 Dec
10.20A	2.0	Clarence	Munyai	RSA-J	20.2.98	4 Mar
10.20	2.0	Devin	Quinn	USA	8.6.96	22 Apr
10.20	2.0	Sam	Effah	CAN	29.12.88	14 May
10.20	1.6	David	Winters	USA	19.2.94	25 May
10.20	1.9	Takumi	Kuki	JPN	18.5.92	4 Jun
10.20	1.3	Raheem	Chambers	JAM	6.10.97	7 Jun
10.20	0.8	Oshane	Bailey	JAM	9.8.89	23 Jun
10.20	0.5	Kenroy	Anderson	JAM	27.6.87	23 Jun
10.20	0.3	Kim	Collins	SKN	5.4.76	9 Jul
10.20	0.0		Yang Chun-Han	TPE	1.1.97	24 Aug
10.21	2.0	Riak	Reese	USA	23.11.94	22 Apr
10.21	2.0	Deji	Tobais	GBR	31.10.91	28 Apr
10.21	0.3	Keitavious	Walter	USA	16.4.96	29 Apr
10.21	2.0	Kyle	de Escofet	GBR	4.10.96	2 Jun
10.21	1.6	Samuel	Osewa	GBR	17.4.91	2 Jun
10.21A	-0.3	Simon	Magakwe	RSA	25.5.85	3 Jun
10.21A	0.6	Ngoni	Makusha	ZIM	11.3.87	10 Jun
10.21	-0.4	Cordero	Gray	USA	9.5.89	10 Jun
10.21	-1.3	Shavez	Hart	BAH	6.9.92	10 Jun
10.21	1.1	Romell	Glave	JAM/GBR-J	11.11.99	17 Jun
10.21A	0.0		Xu Haiyang	CHN	2.11.92	25 Jun
10.21	0.6	Marvin	René	FRA	11.4.95	26 Jun
10.21	1.6	Joel	Fearon	GBR	11.10.88	22 Jul
10.22	1.6	Joshua	Clarke	AUS	19.5.95	19 Feb
10.22A	-3.2	Sydney	Siame	ZAM	7.10.97	11 Mar
10.22	0.9	Levi	Cadogan	BAR	8.11.95	25 Mar
10.22	1.6	Donte	Jackson	USA	8.11.95	29 Apr
10.22	1.8	Ryan	Clark	USA	14.9.96	12 May
10.22	0.9	Kalon	Barnes	USA-J	16.12.99	13 May
10.22	1.6	Kenshard	Hamilton	USA	25.6.93	25 May
10.22	1.9	Tatsuro	Suwa	JPN	17.8.94	4 Jun
10.22	0.5	Bruno	de Barros	BRA	7.1.87	9 Jun
10.22	-1.9	Chris	Royster	USA	26.1.92	10 Jun
10.22	0.4	Trayvon	Bromell	USA	10.7.95	22 Jun
10.22	2.0	Ángel David	Rodríguez	ESP	25.4.80	14 Jul
10.22		Hasan	Taftian	IRI	4.5.93	27 Sep
10.23	0.1	Ameer	Webb	USA	19.3.91	15 Apr
10.23	0.6	Cristofer	Valdez	DOM	1.11.94	4 May
10.23	0.2	Akeem	Haynes	CAN	3.11.92	17 May
10.23	0.6	Aleixo Platini	Menga	GER	29.9.87	25 May
10.23	1.9	Kenji	Fujimitsu	JPN	1.5.86	4 Jun
10.23	0.5	Andrew	Robertson	GBR	17.12.90	11 Jun
10.23A	1.9	Sergiy	Smelyk	UKR	19.4.87	11 Jun
10.23	0.6	Daisuke	Miyamoto	JPN-J	17.4.99	16 Jun
10.23	2.0	Denis	Dimitrov	BUL	10.2.94	8 Jul
10.23	-1.2	Lebokeng	Sesele	RSA	10.12.90	9 Jul
10.23	-1.2	Adama	Jammeh	GAM	10.6.93	15 Jul
10.23	1.6	Adam	Thomas	GBR	15.4.95	22 Jul
10.23	0.9	Abdallah Akbar	Mohamed	KSA	1.6.97	4 Aug
10.24	1.0	Quentin	Butler	USA	18.9.92	1 Apr
10.24	0.4	Tevin	Hester	USA	10.1.94	28 Apr
10.24A	0.2	Yoandry	Andújar	DOM	5.7.90	29 Apr
10.24	0.4		Wu Zhiqiang	CHN	10.4.94	16 May
10.24	0.2	Daniel	Bailey	ANT	9.9.86	10 Jun
10.24	0.5	Khairul Hafiz	Jantan	MAS-J	22.7.98	7 Jul
10.25	1.6	Jhevaughn	Matherson	JAM-J	27.2.99	4 Mar
10.25	0.7	Kevaughn	Rattray	JAM	16.4.96	20 May
10.25	-0.1	Joseph	Dewar	GBR	27.1.96	17 Jun
10.25	0.1	Pascal	Mancini	SUI	18.4.89	6 Jul
10.25	2.0	Barakat	Al-Harthi	OMA	15.6.88	8 Jul
10.25	1.3	Yusuke	Uozato	JPN	10.5.94	9 Jul
10.25	-0.9	Emmanuel	Yeboah	GHA	10.8.97	23 Aug
10.26	-0.3	Roberto	Skyers	CUB	12.11.91	3 Mar
10.26	-0.5	Micah	Larkins	USA	8.12.94	18 Mar
10.26	1.0	Markesh	Woodson	USA	6.9.93	1 Apr
10.26	0.0	Wilfried	Koffi	CIV	24.9.89	21 Apr
10.26	0.9	Leon	Powell	USA	1.9.96	30 Apr
10.26	0.9	Vladislav	Grigoryev	KAZ	10.1.97	13 May
10.26A	1.0	Cravorkian	Carson	USA	.96	14 May
10.26	-1.9	Joe	Morris	USA	4.10.89	10 Jun
10.26	0.2	Michael	Pohl	GER	18.11.89	8 Jul
10.26	0.8	Jonathan	Quarcoo	NOR	13.10.96	13 Jul
10.26	0.4	Hayato	Suda (198)	JPN	23.10.94	7 Oct
10.27		ten men				

Doubtful timing

Mark	Wind	Name		Nat	Born	Pos	Meet	Venue	Date
9.88A	0.2	Sydney	Siame	ZAM	7.10.97	1		Lusaka	8 Apr
10.11A	0.2	Chidamba	Hazemba	ZAM	.97	2		Lusaka	8 Apr
10.14	-1.1	Chevaughn	Walsh	ANT	29.12.87	1		Houston	25 May

Wind assisted

Mark	Wind	Name		Nat	Born	Pos	Meet	Venue	Date
9.69	4.8	Andre	De Grasse	CAN	10.11.94	1	DL	Stockholm	18 Jun
9.84	4.8	Ben Youssef	Meité	CIV	11.11.86	2	DL	Stockholm	18 Jun
9.86	2.4	Ronnie	Baker	USA	15.10.93	1	Pre	Eugene	27 May
9.89	4.8	Ryan	Shields	JAM	12.5.83	3	DL	Stockholm	18 Jun
9.90	4.4	Harry	Aikines-Aryeetey	GBR	29.8.88	1		Clermont	15 Apr
9.90	4.5	Cameron	Burrell	USA	11.9.94	1h1	NCAA-W	Austin	25 May
9.90	2.8	Jeff	Demps	USA	8.1.90	1		Tampa	26 May
9.91	4.1		Xie Zhenye	CHN	17.8.93	1h8		Clermont	15 Apr
9.92	2.4		Su Bingtian	CHN	29.8.89	2	Pre	Eugene	27 May
9.92	4.8	Yunier	Pérez	CUB/ESP	16.2.85	3	DL	Stockholm	18 Jun
9.93	4.4	Ojie	Edoburun	GBR	2.6.96	2		Clermont	15 Apr
9.93	3.2		Coleman			1		Baton Rouge	29 Apr
9.93	?	Emmanuel	Matadi	LBR	15.4.91	1		San Marcos	13 Jun
9.94	4.0	Damarcus	Simpson	USA	14.7.93	1h3	NCAA-W	Austin	25 May

Mark	Wind	Name		Nat	Born	Pos	Meet	Venue	Date
9.94	4.5	Shuhei	Tada	JPN	24.6.96	1s1		Hiratsuka	10 Jun
9.94	2.2	Tyson	Gay	USA	9.8.82	1		Montverde	10 Jun
9.95	4.3	Noah	Lyles	USA	18.7.97	1h2		Clermont	15 Apr
9.95	2.1		Burrell			1q2	NCAA-W	Austin	26 May
9.95	2.4	Chijindu	Ujah	GBR	5.3.94	3	Pre	Eugene	27 May
9.95	2.2	Isiah	Young	USA	5.1.90	2		Montverde	10 Jun
9.96	4.0	Kenzo	Cotton	USA	13.5.96	2h3	NCAA-W	Austin	25 May
9.97	5.1	Gavin	Smellie	CAN	26.6.86	1h16		Clermont	15 Apr
9.97	3.2	Lawrence	Crawford	USA	15.5.97	2		Baton Rouge	29 Apr
9.97	2.2	Brandon	Carnes	USA	6.3.95	1		Wichita	14 May
9.97	3.1	Jaylen	Bacon	USA	5.8.96	1q1	NCAA-W	Austin	26 May
9.98	5.1	Aska	Cambridge	JPN	31.5.93	2h16		Clermont	15 Apr
9.98	7.9	Keitavious	Walter	USA	16.4.96	1		Oxford, MS	6 May
9.98	2.8	Aaron	Brown	CAN	27.5.92	2		Tampa	26 May
9.98	3.7	Kyree	King	USA	9.7.94	1q3	NCAA-W	Austin	26 May
9.98	2.4	Michael	Rodgers	USA	24.4.85	6	Pre	Eugene	27 May
9.99	2.1	Kendal	Williams	USA	23.9.95	1	TexR	Austin	1 Apr
9.99	4.8	Julian	Reus	GER	29.4.88	5	DL	Stockholm	18 Jun
10.00	5.1	Alonso	Edward	PAN	8.12.89	1	FlaR	Gainesville	31 Mar
10.00	2.7	LeShon	Collins	USA	11.12.93	1	TexR	Austin	1 Apr
10.00	2.7	Elijah	Hall	USA	22.8.94	1	PennR	Philadelphia	29 Apr
10.00	2.2	Walter	Dix	USA	31.1.86	3		Montverde	10 Jun
10.00	4.8	Churandy	Martina	NED	3.7.84	6	DL	Stockholm	18 Jun
10.01	3.0	Charles	Silmon	USA	4.7.91	2rC		Austin	29 Apr
10.02A	3.2	Emre Zafer	Barnes	TUR	7.11.88	1		Erzurum	11 Jun
10.03	3.8	Maxwell	Willis	USA-J	2.9.98	1h3	Big 12	Lawrence	13 May
10.03	5.3	Jalen	Miller	USA	17.6.95	1	Big 12	Lawrence	14 May
10.03	2.4	Adam	Gemili	GBR	6.10.93	7	Pre	Eugene	27 May
10.03A	3.2	Jak Ali	Harvey	TUR	5.4.89	2		Erzurum	11 Jun
10.03	3.4		Kim Kuk-young	KOR	19.4.91	1	NSF	Chongju	22 Oct
10.04	5.1	Kemar	Hyman	CAY	11.10.89	2	FlaR	Gainesville	31 Mar
10.04	5.0	Remontay	McClain	USA	21.9.92	1		Redlands	18 May
10.04	2.4	Jason	Rogers	SKN	31.8.91	1	NC	Basseterre	17 Jun
10.05	4.2	McKinley	West	USA	.96	1h8		Wichita	15 Apr
10.05	3.5	Warren	Fraser	BAH	8.7.91	1		Athens, GA	6 May
10.05	4.8	Deshawn	Marshall	USA	1.11.94	1	Big 10	University Park	14 May
10.06	3.2	Roberto	Skyers	CUB	12.11.91	1	NC	La Habana	15 Mar
10.06	5.1	Dentarius	Locke	USA	12.12.89	3	FlaR	Gainesville	31 Mar
10.06	3.2	Tevin	Hester	USA	10.1.94	1rB		Clermont	15 Apr
10.06	3.0	Dedric	Dukes	USA	2.4.92	3rC		Austin	29 Apr
10.06	4.4	Sydney	Siame	ZAM	7.10.97	3h2		Madrid	14 Jul
10.07	3.8	Joseph	Sheffield	USA-J	8.3.99	1		Waco	29 Apr
10.07	2.6	Cravont	Charleston	USA-J	2.1.98	1		Atlanta	14 May
10.07	2.8	J-Mee	Samuels	USA	20.5.87	3		Tampa	26 May
10.08	2.1	Just'N	Thymes	USA	24.1.94	2	TexR	Austin	1 Apr
10.08	2.3	Zharnel	Hughes	GBR	13.7.95	1		Kingston	15 Apr
10.08	5.5	Paulo André	de Oliveira	BRA-J	20.8.98	2rC		Clermont	15 Apr
10.08	4.2	Chris	Jefferson	USA	.96	2h2	NCAA-W	Austin	25 May
10.08	4.8	Alex	Wilson	SUI	19.9.90	7	DL	Stockholm	18 Jun
10.09	2.1	Divine	Oduduru	NGR	7.10.96	1		Lubbock	28 Apr
10.09	4.5	Tayuka	Kawakami	JPN	8.6.95	2s1		Hiratsuka	10 Jun
10.10	?	LaMarion	Arnold	USA	.96	1		El Dorado	8 Apr
10.10	3.1	John	Teeters	USA	19.5.93	1		Norman	22 Apr
10.10	4.8	Xavier	Smith	USA	26.5.96	2	Big 10	University Park	14 May
10.10	2.9	Diogo	Antunes	POR	2.11.92	1	NC	Vagos	10 Jun
10.11	3.4	Joseph	Millar	NZL	24.9.92	1		Auckland	5 Mar
10.11	5.0	Jeremy	Phillips	USA	.93	2		Redlands	18 May
10.11	?	Markesh	Woodson	USA	6.9.93	2		San Marcos	13 Jun
10.11	2.4	Antoine	Adams	SKN	31.8.88	2	NC	Basseterre	17 Jun
10.12	3.5	Desmond	Lawrence	USA	19.12.91	2		Greensboro	15 Apr
10.12	2.5	Cordero	Gray	USA	9.5.89	1		Fayetteville	5 May
10.12	3.7	Ángel David	Rodríguez	ESP	25.4.80	1h1		Salamanca	3 Jun
10.12	4.2	Andrew	Ford-Azonwanna	CAN	29.11.95	1		Windsor	17 Jun
10.13	2.9	Tremayne	Acy	USA	21.1.95	1r2		Baton Rouge	29 Apr
10.13	5.1	Tony	McQuay	USA	16.4.90	4	FlaR	Gainesville	31 Mar
10.13	2.7	Riak	Reese	USA	23.11.94	1		Auburn	22 Apr
10.13	2.1	Danny	Talbot	GBR	1.5.91	2	LI	Loughborough	21 May
10.13	3.8	Javelin	Guidry	USA-J	.98	1		Clovis	3 Jun
10.13	2.2	Likoúrgos-Stéfanos	Tsákonas	GRE	8.3.90	1h3		Gavardo	4 Jun
10.13	2.3	Adrian	Griffith	BAH	11.11.84	1rC		Montverde	10 Jun
10.13	2.5	Moriba	Morain	TTO	8.10.92	1h6	NC	Port of Spain	23 Jun

Mark	Wind	Name		Nat	Born	Date
10.14	3.2	Reynier	Mena	CUB	21.11.96	15 Mar
10.14	4.1	Jaquone	Hoyte	BAR-J	4.2.98	18 Mar
10.14	3.0	Tatenda	Tsumba	ZIM	12.11.91	25 May
10.14	4.5	Keon	Campbell	USA	.95	25 May
10.14	4.2	Mario	Burke	BAR	18.3.97	25 May
10.14	4.6	Yuki	Hirao	JPN	27.4.96	10 Jun
10.14	2.2	Blake	Smith	USA	28.5.93	10 Jun
10.14	2.3	Quentin	Butler	USA	18.9.92	10 Jun
10.14	2.9	Sam	Effah	CAN	29.12.88	15 Jul
10.15A	2.9	Lebokeng	Sesele	RSA	10.12.90	18 Feb
10.15	3.8	Antonio	Alkana	RSA	12.4.90	18 Mar
10.15	4.4	Solomon	Bockarie	NED	18.5.87	15 Apr
10.15	2.3	Chadadyne	Walker	JAM	14.4.97	6 May
10.15	4.5	Yusuke	Tanaka	JPN-J	11.1.98	10 Jun
10.15	4.6	Shuji	Takahashi	JPN	17.5.94	10 Jun
10.15		Diondre	Batson	USA	13.7.92	13 Jun
10.15	2.5	Andrew	Robertson	GBR	17.12.90	16 Aug
10.16	5.1	Emeilo	Ferguson	JAM	16.4.93	15 Apr
10.16	5.2	Antonio	Infantino	ITA	22.3.91	15 Apr
10.16	4.1	Hensley	Paulina	NED	26.6.93	15 Apr
10.16	2.4	Omar	McLeod	JAM	25.4.94	22 Apr
10.16	?	Jeffrey	Hulon	USA-J	4.12.98	29 Apr
10.16	4.2	Roy	Ejiakuekwu	GBR	2.2.95	25 May
10.16	4.2	T.J. (Tarrick)	Brock	USA-J	3.2.98	25 May
10.16	3.8	Cravon	Gillespie	USA	31.7.96	27 May
10.16	4.8	Austin	Hamilton	SWE	29.7.97	18 Jun
10.16A	nwi	Thando	Dlodlo	RSA-J	22.4.99	13 Oct
10.17	3.8	Michael	McGruder	USA	28.2.95	8 Apr
10.17	3.4	Oraine	Palmer	JAM	.95	8 Apr
10.17	3.5	Tosin	Ogunode	QAT	2.3.94	15 Apr
10.17	3.0	Davon	DeMoss	USA	.96	29 Apr
10.17		Kavean	Smith	JAM	12.5.91	6 May
10.17	2.9	Kenji	Fujimitsu	JPN	1.5.86	4 Jun
10.17	4.6	Kotaro	Iwasaki	JPN	14.6.96	10 Jun
10.17	2.4	Brijesh BJ	Lawrence	SKN	27.12.89	17 Jun
10.17	2.8	Jonathan	Quarcoo	NOR	13.10.96	6 Jul
10.17	3.4		Lee Jae-Ha	KOR	14.8.92	22 Oct
10.18	3.2	Shivnarine	Smalling	JAM	28.9.96	8 Apr
10.18	2.7	Caleb	Gabriel	USA	28.12.94	15 Apr
10.18	2.7	Nesta	Carter	JAM	11.10.85	15 Apr
10.18	2.7	Khalil	Henderson	USA	18.11.94	22 Apr
10.18	2.3	Gerald	Phiri	ZAM	6.10.88	10 Jun
10.19	3.4	Aaron	Piper	USA	.95	8 Apr
10.19	3.5	Darrell	Wesh	HAI	21.1.92	15 Apr
10.19	5.8	Kieran	Showler-Davis	GBR	14.11.91	15 Apr
10.19	5.2	Giovanni	Codrington	NED	17.7.88	15 Apr
10.19	3.0	Mookie	Salaam	USA	5.4.90	29 Apr
10.19	7.9	Correion	Mosby	USA	31.1.96	6 May
10.19	5.3	Terrell	Smith	USA	10.10.94	14 May
10.19	4.6	Takayuki	Nishimura	JPN	.95	10 Jun
10.19	2.4	Justin	Walker	USA	30.11.90	10 Jun
10.19	2.2	Abdallah Akbar	Mohamed	KSA	1.6.97	16 Jul
10.19	4.0	Ippei	Takeda	JPN	13.3.97	8 Sep
10.20	2.1	Micah	Larkins	USA	8.12.94	1 Apr
10.20	2.9	Amir	James	USA	7.12.95	8 Apr
10.20	5.5	Alexander	Kosenkow	GER	14.3.77	15 Apr
10.20	2.1	Cristofer	Valdez	DOM	1.11.94	26 May
10.20A	2.1	Karabo	Mothibi	BOT	15.10.96	3 Jun
10.20	2.1	Ben	Bassaw	FRA	9.7.89	17 Jun
10.20	2.8	Joel	Fearon	GBR	11.10.88	1 Jul
10.20	2.8	Samuel	Osewa	GBR	17.4.91	1 Jul
10.20	3.5	Rasheed	Dwyer	JAM	29.1.89	22 Jul
10.20	4.2	Daisuke	Miyamoto	JPN-J	17.4.99	6 Oct
10.21	2.2	Ncincihli	Titi	RSA	15.12.93	31 Mar
10.21A	3.8	Alex	Reece	USA	14.10.93	7 Apr
10.21	4.9	Robert	Hering	GER	14.6.90	15 Apr
10.21	2.7	Kevaughn	Rattray	JAM	16.4.96	15 Apr
10.21	2.9	Benjamin	Williams	CAN	15.5.92	29 Apr
10.21		Kimmari	Roach	JAM	21.9.90	6 May
10.21	2.9	Wayne	Sherbahn	USA	.95	27 May
10.21A	3.4	Heber	Gallegos	MEX	13.4.92	4 Jun
10.21	2.2	Henrik	Larsson	SWE-J	30.9.99	25 Aug
10.22A	2.9	Le Roux	van Tonder	RSA	4.4.88	18 Feb
10.22	?	Travis	Collins	USA	26.2.96	8 Apr
10.22	5.1		Mo Youxue	CHN	10.2.96	15 Apr
10.22	2.7	Hakim	Montgomery	USA	23.6.97	29 Apr
10.22	4.5	Elijah	Ross	USA	.96	29 Apr
10.22	3.1	Hakeem	Lawrence	USA	18.7.94	13 May
10.22	4.8	Karson	Kowalchuk	CAN-J	30.12.98	14 May
10.22	2.3	O'Shea	Wilson	USA	27.10.94	25 May
10.22	2.1	Harlyn	Pérez	CUB	2.6.95	26 May
10.22	3.1	Ja'Maun	Charles	USA	1.10.97	26 May
10.22	2.9	Kabroderan	Handsborough	USA	.93	27 May
10.22	4.2	Bismark	Boateng	CAN	15.3.92	17 Jun
10.22	2.2	Ioannis	Nifadópoulos	GRE	1.11.90	15 Jul
10.23	5.0	Malik	Wilson	USA	12.12.95	8 Apr
10.23	2.8	Darrion	Flowers	USA	12.12.96	15 Apr
10.23	4.0	Charles	Anumnu	USA	24.6.95	13 May
10.23	2.1	César	Ruiz	CUB	18.1.95	26 May
10.23	4.5	Yukitoki	Miyasaki	JPN	29.8.94	10 Jun
10.23	4.5	Yoshihiro	Someya	JPN-J	14.7.98	10 Jun
10.23	2.9	Carlos	Nascimento	POR	12.10.94	10 Jun
10.23	3.0	Adam	Harris	GUY	21.7.87	15 Jul
10.23	2.8	Kenta	Oshima	JPN	3.9.97	8 Sep
10.24	3.7	Roy	Schmidt	GER	30.9.91	15 Apr
10.24	2.5	Joaeph	Amoah	GHA	12.1.97	22 Apr
10.24	2.1	Trevin	Chambers	USA	23.11.97	28 Apr
10.24	2.3	John	Lewis	USA	2.9.96	25 May
10.24	2.7	Panayiótis	Trivizás	GRE	22.11.87	3 Jun
10.24	2.4	Marcus	Duncan	TTO	4.12.86	23 Jun
10.24	2.1	Federico	Cattaneo	ITA	14.7.93	1 Jul
10.24	2.2	Ahmed	Ali	SUD	15.11.93	16 Jul
10.24A	nwi	Maritz	Pieters	RSA-J	.99	13 Oct

Low altitude bests

9.99 -1.2 Simbine 1 DL Doha 5 May
10.11 1.0 Roto 1 Bilbao 24 Jun
10.12 0.9 Erasmus 2 Velenje 20 Jun
10.22 1.5 Siame 13 Jun | 10.25 0.2 Smelyk 6 Jul | 10.21w 3.9 Jobodwana 28 Feb
10.24 1.6 Jammeh 5 Jul | 10.20w 3.2 Sesele 8 Jul | 10.21w 3.8 Reece 13 May

Hand timing

Mark	Wind	Name		Nat	Born	Pos	Meet	Venue	Date
9.9	1.9	Reynier	Mena	CUB	21.11.96			La Habana	24 Feb
9.9	-2.1	Roberto	Skyers	CUB	12.11.91	1h1	NC	La Habana	14 Mar
9.9	-2.1	Edel	Amores	CUB-J	5.10.98	2h1	NC	La Habana	14 Mar
9.9A		Ferdinand	Omanyala	KEN	2.1.96	1h1		Nairobi	11 May
9.9A		Maurice	Wasike	KEN	.93	1		Nairobi	11 May
9.9		Ramil	Guliyev	TUR	29.5.90	1		Ankara	6 Jun

JUNIORS

See main list for top 4 juniors. 11 performances by 6 men to 10.18. Additional marks and further juniors:

Sani Brown 10.05 -0.6 1h2 WCh London (OS) 4 Aug | 10.06 0.5 1s2 NC Osaka 23 Jun
10.06 0.4 1h3 NC Osaka 23 Jun | 10.18 1.8 2 Clay Azusa 14 Apr
Leotlela 10.12A -0.4 1 Pretoria 31 Mar

Mark	Wind	Name		Nat	Born	Pos	Meet	Venue	Date
10.18	1.6	Maxwell	Willis	USA	2.9.98	6s3	NCAA	Eugene	7 Jun
10.18	0.5	Paulo André	de Oliveira	BRA	20.8.98	1	NC	São Bernardo do Campo	9 Jun
10.20A	2.0	Clarence	Munyai	RSA	20.2.98	2		Pretoria	4 Mar
10.22	0.9	Kalon	Barnes	USA	16.12.99	1-HS		Austin	13 May
10.23	0.6	Daisuke	Miyamoto	JPN	17.4.99	1		Kyoto	16 Jun
10.24	0.5	Khairul Hafiz	Jantan (10)	MAS	22.7.98	1s3	AsiC	Bhubaneswar	7 Jul
10.25	1.6	Jhevaughn	Matherson	JAM	27.2.99	1		Kingston	4 Mar
10.27	0.6	Felipe	Bardi dos Santos	BRA	8.10.98	3	NC	São Bernardo do Campo	9 Jun

Mark	Wind	Name		Nat	Born	Pos	Meet	Venue	Date
10.30	1.5	T.J. (Tarrick)	Brock	USA	3.2.98	2h3	TexR	Austin	31 Mar
10.30	1.9	Yusuke	Tanaka	JPN	11.1.98	2		Hiratsuka	10 Jun
10.31	1.4	Caleb	Jolivette	USA	24.9.98	1		Austin	12 May
10.31	1.0	Oliver	Bromby	GBR	30.3.98	2	NC-j	Bedford	17 Jun
10.31	0.2	Samuel	Purola	FIN-Y	19,5,00	1		Mannheim	1 Jul
10.31	1.9	Henrik	Larsson	SWE	30.9.99	1s1	NC	Helsingborg	25 Aug
10.32	1.4	Keishawn	Everly	USA-Y	8.4.00	2		Austin	12 May
10.32	0.3	Kesean	Carter (20)	USA-Y	15.8.00	1		Austin	13 May
10.32	1.5	Isaiah	Cunningham	USA	8.7.99	1		Mission Viejo	13 May
10.32	1.1	Jerod	Elcock	TTO	30.7.98	1	NC-j	Port of Spain	10 Jun
10.32	1.2	Compton	Caesar	GUY	2.1.98	1	NC	Leonara	1 Jul

Wind assisted

See main list for top 7 juniors. 11 performances by 7 men to 10.15w. Additional marks:

Willis 10.04 5.3 3 Big 12 Lawrence 14 May 10.08 2.9 1 Waco 8 Apr

10.07 3.1 1h6 NCAA-W Austin 25 May 10.10 2.1 2q2 NCAA-W Austin 26 May

Mark	Wind	Name		Nat	Born	Pos	Meet	Venue	Date
10.16	?	Jeffrey	Hulon	USA	4.12.98	1		Webster, TX	29 Apr
10.16	4.2	T.J. (Tarrick)	Brock	USA	3.2.98	5h2	NCAA-W	Austin	25 May
10.16A	nwi	Thando	Dlodlo	RSA	22.4.99	1		Mookgohpong	13 Oct
10.20	4.2	Daisuke	Miyamoto	JPN	17.4.99	1		Matsuyama	6 Oct
10.21	2.2	Henrik	Larsson	SWE	30.9.99	2	NC	Helsingborg	25 Aug
10.22	4.8	Karson	Kowalchuk	CAN	30.12.98	4	Big 10	University Park	14 May
10.23	4.5	Yoshihiro	Someya	JPN	14.7.98	5s1		Hiratsuka	10 Jun
10.24A	nwi	Maritz	Pieters	RSA	.99	2		Mookgohpong	13 Oct

150 METRES STRAIGHT

Mark	Wind	Name		Nat	Born	Pos	Meet	Venue	Date
15.04	0.4	Likoúrgos-Stéfanos	Tsákonas	GRE	8.3.90	1		Manchester	26 May

Boston 4 Jun: +1.1 1. Alonso Edward PAN 8.12.89 15.09, 2. Nickel Ashmeade JAM 7.4.90 15.16, 3. Yohan Blake JAM 15.17

200 METRES

Mark	Wind	Name		Nat	Born	Pos	Meet	Venue	Date
19.77	0.0	Isaac	Makwala	BOT	29.9.86	1		Madrid	14 Jul
19.84	1.2	Wayde	van Niekerk	RSA	15.7.92	1		Kingston	10 Jun
19.85	-0.5	Christian	Coleman	USA	6.3.96	1q1	NCAA-E	Lexington	27 May
19.90A	0.5		van Niekerk			1	NC	Potchefstroom	22 Apr
19.90	-0.4	Noah	Lyles	USA	18.7.97	1	DL	Shanghai	13 May
19.95A	1.7	Akani	Simbine	RSA	21.9.93	1		Pretoria	4 Mar
19.97	0.2	Jereem	Richards	TTO	13.1.94	1q3	NCAA-E	Lexington	27 May
19.97	1.0	Yohan	Blake	JAM	26.12.89	1	NC	Kingston	25 Jun
19.98	0.6		Coleman			1	SEC	Columbia, SC	13 May
20.00	0.9		Lyles			1	VD-DLF	Bruxelles	1 Sep
20.01	1.6	Chris	Belcher	USA	29.1.94	1s3	NCAA	Eugene	7 Jun
20.01	0.6	Andre	De Grasse	CAN	10.11.94	1	GGala	Roma	8 Jun
20.01	0.9	Ameer	Webb (10)	USA	19.3.91	2	VD-DLF	Bruxelles	1 Sep
20.02	0.9	Ramil	Guliyev	TUR	29.5.90	3	VD-DLF	Bruxelles	1 Sep
20.03	0.4		De Grasse			1	DL	Rabat	16 Jul
20.04	-0.4	Nethaneel	Mitchell-Blake	GBR	2.4.94	1q2	NCAA-E	Lexington	27 May
20.04	1.6		Richards			1s1	NCAA	Eugene	7 Jun
20.05	-0.6		Richards			1h2	WCh	London	7 Aug
20.06	0.8		Belcher			1h5	NCAA-E	Lexington	26 May
20.07	0.8		Coleman			2h5	NCAA-E	Lexington	26 May
20.08	0.6		Guliyev			1	Isl.Sol	Baku	18 May
20.08	0.7		Mitchell-Blake			1h7	WCh	London(OS)	7 Aug
20.09	0.6		Mitchell-Blake			2	SEC	Columbia, SC	13 May
20.09	-2.3		Webb			1	NC	Sacramento	25 Jun
20.09	-0.1		Guliyev			1	WCh	London(OS)	10 Aug
20.10A	1.7	Clarence	Munyai	RSA-J	20.2.98	2		Pretoria	4 Mar
20.10	0.8		van Niekerk			1		Cape Town	29 Apr
20.10	-0.5		Guliyev			1		Andújar	2 Jun
20.10	-2.3		Coleman			2	NC	Sacramento	25 Jun
20.11	1.2	Rasheed	Dwyer	JAM	29.1.89	2		Kingston	10 Jun
20.11A	0.5	Bernardo	Baloyes	COL	6.1.94	1	NC	Medellín	11 Jun
20.11	-0.1		van Niekerk			2	WCh	London(OS)	10 Aug
20.11	-0.1		Richards			3	WCh	London(OS)	10 Aug
		(33/15)							
20.14	1.7	Ncincihli	Titi	RSA	15.12.93	1		Columbia, SC	15 Apr
20.14	0.9	Isiah	Young	USA	5.1.90	1	Gyulai	Székesfehérvár	4 Jul
20.15	1.3	Aldemir Gomes	da Silva	BRA	8.6.92	1	NC	São Bernardo do Campo	11 Jun
20.16	0.3	Danny	Talbot	GBR	1.5.91	2h3	WCh	London (OS)	7 Aug
20.17	0.9	Aaron	Brown	CAN	27.5.92	4	VD-DLF	Bruxelles	1 Sep
		(20)							

Mark	Wind	Name		Nat	Born	Pos	Meet	Venue	Date
20.18	1.7	Jaylen	Bacon	USA	5.8.96	1h6	NCAA-W	Austin	26 May
20.18	1.2	Warren	Weir	JAM	31.10.89	3		Kingston	10 Jun
20.19	-1.0	Kyle	Greaux	TTO	26.4.88	2	NC	Port of Spain	25 Jun
20.20A	0.5	Tlotliso Gift	Leotlela	RSA-J	12.5.98	3	NC	Potchefstroom	22 Apr
20.20	-0.2		Xie Zhenye	CHN	17.8.93	1	NG	Tianjin	5 Sep
20.21	-2.3	Elijah	Hall	USA	22.8.94	3	NC	Sacramento	25 Jun
20.21	0.9	Christophe	Lemaitre	FRA	11.6.90	5	VD-DLF	Bruxelles	1 Sep
20.22	1.2	Zharnel	Hughes	GBR	13.7.95	4		Kingston	10 Jun
20.24	-0.5	Jaron	Flournoy	USA	24.11.96	2q1	NCAA-E	Lexington	27 May
20.24	-0.7	Fred	Kerley	USA	7.5.95	2	DL	London (OS)	9 Jul
		(30)							
20.25	1.7	Brandon	Carnes	USA	6.3.95	1h1	NCAA-W	Austin	26 May
20.25	-0.5	Teray	Smith	BAH	28.9.94	3q1	NCAA-E	Lexington	27 May
20.25	-0.4	Khalil	Henderson	USA	18.11.94	3q2	NCAA-E	Lexington	27 May
20.27	-0.4	LaShawn	Merritt	USA	27.6.86	2	DL	Shanghai	13 May
20.27	1.6	Kyree	King	USA	9.7.94	2s1	NCAA	Eugene	7 Jun
20.27	-0.5	Churandy	Martina	NED	3.7.84	2	DL	Paris (C)	1 Jul
20.27	-0.3	Lebokeng	Sesele	RSA	10.12.90	1		Kortrijk	8 Jul
20.27	1.3	Alex	Quiñónez	ECU	11.8.89	1	Bol G	Santa Marta	22 Nov
20.28A	0.7	Julius	Morris	MNT	14.4.94	1		El Paso	14 May
20.29	1.0	Julian	Reus	GER	29.4.88	1	NC	Erfurt	9 Jul
		(40)							
20.29	-0.6	Sydney	Siame	ZAM	7.10.97	1h5	WCh	London (OS)	7 Aug
20.30	0.6	Kendal	Williams	USA	23.9.95	4	SEC	Columbia, SC	13 May
20.30	1.7	Aldrich	Bailey	USA	6.2.94	2h1	NCAA-W	Austin	26 May
20.30	0.6	David	Lima	POR	6.9.90	1rB		La Chaux de Fonds	2 Jul
20.31	1.7	Jeffrey	John	FRA	6.6.92	1		Genève	10 Jun
20.32	-0.4	Deshawn	Marshall	USA	1.11.94	4q2	NCAA-E	Lexington	27 May
20.32	1.3	Senoj-Jay	Givans	JAM	30.12.93	2s2	NCAA	Eugene	7 Jun
20.32	-0.2	Marqueze	Washington	USA	29.9.93	1		Mesa	10 Jun
20.32A	0.5	Diego	Palomeque	COL	5.12.93	2	NC	Medellín	11 Jun
20.32	0.3	Abdul Hakim	Sani Brown	JPN-J	6.3.99	1	NC	Osaka	25 Jun
		(50)							
20.33A	1.5	Jamiel	Trimble	USA	25.6.95	1		Logan	13 May
20.33	1.2	Likoúrgos-Stéfanos	Tsákonas	GRE	8.3.90	1h1	ET	Villeneuve d'Ascq	23 Jun
20.33	1.6	Ján	Volko	SVK	2.11.96	1	EC-23	Bydgoszcz	15 Jul
20.34	0.6	Filippo	Tortu	ITA-J	15.6.98	4	GGala	Roma	8 Jun
20.34	0.0	Aleixo Platini	Menga	GER	29.9.87	1		Regensburg	11 Jun
20.35	-0.4	Adam	Gemili	GBR	6.10.93	3	DL	Shanghai	13 May
20.35	0.2	Chadadyne	Walker	JAM	14.4.97	1s2	NC	Kingston	24 Jun
20.37	0.1	Joseph	Millar	NZL	24.9.92	1	NC	Hamilton	19 Mar
20.37	1.3	Dedric	Dukes	USA	2.4.92	1		St Martin	13 May
20.37	1.5	Alex	Wilson	SUI	19.9.90	1		Weinheim	27 May
		(60)							
20.37	0.3	Burkheart	Ellis	BAR	18.9.92	1	NC	Bridgetown	25 Jun
20.37	0.0	Nickel	Ashmeade	JAM	7.4.90	1		Luzern	11 Jul
20.38A	0.0	José Carlos	Herrera	MEX	5.2.86	1		Ciudad de México	11 Feb
20.38	0.2	Nick	Gray	USA	2.6.97	3q3	NCAA-E	Lexington	27 May
20.38	1.6	Gavin	Smellie	CAN	26.6.86	1h6		Windsor	18 Jun
20.38	0.8	Leon	Reid	GBR	26.7.94	3	NC	Birmingham	2 Jul
20.38	0.5	Christopher	Taylor	JAM-J	29.9.99	1	PAm-J	Trujillo	22 Jul
20.39	1.7	Chijindu	Ujah	GBR	5.3.94	1rB		Tempe	8 Apr
20.39	1.5	Maxwell	Willis	USA-J	2.9.98	1h4	NCAA-W	Austin	26 May
20.39	1.1	Kenroy	Anderson	JAM	27.6.87	2s3	NC	Kingston	24 Jun
		(70)							
20.39	0.9	Jonathan	Quarcoo	NOR	13.10.96	1s1	EC-23	Bydgoszcz	15 Jul
20.40	1.7	Paul	Dedewo	USA	4.6.91	2rB		Tempe	8 Apr
20.40A	0.7	Hendrik	Maartens	RSA	24.5.96	1s2	NC	Potchefstroom	22 Apr
20.40	1.5	Mohamed	Yacoub Salem	BRN	1.3.96	1		Manama	10 May
20.40	0.2	Shota	Iizuka	JPN	25.6.91	1h3	NC	Osaka	24 Jun
20.40	-1.0	Ben	Bassaw	FRA	9.7.89	1		La Roche-sur-Yon	5 Jul
20.41	-1.5	Wilfried	Koffi	CIV	24.9.89	1		Claremont	3 Jun
20.41A	1.8	Mike	Otieno	KEN	11.5.93	1	NC	Nairobi	10 Jun
20.41		Julian	Forte	JAM	7.1.93	3s1	NC	Kingston	24 Jun
20.41	0.1	Winston	George	GUY	19.5.87	1		Leonora	15 Jul
		(80)							
20.42	1.8	Roger	Gurski	GER	11.7.97	1		Jena	27 May
20.42	1.2	Sean	McLean	USA	23.3.92	5		Kingston	10 Jun
20.42	-1.3	Sergiy	Smelyk	UKR	19.4.87	1		Kyiv	30 Jun
20.43	0.3	Andrew	Hudson	USA	14.12.96	1rA		Tempe	8 Apr
20.43	1.2	Riak	Reese	USA	23.11.94	1		Auburn	22 Apr

Mark	Wind	Name		Nat	Born	Pos	Meet	Venue	Date
20.43	1.8	Keitavious	Walter	USA	16.4.96	1		Hattiesburg	29 Apr
20.43	0.2	Tevin	Hester	USA	10.1.94	1		Greensboro	14 May
20.44	1.7	Miguel	Francis	GBR	28.2.95	1		Kingston	15 Apr
20.44	-0.1	Walter	Dix	USA	31.1.86	3		Columbia	22 Apr
20.45	-1.0	Brendon	Rodney	CAN	9.4.92	2		St. George's	8 Apr
		(90)							
20.45	1.7	Robin	Vanderbemden	BEL	10.2.94	1		Genève	10 Jun
20.46	0.3	Pavel	Maslák	CZE	21.2.91	1	NC	Trinec	11 Jun
20.47	1.7	Meba-Mickaël	Zézé	FRA	19.5.94	3		Genève	10 Jun
20.47	0.3	Kenji	Fujimitsu	JPN	1.5.86	2	NC	Osaka	25 Jun
20.47	-0.3	Michael	Campbell	JAM	29.11.96	2		Kortrijk	8 Jul
20.48	0.4	Demish	Gaye	JAM	20.1.93	1		Kingston	11 Mar
20.48	0.2	Steven	Gayle	JAM	19.3.94	1		Tallahassee	24 Mar
20.48	1.2	Dentarius	Locke	USA	12.12.89	1		Tallahassee	5 May
20.49	0.4	Chadic	Hinds	JAM	11.8.92	1		Kingston	8 Apr
20.49	0.4	Oshane	Bailey	JAM	9.8.89	2		Kingston	8 Apr
		(100)							
20.49	0.8	Tremayne	Acy	USA	21.1.95	1rB		Baton Rouge	22 Apr
20.49A	0.0	Tatenda	Tsumba	ZIM	12.11.91	1		Provo	13 May
20.49	-0.5	Malik	Moffett	USA	11.4.94	5q1	NCAA-E	Lexington	27 May
20.49	-0.4	Josh	Davis	USA	13.10.95	5q2	NCAA-E	Lexington	27 May
20.49	1.9	Ahmed	Ali	SUD	15.11.93	1	Arab C	Radès	18 Jul

Mark	Wind	Name		Nat	Born	Date
20.50	0.6	Terrel	Cotton	USA	19.7.88	20 May
20.50	-1.0	Dan-Nei	Telesford	TTO	9.9.90	25 Jun
20.50	1.0	Robin	Erewa	GER	24.6.91	9 Jul
20.51A	0.7	Luxolo	Adams	RSA	1.8.96	22 Apr
20.51	0.9	Tyrese	Cooper	USA-Y	21.3.00	27 May
20.51	1.4	Richard	Kilty	GBR	2.9.89	4 Jun
20.51	0.3	Shane	Brathwaite	BAR	8.2.90	25 Jun
20.52	1.3	Josh	Washington	USA	28.8.95	7 Jun
20.52	1.6	Kenzo	Cotton	USA	13.5.96	7 Jun
20.52	2.0	Michael	Mathieu	BAH	24.6.83	8 Jul
20.53	1.7	Carvin	Nkanata	KEN	6.5.91	8 Apr
20.53	0.2	David	Winters	USA	19.2.94	27 May
20.53	-0.5	Tinashe Samuel	Mutanga	ZIM	27.1.93	27 May
20.54	1.1	Chevaughn	Walsh	ANT	29.12.87	5 May
20.54	0.9	Kalon	Barnes	USA-J	16.12.99	27 May
20.55	1.9	Emmanuel	Dasor	GHA	14.9.95	8 Apr
20.56	0.2	John	Lundy	USA	15.3.92	14 May
20.56	1.1	Jak Ali	Harvey	TUR	5.4.89	16 Jul
20.56	0.9		Yang Chun-Han	TPE	1.1.97	25 Oct
20.56	0.4	Nery	Brenes	CRC	25.9.85	14 Dec
20.57A	1.5	Dusty	Fisher	USA	.95	13 May
20.57	2.0	Jamal	Walton	CAY-J	25.11.98	27 May
20.58	1.3	Lalonde	Gordon	TTO	25.11.88	13 May
20.58		Vladislav	Grigoryev	KAZ	10.1.97	14 May
20.58A	0.7	Ventavius	Sears	USA	14.5.95	14 May
20.58	1.2	Nigel	Ellis	JAM	8.8.97	20 May
20.58	1.4	DeTorrian	Green	USA	.96	26 May
20.58	0.9	Panayiátis	Trivizás	GRE	22.11.87	3 Jun
20.58	-1.5	Stirley	Jones	USA	13.12.84	3 Jun
20.58A	0.5	Sibusiso	Matsenjwa	SWZ	2.5.88	10 Jun
20.58	-0.3	Shavez	Hart	BAH	6.9.92	24 Jun
20.58	0.0	Paulo André	de Oliveira	BRA-J	20.8.98	16 Jul
20.58	1.6	Yuki	Koike	JPN	13.5.95	10 Sep
20.59	0.3	Yoshihide	Kiryu	JPN	15.12.95	28 May
20.59	1.7	Antonio	Infantino	ITA	22.3.91	10 Jun
20.59	0.9	Jun	Yamashita	JPN	23.8.97	11 Jun
20.59	0.2	Cejhae	Greene	ANT	6.10.95	22 Jul
20.59	0.6	Samuel	García	ESP	4.12.91	23 Jul
20.60	-1.0	Wallace	Spearmon	USA	24.12.84	8 Apr
20.60	1.7	Jason	Young	JAM	21.3.91	15 Apr
20.60	1.5	Jacarias	Martin	USA	13.1.96	26 May
20.60	-1.5	Daveon	Collins	USA	3.10.92	3 Jun
20.60	0.2	Tyson	Gay	USA	9.8.82	24 Jun
20.60	0.6	Luka	Janezic	SLO	14.11.95	25 Jun
20.60	0.3	Mario	Burke	BAR	18.3.97	25 Jun
20.60	-1.0	Moriba	Morain	TTO	8.10.92	25 Jun
20.61	0.9	Tom	Gamble	AUS	25.11.91	19 Feb
20.61	0.3	Jeremy	Dodson	SAM	30.8.87	15 Apr
20.61	0.3	Just'N	Thymes	USA	24.1.94	15 Apr
20.61	1.7	Chris	Jefferson	USA	.96	14 May
20.61	-0.5	Ryan	Shields	JAM	12.5.83	2 Jun
20.61	1.3	Bruno	de Barros	BRA	7.1.87	11 Jun
20.61	1.3	Derick	Silva	BRA-J	23.4.98	11 Jun
20.61	-0.5	Adama	Jammeh	GAM	10.6.93	15 Jul
20.61	0.3	Alonso	Edward	PAN	8.12.89	7 Aug
20.62		Andre	Ewers	USA/JAM	7.6.95	6 May
20.62	-1.2	Anaso	Jobodwana	RSA	30.7.92	11 Jun
20.62	1.6	Yusuke	Tanaka	JPN-J	11.1.98	10 Sep
20.63	1.0	Clayton	Vaughn	USA	15.5.92	25 Mar
20.63	1.7	Amir	James	USA	7.12.95	8 Apr
20.63	0.3	Remontay	McClain	USA	21.9.92	15 Apr
20.63	0.9	Christian	Sourapas	USA	17.7.96	30 Apr
20.63	1.1	Emmanuel	Matadi	LBR	15.4.91	30 May
20.64	1.7	Rai	Benjamin	ANT	27.7.97	1 Apr
20.64	1.7	Obie	Igbokwe	USA	28.1.97	8 Apr
20.64	0.4	Tyquendo	Tracey	JAM	10.6.93	8 Apr
20.64	-1.0	Cameron	Williams	USA	11.9.95	12 May
20.64	0.1		Bie Ge	CHN	2.8.92	18 May
20.64A		Dennis	Otieno	KEN	15.1.96	10 Jun
20.64	1.7	Eseosa	Desalu	ITA	19.2.94	10 Jun
20.65	1.8	Correion	Mosby	USA	31.1.96	22 Apr
20.65	0.1	McKinley	West	USA	.96	22 Apr
20.65	0.2	Cordero	Gray	USA	9.5.89	5 May
20.65	1.7	Roy	Ejiakuekwu	GBR	2.2.95	26 May
20.65	-0.4	Devin	O'Neal	USA	.94	27 May
20.65	1.2	Shota	Hara	JPN	18.7.92	26 Aug
20.65	0.2	Romario	Williams	JAM	17.11.95	24 Jun
20.66	1.6	Jhevaughn	Matherson	JAM-J	27.2.99	30 Mar
20.66	1.8	Anthony	Schwartz	USA-Y	5.9.00	19 Apr
20.65	-1.0	Emmanuel	Callender	TTO	10.5.84	25 Jun
20.66A	-0.4	Karabo	Mothibi	BOT	15.10.96	14 May
20.66	1.6	Gautier	Dautremer	FRA	14.3.95	15 Jul
20.66	0.3	Liemarvin	Bonevacia	NED	5.4.89	29 Jul
20.67 to 20.69			14 men			

Indoors

Mark	Wind	Name		Nat	Born	Pos	Meet	Venue	Date
20.11			Coleman			1r1	NCAA	College Station	11 Mar
20.36		Just'N	Thymes	USA	24.1.94	2r2	3 NCAA	College Station	11 Mar
20.48		Omar	McLeod	JAM	25.4.94	1		Fayetteville	17 Feb
20.49		Lalonde	Gordon	TTO	25.11.88	1		Boston (A)	28 Jan
20.49		Rondell	Sorrillo	TTO	21.1.86	2		Fayetteville	11 Feb
20.57		Cameron	Williams	USA	11.9.95	1		Boston (A)	19 Feb

Wind assisted

Mark	Wind	Name		Nat	Born	Pos	Meet	Venue	Date
19.86	2.9	Danny	Talbot	GBR	1.5.91	1r2		Clermont	15 Apr
19.87	5.7	Malik	Moffett	USA	11.4.94	1	Big 10	University Park	14 May
19.96	2.1	Elijah	Hall	USA	22.8.94	1		Houston	14 May
19.96	5.7	Nick	Gray	USA	2.6.97	2	Big 10	University Park	14 May

Mark	Wind	Name		Nat	Born	Pos	Meet	Venue	Date
19.96	2.7	Andre	De Grasse	CAN	10.11.94	1	NC	Ottawa	9 Jul
19.98	3.3		Richards			1h5	SEC	Columbia, SC	11 May
19.98	7.1	Ramil	Guliyev	TUR	29.5.90	1	PTS	Samorín	17 Jun
19.99	4.3	Aldrich	Bailey	USA	6.2.94	1		Austin	29 Apr
20.02	2.7	Brendon	Rodney	CAN	9.4.92	2	NC	Ottawa	9 Jul
20.06	4.3	Ronnie	Baker	USA	15.10.93	2		Austin	29 Apr
20.07	3.4	Maxwell	Willis	USA-J	2.9.98	1h1	Big 12	Lawrence	13 May
20.10	4.0		Willis			1	Big 12	Lawrence	14 May
20.10A	3.3	Anaso	Jobodwana	RSA	30.7.92	1		Pretoria	11 Nov
20.12	2.1	Isiah	Young	USA	5.1.90	1s1	WCh	London (OS)	9 Aug
20.13	2.7	Aaron	Brown	CAN	27.5.92	3	NC	Ottawa	9 Jul
20.20	2.7	Kenzo	Cotton	USA	13.5.96	1h5	NCAA-W	Austin	26 May
20.21	3.6	Solomon	Bockarie	NED	18.5.87	1r1		Clermont	15 Apr
20.21	2.9	Gavin	Smellie	CAN	26.6.86	2r2		Clermont	15 Apr
20.22	2.9	Kyree	King	USA	9.7.94	1q1	NCAA-W	Austin	27 May
20.23	5.7	Xavier	Smith	USA	26.5.96	3	Big 10	University Park	14 May
20.24	2.1	Just'N	Thymes	USA	24.1.94	1		San Diego	25 Mar
20.26	2.5	Likoúrgos-Stéfanos	Tsákonas	GRE	8.3.90	1	NC	Pátra	18 Jun
20.29	2.8	Akeem	Bloomfield	JAM	10.11.97	1		Austin	15 Apr
20.30	2.4	Jamiel	Trimble	USA	25.6.95	2q3	NCAA-W	Austin	27 May
20.31	3.2	Paulo André	de Oliveira	BRA-J	20.8.98	1r5		Clermont	15 Apr
20.31	2.3	Josh	Washington	USA	28.8.95	2h1	SEC	Columbia, SC	11 May
20.31	3.1	Tyson	Gay	USA	9.8.82	1		Tampa	26 May
20.32	3.0	Moriba	Morain	TTO	8.10.92	1	NAIA	Gulf Shores, AL	27 May
20.32	2.2	Eseosa	Desalu	ITA	19.2.94	1	NC	Trieste	2 Jul
20.34	3.1	Michael	Mathieu	BAH	24.6.83	2		Tampa	26 May
20.35	8.0	Mohamed	Yacoub Salem	BRN	1.3.96	1	Gulf	Jeddah	15 Apr
20.40	2.3	Ojie	Edoburun	GBR	2.6.96	2rB		Gainesville	28 Apr
20.41	2.2	Remontay	McClain	USA	21.9.92	1		Redlands	18 May
20.41	4.2	Elijah	Morrow	USA	.95	3q2	NCAA-W	Austin	27 May
20.41	3.3	Bruno	de Barros	BRA	7.1.87	1h1	SACh	Asunción	24 Jn
20.42	4.2	Tatenda	Tsumba	ZIM	12.11.91	4q2		Provo	13 May
20.43	2.8	Marcus	Chambers	USA	3.11.94	2	Pac-12	Eugene	14 May
20.43	2.4	Marcus	Lawler	IRL	28.2.95	1		Salamanca	3 Jun
20.44	4.0	Terrell	Smith	USA	10.10.94	3	Big 12	Lawrence	14 May
20.45	6.2	Josh	Elker	USA-J	12.3.98	1		Normal, IL	8 Apr
20.45	2.2	Sibusiso	Matsenjwa	SWZ	2.5.88	1		Réduit	8 Apr
20.45	4.5	Divine	Oduduru	NGR	7.10.96	1		Fort Worth	15 Apr
20.45	2.9	Antonio	Infantino	ITA	22.3.91	3r2		Clermont	15 Apr
20.46	2.9	Yoshihide	Kiryu	JPN	15.12.95	1		Yokohama	28 May

Mark	Wind	Name		Nat	Born	Date
20.48	3.3	Joaeph	Amoah	GHA	12.1.97	25 Mar
20.49	6.2	Devin	Quinn	USA	8.6.96	8 Apr
20.49A	3.0	McKinley	West	USA	.96	8 Apr
20.49	2.4	Jacarias	Martin	USA	13.1.96	27 May
20.52	?	Andre	Ewers	USA	7.6.95	8 Apr
20.52	2.1	Mario	Burke	BAR	18.3.97	14 May
20.52	2.8	Christian	Sourapas	USA	17.7.96	14 May
20.52	2.2	Jeremy	Phillips	USA	.93	18 May
20.52	3.3	Edward	Amaning	GBR	27.10.93	7 Jun
20.54	3.3	Wallace	Spearmon	USA	24.12.84	1 Apr
20.54	8.0	Neseib Salmein	Al-Zaabi	UAE	17.7.88	15 Apr
20.54	2.9	Rohan	Browning	AUS	31.12.97	2 Dec
20.55	4.2	Roy	Ejiakuekwu	GBR	2.2.95	27 May
20.56	2.4	Amir	James	USA	7.12.95	18 Mar
20.56	3.1	Justin	Walker	USA	30.11.90	26 May
20.59	?	LaMarion	Arnold	USA	.96	8 Apr
20.59	4.5	Derrius	Rodgers	USA	15.10.97	15 Apr
20.59	3.3	Mustaqeem	Williams	USA	24.8.95	11 May
20.59	4.0	Ivan	Henry	JAM	16.4.96	14 May
20.59	2.9	Desmond	Mapps	USA	.95	27 May
20.60	2.1	Mateo	Galvan	ITA	24.8.88	23 Jul
20.61	2.2	Rodney	Rowe	USA	17.3.97	31 Mar
20.61	4.6	Michael	McGruder	USA	28.2.95	8 Apr
20.61	4.0	Quantaveon	Poole	USA	11.10.96	15 Apr
20.61	2.7	Rafal	Omelko	POL	16.1.89	21 May
20.61	3.1	Akiyuki	Hashimoto	JPN	18.11.94	9 Jul
20.62	3.4	Lestrod	Roland	SKN	5.9.92	8 Apr
20.62	3.2	James	Dasaolu	GBR	5.9.87	15 Apr
20.63	2.4	Leon	Powell	USA	1.9.96	27 May
20.64	2.7	James	Linde	CAN	18.8.94	9 Jul
20.65	2.1	Davon	DeMoss	USA	.97	14 May
20.65	6.0	Dan	Putnam	GBR	30.12.91	11 Jun
20.66	4.3	Diondre	Batson	USA	13.7.92	29 Apr
20.66	5.7	Duan	Asemota	CAN	.96	14 May

Hand timing

Mark	Wind	Name		Nat	Born	Date
20.3A		Alphas	Kishoyan	KEN	12.10.94	11 May
20.4A		Geoffrey	Kiprotich	KEN	23.11.97	21 May
20.2A	w?	Ferdinand	Omanyala	KEN	2.1.96	20 May

Wind assisted

Mark	Wind	Name		Nat	Born	Date
20.4w	3.3	Kyle	Appel	RSA-J	10.5.98	25 Feb

Low altitude bests

Mark	Wind	Name	Pos	Meet	Venue	Date
20.21	0.9	Simbine	2	Gyulai	Székesfehérvár	4 Jul
20.28	0.5	Leotlela J	1		Cape Town	8 Apr
20.30	1.4	Morris	1h1	NCAA-E	Lexington	26 May
20.31	0.4	Munyai J	5	DL	Rabat	16 Jul
20.36w	2.2	Baloyes	1	SACh	Asunción	25 Jun

20.61 1.0 Maartens 29 Apr   20.61 1.7 Tsumba 27 May

Straight track

Mark	Wind	Name		Nat	Born	Pos	Venue	Date
19.84	0.6		van Niekerk			1	Boston	4 Jun
20.17	0.6	Beejay	Lee	USA	5.3.93	2	Boston	4 Jun

JUNIORS

See main list for top 6 juniors. 11 performances by 6 men to 20.39. Additional marks and further juniors:

Munyai	20.22A 1.1	1	Afr-J	Tiemcen	2 Jul	20.25A 0.5 4 NC Potchefstroom 22 Apr
	20.25A -0.2	1		Pretoria	31 Mar	20.41 0.4 5 DL Rabat 16 Jul

Mark	Wind	Name		Nat	Born	Pos	Meet	Venue	Date
20.51	0.9	Tyrese	Cooper	USA-Y	21.3.00	1-HS	Pre	Eugene	27 May

MEN 2017

Mark	Wind	Name		Nat	Born	Pos	Meet	Venue	Date
20.54	0.9	Kalon	Barnes	USA	16.12.99	2-HSPre		Eugene	27 May
20.57	2.0	Jamal	Walton	CAY	25.11.98	1		Miramar	27 May
20.58	0.0	Paulo André	de Oliveira (10)	BRA	20.8.98	1h5		São Bernardo do Campo	16 Jul
20.61	1.3	Derick	Silva	BRA	23.4.98	3	NC	São Bernardo do Campo	11 Jun
20.62	1.6	Yusuke	Tanaka	JPN	11.1.98	2		Fukui	10 Sep
20.66	1.6	Jhevaughn	Matherson	JAM	27.2.99	1s2		Kingston	30 Mar
20.66	1.8	Anthony	Schwartz	USA-Y	5.9.00	1		Fort Lauderdale	19 Apr
20.71	1.6	Kary	Vincent	USA	27.2.99	1		Austin	12 May
20.71	0.9	Elija	Godwin	USA	1.7.99	3-HSPre		Eugene	27 May
20.76	0.5	Cravont	Charleston	USA	2.1.98	1	ACC	Atlanta	14 May
20.81		Malesala	Senona	RSA	7.3.99	1		Paarl	28 Feb
20.81	-0.9	Toby	Harries	GBR	30.9.98	1	EJ	Grosseto	22 Jul
20.82	1.2	Josh	Eiker (20)	USA	12.3.98	2		Champaign	22 Apr
20.82	0.6	Khance	Meyers	USA	11.1.99	2	Jnr Oly	Ypsilanti	5 Aug

Wind assisted

See main list for top 3 juniors. 7 performances by 2 men to 20.39w. Additional marks to 20.74

Willis 20.10 4.0 1 Big 12 Lawrence 14 May | 20.19 3.4 1 Lubbock 28 Apr

20.22 2.4 1q3 NCAA-W Austin 27 May | 20.36 2.5 1 EWaco 22 Apr

de Oliveira 20.37 2.3 1rB Jones Gainesville 28 Apr

Mark	Wind	Name		Nat	Born	Pos	Meet	Venue	Date
20.71	3.2	Henrik	Larsson	SWE	30.9.99	1	NC	Helsingborg	27 Aug

300 METRES

Mark	Name		Nat	Born	Pos	Meet	Venue	Date
30.81	Wayde	van Niekerk	RSA	15.7.92	1	GS	Ostrava	28 Jun
31.44	Isaac	Makwala	BOT	29.9.86	2	GS	Ostrava	28 Jun
31.61	Clarence	Munyai	RSA-J	20.2.98	3	GS	Ostrava	28 Jun
31.80	Pavel	Maslák	CZE	21.2.91	4	GS	Ostrava	28 Jun
31.89	Luka	Janezic	SLO	14.11.95	1		Slovenska Bistrics	27 May
31.92	Lalonde	Gordon	TTO	25.11.88	1		Liège (NX)	19 Jul
32.00+	Gil	Roberts	USA	15.3.89	1	NC	Sacramento	24 Jun
32.10+	Fred	Kerley	USA	7.5.95	2	NC	Sacramento	24 Jun
32.20	Jonathan	Borlée	BEL	22.2.88	2		Liège (NX)	19 Jul
32.22	Nery	Brenes	CRC	25.9.85	5	GS	Ostrava	28 Jun
32.22	Kévin	Borlée	BEL	22.2.88	3		Liège (NX)	19 Jul
32.23	Rafal	Omelko	POL	16.1.89	6	GS	Ostrava	28 Jun
32.25	Liemarvin	Bonevacia	NED	5.4.89	7	GS	Ostrava	28 Jun

32.45 Julian Jrummi Walsh JPN 18.9.96 17 Mar | 32.55 Jermaine Gayle JAM 23.7.91 19 Jul

32.51 Dylan Borlée BEL 20.9.92 19 Jul | 32.59 Yoshihide Kiryu JPN 15.12.95 17 Mar

Estimated intermediate times in World 400m final London (OS) 8 Aug: van Niekerk 31.6, Thebe 31.9, Gardiner & Allen 32.0, Gaye 32.2.

Indoors

Mark	Name		Nat	Born	Pos	Meet	Venue	Date
31.87A	Noah	Lyles	USA	18.7.97	1r2	NC	Albuquerque	4 Mar
31.92A	Paul	Dedewo	USA	5.6.91	2r2	NC	Albuquerque	4 Mar
31.97	Bralon	Taplin	GRN	8.5.92	1		Ostrava	14 Feb

32.46A Dontavius Wright USA 3.1.94 4 Mar | 32.63A Brycen Spratling USA 10.3.92 4 Mar

400 METRES

Mark	Name		Nat	Born	Pos	Meet	Venue	Date
43.62	Wayde	van Niekerk	RSA	15.7.92	1	Athl	Lausanne	6 Jul
43.70	Fred	Kerley	USA	7.5.95	1q1	NCAA-W	Austin	26 May
43.73		van Niekerk			1	Herc	Monaco	21 Jul
43.84	Isaac	Makwala	BOT	29.9.86	2	Herc	Monaco	21 Jul
43.89	Steven	Gardiner	BAH	12.9.95	1s1	WCh	London(OS)	6 Aug
43.92		Makwala			1rA		Madrid	14 Jul
43.95		Makwala			1	WK-DLF	Zürich	24 Aug
43.98		van Niekerk			1	WCh	London(OS)	8 Aug
44.02	Baboloki	Thebe	BOT	18.3.97	2	Athl	Lausanne	6 Jul
44.03		Kerley			1	NC	Sacramento	24 Jun
44.08		Makwala			3	Athl	Lausanne	6 Jul
44.09		Kerley			1h1	SEC	Columbia, SC	12 May
44.10		Kerley			1	NCAA	Eugene	9 Jun
44.11		Kerley			1s1	NC	Sacramento	23 Jun
44.19	Nathon	Allen	JAM	28.10.95	2s1	WCh	London (OS)	6 Aug
44.22	Gil	Roberts	USA	15.3.89	2	NC	Sacramento	24 Jun
44.22		van Niekerk			1s2	WCh	London(OS)	6 Aug
44.26		Gardiner			1rB		St. George's	8 Apr
44.26		Thebe			3	Herc	Monaco	21 Jul
44.30		Kerley			1	SEC	Columbia, SC	13 May
44.30		Makwala			1s3	WCh	London (OS)	6 Aug
44.33		Roberts			2s1	NC	Sacramento	23 Jun
44.33		Thebe			2s2	WCh	London (OS)	6 Aug
44.41		Gardiner			2	WCh	London(OS)	8 Aug

Mark	Name		Nat	Born	Pos	Meet	Venue	Date
44.47	Wil	London	USA	17.8.97	3	NC	Sacramento	24 Jun
44.47	Vernon	Norwood	USA	10.4.92	4	Athl	Lausanne	6 Jul
44.48	Abdelilah	Haroun (10)	QAT	.97	3	WCh	London(OS)	8 Aug
44.50	Bryshon	Nellum	USA	1.5.89	4	NC	Sacramento	24 Jun
44.51	Tony	McQuay	USA	16.4.90	5	NC	Sacramento	24 Jun
44.51		Kerley			3s1	WCh	London (OS)	6 Aug
44.52		Allen			2	SEC	Columbia, SC	13 May
	(31/12)							
44.53A	Emmanuel	Korir	KEN	15.6.95	1		El Paso	14 May
44.55	Demish	Gaye	JAM	20.1.93	2s3	WCh	London(OS)	6 Aug
44.60	Michael	Norman	USA	3.12.97	3s1	NC	Sacramento	23 Jun
44.66	Michael	Cherry	USA	23.3.95	5	Athl	Lausanne	6 Jul
44.74	Akeem	Bloomfield	JAM	10.11.97	1q2	NCAA-E	Lexington	26 May
44.74	Matthew	Hudson-Smith	GBR	26.10.94	4s2	WCh	London (OS)	6 Aug
44.78	LaShawn	Merritt	USA	27.6.86	2	DL	Doha	5 May
44.79	Kévin	Borlée	BEL	22.2.88	1rB		Madrid	14 Jul
	(20)							
44.84	Luka	Janezic	SLO	14.11.95	6	Herc	Monaco	21 Jul
44.85	My'Lik	Kerley	USA	6.6.96	5s1	NC	Sacramento	23 Jun
44.87	Karsten	Warholm	NOR	28.2.96	1		Florø	10 Jun
44.90	Machel	Cedenio	TTO	6.9.95	1	NC	Port of Spain	24 Jun
44.92	Marcus	Chambers	USA	3.11.94	3s1	NCAA	Eugene	7 Jun
44.95	Kyle	Collins	USA	9.9.94	3h2	NC	Sacramento	22 Jun
44.99	Steven	Gayle	JAM	19.3.94	1q1	NCAA-E	Lexington	26 May
44.99	Jamal	Walton	CAY-J	25.11.98	1	PAm-J	Trujillo	21 Jul
45.00A	Samuel	García	ESP	4.12.91	1		Monachil	7 Jul
45.01	Steven	Champlin	USA	16.2.96	1		Lubbock	28 Apr
	(30)							
45.02	Lalonde	Gordon	TTO	25.11.88	2h1	WCh	London (OS)	6 Aug
45.05	Karabo	Sibanda	BOT-J	2.7.98	4	DL	Doha	5 May
45.07	Nathan	Strother	USA	6.9.95	2q1	NCAA-E	Lexington	26 May
45.08	Bralon	Taplin	GRN	8.5.92	1		Tempe	8 Apr
45.09	Jonathan	Borlée	BEL	22.2.88	2rB		Madrid	14 Jul
45.10	Pavel	Maslák	CZE	21.2.91	4h1	WCh	London (OS)	5 Aug
45.12	Quincy	Hall	USA-J	31.7.98	1	MSR	Torrance	15 Apr
45.13	Paul	Dedewo	USA	5.6.91	1h3	NC	Sacramento	22 Jun
45.14		Guo Zhongze	CHN	7.8.96	1	NG	Tianjin	3 Sep
45.15A	Pieter	Conradie	RSA	20.10.94	1	NC	Potchefstroom	22 Apr
	(40)							
45.16	Winston	George	GUY	19.5.87	1		Leonora	15 Jul
45.16	Óscar	Husillos	ESP	18.7.93	6s1	WCh	London (OS)	6 Aug
45.18	Yoandys	Lescay	CUB	5.1.94	3rB		Madrid	14 Jul
45.19A	Collins	Omae	KEN	9.4.89	1	NC	Nairobi	10 Jun
45.19	Rusheen	McDonald	JAM	17.8.92	4	NC	Kingston	25 Jun
45.19	Steven	Solomon	AUS	16.5.93	1		Stanford	29 Jun
45.20	Zachary	Shinnick	USA-J	8.2.99	1	NC-j	Sacramento	24 Jun
45.21	Raymond	Kibet	KEN	4.2.96	2q3	NCAA-E	Lexington	26 May
45.21	Jereem	Richards	TTO	13.1.94	1		Freeport	22 Jul
45.23	Rafal	Omelko	POL	16.1.89	1		Forbach	28 May
	(50)							
45.23	Samson	Nathaniel	NGR	30.8.97	1		Abuja	3 Jun
45.24	Luguelín	Santos	DOM	12.11.92	1	WUG	Taipei	25 Aug
45.26	Brian	Gregan	IRL	31.12.89	1		Dublin (S)	12 Jul
45.30	Josephus	Lyles	USA-J	22.7.98	2	PAm-J	Trujillo	21 Jul
45.32	Y. Muhammed	Anas	IND	17.9.94	1		New Delhi	15 May
45.32	Aldrich	Bailey	USA	6.2.94	2q2	NCAA-W	Austin	26 May
45.34	Onkabetse	Nkobolo	BOT	22.7.93	2		Forbach	28 May
45.34	Dwayne	Cowan	GBR	1.1.85	3	DL	Birmingham	20 Aug
45.37	Lucas	Carvalho	BRA	16.7.93	1		São Bernardo do Campo	15 Jul
45.38A	Tyrese	Cooper	USA-Y	21.3.00	1		Albuquerque	3 Jun
	(60)							
45.39A	Thapelo	Phora	RSA	21.11.91	1		Potchefstroom	20 May
45.39	Teddy	Atine-Venel	FRA	16.3.85	3		Forbach	28 May
45.39	Brycen	Spratling	USA	10.3.92	1		Montverde	10 Jun
45.40A	Davide	Re	ITA	16.3.93	1		Terminillo	21 Jul
45.41	Christopher	Taylor	JAM-J	29.9.99	1		Kingston	5 Mar
45.41	Renny	Quow	TTO	25.8.87	5rB		Madrid	14 Jul
45.42A	Boniface	Mweresa	KEN	13.11.93	1	UGA Ch	Kampala	20 Jul
45.43A	Emmanuel	Dasor	GHA	14.9.95	2		El Paso	14 May
45.44	Kirani	James	GRN	1.9.92	1		St. George's	8 Apr
45.44	Ricky	Morgan	USA	12.9.95	2q1	NCAA-W	Austin	26 May
	(70)							

Mark	Name		Nat	Born	Pos	Meet	Venue	Date
45.44	Mamadou	Hanne	FRA	6.3.88	1		Bruxelles	9 Jul
45.45	George	Caddick	GBR	29.7.94	3q1	NCAA-W	Austin	26 May
45.45	Mar'yea	Harris	USA	24.11.97	3q3	NCAA-W	Austin	26 May
45.48A	Yilmar Andrés	Herrera	COL	29.4.96	1	NC	Medellín	10 Jun
45.48	Takamasa	Kitagawa	JPN	5.9.96	1h1	NC	Osaka	23 Jun
45.50A	Lucas	Búa	ESP	12.1.94	3		Monachil	7 Jul
45.51A	Alejandro	Perlaza	COL	26.8.94	2	NC	Medellín	10 Jun
45.52	Calvin	Smith	USA	10.12.87	3h1	NC	Sacramento	22 Jun
45.53	Kazushi	Kimura	JPN	17.1.93	1h2	NC	Osaka	23 Jun
45.54	Obie	Igbokwe	USA	28.1.97	1		Fayetteville	22 Apr
	(80)							
45.54	Ali Khamis	Abbas	BRN	30.6.95	1	Isl.Sol	Baku	17 May
45.54	Champ	Page	USA	1.6.94	3q3	NCAA-E	Lexington	26 May
45.54	Donald	Blair-Sanford	ISR	5.2.87	3	Odlozil	Praha	5 Jun
45.55	Ceolamar	Ways	USA	22.11.94	1		Atlanta	14 May
45.55A	Ventavius	Sears	USA	14.5.95	3		El Paso	14 May
45.55	Jonia	McDonald	JAM	16.12.89	1		Montverde	10 Jun
45.55	Nijel	Amos	BOT	15.3.94	3		Lignano	12 Jul
45.55	Alexander	Russo	BRA	26.7.94	2		São Bernardo do Campo	15 Jul
45.55	Hugo	Sousa	BRA	5.3.87	2		São Bernardo do Campo	21 Jul
45.56	Alonzo	Russell	BAH	8.2.92	1rB		Freeport	22 Jul
	(90)							
45.58	Rabah	Yousif	GBR	11.12.86	3	DL	Birmingham	20 Aug
45.60	Janis	Leitis	LAT	13.4.89	2	ET-2	Tel Aviv	24 Jun
45.61	Liemarvin	Bonevacia	NED	5.4.89	7	Athl	Lausanne	6 Jul
45.62	Julian Jrummi	Walsh	JPN	18.9.96	1		Canberra	11 Mar
45.62	Tyler	Terry	USA	3.12.97	1rB		Baton Rouge	22 Apr
45.63	Dontavius	Wright	USA	3.1.94	5h2	NC	Sacramento	22 Jun
45.64A	Ali	Khadivar	IRI	11.11.89	1		Erzurum	11 Jun
45.64	Cameron	Chalmers	GBR	6.2.97	1	NC-23	Bedford	18 Jun
45.65	Jeffrey	Green	USA	18.8.95	2		Atlanta	14 May
45.65	Robin	Vanderbemden	BEL	10.2.94	2		Bruxelles	9 Jul
	(100)							
45.65	Martyn	Rooney	GBR	3.4.87	6rB		Madrid	14 Jul

Mark	Name		Nat	Born	Date
45.66A	Ranti	Dikgale	RSA	12.7.87	12 Apr
45.66	Peter	Matthews	JAM	13.11.89	24 Jun
45.67	Kentaro	Sato	JPN	16.11.94	23 Jun
45.68	Jamari	Rose	JAM	10.8.95	25 Jun
45.68	Warren	Hazel	STK	10.1.96	22 Jul
45.69A	Boitumelo	Masilo	BOT	5.8.95	22 Mar
45.69A	Michael	Saruni	KEN	18.6.95	22 Apr
45.70	Najee	Glass	USA	12.6.94	8 Apr
45.71	Nery	Brenes	CRC	25.9.85	4 Jul
45.72	Izaiah	Brown	USA	1.1.97	22 Apr
45.72	Rai	Benjamin	ANT	27.7.97	30 Apr
45.72A	Va-Sheku	Sheriff	USA	19.12.96	14 May
45.73A	Gaone	Maotoanong	BOT	7.5.91	3 Jun
45.74A	Geoffrey	Kiprotich	KEN	23.11.97	10 Jun
45.74A	Alphas	Kishoyan	KEN	12.10.94	24 Jun
45.75	Philip	Osei	CAN	30.10.90	13 May
45.76	Sean	Bailey	JAM	15.7.97	6 May
45.76	Yuzo	Kanemaru	JPN	18.9.87	23 Jun
45.77	Myles	Pringle	USA	5.9.97	27 May
45.78	Jarrin	Solomon	TTO	11.1.86	28 Apr
45.79	Michael	Berry	USA	10.12.91	15 Apr
45.80	Mazen	Al-Yassin	KSA	8.7.96	10 Sep
45.81	Sedacy	Walden	USA	.96	26 May
45.81	Johannes	Trefz	GER	7.6.92	9 Jul
45.82	Thomas	Jordier	FRA	12.8.94	28 May
45.82	Miloud	Laaredj	ALG	7.11.86	28 May
45.82	Randall	Ceneus	USA	14.12.96	7 Jun
45.82	Jermaine	Gayle	JAM	23.7.91	24 Jun
45.83		Wu Yuang	CHN-J	18.3.98	10 May
45.84	Tomoya	Tamura	JPN	20.8.92	23 Jun
45.84	Collin	King	JAM	6.5.93	24 Jun
45.85	Delano	Williams	GBR	23.12.93	10 Jun
45.85A	Batuhan	Altintas	TUR	24.4.96	11 Jun
45.85	David	Verburg	USA	14.5.91	22 Jun
45.85	Eric	Janise	USA	3.9.93	22 Jun
45.85	Benjamin Lobo	Vedel	DEN	23.9.97	14 Jul
45.86	Lamar	Bruton	USA	26.5.95	26 May
45.86	Sean	Hooper	USA-J	28.10.98	24 Jun
45.87	Champion	Allison	USA-J	5.11.98	13 May
45.88	Kosuke	Horii	JPN	27.4.94	23 Jun
45.88	Taiki	Mihara	JPN	2.9.95	23 Jun
45.89	Ahmed Mubarak	Al-Saadi	OMA	28.2.88	13 Apr
45.89	Richard	Rose	USA	25.2.96	25 May
45.89A	Yevhen	Hutsol	UKR	13.5.90	11 Jun
45.89	Marco	Doodnaughtsingh	JAM	2.11.96	24 Jun
45.92	Kimorie	Shearman	VIN	3.8.92	27 May
45.92	Ludvy	Vaillant	FRA	15.3.95	20 Jun
45.92	Vladimir	Aceti	ITA-J	16.10.98	22 Jul
45.93	Norvel	Mohammed	USA	5.12.94	3 Jun
45.93	Anderson	Henriques	BRA	3.3.92	17 Jun
45.93	Michael	Mathieu	BAH	24.6.83	24 Jun
45.94	Javon	Francis	JAM	14.12.94	11 Mar
45.95	Fitzroy	Dunkley	JAM	20.5.93	22 Apr
45.95	Leander	Forbes	USA-J	6.6.98	27 Apr
45.95	Kunle	Fasasi	NGR	23.6.96	12 May
45.95A	Ashley	Hlungawi	RSA	25.4.91	3 Jun
45.95	Mizuki	Obuchi	JPN	19.2.97	23 Jun
45.96	Derrick	Mokaleng	RSA	18.6.97	26 May
45.97	Hederson	Estefani	BRA	11.9.91	1 Apr
45.97	Rhayko	Schwartz	USA	3.3.97	25 May
45.98	Kajetan	Duszynski	POL	12.5.95	14 Jul
45.99	Fuga	Sato	JPN	1.6.96	23 Jun
46.00	Sadam	Koumi	SUD	6.4.94	15 Apr
46.00	Joel	Burgunder	SUI	20.5.91	22 Jul
46.01	Kerron	Clement	USA	31.10.85	30 Mar
46.01	Daniele	Corsa	ITA	1.10.96	10 Jun
46.02	Patrick	Schneider	GER	30.11.92	9 Jul
46.03	Maurice	Freeman	USA	22.11.93	8 Apr
46.03	Orwin	Emilien	MRI	20.4.95	6 May
46.03	Kota	Wakabayashi	JPN	23.10.97	23 Jun
46.03	Pavel	Ivashko	RUS	16.11.94	29 Jul
46.04	Dajuan	Harding	USA	27.9.96	26 May
46.04	Tymoteusz	Zimny	POL-J	14.3.98	22 Jul
46.06	Mitsuoki	Kawachi	JPN	2.6.97	23 Jun
46.06	Kevon	Nelson	JAM	.92	24 Jun
46.07	Stephan	James	GUY	23.6.93	30 Mar
46.07	Omar	Johnson	JAM	25.11.88	27 May
46.07	Brian	Herron	USA-Y	24.11.00	24 Jun
46.08		Lu Zhiquan	CHN	17.3.94	3 Sep
46.09	Robert	Grant	USA	31.1.96	15 Apr
46.09	Martin	Manley	JAM	10.3.97	20 May
	(182)				

Mark	Name		Nat	Born	Pos	Meet	Venue	Date
Indoors								
45.32	Izaiah	Brown	USA	1.1.97	1	Big 10	Geneva, OH	25 Feb
45.57	Kunle	Fasasi	NGR	23.6.96	2h1	NCAA	College Station	10 Mar
45.59	Sean	Bailey	JAM	15.7.97	1	JUCO	Pittsburg, KS	4 Mar
45.63	Marqueze	Washington	USA	29.9.93	1		Fayetteville	10 Feb

Low altitude bests

45.36 García 3rA Madrid 14 Jul | 45.58 Conradie 1 Marseille 3 Jun
45.40 T Cooper (J) 1 Kissimee 15 Jul | 45.59 Mweresa 4h3 WCh London (O) 5 Aug
45.56 Re 3 ET Villeneuve d'Ascq 24 Jun | 45.59 Dasor 4q3 NCAA-E Lexington 26 May
45.71 Dikgale 24 Jun | 45.77 Perlaza 23 Jun | 45.85 Khadivar 16 May | 45.90 Búa 23 Jul | 46.02 Herrera 23 Jun

Mark	Name		Nat	Born	Pos	Meet	Venue	Date
Hand timing								
45.2A	Geoffrey	Kiprotich	KEN	23.11.97	1		Eldoret	20 May
45.5A	Leonard	Opiny	UGA	12.12.91	2		Eldoret	20 May
45.9	Thandaza	Zwane	SWZ		1	NC	Mavuso	7 May
Prosthetic Limbs: 45.25		Patrick Leeper	USA	31.8.89	7s1	NC	Sacramento	23 Jun

JUNIORS

See main list for top 7 juniors. 13 performances by 6 men to 45.38. Additional marks and further juniors:

Walton 45.053h5 WCh London (OS) 5 Aug | 45.164s3 London (OS) 6 Aug
Sibanda 45.07A1 Sasolburg 28 Mar | 45.20A1 NC Francistown 13 May
45.08A1r3 Potchefstroom 15 Mar | 45.26 1 Orapa 28 Jan
Hall 45.32 1 Stanford 31 Mar

Mark	Name		Nat	Born	Pos	Meet	Venue	Date
45.83		Wu Yuang	CHN	18.3.98	1		Taiyuan	10 May
45.86	Sean	Hooper	USA	28.10.98	3	NC-j	Sacramento	24 Jun
45.87	Champion	Allison (10)	USA	5.11.98	1		Austin	13 May
45.92	Vladimir	Aceti	ITA	16.10.98	1	EJ	Grosseto	22 Jul
45.95	Leander	Forbes	USA	6.6.98	1		Tallahassee	27 Apr
46.04	Tymoteusz	Zimny	POL	14.3.98	2	EJ	Grosseto	22 Jul
46.07	Brian	Herron	USA-Y	24.11.00	4	NC-j	Sacramento	24 Jun
46.10A	Daniel	Mbewe	ZAM	31.12.98	1		Lusaka	25 May
46.13	Jacob	St.Clair	TTO	15.9.98	5		Port of Spain	24 Jun
46.15	Naoki	Kitadani	JPN	12.11.98	3h3	NC	Osaka	23 Jun
46.19	Kenneth	Bednarek	USA	14.10.98	1		Medford	25 May
46.19A	Sean	Burrell	USA-Y	23.2.02	2		Albuquerque	3 Jun
46.20	Zazini	Sokwakhana (20)	RSA-Y	23.9.00	1		Durban	31 Mar

600 METRES

Mark	Name		Nat	Born	Pos	Meet	Venue	Date
1:15.42	Charles	Jock	USA	23.11.89	1		Portland	11 Jun

1:15.74 Mohamed Laalou MAR 29.5.90 5 Jul | 1:15.94 Casimir Loxsom USA 17.3.91 11 Jun
1:15.90 Luguelín Santos DOM 12.11.92 18 Mar | 1:16.01 Harun Abda USA 1.1.90 11 Jun

Mark	Name		Nat	Born	Pos	Meet	Venue	Date
Indoors								
1:14.91	Casimir	Loxsom	USA	17.3.91	1		State College	28 Jan
1:14.96	Isaiah	Harris	USA	18.10.96	2		State College	28 Jan
1:14.97A	Emmanuel	Korir	KEN	15.6.95	1		Albuquerque	20 Jan
1:15.07A	Erik	Sowinski	USA	21.11.89	1	NC	Albuquerque	5 Mar
1:15.23	Daniel	Kuhn	USA	11.8.95	1	Big 10	Geneva OH	25 Feb
1:15.39A	Shaquille	Walker	USA	24.6.93	3	NC	Albuquerque	5 Mar
1:15.55	Nate	Roese	USA	19.9.94	2	Big 10	Geneva OH	25 Feb

1:15.86A Russell Dinkins USA 27.6.89 5 Mar | 1:16.10A Donavan Brazier USA 15.4.97 5 Mar
1:15.96A Christopher Giesting USA 10.12.92 5 Mar | 1:16.36 Duane Solomon USA 28.12.84 28 Jan
1:15.99 Anthony Johnson USA 11.8.95 25 Feb | 1:16.38A Curtis Beach USA 22.7.90 4 Mar
1:16.10 Kyle Langford GBR 2.2.96 15 Feb | 1:16.46A Donte Holmes USA 14.3.89 4 Mar

800 METRES

Mark	Name		Nat	Born	Pos	Meet	Venue	Date
1:43.10	Emmanuel	Korir	KEN	15.6.95	1	Herc	Monaco	21 Jul
1:43.18	Nijel	Amos	BOT	15.3.94	1	DL	London (OS)	9 Jul
1:43.60	Clayton	Murphy	USA	26.2.95	1rA	MSR	Torrance	15 Apr
1:43.73		Korir			1		Berkeley	29 Apr
1:43.86A		Korir			1	WCT	Nairobi	24 Jun
1:43.91		Amos			1	DL	Rabat	16 Jul
1:43.94	Wycliffe	Kinyamal	KEN	2.7.97	1	Quercia	Rovereto	29 Aug
1:43.95	Donavan	Brazier	USA	15.4.97	2	DL	London (OS)	9 Jul
1:44.04A	Kipyegon	Bett	KEN-J	2.1.98	2	WCT	Nairobi	24 Jun
1:44.14		Brazier			1	NC	Sacramento	25 Jun
1:44.2A		Bett			1rA		Nairobi	1 Apr
1:44.24		Amos			1	DL	Paris (C)	1 Jul
1:44.28		Bett			2	DL	Rabat	16 Jul
1:44.36		Bett			2	DL	Paris (C)	1 Jul
1:44.37	Ferguson	Cheruiyot	KEN	30.11.89	2	DL	Paris (C)	1 Jul
1:44.41	Brandon	McBride	CAN	15.6.94	2	Herc	Monaco	21 Jul

Mark	Name		Nat	Born	Pos	Meet	Venue	Date
1:44.43	Asbel	Kiprop	KEN	30.6.89	3	DL	London (OS)	9 Jul
1:44.44	Antoine	Gakémé (10)	BDI	24.12.91	1rA		Madrid	14 Jul
1:44.49		Gakémé			2	Quercia	Rovereto	29 Aug
1:44.50		Amos			1	DL	Birmingham	20 Aug
1:44.53	Isaiah	Harris	USA	18.10.96	2	NC	Sacramento	25 Jun
1:44.53		Amos			1	VD-DLF	Bruxelles	1 Sep
1:44.54		Gakémé			3	Herc	Monaco	21 Jul
1:44.61A	Michael	Saruni	KEN	18.6.95	3	WCT	Nairobi	24 Jun
1:44.62		Brazier			3	DL	Rabat	16 Jul
1:44.62	Amel	Tuka	BIH	9.1.91	3	Quercia	Rovereto	29 Aug
1:44.63		Brazier			1		Tempe	8 Apr
1:44.63	Drew	Windle	USA	22.7.92	1		New York	6 Jul
1:44.66	Erik	Sowinski	USA	21.12.89	2		New York	6 Jul
1:44.67	Pierre-Ambroise	Bosse	FRA	11.5.92	1	WCh	London (OS)	8 Aug
	(30/16)							
1:44.77	Edward	Kemboi	KEN	12.12.91	3		New York	6 Jul
1:44.77	Marcin	Lewandowski	POL	13.6.87	2	VD-DLF	Bruxelles	1 Sep
1:44.80	Alex	Amankwah	USA/GHA	2.3.92	1rA		Marietta, GA	19 May
1:44.8A	Elijah	Manangoi	KEN	5.1.93	1		Nairobi	18 May
	(20)							
1:44.81	Thiago	André	BRA	4.8.95	1	NC	São Bernardo do Campo	11 Jun
1:44.84	Adam	Kszczot	POL	2.9.89	3	VD-DLF	Bruxelles	1 Sep
1:44.86	Willy	Tarbei	KEN-J	30.5.98	1		Kingston	10 Jun
1:44.90	David	Rudisha	KEN	17.12.88	2		Kingston	10 Jun
1:44.9A	Nicholas	Kipkoech	KEN	22.10.92	1		Nairobi	11 May
1:44.9A	Davis	Cheruiyot	KEN		1h2		Nairobi	16 May
1:44.92	Mohamed Ahmed	Hamada	EGY	22.10.92	2rA		Madrid	14 Jul
1:44.98	Andrés	Arroyo	PUR	7.6.95	4		New York	6 Jul
1:44.99	Thijmen	Kupers	NED	4.10.91	1rA	FBK	Hengelo	11 Jun
1:44.99	Elliot	Giles	GBR	26.5.94	5	DL	London (OS)	9 Jul
	(30)							
1:45.00A	Peter	Kiplangat	KEN	6.9.93	1	NC	Nairobi	10 Jun
1:45.0A	Justus	Koech	KEN	.90	2		Nairobi	18 May
1:45.01	Ayanleh	Souleiman	DJI	3.12.92	1		Barcelona	29 Jun
1:45.02	Kevin	López	ESP	12.6.90	2		Barcelona	29 Jun
1:45.04	Jesse	Garn	USA	4.6.93	5		New York	6 Jul
1:45.05	Robert	Biwott	KEN	28.1.96	4	DL	Paris (C)	1 Jul
1:45.06	Álvaro	de Arriba	ESP	2.6.94	4rA		Madrid	14 Jul
1:45.10	Guy	Learmonth	GBR	24.4.92	4	Quercia	Rovereto	29 Aug
1:45.1A	Mathew	Rono	KEN	.92	2		Nairobi	11 May
1:45.13	Andreas	Kramer	SWE	13.4.97	2		Karlstad	25 Jul
	(40)							
1:45.15	Job	Kinyor	KEN	2.9.90	5rA		Madrid	14 Jul
1:45.17	Daniel	Andújar	ESP	14.5.94	6rA		Madrid	14 Jul
1:45.2A	Edwin	Kemboi	KEN	22.8.86	3		Nairobi	11 May
1:45.21A	Bernard	Kipyegon	KEN	19.12.90	5	WCT	Nairobi	24 Jun
1:45.21	Peter	Bol	AUS	22.2.94	1		Mannheim	1 Jul
1:45.22	Marc	Reuther	GER	23.6.96	1		Pfungstadt	5 Jul
1:45.25	Kyle	Langford	GBR	2.2.96	4	WCh	London (OS)	8 Aug
1:45.28	Saúl	Ordóñez	ESP	10.4.94	1		Pamplona	27 Jul
1:45.3A	Cornelius	Tuwei	KEN	.93	1		Machakos	16 Dec
1:45.40	Alfred	Kipketer	KEN	26.12.96	5	DL	Shanghai	13 May
	(50)							
1:45.40	Mohammed	Aman	ETH	10.1.94	2s3	WCh	London (OS)	6 Aug
1:45.4A	Timothy	Sein	KEN	1.2.88	4		Nairobi	18 May
1:45.4A	Solomon	Lekuta	KEN-J	3.10.99	1		Nairobi	14 Jun
1:45.42	Mark	English	IRL	18.3.93	2	DL	Stockholm	18 Jun
1:45.42	Jake	Wightman	GBR	11.7.94	7	DL	London (OS)	9 Jul
1:45.44	Mohamed Amine	Belferrar	ALG	6.2.91	1	DL	Doha	5 May
1:45.46	Abdellatif	El Guesse	MAR	27.2.93	2		Oordegem	27 May
1:45.51	Jesús	López	MEX	2.8.97	1		Culiacan	26 Mar
1:45.54	Andrew	Osagie	GBR	19.2.88	6	Quercia	Rovereto	29 Aug
1:45.58	Ryan	Sánchez	PUR-J	22.6.98	4		Kingston	10 Jun
	(60)							
1:45.6A	Sammy	Kirongo	KEN	4.2.94	1rA		Eldoret	2 Jun
1:45.63	Abdessalem	Ayouni	TUN	16.5.94	4		Oordegem	27 May
1:45.67	Jesús	Gómez	ESP	24.4.91	7rA		Madrid	14 Jul
1:45.68	Shaquille	Walker	USA	24.6.93	4rA		Marietta, GA	19 May
1:45.69	Drew	Piazza	USA	28.1.95	5	NC	Sacramento	25 Jun
1:45.70	Eliud	Rutto	KEN/USA	13.3.94	2rA	MSR	Torrance	15 Apr

Mark	Name		Nat	Born	Pos	Meet	Venue	Date
1:45.70	Michal	Rozmys	POL	13.3.95	1	NC	Bialystok	22 Jul
1:45.7A	Moses	Kipkemboi Kibet	KEN	20.11.94	5		Nairobi	11 May
1:45.71	Devin	Dixon	USA	22.9.97	1	SEC	Columbia, SC	13 May
1:45.72	Samir	Dahmani	FRA	3.4.91	8	Herc	Monaco	21 Jul
	(70)							
1:45.73	Joseph	White	USA	16.11.95	3	NCAA	Eugene	9 Jun
1:45.73	Rynhardt	van Rensburg	RSA	23.3.92	3	DL	Stockholm	18 Jun
1:45.73A	Abu	Mayanja	UGA	9.10.95	1h3	NC	Kampala	19 Jul
1:45.76	Mostafa	Smaïli	MAR	9.1.97	2	DL	Doha	5 May
1:45.78A	Justus	Kiprotich	KEN	.90	3		Nairobi	10 Jun
1:45.79A	Nicholas	Kiplagat	KEN	6.7.95	4	NC	Nairobi	10 Jun
1:45.80A	Jackson	Kivuva	KEN	11.8.88	7	WCT	Nairobi	24 Jun
1:45.87	Edose	Ibadin	USA/NGR	27.2.93	2		Nashville	10 Jun
1:45.9A	Timothy	Kitum	KEN	20.11.94	5rA		Nairobi	1 Apr
1:45.9A	Jonah	Kiprop	KEN-J	22.11.98	1rB		Eldoret	2 Jun
	(80)							
1:46.02A	Lucirio Antonio	Garrido	VEN	8.4.92	1		Medellín	29 Apr
1:46.03	Ryan	Martin	USA	23.3.89	1rA		Concord, MA	1 Jun
1:46.05	Yassine	Hathat	ALG	30.7.91	3	DL	Doha	5 May
1:46.05	Mamush	Lencho	ETH	24.3.96	1rB	FBK	Hengelo	11 Jun
1:46.08	Aymeric	Lusine	FRA	13.9.95	1		Poitiers	14 Jun
1:46.08	Homiyu	Tesfaye	GER	23.6.93	2		Pfungstadt	5 Jul
1:46.09	Giordano	Benedetti	ITA	22.5.89	5	Gyulai	Székesfehérvár	4 Jul
1:46.1A	Jeremiah	Mutai	KEN	27.12.92	6rA		Nairobi	1 Apr
1:46.1A	Kennedy	Chepsiror	KEN	5.6.89	2rA		Eldoret	2 Jun
1:46.13	Leonard	Kosencha	KEN	21.8.94	6rA	FBK	Hengelo	11 Jun
	(90)							
1:46.13	Temam	Tura	ETH-J	1.8.98	2rB	FBK	Hengelo	10 Jun
1:46.14	Joshua	Ralph	AUS	27.10.91	2		Padova	16 Jul
1:46.17	Sho	Kawamoto	JPN	1.3.93	1		Inzai	3 Jun
1:46.17	Nabil	Oussama	MAR	18.2.96	1	Franc	Abidjan	24 Jul
1:46.17	Anthony	Romaniw	CAN	15.9.91	3		Cles	24 Aug
1:46.20	Charles	Simotwo	KEN	6.5.95	1		Merksem	29 Jul
1:46.21	Abraham	Rotich	BRN	26.6.93	6		Barcelona	29 Jun
1:46.24	Riad	El Chenini	TUN	25.3.97	2	Isl.Sol	Baku	18 May
1:46.26	Aman	Wote	ETH	18.4.84	3rB	FBK	Hengelo	11 Jun
1:46.26	Robert	Heppenstall	CAN	28.2.97	3		Washington, DC	15 Jul
	(100)							

Mark	Name		Nat	Born	Date
1:46.28	Artur	Kuciapski	POL	26.12.93	22 Jul
1:46.29	Ibrahim	Al-Zafairi	KUW	8.5.89	5 Aug
1:46.3A	Nobert	Kolombos	KEN-J	13.3.99	18 May
1:46.33	Jacob	Rozani	RSA	24.1.88	20 Jun
1:46.35	Mohamed	Belbachir	ALG	11.1.94	29 Jun
1:46.38	Abedin	Mujezinovic	BIH	2.6.93	7 Jul
1:46.39	Andreas	Bube	DEN	13.7.87	18 Jul
1:46.40	Russell	Dinkins	USA	27.6.89	19 May
1:46.40	Ismael	Debjani	BEL	25.9.90	27 May
1:46.40	James	Bowness	GBR	26.11.91	27 May
1:46.40	Chris	Low	USA	29.8.92	11 Jun
1:46.44	Luke	Mathews	AUS	21.6.95	18 May
1:46.47	Patrick	Joseph	USA	7.9.95	21 Apr
1:46.49	Chris	Giesting	USA	10.12.92	1 Jun
1:46.5A	Boaz	Kiprugut	KEN-J	18.5.98	14 Jun
1:46.51	Joseph	Deng	AUS-J	7.7.98	8 Jul
1:46.54	Charles	Jock	USA	23.11.89	1 Jun
1:46.54	Tadesse	Lemi	ETH-J	20.1.99	11 Jun
1:46.59	Khalid	Benmahdi	ALG	22.10.88	27 May
1:46.61	Jorge Félix	Liranzo	CUB	3.2.94	10 Jun
1:46.61	Pablo	Sánchez-Valladares	ESP	12.11.97	29 Jun
1:46.62	Andy	González	CUB	17.10.87	3 Jun
1:46.62	Abraham	Alvarado	USA	4.8.95	23 Jun
1:46.64	Harun	Abda	USA	1.1.90	1 Jun
1:46.64	Daniel	Rowden	GBR	9.9.97	25 Jul
1:46.65A	Henco	Uys	RSA	4.6.92	22 Apr
1:46.70	Charles	Jones	USA	1.11.95	8 Apr
1:46.7A	Noah	Menjo	KEN-J	.98	1 Apr
1:46.71	Christoph	Kessler	GER	28.4.95	3 Jun
1:46.72	Michael	Rimmer	GBR	3.2.86	11 Jun
1:46.72	Paul	Renaudie	FRA	2.4.90	16 Jul
1:46.75	Konstantin	Kholmogorov	RUS	7.2.96	2 Jul
1:46.76	Quamel	Prince	USA	20.4.94	10 Jun
1:46.76	Kléberson	Davide	BRA	20.7.85	1 Jul
1:46.80	Saúl	Martínez	ESP	12.2.94	8 Jul
1:46.8A	Kumari	Taki	KEN-J	6.5.99	1 Apr
1:46.8A	Cornelius	Kiplangat	KEN	21.12.92	11 May
1:46.8A	Alemu	Mengistu	ETH	.97	18 May
1:46.82	Craig	Engels	USA	1.5.94	29 Jul
1:46.84	Strymar	Livingston	USA	13.12.93	26 May
1:46.84	Boitumelo	Masilo	BOT	5.8.95	11 Jun
1:46.84	Jan	Kubista	CZE	23.9.90	28 Jun
1:46.84	Jamal	Al-Hayrani	QAT	26.5.93	12 Jul
1:46.84	Carl	Soudril	FRA	10.12.90	16 Jul
1:46.84	Rafith	Rodríguez	COL	1.6.89	23 Nov
1:46.86	Alex	Sampao	KEN	31.12.96	4 Jun
1:46.87	Ryan	Manahan	USA	14.7.94	22 Jun
1:46.88	Christian	von Eitzen	GER	1.1.97	30 Aug
1:46.94A	Lutimar	Paes	BRA	14.12.88	29 Apr
1:46.95	Samir	Jamaa	MAR	9.2.90	26 Apr
1:46.96	Zan	Rudolf	SLO	9.5.93	7 Jul
1:46.97	Brad	Mathas	NZL	24.6.93	19 Feb
1:46.97	Markhim	Lonsdale	GBR-J	9.1.99	27 May
1:46.97	Tamás	Kazi	HUN	16.5.85	22 Jul
1:46.98	Lukás	Hodbod	CZE	2.3.96	28 Jun
1:47.00	Colby	Alexander	USA	13.6.91	19 Jul
1:47.01	David	Torrence	PER	26.11.85	15 Apr
1:47.04	Wissam	Al-Masri	PLE	23.11.90	18 May
1:47.07	Derek	Holdsworth	USA	12.2.96	1 Jun
1:47.08	Filip	Snejdr	CZE	16.4.95	14 Jul
1:47.08	Marco	Arop	CAN-J	20.9.98	22 Jul
1:47.09	Brandon	Lasater	USA	9.10.92	19 May
1:47.09	Clay	Lambourne	USA	27.11.95	26 May
1:47.09	Leandro	Paris	ARG	16.2.95	5 Aug
1:47.10	Isaac	Kimeli	BEL	9.3.94	10 Jun
1:47.1A	Ronald	Musagala	UGA	16.12.94	20 May
1:47.1A	Evans	Biwott	KEN		16 Dec
1:47.11A	Tshite	Tshepo	RSA	15.1.97	22 Apr
1:47.12A	Melese	Nberet	ETH-Y	29.1.01	15 Jul
1:47.12	Johnny	Gregorek	USA	7.12.91	29 Jul
1:47.13	Benedikt	Huber	GER	13.10.89	1 Jul
1:47.15	Nasredine	Khatir	FRA	30.1.95	1 Jun
1:47.15	Jan	Petrac	SLO	4.7.95	4 Jun
1:47.16	Konstantin	Tolokonnikov	RUS	26.2.96	26 May

Mark	Name		Nat	Born	Pos	Meet	Venue	Date
1:47.16	Yan	Sloma	BLR	3.5.95				14 Jul
1:47.16A	Tolesa	Bodena	ETH-Y	18.2.00				15 Jul
1:47.16A	Rashid	Etiau	UGA					19 Jul
1:47.17	Sampson	Laari	GHA	3.3.93				10 Jun
1:47.19	Soufiane	El Kabbouri	ITA	5.3.93				7 Jul
1:47.2A	Geoffrey	Rutto	KEN	.95				22 Apr
1:47.23	Stephen	Knuckey	AUS	3.11.94				19 Feb
1:47.26	Mitch	Hechsel	USA	15.3.94				26 May
1:47.28	Carlton	Orange	USA	11.3.97				13 May
1:47.28	Ramzi	Abdenouz	ALG	23.5.93				14 May
1:47.28	Jan	Riedel	GER	14.10.89				11 Jun
1:47.28	Alexis	Miellet	FRA	5.5.95				28 Jun
1:47.28	Hamid	Oualich	FRA	26.4.88				16 Jul
1:47.29	Alex	Rowe	AUS	8.7.92				1 Apr
1:47.29	Domenic	Perretta	USA	25.9.97				21 Apr
1:47.29	Rory	Graham-Watson	GBR	3.6.90				25 Jul
1:47.31A	William	Mothosola	RSA	31.3.90				22 Apr
1:47.31A	Kabelo	Mohlosi	RSA	20.1.93				3 Jun
1:47.32	Blair	Henderson	USA	4.10.94				15 Apr
1:47.33	Anthonio	Mascoll	BAR	17.1.93				12 Jul
1:47.34	Ehab	Chiad Hashim	IRQ	30.3.93				18 May
1:47.34	Chris	O'Hare	GBR	23.11.90				15 Jun
1:47.34	Casimir	Loxsom	USA	17.3.91				6 Jul
1:47.35	Mattia	Moretti	ITA	16.3.92				4 Jun
1:47.36	James	Gilreath	USA	7.8.89				1 Jun
1:47.36	Chadoye (200)	Dawson	JAM	7.2.95				10 Jun
1:47.36	Brannon	Kidder	USA	18.11.93				28 Jun
1:47.36	Curtis	Beach	USA	22.7.90				6 Jul

Indoors

Mark	Name		Nat	Born	Pos	Meet	Venue	Date
1:46.13	Casimir	Loxsom	USA	17.3.91	1		Birmingham	18 Feb
1:46.23	Patrick	Joseph	USA	7.9.95	1		Notre Dame	25 Feb
1:46.42	Daniel	Kuhn	USA	11.8.95				4 Feb
1:47.11	Mateusz	Borkowski	POL	2.4.97				10 Feb
1:47.32	Avery	Bartlett	USA	8.2.97				25 Feb
1:47.33	Carter	Lilly	USA	19.10.95				4 Feb

JUNIORS

See main list for top 6 juniors. 12 performances by 2 men to 1:45.3. Additional marks and further juniors:

	Mark	Pos	Meet	Venue	Date	Mark	Pos	Meet	Venue	Date
Bett 4+	1:44.70	1	DL	Shanghai	13 May	1:45.21	3	WCh	London (OS)	8 Aug
	1:45.02	1s3	WCh	London (OS)	6 Aug	1:45.21	4	VD-DLF	Bruxelles	1 Sep
Tarbei	1:45.04	1		Karlstad	25 Jul	1:45.29	1		Heusden	22 Jul

Mark	Name		Nat	Born	Pos	Meet	Venue	Date
1:46.3A	Nobert	Kolombos	KEN	13.3.99	1		Eldoret	18 May
1:46.5A	Boaz	Kiprugut	KEN	18.5.98	2		Nairobi	14 Jun
1:46.51	Joseph	Deng	AUS	7.7.98	1		Kortrijk	8 Jul
1:46.54	Tadesse	Lemi (10)	ETH	20.1.99	4rB	FBK	Hengelo	11 Jun
1:46.7A	Noah	Menjo	KEN	.98	8rA		Nairobi	1 Apr
1:46.8A	Kumari	Taki	KEN	6.5.99	2rB		Nairobi	1 Apr
1:46.97	Markhim	Lonsdale	GBR	9.1.99	1		Manchester	27 May
1:47.08	Marco	Arop	CAN	20.9.98	2	PAm-J	Trujillo	22 Jul
1:47.12A	Melese	Nberet	ETH-Y	29.1.01	1	WY	Nairobi	15 Jul
1:47.16A	Tolesa	Bodena	ETH-Y	18.2.00	2	WY	Nairobi	15 Jul
1:47.4A	Addisu	Girma	ETH		2	NC-j	Bahir Dar	14 Jan
1:47.59	Cameron	Cooper	USA	18.1.99	1	NC-j	Sacramento	24 Jun
1:47.45	Mouad	Zahafi	MAR	9.5.98	2		Rabat	26 Apr
1:47.74	Ignacio	Fontes (20)	ESP	22.6.98	10		Andújar	2 Jun

1000 METRES

Mark	Name		Nat	Born	Pos	Meet	Venue	Date
2:17.17	Clayton	Murphy	USA	26.2.95	1		Portland	11 Jun
2:18.51	Nicholas	Kipkoech	KEN	22.10.92				28 Jun
2:18.60	Jakub	Holusa	CZE	20.2.88				28 Jun

JUNIOR

Mark	Name		Nat	Born	Pos	Meet	Venue	Date
2:19.08A	George	Kusche	RSA	6.8.98	2		Johannesburg	18 Jan

1500 METRES

Mark	Name		Nat	Born	Pos	Meet	Venue	Date
3:28.80	Elijah	Manangoi	KEN	5.1.93	1	Herc	Monaco	21 Jul
3:29.10	Timothy	Cheruiyot	KEN	20.11.95	2	Herc	Monaco	21 Jul
3:30.77		Cheruiyot			1	DL	Stockholm	18 Jun
3:30.89A	Ronald	Kwemoi	KEN	19.9.95	1	WCT	Nairobi	24 Jun
3:31.05A		Cheruiyot			2	WCT	Nairobi	24 Jun
3:31.34	Sadik	Mikhou	BRN	25.7.90	1	FBK	Hengelo	11 Jun
3:31.49		Mikhou			2	DL	Stockholm	18 Jun
3:31.63	Aman	Wote	ETH	18.4.84	3	DL	Stockholm	18 Jun
3:31.90		Manangoi			1	DL	Doha	5 May
3:32.03A		Manangoi			3	WCT	Nairobi	24 Jun
3:32.20		Wote			1	Athl	Lausanne	6 Jul
3:32.23	Silas	Kiplagat	KEN	20.8.89	2	DL	Doha	5 May
3:32.27	Bethwel	Birgen	KEN	6.8.88	3	DL	Doha	5 May
3:32.32		Mikhou			1	Odlozil	Praha	5 Jun
3:32.34		Kwemoi			3	Herc	Monaco	21 Jul
3:32.48	Filip	Ingebrigtsen	NOR	20.4.93	4	Herc	Monaco	21 Jul
3:32.59	Charles	Simotwo	KEN	6.5.95	2	Athl	Lausanne	6 Jul
3:32.66	Vincent	Kibet (10)	KEN	6.5.91	4	DL	Doha	5 May
3:32.87		Cheruiyot			5	DL	Doha	5 May
3:32.94	Yomif	Kejelcha	ETH	1.8.97	2	FBK	Hengelo	11 Jun
3:32.96		Kiplagat			3	Athl	Lausanne	6 Jul
3:32.97A	Justus	Soget	KEN-J	.99	4	WCT	Nairobi	24 Jun
3:33.17	Asbel	Kiprop	KEN	30.6.89	4	DL	Stockholm	18 Jun

Mark	Name		Nat	Born	Pos	Meet	Venue	Date
3:33.34		Kibet			4	Athl	Lausanne	6 Jul
3:33.41	Matthew	Centrowitz	USA	18.10.89	1		Los Angeles (ER)	18 May
3:33.47	Homiyu	Tesfaye	GER	23.6.93	5	Herc	Monaco	21 Jul
3:33.54		Simotwo			6	Herc	Monaco	21 Jul
3:33.61	Chris	O'Hare	GBR	23.11.90	7	Herc	Monaco	21 Jul
3:33.61		Manangoi			1	WCh	London(OS)	13 Aug
3:33.65	Ronald	Musagala	UGA	16.12.94	3	FBK	Hengelo	11 Jun
		(30/17)						
3:33.70	Ismael	Debjani	BEL	25.9.90	4	FBK	Hengelo	11 Jun
3:33.78	Samuel	Tefera	ETH-J	23.10.99	1	WCT	Hengelo	10 Jun
3:34.04	Marcin	Lewandowski	POL	13.6.87	8	Herc	Monaco	21 Jul
	(20)							
3:34.17	Jake	Wightman	GBR	11.7.94	1	Bisl	Oslo	15 Jun
3:34.19	Mohamed	Farah	GBR	23.3.83	2		Los Angeles (ER)	18 May
3:34.26	Jakub	Holusa	CZE	20.2.88	5	DL	Stockholm	18 Jun
3:34.30	Robert	Biwott	KEN	28.1.96	6	DL	Doha	5 May
3:34.37	Ryan	Gregson	AUS	26.4.90	6	DL	Stockholm	18 Jun
3:34.46	Brahim	Kaazouzi	MAR	15.6.90	1		Bruay-la-Buissière	4 Jul
3:34.47	Teresa	Tolosa	ETH-J	15.6.98	3	WCT	Hengelo	10 Jun
3:34.57	Regasa	Chala	ETH	.97	4	WCT	Hengelo	10 Jun
3:34.67	David	Torrence	PER	26.11.85	8	DL	Stockholm	18 Jun
3:34.70	Adel	Mechaal	ESP	5.12.90	1		Huelva	14 Jun
	(30)							
3:34.70	Ayanleh	Souleiman	DJI	3.12.92	6	Athl	Lausanne	6 Jul
3:34.74	Nick	Willis	NZL	25.4.83	10	Herc	Monaco	21 Jul
3:34.86	Fouad	El Kaam	MAR	27.5.88	3	Odlozil	Praha	5 Jun
3:34.87	Timo	Benitz	GER	24.12.91	8	FBK	Hengelo	11 Jun
3:34.99	Abdelaati	Iguider	MAR	25.3.87	9	DL	Stockholm	18 Jun
3:35.00	Johnny	Gregorek	USA	7.12.91	1		New York	6 Jul
3:35.03	Brahim	Akachab	MAR	9.3.93	1	DL	Rabat	16 Jul
3:35.23	Benson	Seurei	BRN	27.3.84	1		Amiens	10 Jun
3:35.25	Robby	Andrews	USA	29.3.91	2		New York	6 Jul
3:35.28	Thiago	André	BRA	4.8.95	1		Nijmegen	2 Jun
	(40)							
3:35.29	Ben	Blankenship	USA	15.12.89	3		New York	6 Jul
3:35.56	Mahiedine	Mekhissi-Benabbad	FRA	15.3.85	2		Bruay-la-Buissière	4 Jul
3:35.57	Weretew	Eshete	ETH-J	.99	5	WCT	Hengelo	10 Jun
3:35.57	Luke	Mathews	AUS	21.6.95	9	FBK	Hengelo	11 Jun
3:35.72	Charlie	Grice	GBR	7.11.93	7	Odlozil	Praha	5 Jun
3:35.81	Younès	Essalhi	MAR	20.2.93	8	Odlozil	Praha	5 Jun
3:35.85	Marc	Alcalá	ESP	7.11.94	13	Herc	Monaco	21 Jul
3:35.92	Richard	Douma	NED	17.4.93	10	FBK	Hengelo	11 Jun
3:35.95	Craig	Engels	USA	1.5.94	4		New York	6 Jul
3:35.99	Josh	Kerr	GBR	8.10.97	1	Clay	Azusa	14 Apr
	(50)							
3:36.07	Kumari	Taki	KEN-J	6.5.99	11	FBK	Hengelo	11 Jun
3:36.10	Colby	Alexander	USA	13.6.91	5		New York	6 Jul
3:36.14	Sofiane	Selmouni	FRA	22.9.89	14	Herc	Monaco	21 Jul
3:36.34+	Clayton	Murphy	USA	26.2.95	6	Pre	Eugene	27 May
3:36.36	Benjamin	Kigen	KEN	5.7.93	1		Madrid	14 Jul
3:36.37	Michal	Rozmys	POL	13.3.95	9	Odlozil	Praha	5 Jun
3:36.47	Boaz	Kiprugut	KEN-J	18.5.98	12	FBK	Hengelo	11 Jun
3:36.50	Abderrahmane	Anou	ALG	29.1.91	2		Montreuil	1 Jun
3:36.51	Eric	Jenkins	USA	24.11.91	1rB		Los Angeles (ER)	18 May
3:36.55	David	Bustos	ESP	25.8.90	7	DL	London (OS)	9 Jul
	(60)							
3:36.56	Jonathan	Sawe	KEN	22.5.95	1rA		Padova	16 Jul
3:36.60	Kalle	Berglund	SWE	11.3.96	8	DL	London (OS)	9 Jul
3:36.61	Hicham	Oueladha	MAR	31.1.95	3		Bruay-la-Buissière	4 Jul
3:36.65	Kyle	Merber	USA	19.11.90	6		New York	6 Jul
3:36.73	Cristian	Soratos	USA	26.9.92	2rB		Los Angeles (ER)	18 May
3:36.77	Drew	Hunter	USA	5.9.97	3rA		Padova	16 Jul
3:36.8A	Collins	Cheboi	KEN	25.9.87	1		Nairobi	18 May
3:36.81	Ilham Tanui	Özbilen	TUR	5.3.90	2		Huelva	14 Jun
3:36.85	Andrew	Bayer	USA	3.2.90	11	Athl	Lausanne	6 Jul
3:36.87	Jordan	Williamsz	AUS	21.8.92	2		Swarthmore	15 May
	(70)							
3:36.9A	Abednego	Chesebe	KEN	20.6.82	2		Nairobi	18 May
3:36.91	Hillary	Ngetich	KEN	15.9.95	4		Montreuil	1 Jun
3:36.93	Mekonnen	Gebremedhin	ETH	11.10.88	6	WCT	Hengelo	10 Jun
3:36.96	Yoann	Kowal	FRA	28.5.87	7		Marseille	3 Jun

Mark	Name		Nat	Born	Pos	Meet	Venue	Date
3:36.97	Robbie	Fitzgibbon	GBR	23.3.96	4		Nijmegen	2 Jun
3:36.98	Mohamed Ismail	Ibrahim	DJI	1.7.97	1		Kortrijk	8 Jul
3:37.08	Nabil	Oussama	MAR	18.2.96	4		Bruay-la-Buissière	4 Jul
3:37.09	Welde	Tufa	ETH-J	29.3.99	7	WCT	Hengelo	10 Jun
3:37.12	João Capistrano	Bussotti Neves	ITA	10.5.93	8		Marseille	3 Jun
3:37.14	Vladimir	Nikitin	RUS	5.8.92	1	NC	Zhukovskiy	30 Jul
	(80)							
3:37.16	Emanuel	Rolim	POR	30.1.93	3		Oordegem	27 May
3:37.21	Llorenç	Sales	ESP	14.7.88	3		Huelva	14 Jun
3:37.32	Filip	Sasínek	CZE	8.1.96	9		Marseille	3 Jun
3:37.35A	Evans	Kipchumba	KEN	.94	6	WCT	Nairobi	24 Jun
3:37.41	Tamás	Kazi	HUN	16.5.85	3		Lignano	12 Jul
3:37.42	Saïd Aden	Saïd	QAT	–.93	10	DL	Doha	5 May
3:37.43	Haftu	Teklu	ETH	.90	8	WCT	Hengelo	10 Jun
3:37.45	Tom	Marshall	GBR	12.6.89	11	DL	London (OS)	9 Jul
3:37.48	Sam	McEntee	AUS	3.2.92	3		Swarthmore	15 May
3:37.55	Hamish	Carson	NZL	1.11.88	5		Huelva	14 Jun
	(90)							
3:37.57	Peter	Callahan	BEL	1.6.91	4		Oordegem	27 May
3:37.61	Abdelali	Razyn	MAR	1.1.91	2		Kortrijk	8 Jul
3:37.61	Ryan	Hill	USA	31.1.90	3	NA	Heusden-Zolder	22 Jul
3:37.66	Isaac	Kimeli	BEL	9.3.94	4	NA	Heusden-Zolder	22 Jul
3:37.69	Youssouf Hiss	Bachir	DJI	–.87	5	NA	Heusden-Zolder	22 Jul
3:37.75	Andrew	Wheating	USA	21.11.87	4		Los Angeles (ER)	18 May
3:37.79	Sam	Prakel	USA	29.10.94	2		Portland	11 Jun
3:37.84	Carlos Martín	Díaz	CHI	9.7.93	7		Oordegem	27 May
3:37.86	Riley	Masters	USA	5.4.90	3rB		Los Angeles (ER)	18 May
3:37.88	Takieddine	Hedeilli	ALG	6.6.96	2		Bruxelles	9 Jul
	(100)							

Mark	Name		Nat	Born	Date
3:37.91	Charles	Philibert-Thiboutot	CAN	31.12.90	12 Jul
3:37.91	Izaic	Yorks	USA	17.4.94	12 Jul
3:37.92	Jamal	Al-Hayrani	QAT	26.5.93	16 Jul
3:37.93	James	Randon	USA	16.6.94	15 May
3:37.95	Hassan	Mead	USA	28.6.91	18 May
3:37.96	Vincent	Letting	KEN	16.6.93	16 Jul
3:37.97	Jordan	Gusman	AUS	30.1.94	14 Jun
3:37.98	Trevor	Dunbar	USA	29.4.91	16 Jul
3:38.10	Cory	Leslie	USA	24.10.89	15 May
3:38.11	Jerry	Motsau	RSA	12.3.90	9 Jul
3:38.12	Rowan	Axe	GBR	17.5.91	14 Jun
3:38.16	Paul	Robinson	IRL	24.5.91	2 Jun
3:38.2A	Collins	Koros	KEN	.90	11 May
3:38.21	Joshua	Thompson	USA	9.5.93	14 Apr
3:38.28	Florian	Carvalho	FRA	9.3.89	14 Jun
3:38.31	Adam	Kszczot	POL	2.9.89	23 Jul
3:38.35	Adam	Clarke	GBR	3.4.91	2 Jun
3:38.4A	Erick	Kiptanui	KEN	.90	11 May
3:38.46	Rabie	Doukkana	MAR	6.12.87	9 Jul
3:38.49	Isaac	Hockey	AUS	22.8.97	8 Jul
3:38.49	Federico	Bruno	ARG	18.6.93	14 Jul
3:38.52	Lopez	Lomong	USA	1.1.85	11 Jun
3:38.54	Marius	Probst	GER	20.8.95	27 May
3:38.55A	Geoffrey Kibet	Matum	KEN	22.11.87	24 Jun
3:38.56	Gonzalo	García	ESP	26.1.95	14 Jun
3:38.56	Tarik	Moukrime	BEL	3.3.92	4 Jul
3:38.60	Mostafa	Smaïli	MAR	9.1.97	9 Jun
3:38.65	Ali	Hamdi	BEL	2.11.89	9 Jul
3:38.71	Brannon	Kidder	USA	18.11.93	9 Jul
3:38.72	Mac	Fleet	USA	17.10.90	18 May
3:38.73+	Robert	Domanic	USA	10.3.95	1 Jun
3:38.73	Jamal	Hitrane	MAR	1.9.89	10 Jun
3:38.81	Amine	Cheniti	ALG	22.5.93	4 Jul
3:38.83	Rantso	Mokopane	RSA	8.8.94	28 Apr
3:38.85	Tom	Lancashire	GBR	2.7.85	2 Jun
3:38.86	Patrick	Casey	USA	23.5.90	18 May
3:38.92	Gilbert	Kwemoi	KEN	3.10.97	11 Jun
3:38.94	Dumisani	Hlaselo	RSA	8.6.89	28 Apr
3:38.95	Samir	Dahmani	FRA	3.4.91	3 Jun
3:38.96+	Henrik	Ingebrigtsen	NOR	24.2.91	27 May
3:38.96	Andy	Trouard	USA	22.4.94	3 Jun
3:38.96	Travis	Burkstrand	USA	22.7.89	16 Jun
3:38.99	Berihan	Feye	ETH-J	.99	10 Jun
3:39.0A	Zemenu	Addis	ETH-J	15.5.99	21 May
3:39.00	Jonathan	Davies	GBR	28.10.94	14 Jun
3:39.01	Soufiyan	Bouqantar	MAR	30.8.93	25 Apr
3:39.02	Charel	Grethen	LUX	22.6.92	15 Jul
3:39.05	Ben	Saarel	USA	8.3.95	11 Jun
3:39.08	Chris	Hatler	USA	12.10.94	15 May
3:39.23	Jordan	McNamara	USA	7.3.87	16 Jun
3:39.25	Daniel	Winn	USA	30.7.91	11 Jun
3:39.26	Daniel	Estrada	MEX	27.2.90	18 May
3:39.26	Ayoub	Mokhtar	ESP	26.10.96	24 Jun
3:39.28	Rorey	Hunter	AUS	2.2.93	28 Jun
3:39.29	Chad	Noelle	USA	12.4.93	18 May
3:39.39	Matthew	Ramsden	AUS	23.7.97	18 May
3:39.45	Andréas	Dimitrákis	GRE	8.9.90	27 May
3:39.47	Alberto	Imedio	ESP	24.5.91	16 Jul
3:39.53	Charlie	Marquardt	USA	9.7.94	15 May
3:39.54	Edwin	Kiptoo	KEN-J	20.7.98	2 Jun
3:39.54	Grzegorz	Kalinowski	POL	22.9.90	10 Jun
3:39.55	Alexis	Miellet	FRA	5.5.95	1 Jun
3:39.56	David	Ribich	USA	27.12.95	11 Jun
3:39.59	Pieter	Claus	BEL	1.3.93	27 May
3:39.61	Andrew	Butchart	GBR	14.10.91	14 Jun
3:39.64	Craig	Nowak	USA	20.4.94	11 Jun
3:39.65	James	West	GBR	30.1.96	14 Jun
3:39.67	Henry	Wynne	USA	18.4.95	11 Jun
3:39.67A	Bernard	Koros	KEN	7.5.94	24 Jun
3:39.69	Daniel	Herrera	MEX	29.11.92	11 Jun
3:39.71	Robert	Denault	CAN	27.4.93	15 May
3:39.74	Benjamin	Kovács	HUN	24.1.95	5 Jun
3:39.75	Rob	Napolitano	USA	3.11.94	15 May
3:39.78	Martin	Casse	FRA	23.6.90	4 Jul
3:39.82	David	Timlin	USA	10.6.94	16 Jun
3:39.84	Daniel	Huling	USA	16.7.83	19 Jul
3:39.86	Abraham	Rotich	BRN	26.6.93	25 Jun
3:39.92	Jakob	Ingebrigtsen	NOR-Y	19.9.00	18 Jun
3:39.95	Anthony	Kiptoo	KEN	19.8.97	29 Jun
3:40.00	Soufiane	El Kabbouri	ITA	5.3.93	12 Jul
3:40.02	Adam	Pyke	AUS	27.11.95	16 Jul
3:40.10	Yevgeniy	Kunts	RUS	21.4.93	30 Jul
3:40.1A	George	Manangoi	KEN-Y	29.11.00	16 Dec
3:40.12+	Will	Geoghegan	USA	15.7.92	1 Jun
3:40.21	Hicham	Akankam	MAR-J	4.4.98	16 Jul
3:40.22	James	Tenai	KEN	4.4.88	24 Jun
3:40.22	Thomas	Riva	CAN	31.1.92	15 Jul
3:40.28	Levent	Ates	TUR	20.3.91	14 Jun
3:40.29	Viktor	Bakharev	RUS	5.5.94	16 Jun
3:40.30	Liam	Dee	GBR	23.5.96	15 May
3:40.39	Saúl	Ordóñez	ESP	10.4.94	14 Jun
3:40.40	Blake	Haney	USA	29.3.96	7 Jun
3:40.40	Bryan	Cantero	FRA	28.4.91	14 Jun
3:40.42	James	Hansen	AUS	27.11.93	14 Dec

Mark	First	Last	Nat	Born	Date	Mark	First	Last	Nat	Born	Date
3:40.43	Mohad	Abdikadar	ITA	12.6.93	16 Jul	3:40.49	Vincent	Hazeleger	NED	21.8.95	10 Jun
3:40.45	Mohammed	Ahmed	CAN	5.1.91	14 Apr	3:40.49	Marcel	Fehr	GER	20.6.92	9 Jul
						(198)					

Indoors

Mark	Name		Nat	Born	Pos	Meet	Venue	Date
3:37.01+	Edward	Cheserek	KEN	2.2.94	1	in 1M	Boston (A)	26 Feb
3:37.58+	Andrew	Butchart	GBR	14.10.91	1	in 1M	New York (A)	4 Feb

Mark	First	Last	Nat	Born	Date	Mark	First	Last	Nat	Born	Date
3:38.04+	Ford	Palmer	USA	6.10.90	26 Feb	3:39.72	Garrett	Heath	USA	3.11.85	18 Feb
3:38.52	Tom	Lancashire	GBR	2.7.85	10 Feb	3:40.03	Nathan	Brannen	CAN	8.9.82	18 Feb

JUNIORS

See main lists for top 7 juniors. 11 performances by 7 men to 3:37.5. Additional marks and further juniors:

Soget	3:35.04	12	Herc	Monaco	21 Jul	3:36.3A1	Machakos	16 Dec
Tolosa	3:36.03	4		Marseille	4 Jun			
Kiprugut	3:36.59	3		Nijmegen	2 Jun			

Mark	Name		Nat	Born	Pos	Meet	Venue	Date
3:38.99	Berihan	Feye	ETH	.99	9	WCT	Hengelo	10 Jun
3:39.0A	Zemenu	Addis	ETH	15.5.99	3	NC	Addis Ababa	21 May
3:39.54	Edwin	Kiptoo (10)	KEN	20.7.98	2		Somerville	2 Jun
3:39.92	Jakob	Ingebrigtsen	NOR-Y	19.9.00	11	DL	Stockholm	18 Jun
3:40.1A	George	Manangoi	KEN-Y	29.11.00	3		Machakos	16 Dec
3:40.21	Hicham	Akankam	MAR	4.4.98	7	DL	Rabat	16 Jul
3:40.72	Adrián	Ben	ESP	4.8.98	5rB		Huelva	14 Jun
3:41.07	Yani	Khalef	FRA	7.2.98	9		Montreuil	1 Jun
3:41.18	George	Kusche	RSA	6.8.98	4		Durban	28 Feb
3:41.21	Ignacio	Fontes	ESP	22.6.98	6rB		Huelva	14 Jun
3:41.69	Jye	Edwards	AUS	6.3.98	2		Sydney	5 Feb
3:41.9A	Asref	Huadie	ETH	16.9.99	8	NC	Addis Ababa	18 May
3:42.12	Jake	Heyward (20)	GBR	26.4.99	4		Merksem	29 Jul

1 MILE

Mark	Name		Nat	Born	Pos	Meet	Venue	Date
3:49.04	Ronald	Kwemoi	KEN	19.9.95	1	Pre	Eugene	27 May
3:49.08	Elijah	Manangoi	KEN	5.1.93	2	Pre	Eugene	27 May
3:49.64	Timothy	Cheruiyot	KEN	20.11.95	3	Pre	Eugene	27 May
3:51.17	Vincent	Kibet	KEN	6.5.91	4	Pre	Eugene	27 May
3:51.99	Clayton	Murphy	USA	26.2.95	5	Pre	Eugene	27 May
3:51.99	Thiago	André	BRA	4.8.95	1rB	Pre	Eugene	27 May
3:52.77	Abdelaati	Iguider	MAR	25.3.87	6	Pre	Eugene	27 May
3:53.04	Ben	Blankenship	USA	15.12.89	7	Pre	Eugene	27 May
3:53.21	David	Torrence	PER	26.11.85	1		Concord, MA	1 Jun
3:53.23	Filip (10)	Ingebrigtsen	NOR	20.4.93	8	Pre	Eugene	27 May
3:53.34	Chris	O'Hare	GBR	23.11.90	2rB	Pre	Eugene	27 May
3:53.50	Bethwel	Birgen	KEN	6.8.88	9	Pre	Eugene	27 May
3:53.62	Charlie	Grice	GBR	7.11.93	10	Pre	Eugene	27 May
3:53.79	Henrik	Ingebrigtsen	NOR	24.2.91	3rB	Pre	Eugene	27 May
3:53.97	Jakub	Holusa	CZE	20.2.88	4rB	Pre	Eugene	27 May
3:54.39	Fouad	El Kaam	MAR	27.5.88	5rB	Pre	Eugene	27 May
3:54.53	Luke	Mathews	AUS	21.6.95	6rB	Pre	Eugene	27 May
3:54.73	Robert	Domanic	USA	10.3.95	2		Concord, MA	1 Jun
3:54.78	Kyle	Merber	USA	19.11.90	3		Concord, MA	1 Jun
3:54.92	Jake (20/20)	Wightman	GBR	11.7.94	1	DL	Birmingham	20 Aug
3:55.14	Charles	Philibert-Thiboutot	CAN	31.12.90	4		Concord, MA	1 Jun
3:55.23	Andrew	Wheating	USA	21.11.87	7rB	Pre	Eugene	27 May

Mark	First	Last	Nat	Born	Date	Mark	First	Last	Nat	Born	Date
3:55.54	Trevor	Dunbar	USA	29.4.91	1 Jun	3:56.89	Jordan	Williamsz	AUS	21.8.92	20 Aug
3:55.67	Lopez	Lomong	USA	1.1.85	27 May	3:56.90	Ryan	Gregson	AUS	26.4.90	27 May
3:55.79	Morgan	McDonald	AUS	23.4.96	12 Jul	3:57.00	Sean	Tobin	IRL	20.7.94	18 Jul
3:55.89	Sam	Prakel	USA	29.10.94	18 Jul	3:57.02	Chad	Noelle	USA	12.4.93	1 Jun
3:55.97	Stewart	McSweyn	AUS	1.6.95	18 Jul	3:57.23	Jesse	Garn	USA	4.6.93	1 Jun
3:56.13	Daniel	Herrera	MEX	29.11.92	1 Jun	3:57.29	Jrdan	Gusman	AUS	30.1.94	23 Dec
3:56.24	Will	Geoghegan	USA	15.7.92	1 Jun	3:57.38	Colby	Alexander	USA	13.6.91	12 Jul
3:56.29	Jakob	Ingebrigtsen	NOR-Y	19.9.00	15 Jun	3:57.39	Evan	Jager	USA	8.3.89	20 Aug
3:56.41	Nick	Willis	NZL	25.4.83	6 Sep	3:57.50	Johnny	Gregorek	USA	7.12.91	6 Sep
3:56.60	Mohammed	Ahmed	CAN	5.1.91	20 Aug	3:57.59	Silas	Kiplagat	KEN	20.8.89	27 May
3:56.68	Cristian	Soratos	USA	26.9.92	27 May	3:57.59	Patrick	Tiernan	AUS	11.9.94	18 Jul
3:56.71	Graham	Crawford	USA	29.12.92	12 Jul	3:57.66	Hicham	Akankam	MAR-J	4.4..98	15 Jun
3:56.79	Drew	Hunter	USA	5.9.97	12 Jul	3:57.67	Craig	Engels	USA	1.5.94	4 Aug

Indoors

Mark	Name		Nat	Born	Pos	Meet	Venue	Date
3:52.01	Edward	Cheserek	KEN	2.2.94	1		Boston (A)	26 Feb
3:52.22	Kyle	Merber	USA	19.11.90	2		Boston (A)	26 Feb
3:53.15	Johnny	Gregorek	USA	7.12.91	3		Boston (A)	26 Feb
3:53.23	Eric	Jenkins	USA	24.11.91	1	Millrose	New York (A)	11 Feb
3:54.23	Andrew	Butchart	GBR	14.10.91	1		New York (A)	4 Feb
3:54.23	Cristian	Soratos	USA	26.9.92	1rB	Millrose	New York (A)	11 Feb
3:54.92	Ford	Palmer	USA	6.10.90	4		Boston (A)	26 Feb

Mark	Name		Nat	Born	Pos	Meet	Venue	Date
3:55.78	Matthew	Centrowitz	USA	18.10.89				28 Jan
3:55.99	Colby	Alexander	USA	13.6.91				11 Feb
3:56.49	Ryan	Gregson	AUS	26.4.90				15 Feb
3:56.55	Evan	Jager	USA	8.3.89				11 Feb
3:56.89	Joshua	Thompson	USA	9.5.93				11 Feb
3:57.04	Robby	Andrews	USA	29.3.91				11 Feb
3:57.31	Ben	True	USA	29.12.85				28 Jan
3:57.39	Adam	Palamar	CAN	12.3.94				28 Jan
3:57.86	Cory	Leslie	USA	24.10.89				11 Feb
3:57.94	Hamish	Carson	NZL	1.11.88				16 Dec
3:57.99	Daniel	Huling	USA	16.7.83				26 Feb

JUNIORS

Mark	Name		Nat	Born	Pos	Meet	Venue	Date
3:56.29	Jakob	Ingebrigtsen	NOR-Y	19.9.00	1J	Bisl	Oslo	15 Jun
	3:58.07				11rB	Pre	Eugene	27 May
3:57.66	Hicham	Akankam	MAR	4.4..98	2J	Bisl	Oslo	15 Jun
3:58.58	Abdelkarim	Ben Zahra	MAR	27.10.98	3J	Bisl	Oslo	15 Jun
3:59.30	Reed	Brown	USA	6.8.98	3		St. Louis	1 Jun
4:00.16	Cooper	Teare	USA	18.8.99	1J	MSR	Torrance	15 Apr
4:00.2	Jye	Edwards	AUS	6.3.98	4		Melbourne	16 Feb

2000 METRES

Mark	Name		Nat	Born	Pos	Meet	Venue	Date
5:02.82+	Yomif	Kejelcha	ETH	1.8.97	1	in 800m	Doha	5 May

3000 METRES

Mark	Name		Nat	Born	Pos	Meet	Venue	Date
7:28.73	Ronald	Kwemoi	KEN	19.9.95	1	DL	Doha	5 May
7:31.57	Paul	Chelimo	USA	27.10.90	2	DL	Doha	5 May
7:32.27	Yomif	Kejelcha	ETH	1.8.97	3	DL	Doha	5 May
7:32.31	Muktar	Edris	ETH	14.1.94	1	DL	Paris (C)	1 Jul
7:32.88		Kwemoi			2	DL	Paris (C)	1 Jul
7:33.36	Caleb	Ndiku	KEN	9.10.92	4	DL	Doha	5 May
7:33.37		Kejelcha			3	DL	Paris (C)	1 Jul
7:34.96	Joshua	Cheptegei	UGA	12.9.96	4	DL	Paris (C)	1 Jul
7:35.15	Mohamed	Farah	GBR	23.3.83	1	DL	London (OS)	9 Jul
7:35.28	Adel	Mechaal	ESP	5.12.90	5	DL	Paris (C)	1 Jul
7:35.53	Ben	True	USA	29.12.85	6	DL	Paris (C)	1 Jul
7:36.32		Mechaal			2	DL	London (OS)	9 Jul
7:37.56	Andrew	Butchart (10)	GBR	14.10.91	3	DL	London (OS)	9 Jul
7:37.76	Patrick	Tiernan	AUS	11.9.94	4	DL	London (OS)	9 Jul
7:37.82	Abdelaati	Iguider	MAR	25.3.87	1	DL	Rabat	16 Jul
7:38.30	Albert	Rop	BRN	17.7.92	5	DL	Doha	5 May
7:38.33	Davis	Kiplangat	KEN-J	10.7.98	5	DL	London (OS)	9 Jul
7:38.35		Mechaal			2	DL	Rabat	16 Jul
7:38.50	Franklin	Ngelel	KEN	2.3.92	6	DL	London (OS)	9 Jul
7:38.51	Hassan	Mead	USA	28.6.91	7	DL	London (OS)	9 Jul
7:38.64		Farah			1	DL	Birmingham	20 Aug
7:38.65	Soufiyan	Bouqantar	MAR	30.8.93	3	DL	Rabat	16 Jul
7:38.90	Andrew	Bayer	USA	3.2.90	8	DL	London (OS)	9 Jul
7:38.90	Selemon	Barega	ETH-Y	20.1.00	1	Hanz	Zagreb	29 Aug
7:39.28		Tiernan			7	DL	Paris (C)	1 Jul
7:39.57	Yenew	Alamirew	ETH	27.5.90	8	DL	Paris (C)	1 Jul
7:39.91	Zouhaïr	Aouad	BRN	7.4.89	4	DL	Rabat	16 Jul
7:39.97		Kiplangat			2	Hanz	Zagreb	29 Aug
	(28/21)							
7:40.36	Eric	Jenkins	USA	24.11.91	9	DL	London (OS)	9 Jul
7:40.49	Mohammed	Ahmed	CAN	5.1.91	3	Hanz	Zagreb	29 Aug
7:40.55	Illias	Fifa	ESP	16.5.89	5	DL	Rabat	16 Jul
7:41.03	Sam	McEntee	AUS	3.2.92	10	DL	London (OS)	9 Jul
7:41.87	Kemoy	Campbell	JAM	14.1.91	2		Kingston	10 Jun
7:41.88	Brahim	Kaazouzi	MAR	15.6.90	6	DL	Rabat	16 Jul
7:42.19	Ryan	Gregson	AUS	26.4.90	7	DL	Rabat	16 Jul
7:42.22	Nick	Goolab	GBR	30.1.90	11	DL	London (OS)	9 Jul
7:43.20	Edwin	Soi	KEN	3.3.86	9	DL	Rabat	16 Jul
	(30)							
7:43.37	Marc	Scott	GBR	21.12.93	12	DL	London (OS)	9 Jul
7:43.39	Silas	Kiplagat	KEN	20.8.89	5	Hanz	Zagreb	29 Aug
7:43.57	Bethwel	Birgen	KEN	6.8.88	9	DL	Paris (C)	1 Jul
7:43.73	Jacob	Kiplimo	UGA-Y	14.11.00	7	DL	Doha	5 May
7:43.81	Ryan	Hill	USA	31.1.90	13	DL	London (OS)	9 Jul
7:44.24	Collins	Cheboi	KEN	25.9.87	4		Kingston	10 Jun
7:44.33	Jonathan	Ndiku	KEN	18.9.91	11	DL	Paris (C)	1 Jul
7:44.36	Sadik	Mikhou	BRN	25.7.90	1	PNG	Turku	13 Jun
7:44.43	Ben	Blankenship	USA	15.12.89	8	Hanz	Zagreb	29 Aug
7:45.11	Thomas	Curtin	USA	8.8.93	2		Concord, MA	1 Jun
	(40)							

Mark	Name		Nat	Born	Pos	Meet	Venue	Date
7:46.72	Tariq	Al-Amri	KSA	23.12.90	9	DL	Doha	5 May
7:46.89	Lucas	Bruchet	CAN	23.2.91	3		Concord, MA	1 Jun
7:47.42	Donn	Cabral	USA	12.12.89	4		Concord, MA	1 Jun
7:47.47	Brandon	Doughty	USA	14.5.93	5		Concord, MA	1 Jun
7:47.65	Stewart	McSweyn	AUS	1.6.95	3	PNG	Turku	13 Jun
7:47.66	Travis	Mahoney	USA	25.7.90	6		Concord, MA	1 Jun

Mark	Name		Nat	Born	Date
7:48.14	Antonio	Abadía	ESP	2.7.90	9 Jul
7:48.64	Craig	Lutz	USA	7.11.92	1 Jun
7:48.77	Lopez	Lomong	USA	1.1.85	6 Jul
7:48.79	Riley	Masters	USA	5.4.90	9 Jul
7:49.00	Conseslus	Kipruto	KEN	8.12.94	5 May
7:49.12	Graham	Crawford	USA	29.12.92	6 Jul
7:49.17A	Edward	Zakayo	KEN-Y	25.11.01	16 Jul
7:49.75	Hayle	Ibrahimov	AZE	18.1.90	5 May
7:49.84	Dawit	Wolde	ETH	19.5.91	13 Jun
7:49.92	Richard	Ringer	GER	27.2.89	20 Aug
7:50.26	Reid	Buchanan	USA	3.2.93	18 Jul
7:50.47	Collis	Birmingham	AUS	27.12.84	18 Jul
7:50.54	Vincent	Kibet	KEN	6.5.91	16 Jul
7:50.55	Nixon	Chepseba	KEN	12.12.90	10 Jun
7:50.64A	Stanley	Waithaka	KEN-Y	9.4.00	16 Jul
7:50.65	Alfred	Barkach	KEN	2.3.97	10 Jun
7:50.68	Bernard	Muia	KEN	26.5.95	8 Apr
7:51.12	Anthony	Rotich	KEN	.93	6 Jul
7:51.17	Cornelius	Kangogo	KEN	31.12.93	11 Jul
7:51.19	Hélio	Gomes	POR	27.12.84	10 Jun
7:51.26	Simon	Debognies	BEL	16.7.96	10 Jun
7:51.39	Jakub	Holusa	CZE	20.2.88	14 May
7:51.41+	Leonard	Korir	USA	10.12.86	27 May
7:51.48	Amos	Kirui	KEN-J	9.2.98	8 Apr
7:51.48	Altobeli	da Silva	BRA	3.12.90	7 Jul
7:51.55+	Geoffrey	Kamworor	KEN	22.11.92	27 May
7:51.74+	Stephen	Sambu	KEN	7.7.88	27 May
	(73)				

Indoors

Mark	Name		Nat	Born	Pos	Meet	Venue	Date
7:40.80+	Ryan	Hill	USA	31.1.90	1	in 2M	New York (A)	11 Feb
7:43.04	Hagos	Gebrhiwet	ETH	11.5.94	3		Boston (R)	28 Jan
7:44.34	Julian	Oakley	NZL	23.6.93	1		Boston (A)	16 Dec
7:44.55	Mourad	Amdouni	FRA	21.1.88	1		Metz	12 Feb
7:44.65	Vladimir	Nikitin	RUS	5.8.92	1	Winter	Moskva	5 Feb
7:44.73	Hillary	Ngetich	KEN	15.9.95	1		Düsseldorf	1 Feb
7:44.95	Mekonnen	Gebremedhin	ETH	11.10.88	2		Metz	12 Feb
7:45.01+	Lawi	Lalang	KEN	15.6.91	5	in 2M	New York (A)	11 Feb
7:45.28+	Garrett	Heath	USA	3.11.85	6	in 2M	New York (A)	11 Feb
7:45.69+	Matthew	Centrowitz	USA	18.10.89	7	in 2M	New York (A)	11 Feb
7:45.71	Colby	Gilbert	USA	17.3.95	1		Seattle	28 Jan
7:46.06	Dejen	Gebremeskel	ETH	24.11.89	6		Boston (R)	28 Jan
7:46.22	Charles	Philibert-Thiboutot	CAN	31.12.90	2		Seattle	28 Jan
7:46.85	Edward	Cheserek	KEN	2.2.94	1		New York (A)	28 Jan
7:47.18	Nathan	Brannen	CAN	8.9.82	3		Seattle	28 Jan
7:47.66	Dawit	Wolde	ETH	19.5.91	2		Düsseldorf	1 Feb
7:47.82	Justyn	Knight	CAN	19.7.96	2		Ames	10 Feb

Mark	Name		Nat	Born	Date
7:48.39	Hayle	Ibrahimov	AZE	18.1.90	12 Feb
7:49.29	Lee	Emanuel	GBR	24.1.85	4 Feb
7:49.39	Kyle	Merber	USA	19.11.90	28 Jan
7:49.46	Morgan	Pearson	USA	22.9.93	4 Feb
7:49.52	Martin	Hehir	USA	19.12.92	11 Feb
7:49.76	Clayton	Young	USA	14.9.93	28 Jan
7:49.93	Johnny	Gregorek	USA	7.12.91	28 Jan
7:50.78	Marouan	Razine	ITA	9.4.91	7 Feb
7:51.05	Debele	Gezmu	ETH	14.4.96	28 Jan
7:51.19	Morgan	McDonald	AUS	23.4.96	4 Feb
7:51.20	Jack	Keelan	USA	2.2.95	11 Feb
7:51.21	Erik	Peterson	USA	15.6.94	4 Feb
7:51.43	Joe	Klecker	USA	16.11.96	11 Feb
7:51.44	John	Dressel	USA	2.5.97	25 Feb
7:51.51	Scott	Carpenter	USA	19.12.94	11 Feb
7:51.54	Soufiane	El Bakkali	MAR	7.1.96	1 Feb
7:51.90	Drew	Hunter	USA	5.9.97	4 Feb

JUNIORS

See main list for top 3 juniors. 11 performances by 7 men to 7:52.2, Further juniors:

Kiplangat	7:39.97	2	Hanz	Zagreb	29 Aug	7:40.63	3	DL	Birmingham	20 Aug
Barega	7:47.16A	1	WY	Nairobi	16 Jul					
Kirui	7:51.48	2		Tokyo	9 Apr					

Mark	Name		Nat	Born	Pos	Meet	Venue	Date
7:49.17A	Edward	Zakayo	KEN-Y	25.11.01	2	WY	Nairobi	16 Jul
7:50.64A	Stanley	Waithaka	KEN-Y	9.4.00	3	WY	Nairobi	16 Jul
7:51.48	Amos	Kirui	KEN	9.2.98	2		Setagaya	8 Apr
7:52.19+	Aron	Kifle	ERI	20.2.98	7	in 5000	Eugene	27 May
7:52.68	Evans	Keitany	KEN	.98	2		Kawasaki	21 May
7:54.79	Hyuga	Endo	JPN	5.8.98	3		Kitami	9 Jul
7:55.29A	Milkesa	Mengesha (10)	ETH-Y	14.4.00	4	WY	Nairobi	16 Jul
7:59.71A	Robert	Kiprop	KEN-Y	.00	3	WY-T	Nairobi	14 Jun
8:00.0A	Victor	Kurgat	KEN-Y	.01	1h1		Eldoret	25 May

2 MILES INDOORS

Mark	Name		Nat	Born	Pos	Meet	Venue	Date
8:11.33	Ben	True	USA	29.12.85	1	Millrose	New York (A)	11 Feb
8:11.56	Ryan	Hill	USA	31.1.90	2	Millrose	New York (A)	11 Feb
8:12.63	Andrew	Butchart	GBR	14.10.91	3	Millrose	New York (A)	11 Feb
8:13.16	Mohammed	Ahmed	CAN	5.1.91	4	Millrose	New York (A)	11 Feb
8:18.70	Lawi	Lalang	KEN	15.6.91	5	Millrose	New York (A)	11 Feb
8:19.61	Garrett	Heath	USA	3.11.85	6	Millrose	New York (A)	11 Feb
8:21.07	Matthew	Centrowitz	USA	18.10.89	7	Millrose	New York (A)	11 Feb

Mark	Name		Nat	Born	Date
8:26.17	Morgan	Pearson	USA	22.9.93	11 Feb
8:27.10	Ben	Blankenship	USA	15.12.89	11 Feb

+ intermediate time in longer race, A made at an altitude of 1000m or higher, D made in a decathlon, h made in a heat, qf quarter-final, sf semi-final, i indoors, Q qualifying round, r race number, -J juniors, -Y youths (b. 1999 or later)

Mark	Name		Nat	Born	Pos	Meet	Venue	Date

5000 METRES

Mark	Name		Nat	Born	Pos	Meet	Venue	Date
12:55.23	Muktar	Edris	ETH	14.1.94	1	Athl	Lausanne	6 Jul
12:55.58	Selemon	Barega	ETH-Y	20.1.00	2	Athl	Lausanne	6 Jul
12:59.83	Joshua	Cheptegei	UGA	12.9.96	3	Athl	Lausanne	6 Jul
13:00.70	Mohamed	Farah	GBR	23.3.83	1	Pre	Eugene	27 May
13:01.04		Edris			1		Somerville	2 Jun
13:01.21	Yomif	Kejelcha	ETH	1.8.97	2	Pre	Eugene	27 May
13:01.35	Geoffrey	Kamworor	KEN	22.11.92	3	Pre	Eugene	27 May
13:02.84		Cheptegei			4	Pre	Eugene	27 May
13:03.44	Cyrus	Rutto	KEN	21.4.92	2		Somerville	2 Jun
13:04.82	Albert	Rop	BRN	17.7.92	5	Pre	Eugene	27 May
13:06.05		Farah			1	WK-DLF	Zürich	24 Aug
13:06.09		Edris			2	WK-DLF	Zürich	24 Aug
13:06.18		Kejelcha			3	WK-DLF	Zürich	24 Aug
13:06.81	Yenew	Alamirew	ETH	27.5.90	4	Athl	Lausanne	6 Jul
13:07.35		Barega			4	WK-DLF	Zürich	24 Aug
13:08.16	Mohammed	Ahmed (10)	CAN	5.1.91	6	Pre	Eugene	27 May
13:08.62	Paul	Chelimo	USA	27.10.90	1	NC	Sacramento	23 Jun
13:09.93	Birhanu	Yemataw	BRN	27.2.96	1rA	NA	Heusden-Zolder	22 Jul
13:10.11		Chelimo			7	Pre	Eugene	27 May
13:10.13	Dawit	Wolde	ETH	19.5.91	2rA	NA	Heusden-Zolder	22 Jul
13:10.26		Ahmed			5	WK-DLF	Zürich	24 Aug
13:10.83	Ben	True	USA	29.12.85	3rA	NA	Heusden-Zolder	22 Jul
13:11.00		Yemataw			1	ISTAF	Berlin	27 Aug
13:11.20	Hassan	Mead	USA	28.6.91	4rA	NA	Heusden-Zolder	22 Jul
13:11.45	Andrew	Butchart	GBR	14.10.91	8	Pre	Eugene	27 May
13:11.58	Nicholas	Kimeli	KEN-J	29.9.98	2	ISTAF	Berlin	27 Aug
13:11.87	Bashir	Abdi	BEL	10.2.89	5rA	NA	Heusden-Zolder	22 Jul
13:11.88	James	Kibet	KEN	.88	3	ISTAF	Berlin	27 Aug
13:12.73		Butchart			4	ISTAF	Berlin	27 Aug
13:13.00	Stephen	Kissa	UGA	1.12.95	1		Oordegem	27 May
13:13.08		Alamirew			6	WK-DLF	Zürich	24 Aug
	(31/20)							
13:13.16	Fredrick	Kipkosgei	KEN	13.11.96	2		Oordegem	27 May
13:13.23	Betesfa	Getahun	ETH-J	25.9.98	6rA	NA	Heusden-Zolder	22 Jul
13:13.24	Emanuel	Gniki	TAN	18.5.88	7rA	NA	Heusden-Zolder	22 Jul
13:13.30	Eric	Jenkins	USA	24.11.91	9	Pre	Eugene	27 May
13:13.31	Aron	Kifle	ERI-J	20.2.98	10	Pre	Eugene	27 May
13:13.44	Patrick	Tiernan	AUS	11.9.94	11	Pre	Eugene	27 May
13:13.45	Djamal Abdi	Dirieh	DJI	.97	8rA	NA	Heusden-Zolder	22 Jul
13:13.46	Richard	Ringer	GER	27.2.89	5	ISTAF	Berlin	27 Aug
13:13.64	Jacob	Kiplimo	UGA-Y	14.11.00	12	Pre	Eugene	27 May
13:14.06	Soufiyan	Bouqantar	MAR	30.8.93	1		Barcelona	29 Jun
	(30)							
13:14.09	Paul	Tanui	KEN	22.12.90	13	Pre	Eugene	27 May
13:14.52	Amdework	Walelegn	ETH-J	11.3.99	2		Barcelona	29 Jun
13:14.56	Japheth	Korir	KEN	30.6.93	9rA	NA	Heusden-Zolder	22 Jul
13:15.20	Dawit	Fikadu	BRN	29.12.95	4		Barcelona	29 Jun
13:15.53	Zouhaïr	Aouad	BRN	7.4.89	2		Montreuil	1 Jun
13:15.57	Moses	Koech	KEN	5.4.97	5		Barcelona	29 Jun
13:15.83	Morgan	McDonald	AUS	23.4.96	10rA	NA	Heusden-Zolder	22 Jul
13:16.09	Awet	Habte	ERI	29.9.97	3		Carquefou	23 Jun
13:16.16	Aweke	Ayalew	BRN	23.2.93	6		Barcelona	29 Jun
13:16.22	Jonathan	Ndiku	KEN	18.9.91	11rA	NA	Heusden-Zolder	22 Jul
	(40)							
13:16.66	Mathew	Kiptanui	KEN	20.10.94	3		Montreuil	1 Jun
13:16.78	Abadi	Hadis	ETH	6.11.97	1		Hérouville	15 Jun
13:16.98	Brahim	Kaazouzi	MAR	15.6.90	4		Carquefou	23 Jun
13:16.99	Ryan	Hill	USA	31.1.90	3	NC	Sacramento	23 Jun
13:17.27	Solomon	Berihu	ETH-J	2.10.99	2		Hérouville	15 Jun
13:17.38	Leonard	Barsoton	KEN	21.10.94	15	Pre	Eugene	27 May
13:17.39	Illias	Fifa	ESP	16.5.89	3		Oordegem	27 May
13:17.51	Justyn	Knight	CAN	19.7.96	1		Stanford	5 May
13:17.55	Sam	McEntee	AUS	3.2.92	2		Stanford	5 May
13:17.80	Bethwel	Birgen	KEN	6.8.88	4		Montreuil	1 Jun
	(50)							
13:18.00	El Mahjoub	Dazza	MAR	3.3.91	2		Huelva	14 Jun
13:18.09	Davis	Kiplangat	KEN-J	10.7.98	8	ISTAF	Berlin	27 Aug
13:18.30	Getaneh	Molla	ETH	10.1.94	5		Montreuil	1 Jun

Mark	Name		Nat	Born	Pos	Meet	Venue	Date
13:19.12	Wesley	Ledama	KEN-J	2.7.99	2rB	NA	Heusden-Zolder	22 Jul
13:19.20	Polat Kemboi	Arikan	TUR	12.12.90	4		Huelva	14 Jun
13:19.42	Joseph	Ndirangu	KEN	9.9.94	1		Nobeoka	6 May
13:19.88	Josephat	Menjo	KEN	20.8.79	8		Barcelona	29 Jun
13:19.94	Hayle	Ibrahimov	AZE	18.1.90	7		Montreuil	1 Jun
13:19.98	Stewart	McSweyn	AUS	1.6.95	1		Dublin (S)	12 Jul
13:20.02	William	Sitonik	KEN	1.3.94	17	Pre	Eugene	27 May
	(60)							
13:20.16	Sondre Nordstad	Moen	NOR	12.1.91	3rB	NA	Heusden-Zolder	22 Jul
13:20.35	Gabriel	Geay	TAN	10.9.96	3		Stanford	5 May
13:21.26	Cornelius	Kangogo	KEN	31.12.93	1		Bellinzona	18 Jul
13:21.72	Evans	Keitany	KEN-J	27.11.99	3		Nobeoka	6 May
13:21.74	Lopez	Lomong	USA	1.1.85	5	NC	Sacramento	23 Jun
13:21.85	Teressa	Nyakora	ETH	26.2.95	1		Fukagawa	6 Jul
13:21.93	Youssef	Nasir	MAR	15.2.90	9		Barcelona	29 Jun
13:22.04	Leonard	Korir	USA	10.12.86	19	Pre	Eugene	27 May
13:22.18	Soufiane	Bouchikhi	BEL	22.3.90	14rA	NA	Heusden-Zolder	22 Jul
13:22.27	Philemon	Kiplagat	KEN-Y	20.9.01	1		Kitakyushu	3 Nov
	(70)							
13:22.37	Marc	Scott	GBR	21.12.93	4rB	NA	Heusden-Zolder	22 Jul
13:22.65	Andrew	Vernon	GBR	7.1.86	15rA	NA	Heusden-Zolder	22 Jul
13:22.66	Richard	Yator	KEN-J	4.6.98	1		Setagaya	30 Sep
13:22.68	Nicholas	Kosimbei	KEN	10.1.96	20	Pre	Eugene	27 May
13:22.93	Brett	Robinson	AUS	8.5.91	1		Auckland (NS)	26 Feb
13:23.11	Abraham	Kipyatich	KEN	10.5.93	3		Fukagawa	6 Jul
13:23.12	Kirubel	Erassa	USA	17.6.93	1		Portland	11 Jun
13:23.24	Éderson	Pereira	BRA	6.6.90	6		Oordegem	27 May
13:23.51	Biyazen	Alehegn	ETH-J	16.9.99	1		Yokohama	15 Oct
13:23.74	Shadrack	Kipchirchir	USA	22.2.89	1		Los Angeles (ER)	18 May
	(80)							
13:23.79	Stephen	Sambu	KEN	7.7.88	21	Pre	Eugene	27 May
13:24.05	Vladimir	Nikitin	RUS	5.8.92	1		Kazan	2 Jun
13:24.42	Ronald	Kwemoi	KEN	19.9.95	1		Kumamoto	1 Apr
13:24.72	Edward	Cheserek	KEN	2.2.94	4		Stanford	5 May
13:24.83	Yismaw	Ayenew	ETH-J	.98	6		Carquefou	23 Jun
13:24.89	Berhanu	Legesse	ETH	11.9.94	9	WK-DLF	Zürich	24 Aug
13:25.11	David	Bett	KEN	18.10.92	11		Montreuil	1 Jun
13:25.30	Alfred	Barkach	KEN	2.3.97	7		Oordegem	27 May
13:25.33	Tariq	Al-Amri	KSA	23.12.90	7		Carquefou	23 Jun
13:25.55	Abayneh	Degu	ETH-J	1.12.98	1rB		Kumamoto	1 Apr
	(90)							
13:25.55	Thierry	Ndikumwenayo	BDI	26.3.97	3		Bellinzona	18 Jul
13:25.56	Suguru	Osako	JPN	23.5.91	3		Portland	11 Jun
13:25.71	Ali	Kaya	TUR	20.4.94	16rA	NA	Heusden-Zolder	22 Jul
13:25.75	Alexander	Mutiso	KEN	10.9.96	3		Setagaya	30 Sep
13:25.79	Abbabiya	Simbassa	USA	30.6.93	2		Los Angeles (ER)	18 May
13:25.95	Dejen	Gebremeskel	ETH	24.11.89	3		Somerville	2 Jun
13:26.19	Bekele	Shiferaw	ETH	14.10.95	3		Yokohama	15 Oct
13:26.27	Trevor	Dunbar	USA	29.4.91	4		Portland	11 Jun
13:26.38	Daniel	Kipkemoi	KEN	5.7.96	2rB		Kumamoto	1 Apr
13:26.55	Thomas	Curtin	USA	8.8.93	5		Portland	11 Jun
	(100)							

Mark	Name		Nat	Born	Date
13:26.67	Kemoy	Campbell	JAM	14.1.91	9 Aug
13:27.36	Onèsphore	Nzikwinkunda	BDI	8.7.97	27 May
13:27.36	Mogos	Tuemay	ETH	24.5.97	18 Jul
13:27.37	Adel	Mechaal	ESP	5.12.90	27 Aug
13:27.52	Joel	Mwaura	KEN-J	20.1.98	1 Apr
13:27.64	Younès	Essalhi	MAR	20.2.93	16 May
13:27.69	François	Barrer	FRA	8.6.93	23 Jun
13:27.83	Reid	Buchanan	USA	3.2.93	11 Jun
13:27.86	Phillip	Kipyeko	UGA	10.1.95	29 Jun
13:28.00	Alfred	Ngeno	KEN	2.5.97	6 May
13:28.07	Marouan	Razine	ITA	9.4.91	27 May
13:28.24	Edwin	Soi	KEN	3.3.86	2 Jun
13:28.29	Collis	Birmingham	AUS	27.12.84	12 Jul
13:28.56	Kassa	Mekashaw	ETH	19.3.84	6 May
13:28.60	Samuel	Mwangi	KEN	19.9.97	15 Oct
13:28.61	Hiroki	Matsueda	JPN	20.5.93	1 Apr
13:28.78	John	Maina	KEN	14.7.93	6 May
13:28.79	Emmanuel	Bor	USA	14.4.88	11 Jun
13:29.11	David	McNeill	AUS	6.10.86	26 Feb
13:29.28	Ronald	Musagala	UGA	16.12.94	15 Jun
13:29.29	Mohamed	Ibrahim	DJI	1.7.97	16 May
13:29.37	Mekonnen	Gebremedhin	ETH	11.10.88	15 Jun
13:29.79	Charles	Ndungu	KEN	20.2.96	13 Jul
13:29.85	Riley	Masters	USA	5.4.90	5 May
13:29.88	Zouhair	Talbi	MAR	8.4.95	27 May
13:29.90	Ben	Connor	GBR	17.10.92	12 Jul
13:29.94	Martin	Hehir	USA	19.12.92	18 May
13:30.10	Abiyot	Abinet	ETH	10.5.89	21 Oct
13:30.12	Yevgeniy	Rybakov	RUS	27.2.85	25 May
13:30.24	Anatoliy	Rybakov	RUS	27.2.85	25 May
13:30.33	Ibrahim Hassan Bouh		DJI	.96	16 May
13:30.99	Willy	Kwemoi	KEN	8.10.97	13 Jul
13:31.29	Marcel	Fehr	GER	20.6.92	22 Jul
13:31.30	Edward	Waweru	KEN	3.10.90	1 Apr
13:31.35	Ken	Yokote	JPN	27.4.93	1 Apr
13:31.45	Caleb	Ndiku	KEN	9.10.92	27 May
13:31.50	Mamiyo	Nuguse	ETH	13.2.82	3 Jun
13:31.66	David	Njuguna	KEN	6.9.89	21 May
13:31.90	Bernard	Kimani	KEN	10.9.93	6 May
13:31.99	Luc	Bruchet	CAN	23.2.91	22 Jul
13:32.00	Florian	Carvalho	FRA	9.3.89	1 Jun
13:32.00	Tesfu	Tewelde	ERI	21.7.97	23 Jun

Mark	Name		Nat	Born	Date
13:32.01	Rodgers	Chumo	KEN	3.3.97	1 Apr
13:32.15	Diego	Estrada	USA	12.12.89	11 Jun
13:32.16	Tetsuya	Yoroizaka	JPN	20.3.90	29 Apr
13:32.22	Antonio	Abadía	ESP	2.7.90	14 Jun
13:32.42	Muiru	Muthoni	KEN-J	21.3.98	3 Dec
13:32.56	Shuho	Dairokuno	JPN	23.12.92	1 Apr
13:32.64	Cyrus	Kingori	KEN	5.1.97	1 Apr
13:32.87	John	Kariuki	KEN	24.11.97	1 Apr
13:33.14	Kazuya	Shiojiri	JPN	8.11.96	1 Apr
13:33.39	Chris	Derrick	USA	17.10.90	27 May
13:33.48	Nick	Goolab	GBR	30.1.90	27 May
13:33.60	Dewi	Griffiths	GBR	9.8.91	12 Jul
13:33.7A	Mathew	Kimeli	KEN-J	4.1.98	2 Jun
13:33.85	Charles	Ndirangu	KEN	8.2.93	1 Apr
13:33.9A	Geoffrey	Koech	KEN	28.8.93	23 Jun
13:33.95	Daniel	Kitonyi	KEN	12.1.94	3 Dec
13:33.99	Takashi	Ichida	JPN	16.6.92	3 Jun
13:34.28	Mike	Tate	CAN	1.4.95	5 May
13:34.34	Saïd	El Otmani	ITA	14.10.91	27 May
13:34.60	Joe	Stilin	USA	5.12.89	22 Jul
13:34.80	Yuta	Shitara	JPN	18.12.91	1 Apr
13:34.8A	Peter	Kariuki	KEN	.91	11 May
13:34.84	Futsum	Zienasellassie	USA	16.12.92	11 Jun
13:35.00	Hélio	Gomes	POR	27.12.84	14 Jun
13:35.1 9	Ledama	Kisaisa	KEN-J	25.6.98	9 Sep
13:35.29	Keijiro	Mogi	JPN	21.10.95	3 Jun
13:35.5A	Douglas	Kipserem	KEN	.87	11 May
13:35.53	Linus	Kiplagat	BRN	23.12.94	16 May
13:35.61	Simon	Mwangi	KEN	.97	21 May
13:35.69	Govindan	Lakshmanan	IND	5.6.90	9 Aug
13:35.81	Hayato	Seki	JPN	11.4.97	22 Jul
13:35.84	Jakob	Ingebrigtsen	NOR-Y	19.9.00	25 Aug
13:36.03	Craig	Lutz	USA	7.11.92	18 May
13:36.26	Alexander	Monroe	USA	30.3.92	11 Jun
13:36.26	Joeru	Murayama	KEN-J	20.1.99	18 Sep
13:36.36	Juan Antonio	Pérez	ESP	6.11.88	14 Jun
13:36.38	Benuel	Mogeni	KEN-Y	11.3.01	1 Aug
13:36.43	Andy	Trouard	USA	22.4.94	18 May
13:36.5A	Peter	Muindi	KEN	.90	11 May
13:36.52	Yuichiro	Ueno	JPN	29.7.85	29 Apr
13:36.68	David	Elliott	USA	21.7.93	31 Mar
13:36.7A	Franklin	Ngelel	KEN	.92	10 Jun
13:36.73	BCharles	Nzioka	KEN-J	21.9.99	1 Aug
13:37.13	Jonathan	Davies	GBR	28.10.94	23 Jun
13:37.20	Amanal	Petros	GER	17.5.95	27 May
13:37.2A	Wilfred	Kimitei	KEN	11.3.85	13 May
13:37.22	James	Ndiwa	KEN	1.11.97	21 Oct
13:37.23	Jefferson	Abbey	USA	.94	31 Mar
13:37.30	Sam	Stabler	GBR	17.5.92	22 Jul
13:37.31	Malcolm	Hicks	NZL	19.10.87	22 Jul
13:37.48	Julien	Wanders	SUI	18.3.96	27 May
13:37.58	Ramazan	Özdemir	TUR	6.7.91	16 May
13:37.60	Alexander	Yee	GBR-J	18.2.98	27 May
13:37.62	Najibe Marco	Salami	ITA	7.7.85	27 May
13:37.74	Félix	Bour	FRA	25.3.94	27 May
	(197)	200th 13:37.84			

Disqualified - Impeding competitor: 13:06.09 Chelimo – WK-DLF Zürich 24 Aug

Indoors

Mark	Name		Nat	Born	Pos	Meet	Venue	Date
13:04.60	Mohammed	Ahmed	CAN	5.1.91	1		Boston (A)	26 Feb
13:05.85	Eric	Jenkins	USA	24.11.91	2		Boston (A)	26 Feb
13:06.74	Ben	True	USA	29.12.85	3		Boston (A)	26 Feb
13:07.61	Ryan	Hill	USA	31.1.90	4		Boston (A)	26 Feb
13:10.60	Soufiane	El Bakkali	MAR	7.1.96	3		Birmingham	18 Feb
13:11.18	Mourad	Amdouni	FRA	21.1.88	4		Birmingham	18 Feb
13:12.22	William	Kincaid	USA	21.9.92	5		Boston (A)	26 Feb
13:12.27	Lopez	Lomong	USA	1.1.85	6		Boston (A)	26 Feb
13:14.45	Kemoy	Campbell	JAM	14.1.91	7		Boston (A)	26 Feb
13:19.35	Chris	Derrick	USA	17.10.90	8		Boston (A)	26 Feb
13:23.99	Yemaneberhan	Crippa	ITA	15.10.96	5		Birmingham	18 Feb
13:34.85	Colby	Gilbert	USA	17.3.95	2		Seattle	10 Feb

JUNIORS

See main list for top 15 juniors. 17 performances by 9 men to 13:21.5. Additional marks and further juniors:

Barega 2+	13:15.32	1	Montreuil	1 Jun	13:21.50	1h2 WCh London (OS) 9 Aug
Kimeli	13:16.38	1rB NA	Heusden-Zolder	22 Jul		
Walelegn	13:16.28	12 NA	Heusden-Zolder	22 Jul		
Berihu	13:18.00	7	Barcelona	29 Jun		
Kiplangat	13:18.81	6	Montreuil	1 Jun		
Ledama	13:19.96	2	Nobeoka	6 May		

Mark	Name		Nat	Born	Pos	Meet	Venue	Date
13:27.52	Joel	Mwaura	KEN	20.1.99	3rB		Kumamoto	1 Apr
13:32.42	Muiru	Muthoni	KEN	21.3.98	1		Yokohama	3 Dec
13:33.7A	Mathew	Kimeli	KEN	4.1.98	1		Eldoret	2 Jun
13:35.19	Ledama	Kisaisa	KEN	25.6.98	1		Fukui	9 Sep
13:35.84	Jakob	Ingebrigtsen (20)	NOR-Y	19.9.00	1	NC	Sandnes	25 Aug
13:36.26	Joeru	Murayama	KEN	20.1.99	3		Miyoshi	18 Sep

10,000 METRES

Mark	Name		Nat	Born	Pos	Meet	Venue	Date
26:49.51	Mohamed	Farah	GBR	23.3.83	1	WCh	London (OS)	4 Aug
26:49.94	Joshua	Cheptegei	UGA	12.9.96	2	WCh	London (OS)	4 Aug
26:50.60	Paul	Tanui	KEN	22.12.90	3	WCh	London (OS)	4 Aug
26:52.12	Bedan	Karoki	KEN	21.8.90	4	WCh	London (OS)	4 Aug
26:56.11	Jemal	Yimer	ETH	11.9.96	5	WCh	London(OS)	4 Aug
26:57.77	Geoffrey	Kamworor	KEN	22.11.92	6	WCh	London (OS)	4 Aug
26:59.19	Abadi	Hadis	ETH	6.11.97	7	WCh	London(OS)	4 Aug
27:02.35	Mohammed	Ahmed	CAN	5.1.91	8	WCh	London(OS)	4 Aug
27:07.55	Shadrack	Kipchirchir	USA	22.2.89	9	WCh	London (OS)	4 Aug
27:08.26		Hadis			1	FBK	Hengelo	11 Jun
27:08.94	Andamlak	Belihu (10)	ETH-J	20.11.98	10	WCh	London(OS)	4 Aug
27:09.08		Yimer			2	FBK	Hengelo	11 Jun
27:09.92	Aron	Kifle	ERI-J	20.2.98	11	WCh	London (OS)	4 Aug
27:11.08	Abraham	Cheroben	BRN	11.10.92	12	WCh	London (OS)	4 Aug

Mark	Name		Nat	Born	Pos	Meet	Venue	Date
27:12.09		Farah			1	GS	Ostrava	28 Jun
27:14.43	Mathew	Kimeli	KEN-J	4.1.98	2	GS	Ostrava	28 Jun
27:19.86	Yenew	Alamirew	ETH	27.5.90	3	FBK	Hengelo	11 Jun
27:20.18	Leonard	Korir	USA	10.12.86	13	WCh	London (OS)	4 Aug
27:20.57		Belihu			4	FBK	Hengelo	11 Jun
27:20.60	Muktar	Edris	ETH	14.1.94	5	FBK	Hengelo	11 Jun
27:21.09	Timothy	Toroitich	UGA	10.10.91	14	WCh	London (OS)	4 Aug
27:22.33	Moses	Kurong	UGA	7.7.94	6	FBK	Hengelo	11 Jun
27:22.73	Jonathan	Ndiku	KEN	18.9.91	1		Yokohama	11 Nov
27:22.79	William	Sitonik (20)	KEN	1.3.94	2		Yokohama	11 Nov
27:29.81	Patrick	Tiernan	AUS	11.9.94	1		Stanford	5 May
27:30.00		Ahmed			2		Stanford	5 May
27:32.18		Kipchirchir			3		Stanford	5 May
27:32.49	Hassan	Mead	USA	28.6.91	15	WCh	London (OS)	4 Aug
27:32.51	Biyazen	Alehegn	ETH-J	16.9.99	1r1		Machida	25 Nov
27:34.38		Mead			4		Stanford	5 May
27:35.38		Tanui			1		Osaka	23 Sep
	(31/23)							
27:35.67	Birhan	Neberew	ETH	14.8.94	7	FBK	Hengelo	11 Jun
27:37.41	Bernard	Kimani	KEN	10.9.93	1		Abashiri	13 Jul
27:37.62	Abiyot	Abinet	ETH	10.5.89	2r1		Machida	25 Nov
27:38.05	Muiru	Muthoni	KEN-J	21.3.98	3r1		Machida	25 Nov
27:38.61	Rodgers	Chumo Kwemoi	KEN	3.3.97	2		Osaka	23 Sep
27:39.41	John	Maina	KEN	3.8.94	3		Yokohama	11 Nov
27:39.45	Samuel	Cherop	UGA	.97	1		Leiden	17 Jun
	(30)							
27:39.79	El Mahjoub	Dazza	MAR	3.3.91	2		Leiden	17 Jun
27:40.78	James	Rungaru	KEN	14.1.93	3		Osaka	23 Sep
27:41.54	Alexander	Mutiso	KEN	10.9.96	4		Osaka	23 Sep
27:41.97	Yuta	Shitara	JPN	18.12.91	5r1		Machida	25 Nov
27:41.99	Kaan Kigen	Özbilen	TUR	15.1.86	2	Isl.Sol	Baku	20 May
27:42.55	Polat Kemboi	Arikan	TUR	12.12.90	8	FBK	Hengelo	11 Jun
27:45.37	Joel	Mwaura	KEN-J	20.1.99	6		Osaka	23 Sep
27:45.46	Daniel	Kipkemoi	KEN	5.7.96	4		Yokohama	11 Nov
27:45.78	Abbabiya	Simbassa	USA	30.6.93	5		Stanford	5 May
27:45.83	David	Njuguna	KEN	6.9.89	6		Machida	25 Nov
	(40)							
27:46.14	Joseph	Ndirangu	KEN	9.9.94	7		Osaka	23 Sep
27:46.16	Teressa	Nyakora	ETH	26.2.95	1rC		Abashiri	13 Jul
27:46.27	Abdallah	Mande	UGA	10.5.95	3		Leiden	17 Jun
27:46.64	Suguru	Osako	JPN	23.5.91	2		Abashiri	13 Jul
27:47.4A	Leonard	Barsoton	KEN	21.10.94	4	WCT	Nairobi	24 Jun
27:47.59	Soufiyan	Bouqantar	MAR	30.8.93	3	Isl.Sol	Baku	20 May
27:47.87	Kazuya	Shiojiri	JPN	8.11.96	7r1		Machida	25 Nov
27:48.41	Mogos	Tuemay	ETH	24.5.97	9	FBK	Hengelo	11 Jun
27:48.51	Nicholas	Kosimbei	KEN	10.1.96	3		Kobe	23 Apr
27:48.57	Diego	Estrada	USA	12.12.89	6		Stanford	5 May
	(50)							
27:48.59	Zane	Robertson	NZL	14.11.89	16	WCh	London (OS)	4 Aug
27:49.31	Edward	Waweru	KEN	3.10.90	3		Tajimi	14 Oct
27:49.46	El Hassan	El Abbassi	BRN	15.7.79	2		Maia	12 Jul
27:49.62	Hizkel	Tewelde	ERI	15.9.86	17	WCh	London (OS)	4 Aug
27:49.96	Patrick	Mathenge	KEN	2.11.96	8r1		Machida	25 Nov
27:50.72	Minato	Oishi	JPN	19.5.88	9r1		Machida	25 Nov
27:51.08	Daniel	Kitonyi	KEN	12.1.94	5		Yokohama	11 Nov
27:51.61	James	Mwangi	KEN	23.6.84	10r1		Machida	25 Nov
27:52.10	Richard	Yator Kimunyan	KEN-J	6.4.98	6		Yokohama	11 Nov
27:53.58	José Luis	Ostos	PER	9.12.92	7		Stanford	5 May
	(60)							
27:53.84A	Vincent	Rono	KEN	22.12.90	2	NC	Nairobi	10 Jun
27:53.85	Samuel	Mwangi	KEN	19.9.97	11r1		Machida	25 Nov
27:53.99A	Mathew	Kisorio	KEN	16.5.89	3	NC	Nairobi	10 Jun
27:54.41	Ali	Kaya	TUR	20.4.94	4	Isl.Sol	Baku	20 May
27:55.10	Simon	Kariuki	KEN	13.2.92	1		Kobe	22 Apr
27:56.01A	Peter	Kirui	KEN	2.1.88	4	NC	Nairobi	10 Jun
27:56.04A	Fredrick	Moranga	KEN	.95	5	NC	Nairobi	10 Jun
27:57.17A	Stephen	Arita	KEN	26.6.88	6	NC	Nairobi	10 Jun
27:57.47A	Peter	Muindi	KEN	.90	7	NC	Nairobi	10 Jun
27:57.63	Tetsuya	Yoroizaka	JPN	20.3.90	1		Nobeoka	6 May
	(70)							

Mark	Name		Nat	Born	Pos	Meet	Venue	Date
27:58.32A	Emmanuel	Ngatuny	KEN	10.10.92	8	NC	Nairobi	10 Jun
27:58.56	Stanley	Kebenei	USA	6.11.89	8		Stanford	5 May
27:58.69	Andrew	Vernon	GBR	7.1.86	9		Stanford	5 May
27:58.69	Patrick	Mwaka	KEN	2.11.92	3		Gifu	13 May
27:59.76	Takashi	Ichida	JPN	16.6.92	3		Kitakyushu	20 May
28:00.21	Karemi Jeremiah	Thuku	KEN	7.7.94	4		Kitakyushu	20 May
28:01.93	Anatoliy	Rybakov	RUS	27.2.85	1	Znam	Zhukovskiy	1 Jul
28:01.93	Yevgeniy	Rybakov	RUS	27.2.85	2	Znam	Zhukovskiy	1 Jul
28:02.85	Dominic	Nyairo	KEN	22.8.97	2		Kobe	22 Apr
28:03.57	Olivier	Irabaruta	BDI	25.8.90	1		Marina di Carrara	22 Apr
	(80)							
28:03.90	Enoch	Omwamba	KEN	4.4.93	1		Isahaya	14 Oct
28:03.92	Abraham	Kipyatich	KEN	10.5.93	2pm		Abashiri	13 Jul
28:04.51	Ken	Yokote	JPN	27.4.93	3		Kobe	22 Apr
28:04.95	Alfred	Chelangat	KEN	2.4.94	2		Stanford	31 Mar
28:05.54	Tadesse	Tesfahun	ETH-J	.99	10	FBK	Hengelo	11 Jun
28:05.56	Belay	Tilahun	ETH	.95	11	FBK	Hengelo	11 Jun
28:05.96	Richard	Ringer	GER	27.2.89	10		Stanford	5 May
28:06.17	Julien	Wanders	SUI	18.3.96	1		Huelva	8 Apr
28:06.40	Kemoy	Campbell	JAM	14.1.91	3		Stanford	31 Mar
28:07.15	Soufiane	Bouchikhi	BEL	22.3.90	11		Stanford	5 May
	(90)							
28:07.23	Yuichiro	Ueno	JPN	29.7.85	4		Kobe	23 Apr
28:07.26	Mitsunori	Asaoka	JPN	11.1.93	13r1		Machida	25 Nov
28:07.97	Marc	Scott	GBR	21.12.93	12		Stanford	5 May
28:08.04	Hirohito	Inoue	JPN	6.1.93	5		Kitakyushu	20 May
28:08.58	Nguse	Tesfaldet	ERI	10.11.86	4	GS	Ostrava	28 Jun
28:08.60	Martin	Hehir	USA	19.12.92	4		Stanford	31 Mar
28:09.01	Yuki	Sato	JPN	26.11.86	2		Nobeoka	6 May
28:09.29	Ben	Bruce	USA	10.9.82	5		Stanford	31 Mar
28:09.46	Bernard	Kimeli	KEN	10.9.95	5	GS	Ostrava	28 Jun
28:09.98	Onèsphore	Nzikwinkunda	BDI	8.7.97	19	WCh	London (OS)	4 Aug
	(100)							

Mark	Name		Nat	Born	Date
28:10.15	Leul	Gebrselassie	ETH	20.9.937	28 Jun
28:11.02	Erik	Peterson	USA	15.6.94	31 Mar
28:11.80	Jerrell	Mock	USA	24.5.95	31 Mar
28:12.75	Félicien	Muhitira	RWA	4.11.94	22 Apr
28:13.13	Andrew	Lorot	KEN	2.12.97	11 Nov
28:13.58	Bekele	Shiferaw	ETH	14.10.95	25 Nov
28:13.60	Abayneh	Degu	ETH-J	1.12.98	20 May
28:14.19	Guye	Adola	ETH	20.10.90	11 Jun
28:14.67	Stephen	Mokoka	RSA	31.1.85	4 Aug
28:14.79	Ledama	Kisaisa	KEN-J	2.7.99	25 Nov
28:15.12	Sondre Nordstad	Moen	NOR	12.1.91	28 Jun
28:15.58	Bashir	Abdi	BEL	10.2.89	5 May
28:16.01	Shogo	Nakamura	JPN	16.9.92	13 Jul
28:16.07	Dewi	Griffiths	GBR	9.8.91	5 May
28:16.08	Abrar	Osman	ERI	24.6.94	28 Jun
28:16.54	Elroy	Gelant	RSA	25.8.86	28 Feb
28:16.61	Tsubasa	Hayakawa	JPN	2.7.90	23 Apr
28:16.87	Kenta	Murayama	JPN	23.2.93	6 May
28:17.11	Yuki	Muta	JPN	26.5.93	25 Nov
28:17.29	Filimon	Ande	ERI-J	10.2.98	17 Jun
28:17.52	Shota	Onitsuka	JPN	13.9.97	25 Nov
28:18.29	Galen	Rupp	USA	8.5.86	10 Jun
28:18.73	Joseph	Gray	USA	20.1.84	31 Mar
28:19.43	Ryan	Dohner	USA	23.8.91	10 Jun
28:19.89	Watari	Tochigi	JPN	8.5.95	23 Apr
28:19.94	Vincent	Kiprop	KEN	28.4.95	13 Apr
28:20.10	Silas	Naibei	KEN	29.11.95	3 Jun
28:20.90	Alfred	Barkach	KEN	2.3.97	28 Jun
28:21.19	Chiharu	Nakagawa	JPN	8.4.86	14 Oct
28:21.28	Vyacheslav	Shalamov	RUS	8.7.89	1 Jul
28:21.51	Cyrus	Kingori	KEN	5.1.97	22 Apr
28:21.71	Bernard	Muia	KEN	26.5.95	14 Oct
28:21.96	Hiram	Ngatia	KEN	1.1.96	14 Oct
28:22.31	Elkanah	Kibet	USA	2.6.83	10 Jun
28:22.58	Zouhair	Talbi	MAR	8.4.95	17 Jun
28:22.98	Naoya	Takahashi	JPN	28.8.93	20 May
28:23.14	Keiji	Akutsu	JPN	20.3.87	25 Nov
28:23.37	Hayato	Seki	JPN	11.4.97	23 Sep
28:23.54	Noah	Droddy	USA	22.9.90	5 May
28:23.58	Ben	Connor	GBR	17.10.92	17 Jun
28:23.97	Harry	Summers	AUS	19.5.90	25 Nov
28:24.05	Takuya	Fujikawa	JPN	17.12.92	25 Nov
28:24.58	Tatsuya	Oike	JPN	18.5.90	25 Nov
28:25.03	David	McNeill	AUS	6.10.86	5 May
28:25.20	Peter	Mwangi	KEN-J	.99	2 Dec
28:25.27	Atsushi	Yamafuji	JPN	13.3.97	25 Nov
28:25.58	Hiribo	Shano	ETH-J	.99	11 Jun
28:25.76	Yohanes	Gebregergish	ERI	11.1.94	12 Jul
28:25.89	Charles	Ndirangu	KEN	8.2.93	23 Sep
28:26.09A	Isaac	Yego	KEN	.89	1 Dec
28:26.40	Yuma	Hattori	JPN	13.11.93	13 Jul
28:26.7A	Cornelius	Kangogo	KEN	31.12.93	12 May
28:26.74	Kenta	Murozuka	JPN	12.2.86	25 Nov
28:26.86		Duo Bujie	CHN	16.3.87	5 Sep
28:26.9A	Isaac	Yego	KEN	.89	2 Dec
28:27.14	Matt	McClintock	USA	6.1.94	10 Jun
28:27.53	Kazuteru	Onishi	JPN	28.3.87	25 Nov
28:27.69	José Mauricio	González	COL	14.10.88	13 Apr
28:28.11	Chihiro	Miyawaki	JPN	28.8.91	25 Nov
28:28.49	Shun	Inoura	JPN	26.7.92	21 Oct
28:28.63	George	Alex	USA	20.1.90	5 May
28:28.72	Shuho	Dairokuno	JPN	23.12.92	21 Oct
28:28.91	Titus	Wambua	KEN	29.3.94	25 May
28:29.12	Takumi	Yokokawa	JPN-J	30.1.98	23 Sep
28:29.23	Yusuke	Nishiyama	JPN	7.11.94	25 Nov
28:29.74	Hiroyuki	Yamamoto	JPN	30.4.86	13 Jul
28:29.93	Hiroyuki	Ishikawa	JPN	22.1.93	25 Nov
28:30.23	Kazuma	Taira	JPN	5.11.94	25 Nov
28:30.55	Miguel Ángel	Amador	COL	10.6.92	31 Mar
28:30.58	Shinobu	Kubota	JPN	12.10.91	23 Sep
28:30.59	Sho	Nagato	JPN	13.1.97	25 Nov
28:31.16	Antonio	Abadía	ESP	2.7.90	10 Jun
28:31.64	Gen	Hachisuka	JPN	29.11.94	23 Sep
28:31.9A	Thomas	Longosiwa	KEN	14.1.82	12 May
28:32.24	Shuto	Mikami	JPN	25.12.96	25 Nov
	(175) 200th 28:26.15				

JUNIORS

See main list for top 8 juniors. 13 performances (Belihu 2) by 10 men to 28:15.00. Additional marks and further juniors:

Kimeli	27:53.67A	1	NC	Nairobi	10 Jun
Mwaura	27:52.66	1		Kitakyushu	20 May

Mark	Name		Nat	Born	Pos	Meet	Venue	Date
28:13.60	Abayneh	Degu	ETH	1.12.98	6		Kitakyushu	20 May
28:14.79	Ledama	Kisaisa (10)	KEN	2.7.99	16r1		Machida	25 Nov
28:17.29	Filimon	Ande	ERI	10.2.98	4		Leiden	17 Jun
28:25.20	Peter	Mwangi	KEN	.99	3		Tokohama	2 Dec
28:25.58	Hiribo	Shano	ETH	.99	13	FBK	Hengelo	11 Jun
28:29.12	Takumi	Yokokawa	JPN	30.1.98	3		Yokohama	23 Sep
28:32.40	Elijah	Kositany	KEN	20.10.98	3		Konosu	21 Oct
28:36.15	Kiseki	Shiozawa	JPN	17.12.98	4		Konosu	21 Oct
28:36.7A	Josphat	Kipchirchir	KEN	.98	3		Nairobi	12 May
28:44.88	Kazuya	Nishiyama	JPN	5.11.98	3		Fukui	8 Sep
28:46.74	Tasuhiko	Ito	JPN	23.3.98	8r4		Machida	25 Nov
28:46.8A	Robert	Mwei (20)	KEN	11.4.98	2		Tambach	30 Dec
Best European: 30:02.73	Miguel	González	ESP	19.2.98	2rB		Huelva	8 Apr

10 KILOMETRES ROAD

Mark	Name		Nat	Born	Pos	Meet	Venue	Date
27:10	Benard	Kimeli	KEN	10.9.95	1		Praha	9 Sep
27:11	Mathew	Kimeli	KEN-J	4.1.98	2		Praha	9 Sep
27:13	Rhonnex	Kipruto	KEN-J	12.10.99	3		Praha	9 Sep
27:18		B Kimeli			1		Paderborn	15 Apr
27:29	Joshua	Cheptegei	UGA	12.9.96	1		Durban	8 Oct
27:32		M Kimeli			1		Berlin	8 Oct
27:33	Alfred	Barkach	KEN	2.3.97	2		Berlin	8 Oct
Where better than 10,000m track times								
27:42+	Justus	Kangogo	KEN	10.10.95	1	in HMar	Ostia	12 Mar
27:43+	Guye	Adola	ETH	20.10.90		in HMar	Ostia	12 Mar
27:43+	Peter	Ndorobo Kwemoi	KEN	11.8.93		in HMar	Ostia	12 Mar
27:48	Alex	Oloitiptip Korio	KEN	20.12.90	1		Port Gentil	24 Jun
27:48	Ridouane	Harroufi	MAR	30.7.81	1		Mohammedia	9 Jul
27:50+	James	Mwangi	KEN	23.6.84		in HMar	København	17 Sep
27:50+	Jorum	Okumbo	KEN	10.12.97		in HMar	København	17 Sep
27:50+	Albert	Kangogo	KEN	16.8.87		in HMar	København	17 Sep
27:50+	Geoffrey	Yegon	KEN	28.8.88		in HMar	København	17 Sep
27:50+	Fikadu	Haftu	ETH	21.2.94		in HMar	Valencia	22 Oct
27:51+	Abrar	Osman	ERI	24.6.94		in HMar	København	17 Sep
27:51+	Geoffrey	Koech	KEN	28.8.93		in HMar	København	17 Sep
27:51+	Leul	Gebrselassie	ETH	20.9.93		in HMar	Valencia	22 Oct
27:52+	Augustine	Choge	KEN	21.1.87		in HMar	Ra's Al-Khaymah	10 Feb
27:52+	Solomon	Yego	KEN	10.5.87		in HMar	Ra's Al-Khaymah	10 Feb
27:52+	Kenneth	Keter	KEN	4.8.96		in HMar	Ra's Al-Khaymah	10 Feb
27:52	Mohamed	Ziani	MAR	.93	2		Mohammedia	9 Jul
27:53+	Yigrem	Demelash	ETH	28.1.94		in HMar	Ra's Al-Khaymah	10 Feb
27:53	Amos	Kurgat	KEN	7.3.92	5		Praha	9 Sep
27:53	Bekele	Haile	ETH-J	13.5.99	3		Berlin	8 Oct
27:55	Jake	Robertson	NZL	14.11.89	1		New Orleans	15 Apr
27:55	Stephen	Kibet	KEN	9.11.86	1		Cape Elizabeth	5 Aug
27:55	Isaac	Langat	KEN	18.12.94	7		Praha	9 Sep
27:55	Sondre Nordstad	Moen	NOR	12.1.91	8		Praha	9 Sep
27:56	Ben	True	USA	29.12.85	2		Cape Elizabeth	5 Aug
27:56+	Mustapha	El Aziz	MAR	24.12.85		in HMar	Valencia	22 Oct
27:56+	Amanuel	Mesel	ERI	29.12.90		in HMar	Valencia	22 Oct
27:57	Peter	Langat	KEN-J	20.10.98	2		Casablanca	7 May
27:57	Abderrahim	Kachir	MAR	25.9.92	1		Tan-Tan	19 Nov
27:58	Daniel	Chebii	KEN	28.5.85	1		Boston	25 Jun
28:00+	Philip	Kangogo	KEN			in HMar	Ostia	12 Mar
28:00	Japheth	Korir	KEN	30.6.93	2		Prot Gentil	24 Jun
28:02+	Edwin	Kipyego	KEN	16.11.90		in HMar	Ra's Al-Khaymah	10 Feb
28:02+	Shadrack	Korir Kimining	KEN	10.2.96		in HMar	Ra's Al-Khaymah	10 Feb
28:02	Julien	Wanders	SUI	18.3.96	1		Houilles	31 Dec
28:03+	Daniel	Wanjiru	KEN	25.5.92		in HMar	Ra's Al-Khaymah	10 Feb
28:03+	Edwin Kiprop	Kiptoo	KEN	14.8.93		in HMar	Den Haag	12 Mar
28:03	Stephen	Sambu	KEN	7.7.88	2		Boston	25 Jun
28:03	Robert	Mwei	KEN-J	11.4.98	4		Berlin	8 Oct
28:04+	Nguse	Tesfaldet	ERI	10.11.86		in HMar	Ra's Al-Khaymah	10 Feb
28:04+	Leonard	Langat	KEN	7.8.90		in HMar	Den Haag	12 Mat
28:04	Pius Dominic	Ondoro	KEN	3.3.88	1		Mobile	25 Mar
28:05	Sadik	Mikhou	BRN	25.7.90	1		Doha	13 Jan
28:05+	Paul Kipsiele	Koech	KEN	10.11.81		in HMar	Den Haag	12 Mar
28:05	Stephen	Kissa	UGA	1.12.95	2		Durban	8 Oct
28:06+	Gabriel Gerald	Geay	TAN	10.9.96		in HMar	Ra's Al-Khaymah	10 Feb
28:06	John	Wanjiku	KEN	.96	2		Mobile	25 Mar

Mark	Name		Nat	Born	Pos	Meet	Venue	Date
28:06	Dathan	Ritzenhein	USA	30.12.82	1		Manchester	28 May
28:06	John	Langat	KEN	31.12.96	1		Appingedam	24 Jun
28:06	Teshome	Mekonen	ETH	5.8.95	3		Boston	25 Jun
28:06	Abel	Kipchumba	KEN	.94	10		Praha	9 Sep
28:07	Julius	Kogo	KEN	12.8.85	3		Mobile	25 Mar
28:08+	Aziz	Lahbabi	MAR	3.2.91		in HMar	Ústí nad Labem	16 Sep
28:08+	Eliud	Tarus	KEN	3.3.93		in HMar	København	17 Sep
28:08+	Shura	Kitata	ETH	9.6.96		in HMar	København	17 Sep
28:09	Edwin	Rotich	KEN	8.8.88	2		Doha	13 Jan
28:09+	Daniel	Muteti	KEN	10.11.94		in HMar	Den Haag	12 Mar
28:09+	Ismail	Juma	TAN	3.8.91		in HMar	Ústí nad Labem	16 Sep
28:09+	Barselius	Kipyego	KEN	23.7.93		in HMar	Ústí nad Labem	16 Sep
28:09+ +	Josphat	Tanui	KEN	4.2.94		in HMar	Ústí nad Labem	16 Sep
28:09+	Philip	Tarbei	KEN	13.2.94		in HMar	Ústí nad Labem	16 Sep
28:10+	Evans Kipkorir	Cheruiyot	KEN	24.9.91		in HMar	Ústí nad Labem	16 Sep
28:10+	Wilfred	Kimitei	KEN	11.3.85		in HMar	Ústí nad Labem	16 Sep
28:10	Monatcer	Zaghou	MAR	.89	2		Tan-Tan	19 Nov

Mark	Name		Nat	Born	Date
28:12	Mohamed	Ahmani	MAR		19 Nov
28:13	Bernard	Kipkemoi	KEN	.94	15 Apr
28:13+	Simon	Cheprot	KEN	.93	1 May
28:13+	Ambrose	Bor4	KEN	.95	1 May
28:13	Bernard	Lagat	USA	12.12.74	28 May
28:14	D	Fekadu	ETH		8 Apr
28:14	Cornelius	Kangogo	KEN	31.12.93	17 Apr
28:14	Jairus	Birech	KEN	14.12.92	17 Apr
28:14	Patrick	Mwikya	KEN	20.11.94	9 Jul
28:14	Abraham	Kipyatich	KEN	10.5.93	9 Sep
28:14	Leonard	Komon	KEN	10.1.88	1 Oct
28:16	Titus	Mbishei	KEN	28.10.90	24 Jun
28:18	Emmanuel	Kiprono	KEN	.93	15 Apr
28:19	Hicham	Laqouahi	MAR	13.6.89	11 Jan
28:19	Samuel	Chelanga	USA	23.2.85	26 Feb
28:19	James	Kibet	UGA	5.6.86	25 Mar
28:19	Noah	Kigen	KEN	12.6.89	24 Jun
28:20	Elias	Kiptoo	KEN	.92	24 Sep
28:21	Philip	Langat	KEN	23.4.90	26 Feb
28:21	Charles	Nzioka	KEN-J	21.9.99	26 Feb
28:21	Thomas	Longosiwa	KEN	14.1.82	9 Apr
28:21	Zouhair	Talbi	MAR	8.4.95	9 Jul
28:22	Rhonzas	Lokitam	KEN	.96	7 May
28:22	Rhonzas	Kilimo	KEN		7 May
28:22	Hicham	Amghar	MAR	15.5.94	5 Nov
28:23	Geoffrey	Kusuro	UGA	12.2.89	12 Mar
28:23	Amos	Mitei	KEN	24.6.94	9 Sep
28:23+	Morris	Munene Gachaga	KEN	7.4.95	22 Oct
28:23	Maxwell	Rotich	KEN		12 Nov
28:25	Abdennacer	Fathi	MAR	25.1.87	14 May
28:24+	Tadu	Abate	ETH	11.9.97	20 May
28:24+	John	Lotiang	KEN	1.1.91	20 May
28:24+	Amos	Kipruto	KEN	.92	20 May
28:24+	Mourad	El Bannouri	MAR	27.12.79	22 Oct
28:25+	Richard	Mengich	KEN	3.4.89	20 May
28:25	Collis	Birmingham	AUS	27.12.84	28 May
28:25	Dominic	Mibei	KEN	.91	10 Jun
28:25	Kalipus	Lomwai	KEN	.95	10 Jun
28:25	Linus	Kiplagat	BRN	23.12.94	19 Nov
28:26_	William	Kibor	KEN	10.1.85	26 Mar
28:26	Wilson	Kipsang	KEN	15.3.82	28 May
28:27+	Kenneth	Kipkemoi	KEN	2.8.84	5 Feb
28:27+	Meshack	Koech	KEN	.88	26 Mar
28:27	Paul	Kipkorir	KEN	31.5.82	21 May
28:28+	Callum	Hawkins	GBR	22.6.92	5 Feb
28:28+	Daichi	Kamino	JPN	13.9.93	5 Feb
28:29+	Kazuki	Tamura	JPN	16.7.95	5 Feb
28:29+	Adugna	Takele	ETH	26.2.89	10 Feb
28:29	Javier	Guerra	ESP	10.11.83	18 Mar
28:29+	Demeke	Kassaw	ETH		26 Mar
28:29	Haymanot	Alew	ETH	11.11.97	30 Apr
28:29	Daniel	Salel	KEN	11.12.90	25 Jun
28:29	Davis	Kiplangat	KEN-J	10.7.98	1 Oct
28:29+	Kipkemboi	Kiprono	KEN		1 Oct
28:30	Haymanot	Alewe	ETH	11.11.97	7 May
28:30	Mustapha	Houdadi	MAR	5.8.86	14 May

Downhill

Mark	Name		Nat	Born	Pos	Meet	Venue	Date
27:34	Erick	Kiptanui	KEN	.90	1	dh 55m	Madrid	31 Dec
27:44	Abraham	Kiptum	KEN	89	1	dh 70m	Ziwa	9 Dec
27:48	Josphat	Kipchirchir	KEN-J	98	3	dh 70m	Ziwa	9 Dec
27:48	Amos	Kirui	KEN-J	9.2.98	2	dh 55m	Madrid	31 Dec
27:51	Josphat	Bett	KEN	12.6.90	4	dh 70m	Ziwa	9 Dec
28:06	Wilfred	Kimitei	KEN	11.3.85	7	dh 70m	Ziwa	9 Dec

Mark	Name		Nat	Born	Date
28:15	Evans	Kimutai	KEN		9 Dec
28:24	Antonio	Abadía	ESP	2.7.90	31 Dec
28:28	Paul	Melly	KEN	4.1.81	5 Nov
28:30	Stephan	Ogari	KEN	15.10.92	5 Nov

Uncertain distance: Iten 9 Sep: all KEN 1, Jerome Lumbasi 22.5.97 28:19, 2. Gilbert Masai 16.12.89 28:21, 3. Emmanuel Bor .95 28:29

15/20 KILOMETRES ROAD

20k	15k	Name		Nat	Born	Pos	Meet	Venue	Date
	41:16	Joshua	Cheptegei	UGA	12.9.96	1		Nijmegen	19 Nov
	42:00	Mathew	Kimeli	KEN	4.1.98	1		Le Puy-en-Velay	1 May
	42:12+	James	Wangari	KEN	23.3.94		in HMar	København	17 Sep
	42:15+	Geoffrey	Yegon	KEN	28.8.88		in HMar	København	17 Sep
57:05+		Ismail	Juma	TAN	3.8.91		in HMar	Istanbul	30 Apr
57:10	42:32+	Leonard	Langat	KEN	7.8.90		in HMar	Göteborg	20 May
	42:40	Amedwork	Walelegn	ETH-J	11.3.99	2		Nijmegen	19 Nov
	42:43	Noah	Kipkemboi	KEN	.93	3		Nijmegen	19 Nov
57:18	42:48+	Meshack	Koech	KEN	.88		in HMar	Venlo	26 Mar
57:18	42:48+	Kipsang	Kipkemboi	KEN	.90		in HMar	Venlo	26 Mar
57:27	42:44	Wesley	Ledama	KEN-J	28.6.98	1		Tachikawa	14 Oct
	42:44+	Kenneth	Keter	KEN	4.8.96		in HMar	Ústí nad Labem	16 Sep
57:33	42:48	Dominic	Nyairo	KEN	22.8.97	2		Tachikawa	14 Oct
	42:50	Jerome	Okombo	KEN	10.12.97	2		Le Puy-en-Velay	1 May
	42:51	Simon	Cheprot	KEN	.93	3		Le Puy-en-Velay	1 May

Mark		Name		Nat	Born	Pos	Meet	Venue	Date
	42:52	Ambrose	Bore	KEN	.95	4		Le Puy-en-Velay	1 May
57:34+		Josphat	Tanui	KEN	4.2.94		in HMar	Praha	1 Apr
	43:01+	Japheth	Korir	KEN	30.6.93		in HMar	Göteborg	20 May
57:39+		Edwin	Koech	KEN	15.5.83		in HMar	Lisboa	19 Mar
57:40+		Justus	Kangogo	KEN	10.10.95		in HMar	Valencia	22 Oct
57:42+		Barselius	Kipyego	KEN	23.7.93		in HMar	Praha	1 Apr

10 MILES ROAD

10M	15k	10k	Name		Nat	Born	Pos	Venue	Date
45:03	42:04		Rodgers	Chumo Kwemoi	KEN	3.3.97	1	Tilburg	3 Sep
46:06	42:03	28:02	Evans Kiplagat	Chebet	KEN	10.11.88	2	Tilburg	3 Sep
45:38	42:46	28:23	Berhanu	Legesse	ETH	11.9.94	1	Zaandam	17 Sep
45:39	42:25	28:02	Abdallah	Mande	UGA	10.5.95	3	Tilburg	3 Sep
45:45	42:48	28:23	Yenew	Alamirew	ETH	27.5.90	2	Zaandam	17 Sep
45:51	42:46	28:22	Jiksa	Tadesse	ETH		3	Zaandam	17 Sep
45:53	42:47	28:22	Edwin Kiprop	Kiptoo	KEN	14.8.93	4	Zaandam	17 Sep
45:54	42:46	28:23	Leonard	Langat	KEN	7.8.90	5	Zaandam	17 Sep
45:58			Yuka	Shitara	JPN	18.12.91	1	Kosa	3 Dec
46:03	42:48	28:22	Ronald	Kirui	KEN-J	6.12.98	6	Zaandam	17 Sep
46:03	42:48	28:23	Martin	Musau	UGA-J	5.10.98	7	Zaandam	17 Sep

HALF MARATHON

Mark	20k	15k	Name		Nat	Born	Pos	Meet	Venue	Date
58:40	55:51	41:53	Abraham	Cheroben	BRN	11.10.92	1		København	17 Sep
58:48	55:51	41:54	Jorum	Okumbo	KEN	10.12.97	2		København	17 Sep
58:51	55:51	41:54	Alex	Oloitiptip Korio	KEN	20.12.90	3		København	17 Sep
59:10	56:10	42:05	Bedan	Karoki	KEN	21.8.90	1		Ra's Al-Khaymah	10 Feb
59:11	56:14	42:05		Cheroben			1		Valencia	22 Oct
59:14		42:03	Barselius	Kipyego	KEN	23.7.93	1		Ústí nad Labem	16 Sep
59:18		41:55	Guye	Adola	ETH	20.10.90	1		Ostia	12 Mar
59:18	56:17	42:05	Leul	Gebrselassie	ETH	20.9.93	2		Valencia	22 Oct
59:19	56:12	42:06	Yigrem	Demelash	ETH	28.1.94	2		Ra's Al-Khaymah	10 Feb
59:22		42:03	Josphat	Tanui	KEN	4.2.94	2		Ústí nad Labem	16 Sep
59:22	56:17	42:05	Fikadu	Haftu (10)	ETH	21.2.94	3		Valencia	22 Oct
59:25	56:25	41:54	Albert	Kangogo	KEN	16.8.87	4		København	17 Sep
59:26	56:19	42:05	Augustine	Choge	KEN	21.1.87	3		Ra's Al-Khaymah	10 Feb
59:27			Vincent Kipsang	Rono	KEN	11.11.90	1		Lille	2 Sep
59:28	56:25	41:54	Leonard	Barsoton	KEN	21.10.94	5		København	17 Sep
59:30		42:03	Ismail	Juma	TAN	3.8.91	3		Ústí nad Labem	16 Sep
59:31		41:52	Justus	Kangogo	KEN	10.10.95	2		Ostia	12 Mar
59:32			Alex	Kibet	KEN	20.10.90	2		Lille	2 Sep
59:37	56:36	42:26	Tamirat	Tola	ETH	11.8.91	1		Praha	1 Apr
59:46			Berhanu	Legesse	ETH	11.9.94	1		New Delhi	19 Nov
59:48	56:42	42:26	Sondre Nordstad	Moen (20)	NOR	12.1.91	4		Valencia	22 Oct
59:50	56:38	42:05	Solomon	Yego	KEN	10.5.87	4		Ra's Al-Khaymah	10 Feb
59:50	56:43	41:58	Moses	Kurong	UGA	7.7.94	6		København	17 Sep
59:50	56:43	41:58	Geoffrey	Koech	KEN	28.8.93	7		København	17 Sep
59:51			Andamlak	Belihu	ETH-J	20.11.98	2		New Delhi	19 Nov
59:52			Leonard	Korir	USA	10.12.86	3		New Delhi	19 Nov
59:54			Asefa	Mengistu	ETH	18.1.85	4		New Delhi	19 Nov
59:56	56:52	42:20	Geoffrey	Yegon	KEN	28.8.88	1		Den Haag	12 Mar
59:57		42:31	Gilbert	Masai	KEN	16.12.89	1		Berlin	2 Apr
59:58				Okumbo			5		New Delhi	19 Nov
59:59	56:52	42:19	Edwin Kiprop	Kiptoo	KEN	14.8.93	2		Den Haag	12 Mar
60:00	56:55	42:37	Callum	Hawkins	GBR	22.6.92	1		Marugame	5 Feb
			(32/30)							
60:01	56:38		Jake	Robertson	NZL	14.11.89	1		Lisboa	19 Mar
60:04	57:04	42:32	Nguse	Tesfaldet	ERI	10.11.86	5		Ra's Al-Khaymah	10 Feb
60:04	57:00	42:53	Feyisa	Lilesa	ETH	1.2.90	1		New York	19 Mar
60:04			Geoffrey	Kirui	KEN	16.2.93	6		New Delhi	19 Nov
60:05	57:03	42:32	Edwin	Kipyego	KEN	16.11.90	6		Ra's Al-Khaymah	10 Feb
60:06dh			Mohamed	Farah	GBR	23.3.83	1	GNR	South Shields	10 Sep
60:06		42:54	Abraham	Kiptum	KEN	.89	1		Porto	17 Sep
60:07	57:03	42:32	Shadrack	Korir Kimining	KEN	10.2.96	7		Ra's Al-Khaymah	10 Feb
60:07			Meshack	Koech	KEN	.88	3		Lille	2 Sep
60:07		42:54	Marius	Kimutai	KEN	.89	2		Porto	17 Sep
			(40)	GNR – slighly downhill race: 30.5m Necsatle to South Shields						
60:08			Japheth	Korir	KEN	30.6.93	4		Lille	2 Sep
60:08		42:53	Leonard	Langat	KEN	7.8.90	3		Porto	17 Sep
60:10	57:14	42:42	Shura	Kitata	ETH	9.6.96	8		København	17 Sep

Mark			Name		Nat	Born	Pos Meet	Venue	Date
60:11	56:42		James	Mwangi	KEN	23.3.94	2	Lisboa	19 Mar
60:12		42:19	Wilfred	Kimitei	KEN	11.3.85	4	Ústí nad Labem	16 Sep
60:13		42:03	Peter	Ndorobo Kwemoi	KEN	11.8.93	3	Ostia	12 Mar
60:13		42:19	Philip	Tarbei	KEN	13.2.94	5	Ústí nad Labem	16 Sep
60:15		42:19	Aziz	Lahbabi	MAR	3.2.91	6	Ústí nad Labem	16 Sep
60:17		42:29	Yuta	Shitara	JPN	18.12.91	8	Ústí nad Labem	16 Sep
60:19	57:09	41:58	Abrar	Osman	ERI	24.6.94	10	København	17 Sep
			(50)						
60:22	57:12		Terefa	Deleba	ETH-J	20.4.98	2	Istanbul	30 Apr
60:24		42:45	Edwin	Koech	KEN	15.5.83	1	Verona	12 Feb
60:24			Kenneth	Kipkemoi	KEN	2.8.84	4	Venlo	26 Mar
60:24	57:10	42:33	Amos	Kipruto	KEN	.92	2	Göteborg	20 May
60:25	57:17	42:47	Noah	Kigen	KEN	12.6.89	5	Venlo	26 Mar
60:25		42:19	Isaac	Langat	KEN	18.12.94	9	Ústí nad Labem	16 Sep
60:25			Abadi	Hadis	ETH	6.11.97	8	New Delhi	19 Nov
60:28			Mohamed	Ziani	MAR	.93	1	Marrakech	29 Jan
60:28	57:10	42:52	Teshome	Mekonen	ETH	5.8.95	3	New York	19 Mar
60:30			Peter	Kirui	KEN	2.1.88	1	Klagenfurt	20 Aug
			(60)						
60:32			Vincent	Torotich	KEN	.90	2	Berlin	2 Apr
60:34			Getaneh	Molla	ETH	10.1.94	5	Lille	2 Sep
60:37			Joseph	Kiptum	KEN	25.9.87	1	Azkoitia	1 Apr
60:37	57:20		Edwin	Rotich	KEN	8.8.88	3	Istanbul	30 Apr
60:38			Morris	Munene Gachaga	KEN	7.4.95	1	Paris	5 Mar
60:39	57:18	42:32	John	Lotiang	KEN	1.1.91	4	Göteborg	20 May
60:40			Paul	Lonyangata	KEN	12.12.92	2	Paris	5 Mar
60:41			John	Langat	KEN	31.12.96	9	New Delhi	19 Nov
60:44			Moses	Kibet	UGA	23.3.91	2	Klagenfurt	20 Aug
60:45	57:31		Adugna	Takele	ETH	26.2.89	4	Istanbul	30 Apr
			(70)						
60:46	57:36		Tadu	Abate	ETH	11.9.97	4	Lisboa	19 Mar
60:48	57:29	42:28	James	Rungaru	KEN	14.1.93	3	Den Haag	12 Mar
60:50	57:42		Mustapha	El Aziz	MAR	24.12.85	5	Valencia	22 Oct
60:51	57:41		Kaan Kigen	Özbilen	TUR	15.1.86	5	Istanbul	30 Apr
60:51	57:40		Abdallah	Mande	UGA	10.5.95	2	Breda	1 Oct
60:52	57:41		Philip	Langat	KEN	23.4.90	3	Breda	1 Oct
60:53			Dominic	Kiptarus	KEN	3.8.96	6	Lille	2 Sep
60:53			Amanuel	Mesel	ERI	29.12.90	6	Valencia	22 Oct
60:54			Thomas	Kiplagat	KEN		4	Porto	17 Sep
60:55	57:41	42:56	Stephen	Sambu	KEN	7.7.88	4	New York	19 Mar
			(80)						
60:56			Mosinet	Geremew	ETH	12.2.92	1	Yangzhou	23 Apr
60:57			Philip	Kangogo	KEN		4	Ostia	12 Mar
60:57	57:46	43:07	Kenta	Murayama	JPN	23.2.93	5	New York	19 Mar
60:57	58:00	43:39	Alexander	Mutiso	KEN	10.9.96	1	Gifu	23 Apr
60:57	58:00	43:39	Joseph	Ndirangu	KEN	9.9.94	2	Gifu	23 Apr
60:57			Edwin	Kimutai Kiplagat	KEN	19.2.93	2	Karlovy Vary	20 May
60:57			Timothy	Kimeli	KEN	20.1.94	3	Karlovy Vary	20 May
60:57			Wilson	Too	KEN	14.3.91	1	Montbéliard	24 Sep
60:58		42:52	Atsedu	Tsegay	ETH	17.12.91	2	Marugame	5 Feb
60:59	57:49	42:56	Joel	Mwaura	KEN-J	20.1.99	3	Marugame	5 Feb
			(90)						
60:59			Joel	Kimuruer	KEN	21.1.88	3	Barcelona	12 Feb
60:59			Evans Kiprop	Cheruiyot	KEN	10.5.82	4	Karlovy Vary	20 May
61:00		42:37	Abraham	Kipyatich	KEN	10.5.93	4	Marugame	5 Feb
61:01			Vincent	Yator	KEN	11.7.89	6	Istanbul	30 Apr
61:01			Cosmas	Birech	KEN	21.3.86	1	Lugano	21 May
61:02			Nobert	Kigen	KEN	24.1.93	4	Yangzhou	23 Apr
61:03	57:52	42:44	Paul Kipsiele	Koech	KEN	10.11.81	5	Den Haag	12 Mar
61:03			Titus	Mbishei	KEN	28.10.90	2	Azkoitia	1 Apr
61:03			Wilson	Cheruiyot	KEN	12.11.87	2	Krems	17 Sep
61:04	57:51	42:53	Daichi	Kamino	JPN	13.9.93	5	Marugame	5 Feb
			(100)						
61:05	57:51	42:50	Kenneth	Keter	KEN	4.8.96	8	Ra's Al-Khaymah	10 Feb
61:05		42:47	Cornelius	Kangogo	KEN	31.12.93	6	Venlo	26 Mar
61:05			Hillary	Maiyo	KEN	2.10.93	3	Krems	17 Sep

61:07	42:37	Evans Kipkorir	Cheruiyot	KEN	24.9.91	16 Sep
61:09		Tesfaye	Lencho	ETH	.97	14 May
61:10		Kipkemboi	Kiprono	KEN		1 Oct
61:12		Chris	Derrick	USA	17.10.90	19 Mar
61:13	42:53	Suguru	Osako	JPN	23.5.91	5 Feb
61:13	43:04	Gabriel Gerald	Geay	TAN	10.9.96	10 Feb
61:13		Stephen	Muendo	KEN	30.1.92	21 May
61:13		Hizkel	Tewelde	ERI	15.9.86	19 Nov
61:14		Birhan	Neberew	ETH	14.8.94	19 Nov
61:15		Geoffrey	Kusuro	UGA	12.2.89	12 Mar
61:15	42:44	Mathew	Kisorio	KEN	16.5.89	22 Oct
61:17		Fikadu	Tsadik	ETH		15 Jan

Mark		Name		Nat	Born	Date
61:17		Wycliffe	Biwott	KEN	.88	15 Oct
61:17		Aferwerki	Berhane	ERI	6.5.96	19 Nov
61:18		Yohanes	Ghebregergish	ERI	11.1.94	23 Apr
61:19	42:53	William	Kibor	KEN	10.1.85	26 Mar
61:19		Paul	Kuira	KEN	25.1.90	23 Apr
61:20		Fredrik	Moranga	KEN	.95	19 Mar
61:20		Eliud	Mwangi	KEN	12.10.89	1 Apr
61:20	42:44	Eliud	Tarus	KEN	3.3.93	17 Sep
61:21	43:10	Abiyot	Abinet	ETH	10.5.89	12 Feb
61:21+		Nicholas	Korir	KEN	18.11.90	26 Feb
61:21		Reuben	Kerio	KEN	.94	5 Mar
61:21		Stephen	Mokoka	RSA	31.1.85	24 Jun
61:21		El Mahjoub	Dazza	MAR	3.3.91	22 Oct
61:22+		Wilson	Kipsang	KEN	15.3.82	26 Feb
61:22+		Gideon	Kipketer	KEN	10.11.92	26 Feb
61:22+		Dickson	Chumba	KEN	27.10.86	26 Feb
61:22+		Evans Kiplagat	Chebet	KEN	10.11.88	26 Feb
61:23+		Solomon	Deksisa	ETH	11.3.94	26 Feb
61:25		Simon	Kariuki	KEN	13.2.92	19 Nov
61:27		Bernard	Kipyego	KEN	16.7.86	23 Apr
61:29		Peter	Limo	KEN	-.94	12 Feb
61:29+		Eliud	Kipchoge	KEN	5.11.84	24 Sep
61:29+		Vincent	Kipruto	KEN	13.9.87	24 Sep
61:29+		Kenenisa	Bekele	ETH	13.6.82	24 Sep
61:30		Abel	Kirui	KEN	4.6.82	12 Feb
61:30+		Alfers	Lagat	KEN	7.8.86	26 Feb
61:30	42:47	Daniel	Chebii	KEN	28.5.85	12 Mar
61:30		Paul	Mwangi	KEN	2.1.93	21 May
61:30		Elroy	Gelant	RSA	25.8.86	24 Jun
61:31		El Hassan	El Abbassi	BRN	15.7.79	2 Apr
61:33+		Sisay	Lemma	ETH	12.12.90	20 Jan
61:33		Kalipus	Lomwai	KEN	.95	26 Mar
61:33		Dewi	Griffiths	GBR	9.8.91	1 Oct
61:33		Mourad	El Bennouri	MAR	27.12.79	22 Oct
61:34+		Sisay	Jisa	ETH	29.11.82	20 Jan
61:34+		Mule	Wasihun	ETH	20.10.93	20 Jan
61:34		Simon	Muthoni	KEN	27.2.95	19 Mar
61:34		Richard	Mengich	KEN	3.4.89	10 Jun
61:35+		Mark	Lokwanamoi	KEN	1.2.88	20 Jan
61:36+		Tsegaye	Mekonnen	ETH	15.6.95	20 Jan
61:36		Kengo	Suzuki	JPN	11.6.95	5 Mar
61:36		Emanuel	Gniki	TAN	18.5.88	23 Apr
61:37		Abdennacer	Fathi	MAR	25.1.87	29 Jan
61:37		Patrick	Mathenge	KEN	2.11.96	19 Nov
61:38	dh	Tsegay	Tuemay	ERI	20.12.95	4 Jun
61:39		Kennedy	Kipyeko	KEN	12.12.90	23 Apr
61:41		Bisetegn	Masresha	ETH-J	.98	26 Mar
61:42		Mesfin	Alemu	ETH	31.1.89	26 Mar
61:42	dh	Zane	Robertson	NZL	14.11.89	10 Sep
61:43		Julien	Wanders	SUI	18.3.96	19 Mar
61:43		Dereje	Kasaw	ETH		26 Mar
61:43		Reuben	Lemaa	KEN	.87	2 Apr
61:44		Charles	Ndirangu	KEN	8.2.93	14 May
61:45		Birhanu	Yemataw	BRN	27.2.96	14 Jan
61:45		Mohamed	El Aaraby	MAR	12.11.89	29 Jan
61:45		Derara	Hurisa	BRN	12.7.97	23 Apr
61:45		Kennedy	Kibet	KEN	.89	14 May
61:45		Laban	Korir	KEN	30.12.85	20 Aug
61:46		Amos	Mitei	KEN	24.6.94	1 Apr
61:47		Evans	Kiplagat	AZE	5.3.88	30 Apr
61:48		Noah	Droddy	USA	22.9.90	19 Mar
61:48	dh	Juan Luis	Barrios	MEX	24.6.83	4 Jun
61:48		Masresha	Bire	ETH-J	.98	24 Sep
61:48		Precious	Mashele	RSA	13.10.90	19 Nov
61:49		Bernard	Bett	KEN	4.1.93	17 Sep
61:50		Asefa	Tefera	ETH	.93	3 Apr
61:50		Samuel	Kariuki	KEN	13.2.92	23 Apr
61:50		Josphat	Kiptis	KEN	16.11.93	24 Jun
61:50		Bashir	Abdi	BEL	10.2.89	2 Sep
61:50		Nathan	Ayeko	UGA	10.10.93	24 Sep
61:52		Asbel	Kipsang	KEN	10.9.93	2 Sep
61:53	43:28	Taku	Fujimoto	JPN	11.9.89	12 Feb
61:54		Diego	Estrada	USA	12.12.89	19 Mar
61:54		Benjamin	Somikwo	UGA	4.10.96	23 Apr
61:54A		Isaac	Kibet	KEN	5.5.96	19 Nov
61:55		Bernard	Kimani	KEN	10.9.93	12 Mar
61:56+		Azmeraw	Bekele	ETH	22.1.86	20 Jan
61:56		Kazuki	Tamura	JPN	16.7.95	5 Feb
61:56		Philimon	Maritim	KEN	.88	19 Mar
61:56		Félicien	Muhitira	RWA	4.11.94	24 Sep
61:58		Melkhaya	Frans	RSA	2.1.90	24 Jun
61:59		Bernard	Korir	KEN	.92	13 Jan
61:59		Galen	Rupp	USA	8.5.86	1 Apr
61:59		Muiru	Muthoni	KEN-J	27.3.98	14 May
61:59		Ezrah	Sang	KEN	8.6.94	20 Aug
		(200)				

Downhill 100m Eldoret (A) 19 Mar: 2. Joseph Aperumoi KEN 12.1.90 60:54, 4. Timothy Rono KEN 18.9.97 61:11, 5. Donald Mitei KEN 2.4.96 61:21, 6. Daniel Yator KEN .88 61:51

Short course?: At: Casablance (Dar-el-Beida): 29 Oct: 1. Abderrahim Kachir MAR 25.9.92 60:21, 2. Hassan Chani BRN 5.5.88 60:23. 5. Ahmed El Hamazoui MAR 23.3.80 61:43; 12 May: 1. El-Hassan El Abbassi BRN 13.4.84 60:52

JUNIORS

See main list for top 3 juniors

Mark		Name		Nat	Born	Pos	Venue	Date
61:41		Bisetegn	Masresha	ETH-	.98	2	Warszawa	26 Mar
61:48		Masresha	Bire	ETH-	.98	3	Belfort	24 Sep
61:59		Muiru	Muthoni	KEN-	27.3.98	3	Sendai	14 May
62:52		Joshua	Lemushen	BRN	.99	4	Arezzo	29 Oct
63:09	?	Sota	Watanabe	JPN	8.3.98	10	Yokohama	5 Feb

25/30 KILOMETRES ROAD

25k 30k In addition to those shown in Marathon listing

25k	30k	Name		Nat	Born		Venue	Date
1:12:46	1:27:27	Nicholas	Korir	KEN	18.11.90	in Mar	Tokyo	26 Feb
1:12:46		Barselius	Kipyego	KEN	23.7.93	in Mar	Tokyo	26 Feb
1:12:47	1:27:36	Solomon	Deksisa	ETH	11.3.94	in Mar	Tokyo	26 Feb
1:12:50	1:27:26	Wilson	Kipsang	KEN	15.3.82	in Mar	Berlin	24 Sep
1:12:53	1:27:39	Amos	Kipruto	KEN	.92	in Mar	Dubai	20 Jan
1:12:58	1:28:01	Mule	Wasihun	ETH	20.10.93	in Mar	Dubai	20 Jan
1:13:01		Vincent	Yator	KEN	11.7.89	in Mar	Frankfurt	29 Oct
1:13:03	1:28:17	Evans Kiplagat	Chebet	KEN	10.11.88	in Mar	Tokyo	26 Feb
1:13:10	1:28:21	Feyisa	Lilesa	ETH	1.2.90	in Mar	London	23 Apr
1:13:11	1:28:24	Kenenisa	Bekele	ETH	13.6.82	in Mar	Berlin	24 Sep
1:13:18	1:29:23	Cosmas	Birech	KEN	21.3.86	in Mar	Tokyo	26 Feb
1:13:20	1:29:31	Bernard	Koech	KEN	31.1.88	in Mar	Tokyo	26 Feb
	1:28:42	Asefa	Mengistu	ETH	18.1.85	in Mar	London	23 Apr
	1:29:03	Amanuel	Mesel	ERI	29.12.90	in Mar	London	23 Apr
1:13:37		Tsegaye	Mekonnen	ETH	15.6.95	in Mar	Dubai	20 Jan
1:13:42		Albert	Kangogo	KEN	16.8.87	in Mar	Tokyo	26 Feb
1:13:49+	1:29:24	Yuta	Shitara	JPN	18.12.91	in Mar	Tokyo	26 Feb
	1:29:38	Simon	Cheprot	KEN	.93	in Mar	Paris	9 Apr
1:13:55	1:29:57	Birhan	Nebebew	ETH	14.8.94	in Mar	Dubai	20 Jan

Mark	Name		Nat	Born	Pos	Meet	Venue	Date
1:13:55	Azmeraw	Bekele	ETH	22.1.86		in Mar	Dubai	20 Jan

MARATHON

Mark	25k	30k	Name		Nat	Born	Pos	Venue	Date
2:03.32	1:12:50	1:27:24	Eliud	Kipchoge	KEN	5.11.84	1	Berlin	24 Sep
2:03.46	1:12:50	1:27:24	Guye	Adola	ETH	20.10.90	2	Berlin	24 Sep
2:03:58	1:12:47	1:27:27	Wilson	Kipsang	KEN	15.3.82	1	Tokyo	26 Feb
2:04:11	1:12:54	1:27:40	Tamirat	Tola	ETH	11.8.91	1	Dubai	20 Jan
2:05:09		1:29:52	Lawrence	Cherono	KEN	7.8.88	1	Amsterdam	15 Oct
2:05:13		1:29:52	Nobert	Kigen	KEN	24.1.93	2	Amsterdam	15 Oct
2:05:15	1:14:31	1:29:10	Sammy	Kitwara	KEN	26.11.86	1	Valencia	19 Nov
2:05:26		1:29:52	Abraham	Kiptum	KEN	.89	3	Amsterdam	15 Oct
2:05:30			Evans Kiplagat	Chebet	KEN	10.11.88	2	Valencia	19 Nov
2:05:39		1:29:52	Mule	Wasihun (10)	ETH	20.10.93	4	Amsterdam	15 Oct
2:05:43		1:29:52	Amos	Kipruto	KEN	.92	5	Amsterdam	15 Oct
2:05:48	1:13:10	1:28:21	Daniel	Wanjiru	KEN	25.5.92	1	London	23 Apr
2:05:48		1:30:08	Sondre Nordstad	Moen	NOR	12.1.91	1	Fukuoka	3 Dec
2:05:50	1:14:27	1:29:42	Shura	Kitata	ETH	9.6.96	1	Frankfurt	29 Oct
2:05:51	1:12:47	1:27:49	Gideon	Kipketer	KEN	10.11.92	2	Tokyo	26 Feb
2:05:54				Kipruto			1	Seoul	19 Mar
2:05:57	1:13:16	1:28:38	Kenenisa	Bekele	ETH	13.6.82	2	London	23 Apr
2:06:03			Felix	Kandie	KEN	10.4.87	2	Seoul	19 Mar
2:06:04			Marius	Kimutai	KEN	.89	1	Rotterdam	9 Apr
2:06:05			Mark	Korir	KEN	10.1.85	3	Seoul	19 Mar
2:06:07				Kigen			4	Seoul	19 Mar
2:06:09		1:29:35	Mosinet	Geremew	ETH	12.2.92	3	Berlin	24 Sep
2:06:10		1:29:40	Paul	Lonyangata (20)	KEN	12.12.92	1	Paris	9 Apr
2:06:13		1:29:37		Kandie			4	Berlin	24 Sep
2:06:13		1:29:45	Festus	Talam	KEN	20.10.94	1	Eindhoven	8 Oct
2:06:13		1:29:45	Felix	Kirwa	KEN		2	Eindhoven	8 Oct
2:06:14	1:12:51	1:27:33	Vincent	Kipruto	KEN	13.9.87	5	Berlin	24 Sep
2:06:15			Luka	Kanda	KEN	.87	1	Chuncheon	29 Oct
2:06:21				Cherono			2	Rotterdam	9 Apr
2:06:25	1:12:47	1:27:28	Dickson	Chumba	KEN	27.10.86	3	Tokyo	26 Feb
2:06:25			Laban	Korir	KEN	30.12.85	3	Rotterdam	9 Apr
2:06:27			Wilson	Loyanae	KEN	20.11.88	5	Seoul	19 Mar
2:06:38			Deribe	Robi	ETH	20.9.90	3	Valencia	19 Nov
2:06:42	1:13:03	1:28:17		E Chebet			4	Tokyo	26 Feb
2:06:43		1:29:43	Marius (35/30)	Kipserem	KEN	17.5.88	3	Eindhoven	8 Oct
2:06:44			Abera	Kuma	ETH	31.8.90	4	Valencia	19 Nov
2:06:52		1:29:29	Philemon	Rono	KEN	8.2.91	8	Toronto	22 Oct
2:06:54			Felix	Kiprotich	KEN	.88	1	Gyeongju	15 Oct
2:06:56		1:29:42	Kelkile	Gezahegn	ETH	.96	2	Frankfurt	29 Oct
2:06:57		1:29:40	Stephen	Chebogut	KEN	9.1.85	2	Paris	9 Apr
2:07:10		1:29:45	Dejene	Debela	ETH	.95	4	Eindhoven	8 Oct
2:07:10			Stephen	Kiprotich	UGA	18.4.89	2	Fukuoka	3 Dec
2:07:12		1:29:40	Solomon Kirwa	Yego	KEN	10.5.87	3	Paris	9 Apr
2:07:13			Edwin	Koech	KEN	15.5.83	1	Milano	2 Apr
2:07:19			Lucas (40)	Rotich	KEN	16.4.90	5	Rotterdam	9 Apr
2:07:19			Suguru	Osako	JPN	23.5.91	3	Fukuoka	3 Dec
2:07:21		1:29:39	Yitayal	Atnafu	ETH	20.1.93	4	Paris	9 Apr
2:07:21			Benson	Kipruto	KEN	.91	2	Gyeongju	15 Oct
2:07:25			Eliud	Kiptanui	KEN	6.6.89	5	Valencia	19 Nov
2:07:26			Tsegaye	Mekonnen	ETH	15.6.95	1	Hamburg	23 Apr
2:07:32			Mathew	Kisorio	KEN	16.5.89	1	Daegu	2 Apr
2:07:33			Jacob Kibet	Kendagor	KEN	24.8.84	6	Seoul	19 Mar
2:07:34			Samuel	Tsegay	ERI	24.02.88	6	Valencia	19 Nov
2:07:39	1:13:18	1:28:47	Alfers	Lagat	KEN	7.8.86	5	Tokyo	26 Feb
2:07:39			Tesfaye (50)	Abera	ETH	31.3.92	8	Amsterdam	15 Oct
2:07:41	1:13:11	1:28:21	Bedan	Karoki	KEN	21.8.90	3	London	23 Apr
2:07:42		1:29:39	Abayneh	Ayele	ETH	4.11.87	5	Paris	9 Apr
2:07:43			Titus	Ekiru	KEN	2.1.92	1	Sevilla	19 Feb
2:07:45	1:13:11	1:28:21	Abel	Kirui	KEN	4.6.82	4	London	23 Apr
2:07:46		1:29:42	Getu	Feleke	ETH	28.11.86	3	Frankfurt	29 Oct
2:07:48			Tariku	Kebede	ETH	.96	2	Sevilla	19 Feb
2:08:04	1:12:54	1:28:01	Sisay	Lemma	ETH	12.12.90	3	Dubai	20 Jan

Mark			Name		Nat	Born	Pos	Meet	Venue	Date
2:08:06			Julius	Tuwei	KEN		7		Valencia	19 Nov
2:08:09	1:13:22	1:28:56	Sisay	Jisa	ETH	29.11.82	4		Dubai	20 Jan
2:08:10	1:13:18	1:28:47	Bernard	Kipyego	KEN	16.7.86	6		Tokyo	26 Feb
			(60)							
2:08:11			Saïd	Ait-Addi	MAR	29.6.82	8		Valencia	19 Nov
2:08:12			Reuben	Kerio	KEN	.94	1		Kosice	1 Oct
2:08:14		1:30:13	Yohanes	Gebregergish	ERI	11.1.94	7		Tokyo	26 Feb
2:08:14			Robert Kipkorir	Kwambai	KEN	22.11.85	3		Gyeongju	15 Oct
2:08:16			Abdi	Nageeye	NED	2.3.89	9		Amsterdam	15 Oct
2:08:22		1:30:12	Hiroto	Inoue	JPN	6.1.93	8	1 NC	Tokyo	26 Feb
2:08:26			Kipsang	Kipkemboi	KEN	.90	3		Sevilla	19 Feb
2:08:26			Joseph	Aperumoi	KEN	12.1.90	10		Amsterdam	15 Oct
2:08:27			Hayle	Lemi	ETH	13.9.94	1		Xiamen	2 Jan
2:08:27			Geoffrey	Kirui	KEN	16.2.93	1	WCh	London (OS)	6 Aug
			(70)							
2:08:29		1:29:38	Asbel	Kipsang	KEN	10.9.93	6		Paris	9 Apr
2:08:32			Bernard	Koech	KEN	31.1.88	9		Valencia	19 Nov
2:08:35			Stephen	Mokoka	RSA	31.1.85	1		Shanghai	12 Nov
2:08:36			Fikre	Assefa	ETH	18.1.89	2		Kosice	1 Oct
2:08:37	1:13:22	1:28:57	Mark	Lokwanamoi	KEN	1.2.88	5		Dubai	20 Jan
2:08:37			Abele	Abshero	ETH	28.12.90	4		Gyeongju	15 Oct
2:08:38			Ernest	Ngeno	KEN	20.5.95	2		Shanghai	12 Nov
2:08:39		1:29:48	Samuel Kiplimo	Kosgei	KEN	20.1.86	7		Paris	9 Apr
2:08:40			Albert	Korir	KEN	2.3.94	1		Wien	23 Apr
2:08:42			Ishmael	Busendich	KEN	7.7.91	2		Wien	23 Apr
			(80)							
2:08:45			Tsegaye	Kebede	ETH	15.1.87	9		Tokyo	26 Feb
2:08:45		1:29:44	Cosmas	Kipchoge	KEN	21.3.86	5		Eindhoven	8 Oct
2:08:46		1:29:41	Richard	Mengich	KEN	3.4.89	8		Paris	9 Apr
2:08:47			Gebretsadik	Adhana	ETH	16.7.92	1		Praha	7 May
2:08:48			Bazu	Worku	ETH	15.9.90	2		Praha	7 May
2:08:51			Bira	Seboka	ETH	16.11.94	11		Amsterdam	15 Oct
2:08:52			Victor	Kipchirchir	KEN	5.12.87	7		Seoul	19 Mar
2:08:57			Jonah	Chesum	KEN	5.5.89	1		Barcelona	12 Mar
2:08:58			Elisha	Kipchirchir	KEN	.90	2		Chuncheon	29 Oct
2:08:59			Takuya	Noguchi	JPN	2.7.88	1		Gold Coast	2 Jul
			(90)							
2:09:00			Mekuant	Ayenew	ETH	.91	3		Praha	7 May
2:09:01			Robert	Chemosin	KEN	1.2.89	4		Hamburg	23 Apr
2:09:03			Yuta	Shitara	JPN	18.12.91	6		Berlin	24 Sep
2:09:04			Kenneth	Mungara	KEN	7.9.73	2		Gold Coast	2 Jul
2:09:05			Richard	Sigei	KEN	11.5.84	3		Kosice	1 Oct
2:09:05			Evans	Kipchirchir Sambu	KEN	2010.89	5		Gyeongju	15 Oct
2:09:06			Ezekiel	Chebii	KEN	3.1.91	1		Otsu	5 Mar
2:09:08			Dominic	Ruto	KEN	.90	2		Roma	2 Apr
2:09:10			Ezequiel	Omullo	KEN	10.12.87	3		Wien	23 Apr
2:09:10		1:29:54	Alphonce	Felix Simbu	TAN	14.2.92	5		London	23 Apr
			(100)							

Mark	Name		Nat	Born		Date
2:09:12	Hiroyuki	Yamamoto	JPN	30.4.86	26	Feb
2:09:12	Edwin	Kimaiyo	KEN	.86	12	Nov
2:09:13	Benjamin	Bitok	KEN	17.9.80	2	Apr
2:09:13	Anthony	Maritim	KEN	12.11.86	9	Apr
2:09:13	Thomas	Kiplagat Rono	KEN		5	Nov
2:09:18	Yuki	Kawauchi	JPN	5.3.87	2	Jul
2:09:19	Mathew	Kipsaat	KEN		2	Apr
2:09:20	Galen	Rupp	USA	8.5.86	8	Oct
2:09:22	Peter	Some	KEN	5.6.90	2	Apr
2:09:22	Kiprotich	Kirui	KEN	22.12.84	10	Sep
2:09:22	Amanuel	Mesel	ERI	29.12.90	3	Dec
2:09:24	Jacob Chesari	Kirui	KEN	6.4.84	12	Mar
2:09:25	Werkunesh	Seyoum	ETH	.84	2	Apr
2:09:26	Abdiwak	Tura	ETH	.95	5	Nov
2:09:27	Daisuke	Uekado	JPN	11.12.93	3	Dec
2:09:28	Hillary	Kipsambu	KEN	.85	15	Oct
2:09:31 1:27:36	Solomon	Deksisa	ETH	11.3.94	26	Feb
2:09:32	Kentaro	Nakamoto	JPN	7.12.82	5	Feb
2:09:33	Tariku	Bekele	ETH	21.1.87	29	Oct
2:09:37	Fikadu	Kebede	ETH		5	Mar
2:09:39	Sammy	Kigen	KEN	29.9.85	5	Mar
2:09:39	Luka Rotich	Lobuwan	KEN	7.8.88	2	Apr
2:09:39 1:29:44	Martin	Kosgei	KEN	21.3.89	29	Oct
2:09:40	Mohamed	Ayachev Bantte	ETH	23.7.95	15	Oct
2:09:40	Alebachew	Wale	ETH	21.12.80	12	Nov
2:09:42	Henry	Chirchir	KEN	14.5.85	1	Oct
2:09:42	Evans	Kipkoech Korir	KEN	.87	29	Oct
2:09:43	Kenneth	Kiprop Cheborbor	KEN		15	Oct
2:09:44	Samuel	Getachew	ETH	.86	5	Mar
2:09:45	Abdela	Godana	ETH		5	Nov
2:09:46	Yuma	Hattori	JPN	13.11.93	26	Feb
2:09:47	Bernard	Too	KEN	.85	12	Mar
2:09:47	Motlokoa	Nkhabutlane	LES	16.11.84	9	Apr
2:09:48	Douglas	Chebii	KEN	1.11.93	19	Feb
2:09:48	Barnabas	Kiptum	KEN	8.10.86	15	Oct
2:09:49	Afewerk	Mesfin	ETH	12.10.92	19	Mar
2:09:49	Dewi	Griffiths	GBR	9.8.91	29	Oct
2:09:50	Joshua	Kipkorir	KEN	.94	15	Jan
2:09:50	Mohamed	El-Aaraby	MAR	12.11.89	2	Apr
2:09:52	Allan	Kiprono	KEN	15.2.90	9	Apr
2:09:53	Raymond	Choge	KEN	2.1.88	1	Oct
2:09:55	Julius	Keter	KEN	20.10.88	2	Apr
2:09:55	Wycliffe	Biwott	KEN	.88	8	Oct
2:09:55	Wilson	Chebet	KEN	12.7.85	10	Dec
2:09:56	Josphat	Letting	KEN	1.1.88	5	Mar
2:09:56	Elijah	Kemboi	KEN	.84	19	Nov
2:09:57 1:28:21	Ghirmay	Ghebreslassie	ERI	14.11.95	23	Apr
2:09:59	Solomon	Mutai	UGA	22.10.92	5	Mar
2:09:59	Arne	Gabius	GER	22.3.81	29	Oct
2:10:01	Asefa	Mengistu	ETH	18.1.85	17	Sep
2:10:01	Agustino	Sulle	TAN		15	Oct
2:10:01	Yoshiki	Takenouchi	JPN	25.5.92	3	Dec

MEN 2017

Mark	Name		Nat	Born	Pos	Meet	Venue	Date
2:10:03	Micah	Kogo	KEN	3.6.86				9 Apr
2:10:03	Wilfred	Murgor	KEN	12.12.88				12 Nov
2:10:03	Dickson	Tuwei	KEN	31.10.92				10 Dec
2:10:04	Salaheddine	Bounasr	MAR	27.9.90				7 May
2:10:06	Markos	Geneti	ETH	30.5.94				10 Dec
2:10:07	Philip	Kimutai	KEN	10.9.83				9 Apr
2:10:08	Hillary	Kisambu	KEN					5 Mar
2:10:09	Henryk	Szost	POL	20.1.82				29 Oct
2:10:10	Satoru	Sasaki	JPN	16.10.85				5 Mar
2:10:12	Abraham	Kasongor	KEN	.93				9 Apr
2:10:14	Titus	Tuwei	KEN	.94				26 Mar
2:10:14	Emmanuel	Mutai	KEN	12.10.84				19 Nov
2:10:16	Koen	Naert	BEL	3.9.89				9 Apr
2:10:16	Bonsa	Dida	ETH	21.1.95				23 Apr
2:10:17	Meshack	Koech	KEN	.88				9 Apr
2:10:17	Callum	Hawkins	GBR	22.6.92				6 Aug
2:10:19	Ryo	Hashimoto	JPN	26.9.93				2 Jul
2:10:20	Hassan	Chahdi	FRA	7.5.89				9 Apr
2:10:22	Azmeraw	Bekele	ETH	22.1.86				20 Jan
2:10:22	Andrew	Kimutai	KEN	12.8.89				19 Mar
2:10:23	Dereje	Debele	ETH	26.7.86				5 Feb
2:10:23	Vincent	Rono	KEN	22.12.90				2 Apr
2:10:23	Eliud	Barngetuny	KEN	.87				2 Apr
2:10:24	Chala	Dechase	ETH	13.6.84				20 Jan
2:10:24	Hicham	Laqouahi	MAR	13.6.89				29 Jan
2:10:24	Alfonce	Kigen	KEN	.93				23 Apr
2:10:27	Samson	Bungei	KEN	.82				26 Mar
2:10:30	Ryo	Kiname	JPN	22.1.91				5 Feb
2:10:31	Melaku	Belachew	ETH	16.5.90				12 Feb
2:10:31	Seboka	Dibaba Tola	ETH	10.11.87				28 May
2:10:32	Robert	Chemonges	UGA	15.10.97				30 Apr
2:10:33	Mutai	Kipkemei	KEN	25.7.86				9 Apr
2:10:34	Felix	Kimutai	KEN	12.2.89				23 Apr
2:10:36	Suleiman	Simotwo	KEN	21.4.80				23 Apr
2:10:36	Samuel	Theuri	KEN	.84				5 Nov
2:10:38	Vincent	Yator	KEN	11.7.89				10 Dec
2:10:39	Minato	Oishi	JPN	19.5.88				5 Feb
2:10:39	Shadrack	Kipkosgei	KEN	.91				19 Feb
2:10:39	1:29:58 Kipkemoi	Kipsang	KEN	.90				8 Oct
2:10:40	Cosmas	Lagat	KEN	21.10.90				10 Dec
2:10:41	Abdi	Fufa	ETH	.94				5 Nov
2:10:42	Bernard Cheruiyot	Sang	KEN	15.2.81				15 Oct
2:10:43	Michael Njenga	Kunyuga	KEN					23 Apr
2:10:45	Mark Kosgei	Kiptoo	KEN	21.6.76				9 Apr
2:10:46	Michael	Githae	KEN	26.8.94				3 Dec
2:10:48	Levi	Matebo	KEN	3.11.89				28 May
2:10:49	Moses	Kipsiro	UGA	2.9.86				28 May
2:10:49	Tadesse (200)	Mamo	ETH	.91				1 Oct

Downhill 65m at Rennes

Mark	Name		Nat	Born	Date
2:09:45	Josphat	Letting	KEN	–.88	22 Oct
2:09:46	Birhane	Teshome	ETH		22 Oct
2:09:55	Evans	Ruto	KEN	14.1.84	22 Oct
2:10:12	William Kiprono	Yegon	KEN	10.1.83	22 Oct
2:10:16	Belay	Assefa	ETH	17.6.92	22 Oct
2:10:43	Bekele	Adugna	ETH	.89	22 Oct

Illegally paced

Mark	Name		Nat	Born	Pos	Meet	Venue	Date
2:00:25irr	Eliud	Kipchoge	KEN	5.11.84	1		Monza	6 May

JUNIORS

Mark	Name		Nat	Born	Pos	Meet	Venue	Date
2:20:54	Tsegay	Molla	ETH	.98	25		Amsterdam	15 Oct

100 KILOMETRES

Mark	Name		Nat	Born	Pos	Meet	Venue	Date
6:14:18	Tatsuya	Itagaki	JPN	4.1.88	1		Yubetsu	25 Jun
6:29:52	Yasuyuki	Nakamura	JPN	22.1.85	2		Yubetsu	25 Jun
6:33:52	Nao	Kazami	JPN	9.4.83	3		Yubetsu	25 Jun
6:39:13	Minoru	Yoshihara	JPN	6.4.93	4		Yubetsu	25 Jun
6:42:06	Yoshiki	Kawauchi	JPN	5.3.87	1		Shimanto	15 Oct
6:42:45	Lee	Grantham	GBR	11.2.83	1	NC	Partington	21 May
6:43:13	Hideaki	Yamauchi	JPN	16.12.85				25 Jun
6:46:12	Wouter	Decock	BEL	23.9.83				9 Sep
6:46:31	Kaitaro	Toike	JPN	2.9.86				25 Jun
6:48:15	Benedikt	Hoffmann (10)	GER	9.3.85				24 Jun
6:49:52	Koji	Hayasaka	JPN	5.12.83				25 Jun
6:52:08	Hideo	Nojo	JPN	24.12.76				25 Jun

24 HOURS

Mark	Name		Nat	Born	Pos	Meet	Venue	Date
270.870	Yoshihiko	Ishikawa	JPN	25.4.88	1	WCh	Belfast	1 Jul
267.701 t		Liang Jing	CHN	9.3.90	1		Hangzhou	9 Dec
267.187	Sebastian	Bialobrzeski	POL	24.2.89	2	WCh	Belfast	1 Jul
266.938 t		Ishikawa			1		Taipei	3 Dec
266.515	Johan	Steene	SWE	25.12.73	3	WCh	Belfast	1 Jul
265.304 t		Si Guosong	CHN	15.12.80	2		Hangzhou	9 Dec
264.506	Nobuyuki	Takahashi	JPN	1.2.83	4	WCh	Belfast	1 Jul
261.605 t	Toshiro	Naraki	JPN	10.8.76	2		Taipei	3 Dec
260.077	Stephane	Ruel	FRA	21.1.66	5	WCh	Belfast	1 Jul
259.403 t	Norbert	Mihalik	HUN	2.1.82	1		London (TB)	17 Sep
258.662	Florian	Reus (10)	GER	2.3.84	6	WCh	Belfast	1 Jul
258.172	Olivier	Leblond	USA	30.4.72	7	WCh	Belfast	1 Jul
256.800 t	Shingo	Inoue	JPN	27.9.80	3		Hangzhou	9 Dec
256.688 t	Ludovic	Dilmi	FRA	11.4.65	4		Hangzhou	9 Dec
256.246	Andrzej	Radzikowski	POL	1.4.81	1	NC	Lódz	8 Apr
255.375	Tamás (16/15)	Rudolf	HUN	12.12.79	8	WCh	Belfast	1 Jul
254.908	Zoltán	Csécsei	HUN	25.7.84				1 Jul
254.503	Bruno	Batsberg	DEN	14.1.74				1 Jul
253.219	Radek	Brunner	CZE	5.12.74				1 Jul
252.976	Bjørn Tore	Taranger	NOR	23.4.79				1 Jul
252.720	Steve	Slaby	USA	29.1.81				1 Jul
251.087	Toshiro	Naraki	JPN	10.8.76				1 Jul
249.961	Przemyslaw	Basa	POL	16.12.73				1 Jul
249.785	Roman	Elwart	POL	2.6.72				1 Jul
248.778	Jonathan	Olsen	US	18.8.74				1 Apr
248.747	Thierry	Gardent	FRA	23.11.68				8 Oct
248.436	Eoin	Keith	IRL	11.10.68				1 Jul
248.275	Raphael	Gerardin	FRA	12.12.73				1 Jul
245.888	Levente	Halama	HUN	13.7.82				1 Jul
245.793	Guillaume	Laroche	FRA	25.5.76				1 Jul
245.492	Steve	Holyoak	GBR	8.9.64				1 Jul
245.275	Martin	Hokes	CZE	9.11.77				1 Jul

Best track time

Mark	Name		Nat	Born	Date
245.180 t	Andrzej	Radzikowski	POL	1.4.81	3 Dec

Indoors

Mark	Name		Nat	Born	Pos	Meet	Venue	Date
256.443	Bjørn Tore	Taranger	NOR	23.4.79	1	NC	Oslo	26 Nov
249.254	Kim Klitgaard	Sørensen	DEN	6.7.84				26 Feb
245.794	Craig	Holgate	GBR	21.9.76				26 Nov

Mark	Name		Nat	Born	Pos	Meet	Venue	Date

2000 METRES STEEPLECHASE

Mark	Name		Nat	Born	Pos	Meet	Venue	Date
5:18.67	Benjamin	Kigen	KEN	5.7.93	1		Andújar	2 Jun
5:22.10	Barnabas	Kipyego	KEN	12.6.95	2		Andújar	2 Jun
5:28.52A	Leonard	Bett	KEN-Y	3.11.00	1	WY-T	Nairobi	14 Jun
5:29.04	Sebastián	Martos	ESP	20.6.89	3		Andújar	2 Jun
5:29.05	Fernando	Carro	ESP	1.4.92	4		Andújar	2 Jun

JUNIORS

Mark	Name		Nat	Born	Pos	Meet	Venue	Date
5:30.04A	Cleophas	Kandie	KEN-Y	.00	2	WY-T	Nairobi	14 Jun
5:36.82A	Brian	Kipkorir	KEN-Y	.00	3	WY-T	Nairobi	14 Jun

3000 METRES STEEPLECHASE

Mark	Name		Nat	Born	Pos	Meet	Venue	Date
8:01.29	Evan	Jager	USA	8.3.89	1	Herc	Monaco	21 Jul
8:04.63	Conseslus	Kipruto	KEN	8.12.94	1	GGala	Roma	8 Jun
8:04.73		Kipruto			1	VD-DLF	Bruxelles	1 Sep
8:04.83	Soufiane	El Bakkali	MAR	7.1.96	2	VD-DLF	Bruxelles	1 Sep
8:05.12		El Bakkali			1	DL	Rabat	16 Jul
8:05.17		El Bakkali			2	GGala	Roma	8 Jun
8:07.68	Jairus	Birech	KEN	14.12.92	2	Herc	Monaco	21 Jul
8:07.84		Birech			3	GGala	Roma	8 Jun
8:08.30	Stanley	Kebenei	USA	6.11.89	3	Herc	Monaco	21 Jul
8:08.37	Amos	Kirui	KEN-J	9.2.98	4	GGala	Roma	8 Jun
8:10.11		Birech			1		Marseille	3 Jun
8:10.62	Abraham	Kibiwot	KEN	4.6.96	2		Marseille	3 Jun
8:10.91		Birech			2	DL	Rabat	16 Jul
8:11.22	Yemane	Haileselassie	ERI-J	21.2.98	5	GGala	Roma	8 Jun
8:11.38	Benjamin	Kigen	KEN	5.7.93	4	Herc	Monaco	21 Jul
8:11.54		Kigen			1	GS	Ostrava	28 Jun
8:11.71		Jager			3	VD-DLF	Bruxelles	1 Sep
8:11.82	Hillary	Bor (10)	USA	22.11.89	6	GGala	Roma	8 Jun
8:11.93		Kebenei			4	VD-DLF	Bruxelles	1 Sep
8:12.18		Kirui			3	DL	Rabat	16 Jul
8:12.20	Nicholas	Bett	KEN	20.12.96	5	VD-DLF	Bruxelles	1 Sep
8:12.28	Getnet	Wale	ETH-Y	20.7.99	1	FBK	Hengelo	11 Jun
8:13.06		Kigen			6	VD-DLF	Bruxelles	1 Sep
8:13.16		Wale			2	GS	Ostrava	28 Jun
8:13.22	Tafese	Soboka	ETH	29.9.93	2	FBK	Hengelo	11 Jun
8:13.24	Chala	Beyo	ETH	18.1.96	3	FBK	Hengelo	11 Jun
8:13.3A	Kennedy	Njiru	KEN	.87	1		Machakos	16 Dec
8:13.33	Diriba	Tesfaye	ETH-J	11.9.98	4	FBK	Hengelo	11 Jun
8:13.39	Hailemariyam	Amare	ETH	22.2.97	3	GS	Ostrava	28 Jun
8:14.12		Kipruto			1	WCh	London (OS)	8 Aug
	(30/17)							
8:14.13	Barnabas	Kipyego	KEN	12.6.95	7	GGala	Roma	8 Jun
8:14.46	Andrew	Bayer	USA	3.2.90	8	GGala	Roma	8 Jun
8:14.67	Mahiedine	Mekhissi-Benabbad	FRA	15.3.85	3		Marseille	3 Jun
	(20)							
8:15.60	Yoann	Kowal	FRA	28.5.87	10	GGala	Roma	8 Jun
8:18.46	Justus	Lagat	KEN	20.5.96	4		Marseille	3 Jun
8:18.50	Ibrahim	Ezzaydouny	MAR	28.4.91	6	DL	Rabat	16 Jul
8:18.77	Hicham	Sigueni	MAR	30.1.93	2		Huelva	14 Jun
8:19.19	Maksim	Yakushev	RUS	15.3.92	1	NC	Zhukovskiy	29 Jul
8:19.67	Tesfaye	Girma	ETH	24.1.97	12	GGala	Roma	8 Jun
8:19.87A	Brimin	Kipruto	KEN	31.7.85	2	WCT	Nairobi	24 Jun
8:20.20	Bilal	Tabti	ALG	7.6.93	1		Amiens	10 Jun
8:20.28	Mohammed	Tindouft	MAR	12.3.93	2		Amiens	10 Jun
8:20.43	Sebastián	Martos	ESP	20.6.89	3		Huelva	14 Jun
	(30)							
8:20.61	Viktor	Bakharev	RUS	5.5.94	1	Znam	Zhukovskiy	2 Jul
8:20.61	Ezekiel	Kemboi	KEN	25.5.82	4h2	WCh	London (OS)	6 Aug
8:20.76	Takele	Nigatu	ETH-J	.99	6	FBK	Hengelo	11 Jun
8:21.30	Philemon	Kiplagat	KEN-Y	20.9.01	1		Tendo	2 Au
8:21.84	Matt	Hughes	CAN	3.8.89	6	WCh	London (OS)	8 Aug
8:21.92	Jacob	Araptany	UGA	11.2.92	7	FBK	Hengelo	11 Jun
8:22.00	Abdoullah	Bamoussa	ITA	2.6.86	13	GGala	Roma	8 Jun
8:22.94	Osama	Zoghlami	ITA	19.6.94	1		Palermo	12 Sep
8:23.12	Jigisa	Tolosa	ETH	29.3.94	6	GS	Ostrava	28 Jun
8:23.18	Albert	Chemutai	UGA-J	25.11.99	5h2	WCh	London (OS)	6 Aug
	(40)							

Mark	Name		Nat	Born	Pos	Meet	Venue	Date
8:23.2A	Emmanuel	Bett	KEN	14.7.95	1		Nyahururu	6 May
8:23.67	Altobeli	da Silva	BRA	3.12.90	8	DL	Rabat	16 Jul
8:23.68	Krystian	Zalewski	POL	11.4.89	14	GGala	Roma	8 Jun
8:23.93	Lawrence	Kemboi	KEN	15.6.93	6	DL	Stockholm	18 Jun
8:23.98	Clement	Kemboi	KEN	1.2.92	7	DL	Stockholm	18 Jun
8:24.31	Tarik Langat	Akdag	TUR	16.6.88	4		Huelva	14 Jun
8:25.20	Ilgizar	Safiulin	RUS	9.12.92	2		Sochi	25 May
8:25.5A	Felix	Kirong	KEN	.86	1	NC	Nairobi	10 Jun
8:25.64	Alex	Kibet	KEN	20.10.90	1		Doha	25 Apr
8:25.73	Haron	Lagat	USA	15.8.83	5	NC	Sacramento	25 Jun
	(50)							
8:25.75	Donn	Cabral	USA	12.12.89	6	NC	Sacramento	25 Jun
8:25.8A	Micah	Cheserek	KEN	12.10.96	2		Nyahururu	6 May
8:25.84	Younès	Kniya ¶	MAR	15.8.95	1		Rabat	17 May
8:25.9A	Abel	Mutai	KEN	2.10.88	1		Nairobi	11 May
8:26.18	Ala	Zoghlami	ITA	19.6.94	7h1	WCh	London (OS)	6 Aug
8:26.25	Nikolay	Chavkin	RUS	24.4.84	3	NC	Zhukovskiy	29 Jul
8:26.4A	Joash	Kiplimo	KEN	.91	2	NC	Nairobi	10 Jun
8:26.55	Mustapha	Houdadi	MAR	5.8.86	2		Rabat	17 May
8:26.56	Andrey	Farnosov	RUS	9.7.80	4	NC	Zhukovskiy	29 Jul
8:26.75	MJ (Michael)	Erb	USA	2.2.94	7	NC	Sacramento	25 Jun
	(60)							
8:26.81	Jakob	Ingebrigtsen	NOR-Y	19.9.00	1		Kortrijk	8 Jul
8:27.16	Anthony	Rotich	KEN	.93	2		Portland	11 Jun
8:27.34	Yohannes	Chiappinelli	ITA	18.8.97	15	GGala	Roma	8 Jun
8:27.41	Mohamed Ismail	Ibrahim	DJI	1.7.97	6		Huelva	14 Jun
8:27.80	Hichem	Bouchicha	ALG	19.5.89	3		Rehlingen	5 Jun
8:27.86	Ole	Hesselbjerg	DEN	23.4.90	8h1	WCh	London (OS)	6 Aug
8:28.40	Edwin	Kibichy	KEN	2.4.92	1	NCAA	Eugene	9 Jun
8:28.59	José Gregorio	Peña	VEN	12.1.87	2		Kortrijk	8 Jul
8:28.86	Napoleon	Solomon	SWE	14.2.94	3		Kortrijk	8 Jul
8:29.05	Hironori	Tsuetaki	JPN	8.5.93	1		Abashiri	13 Jul
	(70)							
8:29.12	Hamid	Ezzine	MAR	5.10.83	3		Belfort	9 Jun
8:29.2A	Hillary	Kemboi	KEN	.86	5	NC	Nairobi	10 Jun
8:29.24	Daniel	Arce	ESP	22.4.92	1		Oordegem	27 May
8:29.78	Ivan	Lukyanov	RUS	31.1.81	5	NC	Zhukovskiy	29 Jul
8:29.8A	Wilberforce	Koros	KEN		3		Nyahururu	6 May
8:29.92	Fernando	Carro	ESP	1.4.92	8		Huelva	14 Jun
8:29.93	Belayneh	Shimelis	ETH	.96	3		Djibouti	25 Mar
8:30.0A	Daniel	Kipchumba	KEN	12.12.97	6	NC	Nairobi	10 Jun
8:30.06	Rob	Mullett	GBR	31.7.87	3		Los Angeles (ER)	18 May
8:30.1A	Phenus	Kipleting	KEN	.89	3		Nairobi	11 May
	(80)							
8:30.15	Boniface	Sikowo	UGA-J	27.7.99	3		Oordegem	27 May
8:30.17	Zak	Seddon	GBR	28.6.94	1	FlaR	Gainesville	31 Mar
8:30.28	Donnie	Cowart	USA	24.10.85	1		Nashville	10 Jun
8:30.36	Daniel	Huling	USA	16.7.83	3		Portland	11 Jun
8:30.43	Ángel	Mullera	ESP	20.4.84	1		Lloret de Mar	18 Jul
8:30.51	Abdelaziz	Merzougui	ESP	30.8.91	1		Napoli	6 May
8:30.67	Abderraouf	Boubaker	TUN	21.10.88	4		Belfort	9 Jun
8:30.76	Abdelkarim	Ben Zahra	MAR-J	27.10.98	4		Oordegem	27 May
8:30.86	Michael	Jordan	USA	21.5.91	2		Nashville	10 Jun
8:30.87	Mitko	Tsenov	BUL	13.6.93	5		Belfort	9 Jun
	(90)							
8:30.9A	Cleophas	Kandie	KEN-Y	14.8.00	7	NC	Nairobi	10 Jun
8:31.08	Darren	Fahy	USA	14.5.94	2	NCAA	Eugene	9 Jun
8:31.10	Ibrahim	Chakir	ESP	4.9.94	9		Huelva	14 Jun
8:31.17	Dylan	Blankenbaker	USA	6.1.94	3	NCAA	Eugene	9 Jun
8:31.35	Jaouad	Chemlal	MAR	11.4.94	1		Castiglione della Pescaia	14 May
8:31.36	Jonathan	Romeo	ESP	13.8.94	4	NC	Barcelona	23 Jul
8:31.4A	Isaac	Yego	KEN	.89	8	NC	Nairobi	10 Jun
8:31.54	Hillary	Yego	KEN	2.4.92	1		Bursa	7 Jul
8:31.9	Robert	Maiyo	KEN		4		Nyahururu	6 May
8:31.95	Tim	Stegemann	GER	4.8.92	5		Rehlingen	5 Jun
	(100)							

8:32.0A	Festus	Kiprono	KEN	29.12.959	10 Jun
8:32.12	El Mahdi	Lahoufi	ESP	6.11.96	29 Jun
8:32.23	Mike	Hardy	USA	13.1.90	18 May
8:32.27	Emil	Blomberg	SWE	9.4.92	18 May
8:32.34	Isaac	Updike	USA	21.3.92	18 May
8:32.48	Brian	Barraza	USA	16.5.95	22 Apr
8:32.68	Aras	Kaya	TUR	4.4.94	18 May
8:32.68	El Mehdi	Aboujanah	MAR	6.6.87	27 Jul
8:32.7A	Noah	Kiplimo	KEN-Y	.00	6 May
8:32.90	Joshua	Thompson	USA	9.5.93	11 Jun
8:32.92	Scott	Carpenter	USA	19.12.94	9 Jun
8:32.94	Mason	Ferlic	USA	5.8.93	10 Jun

Mark	Name		Nat	Born	Date
8:32.94	Brian	Shrader	USA	22.7.91	23 Jun
8:33.02	Djilali	Bedrani	FRA	1.10.93	21 Jul
8:33.14	John	Koech	BRN	23.8.95	25 Apr
8:33.59	Ieuan	Thomas	GBR	17.7.89	27 May
8:33.68	Will	Gray	GBR	24.1.93	27 May
8:33.76	Hossein	Keyhani	IRI	26.4.90	6 Aug
8:33.89	Caleb	Hoover	USA	22.7.92	21 May
8:33.92	Víctor	Ruiz	ESP	24.6.93	14 Jun
8:33.97	Martin	Grau	GER	26.3.92	28 Jun
8:34.02	Yuri	Floriani	ITA	25.12.81	14 May
8:34.03	Jonathan	Hopkins	GBR	3.6.92	27 May
8:34.08	Antoine	Thibeault	CAN	24.3.94	18 May
8:34.1A	Geoffrey	Ngeno	KEN	11.1.94	10 Jun
8:34.15	Ildar	Nadyrov	RUS	22.4.94	29 Jul
8:34.19	Jamaine	Coleman	GBR	22.9.95	26 May
8:34.19	Tom Erling	Kårbø	NOR	4.2.89	17 Jun
8:34.24	Yuriy	Kloptsov	RUS	22.12.89	29 Jul
8:34.25	Stewart	McSweyn	AUS	1.6.95	10 Jun
8:34.27	Benard	Keter	KEN	.94	9 Jun
8:34.46	Collins	Chebii	KEN	.97	25 Apr
8:34.47A	Rantso	Mokopane	RSA	8.8.94	22 Apr
8:34.57	Abdelhamid	Zerrifi	ALG	20.6.86	3 Jun
8:34.7A	Christopher	Bett	KEN		16 May
8:34.80	Kazuya	Shiojiri	JPN	8.11.96	10 Sep
8:34.89	Solomon	Mehari	ERI	.97	4 Jul
8:34.97	Travis	Mahoney	USA	25.7.90	25 Jun
8:35.01	Yuma	Higashi	JPN	29.11.95	23 Sep
8:35.07	David	Goodman	USA	21.12.88	31 Mar
8:35.10	Yaser Salem	Bagharab	QAT-J	–.98	29 Jun
8:35.3A	Silas	Kitum	KEN	25.5.90	9 Jun
8:35.38	Troy	Fraley	USA	2.4.95	9 Jun
8:35.63	Jorge	Blanco	ESP	15.7.93	14 Jun
8:36.08	Mouname	Sassaoui	MAR	20.3.95	10 Jun
8:36.16	Eric	Peñalver	ESP	23.9.93	14 Jun
8:36.40	Aoi	Matsumoto	JPN	7.9.87	21 May
8:36.40	Emmanuel	Rotich	KEN	.97	26 May
8:36.47	Kent	Pecora	USA	24.11.88	10 Jun
8:36.49	Luke	Musembi	KEN-Y	.00	2 Aug
8:36.55	John	Gay	CAN	.96	18 May
8:36.73	Ahmed	Abdelwahed	ITA	26.5.96	2 Jul
8:36.73	Jordan	Mann	USA	12.1.93	7 Jul
8:36.79	Mark	Parrish	USA	2.12.91	10 Jun
8:37.04	Aaron	Nelson	USA	16.7.92	7 Jul
8:37.08	Brandon	Doughty	USA	14.5.93	7 Jul
8:37.14	Ali	Messaoudi	ALG	13.10.95	27 Aug
8:37.27	Giuseppe	Gerratana	ITA	8.11.92	27 May
8:37.38	Antonio	Abadía	ESP	2.7.90	23 Jul
8:37.41	Adam	Kirk-Smith	GBR	30.1.91	7 Jul
8:37.42	Topi	Raitanen	FIN	7.2.96	27 Aug
8:37.64	Ryuhei	Sakaguchi	JPN	5.4.97	13 Jul
8:37.73	Mohamed Ali	Jelloul	ESP	30.6.94	4 Jul
8:37.78	Soufiane	Elkounia	ITA	11.3.90	14 May
8:37.80	Bryce	Miller	USA	1.5.95	18 May
8:37.92	Tripp	Hurt	USA	30.10.92	23 Jun
8:37.95	Zied	Ben Othman	TUN	21.3.91	17 May
8:38.0	Alvaro	Abreu	DOM	21.7.91	2 Mar
8:38.26	Soufien	Cherni	TUN	8.1.97	8 Jul
8:38.40	Luis Miguel	Borges	POR	4.10.94	14 Jun
8:38.54	Douglas	Musson	GBR	8.4.94	7 Jul
8:38.64	Troy	Reeder	USA	8.8.94	9 Jun
8:38.64	Hashim Salah	Abbas	QAT	15.4.94	14 Jun
8:38.69	Luke	Gunn	GBR	22.3.85	27 May
8:38.84	Louis	Gilavert	FRA-J	1.1.98	27 May
8:38.87	Kosei	Yamaguchi	JPN	19.8.91	23 Apr
8:39.34	Aidan	Tooker	USA-J	26.6.98	26 May
8:39.56	Bailey	Roth	USA	17.1.96	23 Jun
8:39.6A	Kenneth	Rotich	KEN	12.9.91	16 May
8:39.81	Avinash	Sable	IND	13.9.94	27 Sep
		(180)			

JUNIORS

See main list for top 10 juniors. 12 performances by 6 men to 8:22.0. Additional marks and further juniors:

Kirui 2+	8:15.915	Herc	Monaco	21 Jul	8:18.327	VD-DLF	Bruxelles	1 Sep
Haileselassie	8:17.041		Huelva	14 Jun	8:19.198	VD-DLF	Bruxelles	1 Sep
	8:18.292	DL	Stockholm	18 Jun				

Mark	Name		Nat	Born	Pos	Meet	Venue	Date
8:32.7A	Noah	Kiplimo	KEN-Y	.00	5		Nyahururu	6 May
8:35.10	Yaser Salem	Bagharab	QAT	–.98	9		Barcelona	29 Jun
8:36.49	Luke	Musembi	KEN-Y	.00	2		Tendo	2 Aug
8:38.84	Louis	Gilavert	FRA	1.1.98	17		Oordegem	27 May
8:39.34	Aidan	Tooker	USA	26.6.98	5h2	NCAA-E	Lexington	26 May
8:42.15A	Nickson	Kiplagat	KEN	11.5.98	3	Afr-J	Taimcen	29 Jun
8:47.2A	Amsalu	Belaye	ETH		2		Addis Ababa	5 Jan

60 METRES HURDLES INDOORS

Mark	Name		Nat	Born	Pos	Meet	Venue	Date
7.43	Andrew	Pozzi	GBR	15.5.92	1		Birmingham	18 Feb
7.44		Pozzi			1		Karlsruhe	4 Feb
7.44		Pozzi			1h3	NC	Sheffield	11 Feb
7.46	Omar	McLeod	JAM	25.4/94	1	Mill	New York (Armory)	11 Feb
7.48	Orlando	Ortega	ESP	29.7.91	1		Torun	10 Feb
7.49	-	Pozzi			1h1		Karlsruhe	4 Feb
7.51		Ortega			1		Düsseldorf	1 Feb
7.51	Dimitri	Bascou	FRA	20.7.87	2		Düsseldorf	1 Feb
7.51	Pascal	Martinot-Lagarde	FRA	22.9.91	1		Paris	8 Feb
7.51		Pozzi			1	NC	Sheffield	11 Feb
7.51		Ortega			1		Madrid	24 Feb
7.51		Pozzi			1	EI	Beograd	3 Mar
7.51A	Aries	Merritt	USA	24.7.85	1	NC	Albuquerque	5 Mar
	(13/6)							
7.53	Garfield	Darien	FRA	22.12.87	3		Düsseldorf	1 Feb
7.53	Balázs	Baji	HUN	9.6.89	1	NC	Budapest (BH)	19 Feb
7.53	Aurel	Manga	FRA	24.7.92	2	NC	Bordeaux	19 Feb
7.53	Petr	Svoboda	CZE	10.10.84	3	EI	Beograd	3 Mar
	(10)							
7.54A	Aleec	Harris	USA	31.10.90	2	NC	Albuquerque	5 Mar
7.56	Milan	Trajkovic	CYP	17.3.92	1h2	EI	Beograd	3 Mar
7.57	Edward	Lovett	ISV	25.6.92	3	Mill	New York (Armory)	11 Feb
7.58	Grant	Holloway	USA	19.11.97	1	Tyson	Fayetteville	10 Feb
7.59A	Jarret	Eaton	USA	24.6.89	3	NC	Albuquerque	5 Mar
7.61	Chad	Zallow	USA	25.4.97	1		New York (Armory)	4 Feb
7.61	Spencer	Adams	USA	10.9.89	5	Mill	New York (Armory)	11 Feb

Mark	Name		Nat	Born	Pos	Meet	Venue	Date
7.62	Erik	Balnuweit	GER	21.9.88	1	NC	Leipzig	18 Feb
7.63	David	Omoregie	GBR	1.11.95	2		Cardiff	28 Jan
7.63	Michael	Dickson	USA	25.1.97	1		Winston-Salem	4 Feb
	(20)							
7.63	David	King	GBR	13.6.94	2		Birmingham	18 Feb
7.63	Aaron	Mallett	USA	26.9.94	1	Big10	Geneva	25 Feb
7.65	Konstantin	Shabanov	RUS	17.11.89	1		Slavyansk-na-Kubani	22 Jan
7.65	Freddie	Crittenden	USA	3.8.94	1h2	ACC	Notre Dame	24 Feb
7.65	Damian	Czykier	POL	10.8.92	4h2	EI	Beograd	3 Mar
7.66	Dondre	Echols	USA	6.7.93	1		Metz	12 Feb
7.66		Xie Wenjun	CHN	11.7.90	1rA		Xianlin	28 Feb
7.67	Simon	Krauss	FRA	12.2.92	1h2	NC	Bordeaux	19 Feb
7.68	Wilhem	Belocian	FRA	22.6.95	3		Metz	12 Feb
7.68	Greggmar	Swift	BAR	16.2.91	1h		Montreal	18 Feb
	(30)							
7.68	Andreas	Martinsen	DEN	17.7.90	2h3	EI	Beograd	3 Mar
7.69	Benjamin	Sedécias	FRA	18.1.95	1		Reims	31 Jan
7.69A	Chris	Caldwell	USA	6.4.94	1h2		Albuquerque	3 Feb
7.69	Yidiel	Contreras	ESP	27.11.92	3h1		Karlsruhe	4 Feb
7.69	Maximilian	Bayer	GER	5.12.90	1h2	NC	Leipzig	18 Feb
7.69	-David	Kendziera	USA	9.9.94	2	Big10	Geneva	25 Feb
7.69	Nicholas	Anderson	USA	28.4.95	2h2	NCAA	College Station	10 Mar
7.70	Thingalaya	Siddhanth	IND	1.3.91	1		Seattle	14 Jan
7.70	Terence	Somerville	USA	5.11.89	2		Montreal	18 Feb
7.71	Loic	Desbonnes	FRA	26.7.91	1		Nantes	21 Jan
	(40)							
7.71A	Max	Hairston	USA	8.5.94	6	NC	Albuquerque	5 Mar
7.71	Ashtyn	Davis	USA	10.10.96	3h2	NCAA	College Station	10 Mar
7.71	Daniel	Roberts	USA-J	13.4.98	1		Bloomington	8 Dec
7.72	Nicolas	Borome	FRA	7.10.93	2		Eaubonne	21 Jan
7.72A	Braxton	Canady	USA-J	13.1.98	1		Albuquerque	11 Feb
7.72	Wellington	Zaza	LBR	20.1.95	1h2	SEC	Nashville	24 Feb
7.72	Ruebin	Walters	TTO	2.4.95	2h2	SEC	Nashville	24 Feb
7.72	Alexander	Brorsson	SWE	29.5.90	1h2	NC	Växjö	26 Feb
7.72	Koen	Smet	NED	9.8.92	1		Amsterdam	30 Dec
7.73	Marquis	Morris	USA	6.2.96	1		Fayetteville	28 Jan
	(50)							
7.73	Cameron	Hall	USA	12.5.93	1		Clemson	10 Feb
7.73	Hassane	Fofana	ITA	28.4.92	1	NC	Ancona	18 Feb
7.73		Ceng Jianhang	CHN-J	17.9.98	2rA		Xianlin	28 Feb
7.74	Amere	Lattin	USA	17.2.97	1h2	Tyson	Fayetteville	10 Feb
7.74	Andrew	Riley	JAM	6.9.88	7	Mill	New York (Armory)	11 Feb
7.74	Nate	Pozolinski	USA	8.8.95	1		Iowa City	18 Feb
7.74	Alexander	John	GER	3.5.86	2	NC	Leipzig	18 Feb
7.74A	Jamiel	Trimble	USA	25.6.95	1	MWC	Albuquerque	25 Feb
Hand timing								
7.5	Erik	Balnuweit	GER	21.9.88	1		Erfurt	27 Jan
7.5	Martin	Vogel	GER	16.3.92	2		Erfurt	27 Jan

Low altitude bests

7.56	Harris	2	Millrose New York (A)		11 Feb
7.60	Eaton	4	Millrose New York (A)		11 Feb
7.70	Merrit	3		Birmingham	18 Fe

110 METRES HURDLES

Mark	Wind	Name		Nat	Born	Pos	Meet	Venue	Date
12.90	0.7	Omar	McLeod	JAM	25.4.94	1	NC	Kingston	24 Jun
12.96	0.3		McLeod			1	Gyulai	Székesfehérvár	4 Jul
13.01	0.9		McLeod			1	Pre	Eugene	27 May
13.01	0.3	Sergey	Shubenkov	RUS	4.10.90	2	Gyulai	Székesfehérvár	4 Jul
13.04	1.8		McLeod			1	Drake	Des Moines	29 Apr
13.04	0.0		McLeod			1	WCh	London (OS)	7 Aug
13.05	-0.1	Ronald	Levy	JAM	30.10.92	1	DL	Paris (C)	1 Jul
13.09	0.5		McLeod			1	DL	Shanghai	13 May
13.09	0.6	Garfield	Darien	FRA	22.12.87	1	GS	Ostrava	28 Jun
13.09	0.0		Shubenkov			1h1	DL	Paris (C)	1 Jul
13.09	0.0	Aries	Merritt	USA	24.7.85	1	DL	London (OS)	9 Jul
13.10	0.9		Levy			2	Pre	Eugene	27 May
13.10	0.0	Devon	Allen	USA	12.12.94	2h1	DL	Paris (C)	1 Jul
13.10	0.2		McLeod			1s1	WCh	London (OS)	6 Aug
13.11	0.9		Allen			3	Pre	Eugene	27 May
13.11	1.8	Antonio	Alkana	RSA	12.4.90	1	Odlozil	Praha	5 Jun
13.11	0.3		Merritt			3	Gyulai	Székesfehérvár	4 Jul

Mark	Wind	Name		Nat	Born	Pos	Meet	Venue	Date
13.12	0.7		Shubenkov			1	Hanz	Zagreb	29 Aug
13.13	0.9		Merritt			4	Pre	Eugene	27 May
13.13	-0.3		Merritt			1	GGala	Roma	8 Jun
13.13	0.7		Levy			2	NC	Kingston	24 Jun
13.13	0.1		McLeod			1h2	DL	Paris (C)	1 Jul
13.14	-0.1	Andrew	Pozzi	GBR	15.5.92	2	DL	Paris (C)	1 Jul
13.14	0.0		Shubenkov			2	WCh	London (OS)	7 Aug
13.14	0.5		Shubenkov			1	VD-DLF	Bruxelles	1 Sep
13.15	0.5	Orlando	Ortega	ESP	29.7.91	2	DL	Shanghai	13 May
13.15	0.0		Darien			3h1	DL	Paris (C)	1 Jul
13.15	-0.1		Darien			3	DL	Paris (C)	1 Jul
13.15	0.3	Balázs	Baji	HUN	9.6.89	4	Gyulai	Székesfehérvár	4 Jul
13.16	0.1		Merritt			1h3	WCh	London (OS)	6 Aug
		(30/10)							
13.18	0.0	Aleec	Harris	USA	31.10.90	1		Baie-Mahault	17 May
13.19	0.5	Hansle	Parchment	JAM	17.6.90	1		Montreuil	1 Jun
13.25	0.0	Milan	Trajkovic	CYP	17.3.92	2	DL	London (OS)	9 Jul
13.26	0.6	Shane	Brathwaite	BAR	8.2.90	1s2	WCh	London (OS)	6 Aug
13.27	0.5	Aurel	Manga	FRA	24.7.92	3		Montreuil	1 Jun
13.28	1.2	Damian	Czykier	POL	10.8.92	1	EAF	Bydgoszcz	2 Jun
13.30	1.8	Ruebin	Walters	TTO	2.4.95	1h1	NC	Port of Spain	23 Jun
13.31	0.5		Xie Wenjun	CHN	11.7.90	3	DL	Shanghai	13 May
13.32	0.7	Dejour	Russell	JAM-Y	1.4.00	4	NC	Kingston	24 Jun
13.33	-0.5	Yordan	O'Farrill	CUB	9.2.93	1	NC	La Habana	14 Mar
		(20)							
13.33	1.8	Mikel	Thomas	TTO	23.11.87	3	Odlozil	Praha	5 Jun
13.33	1.2	Andrew	Riley	JAM	6.9.88	1		Sotteville-lès-Rouen	7 Jul
13.34	0.0	David	Omoregie	GBR	1.11.95	1h1	ET	Villeneuve d'Ascq	23 Jun
13.34	0.0	Jarret	Eaton	USA	24.6.89	5	DL	London (OS)	9 Jul
13.37	0.2	Devon	Williams	USA	17.1.94	1	SEC	Columbia, SC	13 May
13.37	1.6	Aaron	Mallett	USA	26.9.94	1		Stanford	29 Jun
13.38	1.2	Devon	Hill	USA	26.10.89	1		Gainesville	28 Apr
13.38	0.6	Johnathan	Cabral	CAN	31.12.92	3		St. Martin	13 May
13.39	-0.1	Abdulaziz	Al-Mandeel	KUW	22.5.89	1	NC	Al-Kuwait	18 Apr
13.39	-0.1	Roger	Iribarne	CUB	2.1.96	1	Barr	La Habana	26 May
		(30)							
13.39	1.4	David	Kendziera	USA	9.9.94	1s1	NCAA	Eugene	7 Jun
13.39	0.3		Kim Byung-jun	KOR	15.8.91	1		Bangkok	12 Jun
13.39	-1.7	Grant	Holloway	USA	19.11.97	4	NC	Sacramento	25 Jun
13.40	0.9	David	Oliver	USA	24.4.82	7	Pre	Eugene	27 May
13.40	0.0	Genta	Masuno	JPN	24.5.93	1h2	NC	Osaka	24 Jun
13.40	0.7	Yidiel Islay	Contreras	ESP	27.11.92	4h4	WCh	London (OS)	6 Aug
13.41	0.5	Gregor	Traber	GER	2.12.92	7	DL	Shanghai	13 May
13.41	0.0	Benjamin	Sedecias	FRA	18.1.95	7h1	DL	Paris (C)	1 Jul
13.41	-1.2	Eddie	Lovett	ISV	25.6.92	3h1	WCh	London (OS)	6 Aug
13.42	1.7	Freddie	Crittenden	USA	3.8.94	1		Coral Gables	8 Apr
		(40)							
13.42	0.2	Konstadínos	Douvalídis	GRE	10.3.87	5	ET	Villeneuve d'Ascq	24 Jun
13.44	0.6	Shun-ya	Takayama	JPN	3.9.94	1s1	NC	Osaka	24 Jun
13.44	0.0	Nick	Hough	AUS	20.10.93	1		Liège (NX)	19 Jul
13.45	0.2	Milan	Ristic	SRB	8.8.91	3		New York	6 Jul
13.46	1.4	Matthias	Bühler	GER	2.9.86	1		Mannheim	1 Jul
13.46	-0.3	Petr	Svoboda	CZE	10.10.84	1		Prostejov	24 Sep
13.47	1.4	Isaiah	Moore	USA	12.6.96	2s1	NCAA	Eugene	7 Jun
13.47	0.8	Éder Antônio	de Souza	BRA	15.10.86	1	NC	São Bernardo do Campo	10 Jun
13.48	1.5	Hideki	Omuro	JPN	25.7.90	1		Tsukuba	15 Apr
13.48	-0.1	Yacoub	Al-Yoha	KUW	31.1.93	2	NC	Al-Kuwait	18 Apr
		(50)							
13.48	1.2	David	King	GBR	13.6.94	2		Bydgoszcz	2 Jun
13.48	-0.9	Thingalaya	Siddhanth	IND	1.3.91	1		Mesa	10 Jun
13.49	1.4	Nick	Anderson	USA	28.4.95	3s1	NCAA	Eugene	7 Jun
13.49	0.8	Ludovic	Payen	FRA	18.2.95	1	EC-23	Bydgoszcz	15 Jul
13.49	1.8	Wataru	Yazawa	JPN	26.7.91	1		Hiratsuka	22 Jul
13.50	1.5	Ashtyn	Davis	USA	10.10.96	1	Pac-12	Eugene	14 May
13.50	1.4	Desmond	Palmer	USA	30.7.95	4s1	NCAA	Eugene	7 Jun
13.50	1.0	Andreas	Martinsen	DEN	17.7.90	1		København	20 Jun
13.51	0.8	Eduardo	de Deus	BRA	8.10.95	2	NC	São Bernardo do Campo	11 Jun
13.52	1.2	Gabriel	Constantino	BRA	9.2.95	3		Gainesville	28 Apr
		(60)							
13.52	0.5	Deuce	Carter	JAM	28.9.90	1		Ninove	15 Jul
13.53	0.5	Jeff	Porter	USA	27.11.85	1		Greensboro	14 Apr

Mark	Wind	Name		Nat	Born	Pos	Meet	Venue	Date
13.53	-0.2	Artur	Noga	POL	2.5.88	1h1		Warszawa	27 May
13.53	1.0	Jeffrey	Julmis	HAI	6.1.87	1h2		Montverde	10 Jun
13.53	1.4	Erik	Balnuweit	GER	21.9.88	2		Mannheim	1 Jul
13.53	1.8	Taio	Kanai	JPN	28.9.95	2		Hiratsuka	22 Jul
13.54	-0.2	Damian	Warner	CAN	4.11.89	1D	Hypo	Götzis	28 May
13.54	0.2	Cameron	Hall	USA	12.5.93	6		New York	6 Jul
13.55	-0.1		Ma Lei	CHN	29.6.89	1	NC	Jinan	18 May
13.55	0.9	Dimitri	Bascou	FRA	20.7.87	8	Pre	Eugene	27 May
		(70)							
13.55	-0.5		Chen Kuei-Ju	TPE	22.9.93	2	WUG	Taipei	27 Aug
13.56A	0.0	Tiaan	Smit ¶	RSA	14.3.95	1		Pretoria	12 Apr
13.56	1.8	Spencer	Adams	USA	10.9.89	6	DrakeR	Des Moines	29 Apr
13.56	2.0	Marquis	Morris	USA	6.2.96	1		Los Angeles	30 Apr
13.56	1.1	Nate	Pozolinski	USA	8.8.95	1h1		LaCrosse	12 May
13.56	-0.9	Max	Hairston	USA	8.5.94	2		Mesa	10 Jun
13.57A	-0.6	Ahmad	Al-Moualed	KSA	16.2.88	1h1	NC	Taïf	28 Apr
13.57	0.5		Yang Wei-Ting	TPE	22.9.94	1		Taipei	8 May
13.58	1.2	Alexander	John	GER	3.5.86	1		Weinheim	27 May
13.58	0.7	Rohan	Cole	JAM	28.10.97	7	NC	Kingston	24 Jun
		(80)							
13.58	1.1	Hassane	Fofana	ITA	28.4.92	1	LEAP	Loughborough	22 Jul
13.59	1.4	Khai	Riley-La Borde	GBR	8.11.95	3	LI	Loughborough	21 May
13.59	0.6	Hiroyuki	Sato	JPN	6.8.90	2s1	NC	Osaka	24 Jun
13.60	1.1	Ben	Reynolds	IRL	26.9.90	1r3		Aarhus	2 Jun
13.60	-0.9	Simon	Krauss	FRA	12.2.92	1		La Roche-sur-Yon	5 Jul
13.60	1.8	Anthony Tyrell	Kuriki	JPN	17.9.96	3		Hiratsuka	22 Jul
13.61	1.6	Lloyd	Sicard	USA	31.5.95	1		Fullerton	13 May
13.61	1.0	Spencer	Dunkerley-Offor	USA	6.1.95	3s3	NCAA	Eugene	7 Jun
13.61A	0.0		Zhang Honglin	CHN	12.1.94	2		Guiyang	27 Jun
13.62	-0.1		Jiang Fan	CHN	16.9.89	2	NC	Jinan	18 May
		(80)							
13.62	-0.1	Lorenzo	Perini	ITA	22.7.94	1		Savona	25 May
13.62	1.3	Shusei	Nomoto	JPN	25.10.95	1s3		Hiratsuka	9 Jun
13.63	1.3	Jonathas	Brito	BRA	30.11.92	1h1		Campinas	20 May
13.63	0.2	Ryan	Fontenot	USA	4.5.86	7		New York	6 Jul
13.64	0.8	Silvio Henrique	de Souza	BRA	21.7.93	4	NC	São Bernardo do Campo	10 Jun
13.64	0.0	Shin-ya	Tanaka	JPN	23.6.93	1h4	NC	Osaka	24 Jun
13.65	1.6	Jonathan	Mendes	BRA	14.4.90	2h1		São Bernardo do Campo	1 Apr
13.65	1.2	Gabriel	Odujobi	GBR	15.7.87	1h1		Clermont	13 May
13.65	0.3	Ronnie	Ash	USA	2.7.88	5		Kingston	20 May
13.65A	1.4	Yeison	Rivas	COL	24.9.87	1	NC	Medellín	10 Jun
		(100)							
13.65	0.0	Koen	Smet	NED	9.8.92	4h1	ET	Villeneuve d'Ascq	23 Jun
13.65	-1.6	Jason	Richardson	USA	4.4.86	1h1	NC	Sacramento	24 Jun
13.65	1.8	Sekou	Kaba	CAN	25.8.90	2	NC	Ottawa	8 Jul

Mark	Wind	Name		Nat	Born	Date
13.66	-0.1	Dayron	Robles	CUB	19.11.86	26 May
13.66	0.9	Marcus	Neely	USA	10.2.94	26 May
13.66	0.7	Vitaliy	Parakhonko	BLR	18.8.93	12 Jul
13.66	0.8	Dylan	Caty	FRA	11.1.97	15 Jul
13.67	1.7	Rayzam Shah Wan Sofian		MAS	11.1.88	27 May
13.67	1.3	Shuhei	Ishikawa	JPN	29.5.95	24 Jun
13.67	1.3	Ronald	Forbes	CAY	5.4.85	15 Jul
13.68	1.6	Wellington	Zaza	LBR	20.1.95	22 Apr
13.68	0.5	Chad	Zallow	USA	25.4.97	27 May
13.68	1.2	Jake	Porter	GBR	13.11.93	26 Jul
13.68	-0.1	Rico	Freimuth	GER	14.3.88	12 Aug
13.69	-0.3	Elmo	Lakka	FIN	10.4.93	9 Jun
13.69	0.9	Loïc	Herkenrath	FRA	11.7.94	24 Jun
13.69	1.4	Maximilian	Bayer	GER	5.12.90	1 Jul
13.69	0.9	James	Weaver	GBR	25.7.97	29 Jul
13.71	1.5	Antoine	Lloyd	USA	10.6.96	26 May
13.71	1.1	Lorenzo	Johnson	USA	26.5.93	30 May
13.71A	1.4	Fanor	Escobar	COL	17.12.97	10 Jun
13.71	0.3	Nicolas	Borome	FRA	7.10.93	25 Jun
13.72	2.0	William	Sharman	GBR	12.9.84	28 Apr
13.72A	1.1	Jamiel	Trimble	USA	25.6.95	13 May
13.72	-1.8	Greggmar	Swift	BAR	16.2.91	21 May
13.72A	1.4	Juan Carlos	Moreno	COL	31.1.94	10 Jun
13.72	1.5	Loic	Desbonnes	FRA	26.7.91	20 Jun
13.72	1.8	Ingvar	Moseley	CAN	24.11.91	8 Jul
13.72		Javier	McFarlane	PER	21.10.91	21 Nov
13.73	-0.8	Dondre	Echols	USA	6.7.93	15 Apr
13.73	1.2	Juan	Scott	USA	27.5.97	27 May
13.73	1.7	Brahian	Peña	SUI	3.4.94	27 May
13.73A	0.4	Junior	Mkhatini	RSA	4.1.90	3 Jun
13.74	1.2	Tremayne	Banks	USA	29.7.92	28 Apr
13.74	1.3	Takumu	Furuya	JPN	12.3.97	24 Jun
13.74	-0.6	Rasul	Dabo	POR	14.2.89	14 Jul
13.74	0.6	Konstantin	Shabanov	RUS	17.11.89	28 Jul
13.75	-0.6	Marcus	McWilliams	USA	20.2.97	25 Mar
13.75	2.0	Misana	Viltz	USA	21.2.96	30 Apr
13.75	1.3	Paulo Henrique da Silva		BRA	29.6.95	20 May
13.75	-0.1	Kevin	Mayer	FRA	10.2.92	12 Aug
13.76	1.0	Michael	Nicholls	BAR	6.4.97	14 May
13.77A	-0.1	Ruan	de Vries	RSA	1.2.86	20 May
13.77	1.2	Sebastian	Barth	GER	1.2.93	27 May
13.77	1.6	Trey	Holloway	USA	7.7.94	11 Jun
13.77	1.2	Vladimir	Vukicevic	NOR	6.5.91	13 Jun
13.77	0.2	Edirin	Okoro	GBR	4.4.89	22 Jul
13.78	0.8	Malik	Beverly	USA	.97	29 Apr
13.78	-0.1		Li Haifeng	CHN	20.11.89	18 May
13.78	1.5	Tatsuya	Wado	JPN	4.10.90	4 Jun
13.79	-0.2	Amere	Lattin	USA	17.2.97	1 Apr
13.79	1.2	Martin	Vogel	GER	16.3.92	27 May
13.79	1.9	Genaro	Rodríguez	MEX	10.10.90	17 Jun
13.79	-0.4		Chu Pengfei	CHN	28.12.93	19 Jul
13.79	1.6	Papdemba	Hiramatsu	JPN	15.12.97	10 Sep
13.80	1.2	Shawn	Rowe	JAM	7.12.92	27 May
13.80	1.7	Dario	De Borger	BEL	20.3.92	27 May
13.80	-0.6	Javier	Colomo	ESP	26.3.94	14 Jul
13.81	2.0	Joshua	Hawkins	NZL	9.2.94	19 Feb
13.81	1.3	Marshawn	Scott	USA	.94	15 Apr
13.81	1.4	Robert	Dunning	USA	23.6.97	20 May

Mark	Wind	Name		Nat	Born	Date
13.81	1.0	Tyler	Mason	JAM	15.1.95	27 May
13.81	0.8	João Vitor	de Oliveira	BRA	15.5.92	10 Jun
13.81	-0.8		Lee Jung-joon	KOR	26.3.84	24 Jun
13.81	1.4	Ryota	Fujii	JPN	29.7.96	19 Aug
13.82	0.2	Daniel	Roberts	USA-J	13.4.98	13 May
13.82	1.4	Artem	Makarenko	RUS	23.4.97	10 Jun
13.82	1.8	Brian	Richards	CAN	3.2.89	8 Jul
13.82	0.2	Ogierakhi	Martins	NGR	30.6.91	18 Jul
13.83	2.0	Rafael	Pereira	BRA	8.4.97	23 Apr
13.83	1.3	Kyohei	Furuya	JPN	3.1.96	9 Jun
13.83	1.6	Masahiro	Kagimoto	JPN	29.9.95	9 Jun
13.83	0.0	Masanori	Nishizawa	JPN	16.7.87	24 Jun
13.83	-0.6	Francisco	Javier López	ESP	29.12.89	14 Jul
13.83	0.2	Dominik	Bochenek	POL	14.5.87	23 Jul
13.83	-0.1		Zhao Pengchuan	CHN	28.10.93	2 Sep
13.84A	-0.7	Brendan	Ames	USA	6.10.88	8 Apr
13.84	2.0	Jaron	Thomas	USA	8.1.95	13 May
13.84	1.4	Ricardo	Torres	PUR	13.2.96	10 Jun
13.84	0.0	Kenta	Yamamoto	JPN	17.5.95	24 Jun
13.84	0.0		Ji Wei	CHN	5.2.84	2 Sep
13.84A	-0.2	Alwyn	Bothma	RSA	.97	31 Oct
13.85	2.0	Josh	Thompson	USA	16.1.93	8 Apr
13.85	0.9	John	Rus	USA	.94	5 May
13.85	1.2	Donovan	Robertson	USA	8.11.93	27 May
13.85	1.2	Justin	Veteto	USA	24.3.96	27 May
13.85	1.0	John	Burt	USA	10.2.97	7 Jun
13.85A		William	Mutunga	KEN	17.9.93	10 Jun
13.85	1.0		Ni Mingchao	CHN	20.4.94	8 Jul
13.85	-0.9	Elie	Agot	FRA	9.4.91	16 Jul
13.86	1.4	Jonathan	Ross	USA	.95	22 Apr
13.86	2.0	Tshepo	Lefete	RSA	2.2.92	28 Apr
13.86A	0.9	Jorge	McFarlane	PER	20.2.88	29 Apr
13.86	2.0	Michael	Dickson	USA	25.1.97	14 May
13.86	0.5	Ro-Derick	Spears	USA	14.8.94	27 May
13.86A	0.0		Ceng Jianhang	CHN	28.10.93	27 Jun
13.87	0.8	Blake	Alexander	USA	.95	29 Apr
13.87	1.7	Václav	Sedlák	CZE	6.2.93	11 Jun
13.87	0.7	Stefan	Fennell	JAM	5.11.93	24 Jun

(199)

Wind assisted

Mark	Wind	Name		Nat	Born	Pos	Meet	Venue	Date
13.09	3.5	Orlando	Ortega	ESP	29.7.91	1	DL	Stockholm	18 Jun
13.10	3.5		Shubenkov			2	DL	Stockholm	18 Jun
13.13	5.8	Andrew	Pozzi	GBR	15.5.92	1		Clermont	15 Apr
13.15	2.2		Levy			1		Kingston	15 Apr
13.24	6.2	Aaron	Mallett	USA	26.9.94	1	Big 10	University Park	14 May
13.25	3.5	Shane	Brathwaite	BAR	8.2.90	3	DL	Stockholm	18 Jun
13.34	2.2	Gregor	Traber	GER	2.12.92	1		Mannheim	1 Jul
13.35	2.2	Matthias	Bühler	GER	2.9.86	2		Mannheim	1 Jul
13.37	3.7	Chad	Zallow	USA	25.4.97	1	FlaR	Gainesville	31 Mar
13.37	2.3	Devon	Hill	USA	26.10.89	2rB		Clermont	15 Apr
13.38	5.8	Gabriel	Odujobi	GBR	15.7.87	2		Clermont	15 Apr
13.41	2.2	Jeffrey	Julmis	HAI	6.1.87	1		Fort Lauderdale	19 May
13.42	3.8	Eduardo	de Deus	BRA	8.10.95	1	SAmC	Asunción	23 Jun
13.43	2.7	Ryan	Fontenot	USA	4.5.86	2		San Marcos	1 Apr
13.43	3.8	Thingalaya	Siddhanth	IND	1.3.91	1		San Diego	1 Apr
13.44	2.5	Petr	Svoboda	CZE	10.10.84	1		Praha	27 Aug
13.45	5.5	Spencer	Dunkerley-Offor	USA	6.1.95	1	Big 12	Lawrence	14 May
13.46	2.2	Ricardo	Torres	PUR	13.2.96	2		Fort Lauderdale	19 May
13.46	3.0	Taio	Kanai	JPN	28.9.95	1		Fukui	10 Sep
13.48	3.7	Ronald	Forbes	CAY	5.4.85	1h2		Clermont	15 Apr
13.48	2.2	Erik	Balnuweit	GER	21.9.88	3		Mannheim	1 Jul
13.49A	2.3	Tiaan	Smit ¶	RSA	14.3.95	1		Pretoria	18 Mar
13.49	2.5	Marquis	Morris	USA	6.2.96	2s2	NCAA	Eugene	7 Jun
13.51	2.8	Jeff	Porter	USA	27.11.85	1		Montverde	10 Jun
13.52	3.3	Antoine	Lloyd	USA	10.6.96	1		Lubbock	28 Apr
13.52	2.2	Maximilian	Bayer	GER	5.12.90	3		Mannheim	1 Jul
13.53	2.8	Jason	Richardson	USA	4.4.86	2		Montverde	10 Jun
13.54	3.0	Lorenzo	Perini	ITA	22.7.94	1	NC	Trieste	1 Jul
13.55	3.3	Lloyd	Sicard	USA	31.5.95	2		Irvine	29 Apr
13.55	w?	Spencer	Adams	USA	10.9.89	2		Charlotte, NC	16 Jun
13.56	2.2	Tremayne	Banks	USA	29.7.92	3		Fort Lauderdale	19 May
13.56	3.0	Shuhei	Ishikawa	JPN	29.5.95	2		Fukui	10 Sep
13.59	2.2	Koen	Smet	NED	9.8.92	1		La Chaux de Fonds	2 Jul
13.59	2.7	Shusei	Nomoto	JPN	25.10.95	1	Nambu	Sapporo	9 Jul
13.60	2.4	Jonathas	Brito	BRA	30.11.92	1h1		São Bernardo do Campo	22 Mar
13.60	2.5	Marcus	Neely	USA	10.2.94	4s2	NCAA	Eugene	7 Jun
13.62	2.6	Sekou	Kaba	CAN	25.8.90	q		Windsor	17 Jun
13.64	6.2	Donovan	Robertson	USA	8.11.93	3	Big 10	University Park	14 May

Mark	Wind	Name		Nat	Born	Date
13.66	3.5	Justin	Merlino	AUS	10.12.86	2 Apr
13.66	3.0	Trey	Holloway	USA	7.7.94	8 Apr
13.66A	2.3	Jamiel	Trimble	USA	25.6.95	12 May
13.67A	2.9	Brendan	Ames	USA	6.10.88	5 May
13.67A	2.3	Ruan	de Vries	RSA	1.2.86	18 Mar
13.68	6.8	Ryota	Fujii	JPN	29.7.96	15 Apr
13.68	2.5	Misana	Viltz	USA	21.2.96	27 May
13.68	3.2	Tatsuya	Wado	JPN	4.10.90	4 Jun
13.69A	2.9	Jaron	Thomas	USA	8.1.95	5 May
13.69	3.7	Greggmar	Swift	BAR	16.2.91	6 May
13.69	4.6	Masahiro	Kagimoto	JPN	29.9.95	2 Jul
13.70	2.7	Takumu	Furuya	JPN	12.3.97	9 Jul
13.71	2.6	Ingvar	Moseley	CAN	24.11.91	17 Jun
13.71	3.9	Brian	Richards	CAN	3.2.89	8 Jul
13.72	5.5	Rhys	Phillips	USA/BAR	28.4.93	14 May
13.73	2.6	Amere	Lattin	USA	17.2.97	8 Apr
13.75	2.3	Daniel	Roberts	USA-J	13.4.98	15 Apr
13.75	3.2	John	Burt	USA	10.2.97	27 May
13.76	3.2	Saulius	Rapolas	LTU	15.2.96	20 Jul
13.77	6.2	Justin	Veteto	USA	24.3.96	14 May
13.78	4.0	Daley	Carter	BAR	18.1.94	14 May
13.79	3.0	Patrick	Prince	USA	29.5.97	31 Mar
13.79	3.3	João Vitor	de Oliveira	BRA	15.5.92	29 Apr
13.79	6.2	Jonathan	Tollefson	USA	26.9.96	14 May

Low altitude bests

13.61 -0.6 Al-Moualed 3 AsiC Bhubaneswar 8 Jul

13.69 -0.3 Zhang Honglin 11 May

13.87w 3.8 Jorge McFarlane 23 Jun

Hand timing 13.3 0.0 Yordan O'Farrill CUB 9.2.93 1r1 La Habana 15 Jun

Mark	Wind	Name		Nat	Born	Pos	Meet	Venue	Date

Doubtful timing: Mar 8, Bloemfontein: (0.3) 1, Ruan de Vries RSA 1.2.86 13.23; 2. Junior Mkhatini RSA 4.1.90 13.28; 3. Muntingh Hamman RSA 7.3.90 13.41

Drugs disqualification

Mark	Wind	Name		Nat	Born	Pos	Meet	Venue	Date
13.42A	0.3	Tiaan	Smit ¶	RSA	14.3.95	(1)	NC	Potchefstroom	22 Apr

JUNIORS

Mark	Wind	Name		Nat	Born	Pos	Meet	Venue	Date
13.32	0.7	Dejour	Russell	JAM-Y	1.4.00	4	NC	Kingston	24 Jun
		13.57 0.5 2h2 NC Kingston 24 Jun							
13.82	0.2	Daniel	Roberts	USA-J	13.4.98	6	SEC	Columbia, SC	13 May
		13.89 0.7 3h1 SEC Columbia, SC 12 May			5 performances by 3 men to 13.89				
13.86A	0.0		Ceng Jianhang	CHN	28.10.93	4		Guiyang	27 Jun
13.93	1.5	Braxton	Canaby	USA	13.1.98	2	Pac12	Eugene	14 May
13.93	0.0	Jason	Joseph	SUI	11.10.98	1		Hochdorf	14 May
13.94	0.8	Joseph	Daniels	CAN	12.10.98	5		Guelph	14 Jun
13.95	-0.5	Yoann	Villa	CUB	31.1.98	3	NC	La Habana	14 Mar
13.98	-0.3	Max	Hrelja	SWE	30.1.98	1h1	NC	Helsingborg	26 Aug

Wind assisted

Mark	Wind	Name		Nat	Born	Pos	Meet	Venue	Date
13.75	2.3	Daniel	Roberts	USA-J	13.4.98	3		Austin	15 Apr
13.88	2.4	Joseph	Daniels	CAN	12.10.98	1		New Haven	7 May
13.89	2.3	Braxton	Canaby	USA	13.1.98	2h1	Pac12	Eugene	13 May
13.91	4.0	Jaylan	McConico	USA	17.8.98	3		Wichita	14 May
13.94	3.9	Mason	Weh	USA	14.4.98	2		Abilene	27 Apr

110 Metres Hurdles – 99 cm hurdles

Mark	Wind	Name		Nat	Born	Pos	Meet	Venue	Date
13.21	1.9	Dejour	Russell	JAM-Y	1.4.00	1	N.Sch	Kingston	1 Apr
13.25	0.0	Jason	Joseph	SUI	11.10.98	1		Zofingen	3 Jun
		13.29 1.7 1 Mannheim 1 Jul			13.37 0.6 1h3 Mannheim 1 Jul				
		13.32 0.5 1 NC-j Lausanne 10 Sep			11 performances by 5 men to 13.39				
13.32	-1.8	Eric	Edwards	USA-Y	3.1.00	1	NC-j	Sacramento	23 Jun
		13.33 -0.6 1 PAm-J Trujillo 21 Jul			13.39 1.2 1 Austin 13 May				
13.33	1.4	Joseph	Anderson	USA	30.8.99	1		Clovia	3 Jun
13.35	0.0	Trey	Cunningham	USA	26.8.98	1		Mobile	1 Apr
13.36	-0.6	Anastas	Eliopoulos	CAN	.99	2	PAm-J	Trujillo	21 Jul
13.40	-0.1	Rikuto	Higuchi	JPN	19.8.99	1		Matsuyama	8 Oct
13.43	1.1	Damion	Thomas	JAM-Y	29.6.99	1	TexR	Austin	1 Apr
13.45	1.25	Yoann	Villa	CUB	31.1.98	1		La Habana	24 Feb
13.46	1.6	Max	Hrelja (10)	SWE	30.1.98	1		Skara	6 Jun
13.47	1.4	Sales Junior	Iglin	SUI	27.8.99	1h2		Mannheim	1 Jul
13.47	-0.5	Kentaro	Hiraga	JPN	.99	2		Nagoya	20 Oct
13.48	0.0	Robert	Sakala	GBR	5.2.98	2	EJ	Grosseto	22 Jul
13.48	0.0	Luis	Salort	ESP	26.7.99	3	EJ	Grosseto	22 Jul
13.51	1.7	Noah	Green	USA	23.5.99	1	Jnr Oly	Lawrence	30 Jul
13.51	-0.1	Shinsuke	Izumiya	JPN-Y	26.1.00	3		Matsuyama	8 Oct
13.52	1.9	Orlando	Bennett	JAM	12.10.99	2	N.Sch	Kingston	1 Apr
13.52	1.7	Finlay	Gaio	SUI	15.4.99	2		Mannheim	1 Jul
13.53	1.9	Oquendo	Bernard	JAM-Y	5.5.00	3	N.Sch	Kingston	1 Apr
13.53	1.7	Cameron	Murray	USA	12.12.99	2	Jnr Oly	Lawrence	30 Jul

Wind assisted

Mark	Wind	Name		Nat	Born	Pos	Meet	Venue	Date
13.46		Cary	Poole	USA	29.7.99	1		Newark	15 May
13.50A	3.1	Thabo	Maganyele	RSA	10.1.98	1		Pretoria	18 Mar

200 METRES HURDLES

Mark	Wind	Name		Nat	Born	Pos	Meet	Venue	Date
22.55	1.4	Yoshihiro	Watanabe	JPN	7.1.97	1		Itami	1 Oct

Straight Track

Mark	Wind	Name		Nat	Born	Pos	Meet	Venue	Date
22.48		Johnny	Dutch	USA	20.1.89	1		Manchester	26 May
22.89		Sebastian	Rodger	GBR	29.6.91	2		Manchester	26 May

300 METRES HURDLES

Mark	Wind	Name		Nat	Born	Pos	Meet	Venue	Date
34.87		Kariem	Hussein	SUI	1.4.89	1		Langenthal	25 May
35.45		Alain-Hervé	Mfompkpa	SUI	4.6.96	2		Langenthal	25 May
35.52		Abdelmalik	Lahoulou	ALG	7.5.92	1		Biskra	18 Mar

400 METRES HURDLES

Mark	Wind	Name		Nat	Born	Pos	Meet	Venue	Date
47.80		Kyron	McMaster	IVB	3.1.97	1		Kingston	20 May
48.02		Kerron	Clement	USA	31.10.85	1	DL	London (OS)	9 Jul
48.07			McMaster			1	WK-DLF	Zürich	24 Aug
48.12			McMaster			2	DL	London (OS)	9 Jul
48.13		Quincy	Downing	USA	16.1.93	1		Kingston	10 Jun
48.18		Eric	Futch	USA	25.4.93	1	NC	Sacramento	25 Jun
48.22		Karsten	Warholm	NOR	28.2.96	2	WK-DLF	Zürich	24 Aug
48.24		Yasmani	Copello	TUR	15.4.87	3	DL	London (OS)	9 Jul

Mark	Wind	Name		Nat	Born	Pos	Meet	Venue	Date
48.25			Warholm			1	Bisl	Oslo	15 Jun
48.26		Michael	Stigler	USA	5.4.92	2	NC	Sacramento	25 Jun
48.31A		Aderrahmane	Samba	QAT	5.9.95	1		Sasolburg	28 Mar
48.32			Futch			1	NCAA	Eugene	9 Jun
48.32			Stigler			4	DL	London (OS)	9 Jul
48.33		Rai	Benjamin	ANT	27.7.97	2	NCAA	Eugene	9 Jun
48.35			Clement			1s1	WCh	London (OS)	7 Aug
48.35			Warholm			1	WCh	London (OS)	9 Aug
48.37			Warholm			1	EC-23	Bydgoszcz	16 Jul
48.40		Mamadou Kassé	Hann (10)	FRA	10.10.86	1		Genève	10 Jun
48.43			Warholm			2s1	WCh	London (OS)	7 Aug
48.44		(best la)	Samba			1	DL	Doha	5 May
48.44			Copello			2	Bisl	Oslo	15 Jun
48.44		Timothy TJ	Holmes	USA	2.7.95	3	NC	Sacramento	25 Jun
48.45		Kariem	Hussein	SUI	1.4.89	3	WK-DLF	Zürich	24 Aug
48.46			Warholm			1	ET-1	Vaasa	24 Jun
48.49		Kemar	Mowatt	JAM	12.3.95	3	NCAA	Eugene	9 Jun
48.49			McMaster			1		St. George's	2 Jul
48.49			Copello			2	WCh	London (OS)	9 Aug
48.50		Byron	Robinson	USA	16.2.95	4	NC	Sacramento	25 Jun
48.52		Jaheel	Hyde	JAM	2.2.97	2		Kingston	20 May
48.52			Clement			3	WCh	London (OS)	9 Aug
		(30/15)							
48.59		Juander	Santos	DOM	7.5.95	3s1	WCh	London (OS)	7 Aug
48.60		Kenny	Selmon	USA	27.8.96	4	NCAA	Eugene	9 Jun
48.60		Johnny	Dutch	USA	20.1.89	5	NC	Sacramento	25 Jun
48.63		Bershawn	Jackson	USA	8.5.83	1	DL	Shanghai	13 May
48.76		Javier	Culson	PUR	25.7.84	4		Kingston	20 May
		(20)							
48.77		Jack	Green	GBR	6.10.91	6	DL	London (OS)	9 Jul
48.83		Ricardo	Cunningham	JAM	3.10.80	3	NC	Kingston	23 Jun
48.94		Márcio	Teles	BRA	27.1.94	1	NC	São Bernardo do Campo	11 Jun
48.94		Takatoshi	Abe	JPN	12.11.91	1h2	NC	Osaka	23 Jun
48.94		Rasmus	Mägi	EST	4.5.92	3	Athl	Lausanne	6 Jul
48.95		Thomas	Barr	IRL	24.7.92	3	Bisl	Oslo	15 Jun
49.00		David	Kendziera	USA	9.9.94	4s2	NCAA	Eugene	7 Jun
49.00		Michael	Tinsley	USA	21.4.84	5s2	NC	Sacramento	24 Jun
49.02		Quincy	Hall	USA-J	31.7.98	1	PAm-J	Trujillo	23 Jul
49.03		Yuta	Konishi	JPN	31.7.90	1h1	NC	Osaka	23 Jun
		(30)							
49.05		Abdelmalik	Lahoulou	ALG	7.5.92	1	Arab C	Radès	18 Jul
49.05			Chen Chieh	TPE	8.5.92	2	WUG	Taipei	26 Aug
49.06		Kei	Maeno	JPN	10.5.91	2h1	NC	Osaka	23 Jun
49.13		Hederson	Estefani	BRA	11.9.91	2	NC	São Bernardo do Campo	11 Jun
49.14		Danylo	Brand	SUI	23.2.96	2	EC-23	Bydgoszcz	15 Jul
49.15		Robert	Grant	USA	31.1.96	3	SEC	Columbia, SC	13 May
49.15		Patryk	Dobek	POL	13.2.94	1h1	NC	Bialystok	21 Jul
49.17		Desmond	Palmer	USA	30.7.95	2		Atlanta	14 May
49.19		Andre	Clarke	JAM	6.6.92	4	NC	Kingston	23 Jun
49.22		José	Bencosme de Leon	ITA	16.5.92	1		Orvieto	21 Jul
		(40)							
49.24		Omar	Cisneros	CUB	19.11.89	1		Castellón	4 Jul
49.27A		Cornel	Fredericks	RSA	3.3.90	1		Pretoria	17 Mar
49.28A		Constant	Pretorius	RSA	26.1.94	1		Pretoria	3 Jun
49.29A		Louis 'L.J'	van Zyl	RSA	20.7.85	1		Pretoria	12 Apr
49.30		Victor	Coroller	FRA	21.9.97	2s2	EC-23	Bydgoszcz	15 Jul
49.31		Ludvy	Vaillant	FRA	15.3.95	3	EC-23	Bydgoszcz	16 Jul
49.33		Roxroy	Cato	JAM	1.5.88	5	NC	Kingston	23 Jun
49.33		Ryo	Kajiki	JPN	8.12.95	2h2	NC	Osaka	23 Jun
49.34		Sergio	Fernández	ESP	1.4.93	1		Salamanca	3 Jun
49.35A		Le Roux	Hamman	RSA	6.1.92	1	NC	Potchefstroom	21 Apr
		(50)							
49.35		José Luis	Gaspar	CUB	25.8.95	1r2		La Habana	10 Jun
49.35		Jeffery	Gibson	BAH	15.8.90	1h	NC	Nassau	23 Jun
49.35		Yusuke	Ishida	JPN	25.5.95	1	Nambu	Sapporo	9 Jul
49.36		Shawn	Rowe	JAM	7.12.92	2	PennR	Philadelphia	28 Apr
49.36		Lorenzo	Vergani	ITA	4.9.93	1	NC	Trieste	2 Jul
49.38		Jaak-Heinrich	Jagor	EST	11.5.90	1	NC	Tallinn	23 Jul
49.39		Haron	Koech	KEN	27.1.90	1		Padova	16 Jul
49.39		Takayuki	Kishimoto	JPN	6.5.90	1		Matsuyama	7 Oct

Mark	Name		Nat	Born	Pos	Meet	Venue	Date
49.40	Craig CJ	Allen	USA	14.2.95	2q1	NCAA-W	Austin	26 May
49.40	Yuki	Matsushita	JPN	9.9.91	1h4	NC	Osaka	23 Jun
	(60)							
49.40	Luke	Campbell	GER	22.11.94	1	NC	Erfurt	9 Jul
49.41	Mario	Lambrughi	ITA	5.2.92	1	GGala	Roma	8 Jun
49.43	Yoshihiro	Watanabe	JPN	7.1.97	3h1	NC	Osaka	23 Jun
49.48A	AJ	Boully	USA	1.9.92	1		Logan	13 May
49.48	Hardus	Maritz	NAM	10.5.90	2		Bruxelles	9 Jul
49.49	Isa	Phillips	JAM	22.4.84	1		Baton Rouge	22 Apr
49.49	Jacob	Paul	GBR	6.2.95	8	DL	London (OS)	9 Jul
49.52	Jordin	Andrade	CPV	5.5.92	2rB		Luzern	11 Jul
49.55	Timofey	Chalyy	RUS	7.4.94	1	NC	Zhukovskiy	29 Jul
49.56	Miloud	Rahmouni	ALG	13.12.83	2	Arab C	Radès	18 Jul
	(70)							
49.57	Eric	Cray	PHI	6.11.88	1	AsiC	Bhubaneswar	8 Jul
49.58	Sebastian	Rodger	GBR	29.6.91	4		Genève	10 Jun
49.58	Leandro	Zamora	CUB	11.3.96	2r2		La Habana	10 Jun
49.64	Kazuaki	Yoshida	JPN	31.8.87	2h3	NC	Osaka	23 Jun
49.66		Feng Zhiqiang	CHN-J	14.4.98	1	NG	Tianjin	4 Sep
49.69		Wang Yang	CHN	20.9.96	1h3		Zhengzhou	11 Apr
49.69	Eric	Alejandro	PUR	15.4.86	3		Bruxelles	9 Jul
49.69	Guillermo	Ruggeri	ARG	26.3.92	3h4	WCh	London (OS)	6 Aug
49.70	Nicholas	Bett	KEN	14.6.92	4	DL	Doha	5 May
49.70	Masayuki	Obayashi	JPN	6.2.96	1		Osaka	8 Jul
	(0)							
49.74	Tibor	Koroknai	HUN	24.1.90	1	ET-2	Tel Aviv	24 Jun
49.74	Niall	Flannery	GBR	26.4.91	1	LEAP	Loughborough	22 Jul
49.77	Ian	Dewhurst	AUS	13.11.90	1	NC	Sydney	2 Apr
49.77		Cai Junqi	CHN	11.3.96	1h2		Zhengzhou	11 Apr
49.79	Oleg	Mironov	RUS	5.3.93	2	NCp	Yerino	15 Jul
49.79		Shang Shuo	CHN	1.6.95	2	NG	Tianjin	4 Sep
49.80	Naoya	Nakano	JPN	3.7.94	1h3		Osaka	23 Sep
49.82	William	Wynne	USA	30.1.90	2		Greensboro	4 Jun
49.82	Mohamed Adam	Shoaib	SUD-J	.98	2		Castellón	4 Jul
49.82	Kotaro	Miyao	JPN	12.7.91	5	Nambu	Sapporo	9 Jul
	(90)							
49.83	Curtis	Beach	USA	22.7.90	1		Claremont	3 Jun
49.83	Sheldon	Williams	JAM	17.8.90	2h2	NC	Kingston	22 Jun
49.83	Pavel	Agafonov	RUS	28.8.95	2	NC	Zhukovskiy	29 Jul
49.83	Aleksandr	Skorobogatko	RUS	7.8.94	3	NC	Zhukovskiy	29 Jul
49.84	Cameron	French	NZL	17.5.92	4		Bruxelles	9 Jul
49.85	Leford	Green	JAM	14.11.86	2		Montverde	10 Jun
49.88	Jeshua	Anderson	USA	22.6.89	5		Somerville	2 Jun
49.88A	William	Mutunga	KEN	17.9.93	1	NC	Nairobi	10 Jun
49.88	Felix	Franz	GER	6.5.93	1		Regensburg	11 Jun
49.88	Cory	Poole	USA-J	29.7.99	2	NC-j	Sacramento	24 Jun
	(100)							

Mark	Name		Nat	Born	Date
49.91A	Kefilwe	Mogowane	RSA	11.10.97	3 Jun
49.92	Vít	Müller	CZE	31.8.96	11 Jun
49.92	Tatsuhiro	Yamamoto	JPN	23.4.97	23 Jun
49.93		Yu Chia-Hsuan	TPE	22.1.95	10 Jun
49.93	Wilfried	Happio	FRA-J	22.4.98	23 Jul
49.95	Tom	Burton	GBR	29.10.88	10 Jun
49.96	Alfred	Larry	USA	9.4.93	22 Apr
49.96	Fernando	Vega	MEX-J	19.2.98	23 Jul
49.98	Alfredo	Sepúlveda	CHI	3.8.93	12 Jul
50.00	Mitsuru	Sugai	JPN	7.1.94	23 Jun
50.00	Keisuke	Nozawa	JPN	7.6.91	23 Sep
50.01	Ramfis	Vega	PUR	7.1.94	22 Apr
50.01	Drew	Wiseman	USA	24.8.94	26 May
50.01A	Mark	Ujakpor	ESP	18.1.87	7 Jul
50.03	Paul	Byrne	IRL	18.4.90	9 Jul
50.05	Javan	Gallimore	JAM	7.8.93	22 Jun
50.05	Isak	Andersson	SWE	29.1.96	15 Jul
50.05	Zied	Azizi	TUN	11.6.91	18 Jul
50.05		Quach Cong Lich	VIE	27.8.93	22 Aug
50.07	Masaya	Oda	JPN	11.5.95	14 May
50.09	Ryo	Yamamoto	JPN	21.10.95	12 May
50.09A	Fernando	Martínez	MEX	5.9.93	13 May
50.10	Atsushi	Yamada	JPN	3.7.91	23 Sep
50.11	Saber	Boukamouche	ALG	20.4.92	24 Jun
50.12	Mikael Antonio	de Jesus	BRA	19.8.97	12 Mar
50.12	Thomas	Burns	USA-J	8.12.99	23 Jun
50.13	Lucirio Francisco	Garrido	VEN	4.10.88	22 Jul
50.14	Andre	Colebrook	BAH	8.3.94	26 May
50.15	Marvin	Williams	JAM	13.6.96	22 Jun
50.16	T. Santhosh	Kumar	IND-J	1.1.98	27 Sep
50.17	Amadou	Ndiaye	SEN	6.12.92	24 Jul
50.18	Annsert	Whyte	JAM	10.4.87	13 May
50.18	Taylor	McLaughlin	USA	2.8.97	7 Jun
50.18		Xun Zhizhun	CHN	12.4.92	2 Jul
50.18	Gerber	Blanco	GUA	6.9.93	9 Dec
50.19	Sergio	Esquivel	MEX-J	4.5.99	23 Jul
50.20A	Piet PC	Beneke	RSA	18.7.90	17 Mar
50.21	Rilwan	Alowonle	USA	12.12.93	26 May
50.21	Kern	Alexis	TTO	13.1.94	24 Jun
50.22	M.P.	Jabir	IND	8.6.96	8 Jul
50.23	Amaechi	Morton	NGR	30.10.89	14 Jun
50.23	Nikita	Andriyanov	RUS	7.2.90	15 Jul
50.24	Fabian	Norgrove	BAR	6.2.90	25 Jun
50.25	Jack	Lawrie	GBR	21.2.96	18 Jun
50.26	Hiroki	Miyazaki	JPN	10.12.95	23 Jun
50.28	Isshu	Takada	JPN	27.11.97	23 Jul
50.30	Dmitriy	Koblov	KAZ	30.11.92	8 Jul
50.30	Georg	Fleischhauer	GER	21.10.88	9 Jul
50.30	Thomas	Delmestre	FRA	31.3.91	16 Jul
50.31	Kakeru	Inoue	JPN	19.3.96	10 Jun
50.32	Jaelen	Williams	USA-J	7.7.98	26 May
50.32	Masaki	Toyoda	JPN-J	17.1.98	10 Jun
50.32	Stéphane	Yato	FRA	11.9.92	16 Jul
50.32	Kohei	Miyako	JPN	.97	30 Sep

Mark	Name		Nat	Born	Pos	Meet	Venue	Date
50.33	Ivan	Nuñez	MEX	23.8.97				7 May
50.34	Kion	Joseph	BAR	27.4.94				15 Jul
50.34	Alessandro	Sibilio	ITA-J	27.4.99				23 Jul
50.35	Koichi	Nakaya	JPN	8.7.95				10 Jun
50.35	Maksims	Sincukovs	LAT-J	26.6.98				26 Aug
50.36	Obokhare	Ikpefan	NGR	6.7.95				8 Apr
50.36	Yusuke	Shirao	JPN-J	7.9.99				17 Jun
50.36	Alberth	Bravo	VEN	29.8.87				24 Jun
50.37	Daichi	Inoue	JPN-J	27.4.99				14 May
50.37	Reggie	Wyatt	USA	17.9.90				23 Jun
50.38	Yutaro	Mano	JPN	.96				10 Jun
50.38	Oskari	Mörö	FIN	31.1.93				24 Jun
50.39	Greg	Chiles	USA	2.4.96				26 May
50.39	Kyle	Robinson	JAM	23.9.93				27 May
50.41		Ju Sang-min	KOR	11.3.93				27 Jun
50.41	David José	Pineda	ESP-J	18.3.98				23 Jul
50.42	Yoan	Décimus	FRA	30.11.87				15 Jul
50.43	Hidenori	Arita	JPN	.95				7 May
50.43	Chris	Davis	USA	13.7.89				10 Jun
50.43	Asafe	Virgolino	BRA	30.3.96				23 Jul
50.44	Takafumi	Iwasaki	JPN	8.12.97				20 Aug
50.45	Riki	Ohara	JPN-J	.98				12 May
50.45	Martin	Juránek	CZE	13.3.91				30 May
50.45	Predea	Manounou	FRA	2.7.97				16 Jul
50.46	Jakub	Smolinski	POL	21.7.92				22 Jul
50.47	Yeison	Rivas	COL	24.9.87				23 Nov
50.49	Ken	Kamiya	JPN	.95				15 Jul
50.50		Xu Zhihang	CHN	18.2.97				4 Sep
50.52	Andrés	Silva	URU	27.3.86				9 Apr
50.52	Josef	Robertson	JAM	14.5.87				15 Apr
50.53	Hidekazu	Kobayashi	JPN	17.4.95				16 Jul
50.53	Tim	Rummens	BEL	16.12.87				19 Aug
50.53	Tomoya	Shima	JPN	.96				30 Sep
50.53	Emerson	Chalá	ECU	2.8.91				23 Nov
50.54A	Korey	Smith	USA	27.9.93				12 May
50.55	Andrew	Neal	USA	19.10.94				28 Apr
50.57	Michael	Cochrane	NZL	13.8.91				24 Feb
50.57	Max	Scheible	GER	16.2.93				9 Jul
50.58A	Scott	Mecham	USA	31.3.94				12 May
50.58	Jan	Tesar	CZE	26.3.90				30 May
50.58	Danylo	Danylenko	UKR	10.10.94				7 Jun
50.59	Austin	Corley	USA	10.10.96				14 May
50.59	Amere	Lattin	USA	17.2.97				26 May
50.59	Mickaël	François	FRA	12.3.88				3 Jun
50.59	Kalmon	Stokes	USA	2.12.93				23 Jul
50.60	Robert	Brylinski	POL	2.4.91				4 Jun
50.61	Boniface	Mucheru Tumuti	KEN	2.5.92				5 May
	(200)							

Hand timing

Mark	Name		Nat	Born	Date
50.1A	Kiprono	Kosgei	KEN	.85	18May

Low altitude bests

Mark	Name	Pos	Meet	Venue	Date
49.32	Fredericks	5	Athl	Lausanne	6 Jul
49.35	van Zyl	2	DL	Shanghai	13 May
49.58	Boully	1	TexR	Austin	31 Mar
49.69	Pretorius	3s2	WUG	Taipei	25 Aug
49.70	Hamman	2		La-Chaux-de-Fonds	2 Jul

50.04 Ujakpor 14 Jul   50.28 Mosimanegape 29 Apr

JUNIORS

See main list for top 4 juniors. 10 performances by 5 men to 49.93. Additional marks and further juniors:

Name	Mark	Pos	Meet	Venue	Date	Mark	Pos	Meet	Venue	Date
Hall	49.39	1		Tempe	8 Apr	49.51	1	NC-j	Sacramento	24 Jun
Feng	49.70A	1		Guiyang	26 Jun					
Shoaib	49.85A	1		Potchefstroom	4 Apr	49.93A	2		Sasolburg	28 Mar

Mark	Name		Nat	Born	Pos	Meet	Venue	Date
49.93	Wilfried	Happio	FRA	22.4.98	1	EJ	Grosseto	23 Jul
49.96	Fernando	Vega	MEX	19.2.98	2	PAm-J	Trujillo	23 Jul
50.12	Thomas	Burns	USA	8.12.99	2h1	NC-j	Sacramento	23 Jun
50.16	T. Santhosh	Kumar	IND	1.1.98	1	NC	Chennai	27 Sep
50.19	Sergio	Esquivel	MEX	4.5.99	4	PAm-J	Trujillo	23 Jul
50.32	Jaelen	Williams (10)	USA	7.7.98	1q2	NCAA-E	Lexington	26 May
50.32	Masaki	Toyota	JPN	17.1.98	3s2		Hiratsuka	10 Jun
50.34	Alessandro	Sibilio	ITA	27.4.99	2	EJ	Grosseto	23 Jul
50.35	Maksims	Sincukovs	LAT	26.6.98	1		Lappeenranta	26 Aug
50.36	Yusuke	Shirao	JPN	7.9.99	1	NC	Chiba	17 Jun
50.37	Daichi	Inoue	JPN	27.4.99	1		Tokyo	14 May
50.41	David José	Pineda	ESP	18.3.98	3	EJ	Grosseto	23 Jul
50.45	Riki	Ohara	JPN	.98	2h3		Osaka	12 May
50.70	Charles	Brockman	USA	31.8.99	4	NC-j	Sacramento	24 Jun
50.74	Jauavney	James	JAM	21.12.98	5	PAm-J	Trujillo	23 Jul
50.75	Rasheeme	Griffith (20)	BAR		1		Bridgetown	31 Mar

HIGH JUMP

Mark	Pos	Meet	Venue	Date	Series
2.40	Mutaz Essa Barshim	QAT 24.6.91	1 DL Birmingham	20 Aug	2.20/1 2.24/1 2.28/1 2.31/3 2.34/1 2.39/xx 2.40/1
2.40	1		Eberstadt	27 Aug	2.24/1 2.30/2 2.33/1 2.36/1 2.38/1 2.40/3 2.42/xx 2.44/x
2.38	1	Bisl	Oslo	15 Jun	2.20/1 2.25/1 2.29/1 2.32/1 2.35/3 2.38/2
2.37	1		Opole	4 Jun	2.16/1 2.20/1 2.24/1 2.30/1 2.35/1 2.37/2 2.41/xxx
2.36	1	DL	Doha	5 May	2.19/1 2.23/1 2.26/1 2.29/1 2.31/1 2.33/1 2.35/x 2.36/1
2.36	1	WK-DLF	Zürich	24 Aug	2.16/1 2.20/1 2.24/1 2.28/1 2.31/1 2.33/2 2.36/3
2.35	1	Gulf	Jeddah	15 Apr	
2.35	1	DL	Paris (C)	1 Jul	2.24/1 2.28/1 2.32/2 2.35/1 2.39/xx
2.35	1	WCh	London (OS)	13 Aug	2.22/1 2.25/1 2.29/1 2.32/1 2.35/1 2.40/xxx
2.33	1	DL	Shanghai	13 May	2.24/1 2.27/1 2.33/1 2.37/xxx
2.38	Danil Lysenko	RUS 19.5.97	2 Eberstadt	27 Aug	2.10/1 2.20/1 2.24/1 2.27/1 2.30/1 2.33/1 2.36/2 2.38/1 2.40/xxx
2.34	1	NC-23	Saransk	22 Jun	2.07/1 2.15/1 2.21/1 2.26/1 2.30/1 2.34/3
2.33i	1	Winter	Moskva	5 Feb	2.15/1 2.20/1 2.24/1 2.28/2 2.31/1 2.33/1 2.36/xxx
2.32i	1		Moskva	31 Jan	2.15/1 2.20/1 2.24/1 2.28/1 2.32/2
2.32	1	NC	Zhukovskiy	29 Jul	2.19/1 2.23/1 2.26/2 2.28/1 2.32/1 2.35/xxx
2.32	2	WCh	London (OS)	13 Aug	2.20/1 2.25/1 2.29/2 2.32/1 2.35/xxx
2.35	Mateusz Przybylko	GER 9.3.92	1 Bottrop	25 Jun	2.15/1 2.20/1 2.30/3 2.32/1 2.35/2

Mark		Name		Nat	Born	Pos	Meet	Venue	Date
2.33i		Sylwester	Bednarek	POL	28.4.89	1=		Banská Bystrica	8 Feb
				2.15/1 2.20/1 2.25/1 2.28/1 2.31/2 2.33/2 2.35/xxx					
	2.32i	1 EI	Beograd 5 Mar	2.18/1 2.23/1 2.27/3 2.30/2 2.32/1 2.34/xx 2.35/x					
	2.32	1 GS	Ostrava 28 Jun	2.15/1 2.20/1 2.24/1 2.27/3 2.30/1 2.32/1 2.34/xxx					
2.33i		Derek	Drouin	CAN	6.3.90	1=		Banská Bystrica	8 Feb
				2.15/2 2.20/1 2.25/1 2.28/1 2.31/1 2.33/2 2.35/xxx					
2.33		Maksim	Nedosekov	BLR-J	21.1.98	1	EJ	Grosseto	22 Jul
			2.05/1 2.10/12.14/1	2.17/1 2.20/1 2.22/1 2.24/1 2.26/1 2.28/x 2.30/2 2.33/3 2.35/x					
2.32i		Pavel	Seliverstov	BLR	2.9.96	1		Trinec	11 Feb
				2.21/1 2.27/1 2.30/3 2.32/1 2.34/xxx					
2.32i		Ivan	Ukhov	RUS	29.3.86	1	NC	Moskva	20 Feb
				2.15/1 2.24/1 2.30/1 2.32/2 2.36/x					
	2.32	1	Yerino 10 Jun	2.15/2 2.23/2 2.32/2 2.36/xxx					
2.32		Bohdan	Bondarenko	UKR	30.8.89	2	DL	Paris (C)	1 Jul
				2.20/1 2.28/1 2.32/1 2.35/xxx					
2.32		Majed El Dein	Ghazal	SYR	21.4.87	3	DL	Paris (C)	1 Jul
		(27/10)		2.20/1 2.24/2 2.28/1 2.32/2 2.35/xxx					
2.31i		Ilya	Ivanyuk	RUS	9.3.93	3	Winter	Moskva	5 Feb
2.31i		Donald	Thomas	BAH	1.7.84	4		Banská Bystrica	8 Feb
2.31i		Eric	Kynard	USA	3.2.91	1		Birmingham	18 Feb
2.31		Robbie	Grabarz	GBR	3.10.87	2	DL	Doha	5 May
2.31			Zhang Guowei	CHN	4.6.91	1	NC	Jinan	16 May
2.31		Eure	Yáñez	VEN	20.5.93	1	SAmC	Asunción	23 Jun
2.31		Tihomir	Ivanov	BUL	11.7.94	4=q	WCh	London (OS)	11 Aug
2.30i		Edgar	Rivera	MEX	13.2.91	2		Hustopece	4 Feb
2.30i		Jacorian	Duffield	USA	2.9.92	1	Tyson	Fayetteville	11 Feb
2.30i		Nikita	Anishchenkov	RUS	25.7.92	3	NC	Moskva	20 Feb
		(20)							
2.30		Talles	Silva	BRA	20.8.91	1		São Bernardo do Campo	12 Mar
2.30		Michael	Mason	CAN	30.9.86	1	MSR	Torrance	15 Apr
2.30		Takashi	Eto	JPN	5.2.91	1		Ise	16 Apr
2.30		Nauraj Singh	Randhawa	MAS	27.1.92	1		Singapore	27 Apr
2.30			Wang Yu	CHN	18.8.91	2	DL	Shanghai	13 May
2.30		Eike	Onnen	GER	3.8.82	1		Hannover	14 May
2.30			Woo Sang-hyuk	KOR	23.4.96	1	NC	Kimchun	4 Jun
2.30		Jeron	Robinson	USA	30.4.91	1		Houston	8 Jun
2.30		Ricky	Robertson	USA	19.9.90	1		Chula Vista	17 Jun
2.30		Bryan	McBride	USA	10.12.91	1	NC-23	Sacramento	25 Jun
		(30)							
2.30		Fernando	Ferreira	BRA	13.12.94	1		São Bernardo do Campo	1 Jul
2.30		Andriy	Protsenko	UKR	20.5.88	2	Gyulai	Székesfehérvár	4 Jul
2.30		Tom	Gale	GBR-J	18.12.98	1	CAU	Bedford	29 Jul
2.30		Yuriy	Krymarenko	UKR	11.8.83	1		Volodymyr-Volynskyi	30 Jul
2.29		Gianmarco	Tamberi	ITA	1.6.92	13q	WCh	London (OS)	11 Aug
2.29		Falk	Wendrich	GER	12.6.95	1	WUG	Taipei	25 Aug
2.29		Marco	Fassinotti	ITA	29.4.89	2	WUG	Taipei	25 Aug
2.28i		Dmitriy	Semyonov	RUS	2.8.92	4	Winter	Moskva	5 Feb
2.28i		Lukás	Beer	SVK	23.8.89	2		Banská Bystrica	8 Feb
2.28i			Sun Zhao	CHN	8.2.90	1		Xianlin	23 Feb
		(40)							
2.28i		Silvano	Chesani	ITA	17.7.88	Q	EI	Beograd	4 Mar
2.28i		Matús	Bubeník	SVK	14.11.89	Q	EI	Beograd	4 Mar
2.28			Guo Jinqi	CHN	21.9.92	1		Huaian	3 Apr
2.28		Tequan	Claitt	USA	18.7.97	1		Bowling Green	8 Apr
2.28	7'6"	Vernon	Turner	USA-J	21.8.98	1		Yukon, OK	14 Apr
2.28		Dmitriy	Nabokov	BLR	20.1.96	1		Brest	31 May
2.28		Viktor	Lonskyy	UKR	27.10.95	1	NC	Kropyvnitskiy	8 Jul
2.28		Chris	Baker	GBR	2.2.91	1		Cork	18 Jul
2.28		Luis Joel	Castro	PUR	28.1.91	1		Köln	19 Jul
2.28		Vasilios	Constantinou	CYP	13.9.92	1		Kavála	22 Jul
		(50)							
2.28		Dmytro	Niktiin	UKR-J	31.7.99	2	EJ	Grosseto	22 Jul
2.27i		Jamal	Wilson	BAH	1.9.88	3		Trinec	11 Feb
2.27i		Randall	Cunningham	USA	4.1.96	1		Seattle	25 Feb
2.27		Django	Lovett	CAN	6.7.92	2	MSR	Torrance	15 Apr
2.27			Wang Chen	CHN	27.2.90	2	NG	Tianjin	4 Sep
2.26i		Janick	Klausen	DEN	3.4.93	1		Köln	25 Jan
2.26Ai		Bradley	Adkins	USA	30.12.93	1		Albuquerque	3 Feb
2.26i		Chris	Kandu	GBR	10.9.95	3		Hustopece	4 Feb
2.26i		Naoto	Tobe	JPN	31.3.92	4		Karlsruhe	4 Feb
2.26i		Konstadínos	Baniótis	GRE	6.11.86	4=		Hustopece	4 Feb
		(60)							

Mark	Name		Nat	Born	Pos	Meet	Venue	Date
2.26i	Allan	Smith	GBR	6.11.92	4=		Hustopece	4 Feb
2.26i	Martin	Heindl	CZE	2.6.92	1	NC	Praha (Strom)	25 Feb
2.26i	Trey	Culver	USA	18.7.96	1	NCAA	College Station	11 Mar
2.26i	Kyle	Landon	USA	16.10.94	2	NCAA	College Station	11 Mar
2.26	Hamdi Mahamat	Alamine	QAT	15.4.97	2	Isl.Sol	Baku	19 May
2.26	Norbert	Kobielski	POL	28.1.97	1		Bialystok	18 Jun
2.26	Aleksandr	Asanov	RUS	30.3.96	2	NC-23	Saransk	22 Jun
2.26	Mickaël	Hanany	FRA	25.3.83	1	ET	Villeneuve d'Ascq	24 Jun
2.26	Dmytro	Demyanyuk	UKR	30.6.83	2	NC	Kropyvnitskiy	8 Jul
2.26	Loïc	Gasch	SUI	13.8.94	1	NC	Zürich	22 Jul
	(70)							
2.26		Hsiang Chun-Hsien	TPE	4.9.93	3	WUG	Taipei	25 Aug
2.26i	Keyvan	Ghanbarzadeh	IRI	26.5.90	2	AsiC	Ashgabat	20 Sep
2.25i	Clayton	Brown	JAM	8.12.96	1		Clemson	7 Jan
2.25i	Aleksey	Dmitrik	RUS	12.4.84	2		Chelyabinsk	11 Jan
2.25i	Ailex	Austin	USA	25.11.93	2		Boston	28 Jan
2.25i	Christian	Falocchi	ITA	30.1.97	1	NC-23	Ancona	4 Feb
2.25i	Miguel Ángel	Sancho	ESP	24.4.90	1		Sabadell	5 Feb
2.25i	Fabian	Delryd	SWE	15.10.96	1	v3N	Tampere	11 Feb
2.25i	Raivydas	Stanys	LTU	3.2.87	1		Vilnius	23 Feb
2.25	Manjula Kumara	Wijesekara	SRI	30.1.84	1		Diyagama	8 Apr
	(80)							
2.25A	Chris	Moleya	RSA	27.1.97	1	NC	Potchefstroom	22 Apr
2.25	Tye	Williams	USA	17.8.96	1	PennR	Philadelphia	29 Apr
2.25	Keenon	Laine	USA	12.6.97	1	SEC	Columbia, SC	12 May
2.25	Brandon	Starc	AUS	24.11.93	6=		Kawasaki	21 May
2.25A	Roberto	Vilches	MEX-J	21.5.99	1		Ciudad de México	4 Jun
2.25A	Matthew	Sawe	KEN	2.7.88	1	NC	Nairobi	10 Jun
2.25	Wojciech	Theiner	POL	25.6.86	1	Kuso	Szczecin	10 Jun
2.25	Tobias	Potye	GER	16.3.95	2		Regensburg	11 Jun
2.25	Avion	Jones	USA	31.1.94	1		Charlotte	16 Jun
2.25	Eugenio	Rossi	SMR	6.3.92	1		Nembro	7 Jul
	(90)							
2.25	Breyton	Poole	RSA-Y	23.3.00	1		Cape Town	4 Nov
2.24i	Arseniy	Rasov	RUS	20.6.92	3		Yekaterinburg	7 Jan
2.24i	Dakarai	Hightower	USA	15.7.94	1		Crete, NE	7 Jan
2.24i	Yevgeniy	Korshunov	RUS	11.4.86	5		Volgograd	28 Jan
2.24Ai	Deante	Kemper	USA	27.3.93	1		Flagstaff	4 Feb
2.24i	Christoffe	Bryan	JAM	26.4.96	1	Big 12	Ames	25 Feb
2.24		Lee Hup Wei	MAS	5.5.87	1	AUS Ch	Sydney	1 Apr
2.24		Zhu Gezhen	CHN	14.4.93	3		Zhengzhou	11 Apr
2.24	David	Smith	PUR	2.5.92	1		Atlanta	28 May
2.24	Kris	Kornegay-Gober	USA	6.10.91	5	NC	Sacramento	25 Jun
	(100)							
2.24	Dan	Lazarica	ROU	11.5.92	1	NC	Pitesti	7 Jul
2.24		Cheng Kaiwei	CHN	22.9.95	1		Ordos	19 Jul
2.24		Pai Long	CHN	8.10.89	5	NG	Tianjin	4 Sep
2.24		Yoon Seung-hyun	KOR	1.6.94	1	NSF	Chongju	25 Oct
2.24i	Brenton	Foster	AUS-J	26.2.98	1		Riverdale	2 Dec
2.24	Joel	Baden	AUS	1.2.96	1		Melbourne (Williamstown)	10 Dec

Mark	Name		Nat	Born	Date
2.23i	Lukas	Mihota	GER-J	30.3.99	7 Jan
2.23i	Marius	Dumitrache	ROU	15.6.89	11 Feb
2.23	Mike	Edwards	GBR	11.7.90	25 Mar
2.23	Shelby	McEwen	USA	6.4.96	8 Apr
2.23	Jordan	Wesner	USA	10.6.97	29 Apr
2.23A	Zack	Blackham	USA	10.8.92	29 Apr
2.23	Donte	Nall	USA	27.1.88	17 Jun
2.23	Jakobe	Ford	USA-J	4.9.98	18 Jun
2.23	Mikhail	Veryovkin	RUS	28.6.91	11 Jul
2.23	Tejaswin	Shankar	IND-J	21.12.98	17 Jul
2.23	Adrijus	Glebauskas	LTU	20.11.94	25 Aug
2.23	Dmitriy	Kroyter	ISR	18.2.93	25 Aug
2.23	Mpho	Links	RSA	20.6.96	25 Aug
2.23	Siddarth	Yadav	IND	30.1.93	27 Sep
2.23	Vincent	Bharathi	IND	20.5.94	27 Sep
2.22i	Sergey	Mudrov	RUS	8.9.90	11 Jan
2.22i	Darius	Carbin	USA-J	4.3.98	27 Jan
2.22i	Ken	LeGassey	USA	20.5.94	17 Feb
2.22i	Abdoulaye	Diarra	MLI	27.5.88	19 Feb
2.22i	Andriy	Kovalyov	UKR	11.6.92	19 Feb
2.22i	Mikel	Smith	USA	2.10.93	10 Mar
2.22	Joseph	Baldwin	AUS-J	23.1.98	28 Mar
2.22	Jermaine	Francis	SKN-J	9.3.98	17 Apr
2.22	Ed'Ricus	Williams	USA	6.7.94	28 Apr
2.22	Maciej	Grynienko	POL-J	30.3.98	13 May
2.22	Ryoichi	Akamatsu	JPN	2.5.95	14 May
2.22	Matthew	Roberts	GBR	22.12.84	21 May
2.22	Matthieu	Tomassi	FRA	21.3.95	28 May
2.22	Tzur	Lieberman	ISR	26.1.94	4 Jul
2.22	Alperen	Acet	TUR-J	2.4.98	22 Jul
2.21Ai	Justice	Summerset	USA-J	20.1.98	13 Jan
2.21i	Metin	Dogu	TUR	19.1.97	21 Jan
2.21i	David	Smith	GBR	14.7.91	28 Jan
2.21i	Michael	Burke	USA	23.1.97	28 Jan
2.21i	Dmytro	Yakovenko	UKR	17.9.92	11 Feb
2.21i	Julian	Harvey	USA	17.6.95	24 Feb
2.21i	Oleksandr	Barannikov	UKR	23.1.97	4 Mar
2.21	Trey	McRae	USA	12.7.93	15 Apr
2.21	Guilherme	Cobbo	BRA	1.10.87	30 Apr
2.21	Paulo	Conceição	POR	29.12.93	1 May
2.21	Nicolas	De Luca	ITA	7.4.93	28 May
2.21	Vadym	Kravchuk	UKR	28.10.96	7 Jun
2.21	Gaël	Rotardier	FRA	5.9.94	10 Jun
2.21	Naoto	Hasegawa	JPN	15.11.96	11 Jun
2.21	Eugenio	Meloni	ITA	28.8.94	2 Jul
2.21	Yutaka	Takayama	JPN	8.9.91	15 Jul
2.21	Sarvesh Anil	Kushare	IND	17.6.95	27 Sep
2.21i	Jyles	Etienne	BAH-J	17.3.99	8 Dec

Mark	Name		Nat	Born	Pos	Meet	Venue	Date
2.21i	Semyen	Pozdnyakov (155)	RUS	28.11.92	23	Dec.		

2.20 by 58 men:

i Aleksandr Mrykhin RUS	4.9.96	James Harris USA	18.9.91	Kazuhiro Ota JPN	11.6.95
i Yegor Smolinov RUS	25.6.97	Eric Richards USA-J	1.8.98	Dimón Siverio ESP	2.8.88
i Alhaji Mansaray CAN	27.4.94	Isaiah Holmes USA-J	18.10.98	Jaroslav Bába CZE	2.9.84
i Igor Kopala POL	4.8.97	Michael McCann USA	27.3.95	Mihai Anastasiu ROU	11.3.93
i Benjamin Kirkwood USA	30.12.91	Thiago Julio Alfano Moura BRA	27.11.95	Balasubramanya Chethan IND	18.8.92
i Charles Brown USA	28.5.97	A Keegan Fourie RSA	7.9.91	Adónios Mérlos GRE-J	4.4.99
Alen Melon CRO	25.10.91	Vincent Calhoun USA	25.5.96	Ryad Selloum ALG	12.2.92
i Darryl Sullivan USA	28.12.97	Yuriy Dergachev KAZ	8.11.94	Yu Nakazawa JPN	27.8.96
Luis Joel Zayas CUB	7.6.97	Mohammad R Vazifehdoost IRI	13.10.93	Douwe Amels NED	16.9.91
Jean Carlos Ramírez CUB	2.1.96	Daisuke Nakajima JPN	18.4.95	Péter Bakosi HUN	23.6.93
i Matthew Campbell JAM	20.10.96	Dionte Heath USA	16.5.95	Sean Cate CAN	6.5.94
Roman Loshkaryev KAZ	28.10.96	Luca Wieland GER	7.12.94	Keitaro Fujita JPN	2.10.97
i Chen Ji CHN	27.1.90	Landon Bartel USA	17.2.96	Carlos Layoy ARG	26.2.91
i Janis Vanags LTU	16.6.92	Juozas Baikstys LTU-J	18.3.98	Thomas Carmoy BEL-Y	16.2.00
Yang Lubang CHN	18.6.97	Kabelo Mmono Kgosiemang BOT	7.1.86	Huang Longkang CHN	5.7.95
i Gao Woqi CHN	12.3.95	Andrey Skobeyko BLR	11.6.95	Qiao Yuefeng CHN	26.12.92
i Jin Jiazheng CHN	13.5.97	Nicholas Nava ITA-J	25.5.98	Yu Shisuo CHN	20.2.90
John Dodds AUS-J	24.2.99	Torsten Sanders GER	8.9.94	i Jerin Allen USA	20.11.95
Taira Omata JPN	12.9.89	Arturo Joaquín Abascal MEX	19.6.95	i Javen Reeves USA	4.12.95

Best outdoor marks

2.30	Kynard	1		New York	6 Jul	2.26	Tobe	4	Gyulai	Székesfehérvár	4 Jul
2.30	Ivanyuk	2	NCp	Yerino	15 Jul	2.25	Kandu	1	NC-23	Bedford	17 Jun
2.29	Thomas	3	DL	Doha	5 May	2.24	Culver	1	TexR	Austin	1 Apr
2.29	Rivera	4	WCh	London (OS)	13 Aug	2.24	Ghanbarzadeh	2		Jinhua	24 Apr
2.28	Drouin	1D		Santa Barbara	7 Apr	2.24	Kemper	1		Mesa	10 Jun
2.28	Seliverstov	2		Opole	4 Jun	2.24	A Smith	3		Genève	10 Jun
2.27	Sun Zhao	1		Taipei	30 Apr	2.24	Anishchenkov	1		Chelyabinsk	7 Jul
2.27	Wilson	3=	GS	Ostrava	28 Jun	2.24	Falocchi	2	EC-23	Bydgoszcz	15 Jul

2.23	Dmitrik	26 May	2.21	C Brown	31 Mar	2.21	Kovalyov	17 Jun	2.20	Etiennne	Diarra
2.23	Bubeník	2 Jul	2.21	Cunningham	1 Apr	2.21	Duffield	25 Jun	2.20	Klausen	Rasov
2.22	Adkins	6 May	2.21	Sancho	4 Jun	2.21	Landon	25 Jun	**Low altitude bests**		
2.22	Baniótis	24 Jun	2.21	Bryan	9 Jun	2.21	Yakovenko	30 Jul	2.21	Vilches	23 Jul
2.22	Delryd	15 Jul	2.21	D Smith	10 Jun	2.20	Burke	1 Apr	2.20	Fourie	4 Nov

Drugs disqualification: 2.22i Demar Robinson ¶JAM 13.8.93 (1) Lexington 14 Jan

JUNIORS

See main list for top 7 juniors. 10 performances by 6 men to 2.25. Additional marks and further juniors:

Nedosekov	2.26	1	NC	Grodno	6 Jul	2.25	1	Andújar	2 Jun
Gale	2.28	3	EJ	Grosseto	22 Jul				
Turner	2.26	1		Claremore	24 Mar				

2.23i	Lukas	Mihota	GER-J	30.3.99	1		Essing	7 Jan
2.23	Jakobe	Ford	USA-J	4.9.98	1		Spokane	18 Jun
2.23	Tejaswin	Shankar (10)	IND-J	21.12.98	1		Mangalagiri	17 Jul
2.22i	Darius	Carbin	USA-J	4.3.98	1		Fayetteville	27 Jan
2.22	Joseph	Baldwin	AUS-J	23.1.98	1	NC-j	Sydney	28 Mar
2.22	Jermaine	Francis	SKN-J	9.3.98	1	Carifta	Willemstad	17 Apr
2.22	Maciej	Grynienko	POL-J	30.3.98	1		Wroclaw	13 May
2.22	Alperen	Acet	TUR-J	2.4.98	4	EJ	Grosseto	22 Jul
2.21Ai	Justice	Summerset	USA-J	20.1.98	1		Flagstaff	13 Jan
2.21i	Jyles	Etienne	BAH-J	17.3.99	1		Bloomington	8 Dec
	2.20				1		Huntington Station	6 May
2.20	John	Dodds	AUS-J	24.2.99	1		Brisbane	11 Mar
2.20	Eric	Richards	USA-J	1.8.98	1		Clinton, MS	31 Mar
2.20	Isaiah	Holmes (20)	USA-J	18.10.98	1		Los Angeles	1 Apr
2.20	Juozas	Baikstys	LTU-J	18.3.98	1		Kaunas	19 May
2.20	Nicholas	Nava	ITA-J	25.5.98	1	NC-j	Firenze	11 Jun
2.20	Adónios	Mérlos	GRE-J	4.4.99	1		Kateríni	9 Jul
2.20	Thomas	Carmoy	BEL-Y	16.2.00	1	NC-y	Bertrix	27 Aug

POLE VAULT

6.00i	Piotr	Lisek	POL	16.8.92	1		Potsdam	4 Feb

5.43/1 5.63/1 5.73/2 5.83/2 5.93/2 6.00/2

5.92i	1		Cottbus	25 Jan	5.40/1 5.60/1 5.68/2 5.78/1 5.83/1 5.92/2 6.00/xxx
5.89	2	WCh	London (OS)	8 Aug	5.50/1 5.65/3 5.75/1 5.82/x 5.89/1 5.95/xxx
5.87i	1		Lódz	16 Feb	5.50/2 565/1 5.78/3 5.87/3 5.94/xxx
5.86i	1	ISTAF	Berlin	10 Feb	5.50/1 5.60/1 5.70/1 5.86/2 6.05/xxx
5.85i	1	EI	Beograd	3 Mar	5.35/1 5.50/1 5.60/1 5.71/2 5.81/1 5.86/x 5.91/xx
5.85	1	NC	Bialystok	23 Jul	5.20/1 5.40/1 5.50/1 5.60/1 5.70/1 5.85/2
5.83i	1	NC	Toru_	19 Feb	5.30/1 5.50/1 5.66/2 5.78/1 5.83/1 5.90/xxx
5.82	1	Herc	Monaco	21 Jul	5.42/2 5.60/1 5.72/2 5.82/1 5.87/xxx

6.00	Sam	Kendricks	USA	7.9.92	1	NC	Sacramento	24 Jun

5.40/1 5.50/1 5.60/1 5.65/1 5.70/1 5.75/1 5.80/1 5.91/1 6.00/2

Mark		Name	Nat	Born	Pos	Meet	Venue	Date
	5.95	1 WCh London (OS) 8 Aug	5.50/1 5.65/1 5.75/1 5.82/1 5.89/1 5.95/3 6.01/x					
	5.93	1 Athl Lausanne 6 Jul	5.38/1 5.53/1 5.63/2 5.73/2 5.81/1 5.87/1 5.93/2 6.03/xxx					
	5.88	1 DL Shanghai 13 May	5.25/1 5.40/1 5.50/2 5.60/1 5.70/3 5.78/1 5.83/x 5.88/2 5.93/xx					
	5.87	1 WK-DLF Zürich 24 Aug	5.48/1 5.63/1 5.73/1 5.80/3 5.87/1 5.94/x					
	5.86	1 Pre Eugene 27 May	5.41/1 5.56/1 5.71/2 5.81/1 5.86/1 5.91/xxx					
	5.86	1 ISTAF Berlin 27 Aug	5.36/1 5.51/1 5.61/1 5.71/x 5.81/2 5.86/1 5.91/x					
	5.85Ai	1 NC Albuquerque 4 Mar	5.30/1 5.45/1 5.55/1 5.60/ 2 5.65/1 5.70/1 5.81/1 5.85/1					
	5.82	1 DL Paris (C) 1 Jul	5.37/1 5.52/1 5.62/1 5.72/1 5.77/3 5.82/2					
5.93	Pawel	Wojciechowski	POL	6.6.89	2	Athl	Lausanne	6 Jul
			5.53/1 5.63/1 5.73/1 5.81/3 5.87/2 5.93/3 6.03/xxx					
	5.85i	3 EI Beograd 3 Mar	5.35/1 5.50/1 5.60/1 5.70/2 5.85/3 5.90/xxx					
	5.85	1 DL Rabat 16 Jul	5.40/2 5.60/2 5.70/1 5.85/3					
5.91	Renaud	Lavillenie	FRA	18.9.86	1	Skol	Warszawa	15 Aug
			5.61/3 5.71/2 5.81/1 5.91/2 6.01/xxx					
	5.89	3 WCh London (OS) 8 Aug	5.65/1 5.75/1 5.82/x 5.89/2 5.95/xx 6.01/x					
	5.87	3 Athl Lausanne 6 Jul	5.63/1 5.81/3 5.87/2 5.93/xxx					
	5.83	2 DL Shanghai 13 May	5.40/1 5.60/1 5.70/2 5.78/x 5.83/1 5.88/xx 5.93/x					
5.90	Armand	Duplantis	SWE-J	10.11.99	1	TexR	Austin	1 Apr
			5.35/1 5.50/1 5.65/1 5.80/2 5.90/3					
	5.82i	1 New York (A) 11 Mar	5.31/1 5.55/1 5.71/1 5.82/3 5.86/x					
5.86i	Thiago	Braz da Silva	BRA	16.12.93	1		Rouen	28 Jan
			5.50/1 5.70/2 5.78/1 5.86/2 5.94/xxx					
5.85i	Konstadinos	Filippídis	GRE	26.11.86	2	EI	Beograd	3 Mar
			5.35/2 5.50/1 5.60/1 5.70/1 5.75/x 5.80/2 5.85/1 5.90/xxx					
5.85	Menno	Vloon	NED	11.5.94	1		Zweibrücken	10 Jun
			5.35/1 5.50/1 5.60/2 5.70/2 5.85/1 5.91/xxx					
5.83i	Shawnacy	Barber	CAN	27.5.94	1		Clermont-Ferrand	5 Feb
			5.46/2 5.61/1 5.71/3 5.78/1 5.83/1 5.88/xxx					
5.83	Kévin	Menaldo (10)	FRA	12.7.92	1		Forbach	28 May
			5.35/2 5.55/1 5.70/3 5.83/3 5.91/xx					
5.82		Xue Changrui	CHN	31.5.91	4	WCh	London (OS)	8 Aug
	(33/11)		5.50/1 5.65/1 5.75/1 5.82/1 xxx					
5.80i	Timur	Morgunov	RUS	12.10.96	1		Chelyabinsk	11 Jan
5.80i	Jan	Kudlicka	CZE	29.4.88	4	EI	Beograd	3 Mar
5.80i	Raphael	Holzdeppe	GER	28.9.89	5	EI	Beograd	3 Mar
5.80i	Axel	Chapelle	FRA	24.4.95	6	EI	Beograd	3 Mar
5.80	Michal	Balner	CZE	12.9.82	1=		Hof	24 Jun
5.78	Scott	Houston	USA	11.6.90	1		Charlotte (street)	21 Jul
5.76i	Ivan	Horvat	CRO	17.8.93	1	Balk C	Beograd	25 Feb
5.75	Logan	Cunningham	USA	30.5.91	1		Chula Vista	17 Jun
5.75	Andrew	Irwin	USA	23.1.93	2	NC	Sacramento	24 Jun
	(20)							
5.75	Chris	Nilsen	USA-J	13.1.98	3	NC	Sacramento	24 Jun
5.73	Kurtis	Marschall	AUS	25.4.97	4=	Athl	Lausanne	6 Jul
5.72	Seito	Yamamoto	JPN	11.3.92	1		Ichihara	15 Jul
5.71	Diogo	Ferreira	POR	30.7.90	1		Lisboa (I)	17 Jun
5.71	Arnaud	Art	BEL	28.1.93	3		Leverkusen	27 Jul
5.70i	Georgiy	Gorokhov	RUS	20.4.93	2		Chelyabinsk	11 Jan
5.70i	Ilya	Mudrov	RUS	17.11.91	1		Moskva	18 Jan
5.70Ai	Victor	Weirich	USA	25.10.87	1		Air Force Academy	21 Jan
5.70i	Dmitry	Zhelyabin	RUS	20.5.90	1=		Sankt Peterburg	14 Feb
5.70i	Emmanouíl	Karalís	GRE-J	20.10.99	2	NC	Piréas	19 Feb
	(30)							
5.70	Torben	Laidig	GER	13.3.94	1	TexR	Austin	1 Apr
5.70	Audie	Wyatt	USA	30.4.96	1		Tempe	8 Apr
5.70	Hiroki	Ogita	JPN	30.12.87	1	Oda	Hiroshima	29 Apr
5.70	Matthew	Ludwig	USA	5.7.96	1		Akron, OH	6 May
5.70		Ding Bangchao	CHN	11.10.96	1	NC	Jinan	18 May
5.70	Vladyslav	Malykhin	UKR-J	15.1.98	1		Zary	27 May
5.70	Valentin	Lavillenie	FRA	16.7.91	2	Odlozil	Praha	5 Jun
5.70		Yao Jie	CHN	21.9.90	1		Pierre-Bénite	9 Jun
5.70	Devin	King	USA	12.3.96	4	NC	Sacramento	24 Jun
5.70	Adrián	Vallés	ESP	16.3.95	1		Landau	28 Jun
	(40)							
5.70	Igor	Bychkov	ESP	7.3.87	1		Liège (NX)	19 Jul
5.66i	Deakin	Volz	USA	12.1.97	1		Blacksburg	18 Feb
5.65i	Rutger	Koppelaar	NED	1.5.93	1		Vught	22 Jan
5.65i	Stanley	Joseph	FRA	24.10.91	2		Praha	21 Feb
5.65Ai	Kyle	Pater	USA	24.12.94	1		Albuquerque	25 Feb
5.65i	Malte	Mohr	GER	24.7.86	3		Zweibrücken	25 Feb
5.65Ai	Chris	Pillow	USA	8.7.93	3	NC	Albuquerque	4 Mar

Mark	Name		Nat	Born	Pos	Meet	Venue	Date
5.65	Sergey	Grigoryev	KAZ	24.6.92	1		Busan	13 May
5.65	Baptiste	Boirie	FRA	26.12.92	2		Pontoise	20 Jun
5.65	Masaki	Ejima	JPN-J	6.3.99	2	AsiC	Bhubaneswar	6 Jul
	(50)							
5.63i		Huang Bokai	CHN	26.9.96	1		Nevers	21 Jan
5.63i	Danyil	Kotov	RUS	14.11.95	1	Winter	Moskva	4 Feb
5.63i	Karsten	Dilla	GER	17.7.89	3		Potsdam	4 Feb
5.61i	Nikandros	Stylianou	CYP	22.8.89	3	Balk C	Beograd	25 Feb
5.61	Ernest John	Obiena	PHI	17.11.95	4		Leverkusen	27 Jul
5.61	Bo Kanda Lita	Baehre	GER-J	29.4.99	6		Leverkusen	27 Jul
5.60i	Florian	Gaul	GER	21.9.91	1		Sindelfingen	21 Jan
5.60i	Jeff	Coover	USA	1.12.87	1		Cedar Falls	27 Jan
5.60i	Ivan	Gertleyn	RUS	25.9.87	2	NC	Moskva	20 Feb
5.60i	Mareks	Arents	LAT	6.8.86	8=	EI	Beograd	3 Mar
	(60)							
5.60	Germán	Chiaraviglio	ARG	16.4.87	1		Santa Fé	25 Mar
5.60	Jake	Albright	USA	22.12.93	5	TexR	Austin	1 Apr
5.60	Hussain Asim	Al-Hizam	KSA-J	4.1.98	2		Tempe	8 Apr
5.60	John	Prader	USA	10.2.91	1		Austin	29 Apr
5.60	Yevgeniy	Lukyanenko	RUS	23.1.85	2		Sochi	25 May
5.60	Hendrik	Gruber	GER	28.9.86	3		Zary	27 May
5.60	Augusto	Dutra de Oliveira	BRA	16.7.90	1		São Bernardo do Campo	3 Jun
5.60	Dimítrios	Patsoukákis	GRE	18.3.87	2	NC	Pátra	17 Jun
5.60	Tray	Oates	USA	14.3.95	8	NC	Sacramento	24 Jun
5.60	Tobias	Scherbarth	GER	17.8.85	3		Landau	28 Jun
	(70)							
5.60	Kota	Suzuki	JPN	18.12.95	1		Tsukuba	16 Jul
5.60	Ben	Broeders	BEL	21.6.95	1	EC-23	Bydgoszcz	16 Jul
5.60	Claudio Michel	Stecchi	ITA	23.11.91	2		Liège (NX)	19 Jul
5.57	Chase	Brannon	USA	8.2.91	1		Rock Hill	5 Aug
5.56	Luke	Winder	USA	2.8.95	1		Naperville, IL	17 May
5.56	Rasmus	Jørgensen	DEN	23.1.89	3		Athina	1 Jun
5.55Ai	Mike	Arnold	USA	13.8.90	1		Reno	13 Jan
5.55i	Eirik Greibrokk	Dolve	NOR	5.5.95	1	v3N	Tampere	11 Feb
5.55i	Urho	Kujanpää	FIN	18.5.97	1	NC	Jyväskylä	19 Feb
5.55i	Dominik	Alberto	SUI	28.4.92	5		Zweibrücken	25 Feb
	(80)							
5.55Ai	Max	Babits	USA	30.5.92	6	NC	Albuquerque	4 Mar
5.55	Koki	Kuruma	JPN	25.3.96	1		Yokohama	27 May
5.55	Mathieu	Collet	FRA	15.3.95	2		Pierre-Bénite	9 Jun
5.55	Lukás	Posekany	CZE	30.12.92	2		Kladno	15 Jul
5.55	Aleksandr	Gripich	RUS	21.9.86	3	NC	Zhukovskiy	29 Jul
5.55	Melker	Svärd Jacobsson	SWE	8.1.94	1	vFIN	Stockholm	2 Sep
5.54i	Émile	Denecker	FRA	28.3.92	1eB		Orléans	14 Jan
5.53Ai	Alexandre	Feger	FRA	22.1.90	2		Tignes	6 Jan
5.53i	Alioune	Sène	FRA	3.2.96	3=		Nevers	21 Jan
5.52	Antonio	Ruiz	USA/MEX	4.11.96	1		Houston	5 May
	(90)							
5.52i	Jax	Thoirs	GBR	7.4.93	1		Glasgow	16 Dec
5.51i	Levi	Keller	USA	30.1.86	2		Seatlle	28 Jan
5.51i	Nikólaos	Nerántzis	GRE-J	13.3.98	1	Balk-j	Istanbul	12 Feb
5.51i	Robert	Renner	SLO	8.3.94	4	Balk C	Beograd	25 Feb
5.51	Nate	Richartz	USA	2.11.94	1		Louisville	15 Apr
5.51	Jeff	Rodriguez	USA	3.10.90	1		Abilene	3 May
5.51	Drew	McMichael	USA	25.5.96	2	Big 12	Lawrence	14 May
5.51	Noël	Ost	FRA	15.11.89	1		Bordeaux	1 Jul
5.51	Joel	Leon Benitez	GBR-J	31.8.98	1		Cardiff	12 Jul
5.51	Tomas	Wecksten	FIN	2.11.96	7=		Leverkusen	27 Jul
	(100)							

Mark	Name		Nat	Born	Date
5.50i	Adam	Hague	GBR	29.8.97	8 Jan
5.50i	Anatoliy	Bednyuk	RUS	30.1.89	11 Jan
5.50Ai	Cale	Simmons	USA	5.2.91	21 Jan
5.50i	Jérôme	Clavier	FRA	3.5.83	28 Jan
5.50i	Mateusz	Jerzy	POL	29.3.95	4 Feb
5.50i	Drew	Volz	USA	20.11.92	10 Feb
5.50i	Karol	Pawlik	POL	17.3.94	11 Feb
5.50i	Barrett	Poth	USA	18.4.96	11 Feb
5.50i	Ilya	Prosvirin	RUS	28.2.95	14 Feb
5.50i		Yang Yansheng	CHN	5.1.88	23 Feb
5.50i	Dídac	Salas	ESP	19.5.93	23 Feb
5.50i	Timothy	Ehrhardt	USA	16.3.95	10 Mar
5.50	Garrett	Starkey	USA	7.10.93	8 Apr
5.50		Jin Min-sub	KOR	2.9.92	15 Apr
5.50	Cole	Walsh	USA	14.6.95	15 Apr
5.50	Nikita	Filippov	KAZ	7.10.91	7 Jun
5.50	Luke	Cutts	GBR	13.2.88	10 Jun
5.50	Oleg	Zernikel	GER	16.4.95	18 Jun
5.50	Daichi	Sawano	JPN	16.9.80	23 Jun
5.50		Han Do-hyun	KOR	28.7.94	27 Jun
5.50	Theódorós-Panayiótis	Hrisanthópoulos	GRE	21.6.93	1 Jul
5.50	Fábio	Gomes da Silva	BRA	4.8.83	15 Jul
5.50	Austin	Miller	USA	1.6.94	22 Jul
5.50	Ryo	Tanaka	JPN	10.12.92	2 Sep
5.50		Zhang Wei	CHN	22.3.94	7 Sep
5.50	Angus	Armstrong	AUS	17.3.97	23 Dec
5.49	Nick	Meyer	USA	5.2.95	22 Apr

Mark	Name		Nat	Born	Date
5.47i	Paulo	Benavides	USA	27.7.97	24 Feb
5.47i	Chase	Smith	USA	1.4.97	24 Feb
5.47	Alexandre	Marchand	FRA	23.2.90	7 Jun
5.46i	Damiel	Dossévi	FRA	3.2.83	4 Feb
5.46i	Nick	Maestretti	USA	24.7.93	17 Feb
5.46	Everette	Favor	USA	19.3.94	14May
5.45Ai	Jack	Whitt	USA	12.4.90	13 Jan
5.45Ai	Scott	Marshall	USA	30.6.95	4 Mar
5.45	Leonid	Kivalov	RUS	1.4.88	25May
5.45	Jacob	Wooten	USA	22.4.97	7 Jun
5.45	Sean	Collins	USA	29.8.97	7 Jun
5.45	Charlie	Myers	GBR	12.6.97	10 Jun
5.45	Jules	Cypres	FRA	9.8.97	11 Jun
5.45	Jean	Woloch	FRA	29.3.92	15 Jun
5.45	Alessandro	Sinno	ITA	17.7.94	15 Jun
5.45	Romain	Gavillon	FRA-J	4.11.98	24 Jun
5.45	Robert	Sobera	POL	19.1.91	15 Jul
5.44i	Edi	Maia	POR	10.11.87	11 Feb
5.43i	Max	Eaves	GBR	31.5.88	12 Feb
5.42i	August	Kiles	USA	10.11.95	10 Feb
5.42	Will	Herrscher	USA	23.1.97	28 Apr
5.42	Brandon	Bray	USA	24.4.97	6May
5.42	Bruno	Spinelli	BRA	6.4.97	10May
5.41i	Pascal	Koehl	GER	1.9.91	15 Jan
5.41Ai	Noah	Zorsky	USA	12.10.94	27 Jan
5.41	Nicholas	Homan	USA	24.9.93	15 Apr
5.41	Derick	Hinch	USA	2.2.91	27May
5.41	Deryk	Theodore	CAN	18.8.89	7 Jun
5.41	Sondre	Guttormsen	NOR-J	1.6.99	27 Aug
5.40i	Dmitriy	Lyubushkin	RUS	21.3.94	11 Jan
5.40i	Mikhail	Gelmanov	RUS	18.3.90	11 Jan
5.40i	Harrison	Williams	USA	7.3.96	14 Jan
5.40i	Jacob	Köhler-Baumann	GER	28.11.93	21 Jan
5.40i	Steven	Cahoy	USA	30.7.94	3 Feb
5.40i	Matteo C.	Capello	ITA	22.4.97	5 Feb
5.40i	Niels	Pittomvils	BEL	18.7.92	5 Feb
5.40i	Aaron	Owens	USA	24.9.94	11 Feb
5.40i	Giorgio	Piantella	ITA	6.7.81	18 Feb
5.40i	Niko	Koskinen	FIN	14.7.96	19 Feb
5.40i	Kevin	Mayer	FRA	10.2.92	5 Mar
5.40	Stephen	Clough	AUS	4.11.96	16 Mar
5.40	Pau Gaspar	Tonnesen	ESP	24.10.92	8 Apr
5.40	Shunta	Itsumi	JPN	6.6.94	20May
5.40	Panayiótis	Láskaris	GRE	10.3.92	27May
5.40	Eelco	Sintnicolaas	NED	7.4.87	28May
5.40	Borys	Dzaman	POL	17.9.96	2 Jun
5.40A	K.C.	Lightfoot	USA-J	11.11.99	3 Jun
5.40	Aaron	Unterburger	CAN	12.7.89	3 Jun
5.40	Harry	Coppell	GBR	11.7.96	10 Jun
5.40	Marvin	Caspari	GER	9.8.91	11 Jun
5.40	Thomas	Van Der Plaetsen	BEL	24.12.90	17 Jun
5.40	Mohamed Amin	Romdhana	TUN	27.1.93	18 Jun
5.40	Shota	Doi	JPN	10.4.90	23 Jun
5.40	Shingo	Sawa	JPN	28.9.96	23 Jun
5.40	Albert	Álvarez	ESP	27.4.89	24 Jun
5.40	Lev	Skorish	ISR	12.4.96	5 Jul
5.40	Phatsapong	Umsam-Ang	THA	2.10.97	6 Jul
5.40	Ivan	Yeryomin	UKR	30.5.89	7 Jul
5.40	Nicholas	Southgate	NZL	9.4.94	9 Jul
5.40	Luigi Robert	Colella	ITA	2.4.96	16 Jul
5.40	Tommi	Holttinen	FIN	3.5.97	16 Jul
5.40i	Medhi Amar	Rouana	FRA	30.3.94	9 Dec

(189)

Best outdoor marks

Mark	Name	Pos	Meet	Venue	Date
5.80	Holzdeppe	1=		Hof	24 Jun
5.80	Morgunov	1		Chelyabinsk	7 Jul
5.75	Filippídis	1	NC	Pátra	17 Jun
5.72	Kudlicka	2=	Herc	Monaco	21 Jul
5.72	Chapelle	4	Herc	Monaco	21 Jul
5.72	Barber	6=	Herc	Monaco	21 Jul
5.70	Horvat	1	ET-2	Tel Aviv	25 Jun
5.63	Karalís	2		Athóna	1 Jun
5.61	Dilla	5		Leverkusen	27 Jul
5.60	Koppelaar	1		Leiden	30 Apr
5.60	Braz da Silva	4	DL	Shanghai	13 May
5.60	Gertleyn	2		Zhukovskiy	24 Jun
5.60	Gorokhov	1	Kuts	Moskva	26 Jun
5.60	Kotov	2		Chelyabinsk	7 Jul
5.60	Mudrov	1	NCp	Yerino	14 Jul
5.55	Stylianou	1		Serravalle	1 Jun
5.55	Huang Bokai	3		Pierre-Bénite	9 Jun
5.51	Coover	1		Madison	5 May
5.51	Arents	2		Praha	20 Jun
5.51	Alberto	7=		Leverkusen	27 Jul

Mark	Name	Date
5.50	Hague	7 Feb
5.50	Pater	15 Apr
5.50	Dolve	27 May
5.50	Joseph	10 Jun
5.50	Gaul	10 Jun
5.50	Dennecker	17 Jun
5.50	Renner	20 Jun
5.50	Mohr	24 Jun
5.50	Salas	24 Jun
5.50	Sène	16 Jul
5.50	Deakin Volz	21 Jul
5.46	Nerántzis	1 Jun
5.45	Kujanpää	9 Sep
5.42A	Simmons	5 May
5.41	Poth	15 Apr
5.41	Arnold	27 May
5.41	Feger	1 Jul
5.41	Jerzy	15 Aug
5.40	Weirich	8 Apr
5.40	Maia	1 May
5.40	Benavides	6 May
5.40	Pillow	3 Jun
5.40	Koehl	11 Jun
5.40	Piantella	1 Jul
5.40	Thoirs	2 Jul
5.40	Lyubushkin	7 Jul
5.40	Prosvirin	29 Jul
5.40	Gelmanov	29 Jul

JUNIORS

See main list for top 9 juniors. 20 performances (inc. 6 indoors) by 5 men to 5.65. Additional marks and further juniors:

Name	Mark	Pos	Meet	Venue	Date	Mark	Pos	Meet	Venue	Date
Duplantis 2+	5.75i	1	Mill	New York (A)	11 Feb	5.70i	1		Baton Rouge	18 Feb
	5.73	7	Athl	Lausanne	6 Jul	5.70	2		Jockgrim	12 Jul
	5.72i	1		Baton Rouge	4 Feb	5.70	Q	WCh	London (OS)	6 Aug
	5.71	4	Pre	Eugene	27 May	5.65	1	EJ	Grosseto	23 Jul
Nilsen	5.73	1		Sioux City	21 Apr	5.70	1		Long Beach	13 Apr
	5.70i	1		Fayetteville	11 Feb	5.70	1		Long Beach	15 Apr
	5.70i	1	NCAA	College Station	10 Mar	5.65	1		Tempe	17 Mar

Mark	Name		Nat	Born	Pos	Meet	Venue	Date
5.45	Romain	Gavillon (10)	FRA	4.11.98	2		Moulins	24 Jun
5.41	Sondre	Guttormsen	NOR	1.6.99	1		Meadow Vista	27 Aug
5.40A	K.C.	Lightfoot	USA	11.11.99	1		Albuquerque	3 Jun
5.36i	Riley	Richards	USA	27.5.98	1		College Station	7 Jan
5.36i	Pierre	Cottin	FRA	26.1.98	5		Clermont-Ferrand	4 Feb
5.36	Cole	Riddle	USA	9.4.99	1		Phoenix	11 May
5.35	Sean	Clarke	USA	31.3.98	7q	NCAA-E	Lexington	26 May
5.35	Rashid	Coulibaly	USA	27.12.98	11q	NCAA-W	Austin	26 May
5.35	Eetu	Turakianen	FIN	28.10.98	1		Somero	23 Jun
5.32i	Pål Haugen	Lillefosse	NOR-Y	4.6.01	1		Bergen	9 Dec
	5.31				3		Somero	1 Jul
5.31	Philip	Kass (20)	GER	23.11.98	1		Bremen	20 May
5.31	Robin	Nool	EST	28.10.98	1	NC-j	Rakvere	4 Jul
5.31i	Ethan	Cormont	FRA-Y	29.9.00	1		Nogent-sur-Oise	17 Dec

Symbols/Abbreviations
+ intermediate time in longer race, A made at an altitude of 1000m or higher, D made in a decathlon, h made in a heat, qf quarter-final, sf semi-final, i indoors, Q qualifying round, r race number, -J juniors, -Y youths (b. 2000 or later)

Mark Wind Name Nat Born Pos Meet Venue Date

LONG JUMP

8.65A 1.3 Luvo Manyonga RSA 18.11.91 1 NC Potchefstroom 22 Apr
8.65 p p p p p
8.62A 1.2 1 Pretoria 17 Mar 8.62 8.29/0.3 8.34/1.2 8.34/0.6 p p
8.62 0.8 1 FBK Hengelo 11 Jun 8.60/0.3 x 8.40/0.1 8.46/0.6 x 8.
8.61 0.7 1 DL Shanghai 13 May 8.48/0.2 x 8.49/-0.6 x x 8.61
8.49 -0.7 1 WK-DLF Zürich 24 Aug x 8.31/0.3 x 8.49 p
8.30/-0.2
8.48 0.4 1 WCh London (OS) 5 Aug x 8.48 8.32/1.1 8.29/0.6 8.17 x
8.46A 0.2 1 Bloemfontein 8 Mar 8.37/1.5 8.27/0.0 8.39/0.3 x 8.46 p
8.46A 2.0 1 Tignes 16 Aug x x x x 8.35 8.46
8.33 1.4 * DL Stockholm 18 Jun 8.36w/3.3 8.28w/2.3 2.56 8.33 8.20 8.28/-1.0
8.49A -0.8 Ruswahl Samaai RSA 25.9.91 2 NC Potchefstroom 22 Apr
x 8.05 8.14 8.24 8.01 8.49
8.35 0.2 1 Cape Town 28 Apr 8.21 8.35 x 8.16 x x
8.35 0.4 1 DL Rabat 16 Jul 8.21 8.31/1.1 8.35 p 8.24 8.13
8.34 1.0 2 FBK Hengelo 11 Jun x x 8.08 x 8.34 8.21
8.34 0.5 1 Gyulai Székesfehérvár 4 Jul 8.26 8.26 8.21 p 8.26 8.34
8.32 -0.1 3 WCh London (OS) 5 Aug 8.25 x 8.15 x 8.27/0.1 8.32
8.31 0.0 2 WK-DLF Zürich 24 Aug 8.14 8.23 8.17 8.10 8.31
8.26
8.29 1.3 2 DL Stockholm 18 Jun 8.04 8.29 8.05 7.98 8.11 x
8.44 0.6 Jarrion Lawson USA 6.5.94 2 WCh London (OS) 5 Aug
8.37/0.4 8.43/0.2 8.40/1.2 8.11 8.31/0.5 8.44
8.33 0.7 2 DL Rabat 16 Jul 7.99 8.33 8.00 8.17 x 8.17
8.34 2.0 Tyrone Smith BER 7.8.86 1 Houston 5 May
x 8.01 7.83 8.34 8.03 7.72
8.33 2.0 Maykel Massó CUB-Y 8.5.99 1 Madrid 14 Jul
8.19w 8.33 7.98 x p p
8.32 0.2 Aleksandr Menkov RUS 7.12.90 1 Znam Zhukovskiy 1 Jul
x 7.96 8.14 x 8.05 8.32
8.31 0.8 Shi Yuhao CHN-J 26.9.98 1 Beijing 25 Jun
7.96 8.05 7.94 8.31
8.31A 1.0 Eusebio Cáceres ESP 10.9.91 1 Monachil 7 Jul
8.31 p p p p p
8.31 1.4 Radek Juska CZE 8.3.93 Q WUG Taipei 27 Aug
8.31
8.29 1.3 1 Danek Turnov 23 May 7.70 x 8.29 x 7.80 p
8.30 1.8 Miltiádis Tentóglou GRE-J 18.3.98 1 NC Pátra 18 Jun
6.08w x 7.81w 7.91 8.30 p
8.30A -0.2 Michel Tornéus SWE 26.5.86 2 Monachil 7 Jul
8.12 8.30 p p 8.04 x
8.29 0.7 Damar Forbes JAM 18.9.90 3 FBK Hengelo 11 Jun
7.91 8.08 8.29 8.03 8.13 8.10
8.29A 0.3 Wang Jianan CHN 27.8.96 1 Guiyang 27 Jun
8.03 8.29 p p p p
(30/13)
8.28 2.0 Jeff Henderson USA 19.2.89 5 NC Sacramento 25 Jun
8.28 0.8 Juan Miguel Echevarría CUB-J 11.8.98 2 Madrid 14 Jul
8.28 1.1 Huang Changzhou CHN 20.8.94 1 NG Tianjin 6 Sep
8.22 0.1 Gao Xinglong CHN 12.3.94 2 DL Shanghai 13 May
8.22 1.5 Zarck Visser RSA 15.9.89 1 Bad Langensalza 17 Jun
8.22 0.2 Artyom Primak RUS 14.1.93 1 NC Zhukovskiy 29 Jul
8.21 1.5 Mike Hartfield USA 29.3.90 1 Hamilton 1 Jul
(20)
8.21 1.8 Henry Frayne AUS 14.4.90 1 La Chaux de Fonds 2 Jul
8.20 1.6 Kevin Ojiaku ITA 20.4.89 1 Torino 21 May
8.19 0.8 Emiliano Lasa URU 25.1.90 1 São Paulo 18 Feb
8.19 0.8 Zhang Yaoguang CHN 21.6.93 4 DL Shanghai 13 May
8.19 1.0 Khotso Mokoena RSA 6.3.85 1 Weinheim 27 May
8.18i Serhiy Nykyforov UKR 6.2.94 Q EI Beograd 3 Mar
8.18 0.3 Greg Rutherford GBR 17.11.86 1 Manchester 26 May
8.18 1.7 Tomasz Jaszczuk POL 9.3.92 1 Biala Podlaska 28 May
8.18 1.8 Marquis Dendy USA 17.11.92 * NC Sacramento 25 Jun
8.18 1.5 Aleksandro Melo BRA 26.9.95 1 Maringá 4 Nov
(30)
8.17i Julian Harvey USA 17.6.95 1 Charleston 24 Feb
8.16 0.8 Yahya Berrabah MAR 13.10.81 1 Fès 30 Apr
8.16 0.0 Ramone Bailey JAM 31.10.91 1 NC Kingston 24 Jun
8.15 2.0 Lazar Anic SRB 14.12.91 1 Slovenska Bistrica 27 May

Mark	Wind	Name		Nat	Born	Pos	Meet	Venue	Date
8.15	0.4	Julian	Howard	GER	3.4.89	1		Oberteuringen	4 Jun
8.14	1.6	Charles	Brown	USA	28.5.97	1	TexR	Austin	1 Apr
8.14	1.1	Kirill	Sukharev	RUS	24.5.92	2	NC	Zhukovskiy	29 Jul
8.13	1.3	Jarvis	Gotch	USA	25.3.92	1	MSR	Torrance	15 Apr
8.13	0.0	Ja'Mari	Ward	USA-J	21.7.98	1	SEC	Columbia, SC	12 May
8.12	0.0	Corey	Crawford	USA	12.12.91	1		Mesa	10 Jun
		(40)							
8.11i		Fyodor	Kiselkov	RUS	3.6.95	2	NC	Moskva	21 Feb
8.11	0.6		Li Jinzhe	CHN	1.9.89	3		Beijing	25 Jun
8.11	0.5		Kim Duk-hyun	KOR	8.12.85	1		Goseong	7 Jul
8.10	0.4		Lin Hung-Min	TPE	7.9.90	1		Hiratsuka	10 Jun
8.10A	0.1	Arttu	Pajulahti	FIN	25.9.91	3		Monachil	7 Jul
8.10	1.3	Rail	Kutuyev	RUS	6.8.96	4	NC	Zhukovskiy	29 Jul
8.09	2.0	Hibiki	Tsuha	JPN-J	21.1.98	1		Fukui	9 Sep
8.08i		Jean-Pierre	Bertrand	FRA	5.11.92	1		Tignes	3 Jan
8.08i		Izmir	Smajlaj	ALB	29.3.93	1	EI	Beograd	4 Mar
8.08	1.7	Tiago	da Silva	BRA	23.10.93	1		Castellón	4 Jul
		(50)							
8.07i		Lamont Marcell	Jacobs	ITA	26.9.94	1	NC-23	Ancona	18 Feb
8.07A	-0.6	Kristian	Pulli	FIN	2.9.94	4		Monachil	7 Jul
8.06	1.9	Natsuki	Yamakawa	JPN	24.7.95	2		Fukui	9 Sep
8.05i		Grant	Holloway	USA	19.11.97	1		Blacksburg	21 Jan
8.05i		Filippo	Randazzo	ITA	27.4.96	2	NC	Ancona	18 Feb
8.05	-1.1	KeAndre	Bates	USA	24.5.96	1	NCAA	Eugene	7 Jun
8.05	0.3	Paulo Sérgio	Oliveira	BRA	1.6.93	1		São Bernardo do Campo	17 Jun
8.05	1.4	Yuki	Hashioka	JPN-J	23.1.99	1	NC	Osaka	24 Jun
8.05	1.3	Sergey	Polyanskiy	RUS	29.10.89	*	NC	Zhukovskiy	29 Jul
8.04	1.6	Thobias	Nilsson Montler	SWE	15.2.96	1		Jacksonville	8 Apr
		(60)							
8.04	1.9	Vladyslav	Mazur	UKR	21.11.96	1	EC-23	Bydgoszcz	14 Jul
8.04	0.8	Daiki	Oda	JPN	15.1.96	1		Tokyo	24 Sep
8.03	-0.1	Fabrice	Lapierre	AUS	17.10.83	2		Boston	4 Jun
8.03	-1.0		Chan Ming Tai	HKG	30.1.95	2	AsiC	Bhubaneswar	9 Jul
8.03	1.9	Yasser	Triki	ALG	24.3.97	1	NC	Alger	28 Jul
8.02	0.3		Li Zhipeng	CHN	1.5.95	2		Zhengzhou	12 Apr
8.02	-0.7	Daniel	Bramble	GBR	14.10.90	1	NC	Birmingham	2 Jul
8.02	1.6	Jakub	Andrzejczak	POL-J	13.6.98	2	EJ	Grosseto	21 Jul
8.01i		Damarcus	Simpson	USA	14.7.93	1		New York (A)	28 Jan
8.01i		Andrew	Howe	ITA	12.5.85	3	NC	Ancona	18 Feb
		(70)							
8.01i		Maksim	Kolesnikov	RUS	28.2.91	3	NC	Moskva	21 Feb
8.01	0.9	Kafétien	Gomis	FRA	23.3.80	*	NC	Marseille	16 Jul
8.00	0.0	Tajay	Gayle	JAM	2.8.96	1		Montego Bay	11 Feb
8.00	0.9	Malik	Moffett	USA	11.4.94	1	Big 10	University Park	13 May
8.00	1.4	Marcos	Chuva	POR	8.8.89	1		Maia	20 May
8.00	1.7	Shin-ichiro	Shimono	JPN	10.10.90	3		Kawasaki	21 May
8.00	1.1	Lucas	Marcelino dos Santos	BRA	4.1.95	2		São Bernardo do Campo	17 Jun
7.99	1.1		Sun Yize	CHN	9.3.96	3		Zhengzhou	12 Apr
7.99	0.4		Tang Gongchen	CHN	24.4.89	5	NG	Tianjin	6 Sep
7.98i		Aleksandr	Petrov	RUS	9.8.86	1		Moskva	10 Jan
		(80)							
7.98		Kendall	Spencer	USA	24.7.91	1		Waltham	3 Jun
7.98	-1.0	Christopher	Ullmann	SUI	21.8.93	2		Oberteuringen	4 Jun
7.98	0.4	Anastásios	Galazoúlas	GRE	2.10.92	1		Pátra	1 Jul
7.97	1.5	Christian	Mitrevski	AUS	12.7.96	*		Canberra	12 Mar
7.97	0.8	Zack	Bazile	USA	7.1.96	2	Big 10	University Park	13 May
7.97	0.5	Melvin	Echard	USA/GRN	29.8.89	3		Mesa	10 Jun
7.97	1.5	Shotaro	Shiroyama	JPN	6.3.95	3	AsiC	Bhubaneswar	9 Jul
7.97A	1.2	Antonmarco	Musso	ITA	30.1.91	1		Sestriere	23 Jul
7.96	1.6	Will	Williams	USA	31.1.95	2	TexR	Austin	1 Apr
7.96	1.9	Almir	dos Santos	BRA	4.9.93	1		Buenos Aires	2 Apr
		(90)							
7.96	-0.1	Pavel	Shalin	RUS	15.3.87	2		Sochi	25 May
7.96	2.0	Jacob	Fincham-Dukes	GBR	12.1.97	3Q	NCAA-W	Austin	25 May
7.96	-0.1	Ankit	Sharma	IND	20.7.92	1		Almaty	25 Jun
7.96	0.8	Héctor	Santos	ESP-J	6.1.98	3	EJ	Grosseto	20 Jul
7.95	0.0	István	Virovecz	HUN	1.12.89	1		Budapest	3 Jun
7.95	-0.5	Kristian	Bäck	FIN	18.7.96	1		Jämsä	1 Jul
7.94i		Andre	Dorsey	USA	11.3.93	1		Nashville	11 Feb
7.94	1.3	Raihau	Maiau	FRA	1.8.92	1		Pierre-Bénite	9 Jun
7.94	1.4	Pavel	Karavayev	RUS	27.8.88	5	NC	Zhukovskiy	29 Jul

Mark	Wind	Name		Nat	Born	Pos	Meet	Venue	Date
7.93i		Travonn (100)	White	USA	3.6.95	2	SEC	Nashville	25 Feb
7.93Ai		Laderrick	Ward	USA	28.12.92	1	NC	Albuquerque	4 Mar
7.93	0.7	Higor	Alves	BRA	23.2.94	1		São Bernardo do Campo	15 Jul

Mark	Wind	Name		Nat	Born	Date
7.92i		Elvijs	Misans	LAT	8.4.89	27 Jan
7.92	1.9	Kemonie	Briggs	USA	21.5.96	15 Apr
7.92	-1.0	Maximilian	Entholzner	GER	18.8.94	13 May
7.92		Lasha	Torgvaidze	GEO	26.5.93	28 May
7.92	1.2	Janis	Leitis	LAT	13.4.89	10 Jun
7.92A	0.0	Daniel	Pineda	CHI	19.9.85	7 Jul
7.92	1.5	Yuhi	Oiwa	JPN	17.2.91	8 Jul
7.92	2.0	Jean Marie	Okutu	ESP	4.8.88	14 Jul
7.92	1.7	Tazuma	Kawashima	JPN	16.8.96	9 Sep
7.91	0.0	José Luis	Mandros	PER-J	12.11.98	3 Jun
7.91		Mohcine	Khoua	MAR-J	26.7.98	12 Jul
7.91		Janaka Prasad	Wimalasiri	SRI	8.9.92	3 Oct
7.90	1.3	Liam	Adcock	AUS	21.6.96	25 Feb
7.90	-0.8	Chris	McBride	USA	24.7.97	22 Apr
7.90	1.5	Isaiah	Holmes	USA-J	18.10.98	13 May
7.90A	0.9	Luis	Rivera	MEX	21.6.87	14 May
7.90			Sapwaturrahman	INA	13.5.94	18 Oct
7.89Ai		Terrell	McClain	USA	10.11.95	10 Feb
7.89	0.6	Dhanuka	Liyana Pathirana	SRI	25.6.93	1 Jun
7.89	0.4	Will	Claye	USA	13.6.91	4 Jun
7.89	0.0	Taras	Neledva	UKR	7.6.92	6 Jun
7.89	1.4	Ronald	Taylor	USA	13.8.90	17 Jun
7.89	0.2	Corentin	Campener	BEL	5.10.90	25 Jun
7.89	-1.0	Feron	Sayers	GBR	15.10.94	2 Jul
7.89			Nguyen Van Cong	VIE	19.6.95	27 Jul
7.89	0.8	Santiago	Cova	VEN	10.8.96	22 Sep
7.88i		Anatoliy	Ryapolov	RUS	31.1.97	11 Feb
7.88	0.3	Shem	James	AUS	12.7.97	25 Feb
7.88		Janry	Ubas	PHI	2.1.94	3 Jun
7.88	0.7	Ifeanyi	Otuonye	TKS	27.6.94	10 Jun
7.88A	-0.4	Andreas	Otterling	SWE	25.5.86	7 Jul
7.88A	-0.5	Maykel	Vidal	CUB-Y	6.1.00	13 Jul
7.88	0.9	Vitaliy	Muravyov	RUS	1.10.93	29 Jul
7.87i			Lu Jiming	CHN	22.1.96	27 Feb
7.87	0.0	Tim	Duckworth	GBR	18.6.96	7 Apr
7.87	1.9		Wang Qicheng	CHN	20.9.92	12 Apr
7.87			Nguyen Tien Trong	VIE	9.3.97	27 Jul
7.87	1.4		Kim Yong-won	KOR-J	7.3.99	22 Oct
7.86i		O'Shea	Wilson	USA	27.10.94	13 Jan
7.86	1.5	Jeremy	Hicks ¶	USA	19.9.86	22 Apr
7.86	0.7	Benjamin	Gföhler	SUI	27.1.94	4 Jun
7.86	0.4	Dino	Pervan	CRO	12.1.91	8 Jul
7.85i		Ionut	Neagoe	ROU	11.6.94	12 Feb
7.85	1.5		Jiang Zhaodan	CHN	19.2.89	12 Apr
7.85	1.0	Eric	Sloan	USA	20.6.94	30 Apr
7.85	2.0	Travis	Riley	JAM	.96	6 May
7.85	0.4	Adam	McMullen	IRL	5.7.90	13 May
7.85	1.4	Damian	Warner	CAN	4.11.89	27 May
7.85	2.0	Cristian	Staicu	ROU	30.7.93	8 Jul

Mark	Wind	Name		Nat	Born	Date
7.85	1.3		Yu Bingcan	CHN-J	21.7.98	8 Jul
7.85	1.8	Vladimir	Bulakhov	BLR-J	23.1.99	20 Jul
7.85	1.7	Mamadou	Guèye	SEN	1.4.86	27 Jul
7.84	1.0	Mihaíl	Mertzanídis-Despotéris	GRE	21.8.87	10 Jun
7.84	1.6	Tomoya	Nomura	JPN	18.3.97	10 Jun
7.84	0.0	Carlton	Lavong	USA	18.6.92	10 Jun
7.84	1.6	Alper	Kulaksiz	TUR	6.4.92	14 Jun
7.84	1.7	Stevens	Dorcelus	CAN	19.5.95	4 Aug
7.83i		Stefano	Tremigliozzi	ITA	7.5.85	18 Feb
7.83i		Steffin	McCarter	USA	19.1.97	10 Mar
7.83i		Andreas	Trajkovski	DEN	18.3.93	10 Mar
7.83i		Devon	Williams	USA	17.1.94	10 Mar
7.83		W.P.Amila	Jayasiri	SRI	24.1.94	30 Mar
7.83	0.9	Laquarn	Nairn	BAH	31.7.96	1 Apr
7.83		Greshan	Dhananjaya	SRI	7.6.97	24 Apr
7.83	1.8	Nikólaos	Kapsís	GRE	5.12.91	20 May
7.83	1.0	Daniel	Gardiner	GBR	25.6.90	10 Jun
7.83		Suthisak	Singkhon	THA	5.10.96	14 Jun
7.83	0.0	José Luis	Despaigne	CUB	1.2.95	15 Jun
7.83	0.1		Bui Van Dong	VIE	23.3.95	24 Aug
7.83	2.0		Ju Eun-jae	KOR	12.6.93	22 Oct
7.82	1.9	Anthony	May	USA	19.9.90	18 Mar
7.82	1.2	Michael	Turner	USA	.94	12 May
7.82A		Kiplagat	Ruto	KEN	1.11.94	17 May
7.82	0.1	Cleiton	Sabino	BRA	9.11.88	20 May
7.82	1.9		Zhu Keqi	CHN-J	4.2.99	4 Jun
7.82		Denis	Eradiri	BUL	24.10.83	8 Jul
7.82i		O'Brien	Wasome	JAM	24.1.97	9 Dec
7.81i		Lutalo	Boyce	USA	11.8.91	9 Feb
7.81i		Marquise	Corbett	USA	.93	25 Feb
7.81		Emeka	Eze	USA	11.3.94	15 Apr
7.81	2.0	Justin	Hall	USA-J	12.2.98	15 Apr
7.81	2.0	Strahinja	Jovancevic	SRB	28.2.93	27 May
7.81	1.9	Masashi	Miyauchi	JPN-J	4.2.98	3 Jun
7.81	1.4	Antonino	Trio	ITA	4.6.93	8 Jun
7.81	2.0	Yann	Randrianasolo	FRA	3.2.94	5 Jul
7.81	0.6		Lin Chia-Hao	TPE	3.6.95	9 Jul
7.81	0.0		Zhang Shuo	CHN		18 Jul
7.81A	1.4	Cheswell	Johnson	RSA	30.9.97	2 Dec
7.80i		Daniel	Solis	ESP	5.11.96	21 Jan
7.80Ai		Austin	Hazel	USA	5.4.94	10 Feb
7.80A	0.4	Johan	van Vuuren	RSA	17.7.96	8 Mar
7.80		Andre	Jefferson	USA	14.5.94	25 Mar
7.80	0.2	Taishi	Endo	JPN	3.9.97	10 May
7.80	0.0	Florian	Oswald	GER	11.4.89	24 Jun
7.80	-0.2	Che	Richards	TTO	8.5.97	24 Jun
7.80	1.2	Guillaume	Victorin	FRA	26.5.90	16 Jul
7.80	1.9	Darcy (199)	Roper	AUS-J	31.3.98	16 Dec

Wind assisted

Mark	Wind	Name		Nat	Born	Pos	Meet	Venue		Date
8.50	4.4	Fabrice	Lapierre	AUS	17.10.83	1		Austin		29 Apr
					x	8.00w	x	p	8.50w	p
8.49	3.7	Jarrion	Lawson	USA	6.5.94	1	NC	Sacramento		25 Jun
					8.18w	8.34w/4.0	x	8.43w/3.6	8.49	8.27/1.4
8.39	3.1	Marquis	Dendy	USA	17.11.92	2	NC	Sacramento		25 Jun
					8.07w	7.98	8.13	8.18	8.33w/3.4	8.39w
8.37	2.8	Jarvis	Gotch	USA	25.3.92	1		Chula Vista		27 May
					x	x	7.95	x	8.37w	x
	8.30w 2.4	4 NC	Sacramento	25 Jun	x	7.73w	8.17w	x	8.30w	x
8.36	3.3		Manyonga	see 8.33 legal		1	DL	Stockholm		18 Jun
8.36	5.0	Damarcus	Simpson	USA	14.7.93	3	NC	Sacramento		25 Jun6
					7.95w	x	x	x	x	8.36w
8.34	2.3	Juan Miguel	Echevarría	CUB-J	11.8.98	1		Padova		16 Jul
					7.88	8.34w	7.97	x	x	x
8.30	4.8	Charles	Brown	USA	28.5.97	1		Fort Worth		15 AprJ
					7.66w	8.09w	8.30w	7.93w	8.25w	8.06w

Mark	Wind	Name		Nat	Born	Pos	Meet	Venue	Date
8.23	3.2	Zarck	Visser	RSA	15.9.89	3		Madrid	14 Jul
8.22	4.4	Mike	Hartfield	USA	29.3.90	2		Chula Vista	27 May
8.22	3.4	Raihau	Maiau	FRA	1.8.92	1	NC	Marseille	16 Jul
8.22A	2.2	Kafétien	Gomis	FRA	23.3.80	2		Tignes	16 Aug
8.16	2.9	Melvin	Echard	USA/GRN	29.8.89	3		Chula Vista	27 May

Mark	Wind	Name		Nat	Born	Pos	Meet	Venue	Date
8.15	2.9	KeAndre	Bates	USA	24.5.96	1	NCAA-E	Lexington	25 May
8.14	2.6	Yuhi	Oiwa	JPN	17.2.91	1		Toyama	6 Aug
8.13	3.0	Sergey	Polyanskiy	RUS	29.10.89	3	NC	Zhukovskiy	29 Jul
8.13	3.3	Janaka Prasad	Wimalasiri	SRI	8.9.92	1		Diyagama	3 Oct
8.09	3.1	Will	Williams	USA	31.1.95	1	NCAA-W	Austin	25 May
8.07	3.2	Yuki	Hashioka	JPN-J	23.1.99	1	Nambu	Sapporo	9 Jul
8.06	4.0	Vladyslav	Mazur	UKR	21.11.96	1		Lutsk	7 May
8.05	2.7	Christian	Mitrevski	AUS	12.7.96	1		Canberra	12 Mar
8.05	2.3	Shin-ichiro	Shimono	JPN	10.10.90	1	Oda	Hiroshima	29 Apr
8.03	2.4	Eric	Sloan	USA	20.6.94	2	NCAA-W	Austin	25 May
8.02	3.4	Jacob	Fincham-Dukes	GBR	12.1.97	5		Fort Worth	15 Apr
8.01	3.9	Justin	Hall	USA-J	12.2.98	6		Fort Worth	15 Apr
8.00A	3.3	Andreas	Otterling	SWE	25.5.86	5		Monachil	7 Jul
7.99	2.5	Kemonie	Briggs	USA	21.5.96	1		Long Beach	4 Mar
7.98	2.1	Abubakar	Mohammed	GHA	5.3.91	1		Austin	15 Apr
7.97	5.9	Laquarn	Nairn	BAH	31.7.96	1		Abilene	27 Apr
7.97	3.4	Dhanuka Liyana	Pathirana	SRI	25.6.93	1	NC	Diyagama	2 Sep
7.97	2.5	Tazuma	Kawashima	JPN	16.8.96	3		Fukui	9 Sep
7.95	2.9	Feron	Sayers	GBR	15.10.94	2	NC	Birmingham	2 Jul
7.94	4.7	Hunter	Veith	USA	14.1.95	2		Lubbock	28 Apr
7.94	2.4	Adam	McMullen	IRL	5.7.90	2		Manchester	16 Aug

Mark	Wind	Name		Nat	Born	Date
7.93	4.0	Harrison	Schrage	USA	14.10.97	28 Apr
7.93	2.6	Jean Marie	Okutu	ESP	4.8.88	14 Jul
7.92	6.9	Yuya	Takamasa	JPN	7.4.95	15 Apr
7.92		Jalen	Reagor	USA-J	2.1.99	20 Apr
7.91A	2.1	Dylan	Cotter	RSA	23.8.91	18 Feb
7.90A	2.2	Cheswell	Johnson	RSA	30.9.97	3 Jun
7.89	3.6	Ifeanyi	Otuonye	TKS	27.6.94	29 Apr
7.89	2.4	Sadeekie	Edie	JAM	28.10.93	6 May
7.88	3.8	José Luis	Despaigne	CUB	1.2.95	4 Mar
7.88	2.7	George	Fields	USA	29.12.86	15 Apr
7.88	2.5	Elvijs	Misans	LAT	8.4.89	4 Jun
7.88	2.2	Emanuel	Archibald	GUY	9.9.94	11 Jun
7.87	2.5	Benjamin	Gföhler	SUI	27.1.94	29 Apr
7.87	2.5	Trumaine	Jefferson	USA	.96	13 May
7.87	2.9	Carlton	Lavong	USA	18.6.92	27 May
7.86	2.9	Antwan	Dickerson	USA	2.2.94	13 May
7.86	2.3	Bryce	Huggins	USA	17.4.97	19 May
7.86	3.3	Mamadou	Guèye	SEN	1.4.86	27 Jul
7.86	3.0		Ju Eun-jae	KOR	12.6.93	22 Oct
7.86	4.5	Darcy	Roper	AUS-J	31.3.98	16 Dec
7.85	2.4	Jaak Joonas	Uudmäe	EST	6.4.94	29 Apr
7.85	3.8	Efe	Uwaifo	GBR	15.5.95	6 May
7.85	3.6	Florian	Oswald	GER	11.4.89	17 Jun
7.85	2.1	Augustin	Bey	FRA	6.6.95	18 Jun
7.84	2.1	G.K.D.Sandaruwan	Piyarathna	SRI	15.4.94	2 Sep
7.83	2.2	Angus	Gould	AUS	8.1.94	2 Apr
7.83	4.9	Corey	Muggler	USA		6 May
7.82	2.8	Roni	Ollikainen	FIN	27.8.90	22 Jul

Best outdoor marks

Mark	Wind	Name	Pos	Meet	Venue	Date
8.04	1.5	Holloway	4		Fort Worth	15 Apr
8.04	0.9	Randazzo	Q	EC-23	Bydgoszcz	13 Jul
8.02	0.6	Kiselkov	2	NCp	Yerino	15 Jul
7.98	0.9	Smajlaj	1	NC	Elbasan	8 Jun
7.97	1.6	Bertrand	3	NC	Marseille	16 Jul
7.94	0.0	Dorsey	1		Athens, GA	6 May
7.93	1.7	Petrov	6	NC	Zhukovskiy	29 Jul

7.92 -0.3 Nykyforov 6 Jul | 7.85 -0.2 Ryapolov 4 Jun | 7.84 -0.1 Lu Jiming 9 May | 7.83 1.1 Misans 10 Jun | 7.82 0.7 White 5 May

Low altitude bests

Mark	Wind	Name	Pos	Meet	Venue	Date
8.23	0.6	Wang Jianan	7	WCh	London (OS)	5 Aug
8.18	0.4	Tornéus	8	WCh	London (OS)	5 Aug
8.08	1.5	Cáceres	1		Salamanca	3 Jun
8.02	0.9	Pulli	1		Lapinlahti	16 Jul
7.94	1.1	Musso	1		Savona	17 Sep
8.17w	2.3	Gomis	2	NC	Marseille	16 Jul
7.95w	2.5	Otterling	2		S'satra	25 May

7.88 1.5 Pajulahti 22 Jul | 7.87 2.0 Otterling 18 Jun | 7.85 1.5 Vidal 27 May | 7.81i McClain 10 Mar | 7.87w 3.3 Pineda 24 Jun

With prosthetics: 8.19 0.9 Markus Rehm GER 22.8.88 1 Erfurt 9 Jul

JUNIORS

See main list for top 9 juniors. 17 performances by 6 men to 8.09. Additional marks and further juniors:

Name	Mark	Wind	Pos	Meet	Venue	Date	Mark	Wind	Pos	Meet	Venue	Date
Massó	8.26	0.8	5	WCh	London (OS)	5 Aug	8.15	0.4	Q	WCh	London (OS)	4 Aug
Shi Yuhao	8.23	-0.3	6	WCh	London (OS)	5 Aug	8.15	0.5	Q	NC-j	Ordos	3 Jun
	8.18	1.3	1		Hong Kong	14 May	8.13	0.5	1	NC-j	Ordos	4 Jun
Echevarría	8.19	1.9	1		Saint-Martin	13 May	8.12	0.0	1	Barr	La Habana	27 May
	8.17	-0.8	1		Monterrey	16 Jun						
Tentóglou	8.16	1.7	1		Kalamáta	27 May	8.10	1.7	1	NC-j	Kateríni	9 Jul

Mark	Wind	Name		Nat	Born	Pos	Meet	Venue	Date
7.91	0.0	José Luis	Mandros (10)	PER	12.11.98	1	SAm-J	Leonora	3 Jun
7.91		Mohcine	Khoua	MAR	26.7.98	1		Casablanca	12 Jul
7.90	1.5	Isaiah	Holmes	USA	18.10.98	2	PAC-12	Eugene	13 May
7.88A	-0.5	Maykel	Vidal	CUB	6.1.00	1	WY	Nairobi	13 Jul
7.87	1.4		Kim Yong-won	KOR	7.3.99	1	NSF-HS	Chongju	22 Oct
7.85	1.3		Yu Bingcan	CHN	21.7.98	3		Dalian	8 Jul
7.85	1.8	Vladimir	Bulakhov	BLR	23.1.99	4	EJ	Grosseto	20 Jul
7.82	1.9		Zhu Keqi	CHN	4.2.99	2	NC-j	Ordos	4 Jun
7.81	2.0	Justin	Hall	USA	12.2.98	*		Fort Worth	15 Apr
7.81	1.9	Masashi	Miyauchi	JPN	4.2.98	1		Tsukuba	3 Jun
7.80	1.9	Darcy	Roper (20)	AUS	31.3.98	*		Brisbane (Nathan)	16 Dec

Wind assisted see main lists for top 3 juniors

Mark	Wind	Name		Nat	Born	Pos	Meet	Venue	Date
7.92		Jalen	Reagor	USA-J	2.1.99	1		Lancaster, TX	20 Apr
7.86	4.5	Darcy	Roper	AUS-J	31.3.98	1		Brisbane (Nathan)	16 Dec

Mark Wind Name Nat Born Pos Meet Venue Date

TRIPLE JUMP

18.11 0.8 Christian Taylor USA 18.6.90 1 Pre Eugene 27 May
17.82w/2.5 17.03 17.54w/4.2 18.11 17.66w/2.6 x
17.68 0.2 1 WCh London(OS) 10 Aug 16.97 17.57/0.2 17.68 17.26 17.38/0.4 17.03
17.57 -1.1 1 GS Ostrava 28 Jun 17.09 17.19 17.57 17.24/-0.6 p 17.05
17.49 -0.6 2 Athl Lausanne 6 Jul 17.35-1.4 17.48/-1.5 17.49/? 17.16 17.43/-1.2 x
17.49 0.1 1 VD-DLF Bruxelles 1 Sep 16.51 17.18 17.22 17.49 17.18 17.11
17.29 0.0 1 DL Paris (C) 1 Jul 17.11 17.29 17.01 17.04 17.13 17.19
17.26 1.3 1 Clay Azusa 14 Apr 16.62w 16.82w 16.84w 16.98 17.18w 17.26
17.25 -0.4 1 DL Doha 5 May 16.42 16.57 17.02 16.81 17.06 17.25
17.20 1.6 1 Kingston 10 Jun
17.91 0.9 Will Claye USA 13.6.91 1 NC Sacramento 23 Jun
17.47/1.4 17.68/0.2 17.79/1.2 17.76/1.2 17.91 p
17.82 1.7 * Pre Eugene 27 May 17.01 17.38/1.5 17.66/1/5 17.82 18.05w/2.4 17.75w/3.3
17.63 -0.1 2 WCh London (OS) 10 Aug 17.54/0.2 17.52/0.6 17.63 17.49/0.4 17.53/0.2 x
17.42A 0.7 1 Tignes 16 Aug 16.24 16.72w 16.77w 16.87 16.90 17.42
17.40 0.5 1 Baie-Mahault 17 May 17.08 17.40
17.35 -0.1 2 VD-DLF Bruxelles 1 Sep x 16.95 17.08 17.35 x 17.28/0.1
17.60 -0.3 Pedro Pablo Pichardo CUB 30.6.93 1 Athl Lausanne 6 Jul
17.44/0.1 17.54/-0.9 16.96 p p 17.60
17.32 0.2 3 VD-DLF Bruxelles 1 Sep 16.87 17.32 17.03 17.17 17.21/0.1 17.06
17.52i Max Hess GER 13.7.96 Q EI Beograd 3 Mar
17.52
17.48 0.0 Chris Benard USA 4.4.90 2 NC Sacramento 23 Jun
17.03 17.23/0.0 17.48 p p p
17.20 0.2 Q WCh London (OS) 7 Aug
17.40 0.4 Andy Díaz CUB 25.12.95 1 NC La Habana 17 Mar
16.90 17.40 x x p x
17.32 1.1 Fabrizio Donato ITA 14.8.76 1 Pierre-Bénite 9 Jun
x 15.56 x 16.89 17.32
17.30A 0.6 Jordan Díaz CUB-Y 23.2.01 1 WY Nairobi 14 Jul
15.99 16.25 17.00 17.30 x p
17.27 1.6 Cristian Nápoles CUB-J 27.11.98 2 NC La Habana 17 Mar
16.66w 17.27 16.06w p x x
17.21 0.2 1 Barr La Habana 28 May x 17.21 x x x x
17.27 0.9 Dong Bin (10) CHN 22.11.88 3 Pre Eugene 27 May
17.27 p p p p p
17.23 -0.4 1 NG Tianjin 3 Sep x 17.11 17.23 x 17.15 16.95
17.25 1.1 Donald Scott USA 23.2.92 3 NC Sacramento 23 Jun
16.77 16.81 17.14 17.25 x 16.32
17.23 0.3 Zhu Yaming CHN 4.5.94 2 NG Tianjin 3 Sep
16.53 17.23 x 17.04 17.08 16.91
17.22 0.6 Cao Shuo CHN 8.10.91 3 NG Tianjin 3 Sep
16.85 17.22 x x 16.53 x
17.20i Lyukman Adams RUS 24.9.88 1 NC Moskva 20 Feb
16.74 17.20 x 16.80 p p
17.20i Melvin Raffin FRA-J 9.8.98 Q EI Beograd 3 Mar
17.20i Nelson Évora POR 20.4.84 1 EI Beograd 5 Mar
(33/16) x 16.92 17.20 x 16.98 x
17.19i Clive Pullen JAM 18.10.94 1 Tyson Fayetteville 11 Feb
17.18 1.7 Wu Ruiting CHN 29.11.95 1 Kawasaki 21 May
17.18 0.4 Nazim Babayev AZE 8.10.97 1 EC-23 Bydgoszcz 16 Jul
17.17 0.2 Artyom Primak RUS 14.1.93 1 NC Zhukovskiy 29 Jul
(20)
17.16 0.2 Alexis Copello AZE 12.8.85 5 WCh London (OS) 10 Aug
17.14 -0.5 Simo Lipsanen FIN 13.9.95 2 EC-23 Bydgoszcz 16 Jul
17.13i Jean-Marc Pontvianne FRA 6.8.94 1 NC Bordeaux 19 Feb
17.12 1.4 Matthew O'Neal USA 10.6.94 1 Tampa 18 Mar
17.08 -1.5 Omar Craddock USA 26.4.91 2 DL Doha 5 May
17.07 -0.1 Lázaro Martínez CUB 3.11.97 1 La Habana 11 Feb
17.05 1.7 Momchil Karailiev BUL 21.5.82 1 Sofia 18 Jun
17.02i Elvijs Misans LAT 8.4.89 4 EI Beograd 5 Mar
17.02 1.7 Yordanys Durañona DMA 16.6.88 1 MEX Ch Monterrey 18 Jun
16.97 0.7 Martin Lamou FRA-J 13.5.99 1 EJ Grosseto 23 Jul
(30)
16.97 0.9 Fabrice Zango BUR 25.6.93 2 WUG Taipei 25 Aug
16.96 0.1 Pablo Torrijos ESP 12.5.92 1 Castellón 10 Jun
16.95i Dmitriy Chizhikov RUS 6.12.93 2 NC Moskva 20 Feb
16.95 1.7 Jhon Freddy Murillo COL 13.7.84 5 Pre Eugene 27 May
16.95 0.4 Dmitriy Sorokin RUS 27.9.92 2 NC Zhukovskiy 29 Jul

Mark	Wind	Name		Nat	Born	Pos	Meet	Venue	Date
16.94i		Aleksandr	Yurchenko	RUS	30.7.92	1	Winter	Moskva	5 Feb
16.94i		Harold	Corréa	FRA	26.6.88	2		Madrid	24 Feb
16.94	2.0	Miguel	van Assen	SUR	30.7.97	1	SAmC	Asunción	25 Jun
16.93	0.8	Georgi	Tsonov	BUL	2.5.93	1		Plovdiv	11 Jun
16.92	1.9	Eric	Sloan	USA	20.6.94	1Q	NCAA-W	Austin	27 May
		(40)							
16.91Ai		Josh	Honeycutt	USA	7.3.89	3	NC	Albuquerque	5 Mar
16.87	1.8	Ryoma	Yamamoto	JPN	14.7.95	*	Oda	Hiroshima	29 Apr
16.87	-0.3	Dimítrios	Tsiámis	GRE	12.1.82	1		Kalamáta	27 May
16.87	0.5	Mateus Daniel	de Sá	BRA	21.11.95	1		São Bernardo do Sul	3 Jun
16.87	0.5	Andrea	Dalla Valle	ITA-J	31.8.99	2	EJ	Grosseto	23 Jul
16.86i			Fang Yaoqing	CHN	20.4.96	1		Xianlin	28 Feb
16.86	1.5	Yoann	Rapinier	FRA	29.9.89	3	NC	Marseille	15 Jul
16.86	0.4	Almir	dos Santos	BRA	4.9.93	1		Porto Alegre	7 Sep
16.85	-0.3	Kevin	Luron	FRA	8.11.91	4	NC	Marseille	15 Jul
16.85	1.0	Yasser	Triki	ALG	24.3.97	1	NC	Alger	29 Jul
		(50)							
16.83	0.0	Alberto	Álvarez	MEX	8.3.91	1		Monterrey	25 Mar
16.81i		KeAndre	Bates	USA	24.5.96	1		Nashville	25 Feb
16.81	-1.4	Nathan	Fox	GBR	21.10.90	1		Clermont	13 May
16.80	0.4	Troy	Doris	GUY	12.4.89	2	GS	Ostrava	28 Jun
16.80	1.4	Benjamin	Compaoré	FRA	5.8.87	*	NC	Marseille	15 Jul
16.80	1.7	Nathan	Douglas	GBR	4.12.82	1		Manchester	16 Aug
16.77	0.2	Muhammad Hakimi	Ismail	MAS	8.4.91	1	SEAG	Kuala Lumpur	23 Aug
16.75i		Chris	Carter	USA	11.3.89	1		Houston	10 Feb
16.75A	0.7	Reneilwe	Aphane	RSA	24.8.90	1		Pretoria	11 Feb
16.75	2.0	Brandon	Roulhac	USA	13.12.83	1		Clermont	15 Apr
		(60)							
16.75		Arpinder	Singh	IND	30.12.92	1	Fed Cup	Patiala	4 Jun
16.74	1.2	Alvaro	Cortez	CHI	27.10.95	1		Santiago de Chile	26 Mar
16.73	1.5	Ben	Williams	GBR	25.1.92	2	ET	Villeneuve d'Ascq	25 Jun
16.70	0.8	Mark Harry	Diones	PHI	3.1.93	1		Ilagan	1 Apr
16.70	-1.2	Tosin	Oke	NGR	1.10.80	2		Clermont	13 May
16.69	1.2	Andrea	Chiari	ITA	12.2.91	3		Pierre-Bénite	9 Jun
16.68i			Xu Xiaolong	CHN	20.12.92	3		Xianlin	24 Feb
16.67	2.0	Felix	Obi	USA	15.6.94	2	TexR	Austin	31 Mar
16.67A		Elijah	Kimitei	KEN	25.12.86	1	NC	Nairobi	10 Jun
16.67		Aleksandro	Melo	BRA	26.9.95	1		São Bernardo do Campo	24 Nov
		(70)							
16.66i			Lu Zhiwei	CHN	4.4.96	4		Xianlin	28 Feb
16.65	0.7	Dmitriy	Plotnitskiy	BLR	26.8.88	1	NC	Grodno	5 Jul
16.64	0.9		Liu Mingxuan	CHN	16.5.97	2		Zhengzhou	13 Apr
16.63	1.8	Adil	Gandou	MAR	18.8.93	1		Forbach	28 May
16.63	0.9	Tomás	Veszelka	SVK	9.7.95	4	EC-23	Bydgoszcz	16 Jul
16.59i		Levon	Aghasyan	ARM	19.1.95	1		Ust-Kamenogorsk	18 Feb
16.59		Mamadou Chérif	Dia	MLI	13.3.85	1		Bamako	3 Jun
16.59	0.2	Karol	Hoffmann	POL	1.6.89	4	GS	Ostrava	28 Jun
16.58i		Clayton	Brown	JAM	8.12.96	3	SEC	Nashville	25 Feb
16.58	1.6	Aleksey	Fyodorov	RUS	25.5.91	1		Sochi	26 May
		(80)							
16.56i		Hayden	McClain	USA	8.10.95	3	Tyson	Fayetteville	11 Feb
16.56	1.7	Igor	Sjunin	EST	4.12.90	1		Viljandi	14 Jul
16.55	-1.2	Olu	Olamigoke	NGR	19.9.90	4		Clermont	13 May
16.55A	-0.5	Khotso	Mokoena	RSA	6.3.85	1		Pretoria	2 Dec
16.54	0.1	Jean	Rosa	BRA	1.2.90	1		Santiago de Chile	9 Apr
16.54	1.3	Vicente	Docavo	ESP	13.2.92	2	NC	Barcelona	22 Jul
16.53i		Adrian	Swiderski	POL	26.9.86	1		Spala	11 Feb
16.53	1.3	Maksim	Nesterenko	BLR	1.9.92	2	NC	Grodno	5 Jul
16.52	0.6	Daniele	Cavazzani	ITA	4.12.92	1		Savona	25 May
16.52		K.V.Rakesh	Babu	IND	20.3.90	1		Jalahalli	25 Aug
		(90)							
16.50	0.9	Seref	Osmanoglu	TUR	2.1.89	1		Ankara	7 Jun
16.49i		O'Brien	Wasome	JAM	24.1.97	3	NCAA	College Station	11 Mar
16.49	0.2	Paulo Sérgio	Oliveira	BRA	1.6.93	3		São Bernardo do Campo	3 Jun
16.49	-0.4	Khaled	Al-Subaie	KUW	1.3.96	2	TUN Ch	Radès	17 Jul
16.48	0.1	Kirill	Kovalenko	RUS	20.1.94	3		Sochi	26 May
16.46	0.1	Ilya	Glazunov	RUS	20.4.94	6		Sochi	26 May
16.45	-1.2	Nonso	Okolo	GBR/NGR	7.12.90	5		Clermont	13 May
16.44	1.3	Jordan	Scott	JAM	29.6.97	1		Charlottesville	21 Apr
16.44	1.9	Marcos	Ruiz	ESP	10.3.95	1		Valencia	3 Jun
16.43	1.6	Muhammad	Halim	ISV	26.10.86	1		Lynchburg	3 May
		(100)							

Mark	Wind	Name		Nat	Born	Pos	Meet	Venue	Date
16.43	0.4	Arturo	Rodríguez	CUB-J	28.4.99	2		La Habana	16 Jun
16.43	0.5	Jonathan	Drack	MRI	6.11.88	1		Carquefou	23 Jun

Mark	Wind	Name		Nat	Born	Date
16.42i		Mike	Sandle	USA	10.6.92	25 Feb
16.41i		Daniele	Greco	ITA	1.3.89	19 Feb
16.41	0.8	Kanagaraj	Kamal Raj	IND-J	3.10.99	20 Nov
16.40	0.1	Quentin	Mouyabi	FRA-J	8.10.98	23 Jul
16.39	1.8	Sanjaya	Jayasinghe	SRI	20.4.82	4 Oct
16.38	1.9	Samuel	Trigg	GBR	1.11.93	27 May
16.38		Tom	Ya'acobov	ISR	30.6.92	25 Jun
16.38	-0.7	Razvan	Grecu	ROU-J	23.12.99	22 Jul
16.37		Mamadou	Guèye	SEN	1.4.86	6 May
16.37		Unnikrishnan	Karthik	IND	3.6.93	4 Jun
16.37	0.5	Marian	Oprea	ROU	6.6.82	7 Jul
16.37		Abderrahim	Zahouani	MAR	21.6.91	9 Jul
16.37	0.1	Pratchaya	Tepparak	THA	1.9.93	23 Aug
16.37		Fabian	Florant	NED	1.2.83	6 Sep
16.36i			Fu Haitao	CHN	1.11.93	24 Feb
16.36i		Rumen	Dimitrov	BUL	19.9.86	3 Mar
16.35	-1.1	Oleksandr	Malosilov	UKR	6.6.97	7 Jun
16.35	1.0	Andrey	Churylo	BLR	195.93	28 Jun
16.34i		Eric	Bethea	USA	8.6.97	11 Feb
16.34	2.0	Necati	Er	TUR	24.2.97	7 Jul
16.34	1.1	Issam	Nima	ALG	8.4.79	29 Jul
16.33i		Julian	Kellerer	AUT	22.8.89	3 Mar
16.33	0.2	Michael	Tiller	USA	17.11.94	27 May
16.33	1.0	Wilbert	Walker	JAM	7.1.85	10 Jun
16.32	0.6	Armani	Wallace	USA	11.2.97	14 May
16.32	0.3	Vladislav	Poluboyarov	RUS	17.4.94	15 Jul
16.30i		Julian	Reid	GBR	23.9.88	11 Feb
16.30i		José Emilio	Bellido	ESP	25.5.87	19 Feb
16.30	1.7	Cervantes	Jackson	USA	11.8.97	26 May
16.30		Malkit	Singh	IND	5.10.88	4 Jun
16.30	0.0	Chengetayi	Mapaya	ZIM-J	19.12.98	1 Jul
16.30	0.0	Abdulla	Aboobacker	IND	17.1.96	18 Jul
16.29i	0.0	Viktor	Kuznetsov	UKR	17.7.86	19 Feb
16.29	2.0	Barden	Adams	USA	21.9.96	14 May
16.29	0.3	Dimítrios	Baltadoúros	GRE	1.10.89	27 May
16.29	1.1	Denis	Obyortyshev	RUS	16.2.97	22 Jun
16.29	0.8	Kaual Kamal	Bento	BRA	10.1.93	16 Jul
16.29	0.7		Kim Duk-hyun	KOR	8.12.85	25 Oct
16.28i		Zlatozar	Atanasov	BUL	12.12.89	4 Feb
16.28A		Edwin	Langat	KEN		10 May
16.28		Leevan	Sands	BAH	16.8.81	28 May
16.27	-1.1	Mutsuki	Harada	JPN	4.2.97	25 Jun
16.26i		Scotty	Newton	USA	19.9.96	10 Feb
16.26i		Vitaliy	Pavlov	RUS	12.1.97	20 Feb
16.26	1.6	José Ernesto	Martínez	CUB	1.1.91	17 Mar
16.26	1.8		Zhang Yaoguang	CHN	21.6.93	13 Apr
16.26A	0.5	Scott	Carter	USA	.94	5 May
16.24	1.4	Sergio	Solanas	ESP	28.4.87	24 Jun
16.24			Nguyen Van Hung	VIE	4.3.89	26 Oct

(151)

Wind assisted

Mark	Wind	Name		Nat	Born	Pos	Meet	Venue	Date
18.05	2.4	Will	Claye	USA	13.6.91	2	Pre	Eugene	27 May
		See 17.82 legal							
17.28	3.1	Matthew	O'Neal	USA	10.6.94	1	TexR	Austin	31 Mar
					16.68w	x	17.04	17.02w x	17.28w
17.24	2.1		Hess			1	NC	Erfurt	8 Jul
17.17	2.5	Alexis	Copello	AZE	12.8.85	4	Pre	Eugene	27 May
16.94	3.3	Brandon	Roulhac	USA	13.12.83	1		New York	11 Jun
16.94	4.7	Benjamin	Compaoré	FRA	5.8.87	2	NC	Marseille	15 Jul
16.91	4.7	Ryoma	Yamamoto	JPN	14.7.95	1	Oda	Hiroshima	29 Apr
16.73	2.5	José Emilio	Bellido	ESP	25.5.87	1		Cartagena	7 May
16.73A	4.1	Jan	Luxa	SLO	11.2.96	1		Sestriere	23 Jul
16.69	4.2	Mamadou Cherif	Dia	MLI	13.3.85	5	FRA Ch	Marseille	15 Jul
16.66	4.0	Hayden	McClain	USA	8.10.95	1	Big 12	Lawrence	14 May
16.65A	3.2	Sergio	Solanas	ESP	28.4.87	1		Monachil	7 Jul
16.55A	4.4	Roger	Haitengi	NAM	12.9.83	2		Johannesburg	18 Feb
16.54	2.3	Fabian	Florant	NED	1.2.83	1	NC	Utrecht	16 Jul
16.50	7.2	Necati	Er	TUR	24.2.97	1		Denizli	9 May
16.43	3.5	Scotty	Newton	USA	19.9.96	2	Big 12	Lawrence	14 May

Mark	Wind	Name		Nat	Born	Date
16.38	2.3	Barden	Adams	USA	21.9.96	27 May
16.36	2.5	Askin	Karaca	TUR	20.10.90	23 Apr
16.32	2.2		Wen Tao	CHN	21.6.96	13 Apr
16.30	4.3	Eduardo	Landeta	ECU	3.6.96	25 Jun
16.30	3.8	Yuma	Okabe	JPN	13.7.90	15 Jul
16.30	3.6	Tuomas	Kaukolahti	FIN	6.5.94	23 Jul
16.29	3.5	Louis-Grégory	Occcin	FRA	2.6.89	7 May
16.29	2.6	Ilya	Potaptsev	RUS	19.4.93	15 Jul
16.28	3.6	Jeffrey	Prothro	USA		29 Apr
16.28	5.5	Damon	McLean	JAM	21.11.90	27 May
16.27	2.5	Ariel	Cabarcas	COL	7.2.92	1 Apr
16.26	2.6	Anaquan	Peterson	USA	19.4.94	14 May
16.26		Andy	Hechavarría	CUB-Y	14.9.00	2 Dec

Best outdoor marks

Mark	Wind	Name	Pos	Meet	Venue	Date
17.19	-0.1	Évora	3	WCh	London (OS)	10 Aug
17.13	0.6	Pontvianne	1		Montgeron	14 May
17.13	1.0	Hess	*	NC	Erfurt	8 Jul
16.85	0.6	Raffin	2		Montgeron	14 May
16.85	0.1	Chizhikov	3	NC	Zhukovskiy	29 Jul
16.83	1.9	Pullen	1	NC	Kingston	22 Jun
16.82	0.7	Adams	2	Znam	Zhukovskiy	2 Jul
16.76	-0.6	Yurchenko	2	NCp	Yerino	15 Jul
16.75	1.3	Bates	*	NCAA	Eugene	9 Jun
		16.76w 2.4	1	NCAA	Eugene	9 Jun
16.74	0.4	Misans	3	GS	Ostrava	28 Jun
16.74	2.0	Honeycutt	2		Gresham	2 Jul
16.58	0.2	Fang Yaoqing	2	NC	Jinan	19 May
16.57	0.7	Xu Xiaolong	3		Huaian	5 Apr
16.53	-0.4	Swiderski	1		Leszno	27 May

Mark	Wind	Name	Date
16.38	1.8	McClain	27 May
16.38	0.4	Greco	15 Jul
16.37	1.9	Lu Zhiwei	13 Apr
16.36	0.1	Corréa	21 May
16.31	1.8	Wasome	31 Mar
16.25	0.6	Sandle	26 May
16.25	0.0	Kuznetsov	7 Jun
16.24	0.2	Dimitrov	11 Jun

Low altitude bests

Mark	Wind	Name	Pos	Meet	Venue	Date
16.66	-0.7	J Díaz	4	NC	La Habana	17 Mar
16.24	1.4	S Carter	3	NCAA	Eugene	9 Jun

Drugs disqualification

Mark	Wind	Name		Nat	Born	Pos	Meet	Venue	Date
17.10		Chris	Carter	USA	11.3.89	1	NC	Albuquerque	5 Mar

JUNIORS

See main list for top 6 juniors. 12 performances (2 indoors) by 5 men to 16.85. Additional marks and further juniors:

Name	Mark	Wind	Pos	Meet	Venue	Date	Mark	Wind	Pos	Meet	Venue	Date
Nápoles 2+	17.16	-0.1	4	WCh	London (OS)	10 Aug	17.00	-0.2	1		Göteborg	11 Jul
	17.06	-0.4	Q	WCh	London (OS)	7 Aug	16.98	1.9	2		La Habana	11 Feb
Raffin 2+	17.04i		1		Aubière	17 Jun	16.92i		5	EI	Beograd	5 Mar

Mark	Wind	Name		Nat	Born	Pos	Meet	Venue	Date
16.41	0.8	Kanagaraj	Kamal Raj	IND-J	3.10.99	1	NC-j	Mangalagiri	20 Nov

Mark	Wind	Name		Nat	Born	Pos	Meet	Venue	Date
16.40	0.1	Quentin	Mouyabi	FRA-J	8.10.98	4	EJ	Grosseto	23 Jul
16.38	-0.7	Razvan	Grecu	ROU-J	23.12.99	Q	EJ	Grosseto	22 Jul
16.30	0.0	Chengetayi	Mapaya (10)	ZIM-J	19.12.98	1	Af-J	Tlemcen	1 Jul
16.21		Arturo	Gómez	CUB-J	28.4.99	1		La Habana	5 Jul
16.15	1.6		Du Mingze	CHN	15.2.99	5	NC	Jinan	19 May
16.14	-0.5	Sergey	Shisha	RUS	28.10.98	1		Maykop	23 May
16.13	0.4	Chiebuka Emmanuel	Ihemeje	ITA	9.10.98	Q	EJ	Grosseto	22 Jul
16.10		Edislay	Hodelín	CUB	31.10.99	2		Las Tunas	5 Jul
16.06	1.6		Kim Jang-woo	KOR	20.8.99	1J	NSF-Un	Chongju	24 Oct
16.04	1.6	Yuta	Takenouchi	JPN	23.4.98	4		Hiratsuka	9 Jun
16.04	0.8	Alexandru	Tache	ROU	5.10.98	1	Balk-J	Pitesti	2 Jul
16.04		Andy	Hechavarría	CUB-Y	14.9.00	3		Las Tunas	5 Jul
16.02	-0.7	Jusniel	Jorrín (20)	CUB-Y	2.2.01	3		La Habana	16 Jun
Wind assisted									
Nápoles		16.92A 3.0 4	Tignes		16 Aug				
16.26		Andy	Hechavarría	CUB-Y	14.9.00	4		Camagüey	2 Dec
16.21	2.2	Isaiah	Griffith	USA	7.2.98	1	NC-j	Sacramento	24 Jun
16.08	2.7	Al Assane	Fofana	FRA	6.3.98	1		Antony	17 Jun
16.06	3.4	Johnny	Montenegro	COL	6.1.99	1		Cartagena, COL	16 Jun

SHOT

Mark	Wind	Name		Nat	Born	Pos	Meet	Venue	Date
22.65		Ryan	Crouser	USA	18.12.92	1	NC	Sacramento	25 Jun
					21.82 22.02 x 21.94 22.01 22.65				
22.47	1	DL	Rabat	16 Jul	21.91 22.21 22.44 x 21.95 22.47				
22.43	1	Pre	Eugene	27 May	21.89 x 21.88 x 22.43 x				
22.39	1	Athl	Lausanne	6 Jul	22.18 x 21.56 22.18 22.39 22.35				
22.37	2	VD-DLF	Bruxelles	31 Aug	22.37 x 22.24 x x 21.92				
22.35	1		Vila Real de Santo A.	26 Aug	22.31 22.24 21.67 x 22.35 x				
22.15	1		Auckland (NS)	26 Feb	21.71 22.03 21.43 22.08 22.15 22.15				
22.11	1	KansR	Lawrence	21 Apr	21.65 21.40 22.03 21.22 21.86 22.11				
22.05	1		Christchurch	19 Feb	21.06 22.05 x 21.01 x 20.90				
21.79	1		Baie-Mahault	17 May	x 21.79 x 20.80 21.67 21.37				
21.77	1		Angers	9 Sep	20.14 20.83 21.53 21.77				
22.57		Joe	Kovacs	USA	28.6.89	1		Tucson	18 May
					22.57 22.10 x 22.26 p p				
22.35	2	NC	Sacramento	25 Jun	x 21.46 20.89 21.63 21.93 22.35				
22.44		Darrell	Hill	USA	17.8.93	1	VD-DLF	Bruxelles	31 Aug
					x 21.07 x 21.28 x 22.44				
21.91	1		Los Angeles (Ww)	8 Apr	20.27 21.91 x x x 20.44				
22.14		Tom	Walsh	NZL	1.3.92	Q	WCh	London (OS)	5 Aug
					22.14				
22.06	1		Bedford	30 Jul	22.06 x x 21.15 x 21.14				
22.04	1		Athens, GA	22 Jul	20.63 21.46 21.41 21.24 22.04 21.83				
22.03	1	WCh	London (OS)	6 Aug	21.38 21.64 21.75 21.70 21.63 22.03				
21.97	2	Athl	Lausanne	6 Jul	21.97 21.70 21.72 21.46 21.59 21.74				
21.83	1	DL	Birmingham	20 Aug	20.75 21.29 x 20.92 20.75 21.83				
21.80	2		Auckland (NS)	26 Feb	21.58 21.55 21.67 21.80 x x				
21.71	2	Pre	Eugene	27 May	21.71 x 21.62 21.20 21.48 x				
22.01		Tomás	Stanek	CZE	13.6.91	1		Schönebeck	2 Jun
					20.27 x 20.29 22.01 21.51 20.35				
22.01	1	Skol	Warszawa	15 Aug	20.61 21.10 20.61 20.88 22.01 x				
21.97i		Konrad	Bukowiecki	POL	17.3.97	1	EI	Beograd	4 Mar
					x 21.97 20.69 20.85 x 20.98				
21.96		O'Dayne	Richards	JAM	14.12.88	2	DL	Rabat	16 Jul
					20.88 x 21.96 x x x				
21.88		Michal	Haratyk	POL	10.4.92	1		Cetniewo	29 Jul
					21.25 21.56 21.45 21.72 21.88 21.88				
21.87		David	Storl	GER	27.7.90	1		Gotha	15 Jul
					x 21.87 21.44 x x p				
21.82		Darlan	Romani	BRA	9.4.91	1		São Bernardo do Campo	3 Jun
		(30/10)			20.43 21.82 x x				
21.65		Ryan	Whiting	USA	24.11.86	2		Athens, GA	22 Jul
21.56		Tsanko	Arnaudov	POR	14.3.92	1	ET-1	Vaasa	24 Jun
21.48		Stipe	Zunic	CRO	13.12.90	1		Slovenska Bistrica	27 May
21.40		Mesud	Pezer	BIH	27.8.94	1		Sokolac	29 Jul
21.36		Aleksandr	Lesnoy	RUS	28.7.88	1		Adler	23 Apr
21.35		Damien	Birkinhead	AUS	8.4.93	2	Hanz	Zagreb	28 Aug
21.31		Ahmed	Hassan	EGY	16.12.95	1	MSR	Torrance	15 Apr
21.30		Filip	Mihaljevic	CRO	31.7.94	1	NCAA	Eugene	7 Jun
21.12		Orazio	Cremona	RSA	1.7.89	1	NC	Potchefstroom	22 Apr

Mark	Name		Nat	Born	Pos	Meet	Venue	Date
21.09i	Maksim	Afonin	RUS	6.1.92	1	NC	Moskva	20 Feb
	(20)							
21.07	Chukwuebuka	Enekwechi	NGR	28.1.93	1		Cork	18 Jul
21.01	Jacko	Gill	NZL	20.12.94	1		Lower Hutt	21 Jan
20.93	Jonathan	Jones	USA	23.4.91	1		Chula Vista	27 May
20.92	Jakub	Szyszkowski	POL	21.8.91	1		Wroclaw	18 Jun
20.91	Josh	Freeman	USA	22.8.94	2	Kans R	Lawrence	21 Apr
20.87i	Asmir	Kolasinac	SRB	15.10.84	1		Beograd	18 Feb
20.86i	Frank	Elemba	CGO	21.7.90	1		Madrid	24 Feb
20.86	Francisco	Belo	POR	27.3.91	1	WUG	Taipei	23 Aug
20.84i	Ladislav	Prásil	CZE	17.5.90	1	NCh	Praha	26 Feb
20.83	Stephen	Mozia	NGR	16.8.93	2		Portland	2 Jul
	(30)							
20.82	Hamza	Alic	BIH	20.1.79	2		Zenica	7 Jun
20.73	Kurt	Roberts	USA	20.2.88	1		Columbia, SC	25 Mar
20.73	Tim	Nedow	CAN	16.10.90	1		Windsor	17 Jun
20.69	Curtis	Jensen	USA	1.11.90	2		Rathdrum, ID	3 Jun
20.63i	Bob	Bertemes	LUX	24.5.93	1		Metz	4 Feb
20.63	Jaco	Engelbrecht	RSA	8.3.87	2	NC	Potchefstroom	22 Apr
20.62	Jordan	Geist	USA-J	21.7.98	1		Tucson	9 Dec
20.61	Andrei	Gag	ROU	7.4.91	Q	WCh	London (OS)	5 Aug
20.57	Carlos	Tobalina	ESP	2.8.85	2		Las Palmas de G.C.	12 Mar
20.52	Aleksey	Nichipor	BLR	10.4.93	1		Minsk	20 Jul
	(40)							
20.47i	Jared	Kern	USA	10.6.95	1		Nashville	11 Feb
20.46	Fedrick	Dacres	JAM	28.2.94	1		Kingston	15 Apr
20.45	Ashinia	Miller	JAM	6.6.93	1		Marietta, GA	28 May
20.45	Germán	Lauro	ARG	2.4.84	2		Andùjar	2 Jun
20.44	Konstantin	Lyadusov	RUS	2.3.88	2	NCp	Yerino	14 Jul
20.43	Borja	Vivas	ESP	26.5.84	1		Torremolinos	12 Jun
20.42	Nick	Vena	USA	16.4.93	1		Princeton	21 Apr
20.40	Tejinder Pal	Singh	IND	13.11.94	1	Fed Cup	Patiala	2 Jun
20.39	Oghenakpobo	Efekoro	NGR	15.7.96	1		Charlottesville	8 Apr
20.33	Denzel	Comenentia	NED	25.11.95	2		Charlottesville	21 Apr
	(50)							
20.31i	David	Pless	USA	19.11.90	2	NC	Albuquerque	4 Mar
20.27	Nikólaos	Skarvélis	GRE	2.2.93	1		Claremont	22 Jul
20.24	Nicolai	Ceban	MDA	4.2.95	2Q	NCAA-W	Austin	26 May
20.22i	Mihaíl	Stamatóyiannis ¶	GRE	20.5.82	1	NC	Pireás	18 Feb
20.22	Willian	Dourado	BRA	6.1.94	1		Campinas	30 Apr
20.22	Magdi Mohamed	Hamza	EGY	30.8.96	2	Odlozil	Praha	5 Jun
20.21	J.C.	Murasky	USA	6.2.93	3		Tucson	18 May
20.19	Ayomidotun	Ogundeji	USA	24.2.96	2		La Jolla	22 Apr
20.18i	Arttu	Kangas	FIN	13.7.93	1	NC	Jyväskylä	19 Feb
20.16	Mikhail	Abramchuk	BLR	15.11.92	2		Brest	31 May
	(60)							
20.15	Nick	Demaline	USA	1.3.96	1Q	NCAA-E	Lexington	26 May
20.14	Coy	Blair	USA	10.6.94	1		Ashland	16 Jun
20.12	Georgi	Ivanov	BUL	13.3.85	1		Balchik	14 May
20.11i	Rafal	Kownatke	POL	24.3.85	3	NC	Torun	19 Feb
20.04	Christian	Jagusch	GER	13.7.92	1		Rostock	10 Jun
20.04	Frédéric	Dagée	FRA	11.12.92	4	ET	Villeneuve d'Ascq	24 Jun
20.00	Ivan	Ivanov	KAZ	3.1.92	1		Almaty	12 Jun
19.96	Josh	Awotunde	USA/NGR	12.6.95	1	PennR	Philadelphia	28 Apr
19.88	Osman Can	Özdevici	TUR	23.8.95	1		Ankara	6 Jun
19.87i	Roger	Steen	USA	17.5.92	5	NC	Albuquerque	4 Mar
	(70)							
19.85	Tomas	Djurovic	MNE	14.2.94	2		Bar	1 May
19.80	Ali	Samari	IRI	7.1.93	1	AsiC	Bhubaneswar	7 Jul
19.79i	Willie	Morrison	USA	23.11.96	1	Big 10	Geneva, OH	25 Feb
19.78	Nedzad	Mulabegovic	CRO	4.2.81	3		Slovenska Bistrica	27 May
19.78	Sebastiano	Bianchetti	ITA	20.1.96	1	NC-23	Firenze	9 Jun
19.76	Aleksey	Kulayev	RUS	7.5.94	4		Adler	23 Apr
19.75i	Matt	Katnik	USA	10.10.96	2		Seattle	25 Feb
19.75i	Garrett	Appier	USA	15.10.92	1		Pittsburg	9 Dec
19.74	Péter	Simon	HUN	18.9.94	1	Pac-10	Eugene	13 May
19.72	Sarunas	Banevicius	LTU	20.11.91	5	WUG	Taipei	23 Aug
	(80)							
19.70	Austin	Droogsma	USA	4.3.95	1	FlaR	Gainesville	1 Apr
19.68	Dennis	Lewke	GER	23.7.93	4		Halle	20 May
19.67i	Mateusz	Mikos	POL	10.4.87	4	NC	Torun	19 Feb

Mark	Name		Nat	Born	Pos	Meet	Venue	Date
19.67	Aleksandr	Bulanov	RUS	26.12.89	4		Yerino	10 Jun
19.64	Kristo	Galeta	EST	9.4.83	1		Tallinn	2 Sep
19.63	Aaron	Castle	USA	7.10.93	1		Tempe	29 Apr
19.62	Alex	Renner	USA	28.12.93	1		Fargo	12 May
19.60i	Daniel	Ståhl	SWE	27.8.92	2	v3N	Tampere	11 Feb
19.58	Om Prakash	Singh	IND	11.1.87	1		Taipei	30 Apr
19.58		Tian Zhizhong	CHN	15.12.92	1		Tianjin	3 Sep
	(90)							
19.56	Sultan	Al-Hebshi	KSA	23.2.83	2	Isl.Sol	Baku	20 May
19.56	Maksim	Sidorov	RUS	13.5.86	5		Adler	26 May
19.55	Abdollah	Jamshidi	IRI		1		Tehran	14 Aug
19.53	Nick	Ponzio	USA	5.1.95	6	NCAA	Eugene	7 Jun
19.51	Ihor	Musiyenko	UKR	22.8.93	1		Lutsk	7 May
19.49	Jan Josef	Jeuschede	GER	23.4.93	1		Böhmenkirch	29 Jul
19.48i		Liu Yang	CHN	29.10.86	1		Beijing	19 Feb
19.47	Pavel	Derkach	RUS	2.11.93	2		Adler	23 Apr
19.47	Kiriáko	Zótos	GRE	17.1.96	1	NC-23	Lárisa	29 Jul
19.46i	Daniele	Secci	ITA	9.3.92	2		Schio	9 Feb
	(100)							
19.46	Jasdeep	Singh	IND	6.10.90	2	Fed Cup	Patiala	2 Jun

Mark	Name		Nat	Born	Date
19.44i	Patrick	Cronie	NED	5.11.89	18 Feb
19.42	Riley	Budde	USA	31.5.95	5 May
19.41	Martin	Stasek	CZE	8.4.89	14 Jun
19.40	Andrzej	Gudro	POL	8.4.94	24 Jun
19.40	Marcus	Thomsen	NOR-J	7.1.98	26 Aug
19.39i	Bodo	Göder	GER	27.6.93	12 Feb
19.39	Viktor	Samolyuk	UKR	5.9.86	14 Jun
19.37i	Darien	Moore ¶	USA	10.6.91	12 Feb
19.35	Leif	Arrhenius	SWE	15.7.86	29 Jul
19.34	Szymon	Mazur	POL-J	2.9.98	1 Jun
19.33	Jan	Parol	POL	11.11.95	24 Jun
19.33	Leonardo	Fabbri	ITA	15.4.97	1 Jul
19.30	Simon	Bayer	GER	23.11.95	14 Jul
19.29		Wang Guangfu	CHN	15.11.87	31 Mar
19.25i	Martin	Novák	CZE	5.10.92	4 Feb
19.24i		Jung Il-woo	KOR	28.3.86	18 Sep
19.23	Patrick	Müller	GER	4.2.96	14 Jul
19.22i	Richard	Chavez	USA	30.7.92	4 Feb
19.22	Corey	Murphy	USA	3.11.96	21 Apr
19.21		Wu Jiaxing	CHN	29.3.90	30 Apr
19.20	Jhon Fredy	Zea	COL	13.1.93	10 Jun
19.18	Naveen	Chikara	IND	14.12.96	2 Jun
19.16	Willian	Braido	BRA	18.3.92	10 Jun
19.15	Burger	Lambrechts	RSA-J	6.8.98	22 Apr
19.15	Andrew	Liskowitz	USA	22.5.97	13 May
19.15		Feng Jie	CHN	18.1.86	3 Sep
19.13	Jon	Yohman	USA	23.8.94	26 May
19.11	Danie	McArthur	USA-J	17.3.98	13 May
19.11	Artyom	Podolskiy	RUS	21.7.93	14 Jul
19.10	Mario	Cota	MEX	11.9.90	22 Apr
19.10	Maris	Urtans	LAT	9.2.81	10 Jun
19.09	José Angel	Pinedo	ESP	30.7.90	14 Jul
19.06i	Brian	Williams	USA	18.12.94	25 Feb
19.04	Sergey	Dementyev	UZB	1.6.90	12 Jun
19.03	T'Mond	Johnson	USA	29.7.97	13 May
19.02	Jacob	Mahin	USA	.93	28 Apr
19.02	Nate	Esparza	USA-J	24.4.98	30 Apr
19.00i	Derrick	Vicars	USA	8.5.89	11 Feb
19.00	Scott	Lincoln	GBR	7.5.93	12 Mar
19.00	Gian Piero	Ragonesi	ITA	19.4.95	1 Apr
19.00	Anton	Tikhomirov	RUS	29.4.88	26 May
19.00	Jason	van Rooyen	RSA	4.2.97	10 Jun
18.99i	Kyle	Felpel	USA	26.7.93	10 Mar
18.99	Kevin	Farley	USA	18.7.93	1 Apr
18.99		Li Jun	CHN	2.1.93	3 Sep
18.98	Lucas	Warning	USA	.95	6 May
18.98	Valentin	Döbler	GER	21.11.96	28 May
18.98	Matus	Olej	SVK	5.7.91	2 Jul
18.98	Frántsi-Anastásios	Latifllári	GRE	8.8.96	29 Jul
18.97	Elijah	Talk	USA	.95	21 Apr
18.94	Grant	Cartwright	USA	19.11.94	13 May
18.94		Ding Weiye	CHN	13.4.90	2 Jul
18.94i	Brett	Neelly	USA	22.11.96	9 Dec
18.93	Kole	Weldon	USA	25.3.92	3 May
18.93	Biaz	Zupancic	SLO	6.4.95	26 Jul
18.92i	Jan	Marcell	CZE	4.6.85	4 Feb
18.91	Gaëtan	Bucki	FRA	9.5.80	21 May
18.90	Macklin	Tudor	USA	13.6.94	13 May
18.89i	Nik	Huffman	USA	.94	17 Feb
18.89	Andrzej	Regin	POL	21.2.94	13 May
18.89	Andrea	Caiaffa	ITA	26.7.95	9 Jun
18.88	Cameron	Cornelius	USA	.95	16 Mar
18.88	Mohamed	Eskandari	IRI	27.7.90	17 Oct
18.87i	Timo	Kööpikkä	FIN	10.5.94	19 Feb
18.87	Mathijs	Damsteegt	NED	26.8.95	16 Jul
18.85i	Nathan	Bultman	USA	6.4.97	4 Feb
18.85	Silas	Ristl	GER	1.4.95	28 May
18.85	Jander	Heil	EST	20.4.97	17 Jun
18.84	Reno	Tuufuli	USA	15.2.96	13 May
18.84	Andrzej	Naszko	POL	9.5.94	4 Jun
18.84		Chang Ming-Huang	TPE	7.8.82	23 Oct
18.83	Sourabh	Vij	IND	14.6.87	11 May
18.83	Nikita	Zhidkov	RUS	29.2.88	26 Jun
18.83	Grigoriy	Kamulya	UZB	31.1.89	8 Oct
18.82i	Erik	Cadée	NED	15.2.84	12 Feb
18.81i	Devon	Patterson	USA	27.4.96	24 Feb
18.80i	David	Schall	USA	1.10.96	10 Feb
18.79	Marco	Fortes	POR	26.9.82	10 Jun
18.78	Conrad	Schwarzkopf	USA	.94	12 May
18.77	Benik	Bonhurst	USA	2.6.96	1 Apr
18.77	Stéphane	Szuster	FRA	4.2.74	23 Jun
18.76i	Vladislav	Tulácek	CZE	9.7.88	22 Jan
18.76	Carles	Nahigian	USA	27.5.94	25 Mar
18.76	Naveen	Kumar Singh	IND	15.5.89	25 Aug
18.73	Valdivino	Nunes	BRA	9.1.95	23 Apr
18.72		Hwang In-sung	KOR	15.8.84	5 Jul
18.72	Itamir	Levi	ISR	11.11.91	21 Dec
18.71	McKay	Johnson	USA-J	15.4.98	4 Mar
18.70i	Avery	Meyers	USA	10.6.93	21 Jan
18.70	Eldred	Henry	IVB	18.9.94	2 Jul
	(191)				

Best outdoor marks

Mark	Name	Pos	Meet	Venue	Date
21.59	Bukowiecki	1	EC-23	Bydgoszcz	14 Jul
21.07	Afonin	1		Moskva	22 Jul
20.72	Elemba	1		Franconville	7 May
20.57	Prásil	1		Kladno	15 Jul
20.27	Pless	3		Rathdrum, ID	4 Jun
20.18	Bertemes	6	ECp-w	Las Palmas GC	12 Mar
19.95	Kangas	1		Kotka	3 Aug
19.70	Steen	8	NC	Sacramento	25 Jun
19.69	Morrison	Q	NCAA-E	Lexington	26 May
19.67	Kownatke	4	NC	Bialystok	23 Jul
19.65	Kern	2		Knoxville	7 Apr
19.65	Mikos	4		Bygoszcz	1 Jun

Mark	Name	Date
19.45	Kolasinac	15 Jul
19.42	Secci	12 Mar
19.23	Jung Il-woo	7 May
19.14	Katnik	25 Jun
19.14	Liu Yang	3 Sep
19.07	Göder	25 May
19.00	Cronie	9 Jul
18.92	Stamatóyiannis ¶	23 May
18.81	Neelly	13 May
18.81	Huffman	7 Jun
18.72	Felpel	15 Apr

Mark	Name		Nat	Born	Pos	Meet	Venue	Date
Drugs disqualification								
20.78i	Darien	Moore ¶	USA	10.6.91	(1)	NC	Albuquerque	4 Mar
		JUNIORS						
20.62	Jordan	Geist	USA	21.7.98	1		Tucson	9 Dec
19.40	Marcus	Thomsen	NOR	7.1.98	1	NC	Sandnes	26 Aug
19.34	Szymon	Mazur	POL	2.9.98	5		Bydgoszcz	1 Jun
19.15	Burger	Lambrechts	RSA	6.8.98	3	NC	Potchefstroom	22 Apr
19.11	Danie	McArthur	USA	17.3.98	4		Atlanta	13 May
19.02	Nate	Esparza	USA	24.4.98	2		Los Angeles	30 Apr
18.51	Kyle	Blignaut	RSA	9.11.99	5	NC	Potchefstroom	22 Apr
18.46	Odisséas	Mouzenídis	GRE	30.6.99	1		Édessa	31 May
18.43	Kevin	Nedrick	JAM	11.1.98	3		Kingston	13 May
18.43	Isaiah	Rogers (10)	USA	28.4.98	2	Big12	Lawrence	13 May
18.14	Giorgi	Mujaridze	GEO	22.3.98	4	ET-3	Marsa	24 Jun
18.13i	Bronson	Osborn	USA	5.7.98	1		Flagstaff	4 Fab
18.08i	Wictor	Petersson	SWE	1.5.98	1		Malmö	29 Jan
18.03	Luke	Grodeska	USA	20.5.98	3		State College	5 May
18.01	Charles	Lenford	USA	17.3.98	19q	NCAA-E	Lexington	26 May
		6 KG SHOT						
22.02	Jordan	Geist	USA	21.7.98	1	PAm-J	Trujillo	23 Jul
	21.89i 1 Greensburg 7 Feb	21.14 1 NC-j Sacramento 23 Jun						
21.36	Marcus	Thomsen	NOR	7.1.98	1	EJ	Grosseto	21 Jul
	21.32 1 Hvidovre 11 Jun	20.88 1 NC-j Bergen 2 Sep						
	20.89 1 Mannheim 1 Jul	11 performances (2 indoor) by 4 men to 20.85						
21.34	Szymon	Mazur	POL	2.9.98	1		Torun	7 Jul
	21.03i 1 NC-j Torun 11 Feb	20.99 1 Werfer Halle 20 May						
20.94	Kevin	Nedrick	JAM	11.1.98	1	NC-j	Kingston	24 Jun
20.80	Adrian	Piperi	USA	20.1.99	2	NC-j	Sacramento	23 Jun
20.67	Odisséas	Mouzenídis	GRE	30.6.99	3	EJ	Grosseto	21 Jul
20.66	Kyle	Blignaut	RSA	9.11.99	1		Potchefstroom	21 Oct
20.47i	Wictor	Petersson	SWE	1.5.98	1		Växjö	3 Mar
	20.11				1		Växjö	13 May
20.44	Burger	Lambrechts	RSA	6.8.98	1		Pretoria	11 Feb
20.26i	Giorgi	Mujaridze (10)	GEO	22.3.98	1		Tbilisi	26 Feb
	19.52				2	Balk-j	Pitesti	1 Jul
20.14	Dmitriy	Karpyuk	BLR	5.11.99	4	EJ	Grosseto	21 Jul
20.03	Valentin	Moll	GER	21.6.99	1		Ulm	6 Aug
19.98	Ryan	Ballantyne	NZL	8.1.99	1		Jacksonville	8 Jul
19.96i	Pascal	Eichler	GER	20.6.98	1	v2N	Halle	4 Mar
	19.92				1		Dresden	18 Jun
19.85	McKay	Johnson	USA	15.4.98	3	NC-j	Sacramento	23 Jun
19.83	Nathan	Esparza	USA	24.4.98	4	NC-j	Sacramento	23 Jun
19.72	Charles	Lenford	USA	17.3.98	5	NC-j	Sacramento	23 Jun
19.67i	Tobias	Köhler	GER	23.8.98	2	v2N	Halle	4 Mar
	19.60				2		Biberach	10 Jul
19.58	Kyle	Mitchell	JAM	16.7.98	2	NC-j	Kingston	24 Jun
19.55	Paulius	Gelaziusm (20)	LTU	20.4.98	2		Mannheim	1 Jul
12 lb (5.44kg) Shot								
23.16	Jordan	Geist	USA	21.7.98	1	N.Sch	Greensboro	17 Jun
	22.81 1 Columbia SC 7 Apr	22.62 1 Saxonburg 1 Apr						
	22.78 1 PennR Philadelphia 28 Apr	22.62 1 Butler 21 Aor						
	22.78 1 Pittsburgh 5 May							
22.85	Adrian	Piperi	USA-Y	20.1.99	1		Katy	4 Mar
22.47	Gabriel	Oladipo	USA	17.4.99	1	Jnr Oly	Ypsilanti	2 Aug

DISCUS

Mark	Name		Nat	Born	Pos	Meet	Venue	Date
71.29	Daniel	Ståhl	SWE	27.8.92	1		Sollentuna	29 Jun

Mark	Pos	Meet	Venue	Date						
					68.88	x	71.29 x	x	62.83	
69.19	2	WCh	London (OS)	5 Aug	x	69.19	66.58	68.57	x	63.06
68.36	1		Salinas	21 Apr	x	68.36 x	67.02	x	66.33	
68.13	2	DL	Stockholm	18 Jun	66.25	67.34	66.88	x	66.95	68.13
68.11	1		Salinas	22 Apr	62.29	59.69	67.11	x	67.44	68.11
68.07	1		Halle	20 May	64.57	x	x	x	68.07	66.94
68.06	1	Bisl	Oslo	15 Jun	62.60	64.95	67.36	65.36	62.58	68.06
67.80	1	NC	Helsingborg	25 Aug	58.33	66.99	65.23	x	67.80	x
67.64	Q	WCh	London (OS)	4 Aug	61.83	67.64				
67.59	1		Borås	7 Jul	66.73	x	x	x	67.59	64.21
67.37	1	vFIN	Stockholm	3 Sep	67.37	61.68	x	62.44	x	x
67.26	1		Karlstad	25 Jul	64.11	66.07	65.47	65.35	58.64	67.26

Mark	Name		Nat	Born	Pos	Meet	Venue	Date
69.21	Andrius	Gudzius	LTU	14.2.91	1	WCh	London (OS)	5 Aug
				67.52	69.21	63.43	x 63.98	67.89
	68.61	1 Kaunas	3 Jun	65.57	64.86	68.61	66.97 x	64.28
	68.16	1 Kuso Szczecin	10 Jun	67.23	68.16	67.27	x 61.82	64.06
	68.16	1 VD-DLF Bruxelles	1 Sep	65.43	66.70	68.16	66.76 x	65.63
	68.04	1 NC Palanga	20 Jul	64.40	x	63.95	67.09 64.77	68.04
	67.62	1 Birstonas	13 May	64.97	63.03	66.05	x 64.66	67.62
	67.38	1 Kaunas	19 Apr	60.96	66.03	66.68	66.38 67.38	63.42
	67.29	3 DL Stockholm	18 Jun	66.16	65.04	66.00	67.29 63.64	64.48
	67.01	Q WCh London (OS)	4 Aug	67.01				
68.88	Fedrick	Dacres	JAM	28.2.94	1		Kingston	11 Feb
				64.97	65.80	66.83	65.10 67.10	68.88
	68.67	1 Kingston	21 Jan	64.31	66.65	65.91	67.04 68.67	x
	68.36	1 DL Stockholm	18 Jun	64.90	67.04	67.00	68.36 65.78	67.23
	67.30	1 Chula Vista	20 Apr	67.30	x	x	62.61 67.02	64.29
	67.10	2 Bisl Oslo	15 Jun	x	61.95	67.10	65.40 64.66	64.36
68.03	Mason	Finley	USA	7.10.90	3	WCh	London (OS)	5 Aug
				67.07	68.03	65.21	37.36 66.59	x
67.68	Piotr	Malachowski	POL	7.6.83	1		Cetniewo	29 Jul
				65.76	66.47	66.18	63.61 67.68	67.22
	67.18	1 ISTAF Berlin	27 Aug	61.61	62.16	x	67.18 64.72	63.86
67.05	Philip	Milanov	BEL	6.7.91	4	DL	Stockholm	18 Jun
	(306)			63.61	66.41	67.05	x 65.34	66.09
66.73	Robert	Urbanek	POL	29.4.87	2		Sollentuna	29 Jun
66.67	Lois Maikel	Martínez	ESP	3.6.81	1		Durango	18 Feb
66.61	Andrew	Evans	USA	25.1.91	2		Chula Vista	20 Apr
66.52	Lukas	Weisshaidinger	AUT	20.2.92	3		Halle	20 May
	(10)							
66.30	Robert	Harting	GER	18.10.84	1	ET	Villeneuve d'Ascq	25 Jun
65.87	Gerd	Kanter	EST	6.5.79	1		Wiesbaden	13 May
65.81	Mauricio	Ortega	COL	4.8.94	1		Leiria	30 Jul
65.72A	Niklas	Arrhenius	SWE	10.9.82	1		Provo	18 Jul
65.67	Zoltán	Kövágó	HUN	10.4.79	1	Gyulai	Székesfehérvár	4 Jul
65.66	Ehsan	Hadadi	IRI	21.1.85	1		Tehran	7 Oct
65.61	Sam	Mattis	USA	19.3.94	2		La Jolla	21 Apr
65.56	Martin	Wierig	GER	10.6.87	2		Wiesbaden	13 May
65.39	Rodney	Brown	USA	21.5.93	1		Rathdrum, ID	2 Jun
	(20)							
65.13	Brian	Williams	USA	18.12.94	1	SEC	Columbia, SC	12 May
65.13	Apostolos	Parellis	CYP	24.7.85	1		Limassol	20 Jul
65.12	Jared	Schuurmans	USA	20.8.87	1		Portland	31 May
65.10	Lolassonn	Djouhan	FRA	18.5.91	1		Saran	29 Apr
65.07	Viktor	Butenko	RUS	10.3.93	1		Adler	7 Feb
65.00	Traves	Smikle	JAM	7.5.92	1		Kingston	11 Jun
64.93	Erik	Cadée	NED	15.2.84	1		Heerhugowaard	12 Jul
64.88	Simon	Pettersson	SWE	3.1.94	1		Södertälje	6 Jun
64.67	Benn	Harradine	AUS	14.10.82	1		Enskede	19 Jul
64.66	David	Wrobel	GER	13.2.91	4		Wiesbaden	13 May
	(30)							
64.55	Marshall	Hall	NZL	7.10.88	1		Salinas	27 May
64.55	Christoph	Harting	GER	4.10.90	5	VD-DLF	Bruxelles	1 Sep
64.30	Alex	Rose	SAM	7.11.91	1	Drake	Des Moines	29 Apr
64.18	Victor	Hogan	RSA	25.7.89	1		Leiria	20 Jul
63.98	Mitch	Cooper	AUS	2.6.95	1	Big 12	Lawrence	14 May
63.97	Sven Martin	Skagestad	NOR	13.1.95	1		Göteborg	2 Jul
63.90	Axel	Härstedt	SWE	28.2.87	1		Malmö	1 May
63.78	Markus	Münch	GER	13.6.86	5		Wiesbaden	13 May
63.77	Mykyta	Nesterenko	UKR	15.4.91	1	NC-w	Mukachevo	15 Feb
63.76	Filip	Mihaljevic	CRO	31.7.94	1	NCAA	Eugene	9 Jun
	(40)							
63.66	Giovanni	Faloci	ITA	13.10.85	1		San Benedetto del Tronto	21 May
63.54	Macklin	Tudor	USA	13.6.94	1	PennR	Philadelphia	29 Apr
63.38	Aleksey	Khudyakov	RUS	31.3.95	1		Moskva	15 May
63.15	Matthew	Denny	AUS	2.6.96	1		Geelong	19 Mar
62.91	Nick	Percy	GBR	5.12.94	1	Big 10	University Park	14 May
62.86	Martin	Kupper	EST	31.5.89	3	ECp-w	Las Palmas	11 Mar
62.76	Jordan	Young	CAN	21.6.93	1	NC	Ottawa	7 Jul
62.75	Róbert	Szikszai	HUN	30.9.94	1		Veszprém	22 Jul
62.68	Zane	Duquemin	GBR	23.9.91	1		Leiria	15 Apr
62.61	Sebastian	Scheffel	GER	17.11.93	2eB		Halle	20 May
	(50)							

Mark	Name		Nat	Born	Pos	Meet	Venue	Date
62.60	Hannes	Kirchler	ITA	22.12.78	1		Tarquinia	1 Jun
62.55	Muhd Irfan	Shamsuddin	MAS	16.8.95	2		Linz	25 May
62.53	Mario	Cota	MEX	11.9.90	1		Chula Vista	14 May
62.53	Chad	Wright	JAM	25.3.91	3		Kingston	20 May
62.51	Reggie	Jagers	USA	13.8.94	2	NCAA	Eugene	9 Jun
62.48	Clemens	Prüfer	GER	13.8.97	3eB		Halle	20 May
62.42	Tavis	Bailey	USA	6.1.92	4		Rathdrum, ID	2 Jun
62.38	Nazzareno	Di Marco	ITA	30.4.85	1		Ascoli	29 Jul
62.35	Vikas	Gowda	IND	5.7.83	2		Chula Vista	27 May
62.28	Jason	Harrell	USA	10.1.91	1		Tucson	18 May
	(60)							
62.22	Essa Mohamed	Al-Zankawi	KUW	17.10.92	1		Jeddah	14 Apr
62.22	Aleksandr	Kirya	RUS	23.3.92	3		Adler	25 May
62.20	Daniel	Jasinski	GER	5.8.89	5	NC	Erfurt	8 Jul
62.17	Viktor	Trus	BLR	11.11.96	1		Brest	12 May
62.16	János	Huszák	HUN	5.2.92	1		Senta	6 May
62.09	Torben	Brandt	GER	19.5.95	2		Halle	21 May
62.06	Reno	Tuufuli	USA	15.2.96	1	NCAA-W	Austin	27 May
62.04	Phillip	Jagers	USA	12.8.95	1		San Antonio	25 Mar
62.01	Francisco	Belo	POR	27.3.91	1	NC	Vagos	11 Jun
61.98	Alin Alexandru	Firfirica	ROU	3.11.95	Q	WUG	Taipei	26 Aug
	(70)							
61.74	Kai	Schmidt	GER	11.2.93	1		Abilene	24 Mar
61.72	Damian	Kaminski	POL	15.12.93	1		Gdansk	3 Jun
61.70	Germán	Lauro	ARG	2.4.84	2	SAmC	Asunción	23 Jun
61.66	Pyry	Niskala	FIN	6.11.90	1		Maalahti	14 Jun
61.56	Julian	Wruck	AUS	6.7.91	1	NC	Sydney	1 Apr
61.52	Bartlomiej	Stój	POL	15.5.96	3		Cetniewo	29 Jul
61.48	Gleb	Sidorchenko	RUS	15.5.86	2	NC	Zhukovskiy	30 Jul
61.44	Kord	Ferguson	USA	19.6.95	2		Baton Rouge	28 Apr
61.43	David	Lucas	USA	6.6.96	2	PennR	Philadelphia	29 Apr
61.34	Maximilian	Klaus	GER	7.2.96	2eB		Wiesbaden	13 May
	(80)							
61.33	Ola Stunes	Isene	NOR	29.1.95	1		Albufeira	20 May
61.29	Michael	Ohakwe	USA	.92	3		Chula Vista	27 May
61.20	Martin	Maric	CRO	19.4.84	1	Balk C	Novi Pazar	16 Jul
61.20	Aleksas	Abromavicius	LTU	6.12.84	2	NC	Palanga	20 Jul
61.15	Brett	Morse	GBR	11.2.89	1		Cheltenham	19 Jul
61.09	Roland	Varga	CRO	22.10.77	2		Velenje	20 Jun
61.04A	Leif	Arrhenius	SWE	15.7.86	1		Draper, UT	10 Jun
60.94	Gudni Valur	Gudnason	ISL	11.10.95	1		Hafnafjördur	22 Jul
60.93	Henning	Prüfer	GER	7.3.96	3eB		Wiesbaden	13 May
60.89	Mustapha Katem	Dagher	IRQ	29.11.95	1	Isl.Sol	Baku	16 May
	(90)							
60.84	Benedikt	Stienen	GER	12.1.92	7		Wiesbaden	13 May
60.77	Nikolay	Sedyuk	RUS	29.4.88	5		Adler	25 May
60.77	Basil	Bingham	JAM	1.9.94	3		Kingston	11 Jun
60.75	Yeóryios	Trémos	GRE	21.3.89	2		Iráklio	27 May
60.74	Yuji	Tsutsumi	JPN	22.12.89	1		Osaka	23 Sep
60.69	Pawel	Pasinski	POL	6.3.93	6	Kuso	Szczecin	10 Jun
60.35	Ivan	Panasyuk	UKR	8.10.91	1	NC	Kropyvnystkiy	8 Jul
60.34	Emmanuel	Onyia	JAM	16.6.93	3	PennR	Philadelphia	29 Apr
60.33	Aleksandr	Dobrenkiy	RUS	11.3.94	2	Znam	Zhukovskiy	1 Jul
60.31	Moaaz Mohamed	Ibrahim	QAT-J	8.2.99	4	POL Ch	Bialystok	22 Jul
60.31	Frank	Casañas	ESP	18.10.78	4		Leiria	29 Jul
	(100)							

Mark	Name		Nat	Born	Date
60.28	Greg	Thompson	GBR	5.5.94	5 May
60.28	Jan	Marcell	CZE	4.6.85	12 Jul
60.14	Andreas	Christou	CYP	14.4.93	16 Jul
60.10	Marek	Bárta	CZE	8.12.92	14 May
60.03	Tim	Nedow	CAN	16.10.90	7 Jul
60.01	Nicolai	Ceban	MDA	4.2.95	1 Apr
60.01	Jorge	Fernández	CUB	2.10.87	27 May
59.99		Wu Jian	CHN	25.5.86	27 Mar
59.98	Giulio	Anesa	ITA	7.7.96	14 May
59.90	Douglas	dos Reis	BRA	9.12.95	22 Mar
59.80	Mohammed	Samimi	IRI	29.3.87	6 Jul
59.78	Justin	Ramirez	USA	3.11.93	28 May
59.73	Péter	Savanyú	HUN	26.6.87	6 May
59.72	Aleksey	Sysoyev	RUS	8.8.85	30 Jul
59.70	Martin	Markovic	CRO	13.1.96	11 Jun
59.67	Stephen	Mozia	NGR	16.8.93	14 May
59.63	Joe	Williams	USA	21.8.94	13 Apr
59.63	Artyom	Podolskiy	RUS	21.7.93	8 Jul
59.55	Hayden	Reed	USA	4.4.94	13 Apr
59.53	Josh	Syrotchen	USA	19.4.94	1 Apr
59.37	Victor	Gardenkrans	SWE	30.7.95	9 Dec
59.36	Ryan	Hunter-Simms	USA	20.12.93	29 Apr
59.33	Alan	Toward	GBR	31.10.92	26 Feb
59.27	Wojciech	Praczyk	POL	10.1.93	22 Apr
59.24	Masateru	Yugami	JPN	14.4.93	6 Oct
59.18	Gian Piero	Ragonesi	ITA	19.4.95	25 Mar
59.18	Ihor	Musiyenko	UKR	22.8.93	20 May
59.14		Zhang Menjie	CHN	11.3.92	27 Mar
59.07	Merten	Howe	GER	7.1.97	13 May
59.05	Jacob	Armbrust	USA	22.2.94	25 Mar
58.98	Sultan M.	Al-Dawoodi	KSA	16.6.77	18 Jul
58.96	Martin	Stasek	CZE	8.4.89	3 Jun

Mark	Name		Nat	Born	Date
58.87	Domantas	Poska	LTU	10.1.96	11 Mar
58.78	Duke	Taylor	USA	.94	26 May
58.75	Sajad	Pirigherchman	IRI	22.6.92	30 Apr
58.70	Taylor	Frenia	USA	4.5.94	6 May
58.68	Yevgeniy	Milovatskiy	KAZ	23.3.94	28 Mar
58.65	Jeff	Bartlett	USA	.94	22 Apr
58.59		Tan Shen	CHN	9.3.91	4 Mar
58.59	Mahmoud	Samimi	IRI	18.9.88	13 Apr
58.56	Jaromír	Mazgal	CZE	20.1.93	23 May
58.55	Märt	Israel	EST	23.9.83	11 Jun
58.54	Kyle	Long	USA	14.10.93	14 May
58.53	Shigeyuki	Maisawa	JPN	19.1.93	25 Jun
58.52	Behnam	Shiri	IRI	21.3.93	17 Oct
58.51	Caspar	Hattink	NED	1.6.93	7 Jul
58.50	Josh	Awotunde	USA/NGR	12.6.95	29 Apr
58.46	Sergiu	Ursu ¶	ROU	26.4.80	28 Feb
58.46	Federico	Apolloni	ITA	14.3.87	11 Jul
58.43	Courtland	Clavette	USA	4.7.93	29 Apr
58.43	János	Káplár	HUN	8.2.94	14 May
58.42	Konrad	Bukowiecki	POL	17.3.97	2 Jul
58.38	Stefan	Mura	MDA	2.7.97	27 May
58.37	Austin	Hogan	USA	26.11.96	12 May
58.32	Dharamraj	Yadav	IND	26.1.91	3 Jun
58.26	Jayson	Kovar	USA	30.4.94	27 May
58.25	Luke	Vaughn	USA	24.8.94	3 Jun
58.24	Ahmed Mohamed Dheeb		QAT	29.9.85	16 May
58.23	Grant	Cartwright	USA	19.11.94	14 May
58.22	Matthew	Zajac	USA	23.1.96	12 May
58.16	Ronald	Julião	BRA	16.6.85	20 Apr
58.15	Ricky	Nelson	USA	21.3.97	8 Apr
58.14	Kole	Weldon	USA	25.3.92	13 Jun
58.13	Shaun	Haughton	JAM	16.1.85	8 Apr
58.12	Isaac	Holtz	USA	.95	14 May
58.09	Jakob	Gardenkrans	SWE	15.8.97	8 Apr
58.03	Jordan	Guehaseim	FRA	16.6.97	8 Jul
58.00	Denzel (168)	Comenentia	NED	25.11.95	6 May

Downhill: Oostende 3 Jun: 3. Stephan Dekker NED 17.2.78 62.40, 4. Tomás Vonavka CZE 4.1.90 59.50

JUNIORS

Mark	Name		Nat	Born	Pos	Meet	Venue	Date
60.31	Mouad M.	Ibrahim	QAT-J	8.2.99	4	POL Ch	Bialystok	22 Jul
	58.94 3 Arab Radès 18 Jul				57.68 7		Velenje	20 Jun
57.03	Henrik	Jansen	GER	19.5.98	3		Halle	19 Jan
56.93	Félix	Valle	CUB	3.4.98	1		La Habana	4 Mar
56.52	Oskar	Stachnik	POL	1.3.98	6	Skol	Cetniewo	29 Jul
55.99	Roje	Stona	JAM	26.2.99	4		Kingston	3 Jun
55.67	Christoforos	Genethli	CYP	19.1.98	1		Nicosia	23 May
55.52	Ángel	Álvarez	CUB-Y	25.2.00	2		La Habana	4 Mar
55.27	Patrick	Duvenage	RSA	17.2.98	1		Pretoria	31 Mar
54.93	Werner	Visser	RSA	27.2.98	1		Pretoria	30 Jan

1.75 KG DISCUS

Mark	Name		Nat	Born	Pos	Meet	Venue	Date
66.41	Roje	Stona	JAM	26.2.99	1	Carifta	Willemstad	15 Apr
	61.85 1 N.Sch Kingston 30 Mar				8 performances by 6 men over 61.50			
64.63	Turner	Washington	USA	10.2.99	1		Rathdrum	2 Jun
63.73	Henrik	Janssen	GER	19.5.98	1	v2N-j	Halle	4 Mar
	62.06 1 Halle 4 Feb							
62.09	Claudio	Romero	CHI-Y	10.7.00	1	PAm-J	Tujillo	21 Jul
62.01	Oskar	Stachnik	POL	1.3.98	1	EJ	Grosseto	23 Jul
61.65	Mouad Mohamed	Ibrahim	QAT-Y	8.2.99	1		Czestochowa	28 Jul
61.35	Christoforos	Genethli	CYP	19.1.98	1	Balk-J	Pitesti	2 Jul
61.06	Gleb	Zhuk	BLR	24.3.98	1	NC-j	Brest	29 Jun
61.00	Georgios	Koniarakis	CYP-Y	7.2.99	1	NC-j	Nicosia	29 Apr
60.66	Wictor	Petersson (10)	SWE	1.5.98	1	Nordic	Umeå	20 Aug
60.62	Félix	Valle	CUB	3.4.98	1		La Habana	20 May
60.38	Kevin	Nedrick	JAM	11.1.98	2	Carifta	Willemstad	15 Apr
60.37	George	Evans	GBR	21.1.98	1		Leiria	15 Apr
59.97	Gabriel	Oladipo	USA	17.4.99	1	NC-j	Sacramento	24 Jun
59.89	Laris	Kaufmanis	LAT	16.4.98	1	NC-j	Ventspils	2 Jul
59.46	James	Tomlinson	GBR-Y	11.1.00	1		Cardiff	27 Jun
59.46	Patrick	Duvenage	RSA	17.2.98	1	Afr-J	Tiamcen	29 Jun
59.40	Tim	Ader	GER	29.1.99	2		Schönebeck	2 Jun
59.40	Alessio	Mannucci	ITA	7.7.98	1		Siena	16 Sep
59.26	Kristjan	Ceh (20)	SLO	17.2.99	1	NC-j	Ptuj	9 Jul

1.62kg Discus

Mark	Name		Nat	Born	Pos	Venue	Date
69.45	Turner	Washington	USA	10.2.99	1	Tucson	18 May
	68.03 1 Greensboro 18 Jun				66.28 1	Arcadia	8 Apr
	66.63 1 Mesa 3 May				66.00 1	Phoenix	11 May
67.50	Jonah	Wilson	USA	.98	1	Clovis	28 Apr
65.59	Gabriel	Oladipo	USA	17.4.99	1	Dallas	25 Mar
64.90	Elijah	Mason	USA	19.1.99	2	Arcadia	8 Apr
64.14	Jarez	Parks	USA		1	Bradenton	5 May
63.94	Austin	Glynn	USA		1	La Crosse	13 May

HAMMER

Mark	Name		Nat	Born	Pos	Meet	Venue	Date
83.44	Pawel	Fajdek	POL	4.6.89	1	GS	Ostrava	27 Jun5

Mark	Pos	Meet	Venue	Date	1	2	3	4	5	6
83.44					83.44	81.88	x	x	x	79.61
82.64	1	Gyulai	Székesfehérvár	4 Jul	78.05	75.50	80.29	81.19	82.64	80.65
82.40	1	PNG	Turku	13 Jun	81.85	x	80.59	x	x	82.40
82.31	1		Halle	20 May	x	x	77.12	x	82.31	81.68
81.85	1		Cetniewo	29 Jul	x	81.68	x	81.73	81.85	81.31

MEN 2017

Mark	Name			Nat	Born	Pos	Meet	Venue		Date
Fajdek 81.51	1		Kielce	13 May	75.10	76.42	76.75	79.55	81.51	x
81.50	1	Skol	Warszawa	15 Aug	x	79.17	81.50	x	79.77	x
81.39	1		Coral Gables	7 Apr	78.12	81.39	79.65	x	80.92	80.78
80.82	1		Madrid	14 Jul	x	70.90	80.62	x	79.23	80.82
80.53	1	Kuso	Szczecin	10 Jun	x	80.53	79.32	79.46	x	x
80.14	1		Montreuil	1 Jun	80.14	x	x	x	x	79.75
79.81	1	WCh	London (OS)	11 Aug	x	77.09	79.73	79.81	79.40	x
79.16	1	WUG	Taipei	24 Aug	x	72.57	79.16	77.34	x	x
78.67	1	PTS	Samorin	17 Jun	76.90	78.67	75.48	x	x	x
78.64	2	NC	Bialystok	22 Jul	x	x	x	77.04	x	78.64
78.51	1	DL	Birmingham	20 Aug	x	x	x	78.10	x	78.51
78.29	1	ET	Villeneuve d'Ascq	25 Jun	x	x	78.29	x		
80.47	Wojciech		Nowicki	POL	22.2.89	1	NC	Bialystok		22 Jul
					77.97	x	78.96	77.88	x	80.47
80.31	2	GS	Ostrava	27 Jun	77.64	80.31	79.35	80.25	79.41	x
79.38	2		Cetniewo	29 Jul	76.58	79.05	78.12	79.38 -X	78.14	
78.54	2		Kielce	13 May	x	76.26	75.75	78.16	77.56	78.54
78.03	3	WCh	London (OS)	11 Aug	76.36	76.54	78.03	76.19	x	x
77.98	2	Gyulai	Székesfehérvár	4 Jul	76.87	77.98	x	x	77.55	76.62
79.32	Valeriy		Pronkin	RUS	15.6.94	1	NC	Zhukovskiy		29 Jul
					x	76.80	78.43	78.63	79.32	78.16
78.90	1		Adler	25 May	74.67	74.02	78.90	76.41	x	x
78.16	2	WCh	London (OS)	11 Aug	77.00	77.20	75.71	76.25	77.98	78.16
78.85	Bence		Halász	HUN	4.8.97	3	GS	Ostrava		27 Jun
					x	76.05	75.86	75.77	74.80	78.85
78.04	Pavel		Boreysha	BLR	16.2.91	1	DL	Doha		6 May
					74.88	x	x	x	75.04	78.04
78.01	1		Staiki	16 Feb	75.00	75.96	74.85	78.01	76.80	77.80
77.98	2	WUG	Taipei	24 Aug	68.89	x	71.75	x	77.98	73.59
78.00	Esref		Apak	TUR	3.1.82	1		Ankara		6 Jun
					77.13	78.00	77.53	x		
	(31/6)									
77.92	Marcel		Lomnicky	SVK	6.7.87	2		Coral Gables		7 Apr
77.87	Quentin		Bigot ¶	FRA	1.12.92	1	NC	Marseille		14 Jul
77.81	Dilshod		Nazarov	TJK	6.5.82	4	GS	Ostrava		27 Jun
77.72	Mihaíl		Anastasákis	GRE	3.12.94	1		Nikíti		11 Jun
	(10)									
77.70	Serghei		Marghiev	MDA	6.11.92	1	NC	Chisinau		26 May
77.52	Sergey		Kolomoyets	BLR	11.8.89	1		Minsk		16 Jun
77.51	Nick		Miller	GBR	1.5.93	1		Salinas		21 Apr
77.50	Aleksey		Sokirskiy	RUS	16.3.85	5	WCh	London (OS)		11 Aug
77.32	Sergey		Litvinov	RUS	27.1.86	1	Znam	Zhukovskiy		2 Jul
77.24	Wágner		Domingos	BRA	23.6.83	1	SLO Ch	Celje		23 Jul
77.23	Marco		Lingua	ITA	4.6.78	1		Torino		7 May
77.21	Denis		Lukyanov	RUS	14.7.89	2	Znam	Zhukovskiy		2 Jul
76.92	Serhiy		Reheda	UKR	6.2.94	1		Kyiv		21 May
76.84	Krisztián		Pars	HUN	18.2.82	1		Szombathely		29 Apr
	(20)									
76.63	Javier		Cienfuegos	ESP	15.7.90	1	NC-w	Montijo		4 Mar
76.61	Õzkan		Baltaci	TUR	13.2.94	1		Bursa		6 Jul
76.27	Diego		del Real	MEX	6.3.94	1		Mazatlán		8 Apr
76.14	Ashraf Amjad		El-Seify	QAT	20.2.95	1		Doha		26 Apr
76.12			Wang Shizhu	CHN	20.2.89	1	NG	Tianjin		7 Sep
76.08	Zakhar		Makhrosenko	BLR	10.10.91	1		Minsk		14 Jul
75.86	Igors		Sokolovs	LAT	17.8.74	1	NC	Ogre		30 Jul
75.78	Yuriy		Shayunov	BLR	22.10.87	2	NC-w	Staiki		16 Feb
75.73	Simone		Falloni	ITA	26.9.91	1		Lucca		28 May
75.72	Chris		Bennett	GBR	17.12.89	1		Fränkisch-Crumbach		4 Jun
	(30)									
75.64	Mostafa		Al-Gamal	EGY	1.10.88	1		Cairo		14 May
75.53	David		Söderberg	FIN	11.8.79	1		Helsinki		10 Jul
75.31	Henri		Liipola	FIN	24.4.94	1		Somero		8 Sep
75.22	Rudy		Winkler	USA	6.12.94	1		Princeton		16 Jul
75.22	Allan		Wolski	BRA	18.1.90	1		São Bernardo do Campo		16 Jul
75.00	Nikolay		Bashan	RUS	18.11.92	5	Znam	Zhukovskiy		2 Jul
74.89	Hassan Mohamed		Mahmoud	EGY	10.2.84	1		Cairo		22 Jul
74.42	Yevgeniy		Korotovskiy	RUS	21.6.92	4	NC	Zhukovskiy		29 Jul
74.41	Humberto		Mansilla	CHI	22.5.96	1		Hassloch		14 May
74.39	Alex		Young	USA	1.9.94	1		Wallkill		19 Jul
	(40)									

Mark	Name		Nat	Born	Pos	Meet	Venue	Date
74.32	Kibwé	Johnson	USA	17.7.81	1		Tucson	20 May
74.30	Nejc	Plesko	SLO	9.10.92	2		Slovenska Bistrica	27 May
74.28	Joaquín	Gómez	ARG	14.10.96	1		Buenos Aires	9 Dec
74.27	Eivind	Henriksen	NOR	14.9.90	1	NC	Sandnes	26 Aug
74.26	Sean	Donnelly	USA	1.4.93	2		Tucson	20 May
74.20	Gleb	Dudarov	BLR	17.10.96	1	Big 12	Lawrence	12 May
74.20	Eslam Moussad	Seria	EGY	20.2.91	2		Cairo	22 Jul
74.02	Bence	Pásztor	HUN	5.2.95	1		Szombathely	19 Jul
73.87	Reinier	Mejías	CUB	22.9.90	1		La Habana	4 Mar
73.85	Sukhrob	Khodjayev	UZB	21.5.93	1		Tashkent	12 Jun
	(50)							
73.77		Lee Yun-chul	KOR	28.3.82	3	AsiC	Bhubaneswar	8 Jul
73.54	Alexander	Ziegler	GER	7.7.87	1		Fränkisch-Crumbach	15 Jul
73.52	Hlib	Piskunov	UKR-J	25.11.98	2		Nova Kakhovka	1 Apr
73.50	Reza	Moghaddam	IRI	17.11.88	1		Shiraz	13 Apr
73.50	Roberto	Sawyers	CRC	17.10.86	1		Kolin	8 Jul
73.42	Andrey	Romanov	RUS	19.9.94	1		Adler	7 Feb
73.42		Wan Yong	CHN	22.7.87	2	BLR Ch	Grodno	4 Jul
73.40	Taylor	Campbell	GBR	30.6.96	1		Bedford	30 Apr
73.37	Matt	Denny	AUS	2.6.96	1	NC	Sydney	31 Mar
73.34	Oscar	Vestlund	SWE	27.4.93	1		Karlstad	22 Jul
	(60)							
73.25	Ákos	Hudi	HUN	10.8.91	2		Szombathely	15 Apr
73.12	Oleg	Dubitskiy	BLR	14.10.90	2		Minsk	24 Jun
73.05	Colin	Dunbar	USA	27.6.88	4		Fränkisch-Crumbach	4 Jun
72.69	Constantinos	Stathelakos	CYP	30.12.87	1		Nicosia	14 Jul
72.62	Ivan	Aksyonov	RUS	16.8.95	1		Moskva	8 Jul
72.59	Alexej	Mikhailov	GER	12.4.96	1		Leverkusen	27 May
72.57	Adam	Keenan	CAN	26.3.93	1		Phoenix	2 Dec
72.38	Hilmar Örn	Jonsson	ISL	6.5.96	4	NCAA	Eugene	7 Jun
72.35	Matija	Greguric	CRO	17.9.96	1		Brezice	9 Jun
72.22	Aleksey	Korolyov	RUS	5.4.82	4		Sochi	13 May
	(70)							
71.98	Andy	Fryman	USA	3.2.85	1		High Point, NC	1 Apr
71.95	Aleksi	Jaakkola	FIN	17.11.97	2	NC	Seinäjoki	22 Jul
71.88	Ilya	Terentyev	RUS	25.1.95	1		Adler	6 Feb
71.88	Alexandros	Poursanides	CYP	23.1.93	1		Charlottesville	21 Apr
71.85	Darien	Thornton	USA	14.7.94	1		Allendale	12 May
71.84	Anatoliy	Pozdnyakov	RUS	1.2.87	1		Sankt Peterburg	10 Jun
71.83	Alisher	Eshbekov	TJK/RUS	31.5.90	6	Znam	Zhukovskiy	2 Jul
71.82	Ayhan	Apti	BUL	25.4.93	1		Sofia	17 Jun
71.76	Anders	Eriksson	SWE	22.3.94	1		Wakefield, RI	16 Jul
71.75	Denzel	Comenentia	NED	25.11.95	5	NCAA	Eugene	7 Jun
	(80)							
71.73	Mark	Dry	GBR	11.10.87	1	LI	Loughborough	21 May
71.72	Johnnie	Jackson	USA	19.9.94	6	NCAA	Eugene	7 Jun
71.70	Johannes	Bichler	GER	3.7.90	1		Augsburg	23 Jul
71.48	António Vital e	Silva	POR	23.1.88	1		Leiria	23 Jul
71.45	Volodomyr	Myslyvchuk	UKR	25.4.96	1		Mukachevo	12 Apr
71.42	Myhaylo	Kokhan	UKR-Y	22.1.01	1		Kyiv	30 Jun
71.41	Jesse	Lehto	FIN	12.2.93	9	PNG	Turku	13 Jun
71.36	Ryota	Kashimura	JPN	13.8.91	1	NC	Osaka	23 Jun
71.35	Tuomas	Seppänen	FIN	16.5.86	2		Lappeenranta	26 Aug
71.28	Tshepang	Makhethe	RSA	9.2.96	1		Sasolburg	28 Mar
	(90)							
71.28	Andriy	Martynyuk	UKR	25.9.90	2		Uman	12 May
71.18	Yevgeniy	Ivanov	BLR	11.6.92	2		Minsk	13 Jun
71.12	Marco	Bortolato	ITA	11.2.94	2		Trento	27 May
71.09		Qi Dakai	CHN	23.5.87	6		Fränkisch-Crumbach	4 Jun
71.08	Mohsen	Anani	TUN	25.5.85	1		Bruay-la-Buissière	4 Jul
71.00	Libor	Charfreitag	SVK	11.9.77	1		Bratislava	4 Jun
70.98	Joseph	Ellis	GBR	10.4.96	1	Big 10	University Park	12 May
70.93	Caniggia	Raynor	JAM	3.11.90	1	NC	Kingston	24 Jun
70.89	Andreas	Sahner	GER	27.1.85	2	NC	Erfurt	9 Jul
70.82	Tommi	Remes	FIN	20.1.94	4	NC	Seinäjoki	22 Jul
	(100)							

Mark	Name		Nat	Born	Date
70.72	Yevhen	Vynogradov	UKR	30.4.84	6 Jun
70.71	Jordan	Crayon	USA	15.8.94	15 Jun
70.68	Roman	Zholudyev	BLR	8.1.96	13 Jun
70.66	Igor	Buryi	RUS	8.4.93	2 Jul
70.64	Elias	Håkansson	SWE	29.2.92	31 Mar
70.60	Jerome	Vega	PUR	7.7.95	10 Jun
70.59	Miguel Alberto	Blanco	ESP	22.2.96	22 Jul
70.55	Dempsey	McGuigan	IRL	30.8.93	13 Apr
70.53	Chris	Harmse	RSA	31.5.73	22 Apr
70.49	Konstadínos	Kostoglídis	GRE	10.8.90	14 May

MEN 2017

Mark	Name		Nat	Born	Pos Meet	Venue	Date
70.42	Tristan	Schwandke	GER	23.5.92			4 Jun
70.30	Renaldo	Frechou	RSA	4.3.92			22 Apr
70.30	Aaron	Kangas	FIN	3.7.97			1 Jul
70.17	Lukás	Melich	CZE	16.9.80			13 May
70.15	Pedro José	Martin	ESP	12.8.92			7 Jul
70.12	Juho	Saarikoski	FIN	19.5.93			9 Jun
70.10	Yuiy	Kuziv	RUS	29.5.96			22 Apr
70.10	Pyotr	Nekiporets	RUS	6.5.97			17 Feb
70.06	Yudai	Kimura	JPN	19.10.96			15 Sep
70.05	Kunihiro	Sumi	JPN	27.2.94			10 Jun
70.01	Tom	Postema	USA	17.7.89			18 May
70.00	Osian	Jones	GBR	23.6.93			29 Jul
69.93	Alaa Eldin Mohammed	El-Ashry	EGY	6.1.91			17 Mar
69.92	Mattias	Lindberg	SWE	2.1.90			19 Aug
69.90	Conor	McCullough	USA	31.1.91			21 Jul
69.88	Joachim	Koivu	FIN	5.9.88			22 Aug
69.85	Ahmed Amjad	El-Seify	QAT	1.10.96			16 Jul
69.84	Daniel	Roberts	USA	11.12.94			25 May
69.83	Tomás	Kruzliak	SVK	9.2.92			21 Apr
69.80	Chris	Shorthouse	GBR	23.6.88			26 Feb
69.78	Connor	Neu	USA	5.11.92			13 Apr
69.77	Yasmani	Fernández	CUB	7.4.95			10 Feb
69.75	Kaveh	Mousavi	IRI	27.5.85			13 Apr
69.72	Miroslav	Pavlícek	CZE	31.3.87			20 Aug
69.71	Jordan	Young	CAN	21.6.93			7 Jun
69.62	Gleb	Volik	RUS	17.12.96			25 May
69.42	Nikólaos	Gavriilidis	GRE	15.3.95			29 Jul
69.41	Iván	Menglebéi	GRE	25.1.95			29 Jul
69.15	Michael	Bomba	GBR	10.10.86			25 Apr
69.14	Alan	C umming	RSA	21.3.96			19 Sep
69.13	Callum	Brown	GBR	20.7.94			30 Jul
69.10	Maksim	Mitskov	BLR	1.12.95			16 Jun
69.01	Naoki	Uematsu	JPN	3.11.94			20 May
68.97	Igor	Vinichenko ¶	RUS	11.4.84			29 Jul
68.96	Ali Mohamed	Al-Zankawi	KUW	27.2.84			20 Apr
68.96	Adam	Kelly	USA	6.7.97			6 May
68.96	Markus	Kokkonen	FIN	17.5.95			1 Jul
68.86	Jake	Norris	GBR-J	30.6.99			1 Apr
68.83	Craig	Murch	GBR	27.6.93			29 Jul
68.81	Serhiy	Perevoznikov	UKR	7.4.95			1 Apr
68.79	Arkadiusz	Rogowski	POL	30.3.93			24 Sep
68.76	Frédéric	Pouzy	FRA	18.2.83			8 Jul
68.69	Dário	Manso	POR	1.7.82			11 Jun
68.66	Brock	Eager	USA	26.5.96			29 Apr
68.59	Seth	Whitener	USA	17.3.97			25 May
68.57	Salameh Adel	Salem	EGY	10.10.93			22 Jul
68.55	Cameron	Brown	USA	15.3.94			7 Jun
68.48	Huw	Peacock	AUS	12.5.92			14 Oct
68.44		Guo Kun	CHN	28.2.93			25 Jun
68.42	Taiki	Nemoto	JPN	23.3.94			30 Mar
68.34	Thomas	Mardal	NOR	16.4.97			13 Jul
68.32	Maximilian	Becker	GER	22.1.92			20 May
68.32	Erick	Loomis	USA	18.2.96			11 Jun
68.32	Paul	Hützen	GER	7.3.91			22 Jul
68.30	Igor	Yevseyev	RUS	27.3.96			6 Feb
68.29	Dániel	Rába	HUN-J	24.4.98			9 Sep
68.28	Jack	Dalton	AUS	20.5.94			27 May
68.22	Stevan	Veselinovic	SRB	3.9.94			31 Mar
68.19	Joe	Frye	USA	20.7.88			31 Mar
68.04	A.G.	Kruger	USA	18.2.79			21 Apr
68.03	Hiroki	Uchibori	JPN	7.7.95			23 Jun
68.02	Charlie	Ionata	USA	22.1.95			21 Apr
68.02	Aleksandr	Shimanovich	BLR-J	9.2.98			16 Feb
	(173)						

JUNIORS

Mark	Name		Nat	Born	Pos	Meet	Venue	Date
73.52	Hlib	Piskunov	UKR	25.11.98	2		Nova Kakhovka	1 Apr
71.42	Myhaylo	Kokhan	UKR-Y	22.1.01	1		Kyiv	30 Jun
68.86	Jake	Norris	GBR	30.6.99	1		Eton	1 Apr
68.29	Dániel	Rába	HUN	24.4.98	4		Székesfehérvár	9 Sep
68.02	Aleksandr	Shimanovich	BLR	9.2.98	2		Staiki	16 Feb

5 performances by 5 men over 68.00.

Mark	Name		Nat	Born	Pos	Meet	Venue	Date
67.62	Joshua	Hernandez	USA	1.2.98	4q	NCAA-W	Austin	25 May
67.27	Hugo	Tavernier	FRA	1.12.99	6		Forbach	28 May
67.19	Myhaylo	Havrylyuk	UKR	19.10.99	2		Mukachevo	12 Apr
67.08	Alberto	González	ESP	1.6.98	2		Andújar	20 May
66.60	Ragnar	Carlsson (10)	SWE-Y	16.11.00	1		Växjö	27 Jun
66.39	David	Martín	ESP-Y	10.7.00	1		Barcelona	21 Jun
66.20	Batuhan	Hizal	TUR-Y	14.1.00	2		Izmir	11 Feb
65.27	Karel	Haasbroek	RSA	27.2.98	3		Potchefstroom	19 Sep
65.22	Danyil	Danilov	RUS	5.1.98	11		Zhukovskiy	24 Jun

6KG HAMMER

Mark	Name		Nat	Born	Pos	Meet	Venue	Date
81.75	Hlib	Piskunov	UKR	25.11.98	1	EJ	Grosseto	21 Jul
	81.32 1 Werfer Halle 20 May				78.13 Q	EJ	Grosseto	20 Jul
	80.60 1 NC-j Lutsk 26 Jun							
81.73	Aleksandr	Shimanovich	BLR	9.2.98	1		Brest	28 Apr
	80.26 1 NC-wj Minsk (Staiki) 15 Feb				77.74 2	EJ	Grosseto	21 Jul
78.51	Alberto	González	ESP	1.6.98	1		Jaén	15 Jul
78.09	Jake	Norris	GBR	30.6.99	1	LI	Loughborough	21 May
	77.67 1 NC-j Bedford 17 Jun				10 performances by 4 men over 77.70			
76.93	Dániel	Rába	HUN	24.4.98	1	NC-wj	Szombathely	4 Mar
76.66	Danyil	Danilov	RUS	5.1.98	1	NC-wj	Adler	17 Feb
75.91	Joshua	Hernandez	USA	1.2.98	1	NC-j	Sacramento	24 Jun
75.85	Myhaylo	Havrylyuk	UKR	19.10.99	2	NC-j	Lutsk	26 Jun
75.44	Yann	Chaussinand	FRA	11.5.98	1	NC-j	Dreux	2 Jul
74.98	Ragnar	Carlsson (10)	SWE-Y	16.11.00	4	EJ	Grosseto	21 Jun
74.21	Myhaylo	Kokhan	UKR-Y	22.1.01	1	NC-wj	Mukachevo	13 Feb
73.90	Miguel	Zamora	CUB	25.1.99	1	Barr	La Habana	27 May
73.47	Yeóryios	Korakídis	GRE	16.11.98	1	NC-j	Kateríni	8 Jul
73.03	Balázs	Varga	HUN	30.1.98	1		Veszprém	1 May
72.79	Donát	Varga	HUN-Y	8.4.00	2		Szombathely	21 Sep
72.73	Roope	Auvinen	FIN	17.2.98	1		Nurmijärvi	15 Jun
71.76	Dmitriy	Boravkov	BLR	17.6.99	3		Brest	28 Apr
71.74	Carel	Haasbroek	RSA	27.2.98	1	NC-j	Cape Town	8 Apr
71.72	Mihaita	Micu	ROU	27.9.99	2	Werfer	Halle	20 May
71.64	Dan	Morari (20)	MDA	2.5.98	1	Balk-J	Pitesti	1 Jul

Mark	Name		Nat	Born	Pos	Meet	Venue		Date
12 lb (5.44kg) Hammer									
73.97	Michael	Feldman	USA	22.11.99	1		Princeton		16 Jul
72.77	Jordan	Geist	USA	21.7.98	1	N.Sch	Greensboro		17 Jun

JAVELIN

Mark	Name		Nat	Born	Pos	Meet	Venue		Date
94.44	Johannes	Vetter	GER	26.3.93	1		Luzern		11 Jul
				90.75	91.06	93.06	94.44	89.50	x
93.88	1	Thum	18 Au	81.24	93.88	83.85	87.45	88.35	91.67
91.20	Q WCh	London (OS)	10 Aug	91.20					
89.89	1 WCh	London (OS)	12 Aug	89.89	89.78	87.22	x	82.25	87.71
89.85	1 ISTAF	Berlin	27 Aug	78.70	86.06	82.06	85.90	89.85	81.88
89.68	2 DL	Doha	5 May	x	82.53	89.68	84.27	x	86.38
89.42	1	Bad Köstritz	25 Aug	85.28	89.38	89.42	p	88.59	87.35
89.35	1 NC	Erfurt	9 Jul	89.35	82.84	84.59	87.83	89.23	81.84
88.74	1 DL	Paris (C)	1 Jul	88.74	85.76	85.42	84.15	79.45	82.31
88.15	2 GGala	Roma	8 Jun	81.42	80.70	78.70	x	88.15	x
93.90	Thomas	Röhler	GER	30.9.91	1	DL	Doha		5 May
				82.94	85.52	88.12	93.90	p	p
91.53	1 GS	Ostrava	28 Jun	88.08	91.53	91.02	87.01	87.19	x
90.06	1 GGala	Roma	8 Jun	84.81	87.05	87.89	87.70	85.54	90.06
89.45	2	Luzern	11 Jul	82.18	85.04	85.60	89.45	88.47	x
89.17	1 Herc	Monaco	21 Jul	87.06	89.17	x	86.80	x	88.91
88.26	1 PNG	Turku	13 Jun	85.64	88.26	x	p	p	86.25
88.26	4 WCh	London (OS)	12 Aug	87.08	88.26	x	86.14	85.97	86.40
91.36		Cheng Chao-Tsun	TPE	17.10.93	1	WUG	Taipei		26 Aug
				83.91	82.45	x	84.37	x	91.36
91.07	Andreas	Hofmann	GER	16.12.91	2	WUG	Taipei		26 Aug
				83.00	x	85.59-	85.97	88.33	91.07
88.79	1	Offenburg	13 May	84.84	82.26	88.79	85.86	83.12	p
89.73	Jakub	Vadlejch	CZE	10.10.90	2	WCh	London (OS)		12 Aug
				77.10	89.73	85.04	86.23	87.70	83.22
88.50	1 WK-DLF	Zürich	24 Aug	84.40	88.50	84.12	86.86	85.45	86.16
88.02	2 DL	Paris (C)	1 Jul	88.02	83.33	83.83	x	86.85	82.97
87.95	1 ET	Villeneuve d'Ascq	24 Jun	80.55	83.44	87.95	p		
87.91	3 DL	Doha	5 May	83.74-	81.32	83.65	87.91	84.33	87.55
88.32	Petr	Frydrych	CZE	13.1.88	3	WCh	London (OS)		12 Aug
				84.31	80.48	82.94	87.93	87.93	88.32
88.27	Tero	Pitkämaki	FIN	19.12.82	1	ET-1	Vaasa		25 Jun
				x	83.31	88.27	x		
88.09	Marcin	Krukowski	POL	14.6.92	1	NC	Bialystok		21 Jul
				88.09	p	p	p	p	x
88.01	Ioánnis	Kiriazis	GRE	19.1.96	1	TexR	Austin		31 Mar
				88.01	p	p	p	p	p
87.97A	Julius (30/10)	Yego	KEN	4.1.89	1	WCT	Nairobi		24 Jun
86.71	Lars	Hamann	GER	4.4.89	2		Offenburg		13 May
86.64		Huang Shih-Feng	TPE	2.3.92	3	WUG	Taipei		26 Aug
86.61	Keshorn	Walcott	TTO	2.4.93	3	GGala	Roma		8 Jun
86.06	Magnus	Kirt	EST	10.4.90	1		Orimattila		29 Jul
85.85	Julian	Weber	GER	29.8.94	1	ECp-w	Las Palmas		11 Mar
85.63	Neeraj	Chopra	IND	24.12.97	1	Fed Cup	Patiala		2 Jun
85.23	Ahmed Bader	Magour	QAT	3.3.96	4	PNG	Turku		13 Jun
85.07	Rolands	Strobinders	LAT	14.4.92	2		Bad Köstritz		25 Aug
85.01	Pavel	Meleshko	BLR	24.11.92	2		Pärnu		19 Aug
84.81	Anderson (20)	Peters	GRN	21.10.97	1		St. George's		2 Jul
84.78	Edis	Matusevicius	LTU	30.6.96	1		Ogre		25 May
84.62	Bernhard	Seifert	GER	15.2.93	3	NC	Erfurt		9 Jul
84.57	Davinder	Singh Kang	IND	18.12.88	1		Patiala		7 May
84.36	Hamish	Peacock	AUS	15.10.90	1	NC	Sydney		2 Apr
84.09	Rocco	van Rooyen	RSA	23.12.92	1		Parow		18 Mar
83.93	Adrian	Mardare	MDA	20.6.95	1	ET-2	Tel Aviv		25 Jun
83.12	Cyrus	Hostetler	USA	8.8.86	1		East Stroudsburg		9 Jul
83.09	Jaroslav	Jílek	CZE	22.10.89	4		Bad Köstritz		25 Aug
83.08	Norbert	Rivasz-Tóth	HUN	6.5.96	1	EC-23	Bydgoszcz		15 Jul
82.90	Alexandru (30)	Novac	ROU	24.3.97	1		Pitesti		20 May
2.58	Tanel	Laanmäe	EST	29.9.89	4		Luzern		11 Jul
82.44	Benjamin	Langton Burnell	NZL	10.7.92	1		Hamilton		10 Jun
82.29	Vitezslav	Vesely	CZE	27.2.83	1		Kladno		15 Jul

Mark	Name		Nat	Born	Pos	Meet	Venue	Date
82.27	Lukasz	Grzeszczuk	POL	3.3.90	1		Warszawa	20 May
82.19	Waruna Lakshan	Dayarathne	SRI	14.5.88	1		Diyagama	9 Apr
82.13	Ryohei	Arai	JPN	23.6.91	1	NC	Osaka	24 Jun
82.12	Valeriy	Iordan	RUS	14.2.92	1		Adler	23 Apr
82.02	Kim	Amb	SWE	31.7.90	1		Ventspils	3 Jun
82.01	Gabriel	Wallin	SWE	14.10.81	1		Södertälje	6 Jun
82.00	Ansis	Bruns	LAT	30.3.89	1		Jelgava	18 Jun
	(40)							
81.91	Patriks	Gailums	LAT-J	10.5.98	1		Valmiera	12 Jul
81.77	Riley	Dolezal	USA	16.11.85	1	NC	Sacramento	24 Jun
81.74	Paraskevás	Batzávalis	GRE	25.11.94	1	Veniz	Haniá	3 Jun
81.68	Roberto	Bertolini	ITA	9.10.85	1		Nembro	7 Jul
81.27	Bobur	Shokirjanov	UZB	5.12.90	3		Ventspils	3 Jun
81.15A		Liu Qizhen	CHN	17.9.95	1		Guiyang	26 Jun
81.07	Luke	Cann	AUS	17.7.94	1		Townsville	18 Jun
80.85	Kohei	Hasegawa	JPN	1.1.90	4		Kawasaki	21 May
80.83	Braian	Toledo	ARG	8.9.93	2		Raasepori	4 Jun
80.70	Dmitriy	Tarabin	RUS	29.10.91	1		Adler	26 May
	(50)							
80.70	Thomas	van Ophem	NED	6.9.92	1		Castricum	7 Jun
80.52	Cyprian	Mrzygłód	POL-J	2.2.98	1	EJ	Grosseto	22 Jul
80.49A	Phil Mar	van Rensburg	RSA	23.6.89	1		Germiston	18 Mar
80.44	Jiannis	Smaliós	SWE	17.2.87	1		Karlstad	23 Jul
80.37	Dmytro	Kosynskyy	UKR	31.3.89	3		Halle	20 May
80.29	David	Ocampo	MEX	14.2.92	1		Tucson	18 May
80.25	Oliver	Helander	FIN	1.1.97	1	NC-23	Kauhava	6 Aug
80.22	Bartosz	Osewski	POL	20.3.91	1		Kielce	13 May
80.20	Emin	Õncel	TUR	1.5.97	1		Ankara	12 May
80.20	Hubert	Chmielak	POL	19.6.89	2		Cetniewo	29 Jul
	(60)							
80.10	Dejan	Mileusnic	BIH	16.11.91	2		Velenje	20 Jun
80.04		Zhao Qinggang	CHN	24.7.85	1	NG	Tianjin	4 Sep
79.93	Vladislav	Panasenkov	RUS	22.5.96	1		Sochi	14 May
79.91	Michael	Shuey	USA	2.2.94	3		East Stroudsburg	9 Jul
79.91		Ma Qun	CHN	8.2.94	2	NG	Tianjin	4 Sep
79.80	Norbert	Bonvecchio	ITA	14.8.85	1		Conegliano Veneto	16 Jun
79.72A	Arley	Ibargüen	COL	4.12.82	1		Cali	1 Jul
79.68	Teemu	Wirkkala	FIN	14.1.84	Q	NC	Seinäjoki	22 Jul
79.44	Albert	Reynolds	LCA	28.3.88	2		St. George's	2 Jul
79.21	Sami	Peltomäki	FIN	11.1.91	3		Raasepori	4 Jun
	(70)							
79.17	Takuto	Kominami	JPN	26.7.95	2		Hiratsuka	9 Jun
79.01	Sampo	Lehtola	FIN	10.5.89	4		Raasepori	4 Jun
78.80	Dawid	Kosciów	POL	5.6.90	1		Slupsk	27 May
78.80	Markim	Felix	GRN	.97	2	TTO Ch	Port of Spain	25 Jun
78.77	Vladislav	Polyunin	UZB-J	4.12.98	1		Tallinn	16 Aug
78.71	Janeil	Craigg	BAR	29.3.94	1		St. George's	8 Apr
78.70	D.G.Sampath	Ranasinghe	SRI	1.9.88	1		Diyagama	3 Oct
78.66	Ivan	Zaytsev	UZB	7.11.88	2	Isl.Sol	Baku	19 May
78.46	Mart	ten Berge	NED	27.4.91	1		Lisse	13 May
78.41A	Dayron	Márquez	COL	19.11.83	2		Medellín	29 Apr
	(80)							
78.40	Yuriy	Kushniruk	UKR	6.12.94	1		Kyiv	30 Jun
78.32	Kenji	Ogura	JPN	8.6.95	2		Fukui	8 Sep
78.28	Mauro	Fraresso	ITA	13.1.93	10	GGala	Roma	8 Jun
78.21		Bae You-il	KOR	16.6.94	1	NC	Kimchun	4 Jun
78.13	Jonas	Bonewit	GER	30.7.95	3		Vecindario	12 Mar
78.05	Timothy	VanLiew	USA	25.5.90	4		East Stroudsburg	9 Jul
78.00	Arshad	Nadeem	PAK	2.1.97	7	AsiC	Bhubaneswar	9 Jul
77.92	R.M.Sumedha	Ranasinghe	SRI	10.2.91	3	AUS Ch	Sydney	2 Apr
77.91	Toma	Pop	ROU	11.3.92	2	NC-w	Bucuresti	28 Feb
77.91	Ayumu	Ishiyama	JPN	2.6.96	1		Hiroshima	1 Jul
	(90)							
77.88A	Johannes	Grobler	RSA	6.8.97	1		Potchefstroom	20 May
77.82	Gennard	Paul	GRN	.92	1		New Orleans	13 May
77.81A	Chad	Herman	RSA	25.5.92	1		Potchefstroom	15 Mar
77.80	Lassi	Etelätalo	FIN	30.4.88	9	PNG	Turku	13 Jun
77.74	William	White	AUS	27.11.95	7	WUG	Taipei	26 Aug
77.72	Jani	Kiiskilä	FIN	28.12.89	1		Pudasjärvi	22 Jun
77.67	Aleksey	Tovarnov	RUS	21.1.85	2		Adler	26 May
77.66A	Odel	Jainaga	ESP	14.10.97	1		Soria	20 May

Mark	Name		Nat	Born	Pos	Meet	Venue	Date
77.58	David	Carreón	MEX	23.3.94	2		Tucson	20 May
77.57	Josué	Menéndez	MEX	4.5.90	3		Tucson	20 May
	(100)							

Mark	Name		Nat	Born	Date
77.49	Daan	Meijer	NED	17.2.83	17 Jun
77.47	Matti	Mortimore	GBR	16.5.93	31 Mar
77.41	Liam	O'Brien	AUS	13.4.96	2 Apr
77.41	Taisei	Aibara	JPN	18.8.95	8 Sep
77.37	Oleksandr	Nychyporchuk	UKR	14.4.92	15 Feb
77.37	Hiroki	Tahara	JPN	13.6.89	24 Sep
77.20	Reinhardt	van Zyl	RSA	7.2.94	13 May
77.19A	Sindri Hrafn	Gudmundsson	ISL	21.11.95	13 May
77.10	Skirmantas	Simoliunas	LTU	13.3.94	9 May
77.10	Janis	Griva	LAT	23.4.93	25 May
77.08	Matviy	Krutiyenko	UKR	25.11.96	12 Apr
77.08	Vipin	Kasana	IND	4.8.89	15 May
77.03	James	Whiteaker	GBR-J	8.10.98	6 May
77.01	Osmany	Laffita	CUB	14.8.94	19 Feb
77.00	Abhishek	Singh	IND	29.4.94	2 Jun
76.98	Piotr	Lebioda	POL	28.5.92	14 Jun
76.96	McLean	Lipschutz	USA	29.7.94	9 Jul
76.94	Gatis	Cakss	LAT	13.6.95	1 Jul
76.91	Aleksey	Katkavets	BLR-J	7.6.98	22 Jul
76.88	Matija	Kranjc	SLO	12.6.84	20 May
76.87	Amit	Kumar	IND	18.9.92	22 Aug
76.85	Samarjeet	Singh	IND	7.11.88	7 May
76.83	Krystian	Bondarenko	POL	22.10.91	29 Jul
76.82A	Leonel	Laubsher	RSA	29.4.97	31 Mar
76.81	Harry	Hughes	GBR	26.9.97	1 May
76.77	Nicolás	Quijera	ESP	24.6.96	7 Jun
76.77	Vedran	Samac	SRB	22.1.90	7 Jun
76.67	Chris	Mirabelli	USA	6.6.96	29 Apr
76.66	Rhys	Stein	AUS	15.5.96	31 Mar
76.64	Kennosuke	Sogawa	JPN	12.7.94	24 Sep
76.58	Akito	Aragaki	JPN	28.7.91	7 May
76.50	Valeriy	Izotov	BLR	12.4.97	13 Jun
76.47		Hu Hailong	CHN	26.8.88	4 Sep
76.46	Branko	Paukovic	SRB	28.5.91	20 May
76.45	Bilal	Nouali	MAR	26.9.94	20 May
76.45	Shivpal	Singh	IND	6.7.95	2 Jun
76.39	Brent	Lagace	USA	31.5.88	27 May
76.38	Zakhar	Mishchenko	UKR-J	4.1.98	12 Mar
76.36	Jun-ya	Sado	JPN	17.1.97	25 May
76.30	Rajender	Singh Dalvir	IND	5.4.86	7 May
76.23A		Li Yingchang	CHN	22.6.91	26 Jun
76.19A	Tobir	Holtzhauzen	RSA	25.5.87	2 Dec
76.15A		Deng Sheng	CHN	14.11.92	26 Jun
76.13	Kyle	Nielsen	CAN	22.4.89	20 May
76.11	Antonio	Fent	ITA	31.3.88	16 Jun
76.09A	Alex	Kiprotich	KEN	10.10.94	10 May
75.96	Ilya	Shapovalov	RUS	16.1.94	28 Jul
75.96	Gudmundur	Sverrisson	ISL	24.5.90	29 Jul
75.94	Curtis	Thompson	USA	8.2.96	9 Jul
75.91	Keita	Matsufuji	JPN	.96	16 Apr
75.88	George	Zaharia	ROU	3.8.95	3 Jun
75.79	Shu	Mori	JPN	14.11.96	9 Jun
75.79		Long Zexuan	CHN	8.9.94	4 Sep
75.77	Nico	Rensmann	GER	9.10.96	2 Jun
75.76	Majid	Al-Badri	EGY	29.9.95	15 Mar
75.71	Joe	Harris	GBR	23.5.97	29 Jul
75.62	Patrik	Zenúch	SVK	30.12.90	8 May
75.58	Tasuya	Sakamoto	JPN	.96	15 Jul
75.56	Nick	Howe	USA	17.11.89	27 May
75.56		Kim Ye-ram	KOR	2.3.94	24 Oct
75.49	Jarne	Duchateau	BEL	12.11.96	7 Oct
75.40	Yegor	Nikolayev	RUS	5.6.96	26 May
75.40	Erkki	Leppik	EST	18.3.88	16 Sep
75.38	Alexander	Pascal	CAY	24.10.94	7 Jun
75.37	Dmytro	Sheremet	UKR	19.11.92	28 Apr
75.33		Zhi Qiang	CHN	20.2.94	4 Sep
75.30	Genki	Dean	JPN	30.12.91	29 Apr
75.27	Ismet	Pekbak	TUR-J	10.6.99	12 May
75.26	Sondre	Høyland	NOR-J	20.5.98	20 Aug
75.24		Sun Jianjun	CHN	9.6.91	27 Mar
75.23		Jiang Wujun	CHN	28.11.94	11 May
75.22	Ravinder	Singh Khaira	IND	19.3.86	27 Apr
75.21	Mikko	Aalto	FIN	11.3.82	5 Jul
75.15	Teo	Takala	FIN	6.6.94	5 Jul
75.15	Capers	Williamson	USA	13.10.92	9 Jul
75.11	Wojciech	Cwik	POL	20.7.94	23 Sep
75.05	Nils	Fischer	GER	18.10.97	27 May
75.01	Tiago	Aperta	POR	15.1.92	10 Jun
74.98	Vladimir	Kozlov	BLR	20.4.85	13 Jun
74.92	Rikinari	Ishizaka	JPN	.97	18 Mar
74.90	Héctor	Aragues	ESP	4.1.95	1 Jul
74.88	Joseph	Dunderdale	GBR	2.11.94	29 Jul
74.86	Paulo Henrique	Alves da Silva	BRA	28.9.93	11 Jun
74.83A	Hernu	van Vuuren	RSA-J	15.4.98	21 Apr
74.83	Jami	Kinnunen	FIN	31.3.95	29 Jun
74.82A	Emron	Gibbs	GRN	18.5.92	13 May
74.81	Takuma	Nakanishi	JPN	8.4.94	15 Apr
74.81	Örn	Davidsson	ISL	17.3.90	4 Jun
74.74	Ashish	Singh	IND-J	6.3.98	13 Jan
74.72		Choe Duk-young	KOR	11.5.95	8 May
74.71	Lars	Timmermann	NED	19.4.91	11 Jun
74.71	Eetu	Vanhamäki	FIN	3.3.89	21 Jun
74.64	Mikhail	Klimuk	BLR	20.12.96	31 May
74.58	Pedro Henrique	Rodrigues	BRA-J	18.6.99	22 Jul
74.58	Yuya	Mizuno	JPN	.97	8 Sep
74.57	Víctor	Fatecha	PAR	10.3.88	24 Jun
74.52		Park Won-kil	KOR	24.2.90	26 Aug
74.50	Ioánnis	Houlákis	GRE	10.6.88	26 Mar
74.38	Carson	Fuller	USA	9.7.94	13 May
74.35	Toni	Kuusela	FIN	21.1.94	20 Aug
	(200)	ten more ,men over 74m			

JUNIORS

See main list for top 3 juniors. 8 performances by 4 men over 77.00. Additional marks and further juniors:

Mrzyglód	77.56	Q	EJ	Grosseto	20 Jul	77.19	3	Skol Cetniewo	29 Jul
Polyunin	77.64	2		Praha	13 May	77.08	5	Odlozil Praha	5 Jun

Mark	Name		Nat	Born	Pos	Meet	Venue	Date
77.03	James	Whiteaker	GBR	8.10.98	1		Basingstoke	6 May
76.91	Aleksey	Katkavets	BLR	7.6.98	2	EJ	Grosseto	22 Jul
76.38	Zakhar	Mishchenko	UKR	4.1.98	6	ETCpw-J	Vecindario	12 Mar
75.27	Ismet	Pekbak	TUR	10.6.99	2		Ankara	12 May
75.26	Sondre	Høyland	NOR	20.5.98	1	Mordic-j	Umeå	20 Aug
74.83A	Hernu	van Vuuren	RSA	15.4.98	4	NC	Potchefstroom	21 Apr
74.74	Ashish	Singh (10)	IND	6.3.98	1		Coimbatore	13 Jan
74.58	Pedro Henrique	Rodrigues	BRA	18.6.99	1	PAm-J	Trujillo	22 Jul
74.22	Lukas	Moutarde	FRA	1.4.98	3	EJ	Grosseto	22 Jul
74,07	Connor	Warren	AUS	23.2.98	3		Brisbane	26 Feb
74.02	Muhammad	Yasir	PAK	1.5.98	2	NC	Karachi	7 Apr
73.93	Yarovis	Contreras	CUB-Y	25.8.00	2		Las Tunas	19 Feb
73.57	Maru	Quijera	ESP	13.1.98	1	NC-j	Granollers	8 Jul
73.51	Werner	Dames	RSA	1.6.99	1	NC-j	Cape Town	7 Apr
73.45	Ronny A.	Cedeño	CUB	24.1.98	1	Barr	La Habana	28 May
73.28	Jakub	Kubinec	SVK	18.5.98	Q	EJ	Grosseto	20 Jul
72.89	Niklas	Kaul (20)	GER	11.2.98	1		Halle	20 May

INDOOR HEPTATHLON

Mark	Name		Nat	Born	Pos	Meet	Venue	Date
6479	Kevin	Mayer	FRA	10.2.92	1	EI	Beograd	5 Mar
	6.95	7.54 15.66	2.10	7.88	5.40	2:41.08		
6249	Jorge	Ureña	ESP	8.10.93	1	v4N	Praha (Stromovka)	29 Jan
	6.91	7.62 13.96	2.04	7.85	5.00	2:40.06		
6227		Ureña			2	EI	Beograd	5 Mar
	6.94	7.37 14.24	2.10	7.78	5.00	2:43.66		
6188	Adam Sebastian	Helcelet	CZE	27.10.91	1		Praha (Stromovka)	12 Feb
	6.99	7.58 14.78	2.05	7.94	5.10	2:48.31		
6177	Devon	Williams	USA	17.1.94	1	NCAA	College Station	11 Mar
	6.88	7.83 14.11	1.95	7.75	4.76	2:41.26		
6165	Tim	Duckworth	GBR	18.6.96	2	NCAA	College Station	11 Mar
	6.77	7.77 13.09	2.16	8.10	5.26	3:04.24		
6110		Helcelet			3	EI	Beograd	5 Mar
	7.06	7.41 15.25	2.01	7.97	5.00	2:45.00		
6089#*	Luca	Wieland	GER	7.12.94	1		Brookings	3 Dec
	6.92	7.46 14.83	2.10	8.23	4.80	2:46.39		
6063	Dominik	Distelberger	AUT	16.3.90	4	EI	Beograd	5 Mar
	6.94	7.38 13.55	1.98	7.80	5.10	2:42.32		
6051	Karl Robert	Saluri	EST	6.8.93	3	NCAA	College Station	11 Mar
	6.79	7.58 14.41	1.86	8.33	4.96	2:36.92		
6047#		D.Williams			1	SEC	Nashville	25 Feb
	6.80	7.42 14.51	1.94	7.77	4.80	2:48.71		
6015	Fredrik	Samuelsson	SWE	16.2.95	5	EI	Beograd	5 Mar
	7.06	7.40 14.24	2.01	8.18	5.00	2:42.97		
6006		Duckworth			1		Lincoln	4 Feb
	6.81	7.63 13.02	2.16	8.10	5.12	3:10.75		
5996	Hunter	Price	USA	28.8.94	4	NCAA	College Station	11 Mar
	6.94	7.30 13.27	2.04	8.01	4.66	2:37.99		
	(14/10)							
5986	Kristjan	Rosenberg	EST	16.5.94	1		Tallinn	4 Feb
	7.01	7.25 13.62	2.13	8.37	4.87	2:42.96		
5985	Jirí	Sykora	CZE	20.1.95	2		Praha (Stromovka)	12 Feb
	6.99	7.53 14.85	1.96	8.01	4.80	2:48.40		
5984	Mathias	Brugger	GER	6.8.92	1	NC	Hamburg	29 Jan
	7.09	7.30 14.63	1.97	8.22	5.00	2:40.62		
5984	Darko	Pesic	MNE	30.11.92	5	EI	Beograd	5 Mar
	7.22	7.12 16.08	2.01	7.99	4.70	2:38.23		
5976	Lindon	Victor	GRN	28.2.93	5	NCAA	College Station	11 Mar
	6.99	7.23 16.55	2.07	8.43	4.76	2:51.14		
5975	Ashley	Bryant	GBR	17.5.91	2	v4N	Praha (Stromovka)	29 Jan
	7.08	7.79 14.32	1.98	8.10	4.50	2:40.84		
5970	Harrison	Williams	USA	7.3.96	6	NCAA	College Station	11 Mar
	7.02	7.03 13.34	1.95	8.23	5.36	2:39.45		
5966	Niels	Pittomvils	BEL	18.7.92	1		Gent	5 Feb
	7.21	7.09 13.66	1.99	8.10	5.40	2:44.11		
5962	Pavel	Rudnev	RUS	26.10.92	1	NC	Smolensk	16 Feb
	7.09	7.20 12.88	2.05	8.24	5.20	2:42.60		
5902	Maxime	Maugein (20)	FRA	27.9.92	1	NC	Bordeaux	19 Feb
	7.10	7.12 14.03	2.00	8.12	4.75	2:38.14		
5879	Marek	Lukás	CZE	16.7.91	3		Praha (Stromovka)	12 Feb
	7.06	7.11 14.91	1.93	8.09	4.90	2:45.33		
5875	Yevgeniy	Likhanov	RUS	10.10.95	2	NC	Smolensk	16 Feb
	7.14	7.38 14.59	2.08	8.24	4.70	2:51.19		
5858	Jérémy	Lelièvre	FRA	8.2.91	2	NC	Bordeaux	19 Feb
	6.98	7.31 14.87	1.94	8.31	4.45	2:37.75		
5843#	Steven	Bastien	USA	4.3.94	1		Akron	4 Feb
	6.84	7.33 13.00	1.93	8.17	4.75	2:43.98		
5841	Simone	Cairoli	ITA	12.9.90	12	EI	Beograd	5 Mar
	7.04	7.55 12.21	2.04	8.31	4.70	2:40.14		
5834	Benjamin	Gregory	GBR	21.11.90	1		Glasgow	5 Mar
	7.29	7.30 13.22	1.99	8.22	4.97	2:40.92		
5833	Florian	Geffrouais	FRA	5.12.88	3	NC	Bordeaux	19 Feb
	7.12	6.92 15.36	1.91	8.32	4.85	2:38.09		
5832	Liam	Ramsay	GBR	18.11.92	1		Sheffield	8 Jan
	7.00	7.21 13.58	2.05	8.28	4.41	2:38.86		
5824	Bas	Markies	NED	24.7.84	1		Apeldoorn	5 Feb
	7.03	7.07 14.38	1.91	7.95	4.76	2:45.27		
5820	Vasyl	Ivanytskyy (30)	UKR	29.1.91	1	NC	Sumy	18 Feb
	7.03	7.26 13.12	2.04	8.25	4.80	2:47.88		

Mark	Name		Nat	Born	Date	Mark	Name		Nat	Born	Date
5817#	Steele	Wasik	USA	8.12.95	25 Feb	5756	Austin	Jamerson	USA	16.3.95	26 Feb
5815	Tim	Nowak	GER	13.8.95	29 Jan	5754	Andrey	Fomichev	RUS	12.3.96	22 Dec
5814	Roman	Kondratyev	RUS	15.5.95	16 Feb	5747#	Mitch	Modin	USA	12.4.95	25 Feb
5813	Hunter	Veith	USA	14.1.95	26 Feb	5738A	Japheth	Cato	USA	25.12.90	4 Mar
5804#	Wolf	Mahler	USA	26.9.94	25 Feb	5730	Yuriy	Yeremich	BLR	24.10.95	11 Feb
5786	Jonathan	Wells	USA	18.4.96	11 Mar	5723	Andri	Oberholzer	SUI	24.7.96	5 Feb
5780	Artem	Lukyanenko	RUS	30.1.90	16 Feb	5715	Austin	Bahner	USA	7.7.91	4 Feb
5778	Yevgeniy	Sarantsev	RUS	5.2.88	19 Jan	5714	Akihiko	Nakamura	JPN	23.10.90	4 Feb
5770	John	Seals	USA	22.10.95	19 Feb	5714	Aleksey	Cherkasov	RUS	22.10.94	22 Dec
5760	Ruben	Gado	FRA	13.12.93	19 Feb	5712	John	Lane (50)	GBR	29.1.89	8 Jan

DECATHLON

Mark	Name		Nat	Born	Pos	Meet	Venue			Date
8768	Kevin	Mayer	FRA	10.2.92	1	WCh	London (OS)			12 Aug
	10.70/-0.8	7.52/0.0	15.72	2.08	48.26	13.75/-0.1	47.14	5.10	66.10	4:36.73
8663	Rico	Freimuth	GER	14.3.88	1		Ratingen			25 Jun
	10.44w/3.3	7.60/1.5	14.87	2.01	48.76	13.87/0.7	51.56	4.90	62.33	4:37.04
8601	Ilya	Shkurenyov	RUS	11.1.91	1	NC	Smolensk			10 Jun
	10.89/0.7	7.58/0.9	14.15	2.12	49.00	13.95/1.4	44.91	5.30	60.29	4:28.35
8591	Damian	Warner	CAN	4.11.89	1	Hypo	Götzis			28 May
	10.35/0.5	7.85/1.4	14.09	2.03	47.49	13.54/-0.2	44.35	4.70	57.69	4:29.33
8564		Freimuth			2	WCh	London (OS)			12 Aug
	10.53/-0.7	7.48/-0.4	14.85	1.99	48.41	13.68/-0.1	51.17	4.80	62.34	4:41.57
8539(w)	Lindon	Victor	GRN	28.2.93	1	SEC	Columbia, SC			12 May
	10.64w/3.6	7.35w/2.1	15.18	2.05	48.74	14.45/1.8	55.22	4.70	68.97	4:55.91
8539	Eelco	Sintnicolaas	NED	7.4.87	2	Hypo	Götzis			28 May
	10.57/0.5	7.61/0.6	14.62	1.91	48.37	14.16/-1.2	43.52	5.40	62.13	4:30.32
8509	Kurt	Felix	GRN	4.7.88	2		Ratingen			25 Jun
	10.91w/3.3	7.68/-0.8	15.31	2.07	48.67	14.92/0.7	50.59	4.50	72.80	4:43.21
8488	Kai	Kazmirek	GER	28.1.91	3	WCh	London (OS)			12 Aug
	10.91/-0.8	7.64/-0.4	13.78	2.11	47.19	14.66/1.2	45.06	5.10	63.45	4:38.07
8478(w)		Kazmirek			3		Ratingen			25 Jun
	10.85w/3.3	7.50w/2.3	14.63	2.07	47.40	14.62/0.7	45.19	5.20	60.52	4:38.24
8472		Victor			1	TexR	Austin			30 Mar
	10.63/1.3	7.37/1.8	16.52	2.09	48.24	14.94/0.8	53.00	4.30	66.69	4:48.89
8390		Victor			1	NCAA	Eugene			8 Jun
	10.72/-0.1	7.34/2.9	16.31	2.01	49.33	14.78/1.3	53.31	4.61	67.24	4:55.71
8371	Janek	Oiglane	EST	25.4.94	4	WCh	London (OS)			2 Jul
	11.08/-0.2	7.33/-0.1	15.13	2.05	49.58	14.56/-0.5	42.11	5.10	71.73	4:39.24
8365		Freimuth			3	Hypo	Götzis			28 May
	10.53/0.5	7.47w/2.1	15.21	1.94	49.40	13.80/-0.2	49.45	4.80	57.77	4:42.67
8345	Devon	Williams (10)	USA	17.1.94	1		Athens, GA			8 Apr
	10.72/0.3	7.75	14.20	1.96	48.14	13.83/0.1	46.29	4.57	60.26	4:36.79
8335	Adam Sebastian	Helcelet	CZE	27.10.91	4	Hypo	Götzis			28 May
	10.87/1.4	7.32w/2.8	14.89	2.00	49.50	14.19/-0.2	44.35	5.00	68.04	4:43.69
8334	Pieter	Braun	NED	21.1.93	5	Hypo	Götzis			28 May
	10.90w/2.8	7.71/0.5	14.82	2.00	49.09	14.40/-0.2	42.66	5.00	58.49	4:28.14
8309		Warner			5	WCh	London (OS)			12 Aug
	10.50/-0.7	7.44/-0.6	13.45	2.02	47.47	13.63/-0.1	40.67	4.70	56.63	4:28.39
8294	Mathias	Brugger	GER	6.8.92	6	Hypo	Götzis			28 May
	10.89/1.4	7.25/1.6	15.32	1.97	47.29	14.06/1.4	45.08	4.80	57.81	4:34.26
8281	Oleksiy	Kasyanov	UKR	26.8.85	7	Hypo	Götzis			28 May
	10.66/0.5	7.63/1.4	14.64	2.00	48.68	14.03/-0.2	44.99	4.70	54.11	4:33.43
8252		Warner			1		Talence			17 Sep
	10.52/-0.1	7.60/-0.2	14..07	2.02	48.53	13.81/-0.5	42.70	4.65	56.45	4:40.87
8234		Kasyanov			6	WCh	London (OS)			12 Aug
	10.77/-0.7	7.28/-1.1	14.99	2.02	48.64	14.05/-0.1	48.79	4.70	50.82	4:33.86
8227		Felix			7	WCh	London (OS)			12 Aug
	11.08/-0.2	7.46/0.7	15.01	2.08	49.09	14.68/-0.5	45.39	4.50	64.64	4:36.62
8225	Trey	Hardee	USA	7.2.84	1	NC	Sacramento			23 Jun
	10.57/0.9	7.43/0.0	14.91	1.98	49.02	13.97/0.0	48.04	4.90	60.30	5:12.65
8222		Helcelet			8	WCh	London (OS)			12 Aug
	11.28/-1.3	7.03/-0.7	14.57	2.02	49.51	14.38/0.4	44.71	4.90	71.56	4:36.85
8214	Leonel	Suárez	CUB	1.9.87	8	Hypo	Götzis			28 May
	11.08/1.3	7.25w/3.0	14.18	2.00	48.80	14.54/1.0	44.18	4.50	71.88	4:29.14
8201	Luca	Wieland	GER	7.12.94	1	MSR	Azusa			13 Apr
	10.52w/2.4	7.53/1.9	14.89	2.05	48.88	14.43/1.5	44.78	4.80	48.60	4:38.54
8187w	Jefferson	Santos	BRA	30.8.95	1	SAmC	Asunción			24 Jun
	10.77w/3.0	7.48W/4.3	13.88	2.06	49.97	14.57w/2.7	50.41	4.80	55.10	4:43.99
8181		Williams			2	NCAA	Eugene			8 Jun
	10.65/-0.1	7.73/1.3	14.13	1.98	48.16	13.87/1.7	40.72	4.71	57.04	4:46.11

Mark	Name		Nat	Born	Pos	Meet	Venue			Date
8172	Fredrik	Samuelsson	SWE	16.2.95	9	Hypo	Götzis			28 May
	10.81/1.4	7.50/1.8	14.40	2.03	49.26	14.10/1.4	40.03	5.00	56.21	4:39.52
	(30/19)									
8163	Ashley	Bryant (20)	GBR	17.5.91	10	Hypo	Götzis			28 May
	10.89w/2.8	7.70/0.1	14.20	1.97	49.69	14.69/0.6	42.52	4.50	67.54	4:31.86
8155	Zach	Ziemek	USA	23.2.93	2	NC	Sacramento			23 Jun
	10.69/0.9	7.69/2.0	13.57	2.04	50.20	14.84/0.0	42.30	5.30	56.01	4:47.61
8144	Martin	Roe	NOR	1.4.92	1	ET-2	Monzón			2 Jul
	10.79/-1.7	7.33/2.0	15.44	1.92	49.64	15.37/0.3	49.19	4.50	66.13	4:34.60
8130	Artem	Lukyanenko	RUS	30.1.90	2	NC	Smolensk			10 Jun
	11.01/0.7	6.95/-0.3	15.00	2.03	50.01	13.98/1.4	44.67	4.90	58.81	4:37.24
8126w	Geormi	Jaramillo	VEN	6.3.89	2	SAmC	Asunción			24 Jun
	10.70w/3.0	7.76W/5.0	14.46	1.79	48.99	13.96w/2.7	46.37	4.50	62.86	4:45.94
		8039(w) with LJ 7.41/2.1								
8125	Jorge	Ureña	ESP	8.10.93	9	WCh	London (OS)			12 Aug
	11.00/-0.8	7.30/-0.4	13.91	2.08	48.72	14.15/-0.5	36.33	5.00	56.06	4:26.46
8120	Jirí	Sykora	CZE	20.1.95	11	Hypo	Götzis			28 May
	10.88/1.4	7.33w/2.1	14.73	1.97	49.20	14.25/-1.2	47.38	4.80	61.06	4:57.01
8120	Larbi	Bouraada	ALG	10.5.88	1		Kladno			18 Jun
	10.76w/2.3	7.26/0.4	12.40	2.05	48.47	14.26/1.3	40.17	4.80	62.49	4:32.34
8112	Artem	Makarenko	RUS	23.4.97	3	NC	Smolensk			10 Jun
	11.00/0.7	7.03/0.2	14.62	2.03	48.70	13.82/1.4	40.71	5.00	51.55	4:27.99
8102	Pau Gaspar	Tonnesen	ESP	24.10.92	12	Hypo	Götzis			28 May
	11.08w/2.8	7.53/1.9	14.65	2.06	53.62	14.60/-1.2	42.97	5.40	60.86	4:48.90
8046	Dominik	Distelberger	AUT	16.3.90	13	Hypo	Götzis			28 May
	10.73/0.5	7.15/1.1	13.36	1.88	48.16	14.32/1.0	43.08	4.90	60.11	4:35.68
	(30)									
8041	Basile	Rolnin	FRA	21.1.94	4		Ratingen			25 Jun
	11.11/1.8	7.53/1.9	14.65	2.06	53.62	14.60/-1.2	42.97	5.40	60.86	4:48.90
8028	Ituah	Enahoro	GER/NGR	15.12.97	1	vUSA	Düsseldorf			30 Jul
	10.84/-0.5	7.64/0.2	14.44	1.90	48.02	14.86/0.5	46.65	4.45	51.57	4:27.94
8025	Karl Robert	Saluri	EST	6.8.93	13	WCh	London (OS)			12 Aug
	10.55/-0.7	7.49/-1.0	13.98	1.84	47.76	15.36/-0.5	40.43	5.00	57.12	4:31.31
8015	Steve	Bastien	USA	4.3.94	4	NCAA	Eugene			8 Jun
	10.68/0.2	7.43/0.6	12.91	2.04	47.49	14.73/2.0	40.10	4.81	51.42	4:34.31
8010	Yevgeniy	Sarantsev	RUS	5.8.88	1		Adler			3 Sep
	11.31/0.2	7.20/0.7	15.14	2.01	50.21	15.19/0.3	43.17	4.90	63.03	4:33.91
8009	René	Stauss	GER	17.9.87	2	vUSA	Düsseldorf			30 Jul
	11.30/-0.7	7.22/0.5	14.23	2.11	50.76	15.40/1.3	47.21	4.95	58.58	4:37.73
8002A	Friedrich	Pretorius	RSA	4.8.95	1		Pretoria			18 Mar
	10.74/1.8	7.39/1.2	13.30	1.96	49.98	14.61/0.6	41.264:26.15			
8002	Pawel	Wiesiolek	POL	13.8.91	15	Hypo	Götzis			28 May
	10.79/0.5	7.35/1.9	14.19	2.12	50.83	14.52/1.0	44.50	4.50	55.58	4:42.16
7997w	Marek	Lukás	CZE	16.7.91	16	Hypo	Götzis			28 May
	10.94w/2.8	6.99W/5.1	14.21	1.91	50.05	14.62/-1.2	39.98	4.80	70.80	4:32.94
		7967(w) with LJ 6.86w/2.5								
7987	Marcus	Nilsson	SWE	3.5.91	2	ET-1	Monzón			2 Jul
	11.30/-2.0	6.86/0.3	14.87	1.95	50.30	14.81/-0.5	44.85	4.80	65.33	4:26.79
	(40)									
7973	Tim	Duckworth	GBR	18.6.96	2		Athens, GA			9 Apr
	10.62/0.3	7.87	12.25	2.11	49.18	14.64/0.1	40.71	4.97	55.45	5:15.40
7965	John	Lane	GBR	29.1.89	2	MSR	Azusa			13 Apr
	10.73/1.2	7.42w/3.3	13.06	2.05	48.53	14.57/1.5	43.06	5.00	48.68	4:50.54
7956	Elmo	Savola	FIN	10.3.95	3	EC-23	Bydgoszcz			16 Jul
	10.84/0.7	7.29/-0.6	13.97	1.96	49.14	14.21/1.7	37.35	4.70	61.89	4:39.50
7948	Pierce	Lepage	CAN	22.1.96	1	9	Ottawa			5 Jul
	10.59/0.9	7.33/0.3	13.30	2.08	47.79	14.99/0.3	40.53	4.85	50.87	4:48.85
7942	Tim	Nowak	GER	13.8.95	5		Talence			17 Sep
	11.24/0.8	7.25/0.4	13.98	1.96	49.91	14.69/0.2	43.00	4.75	61.39	4:30.50
7937	Cody	Walton	USA	14.6.95	3		Athens, GA			9 Apr
	11.22/0.3	7.20	14.19	1.99	49.77	14.79/0.1	42.35	4.87	68.21	4:55.90
7922	Bastien	Auzeil	FRA	22.10.89	15	WCh	London (OS)			12 Aug
	11.35/-0.2	6.87/0.2	15.23	1.96	50.36	14.59/1.2	46.86	4.80	60.80	4:39.80
7921	Vitaliy	Zhuk	BLR	10.9.96	4	EC-23	Bydgoszcz			16 Jul
	11.37/0.1	6.76/0.1	14.64	1.99	49.40	14.48/1.7	44.25	4.70	62.90	4:34.50
7915	Scott	Filip	USA	28.1.95	2	TexR	Austin			30 Mar
	10.77/1.3	7.41/0.5	13.94	2.00	48.20	14.94/-1.1	39.63	4.70	54.13	4:40.01
7914	Aleksandr	Tabala	RUS	23.5.86	4	NC	Smolensk			10 Jun
	10.59/0.5	6.94/-0.3	15.22	2.06	51.63	14.83/1.5	43.48	5.00	58.72	4:30.20
	(50)									

Mark	Name		Nat	Born	Pos	Meet	Venue			Date
7900	Sergey	Timshin	RUS	25.11.92	5	NC	Smolensk			10 Jun
	11.02/0.7	6.90/0.3	12.94	2.15	49.62	14.44/1.4	40.74	4.70	56.54	4:35.12
7897	Wolf	Mahler	USA	26.9.94	3	TexR	Austin			30 Mar
	10.79/0.2	6.95/1.9	12.67	1.97	48.03	14.66w/2.8	40.89	4.90	50.90	4:21.73
7882	Taylor	Stewart	CAN	11.4.91	2	NC	Ottawa			5 Jul
	10.90/0.9	7.55/0.2	15.09	1.90	51.47	14.28/0.3	46.33	4.65	52.81	4:48.45
7875	Simone	Cairoli	ITA	12.9.90	18	Hypo	Götzis			28 May
	10.79/1.4	7.37/-0.4	13.04	2.03	49.95	14.72/0.6	37.53	4.50	56.36	4:21.14
7873	Akihiko	Nakamura	JPN	23.10.90	1	NC	Nagano			11 Jun
	10.77/1.0	7.56/1.1	11.44	1.90	48.59	14.10/-0.5	36.23	4.90	52.10	4:22.57
7872	Torben	Blech	GER	12.2.95	1		Filderstadt			11 Jun
	10.84/0.8	7.39/0.0	14.94	1.90	50.58	14.90/-2.4	41.59	5.20	58.18	5:03.77
7866	Hunter	Veith	USA	14.1.95	6	NCAA	Eugene			8 Jun
	10.66/0.5	7.71/1.7	12.72	2.01	49.16	14.40/1.3	36.70	4.81	55.95	4:57.64
7864	Román	Gastaldi	ARG	25.9.89	1		São Bernardo do Campo			12 Mar
	10.92/0.4	7.28/-0.6	14.95	2.02	49.84	15.10/-1.2	45.71	4.60	50.95	4:42.82
7858	Maksim	Andraloits	BLR	17.6.97	5	EC-23	Bydgoszcz			16 Jul
	10.98/0.7	7.36/0.9	13.88	1.99	49.23	14.47/1.5	43.89	4.70	51.97	4:47.76
7856	Yevgeniy	Likhanov	RUS	10.1.95	3		Adler			13 May
	11.12	7.59	14.46	2.00	50.48	14.70	42.09	4.50	54.93	4:37.39
	(60)									
7850	Austin	Bahner	USA	7.7.91	1		Dallas			4 Jun
	10.64	7.19/0.0	13.01	1.83	49.67	15.01/0.8	48.35	4.90	56.10	4:44.02
7846	Darko	Pesic	MNE	30.11.92	19	Hypo	Götzis			28 May
	11.25/1.3	7.15w/2.5	15.47	1.94	51.03	14.65/1.4	45.56	4.20	59.56	4:24.73
7843	Jérémy	Lelièvre	FRA	8.2.91	1	NC	Marseille			15 Jul
	11.06/-1.6	7.54/1.2	14.48	1.88	49.28	14.88/-0.8	43.66	4.50	50.62	4:23.41
7839	Ruben	Gado	FRA	13.12.93	2	Franc	Abidjan			26 Jul
	10.96/0.3	7.14/	12.23	1.97	48.79	15.08/1.1	38.80	5.10	57.03	4:30.50
7827	Andri	Oberholzer	SUI	24.7.96	6	EC-23	Bydgoszcz			16 Jul
	11.13/-0.4	7.54/0.1	13.62	2.08	50.99	14.78/1.7	39.42	4.90	51.59	4:40.75
7825	Manuel	Eitel	GER	28.1.97	7		Talence			17 Sep
	10.51/-0.1	7.14/0.0	13.18	1.99	49.62	14.85/0.2	40.01	4.65	57.25	4:42.13
7811	Atsu	Nyamadi	GHA	1.6.94	1		Charlottesville			22 Apr
	11.24/1.2	7.62/1.7	13.71	1.93	50.49	14.71/1.9	45.76	4.40	59.54	4:42.51
7807	Keisuke	Ushiro	JPN	24.7.86	2	NC	Nagano			11 Jun
	11.22w/2.2	6.87/-0.4	14.44	1.93	52.27	14.93/0.6	46.57	4.80	68.74	4:48.48
7804	Willem	Coertzen	RSA	30.12.82	2		Kladno			18 Jun
	11.12w/2.3	7.23/-0.5	13.38	1.90	49.82	14.53/1.3	42.56	4.20	66.77	4:31.11
7802	Taavi	Tsernjavski	EST	4.3.95	1		Arona			4 Jun
	11.16/1.0	7.01/0.8	13.57	1.91	49.31	14.92/0.0	44.54	4.60	61.02	4:32.25
	(70)									
7801(w)	Hunter	Price	USA	28.8.94	3	MSR	Azusa			13 Apr
	10.73/1.8	7.43w/2.3	12.46	1.99	48.65	13.98w/2.4	37.56	4.40	52.55	4:35.99
7801	Vasyl	Ivanytskyy	UKR	29.1.91	4	ET	Tallinn			2 Jul
	11.19/-1.1	7.59w/2.4	12.35	2.01	50.76	14.62/0.8	40.48	4.60	58.44	4:32.26
7799	Ben	Gregory	GBR	21.11.90	1	ESP Ch	Barcelona			23 Jul
	11.30/0.0	7.11w/3.7	13.17	1.87	49.86	14.52/1.3	40.86	5.10	57.79	4:30.37
7780	Dennis	Hutterer	GER	4.5.96	7	EC-23	Bydgoszcz			16 Jul
	11.02/0.7	7.17/-0.9	14.23	1.99	50.05	14.91/-0.3	47.14	4.60	50.87	4:43.30
7779	Cedric	Dubler	AUS	13.1.95	1	NC	Sydney			31 Mar
	10.93/1.2	7.25/-0.4	11.14	2.04	49.56	14.53/0.0	40.43	5.10	54.18	4:48.52
7772	Maksim	Korolyov	RUS	6.1.88	7	NC	Smolensk			10 Jun
	11.21/0.5	6.93/-0.3	14.56	1.94	49.77	15.14/1.5	47.89	4.50	54.73	4:30.01
7764	Gaël	Quérin	FRA	26.6.87	20	Hypo	Götzis			28 May
	11.26w/2.8	7.32/0.5	13.39	1.88	49.09	14.71/-1.2	39.49	4.60	51.22	4:08.90
7762	José Gregorio	Lemus	COL	4.6.91	1	Bol G	Santa Marta			23 Nov
	11.13/0.6	6.66/0.8	16.91	1.91	51.65	14.58/1.2	52.26	4.20	67.50	5:13.72
7756	Santiago	Ford	CUB	25.8.97	1	Barr	La Habana			27 May
	11.32/-0.8 7	.03/-1.5	12.55	2.02	49.66	14.78/-0.3	45.42	4.20	65.26	4:35.17
7746	Kurtis	Brondyke	USA	24.1.89	5	NC	Sacramento			23 Jun
	11.12w/2.3	7.06w/2.2	15.45	1.92	51.44	14.80/-1.1	44.28	4.70	62.20	4:58.12
	(80)									
7745	Robert	Robinson	USA	3.8.87	4	MSR	Azusa			13 Apr
	11.16/1.2	7.39w/2.5	13.03	1.96	48.76	14.36/0.1	43.72	4.40	54.87	4:46.27
7741	Maxime	Maugein	FRA	27.9.92	6	ET	Tallinn			2 Jul
	11.21/-0.1	7.17w/3.7	13.39	1.92	49.20	14.47/1.0	37.91	4.80	51.42	4:21.29
7735	Marvin	Bollinger	GER	7.10.96	5		Filderstadt			11 Jun
	11.10/-0.1	7.18/-0.3	13.71	2.05	51.13	14.96/-0.9	41.23	4.80	52.67	4:37.68
7732	Suthisak	Singkhon	THA	5.10.96	1	AsiC	Bhubaneswar			7 Jul
	11.03/-0.8	7.79/0.9	14.09	1.98	48.70	14.80/0.0	42.78	4.00	60.64	5:07.61

Mark	Name		Nat	Born	Pos	Meet	Venue	Date
7725	TJ	Lawson	USA	25.1.97	9	NCAA	Eugene	8 Jun
	11.01/0.2	7.43/2.0 13.48	2.10	49.46	14.80w/2.5		40.55 4.41 44.96	4:34.11
7720(w)	Markus	Leemet	EST	22.8.93	3	SEC	Columbia, SC	12 May
	10.75w/3.6	7.16/1.7 14.18	1.90	48.36	14.91/1.8		35.89 4.50 59.03	4:39.85
7719	Briander	Rivero	CUB	23.4.91	2	Barr	La Habana	27 May
	11.12/-0.8	7.29/-2.0 13.88	2.05	49.23	14.54/-0.3		45.05 4.20 51.33	4:48.76
7718	Feliks	Shestopalov	RUS	11.3.96	8	NC	Smolensk	10 Jun
	11.23/0.7	7.15/-0.4 12.82	1.94	48.52	14.53/1.4		40.33 4.50 55.79	4:28.34
7717	Dan	Golubovic	USA	29.11.93	6	NC	Sacramento	23 Jun
	11.25/0.9	6.71/0.9 13.16	1.98	50.88	14.95/-1.1		44.87 4.80 61.44	4:36.86
7715(w)	Steele	Wasik	USA	8.12.95	1	Big 12	Lawrence	13 May
	11.00w/3.4	7.27w/2.2 14.04	2.05	50.09	14.36w/2.4		39.66 4.61 59.19	5:14.57
	(90)							
7699	Gabriel	Moore	USA	10.1.96	7	NC	Sacramento	23 Jun
	10.96/0.9	6.97w/2.4 13.54	1.92	49.09	15.03/-0.6		46.50 4.60 54.96	4:46.83
7699	Felix	Hepperle	GER	23.11.89	3	vUSA	Düsseldorf	30 Jul
	11.04/-05	7.16/-0.1 12.51	1.99	48.26	15.19/0.5		37.51 4.85 50.95	4:28.00
7687	Kyle	Cranston	AUS	3.9.92	1	WUG	Taipei	25 Aug
	11.13/-0.4	7.04/0.5 13.76	1.98	48.99	15.11/-0.2		41.53 4.60 56.30	4:42.08
7669	Matthias	Clark	USA	31.5.87	2		Dallas	4 Jun
	11.04	6.99/0.0 13.94	1.92	50.40	15.80/0.8		41.08 4.80 59.50	4:31.26
7666		Guo Qi	CHN	28.12.90	1	NG	Tianjin	7 Sep
	11.47/-0.9	6.89/-1.0 13.54	2.03	50.60	14.44/-0.1		41.49 5.10 52.25	4:48.95
7664	Pavel	Rudnev	RUS	26.10.92	9	NC	Smolensk	10 Jun
	11.07/0.7	6.94/0.1 13.22	2.00	50.72	14.57/1.5		38.68 5.00 48.12	4:30.23
7642	Kimihito	Morimoto	JPN	21.4.93	1		Osaka	11 May
	10.95/-0.4	7.15/0.7 11.04	1.90	48.83	14.90/0.8		40.34 4.70 62.67	4:43.40
7639	Yaroslav	Novitskiy	RUS	4.4.88	10	NC	Smolensk	10 Jun
	11.56/0.5	6.85/-0.3 14.38	2.00	51.80	15.38/1.5		41.82 4.90 65.11	4:47.98
7635	Derek	Jacobus	USA	23.7.95	4	SEC	Columbia, SC	12 May
	10.77w/3.6	7.29/1.4 12.85	1.93	48.34	15.48/0.4		40.41 4.70 47.52	4:34.79
7634	Pablo	Trescoli	ESP	4.3.95	3		Arona	4 Jun
	11.16/1.0	7.11/-0.6 13.09	1.91	49.24	14.68/0.5		39.56 4.00 63.72	4:26.62
	(100)							

Mark	Name		Nat	Born	Date
7631	Dominik	Alberto	SUI	28.4.92	27 Aug
7630	Phil	Bailey	USA	20.7.94	13 Apr
7624	Bas	Markies	NED	24.7.84	2 Jul
7616	Aleksandr	Cherkasov	RUS	22.10.94	13 May
7592	Alec	Diamond	AUS	9.8.97	3 Dec
7591(w)	Juuso	Hassi	FIN	4.4.93	23 Jul
7590	Joe	Delgado	USA	8.1.95	8 Jun
7584	Maxence	Pécatte	FRA	9.1.97	4 Jun
7584	Kazuya	Kawasaki	JPN	14.6.95	7 Jul
7582	Aaron	Booth	NZL	12.9.96	3 Dec
7579	Tsuyoshi	Shimizu	JPN	21.12.93	11 Jun
7579	Benjamin	Fenrich	FRA	11.6.90	18 Jun
7576	Florian	Obst	GER	24.2.93	26 May
7576	Romain	Martin	FRA	12.7.88	23 Jul
7570	Lars Vikan	Rise	NOR	23.11.88	18 Jun
7563	Patrick	Scherfose	GER	28.11.91	30 Jul
7554	Loek	van Zevenbergen	NED	5.8.96	27 Aug
7550(w)	Jonay	Jordán	ESP	12.5.91	7 May
7546w	Shun	Taue	JPN	30.5.97	9 Sep
7538		Hu Yufei	CHN	9.11.93	7 Sep
7536	Jacopo	Zanatta	ITA	21.8.96	16 Jul
7535	Felipe de Jesús	López	MEX	20.2.95	7 May
7533	Sander	Maes	BEL	21.12.92	4 Jun
7530	Mitch	Modin	USA	12.4.95	7 May
7529	Timur	Ehrhardt	USA	16.3.95	22 Apr
7528A	Andy	Preciado	ECU	12.10.97	20 May
7528	Tim	Wunderlich	USA	2.4.87	4 Jun
7527	Rody	de Wolff	NED	9.4.97	16 Jul
7526	Axel	Hubert	FRA	16.2.96	18 Jun
7521	Yevgeniy	Chernov	RUS	9.11.91	13 May
7520	Alex	Soares	BRA	2.2.95	10 Jun
7518	José Miguel	Paulino	DOM	11.11.97	17 Jun
7513	Taylor	Sanderson	USA	2.10.92	4 Jun
7508A	Josh	Cogdill	USA	31.3.94	11 May
7500	Curtis	Mathews	GBR	22.1.92	17 Sep
7494	Jason	Dunn	USA	-.12.92	13 Apr
7494	Thomas	FitzSimons	USA	8.3.89	23 Jun
7489	Risto	Lillemets	EST	20.11.97	11 Jun
7489	Karel	Tilga	EST-J	5.2.98	13 Aug
7487	Mario	Arancón	ESP	29.3.94	4 Jun
7487	Nico	Beckers	GER	3.3.94	25 Jun
7483A	Jackson	Walker	USA	18.1.92	13 May
7481		Gong Kewei	CHN	29.6.94	19 May
7479	Jonas	Fringeli	SUI	12.1.88	27 Aug
7478(w)	Jackson	Lint	USA	6.1.96	22 Apr
7471(w)	William	Dougherty	USA	8.5.95	13 Apr
7467		Chen Xiaohong	CHN	9.2.97	19 May
7467	Sebastian	Ruthström	SWE	4.8.97	2 Jul
7459	Kevin	Fankl	SWE	6.12.95	11 Jun
7451	James	Turner	CAN	4.8.93	10 Jun
7450	Rafael	Noguera	CUB	28.2.97	15 Mar
7450	Sawyer	Smith	USA	.95	23 Apr
7445	Kazuya	Katayama	JPN	14.6.95	11 Jun
7441	Majed Radhi	Al-Sayed	KUW	31.1.93	7 Jul
7439	Kevin	Nielsen	USA	12.1.93	30 Mar
7438	Ashley	Moloney	AUS-Y	13.3.00	24 Sep
7436	Sascha	Menn	GER	6.4.95	11 Jun
7433	Aries	Toledo	PHI	2.11.93	23 Aug
7430	Axel	Martin	FRA	13.4.94	17 Sep
7423(w)	Robert	Rohner	USA	13.10.93	13 Apr
7420	Solomon	Simmons	USA	26.9.93	5 Jul
7417	Kris	Horn	USA	25.4.94	13 May
7413	Tyler	Brendel	USA	24.10.94	7 May
7412	Rik	Taam	NED	17.1.97	28 May
7406	Tanner	McNutt	USA	11.10.94	26 May
7401	Alex	Bloom	USA	19.2.96	13 May
7401	Oscar	Campos	VEN	18.5.92	23 Sep
7400	Harald	Bust	NED	3.6.92	16 Jul
	(168)				

Best non wind-assisted

Mark	Name	Pos	Meet	Venue	Date
7776	J Santos	1	NC	São Bernardo	10 Jun
	11.07/-0.1 7.15/0.0 13.82 2.10 49.64	14.55/0.8		41.59 4.60 51.03	4:46.27

JUNIORS

Mark	Name		Nat	Born	Pos	Meet	Venue	Date
7489	Karel	Tilga	EST-J	5.2.98	2	NC	Tartu	13 Aug
	11.38/-1.0	7.23/1.9 13.85	2.08	50.12	15.22/0.5		40.92 3.77 60.66	4:48.52

Mark	Name			Nat		Born	Pos	Meet	Venue	Date
7438	Ashley	Moloney		AUS-Y		13.3.00	1		Townsville	24 Sep
	10.62/0.6	7.17/1.8	13.17	2.02	48.57	15.22/-0.5	36.42	4.40	47.15	4:59.54
7114	Ondrej	Kopecky		CZE		16.5.98	14	ET-1	Monzón	2 Jul
	11.38/-2.0	6.85/1.2	12.80	1.86	49.94	15.24/-1.2	39.95	4.50	48.76	4:54.49
7084		Choe Dong-hwi		KOR		15.12.98	3	NG	Gongju	24 Oct
	11.11/0.7	7.29/0.9	12.77	1.82	51.88	14.65/-0.9	30.87	4.60	53.16	5:03.57
7066	Yuma	Maruyama		JPN		3.6.98	4		Yokohama	26 May
	11.09/-0.3	7.12/1.7	12.32	1.90	50.85	14.65w/2.6	35.30	3.60	52.46	4:41.53

IAAF JUNIOR SPECIFICATION – WITH 99CM 110MH, 6KG SP, 1.75KG DT

Mark	Name			Nat		Born	Pos	Meet	Venue	Date
8435	Niklas	Kaul		GER		11.2.98	1	EJ	Grosseto	23 Jul
	11.48/-1.3	7.20/1.6	15.37	2.05	48.42	14.55/-0.2	48.49	4.70	68.05	4:15.51
	7946 1	Filderstadt			11 Jun					
	11.33/0.0	6.900.0	15.40	2.05	49.18	14.50/0.0	34.53	4.70	64.34	4:27.15
8141	Johannes	Erm		EST		26.3.98	2	EJ	Grosseto	23 Jul
	11.06/0.7	7.42/-0.3	13.44	1.92	48.17	14.66/0.9	43.61	4.50	54.19	4:28.96
	7753 2	Filderstadt			11 Jun	10 performances by 8 men to 7725				
8002	Karel	Tilga		EST-J		5.2.98	3	EJ	Grosseto	23 Jul
	11.28/-1.3	7.13/1.8	15.66	2.05	49.38	15.01/-1.2	49.34	4.00	66.30	4:40.07
7893	Rafael	Raap		NED		18.3.99	1	NC-j	Emmeloord	14 May
	11.08/0.4	7.25w/2.3	14.41	2.03	49,.85	14.30/0.7	42.83	4.70	50.56	4:37.45
7823	Ludovic	Besson		FRA		27.1.98	4	EJ	Grosseto	23 Jul
	11.05/-2.0	7.09w/2.7	16.69	1.99	49.67	14.39/-1.3	45.74	4.60	47.93	4:53.82
7791	Ondrej	Kopecky		CZE		16.5.98	1		Olomouc	28 May
	11.05/1.7	7.03/-0.3	14.22	1.96	50.30	14.04/0.6	41.73	5.00	48.82	4:43.23
7790	Yuma	Maruyama		JPN		3.6.98	1	NC-j	Nagano	10 Jun
	10.91/1.1	7.30/0.0	13.92	1.97	50.18	13.64/0.1	40.38	4.10	56.98	4:39.06
7725	Dmitriy	Solomatin		RUS		15.4.98	1		Adler	14 May
	11.37/0.5	7.04/0.2	14.62	2.00	49.71	14.84/-1.9	42.86	4.60	50.33	4:29.15
7713	Maximilian	Vollmer		GER		12.3.98	5	EJ	Grosseto	23 Jul
	11.15/-2.0	7.14/1.8	15.14	1.87	48.66	14.81/-0.1	41.51	4.20	59.01	4:34.91
7704(w)	Matas	Adamonis		LTU		26.6.98	1	Baltic	Rakvere	21 May
	11.53w2.5	7.25w/3.5	16.57	1.99	51.96	14.811.75	45.83	4.27	54.35	4:40.82
7641	Makensen	Gletty		FRA		2.4.99	1		Montpelier	14 May
	10.88/1.1	6.94/0.0	15.87	1.93	49.42	14.37/0.7	42.04	4.40	46.23	4:47.86
7620	Jakob	Samuelsson		SWE		19.2.98	1		Landquart	21 May
	11.45/0.7	6.70/0.6	15.89	1.86	51.01	15.52/0.1	48.52	4.50	63.40	4:45.69
7620	Toraiv	Opsal		NOR		9.3.98	6	EJ	Grosseto	23 Jul
	11.27/-1.2	7.13/2.0	14.57	1.96	48.93	15.23/-0.2	37.29	4.60	44.90	4:15.37
7615	Axel	Clément		FRA		16.1.98	2	NC-j	Saint-Renan	18 Jun
	11.21w/3.0	7.02/0.0	13.85	1.97	51.15	15.10/1.3	40.88	4.94	47.26	4:26.54
7565	Clement	Foucat		FRA		8.8.98	4	NC-j	Saint-Renan	18 Jun
	11.06/2.0	7.20/0.0	12.44	1.88	49.83	14.48/1.4	44.49	4.54	41.01	4:20.63
7547	George	Patrick		USA		23.2.98	1	NC-j	Sacramento	23 Jun
	10.75/1.8	7.44/1.1	13.89	1.95	50.40	14.44/-2.1	40.06	4.30	54.44	5:11.99
7544	Karly	Maisonneuve		FRA		10.7.98	5	NC-j	Saint-Renan	18 Jun
	10.93/2.0	6.95/-0.5	14.04	1.94	50.41	14.29/1.4	44.85	4.24	44.36	4:37.27
7541	Manuel	Wagner		GER		8.3.99	7	EJ	Grosseto	23 Jul
	11.33/-1.2	7.33w/2.9	12.26	1.87	49.47	14.79/-0.2	37.50	4.50	55.67	4:23.38
7538	Patryk	Baran		POL		22.4.98	8	EJ	Grosseto	23 Jul
	11.37/-1.2	7.28/1.5	14.34	2.02	52.19	14.34/-0.3	39.66	4.60	55.18	5:02.50
7520	Kristo	Simulask		EST		20.3.98	2	Baltic	Rakvere	21 May
	10.96w/2.5	7.10/0.4	13.91	2.02	51.34	14.911.7	43.74	4.47	44.86	4:45.21

4 X 100 METRES RELAY

Mark	Nat	Team	Pos	Meet	Venue	Date
37.47	GBR	Ujah, Gemili, Talbot, Mitchell-Blake	1	WCh	London (OS)	12 Aug
37.52	USA	Rodgers, Gatlin, Bacon, Coleman	2	WCh	London (OS)	12 Aug
37.70	USA	Rodgers, Gatlin, BJ Lee, Coleman	1h1	WCh	London (OS)	12 Aug
37.76	GBR	Ujah, Gemili, Talbot, Mitchell-Blake	2h1	WCh	London (OS)	12 Aug
37.95	JAM	Tracey, Forte, Campbell, Bolt	1h2	WCh	London (OS)	12 Aug
38.03	FRA	Dutamby, Vicaut, Zézé, Lemaitre	2h2	WCh	London (OS)	12 Aug
38.04	JPN	Tada, Iizuka, Kiryu, Fujimitsu	3	WCh	London (OS)	12 Aug
38.08	GBR	Ujah, Hughes, Talbot, Aikines-Aryeetey	1	ET	Villeneuve d'Ascq	24 Jun
38.15	CAN	Haynes, Brown, Rodney, De Grasse	1	FlaR	Gainesville	1 Apr
38.16	CHN	Wu Zhiqiang, Xie Zhenye, Su Bingtian, Zhang Peimeng	1	NG	Tianjin	7 Sep
38.19	CHN	Wu, Xie, Su, Zhang	1	Herc	Monaco	21 Jul
38.20	CHN	Wu, Xie, Su, Zhang	3h2	WCh	London (OS)	12 Aug
38.21	CAN	Haynes, Brown, Rodney, De Grasse	1h2	W.Rly	Nassau	22 Apr
38.21	JPN	Tada, Iizuka, Kiryu, Cambridge	3h1	WCh	London (OS)	12 Aug
38.22	USA	Bracy, Rodgers, Baker, Gatlin	2h2	W.Rly	Nassau	22 Apr
38.30	GER	Reus, Hering, R Schmidt, Menga	2	ET	Villeneuve d'Ascq	24 Jun

Mark	Nat	Name	Pos	Meet	Venue	Date
38.30	USA	Rodgers, Coleman, Bacon, Belcher	2	Herc	Monaco	21 Jul
38.32	GBR	Ujah, Hughes, Gemili, Talbot	1h3	W.Rly	Nassau	22 Apr
38.34	CHN	Wu, Xie, Su, Zhang	4	WCh	London (OS)	12 Aug
		(21 performances by teams from 8 nations)				
38.44	TUR	Hekimoglu, Harvey, Barnes, Guliyev	4h1	WCh	London (OS)	12 Aug
38.47A	RSA	Bruintjies, Leotlela, Munyai, Simbine (10)	1		Germiston	22 Mar
38.61	TTO	Bledman, Greaux, Morain, Callender	5h1	WCh	London (OS)	12 Aug
38.66	NED	Codrington, Paulina, Bonevacia, Burnet	6h1	WCh	London (OS)	12 Aug
38.86	ANT	C Walsh, T Walsh, Jarvis, Greene	1	TTO Ch	Port of Spain	25 Jun
38.88	AUS	T Williams, Gamble, Andrews, Browning	7h1	WCh	London (OS)	12 Aug
38.90	THA	Namsuwan, Chuangchai, Meenapra, Sathoengram	1	SEAG	Kuala Lumpur	25 Aug
39.01	CUB	H Pérez, Skyers, Carrero, Gaspar	6h2	WCh	London (OS)	12 Aug
39.05	INA	Fadlin, Iswandi, Rimbawan, Bobi	2	SEAG	Kuala Lumpur	25 Aug
39.06	TPE	Wei, Yang, Cheng, Chen	3	WUG	Taipei	28 Aug
39.07	UKR	Kravtsov, Ibrahimov, Suprun, Smelyk	1rB	ET	Villeneuve d'Ascq	24 Jun
39.08	ITA	Infantino, Desalu, Di Franco, Polanco Rijo (20)	3rB	ET	Villeneuve d'Ascq	24 Jun
39.11	SUI	Somasundaram, Mancini, Wilson, Clivaz	1		Weinheim	27 May
39.11	PHI	Lopenea, Bagsit, Cray, Beram	3	SEAG	Kuala Lumpur	25 Aug
39.17	MEX	Gallegos, Moreno, Ramírez, Alanis	4	WUG	Taipei	28 Aug
39.18	BAR	Burke, Gittens, Deshong, B Ellis	2	W.Rly	Nassau	22 Apr
39.18	BAH	Fraser, Hart, Resias, Griffith	3rB	W.Rly	Nassau	22 Apr
39.21	POL	Kopec, Slowikowski, Zalewski, Kuc	4	ET	Villeneuve d'Ascq	24 Jun
39.26	DOM	Valdez, Andújar, De Oleo, Martínez	1	Barr	La Habana	28 May
39.27	MAS	Hanafi, Nyepa, Abdul Manap, Kennedy	4	SEAG	Kuala Lumpur	25 Aug
39.29	POR	Antunes, Lima, Pereira, Nascimento	2	DL	London (OS)	9 Jul
39.34 A	COL	(Valle) Renteria, Chará, Palomeque, Solis (30)	1	NC	Medellín	11 Jun

39.39	CIV	25 Jul	39.42	GRE	24 Jun	39.52	HKG	6 Sep	39.59	ESP	23 Jul
39.40	VEN	23 Nov	39.47	BRA	24 Jun	39.55	BRN	19 May	39.61	SWE	2 Sep
39.41	CZE	23 May	39.48	SKN	1 Jul	39.59	SRI	7 Jul	39.67	FIN	27 Aug

Best at low altitude
39.58 COL 23 Nov

Hand timing

Mark	Nat	Name	Pos	Meet	Venue	Date
38.2 A	TUR	Hekimoglu, Harvey, Barnes, Guliyev	1		Erzurum	10 Jun
38.3 A	UKR	Kravtsov, Smelyk, Suprun, Ibrahimov	2		Erzurum	10 Jun

Mixed nation teams

Mark	Team / Name	Pos	Meet	Venue	Date
38.17	USA/JAM - Trackwired Elite McLeod JAM, J Lawson, M Washington, Spearmon	1	TexR	Austin	1 Apr
38.34	USA/BAR - Univ. of Houston J Lewis, Burke BAR, J Martin, Burrell	1	NCAA	Eugene	9 Jun

JUNIORS

Mark	Nat	Name	Pos	Meet	Venue	Date
39.00	JAM	Calabar HS T Wilson, C Taylor, M Stephens, D Russell	1	PennR	Philedelphia	29 Apr
39.33	USA	Schwartz, Charleston, Hooper, Brock	1	PAm-J	Trujillo	22 Jul
39.48	GER	Skupin-Alfa, Barthel, Petzke, Stubican	1	EJ	Grosseto	23 Jul
39.50	ITA	Zlatan, Artuso, Marchei, Tortu	2	EJ	Grosseto	23 Jul
39.57	JPN	Rakunan HS Wada, Miyamoto, Imoto, Hiraga	2h1		Yokohama	27 Oct
39.59	ESP	Troyano, Retamal, Ambros, S López	3	EJ	Grosseto	23 Jul
39.67	GBR	Ashwell, Bromby, K Jones, E Davis	4	EJ	Grosseto	23 Jul
39.88	FRA	Reppert, Raffin, Zézé, Drame	5	EJ	Grosseto	23 Jul
39.90	TTO	Hislop, Purcell, T Edwards, Elcock	3	PAm-J	Trujillo	22 Jul
39.98	BRA	L dos Santos, G dos Santos, D Silva, F dos Santos	4	PAm-J	Trujillo	22 Jul

4 X 200 METRES RELAY

Mark	Nat	Name	Pos	Meet	Venue	Date
1:19.42	CAN	Smellie, Rodney, De Grasse, Brown	1	W.Rly	Nassau	23 Apr
1:19.88	USA	N Lyles, Lawson, Young, Webb	2	W.Rly	Nassau	23 Apr
1:19.91	CAN	Ajomale, Rodney, De Grasse, A Brown)	1	FlaR	Gainsecille	1 Apr
1:21.09	JAM	Ashmeade, O Bailey, Dyer, Blake	3	W.Rly	Nassau	23 Apr
1:21.11	CAN	Smellie, Rodney, De Grasse, Brown	1h1	W.Rly	Nassau	23 Apr
1:21.39	TTO	Morain, Telesford, Greaux, Callender	4	W.Rly	Nassau	23 Apr

Mixed nation teams

Mark	Team / Name	Pos	Meet	Venue	Date
1:20.74	Altis Ujah GBR, Hart BAH, De Grasse CAN, Webb USA	1	MSR	Torrance	15 Apr
1:20.74	USA/mx Arkansas Un. Ejiakuekwu GBR, Igbokwe, Washington, Cotton	1		Baton Rouge	29 Apr
1:20.80	Star Athletics USA Walker, I Young, Gatlin, Friday	2	FlaR	Gainesville	1 Apr
1:20.82	LSU Cherry USA, Mutanga/ZIM, Flournoy USA, Mitchell-Blake GBR	1r2	TexR	Austin	1 Apr
1:20.87	Track Wired Elite-USA/JAM J Lawson, M Washington, Spearmon, McLeod/JAM	1r1	TexR	Austin	1 Apr
1:21.07	Tumbleeed TC Brown JPN, C Taylor, Gemili GBR, Martina NED	3	FlaR	Gainesville	1 Apr
1:21.17	Houston A Lattin, Burke BAR, Martin, Hall	1	PennR	Philadelphia	29 Apr

+ intermediate time in longer race, A made at an altitude of 1000m or higher, D made in a decathlon, h made in a heat, qf quarter-final, sf semi-final, i indoors, Q qualifying round, r race number
-J juniors (b. 1998 or 1999), -Y youths (b. 2000 or later)

Mark	Nat	Name	Pos	Meet	Venue	Date

4 X 400 METRES RELAY

Mark	Nat	Name	Pos	Meet	Venue	Date
2:58.12	TTO	Solomon 46.1, Richards 43.4, Cedenio 44.41, L. Gordon 44.08	1	WCh	London (OS)	13 Aug
2:58.61	USA	London 44.8, Roberts 44.2, Cherry 44.91, F.Kerley 44.75	2	WCh	London (OS)	13 Aug
2:59.00	GBR	Hudson-Smith 45.4, Cowan 44.3, Yousif 44.97, Rooney 44.42	3	WCh	London (OS)	13 Aug
2:59.23	USA	London 45.3, Nellum 44.8, Cherry 44.36, McQuay 44.80	1h2	WCh	London (OS)	12 Aug
2:59.35	TTO	Quow 45.9, Richards 44.4, Cedenio 44.78, L. Gordon 44.32	2h2	WCh	London (OS)	12 Aug
2:59.47	BEL	D.Borlée 46.0, J.Borlée 44.9, Vanderbemden 44.44, K.Borlée 44.16	3h2	WCh	London (OS)	12 Aug
2:59.95	USA - Texas A&M	Rose 46.4, M.Kerley 44.4, Grant 45.16, F.Kerley 43.96	1s1	NCAA	Eugene	7 Jun
2:59.98	USA - Texas A&M	Rose 46.7, M.Kerley 44.2, Grant 45.11, F.Kerley 43.99	1	NCAA	Eugene	9 Jun
3:00.04	BEL	Vanderbenden 46.4, J.Borlée 44.7, D.Borlée 45.36, K.Borlée 43.60	4	WCh	London (OS)	13 Aug
3:00.10	GBR	Yousif 45.6, Cowan 44.4, Green 45.42, Rooney 44.66	4h2	WCh	London (OS)	12 Aug
3:00.33	USA-J	Herron 45.1, Shinnick 45.1, Hooper 44.73, J Lyles 45.36	1	PAm-J	Trujillo	23 Jul
3:00.65	ESP	Husillos 45.4, Búa 45.3, Echeverry 45.26, García 44.75	5	WCh	London (OS)	13 Aug
3:00.69	USA - Texas A&M	Rose, F.Kerley, Grant 45.30, M.Kerley 45.29	1h1	NCAA-W	Austin	27 May
3:00.72	USA - Texas A&M	Rose, F.Kerley, Grant 45.48, M.Kerley 44.99	1	SEC	Columbia, SC	13 May
3:00.74	USA - Texas A&M	Rose 45.8, F.Kerley 43.7, Dixon 46.22, M.Kerley 44.99	1		Baton Rouge	29 Apr
3:00.93	FRA	Vaillant 45.5, Jordier 45.4, Hanne 44.92, Atine-Vetel 45.11	5h2	WCh	London (OS)	12 Aug
3:01.10	CUB	Collazo 46.6, Chacón 45.2, Pellicier 45.16, Lescay 44.21	6	WCh	London (OS)	13 Aug
3:01.59	POL	Duszynski 46.0, Omelko 44.9, Krawczyk 45.54, Zimny 45.26	7	WCh	London (OS)	13 Aug
3:01.72	ESP	Husillos 45.8, Búa 45.1, Echeverry 45.18, García 45.65	1h1	WCh	London (OS)	12 Aug
		(21 performances by teams from 8 nations)				
3:01.98	JAM	Matthews 45.4, S Gayle 45.4, Rose 45.71, R McDonald 45.44	4h1	WCh	London (OS)	12 Aug
3:02.28	BOT (10)	Makwala 46.14, Baboloki 44.95, Nkobolo 45.39, Sibanda 45.80	2	W.Rly	Nassau	23 Apr
3:02.37	NED	Stuivenberg 46.4, Bonevacia 44.7, Agard 45.63, Blauwhof 45.61	2rB	ET	Villeneuve d'Ascq	25 Jun
3:02.80	IND	Kunhu Muhammed 46.5, Jacob 45.9, Anas 45.35, Rajiv 45.17	5h1	WCh	London (OS)	12 Aug
3:03.04	BAH	Russell 45.9, Mathieu 45.9, Ferguson 45.72, Miller 45.50	6h1	WCh	London (OS)	12 Aug
3:03.31	CZE	Tesar 47.1, Maslak 44.0, Müller 45.85, Sorm 46.43	3rB	ET	Villeneuve d'Ascq	25 Jun
3:03.53A	RSA	45.9 - 46.8 - 45.6 - 45.2	1		Germiston	22 Mar
3:03.6 A	KEN	Defence Forces Pogisho, S Rutto, Kishoyan, Mwereaa	1	NC	Nairobi	10 Jun
3:03.68	COL	Solís 47.1, Palomeque 45.0, Herrera 45.77, Perlaza 45.83	7h1	WCh	London (OS)	12 Aug
3:04.02	BRA	Carvalho 45.5, Russo 46.5, Henriques 46.53, H Sousa 45.51	6h2	WCh	London (OS)	12 Aug
3:04.20	CAN	Harper, Thompson, Franklin, Osei	3	FlaR	Gainesville	1 Apr
3:04.34	DOM (20)	J. Santos 45.7, I. Charles 45.8, M. Charles 46.9, L. Santos 45.9	1	WUG	Taipei	28 Aug
3:04.64	GER	Schneider 46.4, Junker 45.6, Trefz 46.4, C. Schmidt 46.2	3	ET	Villeneuve d'Ascq	25 Jun
3:04.71	ITA	Re, Lorenzi, Leonardi, Corsa	2	NA	Heusden	22 Jul
3:04.72	RUS - Sankt Petersburg	Raflovich, Rudenko, Kukharenko, Filatov	1	NC	Zhukovskiy	30 Jul
3:04.80	SRI	Dhananjaya, Kumarage, Premakumara, Dileep Ruwan	2	AsiC	Bhubaneswar	9 Jul
3:05.08	IRL	O'Donnell, Gregan, Barr, English	2	ET-1	Vaasa	25 Jun
3:05.22	CHN		1	3-N	Ningbo	2 Jul
3:05.49	ALG	Laaredj, Benchaa, Rahmani, Lahoulou	1	Arab	Radès	18 Jul
3:06.03	MEX	Avilés, J López, E Ramírez, Mendoza	1	NC	Monterrey	18 Jun
3:06.04	JPN - Tokai Un.	Furuta, Kitakani, Osaki, Obuchi	1		Yokohama	28 May
3:06.32	VEN (30)	Zulueta, Longart, Padrino, Aguilar	2	Bol G	Santa Marta	24 Nov

3:06.48 THA 9 Jul	3:06.83 TUR 20 May	3:07.62 PAK 20 May	3:08.55 KUW 18 Jul	3:08.65 LAT 25 Jun
3:06.51 TPE 9 Jul	3:07.03 UKR 25 Jun	3:08.23 KSA 18 Jul	3:08.56 SLO 25 Jun	3:08.75 SWE 25 Jun
3:06.79 OMA 9 Jul	3:07.40 VIE 26 Aug	3:08.42 PHI 26 Aug	3:08.58 GRE 25 Jun	

Mixed nation teams

Mark	Nat	Name	Pos	Meet	Venue	Date
3:00.92	USA/TTO - Empire Athletics	Cedenio/TTO, Clemons, McQuay, Gardiner BAH	1	FlaR	Gainesville	1 Apr
3:01.02	USA/GRN/TTO –Altis	D. Wright, Taplin/GRN, Dedewo, Lendore/TTO	1		Tempe	18 Mar

Best at low altitude

Mark	Nat	Name	Pos	Meet	Venue	Date
3:06.36	KEN	Kishoyan, Omae, G Kiprotich, Mweresa	1B	W.Rly	Nassau	23 Apr

JUNIORS

Mark	Nat	Name	Pos	Meet	Venue	Date
3:00.33	USA	Herron 45.1, Shinnick 45.1, Hooper 44.73, J Lyles 45.36	1	PAm-J	Trujillo	23 Jul
3:03.35A	USA	mx S Burrell, T Cooper, Walton CAY, T Burns. S Burrel	1		Albuquerque	3 Jun
3:03.77	JAM	Chambers, Carpenter, James, C Taylor	2	PAm-J	Trujillo	23 Jul
3:08.68	ITA	Aceti, Scotti, Gjetja, Sibilio	1	EJ	Grosseto	23 Jul
3:08.80	JPN	Rakunan HS	1		Kyoto	18 Jun
3:09.04	FRA	Saidy, Andant, Mbaye, Happio	2	EJ	Grosseto	23 Jul
3:09.32	TTO	Martin, St. Clair, J Taylor, King	1	Carifta	Willemstad	17 Apr
3:09.32	POL	Rzezniczak, Walicki, Holub, Zimny	3	EJ	Grosseto	23 Jul
3:09.45	TUR	Kasap, Özyürek, Çalik, Korkmaz	4	EJ	Grosseto	23 Jul
3:09.54	GER	Sanders, Ringel, Niedrig, Schlegel	1		Mannheim	2 Jul

4 X 800 METRES RELAY

Mark	Nat	Name	Pos	Meet	Venue	Date
7:13.16	USA	Kidder 1:47.39, Sowinski 1:48.11, Loxsom 1:48.48, Murphy 1:49.18	1	W.Rly	Nassau	23 Apr
7:13.70	KEN	A Kipketer 1:47.52, K Bett 1:46.73, Kitum 1:49.76, F Cheruiyot 1:49.69	2	W.Rly	Nassau	23 Apr

Mark	Name	Nat	Born	Pos	Meet	Venue	Date
7:13.75	Virginia Tech Gourley GBR, Ciattei, Piazza, Joseph all USA			1	FlaR	Gainesville	1 Apr

4 X 1 MILE RELAY

Mark	Name	Nat	Pos	Venue	Date
16:12.81	Hoka New Jersey/New York Cabral 4:05.4, Palmer 3:59.5, Crawford 4:08.6, Merber 3:59.3	USA	1	New York (A)	17 Feb

3000 METRES TRACK WALK

Mark	First name	Name	Nat	Born	Pos	Meet	Venue	Date
10:54.70	Dane	Bird-Smith	AUS	15.7.92	1		Brisbane	11 Feb
11:10.22	Wayne	Snyman	RSA	8.3.85	2		Brisbane	11 Feb
11:12.45	Nils	Brembach	GER	23.2.93	1		Dessau	16 Jun
11:13.19	Callum	Wilkinson	GBR	14.3.97	1		Leeds	12 Jun
11:14.16	Yohann	Diniz	FRA	1.1.78	1	Déca	Angers	9 Sep
11:14.49	Lebogang	Shange	RSA	1.8.90	1	PTS	Samorín	17 Jun
11:15:26+	Tom	Bosworth	GBR	17.1.90	1	in 5k	Birmingham	2 Jul
11:19.10	Cameron	Corbishley	GBR	31.3.97	2		Leeds	12 Jun
11:26.42	Karl	Junghannß	GER	6.4.96	2		Dessau	16 Jun
11:27.46	Ivan	Losev	UKR	26.1.86	2	PTS	Samorín	17 Jun
11:32.17	Jonathan	Hilbert	GER	21.4.95	2		Dessau	16 Jun
11:35.88	Hagen	Oogle	GER	5.3.92	4		Dessau	16 Jun

5000 METRES TRACK WALK

Mark	First name	Name	Nat	Born	Pos	Meet	Venue	Date
18:43.28	Tom	Bosworth	GBR	17.1.90	1	NC	Birmingham	2 Jul
18:54.27	Álvaro	Martín	ESP	18.6.94	1		Plasencia	28 Jun
18:55.60	Lebogang	Shange	RSA	1.8.90	1		Budapest	30 Jun
18:56.96	Callum	Wilkinson	GBR	14.3.97	2	NC	Birmingham	2 Jul
19:05.97	Eiki	Takahashi	JPN	19.11.92	1		Yuwa	20 May
19:10.78	Daisuke	Matsunaga	JPN	24.3.95	2		Yuwa	20 May
19:21.93	Kai	Kobayashi	JPN	28.2.93	3		Yuwa	20 May

Mark	First name	Name	Nat	Born	Date
19:26.8	Perseus	Karlström	SWE	2.5.90	10 Dec
19:26.86	Federico	Tontodonati	ITA	30.10.89	10 Sep
19:27:99	Yuga	Yamashita	JPN	6.2.96	5 Aug
19:29:84	Hiroto	Jusho	JPN-Y	.00	26 Nov
19:30.75	Luis Alberto	Amezcua	ESP	1.5.92	24 Jun
19:34.68	Takayuki	Tanii	JPN	14.2.83	20 May
19:35.59	Diego	García	ESP	19.1.96	17 Jun
19:35.69	Kevin	Campion	FRA	23.5.88	6 May
19:35.7	Quentin	Rew	NZL	16.7.84	10 Dec
19:35.99	Håvard	Haukenes	NOR	22.4.90	25 Aug

Indoors

Mark	First name	Name	Nat	Born	Pos	Meet	Venue	Date
18:39.47	Tom	Bosworth	GBR	17.1.90	1	NC	Sheffield	12 Feb
18:50.70	Alex	Wright	IRL	19.12.90	1	NC	Dublin	18 Feb
18:59.06	Francesco	Fortunato	ITA	13.12.94	1	NC	Ancona	18 Feb
19:08.82	Christopher	Linke	GER	24.10.88	1	NC	Erfurt	5 Mar
19:12.98	Aléxandros	Papamihaíl	GRE	18.9.88	1	NC	Piréas	18 Feb
19:14.41	Yohann	Diniz	FRA	1.1.78	1	NC	Bordeaux	19 Feb
19:16.67	Nils	Brembach	GER	23.2.93	2	NC	Erfurt	5 Mar
19:18.59	Vito	Minei	ITA	16.6.94	2	NC	Ancona	18 Feb
19:20.83	Callum	Wilkinson	GBR	14.3.97	2		Bratislava	29 Jan

Mark	First name	Name	Nat	Born	Date
19:24.6	Ruslan	Dmytrenko	UKR	22.3.86	9 Jan
19:26.1	Nazar	Kovalenko	UKR	9.2.89	9 Jan
19:29.17	Veli-Matti	Partanen	FIN	28.10.91	18 Feb
19:32.08	João	Vieira	POR	20.7.76	18 Feb
19:33.57	Salih	Korkmaz	TUR	14.4.97	14 Jan
19:35.68	Dawid	Tomala	POL	27.8.89	18 Feb
19:37.18	Leonardo	Dei Tos	ITA	27.4.92	18 Feb
19:37.68	Oleksiy	Kazanin	UKR	22.5.82	11 Feb

JUNIORS

Mark	First name	Name	Nat	Born	Pos	Meet	Venue	Date
19:29:84	Hiroto	Jusho	JPN-Y	.00	1		Higashi-Hiroshima	26 Nov
19:36.99	Masatora	Kawano	JPN	23.10.98	2		Muroran	5 Aug

10,000 METRES TRACK WALK

Mark	First name	Name	Nat	Born	Pos	Meet	Venue	Date
38:24.23	Dane	Bird-Smith	AUS	15.7.92	1	NC	Sydney	31 Mar
38:56.90	Eiki	Takahashi	JPN	19.11.92	1		Osaka	23 Sep
38:57.45	Perseus	Karlström	SWE	2.5.90	1	vFIN	Stockholm	2 Sep
39:03.25	Daisuke	Matsunaga	JPN	24.3.95	2		Osaka	23 Sep
39:06.86	Kai	Kobayashi	JPN	28.2.93	3		Osaka	23 Sep
39:24.49	Toshikazu	Yamanishi	JPN	15.2.96	1		Osaka	13 May
39:39.45	Hagen	Pohle	GER	5.3.92	1	NC	Diez	16 Sep
39:33.77	Isamu	Fujisawa	JPN	12.10.87	4		Osaka	23 Sep
39:44.14	Francesco	Fortunato	ITA	13.12.94	1		Orvieto	23 Apr
39:44.28	Yuga (10)	Yamashita	JPN	6.2.96	1		Kawagoe	25 Dec
39:47.17	Álvaro	Martín	ESP	18.6.94	1	NC	Barcelona	23 Jul
39:47.77	Diego	García	ESP	19.1.96	1		Torrent	1 Jul
39:49.26	Gianluca	Picchiottino	ITA	22.8.96	2		Orvieto	23 Apr
39:50.88	Luis Alberto	Amezcua	ESP	1.5.92	2	NC	Barcelona	23 Jul
39:51.5	Moacir	Zimmermann	BRA	30.12.83	1		Blumenau	17 Jun
39:51.64	Miguel Ángel	López	ESP	3.7.88	1		Cartagena	6 May

Mark	Name		Nat	Born	Pos	Meet	Venue	Date
39:52.45	Sho	Sakazaki	JPN-J	22.2.99	2		Kawagoe	25 Dec
39:57.75	Mohamed	Ameur	ALG	1.11.84	1		Biskra	17 Mar
39:59.87A	Ricardo	Ortiz	MEX	7.2.95	1		Xalapa	7 May
40:01.26A	Noel Ali	Chama	MEX	15.9.97	2		Xalapa	7 May
40:05.52	Eder	Sánchez	MEX	21.5.86	1	POL Ch	Bialystok	22 Jul
40:06.73	Leonardo	Dei Tos	ITA	27.4.92	1		Bolzano	7 May

Mark	Name		Nat	Born	Date	Mark	Name		Nat	Born	Date
40:09.14	Aymen	Sabri	ALG	19.4.94	17 Mar	40:24.60	Massimo	Stano	ITA	27.2.92	23 Apr
40:10.08	Christopher	Linke	GER	24.10.88	16 Sep	40:25.32	Fumitaka	Oikawa	JPN	5.4.95	8 Jan
40:10.33	Mohamed	Meddour	ALG	24.1.90	17 Mar	40:25.62		Yu Wei	CHN	11.9.87	20 May
40:17.91	Artur	Brzozowski	POL	29.3.85	22 Jul	40:26:34	Ryosuke	Kawagishi	JPN	15.6.96	16 Dec
40:21.33	Masatora	Kawano	JPN-J	23.10.98	25 Dec	40:28.48	Koki	Ikeda	JPN-J	3.5.98	9 Sep
40:23.24	Lyès	Khali	ALG	2.8.87	17 Mar	40:29.91	Nils	Brembach	GER	23.2.93	16 Sep

Indoors

Mark	Name		Nat	Born	Pos	Meet	Venue	Date
39:40.97	Aleksandr	Lyakovich	BLR	4.7.89	1	NC	Mogilyov	18 Feb

JUNIORS

Mark	Name		Nat	Born	Pos	Meet	Venue	Date
39:52.45	Sho	Sakazaki	JPN-J	22.2.99	2		Kawagoe	25 Dec
40:21.33	Masatora	Kawano	JPN-J	23.10.98	3		Kawagoe	25 Dec
40:28.48	Koki	Ikeda	JPN-J	3.5.98	2		Fukui	9 Sep
40:37.64	David	Hurtado	ECU	21.4.99	1	PAm-J	Trujillo	21 Jul
40:45.31	Andrés	Olivas	MEX	27.5.98	2	PAm-J	Trujillo	21 Jul
40:54.45	Ryutaro	Yamamoto	JPN	.98	2		Tama	16 Dec
40:47.66	Yasushi	Morita	JPN	6.2.98	1		Osaka	13 May
40:54.28	Katsuji	Suzuki	JPN	31.7.98	7		Fukui	9 Sep
40:59.02	Yutaro	Murayama	JPN	29.9.98	3		Tama	16 Dec
41:12.01A		Zhang Yao	CHN-Y	11.1.00	1	WY	Nairobi	15 Jul
41:24.17A	Salavat	Ilkayev	RUS-Y	14.9.00	2	WY	Nairobi	15 Jul
41:25.78A	Dominic	Ndigiti	KEN-Y	2.4.00	3	WY	Nairobi	15 Jul
41:26.35	Yusuke	Murao	JPN	.98	8		Tama	16 Dec
41:26.65	Sergey	Kozhevnikov	RUS-Y	9.5.01	4	WY	Nairobi	15 Jul

10 KILOMETRES ROAD WALK

Where better than track times above or as intermediate times in second column of 20k lists over page (to 40:30).

Mark	Name		Nat	Born	Pos	Meet	Venue	Date
39:19+	Takumi	Saito	JPN	23.3.93		in 20k	Kobe	19 Feb
39:30	Luis Alberto	Amezcua	ESP	1.5.92	1		San Fernando	4 Feb
39:34+	Tomohiro	Noda	JPN	24.1.96		in 20k	Kobe	19 Feb
39:38		Zhang Jun	CHN-J	20.7.98	1		Huangshan	4 Mar
39:41	David	Hurtado	ECU-J	21.4.99	1	NC	Sucua	15 Apr
39:42	Kevin	Campion	FRA	23.5.88	2		San Fernando	4 Feb
39:48	Lebogang	Shange	RSA	1.8.90	1		Suzhou	25 Sep
39:50		Zheng Ke	CHN-J	10.1.98	2		Huangshan	4 Mar
39:50+	Tom	Bosworth	GBR	17.1.90		in 20k	London	13 Aug
39:51+	Kolothum Thodi	Irfan	IND	8.2.90		in 20k	London	13 Aug
39:52+	Manuel	Soto	COL	28.1.94		in 20k	London	13 Aug
39:53+	Perseus	Karlström	SWE	2.5.90		in 20k	London	13 Aug
40:02		Zhang Hongliang	CHN-J	1.1.99	3		Huangshan	4 Mar
40:02		Song Huazhang	CHN-J	13.2.99	4		Huangshan	4 Mar

Mark	Name		Nat	Born	Date	Mark	Name		Nat	Born	Date
40:12	Serkan	Dogan	TUR	1.4.92	18 Mar	40:24+	Richard	Vargas	VEN	28.12.94	3 Jun
40:12+	Pedro	Gómez	MEX	31.12.90	13 Aug	40:25+	Aleksandr	Lyakhovich	BLR	4.7.89	21 May
40:16+		Wang Rui	CHN	6.1.96	3 Jun	40:28	Masatora	Kawano	JPN-J	23.10.98	19 Feb
40:20+	Krishnan	Ganapathi	IND	29.6.89	19 Mar	40:28		Xu Hao	CHN-J	4.2.99	4 Mar
40:22	Jonathan	Amores	ECU-J	29.8.99	15 Apr	40:30		Yu Yongcai	CHN_J	23.5.98	4 Mar
40:24+	Alex	Wright	IRL	19.12.90	21 May						

JUNIORS

See above for top 5 juniors

Mark	Name		Nat	Born	Pos	Meet	Venue	Date
40:22	Jonathan	Amores	ECU-J	29.8.99	2	NC	Sucua	15 Apr
40:28		Xu Hao	CHN-J	4.2.99	5		Huangshan	4 Mar
40:30		Yu Yongcai	CHN-J	23.5.98	6		Huangshan	4 Mar
40:34	Kouki	Ikeda	JPN	3.5.98	2	NC-j	Kobe	19 Feb
40:34		Luo Jiayu	CHN	3.4.98	7		Huangshan	4 Mar
40:34		Guo Shuqi	CHN	26.8.98	8		Huangshan	4 Mar
40:37		Kim Min-kue	KOR	28.2.99	1		Gongju	24 Oct
40:41		Sun Shuai	CHN	15.9.99	9		Huangshan	4 Mar
40:44		Li Kewen	CHN	7.3.99	10		Huangshan	4 Mar
40:45		Guo Kuizhijia	CHN	20.11.99	11		Huangshan	4 Mar
40:55		Bai Liga	CHN	21.1.98	12		Huangshan	4 Mar
40:56		Cao Wenlong	CHN	4.3.98	13		Huangshan	4 Mar
40:58	José Eduardo	Ortiz	GUA-Y	8.3.00	2	PAm Cp-J	Lima	13 May
40:59	Sho	Sakazaki	JPN	22.2.99	3	NC-j	Kobe	19 Feb
40:59		Zhu Chendong	CHN	16.9.99	14		Huangshan	4 Mar
41:03		Liu Shun	CHN	1.10.98	15		Huangshan	4 Mar
41:08	Leo	Köpp	GER	23.5.98	1	ECp-J	Podébrady	21 May

20 KILOMETRES WALK

Mark 20k	10k	Name		Nat	Born	Pos	Meet	Venue	Date
1:17:54	39:43		Wang Kaihua	CHN	16.2.94	1		Huangshan	4 Mar
1:18:18	39:07	Eiki	Takahashi	JPN	19.11.92	1	NC	Kobe	19 Feb
1:18:23	39:07	Isamu	Fujisawa	JPN	12.10.87	2	NC	Kobe	19 Feb
1:18:26		Sergey	Shirobokov	RUS-J	16.2.99	1	NC-w	Sochi	18 Feb
1:18:51		Sergey	Bakulin	RUS	13.11.86	2	NC-w	Sochi	18 Feb
1:18:53	39:50	Eider	Arévalo	COL	9.3.93	1	WCh	London	13 Aug
1:18:55	39:50		Shirobokov			2	WCh	London	13 Aug
1:18:59	40:20	Christopher	Linke	GER	24.10.88	1		Podébrady	8 Apr
1:19:03	39:08	Toshikazu	Yamanishi	JPN	15.2.96	3	NC	Kobe	19 Feb
1:19:04	39:51	Caio	Bonfim	BRA	19.3.91	3	WCh	London	13 Aug
1:19:12	40:09		Jin Xiangqian (10)	CHN	18.3.97	2		Huangshan	4 Mar
1:19:13	39:32	Kai	Kobayashi	JPN	28.2.93	4	NC	Kobe	19 Feb
1:19:18	40:13	Lebogang	Shange	RSA	1.8.90	4	WCh	London	13 Aug
1:19:21	39:50		Linke			5	WCh	London	13 Aug
1:19:23	40:21		Wang Rui	CHN	6.1.96	3		Huangshan	4 Mar
1:19:25	39:32	Hirooki	Arai	JPN	18.5.88	5	NC	Kobe	19 Feb
1:19:28	40:04		Linke			1	ECp	Podébrady	21 May
1:19:28	39:50	Dane	Bird-Smith	AUS	15.7.92	6	WCh	London	13 Aug
1:19:30	39:50		Wang Kaihua			7	WCh	London	13 Aug
1:19:37			Bird-Smith			1	Oce Ch	Adelaide	19 Feb
1:19:40	39:18	Daisuke	Matsunaga	JPN	24.3.95	1		Nomi	19 Mar
1:19:41	39:50	Álvaro	Martín	ESP	18.6.94	8	WCh	London	13 Aug
1:19:46	40:09	Luis Alberto	Amezcua	ESP	1.5.92	9	WCh	London	13 Aug
1:19:50	39:34		Kim Hyun-sub	KOR	31.5.85	2		Nomi	19 Mar
1:19:57	39:46		Martín			1		La Coruña	3 Jun
1:19:57	39:51	Miguel Ángel	López (20)	ESP	3.7.88	10	WCh	London	13 Aug
1:20:04	39:43	Tomohiro	Noda	JPN	24.1.96	3		Nomi	19 Mar
1:20:04	39:48		Fujisawa			11	WCh	London	13 Aug
1:20:20	39:57	Perseus	Karlström	SWE	2.5.90	2		La Coruña	3 Jun
1:20:21	40:13		López			2	ECp	Podébrady	21 May
		(30/22)							
1:20:25	40:15		Sun Song	CHN	15.12.96	4		Huangshan	4 Mar
1:20:28		Kevin	Campion	FRA	23.5.88	2		Podébrady	8 Apr
1:20:31	39:12	Satoshi	Maruo	JPN	28.11.91	6	NC	Kobe	19 Feb
1:20:33	40:27	Artur	Brzozowski	POL	29.3.85	12	WCh	London	13 Aug
1:20:34	40:16	Diego	García	ESP	19.1.96	13	WCh	London	13 Aug
1:20:35	39:52	Hassanine	Sbaï	TUN	21.1.84	3		La Coruña	3 Jun
1:20:42		Nils	Brembach	GER	23.2.93	15	WCh	London	13 Aug
1:20:45	39:32	Fumitaka	Oikawa	JPN	5.4.95	7	NC	Kobe	19 Feb
		(30)							
1:20:47	40:04	Georgiy	Sheyko	KAZ	24.8.89	4		Nomi	19 Mar
1:20:47		Giorgio	Rubino	ITA	15.4.86	16	WCh	London	13 Aug
1:20:48		Koki	Ikeda	JPN-J	3.5.98	1		Takahata	22 Oct
1:20:49		Pyotr	Bogatyrev	RUS	11.3.91	3	NC-w	Sochi	18 Feb
1:20:52			Zeng Qingcun	CHN	3.4.95	5		Huangshan	4 Mar
1:20:53		Hagen	Pohle	GER	5.3.92	17	WCh	London	13 Aug
1:20:55			Zhong Heng	CHN	7.11.95	6		Huangshan	4 Mar
1:20:56			Yin Jiaxing	CHN	16.3.94	7		Huangshan	4 Mar
1:20:56	39:48	Takumi	Saito	JPN	23.3.93	5		Nomi	19 Mar
1:20:57		Aleksey	Shevchuk	RUS	10.8.97	4	NC-w	Sochi	18 Feb
		(40)							
1:20:58		Tom	Bosworth	GBR	17.1.90	2		Rio Maior	1 Apr
1:20:59	39:55	Kolothum Thodi	Irfan	IND	8.2.90	6		Nomi	19 Mar
1:21:01			Bian Tongda	CHN	1.4.91	2	NG	Tianjin	3 Sep
1:21:06		Wayne	Snyman	RSA	8.3.85	1		Cape Town	5 Aug
1:21:07	40:21		Liu Jianmin	CHN	9.3.88	8		Huangshan	4 Mar
1:21:12		Quentin	Rew	NZL	16.7.84	3	Oce Ch	Adelaide	19 Feb
1:21:12		Aleksandr	Lyakhovich	BLR	4.7.89	1	NCp	Gomel	22 Apr
1:21:13		Manuel	Soto	COL	28.1.94	4		Rio Maior	1 Apr
1:21:16		Benjamin	Thorne	CAN	19.3.93	2		Lima	13 May
1:21:16		Andrés	Chocho	ECU	4.11.83	7		La Coruña	3 Jun
		(50)							
1:21:17		Alex	Wright	IRL	19.12.90	5		Rio Maior	1 Apr
1:21:17		Brian	Pintado	ECU	29.7.95	18	WCh	London	13 Aug
1:21:22		Evan	Dunfee	CAN	28.9.90	5	Oce Ch	Adelaide	19 Feb
1:21:27		Marius	Ziukas	LTU	29.6.85	7	Oce Ch	Adelaide	19 Feb
1:21:29	40:27	Damian	Blocki	POL	28.4.89	20	WCh	London	13 Aug

Mark			Name	Nat	Born	Pos	Meet	Venue	Date
1:21:30			Chen Rui	CHN	11.8.96	9		Huangshan	4 Mar
1:21:32		Timofey	Parkayev	RUS	19.10.97	5	NC-w	Sochi	18 Feb
1:21:34		Erick	Barrondo	GUA	14.6.91	21	WCh	London	13 Aug
1:21:36.64t		Yuga	Yamashita	JPN	6.2.96	1		Koganei	8 Jan
1:21:38	39:55	Devender (60)	Singh	IND	5.12.83	9		Nomi	19 Mar
1:21:42			Su Xianzhen	CHN	26.2.95	10		Huangshan	4 Mar
1:21:43		Kirill	Frolov	RUS	29.9.93	6	NC-w	Sochi	18 Feb
1:21:45	39:59	Takayuki	Tanii	JPN	14.2.83	8	NC	Kobe	19 Feb
1:21:45			Wang Libo	CHN	9.2.97	11		Huangshan	4 Mar
1:21:46			Zhu Guowen	CHN	20.8.97	12		Huangshan	4 Mar
1:21:48			Li Liangyong	CHN	28.5.96	13		Huangshan	4 Mar
1:21:48		Vasiliy	Mizinov	RUS	29.12.97	2	NC	Cheboksary	10 Jun
1:21:52			Yu Wei	CHN	11.9.87	11		La Coruña	3 Jun
1:21:55			Han Jijiang	CHN	20.7.93	14		Huangshan	4 Mar
1:21:55	40:29	José Luis (70)	Doctor	MEX	14.6.96	12		La Coruña	3 Jun
1:21:56		Yerko	Araya	CHI	14.2.86	8	Oce Ch	Adelaide	19 Feb
1:21:56	40:21		Tong Anqi	CHN	29.9.92	15		Huangshan	4 Mar
1:21:59		Pavel	Parshin	RUS	2.1.94	7	NC-w	Sochi	18 Feb
1:21:59			Peng Chen	CHN	8.7.97	16		Huangshan	4 Mar
1:22:00		Omar	Pineda	MEX	2.12.94	3	PAmCp	Lima	13 May
1:22:01		Francesco	Fortunato	ITA	13.12.94	25	WCh	London	13 Aug
1:22:04			Li Tianlei	CHN	13.1.95	17		Huangshan	4 Mar
1:22:07			Li Shijia	CHN	14.1.92	18		Huangshan	4 Mar
1:22:08			Li Jinguo	CHN	4.5.95	19		Huangshan	4 Mar
1:22:08		Karl (80)	Junghanss	GER	6.4.96	3		Naumburg	23 Apr
1:22:09		Vladislav	Saraykin	RUS	3.3.97	8	NC-w	Sochi	18 Feb
1:22:09		Rhydian	Cowley	AUS	4.1.91	9	Oce Ch	Adelaide	19 Feb
1:22:15		Jakub	Jelonek	POL	7.7.85	10	Oce Ch	Adelaide	19 Feb
1:22:16		Ivan	Kakayev	RUS	13.8.97	4	NC	Cheboksary	10 Jun
1:22:17		Callum	Wilkinson	GBR	14.3.97	10	ECp	Podébrady	21 May
1:22:21		Dmitriy	Dyubin	BLR	12.7.90	11	ECp	Podébrady	21 May
1:22:23			Wang Gang	CHN	2.4.91	20		Huangshan	4 Mar
1:22:23			Wei Xubao	CHN	1.2.93	21		Huangshan	4 Mar
1:22:24			Ceng Qingsheng	CHN	3.4.95	22		Huangshan	4 Mar
1:22:26	40:28	Ruslan (90)	Dmytrenko	UKR	22.3.86	27	WCh	London	13 Aug
1:22:27			Cha Jinhong	CHN	27.5.97	23		Huangshan	4 Mar
1:22:28		Eder	Sánchez	MEX	21.5.86	1	NC	Monterrey	17 Jun
1:22:28		Mauricio	Arteaga	ECU	8.8.88	28	WCh	London	13 Aug
1:22:29			Zhang Wanxin	CHN	25.10.96	24		Huangshan	4 Mar
1:22:29		Aurelien	Quinion	FRA	27.1.93	14		La Coruña	3 Jun
1:22:30			Li Peng	CHN	10.11.94	25		Huangshan	4 Mar
1:22:30		Massimo	Stano	ITA	27.2.92	15		La Coruña	3 Jun
1:22:31		Ersin	Tacir	TUR	1.4.85	1	NC	Antalya	11 Feb
1:22:32			Liu Xu	CHN	11.12.94	26		Huangshan	4 Mar
1:22:32.15t		Ryosuke (100)	Kawagishi	JPN	15.6.96	2		Koganei	8 Jan

Mark		Name	Nat	Born	Date
1:22:34		Ma Youshan	CHN	21.9.95	4 Mar
1:22:36	Koichiro	Morioka	JPN	2.4.85	19 Feb
1:22:36		Wang Qin	CHN	8.5.94	3 Sep
1:22:38	Yevgeniy	Zaleski	BLR	18.7.93	22 Apr
1:22:40		Li Jichao	CHN	10.5.96	4 Mar
1:22:40	Robert	Heffernan	IRL	20.2.78	21 May
1:22:42	João	Vieira	POR	20.2.76	21 May
1:22:42	José Maria	Raymundo	GUA	1.9.93	3 Jun
1:22:45	Armando	Merino	MEX	26.11.89	3 Jun
1:22:46	Aléxandros	Papamihaíl	GRE	18.9.88	1 Apr
1:22:48		Li Shuai	CHN	6.1.95	4 Mar
1:22:48		Men Fuqiang	CHN	22.6.92	4 Mar
1:22:48	Nathaniel	Seiler	GER	6.4.96	23 Apr
1:22:48	Pedro	Gómez	MEX	31.12.90	17 Jun
1:22:50A	Horacio	Nava	MEX	20.1.82	12 Mar
1:22:50 39:55	Yuki	Kurumisawa	JPN	11.12.95	19 Mar
1:22:50		Han Yucheng	CHN	16.12.78	4 Sep
1:22:52	Samuel	Gathimba	KEN	26.10.87	13 Aug
1:22:53	Federico	Tontodonati	ITA	30.10.89	26 Mar
1:22:54		Choi Byung-kwang	KOR	7.4.91	13 Aug
1:22:55		Liu Xiaotong	CHN	24.7.97	4 Mar
1:22:57		Yuan Zisheng	CHN	16.12.97	4 Mar
1:22:57	Nazar	Kovalenko	UKR	9.2.89	11 Mar
1:22:58	Krishnan	Ganapathi	IND	29.6.89	18 Feb
1:22:58		Mo Zhenfeng	CHN	28.2.95	4 Mar
1:22:58	Julio César	Salazar	MEX	8.7.93	15 Apr
1:22:59		Li Chenchen	CHN	7.12.97	4 Mar
1:22:59A	Jorge Alejandro	Martinez	MEX	25.10.90	12 Mar
1:22:59	Jean	Blancheteau	FRA	7.1.96	8 Apr
1:23:00		Zhou Yangjun	CHN	17.10.96	4 Mar
1:23:02		Chen Ding	CHN	5.8.92	3 Sep
1:23:03	Gabriel	Bordier	FRA	8.10.97	16 Jul
1:23:03	Ivan	Losev	UKR	26.1.86	13 Aug
1:23:05		Dong Guozhu	CHN	2.8.92	4 Mar
1:23:05	César Augusto	Rodriguez	PER	26.6.97	13 Aug
1:23:07		Jie Jinzhu	CHN	25.7.95	4 Mar
1:23:08	Marco	De Luca	ITA	12.5.81	26 Mar
1:23:09		Zhaxi Yangben	CHN	15.4.96	4 Mar
1:23:10		Zhang Zhi	CHN	22.7.94	4 Mar
1:23:10	Jesús Tadeo	Vega	MEX	23.5.94	13 Aug
1:23:11	Máté	Helebrandt	HUN	12.1.89	30 Apr
1:23:11	Salih	Korkmaz	TUR	14.4.97	16 Jul
1:23:12	Manuel	Bermúdez	ESP	12.12.97	16 Jul
1:23:14	Carl	Dohmann	GER	18.5.90	23 Apr
1:23:16	Aleksey	Golovin	RUS	24.12.88	18 Feb
1:23:16		Zhao Ziyang	CHN	29.7.91	4 Mar

Mark	Name		Nat	Born	Date
1:23:16	Aleksi	Ojala	FIN	9.12.92	20 Jul
1:23:18		Ning Peng	CHN	15.12.97	4 Mar
1:23:20		Yao Biao	CHN	15.4.96	4 Mar
1:23:26	Sergiy	Budza	UKR	6.12.84	21 May
1:23:26	Jonathan	Hilbert	GER	24.1.95	16 Jul
1:23:26	Sho	Sakazaki	JPN-J	22.2.99	22 Oct
1:23:28	Andrea	Agrusti	ITA	30.8.95	16 Jul
1:23:29	Nikolay	Markov	RUS	1.2.95	18 Feb
1:23:29		Yang Liang	CHN	25.4.93	3 Sep
1:23:30	José Alejandro	Barrondo	GUA	16.9.96	13 May
1:23:31	Kirill	Shutov	RUS	24.4.97	18 Feb
1:23:31	Miguel	Carvalho	POR	2.9.94	21 May
1:23:31		Ma Haijun	CHN	24.11.92	3 Sep
1:23:35	Leonardo	Dei Tos	ITA	27.4.92	26 Mar
1:23:40		Huang Cheng	CHN	8.5.97	4 Mar
1:23:41		Wanma Caidan	CHN	5.1.96	4 Mar
1:23:43		Zhao Fujie	CHN	11.11.93	4 Mar
1:23:44	Juan Manuel	Cano	ARG	12.12.87	1 Apr
1:23:46	Serkan	Dogan	TUR	1.4.92	11 Feb
1:23:46	Gianluca	Picchiottino	ITA	22.8.96	26 Mar
1:23:47	Ever	Palma	MEX	18.3.92	7 May
1:23:47	Noel Ali	Chama	MEX	15.9.97	3 Jun
1:23:49		Kim Dae-ho	KOR	30.4.88	19 Mar
1:23:51	Masatora	Kawano	JPN-J	23.10.98	19 Mar
1:23:54		Zhao Qi	CHN	14.1.93	4 Mar
1:23:54	Mohamed	Ragab Saleh	EGY	5.7.94	16 Mar
1:23:55	Kota	Yamada	JPN	27.4.94	1 Jan
1:23:57	Moacir	Zimmerman	BRA	30.12.83	3 Jun
1:23:58	Manish	Singh Rawat	IND	5.5.91	15 Apr
1:24:00		Dai Jianxing	CHN	11.8.96	4 Mar
1:24:01	Oscar	Villavicencio	ECU	5.5.93	15 Apr
1:24:01	Veli-Matti	Partanen	FIN	28.10.91	20 Jul
1:24:02	Yuki	Yamazaki	JPN	16.1.84	1 Jan
1:24:03	Oleksiy	Kazanin	UKR	22.5.82	11 Mar
1:24:03	Cian	McManamon	IRL	11.10.91	21 May
1:24:05	Aleksey	Kudashkin	RUS	1.2.97	18 Feb
1:24:07	Jordy	Jiménez	ECU	11.2.94	15 Apr
1:24:11		Zhang Jun	CHN-J	20.7.98	15 Apr
1:24:11	Isaac	Palma	MEX	26.10.90	6 May
1:24:11	Rafal	Fedaczynski	POL	3.12.80	18 Jun
1:24:13	Maksim	Vakhrushev	RUS	20.1.96	18 Feb
1:24:14		Yan Dexiang	CHN	18.6.93	4 Mar
1:24:19		Jai Bhagwan	IND	26.4.87	18 Feb
1:24:23	Anatole	Ibáñez	SWE	14.11.85	13 Aug
1:24:31	Francisco	Arcilla	ESP	19.1.84	3 Jun
1:24:32	Toru	Yamamoto	JPN	12.7.90	19 Feb
1:24:33	Hironari	Tomatsu	JPN	23.9.93	19 Mar
1:24:33	Rafal	Augustyn	POL	14.5.84	18 Jun
1:24:34	Aleksandr	Shunikhin	RUS	29.11.92	18 Feb
1:24:34	Kazuki	Takahashi	JPN	17.6.96	22 Oct
1:24:36	Eknath	Turambekar	IND-J	8.1.98	18 Feb
1:24:37	Tomofumi	Kanno	JPN	25.4.93	1 Jan
1:24:37	Brendon	Reading	AUS	26.1.89	19 Feb
1:24:38	Matej (200)	Tóth	SVK	10.2.83	22 Apr

Drugs disqualification

Mark	Name		Nat	Born	Pos	Meet	Venue	Date
1:19:48dq	Stanislav	Yemelyanov ¶	RUS	23.10.90	(3)	NC-w	Sochi	18 Feb

JUNIORS

See main list for top 2 juniors, 10 performances by 8 men to 1:26:00. Additional marks and further juniors:

Shirobokov 2+ 1:22:21 12 ECp Podébrady 21 May

Mark	Name		Nat	Born	Pos	Meet	Venue	Date
1:23:26	Sho	Sakazaki	JPN	22.2.99	3		Takahata	22 Oct
1:23:51	Masatora	Kawano	JPN	23.10.98	14		Nomi	19 Mar
1:24:11		Zhang Jun	CHN	20.7.98	5		Taicang	15 Apr
1:24:36	Eknath	Turambekar	IND	8.1.98	5	NC	New Delhi	18 Feb
1:24:55	Andrey	Mertsalov	RUS	19.1.98	16	NC-w	Sochi	18 Feb
1:25:07		Zhou Xiaojun	CHN	9.90.99	5		Taicang	15 Apr
1:25:58	David	Hurtado	ECU	21.4.99	26		La Coruña	3 Jun
1:26:23	Yuta	Koga (10)	JPN	15.7.99	28		Nomi	19 Mar
1:26:29	Ryutaro	Yamamoto	JPN	17.9.98	10		Takahata	22 Oct
1:26:36		Song Huazhang	CHN	13.2.99	13		Suzhou	24 Sep
1:26:44	Yamato	Nakajima	JPN	1.2.98	17	NC	Kobe	19 Feb
1:26:44	Tyler	Jones	AUS	8.4.98	2		Melbourne	17 Dec
1:26:50A	Yohanis	Algaw	ETH	14.8.99	1	NC	Addis Ababa	21 May
1:26:52	Yuhsuke	Naka	JPN	.98	11		Takahata	22 Oct

30-35 KILOMETRES WALK

30 km	35 km	Name		Nat	Born	Pos	Meet	Venue	Date
	2:27:07	Sergey	Sharipov	RUS	14.4.92	1	NC-w	Sochi	18 Feb
	2:28:00	Dementiy	Cheparev	RUS	28.10.92	2	NC-w	Sochi	18 Feb
	2:29:19	Denis	Nizhegorodov	RUS	26.7.80	3	NC-w	Sochi	18 Feb
2:09:51	2:30:58+	Yohann	Diniz	FRA	1.1.78	1	in 50k	London	13 Aug
	2:31:40	Ihor	Hlavan	UKR	25.9.90	1	NC-w	Ivano-Frankivsk	12 Mar
	2:31:58	Roman	Yevstifeyev	RUS	19.9.92	4	NC-w	Sochi	18 Feb
	2:32:23	Ivan	Banzeruk	UKR	9.2.90	2	NC-w	Ivano-Frankivsk	12 Mar
2:12:38			Gao Yingchao	CHN-J	18.1.98	1		Huangshan	5 Mar
2:12:57		Brian	Pintado	ECU	29.7.95	1		Hauppage	22 Oct
	2:34:40	Claudio	Villanueva	ECU	3.8.88	1	NC	Sucua	15 Apr
	2:34:48+	Marco	De Luca	ITA	12.5.81			Grosseto	29 Jan
	2:34:56	Maryan	Zakolnytskyy	UKR	19.8.94	3	NC-w	Ivano-Frankivsk	12 Mar
2:13:09	2:35:20		Yu Wei	CHN	11.9.87		in 50k	London	13 Aug
2:13:09	2:35:20+	Hirooki	Arai	JPN	18.5.88		in 50k	London	13 Aug
2:13:09+	2:36:21	Aleksi	Ojala	FIN	9.12.92		in 50k	London	13 Aug
2:13:10	(2:35:19)	Claudio	Villanueva	ECU	3.8.88		in 50k	London	13 Aug
2:13:10	2:35:20+	Evan	Dunfee	CAN	28.9.90		in 50k	London	13 Aug
2:13:10	2:35:20+	Kai	Kobayashi	JPN	28.2.93		in 50k	London	13 Aug
2:13:10	2:35:21+	Andrés	Chocho	ECU	4.11.83		in 50k	London	13 Aug
2:13:22+			Cheparev				in 50k	Cheboksary	11 Jun
	2:35:35	Valeriy	Litanyuk	UKR	2.4.94	4	NC-w	Ivano-Frankivsk	12 Mar
2:13:45+			Sharipov				in 50k	Cheboksary	11 Jun
2:13:47+		Håvard	Haukenes	NOR	22.4.90		in 50k	London	13 Aug
2:14:09		Jarkko	Kinnunen	FIN	19.1.94	2	NC	Laitala	11 Jun

Mark		Name		Nat	Born	Pos	Meet	Venue	Date
(2:15:01)	2:36:18+	Robert	Heffernan	IRL	20.2.78		in 50k	London	13 Aug
2:14:18	2:36:31+	Satoshi	Maruo	JPN	28.11.91		in 50k	London	13 Aug
2:14:19	2:36:51	Horacio	Nava	MEX	20.1.82		in 50k	London	13 Aug
2:14:21			Niu Wenchao	CHN-J	16.9.98	2		Huangshan	5 Mar
(2:14:41)	2:36:51+	Máté	Helebrandt	HUN	12.1.89		in 50k	London	13 Aug

50 KILOMETRES WALK

Mark	Name		Nat	Born	Pos	Meet	Venue	Date
3:33:12	Yohann	Diniz	FRA	1.1.78	1	WCh	London	13 Aug
3:41:17	Hirooki	Arai	JPN	18.5.88	2	WCh	London	13 Aug
3:41:19	Kai	Kobayashi	JPN	28.2.93	3	WCh	London	13 Aug
3:41:42	Igor	Hlavan	UKR	25.9.90	4	WCh	London	13 Aug
3:43:03	Satoshi	Maruo	JPN	28.11.91	5	WCh	London	13 Aug
3:43:05	Dementiy	Cheparev	RUS	28.10.92	1	NC	Cheboksary	11 Jun
3:43:40	Håvard	Haukenes	NOR	22.4.90	1		Dudince	25 Mar
3:43:56	Máté	Helebrandt	HUN	12.1.89	6	WCh	London	13 Aug
3:44:18	Rafal	Augustyn	POL	14.5.84	7	WCh	London	13 Aug
3:44:35	Perseus	Karlström (10)	SWE	2.5.90	1		Melbourne	17 Dec
3:44:41	Robert	Heffernan	IRL	20.2.78	8	WCh	London	13 Aug
3:44:42		Augustyn			2		Dudince	25 Mar
3:45:02	Marco	De Luca	ITA	12.5.81	9	WCh	London	13 Aug
3:45:09	José	Ojeda Leyver	MEX	12.11.85	1		Naumburg	23 Apr
3:45:21	Carl	Dohmann	GER	18.5.90	10	WCh	London	13 Aug
3:45:28	João	Vieira	POR	20.2.76	11	WCh	London	13 Aug
3:46:03	Evan	Dunfee	CAN	28.9.90	1		Monterrey	19 Mar
3:46:12		Niu Wenbin	CHN	20.1.91	1		Huangshan	5 Mar
3:46:29	Quentin	Rew	NZL	16.7.84	12	WCh	London	13 Aug
3:47:01	Karl	Junghanss	GER	6.4.96	13	WCh	London	13 Aug
3:47:13	Sergey	Sharipov (20)	RUS	14.4.92	2	NC	Cheboksary	11 Jun
3:47:18		Arai			1		Wajima	16 Apr
3:47:20	Aleksi	Ojala	FIN	9.12.92	14	WCh	London	13 Aug
3:47:36		Dunfee			15	WCh	London	13 Aug
3:47:37	Andrés	Chocho	ECU	4.11.83	2		Monterrey	19 Mar
3:47:53	Horacio	Nava	MEX	20.1.82	16	WCh	London	13 Aug
3:48:04	Pedro	Gómez	MEX	31.12.90	3		Dudince	25 Mar
3:48:08	José Ignacio	Díaz	ESP	22.11.79	17	WCh	London	13 Aug
3:48:15	Ivan	Banzeruk	UKR	9.2.90	1	ECp	Podébrady	21 May
3:48:36	Hayato	Katsuki	JPN	28.11.90	1		Takahata	22 Oct
3:48:38		Wu Qianlong	CHN	30.1.90	2		Huangshan	5 Mar
3:48:38		Hlavan			2	ECp	Podébrady	21 May
	(32/28)							
3:48:39	Adrian	Blocki	POL	11.4.90	4		Dudince	25 Mar
3:48:41		Bian Tongda	CHN	1.4.91	3		Huangshan	5 Mar
	(30)							
3:48:45	Luis	Bustamante	MEX	10.6.84	2		Naumburg	23 Apr
3:48:56	Rafal	Fedaczynski	POL	3.12.80	5		Dudince	25 Mar
3:49:00	Veli-Matti	Partanen	FIN	28.10.91	6		Dudince	25 Mar
3:49:07	Michele	Antonelli	ITA	23.5.94	3	ECp	Podébrady	21 May
3:49:27	Claudio	Villanueva	ECU	3.8.88	18	WCh	London	13 Aug
3:49:49	Brendan	Boyce	IRL	15.10.86	4	ECp	Podébrady	21 May
3:50:37	Jorge	Ruiz	COL	17.5.89	20	WCh	London	13 Aug
3:50:38		Luo Dongpo	CHN	23.6.95	4		Huangshan	5 Mar
3:51:35	Luis Fernando	López	COL	3.6.79	2	PAmCp	Lima	14 May
3:52:14	Teodorico	Caporaso	ITA	14.9.87	5	ECp	Podébrady	21 May
	(40)							
3:52:30	Julio César	Salazar	MEX	8.7.93	7		Dudince	25 Mar
3:52:38		Zhang Lin	CHN	11.11.93	5		Huangshan	5 Mar
3:53:01	Damian	Blocki	POL	28.4.89	8		Dudince	25 Mar
3:53:25	Denis	Nizhegorodov	RUS	26.7.80	3	NC	Cheboksary	1 Jun
3:53:50	Maryan	Zakalnytskyy	UKR	19.8.94	6	ECp	Podébrady	21 May
3:54:02		Xu Faguang	CHN	17.5.87	1	NG	Tianjin	7 Sep
3:54:35		Meng Zhongkai	CHN	15.12.97	6		Huangshan	5 Mar
3:54:46		Wang Qin	CHN	8.5.94	1	NG	Tianjin	7 Sep
3:55:13	Nathaniel	Seiler	GER	6.4.96	7	ECp	Podébrady	21 May
3:55:44	Jarkko	Kinnunen	FIN	19.1.84	23	WCh	London	25 Mar
	(50)							
3:56:00	Sandeep	Kumar Sangwan	IND	16.12.86	1	NC	New Delhi	18 Feb
3:56:22		Luo Yadong	CHN	15.1.92	5	NG	Tianjin	7 Sep
3:56:23		Han Yucheng	CHN	16.12.78	7		Huangshan	5 Mar
3:56:34	Yuki	Ito	JPN	12.4.92	2		Takahata	22 Oct

Mark	Name		Nat	Born	Pos	Meet	Venue	Date
3:56:38	Pedro	Isidro	POR	17.7.85	8	ECp	Podébrady	21 May
3:56:39	Francisco	Arcilla	ESP	19.1.84	9	ECp	Podébrady	21 May
3:56:47	Iván	Pajuelo	ESP	27.8.93	10	ECp	Podébrady	21 May
3:56:54	Mathieu	Bilodeau	CAN	27.11.83	25	WCh	London	14 May
3:57:32	Ever	Palma	MEX	18.3.92	9		Dudince	25 Mar
3:57:46	Erick	Barrondo	GUA	14.6.91	1		Salamá	12 Mat
	(60)							
3:58:00	Anders	Hansson	SWE	10.3.92	28	WCh	London	13 Aug
3:58:08	Andrea	Agrusti	ITA	30.8.95	11	ECp	Podébrady	21 May
3:58:14		Yan Dexiang	CHN	18.6.93	8		Huangshan	5 Mar
3:58:28	José Leonardo	Montaña	COL	21.3.92	3	PAmCp	Lima	14 May
3:58:35	Andrey	Hrechkovskyy	UKR	30.8.93	12	ECp	Podébrady	21 May
3:58:44	Tadas	Suskevicius	LTU	22.5.85	10		Dudince	25 Mar
3:59:46		Park Chil-sung	KOR	8.7.82	29	WCh	London	13 Aug
4:00:05		Liu Jian	CHN	19.5.95	9		Huangshan	5 Mar
4:00:28		Cheng Min	CHN	6.7.91	10		Huangshan	5 Mar
4:00:28		Han Jijiang	CHN	20.7.93	7	NG	Tianjin	7 Sep
	(70)							
4:00:39	Federico	Tontodonati	ITA	30.10.89	14	ECp	Podébrady	21 May
4:01:04		Yang Hu	CHN	16.4.95	12		Huangshan	5 Mar
4:01:15		Geng Yudong	CHN	13.6.94	13		Huangshan	5 Mar
4:01:29		Xie Sichao	CHN	28.2.93	14		Huangshan	5 Mar
4:01:32	Shuto	Goto	JPN	26.2.94	3		Takahata	22 Oct
4:01:39	Luis Manuel	Corchete	ESP	14.5.84	15	ECp	Podébrady	21 May
4:01:47		Yang Liang	CHN	25.4.93	15		Huangshan	5 Mar
4:01:56	Artur	Mastianica	LTU	30.7.92	16	ECp	Podébrady	21 May
4:01:57		Wang Hao	CHN	16.8.89	8	NG	Tianjin	7 Sep
4:01:58	Igor	Saharuk	UKR	3.6.88	2	NC	Ivano-Frankivsk	15 Oct
	(80)							
4:02:12	Jitender	Singh Rathore	IND	20.3.89	2	NC	New Delhi	18 Feb
4:02:23	Roman	Yevstifeyev	RUS	19.9.92	4	NC	Cheboksary	11 Jun
4:02:27	Narcis	Mihaila	ROU	4.8.92	31	WCh	London	13 Aug
4:03:36	Florin Alin	Stirbu	ROU	21.4.92	17	ECp	Podébrady	21 May
4:03:45	Cristian	Berdeja	MEX	21.6.81	6		Monterrey	19 Mar
4:03:48		Fang Hongzhen	CHN	6.3.96	16		Huangshan	5 Mar
4:03:55	Valeriy	Litanyuk	UKR	2.4.94	3	NC	Ivano-Frankivsk	15 Oct
4:04:16	Dominic	King	GBR	30.5.83	13		Dudince	25 Mar
4:04:19	Chandan	Singh	IND	8.6.87	3	NC	New Delhi	18 Feb
4:04:29		You Tao	CHN	19.7.97	17		Huangshan	5 Mar
	(90)							
4:04:36		Chen Rui	CHN	11.8.96	2		Taicang	16 Apr
4:04:37		Yang Yingyi	CHN	9.2.95	18		Huangshan	5 Mar
4:04:38		Wang Zhendong	CHN	11.1.91	10	NG	Tianjin	7 Sep
4:04:58	Tomofumi	Kanno	JPN	25.4.93	5		Wajima	16 Apr
4:05:14	Aleksey	Terentyev	RUS	19.7.91	5	NC	Cheboksary	11 Jun
4:05:29	Isaac	Palma	MEX	26.10.90	7		Monterrey	19 Mar
4:05:44		Zhou Shipeng	CHN	9.2.96	19		Huangshan	5 Mar
4:05:49	Jonathan	Hilbert	GER	24.1.95	2	NC	Gleina	14 Oct
4:06:04		Jiang Su	CHN	8.4.95	20		Huangshan	5 Mar
4:06:30		Zhong Xing	CHN	6.3.95	21		Huangshan	5 Mar
	(100)							

Mark	Name		Nat	Born	Date
4:06:42	Hugo	Andrieu	FRA	16.10.92	12 Mar
4:07:10	Maniram	Patel	IND	16.9.91	18 Feb
4:07:16	Ferney	Rojas	COL	30.9.87	13 May
4:07:43		Hou Xuejing	CHN	17.7.97	5 Mar
4:08:03		Ceng Qingsheng	CHN	3.4.95	5 Mar
4:08:22	Gregorio	Angelini	ITA	24.6.96	15 Jan
4:08:22	Ronal	Quispe	BOL	5.3.89	13 Aug
4:08:32	Rolando	Saquipay	ECU	21.7.79	13 May
4:08:39		Liu Rusi	CHN	6.8.91	5 Mar
4:09:15	Dávid	Tokodi	HUN	3.5.91	25 Mar
4:09:40	S. Dhamen	Singh	IND	15.10.89	18 Feb
4:09:55	Toru	Yamamoto	JPN	12.7.90	16 Apr

Addition to 2017 Lists

60 METRES Outdoors

Mark	Wind	Name		Nat	Born	Pos	Venue	Date
6.53	0.2	Andrew	Fisher	BRN	15.12.91	1	Kingston	21 Jan
6.55	0.7	Julian	Forte	JAM	7.1.93	1h3	Kingston	28 Jan
6.55			Xie Zhenye	CHN	17.8.93	1	Shanghai	1 Jul
6.60	0.2	Everton	Clarke	JAM	24.12.92	2	Kingston	21 Jan
6.60	0.7	Kavean	Smith	JAM	12.5.92	3	Kingston	28 Jan
6.60	0.0	Yoshide	Kiryu	JPN	15.12.95	1	Gold Coast	17 Mar
6.62	-0.2	Asafa	Powell	JAM	23.11.82	1	Melbourne	11 Feb
6.63	0.1	Michael	Campbell	JAM	29.11.96	1h1	Kingston	28 Jan

WOMEN'S WORLD LISTS 2017

60 METRES

Mark	Wind	Name		Nat	Born	Pos	Meet	Venue	Date
7.05	1.7	Christania	Williams	JAM	17.10.94	2		Kingston	28 Jan
7.27	1.7	Audrea	Segree	JAM	5.10.90	3		Kingston	28 Jan
7.27	-0.8	Jenna	Prandini	USA	20.11.92	1	Nitro	Melbourne	9 Feb
Wind assisted									
7.25	2.1	Jura	Levy	JAM	4.11.90	1		Kingston	21 Jan
7.27	2.1	Gayon	Evans	JAM	15.1.90	2		Kingston	21 Jan
Indoors									
6.98		Elaine	Thompson	JAM	28.6.92	1		Birmingham	18 Feb
7.06		Asha	Philip	GBR	25.10.90	1	EI	Beograd	5 Mar
7.07A		Hannah	Cunliffe	USA	9.1.96	1		Albuquerque	11 Feb
7.08A		Morolake	Akinosun	USA	17.5.94	1	NC	Albuquerque	5 Mar
7.10		Ewa	Swoboda	POL	26.7.97	2	EI	Beograd	5 Mar
7.11		Barbara	Pierre	USA	28.4.87	1h1		Torun	10 Feb
7.11A		Dezerea	Bryant	USA	27.4.93	2	NC	Albuquerque	5 Mar
		(7/7)							
7.13		Dina	Asher-Smith	GBR	4.12.95	1h1		Karlsruhe	4 Feb
7.13		Ezinne	Okparaebo	NOR	3.3.88	2		Torun	10 Feb
7.14		Rebekka	Haase	GER	2.1.93	1		Erfurt	27 Jan
		(10)							
7.14		Gayon	Evans	JAM	15.1.90	1		Karlsruhe	4 Feb
7.14		Gina	Lückenkemper	GER	21.11.96	1	NC	Leipzig	18 Feb
7.14		Marie Josée	Ta Lou	CIV	18.11.88	1h2	NC	Bordeaux	18 Feb
7.14		Javianne	Oliver	USA	26.12.94	1h2	NCAA	College Station	10 Mar
7.15A		Lekeisha	Lawson	USA	3.6.87	3	NC	Albuquerque	5 Mar
7.16		Stella	Akakpo	FRA	28.2.94	1		Reims	31 Jan
7.16		Mujinga	Kambundji	SUI	17.6.92	3	EI	Beograd	5 Mar
7.17		English	Gardner	USA	22.4.92	1	New Bal	Boston (R)	28 Jan
7.17A		Ashley	Henderson	USA	4.12.95	1	MWC	Albuquerque	25 Feb
7.17		Deajah	Stevens	USA	19.5.95	2h1	NCAA	College Station	10 Mar
		(20)							
7.18A		Schillonie	Calvert-Powell	JAM	27.7.88	1h1		Flagstaff	17 Feb
7.18		Tatjana	Pinto	GER	2.7.92	1s2	NC	Leipzig	18 Feb
7.18		Lisa	Mayer	GER	2.5.96	3	NC	Leipzig	18 Feb
7.18		Christania	Williams	JAM	17.10.94	3		Birmingham	18 Feb
7.18		Aleia	Hobbs	USA	24.2.96	1	SEC	Nashville	25 Feb
7.19		Mikiah	Brisco	USA	14.7.96	1		Fayetteville	28 Jan
7.19		Alexandra	Burghardt	GER	28.4.94	4	NC	Leipzig	18 Feb
7.20		Kristina	Sivkova	RUS	28.2.97	1		Sankt Peterburg	14 Feb
7.20		Andrea	Purica	VEN	21.11.95	2		Ostrava	14 Feb
7.20A		Destiny	Smith-Barnett	USA	26.7.96	1h4	MWC	Albuquerque	24 Feb
		(30)							
7.20			Liang Xiaojing	CHN	7.4.97	1	NGP	Xianlin	27 Feb
7.20		Floriane	Gnafoua	FRA	30.1.96	6	EI	Beograd	5 Mar
7.20		Ariana	Washington	USA	27.8.96	3	NCAA	College Station	11 Mar
7.21		Teahna	Daniels	USA	27.3.97	2		Lexington	21 Jan
7.21		Kristina	Timanovskaya	BLR	19.11.96	1	NC	Mogilyov	18 Feb
7.21A		Mikele	Barber	USA	4.10.80	4	NC	Albuquerque	5 Mar
7.21		Quanesha	Burks	USA	15.3.95	4h1	NCAA	College Station	10 Mar
7.21		Kortnei	Johnson	USA	11.8.97	5h1	NCAA	College Station	10 Mar
7.22		Stephanie	Kalu	NGR	5.8.93	1		Frisco	10 Feb
7.22		Jessica	Young-Warren	USA	6.4.87	3		Ostrava	14 Feb
		(40)							
7.22		Jura	Levy	JAM	4.11.90	2		Lódz	16 Feb
7.22			Yuan Qiqi	CHN	26.10.95	2	NGP	Xianlin	27 Feb
7.24		Crystal	Emmanuel	CAN	27.11.91	1		Montréal	18 Feb
7.25		Chantal	Butzek	GER	25.2.97	4	ISTAF	Berlin	10 Feb
7.25A		Makenzie	Dunmore	USA	7.10.97	3		Albuquerque	11 Feb
7.25		Tawanna	Meadows	USA	4.8.86	2h1		Metz	12 Feb
7.25A		Jerayah	Davis	USA	15.4.96	1h1	MWC	Albuquerque	24 Feb
7.25		Madiea	Ghafoor	NED	9.9.92	1		Amsterdam	30 Dec
7.26		Yasmin	Kwadwo	GER	9.11.90	3		Erfurt	27 Jan
7.26		Remona	Burchell	JAM	15.9.91	1		Norman	28 Jan
		(50)							
7.26		Kianna	Gray	USA	30.12.96	1h4		Lincoln	3 Feb
7.26		Deanna	Hill	USA	13.4.96	1h3		Fayetteville	10 Feb
7.26			Wei Yongli	CHN	11.10.91	3	Millrose	New York (A)	11 Feb
7.26		Flings	Owusu-Agyapong	GHA	16.10.88	2		Athlone	15 Feb

Mark	Wind	Name		Nat	Born	Pos	Meet	Venue	Date
7.26		Anna	Bongiorni	ITA	15.9.93	1s2	NC	Ancona	19 Feb
7.26		Cassondra	Hall	USA	23.9.97	2h3	SEC	Nashville	24 Feb
7.26		Jada	Martin	USA	8.6.95	2h4	SEC	Nashville	24 Feb
7.26		Devynne	Charlton	BAH	26.11.95	1	Big 10	Geneva	25 Feb

Mark	Name		Nat	Born	Date
7.27	Torie	Robinson	USA	11.6.96	10 Feb
7.27	Phylicia	George	CAN	16.11.87	11 Feb
7.27	Jayla	Kirkland	USA-J	13.2.99	12 Mar
7.28A	Jasmine	Todd	USA	23.12.93	4 Feb
7.28	Naomi	Sedney	NED	17.12.94	11 Feb
7.28	Kennadi	Bouyer	USA	1.1.95	11 Feb
7.28	Rosângela	Santos	BRA	20.12.90	16 Feb
7.28	Agata	Forkasiewicz	POL	13.1.94	18 Feb
7.28	Kate	Hall	USA	12.1.97	24 Feb
7.29	Angelica	Collins	USA	21.10.95	4 Feb
7.29	Gabrielle	Thomas	USA	7.12.96	25 Feb
7.29	Barbora	Procházková	CZE	13.12.91	25 Feb
	(70)				

Best at low altitude

Mark	Name	Pos	Meet	Venue	Date
7.12	Bryant	1	Mill	New York (A)	11 Feb
7.13	Cunliffe	1		New York (A)	27 Jan
7.17	Akinosun	2	Mill	New York (A)	11 Feb
7.18	Henderson	3h1	NCAA	College Station	10 Mar
7.20	Lawson	1		Athlone	15 Feb
7.27	Barber				18 Feb
7.29	Dunmore				14 Jan

Drugs disqualification

Mark	Wind	Name		Nat	Born	Pos	Meet	Venue	Date
7.10		Olesya	Povh	UKR	18.10.87	(2)	EI	Beograd	5 Mar

100 METRES

Mark	Wind	Name		Nat	Born	Pos	Meet	Venue	Date
10.71	0.8	Elaine	Thompson	JAM	28.6.92	1	NC	Kingston	23 Jun
10.78	-0.3		Thompson			1	DL	Shanghai	13 May
10.82	0.9	Michelle-Lee	Ahye	TTO	10.4.92	1	NC	Port of Spain	24 Jun
10.83	1.1	Murielle	Ahouré	CIV	23.8.87	1		Montverde	10 Jun
10.84	1.1	Veronica	Campbell-Brown	JAM	15.5.82	2		Montverde	10 Jun
10.84	-0.2		Thompson			1s2	WCh	London (OS)	6 Aug
10.85	2.0	Aleia	Hobbs	USA	24.2.96	1		Baton Rouge	29 Apr
10.85	0.1	Tori	Bowie	USA	27.8.90	1	WCh	London (OS)	6 Aug
10.86	0.1	Marie Josée	Ta Lou	CIV	18.11.88	2	WCh	London (OS)	6 Aug
10.87	0.3		Thompson			1	DL	Rabat	16 Jul
10.88	0.8		Ta Lou			1s1	WCh	London (OS)	6 Aug
10.88	0.9	Kelly-Ann	Baptiste	TTO	14.10.86	2	NC	Port of Spain	24 Jun
10.90	1.6		Bowie			1h2	NC	Sacramento	22 Jun
10.90	0.3		Ta Lou			2	DL	Rabat	16 Jul
10.91	0.1		Thompson			1	DL	Paris (C)	1 Jul
10.91	0.2		Bowie			1s3	WCh	London (OS)	6 Aug
10.91	-0.2	Rosângela	Santos	BRA	20.12.90	2s2	WCh	London (OS)	6 Aug
10.92	0.4		Thompson			1	VD-DLF	Bruxelles	1 Sep
10.93	-1.2		Thompson			1	DL	Birmingham	20 Aug
10.93	0.4		To Lou			2	VD-DLF	Bruxelles	1 Sep
10.94	-0.1	Schillonie	Calvert-Powell (10)	JAM	27.7.88	1h1		Phoenix	10 Jun
10.94	0.3		Bowie			1	NC	Sacramento	23 Jun
10.94	-1.4		Thompson			1	DL	London (OS)	9 Jul
10.94	1.0		Ta Lou			1h2	DL	Birmingham	20 Aug
10.95	0.8	Dafne	Schippers	NED	15.6.92	1	Clay	Azusa	14 Apr
10.95	1.3	Gina	Lückenkemper	GER	21.11.96	1h1	WCh	London (OS)	5 Aug
10.96	0.3	Mikiah	Brisco	USA	14.7.96	1	NCAA	Eugene	10 Jun
10.96	0.1		Ta Lou			2	DL	Paris (C)	1 Jul
10.96	-0.4		Schippers			1h2	DL	London (OS)	9 Jul
10.96	0.1		Schippers			3	WCh	London (OS)	6 Aug
		(30/13)							
10.98	0.7	Morolake	Akinosun	USA	17.5.94	1h4	NC	Sacramento	22 Jun
10.99	1.4	Barbara	Pierre	USA	28.4.87	1h1	NC	Sacramento	22 Jun
10.99	-1.4	Blessing	Okagbare	NGR	9.10.88	3	DL	London (OS)	9 Jul
11.00	0.7	Deajah	Stevens	USA	19.5.95	1	MSR	Torrance	15 Apr
11.01	1.8	Ashley	Henderson	USA	4.12.95	1q1	NCAA-W	Austin	26 May
11.01	1.6	Aaliyah	Brown	USA	6.1.95	2h2	NC	Sacramento	22 Jun
11.03	1.4	Kimberlyn	Duncan	USA	2.8.91	2h1	NC	Sacramento	22 Jun
		(20)							
11.03	0.7	Allyson	Felix	USA	18.11.85	2h4	NC	Sacramento	22 Jun
11.03	0.7	Christania	Williams	JAM	17.10.94	2s2	NC	Kingston	23 Jun
11.04	-0.2	English	Gardner	USA	22.4.92	2h3	NC	Sacramento	22 Jun
11.04	0.8	Simone	Facey	JAM	7.5.85	2	NC	Kingston	23 Jun
11.04	0.8	Tianna	Bartoletta	USA	30.8.85	1	ISTAF	Berlin	27 Aug
11.05	2.0	Destiny	Carter	USA	9.10.92	2		Baton Rouge	29 Apr
11.05	1.4	Jenna	Prandini	USA	20.11.92	3h1	NC	Sacramento	22 Jun
11.06	0.7	Ariana	Washington	USA	27.8.96	2	MSR	Torrance	15 Apr
11.06	1.8	Rebekka	Haase	GER	2.1.93	2h1		Zeulenroda	25 May
11.06	0.3	Teahna	Daniels	USA	27.3.97	3	NCAA	Eugene	10 Jun
		(30)							
11.06	0.8	Jura	Levy	JAM	4.11.90	3	NC	Kingston	23 Jun
11.06	0.9	Khalifa	St. Fort	TTO-J	13.2.98	3	NC	Port of Spain	24 Jun

Mark	Wind	Name		Nat	Born	Pos	Meet	Venue	Date
11.07	0.0	Mujinga	Kambundji	SUI	17.6.92	1		Bellinzona	18 Jul
11.09	0.6	Desiree	Henry	GBR	26.8.95	1rB	Clay	Azusa	14 Apr
11.09	0.7	Kortnei	Johnson	USA	11.8.97	3	MSR	Torrance	15 Apr
11.09	0.8	Natasha	Morrison	JAM	17.11.92	4	NC	Kingston	23 Jun
11.09	0.7	Remona	Burchell	JAM	15.9.91	3s2	NC	Kingston	23 Jun
11.10A	0.3	Carina	Horn	RSA	9.3.89	1s1	NC	Potchefstroom	21 Apr
11.10	0.8	Shashalee	Forbes	JAM	10.5.96	5	NC	Kingston	23 Jun
11.11	1.4	Hannah	Cunliffe	USA	9.1.96	3	Pac 12	Eugene	14 May
		(40)							
11.11	1.9	Semoy	Hackett	TTO	27.11.88	1		Miami	8 Jul
11.12	1.9	Kerron	Stewart	JAM	16.4.84	1h4		Auburn	22 Apr
11.13	0.4	Jonielle	Smith	JAM	30.1.96	1h3	SEC	Columbia SC	12 May
11.13	0.1	Carolle	Zahi	FRA	12.6.94	1	NC	Marseille	15 Jul
11.13	0.8	Dina	Asher-Smith	GBR	4.12.95	2h1		Birmingham	20 Aug
11.14	-0.4	Daryll	Neita	GBR	29.8.96	4h2	DL	London (OS)	9 Jul
11.14	1.3	Asha	Philip	GBR	25.10.90	4h1	WCh	London (OS)	5 Aug
11.14	0.8	Crystal	Emmanuel	CAN	27.11.91	2h2	WCh	London (OS)	5 Aug
11.14	-0.2	Lisa	Mayer	GER	2.5.96	1rB	ISTAF	Berlin	27 Aug
11.16	0.7	Mikele	Barber	USA	4.10.80	5	MSR	Torrance	15 Apr
		(50)							
11.16	2.0	Javianne	Oliver	USA	26.12.94	3		Baton Rouge	29 Apr
11.16	1.2	Tawanna	Meadows	USA	4.8.86	1		New York	6 Jul
11.17	1.4	Deanna	Hill	USA	13.4.96	6h1	NC	Sacramento	22 Jun
11.17	2.0	Sally	Pearson	AUS	19.9.86	1		Brisbane	16 Dec
11.18	1.2	Ángela	Tenorio	ECU	27.1.96	1	Quercia	Rovereto	29 Aug
11.19	1.1	Charonda	Williams	USA	27.3.87	5		Montverde	10 Jun
11.19	1.0	Shaunae	Miller-Uibo	BAH	15.4.94	5h2		Birmingham	20 Aug
11.20	1.6	Candyce	McGrone	USA	24.3.89	4h2	NC	Sacramento	22 Jun
11.21	0.8	Destiny	Smith-Barnett	USA	26.7.96	3	Clay	Azusa	14 Apr
11.21	1.7	Quanesha	Burks	USA	15.3.95	2h1	SEC	Columbia SC	12 May
		(60)							
11.22	1.2	Orphée	Neola	FRA	1.2.91	2		Montgeron	14 May
11.23	1.1	Candace	Hill	USA-J	11.2.99	1h1	NC-j	Sacramento	23 Jun
11.24	0.9	Symone	Mason	USA-J	31.8.99	1		Jacksonville	18 Mar
11.24	1.3	Gabrielle	Thomas	USA	7.12.96	1rB	FlaR	Gainesville	31 Mar
11.24	0.4	Shericka	Jackson	JAM	15.7.94	1		Kingston	6 May
11.24	0.0	Vitória	Rosa	BRA	12.1.96	2	NC	São Bernardo do Campo	9 Jun
11.24	0.2	Ashton	Purvis	USA	12.7.92	2		Phoenix	10 Jun
11.24	1.6	Kevona	Davis	JAM-Y	20.12.01	1	NC-y	Kingston	24 Jun
11.24	0.3	Tatjana	Pinto	GER	2.7.92	1h1		Ninove	15 Jul
11.24	0.6	Ewa	Swoboda	POL	26.7.97	5h6	WCh	London (OS)	5 Aug
		(70)							
11.25	0.8	Naomi	Sedney	NED	17.12.94	1rC	FlaR	Gainesville	31 Mar
11.25	1.8	Danielle	Williams	JAM	14.9.92	2		Greensboro	15 Apr
11.25	0.4	Brenessa	Thompson	GUY	22.7.96	2h3	SEC	Columbia SC	12 May
11.25	1.9	Sina	Mayer	GER	10.4.95	1h2		Regensburg	11 Jun
11.25	1.6	Tiffany	Townsend	USA	14.6.89	6h2	NC	Sacramento	22 Jun
11.25	1.2	Andrea	Purica	VEN	21.11.95	1		Castellón	4 Jul
11.25	0.8	Ivet	Lalova-Collio	BUL	18.5.84	7s1	WCh	London (OS)	6 Aug
11.26A	0.9	Narcisa	Landázuri	ECU	25.11.92	1	Restrepo	Medellín	29 Apr
11.26	0.4	Alexandria	Anderson	USA	28.1.87	1		St-Martin	13 May
11.26	0.8	Shauna	Helps	JAM	23.10.96	1	ACC	Atlanta	14 May
		(80)							
11.26	1.2	Jamile	Samuel	NED	24.4.92	3		Montgeron	14 May
11.26	1.1	Gabriele	Cunningham	USA-J	22.2.98	2h1	NC-j	Sacramento	23 Jun
11.27A	1.1	Cierra	White	USA	29.4.93	1		Canyon	14 May
11.27	-0.4	Dezerea	Bryant	USA	27.4.93	2		Baie-Mahault	17 May
11.27	1.7	Tameka	Williams	SKN	31.8.89	1		St. George's	4 Jun
11.27	-0.9	Ashleigh	Nelson	GBR	20.2.91	2s2	NC	Birmingham	1 Jul
11.27	1.2	Joanna	Atkins	USA	31.1.89	4		New York	6 Jul
11.27	1.6	Salomé	Kora	SUI	8.6.94	1		Bulle	8 Jul
11.28	1.3	Shayla	Sanders	USA	6.1.94	2rB	FlaR	Gainesville	31 Mar
11.28	2.0	Sha'Carri	Richardson	USA-Y	25.3.00	1		Austin	13 May
		(90)							
11.28	1.4	Kristina	Timanovskaya	BLR	19.11.96	1		Ellwangen	20 May
11.28	0.0	Kianna	Gray	USA	30.12.96	2h1	NCAA-E	Lexington	25 May
11.28	1.2	Floriane	Gnafoua	FRA	30.1.96	4		Montreuil	1 Jun
11.28	0.0	Amelie-Sophie	Lederer	GER	22.4.94	2h2	NC	Erfurt	8 Jul
11.29	2.0	Toea	Wisil	PNG	1.1.88	1		Canberra	19 Feb
11.29	2.0	Shavine	Hodges	JAM	22.10.91	2		Athens	6 May
11.29	0.8	Rebekah	Smith	USA-J	1.5.98	2	ACC	Atlanta	14 May

Mark	Wind	Name		Nat	Born	Pos	Meet	Venue	Date
11.29	0.3	Ky	Westbrook	USA	25.2.96	8	NCAA	Eugene	10 Jun
11.29	1.9	Lara	Matheis	GER	2.8.92	2h2		Regensburg	11 Jun
11.29	1.9	Jennifer	Montag	GER-J	11.2.98	2h2		Regensburg	11 Jun
		(100)							
11.29	1.6	Jasmine	Todd	USA	23.12.93	7h2	NC	Sacramento	22 Jun

Mark	Wind	Name		Nat	Born	Date
11.30	0.4	Kate	Hall	USA	12.1.97	12 May
11.30	0.3	Dutee	Chand	IND	3.2.96	15 May
11.30	0.3		Yuan Qiqi	CHN	26.10.95	16 May
11.30	1.6	Briana	Williams	JAM-Y	21.3.02	24 Jun
11.30	0.1	Orlann	Ombissa-Dzangue	FRA	26.5.91	15 Jul
11.30	1.0	Bianca	Williams	GBR	18.12.93	24 Aug
11.31	1.0	Jennifer	Madu	NGR	23.9.94	1 Apr
11.31	0.0	Zakiya	Denoon	TTO	23.1.95	29 Apr
11.31	1.9	Devynne	Charlton	BAH	26.11.95	14 May
11.31	0.8	Torie	Robinson	USA	11.6.96	14 May
11.31	1.7	Reyare	Thomas	TTO	23.11.87	23 Jun
11.31	0.9	Kayelle	Clarke	TTO	28.2.96	24 Jun
11.31	0.8	Ezinne	Okparaebo	NOR	3.3.88	2 Jul
11.31	-0.3	Irene	Siragusa	ITA	23.6.93	24 Aug
11.31	0.1		Wei Yongli	CHN	11.10.91	3 Sep
11.32A	0.2	Janet	Amponsah	GHA	12.4.93	13 May
11.32	0.1	Gayon	Evans	JAM	15.1.90	20 May
11.32	1.8	Leya	Buchanan	CAN	17.8.96	26 May
11.32	0.3	Ana Cláudia	Silva	BRA	6.11.88	9 Jun
11.33	2.0	Melissa	Breen	AUS	17.9.90	19 Feb
11.33	1.0	Ka'Tia	Seymour	USA	3.10.97	27 May
11.33	-0.3	Hrystyna	Stuy	UKR	3.2.88	6 Jun
11.33	0.0	Melanise	Chapman	USA	28.4.91	10 Jun
11.33	1.3	Sarah	Atcho	SUI	1.6.95	18 Jun
11.33	-0.2	Lekeisha	Lawson	USA	3.6.87	22 Jun
11.33	0.6	Viktoriya	Zyabkina	KAZ	4.9.92	24 Jun
11.33	1.7	Keshia	Kwadwo	GER-J	10.7.99	4 Aug
11.34	1.0	Taylor	Bennett	USA	15.1.97	1 Apr
11.34	1.8	India	Brown	USA	29.1.96	15 Apr
11.34A	0.3	Tebogo	Mamathu	RSA	27.5.95	21 Apr
11.34	1.4	Shania	Collins	USA	14.11.96	12 May
11.34	1.9	Chelsea	Francis	USA	14.10.96	14 May
11.34	1.5	Shimayra	Williams	JAM	2.12.95	20 May
11.34	-1.0	Cassondra	Hall	USA	23.9.97	26 May
11.34	0.8	Imani	Lansiquot	GBR	17.12.97	2 Jul
11.35	1.0	Stephanie	Kalu	NGR	5.8.93	1 Apr
11.35	0.9	Jade	Bailey	BAR	10.6.83	8 Apr
11.35	1.7	Kaylor	Harris	USA-J	31.10.98	28 Apr
11.35	0.0	Jenae	Ambrose	BAH	29.12.97	29 Apr
11.35	1.9	Brittany	Brown	USA	18.4.95	14 May
11.35	-0.4	Shalonda	Solomon	USA	19.12.85	17 May
11.35	0.5	Nedian	Vargas	VEN	5.9.94	3 Jun
11.36	1.9	Sabria	Hadley	USA	1.1.95	8 Apr
11.36	0.7	Quanera	Hayes	USA	7.3.92	28 Apr
11.36	0.9	Jacquelyn	Baldwin	USA	17.1.96	13 May
11.36	1.2	Flings	Owusu-Agyapong	GHA	16.10.88	14 May
11.36	0.4	Laura	Müller	GER	11.12.95	27 May
11.36	0.5	Stella	Akakpo	FRA	28.2.94	20 Jun
11.36	0.5	Gina	Bass	GAM	3.5.95	20 Jun
11.36	1.3	Chisato	Fukushima	JPN	27.6.88	9 Jul
11.37	0.9	Phylicia	George	CAN	16.11.87	8 Apr
11.37	1.5	Audrey	Alloh	ITA	21.7.87	25 May
11.37	0.5	Lorène	Bazolo	POR	4.5.83	3 Jun
11.37	0.9	Twanisha	Terry	USA-J	24.1.99	17 Jun
11.37	1.0	Olga	Safronova	KAZ	5.11.91	17 Jun
11.38	2.0	Jada	Baylark	USA	17.10.97	29 Apr
11.38	0.8	Rima	Kashafutdinova	KAZ	24.7.95	13 May
11.39	1.9	Kayla	White	USA	24.9.96	8 Apr
11.39	1.4	Samantha	Henry-Robinson	JAM	25.9.88	15 Apr
11.39A	-1.8	Lydia	Jele	BOT	22.6.90	13 May
11.39	1.2	Corinne	Humphreys	GBR	7.11.91	15 Jun
11.39	-0.2	Grigoría-Emmanouéla	Keramidá	GRE	25.8.90	17 Jun
11.39	0.7	Anna	Bongiorni	ITA	15.9.93	1 Jul
11.39	-0.1	Marika	Popowicz-Drapala	POL	28.4.88	21 Jul
11.40	2.0	Sabrina	Moore	USA	4.4.95	18 Mar
11.40	1.4	Kiara	Parker	USA	28.10.96	8 Apr
11.40	0.0	Brittney	Reese	USA	9.9.86	8 Apr
11.40	1.9	Brianne	Bethel	BAH-J	5.7.98	14 May
11.40	1.0	Dianna	Johnson	JAM	12.11.95	27 May
11.40	0.9	Kamaria	Durant	TTO	24.2.91	24 Jun
11.40	1.9	Cristina	Lara	ESP	5.8.95	22 Jul
11.41	-1.1	Aneka	Brissett	JAM-J	21.3.98	31 Mar
11.41A	-0.2	Alyssa	Conley	RSA	27.4.91	21 Apr
11.41	1.7	Karolina	Zagajewska	POL	5.4.93	26 May
11.41	0.2	Estela	García	ESP	20.3.89	27 May
11.41	0.0-	Lynna	Irby	USA-J	6.12.98	3 Jun
11.41	0.6	Ayodelé	Ikuesan	FRA	15.5.85	11 Jun
11.41	1.8	Lisa	Nippgen	GER	2.4.97	1 Jul
11.41	0.0	Kristina	Sivkova	RUS	28.2.97	2 Jul
11.41	-0.6	Lorraine	Ugen	GBR	22.8.91	16 Jul
11.42	2.0	Amy	Foster	IRL	2.10.88	19 Feb
11.42	1.5	Jerayah	Davis	USA	15.4.96	13 Apr
11.42	1.8	Breana	Norman	USA	14.9.92	15 Apr
11.42	0.8	Kendall	Baisden	USA	5.3.95	6 May
11.42A	0.0	Sunayna	Wahi	SUR	14.8.90	9 May
11.42	1.3	Ajla	Del Ponte	SUI	15.7.96	18 Jun
11.42	-0.7	Alexandra	Burghardt	GER	28.4.94	8 Jul
11.43	1.0	Kynnedy	Flannel	USA-Y	12.7.00	13 May
11.43	1.8	Jeneba	Tarmoh	USA	27.9.89	27 May
11.43	1.1	Kana	Ichikawa	JPN	14.1.91	4 Jun
11.43	0.9	Thelma	Davies	USA-Y	8.5.00	17 Jun
11.44	2.0	Sydney	Howells	USA		18 Mar
11.44	1.0	Cornelia	Halbheer	SUI	16.8.92	3 Jun
11.44	1.9	Lisa Marie	Kwaiye	GER	27.10.96	11 Jun
11.44	0.0	Madiea	Ghafoor	NED	9.9.92	9 Jul
		(196)	four at 11.45			

Wind assisted

Mark	Wind	Name		Nat	Born	Pos	Meet	Venue	Date
10.72	4.5	Tawanna	Meadows	USA	4.8.86	1		Lubbock	6 May
10.75	2.2		Thompson			1		Kingston	15 Apr
10.80	3.3	Tori	Bowie	USA	27.8.90	1h2		Clermont	15 Apr
10.83	4.5	Candyce	McGrone	USA	24.3.89	2		Lubbock	6 May
10.89	2.9	Deajah	Stevens	USA	19.5.95	1q2	NCAA-W	Austin	26 May
10.94	4.1		Baptiste			1h3		Clermont	15 Apr
10.94	4.5	Rebekka	Haase	GER	2.1.93	9h4		Clermont	15 Apr
10.94A	3.0	Destiny	Smith-Barnett	USA	26.7.96	1h3	MWC	Logan	12 May
10.94	2.1	Morolake	Akinosun	USA	17.5.94	1	Pre	Eugene	27 May
10.95	4.4	Alexandria	Anderson	USA	28.1.87	1		Austin	29 Apr
10.95	4.4		Ahye		10.4.92	2		Austin	29 Apr
10.96	2.6		Ahouré		23.8.87	1	FlaR	Gainesville	31 Mar
10.96	2.1		Ahouré			2	Pre	Eugene	27 May
10.96	2.6	Tatjana	Pinto	GER	2.7.92	1		Weinheim	27 May
10.97	5.2	Ariana	Washington	USA	27.8.96	1h3	NCAA-W	Austin	25 May
10.99	4.5	Stephanie	Kalu	NGR	5.8.93	3		Lubbock	6 May
11.00	4.5	Simone	Facey	JAM	7.5.85	10h4		Clermont	15 Apr
11.01	4.6	Naomi	Sedney	NED	17.12.94	1		Clermont	15 Apr
11.01	4.7	Deanna	Hill	USA	13.4.96	1h6	NCAA-W	Austin	25 May
11.02	2.9	Kerron	Stewart	JAM	16.4.84	1		Auburn	22 Apr
11.02	2.6	Lisa	Mayer	GER	2.5.96	2		Weinheim	27 May

Mark	Wind	Name		Nat	Born	Pos	Meet	Venue	Date
11.02	3.4	Ángela	Tenorio	ECU	27.1.96	1	SAmC	Asunción	23 Jun
11.04	4.5	Jamile	Samuel	NED	24.4.92	1h4		Clermont	15 Apr
11.05	4.6	Madiea	Ghafoor	NED	9.9.92	2		Clermont	15 Apr
11.05	2.6	Carina	Horn	RSA	9.3.89	1		Sotteville-lès-Rouen	7 Jul
11.06	5.8	Crystal	Emmanuel	CAN	27.11.91	1rB		Baton Rouge	29 Apr
11.06	2.8	Hannah	Cunliffe	USA	9.1.96	1h2	NCAA-W	Austin	25 May
11.08	2.6	Jonielle	Smith	JAM	30.1.96	1		Austin	15 Apr
11.09	4.6	Charonda	Williams	USA	27.3.87	3		Clermont	15 Apr
11.12	2.5	Lekeisha	Lawson	USA	3.6.87	1		Redlands	18 May
11.12	3.4	Ana Cláudia	Silva	BRA	6.11.88	2	SAmC	Asunción	23 Jun
11.15	2.3	Brenessa	Thompson	GUY	22.7.96	1	Johnson	Waco	22 Apr
11.15	3.9	Gabrielle	Thomas	USA	7.12.96	1		New Haven	7 May
11.15	3.0	Leya	Buchanan	CAN	17.8.96	1h1	Big 12	Lawrence	13 May
11.15	3.7	Alexis	Love	USA	24.4.91	1rB		Tampa	26 May
11.16	2.9	Lorène	Bazolo	POR	4.5.83	1	NC	Vagos	10 Jun
11.17	4.0	Tameka	Williams	SKN	31.8.89	1		San Marcos	31 Mar
11.17	2.1	Gayon	Evans	JAM	15.1.90	3		St. George's	8 Apr
11.18	4.6	Bianca	Williams	GBR	18.12.93	4		Clermont	15 Apr
11.18	2.9	Quanesha	Burks	USA	15.3.95	2		Auburn	22 Apr
11.18	3.4	Andrea	Purica	VEN	21.11.95	3	SAmC	Asunción	23 Jun
11.19	2.6	Shalonda	Solomon	USA	19.12.85	2	FlaR	Gainesville	31 Mar
11.19	5.2	Taylor	Bennett	USA	15.1.97	2h4	NCAA-W	Austin	25 May
11.19	4.7	Jada	Baylark	USA	17.10.97	2h6	NCAA-W	Austin	25 May
11.19	2.9	Kiara	Parker	USA	28.10.96	2q2	NCAA-W	Austin	26 May
11.20	4.3	Ornella	Livingston	JAM	19.5.91	1h2		Greensboro	15 Apr
11.20	2.3	Cambrya	Jones	USA	20.9.90	3h5		Clermont	15 Apr
11.20	2.6	Laura	Müller	GER	11.12.95	3		Weinheim	27 May
11.20	2.1	Dezerea	Bryant	USA	27.4.93	7	Pre	Eugene	27 May
11.21	4.4	Muna	Lee	USA	30.10.81	2		Houston	8 Apr
11.21	4.5	Cierra	White	USA	29.4.93	4		Lubbock	6 May
11.21	2.2	Joanna	Atkins	USA	31.1.89	2		Gresham	2 Jul
11.22	2.1	Cassondra	Hall	USA	23.9.97	2h3	NCAA-E	Lexington	25 May
11.23	2.6	Sarah	Atcho	SUI	1.6.95	1		Langenthal	25 May
11.23	5.2	Ky	Westbrook	USA	25.2.96	3h4	NCAA-W	Austin	25 May
11.23	2.6	Ezinne	Okparaebo	NOR	3.3.88	5		Weinheim	27 May
11.24	4.3	India	Brown	USA	29.1.96	1		Greensboro	6 May
11.24	3.0	Sydney	Conley	USA	11.12.93	2	Big 12	Lawrence	14 May
11.25	4.5		Liang Xiaojing	CHN	7.4.97	3h4		Clermont	15 Apr
11.25	2.8	Narcisa	Landázuri	ECU	25.11.92	3h1	SAmC	Asunción	23 Jun
11.26	2.6	Toea	Wisil	PNG	1.1.88	1h1		Brisbane	11 Feb
11.26	6.5	Nelda	Huggins	IVB	2.2.97	1		Wichita	15 Apr
11.26	2.1	Irene	Siragusa	ITA	23.6.93	1h1		Orvieto	28 May

Mark	Wind	Name		Nat	Born	Date
11.27	2.9	Flings	Owusu-Agyapong	GHA	16.10.88	22 Apr
11.28	4.5	Samantha	Henry-Robinson	JAM	25.9.88	15 Apr
11.28	4.7	Brianne	Bethel	BAH-J	5.7.98	25 May
11.29	4.6	Tahesia	Harrigan	IVB	15.2.82	15 Apr
11.29A	2.1	Alyssa	Conley	RSA	27.4.91	21 Apr
11.29	4.3	Shenel	Crooke	SKN	12.10.93	6 May
11.29	2.8	Tramesha	Hardy	USA	24.3.96	25 May
11.29	3.3	Jennifer	Montag	GER-J	11.2.98	1 Jul
11.30	3.7	Devynne	Charlton	BAH	26.11.95	15 Apr
11.30	5.2	Simone	Glenn	USA	16.5.96	25 May
11.30	3.7	Sabrina	Moore	USA	4.4.95	25 May
11.31	2.5	Lorraine	Ugen	GBR	22.8.91	15 Apr
11.31	3.2	Marije	van Hunenstijn	NED	2.3.95	15 Apr
11.31	4.2	Agata	Forkasiewicz	POL	13.1.94	20 May
11.31	2.1	Symone	Darius	USA-J	1.3.98	25 May
11.32	5.5	Saqukine	Cameron	JAM	21.8.96	15 Apr
11.32	w	Kailei	Collins	USA-Y	11.7.01	29 Apr
11.33	2.8	Arialis	Gandulla	CUB	22.6.95	15 Mar
11.33	2.2	Gina	Bass	GAM	3.5.95	22 Apr
11.33	3.7	Ngozi	Musa	SLE	11.8.96	6 May
11.33A	2.4	Micha	Auzenne	USA	10.6.95	12 May
11.34	6.1	Tamari	Davis	USA-Y	15.2.03	13 May
11.34	2.2	Kaylin	Whitney	USA-J	9.3.98	10 Jun
11.34	3.4	Nedian	Vargas	VEN	5.9.94	23 Jun
11.35	w	Kynnedy	Flannel	USA-Y	12.7.00	29 Apr
11.35	4.5	Mauricia	Prieto	TTO	20.11.95	6 May
11.35	3.9	Montell	Douglas	GBR	24.1.86	7 May
11.35	3.5	Amarachi	Pipi	GBR	26.11.95	13 May
11.35	2.4	Kristina	Sivkova	RUS	28.2.97	28 Jul
11.36A	2.5	Zaidatul	Husniah Zulkifli	MAS	20.8.93	4 Mar
11.36	2.8	Cristina	Lara	ESP	5.8.95	22 Jul
11.37	2.9	Dominique	Bullock	USA	14.5.96	22 Apr
11.37	2.9	Shannon	Ray	USA	31.12.95	22 Apr
11.37	2.6	Cornelia	Halbheer	SUI	16.8.92	25 May
11.38	4.6	Marissa	Kurtimah	CAN	25.5.94	14 May
11.38	4.7	Aaliyah	Birmmingham	USA	2.9.97	25 May
11.38	4.7	Rochene	Smith	JAM	19.4.95	25 May
11.38	2.1	Kana	Ichikawa	JPN	14.1.91	4 Jun
11.38	6.0	Miki	Sugiyama	JPN	-.95	10 Jun
11.39	3.7	Raven	Grant	USA	1.1.97	15 Apr
11.40	2.9	Diamond	Gause	USA	4.4.94	22 Apr

Best at low altitude

11.21 0.5 Horn 4 Gyulai Székesfehérvár 4 Jul

11.30 1.3 Landázuri 21 Nov 11.41 0.5 Conley 4 Jul

11.06w 3.8 Smith-Barnett 1h1 NCAA-W Austin 25 May

Drugs disqualification: 11.26 0.6 Olesya Povh ¶ UKR 18.10.87 (1h2) NC Kropyvnytskiy 6 Jul

JUNIORS

See main list for top 8 juniors. 11 performances by 8 women to 11.29. Additional marks and further juniors:

C Hill 11.24 2.0 1 Athens GA 6 May 11.29 1 Los Angeles 8 Apr

Mason 11.27 0.9 1 NewBal Greensboro 17 Jun

Mark	Wind	Name		Nat	Born	Pos	Meet	Venue	Date
11.30	1.6	Briana	Williams	JAM-Y	21.3.02	2	NC-y	Kingston	24 Jun
11.33	1.7	Keshia	Kwadwo (10)	GER	10.7.99	1		Ulm	4 Aug
11.35	1.7	Kaylor	Harris	USA	31.10.98	1h2		Waco	28 Apr

Mark	Wind	Name		Nat	Born	Pos	Meet	Venue	Date
11.37	0.9	Twanisha	Terry	USA	24.1.99	2	New Bal	Greensboro	17 Jun
11.40	1.9	Brianne	Bethel	BAH	5.7.98	2		Houston	14 May
11.41	-1.1	Aneka	Brissett	JAM	21.3.98	1	N.Sch	Kingston	31 Mar
11.41	0.0-	Lynna	Irby	USA	6.12.98	1		Bloomington	3 Jun
11.43	1.0	Kynnedy	Flannel	USA-Y	12.7.00	1		Austin	13 May
11.43	0.9	Thelma	Davies	USA-Y	8.5.00	3	New Bal	Greensboro	17 Jun
11.46	0.8	Katrin	Fehm	GER	16.4.98	3		Weinheim	27 May
11.46	0.9	Tamara	Clark	USA	9.1.99	4	New Bal	Greensboro	17 Jun
11.47	1.1	Kaylin	Whitney (20)	USA	9.3.98	7		Montverde	10 Jun
Wind assisted									
11.28	4.7	Brianne	Bethel	BAH-J	5.7.98	4h6	NCAA-W	Austin	25 May
11.29	3.3	Jennifer	Montag	GER	11.2.98	1		Mannheim	1 Jul
11.31	2.1	Symone	Darius	USA	1.3.98	3h3	NCAA-E	Lexington	25 May
11.32	w	Kailei	Collins	USA-Y	11.7.01	1		Houston	29 Apr
11.34	6.1	Tamari	Davis	USA-Y	15.2.03	1		Bradenton	13 May
11.34	2.2	Kaylin	Whitney	USA	9.3.98	3h2		Montverde	10 Jun
11.35	w	Kynnedy	Flannel	USA-Y	12.7.00	2		Houston	29 Apr
11.42	4.5	Omotayo	Abolaji	NGR	12.6.98	6		Lubbock	6 May

150 METRES STRAIGHT

Mark	Wind	Name		Nat	Born	Pos	Meet	Venue	Date
16.30	0.1	Tori	Bowie	USA	27.8.90	1		Boston	4 Jun
16.80	0.1	Shalonda	Solomon	USA	19.12.85	2		Boston	4 Jun
16.84	0.1	Tiffany	Townsend	USA	14.6.89	3		Boston	4 Jun

200 METRES

Mark	Wind	Name		Nat	Born	Pos	Meet	Venue	Date
21.77	1.5	Tori	Bowie	USA	27.8.90	1	Pre	Eugene	27 May
21.88	0.1	Shaunae	Miller-Uibo	BAH	15.4.94	1	WK-DLF	Zürich	24 Aug
21.91	1.5		Miller-Uibo			2	Pre	Eugene	27 May
21.98	1.5	Elaine	Thompson	JAM	28.6.92	3	Pre	Eugene	27 May
22.00	0.1		Thompson			2	WK-DLF	Zürich	24 Aug
22.02	1.1	Kyra	Jefferson	USA	23.9.94	1	NCAA	Eugene	10 Jun
22.05	0.8	Dafne	Schippers	NED	15.6.92	1	WCh	London (OS)	11 Aug
22.08	0.8	Marie Josée	Ta Lou	CIV	18.11.88	2	WCh	London (OS)	11 Aug
22.09	-0.3		Bowie			1	Jones	Gainesville	28 Apr
22.09	1.5	Deajah	Stevens	USA	19.5.95	1	Pac 12	Eugene	14 May
22.09	0.1		Thompson			1		Kingston	20 May
22.09	0.1		Ta Lou			3	WK-DLF	Zürich	24 Aug
22.10	-0.5		Schippers			1	Athl	Lausanne	6 Jul
22.15	0.8		Miller-Uibo			3	WCh	London (OS)	11 Aug
22.16	-0.5		Ta Lou			2	Athl	Lausanne	6 Jul
22.19	-2.3		Thompson			1	DL	Doha	5 May
22.21	0.0		Miller-Uibo			1	NC	Nassau	24 Jun
22.22	0.8	Dina	Asher-Smith	GBR	4.12.95	4	WCh	London (OS)	11 Aug
22.25	-0.2		Ta Lou			1	Herc	Monaco	21 Jul
22.29	1.4		Schippers			1	Clay	Azusa	14 Apr
22.30	1.5		Schippers			4	Pre	Eugene	27 May
22.30	-2.5		Stevens			1	NC	Sacramento	25 Jun
22.31	-0.6		Stevens			1	MSR	Torrance	15 Apr
22.31	1.7		Stevens			1s2	NCAA	Eugene	8 Jun
22.31	1.4		Schippers			1	Bisl	Oslo	15 Jun
22.33	1.5	Allyson	Felix	USA	18.11.85	5	Pre	Eugene	27 May
22.34	-0.5		Jefferson			3	Athl	Lausanne	6 Jul
22.36	0.1		Schippers			4	WK-DLF	Zürich	24 Aug
22.37	1.5		Ta Lou			6	Pre	Eugene	27 May
22.39	1.1	Ariana (30/10)	Washington	USA	27.8.96	2	NCAA	Eugene	10 Jun
22.41	1.5	Deanna	Hill	USA	13.4.96	2	Pac 12	Eugene	14 May
22.42	-0.3	Mujinga	Kambundji	SUI	17.6.92	1	NC	Zürich	22 Jul
22.46	0.2	Shericka	Jackson	JAM	15.7.94	3	ISTAF	Berlin	27 Aug
22.47	0.7	Shakima	Wimbley	USA	23.4.95	1rB	Jones	Gainesville	28 Apr
22.50	0.0	Michelle-Lee	Ahye	TTO	10.4.92	1	NC	Port of Spain	25 Jun
22.50	0.0	Crystal	Emmanuel	CAN	27.11.91	1		Cork	18 Jul
22.54	0.6	Kimberlyn	Duncan	USA	2.8.91	1		St-Martin	13 May
22.54A	-1.0	Ashley	Henderson	USA	4.12.95	1	MWC	Logan	13 May
22.54	1.5	Jenna	Prandini	USA	20.11.92	7	Pre	Eugene	27 May
22.55	-0.3	Quanera (20)	Hayes	USA	7.3.92	2	Jones	Gainesville	28 Apr
22.55	1.7	Brittany	Brown	USA	18.4.95	2s2	NCAA	Eugene	8 Jun
22.56	0.4	Gabrielle	Thomas	USA	7.12.96	1q3	NCAA-E	Lexington	27 May

Mark	Wind	Name		Nat	Born	Pos	Meet	Venue	Date
22.56	-0.3	Léa	Sprunger	SUI	5.3.90	2	NC	Zürich	22 Jul
22.58	1.5	Alexandria	Anderson	USA	28.1.87	1		Austin	29 Apr
22.59	0.2	Phyllis	Francis	USA	4.5.92	4	ISTAF	Berlin	27 Aug
22.60	1.6	Veronica	Campbell-Brown	JAM	15.5.82	1	FlaR	Gainesville	30 Mar
22.60	1.0	Felicia	Brown	USA	27.10.93	1		St. George's	8 Apr
22.60	1.5	Hannah	Cunliffe	USA	9.1.96	3	Pac 12	Eugene	14 May
22.61	1.4	Destiny	Carter	USA	9.10.92	1h1	NCAA-E	Lexington	26 May
22.64	0.5	Shalonda	Solomon	USA	19.12.85	3		Kingston	20 May
		(30)							
22.64	1.7	Lisa	Mayer	GER	2.5.96	1		Weinheim	27 May
22.65	-0.8	Laura	Müller	GER	11.12.95	1	NC	Erfurt	9 Jul
22.68	1.8	Candace	Hill	USA-J	11.2.99	1		Los Angeles	8 Apr
22.68	1.1	Murielle	Ahouré	CIV	23.8.87	1	DL	Stockholm	18 Jun
22.69	1.4	Desiree	Henry	GBR	26.8.95	2	Clay	Azusa	14 Apr
22.71	1.0	Tynia	Gaither	BAH	16.3.93	2		St. George's	8 Apr
22.71	0.8	Shashalee	Forbes	JAM	10.5.96	1	NC	Kingston	25 Jun
22.72	-0.3	Tiffany	Townsend	USA	14.6.89	3	Jones	Gainesville	28 Apr
22.74	-0.3	Joanna	Atkins	USA	31.1.89	4	Jones	Gainesville	28 Apr
22.74	0.8	Simone	Facey	JAM	7.5.85	2	NC	Kingston	25 Jun
		(40)							
22.76	1.1	Rebekka	Haase	GER	2.1.93	3	DL	Stockholm	18 Jun
22.77	1.5	Natalliah	Whyte	JAM	9.8.97	2h1	SEC	Columbia SC	11 May
22.77	0.2	Semoy	Hackett	TTO	27.11.88	1		Freeport	22 Jul
22.79	1.5	Kendall	Ellis	USA	8.3.96	1		Los Angeles	18 Mar
22.79	1.1	Aaliyah	Brown	USA	6.1.95	4	NCAA	Eugene	10 Jun
22.80	0.2	Kortnei	Johnson	USA	11.8.97	2q1	NCAA-E	Lexington	27 May
22.80	1.2	Jada	Martin	USA	8.6.95	2q2	NCAA-E	Lexington	27 May
22.80	-0.3	Sada	Williams	BAR	1.12.97	1	NC	Bridgetown	25 Jun
22.81	1.1	Viktoriya	Zyabkina	KAZ	4.9.92	1	NCp	Almaty	14 May
22.81	1.0	Shania	Collins	USA	14.11.96	2h2	NCAA-E	Lexington	26 May
		(50)							
22.81	-2.9	Katarina	Johnson-Thompson	GBR	9.1.93	1H5	Hypo	Götzis	27 May
22.82	1.1	Ivet	Lalova-Collio	BUL	18.5.84	4	DL	Stockholm	18 Jun
22.83	-0.3	Bianca	Williams	GBR	18.12.93	5	Jones	Gainesville	28 Apr
22.84	1.3	Jaevin	Reed	USA-J	2.5.98	1rB		San Antonio	25 Mar
22.84	0.3	Anthonique	Strachan	BAH	22.8.93	3		Kingston	10 Jun
22.84	1.7	Justine	Palframan	RSA	4.11.93	1		Kortrijk	8 Jul
22.86	0.4	Kianna	Gray	USA	30.12.96	2q3	NCAA-E	Lexington	27 May
22.86	1.3	Finette	Agyapong	GBR	1.2.97	1s1	EU23	Bydgoszcz	15 Jul
22.87	1.3	Blessing	Okagbare	NGR	9.10.88	1		Lubbock	28 Apr
22.87	1.8	Taylor	Bennett	USA	15.1.97	1		Lubbock	28 Apr
		(60)							
22.88	1.0	Jura	Levy	JAM	4.11.90	3		St. George's	8 Apr
22.88	-0.1	Jasmine	Camacho-Quinn	PUR	21.8.96	2h6	NCAA-E	Lexington	26 May
22.88	0.4	Sabria	Hadley	USA	1.1.95	4q3	NCAA-E	Lexington	27 May
22.89A	1.8	Najia	Hudspeth	USA	25.10.96	1h2	MWC	Logan	12 May
22.89	0.5	Nercely	Soto	VEN	23.8.90	1	Bol G	Santa Marta	22 Nov
22.90A	0.7	Janet	Amponsah	GHA	12.4.93	1	Conf USA	El Paso	14 May
22.90	1.5	Makenzie	Dunmore	USA	7.10.97	5	Pac 12	Eugene	14 May
22.90	1.3	Sarah	Atcho	SUI	1.6.95	2	EU23	Bydgoszcz	15 Jul
22.91A	1.8	Destiny	Smith-Barnett	USA	26.7.96	2h2	MWC	Logan	12 May
22.92A	0.7	Tobi	Amusan	NGR	23.4.97	2	Conf USA	El Paso	14 May
		(70)							
22.92	1.4	Cassondra	Hall	USA	23.9.97	2h1	NCAA-E	Lexington	26 May
22.92	0.2	India	Brown	USA	29.1.96	4q1	NCAA-E	Lexington	27 May
22.93	0.1	Shimayra	Williams	JAM	2.12.95	2		Kingston	8 Apr
22.93	1.5	Elexis	Guster	USA	7.7.94	6	Pac 12	Eugene	14 May
22.93	1.5	Vitória	Rosa	BRA	12.1.96	1	NC	São Bernardo do Campo	11 Jun
22.93	-0.8	Nadine	Gonska	GER	23.1.90	3	NC	Erfurt	9 Jul
22.94A	1.5	Alyssa	Conley	RSA	27.4.91	1	NC	Potchefstroom	22 Apr
22.94	1.1	Brenessa	Thompson	GUY	22.7.96	1h2	SEC	Columbia SC	11 May
22.94	1.2	Jodean	Williams	JAM	11.11.93	1h3	NC	Kingston	24 Jun
22.94	0.0	Shannon	Hylton	GBR	19.12.96	1	NC	Birmingham	2 Jul
		(80)							
22.95	0.4	Shayla	Sanders	USA	6.1.94	2	FlaR	Gainesville	31 Mar
22.95	1.5	Amarachi	Pipi	GBR	26.11.95	1		Norman	22 Apr
22.95	1.7	Ofonime	Odiong	BRN	13.3.97	1	Isl.Sol	Baku	18 May
22.95	0.5	Candyce	McGrone	USA	24.3.89	5		Kingston	20 May
22.95	0.3	Dezerea	Bryant	USA	27.4.93	4		Kingston	10 Jun
22.95	1.5	Rosângela	Santos	BRA	20.12.90	2	NC	São Bernardo do Campo	11 Jun
22.96	-1.4	Irene	Siragusa	ITA	23.6.93	1	WUG	Taipei	26 Aug

Mark	Wind	Name		Nat	Born	Pos	Meet	Venue	Date
22.97	0.5	Kevona	Davis	JAM-Y	20.12.01	1	NC-y	Kingston	24 Jun
22.97	0.0	Kayelle	Clarke	TTO	28.2.96	2	NC	Port of Spain	25 Jun
22.98	1.3	Jacquelyn (90)	Baldwin	USA	17.1.96	2h5	NCAA-E	Lexington	26 May
22.98	0.0	Gina	Bass	GAM	3.5.95	1		Bruay-la-Buissière	4 Jul
22.99	1.5	Teahna	Daniels	USA	27.3.97	2		Austin	29 Apr
23.00	1.5	Ella	Nelson	AUS	10.5.94	1		Canberra	12 Mar
23.00	1.6	Symone	Mason	USA-J	31.8.99	1	Hayes	Jacksonville	18 Mar
23.00	-0.3	Charonda	Williams	USA	27.3.87	7	Jones	Gainesville	28 Apr
23.00	-0.6	María	Belibasáki	GRE	19.6.91	1		Árgos Orestikó	10 Jun
23.00	1.7	Shavine	Hodges	JAM	22.10.91	2		Kortrijk	8 Jul
23.01	1.9	Courtney	Blanden	USA	12.3.96	1		Auburn	22 Apr
23.01	2.0	Simone	Glenn	USA	16.5.96	2h4	NCAA-W	Austin	26 May
23.03	1.3	Kadecia (100)	Baird	GUY	24.2.95	2rB		San Antonio	25 Mar
23.03A	2.0	Kabange	Mupopo	ZAM	21.9.92	1		Lusaka	8 Apr
23.03	-0.8	Kendall	Baisden	USA	5.3.95	4h2	NC	Sacramento	24 Jun

Mark	Wind	Name		Nat	Born	Date
23.04	-0.2	Gina	Lückenkemper	GER	21.11.96	3 Jun
23.04	-1.0	Maya	Bruney	GBR-J	24.2.98	22 Jul
23.05	1.2	Jenae	Ambrose	BAH	29.12.97	27 May
23.05	1.9	Estelle	Raffai	FRA-J	6.2.98	18 Jun
23.06	0.4	Shauna	Helps	JAM	23.10.96	31 Mar
23.06	2.0	Tramesha	Hardy	USA	24.3.96	14 May
23.07	-0.2	Kori	Carter	USA	3.6.92	17 Mar
23.07	1.3	Briyahna	Desrosiers	USA	11.3.96	25 Mar
23.07	1.9	Diamond	Spaulding	USA	29.9.96	8 Jun
23.07	0.2	Nediam	Vargas	VEN	5.9.94	17 Jun
23.07	0.4		Huang Guifen	CHN	20.8.97	4 Sep
23.08	0.2	Lorène	Bazolo	POR	4.5.83	14 Jul
23.09	0.0	Agata	Zupin	SLO-J	17.3.98	10 Jun
23.11	1.3	Anastasia	Le-Roy	JAM	11.9.87	11 Mar
23.11	0.9	Olga	Safronova	KAZ	5.11.91	13 Jun
23.12	1.1	Stephenie Ann	McPherson	JAM	25.11.88	27 May
23.12	0.0	Kamaria	Durant	TTO	24.2.91	25 Jun
23.12	1.3	Sindija	Buksa	LAT	14.12.97	15 Jul
23.13	1.5	Toea	Wisil	PNG	1.1.88	12 Mar
23.13	1.0	Diamond	Gause	USA	4.4.94	26 May
23.13	0.7	Estela	García	ESP	20.3.89	23 Jun
23.13	0.7	Kristina	Timanovskaya	BLR	19.11.96	6 Jul
23.13	-0.8	Lara	Matheis	GER	2.8.92	9 Jul
23.13	1.7	Kai	Selvon	TTO	13.4.92	15 Jul
23.13	1.3	Fanny	Peltier	FRA	25.5.97	15 Jul
23.14	1.6	Cierra	White	USA	29.4.93	14 May
23.14	2.0	A'Keyla	Mitchell	USA	25.11.95	26 May
23.14	-2.0	Gloria	Hooper	ITA	3.3.92	2 Jul
23.15	-1.4	Gunta	Latiseva-Cudare	LAT	9.3.95	26 Aug
23.16	1.9	De'Shalyn	Jones	USA	5.1.96	14 May
23.16	-0.3	Cornelia	Halbheer	SUI	16.8.92	22 Jul
23.18	1.3	Gayon	Evans	JAM	15.1.90	11 Mar
23.19	1.7	Roneisha	McGregor	JAM	9.10.97	1 Apr
23.20	1.3	Yana	Kachur	UKR	13.1.97	15 Jul
23.21	1.6	Twanisha	Terry	USA-J	24.1.99	18 Mar
23.21	1.5	Destinee	Gause	USA	4.4.94	25 Mar
23.21	0.6	Tamari	Davis	USA-Y	15.2.03	26 May
23.21	1.0	Marie	Veale	USA	17.11.94	26 May
23.22	1.9	Takyera	Roberson	USA-J	7.5.98	22 Apr
23.22	1.9	Jonielle	Smith	JAM	30.1.96	22 Apr
23.22	2.0	Payton	Stumbaugh	USA	29.11.95	11 May
23.22	1.0	Zakiya	Denoon	TTO	23.1.95	3 Jun
23.22		Yekaterina	Renzhina	RUS	18.10.94	16 Jun
23.22	0.2	Cristina	Lara	ESP	5.8.95	17 Jun
23.22	0.2	Mariely	Sánchez	DOM	30.12.88	14 Jul
23.22A		Narcisa	Landázuri	ECU	25.11.92	29 Oct
23.23	0.4	Mikiah	Brisco	USA	14.7.96	8 Apr
23.23	0.2	Precious	Hitchcock	USA	22.9.94	26 May
23.23	-0.7	Cheriece	Hylton	GBR	19.12.96	10 Jun
23.24	0.2	Cameron	Pettigrew	USA	17.4.95	13 May
23.24	1.6	Iza Daniela	Flores	MEX	6.5.94	18 Jun
23.25	1.5	Sharika	Nelvis	USA	10.5.90	29 Apr
23.25	1.0	Tameka	Williams	SKN	31.8.89	5 May
23.25A	0.7	Khadijah	Valentine	CAN	1.2.94	14 May
23.25	-0.6	Grigoría-Emmanouéla	Keramidá	GRE	25.8.90	10 Jun
23.26	0.2	Zola	Golden	USA	20.6.97	25 Mar
23.26	0.5	Riley	Day	AUS-Y	30.3.00	29 Mar
23.26	0.2	Akua	Obeng-Akrofi	GHA	26.6.96	27 May
23.26	0.4	Savannah	Roberson	USA	15.1.96	27 May
23.26	-0.8	Gabriele	Cunningham	USA-J	22.2.98	24 Jun
23.26	-0.8	Jessica-Bianca	Wessolly	GER	11.12.96	9 Jul
23.26	0.7	Maroussia	Pare	FRA	18.7.96	15 Jul
23.26	0.2	Kaylin	Whitney	USA-J	9.3.98	16 Jul
23.27	-0.6	Reyare	Thomas	TTO	23.11.87	4 Jun
23.27	0.3	Carolin	Schäfer	GER	5.12.91	24 Jun
23.27	0.0	Jodie	Williams	GBR	28.9.93	18 Jul
23.27	0.9	Ashlan	Best	CAN-J	11.2.99	22 Jul
23.27	-0.7	Anna	Kielbasinska	POL	26.6.90	19 Feb
23.27A		Ángela	Tenorio	ECU	27.1.96	29 Oct
23.28	1.4	Olivia	Ekponé	USA	5.1.93	8 Apr
23.28	0.7	Robin	Reynolds	USA	22.2.94	28 Apr
23.28	1.7	Karimah	Davis	USA	23.11.98	5 May
23.28	0.5	Rebekah	Smith	USA-J	1.5.98	12 May
23.28	0.7	Jada	Baylark	USA	17.10.97	26 May
23.28	-2.9	Erica	Bougard	USA	26.7.93	27 May
23.28	-0.8	Sha'Carri	Richardson	USA-Y	25.3.00	24 Jun
23.28	0.2	Anyika	Onuora	GBR	28.10.84	14 Jul
23.28	0.0		Yuan Qiqi	CHN	26.10.95	5 Sep
23.29	1.8	Kiana	Horton	USA	29.1.97	28 Apr
23.29	0.4	Tessa	van Schagen	NED	2.2.94	10 Jun
23.29	0.4	Jess (183)	Thornton	AUS-J	12.4.98	3 Dec

Indoors

Mark	Name		Nat	Born	Pos	Meet	Venue	Date
22.53	Hannah	Cunliffe	USA	9.1.96	2	NCAA	College Station	11 Mar
22.94	Ashley	Spencer	USA	8.6.93	1		Lincoln	4 Feb
22.94	Diamond	Spaulding	USA	29.9.96	3h1	NCAA	College Station	10 Mar
23.00	Danyel	White	USA-J	10.2.98	4h1	NCAA	College Station	10 Mar
23.13	Anna	Kielbasinska	POL	26.6.90				19 Feb
23.26	Kamaria	Brown	USA	21.12.92				18 Feb

Wind assisted

Mark	Wind	Name		Nat	Born	Pos	Meet	Venue	Date
21.90	3.1		Miller-Uibo			1		Clermont	15 Apr
22.16	2.5		Stevens			1q1	NCAA-W	Austin	27 May
22.21	3.7	Shalonda	Solomon	USA	19.12.85	1		Montverde	10 Jun
22.30	2.7	Brittany	Brown	USA	18.4.95	1	Big 10	University Park	14 May
22.30	3.8	Deanna	Hill	USA	13.4.96	1q3	NCAA-W	Austin	27 May
22.31	2.1		Stevens			1h2	NCAA-W	Austin	26 May
22.33	3.8		Brown			2q3	NCAA-W	Austin	27 May
22.35	2.5	Ashley	Henderson	USA	4.12.95	2q1	NCAA-W	Austin	27 May
22.39	3.3	Candyce	McGrone	USA	24.3.89	1		Lubbock	6 May
22.41	2.2	Kimberlyn	Duncan	USA	2.8.91	1		Baton Rouge	22 Apr

Mark	Wind	Name		Nat	Born	Pos	Meet	Venue	Date
22.47	3.4	Taylor	Bennett	USA	15.1.97	1	Big 12	Lawrence	14 May
22.49	3.7	Semoy	Hackett	TTO	27.11.88	2		Montverde	10 Jun
22.50	2.4	Kortnei	Johnson	USA	11.8.97	1h5	SEC	Columbia SC	11 May
22.53	3.0	Tatjana	Pinto	GER	2.7.92	1rB		Clermont	15 Apr
22.54	3.1	Joanna	Atkins	USA	31.1.89	2		Clermont	15 Apr
22.54	3.7	Charonda	Williams	USA	27.3.87	3		Montverde	10 Jun
22.55	2.7	Danyel	White	USA-J	10.2.98	1		San Antonio	25 Mar
22.58	3.0	Rebekka	Haase	GER	2.1.93	1rC		Clermont	15 Apr
22.59	2.7	Brenessa	Thompson	GUY	22.7.96	2		San Antonio	25 Mar
22.60A	3.2	Tobi	Amusan	NGR	23.4.97	1		El Paso	22 Apr
22.60	2.7	Aaliyah	Brown	USA	6.1.95	1q2	NCAA-W	Austin	27 May
22.61	3.7	Kaylin	Whitney	USA-J	9.3.98	4		Montverde	10 Jun
22.64	2.1	Diamond	Spaulding	USA	29.9.96	1h3	NCAA-W	Austin	26 May
22.67	2.8	Vitoria Cristina	Rosa	BRA	12.1.96	1	SAmC	Asunción	25 Jun
22.69	3.0	Cambrya	Jones	USA	20.9.90	2rB		Clermont	15 Apr
22.76	2.2	Jada	Martin	USA	8.6.95	2		Baton Rouge	22 Apr
22.78	3.5	Natasha	Hastings	USA	23.7.86	1	TexR	Austin	1 Apr
22.78A	3.2	Stephanie	Kalu	NGR	5.8.93	2		El Paso	22 Apr
22.81	2.7	Savannah	Roberson	USA	15.1.96	2	Big 10	University Park	14 May
22.82	2.1	Alexis	Love	USA	24.4.91	1rB		Tampa	26 May
22.83	4.8	Nadine	Visser	NED	9.2.95	1rD		Clermont	15 Apr
22.83	3.4	Amarachi	Pipi	GBR	26.11.95	2	Big 12	Lawrence	14 May
22.85	2.5	Kendra	Harrison	USA	18.9.92	1		Austin	15 Apr
22.89	2.3	KaTia	Seymour	USA	3.10.97	1h1		Bradenton	5 May
22.90	2.8	Ángela	Tenorio	ECU	27.1.96	2	SAmC	Asunción	25 Jun
22.91	4.8	Zola	Golden	USA	20.6.97	2h2	Big 12	Lawrence	13 May
22.92	2.1	Tramesha	Hardy	USA	24.3.96	3h3	NCAA-W	Austin	26 May
22.93	2.2	Gunta	Latiseva-Cudare	LAT	9.3.95	1h5	WUG	Taipei	25 Aug
22.94	3.5	Jenae	Ambrose	BAH	29.12.97	1rB		Austin	15 Apr
22.94	3.0	Madiea	Ghafoor	NED	9.9.92	2rC		Clermont	15 Apr
22.94	2.6	Kayelle	Clarke	TTO	28.2.96	1h1	NC	Port of Spain	25 Jun
22.95	2.7	Teahna	Daniels	USA	27.3.97	4q2	NCAA-W	Austin	27 May
22.95	2.8	Nedian	Vargas	VEN	5.9.94	3	SAmC	Asunción	25 Jun
22.96	w	Sydney	McLaughlin	USA-J	7.8.99	1		Egg Harbor	3 Jun
22.97	2.1	English	Gardner	USA	22.4.92	4rB	MSR	Torrance	15 Apr
22.98	3.3	Cierra	White	USA	29.4.93	2		Lubbock	6 May
22.98	3.8	Simone	Glenn	USA	16.5.96	4q3	NCAA-W	Austin	27 May
22.99	3.5	Javianne	Oliver	USA	26.12.94	2rB		Austin	15 Apr
22.99	2.7	Aaliyah	Barnes	USA	17.2.95	3	Big 10	University Park	14 May
23.00	3.6	Hannah	Jackson	USA	28.2.97	1		Houston	8 Apr
23.00	3.8	A'Keyla	Mitchell	USA	25.11.95	5q3	NCAA-W	Austin	27 May

Mark	Wind	Name		Nat	Born	Date
23.01	2.6	Shamier	Little	USA	20.3.95	22 Apr
23.01	2.4	Diamond	Gause	USA	4.4.94	11 May
23.04	4.9		Wei Yongli	CHN	11.10.91	15 Apr
23.04	2.7	Carmiesha	Cox	BAH	16.5.95	14 May
23.04	3.8	Estela	García	ESP	20.3.89	22 Jul
23.05	2.3	Devynne	Charlton	BAH	26.11.95	15 Apr
23.05	2.1	Kiara	Parker	USA	28.10.96	26 May
23.06	3.3	Kiana	Horton	USA	29.1.97	13 May
23.06	3.4	Tameka	Williams	SKN	31.8.89	18 Jun
23.06	2.8	Nercely	Soto	VEN	23.8.90	25 Jun
23.08	2.5	Naomi	Sedney	NED	17.12.94	30 Mar
23.08	3.4	Lekeisha	Lawson	USA	3.6.87	18 May
23.10	2.8	LaTessa	Johnson	USA	13.4.97	14 May
23.10	2.1	Lara	Matheis	GER	2.8.92	27 May
23.11	3.4	Toea	Wisil	PNG	1.1.88	11 Feb
23.11	3.8	Jada	Baylark	USA	17.10.97	27 May
23.11	3.7	Robin	Reynolds	USA	22.2.94	10 Jun
23.12	2.6	De'Shalyn	Jones	USA	5.1.96	18 Mar
23.12	2.5	Kamaria	Brown	USA	21.12.92	15 Apr
23.12	2.8	Brianne	Bethel	BAH-J	5.7.98	14 May
23.12	3.2	Alisha	Rees	GBR-J	16.4.99	3 Jun
23.13	4.3	NaAsha	Robinson	USA	23.1.97	13 May
23.14	3.2	Zoey	Clark	GBR	25.10.94	3 Jun
23.15	2.3	Cornelia	Halbheer	SUI	16.8.92	3 Jun
23.16	4.8	Argyana	Bolton	USA		27 May
23.16	2.8	Grigoría-Emmanouéla	Keramidá	GRE	25.8.90	18 Jun
23.16	2.9	Kyra	Constantine	CAN-J	1.8.98	18 Jun
23.17	2.7	Sydney	Howells	USA		25 Mar
23.17	2.4	Destinee	Gause	USA	4.4.94	11 May
23.18	3.6	Tori	Williams	USA	14.12.94	8 Apr
23.18	4.6	Sha'Carri	Richardson	USA-Y	25.3.00	29 Apr
23.20	2.7	Chloe	Abbott	USA-J	25.7.98	14 May
23.20	6.1	Jordan	Lavender	USA	23.7.93	10 Jun
23.20	2.6	Reyare	Thomas	TTO	23.11.87	25 Jun
23.21	2.6	Ashley	Kelly	IVB	25.3.91	25 Jun
23.21	2.8	Natassha	McDonald	CAN	27.1.97	9 Jul
23.22	3.2	Rachel	Misher	USA	4.2.97	28 Apr
23.22	4.8	Leya	Buchanan	CAN	17.8.96	13 May
23.22	3.2	Nicky	van Leeuveren	NED	25.5.90	8 Jul
23.24	2.8	Chelsea	Francis	USA	14.10.96	14 May
23.24	3.3	Libania	Grenot	ITA	12.7.83	26 May
23.25	2.5	Anna	Kielbasinska	POL	26.6.90	17 Jun
23.26	4.3	Tamdra	Lawrence	USA	1.1.97	13 May
23.27	3.5	Lexis	Lambert	USA	12.5.94	15 Apr
23.27	-0.7	Anna	Kielbasinska	POL	26.6.90	23 Jul
23.28	2.9	Michae	Harriott	JAM-Y	1.6.00	1 Apr
23.28	3.3	Maria	Omokwe	NGR-J	13.12.98	11 Jun

Hand timing

Mark	Wind	Name		Nat	Born	Pos	Meet	Venue	Date
22.6	0.4	María	Belibasáki	GRE	19.6.91	1	ET	Villeneuve d'Ascq	25 Jun
22.8	0.4	Anna	Kielbasinska	POL	26.6.90	2	ET	Villeneuve d'Ascq	25 Jun

Mark	Wind	Name		Nat	Born	Date
22.9	0.0	Gladys	Igbinosun	NGR	23.7.93	1 Dec
23.1	0.4	Kristina	Timanovskaya	BLR	19.11.96	25 Jun
23.1	0.4	Estela	García	ESP	20.3.89	25 Jun

Best at low altitude

Mark	Wind	Name	Pos	Meet	Venue	Date
22.66	2.0	Henderson	1h4	NCAA-W	Austin	26 May
23.03	1.2	Conley	2	GS	Ostrava	28 Jun
23.24w	2.7	Hudspeth				22 Apr
23.33w	2.1	Smith-Barnett				26 May

WOMEN 2017

JUNIORS

See main list for top 4 juniors (& 4 wa). 10 performances by 7 women (1 indoor) to 23.05. Additional marks:

C Hill									
	22.76	0.5	1	Atlanta	17 May	22.89	0.4 1	Athens GA	6 May
	22.80	1.4	1	Greensboro	14 May	22.72w	3.7 1	Columbia SC	25 Mar

Mark	Wind	Name		Nat	Born	Pos	Meet	Venue	Date
23.04	-1.0	Maya	Bruney	GBR	24.2.98	1	EJ	Grosseto	22 Jul
23.05	1.9	Estelle	Raffai	FRA	6.2.98	1		Antony	18 Jun
23.09	0.0	Agata	Zupin	SLO	17.3.98	1		Kranj	10 Jun
23.21	1.6	Twanisha	Terry	USA	24.1.99	2	Hayes	Jacksonville	18 Mar
23.21	0.6	Tamari	Davis	USA-Y	15.2.03	1	Pre	Eugene	26 May
23.22	1.9	Takyera	Roberson (10)	USA	7.5.98	4		Auburn	22 Apr
23.26	0.5	Riley	Day	AUS-Y	30.3.00	1	NC-y	Sydney	29 Mar
23.26	-0.8	Gabriele	Cunningham	USA	22.2.98	2	NC-j	Sacramento	24 Jun
23.26	0.2	Kaylin	Whitney	USA	9.3.98	1rB		Padova	16 Jul
23.27	0.9	Ashlan	Best	CAN	11.2.99	1	PAm-J	Trujillo	22 Jul
23.28	0.5	Rebekah	Smith	USA	1.5.98	1h3	ACC	Atlanta	12 May
23.28	-0.8	Sha'Carri	Richardson	USA-Y	25.3.00	3	NC-j	Sacramento	24 Jun
23.29	0.4	Jess	Thornton	AUS	12.4.98	1		Sydney	3 Dec
23.32	1.6	Kishawna	Wallace	JAM-Y	12.11.00	1		Kirkvine	14 Jan
23.32	1.6	Alisha	Rees	GBR	16.4.99	1		Manchester	16 Aug
23.34	2.0	Sashieka	Steele (20)	JAM-Y	8.11.02	2y		Kirkvine	14 Jan
23.34	0.4	Kynnedy	Flannel	USA-Y	12.7.00	1		Austin	13 May
23.34	1.2	Kayla	Davis	USA-Y	21.12.03	1		Greensboro	24 Jun

Wind assisted: 4 performances to 23.00 by 4 women

Mark	Wind	Name		Nat	Born	Pos	Meet	Venue	Date
23.12	2.8	Brianne	Bethel	BAH	5.7.98	2		Houston	14 May
23.12	3.2	Alisha	Rees	GBR	16.4.99	1		Eton	3 Jun
23.16	2.9	Kyra	Constantine	CAN	1.8.98	1		Windsor	18 Jun
23.18	4.6	Sha'Carri	Richardson	USA-Y	25.3.00	1		Commerce	29 Apr
23.20	2.7	Chloe	Abbott	USA	25.7.98	6	Big 10	University Park	14 May
23.28	2.9	Michae	Harriott	JAM-Y	1.6.00	1	N.Sch-y	Kingston	1 Apr
23.28	3.3	Maria	Omokwe	NGR-J	13.12.98	1		Yaoundé	11 Jun
23.33	2.9	Brittany	Anderson	JAM-Y	31.1.01	2	N.Sch-y	Kingston	1 Apr

Straight track

Mark	Wind	Name		Nat	Born	Pos	Meet	Venue	Date
21.76	0.5	Shaunae	Miller-Uibo	BAH	15.4.94	1		Boston	4 Jun
22.50	0.5	Natasha	Hastings	USA	23.7.86	2		Boston	4 Jun

300 METRES

Mark	Name		Nat	Born	Pos	Meet	Venue	Date
35.70	Léa	Sprunger	SUI	5.3.90	1		Langenthal	25 May
36.58	Justyna	Swiety	POL	3.12.92	1		Warszawa	20 May
36.71	Shakima	Wimbley	USA	23.4.95	1	Sidlo	Sopot	16 Aug
36.77	Agata	Zupin	SLO-J	17.3.98	1		Domzale	30 Aug
36.86	Finette	Agyapong	GBR	1.2.97	1r1		London (Nh)	29 May

Mark	Name		Nat	Born	Date	Mark	Name		Nat	Born	Date
36.96	Martyna	Dabrowska	POL	5.4.94	20 May	37.40	Agne	Serksniene	LTU	18.2.88	25 May
37.08	Symone	Mason	USA-J	31.8.99	11 Feb	37.42	Malgorzata	Holub	POL	30.10.92	20 May
37.22A	Caster	Semenya	RSA	7.1.91	28 Mar	37.43	Sarah	Atcho	SUI	1.6.95	20 May
37.31	Adrianna	Janowicz	POL	16.4.95	20 May	37.44A	Amantle	Montsho	BOT	4.7.83	28 Mar
37.33	Agata	Forkasiewicz	POL	13.1.94	14 May	37.46	Amy	Allcock	GBR	24.8.93	7 May

Indoors

Mark	Name		Nat	Born	Pos	Meet	Venue	Date
35.71	Quanera	Hayes	USA	7.3.92	1r1		Clemson	7 Jan
35.71	Shaunae	Miller-Uibo	BAH	15.4.94	1	Millrose	New York (A)	11 Feb
36.12	Sydney	McLaughlin	USA-J	7.8.99	1		Bloomington	8 Dec
36.15A	Phyllis	Francis	USA	4.5.92	1	NC	Albuquerque	4 Mar
36.18A	Joanna	Atkins	USA	31.1.89	2	NC	Albuquerque	4 Mar
36.27	Ashley	Spencer	USA	8.6.93	2	Millrose	New York (A)	11 Feb
36.56A	Candace	Hill	USA-J	11.2.99	1rB	NC	Albuquerque	4 Mar
	36.86				2		Clemson	7 Jan

Mark	Name		Nat	Born	Date	Mark	Name		Nat	Born	Date
36.87	Courtney	Okolo	USA	15.3.94	28 Jan	36.88	Natasha	Hastings	USA	23.7.86	11 Feb
36.87A	Jessica	Beard	USA	8.1.89	4 Mar	36.92	Rebekka	Haase	GER	2.1.93	27 Jan
	37.37				28 Jan	37.47	Carline	Muir	CAN	1.10.87	10 Mar
36.87A	Robin	Reynolds	USA	22.2.94	4 Mar	37.47	Gabrielle	Thomas	USA	7.12.96	2 Dec
	37.22				18 Feb	37.49A	Jordan	Lavender	USA	23.7.93	4 Mar

400 METRES

Mark	Name		Nat	Born	Pos	Meet	Venue	Date
49.46	Shaunae	Miller-Uibo	BAH	15.4.94	1	VD	Bruxelles	1 Sep
49.65	Allyson	Felix	USA	18.11.85	1	DL	London (OS)	9 Jul
49.72	Quanera	Hayes	USA	7.3.92	1	NC	Sacramento	24 Jun
49.77		Miller-Uibo			1	DL	Shanghai	13 May
49.80		Miller-Uibo			1	DL	Rabat	16 Jul
49.86		Miller-Uibo			1	Gyulai	Székesfehérvár	4 Jul
49.88	Salwa Eid	Naser	BRN-J	23.5.98	2	VD	Bruxelles	1 Sep
49.92	Phyllis	Francis	USA	4.5.92	1	WCh	London (OS)	9 Aug
49.96		Francis			2	NC	Sacramento	24 Jun

Mark	Name		Nat	Born	Pos	Meet	Venue	Date
50.00	Kendall	Ellis	USA	8.3.96	3	NC	Sacramento	24 Jun
50.04		Hayes			1		Coral Gables	8 Apr
50.05	Shericka	Jackson	JAM	15.7.94	1	NC	Kingston	25 Jun
50.06		Naser			2	WCh	London (OS)	9 Aug
50.08		Naser			1s2	WCh	London (OS)	7 Aug
50.08		Felix			3	WCh	London (OS)	9 Aug
50.12		Felix			2s2	WCh	London (OS)	7 Aug
50.13	Chrisann	Gordon	JAM	18.9.94	2	NC	Kingston	25 Jun
50.14	Natasha	Hastings	USA	23.7.86	4	NC	Sacramento	24 Jun
50.14	Novlene	Williams-Mills (10)	JAM	26.4.82	3	NC	Kingston	25 Jun
50.20		Francis			1s1	NC	Sacramento	23 Jun
50.24		Ellis			2s1	NC	Sacramento	23 Jun
50.29	Courtney	Okolo	USA	15.3.94	2	DL	London (OS)	9 Jul
50.30		Gordon			1s2	NC	Kingston	24 Jun
50.32A	Lydia	Jele ¶?	BOT	22.6.90	1		Pretoria	25 Mar
50.36	Shakima	Wimbley	USA	23.4.95	5	NC	Sacramento	24 Jun
50.36		Miller-Uibo			1s1	WCh	London (OS)	7 Aug
50.37		Francis			1s3	WCh	London (OS)	7 Aug
50.39		Gordon			1s1	NCAA	Eugene	8 Jun
50.40		Wimbley			1	ACC	Atlanta	14 May
50.40	Shamier	Little	USA	20.3.95	3	DL	London (OS)	9 Jul
	(30/14)							
50.56	Stephenie Ann	McPherson	JAM	25.11.88	2s1	WCh	London (OS)	7 Aug
50.60	Kabange	Mupopo	ZAM	21.9.92	2s3	WCh	London (OS)	7 Aug
50.64	Daina	Harper	USA	26.5.95	6	NC	Sacramento	24 Jun
50.76	Anneisha	McLaughlin-Whilby	JAM	6.1.86	4	NC	Kingston	25 Jun
50.85	Jessica	Beard	USA	8.1.89	7	NC	Sacramento	24 Jun
51.06	Patience	George	NGR	25.11.91	1	NC	Abuja	15 Jul
	(20)							
51.09	Léa	Sprunger	SUI	5.3.90	1		La Chaux-de-Fonds	2 Jul
51.12	Jaide	Stepter	USA	25.4.94	1		Los Angeles (Ww)	8 Apr
51.15	Justyna	Swiety	POL	3.12.92	1	FBK	Hengelo	11 Jun
51.18A	Maximilia	Imali	KEN	8.12.96	1	NC	Nairobi	10 Jun
51.21	Yekaterina	Renzhina	RUS	18.10.94	1	NCp	Yerino	14 Jul
51.25	Christine	Day	JAM	23.8.86	2s2	NC	Kingston	24 Jun
51.28	Nirmala	Sheoran	IND	15.7.95	1	Fed Cup	Patiala	4 Jun
51.28	Amantle	Montsho	BOT	4.7.83	4s3	WCh	London (OS)	7 Aug
51.30	Yinka	Ajayi	NGR	11.8.97	1		Ozoro	18 Jul
51.32	Elexis	Guster	USA	7.7.94	2	Pac 12	Eugene	14 May
	(30)							
51.35	Takyera	Roberson	USA-J	7.5.98	1	NC-j	Sacramento	24 Jun
51.37	Gunta	Latiseva-Cudare	LAT	9.3.95	3h3	WCh	London (OS)	6 Aug
51.38	Anastasia	Le-Roy	JAM	11.9.87	5	NC	Kingston	25 Jun
51.41	Carly	Muscaro	USA	18.5.95	1	Meagher	Halifax	10 Jun
51.42	Makenzie	Dunmore	USA	7.10.97	3h3	NC	Sacramento	22 Jun
51.46	Kemi	Adekoya	BRN	16.1.93	1h3	Isl.Sol	Baku	18 May
51.46	Roxana	Gómez	CUB-J	7.1.99	1	PAm-J	Trujillo	21 Jul
51.51	Floria	Guei	FRA	2.5.90	3	GGala	Roma	8 Jun
51.52	Jaevin	Reed	USA-J	2.5.98	2	NC-j	Sacramento	24 Jun
51.53	Caster	Semenya	RSA	7.1.91	7	DL	Rabat	16 Jul
	(40)							
51.57	Margaret	Bamgbose ¶	NGR	19.10.93	1		São Bernardo do Campo	3 Jun
51.61	Cameron	Pettigrew	USA	17.4.95	3	Pac 12	Eugene	14 May
51.61	Eleni	Artymata	CYP	16.5.86	1		Pátra	1 Jul
51.62	Bianca	Razor	ROU	8.8.94	1	NC	Pitesti	7 Jul
51.62	Carline	Muir	CAN	1.10.87	2		Madrid	14 Jul
51.62	Kseniya	Aksyonova	RUS	14.1.88	1	NC	Zhukovskiy	29 Jul
51.63	Travia	Jones	CAN	12.7.95	1q2	NCAA-E	Lexington	26 May
51.63	Ashley	Kelly	IVB	25.3.91	1		Miami	8 Jul
51.65	Morgan	Mitchell	AUS	3.10.94	1		Canberra	11 Mar
51.66	Brittny	Ellis	USA	1.9.97	2	ACC	Atlanta	14 May
	(50)							
51.67	Sharrika	Barnett	USA	16.4.97	2s2	NCAA	Eugene	8 Jun
51.67	Emily	Diamond	GBR	11.6.91	7	DL	London (OS)	9 Jul
51.70	Verone	Chambers	JAM	16.12.88	1		Kingston	8 Apr
51.71	Lisanne	de Witte	NED	10.9.92	1	ET	Villeneuve d'Ascq	24 Jun
51.71	Iga	Baumgart	POL	11.4.89	1	NC	Bialystok	22 Jul
51.72	Ruth Sophia	Spelmeyer	GER	19.9.90	1h2	NC	Erfurt	8 Jul
51.76	Malgorzata	Holub	POL	30.10.92	1	WUG	Taipei	25 Aug
51.80		Yang Huizhen	CHN	13.8.92	1	NG	Tianjin	3 Sep

Mark	Name		Nat	Born	Pos	Meet	Venue	Date
51.81	Amalie Hammild	Iuel	NOR	17.4.94	1		Los Angeles	18 Mar
51.81	Ekundayo	Sogbesan	USA	29.3.92	4h2	NC	Sacramento	22 Jun
	(60)							
51.81	Anyika	Onuora	GBR	28.10.84	3		Madrid	14 Jul
51.81	Zoey	Clark	GBR	25.10.94	7s3	WCh	London (OS)	7 Aug
51.82A	Christine	Botlogetswe	BOT	1.10.95	2		Francistown	13 May
51.83	Justine	Palframan	RSA	4.11.93	2	WUG	Taipei	25 Aug
51.86	Iríni	Vasilíou	GRE	18.3.90	2		Pátra	1 Jul
51.87	Maria Benedicta	Chigbolu	ITA	27.7.89	1		Orvieto	28 May
51.88	Sydney	McLaughlin	USA-J	7.8.99	1		Egg Harbor	3 Jun
51.89	Anastasiya	Bryzhina	UKR-J	9.1.98	1		Lutsk	6 Jun
51.90	Domonique	Williams	TTO	8.8.94	2q2	NCAA-E	Lexington	26 May
51.90	Kendall	Baisden	USA	5.3.95	4		Gresham	2 Jul
	(70)							
51.90	Cátia	Azevedo	POR	9.3.94	4		Madrid	14 Jul
51.91	Geisa	Coutinho	BRA	1.6.80	2		São Bernardo do Campo	3 Jun
51.91	Deborah	Sananés	FRA	26.10.95	2		Genève	10 Jun
51.92	Elea Mariama	Diarra	FRA	8.3.90	1	NC	Marseille	16 Jul
51.93	Georganne	Moline	USA	6.3.90	1		Tucson	18 Mar
51.94	Janieve	Russell	JAM	14.11.93	1		Kingston	15 Apr
51.94	Anita	Horvat	SLO	7.9.96	1h2	EU23	Bydgoszcz	14 Jul
51.98	Tamara	Salaski	SRB	16.10.88	1		Kragujevac	23 Jul
51.99	Tovea	Jenkins	JAM	27.10.92	1		Charlotte	8 Apr
51.99	Shae	Anderson	USA-J	7.4.99	1	MSR	Torrance	15 Apr
	(80)							
51.99	Emerald	Egwim	USA/NGR	27.11.95	1h1	Big 10	University Park	13 May
52.00	Claudia	Francis	USA	14.11.93	1	FlaR	Gainesville	30 Mar
52.00	Mikele	Barber	USA	4.10.80	2		Los Angeles (Ww)	8 Apr
52.00	Aiyanna	Stiverne	CAN	20.2.95	1q1	NCAA-E	Lexington	26 May
52.00	NaAsha	Robinson	USA	23.1.97	3q2	NCAA-E	Lexington	26 May
52.01	Martyna	Dabrowska	POL	5.4.94	1		Bialystok	18 Jun
52.02	Zola	Golden	USA	20.6.97	5h1	NC	Sacramento	22 Jun
52.03A	Wenda	Nel	RSA	30.7.88	1		Pretoria	13 May
52.03	Abike	Egbeniyi	NGR	23.10.94	2		Ozoro	18 Jul
52.04	Laura	Müller	GER	11.12.95	1h1	ET	Villeneuve d'Ascq	23 Jun
	(90)							
52.05	Junelle	Bromfield	JAM-J	8.2.98	2		Kingston	20 May
52.05	Dawnalee	Loney	JAM	15.5.96	1rB		Kingston	10 Jun
52.05	Arria	Minor	USA-Y	9.2.01	3	NC-j	Sacramento	24 Jun
52.07	Rachel	Misher	USA	4.2.97	4q2	NCAA-E	Lexington	26 May
52.08	Taylor	Washington	USA	6.5.93	4	Gyulai	Székesfehérvár	4 Jul
52.11	Yana	Glotova	RUS	8.4.95	1	NC-23	Saransk	21 Jun
52.13	Shaquania	Dorsett	BAH	16.9.97	2q1	NCAA-E	Lexington	26 May
52.14A	Veronica	Mutua	KEN	2.2.92	2	NC	Nairobi	10 Jun
52.15	Micha	Powell	CAN	12.1.95	3q1	NCAA-E	Lexington	26 May
52.15	Laura	de Witte	NED	7.8.95	2h1	EU23	Bydgoszcz	14 Jul
	(100)							

Mark			Nat	Born	Date
52.16	Lexis	Lambert	USA	12.5.94	23 Jun
52.16	Djénébou	Danté	MLI	7.8.89	16 Jul
52.16	Jordan	Lavender	USA	23.7.93	22 Jul
52.17	Amina	Seyni	NIG		9 Sep
52.17	Anneliese	Rubie	AUS	22.4.92	16 Dec
52.18	Estelle	Perrossier	FRA	12.1.90	16 Jul
52.19	Perri	Shakes-Drayton	GBR	21.12.88	29 Aug
52.20	Bobby-Gaye	Wilkins-Gooden	JAM	10.9.88	10 Jun
52.20	Tiffany	James	JAM	31.1.97	24 Jun
52.20	Natassha	McDonald	CAN	27.1.97	8 Jul
52.22	Brionna	Thomas	USA	21.3.96	26 May
52.24	Courtney	Blanden	USA	12.3.96	14 May
52.24	Glory Nathaniel	Onome	NGR	23.1.96	15 Jul
52.25	Kateryna	Klymyuk	UKR	2.6.95	6 Jun
52.25	Syaira	Richardson	USA-J	29.10.98	24 Jun
52.26	Ristananna	Tracey	JAM	9.5.92	13 May
52.27	Maggie	Barrie	USA/SLE	29.5.96	26 May
52.27	Madiea	Ghafoor	NED	9.9.92	16 Jul
52.28	Briyahna	Desrosiers	USA	11.3.96	15 Apr
52.29	Agata	Zupin	SLO-J	17.3.98	20 Jun
52.31	Andrea	Miklos	ROU-J	17.4.99	22 Jul
52.32	Margaret	Adeoye	GBR	22.4.85	29 Aug
52.33	Mary	Bergman	USA		27 May
52.34	Iveta	Putalová	SVK	24.3.88	11 Jun
52.34	Hannah	Waller	USA-J	22.6.98	24 Jun
52.35	Patrycja	Wyciszkiewicz	POL	8.1.94	14 Jun
52.36	Kala	Funderburk	USA	14.9.92	14 May
52.36	Eilidh	Doyle	GBR	20.2.87	14 Jun
52.38	Paola	Moran	MEX	25.2.97	24 Aug
52.39A	Jacinta	Shikanda	KEN	14.7.86	10 Jun
52.41	Robin	Reynolds	USA	22.2.94	30 Mar
52.41	Finette	Agyapong	GBR	1.2.97	15 Aug
52.42	Symone	Mason	USA-J	31.8.99	25 Mar
52.43	Rashan	Brown	BAH	27.11.93	23 Jun
52.43	Nercely	Soto	VEN	23.8.90	21 Nov
52.44	Jaílma	de Lima	BRA	31.12.86	21 Jul
52.45	Eíelina	Ptak	POL	20.3.87	2 Jun
52.45	Aleksandra	Gaworska	POL	7.11.95	2 Jun
52.45		Cheng Chong	CHN	22.9.92	3 Sep
52.47	Akua	Obeng-Akrofi	GHA	26.6.96	26 May
52.48		Nguyen Thi Huyen	VIE	19.5.93	24 Aug
52.51	Shatajah	Wattely	USA		27 May
52.51	Nadine	Gonska	GER	23.1.90	18 Jul
52.54	Kayla	Davis	USA-Y	21.12.03	30 Jul
52.55	Elina	Mikhina	KAZ	16.7.94	30 Apr
52.55	Rushell	Clayton	JAM	18.10.92	15 Jul
52.55A	Leni	Shida	UGA	22.5.94	19 Jul
52.55	Hannah	Williams	GBR-J	23.4.98	22 Jul
52.56	Olivia	James	JAM	1.6.94	14 May
52.56	Nicky	van Leuveren	NED	25.5.90	17 Jun
52.60	Laviai	Nielsen	GBR	13.3.96	27 May
52.60	Mary	Iheke	GBR	19.11.90	24 Jun
52.61	Yelizaveta	Fedoseyeva	RUS	10.8.96	29 Jul
52.62	Stacey-Ann	Williams	JAM-J	8.3.99	11 Mar

Mark Name Nat Born Pos Meet Venue Date

52.63 Dominique Blake JAM 15.2.87 28 May
52.63 Kyra Constantine CAN-J 1.8.98 21 Jul
52.64 Laura Bueno ESP 25.5.93 14 Jul
52.65 Natoya Goule JAM 30.3.91 30 Mar
52.65 Jisna Mathew IND-J 7.1.99 15 May
52.65 Agne Serksniene LTU 18.2.88 22 Jul
52.66 Machettira Raju Poovamma IND 5.6.90 11 May
52.68 Camelia Gal ROU 18.10.92 3 Jun
52.68 Yennifer Padilla COL 1.1.90 23 Jun
52.68 Chloe Abbott USA-J 25.7.98 23 Jun
52.68mx Cheriece Hylton GBR 19.12.96 9 Jul
52.68 Petra Fontanive SUI 10.10.88 3 Sep
52.69 Alesha Kelly JAM 17.9.97 1 Apr
52.69 Yelizaveta Anikiyenko RUS 30.6.94 2 Jul
52.69 Maria Enrica Spacca ITA 20.3.86 7 Jul
52.69 Bendere Oboya AUS-Y 17.4.00 21 Jul
52.70 Candace Hill USA-J 11.2.99 25 Mar
52.72 Ella Connolly AUS-Y 13.7.00 21 Jul
52.73 Derri-Ann Hill JAM 17.11.95 20 May
52.73 Gilda Casanova CUB 19.12.95 26 May
52.73 Malgorzata Curylo POL 13.1.94 24 Jun
52.74 Letícia de Souza BRA 6.5.96 22 Apr
52.74 Tong Cenghuan CHN 29.11.95 17 May
52.74A Barbora Malíková CZE-Y 30.12.01 14 Jul
52.75 Kyra Jefferson USA 23.9.94 25 Mar
52.75 Jennifer Edobi NGR 20.1.96 26 May
52.75 Sparkle McKnight TTO 21.12.91 1 Jul
52.76A Ada Benjamin NGR 18.5.94 14 May
52.76 Svea Köhrbrück GER 16.10.93 9 Jul
52.77 Cassandra Tate USA 11.9.90 22 Apr
52.78 Taylor Sharpe CAN 2.12.96 31 Mar
52.78 Quach Thi Lan VIE 18.10.95 7 Jul
52.79 Alex Gholston USA 3.1.95 31 Mar
(188) 200th 52.85

Indoors

51.61 Sydney McLaughlin USA-J 7.8.99 1 New Bal New York 12 Mar
51.77 Zuzana Hejnová CZE 19.12.86 1 Birmingham 18 Feb
51.84 Sage Watson CAN 20.6.94 1rB NCAA College Station 11 Mar
51.86 Eilidh Doyle GBR 20.2.87 1 Wien 28 Jan
51.90 Laviai Nielsen GBR 13.3.96 2 Birmingham 18 Feb
52.02 Chrishuna Williams USA 31.3.93 2 Fayetteville 10 Feb
52.23 Alex Gholston USA 3.1.95 11 Mar
52.54 Letícia de Souza BRA 6.5.96 10 Feb
52.64 Grace Claxton PUR 19.8.93 26 Feb
52.65 Sparkle McKnight TTO 21.12.91 10 Feb
52.69 Leah Nugent JAM 23.11.92 21 Jan
52.79 Symone Black USA 26.10.95 25 Feb

Hand timed

51.9 Geisa Coutinho BRA 1.6.80 20 May
52.4A Margaret Wambui KEN 15.9.95 29 Apr

Best at low altitude

51.41 Jele ¶? 4h3 WCh London (OS) 6 Aug
52.71 Botlogetswe 8 Apr
52.97 Nel 28 Jun

Running with guide runner: 52.75 Omar Durand CUB 26.11.91 1 ParaWC London (OS) 19 Jul

Drugs disqualification

50.89 Olha Zemlyak ¶ UKR 16.1.90 (3) DL Shanghai 13 May

JUNIORS

See main list for top 9 juniors. 14 performances (1 indoor) by 5 women to 51.80. Additional marks and further juniors:

Naser 3+ 50.57 1h4 WCh London (OS) 7 Aug 51.33 1 Isl Sol Baku 19 May
50.59 1 DL Birmingham 20 Aug
Gómez 51.59 1 Monterrey 17 Jun
Reed 51.67 2s1 NCAA Eugene 8 Jun 51.71 2 PAm-J Trujillo 21 Jul
51.71 1h2 NC-j Sacramento 23 Jun

52.25 Syaira Richardson (10) USA 29.10.98 4 NC-j Sacramento 24 Jun
52.29 Agata Zupin SLO 17.3.98 2 Velenje 20 Jun
52.31 Andrea Miklos ROU 17.4.99 2 EJ Grosseto 22 Jul
52.34 Hannah Waller USA 22.6.98 5 NC-j Sacramento 24 Jun
52.42 Symone Mason USA 31.8.99 1 Miami 25 Mar
52.54 Kayla Davis USA-Y 21.12.03 1 Lawrence 30 Jul
52.55 Hannah Williams GBR 23.4.98 3 EJ Grosseto 22 Jul
52.62 Stacey-Ann Williams JAM 8.3.99 1 Kingston 11 Mar
52.63 Kyra Constantine CAN 1.8.98 3 PAm-J Trujillo 21 Jul
52.65 Jisna Mathew IND 7.1.99 1 NGP New Delhi 15 May
52.68 Chloe Abbott USA 25.7.98 1h1 NC-j Sacramento 23 Jun

500 METRES

1:09.60 Aleksandra Gaworska POL 7.11.95 1 Kraków 6 May

Indoors

1:07.34 Courtney Okolo USA 15.3.94 1 Millrose New York (A) 11 Feb
1:08.40 Sage Watson CAN 20.6.94 1 New York 3 Feb
1:09.05 Carly Muscaro USA 18.5.95 4 Feb
1:09.55 Alysia Montaño USA 23.4.86 11 Feb
1:09.63 Ajee' Wilson USA 8.5.94 14 Jan
1:09.66 Dalilah Muhammad USA 7.2.90 11 Feb

600 METRES

1:21.77 Caster Semenya RSA 7.1.91 1 ISTAF Berlin 27 Aug
1:22.39 Ajee' Wilson USA 8.5.94 2 ISTAF Berlin 27 Aug
1:23.18 Francine Niyonsaba BDI 5.5.93 3 ISTAF Berlin 27 Aug
1:25.78 Noélie Yarigo BEN 26.12.85 4 ISTAF Berlin 27 Aug
1:26.74 Joanna Józwik POL 30.1.91 1 EAF Bydgoszcz 2 Jun
1:27.05 Marina Arzamasova BLR 17.12.87 27 Aug
1:27.5mx Kelsey Stewart GBR 12.2.97 29 Jul
1:27.68 Christina Hering GER 9.10.94 14 May
1:27.82 Paulina Mikiewicz-Lapinska POL 13.7.92 2 Jun
1:27.9mx Revee Walcott-Nolan GBR 6.3.95 29 Jul

Indoors

1:23.84A Wilson 1 NC Albuquerque 5 Mar
1:24.00A Courtney Okolo USA 15.3.94 2 NC Albuquerque 5 Mar

Mark	Name		Nat	Born	Pos	Meet	Venue	Date
1:24.48		Wilson			1		New York (A)	4 Feb
1:25.35	Natoya	Goule	JAM	30.3.91	1		Clemson	17 Feb
1:25.46A	Kendra	Chambers	USA	11.9.90	3	NC	Albuquerque	5 Mar
1:25.89	Marilyn	Okoro	GBR	23.9.84	2		Clemson	28 Jan
1:26.54A	Olicia	Williams	USA	26.2.94	4	NC	Albuquerque	5 Mar
1:26.74	Cecilia	Barowski	USA	7.12.92	2		New York	4 Feb
1:26.97	Raevyn	Rogers	USA	7.9.96	1r4		Seattle	14 Jan

Mark	Name		Nat	Born	Date
1:27.13	Samantha	Watson	USA-J	10.11.99	4 Feb
1:27.16	Lynsey	Sharp	GBR	11.7.90	4 Feb
1:27.38A	McKayla	Fricker	USA	19.4.92	4 Mar
1:27.39	Hanna	Green	USA	16.10.94	18 Feb
1:27.60	Karrington	Winters	USA	14.4.97	25 Feb
1:27.94A	Ce'aira	Brown	USA	4.11.93	4 Mar
1:27.97	Meghan	Manley	USA	3.6.93	4 Feb

800 METRES

Mark	Name		Nat	Born	Pos	Meet	Venue	Date
1:55.16	Caster	Semenya	RSA	7.1.91	1	WCh	London (OS)	13 Aug
1:55.27		Semenya			1	Herc	Monaco	21 Jul
1:55.47	Francine	Niyonsaba	BDI	5.5.93	2	Herc	Monaco	21 Jul
1:55.61	Ajee'	Wilson	USA	8.5.94	3	Herc	Monaco	21 Jul
1:55.84		Semenya			1	WK-DLF	Zürich	24 Aug
1:55.92		Niyonsaba			2	WCh	London (OS)	13 Aug
1:56.61		Semenya			1	DL	Diha	5 May
1:56.65		Wilson			3	WCh	London (OS)	13 Aug
1:56.71		Niyonsaba			2	WK-DLF	Zürich	24 Aug
1:56.81	Sifan	Hassan	NED	1.1.93	4	Herc	Monaco	21 Jul
1:56.82		Niyonsaba			1	Athl	Lausanne	6 Jul
1:56.87	Margaret	Wambui	KEN	15.9.95	3	WK-DLF	Zürich	24 Aug
1:57.01	Melissa	Bishop	CAN	5.8.88	5	Herc	Monaco	21 Jul
1:57.03		Wambui			2	DL	Diha	5 May
1:57.05	Habitam	Alemu	ETH	9.7.97	4	WK-DLF	Zürich	24 Aug
1:57.12		Hassan			5	WK-DLF	Zürich	24 Aug
1:57.38	Charlene	Lipsey	USA	16.7.91	2	Athl	Lausanne	6 Jul
1:57.54		Wambui			4	WCh	London (OS)	13 Aug
1:57.59		Semenya			1	Bisl	Oslo	15 Jun
1:57.68		Bishop			5	WCh	London (OS)	13 Aug
1:57.72		Wilson			1	Hanz	Zagreb	29 Aug
1:57.78		Semenya			1	Pre	Eugene	27 May
1:57.78		Wilson			1	NC	Sacramento	25 Jun
1:57.78	Eunice	Sum	KEN	2.9.88	3	Athl	Lausanne	6 Jul
1:57.88		Wambui			2	Pre	Eugene	27 May
1:57.99		Lipsey			6	WK-DLF	Zürich	24 Aug
1:58.01		Lipsey			2	NC	Sacramento	25 Jun
1:58.01	Lynsey	Sharp (10)	GBR	11.7.90	6	Herc	Monaco	21 Jul
1:58.13		Hassan			4	Athl	Lausanne	6 Jul
1:58.13	Winny	Chebet	KEN	20.12.90	2	Hanz	Zagreb	29 Aug
	(30/11)							
1:58.34	Aleksandra	Gulyayeva	RUS	30.4.94	1	NC	Zhukovskiy	29 Jul
1:58.41	Angelika	Cichocka	POL	15.3.88	6	WCh	London (OS)	13 Aug
1:58.43	Brenda	Martinez	USA	8.9.87	7	Herc	Monaco	21 Jul
1:58.69	Laura	Muir	GBR	9.5.93	5	Athl	Lausanne	6 Jul
1:58.77	Lovisa	Lindh	SWE	9.7.91	6	Athl	Lausanne	6 Jul
1:58.82	Nataliya	Pryshchepa	UKR	11.9.94	8	Athl	Lausanne	6 Jul
1:59.10	Raevyn	Rogers	USA	7.9.96	1	MSR	Torrance	15 Apr
1:59.11	Rose Mary	Almanza	CUB	13.7.92	1		Madrid	14 Jul
1:59.20	Svetlana	Uloga	RUS	23.11.86	2	NC	Zhukovskiy	29 Jul
	(20)							
1:59.30	Kate	Grace	USA	24.10.88	1		Portland	11 Jun
1:59.37	Genzebe	Dibaba	ETH	8.2.91	5	DL	Doha	5 May
1:59.46	Selina	Büchel	SUI	26.7.91	5	Pre	Eugene	27 May
1:59.54	Laura	Roesler	USA	19.12.91	2	MSR	Torrance	15 Apr
1:59.55	Sanne	Verstegen	NED	10.11.85	2		Madrid	14 Jul
1:59.65	Konstanze	Klosterhalfen	GER	18.2.97	1		Pfungstadt	3 Jun
1:59.74	Noélie	Yarigo	BEN	26.12.85	3s1	WCh	London (OS)	11 Aug
1:59.82	Shelayna	Oskan-Clarke	GBR	20.1.90	2	DL	London (OS)	9 Jul
1:59.84	Olha	Lyakhova	UKR	18.3.92	5	DL	Stockholm	18 Jun
1:59.87	Hedda	Hynne	NOR	13.3.90	3	DL	London (OS)	9 Jul
	(30)							
1:59.95	Nelly	Jepkosgei	KEN	14.7.91	1		Rehlingen	5 Jun
1:59.97	Kseniya	Savina	RUS	4.6.89	3	NC	Zhukovskiy	29 Jul
2:00.03	Chrishuna	Williams	USA	31.3.93	3		Madrid	14 Jul
2:00.05	Aníta	Hinriksdóttir	ISL	13.1.96	6	Bisl	Oslo	15 Jun
2:00.17	Yusneysi	Santiusti	ITA	24.12.84	3		Bellinzona	18 Jul

Mark	Name		Nat	Born	Pos	Meet	Venue	Date
2:00.18A	Emily	Jerotich	KEN	13.5.86	3	WCT	Nairobi	24 Jun
2:00.22	Winnie	Nanyondo	UGA	23.8.93	4		Madrid	14 Jul
2:00.26	Adelle	Tracey	GBR	27.5.93	6s1	WCh	London (OS)	11 Aug
2:00.34	Yekaterina	Kupina	RUS	2.2.86	3	NCp	Yerino	15 Jul
2:00.38	Chanelle	Price	USA	22.8.90	3	MSR	Torrance	15 Apr
	(40)							
2:00.43	Hanna	Hermansson	SWE	18.5.89	7s1	WCh	London (OS)	11 Aug
2:00.44	Angela	Petty	NZL	16.8.91	3		Los Angeles (ER)	18 May
2:00.48	Egle	Balciunaite	LTU	31.10.88	6s2	WCh	London (OS)	11 Aug
2:00.53	Hannah	Fields	USA	4.2.93	2		Portland	11 Jun
2:00.56	Natoya	Goule	JAM	30.3.91	2		Nashville	10 Jun
2:00.61	Tola	Kore	ETH	16.1.97	1	FBK	Hengelo	10 Jun
2:00.62	Emily	Richards	USA	21.7.95	3		Nashville	10 Jun
2:00.62	Alexandra	Bell	GBR	4.11.92	8	DL	London (OS)	9 Jul
2:00.65	Samantha	Watson	USA-J	10.11.99	4		Bellinzona	18 Jul
2:00.71	Malika	Akkaoui	MAR	25.12.87	1	Franc	Abidjan	24 Jul
	(50)							
2:00.77	Joanna	Józwik	POL	30.1.91	7	Pre	Eugene	27 May
2:00.77	Mahelet	Mulugeta	ETH	20.3.95	2	FBK	Hengelo	10 Jun
2:00.77	Esther	Guerrero	ESP	7.2.90	5		Madrid	14 Jul
2:00.77	Christina	Hering	GER	9.10.94	5		Bellinzona	18 Jul
2:00.77	Tatyana	Markelova	RUS	19.12.88	1h1	NC	Zhukovskiy	28 Jul
2:00.79	Dorcus	Ajok	UGA	12.7.94	1		Huelva	14 Jun
2:00.80	Halimah	Nakaayi	UGA	16.10.94	2		Barcelona	29 Jun
2:00.84	Ce'aira	Brown	USA	4.11.93	3		New York	6 Jul
2:00.90	Cecilia	Barowski	USA	7.12.92	4		Los Angeles (ER)	18 May
2:00.90	Georgia	Griffith	AUS	5.12.96	3		Portland	11 Jun
	(60)							
2:00.92mx	Katie	Snowden	GBR	9.3.94	1mx		Bromley	14 Aug
2:00.92	Yume	Kitamura	JPN	23.12.95	1		Fukui	10 Sep
2:00.95	Alexa	Efraimson	USA	20.2.97	5		Portland	11 Jun
2:01.10	Kendra	Chambers	USA	11.9.90	5	MSR	Torrance	15 Apr
2:01.2	Sarah	McDonald	GBR	2.8.93	1		Tipton	26 Aug
	2:01.25				7	Hanz	Zagreb	29 Aug
2:01.23	Hannah	England	GBR	6.3.87	6	Hanz	Zagreb	29 Aug
2:01.28	Hanna	Green	USA	16.10.94	1	ACC	Atlanta	14 May
2:01.42	Adanech	Anbesa	ETH-J	23.1.98	3	FBK	Hengelo	10 Jun
2:01.43	Jazmine	Fray	JAM	6.6.97	1		Los Angeles (Ww)	15 Apr
2:01.45	Yelena	Murashova	RUS	5.10.87	5	NC	Zhukovskiy	29 Jul
	(70)							
2:01.46	Keely	Small	AUS-Y	9.6.01	1		Canberra	11 Mar
2:01.46	Yelena	Kotulskaya	RUS	8.8.88	2	Znam	Zhukovskiy	1 Jul
2:01.46A	Jackline	Wambui	KEN-Y	8.2.00	1	WY	Nairobi	16 Jul
2:01.50	Gena	Lofstrand	RSA	23.10.95	2		Luzern	11 Jul
2:01.51	Shea	Collinsworth	USA	18.2.95	1		Tempe	8 Apr
2:01.54	Sofia	Ennaoui	POL	30.8.95	2		Radom	4 Jun
2:01.54	Brooke	Feldmeier	USA	26.1.96	3	NCAA	Eugene	10 Jun
2:01.56	Annie	Leblanc	CAN	29.4.92	6		Portland	11 Jun
2:01.62	Santa	Tkhakur	RUS	23.4.93	4	NCp	Yerino	15 Jul
2:01.64	Jenny	Simpson	USA	23.8.86	8	Hanz	Zagreb	29 Aug
	(80)							
2:01.68	Kenyetta	Iyevbele	USA	22.8.92	2		Concord MA	1 Jun
2:01.72	Brittany	McGowan	AUS	24.4.91	4		Barcelona	29 Jun
2:01.73	Dana	Mecke	USA	20.9.87	5rB	Pre	Eugene	26 May
2:01.74	Lauren	Johnson	USA	4.5.87	1		Lignano	12 Jul
2:01.87	Laura	Weightman	GBR	1.7.91	2		Manchester (Str)	25 Jul
2:01.90	Lora	Storey	AUS	19.10.89	2		Canberra	11 Mar
2:01.92	Marina	Arzamasova	BLR	17.12.87	4h4	WCh	London (OS)	10 Aug
2:01.93	Renée	Eykens	BEL	8.6.96	9	Hanz	Zagreb	29 Aug
2:01.96	Olesya	Muratova	RUS	25.10.92	5	NCp	Yerino	15 Jul
2:01.96	Dina	Aleksandrova	RUS	9.8.92	2h1	NC	Zhukovskiy	28 Jul
	(90)							
2:02.03	Amanda	Eccleston	USA	18.6.90	4		Concord MA	1 Jun
2:02.06	Latavia	Thomas	USA	17.12.88	2		Baie-Mahault	17 May
2:02.06A	Lydia	Cheruto	KEN-Y	23.11.00	2	WY	Nairobi	16 Jul
2:02.07	Kimarra	McDonald	JAM	14.8.87	5		Concord MA	1 Jun
2:02.09	Jacqueline	Fairchild	GBR	3.5.89	3		Manchester (Str)	25 Jul
2:02.10	Clarisse	Moh	FRA	6.12.86	7		Oordegem	27 May
2:02.11	Síofra	Cléirigh Büttner	IRL	21.7.95	1q1	NCAA-E	Lexington	26 May
2:02.13	Lindsey	Butterworth	CAN	27.9.92	2		Ninove	15 Jul
2:02.14	Natalia	Evangelidou	CYP	10.3.91	6		Luzern	11 Jul

Mark	Name		Nat	Born	Pos	Meet	Venue	Date
2:02.14mx	Jessica (100)	Judd	GBR	7.1.95	2		Manchester (Str)	15 Aug

Mark	Name		Nat	Born	Date
2:02.18	Anneliese	Rubie	AUS	22.4.92	18 May
2:02.19	Abbey	de la Motte	AUS	24.2.94	11 Mar
2:02.19A	Eglay	Nalyanya	KEN	28.5.96	10 Jun
2:02.20	Ciara	Mageean	IRL	12.3.92	12 Jul
2:02.26	Gudaf	Tsegay	ETH	23.1.97	13 Jun
2:02.28	Tigist	Ketema	ETH-J	15.9.98	10 Jun
2:02.28	Halyna	Syshko	UKR	7.1.91	15 Jul
2:02.29	Charline	Mathias	LUX	23.5.92	15 Jul
2:02.2A	Selah	Busienei	KEN	27.12.91	10 May
2:02.33	Sadi	Henderson	USA	12.4.96	11 Jun
2:02.34	Abike	Egbeniyi	NGR	23.10.94	26 May
2:02.34	Anastasiya	Kalina	RUS	16.2.94	15 Jul
2:02.36	Shannon	Osika	USA	15.6.93	12 Jul
2:02.38	Darya	Borisevich	BLR	6.4.90	19 Jul
2:02.39	Bianka	Kéri	HUN	19.4.94	16 Jul
2:02.40	Siham	Hilali	MAR	2.5.86	24 Jul
2:02.48	Gabriela	Stafford	CAN	13.9.95	29 Jun
2:02.48	Anastasiya	Nemykina	RUS	13.5.93	15 Jul
2:02.50	Marilyn	Okoro	GBR	23.9.84	31 Mar
2:02.53	Danae	Rivers	USA-J	3.2.98	21 Apr
2:02.55	Cory	McGee	USA	29.5.92	31 Mar
2:02.55	Gayanthika Thushari	Abeyrathne	SRI	23.12.86	9 Apr
2:02.57	Ayano	Shiomi	JPN-J	26.11.99	1 Aug
2:02.58	W.K.L.A.	Nimali	SRI	19.9.89	9 Apr
2:02.59	Marina	Pospelova	RUS	23.7.90	28 Jul
2:02.65	Yekaterina	Rogozina	RUS	21.12.89	1 Jul
2:02.66	Susan	Aneno	UGA	27.7.96	26 May
2:02.67	Rachel	Pocratsky	USA	23.1.97	14 May
2:02.67	Rachel	Weber	USA	7.2.95	26 May
2:02.70	Agnes	Abu	GHA	1.5.92	14 Apr
2:02.70	Megan	Krumpoch	USA	31.8.92	1 Jun
2:02.70	Alena	Brooks	TTO	14.11.91	15 Jul
2:02.7A	Dinke	Ferdesa	ETH-J	28.5.99	15 Jan
2:02.73	Anna	Shchagina	RUS	7.12.91	15 Jul
2:02.74	Ayaka	Kawata	JPN-J	22.8.99	1 Aug
2:02.77	Natalija	Piliusina	LTU	22.10.90	16 Jun
2:02.78	Jenna	Westaway	CAN	19.6.94	11 Jun
2:02.79	Hannah	Segrave	GBR	14.4.95	10 Jun
2:02.86	Tintu	Luka	IND	26.4.89	25 Jun
2:02.87	Carsyn	Koch	USA	5.1.96	12 May
2:02.88A	Josephine	Chelangat	KEN-J	10.10.98	24 Jun
2:02.90	Katherine	Camp	NZL	6.2.92	26 Feb
2:02.96	Paulina	Mikiewicz-Lapinska	POL	13.7.92	22 Jul
2:02.97	Martyna	Galant	POL	26.1.95	22 Jul
2:03.00	Madeline	Kopp	USA	4.4.95	26 May
2:03.00	Zoe	Buckman	AUS	21.12.88	12 Jul
2:03.01	Emily	Lipari	USA	19.11.92	1 Jun
2:03.02	Anastasiya	Tkachuk	UKR	20.4.93	7 Jul
2:03.03	Irene	Baldessari	ITA	21.1.93	12 Jul
2:03.03	Lore	Hoffmann	SUI	25.7.96	29 Aug
2:03.06	Meghan	Manley	USA	3.6.93	1 Jun
2:03.07	Florina	Pierdevara	ROU	29.3.90	3 Jun
2:03.07	Samantha	James	JAM	12.8.94	15 Jul
2:03.09	Corane	Gazeau	FRA	23.10.96	20 Jun
2:03.09	Tatyana	Gudkova	RUS	26.3.85	28 Jul
2:03.09mx	Gesa-Felicitas	Krause	GER	3.8.92	6 Sep
2:03.1A	Judy	Kiyeng	KEN	10.12.94	10 May
2:03.12	Charlene	Thomas	GBR	6.5.82	25 Jul
2:03.17	Dominique	Jackson	USA	10.6.89	18 May
2:03.18	Tatyana	Peredunova	RUS	29.6.96	26 May
2:03.20	Baylee	Mires	USA	10.12.92	18 May
2:03.20	Revee	Walcott-Nolan	GBR	6.3.95	24 Jun
2:03.2A	Esther	Chebet	UGA	10.9.97	4 Mar
2:03.2A	Sara	Vaughn	USA	16.5.86	6 Jul
2:03.22	Alisha	Brown	USA	8.11.92	11 Jun
2:03.23	Jessica	Harris	USA	14.3.96	21 Apr
2:03.23	Trine	Mjåland	NOR	30.6.90	27 May
2:03.25		Wang Chunyu	CHN	17.1.95	24 Apr
2:03.25	Anna	Silvander	SWE	22.6.93	1 Jun
2:03.25	Rachel	Aubry	CAN	18.5.90	10 Jun
2:03.26	Yelena	Korobkina	RUS	25.11.90	8 Jul
2:03.27	Selma	Kajan	AUS	30.7.91	29 Jun
2:03.31	Marta	Pérez	ESP	19.4.93	2 Jun
2:03.32	Caitlin	Collier	USA-J	5.8.99	1 Jun
2:03.35	Nicole	Sifuentes	CAN	30.6.86	28 Jun
2:03.36	Grace	Annear	CAN	–.92	18 May
2:03.37	Mhairi	Hendry	GBR	31.3.96	2 Jul
2:03.38	Kaylee	Dodd	GBR	28.12.95	10 Jun
2:03.38	Kaela	Edwards	USA	8.12.93	7 Jul
2:03.40	Mariya	Zhuravlyova	RUS	7.11.86	28 Jul
2:03.41	Gadese	Ejara	ETH-J	7.7.98	10 Jun
2:03.41	Rosangélica	Escobar	COL	13.11.93	23 Nov
2:03.45	Alicia	Keir	AUS	19.3.91	11 Mar
2:03.45	Olivia	Baker	USA	12.6.96	22 Apr
2:03.46	Lili	Das	IND-J	18.3.98	16 Jul
2:03.49	Maité	Bouchard	CAN	1.1.95?	11 Jun
2:03.50	Charlotte	Mouchet	FRA	5.6.96	3 Jun
2:03.50	Alena (188)	Shukhtuyeva	RUS	7.12.93	28 Jul

Indoors

Mark	Name		Nat	Born	Pos	Meet	Venue	Date
1:59.29	Joanna	Józwik	POL	30.1.91	1		Torun	10 Feb
2:00.69	Jazmine	Fray	JAM	6.6.97	1		Clemson	11 Feb
2:01.36	Justine	Fédronic	FRA	11.5.91	3	Millrose	New York (A)	11 Feb
2:01.42	Shea	Collinsworth	USA	18.2.95	1		Ames	11 Feb
2:01.57	Anastasiya	Tkachuk	UKR	20.4.93	3		Metz	12 Feb
2:02.00	Tigist	Ketema	ETH-J	15.9.98	1		Sabadell	7 Feb

Mark	Name		Nat	Born	Date
2:02.18	Liga	Velvere	LAT	10.2.90	15 Feb
2:02.20	Cory	McGee	USA	29.5.92	27 Jan
2:02.22	Megan	Krumpoch	USA	31.8.92	27 Jan
2:02.54	Anna	Silvander	SWE	22.6.93	27 Jan
2:02.71	Diana	Mezuliáníková	CZE	10.4.92	28 Jan
2:02.74	Stina	Troest	DEN	17.1.94	11 Feb
2:02.89	Aaliyah	Miller	USA-J	28.8.98	11 Feb
2:02.97	Lenka	Masná	CZE	22.4.85	28 Jan
2:03.01	Morgan	Schuetz	USA	8.1.94	11 Feb
2:03.01	Ruby	Stauber	USA	30.9.97	11 Mar
2:03.08	Jasmine	Staebler	USA	11.1.97	11 Feb
2:03.27	Amela	Terzic	SRB	2.1.93	5 Feb
2:03.41	Olivia	Baker	USA	12.6.96	25 Feb

JUNIORS

See main list for top 5 juniors. 11 performances by 6 women (3 **Indoors**) to 2:02.3. Additional mark and further juniors:

Watson	2:00.78	2	BosG	Somerville	2 Jun	2:01.47	3	Pre	Eugene	26 May
	2:00.99	6	NC	Sacramento	25 Jun	2:01.78i	5	Mill	New York (A)	11 Feb

Mark	Name		Nat	Born	Pos	Meet	Venue	Date
2:02.28	Tigist	Ketema	ETH	15.9.98	4	FBK	Hengelo	10 Jun
2:02.53	Danae	Rivers	USA	3.2.98	2		Charlottesville	21 Apr
2:02.57	Ayano	Shiomi	JPN	26.11.99	1		Yamagata	1 Aug
2:02.7A	Dinke	Ferdesa	ETH	28.5.99	2	NC-j	Bahir Dar	15 Jan
2:02.74	Ayaka	Kawata (10)	JPN	22.8.99	2		Yamagata	1 Aug
2:02.88A	Josephine	Chelangat	KEN	10.10.98	4	WCT	Nairobi	24 Jun
2:03.32	Caitlin	Collier	USA	5.8.99	1		St. Louis	1 Jun
2:03.41	Gadese	Ejara	ETH	7.7.98	6	FBK	Hengelo	10 Jun
2:03.46	Lili	Das	IND-	18.3.98	1		Mangalagiri	16 Jul
2:03.66	Sarah	Billings	AUS	7.3.98	4rC		Portland	11 Jun
2:03.66	Carly	Thomas	AUS-Y	26.12.00	3		Melbourne	19 Dec
2:03.90	Hiwot	Mehari	ETH-Y	–.01	7	FBK	Hengelo	10 Jun

Mark	Name		Nat	Born	Pos	Meet	Venue	Date
2:04.2A	Netsanet	Desta	ETH-Y	26.10.00	1		Assela	16 Jun
2:04.22	Victoria	Tachinski	CAN	15.6.99	1	PAm-J	Trujillo	22 Jul
2:04.30	Derlia	Sclabas (20)	SUI-Y	6.11.00	6r2		Belfort	9 Jun
2:02.89i	Aaliyah	Miller	USA	28.8.98	2		Ames	11 Feb

1000 METRES

Mark	Name		Nat	Born	Pos	Meet	Venue	Date
2:35.15	Lovisa	Lindh	SWE	9.7.91	1		Göteborg	11 Jul
2:36.51	Angelika	Cichocka	POL	15.3.88	1		Gliwice	10 Sep

Mark	Name		Nat	Born	Date	Mark	Name		Nat	Born	Date
2:38.13	Hanna	Hermansson	SWE	18.5.89	11 Jul	2:38.49	Sarah	McDonald	GBR	2.8.93	11 Jul
						2:39.82	Simona	Vrzalová	CZE	7.4.88	31 Jul

Indoors

Mark	Name		Nat	Born	Pos	Meet	Venue	Date
2:31.93	Laura	Muir	GBR	9.5.93	1		Birmingham	18 Feb
2:33.06	Genzebe	Dibaba	ETH	8.2.91	1		Madrid	24 Feb
2:36.97	Kate	Grace	USA	24.10.88	2		Birmingham	18 Feb
2:37.97A	Charlene	Lipsey	USA	16.7.91	1	NC	Albuquerque	5 Mar

Mark	Name		Nat	Born	Date	Mark	Name		Nat	Born	Date
2:38.05	Gudaf	Tsegay	ETH	23.1.97	24 Feb	2:39.47	Zoe	Buckman	AUS	21.12.88	18 Feb
2:38.19	Darya	Borisevich	BLR	6.4.90	24 Feb	2:39.76	Aleksandra	Gulyayeva	RUS	30.4.94	7 Jan
2:38.33A	Lauren	Johnson	USA	4.5.87	5 Mar	2:40.14	Mariah	Kelly	CAN	19.8.91	12 Feb
2:38.55	Axumawit	Embaye	ETH	18.10.94	24 Feb	2:40.18A	Hannah	Fields	USA	4.2.93	5 Mar
2:38.72	Sanne	Verstegen	NED	10.11.85	18 Feb						

JUNIOR: 2:40.72i Samantha Watson USA-J 10.11.99 4 NC Albuquerque 4 Mar

1500 METRES

Mark	Name		Nat	Born	Pos	Meet	Venue	Date
3:56.14	Sifan	Hassan	NED	1.1.93	1	FBK	Hengelo	11 Jun
3:56.22		Hassan			1	GGala	Roma	8 Jun
3:57.04	Faith	Kipyegon	KEN	10.1.94	1	VD-DLF	Bruxelles	1 Sep
3:57.10		Hassan			1	DL	Paris (C)	1 Jul
3:57.22		Hassan			2	VD-DLF	Bruxelles	1 Sep
3:57.51		Kipyegon			2	DL	Paris (C)	1 Jul
3:57.82+	Genzebe	Dibaba	ETH	8.2.91	1	Athl	Lausanne	6 Jul
3:58.92	Konstanze	Klosterhalfen	GER	18.2.97	1	ISTAF	Berlin	27 Aug
3:59.16	Winny	Chebet	KEN	20.12.90	2	GGala	Roma	8 Jun
3:59.22		Kipyegon			1	DL	Shanghai	13 May
3:59.30		Klosterhalfen			3	GGala	Roma	8 Jun
3:59.55	Gudaf	Tsegay	ETH	23.1.97	3	DL	Paris (C)	1 Jul
3:59.58		Klosterhalfen			1	NC	Erfurt	9 Jul
3:59.67		Kipyegon			1	Pre	Eugene	27 May
4:00.18		Chebet			3	VD-DLF	Bruxelles	1 Sep
4:00.35+	Laura	Muir	GBR	9.5.93	1	in 1M	London (OS)	9 Jul
4:00.36		Tsegay			4	VD-DLF	Bruxelles	1 Sep
4:00.44+	Hellen	Obiri	KEN	13.12.89	2	in 1M	London (OS)	9 Jul
4:00.46		Obiri			2	Pre	Eugene	27 May
4:00.47		Muir			3	Pre	Eugene	27 May
4:00.49	Meraf	Bahta	SWE	24.6.89	5	VD-DLF	Bruxelles	1 Sep
4:00.52	Dawit	Seyaum (10)	ETH	27.7.96	2	DL	Shanghai	13 May
4:00.59		Bahta			4	GGala	Roma	8 Jun
4:00.70	Jenny	Simpson	USA	23.8.86	6	VD-DLF	Bruxelles	1 Sep
4:00.71	Laura	Weightman	GBR	1.7.91	7	VD-DLF	Bruxelles	1 Sep
4:00.96		Tsegay			1	GS	Ostrava	28 Jun
4:00.98	Besu	Sado	ETH	12.1.96	2	FBK	Hengelo	11 Jun
4:01.32		Chebet			3	FBK	Hengelo	11 Jun
4:01.36		Seyaum			1	DL	Birmingham	20 Aug
4:01.42		Tsegay			5	GGala	Roma	8 Jun
	(30/13)							
4:01.60	Eilish	McColgan	GBR	25.11.90	2	ISTAF	Berlin	27 Aug
4:01.61	Angelika	Cichocka	POL	15.3.88	4	DL	Paris (C)	1 Jul
4:01.75	Rabab	Arrafi	MAR	12.1.91	4	Pre	Eugene	27 May
4:02.25	Susan	Krumins	NED	8.7.86	3	ISTAF	Berlin	27 Aug
4:02.75	Nelly	Jepkosgei	KEN	14.7.91	5	FBK	Hengelo	11 Jun
4:02.75	Brenda	Martinez	USA	8.9.87	3	DL	Rabat	16 Jul
4:02.84	Caster	Semenya	RSA	7.1.91	2h1	WCh	London (OS)	4 Aug
	(20)							
4:03.2A	Beatrice	Chepkoech	KEN	6.7.91	1	NC	Nairobi	10 Jun
4:03.35	Sofia	Ennaoui	POL	30.8.95	3h3	WCh	London (OS)	4 Aug
4:03.36	Malika	Akkaoui	MAR	25.12.87	5	DL	Rabat	16 Jul
4:03.55	Gabriela	Stafford	CAN	13.9.95	5	ISTAF	Berlin	27 Aug
4:03.57+	Ciara	Mageean	IRL	12.3.92	7	in 1M	London (OS)	9 Jul
4:03.59	Kate	Grace	USA	24.10.88	7	Pre	Eugene	27 May
4:03.73	Jessica	Judd	GBR	7.1.95	6h1	WCh	London (OS)	4 Aug
4:03.77	Maureen	Koster	NED	3.7.92	8	GGala	Roma	8 Jun

Mark	Name		Nat	Born	Pos	Meet	Venue	Date
4:03.93	Colleen	Quigley	USA	20.11.92	1		Heusden	22 Jul
4:04.15	Hanna	Klein	GER	6.4.93	2		Heusden	22 Jul
	(30)							
4:04.34	Amanda	Eccleston	USA	18.6.90	3		Heusden	22 Jul
4:04.37	Linden	Hall	AUS	29.6.91	2		Portland	11 Jun
4:04.4A	Judy	Kiyeng	KEN	10.12.94	2	NC	Nairobi	10 Jun
4:04.46	Winfredah	Nzisa	KEN	30.5.97	4		Heusden	22 Jul
4:04.49	Aleksandra	Gulyayeva	RUS	30.4.94	1	Znam	Zhukovskiy	2 Jul
4:04.56	Sara	Vaughn	USA	16.5.86	8h3	WCh	London (OS)	4 Aug
4:04.61	Shannon	Rowbury	USA	19.9.84	9	Pre	Eugene	27 May
4:04.63	Stephanie	Garcia	USA	3.5.88	5		Heusden	22 Jul
4:04.75	Alexa	Efraimson	USA	20.2.97	6		Heusden	22 Jul
4:04.82	Nicole	Sifuentes	CAN	30.6.86	6	ISTAF	Berlin	27 Aug
	(40)							
4:04.90	Yelena	Korobkina	RUS	25.11.90	1	NC	Zhukovskiy	30 Jul
4:04.93	Zoe	Buckman	AUS	21.12.88	8	DL	Rabat	16 Jul
4:04.94	Alemaz	Teshale	ETH-J	5.7.99	6	FBK	Hengelo	11 Jun
4:05.29	Katie	Snowden	GBR	9.3.94	2		Watford	14 Jun
4:05.30	Hannah	Fields	USA	4.2.93	1		Stanford	29 Jun
4:05.47	Meryem	Akdag	TUR	5.8.92	1		Bursa	7 Jul
4:05.48	Sarah	McDonald	GBR	2.8.93	9h3	WCh	London (OS)	4 Aug
4:05.71	Marta	Pen Freitas	POR	31.7.93	1		Greenville	3 Jun
4:05.71	Anastasiya	Kalina	RUS	16.2.94	2	NC	Zhukovskiy	30 Jul
4:05.77	Worknesh	Abye	ETH-J	-.99	7	FBK	Hengelo	11 Jun
	(50)							
4:05.81	Taye	Fantu	ETH-J	29.3.99	10h1	WCh	London (OS)	4 Aug
4:05.82+	Melissa	Courtney	GBR	30.8.93	10	in 1M	London (OS)	9 Jul
4:05.82	Marta	Pérez	ESP	19.4.93	11h1	WCh	London (OS)	4 Aug
4:05.88	Lauren	Johnson	USA	4.5.87	3		Portland	11 Jun
4:06.17	Shannon	Osika	USA	15.6.93	3		Greenville	3 Jun
4:06.20	Adanech	Anbesa	ETH-J	23.1.98	14	GGala	Roma	8 Jun
4:06.20	Siham	Hilali	MAR	2.5.86	10	DL	Rabat	16 Jul
4:06.22	Shelby	Houlihan	USA	8.2.93	10		Birmingham	20 Aug
4:06.30	Amela	Terzic	SRB	2.1.93	1		Huelva	14 Jun
4:06.30	Margherita	Magnani	ITA	26.2.87	8		Heusden	22 Jul
	(60)							
4:06.3A	Loice	Chemnung	KEN	22.2.97	4	NC	Nairobi	10 Jun
4:06.33	Claudia	Bobocea	ROU	11.6.92	7	DL	Shanghai	13 May
4:06.34	Esther	Chebet	UGA	10.9.97	1		Kortrijk	8 Jul
4:06.39	Solange Andreia	Pereira	ESP	12.12.89	11	DL	Rabat	16 Jul
4:06.43	Aníta	Hinriksdóttir	ISL	13.1.96	10	FBK	Hengelo	11 Jun
4:06.92+	Stephanie	Twell	GBR	17.8.89	13	in 1M	London (OS)	9 Jul
4:07.06	Helen Ekarare	Lobun	KEN-J	18.3.99	1		Yamagata	30 Jul
4:07.07	Sheila	Reid	CAN	2.8.89	1		Los Angeles (ER)	18 May
4:07.08	Simona	Vrzalová	CZE	7.4.88	9	ISTAF	Berlin	27 Aug
4:07.15	Katie	Mackey	USA	12.11.87	8	DL	Shanghai	13 May
	(70)							
4:07.23	Yelena	Murashova	RUS	5.10.87	3	NC	Zhukovskiy	30 Jul
4:07.25	Karoline Bjerkeli	Grøvdal	NOR	14.6.90	2		Oordegem	27 May
4:07.29	Emily	Lipari	USA	19.11.92	4		Stanford	29 Jun
4:07.32	Georgia	Griffith	AUS	5.12.96	1		Portland	16 Jun
4:07.38	Danuta	Cieslak	POL	24.12.89	1		Neustadt	2 Jul
4:07.38	Kate	Van Buskirk	CAN	9.6.87	1		Memphis	26 Aug
4:07.66	Violah	Lagat	KEN	13.3.89	3		Los Angeles (ER)	18 May
4:07.66	Anna	Shchagina	RUS	7.12.91	4	Znam	Zhukovskiy	2 Jul
4:07.70	Sasha	Gollish	CAN	27.12.81	4		Los Angeles (ER)	18 May
4:07.72	Jenny	Blundell	AUS	9.5.94	12	DL	Shanghai	13 May
	(80)							
4:07.76	Selah	Busienei	KEN	27.12.91	5		Padova	16 Jul
4:07.79	Darya	Borisevich	BLR	6.4.90	10		Heusden	22 Jul
4:07.90	Sanne	Verstegen	NED	10.11.85	12	FBK	Hengelo	11 Jun
4:07.93	Winnie	Nanyondo	UGA	23.8.93	10	ISTAF	Berlin	27 Aug
4:08.04	Dominique	Scott Efurd	RSA	24.6.92	6		Padova	16 Jul
4:08.17	Diana	Sujew	GER	2.11.90	2		Neustadt	2 Jul
4:08.19	Kristiina	Mäki	CZE	22.9.91	4		Liège (NX)	19 Jul
4:08.22	Megan	Moye	USA	27.3.94	6		New York	6 Jul
4:08.39	Sara	Sutherland	USA	31.1.92	8		Padova	16 Jul
4:08.42	Dani	Jones	USA	21.8.96	4		Portland	11 Jun
	(90)							
4:08.47	Linn	Nilsson	SWE	15.10.90	3		Dublin (S)	12 Jul
4:08.64	Bone	Cheluke	ETH-J	11.11.98	14	FBK	Hengelo	11 Jun

Mark	Name		Nat	Born	Pos	Meet	Venue	Date
4:08.81	Martyna	Galant	POL	26.1.95	1	EAF	Bydgoszcz	2 Jun
4:08.84	Fadwa Sidi	Madane	MAR	20.11.94	2		Barcelona	29 Jun
4:08.84	Caroline	Chepkemoi	KEN	1.3.93	12		Heusden	22 Jul
4:08.85	Mary	Kuria	KEN	29.11.87	6	GS	Ostrava	28 Jun
4:08.95	Rachel	Schneider	USA	18.7.91	6		Los Angeles (ER)	18 May
4:09.03	Lovisa	Lindh	SWE	9.7.91	1		Florø	10 Jun
4:09.08	Katie	Rainsberger	USA-J	18.8.98	2		Portland	16 Jun
4:09.17+	Axumawit (100)	Embaye	ETH	18.10.94	5	in 1M	Lausanne	6 Jul

Mark	Name		Nat	Born	Date
4:09.23	Blanca	Fernández	ESP	1.4.92	14 Jun
4:09.27	Olga	Nitsina	RUS	11.2.89	30 Jul
4:09.29	Regan	Yee	CAN	4.7.95	11 Jun
4:09.32	Charlene	Thomas	GBR	6.5.82	24 Jun
4:09.38	Mariah	Kelly	CAN	19.8.91	28 Jun
4:09.48	Sofie	Van Accom	BEL	7.6.89	22 Jul
4:09.52	Hannah	England	GBR	6.3.87	16 Jul
4:09.73	Anna	Ilyina	RUS	14.8.94	2 Jul
4:09.76	Luiza	Gega	ALB	5.11.88	2 Jun
4:09.80	Nuria	Fernández	ESP	16.8.76	14 Jun
4:09.90	Sarah	MacPherson	CAN	8.5.91	28 Jun
4:09.91	Shuru	Bulo	ETH-J	27.6.98	9 Jul
4:09.91	Sheila	Chelangat	KEN-J	11.4.98	12 Jul
4:09.94	Cory	McGee	USA	29.5.92	13 May
4:10.15	Gloria	Kite	KEN-J	29.12.98	19 Jul
4:10.24	Yekaterina	Sokolova	RUS	16.12.95	2 Jul
4:10.28	Gesa-Felicitas	Krause	GER	3.8.92	11 Jun
4:10.28	Nikki	Hiltz	USA	23.10.94	24 Jun
4:10.30	Melissa	Bishop	CAN	5.8.88	20 May
4:10.30	Adelle	Tracey	GBR	27.5.93	14 Jun
4:10.38	Johanna	Geyer Carles	FRA	10.10.95	3 Jun
4:10.41	Eleanor	Fulton	USA	17.5.93	28 Jun
4:10.42	Heidi	See	AUS	9.8.89	19 Jul
4:10.46	Kaela	Edwards	USA	8.12.93	12 Jul
4:10.52	Beyenu	Degefu	ETH-J	12.7.99	2 Jun
4:10.62	Tori	Tsolis	USA	9.3.93	16 Jun
4:10.68	Charlene	Lipsey	USA	16.7.91	15 Jun
4:10.70	Ann	Mwangi	KEN	8.12.88	21 May
4:10.8A	Margaret	Kipkemboi	KEN	9.2.93	18 May
4:10.89	Dina	Aleksandrova	RUS	9.8.92	2 Jul
4:10.89mx	Renée	Eykens	BEL	8.6.96	11 Aug
	4:13.50	Eykens			2 Jul
4:10.90	Julia	Kick	GER	10.5.90	9 Jul
4:10.91	Karisa	Nelson	USA	12.6.96	5 May
4:10.91	Geneviève	Lalonde	CAN	5.9.91	14 Jun
4:10.92	Elena	Burkard	GER	10.2.92	9 Jul
4:10.93	Annemarie	Schwanz	GER	26.4.93	8 Jun
4:11.00	Amy-Eloise	Neale	GBR	5.8.95	8 Jun
4:11.02	Erica	Digby	CAN	23.4.89	28 Jun
4:11.04	Natalija	Piliusina	LTU	22.10.90	11 Jun
4:11.1	Celliphine	Chespol	KEN-J	23.3.99	9 Jun
4:11.11	Letesenbet	Gidey	ETH-J	20.3.98	15 Jun
4:11.14	Biri	Abera	ETH-Y	29.4.00	15 Jun
4:11.15	Helen	Schlachtenhaufen	USA		27 May
4:11.18	Kim	Conley	USA	14.3.86	18 May
4:11.19	Olivia	Burdon	NZL-J	26.1.98	16 Jun
4:11.27	Ashley	Maton	USA	20.11.93	16 Jun
4:11.34	Mel	Lawrence	USA	29.8.89	11 Jun
4:11.34	Natalia	Evangelidou	CYP	10.3.91	14 Jun
4:11.46	Elise	Cranny	USA	8.5.96	22 Apr
4:11.47	Andrea	Seccafien	CAN	27.8.90	18 May
4:11.47	Liina	Tsernov	EST	28.12.87	16 Jul
4:11.61	Annie	Leblanc	CAN	29.4.92	19 Jul
4:11.63	Lianne	Farber	USA	12.6.92	16 Jun
4:11.67	Jessica	Harris	USA	14.3.96	27 May
4:11.72mx	Stacey	Smith	GBR	4.2.90	5 Jun
4:11.83	Anna Emilie	Møller	DEN	28.7.97	2 Jun
4:11.89	Yelena	Arzhakova	RUS	8.9.89	2 Jul
4:11.89	Emma	Coburn	USA	19.10.90	6 Jul
4:11.92	Jaimie	Phelan	CAN	2.9.95	8 Jun
4:11.92	Dana	Mecke	USA	20.9.87	10 Jun
4:11.97	Rebecca	Mehra	USA	25.10.94	16 Jun
4:11.98	Muriel	Coneo	COL	15.3.87	4 Aug
4:12.00	Delia	Sclabas	SUI-Y	8.11.00	6 Jul
4:12.07	Rhianwedd	Price	GBR	11.8.94	8 Jun
4:12.14	Brittany	McGowan	AUS	24.4.91	10 Jun
4:12.14	Marielle	Hall	USA	28.1.92	15 Jun
4:12.19	Carsyn	Koch	USA	5.1.96	14 Apr
4:12.20	Sandra	Tuei	KEN-J	20.1.98	16 Jul
4:12.28	Jemma	Reekie	GBR-J	6.3.98	2 Jul
4:12.28	Elise	Vanderelst	BEL-J	27.1.98	15 Jul
4:12.29	Gabe	Grunewald	USA	25.6.86	18 May
4:12.35	Alena	Shukhtuyeva	RUS	7.12.93	30 Jul
4:12.39	Jessica	O'Connell	CAN	10.2.89	10 Jun
4:12.49	Ayako	Jinnouchi	JPN	21.1.87	21 May
4:12.50	Danielle	Aragon	USA	1.7.94	27 May
4:12.51	Isabella	Andersson	SWE	13.6.97	10 Jun
4:12.54	Millie	Paladino	USA	18.10.95	27 May
4:12.57	Charline	Mathias	LUX	23.5.92	27 May
4:12.62mx	Alexandra	Bell	GBR	4.11.92	29 Aug
4:12.64	Emilee	Trost	USA	19.9.95	27 May
4:12.67	Amy	Griffiths	GBR	22.3.96	14 Jun
4:12.7A	Hawi	Samuel	ETH-J	1.2.99	17 Jan
4:12.93	Laura	Roesler	USA	19.12.91	18 May
4:12.99	Stephanie	Schappert	USA	25.4.93	18 May
4:12.99	Sarah	Inglis	CAN	28.8.91	10 Jun
4:12.99	Sara	Kuivisto	FIN	18.8.91	17 Jun
4:13.02	Viktoriya	Kushnir	BLR	9.2.93	17 Jun
4:13.10	Nicole	Tully	USA	30.10.86	12 Jul
4:13.11	Alina	Reh	GER	23.5.97	26 Jul
4:13.13	Frances	Schmiede	AUS	4.6.93	27 May
4:13.21	Denise	Krebs	GER	27.6.87	9 Jul
4:13.2A	Eunice	Sum	KEN	2.9.88	15 Apr
4:13.2A	Worknesh	Mulatu	ETH		21 May
4:13.34	Svetlana	Karamasheva	RUS	24.5.88	25 May
4:13.37	Albina	Chinchikeyeva	RUS	17.2.92	2 Jul
4:13.40	Angel	Piccirillo	USA	8.1.94	22 Jun
4:13.41	Marisa	Howard	USA	9.8.92	11 Jun
4:13.43	Christina (200)	Aragon	USA	17.6.97	22 Apr

Indoors

Mark	Name		Nat	Born	Pos	Meet	Venue	Date
3:58.80		Dibaba			1		Torun	10 Feb
4:04.56+	Shannon	Rowbury	USA	19.9.84	2	in 1M	New York (A)	11 Feb
4:04.95	Axumawit	Embaye	ETH	18.10.94	2		Torun	10 Feb
4:06.66	Luiza	Gega	ALB	5.11.88	1		Istanbul	17 Feb

Mark	Name		Nat	Born	Date
4:09.48	Renata	Plis	POL	5.2.85	14 Feb
4:11.43+	Heather	Kampf	USA	19.1.87	11 Feb
4:11.53	Diana	Mezuliáníková	CZE	10.4.92	14 Feb
4:11.54	Yasemin	Can	TUR	11.12.96	17 Feb
4:11.73	Katarzyna	Broniatowska	POL	22.2.90	10 Feb
4:11.93+	Leah	O'Connor	USA	30.8.92	11 Feb
4:12.35+	Elinor	Purrier	USA	20.2.95	11 Feb
4:12.55	Özlem	Kaya	TUR	20.4.90	17 Feb
4:13.19	Genevieve	LaCaze	AUS	4.8.89	15 Feb

JUNIORS

See main list for top 7 juniors. 11 performances by 5 women to 4:08.0. Additional marks and further juniors:

	Mark	Pos	Meet	Venue	Date	Mark	Pos	Meet	Venue	Date
Teshale	4:05.91	7		Heusden	22 Jul	4:07.41	10	DL	Shanghai	13 May
	4:06.67	2		Liège (NX)	19 Jul					
Fantu	4:06.93	2		Marseille	3 Jun	4:07.8A	1	NC	Addis Ababa	21 May
Ambesa	4:07.85	4	GS	Ostrava	28 Jun					

Mark	Name		Nat	Born	Pos	Venue	Date
4:09.91	Shuru	Bulo	ETH	27.6.98	1	Kitami	9 Jul
4:09.91	Sheila	Chelangat	KEN	11.4.98	2	Lignano	12 Jul

Mark	Name		Nat	Born	Pos	Meet	Venue	Date
4:10.15	Gloria	Kite (10)	KEN	29.12.98	8		Liège (NX)	19 Jul
4:10.52	Beyenu	Degefu	ETH	12.7.99	2		Andújar	2 Jun
4:11.1	Celliphine	Chespol	KEN	23.3.99	1		Mombasa	9 Jun
4:11.11	Letesenbet	Gidey	ETH	20.3.98	3		Hérouville	15 Jun
4:11.14	Biri	Abera	ETH-Y	29.4.00	4		Hérouville	15 Jun
4:11.19	Olivia	Burdon	NZL	26.1.98	5		Portland	16 Jun
4:12.00	Delia	Sclabas	SUI-Y	8.11.00	1	Athl-j	Lausanne	6 Jul
4:12.20	Sandra	Tuei	KEN	20.1.98	19		Padova	16 Jul
4:12.28	Jemma	Reekie	GBR	6.3.98	7	NC	Birmingham	2 Jul
4:12.28	Elise	Vanderelst	BEL	27.1.98	2		Ninove	15 Jul
4:12.7A	Hawi	Samuel (20)	ETH	1.2.99	2	NC-j	Bahir Dar	17 Jan

1 MILE

Mark	Name		Nat	Born	Pos	Meet	Venue	Date
4:16.05	Genzebe	Dibaba	ETH	8.2.91	1	Athl	Lausanne	6 Jul
4:16.56	Hellen	Obiri	KEN	13.12.89	1	DL	London (OS)	9 Jul
4:18.03	Laura	Muir	GBR	9.5.93	2	DL	London (OS)	9 Jul
4:19.55	Winny	Chebet	KEN	20.12.90	3	DL	London (OS)	9 Jul
4:19.58	Angelika	Cichocka	POL	15.3.88	4	DL	London (OS)	9 Jul
4:19.98	Jenny	Simpson	USA	23.8.86	5	DL	London (OS)	9 Jul
4:20.88	Laura	Weightman	GBR	1.7.91	6	DL	London (OS)	9 Jul
4:22.40	Ciara	Mageean	IRL	12.3.92	7	DL	London (OS)	9 Jul
4:23.15	Melissa	Courtney	GBR	30.8.93	8	DL	London (OS)	9 Jul
4:23.96	Linden	Hall (10)	AUS	29.6.91	9	DL	London (OS)	9 Jul
4:24.01	Kate	Grace	USA	24.10.88	10	DL	London (OS)	9 Jul
4:24.68	Stephanie	Garcia	USA	3.5.88	11	DL	London (OS)	9 Jul
4:25.15	Nelly	Jepkosgei	KEN	14.7.91	2	Athl	Lausanne	6 Jul
4:25.39	Stephanie	Twell	GBR	17.8.89	12	DL	London (OS)	9 Jul
4:25.89	Claudia	Bobocea	ROU	11.6.92	3	Athl	Lausanne	6 Jul
4:25.89	Katie	Snowden	GBR	9.3.94	13	DL	London (OS)	9 Jul
4:26.42	Malika	Akkaoui	MAR	25.12.87	4	Athl	Lausanne	6 Jul
4:27.51	Margherita	Magnani	ITA	26.2.87	5	Athl	Lausanne	6 Jul
4:27.79	Caroline	Chepkemoi	KEN	1.3.93	6	Athl	Lausanne	6 Jul
4:28.14	Axumawit	Embaye (20)	ETH	18.10.94	7	Athl	Lausanne	6 Jul
4:28.16	Esther	Chebet	UGA	10.9.97	8	Athl	Lausanne	6 Jul
4:28.32	Hannah	Fields	USA	4.2.93	1		Falmouth	19 Aug
4:28.51	Nicole	Sifuentes	CAN	30.6.86	2		Falmouth	19 Aug
4:28.59	Jessica	Judd	GBR	7.1.95	14	DL	London (OS)	9 Jul
4:28.82	Jenny	Blundell	AUS	9.5.94	10	Athl	Lausanne	6 Jul
4:28.84	Emily	Lipari	USA	19.11.92	1		South Huntington	6 Sep
4:28.96	Brenda	Martinez	USA	8.9.87	2		South Huntington	6 Sep

Mark	Name		Nat	Born	Date	Mark	Name		Nat	Born	Date
4:29.21	Lauren	Johnson	USA	4.5.87	19 Aug	4:32.05	Elinor	Purrier	USA	20.2.95	29 Apr
4:29.32	Kate	Van Buskirk	CAN	9.6.87	19 Aug	4:32.06	Genevieve	LaCaze	AUS	4.8.89	6 Sep
4:29.71	Hanna	Klein	GER	6.4.93	12 Jul	4:32.49	Stephanie	Schappert	USA	25.4.93	1 Jun
4:30.06	Blanca	Fernández	ESP	1.4.92	6 Jul	4:32.50	Hanna	Green	USA	16.10.94	29 Apr
4:30.22	Nicole	Tully	USA	30.10.86	1 Jun	4:32.57	Heather	Kampf	USA	19.1.87	19 Aug
4:30.24	Dominique	Scott Efurd	RSA	24.6.92	19 Aug	4:32.66	Rachel	Schneider	USA	18.7.91	4 Aug
4:30.34	Eleanor	Fulton	USA	17.5.93	1 Jun	4:32.77	Marielle	Hall	USA	28.1.92	29 Apr
4:30.60	Sara	Sutherland	USA	31.1.92	10 Aug	4:32.79	Regan	Yee	CAN	4.7.95	10 Aug
4:30.78	Emily	Infeld	USA	21.3.90	6 Sep	4:32.87	Sasha	Gollish	CAN	27.12.81	29 Apr
4:31.56	Heidi	See	AUS	9.8.89	6 Sep	4:33.19	Dana	Mecke	USA	20.9.87	29 Apr
4:31.58	Katie	Mackey	USA	12.11.87	19 Aug	4:33.67	Shannon	Osika	USA	15.6.93	29 Apr
4:31.72	Amanda	Eccleston	USA	18.6.90	4 Aug		(50)				

Indoors

Mark	Name		Nat	Born	Pos	Meet	Venue	Date
4:19.89	Sifan	Hassan	NED	1.1.93	1	Millrose	New York (A)	11 Feb
4:22.93	Kate	Grace	USA	24.10.88	2	Millrose	New York (A)	11 Feb
4:23.05	Shannon	Rowbury	USA	19.9.84	3	Millrose	New York (A)	11 Feb
4:24.16	Shelby	Houlihan	USA	8.2.93	1		Boston (A)	10 Feb
4:24.88	Colleen	Quigley	USA	20.11.92	2		Boston (A)	10 Feb
4:25.62	Rachel	Schneider	USA	18.7.91	3		Boston (A)	10 Feb
4:27.27	Brie	Felnagle	USA	9.12.86	1		Seattle	28 Jan
4:27.67	Cory	McGee	USA	29.5.92	1		Boston (A)	16 Dec
4:28.39	Heather	Kampf	USA	19.1.87	4	Millrose	New York (A)	11 Feb
4:28.47	Dominique	Scott Efurd	RSA	24.6.92	5	Millrose	New York (A)	11 Feb
4:28.75	Kaela	Edwards	USA	8.12.93	6	Millrose	New York (A)	11 Feb

Mark	Name		Nat	Born	Date	Mark	Name		Nat	Born	Date
4:29.44	Elinor	Purrier	USA	20.2.95	11 Feb	4:32.18	Anna	Shchagina	RUS	7.12.91	14 Feb
4:29.54	Alexa	Efraimson	USA	20.2.97	11 Feb	4:32.35	Kerri	Gallagher	USA	31.5.89	21 Jan
4:30.13	Charlene	Lipsey	USA	16.7.91	4 Feb	4:32.55	Danae	Rivers	USA-J	3.2.98	11 Feb
4:31.19	Aleksandra	Gulyayeva	RUS	30.4.94	21 Jan	4:32.73	Anastasiya	Kalina	RUS	16.2.94	21 Jan
4:31.24	Karisa	Nelson	USA	12.6.96	11 Mar	4:33.16	Síofra	Cléirigh Büttner	IRL	21.7.95	10 Feb
4:32.03	Megan	Krumpoch	USA	31.8.92	10 Feb	4:33.80	Jessica	Harris	USA	14.3.96	25 Feb
4:32.06	Sarah	McDonald	GBR	2.8.93	21 Jan	4:33.86	Grace	Barnett	USA	29.6.95	25 Feb

JUNIOR: 4:32.55i Danae Rivers USA-J 3.2.98 1 Seattle 11 Feb

Mark	Name		Nat	Born	Pos	Meet	Venue	Date

2000 METRES

Mark	Name		Nat	Born	Pos	Meet	Venue	Date
5:34.83+	Hellen	Obiri	KEN	13.12.89	1	in 3000	Monaco	21 Jul

Other intermedaiae times in 3000m races in Monaco and BIrmingham not known.

Indoors

Mark	Name		Nat	Born	Pos	Meet	Venue	Date
5:23.75	Genzebe	Dibaba	ETH	8.2.91	1		Sabadell	7 Feb
5:40.57+		Obiri			1	in 3000	Karlsruhe	4 Feb
5:41.5+	Laura	Muir	GBR	9.5.93	2	in 3000	Karlsruhe	4 Feb
5:42.5+	Sifan	Hassan	NED	1.1.9	2	in 3000	Birmingham	18 Feb
5:44.42	Aleksandra	Gulyayeva	RUS	30.4.94	1		Moskva	10 Jan

3000 METRES

Mark	Name		Nat	Born	Pos	Meet	Venue	Date
8:23.14	Hellen	Obiri	KEN	13.12.89	1	Herc	Monaco	21 Jul
8:28.66	Beatrice	Chepkoech	KEN	6.7.91	2	Herc	Monaco	21 Jul
8:28.90	Sifan	Hassan	NED	1.1.93	1	DL	Birmingham	20 Aug
8:29.89	Konstanze	Klosterhalfen	GER	18.2.97	2	DL	Birmingham	20 Aug
8:30.11	Margaret	Kipkemboi	KEN	9.2.93	3	DL	Birmingham	20 Aug
8:30.21		Obiri			4	DL	Birmingham	20 Aug
8:30.64	Laura	Muir	GBR	9.5.93	3	Herc	Monaco	21 Jul
8:31.00	Eilish	McColgan	GBR	25.11.90	5	DL	Birmingham	20 Aug
8:31.39		McColgan			4	Herc	Monaco	21 Jul
8:32.73	Lilian	Rengeruk	KEN	3.5.97	5	Herc	Monaco	21 Jul
8:33.38	Shannon	Rowbury	USA	19.9.84	6	Herc	Monaco	21 Jul
8:33.79		Rengeruk			6	DL	Birmingham	20 Aug
8:34.41	Susan	Krumins (10)	NED	8.7.86	7	DL	Birmingham	20 Aug
8:35.23	Agnes	Tirop	KEN	23.10.95	8	DL	Birmingham	20 Aug
8:35.37		Tirop			7	Herc	Monaco	21 Jul
8:35.77		Rowbury			9	DL	Birmingham	20 Aug
	(16/11)							
8:37.40	Shelby	Houlihan	USA	8.2.93	8	Herc	Monaco	21 Jul
8:37.50	Meraf	Bahta	SWE	24.6.89	9	Herc	Monaco	21 Jul
8:37.58	Karoline Bjerkeli	Grøvdal	NOR	14.6.90	10	Herc	Monaco	21 Jul
8:38.27+	Genzebe	Dibaba	ETH	8.2.91	1	in 5000	Roma	8 Jun
8:38.5e+	Yasemin	Can	TUR	11.12.96	2	in 5000	Roma	8 Jun
8:41.33	Dominique	Scott Efurd	RSA	24.6.92	11	Herc	Monaco	21 Jul
8:41.6e+	Letesenbet	Gidey	ETH-J	20.3.98	1	in 5000	Shanghai	13 May
8:42.2+e	Caroline	Kipkirui	KEN	26.5.94	2	in 5000	Bruxelles	1 Sep
8:43.24mx	Jessica	Judd	GBR	7.1.95	1		Watford	6 Sep
	8:59.60	Judd			1	LI	Loughborough	21 May
	(20)							
8:43.68	Azmera	Gebru	ETH	5.5.92	1		Madrid	14 Jul
8:43.68	Gelete	Burka	ETH	23.1.86	2		Madrid	14 Jul
8:43.72mx	Melissa	Courtney	GBR	30.8.93	2		Watford	6 Sep
8:44.46	Molly	Huddle	USA	31.8.84	10	DL	Birmingham	20 Aug
8:45.3+	Etenesh	Diro	ETH	10.5.91	8	in 5000	Roma	8 Jun
8:45.44	Buze	Diriba	ETH	9.2.94	1	BostonG	Somerville	2 Jun
8:45.94	Sheila	Kiprotich	KEN	27.12.90	2	BostonG	Somerville	2 Jun
8:48.27	Pauline	Kamulu	KEN	16.4.95	1		Fukagawa	6 Jul
8:48.60	Emma	Coburn	USA	19.10.90	11	DL	Birmingham	20 Aug
8:49.61	Riko	Matsuzaki	JPN	24.12.92	1		Kitami	9 Jul
	(30)							
8:50.18	Sandra	Tuei	KEN-J	20.1.98	3		Madrid	14 Jul
8:50.24	Dalilah Abdelkadir	Gosa	BRN-J	27.6.98	3	DL	Stockholm	18 Jun
8:51.02	Rosie	Clarke	GBR	17.11.91	12	DL	Birmingham	20 Aug
8:51.61	Rosemary	Wanjiru	KEN	9.12.94	1		Tokyo (Setagaya)	8 Apr
8:52.59	Joyline	Cherotich	KEN-J	22.3.98	2	Quercia	Rovereto	29 Aug
8:52.74	Stephanie	Garcia	USA	3.5.88	1		New York	6 Jul
8:53.43	Aisha	Praught Leer	JAM	14.12.89	3		Luzern	11 Jul
8:53.44	Sintayehu	Lewetegn	ETH	9.5.96	4		Luzern	11 Jul
8:53.48	Genevieve	LaCaze	AUS	4.8.89	13	DL	Birmingham	20 Aug
8:53.54	Mao	Ichiyama	JPN	29.5.97	2		Kitami	9 Jul
	(40)							
8:53.70	Helen Ekarare	Lobun	KEN-J	18.3.99	1		Yokohama	22 Apr
8:53.99	Courtney	Frerichs	USA	18.1.93	14		Birmingham	20 Aug
8:54.13	Heidi	See	AUS	9.8.89	3	Quercia	Rovereto	29 Aug
8:54.27	Nozomi	Tanaka	JPN-J	4.9.99	1		Matsuyama	9 Oct
8:54.28	Nicole	Tully	USA	30.10.86	2		New York	6 Jul
8:54.60	Sheila	Reid	CAN	2.8.89	1		Cork	18 Jul
8:54.68	Martha	Mokaya	KEN-Y	1.3.00	2		Matsuyama	9 Oct
8:54.88	Akari	Ogasawara	JPN-Y	3.10.00	3		Matsuyama	9 Oct

Mark	Name		Nat	Born	Pos	Meet	Venue	Date
8:54.95	Sarah	van der Wielen	SWE	18.2.95	4	DL	Stockholm	18 Jun
8:54.95	Ana	Lozano	ESP	22.2.91	5		Madrid	14 Jul
	(50)							
8:55.41	Emily	Infeld	USA	21.3.90	5		Luzern	11 Jul
8:55.55	Marielle	Hall	USA	28.1.92	1		Concord MA	1 Jun
8:56.08mx	Harriet	Knowles-Jones	GBR-J	3.4.98	1mx		Watford	3 May
8:56.1A	Behenu	Degefa	ETH-J	12.7.99	1	NC-j	Bahir Dar	17 Jan
8:56.29	Ririka	Hironaka	JPN-Y	24.11.00	4		Matsuyama	9 Oct
8:56.99	Lauren	Paquette	USA	27.6.86	3		Cork	18 Jul
8:57.15	Marisa	Howard	USA	9.8.92	3		New York	6 Jul
8:57.15	Rachel	Cliff	CAN	1.4.88	4		Cork	18 Jul
8:57.30	Katie	Mackey	USA	12.11.87	4	Quercia	Rovereto	29 Aug
8:57.46	Shuru	Bulo	ETH-J	27.6.98	1r2		Isahaya	23 Apr
	(60)							

Mark	Name		Nat	Born	Date
8:57.95	Haftamnesh	Tesfay	ETH	28.4.94	18 Jun
8:58.05+	A6maz	Ayana	ETH	21.11.91	13 Aug
8:58.30	Simona	Vrzalová	CZE	7.4.88	29 Aug
8:58.45	Mary	Manela	KEN-J	-.99	9 Oct
8:58.48	Charlotte	Arter	GBR	18.6.91	18 Jul
8:58.62	Margherita	Magnani	ITA	26.2.87	18 Jun
8:58.63	Fabienne	Schlumpf	SUI	17.11.90	11 Jul
8:58.88	Goytatom	Gebreselassie	ETH	15.1.95	2 Jun
8:58.91	Sarah	Pagano	USA	23.7.91	11 Jul
8:59.22	Alycia	Cridebring	USA	11.1.92	18 Jul
8:59.26	Marta	Pérez	ESP	19.4.93	17 Jun
9:00.04mx	Stephanie	Twell	GBR	17.8.89	31 May
	9:01.04	Twell			21 Jul
9:00.13	Naomi	Mussoni	KEN		13 May
9:00.25	Hisami	Ishii	JPN	10.8.95	18 Jul
9:00.32	Misaki	Onishi	JPN	24.2.85	9 Jul
9:00.48	Megan	Rolland	USA	30.8.88	6 Jul
9:00.70	Tabitha	Kamau	KEN-Y	.00	18 Jun
9:00.92	Cally	Macumber	USA	19.8.90	1 Jun
9:01.10	Elaina	Balouris	USA	17.12.91	11 Jul
9:01.2A	Alemtsehay	Assefa	ETH-J		17 Jan
9:01.24	Sofia	Ennaoui	POL	30.8.95	24 Jun
9:01.36	Yuna	Wada	JPN-J	7.8.99	9 Oct
9:01.43	Miriam	Cherop	KEN-J	25.6.99	2 Jun
9:01.45	Liina	Tsernov	EST	28.12.87	29 Aug
9:01.50	Linn	Nilsson	SWE	15.10.90	18 Jun
9:01.53	Mikuni	Yada	JPN-J	29.10.99	18 Jun
9:01.64	Hanna	Klein	GER	6.4.93	24 Jun
9:01.9A	Aberash	Manasebo	ETH-J		17 Jan
9:03.17	Rina	Nabeshima	JPN	16.12.93	13 May
9:03.37	Ema	Hayashi	JPN-Y	26.1.00	9 Oct
9:03.40	Nuria	Fernández	ESP	16.8.76	24 Jun
9:03.50	Ayuko	Suzuki	JPN	8.10.91	13 May
9:03.76	Rika	Kaseda	JPN-J	2.3.99	9 Jul
9:03.85	Emelia	Gorecka	GBR	29.1.94	29 Aug
9:03.9A	Abeba	Ejegu	ETH-J		17 Jan
9:04.4A	Birhan	Mehretu	ETH-J		17 Jan
9:04.85	Hanami	Sekine	JPN	26.2.96	13 May
	(96)				

Indoors

Mark	Name		Nat	Born	Pos	Meet	Venue	Date
8:26.41	Laura	Muir	GBR	9.5.93	1		Karlsruhe	4 Feb
8:29.41		Obiri			1		Birmingham	18 Feb
8:29.46		Obiri			2		Karlsruhe	4 Feb
8:30.76		Hassan			2		Birmingham	18 Feb
8:37.65	Dawit	Seyaum	ETH	27.7.96	3		Birmingham	18 Feb
8:44.63	Maureen	Koster	NED	3.7.92	6		Birmingham	18 Feb
8:45.29	Sofia	Ennaoui	POL	30.8.95	7		Birmingham	18 Feb
8:45.81	Genevieve	LaCaze	AUS	4.8.89	9		Birmingham	18 Feb
8:45.95	Stephanie	Twell	GBR	17.8.89	10		Birmingham	18 Feb
8:47.26	Kate	Grace	USA	24.10.88	1		Seattle	14 Jan
8:49.52	Axumawit	Embaye	ETH	18.10.94	3		Karlsruhe	4 Feb
8:50.36	Taye	Fantu	ETH-J	29.3.99	1		Eaubonne	10 Feb
8:50.74	Gudaf	Tsegay	ETH	23.1.97	2		Eaubonne	10 Feb
8:51.27	Heather	Kampf	USA	19.1.87	1		New York	4 Feb
8:51.58	Claudia	Bobocea	ROU	11.6.92	5		Karlsruhe	4 Feb
8:52.08	Kate	Van Buskirk	CAN	9.6.87	1	Millrose	New York (A)	11 Feb
8:52.35	Brie	Felnagle	USA	9.12.86	3		Seattle	14 Jan
8:52.53	Luiza	Gega	ALB	5.11.88	3		Eaubonne	10 Feb
8:53.55	Nicole	Sifuentes	CAN	30.6.86	4	New Bal	Boston (R)	28 Jan
8:53.56	Alina	Reh	GER	23.5.97	1	NC	Leipzig	19 Feb
8:54.61	Tori	Gerlach	USA	2.6.94	3	Millrose	New York (A)	11 Feb
8:54.71	Lauren	Paquette	USA	27.6.86	4		Seattle	14 Jan
8:55.21	Charlotta	Fougberg	SWE	19.6.85	3h2	EI	Beograd	3 Mar
8:55.68	Elinor	Purrier	USA	20.2.95	1		Boston (A)	2 Dec
8:55.83	Violah	Lagat	KEN	13.3.89	4	Millrose	New York (A)	11 Feb
8:56.13	Gesa-Felicitas	Krause	GER	3.8.92	2	NC	Leipzig	19 Feb
8:56.14	Leah	O'Connor	USA	30.8.92	5		Seattle	14 Jan
8:56.19	Giulia	Viola	ITA	24.4.91	7	EI	Beograd	5 Mar
8:56.52	Shannon	Osika	USA	15.6.93	5	Millrose	New York (A)	11 Feb
8:56.88	Adanech	Anbesa	ETH-J	23.1.98	3		Mondeville	4 Feb
8:57.24	Emily	Lipari	USA	19.11.92	2		New York	4 Feb

Mark	Name		Nat	Born	Date
8:57.65	Birtukan	Fente	ETH	18.6.89	18 Feb
8:57.86	Hanna	Klein	GER	6.4.93	19 Feb
8:58.06	Kalkidan	Fentie	ETH-J	9.5.98	18 Feb
8:58.20	Nuria	Fernández	ESP	16.8.76	3 Mar
8:58.91	Ancuta	Bobocel	ROU	3.10.87	3 Mar
8:59.34	Yelena	Korobkina	RUS	25.11.90	19 Feb
8:59.84	Yekaterina	Ishova	RUS	17.1.89	19 Feb
9:00.35	Sara	Sutherland	USA	31.1.92	4 Feb
9:00.59mx	Elinor	Kirk	GBR	26.4.89	29 Jan
9:00.73	Anna	Ilyina	RUS	14.8.94	19 Feb
9:00.81	Kate	Maltby	GBR	26.7.85	28 Jan
9:01.10	Renata	Plis	POL	5.2.85	4 Feb
9:01.21	Katie	Rainsberger	USA-J	18.8.98	11 Feb
9:02.19	Katarzyna	Broniatowska	POL	22.2.90	19 Feb
9:02.22	Dani	Jones	USA	21.8.96	11 Feb
9:03.00	Amanda	Eccleston	USA	18.6.90	4 Feb
9:03.03	Heather	MacLean	USA	31.8.95	2 Dec
9:03.21	Svetlana	Kudzelich	BLR	7.5.87	3 Mar

Mark	Name		Nat	Born	Pos	Meet	Venue	Date

Mark	Name		Nat	Born	Date	Mark	Name		Nat	Born	Date
9:03.71	Katherine	Receveur	USA	19.1.96	4 Feb	9:04.05	Natalya	Aristarkhova	RUS	31.10.89	19 Feb
9:03.92	Andrea	Seccafien	CAN	27.8.90	11 Feb	9:04.78	Vanessa	Fraser	USA	27.7.95	11 Feb
9:03.99	Birtukan	Adamu	ETH	29.4.92	18 Feb						

JUNIORS

See main list for top 12 juniors + 2 **Indoors**. 11 performances (1 **Indoors**) by 11 women to 8:56.5 and further juniors:

Mark	Name		Nat	Born	Pos	Meet	Venue	Date
8:58.45	Mary	Manela	KEN	-.99	9	Oct		
9:00.70	Tabitha	Kamau	KEN-Y	.00	1		Kumamoto	18 Jun
9:01.2A	Alemtsehay	Assefa	ETH		2	NC-j	Bahir Dar	17 Jan
9:01.36	Yuna	Wada	JPN	7.8.99	6		Matsuyama	9 Oct
9:01.43	Miriam	Cherop	KEN	25.6.99	4	BostonG	Somerville	2 Jun
9:01.53	Mikuni	Yada	JPN	29.10.99	2		Kumamoto	18 Jun
9:01.9A	Aberash	Manasebo (20)	ETH		3	NC-j	Bahir Dar	17 Jan
Indoors								
8:58.06	Kalkidan	Fentie	ETH	9.5.98	12		Birmingham	18 Feb
9:01.21	Katie	Rainsberger	USA-J	18.8.98	1		Seattle	11 Feb

5000 METRES

Mark	Name		Nat	Born	Pos	Meet	Venue	Date
14:18.37	Hellen	Obiri	KEN	13.12.89	1	GGala	Roma	8 Jun
14:22.47		Obiri			1	DL	Shanghai	13 May
14:25.22	Genzebe	Dibaba	ETH	8.2.91	1	Pre	Eugene	26 May
14:25.88		Obiri			1	VD-DLF	Bruxelles	1 Sep
14:27.55	Caroline	Kipkirui	KEN	26.5.94	2	VD-DLF	Bruxelles	1 Sep
14:31.76	Senbere	Teferi	ETH	3.5.95	2	DL	Shanghai	13 May
14:32.03		Teferi			3	VD-DLF	Bruxelles	1 Sep
14:32.82	Margaret	Kipkemboi	KEN	9.2.93	4	VD-DLF	Bruxelles	1 Sep
14:33.09	Agnes	Tirop	KEN	23.10.95	2	GGala	Roma	8 Jun
14:33.32	Letesenbet	Gidey	ETH-J	20.3.98	3	GGala	Roma	8 Jun
14:34.86		Obiri			1	WCh	London (OS)	13 Aug
14:36.80	Lilian	Rengeruk	KEN	3.5.97	2	Pre	Eugene	26 May
14:36.82	Yasemin	Can	TUR	11.12.96	4	GGala	Roma	8 Jun
14:36.84		Gidey			3	DL	Shanghai	13 May
14:39.33	Beatrice	Chepkoech (10)	KEN	6.7.91	5	VD-DLF	Bruxelles	1 Sep
14:40.29	Etenesh	Diro	ETH	10.5.91	5	GGala	Roma	8 Jun
14:40.35	Almaz	Ayana	ETH	21.11.91	2	WCh	London (OS)	13 Aug
14:41.24	Sifan	Hassan	NED	1.1.93	3	Pre	Eugene	26 May
14:41.55		Dibaba			6	GGala	Roma	8 Jun
14:41.61		Rengeruk			6	VD-DLF	Bruxelles	1 Sep
14:42.73		Hassan			3	WCh	London (OS)	13 Aug
14:42.74		Gidey			7	VD-DLF	Bruxelles	1 Sep
14:43.89		Kipkemboi			7	GGala	Roma	8 Jun
14:44.27		Rengeruk			1		Kortrijk	8 Jul
14:45.95		Kipkemboi			4	DL	Shanghai	13 May
14:47.11	Irene	Cheptai	KEN	4.2.92	8	GGala	Roma	8 Jun
14:47.45		Teferi			4	WCh	London (OS)	13 Aug
14:48.49	Eilish	McColgan	GBR	25.11.90	8	VD-DLF	Bruxelles	1 Sep
14:48.74		Kipkemboi			5	WCh	London (OS)	13 Aug
14:51.25	Susan	Krumins	NED	8.7.86	9	VD-DLF	Bruxelles	1 Sep
	(30/16)							
14:51.38	Konstanze	Klosterhalfen	GER	18.2.97	1		Karlsruhe	19 May
14:52.07	Laura	Muir	GBR	9.5.93	6	WCh	London (OS)	13 Aug
14:53.41	Ruth	Jebet	BRN	17.11.96	1	Isl.Sol	Baku	18 May
14:53.44	Sintayehu	Lewetegn	ETH	9.5.96	2		Kortrijk	8 Jul
	(20)							
14:54.05	Sheila	Kiprotich	KEN	27.12.90	7	WCh	London (OS)	13 Aug
14:54.66	Sheila	Chelangat	KEN-J	11.4.98	3		Kortrijk	8 Jul
14:56.33	Emily	Infeld	USA	21.3.90	2		Heusden	22 Jul
14:56.37	Sofia	Assefa	ETH	14.11.87	6	DL	Shanghai	13 May
14:57.38	Azmera	Gebru	ETH	5.5.92	4		Kortrijk	8 Jul
14:57.55	Shannon	Rowbury	USA	19.9.84	5h1	WCh	London (OS)	10 Aug
14:58.20	Shuru	Bulo	ETH-J	27.6.98	1		Abashiri	13 Jul
14:58.82	Pauline	Kamulu	KEN	16.4.95	2		Abashiri	13 Jul
14:58.99	Shalane	Flanagan	USA	8.7.81	3		Heusden	22 Jul
15:00.37	Shelby	Houlihan	USA	8.2.93	3h2	WCh	London (OS)	10 Aug
	(30)							
15:00.42	Darya	Maslova	KGZ	6.5.95	3	Isl.Sol	Baku	18 May
15:00.44	Karoline Bjerkeli	Grøvdal	NOR	14.6.90	6h2	WCh	London (OS)	10 Aug
15:00.45	Alia Mohamed	Saeed	UAE	18.5.91	4	Isl.Sol	Baku	18 May
15:03.27	Kidsan	Alema	ETH	19.7.95	4		Heusden	22 Jul
15:03.60	Molly	Huddle	USA	31.8.84	7h2	WCh	London (OS)	10 Aug
15:06.01	Gelete	Burka	ETH	23.1.86	4	Pre	Eugene	26 May

Mark	Name		Nat	Born	Pos	Meet	Venue	Date
15:07.19	Kalkidan	Gezahegne	BRN	8.5.91	8h2	WCh	London (OS)	10 Aug
15:07.27	Dera	Dida	ETH	26.10.96	5	Pre	Eugene	26 May
15:08.05	Belaynesh	Oljira	ETH	26.6.90	7	Pre	Eugene	26 May
15:08.24	Laura	Weightman	GBR	1.7.91	1		Los Angeles (ER)	18 May
	(40)							
15:08.29	Natosha	Rogers	USA	7.5.91	2		Los Angeles (ER)	18 May
15:08.59	Andrea	Seccafien	CAN	27.8.90	6		Heusden	22 Jul
15:09.45	Mercyline	Chelangat	UGA	17.12.97	8	DL	Shanghai	13 May
15:09.68	Rosemary	Wanjiru	KEN	9.12.94	1		Osaka	24 Sep
15:10.01	Alina	Reh	GER	23.5.97	9h1	WCh	London (OS)	10 Aug
15:10.90	Emily	Sisson	USA	12.10.91	7		Heusden	22 Jul
15:11.02	Marielle	Hall	USA	28.1.92	11	Pre	Eugene	26 May
15:11.83	Rina	Nabeshima	JPN	16.12.93	9h2	WCh	London (OS)	10 Aug
15:12.06	Fotyen	Tesfay	ETH-J	17.2.98	8		Heusden	22 Jul
15:12.47	Tomoko	Kimura	JPN	12.11.94	1		Yokohama	2 Dec
	(50)							
15:12.63	Madeline	Hills	AUS	15.5.87	9		Heusden	22 Jul
15:13.81	Martha	Mokaya	KEN-Y	1.3.00	2		Nobeoka	6 May
15:14.17	Sarah	Lahti/van der Wielen	SWE	18.2.95	3	EU23	Bydgoszcz	16 Jul
15:14.23	Ana	Lozano	ESP	22.2.91	10h1	WCh	London (OS)	10 Aug
15:14.54	Eloise	Wellings	AUS	9.11.82	10		Heusden	22 Jul
15:14.57	Kim	Conley	USA	14.3.86	12	Pre	Eugene	26 May
15:14.79	Helen Ekarare	Lobun	KEN-J	18.3.99	1		Yokohama	11 Nov
15:14.99	Jessica	O'Connell	CAN	10.2.89	11		Heusden	22 Jul
15:15.82	Goytatom	Gebreselassie	ETH	15.1.95	14	Pre	Eugene	26 May
15:16.65	Stephanie	Twell	GBR	17.8.89	1		Watford	24 Jun
	(60)							
15:16.70	Bontu	Edao Rebitu	BRN	12.12.97	11h1	WCh	London (OS)	10 Aug
15:17.14	Hanna	Klein	GER	6.4.93	2		Karlsruhe	19 May
15:17.91	Stella	Chesang	UGA	1.12.96	1		Nijmegen	2 Jun
15:18.32	Tsige	Abreha	ETH-Y	21.9.00	10	DL	Shanghai	13 May
15:18.57	Sarah	Pagano	USA	23.7.91	4		Los Angeles (ER)	18 May
15:18.69	Karissa	Schweizer	USA	4.5.96	4	NC	Sacramento	23 Jun
15:19.49	Beyenu	Degefu	ETH-J	12.7.99	12	GGala	Roma	8 Jun
15:19.62	Ann	Mwangi	KEN	8.12.88	1	NC	Osaka	25 Jun
15:19.73	Lauren	Paquette	USA	27.6.86	5		Los Angeles (ER)	18 May
15:19.81	Camille	Buscomb	NZL	11.7.90	3		Nijmegen	2 Jun
	(70)							
15:19.91	Riko	Matsuzaki	JPN	24.12.92	2		Stanford	5 May
15:19.96	Grace	Kimanzi	KEN	1.3.92	3		Abashiri	13 Jul
15:20.10	Dominique	Scott Efurd	RSA	24.6.92	13	GGala	Roma	8 Jun
15:20.10	Haftamnesh	Tesfay	ETH	28.4.94	14	GGala	Roma	8 Jun
15:20.11	Yui	Fukuda	JPN	1.6.95	3		Osaka	24 Sep
15:20.50	Ayuko	Suzuki	JPN	8.10.91	3	NC	Osaka	25 Jun
15:22.17	Kate	Van Buskirk	CAN	9.6.87	6		Stanford	5 May
15:22.36	Heidi	See	AUS	9.8.89	1rB		Stanford	5 May
15:22.85	Yuliya	Shmatenko	UKR	10.10.91	1	NC	Kropyvnytskiy	8 Jul
15:23.56	Shuri	Ogasawara	JPN-Y	3.10.00	4	NC	Osaka	25 Jun
	(80)							
15:24.12	Sasha	Gollish	CAN	27.12.81	1		Portland	16 Jun
15:24.17	Mao	Ichiyama	JPN	29.5.97	5		Osaka	24 Sep
15:24.53	Gesa-Felicitas	Krause	GER	3.8.92	12	DL	Shanghai	13 May
15:25.0A	Netsanet	Gudeta	ETH	12.2.91	3	NC	Addis Ababa	21 May
15:25.48	Vanessa	Fraser	USA	27.7.95	7	NC	Sacramento	23 Jun
15:26.00	Ednah	Kurgat	KEN	15.6.95	2rB		Stanford	5 May
15:26.18	Muriel	Coneo	COL	15.3.87	13h2	WCh	London (OS)	10 Aug
15:26.49	Mimi	Belete	BRN	9.6.88	14		Heusden	22 Jul
15:26.56	Amanda	Eccleston	USA	18.6.90	6		Los Angeles (ER)	18 May
15:26.59	Sara	Sutherland	USA	31.1.92	10		Stanford	5 May
	(90)							
15:27.14	Nicole	Tully	USA	30.10.86	9	NC	Sacramento	23 Jun
15:27.6mx	Katrina	Wootton	GBR	2.9.85	1mx		Nottingham	25 Aug
15:27.62	Yukari	Abe	JPN	21.8.89	11		Stanford	5 May
15:28.22	Giulia	Viola	ITA	24.4.91	3rB		Stanford	5 May
15:28.38	Esther	Muthoni	KEN	.96	3		Yokohama	2 Dec
15:28.64	Yuka	Hori	JPN	13.6.96	7		Osaka	24 Sep
15:28.95	Melissa	Courtney	GBR	30.8.93	4rB		Stanford	5 May
15:29.07	Charlotte	Taylor	GBR	17.1.94	13		Stanford	5 May
15:29.26	Lauren	Howarth	GBR	21.4.90	5rB		Stanford	5 May
15:30.28	Mariam	Waithera	KEN	23.12.96	6		Nobeoka	6 May
	(100)							

Mark	Name		Nat	Born	Pos	Meet	Venue	Date
15:30.32	Misaki	Onishi	JPN	24.2.85				13 Jul
15:30.91	Margherita	Magnani	ITA	26.2.87				5 May
15:31.07	Rachel	Cliff	CAN	1.4.88				16 Jun
15:31.21	Liv	Westphal	FRA	22.12.93				22 Jul
15:31.39	Nana	Kuraoka	JPN	13.9.97				13 Jul
15:32.25	Miyuki	Uehara	JPN	22.11.95				13 Jul
15:32.34	Jessica	Tonn	USA	15.2.92				23 Jun
15:32.34	Nozomi	Tanaka	JPN-J	4.9.99				15 Oct
15:32.49	Elaina	Balouris	USA	17.12.91				18 May
15:32.89	Misaki	Kato	JPN	15.6.91				24 Sep
15:32.92	Pamela	Cherotich	KEN	1.1.86				19 Aug
15:33.06	Rachel	Schneider	USA	18.7.91				5 May
15:33.06	Olga	Mazuronak	BLR	14.4.89				31 May
15:33.09	Nicole	Sifuentes	CAN	30.6.86				5 May
15:33.14	Kaori	Morita	JPN	19.9.95				13 Jul
15:33.25	Paulina	Kaczynska	POL	27.7.91				1 Jul
15:33.28	Nazret	Weldu	ERI	–.90				23 Jun
15:33.61	Ryo	Koido	JPN	19.9.97				29 Apr
15:33.86	Yekaterina	Ishova	RUS	17.1.89				25 May
15:34.14	Sandra	Tuei	KEN-J	20.1.98				2 Jun
15:34.17		Kim Do-yeon	KOR	2.9.93				13 Jul
15:34.44	Olga	Kungina	RUS	13.5.86				25 May
15:34.60	Viktoriya	Pohoryelska	UKR	4.8.90				8 Jul
15:34.82	Jessica	Judd	GBR	7.1.95				27 May
15:34.91	Salomé	Nyirarukundo	RWA	20.12.97				2 Jun
15:35.31	Rika	Kaseda	JPN-J	2.3.99				15 Oct
15:35.32	Nanami	Watanabe	JPN-J	24.3.98				23 Dec
15:35.55	Allie	Buchalski	USA	12.1.95				24 Mar
15:36.55	Kalkidan	Fentie	ETH-J	9.5.98				2 Jun
15:36.74		Jeong Da-un	KOR	9.5.97				13 Jul
15:37.12	Azusa	Sumi	JPN	12.8.96				6 Oct
15:37.13A	Meskerem	Mamo	ETH-J	13.4.99				1 Jul
15:37.19	Harumi	Okamoto	JPN-J	7.2.98				23 Dec
15:37.34	Louise	Carton	BEL	16.4.94				22 Jul
15:37.40	Lyudmila	Lebedeva	RUS	23.5.90				25 May
15:37.69	Samantha	Nadel	USA	5.6.94				23 Jun
15:37.82	Keiko	Nogami	JPN	6.12.85				6 Oct
15:37.90	Calli	Thackery	GBR	9.1.93				11 Jun
15:38.81	Lauren	LaRocco	USA	15.2.96				26 Jul
15:38.82	Mai	Nishiwaki	JPN	9.2.93				9 Dec
15:39.04	Saori	Noda	JPN	30.3.93				23 Dec
15:39.11	Misaki	Ogata	JPN	21.2.97				2 Dec
15:39.30	Amy-Eloise	Neale	GBR	5.8.95				31 Mar
15:39.38	Sakiko	Naito	JPN	2.9.94				2 Dec
15:39.43	Kasumi	Nishihara	JPN	1.3.89				9 Dec
15:39.82	Mai	Shoji	JPN	9.12.93				2 Dec
15:39.87	Mikuni	Yada	JPN-J	29.11.99				2 Dec
15:39.95	Sara	Moreira	POR	17.10.85				8 Jul
15:40.15	Charlotte	Arter	GBR	18.6.91				24 Jun
15:40.18	Mel	Lawrence	USA	29.8.89				22 Jul
15:40.37A	Hyvin	Jepkemoi	KEN	13.1.92				24 Jun
15:40.42	Natsuki	Sekiya	JPN	16.5.97				29 Apr
15:40.50	Hawi	Samuel	ETH-J	1.2.99				2 Jun
15:40.5mx	Louise	Small	GBR	27.3.92				16 Sep
	15:42.27							13 May
15:40.69	Fumika	Sasaki	JPN	23.5.93				9 Dec
15:40.73	Maja Møller	Alm	DEN	10.7.88				22 Jul
15:41.23	Erika	Kemp	USA	27.4.91				22 Apr
15:41.28	Brenda	Flores	MEX	4.9.91				15 Apr
15:41.29	Sarah	Inglis	GBR	28.8.91				11 Jun
15:41.34	Miku	Moribayashi	JPN-J	5.9.99				2 Dec
15:41.34	Kanami	Sagayama	JPN-J	9.7.98				9 Dec
15:41.54	Maki	Izumida	JPN-J	22.1.96				2 Dec
15:41.60	Risa	Yokoe	JPN	12.10.94				25 Jun
15:41.66	Alycia	Cridebring	USA	11.1.92				22 Jul
15:41.94	Cavaline	Nahimana	BDI	14.1.97				23 Jun
15:42.06	Rino	Goshima	JPN	29.10.97				6 Oct
15:42.09	Yuka	Kato	JPN-J	.99				2 Dec
15:42.17	Sakie	Arai	JPN	3.6.94				2 Dec
15:42.37	Misaki	Tanabe	JPN	31.8.95				2 Dec
15:42.81	Natasha	Wodak	CAN	17.12.81				11 Jun
15:42.82	Eri	Utsonomiya	JPN	17.6.93				2 Dec
15:43.04	Anna	Ilyina	RUS	14.8.94				28 Jul
15:43.07	Anna	Rohrer	USA	27.2.97				22 Apr
15:43.07	Samira	Mezeghrane	FRA	29.12.79				23 Jun
15:43.18	Moeno	Nakamura	JPN	21.3.90				29 Apr
15:43.49	Naruha	Sato	JPN	2.10.97				2 Dec
15:43.61	Anne-Marie	Blaney	USA	9.9.93				15 Apr
15:43.84	Alsu	Gabdullina	RUS	12.5.94				10 Jun
15:43.97	Chikako	Mori	JPN	25.11.92				24 Sep
15:44.12	Sayaka	Sato	JPN	27.5.94				24 Sep
15:44.14	Misaki	Hayashida	JPN	31.1.96				24 Sep
15:44.34	Emelia	Gorecka	GBR	29.1.94				5 May
15:44.51	Sharon	Lokedi	KEN	10.3.95				16 Jun
15.44.70	Akane	Yabushita	JPN	6.6.91				23 Dec
15:44.75	Gulshat	Fazlitdinova	RUS	28.8.92				28 Jul
15:44.80	Katherine	Receveur	USA	19.1.96				10 Jun
15:44.91	Mao	Kiyota	JPN	12.9.93				6 Oct
	(187)							

Indoors

Mark	Name		Nat	Born	Pos	Meet	Venue	Date
14:49.12	Laura	Muir	GBR	9.5.93	1		Glasgow	4 Jan
15:01.64	Molly	Huddle	USA	31.8.84	1		Boston (A)	26 Feb
15:02.10	Emily	Sisson	USA	12.10.91	2		Boston (A)	26 Feb
15:17.31	Karissa	Schweizer	USA	4.5.96	1		Boston (A)	2 Dec
15:19.03	Ednah	Kurgat	KEN	15.6.95	2		Boston (A)	2 Dec
15:27.36	Erin	Finn	USA	19.11.94	2	NCAA	College Station	10 Mar
15:28.89	Katherine	Receveur	USA	19.1.96	1	Big 10	Geneva	25 Feb
15:28.99	Tessa	Barrett	USA	9.2.96	2	Big 10	Geneva	25 Feb
15:29.83	Anna	Rohrer	USA	27.2.97	3	NCAA	College Station	10 Mar
15:37.03	Weini	Kelati	ERI	1.12.96				2 Dec
15:39.05	Sharon	Lokedi	KEN	10.3.95				2 Dec
15:43.95	Jordann	McDermitt	USA	23.4.96				10 Mar
15:44.45	Grayson	Murphy	USA	28.6.95				2 Dec

JUNIORS

See main list for top 9 juniors. 10 performances by 4 women to 15:13.0. Additional marks and further juniors:

	Mark	Pos	Meet	Venue	Date	Mark	Pos	Meet	Venue	Date
Gidey 3+	14:59.34	1h2	WCh	London (OS)	10 Aug	15:04.99	11	WCh	London (OS)	13 Aug
Bulo	15:12.13	2	Oda	Hiroshima	29 Apr	15:12.36	1		Nobeoka	6 May

Mark	Name		Nat	Born	Pos	Meet	Venue	Date
15:32.34	Nozomi	Tanaka (10)	JPN	4.9.99	1		Fukuroi	15 Oct
15:34.14	Sandra	Tuei	KEN	20.1.98	2		Andújar	2 Jun
15:35.31	Rika	Kaseda	JPN	2.3.99	2		Fukuroi	15 Oct
15:35.32	Nanami	Watanabe	JPN	24.3.98	2		Yokohama	23 Dec
15:36.55	Kalkidan	Fentie	ETH	9.5.98	4		Andújar	2 Jun
15:37.13A	Meskerem	Mamo	ETH	13.4.99	1	Af-J	Tlemcen	1 Jul
15:37.19	Harumi	Okamoto	JPN	7.2.98	3		Yokohama	23 Dec
15:39.87	Mikuni	Yada	JPN	29.11.99	8		Yokohama	2 Dec
15:40.50	Hawi	Samuel	ETH	1.2.99	5		Andújar	2 Jun
15:41.34	Miku	Moribayashi	JPN	5.9.99	9		Yokohama	2 Dec
15:41.34	Kanami	Sagayama (20)	JPN	9.7.98	4		Yamaguchi	9 Dec

10,000 METRES

Mark	Name		Nat	Born	Pos	Meet	Venue	Date
30:16.32	Almaz	Ayana	ETH	21.11.91	1	WCh	London (OS)	5 Aug
30:40.87	Gelete	Burka	ETH	23.1.86	1	FBK	Hengelo	10 Jun

Mark	Name		Nat	Born	Pos	Meet	Venue	Date
30:41.68	Senbere	Teferi	ETH	3.5.95	2	FBK	Hengelo	10 Jun
30:44.57	Belaynesh	Oljira	ETH	26.6.90	3	FBK	Hengelo	10 Jun
30:56.48	Dera	Dida	ETH	26.10.96	4	FBK	Hengelo	10 Jun
31:02.69	Tirunesh	Dibaba	ETH	1.10.85	2	WCh	London (OS)	5 Aug
31:03.50	Agnes	Tirop	KEN	23.10.95	3	WCh	London (OS)	5 Aug
31:05.14	Rahma	Tusa	ETH	14.9.93	5	FBK	Hengelo	10 Jun
31:07.56	Veronica	Nyaruai	KEN	29.10.89	6	FBK	Hengelo	10 Jun
31:11.86	Alice Aprot	Nawowuna (10)	KEN	2.1.94	4	WCh	London (OS)	5 Aug
31:13.06	Meraf	Bahta	SWE	24.6.89	1		Stanford	5 May
31:17.20	Amy	Cragg	USA	21.1.84	2		Stanford	5 May
31:18.20	Yasemin	Can	TUR	11.12.96	1	Isl.Sol	Baku	20 May
31:19.00	Desi Jisa	Mokonin	BRN	12.7.97	7	FBK	Hengelo	10 Jun
31:19.86	Molly	Huddle	USA	31.8.84	1	NC	Sacramento	22 Jun
31:20.24	Susan	Krumins	NED	8.7.86	5	WCh	London (OS)	5 Aug
31:20.45	Emily	Infeld	USA	21.3.90	6	WCh	London (OS)	5 Aug
31:21.11	Irene	Cheptai	KEN	4.2.92	7	WCh	London (OS)	5 Aug
31:22.67		Infeld			2	NC	Sacramento	22 Jun
31:24.78		Huddle			8	WCh	London (OS)	5 Aug
31:25.61	Goytatom	Gebreselassie	ETH	15.1.95	3		Stanford	5 May
31:25.64	Emily	Sisson (20)	USA	12.10.91	3	NC	Sacramento	22 Jun
31:26.36		Sisson			9	WCh	London (OS)	5 Aug
31:27.30	Ayuko	Suzuki	JPN	8.10.91	10	WCh	London (OS)	5 Aug
31:29.71	Zinash	Debebe	ETH	12.10.96	8	FBK	Hengelo	10 Jun
31:31.12	Shalane	Flanagan	USA	8.7.81	4	NC	Sacramento	22 Jun
31:32.53		Sisson			4		Stanford	5 May
31:33.33	Yuka	Takashima	JPN	12.5.88	5		Stanford	5 May
31:35.48		Can			11	WCh	London (OS)	5 Aug
31:35.88	Kim	Conley	USA	14.3.86	6		Stanford	5 May
	(30/25)							
31:37.81	Rose	Chelimo	BRN	12.7.89	2	Isl.Sol	Baku	20 May
31:38.66	Shitaye	Eshete	BRN	21.5.90	12	WCh	London (OS)	5 Aug
31:39.41	Mizuki	Matsuda	JPN	31.5.95	1	NC	Osaka	23 Jun
31:40.48	Mercyline	Chelangat	UGA	17.12.97	13	WCh	London (OS)	5 Aug
31:41.10	Madeline	Hills	AUS	15.5.87	7		Stanford	5 May
	(30)							
31:41.23	Rosemary	Wanjiru	KEN	9.12.94	1		Akita	20 May
31:43.40	Juliet	Chekwel	UGA	25.5.90	1		Marina di Carrara	22 Apr
31:45.02	Camille	Buscomb	NZL	11.7.90	9		Stanford	5 May
31:45.63mx	Katrina	Wootton	GBR	2.9.85	1mx		London (Catford)	3 Sep
	32:27.47	Wootton			3	NC	London (PH)	20 May
31:47.13	Pauline	Kamulu	KEN	16.4.95	2		Akita	20 May
31:47.37	Failuna Abdi	Matanga	TAN	28.10.92	9	FBK	Hengelo	10 Jun
31:48.81	Miyuki	Uehara	JPN	22.11.95	3	NC	Osaka	23 Jun
31:49.01	Mao	Ichiyama	JPN	29.5.97	10		Stanford	5 May
31:49.01	Alia Mohamed	Saeed	UAE	18.5.91	3	Isl.Sol	Baku	20 May
31:54.62	Natosha	Rogers	USA	7.5.91	5	NC	Sacramento	22 Jun
	(40)							
31:55.46	Kaitlin	Goodman	USA	31.1.87	11		Stanford	5 May
31:55.47	Natasha	Wodak	CAN	17.12.81	16	WCh	London (OS)	5 Aug
31:57.23	Darya	Maslova	KGZ	6.5.95	17	WCh	London (OS)	5 Aug
31:57.42	Sitora	Khamidova	UZB	12.5.89	18	WCh	London (OS)	5 Aug
31:58.23	Gebeyanesh	Ayele	ETH	1.5.95	10	FBK	Hengelo	10 Jun
31:58.99	Anna	Rohrer	USA	27.2.97	1		Stanford	31 Mar
31:59.80	Yuka	Hori	JPN	13.6.96	5	NC	Osaka	23 Jun
31:59.88	Stephanie	Bruce	USA	14.1.84	2		Stanford	31 Mar
31:59.94	Kaori	Morita	JPN	19.9.95	1		Yamaguchi	9 Dec
32:00.03	Rachel	Cliff	CAN	1.4.88	20	WCh	London (OS)	5 Aug
	(50)							
32:00.46	Erin	Finn	USA	19.11.94	6	NC	Sacramento	22 Jun
32:03.57	Sara	Moreira	POR	17.10.85	1	ECp	Minsk	10 Jun
32:04.63	Beth	Potter	GBR	27.12.91	1	NC	London (PH)	20 May
32:05.99	Chikako	Mori	JPN	25.11.92	2		Yamaguchi	9 Dec
32:06.22	Doricah	Obare	KEN	10.1.90	12		Stanford	5 May
32:07.11	Anna	Matsuda	JPN	18.4.94	4		Yamaguchi	9 Dec
32:07.62	Carla Salomé	Rocha	POR	25.4.90	1		Maia	12 Jul
32:08.09	Akane	Sekino	JPN	28.7.90	1		Takamatsu	26 Nov
32:08.46	Riko	Matsuzaki	JPN	24.12.92	5		Yamaguchi	9 Dec
32:09.89	Allie	Kieffer	USA	16.9.87	3		Portland	10 Jun
	(60)							
32:10.22	Hanami	Sekine	JPN	26.2.96	13		Stanford	5 May

Mark	Name		Nat	Born	Pos	Meet	Venue	Date
32:10.59	Eilish	McColgan	GBR	25.11.90	3		Stanford	31 Mar
32:10.6A	Pascalia	Kipkoech	KEN	22.12.88	2	NC	Nairobi	9 Jun
32:11.67	Trihas	Gebre	ESP	29.4.90	1		Huelva	8 Apr
32:11.80	Charlotte	Taylor	GBR	17.1.94	4		Stanford	31 Mar
32:13.73	Olga	Mazuronak	BLR	14.4.89	2	ECp	Minsk	10 Jun
32:14.43	Yelena	Sedova	RUS	1.3.90	1	Znam	Zhukovskiy	1 Jul
32:16.23	Stephanie	Twell	GBR	17.8.89	2	NC	London (PH)	20 May
32:16.44	Sakiho	Tsutsui	JPN	19.1.96	2		Kobe	23 Apr
32:16.78	Kellyn	Taylor	USA	22.7.86	5		Stanford	31 Mar
	(70)							
32:17.29	Harumi	Okamoto	JPN-J	7.2.98	6		Yamaguchi	9 Dec
32:18.93	Ancuta	Bobocel	ROU	3.10.87	2		Maia	12 Jul
32:19.18	Rina	Nabeshima	JPN	16.12.93	3		Osaka	22 Sep
32:21.79	Rie	Fujita	JPN	18.10.94	7		Yamaguchi	9 Dec
32:22.51	Elvin	Kibet	KEN	4.2.90	14		Stanford	5 May
32:23.95	Sarah	Pagano	USA	23.7.91	15		Stanford	5 May
32:24.61	Yukari	Abe	JPN	21.8.89	4		Osaka	22 Sep
32:26.3A	Joyciline	Jepkosgei	KEN	8.12.93	1		Nairobi	11 May
32:26.31	Eloise	Wellings	AUS	9.11.82	22	WCh	London (OS)	5 Aug
32:26.93	Yuri	Nozoe	JPN	3.5.96	9		Yamaguchi	9 Dec
	(80)							
32:27.36	Sayaka	Kuwahara	JPN	8.3.93	1		Kitami	9 Jul
32:27.58	Natsumi	Matsushita	JPN	22.1.95	10		Yamaguchi	9 Dec
32:27.88	Catarina	Ribeiro	POR	31.5.90	3		Huelva	8 Apr
32:28.05	Liz	Costello	USA	23.2.88	7	NC	Sacramento	22 Jun
32:29.28	Alice	Wright	GBR	3.11.94	16		Stanford	5 May
32:29.78	Misaki	Kato	JPN	15.6.91	5		Osaka	22 Sep
32:31.22	Celia	Sullohern	AUS	5.7.92	1	Zat	Melbourne	14 Dec
32:34.65	Misuzu	Nakahara	JPN	29.11.94	11		Yamaguchi	9 Dec
32:34.73	Elaina	Balouris	USA	17.12.91	17		Stanford	5 May
32:34.97	Kinsey	Gomez	USA	-.92	4		Portland	10 Jun
	(90)							
32:35.0A	Sheila	Kiprotich	KEN	27.12.90	2		Nairobi	11 May
32:35.06	Jessica	Trengove	AUS	15.8.87	2	Zat	Melbourne	14 Dec
32:35.33	Ai	Inoue	JPN	13.1.90	7	NC	Osaka	23 Jun
32:35.86	Tatiele Roberta	de Carvalho	BRA	22.11.89	18		Stanford	5 May
32:35.86	Risa	Yokoe	JPN	12.10.94	2		Kitami	9 Jul
32:35.93	Ayano	Ikemitsu	JPN	18.4.91	12		Yamaguchi	9 Dec
32:36.03	Beverly	Ramos	PUR	24.8.87	19		Stanford	5 May
32:36.14	Misaki	Tanabe	JPN	31.8.95	13		Yamaguchi	9 Dec
32:36.83	Yuki	Munehisa	JPN	15.12.97	3		Kitami	9 Jul
32:37.21	China	Takano	JPN	30.10.97	14		Yamaguchi	9 Dec
	(100)							

Mark	Name		Nat	Born	Date
32:37.52	Charlotte	Arter	GBR	18.6.91	19 Aug
32:38.98	Shiho	Takechi	JPN	18.8.90	22 Sep
32:39.16	Ai	Hosoda	JPN	27.11.95	23 Apr
32:40.63	Ayaka	Fujimoto	JPN	8.7.97	20 May
32:40.84	Inês	Monteiro	POR	18.5.80	8 Apr
32:41.03	Esma	Aydemir	TUR	1.1.92	10 Jun
32:41.19	Sonia	Samuels	GBR	16.5.79	5 May
32:41.64	Keiko	Nogami	JPN	6.12.85	20 May
32:42.62	Suriya	Loganathan	IND	7.7.90	28 Sep
32:42.93	Jo	Pavey	GBR	20.9.73	20 May
32:43.21	Carolina	Tabares	COL	18.7.86	5 May
32:43.45	Misato	Horie	JPN	10.3.87	23 Apr
32:43.87	Ayaka	Inoue	JPN	19.6.91	9 Jul
32:43.89	Chemtai Lonah	Salpeter	ISR	12.12.88	20 Apr
32:44.19	Clementine	Mukandanga	RWA	8.12.85	22 Apr
32:44.23	Kanayo	Miyata	JPN	14.2.95	23 Jun
32:44.45	Yui	Fukuda	JPN	1.6.95	9 Jul
32:45.92	Michi	Numata	JPN	6.5.89	9 Jul
32:45.95	Salomé	Nyirarukundo	RWA	20.12.97	5 Aug
32:46.10	Sharon	Lokedi	KEN	10.3.95	8 Jun
32:46.37	Sabrina	Mockenhaupt	GER	6.12.80	10 Jun
32:46.74	Mimi	Belete	BRN	9.6.88	10 Jun
32:46.91	Sarah	Lahti/van der Wielen	SWE	18.2.95	14 Jul
32:47.24	Saki	Fukui	JPN	25.3.96	9 Jul
32:47.50	Natsuki	Sekiya	JPN	16.5.97	25 Nov
32:48.59	Ryoko	Kitawaki	JPN	24.10.97	25 Nov
32:48.62	Svetlana	Kudzelich	BLR	7.5.87	10 Jun
32:48.69	Yukari	Ishizawa	JPN	16.4.88	22 Sep
32:49.42	Misaki	Ogata	JPN	20.2.97	25 Nov
32:49.70	Grace	Kimanzi	KEN	1.3.92	6 Jul
32:50.37	Peninah	Lokato	KEN	14.1.85	20 Apr
32:50.40	Sayaka	Mori	JPN	-.96	25 Nov
32:50.70	Bethany	Sachtleben	USA	9.2.92	31 Mar
32:50.91	Maki	Izumida	JPN	22.1.96	25 Nov
32:51.02	Margarita	Hernández	MEX	3.12.85	5 May
32:51.38	Claire	Duck	GBR	29.8.85	20 May
32:51.78	Emma	Mitchell	IRL	2.9.93	20 May
32:51.80	Yuki	Sato	JPN	11.12.96	25 Nov
32:52.37	Lauren	LaRocco	USA	15.2.96	5 May
32:52.83	Hitomi	Mizuguchi	JPN	-.96	25 Nov
32:52.87	Misora	Daido	JPN-J	.98	9 Dec
32:53.91	Honoka	Tanaike	JPN	-.97	9 Jul
32:54.98	Anastasiya	Ivanova	BLR	4.11.82	10 Jun
32:55.06	Iwona	Bernardelli	POL	19.2.85	20 May
32:55.11	Yuko	Kikuchi	JPN	8.6.92	9 Dec
32:56.11	Louise	Small	GBR	27.3.92	20 May
32:56.36	Kenza	Dahmani	ALG	18.11.80	16 Jun
32:56.72	Maho	Shimizu	JPN	-.95	25 Nov
32:56.87	Reina	Iwade	JPN	8.12.94	9 Jul
32:56.87	Yuki	Mitsunobu	JPN	9.11.92	22 Sep
32:57.23	Yuma	Adachi	JPN	19.7.96	9 Jul
32:57.50	Nami	Hashimoto	JPN	8.8.91	9 Jul
32:58.31	Alyssa	Snyder	USA	10.5.97	8 Jun
32:59.52	Jennifer	Nesbitt	GBR	24.1.95	20 May
33:00.24	Jessica	Martin	GBR	1.10.92	20 May
33:00.84	Phoebe	Law	GBR	12.1.97	20 May
33:01.18	Suzuna	Seiyama	JPN	19.9.94	22 Sep
33:03.22	Erin	Clark	USA	28.12.94	8 Jun
33:03.47	Hisami	Ishii	JPN	10.8.95	22 Sep
33:04.79	Akane	Fujihara	JPN	-.96	25 Nov
33:04.9A	Beatrice	Mutai	KEN	19.4.87	9 Jun
33:05.02	Saori	Imamura	JPN	24.3.96	8 Sep
33:05.66		Kim Do-yeon	KOR	2.9.93	6 Jul
33:05.99	Mizuki	Tanimoto	JPN	18.12.94	22 Sep

Mark	Name		Nat	Born	Date
33:06.00	Viktoriya	Polyudina	KGZ	29.6.89	20 May
33:06.03	Regan	Rome	USA	26.3.96	8 Jun
33:06.28	Anna	Belokobylskaya	RUS	10.10.95	1 Jul
33:06.86	Chelsea	Blaase	USA	10.4.94	8 Jun
33:07.28	Katarzyna	Rutkowska	POL	14.1.94	8 Apr
33:07.70	Momoe	Nobuoka	JPN	.97	9 Jul
33:08.06		Wang Jiali	CHN	1.2.86	16 May
33:08.13	Mari	Ozaki	JPN	16.7.75	23 Apr
33:08.2A	Mary	Wangui	KEN-J	12.9.99	23 Jun
33:08.26	Moeno	Shimizu	JPN	20.3.97	23 Apr
33:08.93	Erika	Ikeda	JPN	10.6.91	23 Apr
33:09.13	Mara	Olson	USA	8.3.93	31 Mar
33:09.26	Kayoko	Fukushi	JPN	25.3.82	19 May
33:09.67	Jamie	Kempfer	USA		31 Mar
33:09.67	Caroline	Sang	KEN	22.7.95	8 Jun
	(178)				

JUNIORS

Mark	Name		Nat	Born	Pos	Meet	Venue	Date
32:17.29	Harumi	Okamoto	JPN	7.2.98	6		Yamaguchi	9 Dec
32:52.87	Misora	Daido	JPN	.98	15		Yamaguchi	9 Dec
33:08.2A	Mary	Wangui	KEN-J	12.9.99	6	WCT	Nairobi	23 Jun
33:11.68	Yuka	Kato	JPN	.99	2rB		Kitami	7 Sep
33:13.24	Kako	Okada	JPN	.098	10		Yookhama	25 Nov
33:23.8A	Sandra	Tuei	KEN	20.1.98	6	NC	Nairobi	9 Jun

10 KILOMETRES ROAD

Mark		Name		Nat	Born	Pos	Meet	Venue	Date
29:43		Joyciline	Jepkosgei	KEN	8.12.93	1		Praha	9 Sep
30:04+			Jepkosgei			1	in HMar	Praha	1 Apr
30:05+		Violah	Jepchumba	BRN	23.10.90	2	in HMar	Praha	1 Apr
30:06		Fancy	Chemutai	KEN	20.3.95	2		Praha	9 Sep
30:07+			Jepkosgei			1=	in HMar	Valencia	22 Oct
30:07+			Chemutai			1=	in HMar	Valencia	22 Oct
30:23			Chemutai			1		Appingedam	24 Jun
30:25			Jepchumba			3		Praha	1 Apr
30:28		Sheila	Chepkirui	KEN	27.12.90	4		Praha	9 Sep
30:38		Senbere	Teferi	ETH	3.5.95	1		Tilburg	3 Sep
30:41	P	Mary	Keitany	KEN	18.1.82	1		Cape Elizabeth	5 Aug
30:45		Caroline	Kipkirui	KEN	26.5.94	1		Birmingham	30 Apr
30:56+			Chemutai			3	in HMar	Praha	1 Apr
30:57			Jepchumba			2		Birmingham	30 Apr
30:57+			Jepchumba			1	in HMar	Ústí nad Labem	16 Sep
30:58+		Edith	Chelimo	KEN	16.7.86	1	in HMar	Cardiff	1 Oct
31:00		Agnes	Tirop	KEN	23.10.95	2		Tilburg	3 Sep
31:01	P	Purity	Rionoripo	KEN	10.6.93	2		Cape Elizabeth	5 Aug
31:03			T Dibaba			1		Manchester	28 May
31:07+		Peres	Jepchirchir	KEN	27.9.93	1=	in HMar	Ra's Al-Khaymah	10 Feb
31:07+			Keitany			1=	in HMar	Ra's Al-Khaymah	10 Feb
31:08+			Jepkosgei			3	in HMar	Ra's Al-Khaymah	10 Feb
31:08+		Ruth	Chepngetich	KEN	8.8.94		in Mar	Istanbul	30 Apr
31:08+		Eunice	Jepkirui	BRN	20.5.84		in Mar	Istanbul	30 Apr
31:10+			Jepkosgei			1	in HMar	Gifu	23 Apr

Where better than 10,000m track times P = point-to-point course

Mark		Name		Nat	Born	Pos	Meet	Venue	Date
31:14	P	Meseret	Defar	ETH	19.11.83	3		Cape Elizabeth	5 Aug
31:15		Gladys	Kimaina	KEN	1.3.93	1		Paderborn	15 Apr
31:15	P	Shalane	Flanagan	USA	8.7.81	4		Cape Elizabeth	5 Aug
31:16		Helen	Tola	ETH	21.11.94	1		Lausanne	22 Oct
31:17+dq?		Jemima	Sumgong	KEN	21.12.84		in HMar	Ra's Al-Khaymah	10 Feb
31:17+		Helah	Kiprop	KEN	7.4.85		in HMar	Ra's Al-Khaymah	10 Feb
31:17+		Lucy	Cheruiyot	KEN	4.1.97		in HMar	Valencia	22 Oct
31:20		Mary	Munanu	KEN	12.12.94	1		Hamburg	10 Sep
31:21+		Nancy	Kiprop	KEN	7.7.79		in HMar	Ústí nad Labem	16 Sep
31:23		Sofiya	Shemsu	ETH	12.9.94	2		Paderborn	15 Apr
31:24		Joan	Chelimo	KEN	10.11.88	1		Boston	25 Jun
31:24+		Yvonne	Jelagat Morwa	KEN	12.11.93		in 15k	Le-Puy-en-Velay	1 May
31:25+		Vivian	Cheruiyot	KEN	11.9.83		in Mar	London	23 Apr
31:25		Karoline Bjerkeli	Grøvdal	NOR	14.6.90	1		Hole	21 Oct
31:28		Beatrice	Mutai	KEN	19.4.87	3		Tilburg	3 Sep
31:29+		Gladys	Chesire	KEN	20.2.93		in HMar	Praha	1 Apr
31:29+		Valary	Aiyabei	KEN	8.6.91		in HMar	Praha	1 Apr
31:31+		Betty	Lempus	KEN			in HMar	Milano	19 Mar
31:31+		Florence	Kiplagat	KEN	27.2.87		in Mar	London	23 Apr
31:32+		Aselefech	Mergia	ETH	23.1.85		in Mar	London	23 Apr
31:33+		Worknesh	Degefa	ETH	28.10.90	in Mar		Istanbul	30 Apr
31:33		Mercy	Ngugi	KEN	17.12.88	2		Boston	25 Jun
31:35		Netsanet	Gudeta	ETH	12.2.91	1		Ottawa	27 May
31:35		Stacy	Ndiwa	KEN	6.12.92	1		Houilles	31 Dec
31:37		Mamitu	Daska	ETH	16.10.83	1		New York	9 Apr
31:37		Buze	Diriba	ETH	9.2.94	3		Boston	25 Jun
31:38+		Aberu	Kebede	ETH	12.9.86		in Mar	London	23 Apr

Mark		Name		Nat	Born	Pos	Meet	Venue	Date
31:38		Mercyline	Chelangat	UGA	17.12.97	1		Durban	8 Oct
31:38		Alina	Reh	GER	23.5.97	1		Berlin	8 Oct
31:42+		Gladys	Cherono	KEN	12.5.83		in HMar	Ostia	12 Mar
31:42+		Angela	Tanui	KEN	27.7.92		in HMar	Ostia	12 Mar
31:42+		Rebecca	Kangogo	KEN	-.92		in HMar	Ostia	12 Mar
31:43+		Eunice	Chumba	BRN	23.5.93		in HMar	København	17 Sep
31:43+		Brigid	Kosgei	KEN	20.2.94		in HMar	København	17 Sep
31:43+		Roza	Dereje	ETH	6.5.97		in HMar	København	17 Sep
31:43+		Meskerem	Assefa	ETH	20.9.85		in HMar	København	17 Sep
31:43+		Agnes	Barsosio	KEN	5.8.82		in HMar	København	17 Sep
31:43+		Pascalia	Kipkoech	KEN	22.12.88		in HMar	København	17 Sep
31:43+		Yeshi	Chekole	ERI	-.97		in HMar	København	17 Sep
31:44		Magdalene	Masai	KEN	4.4.93	2		New York	9 Apr
31:46		Alia Saed	Mohammed	UAE	18.5.91	2		Port Gentil	24 Jun
31:47+	P	Muliye	Dekebo	ETH-J	13.3.98		in HMar	Ostia	12 Mar
31:47		Sanae	El Othmani	MAR	20.12.86	1		Casablanca	1 Oct
31:49		Naomi	Rotich	KEN	5.4.94	3		Paderborn	15 Apr
31:50+		Rose	Chelimo	BRN	12.7.89		in HMar	Ra's Al-Khaymah	10 Feb
31:53+		Dorcas	Kimeli	KEN	5.7.97		in HMar	Cardiff	1 Oct
31:54		Stella	Chesang	UGA	1.12.96	2		Berlin	8 Oct
31:55		Monicah	Wanjuhi	KEN	7.11.93	3		New York	9 Apr
31:56+		Jordan	Hasay	USA	21.9.91	8		Praha	1 Apr
32:00		Worknesh	Degefa	ETH	28.10.90	2		Bengaluru	21 May
32:01		Eilish	McColgan	GBR	25.11.90	1		Doha	13 Jan
32:02		Helah	Kiprop	KEN	7.4.85	3		Bengaluru	21 May
32:03		Kaltoum	Bouaasayriya	MAR	23.8.82	1		Tan-Tan	19 Nov
32:03		Shuru	Bulo	ETH-J	27.6.98	1		Okayama	23 Dec
32:07		Eunice	Kioko	KEN	4.10.87	2		Brunssum	2 Apr
32:09		Belaynesh	Tsegaye	ETH	-.97	1		Casablanca	7 May
32:10		Fabienne	Schlumpf	SUI	17.11.90	1		Payerne	26 Feb
32:10	P	Diane	Nukuri	BDI	1.12.84	5		Cape Elizabeth	5 Aug
32:10		Evaline	Chirchir	KEN-J	5.10.98	2		Houilles	31 Dec
32:11		Aliphine	Tuliamuk	USA	5.4.89	5		San Juan	26 Feb
32:11		Susan	Jeptoo	KEN	7.3.87	1		Arras	27 Aug
32:12		Dorcas	Tuitoek	KEN	31.1.96	3		Durban	8 Oct
32:14+		Hiwot	Gebrekidan	ETH	11.5.95		in HMar	Istanbul	30 Apr
32:16		Gladys	Yator	KEN	8.8.92	1		Edinburg	5 Feb
32:16		Risper	Gesabwa	KEN	10.2.89	6		San Juan	26 Feb
32:17		Yui	Fukuda	JPN	1.6.95	1		Yamaguchi	12 Feb
32:17		Pauline	Esikon	KEN	24.12.90	1		Torino	2 Apr
32:17		Etaferahu	Temesgen	ETH	-.89	5		New York	9 Apr
32:18+		Veronicah	Maina	KEN	8.8.89		in HMar	Adana	8 Jan
32:18		Maryanne	Wanjiru	KEN	4.10.86	3		Brunssum	2 Apr

Mark		Name		Nat	Born	Date
32:20		Jackline	Adodonyang	KEN	-.96	15 Apr
32:22		Mary Wangui	Kiguru	KEN	.92	15 Apr
32:22		Dominique	Scott Efurd	RSA	24.6.92	25 Jun
32:22		Valeria	Straneo	ITA	5.4.76	23 Oct
32:22		Damaris	Mutua	KEN	.96	19 Nov
32:22+		Rei	Ohara	JPN	10.8.90	23 Dec
32:23		Edna	Kiplagat	KEN	15.11.79	10 Jun
32:23+		Visiline	Jepkesho	KEN	30.12.89	15 Oct
32:26+		Azmera	Gebru	ETH	5.5.92	22 Oct
32:27		Alena	Shewarge	ETH	9.12.86	5 Feb
32:27		Etenesh	Diro	ETH	10.5.91	3 Sep
32:28	P	Wude	Ayalew	ETH	4.7.87	5 Aug
32:28		Hanna	Klein	GER	6.4.93	31 Dec
32:29		Karolina	Nadolska	POL	6.9.81	15 Apr
32:29+		Valentine	Kipketer	KEN	5.1.93	8 Oct
32:30+		Zeineba	Yimer	ETH-J	17.6.98	1 Oct
32:31+	P	Dibaba	Kuma	ETH	14.9.96	12 Mar
32:31		Birham	Mihretu	ETH-J	-.98	17 Jun
32:31		Laura	Weightman	GBR	1.7.91	31 Dec
32:32		Sinke	Dessie	ETH	11.10.94	9 Apr
32:32		Elizeba	Cherono	NED	6.6.88	20 May
32:32		Chaltu	Negasa	ETH	20.9.92	14 Jul
32:33+		Gebrekidam	Birhan	ETH-J	.98	22 Oct
32:33A		Girmawit	Gebrezere	ETH		26 Na=
32:34		Peninah	Kandie	KEN	22.6.92	24 Jun
32:35+		Margaret	Agai	KEN	10.6.88	20 May
32:36+		Stella	Barsosio	KEN	12.3.93	1 Apr
32:36		Maryanne	Wanjiru	KEN	4.10.86	15 Apr
32:37+		Antonina	Kwambai	KEN	-.92	22 Jan
32:37		Hailu	Haven	ETH		12 Mar
32:37+		Caroline	Rotich	KEN	13.5.84	17 Sep
32:38		Sophie	Duarte	FRA	31.7.81	12 Mar
32:39		Ryo	Koido	JPN	19.9.97	12 Feb
32:39		Alemtsehay	Asefa	ETH		12 Mar
32:39		Joyce	Kiplimo	KEN	28.12.88	10 Sep
32:39		Boulaid	Kaoutar	MAR	10.10.89	17 Sep
32:39		Sokayna	El Mkadam	MAR		24 Sep
32:39A		Fotyen	Tesfey	ETH-J	17.2.98	26 Nov
32:40		Martha	Akeno	KEN	15.12.93	7 May
32:40		Cynthia	Kosgei	KEN	-.93	10 Jun
32:41		Fatiha	Benchatki	MAR	6.12.82	26 Feb
32:41		Samira	Mezeghrane-Saad	FRA	29.12.79	2 Apr
32:41		Tabitha	Wambui	KEN	29.12.83	3 Sep
32:41+		Azusa	Sumi	JPN	12.8.96	23 Dec
32:43+		Sarah	Jebet	KEN	14.7.88	1 Apr
32:45		Joan	Aiyabei	KEN	17.5.79	5 Feb
32:46A		Ruti	Aga	ETH	16.1.94	29 May
32:46+		Sylvia	Kiberenge	KEN	24.2.90	17 Sep
32:47		Ivy	Kibet	KEN	4.2.90	2 Apr
32:47		Fate Geleto	Tola	GER	22.10.87	30 Apr
32:47+		Sara	Hall	USA	15.4.83	17 Sep
32:47		Hajiba	El Hasnaoui	MAR	28.4.88	19 Nov
32:48		Leonidah	Mosop	KEN	10.10.91	17 Jun
32:49		Nancy	Wambua	KEN	29.12.95	25 Mar
32:49		Caroline	Nyaguthii	KEN		24 Sep
32:51+		Elizeba	Cherono	NED	6.6.88	12 Mar
32:51		Emma	Mitchell	IRL	2.9.93	5 Nov
32:52		Sinead	Diver	AUS	17.2.77	18 Jun
32:52+		Sofia	Assefa	ETH	14.11.87	19 Nov
32:52		Kanami	Sagayama	JPN-J	9.7.98	23 Dec
32:53		Fatima	Gardadi	MAR	20.3.92	11 Jan
32:53+		Marion	Limo	KEN	.89	26 Mar
32:53		Christelle	Daunay	FRA	5.12.74	17 Jun
32:53		Mekdes	Woldu	ERI	20.10.92	15 Oct

Mark	Name		Nat	Born	Pos	Meet	Venue	Date
32:53+	Birke	Debele	ETH					19 Nov
32:54	Miku	Moribayashi	JPN-J	5.9.99				5 Mar
32:54	Sule	Utura	ETH	8.2.90				30 Apr
32:54+	Esther	Kakuri	KEN	26.10.94				30 Apr
32:54+	Tejitu	Daba	BRN	20.8.91				30 Apr
32:55+	Meskerem	Seifu	ETH					30 Apr
32:56	Yuka	Miyazaki	JPN	21.8.92				5 Mar
32:56	Himawari	Yuda	JPN	14.10.97				23 Dec
32:57	Kesa	Molotsane	RSA	8.1.92				2 Apr
32:57	Martha	Njoroge	KEN	-.94				15 Apr
32:57	Kuftu	Dadiso	ETH					17 Jun
32:57	Maerugu	Shegae	ETH-J	.98				9 Jul
32:58	Yuko	Matsumoto	JPN-J	.99				5 Mar
32:58	Tish	Jones	GBR	7.9.85				11 Jun
32:59	Bontu Edao	Rebitu	BRN	12.12.97				21 May
32:59	Afera	Godfay	ETH	25.9.91				24 Jun

Downhill

Mark	Name		Nat	Born	Pos	Meet	Venue	Date
30:55	Gelete	Burka	ETH	23.1.86	1		Madrid (55m)	31 Dec
31:06		Tirop			1		Ziwa	9 Dec
31:07	Valary	Aiyabei	KEN	8.6.91	2		Ziwa	9 Dec
31:18	Sandra	Tuei	KEN-J	20.1.98	3		Ziwa	9 Dec
31:27	Stacy	Ndiwa	KEN	6.12.92	4		Ziwa	9 Dec
32:01	Ruth	Jebet	BRN	17.11.96	5		Ziwa	9 Dec
32:46	Mercyline	Cherono	KEN	4.1.92				5 Nov
32:55	Perine	Nengampi	KEN	-.89				9 Dec
32:57	Alyson	Dixon	GBR	24.9.78				31 Dec

Drugs disqualification

Mark	Name		Nat	Born	Date
32:56	Louise	Leballo ¶	RSA	4.12.77	2 Apr

15/20 KILOMETRES ROAD

15k 20k	Name		Nat	Born	Pos	Meet	Venue	Date
47:30+64:11		Jepkosgei			1	in HMar	Gifu	23 Apr
47:47	Yvonne	Jelagat Morwa	KEN	-.93	1		Le Puy-en-Velay	1 May
48:02+64:20	Gladys	Chesire	KEN	20.2.93	4	in HMar	Praha	1 Apr
48:09+	Betty	Lempus	KEN			in HMar	Milano	19 Mar
48:15+65:10	Worknesh	Degefa	ETH	28.10.90		in Mar	Istanbul	30 Apr
48:19		J Chelimo			2		Le Puy-en-Velay	1 May
48:24 65:22	Yvonne	Jelagat Morwa	KEN	12.11.93		in HMar	Praha	1 Apr
48:41	Daisy	Kimeli	KEN	28.11.94	1		Mersin	3 Dec
48:52	Birke	Debele	ETH		1		Nijmegen	19 Nov
48:52	Delvin	Meringor	KEN	1.8.92	2		Mersin	3 Dec
48:54	Mercyline	Chelangat	UGA	17.12.97	2		Nijmegen	19 Nov
48:54	Evaline	Chirchir	KEN-J	5.10.98	3		Nijmegen	19 Nov
48:56	Sofia	Assefa	ETH	14.11.87	4		Nijmegen	19 Nov
49:08	Mary	Munanu	KEN	12.12.94	1		's-Heerenberg	3 Dec
49:11+	Vivian	Kiplagat	KEN	.91		in HMar	Porto	27 Sep
49:18	Mercy	Ngugi	KEN	17.12.88	1		Utica	9 Jul
49:20	Ruti	Aga	ETH	16.1.94	2		Utica	9 Jul
49:21	Gladys	Kimaina	KEN	1.3.93	3		Le Puy-en-Velay	1 May
49:22+66:19	Stella	Barsosio	KEN	12.3.93	8	in HMar	Praha	1 Apr
49:23	Pascalia	Kipkoech	KEN	22.12.88	3		Utica	9 Jul
49:30+67:28	Lucy	Cheruiyot	KEN	4.1.97				1 Apr
49:30	Makda	Harun	ETH	5.9.88				29 Jul
49:33	Mamitu	Daska	ETH	16.10.83				9 Jul
49:41	Buze	Diriba	ETH	9.2.94				9 Jul
49:42	Emily	Infeld	USA	21.3.90				11 Mar
49:47	Neely	Spence Gracey	USA	16.4.90				11 Mar
49:54	Laura	Thweatt	USA	17.12.88				11 Mar
49:56	Goytatom	Gebreselassie	ETH	15.1.95				9 Jul
49:59	Monicah	Wanjuhi	KEN	7.11.93				9 Jul

10 MILES ROAD

Mark	Name		Nat	Born	Pos	Meet	Venue	Date
50:48+	Caroline	Kipkirui	KEN	26.5.94		in Mar	London	23 Apr
50:48+	Mary	Keitany	KEN	18.1.82		in Mar	London	23 Apr
51:16+	Veronica	Nyaruai	KEN	29.10.89		in HMar	Houston	15 Jan
51:16+	Dera	Dida	ETH	26.10.96		in HMar	Houston	15 Jan
51:49	Buze	Diriba	ETH	9.2.94	1		Flint	26 Aug
51:55+	Mamitu	Daska	ETH	16.10.83		in HMar	Houston	15 Jan
51:56	Diana	Kipyokei	KEN		2		Flint	26 Aug
52:16	Goytatom	Gebreselassie	ETH	15.1.95	2		Pittsburgh	5 Nov
52:24	Monicah	Wanjuhi	KEN	7.11.93	3		Flint	26 Aug
52:27	Naomi	Rotich	KEN	5.4.94	1		Schortens	19 Aug
52:30	Joyce	Kiplimo	KEN	28.12.88	2		Schortens	19 Aug
53:06	Caroline	Rotich	KEN	13.5.84				26 Aug
53:08	Mercyline	Chelangat	UGA	17.12.97				17 Sep
53:13	Sofia	Assefa	ETH	14.11.87				17 Sep
53:15	Risa	Takenaka	JPN	6.1.90				17 Sep
53:33	Tabitha	Wambui	KEN	29.12.83				19 Aug
53:33	Mimi	Belete	BRN	9.6.88				17 Sep
53:35	Ancuta	Bobocel	ROU	3.10.87				17 Sep
53:36	Monica	Ngige	KEN					5 Nov
53:37	Hiwot	Gebrekidan	ETH	11.5.95				2 Apr
53:40	Ivy	Kibet	KEN	4.2.90				17 Sep
53:43	Sara	Hall	USA	15.4.83				1 Oct
53:45	Natosha	Rogers	USA	7.5.91				1 Oct

20 KILOMETRES ROAD

And see below in Half Marathon lists

Mark	Name		Nat	Born	Pos	Meet	Venue	Date
65:58+	Muliye	Dekebo	ETH-J	13.3.98		in HMar	Houston	15 Jan
66:02	Gebeyanesh	Ayele	ETH	1.5.95	1		Paris	8 Oct
66:05+	Gladys	Cherono	KEN	12.5.83		in Mar	Berlin	24 Sep
66:16	Susan	Jeptoo	KEN	7.3.87	2		Paris	8 Oct
66:19+	Stella	Barsosio	KEN	12.3.93	8		Praha	1 Apr
66:24+	Vivian	Cheruiyot	KEN	11.9.83		in Mar	Frankfurt	29 Oct
66:27+	Yeshaneh	Ababel	ETH	10.6.90		in HMar	Lisboa	19 Mar
66:40	Gudeta	Bekelech	ETH	.97	3		Paris	8 Oct

HALF MARATHON

Mark	20k	15k	Name		Nat	Born	Pos	Meet	Venue	Date
64:51	61:29	45:58	Joyciline	Jepkosgei	KEN	8.12.93	1		Valencia	22 Oct
64:52	61:25	45:37		Jepkosgei			1		Praha	1 Apr
65:06	61:40	46:32	Peres	Jepchirchir	KEN	27.9.93	1	RAK	Ra's Al-Khaymah	10 Feb
65:13	61:52	46:30	Mary	Keitany	KEN	18.1.82	2	RAK	Ra's Al-Khaymah	10 Feb
65:22	61:50	45:40	Violah	Jepchumba	BRN	23.10.90	2		Praha	1 Apr
65:36	62:02	45:59	Fancy	Chemutai	KEN	20.3.95	2		Valencia	22 Oct
65:52	62:30	46:36	Edith	Chelimo	KEN	16.7.86	1		Cardiff	1 Oct
65:59	dh			Keitany			1	GNR	South Shields	10 Sep
66:06		46:38		Jepchumba			1		Ústí nad Labem	16 Sep
66:08	62:36	46:31		Jepkosgei			3	RAK	Ra's Al-Khaymah	10 Feb
66:11	62:58	47:24	Eunice	Chumba	BRN	23.5.93	1		København	17 Sep
66:19	62:57	46:59	Ruth	Chepngetich	KEN	8.8.94	1		Istanbul	30 Apr
66:25	62:57	47:25	Joan	Chelimo	KEN	10.11.88	2		København	17 Sep
66:35	63:17	47:24	Brigid	Kosgei (10)	KEN	20.2.94	3		København	17 Sep
66:43	63:09	47:07	Jemima	Sumgong ¶?	KEN	21.12.84	4	RAK	Ra's Al-Khaymah	10 Feb
66:46	63:11	46:59	Eunice	Jepkirui	BRN	20.5.84	2		Istanbul	30 Apr
66:50	63:25	47:07	Tirunesh	Dibaba	ETH	1.10.85	5	RAK	Ra's Al-Khaymah	10 Feb
66:53+	63:25	47:15	Caroline	Kipkirui	KEN	26.5.94		in Mar	London	23 Apr
66:54+	63:26	47:45		Keitany				in Mar	London	23 Apr
66:58	63:28	47:08		Chemutai			3		Praha	1 Apr
67:01		47:29	Gladys	Cherono	KEN	12.5.83	1		Ostia	12 Mar
67:12			Almaz	Ayana	ETH	21.11.91	1		New Delhi	19 Nov
67:21			Yeshaneh	Ababel	ETH	10.6.90	2		New Delhi	19 Nov
67:22		47:29	Nancy	Kiprop	KEN	7.7.79	2		Ústí nad Labem	16 Sep
67:23		47:28	Lucy	Cheruiyot	KEN	4.1.97	3		Ústí nad Labem	16 Sep
67:23	63:59	47:41	Roza	Dereje (20)	ETH	6.5.97	4		København	17 Sep
67:26			Netsanet	Gudeta	ETH	12.2.91	3		New Delhi	19 Nov
67:31	63:56	47:34		Cheruiyot			3		Valencia	22 Oct
67:35				Kosgei			1		Verbania	5 Mar
67:42		47:50		Chepngetich			1	Stra	Milano	19 Mar
67:42	64:18	47:42	Meskerem	Assefa	ETH	20.9.85	5		København	17 Sep
			(31/22)	Slightly downhill course: GNR: Newcastle to South Shields 30.5m						
67:43		47:36	Angela	Tanui	KEN	27.7.92	2		Ostia	12 Mar
67:44	dh		Vivian	Cheruiyot	KEN	11.9.83	2	GNR	South Shields	10 Sep
67:48	64:13	47:24	Helah	Kiprop	KEN	7.4.85	6	RAK	Ra's Al-Khaymah	10 Feb
67:49			Gladys	Chesire	KEN	20.2.93	1		Lille	2 Sep
67:50	64:20	48:02	Valary	Aiyabei	KEN	8.6.91	4		Praha	1 Apr
67:54	64:13	47:46	Aselefech	Mergia	ETH	23.1.85		in Mar	London	23 Apr
67:55	64:32	48:21	Jordan	Hasay	USA	21.9.91	6		Praha	1 Apr
67:58	64:19	47:45	Veronica	Nyaruai	KEN	29.10.89	1		Houston	15 Jan
			(30)							
68:04	64:31	48:31	Pauline	Kamulu	KEN	16.4.95	1		Okayama	23 Dec
68:06	64:36	47:57	Dera	Dida	ETH	26.10.96	2		Houston	15 Jan
68:10			Worknesh	Degefa	ETH	28.10.90	5		New Delhi	19 Nov
68:12			Visiline	Jepkesho	KEN	30.12.89	2		Lille	2 Sep
68:15	64:40	48:05	Florence	Kiplagat	KEN	27.2.87	1		Barcelona	12 Feb
68:18	64:45	48:10	Gelete	Burka	ETH	23.1.86	4		Valencia	22 Oct
68:19	64:19	49:09	Molly	Huddle	USA	31.8.84	1		New York	19 Mar
68:19	64:51	48:27	Belaynesh	Oljira	ETH	26.6.90	2		Gifu	23 Apr
68:19			Yvonne	Jelagat Morwa	KEN	-.93	1		Karlovy Vary	20 May
68:21	64:51	49:09	Emily	Sisson	USA	12.10.91	2		New York	19 Mar
			(40)							
68:21			Tejitu	Daba	BRN	20.8.91	3		Lille	2 Sep
68:21	64:49	47:53	Agnes	Barsosio	KEN	5.8.82	6		København	17 Sep
68:23	64:49	47:53	Pascalia	Kipkoech	KEN	22.12.88	7		København	17 Sep
68:27	64:56	48:26	Amy	Cragg	USA	21.1.84	2		Marugame	5 Feb
68:28			Rahma	Tusa	ETH	14.9.93	1		Boulogne-Billancourt	19 Nov
68:37	65:04	48:35	Rose	Chelimo	BRN	12.7.89	7	RAK	Ra's Al-Khaymah	10 Feb
68:38	65:10	48:41	Mercy Wacera	Ngugi	KEN	17.12.88	3		Houston	15 Jan
68:40			Sutume	Asefa	ETH	11.12.94	2		Karlovy Vary	20 May
68:44	65:11	48:59	Naomi	Rotich	KEN	5.4.94	1		Breda	1 Oct
68:46			Meseret	Defar	ETH	19.11.83	1		Philadelphia	17 Sep
			(50)							
69:01	65:15	48:15	Mamitu	Daska	ETH	16.10.83	5		Houston	15 Jan
69:01		47:54	Rebecca	Kangogo	KEN	.92	4		Ostia	12 Mar
69:02			Susan	Jeptoo	KEN	7.3.87	4		Lille	2 Sep
69:05			Vivian	Kiplagat	KEN	.91	2		Verbania	5 Mar

WOMEN 2017

Mark			Name		Nat	Born	Pos	Meet	Venue	Date
69:07	65:35	48:17	Desi Jisa	Mokonin	BRN	12.7.97	8		København	17 Sep
69:09		48:28	Stacy	Ndiwa	KEN	6.12.92	4		Ústí Nad Labem	16 Sep
69:10		48:51	Muliye	Dekebo	ETH-J	13.3.98	5		Ostia	12 Mar
69:12+		49:03	Valentine	Kipketer	KEN	5.1.93		in Mar	Chicago	8 Oct
69:13	65:31	49:11	Diane	Nukuri	BDI	1.12.84	3		New York	19 Mar
69:13	65:42	48:22	Yeshi	Chekole	ERI	.97	9		København	17 Sep
			(60)							
69:13			Parendis	Lekapana	KEN	4.8.91	2		Boulogne-Billancourt	19 Nov
69:13	65:51	49:13	Miyuki	Uehara	JPN	22.11.95	2		Okayama	23 Dec
69:14	65:40	48:52	Mao	Ichiyama	JPN	29.5.97	3		Okayama	23 Dec
69:15		49:07	Mimi	Belete	BRN	9.6.88	1		Verona	12 Feb
69:15			Peninah	Kandie	KEN	22.6.92	1		Remich	24 Sep
69:21	65:51	49:13	Azusa	Sumi	JPN	12.8.96	4		Okayama	23 Dec
69:23		49:12	Monica	Jepkoech	KEN	.85	1		Porto	17 Sep
69:25			Betty	Lempus	KEN	.91	2		Milano	19 Mar
69:26	65:47	48:52	Rei	Ohara	JPN	10.8.90	5		Okayama	23 Dec
69:31			Stella	Barsosio	KEN	12.3.93	1		Limassol	19 Mar
			(70)							
69:37	65:49	49:11	Edna	Kiplagat	KEN	15.11.79	4		New York	19 Mar
69:37	66:10	49:28	Sara	Hall	USA	15.4.83	10		København	17 Sep
69:40+	66:05	49:33	Ruti	Aga	ETH	16.1.94		in Mar	Berlin	24 Sep
69:40+	66:05	49:33	Amane	Beriso	ETH	13.10.91		in Mar	Berlin	24 Sep
69:41			Caroline	Rotich	KEN	13.5.84	2		Philadelphia	17 Sep
69:41			Winfridah	Moseti	KEN	12.11.96	1		Arezzo	29 Oct
69:43	66:25		Mare	Dibaba	ETH	20.10.89	1		Lisboa	19 Mar
69:43	65:59	49:10	Margaret	Agai	KEN	10.6.88	3		Göteborg	20 May
69:45			Diana	Kipyokei	KEN	.94	1		Waterloo IA	9 Sep
69:47			Josephine	Jepkoech	KEN	21.4.89	3		Boulogne-Billancourt	19 Nov
			(80)							
69:48			Helen	Tola	ETH	21.11.94	1		Sarnen	3 Sep
69:49		49:12	Antonina	Kwambai	KEN	–.92	1		Santa Pola	22 Jan
69:49	66:13	49:39	Dibaba	Kuma	ETH	14.9.96	2		Barcelona	12 Feb
69:54			Karolina	Nadolska	POL	6.9.81	1		Poznan	26 Mar
69:55	66:26		Afera	Godfay	ETH	25.9.91	4		Lisboa	19 Mar
69:57+			Aberu	Kebede	ETH	12.9.86		in Mar	London	23 Apr
69:57	66:21		Trihas	Gebre	ESP	29.4.90	6		Valencia	22 Oct
69:58	66:06	48:49	Aliphine	Tuliamuk	USA	5.4.89	7		Houston	15 Jan
69:58	66:19		Sarah	Lahti	SWE	18.2.95	6		New York	19 Mar
70:00	66:32		Meskerem	Amare	ETH	1.10.97	4		Istanbul	30 Apr
			(90)							
70:00	66:27		Birhan	Mihretu	ETH-J	–.98	7		Valencia	22 Oct
70:01	66:19	48:58	Gladys	Yator	KEN	8.8.92	8		Houston	15 Jan
70:07	66:32		Esther	Kakuri	KEN	26.10.94	6		Istanbul	30 Apr
70:08			Tabitha	Wambui	KEN	29.12.83	1		Paderborn	15 Apr
70:09	60:41	49:49	Grace	Kimanzi	KEN	1.3.92	1		Matsue	19 Mar
70:10			Shitaye	Eshete	BRN	21.5.90	1		Trento	1 Oct
70:11	66:39	49:57	Kaori	Morita	JPN	19.9.95	6		Okayama	23 Dec
70:13+			Tadelech	Bekele	ETH	11.4.91	1		Amsterdam	15 Oct
70:14	66:28	49:10	Beatrice	Mutai	KEN	19.4.87	4		Göteborg	20 May
70:15			Viola	Kibiwot	KEN	22.12.83	1		Klagenfurt	20 Aug
			(100)							

Mark		Name		Nat	Born	Date
70:17	66:40	Fabienne	Schlumpf	SUI	17.11.90	12 Mar
70:17		Filomena	Cheyech	KEN	5.7.82	1 Oct
70:19+		Purity	Rionoripo	KEN	10.6.93	9 Apr
70:19+		Yebrqual	Melese	ETH	18.4.90	9 Apr
70:20		Veronicah	Maina	KEN	8.8.89	8 Jan
70:20		Elizeba	Cherono	NED	6.6.88	12 Mar
70:20		Maryanne	Wanjiru	KEN	4.10.86	26 Mar
70:21+	66:44	Eunice	Jepkirui	BRN	20.5.84	12 Mar
70:21+	66:44	Yuka	Ando	JPN	16.3.94	12 Mar
70:21		Filomena	Chepchirchir	KEN	1.12.81	25 Jun
70:22+	66:45	Honami	Maeda	JPN	17.7.96	23 Dec
70:23		Sinayehu	Lewetegn	ETH	9.5.96	8 Oct
70:26		Ayantu	Gemechu	ETH	1.3.92	26 Mar
70:28		Joyline	Koima Loyce	KEN	3.3.88	2 Apr
70:28		Belaynesh	Tsegaye	ETH	–.97	16 Sep
70:28+	66:47	Akane	Sekino	JPN	28.7.90	23 Dec
70:31+	66:46	Sarah	Chepchirchir	KEN	27.7.84	26 Feb
70:31+		Amane	Gobena	ETH	1.9.82	26 Feb
70:31		Eunice	Kioko	KEN	4.10.87	15 Apr
70:31		Askale	Alemaheyu	ETH	11.1.96	25 Jun
70:31		Loganathan	Suriya	IND	7.7.90	19 Nov
70:32+		Birhane	Dibaba	ETH	11.9.93	26 Feb
70:32+		Marta	Lema	ETH	30.12.90	26 Feb
70:32+		Betsy	Saina	KEN	30.6.88	26 Feb
70:35+	66:59	Reina	Iwade	JPN	8.12.94	23 Dec
70:36		Jéssica	Augusto	POR	8.11.81	12 Feb
70:38		Pauline	Njeru	KEN	12.12.88	17 Sep
70:39		Sara	Dossena	ITA	22.11.84	21 May
70:39	dh	Magdalene	Masai	KEN	4.4.93	10 Sep
70:39		Makda	Harun	ETH	5.9.88	15 Oct
70:40	66:20	Azmera	Gebru	ETH	5.5.92	22 Oct
70:42		Sylvia	Kiberenge	KEN	24.2.90	17 Sep
70:43		Lilian	Jelagat	KEN	23.1.89	17 Dec
70:45		Gulume	Tollesa	ETH	11.9.92	23 Apr
70:45		Guteni	Shone	ETH	17.11.91	23 Apr
70:45		Natosha	Rogers	USA	7.5.91	29 Apr
70:46+	67:01	Mao	Kiyota	JPN	12.9.93	12 Mar
70:47		Ai	Utsunomiya	JPN	19.9.95	12 Feb
70:47		Marion	Limo	KEN	.89	26 Mar
70:47		Leonidah	Mosop	KEN	10.10.91	1 Apr
70:48+		Hirut	Tibebu	ETH	13.12.94	7 May
70:50	49:15	Dorcas	Kimeli	KEN	5.7..97	1 Oct
70:52		Pauline	Muchiri	KEN	.89	5 Mar
70:52		Susan	Krumins	NED	8.7.86	26 Mar
70:54+	67:09	Rika	ToKuchi	JPN	2.12.87	29 Jan
70:54		Sabrina	Mkckenhaupt	GER	6.12.80	9 Apr

Mark	Name		Nat	Born	Date	Mark	Name		Nat	Born	Date
70:54	Neely	Spence Gracey	USA	16.4.90	29 Apr	71:15	Milly	Clark	AUS	1.3.89	2 Jul
70:55	Sakiho	Tsutsui	JPN	19.1.96	12 Feb	71:15	Lisa	Weightman	AUS	16.1.79	10 Sep
70:57	Lydia	Rotich	KEN	8.8.88	23 Apr	71:16	Keiko	Nogami	JPN	6.12.85	23 Dec
70:58	Kaoutar	Boulaïd	MAR	10.10.89	22 Oct	71:17	Yui	Okada	JPN	15.3.94	12 Feb
71:00	Lenah	Cherotich	KEN	27.3.88	5 Feb	71:17	Kanade	Furuya	JPN	10.4.96	19 Mar
71:00	Ayaka	Fujimoto	JPN	8.7.97	12 Feb	71:18+	Megertu	Ifa	ETH	20.9.91	23 Apr
71:00	Kejeta	Melat	ETH	-.92	2 Apr	71:20	Sarah	Jebet	KEN	14/7.88	1 Apr
71:02	Zerfie	Limeneh	ETH	10.2.97	23 Apr	71:22	Eva	Vrabcová-Nyvltová	CZE	6.2.86	16 Sep
71:02	Diana	Kipyogei	KEN	-.94	2 Dec	71:22	Yuliya	Shmatenko	UKR	10.10.91	1 Oct
71:03+	Fatuma	Sado	ETH	11.10.91	22 Oct	71:23	Alina	Reh	GER	23.5.97	17 Sep
71:04	Riko	Matsuzaki	JPN	24.12.92	5 Feb	71:26	Biruktayit	Degefa	ETH	29.9.90	17 Jun
71:04	Jip	Vastenburg	NED	21.3.94	22 Oct	71:26	Zinash	Debebe	ETH	1.1.96	2 Sep
71:05	Desiree	Linden	USA	26.7.83	19 Mar	71:29	Charlotte	Purdue	GBR	10.6.91	23 Dec
71:05 49:09	Hiwot	Gebrekidan	ETH	11.5.95	30 Apr	71:30	Salomé	Nyirarukundo	RWA	20.12.97	2 Apr
71:06+	Shure	Demise	ETH	21.1.96	20 Jan	71:30	Sudha	Singh	IND	25.6.86	19 Nov
71:06+	Shuko	Genemo	ETH	-.95	20 Jan	71:31	Bezunesh	Getachew	ETH	-1.97	22 Jan
71:06	Darya	Maslova	KGZ	6.5.95	23 Apr	71:31	Peninah	Arusei	KEN	23.2.79	26 Mar
71:07+	Tigist	Teshome	ETH	11.3.87	20 Jan	71:31	Zeineba	Yimer	ETH-J	17.6.98	1 Oct
71:07	Miho	Shimizu	JPN	13.5.90	5 Feb	71:32 dh	Gemma	Steel	GBR	12.11.85	10 Sep
71:07	Hanae	Tanaka	JPN	12.2.90	14 May	71:32	Christine	Oigo	KEN	-.86	29 Oct
71:09	Anja	Scherl	GER	12.4.86	9 Apr	71:32	Muzumi	Tanimoto	JPN	18.12.94	23 Dec
71:12	Maki	Ashi	JPN	2.7.93	12 Feb	71:33	Kasumi	Yamaguchi	JPN	21.11.97	19 Mar
71:12	Saki	Fukui	JPN	25.3.96	19 Mar	71:34	Felista	Wanjugu	KEN	18.2.90	12 Feb
71:13+	Madaí	Pérez	MEX	2.2.80	8 Oct	71:35	Fionnuala	McCormack	IRL	24.9.84	12 Feb
71:13	Pauline	Esikon	KEN	24.12.90	15 Oct	71:35	Ivy	Kibet	KEN	4.2.90	5 Mar
71:14	Yuri	Nozoe	JPN	3.5.96	12 Feb	71:35+	Lucy	Karimi	KEN	24.2.75	9 Apr
71:14	Ayano	Ikemitsu	JPN	18.4.91	23 Dec	71:35	Aberash	Fayesa	ETH	.95	8 Oct

(200)

Excessively downhill

69:39	Winfridah	Moseti	KEN	12.11.96	1	Torino (108m)	1 Oct
70:12	Biruktayit	Degefa	ETH	29.9.90	1	San Diego (86.5m)	4 Jun

JUNIORS

See main list for top 2 juniors. 7 performances by 6 women to 72:30. Additional marks and further juniors:

Dekebo	69:46	6	Houston	15 Jan	69:59	1	Lugano	21 May
	70:07	5	Istanbul	30 Apr	71:10	2	Tamesna	8 Oct

71:31	Zeineba	Yimer	ETH-J	17.6.98	4	Cardiff	1 Oct
72:06	Yuka	Kato	JPN	.99	19	Okayama	23 Dec
72:29	Dalilah Abdelkadir	Gosa	BRN	27.6.98	1	Belfort	24 Sep

25/30 KILOMETRES ROAD

In addition to those shown in Marathon listing

25k	30k			Nat	Born	Pos	Meet	Venue	Date
1:21:09	1:38:50	Vivian	Cheruiyot	KEN	11.9.83		in Mar	London	23 Apr
1:22:26	1:39:27	Amane	Beriso	ETH	13.10.91		in Mar	Berlin	24 Sep
	1:40:35	Valentine	Kipketer	KEN	5.1.93		in Mar	Chicago	8 Oct
1:23:35	1:40:53	Marta	Lema	ETH	30.12.90		in Mar	Tokyo	26 Feb
1:23:48	1:41:43	Aberu	Kebede	ETH	12.9.86		in Mar	London	23 Apr
1:23:53	1:40:44	Hirut	Tibebu	ETH	13.12.94		in Mar	Praha	7 May
1:24:18	1:41:30	Roza	Dereje	ETH	6.5.97		in Mar	Dubai	20 Jan
	1:42:41	Misaki	Kato	JPN	15.6.91		in Mar	Osaka	29 Jan
1:24:35		Aliphine	Tuliamuk	USA	5.4.89	1	NC	Grand Rapids	13 May
1:25:12		Neely	Spence Gracey	USA	16.4.90	2	NC	Grand Rapids	13 May

MARATHON

Mark	25k	30k			Nat	Born	Pos	Venue	Date
2:17:01	1:19:43	1:36:05	Mary	Keitany	KEN	18.1.82	1	London	23 Apr
2:17:56	1:20:51	1:37:23	Tirunesh	Dibaba	ETH	1.10.85	2	London	23 Apr
2:18:31	1:21:59	1:38:29		Dibaba			1	Chicago	8 Oct
2:19:47	1:23:35	1:40:26	Sarah	Chepchirchir	KEN	27.7.84	1	Tokyo	26 Feb
2:20:22	1:21:59	1:38:29	Brigid	Kosgei	KEN	20.2.94	2	Chicago	8 Oct
2:20:23	1:22:27	1:38:58	Gladys	Cherono	KEN	12.5.83	1	Berlin	24 Sep
2:20:41	1:22:26	1:38:58	Ruti	Aga	ETH	16.1.94	2	Berlin	24 Sep
2:20:53	1:22:27	1:38:58	Valary	Aiyabei	KEN	8.6.91	3	Berlin	24 Sep
2:20:55	1:23:10	1:39:49	Purity	Rionoripo	KEN	10.6.93	1	Paris	9 Apr
2:20:57	1:22:19	1:39:11	Jordan	Hasay	USA	21.9.91	3	Chicago	8 Oct
2:20:59	1:23:09	1:39:48	Agnes	Barsosio (10)	KEN	5.8.82	2	Paris	9 Apr
2:21:17	1:23:46	1:40:41	Eunice	Jepkirui	BRN	20.5.84	1	Nagoya	12 Mar
2:21:19	1:23:35	1:40:27	Birhane	Dibaba	ETH	11.9.93	2	Tokyo	26 Feb
2:21:22	1:23:11	1:39:50	Filomena	Cheyech	KEN	5.7.82	3	Paris	9 Apr
2:21:36	1:23:47	1:40:41	Yuka	Ando	JPN	16.3.94	2	Nagoya	12 Mar
2:21:37	1:23:10	1:39:49	Visiline	Jepkesho	KEN	30.12.89	4	Paris	9 Apr
2:21:54	1:23:29	1:40:27	Tadelech	Bekele	ETH	11.4.91	1	Amsterdam	15 Oct
2:21:57	1:21:23	1:38:19		Aiyabei			1	Praha	7 May
2:22:15	1:23:52	1:40:32	Amane	Beriso	ETH	13.10.91	2	Praha	7 May
2:22:15	1:25:13			Kosgei			1	Honolulu	10 Dec

Mark			Name		Nat	Born	Pos	Meet	Venue	Date
2:22:23	1:23:53	1:40:32		Bekele			3		Praha	7 May
2:22:36	1:24:18	1:40:53	Worknesh	Degefa	ETH	28.10.90	1		Dubai	20 Jan
2:22:36		1:41:18	Ruth	Chepngetich	KEN	8.8.94	1		Istanbul	12 Nov
2:22:40				Jepkesho			2		Istanbul	12 Nov
2:22:43			Roza	Dereje (20)	ETH	6.5.97	1		Shanghai	12 Nov
2:22:51	1:23:11	1:39:49	Yebrqual	Melese	ETH	18.4.90	5		Paris	9 Apr
2:22:51	1:24:05	1:41:03	Helen	Tola	ETH	21.11.94	4		Berlin	24 Sep
2:22:57	1:24:18	1:40:54	Shure	Demise	ETH	21.1.96	2		Dubai	20 Jan
2:23:08	1:20:51	1:38:21	Aselefech	Mergia	ETH	23.1.85	3		London	23 Apr
2:23:09	1:23:35	1:40:27	Amane	Gobena	ETH	1.9.82	3		Tokyo	26 Feb
			(30/25)							
2:23:31			Lydia	Cheromei	KEN	11.5.77	2		Shanghai	12 Nov
2:23:35	1:23:20	1:40:14	Vivian	Cheruiyot	KEN	11.9.83	1		Frankfurt	29 Oct
2:23:35			Hirut	Tibebu	ETH	13.12.94	3		Shanghai	12 Nov
2:23:47	1:24:20	1:41:43	Mao	Kiyota	JPN	12.9.93	3		Nagoya	12 Mar
2:23:59			Gulume	Tollesa	ETH	11.9.92	4		Shanghai	12 Nov
			(30)							
2:24:18			Meskerem	Assefa	ETH	20.9.85	1		Rotterdam	9 Apr
2:24:20			Nancy	Kiprop	KEN	7.7.79	1		Wien	23 Apr
2:24:22	1:25:35	1:42:33	Risa	Shigemoto	JPN	29.8.87	1		Osaka	29 Jan
2:24:27			Eunice	Chumba	BRN	23.5.93	2		Rotterdam	9 Apr
2:24:44	1:24:24	1:41:43	Madaí	Pérez	MEX	2.2.80	4		Chicago	8 Oct
2:24:51			Gladys	Chesire	KEN	20.2.93	2		Amsterdam	15 Oct
2:25:01			Letebrhan	Gebreslasea	ETH	29.10.90	1		Dongying	7 May
2:25:12			Rahma	Tusa	ETH	14.9.93	1		Guangzhou	10 Dec
2:25:15	1:25:51	1:43:01	Lisa	Weightman	AUS	16.1.79	5		London	23 Apr
2:25:17			Lucy	Karimi	KEN	24.2.75	3		Rotterdam	9 Apr
			(40)							
2:25:23			Azmera	Abreha	ETH-J	.98	3		Amsterdam	15 Oct
2:25:29			Margaret	Agai	KEN	10.6.88	5		Shanghai	12 Nov
2:25:30			Jéssica	Augusto	POR	8.11.81	1		Hamburg	23 Apr
2:25:32			Viola	Kibiwot	KEN	22.12.83	4		Amsterdam	15 Oct
2:25:34			Abebech	Afework	ETH	11.12.90	1		Gold Coast	2 Jul
2:25:38	1:25:51	1:42:58	Laura	Thweatt	USA	17.12.88	6		London	23 Apr
2:25:39	1:20:48	1:37:25	Helah	Kiprop	KEN	7.4.85	7		London	23 Apr
2:25:44	1:25:17	1:42:08	Misato	Horie	JPN	10.3.87	2		Osaka	29 Jan
2:25:45			Hiwot	Gebrekidan	ETH	11.5.95	1		Tiberias	6 Jan
2:25:52	1:24:43	1:42:25	Tigist	Tufa	ETH	26.1.87	8		London	23 Apr
			(50)							
2:25:57			Ashete	Bekele	ETH	17.4.88	2		Seoul	19 Mar
2:25:58			Meseret	Mengistu	ETH	6.3.90	1		Xiamen	2 Jan
2:26:06			Shuko	Genemo	ETH	–.95	4		Wien	23 Apr
2:26:09	1:25:45	1:43:12	Sayaka	Kuwahara	JPN	8.3.93	4		Nagoya	12 Mar
2:26:13			Eunice	Jeptoo	KEN	24.6.83	1		Eindhoven	8 Oct
2:26:17			Aberu	Mekuria	ETH	24.12.83	1		Valencia	19 Nov
2:26:19	1:25:36	1:42:40	Hanae	Tanaka	JPN	12.2.90	3		Osaka	29 Jan
2:26:22			Rael	Kguriatukei	KEN	4.4.84	1		Chongqing	19 Mar
2:26:25	1:22:13	1:40:36	Florence	Kiplagat	KEN	27.2.87	9		London	23 Apr
2:26:26	1:23:29	1:41:29	Caroline	Rotich	KEN	13.5.84	5		Amsterdam	15 Oct
			(60)							
2:26:27			Workenesh	Edesa	ETH	11.9.92	2		Xiamen	2 Jan
2:26:29			Jane	Jelagat	KEN	25.11.83	4		Rotterdam	9 Apr
2:26:30			Chemutai	Rionotukei	KEN	4.9.86	2		Dongying	7 May
2:26:31			Angela	Tanui	KEN	27.7.92	5		Wien	23 Apr
2:26:44			Melesech	Tsegaye	ETH	.94	2		Barcelona	12 Mar
2:26:46	1:25:47	1:43:06	Feyse	Tadesse	ETH	19.11.88	5		Praha	7 May
2:26:47			Melkaw	Gizaw	ETH	17.9.90	3		Xiamen	2 Jan
2:26:52			Mercy	Kibarus	KEN	25.2.84	3		Seoul	19 Mar
2:26:53		1:44:13	Serena	Burla	USA	29.7.82	4		Osaka	29 Jan
2:26:53			Shalane	Flanagan	USA	8.7.81	1		New York	5 Nov
			(70)							
2:26:58			Monica	Jepkoech	KEN	1.1.85	1		Porto	5 Nov
2:27:01		1:43:43	Jessica	Trengove	AUS	15.8.87	10		London	23 Apr
2:27:04			Aberash	Fayesa	ETH	.95	3		Barcelona	12 Mar
2:27:08			Ayaka	Fujimoto	JPN	8.7.97	4		Tokyo	26 Feb
2:27:08			Carla Salomé	Rocha	POR	25.4.90	6		Praha	7 May
2:27:11			Rose	Chelimo	BRN	12.7.89	1	WCh	London	6 Aug
2:27:14			Olga	Mazuronak	BLR	14.4.89	2		Valencia	19 Nov
2:27:18			Anne	Cheptanui	KEN	4.11.82	2		Chongqing	19 Mar
2:27:18			Edna	Kiplagat	KEN	15.11.79	2	WCh	London	6 Aug
2:27:18			Amy	Cragg	USA	21.1.84	3	WCh	London	6 Aug
			(80)							

Mark		Name		Nat	Born	Pos	Meet	Venue	Date
2:27:18		Winnie	Jepkorir	KEN	10.6.90	3		Valencia	19 Nov
2:27:21		Sara	Hall	USA	15.4.83	5		Frankfurt	29 Oct
2:27:27		Aberu	Kebede	ETH	12.9.86	11		London	23 Apr
2:27:34		Sheila	Jerotich	KEN	6.6.89	1		Kosice	1 Oct
2:27:35	1:43:03	Hisami	Ishii	JPN	10.8.95	5		Nagoya	12 Mar
2:27:37		Marta	Lema	ETH	30.12.90	5		Tokyo	26 Feb
2:27:37		Naomi Tuei	Chepkorir	KEN	.93	4		Valencia	19 Nov
2:27:39		Tigist	Mamuye	ETH	27.9.90	1		Zhengzhou	26 Mar
2:27:48		Pamela Rotich	Chepkosgei	KEN	.84	1		Daegu	2 Apr
2:27:48		Fate Geleto	Tola	GER	22.10.87	1		Hannover	9 Apr
		(90)							
2:27:49		Merima	Mohammed	BRN	10.6.92	6		Frankfurt	29 Oct
2:27:52		Purity	Changwony	KEN	-.90	2		Ljubljana	29 Oct
2:27:54		Miharu	Shimokado	JPN	24.4.90	6		Nagoya	12 Mar
2:28:05	1:22:35	Valentine	Kipketer	KEN	5.1.93	5		Chicago	8 Oct
2:28:06		Makda	Harun	ETH	5.9.88	1		Sydney	17 Sep
2:28:08		Muluhabt	Tsega	ETH	11.9.89	1		Hangzhou	5 Nov
2:28:08		Mamitu	Daska	ETH	16.10.83	3		New York	5 Nov
2:28:12		Misaki	Kato	JPN	15.6.91	1		Hofu	17 Dec
2:28:14		Stella	Barsosio	KEN	12.3.93	1		Wroclaw	10 Sep
2:28:15		Tinbit	Weldegebril	ETH	.89	2		Hangzhou	5 Nov
		(100)							

Mark		Name		Nat	Born	Date
2:28:24		Kaori	Yoshida	JPN	4.8.81	12 Mar
2:28:29		Priscah	Cherono	KEN	27.6.80	19 Mar
2:28:32		Risa	Takenaka	ke	6.1.90	2 Jul
2:28:32		Anna	Hahner	GER	20.11.89	24 Sep
2:28:34		Catherine	Bertone	ITA	6.5.72	24 Sep
2:28:35		Tsehay	Desalegn	ETH	28.10.91	5 Nov
2:28:35		Kim Hye-gyong		PRK	9.3.93	26 Nov
2:28:36	1:43:17	Shitaye	Eshete	BRN	21.5.90	29 Jan
2:28:39		Loice	Kiptoo	KEN	-.86	2 Apr
2:28:44	1:42:40	Risa	Tanaka	JPN	30.10.79	29 Jan
2:28:44		Anastasiya	Ivanova	BLR	4.11.82	23 Apr
2:28:46		Afera	Godfay	ETH	25.9.91	15 Oct
2:28:47		Truphena	Chepchirchir	KEN	-.90	3 Dec
2:28:48		Diana	Lobacevske	LTU	7.8.80	23 Apr
2:28:48		Honami	Maeda	JPN	17.7.96	27 Aug
2:28:49		Mare	Dibaba	ETH	20.10.89	6 Aug
2:28:51		Kellyn	Taylor	USA	22.7.86	23 Apr
2:28:52	1:43:49	Ai	Utsunomiya	JPN	19.9.95	12 Mar
2:28:52		Georgina	Rono	KEN	19.5.84	7 May
2:28:54		Paula	González	ESP	2.5.85	19 Feb
2:28:54		Megertu	Ifa	ETH	20.9.91	15 Oct
2:28:54		Anja	Scherl	GER	12.4.86	19 Nov
2:28:55		Dire	Tune	ETH	19.5.85	26 Nov
2:28:58		Nataliya	Lehonkova	UKR	27.2.82	29 Oct
2:29:01		Bornes	Kitur	KEN	-.88	17 Sep
2:29:04		Janet	Rono	KEN	8.12.88	19 Mar
2:29:04		Sule	Utura	ETH	8.2.90	22 Oct
2:29:05		Tigist	Girma	ETH	.93	12 Nov
2:29:05		Keiko	Nogami	JPN	6.12.85	26 Nov
2:29:06		Alyson	Dixon	GBR	24.9.78	23 Apr
2:29:07		Elizeba	Cherono	NED	6.6.88	2 Jul
2:29:09		Sylvia	Medugu	KEN	24.2.90	29 Oct
2:29:10		Kebede	Megertu	ETH		26 Mar
2:29:13		Sheila	Chepkoech	KEN	1.1.90	1 Oct
2:29:14		Meseret	Abebayehu	ETH-J	.98	12 Mar
2:29:14		Virginia	Moloney	AUS	6.5.90	2 Jul
2:29:15		Netsanet	Gudeta	ETH	12.2.91	9 Apr
2:29:17		Ayelu	Abebe	ETH	15.9.87	19 Mar
2:29:17		Mulu	Seboka	ETH	24.9.84	7 May
2:29:22			Jo Un-ok	PRK	29.8.92	9 Apr
2:29:23		Charlotte	Purdue	GBR	10.6.91	23 Apr
2:29:25		Helaria	Johannes	NAM	13.8.80	23 Apr
2:29:26	1:24:14	Sutume	Asefa	ETH	11.12.94	22 Oct
2:29:27		Celia	Sullohern	AUS	5.7.92	15 Oct
2:29:29		Katharina	Heinig	GER	22.8.89	29 Oct
2:29:30		Nancy	Koech	KEN	12.11.86	2 Apr
2:29:31		Betty	Lempus	KEN	.91	23 Apr
2:29:34		Sonia	Samuels	GBR	16.5.79	24 Sep
2:29:37		Iwona	Bernardelli	POL	19.2.85	29 Jan
2:29:39		Allie	Kieffer	USA	16.9.87	5 Nov

Mark	Name		Nat	Born	Date
2:29:39	Sara	Dossena	ITA	22.11.84	5 Nov
2:29:41	Eva	Vrabcová-Nyvltová	CZE	6.2.86	5 Nov
2:29:46	Sorome	Negash	ETH		26 Nov
2:29:53	Askale	Alemaheyu	ETH	11.1.96	19 Mar
2:29:54	Agnes	Kiprop	KEN	12.12.79	7 May
2:29:56	Izabela	Trzaskalska	POL	9.1.88	23 Apr
2:29:58	Guteni	Shone	ETH	17.11.91	2 Jan
2:29:58	Anna	Incerti	ITA	19.1.80	2 Apr
2:30:02	Sarah	Jebet	KEN	14.7.88	22 Oct
2:30:03	Viola	Yator	KEN	30.7.93	23 Apr
2:30:03	Shasho	Insermu	ETH	-.93	29 Oct
2:30:04	Worknesh	Alemu	ETH	-.90	5 Mar
2:30:06	Dakebo	Hailemariam	ETH	3.11.96	9 Apr
2:30:06	Bekelech	Daba	ETH	29.12.91	12 Nov
2:30:09	Meseret	Legesse	ETH	28.8.87	2 Jan
2:30:09	Tigist	Teshome	ETH	11.3.87	20 Jan
2:30:09	Recho	Kosgei	KEN		12 Mar
2:30:10	Shiho	Takechi	JPN	18.8.90	12 Mar
2:30:11	Tigist	Abayechew	ETH	22.2.94	10 Sep
2:30:12	Wude	Ayalew	ETH	4.7.87	12 Nov
2:30:18	Ashu	Kasim	ETH	20.10.84	29 Jan
2:30:18	Olha	Kotovska	UKR	5.12.83	2 Apr
2:30:22	Ayelu	Lemma	ETH		21 May
2:30:22	Halima	Hassen	ETH	10.11.92	5 Nov
2:30:23	Bethlehem	Moges	ETH	3.5.91	17 Sep
2:30:24	Katarzyna	Kowalska	POL	7.4.85	9 Apr
2:30:26		He Yinli	CHN	20.9.88	19 Mar
2:30:26	Jane	Kibii	KEN	10.3.85	1 Oct
2:30:29	Sardana	Trofimova	RUS	28.3.88	24 Sep
2:30:31	María Azucena	Díaz	ESP	19.12.82	24 Sep
2:30:38	Zinash	Debebe	ETH	-.96	12 Nov
2:30:42	Tracy	Barlow	GBR	18.6.85	23 Apr
2:30:44	Biruktayit	Degefa	ETH	29.9.90	15 Jan
2:30:44	Asami	Furuse	JPN	17.3.88	29 Jan
2:30:45	Wilma	Arizapana	PER	1.10.82	2 Apr
2:30:45	Natalya	Starkova	RUS	8.11.87	7 May
2:30:46	Aregu	Lechisa	ETH	30.12.85	26 Mar
2:30:49	Pauline	Wangui	KEN	17.7.84	19 Feb
2:30:50	Abeba	Gebremeskel	ETH	-.89	29 Sep
2:30:53	Alina	Prokopyeva	RUS	16.8.85	7 May
2:30:53	Aynalem	Kasahun	ETH	28.11.93	19 Nov
2:30:56	Natalya	Puchkova	RUS	28.1.87	7 May
2:30:57	Susan	Jeptoo	KEN	7.3.87	26 Nov
2:30:58	Peninah	Arusei	KEN	23.2.79	29 Sep
2:31:01	Meseret	Kitata	ETH	8.11.93	24 Dec
2:31:02	Ruth	Wanjiru	KEN	11.9.81	5 Nov
2:31:07	Beatrice	Cherop	KEN	-.86	29 Jan
2:31:09	Souad	Kanbouchia	MAR	12.8.82	2 Apr
2:31:10	Reia	Iwade	JPN	8.12.94	12 Nov
	(200)				

Downhill

Mark	Name		Nat	Born	Pos	Venue	Date
2:21:52	Edna	Kiplagat	KEN	15.11.79	1	Boston	17 Apr
2:22:51	Rose	Chelimo	BRN	12.7.89	2	Boston	17 Apr
2:23:00		Hasay			3	Boston	17 Apr
2:25:06	Desiree	Linden	USA	26.7.83	4	Boston	17 Apr

WOMEN 2017

Mark		Name		Nat	Born	Pos	Meet	Venue	Date
2:26:51		Viola	Jelagat	KEN	20.4.92	1		Rennes	22 Oct

Mark	Name		Nat	Born	Date
2:28:26	Vivian	Kiplagat	KEN	.91	22 Oct
2:30:37	Roberta	Groner	USA	4.1.78	3 Dec
2:30:38	Ayantu	Gemechu	ETH	1.3.92	22 Oct
2:30:53	Carrie	Dimoff	USA	31.5.83	3 Dec
2:30:58	Buzunesh	Deba	ETH	8.9.87	17 Apr
Questionable distance					
2:30:54A	Bayartsogt	Munkhzaya	MGL	10.10.93	20 May

JUNIORS

Mark		Name		Nat	Born	Pos	Meet	Venue	Date
2:29:14		Meseret	Abebayehu	ETH-J	.98	4		Barcelona	12 Mar
2:32:21		Sophia	Chesire	KEN-J	-.98	2		La Rochelle	26 Nov
2:34:05		Bekelu	Beji	ETH	.99	3		Rabat	5 Mar
2:34:18		Bedatu	Hirpa	ETH	28.4.99	1		Athína	12 Nov

100 KILOMETRES

Mark		Name		Nat	Born	Pos	Meet	Venue	Date
7:34:36		Nikolina	Sustic	CRO	24.7.87	1		Firenze	28 Jun
7:35:37		Nele	Alder-Baerens	GER	1.4.78	1	NC	Berlin	24 Jun
7:36:39	t	Camille	Herron	USA	25.12.81	1		Phoenix	9 Dec
7:37:21		Yuri	Kano	JPN	27.10.78	1		Yubetsu	25 Jun
7:44:34			Alder-Baerens			1		Rothenburg	7 Oct
7:46:04		Aiko	Kanematsu	JPN	18.5.80	2		Yubetsu	25 Jun
7:47:18		Laura	Gotti	ITA	14.6.91	2		Firenze	28 Jun
7:49:21		Mikiko	Ota	JPN	28.4.75	3		Yubetsu	25 Jun
7:50:13		Sophia	Sundberg	SWE	5.9.84	3		Winschoten	9 Sep
7:51:03		Caroline	Boller	USA	7.12.74	1	NC	Madison	8 Apr
7:58:38		Frida	Södermark	SWE	5.8.78	1		Borås	7 Jul
7:59:16		Marita	Eisler	AUS	7.3.80	1		Broadbeach	11 Jun

Mark	Name		Nat	Born	Date
8:01:13	Veronika	Jurisic	CRO	6.4.77	28 May
8:01:25	Susan	Harrison	GBR	6.8.71	21 May
8:03:47	Julie	Hamulecki	CAN	21.11.80	8 Apr
8:03:58	Katalin	Nagy	USA	5.5.79	8 Apr
8:05:26	Hisayo	Matsumoto	JPN	.78	25 Jun
8:08:59	Yuko	Kusunose	JPN	29.5.79	25 Jun
8:09:17	Tereza	Zuzanková	CZE	18.9.86	19 Aug
8:09:40	Antje	Krause	GER	1.5.72	26 Mar
8:09:45	Katerina	Kasparová	CZE	6.6.86	9 Sep
8:10:05	Flore	Martinuzzi	FRA	27.4.73	27 May
8:10:37	Gwenaelle	Guillou	FRA	25.9.70	14 Oct

24 HOURS

Mark		Name		Nat	Born	Pos	Meet	Venue	Date
259.991		Patrycja	Bereznowska	POL	17.10.75	1	WCh	Belfast	1 Jul
256.405	t	Courtney	Dauwalter	USA	13.2.85	1		Taipei	3 Dec
256.246			Bereznowska			1	NC	Lódz	8 Apr
251.078		Aleksandra	Niwinska	POL	23.1.86	2	WCh	Belfast	1 Jul
250.622		Katalin	Nagy	USA	5.5.79	3	WCh	Belfast	1 Jul
250.079	t		Dauwalter			1		Riverbank	25 Feb
248.276		Gina	Slaby	USA	16.6.81	4	WCh	Belfast	1 Jul
243.611		Pam	Smith	USA	22.9.74	5	WCh	Belfast	1 Jul
243.119			Niwinska			2	NC	Lódz	8 Apr
238.713		Jessica	Baker	GBR	6.6.82	6	WCh	Belfast	1 Jul
237.841		Antje	Krause	GER	1.5.72	7	WCh	Belfast	1 Jul
236.800	t	Therese	Falk	NOR	5.8.75	1		London (TB)	16 Sep
236.247		Maria	Jansson	SWE	10.7.85	8	WCh	Belfast	1 Jul
236.183		Julia	Fatton	GER	24.4.72	9	WCh	Belfast	1 Jul
234.941		Noora Katarina	Honkala	FIN	1.7.92	10	WCh	Belfast	1 Jul
234.618		Yuri	Matsumoto	JPN	27.2.78	11	WCh	Belfast	1 Jul
233.051		Anne Marie	Geisler Andersen	DEN	15.4.81	12	WCh	Belfast	1 Jul
233.033	t		Shan Ying	CHN	1.12.82	1		Hangzhou	9 Dec
232.257		Antonija	Orlic	CRO	4.11.77	13	WCh	Belfast	1 Jul
230.871	t	Monika	Biegasiewicz	POL	25.5.76	1		Barcelona	16 Dec
230.817			Biegasiewicz			14	WCh	Belfast	1 Jul
		(21/16)							
228.761		Mizuki	Aotani	JPN	5.12.73	15	WCh	Belfast	1 Jul
228.603		Agata	Matejczuk	POL	27.11.81	16	WCh	Belfast	1 Jul
228.581		Amy	Masner	IRL	22.11.73	17	WCh	Belfast	1 Jul
226.220		Sandra	Lundqvist	SWE	5.7.77	19	WCh	Belfast	1 Jul
225.792		Aiko	Kanematsu	JPN	18.5.80	1		Tokyo	11 Nov
225.667	t		Chou Ling-Chun	TPE	28.2.72	2		Hangzhou	9 Dec
225.306		Aneta	Rajda	POL	6.5.76	20	WCh	Belfast	1 Jul

Mark	Name		Nat	Born	Date
223.798	Anna	Grundahl	SWE	6.4.76	1 Jul
223.310	Guro	Skjeggerud	NOR	18.5.73	1 Jul
220.509 t	Wendy	Shaw	TPE	5.10.77	17 Dec
Best track times					
222.192 t	Patrycja	Bereznowska	POL	17.10.75	9 Dec

Indoors

Mark		Name		Nat	Born	Pos	Meet	Venue	Date
231.832		Anna	Grundahl	SWE	6.4.76	1	NOR Ch	Oslo	26 Nov

2000 METRES STEEPLECHASE

Mark		Name		Nat	Born	Pos	Meet	Venue	Date
6:18.43		Viktória	Gyürkés	HUN	15.10.92	1		Debrecen	20 May
6:19.5A		Caren	Chebet	KEN-Y	24.5.99	1	AfrJ-T	Nairobi	14 Jun
6:19.7A		Permela	Jeptoo	KEN-Y	3.12.00	2	AfrJ-T	Nairobi	14 Jun
6:20.33		Fabienne	Schlumpf	SUI	17.11.90	1		Pliezhausen	14 May

Mark	Name		Nat	Born	Pos	Meet	Venue	Date
6:20.8A	Nelly	Kigen	KEN-Y	4.5.01	3	AfrJ-T	Nairobi	14 Jun
6:23.36	Jana	Sussmann	GER	12.10.90	2		Pliezhausen	14 May
6:23.78	Victoria	Mitchell	AUS	25.4.82	1		Sydney	21 Jan
6:26.10A	Mercy	Chepkurui	KEN-Y	16.9.00	2	WY	Nairobi	14 Jul
6:29.75	Zita	Kácser	HUN	2.10.88	2		Debrecen	20 May

JUNIORS

See above for top 4 juniors

Chebet	6:24.80A 1 WY Nairobi 14 Jun			6:29.9A2			Eldoret	26 May
6:30.9A	Etalemahu	Sintayehu	ETH-Y	23.2.01	1		Assefa	15 Jun
6:32.38	Hannah	O'Connor	NZL-Y	9.3.01	1		Imgelwood	8 Mar
6:32.4A	Betty	Kibet	KEN-Y	3.4.00	3		Eldoret	26 May
6:33.35	Anna Mark	Helwigh	DEN-Y	12.3.00	1		København	17 Jun
6:33.4A	Betelihem	Mulat	ETH-Y	21.3.01	2		Assefa	15 Jun
6:33.44	Catherine	Beauchemin	CAN	31.8.98	1		Québec City	5 Aug
6:33.9A	Emily	Cherotich	KEN	31.5.98	1		Mombasa	9 Jun

3000 METRES STEEPLECHASE

Mark	Name		Nat	Born	Pos	Meet	Venue	Date
8:55.29	Ruth	Jebet	BRN	17.11.96	1	WK-DLF	Zürich	24 Aug
8:58.78	Celliphine	Chespol	KEN-J	23.3.99	1	Pre	Eugene	26 May
8:59.84	Beatrice	Chepkoech	KEN	6.7.91	2	WK-DLF	Zürich	24 Aug
9:00.12	Hyvin	Jepkemoi	KEN	13.1.92	1	DL	Doha	5 May
9:00.70		Chepkoech			2	Pre	Eugene	26 May
9:01.57		Chepkoech			2	DL	Doha	5 May
9:01.69		Chepkoech			1	DL	Paris (C)	1 Jul
9:01.99		Jebet			3	DL	Doha	5 May
9:02.58	Emma	Coburn	USA	19.10.90	1	WCh	London (OS)	11 Aug
9:03.52		Jebet			3	Pre	Eugene	26 May
9:03.70	Norah	Tanui	KEN	2.10.95	1	ISTAF	Berlin	27 Aug
9:03.77	Courtney	Frerichs	USA	18.1.93	2	WCh	London (OS)	11 Aug
9:04.03		Jepkemoi			3	WCh	London (OS)	11 Aug
9:04.56		Tanui			1	Hanz	Zagreb	29 Aug
9:04.78		Jebet			1	DL	Shanghai	13 May
9:05.31		Tanui			3	WK-DLF	Zürich	24 Aug
9:05.70		Chespol			4	DL	Doha	5 May
9:06.00		Jepkemoi			2	DL	Paris (C)	1 Jul
9:06.72		Jepkemoi			2	DL	Shanghai	13 May
9:07.06	Sofia	Assefa	ETH	14.11.87	1	FBK	Hengelo	11 Jun
9:07.08		Chespol			3	DL	Shanghai	13 May
9:07.54		Chespol			3	DL	Paris (C)	1 Jul
9:07.96		Coburn			4	Pre	Eugene	26 May
9:10.45		Chepkoech			4	WCh	London (OS)	11 Aug
9:10.95		Jebet			1	DL	Paris (C)	1 Jul
9:11.08		Coburn			1	DL	Paris (C)	1 Jul
9:11.85	Gesa-Felicitas	Krause	GER	3.8.92	2	ISTAF	Berlin	27 Aug
9:13.25	Etenesh	Diro (10)	ETH	10.5.91	6	DL	Paris (C)	1 Jul
9:13.35	Karoline Bjerkeli	Grøvdal	NOR	14.6.90	1	NC	Sandnes	26 Aug
9:13.96		Jebet			5	WCh	London (OS)	11 Aug
	(30/11)							
9:15.97	Colleen	Quigley	USA	20.11.92	3	ISTAF	Berlin	27 Aug
9:19.29	Aisha	Praught Leer	JAM	14.12.89	8	DL	Doha	5 May
9:19.68	Daisy	Jepkemei	KEN	13.2.96	2	Hanz	Zagreb	29 Aug
9:20.00	Habiba	Ghribi	TUN	9.4.84	1	ArabC	Radès	16 Jul
9:20.07	Purity	Kirui	KEN	13.8.91	6	Pre	Eugene	26 May
9:20.22	Joan	Chepkemoi	KEN	24.11.93	3	Hanz	Zagreb	29 Aug
9:21.65	Fabienne	Schlumpf	SUI	17.11.90	3	Bisl	Oslo	15 Jun
9:22.67	Winfred	Yavi	BRN-J	-.99	8	WCh	London (OS)	11 Aug
9:23.99	Fadwa Sidi	Madane	MAR	20.11.94	3	DL	Rabat	16 Jul
	(20)							
9:24.52	Genevieve	LaCaze	AUS	4.8.89	6	ISTAF	Berlin	27 Aug
9:24.97	Birtukan	Adamu	ETH	29.4.92	6	DL	Shanghai	13 May
9:25.04	Stephanie	Garcia	USA	3.5.88	8	Pre	Eugene	26 May
9:25.90	Amina	Bettiche	ALG	14.12.87	2	Isl.Sol	Baku	17 May
9:25.99	Belén	Casetta	ARG	26.9.94	11	WCh	London (OS)	11 Aug
9:26.00	Tigist	Mekonen	BRN	7.7.97	3	Isl.Sol	Baku	17 May
9:26.05	Luiza	Gega	ALB	5.11.88	5	Bisl	Oslo	15 Jun
9:26.09	Tugba	Güvenç	TUR	9.7.94	4	Isl.Sol	Baku	17 May
9:27.72	Peruth	Chemutai	UGA-J	10.7.99	7	DL	Shanghai	13 May

Mark	Name		Nat	Born	Pos	Meet	Venue	Date
9:28.63	Rosefline	Chepngetich	KEN	17.6.97	8	DL	Shanghai	13 May
	(30)							
9:29.99	Geneviève	Lalonde	CAN	5.9.91	13	WCh	London (OS)	11 Aug
9:30.03	Woynshet	Ansa	ETH	9.4.96	3	Gyulai	Székesfehérvár	3 Jul
9:30.92	Marisa	Howard	USA	9.8.92	1	SavoG	Lapinlahti	16 Jul
9:31.07	Caroline	Chepkurui	KEN	12.3.90	4	Gyulai	Székesfehérvár	3 Jul
9:31.61	Leah	O'Connor	USA	30.8.92	6	Hanz	Zagreb	29 Aug
9:32.10	Rosie	Clarke	GBR	17.11.91	7	Hanz	Zagreb	29 Aug
9:33.99	Birtukan	Fente	ETH	18.6.89	6h2	WCh	London (OS)	9 Aug
9:34.30	Anna Emilie	Møller	DEN	28.7.97	9	Bisl	Oslo	15 Jun
9:34.71	Yekaterina	Sokolenko	RUS	13.9.92	8	ISTAF	Berlin	27 Aug
9:34.94	Mel	Lawrence	USA	29.8.89	1		Karlstad	25 Jul
	(40)							
9:36.56	Mariya	Shatalova	UKR	3.3.89	2		Huelva	14 Jun
9:37.00	Katie	Landwehr	USA	23.1.93	2		Göteborg	11 Jul
9:37.06	Özlem	Kaya	TUR	20.4.90	7h2	WCh	London (OS)	9 Aug
9:37.94	Lennie	Waite	GBR	4.5.86	3		Göteborg	11 Jul
9:39.03	Iona	Lake	GBR	15.1.93	8	Hanz	Zagreb	29 Aug
9:39.44	Zita	Kácser	HUN	2.10.88	1		Budapest	2 Sep
9:39.46	Jana	Sussmann	GER	12.10.90	10	ISTAF	Berlin	27 Aug
9:39.55	Maritu	Ketema	ETH-Y	-.00	4	FBK	Hengelo	11 Jun
9:39.96	Maria	Larsson	SWE	24.3.94	4		Göteborg	11 Jul
9:40.30	Irene	Sánchez	ESP	25.9.92	3		Huelva	14 Jun
	(50)							
9:40.51	María José	Pérez	ESP	12.6.92	14	DL	Paris (C)	1 Jul
9:40.65	Emily	Oren	USA	20.9.93	1		Nashville	10 Jun
9:40.66	Viktória	Gyürkés	HUN	15.10.92	2		Lapinlahti	16 Jul
9:40.90	Alex	Wilson	USA	16.6.93	3		Los Angeles (ER)	18 May
9:40.94	Megan	Rolland	USA	30.8.88	3		Lapinlahti	16 Jul
9:41.06	Natalya	Vlasova	RUS	19.7.88	2	NC	Zhukovskiy	29 Jul
9:41.19	Maeva	Danois	FRA	10.3.93	5		Göteborg	11 Jul
9:41.31	Allie	Ostrander	USA	24.12.96	1	NCAA	Eugene	10 Jun
9:41.73	Camilla	Richardsson	FIN	14.9.93	3	Odlozil	Praha	5 Jun
9:41.73	Agrie	Belachew	ETH-J	20.1.99	5	FBK	Hengelo	11 Jun
	(60)							
9:42.14	Charlotta	Fougberg	SWE	19.6.85	14	DL	Doha	5 May
9:42.50	Rachel	Johnson	USA	30.4.93	4		Los Angeles (ER)	18 May
9:42.79	Jessica	Kamilos	USA	3.8.93	2		Nashville	10 Jun
9:43.33	Sarah	Pease	USA	9.11.87	3		Nashville	10 Jun
9:43.34	Erin	Teschuk	CAN	25.10.94	1		Portland	16 Jun
9:43.48	María Teresa	Urbina	ESP	20.3.85	5		Huelva	14 Jun
9:43.63	Maria	Bernard	CAN	6.4.93	2		Portland	16 Jun
9:43.65	Elinor	Purrier	USA	20.2.95	1		Providence RI	15 Apr
9:43.80	Francesca	Bertoni	ITA	29.12.93	4	ET	Villeneuve d'Ascq	24 Jun
9:43.88	Lucie	Sekanová	CZE	5.8.89	5	ET	Villeneuve d'Ascq	24 Jun
	(70)							
9:44.09	Victoria	Mitchell	AUS	25.4.82	1	NC	Sydney	2 Apr
9:44.10	Matylda	Kowal	POL	11.1.89	5	SavoG	Lapinlahti	16 Jul
9:44.13	Alycia	Butterworth	CAN	1.10.92	2	NC	Ottawa	6 Jul
9:44.42	Rima	Chenah	ALG	11.2.96	1		Ninove	15 Jul
9:44.52	Nataliya	Strebkova	UKR	6.3.95	2	EU23	Bydgoszcz	15 Jul
9:46.48	Madison	Boreman	USA-J	10.7.98	2	NCAA	Eugene	10 Jun
9:46.76	Tori	Gerlach	USA	2.6.94	3	NCAA	Eugene	10 Jun
9:46.79	Natalya	Aristarkhova	RUS	31.10.89	3	NC	Zhukovskiy	29 Jul
9:47.59	Anastasiya	Puzakova	BLR	12.12.93	11	DL	Shanghai	13 May
9:48.09	Ophélie	Claude-Boxberger	FRA	18.10.88	12	DL	Shanghai	13 May
	(80)							
9:48.53	Nawal	Yahi	ALG	9.12.91	5		Oordegem	27 May
9:49.23	Chinta	Yadav	IND	26.3.93	1	NC	Chennai	27 Sep
9:49.41	Chikako	Mori	JPN	25.11.92	1	NC	Osaka	24 Jun
9:49.74	Alicja	Konieczek	POL	2.11.94	6		Stanford	5 May
9:49.82	Jamie	Cheever	USA	28.2.87	7h2	NC	Sacramento	22 Jun
9:50.30	Emma	Oudiou	FRA	2.1.95	3	EU23	Bydgoszcz	15 Jul
9:50.4A	Marion	Kibor	KEN	27.9.94	1	NC	Nairobi	10 Jun
9:50.51	Hope	Schmelzle	USA	18.2.95	1s2	NCAA	Eugene	8 Jun
9:50.72	Misaki	Sango	JPN	21.4.89	1		Kobe	23 Apr
9:50.75	Kerry	O'Flaherty	IRL	15.7.81	3		Ninove	15 Jul
	(90)							
9:50.93	Anna	Petrova	RUS	15.7.94	2	Znam	Zhukovskiy	1 Jul
9:51.13	Collier	Lawrence	USA	4.10.86	4		Portland	16 Jun
9:51.38	Caroline	Austin	USA	1.7.91	3		Portland	11 Jun

Mark	Name		Nat	Born	Pos	Meet	Venue	Date
9:51.83	Madeline	Strandemo	USA	12.7.95	1	Big 10	University Park	13 May
9:52.32	Zulema	Arenas	PER	15.11.95	1	Bol G	Santa Marta	23 Nov
9:52.36	Natalya	Leontyeva	RUS	5.7.87	4	NC	Zhukovskiy	29 Jul
9:52.51	Lyudmila	Lebedeva	RUS	23.5.90	5	NC	Zhukovskiy	29 Jul
9:52.68	Rolanda	Bell	PAN	27.10.87	4		Ninove	15 Jul
9:52.79	Carolina	Robles	ESP	4.12.91	2	NC	Barcelona	22 Jul
9:52.89	Sarah (100)	Edwards	USA-J	7.7.98	2h3	NCAA-E	Lexington	26 May

Mark	Name		Nat	Born	Date
9:53.04	Grayson	Murphy	USA	28.6.95	8 Jun
9:53.3A	Caroline	Biwott	KEN	-.92	10 Jun
9:53.67	Tatiane Raquel da Silva		BRA	10.6.90	30 Mar
9:54.69	Anju	Takamizawa	JPN	6.3.96	13 Jul
9:54.77	Eva	Krchová	CZE	10.9.89	15 Jul
9:55.10	Michele	Finn	IRL	16.12.89	3 Jul
9:55.2A	Ann	Gathoni	KEN-J	5.3.98	10 Jun
9:55.59	Katy	Kunc	USA	18.10.95	8 Jun
9:55.72	Lili	Tóth	HUN-J	17.9.98	3 Jul
9:55.78	Aïssé	Sow	FRA	19.8.91	27 May
9:56.18	Ellie	Abrahamson	USA	11.11.95	10 Jun
9:56.33	Bri	Ilarda	AUS	19.2.96	12 May
9:56.47	Stella	Radford	AUS	25.6.95	2 Apr
9:56.53	Etalemahu	Sintayehu	ETH-Y	23.2.01	11 Jun
9:56.57	Claire	Borchers	USA	20.4.96	26 May
9:56.83	Breanna	Colbenson	USA	5.8.95	10 Jun
9:57.02		Zhang Xinyan	CHN	9.2.94	13 Apr
9:57.28	Mariola	Slusarczyk	POL	4.1.90	5 Jun
9:57.37	Claudia	Prisecaru	ROU	2.9.97	15 Jul
9:57.68	Isabel	Mattuzzi	ITA	23.4.95	15 Jul
9:57.70	Aneta	Konieczek	POL	8.6.97	17 Jun
9:57.72	Kristi	Rush	USA		14 Apr
9:57.78	Paige	Campbell	AUS	27.6.96	19 Dec
9:57.89	Alsu	Gabdullina	RUS	12.5.94	29 Jul
9:58.16	Lea	Meyer	GER	16.9.97	15 Jul
9:58.18	Kira	Garry	USA	4.3.93	27 Apr
9:58.22	Erica	Birk	USA		14 Apr
9:58.77	Cornelia	Griesche	GER	28.8.93	27 May
9:58.85	Charlotte	Taylor-Green	GBR	2.4.85	14 Jun
9:58.9A	Fancy	Cherotich	KEN	10.8.90	10 Jun
9:59.47	Sudha	Singh	IND	25.6.86	8 Jul
9:59.86	Aimee	Pratt	GBR	3.10.97	14 Jun
10:00.02	Janelle	Lincks	USA	30.9.93	8 Jun
10:00.32	Emily	Myers	USA	23.5.94	8 Jun
10:00.53	Liane	Weidner	GER	13.8.97	27 May
10:00.79	Lisa	Oed	GER-J	2.1.99	22 Jul
10:00.87		Zhong Xiaoqian	CHN	24.10.97	13 Apr
10:00.99	Alicia	Nelson	USA	20.10.90	31 Mar
10:01.19	Amy	Cashin	AUS	28.7.94	26 May
10:01.2A	Nancy	Kimaiyo	KEN	-.84	12 May
10:01.46	Veerle	Bakker	NED	29.9.97	27 May
10:01.62	Viktoriya	Ivanova	RUS	21.11.91	1 Jul
10:01.71	Paige	Kouba	USA	8.1.94	16 Jun
10:02.02	Nell	Crosby	USA		26 May
10:02.06	Charlotte	Wilson	AUS	2.10.92	19 Dec
10:02.34	Katie	Ingle	GBR	4.3.95	2 Jul
10:02.36	Emily	de a Bruyere	USA	31.3.93	27 May
10:02.53	Rosie	Donegan	AUS	1.7.93	13 May
10:02.64	Hiroe	Yabuta	JPN	-.96	10 Sep
10:02.65	Paige	Stoner	USA	31.1.96	8 Jun
10:02.89	Taylor	Austin	USA	26.3.94	26 May
10:03.32	Tatyana	Shabanova	BLR-J	20.3.98	22 Jul
10:03.4	Maroua	Bouzayani	TUN	26.3.97	3 Jun
10:03.54	Anastasiya	Salova	RUS	28.10.94	29 Jul
10:03.94	U.K. Nilani	Rathnayake	SRI	8.8.90	9 Apr
10:04.18		Xu Shuangshuang	CHN	6.4.96	5 Apr
10:04.19A	Andrea	Ferris	PAN	21.9.87	12 Dec
10:04.26	Lea	Navarro	FRA	28.1.97	27 May
10:04.33	Martina	Merlo	ITA	19.2.93	27 May
10:04.43	Courtney	Wayment	USA-J	4.8.98	31 Mar
10:04.60	Colette	Rampf	GER	23.7.91	26 May
10:04.73	Ayaka	Koike	JPN	9.4.93	24 Jun
10:04.79	Rachel	Schilkowsky	USA	15.4.92	22 Jun
10:04.80	Sümeyye	Erol	TUR	15.6.97	6 Jul
10:05.26	Kako	Okada	JPN-J	12.2.98	24 Jun
10:05.32	Katarzyna	Kowalska	POL	7.4.85	21 Jul
10:05.81	Riho	Takamizawa	JPN	12.4.97	24 Jun
10:05.93	Valeria	Roffino	ITA	9.4.90	14 Jun
10:06.41	Chiara	Scherrer	SUI	24.1.96	15 Jul
10:06.42	Rebeka	Stowe	USA	9.3.90	16 Jun
10:06.46	Anne-Sophie	Vittet	FRA	24.12.88	27 May
10:06.67	Shelby	Brown	USA	9.12.95	26 May
10:06.6A	Emmaculate (173)	Chebet	KEN	-.92	12 May

Drugs disqualification

Mark	Name		Nat	Born	Pos	Meet	Venue	Date
9:20.69	Rosefline	Chepngetich ¶	KEN	17.6.97	(3)	DL	Rabat	16 Jul

JUNIORS

See main list for top 7 juniors. 14 performances by 3 women to 9:35.0. Additional marks and further juniors:

	Mark	Pos	Meet	Venue	Date	Mark	Pos	Meet	Venue	Date
Chespol 4+	9:15.04	6	WCh	London (OS)	11 Aug	9:27.35	1h3	WCh	London (OS)	9 Aug
	9:17.56	8	WK	Zürich	24 Aug	9:34.03A	1	WCT	Nairobi	24 Jun
Yavi	9:22.82	3		Belfort	9 Jun	9:28.00	4h3	WCh	London (OS)	9 Aug
	9:27.61	5	DL	Rabat	16 Jul	9:33.29	2	PNG	Turku	13 Jun

Mark	Name		Nat	Born	Pos	Meet	Venue	Date
9:55.2A	Ann	Gathoni	KEN	5.3.98	3	NC	Nairobi	10 Jun
9:55.72	Lili	Tóth	HUN	17.9.98	10	Gyulai	Székesfehérvár	3 Jul
9:56.53	Etalemahu	Sintayehu (10)	ETH-Y	23.2.01	7	FBK	Hengelo	11 Jun
10:00.79	Lisa	Oed	GER-J	2.1.99	1	EJ	Grosseto	22 Jul
10:03.32	Tatyana	Shabanova	BLR-J	20.3.98	2	EJ	Grosseto	22 Jul
10:04.43	Courtney	Wayment	USA-J	4.8.98	4rC		Stanford	31 Mar
10:05.26	Kako	Okada	JPN-J	12.2.98	5	NC	Osaka	24 Jun
10:07.87	Sage	Hurta	USA-J	23.6.98	2	Pac 12	Eugene	13 May
10:07.91	Derya	Kunur	TUR-J	1.9.99	2	NC	Bursa	14 Jun
10:08.1A	Lomi	Leta	ETH-J		1	NC-j	Bahir Dar	15 Jan
10:08.4A	Mekides	Abebe	ETH-J		2	NC-j	Bahir Dar	15 Jan
10:11.80A	Mekides	Abebe	ETH		1	Afr-J	Tiemcen	2 Jul
10:12.49	Alexa	Lemitre (20)	FRA	10.4.98	1		Pézenas	10 Jun

60 METRES HURDLES

Mark	Wind	Name		Nat	Born	Pos	Meet	Venue	Date
8.08	1.1	Sally	Pearson	AUS	19.9.86	1		Gold Coast	6 Jan
8.19	1.8	Adanaca	Brown	BAH	23.10.93	1		Coral Gables	8 Feb

Indoors

Mark	Name		Nat	Born	Pos	Meet	Venue	Date
7.74A	Kendra	Harrison	USA	18.9.92	1h2	NC	Albuquerque	5 Mar
7.75		Harrison			1		Lexington	21 Jan
7.76		Harrison			1		Karlsruhe	4 Feb

Mark	Name		Nat	Born	Pos	Meet	Venue	Date
7.79	Pamela	Dutkiewicz	GER	28.9.91	1	NC	Leipzig	18 Feb
7.81A		Harrison			1	NC	Albuquerque	5 Mar
7.82	Christina	Manning	USA	29.5.90	1		Athlone	15 Feb
7.82A	Jasmin	Stowers	USA	23.9.91	2	NC	Albuquerque	5 Mar
7.83		Manning			1		Birmingham	18 Feb
7.84	Cindy	Roleder	GER	21.8.89	2	NC	Leipzig	18 Feb
7.85		Harrison			1h3		Lexington	21 Jan
7.85	(11/5)	Roleder			1	ISTAF	Berlin	10 Feb
7.86	Alina	Talay	BLR	14.5.89	1s1	EI	Beograd	3 Mar
7.87A	Sharika	Nelvis	USA	10.5.90	2h1	NC	Albuquerque	5 Mar
7.87	Sasha	Wallace	USA	21.9.95	1h1	NCAA	College Station	10 Mar
7.91	Sally	Pearson	AUS	19.9.86	3		Karlsruhe	4 Feb
7.92	Nadine	Visser	NED	9.2.95	2h2	EI	Beograd	3 Mar
	(10)							
7.92	Hanna	Plotitsyna	UKR	1.1.87	2s1	EI	Beograd	3 Mar
7.93	Phylicia	George	CAN	16.11.87	1		Lódz	16 Feb
7.93	Devynne	Charlton	BAH	26.11.95	2	NCAA	College Station	11 Mar
7.95A	Jackie	Coward	USA	5.11.89	3h2	NC	Albuquerque	5 Mar
7.96	Leah	Nugent	JAM	23.11.92	2		Lexington	21 Jan
7.96	Cindy	Ofili	GBR	5.8.94	5		Karlsruhe	4 Feb
7.96	Andrea	Ivancevic	CRO	21.8.84	1		Torun	10 Feb
7.97	Pedrya	Seymour	BAH	29.5.95	3	NCAA	College Station	11 Mar
7.98	Isabelle	Pedersen	NOR	27.1.92	7		Karlsruhe	4 Feb
7.98	Mikiah	Brisco	USA	14.7.96	1		Fayetteville	10 Feb
	(20)							
7.98A	Tobi	Amusan	NGR	23.4.97	1h2		Albuquerque	10 Feb
7.98	Anne	Zagré	BEL	13.3.90	1		Metz	12 Feb
7.98	Anna	Cockrell	USA	28.8.97	2h1	NCAA	College Station	10 Mar
7.99	Ricarda	Lobe	GER	13.4.94	3	NC	Leipzig	18 Feb
8.00	Tiffani	McReynolds	USA	4.12.91	2		Lódz	16 Feb
8.00	Klaudia	Siciarz	POL	15.3.98	1	NC	Torun	18 Feb
8.01A	Alaysha	Johnson	USA	20.7.96	3		Albuquerque	11 Feb
8.02	Jasmine	Camacho-Quinn	PUR	21.8.96	1	SEC	Nashville	25 Feb
8.02	Rushelle	Burton	JAM	4.12.97	5	NCAA	College Station	11 Mar
8.03	Janay	DeLoach	USA	12.10.85	4	Millrose	New York (A)	11 Feb
	(30)							
8.03	Sharona	Bakker	NED	12.4.90	3		Lódz	16 Feb
8.03	Kendell	Williams	USA	14.6.95	1P3	NCAA	College Station	10 Mar
8.04	Anastasiya	Nikolayeva	RUS	24.9.95	1		Sankt Peterburg	14 Feb
8.04	Elisávet	Pesirídou	GRE	12.2.92	1	NC	Pireás	19 Feb
8.04A	Evonne	Britton	USA	10.10.91	3h1	NC	Albuquerque	5 Mar
8.05	Vanessa	Clerveaux	HAI	17.6.94	2	SEC	Nashville	25 Feb
8.06	Ivana	Loncarek	CRO	8.4.91	1		Linz	10 Feb
8.06	Susanna	Kallur	SWE	16.2.81	1	v3N	Tampere	11 Feb
8.06A	Lorenda	Holston	USA	15.8.95	4		Albuquerque	11 Feb
8.06	Lindsay	Lindley	NGR	6.10.89	3		Metz	12 Feb
	(40)							
8.06	Karolina	Koleczek	POL	15.1.93	2	NC	Torun	18 Feb
8.07	Megan	Simmonds	JAM	18.3.94	4h1		Birmingham	18 Feb
8.08	Dior	Hall	USA	2.1.96	4		Fayetteville	10 Feb
8.08	Nooralotta	Neziri	FIN	9.11.92	1	NC	Jyväskylä	19 Feb
8.09	Raven	Clay	USA	5.10.90	4		Lódz	16 Feb
8.09	Danielle	Williams	JAM	14.9.92	1		Clemson	17 Feb
8.10	Jade	Barber	USA	4.4.93	1h1		Mondeville	4 Feb
8.10A	Kaila	Barber	USA	4.4.93	4	NC	Albuquerque	5 Mar
8.11A	Micha	Auzenne	USA	10.6.95	2		Albuquerque	21 Jan
8.11	Kori	Carter	USA	3.6.92	2p2		Fayetteville	10 Feb
	(50)							
8.11	Caridad	Jerez	ESP	23.1.91	1	NC	Salamanca	19 Feb
8.12	Ebony	Morrison	USA	28.12.94	1	ACC	Notre Dame	25 Feb
8.13	Laura	Valette	FRA	16.2.97	1		Nantes	21 Jan
8.13	Franziska	Hofmann	GER	27.3.94	2		Erfurt	27 Jan
8.13	Yuliya	Kondakova	RUS	4.12.81	2		Sankt Peterburg	14 Feb
8.13	Elvira	German	BLR	9.1.97	1	NC	Mogilyov	19 Feb
8.13	Kimberly	Golding	JAM	15.12.92	1h1	Big 10	Geneva	24 Feb
8.13	Emma	Spagnola	USA	18.3.96	2h1	Big 10	Geneva	24 Feb
8.13	Taliyah	Brooks	USA	8.2.95	P	NCAA	College Station	10 Mar
8.14	Chanel	Brissett	USA	10.8.99	1		State College	25 Feb
	(60)							
8.14	Luca	Kozák	HUN	1.6.96	3h1	EI	Beograd	3 Mar
8.14	Tara	Davis	USA	20.5.99	1	New Bal	New York	12 Mar

Mark	Wind	Name		Nat	Born	Pos	Meet	Venue	Date
8.15		Stephanie	Bendrat	AUT	5.3.91				28 Jan
8.15		Jacklyn	Howell	USA	3.10.96				4 Feb
8.15		Peta Gaye	Williams	JAM	13.9.95				10 Feb
8.15		Sandra	Sogoyou	FRA	15.9.91				18 Feb
8.17		Sandra	Gomis	FRA	21.11.83				21 Jan
8.17		Shanice	Grant	USA	23.5.93				11 Feb
8.17		Ann-Marie	Duffus	JAM	18.12.90				17 Feb
8.17		Reetta	Hurske	FIN	15.5.95				19 Feb
8.17			Wang Dou	CHN	18.5.93				24 Feb

Best at low altitude

Mark	Name	Pos	Venue	Date
7.92	Nelvis	2	Athlone	15 Feb
7.97	Coward	2	Val-de-Reuil	6 Feb
7.99	Stowers	2	Torun	7 Feb
8.00	Amusun	3h1NCAA	College Station	10 Mar
8.05	Johnson	4h1NCAA	College Station	10 Mar
8.11	Britton	1	New York (SI)	18 Feb
8.14	K Barber	1rB	Mondeville	4 Feb
8.15	Holston	1	Manhattan KS	21 Jan

100 METRES HURDLES

Mark	Wind	Name		Nat	Born	Pos	Meet	Venue	Date
12.28	0.1	Kendra	Harrison	USA	18.9.92	1	Gyulai	Székesfehérvár	4 Jul
12.39	0.2		K Harrison			1	DL	London (OS)	9 Jul
12.47	0.9	Jasmin	Stowers	USA	23.9.91	1s1	NC	Sacramento	24 Jun
12.47	-0.1		K Harrison			1h1	DL	London (OS)	9 Jul
12.48	0.2	Sally	Pearson	AUS	19.9.86	2	DL	London (OS)	9 Jul
12.51	-0.2		K Harrison			1	Herc	Monaco	21 Jul
12.52	0.9	Nia	Ali	USA	23.10.88	2s1	NC	Sacramento	24 Jun
12.52	-0.2	Sharika	Nelvis	USA	10.5.90	2	Herc	Monaco	21 Jul
12.53	-0.1		Nelvis			1	Athl	Lausanne	6 Jul
12.53	0.5		Pearson			1s1	WCh	London (OS)	11 Aug
12.54	-1.4		K Harrison			1h4	NC	Sacramento	23 Jun
12.54	1.4	Christina	Manning	USA	29.5.90	1	ISTAF	Berlin	27 Aug
12.55	-0.3		Pearson			1	WK-DLF	Zürich	24 Aug
12.55	-0.3		Nelvis			2	WK-DLF	Zürich	24 Aug
12.56	1.0		K Harrison			1	DrakeR	Des Moines	29 Apr
12.56	0.4	Danielle	Williams	JAM	14.9.92	1	NC	Kingston	25 Jun
12.57	1.6	Tobi	Amusan	NGR	23.4.97	1	NCAA	Eugene	10 Jun
12.57	-0.1		Stowers			2	Athl	Lausanne	6 Jul
12.58	-0.1		Nelvis			1		Baie-Mahault	17 May
12.58	1.6	Jasmine	Camacho-Quinn	PUR	21.8.96	2	NCAA	Eugene	10 Jun
12.58	-2.4		K Harrison			1s2	NC	Sacramento	24 Jun
12.58	-0.1		Manning			3	Athl	Lausanne	6 Jul
12.58	-0.2		Williams			3	Herc	Monaco	21 Jul
12.58	1.4		Williams			2	ISTAF	Berlin	27 Aug
12.59	-2.3		K Harrison			1	DL	Doha	5 May
12.59	0.5		Nelvis			1		St-Martin	13 May
12.59	0.8		Stowers			1	Pre	Eugene	27 May
12.59	0.1		Pearson			1	WCh	London (OS)	12 Aug
12.60	0.9		Nelvis			3s1	NC	Sacramento	24 Jun
12.60	-1.7		K Harrison			1	NC	Sacramento	24 Jun
12.60	-0.6	(31/9)	K Harrison			1h3	WCh	London (OS)	11 Aug
12.61	1.9	Pamela (10)	Dutkiewicz	GER	28.9.91	1		Weinheim	27 May
12.61	-0.1	Kristi	Castlin	USA	7.7.88	5	Athl	Lausanne	6 Jul
12.63	0.4	Megan	Simmonds	JAM	18.3.94	2	NC	Kingston	25 Jun
12.63	0.2	Dawn	Harper Nelson	USA	13.5.84	1s3	WCh	London (OS)	11 Aug
12.64	0.8	Queen	Harrison	USA	10.9.88	2	Pre	Eugene	27 May
12.65	1.6	Rushelle	Burton	JAM	4.12.97	3	NCAA	Eugene	10 Jun
12.69	2.0	Alaysha	Johnson	USA	20.7.96	1	FlaR	Gainesville	31 Mar
12.69	0.4	Yanique	Thompson	JAM	12.3.96	3	NC	Kingston	25 Jun
12.72	1.4	Alina	Talay	BLR	14.5.89	3	ISTAF	Berlin	27 Aug
12.74	1.6	Devynne	Charlton	BAH	26.11.95	5	NCAA	Eugene	10 Jun
12.75	1.6	Tiffany (20)	Porter	GBR	13.11.87	1		Montverde	10 Jun
12.75	0.8	Isabelle	Pedersen	NOR	27.1.92	3	Bisl	Oslo	15 Jun
12.78	0.6	Kori	Carter	USA	3.6.92	1		Tempe	18 Mar
12.78	1.0	Nadine	Visser	NED	9.2.95	1H5	Hypo	Götzis	27 May
12.80	0.9	Bridgette	Owens	USA	14.3.92	5s1	NC	Sacramento	24 Jun
12.81	1.9	Nadine	Hildebrand	GER	20.9.87	2		Weinheim	27 May
12.81	0.1	Nickiesha	Wilson	JAM	28.7.86	1		Kingston	27 May
12.81	1.6	Sasha	Wallace	USA	21.9.95	6	NCAA	Eugene	10 Jun
12.81	0.4	Shimayra	Williams	JAM	2.12.95	5	NC	Kingston	25 Jun
12.82	1.6	Dior	Hall	USA	2.1.96	7	NCAA	Eugene	10 Jun
12.82	-0.1	Kendell (30)	Williams	USA	14.6.95	1H	NC	Sacramento	24 Jun
12.83	0.9	Janay	DeLoach Soukup	USA	12.10.85	6s1	NC	Sacramento	24 Jun
12.84A	0.0	Fabiana	Moraes	BRA	5.6.86	1		Ávila	15 Jul
12.85	-0.3	Mikiah	Brisco	USA	14.7.96	3	TexR	Austin	1 Apr

Mark	Wind	Name		Nat	Born	Pos	Meet	Venue	Date
12.85	0.4	Phylicia	George	CAN	16.11.87	3		St. George's	8 Apr
12.85	0.4	Shermaine	Williams	JAM	4.2.90	6	NC	Kingston	25 Jun
12.89	0.2	Anna	Cockrell	USA	28.8.97	2s3	NCAA	Eugene	8 Jun
12.89	0.9	Hanna	Plotitsyna	UKR	1.1.87	1	NC	Kropyvnytskiy	5 Jul
12.90	1.1	Lindsay	Lindley	NGR	6.10.89	1		Long Beach	15 Apr
12.90	-2.3	Cindy	Roleder	GER	21.8.89	2	DL	Doha	5 May
12.91	1.9	Ricarda	Lobe	GER	13.4.94	3		Weinheim	27 May
		(40)							
12.92A	1.9	Evonne	Britton	USA	10.10.91	2		El Paso	22 Apr
12.92	1.0	Cindy	Ofili	GBR	5.8.94	6	DrakeR	Des Moines	29 Apr
12.93	-0.1	Erica	Bougard	USA	26.7.93	2H	NC	Sacramento	24 Jun
12.94	1.1	Kayla	White	USA	24.9.96	1h4	NCAA-E	Lexington	26 May
12.94	1.8	Mulern	Jean	HAI	25.9.92	1		Jacksonville	3 Jun
12.95	0.5	Tara	Davis	USA-J	20.5.99	1h2	NC-j	Sacramento	23 Jun
12.96	0.6	Anne	Zagré	BEL	13.3.90	1	Jones	Gainesville	28 Apr
12.96	0.4	Peta Gaye	Williams	JAM	13.9.95	1	ACC	Atlanta	14 May
12.96	0.0	Elvira	German	BLR	9.1.97	1		Tomblaine	28 Jun
12.97	1.6	Sharona	Bakker	NED	12.4.90	1		Azusa	14 Apr
		(50)							
12.97A	1.5	Micha	Auzenne	USA	10.6.95	1	MWC	Logan	13 May
12.97	-0.2		Wu Shuijiao	CHN	19.6.91	1	NG	Tianjin	4 Sep
12.98	1.3	Franziska	Hofmann	GER	27.3.94	1		Regensburg	11 Jun
12.98	-0.1	Eefje	Boons	NED	18.7.94	7	Athl	Lausanne	6 Jul
12.99	1.3	Michelle	Jenneke	AUS	23.6.93	1		Canberra	12 Mar
12.99	0.6	Raven	Clay	USA	5.10.90	2	Jones	Gainesville	28 Apr
12.99	0.4	Jeanine	Williams	JAM	28.1.97	2	ACC	Atlanta	14 May
12.99	-1.0	Angela	Whyte	CAN	22.5.80	2		Phoenix	10 Jun
12.99	1.0	Rikenette	Steenkamp	RSA	16.10.92	2	GS	Ostrava	28 Jun
13.00	1.7	Payton	Stumbaugh	USA	29.11.95	1H	SEC	Columbia SC	11 May
		(60)							
13.00	1.7	Jacklyn	Howell	USA	3.10.96	1h5	NCAA-E	Lexington	26 May
13.01	0.2		Kang Ya	CHN	16.3.90	2	NC	Jinan	18 May
13.01	0.4	Tia	Jones	USA-Y	8.9.00	1	PAm-J	Trujillo	21 Jul
13.02	1.2	Jackie	Coward	USA	5.11.89	3		Columbia	15 Apr
13.02	0.0	Eline	Berings	BEL	28.5.86	3		Heusden	22 Jul
13.03	1.4	Kimberly	Golding	JAM	15.12.92	2h2	Big 10	University Park	13 May
13.03	1.1	Ebony	Morrison	USA	28.12.94	2h4	NCAA-E	Lexington	26 May
13.03	-0.4	Elisávet	Pesirídou	GRE	12.2.92	2h1	ET	Villeneuve d'Ascq	23 Jun
13.03	0.3	Hitomi	Shimura	JPN	8.11.90	1s2	NC	Osaka	24 Jun
13.04	-0.4	Laura	Valette	FRA	16.2.97	3h1	ET	Villeneuve d'Ascq	23 Jun
		(70)							
13.05	1.0	Monique	Morgan	JAM	14.10.85	1rB		St-Martin	13 May
13.05	1.4	Anastasiya	Nikolayeva	RUS	24.9.95	1	NC	Zhukovskiy	28 Jul
13.06	0.9	Cortney	Jones	USA-J	18.6.99	1		Tallahassee	24 Mar
13.06	1.0	Brianna	Beahan	AUS	1.11.91	1		Perth	24 Mar
13.06	1.8	Pedrya	Seymour	BAH	29.5.95	1		Charleston IL	1 Apr
13.06	1.1	Yuliya	Kondakova	RUS	4.12.81	1		Sankt Peterburg	17 Jun
13.06	0.4	Ayako	Kimura	JPN	11.6.88	1s1	NC	Osaka	24 Jun
13.07	-0.6	Karolina	Koleczek	POL	15.1.93	1		Genève	10 Jun
13.07	-0.8	Alicia	Barrett	GBR-J	25.3.98	1	NC-j	Bedford	18 Jun
13.07	2.0	Carolin	Schäfer	GER	5.12.91	1H		Ratingen	24 Jun
		(80)							
13.08	0.6	Christie	Moerman	CAN	5.10.86	2h1		Guelph	14 Jul
13.09	2.0	Noemi	Zbären	SUI	12.3.94	1		Langenthal	25 May
13.10	0.0		Jung Hye-lim	KOR	1.7.87	4		Kawasaki	21 May
13.10	0.0	Breana	Norman	USA	14.9.92	6		Kawasaki	21 May
13.10	1.0	Laura	Ikauniece-Admidina	LAT	31.5.92	3H5	Hypo	Götzis	27 May
13.10	1.5	Cassandra	Lloyd	USA	27.1.90	2h1		Montverde	10 Jun
13.10	1.1	Luca	Kozák	HUN	1.6.96	2rB	Gyulai	Székesfehérvár	4 Jul
13.10	1.1	Gréta	Kerekes	HUN	9.10.92	3rB	Gyulai	Székesfehérvár	4 Jul
13.10	-0.6	Deborah	John	TTO	10.4.90	2r1		Freeport	22 Jul
13.11	0.1	Skylar	Ross Ransom	USA	19.2.95	3s1	NCAA	Eugene	8 Jun
		(90)							
13.11	1.5	Ladonna	Richards	JAM	1.1.92	3h1		Montverde	10 Jun
13.12	-0.4	Gabrielle	McDonald	JAM-J	14.3.98	1	N.Sch	Kingston	1 Apr
13.12	1.9	Chanel	Brissett	USA-J	10.8.99	2	New Bal	Greensboro	16 Jun
13.12	0.9	Jade	Barber	USA	4.4.93	8s1	NC	Sacramento	24 Jun
13.12	1.2	Andrea Carolina	Vargas	CRC	28.5.96	1	C.AmG	Managua	10 Dec
13.13	0.5		Wang Dou	CHN	18.5.93	1	NGP	Taiyuan	11 May
13.13	1.1	Vanessa	Clerveaux	HAI	17.6.94	1		Guelph	14 Jun
13.13	1.6	Tia	Thevenin	CAN	7.9.96	2h3	NC	Ottawa	8 Jul

Mark	Wind	Name		Nat	Born	Pos	Meet	Venue	Date
13.14	1.7	Taliyah (100)	Brooks	USA	8.2.95	2H	SEC	Columbia SC	11 May
13.14	1.0	Kierre	Beckles	BAR	21.5.90	3rB		St-Martin	13 May
13.14	0.2	Tonea	Marshall	USA-J	17.12.98	2q2	NCAA-E	Lexington	27 May
13.14	1.0	Sandra	Gomis	FRA	21.11.83	4		Montreuil	1 Jun
13.14	-1.8	Alexis	Perry	USA	8.8.94	3h1	NC	Sacramento	23 Jun
13.14	1.1	Stephanie	Bendrat	AUT	5.3.91	1h1		Ried	30 Jun

Mark	Wind	Name		Nat	Born	Date
13.15A	1.5	Taylor	Pegram	USA	14.1.96	13 May
13.15	0.1	Solène	Ndama	FRA-J	23.9.98	22 Jul
13.16	-0.4	Janeek	Brown	JAM-J	14.5.98	1 Apr
13.16	1.6	Ashlea	Maddex	CAN	16.12.92	8 Jul
13.17	1.0	Kaila	Barber	USA	4.4.93	12 May
13.17	1.4	Irina	Reshetkina	RUS	30.1.89	28 Jul
13.18	1.4	Veronika	Chervinskaya	RUS-J	24.8.98	28 Jul
13.18	0.5	Masumi	Aoki	JPN	16.4.94	9 Oct
13.19A	0.6	Maribel	Caicedo	ECU	1.4.98	29 Apr
13.19	1.5	Anamaria	Nesteriuc	ROU	29.11.93	16 Jul
13.19	0.8	Génesis	Romero	VEN	6.11.95	21 Nov
13.20	1.8	Veronica	Borsi	ITA	13.6.87	28 May
13.20	1.8	Micol	Cattaneo	ITA	14.5.82	1 Jul
13.21	1.9	Karelle	Edwards	CAN	30.3.90	29 Apr
13.21	1.4	Emma	Spagnola	USA	18.3.96	13 May
13.22	1.5	Cyrena	Samba-Mayela	FRA-Y	31.10.00	21 May
13.22	1.3	Pauline	Salies	FRA	18.9.97	20 Jun
13.23A	0.9	Claudia	Heunis	RSA	1.5.89	25 Mar
13.23	0.8	Brandeé	Johnson	USA-J	3.4.98	28 Apr
13.23	1.2	Yasmin	Miller	GBR	24.5.95	27 May
13.23	-0.1	Ilionis	Guillaume	FRA-J	13.1.98	3 Jun
13.24	0.4	Ivanique	Kemp	BAH	11.6.91	8 Apr
13.24	0.8	Elisa Maria	Di Lazzaro	ITA-J	5.6.98	25 May
13.24	1.2	Elin	Westerlund	SWE	4.2.90	6 Jun
13.24	1.1	Ivana	Loncarek	CRO	8.4.91	30 Jun
13.25	1.2	Kyra	Atkins	USA	1.9.92	12 May
13.25	0.2	Brittley	Humphrey	USA-J	6.3.98	27 May
13.25		Mariya	Aglitskaya	RUS	20.6.91	16 Jun
13.25	1.9	Marthe	Koala	BUR	8.3.94	17 Jun
13.25	1.9	Pauline	Lett	FRA	8.10.91	18 Jun
13.25		Vashanti	Simmons	BAH-J	.98	24 Jun
13.25	0.5	Lotta	Harala	FIN	26.3.92	12 Jul
13.26	1.6	Alexus	Jimson-Miller	USA	8.2.95	13 May
13.26	1.2	Courtney	Nelson	USA	12.9.95	26 May
13.27	1.5	MacKenzie	Hill	USA	5.1.86	6 May
13.27A	1.5	Mofiyinfoluwa	Olusola	USA	23.8.96	13 May
13.27	0.4	Klaudia	Siciarz	POL-J	15.3.98	20 May
13.27	1.6	Klaudia	Sorok	HUN-J	21.2.98	10 Jun
13.27	1.4	Anna	Vatropina	RUS	5.10.90	28 Jul
13.28	0.1	Brittney	Trought	USA	15.10.96	8 Jun
13.28	-0.4	Katerina	Cachová	CZE	26.2.90	10 Jun
13.29	1.0	Caitlyn	Little	USA-J	24.8.99	8 Apr
13.29A	1.5	Sierra	Brabham-Lawrence	USA	11.7.97	13 May
13.29	1.2	Katarina	Johnson-Thompson	GBR	9.1.93	27 May
13.29	1.6	Melia	Cox	USA	23.11.92	17 Jun
13.29	0.1	Alice	Decaux	FRA	10.4.85	25 Jun
13.30	1.9	Lorenda	Holston	USA	15.8.95	29 Apr
13.30	1.9	Megan	George	USA	5.4.95	29 Apr
13.30	0.5	Deshaunda	Morrison	CAN	16.12.95	14 May
13.30	0.1	Jabreuna	Brimlett	USA	14.7.97	27 May
13.30	1.0	Rosvitha	Okou	CIV	5.9.86	1 Jun
13.30	0.9	Lavonne	Idlette	DOM	31.10.85	10 Jun
13.30	2.0	Reetta	Hurske	FIN	15.5.95	22 Jul
13.31	1.8	Antoinette	Nana Djimou	FRA	2.8.85	21 May
13.31	1.2	Grit	Sadeiko	EST	29.7.89	27 May
13.31	0.9	Beate	Schrott	AUT	15.4.88	27 May
13.31	0.0	Anouk	Vetter	NED	4.2.93	5 Aug
13.32	0.7	Chastity	Stewart	USA		29 Apr
13.32	1.9	Kaylah	Robinson	USA-J	27.6.99	29 Apr
13.32	0.9	Chantel	Ray	USA	3.1.96	13 May
13.32	0.2	Danielle	Phillips	USA	18.7.95	27 May
13.32	1.3	Coralie	Comte	FRA	15.10.95	20 Jun
13.32	1.0	Lucie	Koudelová	CZE	6.7.94	28 Jun
13.32	1.6	Viivi	Avikainen	FIN	7.9.87	29 Jun
13.32	1.4	Yekaterina	Bleskina	RUS	29.1.93	28 Jul
13.33	-1.0	Amoi	Brown	JAM-J	11.1.99	5 Mar
13.33	-0.9	Amber	Hughes	USA	23.8.94	12 May
13.33	0.9	Savannah	Roberson	USA	15.1.96	13 May
13.33	-0.6	Sandra	Sogoyou	FRA	15.9.91	10 Jun
13.34	0.6	Lutisha	Bowen	PAN	9.7.90	28 Apr
13.34	0.8	Nicole	Setterington	CAN	18.4.95	28 Apr
13.34	-0.7	Nafissatou	Thiam	BEL	19.8.94	27 May
13.34	1.3	Eriko	Soma	JPN	30.9.91	4 Jun
13.34	1.0	Hanna	Chubkovtsova	UKR	20.4.94	5 Jul
13.34	2.0	Monika	Zapalska	GER	24.5.94	22 Jul
13.34	0.5	Marzia	Caravelli	ITA	23.10.81	24 Sep
13.35	0.1	Fiona	Morrison	NZL	24.10.88	18 Mar
13.35	0.8	Stefani	Kerrison	USA	7.6.96	28 Apr
13.35		Tiffany	Flynn	USA	2.9.95	28 Apr
13.35	-0.6	Chisato	Kiyoyama	JPN	24.7.91	7 May
13.35	1.2	Jocselyn	Powell	USA	24.10.95	13 May
13.35	1.3	Stanislava	Lajcáková	SVK	20.4.96	17 Jun
13.35	1.9	Odile	Ahouanwanou	BEN	5.1.91	17 Jun
13.35	0.3	Petra (188)	Répási	HUN	30.1.96	17 Jun

Wind assisted

Mark	Wind	Name		Nat	Born	Pos	Meet	Venue	Date
12.53	2.3		Pearson			1	NC	Sydney	2 Apr
12.54	2.3		K Harrison			1		Austin	15 Apr
12.57	4.5	Nadine	Visser	NED	9.2.95	1		Clermont	15 Apr
12.57	4.5		Amusan			1q3	NCAA-W	Austin	27 May
12.67	3.6	Devynne	Charlton	BAH	26.11.95	1	Big 10	University Park	14 May
12.68	2.6	Alaysha	Johnson	USA	20.7.96	1h5	NCAA-W	Austin	26 May
12.81	5.5	Sharona	Bakker	NED	12.4.90	2rB	FlaR	Gainesville	31 Mar
12.83	5.5	Leah	Nugent	JAM	23.11.92	3rB	FlaR	Gainesville	31 Mar
12.83	5.3	Evonne	Britton	USA	10.10.91	1		Lubbock	6 May
12.83	3.7	Tara	Davis	USA-J	20.5.99	1		Clovis	3 Jun
12.87	3.8	Raven	Clay	USA	5.10.90	1h1		Clermont	15 Apr
12.87	5.0	Kimberly	Golding	JAM	15.12.92	1		Austin	29 Apr
12.87	3.5	Ariel	Jones	USA	18.7.95	2	Big 12	Lawrence	14 May
12.90	2.2	Erica	Bougard	USA	26.7.93	1r1		Chula Vista	17 Jun
12.90	3.1	Mulern	Jean	HAI	25.9.92	1		Fort Lauderdale	15 Jul
12.92	2.1	Rikenette	Steenkamp	RSA	16.10.92	1		La Chaux-de-Fonds	2 Jul
12.94	2.5	Kaila	Barber	USA	4.4.93	2	EAF	Bydgoszcz	2 Jun
12.95A	2.9	Micha	Auzenne	USA	10.6.95	1h2	MWC	Logan	12 May
12.95	2.2	Angela	Whyte	CAN	22.5.80	1h1	NC	Ottawa	8 Jul
12.95	2.3	Elvira	German	BLR	9.1.97	2	EU23	Bydgoszcz	15 Jul
12.96	2.3	Brianna	Beahan	AUS	1.11.91	2	NC	Sydney	2 Apr
12.96	2.8	Ebony	Morrison	USA	28.12.94	2h2	Jones	Gainesville	28 Apr
12.97	2.5	Gréta	Kerekes	HUN	9.10.92	1		Debrecen	20 May
12.98	3.7	Kaylah	Robinson	USA-J	27.6.99	2		Clovis	3 Jun
12.99	3.5	Olivia	Haggerty	USA	22.6.95	3	Big 12	Lawrence	14 May

Mark		Name		Nat	Born	Pos	Meet	Venue	Date
12.99	2.5	Luca	Kozák	HUN	1.6.96	2		Debrecen	20 May
12.99	3.7	Ayako	Kimura	JPN	11.6.88	1		Tottori	4 Jun
13.01	3.1	Vanessa	Clerveaux	HAI	17.6.94	2		Fort Lauderdale	15 Jul
13.02	3.6	Emma	Spagnola	USA	18.3.96	3	Big 10	University Park	14 May
13.04A	w?	Maribel	Caicedo	ECU-J	1.4.98	1	NC-j	Quito	7 Apr
13.04	2.8	Brittney	Trought	USA	15.10.96	2q1	NCAA-W	Austin	27 May
13.04	3.6	Nikkita	Holder	CAN	7.5.87	1	Ontario	Windsor	17 Jun
13.04	3.6	Karelle	Edwards	CAN	30.3.90	2	Ontario	Windsor	17 Jun
13.05	4.5	Lorenda	Holston	USA	15.8.95	4q3	NCAA-W	Austin	27 May
13.08	3.5	Ashley	Miller	USA-J	17.2.98	5	Big 12	Lawrence	14 May
13.09	3.6	Chantel	Ray	USA	3.1.96	4	Big 10	University Park	14 May
13.11A	2.1	Taylor	Pegram	USA	14.1.96	1h1	MWC	Logan	12 May
13.12	2.9	Amber	Hughes	USA	23.8.94	1	OVC	Jacksonville	13 May
13.12	2.8	Lotta	Harala	FIN	26.3.92	1	NC	Seinäjoki	22 Jul

Mark	Wind	Name		Nat	Born	Date
13.13	2.3	Lavonne	Idlette	DOM	31.10.85	8 Apr
13.13	2.3	Courtney	Robinson	USA	18.4.95	15 Apr
13.14	4.9	Brandeé	Johnson	USA-J	3.4.98	31 Mar
13.14	2.3	Jayla	Stewart	USA	23.7.97	29 Apr
13.14	5.4	Mary	Young	USA	6.5.96	14 May
13.15	2.6	Jasmine	Barge	USA	2.1.97	28 Apr
13.16	2.3	Yasmin	Miller	GBR	24.5.95	18 Jun
13.16	2.9	Génesis	Romero	VEN	6.11.95	23 Jun
13.17	4.0	Adanaca	Brown	BAH	23.10.93	31 Mar
13.17	5.4	Nikki	Larch-Miller	USA	13.8.94	14 May
13.17	3.1	Melia	Cox	USA	23.11.92	27 May
13.18	2.3	Fiona	Morrison	NZL	24.10.88	2 Apr
13.18	5.0	Jessica	Duckett	USA	22.1.97	29 Apr
13.18	3.4	Deshaunda	Morrison	CAN	16.12.95	26 May
13.20	2.4	Mofiyinfoluwa	Olusola	USA	23.8.96	27 May
13.20	2.1	Elin	Westerlund	SWE	4.2.90	6 Jun
13.21	3.6	Savannah	Roberson	USA	15.1.96	14 May
13.21	5.5	Sandra	Sogoyou	FRA	15.9.91	28 May
13.22	2.9	Jabreuna	Brimlett	USA	14.7.97	13 May
13.23	3.7	Cha'mia	Rothwell	USA-J	18.4.98	6 May
13.23	5.5	Clémence	Vifquin	FRA	9.6.86	28 May
13.23	2.8	Reetta	Hurske	FIN	15.5.95	22 Jul
13.24	5.2	Chastity	Stewart	USA	2.5.93	27 Apr
13.24	2.6	Shanice	Grant	USA	23.5.93	11 Jun
13.25	4.0	Taylor	Larch-Miller	USA	13.8.94	13 May
13.25	3.8	Annimari	Korte	FIN	8.4.88	12 Jul
13.28	4.7	Malia	Cox	USA	23.11.93	13 Apr
13.28	2.8	Lutisha	Bowen	PAN	9.7.90	28 Apr
13.28	2.6	Valerie	Thames	USA	27.2.95	26 May
13.29	4.1	Chisato	Kiyoyama	JPN	24.7.91	29 Apr
13.29	2.4	Chinyere	Njoku	USA	24.2.97	27 May
13.31	6.5	Sophie	Yorke	GBR-J	7.7.98	11 Jun
13.32	2.8	Tawnie	Moore	USA	27.8.95	27 May
13.33	5.0	Mariam	Abdul-Rashid	CAN	21.9.97	29 Apr
13.34	2.3	Elizabeth	Clay	AUS	9.5.95	2 Apr
13.35A	2.1	Andrenette	Knight	JAM	19.11.96	12 May
13.35	2.3	Megu	Hemphill	JPN	23.5.96	9 Jun

Best at low altitude

12.97	1.7	Britton	4		New York	6 Jul
13.03	1.1	Moraes	1	Gyulai	Székesfehérvár	4 Jul
12.86w	2.9		1	SAmC	Asunción	23 Jun
13.19	0.1	Auzenne				22 Apr
13.31	2.0	Romero				25 Mar
13.34	1.9	Caicedo				29 Apr

Doubtful timing: 13.27A 0.3 Maryke Brits RSA 25.2.94 2 Bloemfontein 8 Mar

Hand timing: 12.8 Hanna Plotitsyna UKR 1.1.87 1 Vinntysa 20 May

JUNIORS

See main list for top 7 juniors. 11 performances by 5 women to 13.07. Additional marks and further juniors:

	Mark	Wind	Pos	Meet	Venue	Date	Mark	Wind	Pos	Meet	Venue	Date
T Davis	13.01	1.0	1		Arcadia	8 Apr	13.05	0.4	2	PAm-J	Trujillo	21 Jul
	13.01	-0.7	1	NC-j	Sacramento	23 Jun						
T Jones	13.02	-0.7	2	NC-j	Sacramento	23 Jun	13.03	1.9	1	N.Bal	Greensboro	16 Jun
Barrett	13.07	0.5	1h1	NC-j	Bedford	18 Jun						

Mark	Wind	Name		Nat	Born	Pos	Meet	Venue	Date
13.15	0.1	Solène	Ndama	FRA	23.9.98	1	EJ	Grosseto	22 Jul
13.16	-0.4	Janeek	Brown	JAM	14.5.98	2	N.Sch	Kingston	1 Apr
13.18	1.4	Veronika	Chervinskaya (10)	RUS	24.8.98	3	NC	Zhukovskiy	28 Jul
13.22	1.5	Cyrena	Samba-Mayela	FRA-Y	31.10.00	1rB		Toulouse	21 May
13.23	0.8	Brandeé	Johnson	USA	3.4.98	2r2	Jones	Gainesville	28 Apr
13.23	-0.1	Ilionis	Guillaume	FRA	13.1.98	2		Marseille	3 Jun
13.24	0.8	Elisa Maria	Di Lazzaro	ITA	5.6.98	1		Savona	25 May
13.25	0.2	Brittley	Humphrey	USA	6.3.98	5q3	NCAA-E	Lexington	27 May
13.25		Vashanti	Simmons	BAH	.98	4	NC	Nassau	24 Jun
13.27	0.4	Klaudia	Siciarz	POL	15.3.98	1		Kraków	20 May
13.27	1.6	Klaudia	Sorok	HUN	21.2.98	2	NC	Székesfehérvár	10 Jun
13.29	1.0	Caitlyn	Little	USA	24.8.99	2		Arcadia	8 Apr
13.32	1.9	Kaylah	Robinson (20)	USA	27.6.99	1		Sacramento (ARC)	29 Apr

Wind assisted see main list for 4 juniors. 2 performances by 2 women to 13.05

Mark	Wind	Name		Nat	Born	Pos	Meet	Venue	Date
13.14	4.9	Brandeé	Johnson	USA-J	3.4.98	1rC	FlaR	Gainesville	31 Mar
13.23	3.7	Cha'mia	Rothwell	USA-J	18.4.98	1h1		New Haven	6 May
13.31	6.5	Sophie	Yorke	GBR-J	7.7.98	1		Nuneaton	11 Jun

200 METRES HURDLES

Mark	Wind	Name		Nat	Born	Pos	Venue	Date
25.79	-0.6	Lauren	Wells	AUS	3.8.88	1	Canberra	22 Jan
26.27	-0.6	Zuzana	Hejnová	CZE	19.12.86	1h1	Domazlice	15 Sep
26.43	0.3	Noemi	Zbären	SUI	12.3.94	1	Basel	20 May
26.82	-0.6	Denisa	Rosolová	CZE	21.8.86	2h1	Domazlice	15 Sep
26.94	0.3	Yasmin	Giger	SUI-J	6.11.99	2	Basel	20 May

Irregular timing

Mark	Wind	Name		Nat	Born	Pos	Venue	Date
25.81	-1.5	Zuzana	Hejnová	CZE	19.12.86	1h1	Kutná Hora	13 Sep
26.44	-1.5	Denisa	Rosolová	CZE	21.8.86	2h1	Kutná Hora	13 Sep

Mark		Name		Nat	Born	Pos	Meet	Venue	Date

200 METRES HURDLES STRAIGHT

Mark	Wind	Name		Nat	Born	Pos	Meet	Venue	Date
26.00	-0.2	Shamier	Little	USA	20.3.95	1		Boston	4 Jun
26.12	-0.2	Gianna	Woodruff	PAN	18.11.93	2		Boston	4 Jun
26.43	-0.2	Cassandra	Tate	USA	11.9.90	3		Boston	4 Jun
26.48	-0.2	Kierre	Beckles	BAR	21.5.90	4		Boston	4 Jun

300 METRES HURDLES

Mark	Name		Nat	Born	Pos	Meet	Venue	Date
38.90	Sydney	McLaughlin	USA-J	7.8.99	1		Arcadia	8 Apr
38.98	Zuzana	Hejnová	CZE	19.12.86	1		Cheb	27 Jul
39.29	Léa	Sprunger	SUI	5.3.90	1		Basel	20 May
39.61	Petra	Fontanive	SUI	10.10.88	2		Basel	20 May
39.73	Ayomide	Folorunso	ITA	17.10.96	1		Milano	16 Sep
39.8h	Joanna	Linkiewicz	POL	2.5.90	1h2		Pliezhausen	14 May

400 METRES HURDLES

Mark	Name		Nat	Born	Pos	Meet	Venue	Date
52.64	Dalilah	Muhammad	USA	7.2.90	1	NC	Sacramento	25 Jun
52.75	Shamier	Little	USA	20.3.95	2	NC	Sacramento	25 Jun
52.95	Kori	Carter	USA	3.6.92	3	NC	Sacramento	25 Jun
53.07		Carter			1	WCh	London (OS)	10 Aug
53.11	Ashley	Spencer	USA	8.6.93	4	NC	Sacramento	25 Jun
53.14	Georganne	Moline	USA	6.3.90	5	NC	Sacramento	25 Jun
53.36		Carter			1	Herc	Monaco	21 Jul
53.38		Spencer			1	Pre	Eugene	27 May
53.44		Little			2	Pre	Eugene	27 May
53.50		Muhammad			2	WCh	London (OS)	10 Aug
53.74	Ristananna	Tracey	JAM	9.5.92	3	WCh	London (OS)	10 Aug
53.78		Little			1s1	NC	Sacramento	24 Jun
53.82	Sydney	McLaughlin	USA-J	7.8.99	6	NC	Sacramento	25 Jun
53.84		Moline			2s1	NC	Sacramento	24 Jun
53.89		Muhammad			1	VD	Bruxelles	1 Sep
53.90		Spencer			1	Athl	Lausanne	6 Jul
53.93	Zuzana	Hejnová	CZE	19.12.86	2	VD	Bruxelles	1 Sep
53.95		Muhammad			1s2	NC	Sacramento	24 Jun
54.02	Janieve	Russell	JAM	14.11.93	1	DL	London (OS)	9 Jul
54.02		Little			2	Herc	Monaco	21 Jul
54.03		McLaughlin			1		Egg Harbor	2 Jun
54.04		Carter			2s2	NC	Sacramento	24 Jun
54.09		Moline			3	Pre	Eugene	27 May
54.10		Moline			1		Tucson	20 May
54.13		Hejnová			1	WK-DLF	Zürich	24 Aug
54.14		Russell			1	GGala	Roma	8 Jun
54.18		Hejnová			1	DL	Birmingham	20 Aug
54.20		Hejnová			4	WCh	London (OS)	10 Aug
54.20		Muhammad			2	DL	Birmingham	20 Aug
54.21	(30/9)	Little			1		Kingston	10 Jun
54.29	Rhonda (10)	Whyte	JAM	6.11.90	1	NC	Kingston	23 Jun
54.29	Léa	Sprunger	SUI	5.3.90	2	Athl	Lausanne	6 Jul
54.35	Sara Slott	Petersen	DEN	9.4.87	2	GGala	Roma	8 Jun
54.36	Eilidh	Doyle	GBR	20.2.87	3	Athl	Lausanne	6 Jul
54.52	Sage	Watson	CAN	20.6.94	1	NCAA	Eugene	10 Jun
54.54	Leah	Nugent	JAM	23.11.92	3	NC	Kingston	23 Jun
54.56	Petra	Fontanive	SUI	10.10.88	1		Genève	10 Jun
54.57	Kemi	Adekoya	BRN	16.1.93	2	Gyulai	Székesfehérvár	4 Jul
54.58	Wenda	Nel	RSA	30.7.88	3	GGala	Roma	8 Jun
54.59	Cassandra	Tate	USA	11.9.90	2	DL	London (OS)	9 Jul
54.87	Yadisleidy (20)	Pedroso	ITA	28.1.87	5	DL	London (OS)	9 Jul
54.96	Jaide	Stepter	USA	25.4.94	3		Baie-Mahault	17 May
55.01	Nikita	Tracey	JAM	18.9.90	3h1	NC	Kingston	22 Jun
55.14	Anna	Cockrell	USA	28.8.97	8	NC	Sacramento	25 Jun
55.30	Glory Nathaniel	Onome	NGR	23.1.96	3h5	WCh	London (OS)	7 Aug
55.38	Amalie Hammild	Iuel	NOR	17.4.94	1		Baton Rouge	8 Apr
55.38	Kaliese	Spencer	JAM	6.5.87	4h1	NC	Kingston	22 Jun
55.41	Denisa	Rosolová	CZE	21.8.86	3h1	WCh	London (OS)	7 Aug
55.42	Tia Adana	Belle	BAR	16.6.96	1	NCAA-II	Bradenton	27 May
55.42	Joanna	Linkiewicz	POL	2.5.90	2	Odlozil	Praha	5 Jun
55.46	Sparkle (30)	McKnight	TTO	21.12.91	4h1	WCh	London (OS)	7 Aug

Mark	Name		Nat	Born	Pos	Meet	Venue	Date
55.50	Kymber	Payne	USA	4.6.96	1q3	NCAA-E	Lexington	26 May
55.50	Olena	Kolesnychenko	UKR	3.6.93	1		Lutsk	7 Jun
55.51	Turquoise	Thompson	USA	31.7.91	5s2	NC	Sacramento	24 Jun
55.63	Ayomide	Folorunso	ITA	17.10.96	1	WUG	Taipei	25 Aug
55.70	Valeriya	Khramova	RUS	13.8.92	1	Znam	Zhukovskiy	1 Jul
55.72	Jackie	Baumann	GER	24.8.95	3		Genève	10 Jun
55.76	Gianna	Woodruff	PAN	18.11.93	2		Tucson	20 May
55.78	Autumne	Franklin	USA	20.7.94	3		Tucson	20 May
55.83	Marzia	Caravelli	ITA	23.10.81	8	GGala	Roma	8 Jun
55.85	Noelle	Montcalm	CAN	3.4.88	4		Genève	10 Jun
	(40)							
55.90	Yasmin	Giger	SUI-J	6.11.99	1	EJ	Grosseto	23 Jul
55.96	Agata	Zupin	SLO-J	17.3.98	2	EJ	Grosseto	23 Jul
55.97	Lauren	Wells	AUS	3.8.88	1		Canberra	11 Mar
55.97	Tyler	Brockington	USA	6.2.94	1	SEC	Columbia SC	13 May
55.99		Wang Huan	CHN	21.9.94	1	NG	Tianjin	4 Sep
56.01	Ugonna	Ndu	NGR	27.6.91	1	Jones	Gainesville	28 Apr
56.01	Symone	Black	USA	26.10.95	1	Big 10	University Park	14 May
56.02	Zurian	Hechavarría	CUB	10.8.95	1		La Habana	20 May
56.02		Xiao Xia	CHN	6.6.91	2	NG	Tianjin	4 Sep
56.06		Nguyen Thi Huyen	VIE	19.5.93	1	SEAG	Kuala Lumpur	22 Aug
	(50)							
56.07	Viktoriya	Tkachuk	UKR	8.11.94	1		Minsk	14 Jul
56.07	Vera	Rudakova	RUS	20.3.92	2	NC	Zhukovskiy	29 Jul
56.08	Aminat Youssef	Odeyemi	BRN	27.6.97	2		Manama	10 May
56.08	Jessica	Turner	GBR	8.8.95	2	EU23	Bydgoszcz	16 Jul
56.10	Yanique	Haye-Smith	JAM	22.3.90	1		Greensboro	15 Apr
56.10	Grace	Claxton	PUR	19.8.93	3h2	NC	Kingston	22 Jun
56.11	Kaila	Barber	USA	4.4.93	4h1	NC	Sacramento	23 Jun
56.14	Meghan	Beesley	GBR	15.11.89	2	LEAP	Loughborough	22 Jul
56.17	Jade	Miller	USA	13.1.95	1q2	NCAA-E	Lexington	26 May
56.18	Line	Kloster	NOR	27.2.90	3	LEAP	Loughborough	22 Jul
	(60)							
56.20	Sashel	Brown	JAM	20.1.94	1		Auburn	22 Apr
56.23A	Melissa	Gonzalez	COL	24.6.94	1h2	NC	Medellín	10 Jun
56.31	Emilia	Ankiewicz	POL	22.11.90	1		Plock	16 Jul
56.32	Sayaka	Aoki	JPN	15.12.86	1		Yuwa	21 May
56.32	Katrina	Seymour	BAH	7.1.93	3q3	NCAA-E	Lexington	26 May
56.35	Lisa	Meneau	USA	–.95	4q3	NCAA-E	Lexington	26 May
56.37	Nnenya	Hailey	USA	23.2.94	5h3	NC	Sacramento	23 Jun
56.37	Arna Stefanía	Gudmundsdóttir	ISL	1.9.95	3	EU23	Bydgoszcz	16 Jul
56.44	Ariel	Jones	USA	18.7.95	2q1	NCAA-W	Austin	26 May
56.45	Phara	Anacharsis	FRA	17.12.83	3	Odlozil	Praha	5 Jun
	(70)							
56.49	Viivi	Lehikoinen	FIN-J	27.8.99	3	EJ	Grosseto	23 Jul
56.52	Maeva	Contion	FRA	31.5.92	1		Saint-Égrève	25 Jun
56.53	Gabrielle	McDonald	JAM-J	14.3.98	1	N.Sch	Kingston	31 Mar
56.59	Caryl	Granville	GBR	24.9.89	5	LEAP	Loughborough	22 Jul
56.61	Montayla	Holder	USA	7.2.94	2		Tucson	8 Apr
56.61	Rushell	Clayton	JAM	18.10.92	5h1	NC	Kingston	22 Jun
56.65	Nicolee	Foster	JAM-J	11.1.98	2	N.Sch	Kingston	31 Mar
56.65	Brandeé	Johnson	USA-J	3.4.98	1	PAm-J	Trujillo	23 Jul
56.66	Toria	Levy	USA	5.10.94	2q2	NCAA-E	Lexington	26 May
56.67	Kiah	Seymour	USA	11.1.94	1		Austin	15 Apr
	(80)							
56.68	Ka'lynn	Jupiter	USA	12.1.95	2h2	SEC	Columbia SC	11 May
56.73A	Vera	Barbosa	POR	13.1.89	1		Monachil	7 Jul
56.74	Claudia	Francis	USA	14.11.93	4h2	NC	Sacramento	23 Jun
56.75	Zudikey	Rodríguez	MEX	14.3.87	1	NC	Monterrey	18 Jun
56.75	Axelle	Dauwens	BEL	1.12.90	1	NC	Bruxelles	2 Jul
56.76	Jaílma	de Lima	BRA	31.12.86	1	NC	São Bernardo do Campo	11 Jun
56.84	Ilaria	Vitale	ITA	25.5.90	1		Codroipo	2 Jun
56.87	Aleksandra	Gaworska	POL	7.11.95	1		Radom	4 Jun
56.92	Djamila	Böhm	GER	15.7.94	1	NC	Erfurt	9 Jul
56.93	Aurélie	Chaboudez	FRA	9.5.93	2	NC	Marseille	15 Jul
	(90)							
56.96	Manami	Kira	JPN	23.10.91	2		Yuwa	21 May
56.97	Christine	Salterberg	GER	9.6.94	1		Rhede	29 Jul
56.98		Wu Xueting	CHN	20.8.95	3	NG	Tianjin	4 Sep
56.99	Nenah	De Coninck	BEL	2.9.96	2s2	EU23	Bydgoszcz	15 Jul
57.00	Linda	Olivieri	ITA-J	14.7.98	4	EJ	Grosseto	23 Jul

Mark	Name		Nat	Born	Pos	Meet	Venue	Date
57.01		Huang Yan	CHN	12.1.96	1	NC	Jinan	18 May
57.01	Xahria	Santiago	CAN-J	9.10.99	2	PAm-J	Trujillo	23 Jul
57.02	Shannon	Kalawan	JAM	25.11.97	1		Kingston	8 Apr
57.02	Fiorella	Chiappe	ARG	1.1.96	3	SAmC	Asunción	24 Jun
57.03	Anna Sjoukje (100)	Runia	NED	19.2.95	1	ACC	Atlanta	14 May

Mark	Name		Nat	Born	Date
57.05	Margo	Van Puyvelde	BEL	21.12.95	2 Jul
57.12	Kiana	Hawn	USA	5.12.95	26 May
57.16	Andrenette	Knight	JAM	19.11.96	26 May
57.21	Danielle	Dowie	JAM	5.5.92	22 Jun
57.21	Anu	Raghavan	IND	20.4.93	15 Jul
57.22	Eri	Utsunomiya	JPN	11.4.93	21 May
57.24	Bryiana	Richardson	USA	26.1.95	26 May
57.25	Damajahnee	Birch	USA	29.1.97	11 May
57.27	Sanique	Walker	JAM-Y	8.4.00	31 Mar
57.29	Yelena	Zuykevich	RUS	26.2.90	15 Jul
57.30	Klaudia	Zurek	POL	22.9.91	4 Jun
57.31	Kirsten	McAslan	GBR	1.9.93	30 Jul
57.32	Abigail	Lewis	JAM	7.5.93	15 Jul
57.36	Markeeta	Thomas	USA	29.7.97	14 May
57.40	Yelizaveta	Anikiyenko	RUS	30.6.94	26 Jun
57.43	Geisa	dos Santos	BRA	13.10.92	11 Jun
57.51	Jauna	Murmu	IND	16.8.90	1 Jun
57.51	De'Andreah	Young	USA-J	16.1.98	18 Jun
57.52A	Anneri	Moolman	RSA	9.8.90	4 Mar
57.54	Taysia	Radoslav	CAN	17.9.96	26 May
57.55	Masai	Russell	USA-Y	17.6.00	24 Jun
57.58	Elif	Yildirim	TUR	11.2.90	17 May
57.59	Jasmine	Barge	USA	2.1.97	28 Apr
57.59	Merdzhan	Ishanguliyeva	KAZ	21.1.88	18 Jun
57.60	Alena	Musaleva	RUS	8.2.93	1 Jul
57.61	Déborah	Rodríguez	URU	2.12.92	7 Aug
57.62	Ese	Okoro	GBR	4.7.90	2 Jul
57.63	Alethia	Marrero	PUR	13.5.95	14 May
57.63	Anais	Seiller	FRA	26.6.97	27 May
57.64	Brenna	Detra	USA	-.95	12 May
57.64	M.	Arpitha	IND	11.2.93	1 Jun
57.64	Rebecca	Sartori	ITA	22.5.97	15 Jul
57.65A	Brenna	Porter	USA		12 May
57.65	Kelsey	Balkwill	CAN	19.9.92	9 Jul
57.68	Jean-Marie	Senekal	RSA	11.12.92	29 Apr
57.68	Valentina	Cavalleri	ITA	8.12.95	15 Jul
57.69	Farah	Clerc	FRA	31.7.90	10 Jun
57.75		Yang Qiao	CHN	15.7.96	18 May
57.76	Irina	Takuntseva	RUS	14.11.90	28 Jul
57.82	Shiann	Salmon	JAM-J	31.3.99	31 Mar
57.82	Jessica	Duckett	USA	1.1.97	14 May
57.83	Joanna	Banach	POL	28.8.92	22 Jul
57.84	Deonca	Bookman	USA	29.10.95	26 May
57.84	Anaïs	Lufutucu	FRA	24.4.92	24 Jun
57.86	Candice	McLeod	JAM	15.11.96	15 Apr
57.86	Aisha	Naibe-Wey	SLE	3.8.93	25 Jun
57.86	Johanna	Holmén Svensson	SWE	7.3.95	14 Jul
57.86	Hanne	Claes	BEL	4.8.91	19 Aug
57.87	Nora	McKiver	USA	4.6.95	14 May
57.87	Kana	Koyama	JPN-J	16.12.98	24 Jun
57.87	Lina	Nielsen	GBR	13.3.96	22 Jul
57.88	Emma	Spagnola	USA	18.3.96	14 May
57.88	Sara	Gallego	ESP-Y	21.10.00	23 Jul
57.90	Jonna	Berghem	FIN	25.2.93	25 Aug
57.94	Zeney	van der Walt	RSA-Y	22.5.00	8 Apr
57.94	Andreia	Crespo	POR	9.4.93	25 Jun
57.96	Ranae	McKenzie	JAM	28.10.96	26 May
57.97	Ekateríni	Daláka	GRE	20.8.92	13 May
57.98	Genevieve	Cowie	AUS	26.4.95	9 Dec
58.00	Alesha	Love	USA	20.3.94	22 Apr
58.00	Jessie (161)	Knight	GBR	15.6.94	2 Jul

Best at low altitude

56.29 M González 2 SAmC Asunción 24 Jun | 56.86 Barbosa 2 Bruay-La-Buissière 4 Jul

JUNIORS

See main list for top 9 juniors. 13 performances by 5 women to 56.53. Additional marks and further juniors:

	Mark	Pos	Meet	Venue	Date	Mark	Pos	Meet	Venue	Date
McLaughlin	54.22	1	N.Bal	Greensboro	16 Jun	55.52	1		Egg Harbor	26 May
2+	54.76	3s2	NC	Sacramento	24 Jun	56.15	1		Westfield	22 Apr
	55.41	2h3	NC	Sacramento	23 Jun					
Zupin	56.49	1		Maribor	27 Aug	56.52	1s2	EJ	Grosseto	23 Jul

Mark	Name		Nat	Born	Pos	Meet	Venue	Date
57.27	Sanique	Walker (10)	JAM-Y	8.4.00	3	N.Sch	Kingston	31 Mar
57.51	De'Andreah	Young	USA	16.1.98	2	New Bal	Greensboro	18 Jun
57.55	Masai	Russell	USA-Y	17.6.00	2	NC-j	Sacramento	24 Jun
57.82	Shiann	Salmon	JAM-J	31.3.99	4	N.Sch	Kingston	31 Mar
57.87	Kana	Koyama	JPN-J	16.12.98	2h1	NC	Osaka	24 Jun
57.88	Sara	Gallego	ESP-Y	21.10.00	1	NC	Barcelona	23 Jul
57.94	Zeney	van der Walt	RSA-Y	22.5.00	1	NC-y	Cape Town	8 Apr
58.20	Brooklynn	Broadwater	USA-J	23.6.98	5q2	NCAA-E	Lexington	26 May
58.21	Gontse	Morake	RSA-Y	16.6.01	2	NC-y	Cape Town	8 Apr
58.40	Natalia	Wosztyl	POL	28.8.99	6	EJ	Grosseto	23 Jul
58.33	Lucie	Kruparová	CZE-J	11.7.99	5	EJ	Grosseto	23 Jul

HIGH JUMP

Mark	Name		Nat	Born	Pos	Meet	Venue	Date
2.06	Mariya	Lasitskene	RUS	14.1.93	1	Athl	Lausanne	6 Jul

1.84/1 1.90/1 1.93/1 1.96/2 2.01/1 2.06/2 2.10/xxx

Mark	Pos	Meet	Venue	Date	Series
2.05	1	Herc	Monaco	21 Jul	1.85/1 1.90/1 1.94/1 1.97/1 2.00/1 2.05/2 2.08/x
2.04	1	FBK	Hengelo	11 Jun	1.85/2 1.90/1 1.94/1 2.00/1 2.04/1 2.10/xxx
2.03i	1	NC	Moskva	21 Feb	1.80/1 1.84/1 1.88/1 1.91/1 1.94/2 2.01/3 2.03/1
2.03	1	Pre	Eugene	27 May	1.84/1 1.88/1 1.92/1 1.95/1 1.98/2 2.03/3
2.03	1	WCh	London (OS)	12 Aug	1.84/1 1.88/1 1.92/1 1.95/1 1.97/1 1.99/x 2.01/1 2.03/1 2.08/xxx
2.02	1	VD-DLF	Bruxelles	1 Sep	1.84/1 1.88/1 1.91/1 1.94/1 1.97/2 2.02/3 2.08/xxx
2.01	1	NCp	Yerino	14 Jul	1.80/1 1.84/1 1.88/1 1.91/1 1.94/3 2.01/2 2.05/xxx
2.00i	1		Moskva	18 Jan	1.80/1 1.84/2 1.88/2 1.95/1 1.98/1 2.00/1
2.00	1		Opole	4 Jun	1.82/1 1.86/1 1.90/1 1.93/1 2.00/3 2.04/xxx
2.00	1	GGala	Roma	8 Jun	1.85/1 1.88/1 1.91/1 1.94/1 1.96/1 1.98/1 2.00/2 2.05/xxx
2.00	1	DL	Stockholm	18 Jun	1.85/1 1.90/1 1.94/1 1.97/1 2.00/1 2.06/xxx
2.00	1		Zhukovskiy	24 Jun	1.84/1 1.87/1 1.91/1 1.96/1 2.00/3
2.00	1	DL	London (OS)	9 Jul	1.85/2 1.90/1 1.94/1 1.97/2 2.00/2 2.03/x 2.08/xx

WOMEN 2017

Mark	Name		Nat	Born	Pos	Meet	Venue	Date
	2.00 1	Padova	16 Jul	1.85/2 1.88/1 1.91/1 1.94/1 1.96/3 1.98/1 2.00/1 2.08/xxx				
	2.00i 1	Minsk	23 Dec					
2.01i	Airine	Palsyte	LTU	13.7.92	1	EI	Beograd	4 Mar
				1.80/1 1.85/1 1.89/1 1.92/1 1.94/1 1.96/1 2.01/2				
2.01	Yuliya	Levchenko	UKR	28.11.97	2	WCh	London (OS)	12 Aug
				1.84/1 1.88/1 1.92/1 1.95/1 1.97/1 1.99/1 2.01/2 2.03/xxx				
2.00	Marie-Laurence	Jungfleisch	GER	7.10.90	1		Eberstadt	26 Aug
				1.80/1 1.84/2 1.88/1 1.91/1 1.94/2 1.96/2 2.00/3 2.02/xxx				
1.99	Vashti	Cunningham	USA-J	18.1.98	1	NC	Sacramento	23 Jun
				1.85/1 1.88/1 1.91/1 1.94/1 1.99/2 2.02/xxp				
1.99	Kamila	Licwinko	POL	22.3.86	3	WCh	London (OS)	12 Aug
				1.84/1 1.88/1 1.92/2 1.95/2 1.97/3 1.99/1 2.01/xx 2.03/x				
	1.98 2	Padova	16 Jul	1.85/1 1.88/2 1.91/1 1.94/3 1.98/2 2.00/xxx				
1.98i	Ruth	Beitia	ESP	1.4.79	1		Madrid	24 Feb
				1.85/1 1.89/1 1.92/1 1.95/2 1.98/1 2.01/xxx				
1.98	Nafissatou	Thiam	BEL	19.8.94	1H	Hypo	Götzis	27 May
1.97i		Licwinko			1		Lódz	16 Feb
1.97	Oksana	Okuneva	UKR	14.3.90	1	NC	Kropyvnytskiy	6 Jul
1.97	eight more outdoors: Licwinko & Cunningham 2, Lasitskene, Jungfleisch, Levchenko & Okuneva 1 (34/9)							
1.96	Morgan	Lake	GBR	12.5.97	1	NC	Birmingham	1 Jul
	(10)							
1.96	Inika	McPherson	USA	29.9.86	1		Madrid	14 Jul
1.95	Katarina	Johnson-Thompson	GBR	9.1.93	2H	Hypo	Götzis	27 May
1.95	Iryna	Herashchenko	UKR	10.3.95	1	NC-23	Kropyvnytskiy	22 Jun
1.95	Yorgelis	Rodríguez	CUB	25.1.95	2H	WCh	London (OS)	5 Aug
1.95	Kateryna	Tabashnyk	UKR	15.6.94	1	Quercia	Rovereto	29 Aug
1.94	Liz	Patterson	USA	9.6.88	2	MSR	Torrance	15 Apr
1.94	Irina	Gordeyeva	RUS	9.10.86	1		Sochi	26 May
1.94	Chaunté	Lowe	USA	12.1.84	1		Montverde	10 Jun
1.94	Sofie	Skoog	SWE	7.6.90	3	DL	Stockholm	18 Jun
1.94	Alessia	Trost	ITA	8.3.93	3=	ET	Villeneuve d'Ascq	25 Jun
	(20)							
1.94	Michaela	Hrubá	CZE-J	21.2.98	3=	ET	Villeneuve d'Ascq	25 Jun
1.94	Erika	Kinsey	SWE	10.3.88	3	DL	London (OS)	9 Jul
1.94	Svetlana	Shkolina	RUS	9.3.86	2	NC	Zhukovskiy	28 Jul
1.93i	Madeline	Fagan	USA	4.6.96	1	NCAA	College Station	10 Mar
1.92i	Jossie	Graumann	GER	18.3.94	1		Unna	22 Jan
1.92i	Ana	Simic	CRO	5.5.90	2		Cottbus	25 Jan
1.92	Levern	Spencer	LCA	23.6.84	1		Baie-Mahault	17 May
1.92	Kristina	Korolyova	RUS	6.11.90	2		Sochi	26 May
1.92	Erika	Furlani	ITA	2.1.96	1		Rieti	24 Jun
1.92	Erica	Bougard	USA	26.7.93	1H	NC	Sacramento	24 Jun
	(30)							
1.92	Alyx	Treasure	CAN	15.5.92	1	NC	Ottawa	9 Jul
1.92A	Yaroslava	Mahuchikh	UKR-Y	19.9.01	1	WY	Nairobi	14 Jul
1.92	Mirela	Demireva	BUL	28.9.89	Q	WCh	London (OS)	10 Aug
1.91i	Svetlana	Nikolenko	RUS	26.9.91	2		Chelyabinsk	11 Jan
1.91i	Linda	Sandblom	FIN	18.10.89	1	NC	Jyväskylä	19 Feb
1.91i	Natalya	Aksenova	RUS	6.6.97	3	NC	Moskva	21 Feb
1.91i		Zheng Xingjuan	CHN	20.3.89	1	NGP	Xianlin	28 Feb
1.91	Brigetta	Barrett	USA	24.12.90	1		Long Beach	15 Apr
1.91	Marusa	Cernjul	SLO	30.6.92	1		Lincoln	6 May
1.91	Kimberly	Williamson	JAM	2.10.93	2		Manhattan, KS	6 May
	(40)							
1.91	Marija	Vukovic	MNE	21.1.92	1	CSSE	Serravalle	30 May
1.91	Kristina	Gavrilyuk	RUS	14.5.94	1		Smolensk	9 Jun
1.91	Marina	Smolyakova	RUS	20.6.89	1		Irkutsk	10 Jun
1.91	Tatiána	Goúsin	GRE	26.1.94	2	NCAA	Eugene	10 Jun
1.91	Lissa	Labiche	SEY	18.2.93	1	Franc	Abidjan	26 Jul
1.90i	Yuliya	Chumachenko	UKR	2.10.94	2		Kyiv	10 Jan
1.90	Eleanor	Patterson	AUS	22.5.96	1		Melbourne	28 Jan
1.90i	Logan	Boss	USA	4.8.97	3	NCAA	College Station	10 Mar
1.90i	Stacey	Destin	USA	7.11.96	1P	NCAA	College Station	10 Mar
1.90	Nadezhda	Dusanova	UZB	17.11.87	1		Liège	6 May
	(50)							
1.90A	Kaysee	Pilgrim	USA	11.7.95	1	MWC	Logan	13 May
1.90	Irina	Iliyeva	RUS	22.12.95	1		Moskva	1 Jun
1.90	Yelizaveta	Simanovich	BLR-J	11.10.98	1	NC-j	Brest	28 Jun
1.90	Nicola	McDermott	AUS	28.12.96	1		Brisbane	16 Jul
1.90	Tonje	Angelsen	NOR	17.1.90	1		Oslo	19 Jul
1.90	Maja	Nilsson	SWE-J	8.12.99	1	NC-j	Gävle	12 Aug

Mark	Name		Nat	Born	Pos	Meet	Venue	Date
1.90		Wang Yang	CHN	14.2.89	1	NG	Tianjin	3 Sep
1.90	Bianca	Salming	SWE-J	22.11.98	1H	NC	Linköping	9 Sep
1.89i	Emma	Green	SWE	8.12.84	1		Ulvsunda	28 Jan
1.89i	Serena	Capponcelli	ITA	24.1.89	1		Gent	29 Jan
	(60)							
1.89i	Alina	Shukh	UKR-J	12.2.99	1P		Tallinn	4 Feb
1.89i	Doreen	Amata	NGR	6.5.88	8=		Banská Bystrica	8 Feb
1.89i	Bethan	Partridge	GBR	11.7.90	1=	NC	Sheffield	11 Feb
1.89i	Mariya	Zhodzik	BLR	19.8.97	1	NC	Mogilyov	18 Feb
1.89i	Ekaterina	Krasovskiy	AUT	13.7.84	1	NC	Wien	19 Feb
1.89	Mariya	Pavlova	RUS	21.5.96	1=H		Adler	12 May
1.89	Margarita	Korneychuk	RUS	21.2.95	1=H		Adler	12 May
1.89	Karina	Taranda	BLR-J	10.2.99	1	NCp	Brest	31 May
1.88i	Yekaterina	Stepanova	RUS	24.7.94	2		Irkutsk	15 Jan
1.88i	Laura	Gröll	GER-J	11.4.98	1		München	21 Jan
	(70)							
1.88i	Katarina	Mögenburg	NOR	16.6.91	2		Unna	22 Jan
1.88i	Prisca	Duvernay	FRA	26.5.91	1		Lyon	28 Jan
1.88i	Yevgeniya	Kononova	RUS	28.9.89	6	NC	Moskva	21 Feb
1.88i	Natalya	Baluyeva	RUS	24.12.92	7	NC	Moskva	21 Feb
1.88	Hannah	Joye	AUS	4.1.96	1		Brisbane	23 Feb
1.88i	Eleonora	Omoregie	ITA	22.5.96	1	ACC	Notre Dame	24 Feb
1.88	Zoe	Timmers	AUS	25.5.89	1		Canberra	11 Mar
1.88	Amina	Smith	USA	10.1.92	3	MSR	Torrance	15 Apr
1.88		Yeung Man Wai	HKG	18.9.94	1	AsiGP	Taipei	30 Apr
1.88	Margarita	Mazina	RUS	7.7.95	2		Moskva	1 Jun
	(80)							
1.88	Urszula	Gardzielewska	POL	21.7.88	1		Wroclaw	18 Jun
1.88	Claire	Orcel	BEL	21.12.97	2	Franc	Abidjan	26 Jul
1.88	Ximena	Esquivel	MEX	22.8.97	4=	WUG	Taipei	28 Aug
1.87Ai	Shelley	Spires	USA	19.3.96	1		Air Force Academy	21 Jan
1.87i	Yana	Maksimova	BLR	9.1.89	1P	NCp	Minsk	10 Feb
1.87i	Elena	Vallortigara	ITA	21.9.91	1	NC	Ancona	18 Feb
1.87i	Ivona	Dadic	AUT	29.12.93	3P	EI	Beograd	3 Mar
1.87	Imke	Onnen	GER	17.8.94	1		Kassel	25 May
1.87	Aneta	Rydz	POL	30.3.94	1		Lódz	26 May
1.87	Swapna	Barman	IND	29.10.96	1H	Fed Cup	Patiala	3 Jun
	(90)							
1.87	Barbara	Szabó	HUN	17.2.90	1	NC	Székesfehérvár	11 Jun
1.87	Lada	Pejchalová	CZE-J	15.11.98	1	NC-j	Jablonec	24 Jun
1.87	Eliska	Klucinová	CZE	14.4.88	1H	ET-1	Monzón	1 Jul
1.87	Yelena	Kulichenko	RUS-Y	28.7.02	2	EYOF	Györ	29 Jul
1.87i	Tatyana	Yermachenkova	RUS-J	9.9.98	1		Sankt Peterburg	23 Dec

Mark	Name		Nat	Born	Date
1.86i	Lara	Omerzu	SLO-J	10.2.98	4 Feb
1.86i	Marine	Vallet	FRA	9.9.93	18 Feb
1.86	Maya	Pressley	USA	1.2.91	22 Apr
1.86	Carolin	Schäfer	GER	5.12.91	27 May
1.86	Mariya	Shulgina	BLR	14.8.89	31 May
	(100)				
1.86	Liliya	Klintsova	UKR	12.7.97	6 Jun
1.86	Emma	Nuttall	GBR	23.4.92	10 Jun
1.86	Darya	Kuchyna	UKR	14.6.93	29 Jun
1.86	Desirée	Rossit	ITA	19.3.94	1 Jul
1.86	Tána	Dunajská	SVK	25.7.92	2 Jul
1.86	Salome	Lang	SUI	18.11.97	16 Jul
1.86	Nikki	Manson	GBR	15.10.94	30 Jul
1.86	Mikella	Lefebvre-Oatis	CAN-J	18.4.98	1 Aug
1.86	Valentina	Ulyanova	RUS-Y	9.2.00	4 Aug
1.86	Alysha	Burnett	AUS	4.1.97	26 Aug
1.855 6'1"	Jelena	Rowe	USA-J	1.8.99	22 Apr
1.85i	Clarissa	Cutliff	USA	13.5.97	7 Jan
1.85Ai	Lisanne	Hagens	NED	4.8.95	13 Jan
1.85i	Kandie	Bloch-Jones	USA	21.4.95	14 Jan
1.85i	Priscilla	Frederick	ANT	14.2.89	14 Jan
1.85i	Nicole	Greene	USA	2.5.97	21 Jan
1.85i	Hanna	Gorodskaya	BLR	31.1.93	25 Jan
1.85i	Jeannelle	Scheper	LCA	21.11.94	28 Jan
1.85i	Zarriea	Willis	USA	14.11.96	11 Feb
1.85i	Anabela	Neto	POR	25.3.91	11 Feb
1.85i	Hannelore	Desmet	BEL	25.2.89	18 Feb
1.85i	Aleksandra	Nowakowska	POL-J	23.4.98	19 Feb
1.85	Julia Cristina	Silva	BRA	19.1.95	12 Mar
1.85	Chelsie	Decoud	USA	28.6.96	31 Mar
1.85	Kendell	Williams	USA	14.6.95	8 Apr
1.85	Sharon	Day-Monroe	USA	9.6.85	15 Apr
1.85A	Julia	du Plessis	RSA	27.5.96	22 Apr
1.85i	Saniel	Atkinson Grier	JAM	2.7.91	28 Apr
1.85	Taylor	Wiebke	USA	2.6.97	29 Apr
1.85	Liz	Evans	USA	1.12.90	12 May
1.85	Nadezhda	Dubovitskaya	KAZ-J	12.3.98	16 May
1.85	Anne	Klebsch	GER	20.2.96	20 May
1.85	Sommer	Lecky	IRL-Y	14.6.00	20 May
1.85	Laura	Salin-Eyike	FRA	14.6.95	26 May
1.85	Venelina	Veneva-Mateeva	BUL	13.6.74	7 Jun
1.85	Elodie	Tshilumba	LUX-J	1.5.98	9 Jun
1.85	Martyna	Lewandowska	POL-Y	26.10.00	11 Jun
1.85A	María Fernanda	Murillo	COL-J	21.1.99	11 Jun
1.85	Marlies	van Haaren	NED	6.3.90	17 Jun
1.85	Nikki	Woudstra	NED	6.5.88	18 Jun
1.85	Jenna	Rogers	USA-Y	18.4.02	18 Jun
1.85	Safina	Sadullayeva	UZB-J	4.3.98	25 Jun
1.85	Györgyi	Zsivoczky-Farkas	HUN	13.2.85	16 Sep
1.84i	Tatyana	Odineva	RUS	23.5.83	18 Jan
1.84Ai	Andrea	Stapleton	USA	.96	21 Jan
1.84i	Jailah	Mason	USA	12.9.96	21 Jan
1.84i	Janae	Moffitt	USA	9.1.97	28 Jan
1.84i	Quamecha	Morrison	USA	22.11.96	17 Feb
1.84i		Wang Xueyi	CHN	3.8.91	24 Feb
1.84i	Taliyah	Brooks	USA	8.2.95	10 Mar
1.84	Paige	Wilson	AUS-J	15.7.99	28 Mar
1.84	Hanna	Van Hessche	BEL	5.7.91	6 May
1.84	Claire	Kieffer-Wright	USA	27.9.95	13 May
1.84A	Nicole	Wadden	CAN	.93	13 May
1.84	Mareike	Max	GER-J	19.8.98	21 May
1.84	Isis	Guerra	CUB-J	11.11.99	27 May
1.84	Meike	Reimer	GER-J	21.10.98	5 Jun
1.84	Leonoe	Reuter	GER-J	6.1.98	5 Jun

Mark	Name		Nat	Born	Pos	Meet	Venue	Date
1.84	Yelizaveta	Kamenets	RUS-J	28.12.99				10 Jun
1.84	Luca	Renner	HUN-J	30.11.98				17 Jun
1.84	Yekaterina	Lobakina	RUS	4.2.88				28 Jun
1.84	Nadine	Broersen	NED	29.4.90				1 Jul
1.84	Patrycja	Skoczylas	POL-J	4.2.99				8 Jul
1.84		Deng Siyi	CHN	21.8.97				19 Jul
1.84	Mariya	Nizhegorodtseva	RUS-Y	14.12.00				4 Aug
1.84	Vilena	Komarova	RUS-Y	26.12.01				4 Aug
1.84	Adelina	Kholikova	RUS-Y	18.12.02				4 Aug
	(167)							

Best outdoors

Mark	Name	Pos	Meet	Venue	Date
1.94	Beitia	2		Madrid	14 Jul
1.92	Graumann	1		Regensburg	11 Jun
1.92	Palsyte	Q	WCh	London (OS)	10 Aug
1.91	Zheng Xingjuan	1	NGP	Zhengzhou	13 Apr
1.91	Fagan	1	NCAA	Eugene	10 Jun
1.90	Simic	3		Bühl	30 Jun
1.89	Boss	1		Tuscaloosa	8 Apr
1.89	Chumachenko	1	EAF	Bydgoszcz	2 Jun
1.88	Kononova	3		Sochi	26 May
1.88	Aksenova	2		Yerino	10 Jun
1.88	Amata	1		Orvieto	21 Jul
1.87A	Spires	2	MWC	Logan	13 May
1.87	Duvernay	1	NC	Marseille	15 Jul
1.87	Shukh	1H	EJ	Grosseto	20 Jul
1.87	Nikolenko	5	NC	Zhukovskiy	28 Jul

Mark	Name	Date	Mark	Name	Date	Mark	Name	Date	Mark	Name	Date
1.86	Zhodzik	31 May	1.85	Neto	6 May	1.85	Atkinson Grier	25 Jun	1,84	Destin	12 May
1.86	Vallortigara	16 Jun	1.85	Partridge	21 May	1.85	Yermachenkova	7 Jul	1.84	Sandblom	13 Jun
1.86	Capponcelli	5 Aug	1.85	Vallet	21 May	1.84	Maksimova	28 Apr	1.84	Krasovskiy	25 Jul
1.85	Hagens	8 Apr	1.85	Nowakowska	11 Jun	1.84	Wang Xueyi	11 May	1.84	Odineva	28 Jul

JUNIORS

See main list for top 12 juniors. 10 performances (inc. 1 indoor) by 2 women to 1.93. Additional marks and further juniors:

Name	Mark	Pos	Meet	Venue	Date	Mark	Pos	Meet	Venue	Date
Cunningham	1.97	2	DL	London (OS)	9 Jul	1.95	3	Pre	Eugerne	27 May
	1.97	3	Herc	Monaco	21 Jul	1.94	1	MSR	Torrance	15 Apr
	1.96Ai	1	NC	Albuquerque	5 Mar	1.93	1	PennR	Philadelphia	29 Apr
Hrubá	1.94	4	DL	London (OS)	9 Jul	1.93	1	EJ	Grosseto	23 Jul

Mark		Name		Nat	Born	Pos	Meet	Venue	Date
1.86i		Lara	Omerzu	SLO	10.2.98	1	NC-j	Celje	4 Feb
1.86		Mikella	Lefebvre-Oatis	CAN	18.4.98	1		Winnipeg	1 Aug
1.86		Valentina	Ulyanova	RUS-Y	9.2.00	2		Maykop	4 Aug
1.855	6'1"	Jelena	Rowe	USA	1.8.99	1		Glen Ellyn	22 Apr
1.85i		Aleksandra	Nowakowska	POL	23.4.98	2	NC	Torun	19 Feb
		1.85				3		Kutno	11 Jun
1.85		Nadezhda	Dubovitskaya	KAZ	12.3.98	1		Almaty	16 May
1.85		Sommer	Lecky	IRL-Y	14.6.00	1		Antrim	20 May
1.85		Elodie	Tshilumba	LUX	1.5.98	1		Pierre-Bénite	9 Jun
1.85		Martyna	Lewandowska	POL-Y	26.10.00	2		Kutno	11 Jun
1.85A		María Fernanda	Murillo	COL	21.1.99	1	NC	Medellín	11 Jun
1.85		Jenna	Rogers	USA-Y	18.4.02	1	New Bal	Greensboro	18 Jun
1.85		Safina	Sadullayeva	UZB	4.3.98	1	Kozanov	Almaty	25 Jun
1.85		*Best out*	Yermachenkova	RUS		1		Sankt Peterburg	7 Jul

POLE VAULT

Mark	Pos	Meet	Venue	Date	Series
4.91	Ekateríni Stefanídi	GRE 4.2.90	1 WCh London (OS)	6 Aug	4.65/1 4.75/1 4.82/1 4.89/x 4.91/1 5.02/xxx
4.87i	1	WK	Zürich	23 Aug	4.62/1 4.72/1 4.77/1 4.82/x 4.87/1 4.92/xxx
4.85i	1	EI	Beograd	4 Mar	4.55/2 4.65/1 4.80/1 4.85/1 4.91/xxx
4.85	1	GGala	Roma	8 Jun	4.65/1 4.75/1 4.85/1 5.07/xxx
4.85	1	VD-DLF	Bruxelles	1 Sep	4.65/1 4.75/2 4.85/1 4.92/xxx
4.82i	1	Mill	New York (A)	11 Feb	4.52/1 4.62/1 4.72/1 4.82/1 4.92/xxx
4.81	1	NC	Pátra	18 Jun	4.60/1 4.70/1 4.81/1 4.91/xxx
4.81	1	DL	London (OS)	9 Jul	4.65/1 4.73/2 4.81/1 4.91/xxx
4.80	1	DL	Doha	5 May	4.55/1 4.65/2 4.75/1 4.80/1 4.85/xxx
4.75	1	DL	Birmingham	20 Aug	4.61/1 4.68/2 4.75/2 4.88/xxx
4.87i	Sandi Morris	USA 8.7.92	2 WK Zürich	23 Aug	4.52/1 4.62/1 4.72/3 4.77/1 4.82/1 4.87/1 4.92/xxx
4.84	1		Houston	25 May	??
4.80	1	NC	Sacramento	25 Jun	4.40/1 4.55/1 4.65/2 4.70/1 4.75/1 4.80/1 4.90/xxx
4.80	1		Beckum	27 Aug	4.43/1 4.50/1 4.60/2 4.65/1 4.70/2 4.75/1 4.80/2 4.92/x
4.76	1		Sotteville-lès-Rouen	7 Jul	4.40/1 4.50/1 4.60/1 4.70/1 4.76/2 4.86/xxx
4.75	2	DL	Doha	5 May	4.45/1 4.55/2 4.65/2 4.75/2 4.80/x 4.85/xx
4.75	1		Greenville	19 Jul	4.38/1 4.53/1 4.63/2 4.75/2 4.86/xxx
4.75	2	WCh	London (OS)	6 Aug	4.45/1 4.55/1 4.65/1 4.75/1 4.82/x 4.89/xx
4.75	2	VD-DLF	Bruxelles	1 Sep	4.55/1 4.65/1 4.75/1 4.85/xxx
4.83	Jenn Suhr	USA 5.2.82	1 Austin	15 Apr	4.63/1 4.68/2 4.74/2 4.83/3 5.07/xxx
4.81i	1		Kent	14 Jan	4.60/3 4.71/2 4.81/1 5.07/x
4.76	1		Houston	5 May	4.60/2 4.76/3 4.91/xxx
4.82	Eliza McCartney	NZL 11.12.96	1 Auckland (NS)	26 Feb	4.40/1 4.50/2 4.70/1 4.82/2 4.90/xxx
4.75	3	GGala	Roma	8 Jun	4.40/2 4.55/1 4.65/2 4.75/3 4.85/xxx
4.81	Yarisley Silva	CUB 1.6.87	1 Bisl Oslo	15 Jun	4.55/2 4.65/1 4.75/x 4.81/1 4.92/xxx
4.75	2	GGala	Roma	8 Jun	4.40/1 4.55/3 4.65/1 4.75/1 4.85/xxx

Mark	Name		Nat	Born	Pos	Meet	Venue	Date
4.81	Holly	Bradshaw	GBR	2.11.91	1		Rottach-Egern	15 Jul
				4.45/2 4.55/2 4.65/1 4.73/1 4.81/2 4.90/xx				
	4.80	1 Manchester 26 May		4.50/3 4.62/2 4.72/1 4.80/1				
4.75i	Lisa	Ryzih	GER	27.9.88	2	EI	Beograd	4 Mar
				4.40/1 4.55/1 4.65/1 4.70/1 4.75/1 4.80/x 4.85/xx				
4.75	Anzhelika	Sidorova	RUS	28.6.91	2	Bisl	Oslo	15 Jun
				4.40/2 4.65/3 4.75/1 4.81/xxx				
4.75	Alysha	Newman	CAN	29.6.94	2		Beckum	27 Aug
				4.34/2 4.50/1 4.60/1 4.70/2 4.75/3 4.80/xx				
	4.75	3 VD-DLF Bruxelles 1 Sep		4.30/2 4.45/1 4.55/1 4.65/1 4.75/2 4.85/xxx				
	(32/9)							
4.73	Nicole	Büchler	SUI	17.12.83	2	DL	London (OS)	9 Jul
	(10)							
4.73	Katie	Nageotte	USA	30.6.91	2		Rottach-Egern	15 Jul
4.71	Michaela	Meijer	SWE	30.7.93	1		Göteborg	2 Jul
4.67	Olga	Mullina	RUS	1.8.92	1		Kuortane	17 Jun
4.66Ai	Wilma	Murto	FIN-J	11.6.98	1		Tignes	6 Jan
4.65Ai	Mary	Saxer	USA	21.6.87	3	NC	Albuquerque	5 Mar
4.65	Morgann	LeLeux Romero	USA	14.11.92	1		Hattiesburg	28 Apr
4.65i	Kristen	Hixson	USA	1.7.92	3	DrakeR	Des Moines	28 Apr
4.65	Anicka	Newell	CAN	5.8.93	1		San Marcos	13 Jun
4.65	Angelica	Bengtsson	SWE	8.7.93	2	DL	Stockholm	18 Jun
4.65	Robeilys	Peinado	VEN	26.11.97	3	DL	Stockholm	18 Jun
	(20)							
4.61	Annie	Rhodes-Johnigan	USA	13.5.95	1	Big 12	Lawrence	13 May
4.61	Romana	Malácová	CZE	15.5.87	1		Praha	20 Jun
4.61	Angelica	Moser	SUI	9.10.97	1	NC	Zürich	22 Jul
4.61i	Angelina	Krasnova	RUS	7.2.91	1		Moskva	24 Dec
4.60i	Lexi	Weeks	USA	20.11.96	1		Fayetteville	17 Feb
4.60Ai	Kortney	Ross	USA	26.7.92	4	NC	Albuquerque	5 Mar
4.60	Megan	Clark	USA	10.6.94	2	TexR	Austin	1 Apr
4.60	Emily	Grove	USA	22.5.93	1		Sioux City	21 Apr
4.60	Ninon	Guillon-Romarin	FRA	15.4.95	1		Pierre-Bénite	9 Jun
4.60	Irina	Zhuk	BLR	26.1.93	2	ET	Villeneuve d'Ascq	24 Jun
	(30)							
4.60	Maryna	Kylypko	UKR	10.11.95	1	NC	Kropyvnytskiy	6 Jul
4.57i	Tori	Weeks	USA	20.11.96	1	SEC	Nashville	24 Feb
4.56	Jirina	Ptácníková	CZE	20.5.86	2		Praha	20 Jun
4.55i	Minna	Nikkanen	FIN	9.4.88	2		Karlsruhe	4 Feb
4.55	Nina	Kennedy	AUS	5.4.97	1	WA	Perth	24 Feb
4.55i	Lisa	Gunnarsson	SWE-J	20.8.99	6=	EI	Beograd	4 Mar
4.55Ai	Kristen	Brown	USA	26.5.92	5	NC	Albuquerque	5 Mar
4.55	Sydney	Clute	USA	15.11.93	1		Tempe	25 Mar
4.55	Silke	Spiegelburg	GER	17.3.86	2	NC	Erfurt	8 Jul
4.55	Friedelinde	Petershofen	GER	19.8.95	3	NC	Erfurt	8 Jul
	(40)							
4.51i	Annika	Roloff	GER	10.3.91	1		Potsdam	3 Feb
4.51	Elizabeth	Parnov	AUS	9.5.94	1		Perth	24 Mar
4.50i	Polina	Knoroz	RUS-J	20.7.99	4	NC	Moskva	19 Feb
4.50		Ren Mengqian	CHN	4.10.93	1	NC	Jinan	17 May
4.50		Li Ling	CHN	6.7.89	2	NC	Jinan	17 May
4.50	Olivia	Gruver	USA	29.7.97	1	NCAA	Eugene	8 Jun
4.50	Amálie	Svábíková	CZE-J	22.11.99	2	NC	Trinec	11 Jun
4.50	Tina	Sutej	SLO	7.11.88	1	ET-2	Tel Aviv	24 Jun
4.50	Alina	McDonald	USA	1.1.97	1		Rock Hill	1 Jul
4.48	Allie	Koressel	USA	2.3.91	1		Chula Vista	17 Jun
	(50)							
4.47	Sophie	Gutermuth	USA	2.11.92	1		Knoxville	10 Jun
4.46	Fanny	Smets	BEL	21.4.86	3		Leverkusen	27 Jul
4.45i	Lakan	Taylor	USA	21.6.95	1	NCAA	College Station	11 Mar
4.45	Jill	Marois	USA	8.6.94	1		Boone	29 Apr
4.45	Kylie	Hutson	USA	27.11.87	1		Chula Vista	14 May
4.45	Aksana	Gataullina	RUS-Y	17.7.00	2		Maykop	22 May
4.45		Xu Huiqin	CHN	4.9.93	1		Bron	6 Jul
4.45	Kelsie	Ahbe	CAN	6.7.91	3	NC	Ottawa	8 Jul
4.45	Martina	Schultze	GER	12.9.90	4	NC	Erfurt	8 Jul
4.45	Justyna	Smietanka	POL	24.9.94	4		Rottach-Egern	15 Jul
	(60)							
4.43i	Anjuli	Knäsche	GER	18.10.93	2		Zweibrücken	25 Feb
4.43	Emily	Presley	USA	22.1.97	1		Bolivar	6 May
4.42i	Kally	Long	USA	28.8.95	1		College Station	14 Jan

Mark	Wind	Name		Nat	Born	Pos	Meet	Venue	Date
4.42		Femke	Pluim	NED	10.5.94	2		Mössingen	29 Jul
4.42		Katharina	Bauer	GER	12.6.90	1		Wipperfürth	20 Aug
4.42		Saga	Andersson	FIN-Y	30.3.00	1		Tampere	25 Aug
4.41Ai		Marion	Lotout	FRA	19.11.89	3		Tignes	6 Jan
4.41		Rachel	Baxter	USA-J	5.4.99	1	PAm-J	Trujillo	21 Jul
4.40i		Mariya	Zakharutkina	RUS	14.8.96	1		Chelyabinsk	11 Jan
4.40		Olivia	McTaggart	NZL-Y	9.1.00	1		Hastings	14 Jan
		(70)							
4.40i		Marta	Onofre	POR	28.1.91	1		Jamor	25 Jan
4.40i		Victoria	von Eynatten	GER	6.10.91	5		Karlsruhe	4 Feb
4.40i		Tatyana	Shvydkina	RUS	8.5.90	3		Moskva	7 Feb
4.40i		Alyona	Lutkovskaya	RUS	15.3.96	1	NC-23	Sankt Peterburg	10 Feb
4.40Ai		Jacqueline	Williams	USA	13.11.94	9	NC	Albuquerque	5 Mar
4.40i		Lucy	Bryan	GBR	22.5.95	4	NCAA	College Station	11 Mar
4.40			Chen Qiaoling	CHN-J	22.11.99	1	NGP	Zhengzhou	12 Apr
4.40			Song Tingting	CHN	8.10.93	3	NC	Jinan	17 May
4.40		Sonia	Malavisi	ITA	31.10.94	1		Rieti	21 May
4.40		Yana	Hladiychuk	UKR	21.5.93	1		Lutsk	6 Jun
		(80)							
4.40		Kristina	Owsinski	USA	16.2.93	5	NCAA	Eugene	8 Jun
4.40		Kamila	Przybyla	POL	3.5.96	4	EU23	Bydgoszcz	15 Jul
4.38		Desiree	Freier	USA	24.7.96	3		Waco	8 Apr
4.38		Helen	Falda	ITA	13.2.96	3		Austin	15 Apr
4.36i		Jade	Ive	GBR	22.1.92	1		Sutton	19 Feb
4.35i		Kayla	Caldwell	USA	19.6.91	1		Hillsdale	3 Feb
4.35i		Maria Eleonor	Tavares	POR	24.9.85	2	NC	Bordeaux	18 Feb
4.35i		Nikol	Jiroutová	CZE	30.3.92	3	NC	Praha (Strom)	26 Feb
4.35		Madison	Heath	USA	3.11.95	6		Long Beach	13 Apr
4.35		Elizabeth	Quick	USA	14.11.94	4=		Long Beach	15 Apr
		(90)							
4.35		Bonnie	Draxler	USA	13.10.95	4=		Long Beach	15 Apr
4.35		Eléni-Klaoúdia	Pólak	GRE	9.9.96	1		Athína (E)	22 Apr
4.35		Stélla-Iró	Ledáki	GRE	18.7.88	1		Iráklio	14 May
4.35		Sally	Peake	GBR	8.2.86	3		Rehlingen	5 Jun
4.35		Anastasiya	Sadovnikova	RUS	22.6.95	3	NC-23	Saransk	20 Jun
4.35		Regine	Kramer	GER	5.4.93	1cB		Rottach-Egern	14 Jul
4.35		Lene	Retzius	NOR	4.1.96	6	EU23	Bydgoszcz	15 Jul
4.35		Molly	Caudery	GBR-Y	17.3.00	2	EJ	Grosseto	22 Jul
4.33i		Emily	Gunderson	USA	16.8.96	5	SEC	Nashville	24 Feb
4.33		Karla	da Silva	BRA	12.11.84	1		São Bernardo do Campo	3 May
		(100)							

Mark	Name		Nat	Born	Date
4.32i	Buse	Arıkazan	TUR	8.7.94	17 Feb
4.32i	Courtney	Crandall	USA	17.3.94	24 Feb
4.32	Angela	Wald	GER	8.9.92	22 Jul
4.32	Killiana	Heymans	NED	24.1.97	19 Aug
4.31i	Lilli	Schnitzerling	GER	5.12.93	3 Feb
4.31	Laura	Taylor	USA	22.4.96	13 May
4.31	Solène	Guiloineau	FRA	17.3.92	20 Jun
4.31	Mallaury	Sautereau	FRA	1.8.96	24 Jun
4.31A	Carla	Franch	ESP	25.10.89	15 Jul
4.30i	Lyudmila	Petrova	RUS	15.12.93	11 Jan
4.30i	Lyudmila	Yeryomina	RUS	8.8.91	14 Jan
4.30	Carmelita	Correa	MEX	5.12.88	21 Jan
4.30i	Yelizaveta	Bondarenko	RUS-J	1.7.99	28 Jan
4.30i	Marion	Buisson	FRA	19.2.88	28 Jan
4.30	Sarah	Bell	USA	20.9.94	7 Apr
4.30	Katherine	Pitman	USA	.94	17 May
4.30	Cátia	Pereira	POR	5.7.89	21 May
4.30	Kathryn	Tomczak	USA	17.7.97	25 May
4.30	Stefanie	Dauber	GER	31.7.87	3 Jun
4.30	Alyssa	Applebee	USA	12.1.94	8 Jun
4.30	Miren	Bartolomé	ESP-J	2.1.98	17 Jun
4.30	Tomomi	Abiko	JPN	17.3.88	24 Jun
4.30	Jacqueline	Otchere	GER	5.5.96	24 Jun
4.30	Melissa	Gergel	USA	24.4.89	15 Jul
4.30	Jade	Vigneron	FRA	6.9.91	15 Jul
4.30	Maialen	Axpe	ESP	4.5.93	27 Jul
4.27i	Allison	Harris	CAN	16.5.95	18 Feb
4.27i	Rebeka	Silhanová	CZE	22.3.95	21 Feb
4.27	Allison	Stokke	USA	22.3.89	29 Apr
4.25i	Aurélie	De Ryck	BEL	17.12.92	29 Jan
4.25	Ariel	Lieghio	USA	8.3.92	28 Apr
4.25	Roberta	Bruni	ITA	8.3.94	27 May
4.25	Malen	Ruiz de Azua	ESP	17.11.95	10 Jun
4.25	Henrietta	Paxton	GBR	19.9.83	21 Jun
4.25	Paige	Ridout	CAN	18.9.92	25 Jun
4.25	Elisa	Molinarolo	ITA	29.1.94	2 Jul
4.25	Desiree	Singh	GER	17.8.94	8 Jul
4.25i	Demet	Parlak	TUR	26.7.96	23 Dec
4.25i	Carolina	Carmichael	USA	28.4.94	2 Dec
4.24i	Ariana	Ince	USA	14.3.89	18 Feb
4.23i	Shay	Petty	USA	1.1.96	11 Feb
4.23	Anna	Eaton	USA	24.12.96	29 Apr
4.23	Joana	Ribeiro Costa	BRA	15.8.81	3 May
4.23	Malin	Dahlström	SWE	26.8.89	2 Jul
4.22Ai	Lindsey	Murray	USA	22.7.96	4 Feb
4.22i	Nusa	Maver	SLO	20.8.94	10 Feb
4.22Ai	Greta	Wagner	USA	20.7.96	11 Feb
4.22	Carson	Dingler	USA-J	14.5.99	25 Mar
4.22	Marissa	Kalsey	USA	23.3.94	25 May
4.21	Alexis	Romero	USA	29.6.96	13 May
4.21	Meagan	Gray	USA	15.8.97	13 May
4.21	Elien	De Vocht	BEL	18.7.95	3 Jun
4.21	Aneta	Morysková	CZE	19.9.92	20 Jun
4.20i	Lauren	Chorny	USA	22.6.93	14 Jan
4.20i	Nina	Klyuzheva	RUS	23.11.97	14 Jan
4.20i	Alina	Vishnevskaya	BLR	6.2.96	17 Jan
4.20i	Samantha	Tollerud	USA	6.2.96	28 Jan
4.20i	Gil	Le Bris-Finot	FRA	29.11.95	18 Feb
4.20Ai	Marissa	Berry	USA	18.5.97	24 Feb
4.20i	Taylor	Amann	USA	6.5.96	25 Feb
4.20i	Katie	Jones	USA-J	13.7.99	12 Mar
4.20	Laura	Marty	USA	29.12.97	13 Apr
4.20	Hannah	Sailar	USA	13.7.94	15 Apr
4.20	Diamara	Planell	PUR	16.2.93	15 Apr
4.20	Alexis	Paine	USA	12.10.90	22 Apr
4.20	Jessie	Johnson	USA	21.11.93	22 Apr
4.20	Anastasiya	Savchenko	RUS	15.11.89	16 May
4.20	Tatyana	Stetsyuk	RUS	27.8.92	21 May

Mark	Wind	Name		Nat	Born	Pos	Meet	Venue	Date
4.20		Allison	Jeffries	USA	20.2.95				25 May
4.20		Andrianna	Jacobs	USA	5.9.97				25 May
4.20		Lauren	Martinez	USA	16.10.96				25 May
4.20		Elleyse	Garrett	USA	5.9.96				25 May
4.20		Kayla	Smith	USA	3.1.91				25 May
4.20		Madison	Mills	USA	18.1.94				25 May
4.20		Reece	Timmons	USA					25 May
4.20		Laura	Weyrowitz	GER	28.9.94				27 May
4.20		Hulda	Thorsteinsdóttir	ISL	10.6.91				30 May
4.20		Charlotte	Gaudy	FRA	6.11.96				4 Jun
4.20		Darya	Ignatova	RUS	16.2.95				4 Jun
4.20		Zsófia	Siskó	HUN	8.10.94				24 Jun
4.20		Megumi	Nakada	JPN	6.12.88				24 Jun
4.20		Irina	Ivanova	RUS	19.4.96				8 Jul
4.20		Pascale	Stöcklin	SUI	5.2.97				13 Jul
4.20A			Niu Chunge	CHN-Y	14.2.00				15 Jul
4.20		Dorra	Mahfoudhi	TUN	7.8.93				24 Jul
		(184)	200th 4.16						

Best outdoors

Mark	Name	Pos	Meet	Venue	Date
4.73	Ryzih	3		Rottach-Egern	15 Jul
4.60	Hixson	2		Chula Vista	27 May
4.60	Krasnova	1	Kuts	Moskva	26 Jun
4.55	L Weeks	1		Fayetteville	5 May
4.55	T Weeks	2		Fayetteville	5 May
4.55	Gunnarsson	2		Blois	17 Jun
4.55	Ross	1		Long Beach	15 Apr
4.55	Saxer	6	NC	Sacramento	25 Jun
4.51	Brown	1		Chula Vista	20 Apr
4.51	Roloff	2		Leverkusen	27 Jul
4.45	Knoroz	1		Maykop	22 May
4.45	Nikkanen	1	NC	Seinajöki	23 Jul
4.40	Long	7	TexR	Austin	1 Apr
4.40	Lotout	1		Aix-les-Bains	21 May
4.40	Knäsche	1		Zweibrücken	10 Jun
4.40	von Eynatten	1		Wipperfürth	15 Jun
4.40	Lutkovskaya	2		Moskva	7 Jul
4.40	Shvydkina	2	NCp	Yerino	15 Jul
4.40	Bryan	3	EU23	Bydgoszcz	15 Jul
4.40	Onofre	3	WUG	Taipei	26 Aug
4.35	Zakharutkina	2	NC-23	Saransk	20 Jun
4.35	Tavares	3		Aulnay-sous-Bois	5 Jul

Mark	Name	Nat	Date
4.31	Taylor	USA	15 Apr
4.30	Buisson	FRA	15 Jul
4.30	Bondarenko	RUS-J	28 Jul
4.23	Harris	CAN	6 May
4.20	Gunderson	USA	25 May
4.20	Amann	USA	25 May
4.20	Wagner	USA	25 May
4.20	Jiroutová	CZE	11 Jun
4.20	Parlak	TUR	13 Jul
4.20	Ive	GBR	16 Jul
4.18	Petty	USA	15 Apr
4.18	Watson	USA	6 May
4.18	Carmichael	USA	6 May

JUNIORS

See main list for top 10 juniors. 10 performances (inc. 5 indoors) by 4 women to 4.50. Additional marks:

Murto	4.52i	1		Zweibrücken	25 Feb				
Gunnarsson 2	4.51i	1	NC	Bordeaux	18 Feb	4.50	4=		Montreuil 11 Jun
	4.51	1		Moulins	24 Jun	4.50	1	FRA Ch	Marseille 15 Jul

Mark	Name		Nat	Born	Pos	Meet	Venue	Date
4.30i	Yelizaveta	Bondarenko	RUS	1.7.99	4		Volgograd	28 Jan
	4.30				4	NC	Zhukovskiy	28 Jul
4.30	Miren	Bartolomé	ESP-	2.1.98	1		Ciudad Real	17 Jun
4.22	Carson	Dingler	USA	14.5.99	1		Tallahassee	25 Mar
4.20i	Katie	Jones	USA	13.7.99	1	New Bal	New York	12 Mar
4.20A		Niu Chunge	CHN-Y	14.2.00	1	WY	Nairobi	15 Jul
4.19	Anna	Watson	USA	3.5.99	1	New Bal	Greensboro	17 Jun
4.17i	Andrea	Willis	USA	26.7.98	1		Lawrence	2 Dec
4.15i		Wu Zuocheng	CHN	26.5.99	3	NGP	Xianlin	27 Feb
	4.15				5		Huaian	4 Apr
4.15A	Leni Freyja	Wildgrube	GER-Y	1.1.01	2	WY	Nairobi	15 Jul
4.15	Elina	Lampela	FIN-J	18.2.98	1	Nord-J	Umeå	20 Aug
4.15 best out	Wilma	Murto	FIN	11.6.98	3	EJ	Grosseto	22 Jul

LONG JUMP

Mark	Wind	Name		Nat	Born	Pos	Meet	Venue	Date
7.24i		Ivana	Spanovic	SRB	10.5.90	1	EI	Beograd	5 Mar
					x 7.16 7.24 7.17 x 6.73				
7.03i		Q EI	Beograd	4 Mar	7.03				
6.96i		1 Balk	Beograd	25 Feb	6.72 6.79 6.96 p p p				
6.96	0.1	4 WCh	London (OS)	11 Aug	x 6.96 6.77/-0.9 x x 6.91/0.5				
6.88	-0.1	2 DL	London (OS)	9 Jul	6.88 p p p p p				
6.87i		1 ISTAF	Berlin	10 Feb	6.60 6.83 6.62 6.87 6.87 6.73				
7.13	2.0	Brittney	Reese	USA	9.9.86	1		Chula Vista	17 Jun
					x x 7.13 x p p				
7.02	0.1	1 WCh	London (OS)	11 Aug	6.75/-0.6 x 7.02/0.1 x x x				
7.01	1.4	1 Pre	Eugene	26 May	6.88/2.0 7.01 x x 6.79/0.7 x				
6.98	-0.2	1	Baie-Mahault	17 May	x 6.41 x x 6.61 6.98				
6.86	-0.6	* NC	Sacramento	24 Jun	6.70 x 6.80/1.3 6.59 6.98w/2.1 6.86/-0.6				
7.01	0.5	Tianna	Bartoletta	USA	30.8.85	*	NC	Sacramento	24 Jun
					7.01/0.5 6.85/0.9 6.73 7.01/1.3 6.78w 7.05w/3.0				
7.01	0.8	1 DL	London (OS)	9 Jul	6.64 6.57 6.52 6.71/-0.5 7.01 p				
6.97	0.2	3 WCh	London (OS)	11 Aug	6.56 6.60 x 6.64 6.88/1.1 6.97				
6.83	1.4	2 Pre	Eugene	26 May	6.34w 6.83 6.66 6.65 6.57 x				
7.00	-0.3	Darya	Klishina	RUS	15.1.91	2	WCh	London (OS)	11 Aug
					6.78/0.2 6.88/0.2 x 6.91/0.8 7.00 6.83/0.4				
6.84i		4 EI	Beograd	5 Mar	6.62 6.79 6.52 6.80 6.68 6.84				
6.83i		Q EI	Beograd	4 Mar	x 6.59 6.83				
6.97i		Lorraine	Ugen	GBR	22.8.91	2	EI	Beograd	5 Mar
					6.75 6.97 x x 6.58 x				
6.80i		Q EI	Beograd	4 Mar	6.80				

WOMEN 2017

Mark	Wind	Name		Nat	Born	Pos	Meet	Venue	Date
6.94i		Claudia	Salman-Rath	GER	25.4.86	3	EI	Beograd	5 Mar
					6.84 6.71 6.65 6.67 6.94 6.87				
	6.86	1.7 1H	Götzis	28 May	??				
6.92	1.7	Christabel	Nettey	CAN	2.6.91	*		Chula Vista	17 Jun
					6.80w/3.1 6.66 6.94w/2.4 6.80/2.0 6.72 6.92/1.7				
6.90i		Sha'Keela	Saunders	USA	18.12.93	1	NCAA	College Station	10 Mar
					6.42 6.70 6.55 x 6.62 6.90				
	6.82i	1 SEC	Nashville	25 Feb	6.67 6.59 x 6.56 6.82 6.55				
6.85	0.9	Yelena	Sokolova	RUS	23.7.86	1	NC	Zhukovskiy	29 Jul
					6.75 6.82/0.1 6.85 6.74 6.80/0.8 6.83/-0.3				
	6.82	0.8 1 Znam	Zhukovskiy	2 Jul	6.60 6.82 6.76 6.50 6.55 6.60				
6.83	1.2	Jasmine	Todd (10)	USA	23.12.93	*		Chula Vista	17 Jun
					6.84w/2.4 6.58 6.83 p p p				
6.83	0.5	Quanesha	Burks	USA	15.3.95	1		New York	6 Jul
					6.24 6.32 6.83 6.53 p p				
	6.82	0.2 1 SEC	Columbia SC	12 May	6.82 x p 6.28 6.73 6.82/0.0				
		(30/11)							
6.79i		Ksenija	Balta	EST	1.11.86	5	EI	Beograd	5 Mar
6.79	0.2	Alexandra	Wester	GER	21.3.94	1		Garbsen	21 May
6.79	-0.6	Brooke	Stratton	AUS	12.7.93	3	DL	London (OS)	9 Jul
6.78	-0.3	Alina	Rotaru	ROU	5.6.93	1		Gammertingen	16 Jun
6.77	0.8	Blessing	Okagbare	NGR	9.10.88	2	Gyulai	Székesfehérvár	4 Jul
6.75	-0.8	Katarina	Johnson-Thompson	GBR	9.1.93	4	DL	London (OS)	9 Jul
6.74A	-0.6	Jessamyn	Sauceda	MEX	22.5.89	1		Ciudad de México	7 May
6.73	1.9	Tara	Davis	USA-J	20.5.99	1		Clovis	3 Jun
6.73	0.4	Shara	Proctor	GBR	16.9.88	1	BostonG	Somerville	4 Jun
		(20)							
6.73	-0.6	Kate	Hall	USA	12.1.97	1	NCAA	Eugene	8 Jun
6.72i		Keturah	Orji	USA	5.3.96	3	SEC	Nashville	24 Feb
6.72	0.7	Rougui	Sow	FRA	7.6.95	1		Athens	7 Apr
6.72	-0.8	Khaddi	Sagnia	SWE	20.4.94	1		Göteborg	1 Jul
6.72A	1.7	Laura	Strati	ITA	3.10.90	1		Ávila	15 Jul
6.72	0.3	Lauma	Griva	LAT	27.10.84	1		Novo Mesto	19 Jul
6.71i		Jazmin	Sawyers	GBR	21.5.94	2		Birmingham	18 Feb
6.71i		Maryna	Bekh	UKR	18.7.95	Q	EI	Beograd	4 Mar
6.69	1.6	Eliane	Martins	BRA	26.5.86	1	NC	São Bernardo do Campo	10 Jun
6.68	1.9	Naa	Anang	AUS	10.3.95	1		La Chaux-de-Fonds	2 Jul
		(30)							
6.68	1.8	Svetlana	Biryukova	RUS	1.4.91	1	NCp	Yerino	15 Jul
6.68	0.1	Lanae-Tava	Thomas	USA-Y	28.1.01	1		Lawrence	26 Jul
6.68	0.2		Bui Thi Thu Thao	VIE	29.4.92	1	SEAG	Kuala Lumpur	25 Aug
6.67i		Chantel	Malone	IVB	2.12.91	4	ISTAF	Berlin	10 Feb
6.67	0.7	Kylie	Price	USA	1.10.93	1		Los Angeles (ER)	6 May
6.67	-1.9	Bianca	Stuart	BAH	17.5.88	1		Atlanta	28 May
6.67	1.7		Lu Minjia	CHN	29.12.92	1	v2N	Ningbo	2 Jul
6.66	2.0	Savannah	Carson	USA	30.3.95	1		Louisville	15 Apr
6.66	1.9	Sydney	Conley	USA	11.12.93	*q	NCAA-W	Austin	25 May
6.66	0.5	Háido	Alexoúli	GRE	29.3.91	1		Pátra	1 Jul
		(40)							
6.66	1.8	Angela	Morosanu	ROU	26.7.86	2	NC	Pitesti	9 Jul
6.66	-0.2	Éloyse	Lesueur	FRA	15.7.88	1		Liège (NX)	19 Jul
6.66	0.2	Nektaria	Panagi	CYP	20.3.90	1		Kavála	22 Jul
6.65	1.3	Juliet	Itoya	ESP	17.8.86	1		Castellón	10 Jun
6.65	0.1	Anna	Misochenko	RUS	15.4.92	3	NC	Zhukovskiy	29 Jul
6.64	2.0	Ese	Brume	NGR	20.1.96	*		Denizli	10 May
6.64	0.8	Laura	Ikauniece-Admidina	LAT	31.5.92	2H	Hypo	Götzis	28 May
6.64	0.2	Shanice	McPherson	JAM	12.3.94	2		Phoenix	10 Jun
6.62	0.3	Mariya	Gromysheva	RUS	10.1.90	1		Maykop	4 Jun
6.62	1.4	Concepción	Montaner	ESP	14.1.81	2		Castellón	10 Jun
		(50)							
6.62	-0.2	Malaika	Mihambo	GER	3.2.94	3	NC	Erfurt	8 Jul
6.61A		Evelyn	Aguilar	COL	3.1.93	1		Bogotá	22 Apr
6.61	1.8	Stachia	Reuwsaat	USA	23.11.94	1	Scott	Irvine	28 Apr
6.61	-0.7	Jéssica Carolina	dos Reis	BRA	17.3.93	1		São Bernardo do Campo	3 Jun
6.61	0.0	Melanie	Bauschke	GER	14.7.88	3		Oberteuringen	4 Jun
6.61	0.1	Maryse	Luzolo	GER	13.3.95	4		Oberteuringen	4 Jun
6.61	-0.6	Sosthene Taroum	Moguenara	GER	17.10.89	2		Bad Langensalza	17 Jun
6.61	1.4	Malaina	Payton	USA	16.10.91	4		Chula Vista	17 Jun
6.59i		Marina	Buchelnikova	RUS	8.2.94	2	Winter	Moskva	5 Feb
6.59	1.0	Lynique	Prinsloo	RSA	30.3.91	1		Cape Town	29 Apr
		(60)							

Mark	Wind	Name		Nat	Born	Pos	Meet	Venue	Date
6.59	-0.2	Erica	Bougard	USA	26.7.93	3H	Hypo	Götzis	28 May
6.58	0.1	Konomi	Kai	JPN	10.7.93	1		Higashimatsuyama	5 May
6.58	1.7	Jhoanmy	Luque	VEN	20.12.95	*q	NCAA-W	Austin	25 May
6.58	2.0	Brittney	Howell	JAM	1.9.92	2		Chula Vista	27 May
6.57i		Heather	Arneton	FRA-Y	27.7.02	1		Eaubonne	15 Jan
6.57	0.9	Carolin	Schäfer	GER	5.12.91	4H	Hypo	Götzis	28 May
6.57	-0.5	Nafissatou	Thiam	BEL	19.8.94	1H	WCh	London (OS)	6 Aug
6.56i		Yariagnis	Argüelles	CUB	18.4.84	1		Madrid	2 Feb
6.56	1.8	Milica	Gardasevic	SRB-J	28.9.98	1	Balk-J	Pitesti	2 Jul
6.56	0.1	Yanis	David	FRA	12.12.97	1	EU23	Bydgoszcz	16 Jul
		(70)							
6.55i			Zhou Xiaoxue	CHN	19.6.92	1	NGP	Xianlin	27 Feb
6.55	0.7	Destiny	Carter	USA	9.10.92	3		Baton Rouge	28 Apr
6.55	2.0	Wurrie	Njadoe	USA	14.8.97	2	Big 12	Lawrence	13 May
6.55	0.1	Darrielle	McQueen	USA	29.5.96	5q	NCAA-E	Lexington	25 May
6.55	1.4	Anna	Bühler	GER	3.6.97	2		Weinheim	27 May
6.55	0.2	Nayana	James	IND	18.10.95	1	Fed Cup	Patiala	2 Jun
6.55	1.9	Krystyna	Hryshutyna	UKR	21.3.92	2		Lutsk	6 Jun
6.55		Jana	Veldáková	SVK	3.6.81	1	ET-2	Tel Aviv	25 Jun
6.54	0.7	Rebecca	Chapman	GBR	27.9.92	2	NC	Birmingham	2 Jul
6.54	0.5	Narayanan V.	Neena	IND	2.5.91	2	AsiC	Bhubaneswar	6 Jul
		(80)							
6.53	0.1	Julienne	McKee	USA	6.12.91	2		Fairburn	28 May
6.52i		Kendell	Williams	USA	14.6.95	1		College Station	21 Jan
6.52	1.5	Mara	Griva	LAT	4.8.89	1		Valmiera	11 Jun
6.52A	0.1	Malin	Marmbrandt	SWE	29.4.85	1		Monachil	7 Jul
6.52	1.3	Marthe	Koala	BUR	8.3.94	1	Franc	Abidjan	26 Jul
6.52	0.9	Lauren	Wells	AUS	3.8.88	*		Brisbane	16 Dec
6.51		Tamara	Myers	BAH	27.7.93	1		Kingston	21 Jan
6.51i			Xu Xiaoling	CHN	13.5.92	3	NGP	Xianlin	27 Feb
6.50	0.1	Olga	Rypakova	KAZ	30.11.84	1	NCp	Almaty	13 May
6.50	1.8	Taliyah	Brooks	USA	8.2.95	1H	NCAA	Eugene	10 Jun
		(90)							
6.50	1.4	Yorgelis	Rodríguez	CUB	25.1.95	1		Bilbao	24 Jun
6.49	1.7	Anna	Jagaciak Michalska	POL	10.2.90	1		Lódz	20 May
6.49	1.8	Aiga	Grabuste	LAT	24.3.88	3		Kawasaki	21 May
6.49A		Natalie	Aranda	PAN	22.2.95	1		Medellín	30 Sep
6.48	-1.9	Irisdaymi	Herrera	CUB	18.4.92	*		La Habana	4 Mar
6.48	1.4	Je'Nia	Sears	USA	15.4.93	1		Redlands	18 May
6.48	0.4	Nadia	Akpana Assa	NOR	22.12.95	1		Göteborg	10 Jun
6.48	1.6	Fátima	Diame	ESP	22.9.96	1		Castellón	15 Jun
6.48A	1.0	Macarena	Reyes	CHI	30.3.84	2		Monachil	7 Jul
6.48	1.3	Yelena	Mashinistova	RUS	29.3.94	4	NCp	Yerino	15 Jul
		(100)							

Mark	Wind	Name		Nat	Born	Date
6.47i		Tania	Vicenzino	ITA	1.4.86	18 Feb
6.47	1.0	Paula	Álvarez	CUB	11.9.95	17 Mar
6.47	1.2	Kynnedy	Flannel	USA-Y	12.7.00	13 May
6.47	1.5	Neja	Filipic	SLO	22.4.95	27 May
6.47	0.8	Evelise	Veiga	POR	3.3.96	1 Jul
6.47	0.5	Maria Natalia	Londa	INA	29.10.90	25 Aug
6.46i		Nadja	Käther	GER	29.9.88	10 Feb
6.46	0.6	Tânia	da Silva	BRA	17.12.86	4 Mar
6.46	1.8	Charrie	Dennard	USA		28 Apr
6.46	-0.3	Jessica	Noble	JAM	5.2.97	23 Jun
6.45	1.7	Fatim	Affessi	SUI	8.7.93	25 May
6.45	1.6	Tierra	Williams	USA	10.6.95	25 May
6.45	0.0	Polina	Lukyanenkova	RUS-J	15.7.98	4 Jun
6.45	-0.8		Chen Ting	CHN	28.8.97	17 Jul
6.45	0.0	Marestella	Sunang	PHI	20.2.81	25 Aug
6.45	0.8		Wang Qingling	CHN	14.1.93	3 Sep
6.44i		Paraskeví	Papahrístou	GRE	17.4.89	4 Feb
6.44	1.2	Hanne	Maudens	BEL	12.3.97	14 Jul
6.44	1.6	Chelsea	Jaensch	AUS	6.1.85	16 Dec
6.43i		Samara	Spencer	JAM	30.10.96	13 Jan
6.43i		Veronika	Shutkova	BLR	26.5.86	19 Feb
6.43i			Wang Rong	CHN	1.7.96	23 Feb
6.43	0.9	Aasha	Marler	USA	24.12.92	17 Jun
6.43	1.5	Alexis	Faulknor	USA	22.9.94	17 Jun
6.42Ai		Jessie	Gaines	USA	12.8.90	4 Mar
6.42	0.6	Todea-Kay	Willis	JAM	23.11.88	25 Mar
6.42	1.0	Jogaile	Petrokaite	LTU	30.9.95	20 Jul
6.42	1.0	Jessica	Penney	AUS	21.12.87	17 Dec
6.41i		Ivona	Dadic	AUT	29.12.93	3 Mar
6.41	-0.1	Sydnei	Murphy	USA	12.12.96	1 Apr
6.41	0.0	Ayana	Gales	USA	-.94	28 Apr
6.41	0.9	Petra	Farkas	HUN-J	30.4.99	11 Jun
6.41	1.3	Olatz	Arrieta	ESP	1.12.90	1 Jul
6.41	0.8	Milena	Mitkova	BUL	26.1.90	4 Jul
6.41	1.0	Tabea	Christ	GER-J	5.5.98	23 Jul
6.40A	0.6	Alejandra	Maldonado	MEX	18.4.92	16 Apr
6.40	-1.2	Cidae'a	Woods	USA	26.6.96	12 May
6.40	0.0	Zhanna	Zelikova	RUS	22.2.95	4 Jun
6.40	1.2	Viktoriya	Samitova	RUS	9.9.94	29 Jul
6.39i		Jana	Koresová	CZE	8.4.81	29 Jan
6.39i		Nathalie	Buschung	GER	2.3.96	1 Feb
6.39i		Tyra	Gittens	TTO-J	6.6.98	4 Feb
6.39i		Jahisha	Thomas	GBR	22.11.94	10 Feb
6.39i		Lisa	Maihöfer	GER-J	28.10.98	4 Mar
6.39	0.1	Tissanna	Hickling	JAM-J	7.1.98	11 Mar
6.39	0.0	Rellie	Kaputin	PNG	12.3.93	23 Apr
6.39	0.5	Haoua	Kessely	FRA	2.2.88	9 Jun
6.39	0.0	Annika	Gärtz	GER	24.8.94	8 Jul
6.39	0.8	Parinya	Chuaemaroeng	THA	16.12.97	27 Jul
6.38i		Györgyi	Zsivoczky-Farkas	HUN	13.2.85	3 Mar
6.38Ai		Kenyattia	Hackworth	USA	15.9.93	4 Mar
6.38	0.0	Tay-Leiha	Clark	AUS-J	8.2.98	12 Mar
6.38	1.4	Nataliyah	Friar	USA	3.4.95	28 Apr
6.38	0.9	Diána	Lesti	HUN-J	30.3.98	18 Jun
6.38		Yekaterina	Lobakina	RUS	4.2.88	27 Jun
6.38	0.3	Celina	Leffler	GER	9.4.96	14 Jul
6.37	0.9	Lucia	Slanicková	SVK	8.11.88	23 May
6.37	1.2	María del	Mar Jover	ESP	21.4.88	10
Jun6.37		Kaiza	Karlén	SWE-J	4.12.98	20 Jun
6.37A	0.4		Gong Luying	CHN-Y	22.2.00	16 Jul

Mark	Wind	Name		Nat	Born	Date
6.36i		Yekaterina	Khalyutina	RUS	16.1.91	20 Feb
6.36i		Baileh	Simms	USA	26.4.95	24 Feb
6.36	0.0		Fu Bingling	CHN	1.1.92	10 May
6.36	1.0	Paola	Mautino	PER	1.6.90	27 May
6.36	2.0	Anastasiya	Metelskaya	BLR	16.3.95	31 May
6.36	0.7	Susana	Hernández	MEX-J	18.1.99	18 Jun
6.36	0.3	Caroline	Agnou	SUI	26.5.96	14 Jul
6.35i		Yekaterina	Solovyova	RUS	23.11.95	5 Feb
6.35	1.9	Der'Renae	Freeman	USA	15.4.94	18 Mar
6.35A	0.4	Maya	Evans	USA-J	12.6.99	12 May
6.35	0.0	Gabrielle	Farquharson	USA	2.12.92	26 May
6.35	0.2	Matilda	Bogdanoff	FIN	8.10.90	9 Jun
6.35	-0.6	Anne-Mari	Lehtiö	FIN	6.9.95	1 Jul
6.35	0.2	Martha	Traoré	DEN	8.1.95	15 Jul
6.35	-0.3	Ottavia	Cestonaro	ITA	12.1.95	15 Jul
		(175)				

Wind assisted

Mark	Wind	Name		Nat	Born	Pos	Meet	Venue	Date
7.05	3.0	Tianna	Bartoletta	USA	30.8.85	1	NC	Sacramento	24 Jun
6.98	2.1		Reese			2	NC	Sacramento	24 Jun
6.94	2.4	Christabel	Nettey	CAN	2.6.91	2		Chula Vista	17 Jun
					6.80w	6.66	6.94w	6.80 6.72	6.92
6.93	4.3	Éloyse	Lesueur	FRA	15.7.88	1	NC	Marseille	14 Jul
					6.73w	6.93w	6.84w/2.7	x x	6.78w
6.92	3.0	Sha'Keela	Saunders	USA	18.12.93	3	NC	Sacramento	24 Jun6
					6.66	x	6.57	6.77/-0.8 6.92w	6.58
6.90	2.1	Quanesha	Burks	USA	15.3.95	1		Baton Rouge	28 Apr
					6.28w	6.90w	6.76	6.65 6.62	6.77/1.3
6.84	2.4	Jasmine	Todd	USA	23.12.93	3		Chula Vista	17 Jun
6.81	2.2	Sydney	Conley	USA	11.12.93	1q	NCAA-W	Austin	25 May
6.80	2.6	Tara	Davis	USA-J	20.5.99	1		Norwalk	20 May
6.70	2.4	Chantel	Malone	IVB	2.12.91	1	NC	Port of Spain	25 Jun
6.68	2.1	Ese	Brume	NGR	20.1.96	1		Denizli	10 May
6.68	3.5	Fatim	Affessi	SUI	8.7.93	1	NCAA-II	Bradenton	25 May
6.67	2.8	Wurrie	Njadoe	USA	14.8.97	2q	NCAA-W	Austin	25 May
6.66	3.0	Todea-Kay	Willis	JAM	23.11.88	1		Kingston	25 Feb
6.63	3.1	Brittney	Howell	JAM	1.9.92	1		Chula Vista	14 May
6.63	2.8	Jhoanmy	Luque	VEN	20.12.95	3q	NCAA-W	Austin	25 May
6.62	3.4	Anna	Bühler	GER	3.6.97	Q	EU23	Bydgoszcz	15 Jul
6.62	2.2	Milica	Gardasevic	SRB-J	28.9.98	Q	EJ	Grosseto	22 Jul
6.61	3.5	Tamara	Myers	BAH	27.7.93	2		Kingston	25 Feb
6.60	2.8	Chelsea	Jaensch	AUS	6.1.85	1		Brisbane	16 Dec
6.59	3.3	Paula Beatriz	Álvarez	CUB	11.9.95	1	NC	La Habana	17 Mar
6.59	3.7	Aasha	Marler	USA	24.12.92	2		Chula Vista	14 May
6.58	3.5	Irisdaymi	Herrera	CUB	18.4.92	2	NC	La Habana	17 Mar
6.58	3.1	Samiyah	Samuels	USA	2.10.97	1		Houston	13 May
6.58	2.5	Krystyna	Hryshutyna	UKR	21.3.92	2	PTS	Samorín	17 Jun
6.57	6.2	Kenyattia	Hackworth	USA	15.9.93	1		Waco	8 Apr
6.55	3.8	Viershanie	Latham	USA	1.8.95	1		Lubbock	28 Apr
6.54	2.6	Haoua	Kessely	FRA	2.2.88	2	NC	Marseille	14 Jul
6.54	2.6	Lauren	Wells	AUS	3.8.88	2		Brisbane	16 Dec
6.53	2.1	Rellie	Kaputin	PNG	12.3.93	2	NCAA-II	Bradenton	25 May
6.51	3.0	Katerina	Cachová	CZE	26.2.90	1H		Kladno	18 Jun
6.51	7.3	Macarena	Reyes	CHI	30.3.84	2	SAmC	Asunción	24 Jun
6.50	2.3	Milena	Mitkova	BUL	26.1.90	2		Castellón	4 Jul
6.49	2.7	Olatz	Arrieta	ESP	1.12.90	1		Palencia	8 Jul
6.48	3.5	Celeste	Mucci	AUS-J	11.8.99	1H		Sydney	3 Dec

Mark	Wind	Name		Nat	Born	Date
6.46	2.9	Filippa	Fotopoulou	CYP	20.12.96	28 Apr
6.46	2.3	Der'Renae	Freeman	USA	15.4.94	29 Apr
6.45	4.0	Annika	Gärtz	GER	24.8.94	10 Jun
6.44	2.3	Diána	Lesti	HUN-J	30.3.98	4 Jun
6.43	3.0	Allanah	McCorkle	USA	16.2.94	13 May
6.43	2.1	Angelica	Berriot	FRA-J	2.7.99	24 Jun
6.43	2.5	Tissanna	Hickling	JAM-J	7.1.98	24 Jun
6.41	3.0	Tonye'cia	Burks	USA	29.4.96	8 Apr
6.41	3.3	Nina	Schultz	CAN-J	12.11.98	13 May
6.40	4.8	Kelsey	Berryman	NZL	4.2.92	18 Mar
6.40	2.4	Lucia	Slanicková	SVK	8.11.88	23 May
6.40	2.2	Zuliat	Alli	USA	8.12.97	25 May
6.39A	2.1	Maryke	Brits	RSA	25.2.94	22 Apr
6.39	3.6	Kiara	Williams	USA	15.9.96	28 Apr
6.39A	3.7	Destiny	Longmire	USA-J	6.2.98	12 May
6.39A	2.5	Paola	Mautino	PER	1.6.90	21 May
6.39	4.6	Rhesa	Foster	USA-J	25.5.98	25 May
6.39	2.4	Kaiza	Karlén	SWE-J	4.12.98	27 Aug
6.39	3.0	Erika	Tsujimoto	JPN	20.4.95	8 Sep
6.39	3.0	Katerina	Dvoráková	CZE	10.5.97	9 Sep
6.38	3.1	Baileh	Simms	USA	26.4.95	25 May
6.37	2.7	Mariah	Ririnui	NZL	29.6.92	12 Mar
6.37	3.7	Keila	Costa	BRA	6.2.83	4 Nov
6.36	3.0	Sachiko	Masumi	JPN	20.12.84	23 Apr
6.36	4.8	Tamaka	Shimizu	JPN	22.6.91	23 Apr
6.35	2.5	Polina	Lukyanenkova	RUS-J	15.7.98	21 Jun

Best outdoors

Mark	Wind	Name	Pos	Meet	Venue	Date
6.79	1.2	Saunders	2		Baton Rouge	28 Apr
6.78	0.3	Ugen	3	Pre	Eugene	26 May
6.67	-0.6	Malone	1		St. George's	1 Jul
6.63		Strati	1	Kuso	Szczecin	10 Jun
		6.70w 5.5	1		Salamanca	3 Jun
6.59	1.1	Orji	4q	NCAA-E	Lexington	25 May
		6.71w 2.2	2	NCAA	Eugene	8 Jun
6.59	0.0	Bekh	1	NC	Kropyvnytskiy	6 Jul
		6.63w 2.1	Q	EU23	Bydgoszcz	15 Jul
6.56	0.0	Arneton	1		Angoulême	8 Jul
6.53	1.1	Sawyers	1		Bedford	29 May
		6.55w 2.8	4		Göteborg	11 Jul
6.52	0.0	Buchelnikova	2		Yerino	10 Jun
6.51	-0.3	Xu Xiaoling	2	NG	Tianjin	7 Sep
6.49	1.9	K Williams	1H	NC	Sacramento	25 Jun

Mark	Wind	Name	Date
6.45	1.6	Zhou Xiaoxue	3 Apr
6.41	0.4	Gaines	21 May
6.40	0.9	Argüelles	3 Jun
6.36	0.9	Koresová	29 Jul
6.37	0.7	Dadic	30 Jun
6.35w	2.2	J Thomas	25 May

Best at low altitude

Mark	Wind	Name	Pos	Venue	Date
6.48	-1.0	Sauceda	1	Monterrey	24 Mar
6.48	1.3	Marmbrandt	2	Göteborg	1 Jul

Mark	Wind	Name		Nat	Born	Pos	Meet	Venue	Date

6.46 1.8 Aguilar 29 Apr | 6.41 Reyes 4 Jun | 6.35 -0.2 Gong Yuling 19 Apr
6.46 1.2 Aranda 23 Nov |

JUNIORS

See main list for top 4 juniors. 13 performances (inc. 4 indoors) by 4 women to 6.47. Additional marks and further juniors:

T Davis 6.68i 1 Frisco 10 Feb 6.47Ai 1 Pocatello 18 Feb
6.63 1.6 1 NC-J Sacramento 23 Jun 6.47i 1 New York (A) 11 Mar
6.62 -1.5 1 Moorpark 28 Apr 6.47 1.1 1 Norwalk 20 May
6.61 1.1 * Sacramento 24 Jun
Gardasevic 6.50 1.9 1 Budapest 19 Aug Arneton in & out

Mark	Wind	Name		Nat	Born	Pos	Meet	Venue	Date
6.47	1.2	Kynnedy	Flannel	USA-Y	12.7.00	1		Austin	13 May
6.45	0.0	Polina	Lukyanenkova	RUS	15.7.98	2		Maykop	4 Jun
6.41	0.9	Petra	Farkas	HUN	30.4.99	1	NC	Székesfehérvár	11 Jun
6.41	1.0	Tabea	Christ	GER	5.5.98	2	EJ	Grosseto	23 Jul
6.39i		Tyra	Gittens	TTO	6.6.98	1		Nashville	4 Feb
6.39i		Lisa	Maihöfer (10)	GER	28.10.98	1	v2N-j	Halle	4 Mar
6.39	0.1	Tissanna	Hickling	JAM	7.1.98	1		Kingston	11 Mar
6.38	0.0	Tay-Leiha	Clark	AUS	8.2.98	3		Canberra	12 Mar
6.38	0.9	Diána	Lesti	HUN	30.3.98	1	NC-j	Budapest	18 Jun
6.37		Kaiza	Karlén	SWE	4.12.98	1		Velenje	20 Jun
6.37A	0.4		Gong Luying	CHN-Y	22.2.00	1	WY	Nairobi	16 Jul
6.36	0.7	Susana	Hernández	MEX	18.1.99	1	NC	Monterrey	18 Jun
6.35A	0.4	Maya	Evans	USA	12.6.99	1		Longmont	12 May
6.33	1.1	Martina	Aliventi	ITA	6.8.98	Q	EJ	Grosseto	22 Jul
6.32	2.0	Andrea	Thompson	AUS	2.10.98	5		Canberra	12 Mar
6.32		Maja	Bedrac (20)	SLO	10.9.99	3		Velenje	20 Jun

Wind assisted 3 performances by 3 women to 6.48

T Davis 6.64w 2.9 5 NC Sacramento 24 Jun 6.51w 2.4 1 PAm-J Trujillo 21 Jul

Mark	Wind	Name		Nat	Born	Pos	Meet	Venue	Date
6.44	2.3	Diána	Lesti	HUN	30.3.98	1		Budapest	4 Jun
6.43	2.1	Angelica	Berriot	FRA	2.7.99			Moulins	24 Jun
6.43	2.5	Tissanna	Hickling	JAM	7.1.98	1	NC-j	Kingston	24 Jun
6.41	3.3	Nina	Schultz	CAN	12.11.98	5	Big 12	Lawrence	13 May
6.39A	3.7	Destiny	Longmire	USA	6.2.98	1	MWC	Logan	12 May
6.39	4.6	Rhesa	Foster	USA	25.5.98	6q	NCAA-W	Austin	25 May
6.39	2.4	Kaiza	Karlén	SWE	4.12.98	2	NC	Helsingborg	27 Aug
6.35	2.5	Polina	Lukyanenkova	RUS	15.7.98	1	NC-23	Saransk	21 Jun

TRIPLE JUMP

14.96 -0.3 Yulimar Rojas VEN 21.10.95 1 Andújar 2 Jun
14.46/-0.3 14.45/0.3 14.60/-0.8 14.74/0.4 14.82/0.2 14.96
14.91 0.4 1 WCh London (OS) 7 Aug 14.55/0.5 14.82/0.8 14.83/0.4 13.69 14.91 14.50/-0.3
14.84 0.6 1 GGala Roma 8 Jun x 14.76/1.1 14.08 14.82/0.9 14.84 14.65/0.1
14.83 -0.4 2 Herc Monaco 21 Jul 14.44/-1.3 14.72/-0.8 14.46/-0.3 x 14.25 14.83
14.79i 1 Madrid 28 Jan 14.01 14.61 14.79 x
14.67 1.2 1 Baie-Mahault 17 May 14.31 14.67 14.47/0.9 x x
14.62 0.9 1 Castellón 10 Jun 14.44/1.0 14.53/0.4 14.62 14.25
14.52 -0.8 Q WCh London (OS) 7 Aug 14.17 14.52
14.52 0.8 2 WK-DLF Zürich 24 Aug x 14.24 14.43 14.20 14.52 14.39
14.89 0.9 Caterine Ibargüen COL 12.2.84 2 WCh London (OS) 7 Aug
14.67 14.69/0.4 14.89 14.80/0.3 14.71/-1.0 14.88/0.5
14.86 -0.5 1 Herc Monaco 21 Jul x 14.38 14.43/-0.5 14.34 14.67/-0.4 14.86
14.78 0.0 2 GGala Roma 8 Jun 14.43/0.6 x 14.57/0.8 14.69/0.1 14.68/-0.2 14.78
14.51 -0.3 1 DL Rabat 16 Jul 13.91 14.33 14.51 14.21 14.16 14.12
14.51 0.0 1 DL Birmingham 16 Aug 14.01 14.21 13.89 14.30 14.44/0.5 14.51
14.49 0.0 1 Madrid 14 Jul 13.68 14.03 14.27 14.30 14.46 14.49
14.48 -0.2 3 WK-DLF Zürich 24 Aug 14.13 14.11 14.47/-0.1 14.22 14.46/0.4 14.48
14.43 0.2 1 Kingston 20 May ??
14.77 0.9 Olga Rypakova KAZ 30.11.84 3 WCh London (OS) 7 Aug
14.45/0.4 x 14.77 14.32 14.52/0.2 14.36
14.64 0.1 3 GGala Roma 8 Jun 14.24 14.64 14.45/1.4 14.15 x 14.26
14.57 1.1 Q WCh London (OS) 7 Aug 14.57
14.55 -0.2 1 WK-DLF Zürich 24 Aug 14.48/-0.3 14.38 14.03 14.55 14.44 14.31
14.45 1.0 1 NCp Almaty 14 May x 14.33 x 14.45 14.29 x
14.56 0.7 Núbia Soares BRA 26.3.96 1 NC São Bernardo do Campo 11 Jun
x 14.56 x x 14.56/0.8 14.39
14.54 -0.1 Kimberly Williams JAM 3.11.88 3 Herc Monaco 21 Jul
14.22 14.54 14.36 14.11 14.53/-0.7 14.10
14.44 0.1 2 DL Birmingham 16 Aug 13.99 14.44 14.29 14.44/0.7 14.04 14.36
14.45 0.2 Liadagmis Povea CUB 6.2.96 1 Barr La Habana 26 May
13.64 14.26 13.77 14.38 x 14.45
14.45 0.2 Shanieka Ricketts JAM 2.2.92 1 Hanz Zagreb 29 Aug
14.06 14.45 14.12 14.04 14.19 14.11

Mark	Wind	Name		Nat	Born	Pos	Meet	Venue	Date
14.43	??	Elena Andreea	Panturoiu	ROU	24.2.95	1		Cluj Napoca	3 Jun
14.42	1.0	Patrícia	Mamona	POR	21.11.88	4	GGala	Roma	8 Jun
					14.08 14.42 x x x x				
14.42	1.2	Hanna	Minenko	ISR	25.9.89	4	WCh	London (OS)	7 Aug
		(30/10)			14.11 14.04 14.29 x 14.42 13.97				
14.40	-0.1	Kristin	Gierisch	GER	20.8.90	1	NC	Erfurt	9 Jul
14.39	0.6	Jeanine	Assani Issouf	FRA	17.8.92	*	NC	Marseille	16 Jul
14.35	1.4	Neele	Eckhardt	GER	2.7.92	1		Göttingen	11 Jun
14.35	0.6	Susana	Costa	POR	22.9.84	Q	WCh	London (OS)	5 Aug
14.32i		Keturah	Orji	USA	5.3.96	1	SEC	Nashville	25 Feb
14.30	-0.1	Anna	Krylova	RUS	3.10.85	1		Sochi	26 May
14.29	1.9	Anna	Jagaciak Michalska	POL	10.2.90	1		Bursa	6 Jul
14.27i		Jenny	Elbe	GER	18.4.90	Q	EI	Beograd	3 Mar
14.24i		Paraskeví	Papahrístou	GRE	17.4.89	3	EI	Beograd	4 Mar
14.23	1.4	Ana	Peleteiro	ESP	2.12.95	7	WCh	London (OS)	7 Aug
		(20)							
14.21	1.1	Darya	Nidbaykina	RUS	26.12.94	1	NC	Zhukovskiy	30 Jul
14.20	1.7	Thea	LaFond	DMA	5.4.94	1	PennR	Philadelphia	29 Apr
14.19	-0.2	Gabriela	Petrova	BUL	29.6.92	1		Plovdiv	8 Jul
14.18i		Kristiina	Mäkelä	FIN	20.11.92	Q	EI	Beograd	3 Mar
14.15	1.2	Dovile	Dzindzaletaite	LTU	14.7.93	1		Padova	16 Jul
14.15	0.1		Vu Thi Men	VIE	10.7.90	1	SEAG	Kuala Lumpur	23 Aug
14.13	2.0	Tânia	da Silva	BRA	17.12.86	2	NC	São Bernardo do Campo	11 Jun
14.10	1.2	Éloyse	Lesueur	FRA	15.7.88	1		Dijon	21 May
14.06	1.7	Dariya	Derkach	ITA	27.3.93	1		Orvieto	28 May
14.05A	0.1	Liuba M.	Zaldívar	CUB	5.4.93	1	NC	Cuenca	20 May
		(30)							
14.04	1.9	Irina	Gumenyuk	RUS	6.1.88	2		Sochi	26 May
14.03	1.0	Tamara	Myers	BAH	27.7.93	2	PennR	Philadelphia	29 Apr
14.03	0.4	Fátima	Diame	ESP	22.9.96	2		Torrent	2 Jul
14.03	0.9	Tori	Franklin	USA	7.10.92	13q	WCh	London (OS)	5 Aug
14.02i		Olha	Saladukha	UKR	4.6.83	1	NC	Sumy	19 Feb
14.00i		Viktoriya	Prokopenko	RUS	17.4.91	2	NC	Moskva	21 Feb
14.00	1.1	Irina	Vaskovskaya	BLR	2.4.91	1	NC	Grodno	6 Jul
13.98	0.2	Rouguy	Diallo	FRA	5.2.95	*	EU23	Bydgoszcz	14 Jul
13.97	0.9	Natalya	Yevdokimova	RUS	7.9.93	2	Znam	Zhukovskiy	1 Jul
13.94	0.0	Mariya	Ovchinnikova	KAZ-J	19.10.98	1	Kozanov	Almaty	24 Jun
		(40)							
13.94	1.3	Violetta	Skvortsova	BLR-J	15.4.98	*	EJ	Grosseto	21 Jul
13.93i		Yanis	David	FRA	12.12.97	1		Fayetteville	11 Feb
13.93i			Rao Fan	CHN	1.1.96	1	NGP	Xianlin	28 Feb
13.93	0.9	Nadia	Eke	GHA	11.1.93	2		St-Martin	13 May
13.88	-0.1		Wang Wupin	CHN	18.1.91	1	NG	Tianjin	4 Sep
13.86i		Cristina	Bujin	ROU	12.4.88	2	NC	Bucuresti	18 Feb
13.84		Ana José	Tima	DOM	10.10.89	1		Santo Domingo	15 Jun
13.83i			Chen Ting	CHN	28.8.97	1	NGP	Xianlin	24 Feb
13.82	1.5	Shara	Proctor	GBR	16.9.88	1	Clay	Azusa	14 Apr
13.82	-0.4	Aina	Griksaite	LTU	23.11.94	1		Kaunas	3 Jun
		(50)							
13.82	0.4	Dana	Veldáková	SVK	3.6.81	3		Marseille	3 Jun
13.79	-0.9	Olesya	Ivanenko	RUS	6.10.82	5	NC	Zhukovskiy	30 Jul
13.77	1.0		Wang Rong	CHN	1.7.96	2	NGP	Taiyuan	11 May
13.77	1.8	Nathalie	Marie-Nély	FRA	24.11.86	3		Forbach	28 May
13.77	-0.4	Irina	Ektova	KAZ	8.1.87	2	Kozanov	Almaty	24 Jun
13.76i			Deng Linuo	CHN	16.3.92	2	NGP	Xianlin	28 Feb
13.76	0.4	Yekaterina	Ektova	KAZ	30.8.92	2	NCp	Almaty	14 May
13.76	1.9	Sanna	Nygård	FIN	22.3.88	2	NC	Seinäjoki	22 Jul
13.75i		Shardia	Lawrence	JAM	31.12.95	2		Fayetteville	11 Feb
13.73	-0.3		Li Yanmei	CHN	6.2.90	1	NGP	Zhengzhou	12 Apr
		(60)							
13.73	-0.5	Lucie	Májková	CZE	9.7.88	4	ET	Villeneuve d'Ascq	24 Jun
13.72	1.2	Davisleidis L.	Velazco	CUB-J	4.9.99	2	NC	La Habana	16 Mar
13.71	0.0	Valentina	Kosolapova	RUS	11.7.97	1		Maykop	5 Jun
13.69	1.3	Birte	Damerius	GER	13.12.91	2		Berlin	25 Jun
13.68	1.0	Iana	Amsterdam	GUY	14.11.95	1	TexR	Austin	31 Mar
13.68			Bui Thi Thu Thao	VIE	29.4.92	1	NC	Ho Chi Minh	23 Oct
13.67	1.7	Patricia	Sarrapio	ESP	16.11.82	2		Andújar	2 Jun
13.66	-0.9		Li Xiaohong	CHN	8.1.95	3	NGP	Taiyuan	11 May
13.66	-0.5		Zhou Minjuan	CHN	22.4.96	4	NGP	Taiyuan	11 May
13.66	0.7	Ilionis	Guillaume	FRA-J	13.1.98	2		Nice	18 Jun
		(70)							

Mark	Wind	Name		Nat	Born	Pos	Meet	Venue	Date
13.66	1.7	Ottavia	Cestonaro	ITA	12.1.95	2	NC	Trieste	2 Jul
13.65i		Jhoanmy	Luque	VEN	20.12.95	1	Big 12	Ames	25 Feb
13.64i		Athanasía	Pérra	GRE	2.2.83	2	NC	Pireás	19 Feb
13.64	1.4	H.D. Viduka	Lakshani	SRI	28.12.96	1		Diyagama	9 Apr
13.64	1.7	Diana	Zagainova	LTU	20.6.97	2		Kaunas	3 Jun
13.64	0.4	Naomi	Ogbeta	GBR-J	18.4.98	1	NC	Birmingham	1 Jul
13.64A	0.0		Tan Qiujiao	CHN-Y	28.5.00	1	WY	Nairobi	15 Jul
13.64	1.1	Aleksandra	Nacheva	BUL-Y	20.8.01	4	EJ	Grosseto	21 Jul
13.63	0.0	Ayanna	Alexander	TTO	20.7.82	2	NC	Port of Spain	24 Jun
13.63	1.0	Parinya (80)	Chuaemaroeng	THA	16.12.97	1		Songkhla	26 Jul
13.63i		Marie-José	Ebwea Bile	FRA	7.2.97	1		Bloomingtob	8 Dec
13.62	0.5	Amber	Hughes	USA	23.8.94	1		Jacksonville	8 Apr
13.62	2.0	Andrea	Geubelle	USA	21.6.91	*		Chula Vista	27 May
13.61	0.1	Sokhna	Galle	FRA	23.4.94	6		Forbach	28 May
13.61	1.5	Jessie	Maduka	GER	23.4.96	1	NC-23	Leverkusen	18 Jun
13.61	0.0	Mariya	Suntsova	RUS	27.12.95	6	Znam	Zhukovskiy	1 Jul
13.61	-0.7	Carmen	Toma	ROU	28.3.89	1	NC	Pitesti	7 Jul
13.61	0.4	Mara	Griva	LAT	4.8.89	1	NC	Ogre	29 Jul
13.60	-0.2	Kristína	Alvertsián	GRE	4.7.90	2	NC	Pátra	17 Jun
13.60	1.1	Amy (90)	Zongo-Filet	FRA	4.10.80	4	NC	Marseille	16 Jul
13.60	1.9	Laura	Samuel	GBR	19.2.91	1		Manchester (SC)	16 Aug
13.59	0.6	Yorsiris	Urrutia	COL	26.6.86	1		Gurabo	27 May
13.59	0.3	Caroline	Ehrhardt	CAN	6.2.92	*	Franc	Abidjan	24 Jul
13.59	0.5		Fu Luna	CHN	3.5.95	2	WUG	Taipei	27 Aug
13.58	1.6	Joëlle	Mbumi	CMR	25.5.86	2	Franc	Abidjan	24 Jul
13.57	1.8	Danylle	Kurywchak	USA	15.7.94	1		Turlock	25 Mar
13.56i		Petra	Koren	SLO	30.7.93	1	NC	Celje	18 Feb
13.56A	1.7	Latavia	Coombs	JAM	1.1.95	1		Hobbs	15 Apr
13.56	0.2	Kateryna	Popova	UKR	7.8.96	1		Lutsk	7 Jun
13.56	1.1	Maéva (100)	Phesor	FRA	4.9.97	Q	EU23	Bydgoszcz	13 Jul
13.56	0.3		Wang Huiqin	CHN	7.2.90	Q	NG	Tianjin	3 Sep

Mark	Wind	Name		Nat	Born	Date
13.55i		Merilyn	Uudmäe	EST	26.3.91	3 Mar
13.55A	0.5	Kelly	Kingwell	RSA	22.1.91	21 Apr
13.55	-1.7	Ruslana	Tsyhotska	UKR	23.3.86	8 Jul
13.55	-0.4		Chen Mudan	CHN	4.10.93	3 Sep
13.54i		Simone	Charley	USA	4.2.95	25 Feb
13.53i		Andriana	Bânova	BUL	1.5.87	22 Jan
13.53i		Tiffany	Flynn	USA	2.9.95	25 Feb
13.53	1.4	Tonye'cia	Burks	USA	29.4.96	15 Apr
13.52	-0.5	Maria Natalia	Londa	INA	29.10.90	23 Aug
13.51i		Kseniya	Detsuk	BLR	23.4.86	11 Feb
13.51	1.5	Chaquinn	Cook	USA	10.7.97	27 May
13.50	1.7	Viershanie	Latham	USA	1.8.95	15 Apr
13.50	1.9	Tähti	Alver	EST	4.12.94	22 Jul
13.50	-0.9		Yang Yang	CHN-Y	23.8.01	4 Sep
13.48	1.8	Kaede	Miyasaka	JPN	12.12.92	24 Jun
13.48	-0.9	Kirthana	Ramasamy	MAS	20.1.97	24 Jun
13.47i		Irina	Konstants	RUS	1.3.90	21 Feb
13.47i			Chen Jie	CHN-J	2.3.98	28 Feb
13.47i		Natasha	Dicks	USA	6.7.95	11 Mar
13.47	0.0	Blessing	Ufodiama	USA	28.11.81	3 Jun
13.46i		Marshay	Ryan	USA	4.2.95	25 Feb
13.45i			Peng Mengyuan	CHN	5.9.96	24 Feb
13.45	0.0	Svetlana	Biryukova	RUS	1.4.91	30 Jul
13.45	1.0		Renu	IND-J	–.98	18 Nov
13.44i		Darrielle	McQueen	USA	29.5.96	11 Feb
13.44	-0.3	Sineade	Gutzmore	GBR	9.10.86	1 Jul
13.44	0.2		Li Ying	CHN	29.3.94	4 Sep
13.43	1.5	Angela	Barrett	GBR	25.12.85	16 Aug
13.43	1.4	Paola	Borovic	CRO	26.6.95	9 Sep
13.42	1.5	Tierra	Williams	USA	10.6.95	28 Apr
13.42	0.9	Nellickal Varkey	Sheena	IND	22.11.92	8 Jul
13.42	-0.4	Diana	Adasko	RUS-J	18.1.99	30 Jul
13.40A	0.7	Ivonne	Rangel	MEX	24.8.93	14 May
13.39	1.2	Aleksandra	Malafeyeva	BLR-J	12.9.98	29 Jun
13.38i		Cristina	Sandu	ROU	4.3.90	18 Feb
13.38	1.4	Angela	Mercurio	CAN	7.4.96	27 May
13.38	-0.4	Olga	Velmyakina	RUS	3.8.92	1 Jul
13.37	1.5	Tissanna	Hickling	JAM-J	7.1.98	10 Jun
13.37	1.5	Jaimie	Robinson	USA-J	26.5.99	24 Jun
13.37A	0.1		Zhao Jing	CHN	2.6.96	26 Jun
13.36	0.1	Dannielle	Gibson	BAH	5.4.96	10 Jun
13.36	2.0	Toni	Smith	USA	13.10.84	17 Jun
13.35i		Sasa	Babsek	SLO	27.3.92	18 Feb
13.35	0.0	Iryna	Nikolayeva	UKR	20.1.84	7 Jun
13.34	1.3	Malin	Marmbrandt	SWE	29.4.85	25 May
13.34	1.6	Krisztina	Hoffer	HUN	6.8.90	10 Jun
13.34	0.3	Janne	Nielsen	DEN	8.6.93	10 Jun
13.34	1.9	Klaudia	Kaczmarek	GER	13.3.90	9 Jul
13.32i		Sha'Keela	Saunders	USA	18.12.93	25 Feb
13.32	1.2	Cemre	Bitgin	TUR	21.1.96	22 Apr
13.32	1.6	Yekaterina	Sariyeva	AZE	18.12.95	9 Jun
13.32	1.0	Santa	Matule	LAT	13.12.92	10 Jun
13.31A	1.2	Heather	Arneton	FRA-Y	27.7.02	22 Apr
13.30	0.6	Megan	O'Riley	AUS	18.3.89	1 Apr
13.30	1.5	Brianna	Richardson	USA	9.9.94	22 Apr
13.30	-0.3	Maria (158)	Purtsa	GER	18.8.95	9 Jul

Wind assisted

Mark	Wind	Name		Nat	Born	Pos	Meet	Venue	Date
14.60	5.1	Kimberly	Williams	JAM	3.11.88	1	NC	Kingston	25 Jun
					14.28	14.27	14.60w	p p	p
14.48	2.6	Jeanine	Assani Issouf	FRA	17.8.92	1	NC	Marseille	16 Jul
					14.02	14.48w	14.39	14.07 x	14.
14.42	4.2		Soares			1	SAmC	Asunción	23 Jun
14.21	2.4	Violetta	Skvortsova	BLR-J	15.4.98	1	EJ	Grosseto	21 Jul
14.01	2.3	Irina	Vaskovskaya	BLR	2.4.91	1	NCp	Brest	1 Jun
13.99	3.7	Rouguy	Diallo	FRA	5.2.95	3	EU23	Bydgoszcz	14 Jul
13.98A	4.0	Dana	Veldáková	SVK	3.6.81	1		Sestriere	23 Jul

Mark	Wind	Name		Nat	Born	Pos	Meet	Venue	Date
13.97	2.2	Ilionis	Guillaume	FRA-J	13.1.98	2	EJ	Grosseto	21 Jul
13.96	2.3	Andrea	Geubelle	USA	21.6.91	1		Chula Vista	27 May
13.83	2.8	Caroline	Ehrhardt	CAN	6.2.92	1	Franc	Abidjan	24 Jul
13.80	3.6	Jhoanmy	Luque	VEN	20.12.95	1	Big 12	Lawrence	14 May
13.79	3.4	Shardia	Lawrence	JAM	31.12.95	2	Big 12	Lawrence	14 May
13.76	6.0	Dannielle	Gibson	BAH	5.4.96	1	Big 10	University Park	14 May
13.72	4.4	María	Vicente	ESP-Y	28.3.01	1	EYOF	Györ	28 Jul
13.70	3.0	Blessing	Ufodiama	USA	28.11.81	1	Scott	Irvine	29 Apr
13.69	2.6	Marie-José	Ebwea-Bile	FRA	7.2.97	2	NCAA	Eugene	10 Jun
13.68	4.5	Danique	Bryan	JAM	5.10.95	3	Big 12	Lawrence	14 May
13.68	3.0	Naomi	Ogbeta	GBR-J	18.4.98	3	EJ	Grosseto	21 Jul
13.67	3.3	Viershanie	Latham	USA	1.8.95	1	Johnson	Waco	22 Apr
13.65	4.4	Carmen	Toma	ROU	28.3.89	1	BalkC	Novi Pazar	15 Jul
13.64	2.7	Yorsiris	Urrutia	COL	26.6.86	3	SAmC	Asunción	23 Jun
13.59	4.0	Brianna	Richardson	USA	9.9.94	4	Big 12	Lawrence	14 May
13.58	3.0	Keila	Costa	BRA	6.2.83	3	NC	São Bernardo do Campo	11 Jun
13.58	2.1	Kaede	Miyasaka	JPN	12.12.92	1		Matsuyama	8 Oct

Mark	Wind	Name		Nat	Born	Date
13.54	3.1	Rachel	Toliver	USA	20.11.94	28 Apr
13.52	2.9	Silvia	La Tella	ITA	11.8.95	2 Jul
13.51		Jamie	Robinson	USA-J	26.5.99	18 Jun
13.50A	3.4	Giselly Andrea	Landazuri	COL	8.8.92	10 Jun
13.48	4.6	Cemre	Bitgin	TUR	21.1.96	8 May
13.48	2.9	Janne	Nielsen	DEN	8.6.93	21 May
13.40A	3.0	Patience	Ntshingila	RSA	26.8.89	18 Feb
13.39	2.1	Tissanna	Hickling	JAM-J	7.1.98	31 Mar
13.39	3.7	Evelise	Veiga	POR	3.3.96	11 Jun
13.32	2.5	Aliyah	Johnson	AUS	16.12.96	21 Apr

Best outdoors

Mark	Wind	Name	Pos	Meet	Venue	Date
14.31	0.1	Orji	1		Athens GA	6 May
14.24	0.4	Papahrístou	1	ET	Villenuve d'Ascq	24 Jun
14.00	0.8	Prokopenko	2	NC	Zhukovskiy	30 Jul
13.97	0.5	Saladukha	1		Athína (F)	31 May
13.92	0.6	Mäkelä	16q	WCh	London (OS)	5 Aug
13.85	-0.2	Bujin	2	ROU IC	Cluj Napoca	3 Jun
13.78	-0.2	David	4	EU23	Bydgoszcz	14 Jul
		13.92w 3.3	1		Fort Worth	15 Apr
13.66	1.7	Lawrence	1		Austin	14 Apr
13.60	0.0	Chen Ting	Q	NG	Tianjin	3 Sep

Mark	Wind	Name	Date
13.54	1.7	Luque	23 Jun
13.53	-0.1	Deng Linuo	12 Apr
13.51	0.6	Rao Fan	4 Apr
13.47	0.3	Flynn	27 May
13.46	-0.3	Chen Jie	11 May
13.45	0.4	Pérra	30 Apr
13.45	-0.4	Ryan	27 May
13.45		Konstants	28 Jun
13.39	-0.2	Ebwea Bile	27 May
13.39	1.2	Uudmäe	24 Jun
		13.43w 2.1	4 Jun
13.38	0.5	Dicks	27 May
13.37	1.0	McQueen	27 May

Best at low altitude

Mark	Wind	Name	Pos	Meet	Venue	Date
13.95	0.5	Zaldívar	1		Castres	26 Jul
13.30	0.0	Zhao Jing	8	NGP	Taiyuan	11 May

JUNIORS

See main list for top 7 juniors (and 3 wa). 12 performance (inc. 2 indoors) by 7 women to 13.64. Additional marks:

Name	Mark	Wind	Pos	Meet	Venue	Date
Ovchinnikova	13.72	1.1	1	AsiC	Bhubaneswar	8 Jul
Skvortsova	13.71	1.2	1		Valmiera	10 Jun
	13.69i		2	NC	Mogilyov	18 Feb
	13.69i		1	v7N	Minsk	25 Feb
	13.80w	3.6	2	NCp	Brest	1 Jun
Guillaume	13.65	1.4	*	EJ	Groseto	21 Jul

Mark	Wind	Name		Nat	Born	Pos	Meet	Venue	Date
13.50	-0.9		Yang Yang	CHN-Y	23.8.01	4	NG	Tianjin	4 Sep
13.47i			Chen Jie	CHN-J	2.3.98	3	NGP	Xianlin	28 Feb
13.45	1.0		Renu (10)	IND	–.98	1	NC-j	Mangalagiri	18 Nov
13.42	-0.4	Diana	Adasko	RUS	18.1.99	8	NC	Zhukovskiy	30 Jul
13.39	1.2	Aleksandra	Malafeyeva	BLR	12.9.98	1	NC-j	Brest	29 Jun
13.37	1.5	Tissanna	Hickling	JAM	7.1.98	4		Kingston	10 Jun
13.37	1.5	Jaimie	Robinson	USA	26.5.99	1	NC-j	Sacramento	24 Jun
13.31A	1.2	Heather	Arneton	FRA-Y	27.7.02	1		El Paso	22 Apr
13.29	0.9	Jasmine	Moore	USA-Y	1.5.01	1		Greensboro	16 Jun
13.29A	1.6	Zulia	Hernández	CUB-Y	12.12.01	3	WY	Nairobi	15 Jul
13.26	0.9	Tey-Leiha	Clark	AUS	8.2.98	2	NC	Sydney	1 Apr
13.23	-1.5	Tiffany	March	USA	13.12.99	1		Newport News	3 Jun
13.23	2.0	Agnieszka	Bednarek (20)	POL	14.6.98	1	NC-j	Torun	9 Jul

Wind assisted 5 performances by 4 women to 13.68

Mark	Wind	Name		Nat	Born	Pos	Meet	Venue	Date
Velazco 13.69	2.1					32	Barr	La Habana	26 May
13.51		Jamie	Robinson	USA	26.5.99	1		Belvidere	18 Jun
13.39	2.1	Tissanna	Hickling	JAM	7.1.98	1	N.Sch	Kingston	31 Mar

SHOT

Mark	Name	Nat	Born	Pos	Venue	Date
20.11	Gong Lijiao	CHN	24.1.89	1	Böhmenkirch	28 Jul

19.22 19.71 19.58 19.49 20.11 19.44

Mark	Pos	Meet	Venue	Date	1	2	3	4	5	6
19.94	1	WCh	London (OS)	9 Aug	19.16	19.35	19.03	x	19.94	19.89
19.46	1	DL	Shanghai	13 May	18.35	18.81	18.98	18.99	19.29	19.46
19.46	1	NG	Tianjin	6 Sep	18.76	18.75	19.14	19.08	19.16	19.46
19.60	1	WK-DLF	Zürich	24 Aug	18.81	19.22	19.39	19.52	19.60	19.19
19.56	1	GGala	Roma	8 Ju	19.24	19.35	19.18	19.50	19.56	19.53
19.19	1		Guiyang	27 Jun	18.79	19.10	19.10	x	19.15	19.19
19.18	1	NC	Jinan	19 May	x	18.63	18.59	18.76	19.18	18.83
19.14	1	DL	Paris (C)	1 Jul	18.56	18.68	18.82	18.92	18.95	19.14
18.97	Q	WCh	London (OS)	8 Aug	18.97					

Mark	Name		Nat	Born	Pos	Meet	Venue	Date
19.76	Raven	Saunders	USA	15.5.96	1	NC	Sacramento	24 Jun
				18.30 17.75 x 18.58 x 19.76				
	19.56i 1 NCAA	College Station	10 Mar	18.31 17.98 18.04 19.20 18.10 19.56				
	19.20 1	Athens, GA	21 Jul	17.73 18.26 17.68 17.75 19.20 19.17				
	19.10i 1	Nashville	14 Jan	x 15.44 19.10 18.61 x x				
	19.07i 1 SEC	Nashville	24 Feb	17.10 19.07 18.48 18.43 x 18.50				
19.64	Dani	Bunch	USA	16.5.91	2	NC	Sacramento	24 Jun
				18.92 19.18 x x 19.64 19.57				
	19.12 1	West Lafayette	22 Apr	18.10 18.51 18.57 19.12 x x				
	18.98 2 DL	Shanghai	13 May	18.25 18.22 18.46 18.98 18.86 18.86				
19.63	Anita	Márton	HUN	15.1.89	1		Drazevina	30 Apr
				17.77 18.68 19.11 18.56 19.46 19.63				
	19.49 2 WCh	London (OS)	9 Aug	18.50 18.89 18.65 18.33 18.54 19.49				
	19.48 1 Gyulai	Székesfehérvár	4 Jul	18.27 19.23 18.58 18.64 19.48 19.23				
	19.28i 1 EI	Beograd	3 Mar	18.67 18.96 19.24 x 18.46 19.28				
	19.05 1	Bar	1 May	17.89 18.89 18.68 19.05 18.64 19.01				
	18.99 2 DL	Doha	5 May	17.42 18.52 18.33 x 18.44 18.99				
	18.97i 1	Birmingham	18 Feb	17.27 18.20 18.76 17.88 18.97 18.11				
19.34	Michelle	Carter	USA	12.10.85	3	NC	Sacramento	24 Jun
				18.86 18.68 19.25 19.28 19.01 19.34				
	19.32 1 DL	Doha	5 May	18.86 x 19.32 18.74 18.47 18.46				
	19.14 3 WCh	London (OS)	9 Aug	18.82 18.86 19.14 19.03 x 18.97				
	19.03i 1 NC	Albuquerque	5 Mar	17.25 19.03 18.21 18.89 18.69 19.01				
	18.97 1	Gresham	2 Jul	18.13 18.28 18.77 18.97 x 18.70				
19.15	Danniel	Thomas-Dodd	JAM	11.11.92	1	NCAA	Eugene	8 Jun
				17.99 18.13 18.95 18.39 18.83 19.15				
19.01	Alyona	Dubitskaya	BLR	25.1.90	1	NCp	Brest	31 May
	(32/7)			x 18.61 x 18.72 18.67 19.01				
18.92	Yaniuvis	López	CUB	1.2.86	1		La Habana	30 Jun
18.89	Monique	Riddick	USA	8.11.89	4	NC	Sacramento	24 Jun
18.83	Dimitriana	Surdu	MDA	12.5.94	1	NC	Tiraspol	28 May
	(10)							
18.72i	Felisha	Johnson	USA	24.7.89	1		Indianapolis	11 Feb
18.66	Melissa	Boekelman	NED	11.5.89	1		Merksem	29 Jul
18.58	Brittany	Crew	CAN	3.6.94	2		Tucson	20 May
18.54i	Jeneva	Stevens	USA	28.10.89	1		Birmingham AL	21 Jan
18.50i	Christina	Schwanitz	GER	24.12.85	1	NC	Leipzig	18 Feb
18.48	Brittany	Smith	USA	25.3.91	1		Rathdrum	3 Jun
18.47	Yuliya	Leontyuk	BLR	31.1.84	3	WK	Zürich	24 Aug
18.46	Sara	Gambetta	GER	18.2.93	1		Gotha	15 Jul
18.37	Auriole	Dongmo	CMR	3.8.90	2		São Bernardo do Campo	3 Jun
18.36i	Radoslava	Mavrodieva	BUL	13.3.87	2	EI	Beograd	3 Mar
	(20)							
18.36	Jessica	Woodard	USA	4.2.95	1	Big 12	Lawrence	13 May
18.34		Gao Yang	CHN	1.3.93	1		Neubrandenburg	26 Jul
18.28	Úrsula	Ruiz	ESP	11.8.83	1	NC	Barcelona	22 Jul
18.24	Paulina	Guba	POL	14.5.91	1		København	20 Jun
18.23		Guo Tianqian	CHN	1.6.95	3	NGPF	Guiyang	27 Jun
18.22	Olha	Holodna	UKR	14.11.91	1		Kyiv	14 Jun
18.21	Fanny	Roos	SWE	2.1.95	1		Uppsala	5 Sep
18.18		Bian Ka	CHN	5.1.93	4	DL	Shanghai	13 May
18.16		Liu Xiangrong	CHN	6.6.88	2		Neubrandenburg	26 Jul
18.12i	Maggie	Ewen	USA	23.9.94	1		Albuquerque	11 Feb
	(30)							
18.12	Erin	Farmer	USA	11.8.95	1q	NCAA-W	Austin	27 May
18.09i	Claudine	Vita	GER	19.9.96	5	EI	Beograd	3 Mar
18.08	Geisa	Arcanjo	BRA	19.9.91	1	NC	São Bernardo do Campo	11 Jun
18.06	Alyona	Bugakova	RUS	24.4.97	1		Sochi	14 May
18.05	Anna	Avdeyeva	RUS	6.4.85	1	NC	Zhukovskiy	28 Jul
18.04	Emel	Dereli	TUR	25.2.96	1	NC	Bursa	15 Jun
18.00	Yevgeniya	Solovyova	RUS	28.6.86	1		Adler	26 May
17.99	Natalia	Ducó	CHI	31.1.89	1	Bol G	Santa Marta	21 Nov
17.98	Emmonnie	Henderson	USA	5.11.94	1		Louisville	15 Apr
17.96	Cleopatra	Borel	TTO	10.3.79	5	DL	Doha	5 May
	(40)							
17.93	Kelsey	Card	USA	20.8.92	1		La Jolla	22 Apr
17.93		Song Jiayuan	CHN	15.9.97	5	NG	Tianjin	6 Sep
17.90	Klaudia	Kardasz	POL	2.5.96	2	WUG	Taipei	27 Aug
17.88	Irina	Tarasova	RUS	15.4.87	2		Adler	26 May
17.87	Halyna	Obleshchuk/Turchyn	UKR	23.2.89	1		Lutsk	7 Jun
17.87	Sandra	Lemus	COL	1.1.89	2	Bol G	Santa Marta	21 Nov

Mark	Name		Nat	Born	Pos	Meet	Venue	Date
17.86	Janeah	Stewart	USA	21.7.96	1		Knoxville	7 Apr
17.79	Chase	Ealey	USA	20.7.94	4		Tucson	18 May
17.78i	Brittany	Mann	USA	16.4.94	3	NCAA	College Station	10 Mar
17.77i	Stamatía	Skarvélis	GRE	17.8.95	1		Bloomington	8 Dec
	(50)							
17.76i	Jessica	Cérival	FRA	20.1.82	6q	EI	Beograd	3 Mar
17.76	Valeriya	Zyryanova	RUS	12.8.90	3		Adler	26 May
17.76	Jessica	Ramsey	USA	26.7.91	3		Rathdrum	3 Jun
17.75	Rachel	Fatherly	USA	20.4.94	1		Shrewsbury	7 Jun
17.74	Taryn	Suttie	CAN	7.12.90	3		Tucson	20 May
17.71	Viktoryia	Kolb	BLR	26.10.93	3	NCp	Brest	31 May
17.70	Alyssa	Wilson	USA-J	20.2.99	1	PAm-J	Trujillo	21 Jul
17.69	Noora Salem	Jassem	BRN	27.11.96	7	DL	Doha	5 May
17.68i	Alina	Kenzel	GER	10.8.97	2		Rochlitz	5 Feb
17.62i	McKenzie	Warren	USA	3.12.93	1		Seattle	11 Feb
	(60)							
17.61		Geng Shuang	CHN	9.7.93	2	NGP	Chengdu	27 Mar
17.61	Lena	Urbaniak	GER	31.10.92	1		Rechberghausen	28 May
17.60	Whitney	Ashley	USA	18.2.89	4		Rathdrum	3 Jun
17.57i	Christina	Hillman	USA	6.10.93	6	NC	Albuquerque	5 Mar
17.51	Vera	Kunova	RUS	2.4.90	4	Znam	Zhukovskiy	1 Jul
17.49	Ashlie	Blake	USA	7.6.96	3q	NCAA-W	Austin	27 May
17.47i	Lloydricia	Cameron	USA	8.4.96	1		Blacksburg	21 Jan
17.47	Rachel	Wallader	GBR	1.9.89	4	ECp-w	Las Palmas	11 Mar
17.43	Cassie	Wertman	USA	14.6.93	2	FlaR	Gainesville	1 Apr
17.38	María Belén	Toimil	ESP	5.5.94	1		Pontevedra	15 Jul
	(70)							
17.37i	Austra	Skujyte	LTU	12.8.79	9q	EI	Beograd	3 Mar
17.36	Danielle	Waldner	USA	27.4.96	1		Fargo	12 May
17.35i	Cion	Hicks	USA	14.10.94			Fayetteville	11 Feb
17.34i	Josephine	Terlecki	GER	17.2.86	4		Sassnitz	12 Feb
17.30	Chiara	Rosa	ITA	28.1.83			Ferrara	27 May
17.29	Gleneve	Grange	JAM	6.7.95	2	ACC	Atlanta	13 May
17.24	Julia	Ritter	GER-J	13.5.98	1	EJ	Grosseto	22 Jul
17.18i	Aaliyah	Pete	USA	15.3.95	1	MWC	Albuquerque	25 Feb
17.18	Alena	Pasechnik	BLR	17.4.95	1		Minsk	13 Jun
17.17i	Kiley	Sabin	USA	28.4.96	1		Madison	21 Jan
	(80)							
17.15	Maria Fernanda	Orozco	MEX-J	25.1.98	1		Monterrey	29 May
17.14	Yekaterina	Burmistrova	RUS	18.8.90	3		Sochi	14 May
17.13	Amelia	Strickler	GBR	24.1.94	6	WUG	Taipei	27 Aug
17.12	Lívia	Avancini	BRA	8.5.92	1		São Bernardo do Campo	23 Apr
17.11i	Katharina	Maisch	GER	12.6.97	3	NC	Leipzig	18 Feb
17.08i	Torie	Owers	NZL	6.3.94	1		Seattle	25 Feb
17.08	Haley	Teel	USA	20.6.96	2		Baton Rouge	29 Apr
17.07	Toni	Tupper	USA	3.11.95	5q	NCAA-W	Austin	27 May
17.06i	Agnieszka	Maluskiewicz	POL	18.3.89	2	NC	Torun	18 Feb
17.06		Meng Qianqian	CHN	6.1.91	7	NG	Tianjin	6 Sep
	(90)							
17.05	Sarah	Schmidt	GER	9.7.97	5		Schönebeck	2 Jun
17.04	Sarah	Howard	CAN	11.10.93	2		Knoxville	7 Apr
17.03	Sophie	McKinna	GBR	31.8.94	5	ECp-w	Las Palmas	11 Mar
17.01i	Irina	Kirichenko	RUS	18.5.87	1		Irkutsk	14 Jan
17.00	Lena	Giger	USA	7.6.96	6q	NCAA-W	Austin	27 May
16.97	Ischke	Senekal	RSA	8.1.93	1	NC	Potchefstroom	21 Apr
16.94		Dong Yangzi	CHN	22.10.92	7	NGPF	Guiyang	27 Jun
16.93i	Giedre	Kupstyte	LTU	9.3.92	1		Vilnius	28 Jan
16.92	Yiliena	Otamendi	CUB	12.4.96	1		Las Tunas	18 Feb
16.92	Mel	Herl	USA	14.2.94	1		Seward	12 May
	(100)							

Mark	Name		Nat	Born	Date
16.90i	Jessica	Inchude	GBS	25.3.96	11 Feb
16.90	Portious	Warren	TTO	2.3.96	4 May
16.89i	Anna	Rüh	GER	17.6.93	18 Feb
16.89	Jorinde	van Klinken	NED-Y	2.2.00	22 Jul
16.86	Tanya	Sapa	USA	13.6.95	25 Mar
16.84i	Nikki	Okwelogu	NGR	5.5.95	29 Jan
16.83	Alysiah	Whittaker	USA	17.3.95	13 May
16.81		Lee Mi-young	KOR	19.8.79	2 Jul
16.80i	Amber	Monroe	USA	14.10.93	18 Feb
16.79	Annette	Echikunwoke	USA	29.7.96	15 Apr
16.78	Kearsten	Peoples	USA	20.12.91	20 May
16.78	Samantha	Noennig	USA-J	28.7.98	23 Jun
16.77	Evaggelía	Sofáni	GRE	28.1.85	23 Apr
16.77	Keely	Medeiros	BRA	30.4.87	3 Jun
16.76	Natalya	Troneva	RUS	24.3.93	26 May
16.75	Emmaline	Berg	USA	27.9.91	24 Mar
16.71i	Sade	Olatoye	USA	25.1.97	24 Feb
16.69	Michaela	Dendinger	USA	9.5.95	27 May
16.68		Rong Jun	CHN	7.4.89	19 May
16.67	Elena	Bruckner	USA-J	14.4.98	29 Apr
16.66	Julie	Lange	USA	21.7.95	1 Apr
16.64	Khayla	Dawson	USA-J	18.3.98	15 Apr
16.64	Divine	Oladipo	GBR-J	5.10.98	22 Apr
16.59i	Trine	Mulbjerg	DEN	23.4.90	18 Feb

Mark	Name		Nat	Born	Date
16.59	Christine	Bohan	USA	14.7.95	8 Jun
16.57	Nanaka	Kori	JPN	2.5.97	8 Sep
16.57	Ahymara	Espinoza	VEN	28.5.85	21 Nov
16.56i	Laura	Jokeit	GER	16.8.95	5 Feb
16.53i	Yelena	Bezruchenko	RUS	23.7.96	10 Feb
16.53i	Sarah	Mitton	CAN	20.6.96	2 Dec
16.52	Eden	Francis	GBR	19.10.88	3 Jun
16.50i	Nickolette	Dunbar	USA-J	5.4.98	17 Feb
16.49	Anna	Niedbala	POL-J	10.7.98	29 Jul
16.47	Yelena	Smolyanova	UZB	16.2.86	11 May
16.47	Aya	Ota	JPN	13.4.95	14 May
16.47		Zhang Linru	CHN-J	23.9.99	19 May
16.46	Angela	Rivas	COL	13.8.89	25 Mar
16.43	Obeng	Marfo	CAN	11.4.96	14 May
16.40	Katelyn	Daniels	USA	11.4.95	24 Mar
16.38i	Tori	Bliss	USA	1.12.92	4 Feb
16.37	Brittany	Cox	USA	18.4.88	15 Apr
16.35i	Lenuta	Burueana	ROU	29.4.96	29 Jan
16.35i	Aliyah	Gustafson	USA	3.5.95	8 Dec
16.34		Sun Yue	CHN-Y	19.6.01	27 May
16.34	Magdalena	Zebrowska	POL	11.1.91	21 Jul
16.33	Ashley	Davis	USA	10.5.85	6 May
16.31i	Jolien	Boumkwo	BEL	27.8.93	29 Jan
16.30i	Alyssa	Robinson	USA	10.5.95	28 Jan
16.29i	Kätlin	Piirimäe	EST	8.11.95	3 Mar
16.28	Kathleen	Young	USA-J	31.7.99	3 Jun
16.27	Meia	Gordon	USA-J	12.3.98	13 May
16.27	Adele	Nicoll	GBR	28.9.96	21 May
16.26	Gabriella	Fella	CYP-J	21.1.98	29 Apr
16.24	Jessica	Schilder	NED-J	19.3.99	15 Jul
16.23i	Indi	Jackson	USA		18 Feb
16.22	Brianna	Cueva	USA	6.6.95	12 May
16.19i	Maja	Slepowronska	POL-J	2.12.98	12 Feb
16.19	Tochi	Nlemchi	USA	–.95	18 Mar
16.19	Ivana	Gallardo	CHI	20.3.93	9 Apr
16.18	Saily	Viart	CUB	10.9.95	27 May
16.16i	LaPorscha	Wells	USA	25.10.94	22 Jan
16.16i	Makenzie	Wheat	USA	25.8.94	10 Feb
16.16	Lauren	Evans	USA		27 May
16.14		Xu Jiaqi	CHN	3.2.95	27 Jun
16.13		Chen Xiarong	CHN-J	21.12.98	13 Apr
16.13	Michaela	Walsh	IRL-J	17.12.98	17 Jun
16.07	Viktoriya	Klochko	UKR	2.9.92	5 Jul
16.06i	Breana	Jemison	USA	11.12.93	21 Jan
16.06i	Kristine	Hanks	USA	–.95	10 Feb
16.06i		Wang Xiaoyun	CHN	7.12.93	20 Feb
16.05		Jiang Yue	CHN-J	6.10.98	5 Jun
16.04	Yemisi	Ogunleye	GER-J	3.10.98	28 May
16.04		Lee Su-kyung	KOR	15.2.93	22 Oct
16.00	Anouk	Vetter	NED	4.2.93	13 May
16.00i	Jaynee	Corbett	USA		1 Dec
15.99	Brashe	Wood	USA		14 May
15.99		Lin Chia-Ying	TPE	5.11.82	24 Oct
15.98i	Taylor	Potts	USA	1.7.95	25 Feb
15.96i	Ásdís	Hjálmsdóttir	ISL	28.10.85	18 Feb
15.96	Brenn	Flint	USA	9.6.97	27 May
(180)					

Best outdoors

Mark	Name	Pos	Meet	Venue	Date
18.64	Johnson	5	NC	Sacramento	24 Jun
18.48	Stevens	1		Kawasaki	21 May
17.81	Mavrodieva	2	ET-1	Vaasa	25 Jun
17.72	Ewen	2q	NCAA-W	Austin	27 May
17.62	Vita	1		Neubrandenburg	17 May
17.61	Kenzel	1c2		Schapbach	25 Jun
17.50	Cérival	2	ECp-w	Las Palmas	11 Mar
17.49	Mann	3	NCAA	Eugene	8 Jun
17.48	Hillman	5		Rathdrum	4 Jun
17.39	M Warren	6		Tucson	20 May
17.39	Cameron	5q	NCAA-E	Lexington	27 May
17.33	Hicks	2	Big 12	Lawrence	13 May
16.98	Pete	1	MWC	Logan	13 May
16.98	Maisch	6		Osterode	9 Jun

Mark	Name	Date
16.89	Terlecki	9 Jul
16.76	Skarvélis	18 Jun
16.74	Owers	30 Apr
16.69	Olatoye	14 May
16.65	Sabin	14 May
16.60	Inchude	23 Jun
16.50	Skujyte	2 Jun
16.45	Okwelogu	7 May
16.43	Dunbar	27 May
16.32	Mitton	27 Aug
16.30	Robinson	25 Mar
16.30	Kupstyte	27 May
16.17	Maluskiewicz	12 May
16.09	Bezruchenko	20 Jun
16.07	Piirimäe	15 Jul
15.96	Jackson	8 Apr

Pending doping case

Mark	Name		Nat	Born	Pos	Meet	Venue	Date
18.86	Manpreet	Kaur ¶	IND	6.7.90	(1)	AsiGP	Jinhua	24 Apr

JUNIORS

See main list for top 3 juniors. 10 performances (4 indoors) by 4 women to 16.89. Additional marks and further juniors:

Name	Mark	Pos	Venue	Date	Mark	Pos	Venue	Date
Wilson	17.51i	1	New York (A)	28 Feb	17.13i	1	Toms River	11 Jan
	17.40	1	Jackson NJ.	13 May	17.02i	1	Farmingdale	24 Jan
Orozco	17.13	7	Tucson	20 May	17.05	7	Tucson	18 May

Mark	Name		Nat	Born	Pos	Meet	Venue	Date
16.89	Jorinde	van Klinken	NED-Y	2.2.00	2	EJ	Grosseto	22 Jul
16.78	Samantha	Noennig	USA	28.7.98	1	NC-j	Sacramento	23 Jun
16.67	Elena	Bruckner	USA	14.4.98	1		Austin	29 Apr
16.64	Khayla	Dawson	USA	18.3.98	2		Louisville	15 Apr
16.64	Divine	Oladipo	GBR	5.10.98	2		Princeton	22 Apr
16.50i	Nickolette	Dunbar	USA	5.4.98	1		Baton Rouge	17 Feb
16.49	Anna	Niedbala (10)	POL	10.7.98	2	Skol	Cetniewo	29 Jul
16.47		Zhang Linru	CHN	23.9.99	7	NC	Jinan	19 May
16.34		Sun Yue	CHN-Y	19.6.01	1		Neubrandenburg	27 May
16.28	Kathleen	Young	USA	31.7.99	1		Rathdrum	3 Jun
	15.84				1		Moweaqua	28 Apr
16.27	Meia	Gordon	USA	12.3.98	3	Big 12	Lawrence	13 May
16.26	Gabriella	Fella	CYP	21.1.98	1	NC-j	Nicosia	29 Apr
16.24	Jessica	Schilder	NED	19.3.99	2	NC	Utrecht	15 Jul
16.19i	Maja	Slepowronska	POL	2.12.98	1	NC-j	Torun	12 Feb
16.13		Chen Xiarong	CHN	21.12.98	5	NGP	Zhengzhou	13 Apr
16.13	Michaela	Walsh	IRL	17.12.98	1	Eng-j	Bedford	17 Jun
16.05		Jiang Yue (20)	CHN	6.10.98	2	NC-j	Ordos	5 Jun

DISCUS

Mark	Name		Nat	Born	Pos	Meet	Venue	Date
71.41	Sandra	Perkovic	CRO	21.6.90	1		Bellinzona	18 Jul

					69.08	71.41	65.77	66.87	69.02	70.05
70.83	1	Hanz	Zagreb	29 Aug	x	63.31	66.90	68.07	70.83	70.44
70.31	1	WCh	London (OS)	13 Aug	69.30	70.31	70.28	69.81	x	x
70.23	1	NC-w	Split	25 Feb	64.08	69.24	69.99	69.81	x	x
69.67	Q	WCh	London (OS)	11 Aug	x	69.67				

WOMEN 2017

Mark	Name		Nat	Born	Pos	Meet	Venue	Date

Perkovic 69.58 1 Velenje 20 Jun 64.15 67.62 x 69.58 69.53 68.74
68.82 1 VD-DLF Bruxelles 1 Sep 60.43 x 68.82 x 68.68 x
68.30 2 Sotteville-lès-Rouen 7 Jul 65.73 68.04 67.80 x 68.30 x
67.75 2 DL Stockholm 18 Jun 67.61 x x x 67.75 x
67.51 1 DL Birmingham 20 Aug 61.78 62.49 67.22 x x 67.51
66.94 1 DL Shanghai 13 May 62.73 66.94 x x x x
66.79 1 Bisl Oslo 15 Jun x 65.37 x 66.79 64.92 64.83
69.64 Dani Stevens AUS 26.5.88 2 WCh London (OS) 13 Aug
64.23 65.46 x 66.82 66.59 69.64
68.29 1 Bad Köstritz 25 Aug x 63.08 68.29 x 65.31 65.47
66.78 1 Sydney 25 Feb 63.13 x x 63.51 65.84 66.78
66.78 1 Geelong 19 Mar 61.56 x 65.11 x 66.78 66.50
66.47 2 DL Shanghai 13 May 63.53 x 66.47 63.82 65.18 61.06
65.85 2 VD-DLF Bruxelles 1 Sep 65.85 x x 63.84 x 63.75
69.19 Yaimé Pérez CUB 29.5.91 1 Sotteville-lès-Rouen 7 Jul
65.39 66.10 66.08 67.33 65.70 69.19
67.92 1 DL Stockholm 18 Jun 67.92 64.83 x 65.67 66.87 64.06
67.50 1 Bilbao 24 Jun 62.30 67.50 60.98 66.10 x 67.28
66.24 2 Bisl Oslo 15 Jun 66.24 x 65.06 65.51 x 65.40
65.83 1 Barr La Habana 26 May 63.08 64.92 64.55 65.51 65.83 65.78
67.04 Denia Caballero CUB 13.1.90 1 Leiria 30 Jul
x 64.21 x 67.04 x x
66.51 1 Leiria 29 Jul 66.51 65.51 x 62.37 x x
65.76 3 DL Shanghai 13 May 65.76 62.99 x x x 62.54
66.21 Mélina Robert-Michon FRA 18.7.79 3 WCh London (OS) 13 Aug
65.49 62.54 x 61.88 65.39 66.21
65.81 Gia Lewis-Smallwood USA 1.4.79 1 Rathdrum 2 Jun
63.48 63.32 61.12 65.81 x 63.53
65.76 Nadine Müller GER 21.11.85 1 Werfer Halle 20 May
62.82 62.10 63.13 64.09 63.47 65.76
65.74 3 DL Stockholm 18 Jun 62.09 62.63 65.74 65.72 62.29 62.20
(30/7)

Mark	Name		Nat	Born	Pos	Meet	Venue	Date
64.69	Valarie	Allman	USA	23.2.95	1		Stanford	22 Apr
64.68	Andressa	de Morais	BRA	21.12.90	1	SAmC	Asunción	23 Jun
64.56		Su Xinyue	CHN	8.11.91	1	NG	Tianjin	5 Sep
	(10)							
64.46		Feng Bin	CHN	3.4.94	2	NG	Tianjin	5 Sep
64.45	Claudine	Vita	GER	19.9.96	1		Neubrandenburg	27 May
64.09	Nataliya	Semenova	UKR	7.7.82	1		Kyiv	30 Jun
63.90	Anna	Rüh	GER	17.6.93	3	Werfer	Halle	20 May
63.85	Whitney	Ashley	USA	18.2.89	1		La Jolla	21 Apr
63.63	Julia	Harting	GER	1.4.90	1	NC	Erfurt	9 Jul
63.18	Shanice	Craft	GER	15.5.93	3		Schönebeck	2 Jun
62.90		Chen Yang	CHN	10.7.91	2	NGP	Huaian	4 Apr
62.89	Kristin	Pudenz	GER	9.2.93	3		Wiesbaden	13 May
62.73	Kellion	Knibb	JAM	25.12.93	1	NC	Kingston	23 Jun
	(20)							
62.64	Yelena	Panova	RUS	2.3.87	1	NC-w	Adler	16 Feb
62.63	Irina	Rodrigues	POR	5.2.91	2		Leiria	29 Jul
62.59	Shadae	Lawrence	JAM	31.12.95	1	Big 12	Lawrence	14 May
62.58		Lu Xiaoxin	CHN	22.2.89	4	NG	Tianjin	5 Sep
62.30	Fernanda Raquel	Borges	BRA	26.7.88	2		Leiria	30 Jul
62.15	Jade	Lally	GBR	30.3.87	1		Sydney	5 Feb
61.66	Tara-Sue	Barnett	JAM	9.10.93	2		Tucson	18 May
61.57	Dragana	Tomasevic	SRB	4.6.82	1	NC	Krusevac	10 Jun
61.53	Hrisoúla	Anagnostopoúlou	GRE	27.8.91	1		Kavála	22 Jul
61.48	Zinaida	Sendriüte	LTU	20.12.84	Q	WCh	London (OS)	11 Aug
	(30)							
61.35	Liz	Podominick	USA	5.12.84	1		Chula Vista	14 May
61.16	Kelsey	Card	USA	20.8.92	2		La Jolla	21 Apr
61.07	Sabina	Asenjo	ESP	3.8.86	4		Leiria	30 Jul
60.83		Yang Yanbo	CHN	9.3.90	5	NG	Tianjin	5 Sep
60.79	Summer	Pierson	USA	3.9.78	1		Salinas	27 May
60.65		Tan Jian	CHN	20.1.88	6	NG	Tianjin	5 Sep
60.51	Maggie	Ewen	USA	23.9.94	2		Chula Vista	20 Apr
60.29	Pauline	Pousse	FRA	17.9.87	2		Montgeron	14 May
60.13	Karen	Gallardo	CHI	6.3.84	1		Santiago de Chile	18 Mar
59.94	Taryn	Gollshewsky	AUS	18.5.93	1		Brisbane	14 Jan
	(40)							
59.69	Zaneta	Glanc	POL	11.3.83	1		Lódz	20 May
59.38	Kayla	Hopkins	USA	23.4.96	2q	NCAA-W	Austin	26 May

Mark	Name		Nat	Born	Pos	Meet	Venue	Date
59.37	Laulauga	Tausaga-Collins	USA-J	22.5.98	3q	NCAA-W	Austin	26 May
59.31	Danniel	Thomas-Dodd	JAM	11.11.92	1	MAC	Kalamazoo	13 May
59.31	Yuliya	Maltseva	RUS	30.11.90	2		Adler	25 May
59.23	Daria	Zabawska	POL	16.4.95	2q	EU23	Bydgoszcz	13 Jul
58.97	Venique	Harris	JAM	29.2.96	5		Chula Vista	20 Apr
58.90A	Eliska	Stanková	CZE	11.11.84	1		Potchefstroom	4 Apr
58.84	Isheka	Binns	JAM	9.1.96	2	NC	Kingston	23 Jun
58.75	Katelyn	Daniels	USA	11.4.95	1		Ashland	15 Jun
	(50)							
58.75	Samantha	Hall	JAM	19.4.93	3	NC	Kingston	23 Jun
58.62	Lidia	Augustyniak	POL	14.5.94	2		Kielce	13 May
58.57	Anita	Márton	HUN	15.1.89	1		Debrecen	21 May
58.48	Rachel	Dincoff	USA	24.12.93	7		Rathdrum	2 Jun
58.48	Veronika	Domjan	SLO	3.9.96	3	EU23	Bydgoszcz	14 Jul
58.41		Liang Yan	CHN	2.1.95	3	NGP	Chengdu	31 Mar
58.38		Xie Yuchen	CHN	12.5.96	3	NGP	Huaian	4 Apr
58.24		Yang Fei	CHN	20.7.87	2	NC	Jinan	18 May
58.23	Gabi	Jacobs	USA	20.8.96	5q	NCAA-W	Austin	26 May
58.07	Natalya	Shirobokova	RUS	18.1.94	2	NC	Zhukovskiy	28 Jul
	(60)							
58.06	Daisy	Osakue	ITA	16.1.96	1		Boissano	27 Jul
58.05	Valentina	Aniballi	ITA	19.4.84	1		Rieti	14 Jun
58.01	Svetlana	Serova	BLR	28.8.86	1		Mogilyov	20 Jan
57.97	Corinne	Nugter	NED	28.3.92	Q	NC	Utrecht	14 Jul
57.88	Kimberley	Mulhall	AUS	9.1.91	2		Geelong	19 Mar
57.66	Lidia	Cansian	BRA	8.1.92	3		São Bernardo do Campo	3 May
57.57	Yuliya	Savinova	RUS	28.6.94	4		Adler	25 May
57.55	Te Rina	Keenan	NZL	29.9.90	1		Hamilton	4 Feb
57.53	Eden	Francis	GBR	19.10.88	1		Nuneaton	11 Jun
57.51	Sarah	Thornton	USA	29.8.86	1		Chelmsford	7 Jun
	(70)							
57.46	Joanna	Wisniewska	POL	24.5.72	4	NC	Bialystok	23 Jul
57.39	Salla	Sipponen	FIN	13.3.95	1		Kokemäki	1 Jul
57.38	Marike	Steinacker	GER	4.3.92	6		Wiesbaden	13 May
57.32	Kristina	Rakocevic	MNE-J	13.6.98	1		Bar	18 Jun
57.21	Stefania	Strumillo	ITA	14.10.89	1		Arezzo	25 Jun
57.16	Cion	Hicks	USA	14.10.94	2	Big 12	Lawrence	14 May
57.10	Alexandra	Emilianov	MDA-J	19.9.99	1	NC-w	Chisinau	5 Feb
57.05	Mel	Herl	USA	14.2.94	1		Kearney	15 Apr
57.02	Agnes	Esser	CAN	22.8.95	1	KansR	Lawrence	22 Apr
57.02	Gleneve	Grange	JAM	6.7.95	2	ACC	Atlanta	14 May
	(80)							
57.01	Rocío	Comba	ARG	14.7.87	1		Resistencia	13 May
56.84	Serena	Brown	BAH-J	15.9.98	1		Baton Rouge	28 Apr
56.82	Subenrat	Insaeng	THA	10.2.94	2	AsiC	Bhubaneswar	9 Jul
56.80	Anna	Jelmini	USA	15.7.90	2	Scott	Irvine	29 Apr
56.80	Yekaterina	Burmistrova	RUS	18.8.90	1		Sankt Peterburg	27 Jun
56.75	Micaela	Hazlewood	USA	18.6.95	1		Louisville	15 Apr
56.75	Sarah	Hillman	USA	1.1.97	1		Newark	6 May
56.66	Julie	Hartwig	GER	30.6.94	7		Wiesbaden	13 May
56.64	Jessica	Woodard	USA	4.2.95	6q	NCAA-W	Austin	26 May
56.52	Liliana	Cá	POR	5.11.86	1		Leiria	22 Jun
	(90)							
56.39	Janeah	Stewart	USA	21.7.96	3	FlaR	Gainesville	31 Mar
56.37	Svetlana	Saykina	RUS	10.7.85	2	NC-w	Adler	16 Feb
56.30	June	Kintana	ESP	12.4.95	4	EU23	Bydgoszcz	14 Jul
56.25	Julia	Bremser	GER	27.4.82	1		Frankenberg	28 May
56.16	Izabela	da Silva	BRA	2.8.95	4		São Bernardo do Campo	3 May
56.11	Siositina	Hakeai	NZL	1.3.94	Q	AUS Ch	Sydney	31 Mar
56.08	Brianna	Cueva	USA	6.6.95	8		La Jolla	21 Apr
56.07	Viktoriya	Klochko	UKR	2.9.92	2	NC-w	Mukachevo	15 Feb
56.04	Ischke	Senekal	RSA	8.1.93	Q	WUG	Taipei	23 Aug
55.99	Alexandra	Morgan	ASA	19.5.91	8		Rathdrum	2 Jun
	(100)							

Mark	Name		Nat	Born	Date
55.95	Kamalpreet	Kaur	IND	4.3.96	23 Aug
55.93	Alex	Meyer	USA	8.4.96	25 Mar
55.93	Alex	Collatz	USA	25.5.93	29 Apr
55.88	Andrea	Alarcón	ESP	3.12.94	12 Mar
55.80	Meia	Gordon	USA-J	12.3.98	14 May
55.70	Giada	Andreutti	ITA	16.2.95	11 May
55.68	Kätlin	Tõllasson	EST	4.6.93	28 Jun
55.66		Li Tsai-Yi	TPE	3.12.89	30 Apr
55.61	Rosalina	Alvarez	CUB	3.1.97	14 Mar
55.56	Nikki	Okwelogu	NGR	5.5.95	26 May
55.51	Ailén	Armada	ARG-J	3.10.98	22 Apr
55.48	Alyssa	Wilson	USA-J	20.2.99	6 May
55.43	Julia	Ritter	GER-J	13.5.98	20 May
55.42	Irène	Donzelot	FRA	8.12.88	16 Jul
55.38	Sabine	Rumpf	GER	18.3.83	13 May
55.32	Katelyn	Weimerskirch	USA	28.2.94	26 May

Mark	Name		Nat	Born	Date
55.20	Melanie	Pingeon	FRA	4.11.86	24 Jun
55.19	Alena	Belyakova	RUS-J	21.12.98	15 Jul
55.18	Paula	Ferrándiz	ESP	4.1.96	24 Jun
55.17	Katrine	Bebe	DEN	27.1.91	9 Jul
55.16	Michelle	Wallerstedt	USA	15.4.94	26 May
55.15	Becky	Famurewa	USA	24.2.94	13 May
55.08	Claudia	Ababio	GHA	15.10.96	8 Apr
55.08	Chinwe	Okoro	NGR	20.6.89	29 Apr
55.07	Barbara	Coward	USA	,97	11 Mar
54.95	Lloydricia	Cameron	USA	8.4.96	25 Mar
54.91	Raven	Saunders	USA	15.5.96	25 Mar
54.91	Kirsty	Law	GBR	11.10.86	19 Jul
54.91	Vanessa	Kamga	SWE-J	19.11.98	15 Aug
54.74	Aixa	Middleton	PAN	6.2.88	22 Nov
54.72	Natalina	Capoferri	ITA	6.11.92	14 May
54.71	Mariya	Ogritsko	RUS	1.3.94	10 Jun
54.67	Helena	Leveelahti	FIN-J	30.9.99	20 Jul
54.65	Stephanie	Brown Trafton	USA	1.12.79	21 Apr
54.64	Elena	Bruckner	USA-J	14.4.98	1 Apr
54.64	Mariah	Garcia	USA	26.12.93	21 Apr
54.62	Ieva	Zarankaite	LTU	23.11.94	14 May
54.60	Melissa	Ausman	USA	26.4.95	2 Jun
54.55	Johana	Martínez	COL	9.9.86	18 Mar
54.55	Emmonnie	Henderson	USA	5.11.94	26 May
54.54	Rachel	Andres	CAN	21,4,87	18 Jun
54.53		Wang Jiangmei	CHN	5.10.96	12 Apr
54.49	Ivana	Muzaric	CRO	9.6.96	22 Apr
54.43	Jontavia	Dykes	USA	1.1.95	26 May
54.37	Shanice	Love	JAM	9.6.97	10 Jun
54.36	Marie-Francine	Mvoto Abeng	FRA	3.1.87	16 Jul
54.34		Li Shanshan	CHN	6.1.92	30 Mar
54.33	Molli	Detloff	USA	15.1.96	18 Mar
54.31	Anastasiya	Vityugova	RUS	13.3.97	22 Apr
54.30		Gu Siyu	CHN	11.2.93	3 Sep
54.27	Amy	Holder	GBR	4.8.96	29 May
54.27	Monika	Nowak	POL	11.7.95	13 Jul
54.19	Fiona	Richards	JAM-J	20.11.98	15 Apr
54.18	Katarzyna	Mos	POL	20.12.94	14 Jun
54.15	Sasha Gaye	Marston	JAM	26.2.93	21 Apr
54.14	Ashley	Anumba	USA-J	11.6.99	2 Jun
54.11	Seema	Antil	IND	27.7.83	28 Dec
54.11	Julie	Lange	USA	21.7.95	22 Apr
54.10	Zakiya	Rashid	USA	1.2.97	31 Mar
54.08	Mariya	Telushkina	KAZ	3.4.94	13 Jun
54.06	Stamatía	Skarvélis	GRE	17.8.95	28 Apr
54.03	Lisa Brix	Pedersen	DEN	16.5.96	2 Sep
54.02	Nanaka	Kori	JPN	2.5.97	27 May
53.97		Yang Huanhuan	CHN-Y	3.1.00	19 Aug
53.95	Marija	Tolj	CRO-J	29.11.99	10 Jun
53.94	Pamela	Amaechi	USA-J	12.3.99	3 Jun
53.92	Norma	Cunigan	USA	25.6.97	25 May
53.90	Aleksandra	Grubba	POL	19.6.96	20 May
53.88	Karolina	Urban	POL-J	18.10.98	21 Jul
53.86	Josie	Natrasevschi	USA	13.8.96	7 May
53.79	Androniki	Lada	CYP	19.4.91	12 Mar
53.77	Jorinde	van Klinken	NED-Y	2.2.00	21 May
53.71	Fanny	Roos	SWE	2.1.95	27 Aug
53.68	Alma	Pollorena (174)	MEX-J	17.9.98	22 Jul

JUNIORS

See main list for top 4 juniors. 10 performances by 4 women to 55.90. Additional marks and further juniors:

Tausaga-Collins	59.29	1	PAm-J	Trujillo	22 Jul	56.10	4	FlaR	Gainesville	31 Mar
Rakocevic	56.05	1		Bar	18 Mar					
Emilianov	56.38	1	EJ	Grosseto	21 Jul	55.91	1	NC	Tiraspol	27 May
	56.35	1	Balk-J	Pitesti	1 Jul					

Mark	Name		Nat	Born	Pos	Meet	Venue	Date
55.80	Meia	Gordon	USA	12.3.98	3	Big 12	Lawrence	14 May
55.51	Ailén	Armada	ARG	3.10.98	1		Mar del Plata	22 Apr
55.48	Alyssa	Wilson	USA	20.2.99	1		Glassboro	6 May
55.43	Julia	Ritter	GER	13.5.98	1	Werfer-j	Halle	20 May
55.19	Alena	Belyakova	RUS	21.12.98	4	NCp	Yerino	15 Jul
54.91	Vanessa	Kamga (10)	SWE	19.11.98	1		Huddinge	15 Aug
54.67	Helena	Leveelahti	FIN	30.9.99	Q	EJ	Grosseto	20 Jul
54.64	Elena	Bruckner	USA	14.4.98	1	TexR	Austin	1 Apr
54.19	Fiona	Richards	JAM	20.11.98	1	Carifta	Willemstad	15 Apr
54.14	Ashley	Anumba	USA	11.6.99	1		Clovis	2 Jun
53.97		Yang Huanhuan	CHN-Y	3.1.00	1	NGY	Weinan	19 Aug
53.95	Marija	Tolj	CRO	29.11.99	1		Zagreb	10 Jun
53.94	Pamela	Amaechi	USA	12.3.99	2		Clovis	3 Jun
53.88	Karolina	Urban	POL	18.10.98	2	EJ	Grosseto	21 Jul
53.77	Jorinde	van Klinken	NED-Y	2.2.00	1	Werfer-y	Halle	21 May
53.68	Alma	Pollorena (20)	MEX	17.9.98	2	PAm-J	Trujillo	22 Jul

HAMMER

Mark											
82.87	Anita		Wlodarczyk	POL	8.8.85	1	Skol	Cetniewo		29 Jul	
					80.42	82.87	80.69	80.73	81.63	x	
	80.79	1	NC	Bialystok	23 Jul	70.18	78.59	78.63	80.79	78.52	78.35
	79.80	1	Skol	Warszawa	15 Aug	76.60	79.80	77.30	79.23	77.33	77.99
	79.73	1	DL	Doha	6 May	76.46	x	79.73	x	79.06	77.32
	79.72	1	GS	Ostrava	27 Jun	75.62	79.68	79.07	79.72	76.76	79.27
	78.00	1		São Bernardo do Campo	3 Jun	75.46	78.00	x	75.88		
	77.90	1	WCh	London (OS)	7 Aug	70.45	x	71.94	77.39	77.90	73.91
	77.77	1	Gyulai	Székesfehérvár	3 Jul	75.47	77.67	77.77	77.39	77.34	73.82
	77.07	1	Kuso	Szczecin	10 Jun	77.07	76.48	77.00	x	76.48	75.98
	76.32	1	Werfer	Halle	20 May	72.65	76.32	75.08	74.52	73.98	73.62
	75.69	1		Forbach	28 May	71.76	74.78	74.78	73.64	73.54	75.69
	75.45	1	PTS	Samorín	17 Jun	x	75.11	73.86	74.86	75.45	x
	74.61	Q	WCh	London (OS)	5 Aug	74.61					
76.85	Malwina		Kopron	POL	16.11.94	1	WUG	Taipei		26 Aug	
					76.85	x	74.78	x	x	73.78	
	75.40	2	Skol	Warszawa	15 Aug	74.73	x	75.40	73.00	x	70.71
	75.11	2	NC	Bialystok	23 Jul	75.11	74.72	73.57	73.76	x	72.86
	74.97	Q	WCh	London (OS)	7 Aug	74.97					
	74.76	3	WCh	London (OS)	7 Aug	74.76	x	x	x	69.90	71.66

Mark	Name		Nat	Born	Pos	Meet	Venue	Date
76.77	Gwen	Berry	USA	29.6.89	1		Oxford, USA	6 May
				76.77 76.04 72.27 x x 74.81				
	74.77 1 NC Sacramento		25 Jun	71.73 74.77 72.31 74.44 72.29 73.45				
	74.62 1 MSR Walnut		13 Apr	x 73.17 74.41 x 74.62 73.62				
76.25		Wang Zheng	CHN	14.12.87	2	GS	Ostrava	27 Jun
75.48		Zhang Wenxiu	CHN	22.3.86	1	NG	Tianjin	6 Sep
				74.76 x 75.48 x x 72.42				
75.29	Hanna	Skydan	AZE	14.5.92	1	Isl.Sol	Baku	16 May
				??				
75.09	Joanna	Fiodorow	POL	4.3.89	2	Skol	Cetniewo	29 Jul
				x 74.06 x 73.39 75.09 72.81				
74.94	Hanna	Malyshik	BLR	4.2.94	1	NCp	Brest	1 Jun
74.91	DeAnna	Price	USA	8.6.93	1		Sacramento (CS)	10 Jun
	(30/9)			70.91 71.75 x 74.91 73.81 73.47				
74.56	Maggie	Ewen	USA	23.9.94	2	NC	Sacramento	25 Jun
	(10)							
73.97	Sophie	Hitchon	GBR	11.7.91	2		Kawasaki	21 May
73.80	Zalina	Petrivskaya	MDA	5.2.88	1	NC-w	Chisinau	4 Feb
73.58	Amber	Campbell	USA	5.6.81	4	NC	Sacramento	25 Jun
72.69	Alexandra	Tavernier	FRA	13.12.93	Q	WCh	London (OS)	5 Aug
72.53	Iryna	Klymets	UKR	4.10.94	1		Kyiv	21 May
72.50	Jillian	Weir	CAN	9.2.93	1		Tucson	18 May
72.37	Alyona	Shamotina	UKR	27.12.95	1		Kyiv	30 Jun
72.27		Luo Na	CHN	8.10.93	2	NG	Tianjin	6 Sep
72.06	Amanda	Bingson	USA	20.2.90	2	MSR	Torrence	13 Apr
71.88	Kıvılcım	Salman-Kaya	TUR	27.3.92	1		Bursa	7 Jul
	(20)							
71.73	Yelizaveta	Tsareva	RUS	15.3.93	1		Zhukovskiy	24 Jun
71.68		Liu Tingting	CHN	29.1.90	3	NG	Tianjin	6 Sep
71.58	Marina	Nikisenko	MDA	28.6.86	2	NC	Chisinau	26 May
71.56	Jeneva	Stevens	USA	28.10.89	1		Rathdrum	3 Jun
71.52	Ida	Storm	SWE	26.12.91	2		Fränkisch-Crumbach	4 Jun
71.40	Yelena	Krechik	BLR	20.7.87	1		Minsk	13 Jun
71.34	Katerina	Safránková	CZE	8.6.89	8	WCh	London (OS)	7 Aug
71.27	Réka	Gyurátz	HUN	31.5.96	1		Szombathely	21 Jun
71.25	Susen	Küster	GER	27.7.94	1		Halle	21 Jul
71.18	Iryna	Novozhylova	UKR	7.1.86	1		Kyiv	14 Jun
	(30)							
71.06	Kathrin	Klaas	GER	6.2.84	2	ECp-w	Las Palmas	11 Mar
70.35	Julia	Ratcliffe	NZL	14.7.93	1		Princeton	16 Jul
70.30	Carolin	Paesler	GER	16.12.90	1		Fränkisch-Crumbach	15 Jul
70.26	Berta	Castells	ESP	24.1.84	1		Manresa	15 Jul
70.18	Jennifer	Dahlgren	ARG	27.8.84	1		Buenos Aires	22 Apr
70.01	Marinda	Petersson	SWE	3.2.95	4	Werfer	Halle	20 May
69.60	Katarzyna	Furmanek	POL	19.2.96	5	Kuso	Szczecin	10 Jun
69.44	Bianca	Ghelber-Perie	ROU	1.6.90	1	NC	Pitesti	7 Jul
69.32	Sofiya	Palkina	RUS-J	9.6.98	2		Zhukovskiy	16 Jun
69.16	Heavin	Warner	USA	4.3.93	6	NC	Sacramento	25 Jun
	(40)							
69.10	Nataliya	Zolotuhina	UKR	4.1.85	2		Kyiv	30 Jun
68.90	Nikola	Lomnická	SVK	16.9.88	1		Szombathely	19 Jul
68.66	Alex	Hulley	AUS	24.7.97	1		Sydney	6 Aug
68.62	Brooke	Andersen	USA	23.8.95	2	NCAA	Eugene	8 Jun
68.55	Merja	Korpela	FIN	15.5.81	1		Kaustinen	1 Jul
68.55	Tereza	Králová	CZE	22.10.89	1		Kladno	15 Jul
68.44	Laura	Igaune	LAT	2.10.88	1		Durham	21 Apr
68.37	Britney	Henry	USA	17.10.84	7	NC	Sacramento	25 Jun
68.36	Jessica	Ramsey	USA	26.7.91	2		Tucson	18 May
68.27	Krista	Tervo	FIN	15.11.97	2		Kaustinen	1 Jul
	(50)							
68.24	Sara	Fantini	ITA	16.9.97	1		Modena	2 Jun
68.15	Tugçe	Sahutoglu	TUR	1.5.88	2		Bursa	7 Jul
68.01	Sultana	Frizell	CAN	24.10.84	4		Tucson	20 May
67.86	Martina	Hrasnová	SVK	21.3.83	2	NC	Banská Bystrica	1 Jul
67.70	Alina	Shayunova	BLR	2.3.90	2	NCp	Brest	1 Jun
67.66	Alina	Duran	USA	28.3.90	2		Princeton	16 Jul
67.57	Iryna	Sekachyova	UKR	21.7.76	4		Kyiv	14 Jun
67.55	Cintia	Gergelics	HUN	16.11.91	2		Szombathely	29 Apr
67.45	Laura	Redondo	ESP	3.7.88	1		Barcelona	5 Feb
67.42	Beatrice Nedberge	Llano	NOR	14.12.97	3	NCAA	Eugene	8 Jun
	(60)							

Mark	Name		Nat	Born	Pos	Meet	Venue	Date
67.39	Anna Maria	Orel	EST	11.12.96	1	NC	Tallinn	23 Jul
67.31	Anna	Bulgakova	RUS	17.1.88	2		Adler	7 Feb
67.22	Camille	Sainte-Luce	FRA	18.4.96	1		Eaubonne	14 Jun
67.20	Katerina	Skypalová	CZE-J	20.2.99	1	NC-23	Praha	2 Sep
67.15		Wang Lu	CHN	22.12.91	2	NC	Jinan	18 May
67.08	Johanna	Salmela	FIN	6.11.90	4	vSWE	Stockholm	3 Sep
67.02	Mariana Grasielly	Marcelino	BRA	16.7.92	1	NC	São Bernardo do Campo	9 Jun
66.97	Janee'	Kassanavoid	USA	19.1.95	1		Austin	14 Apr
66.90	Lara	Nielsen	AUS	19.12.92	1		Sydney	26 Feb
66.80	Charlene	Woitha	GER	21.8.93	5		Fränkisch-Crumbach	4 Jun
	(70)							
66.68	Carly	Fehringer	USA	9.11.91	1		Kearney	15 Apr
66.66	Freya	Block	USA	6.2.95	3q	NCAA-W	Austin	25 May
66.50	Johana	Moreno	COL	15.4.85	1	NC	Medellín	10 Jun
66.46	Rachel	Hunter	GBR	30.8.93	1		Loughborough	26 Feb
66.35	Trude	Raad	NOR	27.4.90	1		Samsun	23 Jul
66.31	Rosa	Rodríguez	VEN	2.7.86	1	Bol G	Santa Marta	24 Nov
66.11	Anastasiya	Maslova	BLR	16.10.97	2		Minsk	13 Jun
66.06	Veronika	Kanuchová	SVK	19.4.93	3	NC	Banská Bystrica	1 Jul
65.89	Lauren	Stuart	CAN	16.11.91	2		Tempe	7 Apr
65.85	Ayamey	Medina	CUB-J	21.2.98	1		La Habana	25 Feb
	(80)							
65.83		Yan Ni	CHN	7.2.93	4	NGP	Chengdu	27 Mar
65.83	Iliána	Korosídou	GRE	14.1.95	1		Thessaloníki	27 May
65.82	Monique	Griffiths	USA	10.8.94	1	Big West	Fullerton	12 May
65.81	Natalya	Pospelova	RUS	28.6.96	3	NC	Zhukovskiy	28 Jul
65.78	Viktoriya	Sadova	RUS	18.3.93	3		Adler	25 May
65.75	Sophie	Gimmler	GER	18.3.96	1		Fränkisch-Crumbach	4 Jun
65.67	Anastasiya	Shkuratova	RUS-J	29.12.99	3		Zhukovskiy	24 Jun
65.63	Mayra	Gaviria	COL	22.5.97	1		Bogotá	22 Apr
65.39	LaPorscha	Wells	USA	25.10.94	2	FlaR	Gainesville	31 Mar
65.32	Carys	Parry	GBR	24.7.81	1	Welsh	Cardiff	10 Jun
	(90)							
65.27	Mel	Herl	USA	14.2.94	1	NCAA-II	Bradenton	26 May
65.26	Stamatía	Skarvélis	GRE	17.8.95	1		Baton Rouge	28 Apr
65.25	Sarita	Prakash Singh	IND	26.10.89	1	Fed Cup	Patiala	1 Jun
65.21	Akane	Watanabe	JPN	13.8.91	8		Kawasaki	21 May
65.04	Laëtitia	Bambara	BUR	30.3.84			Bobigny	7 Jan
64.98	Molli	Detloff	USA	15.1.96	5q	NCAA-W	Austin	25 May
64.97	Bianca	Lazar	ROU	24.2.93	2	NC-w	Bucuresti	28 Feb
64.96	Agata	Zienkowicz	POL	17.12.95	1		Zielona Góra	25 May
64.91	Katelyn	Weimerskirch	USA	28.2.94	6q	NCAA-W	Austin	25 May
64.86	Eleni	Larsson	SWE	4.4.93	3cB	ECp-w	Las Palmas	11 Mar
	(100)							

Mark	Name		Nat	Born	Date
64.71	Osarumen	Odeh	ESP	15.11.95	27 Jul
64.70	Rymma	Filimoshkina	UKR	15.4.86	1 Apr
64.69	Janeah	Stewart	USA	21.7.96	31 Mar
64.69	Emma	Thor	SWE	20.11.97	31 Mar
64.61	Suvi	Koskinen	FIN	24.4.97	18 Feb
64.61	Nicole	Zihlmann	SUI	30.7.86	4 Jun
64.59	Inga	Linna	FIN	21.2.95	1 Jul
64.53	Éva	Orbán	HUN	29.11.84	1 May
64.48	Vanessa	Sterckendries	BEL	15.9.95	5 Jun
64.44	Nicole	Bradley	NZL	23.4.92	16 Dec
64.35	Marika	Kaczmarek	POL	25.4.96	1 Jul
64.25	Grete	Ahlberg	SWE-J	29.5.98	3 Sep
64.19	Tatyana	Kachegina	RUS	6.2.89	1 Jul
64.14	Helene Sofie	Ingvaldsen	NOR	22.6.96	25 May
64.11	Lisa	Wilson	USA	29.3.88	30 Apr
64.03	Whitney	Simmons	USA		27 May
64.01	Temilola	Ogunrinde	USA	29.2.96	25 May
63.96	Claudia	Stravs	SLO	11.2.94	27 May
63.96	Zeliha	Uzunbilek	TUR	10.6.91	15 Jun
63.95	Soukana	Zakkour	MAR	13.10.93	19 Mar
63.91	Annette	Echikunwoke	USA	29.7.96	15 Apr
63.89	Francesca	Massobrio	ITA	9.7.93	8 Jul
63.88	Anamari	Kozul	CRO	20.1.96	27 May
63.86		Zong Dan	CHN	19.1.95	25 Jun
63.82	Letitia	Janse van Vuuren	RSA	24.4.96	28 Mar
63.77	Viktoriya	Sakhno	UKR	18.12.97	14 Jun
63.75	Jolien	Boumkwo	BEL	27.8.93	2 Jul
63.56	Anastasiya	Mazurina	BLR	21.2.93	28 Apr
63.54	Michaela	Dendinger	USA	9.5.95	12 May
63.47	Jenni	Penttilä	FIN	9.3.91	1 Jul
63.46	Frida	Bååth	SWE	5.7.97	20 May
63.45	Pavla	Kuklová	CZE	1.11.96	8 Jun
63.43	Erin	Reese	USA	14.1.95	22 Apr
63.42	Camryn	Rogers	CAN-J	7.6.99	23 Jul
63.41	Alison	Ondrusek	USA	22.1.96	7 Apr
63.41	Sarah	Holt	GBR	17.4.87	22 Jul
63.34	Alena	Lysenko	RUS	3.2.88	28 Jul
63.32	Hitomi	Katsuyama	JPN	21.5.94	23 Jun
63.26	Wendy	Koolhaas	NED	2.1.80	3 Jun
63.20		Zhou Mengyuan	CHN-J	3.9.99	3 Jun
63.19	Kinga	Lepkowska	POL	30.4.97	27 May
63.17	Linnéa	Jönsson	SWE	1.10.95	12 May
63.15	Danielle	McConnell	AUS	11.1.94	25 May
63.13		Li Yumao	CHN	28.3.93	31 Mar
63.09	Eva	Mustafic	CRO-J	27.2.98	22 Jul
63.07	Anastasiya	Borodulina	RUS-J	7.11.98	6 Feb
63.05	Jessica	Mayho	GBR	14.6.93	22 Apr
63.02	Kati	Ojaloo	EST	31.1.90	1 Jul
63.01	Michaela	Walsh	IRL-J	17.12.98	1 Jul
62.98	Anna	Zayanchovskaya	BLR	9.7.96	16 Feb
62.98	Kelcey	Bedard	USA	10.4.96	5 May
62.97	Myra	Perkins	GBR	21.1.92	16 Jul
62.96	Christina	Jones	GBR	5.4.90	13 May
62.89	Lenka	Valesová	CZE	11.8.85	15 Jul
62.86	Hana	Feilzer	USA	8.8.96	13 May
62.81		Shang Ningyu	CHN-J	26.5.98	27 Mar
62.79	Jennifer	Batu	CGO	24.10.93	27 Jul
62.78		Xu Xinying	CHN	17.2.97	11 Apr
62.78	Jasmine	Manigault	USA	15.5.95	14 Apr
62.74	Lucy	Marshall	GBR	28.11.81	10 Jun

Mark	Name		Nat	Born	Date
62.73	Katharina	Mähring	GER	12.6.95	21 May
62.73	Aleksandra	Smiech	POL	2.10.97	23 Jul
62.72		Xie Qiao	CHN	12.3.94	30 Mar
62.69	Jamesia	Milton	USA	13.3.94	12 May
62.67	Tiina	Rinnekari	FIN	24.10.96	29 Jun
62.63	Zouina	Bouzebra	ALG	3.10.90	21 May
62.56	Aleksandra	Kokowska	POL	28.4.95	28 May
62.51	Destiney	Coward	USA		12 May
62.38	Sina Mai	Holthuijsen	NED	17.7.96	17 Jun
62.36	Melissa	Coquillas	FRA-J	2.1.98	7 May
62.33	Lorelei	Taillandier	FRA	8.8.91	6 May
62.29	Anna Paula	Pereira	BRA	7.8.86	30 Apr
62.28	Aline	Salut	FRA	30.7.92	7 May
62.28		Chen Luxia	CHN	14.3.93	9 May
62.27	Johanna	Witka	FIN-J	21.12.98	9 Aug
62.23	Audrey	Ciofani	FRA	13.3.96	7 Oct
62.07	Susan	McKelvie	GBR	15.6.85	6 May
62.04	Sarah	Pate	USA		22 Apr
62.04	Nadia	Maffo	ITA	6.6.96	28 Apr
62.03	Leia	Mistowski	USA	8.11.96	5 May
62.02	Suzuka	Asada	JPN	18.10.87	23 Jun
	(180)				

Irregular conditions

64.62	Anamari	Kozul	CRO	20.1.96	4 Jun

JUNIORS

See main list for top 4 juniors. 11 performances by 1 woman to 67.60. Additional marks and further juniors:

Palkina	69.19	2		Zhukovskiy	24 Jun	68.56	1		Adler	6 Feb
	68.90	2	NCp	Yerino	15 Jul	68.42	2	NC	Zhukovskiy	28 Jul
	68.82	1	NC-wj	Adler	16 Feb	68.15	1		Maykop	22 May
	68.74	2	Znam	Zhukovskiy	1 Jul	67.93	1	NC-23	Saransk	21 Jun
	68.59	1	NC-19	Kaluga	3 Jul	67.91	2		Adler	25 May

64.25	Grete	Ahlberg	SWE	29.5.98	5	vFIN	Stockholm	3 Sep
63.42	Camryn	Rogers	CAN	7.6.99	1	PAm-J	Trujillo	23 Jul
63.20		Zhou Mengyuan	CHN	3.9.99	1	NC-j	Ordos	3 Jun
63.09	Eva	Mustafic	CRO	27.2.98	2	EJ	Grosseto	22 Jul
63.07	Anastasiya	Borodulina	RUS	7.11.98	2j		Adler	6 Feb
63.01	Michaela	Walsh (10)	IRL	17.12.98	1	NC-j	Tullamore	1 Jul
62.81		Shang Ningyu	CHN	26.5.98	6	NGP	Chengdu	27 Mar
62.36	Melissa	Coquillas	FRA	2.1.98	1		Bordeaux	7 May
62.27	Johanna	Witka	FIN	21.12.98	1		Turku	9 Aug
61.50	Joy	McArthur	USA	5.7.99	1		Chula Vista	27 May
61.47	Ana Adela	Stanciu	ROU-Y	13.6.00	1	Balk-J	Pitesti	2 Jul
61.25	Anna	Grigoryeva	RUS	14.8.98	2	NC-wj	Adler	16 Feb
60.99	Grace	Wong Xiu Mei	MAS-Y	18.1.00	1		Mokpo	7 Apr
60.84	Valeriya	Ivanenko	UKR-Y	16.8.01	1		Nova Kakhovka	1 Apr
60.83	Mariana	García	CHI	19,3,99	4		Buenos Aires	30 Mar
60.61	Kiira	Väänänen (20)	FIN	6.1.99	2		Kaustinen	29 Jun

JAVELIN

68.43	Sara			Kolak	CRO	22.6.95	1	Athl	Lausanne		6 Jul
						63.94	64.64	66.65	x	65.78	68.43
	67.83	2	DL	London (OS)	9 Jul	56.63	66.79	67.83	65.24	60.09	65.64
	65.12	1	EU23	Bydgoszcz	16 Jul	63.12	65.12	x	61.22	61.02	64.69
	64.95	4	WCh	London (OS)	8 Aug	x	64.95	x	57.38	63.50	x
	65.23	1	NC-w	Split	25 Feb	61.21	61.39	x	62.54	62.06	65.23
	64.64	3	Pre	Eugene	26 May	x	60.66	64.64	58.83	62.07	x
68.26	Barbora			Spotáková	CZE	30.6.81	1	DL	London (OS)		9 Jul
						62.62	65.42	65.79	66.34	p	68.26
	67.40	2	Athl	Lausanne	6 Jul	67.40	63.50	p	62.12	x	64.59
	66.76	1	WCh	London (OS)	8 Aug	58.48	66.76	x	65.64	62.57	63.75
	65.54	1	WK	Zürich	24 Aug	x	62.85	61.10	65.54		
	65.14	1	ET	Villeneuve d'Ascq	25 Jun	62.17	63.81	x	65.14		
67.59				Lu Huihui	CHN	26.6.89	Q	WCh	London (OS)		6 Aug
						67.59					
	65.26	3	WCh	London (OS)	8 Aug	62.71	62.44	61.95	60.87	65.26	58.30
67.21	Eda			Tugsuz	TUR	27.3.97	1	Isl.Sol	Baku		18 May
						67.21	x	p	p	p	p
	64.87	1		Ankara	6 Jun	x	64.87	p	p		
66.47				Liu Shiying	CHN	24.9.93	1		Kawasaki		21 May
						63.75	63.00	66.47	x	x	p
	65.47	1	NGP	Chengdu	27 Mar	65.47	60.37	p	p	p	p
	65.21	2	Pre	Eugene	26 May	61.26	58.20	65.21	x	p	p
	64.72	Q	WCh	London (OS)	6 Aug	x	58.89	64.72			
66.30	Tatyana			Kholodovich	BLR	21.6.91	1	Pre	Eugene		26 May
						66.30	63.30	65.10	66.02	63.57	64.58
	65.88	1	NC-w	Minsk (Staiki)	16 Feb	62.10	65.88	x	p	63.26	65.88
	65.60	1		Brest	28 Apr	64.74	65.60	65.34	64.54	c	64.52
	65.03	1	PNG	Turku	13 Jun	64.62	62.42	65.03	62.45	x	61.73
	64.60	2	ET	Villeneuve d'Ascq	25 Jun	64.60	62.67	x	60.90		
66.25				Li Lingwei	CHN	26.1.89	2	WCh	London (OS)		9 Aug
						61.81	63.01	66.25	65.38	x	64.88
66.12	Kathryn			Mitchell	AUS	10.7.82	3	Athl	Lausanne		6 Jul
						61.71	60.74	64.91	61.94	66.12	61.11

WOMEN 2017

Mark	Name		Nat	Born	Pos	Meet	Venue	Date
65.64	Martina	Ratej	SLO	2.11.81	Q	WCh	London (OS)	6 Aug
				65.64				
64.85	3 DL	London (OS)	9 Jul	57.92	64.85	x	x x	58.51
65.37	Katharina	Molitor (10)	GER	8.11.83	Q	WCh	London (OS)	6 Aug
				61.76	65.37			
64.80	Kara	Winger	USA	10.4.86	1		Austin	14 Apr
	(31/11)			64.80	x	59.12	x 63.07	60.89)
64.53	Kelsey-Lee	Roberts	AUS	21.9.91	2	WK	Zürich	24 Aug
64.47	Liz	Gleadle	CAN	5.12.88	4	DL	London (OS)	9 Jul
64.47	Anete	Kocina	LAT	5.2.96	2	EU23	Bydgoszcz	16 Jul
64.18	Christin	Hussong	GER	17.4.94	1		Luzern	11 Jul
63.92	Madara	Palameika	LAT	18.6.87	1		Jelgava	18 Jun
63.49A	Sunette	Viljoen	RSA	6.1.83	1	NC	Potchefstroom	21 Apr
63.43	Ásdís	Hjálmsdóttir	ISL	28.10.85	1		Joensuu	12 Jul
63.31	Marcelina	Witek	POL	2.6.95	1	WUG	Taipei	25 Aug
63.28	Sigrid	Borge	NOR	3.12.95	1		Bærum	17 Jun
	(20)							
63.07	Margaryta	Dorozhon	ISR	4.9.87	1	Macc	Jerusalem	13 Jul
62.52	Laila	Silva-Domingos	BRA	30.7.82	1	NC	São Bernardo do Campo	11 Jun
62.48	Flor Dennis	Ruiz	COL	24.1.91	1	Bol G	Santa Marta	24 Nov
62.37	Marina	Saito	JPN	15.10.95	2	WUG	Taipei	25 Aug
62.24	Nikola	Ogrodníková	CZE	18.8.90	4	Odlozil	Praha	5 Jun
62.02	Vera	Rebrik	RUS	25.2.89	1	NCp	Yerino	14 Jul
61.95	Yuki	Ebihara	JPN	28.10.85	1	Nambu	Sapporo	9 Jul
61.86	Annu	Rani	IND	29.8.92	1	Fed Cup	Patiala	4 Jun
61.38	Ariana	Ince	USA	14.3.89	1		East Stroudsburg	9 Jul
61.32	Liina	Laasma	EST	13.1.92	1		Tallinn	19 May
	(30)							
61.32		Zhang Li	CHN	17.1.89	3	NG	Tianjin	3 Sep
61.24		Du Xiaowei	CHN	11.8.87	Q	NG	Tianjin	2 Sep
61.07	Haruka	Kitaguchi	JPN-J	16.3.98	1		Matsuyama	8 Oct
60.98	Jenni	Kangas	FIN	3.7.92	3	WUG	Taipei	25 Aug
60.68	Anna	Wessman	SWE	9.10.89	1		Linköping	25 May
60.55	Lina	Müze	LAT	4.12.92	3	NC	Ogre	29 Jul
60.48	Hanna	Hatsko-Fedusova	UKR	3.10.90	1		Kyiv	30 Jun
60.24	Liveta	Jasiūnaite	LTU	26.7.94	1	NC	Palanga	21 Jul
60.03	Risa	Miyashita	JPN	26.4.84	4		Kawasaki	21 May
59.94	Mikako	Yamashita	JPN	3.5.97	2		Matsuyama	8 Oct
	(40)							
59.35	Viktoriya	Yermakova	BLR	18.1.95	Q	EU23	Bydgoszcz	15 Jul
59.32	Nafissatou	Thiam	BEL	19.8.94	1H	Hypo	Götzis	28 May
59.28	Zahra	Bani	ITA	31.12.79	1		Rieti	12 Feb
59.23	Sofía	Ifantídou	GRE	5.1.85	1	NC	Pátra	17 Jun
59.21		Su Lingdan	CHN	12.1.97	1		Jinan	4 Mar
59.10	Yuka	Mori	JPN	21.7.92	4	NC	Osaka	24 Jun
59.03	Daniela Mieko	Nisimura	BRA	26.3.94	1		São Bernardo do Campo	25 Mar
58.97	Sofi	Flink	SWE	8.7.95	7	PNG	Turku	13 Jun
58.95	Oona	Sormunen	FIN	2.8.89	2		Lahti	9 Jun
58.90	Yulenmis	Aguilar	CUB	3.8.96	1	NC	La Habana	16 Mar
	(50)							
58.79	Annabella	Bogdán	HUN	7.4.92	1	NC	Székesfehérvár	10 Jun
58.76	Margaux	Nicollin	FRA	1.5.95	1		Vénissieux	12 Feb
58.76	Irena	Sedivá	CZE	19.1.92	1	NCAA	Eugene	8 Jun
58.72	Lisanne	Schol	NED	22.6.91	1	NC	Utrecht	16 Jul
58.58	Marija	Vucenovic	SRB	3.4.93	2	NCAA	Eugene	8 Jun
58.55	Heidi	Nokelainen	FIN	30.9.90	2		Pihtipudas	2 Jul
58.51	Coralys	Ortiz	PUR	16.4.85	6	Odlozil	Praha	5 Jun
58.49	Réka	Szilágyi	HUN	19.1.96	1		Vác	1 Oct
58.41	Anouk	Vetter	NED	4.2.93	1H	WCh	London (OS)	6 Aug
58.34	Victoria	Hudson	AUT	28.5.96	1		Wien	15 Aug
	(60)							
58.33	Tetyana	Fetiskina	UKR	11.9.94	2		Kyiv	30 Jun
58.31	Géraldine	Ruckstuhl	SUI-J	24.2.98	2H	Hypo	Götzis	28 May
58.28	Tatyana	Korzh	BLR	17.3.93	2		Brest	28 Apr
58.23	Rebekah	Wales	USA	2.10.95	1	SEC	Columbia SC	13 May
58.18	Christine	Winkler	GER	4.5.95	1		Offenburg	13 May
58.15	Kelechi	Nwanaga	NGR	24.12.97	1		Ozoro	18 Jul
58.11	H.L. Dilhani	Lekamge	SRI	14.1.87	2	AsiC	Bhubaneswar	6 Jul
58.00	Anna	Tarasyuk	BLR	30.10.97	6	EU23	Bydgoszcz	16 Jul
57.97	Lidia	Parada	ESP	11.6.93	1	NC	Barcelona	22 Jul
57.95	Estefany	Chacón (70)	VEN	1.11.97	1	NC	Barinas	24 Sep

Mark		Name	Nat	Born	Pos	Meet	Venue	Date
57.84	Bernarda	Letnar	SLO	26.12.89	2		Celje	21 May
57.77	Rafaela	Gonçalves	BRA	27.11.91	2		São Bernardo do Campo	13 May
57.67	Kiho	Kuze	JPN	28.3.95	1		Osaka	21 May
57.64	Indre	Jakubaityte	LTU	24.1.76	4		Jelgava	18 Jun
57.58		Yang Xinli ¶	CHN	7.2.88	4	NGP	Chengdu	27 Mar
57.44	Shiori	Toma	JPN	7.2.96	1		Miyazaki	18 Aug
57.32		Zhu Dandan	CHN	1.3.94	4	NC	Jinan	17 May
57.21	Paola	Padovan	ITA	4.12.95	1	NC-23	Firenze	9 Jun
57.16	Simona	Dobilaite	LTU	23.5.95	2		Riga	19 May
57.02	Jo-Ané	van Dyk	RSA	3.10.97	9	WUG	Taipei	25 Aug
	(80)							
56.96	Dana	Bergrath	GER	24.4.94	1		Pfungstadt	2 Aug
56.93	Ashley	Pryke	CAN	7.7.97	3	NCAA	Eugene	8 Jun
56.92	Jelena	Jaakkola	FIN	7.3.89	3		Vantaa	27 May
56.91	Eloah Caetano	Scramin	BRA	8.6.96	3	NC	São Bernardo do Campo	11 Jun
56.89	Arantxa	Moreno	ESP	16.1.95	1		Pamplona	27 Jul
56.88	Svetlana	Pechnikova	RUS	6.9.94	2	NC-w	Adler	17 Feb
56.84	Nikol	Tabacková	CZE-J	24.1.98	1		Breclav	6 May
56.84	Tori	Peeters	NZL	17.5.94	1		Dunedin	28 Oct
56.82	Hitomi	Sukenaga	JPN	4.5.88	7	NC	Osaka	24 Jun
56.61	Alexie	Alais	FRA	9.10.94	1		St-Louis	16 Jun
	(90)							
56.57		Yu Yuzhen	CHN-J	5.3.98	2	NGP	Chengdu	31 Mar
56.54	Alina	Shukh	UKR-J	12.2.99	3		Lutsk	6 Jun
56.47	Jatta-Mari	Jääskeläinen	FIN	27.2.94	3		Raasepori	4 Jun
56.46		Chen Chen	CHN	19.1.96	3	NGP	Taiyuan	9 May
56.44	Sae	Takemoto	JPN-J	1.1.99	1		Yamagata	1 Aug
56.32	Laura	Ikauniece-Admidina	LAT	31.5.92	2		Tallinn	19 May
56.31	Hiroko	Takigawa	JPN	25.7.94	3		Hiratsuka	9 Jun
56.24	Klaudia	Maruszewska	POL	28.8.97	6		Ogre	25 May
56.24		Kim Kyung-ae	KOR	5.3.88	1	NSF	Chongju	23 Oct
56.20	Saara	Lipsanen	FIN	13.9.95	1	NC-23	Kauhava	4 Aug
	(100)							

Mark		Name	Nat	Born	Date
56.15	Carolina	Visca	ITA-Y	31.5.00	28 Apr
56.12	Sanni	Utriainen	FIN	5.2.91	2 Jul
56.08	Nuttha	Nacharn	THA	4.6.90	12 Jun
56.06	Malin	Haglund	SWE	25.10.88	26 Aug
56.03		Jin Pingping	CHN	23.8.93	3 Sep
55.94	Maggie	Malone	USA	30.12.93	20 May
55.94	Alexia	Kogut Kubiak	FRA	22.1.88	21 Jun
55.88	Poonam	Rani	IND	10.5.94	27 Sep
55.80	Marisleisys	Duarthe	CUB-Y	17.9.00	28 May
55.79		Wu You	CHN	18.12.92	3 Sep
55.74	Laura	Whittingham	GBR	6.6.86	29 Aug
55.71	Sanobar	Erkinova	UZB-J	16.12.98	29 Mar
55.60	Mackenzie	Little	AUS	22.12.96	31 Mar
55.55	Valeriya	Kuchina	RUS-J	12.8.98	23 Apr
55.47	Berivan	Sakır	TUR	22.9.93	19 Feb
55.47	Katie	Reichert	USA	22.8.93	14 Apr
55.47	Theodóra	Arabatzí	GRE	2.5.97	29 Jul
55.37	Audrey	Malone	USA	16.6.95	17 Mar
55.37		Peng Juanhong	CHN	8.8.93	17 May
55.31	Madalaine	Stulce	USA	15.8.96	13 May
55.25		Cai Qing	CHN-Y	8.3.00	17 May
55.25	Luz Mariana	Castro	MEX	23.1.97	17 Jun
55.24	Kseniya	Zybina	RUS	1.2.89	29 Jul
55.23		Suh Hae-an	KOR	1.7.85	23 Oct
55.22	Mariya	Safonova	RUS	28.10.94	23 Apr
55.16	Kim	Hamilton	USA	28.11.85	7 Apr
55.16A	Maria Lucelly	Murillo	COL	5.5.91	1 Jul
55.03	Suman	Devi	IND	15.7.85	4 Jun
55.03	Jarmila	Jurkovicová	CZE	9.2.81	2 Jul
54.94	Orie	Ushiro	JPN	24.8.90	8 Oct
54.88	Mahiro	Osa	JPN-J	26.11.99	20 Mar
54.86	Laura	Paredes	PAR	30.8.96	23 Jun
54.77	Sara	Jemai	ITA	12.4.92	17 Sep
54.69	Hirono	Nakata	JPN	.97	23 Jul
54.68	Tatjana	Mirkovic	SRB	10.8.90	23 Jul
54.67	Luziana	Tomé	BRA	1.8.85	11 Jun
54.60	Kato	Van Den Brulle	BEL	29.10.96	7 May
54.54	Kathryn	Brooks	AUS	11.11.97	26 Feb
54.50	Yuka	Kuwazoe	JPN-J	1.2.99	6 May
54.48	Brittni	Wolczyk	CAN	10.9.97	14 May
54.46	Kamila	Zdybal	POL	18.3.94	21 Jul
54.44	Katja	Mihelic	SLO	11.7.95	11 Mar
54.40	Jaimee	Springer	CAN	21.2.92	7 Jul
54.40		Jiang Chenxi	CHN		17 Jul
54.39		Li Huei-Chun	TPE-J	12.5.99	6 Jul
54.30	Elina	Kinnunen	FIN-J	5.1.99	4 Jun
54.29	Eleonora	Bacciotti	ITA	13.12.89	23 Apr
54.28	Marta	Kakol	POL	25.2.92	17 Jun
54.26	Katelyn	Gochenour	USA-J	23.2.98	8 Jun
54.24	Lyubov	Zhatkina	RUS	30.3.90	14 Jan
54.24		Dai Qianqian	CHN-Y	23.8.00	30 Mar
54.23		Chang Chunfeng	CHN	4.5.88	4 Apr
54.20	Svetlana	Parfyonova	BLR	30.10.87	16 Feb
54.19	Ikumi	Tatebayashi	JPN	.96	8 Oct
54.18	Stephanie	Wrathall	NZL	25.12.89	19 Nov
54.14	Gundega	Griva	LAT	8.4.91	23 Aug
54.09A	Merly	Cabrera	COL	29.8.96	1 Oct
54.04	Mirell	Luik	EST	3.1.97	22 Jul
54.02	Arina	Demeshenok	BLR	25.7.96	5 Jul
54.00	Haruka	Matoba	JPN	24.4.87	18 Mar
54.00	Julieth	Angulo	ECU-Y	2.1.01	4 Jun
53.96		Sun Xiaomei	CHN	2.12.96	11 Apr
53.90		Zhuoma Renqing	CHN	9.6.99	27 Mar
53.82	Mathilde	Andraud	FRA	28.4.89	14 Jul
53.82	Kanaki	Asano	JPN	1.1.96	8 Sep
53.81	Kristina	Kristianslund	NOR	25.6.93	26 Aug
53.80		Han Hyo-hee	KOR	3.6.86	7 Jul
53.78	Momone	Ueda	JPN-J	1.1.99	15 Jun
53.77	Estefanía	López	ESP	10.7.94	8 Apr
53.76	Sharmila	Kumari	IND	2.3.95	27 Sep
53.68	Elisabeth	Lithell	SWE	19.2.90	6 Jun
53.64	Laura	Pesola	FIN	12.5.96	4 Aug
53.59	Carolin	Näslund	SWE-J	23.1.98	6 Jun
53.56	Yekaterina	Starygina	RUS	26.8.95	14 Jul
53.54	Nika	Ouellette	USA	23.4.92	22 Jun
53.52 ?	Jo	Blair	GBR	1.3.86	29 Apr
53.50	Daliadiz	Ortiz	PUR	6.10.94	13 May
53.49	Monique	Cilione	AUS	19.11.94	18 Feb
53.48		Lee Hye-lim	KOR	6.3.89	4 Jun
53.47	Dalila	Rugama	NCA	9.4.84	10 Dec
53.44	Franja	Zelimorski	CRO-J	13.11.98	1 Jul
53.41	Julia	Valtanen	FIN-Y	6.5.01	4 Jun

Mark	Name		Nat	Born	Date
53.41	Lisa	Weißbach	GER-Y	10.2.98	11 Jun
53.39	Riko	Nishimura	JPN	1.11.93	18 Oct
53.38	Marcella	Liiv	EST-J	17.6.98	10 Sep
53.37	Kylee	Carter	USA	10.6.97	24 Mar
53.28	Kisumi	Miyamoto	JPN	4.5.91	29 Apr
53.25	Mayu	Oshiro	JPN	.96	23 Jul
53.20	Antoinette	Nana Djimou	FRA	2.8.85	14 Jul
53.18	Alyssa	Olin	USA	14.7.96	14 Apr
53.17	Athanasía	Kókkali	GRE	26.8.97	22 Jul
53.14	Akane	Koyama	JPN	2.9.96	9 Jun
53.12	Sarah	Blake	USA	30.6.97	13 May
53.11	Mercedes	Chilla	ESP	19.1.80	10 Jun
53.09	Haley	Crouser	USA	11.2.94	8 Jun
53.09		Bui Thi Xuan	VIE	29.12.89	27 Oct
53.07	Yuji	Katsuno	JPN	8.5.96	3 Nov
53.05	Krista	Woodward	CAN	22.11.84	28 Jun
53.05	Rosmary	Luján	VEN	10.10.93	24 Sep
53.04	Anastasiya (200)	Zaytseva	UZB	20.9.92	29 Mar
53.03	Channing	Wilson	USA	2.8.93	22 Jun
53.02	Violene	Granger	FRA	18.7.94	16 Jun
53.00	Suvi	Kemppainen	FIN-J	25.1.98	2 Jul

JUNIORS

See main list for top 6 juniors. 10 performances by 4 women to 56.57. Additional marks and further juniors:

Kitaguchi	60.49	1	Fukui	8 Sep	57.96	Q	WUG	Taipei	23 Aug
	59.59	5	Kawasaki	21 May	57.74	6	NC	Osaka	24 Jun
	59.08	2	Hiratsuka	9 Jun	57.46	1		Hiratsuka	22 Jul

Mark	Name		Nat	Born	Pos	Meet	Venue	Date
56.15	Carolina	Visca	ITA-Y	31.5.00	1		Firenze	28 Apr
55.80	Marisleisys	Duarthe	CUB-Y	17.9.00	1	Barr	La Habana	28 May
55.71	Sanobar	Erkinova	UZB	16.12.98	1	NC-j	Tashkent	29 Mar
55.55	Valeriya	Kuchina (10)	RUS	12.8.98	1j		Adler	23 Apr
55.25		Cai Qing	CHN-Y	8.3.00	6	NC	Jinan	17 May
54.88	Mahiro	Osa	JPN-J	26.11.99	1		Wakayama	20 Mar
54.50	Yuka	Kuwazoe	JPN-J	1.2.99	1		Tsukuba	6 May
54.39		Li Huei-Chun	TPE-J	12.5.99	6	AsiC	Bhubaneswar	6 Jul
54.30	Elina	Kinnunen	FIN-J	5.1.99	4		Raasepori	4 Jun
54.26	Katelyn	Gochenour	USA-J	23.2.98	6	NCAA	Eugene	8 Jun
54.24		Dai Qianqian	CHN-Y	23.8.00	7q	NGP	Chengdu	30 Mar
54.00	Julieth	Angulo	ECU-Y	2.1.01	1	SAm-J	Leonora	4 Jun
53.78	Momone	Ueda	JPN-J	1.1.99	1		Fukuoka	15 Jun
53.59	Carolin	Näslund (230)	SWE-J	23.1.98	3		Södertälje	6 Jun

INDOOR PENTATHLON

Mark	Name		Nat	Born	Pos	Meet	Venue	Date
4870	Nafissatou	Thiam	BEL	19.8.94	1	EI	Beograd	3 Mar
	8.23 1.96 15.29 6.37 2:24.44							
4767	Ivona	Dadic	AUT	29.12.93	2	EI	Beograd	3 Mar
	8.45 1.87 13.93 6.41 2:14.13							
4723	Györgyi	Zsivoczky-Farkas	HUN	13.2.85	3	EI	Beograd	3 Mar
	8.47 1.81 14.95 6.38 2:15.86							
4686#	Kendell	Williams	USA	14.6.95	1	SEC	Nashville	25 Feb
	8.04 1.84 12.66 6.49 2:19.65							
4682		Williams			1	NCAA	College Station	10 Mar
	8.03 1.78 12.96 6.43 2:15.61							
4631	Xénia	Krizsán	HUN	13.1.93	4	EI	Beograd	3 Mar
	8.30 1.81 14.24 6.09 2:15.08							
4582	Nadine	Broersen	NED	29.4.90	5	EI	Beograd	3 Mar
	8.42 1.81 14.59 6.19 2:20.63							
4580	Taliyah	Brooks	USA	8.2.95	2	NCAA	College Station	10 Mar
	8.13 1.84 11.97 6.33 2:22.39							
4558A	Erica	Bougard	USA	26.7.93	1	NC	Albuquerque	3 Mar
	8.21 1.87 11.97 6.18 2:18.41							
4550	Alina	Shukh	UKR-J	12.2.99	1		Zaporizhzhya	27 Jan
	8.85 1.88 14.27 6.04 2:17.69							
4542		Shukh			1		Tallinn	4 Feb
	8.98 1.89 13.81 6.12 2:16.84							
4533		Krizsán			1	NC	Budapest (BH)	11 Feb
	8.42 1.73 14.31 6.17 2:15.23							
4520		Dadic			1	NC	Wien	5 Feb
	8.51 1.76 13.17 6.24 2:13.53							
4486	Verena	Preiner (10)	AUT	1.2.95	1		Linz	15 Jan
	8.65 1.72 14.21 6.06 2:11.21							
4478		Preiner			6	EI	Beograd	3 Mar
	8.45 1.72 14.14 5.86 2:10.26							
4476		Williams			1		Fayetteville	27 Jan
	8.17 1.82 12.05 6.20 2:21.28							
4473	Lecabela	Quaresma	POR	26.12.89	1	NC	Bordeaux	18 Feb
	8.54 1.76 14.29 6.06 2:17.60							
4452	Yana	Maksimova	BLR	9.1.89	1		Mogilyov	25 Jan
	8.94 1.85 14.71 5.93 2:20.29							
4450#		Brooks			2	SEC	Nashville	25 Feb
	8.14 1.69 11.53 6.30 2:22.22							

Mark		Name	Nat	Born	Pos	Meet	Venue	Date
4444		Quaresma			7	EI	Beograd	3 Mar
	8.52 1.78 14.25 5.82 2:16.49							
4438		Maksimova			8	EI	Beograd	3 Mar
	8.85 1.87 14.01 5.69 2:16.00							
4428	Nadine	Visser	NED	9.2.95	1	NC	Apeldoorn	5 Feb
	8.01 1.68 13.61 6.18 2:21.90							
4409	Lucie	Slanicková	SVK	8.11.88	9	EI	Beograd	3 Mar
	8.60 1.78 11.30 6.35 2:15.40							
4404A	Sharon	Day-Monroe	USA	9.6.85	2	NC	Albuquerque	3 Mar
	8.56 1.75 14.44 5.85 2:17.55							
	(24/15)							
4389	Bianca	Salming	SWE-J	22.11.98	10	EI	Beograd	3 Mar
	8.87 1.81 13.59 5.67 2:11.44							
4379#	Leigha	Brown	USA	19.9.94	3	SEC	Nashville	25 Feb
	8.41 1.75 13.05 5.91 2:16.41							
	4257				3		Fayetteville	27 Jan
	8.58 1.73 12.75 5.77 2:16.23							
4376#	Barbara	Nwaba	USA	18.1.89	1		Seattle	27 Jan
	8.50 1.82 13.93 5.38 2:14.33							
4367	Mariya	Pavlova	RUS	21.5.96	1	NC	Smolensk	15 Feb
	8.62 1.84 12.95 5.90 2:21.47							
4340	Nina	Schultz	CAN-J	12.11.98	3	NCAA	College Station	10 Mar
	8.41 1.81 12.14 6.18 2:26.55							
(20)								
4319	Michelle	Atherley	USA	9.12.95	4	NCAA	College Station	10 Mar
	8.21 1.75 12.69 5.67 2:17.05							
4309	Elena	Panturoiu	ROU	24.2.95	1	NC	Bucuresti	11 Feb
	8.60 1.80 11.61 6.06 2:19.33							
4302	Caroline	Agnou	SUI	26.5.96	1	NC	Magglingen	5 Feb
	8.51 1.72 14.30 5.86 2:22.72							
4301	Laura	Arteil	FRA	9.10.93	12	EI	Beograd	3 Mar
	8.75 1.72 14.46 6.14 2:18.11							
4297	Noor	Vidts	BEL	30.5.96	1	NC	Gent	5 Feb
	8.60 1.70 12.68 6.21 2:19.85							
4291A	Brittney	Howell	USA	1.9.92	1		Albuquerque	3 Feb
	8.62 1.79 11.52 6.44 2:28.13							
4284	Hanna	Gorodskaya	BLR	31.1.93	2		Mogilyov	25 Jan
	8.82 1.85 13.32 5.77 2:24.30							
4278	Kelsey	Herman	USA	15.6.96	2		Fayetteville	27 Jan
	8.52 1.79 12.38 6.17 2:28.55							
4256	Esther	Turpin	FRA	29.4.96	1	NC-23	Rennes	4 Feb
	8.43 1.68 12.63 6.04 2:19.56							
4248	Odile	Ahouanwanou	BEN	5.1.91	2	FRA Ch	Bordeaux	18 Feb
	8.36 1.67 14.83 5.92 2:28.89							
(30)								

Mark	Name		Nat	Born	Date
4221	Géraldine	Ruckstuhl	SUI-J	24.2.98	5 Feb
4211A	Sami	Spenner	USA	21.3.91	3 Mar
4210	Mareike	Arndt	GER	29.1.92	29 Jan
4204	Jaclyn	Siefring	USA	30.9.95	4 Feb
4202	Niki	Oudenaarden	CAN	14.1.94	24 Feb
4198	Jordan	Gray	USA	22.4.93	8 Dec
4197	Mariya	Gromysheva	RUS	10.1.90	19 Ja
4188	Izabela	Mikolajczyk	POL	4.9.90	29 Jan
4187	Louisa	Grauvogel	GER	28.9.96	24 Feb
4186	Stacey	Destin	USA	7.11.96	10 Mar
4185A	Lindsay	Lettow	USA	6.6.90	3 Mar
4180	Solène	Ndama	FRA-J	23.9.98	4 Feb
4178	Yelena	Yermolina	RUS	2.2.89	15 Feb
4162	Georgia	Ellenwood	CAN	5.8.95	10 Mar
4155	Jessica	Taylor-Jemmett	GBR	27.6.88	29 Jan
4154	Weronika	Grzelak	POL	19.3.97	29 Jan
4154		Wang Qingling	CHN	14.1.93	24 Feb
4151	Holly	Hankenson	USA	4.6.95	23 Feb
4103	Jo	Rowland	GBR	29.12.89	5 Mar
	(49)				

WOMEN 2017

HEPTATHLON

Mark		Name	Nat	Born	Pos	Meet	Venue	Date
7013	Nafissatou	Thiam	BEL	19.8.94	1	Hypo	Götzis	28 May
	13.34/-0.7 1.98 14.51 24.40/-1.6			6.56/0.8		59.32	2:15.24	
6836	Carolin	Schäfer	GER	5.12.91	2	Hypo	Götzis	28 May
	13.09/1.0 1.86 14.76 23.36/0.7			6.57/0.9		49.80	2:14.7	
6815	Laura	Ikauniece-Admidina	LAT	31.5.92	3	Hypo	Götzis	28 May
	13.10/1.0 1.77 13.53 23.49/-2.9			6.64/0.8		56.17	2:11.76	
6784		Thiam			1	WCh	London (OS)	6 Aug
	13.54/0.0 1.95 15.17 24.57/0.0			6.57/-0.5		53.93	2:21.42	
6696		Schäfer			2	WCh	London (OS)	6 Aug
	13.09/0.0 1.86 14.84 23.58/-0.2			6.20/-0.7		49.99	2:15.34	
6691	Katarina	Johnson-Thompson	GBR	9.1.93	4	Hypo	Götzis	28 May
	13.29/1.2 1.95 12.72 22.81/-2.9			6.53/0.7		39.98	2:11.12	
6667		Schäfer			1		Ratingen	25 Jun
	13.07/2.0 1.84 13.84 23.27/0.3			6.37/0.2		50.34	2:17.56	
6636	Anouk	Vetter	NED	4.2.93	3	WCh	London (OS)	6 Aug
	13.31/0.0 1.77 15.09 24.36/-0.4			6.32/-1.0		58.41	2:19.43	

Mark	Name		Nat	Born	Pos	Meet	Venue	Date
6594	Yorgelis	Rodríguez	CUB	25.1.95	4	WCh	London (OS)	6 Aug
	13.60/-0.3	1.95	13.45	24.42/-0.4	6.23/-0.6	47.41	2:10.48	
6580	Claudia	Salman-Rath	GER	25.4.86	5	Hypo	Götzis	28 May
	13.51/1.2	1.74	14.00	23.62/0.7	6.86/1.7	39.67	2:05.54	
6564	Kendell	Williams	USA	14.6.95	1	NC	Sacramento	25 Jun
	12.82/-0.1	1.83	13.01	23.50/0.2	6.49/1.9	44.97	2:16.46	
6558		Johnson-Thompson			5	WCh	London (OS)	6 Aug
	13.33/0.0	1.80	12.47	22.86/-0.2	6.56/-0.1	41.72	2:08.10	
6557	Erica	Bougard	USA	26.7.93	2	NC	Sacramento	25 Jun
	12.93/-0.1	1.92	11.98	23.40/0.2	6.36/1.1	40.96	2:11.51	
6502		Bougard			6	Hypo	Götzis	28 May
	13.57/1.0	1.83	12.45	23.28/-2.9	6.59/-0.2	40.85	2:08.68	
6497		Vetter			7	Hypo	Götzis	28 May
	13.32/1.2	1.71	15.54	24.21/0.7	6.19/0.0	55.43	2:20.20	
6446		Rodríguez			8	Hypo	Götzis	28 May
	13.80/-0.7	1.86	14.09	24.16/-2.9	6.06/1.6	48.25	2:12.65	
6421	Sharon	Day-Monroe (10)	USA	9.6.85	3	NC	Sacramento	25 Jun
	13.50/-0.1	1.83	15.49	24.94/0.8	5.89/1.6	50.12	2:15.14	
6417	Ivona	Dadic	AUT	29.12.93	6	WCh	London (OS)	6 Aug
	13.68/-0.3	1.80	13.82	24.11/-0.2	5.98/-0.4	52.29	2:13.44	
6390	Xénia	Krizsán	HUN	13.1.93	9	Hypo	Götzis	28 May
	13.72/-0.7	1.80	14.29	25.03/-1.6	6.09/1.1	49.81	2:10.04	
6381	Alina	Shukh	UKR-J	12.2.99	1	EJ	Grosseto	21 Jul
	14.46/-1.7	1.87	13.87	25.97/0.3	6.33w/3.2	54.51	2:13.52	
6370	Nadine	Visser	NED	9.2.95	7	WCh	London (OS)	6 Aug
	12.85/0.0	1.77	12.96	23.73/-0.2	6.30/-0.6	42.26	2:14.74	
6363		Vetter			1	Décastar	Talence	17 Sep
	13.60/-0.5	1.73	14.86	24.21w/3.1	6.18/0.0	52.49	2:20.99	
6362		Salman-Rath			8	WCh	London (OS)	6 Aug
	13.52/0.0	1.74	12.84	23.92/-0.2	6.55/-0.2	40.70	2:07.37	
6357	Géraldine	Ruckstuhl	SUI-J	24.2.98	2	EJ	Grosseto	21 Jul
	13.98/-1.5	1.81	13.54	24.74/0.1	5.97/1.1	54.32	2:12.56	
6356		Krizsán			9	WCh	London (OS)	6 Aug
	13.70/-0.3	1.77	14.14	25.15/-0.3	5.93/-0.5	51.25	2:07.17	
6355		Visser			10	Hypo	Götzis	28 May
	12.78/1.0	1.74	12.85	23.46/-2.9	6.27/0.7	42.81	2:15.24	
6354		Williams			1		Athens GA	9 Apr
	13.17/1.1	1.85	12.85	23.90/0.0	6.35/-0.3	41.84	2:18.40	
6337(w)	Katerina	Cachová	CZE	26.2.90	1		Kladno	18 Jun
	13.28/1.9	1.68	13.17	24.24w/2.6	6.51w/3.0	46.75	2:13.05	
6330	Caroline	Agnou	SUI	26.5.96	1	EU23	Bydgoszcz	14 Jul
	13.61/-0.3	1.72	14.77	24.36/-0.1	6.36/0.3	46.19	2:16.06	
6326	Nadine	Broersen	NED	29.4.90	1	ET-1	Monzón	2 Jul
	13.78/0.8	1.84	14.35	25.33/1.8	6.19/0.0	51.10	2:19.93	
	(30/18)							
6313	Eliska	Klucinová	CZE	14.4.88	10	WCh	London (OS)	6 Aug
	14.03/-0.3	1.86	14.80	24.72/0.0	6.16/-0.5	41.91	2:13.00	
6311	Antoinette	Nana Djimou (20)	FRA	2.8.85	11	Hypo	Götzis	28 May
	13.32/1.0	1.68	15.16	24.57/-1.6	6.33/0.4	50.19	2:22.64	
6280	Grit	Sadeiko	EST	29.7.89	13	Hypo	Götzis	28 May
	13.31/1.2	1.74	13.89	24.69/-1.8	6.17/-0.2	48.35	2:16.86	
6232	Verena	Preiner	AUT	1.2.95	2	EU23	Bydgoszcz	14 Jul
	13.79/-0.3	1.72	13.97	24.36/-0.1	5.84/0.9	49.56	2:10.72	
6230(w)	Marthe	Koala	BUR	8.3.94	3		Kladno	18 Jun
	13.25/1.9	1.77	13.59	24.24w/2.6	6.22w/2.1	41.52	2:17.15	
6228	Evelyn	Aguilar	COL	3.1.93	1		Firenze	29 Apr
	13.95/0.6	1.72	13.25	24.32/-0.2	6.46/1.8	47.02	2:16.31	
6174	Lecabela	Quaresma	POR	26.12.89	4		Kladno	18 Jun
	13.56/1.9	1.80	14.61	24.98/0.0	6.06/0.8	37.18	2:11.03	
6131(w)	Odile	Ahouanwanou	BEN	5.1.91	5		Kladno	18 Jun
	13.35/1.9	1.71	14.70	24.13w/2.3	5.83w/2.1	45.26	2:20.45	
6129	Alex	Gochenour	USA	17.2.93	4	NC	Sacramento	25 Jun
	13.41/-0.1	1.68	13.91	24.22/0.8	6.15/1.5	40.35	2:13.21	
6113	Hanne	Maudens	BEL	12.3.97	15	Hypo	Götzis	28 May
	14.14/0.0	1.77	12.53	24.33/-1.8	6.30/0.7	40.45	2:11.09	
6106	Mareike	Arndt	GER	29.1.92	3		Ratingen	25 Jun
	13.44/2.0	1.63	14.75	23.89/0.3	6.01/-0.4	44.25	2:18.87	
6103	Lucia	Slanicková	SVK	8.11.88	6		Kladno	18 Jun
	13.97/1.3	1.77	11.08	24.30w/2.3	6.31/1.6	43.81	2:11.71	
	(30)							

Mark	Name		Nat	Born	Pos	Meet	Venue	Date
6099	Taliyah	Brooks	USA	8.2.95	1	SEC	Columbia SC	12 May
	13.14/1.7	1.80 11.99 23.88/1.3		6.40/1.5		36.40	2:22.29	
6083	Sarah	Lagger	AUT-J	3.9.99	3	EJ	Grosseto	21 Jul
	14.31/-1.5	1.78 13.26 25.08/0.1		6.21/1.3		44.02	2:13.70	
6070	Celina	Leffler	GER	9.4.96	3	EU23	Bydgoszcz	14 Jul
	13.74/-0.3	1.75 14.09 23.99w/2.1		6.38/0.3		35.16	2:20.81	
6050	Laura	Arteil	FRA	9.10.93	1		Oyonnax	28 May
	13.99/0.1	1.67 14.42 24.52/0.6		6.15/0.9		43.98	2:17.42	
6050	Györgyi	Zsivoczky-Farkas	HUN	13.2.85	17	WCh	London (OS)	6 Aug
	14.05/-0.3	1.77 13.75 25.38/-0.3		5.94/-0.8		44.95	2:13.44	
6040	Tamara	de Souza	BRA	8.9.93	1	NC	São Bernardo do Campo	11 Jun
	13.88/0.5	1.77 14.56 24.48/0.8		5.99/0.1		44.20	2:26.0	
6033		Wang Qingling	CHN	14.1.93	1	NG	Tianjin	3 Sep
	13.59/0.6	1.72 12.89 24.63/0.1		6.45/0.8		40.51	2:21.15	
6024	Noor	Vidts	BEL	30.5.96	18	Hypo	Götzis	28 May
	14.11/0.0	1.74 13.95 24.21/-1.6		6.02/0.0		36.44	2:10.96	
6023	Payton	Stumbaugh	USA	29.11.95	2	SEC	Columbia SC	12 May
	13.00/1.7	1.71 11.08 23.22/2.0		6.10w/2.3		37.28	2:15.91	
6021	Nina	Schultz	CAN-J	12.11.98	1		Tucson	7 Apr
	13.83/-0.5	1.75 12.19 24.43/1.8		6.04/0.0		46.09	2:18.75	
	(40)							
6013	Niamh	Emerson	GBR-J	22.4.99	4	EJ	Grosseto	21 Jul
	14.01/-1.7	1.81 12.40 24.64/0.1		6.09w/2.7		38.23	2:12.60	
6007	Caroline	Klein	GER	4.3.96	1-22		Filderstadt	11 Jun
	13.73/0.0	1.78 13.44 24.66/-0.5		5.99/0.6		45.56	2:26.14	
6000	Niki	Oudenaarden	CAN	14.1.94	1	PAmCp	Ottawa	5 Jul
	14.32/1.6	1.70 14.03 24.94/0.5		6.04/0.1		45.54	2:15.41	
5999	Angela	Whyte	CAN	22.5.80	1		Woerden	27 Aug
	13.24/1.1	1.70 12.79 24.54/2.0		6.05/0.3		41.80	2:18.39	
5986	Daryna	Sloboda	UKR	19.6.95	1	NC	Lutsk	7 Jun
	14.48/-1.4	1.79 13.48 24.70/0.5		5.88/-1.6		40.50	2:11.44	
5986	Sami	Spenner	USA	21.3.91	2	PAmCp	Ottawa	5 Jul
	14.24/1.6	1.76 12.39 24.39/0.5		5.90/1.7		42.71	2:11.42	
5942	Swapana	Barman	IND	29.10.96	1	AsiC	Bhubaneswar	9 Jul
	13.99/-.6	1.86 11.39 26.11/-0.5		6.03/0.7		45.03	2:16.20	
5940	Esther	Turpin	FRA	29.4.96	4	EU23	Bydgoszcz	14 Jul
	13.54/-0.3	1.69 12.38 24.89/-0.1		6.02/-0.7		42.36	2:14.36	
5924w	Emilyn	Dearman	USA	1.1.95	1		San Angelo	7 Apr
	13.43w/2.3	1.78 12.25 24.85/1.9		5.95w/4.4		39.57	2:18.86	
5907	Megu	Hemphill	JPN	23.5.96	1	NC	Nagano	11 Jun
	13.35w/2.3	1.71 11.13 24.87/0.2		6.06w/2.6		45.02	2:19.32	
	(50)							
5901	Yana	Maksimova	BLR	9.1.89	2		Firenze	29 Apr
	14.51/0.6	1.84 14.16 26.45/-0.4		5.59/-0.1		45.93	2:14.84	
5895	Izabela	Mikolajczyk	POL	4.9.90	1	NC	Kraków	4 Jun
	13.88/0.7	1.82 12.31 24.88/0.9		6.04/1.6		40.13	2:22.90	
5895	Mariya	Pavlova	RUS	21.5.96	1		Adler	3 Sep
	13.99/0.5	1.81 12.28 25.30/0.3		6.00/0.9		39.79	2:16.50	
5894	Bianca	Salming	SWE-J	22.11.98	1	v2N	Kuortane	11 Jun
	14.83/0.0	1.89 13.57 26.47/-0.2		5.72/0.0		41.74	2:11.08	
5890	Lisa	Linnell	SWE	30.4.91	2	v2N	Kuortane	11 Jun
	14.21/0.2	1.77 12.43 25.22/-0.6		6.21/1.4		36.72	2:12.80	
5889	Lindsay	Schwartz	USA	23.4.90	5	NC	Sacramento	25 Jun
	13.58/-0.1	1.65 13.06 24.12/2.0		5.73w/3.2		41.07	2:14.53	
5888	Mariya	Gromysheva	RUS	10.1.90		nC	Smolensk	11 Jun
	13.67/1.7	1.75 12.48 24.43/0.0		6.06/0.0		38.02	2:20.53	
5882	Anna	Maiwald	GER	21.7.90	4		Ratingen	25 Jun
	13.43/2.0	1.69 14.03 24.63/0.3		5.49/-1.5		44.49	2:20.88	
5873	Katie	Stainton	GBR	8.1.95	7		Kladno	18 Jun
	14.12/1.3	1.68 11.80 24.22/2.6		5.98/1.0		43.18	2:14.27	
5872	Mari	Klaup	EST	27.2.90	21	Hypo	Götzis	28 May
	13.95/0.0	1.83 12.06 25.62/-2.1		5.78/0.0		47.07	2:22.60	
	(60)							
5870	Celeste	Mucci	AUS-J	11.8.99	1		Sydney	3 Dec
	13.58/0.2	1.70 12.17 24.78/1.2		6.48w/3.5		42.32	2.28.22	
5869(w)	Kaylee	Hinton	USA	19.4.97	1	Big 12	Lawrence	13 May
	13.48w/3.2	1.79 10.19 24.01w/2.9		6.15/2.1		36.27	2:19.10	
5852(w)	Leigha	Brown	USA	19.9.94	3	SEC	Columbia SC	12 May
	13.57/2.0	1.74 13.31 24.19/2.0		5.77/2.3		35.34	2:18.81	
5845	Chari	Hawkins	USA	21.5.91	1		Santa Barbara	13 May
	13.83/-1.1	1.78 12.18 25.06/-0.2		5.98/0.3		39.85	2:19.69	

Mark	Name		Nat	Born	Pos	Meet	Venue	Date
5840	Karin	Strametz	AUT-J	18.4.98	23	Hypo	Götzis	28 May
	13.85/-0.7	1.68 11.71	25.20/-1.8	6.11/1.2		42.86	2:14.93	
5835	Alysha	Burnett	AUS	4.1.97	2	WUG	Taipei	27 Aug
	14.60/-1.4	1.86 12.46	25.92/-0.2	6.09/0.8		46.26	2:27.45	
5832A	Elizabeth	Dadzie	GHA	21.3.93	1	Conf USA	El Paso	13 May
	13.47/1.6	1.67 11.67	24.59/0.0	6.34/0.0		39.56	2:23.26	
5830	Allison	Reaser	USA	9.9.92	6	NC	Sacramento	25 Jun
	13.65/-0.1	1.65 11.99	23.86/2.0	5.79/1.5		39.53	2:13.87	
5821	Yelizaveta	Aksyonova	RUS	10.7.96	3		Adler	13 May
	14.07/1.6	1.80 13.41	25.13/2.0	5.70/-2.1		39.37	2:19.43	
5820	Kelsey	Herman	USA	15.6.96	4	SEC	Columbia SC	12 May
	13.45/1.7	1.77 11.90	23.91/2.0	6.01/1.4		35.34	2:25.76	
	(70)							
5815	Fiorella	Chiappe	ARG	1.1.96	1		Buenos Aires	5 Mar
	13.72/0.2	1.76 11.33	24.70w/2.7	6.25/0.5		33.41	2:16.68	
5813	Ellen	Sprunger	SUI	5.8.86	4	ET	Tallinn	2 Jul
	14.22/-0.8	1.63 12.68	24.50/-4.7	6.24/0.0		40.78	2:18.03	
5812	Vanessa	Spínola	BRA	5.3.90	2	NC	São Bernardo do Campo	11 Jun
	14.04/0.5	1.71 13.24	24.28/0.8	5.74/-0.5		40.58	2:19.8	
5801	Elizabeth	Morland	IRL-J	3.3.98	5	EJ	Grosseto	21 Jul
	13.94/-1.5	1.75 11.47	24.76/-1.2	6.01/-0.1		43.74	2:23.93	
5798	Margarita	Korneychuk	RUS	21.2.95	4		Adler	13 May
	14.56/1.6	1.89 11.90	26.06/2.0	6.12/-0.8		37.58	2:18.07	
5798	Purnima	Hembram	IND	10.7.93	3	AsiC	Bhubaneswar	9 Jul
	13.75/-0.6	1.71 11.84	24.86/-0.5	5.97/-0.7		39.08	2:16.21	
5794	Cassandre	Aguessy-Thomas	FRA	1.9.97	9	EU23	Bydgoszcz	14 Jul
	13.87w/2.6	1.75 12.27	24.5w9/2.1	6.20/0.2		37.07	2:25.21	
5785	Luisaris	Toledo	VEN	29.2.92	1	Bol G	Santa Marta	24 Nov
	14.35/1.8	1.67 12.73	24.93/2.0	6.03w/2.2		42.66	2:17.39	
5784w	Austra	Skujyte	LTU	12.8.79	2	ET-2	Monzón	2 Jul
	14.42/1.4	1.69 16.08	26.53w/5.1	5.77/0.5		47.27	2:25.46	
5784	Adrianna	Sulek	POL-J	3.4.99	7	EJ	Grosseto	21 Jul
	14.10/-1.5	1.78 12.38	24.30/0.1	6.15/0.1		33.35	2:22.29	
	(80)							
5783	Rachael	McIntosh	CAN	17.1.91	3	PAmCp	Ottawa	5 Jul
	14.51/1.3	1.70 12.48	25.55/-0.1	5.95/0.4		43.26	2:12.62	
5779	Yusleidys	Mendieta	CUB	17.2.94		NC	La Habana	16 Mar
	13.53/1.7	1.75 13.50	23.87/1.5	5.72w/2.3		42.50	2:39.09	
5774	Lindsay	Lettow	USA	6.6.90	8	NC	Sacramento	25 Jun
	14.10/-0.1	1.68 11.84	24.95/2.0	6.14w/2.5		42.64	2:19.74	
5767	Jessica	Taylor-Jemmett	GBR	27.6.88	7	Décastar	Talence	17 Sep
	13.98/-0.2	1.64 12.85	23.72w/3.1	5.81/-0.3		37.26	2:16.58	
5759	Kate	O'Connor	IRL-Y	12.12.00	8	EJ	Grosseto	21 Jul
	15.06/-0.2	1.78 12.90	25.24/-1.2	5.75/1.3		43.30	2:15.87	
5755	Marisa Vaz	Carvalho	POR-J	19.11.99	1		Arona	4 Jun
	13.66/-0.3	1.64 12.89	24.61/0.4	6.13/1.3		34.44	2:17.97	
5752	Portia	Bing	NZL	17.4.93	2	NC	Sydney	31 Mar
	13.98/1.0	1.69 13.01	24.77/-0.3	5.64/0.8		39.59	2:14.98	
5751	Giovana	Cavaleti	BRA	13.1.89	3	NC	São Bernardo do Campo	11 Jun
	13.86/0.5	1.71 12.60	24.39/0.8	6.03/-0.2		35.19	2:21.21	
5750	Jaclyn	Siefring	USA	30.9.95	3	MSR	Azusa	13 Apr
	14.01/0.7	1.63 12.46	24.65/1.4	5.93w/2.2		39.87	2:14.62	
5747	Jutta	Heikkinen	FIN	27.10.94	1	NC	Seinäjoki	22 Jul
	14.00/1.2	1.68 12.72	25.27/1.2	5.82/2.1		44.02	2:19.67	
	(90)							
5745	Sofía	Ifantídou	GRE	5.1.85	1	NC	Sérres	28 May
	14.03/-0.7	1.63 13.47	26.17/1.0	5.85/-0.4		54.14	2:28.25	
5737	Rimma	Hordiyenko	UKR	30.12.95	2	NC	Lutsk	7 Jun
	13.99/-1.4	1.79 13.70	25.48/0.5	6.00/0.7		36.18	2:27.08	
5733	Adriana	Rodríguez	CUB-J	12.7.99	1	PAm-J	Trujillo	23 Jul
	13.37/-0.2	1.72 12.04	24.00/0.2	6.00/0.8		35.31	2:28.50	
5731	Diane	Marie-Hardy	FRA	19.2.96	2		Oyonnax	28 May
	14.18/1.8	1.67 11.81	24.77/0.6	6.02/0.4		36.99	2:11.92	
5730(w)	Arna Stefanía	Gudmundsdóttir	ISL	1.9.95	1		Akureyri	12 Aug
	13.80w/2.1	1.70 10.96	24.34w/2.6	5.67/1.6		42.35	2:18.88	
5726	Sophie	Hamann	GER	12.8.96	3-22		Filderstadt	11 Jun
	13.72/0.0	1.78 11.30	24.86/-0.5	5.95/0.4		32.60	2:15.92	
5717	Veronica	Torr	NZL	17.5.87	1		Canberra	22 Jan
	13.81/0.6	1.70 13.15	25.13/0.6	6.11/0.0		40.64	2:30.91	
5716	Jana	Novotná	CZE-J	26.1.99	9	EJ	Grosseto	21 Jul
	14.14/-1.7	1.75 12.16	25.30/-1.2	6.02/1.2		36.10	2:17.29	

Mark	Name		Nat	Born	Pos	Meet	Venue	Date
5715	Tiffeny	Parker	USA	8.6.88	5		Düsseldorf	30 Jul
	14.09/-1.9	1.80 13.42 26.04/0.6		5.80/-1.2		50.00	2:40.02	
5703	Martha Valeria	Araujo	COL	12.5.96	2	Bol G	Santa Marta	24 Nov
	14.04/1.8	1.61 11.92 25.64/2.0		6.16/		47.21	2:22.26	
	(100)							

Mark	First name	Name	Nat	Born	Date
5697	Nicole	Wadden	CAN	1.1.93	30 Mar
5694	Vanessa	Grimm	GER	22.4.97	25 Jun
5692	Melissa-Maree	Farrington	AUS	28.5.95	13 May
5687	Holly	McArthur	GBR-J	20.12.99	21 Jul
5671	Lucia	Mokrásová	SVK	27.3.94	30 Mar
5671	Riley	Cooks	USA	6.12.93	6 May
5664	Annik	Kälin	SUI-Y	27.4.00	27 Aug
5661	Sophie	Stanwell	AUS	8.6.91	3 Dec
5660	Stanislava	Lajcáková	SVK	20.4.96	21 May
5658	Alissa	Brooks-Johnson	USA	1.8.95	10 Jun
5657	Solène	Ndama	FRA-J	23.9.98	18 Jun
5641	Jordan	Gray	USA	22.4.93	13 May
5640	Breanne	Borman	USA	29.12.93	13 May
5636	Madeline	Holmberg	USA	26.10.96	22 Apr
5634	Yekaterina	Netsvetayeva	BLR	26.6.89	28 May
5633	Liksy	Joseph	IND	17.2.90	9 Jul
5624	Lisanne	Drost	NED	27.8.91	28 May
5621		Shen Muhan	CHN	5.1.97	3 Sep
5616	Louisa	Grauvogel	GER	28.9.96	9 Apr
5614	Jo	Rowland	GBR	29.12.89	29 Apr
5610	Léa	Fleury	FRA	8.2.96	14 May
5610	Iryna	Rofe-Beketova	UKR-J	18.9.98	21 Jul
5607	Juanita	Webster-Freeman	USA	13.11.96	5 Jul
5597	Hertta	Heikkinen	FIN	27.10.94	11 Jun
5591	Crystiane	Barroso	BRA	26.8.88	11 Jun
5591	Erika	Wärff	SWE-Y	16.7.00	21 Jul
5586	Eri	Utsunomiya	JPN	11.4.93	9 Jul
5585	Yuki	Yamasaki	JPN	6.6.95	14 May
5585	Paulina	Ligarska	POL	9.4.96	14 Jul
5584(w)	Jenna	Pfeiffer	USA	23.2.94	13 May
5584	Alysbeth	Félix	PUR	7.3.93	6 Aug
5579	Carmen	Romero	ESP	4.3.91	23 Jul
5578		Du Jiani	CHN-J	9.10.99	5 Apr
5576	Estefanía	Fortes	ESP	25.4.87	23 Jul
5574	Malin	Skogström	SWE	8.4.95	14 Jul
5574	Kristina	Korolyova	RUS	6.11.90	3 Sep
5570	Tori	West	AUS	14.10.95	3 Dec
5568	Marion	Milan	FRA	5.1.95	28 May
5567	Yuliya	Rout	BLR	22.1.95	2 Jul
5556	Holly	Hankenson	USA	4.6.95	30 Mar
5554w	Sarah	Chauchard	FRA	13.3.91	6 Apr
5554	Elodie	Jakob	SUI	8.10.93	27 Aug
5553	Gavyn	Yetter	USA		13 May
5553	Lyubov	Tkach	RUS	18.2.93	13 May
5551	Nikki	Larch-Miller	USA	13.8.94	12 Apr
5551	Tori	Usgaard	USA	1.11.94	13 Apr
5551	Kara	Hallock	USA	20.4.94	7 May
5550	Carmen	Ramos	ESP-J	18.6.98	4 Jun
5546	Michelle	Oud	NED	19.7.96	28 May
5540	Rose	Jackson	USA	12.5.95	24 Mar
5527	Anna	Kerbachová	CZE-Y	5.3.00	18 Jun
5525	Saga	Kivekäs	FIN	6.5.97	11 Jun
5515	Patrycja	Adamczyk	POL-J	19.5.99	4 Jun
5512	Lisa	Maihöfer	GER-J	28.10.98	11 Jun
5507	Fiona	Espagnet	FRA	30.4.97	18 Jun
5501	Viktoriya	Vaseykina	RUS	19.3.97	13 May
5496	Maria	Huntington	FIN	13.3.97	2 Jul
5490w	Tyra	Gittens	TTO-J	6.6.98	4 Jul
5489	Lovisa	Östervall	SWE	9.3.97	10 Sep
5488(w)	María Rún	Gunnlaugsdóttir	ISL	19.2.93	12 Aug
5487	Céline	Albisser	SUI	5.5.96	14 Jul
5475	Miia	Sillman	FIN	3.6.95	11 Jun
5475	Ida	Marcussen	NOR	1.11.87	18 Jun
5473	Ella	Vedeneyeva	RUS-J	30.11.98	14 May
5469	Kami	Norton	USA	16.9.95	26 May
5465		Pang Yuting	CHN	28.5.95	20 Jul
5461		Liu Ya-Chun	TPE	20.9.93	10 May
5457	Elisa	Pineau	FRA-J	26.10.98	18 Jun
5453	Janika	Baarck	GER-J	1.9.99	11 Jun
5451A	Stella	Clemens	GER	6.8.97	11 May
5445(w)	Jessica	Rautelin	FIN	16.1.97	22 Jul
5444	Zoe	Hughes	GBR-J	1.2.98	13 Apr
5444	Kira	Biesenbach	GER	7.10.92	25 Jun
5443(w)	Maya	Neal	LBR	22.12.96	12 May
5442	Margit	Kalk	EST-J	16.6.99	21 May
5442	Barbora	Dvoráková	CZE	10.5.97	18 Jun
5442	Jade	O'Dowda	GBR-J	9.9.99	17 Sep
5439	Sandra	Böll	DEN	6.11.94	30 Jul
5438	Christina	Chenault	USA	22.12.96	13 Apr
5438	Brittany	Kelly	USA	5.12.95	12 May
5437	Sveva	Gerevini	ITA	31.5.96	14 Jul
5436	Lucy	Turner	GBR	14.2.97	28 May
5433	Andrea	Medina	ESP	26.4.96	23 Jul
5430	Sunisa	Khotseemueang	THA	8.4.93	25 Aug
5425	Frida	Thorsås	NOR	31.1.94	8 Apr
5425	Katerina	Dvoráková	CZE	10.5.97	18 Jun
5422	Yanira	Soto	ESP	21.8.88	4 Jun
5420(w)	Liz	Harper	USA	1.5.95	13 Apr
5410	Patricia	Ortega	ESP	18.4.94	23 Jul
5407	Janel	Conley	USA	14.4.94	20 Apr
5404	Kiara	Reddingius	AUS	2.1.92	5 Feb
5404	Barbora	Zatloukalová	CZE	3.6.97	14 Jul
5400	Estefanía	García	DOM	2.2.91	28 May
	(193)				

Best non wind assisted

Mark	First name	Name	Nat	Born	Date
5625	Emilyn	Dearman	USA	1.1.95	26 May

JUNIORS

See main list for top 14 juniors. 11 performances by 5 women to 6013. Additional marks and further juniors:

	Mark	Pos	Meet	Venue				Date
Shukh	6208	1	ET	Tallinn				2 Jul
	14.64/-3.2		1.81	13.47	26.14/-2.8	6.10/1.1	55.95	2:12.61
	6106	16	Hypo	Götzis				28 May
	14.78/0.0		1.80	13.16	26.77/-2.1	6.29/1.7	52.92	2:12.31
	6075	14	WCh	London (OS)				6 Aug
	14.32/0.3		1.83	13.75	26.59/-0.3	5.85/0.1	52.93	2:15.84
Ruckstuhl	6291	12	Hypo	Götzis				28 May
	13.96/0.0		1.77	13.89	24.80/-2.1	5.78/0.9	58.31	2:16.68
	6230	11	WCh	London (OS)				6 Aug
	13.80/0.3		1.80	13.36	24.84/0.0	5.82/0.5	52.15	2:14.85
	6134	2	ET	Tallinn				2 Jul
	14.36/-3.2		1.78	12.68	25.04/-2.8	6.06/1.5	53.72	2:17.04

Mark	Name		Nat	Born	Pos	Meet	Venue	Date
5687	Holly	McArthur	GBR-J	20.12.99	11	EJ	Grosseto	21 Jul
	13.93/-1.5	1.63 11.47 24.59/0.1		5.91/1.0		37.25	2:11.71	
5664	Annik	Kälin	SUI-Y	27.4.00	1	NC-j	Payerne	27 Aug
	13.86/-0.1	1.75 12.23 25.13/-1.5		6.00/-0.1		44.27	2:37.65	
5657	Solène	Ndama	FRA-J	23.9.98	1	NC-j	Saint-Renan	18 Jun
	13.25/0.0	1.74 11.89 24.98/1.4		5.71/1.9		32.51	2:18.91	
5610	Iryna	Rofe-Beketova	UKR-J	18.9.98	12	EJ	Grosseto	21 Jul
	14.22/-1.5	1.81 12.84 25.76/-0.4		5.93/1.3		35.66	2:27.44	
5591	Erika	Wärff	SWE-Y	16.7.00	13	EJ	Grosseto	21 Jul
	14.49/1.2	1.81 11.81 25.57/-1.2		5.76/0.7		41.25	2:26.47	

Mark	Name	Nat	Born	Pos	Meet	Venue	Date
5578	Du Jiani	CHN-J	9.10.99	1	NGP	Huaian	5 Apr
	14.39/-1.8 1.72 13.47 25.26/-1.1 6.08/1.0 34.96 2:28.77						

4 X 100 METRES RELAY

Mark	Nat	Team	Pos	Meet	Venue	Date
41.82	USA	A.Brown, Felix, Akinosun, Bowie	1	WCh	London (OS)	12 Aug
41.84	USA	A.Brown, Felix, Akinosun, Washington	1h1	WCh	London (OS)	12 Aug
41.85	JAM	C Williams, Levy, Facey, Thompson	1	WK	Zürich	24 Aug
41.86	GBR	Philip, Henry, Asher-Smith, Neita	2	WK	Zürich	24 Aug
41.93	GBR	Philip, Henry, Asher-Smith, Neita	2h1	WCh	London (OS)	12 Aug
42.12	USA	Un of Oregon Dunmore, Stevens, Cunliffe, Washington	1	MSR	Torrance	14 Apr
42.12	USA	LSU Brisco, K Johnson, Martin, Hobbs	1		Baton Rouge	29 Apr
42.12	GBR	Philip, Henry, Asher-Smith, Neita	2	WCh	London (OS)	12 Aug
42.14	USA	LSU Brisco, K Johnson, Martin, Hobbs	2	MSR	Torrance	14 Apr
42.17	GER	Burghardt, Mayer, Lückenkemper, Haase	1	ISTAF	Berlin	27 Aug
42.19	JAM	Levy, Morrison, Facey, Forbes	3	WCh	London (OS)	12 Aug
42.25	JAM	C Williams, Stewart, Evans, Thompson	1	PennR	Philadelphia	29 Apr
42.25	GER	Burghardt, Mayer, Lückenkemper, Haase	1	FBK	Hengelo	11 Jun
42.32	USA	LSU Brisco, K Johnson, Martin, Hobbs	1h1	NCAA-E	Lexington	27 May
42.32	GER	Burghardt, Mayer, Lückenkemper, Haase	3	WK	Zürich	24 Aug
42.34	USA	Un of Oregon Stevens, Dunmore, Cunliffe, Washington	1	FlaR	Gainesville	1 Apr
42.34	USA	Bartoletta, Felix, Gardner, A Brown	1	Herc	Monaco	21 Jul
42.34	GER	Pinto, Mayer, Lückenkemper, Haase	1h2	WCh	London (OS)	12 Aug
42.35	USA	Un of Oregon Johnson, Stevens, Dunmore, Washington	1	PennR	Philadelphia	28 Apr
42.36	GER	Pinto, Mayer, Lückenkemper, Haase	4	WCh	London (OS)	12 Aug
42.42	USA	Bryant, Duncan, Gardner, Akinosun	2	PennR	Philadelphia	29 Apr
42.47	GER	Matheis, Burghardt, Lückenkemper, Haase	1r1	ET	Villeneuve d'Ascq	24 Jun
42.50	SUI	Del Ponte, Atcho, Kambundji, Kora	3h1	WCh	London (OS)	12 Aug
42.50	JAM	C Williams, Morrison, Levy, Forbes	2h2	WCh	London (OS)	12 Aug
		(24 performances by teams from 5 nations)				
42.59		Su Minxiang (CHN) Ge Manqi, Lin Huijun, Jiang Lan, Wei Yongli	1	NG	Tianjin	7 Sep
42.62	TTO	Hackett, Ahye, St.Fort, Baptiste	6	WCh	London (OS)	12 Aug
42.63	BRA	Krasucki, A C Silva, Rosa, R Santos	7	WCh	London (OS)	12 Aug
42.64	NED	Ghafoor, Schippers, Sedney, Samuel	4h1	WCh	London (OS)	12 Aug
42.92	FRA	Ombissa, Ikuesan, Pare, Zahi	5h1	WCh	London (OS)	12 Aug
	(10)					
43.03	KAZ	Kashafutdinova, Zyabkina, Golendova, Safronova	1	Kozanov	Almaty	24 Jun
43.07	POL	Ciba, Popowicz-Drabala, Kielbasinska, Swoboda	2r1	ET	Villeneuve d'Ascq	24 Jun
43.21	ITA	Hooper, Siragusa, Bongiorni, Alloh	4	Athl	Lausanne,	6 Jul
43.68	GHA	Owusu-Agyepong, Acheampong, Obeng-Akrofi, Amponsah	6h1	WCh	London (OS)	12 Aug
43.84	NGR	Osuji, P George, Duncan, Madu	2		Port of Spain	25 Jun
43.88	ESP	Sevilla, Furundarena, García, Lara	5	Athl	Lausanne,	6 Jul
43.88	VIE	Le Thi Mong Tuyen, Do Thi Quyen, Tran,Thi Yen Hoa, Le Tu Chinh	1	SEAG	Kuala Lumpur	25 Aug
43.94	ECU	Angulo, Landázuri, Cifuentes, Tenorio	7h1	WCh	London (OS)	12 Aug
44.01	BAH	Parker, Bethel, Carter, Gaither	6	W.Rly	Nassau	23 Apr
44.03	IVB	Harrigan, Kelly, Moses, King	3		Port of Spain	25 Jun
	(20)					
44.05	CAN	Jacques, Emmanuel, Davis, Rowe	5		Baton Rouge	29 Apr
44.07	CZE	Seidlová, Procházková, Slaninová, Domská	1	Danek	Turnov	23 May
44.07	AUS	Whittaker, Beahan, Pearson, Breen	1		Brisbane	15 Dec
44.15	VEN	Vargas, Purica, Romero, Soto	1	Bol G	Santa Marta	23 Nov
44.20	GRE	Keramidá, Pesirídou, Daláka, Belibasáki	3r2	ET	Villeneuve d'Ascq	24 Jun
44.22	CIV	Ziketh, Gaha, Gouénon, Ta Lou	1	Franc	Abidjan	25 Jul
44.31	IRL	Scott, Mawdsley, Akpe-Moses, Neville	6	Athl	Lausanne	6 Jul
44.47	HUN	Nguyen, Kaptur, G Kerekes, Sorok	2		Budapest	3 Jun
44.50	COL	Alcázar, Padilla, Obregón, Palacios	2	SAmC	Asunción	24 Jun
44.51	RUS	Moskva Sivkov, Panteleyeva, Polyakova, Kuzina	1	NC	Zhukovskiy	30 Jul
	(30)					

44.56	JPN	28 Aug	44.60	DOM	17 Jun	44.63	SWE	2 Sep	44.81	BEL-J	23 Jul	44.87	TPE	30 Apr
44.57	IND	7 Jul	44.62	THA	25 Aug	44.78	FIN	2 Sep	44.81	PHI	25 Aug	44.96	SIN	25 Aug
						44.79	MEX	28 Aug	44.85A	RSA	22 Mar	44.98	BRN	19 May

Drugs disqualification

Mark	Nat	Team	Pos	Meet	Venue	Date
43.09	UKR	Povh ¶, Stuy, Kavchur, Bryzgina	(1r2)	ET	Villeneuve d'Ascq	24 Jun

JUNIORS

Mark	Nat	Team	Pos	Meet	Venue	Date
43.27	GER	Fehm, Kwadwo, Junk, Montag	1h3	EJ	Grosseto	23 Jul
		43.44 1 EJ Grosseto 23 Jul 43.84 (1 Griephan) 1r2 Mannheim 2 Jul				
43.96	JAM	Edwin Allen School Cameron, K davis, S Clarke, Moody	1	PennR	Philadelphia	28 Apr
44.03	FRA	De La Taille, Mingas, Raffai, Mignon	2	EJ	Grosseto	23 Jul
44.07	USA	Cunningham, Smith, Richardson, T Davis	1	PAm-J	Trujillo	22 Jul
44.17	GBR	Carr, Rees, Bruney, Okoli	3	EJ	Grosseto	23 Jul
44.32	IRL	Scott, Mawdsley, Akpe-Moses, Neville	1h1	EJ	Grosseto	23 Jul

Mark	Nat	Name	Pos	Meet	Venue	Date
44.61	SUI	Goll, Mantingh, Vancardo, Reinle	2h3	EJ	Grosseto	23 Jul
44.64	NED	Klaver, Bouma, Jansen, van den Wildenberg	3h3	EJ	Grosseto	23 Jul
44.81	BEL	Bauwens, Tchapda, Ferauge, Claus	2h2	EJ	Grosseto	23 Jul
44.84	CHN	Gomg Luying, Zhu Cuiwei, Tao Yanan, Feng Lulu	1		Weinan	19 Aug
44.94	ESP	Bestue, Urquia, Verdó, Marco	3h1	EJ	Grosseto	23 Jul

4 X 200 METRES RELAY

Mark	Team	Name	Pos	Meet	Venue	Date
1:28.77	Tumbleweed, TC	Henry GBR, Onuora GBR, Bartoletta USA, Schippers NED	1	FlaR	Gainesville	1 Apr
1:28.78	Un of Oregon USA	Dunmore, Cunliffe, Stevens, Washington	2	FlaR	Gainesville	1 Apr
1:29.04	JAM	Levy, Jackson, Forbes, Thompson	1	W.Rly	Nassau	22 Apr
1:29.71	Pure Athletics	Latvala FIN, Miller-Uibo BAH, Baptiste TTO, Bowie USA	3	FlaR	Gainesville	1 Apr
1:29.86	Empire Athletics USA	Solomon, McCorory, Ch.Williams, F.Brown	4	FlaR	Gainesville	1 Apr
1:29.89	Texas A&M USA	Spaulding, B.Thompson GUY, Reed, White	1	TexR	Austin	1 Apr
1:30.60	LSU USA	Cas.Hall, Mosher,iK.Johnson, Martin	1		Baton Rouge	29 Apr
1:30.68	GER	Matheis, Pinto, Haase, Luckenkemper	2	W.Rly	Nassau	22 Apr
1:30.87	USA	Bryant, Townsend, F Brown, Solomon	3	W.Rly	Nassau	22 Apr
1:31.00	Star Athletics	Ahouré CIV, Love, McGrone, Whitney all US	5	FlaR	Gainesville	1 Apr
Other nations						
1:32.62	TTO	Durant, Hackett, Thomas, Ahye	3h1	WRly	Nassau	22 Apr
1:33.00	CAN	Emmanuel, Hyacinthe, Jacques, Bingham	6	FlaR	Gainesville	1 Apr

4 X 400 METRES RELAY

Mark	Nat	Name	Pos	Meet	Venue	Date
3.19.02	USA	Hayes 50.4, Felix 48.7, Wimbley 49.58, Francis 50.28	1	WCh	London (OS)	13 Aug
3:21.66	USA	Hayes 50.5, Ellis 50.9, Wimbley 49.41, Hastings 50.80	1h1	WCh	London (OS)	13 Aug
3:23.13	Un of Oregon USA	Dunmore 51.7, Stevens 50.8, Guster 50.8-0, Rogers 49.77	1	NCAA	Eugene	10 Jun
3.23.64	JAM	Le Roy 51.6, McLaughlin-Whilby 50.7, Gordon 50.49, McPherson 50.82	1h2	WCh	London (OS)	12 Aug
3:24.36	USA	P Francis 50.42, A Spencer 50.92, Q Hayes 50.66, Hastings 52.36	1	W.Rly	Nassau	23 Apr
3:24.72	Un of Oregon USA	Guster, Rogers, Dunmore 51.18, Stevens 51.03	1	NCAA	Eugene	10 Jun
3.24.74	GBR	Clark 51.5, Nielsen 50.4, Shakes-Drayton 52.10, Diamond 50.71	2h1	WCh	London (OS)	12 Aug
3.25.00	GBR	Clark 51.5, Laviai Nielsen 51.0, Doyle 51.56, Diamond 50.96	2	WCh	London (OS)	13 Aug
3:25.40	NGR	P George 51.5, Nathaniel 51.3, Egwim 52.10, Ajayi 50.47	2h2	WCh	London (OS)	12 Aug
3.25.41	POL	Holub 51.6, Baumgart 51.0, Gaworska 51.66, Swiety 51.17	3	WCh	London (OS)	13 Aug
3:26.07	Un of Oregon USA	Waller, Guster, Dunmore, Rogers	1	FlaR	Gainesville	1 Apr
3.26.24	GER	Spelmeyer 51.7, Gonska 51.6, Köhrbrück 51.89, Müller 51.10	3h2	WCh	London (OS)	12 Aug
3.26.47	POL	Holub 51.9, Wyciszkiewicz 51.8, Dabrowska 51.93, Baumgart 50.79	4h2	WCh	London (OS)	12 Aug
3.26.56	FRA	Perrossier 53.0, Sananes 51.4, Raharolahy 51.28, Diarra 51.01	4	WCh	London	13 Aug
3:26.72	NGR	P George 51.4, Egbeniyi 53.0, Nathaniel 51.45, Ajayi 50.93	5	WCh	London (OS)	13 Aug
3.26.75	POL	Holub, Baumgart, Wycoszkiewicz, Swiety	1	WUG	Taipei	28 Aug
3.26.90	BOT	Botlogetswe 52.5, Jele 51.0, Moroko 52.12, Montsho 51.25	3h1	WCh	London (OS)	12 Aug
	(17/8)					
3.27.81	ITA	Chigbolu 51.8, Spacca 51.9, Grenot 52.11, Folorunso 52.00	5h2	WCh	London (OS)	12 Aug
3:28.02	AUS	Rubie 52.2, Connolly 52.2, Wells 52.60, Mitchell 51.07	5h1	WCh	London (OS)	12 Aug
	(10)					
3:28.47	CAN	Muir 52.5, Stiverne 51.2, T Jones 51.93, N McDonald 52.81	6h1	WCh	London (OS)	12 Aug
3.30.84	MEX	Brito, Medina, Z Rodríguez, Morán	1	NC	Monterrey	18 Jun
3:30.95	CHN	Su Lu Xiangchuan Huang Guifen, Cheng Chong, Pan Gaoqin, Yang Huizhen	1	NG	Tianjin	7 Sep
3.31.34	IND	Majumdar, Poovamma, Mathew, Sheoran	1	AsiC	Bhubaneswar	9 Jul
3.31.79	NED	Runia, Li. de Witte 51.1e, La. de Witte, Hovenkamp	1r2	ET	Villeneuve d'Ascq	25 Jun
3.31.83	ROU	Gal, Miklos, Pap-Pastor, Razor	1r1	ET-1	Vaasa	25 Jun
3.31.83	RUS	Moskva Kotlyarva, Anikiyenko, Kuznetsova, Luzina	1	NC	Zhukovskiy	30 Jul
3.32.05	CUB	Hechavarría, Almanza, Gómez, Casanova	1	Barr	La Habana	28 May
3.32.65	IRL	Denny, Healy, Bromell, Mawdsley	2r1	ET-1	Vaasa	25 Jun
3.32.80	GRE	Mourtá, A Vasilíou, Férra, I Vasilíou	2r2	ET	Villeneuve d'Ascq	25 Jun
	(20)					
3.32.96	BRN	Naser, Odiong, Odeyemi, Adekoya	1	Isl.Sol	Baku	20 May
3.33.00	BRA	de Lima, J da Silva, J dos Santos, Coutinho	1	SAmC	Asunción	25 Jun
3.33.10	SUI	Fontanive, L Sprunger, Giger, Büchel	1r1	ET-1	Vaasa	25 Jun
3.33.22	VIE	Ng. Thi Oanh, Quach Thi Lan, Hoang Thi Minh Hanh, Ng. Thi Huyen	2	AsiC	Bhubaneswar	9 Jul
3.33.70	ESP	Sánchez, Bueno, Bokesa, Moreno	3r2	ET	Villeneuve d'Ascq	25 Jun
3.33.92	COL	Chávez, Escobar, Balanta, Padilla	2	SAmC	Asunción	25 Jun
3.34.05	SVK	Ledecká, Slanicková, Stuková, Putalová	1	ET-2	Tel Aviv	25 Jun
3:34.19	SLO	Zupin, Smonkar, Benko, Horvat	2	ET-2	Tel Aviv	25 Jun
3:34.3A	Prisons KEN	Michira, Adijah, Ndungwa, Wambui	1		Nairobi	10 Jun
3:34.40	BAH	Miller-Uibo 50.25, Strachan, Amertil, R Brown	4h2	W.Rly	Nassau	22 Apr
	(30)					

3.34.76 IVB 2 Jul	3.35.77 HUN 25 Jun	3.37.18 SRB 25 Jun	3.37.48 GRN 2 Jul	3.37.95 KAZ 9 Jul
3.35.41 CZE 25 Jun	3.36.00 JPN 29 Oct	3.37.20 SWE 25 Jun	3.37.82 FIN 25 Jun	3.38.28 BLR 25 Jun
3.35.69 LTU 25 Jun	3.36.44 POR 25 Jun	3.37.30 CRO 25 Jun	3.37.82 RSA 12 Aug	3.38.63 THA 9 Jul
		3:37.3A ETH 21 May	3.37.93 CHI 24 Nov	3.38.80 BEL 25 Jun

Mark	Name	Nat	Born	Pos	Meet	Venue	Date

Mixed nation teams

Mark	Team	Runners	Pos	Meet	Venue	Date
3:23.35	USC	Pettigrew USA 51.6, Iuel NOR 50.9, D Hil USA 51.22, Ellis USA 49.63	2	NCAA	Eugene	10 Jun
3:26.09	USC	Pettigrew USA, Iuel NOR, Cockrell USA 53.13, Ellis USA 50.45	1h1	NCAA-W	Austin	27 May
3:26.27	USA	Pettigrew 53.0, Iuel NOR 51.5, Hill 51.37, Ellis 50.43	1	TexR	Austin	1 Apr
3:26.99	LSU USA	Misher, Martin, Payne, T Jones CAN	3	NCAA	Eugene	10 Jun

Drugs disqualification

Mark	Team	Runners	Pos	Meet	Venue	Date
3:28.02	UKR	Klymyuk 53.5e, Lyakhova 51.2e, Bryzgina 52.12, Zemlyak ¶ 51.28	(2r1)	ET	Villeneuve d'Ascq	25 Jun

JUNIORS

Mark	Team	Runners	Pos	Meet	Venue	Date
3:28.57	USA	Richardson, Reed, Minor, Roberson	1	PAm-J	Trujillo	23 Jul
3:32.82	UKR	Avramchuk 55.0, Koba 52.3, Marchak 52.97, Bryzhina 52.63	1	EJ	Grosseto	23 Jul
3:33.08	GER	Aniteye, Gerlach, A Schmidt, Schwab	2	EJ	Grosseto	23 Jul
3:33.19	CAN	Santiago, Tachinski, Best, Constantine	2	PAm-J	Trujillo	23 Jul
3:33.68	GBR	M Edwards 55.4, Bruney 51.7, E Barrett 53.73, H Williams 52.98	3	EJ	Grosseto	23 Jul
3:33.99	JAM	Hydel Schools. McGregor, Salmon, Young, Brooks	1	PennR	Philadelphia	28 Apr
3:34.48	POL	Wosztyl, Lozowska, Martyna, Kaczmarek	4	EJ	Grosseto	23 Jul
3:34.54	FRA	Kandissounon, Mignon, Jean, Amaro	5	EJ	Grosseto	23 Jul
3:35.86	ITA	Borga, Oliveiri, Vandi, Verderio	6	EJ	Grosseto	23 Jul
3:38.20	JPN	Higashi-Osaka-dai Kelal HS E Fukishima, Miyade, Onishi, Kawata	3	NC	Yokohama	29 Oct
3:39.33	FIN	Pulkkinen, Mattila, Lassfolk, Lehikoinen	7	EJ	Grosseto	23 Jul

4 X 800 METRES RELAY

Mark	Team	Runners	Pos	Meet	Venue	Date
8.16.36	USA	Price 2:01.73, C.Williams 2:03.72, Roesler 2:03.05, Lipsey 2:07.86	1	W.Rly	Nassau	22 Apr
8.20.07	BLR	Borisevich 2:02.64, I.Usovich 2:04.37, Kushnir 2:04.54, Arzamasova 2:08.52	2	W.Rly	Nassau	22 Apr
8.21.08	AUS	Storey 2:02.07, de la Motte 2:02.66, Buckman 2:08.28, See 2:08.07	3	W.Rly	Nassau	22 Apr

DISTANCE MEDLEY RELAY

Indoors

Mark	Team	Runners	Pos	Venue	Date
10:40.31	USA	Coburn 3:18.40, McLaughlin 52.32, Martinez 2:01.94, Simpson 4:27.66	1	Boston (R)	28 Jan
10:48.77	Un. of Oregon	Burdon'3:20.56, Horsley' 53.76, Rogers 2:03.53, Rainsberger 4:30.92	1	New York (A)	27 Jan
10:49.39	New Balance Europe	Silvander SWE 3:18.77, Lisanne de Witte NED 52.43, Guerrero ESP 2:04.29, McDonald GBR 4:33.91	2	Boston (R)	28 Jan

4 X 1500 METRES RELAY

Mark	Team	Runners	Pos	Meet	Venue	Date
17.25.85	Villanova USA	Burda, Piccirillo, Hutchinson CAN, Cleirigh-Buttner IRL	1	PennR	Philadelphia	28 Apr

4 X 100 METRES HURDLES RELAY

Mark	Team	Runners	Pos	Meet	Venue	Date
53.13	LSU USA	Phillips, Humphrey, Brisco, Marshall	1		Baton Rouge	29 Apr
53.82	Mississippi State University	Lott, Flynn, Broghton, Tillman	1	FlaR	Gainesville	1 Apr

3000 METRES WALK

Mark	Name		Nat	Born	Pos	Meet	Venue	Date
12:16.10	Laura	García-Caro	ESP	16.4.95	1		Huelva	14 Jun
12:26.45	Bethan	Davies	GBR	7.11.90	1	Welsh	Cardiff	10 Jun
12:32.07	Teresa	Zurek	GER-J	29.7.98	1		Dessau	16 Jun
12:35.62	Émilie	Menuet	FRA	27.11.91	1		Blois	7 May
12:36.83	Ainhoa	Pinedo	ESP	17.2.83	2		Huelva	14 Jun
12:37.82	Alana	Barber	NZL	8.7.87	1		Auckland	5 Mar
Indoors								
12:08.83i	Antonella	Palmisano	ITA	6.8.91	1	NC	Ancona	18 Feb

JUNIORS

Mark	Name		Nat	Born	Pos	Meet	Venue	Date
12:46.34mx	Katie	Hayward	AUS-Y	23.7.00	1		Brisbane	11 Nov

5000 METRES WALK

Mark	Name		Nat	Born	Pos	Meet	Venue	Date
21:02.42	Lidia	Sánchez-Puebla	ESP	17.7.96	1		Plasencia	28 Jun
21:02.72	Viktória	Madarász	HUN	12.5.85	1		Budapest	30 Jun
21:17.58	Julia	Takacs	ESP	29.6.89	2		Plasencia	28 Jun
21:21.52	Bethan	Davies	GBR	7.11.90	1	NC	Birmingham	2 Jul
21:23.85	Chahineze	Nasri	TUN	3.6.96	1		Blois	17 Jun
21:25.25	Mária	Pérez	ESP	29.4.96	1		Cartagena	6 May
21:26.05	Émilie	Menuet	FRA	27.11.91	2		Blois	17 Jun
21:28.23mx	Kumiko	Okada	JPN	17.10.91	1		Yuwa	20 May

Mark	Name		Nat	Born	Date
21:33.44	Nanako	Fujii	JPN-J	7.5.99	9 Oct
21:46.77	Valentina	Trapletti	ITA	12.7.85	23 Sep
21:50.45i	Sofiya	Brodatskaya	RUS	4.10.95	23 Feb
21:51.29	Katie	Hayward	AUS-Y	23.7.00	14 Oct

JUNIORS

Mark	Name		Nat	Born	Pos	Meet	Venue	Date
21:33.44	Nanako	Fujii	JPN-J	7.5.99	1		Matsuyama	9 Oct
21:51.29	Katie	Hayward	AUS-Y	23.7.00	1		Brisbane	14 Oct
22:21.51	Teresa	Zurek	GER	29.7.98	1		Ulm	4 Aug
22:25.16A	Glenda	Morejón	ECU-Y	30.5.00	1	NC-j	Cuenca	26 Aug

See also 20km list for many intermediate 10k times.

10 KILOMETRES WALK

Mark		Name	Nat	Born	Pos	Meet	Venue	Date
41:57.29t	Antonella	Palmisano	ITA	6.8.91	1		Orvieto	23 Apr
42:46		Qieyang Shenjie	CHN	11.11.90	1		Suzhou	25 Sep
42:56.74 t	Viktória	Madarász	HUN	12.5.85	1		Budapest	3 Sep
43:03	Érica	de Sena	BRA	3.5.85	2		Suzhou	25 Sep
43:05		Nie Jingjing	CHN	1.3.88	3		Suzhou	25 Sep
43:16	Sandra	Arenas	COL	17.9.93	4		Suzhou	25 Sep
43:18.72 t	Ana	Cabecinha	POR	29.4.84	1	NC	Vagos	10 Jun
43:23	Kimberley	García	PER	19.10.93	5		Suzhou	25 Sep
43:27		Palmisano			6		Suzhou	25 Sep
43:40		Ge Sangzhuoma	CHN-J	16.7.98	1	NGP-j	Huangshan	4 Mar
43:40		Yang Liujing	CHN-J	22.8.98	2	NGP-j	Huangshan	4 Mar
43:42		Li Maocuo	CHN	20.10.92	7		Suzhou	25 Sep
43:46.06 t	Inês	Henriques	POR	1.5.80	2	NC	Vagos	10 Jun
43:56.95 t	Eleonora	Giorgi	ITA	14.9.89	1	NC	Trieste	30 Jun
43:59	Nadiya	Borovska	UKR	25.2.81	8		Suzhou	25 Sep
44:04.94 t	Valentina	Trapletti	ITA	12.7.85	2	NC	Trieste	30 Jun
44:05+	Paola	Pérez	ECU	21.12.89		in 20k	Lima	13 May
44:05		Ma Zhenxia	CHN-J	1.8.98	1	NG-j	Tianjin	4 Sep
44:10+	Klavdiya	Afanasyeva	RUS	15.1.96		in 20k	London	13 Aug
44:14		Su Wenxiu	CHN-J	28.6.98	2	NG-j	Tianjin	4 Sep
44:16		Xiao Han	CHN-J	12.11.98	3	NG-j	Tianjin	4 Sep
44:18	Brigita	Virbalyte-Dimsiene	LTU	1.2.85	1		Gdansk	26 Aug
44:19		Ma Li	CHN-Y	15.1.00	4	NG-j	Tianjin	4 Sep
44:21		Yang Weiwei	CHN-J	3.8.99	3	NGP-j	Huangshan	4 Mar
44:26+	Laura	García-Caro	ESP	16.4.95		in 20k	Podébrady	21 May
44:28		Shi Yuxia	CHN-J	1.1.99	6	NG-j	Tianjin	4 Sep
44:31		Xue Ke	CHN-J	14.3.98	7	NG-j	Tianjin	4 Sep
44:33		Qiji Zhuoma	CHN-J	27.5.98	8	NG-j	Tianjin	4 Sep
44:33.5 t	Khushbir	Kaur	IND	9.7.93	1		Dehradun	27 Dec
44:36	Julia	Takacs	ESP	29.6.89	10		Suzhou	25 Sep
44:40.79At	Guadalupe	Sánchez	MEX	4.8.95	1		Xalapa	7 May
44:42	Amanda	Cano	ESP	19.8.94	1		Castellón	11 Feb
44:43.89 t	Alegna	González	MEX-J	2.1.99	1	PAm-J	Trujillo	23 Jul
44:48	Émilie	Menuet	FRA	27.11.91	1		San Fernando	4 Feb
44:50.80 t	Kumiko	Okada	JPN	17.10.91	1		Abashiri	13 Jul
44:55		Zhang Xiaole	CHN-Y	17.1.00	1	NGP-y	Huangshan	4 Mar
44:55+		Wang Yingliu	CHN	1.3.92		in 20k	La Coruña	3 Jun
44:57+	Regan	Lamble	AUS	14.10.91		in 20k	London	13 Aug
44:58	Chiaki	Asada	JPN	21.1.91	1		Tokyo	1 Jan
44:58	Meryem	Bekmez	TUR-Y	31.7.00	1		Antalya	11 Feb
45:01+	Olga	Shargina	RUS	24.7.96		in 20k	Cheboksary	10 Jun
45:01.77t	Nadezhda	Mokeyeva	RUS	10.1.96	1		Kazan	1 Jun
45:07		Wu Quanming	CHN-J	1.1.99	9	NG-j	Tianjin	4 Sep
45:09	Teresa	Zurek	GER-J	29.7.98	1		Naumburg	23 Apr
45:13	María	Larios	ESP	29.10.92	2		Castellón	11 Feb
45:14.91 t	Chahineze	Nasri	TUN	3.6.96			Balma	3 Dec
45:16	Glenda Estefanía	Morejón	ECU-Y	30.5.00	1		Hauppauge	22 Oct
45:21+	Janeth	Guamán	ECU	15.1.88		in 20k	La Coruña	3 Jun
45:27		Han Longmei	CHN-Y	1.6.00	2	NGP-y	Huangshan	4 Mar

Mark		Name	Nat	Born	Date
45:31.40t	Maria	Michta-Coffey	USA	23.6.86	30 Jul
45:40A	Vivian	Castillo	MEX-J	10.6.98	12 Mar
45:43.02t	Sibilla	Di Vincenzo	ITA	22.1.83	23 Apr
45:44		Li Leilei	CHN	18.8.89	25 Sep
45:49.80t	Rena	Goto	JPN	6.9.95	10 Sep
45:51.09t	Katie	Hayward	AUS-Y	23.7.00	31 Mar
45:52	Valeria	Ortuño	MEX-J	27.5.98	19 Mar
45:52.92t	Maria Fernanda	Montoya	COL-J	11.3.98	23 Jul
45:54	Claire	Tallent	AUS	7.6.81	25 Sep
45:55	Khrystyna	Yudkina	UKR	4.12.84	29 Oct
45:59.48t	Rachelle	De Orbeta	PUR-Y	27.3.00	29 Jan
46:02.68+ t	Nicole	Colombi	ITA	29.12.95	21 Oct
46:03A+	Maritza Rafaela	Poncio	GUA	3.12.94	12 Mar
46:03.25t	Barbara	Kovács	HUN	26.7.93	14 May
46:03.35A t	Andrea	Martínez	MEX	4.5.88	7 May
46:04+	Mária	Czáková	SVK	2.10.88	13 Aug
46:05		Zhang Yidan	CHN-J	24.12.99	4 Mar
46:05+	Miranda	Melville	USA	20.3.89	13 Aug
46:07+	Grace	Wanjiru	KEN	10.1.79	13 Aug
46:08.97t	Edna	Barros	POR	18.12.96	1 Jul
46:09+	Déspina	Zapounídou	GRE	5.10.85	13 Aug
46:09.5A	Yehualye	Beletew	ETH-J	31.7.98	16 Jan
46:11+	Anezka	Drahotová	CZE	22.7.95	8 Apr
46:13		Wang Jiahui	CHN-J	1.1.98	4 Mar
46:13.08t	Mara	Ribeiro	POR	11.5.95	1 Jul
46:14+	Johana	Ordóñez	ECU	12.12.87	13 May
46:14+	Viktoryia	Roshchupkina	BLR	23.5.95	8 Apr
46:17	Ayse	Tekdal	TUR-J	3.4.99	11 Feb
46:18+	Tatyana	Mineyeva	RUS	10.8.90	10 Jun
46:18.6At	Askale	Tiksa	ETH	21.7.94	5 Jan
46:20+		Gao Ni	CHN	14.9.91	4 Mar
46:21+		Lee Da-seul	KOR	8.11.96	19 Mar
46:22		Li Jie	CHN-J	1.4.99	4 Mar
46:22.4 t	Baby	Soumya	IND		27 Dec
46:23	Ileana	García	MEX-J	24.3.98	19 Mar
46:24.07t	Rachel	Tallent	AUS	20.2.93	31 Mar
46:24.85t	Katarzyna	Golba	POL	21.12.89	29 Jan
46:26.21t	Amanda	Cano	ESP	19.8.94	22 Jul

Best track times

Mark		Name	Nat	Born	Pos	Meet	Venue	Date
44:36.63	Julia	Takacs	ESP	29.6.89	1	NC	Barcelona	22 Jul
45:29.06 t	Regan	Lamble	AUS	14.10.91	2		Canberra	29 Jan

Mark	Name		Nat	Born	Pos	Meet	Venue	Date

Mark	First	Name	Nat	Born	Date	Mark	First	Name	Nat	Born	Date
45:52.62	Brigita	Virbalyte-Dimsiene	LTU	1.2.85	29 Jan	46:13.79	Lidia	Sánchez-Puebla	ESP	17.7.96	22 Jul
45:56.89t	Kaori	Kawazoe	JPN	30.5.95	13 May	46:21.11t	Yuki	Yoshizumi	JPN	7.1.96	26 Mar

Indoors

Mark	First	Name	Nat	Born	Pos	Meet	Venue	Date
45:26.82i	Viktoriya	Roshchupkina	BLR	14.5.95	1	NC	Mogilyov	18 Feb
46:21.44i	Anastasiya	Rodikina	BLR	29.8.94	2	NC	Mogilyov	18 Feb

JUNIORS

See main list for top 17 juniors. 12 performances by 10 women to 44:45. Additional performances:

Yang Liujing 44:21 5 NG-j Tianjin 4 Sep
Su Wenxiu 44:36 4 NGP-j Huangshan 4 Mar

Mark	First	Name	Nat	Born	Pos	Meet	Venue	Date
45:40A	Vivian	Castillo	MEX-J	10.6.98	2		Juarez	12 Mar
45:51.09 t	Katie	Hayward	AUS-Y	23.7.00	1	NC	Sydney	31 Mar
45:52	Valeria	Ortuño	MEX-J	27.5.98	2		Monterrey	19 Mar

20 KILOMETRES WALK

Mark	Split	First	Name	Nat	Born	Pos	Meet	Venue	Date
1:25:18		Yelena	Lashmanova	RUS	9.4.92	1	NC-w	Sochi	18 Feb
1:25:22		Yekaterina	Medvedyeva	RUS	29.3.94	2	NC-w	Sochi	18 Feb
1:26:18	44:10		Yang Jiayu	CHN	18.2.96	1	WCh	London	13 Aug
1:26:19	44:10	María Guadalupe	González	MEX	9.1.89	2	WCh	London	13 Aug
1:26:27		Sofiya	Brodatskaya	RUS	4.10.95	3	NC-w	Sochi	18 Feb
1:26:28	43:29		Lu Xiuzhi	CHN	26.10.93	1	NGP	Huangshan	4 Mar
1:26:29	43:27		Wang Na	CHN	29.5.95	2	NGP	Huangshan	4 Mar
1:26:35	43:28		Yang Jiayu			3	NGP	Huangshan	4 Mar
1:26:36	44:10	Antonella	Palmisano	ITA	6.8.91	3	WCh	London	13 Aug
1:26:59	44:10	Erica	de Sena	BRA	3.5.85	4	WCh	London	13 Aug
1:27:43	44:37		Lashmanova			1	NC	Cheboksary	10 Jun
1:27:50	44:37		Medvedyeva			2	NC	Cheboksary	10 Jun
1:27:53	44:37	Mariya	Ponomaryova (10)	RUS	18.6.95	3	NC	Cheboksary	10 Jun
1:27:57	44:21		Palmisano			1	ECp	Podébrady	21 May
1:28:02	44:37		Brodatskaya			4	NC	Cheboksary	10 Jun
1:28:09	43:52		M G González			1	PAmCp	Lima	13 May
1:28:10	44:10	Sandra	Arenas	COL	17.9.93	5	WCh	London	13 Aug
1:28:15	43:31		Wang Yingliu	CHN	1.3.92	4	NGP	Huangshan	4 Mar
1:28:29	44:37	Klavdiya	Afanasyeva	RUS	15.1.96	5	NC	Cheboksary	10 Jun
1:28:29	44:46		Yang Jiayu			1	NG	Tianjin	3 Sep
1:28:32		Tatyana	Mineyeva	RUS	10.8.90	4	NC-w	Sochi	18 Feb
1:28:33	44:46		Qieyang Shenjie	CHN	11.11.90	2	NG	Tianjin	3 Sep
1:28:34	43:29		Nie Jingjing	CHN	1.3.88	5	NGP	Huangshan	4 Mar
1:28:37	44:57		Duan Dandan	CHN	23.5.95	6	NGP	Huangshan	4 Mar
1:28:43			Nie Jingjing			1	NG	Tianjin	4 Sep
1:28:44	43:33		La Mao	CHN	17.12.96	7	NGP	Huangshan	4 Mar
1:28:45	44:57		Yang Peili	CHN	7.8.94	8	NGP	Huangshan	4 Mar
1:28:46			Duan Dandan			2	NG	Tianjin	4 Sep
1:28:50			Liang Rui	CHN	18.6.94	3	NG	Tianjin	4 Sep
1:28:55	44:57		Liang Rui			9	NGP	Huangshan	4 Mar
		(30/20)							
1:28:57	44:10	Ana	Cabecinha	POR	29.4.84	6	WCh	London	13 Aug
1:29:06		Paola	Pérez	ECU	21.12.89	1		Sucua	15 Apr
1:29:13	44:10	Kimberley	García	PER	19.10.93	7	WCh	London	13 Aug
1:29:14	43:29		Ni Yuanyuan	CHN	6.4.95	10	NGP	Huangshan	4 Mar
1:29:19			Chen Chen	CHN	25.8.95	11	NGP	Huangshan	4 Mar
1:29:27	44:57		He Qin	CHN	23.3.92	12	NGP	Huangshan	4 Mar
1:29:29	44:36	Laura	García-Caro	ESP	16.4.95	9	WCh	London	13 Aug
1:29:33		María	Pérez	ESP	29.4.96	10	WCh	London	13 Aug
1:29:40	44:30	Kumiko	Okada	JPN	17.10.91	1	NC	Kobe	19 Feb
1:29:42	44:39		Ji Yefang	CHN	4.3.96	13	NGP	Huangshan	4 Mar
		(30)							
1:29:50	45:02	Ainhoa	Pinedo	ESP	17.2.83	2		La Coruña	3 Jun
1:29:56		Olga	Shargina	RUS	24.7.96	6	NC-w	Sochi	18 Feb
1:29:58	44:33	Regan	Lamble	AUS	14.10.91	1	Oce Ch	Adelaide	19 Feb
1:30:00	44:30	Sandra	Galvis	COL	28.6.86	1		Podébrady	8 Apr
1:30:01	44:54	Mirna	Ortiz	GUA	28.2.87	11	WCh	London	13 Aug
1:30:05	44:53	Viktória	Madarász	HUN	12.5.85	12	WCh	London	13 Aug
1:30:11	44:51	Inna	Kashyna	UKR	27.9.91	4	ECp	Podébrady	21 May
1:30:14		Julia	Takacs	ESP	29.6.89	1		Naumburg	23 Apr
1:30:26	44:48	Nadiya	Borovska	UKR	25.2.81	5	ECp	Podébrady	21 May
1:30:34	45:09	Eleonora	Giorgi	ITA	14.9.89	14	WCh	London	13 Aug
		(40)							
1:30:35	45:11	Valentina	Trapletti	ITA	12.7.85	15	WCh	London	13 Aug
1:30:44	45:01	Inês	Henriques	POR	1.5.80	4		La Coruña	3 Jun

Mark		Name		Nat	Born	Pos	Meet	Venue	Date
1:30:45	45:13	Brigita	Virbalyte-Dimsiene	LTU	1.2.85	16	WCh	London	13 Aug
1:30:51	45:01	Lidia	Sánchez-Puebla	ESP	17.7.96	5		La Coruña	3 Jun
1:31:00			Zhou Kang	CHN	24.12.89	14	NGP	Huangshan	4 Mar
1:31:00	45:57		Li Maocuo	CHN	20.10.92	15	NGP	Huangshan	4 Mar
1:31:14	44:46	Yeseida	Carrillo	COL	22.10.93	2		Podébrady	8 Apr
1:31:21	45:17		Xie Lijuan	CHN	14.5.93	16	NGP	Huangshan	4 Mar
1:31:22			Hou Yongbo	CHN	15.9.94	8	NG	Tianjin	4 Sep
1:31:23	45:24	Bekki	Smith	AUS	25.11.86	3	Oce Ch	Adelaide	19 Feb
		(50)							
1:31:23	45:30	Zivile	Vaiciukeviciute	LTU	3.4.96	19	WCh	London	13 Aug
1:31:23			Yin Hang	CHN	7.2.97	9	NG	Tianjin	4 Sep
1:31:23			Sun Huanhuan	CHN	15.3.90	10	NG	Tianjin	4 Sep
1:31:27			Li Ping	CHN	7.1.94	11	NG	Tianjin	4 Sep
1:31:31	46:22		Wang Yalan	CHN	19.2.93	17	NGP	Huangshan	4 Mar
1:31:31		Janeth	Guamán	ECU	15.1.88	2		Sucua	15 Apr
1:31:32	46:20		Ma Yiming	CHN	10.9.97	18	NGP	Huangshan	4 Mar
1:31:34	45:29	Ángela	Castro	BOL	21.2.93	23	WCh	London	13 Aug
1:31:36	46:20		Ma Faying	CHN	30.8.93	19	NGP	Huangshan	4 Mar
1:31:37			Mao Yanxue	CHN	15.2.94	20	NGP	Huangshan	4 Mar
		(60)							
1:31:48		Nadezhda	Sergeyeva	RUS	6.11.94	7	NC-w	Sochi	18 Feb
1:31:48	46:08	Valeria	Ortuño	MEX-J	27.5.98	4		Podébrady	8 Apr
1:31:50	45:37	Amanda	Cano	ESP	19.8.94	4		Mérida	2 Apr
1:31:56	46:22		Yang Mingxia	CHN	13.1.90	22	NGP	Huangshan	4 Mar
1:32:00		Émilie	Menuet	FRA	27.11.91	1	NC	La Roche-sur-Yon	12 Mar
1:32:03	45:14	Antigóni	Drisbióti	GRE	21.3.84	24	WCh	London	13 Aug
1:32:12	45:51	Chiaki	Asada	JPN	21.1.91	2		Nomi	19 Mar
1:32:14	45:29	Maria	Michta-Coffey	USA	23.6.86	25	WCh	London	13 Aug
1:32:16	46:20		Xiao Xianghua	CHN	19.2.97	23	NGP	Huangshan	4 Mar
1:32:21		Yuliya	Turova	RUS	9.6.97	8	NC-w	Sochi	18 Feb
		(70)							
1:32:22	45:31	Anastasiya	Yatsevich	BLR	18.1.85	26	WCh	London	13 Aug
1:32:23	45:24	Alana	Barber	NZL	8.7.87	4	Oce Ch	Adelaide	19 Feb
1:32:23	45:51	Yuki	Yoshizumi	JPN	7.1.96	3		Nomi	19 Mar
1:32:31	46:17	Maria	Larios	ESP	29.10.92	8		La Coruña	3 Jun
1:32:32	44:58		Gao Shan	CHN	8.4.95	24	NGP	Huangshan	4 Mar
1:32:33	45:52	Gemma	Bridge	GBR	17.5.93	1		Leeds	25 Jun
1:32:39	46:08	Monika	Vaiciukeviciute	LTU	3.4.96	5		Podébrady	8 Apr
1:32:40	46:13	Annabel	Orjuela	COL	24.7.88	6	PAmCp	Lima	13 May
1:32:40A		Yehualye	Beletew	ETH-J	31.7.98	1	NC	Addis Ababa	21 May
1:32:44		Anastasiya	Yevacheva	RUS	20.11.97	9	NC-w	Sochi	18 Feb
		(80)							
1:32:44		Magaly	Bonilla	ECU	8.2.92	3		Sucua	15 Apr
1:32:44	45:42	Barbara	Kovács	HUN	26.7.93	27	WCh	London	13 Aug
1:32:50	45:39	Rena	Goto	JPN	6.9.95	2	NC	Kobe	19 Feb
1:32:52		Johana	Ordóñez	ECU	12.12.87	4		Sucua	15 Apr
1:32:57		Aleksandra	Bushkova	RUS	13.1.97	10	NC-w	Sochi	18 Feb
1:33:04		Miranda	Melville	USA	20.3.89	2		Philadelphia	2 Apr
1:33:04	45:53	Bethan	Davies	GBR	7.11.90	3		Leeds	25 Jun
1:33:09	45:40	Kaori	Kawazoe	JPN	30.5.95	4		Nomi	19 Mar
1:33:16	45:26	Sae	Matsumoto	JPN	15.5.93	3	NC	Kobe	19 Feb
1:33:16	46:22		Zhao Wenli	CHN	11.12.96	25	NGP	Huangshan	4 Mar
		(90)							
1:33:16	46:18		Ma Zhenxia	CHN-J	1.8.98	9		La Coruña	3 Jun
1:33:16		Viktoryia	Roshchupkina	BLR	23.5.95	4	EU23	Bydgoszcz	16 Jul
1:33:18	46:11	Anezka	Drahotová	CZE	22.7.95	6		Podébrady	8 Apr
1:33:26	46:27	Mária	Czáková	SVK	2.10.88	2		Lugano	19 Mar
1:33:27			Chen Zhen	CHN	3.11.94	26	NGP	Huangshan	4 Mar
1:33:28A	45:22	María Guadalupe	Sánchez	MEX	4.8.95	7		Ciudad Juárez	12 Mar
1:33:29	45:41		Jeon Yang-eun	KOR	24.5.88	30	WCh	London	13 Aug
1:33:31	46:20		Dong Genmiao	CHN	16.7.94	27	NGP	Huangshan	4 Mar
1:33:32		Eleonora	Dominici	ITA	22.2.96	5	EU23	Bydgoszcz	16 Jul
1:33:35		Karla	Jaramillo	ECU	21.1.97	5		Sucua	15 Apr
		(100)							

Mark		Name		Nat	Born	Date
1:33:39			Jiang Shanshan	CHN	28.2.97	15 Apr
1:33:46	45:40	Andreea	Arsine	ROU	14.9.88	13 Aug
1:33:48			Mao Yanqiu	CHN	7.10.96	4 Mar
1:33:51	46:18	Maritza Rafaela	Poncio	GUA	3.12.94	3 Jun
1:33:52			Zhang Xin	CHN	17.8.89	4 Mar
1:33:58	45:41	Nadezhda	Mokeyeva	RUS	10.1.96	10 Jun
1:33:59	45:45	Valentyna	Myronchuk	UKR	10.8.94	13 Aug
1:33:59		Claire	Tallent	AUS	7.6.81	17 Dec
1:34:01		Khushbir	Kaur	IND	9.7.93	15 Apr
1:34:05		Anastasiya	Kalashnikova	RUS	29.6.97	18 Feb
1:34:15A		Grace	Wanjiru	KEN	10.1.79	10 May
1:34:16		Katarzyna	Golba	POL	21.12.89	19 Mar
1:34:17	46:17		Li Qiuye	CHN	2.12.93	4 Mar
1:34:18		Jemima	Montag	AUS-J	15.2.98	17 Dec
1:34:24		Emilia	Lehmeyer	GER	11.4.97	16 Jul
1:34:25	46:22	Lizbeth	Silva	MEX	30.9.89	23 Apr

Mark		Name	Nat	Born	Date
1:34:26	Déspina	Zapounídou	GRE	5.10.85	21 May
1:34:33A	Mayra Carolina	Herrera	GUA	20.12.88	12 Feb
1:34:35		Cun Hailu	CHN	15.8.97	4 Mar
1:34:37		Li Leilei	CHN	18.8.89	3 Sep
1:34:40	Kristina	Mikhaylova	RUS	16.10.92	18 Feb
1:34:41	Nadezda	Dorozhuk	BLR	23.1.90	22 Apr
1:34:42	46:09	Zhang Lifang	CHN	6.12.97	4 Mar
1:34:43	Rita	Récsei	HUN	30.1.96	30 Apr
1:34:44		Yang Lei	CHN	29.11.95	4 Sep
1:34:45		Zhao Qianyuan	CHN	11.3.95	4 Mar
1:34:48		Zhang Xuhong	CHN	2.1.94	4 Mar
1:34:49		Zhou Yumei	CHN	11.11.94	4 Mar
1:34:49	Anél	Oosthuizen	RSA	22.4.95	8 Apr
1:34:50	Ana Veronica	Rodean	ROU	23.6.84	13 Aug
1:34:52	Chahineze	Nasri	TUN	3.6.96	12 Mar
1:34:58		Chen Yumin	CHN	8.2.97	4 Sep
1:34:59	Diana	Cacciotti	ITA	2.12.95	3 Jun
1:35:04	Jessica	Ching Siu Nga	HKG	11.2.87	13 Aug
1:35:07		Yang Fuyao	CHN	6.12.96	4 Mar
1:35:07	Marine	Quennehen	FRA	1.8.91	8 Apr
1:35:09	Elisa	Neuvonen	FIN	19.3.91	8 Apr
1:35:16	Ai	Michiguchi	JPN	3.6.88	19 Feb
1:35:16		Zhou Tao	CHN	18.11.97	4 Sep
1:35:22		Wang Chen	CHN	18.2.94	4 Mar
1:35:23	Milángela	Rosales	VEN	21.2.87	13 May
1:35:25	Olena	Mizernyuk	UKR	23.11.95	12 Mar
1:35:27		Zhao Fenyan	CHN	21.7.96	4 Mar
1:35:28	Anett	Torma	HUN	2.4.84	30 Apr
1:35:28		Tong Lingling	CHN	25.1.92	4 Sep
1:35:35A 46:09	Ilse	Guerrero	MEX	24.3.93	12 Mar
1:35:39		Tang Caihong	CHN	29.4.96	4 Sep
1:35:44	Reykhan	Kagramanova	RUS	1.6.97	18 Feb
1:35:44	Paulina	Buziak	POL	16.12.86	22 Apr
1:35:45	Regina	Rykova	KAZ	12.12.91	19 Mar
1:35:45	Mara	Ribeiro	POR	11.5.95	21 May
1:35:47		Jiang Pengqin	CHN	5.9.95	4 Mar
1:35:47A	Ayalnesh	Dejene	ETH-J	20.1.98	21 May
1:35:55	Nicole	Colombi	ITA	29.12.95	15 Oct
1:35:56		Wang Lixue	CHN	15.12.96	4 Mar
1:35:58	Chiaki	Yamato	JPN	20.11.90	19 Feb
1:36:10.0t	Jéssica	Hancco	PER	10.9.95	30 Sep
1:36:14		Wang Zhenzhen	CHN	3.2.95	4 Mar
1:36:15	Yukiho	Mizoguchi	JPN	6.12.97	22 Oct
1:36:20	Liliya	Stepanova	RUS	13.11.96	18 Feb
1:36:21	Kristina	Saltanovic	LTU	20.2.75	4 Mar
1:36:23		Chi Meijiao	CHN	28.6.96	4 Mar
1:36:26		Zhang Yan	CHN	3.1.97	4 Mar
1:36:26	Rachel	Tallent	AUS	20.2.93	3 Jun
1:36:28	Mar	Juárez	ESP	27.9.93	3 Jun
1:36:40		Lee Da-seul	KOR	8.11.96	24 Oct
1:36:46A	Askale	Tiksa	ETH	21.7.94	21 May
1:36:47		Kang Jinzi	CHN	25.1.90	4 Sep
1:36:48	Tamara	Havrylyuk	UKR	14.12.95	12 Mar
1:36:49	Serena	Sonoda	JPN-J	10.9.96	19 Feb
1:36:50	Masumi	Fuchise	JPN	2.9.86	19 Mar
1:36:58	Anastasiya	Taushkanova	RUS	25.3.96	18 Feb
1:37:00	Amandine	Marcou	FRA	26.4.92	8 Apr
1:37:06	Alina	Tsviliy	UKR	18.9.94	12 Mar
1:37:06	Clara	Smith	AUS-J	9.3.98	17 Dec
1:37:10	Laura	Polli	SUI	7.9.83	8 Apr
1:37:12	Anastasiya	Rodkina	BLR	28.8.94	22 Apr
1:37:12.0t	Leidy	Guerra	PER-J	27.9.98	30 Sep
1:37:14	Saskia	Feige	GER	13.8.97	23 Apr
1:37:19	Yekaterina	Lyubushkina	RUS	19.9.95	18 Feb
1:37:21	Khrystyna	Yudkina	UKR	4.12.84	12 Mar
1:37:23	Edna	Barros	POR	18.12.96	3 Jun
1:37:39	Heather	Lewis	GBR	25.10.93	19 Mar
1:37:42	Priyanka	Goswami	IND	10.3.96	19 Mar
1:37:44	Cisiane	Lopes	BRA	17.2.83	1 Apr
1:37:53		Lei Fei	CHN	8.8.97	4 Mar
1:37:53	Kseniya	Radko	UKR	18.8.94	12 Mar
1:37:54	Kristina	Lyubushkina	RUS	19.9.95	18 Feb
1:37:54	Dana	Aydosova	KAZ	5.5.95	3 Jun
1:37:56	Jessica	Pickles	AUS	6.2.94	19 Feb
1:37:59	Corinne (192)	Baudoin	FRA	22.2.80	8 Apr

Irregular

1:33:35	Taika	Nummi	FIN	12.10.97	6 May

Best track times

Mark		Name	Nat	Born	Pos	Meet	Venue	Date
1:32:26.0t	Paola	Pérez	ECU	21.12.89	1	SAmC	Asunción	24 Jun
1:32:35.2t	Ángela	Castro	BOL	21.2.93	2	SAmC	Asunción	24 Jun
1:33:51.2At	Sandra	Arenas	COL	17.9.93	1	NC	Medellín	10 Jun
1:36:21.3At	Annabel	Orjuela	COL	24.7.88	2	NC	Medellín	10 Jun

JUNIORS

See main list for top 3 juniors. 7 performances by 5 women to 1:36:00. Additional performance:

Belete	1:33:33	10	Suzhou	24 Sep
Ortuño	1:35:47A	11	Ciudad Juárez	12 Mar

Mark		Name	Nat	Born	Pos	Meet	Venue	Date
1:34:18	Jemima	Montag	AUS	15.2.98	3		Melbourne	17 Dec
1:36:49	Serena	Sonoda	JPN	10.9.96	8	NC	Kobe	19 Feb
1:37:06	Clara	Smith	AUS	9.3.98	5		Melbourne	17 Dec
1:37:12.0t	Leidy	Guerra	PER	27.9.98	2	NCp	Lima	30 Sep
1:39:29		Yan Peirong	CHN	26.9.99	12	NG	Tianjin	3 Sep
1:39:53	Akane	Tamaki	JPN-Y	.00	19		Nomi	19 Mar
1:39:53	Shione	Honma (10)	JPN	.98	6		Takaata	22 Oct

50 KILOMETRES WALK

50k	30k	35k		Name	Nat	Born	Pos	Meet	Venue	Date
4:05:56	2:26:35	2:50:52	Inês	Henriques	POR	1.5.80	1	WCh	London	13 Aug
4:08:26	2:26:10	2:50:09		Henriques			1		Porto de Mós	15 Jan
4:08:58	2:26:39	2:51:42		Yin Hang	CHN	7.2.97	2	WCh	London	13 Aug
4:15:42			Mayra Carolina	Herrera	GUA	20.12.88	1		Owego	9 Sep
4:20:49	2:34:22	2:59:53		Yang Shuqing	CHN	30.8.96	3	WCh	London	13 Aug
4:21:51	2:34:43	3:00:43	Kathleen	Burnett	USA	10.7.88	4	WCh	London	13 Aug
4:22:22	2:32:27			Yin Hang			1	NGP	Huangshan	5 Mar
4:26:37				Burnett			1	NC	Santee	28 Jan
4:27:24	2:34:52			Yang Shuqing			2	NGP	Huangshan	5 Mar
4:29:33			Erin	Talcott	USA	21.5.78	2	NC	Santee	28 Jan
4:32:14	2:43:46			Jiang Shanshan	CHN	28.2.97	3	NGP	Huangshan	5 Mar
4:32:14	2:41:48	3:08:22	Khrystyna	Yudkina	UKR	4.12.84	1	NC	Ivano-Frankivsk	15 Oct
4:34:49	2:39:31	3:07:51	Kseniya	Radko	UKR	18.8.94	2	NC	Ivano-Frankivsk	15 Oct
4:36:40	2:43:46			Wang Lixue (10)	CHN	15.12.96	4	NGP	Huangshan	5 Mar
4:37:55	2:41:28	3:09:59	Vasylyna	Vitovshchyk	UKR	30.4.90	3	NC	Ivano-Frankivsk	15 Oct
4:38:48	2:43:46			Wang Dan	CHN	11.1.95	5	NGP	Huangshan	5 Mar

Mark			Name		Nat	Born	Pos	Meet	Venue	Date
4:38:56				Yang Shuqing			1	NGP	Xi'an	18 Jun
4:39:28			Nair	da Rosa	BRA	22.3.80	1	PAmCp	Lima	14 May
4:40:02				Tang Caihong	CHN	29.4.96	2	NGP	Zhengzhou	22 May
4:41:55	2:52:47	3:21:02	Dusica (20/15)	Topic	SRB	11.1.82	4	NC	Ivano-Frankivsk	15 Oct
4:41:58			Agnieszka	Ellward	POL	26.3.89	1		Gleina	14 Oct
4:42:27				Li Qiuye	CHN	2.12.93	2	NGP	Xi'an	18 Jun
4:44:01				Zhao Huimin	CHN	12.10.93	3	NGP	Xi'an	18 Jun
4:48:26	2:44:32	3:13:22	María Dolores	Marcos	ESP	18.8.79	1		Naumburg	23 Apr
4:49:45			Yoci	Caballero	PER	2.2.93	2	PAmCp	Lima	14 May
4:54:12			Susan	Randall	USA	6.9.74	3	NC	Santee	28 Jan
4:54:20				Ma Lingyu	CHN	6.1.95	4	NGP	Xi'an	18 Jun
4:54:33			Natalie	le Roux	RSA	10.6.80	1		George	21 Oct
4:59:12				Zhu Chunyan	CHN	3.6.92	4	NGP	Zhengzhou	22 May
4:59:14				Guo Runfeng	CHN	9.5.95	5	NGP	Xi'an	18 Jun
5:00:37			Viktoriya	Pchelintseva	UKR	15.2.97	5	NC	Ivano-Frankivsk	15 Oct
5:02:33			Erica (27)	Morales	MEX	10.12.86	1		Monterrey	19 Mar

Late Amendments to 2017 Lists

Men: 100m: 10.24w 4.0 Ryichiro Sakai JPN-J .98 1 Osaka 14 Sep
300m: 32.47 Kenji Fukumitsu JPN 23 Apr
10km: 28:22 Fantahun Hunegnaw ETH 8 Zaandam 17 Sep
15km: 42:53+ Jonathan Ndiku KEN in HMar Marugame 5 Feb
HMar: 61:16 Kassa Mekashaw ETH 19.3.84 20 Mar
Women: 3000m: 8:44.2+ Irene Cheptai 4.2.92 7 in 5000 Roma 8 Jun; 9:00.0+ Berhenu Degefa 8 Jun
15km: 49:46+ Grace Kimanzi KEN 1.3.92 in HMar Okayama 23 Dec

100th bests on Trends pages: Men: 5000m 13:26.55, 10,000m: 28:09.98, 3000mSt 8:31.95

Base standards: Men: 5000m 185, 3000mSt 180; **Women:** JT 203

Some notes on Lists

World Lists 2017

No Finnish men appear in the senior world lists for running events on the flat in 2017.

All-time lists

No changes made in 2017 to top 50 performers or 30 performances men's 5000m or hammer, women's 400m – only one for men's 3000m steeplechase, 400m hurdles, high jump.

Women's shot – highest change to all-time list: Raven Saunders 19.76 to 97th.

In contrast: the top of the women's half marathon lists were transformed so that by the end of the year, 6 of the all-time top 10 performances and 13 of the top 30 were run in 2017.

Further Additions and Corrections

Nationality change

Edose Ibadin USA NGR 1 Aug 17

Name changes

Rhianwedd Price-Weimer GBR, Brianna Rollins-McNeal USA

Championships corrections:

Bolivar Games: W 3000mSt: Zulema Arenas
European Team: drugs dq : W 400m: (2) Zemlyak, so. 2. Müller, 3. Ida Baumgart POL 52.18; 4x100m: (3) UKR so 3. ITA 43.38; 4x400m: (2) UKR so: 2. GER, 3. GBR
South American Champs W 1500m & 3000mSt : Zulema Arenas, HJ: 3. Júlia Cristina dos Santos

Drugs Bans

Add to 2016:
Olesya Povh UKR 4y with all results annulled from 15 June 2016 (inc 2nd and POL 2nd at 4x400m in European Team 2017); Olha Zemlyak UKR 8y with all results annulled from 5 July 2016
Further IAAF Drugs bans list (March 2018)
In 2013: 4y: Lutfiye Kaya TUR (7 Sep)
In 2016: 4y: Omer Tuncer TUR (16 Nov)
In 2017: 4y: David Burrell GBR (23 Aug), Younés Kniya MAR (9 Jul), Jithin Paul IND (17 Apr), D Sreekanth IND (15 May); 2y: Cecilia Raath RSA (4 Jun), 5m: Stefano Cadoni ITA (22 Jul).

ADD OBITUARY 2017

Suzanne ALLDAY (née Farmer) (later GOODISON (b. 26 Nov 1934 Shoreham-by-Sea) died in Chichester on 26 July 2017. She competed in 35 internationals for Britain at shot and discus 1951-64, including at the Olympic Games of 1952, 1960 and 1964, European Championships in 1958 (5th SP/10th DT) and 1962 (10th/15th), and at three Commonwealth Games 1954 (6/2, also 6th javelin), 1958 (2/1) and 1962 (3/4). She was WAAA champion at shot 1954, 1956 and 1958-61 and at discus 1952-3, 1956 and 1958-61. She set eight UK records at shot from 13.33 (1956) to 15.18 (1964) and ten at discus from 40.37 (1952) to 47.70 (1958).

Obituary 2018

Chala ADUGNA Bekele (Ethiopia) (b. 1989) died during a training session on 2 March. He was electrocuted when he accid–entally touched a downed power line. He was second in the Hannover Marathon in 2015 in his pb of 2:09:42. Other pbs: HMar 62:56 (2014), 3000mSt 8:55.1A (2015).

Peter Charles **ALLDAY** (Great Britain & NI) (b. 27 Jun 1927 Wandsworth, London) on 10 March in Bexhill-on-Sea. A founder member of the Hammer Circle. he competed in 14 internationals for Britain 1952-62, including 21st in 1952 and 9th in 1956 at the Olympic Games and 18th at the 1958 Europeans. After 5th in 1954 he was the bronze medallist at the 1958 Commonwealth Games, and was AAA champion in 1956 (2nd 1953, 3rd 1951-2, 1955, 1962), CAU champion 1950-1 and Southern 1950-1, 1953-5, 1958, 1962. His pb was a UK record 59.61 in 1956. He married Suzanne Farmer, who as Sue Allday was Britain's top shot putter and discus thrower for several years.

Irina Anatolyevna **BEGLYAKOVA** (USSR/Russia) (b. 26 Feb 1933) (later Chelnaya) in March. At the discus she won silver medals at the 1952 Olympic Games and 1954 European Championships and was 4th at the 1958 Europeans. She was the World University Games champion in 1957 (and also 1st in 1954 and 2nd in 1955 and 1957 at the UIE event). She did not win a USSR title but was 2nd in 1957 and 3rd in 1955-6 and 1958. She was third on the world list in 1955 and 1956 (pb 52.71). She worked as a doctor in Moscow.

Edwin William **CARR** Jr. (Australia) (b. 23 Sep 1928) on 25 March. Australian champion at 440y 1949-50 and 1952, he competed at 200m (qf), 400m (ht) and both relays at the 1952 Olympic Games and was the Empire Games champion at 440y and 4x440y in 1950. Pbs: 220y 21.5 (1951), 440y 47.6 (1949). He was the son of Edwin 'Slip' Carr (1899-1971), who competed at 100m and 200m at the 1924 Olympic Games and also played for Australia at rugby union.

Guy CURY (France) (b. 21 Mar 1930 Saint-Marcellin) on 17 March in Saint-Paul-Trois-Châteaux. At 400m hurdles he was 4th at the 1954 European Championships and reached the semi-finals at the 1956 Olympic Games He was French champion in 1953 and 1955-6 and had 23 internationals 1949-56. He set national records at 200mh 24.3 (1955) and 400mh 51.6 and 51.5 (1956). Other pbs: 200m 22.1 (1954), 400m 49.0 (1955), 110mh 14.9 (1956, HJ 1.80 (1953).

Dr **David** Edward **MARTIN** on 28 February in Decatur, Georgia at the age of 78. He was a world-leading exercise physiologist and worked on USATF's heat-training programme at the 2004 Olympics as well as with many top athletes such as Sebastian Coe, Arturo Barrios and Steve Scott. He wrote five books on running and many articles in coaching and scientific journals. He was a valued contributor for many years to the International Athletics Annual and annually compiled detailed marathon statistics, including all male performances better than 2:20 and women better than 2:50. With Roger Gynn he wrote "The Marathon Footrace" (1979), the seminal history of the event, and with Peter Coe "Better Training for Distance Runners" (2000). He worked at Georgia State University from 1970 and on his retirement was awarded the title of Professor Emeritus in the School of Allied Health Sciences.

Milan MATOS (Cuba) (b. 12 Nov 1949 Guantanamo) on 16 March in Havana. A long jumper, he competed (dnq) at the 1972 and 1976 Olympic Games and was CAC champion in 1975 with silver medals at the Central American & Caribbean Games in 1974 and 1978. He set Cuban records at 7.89A (1972) and 7.96 (1975). He became a top coach, notably of the jumpers Iván Pedroso, Yargelis Savigne and Mabel Gay.

Paavo NIEMELÄ (Finland) (b. 3 Apr 1936 Tyrnävä) on 19 February in Oulu. The third Finn to exceed 80m for the javelin, his pb 80.33 came in the 1963 Finnish Champs in Turku, looking to win until Pauli Nevala´s last-round 80.54. Just 1.69m tall and weighing 70 kilos, forester Niemelä is still one of the shortest men ever to achieve 80m. In his big year of 1963 he had three international dual matches. Over 40 years later he made a comeback, throwing a world best in the M70 age group.

Milica RAJKOV-NINKOV (Serbia) (b. 18 Apr 1936) on 1 January. Yugoslav champion at 400m 1957-9, 800m 1957-63 and cross-country 1961-62, and also Balkan champion at 800m in 1957 and 1963, competing at the European Championships in 1958 and 1962. Four YUG records at 800m from 2:12.3 (1957) to 2:09.9 (1963) with 400m pb 58.1 (1964). She became a professor of history in Novi Sad.

MEN'S INDEX 2017

Athletes included are those ranked in the top 100s at standard (World Championships) events (plus shorter lists for 1000m, 1M, 2000m and 3000m). Those with detailed biographical profiles are indicated in first column by:
* in this year's Annual, ^ featured in a previous year's Annual.

Name		Nat	Born	Ht/Wt	Event	2017 Mark	Pre-2017 Best
* Amos	Nijel	BOT	15.3.94	179/60	400	45.55	45.56- 14
					800	1:43.18	1:41.73- 12
Anani	Mohsen	TUN	25.5.85	187/117	HT	71.08	77.36- 10
Anas	Y. Muhammed	IND	17.9.94	176/64	400	45.32	45.40- 16
Anastasákis	Mihaíl	GRE	3.12.94	183/92	HT	77.72	77.08- 16
Anderson	Jeshua	USA	22.6.89	187/84	400h	49.88	47.93- 11
Anderson	Kenroy	JAM	27.6.87	178/75	200	20.39	20.54- 12
Anderson	Nick	USA	28.4.95	186/77	110h	13.49	13.60, 13.59w- 15
Andrade	Jordin	CPV	5.5.92	183/73	400h	49.52	49.24- 15
Andraloits	Maksim	BLR	17.6.97		Dec	7858	
André	Thiago	BRA	4.8.95	177/62	800	1:44.81	1:45.99- 14
1500	3:35.28		3:35.90- 15		1M	3:51.99	-0-
^ Andrews	Robby	USA	29.3.91	177/68	1500	3:35.25	3:34.78- 12
Andrzejczak	Jakub	POL-J	13.6.98	175/60	LJ	8.02	7.86- 16
Andújar	Daniel	ESP	14.5.94	183/78	800	1:45.17	1:45.61- 16
Anic	Lazar	SRB	14.12.91	188/78	LJ	8.15	7.98- 16
Anishchenkov	Nikita	RUS	25.7.92	188/80	HJ	2.30i, 2.24	2.30- 11
Anou	Abderrahmane	ALG	29.1.91	172/60	1500	3:36.50	3:35.2- 11
Antonelli	Michele	ITA	23.5.94	177/64	50kW	3:49:07	3:53:08- 16
Antunes	Diogo	POR	2.11.92	178/65	100	10.27, 10.10w	10.29- 16
Aouad	Zouhaïr	BRN	7.4.89	179/61	3000	7:39.91	7:45.80- 16
					5000	13:15.53	13:14.16- 16
^ Apak	Esref	TUR	3.1.82	186/105	HT	78.00	81.45- 05
Aperumoi	Joseph	KEN	12.1.90		Mar	2:08:26	2:20:42- 12
Aphane	Reneilwe	RSA	24.8.90	175/73	TJ	16.75A	16.10A- 16, 16.02, 16.21Aw- 15
Appier	Garrett	USA	15.10.92	197/114	SP	19.75i	20.79- 16
Apti	Ayhan	BUL	25.4.93	183/98	HT	71.82	70.19- 16
* Arai	Hirooki	JPN	18.5.88	180/62	20kW	1:19:25	1:19:54- 16
					50kW	3:41:17	3:40:20- 15
^ Arai	Ryohei	JPN	23.6.91	183/96	JT	82.13	86.83- 14
^ Araptany	Jacob	UGA	11.2.92	168/58	3kSt	8:21.92	8:14.48- 12
Araya	Yerko	CHI	14.2.86	174/59	20kW	1:21:56	1:20:47.2t- 11
Arce	Daniel	ESP	22.4.92	187/72	3kSt	8:29.24	9:05.37- 10
Arcilla	Francisco	ESP	19.1.84	171/62	50kW	3:56:39	3:55:06- 16
Arents	Mareks	LAT	6.8.86	190/90	PV	5.60i, 5.51	5.70- 16
* Arévalo	Eider	COL	9.3.93	165/58	20kW	1:18:53	1:19:45- 13
* Arikan	Polat Kemboi	TUR	12.12.90	173/62	5000	13:19.20	13:05.98- 11
					10k	27:42.55	27:35.50- 16
Arita	Stephen	KEN	26.6.88	165/54	10k	27:57.17A	27:55.17A- 15
Arnaudov	Tsanko	POR	14.3.92	192/118	SP	21.56	21.06- 15
Arnold	LaMarion	USA	.96	175/68	100	10.10w	10.35w- 16
Arnold	Mike	USA	13.8.90	190/84	PV	5.55Ai, 5.41	5.77Ai- 16, 5.72A- 15, 5.70- 13
Arrhenius	Leif	SWE	15.7.86	192/120	DT	61.04A	64.46- 11
Arrhenius	Niklas	SWE	10.9.82	192/125	DT	65.72A	66.22- 11
Arroyo	Andrés	PUR	7.6.95	171/61	800	1:44.98	1:45.78- 16
Art	Arnaud	BEL	28.1.93	185/83	PV	5.71	5.65- 15
Arteaga	Mauricio	ECU	8.8.88	173/65	20kW	1:22:28	1:21:08- 16
Asanov	Aleksandr	RUS	30.3.96		HJ	2.26	2.21- 15
Asaoka	Mitsunori	JPN	11.1.93	162/50	10k	28:07.26	27:59.72- 16
* Ash	Ronnie	USA	2.7.88	188/86	110h	13.65	12.99- 14, 12.98w- 10
* Ashmeade	Nickel	JAM	7.4.90	184/87	200	20.37	19.85- 12
Assefa	Fikre	ETH	18.1.89		Mar	2:08:36	2:10:01- 15
Atine-Venel	Teddy	FRA	16.3.85	184/77	400	45.39	45.54- 08
Atnafu	Yitayal	ETH	20.1.93	172/55	Mar	2:07:21	2:08:53- 16
* Augustyn	Rafal	POL	14.5.84	178/71	50kW	3:44:18	3:43:22- 16
Austin	Ailex	USA	25.11.93	201/82	HJ	2.25i	2.19- 16
Auzeil	Bastien	FRA	22.10.89	190/82	Dec	7922	8191- 16
Awotunde	Josh	USA/NGR	12.6.95	188/107	SP	19.96	20.11- 16
Ayalew	Aweke	BRN	23.2.93	182/64	5000	13:16.16	13:05.00- 13
Ayele	Abayneh	ETH	4.11.87	175/57	Mar	2:07:42	2:06:45- 16
Ayenew	Mekuant	ETH	.91		Mar	2:09:00	2:10:05- 13
Ayenew	Yismaw	ETH-J	.98		5000	13:24.83	-0-
Ayouni	Abdessalem	TUN	16.5.94	187/79	800	1:45.63	1:45.98 -16
* Babayev	Nazim	AZE	8.10.97	185/70	TJ	17.18	17.04- 15
Babits	Max	USA	30.5.92	185/70	PV	5.55Ai	5.51i- 14, 5.41- 15
Babu	K.V.Rakesh	IND	20.3.90		TJ	16.52	16.29- 15
Bachir	Youssouf Hiss	DJI	–.87	178/70	1500	3:37.69	3:36.96- 15
Bäck	Kristian	FIN	18.7.96	193/83	LJ	7.95	7.95, 7.96w- 16
Bacon	Jaylen	USA	5.8.96	183/75	100	10.00, 9.97w	10.10- 15
					200	20.18	20.71- 15
Baden	Joel	AUS	1.2.96	190/70	HJ	2.24	2.29- 14

	Name		Nat	Born	Ht/Wt	Event	2017 Mark	Pre-2017 Best
	Bae You-il		KOR	16.6.94		JT	78.21	74.10- 15
	Baehre	Bo Kanda Lita	GER-J	29.4.99	185/79	PV	5.61	5.30- 16
	Bahner	Austin	USA	7.7.91	188/81	Dec	7850	7847w- 13, 7776- 16
	Bailey	Aldrich	USA	6.2.94	183/70	200	20.30, 19.99w	20.30, 20.16w- 15
						400	45.32	45.19- 12
	Bailey	Oshane	JAM	9.8.89	168/64	200	20.49	20.42- 16
	Bailey	Ramone	JAM	31.10.91	179/77	LJ	8.16	7.80- 15
	Bailey	Sean	JAM	15.7.97	183/73	400	45.59i, 45.76	46.51- 16
	Bailey	Tavis	USA	6.1.92	190/134	DT	62.42	65.82- 16
*	Bailey-Cole	Kemar	JAM	10.1.92	195/86	100	10.06	9.92- 15
*	Baji	Balázs	HUN	9.6.89	192/84	110h	13.15	13.28- 16
	Baker	Chris	GBR	2.2.91	197/84	HJ	2.28	2.36i, 2.29- 16
*	Baker	Ronnie	USA	15.10.93	178/75	100	9.98, 9.86w	10.05, 9.94w- 15
						200	20.06w	20.60Ai, 20.64- 16
	Bakharev	Viktor	RUS	5.5.94	184/70	3kSt	8:20.61	8:25.34- 16
*	Bakulin	Sergey	RUS	13.11.86	169/58	20kW	1:18:51	1:18:18- 08
	Balner	Michal	CZE	12.9.82	193/78	PV	5.80	5.82- 15
	Balnuweit	Erik	GER	21.9.88	189/75	110h	13.53, 13.48w	13.44, 13.32w-13
	Baloyes	Bernardo	COL	6.1.94	177/66	200	20.11A, 20.36w	20.43,20.35Aw- 14, 20.37A-15
	Baltaci	Özkan	TUR	13.2.94	187/111	HT	76.61	75.77- 16
	Bamoussa	Abdoullah	ITA	2.6.86	170/59	3kSt	8:22.00	8:32.54- 16
	Banevicius	Sarunas	LTU	20.11.91	188/105	SP	19.72	19.63i- 15, 19.50- 13
^	Baniótis	Konstadínos	GRE	6.11.86	202/80	HJ	2.26i, 2.22	2.34- 13
	Banks	Tremayne	USA	29.7.92	178/70	110h	13.74, 13.56w	13.62, 13.57w- 15
*	Banzeruk	Ivan	UKR	9.2.90	180/70	50kW	3:48:15	3:44:49- 14
*	Barber	Shawnacy	CAN	27.5.94	190/82	PV	5.83i, 5.72	6.00Ai- 16, 5.93- 15
*	Barega	Selemon	ETH-Y	20.1.00	173/59	3000	7:38.90	-
						5000	12:55.58	13:21.21- 16
	Barkach	Alfred	KEN	2.3.97	167/52	5000	13:25.30	13:48.30- 16
	Barnes	Emre Zafer	TUR	7.11.88	178/73	100	10.17, 10.02Aw	10.12- 16
*	Barr	Thomas	IRL	24.7.92	183/73	400h	48.95	47.97- 16
^	Barrondo	Erick	GUA	14.6.91	172/60	20kW	1:21:34	1:18:15- 12
						50kW	3:57:46	3:41:089- 13
^	de Barros	Bruno	BRA	7.1.87	178/70	200	20.61, 20.41w	20.16- 11
*	Barshim	Mutaz Essa	QAT	24.6.91	192/70	HJ	2.40	2.43- 14
*	Barsoton	Leonard	KEN	21.10.94	166/56	5000	13:17.38	13:16.25- 15
	10k	27:47.4A		27:20.74- 14		HMar	59:28	
*	Bascou	Dimitri	FRA	20.7.87	182/79	110h	13.55	13.12, 13.05w- 16
	Bashan	Nikolay	RUS	18.11.92	182/95	HT	75.00	72.61- 16
	Bassaw	Ben	FRA	9.7.89	184/80	200	20.40	20.43- 14
	Bastien	Steve	USA	4.3.94	183/76	Dec	8015	7917- 16
	Bates	KeAndre	USA	24.5.96	181/75	LJ	8.05, 8.15w	8.11, 8.32w- 16
						TJ	16.81i, 16.75, 16.76w	16.63, 16.73w- 16
	Batson	Diondre	USA	13.7.92	188/75	100	10.16	9.94, 9.86w- 15
	Batzávalis	Paraskevás	GRE	25.11.94	185/100	JT	81.74	85.95- 16
	Bayer	Andrew	USA	3.2.90	180/60	1500	3:36.85	3:34.47- 13
	3000	7:38.90		7:42.33i- 16, 7:43.84- 13		3kSt	8:14.46	8:16.11- 16
	Bayer	Maximilian	GER	5.12.90	181/73	110h	13.69, 13.52w	13.43- 16
	Bazile	Zack	USA	7.1.96	180/74	LJ	7.97	7.58, 7.69w- 16
	Beach	Curtis	USA	22.7.90	183/75	400h	49.83	49.87- 16
*	Bednarek	Sylwester	POL	28.4.89	198/75	HJ	2.33i, 2.32	2.32- 09
	Beer	Lukás	SVK	23.8.89	186/73	HJ	2.28i	2.26- 14
*	Bekele	Kenenisa	ETH	13.6.82	162/54	Mar	2:05:57	2:03:03- 16
	Belcher	Chris	USA	29.1.94	175/75	100	9.93	10.07- 16
						200	20.01	20.39- 16
	Belferrar	Mohamed Amine	ALG	6.2.91	180/69	800	1:45.44	1:45.01- 16
*	Belihu	Andamlak	ETH-J	20.11.98	181/62	10k	27:08.94	-0-
						HMar	59:51	-0-
	Bellido	José Emilio	ESP	25.5.87	180/68	TJ	16.30i, 16.73w	16.80A, 16.65- 12
	Belo	Francisco	POR	27.3.91	193/120	SP	20.86	19.58- 16
						DT	62.01	56.15- 15
	Ben Zahra	Abdelkarim	MAR-J	27.10.98	182/64	3kSt	8:30.76	8:34.28- 16
*	Benard	Chris	USA	4.4.90	190/79	TJ	17.48	17.21- 16
	Bencosme de Leon	José	ITA	16.5.92	187/77	400h	49.22	49.33- 12
	Benedetti	Giordano	ITA	22.5.89	189/67	800	1:46.09	1:44.67- 13
	Benitz	Timo	GER	24.12.91	170/56	1500	3:34.87	3:34.94- 14
	Benjamin	Rai	ANT	27.7.97	191/77	400h	48.33	49.82- 16
	Bennett	Chris	GBR	17.12.89	188/115	HT	75.72	76.45- 16
	Berdeja	Cristian	MEX	21.6.81	169/58	50kW	4:03:45	3:50:19- 15
	Berglund	Kalle	SWE	11.3.96	179/62	1500	3:36.60	3:41.00- 16
	Berihu	Solomon	ETH-J	2.10.99	172/55	5000	13:17.27	13:12.67- 16

Name		Nat	Born	Ht/Wt	Event	2017 Mark	Pre-2017 Best
^ Berrabah	Yahya	MAR	13.10.81	186/75	LJ	8.16	8.40- 09
Bertemes	Bob	LUX	24.5.93	187/118	SP	20.63i, 20.18	20.56i- 15, 20.14- 16
Bertolini	Roberto	ITA	9.10.85	187/100	JT	81.68	81.05- 16
Bertrand	Jean-Pierre	FRA	5.11.92	180/71	LJ	8.08i, 7.97	8.03- 16
Bett	David	KEN	18.10.92	160/52	5000	13:25.11	13:06.06- 10
Bett	Emmanuel	KEN	14.7.95	170/55	3kSt	8:23.2A	
* Bett	Kipyegon	KEN-J	2.1.98	182/70	800	1:44.04A	1:43.76- 16
* Bett	Nicholas	KEN	20.12.96	172/52	3kSt	8:12.20	8:10.07- 16
* Bett	Nicholas	KEN	14.6.92	186/77	400h	49.70	47.79- 15
Beyo	Chala	ETH	18.1.96	174/57	3kSt	8:13.24	8:17.84- 16
Bian Tongda		CHN	1.4.91	170/58	20kW	1:21:01	1:19:34- 13
					50kW	3:48:41	3:59:30- 15
Bianchetti	Sebastiano	ITA	20.1.96	188/125	SP	19.78	19.78- 16
Bichler	Johannes	GER	3.7.90	186/95	HT	71.70	71.02- 16
* Bigot ¶	Quentin	FRA	1.12.92	179/95	HT	77.87	78.58- 14
Bilodeau	Mathieu	CAN	27.11.83	185/73	50kW	3:56:54	3:53:56- 16
Bingham	Basil	JAM	1.9.94	185/102	DT	60.77	58.12- 16
* Bird-Smith	Dane	AUS	15.7.92	178/66	20kW	1:19:28	1:19:37- 16
Birech	Cosmas	KEN	21.3.86	176/63	HMar	61:01	60:23- 15
* Birech	Jairus	KEN	14.12.92	170/56	3kSt	8:07.68	7:58.41- 14
* Birgen	Bethwel	KEN	6.8.88	178/64	1500	3:32.27	3:30.77- 13
					1M	3:53.50	3:50.42- 13
					3000	7:43.57	7:32.48- 16
					5000	13:17.80	13:04.66- 16
Birkinhead	Damien	AUS	8.4.93	190/130	SP	21.35	21.21- 16
* Biwott	Robert	KEN	28.1.96	180/68	800	1:45.05	1:43.56- 15
					1500	3:34.30	3:30.10- 15
Blair	Coy	USA	10.6.94	190/130	SP	20.14	19.45- 15
Blair-Sanford	Donald	ISR	5.2.87	193/84	400	45.54	45.04- 15
* Blake	Yohan	JAM	26.12.89	181/79	100	9.90	9.69- 12
					200	19.97	19.26- 11
Blankenbaker	Dylan	USA	6.1.94	183/64	3kSt	8:31.17	8:34.69- 16
Blankenship	Ben	USA	15.12.89	173/61	1500	3:35.29	3:34.26- 16
					1M	3:53.04	3:53.83- 16, 3:53.13i- 15
					3000	7:44.43	7:38.08- 15
Blech	Torben	GER	12.2.95	183/84	Dec	7872	7541- 16
^ Bledman	Keston	TTO	8.3.88	183/75	100	10.08	9.86, 9.85w- 12
Blocki	Adrian	POL	11.4.90	173/63	50kW	3:48:39	3:47:16- 16
Blocki	Damian	POL	28.4.89	180/65	20kW	1:21:29	1:26:06- 14
					50kW	3:53:01	3:51:32- 13
Bloomfield	Akeem	JAM	10.11.97	188/77	200	20.29w	20.66- 16
					400	44.74	44.93- 15
Bockarie	Solomon	NED	18.5.87	170/64	200	20.21w	20.37- 16
Bogatyrev	Pyotr	RUS	11.3.91		20kW	1:20:49	1:19:36- 13
Boirie	Baptiste	FRA	26.12.92	171/65	PV	5.65	5.60- 16
Bol	Peter	AUS	22.2.94	168/57	800	1:45.21	1:45.41- 16
Bollinger	Marvin	GER	7.10.96		Dec	7735	7208- 16
* Bolt	Usain	JAM	21.8.86	196/88	100	9.95	9.58- 09
* Bondarenko	Bohdan	UKR	30.8.89	197/80	HJ	2.32	2.42- 14
Bonevacia	Liemarvin	NED	5.4.89	180/81	400	45.61	44.72- 15
Bonewit	Jonas	GER	30.7.95	191/85	JT	78.13	76.54- 15
* Bonfim	Caio	BRA	19.3.91	170/58	20kW	1:19:04	1:19:42- 16
Bonvecchio	Norbert	ITA	14.8.85	183/82	JT	79.80	80.37- 14
* Bor	Hillary	USA	22.11.89	168/57	3kSt	8:11.82	8:13.68- 16
* Boreysha	Pavel	BLR	16.2.91	193/120	HT	78.04	78.60- 16
* Borlée	Jonathan	BEL	22.2.88	180/70	400	45.09	44.43- 12
* Borlée	Kévin	BEL	22.2.88	180/71	400	44.79	44.56- 12
Bortolato	Marco	ITA	11.2.94	189/107	HT	71.12	72.17- 16
* Bosse	Pierre-Ambroise	FRA	11.5.92	185/68	800	1:44.67	1:42:53- 14
* Bosworth	Tom	GBR	17.1.90	184/64	20kW	1:20:58	1:20:13- 16
Boubaker	Abderraouf	TUN	21.10.88		3kSt	8:30.67	8:36.70- 11
Bouchicha	Hichem	ALG	19.5.89	183/70	3kSt	8:27.80	8:20.11- 13
Bouchikhi	Soufiane	BEL	22.3.90	168/52	5000	13:22.18	13:33.09- 12
					10k	28:07.15	28:11.04- 16
Boully	AJ	USA	1.9.92	188/75	400h	49.48A, 49.58	50.76A- 16
Bouqantar	Soufiyan	MAR	30.8.93	170/50	3000	7:38.65	7:43.33- 14
					5000	13:14.06	13:19.59- 12
					10k	27:47.59	28:57.82- 13
* Bouraada	Larbi	ALG	10.5.88	187/84	Dec	8120	8521- 16
Boyce	Brendan	IRL	15.10.86	183/76	50kW	3:49:49	3:48:55- 15
Bramble	Daniel	GBR	14.10.90	178/76	LJ	8.02	8.21- 15
Brand	Danylo	SUI	23.2.96	181/73	400h	49.14	50.79- 16
Brandt	Torben	GER	19.5.95	190/105	DT	62.09	57.46- 16
Brannen	Nathan	CAN	8.9.82	175/59	3000	7:47.18i	7:47.90i- 06, 7:48.98- 13
Brannon	Chase	USA	8.2.91	183/75	PV	5.57	5.51- 16

Name		Nat	Born	Ht/Wt	Event	2017 Mark	Pre-2017 Best
* Brathwaite	Shane	BAR	8.2.90	185/75	110h	13.26, 13.25w	13.21- 15
Braun	Pieter	NED	21.1.93	182/80	Dec	8334	8197- 15
* Braz da Silva	Thiago	BRA	16.12.93	193/84	PV	5.86i, 5.60	6.03- 16
* Brazier	Donavan	USA	15.4.97	188/73	800	1:43.95	1:43.55- 16
Brembach	Nils	GER	23.2.93	184/68	20kW	1:20:42	1:20:58- 16
Briggs	Kemonie	USA	21.5.96	188/77	LJ	7.92, 7.99w	7.64, 7.98w- 16
Brito	Jonathas	BRA	30.11.92	187/75	110h	13.63, 13.60w	13.73, 13.69w- 14
Broeders	Ben	BEL	21.6.95	178/75	PV	5.60	5.61- 16
Brondyke	Kurtis	USA	24.1.89	198/93	Dec	7746	7795- 16
Brown	Aaron	CAN	27.5.92	185/79	100	10.15, 9.98w	9.96, 9.95w- 16
					200	20.17, 20.13w	20.00- 16
Brown	Charles	USA	28.5.97	173/64	LJ	8.14, 8.30w	7.83- 16
Brown	Clayton	JAM	8.12.96	184/77	HJ	2.25i, 2.21	2.20- 15
					TJ	16.58i	16.17- 15
Brown	Izaiah	USA	1.1.97	186/77	400	45.32i	
Brown	Rodney	USA	21.5.93	183/109	DT	65.39	66.00- 16
Brown	Tony	USA	13.7.95	183/88	100	10.12	10.53, 10.45w- 13
Bruce	Ben	USA	10.9.82	185/68	10k	28:09.29	28:25.32- 16
Bruchet	Lucas	CAN	23.2.91	175/60	3000	7:46.89	7:51.56i- 16, 7:57.41- 15
Brugger	Mathias	GER	6.8.92	189/90	Dec	8294	8009- 15
Bruintjies	Henricho	RSA	16.7.93	178/70	100	10.06	9.97- 15, 9.89w- 16
Bruns	Ansis	LAT	30.3.89	182/93	JT	82.00	81.28- 14
Bryan	Christoffe	JAM	26.4.96	193/75	HJ	2.24i, 2.21	2.28i- 15, 2.25- 16
Bryant	Ashley	GBR	17.5.91	180/82	Dec	8163	8141- 14
Brzozowski	Artur	POL	29.3.85	173/67	20kW	1:20:33	1:22:11- 16
Búa	Lucas	ESP	12.1.94	185/70	400	45.50A	45.98- 15
Bubeník	Matús	SVK	14.11.89	197/78	HJ	2.28i, 2.23	2.31i, 2.29- 15
Bühler	Matthias	GER	2.9.86	189/74	110h	13.46, 13.35w	13.34- 12, 13.20w- 14
* Bukowiecki	Konrad	POL	17.3.97	191/140	SP	21.97i, 21.59	21.14- 16
Bulanov	Aleksandr	RUS	26.12.89	193/120	SP	19.67	19.92i ,19.81-13
Burke	Mario	BAR	18.3.97	175/64	100	10.17	10.21 - 15
Burrell	Cameron	USA	11.9.94	173/68	100	9.93, 9.90w	10.16- 16, 10.07w- 13
Busendich	Ishmael	KEN	7.7.91		Mar	2:08:42	2:08:20- 16
Bussotti Neves	João Capistrano	ITA	10.5.93	180/60	1500	3:37.12	3:37.90- 16
Bustamante	Luis	MEX	10.6.84		50kW	3:48:45	3:52:17A-15
Bustos	David	ESP	25.8.90	182/65	1500	3:36.55	3:34.77- 12
* Butchart	Andrew	GBR	14.10.91	175/64	1500	3:37.58+i	3:44.57- 15
1M	3:54.23i		4:05.40- 13		3000	7:37.56	7:45.00- 16
2M	8:12.63i				5000	13:11.45	13:08.61- 16
^ Butenko	Viktor	RUS	10.3.93	196/116	DT	65.07	65.97- 13
Bychkov	Igor	ESP	7.3.87	189/80	PV	5.70	5.65- 13
Cabral	Donn	USA	12.12.89	175/60	3000	7:47.42	7:47.18i- 16, 7:53.48- 12
					3kSt	8:25.75	8:13.37- 15
Cabral	Johnathan	CAN	31.12.92	193/82	110h	13.38	13.35- 16, 13.22w- 15
^ Cáceres	Eusebio	ESP	10.9.91	175/68	LJ	8.31A, 8.08	8.37- 13
Caddick	George	GBR	29.7.94	192/84	400	45.45	45.90- 15
^ Cadée	Erik	NED	15.2.84	201/120	DT	64.93	67.30- 12
Cai Junqi		CHN	11.3.96	177/62	400h	49.77	50.61- 15
Cairoli	Simone	ITA	12.9.90	183/77	Dec	7875	7616- 16
Callahan	Peter	BEL	1.6.91	183/68	1500	3:37.57	3:37.87- 16
Callender	Emmanuel	TTO	10.5.84	184/79	100	10.10	10.05- 09
Cambridge	Aska	JPN	31.5.93	180/76	100	10.08, 9.98w	10.10- 16
Campbell	Kemoy	JAM	14.1.91	165/57	3000	7:41.87	7:40.79i- 16
5000	13:14.45i		13:20.39- 15		10k	28:06.40	28:45.84- 15
Campbell	Luke	GER	22.11.94	183/77	400h	49.40	50.36- 14
Campbell	Michael	JAM	29.11.96	178/73	100	10.07	10.43- 16
					200	20.47	20.81- 16
Campbell	Taylor	GBR	30.6.96	191/95	HT	73.40	72.70- 16
Campion	Kevin	FRA	23.5.88	183/63	20kW	1:20:28	1:20:39- 14
Cann	Luke	AUS	17.7.94	183/90	JT	81.07	80.27- 16
* Cao Shuo		CHN	8.10.91	183/69	TJ	17.22	17.35- 12
Caporaso	Teodorico	ITA	14.9.87	166/60	50kW	3:52:14	3:48:29- 16
Carnes	Brandon	USA	6.3.95	175/73	100	10.06, 9.97w	10.33, 10.06w -16
					200	20.25	20.80, 20.31w- 15
Carreón	David	MEX	23.3.94		JT	77.58	77.00- 16
Carro	Fernando	ESP	1.4.92	175/67	3kSt	8:29.92	8:21.78- 15
Carson	Hamish	NZL	1.11.88	181/66	1500	3:37.55	3:36.25- 16
* Carter	Chris	USA	11.3.89	186/80	TJ	16.75i, 17.10dq	17.18- 16
Carter	Deuce	JAM	28.9.90	182/75	110h	13.52	13.20- 16
Carvalho	Lucas	BRA	16.7.93	183/73	400	45.37	45.98- 16
^ Casañas	Frank	ESP	18.10.78	187/115	DT	60.31	67.91- 08

Name		Nat	Born	Ht/Wt	Event	2017 Mark	Pre-2017 Best
Castle	Aaron	USA	7.10.93	183/105	SP	19.63	19.17i, 18.97- 15
Castro	Luis Joel	PUR	28.1.91	195/72	HJ	2.28	2.29- 16
* Cato	Roxroy	JAM	1.5.88	183/76	400h	49.33	48.48- 14
Cavazzani	Daniele	ITA	4.12.92	186/75	TJ	16.52	16.52- 14
Ceban	Nicolai	MDA	4.2.95	191/115	SP	20.24	19.25i- 16, 18.51- 15
* Cedenio	Machel	TTO	6.9.95	183/70	400	44.90	44.01- 16
Ceng Qingsheng		CHN	3.4.95		20kW	1:22:24	1:24:36- 16
* Centrowitz	Matthew	USA	18.10.89	175/61	1500	3:33.41	3:30.40- 15
3000	7:45.69+i		7:40.74i- 16		2M	8:21.07i	8:41.55- 07
Cha Jinhong		CHN	27.5.97		20kW	1:22:27	1:26:29- 16
Chakir	Ibrahim	ESP	4.9.94	178/62	3kSt	8:31.10	8:33.35- 16
Chala	Regasa	ETH	.97		1500	3:34.57	3:37.24- 15
Chalmers	Cameron	GBR	6.2.97	182/75	400	45.64	46.51- 16
Chalyy	Timofey	RUS	7.4.94	190/79	400h	49.55	48.57- 16
Chambers	Marcus	USA	3.11.94	178/75	200	20.43w	20.94- 16, 20.71w- 15
					400	44.92	44.95- 15
Champlin	Steven	USA	16.2.96	183/79	400	45.01	45.92- 15
Chan Ming Tai		HKG	30.1.95	175/65	LJ	8.03	8.12- 16
* Chapelle	Axel	FRA	24.4.95	182/77	PV	5.80i, 5.72	5.65- 16
^ Charfreitag	Libor	SVK	11.9.77	191/117	HT	71.00	81.81- 03
Charleston	Cravont	USA-J	2.1.98	180/73	100	10.07w	10.38- 15
Chavkin	Nikolay	RUS	24.4.84	183/70	3kSt	8:26.25	8:22.81- 12
* Chebet	Evans Kiplagat	KEN	10.11.88	170/60	Mar	2:05:30	2:05:31- 16
Chebii	Ezekiel	KEN	3.1.91		Mar	2:09:06	2:06:07- 16
Chebogut	Stephen	KEN	9.1.85		Mar	2:06:57	2:05:52- 15
^ Cheboi	Collins	KEN	25.9.87	175/64	1500	3:36.8A	3:30.34- 15
					3000	7:44.24	7:45.32- 16
Chelangat	Alfred	KEN	2.4.94	170/57	10k	28:04.95	29:27.88- 16
* Chelimo	Paul	USA	27.10.90	171/57	3000	7:31.57	7:37.98- 16
					5000	13:08.62	13:03.90- 16
Chemlal	Jaouad	MAR	11.4.94	177/59	3kSt	8:31.35	8:19.22- 13
Chemosin	Robert	KEN	1.2.89		Mar	2:09:01	2:08:05- 15
Chemutai	Albert	UGA-J	25.11.99	185/65	3kSt	8:23.18	8:37.76- 16
Chen Chieh		TPE	8.5.92	183/68	400h	49.05	49.05- 15
Chen Kuei-Ju		TPE	22.9.93	188/79	110h	13.55	13.68- 15
Chen Rui		CHN	11.8.96		20kW	1:21:30	1:23:07- 16
					50kW	4:04:36	4:14:59- 16
* Cheng Chao-Tsun		TPE	17.10.93	182/88	JT	91.36	81.78- 15
Cheng Kaiwei		CHN	22.9.95		HJ	2.24	2.14- 16
Cheng Min		CHN	6.7.91		50kW	4:00:28	3:58:38- 16
Cheparev	Dementiy	RUS	28.10.92		50kW	3:43:05	
Chepsiror	Kennedy	KEN	5.6.89		800	1:46.1A	1:50.2 -16
* Cheptegei	Joshua	UGA	12.9.96	179/61	3000	7:34.96	7:56.07+- 16
5000	12:59.83		13:00.60- 16		10k	26:49.94	27:10.06- 16
Cheroben	Abraham	BRN	11.10.92	174/58	10k	27:11.08	27:31.86- 16
* Cheroben	Abraham	BRN	11.10.92	174/58	HMar	58:40	58:48- 14
* Cherono	Lawrence	KEN	7.8.88	170/55	Mar	2:05:09	2:07:24- 16
Cherop	Samuel	UGA	.97		10k	27:39.45	-0-
* Cherry	Michael	USA	23.3.95	186/75	400	44.66	44.81- 16
Cheruiyot	Davis	KEN			800	1:44.9A	
Cheruiyot	Evans Kiprop	KEN	10.5.82	168/52	HMar	60:59	59:05- 07
* Cheruiyot	Ferguson	KEN	30.11.89	183/73	800	1:44.37	1:42.84- 14
* Cheruiyot	Timothy	KEN	20.11.95	178/64	1500	3:29.10	3:31.34- 16
					1M	3:49.64	3:53.17- 16
Cheruiyot	Wilson	KEN	12.11.87		HMar	61:03	61:55- 16
Chesani	Silvano	ITA	17.7.88	190/75	HJ	2.28i	2.33i, 2.31 -13
Chesebe	Abednego	KEN	20.6.82	174/62	1500	3:36.9A	3:35.02A- 12
* Cheserek	Edward	KEN	2.2.94	168/57	1500	3:37.01+i	3:36.50- 14
1M	3:52.01i		3:56.43i- 15, 4:03.29- 11		3000	7:46.85i	7:40.51i- 16
5000	13:24.72		13:18.71- 14				
Cheserek	Micah	KEN	12.10.96		3kSt	8:25.8A	9:03.76A-14
Chesum	Jonah	KEN	5.5.89		Mar	2:08:57	-0-
Chiappinelli	Yohannes	ITA	18.8.97	171/55	3kSt	8:27.34	8:32.66- 16
Chiaraviglio	Germán	ARG	16.4.87	192/77	PV	5.60	5.75- 15
Chiari	Andrea	ITA	12.2.91	186/70	TJ	16.69	16.85i, 16.83- 12
^ Chizhikov	Dmitriy	RUS	6.12.93	194/85	TJ	16.95i, 16.85	17.20- 15
Chmielak	Hubert	POL	19.6.89	188/88	JT	80.20	82.58- 14
* Chocho	Andrés	ECU	4.11.83	167/67	20kW	1:21:16	1:20:07- 16
					50kW	3:47:37	3:42:57A- 16
* Choge	Augustine	KEN	21.1.87	162/53	HMar	59:26	60:01- 16
* Chopra	Neeraj	IND	24.12.97	184/80	JT	85.63	86.48- 16

Name		Nat	Born	Ht/Wt	Event	2017 Mark	Pre-2017 Best
* Chumba	Dickson	KEN	27.10.86	167/50	Mar	2:06:25	2:04:32- 14
Chumo Kwemoi	Rodgers	KEN	3.3.97	165/49	10k	27:38.61	27:25.23- 16
Chuva	Marcos	POR	8.8.89	183/73	LJ	8.00	8.34- 11
Cienfuegos	Javier	ESP	15.7.90	193/134	HT	76.63	76.71- 13
Cisneros	Omar	CUB	19.11.89	186/80	400h	49.24	47.93- 13
Claitt	Tequan	USA	18.7.97	188/81	HJ	2.28	2.17- 16
Clark	Matthias	USA	31.5.87	181/78	Dec	7669	7785- 09
Clarke	Andre	JAM	6.6.92	190/79	400h	49.19	49.64- 16
Clarke	Everton	JAM	24.12.92	172/70	100	10.12	10.08- 16
* Claye	Will	USA	13.6.91	180/68	TJ	17.91, 18.05w	17.76- 16
* Clement	Kerron	USA	31.10.85	188/84	400h	48.02	47.24- 05
Coertzen	Willem	RSA	30.12.82	186/80	Dec	7804	8398- 15
Cole	Rohan	JAM	28.10.97	184/75	110h	13.58	13.67- 16
* Coleman	Christian	USA	6.3.96	175/75	100	9.82	9.95- 16
					200	19.85	20.26- 16
Collet	Mathieu	FRA	15.3.95	180/72	PV	5.55	5.51- 16
Collins	Kyle	USA	9.9.94	183/77	400	44.95	45.33- 16
Collins	LeShon	USA	11.12.93	179/73	100	10.11, 10.00w	10.15- 16
Comenentia	Denzel	NED	25.11.95	186/114	SP	20.33	19.53- 16
					HT	71.75	69.42- 16
^ Compaoré	Benjamin	FRA	5.8.87	189/86	TJ	16.80, 16.94w	17.48- 14
Conradie	Pieter	RSA	20.10.94	182/73	400	45.15A, 45.58	45.86- 16
Constantino	Gabriel	BRA	9.2.95	186/77	110h	13.52	13.50- 16
Constantinou	Vasilios	CYP	13.9.92	173/60	HJ	2.28	2.28i, 2.25- 16
Contreras	Yidiel Islay	ESP	27.11.92	185/78	110h	13.40	13.35- 15
Cooper	Mitch	AUS	2.6.95	196/115	DT	63.98	62.56- 16
Cooper	Tyrese	USA-Y	21.3.00	183/75	400	45.38A, 45.40	45.23- 16
Coover	Jeff	USA	1.12.87	185/77	PV	5.60i, 5.51	5.68i- 15, 5.60- 13
* Copello	Alexis	AZE	12.8.85	185/80	TJ	17.16, 17.17w	17.68A- 11, 17.65, 17.69w- 09
* Copello	Yasmani	TUR	15.4.87	196/86	400h	48.24	47.92- 16
Corchete	Luis Manuel	ESP	14.5.84	185/74	50kW	4:01:39	3:59:58- 12
Coroller	Victor	FRA	21.9.97	181/65	400h	49.30	50.13- 15
Corréa	Harold	FRA	26.6.88	190/78	TJ	16.94i, 16.36	17.08, 17.11w- 16
Cortez	Alvaro	CHI	27.10.95	188/82	TJ	16.74	16.52- 15
Cota	Mario	MEX	11.9.90	188/115	DT	62.53	63.35- 16
Cotton	Kenzo	USA	13.5.96	185/87	100	10.11, 9.96w	10.07- 16
					200	20.52, 20.20w	20.35- 16
Cowan	Dwayne	GBR	1.1.85	188/82	400	45.34	46.02- 16
Cowart	Donnie	USA	24.10.85	170/60	3kSt	8:30.28	8:23.38- 16
Cowley	Rhydian	AUS	4.1.91	181/65	20kW	1:22:09	1:22:07- 16
* Craddock	Omar	USA	26.4.91	178/79	TJ	17.08	17.53- 15
Craigg	Janeil	BAR	29.3.94		JT	78.71	75.62- 16
Cranston	Kyle	AUS	3.9.92	186/83	Dec	7687	7703- 16
Crawford	Corey	USA	12.12.91	190/86	LJ	8.12	8.22i- 14, 7.92, 7.93w- 16
Crawford	Lawrence	USA	15.5.97	175/70	100	9.97w	10.48- 16
Cray	Eric	PHI	6.11.88	176/73	400h	49.57	48.98- 16
Cremona	Orazio	RSA	1.7.89	192/130	SP	21.12	20.63- 14
Crippa	Yemaneberhan	ITA	15.10.96	179/62	5000	13:23.99i	13:36.65- 16
Crittenden	Freddie	USA	3.8.94	183/73	110h	13.42	13.48, 13.43w- 16
* Crouser	Ryan	USA	18.12.92	201/120	SP	22.65	22.52- 16
* Culson	Javier	PUR	25.7.84	198/79	400h	48.76	47.72- 10
Culver	Trey	USA	18.7.96	193/75	HJ	2.26i, 2.14	2.26- 16
Cunningham	Logan	USA	30.5.91	183/80	PV	5.75	5.71, 5.80dh- 16
Cunningham	Randall	USA	4.1.96	196/84	HJ	2.27i, 2.21	2.26i, 2.25- 16
Cunningham	Ricardo	JAM	3.10.80	183/78	400h	48.83	49.66- 16
Curtin	Thomas	USA	8.8.93	173/61	3000	7:45.11	7:52.92i-15
					5000	13:26.55	13:27.64- 16
Czykier	Damian	POL	10.8.92	186/73	110h	13.28	13.32, 13.31w- 16
* Dacres	Fedrick	JAM	28.2.94	191/104	SP	20.46	18.99- 14
					DT	68.88	68.02- 16
Dagée	Frédéric	FRA	11.12.92	192/108	SP	20.04	19.87- 15
Dagher	Mustapha Katem	IRQ	29.11.95	194/110	DT	60.89	60.60- 15
Dahmani	Samir	FRA	3.4.91	183/65	800	1:45.72	1:44.07- 16
Dalla Valle	Andrea	ITA-J	31.8.99	183/73	TJ	16.87	15.81- 16
* Darien	Garfield	FRA	22.12.87	187/76	110h	13.09	13.15- 12
^ Dasaolu	James	GBR	5.9.87	180/75	100	10.06	9.91- 13
Dasor	Emmanuel	GHA	14.9.95	180/68	400	45.43A, 45.59	45.61A -15, 45.82- 16
Davis	Ashtyn	USA	10.10.96	178/82	110h	13.50	13.73- 16
Davis	Josh	USA	13.10.95	183/84	200	20.49	21.19w- 16
Dayarathne	Waruna Lakshan	SRI	14.5.88	180/90	JT	82.19	78.52- 16
Dazza	El Mahjoub	MAR	3.3.91		5000	13:18.00	13:24.54- 16
					10k	27:39.79	29:45.70- 16

Name		Nat	Born	Ht/Wt	Event	2017 Mark	Pre-2017 Best
de Arriba	Álvaro	ESP	2.6.94	180/65	800	1:45.06	1:45.93 -16
de Deus	Eduardo	BRA	8.10.95	187/82	110h	13.51, 13.42w	13.56- 16
* De Grasse	Andre	CAN	10.11.94	180/73	100	10.01, 9.69w	9.91- 16, 9.75w- 15
					200	20.01, 19.96w	19.80- 16, 19.58w- 15
* De Luca	Marco	ITA	12.5.81	189/72	50kW	3:45:02	3:44:47- 16
de Vries	Ruan	RSA	1.2.86	187/88	110h	13.77A, 13.23Adt	
							13.59A,13.67- 13, 13.57Aw- 15
Debela	Dejene	ETH	.95	180/62	Mar	2:07:10	2:10:13- 16
Debjani	Ismael	BEL	25.9.90	175/61	1500	3:33.70	3:35.62- 16
Dedewo	Paul	USA	4.6.91	185/73	200	20.40	20.53- 16
					400	45.13	45.41- 15
Degu	Abayneh	ETH-J	1.12.98	176/59	5000	13:25.55	13:43.33- 16
del Real	Diego	MEX	6.3.94	185/103	HT	76.27	77.49- 16
Deleba	Terefa	ETH-J	20.4.98		HMar	60:22	61:55- 16
Delryd	Fabian	SWE	15.10.96	205/87	HJ	2.25i, 2.22	2.17- 15
Demaline	Nick	USA	1.3.96	188/127	SP	20.15	18.80i, 18.38- 16
Demelash	Yigrem	ETH	28.1.94	167/52	HMar	59:19	59:48- 16
^ Demps	Jeff	USA	8.1.90	175/77	100	10.03, 9.90w	10.01- 08, 9.96w- 10
^ Demyanyuk	Dmytro	UKR	30.6.83	200/86	HJ	2.26	2.35- 11
* Dendy	Marquis	USA	17.11.92	190/75	LJ	8.18, 8.39w	8.42- 16, 8.68w- 15
Denecker	Émile	FRA	28.3.92	198/87	PV	5.54i, 5.50	5.63- 11
Denny	Matthew	AUS	2.6.96	195/115	DT	63.15	65.37- 16
					HT	73.37	70.52- 15
Derkach	Pavel	RUS	2.11.93		SP	19.47	18.68- 16
Derrick	Chris	USA	17.10.90	180/64	5000	13:19.35i	13:08.04- 13
Desalu	Eseosa	ITA	19.2.94	179/69	200	20.64, 20.32w	20.31- 16
Dewhurst	Ian	AUS	13.11.90	185/73	400h	49.77	49.52- 14
Di Marco	Nazzareno	ITA	30.4.85	195/105	DT	62.38	61.19- 16
Dia	Mamadou Chérif	MLI	13.3.85	182/70	TJ	16.59, 16.69w	16.55- 15
* Díaz	Andy	CUB	25.12.95	191/80	TJ	17.40	16.81- 15
Díaz	Carlos Martín	CHI	9.7.93	174/58	1500	3:37.84	3:37.82- 16
Díaz	Jordan	CUB-Y	23.2.01	192/73	TJ	17.30A, 16.66	15.65- 16
Díaz	José Ignacio	ESP	22.11.79	168/53	50kW	3:48:08	3:51:09- 05
Dilla	Karsten	GER	17.7.89	189/80	PV	5.63i, 5.61	5.73i, 5.72- 11
Ding Bangchao		CHN	11.10.96	188/75	PV	5.70	5.15- 16
* Diniz	Yohann	FRA	1.1.78	185/69	50kW	3:33:12	3:32:33- 14
Diones	Mark Harry	PHI	3.1.93	183/72	TJ	16.70	16.29- 16
Dirieh	Djamal Abdi	DJI	.97	170/60	5000	13:13.45	13:21.50- 16
Distelberger	Dominik	AUT	16.3.90	182/77	Dec	8046	8175- 16
^ Dix	Walter	USA	31.1.86	178/84	100	10.19, 10.00w	9.88- 10, 9.80w- 08
					200	20.44	19.53- 11
Dixon	Devin	USA	22.9.97	196/82	800	1:45.71	1:49.52- 16
Djouhan	Lolassonn	FRA	18.5.91	188/118	DT	65.10	61.95- 16
Djurovic	Tomas	MNE	14.2.94	190/98	SP	19.85	19.55- 16
* Dmitrik	Aleksey	RUS	12.4.84	191/69	HJ	2.25i, 2.23	2.40i- 14, 2.36- 11
^ Dmytrenko	Ruslan	UKR	22.3.86	180/68	20kW	1:22:26	1:18:37- 14
* Dobek	Patryk	POL	13.2.94	183/75	400h	49.15	48.40- 15
Dobrenkiy	Aleksandr	RUS	11.3.94	195/110	DT	60.33	60.81- 16
Docavo	Vicente	ESP	13.2.92	182/72	TJ	16.54	16.72- 12
Doctor	José Luis	MEX	14.6.96		20kW	1:21:55	1:23:29- 16
Dohmann	Carl	GER	18.5.90	182/62	50kW	3:45:21	3:47:57- 16
Dolezal	Riley	USA	16.11.85	188/100	JT	81.77	83.50- 13
Dolve	Eirik Greibrokk	NOR	5.5.95	185/80	PV	5.55i, 5.50	5.66- 16
Domanic	Robert	USA	10.3.95	186/70	1M	3:54.73	4:00.19I-16
Domingos	Wágner	BRA	23.6.83	183/126	HT	77.24	78.63- 16
* Donato	Fabrizio	ITA	14.8.76	189/82	TJ	17.32	17.73i- 11, 17.60- 00, 17.63w- 12
* Dong Bin		CHN	22.11.88	179/67	TJ	17.27	17.58- 16
Donnelly	Sean	USA	1.4.93	183/107	HT	74.26	74.35- 16
Doris	Troy	GUY	12.4.89	174/73	TJ	16.80	17.18- 16
Dorsey	Andre	USA	11.3.93	186/77	LJ	7.94i, 7.94	7.79, 7.87w- 16
					TJ	16.86	15.89- 16
Doughty	Brandon	USA	14.5.93	180/61	3000	7:47.47	7:56.91i-15
^ Douglas	Nathan	GBR	4.12.82	183/71	TJ	16.80	17.64- 05
Douma	Richard	NED	17.4.93	184/67	1500	3:35.92	3:35.77- 16
Dourado	Willian	BRA	6.1.94	188/109	SP	20.22	19.01- 16
Douvalídis	Konstadínos	GRE	10.3.87	184/78	110h	13.42	13.33- 15
Downing	Quincy	USA	16.1.93	185/75	400h	48.13	49.32- 16
Drack	Jonathan	MRI	6.11.88	184/77	TJ	16.43	16.96, 17.05w- 15
Droogsma	Austin	USA	4.3.95	190/132	SP	19.70	18.93- 15
* Drouin	Derek	CAN	6.3.90	195/80	HJ	2.33i, 2.28	2.40- 14
Dry	Mark	GBR	11.10.87	184/110	HT	71.73	76.93- 15

	Name		Nat	Born	Ht/Wt	Event	2017 Mark	Pre-2017 Best
	Dubitskiy	Oleg	BLR	14.10.90	184/100	HT	73.12	76.67- 15
	Dubler	Cedric	AUS	13.1.95	190/82	Dec	7779	8114- 16
	Duckworth	Tim	GBR	18.6.96	185/80	Dec	7973	7709- 16
	Dudarov	Gleb	BLR	17.10.96	196/109	HT	74.20	72.86- 16
	Duffield	Jacorian	USA	2.9.92	190/79	HJ	2.30i, 2.21	2.34- 15
*	Dukes	Dedric	USA	2.4.92	180/70	100	10.06w	10.13- 16
						200	20.37	19.97- 14, 19.86w- 15
	Dunbar	Colin	USA	27.6.88	190/115	HT	73.05	73.56- 15
	Dunbar	Trevor	USA	29.4.91	180/70	5000	13:26.27	13:26.90- 14
*	Dunfee	Evan	CAN	28.9.90	186/68	20kW	1:21:22	1:20:13- 14
						50kW	3:46:03	3:41:38- 16
	Dunkerley-Offor	Spencer	USA	6.1.95	196/88	110h	13.61, 13.45w	13.58, 13.45w- 15
*	Duplantis	Armand	SWE-J	10.11.99	181/68	PV	5.90	5.51- 16
	Duquemin	Zane	GBR	23.9.91	185/110	DT	62.68	63.46- 12
	Durañona	Yordanys	DMA	16.6.88	188/75	TJ	17.02	17.20A- 14, 17.02, 17.28w- 09
*	Dutch	Johnny	USA	20.1.89	180/82	400h	48.60	47.63- 10
^	Dutra de Oliveira	Augusto	BRA	16.7.90	180/70	PV	5.60	5.82- 13
*	Dwyer	Rasheed	JAM	29.1.89	188/80	200	20.11	19.80- 15
	Dyubin	Dmitriy	BLR	12.7.90		20kW	1:22:21	1:21:09- 14
*	Eaton	Jarret	USA	24.6.89	183/82	110h	13.34	13.25- 16
	Echard	Melvin	USA/GRN	29.8.89	183/75	LJ	7.97, 8.16w	7.92- 16, 8.09w- 11
*	Echevarría	Juan Miguel	CUB-J	11.8.98	186/76	LJ	8.28, 8.34w	8.05- 15, 8.15w- 16
	Edoburun	Ojie	GBR	2.6.96	183/77	100	10.12, 9.93w	10.16- 14, 10.02w- 16
						200	20.40w	20.87, 20.50w- 16
*	Edris	Muktar	ETH	14.1.94	172/57	3000	7:32.31	7:33.28- 16
	5000	12:55.23	12:54.83- 14			10k	27:20.60	27:17.18- 15
*	Edward	Alonso	PAN	8.12.89	183/73	100	10.00w	10.02-14. 9.97w- 09
	Efekoro	Oghenakpobo	NGR	15.7.96	190/138	SP	20.39	19.57- 16
	Eitel	Manuel	GER	28.1.97	180/80	Dec	7825	-0-
	Ejima	Masaki	JPN-J	6.3.99	189/75	PV	5.65	5.46- 16
	Ekiru	Titus	KEN	2.1.92		Mar	2:07:43	-0-
	El Abbassi	El Hassan	BRN	15.7.79	171/54	10k	27:49.46	27:25.02- 15
	El Aziz	Mustapha	MAR	24.12.85	175/60	HMar	60:50	-16
*	El Bakkali	Soufiane	MAR	7.1.96	188/70	5000	13:10.60i	13:47.76- 14
						3kSt	8:04.83	8:14.35- 16
	El Chenini	Riad	TUN	25.3.97	180/66	800	1:46.24	1:47.11- 16
	El Guesse	Abdellatif	MAR	27.2.93	186/68	800	1:45.46	1:45.78- 15
	El Kaam	Fouad	MAR	27.5.88	177/62	1500	3:34.86	3:33.71- 13
						1M	3:54.39	3:54.21- 14
*	El-Seify	Ashraf Amjad	QAT	20.2.95	183/100	HT	76.14	78.19- 16
	Elemba	Frank	CGO	21.7.90	200/115	SP	20.86i, 20.72	21.20- 16
*	Elker	Josh	USA-J	12.3.98	186/79	200	20.45w	21.05- 15, 20.83w- 16
	Ellis	Burkheart	BAR	18.9.92	175/64	200	20.37	20.36- 16
	Ellis	Joseph	GBR	10.4.96	181/102	HT	70.98	68.25- 16
	Ellis	Nigel	JAM	8.8.97	186/77	100	10.17	10.16- 16
	Enahoro	Ituah	GER/NGR	15.12.97	188/82	Dec	8028	-0-
	Enekwechi	Chukwuebuka	NGR	28.1.93	181/107	SP	21.07	20.37- 16
	Engelbrecht	Jaco	RSA	8.3.87	200/125	SP	20.63	20.45- 15
	Engels	Craig	USA	1.5.94	187/73	1500	3:35.95	3:37.66- 16
	English	Mark	IRL	18.3.93	187/76	800	1:45.42	1:44.84- 13
	Er	Necati	TUR	24.2.97		TJ	16.34, 16.50w	16.06- 16
	Erasmus	Emile	RSA	3.4.92	186/84	100	10.08A, 10.12	10.21A, 10.23- 16
	Erassa	Kirubel	USA	17.6.93	172/61	5000	13:23.12	13:27.55- 14
	Erb	MJ (Michael)	USA	2.2.94	184/73	3kSt	8:26.75	8:34.13- 16
	Eriksson	Anders	SWE	22.3.94	190/100	HT	71.76	71.14- 16
	Eshbekov	Alisher	TJK/RUS	31.5.90	190/114	HT	71.83	69.85- 16
	Eshete	Weretew	ETH-J	.99		1500	3:35.57	
	Essalhi	Younès	MAR	20.2.93	181/68	1500	3:35.81	3:35.52- 13
	Estefani	Hederson	BRA	11.9.91	184/75	400h	49.13	49.40- 15
	Estrada	Diego	USA	12.12.89	180/61	10k	27:48.57	27:30.53- 15
	Etelätalo	Lassi	FIN	30.4.88	193/90	JT	77.80	84.98- 14
	Eto	Takashi	JPN	5.2.91	183/68	HJ	2.30	2.29- 16
	Evans	Andrew	USA	25.1.91	198/110	DT	66.61	66.37- 14
*	Évora	Nelson	POR	20.4.84	181/70	TJ	17.20i, 17.19	17.74- 07, 17.82w- 09
	Ewers	Andre	USA	7.6.95	173/64	100	10.13	10.25- 16
	Ezzaydouny	Ibrahim	MAR	28.4.91	181/65	3kSt	8:18.50	8:27.43- 15
	Ezzine	Hamid	MAR	5.10.83	174/60	3kSt	8:29.12	8:09.72- 07
	Fahy	Darren	USA	14.5.94	178/61	3kSt	8:31.08	8:35.25- 15
*	Fajdek	Pawel	POL	4.6.89	186/118	HT	83.44	83.93- 15
	Falloni	Simone	ITA	26.9.91	187/110	HT	75.73	73.78- 16
	Falocchi	Christian	ITA	30.1.97	193/77	HJ	2.25i, 2.24	2.15- 15

Name		Nat	Born	Ht/Wt	Event	2017 Mark	Pre-2017 Best
Faloci	Giovanni	ITA	13.10.85	193/108	DT	63.66	64.77- 13
Fang Hongzhen		CHN	6.3.96		50kW	4:03:48	4:02:01- 16
Fang Yaoqing		CHN	20.4.96	182/70	TJ	16.86i, 16.58	16.55- 15
* Farah	Mohamed	GBR	23.3.83	175/65	1500	3:34.19	3:28.81- 13
3000	7:35.15		7:32.62- 16		5000	13:00.70	12:53.11- 11
10k	26:49.51		26:46.57- 11		HMar	60:06dh	59:32, 59:22dh- 15
Farnosov	Andrey	RUS	9.7.80	182/66	3kSt	8:26.56	8:21.95- 11
Fasasi	Kunle	NGR	23.6.96	183/75	400	45.57i	45.43- 16
* Fassinotti	Marco	ITA	29.4.89	190/71	HJ	2.29	2.35i- 16, 2.33- 15
Fedaczynski	Rafal	POL	3.12.80	168/61	50kW	3:48:56	3:46:05- 11
Feger	Alexandre	FRA	22.1.90	179/74	PV	5.53Ai, 5.41	5.60- 14
Feleke	Getu	ETH	28.11.86		Mar	2:07:46	2:04:50- 12
* Felix	Kurt	GRN	4.7.88	190/88	Dec	8509	8323- 16
Felix	Markim	GRN	.97	190/91	JT	78.80	69.41- 16
* Felix Simbu	Alphonce	TAN	14.2.92		Mar	2:09:10	2:09:19- 16
Feng Zhiqiang		CHN-J	14.4.98	184/73	400h	49.66	50.62- 16
Ferguson	Kord	USA	19.6.95	198/109	DT	61.44	60.13- 16
Fernández	Sergio	ESP	1.4.93	188/70	400h	49.34	48.87- 16
Ferreira	Diogo	POR	30.7.90	175/77	PV	5.71	5.67- 14
Ferreira	Fernando	BRA	13.12.94	188/57	HJ	2.30	2.26- 15
Fifa	Illias	ESP	16.5.89	174/55	3000	7:40.55	7:47+- 15, 7:49.13- 14
					5000	13:17.39	13:05.61- 15
Fikadu	Dawit	BRN	29.12.95		5000	13:15.20	13:23.03- 16
Filip	Scott	USA	28.1.95	188/85	Dec	7915	7876- 16
* Filippídis	Konstadinos	GRE	26.11.86	188/73	PV	5.85i, 5.75	5.91- 15
Fincham-Dukes	Jacob	GBR	12.1.97	185/72	LJ	7.96, 8.02w	7.75- 15
* Finley	Mason	USA	7.10.90	203/136	DT	68.03	66.72- 16
Firfirica	Alin Alexandru	ROU	3.11.95	196/108	DT	61.98	65.03- 16
Fisher	Andrew	BRN	15.12.91	168/64	100	10.12	9.94- 15
Fitzgibbon	Robbie	GBR	23.3.96	183/70	1500	3:36.97	3:39.03- 16
Flannery	Niall	GBR	26.4.91	178/70	400h	49.74	48.80- 14
Florant	Fabian	NED	1.2.83	176/73	TJ	16.37, 16.54w	16.92- 16
Flournoy	Jaron	USA	24.11.96	183/77	200	20.24	20.69, 20.53w- 16
Fofana	Hassane	ITA	28.4.92	187/77	110h	13.58	13.52- 16
Fontenot	Ryan	USA	4.5.86	188/75	110h	13.63, 13.43w	13.44- 13, 13.39w -12
* Forbes	Damar	JAM	18.9.90	185/77	LJ	8.29	8.25, 8.35w- 13
Forbes	Ronald	CAY	5.4.85	192/86	110h	13.67, 13.48w	13.36- 16, 13.24w- 11
Ford	Santiago	CUB	25.8.97	184/81	Dec	7756	7112- 15
Ford-Azonwanna	Andrew	CAN	29.11.95	173/64	100	10.12w	10.27- 15
* Forte	Julian	JAM	7.1.93	186/73	100	9.91	10.03- 14, 9.94w- 16
					200	20.41	19.97- 16
Fortunato	Francesco	ITA	13.12.94	178/51	20kW	1:22:01	1:22:57- 16
Foster	Brenton	AUS-J	26.2.98	191/	HJ	2.24i	2.09- 14
Fox	Nathan	GBR	21.10.90	186/84	TJ	16.81	16.69- 14
* Francis	Miguel	GBR	28.2.95	186/75	200	20.44	19.88, 19.67dt- 16
Franz	Felix	GER	6.5.93	193/78	400h	49.88	48.96- 14
Fraresso	Mauro	ITA	13.1.93	191/95	JT	78.28	73.41- 14
Fraser	Warren	BAH	8.7.91	168/68	100	10.18. 10.05w	10.14- 14
^ Frayne	Henry	AUS	14.4.90	187/72	LJ	8.21	8.27- 12
^ Fredericks	Cornel	RSA	3.3.90	178/70	400h	49.27A, 49.32	48.14- 11
Freeman	Josh	USA	22.8.94	193/134	SP	20.91	20.15- 15
* Freimuth	Rico	GER	14.3.88	196/92	Dec	8663	8561- 15
French	Cameron	NZL	17.5.92	180/73	400h	49.84	49.72- 15
Frolov	Kirill	RUS	29.9.93		20kW	1:21:43	1:21:11- 15
* Frydrych	Petr	CZE	13.1.88	198/99	JT	88.32	88.23- 10
Fryman	Andy	USA	3.2.85	188/130	HT	71.98	73.90- 14
Fujimitsu	Kenji	JPN	1.5.86	182/70	200	20.47	20.13- 15
Fujisawa	Isamu	JPN	12.10.87	165/53	20kW	1:18:23	1:18:45- 16
* Futch	Eric	USA	25.4.93	175/70	400h	48.18	48.91- 16
^ Fyodorov	Aleksey	RUS	25.5.91	184/73	TJ	16.58	17.42- 15
Gado	Ruben	FRA	13.12.93	180/73	Dec	7839	7720- 16
* Gag	Andrei	ROU	7.4.91	195/118	SP	20.61	21.06- 16
Gailums	Patriks	LAT-J	10.5.98	192/85	JT	81.91	74.02- 16
* Gakémé	Antoine	BDI	24.12.91	170/57	800	1:44.44	1:44.09- 15
Galazoúlas	Anastásios	GRE	2.10.92	182/68	LJ	7.98	7.82, 7.91dq- 15
Gale	Tom	GBR-J	18.12.98	197/82	HJ	2.30	2.18- 16
Galeta	Kristo	EST	9.4.83	190/94	SP	19.64	19.78- 16
Gandou	Adil	MAR	18.8.93	187/69	TJ	16.63	16.55- 12
* Gao Xinglong		CHN	12.3.94	181/65	LJ	8.22	8.34- 15
García	Diego	ESP	19.1.96	174/60	20kW	1:20:34	1:21:36- 16
García	Samuel	ESP	4.12.91	194/84	400	45.00A, 45.36	45.50- 14

Name		Nat	Born	Ht/Wt	Event	2017 Mark	Pre-2017 Best
* Gardiner	Steven	BAH	12.9.95	188/75	400	43.89	44.27- 15
Garn	Jesse	USA	4.6.93	179/61	800	1:45.04	1:47.03, 1:46.98i -15
Garrido	Lucirio Antonio	VEN	8.4.92	184/75	800	1:46.02A	1:46.60- 14
Gasch	Loïc	SUI	13.8.94	192/78	HJ	2.26	2.23- 16
Gaspar	José Luis	CUB	25.8.95	188/72	400h	49.35	49.17- 16
Gastaldi	Román	ARG	25.9.89	187/86	Dec	7864	7826A- 11, 7882w- 15
* Gatlin	Justin	USA	10.2.82	185/79	100	9.92	9.74- 15
Gaul	Florian	GER	21.9.91	182/78	PV	5.60i, 5.50	5.77-16
* Gay	Tyson	USA	9.8.82	180/73	100	10.17, 9.94w	9.69- 09, 9.68w- 08
					200	20.60, 20.31w	19.58- 09
* Gaye	Demish	JAM	20.1.93	188/77	200	20.48	20.82- 16
					400	44.55	45.30- 16
Gayle	Steven	JAM	19.3.94	179/70	200	20.48	21.16A- 13
					400	44.99	45.67- 15
Gayle	Tajay	JAM	2.8.96		LJ	8.00	7.54- 16
Geay	Gabriel	TAN	10.9.96	176/61	5000	13:20.35	13:25.66- 16
Gebregergish	Yohanes	ERI	11.1.94		Mar	2:08:14	-0-
^ Gebremedhin	Mekonnen	ETH	11.10.88	180/64	1500	3:36.93	3:31.45- 12
3000	7:44.95i		7:41.42- 11		5000	13:29.37	-0-
* Gebremeskel	Dejen	ETH	24.11.89	178/53	3000	7:46.06i	7:34.14i- 12, 7:45.9- 10
					5000	13:25.95	12:46.81- 12
* Gebrhiwet	Hagos	ETH	11.5.94	167/65	3000	7:43.04i	7:30.36- 13
Gebrselassie	Leul	ETH	20.9.93	170/55	HMar	59:18	60:34- 15
Geist	Jordan	USA-J	21.7.98	188/125	SP	20.62	20.83i- 16
* Gemili	Adam	GBR	6.10.93	178/73	100	10.08, 10.03w	9.97- 15
					200	20.35	19.97- 16
Geng Yudong		CHN	13.6.94		50kW	4:01:15	4:00:50- 16
George	Winston	GUY	19.5.87	174/66	200	20.41	20.53, 20.42w- 16, 20.4- 14
					400	45.16	45.25- 15
* Geremew	Mosinet	ETH	12.2.92	174/57	HMar	60:56	-14
					Mar	2:06:12	-0-
Gertleyn	Ivan	RUS	25.9.87	184/75	PV	5.60i, 5.60	5.70- 15
Getahun	Betesfa	ETH-J	25.9.98	165/50	5000	13:13.23	
Gezahegn	Kelkile	ETH	.96		Mar	2:06:56	2:08:56- 16
Ghanbarzadeh	Keyvan	IRI	26.5.90	193/78	HJ	2.26i, 2.24	2.26- 12
* Ghazal	Majed El Dein	SYR	21.4.87	193/70	HJ	2.32	2.36- 16
^ Gibson	Jeffery	BAH	15.8.90	186/79	400h	49.35	48.17- 15
Gilbert	Colby	USA	17.3.95	178/57	3000	7:45.71i	7:49.25i- 15, 8:11.73- 15
Giles	Elliot	GBR	26.5.94	173/64	800	1:44.99	1:45.54- 16
* Gill	Jacko	NZL	20.12.94	190/118	SP	21.01	20.83- 16
Girma	Tesfaye	ETH	24.1.97		3kSt	8:19.67	8:16.14- 16
^ Gittens	Ramon	BAR	20.7.87	180/77	100	10.16	10.02- 13, 10.0A1w- 15
Givans	Senoj-Jay	JAM	30.12.93	178/73	100	10.02	9.96- 16, 9.90w- 14
					200	20.32	20.47- 15, 20.28w- 14
Glazunov	Ilya	RUS	20.4.94		TJ	16.46	16.34i, 16.27- 16
Gniki Gisamoda	Emanuel	TAN	18.5.88	164/50	5000	13:13.24	
Golubovic	Dan	USA	29.11.93	194/86	Dec	7717	7139- 16
Gómez	Jesús	ESP	24.4.91	178/60	800	1:45.67	1:46.83- 15
Gómez	Joaquín	ARG	14.10.96	178/95	HT	74.28	71.50- 16
Gómez	Pedro	MEX	31.12.90	175/64	50kW	3:48:04	3:53:23- 16
Gomis	Kafétien	FRA	23.3.80	183/67	LJ	8.01, 8.22Aw, 8.17w	8.26- 15
Goolab	Nick	GBR	30.1.90	181/65	3000	7:42.22	8:08.01i- 16, 8:14.59- 13
* Gordon	Lalonde	TTO	25.11.88	188/83	400	45.02	44.52- 12
Gorokhov	Georgiy	RUS	20.4.93	183/75	PV	5.70i, 5.60	5.70i- 16, 5.65- 15
Gotch	Jarvis	USA	25.3.92	185/73	LJ	8.13, 8.37w	8.24, 8.35w- 16
Goto	Shuto	JPN	26.2.94		50kW	4:01:32	3:59:23- 15
^ Gowda	Vikas	IND	5.7.83	196/115	DT	62.35	66.28- 12
* Grabarz	Robbie	GBR	3.10.87	192/87	HJ	2.31	2.37- 12
Grant	Robert	USA	31.1.96	180/76	400h	49.15	49.36- 16
Gray	Cordero	USA	9.5.89	173/68	100	10.21, 10.12w	10.11- 12, 10.03w- 14
Gray	Nick	USA	2.6.97	181/66	200	20.38, 19.96w	20.45- 16
Greaux	Kyle	TTO	26.4.88	190/80	100	10.16	10.27- 16
					200	20.19	20.42- 15
Green	Jack	GBR	6.10.91	187/82	400h	48.77	48.60- 12
Green	Jeffrey	USA	18.8.95	183/75	400	45.65	45.82- 15
Green	Leford	JAM	14.11.86	186/79	400h	49.85	48.47- 10
Greene	Cejhae	ANT	6.10.95	174/68	100	10.05	10.01- 16
Gregan	Brian	IRL	31.12.89	190/85	400	45.26	45.53- 13
Gregorek	Johnny	USA	7.12.91	178/61	1500	3:35.00	3:36.04- 16
1M	3:53.15i, 3:57.00		3:55.27- 16		3000	7:49.93i	7:54.85i- 15
Gregory	Ben	GBR	21.11.90	184/82	Dec	7799	7882- 16

MEN'S INDEX

Name		Nat	Born	Ht/Wt	Event	2017 Mark	Pre-2017 Best
* Gregson	Ryan	AUS	26.4.90	184/68	1500	3:34.37	3:31.06- 10
1M	3:56.90		3:42.24- 10		3000	7:42.19	7:44.90- 16
Greguric	Matija	CRO	17.9.96	187/90	HT	72.35	72.24- 16
Grice	Charlie	GBR	7.11.93	182/68	1500	3:35.72	3:33.60- 16
					1M	3:53.62	3:52.64- 16
Griffith	Adrian	BAH	11.11.84	178/75	100	10.13w	10.11- 16, 10.03w- 14
^ Grigoryev	Sergey	KAZ	24.6.92	178/65	PV	5.65	5.50- 14
Gripich	Aleksandr	RUS	21.9.86	190/80	PV	5.55	5.85i- 15, 5.75- 09
Grobler	Johannes	RSA	6.8.97	176/79	JT	77.88A	80.59- 16
Gruber	Hendrik	GER	28.9.86	192/82	PV	5.60	5.75i- 13, 5.70- 10
Grzeszczuk	Lukasz	POL	3.3.90	189/95	JT	82.27	84.77- 14
Gudnason	Gudni Valur	ISL	11.10.95	198/115	DT	60.94	63.50- 15
* Gudzius	Andrius	LTU	14.2.91	200/130	DT	69.21	66.11- 14, 67.96dh- 16
Guidry	Javelin	USA-J	.98	178/82	100	10.13w	10.41- 16
* Guliyev	Ramil	TUR	29.5.90	187/73	100	9.97, 9.9h	10.07- 16
					200	20.02, 19.98w	19.88- 15
Guo Jinqi		CHN	21.9.92	195/75	HJ	2.28	2.25- 16
Guo Qi		CHN	28.12.90	190/80	Dec	7666	7804- 14
Guo Zhongze		CHN	7.8.96	185/75	400	45.14	45.66- 15
Gurski	Roger	GER	11.7.97	174/73	200	20.42	20.64- 16
Habte	Awet	ERI	29.9.97		5000	13:16.09	13:24.40- 16
* Hadadi	Ehsan	IRI	21.1.85	193/125	DT	65.66	69.32- 08
* Hadis	Abadi	ETH	6.11.97	170/63	5000	13:16.78	13:02.49- 16
10k	26:59.19		26:57.88- 16		HMar	60:25	-0-
Haftu	Fikadu	ETH	21.2.94		HMar	59:22	61:02- 16
Haileselassie	Yemane	ERI-J	21.2.98	175/57	3kSt	8:11.22	8:22.52- 16
Hairston	Max	USA	8.5.94	185/79	110h	13.56	13.74- 14, 13.62w- 16
Haitengi	Roger	NAM	12.9.83	184/80	TJ	16.55Aw	16.78A, 16.48- 16, 16.74w- 10
* Halász	Bence	HUN	4.8.97	188/93	HT	78.85	73.97- 16
Halim	Muhammad	ISV	26.10.86	193/84	TJ	16.43	16.99- 16
Hall	Cameron	USA	12.5.93	190/100	110h	13.54	13.61- 15
* Hall	Elijah	USA	22.8.94	174/68	100	10.11, 10.00w	10.15- 16
					200	20.21, 19.96w	20.37A- 16, 20.60- 13
Hall	Justin	USA-J	12.2.98		LJ	7.81, 8.01w	7.29w- 16
Hall	Marshall	NZL	7.10.88	198/111	DT	64.55	59.87- 15
Hall	Quincy	USA-J	31.7.98	185/75	400	45.12	46.98- 16
					400h	49.02	52.19- 14
Hamada	Mohamed Ahmed	EGY	22.10.92	176/64	800	1:44.92	1:44.98- 12
Hamann	Lars	GER	4.4.89	187/88	JT	86.71	85.79- 16
Hamman	Le Roux	RSA	6.1.92	186/69	400h	49.35A, 49.70	49.24A, 49.60- 16
Hamza	Magdi Mohamed	EGY	30.8.96	189/115	SP	20.22	20.32- 16
Han Jijiang		CHN	20.7.93		20kW	1:21:55	1:23:32- 16
					50kW	4:00:28	4:03:16- 15
^ Han Yucheng		CHN	16.12.78	177/59	50kW	3:56:23	3:36:20- 05
Hanany	Mickaël	FRA	25.3.83	198/84	HJ	2.26	2.34- 14
Hann	Mamadou Kassé	FRA	10.10.86	189/79	400h	48.40	48.50- 13
Hanne	Mamadou	FRA	6.3.88	186/72	400	45.44	45.56- 15
Hansson	Anders	SWE	10.3.92	177/67	50kW	3:58:00	4:01:23A- 16
Hara	Shota	JPN	18.7.92	180/75	100	10.13	10.31- 16
* Haratyk	Michal	POL	10.4.92	194/136	SP	21.88	21.35i, 21.23- 16
^ Hardee	Trey	USA	7.2.84	196/95	Dec	8225	8790- 09
* Haroun	Abdelilah	QAT	.97	178/73	400	44.48	44.27- 15
^ Harradine	Benn	AUS	14.10.82	198/115	DT	64.67	68.20- 13
Harrell	Jason	USA	10.1.91	188/109	DT	62.28	62.12- 16
* Harris	Aleec	USA	31.10.90	185/77	110h	13.18	13.11- 15
Harris	Isaiah	USA	18.10.96	182/70	800	1:44.53	1:45.76- 16
Harris	Mar'yea	USA	24.11.97	174/66	400	45.45	45.76- 16
Härstedt	Axel	SWE	28.2.87	197/130	DT	63.90	66.03- 16
* Hartfield	Mike	USA	29.3.90	190/77	LJ	8.21, 8.22w	8.34- 16, 8.42w- 15
* Harting	Christoph	GER	4.10.90	207/120	DT	64.55	68.37- 16
* Harting	Robert	GER	18.10.84	201/127	DT	66.30	70.66- 12
* Harvey	Jak Ali	TUR	5.4.89	182/73	100	10.06, 10.03Aw	9.92A- 16, 10.01- 15
Harvey	Julian	USA	17.6.95	183/77	LJ	8.17i	7.89i, 7.91w- 16
Hasegawa	Kohei	JPN	1.1.90	184/102	JT	80.85	81.55- 16
Hashioka	Yuki	JPN-J	23.1.99	176/64	LJ	8.05, 8.07w	7.75- 16
Hassan	Ahmed	EGY	16.12.95	193/118	SP	21.31	18.73- 16
Hathat	Yassine	ALG	30.7.91	180/68	800	1:46.05	1:44.81- 16
* Haukenes	Håvard	NOR	22.4.90	180/68	50kW	3:43:40	3:46:33- 16
Hawkins	Callum	GBR	22.6.92	179/62	HMar	60:00	62:39, 60:24sh- 16
Heath	Garrett	USA	3.11.85	178/65	3000	7:45.28+i	7:37.40i- 14, 7:37.97- 15
1500	3:39.72i		3:34.12- 13		2M	8:19.61i	8:27.99i- 15, 8:29.43- 12

	Name		Nat	Born	Ht/Wt	Event	2017 Mark	Pre-2017 Best
	Hedeilli	Takieddine	ALG	6.6.96	183/64	1500	3:37.88	3:42.22- 16
*	Heffernan	Robert	IRL	20.2.78	173/55	50kW	3:44:41	3:37:54- 12
	Hehir	Martin	USA	19.12.92	182/64	10k	28:08.60	28:27.70- 15
	Heindl	Martin	CZE	2.6.92	206/93	HJ	2.26i	2.22- 15
	Helander	Oliver	FIN	1.1.97	195/85	JT	80.25	76.28- 15
*	Helcelet	Adam Sebastian	CZE	27.10.91	187/86	Dec	8335	8291- 16
	Helebrandt	Máté	HUN	12.1.89	174/60	50kW	3:43:56	3:53:54- 16
*	Henderson	Jeff	USA	19.2.89	178/82	LJ	8.28	8.52- 15, 8.59w- 16
	Henderson	Khalil	USA	18.11.94	188/75	200	20.25	20.29- 15, 20.20w- 16
	Henriksen	Eivind	NOR	14.9.90	191/116	HT	74.27	75.57- 12
	Heppenstall	Robert	CAN	28.2.97	183/73	800	1:46.26	1:46.78- 16
	Hepperle	Felix	GER	23.11.89		Dec	7699	7618- 14
	Herman	Chad	RSA	25.5.92	186/96	JT	77.81A	77.67A- 15
	Herrera	José Carlos	MEX	5.2.86	187/77	200	20.38A	20.17- 16
	Herrera	Yilmar Andrés	COL	29.4.96	175/65	400	45.48A, 46.02	48.03- 15
*	Hess	Max	GER	13.7.96	186/79	TJ	17.52i, 17.13, 17.24w	17.20- 16
	Hesselbjerg	Ole	DEN	23.4.90	183/70	3kSt	8:27.86	8:30.51- 16
	Hester	Tevin	USA	10.1.94	170/66	100	10.06w	10.05, 9.87w- 15
						200	20.43	20.13- 16
	Hightower	Dakarai	USA	15.7.94	183/68	HJ	2.24i	2.25- 16
	Hilbert	Jonathan	GER	24.1.95	175/62	50kW	4:05:49	-0-
*	Hill	Darrell	USA	17.8.93	193/135	SP	22.44	21.63- 16
	Hill	Devon	USA	26.10.89	185/75	110h	13.38, 13.37w	13.35- 12, 13.32w- 13
*	Hill	Ryan	USA	31.1.90	176/60	1500	3:37.61	3:35.59- 16
	3000	7:40.80+i, 7:43.81		7:30.93- 16		2M	8:11.56i	8:26.72i- 15
	5000	13:07.61i, 13:16.99		13:05.69- 15				
	Hinds	Chadic	JAM	11.8.92	183/75	200	20.49	20.69- 16
*	Hlavan	Igor	UKR	25.9.90	172/62	50kW	3:41:42	3:40:39- 13
*	Hoffmann	Karol	POL	1.6.89	197/80	TJ	16.59	17.16- 16
*	Hofmann	Andreas	GER	16.12.91	195/108	JT	91.07	86.14- 15
	Hogan	Victor	RSA	25.7.89	198/108	DT	64.18	65.33- 13, 67.62dq- 16
*	Holloway	Grant	USA	19.11.97	188/82	110h	13.39	-0-
						LJ	8.05i, 8.04	7.91i- 16, 7.84- 15
*	Holmes	Timothy TJ	USA	2.7.95	182/73	400h	48.44	49.31- 16
*	Holusa	Jakub	CZE	20.2.88	183/72	1500	3:34.26	3:33.36- 16
						1M	3:53.97	3:53.46- 15
*	Holzdeppe	Raphael	GER	28.9.89	181/78	PV	5.80i, 5.80	5.94- 15
	Honeycutt	Josh	USA	7.3.89	182/73	TJ	16.91Ai, 16.74	16.83- 14
	Horvat	Ivan	CRO	17.8.93	188/77	PV	5.76i, 5.70	5.70- 15
	Hostetler	Cyrus	USA	8.8.86	190/95	JT	83.12	83.83- 16
	Houdadi	Mustapha	MAR	5.8.86		3kSt	8:26.55	8:30.0 - 15
	Hough	Nick	AUS	20.10.93	191/86	110h	13.44	13.42- 15
	Houston	Scott	USA	11.6.90	193/79	PV	5.78	5.65, 5.70irr- 16
	Howard	Julian	GER	3.4.89	178/75	LJ	8.15	8.07, 8.13w- 13
^	Howe	Andrew	ITA	12.5.85	184/73	LJ	8.01i	8.47- 07
	Hrechkovskyy	Andrey	UKR	30.8.93	174/55	50kW	3:58:35	3:49:06- 14
	Hsiang Chun-Hsien		TPE	4.9.93	186/70	HJ	2.26	2.29- 15
	Huang Bokai		CHN	26.9.96	183/75	PV	5.63i, 5.55	5.75i- 16, 5.50 - 15
*	Huang Changzhou		CHN	20.8.94	183/66	LJ	8.28	8.21i- 16, 8i.17- 15
	Huang Shih-Feng		TPE	2.3.92	178/88	JT	86.64	83.82- 16
	Hudi	Ákos	HUN	10.8.91	185/95	HT	73.25	76.93- 13
	Hudson	Andrew	USA	14.12.96	180/73	200	20.43	20.64- 14
*	Hudson-Smith	Matthew	GBR	26.10.94	194/78	400	44.74	44.48- 16
*	Hughes	Matt	CAN	3.8.89	180/64	3kSt	8:21.84	8:11.64- 13
*	Hughes	Zharnel	GBR	13.7.95	190/79	100	10.12, 10.08w	10.10- 16
						200	20.22	20.02- 15
^	Huling	Daniel	USA	16.7.83	183/68	3kSt	8:30.36	8:13.29- 10
	Hunter	Drew	USA	5.9.97	175/61	1500	3:36.77	3:41.85+-16
	Husillos	Óscar	ESP	18.7.93	176/73	400	45.16	48.74- 12
*	Hussein	Kariem	SUI	1.4.89	190/77	400h	48.45	48.45- 15
	Huszák	János	HUN	5.2.92	197/118	DT	62.16	64.89- 16
	Hutterer	Dennis	GER	4.5.96	193/89	Dec	7780	7513- 16
*	Hyde	Jaheel	JAM	2.2.97	180/73	400h	48.52	48.81- 16
	Hyman	Kemar	CAY	11.10.89	178/74	100	10.15, 10.04w	9.95- 12, 9.85Aw- 15
	Ibadin	Edose	USA/NGR	27.2.93	172/64	800	1:45.87	1:46.31- 16
	Ibargüen	Arley	COL	4.12.82	182/85	JT	79.72A	81.23A- 16, 81.07- 09
	Ibrahim	Moaaz Mohamed	QAT-J	8.2.99	186/95	DT	60.31	
	Ibrahim	Mohamed Ismail	DJI	1.7.97	171/60	1500	3:36.98	3:37.08- 15
	5000	13:29.29		-0-		3kSt	8:27.41	8:23.77- 16
^	Ibrahimov	Hayle	AZE	18.1.90	168/58	5000	13:19.94	13:09.17- 14
	Ichida	Takashi	JPN	16.6.92	163/48	10k	27:59.76	27:53.59- 16

	Name		Nat	Born	Ht/Wt	Event	2017 Mark	Pre-2017 Best
	Igbokwe	Obie	USA	28.1.97	181/73	400	45.54	46.22- 15
*	Iguider	Abdelaati	MAR	25.3.87	170/52	1500	3:34.99	3:28.79- 15
	1M	3:52.77		3:49.09- 14		3000	7:37.82	7:30.09- 16
	Iizuka	Shota	JPN	25.6.91	185/80	100	10.08	10.22- 13
						200	20.40	20.11- 16
	Ikeda	Koki	JPN-J	3.5.98		20kW	1:20:48	-0-
	Infantino	Antonio	ITA	22.3.91	182/73	200	20.59, 20.45w	20.53- 16
*	Ingebrigtsen	Filip	NOR	20.4.93	187/75	1500	3:32.48	3:32.43- 16
						1M	3:53.23	3:55.02- 16
*	Ingebrigtsen	Henrik	NOR	24.2.91	180/69	1M	3:53.79	3:50.72- 14
	Ingebrigtsen	Jakob	NOR-Y	19.9.00	181/65	3kSt	8:26.81	-0-
	Inoue	Hirohito	JPN	6.1.93	164/53	10k	28:08.04	28:12.96- 15
	Inoue	Hiroto	JPN	6.1.93	164/53	Mar	2:08:22	2:12:56- 16
	Iordan	Valeriy	RUS	14.2.92	182/84	JT	82.12	83.56- 13
	Irabaruta	Olivier	BDI	25.8.90	171/61	10k	28:03.57	27:55.92- 16
	Irfan	Kolothum Thodi	IND	8.2.90	172/55	20kW	1:20:59	1:20:21- 12
	Iribarne	Roger	CUB	2.1.96	183/68	110h	13.39	13.53- 16
	Irwin	Andrew	USA	23.1.93	190/84	PV	5.75	5.75i- 15, 5.72- 12
	Isene	Ola Stunes	NOR	29.1.95	193/106	DT	61.33	61.36- 16
	Ishida	Yusuke	JPN	25.5.95	183/70	400h	49.35	50.32- 16
	Ishikawa	Shuhei	JPN	29.5.95		110h	13.67, 13.56w	13.88- 16
	Ishiyama	Ayumu	JPN	2.6.96	179/91	JT	77.91	73.11- 16
	Isidro	Pedro	POR	17.7.85	175/58	50kW	3:56:38	3:55:44- 15
	Ismail	Muhammad Hakimi	MAS	8.4.91	188/80	TJ	16.77	16.76- 15
	Ito	Yuki	JPN	12.4.92		50kW	3:56:34	3:55:54- 15
	Ivanov	Georgi	BUL	13.3.85	187/130	SP	20.12	21.09- 13
	Ivanov	Ivan	KAZ	3.1.92	202/144	SP	20.00	20.51i-dm, 19.63- 16
	Ivanov	Tihomir	BUL	11.7.94	198/77	HJ	2.31	2.29- 16
	Ivanov	Yevgeniy	BLR	11.6.92		HT	71.18	69.90- 16
	Ivanytskyy	Vasyl	UKR	29.1.91	186/80	Dec	7801	7683- 16
	Ivanyuk	Ilya	RUS	9.3.93	183/75	HJ	2.31i, 2.30	2.30- 15
	Jaakkola	Aleksi	FIN	17.11.97	192/117	HT	71.95	73.77- 16
*	Jackson	Bershawn	USA	8.5.83	173/69	400h	48.63	47.30- 05
	Jackson	Johnnie	USA	19.9.94	188/109	HT	71.72	66.17- 16
	Jacobs	Lamont Marcell	ITA	26.9.94	184/73	LJ	8.07i	8.03i- 15, 7.95, 8.48w- 16
	Jacobus	Derek	USA	23.7.95	185/86	Dec	7635	7356- 16
*	Jager	Evan	USA	8.3.89	185/65	3kSt	8:01.29	8:00.45- 15
	Jagers	Phillip	USA	12.8.95	183/95	DT	62.04	62.71- 16
	Jagers	Reggie	USA	13.8.94	185/100	DT	62.51	61.64- 16
	Jagor	Jaak-Heinrich	EST	11.5.90	190/80	400h	49.38	49.37- 15
	Jagusch	Christian	GER	13.7.92	190/110	SP	20.04	20.10- 15
	Jainaga	Odel	ESP	14.10.97	193/80	JT	77.66A	69.27- 16
*	James	Kirani	GRN	1.9.92	185/74	400	45.44	43.74- 14
	Jamshidi	Abdollah	IRI			SP	19.55	18.93- 13
	Janezic	Luka	SLO	14.11.95	192/83	400	44.84	45.07- 16
	Jaramillo	Geormi	VEN	6.3.89	185/80	Dec	8126w, 8039(w)	7679A-11
*	Jasinski	Daniel	GER	5.8.89	207/125	DT	62.20	67.16- 16
	Jaszczuk	Tomasz	POL	9.3.92	195/83	LJ	8.18	8.15- 14
	Jefferson	Chris	USA	.96	180/74	100	10.08w	10.64, 10.62w- 15
	Jelonek	Jakub	POL	7.7.85	184/71	20kW	1:22:15	1:21:05- 12
	Jenkins	Eric	USA	24.11.91	170/61	1500	3:36.51	3:35.94- 16
	1M	3:53.23i		3:57.09- 15		3000	7:40.36	7:39.43i- 16, 7:41.79- 15
	5000	13:05.85i, 13:13.30		13:07.33- 15				
	Jensen	Curtis	USA	1.11.90	193/130	SP	20.69	20.33- 14
	Jeuschede	Jan Josef	GER	23.4.93	187/110	SP	19.49	19.31- 15
	Jiang Fan		CHN	16.9.89	188/75	110h	13.62	13.47- 11
	Jiang Su		CHN	8.4.95		50kW	4:06:04	4:04:19- 16
	Jílek	Jaroslav	CZE	22.10.89	183/85	JT	83.09	83.19- 16
	Jin Xiangqian		CHN	18.3.97		20kW	1:19:12	-0-
	Jisa	Sisay	ETH	29.11.82		Mar	2:08:09	2:06:27- 12
*	Jobodwana	Anaso	RSA	30.7.92	187/71	100	10.16A	10.10 -13
						200	20.10Aw	19.87- 15
	John	Alexander	GER	3.5.86	185/77	110h	13.58	13.35- 09
	John	Jeffrey	FRA	6.6.92	184/67	200	20.31	20.38- 15
	Johnson	Kibwé	USA	17.7.81	189/108	HT	74.32	80.31- 11
	Jones	Avion	USA	31.1.94	190/75	HJ	2.25	2.31- 16
	Jones	Jonathan	USA	23.4.91	183/127	SP	20.93	20.92- 15
	Jonsson	Hilmar Örn	ISL	6.5.96	183/107	HT	72.38	72.12- 16
	Jordan	Michael	USA	21.5.91	178/64	3kSt	8:30.86	8:35.30- 16
	Jørgensen	Rasmus	DEN	23.1.89	180/75	PV	5.56	5.65- 13
	Joseph	Patrick	USA	7.9.95	175/64	800	1:46.23i	

Name		Nat	Born	Ht/Wt	Event	2017 Mark	Pre-2017 Best
Joseph	Stanley	FRA	24.10.91	181/70	PV	5.65i, 5.50	5.75- 16
Julmis	Jeffrey	HAI	6.1.87	183/80	110h	13.53, 13.41w	13.47- 16, 13.38w- 11
Juma	Ismail	TAN	3.8.91		HMar	59:30	62:42- 13
Junghanss	Karl	GER	6.4.96	178/59	20kW	1:22:08	1:23:53- 16
					50kW	3:47:01	3:52:46- 16
* Juska	Radek	CZE	8.3.93	195/82	LJ	8.31	8.15- 15
Kaazouzi	Brahim	MAR	15.6.90	179/62	1500	3:34.46	3:35.76- 16
3000	7:41.88		7:46.58- 16		5000	13:16.98	-0-
Kaba	Sekou	CAN	25.8.90	190/82	110h	13.65, 13,62w	13.43- 15
Kajiki	Ryo	JPN	8.12.95	176/62	400h	49.33	50.71- 16
Kakayev	Ivan	RUS	13.8.97		20kW	1:22:16	-0-
Kamino	Daichi	JPN	13.9.93	164/42	HMar	61:04	61:21- 15
Kaminski	Damian	POL	15.12.93	192/91	DT	61.72	59.71- 16
* Kamworor	Geoffrey	KEN	22.11.92	168/54	5000	13:01.35	12:59.98- 16
10k	26:57.77		26:52.65- 15		Mar	2:10:53	2:06:12- 12
Kanai	Taio	JPN	28.9.95	179/65	110h	13.53, 13.46w	13.74, 13.61w- 16
Kanda	Luka	KEN	.87		Mar	2:06:15	2:07:20- 15
Kandie	Cleophas	KEN-Y	14.8.00		3kSt	8:30.9A	9:04.1A- 16
* Kandie	Felix	KEN	10.4.87	178/62	Mar	2:06:03	2:06:25- 16
Kandu	Chris	GBR	10.9.95	197/79	HJ	2.26i, 2.25	2.26i- 15, 2.24- 14
Kangas	Arttu	FIN	13.7.93	186/108	SP	20.18i, 19.95	20.30- 16
Kangogo	Albert	KEN	16.8.87		HMar	59:25	59:29- 16
Kangogo	Cornelius	KEN	31.12.93	186/62	5000	13:21.26	13:10.80- 16
Kangogo	Justus	KEN	10.10.95	173/55	HMar	59:31	61:16- 15
Kangogo	Philip	KEN			HMar	60:57	-0-
Kanno	Tomofumi	JPN	25.4.93		50kW	4:04:58	3:54:24- 15
* Kanter	Gerd	EST	6.5.79	196/125	DT	65.87	73.38- 06
Karailiev	Momchil	BUL	21.5.82	188/75	TJ	17.05	17.41- 09
* Karalís	Emmanouíl	GRE-J	20.10.99	183/75	PV	5.70i, 5.63	5.55- 16
Karavayev	Pavel	RUS	27.8.88	185/74	LJ	7.94	8.08- 11
Kariuki	Simon	KEN	13.2.92	171/54	10k	27:55.10	27:53.50- 16
* Karlström	Perseus	SWE	2.5.90	184/73	20kW	1:20:20	1:19:11- 16
					50kW	3:44:35	3:52:43- 13
* Karoki	Bedan	KEN	21.8.90	169/53	10k	26:52.12	26:52.36- 14
HMar	59:10		59:14- 15		Mar	2:07:41	-0-
Kashimura	Ryota	JPN	13.8.91	175/115	HT	71.36	70.81- 16
* Kasyanov	Oleksiy	UKR	26.8.85	191/87	Dec	8281	8479- 09
Katnik	Matt	USA	10.10.96	190/127	SP	19.75i, 19.14	18.79- 16
Katsuki	Hayato	JPN	28.11.90	168/58	50kW	3:48:36	3:52:07- 16
Kawagishi	Ryosuke	JPN	15.6.96	177/59	20kW	1:22:32.15	1:23:41.46t- 16
Kawakami	Tayuka	JPN	8.6.95		100	10.09w	10.33- 15, 10.19w- 14
Kawamoto	Sho	JPN	1.3.93	175/68	800	1:46.17	1:45.97 -16
Kawashima	Tazuma	JPN	16.8.96		LJ	7.92, 7.97w	7.59- 16
* Kaya	Ali	TUR	20.4.94	171/55	5000	13:25.71	13:00.31- 15
					10k	27:54.41	27:24.09- 15
Kazi	Tamás	HUN	16.5.85	179/70	1500	3:37.41	3:38.95- 16
* Kazmirek	Kai	GER	28.1.91	189/91	Dec	8488	8580- 16
Kebede	Tariku	ETH	.96		Mar	2:07:48	2:12:07- 16
Kebede	Tsegaye	ETH	15.1.87	158/50	Mar	2:08:45	2:04:38- 12
* Kebenei	Stanley	USA	6.11.89	174/61	10k	27:58.56	29:33.58- 14
					3kSt	8:08.30	8:18.52- 16
Keenan	Adam	CAN	26.3.93	180/102	HT	72.57	70.14- 16
Keitany	Evans	KEN-J	27.11.99		5000	13:21.72	
* Kejelcha	Yomif	ETH	1.8.97	186/58	1500	3:32.94	-0-
3000	7:32.27		7:28.19- 16		5000	13:01.21	12:53.98- 15
Keller	Levi	USA	30.1.86	183/82	PV	5.51i	5.61- 16
* Kemboi	Clement	KEN	1.2.92	180/65	3kSt	8:23.98	8:10.65- 16
Kemboi	Edward	KEN	12.12.91	170/57	800	1:44.77	1:45.58- 15
Kemboi	Edwin	KEN	22.8.86		800	1:45.2A	1:45.4A- 15
* Kemboi	Ezekiel	KEN	25.5.82	175/62	3kSt	8:20.61	7:55.76- 11
Kemboi	Hillary	KEN	.86		3kSt	8:29.2A	8:22.26- 14
Kemboi	Lawrence	KEN	15.6.93	170/57	3kSt	8:23.93	8:17.79- 16
Kemper	Deante	USA	27.3.93	181/70	HJ	2.24Ai, 2.24	2.27Ai- 16, 2.23- 14
Kendagor	Jacob Kibet	KEN	24.8.84	158/50	Mar	2:07:33	2:07:47- 15
* Kendricks	Sam	USA	7.9.92	189/79	PV	6.00	5.92- 16
Kendziera	David	USA	9.9.94	190/84	110h	13.39	13.67, 13.56w- 15
					400h	49.00	49.56- 15
Kerio	Reuben	KEN	.94		Mar	2:08:12	2:09:05- 16
* Kerley	Fred	USA	7.5.95	188/86	200	20.24	20.61- 16
					400	43.70	45.10- 16
Kerley	My'Lik	USA	6.6.96	193/75	400	44.85	45.98- 16

Name		Nat	Born	Ht/Wt	Event	2017 Mark	Pre-2017 Best
Kern	Jared	USA	10.6.95	185/125	SP	20.47i, 19.65	18.62- 16
Kerr	Josh	GBR	8.10.97	186/73	1500	3:35.99	3:41.08- 16
Khadivar	Ali	IRI	11.11.89	180/73	400	45.64A, 45.85	
Khodjayev	Sukhrob	UZB	21.5.93	186/105	HT	73.85	78.22- 15
Khudyakov	Aleksey	RUS	31.3.95	191/95	DT	63.38	62.23- 16
Kibet	Alex	KEN	20.10.90	172/52	HMar	59:32	-0-
					3kSt	8:25.64	8:18.28- 16
Kibet	James	KEN	.88		5000	13:11.88	13:36.7A- 15
Kibet	Moses	UGA	23.3.91	165/55	HMar	60:44	61:37- 16
Kibet	Raymond	KEN	4.2.96	188/80	400	45.21	45.39A, 45.66- 15
* Kibet	Vincent	KEN	6.5.91	173/57	1500	3:32.66	3:31.96 -14
1M	3:51.17		3:52.15- 14		3000	7:50.54	7:44.87i- 16, 7:58.9- 14
Kibichy	Edwin	KEN	2.4.92	183/73	3kSt	8:28.40	8:30.71- 16
* Kibiwot	Abraham	KEN	4.6.96	175/55	3kSt	8:10.62	8:09.25- 16
* Kifle	Aron	ERI-J	20.2.98	170/55	5000	13:13.31	13:13.39- 16
					10k	27:09.92	27:26.20- 16
* Kigen	Benjamin	KEN	5.7.93	173/57	1500	3:36.36	3:42.4A- 14
2kSt	5:18.67				3kSt	8:11.38	-0-
Kigen	Noah	KEN	12.6.89		HMar	60:25	64:32A-16
Kigen	Nobert	KEN	24.1.93		HMar	61:02	-16
					Mar	2:05:13	2:09:19- 16
Kiiskilä	Jani	FIN	28.12.89	180/81	JT	77.72	78.41- 16
Kim Byung-jun		KOR	15.8.91	190/80	110h	13.39	13.43- 14
Kim Duk-hyun		KOR	8.12.85	180/70	LJ	8.11	8.20, 8.41w- 09
* Kim Hyun-sub		KOR	31.5.85	175/53	20kW	1:19:50	1:19:13- 15
Kim Kuk-young		KOR	19.4.91	172/60	100	10.07, 10.03w	10.16- 15
Kimani	Bernard	KEN	10.9.93	172/54	10k	27:37.41	27:36.60- 14
Kimeli	Bernard	KEN	10.9.95	170/52	10k	28:09.46	
Kimeli	Isaac	BEL	9.3.94	175/59	1500	3:37.66	3:37.79- 16
Kimeli	Mathew	KEN-J	4.1.98	168/53	10k	27:14.43	28:19.4A- 16
Kimeli	Nicholas	KEN-J	29.9.98		5000	13:11.58	13:44.4A -16
Kimeli	Timothy	KEN	20.1.94		HMar	60:57	63:48- 16
Kimitei	Elijah	KEN	25.12.86	183/81	TJ	16.67A	16.66A, 16.28- 12
Kimitei	Wilfred	KEN	11.3.85	172/57	HMar	60:12	62:10- 14
Kimura	Kazushi	JPN	17.1.93	181/65	400	45.53	45.96- 15
Kimuruer	Joel	KEN	21.1.88		HMar	60:59	
Kimutai	Marius	KEN	.89	167/57	HMar	60:07	64:27- 16
					Mar	2:06:04	2:05:47- 16
Kimutai Kiplagat	Edwin	KEN	19.2.93		HMar	60:57	-0-
Kincaid	William	USA	21.9.92	173/55	5000	13:12.22i	13:27.32- 16
King	David	GBR	13.6.94	186/77	110h	13.48	13.54, 13.4- 16
King	Devin	USA	12.3.96	185/75	PV	5.70	5.70- 16
King	Dominic	GBR	30.5.83	179/60	50kW	4:04:16	3:55:48- 16
King	Kyree	USA	9.7.94	181/68	100	10.00, 9.98w	10.23, 10.11w- 15
					200	20.27, 20.22w	20.51- 15, 20.37w- 16
Kinnunen	Jarkko	FIN	19.1.84	187/69	50kW	3:55:44	3:46:25- 12
Kinyamal	Wycliffe	KEN	2.7.97	186/75	800	1:43.94	1:46.8A- 16
Kinyor	Job	KEN	2.9.90	176/68	800	1:45.15	1:43.76- 12
Kipchirchir	Elisha	KEN	.90		Mar	2:08:58	2:10:45- 16
Kipchirchir	Shadrack	USA	22.2.89	175/60	5000	13:23.74	13:18.52- 16
					10k	27:07.55	27:36.79- 14
Kipchirchir	Victor	KEN	5.12.87		Mar	2:08:52	2:07:39- 16
Kipchirchir Sambu	Evans	KEN	2010.89		Mar	2:09:05	2:10:28- 16
Kipchoge	Cosmas	KEN	21.3.86	176/63	Mar	2:08:45	
* Kipchoge	Eliud	KEN	5.11.84	167/52	Mar	2:03.32, 2:00:25irr	2:03:05- 16
Kipchumba	Daniel	KEN	12.12.97	167/55	3kSt	8:30.0A	8:37.9A- 16
Kipchumba	Evans	KEN	.94		1500	3:37.35A	3:44.4A- 16
Kipkemboi	Kipsang	KEN	.90		Mar	2:08:26	2:13:05- 11
Kipkemboi Kibet	Moses	KEN	20.11.94	177/60	800	1:45.7A	1:45.83- 13
Kipkemoi	Daniel	KEN	5.7.96	170/52	5000	13:26.38	13:27.44- 15
					10k	27:45.46	27:53.19- 15
* Kipkemoi	Kenneth	KEN	2.8.84	165/54	HMar	60:24	59:01- 14
* Kipketer	Alfred	KEN	26.12.96	169/61	800	1:45.40	1:42.87- 16
* Kipketer	Gideon	KEN	10.11.92	178/57	Mar	2:05:51	2:08:14- 12
Kipkoech	Nicholas	KEN	22.10.92	168/57	800	1:44.9A	1:43.37A-16
Kipkosgei	Fredrick	KEN	13.11.96	170/57	5000	13:13.16	13:15.59- 16
Kiplagat	Nicholas	KEN	6.7.95		800	1:45.79A	
Kiplagat	Philemon	KEN-Y	20.9.01	187/68	5000	13:22.27	
					3kSt	8:21.30	
* Kiplagat	Silas	KEN	20.8.89	170/57	1500	3:32.23	3:27.64 -14
					3000	7:43.39	7:39.94- 10

Name		Nat	Born	Ht/Wt	Event	2017 Mark	Pre-2017 Best
Kiplagat	Thomas	KEN			HMar	60:54	63:17- 16
Kiplangat	Davis	KEN-J	10.7.98		3000	7:38.33	7:48.04- 16
					5000	13:18.09	13:16.35- 16
Kiplangat	Peter	KEN	6.9.93	186/75	800	1:45.00A	1:45.04A- 16
Kipleting	Phenus	KEN	.89		3kSt	8:30.1A	8:21.23- 16
Kiplimo	Jacob	UGA-Y	14.11.00	168/55	3000	7:43.73	7:52.94- 16
					5000	13:13.64	13:19.54- 16
Kiplimo	Joash	KEN	.91		3kSt	8:26.4A	8:24.26A- 15
* Kiprop	Asbel	KEN	30.6.89	186/70	800	1:44.43	1:43.15- 11
					1500	3:33.17	3:26.69- 15
Kiprop	Jonah	KEN-J	22.11.98		800	1:45.9A	1:47.9A- 16
Kiprotich	Felix	KEN	.88		Mar	2:06:54	2:06:58- 16
Kiprotich	Geoffrey	KEN	23.11.97	178/64	400	45.74A, 45.2A	45.66A- 16
Kiprotich	Justus	KEN	.90		800	1:45.78A	
* Kiprotich	Stephen	UGA	18.4.89	172/56	Mar	2:07:10	2:06:33- 15
Kiprugut	Boaz	KEN-J	18.5.98	173/61	1500	3:36.47	3:39.5 - 16
Kipruto	Amos	KEN	.92		HMar	60:24	61:09- 16
					Mar	2:05:43	2:08:12- 16
Kipruto	Benson	KEN	.91		Mar	2:07:21	2:13:24- 16
* Kipruto	Brimin	KEN	31.7.85	176/54	3kSt	8:19.87A	7:53.64- 11
* Kipruto	Conseslus	KEN	8.12.94	171/55	3kSt	8:04.63	8:00.12- 16
Kipruto	Vincent	KEN	13.9.87	172/57	Mar	2:06:14	2:05:13- 10
Kipsang	Asbel	KEN	10.9.93		Mar	2:08:29	2:07:30- 16
* Kipsang	Wilson	KEN	15.3.82	178/59	Mar	2:03:58	2:03:13- 16
Kipserem	Marius	KEN	17.5.88		Mar	2:06:43	2:06:11- 16
* Kiptanui	Eliud	KEN	6.6.89	169/55	Mar	2:07:25	2:05:21- 15
Kiptanui	Mathew	KEN	20.10.94		5000	13:16.66	13:14.06- 16
Kiptarus	Dominic	KEN	3.8.96	168/52	HMar	60:53	-0-
Kiptoo	Edwin Kiprop	KEN	14.8.93		HMar	59:59	59:26- 15
Kiptum	Abraham	KEN	.89		HMar	60:06	59:36- 16
Kiptum	Abraham	KEN	.89		Mar	2:05:26	2:11:36- 15
Kiptum	Joseph	KEN	25.9.87		HMar	60:37	60:17- 15
Kipyatich	Abraham	KEN	10.5.93	176/50	5000	13:23.11	
10k	28:03.92		-0-		HMar	61:00	60:03- 15
Kipyego	Barnabas	KEN	12.6.95	176/57	3kSt	8:14.13	8:09.13- 16
Kipyego	Barselius	KEN	23.7.93		HMar	59:14	59:15- 16
^ Kipyego	Bernard	KEN	16.7.86	160/50	Mar	2:08:10	2:06:22- 14
Kipyego	Edwin	KEN	16.11.90	178/52	HMar	60:05	59:30- 15
Kipyegon	Bernard	KEN	19.12.90	181/65	800	1:45.21A	1:45.68- 15
Kirchler	Hannes	ITA	22.12.78	191/113	DT	62.60	65.01- 07
Kiriazis	Ioánnis	GRE	19.1.96	194/98	JT	88.01	87.14- 16
Kirong	Felix	KEN	.86	175/62	3kSt	8:25.5A	8:37.2A- 15
Kirongo	Sammy	KEN	4.2.94	176/62	800	1:45.6A	1:45.3A- 14, 1:45.38 -14
* Kirt	Magnus	EST	10.4.90	192/89	JT	86.06	86.65- 15
* Kirui	Abel	KEN	4.6.82	177/62	Mar	2:07:45	2:05:04- 09
Kirui	Amos	KEN-J	9.2.98	169/54	3kSt	8:08.37	8:20.43- 16
Kirui	Geoffrey	KEN	16.2.93	158/50	HMar	60:04	59:38- 15
					Mar	2:08:27	2:06:27- 16
Kirui	Peter	KEN	2.1.88	182/66	10k	27:56.01A	27:25.63- 11
					HMar	60:30	59:22- 14
Kirwa	Felix	KEN			Mar	2:06:13	2:14:42- 15
Kirya	Aleksandr	RUS	23.3.92	187/102	DT	62.22	61.02- 16
Kiryu	Yoshihide	JPN	15.12.95	175/69	100	9.98	10.01- 13, 9.87w- 15
					200	20.59, 20.46w	20.41- 13
Kiselkov	Fyodor	RUS	3.6.95	176/73	LJ	8.11i, 8.02	7.97- 16
Kishimoto	Takayuki	JPN	6.5.90	171/61	400h	49.39	48.41- 12
^ Kisorio	Mathew	KEN	16.5.89	178/62	10k	27:53.99A	26:54.25- 11
					Mar	2:07:32	2:06:33- 15
Kissa	Stephen	UGA	1.12.95	174/61	5000	13:13.00	13:45.59A-15
Kitagawa	Takamasa	JPN	5.9.96	177/70	400	45.48	45.52- 15
Kitata	Shura	ETH	9.6.96		HMar	60:10	62:50+-15
					Mar	2:05:50	2:08:53- 15
Kitonyi	Daniel	KEN	12.1.94	165/51	10k	27:51.08	27:49.89- 16
* Kitum	Timothy	KEN	20.11.94	172/60	800	1:45.9A	1:42.53- 12
* Kitwara	Sammy	KEN	26.11.86	177/54	Mar	2:05:15	2:04:28- 14
^ Kivuva	Jackson	KEN	11.8.88	172/59	800	1:45.80A	1:43.72- 10
Klaus	Maximilian	GER	7.2.96	193/105	DT	61.34	55.42- 16
Klausen	Janick	DEN	3.4.93	178/72	HJ	2.26i, 2.20	2.27i, 2.25- 11
Knight	Justyn	CAN	19.7.96	171/59	3000	7:47.82i	7:48.71i- 16
					5000	13:17.51	13:26.36- 16
Kniya ¶	Younès	MAR	15.8.95		3kSt	8:25.84	8:29.7- 15

	Name		Nat	Born	Ht/Wt	Event	2017 Mark	Pre-2017 Best
	Kobayashi	Kai	JPN	28.2.93	165/53	20kW	1:19:13	1:19:12- 15
						50kW	3:41:19	3:42:08- 16
	Kobielski	Norbert	POL	28.1.97	202/80	HJ	2.26	2.22I- 16, 2.19- 15
	Koech	Bernard	KEN	31.1.88	165/50	Mar	2:08:32	2:04:53- 13
	Koech	Edwin	KEN	15.5.83		HMar	60:24	59:54- 15
						Mar	2:07:13	2:09:04- 14
	Koech	Geoffrey	KEN	28.8.93		HMar	59:50	61:44- 15
*	Koech	Haron	KEN	27.1.90	188/79	400h	49.39	48.49- 16
	Koech	Justus	KEN	.90	183/70	800	1:45.0A	1:50.1A- 15
	Koech	Meshack	KEN	.88		HMar	60:07	61:39+- 16
	Koech	Moses	KEN	5.4.97	168/52	5000	13:15.57	13:15.56- 15
*	Koech	Paul Kipsiele	KEN	10.11.81	168/57	HMar	61:03	-0-
	Koffi	Wilfried	CIV	24.9.89	186/80	200	20.41	20.25- 14
	Kokhan	Myhaylo	UKR-Y	22.1.01	182/103	HT	71.42	-0-
*	Kolasinac	Asmir	SRB	15.10.84	186/137	SP	20.87i, 19.45	21.58- 15
	Kolesnikov	Maksim	RUS	28.2.91		LJ	8.01i	7.91i- 16, 7.87, 7.95w- 15
	Kolomoyets	Sergey	BLR	11.8.89	191/110	HT	77.52	77.52- 11
	Kominami	Takuto	JPN	26.7.95	172/83	JT	79.17	75.85- 16
	Konishi	Yuta	JPN	31.7.90	182/70	400h	49.03	49.41- 11
	Koppelaar	Rutger	NED	1.5.93	187/73	PV	5.65i, 5.60	5.53- 16
	Korir	Albert	KEN	2.3.94		Mar	2:08:40	2:10:08- 16
*	Korir	Emmanuel	KEN	15.6.95	177/64	400	44.53A	
						800	1:43.10	1:46.94- 16
	Korir	Japheth	KEN	30.6.93	168/55	5000	13:14.56	13:11.44i- 12, 13:17.18- 11
						HMar	60:08	61:00- 16
	Korir	Laban	KEN	30.12.85		Mar	2:06:25	2:05:54- 16
*	Korir	Leonard	USA	10.12.86	173/61	5000	13:22.04	13:15.45- 13
	10k	27:20.18	27:29.40- 11HMar			59:52	61:06- 15	
	Korir	Mark	KEN	10.1.85	175/59	Mar	2:06:05	2:05:49- 15
	Korir Kimining	Shadrack	KEN	10.2.96	170/54	HMar	60:07	60:53- 16
	Kornegay-Gober	Kris	USA	6.10.91	188/74	HJ	2.24	2.24i- 12, 2.23- 16
	Koroknai	Tibor	HUN	24.1.90	190/77	400h	49.74	50.25- 14
	Korolyov	Aleksey	RUS	5.4.82	190/118	HT	72.22	79.36- 08
	Korolyov	Maksim	RUS	6.1.88		Dec	7772	7521- 15
	Koros	Wilberforce	KEN			3kSt	8:29.8A	8:41.8A- 16
	Korotovskiy	Yevgeniy	RUS	21.6.92	184/102	HT	74.42	74.46- 16
	Korshunov	Yevgeniy	RUS	11.4.86	193/84	HJ	2.24i	2.29i- 14, 2.26- 15
	Kosciów	Dawid	POL	5.6.90	193/95	JT	78.80	77.48- 15
^	Kosencha	Leonard	KEN	21.8.94	174/60	800	1:46.13	1:45.4A- 16
	Kosgei	Samuel Kiplimo	KEN	20.1.86	173/55	Mar	2:08:39	2:06:53- 16
	Kosimbei	Nicholas	KEN	10.1.96	175/59	5000	13:22.68	13:17.08- 16
						10k	27:48.51	27:02.59- 16
	Kosynskyy	Dmytro	UKR	31.3.89	200/105	JT	80.37	84.08- 16
	Kotov	Danyil	RUS	14.11.95	183/73	PV	5.63i, 5.60	5.50- 14
*	Kovacs	Joe	USA	28.6.89	181/132	SP	22.57	22.56- 15
*	Kövágó	Zoltán	HUN	10.4.79	204/127	DT	65.67	69.95- 06
	Kovalenko	Kirill	RUS	20.1.94		TJ	16.48	16.06, 16.13w- 16
*	Kowal	Yoann	FRA	28.5.87	172/58	1500	3:36.96	3:33.75- 11
						3kSt	8:15.60	8:12.53- 13
	Kownatke	Rafal	POL	24.3.85	189/133	SP	20.11i, 19.67	20.37- 16, 20.13- 13
	Kramer	Andreas	SWE	13.4.97	183/68	800	1:45.13	1:47.24- 16
	Krauss	Simon	FRA	12.2.92	182/77	110h	13.60	13.50- 14, 13.41w- 13
	Krukowski	Marcin	POL	14.6.92	182/92	JT	88.09	85.20- 15
^	Krymarenko	Yuriy	UKR	11.8.83	187/65	HJ	2.30	2.34i- 07, 2.34- 13
*	Kszczot	Adam	POL	2.9.89	178/64	800	1:44.84	1:43.30- 11
*	Kudlicka	Jan	CZE	29.4.88	184/76	PV	5.80i, 5.72	5.83- 16
	Kujanpää	Urho	FIN	18.5.97	188/80	PV	5.55i, 5.45	5.30- 16
	Kulayev	Aleksey	RUS	7.5.94		SP	19.76	19.94- 16
*	Kuma	Abera	ETH	31.8.90	160/50	Mar	2:06:44	2:05:56- 14
	Kumar Sangwan	Sandeep	IND	16.12.86	183/68	50kW	3:56:00	3:56:22- 14
	Kupers	Thijmen	NED	4.10.91	180/65	800	1:44.99	1:45.23 -16
^	Kupper	Martin	EST	31.5.89	195/108	DT	62.86	66.67- 15
	Kuriki	Anthony Tyrell	JPN	17.9.96		110h	13.60	13.84- 16
	Kurong	Moses	UGA	7.7.94	165/52	10k	27:22.33	27:27.43- 16
						HMar	59:50	65:09- 14
	Kuruma	Koki	JPN	25.3.96	182/73	PV	5.55	5.40- 16
	Kushniruk	Yuriy	UKR	6.12.94	180/92	JT	78.40	75.05- 12
	Kutuyev	Rail	RUS	6.8.96		LJ	8.10	7.65- 16
	Kwambai	Robert Kipkorir	KEN	22.11.85		Mar	2:08:14	2:08:03- 16
*	Kwemoi	Ronald	KEN	19.9.95	180/68	1500	3:30.89A	3:28.81 -14
	1M	3:49.04 3:52.57- 15		3000	7:28.73			5000 13:24.42 13:16.14- 15

	Name		Nat	Born	Ht/Wt	Event	2017 Mark	Pre-2017 Best
*	Kynard	Eric	USA	3.2.91	193/86	HJ	2.31i, 2.30	2.37- 13
	Laanmäe	Tanel	EST	29.9.89	183/94	JT	82.58	85.04- 16
	Lagat	Alfers	KEN	7.8.86		Mar	2:07:39	2:06:48- 15
	Lagat	Haron	USA	15.8.83	185/72	3kSt	8:25.73	8:15.80- 11
	Lagat	Justus	KEN	20.5.96	168/55	3kSt	8:18.46	8:22.5A- 16
	Lahbabi	Aziz	MAR	3.2.91	169/55	HMar	60:15	59:14- 14
	Lahoulou	Abdelmalik	ALG	7.5.92	180/70	400h	49.05	48.62- 16
	Laidig	Torben	GER	13.3.94	187/82	PV	5.70	5.62i, 5.60- 16
	Laine	Keenon	USA	12.6.97	193/79	HJ	2.25	2.20- 16
	Lalang	Lawi	KEN	15.6.91	170/58	3000	7:45.01+i	7:36.44- 14
						2M	8:18.70i	
	Lambrughi	Mario	ITA	5.2.92	184/75	400h	49.41	49.35- 16
	Lamou	Martin	FRA-J	13.5.99	182/70	TJ	16.97	16.34i, 16.15, 16.46w- 16
	Landon	Kyle	USA	16.10.94	193/77	HJ	2.26i, 2.21	2.26- 16
	Lane	John	GBR	29.1.89	186/88	Dec	7965	7922- 14
	Langat	Isaac	KEN	18.12.94		HMar	60:25	61:36- 14
	Langat	John	KEN	31.12.96	170/63	HMar	60:41	
	Langat	Leonard	KEN	7.8.90	175/58	HMar	60:08	59:18- 16
	Langat	Philip	KEN	23.4.90		HMar	60:52	60:04- 15
	Langford	Kyle	GBR	2.2.96	183/66	800	1:45.25	1:45.78 -15
	Langton Burnell	Benjamin	NZL	10.7.92	183/82	JT	82.44	79.80- 16
*	Lapierre	Fabrice	AUS	17.10.83	179/66	LJ	8.03, 8.50w	8.40, 8.78w- 10
	Lasa	Emiliano	URU	25.1.90	180/75	LJ	8.19	8.16- 16, 8.17w- 15
^	Lauro	Germán	ARG	2.4.84	185/127	SP	20.45	21.26- 13
						DT	61.70	63.55- 12
*	Lavillenie	Renaud	FRA	18.9.86	177/71	PV	5.91	6.16i- 14, 6.05- 15
	Lavillenie	Valentin	FRA	16.7.91	170/66	PV	5.70	5.80i- 15, 5.71- 16
	Lawler	Marcus	IRL	28.2.95	185/77	200	20.71, 20.43w	20.74- 15
	Lawrence	Desmond	USA	19.12.91	178/77	100	10.12w	10.08- 16
*	Lawson	Jarrion	USA	6.5.94	188/75	100	10.03	10.04, 9.9, 9.90w- 15
						LJ	8.44, 8.49w	8.58- 16
	Lawson	TJ	USA	25.1.97	193/84	Dec	7725	
	Lazarica	Dan	ROU	11.5.92		HJ	2.24	2.20- 15
	Learmonth	Guy	GBR	24.4.92	184/73	800	1:45.10	1:46.65 -15
	Ledama	Wesley	KEN-J	2.7.99	173/57	5000	13:19.12	13:23.34- 16
	Lee	Beejay (Bernard)	USA	5.3.93	168/72	100	10.05	9.99, 9.94w- 15
						200	20.69, 20.17St	20.11- 15
	Lee Hup Wei		MAS	5.5.87	178/62	HJ	2.24	2.27 -08
	Lee Yun-chul		KOR	28.3.82	188/110	HT	73.77	72.98- 13
	Leemet	Markus	EST	22.8.93	178/75	Dec	7720(w)	7549- 15
	Legesse	Berhanu	ETH	11.9.94	168/55	5000	13:24.89	13:08.88- 14
						HMar	59:46	59:20- 15
	Lehata	Mosito	LES	8.4.89	177/69	100	10.11	10.11- 15, 10.04w- 16
	Lehto	Jesse	FIN	12.2.93	180/85	HT	71.41	73.09- 16
	Lehtola	Sampo	FIN	10.5.89	188/82	JT	79.01	83.77- 11
	Leitis	Janis	LAT	13.4.89	188/70	400	45.60	45.88- 12
	Lekuta	Solomon	KEN-J	3.10.99	178/61	800	1:45.4A	1:48.3A- 16
	Lelièvre	Jérémy	FRA	8.2.91	193/82	Dec	7843	7911- 12
*	Lemaitre	Christophe	FRA	11.6.90	189/74	200	20.21	19.80- 11
*	Lemi	Hayle	ETH	13.9.94	172/56	Mar	2:08:27	2:04:33- 16
*	Lemma	Sisay	ETH	12.12.90	170/57	Mar	2:08:04	2:05:16- 16
	Lemus	José Gregorio	COL	4.6.91	191/93	Dec	7762	7097- 12
	Lencho	Mamush	ETH	24.3.96		800	1:46.05	1:46.84- 16
	Leon Benitez	Joel	GBR-J	31.8.98	181/75	PV	5.51	5.25i- 16, 5.10- 15
	Leotlela	Tlotliso Gift	RSA-J	12.5.98	180/70	100	10.12A	10.20- 15
						200	20.20A, 20.28	20.47A, 20.58- 16
	Lepage	Pierce	CAN	22.1.96	201/91	Dec	7948	8027- 16
	Lescay	Yoandys	CUB	5.1.94	181/77	400	45.18	45.00- 16
*	Lesnoy	Aleksandr	RUS	28.7.88	194/116	SP	21.36	21.40- 14
*	Levy	Ronald	JAM	30.10.92	181/73	100	10.17	10.48- 12, 10.10w- 16
						110h	13.05	13.50- 16
*	Lewandowski	Marcin	POL	13.6.87	180/64	800	1:44.77	1:43.72- 15
						1500	3:34.04	3:37.37i- 14, 3:37.69- 16
	Lewke	Dennis	GER	23.7.93	193/118	SP	19.68	19.47- 16
	Li Jinguo		CHN	4.5.95		20kW	1:22:08	1:27:55- 13
^	Li Jinzhe		CHN	1.9.89	188/64	LJ	8.11	8.47- 14
	Li Liangyong		CHN	28.5.96		20kW	1:21:48	1:26:20- 15
	Li Peng		CHN	10.11.94		20kW	1:22:30	1:26:17- 13
	Li Shijia		CHN	14.1.92		20kW	1:22:07	1:20:54- 13
	Li Tianlei		CHN	13.1.95	173/63	20kW	1:22:04	1:20:57- 15
	Li Zhipeng		CHN	1.5.95		LJ	8.02	7.92i, 7.86- 15

Name		Nat	Born	Ht/Wt	Event	2017 Mark	Pre-2017 Best
Liipola	Henri	FIN	24.4.94	188/105	HT	75.31	72.12- 16
Likhanov	Yevgeniy	RUS	10.1.95	187/82	Dec	7856	7869- 15
* Lilesa	Feyisa	ETH	1.2.90	158/50	HMar	60:04	59:22- 12
Lima	David	POR	6.9.90	186/75	100	10.05	10.29, 10.20w- 16
Lima	David	POR	6.9.90	186/75	200	20.30	20.62, 20.60w- 16
Lin Hung-Min		TPE	7.9.90	177/73	LJ	8.10	8.04- 16
^ Lingua	Marco	ITA	4.6.78	179/118	HT	77.23	79.97- 08
* Linke	Christopher	GER	24.10.88	191/66	20kW	1:18:59	1:19:19- 16
Lipsanen	Simo	FIN	13.9.95	191/72	TJ	17.14	16.23i, 16.19- 16, 16.62w- 15
* Lisek	Piotr	POL	16.8.92	194/96	PV	6.00i, 5.89	5.90i- 15, 5.82- 14
Litanyuk	Valeriy	UKR	2.4.94	175/75	50kW	4:03:55	3:58.33- 16
* Litvinov	Sergey	RUS	27.1.86	185/110	HT	77.32	80.98- 12
Liu Jian		CHN	19.5.95		50kW	4:00:05	3:47:51- 16
Liu Jianmin		CHN	9.3.88	183/68	20kW	1:21:07	1:19:34- 13
Liu Mingxuan		CHN	16.5.97		TJ	16.64	16.38, 16.39w- 16
Liu Qizhen		CHN	17.9.95	182/95	JT	81.15A	77.91- 16
Liu Xu		CHN	11.12.94		20kW	1:22:32	1:23:00- 13
Liu Yang		CHN	29.10.86	190/110	SP	19.48i, 19.14	19.77- 13
Lloyd	Antoine	USA	10.6.96	188/75	110h	13.71, 13.52w	13.69- 16
Locke	Dentarius	USA	12.12.89	170/68	100	10.16, 10.06w	9.96, 9.91w- 13
					200	20.48	20.57- 16
Lokwanamoi	Mark	KEN	1.2.88		Mar	2:08:37	2:14:08A-16
* Lomnicky	Marcel	SVK	6.7.87	177/106	HT	77.92	79.16- 14
Lomong	Lopez	USA	1.1.85	178/67	5000	13:12.27i, 13:21.74	13:07.00i- 13, 13:07.95- 14
* London	Wil	USA	17.8.97	183/68	400	44.47	45.27- 16
Lonskyy	Viktor	UKR	27.10.95	184/65	HJ	2.28	2.23i- 16, 2.20- 15
Lonyangata	Paul	KEN	12.12.92	170/55	HMar	60:40	59:53- 12
					Mar	2:06:10	2:07:14- 15
López	Jesús	MEX	2.8.97	182/66	800	1:45.51	1:46.57- 16
López	Kevin	ESP	12.6.90	172/60	800	1:45.02	1:43.74- 12
^ López	Luis Fernando	COL	3.6.79	173/60	50kW	3:51:35	3:55:43- 14
* López	Miguel Ángel	ESP	3.7.88	181/70	20kW	1:19:57	1:19:14- 15
Lotiang	John	KEN	1.1.91		HMar	60:39	60:16- 13
Lovett	Django	CAN	6.7.92	193/72	HJ	2.27	2.23- 16
Lovett	Eddie	ISV	25.6.92	181/73	110h	13.41	13.31A- 15, 13.39, 13.29w- 13
Loxsom	Casimir	USA	17.3.91	183/64	800	1:46.13i, 1:47.34	1:44.92- 15
* Loyanae	Wilson	KEN	20.11.88		Mar	2:06:27	2:05:13- 16
Lu Zhiwei		CHN	4.4.96		TJ	16.66i, 16.37	16.46- 16
Lucas	David	USA	6.6.96	188/105	DT	61.43	60.75- 16
Ludwig	Matthew	USA	5.7.96	183/86	PV	5.70	5.46- 16
Lukás	Marek	CZE	16.7.91	180/75	Dec	7997w, 7967(w)	7903- 16
Lukyanenko	Artem	RUS	30.1.90	193/84	Dec	8130	8177- 13
Lukyanenko	Yevgeniy	RUS	23.1.85	190/79	PV	5.60	6.01- 08
Lukyanov	Denis	RUS	14.7.89	190/115	HT	77.21	79.61- 13
Lukyanov	Ivan	RUS	31.1.81	178/67	3kSt	8:29.78	8:18.97- 08
Luo Dongpo		CHN	23.6.95		50kW	3:50:38	3:56:46- 15
Luo Yadong		CHN	15.1.92		50kW	3:56:22	3:48:48- 15
Luron	Kevin	FRA	8.11.91	184/80	TJ	16.85	16.63- 15, 16.89w- 16
Lusine	Aymeric	FRA	13.9.95	174/62	800	1:46.08	1:47.99- 16
Luxa	Jan	SLO	11.2.96	189/78	TJ	16.23, 16.73Aw	15.63- 16, 15.96w- 14
Lyadusov	Konstantin	RUS	2.3.88	190/125	SP	20.44	20.88i, 20.62- 16
Lyakhovich	Aleksandr	BLR	4.7.89	171/65	20kW	1:21:12	1:21:14- 16
Lyles	Josephus	USA-J	22.7.98	184/73	400	45.30	45.46A, 45.77- 15
* Lyles	Noah	USA	18.7.97	180/70	100	9.95w	10.14, 10.07w-15, 9.9- 16
					200	19.90	20.09, 20.04w- 16
* Lysenko	Danil	RUS	19.5.97	192/73	HJ	2.38	2.31i, 2.30- 16
Ma Lei		CHN	29.6.89		110h	13.55	13.82- 15
Ma Qun		CHN	8.2.94		JT	79.91	79.39- 15
Maartens	Hendrik	RSA	24.5.96	183/75	200	20.40A, 20.61	20.51A, 20.2Aw- 16
Maeno	Kei	JPN	10.5.91	180/67	400h	49.06	50.27- 13
* Mägi	Rasmus	EST	4.5.92	188/74	400h	48.94	48.40- 16
* Magour	Ahmed Bader	QAT	3.3.96	190/90	JT	85.23	84.74- 16
Mahler	Wolf	USA	26.9.94	180/77	Dec	7897	7650- 15
Mahmoud	Hassan Mohamed	EGY	10.2.84	188/110	HT	74.89	78.39- 16
Mahoney	Travis	USA	25.7.90	175/61	3000	7:47.66	7:52.09i-14
Maiau	Raihau	FRA	1.8.92	184/77	LJ	7.94, 8.22w	8.02i- 16, 7.98, 8.14w- 15
Maina	John	KEN	3.8.94	179/53	10k	27:39.41	27:21.97- 16
Maiyo	Robert	KEN			3kSt	8:31.9	9:08.0A- 16
Makarenko	Artem	RUS	23.4.97	183/79	Dec	8112	7318- 16
Makhethe	Tshepang	RSA	9.2.96	180/86	HT	71.28	70.26- 16
Makhrosenko	Zakhar	BLR	10.10.91	182/105	HT	76.08	77.41- 16

Name		Nat	Born	Ht/Wt	Event	2017 Mark	Pre-2017 Best
* Makwala	Isaac	BOT	29.9.86	183/79	200	19.77	19.96, 19.7A- 14
					400	43.84	43.72- 15
* Malachowski	Piotr	POL	7.6.83	194/135	DT	67.68	71.84- 13
Mallett	Aaron	USA	26.9.94	188/79	110h	13.37, 13.24w	13.48- 16, 13.40w- 15
Malykhin	Vladyslav	UKR-J	15.1.98	184/76	PV	5.70	5.55- 16
* Manangoi	Elijah	KEN	5.1.93	181/65	800	1:44.8A	1:45.1A- 16
1500	3:28.80		3:29.67- 15		1M	3:49.08	3:52.04- 16
Mande	Abdallah	UGA	10.5.95	166/52	10k	27:46.27	28:12.72- 15
					HMar	60:51	
Manga	Aurel	FRA	24.7.92	188/75	110h	13.27	13.33, 13.25w- 16
Mansilla	Humberto	CHI	22.5.96	180/100	HT	74.41	72.67- 16
* Manyonga	Luvo	RSA	18.11.91	185/65	LJ	8.65A, 8.62	8.48- 16
Marcelino dos Santos	Lucas	BRA	4.1.95	175/64	LJ	8.00	7.81- 14
Mardare	Adrian	MDA	20.6.95	193/92	JT	83.93	78.48- 16
* Marghiev	Serghei	MDA	6.11.92	194/99	HT	77.70	78.72- 15
Maric	Martin	CRO	19.4.84	196/115	DT	61.20	67.92- 14
Maritz	Hardus	NAM	10.5.90	190/79	400h	49.48	50.14A- 15, 50.38- 14
Márquez	Dayron	COL	19.11.83	181/93	JT	78.41A	82.39A- 16
* Marschall	Kurtis	AUS	25.4.97	188/78	PV	5.73	5.70- 16
Marshall	Deshawn	USA	1.11.94	185/73	100	10.05w	10.50- 16
					200	20.32	
Marshall	Tom	GBR	12.6.89	174/59	1500	3:37.45	3:39.41- 16
Martin	Ryan	USA	23.3.89	185/68	800	1:46.03	1:44.77- 12
* Martín	Álvaro	ESP	18.6.94	181/62	20kW	1:19:41	1:19:36- 16
* Martina	Churandy	NED	3.7.84	178/75	100	10.19, 10.00w	9.91- 12, 9.76Aw- 06
					200	20.27	19.81- 16
* Martínez	Lázaro	CUB	3.11.97	192/85	TJ	17.07	17.24- 14
Martínez	Lois Maikel	ESP	3.6.81	183/123	DT	66.67	67.45- 05
Martinsen	Andreas	DEN	17.7.90	190/82	110h	13.50	13.55- 15
Martos	Sebastián	ESP	20.6.89	178/63	3kSt	8:20.43	8:18.31- 14
Martynyuk	Andriy	UKR	25.9.90	184/110	HT	71.28	77.70- 12
* Maruo	Satoshi	JPN	28.11.91	175/60	20kW	1:20:31	1:19:42- 15
					50kW	3:43:03	4:02:36- 16
Masai	Gilbert	KEN	16.12.89		HMar	59:57	59:31- 16
* Maslák	Pavel	CZE	21.2.91	176/67	200	20.46	20.49- 13
					400	45.10	44.79- 14
Mason	Michael	CAN	30.9.86	188/67	HJ	2.30	2.33- 15
* Massó	Maykel	CUB-Y	8.5.99	178/69	LJ	8.33	8.28- 16
Masters	Riley	USA	5.4.90	185/73	1500	3:37.86	3:36.49- 15
Mastianica	Artur	LTU	30.7.92	173/63	50kW	4:01:56	4:04:49- 16
Masuno	Genta	JPN	24.5.93	182/76	110h	13.40	13.58- 14, 13.51w- 16
Matadi	Emmanuel	LBR	15.4.91	183/85	100	10.18, 9.93w	10.14, 9.97w- 16
Mathenge	Patrick	KEN	2.11.96	169/53	10k	27:49.96	27:54.98- 15
Mathews	Luke	AUS	21.6.95	188/75	1500	3:35.57	3:35.99- 16
800	1:46.44		1:45.16- 16		1M	3:54.53	3:56.7- 16
Mathieu	Michael	BAH	24.6.83	180/78	200	20.52, 20.34w	20.16- 12
Matsenjwa	Sibusiso	SWZ	2.5.88	180/82	200	20.58A, 20.67, 20.45w	20.63- 16
* Matsunaga	Daisuke	JPN	24.3.95	174/58	20kW	1:19:40	1:18:53- 16
Matsushita	Yuki	JPN	9.9.91	176/64	400h	49.40	49.10- 16
Mattis	Sam	USA	19.3.94	185/100	DT	65.61	67.45- 16
Matusevicius	Edis	LTU	30.6.96	184/79	JT	84.78	81.28- 16
Maugein	Maxime	FRA	27.9.92	182/81	Dec	7741	7801- 15
Mayanja	Abu	UGA	9.10.95	172/63	800	1:45.73A	1:46.82A-16
* Mayer	Kevin	FRA	10.2.92	186/77	Dec	8768	8834- 16
Mazur	Vladyslav	UKR	21.11.96	173/64	LJ	8.04, 8.06w	7.96- 16
^ Mbishei	Titus	KEN	28.10.90	178/59	HMar	61:03	59:55- 14
* McBride	Brandon	CAN	15.6.94	195/75	800	1:44.41	1:43.95- 16
McBride	Bryan	USA	10.12.91	188/77	HJ	2.30	2.30- 15
McClain	Hayden	USA	8.10.95	183/75	TJ	16.56i, 16.38, 16.66w	16.01- 15, 16.10w- 16
McClain	Remontay	USA	21.9.92	188/85	100	10.14, 10.04w	10.07, 9.82w- 15
					200	20.63, 20.41w	20.12- 15
McDonald	Jonia	JAM	16.12.89	190/77	400	45.55	45.61- 16
McDonald	Morgan	AUS	23.4.96	183/66	5000	13:15.83	13:29.79- 16
* McDonald	Rusheen	JAM	17.8.92	175/73	400	45.19	43.93- 15
McEntee	Sam	AUS	3.2.92	190/75	1500	3:37.48	3:36.81- 12
3000	7:41.03		7:48.35 -15		5000	13:17.55	13:20.72- 16
McLean	Sean	USA	23.3.92	185/79	100	10.13	10.01- 15
					200	20.42	20.24- 16
* McLeod	Omar	JAM	25.4.94	180/73	110h	12.90	12.97- 15
* McMaster	Kyron	IVB	3.1.97	187/79	400h	47.80	49.56- 16
McMichael	Drew	USA	25.5.96	186/79	PV	5.51	5.23- 15

	Name		Nat	Born	Ht/Wt	Event	2017 Mark	Pre-2017 Best
	McMullen	Adam	IRL	5.7.90	197/87	LJ	7.85, 7.94w	7.84- 16
*	McQuay	Tony	USA	16.4.90	180/70	100	10.13w	10.22- 13, 10.13w- 14
						400	44.51	44.24- 16
	McSweyn	Stewart	AUS	1.6.95	184/65	3000	7:47.65	7:54.43- 16
	1M	3:55.97		5000	13:19.98	13:41.74- 16		
	Mead	Hassan	USA	28.6.91	174/61	3000	7:38.51	7:38.85i- 16, 7:46.18- 13
	5000	13:11.20		13:02.80- 14		10k	27:32.49	27:33.04- 15
*	Mechaal	Adel	ESP	5.12.90	184/67	1500	3:34.70	3:35.24- 16
	3000	7:35.28		7:39.51- 16		5000	13:27.37	13:15.40- 16
*	Meité	Ben Youssef	CIV	11.11.86	179/70	100	9.97, 9.84w	9.96, 9.95w- 16
	Mejías	Reinier	CUB	22.9.90	178/98	HT	73.87	75.98- 13
*	Mekhissi-Benabbad	Mahiedine	FRA	15.3.85	190/75	1500	3:35.56	3:33.12- 13
						3kSt	8:14.67	8:00.09- 13
	Mekonen	Teshome	ETH	5.8.95		HMar	60:28	60:27- 15
*	Mekonnen	Tsegaye	ETH	15.6.95	174/56	Mar	2:07:26	2:04:46- 16
	Meleshko	Pavel	BLR	24.11.92	187/90	JT	85.01	80.96- 15
	Melo	Aleksandro	BRA	26.9.95	179/56	LJ	8.18	8.12- 15
						TJ	16.67	16.53- 16
	Mena	Reynier	CUB	21.11.96	174/79	100	10.17, 9.9h	10.17, 10.08w- 15, 10.1h- 13
*	Menaldo	Kévin	FRA	12.7.92	176/66	PV	5.83	5.81- 15
	Mendes	Jonathan	BRA	14.4.90	187/80	110h	13.65	13.53- 14, 13.5- 13
	Menéndez	Josué	MEX	4.5.90		JT	77.57	76.36- 16
	Meng Zhongkai		CHN	15.12.97		50kW	3:54:35	
	Menga	Aleixo Platini	GER	29.9.87	187/78	200	20.34	20.27- 16
	Mengich	Richard	KEN	3.4.89	187/68	Mar	2:08:46	2:10:39- 16
	Mengistu	Asefa	ETH	18.1.85	172/57	HMar	59:54	61:36- 13
^	Menjo	Josephat	KEN	20.8.79	168/50	5000	13:19.88	12:55.95- 10
*	Menkov	Aleksandr	RUS	7.12.90	178/74	LJ	8.32	8.56- 13
	Merber	Kyle	USA	19.11.90	180/64	1500	3:36.65	3:34.54- 15
	1M	3:52.22i, 3:54.78		3:54.57- 16		3000	7:49.39i	7:50.41i- 16, 7:52.95- 15
*	Merritt	Aries	USA	24.7.85	182/70	110h	13.09	12.80- 12
*	Merritt	LaShawn	USA	27.6.86	188/82	200	20.27	19.74- 16
						400	44.78	43.65- 15
	Merzougui	Abdelaziz	ESP	30.8.91	177/62	3kSt	8:30.51	8:18.03- 12
	Mesel	Amanuel	ERI	29.12.90	175/57	HMar	60:53	60:10- 13
	Mihaila	Narcis	ROU	4.8.92	183/73	50kW	4:02:27	4:02:46- 16
*	Mihaljevic	Filip	CRO	31.7.94	201/113	SP	21.30	20.87i, 20.71- 16
						DT	63.76	63.11- 15
	Mikhailov	Alexej	GER	12.4.96	185/105	HT	72.59	70.58- 16
*	Mikhou	Sadik	BRN	25.7.90	174/61	1500	3:31.34	3:32.30- 16
						3000	7:44.36	7:39.02- 16
	Mikos	Mateusz	POL	10.4.87	198/134	SP	19.67i, 19.65	20.18- 16
*	Milanov	Philip	BEL	6.7.91	191/118	DT	67.05	67.26, 68.44dh- 16
	Mileusnic	Dejan	BIH	16.11.91	183/84	JT	80.10	81.63- 16
	Millar	Joseph	NZL	24.9.92	190/82	100	10.18, 10.11w	10.32, 10.21w- 13
						200	20.37	20.77- 16
	Miller	Ashinia	JAM	6.6.93	189/100	SP	20.45	20.31i- 15, 20.02- 16
	Miller	Jalen	USA	17.6.95	175/77	100	10.03w	10.12- 15
*	Miller	Nick	GBR	1.5.93	188/112	HT	77.51	77.55- 15
	Minzie	Jevaughn	JAM	20.7.95	173/66	100	10.15	10.02- 16
	Mironov	Oleg	RUS	5.3.93	188/79	400h	49.79	50.01- 14
	Misans	Elvijs	LAT	8.4.89	182/73	TJ	17.02i, 16.74	16.77- 16
*	Mitchell-Blake	Nethaneel	GBR	2.4.94	188/79	100	9.99	10.09- 16
						200	20.04	19.95-16
	Mitrevski	Christian	AUS	12.7.96	185/77	LJ	7.97, 8.05w	7.92- 16
	Miyao	Kotaro	JPN	12.7.91	172/72	400h	49.82	49.67- 16
	Mizinov	Vasiliy	RUS	29.12.97		20kW	1:21:48	-0-
	Mkhatini	Junior	RSA	4.1.90	182/75	110h	13.73A, 13.28Adt	
*	Moen	Sondre Nordstad	NOR	12.1.91	178/62	5000	13:20.16	13:30.22- 11
	HMar	59:48		62:19- 16		Mar	2:05:48	2:12:54- 15
	Moffett	Malik	USA	11.4.94	188/75	200	20.49, 19.87w	21.05, 20.73w- 16
						LJ	8.00	7.62- 15
	Moghaddam	Reza	IRI	17.11.88	197/128	HT	73.50	73.08- 15
	Mohammed	Abubakar	GHA	5.3.91		LJ	7.98w	7.69A- 16
^	Mohr	Malte	GER	24.7.86	192/84	PV	5.65i, 5.50	5.91- 12
*	Mokoena	Khotso	RSA	6.3.85	190/73	LJ	8.19	8.50- 09
						TJ	16.55A	17.35- 14
	Mokoka	Stephen	RSA	31.1.85	156/50	Mar	2:08:35	2:07:40- 15
	Moleya	Chris	RSA	27.1.97	189/62	HJ	2.25A	2.23A- 16
	Molla	Getaneh	ETH	10.1.94	171/55	5000	13:18.30	13:05.59- 16
						HMar	60:34	-0-

Name		Nat	Born	Ht/Wt	Event	2017 Mark	Pre-2017 Best
Montaña	José Leonardo	COL	21.3.92	168/61	50kW	3:58:28	3:52:48- 16
Moore	Gabriel	USA	10.1.96	190/88	Dec	7699	7097- 16
Moore	Isaiah	USA	12.6.96	183/79	110h	13.47	13.68, 13.54w- 16
Moore ¶	Darien	USA	10.6.91	185/105	SP	20.78i dq	20.33- 16
Morain	Moriba	TTO	8.10.92	177/70	100	10.19, 10.13w	10.22- 12, 10.09w- 16
					200	20.60, 20.32w	20.77- 12, 20.76w- 16
Moranga	Fredrick	KEN	.95		10k	27:56.04A	28:59.0A- 15
Morgan	Ricky	USA	12.9.95	175/70	400	45.44	45.54- 16
* Morgunov	Timur	RUS	12.10.96	188/77	PV	5.80i, 5.80	5.80i, 5.60- 16
Morimoto	Kimihito	JPN	21.4.93		Dec	7642	7469w- 16
Morris	Julius	MNT	14.4.94	178/68	100	10.15A	10.23A, 10.06Aw- 15, 10.33- 16
					200	20.28A, 20.30	20.45A- 15,20.52- 14, 20.44w- 16
Morris	Marquis	USA	6.2.96	190/79	110h	13.56, 13.49w	13.77- 15
Morrison	Willie	USA	23.11.96	184/120	SP	19.79i, 19.69	19.47i, 19.27- 16
Morrow	Elijah	USA	.95	178/77	200	20.67, 20.41w	20.61- 16
Morse	Brett	GBR	11.2.89	191/114	DT	61.15	66.84- 13
* Mowatt	Kemar	JAM	12.3.95	188/77	400h	48.49	50.66- 16
Mozia	Stephen	NGR	16.8.93	190/114	SP	20.83	21.76- 16
Mrzygłód	Cyprian	POL-J	2.2.98	185/73	JT	80.52	74.90- 16
Mudrov	Ilya	RUS	17.11.91	190/79	PV	5.70i, 5.60	5.80- 16
Muindi	Peter	KEN	.90		10k	27:57.47A	-0-
Mulabegovic	Nedzad	CRO	4.2.81	190/120	SP	19.78	20.67- 14
Mullera	Ángel	ESP	20.4.84	175/62	3kSt	8:30.43	8:13.71- 12
Mullett	Rob	GBR	31.7.87	183/68	3kSt	8:30.06	8:22.42- 16
Münch	Markus	GER	13.6.86	207/130	DT	63.78	66.87- 11
Munene Gachaga	Morris	KEN	7.4.95		HMar	60:38	60:35- 16
Mungara	Kenneth	KEN	7.9.73	170/52	Mar	2:09:04	2:07:36- 11
* Munyai	Clarence	RSA-J	20.2.98	176/66	200	20.10A, 20.31	20.36A, 20.40, 20.33Aw- 16
Murasky	J.C.	USA	6.2.93	203/123	SP	20.21	20.21- 16
Murayama	Kenta	JPN	23.2.93	176/55	HMar	60:57	60:50- 14
* Murillo	Jhon Freddy	COL	13.7.84	183/84	TJ	16.95	17.09- 16
* Murphy	Clayton	USA	26.2.95	182/68	800	1:43.60	1:42.93- 16
					1000	2:17.17	2:20.12- 16
					1500	3:36.34+	3:36.23- 16
					1M	3:51.99	3:57.11i- 16
Musagala	Ronald	UGA	16.12.94	176/61	1500	3:33.65	3:35.02- 15
Musiyenko	Ihor	UKR	22.8.93	186/128	SP	19.51	18.20i, 17.84- 16
Musso	Antonmarco	ITA	30.1.91	184/73	LJ	7.97A, 7.94	7.79, 7.83w- 16
^ Mutai	Abel	KEN	2.10.88	172/73	3kSt	8:25.9A	8:01.67- 12
Mutai	Jeremiah	KEN	27.12.92	173/60	800	1:46.1A	1:43.9A- 13
Muthoni	Muiru	KEN-J	21.3.98	167/55	10k	27:38.05	-0-
Mutiso	Alexander	KEN	10.9.96	171/52	5000	13:25.75	13:21.90- 16
					10k	27:41.54	27:39.25- 16
					HMar	60:57	60:59- 16
Mutunga	William	KEN	17.9.93	178/70	400h	49.88A	49.43- 15
Mwaka	Patrick	KEN	2.11.92	165/45	10k	27:58.69	27:33.14- 11
Mwangi	James	KEN	23.6.84	175/58	10k	27:51.61	27:49.27- 09
					HMar	60:11	59:07- 16
Mwangi	Samuel	KEN	19.9.97	169/51	10k	27:53.85	27:45.27- 16
Mwaura	Joel	KEN-J	20.1.99	173/55	5000	13:27.52	-0-
					10k	27:45.37	-0-
					HMar	60:59	-0-
* Mweresa	Boniface	KEN	13.11.93	170/70	400	45.42A, 45.59	45.01- 15
Myslyvchuk	Volodomyr	UKR	25.4.96	191/94	HT	71.45	68.62- 16
Nabokov	Dmitriy	BLR	20.1.96	186/69	HJ	2.28	2.29i- 16, 2.25- 15
Nadeem	Arshad	PAK	2.1.97		JT	78.00	78.33- 16
Nageeye	Abdi	NED	2.3.89	165/54	Mar	2:08:16	2:10:24- 15
Nairn	Laquarn	BAH	31.7.96	178/64	LJ	7.83, 7.97w	7.61, 7.65w- 15
Nakamura	Akihiko	JPN	23.10.90	180/73	Dec	7873	8180- 16
Nakano	Naoya	JPN	3.7.94	175/64	400h	49.80	49.51- 16
* Nápoles	Cristian	CUB-J	27.11.98	181/80	TJ	17.27	16.92- 16
Nasir	Youssef	MAR	15.2.90		5000	13:21.93	-0-
Nathaniel	Samson	NGR	30.8.97	183/75	400	45.23	45.80- 15
^ Nava	Horacio	MEX	20.1.82	175/62	50kW	3:47:53	3:42:51- 14
* Nazarov	Dilshod	TJK	6.5.82	187/115	HT	77.81	80.71- 13
* Ndiku	Caleb	KEN	9.10.92	183/68	3000	7:33.36	7:30.99- 12
* Ndiku	Jonathan	KEN	18.9.91	173/60	3000	7:44.33	7:39.63- 14
					5000	13:16.22	13:11.99- 09
					10k	27:22.73	27:11.23- 16
Ndikumwenayo	Thierry	BDI	26.3.97	163/50	5000	13:25.55	13:26.24- 16
Ndirangu	Joseph	KEN	9.9.94	168/49	5000	13:19.42	13:23.43- 16
					10k	27:46.14	27:57.57- 16
					HMar	60:57	60:30- 15
Ndorobo Kwemoi	Peter	KEN	11.8.93		HMar	60:13	60:13- 16
Neberew	Birhan	ETH	14.8.94	172/55	10k	27:35.67	27:14.34- 13
Nedosekov	Maksim	BLR-J	21.1.98	188/70	HJ	2.33	2.20- 16
* Nedow	Tim	CAN	16.10.90	198/125	SP	20.73	21.33i- 16, 20.98- 14

	Name		Nat	Born	Ht/Wt	Event	2017 Mark	Pre-2017 Best
	Neely	Marcus	USA	10.2.94	188/82	110h	13.66, 13.60w	13.83, 13.70w- 16
*	Nellum	Bryshon	USA	1.5.89	183/79	400	44.50	44.65- 15
	Nerántzis	Nikólaos	GRE-J	13.3.98	183/67	PV	5.51i, 5.46	5.41- 16
	Nesterenko	Maksim	BLR	1.9.92	193/82	TJ	16.53	16.85- 16
	Nesterenko	Mykyta	UKR	15.4.91	210/136	DT	63.77	66.23- 16
	Newton	Scotty	USA	19.9.96		TJ	16.26i, 16.43w	15.85- 16
	Ngatuny	Emmanuel	KEN	10.10.92		10k	27:58.32A	28:08.4A- 15
	Ngelel	Franklin	KEN	2.3.92	172/57	3000	7:38.50	
	Ngeno	Ernest	KEN	20.5.95		Mar	2:08:38	2:07:49- 16
	Ngetich	Hillary	KEN	15.9.95	171/57	1500	3:36.91	3:32.97- 16
						3000	7:44.73i	7:45.22- 16
	Nichipor	Aleksey	BLR	10.4.93	193/115	SP	20.52	19.75- 16
	Nigatu	Takele	ETH-J	.99		3kSt	8:20.76	8:56.0A- 15
	Nikitin	Vladimir	RUS	5.8.92	168/60	1500	3:37.14	3:40.74- 16
						3000	7:44.65i	7:51.21i- 16
						5000	13:24.05	13:30.06- 16
	Niktiin	Dmytro	UKR-J	31.7.99	199/82	HJ	2.28	2.16- 16
	Nilsen	Chris	USA-J	13.1.98	196/84	PV	5.75	5.60- 16
	Nilsson	Marcus	SWE	3.5.91	185/90	Dec	7987	8104(w)- 13
	Nilsson Montler	Thobias	SWE	15.2.96	183/73	LJ	8.04	7.68- 15
	Niskala	Pyry	FIN	6.11.90	191/105	DT	61.66	61.58- 16
	Niu Wenbin		CHN	20.1.91		50kW	3:46:12	3:48:32- 16
*	Nizhegorodov	Denis	RUS	26.7.80	180/61	50kW	3:53:25	3:34:14- 08
	Njiru	Kennedy	KEN	.87		3kSt	8:13.3A	8:31.4A- 13
	kuna	David	KEN	6.9.89	176/60	10k	27:45.83	27:49.57- 16
	Nkobolo	Onkabetse	BOT	22.7.93	183/74	400	45.34	45.10- 15
	Noda	Tomohiro	JPN	24.1.96	174/58	20kW	1:20:04	1:20:08- 15
^	Noga	Artur	POL	2.5.88	195/82	110h	13.53	13.26- 13, 13.20w- 10
	Noguchi	Takuya	JPN	2.7.88	173/63	Mar	2:08:59	2:12:29- 15
	Nomoto	Shusei	JPN	25.10.95	185/68	110h	13.62, 13.59w	14.00- 16
*	Norman	Michael	USA	3.12.97	183/73	400	44.60	45.19- 15
*	Norwood	Vernon	USA	10.4.92	187/77	400	44.47	44.44- 15
	Novac	Alexandru	ROU	24.3.97	186/84	JT	82.90	78.66- 16
	Novitskiy	Yaroslav	RUS	4.4.88		Dec	7639	7594- 16
	Nowak	Tim	GER	13.8.95	183/78	Dec	7942	7838- 16
*	Nowicki	Wojciech	POL	22.2.89	196/112	HT	80.47	78.71- 15
	Nyairo	Dominic	KEN	22.8.97	167/49	10k	28:02.85	27:56.47- 16
	Nyakora	Teressa	ETH	26.2.95	171/54	5000	13:21.85	13:23.66- 16
						10k	27:46.16	27:38.93- 15
	Nyamadi	Atsu	GHA	1.6.94	190/85	Dec	7811	7800- 16
	Nykyforov	Serhiy	UKR	6.2.94	194/83	LJ	8.18i, 7.92	8.11, 8.18w- 16
	Nzikwinkunda	Onèsphore	BDI	8.7.97		10k	28:09.98	
^	O'Farrill	Yordan	CUB	9.2.93	183/78	110h	13.33, 13.3h	13.19, 12.9- 14
	O'Hare	Chris	GBR	23.11.90	174/60	1500	3:33.61	3:34.83- 15
						1M	3:53.34	3:52.91i- 16, 3:56.35- 15
	O'Neal	Matthew	USA	10.6.94	185/74	TJ	17.12, 17.28w	16.92, 17.01w- 16
	Oakley	Julian	NZL	23.6.93	176/61	3000	7:44.34i	8:17.41i- 16
	Oates	Tray	USA	14.3.95	186/79	PV	5.60	5.65- 16
	Obayashi	Masayuki	JPN	6.2.96		400h	49.70	50.15- 16
	Oberholzer	Andri	SUI	24.7.96		Dec	7827	-0-
	Obi	Felix	USA	15.6.94	188/79	TJ	16.67	16.44- 16
	Obiena	Ernest John	PHI	17.11.95	187/75	PV	5.61	5.55- 16
	Ocampo	David	MEX	14.2.92	182/84	JT	80.29	79.84- 16
	Oda	Daiki	JPN	15.1.96	180/73	LJ	8.04	7.93- 16
	Oduduru	Divine	NGR	7.10.96	175/70	100	10.09w	10.25, 10.23w, 10.0- 16
						200	20.45w	20.34- 16
	Odujobi	Gabriel	GBR	15.7.87	183/79	110h	13.65, 13.38w	13.64, 13.57w- 16
	Ogho-Oghene	Egwero	NGR	26.11.88	171.66	100	10.17	10.06- 11, 10.0- 08
	Ogita	Hiroki	JPN	30.12.87	186/80	PV	5.70	5.70- 13
	Ogundeji	Ayomidotun	USA	24.2.96	186/111	SP	20.19	19.19- 16
^	Ogunode	Femi Seun	QAT	15.5.91	183/79	100	10.13	9.91- 15
	Ogura	Kenji	JPN	8.6.95	180/80	JT	78.32	75.77- 16
	Ohakwe	Michael	USA	.92	190/107	DT	61.29	59.47- 16
*	Oiglane	Janek	EST	25.4.94	182/78	Dec	8371	7945- 15
	Oikawa	Fumitaka	JPN	5.4.95		20kW	1:20:45	1:20:55- 16
	Oishi	Minato	JPN	19.5.88	162/48	10k	27:50.72	27:48.56- 16
	Oiwa	Yuhi	JPN	17.2.91	173/62	LJ	7.92, 8.14w	7.91, 7.98w- 15
	Ojala	Aleksi	FIN	9.12.92	180/62	50kW	3:47:20	3:46:25- 16
	Ojeda Leyver	José	MEX	12.11.85	164/52	50kW	3:45:09	3:49:16A- 11
	Ojiaku	Kevin	ITA	20.4.89	195/78	LJ	8.20	7.91i, 7.90- 13, 7.97w- 16
^	Oke	Tosin	NGR	1.10.80	178/77	TJ	16.70	17.23- 12
	Okolo	Nonso	GBR/NGR	7.12.90	187/77	TJ	16.45	16.06- 14, 16.28w- 16

Name		Nat	Born	Ht/Wt	Event	2017 Mark	Pre-2017 Best
Okumbo	Jorum	KEN	10.12.97		HMar	58:48	-0-
Olamigoke	Olu	NGR	19.9.90	178/68	TJ	16.55	16.98- 15
de Oliveira	Paulo André	BRA-J	20.8.98	183/75	100	10.18, 10.08w	10.26- 16
					200	20.58, 20.31w	20.75- 16
Oliveira	Paulo Sérgio	BRA	1.6.93	185/65	LJ	8.05	8.13- 14
					TJ	16.49	16.52- 16
^ Oliver	David	USA	24.4.82	188/93	110h	13.40	12.89- 10
Oloitiptip Korio	Alex	KEN	20.12.90	176/58	HMar	58:51	59:28- 15
Omae	Collins	KEN	9.4.89	179/75	400	45.19A	46.00A- 16
Omanyala	Ferdinand	KEN	2.1.96		100	9.9A	10.38A-16
Omelko	Rafal	POL	16.1.89	195/75	400	45.23	45.14- 16
Omoregie	David	GBR	1.11.95	185/84	110h	13.34	13.24- 16
Omullo	Ezequiel	KEN	10.12.87		Mar	2:09:10	2:08:55- 16
Omuro	Hideki	JPN	25.7.90	180/69	110h	13.48	13.52- 16
Omwamba	Enoch	KEN	4.4.93	168/54	10k	28:03.90	28:00.33- 14
Õncel	Emin	TUR	1.5.97	186/100	JT	80.20	79.42- 16
^ Onnen	Eike	GER	3.8.82	194/83	HJ	2.30	2.34- 07
Onyia	Emmanuel	JAM	16.6.93	185/105	DT	60.34	56.52- 16
Opiny	Leonard	UGA	12.12.91		400	45.5A	45.66A- 16
Ordóñez	Saúl	ESP	10.4.94	178/63	800	1:45.28	1:47.13- 15
Ortega	Mauricio	COL	4.8.94	184/102	DT	65.81	65.84, 67.45dh- 16
* Ortega	Orlando	ESP	29.7.91	185/70	110h	13.15, 13.09w	12.94- 15
^ Osagie	Andrew	GBR	19.2.88	189/72	800	1:45.54	1:43.77- 12
Osako	Suguru	JPN	23.5.91	170/53	5000	13:25.56	13:08.40- 15
10k 27:46.64	27:38.31- 13				Mar	2:07:19	-0-
Osewski	Bartosz	POL	20.3.91	194/104	JT	80.22	83.89- 12
^ Osman	Abrar	ERI	24.6.94	173/55	HMar	60:19	60:39- 15
Osmanoglu	Seref	TUR	2.1.89	176/58	TJ	16.50	17.72- 11
Ost	Noël	FRA	15.11.89	189/82	PV	5.51	5.51i, 5.50- 15
Ostos	José Luis	PER	9.12.92	160/50	10k	27:53.58	27:54.80- 16
Otieno	Mark	KEN	11.5.93	178/68	100	10.14A	10.39A- 16, 10.41- 15
					200	20.41A	
Otterling	Andreas	SWE	25.5.86	183/80	LJ	8.00Aw, 7.87,7.95w	8.12i- 16, 8.06, 8.13w- 15
Oueladha	Hicham	MAR	31.1.95		1500	3:36.61	3:39.68- 15
Oussama	Nabil	MAR	18.2.96	170/60	800	1:46.17	1:49.95- 13
					1500	3:37.08	3:40.07- 14
^ Özbilen	Ilham Tanui	TUR	5.3.90	177/60	1500	3:36.81	3:31.30- 13
* Özbilen	Kaan Kigen	TUR	15.1.86	170/54	10K	27:41.99	27:03.49- 12
					HMar	60:51	-11
Özdevici	Osman Can	TUR	23.8.95	191/110	SP	19.88	18.96- 16
Page	Champ	USA	1.6.94	174/64	400	45.54	45.74- 16
Pai Long		CHN	8.10.89		HJ	2.24	2.28- 12
Pajuelo	Iván	ESP	27.8.93	171/60	50kW	3:56:47	4:11:43- 14
Pajulahti	Arttu	FIN	25.9.91	182/75	LJ	8.10A, 7.88	7.92- 14
Palma	Ever	MEX	18.3.92	176/66	50kW	3:57:32	-0-
Palma	Isaac	MEX	26.10.90	174/59	50kW	4:05:29	
Palmer	Desmond	USA	30.7.95	196/84	110h	13.50	13.83, 13.81w- 16
					400h	49.17	49.41- 15
Palmer	Ford	USA	6.10.90	180/64	1M	3:54.92i	3:55.60- 16
Palomeque	Diego	COL	5.12.93	176/68	100	10.11	10.22A- 15, 10.07Aw- 16
					200	20.32A	20.50A, 20.70w- 15, 20.79- 16
Panasenkov	Vladislav	RUS	22.5.96	190/95	JT	79.93	75.70- 16
Panasyuk	Ivan	UKR	8.10.91	188/118	DT	60.35	63.39- 14
* Parchment	Hansle	JAM	17.6.90	196/90	110h	13.19	12.94- 14
* Parellis	Apostolos	CYP	24.7.85	186/110	DT	65.13	65.69- 16
Park Chil-sung		KOR	8.7.82	173/61	50kW	3:59:46	3:45:55-12
Parkayev	Timofey	RUS	19.10.97		20kW	1:21:32	-0-
* Pars	Krisztián	HUN	18.2.82	188/113	HT	76.84	82.69- 14
Parshin	Pavel	RUS	2.1.94	171/55	20kW	1:21:59	1:21:55- 14
Partanen	Veli-Matti	FIN	28.10.91	178/62	50kW	3:49:00	3:49:02- 15
Pasinski	Pawel	POL	6.3.93	196/115	DT	60.69	61.46- 15
Pásztor	Bence	HUN	5.2.95	186/95	HT	74.02	75.74- 15
Pater	Kyle	USA	24.12.94	180/77	PV	5.65Ai, 5.50	5.41Ai, 5.40- 16
Pathirana	Dhanuka Liyana	SRI	25.6.93		LJ	7.89, 7.97w	7.94- 16
Patsoukákis	Dimítrios	GRE	18.3.87	180/70	PV	5.60	5.62- 14
Paul	Gennard	GRN	.92	186/97	JT	77.82	
Paul	Jacob	GBR	6.2.95	180/73	400h	49.49	50.17- 16
Payen	Ludovic	FRA	18.2.95	185/80	110h	13.49	13.69- 16
Peacock	Hamish	AUS	15.10.90	186/96	JT	84.36	84.39- 16
Peltomäki	Sami	FIN	11.1.91	180/87	JT	79.21	80.36- 14
Peña	José Gregorio	VEN	12.1.87	163/60	3kSt	8:28.59	8:20.87- 13

Name		Nat	Born	Ht/Wt	Event	2017 Mark	Pre-2017 Best
Peng Chen		CHN	8.7.97		20kW	1:21:59	1:29:43- 16
Percy	Nick	GBR	5.12.94	190/105	DT	62.91	63.38- 16
Pereira	Éderson	BRA	6.6.90		5000	13:23.24	13:37.69- 16
Pérez	Yunier	CUB/ESP	16.2.85	175/70	100	10.00, 9.92w	10.22- 09
Perini	Lorenzo	ITA	22.7.94	186/72	110h	13.62, 13.54w	13.67- 16
Perlaza	Alejandro	COL	26.8.94	180/60	400	45.51A, 45.77	45.45A/45.81- 16
Pesic	Darko	MNE	30.11.92	189/89	Dec	7846	7827- 16
Peters	Anderson	GRN	21.10.97	187/84	JT	84.81	79.65- 16
Petrov	Aleksandr	RUS	9.8.86	187/79	LJ	7.98i, 7.93	8.20- 11
Pettersson	Simon	SWE	3.1.94	198/105	DT	64.88	63.10- 16
* Pezer	Mesud	BIH	27.8.94	198/120	SP	21.40	20.58- 16
Philibert-Thiboutot	Charles	CAN	31.12.90	176/62	1500	3:37.91	3:34.23- 15
1M	3:55.14		3:54.52- 15		3000	7:46.22i	7:53.99i- 15
Phillips	Isa	JAM	22.4.84	193/84	400h	49.49	48.05- 09
Phillips	Jeremy	USA	.93	183/75	100	10.11w	10.58- 16, 10.35w- 15
Phora	Thapelo	RSA	21.11.91	183/77	400	45.39A	45.64, 46.50- 16
Piazza	Drew	USA	28.1.95	185/73	800	1:45.69	1:47.28i- 16, 1:47.66- 15
* Pichardo	Pedro Pablo	CUB	30.6.93	185/71	TJ	17.60	18.08- 15
Pillow	Chris	USA	8.7.93	190/82	PV	5.65Ai, 5.40	5.60i- 15, 5.50- 14
Pineda	Omar	MEX	2.12.94	172/60	20kW	1:22:00	1:19:20- 16
Pintado	Brian	ECU	29.7.95	168/57	20kW	1:21:17	1:21:49- 16
Piskunov	Hlib	UKR-J	25.11.98	182/96	HT	73.52	71.53- 16
* Pitkämaki	Tero	FIN	19.12.82	195/92	JT	88.27	91.53- 05
Plesko	Nejc	SLO	9.10.92	186/97	HT	74.30	73.63- 15
Pless	David	USA	19.11.90	191/109	SP	20.31i, 20.27	20.37- 16
Plotnitskiy	Dmitriy	BLR	26.8.88	189/80	TJ	16.65	16.91- 10
Pohle	Hagen	GER	5.3.92	177/64	20kW	1:20:53	1:19:58- 16
Polyanskiy	Sergey	RUS	29.10.89	180/75	LJ	8.05, 8.13w	8.20- 15
Polyunin	Vladislav	UZB-J	4.12.98		JT	78.77	72.87- 16
Pontvianne	Jean-Marc	FRA	6.8.94	170/60	TJ	17.13i, 17.13	16.81- 15
Ponzio	Nick	USA	5.1.95	183/132	SP	19.53	19.53- 15
Poole	Breyton	RSA-Y	23.3.00	172/58	HJ	2.25	2.05- 16
Poole	Cory	USA-J	29.7.99	185/70	400h	49.88	51.56- 16
Pop	Toma	ROU	11.3.92	182/72	JT	77.91	74.71- 16
^ Porter	Jeff	USA	27.11.85	183/84	110h	13.53, 13.51w	13.08- 12
Posekany	Lukás	CZE	30.12.92	183/79	PV	5.55	5.55- 16
Potye	Tobias	GER	16.3.95	195/67	HJ	2.25	2.23- 14
Poursanides	Alexandros	CYP	23.1.93	188/110	HT	71.88	70.08- 15
* Powell	Asafa	JAM	23.11.82	190/88	100	10.08	9.72- 08
Pozdnyakov	Anatoliy	RUS	1.2.87	184/101	HT	71.84	79.06- 13
Pozolinski	Nate	USA	8.8.95	186/82	110h	13.56	13.66- 16
* Pozzi	Andrew	GBR	15.5.92	186/79	110h	13.14, 13.13w	13.19- 16
Prader	John	USA	10.2.91	178/73	PV	5.60	5.67- 13
Prakel	Sam	USA	29.10.94	176/61	1500	3:37.79	3:38.43- 16
^ Prásil	Ladislav	CZE	17.5.90	198/125	SP	20.84i, 20.57	21.47- 13
Prescod	Reece	GBR	29.2.96	193/75	100	10.03	10.04- 16
Pretorius	Constant	RSA	26.1.94	184/80	400h	49.28A, 49.69	50.00- 16
Pretorius	Friedrich	RSA	4.8.95	187/84	Dec	8002A	7780- 16
Price	Hunter	USA	28.8.94	190/84	Dec	7801(w)	6810- 16
Primak	Artyom	RUS	14.1.93	190/77	LJ	8.22	7.88- 12
					TJ	17.17	16.76- 12, 16.79w- 14
* Pronkin	Valeriy	RUS	15.6.94	195/115	HT	79.32	76.80- 15
* Protsenko	Andriy	UKR	20.5.88	194/80	HJ	2.30	2.40- 14
Prüfer	Clemens	GER	13.8.97	198/113	DT	62.48	61.62- 16
Prüfer	Henning	GER	7.3.96	201/125	DT	60.93	60.89- 16
* Przybylko	Mateusz	GER	9.3.92	195/72	HJ	2.35	2.30- 15
Pullen	Clive	JAM	18.10.94	175/73	TJ	17.19i, 16.83	16.90- 16
Pulli	Kristian	FIN	2.9.94	189/71	LJ	8.07A, 8.02	7.92A- 16, 7.89- 14
Qi Dakai		CHN	23.5.87	185/120	HT	71.09	74.19- 13
Quarcoo	Jonathan	NOR	13.10.96	180/70	200	20.39	20.94, 20.91w- 16
Quérin	Gaël	FRA	26.6.87	182/76	Dec	7764	8194- 14
Quinion	Aurelien	FRA	27.1.93	178/62	20kW	1:22:29	1:24:05- 16
Quiñónez	Alex	ECU	11.8.89	176/65	100	10.13	10.09A, 10.22- 13
					200	20.27	20.28- 12
^ Quow	Renny	TTO	25.8.87	170/66	400	45.41	44.53- 09
Raffin	Melvin	FRA-J	9.8.98	183/65	TJ	17.20i, 16.85	16.47, 16.93w- 16
Rahmouni	Miloud	ALG	13.12.83	175/70	400h	49.56	49.24- 15
Ralph	Joshua	AUS	27.10.91	185/70	800	1:46.14	1:45.79 -15
Ranasinghe	D.G.Sampath	SRI	1.9.88	178/87	JT	78.70	76.91- 16
Ranasinghe	R.M.Sumedha	SRI	10.2.91	182/82	JT	77.92	83.04- 15
Randazzo	Filippo	ITA	27.4.96	180/68	LJ	8.05i, 8.04	7.76- 15

Name		Nat	Born	Ht/Wt	Event	2017 Mark	Pre-2017 Best
Randhawa	Nauraj Singh	MAS	27.1.92	193/68	HJ	2.30	2.29- 16
^ Rapinier	Yoann	FRA	29.9.89	182/70	TJ	16.86	17.45- 13
Rasov	Arseniy	RUS	20.6.92	193/80	HJ	2.24i, 2.20	2.28- 14
Raynor	Caniggia	JAM	3.11.90	183/109	HT	70.93	70.91- 16
Razyn	Abdelali	MAR	1.1.91	165/59	1500	3:37.61	3:39.20- 15
Re	Davide	ITA	16.3.93	173/64	400	45.40A, 45.56	46.00- 14
Reese	Riak	USA	23.11.94	180/68	100	10.21, 10.13w	10.51- 13, 10.22w- 16
					200	20.43	20.73- 14
Reheda	Serhiy	UKR	6.2.94	190/100	HT	76.92	73.58- 16
Reid	Leon	GBR	26.7.94	173/66	200	20.38	20.62- 13
Remes	Tommi	FIN	20.1.94	183/98	HT	70.82	72.55- 16
Renner	Alex	USA	28.12.93	196/125	SP	19.62	19.01- 16
Renner	Robert	SLO	8.3.94	182/75	PV	5.51i, 5.50	5.70- 15
Reus	Julian	GER	29.4.88	177/73	100	10.10, 9.99w	10.01- 16, 10.00w- 13
					200	20.29	20.36- 13, 20.23w- 16
Reuther	Marc	GER	23.6.96	190/77	800	1:45.22	1:46.19- 16
Rew	Quentin	NZL	16.7.84	175/63	20kW	1:21:12	1:21:54- 16
					50kW	3:46:29	3:48:48- 15
Reynolds	Albert	LCA	28.3.88	178/82	JT	79.44	77.71A- 15
Reynolds	Ben	IRL	26.9.90	188/77	110h	13.60	13.48- 15
* Richards	Jereem	TTO	13.1.94	183/66	200	19.97	20.58- 14
					400	45.21	45.91- 15
* Richards	O'Dayne	JAM	14.12.88	177/120	SP	21.96	21.69- 15
^ Richardson	Jason	USA	4.4.86	186/73	110h	13.65, 13.53w	12.98- 12
Richartz	Nate	USA	2.11.94	186/77	PV	5.51	5.46i- 16, 5.25- 15
* Riley	Andrew	JAM	6.9.88	188/80	110h	13.33	13.14- 13
Riley-La Borde	Khai	GBR	8.11.95	186/94	110h	13.59	13.60- 16
Ringer	Richard	GER	27.2.89	182/63	5000	13:13.46	13:10.94- 15
3000	7:49.92	7:46.18i- 15, 7:46.59- 16			10k	28:05.96	28:28.96- 14
Ristic	Milan	SRB	8.8.91	186/72	110h	13.45	13.39- 16
Rivas	Yeison	COL	24.9.87	175/64	110h	13.65A	13.36A, 13.65- 16
Rivasz-Tóth	Norbert	HUN	6.5.96	182/86	JT	83.08	79.47- 16
* Rivera	Edgar	MEX	13.2.91	191/80	HJ	2.30i, 2.29	2.30i, 2.29- 16
Rivero	Briander	CUB	23.4.91	189/91	Dec	7719	7709- 16
* Roberts	Gil	USA	15.3.89	188/81	400	44.22	44.53- 14
* Roberts	Kurt	USA	20.2.88	191/127	SP	20.73	21.57i- 16, 21.47- 14
Robertson	Donovan	USA	8.11.93	181/73	110h	13.85, 13.64w	13.70- 14, 13.62w- 15
Robertson	Jake	NZL	14.11.89	180/65	HMar	60:01	-0-
Robertson	Ricky	USA	19.9.90	178/70	HJ	2.30	2.32- 12
^ Robertson	Zane	NZL	14.11.89	180/65	10k	27:48.59	27:33.67- 16
Robi	Deribe	ETH	20.9.90		Mar	2:06:38	2:05:58- 15
Robinson	Brett	AUS	8.5.91	173/57	5000	13:22.93	13:18.96- 13
Robinson	Byron	USA	16.2.95	175/73	400h	48.50	48.65- 16
Robinson	Jeron	USA	30.4.91	193/73	HJ	2.30	2.31- 15
Robinson	Robert	USA	3.8.87	196/91	Dec	7745	7526- 10
Rodger	Sebastian	GBR	29.6.91	188/75	400h	49.58	49.19- 13
* Rodgers	Michael	USA	24.4.85	178/73	100	10.00, 9.98w	9.85- 11, 9.80w- 14
Rodney	Brendon	CAN	9.4.92	190/84	200	20.45, 20.02w	19.96- 16
Rodriguez	Jeff	USA	3.10.90	190/86	PV	5.51	5.40- 12
Rodríguez	Ángel David	ESP	25.4.80	178/66	100	10.22, 10.12w	10.14- 08
Rodríguez	Arturo	CUB-J	28.4.99	192/78	TJ	16.43	16.01- 16
Roe	Martin	NOR	1.4.92	187/86	Dec	8144	7875- 15
Rogers	Jason	SKN	31.8.91	173/66	100	10.18,10.04w	10.01- 13, 9.98Aw- 15, 10.0- 16
* Röhler	Thomas	GER	30.9.91	192/92	JT	93.90	91.28- 16
Rolim	Emanuel	POR	30.1.93	184/68	1500	3:37.16	3:38.66- 14
Rolnin	Basile	FRA	21.1.94	194/83	Dec	8041	8087- 16
* Romani	Darlan	BRA	9.4.91	188/140	SP	21.82	21.02- 16
Romaniw	Anthony	CAN	15.9.91	178/68	800	1:46.17	1:45.60- 13
Romanov	Andrey	RUS	19.9.94	180/90	HT	73.42	74.60- 16
Romeo	Jonathan	ESP	13.8.94	174/59	3kSt	8:31.36	8:40.89- 16
Rono	Mathew	KEN	.92	173/60	800	1:45.1A	1:45.88A- 16
Rono	Philemon	KEN	8.2.91		Mar	2:06:52	2:07:07- 14
Rono	Vincent	KEN	22.12.90	165/55	10K	27:53.84A	27:52.19- 11
Rono	Vincent Kipsang	KEN	11.11.90	165/55	HMar	59:27	60:52- 15
^ Rooney	Martyn	GBR	3.4.87	198/78	400	45.65	44.45- 13
* Rop	Albert	BRN	17.7.92	176/55	3000	7:38.30	7:32.02- 16
					5000	13:04.82	12:51.96- 13
Rosa	Jean	BRA	1.2.90	188/78	TJ	16.54	16.80- 15, 16.82w- 13
Rose	Alex	SAM	7.11.91	188/127	DT	64.30	65.74- 16
Rossi	Eugenio	SMR	6.3.92	192/72	HJ	2.25	2.27- 15
^ Rotich	Abraham	BRN	26.6.93	183/64	800	1:46.21	1:43.13- 12

	Name		Nat	Born	Ht/Wt	Event	2017 Mark	Pre-2017 Best
	Rotich	Anthony	KEN	.93	174/60	3kSt	8:27.16	8:21.19- 13
	Rotich	Edwin	KEN	8.8.88	168/50	HMar	60:37	-16
^	Rotich	Lucas	KEN	16.4.90	171/57	Mar	2:07:19	2:07:17- 15
	Roto	Thando	RSA	26.9.95	173/68	100	9.95A, 10.11	10.27A, 10.28, 10.15w- 16
^	Roulhac	Brandon	USA	13.12.83	188/73	TJ	16.75, 16.94w	17.26, 17.44w- 09
	Rowe	Shawn	JAM	7.12.92	193/84	400h	49.36	49.93- 16
	Rozmys	Michal	POL	13.3.95	187/72	800	1:45.70	1:46.85- 16
						1500	3:36.37	3:38.35- 16
	Rubino	Giorgio	ITA	15.4.86	174/56	20kW	1:20:47	1:19:37- 09
*	Rudisha	David	KEN	17.12.88	189/73	800	1:44.90	1:40.91- 12
	Rudnev	Pavel	RUS	26.10.92		Dec	7664	7659- 15
	Ruggeri	Guillermo	ARG	26.3.92	183/77	400h	49.69	50.85- 16
	Ruiz	Antonio	USA/MEX	4.11.96	178/75	PV	5.52	5.18- 15
	Ruiz	Jorge	COL	17.5.89	167/57	50kW	3:50:37	3:51:42- 16
	Ruiz	Marcos	ESP	10.3.95	183/69	TJ	16.44	15.81- 16
	Rungaru	James	KEN	14.1.93	174/58	10k	27:40.78	27:22.53- 11
						HMar	60:48	60:12- 15
	Russell	Alonzo	BAH	8.2.92	183/75	400	45.56	45.25- 16
	Russell	Dejour	JAM-Y	1.4.00	185/79	110h	13.32	-0-
	Russo	Alexander	BRA	26.7.94	173/61	400	45.55	46.15- 14
*	Rutherford	Greg	GBR	17.11.86	188/84	LJ	8.18	8.51- 14
	Ruto	Dominic	KEN	.90		Mar	2:09:08	2:09:28- 16
	Rutto	Cyrus	KEN	21.4.92	173/52	5000	13:03.44	13:12.91- 13
	Rutto	Eliud	KEN/USA	13.3.94	175/64	800	1:45.70	1:45.37- 14
	Rybakov	Anatoliy	RUS	27.2.85	160/51	10k	28:01.93	28:03.59- 14
	Rybakov	Yevgeniy	RUS	27.2.85	160/51	10k	28:01.93	28:05.75- 08
	de Sá	Mateus Daniel	BRA	21.11.95	183/73	TJ	16.87	16.63- 16
	Safiulin	Ilgizar	RUS	9.12.92	183/64	3kSt	8:25.20	8:18.49- 15
	Saharuk	Igor	UKR	3.6.88	179/63	50kW	4:01:58	3:50:49- 14
	Sahner	Andreas	GER	27.1.85	175/100	HT	70.89	71.67- 10
	Saïd	Saïd Aden	QAT	–.93		1500	3:37.42	3:37.29i- 16, 3:40.81- 16
	Saito	Takumi	JPN	23.3.93	178/61	20kW	1:20:56	1:19:44- 16
	Salazar	Julio César	MEX	8.7.93	176/65	50kW	3:52:30	-0-
	Sales	Llorenç	ESP	14.7.88	179/67	1500	3:37.21	3:38.64- 15
	Saluri	Karl Robert	EST	6.8.93	178/75	Dec	8025	8108- 16
*	Samaai	Ruswahl	RSA	25.9.91	178/73	LJ	8.49A, 8.35	8.38, 8.40w- 16
	Samari	Ali	IRI	7.1.93	189/118	SP	19.80	19.09i, 19.08- 16
*	Samba	Aderrahmane	QAT	5.9.95	186/75	400h	48.31A, 48.44	-0-
*	Sambu	Stephen	KEN	7.7.88	169/55	5000	13:23.79	13:13.74i- 12, 13:21.14- 16
	3000	7:51.74		7:51.59i- 12		HMar	60:55	60:41- 13
	Samuels	J-Mee	USA	20.5.87	172/76	100	10.07w	10.03- 10
	Samuelsson	Fredrik	SWE	16.2.95	185/80	Dec	8172	7884- 15
	Sánchez	Éder	MEX	21.5.86	176/67	20kW	1:22:28	1:18:34- 08
	Sánchez	Ryan	PUR-J	22.6.98	179/64	800	1:45.58	1:46.99- 16
	Sancho	Miguel Ángel	ESP	24.4.90	180/67	HJ	2.25i, 2.21	2.27i- 09, 2.26- 11
*	Sani Brown	Abdul Hakim	JPN-J	6.3.99	188/78	100	10.05	10.22- 16
						200	20.32	20.34A, 20.35- 15
*	dos Santos	Almir	BRA	4.9.93	188/79	LJ	7.96	7.74- 16
	Santos	Héctor	ESP-J	6.1.98	180/64	LJ	7.96	7.56, 7.78w- 16
	Santos	Jefferson	BRA	30.8.95	178/76	Dec	8187w, 7776	7958- 16
	Santos	Juander	DOM	7.5.95	188/79	400h	48.59	49.43- 16
*	Santos	Luguelín	DOM	12.11.92	173/61	400	45.24	44.11- 15
	Sarantsev	Yevgeniy	RUS	5.8.88	188/85	Dec	8010	8123- 14
	Saraykin	Vladislav	RUS	3.3.97		20kW	1:22:09	-0-
*	Saruni	Michael	KEN	18.6.95	175/61	800	1:44.61A	
	Sasínek	Filip	CZE	8.1.96	181/62	1500	3:37.32	3:36.32- 16
	Sato	Hiroyuki	JPN	6.8.90	182/72	110h	13.59	13.61- 13, 13.59w- 12
	Sato	Yuki	JPN	26.11.86	179/60	10k	28:09.01	27:38.25- 09
	Savola	Elmo	FIN	10.3.95	189/77	Dec	7956	7743- 15
	Sawe	Jonathan	KEN	22.5.95	176/64	1500	3:36.56	3:38.51- 15
	Sawe	Matthew	KEN	2.7.88	190/70	HJ	2.25A	2.25A, 2.20- 15, 2.22i- 16
	Sawyers	Roberto	CRC	17.10.86	189/107	HT	73.50	77.15- 16
	Sayers	Feron	GBR	15.10.94	186/77	LJ	7.95w	7.80- 13
	Sbaï	Hassanine	TUN	21.1.84	176/60	20kW	1:20:35	1:20:19- 11
	Scheffel	Sebastian	GER	17.11.93	193/114	DT	62.61	61.18- 16
^	Scherbarth	Tobias	GER	17.8.85	195/84	PV	5.60	5.76i- 09, 5.75- 16
	Schmidt	Kai	GER	11.2.93	193/118	DT	61.74	56.23- 16
	Schuurmans	Jared	USA	20.8.87	198/118	DT	65.12	66.10- 15
	Schwartz	Anthony	USA-Y	5.9.00	183/78	100	10.15	10.37, 10.26w- 16
	Scott	Donald	USA	23.2.92	183/84	TJ	17.25	17.02- 16
	Scott	Jordan	JAM	29.6.97	175/73	TJ	16.44	16.01, 16.61w- 16

Name		Nat	Born	Ht/Wt	Event	2017 Mark	Pre-2017 Best
Scott	Marc	GBR	21.12.93	173/59	3000	7:43.37	7:55.37i-15
5000	13:22.37		13:36.81- 15		10k	28:07.97	28:30.33- 15
Sears	Ventavius	USA	14.5.95	183/64	400	45.55A	46.82- 16
Seboka	Bira	ETH	16.11.94		Mar	2:08:51	-0-
Secci	Daniele	ITA	9.3.92	193/110	SP	19.46i, 19.42	19.56i- 15, 19.33- 16
Seddon	Zak	GBR	28.6.94	179/61	3kSt	8:30.17	8:33.09- 16
Sedecias	Benjamin	FRA	18.1.95	177/78	110h	13.41	13.45- 16
Sedyuk	Nikolay	RUS	29.4.88	198/115	DT	60.77	64.72- 08
Seifert	Bernhard	GER	15.2.93	190/88	JT	84.62	82.42- 13
Seiler	Nathaniel	GER	6.4.96	175/65	50kW	3:55:13	3:58:03- 16
Sein	Timothy	KEN	1.2.88	178/64	800	1:45.4A	1:45.48A- 16
Seliverstov	Pavel	BLR	2.9.96	197/77	HJ	2.32i, 2.28	2.30- 16
Selmon	Kenny	USA	27.8.96	188/82	400h	48.60	49.31- 16
Selmouni	Sofiane	FRA	22.9.89	189/75	1500	3:36.14	3:40.01- 15
Semyonov	Dmitriy	RUS	2.8.92	195/77	HJ	2.28i	2.31i- 15, 2.28- 14
Sène	Alioune	FRA	3.2.96	185/69	PV	5.53i, 5.50	5.60- 16
Seppänen	Tuomas	FIN	16.5.86	180/107	HT	71.35	76.20- 16
Seria	Eslam Moussad	EGY	20.2.91		HT	74.20	69.25- 14
Sesele	Lebokeng	RSA	10.12.90	181/68	200	20.27	20.80A, 20.87- 16
Seurei	Benson	BRN	27.3.84	172/62	1500	3:35.23	3:31.61- 12
Shalin	Pavel	RUS	15.3.87	175/73	LJ	7.96	8.25- 10, 8.33w- 11
Shamsuddin	Muhd Irfan	MAS	16.8.95	189/102	DT	62.55	59.29- 16
Shang Shuo		CHN	1.6.95	180/68	400h	49.79	49.97- 16
* Shange	Lebogang	RSA	1.8.90	160/56	20kW	1:19:18	1:20:06- 16
Sharipov	Sergey	RUS	14.4.92		50kW	3:47:13	3:46:51- 16
Sharma	Ankit	IND	20.7.92	178/68	LJ	7.96	8.04- 15
Shayunov	Yuriy	BLR	22.10.87	189/120	HT	75.78	80.72- 09
Sheffield	Joseph	USA-J	8.3.99	184/73	100	10.07w	10.49, 10.40w- 16
Shestopalov	Feliks	RUS	11.3.96		Dec	7718	7835- 16
Shevchuk	Aleksey	RUS	10.8.97		20kW	1:20:57	1:25:13- 16
Sheyko	Georgiy	KAZ	24.8.89	183/70	20kW	1:20:47	1:21:34- 15
* Shi Yuhao		CHN-J	26.9.98	178/61	LJ	8.31	8.30- 16
Shields	Ryan	JAM	12.5.83	188/82	100	10.16, 9.89w	10.27- 11, 10.21w- 10
Shiferaw	Bekele	ETH	14.10.95	171/54	5000	13:26.19	13:37.41- 16
Shimelis	Belayneh	ETH	.96		3kSt	8:29.93	8:28.01- 16
Shimono	Shin-ichiro	JPN	10.10.90	177/64	LJ	8.00, 8.05w	8.11- 15
Shinnick	Zachary	USA-J	8.2.99	180/73	400	45.20	47.19- 15
Shiojiri	Kazuya	JPN	8.11.96	170/54	10k	27:47.87	28:42.56- 16
* Shirobokov	Sergey	RUS-J	16.2.99		20kW	1:18:26	1:22:31- 16
Shiroyama	Shotaro	JPN	6.3.95	178/64	LJ	7.97	8.01- 16
Shitara	Yuta	JPN	18.12.91	170/48	10k	27:41.97	27:42.71- 15
HMar	60:17		61:48- 12		Mar	2:09:03	-0-
* Shkurenyov	Ilya	RUS	11.1.91	191/82	Dec	8601	8538- 15
Shoaib	Mohamed Adam	SUD-J	.98	184/73	400h	49.82	51.10- 15
Shokirjanov	Bobur	UZB	5.12.90	193/99	JT	81.27	84.24- 15
* Shubenkov	Sergey	RUS	4.10.90	190/75	110h	13.01	12.98- 15, 12.7- 16
Shuey	Michael	USA	2.2.94	196/93	JT	79.91	76.02- 14
Siame	Sydney	ZAM	7.10.97	173/64	100	10.22, 9.88Adt, 10.06w	10.26, 10.18- 15
					200	20.29	20.53A- 15
* Sibanda	Karabo	BOT-J	2.7.98	192/79	400	45.05	44.25- 16
Sicard	Lloyd	USA	31.5.95	178/73	110h	13.61, 13.55w	13.60- 15
Siddhanth	Thingalaya	IND	1.3.91	193/87	110h	13.48, 13.43w	13.54, 13.47w- 16
Sidorchenko	Gleb	RUS	15.5.86	197/110	DT	61.48	62.55- 13
Sidorov	Maksim	RUS	13.5.86	190/126	SP	19.56	21.51- 12
Sigei	Richard	KEN	11.5.84		Mar	2:09:05	2:08:28- 15
Sigueni	Hicham	MAR	30.1.93	175/55	3kSt	8:18.77	8:16.54- 15
Sikowo	Boniface	UGA-J	27.7.99		3kSt	8:30.15	8:57.7A- 15
Silmon	Charles	USA	4.7.91	175/72	100	10.10, 10.01w	9.98, 9.85w- 13
da Silva	Aldemir Gomes	BRA	8.6.92	179/67	200	20.15	20.32- 14
da Silva	Altobeli	BRA	3.12.90	181/60	3kSt	8:23.67	8:26.30- 16
Silva	António Vital e	POR	23.1.88	183/110	HT	71.48	70.06- 16
da Silva	Tiago	BRA	23.10.93	176/73	LJ	8.08	8.09- 14
Silva	Talles	BRA	20.8.91	190/78	HJ	2.30	2.29- 16
Simbassa	Abbabiya	USA	30.6.93	176/61	5000	13:25.79	13:29.51- 16
					10k	27:45.78	28:42.56- 14
* Simbine	Akani	RSA	21.9.93	174/67	100	9.92A, 9.99	9.89 -16
					200	19.95A, 20.21	20.16- 16
Simmons	Cale	USA	5.2.91	178/70	PV	5.50Ai	5.72A, 5.65- 16
Simon	Péter	HUN	18.9.94	187/118	SP	19.74	19.30- 16
* Simotwo	Charles	KEN	6.5.95	173/59	800	1:46.20	1:47.46A- 14
					1500	3:32.59	3:35.86A-15

Name		Nat	Born	Ht/Wt	Event	2017 Mark	Pre-2017 Best
Simpson	Damarcus	USA	14.7.93	175/68	100	10.12, 9.94w	10.47- 16, 10.46Aw- 15
					LJ	8.01i, 8.36w	8.12- 16
Singh	Arpinder	IND	30.12.92	188/80	TJ	16.75	17.17- 14
Singh	Chandan	IND	8.6.87		50kW	4:04:19	4:09:51- 16
Singh	Devender	IND	5.12.83		20kW	1:21:38	1:20:21- 16
Singh	Jasdeep	IND	6.10.90	192/120	SP	19.46	18.92- 16
Singh	Om Prakash	IND	11.1.87	198/130	SP	19.58	20.69- 12
Singh	Tejinder Pal	IND	13.11.94	193/120	SP	20.40	19.93- 16
Singh Kang	Davinder	IND	18.12.88	178/92	JT	84.57	80.21- 16
Singh Rathore	Jitender	IND	20.3.89		50kW	4:02:12	4:08:36- 16
Singkhon	Suthisak	THA	5.10.96	189/78	Dec	7732	7082- 16
* Sintnicolaas	Eelco	NED	7.4.87	186/81	Dec	8539	8506- 12
* Sitonik	William	KEN	1.3.94	165/52	5000	13:20.02	13:19.83- 13
					10k	27:22.79	26:54.66- 16
Sjunin	Igor	EST	4.12.90	173/70	TJ	16.56	16.86- 10
Skagestad	Sven Martin	NOR	13.1.95	201/118	DT	63.97	65.20- 16
Skarvélis	Nikólaos	GRE	2.2.93	185/121	SP	20.27	20.61- 16
Skeen	Odean	JAM	28.8.94	181/75	100	9.98	10.14, 10.12w- 14
Skorobogatko	Aleksandr	RUS	7.8.94	186/78	400h	49.83	49.33- 16
Skyers	Roberto	CUB	12.11.91	187/83	100	10.06w, 9.9h	10.11- 16, 9.9dt- 10
Sloan	Eric	USA	20.6.94	185/77	LJ	7.85, 8.03w	7.85i- 16, 7.82, 7.88w- 15
					TJ	16.92	17.03i- 16, 16.31- 14
Smaïli	Mostafa	MAR	9.1.97	172/61	800	1:45.76	1:45.05- 16
Smajlaj	Izmir	ALB	29.3.93	184/75	LJ	8.08i, 7.98	8.03-16
Smaliós	Jiannis	SWE	17.2.87	192/90	JT	80.44	81.89- 16
Smellie	Gavin	CAN	26.6.86	180/75	100	10.12, 9.97w	10.09, 10.05w- 15
					200	20.38, 20.21w	20.43- 16, 20.16w- 15
Smelyk	Sergiy	UKR	19.4.87	178/74	200	20.42	20.30- 14
Smet	Koen	NED	9.8.92	186/74	110h	13.65, 13.59w	13.58, 13.52w- 13
Smikle	Traves	JAM	7.5.92	201/95	DT	65.00	67.12- 12
Smit ¶	Tiaan	RSA	14.3.95	188/82	110h	13.56A, 13.49Aw, 13.42dq	13.78- 16
Smith	Allan	GBR	6.11.92	198/84	HJ	2.26i, 2.24	2.29i- 15, 2.26- 13
Smith	Calvin	USA	10.12.87	180/75	400	45.52	44.81- 10
Smith	David	PUR	2.5.92	183/73	HJ	2.24	2.29- 16
Smith	Teray	BAH	28.9.94	185/77	200	20.25	20.34- 15
Smith	Terrell	USA	10.10.94	182/75	200	20.71, 20.44w	20.51- 15, 20.44w- 16
Smith	Tyrone	BER	7.8.86	183/70	LJ	8.34	8.22- 10
Smith	Xavier	USA	26.5.96	175/70	100	10.10w	10.59, 10.45w- 16
					200	20.23w	20.96- 16
Snyman	Wayne	RSA	8.3.85	177/64	20kW	1:21:06	1:20:46- 16
Soboka	Tafese	ETH	29.9.93	176/60	3kSt	8:13.22	8:17.75- 16
* Söderberg	David	FIN	11.8.79	185/100	HT	75.53	78.83- 03
Soget	Justus	KEN-J	.99	178/61	1500	3:32.97A	
* Soi	Edwin	KEN	3.3.86	172/55	3000	7:43.20	7:27.55- 11
* Sokirskiy	Aleksey	RUS	16.3.85	185/108	HT	77.50	78.91- 12
^ Sokolovs	Igors	LAT	17.8.74	187/110	HT	75.86	80.14- 09
Solanas	Sergio	ESP	28.4.87	194/83	TJ	16.24, 16.65Aw	16.68A, 16.52- 15
Solomon	Napoleon	SWE	14.2.94	168/54	3kSt	8:28.86	8:41.23- 16
^ Solomon	Steven	AUS	16.5.93	186/73	400	45.19	44.97- 12
Soratos	Cristian	USA	26.9.92	175/64	1500	3:36.73	3:39.33- 16
					1M	3:54.23i, 3:56.68	3:55.27i- 15
* Sorokin	Dmitriy	RUS	27.9.92	176/73	TJ	16.95	17.29- 15
Sorrillo	Rondell	TTO	21.1.86	178/62	100	10.15	9.99- 16
Soto	Manuel	COL	28.1.94	174/60	20kW	1:21:13	1:20:36- 16
* Souleiman	Ayanleh	DJI	3.12.92	172/60	800	1:45.01	1:42.97- 15
					1500	3:34.70	3:29.58 -14
Sousa	Hugo	BRA	5.3.87	188/77	400	45.55	45.09- 14
de Souza	Éder Antônio	BRA	15.10.86	189/85	110h	13.47	13.46- 15
de Souza	Silvio Henrique	BRA	21.7.93		110h	13.64	13.99- 16
Sowinski	Erik	USA	21.12.89	186/70	800	1:44.66	1:44.58 -14
Spencer	Kendall	USA	24.7.91	178/73	LJ	7.98	8.16A, 8.01i- 12, 7.85- 16
Spratling	Brycen	USA	10.3.92	175/68	400	45.39	45.09- 14
* Ståhl	Daniel	SWE	27.8.92	200/150	SP	19.60i	19.38- 16
					DT	71.29	68.72- 16
Stamatóyiannis ¶	Mihaíl	GRE	20.5.82	188/112	SP	20.22i, 18.92	20.36i- 10, 20.17- 11
* Stanek	Tomás	CZE	13.6.91	190/127	SP	22.01	21.30i, 21.26- 16
Stano	Massimo	ITA	27.2.92	179/63	20kW	1:22:30	1:22:16- 15
Stanys	Raivydas	LTU	3.2.87	184/77	HJ	2.25i	2.31- 12
Starc	Brandon	AUS	24.11.93	188/73	HJ	2.25	2.31- 15
Stathelakos	Constantinos	CYP	30.12.87	181/105	HT	72.69	75.32- 15
Stauss	René	GER	17.9.87	190/80	Dec	8009	7907- 15

	Name		Nat	Born	Ht/Wt	Event	2017 Mark	Pre-2017 Best
	Stecchi	Claudio Michel	ITA	23.11.91	184/82	PV	5.60	5.60- 12
	Steen	Roger	USA	17.5.92	185/118	SP	19.87i, 19.70	19.97- 16
	Stegemann	Tim	GER	4.8.92	179/63	3kSt	8:31.95	8:39.97- 16
	Stewart	Taylor	CAN	11.4.91	185/89	Dec	7882	7225- 16
	Stienen	Benedikt	GER	12.1.92	196/110	DT	60.84	60.32- 16
*	Stigler	Michael	USA	5.4.92	178/70	400h	48.26	48.44- 15
	Stirbu	Florin Alin	ROU	21.4.92		50kW	4:03:36	4:34:40- 16
	Stój	Bartlomiej	POL	15.5.96	193/115	DT	61.52	64.64- 16
*	Storl	David	GER	27.7.90	199/122	SP	21.87	22.20- 15
	Strobinders	Rolands	LAT	14.4.92	193/90	JT	85.07	83.37- 15
	Strother	Nathan	USA	6.9.95	183/70	400	45.07	45.07- 16
	Stylianou	Nikandros	CYP	22.8.89	179/72	PV	5.61i, 5.55	5.52- 14
*	Su Bingtian		CHN	29.8.89	172/64	100	10.03, 9.92w	9.99- 15
	Su Xianzhen		CHN	26.2.95		20kW	1:21:42	1:22:58- 15
*	Suárez	Leonel	CUB	1.9.87	181/78	Dec	8214	8654- 09
	Sukharev	Kirill	RUS	24.5.92	183/75	LJ	8.14	8.13- 14
	Sun Song		CHN	15.12.96		20kW	1:20:25	1:21:51- 16
	Sun Yize		CHN	9.3.96	186/73	LJ	7.99	7.55- 16
	Sun Zhao		CHN	8.2.90	193/83	HJ	2.28i, 2.27	2.25- 12
	Suskevicius	Tadas	LTU	22.5.85	175/65	50kW	3:58:44	3:51:58- 14
	Suzuki	Kota	JPN	18.12.95	176/72	PV	5.60	5.51- 16
	Svärd Jacobsson	Melker	SWE	8.1.94	188/78	PV	5.55	5.70- 16
^	Svoboda	Petr	CZE	10.10.84	195/83	110h	13.46, 13.44w	13.27- 10
	Swiderski	Adrian	POL	26.9.86	188/74	TJ	16.53i, 16.53	16.81- 15
	Sykora	Jirí	CZE	20.1.95	191/92	Dec	8120	8121- 16
	Szikszai	Róbert	HUN	30.9.94	200/118	DT	62.75	63.20- 14
	Szyszkowski	Jakub	POL	21.8.91	193/145	SP	20.92	20.55- 15
	Tabala	Aleksandr	RUS	23.5.86	186/87	Dec	7914	8070- 12
	Tabti	Bilal	ALG	7.6.93	175/60	3kSt	8:20.20	8:20.26- 16
	Tacir	Ersin	TUR	1.4.85	170/61	20kW	1:22:31	1:22:19- 16
	Tada	Shuhei	JPN	24.6.96	176/66	100	10.07, 9.94w	10.25- 16
*	Takahashi	Eiki	JPN	19.11.92	175/56	20kW	1:18:18	1:18:03- 15
	Takayama	Shun-ya	JPN	3.9.94	183/71	110h	13.44	13.58- 16
	Takele	Adugna	ETH	26.2.89	170/55	HMar	60:45	-16
	Taki	Kumari	KEN-J	6.5.99	172/59	1500	3:36.07	3:36.38A- 15
	Talam	Festus	KEN	20.10.94		Mar	2:06:13	2:06:26- 16
*	Talbot	Danny	GBR	1.5.91	184/73	100	10.13w	10.15- 16
						200	20.16, 1.86w	20.25- 16
*	Tamberi	Gianmarco	ITA	1.6.92	189/71	HJ	2.29	2.39- 16
	Tanaka	Shin-ya	JPN	23.6.93	183/73	110h	13.64	13.89, 13.81w- 15
	Tang Gongchen		CHN	24.4.89	185/71	LJ	7.99	8.17- 15
*	Tanii	Takayuki	JPN	14.2.83	167/57	20kW	1:21:45	1:20:39- 04
	Tanui	Josphat	KEN	4.2.94		HMar	59:22	-0-
*	Tanui	Paul	KEN	22.12.90	172/54	5000	13:14.09	12:58.69- 15
						10k	26:50.60	26:50.63- 11
*	Taplin	Bralon	GRN	8.5.92	180/73	400	45.08	44.38- 16
*	Tarabin	Dmitriy	RUS	29.10.91	176/85	JT	80.70	88.84- 13
	Tarbei	Philip	KEN	13.2.94		HMar	60:13	-0-
	Tarbei	Willy	KEN-J	30.5.98	180/64	800	1:44.86	1:44.51A- 15
*	Taylor	Christian	USA	18.6.90	190/75	TJ	18.11	18.21- 15
	Taylor	Christopher	JAM-J	29.9.99	178/70	200	20.38	20.78- 15
						400	45.41	45.27A, 45.55- 15
	Teeters	John	USA	19.5.93	183/82	100	10.10w	10.00- 16, 9.91w- 14
*	Tefera	Samuel	ETH-J	23.10.99	171/52	1500	3:33.78	3:43.0A- 16
	Teklu	Haftu	ETH	.90		1500	3:37.43	3:40.66- 16
	Teles	Márcio	BRA	27.1.94	180/68	400h	48.94	49.09- 16
	ten Berge	Mart	NED	27.4.91	186/86	JT	78.46	77.97- 16
	Tentóglou	Miltiádis	GRE-J	18.3.98	187/70	LJ	8.30	8.19- 16
	Terentyev	Aleksey	RUS	19.7.91		50kW	4:05:14	4:09:16- 13
	Terentyev	Ilya	RUS	25.1.95	184/100	HT	71.88	71.82- 16
	Terry	Tyler	USA	3.12.97	191/79	400	45.62	-0-
	Tesfahun	Tadesse	ETH-J	.99	176/60	10k	28:05.54	-0-
	Tesfaldet	Nguse	ERI	10.11.86	180/56	10k	28:08.58	27:28.10- 12
						HMar	60:04	59:39- 14
	Tesfaye	Diriba	ETH-J	11.9.98	185/66	3kSt	8:13.33	
*	Tesfaye	Homiyu	GER	23.6.93	183/66	800	1:46.08	1:46.40- 13
						1500	3:33.47	3:31.98- 14
	Tewelde	Hizkel	ERI	15.9.86	173/57	10k	27:49.62	27:30.50- 16
*	Thebe ?186/77	Baboloki	BOT	18.3.97	178/68	400	44.02	44.22A, 44.69- 16
	Theiner	Wojciech	POL	25.6.86	187/74	HJ	2.25	2.32- 14
	Thoirs	Jax	GBR	7.4.93	195/90	PV	5.52i	5.65- 15

MEN'S INDEX

	Name		Nat	Born	Ht/Wt	Event	2017 Mark	Pre-2017 Best
*	Thomas	Donald	BAH	1.7.84	190/75	HJ	2.31i, 2.29	2.37- 16
	Thomas	Mikel	TTO	23.11.87	182/77	110h	13.33	13.17- 15
^	Thorne	Benjamin	CAN	19.3.93	180/57	20kW	1:21:16	1:19:55- 16
	Thornton	Darien	USA	14.7.94	183/100	HT	71.85	73.26- 16
	Thuku	Karemi Jeremiah	KEN	7.7.94	176/62	10k	28:00.21	27:28.27- 14
	Thymes	Just'N	USA	24.1.94	180/70	100	10.14, 10.08w	10.18 -14
						200	20.36i, 20.24w	20.46- 15
	Tian Zhizhong		CHN	15.12.92	196/128	SP	19.58	19.61- 15
	Tiernan	Patrick	AUS	11.9.94	183/68	3000	7:37.76	7:48.55i, 7:54.12- 16
	5000	13:13.44		13:20.88- 16		10K	27:29.81	27:59.74- 16
	Tilahun	Belay	ETH	.95	178/62	10k	28:05.56	27:11.83- 16
	Timshin	Sergey	RUS	25.11.92	183/79	Dec	7900	7984- 15
	Tindouft	Mohammed	MAR	12.3.93		3kSt	8:20.28	8:30.23- 16
*	Tinsley	Michael	USA	21.4.84	185/74	400h	49.00	47.70- 13
	Titi	Ncincihli	RSA	15.12.93	167/61	200	20.14	20.48, 20.41A- 14
	Tobalina	Carlos	ESP	2.8.85	187/127	SP	20.57	20.50i- 16, 20.32- 14
	Tobe	Naoto	JPN	31.3.92	194/74	HJ	2.26i, 2.26	2.31- 14
*	Tola	Tamirat	ETH	11.8.91	181/59	HMar	59:37	60:06- 16
						Mar	2:04:11	2:06:17- 14
	Toledo	Braian	ARG	8.9.93	187/100	JT	80.83	83.32- 15
	Tolosa	Jigisa	ETH	29.3.94	188/70	3kSt	8:23.12	8:21.33- 16
	Tolosa	Teresa	ETH-J	15.6.98	177/60	1500	3:34.47	3:40.9A- 16
	Tong Anqi		CHN	29.9.92		20kW	1:21:56	1:22:46- 13
	Tonnesen	Pau Gaspar	ESP	24.10.92	196/89	Dec	8102	8247- 15
	Tontodonati	Federico	ITA	30.10.89	169/55	50kW	4:00:39	3:49:27- 15
	Too	Wilson	KEN	14.3.91	165/52	HMar	60:57	62:48- 16
*	Tornéus	Michel	SWE	26.5.86	184/70	LJ	8.30A, 8.18	8.44A- 16, 8.30i- 15, 8.22- 12
	Toroitich	Timothy	UGA	10.10.91	169/57	10k	27:21.09	27:31.07- 13
	Torotich	Vincent	KEN	.90		HMar	60:32	64:14- 13
	Torrence	David	PER	26.11.85	175/61	1500	3:34.67	3:33.23- 13
						1M	3:53.21	3:52.01- 12
	Torres	Ricardo	PUR	13.2.96	181/70	110h	13.84, 13.46w	13.79A, 13.83- 16
	Torrijos	Pablo	ESP	12.5.92	187/78	TJ	16.96	17.04i- 15, 16.89A- 16, 16.87- 14
	Tortu	Filippo	ITA-J	15.6.98	182/68	100	10.15	10.19- 16
						200	20.34	20.92- 15
	Tovarnov	Aleksey	RUS	21.1.85	183/86	JT	77.67	82.54- 13
	Traber	Gregor	GER	2.12.92	189/77	110h	13.41, 13.34w	13.21- 16
	Tracey	Tyquendo	JAM	10.6.93	179/75	100	10.12	10.14- 15
	Trajkovic	Milan	CYP	17.3.92	187/72	110h	13.25	13.31- 16
	Trémos	Yeóryios	GRE	21.3.89	197/118	DT	60.75	63.00- 14
	Trescoli	Pablo	ESP	4.3.95	197/85	Dec	7634	7314- 16
	Triki	Yasser	ALG	24.3.97	186/70	LJ	8.03	7.81- 16
						TJ	16.85	16.01- 16
	Trimble	Jamiel	USA	25.6.95	188/82	200	20.33A, 20.30w	20.12- 16
*	True	Ben	USA	29.12.85	183/70	3000	7:35.53	7:36.59- 13
	5000	13:06.81		12:48.77- 12		10k	27:19.86	-0-
	Trus	Viktor	BLR	11.11.96	197/110	DT	62.17	57.20- 16
	Tsákonas	Likoúrgos-Stéfanos	GRE	8.3.90	184/67	100	10.16, 10.13w	10.23- 16, 10.22w- 14
						200	20.33, 20.26w	20.09- 15
	Tsegay	Atsedu	ETH	17.12.91		HMar	60:58	-12
	Tsegay	Samuel	ERI	24.02.88	176/55	Mar	2:07:34	2:07:28- 11
	Tsenov	Mitko	BUL	13.6.93	185/64	3kSt	8:30.87	8:20.87- 14
	Tsernjavski	Taavi	EST	4.3.95	196/86	Dec	7802	7487- 14
	Tsiámis	Dimítrios	GRE	12.1.82	178/67	TJ	16.87	17.55- 06
	Tsonov	Georgi	BUL	2.5.93	172/66	TJ	16.93	17.03, 17.11w- 15
	Tsuetaki	Hironori	JPN	8.5.93	175/60	3kSt	8:29.05	8:29.78- 16
	Tsuha	Hibiki	JPN-J	21.1.98	168/65	LJ	8.09	7.69, 7.86w- 16
	Tsumba	Tatenda	ZIM	12.11.91	175/73	200	20.49A, 20.42w	20.44- 16
	Tsutsumi	Yuji	JPN	22.12.89	184/107	DT	60.74	60.05- 14
	Tudor	Macklin	USA	13.6.94	188/109	DT	63.54	62.50- 16
	Tuemay	Mogos	ETH	24.5.97	178/62	10K	27:48.41	-0-
	Tufa	Welde	ETH-J	29.3.99		1500	3:37.09	3:41.74- 15
*	Tuka	Amel	BIH	9.1.91	187/77	800	1:44.62	1:42.51- 15
	Tura	Temam	ETH-J	1.8.98		800	1:46.13	1:47.7A - 16
	Turner	Vernon	USA-J	21.8.98	188/77	HJ	2.28	2.25- 16
	Tuufuli	Reno	USA	15.2.96	190/120	DT	62.06	60.71- 16
	Tuwei	Cornelius	KEN	.93		800	1:45.3A	
	Tuwei	Julius	KEN			Mar	2:08:06	2:16:12- 16
	Ueno	Yuichiro	JPN	29.7.85	181/61	10k	28:07.23	28:01.71- 14
*	Ujah	Chijindu	GBR	5.3.94	180/75	100	9.97, 9.95w	9.96- 14
						200	20.39	20.47- 15

Name		Nat	Born	Ht/Wt	Event	2017 Mark	Pre-2017 Best
* Ukhov	Ivan	RUS	29.3.86	192/83	HJ	2.32	2.42i, 2.41- 14
Ullmann	Christopher	SUI	21.8.93	182/73	LJ	7.98	7.76- 15, 7.92w- 16
* Urbanek	Robert	POL	29.4.87	200/120	DT	66.73	66.93- 12
Ureña	Jorge	ESP	8.10.93	178/82	Dec	8125	7985- 16
Ushiro	Keisuke	JPN	24.7.86	196/95	Dec	7807	8308- 14
* Vadlejch	Jakub	CZE	10.10.90	190/93	JT	89.73	88.02- 16
Vaillant	Ludvy	FRA	15.3.95	180/64	400h	49.31	50.32- 16
Vallés	Adrián	ESP	16.3.95	190/76	PV	5.70	5.65- 15
van Assen	Miguel	SUR	30.7.97	176/75	TJ	16.94	16.37- 15
* van Niekerk	Wayde	RSA	15.7.92	183/73	100	9.94	9.98A- 16
200 19.84			19.94- 15		400	43.62	43.03- 16
van Ophem	Thomas	NED	6.9.92	195/95	JT	80.70	72.03- 15
van Rensburg	Phil Mar	RSA	23.6.89	188/86	JT	80.49A	78.88- 16
van Rensburg	Rynhardt	RSA	23.3.92	184/70	800	1:45.73	1:45.33- 16
van Rooyen	Rocco	RSA	23.12.92	188/93	JT	84.09	85.39- 15
* van Zyl	Louis 'L.J'	RSA	20.7.85	186/75	400h	49.29A, 49.35	47.66- 11
Vanderbemden	Robin	BEL	10.2.94	183/72	200	20.45	20.83- 16
					400	45.65	45.98- 16
VanLiew	Timothy	USA	25.5.90	190/95	JT	78.05	79.62- 16
Varga	Roland	CRO	22.10.77	196/125	DT	61.09	67.38- 02
Vaughn	Clayton	USA	15.5.92	173/77	100	10.04	9.93- 15
Veith	Hunter	USA	14.1.95	185/79	LJ	7.94w	7.22- 14, 7.69w- 16
					Dec	7866	7300- 16
Vena	Nick	USA	16.4.93	194/120	SP	20.42	20.39- 14
Vergani	Lorenzo	ITA	4.9.93	188/78	400h	49.36	50.65- 16
Vernon	Andrew	GBR	7.1.86	178/65	5000	13:22.65	13:11.50- 14
					10k	27:58.69	27:42.62- 15
* Vesely	Vitezslav	CZE	27.2.83	186/94	JT	82.29	88.34- 12
Vestlund	Oscar	SWE	27.4.93	189/110	HT	73.34	72.20- 15
Veszelka	Tomás	SVK	9.7.95	183/79	TJ	16.63	16.33- 16
* Vetter	Johannes	GER	26.3.93	188/105	JT	94.44	89.57- 16
* Vicaut	Jimmy	FRA	27.2.92	188/83	100	9.97	9.86- 15
* Victor	Lindon	GRN	28.2.93	191/90	Dec	8539(w)	8446- 16
^ Vieira	João	POR	20.2.76	174/58	50kW	3:45:28	3:45:17- 12
Vilches	Roberto	MEX-J	21.5.99	193/84	HJ	2.25A, 2.21	2.18- 16
Villanueva	Claudio	ECU	3.8.88	168/55	50kW	3:49:27	3:50:29- 13
Virovecz	István	HUN	1.12.89	176/73	LJ	7.95	7.81- 16, 7.82w- 12
* Visser	Zarck	RSA	15.9.89	178/70	LJ	8.22, 8.23w	8.41- 15
^ Vivas	Borja	ESP	26.5.84	203/140	SP	20.43	21.07- 14
Vloon	Menno	NED	11.5.94	177/77	PV	5.85	5.58- 16
Volko	Ján	SVK	2.11.96	179/75	100	10.15	10.33, 10.30w- 16
					200	20.33	20.69- 16
Volz	Deakin	USA	12.1.97	178/75	PV	5.66i, 5.50	5.65- 16
* Walcott	Keshorn	TTO	2.4.93	188/90	JT	86.61	90.16- 15
Wale	Getnet	ETH-Y	20.7.99	178/60	3kSt	8:12.28	8:22.83- 16
Walelegn	Amdework	ETH-J	11.3.99	167/52	5000	13:14.52	
Walker	Chadadyne	JAM	14.4.97	183/75	100	10.16	10.45- 14
					200	20.35	20.97- 15
Walker	Shaquille	USA	24.6.93	178/70	800	1:45.68	1:44.99- 16
Wallin	Gabriel	SWE	14.10.81	193/93	JT	82.01	83.23- 13
Walsh	Chevaughn	ANT	29.12.87	178/75	100	10.17	10.31, 10.21w- 15
Walsh	Julian Jrummi	JPN	18.9.96	175/75	400	45.62	45.35- 16
* Walsh	Tom	NZL	1.3.92	186/123	SP	22.14	22.21- 16
Walter	Keitavious	USA	16.4.96	178/77	100	10.21, 9.98w	10.21A, 10.37, 10.15w- 16
					200	20.43	20.57- 16
Walters	Ruebin	TTO	2.4.95	184/70	110h	13.30	13.60- 16, 13.53w- 15
Walton	Cody	USA	14.6.95	188/89	Dec	7937	7620w- 16
Walton	Jamal	CAY-J	25.11.98	190/77	400	44.99	45.99A- 15. 46.08- 16
Wan Yong		CHN	22.7.87	188/107	HT	73.42	74.74- 15
Wanders	Julien	SUI	18.3.96	173/60	10k	28:06.17	29:10.17- 16
Wang Chen		CHN	27.2.90	193/65	HJ	2.27	2.26- 09
Wang Gang		CHN	2.4.91		20kW	1:22:23	1:20:31- 13
Wang Hao		CHN	16.8.89	180/65	50kW	4:01:57	3:41:55- 09
* Wang Jianan		CHN	27.8.96	178/61	LJ	8.29A, 8.23	8.25- 15
* Wang Kaihua		CHN	16.2.94	180/65	20kW	1:17:54	1:19:49- 15
Wang Libo		CHN	9.2.97		20kW	1:21:45	1:27:58- 16
Wang Qin		CHN	8.5.94		50kW	3:54:46	3:50:16- 16
Wang Rui		CHN	6.1.96		20kW	1:19:23	1:21:23- 16
Wang Shizhu		CHN	20.2.89	184/100	HT	76.12	75.20- 13
Wang Yang		CHN	20.9.96	181/65	400h	49.69	50.21- 16
Wang Yu		CHN	18.8.91	192/73	HJ	2.30	2.33- 13

Name		Nat	Born	Ht/Wt	Event	2017 Mark	Pre-2017 Best
^ Wang Zhendong		CHN	11.1.91	180/65	50kW	4:04:38	3:41:02- 16
* Wanjiru	Daniel	KEN	25.5.92	174/58	Mar	2:05:48	2:05:21- 16
Ward	Ja'Mari	USA-J	21.7.98	175/68	LJ	8.13	7.96- 16
Ward	Laderrick	USA	28.12.92	173/68	LJ	7.93Ai	8.00- 14, 8.14w- 15
* Warholm	Karsten	NOR	28.2.96	187/78	400	44.87	46.23- 15, 45.8- 16
					400h	48.22	48.49- 16
* Warner	Damian	CAN	4.11.89	185/83	110h	13.54	13.27- 15
					LJ	7.85	8.04- 16
					Dec	8591	8695- 15
Washington	Josh	USA	28.8.95	175/68	200	20.52, 20.31w	20.70, 20.63w- 16
Washington	Marqueze	USA	29.9.93	188/84	100	10.07	10.19- 16
					200	20.32	20.54, 20.49w- 16
					400	45.63i	45.99- 15, 45.72i -16
Wasihun	Mule	ETH	20.10.93		Mar	2:05:39	2:05:44- 16
Wasik	Steele	USA	8.12.95	196/86	Dec	7715(w)	7521- 15
Wasike	Maurice	KEN	.93		100	9.9A	10.77A-13
Wasome	O'Brien	JAM	24.1.97	177/64	TJ	16.49i, 16.31	16.39- 16
Watanabe	Yoshihiro	JPN	7.1.97	170/59	400h	49.43	49.96- 16
Waweru	Edward	KEN	3.10.90	178/58	10k	27:49.31	27:13.94- 10
Ways	Ceolamar	USA	22.11.94	182/73	400	45.55	45.49- 15
* Webb	Ameer	USA	19.3.91	175/75	200	20.01	19.85- 16
* Weber	Julian	GER	29.8.94	190/94	JT	85.85	88.29- 16
Weckstén	Tomas	FIN	2.11.96	182/76	PV	5.51	5.50- 16
Wei Xubao		CHN	1.2.93		20kW	1:22:23	1:21:46- 16
^ Weir	Warren	JAM	31.10.89	178/75	200	20.18	19.79- 13
Weirich	Victor	USA	25.10.87	188/86	PV	5.70Ai, 5.40	5.66Ai- 15, 5.60- 14
* Weisshaidinger	Lukas	AUT	20.2.92	196/136	DT	66.52	67.24- 15
Wendrich	Falk	GER	12.6.95	194/75	HJ	2.29	2.24- 12
West	McKinley	USA	.96	173/66	100	10.05w	10.41, 10.38w- 16
^ Wheating	Andrew	USA	21.11.87	195/77	1500	3:37.75	3:30.90- 10
					1M	3:55.23	3:51.74- 10
White	Joseph	USA	16.11.95	178/61	800	1:45.73	1:46.66- 16
White	Travonn	USA	3.6.95	178/70	LJ	7.93i, 7.82	8.04- 14
White	William	AUS	27.11.95	188/86	JT	77.74	73.55- 12
* Whiting	Ryan	USA	24.11.86	191/134	SP	21.65	22.28- 13
Wieland	Luca	GER	7.12.94	185/82	Dec	8201	7784w- 16
* Wierig	Martin	GER	10.6.87	202/127	DT	65.56	68.33- 12
Wiesiolek	Pawel	POL	13.8.91	194/84	Dec	8002	8140- 15
Wightman	Jake	GBR	11.7.94	173/60	800	1:45.42	1:47.13- 16
					1500	3:34.17	3:35.49- 14
					1M	3:54.92	3:54.20- 16
Wijesekara	Manjula Kumara	SRI	30.1.84	183/73	HJ	2.25	2.27- 04
Wilkinson	Callum	GBR	14.3.97		20kW	1:22:17	-0-
Williams	Ben	GBR	25.1.92	183/73	TJ	16.73	16.74- 15
Williams	Brian	USA	18.12.94	188/109	DT	65.13	63.23- 16
Williams	Devon	USA	17.1.94	190/84	110h	13.37	13.94- 16
					Dec	8345	8116- 16
Williams	Kendal	USA	23.9.95	180/73	100	10.06, 9.99w	10.06- 16, 9.98w- 15
					200	20.30	20.26- 15, 20.11w- 16
Williams	Sheldon	JAM	17.8.90	184/73	400h	49.83	51.71- 15
Williams	Tye	USA	17.8.96	190/82	HJ	2.25	2.11i, 2.10 -16
Williams	Will	USA	31.1.95	183/79	LJ	7.96, 8.09w	8.03- 15
Williamsz	Jordan	AUS	21.8.92	172/64	1500	3:36.87	3:36.74- 12
Willis	Maxwell	USA-J	2.9.98	170/64	100	10.18, 10.03w	10.53- 15, 10.35Aw- 16
					200	20.39, 20.07w	20.71A- 16, 20.55Aw- 15
* Willis	Nick	NZL	25.4.83	183/68	1500	3:34.74	3:29.66- 15
Wilson	Alex	SUI	19.9.90	182/79	100	10.11, 10.08w	10.12- 13
					200	20.37	20.51- 11, 20.43w- 12
Wilson	Jamal	BAH	1.90.88	188/68	HJ	2.27i, 2.27	2.31i, 2.30- 16
Wimalasiri	Janaka Prasad	SRI	8.9.92	173/63	LJ	7.91, 8.13w	8.15- 16
Winder	Luke	USA	2.8.95	185/75	PV	5.56	5.52i, 5.51- 16
Windle	Drew	USA	22.7.92	183/73	800	1:44.63	1:45.65- 16
Winkler	Rudy	USA	6.12.94	186/102	HT	75.22	76.76- 16
^ Wirkkala	Teemu	FIN	14.1.84	187/85	JT	79.68	87.23- 09
* Wojciechowski	Pawel	POL	6.6.89	190/81	PV	5.93	5.91- 11
Wolde	Dawit	ETH	19.5.91	169/54	3000	7:47.66i, 7:49.84	7:41.69i- 16, 7:42.65- 11
					5000	13:10.13	13:17.04- 14
Wolski	Allan	BRA	18.1.90	185/110	HT	75.22	73.52- 15
Woo Sang-hyuk		KOR	23.4.96	187/66	HJ	2.30	2.29- 16
Woodson	Markesh	USA	6.9.93	168/64	100	10.26, 10.11w	10.05- 16
Worku	Bazu	ETH	15.9.90	170/52	Mar	2:08:48	2:05:25- 10
* Wote	Aman	ETH	18.4.84	181/64	800	1:46.26	1:44.99- 13
					1500	3:31.63	3:29.91- 14
Wright	Alex	IRL	19.12.90	173/64	20kW	1:21:17	1:21:56- 16

Name		Nat	Born	Ht/Wt	Event	2017 Mark	Pre-2017 Best
Wright	Chad	JAM	25.3.91	188/110	DT	62.53	65.03- 15
Wright	Dontavius	USA	3.1.94	178/68	400	45.63	45.12- 16
Wrobel	David	GER	13.2.91	195/125	DT	64.66	63.51, 64.93dh- 16
^ Wruck	Julian	AUS	6.7.91	198/125	DT	61.56	68.16- 13
Wu Qianlong		CHN	30.1.90	176/62	50kW	3:48:38	3:47:35- 15
Wu Ruiting		CHN	29.11.95		TJ	17.18	16.83 -15
Wyatt	Audie	USA	30.4.96	190/84	PV	5.70	5.65, 5.70dh- 16
Wynne	William	USA	30.1.90	183/75	400h	49.82	49.31- 09
Xie Sichao		CHN	28.2.93		50kW	4:01:29	3:49:57- 15
* Xie Wenjun		CHN	11.7.90	188/77	110h	13.31	13.23- 14
Xie Zhenye		CHN	17.8.93	185/80	100	10.04, 9.91w	10.08- 16
					200	20.20	20.44- 14
Xu Faguang		CHN	17.5.87	178/69	50kW	3:54:02	3:42:20- 11
Xu Xiaolong		CHN	20.12.92	185/70	TJ	16.68i, 16.57	16.93- 15
* Xue Changrui		CHN	31.5.91	183/60	PV	5.82	5.81i- 16, 5.80- 14
Yacoub Salem	Mohamed	BRN	1.3.96	175/68	200	20.40, 20.35w	20.19- 16
Yakushev	Maksim	RUS	15.3.92	173/61	3kSt	8:19.19	8:26.21- 16
Yamagata	Ryota	JPN	10.6.92	176/70	100	10.00	10.03- 16
Yamakawa	Natsuki	JPN	24.7.95	178/73	LJ	8.06	8.00- 16
Yamamoto	Ryoma	JPN	14.7.95	179/66	TJ	16.87, 16.91w	16.68- 16
Yamamoto	Seito	JPN	11.3.92	181/70	PV	5.72	5.77Ai- 16, 5.75- 13
Yamanishi	Toshikazu	JPN	15.2.96	164/53	20kW	1:19:03	1:20:50- 16
Yamashita	Yuga	JPN	6.2.96		20kW	1:21:36.64	1:23:06- 14
Yan Dexiang		CHN	18.6.93		50kW	3:58:14	4:14:29- 13
Yáñez	Eure	VEN	20.5.93	194/77	HJ	2.31	2.27- 14
Yang Hu		CHN	16.4.95		50kW	4:01:04	4:19:25- 16
Yang Liang		CHN	25.4.93		50kW	4:01:47	4:05:01- 15
Yang Wei-Ting		TPE	22.9.94	182/73	110h	13.57	13.61- 16
Yang Yingyi		CHN	9.2.95		50kW	4:04:37	4:11:53- 15
Yao Jie		CHN	21.9.90	188/85	PV	5.70	5.70- 16
Yator	Richard	KEN-J	4.6.98	173/47	5000	13:22.66	13:51.3A- 16
Yator	Vincent	KEN	11.7.89	172/55	HMar	61:01	-15
Yator Kimunyan	Richard	KEN-J	6.4.98	173/47	10k	27:52.10	-0-
Yazawa	Wataru	JPN	26.7.91	179/73	110h	13.49	13.47- 16
* Yego	Hillary	KEN	2.4.92	178/60	3kSt	8:31.54	8:03.57- 13
Yego	Isaac	KEN	.89		3kSt	8:31.4A	8:32.48A- 15
* Yego	Julius	KEN	4.1.89	175/90	JT	87.97A	92.72- 15
* Yego	Solomon Kirwa	KEN	10.5.87	175/58	HMar	59:50	58:44- 16
					Mar	2:07:12	2:08:31- 16
Yegon	Geoffrey	KEN	28.8.88		HMar	59:56	59:44- 16
Yemataw	Birhanu	BRN	27.2.96	167/54	5000	13:09.93	13:09.26- 16
^ Yemelyanov ¶	Stanislav	RUS	23.10.90	175/62	20kW	1:19:48dq	1:19:43- 10
Yevstifeyev	Roman	RUS	19.9.92		50kW	4:02:23	3:45:41- 14
* Yimer	Jemal	ETH	11.9.96	163/48	10k	26:56.11	28:08.92- 16
Yin Jiaxing		CHN	16.3.94		20kW	1:20:56	1:21:07- 12
Yokote	Ken	JPN	27.4.93	165/54	10k	28:04.51	27:58.40- 15
Yoon Seung-hyun		KOR	1.6.94	194/74	HJ	2.24	2.32- 15
Yoroizaka	Tetsuya	JPN	20.3.90	166/52	10k	27:57.63	27:29.74- 15
Yoshida	Kazuaki	JPN	31.8.87	180/73	400h	49.64	49.45- 09
You Tao		CHN	19.7.97		50kW	4:04:29	-0-
Young	Alex	USA	1.9.94	188/105	HT	74.39	72.47- 16
* Young	Isiah	USA	5.1.90	183/75	100	9.97, 9.95w	9.99- 13, 9.82w- 15
					200	20.14, 20.12w	19.86- 13, 19.75w- 15
Young	Jordan	CAN	21.6.93	190/113	DT	62.76	62.27- 15
^ Yousif	Rabah	GBR	11.12.86	183/75	400	45.58	44.54- 15
* Yu Wei		CHN	11.9.87	180/60	20kW	1:21:52	1:19:07- 13
Yurchenko	Aleksandr	RUS	30.7.92	182/73	TJ	16.94i, 16.76	16.81i- 15, 16.67- 13
Zakalnytskyy	Maryan	UKR	19.8.94	180/65	50kW	3:53:50	3:56:30- 16
Zalewski	Krystian	POL	11.4.89	183/67	3kSt	8:23.68	8:16.20- 14
Zallow	Chad	USA	25.4.97	178/73	110h	13.68, 13.37w	13.92- 16
Zamora	Leandro	CUB	11.3.96	186/75	400h	49.58	50.52- 15
Zango	Fabrice	BUR	25.6.93	180/75	TJ	16.97	16.81, 16.84w- 16
Zaytsev	Ivan	UZB	7.11.88	190/98	JT	78.66	85.03- 12
Zeng Qingcun		CHN	3.4.95		20kW	1:20:52	1:22:19- 16
Zézé	Meba-Mickaël	FRA	19.5.94	174/61	200	20.47	20.49- 16
* Zhang Guowei		CHN	4.6.91	200/77	HJ	2.31	2.38- 15
Zhang Honglin		CHN	12.1.94	188/82	110h	13.61A, 13.69	13.53- 15
^ Zhang Lin		CHN	11.11.93	175/55	50kW	3:52:38	3:44:39- 15
Zhang Wanxin		CHN	25.10.96		20kW	1:22:29	1:25:04- 16
Zhang Yaoguang		CHN	21.6.93		LJ	8.19	8.09i, 8.01- 16
Zhao Qinggang		CHN	24.7.85	184/93	JT	80.04	89.15- 14

	Name		Nat	Born	Ht/Wt	Event	2017 Mark	Pre-2017 Best
	Zhelyabin	Dmitry	RUS	20.5.90	187/75	PV	5.70i	5.65- 12
	Zhong Heng		CHN	7.11.95		20kW	1:20:55	1:25:03- 16
	Zhong Xing		CHN	6.3.95		50kW	4:06:30	4:10:45- 16
	Zhou Shipeng		CHN	9.2.96		50kW	4:05:44	4:11:35- 16
	Zhu Gezhen		CHN	14.4.93		HJ	2.24	2.20- 15
	Zhu Guowen		CHN	20.8.97		20kW	1:21:46	1:26:22- 16
	Zhu Yaming		CHN	4.5.94	187/74	TJ	17.23	16.97- 16
	Zhuk	Vitaliy	BLR	10.9.96		Dec	7921	7400- 16
	Ziani	Mohamed	MAR	.93		HMar	60:28	62:50- 15
	Ziegler	Alexander	GER	7.7.87	180/98	HT	73.54	76.29- 14
*	Ziemek	Zach	USA	23.2.93	190/77	Dec	8155	8413- 16
	Ziukas	Marius	LTU	29.6.85	185/70	20kW	1:21:27	1:22:09- 14
	Zoghlami	Ala	ITA	19.6.94	180/57	3kSt	8:26.18	8:37.11- 15
	Zoghlami	Osama	ITA	19.6.94	182/58	3kSt	8:22.94	8:32.20- 16
	Zótos	Kiriáko	GRE	17.1.96	187/100	SP	19.47	18.19- 16
*	Zunic	Stipe	CRO	13.12.90	188/115	SP	21.48	21.11i- 15, 20.70- 16

WOMEN'S INDEX 2017

Athletes included are those ranked in the top 100s at standard (World Championships) events (plus shorter lists for 1000m, 1M, 2000m and 3000m). Those with detailed biographical profiles are indicated in first column by:
* in this year's Annual, ^ featured in a previous year's Annual.

	Ababel	Yeshaneh	ETH	10.6.90	157/42	HMar	67:21	67:52- 16
	Abe	Yukari	JPN	21.8.89	154/48	5000	15:27.62	15:22.29- 16
						10000	32:24.61	32:26.84- 16
	Abreha	Azmera	ETH-J	.98	162/45	Mar	2:25:23	
	Abreha	Tsige	ETH-Y	21.9.00	162/48	5000	15:18.32	
	Abye	Workneshs	ETH-J	-.99	168/52	1500	4:05.77	
	Adamu	Birtukan	ETH	29.4.92	164/49	3kSt	9:24.97	9:20.37- 11
*	Adekoya	Kemi	BRN	16.1.93	168/57	400	51.46	50.72- 16
						400h	54.57	54.12- 15
	Afanasyeva	Klavdiya	RUS	15.1.96		20kW	1:28:29	1:26:47- 16
	Afework	Abebech	ETH	11.12.90	152/42	Mar	2:25:34	2:23:33- 15
	Affessi	Fatim	SUI	8.7.93	177/64	LJ	6.45, 6.68w	6.38- 15
	Aga	Ruti	ETH	16.1.94	159/45	HMar	69:40+	68:07- 16
						Mar	2:20:41	2:24:41- 16
	Agai	Margaret	KEN	10.6.88	154/44	HMar	69:43	69:57- 15
						Mar	2:25:29	2:23:28- 13
	Agnou	Caroline	SUI	26.5.96	171/65	Hep	6330	6123- 15
	Aguessy-Thomas	Cassandre	FRA	1.9.97	174/60	Hep	5794	5297- 16
	Aguilar	Evelyn	COL	3.1.93	170/62	LJ	6.61A, 6.46	6.23- 16
						Hep	6228	6270A, 6263- 16
	Aguilar	Yulenmis	CUB	3.8.96	167/70	JT	58.90	63.86- 15
	Agyapong	Finette	GBR	1.2.97	173/57	200	22.86	23.55- 16
	Ahbe	Kelsie	CAN	6.7.91	170/63	PV	4.45	4.55- 16
	Ahouanwanou	Odile	BEN	5.1.91	178/71	Hep	6131(w)	5751- 15
*	Ahouré	Murielle	CIV	23.8.87	167/57	100	10.83	10.78- 16
						200	22.68	22.24- 13
*	Ahye	Michelle-Lee	TTO	10.4.92	168/59	100	10.82	10.85- 14
						200	22.50	22.25- 16, 22/01w- 15
	Aiyabei	Valary	KEN	8.6.91	156/42	HMar	67:50	69:33- 16
						Mar	2:20:53	2:24:48- 16
	Ajayi	Yinka	NGR	11.8.97	163/54	400	51.30	52.27- 16
	Ajok	Dorcus	UGA	12.7.94	162/65	800	2:00.79	2:02.04A- 14
	Akdag	Meryem	TUR	5.8.92	171/51	1500	4:05.47	4:10.59- 16
*	Akinosun	Morolake	USA	17.5.94	165/54	100	10.98, 10.94w	10.95- 16, 10.94w- 15
*	Akkaoui	Malika	MAR	25.12.87	160/46	800	2:00.71	1:57.64- 13
	1500	4:03.36		4:04.49- 15		1M	4:26.42	
	Akpana Assa	Nadia	NOR	22.12.95	176/57	LJ	6.48	6.53- 16
	Aksenova	Natalya	RUS	6.6.97		HJ	1.91i, 1.88	1.92- 16
	Aksyonova	Kseniya	RUS	14.1.88	177/60	400	51.62	49.92- 10
	Aksyonova	Yelizaveta	RUS	10.7.96		Hep	5821	
	Alais	Alexie	FRA	9.10.94	168/68	JT	56.61	57.81- 16
	Aleksandrova	Dina	RUS	9.8.92	160/50	800	2:01.96	2:02.49- 16
	Alema	Kidsan	ETH	19.7.95		5000	15:03.27	15:39.27- 16
*	Alemu	Habitam	ETH	9.7.97	171/52	800	1:57.05	1:58.99- 16
	Alexander	Ayanna	TTO	20.7.82	172/65	TJ	13.63	14.40- 14
	Alexoúli	Háido	GRE	29.3.91	179/59	LJ	6.66	6.78- 16
*	Ali	Nia	USA	23.10.88	170/64	100h	12.52	12.48- 13
	Allman	Valarie	USA	23.2.95	183/70	DT	64.69	61.42- 16
*	Almanza	Rose Mary	CUB	13.7.92	166/53	800	1:59.11	1:57.70- 15

Name		Nat	Born	Ht/Wt	Event	2017 Mark	Pre-2017 Best
Álvarez	Paula Beatriz	CUB	11.9.95	164/58	LJ	6.47, 6.59w	6.48- 13
Alvertsián	Kristína	GRE	4.7.90	175/62	TJ	13.60	13.50- 16
Amare	Meskerem	ETH	1.10.97	155/43	HMar	70:00	73:41- 16
Amata	Doreen	NGR	6.5.88	185/55	HJ	1.89i, 1.88	1.95- 08
Ambrose	Jenae	BAH	29.12.97	160/52	200	23.05, 22.94w	23.43- 16
Amponsah	Janet	GHA	12.4.93	167/52	200	22.90A	22.99- 16
Amsterdam	Iana	GUY	14.11.95	168/55	TJ	13.68	13.10- 15
Amusan	Tobi	NGR	23.4.97	164/52	200	22.92A, 22.60Aw	23.24A, 23.27- 16
					100h	12.57	12.83A,12.91, 12.79w- 16
Anacharsis	Phara	FRA	17.12.83	177/60	400h	56.45	55.84- 16
Anagnostopoúlou	Hrisoúla	GRE	27.8.91	176/79	DT	61.53	61.40- 15
Anang	Naa	AUS	10.3.95	165/54	LJ	6.68	6.55- 15
Anbesa	Adanech	ETH-J	23.1.98	160/48	800	2:01.42	
1500	4:06.20		4:05.22- 16		3000	8:56.88i	
Andersen	Brooke	USA	23.8.95	170/84	HT	68.62	65.50- 16
^ Anderson	Alexandria	USA	28.1.87	175/60	100	11.26, 10.95w	10.91- 13, 10.88w- 12
					200	22.58	22.60- 09
Anderson	Shae	USA-J	7.4.99	170/57	400	51.99	55.69- 16
Andersson	Saga	FIN-Y	30.3.00	168/53	PV	4.42	4.16- 16
Ando	Yuka	JPN	16.3.94	160/42	Mar	2:21:36	
^ Angelsen	Tonje	NOR	17.1.90	179/62	HJ	1.90	1.97- 12
Aniballi	Valentina	ITA	19.4.84	176/85	DT	58.05	58.55- 15
Ankiewicz	Emilia	POL	22.11.90	178/64	400h	56.31	55.89- 16
Ansa	Woynshet	ETH	9.4.96	158/42	3kSt	9:30.03	9:37.85- 16
Aoki	Sayaka	JPN	15.12.86	163/51	400h	56.32	55.94- 08
Aranda	Natalie	PAN	22.2.95	175/85	LJ	6.49A, 6.46	6.03- 15
Araujo	Martha Valeria	COL	12.5.96	168/	Hep	5703	4820- 16
Arcanjo	Geisa	BRA	19.9.91	180/92	SP	18.08	19.02- 12
* Arenas	Sandra	COL	17.9.93	160/50	20kW	1:28:10, 1:33:51.2At	1:29:31- 16
Arenas	Zulema	PER	15.11.95	169/58	3kSt	9:52.32	9:52.88- 16
Argüelles	Yariagnis	CUB	18.4.84	173/55	LJ	6.56i, 6.49	6.70A- 15, 6.66- 09
Aristarkhova	Natalya	RUS	31.10.89	163/46	3kSt	9:46.79	9:30.64- 13
Arndt	Mareike	GER	29.1.92	185/70	Hep	6106	5765- 16
Arneton	Heather	FRA-Y	27.7.02	174/57	LJ	6.57i, 6.56	6.11, 6.45w- 18
* Arrafi	Rabab	MAR	12.1.91	167/54	1500	4:01.75	4:02.71- 14
Arrieta	Olatz	ESP	1.12.90	176/70	LJ	6.41, 6.49w	6.61A, 6.37- 16
Arteil	Laura	FRA	9.10.93	170/61	Hep	6050	5812- 14
Artymata	Eleni	CYP	16.5.86	178/58	400	51.61	
* Arzamasova	Marina	BLR	17.12.87	173/57	800	2:01.92	1:57.54- 15
Asada	Chiaki	JPN	21.1.91		20kW	1:32:12	1:30:44- 16
Asefa	Sutume	ETH	11.12.94	153/42	HMar	68:40	68:47- 15
Asenjo	Sabina	ESP	3.8.86	181/95	DT	61.07	61.89- 16
* Asher-Smith	Dina	GBR	4.12.95	165/55	100	11.13	10.99- 15
					200	22.22	22.07- 15
* Ashley	Whitney	USA	18.2.89	183/93	SP	17.60	17.62i- 16, 17.00- 14
					DT	63.85	64.80- 15
Assani Issouf	Jeanine	FRA	17.8.92	169/57	TJ	14.39, 14.48w	14.40- 16
* Assefa	Meskerem	ETH	20.9.85	155/43	HMar	67:42	69:10- 14
					Mar	2:24:18	2:25:11- 15
* Assefa	Sofia	ETH	14.11.87	171/58	5000	14:56.37	15:59.74- 07
					3kSt	9:07.06	9:09.00- 12
Atcho	Sarah	SUI	1.6.95	180/63	100	11.33, 11.23w	11.62- 15
					200	22.90	23.30- 16
* Atkins	Joanna	USA	31.1.89	180/64	100	11.27, 11.21w	11.02- 14, 10.99w- 16
					200	22.74, 22.54w	22.27, 22.19w- 14
* Augusto	Jéssica	POR	8.11.81	165/46	Mar	2:25:30	2:24:25- 14
Augustyniak	Lidia	POL	14.5.94	187/84	DT	58.62	59.36- 16
Austin	Caroline	USA	1.7.91	158/52	3kSt	9:51.38	10:05.04- 16
Auzenne	Micha	USA	10.6.95	161/52	100h	12.97A, 12.95Aw, 13.19	13.27, 13.18w- 16
Avancini	Lívia	BRA	8.5.92		SP	17.12	16.47- 16
Avdeyeva	Anna	RUS	6.4.85	171/100	SP	18.05	20.07- 09
* Ayana	Almaz	ETH	21.11.91	165/50	5000	14:40.35	14:12.59- 16
10000	30:16.32		29:17.45- 16		HMar	67:12	
Ayele	Gebeyanesh	ETH	1.5.95		10000	31:58.23	33:22.5- 15
Azevedo	Cátia	POR	9.3.94	170/50	400	51.90	51.63- 16
* Bahta	Meraf	SWE	24.6.89	177/51	1500	4:00.49	4:01.34- 14
3000	8:37.50		8:43.08- 16		10000	31:13.06	33:11.45- 16
Baird	Kadecia	GUY	24.2.95	167/52	200	23.03	23.38- 16, 23.13w- 14
^ Baisden	Kendall	USA	5.3.95	176/61	200	23.03	22.80- 15
					400	51.90	50.46- 14
Bakker	Sharona	NED	12.4.90	170/63	100h	12.97, 12.81w	12.85- 14

Name		Nat	Born	Ht/Wt	Event	2017 Mark	Pre-2017 Best
Balciunaite	Egle	LTU	31.10.88	175/60	800	2:00.48	1:59.29- 10
Baldwin	Jacquelyn	USA	17.1.96	163/52	200	22.98	23.71- 16
Balouris	Elaina	USA	17.12.91	173/52	10000	32:34.73	32:27.28- 16
^ Balta	Ksenija	EST	1.11.86	168/53	LJ	6.79i	6.87i- 09, 6.87- 10
Baluyeva	Natalya	RUS	24.12.92		HJ	1.88i	1.88i- 16
Bambara	Laëtitia	BUR	30.3.84	180/75	HT	65.04	68.59- 16
Bamgbose ¶	Margaret	NGR	19.10.93	162/52	400	51.57	51.11- 16
Bani	Zahra	ITA	31.12.79	173/71	JT	59.28	62.75- 05
* Baptiste	Kelly-Ann	TTO	14.10.86	160/54	100	10.88	10.84- 10, 10.83dq- 13
Barber	Alana	NZL	8.7.87	163/52	20kW	1:32:23	1:32:48- 16
Barber	Jade	USA	4.4.93	170/64	100h	13.12, 12.94w	12.85, 12.70w- 15
Barber	Kaila	USA	4.4.93	163/54	400h	56.11	55.53- 16
^ Barber	Mikele	USA	4.10.80	160/50	100	11.16	11.02- 07, 10.96w- 11
					400	52.00	50.63- 01
Barbosa	Vera	POR	13.1.89	168/58	400h	56.73A, 56.86	55.22- 12
Barman	Swapna	IND	29.10.96	164/52	HJ	1.87	1.78- 14
					Hep	5942	5400- 14
Barnes	Aaliyah	USA	17.2.95		200	22.99w	23.31- 15
Barnett	Sharrika	USA	16.4.97	168/52	400	51.67	52.25- 15
Barnett	Tara-Sue	JAM	9.10.93	178/81	DT	61.66	61.28- 16
Barowski	Cecilia	USA	7.12.92	170/59	800	2:00.90	2:02.14- 14
Barrett	Alicia	GBR-J	25.3.98	165/55	100h	13.07	13.15- 16
Barrett	Brigetta	USA	24.12.90	183/64	HJ	1.91	2.04- 13
Barrett	Tessa	USA	9.2.96	160/48	5000	15:28.99i	15:46.08i, 16:06.19- 16
Barsosio	Agnes	KEN	5.8.82	159/44	HMar	68:21	70:50- 15
					Mar	2:20:59	2:24:03- 13
Barsosio	Stella	KEN	12.3.93		HMar	69:31	72:18- 16
					Mar	2:28:14	2:33:13- 16
* Bartoletta	Tianna	USA	30.8.85	168/60	100	11.04	10.78- 16
					LJ	7.01, 7.05w	7.17- 16
Bass	Gina	GAM	3.5.95	164/52	200	22.98	22.92- 16
Bauer	Katharina	GER	12.6.90	179/68	PV	4.42	4.65- 15
Baumann	Jackie	GER	24.8.95	172/57	400h	55.72	56.19- 16
Baumgart	Iga	POL	11.4.89	178/57	400	51.71	52.02- 15
Bauschke	Melanie	GER	14.7.88	178/62	LJ	6.61	6.83- 09
Baxter	Rachel	USA-J	5.4.99	163/52	PV	4.41	4.34- 16
Baylark	Jada	USA	17.10.97		100	11.38, 11.19w	11.73- 16
Bazolo	Lorène	POR	4.5.83	170/53	100	11.37, 11.16w	11.21- 16
Beahan	Brianna	AUS	1.11.91	168/57	100h	13.06, 12.96w	13.03- 16
^ Beard	Jessica	USA	8.1.89	168/57	400	50.85	50.56- 09
Beckles	Kierre	BAR	21.5.90	169/54	100h	13.14	12.88- 15
Beesley	Meghan	GBR	15.11.89	167/63	400h	56.14	54.52- 15
^ Beitia	Ruth	ESP	1.4.79	192/71	HJ	1.98i, 1.94	2.01- 07
Bekele	Ashete	ETH	17.4.88	169/52	Mar	2:25:57	2:23:43- 15
* Bekele	Tadelech	ETH	11.4.91	154/40	HMar	70:13+	68:38- 13
					Mar	2:21:54	2:22:51- 15
Bekh	Maryna	UKR	18.7.95	174/59	LJ	6.71i, 6.58, 6.63w	6.93- 16
Belachew	Agrie	ETH-J	20.1.99	164/48	3kSt	9:41.73	9:37.17- 16
^ Belete	Mimi	BRN	9.6.88	169/55	5000	15:26.49	14:54.71- 15
10k	32:46.74				HMar	69:15	
Beletew	Yehualye	ETH-J	31.7.98	165/52	20kW	1:32:40A	1:31:58- 16
Belibasáki	María	GRE	19.6.91	174/54	200	23.00, 22.6h	23.03- 16
Bell	Alexandra	GBR	4.11.92	166/55	800	2:00.62	2:00.53- 16
Bell	Rolanda	PAN	27.10.87	160/48	3kSt	9:52.68	9:47.16- 15
Belle	Tia Adana	BAR	16.6.96	178/59	400h	55.42	55.82- 16
Bendrat	Stephanie	AUT	5.3.91	164/52	100h	13.14	13.11- 16
* Bengtsson	Angelica	SWE	8.7.93	164/53	PV	4.65	4.70- 15
Bennett	Taylor	USA	15.1.97	170/59	100	11.34, 11.19w	11.33- 16
					200	22.87, 22.47w	22.71- 16
Bergrath	Dana	GER	24.4.94	168/70	JT	56.96	54.96- 16
Berings	Eline	BEL	28.5.86	162/53	100h	13.02	12.87- 14
Beriso	Amane	ETH	13.10.91	165/52	HMar	69:40+	68:43- 15
					Mar	2:22:15	2:20:48- 16
Bernard	Maria	CAN	6.4.93	165/53	3kSt	9:43.63	9:44.81- 16
* Berry	Gwen	USA	29.6.89	176/80	HT	76.77	73.81- 13
Bertoni	Francesca	ITA	29.12.93	163/48	3kSt	9:43.80	9:58.10- 16
Bettiche	Amina	ALG	14.12.87	161/44	3kSt	9:25.90	9:29.20- 14
Bian Ka		CHN	5.1.93	182/115	SP	18.18	18.71- 15
Bing	Portia	NZL	17.4.93	179/65	Hep	5752	6102- 15
* Bingson	Amanda	USA	20.2.90	170/89	HT	72.06	75.73- 13
Binns	Isheka	JAM	9.1.96	175/77	DT	58.84	53.62- 16

Name		Nat	Born	Ht/Wt	Event	2017 Mark	Pre-2017 Best
Biryukova	Svetlana	RUS	1.4.91	180/72	LJ	6.68	6.98i- 14, 6.72, 6.85w- 12
Bishop	Melissa	CAN	5.8.88	173/57	800	1:57.01	1:57.02- 16
Black	Symone	USA	26.10.95	158/50	400h	56.01	56.03- 16
Blake	Ashlie	USA	7.6.96	178/105	SP	17.49	16.50i- 16, 15.87- 12
Blanden	Courtney	USA	12.3.96	168/52	200	23.01	23.79- 16
Block	Freya	USA	6.2.95	168/82	HT	66.66	60.89- 16
Blundell	Jenny	AUS	9.5.94	164/49	1500	4:07.72	4:04.62- 16
					1M	4:28.82	4:36.5- 14
Bobocea	Claudia	ROU	11.6.92	176/53	1500	4:06.33	4:08.64- 16
1M	4:25.89				3000	8:51.58i	9:03.42i, 9:11.39- 15
Bobocel	Ancuta	ROU	3.10.87	163/52	10000	32:18.93	
Boekelman	Melissa	NED	11.5.89	176/86	SP	18.66	18.36- 16
Bogdán	Annabella	HUN	7.4.92		JT	58.79	56.99- 16
Böhm	Djamila	GER	15.7.94	175/58	400h	56.92	57.75- 16
Bonilla	Magaly	ECU	8.2.92	152/54	20kW	1:32:44	1:34:25- 16
Boons	Eefje	NED	18.7.94	176/68	100h	12.98	13.07- 16
* Borel	Cleopatra	TTO	10.3.79	168/93	SP	17.96	19.42- 11
Boreman	Madison	USA-J	10.7.98	170/57	3kSt	9:46.48	
Borge	Sigrid	NOR	3.12.95	181/82	JT	63.28	59.33- 16
Borges	Fernanda Raquel	BRA	26.7.88	165/65	DT	62.30	64.01- 14
Borisevich	Darya	BLR	6.4.90	170/52	1500	4:07.79	4:08.95- 16
Borovska	Nadiya	UKR	25.2.81	163/50	20kW	1:30:26	1:30:03- 12
Boss	Logan	USA	4.8.97	173/61	HJ	1.90i, 1.89	1.82- 16
Botlogetswe	Christine	BOT	1.10.95	172/55	400	51.82A, 52.71	52.15A, 52.37- 16
* Bougard	Erica	USA	26.7.93	168/57	100h	12.93, 12.90w	12.99- 15
HJ 1.92	1.88- 15	LJ	6.59		6.39- 13	Hep 6557	6288- 15
* Bowie	Tori	USA	27.8.90	175/61	100	10.85, 10.80w	10.78- 16, 10.72w- 15
			200	21.77	21.99- 16		
* Bradshaw	Holly	GBR	2.11.91	175/68	PV	4.81	4.87i, 4.71- 12
Bremser	Julia	GER	27.4.82	176/78	DT	56.25	59.84- 11
Bridge	Gemma	GBR	17.5.93		20kW	1:32:33	
Brisco	Mikiah	USA	14.7.96	165/54	100	10.96	11.24- 16
					100h	12.85	13.10, 13.02w- 16
Brissett	Chanel	USA-J	10.8.99	163/52	100h	13.12	12.95- 16
Britton	Evonne	USA	10.10.91	173/59	100h	12.92A, 12.97, 12.83w	12.87- 16
Brockington	Tyler	USA	6.2.94	171/57	400h	55.97	56.45- 16
Brodatskaya	Sofiya	RUS	4.10.95		20kW	1:26:27	1:32:02- 15
* Broersen	Nadine	NED	29.4.90	171/62	Hep	6326	6539- 14
Bromfield	Junelle	JAM-J	8.2.98	176/59	400	52.05	51.74- 16
Brooks	Taliyah	USA	8.2.95	176/60	100h	13.14	13.21, 13.16w- 16
LJ	6.50		6.39- 16		Hep	6099	5991- 16
Brown	Aaliyah	USA	6.1.95	173/60	100	11.01	11.08- 15
					200	22.79, 22.60w	22.76, 22.66w- 15
Brown	Brittany	USA	18.4.95	164/55	200	22.55, 22.30w	22.89- 15
Brown	Ce'aira	USA	4.11.93	168/55	800	2:00.84	2:02.82- 16
Brown	Felicia	USA	27.10.93	168/57	200	22.60	22.26, 22.19w- 16
Brown	India	USA	29.1.96	165/64	100	11.34, 11.24w	11.43- 15
					200	22.92	23.26, 23/08w- 16
Brown	Kristen	USA	26.5.92	167/57	PV	4.55Ai, 4.51	4.70- 16
Brown	Leigha	USA	19.9.94	183/65	Hep	5852(w)	5677- 16
Brown	Sashel	JAM	20.1.94	165/52	400h	56.20	57.34- 15
Brown	Serena	BAH-J	15.9.98		DT	56.84	52.73- 16
Bruce	Stephanie	USA	14.1.84	165/49	10000	31:59.88	32:14.42- 16
* Brume	Ese	NGR	20.1.96	167/58	LJ	6.64, 6.68w	6.83- 16
Bryan	Danique	JAM	5.10.95		TJ	13.68w	12.41- 16
Bryan	Lucy	GBR	22.5.95	162/48	PV	4.40i, 4.40	4.40- 13
Bryant	Dezerea	USA	27.4.93	157/50	100	11.27, 11.20w	11.00- 15, 10.96w- 14
					200	22.95	22.18- 15
Bryzhina	Anastasiya	UKR-J	9.1.98	172/51	400	51.89	53.45- 16
Buchanan	Leya	CAN	17.8.96	180/65	100	11.15w	11.49- 16, 11.46w- 15
* Büchel	Selina	SUI	26.7.91	168/55	800	1:59.46	1:57.95- 15
Buchelnikova	Marina	RUS	8.2.94		LJ	6.59i, 6.52	6.59- 16
* Büchler	Nicole	SUI	17.12.83	160/56	PV	4.73	4.80i, 4.78- 16
^ Buckman	Zoe	AUS	21.12.88	172/55	1500	4:04.93	4:03.22- 16
Bugakova	Alyona	RUS	24.4.97	187/95	SP	18.06	17.94- 16
Bühler	Anna	GER	3.6.97	183/61	LJ	6.55, 6.62w	6.47- 16
Bui Thi Thu Thao		VIE	29.4.92	162/53	LJ	6.68	6.65- 15
					TJ	13.68	13.14- 16
^ Bujin	Cristina	ROU	12.4.88	171/52	TJ	13.86i, 13.85	14.42- 09
* Bulgakova	Anna	RUS	17.1.88	173/90	HT	67.31	76.17- 13

Name		Nat	Born	Ht/Wt	Event	2017 Mark	Pre-2017 Best
Bulo	Shuru	ETH-J	27.6.98	159/44	3000	8:57.46	9:01.12A- 15
					5000	14:58.20	15:13.07- 16
* Bunch	Dani	USA	16.5.91	178/95	SP	19.64	18.89- 15
Burchell	Remona	JAM	15.9.91	166/52	100	11.09	11.03, 10.95w- 14
* Burka	Gelete	ETH	23.1.86	165/45	3000	8:43.68	8:25.92- 06
					5000	15:06.01	14:31.20- 07
					10000	30:40.87	30:26.66- 16
					HMar	68:18	69:32- 16
* Burks	Quanesha	USA	15.3.95	160/55	100	11.21, 11.18w	11.52- 14
					LJ	6.83, 6.90w	6.93A, 6.84, 6.91w- 15
Burla	Serena	USA	29.7.82	158/45	Mar	2:26:53	2:28:01- 13
Burmistrova	Yekaterina	RUS	18.8.90		SP	17.14	17.02- 16
					DT	56.80	57.32- 15
Burnett	Alysha	AUS	4.1.97		HJ	1.86	1.83- 16
					Hep	5835	5547- 16
Burnett	Kathleen	USA	10.7.88		50kW	4:21:51	4:39:42- 14
Burton	Rushelle	JAM	4.12.97	175/61	100h	12.65	12.87- 16
Buscomb	Camille	NZL	11.7.90	164/51	5000	15:19.81	15:28.78- 15
					10000	31:45.02	32:26.36- 15
Bushkova	Aleksandra	RUS	13.1.97		20kW	1:32:57	
Busienei	Selah	KEN	27.12.91	177/57	1500	4:07.76	4:06.28A- 16
Butterworth	Alycia	CAN	1.10.92	170/55	3kSt	9:44.13	9:41.26- 16
Butterworth	Lindsey	CAN	27.9.92	175/60	800	2:02.13	2:02.67- 16
Cá	Liliana	POR	5.11.86		DT	56.52	59.33- 10
* Caballero	Denia	CUB	13.1.90	175/73	DT	67.04	70.65- 15
Caballero	Yoci	PER	2.2.93		50kW	4:49:45	
Cabecinha	Ana	POR	29.4.84	168/52	20kW	1:28:57	1:27:46- 08
* Cachová	Katerina	CZE	26.2.90	173/63	LJ	6.51w	6.40- 08
					Hep	6337(w)	6328- 16
Caicedo	Maribel	ECU-J	1.4.98	168/61	100h	13.19A, 13.04Aw	13.41A- 16, 13.47- 15
Caldwell	Kayla	USA	19.6.91	163/57	PV	4.35i	4.50i- 15, 4.40A- 13
^ Calvert-Powell	Schillonie	JAM	27.7.88	166/57	100	10.94	11.05- 11
Camacho-Quinn	Jasmine	PUR	21.8.96	180/73	200	22.88	22.87, 22.70w- 16
					100h	12.58	12.69, 12.54w- 16
Cameron	Lloydricia	USA	8.4.96	186/111	SP	17.47i, 17.39	17.06- 16
* Campbell	Amber	USA	5.6.81	170/91	HT	73.58	74.03- 16
* Campbell-Brown	Veronica	JAM	15.5.82	163/61	100	10.84	10.76- 11
					200	22.60	21.74- 08
* Can	Yasemin	TUR	11.12.96	166/49	3000	8:38.5e+	8:48.8+- 16
					5000	14:36.82	14:37.61- 16
					10000	31:18.20	30:26.41- 16
Cano	Amanda	ESP	19.8.94	166/51	20kW	1:31:50	1:35:14- 15
Cansian	Lidia	BRA	8.1.92	180/100	DT	57.66	57.12- 16
Capponcelli	Serena	ITA	24.1.89	183/68	HJ	1.89i, 1.86	1.87- 08
Caravelli	Marzia	ITA	23.10.81	177/63	400h	55.83	55.69- 16
Card	Kelsey	USA	20.8.92	178/116	SP	17.93	18.56- 16
					DT	61.16	63.52- 16
Carrillo	Yeseida	COL	22.10.93	168/52	20kW	1:31:14	1:32:45- 16
Carson	Savannah	USA	30.3.95	163/50	LJ	6.66	6.44- 16
Carter	Destiny	USA	9.10.92	170/55	100	11.05	11.35, 11.11w- 16
					200	22.61	22.97, 22.41w- 16
					LJ	6.55	6.51- 16
* Carter	Kori	USA	3.6.92	165/57	100h	12.78	12.76- 13
					400h	52.95	53.21- 13
* Carter	Michelle	USA	12.10.85	175/107	SP	19.34	20.63- 16
Carvalho	Marisa Vaz	POR-J	19.11.99		Hep	5755	
Casetta	Belén	ARG	26.9.94	163/50	3kSt	9:25.99	9:42.93- 16
Castells	Berta	ESP	24.1.84	174/79	HT	70.26	70.52- 16
* Castlin	Kristi	USA	7.7.88	170/75	100h	12.61	12.50- 16, 12.48w- 12
Castro	Ángela	BOL	21.2.93	160/54	20kW	1:31:34, 1:32:35.2t	1:30:33- 16
Caudery	Molly	GBR-Y	17.3.00	166/57	PV	4.35	4.06- 16
Cavaleti	Giovana	BRA	13.1.89	181/70	Hep	5751	5808- 16
Cérival	Jessica	FRA	20.1.82	187/120	SP	17.76i, 17.50	17.99i- 11, 17.87- 09
Cernjul	Marusa	SLO	30.6.92	177/56	HJ	1.91	1.93- 16
Cestonaro	Ottavia	ITA	12.1.95	176/68	TJ	13.66	13.76- 15
Chaboudez	Aurélie	FRA	9.5.93	173/60	400h	56.93	55.51- 15
Chacón	Estefany	VEN	1.11.97	170/66	JT	57.95	55.16- 15
Chambers	Kendra	USA	11.9.90	161/48	800	2:01.10	2:00.76- 16
Chambers	Verone	JAM	16.12.88		400	51.70	52.28- 12
Changwony	Purity	KEN	-.90	157/42	Mar	2:27:52	2:29:32- 16
Chapman	Rebecca	GBR	27.9.92		LJ	6.54	6.23i- 15, 6.17- 14
Charlton	Devynne	BAH	26.11.95	161/54	100h	12.74, 12.67w	13.00- 15
Chebet	Esther	UGA	10.9.97	160/48	1500	4:06.34	4:17.72- 15
					1M	4:28.16	

Name		Nat	Born	Ht/Wt	Event	2017 Mark	Pre-2017 Best
* Chebet	Winny	KEN	20.12.90	165/50	800	1:58.13	1:59.30- 13
1500	3:59.16		4:02.66- 16		1M	4:19.55	
Cheever	Jamie	USA	28.2.87	175/55	3kSt	9:49.82	9:29.13- 13
Chekole	Yeshi	ERI	.97		HMar	69:13	72:17- 15
Chekwel	Juliet	UGA	25.5.90	165/52	10000	31:43.40	31:37.99- 16
Chelangat	Mercyline	UGA	17.12.97	160/45	5000	15:09.45	15:34.09- 16
					10000	31:40.48	
Chelangat	Sheila	KEN-J	11.4.98	158/52	5000	14:54.66	15:42.0A- 16
Chelimo	Edith	KEN	16.7.86	165/50	HMar	65:52	69:45- 16
Chelimo	Joan	KEN	10.11.88		HMar	66:25	71:52- 14
* Chelimo	Rose	BRN	12.7.89	162/45	10000	31:37.81	
HMar	68:37		68:08- 16		Mar	2:27:11, 2:22:51dh	2:24:14- 16
Cheluke	Bone	ETH-J	11.11.98		1500	4:08.64	
Chemnung	Loice	KEN	22.2.97	158/42	1500	4:06.3A	4:24.08- 15
* Chemutai	Fancy	KEN	20.3.95	163/52	HMar	65:36	
Chemutai	Peruth	UGA-J	10.7.99	165/50	3kSt	9:27.72	9:31.03- 16
Chen Chen		CHN	19.1.96		JT	56.46	52.72- 14
Chen Chen		CHN	25.8.95		20kW	1:29:19	1:34:48- 16
Chen Qiaoling		CHN-J	22.11.99		PV	4.40	4.30- 16
Chen Ting		CHN	28.8.97		TJ	13.83i, 13.60	13.85- 16
* Chen Yang		CHN	10.7.91	180/97	DT	62.90	63.61- 16
Chen Zhen		CHN	3.11.94		20kW	1:33:27	1:32:28- 13
Chenah	Rima	ALG	11.2.96	160/52	3kSt	9:44.42	10:06.96- 16
* Chepchirchir	Sarah	KEN	27.7.84	165/49	Mar	2:19:47	2:24:13- 16
Chepkemoi	Caroline	KEN	1.3.93	158/45	1500	4:08.84	4:05.31- 15
					1M	4:27.79	
Chepkemoi	Joan	KEN	24.11.93	163/48	3kSt	9:20.22	9:42.77- 15
* Chepkoech	Beatrice	KEN	6.7.91	171/57	1500	4:03.2A	4:03.28- 15
3000	8:28.66	see St	5000	14:39.33	3kSt	8:59.84	9:10.86- 16
Chepkorir	Naomi Tuei	KEN	.93		Mar	2:27:37	2:30:14- 16
Chepkosgei	Pamela Rotich	KEN	.84		Mar	2:27:48	2:28:06- 16
* Chepkurui	Caroline	KEN	12.3.90	169/52	3kSt	9:31.07	9:28.81- 16
Chepngetich	Rosefline	KEN	17.6.97	166/55	3kSt	9:28.63	9:25.91- 15
Chepngetich	Ruth	KEN	8.8.94	160/44	HMar	66:19	74:13- 16
					Mar	2:22:36	
Chepngetich ¶	Rosefline	KEN	17.6.97	166/55	3kSt	9:20.69dq	9:25.91- 15
* Cheptai	Irene	KEN	4.2.92	160/45	5000	14:47.11	14:43.42- 16
3000	8:44.2+		8:48.03- 15		10000	31:21.11	31:15.38- 16
Cheptanui	Anne	KEN	4.11.82		Mar	2:27:18	2:28:22- 10
Cheromei	Lydia	KEN	11.5.77	162/47?	Mar	2:23:31	2:21:30- 12
* Cherono	Gladys	KEN	12.5.83	161/45	HMar	67:01	66:07- 16
					Mar	2:20:23	2:19:25- 15
Cherotich	Joyline	KEN-J	22.3.98	160/44	3000	8:52.59	
Cheruiyot	Lucy	KEN	4.1.97		HMar	67:23	68:17- 16
* Cheruiyot	Vivian	KEN	11.9.83	155/38	HMar	67:44dh	67:54- 16
					Mar	2:23:35	0
Cheruto	Lydia	KEN-Y	23.11.00	162/48	800	2:02.06A	
Chesang	Stella	UGA	1.12.96	161/47	5000	15:17.91	15:10.30- 16
Chesire	Gladys	KEN	20.2.93	162/47	HMar	67:49	66:57- 16
					Mar	2:24:51	
* Chespol	Celliphine	KEN-J	23.3.99	163/48	3kSt	8:58.78	9:24.73- 16
* Cheyech	Filomena	KEN	5.7.82	165/49	Mar	2:21:22	2:22:44- 14
Chiappe	Fiorella	ARG	1.1.96	174/59	400h	57.02	58.90- 16
					Hep	5815	5568- 14
Chigbolu	Maria Benedicta	ITA	27.7.89	172/53	400	51.87	51.67- 15
Chuaemaroeng	Parinya	THA	16.12.97	165/50	TJ	13.63	12.78- 16
Chumachenko	Yuliya	UKR	2.10.94	185/65	HJ	1.90i, 1.89	1.93i- 16, 1.92- 15
Chumba	Eunice	BRN	23.5.93	160/46	HMar	66:11	68:04- 16
					Mar	2:24:27	2:25:00- 16
* Cichocka	Angelika	POL	15.3.88	169/54	800	1:58.41	1:58.97- 16
1000	2:36.51 2:34.84- 16	1500	4:01.61	4:03.06- 15	1M	4:19.58	4:25.39- 16
Cieslak	Danuta	POL	24.12.89	167/58	1500	4:07.38	4:06.58- 16
Clark	Megan	USA	10.6.94	167/57	PV	4.60	4.63- 16
Clark	Zoey	GBR	25.10.94	168/54	400	51.81	52.58- 16
Clarke	Kayelle	TTO	28.2.96	175/59	200	22.97, 22.94w	23.16A, 23.12w- 16
Clarke	Rosie	GBR	17.11.91	170/57	3000	8:51.02	9:10.99i- 14, 9:15.04- 16
					3kSt	9:32.10	9:51.97- 16
Claude-Boxberger	Ophélie	FRA	18.10.88	169/54	3kSt	9:48.09	9:34.96- 16
Claxton	Grace	PUR	19.8.93	167/52	400h	56.10	55.85- 16
Clay	Raven	USA	5.10.90	168/59	100h	12.99, 12.87w	12.93- 16
Clayton	Rushell	JAM	18.10.92	175/61	400h	56.61	56.29- 15

Name		Nat	Born	Ht/Wt	Event	2017 Mark	Pre-2017 Best
Cléirigh Büttner	Síofra	IRL	21.7.95	159/50	800	2:02.11	2:01.98- 16
Clerveaux	Vanessa	HAI	17.6.94	170.59	100h	13.13, 13.01w	13.15- 16
Cliff	Rachel	CAN	1.4.88	163/47	3000	8:57.15	9:50.59- 06
					10000	32:00.03	32:21.98- 16
Clute	Sydney	USA	15.11.93	170/58	PV	4.55	4.42- 16
* Coburn	Emma	USA	19.10.90	173/55	3000	8:48.60	8:59.76- 15
					3kSt	9:02.58	9:07.63- 16
Cockrell	Anna	USA	28.8.97	178/	100h	12.89	13.17- 16
					400h	55.14	55.20- 16
Collins	Shania	USA	14.11.96	171/59	200	22.81	23.23- 15
Collinsworth	Shea	USA	18.2.95	175/59	800	2:01.42i, 2:01.51	2:02.83- 16
Comba	Rocío	ARG	14.7.87	175/78	DT	57.01	62.77- 13
Coneo	Muriel	COL	15.3.87	160/49	5000	15:26.18	16:35.71- 14
Conley	Alyssa	RSA	27.4.91	175/60	200	22.94A, 23.03	22.84- 16
Conley	Kim	USA	14.3.86	160/49	5000	15:14.57	15:08.61- 14
					10000	31:35.88	31:48.71- 14
Conley	Sydney	USA	11.12.93	176/60	100	11.41A, 11.24w	11.54, 11.28w- 15
					LJ	6.66, 6.81w	6.48, 6.60w- 15
Contion	Maeva	FRA	31.5.92	167/55	400h	56.52	56.03- 15
Coombs	Latavia	JAM	1.1.95		TJ	13.56A	12.68- 14
^ Costa	Keila	BRA	6.2.83	170/62	TJ	13.58w	14.58- 13, 15.10w- 07
Costa	Susana	POR	22.9.84	178/65	TJ	14.35	14.34- 16
Costello	Liz	USA	23.2.88	160/45	10000	32:28.05	31:43.79- 16
Courtney	Melissa	GBR	30.8.93	170/54	1500	4:05.82+	4:07.55- 16
					1M	4:23.15	4:35.48i- 15, 4:52.11- 07
					3000	8:43.72mx	9:03.63mx, 9:13.87- 16
					5000	15:28.95	16:13.45- 15
Coutinho	Geisa	BRA	1.6.80	161/55	400	51.91, 51.9h	51.08- 11
Coward	Jackie	USA	5.11.89	167/55	100h	13.02	12.68- 16, 12.67w- 13
* Craft	Shanice	GER	15.5.93	185/89	DT	63.18	65.88- 14
* Cragg	Amy	USA	21.1.84	163/46	10000	31:17.20	31:10.69- 12
					HMar	68:27	69:50- 16
					Mar	2:27:18	2:27:03- 14
Crew	Brittany	CAN	3.6.94	176/111	SP	18.58	18.06- 16
Cueva	Brianna	USA	6.6.95	175/84	DT	56.08	54.96- 16
Cunliffe	Hannah	USA	9.1.96	169/55	100	11.11, 11.06w	10.99- 16
					200	22.53i, 22.60	22.49- 16
Cunningham	Gabriele	USA-J	22.2.98	165/52	100	11.26	11.64- 16
* Cunningham	Vashti	USA-J	18.1.98	185/66	HJ	1.99	1.99i, 1.97- 16
Czáková	Mária	SVK	2.10.88	165/60	20kW	1:33:26	1:32:23- 15
da Silva	Izabela	BRA	2.8.95	178/95	DT	56.16	58.81- 15
da Silva	Karla	BRA	12.11.84	168/58	PV	4.33	4.53- 13
da Silva	Tânia	BRA	17.12.86	178/59	TJ	14.13	14.11- 07
Daba	Tejitu	BRN	20.8.91	162/44	HMar	68:21	71:17- 16
Dabrowska	Martyna	POL	5.4.94	174/50	400	52.01	52.23- 15
* Dadic	Ivona	AUT	29.12.93	179/65	HJ	1.87i	1.80- 12
					LJ	6.41i, 6.37	6.49- 16
					Hep	6417	6408- 16
Dadzie	Elizabeth	GHA	21.3.93	183/66	Hep	5832A	5730- 16
^ Dahlgren	Jennifer	ARG	27.8.84	180/115	HT	70.18	73.74- 10
Damerius	Birte	GER	13.12.91	170/57	TJ	13.69	13.60- 16
Daniels	Katelyn	USA	11.4.95	178/93	DT	58.75	60.54- 16
Daniels	Teahna	USA	27.3.97	165/55	100	11.06	11.21- 16, 11.15w- 15
					200	22.99, 22.95w	23.56- 15
Danois	Maeva	FRA	10.3.93	165/53	3kSt	9:41.19	9:40.19- 16
* Daska	Mamitu	ETH	16.10.83	164/45	HMar	69:01	66:28- 15
					Mar	2:28:08	2:21:59- 11
Dauwens	Axelle	BEL	1.12.90	171/62	400h	56.75	55.56- 14
David	Yanis	FRA	12.12.97	169/58	LJ	6.56	6.48- 16
					TJ	13.93i, 13.78, 13.92w	13.65-15
Davies	Bethan	GBR	7.11.90		20kW	1:33:04	1:33:48- 16
Davis	Kevona	JAM-Y	20.12.01	170/60	100	11.24	11.63- 16
					200	22.97	23.91- 16
Davis	Tara	USA-J	20.5.99	168/59	100h	12.95, 12.83w	13.48- 15
					LJ	6.73, 6.80w	6.41A- 15, 6.27, 6.31w- 16
* Day	Christine	JAM	23.8.86	168/51	400	51.25	50.14- 15
^ Day-Monroe	Sharon	USA	9.6.85	175/70	Hep	6421	6550- 13
de Carvalho	Tatiele Roberta	BRA	22.11.89	156/50	10000	32:35.86	32:09.14- 16
De Coninck	Nenah	BEL	2.9.96	171/57	400h	56.99	56.27- 16
de Lima	Jaílma	BRA	31.12.86	174/65	400h	56.76	56.00- 11
de Morais	Andressa	BRA	21.12.90	178/100	DT	64.68	64.21- 12
* de Sena	Erica	BRA	3.5.85	168/55	20kW	1:26:59	1:27:18- 16
de Souza	Tamara	BRA	8.9.93	185/76	Hep	6040	5962- 14
de Witte	Laura	NED	7.8.95	173/61	400	52.15	52.70- 16

Name		Nat	Born	Ht/Wt	Event	2017 Mark	Pre-2017 Best
de Witte	Lisanne	NED	10.9.92	175/65	400	51.71	52.14- 16
Dearman	Emilyn	USA	1.1.95	173/62	Hep	5924w, 5625	5363- 16
Debebe	Zinash	ETH	12.10.96		10000	31:29.71	
* Defar	Meseret	ETH	19.11.83	155/42	HMar	68:46	66:09- 13
Degefa	Behenu	ETH-J	12.7.99		3000	8:56.1A	
* Degefa	Worknesh	ETH	28.10.90	159/42	HMar	68:10	66:14- 16
					Mar	2:22:36	
Degefu	Beyenu	ETH-J	12.7.99	165/48	5000	15:19.49	
Dekebo	Muliye	ETH-J	13.3.98		HMar	69:10	69:52- 16
^ DeLoach Soukup	Janay	USA	12.10.85	165/59	100h	12.83	12.84- 15
* Demireva	Mirela	BUL	28.9.89	180/58	HJ	1.92	1.97- 16
* Demise	Shure	ETH	21.1.96	168/54	Mar	2:22:57	2:20:59- 15
Deng Linuo		CHN	16.3.92	165/44	TJ	13.76i, 13.53	13.92- 13
* Dereje	Roza	ETH	6.5.97	168/52	HMar	67:23	
					Mar	2:22:43	2:26:18- 16
Dereli	Emel	TUR	25.2.96	181/110	SP	18.04	18.57- 16
Derkach	Dariya	ITA	27.3.93	167/56	TJ	14.06	14.15- 16
Destin	Stacey	USA	7.11.96	168/52	HJ	1.90i	1.81- 16
Detloff	Molli	USA	15.1.96		HT	64.98	60.47- 15
Diallo	Rouguy	FRA	5.2.95	168/52	TJ	13.98, 13.99w	14.20, 14.44w- 14
Diame	Fátima	ESP	22.9.96	170/52	LJ	6.48	6.46- 15
					TJ	14.03	12.83- 16
Diamond	Emily	GBR	11.6.91	173/57	400	51.67	51.23- 16
Diarra	Elea Mariama	FRA	8.3.90	175/56	400	51.92	52.23- 16
* Dibaba	Birhane	ETH	11.9.93	159/44	Mar	2:21:19	2:22:30- 14
* Dibaba	Genzebe	ETH	8.2.91	168/52	800	1:59.37	
1000	2:33.06i		2:35.6+- 15		1500	3:57.82+	3:50.07- 15
1M	4:16.05		4:13.31i, 4:14.30- 16		2000	5:23.75i	5:27.50- 14
3000	8:38.27+		8:16.60i, 8:26.21- 14		5000	14:25.22	14:15.41- 15
* Dibaba	Mare	ETH	20.10.89	152/40	HMar	69:43	67:13- 10
* Dibaba	Tirunesh	ETH	1.10.85	155/44	10000	31:02.69	29:42.56- 16
HMar	66:50		66:56- 13		Mar	2:17:56	2:20:35- 14
Dida	Dera	ETH	26.10.96	155/42	5000	15:07.27	14:42.84- 16
10000	30:56.48				HMar	68:06	
Dincoff	Rachel	USA	24.12.93	180/46	DT	58.48	55.80- 15
* Diriba	Buze	ETH	9.2.94	160/43	3000	8:45.44	8:39.65- 12
* Diro	Etenesh	ETH	10.5.91	169/47	5000	14:40.29	14:33.30- 16
3000	8:45.3+		8:38.32- 16		3kSt	9:13.25	9:14.07- 12
Dobilaite	Simona	LTU	23.5.95	172/62	JT	57.16	54.03- 14
Dominici	Eleonora	ITA	22.2.96		20kW	1:33:32	1:38:22- 16
Domjan	Veronika	SLO	3.9.96	178/94	DT	58.48	60.11- 16
Dong Genmiao		CHN	16.7.94		20kW	1:33:31	1:31:59- 14
Dong Yangzi		CHN	22.10.92		SP	16.94	16.96i, 16.80- 16
Dongmo	Auriole	CMR	3.8.90	173/95	SP	18.37	17.92- 16
^ Dorozhon	Margaryta	ISR	4.9.87	180/75	JT	63.07	64.56- 15
Dorsett	Shaquania	BAH	16.9.97	160/52	400	52.13	52.50- 16
dos Reis	Jéssica Carolina	BRA	17.3.93	160/50	LJ	6.61	6.69- 16
* Doyle	Eilidh	GBR	20.2.87	172/59	400	51.86i, 52.36	51.45i, 51.83- 13
					400h	54.36	54.09- 16
^ Drahotová	Anezka	CZE	22.7.95	183/63	20kW	1:33:18	1:26:53- 15
Draxler	Bonnie	USA	13.10.95	155/48	PV	4.35	4.29- 16
Drisbióti	Antigóni	GRE	21.3.84	162/52	20kW	1:32:03	1:30:56- 16
Du Xiaowei		CHN	11.8.87	180/72	JT	61.24	61.89- 12
Duan Dandan		CHN	23.5.95		20kW	1:28:37	1:32:21- 15
* Dubitskaya	Alyona	BLR	25.1.90	182/77	SP	19.01	19.03- 14
Ducó	Natalia	CHI	31.1.89	177/95	SP	17.99	18.80- 12
Dunajská	Tána	SVK	25.7.92		HJ	1.86	1.78- 09
* Duncan	Kimberlyn	USA	2.8.91	173/59	100	11.03	10.96, 10.94w- 12
					200	22.54, 22.41w	22.19- 12, 21.80w- 13
Dunmore	Makenzie	USA	7.10.97	170/65	200	22.90	23.67- 16
					400	51.42	52.51- 16
Duran	Alina	USA	28.3.90	170/88	HT	67.66	66.79- 16
Dusanova	Nadezhda	UZB	17.11.87	174/56	HJ	1.90	1.96i, 1.95- 09
* Dutkiewicz	Pamela	GER	28.9.91	170/63	100h	12.61	12.85- 16
Duvernay	Prisca	FRA	26.5.91	180/60	HJ	1.88i, 1.87	1.81- 16
Dzindzaletaite	Dovile	LTU	14.7.93	168/58	TJ	14.15	14.23- 15, 14.26w- 14
Ealey	Chase	USA	20.7.94	178/84	SP	17.79	18.46- 16
Ebihara	Yuki	JPN	28.10.85	164/68	JT	61.95	63.80- 15
Ebwea Bile	Marie-José	FRA	7.2.97	178/73	TJ	13.63i, 13.39, 13.69w	13.31- 13
Eccleston	Amanda	USA	18.6.90	160/50	800	2:02.03	2:02.14- 16
1500	4:04.34		4:03.25- 16		5000	15:26.56	15:44.14- 16

Name		Nat	Born	Ht/Wt	Event	2017 Mark	Pre-2017 Best
Eckhardt	Neele	GER	2.7.92	168/52	TJ	14.35	13.93- 16, 13.98w- 14
Edao Rebitu	Bontu	BRN	12.12.97	162/47	5000	15:16.70	15:25.12- 16
Edesa	Workenesh	ETH	11.9.92		Mar	2:26:27	2:24:04- 16
Edwards	Kaela	USA	8.12.93	165/52	1M	4:28.75i	4:32.14i- 16
Edwards	Karelle	CAN	30.3.90	170/55	100h	13.21, 13.04w	13.33- 16, 13.24w- 15
Edwards	Sarah	USA-J	7.7.98		3kSt	9:52.89	
Efraimson	Alexa	USA	20.2.97	170/57	800	2:00.95	2:00.99- 16
1500	4:04.75		4:03.39- 15		1M	4:29.54i	4:27.39- 16
Egbeniyi	Abike	NGR	23.10.94	172/57	400	52.03	54.58- 13
Egwim	Emerald	USA/NGR	27.11.95	167/55	400	51.99	53.70- 15
Ehrhardt	Caroline	CAN	6.2.92		TJ	13.59, 13.83w	13.08- 15
Eke	Nadia	GHA	11.1.93	170/59	TJ	13.93	13.82- 16
Ektova	Irina	KAZ	8.1.87	172/63	TJ	13.77	14.48- 11
Ektova	Yekaterina	KAZ	30.8.92	169/59	TJ	13.76	14.16- 16
Elbe	Jenny	GER	18.4.90	180/62	TJ	14.27i	14.28- 16, 14.38w- 15
Ellis	Brittny	USA	1.9.97	170/57	400	51.66	53.49- 14
* Ellis	Kendall	USA	8.3.96	173/59	200	22.79	23.32- 16
					400	50.00	51.82- 16
Ellward	Agnieszka	POL	26.3.89		50kW	4:41:58	-0-
* Embaye	Axumawit	ETH	18.10.94	160/50	1500	4:09.17+	4:02.35- 14
1500	4:04.95i 4:02.35- 14	1M	4:28.14	4:23.50i, 4:26.84- 15	3000	8:49.52i	8:51.82- 15
Emerson	Niamh	GBR-J	22.4.99	175/60	Hep	6013	0
Emilianov	Alexandra	MDA-J	19.9.99	183/79	DT	57.10	58.09- 16
Emmanuel	Crystal	CAN	27.11.91	170/59	100	11.14, 11.06w	11.26- 16, 11.16w- 13
					200	22.50	22.80- 16
^ England	Hannah	GBR	6.3.87	177/54	800	2:01.23	1:59.66- 12
* Ennaoui	Sofia	POL	30.8.95	158/43	800	2:01.54	2:00.11- 15
1500	4:03.35		4:01.00- 16		3000	8:45.29i	8:49.07i- 16, 8:59.44- 14
^ Eshete	Shitaye	BRN	21.5.90	164/51	10000	31:38.66	30:47.25- 12
					HMar	70:10	70:14- 15
Esquivel	Ximena	MEX	22.8.97	175/57	HJ	1.88	1.90A- 16
Esser	Agnes	CAN	22.8.95	183/86	DT	57.02	57.91- 16
Evangelidou	Natalia	CYP	10.3.91	170/56	800	2:02.14	2:02.10- 16
Evans	Gayon	JAM	15.1.90	158/50	100	11.32, 11.17w	11.24- 16
* Ewen	Maggie	USA	23.9.94	178/79	SP	18.12i, 17.72	16.85i, 16.82- 16
DT	60.51		59.28- 16		HT	74.56	70.50- 16
Eykens	Renée	BEL	8.6.96	171/56	800	2:01.93	2:00.00- 16
* Facey	Simone	JAM	7.5.85	162/53	100	11.04, 11.00w	10.95A- 08, 11.00-16
					200	22.74	22.25- 08
Fagan	Madeline	USA	4.6.96	182/60	HJ	1.93i, 1.91	1.86- 16
Fairchild	Jacqueline	GBR	3.5.89	164/52	800	2:02.09	2:04.92- 16
Falda	Helen	ITA	13.2.96		PV	4.38	4.10i, 4.05- 16
Fantini	Sara	ITA	16.9.97	170/72	HT	68.24	62.44- 16
Fantu	Taye	ETH-J	29.3.99	162/46	1500	4:05.81	4:05.84- 16
					3000	8:50.36i	
Farmer	Erin	USA	11.8.95	183/107	SP	18.12	17.80- 16
Fatherly	Rachel	USA	20.4.94	180/86	SP	17.75	17.27i- 16, 17.15- 15
Fayesa	Aberash	ETH	.95		Mar	2:27:04	2:32:30- 15
Fédronic	Justine	FRA	11.5.91	168/54	800	2:01.36i	1:59.86- 16
Fehringer	Carly	USA	9.11.91	168/93	HT	66.68	65.47- 15
Feldmeier	Brooke	USA	26.1.96	167/55	800	2:01.54	2:03.13- 15
* Felix	Allyson	USA	18.11.85	168/57	100	11.03	10.89- 12
200	22.33		21.69- 12		400	49.65	49.26- 15
Felnagle	Brie	USA	9.12.86	170/57	1M	4:27.27i	4:29.84- 14, 4:28.90irr- 13
					3000	8:52.35i	8:51.38- 12
* Feng Bin		CHN	3.4.94	184/95	DT	64.46	65.14- 16
Fente	Birtukan	ETH	18.6.89	166/50	3kSt	9:33.99	9:24.91- 15
Fetiskina	Tetyana	UKR	11.9.94	172/64	JT	58.33	58.53- 16
Fields	Hannah	USA	4.2.93	174/55	800	2:00.53	2:03.89- 16
1500	4:05.30		4:11.00- 15		1M	4:28.32	4:31.4- 15
Finn	Erin	USA	19.11.94	160/52	5000	15:27.36i	15:23.16i- 16, 15:26.08- 14
					10000	32:00.46	31:51.84- 16
* Fiodorow	Joanna	POL	4.3.89	169/89	HT	75.09	74.39- 14
* Flanagan	Shalane	USA	8.7.81	165/50	5000	14:58.99	14:44.80- 07
10000	31:31.12		30:22.22- 08		Mar	2:26:53	2:21:14- 14
Flink	Sofi	SWE	8.7.95	168/71	JT	58.97	61.96- 13
Folorunso	Ayomide	ITA	17.10.96	170/55	400h	55.63	55.50- 16
Fontanive	Petra	SUI	10.10.88	170/60	400h	54.56	56.09- 15
Forbes	Shashalee	JAM	10.5.96	160/55	100	11.10	11.17- 16
					200	22.71	23.28- 16
Foster	Nicolee	JAM-J	11.1.98	159/50	400h	56.65	56.99- 16

	Name		Nat	Born	Ht/Wt	Event	2017 Mark	Pre-2017 Best
	Fougberg	Charlotta	SWE	19.6.85	165/51	3000	8:55.21i	8:58.56- 14
						3kSt	9:42.14	9:23.96- 14
	Francis	Claudia	USA	14.11.93	165/55	400	52.00	51.55- 16
						400h	56.74	55.55- 16
	Francis	Eden	GBR	19.10.88	178/85	DT	57.53	59.78- 11
*	Francis	Phyllis	USA	4.5.92	178/61	200	22.59	22.50- 16
						400	49.92	49.94- 16
	Franklin	Autumne	USA	20.7.94	162/54	400h	55.78	54.65- 16
	Franklin	Tori	USA	7.10.92	173/55	TJ	14.03	13.66, 13.54- 16
	Fraser	Vanessa	USA	27.7.95	168/52	5000	15:25.48	15:41.64- 16
	Fray	Jazmine	JAM	6.6.97	165/48	800	2:00.69i, 2:01.43	2:03.25- 16
	Freier	Desiree	USA	24.7.96	152/52	PV	4.38	4.45- 14
*	Frerichs	Courtney	USA	18.1.93	170/62	3000	8:53.99	
						3kSt	9:03.77	9:20.92- 16
^	Frizell	Sultana	CAN	24.10.84	183/110	HT	68.01	75.73- 14
	Fu Luna		CHN	3.5.95		TJ	13.59	13.37, 13.59w- 14
	Fujimoto	Ayaka	JPN	8.7.97	156/38	Mar	2:27:08	2:47:31- 16
	Fujita	Rie	JPN	18.10.94	156/	10000	32:21.79	33:466mx- 14
	Fukuda	Yui	JPN	1.6.95	162/47	5000	15:20.11	15:30.15- 16
	Furlani	Erika	ITA	2.1.96	174/51	HJ	1.92	1.91- 16
	Furmanek	Katarzyna	POL	19.2.96	174/76	HT	69.60	67.11- 16
	Gaither	Tynia	BAH	16.3.93	158/50	200	22.71	22.54- 16
	Galant	Martyna	POL	26.1.95	171/56	1500	4:08.81	4:14.88- 16
	Gallardo	Karen	CHI	6.3.84	175/95	DT	60.13	61.10- 15
	Galle	Sokhna	FRA	23.4.94	165/50	TJ	13.61	13.42, 13.62w- 11
	Galvis	Sandra	COL	28.6.86	165/60	20kW	1:30:00	1:31:15- 14
	Gambetta	Sara	GER	18.2.93	183/70	SP	18.46	17.95- 16
	Gao Shan		CHN	8.4.95		20kW	1:32:32	1:33:34- 13
*	Gao Yang		CHN	1.3.93	178/110	SP	18.34	19.20- 16
*	Garcia	Stephanie	USA	3.5.88	168/52	1500	4:04.63	4:05.39- 15
	1M	4:24.68	4:28.47i- 16, 4:28.84- 15			3000	8:52.74	8:53.20i- 16, 8:58.09- 14
	3kSt	9:25.04	9:19.48- 16					
	García	Estela	ESP	20.3.89	174/55	200	23.1h	23.17- 16
*	García	Kimberley	PER	19.10.93	167/44	20kW	1:29:13	1:29:38- 16
	García-Caro	Laura	ESP	16.4.95	165/56	20kW	1:29:29	1:29:32- 15
	Gardasevic	Milica	SRB-J	28.9.98	175/59	LJ	6.56, 6.62w	6.30i- 16, 6.23- 15
*	Gardner	English	USA	22.4.92	162/50	100	11.04	10.74- 16
						200	22.97w	22.62- 13
	Gardzielewska	Urszula	POL	21.7.88	177/55	HJ	1.88	1.93i- 16, 1.89- 15
	Gataullina	Aksana	RUS-Y	17.7.00		PV	4.45	4.20- 16
	Gaviria	Mayra	COL	22.5.97	170/65	HT	65.63	62.18- 16
	Gavrilyuk	Kristina	RUS	14.5.94		HJ	1.91	1.81- 14
	Gaworska	Aleksandra	POL	7.11.95	168/51	400h	56.87	58.62- 16
	Gebre	Trihas	ESP	29.4.90	163/46	10000	32:11.67	32:03.39- 13
						HMar	69:57	73:46- 11
	Gebrekidan	Hiwot	ETH	11.5.95	156/44	Mar	2:25:45	2:34:45- 16
	Gebreselassie	Goytatom	ETH	15.1.95	152/42	5000	15:15.82	14:57.33- 15
						10000	31:25.61	31:14.52- 16
	Gebreslasea	Letebrhan	ETH	29.10.90	155/40	Mar	2:25:01	2:25:24- 15
	Gebru	Azmera	ETH	5.5.92	160/45	3000	8:43.68	8:40.01- 12
						5000	14:57.38	14:58.23- 12
*	Gega	Luiza	ALB	5.11.88	166/56	1500	4:06.66i	4:02.63- 15
	3000	8:52.53i		8:53.78- 16		3kSt	9:26.05	9:28.52- 16
	Genemo	Shuko	ETH	-.95		Mar	2:26:06	2:24:31- 16
	Geng Shuang		CHN	9.7.93		SP	17.61	18.06i, 17.87- 16
	George	Patience	NGR	25.11.91	176/61	400	51.06	50.71- 15
*	George	Phylicia	CAN	16.11.87	178/65	100h	12.85	12.65- 12
	Gergelics	Cintia	HUN	16.11.91		HT	67.55	66.89- 16
	Gerlach	Tori	USA	2.6.94	167/50	3000	8:54.61i	9:10.76i- 14, 9:37.72- 13
						3kSt	9:46.76	9:53.98- 15
	German	Elvira	BLR	9.1.97	168/54	100h	12.96, 12.95w	12.85- 16
	Geubelle	Andrea	USA	21.6.91	165/57	TJ	13.62, 13.96w	14.18i- 13,14.15- 16,14.17w- 12
	Gezahegne	Kalkidan	BRN	8.5.91	154/44	5000	15:07.19	
	Ghafoor	Madiea	NED	9.9.92	169/53	100	11.44, 11.05w	11.50- 14, 11.39w- 13
						200	22.94w	23.82- 14
^	Ghelber-Perie	Bianca	ROU	1.6.90	170/70	HT	69.44	73.52- 10
*	Ghribi	Habiba	TUN	9.4.84	170/57	3kSt	9:20.00	9:05.36- 15
	Gibson	Dannielle	BAH	5.4.96		TJ	13.36, 13.76w	13.54- 16
*	Gidey	Letesenbet	ETH-J	20.3.98	163/48	1500	4:11.11	
	3000	8:41.6e+		8:53.3+- 16		5000	14:33.32	14:45.63- 16
*	Gierisch	Kristin	GER	20.8.90	178/69	TJ	14.40	14.46i, 14.38, 14.46w- 15

Name		Nat	Born	Ht/Wt	Event	2017 Mark	Pre-2017 Best
Giger	Lena	USA	7.6.96		SP	17.00	16.25- 16
Giger	Yasmin	SUI-J	6.11.99	180/60	400h	55.90	58.39- 16
Gimmler	Sophie	GER	18.3.96	178/81	HT	65.75	63.99- 16
* Giorgi	Eleonora	ITA	14.9.89	163/52	20kW	1:30:34	1:26:17- 15
Gizaw	Melkaw	ETH	17.9.90	163/48	Mar	2:26:47	2:24:28- 16
^ Glanc	Zaneta	POL	11.3.83	187/86	DT	59.69	65.34- 12
* Gleadle	Liz	CAN	5.12.88	183/95	JT	64.47	64.83- 15
Glenn	Simone	USA	16.5.96	172/60	200	23.01, 22.98w	23.48- 15, 23.17w- 16
Glotova	Yana	RUS	8.4.95	166/54	400	52.11	52.58- 15
Gnafoua	Floriane	FRA	30.1.96	158/60	100	11.28	11.19- 16
* Gobena	Amane	ETH	1.9.82	163/48	Mar	2:23:09	2:21:51- 16
Gochenour	Alex	USA	17.2.93	183/70	Hep	6129	6027w- 15, 5962- 16
Godfay	Afera	ETH	25.9.91	156/42	HMar	69:55	68:32- 16
Golden	Zola	USA	20.6.97	163/52	200	23.26, 22.91w	24.17- 16
					400	52.02	52.82- 14
Golding	Kimberly	JAM	15.12.92	168/55	100h	13.03, 12.87w	13.25, 13.11w- 16
Gollish	Sasha	CAN	27.12.81	165/52	1500	4:07.70	4:07.08- 15
1M 4:32.87 4:40.54- 14					5000	15:24.12	15:35.16- 16
Gollshewsky	Taryn	AUS	18.5.93	184/80	DT	59.94	60.27- 16
Gomez	Kinsey	USA	-.92	167/54	10000	32:34.97	33:18.00- 16
Gómez	Roxana	CUB-J	7.1.99	169/54	400	51.46	52.24- 16
Gomis	Sandra	FRA	21.11.83	165/53	100h	13.14	12.79- 16
Gonçalves	Rafaela	BRA	27.11.91	168/70	JT	57.77	56.60- 14
* Gong Lijiao		CHN	24.1.89	174/110	SP	20.11	20.43- 16
Gonska	Nadine	GER	23.1.90	169/57	200	22.93	22.79- 16
Gonzalez	Melissa	COL	24.6.94	168/66	400h	56.23A, 56.29	57.78- 15
* González	María Guadalupe	MEX	9.1.89	162/48	20kW	1:26:19	1:26:17- 16
Goodman	Kaitlin	USA	31.1.87	158/42	10000	31:55.46	32:09.82- 15
* Gordeyeva	Irina	RUS	9.10.86	185/55	HJ	1.94	2.04- 12
* Gordon	Chrisann	JAM	18.9.94	164/52	400	50.13	51.02- 16
Gosa	Dalilah Abdelkadir	BRN-J	27.6.98	159/42	3000	8:50.24	8:46.42- 16
Goto	Rena	JPN	6.9.95	160/47	20kW	1:32:50	1:31:00- 16
Goule	Natoya	JAM	30.3.91	160/50	800	2:00.56	1:59.38- 16
Goúsin	Tatiána	GRE	26.1.94	188/63	HJ	1.91	1.87i- 15, 1.86- 14
^ Grabuste	Aiga	LAT	24.3.88	178/66	LJ	6.49	6.82i- 15, 6.69, 6.75w- 14
* Grace	Kate	USA	24.10.88	173/55	800	1:59.30	1:58.28- 16
1000 2:36.97i					1500	4:03.59	4:05.65- 16
1M 4:22.93i, 4:24.01 4:28.30i- 16					3000	8:47.26i	8:55.06i- 13
Grange	Gleneve	JAM	6.7.95	170/75	SP	17.29	14.92- 16
					DT	57.02	59.03- 16
Granville	Caryl	GBR	24.9.89	168/55	400h	56.59	57.19- 13
Graumann	Jossie	GER	18.3.94	175/58	HJ	1.92i, 1.92	1.90- 16
Gray	Kianna	USA	30.12.96	171/57	100	11.28	11.20, 11.22w- 16
					200	22.86	22.79, 22.58w- 16
Green	Emma	SWE	8.12.84	180/62	HJ	1.89i	1.98- 08
Green	Hanna	USA	16.10.94	168/59	800	2:01.28	2:01.17- 15
Griffith	Georgia	AUS	5.12.96	163/50	800	2:00.90	2:04.00- 14
					1500	4:07.32	4:13.55- 16
Griffiths	Monique	USA	10.8.94	170/75	HT	65.82	65.60- 16
Griksaite	Aina	LTU	23.11.94	168/52	TJ	13.82	
Griva	Lauma	LAT	27.10.84	181/62	LJ	6.72	6.86- 11
Griva	Mara	LAT	4.8.89	171/57	LJ	6.52	6.59, 6.70w- 11
					TJ	13.61	13.81- 11
Gröll	Laura	GER-J	11.4.98	183/64	HJ	1.88i	1.83- 16
Gromysheva	Mariya	RUS	10.1.90		LJ	6.62	6.48- 08
					Hep	5888	5970- 16
* Grøvdal	Karoline Bjerkeli	NOR	14.6.90	167/52	1500	4:07.25	4:09.03- 16
3000 8:37.58 8:39.47- 16 5000 15:00.44 14:57.53- 16 3kSt 9:13.35 9:33.19- 07							
Grove	Emily	USA	22.5.93	168/61	PV	4.60	4.51Ai- 14, 4.50- 16
Gruver	Olivia	USA	29.7.97	170/64	PV	4.50	4.30- 16
Guamán	Janeth	ECU	15.1.88	155/47	20kW	1:31:31	1:35:07- 16
Guba	Paulina	POL	14.5.91	180/90	SP	18.24	18.63i- 16, 17.95- 15
* Gudeta	Netsanet	ETH	12.2.91	162/45	5000	15:25.0A	15:31.25- 15
					HMar	67:26	67:31- 15
Gudmundsdóttir	Arna Stefanía	ISL	1.9.95	175/59	400h	56.37	56.08- 16
					Hep	5730(w)	5383- 13
* Guei	Floria	FRA	2.5.90	166/53	400	51.51	50.84- 16
Guerrero	Esther	ESP	7.2.90	160/57	800	2:00.77	2:01.20- 16
Guillaume	Ilionis	FRA-J	13.1.98	178/64	TJ	13.66, 13.97w	13.37, 13.46w- 16
Guillon-Romarin	Ninon	FRA	15.4.95	163/53	PV	4.60	4.40- 16

Name		Nat	Born	Ht/Wt	Event	2017 Mark	Pre-2017 Best
Gulyayeva	Aleksandra	RUS	30.4.94	173/59	800	1:58.34	2:00.24- 16
1M 4:31.19i					1500	4:04.49	4:09.30- 16
^ Gumenyuk	Irina	RUS	6.1.88	176/59	TJ	14.04	14.58- 13
Gunderson	Emily	USA	16.8.96		PV	4.33i	4.14- 15
Gunnarsson	Lisa	SWE-J	20.8.99	171/57	PV	4.55i, 4.55	4.50- 16
Guo Tianqian		CHN	1.6.95	180/110	SP	18.23	18.59- 15
Guster	Elexis	USA	7.7.94	171/60	200	22.93	23.03- 16
					400	51.32	51.85- 16
Gutermuth	Sophie	USA	2.11.92		PV	4.47	4.41i- 16, 4.35- 15
Güvenç	Tugba	TUR	9.7.94	166/50	3kSt	9:26.09	9:33.34- 15
Gyurátz	Réka	HUN	31.5.96	175/70	HT	71.27	70.39- 15
Gyürkés	Viktória	HUN	15.10.92	172/61	3kSt	9:40.66	9:49.70- 16
Haase	Rebekka	GER	2.1.93	170/57	100	11.06, 10.94w	11.21- 15, 10.98w- 16
					200	22.76, 22.58w	22.95- 15
Hackett	Semoy	TTO	27.11.88	173/70	100	11.11	11.07- 16. 11.04dq- 12, 10.98w- 11
					200	22.77,22.49w	22.51A- 15,22.55- 12,22.14w- 11
Hackworth	Kenyattia	USA	15.9.93	168/55	LJ	6.38Ai, 6.57w	6.81- 16
Hadley	Sabria	USA	1.1.95	157/50	200	22.88	23.04- 15
Haggerty	Olivia	USA	22.6.95	160/52	100h	12.99w	13.25- 16
Hailey	Nnenya	USA	23.2.94	165/54	400h	56.37	54.98- 16
Hakeai	Siositina	NZL	1.3.94	182/105	DT	56.11	59.81- 15
Hall	Cassondra	USA	23.9.97	170/59	100	11.34, 11.22w	11.47- 15, 11.37w- 16
					200	22.92	23.24- 15
Hall	Dior	USA	2.1.96	168/55	100h	12.82	12.74- 15
Hall	Kate	USA	12.1.97	173/64	LJ	6.73	6.83- 15
Hall	Linden	AUS	29.6.91	167/51	1500	4:04.37	4:01.78- 16
					1M	4:23.96	4:34.94i- 14
Hall	Marielle	USA	28.1.92	160/52	3000	8:55.55	8:54.48- 14
					5000	15:11.02	15:06.45- 15
Hall	Samantha	JAM	19.4.93	178/77	DT	58.75	58.50- 15
Hall	Sara	USA	15.4.83	163/48	HMar	69:37	70:07- 16
					Mar	2:27:21	2:30:06- 16
Hamann	Sophie	GER	12.8.96		Hep	5726	5600- 16
Harala	Lotta	FIN	26.3.92	170/56	100h	13.25, 13.12w	13.41- 16
Hardy	Tramesha	USA	24.3.96		200	23.06, 22.92w	23.54- 15
Harper	Daina	USA	26.5.95	178/64	400	50.64	52.36- 16
* Harper Nelson	Dawn	USA	13.5.84	168/61	100h	12.63	12.37- 12, 123.36w- 09
Harris	Venique	JAM	29.2.96	173/79	DT	58.97	52.61- 16
* Harrison	Kendra	USA	18.9.92	163/52	200	22.85w	23.00- 16
					100h	12.28	12.20- 16
* Harrison	Queen	USA	10.9.88	170/60	100h	12.64	12.43- 13
* Harting	Julia	GER	1.4.90	192/95	DT	63.63	68.49- 16
Hartwig	Julie	GER	30.6.94	188/75	DT	56.66	58.03- 16
Harun	Makda	ETH	5.9.88		Mar	2:28:06	2:26:46- 12
* Hasay	Jordan	USA	21.9.91	163/45	HMar	67:55	
					Mar	2:20:57	0
* Hassan	Sifan	NED	1.1.93	170/49	800	1:56.81	1:58.50- 15
1500 3:56.14			3:56.05- 15		1M	4:19.89i	4:18.20- 15
3000 8:28.90			8:29.38- 14		5000	14:41.24	14:59.23- 14
* Hastings	Natasha	USA	23.7.86	173/63	200	22.78w, 22.50St	22.57- 16
					400	50.14	49.84- 07
Hatsko-Fedusova	Hanna	UKR	3.10.90	174/73	JT	60.48	67.29- 14
Hawkins	Chari	USA	21.5.91	170/57	Hep	5845	5956- 16
Haye-Smith	Yanique	JAM	22.3.90	170/55	400h	56.10	56.17- 16
* Hayes	Quanera	USA	7.3.92	172/59	200	22.55	22.89- 16, 22.81w- 15
					400	49.72	49.91- 16
Hazlewood	Micaela	USA	18.6.95	175/77	DT	56.75	55.77- 16
He Qin		CHN	23.3.92		20kW	1:29:27	1:27:42- 13
Heath	Madison	USA	3.11.95	173/59	PV	4.35	4.30- 16
Hechavarría	Zurian	CUB	10.8.95	164/58	400h	56.02	55.97- 15
Heikkinen	Jutta	FIN	27.10.94	171/63	Hep	5747	5715- 15
* Hejnová	Zuzana	CZE	19.12.86	170/54	400	51.77i	51.27i, 51.90- 13
					400h	53.93	52.83- 13
Helps	Shauna	JAM	23.10.96	166/52	100	11.26	11.50- 14
Hembram	Purnima	IND	10.7.93	167/57	Hep	5798	5706- 16
Hemphill	Megu	JPN	23.5.96	167/57	Hep	5907	5882- 16
Henderson	Ashley	USA	4.12.95	168/59	100	11.01	11.21,10.96w- 16
					200	22.54A, 22.66, 22.35w	22.64- 16
Henderson	Emmonnie	USA	5.11.94	188/84	SP	17.98	17.09- 15
* Henriques	Inês	POR	1.5.80	156/48	20kW	1:30:44	1:29:00- 16
					50kW	4:05:56	

	Name		Nat	Born	Ht/Wt	Event	2017 Mark	Pre-2017 Best
	Henry	Britney	USA	17.10.84	178/84	HT	68.37	71.27- 10
*	Henry	Desiree	GBR	26.8.95	172/60	100	11.09	11.06- 16, 11.04w- 14
						200	22.69	22.46- 16
	Herashchenko	Iryna	UKR	10.3.95	181/62	HJ	1.95	1.95i- 14, 1.94- 15
	Hering	Christina	GER	9.10.94	185/62	800	2:00.77	1:59.54- 15
	Herl	Mel	USA	14.2.94		SP	16.92	15.25- 16
	DT	57.05		51.82- 15		HT	65.27	
	Herman	Kelsey	USA	15.6.96	175/64	Hep	5820	5495- 16
	Hermansson	Hanna	SWE	18.5.89	175/62	800	2:00.43	2:03.32- 16
	Herrera	Irisdaymi	CUB	18.4.92	167/66	LJ	6.48, 6.58w	6.56- 14
	Herrera	Mayra Carolina	GUA	20.12.88	163/54	50kW	4:15:42	
	Hicks	Cion	USA	14.10.94	178/64	SP	17.35i, 17.33	17.39i, 17.09- 16
						DT	57.16	54.25- 16
	Hilali	Siham	MAR	2.5.86	161/58	1500	4:06.20	4:01.33- 11
	Hildebrand	Nadine	GER	20.9.87	158/51	100h	12.81	12.64- 16
*	Hill	Candace	USA-J	11.2.99	175/59	100	11.23	10.98- 15
						200	22.68	22.43A- 15, 22.76, 22.38w- 16
	Hill	Deanna	USA	13.4.96	168/55	100	11.17, 11.01w	11.21- 16
						200	22.41, 22.30w	22.60- 16
	Hillman	Christina	USA	6.10.93	178/84	SP	17.57i, 17.48	18.15i, 17.73- 14
	Hillman	Sarah	USA	1.1.97	183/105	DT	56.75	51.89- 16
*	Hills	Madeline	AUS	15.5.87	174/53	5000	15:12.63	15:04.05- 16
						10000	31:41.10	32:44.71- 14
	Hinriksdóttir	Aníta	ISL	13.1.96	161/50	800	2:00.05	2:00.14- 16
						1500	4:06.43	4:15.14- 14
	Hinton	Kaylee	USA	19.4.97	175/64	Hep	5869(w)	5349- 16
	Hironaka	Ririka	JPN-Y	24.11.00	164/47	3000	8:56.29	9:00.81- 16
*	Hitchon	Sophie	GBR	11.7.91	170/74	HT	73.97	74.54- 16
	Hixson	Kristen	USA	1.7.92	170/60	PV	4.65i, 4.60	4.65- 16
	Hjálmsdóttir	Ásdís	ISL	28.10.85	175/65	JT	63.43	62.77- 12
	Hladiychuk	Yana	UKR	21.5.93	174/63	PV	4.40	4.20- 16
	Hobbs	Aleia	USA	24.2.96	172/59	100	10.85	11.13- 15
	Hodges	Shavine	JAM	22.10.91	168/55	100	11.29	11.33A- 14, 11.53- 15
						200	23.00	23.45A- 14, 23.51, 23.43w- 13
	Hofmann	Franziska	GER	27.3.94	175/69	100h	12.98	12.87- 14
	Holder	Montayla	USA	7.2.94	160/51	400h	56.61	56.70- 16
	Holder	Nikkita	CAN	7.5.87	170/59	100h	13.04w	12.80- 12
	Holodna	Olha	UKR	14.11.91	183/93	SP	18.22	18.72- 13
	Holston	Lorenda	USA	15.8.95	170/57	100h	13.30, 13.05w	13.26- 16
	Holub	Malgorzata	POL	30.10.92	168/56	400	51.76	51.67- 16
	Hopkins	Kayla	USA	23.4.96	174/85	DT	59.38	54.08- 16
	Hordiyenko	Rimma	UKR	30.12.95	172/63	Hep	5737	5489- 14
	Hori	Yuka	JPN	13.6.96	155/40	5000	15:28.64	15:23.53- 16
						10000	31:59.80	
	Horie	Misato	JPN	10.3.87	168/49	Mar	2:25:44	2:26:40- 16
	Horn	Carina	RSA	9.3.89	169/56	100	11.10A, 11.21, 11.05w	11.06- 15
	Horvat	Anita	SLO	7.9.96	174/56	400	51.94	53.47- 16
	Hou Yongbo		CHN	15.9.94		20kW	1:31:22	1:28:30- 15
*	Houlihan	Shelby	USA	8.2.93	160/54	1500	4:06.22	4:03.39- 16
	1M	4:24.16i		4:28.71i, 4:31.79- 15		3000	8:37.40	9:01.11i- 16, 9:28.94- 15
	5000	15:00.37		15:06.14- 16				
	Howard	Marisa	USA	9.8.92	160/53	3000	8:57.15	
						3kSt	9:30.92	9:37.84- 15
	Howard	Sarah	CAN	11.10.93		SP	17.04	16.99- 15
	Howarth	Lauren	GBR	21.4.90	168/52	5000	15:29.26	15:44.28- 16
	Howell	Brittney	JAM	1.9.92	170/55	LJ	6.58, 6.63w	6.37- 14
	Howell	Jacklyn	USA	3.10.96	160/52	100h	13.00	12.90, 12.87w- 16
*	Hrasnová	Martina	SVK	21.3.83	176/75	HT	67.86	76.90- 09
*	Hrubá	Michaela	CZE-J	21.2.98	191/75	HJ	1.94	1.95i, 1.93- 16
	Hryshutyna	Krystyna	UKR	21.3.92	176/59	LJ	6.55, 6.58w	6.81- 15
	Huang Yan		CHN	12.1.96		400h	57.01	56.48- 16
*	Huddle	Molly	USA	31.8.84	163/48	3000	8:44.46	8:42.99- 13
	5000	15:01.64i, 15:03.60		14:42.64- 14		10000	31:19.86	30:13.17- 16
	HMar	68:19		67:41- 16				
	Hudson	Victoria	AUT	28.5.96	169/64	JT	58.34	52.68- 15
	Hudspeth	Najia	USA	25.10.96	165/52	200	22.89A	23.69- 16
	Huggins	Nelda	IVB	2.2.97	164/50	100	11.26w	11.59- 14
	Hughes	Amber	USA	23.8.94	175/60	100h	13.33, 13.12w	13.27, 13.26w- 15
						TJ	13.62	13.46m 13.50w- 16
	Hulley	Alex	AUS	24.7.97	171/90	HT	68.66	65.75- 16
	Hunter	Rachel	GBR	30.8.93	176/100	HT	66.46	66.30- 14

	Name		Nat	Born	Ht/Wt	Event	2017 Mark	Pre-2017 Best
*	Hussong	Christin	GER	17.4.94	187/82	JT	64.18	66.41- 16
^	Hutson	Kylie	USA	27.11.87	165/57	PV	4.45	4.75Ai, 4.70- 13
	Hylton	Shannon	GBR	19.12.96	168/52	200	22.94	22.94, 22.73w- 15
	Hynne	Hedda	NOR	13.3.90	172/57	800	1:59.87	2:00.94- 16
*	Ibargüen	Caterine	COL	12.2.84	181/65	TJ	14.89	15.31- 14
	Ichiyama	Mao	JPN	29.5.97	157/42	3000	8:53.54	9:13.09- 16
	5000 15:24.17 15:44.33- 16			10000 31:49.01		32:15.73- 16	HMar 69:14	
	Ifantídou	Sofía	GRE	5.1.85	164/53	JT	59.23	57.50- 15
						Hep	5745	6113- 15
	Igaune	Laura	LAT	2.10.88	170/70	HT	68.44	68.94- 12
	Igbinosun	Gladys	NGR	23.7.93		200	22.9h	23.60- 12
*	Ikauniece-Admidina	Laura	LAT	31.5.92	179/60	100h	13.10	13.07- 16
	LJ 6.64 6.32- 15		JT 56.32			55.93- 16	Hep 6815	6622- 16
	Ikemitsu	Ayano	JPN	18.4.91	161/48	10000	32:35.93	32:53.91- 16
	Iliyeva	Irina	RUS	22.12.95	180/58	HJ	1.90	1.92- 15
	Imali	Maximilia	KEN	8.12.96	169/59	400	51.18A	
	Ince	Ariana	USA	14.3.89	180/75	JT	61.38	59.84- 15
*	Infeld	Emily	USA	21.3.90	163/48	3000	8:55.41	8:41.43- 13
	5000 14:56.33 15:00.91i- 16, 15:07.18- 15					10000	31:20.45	31:26.94- 16
	Inoue	Ai	JPN	13.1.90	158/44	10000	32:35.33	32:07.56- 16
	Insaeng	Subenrat	THA	10.2.94	183/105	DT	56.82	61.12- 16
	Ishii	Hisami	JPN	10.8.95	158/42	Mar	2:27:35	
	Itoya	Juliet	ESP	17.8.86	174/63	LJ	6.65	6.79- 16
	Iuel	Amalie Hammild	NOR	17.4.94	180/59	400	51.81	52.52i, 52.85- 16
						400h	55.38	55.79- 16
	Ivanenko	Olesya	RUS	6.10.82	165/56	TJ	13.79	14.54i- 08, 14.50- 06
	Ive	Jade	GBR	22.1.92		PV	4.36i	4.15- 16
	Iyevbele	Kenyetta	USA	22.8.92	181/61	800	2:01.68	2:02.43- 15
	Jaakkola	Jelena	FIN	7.3.89	172/76	JT	56.92	58.89- 08
	Jääskeläinen	Jatta-Mari	FIN	27.2.94	165/61	JT	56.47	51.86- 14
	Jackson	Hannah	USA	28.2.97		200	23.33, 23.00w	23.59- 15
*	Jackson	Shericka	JAM	15.7.94	174/59	100	11.24	
	200 22.46			22.84- 13		400	50.05	49.83- 16
	Jacobs	Gabi	USA	20.8.96	173/82	DT	58.23	53.24- 16
	Jaensch	Chelsea	AUS	6.1.85	168/55	LJ	6.44, 6.60w	6.70- 16, 6.74w- 15
*	Jagaciak Michalska	Anna	POL	10.2.90	178/68	LJ	6.49	6.74- 10
						TJ	14.29	14.33, 14.40w- 16
	Jakubaityte	Indre	LTU	24.1.76	177/70	JT	57.64	63.65- 07
	James	Nayana	IND	18.10.95		LJ	6.55	5.94- 12
	Jaramillo	Karla	ECU	21.1.97	160/58	20kW	1:33:35	1:45:36- 15
	Jasiünaite	Liveta	LTU	26.7.94	174/68	JT	60.24	61.32- 16
	Jassem	Noora Salem	BRN	27.11.96	175/90	SP	17.69	15.24- 15
	Jean	Mulern	HAI	25.9.92	168/57	100h	12.94, 12.90w	13.01- 16
*	Jebet	Ruth	BRN	17.11.96	165/49	5000	14:53.41	16:16.1- 13
						3kSt	8:55.29	8:52.78- 16
*	Jefferson	Kyra	USA	23.9.94	165/57	200	22.02	22.24- 15
	Jelagat	Jane	KEN	25.11.83		Mar	2:26:29	2:34:18- 16
	Jelagat	Viola	KEN	20.4.92	154/42	Mar	2:26:51dh	2:35:03- 16
	Jelagat Morwa	Yvonne	KEN	-.93		HMar	68:19	
	Jele ¶?	Lydia	BOT	22.6.90	172/54	400	50.32A, 51.41	51.50A, 52.14- 16
	Jelmini	Anna	USA	15.7.90	176/86	DT	56.80	60.80- 10
	Jenkins	Tovea	JAM	27.10.92	172/60	400	51.99	52.42- 15
	Jenneke	Michelle	AUS	23.6.93	172/63	100h	12.99	12.82- 15
	Jeon Yang-eun		KOR	24.5.88	157/43	20kW	1:33:29	1:30:35- 15
	Jepchirchir	Peres	KEN	27.9.93	153/40	HMar	65:06	66:39- 16
*	Jepchumba	Violah	BRN	23.10.90	172/52	HMar	65:22	65:51- 16
	Jepkemei	Daisy	KEN	13.2.96	167/50	3kSt	9:19.68	9:38.16- 15
*	Jepkemoi	Hyvin	KEN	13.1.92	156/45	3kSt	9:00.12	9:00.01- 16
	Jepkesho	Visiline	KEN	30.12.89	160/45	HMar	68:12	69:43- 16
						Mar	2:21:37	2:24:44- 15
*	Jepkirui	Eunice	BRN	20.5.84	158/45	HMar	66:46	68:06- 16
						Mar	2:21:17	2:21:41- 12
	Jepkoech	Josephine	KEN	21.4.89		HMar	69:47	68:53- 13
	Jepkoech	Monica	KEN	.85		HMar	69:23	69:12- 12
						Mar	2:26:58	2:28:56- 16
	Jepkorir	Winnie	KEN	10.6.90		Mar	2:27:18	2:27:57- 14
*	Jepkosgei	Joyciline	KEN	8.12.93	156/52	10000	32:26.3A	31:28.28- 16
						HMar	64:51	69:07- 16
	Jepkosgei	Nelly	KEN	14.7.91	164/53	800	1:59.95	1:59.40- 13
	1500 4:02.75			4:04.26- 16		1M	4:25.15	4:39.09- 16
	Jeptoo	Eunice	KEN	24.6.83		Mar	2:26:13	2:32:36- 16

Name		Nat	Born	Ht/Wt	Event	2017 Mark	Pre-2017 Best
Jeptoo	Susan	KEN	7.3.87		HMar	69:02	70:49- 16
Jerotich	Emily	KEN	13.5.86	155/44	800	2:00.18A	2:00.0A- 16
Jerotich	Sheila	KEN	6.6.89		Mar	2:27:34	
Ji Yefang		CHN	4.3.96		20kW	1:29:42	1:31:06- 14
Jiang Shanshan		CHN	28.2.97		50kW	4:32:14	
Jiroutová	Nikol	CZE	30.3.92		PV	4.35i	4.15- 16
John	Deborah	TTO	10.4.90	175/64	100h	13.10	13.07- 16
Johnson	Alaysha	USA	20.7.96	160/52	100h	12.69, 12.68w	12.96- 16
Johnson	Brandeé	USA-J	3.4.98	163/52	400h	56.65	56.16- 16
Johnson	Felisha	USA	24.7.89	185/105	SP	18.72i, 18.64	19.26- 16
Johnson	Kortnei	USA	11.8.97	165/52	100	11.09	11.27, 11.13w- 16
					200	22.80, 22.50w	22.78, 22.67w- 16
Johnson	Lauren	USA	4.5.87	170/52	800	2:01.74	2:01.59- 16
					1500	4:05.88	4:04.17- 15
Johnson	Rachel	USA	30.4.93	165/50	3kSt	9:42.50	9:41.56- 14
* Johnson-Thompson	Katarina	GBR	9.1.93	183/70	200	22.81	22.79- 16
HJ 1.95 1.98- 16 LJ 6.75 6.93i- 15, 6.92- 14 Hep 6691 6682- 14							
Jones	Ariel	USA	18.7.95	165/52	100h	12.87w	13.29, 13.14w- 16
					400h	56.44	56.55- 16
Jones	Cambrya	USA	20.9.90	171/64	100	11.20w	11.33- 12
					200	22.69w	22.72- 12
Jones	Cortney	USA-J	18.6.99	168/55	100h	13.06	13.40- 16
Jones	Dani	USA	21.8.96	165/54	1500	4:08.42	4:13.44- 16
Jones	Tia	USA-Y	8.9.00	163/52	100h	13.01	12.84- 16
Jones	Travia	CAN	12.7.95	175/61	400	51.63	53.08- 16
Joye	Hannah	AUS	4.1.96	177/63	HJ	1.88	1.92- 15
* Józwik	Joanna	POL	30.1.91	168/53	800	1:59.29i, 2:00.77	1:58.35- 15
Judd	Jessica	GBR	7.1.95	178/60	800	2:02.14mx	1:59.77- 14
500 4:03.73 4:09.56- 15					1M	4:28.59	4:39.49- 16
3000 8:43.24 mx, 8:59.60 9:08.13i- 15, 9:08.5- 11							
Jung Hye-lim		KOR	1.7.87	167/52	100h	13.10	13.04, 12.86w- 16
* Jungfleisch	Marie-Laurence	GER	7.10.90	181/68	HJ	2.00	2.00- 16
Jupiter	Ka'lynn	USA	12.1.95	168/57	400h	56.68	56.63- 16
Kácser	Zita	HUN	2.10.88		3kSt	9:39.44	9:48.06- 16
Kai	Konomi	JPN	10.7.93	153/50	LJ	6.58	6.84- 15
Kakuri	Esther	KEN	26.10.94		HMar	70:07	73:04- 16
Kalawan	Shannon	JAM	25.11.97	168/52	400h	57.02	56.29- 16
Kalina	Anastasiya	RUS	16.2.94	162/50	1500	4:05.71	4:05.67- 16
Kalu	Stephanie	NGR	5.8.93	156/52	100	11.35, 10.99w	11.33- 13. 11.15w- 14
					200	22.78Aw	23.57- 15, 23.21w- 14
* Kambundji	Mujinga	SUI	17.6.92	168/59	100	11.07	11.07- 15
					200	22.42	22.64- 15
Kamilos	Jessica	USA	3.8.93	158/48	3kSt	9:42.79	9:41.28- 16
Kampf	Heather	USA	19.1.87	162/53	1M	4:28.39i, 4:32.57	4:27.23- 16
1500 4:11.53+i 4:04.46- 16					3000	8:51.27i	8:58.34i- 16
* Kamulu	Pauline	KEN	16.4.95	154/45	3000	8:48.27	9:10.84- 15
5000 14:58.82 15:26.51- 16 10000 31:47.13 31:56.70- 16 HMar 68:04 69:44- 15							
Kandie	Peninah	KEN	22.6.92		HMar	69:15	73:58- 14
Kang Ya		CHN	16.3.90	168/50	100h	13.01	13.12, 13.10w- 15
Kangas	Jenni	FIN	3.7.92	178/74	JT	60.98	60.70- 16
Kangogo	Rebecca	KEN	.92	161/45	HMar	69:01	68:21- 15
Kanuchová	Veronika	SVK	19.4.93	170/69	HT	66.06	69.48- 16
Kaputin	Rellie	PNG	12.3.93		LJ	6.39, 6.53w	5.97- 15
Kardasz	Klaudia	POL	2.5.96	179/77	SP	17.90	16.80- 15
Karimi	Lucy	KEN	24.2.75	164/45	Mar	2:25:17	2:24:46- 16
Kashyna	Inna	UKR	27.9.91	162/49	20kW	1:30:11	1:30:17- 14
Kassanavoid	Janee'	USA	19.1.95	175/79	HT	66.97	61.46- 16
Kato	Misaki	JPN	15.6.91	155/40	10000	32:29.78	31:59.72- 16
					Mar	2:28:12	2:31:04- 16
Kaur ¶	Manpreet	IND	6.7.90	170/89	SP	18.86dq?	17.96- 15
Kawazoe	Kaori	JPN	30.5.95	158/48	20kW	1:33:09	1:34:21- 16
Kaya	Özlem	TUR	20.4.90	160/49	3kSt	9:37.06	9:30.23- 15
^ Kebede	Aberu	ETH	12.9.86	163/50	HMar	69:57+	67:39- 09
					Mar	2:27:27	2:20:30- 12
Keenan	Te Rina	NZL	29.9.90	180/84	DT	57.55	60.78- 15
* Keitany	Mary	KEN	18.1.82	158/45	HMar	65:13	65:39dh- 14, 66:02- 16
					Mar	2:17:01	2:18:37- 12
Kelly	Ashley	IVB	25.3.91	173/75	400	51.63	52.29- 16
Kennedy	Nina	AUS	5.4.97	166/57	PV	4.55	4.59- 15
Kenzel	Alina	GER	10.8.97	181/83	SP	17.68i, 17.61	17.58- 16
Kerekes	Gréta	HUN	9.10.92	164/54	100h	13.10, 12.97w	13.15- 16

	Name		Nat	Born	Ht/Wt	Event	2017 Mark	Pre-2017 Best
	Kessely	Haoua	FRA	2.2.88	178/72	LJ	6.39, 6.54w	6.58- 16
	Ketema	Maritu	ETH-Y	-.00		3kSt	9:39.55	10:26.5- 15
	Ketema	Tigist	ETH-J	15.9.98		800	2:02.00i	2:02.28- 17
	Kguriatukei	Rael	KEN	4.4.84		Mar	2:26:22	2:25:23- 11
	Khamidova	Sitora	UZB	12.5.89	166/50	10000	31:57.42	31:57.77- 16
*	Kholodovich	Tatyana	BLR	21.6.91	181/83	JT	66.30	66.34- 16
	Khramova	Valeriya	RUS	13.8.92	170/60	400h	55.70	55.80- 14
	Kibarus	Mercy	KEN	25.2.84	155/42	Mar	2:26:52	2:27:06- 15
	Kibet	Elvin	KEN	4.2.90	153/42	10000	32:22.51	32:40.22- 14
*	Kibiwot	Viola	KEN	22.12.83	157/45	HMar	70:15	
						Mar	2:25:32	
	Kibor	Marion	KEN	27.9.94	158/52	3kSt	9:50.4A	9:46.29- 15
	Kieffer	Allie	USA	16.9.87	163/50	10000	32:09.89	32:25.69- 12
	Kielbasinska	Anna	POL	26.6.90	170/55	200	23.13i, 23.27, 22.8h	
	Kim Kyung-ae		KOR	5.3.88	163/62	JT	56.24	58.77- 15
	Kimanzi	Grace	KEN	1.3.92	162/46	5000	15:19.96	15:16.44- 16
						HMar	70:09	70:17- 13
	Kimura	Ayako	JPN	11.6.88	168/53	100h	13.06, 12.99w	13.03, 13.02w- 13
	Kimura	Tomoko	JPN	12.11.94	154/43	5000	15:12.47	15:18.08- 16
^	Kinsey	Erika	SWE	10.3.88	185/68	HJ	1.94	1.97- 15
	Kintana	June	ESP	12.4.95	175/74	DT	56.30	55.66- 14
*	Kipkemboi	Margaret	KEN	9.2.93	162/45	3000	8:30.11	8:37.54- 16
						5000	14:32.82	14:47.24- 16
*	Kipketer	Valentine	KEN	5.1.93		HMar	69:12+	68:21- 11
						Mar	2:28:05	2:23:02- 13
*	Kipkirui	Caroline	KEN	26.5.94	162/47	3000	8:42.2+e	8:58.63- 11
						5000	14:27.55	15:24.66- 11
						HMar	66:53+	
	Kipkoech	Pascalia	KEN	22.12.88	153/42	10000	32:10.6A	32:59.2- 13
						HMar	68:23	67:17- 12
*	Kiplagat	Edna	KEN	15.11.79	163/47	HMar	69:37	67:41- 12
						Mar	2:27:18, 2:21:52dh	2:19:50- 12
*	Kiplagat	Florence	KEN	27.2.87	155/42	HMar	68:15	65:09- 15
						Mar	2:26:25	2:19:44- 11
	Kiplagat	Vivian	KEN	.91		HMar	69:05	79:35- 16
*	Kiprop	Helah	KEN	7.4.85	164/48	HMar	67:48	67:39- 13
						Mar	2:25:39	2:21:27- 16
	Kiprop	Nancy	KEN	7.7.79	164/48	HMar	67:22	71:34- 16
						Mar	2:24:20	2:25:13- 16
*	Kiprotich	Sheila	KEN	27.12.90	163/48	3000	8:45.94	
						5000	14:54.05	15:05.45- 16
						10000	32:35.0A	35:49.8- 16
*	Kipyegon	Faith	KEN	10.1.94	157/42	1500	3:57.04	3:56.41- 16
	Kipyokei	Diana	KEN	.94		HMar	69:45	68:38- 16
	Kira	Manami	JPN	23.10.91	174/61	400h	56.96	56.63- 14
	Kirichenko	Irina	RUS	18.5.87		SP	17.01i	18.35i, 17.93- 16
*	Kirui	Purity	KEN	13.8.91	162/47	3kSt	9:20.07	9:17.74- 15
	Kitaguchi	Haruka	JPN-J	16.3.98	178/80	JT	61.07	61.38- 16
	Kitamura	Yume	JPN	23.12.95	163/48	800	2:00.92	2:04.57- 16
	Kiyeng	Judy	KEN	10.12.94	160/45	1500	4:04.4A	4:05.45A- 16
	Kiyota	Mao	JPN	12.9.93	156/42	Mar	2:23:47	2:24:32- 16
*	Klaas	Kathrin	GER	6.2.84	168/72	HT	71.06	76.05- 12
	Klaup	Mari	EST	27.2.90	180/58	Hep	5872	6023(w)- 15, 6002- 13
	Klein	Caroline	GER	4.3.96	178/67	Hep	6007	5842- 16
	Klein	Hanna	GER	6.4.93	172/55	1500	4:04.15	4:08.56- 16
						5000	15:17.14	15:27.09- 16
	Klintsova	Liliya	UKR	12.7.97	176/56	HJ	1.86	1.83- 16
*	Klishina	Darya	RUS	15.1.91	180/57	LJ	7.00	7.05- 11
	Klochko	Viktoriya	UKR	2.9.92	187/120	DT	56.07	58.01- 15
	Kloster	Line	NOR	27.2.90	175/59	400h	56.18	
*	Klosterhalfen	Konstanze	GER	18.2.97	174/48	800	1:59.65	2:01.55- 16
						1500	3:58.92	4:06.91- 16
						3000	8:29.89	8:46.74- 16
						5000	14:51.38	15:16.98- 16
	Klucinová	Eliska	CZE	14.4.88	177/69	HJ	1.87	1.90- 14
						Hep	6313	6460- 14
	Klymets	Iryna	UKR	4.10.94	169/71	HT	72.53	72.23- 16
	Knäsche	Anjuli	GER	18.10.93	169/61	PV	4.43i, 4.40	4.55- 16
	Knibb	Kellion	JAM	25.12.93	193/93	DT	62.73	61.44- 16
	Knoroz	Polina	RUS-J	20.7.99	175/60	PV	4.50i, 4.45	4.35- 16
	Knowles-Jones	Harriet	GBR-J	3.4.98		3000	8:56.08mx	9:23.76- 14
	Koala	Marthe	BUR	8.3.94	174/68	LJ	6.52	6.16- 15
						Hep	6230(w)	5952- 16
	Kocina	Anete	LAT	5.2.96	176/65	JT	64.47	60.01- 15
*	Kolak	Sara	CRO	22.6.95	170/74	JT	68.43	66.18- 16

	Name		Nat	Born	Ht/Wt	Event	2017 Mark	Pre-2017 Best
	Kolb	Viktoryia	BLR	26.10.93	182/90	SP	17.71	17.47- 15
	Koleczek	Karolina	POL	15.1.93	169/51	100h	13.07	12.91, 12.87w- 15
	Kolesnychenko	Olena	UKR	3.6.93	172/58	400h	55.50	55.48- 16
	Kondakova	Yuliya	RUS	4.12.81	170/64	100h	13.06	12.73- 13
	Konieczek	Alicja	POL	2.11.94	159/41	3kSt	9:49.74	10:23.61- 13
	Kononova	Yevgeniya	RUS	28.9.89	175/53	HJ	1.88i, 1.88	1.92- 12
*	Kopron	Malwina	POL	16.11.94	169/89	HT	76.85	72.74- 16
	Kora	Salomé	SUI	8.6.94	173/66	100	11.27	11.45- 16
	Kore	Tola	ETH	16.1.97		800	2:00.61	2:02.75- 15
	Koren	Petra	SLO	30.7.93	170/59	TJ	13.56i	13.82- 16
	Koressel	Allie	USA	2.3.91	168/57	PV	4.48	4.46- 16
	Korneychuk	Margarita	RUS	21.2.95		HJ	1.89	1.84- 16
						Hep	5798	5499- 16
	Korobkina	Yelena	RUS	25.11.90	163/47	1500	4:04.90	4:05.18- 13
	Korolyova	Kristina	RUS	6.11.90	183/68	HJ	1.92	1.91- 15
	Korosídou	Iliána	GRE	14.1.95	175/72	HT	65.83	66.68- 16
	Korpela	Merja	FIN	15.5.81	170/75	HT	68.55	69.56- 09
	Korzh	Tatyana	BLR	17.3.93	175/75	JT	58.28	62.10- 16
*	Kosgei	Brigid	KEN	20.2.94	163/46	HMar	66:35	74:08- 16
						Mar	2:20:22	2:24:45- 16
	Kosolapova	Valentina	RUS	11.7.97		TJ	13.71	13.43- 15, 13.74w- 16
*	Koster	Maureen	NED	3.7.92	175/56	1500	4:03.77	3:59.79- 15
						3000	8:44.63i	8:48.46mx- 16, 8:49.18i- 16
	Kotulskaya	Yelena	RUS	8.8.88	174/61	800	2:01.46	1:57.77- 12
	Kovács	Barbara	HUN	26.7.93	167/52	20kW	1:32:44	1:35:10- 16
	Kowal	Matylda	POL	11.1.89	165/54	3kSt	9:44.10	9:35.13- 16
	Kozák	Luca	HUN	1.6.96	166/55	100h	13.10, 12.99w	13.20- 16
	Králová	Tereza	CZE	22.10.89	175/85	HT	68.55	70.21- 13
	Kramer	Regine	GER	5.4.93	168/59	PV	4.35	4.40- 16
*	Krasnova	Angelina	RUS	7.2.91	168/55	PV	4.61i, 4.60	4.70- 13
	Krasovskiy	Ekaterina	AUT	13.7.84	175/60	HJ	1.89i	1.94- 06
*	Krause	Gesa-Felicitas	GER	3.8.92	167/55	3000	8:56.13i	8:49.43i- 16, 9:02.04- 15
	5000	15:24.53				3kSt	9:11.85	9:18.41- 16
	Krechik	Yelena	BLR	20.7.87	174/73	HT	71.40	72.06- 15
*	Krizsán	Xénia	HUN	13.1.93	171/62	Hep	6390	6322- 15
	Krumins	Susan	NED	8.7.86	170/54	1500	4:02.25	4:05.38- 13
*	3000	8:34.41	8:36.08- 14	5000	14:51.25	15:00.69- 16	10000 31:20.24	31:31.97- 15
^	Krylova	Anna	RUS	3.10.85	177/65	TJ	14.30	14.40- 12
	Kuchyna	Darya	UKR	14.6.93	178/58	HJ	1.86	1.86- 16
	Kulichenko	Yelena	RUS-Y	28.7.02		HJ	1.87	
	Kuma	Dibaba	ETH	14.9.96		HMar	69:49	69:21- 16
	Kunova	Vera	RUS	2.4.90		SP	17.51	17.48- 15
	Kupina	Yekaterina	RUS	2.2.86	172/59	800	2:00.34	1:59.21- 13
	Kupstyte	Giedre	LTU	9.3.92	182/80	SP	16.93i, 16.30	16.72- 16
	Kurgat	Ednah	KEN	15.6.95	169/50	5000	15:19.03i, 15:26.00	15:48.63- 16
	Kuria	Mary	KEN	29.11.87	157/48	1500	4:08.85	4:03.18- 12
	Kurywchak	Danylle	USA	15.7.94		TJ	13.57	12.65- 16
	Küster	Susen	GER	27.7.94	165/69	HT	71.25	66.44- 16
	Kuwahara	Sayaka	JPN	8.3.93	162/45	10000	32:27.36	32:14.43- 15
						Mar	2:26:09	2:25:09- 16
	Kuze	Kiho	JPN	28.3.95	165/58	JT	57.67	58.98- 13
	Kwambai	Antonina	KEN	–.92		HMar	69:49	72:28- 16
	Kylypko	Maryna	UKR	10.11.95	165/60	PV	4.60	4.65- 16
	La Mao		CHN	17.12.96		20kW	1:28:44	1:31:46- 16
	Laasma	Liina	EST	13.1.92	178/77	JT	61.32	63.65- 16
	Labiche	Lissa	SEY	18.2.93	172/52	HJ	1.91	1.92A- 15
*	LaCaze	Genevieve	AUS	4.8.89	168/54	3000	8:45.81i, 8:53.48	8:52.28- 16
						3kSt	9:24.52	9:14.28- 16
	LaFond	Thea	DMA	5.4.94	173/65	TJ	14.20	13.61i, 13.41, 13.70w- 16
	Lagat	Violah	KEN	13.3.89	165/49	1500	4:07.66	4:04.10- 15
						3000	8:55.83i	8:52.34- 13
	Lagger	Sarah	AUT-J	3.9.99	174/60	Hep	6083	5960- 16
	Lahti/van der Wielen	Sarah	SWE	18.2.95	177/57	5000	15:14.17	15:10.76- 16
	10k	32:46.91	31:28.43- 16			HMar	69:58	
	Lake	Iona	GBR	15.1.93	160/50	3kSt	9:39.03	9:56.64- 15
*	Lake	Morgan	GBR	12.5.97	178/64	HJ	1.96	1.94- 15
	Lakshani	H.D. Viduka	SRI	28.12.96		TJ	13.64	13.49- 15
	Lally	Jade	GBR	30.3.87	183/81	DT	62.15	65.10- 16
	Lalonde	Geneviève	CAN	5.9.91	167/47	3kSt	9:29.99	9:30.24- 16
	Lalova-Collio	Ivet	BUL	18.5.84	168/55	100	11.25	10.77- 04
*						200	22.82	22.32- 15

	Name		Nat	Born	Ht/Wt	Event	2017 Mark	Pre-2017 Best
	Lamble	Regan	AUS	14.10.91	174/55	20kW	1:29:58	1:29:33- 16
	Landázuri	Narcisa	ECU	25.11.92	160/52	100	11.26A, 11.30, 11.25w	11.26A, 11.27- 16
	Landwehr	Katie	USA	23.1.93	168/64	3kSt	9:37.00	9:41.22- 16
	Lang	Salome	SUI	18.11.97		HJ	1.86	1.87i, 1.86- 16
	Larios	Maria	ESP	29.10.92	164/49	20kW	1:32:31	1:35:56- 16
	Larsson	Eleni	SWE	4.4.93	186/100	HT	64.86	68.76- 15
	Larsson	Maria	SWE	24.3.94	179/55	3kSt	9:39.96	9:50.16- 16
*	Lashmanova	Yelena	RUS	9.4.92	170/48	20kW	1:25:18	1:24:58- 16
*	Lasitskene	Mariya	RUS	14.1.93	182/60	HJ	2.06	2.01- 15
	Latham	Viershanie	USA	1.8.95		LJ	6.55w	6.14- 16
						TJ	13.50, 13.67w	13.31, 13.60w- 16
	Latiseva-Cudare	Gunta	LAT	9.3.95	179/68	200	23.15, 22.93w	23.65- 16
						400	51.37	52.17- 15
	Lawrence	Collier	USA	4.10.86	163/52	3kSt	9:51.13	9:50.47- 15
	Lawrence	Mel	USA	29.8.89	167/52	3kSt	9:34.94	9:36.35- 16
	Lawrence	Shadae	JAM	31.12.95	173/84	DT	62.59	61.18- 16
	Lawrence	Shardia	JAM	31.12.95		TJ	13.75i, 13.66, 13.79w	13.28- 16
	Lawson	Lekeisha	USA	3.6.87	168/57	100	11.33, 11.12w	11.06- 15
	Lazar	Bianca	ROU	24.2.93	166/74	HT	64.97	65.48- 16
	le Roux	Natalie	RSA	10.6.80		50kW	4:54:33	
	Le-Roy	Anastasia	JAM	11.9.87	172/57	400	51.38	50.84- 14
	Lebedeva	Lyudmila	RUS	23.5.90	165/48	3kSt	9:52.51	9:36.56- 15
	Leblanc	Annie	CAN	29.4.92	170/57	800	2:01.56	2:01.87- 15
	Ledáki	Stélla-Iró	GRE	18.7.88	170/58	PV	4.35	4.50- 12
	Lederer	Amelie-Sophie	GER	22.4.94	173/60	100	11.28	11.46- 16
^	Lee	Muna	USA	30.10.81	173/50	100	11.21w	10.85- 08, 10.78w- 09
	Lefebvre-Oatis	Mikella	CAN-J	18.4.98		HJ	1.86	1.77- 15
	Leffler	Celina	GER	9.4.96	174/61	Hep	6070	5846- 14
	Lehikoinen	Viivi	FIN-J	27.8.99	171/54	400h	56.49	57.65- 16
	Lekamge	H.L. Dilhani	SRI	14.1.87	167/61	JT	58.11	56.92- 16
	Lekapana	Parendis	KEN	4.8.91		HMar	69:13	69:49- 16
	LeLeux Romero	Morgann	USA	14.11.92	170/61	PV	4.65	4.60- 16
	Lema	Marta	ETH	30.12.90		Mar	2:27:37	2:24:32- 16
	Lempus	Betty	KEN	.91		HMar	69:25	71:51- 16
	Lemus	Sandra	COL	1.1.89	170/102	SP	17.87	18.03- 13
	Leontyeva	Natalya	RUS	5.7.87	168/48	3kSt	9:52.36	10:01.70- 16
*	Leontyuk	Yuliya	BLR	31.1.84	185/80	SP	18.47	19.79- 08
^	Lesueur	Éloyse	FRA	15.7.88	181/65	LJ	6.66, 6.93w	6.92- 14, 7.04w- 12
						TJ	14.10	
	Letnar	Bernarda	SLO	26.12.89	177/72	JT	57.84	56.51- 11
	Lettow	Lindsay	USA	6.6.90	175/62	Hep	5774	6098- 16
*	Levchenko	Yuliya	UKR	28.11.97	179/60	HJ	2.01	1.95- 16
*	Levy	Jura	JAM	4.11.90	157/50	100	11.06	11.10, 11.07w- 11
						200	22.88	22.76- 11
	Levy	Toria	USA	5.10.94	165/50	400h	56.66	57.05- 16
	Lewetegn	Sintayehu	ETH	9.5.96	161/48	3000	8:53.44	9:02.98- 15
						5000	14:53.44	15:06.49- 16
*	Lewis-Smallwood	Gia	USA	1.4.79	183/93	DT	65.81	69.17- 14
*	Li Ling		CHN	6.7.89	180/65	PV	4.50	4.70i- 16, 4.66- 15
*	Li Lingwei		CHN	26.1.89	172/75	JT	66.25	65.11- 12
	Li Maocuo		CHN	20.10.92		20kW	1:31:00	1:31:55- 14
	Li Ping		CHN	7.1.94		20kW	1:31:27	1:33:39- 15
	Li Qiuye		CHN	2.12.93		50kW	4:42:27	
	Li Xiaohong		CHN	8.1.95	178/87	TJ	13.66	14.20- 15
	Li Yanmei		CHN	6.2.90	171/56	TJ	13.73	14.35- 11
	Liang Rui		CHN	18.6.94		20kW	1:28:50	1:28:43- 16
	Liang Xiaojing		CHN	7.4.97	156/48	100	11.25w	11.52- 15
	Liang Yan		CHN	2.1.95	171/73	DT	58.41	62.01- 13
*	Licwinko	Kamila	POL	22.3.86	183/66	HJ	1.99	2.02i, 1.99- 15
	Linden	Desiree	USA	26.7.83	157/44	Mar	2:25:06dh	2:22:38dh- 11, 2:25:55- 12
	Lindh	Lovisa	SWE	9.7.91	169/56	800	1:58.77	1:59.41- 16
	1000	2:35.15		2:36.04- 16		1500	4:09.03	4:14.10- 16
	Lindley	Lindsay	NGR	6.10.89	173/63	100h	12.90	12.97- 15
	Linkiewicz	Joanna	POL	2.5.90	172/55	400h	55.42	55.25- 16
	Linnell	Lisa	SWE	30.4.91	175/66	Hep	5890	5888- 13
	Lipari	Emily	USA	19.11.92	153/48	1500	4:07.29	4:12.17- 13
	1M	4:28.84		4:31.68i- 16, 4:32.4- 15		3000	8:57.24i	9:08.91i- 13, 9:34.52- 10
	Lipsanen	Saara	FIN	13.9.95	178/65	JT	56.20	53.34- 16
*	Lipsey	Charlene	USA	16.7.91	168/57	800	1:57.38	2:00.60- 15
						1000	2:37.97Ai	2:40.79i- 15

	Name		Nat	Born	Ht/Wt	Event	2017 Mark	Pre-2017 Best
*	Little	Shamier	USA	20.3.95	163/52	400	50.40	51.06- 14
						400h	52.75	53.51- 16
*	Liu Shiying		CHN	24.9.93	179/76	JT	66.47	65.64- 16
	Liu Tingting		CHN	29.1.90	178/87	HT	71.68	73.06- 14
	Liu Xiangrong		CHN	6.6.88	185/119	SP	18.16	19.24- 12
	Livingston	Ornella	JAM	19.5.91	168/55	100	11.20w	11.37- 16
	Llano	Beatrice Nedberge	NOR	14.12.97	169/90	HT	67.42	67.86- 16
	Lloyd	Cassandra	USA	27.1.90	163/54	100h	13.10	12.86- 16
	Lobe	Ricarda	GER	13.4.94	171/59	100h	12.91	13.01- 16
	Lobun	Helen Ekarare	KEN-J	18.3.99	170/46	1500	4:07.06	4:12.90- 16
	3000	8:53.70		8:55.06- 16		5000	15:14.79	15:12.89- 16
	Lofstrand	Gena	RSA	23.10.95	162/52	800	2:01.50	2:04.60- 13
	Lomnická	Nikola	SVK	16.9.88	168/70	HT	68.90	71.58- 14
	Loney	Dawnalee	JAM	15.5.96	181/62	400	52.05	52.35- 16
	Long	Kally	USA	28.8.95	180/62	PV	4.42i, 4.40	4.32- 16
	López	Yaniuvis	CUB	1.2.86	180/71	SP	18.92	18.81- 09
	Lotout	Marion	FRA	19.11.89	165/54	PV	4.41Ai, 4.40	4.60- 13
	Love	Alexis	USA	24.4.91	168/57	100	11.15w	11.28- 12, 11.25w- 16
						200	23.34, 22.82w	22.63- 16
*	Lowe	Chaunté	USA	12.1.84	175/60	HJ	1.94	2.05- 10
	Lozano	Ana	ESP	22.2.91	174/53	3000	8:54.95	9:30.15- 16
						5000	15:14.23	
*	Lu Huihui		CHN	26.6.89	171/68	JT	67.59	66.13- 15
	Lu Minjia		CHN	29.12.92	172/58	LJ	6.67	6.74- 09
	Lu Xiaoxin		CHN	22.2.89	184/90	DT	62.58	63.27- 13
-	Lu Xiuzhi		CHN	26.10.93	167/52	20kW	1:26:28	1:25:12- 15
	Lückenkemper	Gina	GER	21.11.96	170/58	100	10.95	11.04- 16
	Luo Na		CHN	8.10.93	173/75	HT	72.27	69.81- 14
	Luque	Jhoanmy	VEN	20.12.95	158/52	LJ	6.58, 6.63w	6.36- 15
						TJ	13.65i, 13.54, 13.80w	13.37- 16
	Lutkovskaya	Alyona	RUS	15.3.96	164/55	PV	4.40i, 4.40	4.61- 15
	Luzolo	Maryse	GER	13.3.95	169/54	LJ	6.61	6.59- 16
	Lyakhova	Olha	UKR	18.3.92	174/55	800	1:59.84	1:58.64- 15
	M González		COL			400h	56.29	
	Ma Faying		CHN	30.8.93		20kW	1:31:36	1:33:39- 15
	Ma Lingyu		CHN	6.1.95		50kW	4:54:20	4:48:12- 16
	Ma Yiming		CHN	10.9.97		20kW	1:31:32	1:47:37- 16
	Ma Zhenxia		CHN-J	1.8.98		20kW	1:33:16	
	Mackey	Katie	USA	12.11.87	165/53	1500	4:07.15	4:03.81- 15
	1M	4:31.58		4:25.48- 16		3000	8:57.30	8:46.58- 16
	Madane	Fadwa Sidi	MAR	20.11.94	162/50	1500	4:08.84	4:18.62- 14
						3kSt	9:23.99	9:27.87- 15
	Madarász	Viktória	HUN	12.5.85	153/46	20kW	1:30:05	1:30:47- 16
	Maduka	Jessie	GER	23.4.96	183.69	TJ	13.61	13.16- 16
	Mageean	Ciara	IRL	12.3.92	168/56	1500	4:03.57+	4:01.46- 16
	800	2:02.20		2:00.79- 16		1M	4:22.40	4:28.40i- 16, 4:30.64- 15
	Magnani	Margherita	ITA	26.2.87	161/45	1500	4:06.30	4:06.05- 14
						1M	4:27.51	
	Mahuchikh	Yaroslava	UKR-Y	19.9.01	165/45	HJ	1.92A	1.76- 16
	Maisch	Katharina	GER	12.6.97	177/78	SP	17.11i, 16.98	16.65- 16
	Maiwald	Anna	GER	21.7.90	176/62	Hep	5882	6111- 15
	Májková	Lucie	CZE	9.7.88	182/66	TJ	13.73	13.93- 16
	Mäkelä	Kristiina	FIN	20.11.92	185/67	TJ	14.18i, 13.92	14.24- 16
	Mäki	Kristiina	CZE	22.9.91	170/50	1500	4:08.19	4:08.68- 16
	Maksimova	Yana	BLR	9.1.89	182/70	HJ	1.87i	1.95i- 15, 1.91- 12
						Hep	5901	6198- 12
	Malácová	Romana	CZE	15.5.87	164/57	PV	4.61	4.62i, 4.55- 16
	Malavisi	Sonia	ITA	31.10.94	173/67	PV	4.40	4.51- 16
	Malone	Chantel	IVB	2.12.91	175/62	LJ	6.67i, 6.67, 6.70w	
								6.69A- 15, 6.65- 13, 6.66w- 12
	Maltseva	Yuliya	RUS	30.11.90	187/84	DT	59.31	63.48- 15
	Maluskiewicz	Agnieszka	POL	18.3.89	175/83	SP	17.06i, 16.17	17.20- 14
*	Malyshik	Hanna	BLR	4.2.94	175/90	HT	74.94	72.78- 16
*	Mamona	Patrícia	POR	21.11.88	168/53	TJ	14.42	14.65- 16
	Mamuye	Tigist	ETH	27.9.90		Mar	2:27:39	2:36:49- 11
	Mann	Brittany	USA	16.4.94	173/98	SP	17.78i, 17.49	17.49- 16
*	Manning	Christina	USA	29.5.90	163/54	100h	12.54	12.68, 12.57w- 12
	Manson	Nikki	GBR	15.10.94		HJ	1.86	1.81- 16
	Mao Yanxue		CHN	15.2.94		20kW	1:31:37	1:29:47- 15
	Marcelino	Mariana Grasielly	BRA	16.7.92	168/77	HT	67.02	64.90- 16
	Marcos	María Dolores	ESP	18.8.79	160/60	50kW	4:48:26	

	Name		Nat	Born	Ht/Wt	Event	2017 Mark	Pre-2017 Best
	Marie-Hardy	Diane	FRA	19.2.96	166/59	Hep	5731	5390- 16
	Marie-Nély	Nathalie	FRA	24.11.86	175/66	TJ	13.77	14.03- 12
	Markelova	Tatyana	RUS	19.12.88	166/59	800	2:00.77	1:58.55- 12
	Marler	Aasha	USA	24.12.92		LJ	6.43, 6.59w	6.19- 16
	Marmbrandt	Malin	SWE	29.4.85	166/58	LJ	6.52A, 6.48	6.50, 6.52w- 16
	Marois	Jill	USA	8.6.94	175/59	PV	4.45	4.22- 16
	Marshall	Tonea	USA-J	17.12.98	178/75	100h	13.14	13.04- 16
	Martin	Jada	USA	8.6.95	170/55	200	22.80, 22.76w	22.60, 22.41w- 16
*	Martinez	Brenda	USA	8.9.87	163/52	800	1:58.43	1:57.91- 13
	1500	4:02.75		4:00.94- 13		1M	4:28.96	4:26.76- 12
	Martins	Eliane	BRA	26.5.86	160/49	LJ	6.69	6.72- 16, 6.73w- 15
*	Márton	Anita	HUN	15.1.89	171/84	SP	19.63	19.87- 16
						DT	58.57	60.94- 16
	Maruszewska	Klaudia	POL	28.8.97	180/72	JT	56.24	57.59- 16
	Mashinistova	Yelena	RUS	29.3.94		LJ	6.48	6.67- 15
	Maslova	Anastasiya	BLR	16.10.97		HT	66.11	66.38- 16
	Maslova	Darya	KGZ	6.5.95	170/50	5000	15:00.42	15:42.82- 15
						10000	31:57.23	31:36.90- 16
	Mason	Symone	USA-J	31.8.99	161/55	100	11.24	11.65- 14
						200	23.00	23.37- 15
	Matanga	Failuna Abdi	TAN	28.10.92	148/37	10000	31:47.37	33:32.8- 14
	Matheis	Lara	GER	2.8.92	168/55	100	11.29	11.70- 15
	Matsuda	Anna	JPN	18.4.94	159/43	10000	32:07.11	32:54.41- 16
	Matsuda	Mizuki	JPN	31.5.95	158/46	10000	31:39.41	31:59.12- 16
	Matsumoto	Sae	JPN	15.5.93		20kW	1:33:16	1:34:47- 16
	Matsushita	Natsumi	JPN	22.1.95	158/46	10000	32:27.58	
	Matsuzaki	Rico	JPN	24.12.92	157/44	3000	8:49.61	9:06.95- 14
	5000	15:19.91		15:18.95- 14		10000	32:08.46	31:44.86- 15
	Maudens	Hanne	BEL	12.3.97	178/64	Hep	6113	5881- 16
	Mavrodieva	Radoslava	BUL	13.3.87	178/86	SP	18.36i, 17.81	18.67- 13
	Mayer	Lisa	GER	2.5.96	171/57	100	11.14, 11.02w	11.25, 11.04w- 16
						200	22.64	22.86- 16
	Mayer	Sina	GER	10.4.95		100	11.25	11.51- 16
	Mazina	Margarita	RUS	7.7.95		HJ	1.88	1.88- 15
*	Mazuronak	Olga	BLR	14.4.89	176/56	10000	32:13.73	32:31.15- 14
						Mar	2:27:14	2:23:54- 16
	Mbumi	Joëlle	CMR	25.5.86	170/63	TJ	13.58	14.16- 15
*	McCartney	Eliza	NZL	11.12.96	179/65	PV	4.82	4.80- 16
*	McColgan	Eilish	GBR	25.11.90	176/59	1500	4:01.60	4:03.74- 16
	3000	8:31.00 8:43.27- 16		5000	14:48.49	15:05.00- 16	10000 32:10.59	0
	McDermott	Nicola	AUS	28.12.96	186/63	HJ	1.90	1.88- 15
	McDonald	Alina	USA	1.1.97	168/57	PV	4.50	4.32- 16
	McDonald	Gabrielle	JAM-J	14.3.98	159/52	100h	13.12	13.94- 16
						400h	56.53	
	McDonald	Kimarra	JAM	14.8.87	170/55	800	2:02.07	2:02.08- 15
	McDonald	Sarah	GBR	2.8.93	167/50	800	2:01.2, 2:01.25	2:01.10- 16
						1500	4:05.48	4:07.18- 16
	McGee	Cory	USA	29.5.92	168/52	1M	4:27.67i	4:28.55- 16
	McGowan	Brittany	AUS	24.4.91	163/49	800	2:01.72	2:01.26- 14
*	McGrone	Candyce	USA	24.3.89	168/59	100	11.20, 10.83w	11.00, 10.91w- 15
						200	22.95, 22.39w	22.01- 15
	McIntosh	Rachael	CAN	17.1.91	174/62	Hep	5783	5789- 14
	McKee	Julienne	USA	6.12.91	167/52	LJ	6.53	6.68, 6.70w- 15
	McKinna	Sophie	GBR	31.8.94	172/95	SP	17.03	17.14- 16
	McKnight	Sparkle	TTO	21.12.91	165/55	400h	55.46	55.41- 15
*	McLaughlin	Sydney	USA-J	7.8.99	174/61	200	22.96w	23.53- 16
	400	51.61i, 51.88		51.84- 16		400h	53.82	54.15- 16
^	McLaughlin-Whilby	Anneisha	JAM	6.1.86	152/50	400	50.76	51.03- 16
*	McPherson	Inika	USA	29.9.86	163/55	HJ	1.96	1.96, 2.00dq- 14
	McPherson	Shanice	JAM	12.3.94	158/52	LJ	6.64	6.52- 15
*	McPherson	Stephenie Ann	JAM	25.11.88	168/55	400	50.56	49.92- 13
	McQueen	Darrielle	USA	29.5.96	170/57	LJ	6.55	6.51i, 6.35- 16
	McTaggart	Olivia	NZL-Y	9.1.00	172/62	PV	4.40	4.30- 16
	Meadows	Tawanna	USA	4.8.86	168/55	100	11.16, 10.72w	11.11- 14
	Mecke	Dana	USA	20.9.87	158/48	800	2:01.73	2:00.76- 15
	Medina	Ayamey	CUB-J	21.2.98	164/73	HT	65.85	68.98- 16
*	Medvedyeva	Yekaterina	RUS	29.3.94		20kW	1:25:22	1:26:40- 16
	Meijer	Michaela	SWE	30.7.93	172/63	PV	4.71	4.62- 16
	Mekonen	Tigist	BRN	7.7.97	171/70	3kSt	9:26.00	9:20.65- 15
	Mekuria	Aberu	ETH	24.12.83		Mar	2:26:17	2:25:30- 15
*	Melese	Yebrqual	ETH	18.4.90	164/55	Mar	2:22:51	2:23:23- 15

Name		Nat	Born	Ht/Wt	Event	2017 Mark	Pre-2017 Best
Melville	Miranda	USA	20.3.89	160/54	20kW	1:33:04	1:31:42- 16
Mendieta	Yusleidys	CUB	17.2.94	180/66	Hep	5779	6024- 13
Meneau	Lisa	USA	–.95	164/52	400h	56.35	57.90- 16
Meng Qianqian		CHN	6.1.91	178/85	SP	17.06	18.31- 11
Mengistu	Meseret	ETH	6.3.90	161/47	Mar	2:25:58	2:23:26- 15
Menuet	Émilie	FRA	27.11.91	155/44	20kW	1:32:00	1:31:38- 16
* Mergia	Aselefech	ETH	23.1.85	168/51	HMar	67:54	67:21- 11
					Mar	2:23:08	2:19:31- 12
Michta-Coffey	Maria	USA	23.6.86	165/51	20kW	1:32:14	1:30:49- 14
* Mihambo	Malaika	GER	3.2.94	170/52	LJ	6.62	6.95- 16
Mihretu	Birhan	ETH-J	–.98		HMar	70:00	
Mikolajczyk	Izabela	POL	4.9.90	175/63	Hep	5895	5968- 12
Miller	Ashley	USA-J	17.2.98	162/52	100h	13.08w	13.22, 13.18w- 16
Miller	Jade	USA	13.1.95	168/57	400h	56.17	55.75- 16
* Miller-Uibo	Shaunae	BAH	15.4.94	185/69	100	11.19	11.19- 16
200	21.88, 21.76St		22.05- 16		400	49.46	49.44- 16
* Minenko	Hanna	ISR	25.9.89	178/61	TJ	14.42	14.78- 15
Mineyeva	Tatyana	RUS	10.8.90		20kW	1:28:32	1:28:09- 11
Minor	Arria	USA-Y	9.2.01	168/52	400	52.05	52.50- 16
Misher	Rachel	USA	4.2.97	163/54	400	52.07	52.98- 16
Misochenko	Anna	RUS	15.4.92		LJ	6.65	6.76i, 6.69- 16
Mitchell	A'Keyla	USA	25.11.95	173/60	200	23.14, 23.00w	22.94- 16, 22.84w- 15
* Mitchell	Kathryn	AUS	10.7.82	168/72	JT	66.12	66.10- 14
Mitchell	Morgan	AUS	3.10.94	177/64	400	51.65	51.25- 16
Mitchell	Victoria	AUS	25.4.82	164/48	3kSt	9:44.09	9:30.84- 06
Mitkova	Milena	BUL	26.1.90		LJ	6.41, 6.50w	6.45- 15
Miyasaka	Kaede	JPN	12.12.92	160/48	TJ	13.48, 13.58w	13.52- 16
Miyashita	Risa	JPN	26.4.84	171/71	JT	60.03	60.86- 16
Moerman	Christie	CAN	5.10.86	172/62	100h	13.08	13.14A, 12.91Aw- 15, 12.96w-n16
Mögenburg	Katarina	NOR	16.6.91	191/65	HJ	1.88i	1.90- 15
* Moguenara	Sosthene Taroum	GER	17.10.89	182/68	LJ	6.61	7.16- 16
Moh	Clarisse	FRA	6.12.86	163/54	800	2:02.10	2:01.43- 13
Mohammed	Merima	BRN	10.6.92		Mar	2:27:49	2:23:06- 10
Mokaya	Martha	KEN-Y	1.3.00	150/42	3000	8:54.68	9:06.29- 16
					5000	15:13.81	
Mokonin	Desi Jisa	BRN	12.7.97	163/48	10000	31:19.00	
					HMar	69:07	71:40- 16
Moline	Georganne	USA	6.3.90	178/59	400	51.93	52.08- 15
*					400h	53.14	53.72- 13
* Molitor	Katharina	GER	8.11.83	182/76	JT	65.37	67.69- 15
Møller	Anna Emilie	DEN	28.7.97	166/52	3kSt	9:34.30	9:32.68- 16
Montag	Jennifer	GER-J	11.2.98	165/48	100	11.29	11.84- 16
^ Montaner	Concepción	ESP	14.1.81	170/56	LJ	6.62	6.92- 05
Montcalm	Noelle	CAN	3.4.88	166/53	400h	55.85	55.81- 14
* Montsho	Amantle	BOT	4.7.83	173/57	400	51.28	49.33- 13
Moraes	Fabiana	BRA	5.6.86	170/56	100h	12.84A, 13.03, 12.86w	12.91- 16
* Moreira	Sara	POR	17.10.85	168/51	10000	32:03.57	31:12.93- 15
Moreno	Arantxa	ESP	16.1.95	173/67	JT	56.89	56.76- 15
Moreno	Johana	COL	15.4.85	177/96	HT	66.50	69.80- 09
Morgan	Alexandra	ASA	19.5.91		DT	55.99	52.95- 15
Morgan	Monique	JAM	14.10.85	168/60	100h	13.05	12.80- 16
Mori	Chikako	JPN	25.11.92	159/43	10000	32:05.99	33:31.22- 14
					3kSt	9:49.41	9:45.27- 16
Mori	Yuka	JPN	21.7.92		JT	59.10	59.22- 12
Morita	Kaori	JPN	19.9.95	160/44	10000	31:59.94	0
					HMar	70:11	
Morland	Elizabeth	IRL-J	3.3.98		Hep	5801	5545- 16
^ Morosanu	Angela	ROU	26.7.86	178/57	LJ	6.66	
* Morris	Sandi	USA	8.7.92	174/65	PV	4.87i/4.84	5.00- 16
Morrison	Ebony	USA	28.12.94	165/57	100h	13.03, 12.96w	12.76- 16
* Morrison	Natasha	JAM	17.11.92	170/57	100	11.09	10.96- 15
Moser	Angelica	SUI	9.10.97	168/63	PV	4.61	4.57- 16
Moseti	Winfridah	KEN	12.11.96		HMar	69:41	72:57- 16
Moye	Megan	USA	27.3.94	168/52	1500	4:08.22	4:11.91- 16
Mucci	Celeste	AUS-J	11.8.99		LJ	6.48w	5.91- 16
					Hep	5870	
* Muhammad	Dalilah	USA	7.2.90	170/62	400h	52.64	52.88- 16
Muir	Carline	CAN	1.10.87	173/65	400	51.62	51.05- 16
* Muir	Laura	GBR	9.5.93	162/54	800	1:58.69	2:00.42- 15
1000	2:31.93i	2:40.5- 16	1500	4:00.35+	3:55.22- 16	1M 4:18.03	4:19.12- 16
3000	8:26.41i, 8:30.64		8:38.47- 15		5000	14:49.12i, 14:52.07	15:53.68- 13

Name		Nat	Born	Ht/Wt	Event	2017 Mark	Pre-2017 Best
Mulhall	Kimberley	AUS	9.1.91		DT	57.88	58.53- 16
Müller	Laura	GER	11.12.95	172/57	100	11.36, 11.20w	11.37- 16
200	22.65		22.81- 16		400	52.04	51.69- 16
* Müller	Nadine	GER	21.11.85	193/90	DT	65.76	68.89- 12
Mullina	Olga	RUS	1.8.92	166/60	PV	4.67	4.65- 16
Mulugeta	Mahelet	ETH	20.3.95	164/52	800	2:00.77	2:04.3- 14
Munehisa	Yuki	JPN	15.12.97		10000	32:36.83	31:58.46- 16
* Mupopo	Kabange	ZAM	21.9.92	170/57	200	23.03A	23.35- 14
					400	50.60	50.22- 15
Murashova	Yelena	RUS	5.10.87	163/52	800	2:01.45	2:02.40- 14
					1500	4:07.23	4:21.36- 13
Muratova	Olesya	RUS	25.10.92		800	2:01.96	2:03.48i- 15, 2:04.21- 16
Murto	Wilma	FIN-J	11.6.98	182/68	PV	4.66Ai	4.71i, 4.52- 16
Muscaro	Carly	USA	18.5.95	164/54	400	51.41	51.17- 16
Mutai	Beatrice	KEN	19.4.87	152/38	HMar	70:14	69:30- 14
Muthoni	Esther	KEN	.96		5000	15:28.38	
Mutua	Veronica	KEN	2.2.92		400	52.14A	54.26- 15
Müze	Lina	LAT	4.12.92	181/75	JT	60.55	62.09- 16
Mwangi	Ann	KEN	8.12.88	172/51	5000	15:19.62	15:05.34- 09
Myers	Tamara	BAH	27.7.93	173/66	LJ	6.51, 6.61w	6.39- 14
					TJ	14.03	13.60, 13.77w- 16, 13.78Aw- 15
Nabeshima	Rina	JPN	16.12.93	160/46	5000	15:11.83	15:22.34- 16
					10000	32:19.18	33:08.0- 14
Nacheva	Aleksandra	BUL-Y	20.8.01		TJ	13.64	12.25- 16
Nadolska	Karolina	POL	6.9.81	165/54	HMar	69:54	70:36- 11
* Nageotte	Katie	USA	30.6.91	168/59	PV	4.73	4.63i, 4.60- 16
Nakaayi	Halimah	UGA	16.10.94	160/55	800	2:00.80	1:59.78- 16
Nakahara	Misuzu	JPN	29.11.94	160/43	10000	32:34.65	
* Nana Djimou	Antoinette	FRA	2.8.85	175/69	Hep	6311	6576- 12
Nanyondo	Winnie	UGA	23.8.93	164/48	800	2:00.22	1:58.63- 14
					1500	4:07.93	4:17.13- 15
* Naser	Salwa Eid	BRN-J	23.5.98	167/50	400	49.88	50.88- 16
* Nawowuna	Alice Aprot	KEN	2.1.94	174/55	10000	31:11.86	29:53.51- 16
Ndiwa	Stacy	KEN	6.12.92		HMar	69:09	
Ndu	Ugonna	NGR	27.6.91	169/54	400h	56.01	56.12- 13
Neena	Narayanan V.	IND	2.5.91		LJ	6.54	6.66- 16
Neita	Daryll	GBR	29.8.96	172/61	100	11.14	11.23- 16
* Nel	Wenda	RSA	30.7.88	169/52	400	52.03A, 52.97	52.09A, 53.02- 15
					400h	54.58	54.37- 15
Nelson	Ashleigh	GBR	20.2.91	175/69	100	11.27	11.19, 11.15w- 14
Nelson	Ella	AUS	10.5.94	169/56	200	23.00	22.50- 16
* Nelvis	Sharika	USA	10.5.90	178/64	100h	12.52	12.34- 15
Neola	Orphée	FRA	1.2.91	162/46	100	11.22	11.51- 16
* Nettey	Christabel	CAN	2.6.91	162/59	LJ	6.92, 6.94w	6.99- 15
Newell	Anicka	CAN	5.8.93	175/64	PV	4.65	4.50- 16
* Newman	Alysha	CAN	29.6.94	179/67	PV	4.75	4.61- 16
* Ngugi	Mercy Wacera	KEN	17.12.88	155/	HMar	68:38	66:29- 16
Nguyen Thi Huyen		VIE	19.5.93	162/52	400h	56.06	56.15- 15
Ni Yuanyuan		CHN	6.4.95		20kW	1:29:14	1:29:53- 16
Nicollin	Margaux	FRA	1.5.95	185/72	JT	58.76	59.73- 15
Nidbaykina	Darya	RUS	26.12.94	168/57	TJ	14.21	13.72i- 16, 13.70- 15
Nie Jingjing		CHN	1.3.88	168/45	20kW	1:28:34	1:27:51- 15
Nielsen	Lara	AUS	19.12.92	168/80	HT	66.90	66.37- 15
Nielsen	Laviai	GBR	13.3.96	168/54	400	51.90i	52.25- 15
Nikisenko	Marina	MDA	28.6.86	185/85	HT	71.58	72.53- 09
Nikkanen	Minna	FIN	9.4.88	169/53	PV	4.55i, 4.45	4.61i- 16, 4.60- 15
Nikolayeva	Anastasiya	RUS	24.9.95	166/52	100h	13.05	13.25- 15
Nikolenko	Svetlana	RUS	26.9.91	182/60	HJ	1.91i, 1.87	1.88- 16
Nilsson	Linn	SWE	15.10.90	169/55	1500	4:08.47	4:11.19- 15
Nilsson	Maja	SWE-J	8.12.99	183/65	HJ	1.90	1.82- 16
Nisimura	Daniela Mieko	BRA	26.3.94	174/81	JT	59.03	54.87- 14
* Niyonsaba	Francine	BDI	5.5.93	161/56	800	1:55.47	1:56.24- 16
Njadoe	Wurrie	USA	14.8.97	170/57	LJ	6.55, 6.67w	6.03- 16
Nokelainen	Heidi	FIN	30.9.90	170/68	JT	58.55	62.13- 16
Norman	Breana	USA	14.9.92	174/63	100h	13.10	13.07- 16
Novotná	Jana	CZE-J	26.1.99		Hep	5716	
Novozhylova	Iryna	UKR	7.1.86	175/87	HT	71.18	74.10- 12
Nozoe	Yuri	JPN	3.5.96	150/38	10000	32:26.93	
* Nugent	Leah	JAM	23.11.92	168/62	100h	12.83w	13.11- 15
					400h	54.54	54.45- 16
Nugter	Corinne	NED	28.3.92	182/80	DT	57.97	56.74- 16

	Name		Nat	Born	Ht/Wt	Event	2017 Mark	Pre-2017 Best
	Nukuri	Diane	BDI	1.12.84	175/54	HMar	69:13	69:12- 13
	Nuttall	Emma	GBR	23.4.92	184/64	HJ	1.86	1.88i- 14, 1.87- 13
	Nwanaga	Kelechi	NGR	24.12.97	170/59	JT	58.15	53.52- 16
	Nyaruai	Veronica	KEN	29.10.89	165/43	10000	31:07.56	32:22.22- 14
						HMar	67:58	68:06- 16
	Nygård	Sanna	FIN	22.3.88	176/60	TJ	13.76	13.73- 15
	Nzisa	Winfredah	KEN	30.5.97	158/48	1500	4:04.46	4:09.25- 16
	O'Connell	Jessica	CAN	10.2.89	158/48	5000	15:14.99	15:06.44- 15
	O'Connor	Kate	IRL-Y	12.12.00		Hep	5759	
	O'Connor	Leah	USA	30.8.92	171/55	3000	8:56.14i	8:59.44i- 16
						3kSt	9:31.61	9:18.85- 16
	O'Flaherty	Kerry	IRL	15.7.81	167/52	3kSt	9:50.75	9:42.61- 15
	Obare	Doricah	KEN	10.1.90	162/48	10000	32:06.22	31:37.07- 10
*	Obiri	Hellen	KEN	13.12.89	155/45	1500	4:00.44+	3:57.05- 14
	1M	4:16.56				2000	5:34.83+	5:37.7- 14
	3000	8:23.14		8:20.68- 14		5000	14:18.37	14:25.78- 16
	Obleshchuk/Turchyn	Halyna	UKR	23.2.89	177/94	SP	17.87	19.40- 14
	Odeyemi	Aminat Youssef	BRN	27.6.97	168/60	400h	56.08	56.94- 16
	Odiong	Ofonime	BRN	13.3.97	168/60	200	22.95	22.74- 16
*	Ofili	Cindy	GBR	5.8.94	172/60	100h	12.92	12.60- 15
	Ogasawara	Akari	JPN-Y	3.10.00	161/42	3000	8:54.88	9:05.15- 16
	Ogasawara	Shuri	JPN-Y	3.10.00	161/42	5000	15:23.56	15:29.32- 16
	Ogbeta	Naomi	GBR-J	18.4.98	180/64	TJ	13.64, 13.68w	12.99i- 16, 12.98- 15
	Ogrodníková	Nikola	CZE	18.8.90	175/73	JT	62.24	60.04- 14
	Ohara	Rei	JPN	10.8.90	165/47	HMar	69:26	69:17- 15
	Okada	Kumiko	JPN	17.10.91	158/44	20kW	1:29:40	1:29:40- 16
*	Okagbare	Blessing	NGR	9.10.88	180/68	100	10.99	10.79, 10.75w- 13
	200	22.87		22.23- 14		LJ	6.77	7.00. 7.14w- 13
	Okamoto	Harumi	JPN-J	7.2.98	160/44	10000	32:17.29	
*	Okolo	Courtney	USA	15.3.94	168/54	400	50.29	49.71- 16
	Okparaebo	Ezinne	NOR	3.3.88	164/56	100	11.31, 11.23w	11.10- 12, 11.0- 15
*	Okuneva	Oksana	UKR	14.3.90	175/61	HJ	1.97	1.98- 14
	Oliver	Javianne	USA	26.12.94	160/52	100	11.16	11.29, 11.16w- 16
						200	22.99w	23.68- 16
	Olivieri	Linda	ITA-J	14.7.98	167/52	400h	57.00	59.03- 15
*	Oljira	Belaynesh	ETH	26.6.90	160/47	5000	15:08.05	14:42.57- 16
	10000	30:44.57		30:26.70- 12		HMar	68:19	67:27- 11
	Omerzu	Lara	SLO-J	10.2.98	183/63	HJ	1.86i	1.85- 15
	Omoregie	Eleonora	ITA	22.5.96	175/58	HJ	1.88i	1.86i- 15, 1.86- 16
	Onnen	Imke	GER	17.8.94	190/66	HJ	1.87	1.89- 15
	Onofre	Marta	POR	28.1.91	171/65	PV	4.40i, 4.40	4.51i, 4.38- 16
	Onome	Glory Nathaniel	NGR	23.1.96	169/6	400h	55.30	57.44- 15
	Onuora	Anyika	GBR	28.10.84	175/69	400	51.81	50.87- 15
	Orcel	Claire	BEL	21.12.97		HJ	1.88	1.84- 16
	Ordóñez	Johana	ECU	12.12.87	166/52	20kW	1:32:52	1:34:30- 08
	Orel	Anna Maria	EST	11.12.96	171/70	HT	67.39	68.71- 16
	Oren	Emily	USA	20.9.93	175/60	3kSt	9:40.65	9:50.54- 16
*	Orji	Keturah	USA	5.3.96	166/61	LJ	6.72i, 6.59	6.63- 15
						TJ	14.32i, 14.31	14.71- 16
	Orjuela	Annabel	COL	24.7.88	150/43	20kW	1:32:40	1:32:54- 16
	Orozco	Maria Fernanda	MEX-J	25.1.98	177/105	SP	17.15	16.92- 16
	Ortiz	Coralys	PUR	16.4.85	178/61	JT	58.51	60.37- 16
	Ortiz	Mirna	GUA	28.2.87	158/44	20kW	1:30:01	1:28:32- 13
	Ortuño	Valeria	MEX-J	27.5.98		20kW	1:31:48	1:36:40- 16
	Osakue	Daisy	ITA	16.1.96	181/74	DT	58.06	52.80- 16
	Osika	Shannon	USA	15.6.93	161/48	1500	4:06.17	4:09.08- 16
	800	2:02.36		2:07.03- 16		3000	8:56.52i	9:19.10i- 15, 9:24.68- 13
*	Oskan-Clarke	Shelayna	GBR	20.1.90	167/54	800	1:59.82	1:58.86- 15
	Ostrander	Allie	USA	24.12.96	158/45	3kSt	9:41.31	
	Otamendi	Yiliena	CUB	12.4.96	174/75	SP	16.92	16.90- 16
	Oudenaarden	Niki	CAN	14.1.94		Hep	6000	5774w- 13, 5721- 14
	Oudiou	Emma	FRA	2.1.95	172/54	3kSt	9:50.30	9:44.74- 15
	Ovchinnikova	Mariya	KAZ-J	19.10.98	178/60	TJ	13.94	13.60, 13.67w- 16
	Owens	Bridgette	USA	14.3.92	163/52	100h	12.80	12.71- 12, 12.62w- 14
	Owers	Torie	NZL	6.3.94	170/80	SP	17.08i, 16.74	17.50- 16
	Owsinski	Kristina	USA	16.2.93	172/60	PV	4.40	4.40- 15
	Padovan	Paola	ITA	4.12.95	181/68	JT	57.21	54.99- 16
	Paesler	Carolin	GER	16.12.90	167/72	HT	70.30	70.76- 14
	Pagano	Sarah	USA	23.7.91	160/47	5000	15:18.57	15:26.79- 16
	3000	8:58.91				10000	32:23.95	32:16.03- 16
*	Palameika	Madara	LAT	18.6.87	185/76	JT	63.92	66.18- 16

	Name		Nat	Born	Ht/Wt	Event	2017 Mark	Pre-2017 Best
	Palframan	Justine	RSA	4.11.93	165/64	200	22.84	22.96, 22.92w- 15
						400	51.83	51.27- 15
	Palkina	Sofiya	RUS-J	9.6.98		HT	69.32	65.96- 16
*	Palmisano	Antonella	ITA	6.8.91	166/49	20kW	1:26:36	1:27:51- 14
*	Palsyte	Airine	LTU	13.7.92	186/62	HJ	2.01i, 1.92	1.98- 14
	Panagi	Nektaria	CYP	20.3.90	165/52	LJ	6.66	6.62- 15
	Panova	Yelena	RUS	2.3.87	185/95	DT	62.64	63.22- 15
*	Panturoiu	Elena Andreea	ROU	24.2.95	170/57	TJ	14.43	14.33- 16
*	Papahrístou	Paraskeví	GRE	17.4.89	170/53	TJ	14.24i, 14.24	14.73- 16, 14.77w- 12
	Paquette	Lauren	USA	27.6.86	163/45	3000	8:45.71i, 8:56.99	8:57.78i- 16, 9:11.87- 14
						5000	15:19.73	15:14.45- 16
	Parada	Lidia	ESP	11.6.93	174/70	JT	57.97	59.03- 15
	Parker	Kiara	USA	28.10.96	167/57	100	11.40, 11.19w	11.39, 11.31w- 16
	Parker	Tiffeny	USA	8.6.88	170/60	Hep	5715	5951- 16
	Parnov	Elizabeth	AUS	9.5.94	175/57	PV	4.51	4.50- 12
	Parry	Carys	GBR	24.7.81	173/72	HT	65.32	66.80- 14
	Partridge	Bethan	GBR	11.7.90	178/60	HJ	1.89i, 1.85	1.87- 15
	Pasechnik	Alena	BLR	17.4.95		SP	17.18	16.94i, 16.72- 16
^	Patterson	Eleanor	AUS	22.5.96	182/66	HJ	1.90	1.96- 13
	Patterson	Liz	USA	9.6.88	183/65	HJ	1.94	1.93- 16
	Pavlova	Mariya	RUS	21.5.96		HJ	1.89	1.82- 14
						Hep	5895	5613- 15
	Payne	Kymber	USA	4.6.96	168/54	400h	55.50	56.38- 16
	Payton	Malaina	USA	16.10.91	163/52	LJ	6.61	6.53- 16, 6.56w- 12
	Peake	Sally	GBR	8.2.86	164/57	PV	4.35	4.42i- 12, 4.40- 16
*	Pearson	Sally	AUS	19.9.86	166/60	100	11.17	11.14- 07
						100h	12.48	12.28- 11
	Pease	Sarah	USA	9.11.87	166/52	3kSt	9:43.33	9:40.94- 16
	Pechnikova	Svetlana	RUS	6.9.94		JT	56.88	52.95- 15
	Pedersen	Isabelle	NOR	27.1.92	168/54	100h	12.75	12.86- 16
	Pedroso	Yadisleidy	ITA	28.1.87	168/51	400h	54.87	54.54- 13
	Peeters	Tori	NZL	17.5.94	174/67	JT	56.84	55.14- 15
	Pegram	Taylor	USA	14.1.96	162/54	100h	13.15A, 13.11Aw	13.61- 16
*	Peinado	Robeilys	VEN	26.11.97	178/62	PV	4.65	4.60- 15
	Pejchalová	Lada	CZE-J	15.11.98	181/60	HJ	1.87	1.90- 16
*	Peleteiro	Ana	ESP	2.12.95	171/52	TJ	14.23	14.17- 12
	Pen Freitas	Marta	POR	31.7.93	153/46	1500	4:05.71	4:06.54- 16
	Pereira	Solange Andreia	ESP	12.12.89	168/49	1500	4:06.39	4:08.29- 16
	Pérez	Madaí	MEX	2.2.80	158/44	Mar	2:24:44	2:22:59- 06
	Pérez	María	ESP	29.4.96	156/48	20kW	1:29:33	1:33:44- 16
	Pérez	María José	ESP	12.6.92	159/48	3kSt	9:40.51	9:48.97- 16
	Pérez	Marta	ESP	19.4.93	169/53	1500	4:05.82	4:10.43- 16
	Pérez	Paola	ECU	21.12.89	148/55	20kW	1:29:06, 1:32:26.0t	1:31:53- 15
*	Pérez	Yaimé	CUB	29.5.91	174/78	DT	69.19	68.86- 16
*	Perkovic	Sandra	CRO	21.6.90	183/80	DT	71.41	71.08- 14
	Pérra	Athanasía	GRE	2.2.83	167/55	TJ	13.64i, 13.45	14.71- 12
	Perry	Alexis	USA	8.8.94	170/57	100h	13.14	12.90, 12.87w- 16
	Pesirídou	Elisávet	GRE	12.2.92	174/55	100h	13.03	12.93- 16
	Pete	Aaliyah	USA	15.3.95		SP	17.18i, 16.98	16.95-15
*	Petersen	Sara Slott	DEN	9.4.87	171/57	400h	54.35	53.55- 16
	Petershofen	Friedelinde	GER	19.8.95	181/68	PV	4.55	4.33i, 4.30- 16
	Petersson	Marinda	SWE	3.2.95	166/76	HT	70.01	69.43- 16
*	Petrivskaya	Zalina	MDA	5.2.88	174/90	HT	73.80	74.21- 16
	Petrova	Anna	RUS	15.7.94	163/53	3kSt	9:50.93	9:53.13- 16
*	Petrova	Gabriela	BUL	29.6.92	167/61	TJ	14.19	14.66, 14.85w- 15
	Pettigrew	Cameron	USA	17.4.95	178/60	400	51.61	53.28- 15
	Petty	Angela	NZL	16.8.91	164/55	800	2:00.44	1:59.06- 15
	Phesor	Maéva	FRA	4.9.97	178/71	TJ	13.56	13.09- 15
*	Philip	Asha	GBR	25.10.90	163/54	100	11.14	11.10- 15
*	Pierre	Barbara	USA	28.4.87	160/57	100	10.99	10.85- 13
	Pierson	Summer	USA	3.9.78	180/84	DT	60.79	61.23- 15, 61.25dh- 09
	Pilgrim	Kaysee	USA	11.7.95	185/66	HJ	1.90A	1.85- 16
	Pinedo	Ainhoa	ESP	17.2.83	171/60	20kW	1:29:50	1:31:58- 15
	Pinto	Tatjana	GER	2.7.92	170/56	100	11.24, 10.96w	11.00- 16
						200	23.32i, 22.53w	23.02- 15
	Pipi	Amarachi	GBR	26.11.95	172/60	200	22.95, 22.83w	23.20- 16
	Plotitsyna	Hanna	UKR	1.1.87	182/68	100h	12.89, 12.8h	12.93- 14, 12.91w- 13
	Pluim	Femke	NED	10.5.94	180/62	PV	4.42	4.55- 15
	Podominick	Liz	USA	5.12.84	188/86	DT	61.35	63.87- 15
	Pólak	Eléni-Klaoúdia	GRE	9.9.96	174/61	PV	4.35	4.10- 16
*	Ponomaryova	Mariya	RUS	18.6.95		20kW	1:27:53	1:26:46- 16

	Name		Nat	Born	Ht/Wt	Event	2017 Mark	Pre-2017 Best
	Popova	Kateryna	UKR	7.8.96	176/60	TJ	13.56	13.31- 16
*	Porter	Tiffany	GBR	13.11.87	172/62	100h	12.75	12.51- 14, 12.47w- 12
	Pospelova	Natalya	RUS	28.6.96		HT	65.81	64.35- 16
	Potter	Beth	GBR	27.12.91	168/48	10000	32:04.63	32:03.45- 16
	Pousse	Pauline	FRA	17.9.87	184/84	DT	60.29	62.68- 16
	Povea	Liadagmis	CUB	6.2.96	165/61	TJ	14.45	14.56- 16
^	Povh ¶	Olesya	UKR	18.10.87	169/63	100	11.26dq	11.08- 12, 11.0- 14
	Powell	Micha	CAN	12.1.95	168/55	400	52.15	51.97- 16
	Prakash Singh	Sarita	IND	26.10.89		HT	65.25	61.81- 16
*	Prandini	Jenna	USA	20.11.92	172/59	100	11.05	10.92- 15, 10.81w- 16
						200	22.54	22.20, 22.18w- 15
	Praught Leer	Aisha	JAM	14.12.89	173/55	3000	8:53.43	9:00.67- 14
						3kSt	9:19.29	9:31.75- 16
	Preiner	Verena	AUT	1.2.95	177/64	Hep	6232	6050- 16
	Presley	Emily	USA	22.1.97	166/59	PV	4.43	4.05- 16
	Pressley	Maya	USA	1.2.91	175/60	HJ	1.86	1.92- 13
^	Price	Chanelle	USA	22.8.90	166/53	800	2:00.38	1:59.10- 15
*	Price	DeAnna	USA	8.6.93	172/109	HT	74.91	73.09- 16
	Price	Kylie	USA	1.10.93	178/64	LJ	6.67	6.54, 6.66w- 16
	Prinsloo	Lynique	RSA	30.3.91	165/54	LJ	6.59	6.81- 13
*	Proctor	Shara	GBR	16.9.88	174/56	LJ	6.73	7.07- 15
						TJ	13.82	13.88i- 10, 13.74- 09
	Prokopenko	Viktoriya	RUS	17.4.91	174/60	TJ	14.00i, 14.00	14.28- 16
	Pryke	Ashley	CAN	7.7.97		JT	56.93	50.32- 16
*	Pryshchepa	Nataliya	UKR	11.9.94	163/49	800	1:58.82	1:58.60- 16
	Przybyla	Kamila	POL	3.5.96	170/54	PV	4.40	4.30- 15
^	Ptácníková	Jirina	CZE	20.5.86	175/69	PV	4.56	4.76- 13
	Pudenz	Kristin	GER	9.2.93	180/92	DT	62.89	62.61- 15
	Purica	Andrea	VEN	21.11.95	179/65	100	11.25, 11.18w	11.29A- 14,11.45, 11.1A- 16
	Purrier	Elinor	USA	20.2.95	160/50	3000	8:55.68i	9:29.29i- 16
						3kSt	9:43.65	9:47.17- 16
	Purvis	Ashton	USA	12.7.92	173/60	100	11.24	11.17- 10
	Puzakova	Anastasiya	BLR	12.12.93	161/45	3kSt	9:47.59	9:42.91- 16
	Qieyang Shenjie		CHN	11.11.90	160/50	20kW	1:28:33	1:25:16- 12
*	Quaresma	Lecabela	POR	26.12.89	172/67	Hep	6174	5802- 16
	Quick	Elizabeth	USA	14.11.94	178/63	PV	4.35	4.35i, 4.22- 16
*	Quigley	Colleen	USA	20.11.92	173/59	1500	4:03.93	4:11.61- 15
	1M	4:24.88i		4:29.67i- 15		3kSt	9:15.97	9:20.00- 16
	Raad	Trude	NOR	27.4.90	167/75	HT	66.35	65.03- 15
	Radko	Kseniya	UKR	18.8.94	162/49	50kW	4:34:49	4:39:09- 16
	Rainsberger	Katie	USA-J	18.8.98	175/57	1500	4:09.08	4:12.62- 16
	Rakocevic	Kristina	MNE-J	13.6.98	189/79	DT	57.32	58.30- 16
	Ramos	Beverly	PUR	24.8.87	163/51	10000	32:36.03	33:51.54- 09
	Ramsey	Jessica	USA	26.7.91	165/85	SP	17.76	18.42- 15
						HT	68.36	69.47- 15
	Randall	Susan	USA	6.9.74		50kW	4:54:12	4:42:34- 14
	Rani	Annu	IND	29.8.92	165/63	JT	61.86	60.01- 16
	Rao Fan		CHN	1.1.96	170/59	TJ	13.93i, 13.51	13.61i, 13.56- 16
	Ratcliffe	Julia	NZL	14.7.93	171/66	HT	70.35	70.75- 16
*	Ratej	Martina	SLO	2.11.81	178/69	JT	65.64	67.16- 10
	Ray	Chantel	USA	3.1.96	162/50	100h	13.31, 13.09w	13.33- 16
	Razor	Bianca	ROU	8.8.94	167/50	400	51.62	50.37- 15
	Reaser	Allison	USA	9.9.92	171/61	Hep	5830	5990- 16
*	Rebrik	Vera	RUS	25.2.89	176/65	JT	62.02	67.30- 16
	Receveur	Katherine	USA	19.1.96	155/44	5000	15:28.89i, 15:44.80	16:51.63- 16
	Redondo	Laura	ESP	3.7.88	165/80	HT	67.45	69.59- 13
	Reed	Jaevin	USA-J	2.5.98	167/55	200	22.84	24.34- 16
	Reed	Jaevin	USA-J	2.5.98	167/55	400	51.52	53.32- 16
*	Reese	Brittney	USA	9.9.86	170/61	LJ	7.13	7.31- 16
	Reh	Alina	GER	23.5.97	174/52	3000	8:53.56i	9:00.58i- 16, 9:05.07- 14
						5000	15:10.01	15:41.62- 16
	Reid	Sheila	CAN	2.8.89	166/52	1500	4:07.07	4:02.96- 13
						3000	8:54.60	8:44.02- 13
	Ren Mengqian		CHN	4.10.93	175/62	PV	4.50	4.50- 15
*	Rengeruk	Lilian	KEN	3.5.97	161/44	3000	8:32.73	8:53.41- 14
						5000	14:36.80	16:04.61A- 15
	Renzhina	Yekaterina	RUS	18.10.94	172/57	400	51.21	51.49- 15
	Retzius	Lene	NOR	4.1.96		PV	4.35	4.32- 16
	Reuwsaat	Stachia	USA	23.11.94	172/59	LJ	6.61	6.46- 16
	Reyes	Macarena	CHI	30.3.84	167/52	LJ	6.48A, 6.41, 6.51w	6.60- 12
	Rhodes-Johnigan	Annie	USA	13.5.95	173/64	PV	4.61	4.45- 16

Name		Nat	Born	Ht/Wt	Event	2017 Mark	Pre-2017 Best
Ribeiro	Catarina	POR	31.5.90	167/50	10000	32:27.88	32:31.18- 16
Richards	Emily	USA	21.7.95	170/52	800	2:00.62	2:05.54- 16
Richards	Ladonna	JAM	1.1.92	165/54	100h	13.11	13.19- 12
Richardson	Brianna	USA	9.9.94	176/	TJ	13.30, 13.59w	13.34- 15
Richardson	Sha'Carri	USA-Y	25.3.00	168/52	100	11.28	11.34A- 16
Richardsson	Camilla	FIN	14.9.93	174/52	3kSt	9:41.73	9:46.34- 15
* Ricketts	Shanieka	JAM	2.2.92	182/66	TJ	14.45	14.57- 16
Riddick	Monique	USA	8.11.89	168/84	SP	18.89	17.73- 16
Rionoripo	Purity	KEN	10.6.93	165/48	Mar	2:20:55	2:24:47- 16
Rionotukei	Chemutai	KEN	4.9.86		Mar	2:26:30	2:34:38- 16
Ritter	Julia	GER-J	13.5.98	180/95	SP	17.24	16.30i, 15.89- 16
Roberson	Savannah	USA	15.1.96		200	23.26, 22.81w	23.42, 22.98w- 16
Roberson	Takyera	USA-J	7.5.98	168/57	400	51.35	53.90- 15
* Robert-Michon	Mélina	FRA	18.7.79	180/85	DT	66.21	66.73- 16
* Roberts	Kelsey-Lee	AUS	21.9.91	175/70	JT	64.53	63.92- 14
Robinson	Kaylah	USA-J	27.6.99	158/50	100h	13.32, 12.98w	13.53- 16
Robinson	NaAsha	USA	23.1.97	168/54	400	52.00	53.15- 16
Robles	Carolina	ESP	4.12.91	163/49	3kSt	9:52.79	9:59.18- 16
Rocha	Carla Salomé	POR	25.4.90	158/48	10000	32:07.62	32:05.82- 16
					Mar	2:27:08	
Rodrigues	Irina	POR	5.2.91	181/81	DT	62.63	63.96- 16
Rodríguez	Adriana	CUB-J	12.7.99		Hep	5733	5925- 16
^ Rodríguez	Rosa	VEN	2.7.86	180/85	HT	66.31	73.64- 13
* Rodríguez	Yorgelis	CUB	25.1.95	173/66	HJ	1.95	1.87- 16
LJ	6.50		6.35- 14		Hep	6594	6481- 16
Rodríguez	Zudikey	MEX	14.3.87	168/56	400h	56.75	55.78A- 14, 56.10- 10
Roesler	Laura	USA	19.12.91	168/54	800	1:59.54	1:59.04- 14
Rogers	Natosha	USA	7.5.91	164/48	5000	15:08.29	15:28.56- 16
					10000	31:54.62	31:59.21- 12
Rogers	Raevyn	USA	7.9.96	171/64	800	1:59.10	1:59.71- 15
Rohrer	Anna	USA	27.2.97	170/50	5000	15:29.83i	15:32.03i, 15:49.42- 16
					10000	31:58.99	
* Rojas	Yulimar	VEN	21.10.95	189/75	TJ	14.96	15.02- 16
* Roleder	Cindy	GER	21.8.89	178/68	100h	12.90	12.59- 15
Rolland	Megan	USA	30.8.88	173/57	3kSt	9:40.94	9:35.31- 16
Roloff	Annika	GER	10.3.91	168/58	PV	4.51i, 4.51	4.60- 16
Roos	Fanny	SWE	2.1.95	173/78	SP	18.21	17.58- 16
^ Rosa	Chiara	ITA	28.1.83	178/95	SP	17.30	19.15-07
da Rosa	Nair	BRA	22.3.80		50kW	4:39:28	
Rosa	Vitória	BRA	12.1.96	170/56	100	11.24	11.36A- 15
					200	22.93	23.11, 23.10w- 15
Rosa	Vitoria Cristina	BRA	12.1.96	170/56	200	22.93, 22.67w	23.11- 15
Roshchupkina	Viktoryia	BLR	23.5.95		20kW	1:33:16	1:34:18- 15
^ Rosolová	Denisa	CZE	21.8.86	175/63	400h	55.41	54.24- 12
Ross	Kortney	USA	26.7.92	180/64	PV	4.60Ai, 4.55	4.43- 16
Ross Ransom	Skylar	USA	19.2.95	160/52	100h	13.11	13.28, 13.18w- 16
Rossit	Desirée	ITA	19.3.94	181/53	HJ	1.86	1.97- 16
* Rotaru	Alina	ROU	5.6.93	175/54	LJ	6.78	6.75- 15
Rotich	Caroline	KEN	13.5.84	161/45	HMar	69:41	68:52- 11
					Mar	2:26:26	2:23:22- 12
Rotich	Naomi	KEN	5.4.94		HMar	68:44	70:28- 16
* Rowbury	Shannon	USA	19.9.84	165/52	1500	4:04.56+I, 4:04.61	3:56.29- 15
1M	4:23.05i 4:20.34- 08		3000	8:33.38	8:29.93- 14	5000 14:57.55	14:38.92- 16
Ruckstuhl	Géraldine	SUI-J	24.2.98	175/64	JT	58.31	53.38- 16
					Hep	6357	5835- 16
Rudakova	Vera	RUS	20.3.92	175/57	400h	56.07	54.48- 16
* Rüh	Anna	GER	17.6.93	184/74	DT	63.90	66.14- 15
Ruiz	Flor Dennis	COL	24.1.91	171/67	JT	62.48	63.84A- 16
Ruiz	Úrsula	ESP	11.8.83	170/84	SP	18.28	17.99- 12
Runia	Anna Sjoukje	NED	19.2.95		400h	57.03	
* Russell	Janieve	JAM	14.11.93	175/63	400	51.94	51.17- 16
					400h	54.02	53.96- 16
Rydz	Aneta	POL	30.3.94	175/56	HJ	1.87	1.86- 15
* Rypakova	Olga	KAZ	30.11.84	178/53	LJ	6.50	6.85- 07
					TJ	14.77	15.25- 10
* Ryzih	Lisa	GER	27.9.88	179/60	PV	4.75i, 4.73	4.73- 16
Sabin	Kiley	USA	28.4.96	181/100	SP	17.17i, 16.65	15.79- 16
Sadeiko	Grit	EST	29.7.89	172/62	Hep	6280	6221- 13
* Sado	Besu	ETH	12.1.96	172/56	1500	4:00.98	3:59.47- 16
Sadova	Viktoriya	RUS	18.3.93		HT	65.78	64.36- 14
Sadovnikova	Anastasiya	RUS	22.6.95	174/61	PV	4.35	4.45i, 4.40- 15

	Name		Nat	Born	Ht/Wt	Event	2017 Mark	Pre-2017 Best
	Saeed	Alia Mohamed	UAE	18.5.91	164/53	5000	15:00.45	15:24.94- 14
						10000	31:49.01	31:10.25- 16
	Safránková	Katerina	CZE	8.6.89	191/105	HT	71.34	72.47- 16
*	Sagnia	Khaddi	SWE	20.4.94	173/63	LJ	6.72	6.78- 15
	Sahutoglu	Tugçe	TUR	1.5.88	180/120	HT	68.15	74.17- 12
	Sainte-Luce	Camille	FRA	18.4.96	180/84	HT	67.22	65.96- 16
	Saito	Marina	JPN	15.10.95	164/64	JT	62.37	58.21- 16
*	Saladukha	Olha	UKR	4.6.83	175/55	TJ	14.02i, 13.97	14.99- 12, 15.06w- 11
	Salaski	Tamara	SRB	16.10.88	166/54	400	51.98	51.89- 16
	Salman-Kaya	Kıvılcım	TUR	27.3.92	167/80	HT	71.88	72.55- 12
*	Salman-Rath	Claudia	GER	25.4.86	175/65	LJ	6.94i, 6.86	6.73, 6.84w- 15
						Hep	6580	6462- 13
	Salmela	Johanna	FIN	6.11.90	172/76	HT	67.08	65.83- 15
	Salming	Bianca	SWE-J	22.11.98	178/67	HJ	1.90	1.83- 16
						Hep	5894	5840- 16
	Salterberg	Christine	GER	9.6.94	178/59	400h	56.97	57.55- 14
	Samuel	Jamile	NED	24.4.92	168/57	100	11.26, 11.04w	11.12- 14
	Samuel	Laura	GBR	19.2.91	165/68	TJ	13.60	14.09- 14
	Samuels	Samiyah	USA	2.10.97		LJ	6.58w	6.48i, 6.44- 16
	Sananés	Deborah	FRA	26.10.95	171/52	400	51.91	51.75- 16
	Sánchez	Irene	ESP	25.9.92	173/57	3kSt	9:40.30	9:53.65- 15
	Sánchez	María Guadalupe	MEX	4.8.95	165/48	20kW	1:33:28A	1:31:31- 16
	Sánchez-Puebla	Lidia	ESP	17.7.96	169/52	20kW	1:30:51	1:34:58- 15
	Sandblom	Linda	FIN	18.10.89	176/62	HJ	1.91i, 1.84	1.93- 16
	Sanders	Shayla	USA	6.1.94	168/55	100	11.28	11.13- 16
						200	22.95	22.77- 16
	Sango	Misaki	JPN	21.4.89	165/46	3kSt	9:50.72	9:49.85- 14
	Santiago	Xahria	CAN-J	9.10.99	165/50	400h	57.01	56.79- 15
	Santiusti	Yusneysi	ITA	24.12.84	161/48	800	2:00.17	1:58.53- 12
*	Santos	Rosângela	BRA	20.12.90	165/55	100	10.91	11.04, 11.01w- 15
						200	22.95	22.77- 15
	Sarrapio	Patricia	ESP	16.11.82	168/58	TJ	13.67	14.16A- 16, 14.10- 10, 14.30w- 12
	Sauceda	Jessamyn	MEX	22.5.89	173/60	LJ	6.74A, 6.48	6.39, 6.43w- 16
*	Saunders	Raven	USA	15.5.96	165/125	SP	19.76	19.35- 16
*	Saunders	Sha'Keela	USA	18.12.93	168/59	LJ	6.90i, 6.79, 6.92w	6.89- 16
	Savina	Kseniya	RUS	4.6.89		800	1:59.97	2:02.37- 14
	Savinova	Yuliya	RUS	28.6.94		DT	57.57	52.15- 16
^	Sawyers	Jazmin	GBR	21.5.94	167/52	LJ	6.71i, 6.53, 6.55w	6.75, 6.86w- 16
^	Saxer	Mary	USA	21.6.87	169/57	PV	4.65Ai, 4.55	4.71Ai- 14, 4.70- 13
	Saykina	Svetlana	RUS	10.7.85	177/82	DT	56.37	63.42- 08
*	Schäfer	Carolin	GER	5.12.91	176/66	100h	13.07	13.12- 16
	HJ 1.86	1.84- 14	LJ	6.57			6.31- 16 Hep 6836	6557- 16
*	Schippers	Dafne	NED	15.6.92	179/68	100	10.95	10.81- 15
						200	22.05	21.63- 15
	Schlumpf	Fabienne	SUI	17.11.90	183/62	3kSt	9:21.65	9:30.54- 16
	Schmelzle	Hope	USA	18.2.95	167/54	3kSt	9:50.51	10:10.90- 16
	Schmidt	Sarah	GER	9.7.97	182/85	SP	17.05	16.45i, 16.42- 16
	Schneider	Rachel	USA	18.7.91	168/52	1500	4:08.95	4:06.90- 15
	1M 4:25.62i, 4:32.66	4:28.50i- 16, 4:31.04- 15				5000	15:33.06	16:04.09- 15
	Schol	Lisanne	NED	22.6.91	176/63	JT	58.72	57.50- 11
	Schultz	Nina	CAN-J	12.11.98	178/64	Hep	6021	5639- 16
	Schultze	Martina	GER	12.9.90	172/62	PV	4.45	4.50- 13
*	Schwanitz	Christina	GER	24.12.85	180/103	SP	18.50i	20.77- 15
	Schwartz	Lindsay	USA	23.4.90	178/64	Hep	5889	6036- 16
	Schweizer	Karissa	USA	4.5.96	164/50	5000	15:17.31i, 15:18.69	15:58.09- 16
	Scott Efurd	Dominique	RSA	24.6.92	160/50	1500	4:08.04	4:08.65- 15
	1M 4:28.47i	4:31.57i- 16	3000	8:41.33			8:46.65- 16 5000 15:20.10	15:25.10- 16
	Scramin	Eloah Caetano	BRA	8.6.96		JT	56.91	53.49- 15
	Sears	Je'Nia	USA	15.4.93	168/55	LJ	6.48	6.63- 16
	Seccafien	Andrea	CAN	27.8.90	152/46	5000	15:08.59	15:17.81- 16
	Sedivá	Irena	CZE	19.1.92	173/70	JT	58.76	59.89- 15
	Sedney	Naomi	NED	17.12.94	170/61	100	11.25, 11.01w	11.34- 15
	Sedova	Yelena	RUS	1.3.90	170/55	10000	32:14.43	32:13.44- 16
	See	Heidi	AUS	9.8.89	168/52	3000	8:54.13	8:55.20i- 15
	1500 4:10.42			4:08.15- 15		5000	15:22.36	16:09.10- 13
^	Sekachyova	Iryna	UKR	21.7.76	163/70	HT	67.57	74.52- 08
	Sekanová	Lucie	CZE	5.8.89	170/57	3kSt	9:43.88	9:41.84- 15
	Sekine	Hanami	JPN	26.2.96	156/43	10000	32:10.22	31:22.92- 16
	Sekino	Akane	JPN	28.7.90		10000	32:08.09	32:53.44- 11
^	Semenova	Nataliya	UKR	7.7.82	178/85	DT	64.09	64.70- 08

	Name		Nat	Born	Ht/Wt	Event	2017 Mark	Pre-2017 Best
*	Semenya	Caster	RSA	7.1.91	170/64	400	51.53	50.40- 16
	800	1:55.16		1:55.28- 16		1500	4:02.84	4:01.99- 16
*	Sendriüte	Zinaida	LTU	20.12.84	188/89	DT	61.48	65.97- 13
	Senekal	Ischke	RSA	8.1.93	175/110	SP	16.97	16.59- 16
						DT	56.04	56.86- 16
	Sergeyeva	Nadezhda	RUS	6.11.94		20kW	1:31:48	1:29:57- 16
	Serova	Svetlana	BLR	28.8.86	178/92	DT	58.01	62.23- 13
	Seyaum	Dawit	ETH	27.7.96	161/49	1500	4:00.52	3:58.09- 16
*						3000	8:37.65i	
	Seymour	KaTia	USA	3.10.97	164/50	200	23.37, 22.89w	23.26- 16
	Seymour	Katrina	BAH	7.1.93	170/61	400h	56.32	56.86- 16
	Seymour	Kiah	USA	11.1.94	178/64	400h	56.67	54.67- 16
*	Seymour	Pedrya	BAH	29.5.95	168/57	100h	13.06	12.64- 16
	Shamotina	Alyona	UKR	27.12.95	178/88	HT	72.37	68.96- 15
	Shargina	Olga	RUS	24.7.96		20kW	1:29:56	1:32:22- 16
*	Sharp	Lynsey	GBR	11.7.90	175/60	800	1:58.01	1:57.69- 16
	Shatalova	Mariya	UKR	3.3.89	169/56	3kSt	9:36.56	9:30.89- 16
	Shayunova	Alina	BLR	2.3.90		HT	67.70	70.31- 12
	Shchagina	Anna	RUS	7.12.91	166/54	1500	4:07.66	4:01.46- 15
	Sheoran	Nirmala	IND	15.7.95	166/52	400	51.28	51.48- 16
	Shigemoto	Risa	JPN	29.8.87	168/50	Mar	2:24:22	2:23:23- 12
	Shimokado	Miharu	JPN	24.4.90	161/46	Mar	2:27:54	2:39:21- 16
	Shimura	Hitomi	JPN	8.11.90	167/53	100h	13.03	13.02- 13
	Shirobokova	Natalya	RUS	18.1.94	173/79	DT	58.07	60.46- 16
^	Shkolina	Svetlana	RUS	9.3.86	187/66	HJ	1.94	2.03- 13
	Shkuratova	Anastasiya	RUS-J	29.12.99		HT	65.67	
	Shmatenko	Yuliya	UKR	10.10.91	163/50	5000	15:22.85	15:30.12- 16
*	Shukh	Alina	UKR-J	12.2.99	175/60	HJ	1.89i, 1.87	1.92- 16
	JT	56.54		51.52- 16		Hep	6381	6099- 16
	Shulgina	Mariya	BLR	14.8.89		HJ	1.86	1.90i- 14, 1.86- 10
	Shvydkina	Tatyana	RUS	8.5.90	171/62	PV	4.40i, 4.40	4.50I, 4.45-15
*	Sidorova	Anzhelika	RUS	28.6.91	170/52	PV	4.75	4.85- 16
	Siefring	Jaclyn	USA	30.9.95	168/61	Hep	5750	5627(w)- 16
	Sifuentes	Nicole	CAN	30.6.86	173/57	1500	4:04.82	4:03.97- 16
	1M	4:28.51		4:28.97i- 14, 4:31.98- 11		3000	8:53.55i	8:46.25- 16
	Silva	Ana Cláudia	BRA	6.11.88	158/55	100	11.32, 11.12w	11.01- 15, 10.93w- 13
*	Silva	Yarisley	CUB	1.6.87	169/68	PV	4.81	4.91- 15
	Silva-Domingos	Laila	BRA	30.7.82	180/80	JT	62.52	61.70- 16
	Simanovich	Yelizaveta	BLR-J	11.10.98	178/60	HJ	1.90	1.75- 16
*	Simic	Ana	CRO	5.5.90	177/58	HJ	1.92i, 1.90	1.95- 15
	Simmonds	Megan	JAM	18.3.94	159/48	100h	12.63	12.79- 16
*	Simpson	Jenny	USA	23.8.86	165/50	800	2:01.64	2:00.45- 13
	1500	4:00.70		3:57.22- 14		1M	4:19.98	4:22.18- 15
	Sipponen	Salla	FIN	13.3.95	178/73	DT	57.39	56.85- 16
	Siragusa	Irene	ITA	23.6.93	161/49	100	11.31, 11.26w	11.43, 11.36w- 14
						200	22.96	23.27- 14
*	Sisson	Emily	USA	12.10.91	165/47	10000	31:25.64	31:38.03- 15
	5000	15:02.10i, 15:10.90		15:12.22i- 15, 15:24.63- 16		HMar	68:21	
	Skarvélis	Stamatía	GRE	17.8.95	173/80	SP	17.77i, 16.76	16.75- 16
						HT	65.26	61.05- 16
*	Skoog	Sofie	SWE	7.6.90	181/65	HJ	1.94	1.94- 16
^	Skujyte	Austra	LTU	12.8.79	188/80	SP	17.37i, 16.50	17.86- 09
						Hep	5784w	6599- 12
	Skvortsova	Violetta	BLR-J	15.4.98	178/58	TJ	13.94, 14.21w	13.45- 16
*	Skydan	Hanna	AZE	14.5.92	183/114	HT	75.29	74.21- 12
	Skypalová	Katerina	CZE-J	20.2.99		HT	67.20	59.90- 16
	Slanicková	Lucia	SVK	8.11.88	179/65	Hep	6103	5780- 12
	Sloboda	Daryna	UKR	19.6.95	182/68	Hep	5986	5715- 16
	Small	Keely	AUS-Y	9.6.01		800	2:01.46	2:08.17- 15
	Smets	Fanny	BEL	21.4.86	173/59	PV	4.46	4.40- 13
	Smietanka	Justyna	POL	24.9.94	178/60	PV	4.45	4.40- 16
	Smith	Amina	USA	10.1.92	175/59	HJ	1.88	1.91- 16
	Smith	Bekki	AUS	25.11.86	165/46	20kW	1:31:23	1:29:49- 16
^	Smith	Brittany	USA	25.3.91	178/89	SP	18.48	19.01i, 18.96- 15
	Smith	Jonielle	JAM	30.1.96	171/59	100	11.13, 11.08w	11.32, 11.17w- 14
	Smith	Rebekah	USA-J	1.5.98	163/52	100	11.29	11.88- 15
	Smith-Barnett	Destiny	USA	26.7.96	167/54	100	11.21, 10.94Aw, 11.06w	11.40- 14,11.32w- 16
						200	22.91A	23.75- 14
	Smolyakova	Marina	RUS	20.6.89	188/65	HJ	1.91	1.90- 13
	Snowden	Katie	GBR	9.3.94	167/52	800	2:00.92mx	2:01.77- 15
	1500	4:05.29		4:13.06mx- 16, 4:17.29- 15		1M	4:25.89	

	Name		Nat	Born	Ht/Wt	Event	2017 Mark	Pre-2017 Best
	Soares	Núbia	BRA	26.3.96	176/52	TJ	14.56	14.22- 14
	Sogbesan	Ekundayo	USA	29.3.92	170/57	400	51.81	52.01- 16
	Sokolenko	Yekaterina	RUS	13.9.92	164/50	3kSt	9:34.71	9:25.77- 15
*	Sokolova	Yelena	RUS	23.7.86	170/61	LJ	6.85	7.07- 12
*	Solomon	Shalonda	USA	19.12.85	169/56	100	11.35, 11.19w	10.90- 10
						200	22.64, 22.21w	22.15- 11
	Solovyova	Yevgeniya	RUS	28.6.86	185/90	SP	18.00	18.71i- 12, 18.50- 16
	Song Jiayuan		CHN	15.9.97	179/90	SP	17.93	17.56- 16
	Song Tingting		CHN	8.10.93		PV	4.40	4.30- 15
	Sormunen	Oona	FIN	2.8.89	165/72	JT	58.95	60.56- 13
	Soto	Nercely	VEN	23.8.90	169/55	200	22.89	22.53- 12
	Sow	Rougui	FRA	7.6.95	170/58	LJ	6.72	6.58- 16
	Spagnola	Emma	USA	18.3.96	167/57	100h	13.21, 13.02w	13.43, 13.20w- 16
*	Spanovic	Ivana	SRB	10.5.90	176/65	LJ	7.24i	7.10- 16
	Spaulding	Diamond	USA	29.9.96	163/57	200	23.07, 22.94i, 22.64w	23.21- 15, 23.00Aw- 14
	Spelmeyer	Ruth Sophia	GER	19.9.90	173/60	400	51.72	51.43- 16
*	Spencer	Ashley	USA	8.6.93	168/54	200	22.94i	22.92, 22.69w- 14
						400h	53.11	53.72- 16
*	Spencer	Kaliese	JAM	6.5.87	175/63	400h	55.38	52.79- 11
*	Spencer	Levern	LCA	23.6.84	180/54	HJ	1.92	1.98- 10
	Spenner	Sami	USA	21.3.91	168/59	Hep	5986	6019(w)- 15, 6003- 14
*	Spiegelburg	Silke	GER	17.3.86	173/64	PV	4.55	4.82- 12
	Spínola	Vanessa	BRA	5.3.90	178/68	Hep	5812	6188- 16
	Spires	Shelley	USA	19.3.96		HJ	1.87Ai. 1.87A	1.79A- 16
*	Spotáková	Barbora	CZE	30.6.81	182/80	JT	68.26	72.28- 08
	Sprunger	Ellen	SUI	5.8.86	172/62	Hep	5813	6124- 12
*	Sprunger	Léa	SUI	5.3.90	183/69	200	22.56	22.38- 16
	400	51.09	52.36i- 16, 53.49- 14			400h	54.29	54.92- 16
	St. Fort	Khalifa	TTO-J	13.2.98	168/52	100	11.06	11.16- 16
	Stafford	Gabriela	CAN	13.9.95	165/53	1500	4:03.55	4:06.53- 16
	Stainton	Katie	GBR	8.1.95	174/62	Hep	5873	5777(w), 5763- 16
	Stanková	Eliska	CZE	11.11.84	181/82	DT	58.90A	60.48- 16
	Steenkamp	Rikenette	RSA	16.10.92	169/55	100h	12.99, 12.92w	13.16- 14
*	Stefanídi	Ekateríni	GRE	4.2.90	172/63	PV	4.91	4.90i, 4.86- 16
	Steinacker	Marike	GER	4.3.92	184/80	DT	57.38	59.03- 15
	Stepanova	Yekaterina	RUS	24.7.94		HJ	1.88i	1.88- 16
	Stepter	Jaide	USA	25.4.94	173/64	400	51.12	50.91- 16
						400h	54.96	54.95- 16
*	Stevens	Dani	AUS	26.5.88	182/82	DT	69.64	67.99- 14
*	Stevens	Deajah	USA	19.5.95	172/60	100	11.00, 10.89w	11.18, 11.04w- 16
						200	22.09	22.25- 16
*	Stevens	Jeneva	USA	28.10.89	178/102	SP	18.54i, 18.48	19.11- 16
						HT	71.56	74.77- 13
	Stewart	Janeah	USA	21.7.96	183/102	SP	17.86	16.31- 16
						DT	56.39	50.79- 16
^	Stewart	Kerron	JAM	16.4.84	175/61	100	11.12, 11.02w	10.75- 09
	Stiverne	Aiyanna	CAN	20.2.95	168/55	400	52.00	52.08- 16
	Storey	Lora	AUS	19.10.89	170/54	800	2:01.90	2:01.67- 16
	Storm	Ida	SWE	26.12.91	190/95	HT	71.52	69.13- 14
*	Stowers	Jasmin	USA	23.9.91	175/64	100h	12.47	12.35- 15
*	Strachan	Anthonique	BAH	22.8.93	168/57	200	22.84	22.32- 13
	Strametz	Karin	AUT-J	18.4.98		Hep	5840	5666- 16
	Strandemo	Madeline	USA	12.7.95	167/55	3kSt	9:51.83	10:03.52- 16
	Strati	Laura	ITA	3.10.90	171/58	LJ	6.72A, 6.63, 6.70w	6.59- 16
*	Stratton	Brooke	AUS	12.7.93	168/58	LJ	6.79	7.05- 16
	Strebkova	Nataliya	UKR	6.3.95	167/50	3kSt	9:44.52	9:57.56- 16
	Strickler	Amelia	GBR	24.1.94	167/102	SP	17.13	16.91i, 16.72- 15
	Strumillo	Stefania	ITA	14.10.89	182/81	DT	57.21	59.80- 16
	Stuart	Bianca	BAH	17.5.88	168/52	LJ	6.67	6.83- 15, 6.91w- 11
	Stuart	Lauren	CAN	16.11.91	168/79	HT	65.89	67.56- 15
	Stumbaugh	Payton	USA	29.11.95	170/65	100h	13.00	12.83- 16
						Hep	6023	5985(w)- 16
	Su Lingdan		CHN	12.1.97		JT	59.21	57.32- 16
*	Su Xinyue		CHN	8.11.91	179/70	DT	64.56	65.59- 16
*	Suhr	Jenn	USA	5.2.82	180/64	PV	4.83	5.03i- 16, 4.92- 08
	Sujew	Diana	GER	2.11.90	166/52	1500	4:08.17	4:05.62- 13
	Sukenaga	Hitomi	JPN	4.5.88	168/76	JT	56.82	58.51- 15
	Sulek	Adrianna	POL-J	3.4.99	173/62	Hep	5784	0
	Sullohern	Celia	AUS	5.7.92	158/45	10000	32:31.22	33:05.89- 14
*	Sum	Eunice	KEN	2.9.88	172/53	800	1:57.78	1:56.99- 15
^	Sumgong ¶?	Jemima	KEN	21.12.84	158/45	HMar	66:43	66:58- 16

Name		Nat	Born	Ht/Wt	Event	2017 Mark	Pre-2017 Best
Sumi	Azusa	JPN	12.8.96	169/49	HMar	69:21	
Sun Huanhuan		CHN	15.3.90	161/50	20kW	1:31:23	1:27:36- 13
Suntsova	Mariya	RUS	27.12.95	172/60	TJ	13.61	13.32- 14
Surdu	Dimitriana	MDA	12.5.94		SP	18.83	17.85- 16
Sussmann	Jana	GER	12.10.90	166/47	3kSt	9:39.46	9:41.05- 16
^ Sutej	Tina	SLO	7.11.88	173/59	PV	4.50	4.71i- 14, 4.61- 11
Sutherland	Sara	USA	31.1.92	175/66	1500	4:08.39	4:06.43- 16
					5000	15:26.59	16:04.15- 12
Suttie	Taryn	CAN	7.12.90	182/95	SP	17.74	17.88- 16
Suzuki	Ayuko	JPN	8.10.91	154/38	5000	15:20.50	15:08.29- 15
					10000	31:27.30	31:18.16- 16
Svábíková	Amálie	CZE-J	22.11.99	172/60	PV	4.50	4.30- 16
Swiety	Justyna	POL	3.12.92	170/56	400	51.15	51.62- 16
Swoboda	Ewa	POL	26.7.97	164/55	100	11.24	11.12, 11.10w- 16
Szabó	Barbara	HUN	17.2.90	175/59	HJ	1.87	1.94- 15
Szilágyi	Réka	HUN	19.1.96		JT	58.49	59.39- 16
* Ta Lou	Marie Josée	CIV	18.11.88	159/57	100	10.86	10.86- 16
					200	22.08	22.21- 16
Tabacková	Nikol	CZE-J	24.1.98		JT	56.84	56.19- 16
Tabashnyk	Kateryna	UKR	15.6.94	178/62	HJ	1.95	1.90- 13
* Tadesse	Feyse	ETH	19.11.88	167/53	Mar	2:26:46	2:20:27- 14
^ Takacs	Julia	ESP	29.6.89	171/53	20kW	1:30:14	1:28:44- 13
Takano	China	JPN	30.10.97		10000	32:37.21	
Takashima	Yuka	JPN	12.5.88	153/42	10000	31:33.33	31:35.76- 16
Takemoto	Sae	JPN-J	1.1.99	160/59	JT	56.44	52.74- 16
Takigawa	Hiroko	JPN	25.7.94	155/55	JT	56.31	56.79- 16
* Talay	Alina	BLR	14.5.89	164/54	100h	12.72	12.63- 16
Talcott	Erin	USA	21.5.78		50kW	4:29:33	4:33:23- 12
Tan Jian		CHN	20.1.88	179/80	DT	60.65	64.45- 12
Tan Qiujiao		CHN-Y	28.5.00		TJ	13.64A	12.75- 15
Tanabe	Misaki	JPN	31.8.95	160/46	10000	32:36.14	
Tanaka	Hanae	JPN	12.2.90	160/48	Mar	2:26:19	
Tanaka	Nozomi	JPN-J	4.9.99	153/43	3000	8:54.27	9:01.16- 16
Tang Caihong		CHN	29.4.96		50kW	4:40:02	
Tanui	Angela	KEN	27.7.92	155/42	HMar	67:43	67:16- 16
					Mar	2:26:31	
* Tanui	Norah	KEN	2.10.95	157/45	3kSt	9:03.70	9:25.07- 16
Taranda	Karina	BLR-J	10.2.99	181/60	HJ	1.89	1.78- 16
^ Tarasova	Irina	RUS	15.4.87	183/110	SP	17.88	19.35- 12
Tarasyuk	Anna	BLR	30.10.97	183/75	JT	58.00	56.40- 16
* Tate	Cassandra	USA	11.9.90	174/64	400h	54.59	54.01- 15
Tausaga-Collins	Laulauga	USA-J	22.5.98	188/105	DT	59.37	50.70- 16
Tavares	Maria Eleonor	POR	24.9.85	164/55	PV	4.35i, 4.35	4.50- 11
* Tavernier	Alexandra	FRA	13.12.93	170/82	HT	72.69	74.39- 15
Taylor	Charlotte	GBR	17.1.94	159/45	5000	15:29.07	16:05.88- 16
					10000	32:11.80	33:25.09- 16
Taylor	Kellyn	USA	22.7.86	167/52	10000	32:16.78	31:40.70- 16
Taylor	Lakan	USA	21.6.95	160/52	PV	4.45i, 4.31	4.31Ai- 15, 4.27- 15
Taylor-Jemmett	Jessica	GBR	27.6.88	172/63	Hep	5767	5913(w)- 16
Teel	Haley	USA	20.6.96		SP	17.08	16.32- 16
* Teferi	Senbere	ETH	3.5.95	159/45	5000	14:31.76	14:29.82- 16
					10000	30:41.68	30:40.59- 16
Tenorio	Ángela	ECU	27.1.96	167/59	100	11.18, 11.02w	10.99- 15
					200	23.27A, 22.90w	22.84A, 22.86, 22.59w- 15
Terlecki	Josephine	GER	17.2.86	182/78	SP	17.34i, 16.89	18.87- 12
Tervo	Krista	FIN	15.11.97	165/64	HT	68.27	64.63- 16
Terzic	Amela	SRB	2.1.93	169/51	1500	4:06.30	4:04.77- 15
Teschuk	Erin	CAN	25.10.94	168/54	3kSt	9:43.34	9:40.07- 15
Tesfay	Fotyen	ETH-J	17.2.98	154/40	5000	15:12.06	
Tesfay	Haftamnesh	ETH	28.4.94	162/48	5000	15:20.10	15:10.85- 16
Teshale	Alemaz	ETH-J	5.7.99	163/48	1500	4:04.94	4:16.66- 15
Thevenin	Tia	CAN	7.9.96		100h	13.13	13.57- 16
* Thiam	Nafissatou	BEL	19.8.94	184/69	HJ	1.98	1.98- 16
					LJ	6.57	6.58- 16
					JT	59.32	53.13- 16
					Hep	7013	6810- 16
Thomas	Gabrielle	USA	7.12.96	170/57	100	11.24, 11.15w	11.30- 16
					200	22.56	22.47, 22.37w- 16
Thomas	Lanae-Tava	USA-Y	28.1.01		LJ	6.68	6.19, 6.29w- 16
Thomas	Latavia	USA	17.12.88	173/57	800	2:02.06	1:59.67- 11
* Thomas-Dodd	Danniel	JAM	11.11.92	168/91	SP	19.15	17.76- 15
					DT	59.31	59.38- 14

Name		Nat	Born	Ht/Wt	Event	2017 Mark	Pre-2017 Best
Thompson	Brenessa	GUY	22.7.96	163/52	100	11.25, 11.5w	11.14- 16
					200	22.94, 22.59w	22.99- 16
* Thompson	Elaine	JAM	28.6.92	169/57	100	10.71	10.70- 16
					200	21.98	21.66- 15
Thompson	Turquoise	USA	31.7.91	178/66	400h	55.51	54.99- 13
Thompson	Yanique	JAM	12.3.96	163/55	100h	12.69	13.33, 13.21w- 15
Thornton	Sarah	USA	29.8.86	174/79	DT	57.51	56.55- 15
Thweatt	Laura	USA	17.12.88	168/52	Mar	2:25:38	2:28:23- 15
Tibebu	Hirut	ETH	13.12.94		Mar	2:23:35	2:30:58- 15
Tima	Ana José	DOM	10.10.89	168/56	TJ	13.84	14.22- 16
Timanovskaya	Kristina	BLR	19.11.96	167/54	100	11.28	11.46- 16
Timmers	Zoe	AUS	25.5.89	176/56	HJ	1.88	1.87- 16
* Tirop	Agnes	KEN	23.10.95	165/50	3000	8:35.23	8:39.13- 13
Tkachuk	Anastasiya	UKR	20.4.93	170/58	800	2:01.57i	2:00.21- 15
Tkachuk	Viktoriya	UKR	8.11.94	178/69	400h	56.07	55.32- 16
Tkhakur	Santa	RUS	23.4.93	160/50	800	2:01.62	2:01.21- 16
* Todd	Jasmine	USA	23.12.93	165/55	100	11.29	10.92, 10.86w- 15
					LJ	6.83, 6.84w	6.84- 15
Toimil	María Belén	ESP	5.5.94	175/89	SP	17.38	16.31- 15
Tola	Fate Geleto	GER	22.10.87		Mar	2:27:48	2:25:14- 12
Tola	Helen	ETH	21.11.94	166/50	HMar	69:48	71:27- 15
					Mar	2:22:51	2:29:21- 16
Toledo	Luisaris	VEN	29.2.92	175/60	Hep	5785	
Tollesa	Gulume	ETH	11.9.92	155/42	Mar	2:23:59	2:23:12- 15
Toma	Carmen	ROU	28.3.89	168/50	TJ	13.61, 13.65w	14.29- 09, 14.56w- 13
Toma	Shiori	JPN	7.2.96		JT	57.44	56.17- 16
^ Tomasevic	Dragana	SRB	4.6.82	175/80	DT	61.57	63.63- 06
Topic	Dusica	SRB	11.1.82		50kW	4:41:55	0
Torr	Veronica	NZL	17.5.87	175/61	Hep	5717	6051- 16
Townsend	Tiffany	USA	14.6.89	163/50	100	11.25	11.08- 15, 11.03w- 16
					200	22.72	22.26- 13
Tracey	Adelle	GBR	27.5.93	164/50	800	2:00.26	2:00.04mx- 16, 2:01.10- 15
Tracey	Nikita	JAM	18.9.90	173/63	400h	55.01	55.18- 14
* Tracey	Ristananna	JAM	9.5.92	170/61	400h	53.74	54.15- 16
Trapletti	Valentina	ITA	12.7.85	172/56	20kW	1:30:35	1:31:28- 16
Treasure	Alyx	CAN	15.5.92	181/	HJ	1.92	1.94- 16
Trengove	Jessica	AUS	15.8.87	168/54	10000	32:35.06	33:08.26- 13
					Mar	2:27:01	2:27:45- 15
* Trost	Alessia	ITA	8.3.93	188/68	HJ	1.94	2.00i, 1.98- 13
Trought	Brittney	USA	15.10.96		100h	13.28, 13.04w	13.79- 16
Tsareva	Yelizaveta	RUS	15.3.93	177/82	HT	71.73	71.35- 15
Tsega	Muluhabt	ETH	11.9.89	165/54	Mar	2:28:08	2:29:17- 14
* Tsegay	Gudaf	ETH	23.1.97	159/45	1500	3:59.55	4:00.18- 16
800	2:02.26		1:59.77- 16		3000	8:50.74i	
Tsegaye	Melesech	ETH	.94		Mar	2:26:44	2:28:57- 16
Tsutsui	Sakiho	JPN	19.1.96	154/38	10000	32:16.44	
Tuei	Sandra	KEN-J	20.1.98	160/45	3000	8:50.18	8:55.77- 16
Tufa	Tigist	ETH	26.1.87	155/40	Mar	2:25:52	2:21:52- 14
Tugsuz	Eda	TUR	27.3.97	171/68	JT	67.21	58.95- 16
Tuliamuk	Aliphine	USA	5.4.89	163/50	HMar	69:58	69:16- 13
Tully	Nicole	USA	30.10.86	156/45	3000	8:54.28	8:55.48- 14
1M	4:30.22		4:29.78- 16		5000	15:27.14	15:04.08- 16
Tupper	Toni	USA	3.11.95		SP	17.07	16.14- 16
Turner	Jessica	GBR	8.8.95	172/59	400h	56.08	57.00- 16
Turova	Yuliya	RUS	9.6.97		20kW	1:32:21	
Turpin	Esther	FRA	29.4.96	174/54	Hep	5940	5591- 16
Tusa	Rahma	ETH	14.9.93	162/46	10000	31:05.14	
HMar	68:28		72:21- 15		Mar	2:25:12	2:28:49- 16
^ Twell	Stephanie	GBR	17.8.89	168/54	1500	4:06.92+	4:02.54- 10
1M	4:25.39		4:28.16- 07		3000	8:45.95i	8:40.98- 16
5000	15:16.65		14:54.08- 10		10000	32:16.23	0
Uehara	Miyuki	JPN	22.11.95	154/39	10000	31:48.81	31:38.80- 16
					HMar	69:13	
Ufodiama	Blessing	USA	28.11.81	178/61	TJ	13.47, 13.70w	14.06- 11
* Ugen	Lorraine	GBR	22.8.91	178/64	LJ	6.97i, 6.78	6.93i- 16, 6.92, 6.96w- 15
Uloga	Svetlana	RUS	23.11.86	162/55	800	1:59.20	1:59.88- 16
Ulyanova	Valentina	RUS-Y	9.2.00		HJ	1.86	1.82- 15
Urbaniak	Lena	GER	31.10.92	175/95	SP	17.61	18.32i, 18.02- 16
Urbina	María Teresa	ESP	20.3.85	177/53	3kSt	9:43.48	9:41.95- 09
^ Urrutia	Yorsiris	COL	26.6.86	175/61	TJ	13.59, 13.64w	14.58- 14
Vaiciukeviciute	Monika	LTU	3.4.96		20kW	1:32:39	1:34:00- 16

	Name		Nat	Born	Ht/Wt	Event	2017 Mark	Pre-2017 Best
	Vaiciukeviciute	Zivile	LTU	3.4.96	164/54	20kW	1:31:23	1:35:33- 16
	Valette	Laura	FRA	16.2.97	174/60	100h	13.04	13.19- 16
	Vallet	Marine	FRA	9.9.93	174/56	HJ	1.86i	1.88- 16
	Vallortigara	Elena	ITA	21.9.91	179/56	HJ	1.87i, 1.86	1.91- 10
	Van Buskirk	Kate	CAN	9.6.87	178/60	1500	4:07.38	4:05.38- 14
	3000	8:52.08i		9:12.57i- 14		5000	15:22.17	15:29.72- 13
	van der Wielen	Sarah	SWE	18.2.95	177/57	3000	8:54.95	8:50.97- 16
	van Dyk	Jo-Ané	RSA	3.10.97	171/63	JT	57.02	57.32- 16
	Vargas	Andrea Carolina	CRC	28.5.96		100h	13.12	
	Vargas	Nedian	VEN	5.9.94	160/48	200	23.07, 22.95w	23.46- 16
	Vasilíou	Iríni	GRE	18.3.90	168/57	400	51.86	52.12- 16
	Vaskovskaya	Irina	BLR	2.4.91	179/65	TJ	14.00, 14/01w	14.19- 16
	Vaughn	Sara	USA	16.5.86	155/48	1500	4:04.56	4:08.34- 12
	Velazco	Davisleidis L.	CUB-J	4.9.99	170/60	TJ	13.72	14.08- 16
^	Veldáková	Dana	SVK	3.6.81	182/68	TJ	13.82, 13.98Aw	14.51- 08, 14.59w- 10
	Veldáková	Jana	SVK	3.6.81	177/59	LJ	6.55	6.75- 16, 6.88w- 10
	Verstegen	Sanne	NED	10.11.85	168/53	800	1:59.55	1:59.29- 16
						1500	4:07.90	4:12.40- 16
*	Vetter	Anouk	NED	4.2.93	177/62	JT	58.41	55.76- 16
	100h	13.31		13.29- 16		Hep	6636	6626- 16
	Vicente	María	ESP-Y	28.3.01	176/63	TJ	13.72w	12.83, 12.85w- 16
	Vidts	Noor	BEL	30.5.96	177/70	Hep	6024	5851- 16
*	Viljoen	Sunette	RSA	6.1.83	168/64	JT	63.49A	69.35- 12
	Viola	Giulia	ITA	24.4.91	162/45	3000	8:56.19i	8:56.23i- 15, 9:01.33- 14
						5000	15:28.22	15:38.47- 15
	Virbalyte-Dimsiene	Brigita	LTU	1.2.85	165/50	20kW	1:30:45	1:30:20- 15
*	Visser	Nadine	NED	9.2.95	175/63	200	22.83w	23.62- 15
	100h	12.78, 12.57w		12.81- 15		Hep	6370	6467- 15
	Vita	Claudine	GER	19.9.96	179/81	SP	18.09i, 17.62	17.90- 16
						DT	64.45	62.77- 16
	Vitale	Ilaria	ITA	25.5.90	162/52	400h	56.84	57.99- 16
	Vitovshchyk	Vasylyna	UKR	30.4.90	166/54	50kW	4:37:55	4:44:35- 16
	Vlasova	Natalya	RUS	19.7.88	164/48	3kSt	9:41.06	9:31.95- 16
	von Eynatten	Victoria	GER	6.10.91	174/54	PV	4.40i, 4.40	4.51i- 15, 4.30- 11
	Vrzalová	Simona	CZE	7.4.88	168/52	1500	4:07.08	4:13.54- 16
	Vu Thi Men		VIE	10.7.90	170/57	TJ	14.15	13.70- 15
	Vucenovic	Marija	SRB	3.4.93	172/70	JT	58.58	57.81- 16
	Vukovic	Marija	MNE	21.1.92	194/69	HJ	1.91	1.95- 16
	Waite	Lennie	GBR	4.5.86	172/59	3kSt	9:37.94	9:35.91- 16
	Waithera	Mariam	KEN	23.12.96	169/49	5000	15:30.28	15:20.94- 16
	Waldner	Danielle	USA	27.4.96	175/86	SP	17.36	15.94i, 15.93- 16
	Wales	Rebekah	USA	2.10.95	178/70	JT	58.23	55.04- 16
	Wallace	Sasha	USA	21.9.95	175/64	100h	12.81	12.95, 12.81w- 16
	Wallader	Rachel	GBR	1.9.89	180/87	SP	17.47	17.53- 16
	Wambui	Jackline	KEN-Y	8.2.00	171/57	800	2:01.46A	
*	Wambui	Margaret	KEN	15.9.95	175/66	800	1:56.87	1:56.89- 16
	Wambui	Tabitha	KEN	29.12.83	162/62	HMar	70:08	74:00- 10
	Wang Dan		CHN	11.1.95		50kW	4:38:48	4:38:56- 16
	Wang Dou		CHN	18.5.93	167/56	100h	13.13	13.09- 13
	Wang Huan		CHN	21.9.94	168/54	400h	55.99	56.44- 16
	Wang Huiqin		CHN	7.2.90	168/52	TJ	13.56	14.16- 12
	Wang Lixue		CHN	15.12.96		50kW	4:36:40	4:46:50- 16
	Wang Lu		CHN	22.12.91	178/83	HT	67.15	69.39- 13
*	Wang Na		CHN	29.5.95		20kW	1:26:29	1:28:21- 16
	Wang Qingling		CHN	14.1.93	170/58	Hep	6033	5873- 14
	Wang Rong		CHN	1.7.96		TJ	13.77	14.09i- 13, 13.98- 14
	Wang Wupin		CHN	18.1.91		TJ	13.88	14.10- 15
	Wang Yalan		CHN	19.2.93		20kW	1:31:31	1:33:43- 16
	Wang Yang		CHN	14.2.89	185/65	HJ	1.90	1.92- 12
	Wang Yingliu		CHN	1.3.92		20kW	1:28:15	1:30:20- 15
*	Wang Zheng		CHN	14.12.87	174/108	HT	76.25	77.68- 14
	Wanjiru	Rosemary	KEN	9.12.94	159/44	3000	8:51.61	8:48.44- 14
	5000	15:09.68		15:15.14- 16		10000	31:41.23	
	Warner	Heavin	USA	4.3.93	180/86	HT	69.16	69.33- 16
	Warren	McKenzie	USA	3.12.93	176/105	SP	17.62i, 17.39	17.14- 16
*	Washington	Ariana	USA	27.8.96	175/59	100	11.06, 10.97w	11.01, 10.95w- 16
						200	22.39	22.21- 16
*	Washington	Taylor	USA	6.5.93	175/64	400	52.08	50.25- 16
	Watanabe	Akane	JPN	13.8.91	173/75	HT	65.21	66.79- 16
*	Watson	Sage	CAN	20.6.94	175/62	400	51.84i	52.01- 16
						400h	54.52	54.82- 16

WOMEN'S INDEX

Name		Nat	Born	Ht/Wt	Event	2017 Mark	Pre-2017 Best
Watson	Samantha	USA-J	10.11.99	174/57	800	2:00.65	2:02.91- 16
Weeks/Jacobus	Lexi	USA	20.11.96	167/60	PV	4.60i, 4.55	4.70- 16
Weeks/Hoggard	Tori	USA	20.11.96	167/	PV	4.57i, 4.55	4.40- 16
* Weightman	Laura	GBR	1.7.91	172/58	800	2:01.87	2:02.52- 12
1500 4:00.71 4:00.17- 14	1M 4:20.88				5000	15:08.24 0	
Weightman	Lisa	AUS	16.1.79	157/44	Mar	2:25:15	2:26:05- 13
Weimerskirch	Katelyn	USA	28.2.94		HT	64.91	60.41- 16
Weir	Jillian	CAN	9.2.93	177/78	HT	72.50	69.65- 16
Weldegebril	Tinbit	ETH	.89		Mar	2:28:15	2:34:40- 15
Wellings	Eloise	AUS	9.11.82	167/44	5000	15:14.54	14:54.11- 06
					10000	32:26.31	31:14.94- 16
Wells	LaPorscha	USA	25.10.94	175/86	HT	65.39	61.02- 16
Wells	Lauren	AUS	3.8.88	179/86	400h	55.97	55.08- 13
					LJ	6.52, 6.54w	
Wertman	Cassie	USA	14.6.93	178/86	SP	17.43	17.68i- 16, 17.26- 14
Wessman	Anna	SWE	9.10.89	164/70	JT	60.68	61.42- 16
Westbrook	Ky	USA	25.2.96	175/64	100	11.29, 11.23w	11.17, 11.11w- 15
* Wester	Alexandra	GER	21.3.94	180/64	LJ	6.79	6.95i, 6.79, 7.00w- 16
White	Cierra	USA	29.4.93	165/52	100	11.27A, 11.21w	11.09- 13, 11.07w- 15
					200	23.14, 22.98w	22.84, 22.65w- 15
White	Danyel	USA-J	10.2.98		200	23.00i, 22.55w	23.29, 23.26w- 16
White	Kayla	USA	24.9.96	165/52	100h	12.94	13.37- 16
^ Whitney	Kaylin	USA-J	9.3.98	167/57	200	22.61w	22.47- 15
^ Whyte	Angela	CAN	22.5.80	170/56	100h	12.99, 12.95w	12.63- 07, 12.52w- 13
					Hep	5999	6018- 14
Whyte	Natalliah	JAM	9.8.97	165/52	200	22.77	23.36- 14
Whyte	Rhonda	JAM	6.11.90	170/55	400h	54.29	55.58- 16
Williams	Bianca	GBR	18.12.93	167/55	100	11.30, 11.18w	11.17- 14
					200	22.83	22.58- 14
Williams	Charonda	USA	27.3.87	167/55	100	11.19, 11.09w	11.07- 13, 10.95w-12
					200	23.00, 22.54w	22.32- 15
Williams	Chrishuna	USA	31.3.93	161/54	400	52.02i	52.13- 16
					800	2:00.03	1:59.59- 16
* Williams	Christania	JAM	17.10.94	157/52	100	11.03	10.96- 16
* Williams	Danielle	JAM	14.9.92	168/59	100	11.25	11.24A, 11.41, 11.35w- 13
					100h	12.56	12.57- 15
Williams	Domonique	TTO	8.8.94	165/52	400	51.90	52.65- 16
Williams	Jacqueline	USA	13.11.94		PV	4.40Ai	4.31- 16
Williams	Jeanine	JAM	28.1.97	168/57	100h	12.99	13.59- 16, 13.40w- 15
Williams	Jodean	JAM	11.11.93	175/65	200	22.94	23.05- 15
* Williams	Kendell	USA	14.6.95	173/64	100h	12.82	12.83- 16
LJ 6.52i, 6.49	6.54, 6.46- 15				Hep	6564	6402- 16
* Williams	Kimberly	JAM	3.11.88	169/66	TJ	14.54, 14.60w	14.62, 14.78w- 13
Williams	Peta Gaye	JAM	13.9.95	171/64	100h	12.96	13.26- 16
Williams	Sada	BAR	1.12.97	178/63	200	22.80	22.61- 16
Williams	Shermaine	JAM	4.2.90	174/62	100h	12.85	12.78, 12.65w- 12
Williams	Shimayra	JAM	2.12.95	170/56	200	22.93	23.05- 16
					100h	12.81	13.89- 16
Williams	Tameka	SKN	31.8.89	165/52	100	11.27, 11.17w	11.18- 12
* Williams-Mills	Novlene	JAM	26.4.82	170/57	400	50.14	49.63- 06
Williamson	Kimberly	JAM	2.10.93	168/57	HJ	1.91	1.90- 15
Willis	Todea-Kay	JAM	23.11.88		LJ	6.42, 6.66w	6.37- 12
* Wilson	Ajee'	USA	8.5.94	169/55	800	1:55.61	1:57.67- 14
Wilson	Alex	USA	16.6.93	170/55	3kSt	9:40.90	9:50.07- 16
Wilson	Alyssa	USA-J	20.2.99	178/91	SP	17.70	17.01i, 17.00- 16
Wilson	Nickiesha	JAM	28.7.86	174/66	100h	12.81	12.79- 09, 12.63w- 08
* Wimbley	Shakima	USA	23.4.95	178/61	200	22.47	22.43- 15
					400	50.36	50.84- 15
* Winger	Kara	USA	10.4.86	183/86	JT	64.80	66.67- 10
Winkler	Christine	GER	4.5.95	178/70	JT	58.18	53.74- 14
Wisil	Toea	PNG	1.1.88	168/63	100	11.29, 11.26w	11.29- 16
^ Wisniewska	Joanna	POL	24.5.72	178/84	DT	57.46	63.97- 99
Witek	Marcelina	POL	2.6.95	173/67	JT	63.31	61.48- 16
* Wlodarczyk	Anita	POL	8.8.85	176/90	HT	82.87	82.98- 16
Wodak	Natasha	CAN	17.12.81	160/45	10000	31:55.47	31:41.59- 15
Woitha	Charlene	GER	21.8.93	178/77	HT	66.80	70.98- 16
Woodard	Jessica	USA	4.2.95	178/86	SP	18.36	17.88- 16
					DT	56.64	54.20- 16
Woodruff	Gianna	PAN	18.11.93	170/57	400h	55.76	57.34- 16
Wootton	Katrina	GBR	2.9.85	166/51	5000	15:27.6mx	15:30.82- 13
					10000	31:45.63mx/32:27.47	33:07.93- 16

	Name		Nat	Born	Ht/Wt	Event	2017 Mark	Pre-2017 Best
	Wright	Alice	GBR	3.11.94	161/48	10000	32:29.28	32:36.11- 16
	Wu Shuijiao		CHN	19.6.91	161/53	100h	12.97	12.72- 14
	Wu Xueting		CHN	20.8.95		400h	56.98	58.10- 15
	Xiao Xia		CHN	6.6.91	174/54	400h	56.02	56.25- 13
	Xiao Xianghua		CHN	19.2.97		20kW	1:32:16	
	Xie Lijuan		CHN	14.5.93		20kW	1:31:21	1:29:14- 15
	Xie Yuchen		CHN	12.5.96	179/79	DT	58.38	58.30- 16
	Xu Huiqin		CHN	4.9.93	175/55	PV	4.45	4.40- 11
	Xu Xiaoling		CHN	13.5.92		LJ	6.51i, 6.51	6.66i- 16, 6.63- 12
	Yadav	Chinta	IND	26.3.93		3kSt	9:49.23	10:32.88- 16
	Yahi	Nawal	ALG	9.12.91		3kSt	9:48.53	9:53.63- 16
	Yamashita	Mikako	JPN	3.5.97	168/70	JT	59.94	58.59- 15
	Yan Ni		CHN	7.2.93	176/62	HT	65.83	68.56- 16
	Yang Fei		CHN	20.7.87	186/90	DT	58.24	60.43- 12
	Yang Huizhen		CHN	13.8.92	168/55	400	51.80	51.98- 15
*	Yang Jiayu		CHN	18.2.96	163/48	20kW	1:26:18	1:28:12- 16
	Yang Mingxia		CHN	13.1.90	163/44	20kW	1:31:56	1:28:56- 08
	Yang Peili		CHN	7.8.94		20kW	1:28:45	1:34:21- 16
	Yang Shuqing		CHN	30.8.96		50kW	4:20:49	4:56:44- 16
	Yang Xinli ¶		CHN	7.2.88		JT	57.58	61.92- 15
	Yang Yanbo		CHN	9.3.90	183/89	DT	60.83	63.32- 12
	Yarigo	Noélie	BEN	26.12.85	165/52	800	1:59.74	1:59.12- 16
	Yator	Gladys	KEN	8.8.92		HMar	70:01	68:39- 16
	Yatsevich	Anastasiya	BLR	18.1.85	158/48	20kW	1:32:22	1:29:30- 11
	Yavi	Winfred	BRN-J	-.99	157/48	3kSt	9:22.67	10:21.4- 15
	Yermachenkova	Tatyana	RUS-J	9.9.98		HJ	1.87i	1.84- 15
	Yermakova	Viktoriya	BLR	18.1.95		JT	59.35	52.82- 14
	Yeung Man Wai		HKG	18.9.94	172/56	HJ	1.88	1.83- 16
	Yevacheva	Anastasiya	RUS	20.11.97		20kW	1:32:44	
	Yevdokimova	Natalya	RUS	7.9.93	164/50	TJ	13.97	13.88- 15
*	Yin Hang		CHN	7.2.97	161/50	20kW	1:31:23	1:34:25- 16
						50kW	4:08:58	
	Yokoe	Risa	JPN	12.10.94	164/40	10000	32:35.86	32:24.87- 16
	Yoshizumi	Yuki	JPN	7.1.96	167/51	20kW	1:32:23	1:43:42- 16
	Yu Yuzhen		CHN-J	5.3.98		JT	56.57	54.81- 16
	Yudkina	Khrystyna	UKR	4.12.84	169/59	50kW	4:32:14	
	Zabawska	Daria	POL	16.4.95	185/92	DT	59.23	60.23- 15
	Zagainova	Diana	LTU	20.6.97	179/62	TJ	13.64	13.06- 16
	Zagré	Anne	BEL	13.3.90	176/69	100h	12.96	12.71- 15
	Zahi	Carolle	FRA	12.6.94	170/66	100	11.13	11.28- 16
	Zakharutkina	Mariya	RUS	14.8.96		PV	4.40i, 4.35	4.35- 16
	Zaldívar	Liuba M.	CUB	5.4.93	161/54	TJ	14.05A, 13.95	14.51A- 16, 14.20- 13
	Zbären	Noemi	SUI	12.3.94	177/65	100h	13.09	12.71- 15
^	Zemlyak ¶	Olha	UKR	16.1.90	165/56	400	50.89dq	50.75- 16
	Zhang Li		CHN	17.1.89	174/65	JT	61.32	65.47- 14
*	Zhang Wenxiu		CHN	22.3.86	182/108	HT	75.48	77.33- 14
	Zhao Huimin		CHN	12.10.93		50kW	4:44:01	
	Zhao Wenli		CHN	11.12.96		20kW	1:33:16	1:36:34- 16
	Zheng Xingjuan		CHN	20.3.89	184/60	HJ	1.91i, 1.91	1.96- 14
	Zhodzik	Mariya	BLR	19.8.97		HJ	1.89i, 1.86	1.83- 16
	Zhou Kang		CHN	24.12.89	165/54	20kW	1:31:00	1:30:58- 13
	Zhou Minjuan		CHN	22.4.96		TJ	13.66	13.03- 15
	Zhou Xiaoxue		CHN	19.6.92		LJ	6.55i, 6.45	6.55- 15
	Zhu Dandan		CHN	1.3.94		JT	57.32	59.19- 16
	Zhuk	Irina	BLR	26.1.93	166/60	PV	4.60	4.51- 16
	Zienkowicz	Agata	POL	17.12.95	176/80	HT	64.96	58.78- 16
	Zolotuhina	Nataliya	UKR	4.1.85	180/79	HT	69.10	72.22- 11
	Zongo-Filet	Amy	FRA	4.10.80	165/52	TJ	13.60	14.03- 08
*	Zsivoczky-Farkas	Györgyi	HUN	13.2.85	170/58	Hep	6050	6442- 16
	Zupin	Agata	SLO-J	17.3.98	176/59	400h	55.96	59.86- 16
	Zyabkina	Viktoriya	KAZ	4.9.92	170/55	200	22.81	22.77- 15, 22.66dt- 16
	Zyryanova	Valeriya	RUS	12.8.90		SP	17.76	17.67- 16

WORLD INDOOR LISTS 2018 – MEN

60 METRES

Note: including some marks from December 2017 (*), # Oversized track (over 200m)

6.34A	Christian	Coleman	USA	6.3.96	1	NC	Albuquerque	18 Feb
6.40A	Ronnie	Baker	USA	15.10.93	2	NC	Albuquerque	18 Feb
6.42		Su Bingtian	CHN	29.8.89	2	WI	Birmingham	3 Mar
6.48		Xu Zhouzheng	CHN	26.12.95	1	NGPF	Beijing	23 Mar
6.50A	Mike	Rodgers	USA	24.4.85	3	NC	Albuquerque	18 Feb
6.51A	Hassan	Taftian	IRI	4.5.93	1	AsiC	Tehran	1 Feb
6.51A	Bryce	Robinson	USA	13.11.93	2h1	NC	Albuquerque	17 Feb
6.52	Andre	Ewers	USA	7.6.95	1		Iowa City	20 Jan
6.52	Yunier	Pérez	ESP	16.2.85	2		Düsseldorf	6 Feb
6.52A	Blake	Smith	USA	28.5.93	2h3	NC	Albuquerque	17 Feb
6.52		Xie Zhenye	CHN	17.8.93	4	WI	Birmingham	3 Mar
6.52	Elijah	Hall	USA	22.8.94	1	NCAA	College Station	10 Mar
6.53	Chijindu	Ujah	GBR	5.3.94	1r4		London (Nh)	7 Feb
6.53	Raheem	Chambers	JAM	6.10.97	2	NCAA	College Station	10 Mar
6.54A	Kirk	Wilson	USA	27.5.91	1		Flagstaff AZ	3 Feb
6.54	Everton	Clarke	JAM	24.12.92	2		Karlsruhe	3 Feb
6.54A	Brandon	Carnes	USA	6.3.95	2h2	NC	Albuquerque	17 Feb
6.54A	Jeff	Demps	USA	8.1.90	3s1	NC	Albuquerque	18 Feb
6.55	Jeryl	Brazil	USA	28.3.94	1		Baton Rouge	2 Feb
6.55	Ben Youssef	Meité	CIV	11.11.86	1h3		Metz	11 Feb
6.55	Emre Zafer	Barnes	TUR	7.11.88	1		Istanbul	18 Feb
6.55	Demek	Kemp	USA	26.4.96	3	NCAA	College Station	10 Mar
6.56	Ojie	Edoburun	GBR	2.6.96	4	GP	Glasgow	25 Feb
6.57	Tevin	Hester	USA	10.1.94	2		Clemson	19 Jan
6.57	Arthur Gue	Cissé	CIV	29.12.96	1r4		Reims	31 Jan
6.57	Christophe	Lemaitre	FRA	11.6.90	1h3		Mondeville	3 Feb
6.57	Noah	Lyles	USA	18.7.97	3	GP	Boston (R)	10 Feb
6.57	Ján	Volko	SVK	2.11.96	1		Torun	15 Feb
6.58	Divine	Oduduru	NGR	7.10.96	1		Lubbock	3 Feb

6.59	Kenzo	Cotton	USA	13.5.96	9 Feb
6.59	Kimmari	Roach	JAM	21.9.90	11 Feb
6.59	Andrew	Fisher	BRN	15.12.91	15 Feb
6.59	Adam	Gemili	GBR	6.10.93	25 Feb
6.59	Sean	Safo-Antwi	GHA	31.10.90	3 Mar
6.59	Jaylen	Mitchell	USA		9 Mar
6.59	Anthony	Schwartz	USA-J	5.9.00	11 Mar
6.59		Quan Yingrui	CHN	18.11.97	23 Mar
6.60	John	Otugade	GBR	24.1.95	13 Jan
6.60A	Tre	James	USA	1.1.96	19 Jan
6.60	Abdullah Abkar	Mohammed	KSA	1.6.97	3 Feb
6.60	Kim	Collins	SKN	5.4.76	3 Feb
6.60	Julian	Reus	GER	29.4.88	9 Feb
6.60	Zdenek	Stromsík	CZE	25.11.94	10 Feb
6.60	Emeilo	Ferguson	JAM	16.4.93	10 Feb
6.60	Jalen	Miller	USA	17.6.95	10 Feb
6.60A	John	Teeters	USA	19.5.93	18 Feb
6.60A	Desmond	Lawrence	USA	19.12.91	18 Feb
6.60	Jaylen	Bacon	USA	5.8.96	19 Feb
6.60	Derrius	Rodgers	USA	15.10.97	25 Feb
6.60	Bolade	Ajomale	CAN	31.8.95	9 Mar
6.60		Liang Jinsheng	CHN	12.1.96	11 Mar

Best at low altitude

6.37	Coleman	1		Clemson	19 Jan
6.43	Baker	3	WI	Birmingham	3 Mar
6.52	Rodgers	3		Düsseldorf	6 Feb
6.53	Taftian	5	WI	Birmingham	3 Mar
6.56	Robinson	3	GP	Glasgow	25 Feb

200 METRES

20.02	Elijah	Hall	USA	22.8.94	1	NCAA	College Station	10 Mar
20.18	Divine	Oduduru	NGR	7.10.96	1		Lubbock	3 Feb
20.34	Rai	Benjamin	ANT	27.7.97	1rB	NCAA	College Station	10 Mar
20.42	Andrew	Hudson	USA	14.12.96	2		Lubbock	3 Feb
20.45	Ncincihli	Titi	RSA	15.12.93	1		Clemson	20 Jan
20.45#	Nick	Gray	USA	2.6.97	1	Big 10	Geneva OH	24 Feb
20.52A	Jereem	Richards	TTO	13.1.94	1		Albuquerque	3 Feb
20.53	Christophe	Lemaitre	FRA	11.6.90	1		Metz	11 Feb
20.55	Mustaqeem	Williams	USA	24.8.95	1	SEC	College Station	25 Feb
20.55	Jaron	Flournoy	USA	24.11.96	1h2	NCAA	College Station	9 Mar
20.56#	Terrance	Laird	USA	12.10.98	2	Big 10	Geneva OH	24 Feb

20.60	Andre	Ewers	USA	7.6.95	24 Feb
20.61	Kenzo	Cotton	USA	13.5.96	25 Feb
20.64	Marqueze	Washington	USA	29.9.93	12 Jan
20.64	Karol	Zalewski	POL	7.8.93	18 Feb
20.65	Mickael-Méba	Zeze	FRA	19.5.94	18 Feb
20.65	Khance	Meyers	USA	11.1.99	3 Mar
20.67	Bolade	Ajomale	CAN	31.8.95	25 Feb
20.68	Fred	Kerley	USA	7.5.95	12 Jan
20.68	Óscar	Husillos	ESP	18.7.93	17 Feb
20.68#	Divine	Oduduru	NGR	7.10.96	24 Feb
20.69	Obie	Igbokwe	USA	28.1.97	16 Feb

300 METRES

32.10	Jereem	Richards	TTO	13.1.94	1	GP	Boston (R)	10 Feb
32.39	Óscar	Husillos	ESP	18.7.93	1		Salamanca	20 Jan
32.50	Bralon	Taplin	GRN	8.5.92	2	GP	Boston (R)	10 Feb
32.51	Steven	Gardiner	BAH	12.9.95	1		Birmingham AL	12 Jan
32.52	Pavel	Maslák	CZE	21.2.91	1r2		Ostrava	25 Jan
32.60	Karol	Zalewski	POL	7.8.93	2r2		Ostrava	25 Jan
32.64	Brian	Herron	USA-J	24.11.00	1		Lynchburg	19 Jan
32.80	Benjamin Lobo	Vedel	DEN	23.9.97	1		Clemson	6 Jan

400 METRES

44.85	Fred	Kerley	USA	7.5.95	1r2	NCAA	College Station	11 Mar
44.52	Michael	Norman	USA	3.12.97	1	NCAA	College Station	10 Mar
44.86	Akeem	Bloomfield	JAM	10.11.97	1rB	NCAA	College Station	10 Mar
44.88	Bralon	Taplin	GRN	8.5.92	1		College Station	3 Feb
45.16	Mylik	Kerley	USA	6.6.96	2	NCAA	College Station	10 Mar
45.18A	Fred	Kerley	USA	7.5.95	1h2	NC	Albuquerque	17 Feb
45.24	Marqueze	Washington	USA	29.9.93	1rE		Fayetteville	9 Feb
45.24	Kahmari	Montgomery	USA	16.8.97	3	NCAA	College Station	10 Mar
45.27	Nathon	Allen	JAM	28.10.95	2rB	NCAA	College Station	10 Mar
45.38	Obie	Igbokwe	USA	28.1.97	2rE		Fayetteville	9 Feb
45.44	Steven	Solomon	AUS	16.5.93	1h9		Clemson	23 Feb
45.47	Pavel	Maslák	CZE	21.2.91	1	WI	Birmingham	3 Mar
45.50A	Dontavius	Wright	USA	3.1.94	1		Albuquerque	10 Feb
45.53A	Michael	Cherry	USA	23.3.95	1	NC	Albuquerque	18 Feb
45.56	Nathan	Strother	USA	6.9.95	2		Clemson	10 Feb
45.58A	Vernon	Norwood	USA	10.4.92	2h2	NC	Albuquerque	17 Feb
45.59	Karsten	Warholm	NOR	28.2.96	1	NC	Rud	3 Feb
45.59A	Aldrich	Bailey	USA	6.2.94	1rB	NC	Albuquerque	18 Feb
45.61A	Paul	Dedewo	USA	5.6.91	2rB	NC	Albuquerque	18 Feb

45.68	Derrick	Mokaleng	RSA	18.6.97	10 Mar
45.69	Óscar	Husillos	ESP	18.7.93	2 Mar
45.80	Gil	Roberts	USA	15.3.89	10 Feb
45.81	Zach	Shinnick	USA	8.2.98	10 Mar
45.82	Jeffrey	Green	USA	18.8.95	24 Feb
45.84	Robert	Grant	USA	31.1.96	24 Feb
45.85	Deon	Lendore	TTO	28.10.92	3 Feb
45.91A	Brycen	Spratling	USA	10.3.92	18 Feb
45.95	Wil	London	USA	17.8.97	9 Feb
45.97	Steven	Champlin	USA	16.2.96	10 Feb
45.97	Javon	Francis	JAM	14.12.94	10 Feb
Oversized track					
45.93	Myles	Pringle	USA	5.9.97	10 Mar
45.94	Rai	Benjamin	ANT	27.7.97	24 Feb
45.95	Mar'yea	Harris	USA	24.11.97	3 Feb
45.96	Ricky	Morgan	USA	7.1.96	24 Feb

600 METRES: 1:14.79A Michael Saruni KEN 18.6.95 1 Albuquerque 20 Jan

800 METRES

1:44.21	Emmanuel	Korir	KEN	15.6.95	1	Millrose	New York (Arm)	3 Feb
1:45.10A	Donavan	Brazier	USA	15.4.97	1	NC	Albuquerque	18 Feb
1:45.15	Michael	Saruni	KEN	18.6.95	1	NCAA	College Station	10 Mar
1:45.43	Álvaro	de Arriba	ESP	2.6.94	1		Salamanca	3 Feb
1:45.46	Elliot	Giles	GBR	26.5.94	2h1	WI	Birmingham	2 Mar
1:45.52	Drew	Windle	USA	22.7.92	3h1	WI	Birmingham	2 Mar
1:45.96	Mostafa	Smaïli	MAR	9.1.97	1rC		Gent	10 Feb
1:46.08	Isaiah	Harris	USA	18.10.96	2	NCAA	College Station	10 Mar
1:46.33	Amel	Tuka	BIH	9.1.91	2rC		Gent	10 Feb
1:46.43	Kyle	Langford	GBR	2.2.96	4	Millrose	New York (Arm)	3 Feb
1:46.47	Adam	Kszczot	POL	2.9.89	1		Düsseldorf	6 Feb
1:46.49	Sam	Ellison	USA	5.12.92	1		Boston (Allston)	10 Feb
1:46.51	Marc	Reuther	GER	23.6.96	1		Erfurt	27 Jan
1:46.52	Nicholas	Kipkoech	KEN	22.10.92	1rB		Düsseldorf	6 Feb
1:46.54	Wycliffe	Kinyamal	KEN	2.7.97	2rB		Düsseldorf	6 Feb
1:46.57	Erik	Sowinski	USA	21.12.89	3rB		Düsseldorf	6 Feb
1:46.61	Clayton	Murphy	USA	26.2.95	5	Millrose	New York (Arm)	3 Feb
1:46.83	Christian	Harrison	USA	27.9.93	1		Boston (Allston)	25 Feb
1:46.87	Andreas	Kramer	SWE	13.4.97	2		Düsseldorf	6 Feb
1:46.88	Robert	Heppenstall	CAN	28.2.97	3	NCAA	College Station	10 Mar

1:46.90	Marcin	Lewandowski	POL	13.6.87	3 Feb
1:46.96	Saul	Ordóñez	ESP	10.4.94	3 Feb
1:46.99	Russell	Dinkins	USA	27.6.89	10 Feb
1:47.02	Andrew	Osagie	GBR	19.2.88	3 Feb
1:47.04	Neil	Gourley	GBR	7.2.95	24 Feb
1:47.09#	Bryce	Hoppel	USA	1.1.97	10 Feb
1:47.14	John	Lewis	USA	18.1.96	24 Feb
1:47.23#	Thomas	Staines	GBR	22.2.98	10 Mar

1000 METRES: 2:18.94 Thijmen Kupers NED 4.10.91 1 Apeldoorn 27 Jan

1500 METRES

3:33.76+	Edward	Cheserek	KEN	2.2.94			Boston (Allston)	9 Feb
3:35.39	Ayanleh	Souleiman	DJI	3.12.92	1		Liévin	13 Feb
3:35.79	Abdelaati	Iguider	MAR	25.3.87	2		Liévin	13 Feb
3:36.05	Samuel	Tefera	ETH-J	23.10.99	1		Val-de-Reuil	27 Jan
3:36.86	Vincent	Kibet	KEN	6.5.91	1		Düsseldorf	6 Feb
3:36.95	Brahim	Kaazouzi	MAR	15.6.90	3		Liévin	13 Feb
3:37.03	Chris	O'Hare	GBR	23.11.90	1	GP	Boston (R)	10 Feb
3:37.41	Taresa	Tolosa	ETH	15.6.98	1		Torun	15 Feb
3:37.43	Jake	Wightman	GBR	11.7.94	2	GP	Boston (R)	10 Feb
3:37.67	Marcin	Lewandowski	POL	13.6.87	2		Torun	15 Feb
3:37.76	Bethwel	Birgen	KEN	6.8.88	1	GP	Glasgow	25 Feb
3:37.91	Jakub	Holusa	CZE	20.2.88	3		Torun	15 Feb
3:38.00	Ryan	Gregson	AUS	26.4.90	3	GP	Glasgow	25 Feb
3:38.35	Aman	Wote	ETH	18.4.84	2		Düsseldorf	6 Feb
3:38.47	Justus	Soget	KEN-J	22.10.99	4		Val-de-Reuil	27 Jan

3:38.48	Sadik	Mikhou	BRN	25.7.90	13	Feb
3:38.53+	Craig	Engels	USA	1.5.94	10	Feb
3:39.05	Charles Da'Vall	Grice	GBR	7.11.93	15	Feb
3:39.17+	Brannon	Kidder	USA	18.11.93	10	Feb
3:39.19+	Ben	Blankenship	USA	15.12.88	3	Feb
3:39.27	Valentin	Smirnov	RUS	13.2.86	14	Feb
3:39.45	Marc	Alcalá	ESP	7.11.94	13	Feb
3:39.52	Vladimir	Nikitin	RUS	5.8.92	14	Feb

1 MILE

3:49.44	Edward	Cheserek	KEN	2.2.94	1		Boston (Allston)	9 Feb
3:53.40	Izaic	Yorks	USA	17.4.94	1		Boston (Allston)	25 Feb
3:53.93	Craig	Engels	USA	1.5.94	1		Boston (Allston)	10 Feb
3:54.14	Chris	O'Hare	GBR	23.11.90	1	Millrose	New York (Arm)	3 Feb
3:54.72	Josh	Kerr	GBR	8.10.97	2	Millrose	New York (Arm)	3 Feb
3:54.77	Ben	Blankenship	USA	15.12.88	3	Millrose	New York (Arm)	3 Feb
3:55.10	Julian	Oakley	NZL	23.6.93	2		Boston (Allston)	10 Feb
3:55.23	Henry	Wynne	USA	18.4.95	2		Boston (Allston)	25 Feb
3:55.52	Shadrack	Kipchirchir	USA	22.2.89	1		Boston (Allston)	27 Jan

3:55.77	Peter	Callahan	BEL	1.6.91	25	Feb
3:55.82	Justyn	Knight	CAN	19.7.96	27	Jan
3:56.06	Valentin	Smirnov	RUS	13.2.86	4	Feb
3:56.06	Brannon	Kidder	USA	18.11.93	25	Feb
3:56.44	Vladimir	Nikitin	RUS	5.8.92	4	Feb
3:56.47	Charles Da'Vall	Grice	GBR	7.11.93	3	Feb
3:56.89#	Sam	Prakel	USA	29.10.94	10	Feb
3:56.95#	Yomif	Kejelcha	ETH	1.8.97	27	Jan

3000 METRES

7:36.64	Selemon	Barega	ETH	20.1.00	1		Liévin	13 Feb
7:37.91	Hagos	Gebrhiwet	ETH	11.5.94	1		Karlsruhe	3 Feb
7:38.67	Yomif	Kejelcha	ETH	1.8.97	2		Karlsruhe	3 Feb
7:38.74	Edward	Cheserek	KEN	2.2.94	1	GP	Boston (R)	10 Feb
7:39.09	Justus	Soget	KEN-J	22.10.99	1	GP	Glasgow	25 Feb
7:39.10	Paul	Chelimo	USA	27.10.90	2	GP	Glasgow	25 Feb
7:39.92	Abdelaati	Iguider	MAR	25.3.87	3		Karlsruhe	3 Feb
7:40.12	Davis	Kiplangat	KEN	10.7.98	4	GP	Glasgow	25 Feb
7:40.14	Adel	Mechaal	ESP	5.12.90	4		Karlsruhe	3 Feb
7:40.56	Bethwel	Birgen	KEN	6.8.88	5		Karlsruhe	3 Feb
7:40.69	Muktar	Edris	ETH	14.1.94	2		Liévin	13 Feb
7:41.39	Sadik	Mikhou	BRN	25.7.90	6		Karlsruhe	3 Feb
7:41.88	Soufiane	El Bakkali	MAR	7.1.96	3		Liévin	13 Feb
7:41.97	Paul	Koech	KEN	1.1.91	4		Liévin	13 Feb
7:42.02	Edwin	Soi	KEN	3.3.86	7		Karlsruhe	3 Feb
7:42.14	Gemechu	Dida	ETH-J	12.9.99	5	GP	Glasgow	25 Feb
7:42.34	Albert	Rop	BRN	17.7.92	5		Liévin	13 Feb
7:42.71	Shadrack	Kipchirchir	USA	22.2.89	1		Boston (Allston)	27 Jan
7:42.78	Dejen	Gebremeskel	ETH	24.11.89	3	GP	Boston (R)	10 Feb
7:42.82	Vladimir	Nikitin	RUS	5.8.92	1		Yekaterinburg	7 Jan
7:44.03	Birhanu	Yemataw	BRN	27.2.96	4h1	WI	Birmingham	2 Mar
7:44.34*	Julian	Oakley	NZL	23.6.93	1		Boston MA	16 Dec
7:44.58	Mohammed Ayoub	Tiouali	BRN	26.5.91	1		Ostrava	25 Jan
7:44.77	Benjamin	Kigen	KEN	5.7.93	2		Ostrava	25 Jan
7:44.93	Emmanuel	Bor	USA	14.4.88	2		Boston (Allston)	27 Jan
7:45.07	Youness	Essalhi	MAR	20.2.93	6h1	WI	Birmingham	2 Mar
7:45.34	Tilahun	Haile	ETH	1.1.99	3		Ostrava	25 Jan

7:45.86	Justyn	Knight	CAN	19.7.96	3	Feb
7:45.96	Djamal Abdi	Dirieh	DJI	1.1.97	3	Feb
7:46.65	Ryan	Hill	USA	31.1.90	3	Feb
7:47.19	Woody	Kincaid	USA	21.9.92	3	Feb
7:47.21	Andrew	Butchart	GBR	14.10.91	3	Feb
7:47.22	Hamish	Carson	NZL	1.11.88	3	Feb
7:47.36	Garrett	Heath	USA	3.11.85	3	Feb
7:47.43	Kemoy	Campbell	JAM	14.1.91	3	Feb
7:47.48	Kirubel	Erassa	USA	17.6.93	27	Jan
7:47.54	Andy	Bayer	USA	3.2.90	3	Feb
7:47.57	Birhan	Melesse	ETH-J	12.9.99	25	Jan
7:48.75	Youssouf Hiss	Bachir	DJI	1.1.87	25	Jan

60 METRES HURDLES

7.42	Grant	Holloway	USA	19.11.97	1		Clemson	10 Feb
7.43A	Jarret	Eaton	USA	24.6.89	1	NC	Albuquerque	18 Feb
7.46	Omar	McLeod	JAM	25.4.94	1h2		Clemson	10 Feb
7.46A	Aries	Merritt	USA	24.7.85	2	NC	Albuquerque	18 Feb
7.46	Andy	Pozzi	GBR	15.5.92	1	WI	Birmingham	4 Mar
7.49A	Devon	Allen	USA	12.12.94	3	NC	Albuquerque	18 Feb
7.49	Ronald	Levy	JAM	30.10.92	1	GP	Glasgow	25 Feb
7.51	Petr	Svoboda	CZE	10.10.84	1		Jablonec	20 Jan
7.51	Milan	Trajkovic	CYP	17.3.92	1s3	WI	Birmingham	4 Mar
7.52	Pascal	Martinot-Lagarde	FRA	22.9.91	2s3	WI	Birmingham	4 Mar
7.53	Aurel	Manga	FRA	24.7.92	1	NC	Liévin	17 Feb
7.57	Ahmad	Al-Moualed	KSA	16.2.88	1h1		Mondeville	3 Feb
7.57A	Brendan	Ames	USA	6.10.88	4	NC	Albuquerque	18 Feb
7.58	Roger V.	Iribarne	CUB	2.1.96	2s2	WI	Birmingham	4 Mar
7.60	Aleec	Harris	USA	31.10.90	3		Clemson	10 Feb
7.60	Erik	Balnuweit	GER	21.9.88	1 h2		Chemnitz	10 Feb
7.60	Balázs	Baji	HUN	9.6.89	2		Torun	15 Feb
7.60	Gabriel	Constantino	BRA	9.2.95	1		São Caetano do Sul	17 Feb
7.60	Antoine	Lloyd	USA	10.6.96	2	NCAA	College Station	10 Mar

7.61	Ruebin	Walters	TTO	2.4.95	4		Clemson	10 Feb
7.62	Johnathan	Cabral	CAN	31.12.92	2		Mondeville	3 Feb

7.63	Simon	Krauss	FRA	12.2.92	31 Jan
7.63	David	King	GBR	13.6.94	11 Feb
7.63	Ashtyn	Davis	USA	10.10.96	10 Mar
7.64A	Josh	Thompson	USA	16.1.93	17 Feb
7.64	Jaylan	McConico	USA	17.8.98	25 Feb
7.64	Jovaine	Atkinson	JAM	6.12.95	9 Mar
7.65*	Chad	Zallow	USA	25.4.97	1 Dec
7.65	Freddie	Crittenden	USA	3.8.94	13 Jan
7.65	Koen	Smet	NED	9.8.92	3 Feb
7.65	Konstantin	Shabanov	RUS	17.11.89	13 Feb
7.65		Ceng Jianhang	CHN	17.9.98	24 Mar
7.66	Ludovic	Payen	FRA	18.2.95	13 Feb
7.66	Hassane	Fofana	ITA	28.4.92	17 Feb
7.66A	Aaron	Mallett	USA	26.9.94	18 Feb
7.66	Konstadínos	Douvalídis	GRE	10.3.87	3 Mar

Best at low altitude

7.47	Eaton	1		Reims	31 Jan
7.50	Allen	1	Millrose	New York (Arm)	3 Feb
7.53	Merritt	3	Millrose	New York (Arm)	3 Feb

HIGH JUMP

2.38A	Mutaz Essa	Barshim	QAT	24.6.91	1	AsiC	Tehran	1 Feb
2.37	Danil	Lysenko	RUS	19.5.97	1		Hustopece	27 Jan
2.35	Ivan	Ukhov	RUS	29.3.86	1		Moskva	31 Jan
2.33	Trey	Culver	USA	18.7.96	1		Lubbock	13 Jan
2.33	Sylwester	Bednarek	POL	28.4.89	2		Trinec	30 Jan
2.33	Vernon	Turner	USA	21.8.98	1		Fayetteville	10 Feb
2.32	Dmitriy	Nabokov	BLR	20.1.96	1		Minsk	3 Mar
2.31	Erik	Kynard	USA	3.2.91	1		Manhattan KS	3 Feb
2.31		Wang Yu	CHN	18.8.91	1		Banská Bystrica	6 Feb
2.31	Donald	Thomas	BAH	1.7.84	3		Banská Bystrica	6 Feb
2.31	Jamal	Wilson	BAH	1.9.88	1		Birmingham AL	9 Feb
2.31	Ilya	Ivanyuk	RUS	9.3.93	3	NC	Moskva	13 Feb
2.31	Maksim	Nedasekov	BLR	21.1.98	1	NC	Mogilyov	17 Feb
2.30	Robbie	Grabarz	GBR	3.10.87	1		Birmingham	6 Jan
2.30	Jeron	Robinson	USA	30.4.91	1		Houston	12 Jan
2.30	Matús	Bubeník	SVK	14.11.89	1cB		Hustopece	27 Jan
2.30	Mateusz	Przybylko	GER	9.3.92	1	NC	Dortmund	18 Feb
2.29	Django	Lovett	CAN	6.7.92	1		Seattle	27 Jan
2.29	Andrii	Protsenko	UKR	20.5.88	1	NC	Sumy	10 Feb
2.29	Randall	Cunningham	USA	4.1.96	1	NCAA	College Station	10 Mar
2.29	Shelby	McEwen	USA	6.4.96	3	NCAA	College Station	10 Mar

2.28	Viktor	Lonskyy	UKR	27.10.95	23 Dec
2.28	Edgar	Rivera	MEX	13.2.91	27 Jan
2.28	Tihomir	Ivanov	BUL	11.7.94	4 Feb
2.28	Semen	Pozdnyakov	RUS	28.11.92	13 Feb
2.28	Tejaswin	Shankar	IND	21.12.98	24 Feb
2.27	Keenon	Laine	USA	12.6.97	6 Jan
2.26	Douwe	Amels	NED	16.9.91	20 Jan
2.26	Fabian	Delryd	SWE	15.10.96	21 Jan
2.26	Aleksey	Dmitrik	RUS	12.4.84	21 Jan
2.26	Talles Frederico	Silva	BRA	20.8.91	3 Feb
2.26	Andrey	Skobeyko	BLR	11.6.95	3 Feb
2.26	Naoto	Tobe	JPN	31.3.92	10 Feb

POLE VAULT

5.93	Sam	Kendricks	USA	7.9.92	1		Clermont-Ferrand	25 Feb
5.93	Renaud	Lavillenie	FRA	18.9.86	2		Clermont-Ferrand	25 Feb
5.91	Piotr	Lisek	POL	16.8.92	1		Torun	15 Feb
5.90	Thiago	Braz	BRA	16.12.93	1		Rouen	10 Feb
5.88	Raphael	Holzdeppe	GER	28.9.89	1		Karlsruhe	3 Feb
5.88	Paweł	Wojciechowski	POL	6.6.89	3		Clermont-Ferrand	25 Feb
5.88	Axel	Chapelle	FRA	24.4.95	4		Clermont-Ferrand	25 Feb
5.88	Armand	Duplantis	SWE-J	10.11.99	5		Clermont-Ferrand	25 Feb
5.88	Kévin	Menaldo	FRA	12.7.92	7		Clermont-Ferrand	25 Feb
5.85	Konstadínos	Filippídis	GRE	26.11.86	1		Madrid	8 Feb
5.85	Timur	Morgunov	RUS	27.10.96	1	NC	Moskva	13 Feb
5.83A	Scott	Houston	USA	11.6.90	1	NC	Albuquerque	17 Feb
5.81	Shawnacy	Barber	CAN	27.5.94	8		Clermont-Ferrand	25 Feb
5.80	Dmitriy	Zhelyabin	RUS	20.5.90	1	Mosc Ch	Moskva	25 Jan
5.80	Chris	Nilsen	USA	13.1.98	1		Lincoln NE	16 Feb
5.80	Kurtis	Marschall	AUS	25.4.97	4	WI	Birmingham	4 Mar
5.80	Emmanouíl	Karalís	GRE-J	20.10.99	5	WI	Birmingham	4 Mar
5.78'A	Devin	King	USA	12.3.96	2		Reno	12 Jan
5.78	Melker	Svärd Jacobsson	SWE	8.1.94	1	v3N	Uppsala	11 Feb
5.78A	Mike	Arnold	USA	13.8.90	3	NC	Albuquerque	17 Feb
5.75		Xue Changrui	CHN	31.5.91	1		Liévin	13 Feb
5.72	Valentin	Lavillenie	FRA	16.7.91	2	NC	Liévin	18 Feb
5.70	Menno	Vloon	NED	11.5.94	4		Düsseldorf	6 Feb
5.70	Hussain Asim	Al-Hizam	KSA	4.1.98	1	NCAA	College Station	9 Mar
5.67	Andrew	Irwin	USA	23.1.93	1		Fayetteville	12 Jan
5.66	Matt	Ludwig	USA	5.7.96	1		University Park	27 Jan
5.66	Stanley	Joseph	FRA	24.10.91	1		Clermont-Ferrand	24 Feb
5.65	Georgiy	Gorokhov	RUS	20.4.93	2		Moskva	17 Jan
5.65	Adam	Hague	GBR	29.8.97	1	NC	Birmingham	18 Feb
5.65	Ben	Broeders	BEL	21.6.95	1		Bad Oeynhausen	22 Feb
5.65	Ilya	Mudrov	RUS	17.11.91	2=		Sankt Peterburg	23 Feb
5.63A	Tray	Oates	USA	14.3.95	4	NC	Albuquerque	17 Feb

5.62		Yao Jie	CHN	21.9.90	1		Rennes	27 Jan
5.62	Arnaud	Art	BEL	28.1.93	2		Rennes	27 Jan
5.62	Ivan	Horvat	CRO	17.8.93	1		Beograd	21 Feb
5.61	Adrián	Valles	ESP	16.3.95	1		Notre Dame	20 Jan
5.61	Gordon	Porsch	GER	11.3.95	1		Sindelfingen	11 Feb

5.60	Vladyslav	Malykhin	UKR	15.1.98	9	Jan
5.60	Bo Kanda	Lita Baehre	GER	29.4.99	20	Jan
5.60	Tim	Ehrhardt	USA	16.3.95	3	Feb
5.60	Karsten	Dilla	GER	17.7.89	6	Feb
5.60A	Garrett	Starkey	USA	7.10.93	10	Feb
5.60	Jacob	Wooten	USA	22.4.97	10	Feb
5.60	Kevin	Mayer	FRA	10.2.92	10	Feb
5.60	Seito	Yamamoto	JPN	11.3.92	25	Feb
5.60	Deakin	Volz	USA	12.1.97	9	Mar
5.58'A	Nate	Richartz	USA	2.11.94	12	Jan
5.58	Daniel	Clemens	GER	28.4.92	18	Feb
5.57*	Jake	Albright	USA	22.12.93	2	Dec
5.56	Anton	Ivakin	RUS	3.2.91	17	Jan
5.56	Eirik Greibrokk	Dolve	NOR	5.5.95	24	Jan
5.55	five men					

' = long pegs

LONG JUMP

8.46	Juan Miguel	Echevarría	CUB	11.8.98	1	WI	Birmingham	2 Mar
8.44	Luvo	Manyonga	RSA	18.11.91	2	WI	Birmingham	2 Mar
8.42	Marquis	Dendy	USA	17.11.92	3	WI	Birmingham	2 Mar
8.38A	Jarrion	Lawson	USA	6.5.94	1	NC	Albuquerque	17 Feb
	8.14				4	WI	Birmingham	2 Mar
8.23	Aleksandr	Menkov	RUS	7.12.90	1	NC	Moskva	14 Feb
8.19	Will	Williams	USA	31.1.95	1	NCAA	College Station	9 Mar
8.19		Huang Changzhou	CHN	20.8.94	1	NGP	Xianlin	11 Mar
8.18A	Mike	Hartfield	USA	29.3.90	3	NC	Albuquerque	17 Feb
8.16A		Shi Yuhao	CHN	26.9.98	1	AsiC	Tehran	3 Feb
	8.13				1	GP	Glasgow	25 Feb
8.14A	Jarvis	Gotch	USA	25.3.92	4	NC	Albuquerque	17 Feb
8.13	Zack	Bazile	USA	7.1.96	1		Nashville	10 Feb
8.13	Grant	Holloway	USA	19.11.97	2	NCAA	College Station	9 Mar
8.12	Paulo Sérgio	de Oliveira	BRA	1.6.93	1		São Caetano do Sul	17 Feb
8.12	Charles	Brown	USA	28.5.97	3	NCAA	College Station	9 Mar
8.09	Cristian Iulian	Staicu	ROU	30.7.93	1	NC	Bucuresti	4 Feb
8.07	Damar	Forbes	JAM	11.9.90	1		Iowa City	20 Jan
8.05	Ruswahl	Samaai	RSA	25.9.91	6	WI	Birmingham	2 Mar
8.02	Corion	Knight	USA		1		Fayetteville	9 Feb
8.02	Artyom	Primak	RUS	14.1.93	2	NC	Moskva	14 Feb
8.00	Max	Heß	GER	13.7.96	1		Chemnitz	20 Jan
7.99	Adam	McMullen	IRL	5.7.90	1	NC	Dublin	18 Feb
7.99	Radek	Juska	CZE	8.3.93	1	NC	Praha	18 Feb
7.97	Ja'Mari	Ward	USA	21.3.98	1		Columbia MO	16 Feb
7.97	Eusebio	Cáceres	ESP	10.9.91	1	NC	Valencia	17 Feb
7.96	Jordan	Downs	USA		1		Marion IN	10 Feb
7.96	Serhii	Nykyforov	UKR	6.2.94	1	NC	Sumy	10 Feb
7.96	Steffin	McCarter	USA	19.1.97	1	Big 12	Ames	23 Feb

7.95	Miltiádis	Tentóglou	GRE	18.3.98	11	Feb
7.94	Alper	Kulaksız	TUR	6.4.92	18	Jan
7.94	Benjamin	Gföhler	SUI	27.1.94	4	Feb
7.93	Scotty	Newton	USA	19.9.96	23	Feb
7.90	Andre	Dorsey	USA	11.3.93	20	Jan
7.90	Thobias	Nilsson Montler	SWE	15.2.96	28	Jan
7.90	Filippo	Randazzo	ITA	27.4.96	3	Feb
7.90	KeAndre	Bates	USA	24.5.96	9	Mar

TRIPLE JUMP

17.43	Will	Claye	USA	13.6.91	1	WI	Birmingham	3 Mar
17.41	Almir	dos Santos	BRA	4.9.93	2	WI	Birmingham	3 Mar
17.40	Nelson	Évora	POR	20.4.84	3	WI	Birmingham	3 Mar
17.23	Fabrice	Zango	BUR	25.6.93	1		Val-de-Reuil	27 Jan
17.20A	Chris	Carter	USA	11.3.89	2	NC	Albuquerque	18 Feb
	17.15				5	WI	Birmingham	3 Mar
17.19	Pedro Pablo	Pichardo	POR	30.6.93	1		Pombal	18 Feb
17.18	Omar	Craddock	USA	26.4.91	1		Fayetteville	10 Feb
17.17	Alexis	Copello	AZE	12.8.85	4	WI	Birmingham	3 Mar
17.12	Aleksandr	Yurchenko	RUS	30.7.92	1		Moskva	3 Feb
17.06	Donald	Scott	USA	23.2.92	1		Ann Arbor	13 Jan
17.02	Cristian Atanay	Nápoles	CUB	27.11.98	2		Liévin	13 Feb
16.94	Fabrizio	Donato	ITA	14.8.76	1	NC	Ancona	18 Feb
16.93A	Chris	Benard	USA	4.4.90	4	NC	Albuquerque	18 Feb
	16,63				1		Lubbock	27 Jan
16.89	Martin	Lamou	FRA	13.5.99	1	NC	Liévin	18 Feb
16.87	Dmitriy	Chizhikov	RUS	6.12.93	1	NC	Moskva	13 Feb
16.87		Zhu Yaming	CHN	4.5.94	7	WI	Birmingham	3 Mar
16.84	Max	Heß	GER	13.7.96	1	NC	Dortmund	18 Feb
16.84		Dong Bin	CHN	22.11.88	8	WI	Birmingham	3 Mar
16.82	O'Brien	Wasome	JAM	24.1.97	1	NCAA	College Station	10 Mar
16.78	Vitaliy	Pavlov	RUS	12.1.97	1	NC-23	Sankt-Peterburg	22 Feb
16.77	Nathan	Douglas	GBR	4.12.82	1	NC	Birmingham	18 Feb
16.76	Pablo	Torrijos	ESP	12.5.92	4		Liévin	13 Feb
16.72	Aleksey	Fyodorov	RUS	25.5.91	2	NC	Moskva	13 Feb

16.71	Clive	Pullen	JAM	18.10.94	2		Fayetteville	10 Feb
16.69	Momchil	Karailiev	BUL	21.5.82	1	NC	Sofia	4 Feb
16.69	Karol	Hoffmann	POL	1.6.89	4		Torun	15 Feb
16.69A	Matthew	O'Neal	USA	10.6.94	6	NC	Albuquerque	18 Feb
16.67	KeAndre	Bates	USA	24.5.96	2	NCAA	College Station	10 Mar
16.66		Xu Xiaolong	CHN	20.12.92	1	NGP	Xi'an	12 Mar

16.65	Dmitriy	Sorokin	RUS	27.9.92	13 Feb	16.55	Dmitriy	Platnitskiy	BLR	26.8.88	16 Feb
16.63	Scotty	Newton	USA	19.9.96	24 Feb	16.55	Elvijs	Misans	LAT	4.8.89	3 Mar
16.61	Necati	Er	TUR	24.2.97	18 Jan	16.54	Julian	Reid	GBR	23.9.88	18 Feb
16.60	Marian	Oprea	ROU	6.6.82	20 Jan	16.52	Denis	Obyortyshev	RUS	16.2.97	17 Jan
16.56	Marcos	Ruiz	ESP	10.3.95	28 Jan	16.50	Kevin	Luron	FRA	8.11.91	18 Feb

SHOT

22.31	Tom	Walsh	NZL	1.3.92	1	WI	Birmingham	3 Mar
22.17	Tomás	Stanek	CZE	13.6.91	1		Düsseldorf	6 Feb
22.00	Konrad	Bukowiecki	POL	17.3.97	1		Torun	15 Feb
21.47	Michał	Haratyk	POL	10.4.92	1	NC	Torun	18 Feb
21.45	Jordan	Geist	USA	21.7.98	1		Seattle	27 Jan
21.44	David	Storl	GER	27.7.90	2	WI	Birmingham	3 Mar
21.39	Maksim	Afonin	RUS	6.1.92	1	NC	Moskva	13 Feb
21.37	Darlan	Romani	BRA	9.4.91	4	WI	Birmingham	3 Mar
21.33	Josh	Awotunde	USA/NGR	12.6.95	1	SEC	College Station	25 Feb
21.27	Tsanko	Arnaudov	POR	14.3.92	1	Club Ch	Pombal	18 Feb
21.15	Mesud	Pezer	BIH	27.8.94	5	WI	Birmingham	3 Mar
21.13	Stipe	Zunic	CRO	13.12.90	2		Düsseldorf	6 Feb
21.06	Darrell	Hill	USA	17.8.93	6	WI	Birmingham	3 Mar
21.05	Aleksandr	Lesnoy	RUS	28.7.88	2	NC	Moskva	13 Feb
21.03	Ryan	Whiting	USA	24.11.86	7	WI	Birmingham	3 Mar
20.89	Chuk	Enekwechi	NGR	28.1.93	1		West Lafayette	27 Jan
20.86	Mostafa Amer	Hassan	EGY	16.12.95	1	NCAA	College Station	9 Mar
20.82	Tim	Nedow	CAN	16.10.90	1		Toronto	3 Feb
20.68	Nick	Vena	USA	16.4.93	1		West Long Branch	27 Jan
20.60	Andrei	Gag	ROU	27.4.91	1		Istanbul	18 Feb
20.44	Denzel	Comenentia	NED	25.11.95	1		Clemson	10 Feb
20.42	Ashinia	Miller	JAM	6.6.93	2		University Park	27 Jan
20.40	Aleksey	Nichipor	BLR	10.4.93	1		Mogilyov	25 Jan
20.36	Frederic	Dagee	FRA	11.12.92	1		Nice	12 Jan
20.27	Borja	Vivas	ESP	26.5.84	1	NC	Valencia	17 Feb
20.24	Nick	Demaline	USA	1.3.96	1	Big 10	Geneva OH	23 Feb
20.19	Curtis	Jensen	USA	1.11.90	1		Superior WI	10 Feb
20.18	Hamza	Alic	BIH	20.1.79	2		Beograd	21 Feb
20.15	Nikólaos	Skarvélis	GRE	2.2.93	3	BalkC	Istanbul	17 Feb
20.14	Patrick	Müller	GER	4.2.96	1		Neubrandenburg	20 Jan
20.12	Carlos	Tobalina	ESP	2.8.85	1	Club Ch	Valencia	27 Jan
20.11	Asmir	Kolasinac	SRB	15.10.84	3		Beograd	21 Feb
20.10	Austin	Droogsma	USA	4.3.95	1		Notre Dame	17 Feb
20.06	Kord	Ferguson	USA	19.6.95	2	SEC	College Station	25 Feb

19.96	Josh	Freeman	USA	22.8.94	3 Feb	19.71	Franck	Elemba	CGO	21.7.90	17 Feb
19.95	Leonardo	Fabbri	ITA	15.4.97	13 Jan	19.67	Marcus	Thomsen	NOR	7.1.98	11 Feb
19.95	Konstantin	Lyadusov	RUS	2.3.88	4 Feb	19.64	Coy	Blair	USA	10.6.94	20 Jan
19.95	Jared	Kern	USA	10.6.95	16 Feb	19.64	McKay	Johnson	USA	15.4.98	27 Jan
19.93A	Jon	Jones	USA	23.4.91	18 Feb	19.62	Payton	Otterdahl	USA	2.4.96	27 Jan
19.93	O'Dayne	Richards	JAM	14.12.88	3 Mar	19.62	Nick	Ponzio	USA	4.1.95	24 Feb
19.90	Arttu	Kangas	FIN	13.7.93	18 Feb	19.60	Tobias	Dahm	GER	23.5.87	10 Feb
19.83	Adrian	Piperi	USA-J	20.1.99	27 Jan	19.59	Bob	Bertemes	LUX	24.5.93	4 Feb
19.81	Ivan	Ivanov	KAZ	3.1.92	11 Jan	19.59	Kiriákos	Zótos	GRE	17.1.96	10 Feb
19.75	Garrett	Appier	USA	15.10.92	9 Dec	19.56	Martin	Novák	CZE	5.10.92	18 Feb
19.75	Mikhail	Abramchuk	BLR	22.9.92	16 Feb	19.55	David	Pless	USA	19.11.90	13 Jan
19.73	Jakub	Szyszkowski	POL	21.8.91	18 Feb	19.50	Willie	Morrison	USA	23.11.96	8 Dec

DISCUS

63.91	Lukas	Weißhaidinger	AUT	20.2.92	1	ISTAF	Berlin	26 Jan
62.32	Robert	Harting	GER	18.10.84	2	ISTAF	Berlin	26 Jan

61.86	Daniel	Jasinski	GER	5.8.89	26 Jan	61.60	Simon	Pettersson	SWE	3.1.94	3 Feb

WEIGHT

24.02	David	Lucas	USA	6.6.96	1	NCAA	College Station	10 Mar
23.84	Conor	McCullough	USA	31.1.91	1	NC	Albuquerque	17 Feb
23.83	Josh	Davis	USA	23.9.95	1		Clemson	23 Feb
23.71	Demzel	Comenentia	NED	25.11.95	1	SEC	College Station	24 Feb
23.64	Joe	Ellis	GBR	10.4.96	1	Big10	Geneva NH	24 Feb
23.57	Colin	Dunbar	USA	27.6.88	1		Albuquerque	3 Feb
23.50	Alex	Young	USA	1.9.94	2	NC	Albuquerque	17 Feb

23.46	Sean	Donnelly	USA	1.4.93	17 Feb	22.83	Daniel	Haugh	USA	3.5.95	10 Mar
22.99	Alton	Clay	USA	6.9.98	20 Feb	22.52	Michael	Shanahan	USA	5.12.94	3 Mar
22.87	Grant	Cartwright	USA	19.11.94	24 Feb	22.49	Alex	Hill	USA		24 Feb

HEPTATHLON

6348	Kevin	Mayer	FRA	10.2.92	1	WI	Birmingham	3 Mar
	6.85	7.55	15.67	2.02	7.83	5.00	2:39.64	
6343	Damian	Warner	CAN	4.11.89	2	WI	Birmingham	3 Mar
	6.74	7.39	14.90	2.02	7.67	4.90	2:37.12	
6265	Maicel	Uibo	EST	27.12.92	3	WI	Birmingham	3 Mar
	7.20	7.41	14.30	2.17	8.19	5.30	2:38.51	
6238	Kai	Kazmirek	GER	28.1.91	4	WI	Birmingham	3 Mar
	7.15	7.68	14.55	2.05	7.95	5.20	2:42.15	
6188	Tim	Duckworth	GBR	18.6.96	1	NCAA	College Station	10 Mar
	6.84	7.74	13.59	2.17	8.23	5.16	2:56.23	
6090	Hunter	Veith	USA	14.1.95	2	NCAA	College Station	10 Mar
	6.90	7.54	13.39	2.08	7.99	4.76	2:43.33	
6081	Tyler	Adams	USA	11.2.96	3	NCAA	College Station	10 Mar
	6.99	7.38	12.12	2.20	7.97	4.56	2:36.14	
6043	Zach	Ziemek	USA	23.2.93	1		Lincoln NE	3 Feb
	6.89	7.10	14.02	2.03	8.08	5.27	2:49.95	
6021	Jan	Dolezal	CZE	6.6.96	1	NC	Praha (Strom)	11 Feb
	7.01	7.59	14.31	1.99	7.96	4.90	2:49.42	
6016	Oleksiy	Kasyanov	UKR	26.8.85	1		Aubière	14 Jan
	6.92	7.45	13.78	2.02	7.80	4.66	2.46.22	
6014	Ruben	Gado	FRA	13.12.93	1	v4Nat	Madrid	28 Jan
	6.99	7.33	12.91	2.00	8.32	5.30	2:40.96	
5997	Eelco	Sintnicolaas	NED	7.4.87	5	WI	Birmingham	3 Mar
	6.96	7.15	14.09	1.90	7.97	5.30	2:45.93	
5988	Johannes	Erm	EST	26.3.98	4	NCAA	College Station	10 Mar
	7.11	7.64	13.77	1.99	8.38	4.96	2:39.45	
5980	Samuel	Remédios	POR	24.2.92	1	NC	Pombal	11 Feb
	6.92	7.52	13.70	2.03	7.98	5.00	2:57.33	
5973	Dominik	Distelberger	AUT	16.3.90	1	NC	Wien	4 Feb
	6.93	7.40	12.84	1.95	7.96	4.90	2:40.42	
5951	Adam Sebastian	Helcelet	CZE	27.10.91	2	NC	Praha (Strom)	11 Feb
	7.05	7.41	14.65	2.05	7.97	4.60	2:48.98	
5951	Martin	Roe	NOR	1.4.92	1		Sandnes	4 Mar
	6.92	7.81	15.71	1.90	8.43	4.80	2:51.03	
5935A	Jeremy	Taiwo	USA	15.1.90	1	NC	Albuquerque	17 Feb
	7.15	7.10	12.75	2.10	8.19	5.05	2:41.36	
5934	T.J.	Lawson	USA	25.1.97	5	NCAA	College Station	10 Mar
	7.09	7.40	14.46	2.02	8.36	4.76	:40.89	
5923A	Wolf	Mahler	USA	26.9.94	2	NC	Albuquerque	17 Feb
	6.99	7.24	13.07	1.92	8.18	5.15	2:40.43	
5908	Fredrik	Samuelsson	SWE	16.2.95	1	NC	Norrköping	11 Feb
	(7.09	7.28	13.43	2.08	8.14	4.85	2:47.44	
5906	Tim	Nowak	GER	13.8.95	2		Aubière	14 Jan
	7.23	6.96	14.30	2.02	7.80	4.66	2.46.22	
5904	Artem	Makarenko	RUS	23.4.97	1	NC	Smolensk	15 Feb
	6.91	7.05	13.85	2.02	7.81	4.60	2:46.53	
5874	Gabriel	Moore	USA	10.1.96	6	NCAA	College Station	10 Mar
	6.94	7.33	14.38	1.99	8.11	4.46	2:44.01	

5866	Karl Robert	Saluri	EST	6.8.93	27 Jan
5866	Marcus	Nilsson	SWE	3.5.91	11 Feb
5864	Maxence	Pecatte	FRA	9.1.97	17 Feb
5842A	Devon	Williams	USA	17.1.94	17 Feb
5825	Romain	Martin	FRA	12.7.88	28 Jan
5824	Marek	Lukás	CZE	16.7.91	11 Feb
5810	Bastien	Auzeil	FRA	22.10.89	17 Feb
5810#	Trent	Nytes	USA	21.12.95	24 Feb
5807	Manuel	Eitel	GER	28.1.97	14 Jan
5804	Hans-Christian	Hausenberg	EST	18.9.98	3 Feb

3000 METRES WALK

10:30.28	Tom	Bosworth	GBR	17.1.90	1	GP	Glasgow	25 Feb
10:49.33	Christopher	Linke	GER	24.10.88	1		Erfurt	9 Feb
10:52.15	Nils	Brembach	GER	23.2.93	2		Erfurt	9 Feb
10:52.77	Callum	Wilkinson	GBR	14.3.97	2	GP	Glasgow	25 Feb
10:56.30	Marius	Ziukas	LTU	29.6.85	3	GP	Glasgow	25 Feb
10:58.89	Dawid	Tomala	POL	27.8.89	4	GP	Glasgow	25 Feb
11:06.57	Diego	García	ESP	19.1.96	5	GP	Glasgow	25 Feb

5000 METRES WALK

18:28.70	Tom	Bosworth	GBR	17.1.90	1	NC	Birmingham	18 Feb
18:52.94	Ruslan	Dmytrenko	UKR	22.3.86	1		Kyiv	9 Jan
18:55.26	Francesco	Fortunato	ITA	13.12.94	1	NC	Ancona	17 Feb
18:58.27	Marius	Ziukas	LTU	29.6.85	1	NC	Klaipeda	17 Feb
18:59.62	Alex	Wright	IRL	19.12.90	1	NC	Dublin	17 Feb
19:02.59	Ivan	Losev	UKR	26.1.86	2		Kyiv	9 Jan
19:10.13	Nils	Brembach	GER	23.2.93	1		Erfurt	2 Mar

WORLD INDOOR LISTS 2018 – WOMEN

60 METRES

6.97	Murielle	Ahouré	CIV	23.8.87	1	WI	Birmingham	2 Mar
7.02A	Javianne	Oliver	USA	26.12.94	1	NC	Albuquerque	18 Feb
	7.10				4s1	WI	Birmingham	2 Ma
7.03	Mujinga	Kambundji	SUI	17.6.92	1	NC	Magglingen	17 Feb
7.05	Marie Josée	Ta Lou	CIV	18.11.88	2	WI	Birmingham	2 Mar
7.06	Tatjana	Pinto	GER	2.7.92	1	NC	Dortmund	17 Feb
7.07	Elaine	Thompson	JAM	28.6.92	2s1	WI	Birmingham	2 Mar
7.07	Aleia	Hobbs	USA	24.2.96	1	NCAA	College Station	10 Mar
7.08A	Mikiah	Brisco	USA	14.7.96	1		Albuquerque	3 Feb
	7.10				1	SEC	College Station	25 Feb
7.08	Dina	Asher-Smith	GBR	4.12.95	1h1	GP	Glasgow	25 Feb
7.09	Carina	Horn	RSA	9.3.89	2		Metz	11 Feb
7.09	Dafne	Schippers	NED	15.6.92	1	NC	Apeldoorn	17 Feb
7.11	Gina	Lückenkemper	GER	21.11.96	1		Dortmund	21 Jan
7.11	Carolle	Zahi	FRA	12.6.94	1h4	WI	Birmingham	2 Mar
7.12	Lisa	Mayer	GER	2.5.96	2		Karlsruhe	3 Feb
7.12	Asha	Philip	GBR	25.10.90	3		Karlsruhe	3 Feb
7.12	Natalliah	Whyte	JAM	9.8.97	3	NCAA	College Station	10 Mar
7.13	Remona	Burchell	JAM	15.9.91	1		Mondeville	3 Feb
7.13	Michelle-Lee	Ahye	TTO	10.4.92	6	WI	Birmingham	2 Mar
7.14	Tori	Bowie	USA	27.8.90	2	Millrose	New York (Arm)	3 Feb
7.14	Christania	Williams	JAM	17.10.94	4	GP	Glasgow	25 Feb
7.15	Jonielle	Smith	JAM	30.1.96	1h1	NCAA	College Station	9 Mar
7.17	Ezinne	Okparaebo	NOR	3.3.88	5		Karlsruhe	3 Feb
7.17	Jamile	Samuel	NED	24.4.92	2	NC	Apeldoorn	17 Feb
7.17	Kate	Hall	USA	12.1.97	2h1	NCAA	College Station	9 Mar
7.18	Kortnei	Johnson	USA	11.8.97	1		Fayetteville	27 Jan
7.18	Morolake	Akinuson	USA	17.5.94	1h1		Lubbock	27 Jan
7.18A	Makenzie	Dunmore	USA	7.10.97	1		Albuquerque	10 Feb
7.18	Ewa	Swoboda	POL	26.7.97	4		Torun	15 Feb

7.19A	Ashley	Henderson	USA	4.12.95	10 Feb
7.19A	Destiny	Carter	USA	9.10.92	18 Feb
7.20A		Liang Xiaojing	CHN	7.4.97	2 Feb
7.20	Rosângela	Santos	BRA	20.12.90	13 Feb
7.20	Quanesha	Burks	USA	15.3.95	25 Feb
7.21	Imani	Lansiquot	GBR	17.12.97	15 Feb
7.21	Kelly-Ann	Baptiste	TTO	14.10.86	2 Mar
7.21	Cassondra	Hall	USA	23.9.97	9 Mar
7.21		Wei Yongli	CHN	11.10.91	11 Mar
7.22	Orlann	Ombissa-Dzangue	FRA	26.5.91	31 Jan
7.22	Jada	Baylark	USA	17.10.97	9 Feb
7.22	Simone	Facey	JAM	7.5.85	15 Feb
7.22	Naomi	Sedney	NED	17.12.94	17 Feb
7.22A	Teahna	Daniels	USA	27.3.97	18 Feb
7.22	Twanisha	Terry	USA-J	24.1.99	9 Mar
7.23	Anna	Kiełbasinska	POL	26.6.90	4 Feb
7.23	Rebekka	Haase	GER	2.1.93	10 Feb
7.23	Klára	Seidlová	CZE	10.3.94	17 Feb
7.24	Deajah	Stevens	USA	19.5.95	26 Jan
7.24	Barbara	Pierre	USA	28.4.87	3 Feb
7.24	Daryll	Neita	GBR	29.8.96	17 Feb
7.24	Ajla	Del Ponte	SUI	15.7.96	17 Feb
7.24	Jayla	Kirkland	USA-J	13.2.99	24 Feb
7.24	Ka'tia	Seymour	USA	3.10.97	24 Feb
7.24	Anna	Bongiorni	ITA	15.9.93	2 Mar
7.25	seven women				

200 METRES

22.38	Gabrielle	Thomas	USA	7.12.96	1	NCAA	College Station	10 Mar
22.41	Ashley	Henderson	USA	4.12.95	1rB	NCAA	College Station	10 Mar
22.55	Lynna	Irby	USA	6.12.98	2	NCAA	College Station	10 Mar
22.68	Sydney	McLaughlin	USA	7.8.99	2h3	NCAA	College Station	9 Mar
22.81	Mikiah	Brisco	USA	14.7.96	1rB	SEC	College Station	25 Feb
22.82	Deanna	Hill	USA	13.4.96	1		Clemson	10 Feb
22.83	Kayelle	Clarke	TTO	28.2.96	2rB	SEC	College Station	25 Feb
22.85	Ka'tia	Seymour	USA	3.10.97	1		Clemson	24 Feb
22.88	Léa	Sprunger	SUI	5.3.90	1	NC	Magglingen	18 Feb
22.88	Kortnei	Johnson	USA	11.8.97	1h4	SEC	College Station	24 Feb
22.99	Payton	Chadwick	USA	29.11.95	1rB		Fayetteville	27 Jan
22.99	Kendall	Ellis	USA	8.3.96	2rB		Clemson	10 Feb

23.00	Jasmine	Camacho-Quinn	PUR	21.8.96	10 Feb
23.02	Quanera	Hayes	USA	7.3.92	12 Jan
23.02	María	Belibasáki	GRE	19.6.91	11 Feb
23.02	Shauna	Helps	JAM	23.10.96	24 Feb

300 METRES

335.45	Shaunae	Miller-Uibo	BAH	15.4.94	1	Millrose	New York (Arm)	3 Feb
36.12	Sydney	McLaughlin	USA	7.8.99	1		Bloomington IN	8 Dec
36.73	Lynna	Irby	USA	6.12.98	1		Clemson	6 Jan

36.85	Phyllis	Francis	USA	4.5.92	3 Feb
36.89	Sarah	Atcho	SUI	1.6.95	11 Feb
36.96	Gunta	Latiseva-Cudare	LAT	9.3.95	13 Feb
36.98	Shamier	Little	USA	20.3.95	3 Feb

400 METRES

50.34	Kendall	Ellis	USA	8.3.96	1	NCAA	College Station	10 Mar
50.36	Sydney	McLaughlin	USA-J	7.8.99	1rB	NCAA	College Station	10 Mar
50.55	Courtney	Okolo	USA	15.3.94	1	WI	Birmingham	3 Mar
50.62	Lynna	Irby	USA	6.12.98	2	SEC	College Station	25 Feb

51.07	Sharrika	Barnett	USA	16.4.97	2rB	NCAA	College Station	10 Mar
51.17A	Shakima	Wimbley	USA	23.4.95	2	NC	Albuquerque	18 Feb
	51.24				1s1	WI	Birmingham	2 Mar
51.19A	Phyllis	Francis	USA	4.5.92	1rB	NC	Albuquerque	18 Feb
	52.00				1	GP	Glasgow	25 Feb
51.28	Léa	Sprunger	SUI	5.3.90	1		Torun	15 Feb
51.39	Georganne	Moline	USA	6.3.90	1		Lubbock	10 Feb
51.46A	Quanera	Hayes	USA	7.3.92	3rB	NC	Albuquerque	18 Feb
	51.82				1		Fayetteville	8 Feb
51.56	Brionna	Thomas	USA	21.3.96	3rB	NCAA	College Station	10 Mar
51.60	Eilidh	Doyle	GBR	20.2.87	3	WI	Birmingham	3 Mar
51.68	Briana	Guillory	USA	21.11.97	4rB	NCAA	College Station	10 Mar
51.78	Justyna	Swiety-Ersetic	POL	3.12.92	2		Torun	15 Feb
51.87A	Joanna	Atkins	USA	31.1.89	3	NC	Albuquerque	18 Feb
52.07	Amarachi	Pipi	GBR	26.11.95	3h4	NCAA	College Station	9 Mar
52.08	Phil	Healy	IRL	19.11.94	1		Wien	27 Jan
52.11A	Natasha	Hastings	USA	23.7.86	2h1	NC	Albuquerque	17 Feb
52.12	Tovea	Jenkins	JAM	27.10.92	2		Clemson	10 Feb
52.12	Zoey	Clark	GBR	25.10.94	2	NC	Birmingham	18 Feb
52.18	Stephenie Ann	McPherson	JAM	25.11.88	1h5	WI	Birmingham	2 Mar

52.20	Morgan	Burks-Magee	USA	6.3.99	24 Feb
52.21	Madiea	Ghafoor	NED	9.9.92	18 Feb
52.22	Anita	Horvat	SLO	7.9.96	8 Feb
52.23A	Jaide	Stepter	USA	25.4.94	18 Feb
52.27	María	Belibasáki	GRE	19.6.91	2 Mar
52.29A	Jessica	Beard	USA	8.1.89	18 Feb
52.35	Carly	Muscaro	USA	18.5.95	27 Jan
52.44A	Hannah	Waller	USA	22.6.98	10 Feb
52.49	Chloe	Abbott	USA	25.7.98	9 Feb

Oversized track

52.24	Raevyn	Rogers	USA	7.9.96	27 Jan
52.39A	Jasmine	Malone	USA	19.9.96	24 Feb

600 METRES

1:26.65#	Jahneya	Mitchell	USA		1	Big 10	Geneva OH	24 Feb
1:26.75#	Titania	Markland	JAM	1.2.94	2	Big 10	Geneva OH	24 Feb
1:26.99	Chrishuna	Williams	USA	31.3.93	1		Fayetteville	12 Jan

800 METRES

1:58.31	Francine	Niyonsaba	BDI	5.5.93	1	WI	Birmingham	4 Mar
1:58.99	Ajee'	Wilson	USA	8.5.94	2	WI	Birmingham	4 Mar
1:59.69	Laura	Muir	GBR	9.5.93	1	Scot Ch	Glasgow	28 Jan
1:59.69	Habitam	Alemu	ETH	9.7.97	1		Liévin	13 Feb
1:59.81	Shelayna	Oskan-Clarke	GBR	20.1.90	3	WI	Birmingham	4 Mar
1:59.86	Natoya	Goule	JAM	30.3.91	1		Clemson	20 Jan
1:59.99A	Raevyn	Rogers	USA	7.9.96	1h2	NC	Albuquerque	17 Feb
2:00.48	Margaret	Wambui	KEN	15.9.95	2		Liévin	13 Feb
2:00.70	Angelika	Cichocka	POL	15.3.88	3		Liévin	13 Feb
2:00.86	Ce'aira	Brown	USA	4.11.93	1		Boston (Allston)	25 Feb
2:01.08	Olha	Lyakhova	UKR	18.3.92	2		Torun	15 Feb
2:01.22	Jenna	Westaway	CAN	19.6.94	1	GP	Boston (R)	10 Feb
2:01.30	Mhairi	Hendry	GBR	31.3.96	2	NC	Birmingham	18 Feb
2:01.49A	Kaela	Edwards	USA	8.12.93	2h2	NC	Albuquerque	17 Feb
2:01.55	Sabrina	Southerland	USA	18.12.95	1	NCAA	College Station	10 Mar
2:01.61	Cecilia	Barowski	USA	7.12.92	2		Boston (Allston)	25 Feb
2:01.68	Nelly	Jepkosgei	KEN	14.7.91	1		Metz	11 Feb
2:01.80	Selina	Büchel	SUI	26.7.91	3		Torun	15 Feb
2:01.89A	Charlene	Lipsey	USA	16.7.91	2h3	NC	Albuquerque	17 Feb
2:02.01	Liga	Velvere	LAT	10.2.90	1	GP	Glasgow	25 Feb

2:02.03	Noélie	Yarigo	BEN	26.12.85	13 Feb
2:02.20	Lynsey	Sharp	GBR	11.7.90	10 Feb
2:02.22A	Hanna	Green	USA	16.10.94	17 Feb
2:02.29	Danaïd	Prinsen	NED	20.8.97	21 Feb
2:02.30	Jazmine	Fray	JAM	6.6.97	27 Jan
2:02.30	Agnes	Abu	GHA	1.5.92	25 Feb
2:02.34	Cynthia	Anais	FRA	18.1.88	11 Feb
2:02.39	Emily	Jerotich	KEN	13.5.86	3 Feb
2:02.42	Yekaterina	Kupina	RUS	2.2.86	4 Feb
2:02.46	Síofra	Cléirigh Büttner	IRL	21.7.95	10 Mar
2:02.49	Rabab	Arrafi	MAR	12.1.91	27 Jan
2:02.60	Hedda	Hynne	NOR	13.3.90	15 Feb

1500 METRES

3:57.45	Genzebe	Dibaba	ETH	8.2.91	1		Karlsruhe	3 Feb
4:02.21	Beatrice	Chepkoech	KEN	6.7.91	1	GP	Glasgow	25 Feb
4:04.00	Konstanze	Klosterhalfen	GER	18.2.97	2		Karlsruhe	3 Feb
4:04.38	Dawit	Seyaum	ETH	27.7.96	1	GP	Boston (R)	10 Feb
4:04.76	Rabab	Arrafi	MAR	12.1.91	1		Torun	15 Feb
4:04.89	Meraf	Bahta	SWE	24.6.89	2		Torun	15 Feb
4:04.95	Aisha	Praught Leer	JAM	14.12.89	2	GP	Boston (R)	10 Feb
4:05.04	Hellen	Obiri	KEN	13.12.89	3		Torun	15 Feb
4:05.36	Alemaz	Teshale	ETH-J	5.7.99	4		Torun	15 Feb
4:05.37	Laura	Muir	GBR	9.5.93	1	Univ Ch	Glasgow	10 Feb
4:05.46	Sifan	Hassan	NED	1.1.93	1h3	WI	Birmingham	2 Mar
4:05.51	Habitam	Alemu	ETH	9.7.97	5		Torun	15 Feb
4:05.64	Axumawit	Embaye	ETH	18.10.94	6		Torun	15 Feb
4:05.81	Winny	Chebet	KEN	20.12.90	2h3	WI	Birmingham	2 Mar

4:05.91	Gudaf	Tsegay	ETH	23.1.97	3	GP	Boston (R)	10 Feb
4:06.21	Shelby	Houlihan	USA	8.2.93	4h3	WI	Birmingham	2 Mar
4:06.35	Angelika	Cichocka	POL	15.3.88	2		Düsseldorf	6 Feb
4:07.25	Dominique	Scott Efurd	RSA	24.6.92	4	GP	Boston (R)	10 Feb
4:07.62	Sarah	McDonald	GBR	2.8.93	5	GP	Boston (R)	10 Feb
4:07.71	Linn	Nilsson	SWE	15.10.90	7		Torun	15 Feb
4:08.07	Eilish	McColgan	GBR	25.11.90	3		Madrid	8 Feb
4:08.33	Diana	Sujew	GER	2.11.90	4		Düsseldorf	6 Feb
4:08.49	Aleksandra	Gulyayeva	RUS	30.4.94	1	NC	Moskva	14 Feb
4:08.70	Sofia	Ennaoui	POL	30.8.95	8		Torun	15 Feb
4:08.84	Cory	McGee	USA	29.5.92	6	GP	Boston (R)	10 Feb
4:09.24	Marta	Pérez	ESP	19.4.93	7		Madrid	8 Feb
4:09.25	Yelena	Korobkina	RUS	25.11.90	1		Moskva	4 Feb
4:09.31	Malika	Akkaoui	MAR	25.12.87	9		Torun	15 Feb
4:09.31	Colleen	Quigley	USA	20.11.92	2h2	WI	Birmingham	2 Mar
4:09.42	Kate	Van Buskirk	CAN	9.6.87	3h2	WI	Birmingham	2 Mar
4:09.47	Ciara	Mageean	IRL	12.3.92	8	GP	Boston (R)	10 Feb
4:09.54	Aníta	Hinriksdóttir	ISL	13.1.96	5		Düsseldorf	6 Feb
4:09.94	Gabriela	Stafford	CAN	13.9.95	5h1	WI	Birmingham	2 Mar
4:09.99	Nelly	Jepkosgei	KEN	14.7.91	3		Liévin	13 Feb

4:10.05	Stacey	Smith	GBR	4.2.90	25 Feb
4:10.09	Katie	Snowden	GBR	9.3.94	10 Feb
4:10.12	Hanna	Klein	GER	6.4.93	3 Feb
4:10.14	Josephine	Chelangat	KEN	10.10.98	6 Feb
4:10.21+	Elinor	Purrier	USA	20.2.95	9 Feb
4:10.24	Shannon	Osika	USA	15.6.93	27 Jan
4:10.36	Simona	Vrzalová	CZE	7.4.88	15 Feb
4:10.36	Luiza	Gega	ALB	5.11.88	18 Feb
4:10.37	Claudia	Bobocea	ROU	11.6.92	6 Feb
4:10.38	Rachel	Schneider	USA	18.7.91	27 Jan
4:10.52	Zoe	Buckman	AUS	21.12.88	25 Feb
4:10.68	Karissa	Schweizer	USA	4.5.96	27 Jan
4:10.85	Gesa-Felicitas	Krause	GER	3.8.92	25 Feb
4:11.25	Hannah	England	GBR	6.3.87	10 Feb
4:11.57	Feyisa	Adanech	ETH	23.1.98	13 Feb
4:11.59+	Marta	Pen	POR	31.7.93	9 Feb
4:11.66	Daryia	Barysevich	BLR	6.4.90	18 Feb
4:12.02	Marina	Pospelova	RUS	23.7.90	14 Feb

1 MILE

4:26.55	Elinor	Purrier	USA	20.2.95	1		Boston (Allston)	9 Feb
4:26.92	Kate	Van Buskirk	CAN	9.6.87	1		New York (Arm)	27 Jan
4:27.30	Rachel	Schneider	USA	18.7.91	2		New York (Arm)	27 Jan
4:27.44	Gabriela	Stafford	CAN	13.9.95	2		Boston (Allston)	9 Feb
4:27.54	Karissa	Schweizer	USA	4.5.96	3		New York (Arm)	27 Jan
4:27.55	Shannon	Osika	USA	15.6.93	4		New York (Arm)	27 Jan
4:27.67	Cory	McGee	USA	29.5.92	1		Boston MA	16 Dec
4:27.69	Nicole	Sifuentes	CAN	30.6.86	1		Ann Arbor	13 Jan
4:29.65	Marta	Pen	POR	31.7.93	3		Boston (Allston)	9 Feb

4:30.05	Colleen	Quigley	USA	20.11.92	3 Feb
4:30.08	Kate	Grace	USA	24.10.88	3 Feb
4:30.98	Nicole	Tully	USA	30.10.86	25 Feb
4:30.99	Ciara	Mageean	IRL	12.3.92	3 Feb
4:31.09	Becca	Addison	USA	28.5.91	25 Feb
4:31.29#	Elise	Cranny	USA	8.5.96	24 Feb
4:31.63	Lauren	Johnson	USA	4.5.87	3 Feb
4:31.66	Lucia	Stafford	CAN	1.1.98	27 Jan

2000 METRES

5:39.69+	Genzebe	Dibaba	ETH	8.2.91	1		Sabadell	13 Feb
5:41.10	Yelena	Korobkina	RUS	25.11.90	1		Yekaterinburg	7 Jan

3000 METRES

8:31.23	Genzebe	Dibaba	ETH	8.2.91	1		Sabadell	13 Feb
8:34.45#	Sifan	Hassan	NED	1.1.93	1		Seattle	27 Jan
8:36.01	Shelby	Houlihan	USA	8.2.93	1rB		Boston (Allston)	3 Feb
8:36.01	Konstanze	Klosterhalfen	GER	18.2.97	1	NC	Dortmund	18 Feb
8:37.21mx	Laura	Muir	GBR	9.5.93	1		Glasgow	7 Jan
	8:45.78				1	GP	Birmingham	1 Mar
8:38.81	Hellen	Obiri	KEN	13.12.89	1		Ostrava	25 Jan
8:39.15	Beatrice	Chepkoech	KEN	6.7.91	2		Ostrava	25 Jan
8:39.55	Taye	Fantu	ETJ	29.3.99	3		Ostrava	25 Jan
8:40.20	Marielle	Hall	USA	28.1.92	2rB		Boston (Allston)	3 Feb
8:40.31	Jenny	Simpson	USA	23.8.86	1	GP	Boston (R)	10 Feb
8:41.08	Fotyen	Tesfay	ETH	17.2.98	2	GP	Boston (R)	10 Feb
8:41.10	Aisha	Praught Leer	JAM	14.12.89	1	Millrose	New York (Arm)	3 Feb
8:41.16	Emma	Coburn	USA	19.10.90	2	Millrose	New York (Arm)	3 Feb
8:41.18	Dominique	Scott Efurd	RSA	24.6.92	3	Millrose	New York (Arm)	3 Feb
8:41.60	Karissa	Schweizer	USA	4.5.96	4	Millrose	New York (Arm)	3 Feb
8:41.94	Stephanie	Twell	GBR	17.8.89	3	GP	Boston (R)	10 Feb
8:42.46	Meraf	Bahta	SWE	24.6.89	1		Madrid	8 Feb
8:43.15	Katie	Mackey	USA	12.11.87	5	Millrose	New York (Arm)	3 Feb
8:43.28#	Shalane	Flanagan	USA	8.7.81	2		Seattle	27 Jan
8:43.56	Meskerem	Mamo	ETH-J	1.1.99	3		Madrid	8 Feb
8:47.30	Rosie	Clarke	GBR	17.11.91	4		Madrid	8 Feb
8:47.81	Lauren	Paquette	USA	27.6.86	6	Millrose	New York (Arm)	3 Feb
8:48.99	Ruth	Jebet	BRN	17.11.96	5		Ostrava	25 Jan

8:49.02	Kate	Van Buskirk	CAN	9.6.87	7	Millrose	New York (Arm)	3 Feb
8:49.78	Geneviève	Lalonde	CAN	5.9.91	5	GP	Boston (R)	10 Feb
8:49.89	Norah	Tanui	KEN	2.10.95	6		Ostrava	25 Jan
8:50.80	Hawi	Feysa	ETH-J	1.2.99	5		Madrid	8 Feb
8:50.87	Eilish	McColgan	GBR	25.11.90	2	NC	Birmingham	17 Feb
8:50.96	Mel	Lawrence	USA	29.8.89	8	Millrose	New York (Arm)	3 Feb
8:51.07	Emily	Lipari	USA	19.11.92	9	Millrose	New York (Arm)	3 Feb

8:51.90	Yelena	Korobkina	RUS	25.11.90	12 Feb
8:53.63	Sofia	Ennaoui	POL	30.8.95	25 Jan
8:53.97	Claudia	Bobocea	ROU	11.6.92	25 Jan
8:54.08	Gesa-Felicitas	Krause	GER	3.8.92	18 Feb
8:54.35	Allie	Ostrander	USA	24.12.96	10 Mar
8:54.56	Margherita	Magnani	ITA	26.2.87	25 Jan
8:55.10	Melissa	Courtney	GBR	30.8.93	7 Jan
8:55.68	Elinor	Purrier	USA	20.2.95	2 Dec

5000 METRES

15:13.76	Emily	Sisson	USA	12.10.91	1		Boston (Allston)	25 Feb
15:15.52#	Emily	Infeld	USA	21.3.90	1		Seattle	10 Feb
15:15.64#	Gwen	Jorgensen	USA	25.4.86	2		Seattle	10 Feb
15:17.31*	Karissa	Schweizer	USA	4.5.96	1		Boston (Allston)	2 Dec
15:19.03*	Ednah	Kurgat	KEN		2		Boston (Allston)	2 Dec

60 METRES HURDLES

7.70A	Sharika	Nelvis	USA	10.5.90	1	NC	Albuquerque	18 Feb
7.70	Kendra	Harrison	USA	18.9.92	1	WI	Birmingham	3 Mar
7.73A	Christina	Manning	USA	29.5.90	3	NC	Albuquerque	18 Feb
7.83	Pamela	Dutkiewicz	GER	28.9.91	3		Düsseldorf	6 Feb
7.83	Nadine	Visser	NED	9.2.95	1s3	WI	Birmingham	3 Mar
7.84	Cindy	Roleder	GER	21.8.89	3		Karlsruhe	3 Feb
7.86	Isabelle	Pedersen	NOR	27.1.92	3s3	WI	Birmingham	3 Mar
7.88	Alina	Talay	BLR	14.5.89	4		Karlsruhe	3 Feb
7.88A	Jasmin	Stowers	USA	23.9.91	3s2	NC	Albuquerque	18 Feb
7.89A	Tobi	Amusan	NGR	23.4.97	1s3		Albuquerque	20 Jan
7.89	Devynne	Charlton	BAH	26.11.95	2s1	WI	Birmingham	3 Mar
7.91A	Queen	Harrison	USA	10.9.88	5	NC	Albuquerque	18 Feb
7.92	Sally	Pearson	AUS	19.9.86	3s2	WI	Birmingham	3 Mar
7.93	Payton	Chadwick	USA	29.11.95	1h2	NCAA	College Station	9 Mar
7.93	Anna	Cockrell	USA	28.8.97	2	NCAA	College Station	10 Mar
7.94A	Dior	Hall	USA	2.1.96	1s2		Albuquerque	20 Jan
7.94A	Kristi	Castlin	USA	7.7.88	2h3	NC	Albuquerque	17 Feb
7.94A	Bridgette	Owens	USA	14.3.92	7	NC	Albuquerque	18 Feb
7.95	Jasmine	Camacho-Quinn	PUR	21.8.96	2		Clemson	10 Feb
7.98A	Erica	Bougard	USA	26.7.93	1P	NC	Albuquerque	16 Feb
7.98	Tara	Davis	USA-J	20.5.99	1h1	NCAA	College Station	9 Mar
7.99	Nadine	Hildebrand	GER	20.9.87	7		Karlsruhe	3 Feb
8.00A	Kori	Carter	USA	3.6.92	3h3	NC	Albuquerque	17 Feb
8.00A	Tiffani	McReynolds	USA	4.12.91	4s2	NC	Albuquerque	18 Feb
8.01	Hanna	Plotitsyna	UKR	1.1.87	3		Torun	15 Feb

8.02	Jeanine	Williams	JAM	28.1.97	19 Jan
8.02	Stephanie	Bendrat	AUT	5.3.91	18 Feb
8.02	Cortney	Jones	USA-J	18.6.99	10 Mar
8.03	Nooralotta	Neziri	FIN	9.11.92	11 Feb
8.03	Alaysha	Johnson	USA	20.7.96	24 Feb
8.04	Tonea	Marshall	USA	17.12.98	9 Feb
8.04A	Jade	Barber	USA	4.4.93	18 Feb
8.04	Lindsay	Lindley	NGR	6.10.89	21 Feb
8.04	Janeek	Brown	JAM	14.5.98	25 Feb
8.05	Gabriele	Cunningham	USA	22.2.98	10 Feb
8.05	Eline	Berings	BEL	28.5.86	10 Feb
8.05	Elvira	Herman	BLR	9.1.97	17 Feb
8.05	Taliyah	Brooks	USA	8.2.95	10 Mar
8.05	Tia	Jones	USA-J	8.9.00	11 Mar
8.05	Grace	Stark	USA-Y	6.5.01	11 Mar
8.06	Kayla	White	USA	24.9.96	10 Mar

Best at low altitude

7.77	Manning	1		Düsseldorf	6 Feb
7.80	Nelvis	1		Karlsruhe	3 Feb
7.90	Amusun	1	Mil	New York (Arm)	3 Feb
7.98	Stowers	3	GP	Boston (R)	10 Feb
7.98	Hall	4		Fayetteville	27 Jan
8.00	Q Harrison	4	GP	Boston (R)	10 Feb
8.00	Castlin	5	GP	Boston (R)	10 Feb
8.06	Owens	1		Seattle	27 Jan

HIGH JUMP

2.04	Mariya	Lasitskene	RUS	14.1.93	1		Volgograd	27 Jan
1.97	Yuliya	Levchenko	UKR	28.11.97	1		Kyiv	10 Jan
1.97A	Vashti	Cunningham	USA	18.1.98	1	NC	Albuquerque	18 Feb
1.95	Levern	Spencer	LCA	23.6.84	1		Trinec	30 Jan
1.95	Mirela	Demireva	BUL	28.9.89	1		Karlsruhe	3 Feb
1.93	Iryna	Herashchenko	UKR	10.3.95	1		Ostrava	25 Jan
1.93	Michaela	Hrubá	CZE	21.2.98	2		Ostrava	25 Jan
1.93	Katarina	Johnson-Thompson	GBR	9.1.93	1		Eaubonne	9 Feb
1.93	Yuliya	Chumachenko	UKR	2.10.94	2	NC	Sumy	10 Feb
1.93	Alessia	Trost	ITA	8.3.93	3	WI	Birmingham	1 Mar
1.93	Morgan	Lake	GBR	12.5.97	4	WI	Birmingham	1 Mar
1.92*	Kateryna	Tabashnyk	UKR	15.6.94	2		Minsk	23 Dec
1.92	Logan	Boss	USA	4.8.97	1		Cambridge MA	2 Feb
1.92	Nadezhda	Dusanova	UZB	17.11.87	1		Brno	7 Feb
1.92	Ana	Simic	CRO	5.5.90	1	BalkC	Istanbul	17 Feb

1.92	Erika	Kinsey	SWE	10.3.88	1	NC	Gävle	18 Feb
1.91A	Liz	Patterson	USA	9.6.88	1		Air Force Academy	27 Jan
1.91	Sofie	Skoog	SWE	7.6.90	6		Banská Bystrica	6 Feb
1.91A	Inika	McPherson	USA	29.9.86	2	NC	Albuquerque	18 Feb
1.90	Serena	Capponcelli	ITA	24.1.89	1		Gent	6 Jan
1.90	Yaroslava	Mahuchikh	UKR-Y	19.9.01	1		Sumy	16 Jan
1.90	Marija	Vukovic	MNE	21.1.92	2		Brno	7 Feb
1.90	Nafissatou	Thiam	BEL	19.8.94	4		Eaubonne	9 Feb
1.90	Nikki	Manson	GBR	15.10.94	1	Univ Ch	Glasgow	10 Feb
1.90	Alyx	Treasure	CAN	15.5.92	1		Ann Arbor	16 Feb

1.89	Marie-Laurence	Jungfleisch	GER	7.10.90	3 Feb
1.89	Zarriea	Willis	USA	14.11.96	10 Feb
1.89	Maja	Nilsson	SWE-J	8.12.99	11 Feb
1.89	Tonje	Angelsen	NOR	17.1.90	11 Feb
1.89A	Erica	Bougard	USA	26.7.93	16 Feb
1.89	Karina	Taranda	BLR-J	10.2.99	17 Feb
1.89	Lada	Pejchalová	CZE	15.11.98	18 Feb
1.88	Nicole	Greene	USA	2.5.97	13 Jan
1.88	Yevgeniya	Kononova	RUS	28.9.89	4 Feb
1.88	Tatyana	Yermachenkova	RUS	9.9.98	4 Feb
1.88	Jeannelle	Scheper	LCA	21.11.94	10 Feb
1.88	Doreen	Amata	NGR	6.5.88	10 Feb
1.88	Chelsie	Decoud	USA	28.6.96	20 Feb
1.88	Yorgelis	Rodríguez	CUB	25.1.95	2 Mar
1.88		Hu Linpeng	CHN	29.12.95	8 Mar
1.87	three women				

POLE VAULT

4.95	Sandi	Morris	USA	8.7.92	1	WI	Birmingham	3 Mar
4.91A	Katie	Nageotte	USA	30.6.91	1	NC	Albuquerque	18 Feb
4.90	Anzhelika	Sidorova	RUS	28.6.91	2	WI	Birmingham	3 Mar
4.83	Ekateríni	Stefanídi	GRE	4.2.90	1		Liévin	13 Feb
4.81	Jenn	Suhr	USA	5.2.82	1		Toronto	20 Jan
4.75	Eliza	McCartney	NZL	11.12.96	4	WI	Birmingham	3 Mar
4.72	Ninon	Guillon-Romarin	FRA	15.4.95	3		Clermont-Ferrand	25 Feb
4.70	Alysha	Newman	CAN	29.6.94	6	WI	Birmingham	3 Mar
4.67	Olivia	Gruver	USA	29.7.97	1	SEC	College Station	24 Feb
4.66	Lexi	Jacobus	USA	20.11.96	1	NCAA	College Station	10 Mar
4.65	Nikoléta	Kiriakopoúlou	GRE	21.3.86	2	GP	Glasgow	25 Feb
4.62	Kristen	Hixson	USA	1.7.92	1		Notre Dame	3 Feb
4.62	Maryna	Kylypko	UKR	10.11.95	4		Clermont-Ferrand	25 Feb
4.62	Lisa	Ryzih	GER	27.9.88	6		Clermont-Ferrand	25 Feb
4.62	Irina	Zhuk	BLR	26.1.93	7		Clermont-Ferrand	25 Feb
4.62	Nina	Kennedy	AUS	5.4.97	8		Clermont-Ferrand	25 Feb
4.61A	Morgann	LeLeux	USA	14.11.92	4	NC	Albuquerque	18 Feb
4.61	Tori	Hoggard	USA	20.11.96	2	NCAA	College Station	10 Mar
4.60*	Angelina	Krasnova	RUS	7.2.91	1		Moskva	19 Dec
4.60A	Anicka	Newell	CAN	5.8.93	1		Albuquerque	10 Feb
4.60	Holly	Bradshaw	GBR	2.11.91	2		Rouen	10 Feb
4.60	Yarisley	Silva	CUB	1.6.87	7	WI	Birmingham	3 Mar
4.60	Olga	Mullina	RUS	1.8.92	9	WI	Birmingham	3 Mar
4.57	Annie	Rhodes-Johnigan	USA	13.5.95	1		Lovejoy	20 Jan
4.55	Jirina	Ptácníková	CZE	20.5.86	1		Praha	13 Feb
4.55	Aksana	Gataullina	RUS-J	17.7.00	1		Sankt Peterburg	23 Feb
4.52	Katharina	Bauer	GER	12.6.90	1		Dortmund	21 Jan
4.51	Friedelinde	Petershofen	GER	19.8.95	3		Potsdam	19 Jan
4.51A	Kristen	Brown	USA	26.5.92	5	NC	Albuquerque	18 Feb
4.50	Anjuli	Knäsche	GER	18.10.93	1		Hamburg	4 Feb
4.50	Polina	Knoroz	RUS-J	20.7.99	2		Sankt Peterburg	23 Feb
4.50	Angelica	Bengtsson	SWE	8.7.93	11	WI	Birmingham	3 Mar
4.50		Li Ling	CHN	6.7.89	1	NGPF	Beijing	24 Mar

4.47A	Megan	Clark	USA	10.6.94	20 Jan
4.47	Lucy	Bryan	GBR	22.5.95	3 Feb
4.46	Lisa	Gunnarsson	SWE-J	20.8.99	27 Jan
4.45	Michaela	Meijer	SWE	30.7.93	27 Jan
4.45	Tatyana	Shvydkina	RUS	8.5.90	4 Feb
4.45	Alyona	Lutkovskaya	RUS	15.3.96	4 Feb
4.45	Minna	Nikkanen	FIN	9.4.88	11 Feb
4.45	Femke	Pluim	NED	10.5.94	17 Feb
4.42	Romana	Malácová	CZE	15.5.87	25 Jan
4.42	Kortney	Ross	USA	26.7.92	27 Jan
4.42	Eléni-Klaoúdia	Pólak	GRE	9.9.96	3 Feb
4.41	Marion	Fiack	FRA	13.10.92	13 Jan
4.41	Martina	Schultze	GER	12.9.90	19 Jan
4.41	Angelica	Moser	SUI	9.10.97	20 Jan
4.41	Desiree	Freier	USA	24.7.96	10 Mar
4.40	Alina	McDonald	USA	1.1.97	2 Dec
4.40	Irina	Ivanova	RUS	19.4.96	11 Jan
4.40	Saga	Andersson	FIN-J	30.3.00	17 Feb
4.40	Maialen	Axpe	ESP	4.5.93	24 Feb
4.40		Chen Qiaoling	CHN-J	22.11.99	7 Mar

LONG JUMP

6.96	Ivana	Spanovic	SRB	10.5.90	1	WI	Birmingham	4 Mar
6.92	Khaddi	Sagnia	SWE	20.4.94	1	GP	Glasgow	25 Feb
6.89	Brittney	Reese	USA	9.9.86	2	WI	Birmingham	4 Mar
6.85	Sosthene Taroum	Moguenara	GER	17.10.89	3	WI	Birmingham	4 Mar
6.81	Quanesha	Burks	USA	15.3.95	4	WI	Birmingham	4 Mar
6.73	Kate	Hall	USA	12.1.97	1	NCAA	College Station	9 Mar
6.72	Malaika	Mihambo	GER	3.2.94	1		Karlsruhe	3 Feb
6.71	Katarina	Johnson-Thompson	GBR	9.1.93	1	NC	Birmingham	17 Feb
6.69	Éloyse	Lesueur-Aymonin	FRA	15.7.88	1	NC	Liévin	18 Feb
6.67	Maryna	Bekh	UKR	18.7.95	1	NC	Sumy	10 Feb

6.65		Wang Qingling	CHN	14.1.93	1	NGP	Xianlin	11 Mar
6.64	Krystyna	Hryshutyna	UKR	21.3.92	2	NC	Sumy	10 Feb
6.63	Ksenija	Balta	EST	1.11.86	1	NC	Tallinn	18 Feb
6.63	Christabel	Nettey	CAN	2.6.91	7	WI	Birmingham	4 Mar
6.61	Yelena	Sokolova	RUS	23.7.86	1	NC	Moskva	13 Feb
6.61	Tianna	Bartoletta	USA	30.8.85	6	GP	Glasgow	25 Feb
6.60	Lanae-Tava	Thomas	USA-Y	28.1.01	1		Houghton	20 Jan
6.59	Chanice	Porter	JAM	25.5.94	2		Clemson	10 Feb
6.58	Yariagnis	Argüelles	CUB	18.4.84	1		Dortmund	21 Jan
6.57	Taliyah	Brooks	USA	8.2.95	1		Fayetteville	9 Feb
6.56	Yelena	Mashinistova	RUS	29.3.94	1	Mosc Ch	Moskva	24 Jan
6.56	Nadja	Käther	GER	29.9.88	1	ISTAF	Berlin	26 Jan
6.53	Keturah	Orji	USA	5.3.96	2	SEC	College Station	24 Feb

6.52	Lauma	Griva	LAT	27.10.84	9 Feb	6.49	Yanis	David	FRA	12.12.97	24 Feb
6.52	Tania	Vicenzino	ITA	1.4.86	17 Feb	6.48	Bianca	Stuart	BAH	17.5.88	28 Jan
6.51	Darrielle	McQueen	USA	29.5.96	24 Feb	6.48	Alina	Rotaru	ROU	5.6.93	25 Feb
6.50	Tara	Davis	USA	20.5.99	9 Mar	6.47	three women				

TRIPLE JUMP

14.63	Yulimar	Rojas	VEN	21.10.95	1	WI	Birmingham	3 Mar
14.53	Keturah	Orji	USA	5.3.96	1		Clemson	20 Jan
14.48	Kimberly	Williams	JAM	3.11.88	2	WI	Birmingham	3 Mar
14.44	Viktoriya	Prokopenko	RUS	17.4.91	1		Moskva	3 Feb
14.40	Ana	Peleteiro	ESP	2.12.95	3	WI	Birmingham	3 Mar
14.33	Elena	Pan□uroiu	ROU	24.2.95	4	WI	Birmingham	3 Mar
14.30	Irina	Vaskovskaya	BLR	2.4.91	1	NCp	Gomel	3 Feb
14.25	Paraskeví	Papahrístou	GRE	17.4.89	1		Val-de-Reuil	27 Jan
14.22	Rouguy	Diallo	FRA	5.2.95	2		Val-de-Reuil	27 Jan
14.15A	Tori	Franklin	USA	7.10.92	1	NC	Albuquerque	17 Feb
	14.03				8	WI	Birmingham	3 Mar
14.13	Dovile	Dzindzaletaite	LTU	14.7.93	3		Madrid	8 Feb
14.13	Neele	Eckhardt	GER	2.7.92	1	NC	Dortmund	17 Feb
14.11	Yekaterina	Koneva	RUS	25.9.88	2		Moskva	3 Feb
14.11	Yanis	David	FRA	12.12.97	2	SEC	College Station	25 Feb
14.08	Thea	Lafond	DMA	5.4.94	1		University Park	17 Feb
14.07	Patricia	Sarrapio	ESP	16.11.82	5		Madrid	8 Feb
14.07	Ilionis	Guillaume	FRA	13.1.98	1	NC	Liévin	17 Feb
14.06	Jeanine	Assani Issouf	FRA	17.8.92	2	NC	Liévin	17 Feb
14.02	Anna	Krylova	RUS	3.10.85	3		Moskva	3 Feb
14.02	Natalya	Yevdokimova	RUS	7.9.93	4		Moskva	3 Feb
14.00	Nubia	Soares	BRA	26.3.96	9	WI	Birmingham	3 Mar
13.93	Shanieka	Ricketts	JAM	2.2.92	10	WI	Birmingham	3 Mar
13.91	Marie-José	Ebwea Bile	FRA	7.2.97	3	SEC	College Station	25 Feb
13.91	Gabriela	Petrova	BUL	29.6.92	11	WI	Birmingham	3 Mar

13.89	Irina	Ektova	KAZ	8.1.87	16 Jan	13.78A	Andrea	Geubelle	USA	21.6.91	17 Feb
13.86	Kristiina	Mäkelä	FIN	20.11.92	18 Feb	13.78		Wang Rong	CHN	1.7.96	12 Mar
13.85	Olha	Saladukha	UKR	4.6.83	11 Feb	13.75	Tähti	Alver	EST	4.12.94	10 Feb
13.85		Rao Fan	CHN	1.1.96	8 Mar	13.69		Chen Jie	CHN	2.3.98	8 Mar
13.82	Darya	Nidbaykina	RUS	26.12.94	3 Feb	13.68	Johanmy	Luque	VEN	20.12.95	10 Mar
13.81	Jessie	Maduka	GER	23.4.96	17 Feb	13.65	Ruslana	Tsyhotska	UKR	23.3.86	27 Jan
13.79	Violetta	Skvortsova	BLR	15.4.98	27 Jan	13.65	Naomi	Ogbeta	GBR	18.4.98	18 Feb

SHOT

19.62	Anita	Márton	HUN	15.1.89	1	WI	Birmingham	2 Mar
19.53		Gong Lijiao	CHN	24.1.89	1	NGPF	Beijing	24 Mar
19.22	Danniel	Thomas-Dodd	JAM	11.11.92	2	WI	Birmingham	2 Mar
19.20	Maggie	Ewen	USA	23.9.94	1		Albuquerque	10 Feb
18.77	Paulina	Guba	POL	14.5.91	1	NC	Torun	17 Feb
18.77		Gao Yang	CHN	1.3.93	4	WI	Birmingham	2 Mar
18.55	Jeneva	Stevens	USA	28.10.89	1	NC	Montréal	10 Feb
18.28	Irina	Tarasova	RUS	15.4.87	1		Moskva	4 Feb
18.21	Alyona	Dubitskaya	BLR	25.1.90	6	WI	Birmingham	2 Mar
18.20	Brittany	Crew	CAN	3.6.94	2	NC	Montréal	10 Feb
18.19	Yaniuvis	López	CUB	1.2.86	7	WI	Birmingham	2 Mar
18.18	Dani	Hill	USA	16.5.91	1		Allendale MI	9 Feb
18.14	Emmonnie	Henderson	USA	5.11.94	1		Clemson	24 Feb
17.98	Erin	Farmer	USA	11.8.95	2	NC	Albuquerque	17 Feb
17.88	Fanny	Roos	SWE	2.1.95	1	IDM	Växjö	4 Feb
17.85	Radoslava	Mavrodieva	BUL	13.3.87	1	BalkC	Istanbul	17 Feb
17.83	Dimitriana	Surdu	MDA	12.5.94	1	NC	Chisinau	3 Feb
17.83	Jessica	Ramsey	USA	26.7.91	1		Nashville	10 Feb
17.83		Guo Tianqian	CHN	1.6.95	1	NGP	Dalian	8 Mar
17.81	McKenzie	Warren	USA	3.12.93	1		Seattle	27 Jan
17.80	Cleopatra	Borel	TTO	10.3.79	9	WI	Birmingham	2 Mar

17.78	Lena	Giger	USA	7.6.96	10	Feb
17.77	Stamatía	Skarvélis	GRE	17.8.95	8	Dec
17.76		Bian Ka	CHN	5.1.93	24	Mar
17.71	Klaudia	Kardasz	POL	2.5.96	10	Feb
17.67	Felisha	Johnson	USA	24.7.89	3	Feb
17.65	Lloydricia	Cameron	USA	8.4.96	24	Feb
17.63	Janeah	Stewart	USA	21.7.96	24	Feb
17.58	Jessica	Woodard	USA	4.2.95	10	Feb
17.57	Chase	Ealey	USA	20.7.94	17	Feb
17.53	Monique	Riddick	USA	8.11.89	10	Feb

WEIGHT

25.27	Gwen	Berry	USA	29.6.89	1		Nashville	10 Feb
24.78	Annette	Echikunwoke	USA	29.7.96	1		Columbus	16 Feb
24.51	DeAnna	Price	USA	8.6.93	1	NC	Albuquerque	18 Feb
24.37	Kaitlyn	Long	USA	25.4.96	1	Big 10	Geneva OH	24 Feb
24.24	Jeneva	Stevens	USA	28.10.89	2		Nashville	20 Jan
24.12	Janeah	Stewart	USA	21.7.96	2		Nashville	10 Feb
23.84	Sade	Olatoye	USA	25.1.97	2	Big 10	Geneva OH	24 Feb
23.72	Ida	Storm	SWE	26.12.91	1	NC	Gävle	18 Feb
23.42	Tiffany	Okieme	USA	8.1.94	4	NC	Albuquerque	18 Feb
22.74	Jessica	Ramsey	USA	26.7.91	4		Nashville	10 Feb

22.27	Stamatía	Skarvélis	GRE	17.8.95	13	Jan
22.26	Maggie	Ewen	USA	23.9.94	10	Feb
22.25	Brooke	Andersen	USA	23.8.95	24	Feb
22.08	Felisha	Johnson	USA	24.7.89	27	Jan

PENTATHLON

4760A	Erica	Bougard	USA	26.7.93	1	NC	Albuquerque	16 Feb
	7.98	1.89	12.76	6.20	2:13.77			
4750	Katarina	Johnson-Thompson	GBR	9.1.93	1	WI	Birmingham	2 Mar
	8.36	1.91	12.68	6.50	2:16.63			
4700	Ivona	Dadic	AUT	29.12.93	2	WI	Birmingham	2 Mar
	8.32	1.82	14.27	6.40	2:17.82			
4663	Eliska	Klucinová	CZE	14.4.88	1	NC	Praha (Strom)	11 Feb
	8.51	1.84	14.52	6.26	2:17.34			
4637	Yorgelis	Rodríguez	CUB	25.1.95	3	WI	Birmingham	2 Mar
	8.57	1.88	14.15	6.15	2:17.70			
4583	Xénia	Krizsán	HUN	13.1.93	1	NC	Budapest	10 Feb
	8.39	1.79	14.21	6.14	2:16.2			
4572	Taliyah	Brooks	USA	8.2.95	1	NCAA	College Station	9 Mar
	8.05	1.84	12.16	6.36	2:22.44			
4508A	Kendell	Williams	USA	14.6.95	2	NC	Albuquerque	16 Feb
	8.11	1.74	12.55	6.38	2:19.22			
4502	Nina	Schultz	CAN	12.11.98	1		Lubbock	9 Feb
	8.28	1.82	11.61	6.39	2:19.79			
4472	Alina	Shukh	UKR	12.2.99	1	NC	Sumy	9 Feb
	8.88	1.85	13.48	6.05	2:16.47			
4464	Katerina	Cachová	CZE	26.2.90	2	NC	Praha (Strom)	11 Feb
	8.34	1.75	12.20	6.31	2:16.21			
4456	Antoinette	Nana Djimou	FRA	2.8.85	2	v4N	Madrid	28 Jan
	8.30	1.72	14.88	6.19	2:25.15			
4455	Géraldine	Ruckstuhl	SUI	24.2.98	1		Magglingen	4 Feb
	8.64	1.81	13.74	5.93	2:16.50			
4446	Noor	Vidts	BEL	30.5.96	1	NC	Gent	4 Feb
	8.54	1.76	13.87	6.18	2:20.25			
4440	Caroline	Agnou	SUI	26.5.96	2		Magglingen	4 Feb
	8.55	1.69	14.48	6.34	2:21.03			
4424	Lecabela	Quaresma	POR	26.12.89	8	WI	Birmingham	2 Mar
	8.51	1.76	14.12	6.01	2:19.85			
4405A	Alex	Gochenour	USA	17.2.93	3	NC	Albuquerque	16 Feb
	8.35	1.71	13.91	6.01	2:18.27			
4385	Adrianna	Sułek	POL-J	3.4.99	1	NC	Torun	17 Feb
	8.52	1.83	12.26	5.98	2:19.14			
4381	Georgia	Ellenwood	CAN	5.8.95	3	NCAA	College Station	9 Mar
	8.55	1.78	12.31	5.96	2:14.28			
4377	Solène	Ndama	FRA	23.9.98	1		Lyon	3 Feb
	8.15	1.74	12.82	5.82	2:16.66			
4365	Jaclyn	Siefring	USA	30.9.95	4	NCAA	College Station	9 Mar
	8.67	1.69	12.72	6.19	2:14.64			
4364	Esther	Turpin	FRA	29.4.96	1	NC	Liévin	17 Feb
	8.35	1.69	13.22	6.09	2:17.88			
4353	Yana	Maksimova	BLR	9.1.89	1	NCp	Gomel	3 Feb
	8.77	1.80	14.14	5.68	2:17.32			

4335	Yelizaveta	Aksyonova	RUS	10.7.96	14	Feb
4328	Györgyi	Zsivoczky-Farkas	HUN	13.2.85	10	Feb
4323	Rimma	Hordiyenko	UKR	30.12.95	9	Feb
4320	Lucia	Vadlejch	SVK	8.11.88	11	Feb
4319	Sarah	Lagger	AUT	3.9.99	4	Feb
4318	Louisa	Grauvogel	GER	28.9.96	9	Mar
4303	Bianca	Salming	SWE	22.11.98	11	Feb
4300	Karin	Strametz	AUT	18.4.98	4	Feb
4291	Jo	Rowland	GBR	29.12.89	28	Jan
4269	Niki	Oudenaarden	CAN	14.1.94	19	Jan
4264	Aleksandra	Butvina	RUS	14.2.86	14	Feb
4260A	Emilyn	Dearman	USA	1.1.95	16	Feb

3000 METRES WALK: 11:55.30 Antonella Palmisano ITA 6.8.91 1 NC Ancona 17 Feb

5000 METRES WALK: 21:25.3 Bethan Davies GBR 7.11.90 1 NC Birmingham 18 Feb

WORLD INDOOR CHAMPIONSHIPS 2018

Birmingham, GBR 1-4 March

The 17th edition of the IAAF World Indoor Championships, was a great success, showing onec again that there is nothing like real Championships action, where performances matter to all. Genzebe Dibaba, who has been the queen of indoor athletics for some years, won a marvellous double to take her World Indoor gold tally to five. She produced sensationally fast long drives to the finish (4:03.12 for the second half of the 3000m and 1:59.82 for the last 800m of the 1500m), but terribly slow starts to the races meant that the championships records were not threatened in those events and the tactics of most in the men's 1500m and 3000m were simply deplorable. There were, however, six new marks, three each for men and women. Most notably Christian Coleman lived up to all expectation with 6.37 for 60m, a time probably intrinsically better even than his world record of 6.34 as that was achieved at high altitude. Kendra Harrison put aside her previous disappointments in major championships to win the 60m hurdles in 7.70 and on the track there were also new records in both 4x400m finals with Poland causing a major upset to defeat the USA in the men's race and set the one world indoor record of the meeting

As usual the field events featured higher quality fields than most of the track events, and one just wishes that the IAAF and other athletics authorities would realise that spectators very often enjoy these events more than fleeting track action. Here new championship records were set by Tom Walsh, 22.31 in the shot, and Sandi Morris, 4.95 in the pole vault, in both of which there was great depth of performance. There was also especially exciting close action in the men's pole vault, long jump and triple jump and in the women's long jump.

Renaud Lavillenie's pole vault win at 5.90 took his World Indoor gold tally to three, a one-event tally matched by Pavel Maslák at 400m and Dibaba at 3000m. There were world-leading marks at 14 events in all.

There were 22 disqualifications. Apart from false starts, many athletes were disqualified for stepping on or over their inside line in races. All five went out in heat 3 of the men's 400m, and also the first two in the final. The format for the shot and horizontal jumps was that after three rounds the field as normal was reduced to eight, but here only the top four after the fifth round were offered a sixth attempt – a stupid exerceise in attempting to increase excitement that fell very flat.

MEN

60 Metres (3)

1. Christian Coleman USA	6.37*
2. Su Bingtian CHN	6.42
3. Ronnie Baker USA	6.44
4, Xie Zhenye CHN	6.52
5. Hassan Taftian IRI	6.53
6. Ján Volko SVK	6.59
7. Sean Safo-Antwi GHA	6.60
8. Emre Zafer Barnes TUR	6.64

400 Metres (2-2-3)

1. Pavel Maslák CZE	45.47
2. Michael Cherry USA	45.84
3. Deon Lendore TTO	46.37
4. Aldrich Bailey Jr USA	46.44
dq. Óscar Husillos ESP	(44.92)
dq. Luguelín Santos DOM	(45.09)

800 Metres (2-3)

1. Adam Kszczot POL	1:47.47
2. Drew Windle USA	1:47.99
3. Saúl Ordóñez ESP	1:48.01
4. Elliot Giles GBR	1:48.22
5. Álvaro de Arriba ESP	1:48.51
6. Mostafa Smaili MAR	1:48.75

1500 Metres (3-4)

1. Samuel Tefera ETH-J	3:58.19
2. Marcin Lewandowski POL	3:58.39
3. Abdelaati Iguider MAR	3:58.43
4. Aman Wote ETH	3:58.64
5. Ben Blankenship USA	3:58.89
6. Jake Wightman GBR	3:58.91
7. Craig Engels USA	3:58.92
8. Chris O'Hare GBR	4:00.65
9. Vincent Kibet KEN	4:02.32

3000 Metres (2-4)

1. Yomif Kejelcha ETH	8:14.41
2. Selemon Barega ETH-J	8:15.59
3. Bethwel Birgen KEN	8:15.70
4, Hagos Gebrhiwet ETH	8:15.76
5. Adel Mechaal ESP	8:16.13
6. Younès Essalhi MAR	8:16.63
7. Davis Kiplangat KEN	8:18.03
8. Clemens Bleistein GER	8:18.24
9. Julian Oakley NZL	8:18.60
10. Birhanu Yemataw BRN	8:18.89

60 Metres Hurdles (3-4-4)

1. Andrew Pozzi GBR	7.46
2. Jarret Eaton USA	7.47
3. Aurel Manga FRA	7.54
4. Aries Merritt USA	7.56
5. Pascal Martinot-Lagarde FRA	7.68
6. Gabriel Constantino BRA	7.71
7. Roger Iribarne CUB	7.77
dq (fs) Milan Trajkovic CYP	–

High Jump (1)

1. Danil Lysenko ANA/RUS	2.36
2. Mutaz Essa Barshim QAT	2.33
3. Mateusz Przybylko GER	2.29
4. Erik Kynard USA	2.29
5. Sylwester Bednarek POL	2.25
6= Wang Yu CHN	2.20
6= Donald Thomas BAH	2.20
6= Maksim Nedasekov BLR	2.20

Pole Vault (4)

1. Renaud Lavillenie FRA	5.90
2. Sam Kendricks USA	5.85
3. Piotr Lisek POL	5.85
4. Kurtis Marschall AUS	5.80
5= Raphael Holzdeppe GER	5.80
5= Emmanouíl Karalís GRE-J	5.80
7= Armand Duplantis SWE-J	5.70
7= Konstadínos Filippídis GRE	5.70

Long Jump 2)

1. Juan Miguel Echevarría CUB	8.46
2. Luvo Manyonga RSA	8.44
3. Marquis Dendy USA	8.42
4. Jarrion Lawson USA	8.14
5. Shi Yuhao CHN	8.12
6. Ruswahl Samaai RSA	8.05
7. Radek Juska CZE	7.99
8. Eusebio Cáceres ESP	7.91

Triple Jump (3)

1. Will Claye USA	17.43
2. Almir dos Santos BRA	17.41
3. Nelson Évora POR	17.40
4. Alexis Copello AZE	17.17
5. Chris Carter USA	17.15
6. Fabrice Zango BUR	17.11
7. Zhu Yaming CHN	16.87
8. Dong Bin CHN	16.84

Shot (3)

1. Tomas Walsh NZL	22.31*
2. David Storl GER	21.44
3. Tomás Stanek CZE	21.44
4. Darlan Romani BRA	21.37
5. Mesud Pezer BIH	21.15
6. Darrell Hill USA	21.06
7. Ryan Whiting USA	21.03
8. Konrad Bukowiecki POL	20.99

Heptathlon (2/3)

1. Kevin Mayer FRA	6348
2. Damian Warner CAN	6343

3. Maicel Uibo EST 6265
4. Kai Kazmirek GER 6238
5. Eelco Sintnicolaas NED 5997
6. Zach Ziemek USA 5941
7. Ruben Gado FRA 5927
8. Dominik Distelberger AUT 5908
9. Jan Dolezal CZE 5775

4 x 400 Metres (3-4)
1. POL 3:01.77* WR
K Zalewski 45.73, R Omelko 45.17, L Krawczuk 45.87, J Krzewina 45.00
2. USA 3:01.97
F Kerley 44.85, M Cherry 45.34, A Bailey Jr 46.11, V Norwood 45.67
3. BEL 3:02.51
D Borlée 46.40, J Borlée 45.42, J Sacoor 45.83, K Borlée 44.86
4. TTO 3:02.52
5. CZE 3:04.87
6. GBR 3:05.08

WOMEN

60 Metres (2)
1. Murielle Ahouré CIV 6.97
2. Marie Josée Ta Lou CIV 7.05
3. Mujinga Kambundji SUI 7.05
4. Elaine Thompson JAM 7.08
5. Dafne Schippers NED 7.10
6. Michelle-Lee Ahye TTO 7.13
7. Carole Zahi FRA 7.19
8. Remona Burchell JAM 7.50

400 Metres (2-2-3)
1. Courtney Okolo USA 50.55
2. Shakima Wimbley USA 51.47
3. Eilidh Doyle GBR 51.60
4. Justyna Swiety-Ersetic POL 51.85
5. Tovea Jenkins JAM 52.12
6. Zoey Clark GBR 52.16

800 Metres (3-4)
1. Francine Niyonsaba BDI 1:58.31
2. Ajee' Wilson USA 1:58.99
3. Shelayna Oskan-Clarke GBR 1:59.81
4. Habitam Alemu ETH-J 2:01.10
5. Raevyn Rogers USA 2:01.44
6. Selina Büchel SUI 2:03.01

1500 Metres (2-3)
1. Genzebe Dibaba ETH 4:05.27
2. Laura Muir GBR 4:06.23
3. Sifan Hassan NED 4:07.26
4. Shelby Houlihan USA 4:11.93
5. Winny Chebet KEN 4:12.08
6. Aisha Praught Leer JAM 4:12.86
7. Beatrice Chepkoech KEN 4:13.59
8. Rababe Arrafi MAR 4:14.94
9. Colleen Quigley USA 4:15.97
10. Meraf Bahta SWE 4:23.05

ANA = Authorised neutral athlete

3000 Metres (1)
1. Genzebe Dibaba ETH 8:45.05
2. Sifan Hassan NED 8:45.68
3. Laura Muir GBR 8:45.78
4. Hellen Obiri KEN 8:49.66
5. Shelby Houlihan USA 8:50.38
6. Taye Fantu ETH-J 8:50.54
7. Konstanze Klosterhalfen GER 8:51.79
8. Katie Mackey USA 8:56.62

60 Metres Hurdles (2-3-3)
1, Kendra Harrison USA 7.70*
2. Christina Manning USA 7.79
3. Nadine Visser NED 7.84
4. Sharika Nelvis USA 7.86
5. Cindy Roleder GER 7.87
6. Isabelle Pedersen NOR 7.94
7. Tobi Amusan NGR 8.05
8. Devynne Charlton BAH 8.18

High Jump (1)
1. Mariya Lasitskene ANA/RUS 2.01
2. Vashti Cunningham USA-J 1.93
3. Alessia Trost ITA 1.93
4. Morgan Lake GBR 1.93
5. Yuliya Levchenko UKR 1.89
6. Mirela Demireva BUL 1.89
7= Iryna Herashchenko UKR 1.84
7= Erika Kinsey SWE 1.84
7= Inika McPherson USA 1.84

Pole Vault (3)
1. Sandi Morris USA 4.95*
2. Anzhelika Sidorova ANA/RUS 4.90
3. Ekateríni Stefanídi GRE 4.80
4. Eliza McCartney NZL 4.75
5. Katie Nageotte USA 4.70
6. Alysha Newman CAN 4.70
7. Yarisley Silva CUB 4.60
8. Nina Kennedy AUS 4.60
9. Olga Mullina ANA/RUS 4.60

Long Jump (4
1. Ivana Spanovic SRB 6.96
2. Brittney Reese USA 6.89
3. Sosthene Moguenara GER 6.85
4. Quanesha Burks USA 6.81
5. Malaika Mihambo GER 6.64
6. Khaddi Sagnia SWE 6.64
7. Christabel Nettey CAN 6.63
8. Ksenija Balta EST 6.57

Triple Jump (3)
1. Yulimar Rojas VEN 14.63
2. Kimberly Williams JAM 14.48
3. Ana Peleteiro ESP 14.40
4. Elena Panturoiu ROU 14.33
5. Keturah Orji USA 14.31
6. Paraskevi Papahrístou GRE 14.05
7. Viktoriya Prokopenko ANA/RUS 14.05
8. Tori Franklin USA 14.03

Shot (2)
1. Anita Márton HUN 19.62
2. Danniel Thomas-Dodd JAM 19.22
3. Gong Lijiao CHN 19.08
4. Gao Yang CHN 18.77
5. Paulina Guba POL 18.54
6. Alyona Dubitskaya BLR 18.21
7. Yaniuvis López CUB 18.19
8. Jeneva Stevens USA 18.18

Pentathlon (2)
1. Katarina Johnson-Thompson GBR 4750
2. Ivona Dadic AUT 4700
3. Yorgelís Rodríguez CUB 4637
4. Eliska Klucinová CZE 4579
5. Erica Bougard USA 4571
6. Xénia Krizsán HUN 4559
7. Alina Shukh UKR-J 4466
8. Lecabela Quaresma POR 4424
9. Kendell Williams USA 4414
10. Caroline Agnou SUI 4397

4 x 400 Metres (2)
1. USA 3:23.85*
Q Hayes 51.51, G Moline 50.87, S Wimbley 51.29, C Okolo 50.18
2. POL 3:26.09
J Swiety-Ersetic 52.18, P Wyciszkiewicz 50.97, A Gaworska 51.31, M Holub-Kowalik 51.63
3. GBR 3:29.38
M Beesley 52.99, H Williams 51.91, A Allcock 52.12, Z Clark 52.36
4. UKR 3:31.32
5. ITA 3:31.55
dq. JAM (3:24.16)

Leading Nations – Medals & Points

Nation	G	S	B	Points
USA	6	10	2	207
GBR	2	1	4	67
ETH	4	1	0	57
POL	2	2	1	50
GER	-	1	2	38
CHN	-	1	1	32
FRA	2	-	1	30
JAM	-	2	-	27
NED	-	1	2	27
CZE	1	-		25
ESP	-	-	2	21
CUB	1	-	1	20
KEN	-	-	1	19
CIV	1	1	-	15
BRA	-	1	-	15
GRE	-	-	1	14
TTO	-	-	1	14
NZL	1	-	-	13
MAR	-	-	1	13
UKR	-	-	-	12.5

13 nations won gold, 32 medals and 48 placed in top 8

ASIAN INDOOR CHAMPIONSHIPS 2018

February 1-2, Tehran, Iran. **Men:** 60m: Hassan Taftian IRI 6.51*, 400m: Abdelilah Haroun QAT 46.37, 800m: Abubaker Abdallah QAT 1:51.98, 1500m: Amir Moradi IRI 3:53.78, 3000m: Hosein Keyhani IRI 8:37.68, 60mh: Abdulaziz Al-Mandeel KUW 7.71 HJ: Mutaz Essa Barshim QAT 2.38*, PV: Nikita Filippov KAZ 5.20, LJ: Shi Yuhao 8.16, TJ: Khalid Al-Subaie KUW 16.26, SP: Ali Samari IRI 19.42, Hep: Majed Al-Sayed KUW 5228, 4x400m: QAT 3:10.08. **Women**: 60m: Liang Xiaojing CHN 7.20*, 400m: Svetlana Golendova KAZ 53.28, 800m: Wang Chunyu CHN 2:09.30, 1500m: Gayanthika T. Abeyrathne SRI 4:26.83, 3000m: Tatyana Neroznak KAZ 9:33.65, 60mh: Aygerim Shynazbekova KAZ 8.32, HJ: Nadiya Dusanova UZB 1.87, PV: Anastasiya Yermakova KAZ 3.70, LJ: Bui Thi Thu Thao VIE 6.20, TJ: Irina Ektova KAZ 13.79, SP: Yelena Smolyanova UZB 15.54, Pen: Sepideh Tavakoli IRI 4038, 4x400m: KAZ 3:41.67. **Medal table leaders**: KAZ 7G-4S-1B, IRI 5-9-10, QAT 4-3-2, CHN 3-2-1, KUW 3-1-2, UZB 2-1-9, SRI & VIE 1-0-3, 13 nations won medals. ** Championship records*

IAAF World Half Marathon Championships 2018

At Valencia, Spain 24 March

Men
1. Geoffrey Kamworor KEN 60:02
2. Abraham Cheroben BRN 60:22
3. Aron Kifle ERI 60:31
4. Jemal Yimer ETH 60:33
5. Getaneh Molla ETH 60:47
6. Betesfa Getahun ETH 60:54
7. Amanuel Mesel ERI 60:58
8. Julien Wanders SUI 61:03
9. Kaan Kigen Özbilen TUR 61:05
10. Leul Gebresilase ETH 61:07
11. Aweke Ayalew BRN 61:09
12. Leonard Barsoton KEN 61:14
13. Albert Rop BRN 61:21
14. Samuel Chelanga USA 61:23
15. Barselius Kipyego KEN 61:24

Teams: (3 to score) 1. ETH 3:02:14; 2. KEN 3:02:40; 3. BRN 3:02:52; 4. ERI 3:03:03; 5. UGA 3:06:15; 6. RSA 3:07:16; 7. USA 3:07:38; 8. ESP 3:08:29; 9. PER 3:08:35; 10. ISR 3:08:47; 11. GBR 3:08:57; 12. JPN 3:09:15; 13. FRA 3:10:20; 14. AUS 3:11:49; 15. ECU 3:11:53; 23 teams finished

Women
1. Netsanet Gudeta ETH 66:1
2. Joyciline Jepkosgei KEN 66:54
3. Pauline Kamulu KEN 66:56
4. Eunice Chumba BRN 67:17
5. Zeineba Yimer ETH 68:07
6. Meseret Belete ETH 68:09
7. Desi Jisa Mokonin BRN 68:10
8. Bekelech Gudeta ETH 68:12
9. Dalilah Abdulkadir BRN 68:12
10. Shitaye Eshete BRN 68:25
11. Zinash Mekonnen ETH 68:30
12. Lonah Salpeter ISR 68:58
13. Ruth Chepngetich KEN 69:12
14. Rose Chelimo BRN 70:20
15. Ancuta Bobocel ROU 70:21

Teams: 1. ETH 3:22:27; 2. KEN 3:23:02; 3. BRN 3:23:39; 4. JPN 3:33:57; 5. ERI 3:35:09; 6. BLR 3:35:43; 7. GBR 3:35:48; 8. PER 3:35:52; 9. USA 3:39:11; 10. CAN 3:39:19; 19 teams finished.

African Cross-Country Championships 2018

At Chlef. Algeria March 17

Men 10k
1. Alfred Barkach KEN 30:47
2. Julius Kogo KEN 30:47
3. Thomas Akeyo UGA 30:47
4. Enyew Mekonnen ETH 31:01
5. Emmanuel Bor KEN 31:19
6. Phillip Kipyeko UGA 31:19
7. John Chepkwony KEN 31:22
8. Filmon Ande ERI 31:23
9. Mande Bushendich UGA 31:26
10. Berhane Tesfay ERI 31:28

Team: 1. KEN 16; 2. UGA 30; 3. ERI 58; 4. ETH 57; 5. ALG 83; 6. RSA 92

Junior men 8k
1. Rhonnex Kipruto KEN 25:01
2. Stanley Waithaka KEN 25:06
3. Solomon Berihu ETH 25:08
4. Berehanu Wendim ETH 25:11
5. Milkesa Mengesha ETH 25:13
6. Vincent Kipkemoi KEN 25:14

Team: 1. KEN 16, 2. ETH 22, 3. ERI 68

Women 10k
1. Celliphine Chespol KEN 35:10
2. Margaret Chelimo KEN 35:13
3. Yeshi Kalayu ETH 35:26
4. Stacy Ndiwa KEN 35:27
5. Stella Chesang UGA 35:30
6. Sandra Chebet KEN 35:47
7. Mercyline Chelangat UGA 35:53
8. Alamrew tirusew ETH 35:57
9. Rosemary Wanjiru KEN 36:01
10. Gete Alemayehu ETH 36:08

Team: 1. KEN 13; 2,ETH 32; 3. UGA 89; 4. ALG 80

Junior Women 6k
1. Girmawit Gebregziabher ETH 19:44
2. Tsige Gebreselama ETH 19:58
3. Helen Lobun KEN 19:59
4. Agnes Jebet KEN 20:06
5. Roselidah Jepketer KEN 20:08
6. MIriam Cherop KEN 21:06

Team: 1. KEN 18, 2. ETH 19, 3. UGA 72

Mixed relay: 1. ETH 23:52; 2. KEN 24:15; 3. MAR 25:07

Asian Cross-Country Championships 2018

At Guiyang. China March 15

Men 12k
1. Peng Jianhua CHN 38:22
2. Kazuya Nishiyama JPN 38:26
3. Shunsuke Imanishi JPN 38:28
4. Kosei Yamaguchi JPN 38:37
5. Damuzhen Ciwang CHN 39:07
6. Tazuma Kazuma JPN 39:11

Team: 1. JPN 9, 2. CHN 16, 3. IRI 32, 4. IND 34, 5. TPE 63

Overall Medals: JPN 5 G, 4 S, 3 B CHN 3-4-0. IND & IRI 0-0-2

Junior Men 8k
1. Suolang Cairen CHN 25:35
2. Yuhi Nakaya JPN 25:39
3. Ren Tazawa JPN 25:42

Team: 1,. JPN 9, 2. CHN 19, 3. IRI 31

Women 8k
1. Li Dan CHN 28:03
2. Yukari Abe JPN 28:06
3. Sanjivani Jadhav IND 28:19
4. Nanami Watanabe JPN 28:27
5. Zhang Xinyan CHN 28:41
6. Yuka Hori JPN 28:4w

Team: 1. JPN 12. 2. CHN 14, 3. IND 28

Junior Women 6k
1. Yuna Wada JPN 20:43
2. Riraka Hironaka JPN 20:45
3. Tomomi Takematsu JPN 20:48

Team: 1 JPN 6, 2. CHN 20

World Indoor Tour Winners 2018

Men: 60: Su Bingtian; 800: Adam Kszczot; 3000: Yomif Kejelcha; PV: Piotr Lisek; TJ: Nelson Évora; SP: Tomás Stanek; **Women** 400: Léa Sprunger; 1500: Beatrice Chepkoech; 60H: Christina Manning; HJ: Mariya Lasitskene; LJ: Sosthene Moguenara.